KU-189-131

# CHILDREN'S ILLUSTRATED DICTIONARY

INTRODUCTION

# CHILDREN'S ILLUSTRATED DICTIONARY

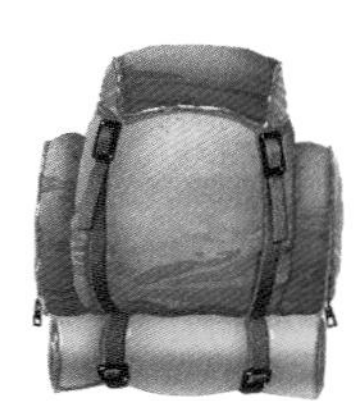

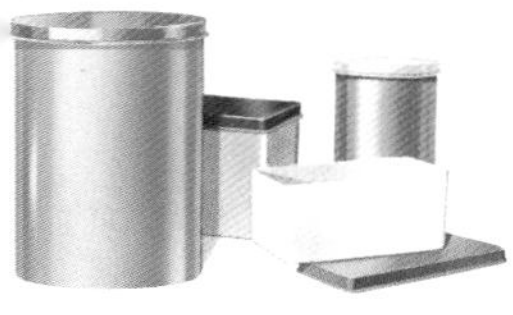

p

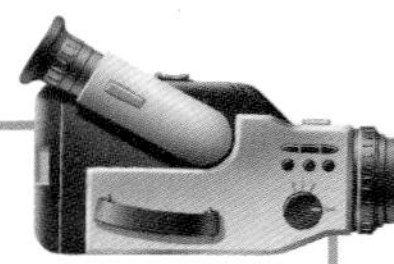

Authors
John Grisewood, Neil Morris, Ting Morris

This is a Parragon Book
This edition published in 2003
Parragon, Queen Street House, 4 Queen Street, Bath, BA1 1HE, UK

Copyright © Parragon 1999

All rights reserved. No part of this publication may be reproduced, stored in a retrieval system, or transmitted by any other means, electronic, mechanical, photocopying, recording, or otherwise, without the prior permission of the copyright holder.

ISBN 1-40541-627-0

Printed in Dubai

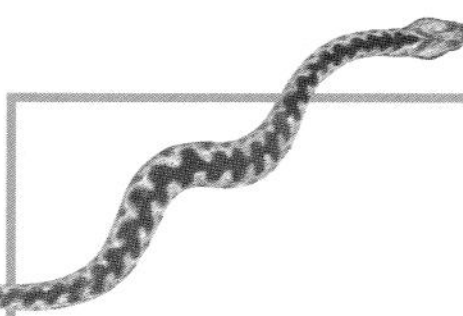

# Introduction

Have you ever played the game in which you try to describe something in words only – without using any gestures – and other people have to work out what you are describing? How would you describe a horse or a television?

This dictionary describes a horse as follows: 'a big, four-legged animal with hooves, a long mane and a tail, which can be used for riding or for pulling things like carts and ploughs'. The television is described as 'a box-shaped instrument that receives programmes that have been broadcast, and shows them on a screen as moving pictures with sound'.

That is exactly what a dictionary does. It tells us what words mean. A good dictionary should describe things well by being clear and concise. If a word has two or more meanings, it should tell us. 'Post', for example, has two quite different meanings: firstly, mail (letters, parcels etc.) and secondly, a pole, like a telegraph pole. The noun 'bear' is an animal but the verb means 'to carry or support'.

A good dictionary has certain other features:

It tells you how words are spelled ('accommodation' has two 'c's and two 'm's).

It tells you how awkward words are pronounced ('gnome', 'handkerchief', 'scythe', 'qualm', 'typhoon', for example).

It tells you what the part of speech is. Is it a noun, verb, adjective or adverb?

This is useful. For instance, the noun 'object' meaning 'a thing' is pronounced '**ob**-ject' but the verb, meaning 'to protest' is pronounced 'ob-**ject**'.

It provides example sentences or phrases to help you understand how a word should be used. For instance: 'This is just (exactly) the colour I'm looking for' and 'There's just about (almost not) enough to eat.'

To be really useful, a dictionary must be up-to-date. New words enter the language and old words may die or acquire a new meaning. If you looked at a dictionary that is only a few years old, you probably would not find the second definition of 'mouse': 'a small device on your desk that you move on the surface with your hand to control the position of the cursor on a computer screen'. And the word 'cursor' in the definition would probably not be in the dictionary.

This dictionary has some other features that make it rather special:

- It is superbly illustrated with photographs, diagrams and drawings that complement the definitions and add more visual information.
- Special notice-board panels provide fascinating facts on such things as word histories, spelling, grammar and homophones plus much general information associated with a particular word.

We hope you will find this dictionary both useful and interesting. How would you describe it – without using gestures?

*John Grisewood, Neil Morris, Ting Morris*

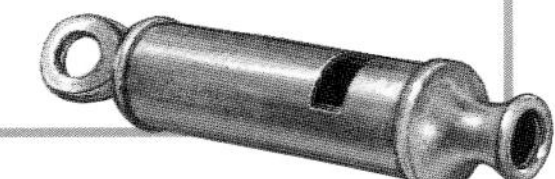

# How to use this dictionary

All the entries are in alphabetical order. A page letter or thumb-index shows you the pages on which all the entries beginning with the same letter appear. A guide word at the top outside corner of each page also helps you find the word you're looking for.

The guide word on the left-hand page gives the first word on that page and the guide word on the right gives the last.

## Parts of speech

These show how words behave in a sentence. They are: adjective, adverb, conjunction, noun, preposition, pronoun, verb. Look up the entry in the dictionary to find out more about each of these parts of speech.

## Headwords

Headwords or entries are printed in bold, black type. Other forms of the same word (related words) are in less bold type, for example: **baptize** *verb*. **baptism** *noun*. **baptismal** *adjective*.

## Derivatives

Derivatives or other irregular forms of the headword are shown in brackets as in the verb give (give, gives, giving, gave), the noun goose (geese) and the adjective big (bigger, biggest). Regular forms are not given, for example, dog (dogs).

## Pronunciation

For some of the more difficult words there is a guide to how to say it correctly, for example: **gnash** *verb* (say nash).

## Definition

This tells you what a word means. If a word has more than one meaning, each meaning is numbered. For example: temple noun 1 a building... 2 the flat part on either side of your head...

---

**chariot**

**C**

**chariot** *noun* an ancient horse-drawn vehicle with two wheels, used in battles and races.

Around 1200 BC the Hittites, who lived in modern-day Turkey, used chariots for warfare.

**charity** *noun* 1 an organization that helps those who need it. *A charity for stray cats.* 2 kindness towards others.

**charm** *noun* 1 the ability to be attractive and to please. *He used all his charm to win her over.* 2 an act, saying or object that has magical powers. 3 an ornament on a bracelet or chain. **charm** *verb* 1 *He charmed her with his flattery.* 2 to control something by using magical powers.

**charming** *adjective* delightful, pleasing. *She is a charming person.*

**chart** *noun* 1 a map of the sea and coast or sky and stars. 2 a map with special information in curves and graphs. *A weather chart.* 3 a list of information in a particular order. *The charts list the most popular records.* **chart** *verb*. *Explorers charted the coastline.*

**chase** *verb* to go after somebody or something in order to try and catch them or make them go away. *The cat chased the mouse.* **chase** *noun*.

**chasm** *noun* 1 a deep crack in the ground. 2 a large difference between two things or groups. *The chasm between us widened.*

**chat** *noun* a friendly talk. **chat** *verb*. *We chatted all afternoon.*

**chat show** *noun* a TV or radio programme in which famous people are interviewed.

**chatter** *verb* 1 to talk non-stop about unimportant things. 2 to make a rattling sound. *His teeth were chattering with cold.*

**chauffeur** *noun* (say **shoh**-fer) a person employed to drive somebody's car.

The chauffeur wears a smart uniform and waits by his employer's car.

**AMAZING FACT**

Cheetahs can reach speeds of up to 60 mph (100kph) over short distances when chasing gazelles.

Tartan is a traditional Scottish fabric pattern, based on colourful overlaid checks.

**WORD HISTORY**

*The original 'chauffeur', in French, was not a driver but a stoker or fireman, who put coal on the furnace of a steam engine. Early motor cars gave off a lot of smoke and steam, so their drivers were jokingly called stokers.*

**chauvinist** *noun* (say **shoh**-vin-ist) a person who shows great prejudice, especially against women. *He's a real male chauvinist.*

**cheap** *adjective* 1 not costing very much. *Food is cheaper in Portugal than in Spain.* 2 of poor quality, not very good. *Cheap housing is hard to come by.*

**cheat** *verb* to lie or trick somebody, often in order to do well. *He always cheats in exams.* **cheat** *noun* 1 a person who cheats. 2 a dishonest action.

**check** *noun* 1 an examination to find out if something is correct. *He made a thorough check.* 2 keeping somebody or something under control. *It's impossible to keep the disease in check.* 3 in chess the position of the king when under attack.

**check** *noun* a pattern of squares in different colours. **checked** *adjective*.

**check** *verb* 1 to make sure something is correct or satisfactory. *Have you checked the bill?* 2 to hold back or stop doing something. *The bad weather checked their progress.* **check in** to register at a hotel or report at an airport. *You have to check in an hour before take-off.* **check out** to pay the bill and leave a hotel.

**checkout** *noun* a place in a supermarket where goods are packed and paid for.

**check-up** *noun* a medical examination.

**cheek** *noun* the side of the face below the eye. *Rosy cheeks are a sign of health.*

**cheek** *noun* rude behaviour. **cheeky** *adjective*. *Don't be cheeky to your mother!*

**cheer** *noun* 1 a shout of praise or happiness. *The crowd gave a big cheer.* 2 If you are full of cheer, you are very happy. **cheer** *verb*. *The fans cheered wildly throughout the match.* **cheer up** to become happy and stop feeling sad.

**cheerful** *adjective* 1 looking, sounding and feeling happy. 2 something pleasant, that makes you happy. **cheerfully** *adverb*.

**cheese** *noun* a soft or hard food made from milk. *Let's have bread and cheese for lunch.*

**cheetah** *noun* a wild animal, like a big spotted cat. Cheetahs are the fastest land animals in the world.

72

## Illustrations

The illustrations have been carefully selected to extend and complement the definitions. All have informative captions or labels. 'A good picture,' they say, 'is worth a thousand words.'

## Phrasal verbs

Phrasal verbs are included as a distinct part of many definitions. They are simple verbs like make, get, go, together with an adverb or preposition (as in get up, get away, get on etc.). They function like a single word but the meaning cannot be worked out from the literal meaning of the words. The ability to use and understand phrasal verbs is very important in writing and speaking clear English.

chip

C

**chef** *noun* a cook in a restaurant.

A chef has to deal with many pans at once. His job is both hot and demanding.

**chemical** *adjective* used in, made by or connected with chemistry. **chemical** *noun*. **chemically** *adverb*.

**chemist** *noun* 1 a trained person who makes up and sells medicines. 2 a shop selling medicines and toilet articles. 3 a scientist who specializes in chemistry.

**chemistry** *noun* the study of how substances are made up and how they react with other substances.

**cheque** *noun* a printed form telling the bank to pay money from your account to the person you have written the cheque to. *Can I pay by cheque?*

**cherry** (cherries) *noun* 1 a small round fruit with a stone. Ripe cherries are red. 2 the tree on which cherries grow.

**chess** *noun* a game for two players in which each player moves pieces on a chessboard.

**chest** *noun* the upper front part of the body enclosing the heart and the lungs.

**chest** *noun* a big, strong box for keeping things in. *A treasure chest.*

**chestnut** *noun* 1 a reddish brown nut inside a prickly green case. 2 the tree on which these nuts grow. **chestnut** *adjective* having a reddish-brown colour. *Chestnut hair.*

When the chestnut is ripe, the case falls to the ground and splits open. The shiny nuts roll out.

**chest of drawers** *noun* a piece of furniture with a set of drawers.

**chew** *verb* to move food about in your mouth and grind it with your teeth, so it is easy to swallow. **chew over** to think about something very carefully.

**chewing gum** *noun* a sweet gum that you chew and don't swallow.

**chick** *noun* a young bird.

**DID YOU KNOW?**

*China has a population of more than 1,200 million, more people than any other country in the world. Yet China has a smaller area than either Russia or Canada.*

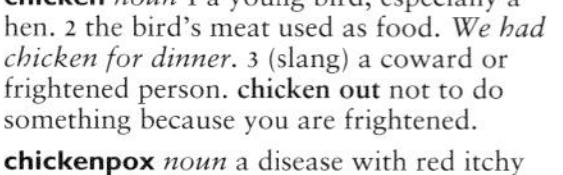

**chicken** *noun* 1 a young bird, especially a hen. 2 the bird's meat used as food. *We had chicken for dinner.* 3 (slang) a coward or frightened person. **chicken out** not to do something because you are frightened.

**chickenpox** *noun* a disease with red itchy spots on the skin.

**chief** *noun* a leader or highest official. **chief** *adjective* most important. **chiefly** *adverb*.

**chilblain** *noun* a painful swelling or sore in the fingers or toes caused by extreme cold.

**child** (children) *noun* 1 a young boy or girl. 2 a son or daughter.

**childhood** *noun* the time when you are a child. *Now he's old, he often thinks back to his childhood.*

**childish** *adjective* behaving like a child, often in silly way. *It's very childish to shout and scream like that.*

**children** plural of child.

**Chile** *noun* a country in South America.

Chile is a long thin country that runs along the backbone of South America.

**chill** *noun* 1 an unpleasant coldness. *In the morning there is often a chill in the air.* **chilly** *adjective*. 2 an illness caused by cold in which you might have a temperature, a headache and feel shivery. 3 a feeling of fear and doom. **chill** *verb* 1 to make something colder. 2 to become cold with fear. **chilling** *adjective*. *A chilling film.*

**chimney** *noun* a hollow passage in a roof through which smoke goes up into the air.

**chimpanzee** *noun* an African ape.

**chin** *noun* the front of the lower jaw.

**china** *noun* 1 a kind of fine white clay. 2 cups, saucers, plates and ornaments made of china. *The china cupboard.*

**China** *noun* a country in East Asia.

**Chinese** *noun* a person who comes from China. **Chinese** *adjective*. *An excellent Chinese restaurant.*

**chip** *noun* 1 a fried strip of potato. *We bought fish and chips.* 2 a small piece of wood, brick or paint, broken off something. 3 a crack that has been left in a cup or glass, when a small piece has been broken off. 4 a flat plastic counter used as money in games. 5 a very small electronic circuit in a computer. *A silicon chip.* **have a chip on your shoulder** to be rude or behave badly, because you think you have been treated unfairly in the past. **chip** (chipping, chipped) *verb* to damage something by breaking off a small piece of it. *I'm afraid I've chipped a plate.* **chip in** 1 to interrupt a conversation. 2 to give money to a fund, so that something can be paid for by a number of people.

73

## Examples of use

A sentence or phrase may be given to show how to use the word correctly.

## Gazetteer

The dictionary is also a useful mini-gazetteer. It includes as 'definition' all the countries of the world and their capitals, from Abu Dhabi, capital of the United Arab Emirates, to Zimbabwe, a country in Africa.

## Notice-board

The narrow centre column has been used as a kind of notice-board on which to 'pin' different kinds of notes – tips, words of advice and warnings about problem words and how to use them well. There are notes on grammar and spelling, on confusable words ('lightening' and 'lightning', for example), on how to make new words by building them with prefixes, as well as notes on the history of words and an interesting series of asides called 'Did you know'.

A

# Aa

**aardvark** *noun* an African mammal with a long snout and a long sticky tongue that it uses for catching insects.

**abacus** (abacuses) *noun* a frame with beads that slide along wires, used for counting.

**abandon** *verb* 1 to leave someone or something without returning. *They abandoned the sinking boat.* 2 to stop doing something. *She abandoned her search when it got dark.*

**abbey** *noun* a church and a group of buildings where monks or nuns live, work and pray.

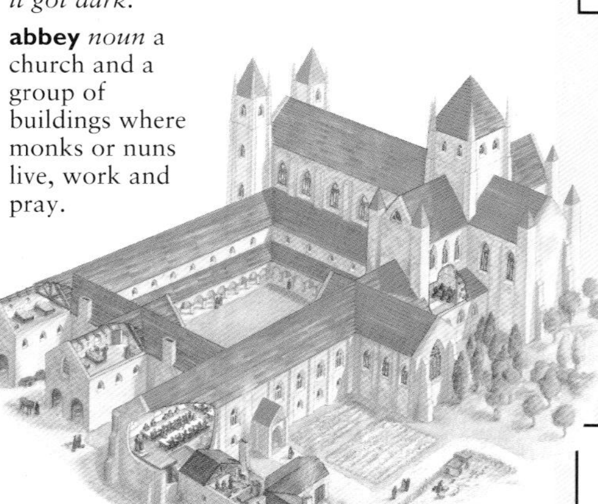

Some large abbeys were like walled towns, where the monks or nuns lived in seclusion from the rest of the world.

**abbot** *noun* the head of an abbey of monks.

**abbreviation** *noun* a short way of writing a word or group of words. *Maths is an abbreviation for mathematics.* **abbreviated** *adjective.*

**abdicate** *verb* to give up a position, especially that of king or queen. **abdication** *noun.*

**abdomen** *noun* 1 the part of the body that contains the stomach. 2 the back part of an insect's body.

Dragonfly larva

An insect's body is clearly divided into head, thorax and abdomen.

### WORD HISTORY

*Dutch settlers in South Africa gave the aardvark its name. It means 'earth pig', although an aardvark is really a type of anteater.*

### DID YOU KNOW?

*Abbreviations such as Mr and Dr that end in the final letter of the word do not need a full stop. Abbreviations of names of countries and organizations, e.g. USA and EU, do not usually have full stops either.*

**abhor** (abhors, abhorring, abhorred) *verb* to look on something with horror and hate. **abhorrence** *noun.*

**ability** *noun* the power or skill to do something. *Cats have the ability to see in the dark.*

**able** *adjective* 1 having the power, time, opportunity etc. to do something. *I wasn't able to leave work early.* 2 clever or skilled. *An able cook.* **ably** *adverb.*

**abnormal** *adjective* strange, peculiar and not normal. *It's abnormal for it to snow in summer.* **abnormality** *noun.*

**aboard** *adverb, preposition* in or on a ship, bus, train or aeroplane. *The ferry is leaving. All aboard!*

**abolish** (abolishes, abolishing, abolished) *verb* to get rid of or put an end to. *Capital punishment was abolished years ago.* **abolition** *noun.*

**abominable** *adjective* bad and very unpleasant. **abominably** *adverb. He was rude and noisy and behaved abominably.*

**aborigine** (or now preferred) **aboriginal** *noun* (say ab-or-**ij**-in-ee and ab-or-**ij**-in-ul) one of the original people who lived in Australia. **aboriginal** *adjective.*

The art of Australian aboriginals often recalls their ancient myths and legends with bold patterns and pictures of animals.

**abortion** *noun* ending a woman's pregnancy by removing the foetus from her womb. **abort** *verb.*

**abortive** *adjective* unsuccessful. *An abortive attempt to seize power.*

**about** *preposition* 1 concerning, in connection with. *The film is about space travel.* 2 near to. *I'll ring you at about six o'clock.* 3 all round. *Old papers were scattered about the room.* **about** *adverb* all over the place. *The dogs were dashing about.*

**above** *preposition* 1 higher than. *A bee is buzzing above my head.* 2 more than. *Above normal temperature.* **above** *adverb* overhead. *Look at the sky above.*

**abreast** *adverb* side by side and facing the same way. *The boys marched four abreast.*

**abridge** *verb* to make a book etc. shorter. **abridged** *adjective. The abridged novels of Dickens.* **abridgement** *noun.*

**abroad** *adverb* in another country. *Holidays abroad.*

**abrupt** *adjective* 1 sudden and unexpected. *The bus came to an abrupt stop.* 2 rude and unfriendly. *An abrupt answer.*

**abscess** *noun* (say **ab**-sess) a swelling on the body containing a yellow liquid called pus.

**abseil** *verb* (say **ab**-sail) to lower yourself down a cliff by holding on to ropes.

Henry abseiled slowly down the cliff face.

**absent** *adjective* not there but away. *Anne was absent from school because she had a cold.* **absence** noun.

**absent-minded** *adjective* forgetful or not paying attention.

**absolute** *adjective* 1 complete. *I'm telling the absolute truth.* 2 unlimited. *Dictators have absolute power to do what they want.*

**absorb** *verb* 1 to soak up a liquid. *Sponges absorb water.* **absorbent** *adjective.* 2 to take up somebody's attention. *She is absorbed in her work.* **absorbing** *adjective.*

Litmus paper absorbs liquid and turns pink if the liquid is acid. It turns blue if the liquid is alkaline. This experiment is called the litmus test.

**abstain** *verb* 1 to keep yourself from doing something, especially if it is something you enjoy. *She abstained from drinking alcohol.* **abstinence** *noun.* 2 to choose not to vote in an election. **abstention** *noun.*

**abstract** *adjective* concerned with thoughts and ideas rather than real things.

**WORD BUILDER**

*The suffix '-able' can be added to certain verbs and nouns to form adjectives, e.g. 'adaptable' and 'advisable'. But some adjectives end in '-ible', e.g. 'audible', 'credible' and 'edible'. This has given rise to a lot of confusion and misspellings!*

**AMAZING FACT**

In the 1950s a group of playwrights founded a type of drama called the Theater of the Absurd which examined the meaning of life. They included Beckett, Ionesco and Pinter.

**abstract** *noun* a noun that is concerned with qualities and ideas. *Love and courage are abstract nouns.* The opposite of 'abstract' is 'concrete'.

**absurd** *adjective* stupid and ridiculous. **absurdity** *noun.*

**Abu Dhabi** *noun* the capital of the United Arab Emirates.

Locals hunt for bargains in this shopping bazaar in Abu Dhabi, United Arab Emirates.

**Abuja** *noun* the capital of Nigeria.

**abundant** *adjective* available in large amounts, plentiful. *Abundant supplies of fruit.* **abundance** *adjective.*

**abuse** *verb* (say a-**bewz**) 1 to treat a person or an animal in an unkind or violent way. 2 to misuse or use in a wrong way.

**abuse** *noun* (say a-**bewss**) 1 rude or cruel words. 2 the wrong and harmful use of something. *Drug abuse.* **abusive** *adjective.*

**abysmal** *adjective* very bad. *What an abysmal film!*

**abyss** *noun* a very deep pit.

**academic** *adjective* concerned with education and learning. *Academic studies.* **academic** *noun.*

Academics wearing traditional gowns talk outside a college at Oxford University.

**academy** *noun* a school or college, especially one for training in a particular subject. *The Academy of Speech and Drama.*

**accelerate** *verb* to go faster and faster. **acceleration** *noun.*

**accelerator** *noun* a pedal that you press with your foot to make a motor vehicle go faster.

A

**accent** *noun* (say **ak**-sent) 1 a way of pronouncing a language in a particular region or country. *An American accent.* 2 a mark that is put above or below a letter of the alphabet in some languages to show you how to pronounce it. **accent** *verb* (say ak-**sent**) to pronounce a syllable in a word with more force. *You accent the second syllable in 'tomato'.*

**accentuate** *verb* to emphasize or to make more noticeable.

**accept** *verb* 1 to take something that is offered. 2 to agree to or say yes to something. *I accept your decision.* 3 to believe something to be true. *You must accept that abseiling is dangerous.* **acceptance** *noun.*

**acceptable** *adjective* satisfactory. *Your homework is not acceptable.*

**access** *noun* a way to get into a place. *The access to the castle is over the drawbridge.*

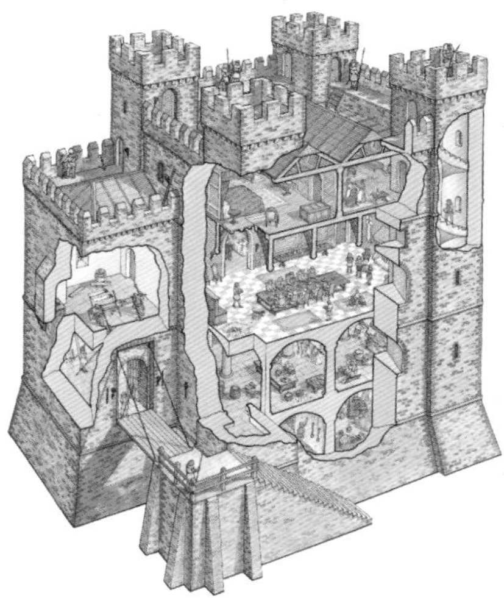

People must cross a drawbridge to gain access to this fortress.

**accessible** *adjective* easy to approach or to reach.

**accessory** *noun* 1 an extra part that goes with the main part. 2 somebody who helps to carry out a crime.

**accident** *noun* an unexpected and usually unpleasant happening, especially one in which people are hurt. *An aeroplane accident.*

**accidental** *adjective* by chance and not on purpose. **accidentally** *adverb.*

**accommodate** *verb* to provide a place for somebody to live. **accommodation** *noun.*

**accompany** (accompanies, accompanying, accompanied) *verb* 1 to go along with somebody or something. 2 to play a musical instrument while somebody else sings or dances. **accompanist** *noun.*

**AMAZING FACT**

Everyone who speaks has an accent, although it may not seem like it unless the accent is different from ours.

We often make judgements about people based on their accents – without realizing that we are doing it.

We may also form opinions of people's character based on how quickly they speak, how loudly they speak and how much they speak.

**SPELLING NOTE**

*'Accommodation' has two 'c's and two 'm's. There is no plural form.*

**AMAZING FACT**

The accordion was invented in Vienna, Austria in 1829 by Cyrill Damien.

**accomplice** *noun* a person who helps somebody carry out a crime.

**accomplish** *verb* to succeed in completing something. **accomplishment** *noun.*

A student who has accomplished a degree is awarded a certificate.

**accomplished** *adjective* talented or skilful at something. *An accomplished violinist.*

**according to** *preposition* as said by or in the opinion of somebody. *According to Jack, the visit has been postponed.* 2 in a suitable way. *Your pension is bigger according to how many years you've worked.*

**accordingly** *adverb* therefore, as a result.

**accordion** *noun* a portable musical instrument that you play by pressing keys and squeezing bellows to force air through reeds.

The accordion is a popular musical instrument in Madeira, Portugal.

**account** *noun* 1 a description of something. *There was a full account of the accident in the papers.* 2 the money that a person keeps in a bank. *Which bank is your account with?* 3 a bill or a record of money received or owed. **on account of** because of. *She stayed at home on account of the strike.* **by all accounts** according to what other people say.

**account** *verb* To account for means to give an explanation or reason for something. *How do you account for this broken window?*

**accountant** *noun* a person whose job it is to look after money and the accounts of businesses or people.

**Accra** *noun* the capital of Ghana.

**accumulate** *verb* to collect things in large quantities or to let things pile up. Dad has accumulated a pile of magazines over the years. **accumulation** *noun*.

**accurate** *adjective* correct and exact. **accuracy** *noun*.

For accurate measurement of time, athletes use a stopwatch.

**accuse** *verb* to blame and say that somebody has done something wrong. **accusation** *noun*.

**accustomed** *adjective* used to something. *It will take a little time to get accustomed to your new computer.*

**ace** *noun* 1 a playing card with a single symbol on it. *The ace of spades.* 2 a person who is very skilled at something. *He was a diving ace.*

**ache** *noun* a pain that goes on hurting for a long time. **ache** *verb* to hurt. *I'm aching badly all over.*

**achieve** *verb* to do or finish something successfully, especially after trying hard. **achievement** *noun*.

**acid** *noun* a chemical substance that can dissolve metals and turn blue litmus paper pink. **acidic** *adjective*.

**acid** *adjective* a sharp, sour taste. *Lemons have an acid taste.*

**acid rain** *noun* rain that contains chemicals from factories and cars and that damages plants and rivers.

Trees damaged by acid rain are unable to produce leaves, and so slowly die.

**DID YOU KNOW?**

*Some common acronyms are 'laser' (light amplification by stimulated emission of radiation), 'Nato' (North Atlantic Treaty Organization), 'radar' (radio detection and ranging) and 'sonar' (sound navigation ranging).*

**acknowledge** *verb* to admit or agree that something is true. *She acknowledged that she'd been badly mistaken.* **acknowledgement** *noun*.

**acne** *noun* a lot of red pimples on the face, especially common in young people.

**acorn** *noun* the nut or seed of an oak tree.

Acorns are a favourite food of squirrels. They bury them to provide a stock of winter food.

**acoustics** *plural noun* 1 the science of sound. 2 the effect a room has on the quality of sounds you hear in it. **acoustic** *adjective*. *An acoustic guitar.*

**acquaintance** *noun* 1 a person you know, but not a close friend. 2 a knowledge of something. *I have some acquaintance with the Japanese language.*

**acquire** *verb* to get something, especially by your own efforts.

**acre** *noun* an area of land equal to 4,047 square metres.

**acrobat** *noun* a person who is skilled in doing difficult and exciting gymnastic actions (acrobatics), especially at a circus. **acrobatic** *adjective*.

Trapeze artists are among the most daring of circus acrobats, swinging high over the ring, often without a safety net.

**acronym** *noun* a word made from the first letter of other words, such as VAT (Value Added Tax).

**acrophobia** *noun* a fear of great heights.

**across** *adverb, preposition* from one side of something to the other. *It measures almost 3 metres across.*

**act** *verb* 1 to do something. *She acted quickly to rescue the child from the blazing car.* 2 to perform a part in a play or film. **acting** *noun*. 3 to behave. *He's acting in a peculiar way.*

**act** *noun* 1 something that somebody does. *A kind act.* 2 a part of a play. 3 an Act of Parliament, a law passed by the government.

**action** *noun* 1 something that is done. *His fast action prevented the fire from spreading.* 2 a gesture or physical movement. 3 a law suit. 4 a battle. *He was killed in action.* **take action** to do something. **out of action** not working.

**active** *adjective* busy and full of energy. The opposite of 'active' is 'inactive'.

**activity** *noun* 1 lively action and movement. *The market is full of activity.* 2 something that people do, for example a hobby or playing games.

**actor** *noun* a man who performs in plays, in films or on television.

These actors are performing on stage against a painted backdrop.

**actress** *noun* a woman who performs in plays, in films or on television.

**actually** *adverb* really, in fact. *Did you actually talk to the president?*

**acute** *adjective* 1 severe and great. *An acute shortage of water.* 2 sharp. *Acute toothache.*

**acute accent** a sloping symbol placed over a vowel in some languages to show how it is pronounced, e.g. é in café.

**acute angle** an angle of less than 90°.

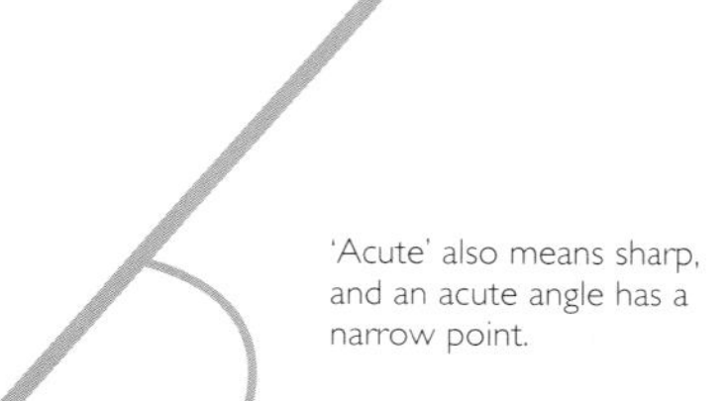

'Acute' also means sharp, and an acute angle has a narrow point.

**AD** *abbreviation* Anno Domini, the Latin words meaning 'in the year of our Lord', used for all dates after the birth of Jesus Christ.

**adamant** *adjective* unwilling to change your mind. *He's adamant that he will go.*

**AMAZING FACT**

Some species of adder, although they are poisonous, are so small that they can only bite humans in very delicate places, such as the skin between the toes or fingers.

The adder has a distinctive zigzag pattern along its back.

**DID YOU KNOW?**

*By tradition the abbreviation 'AD' is placed before the year number, e.g. AD 2006, whereas 'BC' (standing for Before Christ) follows the year number, e.g. 20 BC.*

**adapt** *verb* to change or make something suitable for a new situation or purpose. *We adapted the old shed into an office.* **adaptable** *adjective.*

**adaptor** *noun* a device that can connect two or more electrical plugs to one socket.

**add** *verb* to put two or more things together. *If you add four and three you get seven.* **addition** *noun.* The opposite of 'add' is 'subtract'.

**adder** *noun* a small snake, also sometimes known as a viper.

**addict** *noun* somebody who likes or needs something (especially harmful drugs) so much that they cannot give it up.

**addiction** *noun* something that people find it hard to do without, especially harmful drugs. **addictive** *adjective.*

**Addis Ababa** *noun* the capital of Ethiopia.

**additional** *adjective* extra, more than usual. *It was so cold she put on an extra jersey.*

**address** *noun* the name of the house, street and town where somebody lives. **address** *verb* to write an address on an envelope, parcel etc.

If the address on a letter contains a postcode, it can get to its destination more quickly.

**adenoids** *plural noun* soft lumps of flesh at the back of your nose, which sometimes swell and make it difficult to breathe.

**adequate** *adjective* just enough, suitable. *Adequate food supplies.*

**adhere** *verb* to stick. *Please adhere strictly to the rules.*

**adhesive** *noun* a substance, like glue, that sticks things together. **adhesive** *adjective* sticky. *Adhesive tape.*

**adjacent** *adjective* very close or next to. *The playing fields are adjacent to the school.*

The settlers built their wooden homes adjacent to each other.

**adjective** *noun* a word that tells us something about nouns. In the phrase 'big, brown bear' the words 'big' and 'brown' are adjectives that describe the noun 'bear'.

**adjust** *verb* to arrange or change something slightly so as to improve it. *She adjusted the curtains.* **adjustment** *noun.*

**administer** *verb* 1 to be in charge of and manage. *She administers the company's finances.* 2 to give out. *The nurse who was on duty always administered the medicine at the correct time.*

**administration** *noun* 1 the management of a company etc. 2 the government of a country. *The last Liberal administration.* **administrate** *verb* to admininster.

**admirable** *adjective* very good and worthy of being admired. *An admirable achievement.*

**admiral** *noun* a very senior officer in the navy.

Admiral Lord Nelson was the hero of the Battle of Trafalgar.

**admire** *verb* 1 to like and to think somebody or something is very good, to respect. *They admired him for his courage.* 2 to look at something with pleasure. *We admired the view.* **admiration** *noun.*

**DID YOU KNOW?**

*'Admission' usually refers to permission to enter a public place, or the price of a ticket for entry. 'Admittance' is a more formal word for the act of entering a private place not usually open to the public.*

**admission** *noun* 1 permission to enter somewhere. *Admission is by invitation only.* 2 the price charged to enter a place. *Admission is free.* 3 a statement that something is true. *She was guilty by her own admission.*

Tickets give admission to National Trust properties.

**admit** (admits, admitting, admitted) *verb* 1 to agree or own up that something is true. *They admitted they were wrong.* 2 to let somebody enter.

**adobe** *noun* 1 a clay brick hardened in the Sun. 2 a building made of such brick.

**adolescent** *noun* a young person who is changing from a child to an adult. **adolescence** *noun.*

**adopt** *verb* to take somebody's child into your home and make it legally your own son or daughter. **adoption** *noun.*

**adore** *verb* to love and admire somebody very much. **adoration** *noun.*

**adorn** *verb* to decorate something to make it look pretty.

**adrift** *adverb* floating and drifting without being secured. *The yacht was adrift.*

This boat has broken free of its moorings and is adrift near dangerous rocks.

**adult** *noun* a grown-up person or animal. **adult** *adjective* grown-up. **adulthood** *noun.*

**adulterate** *verb* to spoil something by adding to it something that is less good or harmful. **adulteration** *noun.*

A

**advance** *verb* 1 to move forward. *The army advanced towards the enemy.* **advance** *noun.* 2 to suggest an idea. *The detective advanced a new theory.*

**advance** *noun* 1 progress. *Medicine has made great advances.* 2 a loan of money. **in advance** before a certain date.

**advantage** *noun* something that helps you to succeed and perhaps do better than others. *It's a great advantage to be able to speak Japanese.* **take advantage of** to make use of a person or situation to help yourself.

**advent** *noun* 1 the beginning or arrival of something. *The advent of television.* 2 the four weeks before Christmas in the Christian Church.

**adventure** *noun* a happening that is exciting and perhaps dangerous. **adventurous** *adjective. She led an adventurous life in Africa.*

The South Pole was first reached by a Norwegian, Roald Amundsen, in 1911. The expedition was the greatest adventure of his life.

**adverb** *noun* a word that tells us more about a verb, an adjective or another adverb. In the sentence 'My grandmother talks very quickly,' the words 'very' and 'quickly' are adverbs.

**advertise** *verb* to tell people in a newspaper, on television etc. about something that is for sale.

**advertisement** *noun* a notice in a newspaper, on a hoarding, on television etc. that advertises something.

**advice** *noun* a helpful suggestion made to somebody about what they should do.

**SPELLING NOTE**

*'Advertise' is one of the words in British English ending in '–ise' that must never be spelled with '–ize'. Other words are 'despise', 'supervise', 'surprise' and 'televise'.*

A television mast or aerial placed on high ground ensures good reception for viewers and listeners in the surrounding area.

**AMAZING FACT**

Roald Amundsen was beaten to the North Pole by Robert Peary, a US polar explorer, the year before he succeeded in being the first person to reach the South Pole in 1911.

**SPELLING NOTE**

*Try not to confuse 'advice' with a 'c' (the noun) and 'advise' with an 's' (the verb).*

**advisable** *adjective* sensible and worth doing. *It's advisable to get an early night before setting off on holiday.*

**advise** *verb* to recommend and tell somebody what you think they ought to do. *The dentist advised me to brush my teeth twice a day.* **adviser** *noun.*

**aerial** *noun* a device such as a metal rod or wire that transmits or receives radio or television signals.

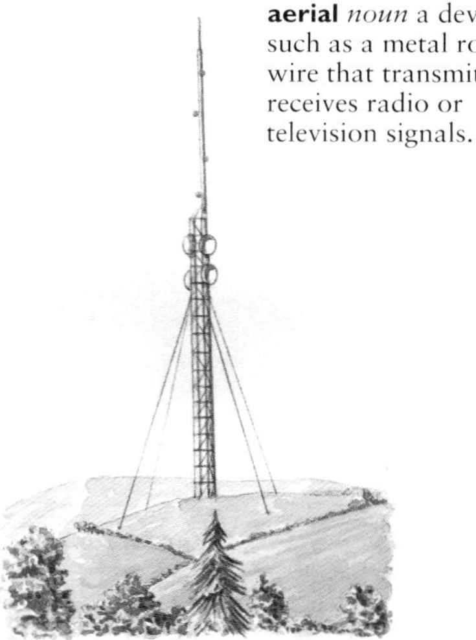

**aerobics** *plural noun* energetic physical exercises performed to music.

**aerodynamics** *plural noun* the science of objects moving through the air. **aerodynamic** *adjective.*

The aerodynamic shape of the Bullet train enables it to reach an average speed of 160 kph.

**aeronautics** *plural noun* the science of designing and building aircraft.

**aeroplane** *noun* a machine with wings that flies through the air carrying passengers or freight, driven by one or more engines.

**aerosol** *noun* a container that holds a liquid such as paint under pressure and lets it out as a fine spray.

**affair** *noun* 1 an event. *A barbecue is usually an informal affair.* 2 a relationship between two people, usually temporary. *A passionate love affair.*

**affairs** *plural noun* business and things that have to be done.

**affect** *verb* to influence or to cause a change in something. *The cold weather affects her health really badly.*

**affected** *adjective* pretended, not natural or sincere. *An affected smile.*

**affection** *noun* a feeling of love for somebody. **affectionate** *adjective.*

**affluent** *adjective* wealthy. **affluence** *noun.*

**afford** *verb* to have enough money to buy something.

**afforestation** *noun* the covering of land with forest. The opposite of 'afforestation' is 'deforestation'.

**Afghanistan** *noun* a country in central Asia.

**afloat** *adjective, adverb* floating on water or another liquid.

**afraid** *adjective* 1 frightened. *Are you afraid of the dark?* 2 apologetic. *I'm afraid you'll have to wait outside.*

**Africa** *noun* one of the Earth's seven continents.

Africa is a vast continent with deserts, high mountains, lush rainforests and grassy plains.

**African** *noun* a person who comes from Africa. **African** *adjective. An African sportswoman.*

**aft** *adverb* towards the back or stern of a ship or an aircraft. *The captain went aft.*

The plan shows the two flagpoles at the aft of the boat.

**after** *preposition* 1 later. *Come round after school.* 2 following behind. *The lamb ran after her.* **after** *adverb* later. *I met her the day after.*

**SPELLING NOTE**

*'Agenda' is a noun with a Latin plural ending (the singular form is 'agendum'). However, it is used as a singular noun. 'What's on the agenda for today?'*

**afternoon** *noun* the part of the day between midday and the evening.

**afterwards** *adverb* later. *We swam first and had breakfast afterwards.*

**again** *adverb* once more. *Please would you sing it again.*

**against** *preposition* 1 touching or next to something. *She propped the ladder against the wall.* 2 opposed to *They are against all hunting.* 3 in opposition to. *Who are you playing against tomorrow?*

**agate** *noun* a semi-precious stone striped with different colours.

This flint was used as a tool during the Iron Age.

**age** *noun* 1 the length of time that somebody has lived or that something has existed. *What age are you?* 2 a length of time in history. *The Iron Age.* **age** *verb* to become old.

**aged** *adjective* 1 (say ay-jid) very old. *An aged witch.* 2 ( rhymes with 'paged') having a certain age. *A woman aged 50.*

**ageism** *noun* unfair treatment of somebody because of their age.

**ageless** *adjective* showing no signs of getting old.

**agenda** *noun* a list of things that are to be discussed at a meeting.

**agent** *noun* 1 a person who organizes things and does business for other people. *A travel agent.* 2 a spy.

The secret agent has a glamorous image thanks to fictional characters like James Bond.

**aggression** *noun* forcefulness, or an attack without being provoked.

A

**aggressive** *adjective* violent and likely to attack people. *An aggressive dog.* **aggressor** *noun.*

**agile** *adjective* nimble. Moving quickly and easily. **agility** *noun.*

The ballet dancer displayed astonishing agility.

**agitate** *verb* 1 to make somebody nervous or worried. *She was agitated because she was late.* 2 to campaign or argue strongly for something. *They agitated for bigger pensions.* **agitator** *noun.*

**agitation** *noun* 1 a strong feeling of worry. 2 a campaign or protest.

**ago** *adverb* in the past. *Napoleon lived years ago.*

**agonizing** *adjective* very painful.

**agony** *noun* great pain or suffering.

**agoraphobia** *noun* (say agra-**foh**-bee-uh) a great fear of open spaces.

**agree** *verb* 1 to say 'yes' to something. *Angela agreed to babysit.* 2 to share the same ideas or opinions about something. *We all agree that cruelty is wrong.* **agree with** to be good for or to suit. *Curry doesn't agree with him.*

**agreeable** *adjective* pleasant. *An agreeable evening.*The opposite of 'agreeable' is 'disagreeable'.

**agreement** *noun* a promise or an understanding between two or more people, countries etc.

**agriculture** *noun* farming. **agricultural** *adjective.*

**DID YOU KNOW?**

*Do not use 'ago' with 'since' – you should use either one or the other. 'It's years since I last went to Greece,' or 'It was years ago that I last went to Greece.'*

Agriculture began when humans realized that sowing seeds would yield food crops. They settled to farm because it was more efficient than gathering food. Agriculture has shaped our land – not always for the better.

**aground** *adverb* If a boat runs aground, it touches the bottom of the sea or lake and cannot move.

**ahead** *adverb* 1 in front of. *She walked ahead.* 2 in the future. *Plan ahead.*

**aid** *verb* to help. **aid** *noun* 1 help or support, something that helps you do something. *He walks with the aid of a stick.* 2 money, food etc. for people in need.

**Aids** *noun* (short for or an acronym for acquired immune deficiency syndrome) a serious illness that destroys the body's natural defences (immunity) against disease and infection.

**ailment** *noun* an illness that is not very serious.

**aim** *verb* 1 to point at something, especially with a weapon. *He aimed the gun at the target.* 2 to plan or try to do something. *Alan aims to be the finest athlete in his school.* **aim** *noun* line of sighting. *He took aim.*

An archer takes careful aim. He fires arrows that are stored in a quiver belted to his waist.

**aimless** *adjective* without any purpose. *An aimless existence.*

**air** *noun* 1 the invisible mixture of gases that surrounds us and which we breathe. 2 general appearance or impression. *You have an air of calm about you.* 3 a tune. *The Londonderry Air.*

**air-conditioning** *noun* a system of controlling a building's temperature and keeping it cool in summer. **air-conditioner** *noun.* **air-conditioned** *adjective.*

**aircraft** any machine that flies, such as an aeroplane, glider or helicopter.

**aircraft carrier** *noun* a warship with a large deck from which aircraft can take off and land.

**airfield** *noun* a place where aircraft take off and land.

A plane lifts off the runway at an airfield. In the background are the airport buildings, including the control tower.

**airforce** *noun* the part of a country's forces that uses aircraft for fighting.

**airline** *noun* a company that owns aircraft and provides a regular service.

**airport** *noun* a place you leave from or arrive at when travelling by aeroplane.

**airscrew** *noun* an aircraft's propeller.

**airship** *noun* a large balloon with engines and that can be steered. Airships have a compartment beneath for carrying passengers or freight.

**airtight** *adjective* tightly sealed so that no air can get in or out. *Food can be preserved in airtight containers.*

**airy** (airier, airiest) *adjective* full of fresh air. *A large, airy room.*

The window is open, so a breeze can blow in, making the room cool and airy.

**aisle** *noun* (rhymes with 'pile') 1 a narrow passage where you can walk between rows of seats in an aeroplane, cinema etc., or rows of shelves in a supermarket.

**AMAZING FACT**

HMS Hermes, which was completed in 1913, was the first purpose-designed aircraft carrier.

**WORD HISTORY**

*'Alcohol' is one of a number of words that we have taken from Arabic. Others include 'algebra', 'assassin' and 'sofa'.*

**ajar** *adverb, adjective* When a door or window is slightly open, it is ajar.

**alarm** *verb* to make somebody suddenly afraid or anxious that something bad will happen. *They were alarmed to see smoke pouring out of their house.*

**alarm** *noun* 1 a sudden fear or danger. 2 a bell, buzzer etc. that warns people of danger. *A fire alarm.*

**Albania** *noun* a country in southeastern Europe.

The Albanian flag shows a black eagle against a red ground.

**Albanian** *noun* a person who comes from Albania. **Albanian** *adjective. Albanian wine.*

**albatross** (albatrosses) *noun* a large white seabird with long wings.

**album** *noun* 1 a blank book in which to keep photographs, stamps etc. 2 a CD or tape or record with a collection of songs.

Keeping a photograph album is a good way to record your family's history.

**alchemy** *noun* (say **al**-kem-ee) the medieval science of trying to turn metals into gold. **alchemist** *noun.*

**alcohol** *noun* 1 a colourless chemical liquid that catches fire quickly. 2 drinks such as beer, whisky and wine that contain alcohol and which can make people drunk.

**alcoholic** *adjective* containing alcohol. *alcoholic drink.* **alcoholic** *noun* a person who is addicted to alcohol and cannot stop drinking it.

**alcove** *noun* a recess or a small part of a room with the wall set back.

**ale** *noun* a kind of beer.

**alert** *verb* to warn people of a possible danger. *The doctor alerted her to the danger of eating too much.*

**alert** *adjective* quick-thinking and watchful of what is going on. **on the alert** ready for any possible danger.

**algae** *noun* (say **al**-ghee) water plants such as seaweed that have no root or stem.

**algebra** *noun* a branch of mathematics that uses symbols and letters to represent numbers. 3X + Y = 10 is an example of an algebraic equation.

**Algeria** *noun* a country in Africa.

The Algerian flag shows a red star and crescent moon against a green and white ground.

**Algiers** *noun* the capital of Algeria.

**alias** *noun* (say **ail**-ee-uss) a false or pretended name. **alias** *adverb* also known as. *Ron Chalky, alias Ronald White.*

**alibi** *noun* (say **al**-ee-beye) a proof or claim that a person charged with a crime was somewhere else when it was committed.

**alien** *noun* 1 a foreigner or stranger 2 a creature from space. **alien** *adjective. An alien being.*

It's difficult to imagine what an alien creature from outer space might look like....

**alight** *adjective* on fire, burning.

**alike** *adjective* similar. *The brothers are very alike.* **alike** *adverb* equally. *She treats them all alike.*

**alive** *adjective* living, not dead. **alive** *adverb* full of life.

**alkali** (alkalis) *noun* a chemical substance that can turn pink litmus paper blue. It reacts with acid to form a salt.

**SPELLING NOTE**

*'Allege' is a word that is often misspelt. People often put '–edge' at the end instead of just '–ege'.*

Some people suffer from allergies that cause them difficulty in breathing. They can often get relief by using an inhaler to breathe in a fine spray of medicine.

You can tell an alligator from a crocodile, because when an alligator shuts its mouth, the fourth pair of teeth on the lower jaw disappears into pits in the upper jaw. A crocodile's teeth stick out when its mouth is shut!

**all** *adjective* the whole amount or number. *All babies sleep a lot.* **all** *adverb* completely. *He was dressed all in black.* **all along** all the time. **all at once** 1 suddenly. *All at once the house shook.* 2 all at the same time. *Try not to spend it all at once.* **after all** all things considered. *After all he's no longer young.*

**Allah** *noun* the name given to God in the Islamic religion.

**allege** *verb* (say al-**edge**) to say that something is true or that somebody has done something, usually without having any proof. **allegation** (say al-eg-**ay**-shun) *noun.*

**allergy** *noun* an illness caused by substances such as dust, fur or certain foods, which do not normally make people ill. **allergic** *adjective* reacting badly to. *Andy is allergic to eggs.*

**alley** (alleys) *noun* a very narrow street with only one way out. **a blind alley** a situation without a way out.

**alliance** *noun* a union or friendly agreement between two or more different countries, political parties etc.

**alligator** *noun* a large reptile with a long body and tail, sharp teeth and strong jaws. Alligators are similar to crocodiles and live in rivers in the southern states of the US.

**alliteration** *noun* the repetition of the same sound at the beginning of each word in a phrase or sentence. *The Sun sank slowly.*

**allocate** *verb* to share out or to set aside something for a particular purpose. *The charity allocated £1,000 for the children's home.* **allocation** *noun.*

**allotment** *noun* a piece of land that people can rent for growing vegetables etc.

**allow** *verb* to permit or let somebody do something. *Nobody is allowed to smoke on public transport.*

**allowance** *noun* a fixed amount of money that is paid to somebody regularly. **make allowances for** to take someone's circumstances into account.

**alloy** (alloys) *noun* a metal made from mixing other metals. **alloy** *verb* to mix metals together.

AMAZING FACT

Alliteration is a powerful poetic device but many of familiar phrases and cliches are also examples of alliteration.

For example:
She's 'cool as a cucumber'.
He's 'fit as a fiddle'.

Some knives and forks are made of alloy.

**all right** *adjective* If you are all right, you are not ill, hurt or in difficulties. **all right!** *interjection* a phrase you can say when you agree to something. *'Will you do the washing up?' 'Oh, all right.'*

**allude** *verb* to talk about something in an indirect way or to mention it in passing. **allusion** *noun.*

**alluring** *adjective* very attractive, appealing and charming.

**alluvium** *noun* fertile soil washed down by rivers and floods.

**ally** *noun* (say **al**-eye) a country or person that helps and supports another. *America, France and Great Britain were allies in World War II.*

**almanac** *noun* a kind of calendar or book with information about the movements of the Moon and stars.

**Almaty** *noun* the capital of Kazakhstan.

**almond** *noun* the oval nut that grows on the almond tree.

Almonds are a nutritious source of food.

WORD HISTORY

*The word 'alphabet' comes from the first two letters of the Greek alphabet, 'alpha' and 'beta'.*

SPELLING NOTE

*Don't confuse 'already' with 'all ready' – 'Are you all ready to go?*

**almost** *adjective* very nearly but not quite. *Arthur is almost as tall as Angela.*

**alone** *adjective, adverb* with no other people, by yourself.

**along** *preposition, adverb* 1 from one end to the other. *They drove along the road.* 2 in the company of. *He brought his sister along.*

**alongside** *preposition, adverb* next to and by the side of. *He put the bench alongside the wall.*

**aloud** *adverb* in a voice loud enough to be heard. *Archie read the letter aloud.*

The teacher is reading aloud from a storybook to a group of children.

**alphabet** *noun* all the letters we use to write words, arranged in order. *Our alphabet begins with A and ends with Z.*

Aa Bb Cc Dd Ee
Ff Gg Hh Ii Jj
Kk Ll Mm Nn
Oo Pp Qq Rr Ss
Tt Uu Vv Ww
Xx Yy Zz

Our alphabet has 26 letters.

**alphabetical** *adjective* in order according to the alphabet. *The words in this dictionary are arranged in alphabetical order.*

**alphabetize** *verb* to put words in the order of the alphabet.

**already** *adverb* before this time. *I've already had my lunch.*

**alsatian** *noun* a large wolf-like breed of dog, also called a German Shepherd, often used as a guard dog and by the police.

**also** *adverb* as well, too. *He can play and also sing, but rather badly.*

A

**altar** *noun* a table used for religious ceremonies in a church or temple.

A cross and two candlesticks stand on the altar.

**alter** *verb* to change or to become different. *The village has altered a lot since my grandmother was a child.*

**alternate** *verb* (say **awl**-ter-nate) to happen by turn or to change first one way and then the other. *Barbara alternates between being happy and sad.* **alternate** *adjective* (say awl-ter-nat) *Alternate weeks of good weather and bad weather.* **alternately** *adverb.*

**alternative** *noun* 1 a choice between two or more things or possibilities. *The alternative to flying is to travel by train.* 2 different from what is usual. *Alternative medicine can involve taking herbs to cure illness.*

**although** *conjunction* even if, in spite of the fact. *Although it was snowing, we drove through the mountains.*

**altitude** *noun* the height above sea level.

**altogether** *adverb* 1 completely. *Are you altogether pleased with the plan?* 2 counting everybody or everything. *There are eight of us altogether.*

**aluminium** *noun* a lightweight silver-coloured metal.

Because aluminium is a very lightweight metal, it is much used in building planes.

**always** *adverb* something that always happens, happens all the time or very often. *Sally Remblance is always smiling.*

**SPELLING NOTE**
*Try not to confuse 'alternate' with 'alternative'.*

**SPELLING NOTE**
*Try not to confuse 'altogether' with 'all together'. 'The puppies sat all together in a line. It was altogether an amusing sight.'*

**a.m.** *abbreviation* the initial letters of the Latin words 'ante meridiem', which mean before noon. 7 a.m. is 7 o'clock in the morning.

**amalgam** *noun* a mixture of metals. *Dentists use an amalgam of mercury and silver to fill teeth.*

**amalgamate** *verb* to combine to make something bigger. *The two companies have amalgamated.* **amalgamation** *noun.*

**amateur** *noun* a person who does something such as paint or play games just for pleasure and not for payment. **amateur** *adjective. Amateur dramatics.*

Amateur dramatics can be fun for anyone who likes dressing up.

**amateurish** *adjective* not professional or skilful. *Debbie turned in a very amateurish design job.*

**amaze** *verb* to surprise or astonish somebody very much. **amazement** *noun. We watched the bungee jumping with fear and amazement.*

**amazing** *adjective* surprising. *What amazing tricks!*

**ambassador** *noun* an important official who represents his or her country abroad.

**amber** *noun* a hard yellowish-red fossil substance that you can see through, used in making jewellery. 2 the yellowish-red colour of amber.

Sometimes you can be lucky enough to find pieces of amber on the beach.

**ambi-** *prefix* meaning 'both'. **ambidextrous** able to use both hands equally well.

A

**ambiguous** *adjective* not clear, having more than one possible meaning. 'They are eating apples' is an ambiguous sentence. It could mean 'the apples are for eating', or 'those people are eating apples.' **ambiguity** *noun* of uncertain meaning.

**ambition** *noun* a very strong wish to do something well or to have success and fame. *Her burning ambition is to be a vet.* **ambitious** *adjective*.

**amble** *verb* to walk slowly. **amble** *noun*.

**ambulance** *noun* a vehicle for carrying people who are ill or injured.

You can often recognize an ambulance by a red cross on a white background.

**ambush** *verb* to wait in hiding in order to attack somebody by surprise. **ambush** *noun*.

**amend** *verb* to alter or correct something slightly in order to improve it. *Some laws are out of date and need amending.* **amendment** *noun*.

**American** *noun* a person who comes from the United States. **American** *adjective* belonging to the United States.

**amiable** *adjective* pleasant and friendly. **amiably** *adverb*.

**Amman** *noun* the capital of Jordan.

**ammonia** *noun* a strong-smelling gas that dissolves in water.

**ammonite** *noun* a fossilized shell shaped like a flat coil.

Ammonites were molluscs, related to squid. This is a fossilized ammonite.

**AMAZING FACT**

The amoeba feeds by flowing around and surrounding its food. It reproduces by splitting in half.

**DID YOU KNOW?**

*The preposition 'among' or 'amongst' is used when talking about more than two people: 'The teacher handed the books among the pupils.' Use 'between' when talking of two people. 'The twins shared the sweets between them.'*

**ammunition** *noun* things such as bullets and shells that can be fired from a gun or other weapon.

**amnesia** *noun* loss of memory.

**amnesty** *noun* a general pardon given by the state to, usually political, prisoners.

**amoeba** *noun* a microscopic, one-celled animal that moves about by constantly changing its shape.

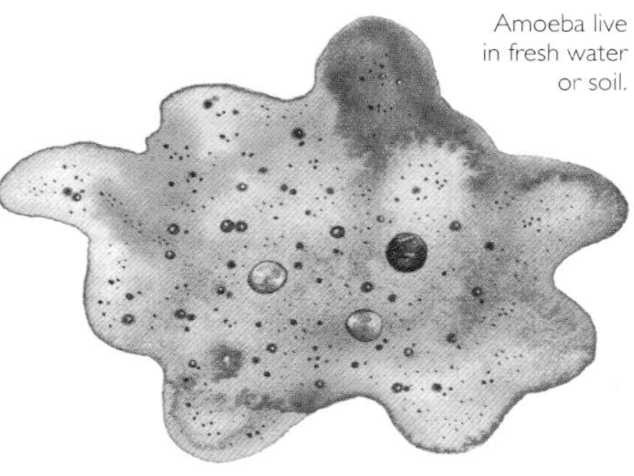

Amoeba live in fresh water or soil.

**among** *or* **amongst** *preposition* 1 in the middle of, surrounded by. *She lived among the islanders.* 2 one of. *Canada is among the biggest countries in the world.* 3 between. *Share these sweets among your friends.*

**amount** *noun* the quantity of something, or how much there is. *A large amount of money was spent on renovating the palace.*

**amount** *verb*. to add up to or be equal to. *The bill amounts to £50.*

**ampersand** *noun* the sign '&' that means 'and'.

**amphibian** *noun* an animal that lives mainly on land and breathes air but breeds in water. Frogs and newts are amphibians. **amphibious** *adjective*.

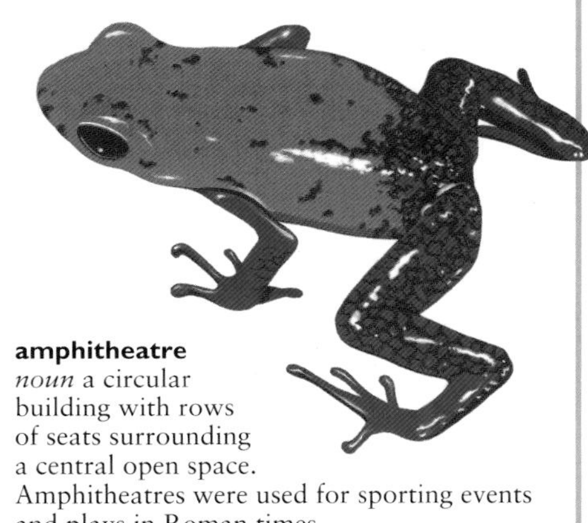

Frogs are amphibians. This is the poison arrow frog that lives in South American rainforests. The bright colours warn predators that they are poisonous and should be left alone.

**amphitheatre** *noun* a circular building with rows of seats surrounding a central open space. Amphitheatres were used for sporting events and plays in Roman times.

**ample** *adjective* more than enough, plenty. *The car has ample room for five passengers.*

A

**amplifier** *noun* an electrical device for making sounds louder.

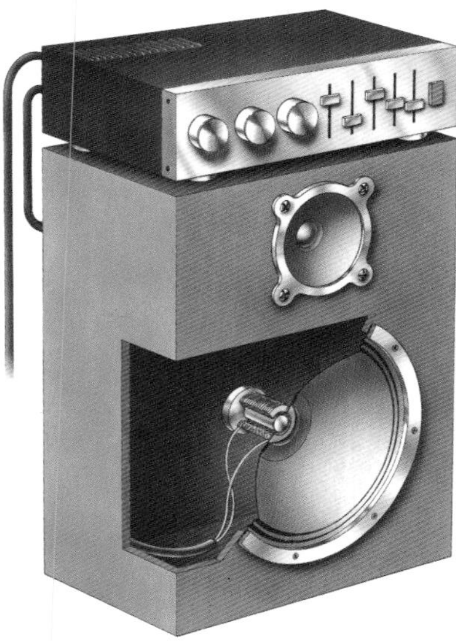

Small electrical signals from the pickup of a record player are strengthened in the amplifierer before being passed to the loudspeaker.

**amplify** (amplifies, amplifying, amplified) *verb* to make louder. **amplification** *noun.*

**amputate** *verb* to cut off a limb because it is diseased or badly broken. *He had his leg amputated in the war.* **amputation** *noun.*

**amputee** *noun* a person who has had a limb amputated.

**Amsterdam** *noun* the capital of the Netherlands.

Amsterdam is a city of fine old buildings and many canals.

**amuse** *verb* to make somebody laugh or smile or to keep them happy and busy. *They amused themselves by drawing, reading and listening to records.*

**amusement** *noun* 1 the feeling of being amused. 2 something that gives enjoyment or entertainment.

**WORD HISTORY**

*The word 'anaemia' comes from Greek words for 'no' ('an') and 'blood'. 'Anaesthetic' comes from the Greek for 'no' and 'feeling', and 'anarchy' from the words 'no' and 'ruler'.*

**SPELLING NOTE**

*In British English the '–yse' ending of 'analyse' should never be replaced with a '–yze' ending.*

**amusing** *adjective* something that is funny. *An amusing story.*

**anaemia** *noun* (say a-**neem**-ya) an illness caused by a shortage of red cells in the blood. **anaemic** *adjective. Anaemic people are always tired and look pale.*

**anaesthetic** *noun* (say an-iss-**thet**-ik) a substance that is given to patients before an operation to stop them feeling pain. **anaesthetize** *verb.*

**anagram** *noun* a word made by changing all the letters of another word. 'Horse' is an anagram of 'shore'.

**analyse** *verb* to examine something in great detail, often to find what it is made of. *She analysed the water and found that it was polluted.* **analysis** *noun.*

**analyst** *noun* a person who analyses something.

**anarchist** *noun* a person who believes there should be no government and no laws.

**anarchy** *noun* disorder and lack of control by the government.

**anatomy** *noun* 1 the structure of the body of an animal or person. 2 the study of the structure of the body of living things.

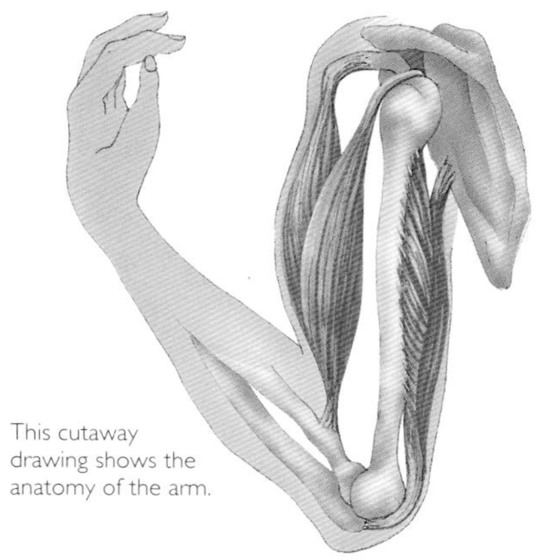

This cutaway drawing shows the anatomy of the arm.

**ancestor** *noun* Your ancestors are members of your family who lived before you. **ancestral** *adjective.*

**ancestry** *noun* all your ancestors, the people you are descended from. *Many Canadians have Scottish ancestry.*

In the Middle Ages a knight's shield displayed his coat of arms and told something of his ancestry.

A

**anchor** *noun* a heavy metal hook that is lowered on a long chain from a boat to lodge in the seabed and stop the boat from moving. *They threw the anchor overboard.*

**ancient** *adjective* (say **ane**-shunt) 1 very old. *Ancient ruins.* 2 of a time long ago. *Ancient Rome was the centre of a great empire.*

The arrangement of the seats and the cages for the wild animals in the Coliseum can tell us a lot about life in ancient Rome, where visiting the amphitheatre was a popular entertainment.

**Andorra** *noun* a country in the Pyrenees Mountains of Europe.

**Andorra la Vella** *noun* the capital of Andorra.

**anecdote** *noun* a very short, amusing story.

**anemone** *noun* a small woodland or garden plant, usually red, blue, white or purple.

**angel** *noun* 1 a spiritual being and messenger from God. 2 a very kind person. *Be an angel and bring me my glasses.* **angelic** *adjective.*

An angel descended from heaven and appeared to the shepherds.

**anger** *noun* a strong feeling you have when you are not pleased with somebody or something, bad temper.

**angle** *noun* a corner, the space between two straight lines that meet.

**angler** *noun* a person who fishes using a rod.

**Angola** *noun* a country in Africa.

The civil war in Angola has left a great many children orphaned.

**DID YOU KNOW?**

*You are usually 'angry' or 'annoyed' with somebody, but you are 'angry' or 'annoyed' at or about something.*

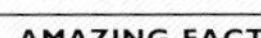

**AMAZING FACT**

Wedding anniversaries have different materials connected to them. The first anniversary is cotton, the fifth is wood and the twentieth is china.

**angry** (angrier, angriest) *adjective* annoyed and feeling full of anger. *I'm very angry with her for being so late.* **angrily** *adverb.*

**anguish** *noun* a very great feeling of sorrow or pain. **anguished** *adjective.*

**animal** *noun* 1 any living creature that is not a plant. 2 all mammals except human beings. **animal kingdom** one of the three basic groups into which all things in nature are divided. The other two are the mineral kingdom and the plant kingdom.

**animate** *adjective* (say **anny**-mut) alive. Animals and plants are animate. The opposite is 'inanimate'. Stones and metals are inanimate.

**animation** *noun* a kind of film, e.g. a cartoon in which photographs of a series of drawings of people and things are shown in quick succession and appear to move.

These three pictures form part of an animation sequence.

**Ankara** *noun* the capital of Turkey.

**ankle** *noun* the joint that connects your leg to your foot.

**annexation** *noun* the act of annexing a territory or of taking possession of it. *The annexation of Poland.*

**annexe** *noun* an additional building joined on to or near the main building. **annexe** *verb* to seize or take possession of.

**annihilate** *verb* to destroy completely. *The volcano annihilated all the farms for miles around.* **annihilation** *noun.*

**anniversary** *noun* a day each year when you remember something special that happened on the same day in a previous year. *A wedding anniversary.*

**announce** *verb* to make known publicly something important. *The king announced his abdication over the radio.* **announcement** *noun.*

**announcer** *noun* a person who makes an announcement. *A radio announcer.*

A

**annoy** *verb* to irritate or make somebody angry. **annoyance** *adjective*.

**annual** *adjective* happening every year or once a year. *Annual medical check-up*. **annual** *noun* 1 a plant that lives for one year only. 2 a book or magazine that appears once a year. **annually** *adverb*.

A birthday is an annual event. Most people are given presents on their birthday.

**anoint** *verb* to smear oil on somebody, usually as part of a religious ceremony.

**anonymous** *adjective* without the name being known or given. *An anonymous author*. **anonymity** *noun*.

**anorak** *noun* a zip-up waterproof jacket with a hood.

**anorexia** *noun* an illness that makes the sufferer afraid of becoming fat and so not want to eat anything. **anorexic** *adjective*.

**another** *adjective* 1 one more *He ate another sweet*. 2 different. *Can you find me a dress in another colour?*

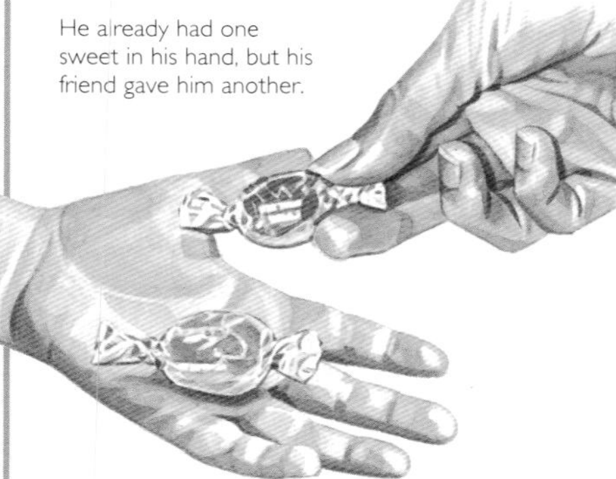

He already had one sweet in his hand, but his friend gave him another.

**answer** *verb* 1 to speak or write in reply to a question or to something that somebody has said. *'Where are you going?' 'To the stables,' she answered*. 2 to respond to a signal etc. *'Can you answer the phone?'*

**answer** *noun* 1 reply. *Have you had an answer to your letter?* 2 a solution. *I can't find an answer to this problem*. **answer back** to give a rude or cheeky reply to somebody.

**answerable** *adjective* responsible for.

**WORD HISTORY**

*'Answer' is made up of two Anglo-Saxon words: 'swear' and 'an' (meaning against). So the whole word meant 'to swear against'. 'Answer' has two synonyms: to reply and to respond.*

**SPELLING NOTE**

*Try not to confuse the prefixes 'ante–' meaning before, e.g. 'anteroom', a small room giving access to another, and 'anti–', against or opposite, e.g. 'anti-aircraft'.*

**answering machine** *noun* a machine that records telephone messages from people who ring you when you are out.

**ant** *noun* a small sociable insect that lives with other ants in an underground colony. **anthill** *noun* a heap of earth made by ants above their nest.

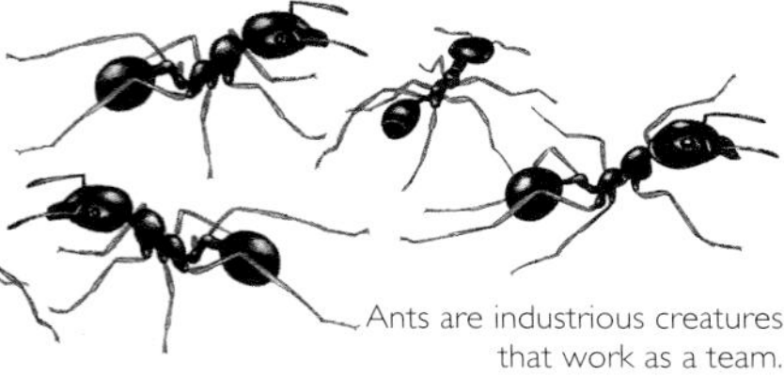

Ants are industrious creatures that work as a team.

**antagonist** *noun* an enemy or opponent.

**antagonize** *verb* to make somebody angry, unfriendly or hostile to you. **antagonism** *noun*. **antagonistic** *adjective*.

**Antananarivo** *noun* the capital of Madagascar.

**Antarctic** *noun* the area around the South Pole. **Antarctic** *adjective*. *An Antarctic expedition with sledges and husky dogs*.

**Antarctica** *noun* one of the Earth's seven continents, situated at the South Pole.

**ante-** *prefix* before. 'Antenuptial' means before marriage and 'antenatal' means before birth.

**anteater** *noun* a toothless mammal from South America that uses its long snout and long sticky tongue to catch ants and other insects on which it feeds.

**antelope** *noun* any one of several kinds of deer-like animals of Africa and Asia. They include gazelles, impala and springboks.

Antelopes are fast running animals that live in South Africa's grassy savanna.

**antenna** (antennae) *noun* 1 one of the feelers on an insect's head. 2 an aerial.

**anthem** *noun* a hymn or a song written for special occasions. 'The Star-Spangled Banner' is the national anthem of the United States.

A

**anther** *noun* part of a flower's stamen where pollen matures.

**anthology** *noun* a collection of poems, stories etc.

**anthropology** *noun* the study of human beings, especially their customs and beliefs.

**anti-** *prefix* against, opposed to, opposite. *Anti-Communist demonstrations.*

**antibiotic** *noun* a powerful medicine that kills harmful bacteria that cause diseases.

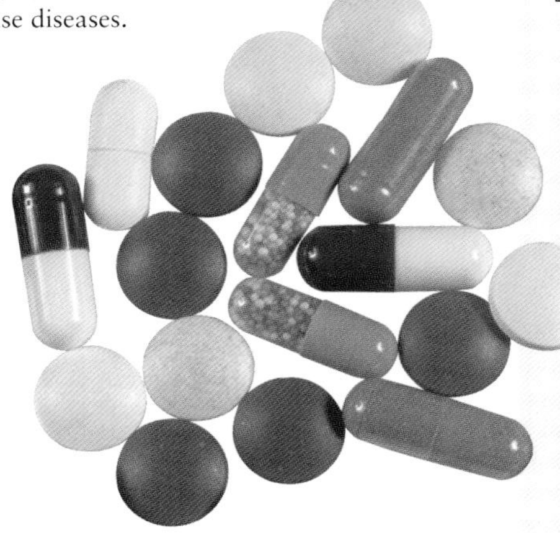

It is important not to take antibiotics too often, or the body will get immune to them.

**AMAZING FACT**

In 1928, Alexander Fleming dicovered that penicillin could kill harmful germs. It was first used extensively in WWII on soldiers with serious wounds and saved many lives.

**anticipate** *verb* to look forward to or expect something to happen. *We anticipated that these books would sell well, so we stocked up.* **anticipation** *noun.*

**anticlockwise** *adjective, adverb* moving in the opposite direction to the hands of a clock. Not clockwise.

**anticyclone** *noun* air moving away from an area of high pressure, usually bringing calm weather. The opposite of 'anticyclone' is 'cyclone'.

**antidote** *noun* a medicine that acts against the harmful effects of poison.

**antifreeze** *noun* a chemical that you put in a car's radiator to stop the water freezing.

**Antigua and Barbuda** *noun* a country in the West Indies.

The colourful flag of Antigua and Barbuda shows that the Sun and the sea are part of everyday life.

**antiquated** *adjective* old and out of date. *Antiquated rules.*

**DID YOU KNOW?**

*The opposite of 'antique' is 'modern'. Another word meaning old is 'antiquated', but whereas 'antique' is old and valuable, 'antiquated' is old and almost laughably useless.*

**antique** *noun* something that is old and also very valuable. **antique** *adjective* valuable, old. *Antique furniture.*

Valuable antiques, like this chest of drawers, are often sold at auctions.

**antiquity** *noun* ancient times, especially the times of Ancient Greece and Rome.

**antiseptic** *noun* a substance that kills harmful germs and prevents infection and disease. **antiseptic** *adjective* clean and germ-killing. *Antiseptic soap.*

**antler** *noun* one of the branching horns on a stag's head.

During the mating season, stags fight by locking antlers until one brings the other to its knees.

**antonym** *noun* a word that has the opposite meaning to another word. 'Hot' is the antonym of 'cold'.

**anus** *noun* the opening at the end of the bowels through which solid food waste leaves the body.

**anxious** *adjective* 1 worried, concerned. **anxiety** *noun.* 2 eager. *Annie is extremely anxious to help.*

**any** *adjective* 1 one of. *Take any record you like.* 2 some. *Is there any pudding left?* 3 at all. *Are you any happier?* 4 every. *Any athlete could jump that fence.* (**anybody anyhow anyone anything anytime anyway anywhere**).

**apart** *adverb* 1 separate and at a distance away from each other. *The two villages are about a mile apart.* 2 into parts or pieces. *Andrea took her bike apart.* **apart from** except for. *Apart from a few showers the weather is lovely.*

**apartment** *noun* a flat (especially US).

A

**apathy** *noun* a lack of interest or feeling.

**ape** *noun* an animal like a monkey but with no tail. Gorillas and chimpanzees are apes.

Gorillas are apes that live in the rainforests of West and Central Africa.

**ape** (apes, aping, aped) *verb* to imitate how somebody behaves, usually in a silly way.

**aperture** *noun* a small hole or opening.

**apex** (apexes) *noun* the highest point.

**aphid** or **aphis** *noun* a tiny insect that damages or kills plants by sucking juices from them.

**Apia** *noun* the capital of Samoa.

**apologize** *verb* to say that you are sorry for doing something. *We apologized sincerely for causing so much trouble.* **apology** *noun.* **apologetic** *adjective.*

**apostle** *noun* one of the original twelve disciples or followers of Christ.

The apostles listened to Christ's teachings and spread the Christian message after his death.

**apostrophe** *noun* (say a-**poss**-tra-fee) a punctuation mark (') that shows that letters have been left out of a word (*we've* for *we have*) or to show the ownership of something (*Margaret's pencil*).

**appal** (appals, appalling, appalled) *verb* to cause horror or shock. *I was appalled by the chairman's rude and unkind remarks.* **appalling** *adjective.*

**apparatus** *noun* the tools or equipment needed for a particular purpose.

**DID YOU KNOW?**

*Apostrophes are often used – for clarity – to form the plural of a number of short words, e.g. do's and dont's, but dos and donts are acceptable too.*

Inflammation of the appendix is common. The usual treatment is to remove the appendix by surgery.

**apparent** *adjective* 1 obvious and easily seen. *It was quite apparent that she was bored.* 2 seeming to be true or real.

**apparition** *noun* a ghost or something that you think you have seen.

**appeal** *verb* 1 to ask for something urgently and seriously. *They appealed for help for the orphans.* 2 to be interesting or attractive. *The plan doesn't appeal to me at all.* **appealing** *adjective.* 3 to ask for a legal decision to be changed by going to a higher court. **appeal** *noun.*

**appear** *verb* 1 to come into view. *He suddenly appeared from behind the wall.* 2 to seem. *Fiona appears to be quite ill.* 3 to take part in. *Actors appear in films and plays.*

**appearance** *noun* 1 the act of coming into view. *The sudden appearance of the bull frightened everybody.* 2 the way somebody or something looks.

**appendicitis** *noun* painful inflammation of the appendix.

**appendix** (appendixes or appendices) *noun* 1 a small tube inside the body at the end of the intestines. 2 additional information after the main text at the end of a book.

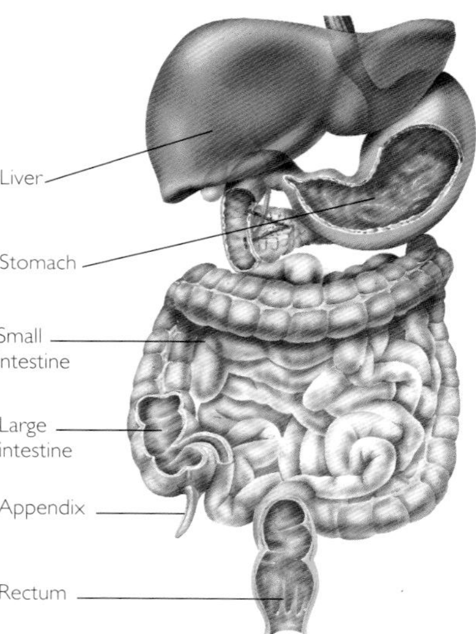


**appetite** *noun* 1 hunger or a desire for food. 2 a desire or enthusiasm.

**appetizing** *adjective* smelling and looking so good that you want to eat it.

**applaud** *verb* to show that you like something by clapping your hands. **applause** *noun.*

**apple** *noun* the hard, round fruit of the apple tree. **in apple pie order** in perfect order.

The Golden Delicious is the most popular apple in the world.

A

**appliance** *noun* a tool or piece of equipment designed to do a specific job, especially in the home, such as a vacuum cleaner.

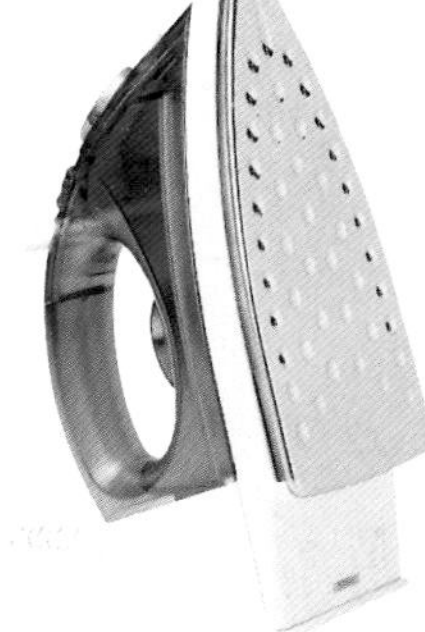

The steam iron is one of the most commonly owned electrical appliances.

**applicant** *noun* a person who applies or asks for something. *There were lots of applicants for the job.*

**apply** (applies, applying, applied) *verb* 1 to ask for something formally. *She applied for the job of editor.* 2 to be relevant or suitable to a person or situation. *These rules apply to everyone.* 3 to spread on. *She applied the ointment to the cut.* **application** *noun.*

**appoint** *verb* to choose somebody to do a job. *Mrs Bartholomew has been appointed chief accountant.*

**appointment** *noun* 1 a job. 2 a time and place that you have arranged to see somebody.

Write your appointments down to help you remember them.

**appreciate** *verb* 1 to know about and understand the value or good points of something. *She appreciates good food.* 2 to be grateful for something. *I appreciate all the valuable help you've given me.* 3 to rise in value. *House prices have appreciated.* **appreciation** *noun.*

**appreciative** *adjective* showing gratitude.

**approach** *verb* 1 to come nearer. *She approached the stray dog.* 2 to speak to somebody about a request or an offer. *Dean approached his uncle to ask for some money towards a new car.*

**approach** *noun* 1 a road or path leading somewhere. 2 the course followed by an aeroplane before landing.

**AMAZING FACT**

Apricots are originally from the Far East. They were cultivated in Armenia for many years and were later introduced to Europe and the US from there.

**WORD HISTORY**

*Like all the months of the year, 'April' comes from a Latin word. It is named after 'Aprilis', meaning to open. April was the second month in the early Roman calendar.*

**approachable** *adjective* easy to talk to and willing to listen. The opposite of 'approachable' is 'unapproachable'.

**appropriate** *adjective* suitable and correct for a certain place or event. *Trainers are appropriate footwear for running.*

**approval** *noun* 1 good opinion. *Does this plan meet with your approval?* 2 permission. *You have to get approval from the council to build a summerhouse.*

**approve** *verb* to agree to, to be in favour of something. *She doesn't approve of my clothes.* The opposite is disapprove.

**approximate** *adjective* nearly but not exactly correct. *What is the approximate length of the Nile?*

**apricot** *noun* a yellowish-orange fruit like a small peach.

Apricots grow best in a warm climate. This fruit is rich in vitamin A.

**April** *noun* the fourth month of the year. April has 30 days. **April fool** somebody who has been fooled by a trick played on them on the morning of 1 April, April Fools' Day.

**apron** *noun* a piece of clothing you wear around the front of your body to protect the clothes underneath when you are cooking or cleaning etc.

**apt** *adjective* 1 suitable. *An apt time to leave.* 2 likely to do something. *He's apt to fall asleep when he's bored.*

**aptitude** *noun* an ability to learn and do something well.

**aqualung** *noun* equipment that divers wear to breathe underwater.

**aquarium** *noun* a glass tank for keeping fish and other water animals, or a building (in a zoo) where many such tanks are kept.

It is fun to breed tropical fish in an aquarium at home.

**aquatic** *adjective* living or growing in water, or to do with water. *Aquatic plants.*

**aqueduct** *noun* a bridge with a canal or pipes for carrying water across a valley etc.

**Arab** *noun* a person who comes from Arabia and other parts of the Middle East and North Africa. **Arabian** *adjective*.

**Arabic** *noun* the language spoken by the Arabs. **Arabic numerals** the numerical figures 1 to 9.

**arable** *adjective* ploughed and suitable for growing crops. *Arable land.*

**arbitrary** *adjective* decided by a person's random opinion and not according to reason or rules. *An arbitrary decision.*

**arc** *noun* 1 a curved line. 2 in geometry, a section of the circumference of a circle.

**arcade** *noun* 1 a row of arches supported on columns. 2 a covered passageway usually with small shops on either side. 3 a place where there are slot machines for games etc. *An amusement arcade.*

**arch** *noun* a curved part of a building, bridge or wall. *verb* to form the shape of a curve. *The rainbow arches across the sky.*

This spectacular arch leads to the Murder Corridor in Alnwick Castle, Northumberland.

**arch-** *prefix* chief or most important. *archbishop.*

**archaeology** or **archeology** *noun* (say ar-kee-**ol**-oh-jee) the study of the past and how people lived, by the examination of remains of buildings, tools etc. **archaeological** *adjective. An archeological dig.* **archaeologist** *noun.*

**DID YOU KNOW?**

*Arabic numerals were originally brought to Europe from India by the Arabs. Before that, people in Europe used Roman numerals: I II III IV V VI VII VIII IX X.*

**archaic** *adjective* (say ar-**kay**-ik) very old or antiquated.

**archer** *noun* a person who shoots with a bow and arrow.

**archery** *noun* a sport in which people shoot at a target with a bow and arrow.

This archer is using a longbow. Nowadays, archery is a popular competitive sport, testing steadiness of aim.

**archipelago** *noun* (say ar-kee-**pel**- agoh) a group of small islands.

**architect** *noun* a person who designs and plans buildings.

**architecture** *noun* 1 the skill or activity of designing buildings. 2 a style of architecture. *Greek architecture.*

**Arctic** *noun* the region around the North Pole. **Arctic** *adjective*.

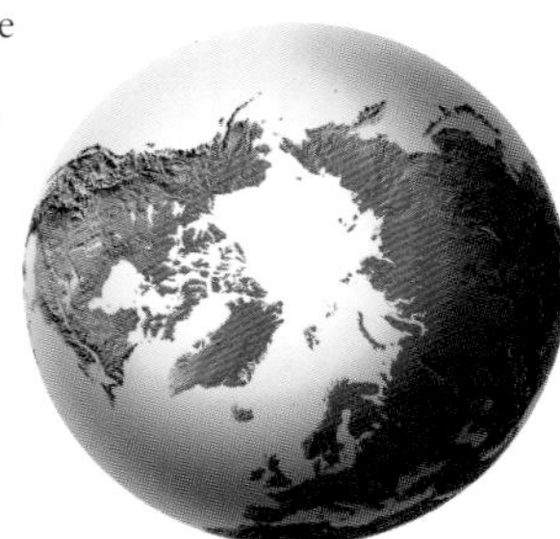

The Arctic Circle is an imaginary line around the northern part of the globe.

**arduous** *adjective* difficult and tiring to do. *Arduous work.*

Stonehenge is a site of special archaeological interest. The stones are said to have been brought across the River Severn to the south of England from the Preselli Mountains in Wales.

A

**area** *noun* 1 the size of a flat surface. *The barn has an area of 15 square metres.* 2 a part of a place. *The residential area of Bristol.* 3 a part of somewhere used for a special purpose. *Non-smoking areas.*

**arena** *noun* a large area with seats around it where you can watch sports and various other entertainments.

**Argentina** *noun* a country in South America.

**Argentinian** *noun* a person who comes from Argentina. **Argentinian** *adjective.*

**argue** *verb* 1 to talk angrily with somebody you disagree with, to quarrel. 2 to give your reasons for or against something. *Mrs Earnshaw argued against joining the club.* **argument** *noun.*

**argumentative** *adjective* often arguing and tending to disagree for the sake of it.

**arid** *adjective* very dry and having little rainfall. Deserts are arid.

**aristocracy** *noun* the nobility, the social class that aristocrats belong to.

**aristocrat** *noun* a person of high social rank and with a title, a nobleman or noblewoman.

**arithmetic** *noun* the study and use of numbers, especially addition, subtraction, division and multiplication.

**ark** *noun* a ship in the Bible that Noah built for his family and animals to live in during the Great Flood.

Tradition tells that one pair of each species of Earth's animals went aboard the ark and survived the flood.

**arm** *noun* 1 the part of your body between your shoulder and your hand. 2 anything shaped like an arm. *The arm of a chair.* **arm in arm** with arms joined in friendship.

**arm** *verb* to supply with weapons (arms). **armed** *adjective* carrying weapons. *The armed forces.*

**armada** *noun* a fleet of ships, especially the fleet that was sent from Spain to attack England in 1588.

**armadillo** (armadillos) *noun* a South American mammal covered with a shell of bony plates.

**WORD HISTORY**

*'Arena' comes from the Latin word for sand. Sand was put on central areas of amphitheatres where Roman gladiators fought.*

**WORD HISTORY**

*'Armadillo' is a Spanish word meaning a small armoured man.*

**armaments** *plural noun* guns, ammunition and other war supplies.

**armchair** *noun* a comfortable chair with supports for the arms.

**Armenia** *noun* a country in West Asia.

**armour** *noun* 1 a strong metal or leather covering that protects a soldier's body in battle. *Knights in armour.* 2 a metal protection for tanks, ships etc. **armoured** *adjective.*

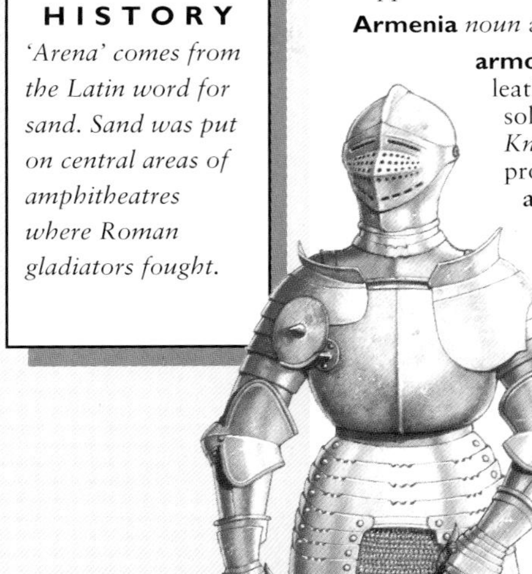

This suit of armour is made of shaped metal plates fitted carefully together. It dates from around 1450. The most expensive suits of armour were decorated with engraved patterns or polished gold.

**armoury** (armouries) *noun* a place in which to store arms.

**armpit** *noun* the hollow place under your shoulder.

**arms** *plural noun* 1 weapons. 2 a coat of arms, a symbol or design on a shield etc. used as the badge of a noble family, city etc. **up in arms** very angry and ready to fight.

**army** *noun* a large number of soldiers who have been trained to fight on land.

**aroma** *noun* a pleasant, distinctive smell. **aromatic** *adjective. The chef liked to use plenty of aromatic herbs.*

**around** *adverb* on all sides. *He looked around but there was nobody there.* **around** *preposition* in all directions, in a circle. *She walked around the room.*

**arouse** *verb* 1 to stir up or excite feelings. *The terrible news aroused great anger in everybody.* 2 to wake somebody up.

**arrange** *verb* 1 to put in a certain order or position. *He arranged his books in alphabetical order.* 2 to plan or prepare something. *Can you arrange a meeting for next week?* **arrangement** *noun.*

**arrest** *verb* 1 to hold somebody as a prisoner. *The police arrested her for shop-lifting.* 2 to stop or prevent. *Progress was arrested because Richard did not bring the digger.* **arrest** *noun.* **arresting** *adjective* attractive, holding your attention.

**arrival** *noun* 1 the act of arriving or reaching a place. 2 a person or thing that has arrived. *The new arrivals were welcomed by the committee.*

**arrive** *verb* to reach somewhere. *They arrived home last night.*

**arrogant** *adjective* having an unpleasantly high opinion of yourself. **arrogance** *noun*.

**arrow** *noun* 1 a stick with a point at one end that you shoot from a bow. 2 a sign that tells you which way to go.

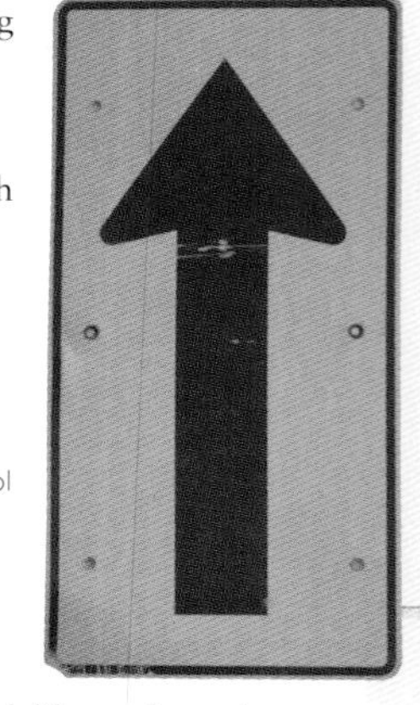

The head of an arrow points in the direction you need to go. An arrow is also a useful symbol meaning 'this way up'.

**arsenic** *noun* a very powerful poison made from a metallic element.

**arson** *noun* the crime of deliberately setting fire to a house etc. **arsonist** *noun* someone who intends criminal damage by fire. *The arsonist was sent to gaol.*

**art** *noun* 1 the ability to create beautiful paintings, sculpture, music, poetry etc. 2 an activity requiring a great skill. *The art of good conversation.* **artful** *adjective* 1 skilful. 2 cunning.

**artery** *noun* one of the thick-walled tubes that carries blood from your heart to all parts of your body.

Artery

The heart's job is to pump blood to the lungs and then all round the body. The right side of the heart takes in blood from the body and pumps it to the lungs. The left side of the heart takes blood filled with oxygen from the lungs and pumps it to the rest of the body.

**DID YOU KNOW?**

*'An' is the form of the indefinite article used before words beginning with a vowel, as in 'an apple', and before words beginning with a vowel sound, as in 'an hour'.*

**arthritis** *noun* a disease that makes joints painful and swollen. **arthritic** *adjective*.

**arthropod** *noun* an animal such as an insect, spider or crab, with a skeleton on the outside of its body.

**article** *noun* 1 an object of some kind. *A belt is an article of clothing.* 2 a piece of writing published in a newspaper etc. 3 the words 'a' or 'an' (indefinite articles) and 'the' (definite article).

**articulate** *adjective* able to express thoughts and feelings clearly in words. **articulate** *verb* to pronounce words clearly.

**articulated lorry** *noun* a lorry made in two parts, a cab and a trailer.

An Australian road train is a very powerful articulated truck that often has several trailers.

**artificial** *adjective* not found in nature but made by people. *These flowers are artificial because they are made of plastic.*

**artillery** *noun* large guns used by the army.

**artist** *noun* a person who can paint, draw or produce other works of art.

This Russian artist has set up his easel outside and is painting from life.

**artiste** *noun* a professional entertainer in a circus, theatre etc.

**artistic** *adjective* liking art or showing skill in creating art. *An artistic family.*

**artistry** *noun* the skill of an artist. *This pianist's artistry is much admired.*

**a.s.a.p.** *abbreviation* as soon as possible.

**ascend** *verb* (say az-**send**) to go or move up, to climb. *The plane ascended quickly after take-off.* **ascent** *noun*. The opposite of 'ascend' is 'descend'.

**ASCII** *abbreviation* American Standard Code for Information Interchange (a computer term).

**ash** (ashes) *noun* the grey powder that is left after something has burned completely. *Wood ash is good for the garden.*

**ash** *noun* a hardwood tree with a silver-grey bark. *A whole forest of ash trees.*

The ash is a fast growing tree that provides a beautiful pale wood often used to make furniture.

The ash is easily recognized by its divided leaves in pairs on the stem.

**ashamed** *adjective* feeling guilty or embarrassed about something.

**Ashkhabat** *noun* the capital of Turkmenistan.

**ashore** *adverb* on shore or land. *The sailors stepped ashore on the island.*

**Asia** *noun* one of the Earth's seven continents.

**Asian** *noun* a person from Asia. **Asian** *adjective. Asian countries include India and Sri Lanka.*

**ask** *verb* 1 to speak in order to get the answer to a question. 2 to make a request or to say that you would like somebody to do something for you. 3 to invite. *Ask him to the meeting on Monday.*

**asleep** *adjective* sleeping. *He was still asleep when I called, although it was after lunch.* The opposite of 'asleep' is 'awake'.

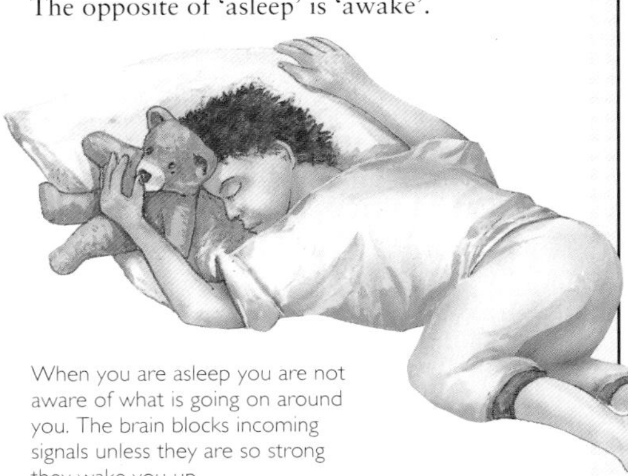

When you are asleep you are not aware of what is going on around you. The brain blocks incoming signals unless they are so strong they wake you up.

**WORD HISTORY**

*The word 'assassin' – and note its two double 's's – comes from an Arabic word meaning an eater of the drug hasish. Many people under the influence of the drug committed murders.*

**AMAZING FACT**

Although aspirin has been used as a painkiller for many years, it was not known how the drug works until recently.

**SPELLING NOTE**

*Try not to confuse 'assent' (meaning agreement) with 'ascent' (meaning a climb or an act of ascending).*

**Asmera** *noun* the capital of Eritrea.

**asp** *noun* a small poisonous snake.

Queen Cleopatra of Egypt is said to have committed suicide by putting an asp to her breast.

**aspect** *noun* a side, feature or look of something. *Let's consider every aspect of the problem before making a decision.*

**asphalt** *noun* a tar-like substance that is used for making road surfaces etc.

**aspiration** *noun* an ambition or goal in life.

**aspirin** *noun* a medicine that helps to ease pain and reduce fever.

**ass** (asses) *noun* 1 a wild donkey. 2 a stupid person.

Asses are used in many countries as beasts of burden.

**assassin** *noun* a person who assassinates or murders. *The assassin was arrested.*

**assassinate** *verb* to murder somebody, especially an important person like a king or president. **assassination** *noun.*

**assault** *verb* to attack someone violently. **assault** *noun. It was a ferocious assault.*

**assemble** *verb* 1 to bring or collect together in one place. *A small crowd assembled in the square.* 2 to put or fit the parts of something together.

**assembly** *noun* 1 a meeting, often regular like a school assembly. 2 putting together different parts of something to make a whole. *A car assembly plant.*

**assent** *verb* to agree to something. **assent** *noun* agreement. *He gave his assent.*

A

**assert** *verb* to declare or state something forcefully so people pay attention. **assertion** *noun. He made a false assertion about me.*

**assess** *verb* to judge the quality or value of something. *He assessed the damages.* **assessment** *noun.*

This wine taster is assessing the quality of a glass of red wine. He must smell the wine as well as taste it.

**asset** *noun* somebody or something that is useful or valuable. *She is good at maths and this is a great asset to the finance company.*

**assist** *verb* to help. **assistance** *noun. Can I be of any assistance?*

The girl is giving her mother valuable assistance with the washing-up.

**assistant** *noun* 1 a person who helps. *My aunt is the head teacher's assistant.* 2 a person who serves in a shop. *A shop assistant must be polite to the customers.*

**associate** *verb* 1 to spend time with a group, to work together. *He associates mainly with sports people.* 2 to connect two things in your mind. *He associates snow with skiing.*

**association** *noun* 1 a club or a group of people working together, an organization. 2 a connection made in your mind.

**assorted** *adjective* of different kinds. Mixed. *We found assorted oddments of clothing strewn all over the lawn.* **assortment** *noun.*

An assortment of sweets usually contains chocolates, toffees and sweets with fruity centres.

**SPELLING NOTE**

*'Asthma' comes from a Greek word meaning panting or breathing hard.*

**assume** *verb* 1 to accept something as true without question, to suppose. *We assumed she had no money because she dressed so badly.* **assumption** *noun.* 2 to take over. *The vice-president assumed absolute control of the country.*

**assurance** *noun* 1 a confident statement or promise. *He gave every assurance that the bridge was safe.* 2 confidence. *She is playing the piano now with more assurance.* 3 insurance.

**assure** *verb* to tell somebody something confidently and definitely. *The nurse assured him that he would soon be better.*

**asterisk** *noun* a small star (*) used in printing.

**astern** *adverb* towards the stern or back of a boat.

**asteroid** *noun* a small planet that orbits the Sun between Mars and Jupiter.

Over 3,200 asteroids have been identified so far. The biggest, Ceres, is 1,000 km across, but most are much smaller.

**asthma** *noun* a chest illness that makes it difficult to breathe. **asthmatic** *adjective.*

**astonish** *verb* to surprise somebody very much, to amaze. **astonishment** *noun.*

**astound** *verb* 1 to surprise or shock somebody very much. *She was astounded to hear that he had failed the final examination.*

**astride** *preposition* with one leg on each side of something. *He sat astride the horse.*

**astrologer** *noun* a person who studies the stars to try to predict the future. *The astrologer predicted a win.* **astrology** *noun*.

**astronaut** *noun* a man or woman who travels in a spacecraft.

Astronauts on the Moon could jump high in heavy spacesuits because the Moon is much smaller than Earth and its gravity is weaker.

**astronomer** *noun* a person who scientifically studies the planets, the stars and other heavenly bodies.

**astronomical** *adjective* 1 concerned with astronomy. 2 very large. *The house prices were astronomical.*

**astronomy** *noun* the scientific study of the planets and stars.

It is not clear who invented the telescope, but Galileo was the first person to put it to use in the study of astronomy.

**astute** *adjective* clever and quick of mind, shrewd. *She is an astute businesswoman.*

**Asuncion** *noun* the capital of Paraguay.

**asylum** *noun* 1 a refuge or a place to shelter from persecution etc. *The refugees were given political asylum.* 2 in the past, a place for treating people with mental illnesses.

**ate** *verb* past tense of eat. *He ate too much.*

**atheism** *noun* the rejection of a belief in God or gods.

**WORD HISTORY**

*Atlas is named after a Greek god who was made to carry the heavens on his shoulders as a punishment for his rebelliousness.*

**atheist** *noun* a person who does not believe in God or gods.

**Athens** *noun* the capital of Greece.

**athlete** *noun* a person who is good at athletics. **athletic** *adjective*.

**athletics** *plural noun* competitive sports such as running, jumping, vaulting and throwing the javelin or discus.

People from many countries compete in athletics championships.

**atlas** (atlases) *noun* a book of maps.

**atmosphere** *noun* 1 the air that surrounds and protects the Earth. 2 the air in a particular place. *The atmosphere in this city is badly polluted.* 3 the general feeling of a place. *The hotel has a warm and friendly atmosphere but is excessively expensive.*

**atoll** *noun* a coral island in the shape of a ring surrounding a lagoon.

**atom** *noun* the smallest possible part of a chemical element that can take part in a chemical reaction. An atom consists of a nucleus surrounded by electrons. **atomic** *adjective*. *Atomic energy.*

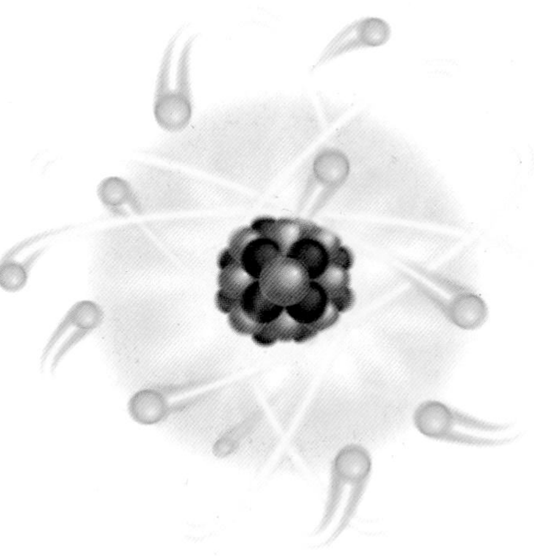

The atom was first split by the New Zealand-British physicist Ernest Rutherford in 1919.

A

**atrocious** *adjective* very bad, terrible. *Atrocious spelling mistakes.*

**atrocity** *noun* a very cruel act, a crime.

**attach** *verb* to fasten or join two things together. *She attached another link to the chain.* **to be attached to** to be very fond of somebody or something.

**attachment** *noun* 1 something extra that can be attached. *The vacuum cleaner has a special attachment for cleaning upholstery.* 2 fondness or friendship.

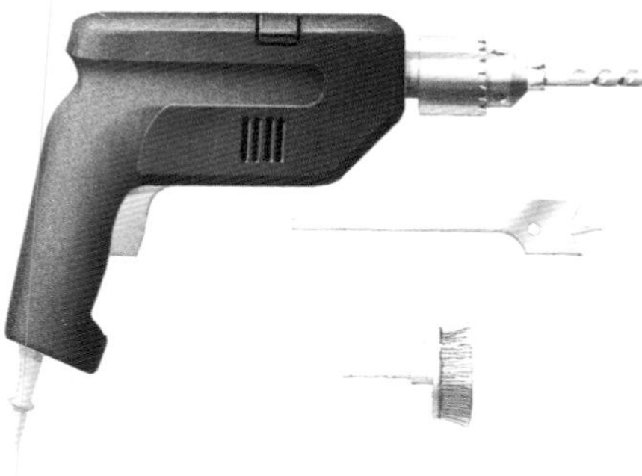

Electric drills usually come with several attachments designed for different jobs.

**attack** *verb* 1 to use violence against a person or place. *The army attacked the village.* 2 to criticize or speak strongly against. *The architects were attacked for their bad design.*

**attack** *noun* 1 a violent attempt to hurt someone or something. 2 a fit or sudden illness. *An asthma attack.*

**attain** *verb* to reach or achieve something, to succeed. *She attained a ripe old age.* **attainment** *noun.* **attainable** *adjective.*

**attempt** *verb* to try to do something. *Jo attempted to climb the tree.* **attempt** *noun.*

**attend** *verb* to be present at a place or happening. *We all attended the public meeting.* **attendance** *noun.* **attend to** 1 to concentrate. *Please attend to what I'm saying.* 2 to deal with or look after. *He attended to the accident victims.*

A crowd is gathering in the square to attend a public meeting.

**SPELLING NOTE**

*Whether words like 'attendance', 'acquaintance' and 'intelligence' should end in '–ance' or in '–ence' causes people a lot of trouble. There are no easy rules. You just have to learn the spelling!*

**attention** *noun* giving thought or care or being interested in something. *She gave all her attention to her studies.* **attract attention** to make somebody notice something.

**attentive** *adjective* 1 taking care to notice or listen. 2 kind and gentle. *He was very attentive to his grandfather's needs.*

**attic** *noun* a room just under the roof of a house.

The attic is well insulated to conserve energy.

**attitude** *noun* an opinion or a way of thinking about somebody or something, a way of behaving. *She has a very mean attitude towards her children.*

**attract** *verb* 1 to like and find somebody or something interesting. *Katie was attracted to the boy next door.* 2 to catch the attention of. *The elephant caught the child's attention and he stopped crying.* 3 to make something come nearer. *Bright flowers attract butterflies.* **attraction** *noun.*

**attractive** *adjective* 1 interesting and pleasing. *An attractive idea.* 2 good-looking. *An attractive boy.*

**aubergine** *noun* (US eggplant) a vegetable with a shiny purple skin.

Aubergines grow in warm climates. They are a favourite vegetable in Mediterranean lands and in the Middle East.

**auburn** *adjective* reddish-brown. *Jill had long auburn hair.*

**auction** *noun* a public sale in which goods are sold to the person who will bid (offer to pay) the highest price. **auction** *verb*.

An auctioneer is someone in charge of an auction. Items such as paintings are sold to the highest bidder.

**audible** *adjective* loud enough to be heard. The opposite of 'audible' is 'inaudible'.

**audience** *noun* a group of people who watch or listen to something. *The play is attracting huge audiences.*

**audio-visual** *adjective* using recorded sound and pictures for teaching etc. *The school's audio-visual equipment includes CDs and cassettes.*

Audio-visual material such as CDs and cassettes make learning more fun.

**audition** *noun* a short performance to test whether an actor, singer or musician is suitable for a particular job.

**auditorium** *noun* the place in a theatre, concert hall etc. where the audience sits.

**August** *noun* the eighth month of the year. August has 31 days.

**aunt** *noun* Your aunt is the sister of your father or mother, or the wife of your uncle.

**au pair** *noun* a young foreign person, usually a young woman, who lives for a short time with a family to learn the language and in return looks after the children and does light housework. *The au pair was looking after three children.*

**AMAZING FACT**

Australia is the smallest continent and the largest island in the world.

**WORD HISTORY**

*August was named in honour of the Roman Emperor, Augustus Caesar.*

**SPELLING NOTE**

*The name 'Australia' comes from the Latin word 'australis', meaning southern.*

**austere** *adjective* simple and without luxury, severe. **austerity** *noun*.

**Australasia** *noun* one of the Earth's seven continents.

**Australia** *noun* a country in Australasia.

**Australian** *noun* a person who comes from Australia. **Australian** *adjective*. *The Australian outback.*

**Austria** *noun* a country in Central Europe.

The red and white stripes of the Austrian flag also appear on the country's eagle crest.

**Austrian** *noun* a person from Austria. **Austrian** *adjective*. *The Austrian alps.*

**authentic** *adjective* real, genuine and not copied. *An authentic painting by Picasso.* **authenticity** *noun*.

The archaeologists found an authentic African mask.

**author** *noun* a person who writes a book, article, poem, play etc.

**authoritative** *adjective* 1 showing power and authority. 2 reliable and coming from somebody in authority. *An authoritative atlas contains up-to-date information.*

**authority** *noun* 1 the power to tell others what to do. *The police have the authority to breathalyze people.* 2 a group or organization that has the power to control what is going on. *The local authority refused our planning application.* 3 an expert. *She's an authority on dolls' houses.*

**authorize** *verb* to give somebody power or permission to do something.

**autism** *noun* an abnormal condition in children in which they are unable to respond to or communicate with people. **autistic** *adjective*.

**auto-** *prefix* self, self-caused, or same.

**autobiography** *noun* a book that somebody writes about her or his own life. **autobiographical** *adjective*.

**autograph** *noun* a person's name written in their own handwriting, a signature. **autograph** *verb*. *The pop star autographed our programmes.*

The autograph of a famous person could one day be worth a lot of money.

**automatic** *adjective* 1 working by itself without the control of a human being. *An automatic central-heating system.* 2 done without thinking about it. *Breathing is automatic.* **automatically** *adverb*.

**automation** *noun* using machines instead of people to do monotonously repetitive jobs in factories etc.

**SPELLING NOTE**

*Try not to confuse 'adverse' (which means harmful or unfavourable) with 'averse' (which means unwilling or disinclined).*

**automobile** *noun* a motor car (mainly US).

**autopsy** *noun* the examination of a body after death, a post-mortem.

**autumn** *noun* the season of the year between summer and winter.

**available** *adjective* 1 obtainable and ready to be used. *Raspberries are not available all the year round.* 2 free to see people. *She'll be available to interview you next week.* **availability** *noun*.

**avalanche** *noun* a huge mass of snow and ice suddenly falling down a mountain.

**avenge** *verb* to harm or punish somebody in return for a wrong they have done to somebody else. *He avenged his father's murder.* **avenger** *noun*.

**average** *noun* in maths, the sum of several amounts divided by the number of amounts. The average of 4+6+9+13 = 8. (4+6+9+13=32 divided by 4 = 8.) **average** *adjective* 1 normal, ordinary. *It's been a very average week.* 2 not extreme or special. *Her work is about average.*

**averse** *adjective* opposed to or disliking. *Averse to hard work.*

**aversion** *noun* a strong dislike. *He has a great aversion to jellyfish.*

**aviary** *noun* a large cage for keeping birds.

**aviation** *noun* the science of building and flying aircraft.

Automobiles are produced in a factory by automation. Robots rather than humans put them together.

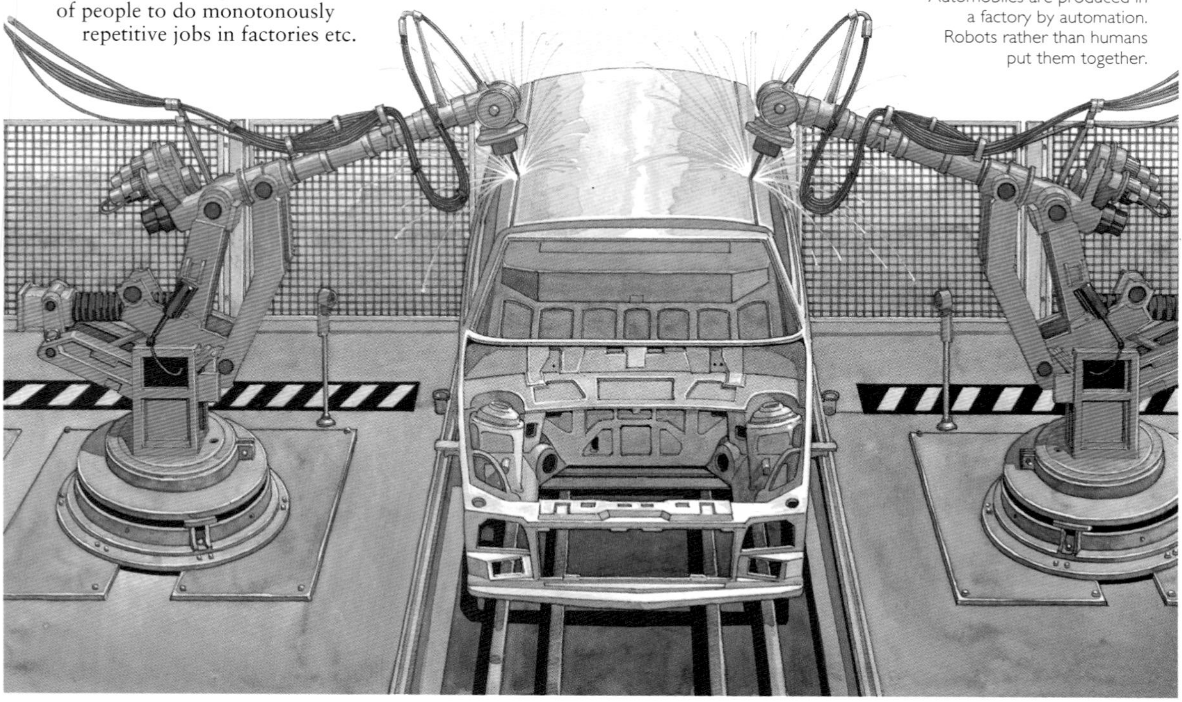

**aviator** *noun* (old-fashioned) an aircraft pilot. *The aviator wore flying goggles and a leather hat with earflaps.*

The Sopwith Camel was flown by British aviators in World War I.

**avid** *adjective* 1 keen, enthusiastic. *An avid reader.* 2 greedy. *The pupil waved her arm in the air, avid for the teacher's attention.*

**await** *verb* to wait for, to expect. *We are awaiting the arrival of the president.*

**awake** *adjective* not sleeping. **awake** (awakes, awaking, awoke, awoken) *verb* to wake up. *I awoke at dawn.*

**award** *noun* something, such as a prize or money, given to somebody for doing well. **award** *verb* to present. *She was awarded first prize for singing.*

She was awarded a gold medal for coming first in the swimming contest.

**aware** *adjective* knowing about. *Andy wasn't aware of the dangers of mountaineering.* **awareness** *noun.*

**away** *adverb* 1 not here, not at home. *He's gone away for a few weeks.* 2 at a distance. *The next town is miles away.* 3 into the distance. *The music faded slowly away.* 4 ceaselessly. *She worked away at her exercises.* **do away with** *verb* to get rid of.

**awe** *noun* a mixture of wonder, fear and respect. *She is in awe of her teacher.* **awe-inspiring** *adjective* causing a feeling of awe. *An awe-inspiring poem.*

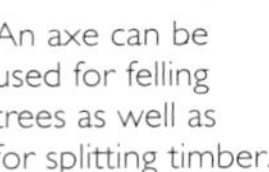

**SPELLING NOTE**

*An award is something that you win or are given for a special reason. 'She was awarded the Nobel peace prize.' A reward is something you get for doing something useful or helpful. 'The police are offering a reward for any information about the accident.'*

**awful** *adjective* 1 very bad or unpleasant. *What an awful smell!* 2 very great. *She's done an awful lot of knitting.*

**awfully** *adverb* very. *I'm awfully sorry.*

**awkward** *adjective* 1 clumsy and embarrassed. *The boy feels awkward among adults.* 2 not convenient. *We are eating, so this is an awkward time to call.* **awkwardness** *noun.*

**awoke** past tense of awake. *He awoke when the alarm went off.*

**axe** *noun* a tool with a sharp blade on a long handle used for chopping wood.

An axe can be used for felling trees as well as for splitting timber.

**axiom** *noun* a statement that everyone generally agrees to be true.

**axis** *noun* 1 a real or imaginary line through the middle of an object around which it spins. *The Earth rotates on its axis, which passes through the North and South Pole.* 2 a line along the side or bottom of a graph.

The Earth tilts on its axis as it spins through space.

**axle** *noun* the rod that goes through the centre of a wheel and on which it turns.

**Azerbaijan** *noun* a country in West Asia.

**azure** *adjective* bright blue like an unclouded sky.

B

# Bb

**babble** *verb* to chatter and talk in a confused and excited way.

**babe** *noun* a baby. *A babe in arms.*

**baboon** *noun* a large monkey from Africa.

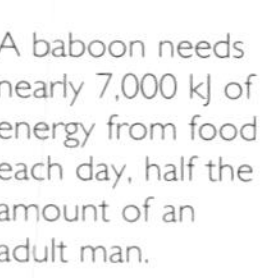

A baboon needs nearly 7,000 kJ of energy from food each day, half the amount of an adult man.

**baby** *noun* a very young child. *The baby's first smile.* **babyish** *adjective.*

**babysitter** *noun* a person who is paid to look after children when their parents are away. **babysit** (babysits, babysitting, babysat) *verb.*

**bachelor** *noun* a man who has never been married. *A bachelor pad.*

**back** *noun* 1 the part of your body along the spine between your shoulders and bottom, also the top part of an animal. *She climbed on to the horse's back.* 2 the opposite side to the front, the part situated behind. **back** *adjective* at the rear. *The back door was wide open and the dog had run away.* **back-breaking** very tiring. *Back-breaking work.*

The staple food in Southeast Asia is rice. Cultivating the paddy fields is back-breaking work.

**back** *adverb* to an earlier place or time. *He thought back to when he was young.*

**AMAZING FACT**

The human backbone, or spinal column, is a flexible S-shaped arrangement allowing us to bend forward and backward and to stand up without falling over.

**SPELLING NOTE**

*The commonest error in spelling 'bachelor' is to put a 't' before the 'ch'.*

**back** *verb* 1 to move backwards. *She backed away from the fierce dog.* 2 to support or help. *Will you back me?* 3 to put money (bet) on an animal etc. *Uncle Ben backed the winning horse in the race.* **back down** to give up or change your mind. **put your back into** to work hard. **back out** to decide not to keep an agreement. *You promised to come to the party. You can't back out now.*

**backbone** *noun* the set of joined bones along the back. The spine.

The backbone is made up of individual bones called vertebrae. They interlock with each other in sliding joints.

**backfire** *verb* to have the opposite result to the one intended. *The plan backfired and the robbery was discovered.*

**background** *noun* 1 the part of a scene or picture that is behind the main objects or people. *The picture shows a lake with mountains in the background.* 2 the different facts that surround an event and which help to explain it. 3 a person's past experience or family history and education. *She comes from a farming background.*

**backpack** *noun* a large bag that climbers, campers etc. carry on their backs. **backpacker** *noun.*

This backpack is ready for the hike. It is stuffed with warm clothes and has a bed-roll strapped beneath it.

**backward** *adjective* 1 towards the back. *A backward look.* 2 slow to learn or develop. *This baby is backward at walking.*

**backwards** *adverb* 1 towards the back. *She took a step backwards and fell over the rug, breaking her leg.* 2 in the reverse way from normal. *Counting backwards.*

**backyard** *noun* a yard with a hard surface at the back of a house. In US a garden with a lawn at the back of a house.

**bacon** *noun* thin slices of salted or dried meat from a pig.

**bacteria** *plural noun* microscopic living things. Some bacteria cause diseases.

B

**bad** (worse, worst) *adjective* 1 not good. Unpleasant. *I've got some bad news.* 2 naughty, wicked. *You're a bad girl to tell so many lies.* 3 harmful. *Eating too many sweets is bad for you.* 4 hurt or in bad health. *I've got a bad leg.* 5 rotten and not good to eat. *The food has gone bad.* 6 serious. *A bad accident.* **go bad** to decay.

**badge** *noun* a piece of cloth, metal or plastic that is pinned or sewn on to clothes, with a picture or message on it. *All employees must wear a badge with their name on it.*

**badger** *noun* a wild animal with grey fur and a black and white striped head. Badgers live in underground holes called sets and are active at night.

Badgers' hands and feet are broad with wide claws for digging.

**badger** *verb* to annoy somebody by pestering them to do something.

**badminton** *noun* a game like tennis that is played by hitting a shuttlecock over a high net with rackets.

**baffle** *verb* to confuse or puzzle. *I was baffled by so many questions and couldn't think of what to say.* **baffling** *adjective*.

**bag** *noun* a container for carrying things. *Never put a plastic bag on your head.*

**baggage** *noun* bags and suitcases that travellers use. Luggage.

**baggy** *adjective* baggy clothes are too big and so hang in loose folds.

**Baghdad** *noun* the capital of Iraq.

**bagpipes** *plural noun* a musical instrument. Air is squeezed from a bag into pipes on which the music is played.

Bagpipe music is traditional in Scotland at Hogmanay, or New Year.

**Bahamas** *noun* a country in the West Indies.

**Bahrain** *noun* a country in Southwest Asia.

**bail** *noun* one of a pair of pieces of wood placed on top of the stumps on a cricket wicket. *The bowler knocked off the bail.*

**AMAZING FACT**

A badger's sett is an elaborate underground network of tunnels and rooms. There are usually several entrances.

**WORD HISTORY**

*'Badminton' is named after Badminton House in England where the game was first played in the middle of the 19th century.*

**bail** *noun* money that is paid to allow somebody accused of a crime to go free until their trial. *She was released on bail for £100,000.*

**bail** *verb* to scoop water from a boat to prevent it sinking. **bail out** (also bale out) to jump from an aircraft, using a parachute.

**bait** *noun* 1 a small amount of food used to attract fish, birds or animals to help you catch them. 2 something that is tempting.

**bake** *verb* to cook in an oven. *He baked a cake for their birthday tea.*

**baker** *noun* a person who works in a bakery and makes and sells bread, cakes etc.

This decorative tile shows a scene in a bakery in Seville, Spain.

**Baku** *noun* the capital of Azerbaijan.

**balance** *verb* to keep something steady and not let it fall over. **balance** *noun*. *Jack has good balance. He can stand on one leg without falling over.*

**balance** *noun* 1 an instrument for weighing things. 2 the amount of money somebody has in the bank.

**balcony** *noun* a platform on the outside wall of a building with a wall or railings around it.

A beautiful girl stands on the balcony waiting for her lover.

**bald** *adjective* (rhymes with 'crawled') with little or no hair on the head. **baldness** *noun*.

**bale** *noun* a large bundle of something soft. *A bale of hay.*

**ball** *noun* 1 a round object used to play games. 2 something that is round in shape. *A cannon ball.* 3 a grand, formal party at which people dance.

**ball bearings** *plural noun* very small steel balls that help different parts of a machine move smoothly against each other.

**ballad** *noun* a poem or song that tells a story. *He sang a romantic ballad.*

**ballerina** *noun* a female ballet dancer.

**ballet** *noun* (say **bal**-ay) a form of highly artistic dancing, usually telling a story, and performed on a stage. **ballet-dancer** *noun*.

**balloon** *noun* 1 a small bag made of thin material such as plastic or rubber and filled with gas. *The children blew up red and blue balloons.* 2 a large bag made of strong material and filled with gas or hot air (hot-air balloon), which carries people in a basket underneath. **balloonist** *noun*.

A colourful hot air balloon drifts through a blue sky.

**ballot** *noun* a way of voting secretly in an election. *The ballot box was full of votes.*

**Bamako** *noun* the capital of Mali.

**bamboo** *noun* a giant tropical grass-like plant with a hollow, woody stem used to make furniture etc.

**ban** (bans, banning, banned) *verb* to forbid or say that something must not be done. *She was banned from driving for six months.* **ban** *noun*.

**banana** *noun* a long tropical fruit with soft white flesh and a yellow skin when ripe.

**band** *noun* a group of musicians or a group of people who get together for a purpose. *A band of hooligans.* **band together** *verb*. *The villagers banded together to stop the motorway being built.*

**band** *noun* a narrow strip of material that goes around something. *An elastic band.*

**bandage** *noun* a strip of material used to tie around an injury or to cover a wound. **bandage** *verb*. *The nurse bandaged his knee.*

**Bandar Seri Begawan** *noun* the capital of Brunei.

**bandit** *noun* a robber who works with others in a group or band. *The travellers were attacked by bandits.*

Gangs of bandits often hide in remote wooded hills and ambush unsuspecting travellers.

### WORD HISTORY

*'Ballot' comes from an Italian word meaning little ball. Little balls were dropped into a container to vote – white for yes, black for no. Hence the expression 'to blackball' or vote against somebody.*

**bang** *noun* 1 a sudden, very loud noise. *She shut the lid with a bang.* 2 a heavy knock. **bang** *verb*. *He banged on the door.*

**banger** *noun* 1 (slang) a sausage. 2 (slang) an old car. 3 a firework that makes a loud banging noise.

**Bangkok** *noun* the capital of Thailand.

Visitors to Bangkok often shop for local produce in Thailand's floating markets.

**Bangladesh** *noun* a country in South Asia.

**Bangui** *noun* the capital of the Central African Republic.

**banish** *verb* to send somebody away, usually from their own country, as a punishment. **banishment** *noun*.

**banister** or **bannister** *noun* a hand-rail along the side of a staircase.

**Banjul** *noun* the capital of Gambia.

**bank** *noun* 1 a place that looks after money for people and which provides financial services. **bank** *verb*. *She banked all her savings.* 2 a place for storing things or leaving things for collection. *A bottle bank.* **bank holiday** in UK a public holiday when banks close. **bank on** to rely on. *You can bank on me. I'll be there.*

**bank** *noun* 1 the sides of a river, lake or canal. 2 a piece of raised, sloping land.

**bankrupt** *adjective* unable to pay debts. **bankruptcy** *noun*.

**banner** *noun* a large flag with a design or message on it, hung up or carried on a pole or between two poles.

The suffragettes carried banners demanding votes for women.

**banquet** *noun* a large, formal dinner, usually for a special occasion. *The mayor held a banquet in honour of the king.*

**baptize** *verb* in the Christian religion, to sprinkle or pour water over a person as a sign that they have become a Christian. To christen. **baptism** *noun*. **baptismal** *adjective*.

**bar** *noun* 1 a long, straight piece of metal or wood. *A cage with iron bars.* 2 a room or a long table or counter in a pub or hotel at which drinks etc. are served. 3 a solid block of something. *A bar of soap.* 4 the equal sections into which music is divided.

**bar** (bars, barring, barred) *verb* 1 to keep out. *Children are barred from the premises.* 2 to block. *She barred the door.*

**Barbados** *noun* a country in the West Indies.

Neptune's trident appears on the flag of the island nation of Barbados.

**barbarian** *noun* a cruel, rough, uncivilized person. In the ancient world barbarians were people who were not Greek or Roman.

**barbaric** or **barbarous** *adjective* brutally cruel. **barbarity** *noun*.

**barbecue** *noun* an outdoor party at which food is cooked on a grill over a charcoal fire. **barbecue** *verb*.

**barbed wire** *noun* fencing wire with sharp spikes sticking out of it.

**barber** *noun* a men's hairdresser.

**bar code** *noun* an arrangement of thick and thin lines and spaces printed on goods in shops, containing information about price, size etc., and which can be 'read' by a computer.

Bar codes save time at a supermarket checkout.

**bare** *adjective* 1 uncovered, naked. *bare arms.* 2 empty. *The removal van has gone and the house is bare.* **bare** *verb* to expose. *The dog bared its teeth.*

**barely** *adverb* scarcely, only just. *She could barely lift the heavy box.*

**bargain** *noun* 1 something that you buy at a price that is cheaper than usual. *This book is a real bargain!* 2 an agreement between two people in return for something.

**bargain** *verb* to haggle or argue over the price of something.

**barge** *noun* a long boat with a flat bottom, used on canals mainly to carry heavy goods.

**barge** *verb* to push your way roughly through people. To bump clumsily into people or things. *Jim barged his way through the crowd and grabbed the money.*

**AMAZING FACT**

Barometers measure the air pressure and interpret its changes. If the pressure is high, that generally means that the weather is good, low pressure signals changing or bad weather.

**WORD HISTORY**

*'Barbarian' comes from the Greek word 'barbaros', meaning foreign. The Greeks invented the word because it resembled the strange sounds of the languages spoken by non-Greeks.*

**SPELLING NOTE**

*Try not to confuse the spellings of 'bare', meaning naked, and 'bear', the verb meaning to support.*

**bark** *noun* the sharp sound made by a dog, fox etc. **bark** *verb*. *The dog barked at the postman and then bit his leg.*

**bark** *noun* the rough, hard covering of the trunk and branches of trees.

**barley** *noun* a grain used for food and in making beer.

**bar mitzvah** *noun* a religious ceremony that takes place on a Jewish boy's 13th birthday to celebrate his becoming an adult.

**barn** *noun* a farm building for keeping animals or storing crops.

**barnacle** *noun* a shellfish that fixes itself firmly to rocks and the sides of boats.

**barometer** *noun* an instrument that measures the air pressure and shows changes in the weather.

The barometer was invented in 1643 by Italian scientist Torricelli, who discovered air pressure.

**baron** *noun* a nobleman or peer of the lowest rank.

**baroness** *noun* the wife of a baron or a noblewoman or peer of the lowest rank.

**baroque** *noun* a highly ornate style of European architecture of the late 16th to early 18th century.

**barracks** *plural noun* buildings where soldiers live.

**barrage** *noun* 1 a dam or barrier built across a river. 2 continuous heavy gunfire. 3 a huge number of something. *A barrage of complaints.*

**barrel** *noun* 1 a large container with curved sides for storing liquids such as beer. *The beer barrels are in the cellar.* 2 the tube of a gun through which a bullet is fired.

**barren** *adjective* the soil of barren land is so poor that crops cannot grow.

**barricade** *noun* a barrier that has been quickly put up to block a road. **barricade** *verb* to block. *The demonstrating students barricaded the streets.*

A barricade hastily put together out of any objects to hand blocks the road.

B

**barrier** *noun* a fence, railing or some other obstacle designed to stop people or things getting past.

**barrow** *noun* 1 a cart that you can push or pull. 2 a cart from which fruit, vegetables etc. are sold in the street.

The builders' barrow is full of sand.

**barrow** *noun* a prehistoric mound of earth and stones over a grave.

**barter** *noun* to exchange goods for other goods rather than for money. To swap.

**base** *noun* 1 the lowest part of something, especially the part on which it stands. *The base of the vase.* 2 the headquarters or main place from which things are controlled. *The expedition returned to base.* **base** *verb. The company is based in Edinburgh.*

**base** *verb* to use something as a basis or starting point. *The new musical is based on a famous novel.*

**baseball** *noun* an American game played with a bat and ball by two teams of nine players.

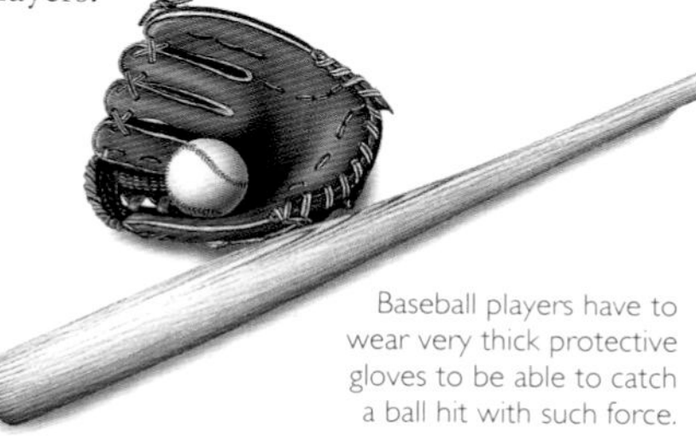

Baseball players have to wear very thick protective gloves to be able to catch a ball hit with such force.

**basement** *noun* a room or an area below the level of the street.

**bashful** *adjective* shy and lacking in confidence. **bashfulness** *noun.*

**basic** *adjective* 1 the most important and necessary. *The basic rules of grammar.* 2 very simple, essential. *Basic needs.*

**basically** *adverb* 1 concerned with what is basic or fundamental. 2 most important.

**basil** *noun* a herb used to flavour food.

**basin** *noun* 1 a large bowl for mixing food. 2 a bowl fixed to a wall in a bathroom where you can wash. 3 A river basin is the area of land it gets its water from.

**AMAZING FACT**

Bats are the only mammal that is capable of genuine flight.

There is great variety among the 2000 + species of bats. Some have wingspans of only about 10 inches while others have a wingspan of up to four or five feet.

Bats have leathery wings and very poor eyesight. They hunt and navigate using ultrasonics and echo-location.

**DID YOU KNOW?**

*'Basically' is far too often used nowadays to mean simply 'importantly' – or even nothing at all. Try to avoid sentences like: 'Basically, I think it's time I went to bed.'*

Cotton and silk can be dyed with brilliant colours to make batik.

**basis** (bases) *noun* the main principle or idea behind something.

**basket** a woven container with a handle.

**basketball** *noun* a game for two teams in which the players try to score points by throwing a ball through a high net at each end of the court.

**bass** *adjective* 1 the lowest sounds in music. *Deep bass notes.* 2 A double bass is a very large violin-shaped instrument that plays very low notes.

**Basseterre** *noun* the capital of St Kitts and Nevis.

**bat** *noun* a mouse-like animal with wings that flies at night hunting for insects.

**bat** *noun* a piece of wood or metal that players use to hit a ball in games like baseball, cricket and table tennis. **bat** (bats, batting, batted) *verb. Nick batted the ball to Jim.*

**batch** *noun* a group of things that were made at one time or have to be dealt with together. *A large batch of letters arrived for my grandmother this morning.*

**bath** *noun* a long, deep container that you fill with water and sit in to wash your whole body. **bath** *verb.*

**bathe** *verb* 1 to go swimming in the sea. 2 to wash a part of the body very gently. *The nurse bathed the wound.* 3 (US) to take a bath or to bath.

**bathroom** *noun* a room with a bath or shower and usually a basin and toilet.

**batik** *noun* an Eastern way of printing designs on cloth by covering parts of the cloth with wax patterns and dyeing the rest.

**baton** *noun* 1 a short, thin stick the conductor uses to beat time for an orchestra or choir. 2 a short stick that is passed from one runner to the next in a relay race.

**battalion** *noun* an army unit made up of smaller units called companies.

**batter** *noun* to hit something heavily again and again. *Battered to death.* **batter** *adjective. A battered old car.*

**batter** *noun* a mixture of flour, milk and eggs for making pancakes etc.

**battery** *noun* 1 a container that makes and stores electricity. You put batteries in things such as radios and torches to make them work. 2 a number of big guns. 3 a large group of small cages in which hens or other animals are kept for the mass production of eggs or meat. *Battery farming.*

**battle** *noun* a fight between two armies or opposing groups. **battle** *verb. She battled against poor health.*

**battleship** *noun* a large, heavily armed warship. *Battleship grey.*

**bay** (bays) *noun* a part of the seashore that curves inwards. An inlet. **bay window** a window that forms a recess by sticking out from the wall of a house. **at bay** facing an enemy and fighting them off. *A stag at bay.*

**bay** *adjective* a reddish-brown colour of a horse. **bay** *noun. This horse is a bay.*

**bayonet** *noun* a knife that can be attached to the end of a rifle.

**bazaar** *noun* 1 a market in Eastern countries. 2 a sale to raise money for something. *A church bazaar.*

**AMAZING FACT**

Bears are omnivores, which means that they eat plants and animals. They do not have very good eyesight but have an excellent sense of smell.

**WORD HISTORY**

*The word 'bayonet' is named after the town of Bayonne in France, where the weapons were originally made.*

**BC** *abbreviation* Before Christ, used for dates before the birth of Jesus Christ. *Alexander the Great died in 323 BC.*

**beach** *noun* the area of sand or pebbles where the land meets the sea.

**beacon** *noun* a light or fire used as a guide or warning. *A beacon was lit on the hilltop.*

**bead** *noun* a small piece of glass or other material with a hole through it, which can be threaded on string or wire to make a necklace etc.

**beak** *noun* the hard pointed outer part of a bird's mouth. *The eagle has a hooked beak.*

**beaker** *noun* 1 a drinking mug without a handle. 2 a glass vessel used for pouring liquids in chemistry.

**beam** *noun* a large, heavy bar of wood, metal or concrete used for supporting the roof or floors of a building.

**beam** *noun* a band or ray of bright light. *The beam from the torch dazzled us.*

**bean** *noun* a plant that produces seeds (beans) that grow in a pod and are eaten as a vegetable. *Broad beans.* **full of beans** lively and full of energy.

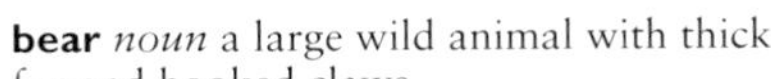

Beans are one of the world's most nutritious foods. Young broad beans can be eaten raw, and even the pods can be made into a soup. Older beans are lightly steamed or boiled.

Men selling beaten metalware wait for their customers. When buying goods at a bazaar it is customary to haggle over the prices.

**bear** *noun* a large wild animal with thick fur and hooked claws.

**bear** (bears, bearing, bore, borne) *verb* 1 to support the weight of something. *That little chair won't bear your heavy weight.* 2 to carry from one place to another. *Seeds borne by the wind.* 3 to produce. *The plum tree bears fruit in the autumn.* 4 to accept or tolerate something unpleasant. *She cannot bear rudeness.* **bear with** to be patient with. *Bear with me and I'll tell you.*

**beard** *noun* the hair on a man's face.

**beast** *noun* 1 a large wild animal. 2 (slang) a cruel, unpleasant person. **beastly** *adjective.*

B

**beat** (beats, beating, beat, beaten) *verb* 1 to hit somebody or something hard and often. *The hail beat against the window.* 2 to stir something with a whisk or fork. *The chef beat the batter.* 3 to defeat or win against somebody. *He always beats me at chess.* 4 to make a regular sound or movement. *The bird was beating its wings.* **beat** *noun* rhythmic knocking. *The beat of the music.*

**beauty** *noun* the quality of something that makes it attractive to look at or listen to. Loveliness. *The inspiring beauty of the lakes and mountains.* **beautiful** *adjective.* **beautifully** *adverb.*

**beaver** *noun* a North American furry wild animal with a broad flat tail and strong front teeth. Beavers cut branches to build dams and homes called lodges in rivers.

A beaver gnaws at a stick in front of its dam. The beaver's staple food is fish.

**because** *conjunction* for the reason that. *The tennis match stopped because it had started to rain.*

**become** (becomes, becoming, became, become) *verb* 1 to come to be. To start feeling. *We became very good friends.* 2 to change into. *Caterpillars become moths and tadpoles develop into frogs.*

**bed** *noun* 1 a piece of furniture to sleep on. 2 the bottom of the sea or a river. 3 an area for growing flowers etc. *Flower bed.*

A bee sucks nectar from a flower. At the same time, it pollinates the flower by carrying pollen on its legs from one bloom to the next.

**WORD HISTORY**

*The word beauty – and take care how you spell it! – comes via the French from the Latin 'bellus'. We usually use the word 'beautiful' to describe women, children and things, but not men. It is more usual to call a man 'handsome' or 'good-looking'.*

There are over 300,000 species of beetle worldwide.

**bedridden** *adjective* permanently in bed because of illness or old age.

**bedroom** *noun* a room to sleep in. *The twins share a bedroom.*

**bedsitter** or **bedsit** *noun* a rented room for eating and sleeping in.

**bee** *noun* a flying insect with a yellow and black body that lives in large groups and makes honey. Some bees can sting.

**beech** *noun* a hardwood tree with a smooth bark. Beeches are deciduous, so their leaves drop in autumn.

**beef** *noun* the meat of cattle.

**beefy** (beefier, beefiest) *adjective* A beefy person is big and has strong muscles.

**beehive** or **hive** *noun* a small wooden house in which bees are kept.

**beeline** *noun* a straight line between two places. **make a beeline for** to go directly and swiftly towards something. *The boys made a beeline for the beach.*

**beer** *noun* an alcoholic drink brewed from malt, barley and hops.

**beeswax** *noun* the wax produced by bees to build the combs in which they store honey.

**beet** or **sugarbeet** *noun* a plant with a bulbous root that can be eaten as a vegetable (beetroot) or that can be used to make sugar.

**beetle** *noun* an insect with hard covers for its wings.

**beetroot** *noun* a variety of beet with a red root that is cooked as a vegetable.

**bedding** *noun* 1 blankets, duvets, sheets etc. for a bed (also bedclothes). 2 straw etc. for animals to lie on.

Water beetles, snails and small fishes are some of the creatures that feed on the bed of the river.

**before** *preposition* 1 earlier than or sooner than now. *The day before yesterday.* 2 in front of. *She stood before the statue.* **before** *adverb* previously. *We've never met before.*

**beg** (begs, begging, begged) *verb* 1 to ask somebody for money or food, especially in the street. *She begged for enough money to buy a bowl of soup.* **beggar** *noun.* 2 to ask for something very earnestly and eagerly. *He begged to be allowed to go swimming.*

**begin** (begins, beginning, began, begun) *verb* to start. *The meeting began at 7 o'clock.* The opposite of 'begin' is 'end'.

**beginner** *noun* a person who is just starting to do or learn something.

When you begin to learn to ride a bike, stabilizers can give you confidence.

**beginning** *noun* the start of something, the origin. *At the beginning of the week.*

**behave** *verb* 1 the way we act or do things is how we behave. *She's been behaving in a funny way lately.* 2 to act in a good or proper way. *You can come with me only if you behave.*

**behaviour** *noun* a way of behaving.

**behind** *preposition* 1 on the other side of or towards the back. *She hid behind the curtain.* 2 not making good progress. *He's behind with his studies.* 3 supporting or encouraging somebody. *We're behind you in your campaign.* **leave behind** *verb* to leave without something. *Peter was always leaving his keys behind.*

**Beijing** *noun* the capital of China.

**being** *noun* a living creature. *The first human beings lived in Africa.*

**Beirut** *noun* the capital of Lebanon.

**Belarus** *noun* a country in eastern Europe.

This is the flag of Belarus, which used to be part of the Soviet Union. The capital of Belarus is Minsk.

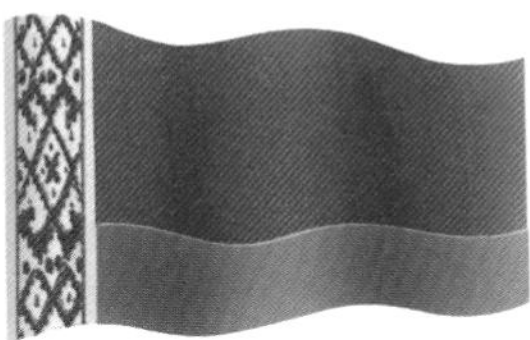

**WORD HISTORY**

*The word 'beggar' may have come from an Old French word 'bégard', a begging monk, named after Lambert e Begue, the founder of an order of nuns.*

**AMAZING FACT**

Belize was the last British mainland colony in the Americas. It gained independence in 1981. Both English and Spanish are spoken in Belize.

**belch** *verb* 1 to let wind from your stomach come noisily out of your mouth, to burp. *It is rude to belch at the table.* 2 to send out gases, fire smoke etc. like a volcano.

**Belfast** *noun* the capital of Northern Ireland.

**belfry** (belfries) *noun* a tower attached to a church, where the bells are hung.

**Belgian** *noun* a person from Belgium. Belgian *adjective. Belgian chocolates.*

**Belgium** *noun* a country in Northwest Europe.

**Belgrade** *noun* the capital of Yugoslavia.

**belief** *noun* 1 the things you believe to be true. The feeling that something is true.

**believe** *verb* 1 to think or feel strongly that something is true or real. *I believe in ghosts.* 2 to think that somebody is telling the truth. 3 to think or have an opinion. *I believe he's coming tomorrow.*

**Belize** *noun* a country in Central America.

**bell** *noun* a hollow metal object shaped like an upside-down cup that makes a ringing sound when struck. Any device that makes a ringing sound. *An electric door bell.*

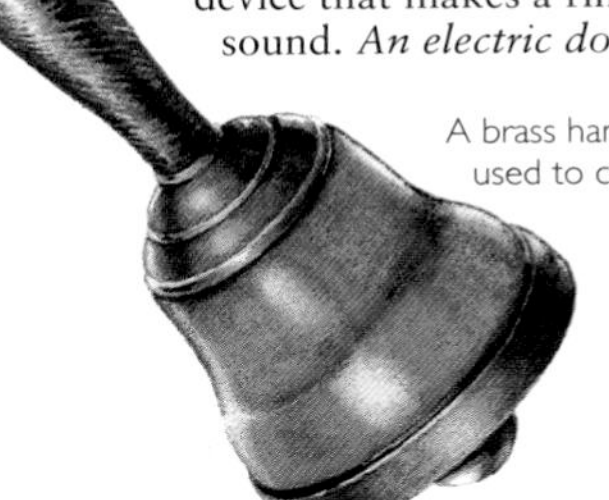

A brass hand bell was used to call children to school.

**bellow** *noun* a deep roaring sound made by a bull. **bellow** *verb. The bull bellowed with rage and the children ran for cover.*

**bellows** *plural noun* an instrument used for pumping air into a fire or a church organ.

To get a fire to light, people used to pump air under it with bellows.

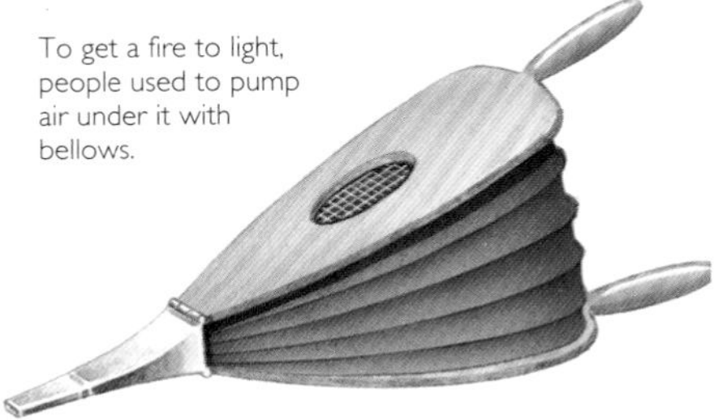

**belly** (bellies) *noun* the abdomen or the part of a person's or animal's body containing the stomach and intestines. *He ate until his belly was full.* **belly button** the navel.

B

**Belmopan** *noun* the capital of Belize.

**belong** *verb* 1 to be the property of somebody. *This book belongs to you, it is yours.* 2 to be a member of a group. *Brian belongs to the bowling club.* 3 to have its right place. *Put the tools back in the cupboard where they belong.*

**belongings** *plural noun* all the things that are yours and which you own.

**below** *preposition* 1 lower than. *Your chin is below your mouth.* 2 less than. *The temperature is below freezing.* **below** *adverb* beneath. *He looked down at the moat below.* The opposite of 'below' is 'above'.

**belt** *noun* 1 a long strap of leather or other material that you wear around your waist. 2 a narrow area of land. *The corn belt.* **belt** *verb* to hit. *He belted me round the ear.*

**bench** *noun* 1 a long wooden seat that two or more people can sit on. 2 a table that people put things on when they work. *A work bench.*

A work bench is an essential piece of furniture for the do-it-yourself enthusiast.

**bend** *verb* 1 to change the shape of something straight so that it curves or is at an angle. 2 something that bends changes direction. *The trees bend in the wind.* 3 to move the top part of your body downwards. *Ben bent down to examine the beetle.*

**beneath** *preposition, adverb* 1 under, below. *The cat was asleep all day beneath the bed.* 2 not worthy or not good enough. *The business executive thought it was beneath him to do the housework.*

**benefit** *noun* 1 an advantage or something that helps you. 2 money that the government pays to people who are ill, unemployed, or very poor. **benefit** (benefits, benefiting, benefited) *verb. She benefited from her seaside holiday and felt much better.*

**Benin** *noun* a country in Africa.

**beret** *noun* (say **bare**-ay) a soft, round, flat cap made of wool.

**Berlin** *noun* the capital of Germany.

**Berne** *noun* the capital of Switzerland.

**SPELLING NOTE**

*Try not to confuse the spelling of the words 'berry' and 'bury', which sound exactly the same.*

**SPELLING NOTE**

*Remember 'i' comes before 'e' except after 'c'. Take care with the spelling of 'besiege' (not to be confused with 'seize'), which is an exception to the 'i' before 'e' rule.*

**berry** *noun* a small, round, juicy fruit with lots of seeds such as a strawberry, blackberry or gooseberry.

Blueberries, raspberries and strawberries make a lovely dessert.

**berserk** *adjective* **go berserk** *verb* to become violently angry.

**berth** *noun* 1 a bed in a ship or train. 2 a place in a port where a ship can be moored.

**beside** *preposition* at the side of, next to. *A house beside the sea.*

**besides** *adverb* as well as. *What games can you play besides rugby?*

**besiege** *verb* to lay siege to a place or surround it with soldiers in order to make it surrender. *The soldiers besieged the castle.*

**best** *adjective, adverb* better than all the others. *The best film I've ever seen.* **best man** a friend of the bridegroom who helps him at his wedding. **best-seller** *noun* a book that sells a very large number of copies.

**bet** (bets, betting, bet or betted) *verb* 1 to forecast the result of a race etc. and to risk money on the result. *She bet £3 on the bay horse.* **bet** *noun* the money risked. 2 to be certain. *I bet I can swim farther than you.*

**betray** *verb* 1 to let somebody down and hurt them by being disloyal. *She betrayed me by giving away all my secrets.* 2 to show signs of your real feelings etc. *His face betrayed his sadness.*

**better** *adjective* 1 something that is better has more good about it but is not the best. 2 recovered from an illness. *When you're better you can go back to school again.*

The patient is sitting up in bed reading, so he must be getting better.

**between** *preposition* 1 in the space or time after one thing and before another. *Between the school and the hospital is a field where we play football between teatime and bedtime.* 2 in shares or parts. *They shared the money between them.* 3 used in comparing. *What's the difference between jam and marmalade?*

**beverage** *noun* a drink.

**beware** *interjection* be careful and look out for something dangerous. *Beware of the bull!*

Bulls can be dangerous, so beware of entering a field with a bull in it.

**bewilder** *verb* to confuse and worry somebody. *He was bewildered by all the street signs.* **bewildering** *adjective*.

**beyond** *preposition* 1 on the other side or farther than. *Don't drive beyond the crossroads.* 2 outside the limit of, past. *The camera is beyond repair.* 3 too difficult or confusing. *Algebra is quite beyond me.*

**Bhutan** *noun* a Himalayan country in South Asia.

Television is banned in mountainous Bhutan and the people are required by law to wear national costume.

**bi-** *prefix* two or twice. **biannual** happening twice a year. **bilateral** with two sides. **bilingual** speaking two languages.

**biased** *adjective* unfairly preferring one side to another, prejudiced. *She's biased against all foreigners.* **bias** *noun*.

**bib** *noun* a cloth or piece of plastic tied under a child's chin to protect its clothes when it is eating.

**Bible** *noun* A sacred book that has two main parts. First, the Old Testament, the holy book of the Jewish religion. Second, the New Testament, which, with the Old Testament, is the holy book of the Christian religion. **biblical** *adjective*.

**AMAZING FACT**

Although we have a saying, 'like a red rag to a bull', it is misleading. Bulls, like most mammals, are colour-blind.

**WORD HISTORY**

*'Billabong' is an Australian aboriginal word that means 'dead river'.*

**bicker** *verb* to quarrel continuously over unimportant things.

**bicycle** *noun* a two-wheeled vehicle that you ride by pushing pedals and steering with handlebars. The short form of bicycle is bike. *I love riding my new bike.*

A bicycle provides an environmentally friendly way of getting about.

**bid** (bids, bidding, bid) *verb* to offer to pay a certain amount of money for something, especially at an auction. *What am I bid for this vase?* **bid** *noun*.

**bid** *noun* an attempt to achieve something. *She's going all out in her bid to become ice-dance champion.*

**big** (bigger, biggest) *adjective* 1 large in size. *Elephants are big.* 2 important. *The big match is on today.* The opposites of 'big' are 'small' and 'unimportant'.

**bigot** *noun* a bigot is somebody who has strong and usually unreasonable views, which they obstinately refuse to change.

**bike** *noun* a bicycle or motorbike.

**bill** *noun* 1 a piece of paper on which is written how much you owe for something. *The gas bill.* 2 a written statement of a proposed new law to be discussed by parliament. 3 in the US, a piece of paper money. *A 10$ bill.*

**bill** *noun* a bird's beak.

**billabong** *noun* in Australia, a pool of water that is left when a river has run dry.

**billiards** *noun* a game played with balls and long sticks (cues) on a cloth-covered table with pockets along the sides and at the corners. *Let's have a game of billiards.*

**billion** *noun* 1 in North America and now generally in UK, a thousand million. 2 previously in UK, a million million.

**billygoat** *noun* a male goat.

**bin** *noun* a container. *A rubbish bin.*

**binary** *adjective* consisting of two parts. **binary system** *noun* a number system used in computers in which only two numbers, 0 and 1, are used.

**bind** (binds, binding, bound) *verb* 1 to tie or fasten together. *He bound the magazines into a bundle with string.* 2 to wrap. *She bound the bruise with a bandage.* 3 to join the pages of a book together and put a cover or binding on it.

**binder** *noun* a stiff cover or folder for holding papers.

**binoculars** *plural noun* an instrument with lenses you look through to make distant things seem closer.

The craters on the surface of the Moon are clearly visible through binoculars.

**biodegradable** *adjective* Things that are biodegradable decay naturally. *Paper is biodegradable.*

**biography** *noun* the story of somebody's life written by somebody else. **biographical** *adjective*. **biographer** *noun* someone who writes a biography.

**biologist** *noun* a person who studies biology. *The biologist examined the newt.*

**biology** *noun* the scientific study of living things. *Human biology.* **biological** *adjective*. **biological warfare** the use of germs as weapons in warfare.

**biped** *noun* an animal with two feet. *Birds and humans are bipeds.*

**biplane** *noun* an aeroplane with two sets of wings. *The biplane looped the loop.*

**bird** *noun* a creature that is covered with feathers, has two legs, two wings and a beak. All female birds lay eggs and most birds can fly. **bird of prey** any bird that kills other birds and small animals for food. *Eagles are birds of prey.* **bird-watcher** *noun* a person who studies birds.

The toucan is a bird that lives in the rainforests of South America.

**WORD HISTORY**

*The word 'biscuit' – a French word – means 'twice cooked' – from the two Latin words 'bis coctus'. Remember the 'u' in the spelling.*

**WORD HISTORY**

*The prefix 'bio–' in words like 'biology', 'biography' and 'biopsy' comes from the Greek word 'bios', meaning 'life'.*

**birth** *noun* being born, the beginning of anything. *The birth of the universe.*

**birth control** *noun* ways of preventing a woman becoming pregnant.

**birthday** *noun* the anniversary or day each year when you celebrate the day you were born. *Birthday cake.*

**biscuit** *noun* a crisp, flat cake.

**bisect** *verb* to divide into two equal parts.

**Bishkek** *noun* the capital of Kyrgyzstan.

**bishop** *noun* 1 a high-ranking priest in some Christian churches, in charge of a diocese or group of churches. 2 a chesspiece in the shape of a bishop's mitre (hat).

**bison** *noun* (*plural* bison) a wild ox (the buffalo of North America).

The bison has been saved from extinction and lives in protected wildlife parks in America.

**Bissau** *noun* the capital of Guinea-Bissau.

**bit** *noun* a very small piece.

**bit** *noun* the metal bar part of a bridle that fits into a horse's mouth.

**bit** *noun* the smallest unit of information, expressed in binary numbers, in a computer.

**bitch** *noun* a female dog.

**bite** (biting, bit, bitten) *verb* 1 to grasp and cut through something with your teeth. 2 to sting. *The gnats have bitten me.* **bite** *noun*. *The insect bite has left a red mark.*

**bitter** *adjective* 1 having a sharp, nasty taste. *Bitter medicine.* 2 angry and full of hatred. *Bitter enemies.* 3 very cold. *We expect bitter weather in the winter months.*

**bizarre** *adjective* strange and unusual.

**black** *adjective* the darkest of colours. *A black cat is thought to bring good luck.* **Black** *noun* a person with black skin.

**blackberry** *noun* the fruit of a wild, prickly bush called a bramble.

**blackbird** *noun* a common European songbird.

**blackboard** *noun* a large board painted in a dark colour for writing on with chalk.

A cat is drawn in white chalk on this child's blackboard.

**blackbox** *noun* an electronic machine on an aircraft that automatically records details of the flight.

**blacken** *verb* to make or become black. *Soot from the fire has blackened the bricks.*

**blackmail** *noun* the crime of trying to get money from somebody by threatening to reveal a secret. **blackmail** *verb. He was arrested for blackmail.* **blackmailer** *noun.*

**blacksmith** *noun* a person who makes things out of metal, including horseshoes.

**bladder** *noun* a bag-like organ in your body where urine collects until it leaves your body.

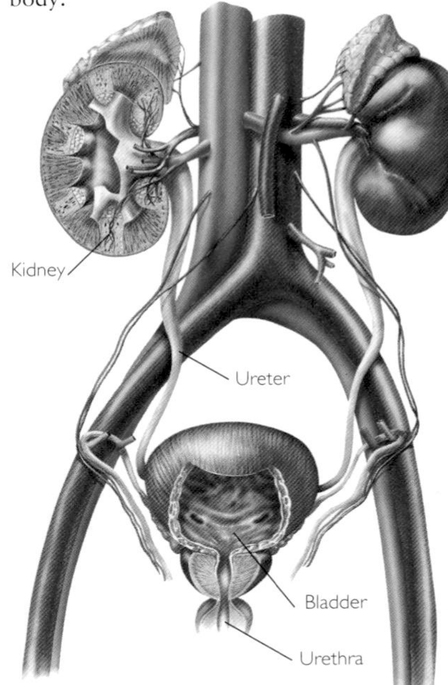


Urine leaves the bladder through the urethra when a circle of muscle relaxes to open the entrance to the tube.

**blade** *noun* 1 the sharp part of an axe, knife, sword etc. 2 a narrow leaf. *A blade of grass.* 3 the flat, thin parts of oars, propellers etc.

### WORD HISTORY

*The 'mail' in 'blackmail' is a Scottish word meaning 'payment', 'tax' or 'tribute'. Blackmail was the tribute in money, corn or cattle demanded by rebel chiefs in the 16th century in return for their protection.*

**blame** *verb* to say that somebody has done something wrong and that it is their fault. *She blamed me for spilling the paint all over the sofa.* **blame** *noun. My sister took the blame.* **blameless** *adjective.*

**blank** *adjective* 1 unmarked, with nothing on it. *A book of blank pages.* 2 empty. *My mind went blank.*

**blanket** *noun* 1 a thick warm covering for a bed. 2 any sort of covering. *A thick blanket of snow lay over the fields.*

**blare** *verb* to make a loud, harsh, unpleasant noise. *The taxi horn blared.*

**blaspheme** *verb* (say blass-**feem**) to speak without respect about God and holy things. To swear. **blasphemy** *noun.* **blasphemous** *adjective.*

**blast** *noun* 1 a sudden strong gust of air or wind. 2 a sudden loud noise, especially the noise of an explosion. *He gave a deafening blast on the trumpet.*

**blast-off** *noun* the moment when a rocket or spacecraft takes off. **blast off** *verb.*

It is always a thrilling moment when a rocket blasts off the launchpad.

**blaze** *noun* a very bright light or fire. *The blaze of the headlights.* **blaze** *verb* to give off bright light. *The fire is blazing.*

**blazer** *noun* a jacket, often coloured with a badge on it, and part of a school uniform.

**bleach** *noun* a strong chemical liquid used to kill germs and to make things such as cloth white. **bleach** *verb* to make white. *He bleached his grey shirt.*

**bleak** *noun* 1 cold, bare and miserable. *The moor is windswept and bleak.* 2 not very hopeful. *Bleak prospects.*

**bleat** *verb* to make a noise like a sheep or goat. *Stop bleating about how terribly hungry you are.* **bleat** *noun.*

**bleed** (bleeds, bleeding, bled) *verb* to lose blood. *A bleeding nose.*

**blend** *verb* 1 to mix things together. *He blended the ingredients into a smooth paste.* 2 When things like colours or sounds come together in a pleasing way, they blend. **blend** *noun. A nice blend of coffee.*

**bless** (blesses, blessing, blessed *or* blest) *verb* to ask God to protect someone or something from harm.

**blew** past tense of blow.

B

**blind** *adjective* not able to see. *Guide dogs for the blind.* **blindness** *noun.*

**blind** *noun* a screen or covering for a window. *Pull up the blind to let in the sun.*

A venetian blind is made up of slats that tilt to allow more or less light into a room.

**blindfold** *noun* a piece of cloth tied over someone's eyes. **blindfold** *verb.*

**blink** *verb* to close and open your eyes again very quickly. *He blinked in the bright light.*

**blinkers** *plural noun* leather flaps placed at the side of a horse's eyes so that it can only see forwards.

**blister** *noun* a sore swelling like a bubble on your skin, filled with liquid, caused by a burn or by rubbing. *A blood blister.*

**blizzard** *noun* a heavy snowstorm with strong winds. *They were lost in the blizzard.*

**block** *verb* to be in the way of, or put something in the way of so that nothing can pass. *A broken-down tractor blocked the road and stopped us from getting home.*

**block** *noun* 1 a lump or solid piece of something with flat sides like a block of wood. 2 a large building or group of buildings. *A block of flats.*

**blockade** *verb* to isolate or cut off a place and stop supplies getting through.

**blockage** *noun* something in, e.g. a pipe, that stops anything passing through.

**blond** *adjective* having fair hair (of a boy or man).

**blonde** *adjective* having fair hair (of a girl or woman).

**blood** *noun* the red liquid that flows around inside the bodies of humans and animals.

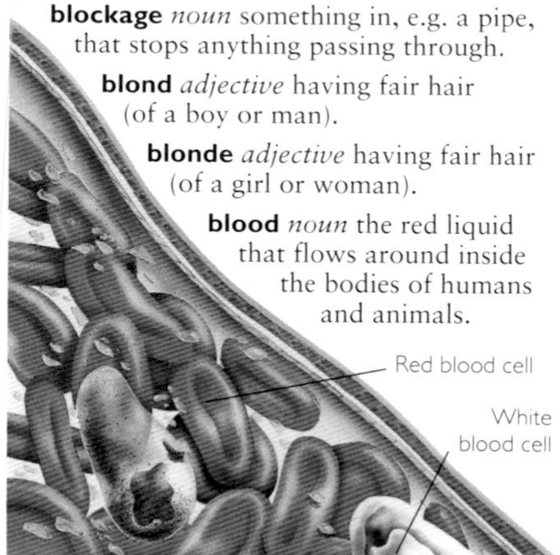

Red blood cell

White blood cell

Each drop of your blood contains up to 5 million red blood cells that give blood its colour.

**DID YOU KNOW?**

*In Australia and New Zealand a 'block' is also a plot of land or settlement. And 'to do your block' means to get very angry.*

**AMAZING FACT**

Wind blows when some air masses are warmer than others.

**blood-curdling** *adjective* terrifying.

**blood donor** *noun* a person who gives some blood to be stored in a blood bank to be given to others in operations etc.

**bloodhound** *noun* a large dog with a keen sense of smell.

**bloodshed** *noun* the loss or spilling of blood in war etc.

**blood-thirsty** *adjective* keen for violence or killing. *A bloodthirsty film.*

**blood vessel** *noun* one of the tubes in your body that blood flows along.

**bloom** *noun* a flower. **bloom** *verb. The roses are blooming.*

The bright red blooms of the poppy are very short-lived.

**blossom** *noun* the flowers that grow on trees in spring. **blossom** *verb* 1 to grow blossom. 2 to grow and improve. *The girl blossomed into a beautiful woman.*

**blot** *noun* 1 a mark or spot made by a spilled drop of ink or paint. 2 a stain or fault that spoils something. **blot** *verb.*

**blouse** *noun* a loose shirt, usually worn by girls and women.

**blow** (blows, blowing, blew, blown) *verb* 1 to push air quickly through your mouth. 2 to move about in or be moved by the wind. *The wind blew the gate shut.* **blow over** to pass or become forgotten. *The fuss will soon blow over.* **blow up** 1 to destroy with an explosion. *Guy Fawkes tried to blow up the Houses of Parliament.* 2 to enlarge. *She blew up the photo.*

It used to be thought that the winds had personalities, both kind and unkind.

**blow** *noun* 1 a hard hit. *A blow to the head.* 2 a cause of unhappiness or disappointment. *Her dad's death was a terrible blow.*

**blubber** *noun* the fat from whales.

**blubber** or **blub** *verb* to cry.

**blue** *noun* the pure colour of a cloudless sky. **blue** *adjective* 1 of the colour blue. 2 sad and miserable. **out of the blue** suddenly. *The money arrived out of the blue.*

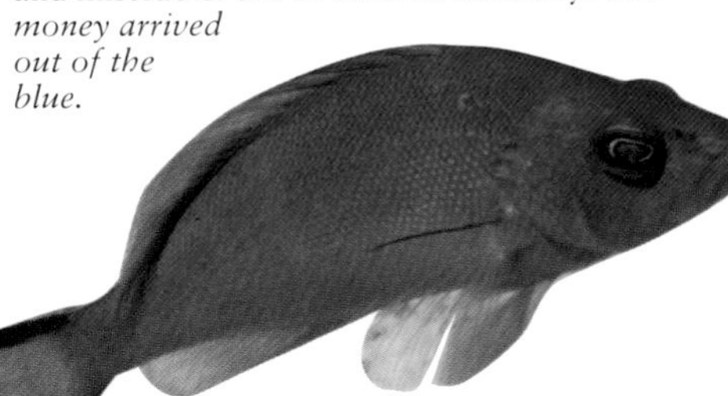

The blue hamlet is one of the world's most beautiful fish.

**blues** *noun* a slow, sad kind of jazz.

**blunder** *noun* a bad and stupid mistake. **blunder** *verb* to stumble or make a clumsy mistake. *He blundered into the room.*

**blunt** *adjective* 1 not sharp. *A blunt knife.* 2 plain and to the point. *The language my father used was very blunt.*

**blur** (blurs, blurring, blurred) *verb* to make something indistinct or less clear. To smear. *The photograph is very blurred.* **blur** *noun* a smear, something that is unclear. *In my memory, the accident is all a blur.*

The sign is blurred. It is not shown in clear focus.

**blurb** *noun* a publisher's description praising a book.

**blurt out** *verb* to say something suddenly and without thinking.

**blush** *verb* to go red in the face, usually because you are shy, embarrassed or ashamed.

**boa constrictor** *noun* a large South American snake that crushes its prey to death by winding its body around it.

**boar** *noun* 1 a male pig. 2 a wild pig.

**board** *noun* 1 a plank or long flat piece of wood or card. 2 a piece of wood or card used for playing games etc. *A chess board.* 3 a group of people who manage an organization. *The company's board of directors met to discuss the merger.*

**DID YOU KNOW?**

*The words 'blush' and 'flush' mean 'to go red in the face'. People blush because they are embarrassed or out of shame or guilt. People who flush may be angry or may have had too much alcohol to drink!*

**board** *verb* to get on an aircraft, ship or train. *We got on board ship and set sail.*

**boarding school** *noun* a school where pupils eat and sleep.

**boast** *verb* to talk proudly about what you possess and how good and clever you think you are in order to impress people, to brag. **boast** *noun*. **boastful** *adjective*.

**boat** *noun* a small vessel for carrying people and things on water. **in the same boat** in the same difficult or unpleasant situation.

A fishing boat is called a trawler. Its nets trawl deep waters to catch fish.

**body** *noun* 1 all the physical parts of a person or animal, both inside and outside. 2 the main part of a body without the limbs. 3 a dead body, a corpse. 4 the main part of something. 5 a group of people. **bodily** *adjective*.

**bodyguard** *noun* a person or group of people who protects someone.

**bog** *noun* soft, wet ground. A marsh.

**bogged down** *adjective* stuck and unable to make progress. *Bogged down with work.* **bog down** *verb*.

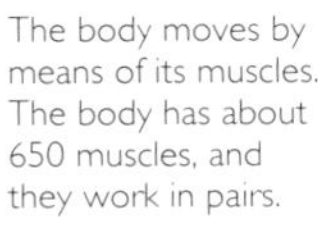

The body moves by means of its muscles. The body has about 650 muscles, and they work in pairs.

**Bogota** *noun* the capital of Colombia.

**bogus** *adjective* false, not genuine.

**boil** *verb* 1 When a liquid boils, it becomes so hot that it bubbles and steams. 2 to cook food in boiling water. *He prefers to eat boiled beef and carrots, like his mother used to make.* **boiling point** the temperature at which a liquid boils.

The pan of boiling water is steaming up the mirror.

**boil** *noun* a red, painful lump under your skin. *He had horrible boils all over his face.*

**boisterous** *adjective* noisy, cheerful and lively. *The children were too boisterous.*

**bold** *adjective* 1 showing no fear, brave. 2 clear, easy to see and impressive. *Bold lettering.* **boldness** *noun.*

**Bolivia** *noun* a country in South America.

**bollard** *noun* a short, thick post in a road to keep traffic away from the area.

**bolt** *noun* 1 a metal bar that slides across to lock a door, window etc. **bolt** *verb. She bolted the door every night.* 2 a metal pin with a screw that fits into a part called a nut to hold things together.

The bolt screws into the nut to make a secure fastening.

**bolt** *verb* 1 to run away suddenly. *The horses bolted.* 2 to eat something very quickly. *Don't bolt your food!*

**bomb** *noun* a weapon containing explosive chemicals that is used to destroy buildings etc. **bomb** *verb. Coventry was badly bombed in the war.* **bombshell** *noun* a surprise. *The news that she had been chosen for the job came as a bombshell.*

**bombard** *verb* 1 to attack with gunfire. 2 to attack or overwhelm. *They bombarded the chairman with difficult questions, but he was unable to give satisfactory answers.*

**WORD HISTORY**

*In the Middle Ages a 'bonfire' was a 'bone fire'. Burning bones as a source of fuel was quite common until the beginning of the 19th century.*

**bone** *noun* any of the hard, white pieces forming the skeleton of a person or animal. **bone idle** very lazy.

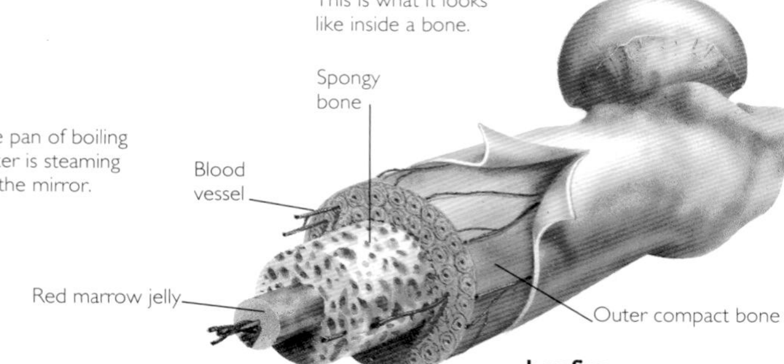


This is what it looks like inside a bone.

**bonfire** *noun* an outdoor fire. *We made a massive bonfire yesterday to burn all the rubbish.*

**bonnet** *noun* 1 the part of a car that covers the engine (US hood). 2 a hat tied under the chin, worn by women or babies.

**bonus** *noun* a reward or extra payment added to your pay.

**bony** (bonier, boniest) *adjective* 1 thin and with little flesh. *A bony cow.* 2 having large bones. 3 full of bones. *This fish is very bony.*

**book** *noun* a set of pages, usually printed, bound together in a cover. *A leather-bound book of poems.*

**book** *verb* to reserve or arrange a place in a theatre, hotel, airline etc. before you need it. *Let's book up to go to Spain.* **booking** *noun.*

**bookcase** *noun* a piece of furniture with shelves for books.

**bookmaker** or **bookie** *noun* a person whose job is to take bets on horses etc.

**bookworm** *noun* a person who likes reading books a lot.

**boom** *noun* 1 a deep, loud sound. *The boom of the guns.* 2 a period of sudden increase. *A boom in computer sales.*

**boomerang** *noun* a curved stick used by Australian aboriginals as a weapon. It is thrown at its target and returns to the thrower if it misses.

Boomerangs are often decorated by aboriginal hunters with beautiful patterns.

**boost** *verb* to increase, push up or encourage. *The advertisement has boosted sales considerably.* **boost** *noun.*

**boot** *noun* 1 a shoe with high sides covering the ankle and sometimes lower leg. *Cowboy boots.* 2 a place in a car where you can put luggage etc. (US trunk).

**boot up** *verb* to turn on a computer.

**booty** *noun* valuable things stolen after a battle. Plunder.

**border** *noun* 1 a frontier or the line along which two countries meet. **border** *verb. Canada borders the United States.* 2 a strip along an edge.

The border between France and Spain runs along the Pyrenees mountains.

**bore** *verb* 1 to pierce or drill a hole into something. 2 to tire through lack of interest. **boring** *adjective* dull. *What a boring book!*

**bore** *noun* a dull person who makes you feel weary. *The boss is a real bore.*

**bore** past tense of bear. *The knight bore a coat of arms on his helmet.*

**boredom** *noun* tiredness caused by dull or monotonous work etc.

**born** *verb* When people or animals are born they start a life of their own. *Mum was born in Singapore in 1970.*

**borrow** *verb* to take something belonging to somebody else and use it for a short time before returning it. **borrower** *noun.* The opposite of 'borrow' is 'lend'.

**Bosnia-Herzegovina** *noun* a country in Southeast Europe.

The flag of Bosnia-Herzegovina shows a blue shield with yellow fleurs-de-lys on a white ground.

**bosom** *noun* a woman's chest or breasts. **bosom friend** a very close friend.

**boss** *noun* a person in charge of workers. **boss** *verb* to tell people what to do.

**bossy** *adjective* enjoying giving orders and telling people what to do. **bossiness** *noun.*

**AMAZING FACT**

Many computer terms are new uses for old words like 'boot' (to start up a computer), 'mouse' (the device that is used alongside the keyboard to work on screen), and 'bookmark' (to record an Internet address on your computer).

**SPELLING NOTE**

*Try not to confuse 'borne', past participle of the verb 'bear', with 'born', which means giving birth.*

**HANDY HINT**

Words that sound alike but that are spelled differently – like 'bough' and 'bow' are called homophones. Be careful not to confuse them when you're writing.

**botany** *noun* the scientific study of plants. **botanist** *noun. She's studying to become a botanist.* **botanical** *adjective.*

Botanical drawings are very delicate and show every detail of the plant.

**both** *adjective, pronoun* the two together, not only one. *Both Jane's grandparents are now dead.*

**bother** *verb* 1 to feel worried or disturbed about something. 2 to be a nuisance or worry somebody. **bother** *noun* nuisance. *I'm sorry to be a bother.* 3 to take care, time and trouble over something. *He can't be bothered to do his homework.*

**Botswana** *noun* a country in Africa.

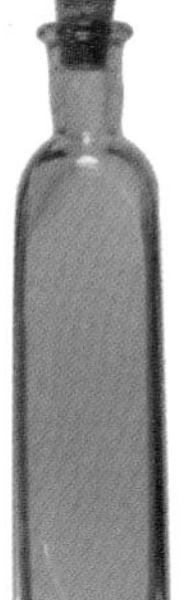

**bottle** *noun* a container made of glass or plastic for holding liquid. **bottle** *verb. He bottled the delicious homemade lemonade.*

This beautiful blue glass bottle has been hand-blown. You can tell this because of irregularities in the glass.

**bottleneck** *noun* a place where a road becomes narrower and traffic cannot flow freely. Anything that slows down work or progress.

**bottle up** *verb* to keep your feelings and thoughts to yourself.

**bottom** *noun* 1 the lowest part or underside of something. *The bottom of the sea.* 2 the part of your body that you sit on. **get to the bottom of** *verb* to solve or explain a mystery etc. *Let's get to the bottom of the problem.*

**bough** *noun* ( rhymes with 'how') a large branch of a tree. *An apple bough.*

**bought** past tense of buy.

**boulder** *noun* a large, round rock.

**bounce** *verb* to spring back after hitting something. *The ball hit the floor and bounced back.* **bounce** *noun.* **bouncy** *adjective. A bouncy castle.*

B

**bound** *verb* to move along by making large leaps. **bound to** certain to. *You're bound to win the competition.* **out of bounds** a place where you are not allowed to go.

**boundary** *noun* a line that marks an edge.

**bouquet** *noun* (say boo-**kay**) a gift of a bunch of flowers.

The bouquet is made up of lovely summer flowers.

**bout** *noun* a short period of something. *A serious bout of ill health.*

**bow** *noun* (rhymes with 'so') 1 a piece of wood curved by a string attached at each end, used in shooting arrows. 2 a long thin stick used for playing stringed instruments such as violins. 3 a knot with loops. *He tied his shoelaces in a neat bow.*

**bow** *noun* (rhymes with 'cow') the front part of a ship.

**bow** *verb* (rhymes with 'cow') 1 to bend your head or the top part of your body forwards. *At the end of the show the actors bowed.* 2 to give in. *They refused to bow to his unreasonable demands.*

**bowels** *plural noun* the intestines in the lower part of your body, which carry waste matter from your body.

**bowl** *noun* a deep, uncovered dish. *A sugar bowl.*

**bowl** *verb* to throw a ball towards the batsman in cricket. **bowl** *noun* a big hard wooden ball used in the game of bowling.

The bowler runs up to the wicket and bowls the cricket ball to the batsman.

**box** *noun* a wooden or cardboard container with straight sides and usually with a lid.

**WORD HISTORY**

*Boxing Day gets its name from the boxes or gifts traditionally given on this day.*

**WORD HISTORY**

*'Boycott' is named after a British estate manager in Ireland whose tenants refused to pay unreasonable rents.*

**DID YOU KNOW?**

*Braille was invented in the 19th century by a Frenchman called Louis Braille.*

**box** *verb* to punch or fight with your fists wearing heavy leather gloves in a sport called boxing. **boxer** *noun. He is a not a heavyweight but a middleweight boxer.*

**boxer** *noun* a short-haired breed of dog related to the bulldog.

**Boxing Day** *noun* the first weekday after Christmas Day.

**boy** (boys) *noun* a male child. **boyhood** *noun* the childhood of a man. *In my boyhood things were different.*

**boycott** *verb* to refuse to have any dealings with somebody, as a protest or to bring about a change.

**boyfriend** *noun* 1 a girl or woman's usual and regular male friend. *She lives with her boyfriend.* 2 a gay man's partner.

**bra** or **brassiere** *noun* a piece of underwear that supports a woman's breasts.

**brace** *noun* 1 something that straightens or supports. *She wears a wire brace on her teeth.* 2 a carpenter's tool for drilling holes. 3 two things of the same kind. *A brace of pheasant.* 4 **braces** *plural noun* straps worn over the shoulders to hold up trousers.

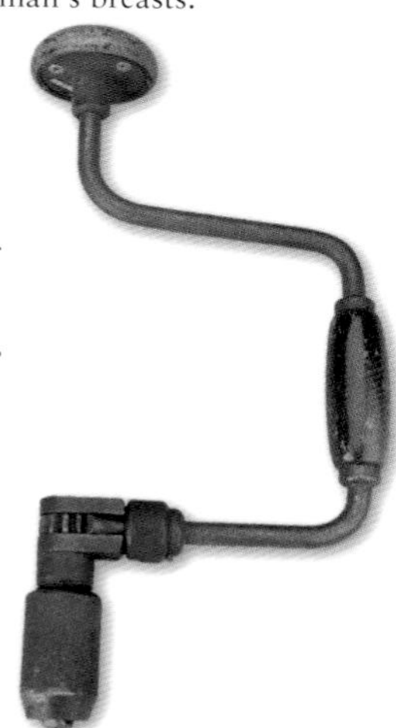

The brace gives the carpenter a good grip for drilling holes.

**brace** *verb* to prepare yourself for something nasty. *He braced himself to go to the dentist and have six fillings.*

**bracelet** *noun* an ornamental band worn around the arm or wrist.

**bracing** *adjective* fresh and strength-giving. *Bracing sea breezes are good for the health.*

**bracket** *noun* 1 a support fixed to a wall for a shelf etc. 2 **brackets** *plural noun* the signs ( ) used in writing or maths to enclose words or symbols. **bracket** *verb* to group together.

**brag** (brags, bragging, bragged) *verb* to boast and talk too proudly about yourself. **braggart** *noun* boaster.

**braid** *noun* 1 a narrow strip of decorative material used for trimming. 2 (mainly North American) a plait of hair. **braid** *verb.*

**Braille** *noun* a system of printing for blind people using raised dots that can be felt and read with the fingers.

B

**brain** *noun* the part inside your head that controls how your body works and which enables you to think and feel.

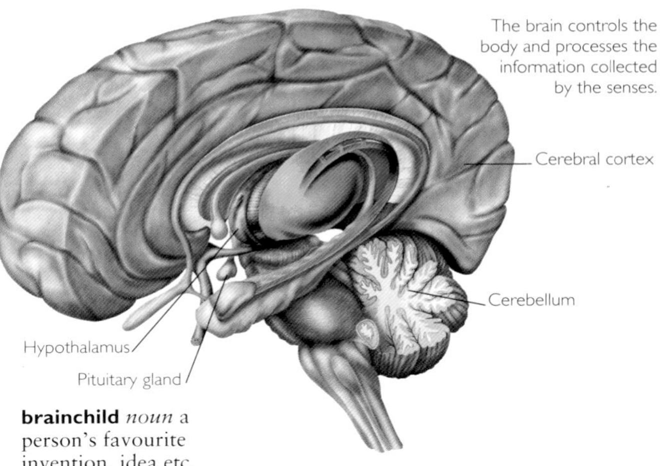

The brain controls the body and processes the information collected by the senses.

**brainchild** *noun* a person's favourite invention, idea etc.

**brainteaser** *noun* a difficult problem or puzzle. *This crossword is a real brainteaser.*

**brainwave** *noun* a good idea.

**brainy** (brainier, brainiest) *adjective* clever and intelligent. *A very brainy pupil.*

**brake** *noun* the part of a vehicle that you use to slow it down or to stop it. *The brakes failed and the car crashed.* **brake** *verb.*

**bramble** *noun* a prickly bush that blackberries grow on.

**bran** *noun* what is left after flour has been made from the grain of wheat, the husks or outside parts of the seed.

**branch** *noun* 1 a part of a tree that sticks out from the trunk. 2 a division of a group or subject. *What branch of science are you studying?* 3 a bank, office or shop belonging to a big organization. *The supermarket has branches in most towns.* **branch** *verb* to divide. *The railway line branches here.* **branch out** to strike out in a new direction. *They've branched out on their own.*

In spring, the branch sprouts new leaves.

**brand** *noun* a particular kind or make of goods. *An expensive brand.* **brand new** *adjective* unused and completely new.

**brandy** *noun* a strong alcoholic drink.

**WORD HISTORY**

*'Brandy' is the shortened form of a Dutch word, 'brandewijn', meaning 'burnt wine'. In fact the wine was not burned but distilled over a fire.*

**Brasilia** *noun* the capital of Brazil.

**brass** *noun* a yellow metal made from mixing two other metals, copper and zinc. **brass band** a group of musicians who play instruments made of brass.

**Bratislava** *noun* the capital of Slovakia.

**brave** *adjective* willing to do dangerous things and face danger, fearless. **bravery** *noun. He was awarded a medal for bravery.*

**brave** *noun* a Native American warrior.

**brawl** *noun* a rowdy quarrel or rough fight. *A drunken brawl.* **brawl** *verb.*

**brawn** *noun* great physical and muscular strength. **brawny** *adjective.*

**bray** *noun* the loud sound that a donkey makes. **bray** *verb.*

**brazen** *adjective* 1 made of brass. 2 without shame. *A brazen lie.*

**Brazil** *noun* a country in South America.

**Brazilian** *noun* a person from Brazil. **Brazilian** *adjective. Brazilian coffee.*

**Brazzaville** *noun* the capital of the Republic of the Congo.

**bread** *noun* a food made from flour, water and yeast and baked in an oven. **breadwinner** the person who earns money for a family to live on.

Brown bread is healthier than white bread because it contains more roughage.

**breadth** *noun* how wide something is from one side to the other.

**break** *verb* 1 to split into pieces, to smash. *The glass fell off the table and broke.* **breakages** *plural noun* things that are broken. *All breakages must be paid for.* 2 to damage something so it does not work. *The radio is broken.* 3 to fail to keep. *He broke his promise.* **break down** 1 If a car breaks down, it stops going because something has gone wrong. 2 If somebody has a breakdown, they cry and are overcome by nervous exhaustion. **break into** to enter a building with force. **break off** to stop doing something. *They broke off for lunch.*

B

**break** *noun* 1 a rest. *You've worked long enough. Take a break.* 2 a sudden change. *A lucky break was well deserved.*

**breaker** *noun* a large wave that crashes against the rocks.

**breakfast** *noun* the first meal of the day. *I like a cooked breakfast.* **breakfast** *verb.*

**breakthrough** *noun* an important achievement or discovery.

**breakwater** *noun* a wall or barrier protecting a harbour or shore from the full force of waves.

**breast** *noun* 1 one of the two soft parts on a woman's chest that produces milk when she has had a baby, the bosom. 2 the chest.

**breath** *noun* the air that you draw in and let out of your lungs. **out of breath** panting. **under your breath** very quietly. *She said it under her breath so they wouldn't hear.*

**breathalyser** *noun* a device that the police ask a person to breathe into to find out how much alcohol is in their blood. **breathalyse** *verb. He was breathalysed by the police.*

**breathe** *verb* to draw air into your lungs through your nose and mouth and send it out again. *Breathe deeply and calm down.*

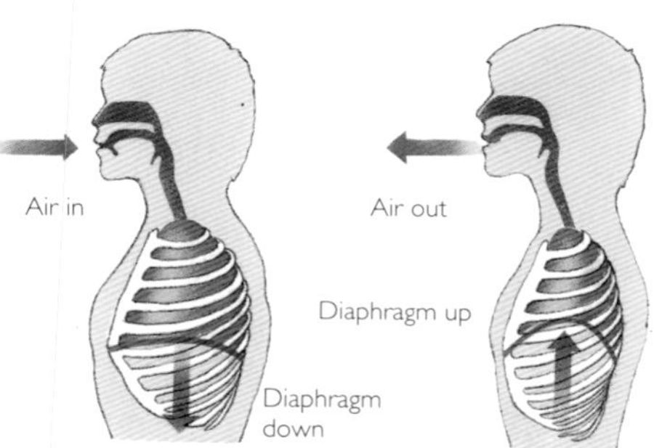


The diaphragm and the muscles between the ribs make you breathe in and out.

**breed** *verb* 1 to mate and produce young. 2 to raise animals to sell. *Tom and Mary breed pigs.* **breed** *noun* animals that mate and produce others of the same kind. *Bloodhounds and collies are breeds of dog.*

The collie is a very popular breed of dog.

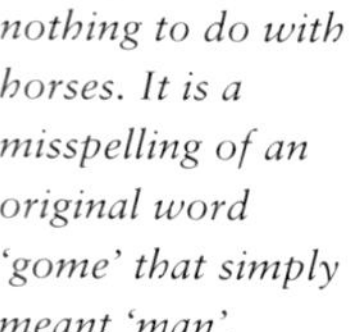

**WORD HISTORY**

*The 'groom' in 'bridegroom' has nothing to do with horses. It is a misspelling of an original word 'gome' that simply meant 'man'.*

**WORD HISTORY**

*'Breathalyser' is a 'blend' word made up of two words put together – 'breath' and 'analyser'. ('Motel', 'Eurovision' and 'smog' are other examples.) Note that in British English the word must always be spelt with '–yse', never '–yze'.*

**breeze** *noun* a soft wind. **breezy** *adjective.*

**brewery** *noun* a place where beer is made (brewed). *Malt is delivered to the brewery.*

**bribe** *noun* a gift or money given to somebody to persuade them to do something unlawful or dishonest. *He gave them a bribe to keep them quiet.* **bribe** *verb.*

**brick** *noun* a small block of hardened clay used for building.

**bride** *noun* a woman who is about to get married. **bridal** *adjective.*

**bridegroom** *noun* a man who is about to get married. *The bridegroom is nervous.*

**bridesmaid** *noun* a girl or young woman who helps the bride on her wedding day.

**bridge** *noun* 1 a structure built over a canal, river, road etc. so that people and vehicles can cross from one side to the other. *A railway bridge.* 2 a high platform from which a ship is steered. *The captain stands on the bridge.* 3 a piece of wood that holds up the strings stretched along a violin, guitar etc. **bridge** *verb. Bridge that gap.*

A bridge carries the road across the river.

**bridge** *noun* a card game for four players.

**Bridgetown** *noun* the capital of Barbados.

**bridle** *noun* the leather straps that fit over a horse's head and to which the reins are attached. *The bridle is part of the tack.*

**brief** *adjective* lasting or taking only a short time. *A brief encounter.*

**brief** *verb* to give instructions, information or advice. *She briefed her staff on the best tactics.* **briefing** *noun.*

**briefcase** *noun* a flat case for papers etc.

**briefs** *plural noun* short underpants or knickers. *His briefs were too tight.*

**bright** *adjective* 1 giving out a lot of strong light. 2 a clear, strong colour. *Bright orange.* 3 clever. *A bright student.* **brightness** *noun. The brightness of the Sun.* The opposite of 'bright' is 'dull' or 'dim' or 'dark'.

**brighten** *verb* to make or become brighter.

**brilliant** *adjective* 1 shining very brightly. *Brilliant stars.* 2 very clever or able. *A brilliant dancer.* **brilliance** *noun.*

The dancers wear brilliant flowers round their necks, heads and ankles.

**brim** *noun* 1 the top of a container. *The glass is full to the brim.* 2 the part of a hat that sticks out.

**brine** *noun* salty water.

**bring** (brings, bringing, brought) *verb* 1 to carry something or to take somebody with you. *Can you bring your CDs when you come?* 2 to cause or start something happening. *The sad story brought tears to his eyes.* **bring back** to cause to return. *Bring back the old days.* **bring up** 1 to look after and educate a child. 2 to mention a subject. *Don't bring up the War.*

**brink** *noun* the edge of a steep place such as a cliff.

**brisk** *adjective* 1 lively and efficient. *Brisk manner.* 2 fast. *A brisk walk by the sea.*

**bristle** *noun* a short, stiff hair on an animal or on a man's unshaven face. **bristly** *adjective.*

**British** *adjective* relating to Great Britain and its people.

**brittle** *adjective* hard and easily broken. *Brittle twigs.*

**broad** *adjective* (rhymes with 'lord') measuring a lot from one side to the other, wide. **broaden** *verb* to make wider. *They are going to broaden the road.*

**broadcast** (broadcasts, broadcasting, broadcast) *verb* to send out a programme by radio or television. **broadcast** *noun.*

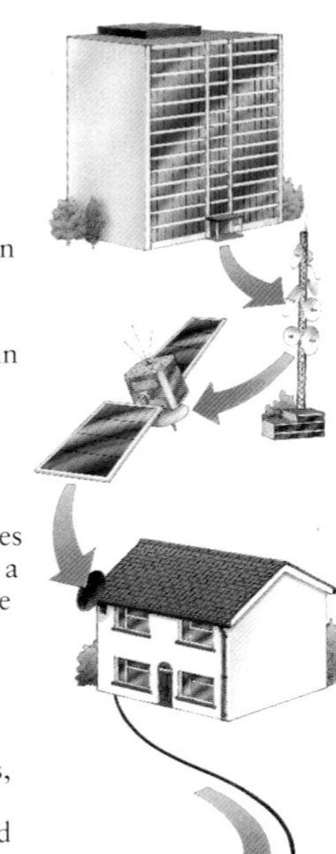

When a television programme is broadcast, the signal leaves the studios and is sent via a transmitter to a satellite in space. The satellite beams the signal to a receiver on your house and into your television set.

**DID YOU KNOW?**

*'Britain' is an abbreviation of 'Great Britain', a country made up of England, Scotland and Wales. The United Kingdom is correctly called the United Kingdom of Great Britain and Northern Ireland. The two kingdoms that united were those of England (and Wales) and Scotland.*

**broad-minded** *adjective* tolerant and accepting opinions and behaviour that you may not agree with.

**broccoli** *noun* a vegetable like a cauliflower with a green stalk and small green flowerheads. *Broccoli is very good for you.*

**brochure** *noun* a pamphlet or small book containing information.

**broke, broken** past and past participle of break.

**bronchitis** *noun* an illness of the lungs that makes you cough a lot.

**bronco** *noun* (US) a wild or half-tamed pony. *The bucking bronco threw off the cowboy who was trying to break him in.*

**bronze** *noun* a reddish-brown metal made by mixing copper and tin. **bronze** *adjective.*

**Bronze Age** *noun* a time in history when people made tools of bronze.

These urns were made by people who lived in the Bronze Age.

**brooch** *noun* (rhymes with 'poach') an ornament that you can pin to your clothes.

**brood** *noun* a family of young birds hatched at the same time. *The mother hen sat on her brood of chicks.* **brood** *verb* 1 to sit on eggs to hatch them. 2 to worry about things for a long time. *Helen was brooding over her poor examination results.*

**brook** *noun* a small stream. *The brook rushed down the mountainside.*

**broom** *noun* a large brush with a long handle for sweeping floors. *A new broom sweeps away old problems.*

**broth** *noun* a thin soup containing vegetables and barley. *The doctor recommended a good thick broth.*

**brother** *noun* a boy or man who has the same parents as you. A half-brother has only one parent the same as you. **brotherly** *adjective. Brotherly love.*

**brother-in-law** *noun* the brother of a person's husband or wife.

**brought** past tense of bring.

B

**brow** *noun* 1 the part of your face between your eyes and the top of your head, forehead. 2 the arch of hair over each eye, eyebrow. 3 the top of a hill.

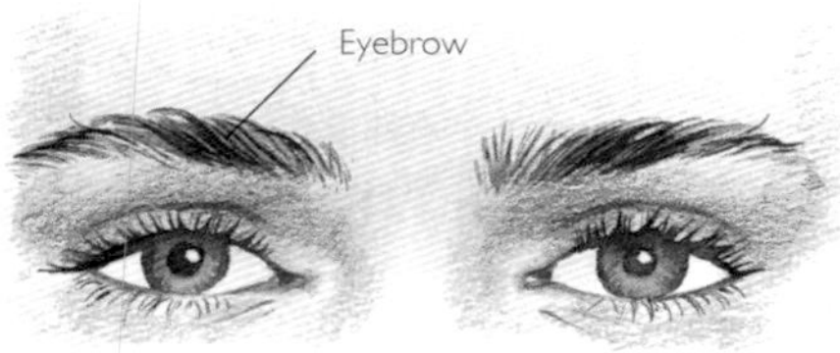


Eyebrows protect the eyes from sweat running into them down the brow.

**brown** *noun, adjective* the colour of wood or chocolate. *As brown as a nut.*

**browned off** *adjective* bored.

**browse** *verb* to glance at things such as books or goods in a shop in a casual way. *He browsed through the catalogues.* **browser** *noun.*

**bruise** *noun* a bluish-black mark on your skin caused by a knock. **bruise** *verb. She bruised her knee when she fell.*

**Brunei** *noun* a country on the island of Borneo, in Southeast Asia.

The flag of Brunei has a red crest on a yellow, black and white ground.

**brush** *noun* a tool with stiff hairs called bristles used for sweeping, painting etc. *A hairbrush.* **brush** *verb* 1 to use a brush. *He brushed the floor.* 2 to touch gently while passing. *The cat brushed against her legs.*

**Brussels** *noun* the capital of Belgium.

**brutal** *adjective* cruel, violent and without feeling. **brutality** *noun.*

**brute** *noun* 1 a cruel person. 2 a wild, savage animal.

**bubble** *noun* a thin ball of liquid filled with air or gas, especially one that floats. *A soap bubble.* **bubble** *verb. The water is bubbling on the stove.* **bubbly** *adjective. Bubbly lemonade.*

**buccaneer** *noun* an old word for pirate.

The buccaneers boarded the ship wielding their daggers. Then they took all the valuables on board.

**SPELLING NOTE**

*Be careful with the spelling of 'Buddha' and 'Buddhism' and note the double 'd' and the position of the 'h'. The word 'Buddha' means 'the enlightened one'.*

**Bucharest** *noun* the capital of Romania.

**buck** *noun* 1 a male deer or rabbit. 2 (slang) a dollar. *That will cost you several bucks.*

**buck** *verb* When a horse bucks it leaps into the air with its head down.

**bucket** *noun* a container with a handle for carrying water etc.

**buckle** *noun* a metal fastener for joining the ends of a belt. **buckle** *verb.*

**bud** *noun* a small, round swelling on a plant that will grow into a leaf or flower. **bud** *verb. The trees are starting to bud.* **budding** *adjective.* **nip in the bud** *expression* to deal with a problem etc. while it is still small.

**Budapest** *noun* the capital of Hungary.

**Buddhism** *noun* the religion founded by the Buddha in the 500s BC. **Buddhist** *adjective, noun. Buddhist monks.*

The young Buddhist monks are praying in the temple. Their heads are shaved and they wear robes dyed with saffron, a valuable crocus flower.

**budge** *verb* to move a little.

**budgerigar** *noun* a small, parrot-like bird, often kept as a pet.

**budget** *noun* a plan of how money should be spent. **budget** *verb.*

**Buenos Aires** *noun* the capital of Argentina.

**buff** *noun* 1 a dull yellow colour. 2 (slang) a person who knows a lot about a subject. *A cricket buff.*

**buffalo** *noun* 1 one of a variety of wild oxen from Asia and Africa with long curved horns. 2 a North American bison.

**buffet** *noun* (say **buh**-fay) a meal set out on a table from which guests help themselves.

**bug** *noun* 1 an insect, especially an unpleasant one. *Bed bugs.* 2 a germ causing a minor illness. *A tummy bug.* 3 a fault in a computer program. 4 a hidden microphone that records conversations.

**bugle** *noun* a brass musical instrument like a small trumpet used mainly in the armed forces. **bugler** *noun.*

**build** (builds, building, built) *verb* to make something by joining different pieces together. *The house that Jack built.*

The truck is at the building site, pouring concrete into the foundations

**build** *noun* the shape and size of a person. *A woman of slender build.*

**builder** *noun* a person who earns a living by putting up buildings.

**building** *noun* a construction such as a house or supermarket with walls and a roof.

**built-up** *adjective* A built-up area is covered with houses, shops and other buildings.

**Bujumbura** *noun* the capital of Burundi.

**bulb** *noun* 1 the roundish part of plants like daffodils and tulips from which the flowers grow. 2 (or **light bulb**) the pear-shaped glass part of an electric lamp that gives the light.

The pressure of the electric current through the bulb's thin wire filament makes it glow.

Wire filament

**Bulgaria** *noun* a country in eastern Europe.

**bulge** *verb* to swell or stick out. *His sack was bulging with presents.*

**DID YOU KNOW?**

*The expression 'like a bull in a china shop' means to behave in a rough, coarse and clumsy way, likely to cause damage.*

**AMAZING FACT**

Early buildings were made from the materials that were most readily available. In Europe, houses were made of woven branches filled with mud. Other cultures used birchbark laid over poles or sometimes animal hides over bones.

**bulk** *noun* 1 great in size. 2 most of. *The bulk of the work has been done.* **bulky** *adjective. A bulky package.*

**bull** *noun* a male cow, elephant, seal or whale. *A bull elephant has huge tusks.*

**bulldog** *noun* a strong, fearless breed of dog. *The fierce bulldog bit the postman.*

**bulldozer** *noun* a powerful vehicle with a big metal blade in front for moving earth and clearing land.

A bulldozer clears up after logging in a sustainable plantation.

**bullet** *noun* the small pointed piece of metal that is fired from a gun.

**bullion** *noun* large bars of gold or silver.

**bull's eye** *noun* the small round centre of a target. *Peter hits the bull's eye every time.*

**bully** *noun* somebody who tries to frighten or hurt a weaker or smaller person. **bully** *verb. The bully was expelled from school.*

**bump** *verb* to collide or knock into something. *Things that go bump in the night.* **bump** *noun.* **bump into** to meet accidentally. *I bumped into Adam.*

**bump** *noun.* a round lump caused by something hitting you. **bumpy** *adjective. A very bumpy road.*

**bumper** *noun* a bar fixed to the front and back of a motor vehicle to protect it from bumps. (US) fender.

**bumptious** *adjective* A bumptious person is full of self-importance.

**bun** *noun* 1 a small, round cake. 2 a round coil of hair at the back of a woman's head.

Buns are made of white flour and sugar and may be iced.

B

**bunch** *noun* 1 a group of things of the same kind tied or joined together. *An enormous bunch of keys.* 2 a group of people. *A nice bunch of kids.* **bunch** *verb.*

**bundle** *noun* a number of things tied loosely together or wrapped in a cloth. *A bundle of old newspapers.* **bundle** *verb* 1 to tie up loosely. 2 to push or hurry away. *The children were bundled into the bus.*

A bundle of towels was tied together with a blue ribbon.

**bungalow** *noun* a house with all the rooms on the ground floor.

**bungee jumping** *noun* a sport in which a person jumps from a great height with elastic ropes tied to their legs to stop them hitting the ground.

**bungle** *verb* to do something awkwardly and badly. **bungler** *noun.*

**bunk** *noun* 1 a narrow bed attached to a wall on a ship, train etc. 2 **bunkbeds** a bed that has one or more beds above or below it. *The children slept in bunkbeds.*

**bunny** *noun* a child's name for a rabbit.

**buoy** *noun* a floating, anchored marker in the sea that warns ships of danger etc.

**buoyant** *adjective* 1 able to float. 2 A buoyant person is cheerful.

The life jacket saved his life by keeping him buoyant.

**burden** *noun* 1 a heavy load. 2 something that is difficult to carry or put up with. *The responsibility is a great burden to him.* **burden** *verb.*

**burglar** *noun* a person who breaks into a building to steal things. **burglary** *noun.* **burgle** *verb.*

**WORD HISTORY**

*'Bungalow' comes from a Hindi word 'bangla', meaning 'a house in the style of Bengal', a region in Northeast India where thatched, single-storey houses are common.*

**burial** *noun* the act of putting a dead body in a grave. *The burial was a sad affair.*

**Burkina Faso** *noun* a country in Africa.

The flag of Burkina Faso has a gold star on a red and green ground.

**burn** (burns, burning, burned or burnt) *verb* 1 to set fire to something. To be destroyed by fire. *He burnt the rubbish.* 2 to hurt or damage with fire. *He burnt his hand very badly while cooking.* **burn** *noun. She has a nasty burn right across her face.*

**burp** *verb* to let wind from your stomach come noisily out of your mouth, to belch. **burp** *noun. He let out a loud burp.*

**burrow** *noun* a hole made in the ground by an animal as a shelter. **burrow** *verb* to dig or make a tunnel. *Lots of rabbits have been burrowing in the field.*

**burst** (burst, bursting, burst) *verb* to explode. To break apart suddenly. *The balloons burst in the heat.* **burst into** *He burst into the room. She burst into tears.*

**Burundi** *noun* a country in Africa.

**bury** (buries, burying, buried) *verb* 1 to put a dead body or thing in the ground. *The dog buried its bone in the garden.* 2 to hide. *He wept and buried his head in his hands.*

**bus** *noun* a large road vehicle for carrying a lot of passengers.

**bush** *noun* a shrub or large plant like a small tree with many branches. **bushy** *adjective. Bushy eyebrows.* **the bush** wild, uncultivated land, especially in Australia. **bushman** a native of the African bush. **bushranger** an outlaw living wild in the Australian outback or bush.

The burning bush threw out such a lot of light that the shepherd was blinded.

B

**business** *noun* (say **biz**-ness) 1 buying and selling goods and services. The company or organization that makes, buys or sells things. *Business is very good at the moment.* 2 concerns, events or situations in general. *What she did is none of your business.*

**businesslike** *adjective* efficient, methodical.

**businessman, businesswoman** a man or woman who works in a business or who owns a business.

**busker** *noun* a singer, musician etc. who performs in the street for money. **busk** *verb*.

**bust** *noun* 1 a statue of a person's head and the top part of the chest. 2 a woman's breasts. *What is your bust size?*

This bust of William Lyon Mackenzie can be seen in Queen's Park, Toronto, Canada.

**bust** *adjective* (slang) 1 broken. *The television is bust.* 2 bankrupt. *The haulage company has gone bust.*

**bustle** *verb* to hurry because you are busy. *He bustled about putting things away.* **bustle** *noun*. *The bustle of the supermarket.*

**busy** (busier, busiest) *adjective* 1 If you are busy, you have a lot to do. *I'm too busy to see you today.* 2 full of people or activity. *A busy office.* **busily** *adverb*. **busybody** *noun* a person who interferes with other people's business and gives unwanted advice.

**butcher** *noun* a person who cuts up meat and sells it.

**butler** *noun* the chief male servant in a house. *The butler's pantry.*

**butt** *verb* to push or hit with the head or horns like a bull or goat, to ram. **butt in** to interrupt. *Don't butt in when I'm talking.*

**butt** *noun* 1 a large barrel. 2 the thick end or handle of a gun etc. 3 the end of a finished cigarette. 4 a person that others joke about or criticize. *I am the butt of all his jokes.*

**butter** *noun* a soft yellow food made from cream and milk. **butter** *verb*. *Please butter the bread and pass it to your Aunt Maud.*

**AMAZING FACT**

There are more than 17,000 varieties of butterfly.

Some species migrate. The monarch butterfly spends the summer months in Canada and the northern US, then flies to southern California and Mexico for the winter.

**WORD HISTORY**

*'Butler' comes from the French 'bouteillier', a man who puts wine into bottles. The Normans brought the word to England at the time of the conquest in 1066.*

**buttercup** *noun* a small plant with yellow petals that grows in fields.

**butterfly** *noun* an insect with large white or colourful wings.

The habitat of many butterflies is under threat because of urban development.

**buttocks** *plural noun* the fleshy parts of your body on which you sit.

**button** *noun* 1 a small, round thing sewn on to clothes to hold them together. 2 a small thing or device that you press to make a machine work. *Which button do I press to get this machine to start printing?*

**buttress** *noun* a support for an outside wall. **buttress** *verb*.

**buy** (buys, buying, bought) *verb* to get something by paying money for it, to purchase. *He bought a new car.*

**buzz** *verb* to make a low humming sound like a bee. *The buzz of many flies.*

**buzzard** *noun* a large bird of prey that hunts other animals for food.

A buzzard glides on a warm air current, waiting to spot its prey.

**byelection** *noun* a special election that is held when an MP dies or resigns.

**bypass** *noun* a road that takes traffic around a town etc. and not through it. **bypass** *verb*.

**bystander** a person who looks on at something but takes no part in it, a spectator. *The bystanders cheered loudly.*

**byte** *noun* a group of bits or units of information in a computer's memory.

# Cc

**cab** *noun* 1 a taxi. 2 the front part of a lorry, train or crane in which the driver sits.

**cabbage** *noun* a large round vegetable with thick green leaves. *A red cabbage has purple leaves that go blue when cooked.*

**cabin** *noun* 1 a small wooden house. *A log cabin.* 2 a room or compartment in a ship or plane.

In Canada, a log cabin in the pine forests makes an ideal holiday home.

**cabinet** *noun* 1 a cupboard used for storing things in. *We keep our documents in a filing cabinet.* 2 **Cabinet** the group of senior ministers who decide on government policy.

**cable** *noun* 1 a thick rope of fibres or wire. 2 a bundle of wires inside a plastic casing through which electricity flows. *An electric cable.* 3 a telegram.

**cable car** *noun* a cabin hanging from a cable which carries people up and down a mountainside.

**cable television** *noun* a system in which TV programmes are sent to sets along electric cables instead of as radio waves.

**cackle** *verb* to laugh in a loud and nasty way. *The witch cackled as she cast her spell.*

**cactus** (cacti) *noun* a fleshy plant covered with spines that grows in hot countries.

**cadge** *verb* to get something by begging for it. *Can I cadge a lift?*

**café** *noun* (say **kaf**-ay) a small restaurant that serves refreshments and light meals.

**cafeteria** *noun* (say kaf-it-**eer**-ee-uh) a self-service restaurant.

**cage** *noun* a container with wires or bars in which animals or birds are kept.

**Cairo** *noun* the capital of Egypt.

**cajole** *verb* to persuade somebody into doing something by flattering them. *He cajoled her into giving him the information.*

**AMAZING FACT**

The forerunner of today's calculator was the abacus – invented about 5000 years ago!

**SPELLING NOTE**

*'Café' is the French word for 'coffee' or 'coffee house' and is usually spelt with an acute accent on the 'e' (é).*

**cake** *noun* a sweet mixture of flour, eggs and sugar baked in an oven. *I had a piece of her birthday cake.* **a piece of cake** really easy.

This gorgeous cake is layered with jam and topped with pink icing, cherries and cream.

**calamity** *noun* a disaster, such as losing all your money. **calamitous** *adjective.*

**calcium** *noun* a chemical substance found in limestone, teeth and bones.

**calculate** *verb* 1 to work out an amount by using numbers. *We calculated that we'd arrive at about 10 o'clock.* 2 to plan. *The ads are calculated to attract students.* **calculation** *noun.*

**calculator** *noun* a small electronic machine for doing sums.

**calendar** *noun* a list that shows the days, weeks and months of the year, so you can look up the date. Calendars also list important events in the year.

**calf** (calves) *noun* a young cow, elephant or whale.

A calf learns to walk in the first couple of hours after birth.

**calf** (calves) *noun* the back part of your leg that is between the knee and the ankle.

**call** *verb* 1 to shout or speak in a loud voice, usually to attract somebody's attention. 2 to tell somebody to come to you. *Why don't you come when I call you?* 3 to telephone. 4 to give a name to somebody or something. *Her brother is called John.* 5 to describe something or somebody. *I wouldn't call her fat.* 6 to get somebody to come. *We had to call the doctor.* 7 to make a short visit. 8 to wake somebody up. *Call me at seven in the morning.* **call** *noun* 1 a shout or cry. 2 a visit. 3 a telephone call. **call for** to collect somebody. *I'll call for you on my way to school.* 2 to require. *This calls for prompt action.* **call off** to stop something. *The meeting was called off.* **call out** 1 to shout. 2 to summon in an emergency. *The fire brigade was called out twice last night.* 3 to order workers to strike.

C

**calling** *noun* an occupation, especially a profession that involves helping others.

**callous** *adjective* not caring about other people's feelings. *His behaviour was selfish and callous.*

**calm** *adjective* 1 not windy. 2 When the sea is calm, it is still and without waves. 3 not excited and not showing any worry. *Please stay calm when we land.* **calm** *noun.*

**calorie** *noun* 1 a unit for measuring the energy that food produces. *One slice of brown bread has 95 calories, which is less than a slice of cake.* 2 a unit of heat.

**calves** plural of calf.

**Cambodia** *noun* a country in Southeast Asia.

**camcorder** *noun* a video camera and recorder all in one.

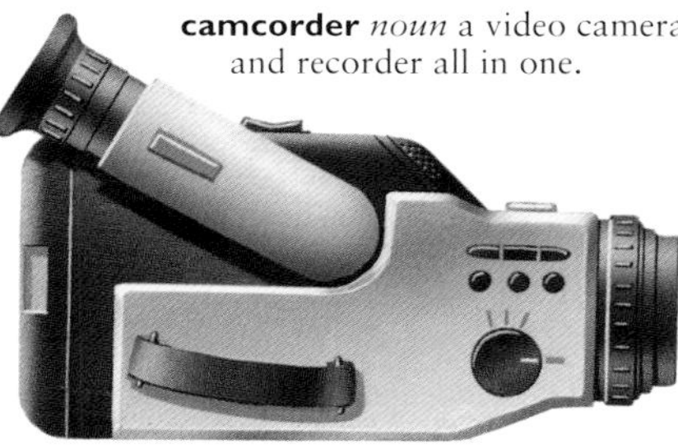

With a camcorder you can film family events such as weddings.

**came** past tense of come.

**camel** *noun* an animal with a long neck and one or two humps on its back. Camels are used in the desert for riding and carrying goods. *A camel train.*

**camera** *noun* an apparatus for taking photographs or making films and television pictures. *Smile at the camera, please!*

**Cameroon** *noun* a country in Africa.

**camouflage** *noun* (say **kam**-off-lahzh) a way of hiding things by making them blend in with their surroundings. *A polar bear's white fur is good camouflage in the snow.* **camouflage** *verb. The enemy camp was well camouflaged behind the bushes.*

**camp** *noun* a place where people live in tents, huts or caravans, usually for a short time. **camp** *verb* to make a camp. **camping** *noun. Scouts and guides go camping.*

Bedouins sit inside a tent made of camel skin at their camp in the North African desert.

**AMAZING FACT**

Canada is the second largest country in the world.

Canada's northern lands reach deep into the frozen Arctic, but most Canadians live in the south, close to the border with America.

**DID YOU KNOW?**

*A one-humped camel is called an Arabian camel or a dromedary. The two-humped animal is a Bactrian camel.*

**campaign** *noun* a series of planned activities to achieve a particular result. *A successful advertising campaign.* **campaign** *verb. He's campaigning for the president.*

**campus** *noun* the grounds of a university or college. *Most first-year students live on campus in halls of residence.*

**can** *noun* a metal container for holding food or drink. *A can of worms.*

**can** (could) *verb* 1 to be able to. *Can you carry that heavy box?* 2 to know how to do something or have the ability to do it. *She can speak German.* 3 to be allowed to do something. *The teacher says we can go home after the break.* 4 a polite way of asking somebody to do something. *Can you tell me the time?*

**Canada** *noun* a country in North America.

**Canadian** *noun* a person who comes from Canada. **Canadian** *adjective. A Canadian film.*

**canal** *noun* 1 a man-made waterway for boats to travel along or to bring water to an area. 2 a tube in a plant or an animal that carries food.

**canary** (canaries) *noun* a small yellow bird that sings.

**Canberra** *noun* the capital of Australia.

**cancel** (cancelling, cancelled) *verb* 1 to say that a planned activity will not take place. *The concert was cancelled because the singer had flu.* 2 to stop an instruction for something. *I decided not to go and cancelled the booking.* 3 to mark a ticket or stamp to stop it from being used again. When you cancel a cheque, it is no longer valid. **cancellation** *noun.* **cancel out** to balance and be equal to each other.

**cancer** *noun* 1 a serious disease in which abnormal growths form in the body. *Smoking can cause lung cancer.* 2 **Cancer** a sign of the zodiac (21 June to 22 July).

**candid** *adjective* honest. If you're candid, you tell the truth even when it is unwelcome. **candour** *noun.*

**candidate** *noun* 1 a person who wants to be chosen for a special position. *The Labour candidate was elected.* 2 a person taking an examination.

**candle** *noun* a stick of wax with a piece of string (a wick) through it, which gives light when it burns.

**candlestick** *noun* a holder for a candle. *Brass candlesticks.*

**candy** (candies) *noun* a sweet.

**cane** *noun* a long thin stick. Cane is the hollow stem from a plant such as bamboo. **cane** *verb* to hit with a cane.

C

**cannabis** *noun* 1 a kind of hemp plant. 2 a drug made from the plant.

**cannibal** *noun* 1 a person who eats other people. 2 an animal that eats its own kind. **cannibalism** *noun*.

**cannon** *noun* a big gun that fires cannon balls.

Cannons were the first guns and appeared in the early 14th century.

**cannot** = can not, see can. *Unfortunately we cannot come to the party.*

**canoe** *noun* a light, long and narrow boat that is moved by using a paddle. **canoe** *verb* to go in a canoe. **canoeing** *noun*.

**can't** short for cannot, see can. 'Can't' is mainly spoken rather than written.

**canteen** *noun* a restaurant in a factory, office, school or college.

**canter** *noun* the movement of a horse, faster than a trot but slower than a gallop. **canter** *verb*.

**canvas** *noun* 1 a strong, rough cloth used for tents, sails and bags. *We spent the night under canvas.* 2 a stretched piece of cloth on which oil paintings are done. 3 an oil painting on canvas. 4 the floor of a boxing or wrestling ring.

**canvass** *verb* to go to people to ask for their vote, support or opinion. *They canvassed the neighbours for support.*

**canyon** *noun* a deep, steep valley, usually with a river running through it.

America's Grand Canyon is regarded as one of the seven wonders of the natural world.

**cap** *noun* 1 a hat with a peak. 2 a lid or top on a bottle or tube. 3 a piece of paper covered with a tiny amount of explosive that makes a bang when used in a toy gun. **cap** *verb* to put a cap or top on something.

**capable** *adjective* having the ability to do something. **capability** *noun*.

**SPELLING NOTE**

*Note that the cloth called canvas has one 's' at the end, while the verb asking for support has two – to canvass. The two words sound exactly the same.*

**AMAZING FACT**

The main difference between a canoe and a kayak is that kayak paddles are double-bladed – one on each side, and canoe paddles are single-bladed.

**capacity** *noun* 1 the amount that can be held. *The stadium has a capacity of 30,000.* If a place is filled to capacity, it is completely full. 2 the ability to do something. *Algebra is beyond my capacity.* 3 a position. *In my capacity as head teacher.*

**cape** *noun* a loose cloak without sleeves and fastened at the neck.

**cape** *noun* a large piece of land going out into the sea. *The Cape of Good Hope is in South Africa.*

**Cape Town** *noun* the legal capital of South Africa.

**Cape Verde** *noun* a country in the Atlantic Ocean off West Africa.

The flag of Cape Verde has a circle of yellow stars on a striped red, blue and white ground.

**capital** *noun* 1 a city where the government of a country is. *Paris is the capital of France.* 2 a letter written or printed in a large form (A, B, C), used at the beginning of a sentence or a name. *Write your name in capitals.* 3 a sum of money used to start up a business, as well as money or property used to make more money. *He put up the capital for the new company.* **capital** *adjective*.

**capitalism** *noun* (say **kap**-it-ul-izm) a system in which a country's trade and industry are controlled by the owners of capital and are run for profit.

**capitalist** *noun* 1 a person who lends his money to businesses, to make more money. 2 a person who supports capitalism. **capitalist** *adjective*.

**capital punishment** *noun* punishment in which the criminal is killed.

**capitulate** *verb* to admit that you have lost and give in under agreed conditions. **capitulation** *noun*.

**capsize** *verb* to overturn in water. *The boat capsized in deep water.*

The friends wait to be rescued on top of the capsized boat.

**capsule** *noun* 1 a pill containing medicine. 2 the seed case of a plant. 3 the part of a spaceship that holds the crew and instruments and can be separated from the craft in space.

**captain** *noun* 1 the leader of a team or group. *Who's the captain of your football team?* 2 a person in command of a ship or an aircraft. 3 an officer in the army or navy. **captain** *verb* to be captain of a sports team.

Captain James Cook and the crew of the *Endeavour* step ashore in New Zealand and meet the Maoris for the first time.

**caption** *noun* 1 words put with a picture to explain what it is about. 2 a heading or short title in a newspaper or magazine.

**captive** *noun* a person or an animal taken prisoner. If you are taken captive, you are taken as a prisoner. **captive** *adjective* kept as a prisoner. **a captive audience** a group of people who have to listen to somebody. *TV viewers are a captive audience for advertisers.* **captivity** *noun.*

**capture** *verb* 1 to make a person or an animal a prisoner. 2 to get something by force, skill, attraction or trickery. *Her beauty captured his heart.* 3 to put data into a computer. 4 to describe something in words or pictures. *The film captures the loneliness of old age.* **capture** *noun* 1 the act of capturing. 2 somebody or something that has been taken by force.

**car** *noun* 1 a car has four wheels and an engine and room for a driver and passengers. Cars drive on roads and motorways. *We usually go by car.* 2 a railway carriage. *This train has a dining car.*

Most cars have the engine at the front.

**Caracas** *noun* the capital of Venezuela.

**carat** *noun* 1 a unit for measuring the weight of precious stones such as diamonds, equal to 0.2 grams. 2 a unit for measuring gold. Pure gold is 24 carats.

**caravan** *noun* 1 a home on wheels in which people live or spend their holidays. Caravans are usually pulled by a car. 2 a group of people travelling across the desert.

**DID YOU KNOW?**

*The phrase 'on the cards' comes from fortune-tellers who predict the future by reading and interpreting special cards.*

**WORD HISTORY**

*The cardigan is named after the Earl of Cardigan, who led the Charge of the Light Brigade in the Crimean War in 1854.*

**carbon** *noun* 1 a substance that is found in all living things. Diamonds and coal are made of carbon. 2 a thin piece of paper with a coloured coating on one side which is put between two sheets of paper for making copies of what is written or typed, also called carbon paper. 3 a copy made by using carbon paper, a carbon copy.

**carbon dioxide** *noun* a gas that is present in the air and is also formed when animals and people breathe out.

**carbon monoxide** *noun* a poisonous gas produced especially by car engines.

**carburettor** *noun* the part of a car engine in which petrol and air are mixed to provide power. *The carburettor needs replacing.*

**carcass** (carcasses) *noun* the body of a dead animal.

Bearded vultures gather at a carcass to feed.

**card** *noun* 1 a folded piece of stiff paper with a picture on the front and a message inside which you send to somebody on special occasions. *A birthday card.* 2 a piece of stiff paper for writing information on. 3 a postcard. 4 a small piece of printed plastic which you use if you have an account at a bank or a shop. *I paid with my credit card.* 5 one of a pack of 52 playing cards, used for games like whist, bridge or poker. *We played cards all afternoon.* **on the cards** likely or possible. **put your cards on the table** to make your plans known.

**cardboard** *noun* thick stiff paper used for making boxes. *A cardboard box.*

**Cardiff** *noun* the capital of Wales.

**cardigan** *noun* a knitted jacket that usually buttons up at the front.

**care** *verb* to be interested and feel that something is important. *We care about the environment.* If you don't care about something, it doesn't matter to you and you don't worry. **care** *noun* 1 serious attention, in an effort to avoid making any mistakes. *She plans her essays with great care.* 2 If you take care of somebody or something, you look after them. 3 a person or object you are responsible for. *Children in care are looked after by the authorities because their parents can't care for them.* 4 worry and sorrow. 5 **care of** (c/o *abbreviation*) written when sending a letter or parcel to somebody who is living at another address.

**care for** 1 to look after somebody or something. 2 to like a person. *Although he's nasty to her, she still cares for him.* If you care for something, you enjoy it. *I don't care for dancing.*

The boy was caring for the orphan lamb.

**career** *noun* 1 a job or profession that you do for a long time and hope to be successful in. *He's chosen a career in teaching.* 2 the development and progress through a person's working life. **career** *verb* to move very fast and in an uncontrolled way. *The car careered into a wall.*

**careful** *adjective* 1 paying attention to what you do in order to avoid danger or damage. *Be careful when crossing the road.* 2 done with care and thought. *A careful report.* **carefully** *adverb*. **carefulness** *noun*.

**careless** *adjective* 1 not paying attention or taking care about something and making mistakes. 2 thoughtless. *Careless driving costs lives.* 3 untroubled and not worried. *She's careless with money.* **carelessly** *adverb*.

**caress** *verb* to stroke or kiss somebody to show your love for them. **caress** *noun* a loving touch.

**cargo** (cargoes) *noun* goods carried in a ship or plane.

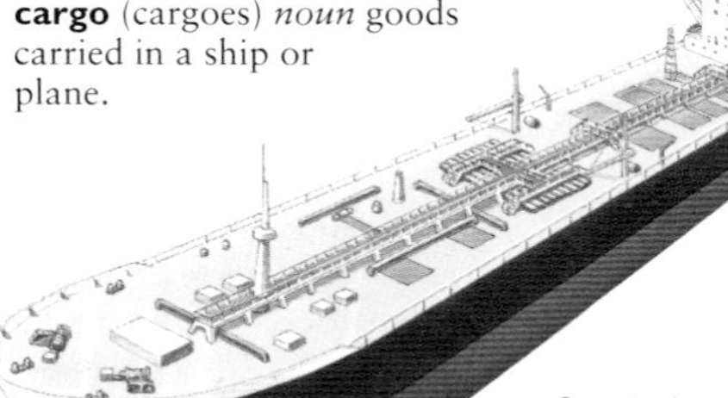

Supertankers designed to carry oil are among the world's biggest cargo ships.

**caricature** *noun* an amusing picture or description of somebody, so that parts of his character seem odder than they really are. **caricature** *verb* to make a caricature of a person. *He's brilliant at caricaturing all sorts of politicians.*

**carnation** *noun* a scented garden flower.

**carnival** *noun* a public festival with music, dance and processions of people in wild make-up and fancy dress.

**AMAZING FACT**

Carnivores generally have very good hearing and eyesight, a keen sense of smell and are able to move fast enough to hunt and catch their prey.

**WORD BUILDING**

*The suffix '-ful' means full of. It is usually spelt with just one 'l'. 'Careful' means full of care or taking care. The suffix '-less' means without, e.g. careless.*

**AMAZING FACT**

Carnival in Latin American countries is a major celebration that may last a full week or more.

In New Orleans, Louisiana, it is known as 'Mardi Gras' and marks the period of festivity before Lent.

**carnivore** *noun* an animal that eats meat. Lions and tigers are carnivores. **carnivorous** *adjective*.

**carol** *noun* a Christmas song.

**carpenter** *noun* a person who makes or repairs wooden things.

**carpet** *noun* a thick woven covering for floors and stairs. **sweep something under the carpet** to keep something secret.

**carriage** *noun* 1 a section of a train for passengers. 2 an old-fashioned passenger vehicle pulled by horses. 3 the cost of carrying goods from one place to another. *Carriage paid.* 4 the movable part of a machine. *The typewriter carriage holds the paper.*

In the 18th century Russians travelled the snowy roads in sledge carriages drawn by a team of horses.

**carrier** *noun* 1 a construction usually fixed to a car or bicycle for carrying things. 2 a person who has a disease and passes it on to others without suffering from it.

**carrion** *noun* the flesh of dead animals.

**carrot** *noun* a plant with an orange root grown as a vegetable.

**carry** (carries, carrying, carried) *verb* 1 to hold something or somebody and go from one place to another. *The porter carried my suitcase.* 2 to hold something up, e.g. a roof or ceiling. 3 to pass something like a disease from one person to another. *Mosquitoes can carry dangerous diseases.* 4 to make sound move through the air. *Her voice carried right to the back of the hall.* 5 to win the support of others in a debate when voting is involved. *The motion was carried by 20 votes to 10.* 6 to print something. *The newspapers carried pictures of the funeral.* 7 to have as a result. *In some countries murder still carries the death penalty.* 8 to keep goods in stock. 9 If somebody carries weight, people respect that person's opinion. **get carried away** to be very excited. **carry on** 1 to continue. *I tried to speak to him but he just carried on reading.* 2 to manage in a difficult situation. 3 to complain and make a fuss about something. *My mother carried on all day about the noise.* 4 (informal) If a person is carrying on with somebody, they are having an affair.

C

**carry out** *verb* to fulfil, to do what you have promised or have been told to do. *We carried out our plan and explored the cave.*

**cart** *noun* a vehicle for carrying goods, usually drawn by a horse. **cart** *verb* 1 to carry in a cart. 2 to carry something heavy and find it tiring. *I don't want to cart those bags around town.*

**carton** *noun* a plastic or cardboard container for food or drink.

**cartoon** *noun* 1 an amusing drawing or set of drawings, often showing something of interest in the news. *There was a funny cartoon about the strike in the newspaper.* 2 an animated film. *Have you seen the latest Disney cartoon?* **cartoonist** *noun.*

**cartridge** *noun* 1 a container holding film for a camera, a tape, a typewriter ribbon or ink for a pen or printer. 2 a tube holding explosive for a bullet. 3 a small case that holds the stylus of a record-player.

**carve** *verb* 1 to make something by cutting a special shape out of wood or stone. *This statue is carved from marble.* **carving** *noun. An African wood carving.* 2 to cut up cooked meat into slices.

**cascade** *noun* a waterfall. **cascade** *verb* to fall in a cascade.

**case** *noun* 1 a container. *A case of wine.* 2 a suitcase. *I packed my case and left.*

Lightweight suitcases are ideal for air travel.

**case** *noun* 1 an event or a situation of a particular kind. *In this case I wouldn't pay the fee.* 2 an event the police are investigating or a question which will be decided on in court. *A murder case.* 3 an example of something bad, or of a disease. *A case of Asian flu.* 4 a patient, a solicitor's client, or a person looked after by a social worker. 5 facts and arguments for and against a plan used in a discussion. *The case for giving up smoking.* 6 in grammar, the change in the form of a word showing how it relates to other words in the sentence. Emma's is the possessive case of Emma. **in case** an action taken in advance referring to a particular thing that might happen. *I've brought a map in case we get lost.* **in any case** anyway. *I'll come in any case.*

**DID YOU KNOW?**

*The first full-length cartoon made as a feature film was Disney's 'Snow White and the Seven Dwarfs', which came out in 1938.*

**cash** *noun* money in coins and notes. *Please pay in cash.* **cash** *verb* When you cash a cheque, you get money for it.

**cash-and-carry** *noun* a large supermarket that sells goods cheaper than other shops.

**cashier** *noun* a person who takes in or pays out money in a bank or shop.

**cashpoint** *noun* an automatic machine, usually in or outside a bank, from which customers can withdraw cash.

**cask** *noun* a container like a barrel for holding liquids.

**casket** *noun* a small box for jewellery or other valuable things.

**cassette** *noun* a small flat plastic container with tape or film inside it.

**cassette recorder** *noun* a machine for recording and playing music and other sounds on cassettes.

Most cassette recorders are manufactured in the Far East.

**cast** *noun* 1 all the actors in a film or play. 2 an object made from liquid metal, plastic or plaster poured into a mould. 3 a hard covering made of plaster that keeps a broken bone in place while it is mending. **cast** *verb* 1 to throw. *The fishermen cast their nets into the sea.* 2 To cast doubt on something means that you're not sure about it. 3 to give your vote in an election. *Have all the votes been cast?* 4 to choose actors for a film or play. 5 to make an object by pouring liquid into a mould and leaving it to harden. *A beautiful figure cast in bronze.* **cast off** 1 to get rid of something. 2 to set off in a boat by untying the rope. 3 In knitting, you cast off when you take the stitches off the needle to finish a piece. **cast on** You cast on when you start knitting something and put the first stitches on to the needle.

**castaway** *noun* a shipwrecked person.

**castle** *noun* 1 a large, strong building with high walls that was built to protect kings, queens and others from their enemies. 2 a chesspiece, also called a rook. *He took the pawn with the castle.*

Robinson Crusoe is the world's most famous fictional castaway.

C

**Castries** *noun* the capital of St Lucia.

**casual** *adjective* 1 happening by chance, without planning. *A casual chat.* 2 relaxed and not doing things very seriously, sometimes seeming uninterested. *The teacher didn't like his casual attitude.* 3 informal. *I wear casual clothes at home.* 4 not permanent or regular. *Casual work.* **casually** *adverb.*

**casualty** *noun* a person who is injured or killed in a war or an accident. *There were five casualties in the car crash.*

**cat** *noun* 1 a small furry pet animal. 2 a large wild animal of the cat family. Lions, tigers and leopards are all big cats. **let the cat out of the bag** to tell a secret.

Today's domestic cat is believed to have originated in Egypt.

**catalogue** *noun* a list of names, places, goods and other things put in a particular order so that they can be found easily. *I buy all my clothes from a catalogue.* **catalogue** *verb* to list something in a catalogue. *The library books are all catalogued.*

**catalyst** *noun* (say **kat**-uh-list) something that causes a change or speeds up an event. One person's actions can also act as a catalyst to others.

**catapult** *noun* 1 a Y-shaped stick with an elastic band, used by children to shoot small stones. 2 an ancient military machine used to hurl stones and rocks at the enemy. **catapult** *verb* to launch, as if from a catapult. *She was catapulted to stardom.*

**cataract** *noun* a large waterfall.

**cataract** *noun* a growth over the eyeball that blurs a person's vision. *My grandfather had a cataract removed.*

The cataract is rushing down the mountainside.

**catarrh** *noun* (say ku-**tar**) an inflammation of the nose and throat similar to a cold.

**catastrophe** *noun* (say ku-**tass**-trof-ee) a disastrous event that causes suffering and great damage. **catastrophic** *adjective. A catastrophic mistake.* **catastrophically** *adverb. It went catastrophically wrong.*

**WORD HISTORY**

*The expression 'to let the cat out of the bag' probably started in market places hundreds of years ago. Traders would sometimes secretly put a cat in a bag and pretend it was a pig, which was worth much more.*

**catch** (catches, catching, caught) *verb* 1 to get hold of an object that is moving through the air. *He threw the ball and I caught it.* 2 to capture an animal or a person after chasing them. *You can catch fish in a net and mice in a trap.* 3 to be in time for a bus or train. *Leave now if you want to catch the train.* 4 to suddenly discover a person doing something wrong. *The teacher caught them smoking in the loo.* 5 to become stuck. *I caught my shirt on a nail.* 6 to manage to hear. *I didn't catch his name.* 7 to become infected by an illness. *The baby caught a cold.* 8 to overtake. *He's only just left, you can still catch him.* 9 If you catch sight of somebody or something, you see them for just a moment. **catch fire** to start burning. **catch somebody's eye** to attract their attention. **catch the post** to post a letter just before the next collection.

Anglers often tend to exaggerate the size of the fish they catch.

**catch** *noun* 1 catching something like a ball. *He saved the game with a brilliant catch.* 2 something caught or worth having. *She's a good catch, I should marry her if you can.* 3 a trick, a hidden difficulty. *That car's too cheap, there must be a catch.* 4 a hook or another method of fastening something or locking a door. *The catch on the door is broken.* 5 a game in which children throw a ball to each other. **catch on** 1 to become popular. *The new fashion soon caught on.* 2 to understand. *I didn't catch on at first.* **catch up** 1 to reach somebody who is in front of you. *You go on, I'll soon catch up with you.* 2 to make up work that you are behind on. *I stayed up late to catch up on my homework.* 3 If something catches up with a person, they have to deal with an unpleasant situation they wanted to avoid. *My laziness caught up with me at last.*

**catcher** *noun* a person or thing that catches. *Grandpa was a mole catcher.*

**catching** *adjective* spreading quickly from one person to another. *Is the disease that you are suffering from very catching?*

**category** *noun* a division or class.

**cater** *verb* 1 to provide food and drink for parties. **caterer** *noun.* 2 to provide whatever is needed. *They don't cater for children.*

**caterpillar** *noun* a small worm-like creature with many legs. *Caterpillars turn into beautiful butterflies.*

Caterpillars are voracious eaters and can do a lot of damage to crops.

**cathedral** *noun* a large church. The main church of a district.

**Catholic** *noun* a member of the Roman Catholic Church. **Catholic** *adjective. Their children go* to a Catholic school. **Catholicism** *noun.*

**catseye** *noun* a spot in the road that reflects cars' lights at night.

These cattle are Friesians. Commercial dairy cows can produce 18 litres of a milk a day.

**cattle** *noun* farm animals, especially cows. Cattle are kept for beef and milk.

**caught** past tense of catch.

**cauliflower** *noun* a vegetable with green leaves and a large head of white flower buds. Only the white part is eaten.

**cause** *noun* 1 a person or thing that makes something happen. *Nobody knows the cause of the fire.* 2 reason. *You've got no cause for complaint.* 3 a purpose for which people work, such as a charity. *The money is for a good cause.* **cause** *verb* to make something happen. *The accident was caused by negligence.*

**causeway** *noun* a raised road or footpath across wet ground.

**caution** *noun* 1 a warning. 2 the act of taking care to avoid danger or making mistakes. **caution** *verb* to give a warning to somebody. **cautious** *adjective.*

**cavalry** *noun* soldiers on horses.

**cave** *noun* an underground hollow, sometimes in the side of a cliff or hill. **cave in** *verb* to fall down. *The roof caved in.*

**caveman** *noun* a person living in a cave. *The caveman killed a mammoth.*

**caving** *noun* exploring caves.

**cavity** *noun* a hole.

**CD** *abbreviation* compact disc.

**CD-ROM** *abbreviation* compact disc read-only memory, a disc used in a computer for reading information.

The CD has largely replaced vinyl records and cassettes.

**cease** *verb* 1 to end. 2 to stop doing something. *Cease this idle chat!*

**ceiling** *noun* 1 the top part of a room forming the upper surface. 2 the highest limit of something.

Some people keep wine in their cellars. Others use them for storing junk.

**DID YOU KNOW?**

*The Celsius scale was invented by the Swedish astronomer Anders Celsius (1701–1744).*

**celebrate** *verb* to do something special to show that a day or an event is important. *We had a party to celebrate granny's 80th birthday.* **celebration** *noun.*

**celebrity** *noun* 1 fame. 2 a famous person.

**celery** *noun* a plant with long stems grown as a vegetable and often eaten raw.

**cell** *noun* 1 a small room in which a prisoner is kept. 2 a small room in which a monk or a nun lives. 3 the smallest part of humans, plants or animals. 4 one of the compartments of a honeycomb. 5 a unit of an apparatus, such as a battery for producing electric current.

**cellar** *noun* an underground room of a building, often used for storing things.

**cello** *noun* (say **chel**-oh) a musical instrument with strings that looks like a very large violin. **cellist** *noun.*

**cellular** *adjective* 1 made up of cells. 2 Cellular blankets are loosely woven and very warm. 3 A cellular phone is a mobile phone.

**Celsius** *adjective* (say **sel**-see-us) from the Celsius scale for measuring temperature. Water boils at 100° Celsius.

**cement** *noun* 1 a grey powder, made from lime and clay, used for building. When cement is mixed with water and left to dry, it becomes hard as stone. 2 a strong glue. **cement** *verb* 1 to cover with cement. *Unfortunately the garden has been cemented over, so we can't plant anything.* 2 to strengthen an agreement or a friendship.

**cemetery** *noun* (say **sem**-et-ree) a place where dead people are buried.

Cents are American coins.

**census** *noun* the official count of population.

**cent** *noun* the 100th part of a dollar and some other currencies. *I've only got a few cents left in my pocket.*

**centenary** *noun* (say sen-**teen**-u-ree) a 100th anniversary.

**centimetre** *noun* a measure of length. There are 100 centimetres in a metre.

**centipede** *noun* a long crawling creature with many legs.

**central** *adjective* 1 in the middle of something, near the centre. 2 most important. *The government's central aim is to improve education.* **centrally** *adverb.*

**Central African Republic** *noun* a country in Africa.

**Central America** *noun* a narrow strip of seven countries between Mexico and South America.

**central heating** *noun* a system of heating buildings from a central boiler through pipes and radiators.

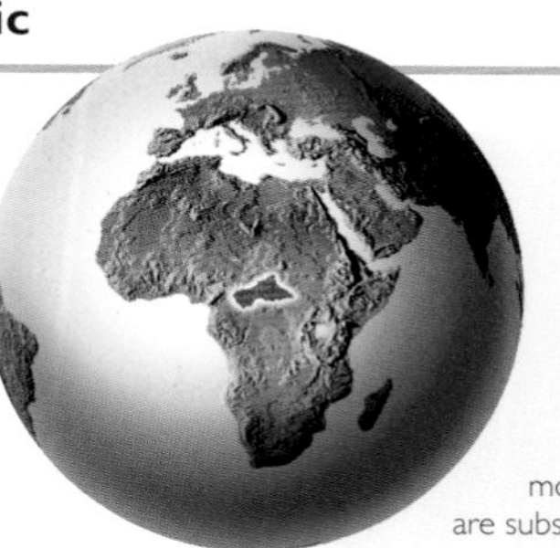

The CAR has diamond mines and rubber plantations, but most of its people are subsistence farmers.

**centre** *noun* 1 the middle part or point, such as the point around which a circle is drawn. *She likes to be the centre of attention.* 2 an important place of interest and great activity. *Cambridge is a centre of learning.* 3 in sport, a player in a team who plays near the middle of the field. **centre** *verb* 1 to put something near or in the middle. 2 to concentrate your thoughts or ideas on something.

**centurion** *noun* (say sent-**yoor**-ee-un) a commander of 100 men in the ancient Roman army.

**century** *noun* 1 a period of 100 years. *The 21st century starts in the year 2000.* 2 in cricket, 100 runs made by a batsman.

**cereal** *noun* 1 any grain such as wheat, rice or maize used for food. 2 a breakfast food make from grain.

**ceremony** *noun* 1 a special event or occasion, such as a wedding. 2 the things said and done during such an occasion. *I don't like all the ceremony at big church weddings.* **ceremonious** *adjective*.

**certain** *adjective* 1 sure, having no doubt. *I'm certain that's right.* If you make certain of something, you find out first. 2 not named. *A certain person was involved in the crime.* 3 some but not much. *He seems to get a certain pleasure out of it.*

**certificate** *noun* an official document giving facts about a person. *A birth certificate.* **certify** *verb*.

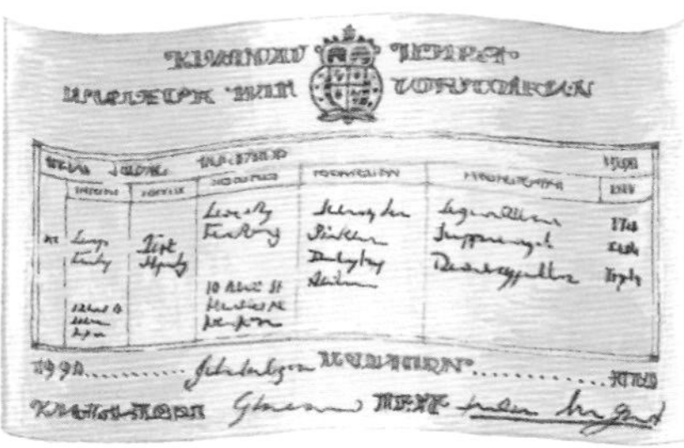

A birth certificate gives proof of identity and entitles its owner to a passport.

**CFC** *abbreviation* chlorofluorocarbon. A substance used in things such as fridges and aerosols. CFCs have caused the ozone layer to shrink.

**SPELLING NOTE**

*'Cereal' is pronounced the same as 'serial', but the two words have completely different meanings. The word for grain comes originally from Ceres, who was the Roman goddess of agriculture.*

**Chad** *noun* a country in Africa.

**chaffinch** *noun* a small songbird.

**chain** *noun* 1 metal rings fitted into one another. *She wore a silver chain around her neck.* 2 a number of connected events, or shops, mountains and restaurants. **chain reaction** a number of events in which each causes the next. **chain-smoke** to smoke all the time. **in chains** kept as a prisoner.

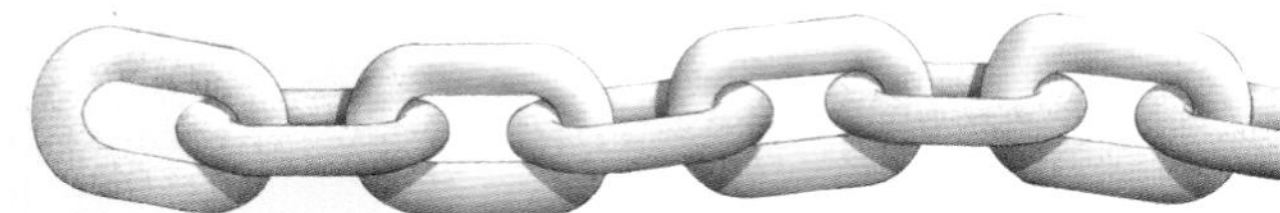

Strong chains such as this one are often used in heavy industry.

**chair** *noun* 1 a seat with legs and a back for one person to sit on. 2 a person in control of a discussion. *Who is in the chair?* **chair** *verb* to chair a meeting.

**chalk** *noun* 1 a soft white stick used for writing and drawing on a blackboard. 2 a soft white rock. Chalk is a common form of limestone.

**challenge** (challenging, challenged) *verb* 1 to demand to have a fight, play a game or run a race to see who is stronger or better. *I challenged my brother to a game of tennis.* 2 to question the truth or rightness of something. **challenge** *noun* 1 a demand to see who is stronger or better. 2 a difficult project which demands effort and willpower. *Mountaineering is a great challenge.* **challenger** *noun*.

**chamber** *noun* 1 a large room used for meetings or for a special purpose. *The House of Lords is the upper chamber of Parliament.* 2 A Chamber of Commerce is a group of people in businesses who work together. 3 an enclosed space in a body or a machine. *The human heart has four chambers.* 4 in old use, a room, especially the bedroom.

**champion** *noun* 1 a person or team who wins a race or game. *A tennis champion.* 2 somebody who speaks or fights for other people and defends ideas. *She is a champion of women's rights.* **champion** *verb*.

The champion was presented with this fine cup by the mayor.

**championship** *noun* a competition to find the best player or team. *Wimbledon is the oldest tennis championship.*

**chance** *noun* 1 something unplanned. *I met her by chance.* 2 the possibility that something might happen. *What are our chances of winning?* 3 an opportunity. *This is your last chance.* If you take a chance, you do something although it might fail. **by any chance** a polite way of asking for something. *You wouldn't have a pencil by any chance?* **chance it** to take a risk.

**chancellor** *noun* a high state official. *The Chancellor of the Exchequer is the country's finance minister.*

**change** *verb* 1 to become different or make something different. *She's changed a lot since I last saw her.* 2 to take something back and get something else instead. *I changed the jeans because they were too tight.* 3 to put on different clothes or coverings. *I always change when I get home from work.* 4 to get off one bus or train and get on to another. *We changed at Oxford.* 5 to give something up and get something else. *I've changed my job.* **change your mind** to come to have another opinion. **change money** to exchange a sum of money for the same amount in coins or notes. **change** *noun* 1 the act of changing or the result of changing. *A change in the weather.* 2 the money returned to the payer when the cost of the goods is less than the amount given. *It costs 50p and you gave her a pound, so you get 50p change.* 3 the same amount of money in coins or smaller notes. *Have you got change for a pound?* 4 A change of clothes is a clean set. **for a change** something different from what usually happens. *Why don't we go out for a pleasant change of scene?*

**channel** *noun* 1 a stretch of water that connects two seas. *The English Channel.* 2 a passage along which water flows. 3 a wavelength for television or radio programmes. *I often watch Channel 5.* **channel** (channelling, channelled) *verb* 1 to form a channel in something. 2 to direct. *He channelled his energy into the new project.*

**chant** *noun* 1 a word or a group of words that is repeated over and over again. 2 a religious song. **chant** *verb.*

**chaos** *noun* a state of disorder and confusion. *The accident caused chaos on the motorway in both directions.*

The holiday traffic threatened to cause chaos on the motorway.

**WORD HISTORY**

*'Chancellor' comes from the Latin word 'cancelli', meaning a lattice or grating. This is because a Roman court official used to stand at a grating to separate the public from judges. Today, the head of a British university and the head of the German government are both chancellors.*

**AMAZING FACT**

'Chaos theory' is the theory that changes in the physical world, and their consequences, are unpredictable.

**chapel** *noun* 1 a small church, sometimes as part of a hospital or school. *A Methodist chapel.* 2 a part of a church with its own altar. 3 the members of a trade union.

**chapter** *noun* 1 a division of a book, usually with its own number or title. 2 a special period in history. 3 all the members of a religious group. **chapter and verse** the exact place where detailed information can be found.

**char** (charring, charred) *verb* to become black from burning.

**character** *noun* 1 the qualities that make a person or a place what they are. *The twins have quite different characters.* 2 a person in a story, film or play. 3 a character is somebody interesting or different from others. *He's a real character.* 4 a letter, number or other symbol. **characteristic** *adjective.* **characterize** *verb.*

The cartoon character gasped with exhaustion as he continued his journey.

**charade** *noun* (say shu-**rahd**) 1 a scene in a game in which players guess words acted out by others. 2 an act that can easily be seen by others to be false or foolish. *The trial was just a charade.*

**charge** *noun* 1 a price asked or paid for goods or a service. 2 a written or spoken statement blaming a person for breaking the law. *He was arrested on a murder charge.* 3 the care and responsibility for a person or thing. If you are in charge of somebody or something, you are in control of them and responsible for them. 4 a sudden attack. 5 an amount of explosive to be fired. 6 electricity in a battery or other electrical apparatus. **take charge** to become responsible for something. *I'll take charge of the children if you do the washing up.*

**charge** *verb* 1 to ask a price for something. *He didn't charge me for the phone call.* 2 to accuse somebody of a crime. 3 to rush forward in an attack. *The bull charged at the crowd and killed three children.* 4 When you charge a battery, it lasts longer. 5 If you are charged with something or charged to do something, you are given a duty or task.

**chariot** *noun* an ancient horse-drawn vehicle with two wheels, used in battles and races.

**charity** *noun* 1 an organization that helps those who need it. *A charity for stray cats.* 2 kindness towards others.

**charm** *noun* 1 the ability to be attractive and to please. *He used all his charm to win her over.* 2 an act, saying or object that has magical powers. 3 an ornament on a bracelet or chain. **charm** *verb* 1 *He charmed her with his flattery.* 2 to control something by using magical powers.

**charming** *adjective* delightful, pleasing. *She is a charming person.*

**chart** *noun* 1 a map of the sea and coast or sky and stars. 2 a map with special information in curves and graphs. *A weather chart.* 3 a list of information in a particular order. *The charts list the most popular records.* **chart** *verb. Explorers charted the coastline.*

**chase** *verb* to go after somebody or something in order to try and catch them or make them go away. *The cat chased the mouse.* **chase** *noun.*

**chasm** *noun* 1 a deep crack in the ground. 2 a large difference between two things or groups. *The chasm between us widened.*

**chat** *noun* a friendly talk. **chat** *verb. We chatted all afternoon.*

**chat show** *noun* a TV or radio programme in which famous people are interviewed.

**chatter** *verb* 1 to talk non-stop about unimportant things. 2 to make a rattling sound. *His teeth were chattering with cold.*

**chauffeur** *noun* (say **shoh**-fer) a person employed to drive somebody's car.

The chauffeur wears a smart uniform and waits by his employer's car.

Around 1200 BC the Hittites, who lived in modern-day Turkey, used chariots for warfare.

**AMAZING FACT**

Cheetahs can reach speeds of up to 60 mph (100kph) over short distances when chasing gazelles.

**WORD HISTORY**

*The original 'chauffeur', in French, was not a driver but a stoker or fireman, who put coal on the furnace of a steam engine. Early motor cars gave off a lot of smoke and steam, so their drivers were jokingly called stokers.*

**chauvinist** *noun* (say **shoh**-vin-ist) a person who shows great prejudice, especially against women. *He's a real male chauvinist.*

**cheap** *adjective* 1 not costing very much. *Food is cheaper in Portugal than in Spain.* 2 of poor quality, not very good. *Cheap housing is hard to come by.*

**cheat** *verb* to lie or trick somebody, often in order to do well. *He always cheats in exams.* **cheat** *noun* 1 a person who cheats. 2 a dishonest action.

**check** *noun* 1 an examination to find out if something is correct. *He made a thorough check.* 2 keeping somebody or something under control. *It's impossible to keep the disease in check.* 3 in chess the position of the king when under attack.

**check** *noun* a pattern of squares in different colours. **checked** *adjective.*

Tartan is a traditional Scottish fabric pattern, based on colourful overlaid checks.

**check** *verb* 1 to make sure something is correct or satisfactory. *Have you checked the bill?* 2 to hold back or stop doing something. *The bad weather checked their progress.* **check in** to register at a hotel or report at an airport. *You have to check in an hour before take-off.* **check out** to pay the bill and leave a hotel.

**checkout** *noun* a place in a supermarket where goods are packed and paid for.

**check-up** *noun* a medical examination.

**cheek** *noun* the side of the face below the eye. *Rosy cheeks are a sign of health.*

**cheek** *noun* rude behaviour. **cheeky** *adjective. Don't be cheeky to your mother!*

**cheer** *noun* 1 a shout of praise or happiness. *The crowd gave a big cheer.* 2 If you are full of cheer, you are very happy. **cheer** *verb. The fans cheered wildly throughout the match.* **cheer up** to become happy and stop feeling sad.

**cheerful** *adjective* 1 looking, sounding and feeling happy. 2 something pleasant, that makes you happy. **cheerfully** *adverb.*

**cheese** *noun* a soft or hard food made from milk. *Let's have bread and cheese for lunch.*

**cheetah** *noun* a wild animal, like a big spotted cat. Cheetahs are the fastest land animals in the world.

**chef** *noun* a cook in a restaurant.

A chef has to deal with many pans at once. His job is both hot and demanding.

**chemical** *adjective* used in, made by or connected with chemistry. **chemical** *noun.* **chemically** *adverb.*

**chemist** *noun* 1 a trained person who makes up and sells medicines. 2 a shop selling medicines and toilet articles. 3 a scientist who specializes in chemistry.

**chemistry** *noun* the study of how substances are made up and how they react with other substances.

**cheque** *noun* a printed form telling the bank to pay money from your account to the person you have written the cheque to. *Can I pay by cheque?*

**cherry** (cherries) *noun* 1 a small round fruit with a stone. Ripe cherries are red. 2 the tree on which cherries grow.

**chess** *noun* a game for two players in which each player moves pieces on a chessboard.

**chest** *noun* the upper front part of the body enclosing the heart and the lungs.

**chest** *noun* a big, strong box for keeping things in. *A treasure chest.*

**chestnut** *noun* 1 a reddish brown nut inside a prickly green case. 2 the tree on which these nuts grow. **chestnut** *adjective* having a reddish-brown colour. *Chestnut hair.*

When the chestnut is ripe, the case falls to the ground and splits open. The shiny nuts roll out.

**chest of drawers** *noun* a piece of furniture with a set of drawers.

**chew** *verb* to move food about in your mouth and grind it with your teeth, so it is easy to swallow. **chew over** to think about something very carefully.

**chewing gum** *noun* a sweet gum that you chew and don't swallow.

**chick** *noun* a young bird.

**DID YOU KNOW?**

*China has a population of more than 1,200 million, more people than any other country in the world. Yet China has a smaller area than either Russia or Canada.*

**chicken** *noun* 1 a young bird, especially a hen. 2 the bird's meat used as food. *We had chicken for dinner.* 3 (slang) a coward or frightened person. **chicken out** not to do something because you are frightened.

**chickenpox** *noun* a disease with red itchy spots on the skin.

**chief** *noun* a leader or highest official. **chief** *adjective* most important. **chiefly** *adverb.*

**chilblain** *noun* a painful swelling or sore in the fingers or toes caused by extreme cold.

**child** (children) *noun* 1 a young boy or girl. 2 a son or daughter.

**childhood** *noun* the time when you are a child. *Now he's old, he often thinks back to his childhood.*

**childish** *adjective* behaving like a child, often in silly way. *It's very childish to shout and scream like that.*

**children** plural of child.

**Chile** *noun* a country in South America.

Chile is a long thin country that runs along the backbone of South America.

**chill** *noun* 1 an unpleasant coldness. *In the morning there is often a chill in the air.* **chilly** *adjective.* 2 an illness caused by cold in which you might have a temperature, a headache and feel shivery. 3 a feeling of fear and doom. **chill** *verb* 1 to make something colder. 2 to become cold with fear. **chilling** *adjective. A chilling film.*

**chimney** *noun* a hollow passage in a roof through which smoke goes up into the air.

**chimpanzee** *noun* an African ape.

**chin** *noun* the front of the lower jaw.

**china** *noun* 1 a kind of fine white clay. 2 cups, saucers, plates and ornaments made of china. *The china cupboard.*

**China** *noun* a country in East Asia.

**Chinese** *noun* a person who comes from China. **Chinese** *adjective. An excellent Chinese restaurant.*

**chip** *noun* 1 a fried strip of potato. *We bought fish and chips.* 2 a small piece of wood, brick or paint, broken off something. 3 a crack that has been left in a cup or glass, when a small piece has been broken off. 4 a flat plastic counter used as money in games. 5 a very small electronic circuit in a computer. *A silicon chip.* **have a chip on your shoulder** to be rude or behave badly, because you think you have been treated unfairly in the past. **chip** (chipping, chipped) *verb* to damage something by breaking off a small piece of it. *I'm afraid I've chipped a plate.* **chip in** 1 to interrupt a conversation. 2 to give money to a fund, so that something can be paid for by a number of people.

C

**chipmunk** *noun* a small American animal like a squirrel with a long bushy tail.

Chipmunks are friendly animals. They often come up to visitors in America's national parks, looking for titbits.

**chirp** *verb* to make a short, sharp sound like a bird or insect.

**Chisinau** *noun* the capital of Moldova.

**chivalry** *noun* (say **shiv**-ul-ree) good manners, helpfulness and polite behaviour, in particular by men towards women. **chivalrous** *adjective*.

**chocolate** *noun* 1 a sweet food made from cocoa beans. *A bar of chocolate.* 2 a sweet covered with a layer of chocolate. *A box of chocolates.* 3 a hot drink made from the powder of crushed cocoa beans.

**choice** *noun* 1 a number of things you can choose from. *There is a choice of three films.* 2 the thing or things you have decided on. *The French film was my choice.* 3 the right, act or possibility of choosing. *My friend had no choice but to come.* **choice** *adjective* of high quality, best. *We only sell choice wines.*

**choir** *noun* a group of people who sing together, e.g. in a church or school.

**choke** *verb* 1 to be unable to breathe properly because something is blocking the air passages. *He choked on a fish bone.* 2 to stop the breathing by pressing on the throat or squeezing the neck. *The victim was choked to death.* 3 If a place is choked with cars or people, it is so full that it is impossible to move.

**choke** *noun* a device controlling the amount of air going into the engine that makes it easier to start a car.

**cholesterol** *noun* (say kol-**est**-er-ol) a fatty substance found in animals and food. Too much cholesterol is bad for the heart.

**choose** (choosing, chose, chosen) *verb* 1 to pick out a person or thing from a greater number. *I chose my favourite music.* 2 to decide to do something. *We chose to stay.*

**chop** (chopping, chopped) *verb* to cut wood or food into small pieces with a chopper, an axe or a knife. **chop and change** to keep changing your mind about what to do. **chop** *noun* 1 a quick, heavy blow with a chopper or an axe. 2 a slice of meat with a bone in it. *A pork chop.*

**SPELLING NOTE**

*It's easy to confuse 'chord' and 'cord', which are pronounced the same. Musicians play chords, and mathematicians use them to connect points on a curve. Both words come from the Latin 'chorda', the string of a musical instrument.*

**AMAZING FACT**

Chocolate originally came from the Aztec people of Mexico who valued it as a drink.

**chopper** *noun* a heavy tool, like an axe, for cutting wood or meat.

**chopsticks** *noun* a pair of thin sticks held in one hand and used by the Chinese and others to eat food.

Lots of trees are cut down every year and made into chopsticks. But other chopsticks are made of plastic.

**chord** *noun* (say kord) a number of musical notes sounded at the same time.

**chord** *noun* (say kord) in geometry, a straight line connecting two points on a curve.

**chore** *noun* (say chor) a small everyday task or duty that is usually boring.

**choreography** *noun* (say ko-ree-**og**-ru-fee) the art of planning and arranging dances for the stage. **choreographer** *noun*.

**chorus** *noun* 1 a group of people who sing together. 2 a part of a song that is repeated after each verse by all the singers. 3 a group of singers or dancers who act together in a show. *She dances in the chorus.* **in chorus** at the same time. **chorus** *verb* to sing or say something at the same time.

**chose** past tense of choose.

**chosen** past participle of choose.

**Christian** *noun* a person who believes in Jesus Christ and his teachings. A member of the Christian Church. **Christian** *adjective* believing in the Christian religion. **Christianity** *noun*.

**Christmas** (Christmases) *noun* the day when people celebrate the birth of Jesus Christ, 25 December. **Christmas Eve** the day before Christmas Day. **Christmas tree** a tree decorated at Christmas time.

Christmas is celebrated throughout the Christian world.

**chrome** *noun* (say krohm) a hard, silver-coloured metal used for covering objects such as taps.

**chronic** *adjective* lasting for a long time. *A chronic illness kept him away from work.*

**chronological** *adjective* arranged in the order in which things happened, according to time. *I've listed the events in strict chronological order.* **chronologically** *adverb.*

**chrysalis** *noun* 1 a butterfly or moth in the stage between being a caterpillar and the time when it flies, also called a pupa. 2 the hard covering of a chrysalis during that time.

Inside this chrysalis a beautiful butterfly is waiting to emerge.

**church** *noun* 1 a building in which Christians pray. 2 a religious service in a church. 3 The Church is a group of people within the Christian religion. *The Pope is head of the Catholic Church throughout the world.*

AMAZING FACT

Inside the chrysalis, the caterpillar's body is broken down by hormones and is gradually replaced with the butterfly's body.

**cigar** *noun* a roll of dried tobacco leaves that people smoke. *Cigars are usually much bigger than cigarettes.*

**cigarette** *noun* finely cut tobacco wrapped in a roll of thin paper which people smoke.

**cinema** *noun* a place where you can watch films. *Let's go to the cinema tonight.*

**cipher** *noun* (say **sy**-fer) a secret way of writing. *Inscribed with strange ciphers.*

**circa** *preposition* about, approximately. *He died circa 1850.*

**circle** *noun* 1 a round flat shape enclosed by a line. Every part of the line is the same distance from the centre. 2 something that makes the shape of a circle. 3 a group of people who like the same thing or have similar interests. *He is well respected in political circles.* 4 seats on the upper floor of a theatre. **circle** *verb* to go round in a circle.

diameter

radius

The diameter of a circle is twice the length of its radius.

**circular** *adjective* 1 round, shaped like a circle. 2 moving in a circle, starting from a point and ending up in the same place. *A circular route.*

**circular** *noun* a printed letter, advertisement or notice sent to a large number of people.

**circulation** *noun* 1 the process of passing something round a number of people. *When will the Euro be put into circulation?* 2 the flow of blood through the body. *She's got poor circulation.* 3 the movement of any substance around a system. *Air circulation.* 4 the number of sold copies of a newspaper or magazine. *This magazine has a high circulation.* **circulate** *verb.*

**circumcision** *noun* cutting off the foreskin of the penis for medical or religious reasons. **circumcise** *verb.*

**circumference** *noun* the line that marks out a circle or the distance all the way around a circular object.

**circumstance** *noun* the conditions connected with an event or person and influencing a particular situation. *Mysterious circumstances surrounded her disappearance.* **in the circumstances** because of the way things are. *I decided it was the best thing to do in the circumstances.* **under no circumstances** never.

**circus** (circuses) *noun* a show with clowns, animals and acrobats in a big tent. *The circus travels from one town to another.*

The large tent that houses a circus is called a big top.

**cistern** *noun* a tank for storing water. *Flush the lavatory and the cistern empties.*

**citizen** *noun* 1 a member of a state. *She's a British citizen.* 2 the inhabitant of a city.

**citrus fruit** *noun* a fruit, such as a lemon, orange, lime or grapefruit, with a sour-sweet taste.

**city** *noun* 1 a large town. 2 *The City of London is a centre for financial matters.*

**civil** *adjective* 1 belonging to the people, not military or religious. *Civil rights include freedom and equality.* 2 The Civil Service includes all government departments, except the armed forces. 3 polite and helpful. *He gave me a civil response.* **civility** *noun.*

Lemons and other citrus fruit grow around the warm Mediterranean Sea.

**civilian** *noun* a person who is not a member of the armed forces.

**civilization** *noun* 1 a society that has reached a high level of education and culture. *The Greek civilization.* 2 the state of making or becoming civilized.

**civilize** *verb* to educate and bring culture to people. *The civilized world.*

**civil war** *noun* a war between people of the same country.

The Battle of Bull Run, which took place in Virginia in 1861, was the first major battle of the American Civil War. Confederate forces (right) defeated the Union army (left).

**claim** *verb* 1 to say that something belongs to you and ask for it. *Who claimed the lost umbrella?* 2 to say that something is a fact. *He claims to have written to me, but I haven't received the letter.* **claim** *noun* 1 *His claim to have written is a lie.* 2 a demand for something you have a right to. *A pay claim.* 3 a piece of ground or property belonging to somebody. **lay claim to something** to say that something belongs to you.

**clan** *noun* a group of families who all come from one common family. *The Scottish clans were gathering for Hogmanay.*

**clap** (clapping, clapped) *verb* 1 to hit your hands together loudly, to show that you are pleased or to attract attention. *Everybody clapped when the music started.* 2 to hit somebody in a friendly way. *He clapped him on the shoulder and said, 'Hello'!* **clap** *noun* 1 the sound of people clapping. 2 a friendly slap. 3 a clap of thunder.

**clarinet** *noun* a wooden musical instrument, shaped like a tube, which you blow into.

The clarinet is a wind instrument that gives a lovely mellow sound.

**clarity** *noun* clearness. *He explained it with such clarity that I understood immediately.*

**clash** *verb* 1 to fight, argue or disagree with somebody. *Gangs of hooligans clashed with the police.* 2 When colours clash, they don't look good together. 3 to take place at the same time and therefore be difficult. *The football clashes with the tennis.* 4 to make a loud sound, like the noise of metal objects being hit together. **clash** *noun.*

**GRAMMAR NOTE**

*There are two types of clauses in grammar. A main clause stands alone and forms a complete sentence, e.g. 'I switched on the light.' A subordinate clause cannot stand on its own and has to go with a main clause to form a sentence, e.g. 'I switched on the light when it got dark.'*

A bird's claws help it grip its perch.

**clasp** *noun* 1 a metal fastener for holding two things or parts of something together. *I can't close my bag because the clasp has broken.* 2 a tight hold with your fingers or arms. **clasp** *verb* to take something in your hand or arms and hold it tightly.

**class** (classes) *noun* 1 a group of pupils or students who are taught together. **in class** during the lesson. *We aren't allowed to talk in class.* 2 people of the same social group. *People used to divide society into upper, middle and lower classes.* 3 people, animals or things that are similar. 4 an examination result. *A first-class degree in History.* 5 good style. *You can see from the way she dresses that she's got class.* **class** *verb* to say that somebody or something belongs to a group of things, to put them in a class. *You can't class all pop music as rubbish.*

**classic** *adjective* 1 of very high quality, outstanding. *A classic novel.* 2 well known and serving as a good example for what is expected. *This is a classic case of measles.* **classic** *noun* 1 a book or film of very high quality. 2 classics is the study of ancient Greek and Roman customs, language and literature.

Students of the classics know that Julius Caesar was murdered on the Ides (15) March by Brutus and Cassius.

**classical** *adjective* 1 thought of as best, because it follows old traditions. Serious and lasting. *I prefer classical ballet to modern dance.* 2 going back to Roman or Greek customs, art and literature. *In classical times, women were often treated as badly as slaves.*

**classroom** *noun* a room in a school or college in which children or students are taught. *The classroom was full of students.*

**clause** *noun* 1 a part of a written agreement or legal document. *It was covered by a clause in the contract written in small print.* 2 a group of words with its own verb forming part of a sentence.

**claustrophobia** *noun* fear of being in a small closed space.

**claw** *noun* 1 a sharp nail on the toe of an animal or bird. *Cats have sharp claws.* 2 Crabs and lobsters catch and hold things with their claws. 3 an instrument like a hook on machines for lifting things. **claw** *verb* to pull and scratch with a claw or hand. *The cat clawed a hole in my tights.*

**clay** *noun* a kind of earth that is soft when it is wet and hard when it is dry. Bricks and pots are made from clay.

The first clay pots were made in Japan around 10,500 BC.

**clean** *adjective* 1 without any dirt or marks. *I put on clean clothes.* 2 not yet used. *Can I have a clean sheet of paper?* 3 fair. *A clean fight.* 4 morally pure, not dirty. *He only tells clean jokes when there are girls about.* **come clean** to decide to be honest about something you've kept as a secret.

**clean** *verb* to make something clean from dirt or dust. *I cleaned the car for you.* **clean up** 1 to make an area or a person clean and tidy again. *Before my parents came back, we cleaned up the mess.* 2 You clean up when you win a bet and take all the money.

**clean** *adverb* completely. *I clean forgot about the money.*

**clear** *adjective* 1 easy to see through. *The water is so clear, you can see the bottom of the lake.* 2 not cloudy. *A clear sky.* 3 easy to understand or hear. *A clear description.* 4 empty, free from blocks, unwanted things or dangers. *A clear road ahead.* 5 free from doubt, guilt or difficulty. *I'm quite clear about my plans.* 6 complete. *Allow three clear days for the cheque to clear.* **make yourself clear** to say something so that it is understood and there is no doubt about your wishes. **clearly** *adverb.*

**clear** *adverb* 1 easily heard or seen. *He said it loud and clear.* 2 out of the way, not near or touching. *Stand clear of the doors.*

**clear** *verb* 1 to become free of something like clouds, traffic or unwanted objects. *The mist has cleared.* 2 *The tablets will clear your headache.* 3 to get past something without touching it. *The horse cleared the fence.* 4 to state that somebody is not guilty. *The jury cleared him of all charges.* 5 to get somebody's permission for something. *You'll have to clear your plans with the manager.* **clear away** to take away things that are no longer needed. **clear off** to go away. **clear up** 1 to stop raining or being cloudy. 2 to tidy up. 3 to solve or settle a mystery or misunderstanding.

**clench** *verb* to close your teeth or fist tightly.

**clergy** *noun* ministers of the Christian Church. *The clergy wear surplices in church.*

**SPELLING NOTE**

*Though pronounced 'clark', the word 'clerk' is spelt with an 'e'. It originally meant a clergyman, and is rather an old-fashioned word in British English. But in America, 'clerk' rhymes with 'Turk' and means a shop assistant.*

**WORD HISTORY**

*'Climax' comes from the Greek for ladder. As you near the top of a series of rungs, you reach the climax.*

Ice cubes are sparkling clear lumps of frozen water.

**clerk** *noun* (rhymes with bark) a person who works in an office, bank or law court and looks after accounts, records and paperwork. *The clerk of the court.*

**clever** *adjective* 1 intelligent and able to learn and understand things quickly. 2 showing skill. *The pocket calculator was a clever invention.* **cleverness** *noun.*

**cliché** *noun* (say **klee**-shay) a phrase that has been used so much that it has become meaningless.

**click** *noun* a short, sharp sound. **click** *verb* 1 *I heard the camera click.* 2 to suddenly understand something. *It suddenly clicked that I had met them before.*

**cliff** *noun* a steep rock-face, usually at the coast. *The white cliffs of Dover.*

Waves hollow out caves in a rocky cliff. Blow holes form above the caves.

**climate** *noun* the weather conditions of a place. *Oranges don't grow in cold climates.*

**climax** *noun* the most important and exciting moment in a story, usually near the end. *The film built up to a climax.*

**climb** *verb* 1 to go up, down or over something. *We climbed over the wall.* 2 to go higher. *Prices have climbed.* 3 to grow upwards. *A rose climbing up the fence.* **climb** *noun. It was a hard climb to the top.*

**climber** *noun* a person or plant that climbs.

**cling** *verb* to hold on to somebody tightly. If you cling to an idea, you keep it firmly in your head and believe in it.

**cling film** *noun* thin plastic material used for wrapping up food.

**clinic** *noun* a place where people go to get medical treatment or advice.

**clip** *noun* a small metal or plastic fastener for holding things together. **clip** *verb.*

**clip** *noun* a short piece of a film or television programme. **clip** *verb* to cut. *Diane clipped the hedge with her shears.*

**cloak** *noun* 1 a loose coat without sleeves that fastens at the neck. 2 a disguise to hide the truth. *Under the cloak of darkness.* **cloak** *verb* to hide or cover secrets.

**clock** *noun* an instrument that tells the time. **turn the clock back** to go back to things or ideas how they were a long time ago. **clock in** *verb* to record the time when you start work. **clock out** to record the time you stop work. *The workers clocked out at 4 p.m.*

No one would be able to sleep through the loud ringing of this alarm clock.

**clockwise** *adjective* moving in the same direction as the hands of the clock. *To switch on, you turn the knob clockwise.*

**clockwork** *noun* a mechanism with wheels and springs that is wound up. **clockwork** *adjective. Clockwork toys.*

**clod** *noun* a lump of earth.

**clog** *noun* a shoe with a wooden sole.

**clog** (clogging, clogged) *verb* to become blocked with grease or dirt. **clog up** *I need a plunger because the sink is clogged up.*

**cloister** *noun* a covered path round a square in a monastery or college.

**clone** *noun* an animal or plant that has been produced in a laboratory from the cells of another animal or plant. A clone looks exactly like the animal it was made from. **clone** *verb.*

**close** *verb* (say klohz) 1 to shut. *She closed the door.* 2 to end. *The offer closes at the end of the month.* **close down** to stop work. *Most of the coal mines have closed down.* **close in** to come nearer and nearer. *Winter is closing in.* **close** *noun* the end of an activity or a period of time.

**close** *noun* (say klohss) 1 an enclosed area around a church. 2 a short street closed at one end. *A close of houses.*

**close** *adjective* (say klohss) 1 near. *My cousins are my close relatives.* 2 trusted and liked. *Sophie is my closest friend.* 3 tight, with little space between, especially in competitions and games. *It was a close contest.* 4 thorough and careful. *A close examination of the document showed that it was a forgery.* 5 warm and stuffy. **closely** *adverb.* **closeness** *noun.*

**close** *adverb* (say klohss) 1 near. *I live quite close.* 2 almost. *Close to 30 years ago.*

The section of the caterpillar that is under the magnifying glass is seen in close-up.

**AMAZING FACT**

The four main types of clouds are called 'cirrus', 'nimbus', 'cumulonimbus' and 'stratus'.

**DID YOU KNOW?**

*Clubs are one of the four suits in a pack of playing cards. The other suits are diamonds, hearts and spades.*

**closed** *adjective* 1 not open. *We could hardly breathe with all the windows closed.* 2 not open to the public, especially a shop or museum. *Closed on Mondays and Wednesdays.* **behind closed doors** in secret.

**closet** *noun* a small room for storing things. **closet** (closeting, closeted) *verb* to shut away. *They were closeted in the study.*

**close-up** *noun* a photograph or film that is taken from very near.

**closure** *noun* the closing down of a factory, shop or other business. *There have been more pit closures in the south of Wales.*

**cloth** *noun* 1 woven fabric used for making clothes, coverings and other things. 2 a piece of material for cleaning, e.g. a dish cloth.

**clothes** *plural noun* things you wear, such as trousers, shirts and dresses.

**clothing** *noun* the clothes people wear. *You'll need waterproof clothing for mountain biking.*

**cloud** *noun* 1 a mass of small drops of water that floats in the sky. *Clouds are usually white or grey.* 2 a mass of smoke or dust in the air. **under a cloud** out of favour, in disgrace. *He had a row and left under a cloud.* **cloud** *verb* to become unclear. **cloudy** *adjective.* **cloud over** *The sky clouded over.*

It was a bright summer's day, but now the sky is beginning to cloud over.

**clover** *noun* a small plant with three leaves on each stalk.

**clown** *noun* 1 a person in a circus or pantomime who wears funny clothes and make-up, and says and does silly things to make people laugh. 2 a person who acts like a clown. **clown** *verb.*

**club** *noun* 1 a group of people who meet because they have the same interests. *My brother has joined the football club.* 2 the place where the club members meet.

**club** *noun* 1 a big, heavy stick with a thick end that can be used for fighting. 2 a specially shaped stick for hitting a golf ball. 3 a playing card with black clover leaves on it. *The king of clubs.* **club** *verb* to hit somebody with a heavy stick. **club together** to give money to share the cost with others. *We all clubbed together to buy a present.*

**clue** *noun* something that helps you to find the answer to a question or problem. *The footprints provided a clue.* **not to have a clue** not to know much about something.

Daffodils grow in clumps as the bulbs under the ground multiply.

**clump** *noun* a group. *A clump of daffodils.* **clump** *verb* to walk with heavy footsteps. *Don't clump about in those big heavy boots.*

**clumsy** *adjective* 1 A clumsy person moves about awkwardly, walks into things, knocks things over and breaks them. 2 tactless and not very skilful. *A clumsy explanation.*

**cluster** *noun* a small group of people or things close together. *A cluster of bright stars.* **cluster** *verb* to form a tight group.

**clutch** (clutches) *noun* 1 a tight hold. If you are in somebody's clutches, they have control over you. 2 the pedal you press in a car while changing gear.

**clutch** *verb* to hold tightly.

**coach** (coaches) *noun* 1 a bus for long-distance journeys. 2 a train carriage designed for passengers. 3 a four-wheeled horse-drawn carriage that was used to carry passengers and mail.

**coach** (coaches) *noun* 1 a person who trains sportspeople. *The football team has a new coach.* 2 a teacher who gives private lessons. **coach** *verb. She was coached by her dad.*

**coal** *noun* 1 a hard black or brown mineral substance from under the earth that gives heat when it is burned. Coal is dug out of mines. 2 a piece of coal.

**coarse** *adjective* 1 rough, not smooth. 2 rude, vulgar. **coarseness** *noun.*

**coast** *noun* land right next to the sea. **coastal** *adjective.* **the coast is clear** there is nobody around to see you or catch you out.

**coastline** *noun* the outline of the coast. *A rocky coastline.*

This coastline has rocky headlands, sandy beaches and two rivers running down to the sea.

**DID YOU KNOW?**

*Real cockneys are born within hearing distance of Bow Bells in London. Some cockneys still use a rhyming slang: 'apples and pears' mean stairs, and your 'plates of meat' are your feet.*

Inside a coconut there is white flesh and a thin milk that makes a refreshing drink.

**coat** *noun* 1 a piece of clothing with sleeves that you wear over other clothes when you go out. 2 an animal's fur or hair. 3 a layer of paint or varnish. *A coat of paint.* **coat** *verb.*

**coating** *noun* a thin covering or layer spread over a surface.

**coax** *verb* to gently try to talk somebody into doing something.

**cobra** *noun* (say **koh**-bruh) a poisonous snake. *A cobra was coiled up in the grass.*

**cobweb** *noun* a spider's web.

**cock** *noun* a male bird.

**cockerel** *noun* a young male bird.

A cockerel has a bright red comb and shiny tail feathers. A cock is usually more colourful than a hen.

**cockney** *noun* 1 a person born in East London. 2 the way people from East London speak.

**cockpit** *noun* a compartment for the pilot of a plane or the driver of a car.

**cocoa** *noun* 1 a brown powder made from cocoa seeds. 2 a hot drink made from cocoa powder and water or milk.

**coconut** *noun* 1 a large round nut with a hard, hairy shell from the coconut palm. 2 the white flesh inside the nut, which is used in cooking and baking.

**cocoon** *noun* a covering of silky threads produced by a caterpillar before it develops into an adult insect.

**cod** (cod) *noun* a large sea-fish. *We had cod and chips for dinner.*

**code** *noun* 1 a set of signals or a system of words, letters or numbers used to write messages. *You can only crack a code if you know the system.* 2 a set of laws or rules. *You must know the Highway Code if you want to pass your driving test.* **code** *verb* You code a message by replacing the letters or numbers in it with other letters or numbers. **coded** *adjective. A coded message.*

**coffee** *noun* 1 a drink made by pouring hot water on to the roasted and ground seeds, called coffee beans, of a tropical plant. *A cup of strong coffee.* 2 the coffee beans or powder the drink is made from.

**coffin** *noun* a box in which a dead person is buried. *A vampire rose up out of the coffin.*

**cog** *noun* one of a number of teeth round the edge of a wheel which is used to move another wheel or part in a machine.

Cogs like these are found in watches as well as in gear boxes.

**cogwheel** *noun* a wheel with cogs.

**coil** *noun* a loop of rope or wire or a series of loops wound into a spiral. **coil** *verb* to wind into a coil. *The snake coiled its body around a tree.* **coil up** to wind round and round.

**coin** *noun* a piece of metal money. **coin** *verb* 1 to manufacture coins. 2 to invent a new word or phrase.

**coincide** *verb* to happen at the same time as something else. *Her holiday coincided with his trip to Italy.*

**coincidence** *noun* a remarkable set of events. *By coincidence they met on the plane to New York.*

**cold** *adjective* 1 not warm, having a low temperature. 2 unfriendly or unkind. *She seems very cold and unloving.* If something leaves you cold, you can't get excited about it. **coldness** *noun*.

**cold** *noun* 1 low temperature, cold weather. *Wrap up warm if you're going out in the cold.* 2 an infectious illness that makes you sneeze and cough. *If you don't wrap up warm, you'll catch a cold.*

**cold-blooded** *adjective* Cold-blooded animals change their body temperature according to the temperature around them. Reptiles are cold-blooded. A cold-blooded person is cruel.

Reptiles like this iguana are cold-blooded. They need to sit on a rock to warm up in the Sun before they get active.

**cold sore** *noun* a blister on the lips or in the mouth. *Philip had a cold sore on his mouth.*

**colic** *noun* a stomach-ache.

**collaborate** *verb* to work together or with someone else on a job. **collaboration** *noun*.

**collapse** *verb* 1 to fall down suddenly. *The roof collapsed in the storm.* 2 If you collapse, you become weak or ill. 3 If a plan collapses, it doesn't work out. 4 to fold up, e.g. a table or chair. **collapse** *noun*. *Disagreements on both sides caused the collapse of the talks.* **collapsible** *adjective*. *Collapsible chairs are easy to store.*

Colombia was named by its Spanish conquerors after Christopher Columbus, the first European to discover it.

Red, blue and yellow are the primary colours from which all other colours can be made.

**collar** *noun* 1 the part of a shirt, dress or coat that stands up or folds down round the neck. 2 a leather band round the neck of a dog, cat or horse. **collar** *verb* to catch somebody. *I collared him just as he was leaving the office.*

**colleague** *noun* a person you work with.

**collect** *verb* 1 to gather from various places. *We collected wood for the fire.* 2 If you collect things, you are interested in them. *I collect comics.* 3 to come together. *People collected around the singer.* 4 to ask for money from people. 5 to fetch. *My sister is collecting the children from school.* 6 When you collect your thoughts, you prepare and calm yourself. **collection** *noun*.

**collector** *noun* a person who collects things. *A stamp collector.*

**college** *noun* a place where people can carry on studying after they have left school.

**collide** *verb* to crash into something. *The two cars collided.* **collision** *noun*.

**Colombia** *noun* a country in South America.

**Colombo** *noun* the capital of Sri Lanka.

**colon** *noun* a mark (:), often put before listing a number of things.

**colon** *noun* the large part of the intestine.

**colonel** *noun* (say **ker**-nul) an army officer in charge of a regiment.

**colony** *noun* 1 a country that is controlled by another more powerful country. 2 a group of people of the same kind living close together. 3 a group of animals living together. *A colony of bees.*

**colossal** *adjective* very large. *There was colossal interest in the new project.*

**colour** *noun* 1 Colour is what you see when light is broken up into parts. Red, blue and green are colours. 2 something seen in all its colours, not just in black and white. 3 the quality that makes things interesting or more exciting. *He'll add a bit of colour to the party.* **colour** *verb* 1 to colour in a picture with crayons. 2 to influence somebody's opinion or feelings. 3 to become red in the face. **coloured** *adjective*.

**colt** *noun* a young male horse.

**column** *noun* 1 a tall stone structure holding up part of a building or standing on its own. A pillar. 2 a long, narrow shape. *A column of smoke.* 3 an article usually written by the same person in a newspaper or magazine. 4 part of a page. *There are three columns on this page.* 5 a group of people or animals that move in a long line.

**coma** *noun* (say **koh**-muh) a state of unconsciousness from which it is difficult to wake up, usually due to illness or an accident.

**comb** *noun* a piece of plastic or metal with a row of teeth for tidying your hair. **comb** *verb* 1 to comb your hair. 2 to search thoroughly. *We combed the house for clues.*

Viking comb

**combination** *noun* 1 a mixture of things. *The members are a good combination of young and old.* 2 a code of numbers or letters for opening a lock.

**combine** *verb* to join together. *It's not always easy to combine work and play.*

**combine harvester** *noun* a machine that reaps and threshes grain.

**combustion** *noun* the process of burning.

**come** (coming, came, come) *verb* 1 to move towards a place or the speaker. 2 to arrive at a particular place or reach something like a decision. *I've come to the conclusion that I don't like meat.* 3 to happen. *How did you come to be invited to the party?* 4 to exist. *The T-shirts come in all colours.* 5 to become. *My laces have come undone.* **come about** to happen. **come across** to meet or find. **come by** to get. **come in** 1 to enter. 2 to become fashionable. 3 to be received. *A report of the accident has just come in.* **come in for** to get a share of something. *She's come in for some criticism.* **come into** to inherit. **come off** 1 to take place or succeed. *Our holiday didn't come off.* 2 to become unfastened. *A button has come off.* 3 to fall from something. *He came off his bike.* **come through** to survive a difficult situation. **come to** 1 *The bill came to £20.* 2 to wake up after having been unconscious. *I was in hospital when I came to.* **come up** 1 to come to attention, be mentioned or discussed. *My question came up at the meeting.* 2 to happen. *An interesting job has come up.* 3 to win. *Your number might come up next time.* **come up against** to meet something, such as a difficult situation. **come up with** to think of. *He came up with a new plan for the school play.*

**comedian** *noun* an actor who plays a funny part or a person who makes people laugh.

**comedy** *noun* a funny play, film or situation.

**comet** *noun* an object travelling across the sky that looks like a star with a bright tail of light.

Spectacular comets are just dirty iceballs a few kilometres across.

**WORD HISTORY**

*'Coma' comes from the Greek for 'deep sleep'. Some people have fully recovered after being in a coma for years.*

**GRAMMAR NOTE**

*We usually write a comma in places where we would make a slight pause if we were speaking the words. A comma can also show that one part of a sentence is separate: 'When you leave, please shut the door'.*

Napoleon was in command of the French navy as well as the French army.

**comfort** *noun* 1 a pleasant and relaxed situation or feeling. 2 kindness and sympathy given to a person who is unhappy. 3 a person or thing that gives hope or makes pain easier for an unhappy person. **comfort** *verb* to make somebody less unhappy. *I tried to comfort her after the accident.* **comforting** *adjective.*

**comfortable** *adjective* 1 relaxing and pleasant to be in or on. *A comfortable chair.* 2 having enough money. *We are comfortable and can afford most things now.* 3 free from pain or worry. *I don't feel comfortable with people I don't know.*

Cats usually like to sit in the most comfortable chair in the house.

**comic** *noun* 1 a magazine with picture stories. 2 a person who makes people laugh or an actor who plays funny parts. **comic** *adjective. A comic strip.*

**comma** *noun* a mark (,) used in writing to show a pause or separate items in a list. *Oranges, apples and pears are all fruit.*

**command** *noun* 1 an order, telling people what to do. *The soldier obeyed the officer's commands.* 2 control. *The troops are under the general's command.* 3 knowledge and ability. *She has a good command of French.* **command** *verb* 1 to order. 2 to be in control and responsible for a person or group. 3 to deserve and get. *Her position commands respect.* **commanding** *adjective.*

**commence** *verb* to begin.

**comment** *noun* an opinion or explanation about an event, a book or a person. *I have made a few comments on your essay.* **comment** *verb.*

**commentary** *noun* 1 opinions and descriptions spoken during an event. *I listened to the exciting commentary on the big match.* 2 a collection of written opinions and explanations on an event, a book or a person. *I read the commentary with interest.*

**commerce** *noun* the buying and selling of goods on a large scale.

C

**commercial** *adjective* 1 used in commerce. 2 profitable, out to make money. *His film is a commercial success.* 3 Commercial television and radio are paid for by advertisements.

**commercial** *noun* an advertisement on television or radio.

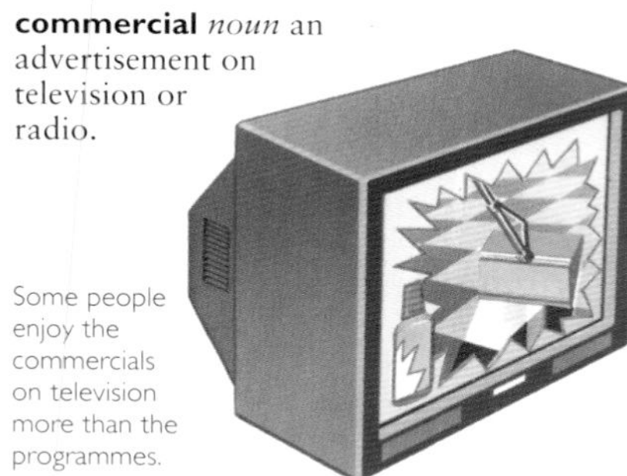

Some people enjoy the commercials on television more than the programmes.

**commit** (committing, committed) *verb* 1 to do something wrong or bad. To commit a crime. 2 to put somebody into care or prison. 3 If you commit yourself to something, you promise to do it. **commitment** *noun*.

**committee** *noun* a group of people chosen by others to carry out special duties.

**common** *adjective* 1 shared by two or more. *It is our common aim to stop the war.* If people have something in common, they share the same interest or are somehow the same. 2 ordinary or happening often. *Smith is a common name.* 3 generally known. *It is common knowledge that smoking is bad for you.* 4 If something is done for the common good, it is done for all people. **common law** unwritten law based on customs. **common sense** good sense and the ability to make the right decision, gained from experience.

**common** *noun* a grassy area where everybody is allowed to go.

**communicate** *verb* to make news, information or your feelings known to other people. *She communicates very well.*

**communication** *noun* 1 sharing and exchanging news or information. 2 a message. 3 Communications are the links between people and places, such as television, radio, telephone, fax, e-mail, roads and railways.

**communism** *noun* a political system in which production is owned and controlled by the state. **communist** *noun*. **communist** *adjective*.

**community** (communities) *noun* 1 people living in one particular place or area. 2 a group of people living together and sharing interests, religion or nationality.

**GRAMMAR NOTE**

*The comparatives of short words add '-er' at the end: 'older', 'younger', 'taller'. Longer words use 'more' in front: 'more beautiful', 'more cowardly', 'more thrilling'. Do not ever use 'more' and '-er' together.*

**commuter** *noun* a person who travels regularly between home and work. **commute** *verb. I commute by train.*

**Comoros** *noun* a country in the Indian Ocean off East Africa.

**compact** *adjective* closely packed and neatly fitted together. *A compact kitchen.*

**compact disc** *noun* a disc from which recorded sound is reproduced. CD stands for compact disc.

**companion** *noun* a person you spend time with. *A travelling companion.*

**company** *noun* 1 being with other people. When you keep somebody company, you stay or go with them. 2 visitors. 3 a business firm. *He works for a toy company.*

**comparative** *adjective* judged by looking and thinking about things, by comparing. *Despite the war raging around them, they live in comparative peace.* **comparatively** *adverb*. **comparative** *noun* the form of an adjective or adverb that shows 'more'. The comparative of 'good' is 'better'.

**compare** *verb* to look at and examine things or people to find out in what ways they are similar or different. *It's cold compared to yesterday.* **comparison** *noun*.

**compartment** *noun* 1 a separate section in a train carriage. 2 a separate part in a bag or box for keeping things in.

You should always take a compass when walking in the mountains, in case a fog descends and you lose your way.

**compass** (compasses) *noun* (say **kum**-puhss) an instrument used for finding directions. The needle of a compass always points north.

**compasses** *noun* a V-shaped instrument used for drawing circles.

**compatible** *adjective* able to exist together or work well with another. *Good holidays at prices compatible with most people's income.* The opposite of compatible is incompatible.

**compel** (compelling, compelled) *verb* to make somebody do something they don't want to do.

**compensate** *verb* to make up for loss, injury or damage, usually by paying money. **compensation** *noun*. *They asked for compensation for their ruined holiday.*

The Muslim community prays to Allah five times a day, not always at a mosque. The most important worship is at noon on Friday.

**compete** *verb* to take part in a game, race or examination.

The fastest cars in the world compete against each other at a Grand Prix race.

**competent** *adjective* able to do something. *She is a competent teacher.*

**competition** *noun* 1 a game, race or other test that people try to win. 2 the act of trying to win or get something. *I was in competition with two other applicants for the job.* In business, competition means trying to get people to buy one thing rather than another. *Competition helps to keep prices down.*

**competitive** *adjective* 1 keen to take part in tests and enjoy competition. 2 Competitive prices are low. *Selling at competitive rates.*

**competitor** *noun* a person, firm or product competing with others.

**compile** *verb* to collect information and put it together in a list or book. *Lots of people helped to compile this dictionary.*

**complain** *verb* to say that you are not happy about something. *The neighbours complained about the noise.*

**complaint** *noun* 1 a statement expressing unhappiness with a particular situation. *He made an official complaint.* 2 an illness.

**complete** *adjective* 1 whole. 2 finished. *When will work on the new house be complete?* 3 total, full. *The party was a complete surprise.* **complete** *verb* to finish doing something or add what is needed. **completion** *noun.*

**complex** *adjective* difficult to understand or explain. *A complex problem.*

Simon could not work out the complex equation his teacher set him.

**complex** *noun* 1 a group of buildings or things connected with each other. *A new housing complex.* 2 an emotional problem that influences a person's behaviour. *If you keep blaming me, I'll get a guilt complex.*

**complexion** *noun* the natural colour and quality of the skin of your face. *She has a beautiful complexion.*

**WORD HISTORY**

*The ancient Greeks believed that the body contained four vital fluids, or humours – blood, phlegm, yellow bile and black bile. Your complexion, from the Latin 'weaving together', showed how your humours were combined.*

**complicated** *adjective* difficult. *A complicated problem.* **complication** *noun.*

**compliment** *noun* an expression of praise and admiration. *He paid her a compliment on her new dress.* **compliment** *verb.*

**component** *noun* a part of a larger object or machine. *The bike's components are made in southern Italy.*

A spark plug is one of the components of a car's engine.

**compose** *verb* 1 to make up or form something. *The firm is composed of managers, secretaries and builders.* 2 to write music or poetry. 3 to make yourself calm. *Compose yourself before you speak.*

**composer** *noun* a person who writes music.

**composition** *noun* 1 a piece of music. 2 an essay or story written at school. 3 the various parts something is made up of. *A chemical composition.*

**comprehend** *verb* to understand. *I don't comprehend.* **comprehension** *noun.*

**comprehensive** *adjective* including everything needed. *The Prime Minister gave a comprehensive explanation of his plans.*

**comprehensive school** *noun* a secondary school for pupils of all abilities.

**compress** *verb* (say kum-**press**) to squeeze something together so it takes up less space.

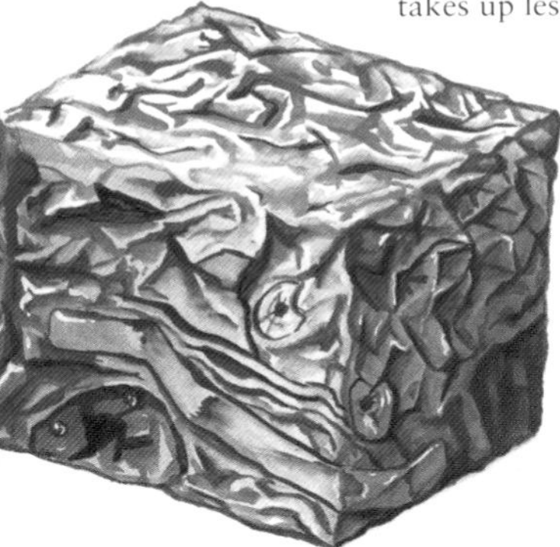

A car crusher can compress a whole car into a small cube for recycling purposes.

**compress** *noun* (say **kom**-press) a soft pad pressed on a wound to stop it bleeding.

**compromise** *noun* the settlement of an argument or differences of opinion by each side accepting less than it had asked for. *After a long discussion we reached a compromise.* **compromise** *verb* 1 *We compromised and went by bus.* 2 If you compromise yourself, you act unwisely or make people doubt you.

C

**compulsive** *adjective* not being able to stop yourself from doing something, even though it is wrong or harmful. *Compulsive liars rarely tell the truth.* **compulsion** *noun.*

**compulsory** *adjective* having to do something. If something is compulsory, it must be done. *Education is compulsory for all children in Europe.* The opposite of compulsory is optional.

**computer** *noun* an electronic machine that can make calculations, store information or control other machines. **computerize** *verb* 1 to store information on a computer. 2 to equip a business with computers.

Businesses and schools have all benefited from the invention of the computer.

**Conakry** *noun* the capital of Guinea.

**concave** *adjective* curved inwards, like the inside of a hollow ball. The opposite of concave is convex.

**conceal** *verb* to hide or keep secret. *The scarf concealed the hideous scar.*

**conceited** *adjective* being too proud of yourself and your abilities. **conceit** *noun.*

**concentrate** *verb* 1 to give all your attention to something. *You must concentrate more on your homework.* 2 to bring or come together. *Industry is concentrated in the north.* **concentrated** *adjective. Concentrated orange juice has to be diluted with water.*

**concentration** *noun* 1 If something needs concentration, it requires all your attention. 2 a gathering. *A concentration of troops at the border.*

**concept** *noun* an idea.

**concern** *noun* 1 something that is very important to you. *Her diet is no concern of mine.* **concern** *verb.* 2 a business. *A very profitable concern.*

**concert** *noun* a musical performance. *They played a symphony at the concert.*

The concert is in full swing, with the conductor directing the percussionist to bang the drums.

**WORD HISTORY**

*'Concave' comes from the Latin 'cavus', a cave. 'Convex' comes from the Latin 'convexus', arched.*

**concise** *adjective* short and to the point, not saying anything unnecessary.

**conclude** *verb* 1 to end. 2 to come to believe something after having thought it over. To decide. *When they didn't ring back, he concluded that they had gone away.*

**conclusion** *noun* 1 an ending. 2 an opinion or judgement. *The jury reached the conclusion that he was guilty.*

**concrete** *noun* building material made by mixing together cement, sand, gravel and water. *A concrete bridge.*

**concrete** *adjective* definite, real. *Can you give me a concrete example?*

**condemn** *verb* 1 to say that you find something wrong and unacceptable. *We condemn violence.* 2 to judge a person guilty or sentence a criminal. 3 to force somebody to suffer. *After her husband's death, she was condemned to a life of loneliness.*

**condense** *verb* 1 to make a speech or piece of writing shorter. *He condensed his report to a few sentences.* 2 to change from gas or vapour into liquid. 3 to become thicker. **condensed** *adjective. Condensed milk.*

The type on the right has been squashed up, or condensed.

CONDENSED

**condition** *noun* 1 the state somebody or something is in. *My bike is in very good condition.* 2 The conditions people live or work in are the surroundings that affect their well-being. *It is impossible to work under these conditions.* 3 something that is dependent on another thing, or necessary for something else. *You can come to stay on condition that you help with the baby.*

**condom** *noun* a rubber covering for the penis used as a means of birth control or to prevent infection.

**conduct** *verb* (say kun-**dukt**) 1 to behave. *They conducted themselves well.* 2 to lead or guide a person. 3 to control or manage a group. *To conduct a meeting.* 4 to direct. *To conduct an orchestra.* 5 to act as a path for electricity or heat.

**conduct** *noun* (say **kon**-dukt) 1 behaviour. *Conduct at school has improved.* 2 the manner in which something is managed.

**conductor** *noun* 1 a person who conducts musicians in an orchestra. 2 a person who collects fares from passengers on buses and trains. 3 something that conducts heat or electricity. *Copper is a good conductor.*

**cone** *noun* 1 a shape with a round base ending in a point at the top. 2 the fruit of pine or fir trees. 3 an ice-cream cone.

Cones are the seed pods of conifers or evergreen trees.

**confuse** *verb* 1 to make a person feel puzzled. To make something difficult to understand. *He confused me with his long explanation.* 2 to get things mixed up. *I'm always confusing her with her sister.*

**confusion** *noun* 1 mixing a thing, person or situation up. 2 a situation where nobody knows what is going on. **confusing** *adjective. A confusing explanation.*

**Congo** *noun* one of two countries in Africa; the Republic of the Congo is also called Congo-Brazzaville; the Democratic Republic of the Congo was fomerly called Zaire.

The flag of the Congo has a diagonal yellow stripe on a green and red ground.

**congratulate** *verb* to tell a person that you are pleased about their success or something that they have done. *My friend congratulated me on passing my driving test.* **congratulation** *noun.*

**conifer** *noun* (say **kon**-if-er) a type of tree that has needle-like leaves and bears its fruit in cones. *A conifer plantation.*

**conjure** (say **kun**-juh) *verb* to do magic tricks. *The magician conjured a large white rabbit out of a hat.* **conjuror** *noun.* a person who does magic tricks. **conjure up** to make something appear.

**conker** *noun* a round brown nut of the horse chestnut tree.

**connect** *verb* 1 to join together. 2 to link by telephone. *Don't hang up, I'm trying to connect you.* 3 to be related or linked. *The families are connected.* **connection** *noun.*

**conquer** *verb* 1 to defeat and take over. To conquer a country. 2 to overcome an illness or a difficult situation. **conqueror** *noun.*

**conquest** *noun* 1 the conquering of something. *The conquest of Mount Everest.* 2 overcoming something.

**conscience** *noun* the part of your mind that tells you if what you are doing is right or wrong. *You have a guilty conscience when you do something wrong.*

**conscious** *adjective* 1 noticing what is happening. *He was conscious of everybody looking at him.* 2 awake. *The patient is not conscious.* **consciousness** *noun.*

**consent** *verb* to agree to do something. **consent** *noun* permission given. *She left school without her parents' consent.*

**DID YOU KNOW?**

*Except for the larch, nearly all conifer trees are evergreen. This means they don't lose their leaves in autumn. Trees that drop their leaves are called deciduous.*

Many of the constellations, such as the Great Bear, were named after mythical creatures.

**consequence** *noun* something that happens as a result of something else. *He dreaded the consequences of his actions.*

**conserve** *verb* to store up, or keep from going bad or being wasted. *We need to conserve energy.* **conservation** *noun.*

**consider** *verb* 1 to think about something in order to make a decision. *I'm considering changing my job.* 2 to regard as. *I consider him an idiot.* **consideration** *noun.* **take into consideration** to allow for something. *I will take your illness into consideration when marking your paper.*

**considerable** *adjective* fairly large. *A considerable amount of money.*

**consist** *verb* to be made up of. *Europe consists of many different countries.*

The Low Countries consist of many islands.

**console** *verb* to give somebody sympathy to make them less sad. **consolation** *noun.*

**consonant** *noun* any of the letters of the alphabet except for the vowels a, e, i, o and u. *How many consonants are in your name?*

**conspiracy** *noun* a secret plan to do something that is against the law. A plot.

**conspirator** *noun* a person who takes part in a conspiracy.

**constant** *adjective* 1 unchanging, fixed. *We were driving at a constant speed.* 2 loyal and faithful. **constancy** *noun.*

**constellation** *noun* a group of stars.

**constipated** *adjective* If you are constipated, you are unable to empty your bowels. **constipation** *noun. Constipation is unpleasant.*

**constituency** *noun* a town or area that elects a Member of Parliament to represent them.

**constitution** *noun* 1 the system of laws that states how a country is governed. *The constitution requires elections to be held every five years.* 2 the general condition of a person's body. 3 the way in which something is made up.

**construct** *verb* to build or put together.

**construction** *noun* 1 a building. 2 the process of building. *The bridge is under construction.* 3 words put together to form a phrase or sentence. *The construction of a sentence.* 4 an explanation. *The wrong construction was put on his behaviour.*

**constructive** *adjective* helpful.

Cranes work from above to finish the construction of this skyscraper.

**consult** *verb* to go to a person or book for information. *Consult a doctor about your illness before it gets any worse.*

**consultant** *noun* a person who gives advice.

**consume** *verb* 1 to eat or drink something. 2 to use up. *The car consumes a lot of petrol.* 3 to destroy. *Fire consumed the entire village in a matter of hours.*

**consumer** *noun* a person who buys and uses goods and services.

**contact** *noun* 1 the process of touching or coming together. Communication. *I'm not in contact with him.* 2 a person. **contact** *verb*. *He's got some useful contacts.*

**contact lens** *noun* a tiny piece of plastic shaped to fit over the eye to make you see better. *Disposable contact lenses.*

**contagious** *adjective* spreading from person to person. *A contagious disease.*

**contain** *verb* to hold. *The book contains all the information you need.*

**container** *noun* 1 a box, barrel or bottle to hold things in. 2 a large metal box used for transporting goods.

Different shaped plastic containers are useful for storing food.

**contemporary** *adjective* 1 happening now, modern. 2 belonging to the past and happening at the same time as something else. *Contemporary politicians were critical of Disraeli.* **contemporary** *noun*. *Our fathers were contemporaries at school.*

**contempt** *noun* lack of respect, thinking that somebody or something is not important. *I hold him in contempt.*

**AMAZING FACT**

The continents, Africa, Asia, Antartica, Europe, Australia, North America and South America, formed a single continent millions of years ago called Pangaea.

**GRAMMAR NOTE**

*Words like 'I've', 'won't' and 'shouldn't' are called contractions. These shorter forms (for 'I have', 'I will not' and 'I should not') use an apostrophe to show where letters have been missed out.*

**content** *adjective* (say kun-**tent**) happy, satisfied. *She was content with her life.*

**content** *noun* (say **kon**-tent) something contained. *The contents had gone off.*

**contents** *plural noun* things contained. *He emptied the contents of the packet.*

**contest** *noun* (say **kon**-test) a struggle or fight in which people take part in order to win. *It was an even contest.*

**contest** *verb* (say kun-**test**) to compete or fight for a place. *To contest an election.*

**continent** *noun* one of Earth's huge land masses. *Europe, Asia and Africa are continents.*

The continent of Antarctica surrounds the South Pole.

**continual** *adjective* without stopping.

**continue** *verb* 1 to go on doing or being something without stopping. 2 to start again after stopping. **continuation** *noun*.

**continuous** *adjective* without a break. **continuity** *noun*.

**contract** *noun* (say **kon**-trakt) a written agreement between people. **contract** *verb* (say kun-**trakt**) 1 *We have been contracted to do the music.* 2 to get a disease. *My sister has contracted German measles.*

**contract** *verb* (say kun-**trakt**) to make or become smaller or shorter. *'Has not' is often contracted to 'hasn't'.* **contraction** *noun*.

**contradict** *verb* to say that something said or written is wrong. *Don't contradict me.* **contradiction** *noun*.

**contrast** *noun* (say **kon**-trast) the difference seen between things when they are compared. *There was a big contrast between their results.* **contrast** *verb* (say kun-**trast**).

**contribute** *verb* 1 to join with others in doing things or giving money to help make something successful. *She contributed towards my success.* 2 to write an article for a newspaper or magazine. **contribution** *noun*. *He made a contribution of £100.*

**control** *noun* the power to influence, make decisions or give orders. **control** *verb* to have control of something. *The teacher can't control the class.*

**convenience** *noun* 1 ease of use. *I always buy frozen food for convenience when I'm busy at work.* 2 a useful appliance, such as a dishwasher. 3 a public lavatory.

**convenient** *adjective* 1 easy to use or suitable. 2 easy to get to. *The flat is convenient for the shops.*

**convent** *noun* a place where nuns live.

**converge** *verb* to come together towards the same point. *The crowds converged on the stadium.*

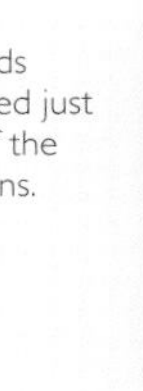

The roads converged just south of the mountains.

**conversation** *noun* a talk between people.

**converse** *verb* to talk. *Let's converse.*

**convex** *adjective* curved outward, like the outside of a ball. The opposite of convex is concave. *A convex mirror.*

**convey** *verb* 1 to carry from one place to another. 2 to make known. *Words cannot convey my sympathy.*

**convict** *verb* (say kun-**vikt**) to find somebody guilty of a crime. *He was convicted of murder.* **convict** *noun* (say **kon**-vikt) a person who has been found guilty.

**convoy** *noun* a group of ships or vehicles travelling together.

**copper** *noun* 1 a reddish-brown metal. Wires are made of copper. 2 a coin. *It only cost a few coppers.* **copper** *adjective. A copper colour.*

**copy** *noun* 1 a thing that looks exactly like another. *Can I have a copy of the picture?* 2 an example of a book, newspaper or magazine of which there are many others. *His copy of the book was torn.* **copy** *verb* 1 to make a copy of something. 2 to do the same as another person. *He's always copying me.*

**coral** *noun* a hard red, pink or white substance formed from the skeletons of tiny sea animals. *A coral necklace.*

A coral reef is a fascinating place for underwater explorers to observe tropical fish.

**cord** *noun* 1 a thick string. 2 wires inside a plastic casing for electrical equipment. 3 a part of the body. *We use our vocal cords to make sounds.*

**corduroy** *noun* thick velvety cotton material with thin ridges. *A corduroy jacket.*

**core** *noun* 1 the hard middle of an apple or pear which contains the pips. 2 the central, most important part of something.

**cork** *noun* 1 the soft, light bark of the cork oak. Cork tiles are used as a floor covering. 2 a stopper for a bottle made of cork or other material.

A convoy of vehicles is heading for the ferry.

**cook** *verb* to make food. **cook** *noun. She's a wonderful cook.*

**cooker** *noun* an apparatus on which food is cooked. *Your tea is in the cooker.*

**cookie** *noun* a biscuit.

**cool** *adjective* 1 between warm and cold. 2 calm. *She manages to keep cool even when she is annoyed.* **cool** *verb* to make or become cool.

**cooperate** *verb* to work together for a common purpose. **cooperation** *noun.*

**cooperative** *adjective* 1 helpful. 2 owned by its members. *A cooperative business.*

**cope** *verb* to deal with something successfully. *She manages to cope with all the family's problems.*

**Copenhagen** *noun* the capital of Denmark.

**WORD BUILDING**

*The prefix 'co-' gives a sense of together. People who cooperate (sometimes spelled with a hyphen, co-operate), work together.*

**corn** *noun* 1 the crop of wheat, barley and other types of grain. *The farmer stored his corn in a barn.* 2 maize. *Corn on the cob.*

**corn** *noun* a painful, hard lump of skin on the foot. *He trod on my corn.*

**corner** *noun* 1 the place where two edges, lines, walls or streets meet. 2 a kick from the corner of a football field. *They scored from a corner.* 3 a region. *The four corners of the world.* **in a corner** in a difficult situation. **corner** *verb* 1 to drive round a corner. 2 to force somebody into a difficult situation. *He finally cornered me about the mistake.*

**cornflakes** *noun* toasted flakes made from corn, usually eaten with milk for breakfast.

**coronation** *noun* the crowning of a king or queen. *We watched the coronation of the new king on television.*

C

**corporal punishment** *noun* punishing a person by beating them.

**corpse** *noun* a dead body.

**correct** *adjective* 1 without any mistakes. 2 proper, most suitable in a particular situation. **correct** *verb* 1 to put something right and mark the mistakes. 2 to point out a person's faults in order to improve their behaviour. **correction** *noun*.

**correspond** *verb* 1 to write letters to each other. 2 to be the same or in agreement with something. *Her report of the accident doesn't correspond with his.* 3 to be like or match closely. *Our prime minister corresponds to their president.*

**correspondence** *noun* 1 writing and exchanging letters. 2 the letters you receive. *A pile of correspondence.* 3 likeness or relationship between particular things.

**corridor** *noun* a passage in a building.

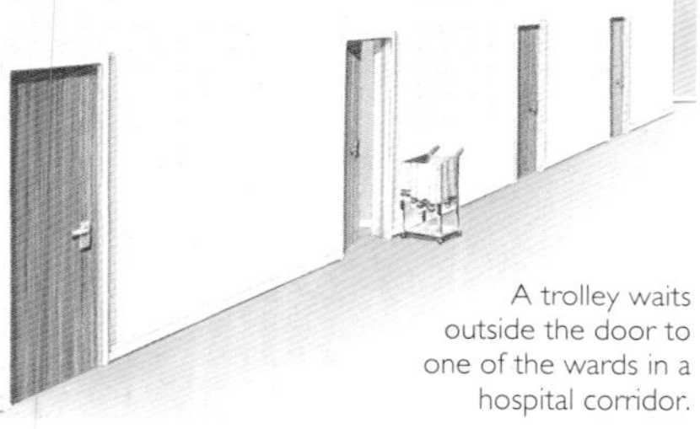

A trolley waits outside the door to one of the wards in a hospital corridor.

**corrode** *verb* to destroy by chemical action or by rust. *Acid corrodes metal.* **corrosion** *noun*. **corrosive** *adjective*.

**corrugated** *adjective* shaped into ridges or folds. *Corrugated paper is used for packing.*

**corrupt** *adjective* immoral or wicked. *The newspaper exposed the corrupt politicians.*

**corrupt** *verb* to make somebody change from good to bad. *Power corrupts.* **corruption** *noun*.

**cosmetics** *noun* substances such as lipstick and eyeshadow, used to beautify the face.

**cosmic** *adjective* related to the universe. *Cosmic rays from outer space.*

The galaxy is surrounded by cosmic dust.

**cosmonaut** *noun* a Russian astronaut.

**cosmos** *noun* (say **koz**-moss) the universe.

**DID YOU KNOW**

*Costa Rica, the 'rich coast', actually has two coastlines. One is on the Pacific Ocean and the other on the Caribbean Sea.*

**GRAMMAR NOTE**

*'Could' is used with another verb to express possibility or permission: 'You could be right.' 'He said we could smoke.' 'Could' is also used to make a polite request: 'Could you help me carry the bags?' 'Could not' is the negative of 'could'. If you could not do it, you were unable to do it.*

**SPELLING NOTE**

*'Council' and 'councillor' have different meanings from 'counsel' and 'counsellor', though they sound exactly the same.*

**cost** *noun* the price of something. **at all costs** no matter what the cost may be. **cost** (costing, cost) *verb* 1 to have a certain price. 2 to cause a loss or disadvantage to somebody. *Drunken driving costs many lives.* 3 to estimate. *The garage costed the repairs at about £100.*

**Costa Rica** *noun* a country in Central America.

The flag of Costa Rica has a coloured emblem on a striped red, blue and white background.

**costly** *adjective* expensive.

**costume** *noun* clothes worn by actors or at a particular time in history. *National costume is worn on historic occasions.*

**cot** *noun* a bed with high sides for a baby or young child.

**cottage** *noun* a small house, especially in the country.

**cotton** *noun* 1 cloth made from the soft white fibres covering the seeds of the cotton plant. 2 a tall tropical plant. 3 cotton thread.

**cotton wool** *noun* soft, fluffy cotton used for putting cream on your skin or cleaning wounds. *A packet of cotton wool.*

**couch** *noun* a sofa. *Sit on the couch.*

**cough** *verb* to push air out of your throat and make a harsh noise. **cough** *noun* 1 the sound of coughing. 2 an illness that makes you cough. *The baby had a nasty cough.*

**could** past tense of can.

**council** *noun* a group of people chosen to make laws and decisions and run a town or county. *The parish council.*

**councillor** *noun* a member of a council.

**counsel** *noun* 1 advice. 2 a group of lawyers acting for somebody in court. **counsel** (counselling, counselled) *verb*. *She counsels families who have problems.*

**counsellor** *noun* a person trained to give advice and help.

**count** *verb* 1 to say numbers in order. *He counted up to 10.* 2 to say or name objects or people to find the total number in a collection. *The teacher counted the children.* 3 to include. *There are four of us, counting me.* 4 to have importance or value. *It's the thought that counts.* 5 to consider. *I count myself lucky.* **count** *noun* 1 counting. 2 a number reached by counting. 3 one of a number of crimes somebody is accused of. *He was found guilty on all counts.* **lose count** not know the exact number.

**count** *noun* a European nobleman equal to an earl. *The count married the countess.*

**counter** *noun* 1 a flat surface like a table on which goods are shown and where customers are served in a shop or bank. 2 a small, flat, round piece of plastic or wood used in board games.

**counter** *verb* 1 to act against something. 2 to meet an attack by hitting back.

**counterfeit** *noun* a copy of something made in order to deceive, a fake. **counterfeit** *adjective. Counterfeit money.* **counterfeit** *verb. It is illegal to counterfeit money.*

**country** *noun* 1 a land with its own people, government and language. 2 all the people who live in a particular country. *The Queen spoke to the country.* 3 land away from towns. *We live in the country.*

**county** (counties) *noun* a region that has its own local government.

**couple** *noun* 1 two people or things. 2 two people who are married or live together.

**couple** *verb* to connect or link together.

**coupon** *noun* a ticket or piece of printed paper allowing the holder to receive goods or information or pay less money for something than usual.

**courage** *noun* the ability to control fear and face danger or difficulty. **courageous** *adjective.* **pluck up courage** to become brave enough to do something.

The lion is known as the king of the jungle because of its great courage.

**courier** *noun* 1 a messenger who takes letters and parcels from one place to another. 2 a person who works for a travel company and looks after tourists.

**course** *noun* 1 lessons or lectures on a particular subject. 2 a series of events or things you can do in a particular situation. 3 the direction or route in which something goes. 4 part of a meal. *What would you like for your main course?* 5 a ground for certain games. *A golf course.* **in the course of** during. **of course** certainly, naturally.

**court** *noun* 1 a place where law cases are heard and judged. 2 a place where a king or queen, their family and officials live. 3 an area for games. *A tennis court.*

**court** *verb* to try and win somebody's love. *He courted her for many years.*

**courtesy** *noun* (say **ker-tuh-see**) polite behaviour. **courteous** *adjective.*

**DID YOU KNOW**

*Your mother's or father's cousin is your cousin once removed. Your grandmother's or grandfather's cousin is your cousin twice removed.*

**cousin** *noun* the child of your uncle or aunt.

**cove** *noun* a small bay on the coast.

They bathed in the sea in the beautiful cove.

**cover** *verb* 1 to put something on or round something else to protect or hide it. *I covered my eyes.* 2 to spread over. *Snow covered the fields.* 3 to travel a certain distance. 4 to be enough money for something. *£10 should cover the petrol.* 5 to deal with or discuss a subject or topic. *The book covers the whole of modern history.* 6 to insure against damage or loss. *The policy doesn't cover jewellery.*

**cover** *noun* 1 a thing put on to cover another thing. 2 the binding of a book or magazine. If you read a book from cover to cover, you read it from beginning to end. 3 something that hides something illegal or shelters you from bad weather. *We had to spend the whole day under cover.* 4 a guarantee from an insurance company against loss or damage. **take cover** to hide or protect yourself.

**cow** *noun* 1 a fully grown female animal that farmers keep for its milk. 2 a female elephant, whale or seal.

**coward** *noun* a person who shows fear and avoids dangerous situations. *Cowards lack courage.* **cowardly** *adjective.*

**cowardice** *noun* cowardly behaviour.

**cowboy** *noun* a man who looks after cattle on a ranch in America.

A cowboy on horseback rounds up a steer that has strayed from the herd.

**cox** (coxes) *noun* a person who steers a rowing boat.

**coy** *adjective* pretending to be shy and modest. *She gave him a coy smile.*

**crab** *noun* a sea animal with a shell-covered body and five pairs of legs.

C

**crack** *verb* 1 to split or make something split. *The hot water cracked the glass.* 2 to make a sudden loud noise. *To crack a whip.* 3 to break down. *After days of questioning, he finally cracked.* **crack a problem** to finally solve a problem. **crack a joke** to tell a joke. **get cracking** to get on with a task. **crack up** to break down. **crack** *noun* 1 a thin line on the surface of a glass or plate, for example, where they have cracked but not come completely apart. 2 a narrow gap. 3 a sudden loud noise. **at the crack of dawn** very early in the morning. **have a crack at something** to try to do something difficult.

**cracker** *noun* 1 a hollow cardboard tube with toys inside that cracks when you pull apart a snap inside it. 2 a firework that explodes with a crack. 3 a thin, dry biscuit.

**cradle** *noun* a small bed for a baby. **from the cradle to the grave** from birth to death.

**cradle** *verb* to hold gently.

**craft** 1 a job that needs skill, especially making things skilfully with your hands. 2 the skill of tricking people. **crafty** *adjective. I wouldn't trust him, he's very crafty.*

**craft** *noun* a ship, boat or plane. *A spacecraft is a craft for travelling in space.*

Sputnik was the first craft ever to be sent into space. It was launched on 4 October 1957.

**cram** (cramming, crammed) *verb* 1 to push lots of things or people into a small space. 2 to fill. *His head was crammed with facts.*

**crane** *noun* 1 a machine for lifting and moving heavy objects. 2 a large bird with a long neck and long legs.

**crane** *verb* to stretch out your neck in order to see something better.

**crash** *noun* 1 a loud noise made by something falling or breaking. 2 a bad accident. 3 a business failure. **crash** *verb* 1 to make a loud noise when falling, or hitting something violently. 2 to hit something and be damaged. *She crashed the car.* 3 to move noisily or break through something with force. *He crashes through the house like an elephant.* 4 to fail, especially in business or money matters. *The stock market crashed.*

**crate** *noun* a box made of wood for putting goods in. *A crate of oranges.*

**DID YOU KNOW?**

*Craters in extinct volcanoes are often filled with water. Most other craters, on Earth and other planets, were caused when meteorites crashed into them.*

**WORD HISTORY**

*'Crafty' used to mean skilful, before it got today's meaning of cunning.*

**AMAZING FACT**

The Whooping Crane was once a common bird in the United States but was hunted nearly to extinction. In 1945 there were only 16 individual birds left. Then a successful breeding program was started and the chicks were reared by humans. But the chicks couldn't be released because they were so used to the humans that fed them. So now the chicks are fed using hand puppets that look like adult cranes.

**crater** *noun* 1 a round hole in the top of a volcano. 2 a round hole in the ground or on the surface of another planet.

**crawl** *verb* 1 to move on your hands and knees with the body close to the ground. 2 to move slowly. *The traffic was crawling along.* 3 to be full of or covered with crawling things. *Don't sit on the grass, it's crawling with ants.* 4 If something makes your skin crawl, it gives you a nasty feeling. **crawl** *noun* 1 a slow crawling movement. 2 a fast swimming stroke.

Babies learn to crawl before they can walk.

**crayon** *noun* a pencil or stick of coloured wax for drawing.

**crazy** *adjective* 1 foolish, mad. 2 very interested or excited. *Crazy about football.* **crazily** *adverb.* **craziness** *noun.*

**creak** *verb* to make a sound, usually when something is moved or moves. **creak** *noun* the sound of wood bending or an unoiled door opening.

**cream** *noun* 1 the fatty part of milk. *We had strawberries and cream.* 2 food that looks and tastes like cream. *Ice-cream.* 3 a soft substance that you put on your skin to make it soft or soothe it. 4 the best part of something. *The cream of society.* **creamy** *adjective.* **cream** *verb* to mix food until it is like cream. **cream** *adjective* a cream colour.

Cream and fruit are two of the ingredients of ice-cream.

**crease** *noun* 1 a line made on cloth, paper or clothes by folding, crushing or pressing. 2 a line on a cricket pitch. **crease** *verb. I can't sit down because my dress will crease.*

**create** *verb* 1 to make something new. *They have created a garden in the desert.* 2 to produce or cause something to happen. *His film created a lot of controversy.*

**creation** *noun* 1 making something. *The creation of great works of art.* 2 a thing created. *All my own creation.*

**creative** *adjective* able to invent and produce new ideas and things.

**creator** *noun* a person who makes or invents something.

**creature** *noun* a living being.

**crèche** *noun* (say kresh) a day nursery for babies and young children.

**credit** *noun* 1 the practice of allowing somebody to buy something and pay for it later. 2 the money a bank or business has agreed somebody can borrow. 3 the time you are allowed to pay a debt. *They gave us a month's credit.* 4 somebody with a good reputation. *He's a credit to the school.* 5 trust. *Don't give any credit to what he says.* 6 Credits are the list of people who helped to make a film or programme. **credit** *verb* 1 to believe. 2 to say that somebody has done something. *She is credited with many achievements.* 3 to increase an account with a sum of money. *We will credit your account with the refund.*

**credit card** *noun* a plastic card you can use to buy goods on credit.

Credit cards are sometimes also called smart cards.

**creditor** *noun* a person money is owed to.

**creed** *noun* a set of beliefs or opinions.

**creek** *noun* a small inlet on the sea coast.

**creep** (crept) *verb* 1 to move slowly and quietly. *She creeps around the house.* 2 to move slowly towards or across something. **creep** *noun* an unpleasant person you dislike. *That creep always flatters the boss.* If someone or something gives you the creeps, they make you feel nervous. **creepy** *adjective. A creepy story.*

**cremate** *verb* to burn a dead body to ashes. **cremation** *noun.*

**crematorium** *noun* a place where people are cremated.

**crescent** *noun* 1 a curved shape like a crescent moon. 2 a curved street.

**crevice** *noun* an opening or crack in a rock.

**crew** *noun* 1 all the people working on a ship, plane or spacecraft. 2 a group of people working together. *A film crew.*

The air crew greet the passengers as they board the plane.

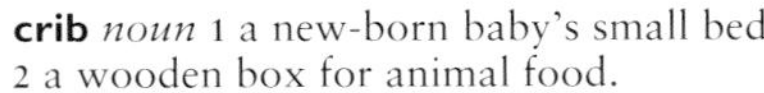

**crib** *noun* 1 a new-born baby's small bed. 2 a wooden box for animal food.

**crib** *verb* to copy somebody else's work and pretend that it is your own.

**cricket** *noun* an outdoor game for teams played with a ball, bats and two wickets.

**cricket** *noun* an insect like a grasshopper.

On warm summer nights you can hear the crickets chirping.

**cried** past tense of cry.

**crime** *noun* 1 an unlawful activity. 2 an action that is wrong, but not a matter for the police. *It would be a crime not to enjoy the sunshine.*

**criminal** *noun* a person who has committed a crime. **criminal** *adjective. A criminal act.*

**crimson** *adjective* purplish red.

**cringe** *verb* to move back with fear.

The poor creature cringed with fear when he heard the man's voice.

**crisis** *noun* a serious or dangerous situation.

**crisp** *adjective* 1 dry and easily broken. *Crisp pastry.* 2 fresh or newly made. *A crisp shirt.* 3 fresh and cold. *A crisp morning.* 4 quick and clear. *A crisp hello.* **crisp** *noun* a thin piece of fried potato.

**critic** *noun* 1 a person who gives his opinion about books, films, music or art. 2 a person who points out mistakes.

**critical** *adjective* 1 finding faults or mistakes. *He made critical remarks about my work.* 2 very important or dangerous. *A critical illness.* **critically** *adverb*.

**criticism** *noun* 1 pointing out faults and mistakes. 2 a critic's opinion on books, films, music or art. **criticize** *verb*.

**croak** *verb* to make a deep low sound. *Frogs croak in spring.* **croak** *noun* a deep hoarse sound.

**Croatia** *noun* a country in Southeast Europe.

The flag of Croatia has a colourful crest on a striped red, blue and white background.

**crockery** *noun* cups, plates and other dishes. *He smashed all their crockery.*

**crocodile** *noun* a large reptile with a long body. Crocodiles live in rivers.

**crocus** *noun* a small plant with white, yellow or purple flowers that grows in spring. *Crocuses grew on the lawn in spring.*

**croissant** *noun* (say **krwah**-sahn) a crescent-shaped bread roll.

**crook** *noun* 1 a shepherd's stick. 2 a dishonest person. 3 the inside of your elbow or knee. *The crook of my arm.*

**crooked** *adjective* 1 not straight, twisted. 2 dishonest, criminal.

**crop** *noun* 1 plants such as grain, fruit or vegetables grown for food. 2 the plants collected at harvest time. 3 a group of things appearing at the same time. *A crop of questions.* **crop** *verb* to cut short. *Cropped hair.* **crop up** to appear or happen. *A problem has cropped up.*

**cross** *noun* 1 a mark that looks like an X. *He marked the place with a cross.* 2 an upright post with another shorter bar across the top or any similar design used for decoration or as jewellery. The cross is an important Christian symbol. 3 a mixture of two animals or plants. *A mule is a cross between a horse and a donkey.*

Christian relics were highly prized in the Byzantine Empire, which began in AD 476. This gold crucifx, or cross, is an example.

**AMAZING FACT**

Although crocodiles' jaws are powerful enough to crush the bones of their prey, they are also sensitive enough to carry their young hatchlings safely to water.

**WORD HISTORY**

*In crossword puzzles, words have to fit both across and down and so cross each other. The first crossword was published in a New York magazine called 'World' in 1913, so the puzzle is not as old as you might think.*

**AMAZING FACT**

The Crown Jewels are a collection of crowns, swords and other valuable articles that belong to the kings and queens of Britain. In 1671, a man called Colonel Blood tried to steal the jewels. He was captured just outside the Tower of London where the Crown jewels were kept.

**cross** *verb* 1 to go across something, or move from one side to another. 2 to draw a line or lines across something. 3 When roads or railways cross, they meet and go across each other. 4 to put one arm, leg or finger on top of the other. *I crossed my fingers for luck.* 5 to mix one animal or plant with another. 6 to oppose somebody's plans or go against somebody's wishes. *If you cross me, I'll get angry.* **cross out** to draw a line through something to show that it is wrong or not wanted.

**cross** *adjective* angry.

**crossing** *noun* 1 a journey by ship to the other side of a sea. 2 a place where people can cross a road or railway. 3 a place where two roads or railways cross.

**crossroads** *noun* a place where two roads meet and cross each other.

**crossword** *noun* a puzzle in which you work out answers to clues and write the answers into numbered squares.

**crouch** *verb* to lower your body close to the ground by bending your knees and back.

**crow** *noun* a large black bird with a loud cry. **as the crow flies** in a straight line. **crow** *verb* to make a loud cry like a crow.

**crowd** *noun* a large group of people in one place. **crowd** *verb* 1 to come together in a large group. 2 to fill completely. *The new museum was crowded with tourists carrying cameras.* 3 to cram in.

**crown** *noun* 1 a headdress like a ring made of gold and jewels, worn by a king or queen. 2 The Crown is the governing power of a monarchy. 3 the top part of your head. 4 an old British coin that is no longer used, worth 25 pence. **crown** *verb* 1 to put a crown on somebody who has become king or queen. 2 to complete something successfully. *Crowned with glory.*

The crown was made of gold and studded with precious jewels.

**crucial** *adjective* (say **kroo**-shuhl) extremely important. *A crucial appointment.*

**crucify** (crucifying, crucified) *verb* to punish by nailing or binding a person to a cross and leaving them to die. **crucifixion** *noun*. The Crucifixion is the death of Jesus Christ on the Cross.

**crude** *adjective* 1 in a raw or natural state. *Crude oil.* 2 rough, not skilfully made. *A crude drawing.* 3 not showing sensitive feeling, vulgar. *Crude jokes.*

**cruel** (crueller, cruellest) *adjective* causing pain or suffering to people or animals. **cruelty** *noun.*

**cruise** *noun* a holiday on a ship visiting a number of places. **cruise** *verb* to move in a car or ship at a comfortable speed.

A cruise in the warm blue waters of the Mediterranean makes a luxurious summer holiday.

**crumb** *noun* a very small piece of bread, cake or biscuit.

**crumble** *verb* 1 to break or fall into lots of small pieces. 2 to come to an end or to nothing. *Her hopes soon crumbled.* **crumble** *noun* cooked fruit covered with a mixture of flour, butter and sugar.

**crumple** *verb* to become full of creases and folds. *She crumpled up the invoice.*

**crunch** *verb* 1 to crush hard food noisily with your teeth. *The dog was crunching a bone.* 2 to make a crushing or breaking noise. **crunch** *noun* 1 crunching. 2 a crunching noise. *The crunch of footsteps on the gravel drive frightened me.* **come to the crunch** to reach a point when a difficult decision has to be made.

**crusade** *noun* 1 an expedition to Palestine made by Christian knights in the Middle Ages. 2 a movement against something bad or for something good. *A crusade against smoking in public places.*

**crust** *noun* 1 the hard surface of something baked, such as bread. 2 a hard surface. *The Earth's crust.*

**crustacean** *noun* (say krust-**ay**-shuhn) an animal with a shell. Crabs and lobsters are crustaceans.

Crabs and other crustaceans have delicately flavoured meat.

**AMAZING FACT**

Cuckoos live in all the continents of the world except Antarctica. There are 136 species of cuckoo in all and 45 of these lay their eggs in the nests of other birds. Their eggs are then incubated, and hatched by the 'adopted' parent.

**crutch** *noun* a stick, with a piece that fits under the arm, which people who have difficulty walking use as a support.

**cry** (cried) *verb* 1 to shed tears from your eyes, because you are unhappy or in pain. 2 to shout or say something loudly. *She cried for help.* **cry** (cries) *noun* 1 a sound you make when you feel excited or frightened. *A cry of pain.* 2 a shout to attract somebody's attention. 3 weeping.

**crypt** *noun* an underground room in a church. *A tryst in the crypt.*

**crystal** *noun* 1 a natural mineral that looks like ice. 2 a shaped piece of this mineral used in jewellery or decoration. 3 high-quality glass, often cut. **crystal** *adjective.*

Crystals are prized for their brilliance and clarity. Some people believe they have the power to heal illness.

**cub** *noun* a young wild animal. *Tiger cubs.*

**Cuba** *noun* a country in the West Indies.

**cube** *noun* 1 an object with six square sides which are all the same size. *A cube of sugar.* 2 the number made by multiplying a number by itself twice. The cube of 2 is 2 x 2 x 2, which makes 8. **cube** *verb* 1 to multiply a number by itself twice. 2 to cut something into cubes. **cubed** *adjective.*

**cubicle** *noun* a small room, especially for changing clothes.

**cuckoo** *noun* 1 a bird that lays its eggs in other birds' nests. 2 the sound a cuckoo makes.

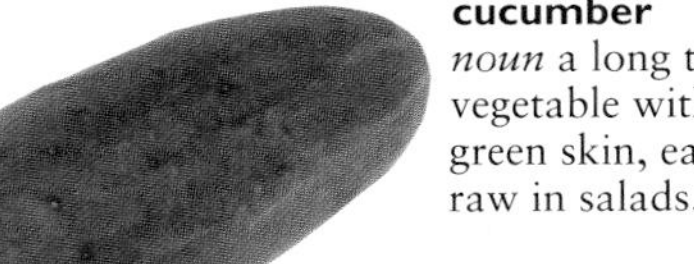

**cucumber** *noun* a long thin vegetable with a green skin, eaten raw in salads.

Cucumbers can be served in salads or sandwiches.

**cud** *noun* the half-eaten food that cows and sheep bring up a number of times, before finally swallowing it.

**cuddle** (cuddled, cuddling) *verb* to hold somebody or something closely in your arms. **cuddle** *noun.* **cuddly** *adjective.*

**cue** *noun* a signal for somebody to do or say something.

**cue** *noun* a long stick for hitting the ball in snooker or pool.

C

**culprit** *noun* a person who has done something wrong.

**cultivate** *verb* 1 to use land to grow crops on. 2 to develop something and make it strong. *He has cultivated a love of art.* **cultivation** *noun.*

In the Philippines rice is cultivated in terraces that were dug out 2,000 years ago.

AMAZING FACT

'Amp' or 'ampere' is the unit of electric current. Our muscles respond to electric impulses from our nerves. The current necessary to raise an arm is about one hundred thousandth of an amp.

**culture** *noun* 1 an understanding of literature, art, music and other activities of the mind. 2 the shared customs and traditions of a group of people at a particular time. *He studied the Inca culture.* 3 a group of cells grown in a laboratory for medical study. 4 raising animals and growing plants. **cultural** *adjective.*

**cultured** *adjective* well educated, with good manners and a knowledge of the arts.

**cunning** *adjective* clever in deceiving others. *He's as cunning as a fox.* **cunning** *noun.*

The fox is an animal renowned for its cunning.

**cup** *noun* 1 a container with a handle for drinking from, or its contents. 2 a metal trophy given as a prize to a winning team or player. 3 anything shaped like a cup. **cup** *verb* to make your hands into a cup shape.

**cupboard** *noun* a piece of furniture with shelves and a door for keeping things in.

**curb** *verb* to keep something under control. *The government has curbed the powers of the police.* curb *noun.*

**cure** (cured, curing) *verb* 1 to make an illness disappear or a person well again. *There are still many diseases that drugs cannot cure.* 2 to stop something bad. *It is impossible to cure his meanness.* 3 to preserve something to make it last longer. *Fish and meat can be cured by drying, smoking or salting.* **cure** *noun. Doctors are searching for a cure for Aids.*

SPELLING NOTE

*'Currant' and 'current' sound the same but are spelt differently. Currants get their name from Corinth, in Greece, where they grew in ancient times. 'Current' comes from the Latin word for to run or flow.*

**curious** *adjective* 1 interested in things and wanting to find out. *I'm curious to know what he said to my mother the other day.* 2 unusual and interesting. *That's a curious story!* **curiosity** *noun.*

**curl** *noun* 1 hair shaped into curves and circles. *Goldilocks had golden curls.* 2 a spiral shape. *A curl of smoke.* **curl** *verb* to twist hair into curls or be in curls. **curl up** 1 to form curls or twists. *The leaves have gone brown and curled up.* 2 to lie with your arms and legs drawn close to the body. *She curled up in front of the fire.*

**curler** *noun* a pin or roller put in the hair to make it curly.

**curly** *adjective* full of curls.

**currant** *noun* 1 a small dried grape used in baking and cooking. 2 a soft red, black or white berry.

**currency** (currencies) *noun* 1 the money used in a country. *The value of foreign currencies is always changing.* 2 the common use of something. If an idea gains currency, more people get used to it and accept it.

Most of the world's currencies are made up of paper notes and metal coins.

**current** *adjective* happening or being used now. *The current fashion for body piercing.*

**current** *noun* 1 water or air moving in one direction. *The river has a strong current.* 2 the flow of electricity. *An electric current.*

**curry** (curries) *noun* food cooked with hot-tasting spices. *An Indian curry.*

**curse** *noun* a word, phrase or sentence asking supernatural powers to harm somebody or something. *There must be a curse on our family, because everything is going wrong.* **curse** *verb* 1 to swear or say rude words because you are angry. 2 to use a curse against somebody.

**cursor** *noun* a small movable point on a computer screen used to identify a position.

**curtain** *noun* 1 a piece of material hung up at a window or door. 2 the heavy sheet of material lowered in front of a theatre stage. 3 something that covers or hides. *A curtain of mist descended on the hills.*

**curve** *verb* to bend. *The road curves at the top of the hill.* **curve** *noun* a bending line, like the edge of a circle. *A curve in the road.* **curvy** *adjective.*

**cushion** *noun* 1 a case filled with soft material to sit on or lean against. 2 anything soft or springy in the shape of a cushion. *We floated on a cushion of air.* **cushion** *verb* to protect from shock, a knock, hardship or change. *The branches must have cushioned his fall.*

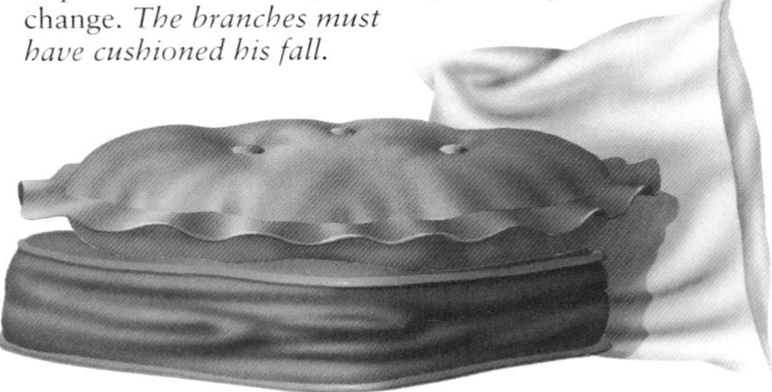

Big soft cushions add to the comfort of any home.

**custody** *noun* 1 the legal right of caring and looking after a child. *The mother was given custody of the children.* 2 imprisonment. **take into custody** to arrest.

**custom** *noun* 1 something which is accepted behaviour among people or that people of a particular society always do. *Different countries have different customs.* 2 regular business given to a shop by customers. *The corner shop lost most of its custom to the new supermarket.*

At the spring festival of Holi, it is the custom for Hindu children to throw coloured powder over each other.

**customer** *noun* a person who buys goods from a shop or uses a bank or other business. *The customer is always right.*

**customs** *plural noun* a place where government officers check your luggage for goods on which you need to pay duty (tax) when your enter or leave a country. *We were stopped at customs.*

**WORD HISTORY**

*'Cute' comes from 'acute,' which itself comes originally from the Latin word for 'sharp'.*

**DID YOU KNOW?**

*Cyclones are usually called hurricanes in Europe and America. In the Far East and the Pacific they are usually called typhoons.*

**cut** (cutting, cut) *verb* 1 to make an a opening in your skin with something sharp. *I cut my finger.* 2 to divide, break or make something shorter with a knife, scissors or another sharp instrument. *I've cut some flowers.* 3 to reduce time, size or quantity. *Shops are cutting prices.* 4 to shorten something. *The film was cut by twenty minutes.* 5 to make a recording. *We cut a disc.* **cut and dried** already decided and impossible to change. **cut back** to reduce. *Factories are cutting back on staff.* **cut in** to interrupt. **cut off** 1 to stop a person while speaking. *He cut me off when I was in the middle of asking a question.* 2 to stop a telephone connection. *We were cut off and the line went dead.* 3 to cut off a flower. 4 to stop the supply. *The electricity was cut off because we couldn't pay the bill.* **cut** *noun* 1 the act of cutting. 2 the result of cutting. *There's a cut in the cloth.* 3 an opening or small wound. 4 a reduction. *A price cut.* 5 a part that is cut out. *I noticed quite a few cuts in the film.* 6 a style or shape. *A good hair cut.* 7 a share. *She promised me a cut of her winnings.*

**cute** *adjective* 1 pretty, attractive. *She's a cute little girl.* 2 clever. *That's a cute idea.*

**cutlery** *noun* knives, forks and spoons.

**cycle** (cycling, cycled) *verb* to ride a bicycle or tricycle. *I usually cycle to school, but today I'm walking.* **cyclist** *noun.*

**cyclone** *noun* (say **seye**-klohn) a tropical storm that moves very fast round a calm central area, a hurricane.

**cygnet** *noun* (say **sig**-nit) a young swan.

**cylinder** *noun* an object or container with a long tubular body.

**cynic** *noun* (say **sin**-ik) a person who sees no good in anything and believes that people always behave in a selfish way. **cynical** *adjective.*

**Cypriot** *noun* a person who comes from Cyprus. **Cypriot** *adjective. A Cypriot dance.*

**Cyprus** *noun* an island country in the eastern Mediterranean Sea.

The island of Cyprus appears in yellow on the country's flag.

**czar** *noun* (say zar) the title of the former emperor of Russia.

**Czech** *noun* (say chek) 1 the language spoken in the Czech Republic. 2 a person who comes from the Czech Republic. **Czech** *adjective. A Czech tennis player.*

**Czech Republic** *noun* a country in eastern Europe.

D

# Dd

**dab** (dabs, dabbing, dabbed) *verb* to touch quickly and gently with something soft. *She dabbed the dirty mark with a damp cloth.*

**dachshund** *noun* a small black or brown dog with a long body and short legs.

**dad** *or* **daddy** (daddies) *noun* an informal word for father.

**daddy-long-legs** *noun* also known as a cranefly, a flying insect with very long legs.

**daffodil** *noun* a tall plant with a yellow, bell-shaped flower that grows from a bulb in spring.

**daft** *adjective* silly or foolish. *You really look daft in that hat!*

**dagger** *noun* a weapon for stabbing that looks like a short, pointed knife.

**Dáil** *noun* the lower house in the parliament of the Republic of Ireland, the equivalent of the British House of Commons.

**daily** *adjective* happening or done every day. **daily** *adverb.* **daily** (dailies) *noun* a newspaper that is published every day except on Sunday.

**dainty** (daintier, daintiest) *adjective* small, pretty and delicate. *Dainty feet.* **daintiness** *noun.* **daintily** *adverb.*

**dairy** (dairies) *noun* a place where milk is put into bottles and where milk products such as butter and cheese are made and sold. **dairy** *adjective.*

**daisy** *noun* a wild flower with a yellow centre and white petals.

**Dakar** *noun* the capital of Senegal.

**dam** *noun* 1 a strong barrier or concrete wall built across a river to hold back the water. 2 the water held back. **dam** (dams, damming, dammed) *verb.*

**damage** *verb* to harm or spoil something. **damage** *noun.* **damaging** *adjective.*

The Aswan Dam in Egypt provides the country with hydroelectric power.

**DID YOU KNOW?**

*'Dáil' is the Irish word for assembly. The Dáil Éireann (Irish Assembly) has 144 members, who are elected every five years.*

**WORD HISTORY**

*Flower names often have an interesting history. 'Daisy' comes from Old English 'day's eye', because it opens in the morning. 'Dandelion' comes from the French 'dent de lion', meaning 'lion's tooth', from the shape of its leaves.*

Graceful Balinese dancers enact a traditional story. Their elaborate costumes are decorated with gold threadwork.

**damages** *noun* money that somebody is paid for injury or harm done to them.

**Damascus** *noun* the capital of Syria.

**damp** *adjective* moist or slightly wet. **dampness** *noun.* **dampen** *verb.*

**dance** *verb* to move your feet and body to the rhythm of music. **dancer** *noun.*

**dance** *noun* 1 a style of dancing with special set steps e.g. a waltz or gavotte. 2 a party at which there is dancing.

**dandelion** *noun* a wild plant with a yellow flower.

**dandruff** *noun* small flakes of dead skin found on the scalp of some people.

**danger** *noun* 1 the chance that something may happen that will cause harm or injury. 2 a situation that is not safe. *The tunnel is in danger of collapsing.* **danger** *interjection. Danger! Falling rocks.* **dangerous** *adjective.*

**dangle** *verb* to swing to and fro or to hang down loosely. *He dangled his legs over the side of the pool.*

**Danish** *adjective* of Denmark or its people. *A Danish ship.* **Danish** *noun.* The language spoken in Denmark.

**dank** *adjective* damp and cold.

**dappled** *adjective* marked with patches or spots of dark and light colours.

**dare** *verb* 1 to be brave enough or rude enough to do or try to do something. *How dare you contradict me!* 2 to challenge somebody to do something brave. *I dare you to jump.* **dare** *noun.*

**daring** *adjective* brave and not afraid to take chances. **daring** *noun.*

**dark** *adjective* 1 with little or no light. **dark** *noun* darkness. 2 not light or fair in colour. *She has dark hair.* **in the dark** not knowing about something. **a dark horse** somebody who may have unexpected, hidden abilities.

**darken** *verb* to make or become dark.

**darn** *verb* to mend a hole in a piece of clothing by sewing threads across it.

**dart** *noun* a small arrow that players throw at a round board marked with numbers in a game called darts.

**dart** *verb* to move suddenly and quickly. *She darted across the road.*

**dash** *verb* to rush somewhere. **dash** *noun.*

**dash** *noun* a short line (–) used in writing.

**dash** *noun* a small amount. *A dash of salt.*

**data** *noun* facts and information.

All the data about the new business venture was presented in a huge sheaf of papers.

**database** *noun* a large amount of information stored on a computer.

**date** *noun* 1 the day, month and/or year of a particular event. 2 an appointment to meet somebody, particularly a boyfriend or girlfriend. **date** *verb* 1 to put a date on a letter etc. 2 to guess or give a date when something was made. *This church dates from 1400.* **out of date** 1 old-fashioned. 2 no longer valid. *An out of date ticket.* **up to date** modern.

**date** *noun* the brown, sticky fruit of the date palm.

**daughter** *noun* somebody's female child.

**daughter-in-law** *noun* the wife of somebody's son.

**daunt** *verb* to make somebody afraid that they won't be able to do something. *He was daunted by the huge task that lay ahead of him.* **daunting** *adjective.*

**dawdle** *verb* to waste time by moving or doing something very slowly.

**dawn** *noun* the beginning of the day when the Sun rises.

At dawn the sky was full of warm apricot coloured light.

**day** (days) *noun* 1 the 24 hours from one midnight to the next midnight. 2 the part of the day from sunrise to sunset when it is light. **call it a day** to stop doing something in order to return to it later.

**daybreak** *noun* dawn.

**daydream** *noun* pleasant, distracting thoughts that some people have when they are awake. **daydream** *verb.*

**GRAMMAR NOTE**

*A dash is usually used to show a pause or an interruption in a sentence. Two dashes – such as these – can act like brackets.*

**SPELLING NOTE**

*Don't confuse the spelling of 'dear', as in 'Dear Mrs Earnshaw', with 'deer', the animal.*

**dazed** *adjective* bewildered and unable to think clearly, perhaps because of a shock.

**dazzle** *verb* 1 to blind briefly or make somebody dazed with a bright light. 2 to amaze or impress somebody. *She was dazzled by his wit.* **dazzling** *adjective.*

**de-** *prefix* By adding de- to a noun or verb it changes the meaning to its opposite or negative. **defrost** to remove ice from something. *Please defrost the fridge.*

**dead** *adjective* no longer alive.

**deadline** *noun* a time or date by which some work or a job must be finished.

**deadlock** *noun* a situation in which people cannot settle a disagreement. *The talks ended in deadlock.*

**deadly** (deadlier, deadliest) *adjective* fatal or likely to kill. *Deadly poison.*

**deaf** *adjective* unable to hear well or to hear at all. **deafness** *noun.*

**deafen** *verb* to make unable to hear because the noise is so loud. **deafening** *adjective.*

**deal** (deals, dealing, dealt) *verb* 1 to do business by buying and selling. *They deal in silver.* 2 to give out cards to people in a card game. **dealer** *noun.* **deal with** 1 to take action to sort out a problem. 2 to be about or concerned with. *This book deals with religion in Africa.*

The cards were dealt into four piles.

**deal** *noun* 1 a business agreement. 2 a bargain. *I got a good deal on this car.*

**dear** *adjective* 1 loved very much. *A dear friend.* 2 the way of beginning a letter before putting the name of the person you are writing to. *Dear Mrs Smith.* 3 costing a lot of money. The opposite of dear is cheap.

**dear** *noun* 1 a person you love or who is loveable. 2 an interjection, used when surprised or angry. *Oh dear, I'm late!*

**death** *noun* the end of life. **put to death** to kill, execute. **frightened/sick to death** very scared/fed up.

**death penalty** *noun* the punishment of death for a person who has committed a crime such as murder.

**death trap** *noun* a building, vehicle or something else that is very dangerous.

**deathly** *adjective, adverb* like death. *Deathly cold hands.*

**debate** *noun* a discussion, especially at a public meeting. **debate** *verb.*

D

**debris** *noun* (say **deb**-ree) scattered pieces of things that have been destroyed, or rubbish. *The debris left after the bomb attack.*

The beach was littered with all kinds of debris.

**debt** *noun* (say det) 1 money you owe somebody. *Pay off your debts before you buy a new car.* If you are in debt, you owe money. 2 a feeling that you owe somebody for something they have done for you. *A debt of gratitude.*

**debtor** *noun* a person who owes money. The opposite of debtor is creditor.

**debug** (debugging, debugged) *verb* 1 to remove faults or problems from a computer. 2 to remove a listening device.

**decade** *noun* a period of ten years. *The first decade of the 21st century.*

**decaffeinated** *adjective* with the caffeine removed. *My grandmother has a heart problem, so she drinks decaffeinated coffee.*

**decapitate** *verb* to cut off someone's head.

**decathlon** *noun* a competition in which athletes take part in ten different events, involving running, jumping, hurdling, shot put, discus, pole vault and javelin.

**decay** *verb* 1 to go bad. *Sugar can decay your teeth.* 2 to lose health or power, to become weak. **decay** *noun. The building is falling into decay.* **decayed** *adjective.*

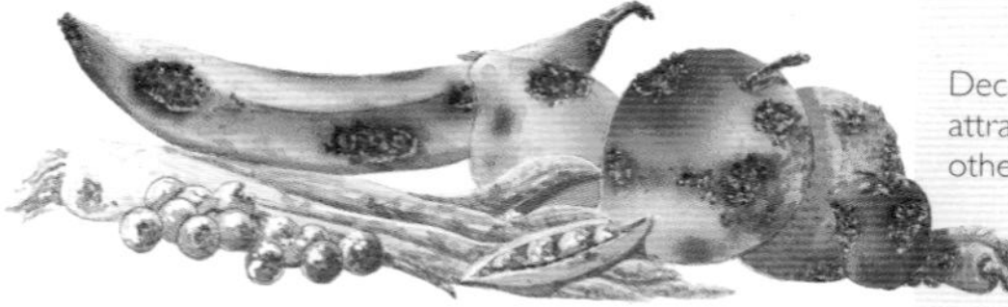

Decaying fruit attracts wasps and other insects.

**deceased** *noun* a person who has recently died. *The deceased was a very rich man.*

**deceit** *noun* being dishonest by making people believe something that is not true. **deceitful** *adjective.*

**deceive** *verb* to make somebody believe something that is not true. *He deceived everybody with his terrible lies.*

**December** *noun* the twelfth month of the year. December has 31 days.

**decent** *adjective* 1 socially acceptable, honest and respectable. 2 acceptable, good. *A decent wage.* **decency** *noun. He had the decency to apologize.*

**deception** *noun* deceiving somebody or being deceived. **deceptive** *adjective. Her charm is very deceptive.*

**WORD HISTORY**

*A decibel is actually a tenth of a bel, which is rarely used. The unit was named after Alexander Graham Bell (1847–1922), the inventor of the telephone.*

**WORD BUILDING**

*The prefix 'deci–', as in 'decibel' and 'decimal', comes from the Latin 'decimus', which means tenth.*

**decibel** *noun* (say **dess**-ib-el) a unit for measuring the loudness of sound.

**decide** *verb* 1 to do something after thinking about it; to make up your mind. *I've decided to go away.* 2 to settle something or bring it to an end. *Lack of money decided the issue.*

**decided** *adjective* clear and definite, easily seen. *You have a decided advantage.*

**deciduous** *adjective* (say dis-**id**-yoo-us) deciduous trees shed their leaves every autumn. (Trees that never shed their leaves are called evergreen.)

**decimal** *adjective* counting units in tens. *Decimal currency.* The dot in a decimal fraction (such as 1·5) is called a decimal point. **decimal** *noun.*

**decipher** *verb* (say dis-**eye**-fer) to work something out that is difficult to read or understand. *I can't decipher his writing.*

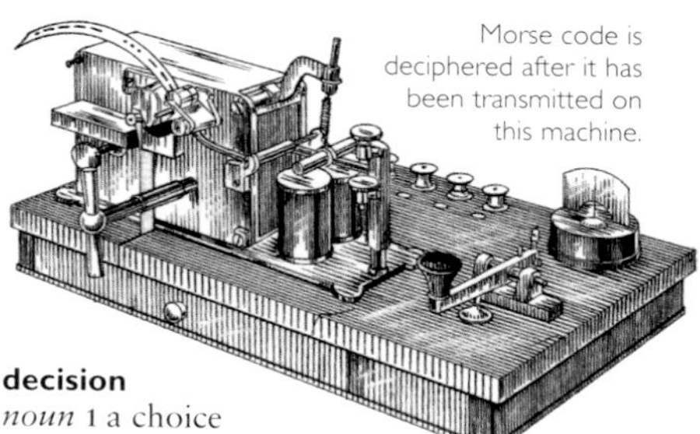

Morse code is deciphered after it has been transmitted on this machine.

**decision** *noun* 1 a choice made about what should be done. Deciding. *She made the right decision.* 2 the ability to decide and act quickly.

**decisive** *adjective* 1 full of decision and acting quickly. 2 having a definite result or making certain that there will be a particular result. *A decisive victory.* **decisively** *adverb.*

**deck** *noun* 1 a floor on a ship or bus. 2 a piece of equipment for playing records on or tapes in. *A tape deck.* 3 a pack. *A deck of playing cards.*

**declaration** *noun* something declared. *A declaration of war.*

**declare** *verb* 1 to make known or say something clearly. *I have declared my support.* 2 to tell Customs that you have bought goods abroad or tell the tax office about your income.

**decline** *verb* 1 to refuse politely. *We declined the invitation.* 2 to become smaller, weaker or worse. *Her health is declining rapidly.* **decline** *noun* a gradual loss of strength or importance.

**decode** *verb* to work out the meaning of a code. *He tried to decode the message.*

**decompose** *verb* to rot or decay after having died. **decomposition** *noun.*

D

**decorate** *verb* 1 to make something look more attractive by adding things to it. *The cake was decorated with sweets.* 2 When you decorate a room, you paint or wallpaper it. 3 to give somebody a medal. *The soldier was decorated for bravery.* **decoration** *noun.*

The decorator is wearing rubber gloves to protect her hands against the paint.

**decorator** *noun* a person who paints houses or paints and wallpapers rooms.

**decrease** *verb* to become smaller or weaker. *The number of voluntary workers is sadly decreasing.* **decrease** *noun.* **decreasing** *adjective.*

**decree** *noun* an official order or decision, especially by a ruler or a government. **decree** *verb. The king decreed an end to the war.*

**decrepit** *adjective* very old and in bad condition. *A decrepit old man.*

**dedicate** *verb* 1 to give a lot of time and effort to something. *She dedicates her life to prayer.* 2 to declare a book or performance to be in honour of somebody. *I dedicated this book to my mother.* **dedication** *noun.*

**dedicated** *adjective* devoted to something or somebody. *Dedicated to her job.*

**deduce** *verb* to work something out by looking at the facts and reaching a conclusion. *They have been silent all year, and from this I deduce that they must have moved away.* **deduction** *noun.*

**deed** *noun* 1 something done, especially a good deed. 2 The deeds of a house are the official documents given to its owner.

**deep** *adjective* 1 going a long way down from the surface. *A deep hole.* 2 measured from back to front. *The drawers are 20 centimetres deep.* 3 serious, strong or to a great extent. *Deep feelings* 4 low. *A deep voice.* **deeply** *adverb.* **deep in thought** thinking very hard about something.

**deep-freeze** *noun* a refrigerator for keeping frozen food in, a freezer.

**deer** (*plural* deer) *noun* a large fast animal. Male deer usually have antlers.

A male red deer has magnificent antlers. It uses them to attract a mate and to fight off other stags.

Two of these pots are perfect, but the middle one is cracked and broken. This may be due to a defect in manufacturing techniques.

**DID YOU KNOW?**

*Male deer (note that the plural word stays the same, like sheep) are called stags, bucks or harts. Female deer are called hinds or does. Deer range in size from the small Pudu of South America to the huge elk of northern Europe, Asia and North America.*

**deface** *verb* to spoil something, especially a wall or a notice, by scribbling all over it. *The white wall was defaced with graffiti.*

**default** *verb* to fail to do something you have agreed to do. **default** *noun.* If you win a game by default, you have won because the other player has not turned up.

**defeat** *verb* 1 to beat. *Chelsea were defeated in the final.* 2 to cause to fail. *My hopes were defeated.* 3 to be too difficult to solve. *The problem defeated me.* **defeat** *noun.*

**defect** *noun* (say **dee**-fekt) a fault or imperfection. *His radio had a defect.*

**defect** *verb* (say di-**fekt**) to leave your own country, party or army and join the other side. **defector** *noun.*

**defective** *adjective* having faults, not working properly.

**defence** *noun* 1 something used for defending or protecting. *The trees act as a defence against the wind.* 2 the act or action of defending. 3 the arguments put forward by a defendant in court. 4 the lawyers representing an accused person in a trial. 5 a group of players in a team who try to stop the opposition from scoring.

**defend** *verb* 1 to protect, guard or speak in support, especially when attacked. She is always defending her little brother. 2 to try to prove in court that an accused person is not guilty. 3 to play in a position that stops an opponent from scoring points or goals. If a champion defends her title, she wants to win to keep it. **defender** *noun.*

**defendant** *noun* a person who has been accused of a crime.

**defensive** *adjective* 1 used for defending. *Defensive weapons.* 2 behaving in an unsure or threatened way. *She is very defensive about her friends.* **on the defensive** behaving as if expecting an attack.

**defer** (defers, deferring, deferred) *verb* 1 to arrange that something will take place at a later date. *She deferred her studies for a year.* 2 to agree with a person or an opinion out of respect.

**defiance** *noun* openly refusing to obey. If you act in defiance of something, you do something although it is forbidden. **defiant** *adjective. Defiant teenagers stay out late.*

**deficient** *adjective* lacking in a particular thing, short of something. **deficiency** *noun. A deficiency in vitamin C.*

D

**define** *verb* to say exactly what something is or explain what a word means. *Let's define the problem.* **definition** *noun.*

**definite** *adjective* firm and unlikely to change. *I need a definite answer.* **definite article** the word 'the' is the definite article. ('A' and 'an' are indefinite articles.) **definitely** *adverb.*

**deforestation** *noun* the cutting down of forests.

Deforestation is a huge problem in the Amazon, where more trees are felled every day to make way for building and farming land.

**deformed** *adjective* abnormally shaped. **deformity** *noun.*

**defrost** *verb* 1 to get rid of ice or frost, especially in a refrigerator or on a windscreen. 2 When you defrost food, it becomes unfrozen.

**defuse** *verb* 1 to remove the fuse from an unexploded bomb so it cannot explode. 2 to make a situation less dangerous. *He defused the situation by apologizing.*

**defy** (defies, defying, defied) *verb* 1 to refuse to obey. *Criminals defy the law.* 2 to challenge somebody to do something that seems impossible. *I defy you to swim across the river.* 3 to be impossible to understand or solve. *The problem defies solution.*

**degree** *noun* 1 a unit for measuring temperature, usually written with a degree sign (°). 2 a unit of measurement of angles. *A right angle is a 90° angle.* 3 the extent or amount of feeling. *I admire him to a degree.* 4 an academic grade given by a university or a college to a person who has finished a course or passed an examination. *A degree in German.* **by degrees** gradually.

**deity** (deities) *noun* (say **day**-it-ee) a god or goddess. *They worshipped several deities.*

**delay** *verb* 1 to put something off until later. *We have decided to delay the meeting until the middle of this afternoon.* 2 to make somebody or something late.

**delete** *verb* to cross out something written or printed.

**deliberate** *adjective* (say dil-**ib**-er-ut) 1 planned, done on purpose and not by accident. *A deliberate lie.* 2 slow and careful, especially when moving or speaking. **deliberately** *adverb.*

**WORD HISTORY**

*The delta of a river got its name from its triangular shape. It was named after the shape of the Greek letter D.*

**deliberate** *verb* (say dil-ib-er-**ayt**) to think carefully. **deliberation** *noun* careful consideration of a subject.

**delicacy** (delicacies) *noun* 1 something soft, fine and graceful. 2 something that needs careful and tactful handling. *He didn't appreciate the delicacy of the situation.* 3 delicious and often expensive food.

**delicate** *adjective* 1 soft, fine and graceful. *Delicate silk.* 2 fragile, easily broken or becoming ill easily. *A delicate child.* 3 not strong, especially when talking about colour, taste or smell. *A delicate flavour.* 4 needing careful treatment or tactful handling. *Don't mention her old boyfriend, it's a delicate subject.* **delicately** *adverb.*

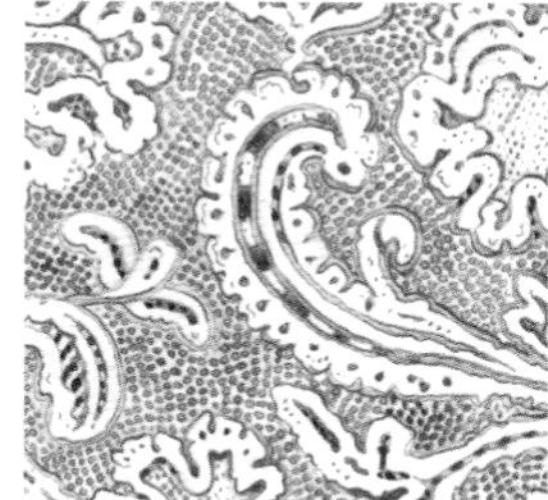

Lace is a strong yet very delicate fabric.

**delicatessen** *noun* a shop or section of a supermarket selling cooked meats, cheeses and other prepared foods.

**delicious** *adjective* giving great pleasure, having a pleasant taste or smell. *The food was delicious.*

**delight** *noun* great pleasure. *To our delight the exam was cancelled.* **delight** *verb* to give or feel a lot of pleasure. **be delighted** *I'd be delighted to come to Marianne's party.* **delightful** *adjective.*

**deliver** *verb* 1 to take something, especially goods or messages, to somebody's house or office. *The postman delivered the letters.* 2 to give a speech. 3 to help with the birth of a baby. *The baby was delivered this morning.* **delivery** *noun.*

**delta** *noun* 1 the Greek letter D (written Δ). 2 the fan-shaped area at the mouth of a river, where it splits up into many channels. *The Nile delta.*

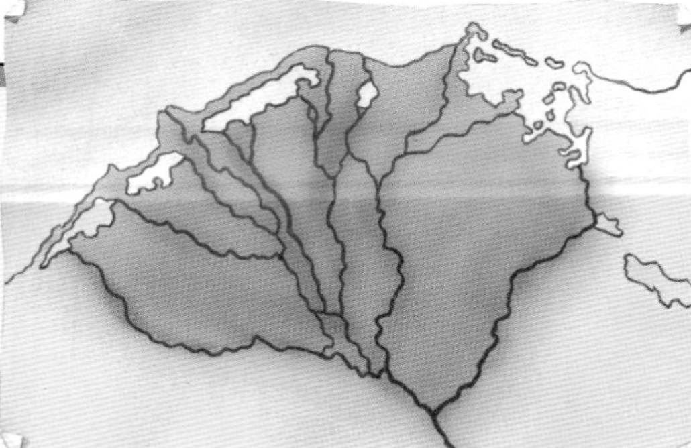

At the delta of a river a lot of silt flows into the sea.

**deluge** *noun* 1 a heavy fall of rain, a great flood. 2 things arriving in large numbers. *We had a deluge of applications for the job we advertised.* **deluge** *verb.*

**demand** *verb* 1 to ask for something firmly, as if ordering it. *I demand an explanation.* 2 to need. *Teaching demands a lot of patience.* **demand** *noun* 1 a firm request. 2 a desire to buy or get something. **in demand** wanted. *Mobile phones are in great demand even though expensive to run.*

**demanding** *adjective* needing attention, time or energy. *Looking after small children is a very demanding job.*

**demo** (demos) *noun* a demonstration.

**democracy** *noun* 1 a system of government in which people elect the leaders of their country. 2 a country governed by democracy. **democrat** *noun.* **democratic** *adjective. A democratic decision.*

**demolish** *verb* to pull down old buildings or destroy something. **demolition** *noun. Demolition work began early.*

The crane operator began the demolition work and soon the old house began to crumble.

**demon** *noun* a devil or evil spirit.

**demonstrate** *verb* 1 to show how something works or prove a point by giving examples. 2 to take part in a march or meeting, to show support for a cause. *The students are demonstrating against grant cuts.* **demonstration** *noun.*

**demonstrative** *adjective* showing your feelings. *He rarely kisses his children, he is not a very demonstrative father.* 'This', 'that', 'these', 'those' are **demonstrative adjectives**. They are used to point out a person or thing.

**den** *noun* 1 the home of a fox or wolf. 2 a person's private room. *He invited me to a game of billiards in his den.*

**denial** *noun* 1 denying or refusing something. *A denial of justice.* 2 saying that something somebody is accused of is not true. *He printed a denial in the newspaper.*

**Denmark** *noun* a Scandinavian country in Europe.

The flag of Denmark has a white cross against a red background.

**AMAZING FACT**

George Washington, the first President of the United States, wore dentures, or false teeth. Several sets are on show at the Smithsonian Institution in Washington, DC. Early dentures were made of various materials including ivory and wood.

**DID YOU KNOW?**

*Denmark is a small country, made up of a peninsula and about 100 inhabited islands. The island of Greenland, thousands of kilometres away, belongs to Denmark and is over 50 times bigger than the mother country.*

**denounce** *verb* to speak or write against somebody. *He was denounced as a traitor.* **denunciation** *noun.*

**dense** *adjective* 1 thick, crowded together or difficult to see through. *A dense forest.* 2 stupid. **density** *noun.*

**dent** *noun* a hollow in a hard surface made by a collision or by pressure. *There was a big dent in the side of the car.* **dent** *verb* to make a dent.

**dental** *adjective* of or for the teeth. *Free dental treatment for children.* A dental surgeon is a dentist.

**dentist** *noun* a person trained to treat people's teeth.

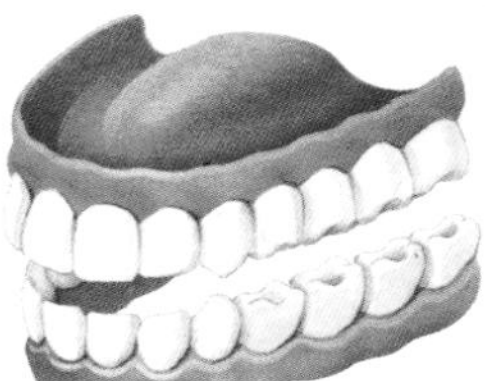

**dentures** *plural noun* false teeth.

Some people take out their dentures and put them in a glass beside the bed overnight.

**depart** *verb* to go away, leave. *The train to Oxford is about to depart from platform three.* **departure** *noun.*

**department** *noun* a part of a large business, government, college or shop.

**department store** *noun* a large shop in which all sorts of goods are sold in different departments.

**depend** *verb* 1 If you depend on somebody or something, you need them. *Our group depends on your help.* 2 to trust somebody or rely on something. *You can always depend on me.* 3 to vary according to circumstances. *The success of the trip will depend on the weather.* **it depends** said when you are not sure about what will happen. *'Are you going to the cinema?' 'I don't know. It depends.'*

**deport** *verb* to send an unwanted person out of a country. **deportation** *noun.*

**deposit** *noun* 1 a sum of money paid into a bank account. *I'd like to make a deposit, please.* 2 money paid as part payment for something. *If you want to order the goods, you will have to pay a deposit.* 3 a layer of a substance left somewhere. *There were deposits of sugar at the bottom of the bottle.* 4 a natural layer of sand, coal or rock. **deposit** *verb* 1 to put something down. *Sand was deposited by the wind.* 2 to pay money as a deposit.

**depot** *noun* (say **dep**-oh) 1 a place for storing goods. 2 a place where buses or trains are parked and repaired.

**depressed** *adjective* very sad. **depression** *noun. She felt depressed and anxious.*

**deprive** *verb* to take or keep something away from somebody. *The children have been deprived of love.*

**depth** *noun* the distance between the top and bottom surfaces or the distance from the front to the back of something. How deep something is. **in depth** thoroughly, looking at all aspects. **out of your depth** 1 to be in water that is too deep to stand in. 2 to try and do something that is too difficult.

Divers wear special breathing apparatus so they can explore the ocean depths.

**derive** *verb* 1 to get from. *She derives great satisfaction from her work.* 2 to come from. *The word democracy derives from the Greek for 'people'.*

**descend** *verb* to go down. **be descended from** to be related to and come from a certain family. **descent** *noun.*

**descendant** *noun* a person or an animal related to another who lived a long time ago. *She is a descendant of Mary Stuart.*

**describe** *verb* 1 to say what something or somebody is like. 2 to mark out. *To describe a circle.* **description** *noun.* **descriptive** *adjective.*

**desert** (say **dez**-ut) *noun* a large sand-covered area of land where very little rain ever falls.

The cactus can survive in the harsh conditions of the desert. It stores water in its thick stems and its spines protect it against getting eaten by animals.

**SPELLING NOTE**

*They sound the same but they are spelt differently: 'desert' is an empty area, 'dessert' (with two 's's) is a pudding.*

**desert** (say diz-**ert**) *verb* 1 to go away with no intention of returning, to abandon. *He deserted his wife and children.* 2 to run away from military service. **desertion** *noun. The soldier was accused of desertion.* **deserter** *noun.* **deserted** *adjective* empty, abandoned.

**deserts** *plural noun* what somebody deserves. *He got his just deserts.*

**deserve** *verb* to be worthy of something. *He deserves to win after all the hard training he has done.*

**desiccate** *verb* to dry. *Desiccated coconut.*

**design** *noun* 1 a drawing that shows how something is to be made or built. *He showed the designs for his new fashion collection.* 2 the way something is made or built. *I don't like the design of the car.* 3 a pattern of shapes to decorate something. *Curtains with a floral design.* 4 a thought-out plan. **design** *verb* 1 to invent the look of something. *He designs for a jeweller.* 2 to plan. *This dictionary is designed for children.* **designer** *noun.*

**desire** *noun* a strong wish for something. *I have no desire to meet him.* **desire** *verb.*

**desk** *noun* a table at which you sit to read, write and work.

**despair** *noun* a complete loss of hope. **despair** *verb. He quite despaired of ever seeing her again.*

**despatch** see dispatch.

**despise** *verb* If you despise somebody, you think that they are worthless.

**dessert** *noun* (say diz-**ert**) sweet food eaten at the end of a meal.

**destination** *noun* the place to which a person or thing is going.

**destiny** *noun* 1 Your destiny is what will happen to you in your life. *It was her destiny to marry the king.* 2 the force that controls your life. Fate. **destine** *verb. They were destined to meet again.*

**destroy** *verb* to ruin something, or break it to pieces. *The criminals destroyed all the vital evidence before their capture.* **destruction** *noun.* **destructive** *adjective.*

**detail** *noun* a small point or fact. *The police officer noted down the essential details.* **detailed** *adjective.*

**detective** *noun* a person, especially a police officer, whose job it is to find out what has happened in a crime.

**deteriorate** *verb* to become worse. *Her health has deteriorated within the last year.* **deterioration** *noun.*

**determined** *adjective* having firmly decided to do something in order to be successful. *She is determined to win the tennis tournament.* **determination** *noun.*

**devastate** *verb* 1 to destroy or damage. *The floods have devastated the whole area.* 2 to shock. *I was devastated when he gave me the terrible news.* **devastation** *noun.*

**develop** *verb* 1 to grow or become bigger. *Her small company soon developed into a major business.* 2 to come into existence, to become more serious. *She has developed a huge appetite.* 3 to make prints from a photographic film. 4 to use an area of land for building houses, shops and factories. **development** *noun.*

**device** *noun* something made or built for a particular purpose. *She has invented an unusual listening device.*

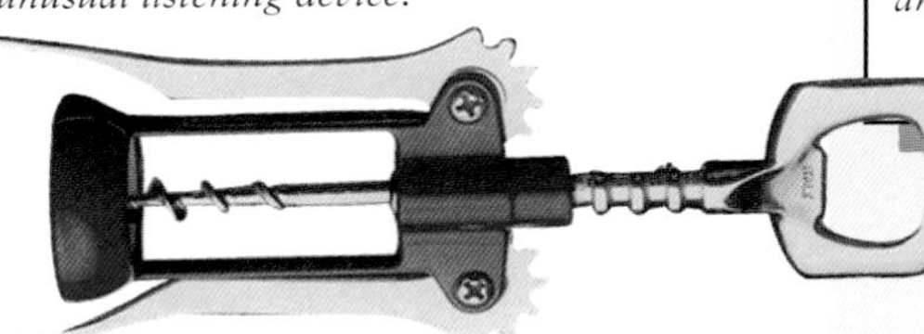

A corkscrew is a device for opening bottles.

**devise** *verb* to invent or think up. *He devised a cunning plan.*

**devote** *verb* to spend time or energy on something or somebody. *He devotes all his spare time to football.* **devotion** *noun.*

**devour** *verb* to eat greedily.

**dew** *noun* tiny drops of water that form during the night on the ground or cool surfaces. *Dew lay on the grass.*

**Dhaka** *noun* the capital of Bangladesh.

**diabetes** *noun* (say die-uh-**bee**-teez) an illness in which there is too much sugar in a person's blood. **diabetic** *adjective* (say die-uh-**bet**-ik). *Diabetic marmalade.*

**diagnose** *verb* to find out what is wrong with a person and what illness they might have. *The doctor diagnosed a case of measles.* **diagnosis** *noun.*

**diagonal** *adjective* (say die-**ag**-un-ul) A diagonal line goes in a slanting direction, joining opposite corners. **diagonal** *noun* a straight line going diagonally across.

**diagram** *noun* a simple drawing that shows the parts of something, often used to explain how things work.

**dial** *noun* an indicator, like a clock face or a meter, with numbers or letters around it. **dial** (dials, dialling, dialled) *verb* to ring a telephone number by turning a dial or pressing buttons.

**DID YOU KNOW**

*Diamond is made of carbon and is the hardest mineral in the world. Because of this, diamonds are used in cutting and grinding tools.*

**AMAZING FACT**

Dr Samuel Johnson (1700–84) wrote one of the first major dictionaries of the English language.

**dialect** *noun* a form of language spoken in a particular region, which has different words and pronunciation from other forms of the same language.

**dialysis** *noun* (say die-**al**-iss-iss) a process of removing harmful products from the blood, especially when the kidneys are not functioning properly.

**diameter** *noun* (say die-**am**-it-er) the length of a straight line going from side to side through the centre of a circle or sphere.

**diamond** *noun* 1 a very hard precious stone that looks like cut glass. 2 a shape with four straight sides of equal length that stands on one of its points. 3 a playing card with red diamond shapes on it. *The ace of diamonds.* **diamond** *adjective.*

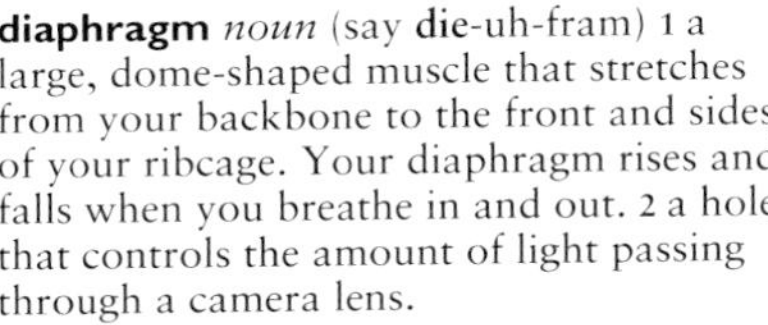

A diamond is a beautiful clear and sparkling stone.

**diaphragm** *noun* (say **die**-uh-fram) 1 a large, dome-shaped muscle that stretches from your backbone to the front and sides of your ribcage. Your diaphragm rises and falls when you breathe in and out. 2 a hole that controls the amount of light passing through a camera lens.

**diary** (diaries) *noun* 1 a book with spaces for each day of the year used for writing down appointments. 2 a book for keeping a record of daily events.

**dice** *noun* ('Dice' is the plural of 'die', but is used as both singular and plural.) a small six-sided cube marked with dots from one to six on each of its sides, used in board games and gambling.

Dice are used in many games of chance.

**dice** *verb* to cut something, especially food, into cubes.

**dictate** *verb* 1 to say aloud what somebody should write down. *She dictated a letter to her secretary.* **dictation** *noun.* 2 to give orders. *I won't be dictated to by my parents.*

**dictator** *noun* a ruler who has total power over a country. Most dictators take power by force. *A ruthless dictator ran the country.*

**dictionary** *noun* a book in which words are listed in alphabetical order, from A to Z. You look up a word in the dictionary to find out what it means and how to spell it.

D

**did** past tense of do.

**die** singular of dice.

**die** *noun* a block of hard metal for pressing coins and other metal or plastic objects into shape. *This component was cast in a die.*

**die** (dies, dying, died) *verb* 1 to stop living. *She died of cancer.* 2 to come to an end or disappear. *My love will never die.* **die down** to become less strong. *The noise eventually died down.* **die for** to want something very much. *I'm dying for a drink.*

**diesel** *noun* 1 a vehicle that has a diesel engine. 2 fuel for a diesel engine.

A diesel engine is more economical and less polluting than a petrol engine.

**diet** *noun* 1 the sort of food usually eaten by a person or an animal. *A healthy diet.* 2 special kinds of food eaten in order to be healthy or to lose weight. *I'm on a very strict diet.* **diet** *verb.*

**difference** *noun* 1 being different. A way of being unlike each other. *The difference between boys and girls.* 2 the amount left between two numbers when one is subtracted from the other. *The difference between 10 and 4 is 6.* 3 When people have their differences, they have a disagreement. 4 When something makes a difference, it is important. *It makes no difference to me.*

**different** *adjective* 1 not the same. *Every time I see her, she has a different boyfriend.* 2 various. *The dress comes in different colours.*

These two houses are the same, but they have different coloured doors and different windows.

**difficult** *adjective* 1 not easy, hard to do or understand. 2 a difficult person is somebody who is not easily pleased and hard to get on with. **difficulty** (difficulties) *noun.*

**dig** (digs, digging, dug) *verb* 1 to make a hole in the ground, usually by moving soil. *To dig the garden.* 2 to poke or push in. *Don't dig your knife into the cake.* **dig up** 1 to remove something from the soil. *I dug up the bush.* 2 to discover something. *The newspapers have dug up another scandal.*

**AMAZING FACT**

The human digestive tract is approximately eight to ten metres long.

**WORD HISTORY**

*A diesel (car or locomotive) has a diesel engine that burns diesel oil. They were all named after Rudolf Diesel (1858–1913), a German engineer.*

**AMAZING FACT**

Dinosaurs died out about 65 million years ago but, although there are several theories, no one knows why.

**dig** *noun* 1 a small push or poke. *She gave him a dig in the ribs.* 2 an archaeological site. 3 a remark against a person, intended to upset. *That teacher loves having a dig at me.*

**digest** (say die-**jest**) *verb* 1 to make food change so the body can use it. *Fruit is easy to digest.* 2 to take in information and think it over. **digestion** *noun.*

**digest** (say **die**-jest) *noun* a summary of information or news.

**digit** *noun* 1 any of the numbers from 0 to 9. 2 a finger or toe.

**digital** *adjective* 1 giving a reading by displaying numbers rather than by moving hands. *A digital clock.* 2 working with signals or information represented by numbers. *A digital recording.*

The watch is digital. It has no hands.

**dilemma** *noun* a difficult situation in which you have to choose between two or more possible actions.

**dilute** *verb* to make a liquid weaker or thinner by mixing it with water or other liquid. *I like to dilute my orange juice.*

**dim** (dimmer, dimmest) *adjective* 1 not bright or clear, difficult to see. *The light was very dim.* 2 stupid.

**dim** (dims, dimming, dimmed) *verb* to make something dim. *Dim the lights.*

**dime** *noun* an American 10 cent coin.

**dimension** *noun* 1 a measurement, especially of length, height or width. *The exact dimensions of the room.* 2 The dimensions of a problem are the extent and importance of it.

**diminish** *verb* to become smaller.

**din** *noun* a loud, annoying noise.

**dine** *verb* to have dinner. **dine out** to eat in a restaurant or at friends.

**dinghy** (dinghies) *noun* (say **ding**-ee) a small boat, especially an inflatable rubber boat.

**dingy** (dingier, dingiest) *adjective* (say **din**-jee) dark, depressing and dirty-looking. *He's got a dingy little room.*

**dining room** *noun* a room where people have their meals.

**dinner** *noun* the main meal of the day.

**dinner party** *noun* a party at which guests eat dinner together.

**dinosaur** *noun* a large extinct reptile that lived in prehistoric times.

D

**dip** (dips, dipping, dipped) *verb* 1 to put into a liquid. *He dipped his biscuit in the tea.* 2 to move downward or drop slightly. *The Sun dipped below the horizon.*

**dip** *noun* 1 a downward slope or slight drop. 2 a quick swim or bathe. *A dip in the sea.* 3 a creamy mixture that is eaten with raw vegetables or biscuits.

**diplomacy** *noun* 1 the building of relations between countries and different people. 2 the skill of doing and saying the right thing at the right time. *She handled the delicate situation with tact and diplomacy.*

**diplomat** *noun* 1 a government official who represents their country in another country. Diplomats usually work in an embassy. 2 a tactful person. **diplomatic** *adjective*. **diplomatically** *adverb*.

**direct** *adjective* 1 straight towards a place. *A direct flight.* 2 honest and frank. *Please give me a direct answer.* 3 exact. *The direct opposite.* **directly** *adverb*.

**direct** *verb* 1 to tell somebody the way. *Can you direct me to the station?* 2 to order somebody to do something. 3 to organize and manage something. *Who is directing the new Batman film?* **director** *noun*.

**direction** *noun* 1 the course in which a person or thing is moving or the line they are pointing in. *What direction is the reform taking?* 2 control or management. *The film was made under his direction.*

**directions** *plural noun* instructions on how to do, use or find something. *Can you give me directions?*

The arms of the signpost point in the directions of some of the world's most famous cities.

**dirt** *noun* earth, soil, or anything that is not clean.

**dirty** (dirtier, dirtiest) *adjective* 1 not clean. *My hands are dirty.* 2 vulgar. *Dirty jokes.* 3 mean, unfair. *That was a dirty trick.*

**dis-** *prefix* forming the opposite of a word. Dishonest is the opposite of honest.

**SPELLING NOTE**

*A disc is thin, flat and circular. It is sometimes spelt 'disk', and this is the usual spelling for computer storage devices, such as hard and floppy disks.*

**disabled** *adjective* physically or mentally unable to do something. *There are special parking spaces reserved for disabled people.* **disability** *noun*.

**disadvantage** *noun* a condition that causes problems and makes success difficult. The opposite of advantage. *You are at a disadvantage if you can't use a computer.*

**disagree** *verb* to have different opinions and so not agree. If food disagrees with you, it makes you feel ill. **disagreement** *noun*.

**disappear** *verb* to stop being seen, to go out of sight. **disappearance** *noun*.

**disappoint** *verb* to fail to come up to somebody's hopes or expectations. *My parents were disappointed in me.* **disappointment** *noun*.

**disaster** *noun* 1 an unexpected event that causes great damage and suffering. *Floods and earthquakes are natural disasters.* 2 a failure, something unsuccessful. *Our holiday was a disaster.* **disastrous** *adjective*.

**disc** *noun* 1 a gramophone record. 2 a round flat object. 3 a layer of cartilage between the bones in your back. *She's suffering from a slipped disc.*

**disc jockey** or usually **DJ** *noun* a person who plays records and tapes on radio, TV, or in discos and clubs.

**disciple** *noun* a person who believes in and follows the teachings of a leader. *Jesus and all his disciples sat in a circle.*

**discontinue** (discontinues, discontinuing, discontinued) *verb* to stop something.

**discover** *verb* 1 to find or find out. 2 to be the first person to find something. *Christopher Columbus was the first European to discover America.* **discovery** *noun*.

Marco Polo is believed to have discovered spaghetti. He ate it in the form of noodles while exploring China.

**discreet** *adjective* 1 tactful in what you say or do. 2 not attracting a lot of attention. *Discreet pastel colours.* **discretion** *noun*.

**discriminate** *verb* 1 to notice a difference between two or more things. *We must discriminate between right and wrong.* 2 to treat things or people differently. If you discriminate against somebody, you treat them unfairly. **discrimination** *noun*. *Racial discrimination is a crime.*

**discuss** *verb* to talk about something. *I often discuss politics while drinking coffee with my friends.* **discussion** *noun*.

**disguise** *verb* to make somebody or something look or sound different so they are not recognized by other people. *The prince disguised himself as a servant.* **disguise** *noun. She wore a red wig as a disguise.* **in disguise** disguised.

If you wear this cunning disguise to school, none of your friends will know who you are.

**disgust** *noun* a feeling of strong dislike caused by an unpleasant smell, sight or sound. *He left the meeting room in utter disgust.* **disgust** *verb.*

**disgusting** *adjective* very unpleasant. *Wendy noticed a truly disgusting smell.*

**dish** (dishes) *noun* 1 a shallow bowl for food. 2 part of a meal. **do the dishes** to wash up. **dish up** to serve food.

**dishevelled** *adjective* (say di-**shev**-uld) untidy, especially somebody's hair or clothes. *The bed was dishevelled.*

**dishonest** *adjective* not honest. *It is dishonest to cheat.* **dishonestly** *adverb.*

**dishwasher** *noun* a machine that automatically washes dishes.

**disinfectant** *noun* a substance used to destroy germs.

**disk** *noun* a flat round object for storing information, used in computing.

**dislike** *verb* to not like. *I dislike long car journeys intensely.* **dislike** *noun.*

**disloyal** *adjective* not loyal. *He was disloyal to his regiment.* **disloyally** *adverb.*

**dismay** *noun* a feeling of worry and disappointment. **dismay** *verb.* **dismayed** *adjective. I was dismayed at her truly pathetic attitude.*

**dismiss** *verb* 1 to send somebody away or tell a person that they will no longer have a job. *He was dismissed for constantly being late for work.* 2 to stop thinking about something or somebody or considering an idea. *We dismissed the idea.* **dismissal** *noun.*

**disobedience** *noun* not doing what you are told to. Not obeying. **disobedient** *adjective.*

**dispatch** *verb* to send somebody or something off to a destination. *The message was dispatched early this morning.*

**dispatch** *noun* an official report.

**dispense** *verb* to give out. *The chemist dispenses medicines.* **dispenser** *noun. A cash dispenser outside the bank.*

**WORD HISTORY**

*'Disgust' and 'disgusting' come from the Latin 'gustus', meaning taste. The prefix 'dis–' shows the opposite, so disgusting food is food that doesn't taste very good.*

**display** *verb* 1 to put something in a place so it can easily be seen. *The shop displayed the new range in the window.* 2 to show. *He displayed his ignorance.* **display** *noun.*

**dispute** *noun* a quarrel between people. *The dispute over university grants.* **in dispute** being argued about.

**dispute** *verb* 1 to argue or quarrel. 2 to say that something is not true, to raise objections. *I don't dispute that the homeless need our support.*

**disqualify** (disqualifies, disqualifying, disqualified) *verb* to stop somebody from doing something because they have broken the rules. **disqualification** *noun. He took his disqualification badly.*

**disrupt** *verb* to bring into disorder and prevent something from continuing normally. **disruption** *noun.*

**dissatisfied** *adjective* not satisfied.

**dissect** (say dis-**sekt**) *verb* to cut something up in order to examine it, especially a dead animal or plant. **dissection** *noun.*

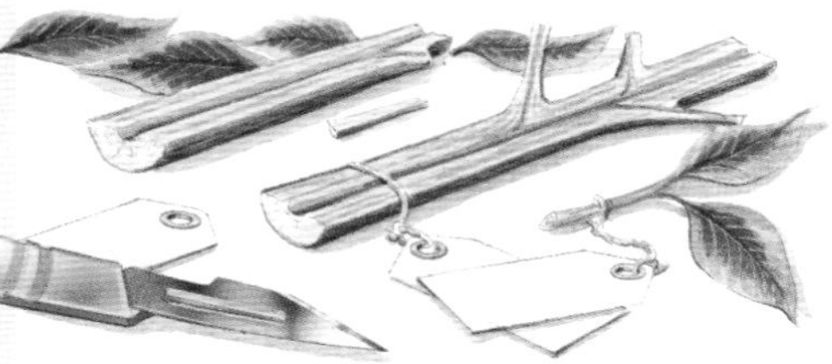

Part of the botanist's job was to dissect the plants for research purposes.

**distance** *noun* the amount of space between two places. *My new flat is within easy walking distance of the office.* **in the distance** far away. **from a distance** a long way away from something in space or time. **distant** *adjective.*

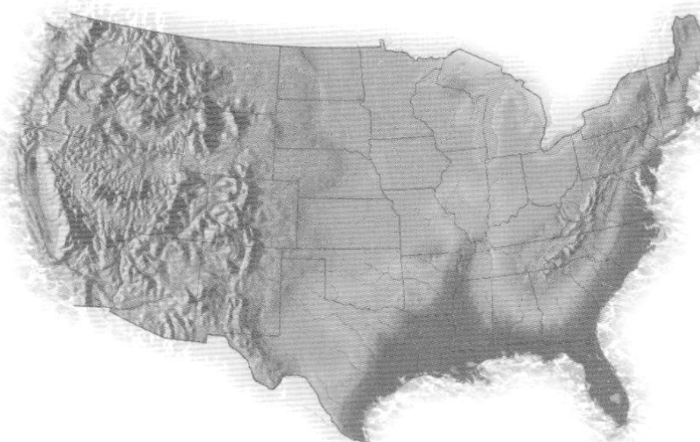

From one side of North America to the other is a huge distance to travel.

**distinct** *adjective* 1 easily heard or seen. *I noticed a distinct bruise on his leg.* 2 clearly different. **distinctly** *adverb.*

**distinction** *noun* 1 a clear difference. 2 excellence, or an award for excellence. *She got a distinction in her exam.*

**distinguish** *verb* 1 to make or notice differences between things. *I can't distinguish one from the other.* 2 to show excellence. *He distinguished himself by his bravery in the face of the enemy.*

**district** *noun* a part of a town or country.

**disturb** *verb* 1 to spoil somebody's rest or interrupt what they are doing. *That noise disturbs my concentration.* 2 to cause somebody to be upset or worried. 3 to move things from their position. *Nothing in the room had been disturbed.* **disturbance** *noun.*

**ditch** (ditches) *noun* a channel dug in the ground for water to flow along.

**ditch** *verb* to get rid of or leave behind. *The robbers ditched their get-away car.*

**dive** *verb* 1 to plunge head first into the water. *She dived off the top board.* 2 to swim under water. *They went diving for pearls.* 3 to go down steeply. *The eagle dived from a great height.* 4 to move quickly and suddenly. *He dived for cover.* **diver** *noun.*

Diving is a skill that requires courage and stamina. It can sometimes be dangerous.

**divert** *verb* 1 to turn something in another direction. *The traffic has been diverted because of road works.* 2 to turn somebody's attention away from something else. 3 to amuse or entertain. **diversion** *noun.*

**divide** *verb* 1 to split up or be separated into smaller parts. *We divided the sweets between us.* 2 in maths, to find out how many times one number is contained in another. *Divide 12 by 3.*

**division** *noun* 1 the process or result of dividing or being divided. *We have a fair division of work in our family.* 2 in maths, the process of dividing one number by another. 3 a vote in parliament which separates members into two sections. 4 a group having a special purpose within an organization. *The soccer team were relegated to the second division.*

**divorce** *noun* the legal ending of a marriage. **divorce** *verb* 1 to end a marriage. 2 to separate things. *He has become divorced from reality.*

**WORD HISTORY**

*'Diwali' comes from the ancient Sanskrit for 'row of lights'. During the festival, which is celebrated in October or November, lamps are lit in honour of the Hindu god Rama.*

**Diwali** (say di-**wah**-lee) *noun* a Hindu religious festival.

This girl is celebrating Diwali by burning candles.

**DIY** *abbreviation* do-it-yourself.

**dizzy** (dizzier, dizziest) *adjective* feeling that everything is going round and round. *I felt dizzy after the roller-coaster ride.*

**Djibouti** *noun* a country in Africa, and its capital city.

The flag of Djibouti is blue, green and white with a red star.

**do** (does, doing, did, done) *verb* 1 to carry out or deal with something, perform an action or activity. *I'm doing the cooking.* 2 to be enough. *That will do.* 3 in questions with another verb. *Do you know him?* 4 in statements with 'not' forming the negative. *I do not know him.* 5 to stress something. *He hasn't received the invitation, but I did send him one.* 6 instead of repeating a verb that has already been used. *We earn as much money as they do.* 7 at the end of a statement to form a question. *He won the match, didn't he?* **do away with** to get rid of. **do up** 1 to fasten. *Do up your laces.* 2 to repair or improve. *They are doing up the house.*

**dock** *noun* a place where ships are loaded and unloaded or repaired. **docker** *noun* a worker at the docks.

**dock** *verb* 1 to come or go into dock. *The ship docked at Dover.* 2 to join with another spacecraft in space. 3 to take money away, especially wages. *Our pay was docked.*

**dock** *noun* the place in a court where the accused person stands.

**dock** *noun* a plant with broad leaves that grows as a weed.

D

**doctor** *noun* 1 a person who treats people who are ill. 2 an academic title, a high university degree. *A Doctor of Law.*

**document** (say **dock**-you-munt) *noun* an official piece of paper giving proof or information about something. **document** (say **dock**-you-ment) *verb. To document the past we have used records from the library.*

**dodge** *verb* to move away quickly in order to avoid being hit or seen.

**Dodoma** *noun* the capital of Tanzania.

**doe** *noun* a female deer, rabbit or hare.

**dog** *noun* an animal that is kept as a pet. Dogs bark.

**Doha** *noun* the capital of Qatar.

**dole** *noun* a weekly payment made to unemployed people. *He's on the dole.*

**doll** *noun* a child's toy that looks like a baby girl or boy. *A Barbie doll.*

**dollar** *noun* money used in the USA, Canada and some other countries.

**dolphin** *noun* a sea animal like a small whale with a long nose. Dolphins are mammals and breathe through a blowhole.

**dome** *noun* a round roof on a building. A dome is shaped like half a ball.

**Dominica** *noun* a country in the West Indies.

**Dominican Republic** *noun* a country in the West Indies. The eastern part of the island of Hispaniola.

The flag of the Dominican Republic has a white cross on a red and blue quartered ground. A colourful crest lies at its centre.

**domino** *noun* a small rectangular piece of wood or plastic marked with two sets of spots used for playing an old game called dominoes. *She beat me at dominoes.*

**donate** *verb* to give something, especially money, to a good cause. *I donated some money to charity.* **donation** *noun.*

**WORD HISTORY**

*'Dormant', 'dormitory' and 'dormouse' all come from the Latin word 'dormire', to sleep. The dormouse is probably called a 'sleeping mouse' because it has a long winter sleep, or hibernation.*

Dolphins are among the most friendly and intelligent of animals.

**done** past tense of do.

**done** *adjective* **not done** socially not acceptable.

**donkey** (donkeys) *noun* an animal like a small horse with long ears.

**door** *noun* a movable flat surface that opens or closes the entrance to a building, room or cupboard. **answer the door** to open the door to a visitor.

**door-to-door** *adjective* visiting homes to sell something. *A door-to-door salesman.*

**dormant** *adjective* not active. *A dormant volcano is no longer dangerous.*

**dormitory** (dormitories) *noun* a room with a number of beds for people to sleep in, especially in a school or hostel.

**dormouse** (dormice) *noun* a woodland animal like a large mouse with a long furry tail. *As sleepy as a dormouse.*

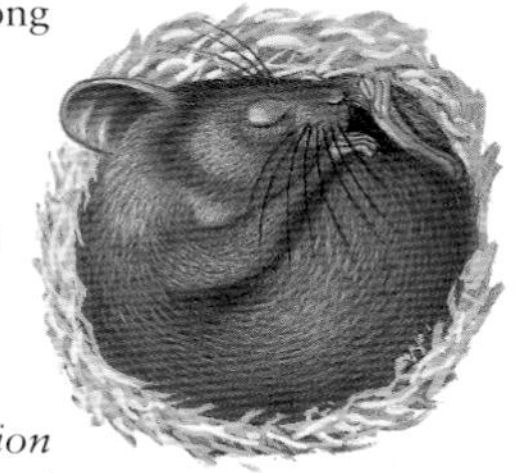

The dormouse was a delicacy roasted with honey in Roman times.

**DOS** *abbreviation* disk operating system (in a computer).

**dose** *noun* the amount of medicine to be taken at one time. **dose** *verb. I dosed myself with aspirin against the flu.*

**dot** *noun* a small spot. **dot** *verb* to mark or cover with dots. **dotted** *adjective.*

**double** *adjective* 1 twice as much or twice as many. *A double portion of spaghetti.* 2 for two people or things. *A double bed.* 3 having two parts. *Double glazing.* 4 having two different uses. *A word with a double meaning.* **doubly** *adverb.*

**double** *noun* 1 a double thing, an amount or size that is twice as large. *I paid £5 for it and sold it for double.* 2 a person or thing that looks exactly like another. *He's his father's double.* **double** *verb* 1 to become twice as large, strong or fast. *Sales have doubled in the last year.* 2 to have a second use. *My bedroom doubles as a study.*

D

**doubt** *noun* a feeling of not being sure about something. *There's no doubt that he'll pass the exam.* **doubt** *verb* to feel doubt. **doubtful** *adjective.*

**doughnut** *noun* a round cake or ring fried in hot fat and covered with sugar.

**dove** *noun* a bird like a pigeon.

**dowdy** (dowdier, dowdiest) *adjective* not fashionable, dull. *Dowdy clothes.*

**down** *adverb, preposition* 1 towards, at or into a lower position. *Could you get the book down from the shelf?* 2 in a lower place or from one place to another. *We walked down to the shops.* 3 to a smaller size, grade or standard. *Prices are down.* 4 to put something in writing. *To take down notes.* 5 on to a surface. *Sit down.*

**down** *noun* 1 a bird's soft feathers. 2 fine soft hair. *The down on the baby's head.*

**downcast** *adjective* 1 sad, depressed. 2 looking downwards, especially when feeling sad. *With downcast eyes.*

**downfall** *noun* 1 a fall from power, ruin. *Drink was his downfall.* 2 a fall of rain, a downpour.

**downstairs** *adverb, adjective* to, at or in a lower floor. *I'll wait downstairs.*

Downstairs there is a sitting room that leads off the kitchen.

**doze** *verb* to sleep lightly or be half asleep.

**dozen** *noun* 1 twelve. *A dozen eggs.* 2 lots of. *I've asked him dozens of times.*

**Dr** *abbreviation* doctor.

**drab** (drabber, drabbest) *adjective* not colourful, dull.

**drag** (drags, dragging, dragged) *verb* 1 to pull a heavy load along or pull somebody roughly. *He dragged the case across the street.* 2 to go on slowly, to seem to last a long time. *The meeting dragged on.* 3 to move along while touching the ground or search for something by pulling a heavy net along the bottom of a river or lake. *Her dress dragged in the mud.*

**dragon** *noun* an imaginary animal or monster in children's stories that has scales and wings and breathes fire.

**WORD HISTORY**

*The imaginary dragon comes from the Greek 'drakon', meaning serpent or snake. Although it is usually shown as a fierce creature, the dragon appears on the flag of Wales and stands for good luck in China.*

**dragonfly** (dragonflies) *noun* an insect with a long body and two pairs of large thin wings. *The dragonflies darted and hovered over the pond in the warm summer sun.*

The wings of a dragonfly shimmer in the sunlight with rainbow colours.

**drain** *noun* 1 a pipe that carries away water or other unwanted liquid. 2 something that uses up time, money or energy. *Her sons are a drain on her purse.* **drain** *verb* 1 to flow away slowly. 2 to make weak or take away strength. 3 to empty or become dry or empty. *He drained the glass in one gulp, then threw it in the hearth and made a wish.*

**drake** *noun* a male duck.

**drama** *noun* 1 a play for the theatre, television or radio. 2 the study of plays, their writing, presentation and performance. 3 exciting real-life events or an emotional situation. *Our visit turned into a big drama when the house caught fire.*

**dramatic** *adjective* 1 impressive, exciting. *The new government has made some dramatic changes.* 2 showing feeling in a lively way. *His speech was very dramatic, but not many people appreciated it.*

**drank** past tense of drink.

**drastic** *adjective* having a strong and often violent effect. *A drastic decision had to be taken to save the day.*

The dragon is a mythical beast that can fly and breathe fire.

D

**draw** (draws, drawing, drew, drawn) *verb* 1 to make pictures, patterns or diagrams with a pencil or pen. 2 to pull something heavy along. *Two horses drew the carriage.* 3 to pull something out of a place, to take out. *To draw money out of the bank.* 4 to attract. *The concert drew a large crowd.* 5 to come or move in the direction mentioned. *Our holiday is drawing to an end.* 6 to end a game or contest with the same points on both sides. *Arsenal and Spurs drew two all.* 7 to form an idea. *To draw a conclusion.* **draw ahead** to move in front of somebody. **draw the curtains** to open or close the curtains. **draw up** 1 to come near and stop. *A car drew up outside my door.* 2 to prepare, especially a report or document.

**draw** *noun* 1 equal marks in a game or contest. 2 the drawing of lottery tickets. *The luck of the draw.*

**drawback** *noun* a disadvantage, something that can cause trouble or difficulty. *The high price is a drawback.*

**drawbridge** *noun* a bridge over a moat or river that can be pulled up by chains to protect a castle or let ships pass.

**drawer** *noun* 1 a box-like container which is part of a cupboard or a table that slides in and out. 2 a person who writes out and signs a cheque.

**drawing** *noun* 1 making pictures with a pen or pencil. 2 a picture made by drawing.

I pinned the drawing of our house on the wall.

**drawing pin** *noun* a short pin with a flat top used for fastening papers to a flat surface. *Please pass me four drawing pins.*

**drawn** past tense of draw.

**dread** *noun* great fear. **dread** *verb* to fear something greatly. *I dread the exam.* **dreadful** *adjective. A dreadful headache.*

**dreadlocks** *plural noun* hair worn in tight plaits. *Bob Marley's dreadlocks.*

**DID YOU KNOW?**

*When you are dreaming, your eyes move about rapidly behind your closed eyelids. Experts believe that most people dream every night, but they do not always remember their dreams.*

**AMAZING FACT**

In drawing, the point where receding parallel lines seem to meet when you look at them in perspective is called the Vanishing Point.

**dream** *noun* 1 thoughts, feelings and pictures you see or live through while you are asleep. A bad dream is called a nightmare. 2 something ideal you think about and that you would like to come true. *It's my dream to sail around the world.* 3 something beautiful. *She dances like a dream.* **dream** (dreams, dreaming, dreamt or dreamed) *verb* 1 to have a dream or dreams while sleeping. 2 to imagine that something you want might happen. *I dream of winning the lottery.* **dreamer** *noun.*

**dredge** *verb* to dredge a river means to clear it by removing mud. **dredger** *noun* a boat or barge used for dredging.

**drench** *verb* to make or be very wet. *We were caught in a storm and got drenched.*

**dress** (dresses) *noun* 1 a piece of clothing with a top and a skirt for a woman or a girl. 2 clothing in general. *The children wore national dress.*

This Bulgarian woman is wearing national dress.

**dress** *verb* 1 to put on clothes. 2 to wear clothes. *She was dressed in black.* 3 to add sauce to food. *I haven't dressed the salad.* 4 to cover with a bandage. *To dress a wound.* 5 to arrange goods for display. *To dress a shop window.* **dress up** 1 to put on smart clothes. 2 to wear something else for fun, to put on clothes in a game. *The children dressed up as pirates.* **get dressed** to put on clothes.

**dresser** *noun* 1 a kitchen sideboard with shelves above for displaying dishes. 2 a person who is employed to help actors and actresses to dress for the stage.

The jugs, plates and dishes were displayed on the kitchen dresser.

**dressing** *noun* 1 a bandage for covering a wound. 2 a sauce for food. *Salad dressing.*

**dressing gown** *noun* a robe worn over pyjamas or a nightie.

**drew** past tense of draw.

**dribble** *verb* 1 to let drops of spit (saliva) trickle out of your mouth. *Babies dribble.* 2 to move the ball forward with short kicks. *He dribbled into the penalty area.*

**dried** past tense of dry.

**drier** *noun* a device for drying hair or clothes. *The hair drier blows hot or cold.*

**drift** *verb* 1 to float or be carried along gently by the wind or waves. 2 to move about without a plan. *She just drifts from one job to another.*

**drift** *noun* 1 sand or snow that the wind has blown into a pile. 2 a general movement or the direction in which something is moving. *There is a drift away from higher education.* 3 the meaning of something, especially a speech. *I didn't catch the drift of their discussion.*

**drill** *noun* 1 a tool for making holes. *A dentist's drill.* 2 practising an emergency routine. *We had a fire drill this morning.* 3 training by repeating an exercise. *They have a lot of drill in the army.* **drill** *verb* 1 to drill a hole. 2 to do something repeatedly. *We were drilled to say 'thank you'.*

The driver pulled the lever and the powerful drill began to bite into the road.

**drink** (drinks, drinking, drank, drunk) *verb* 1 to swallow liquid. *You should drink plenty of water.* 2 to drink too much alcohol. *He drinks too much.* **drink** *noun* 1 something you drink. *A drink of water.* 2 alcohol, an alcoholic drink. *He's very fond of drink.*

**drip** (drips, dripping, dripped) *verb* to fall slowly or let something fall in small drops. *The tap is dripping.* **drip** *noun* 1 a drop of liquid falling, the sound of falling drops. 2 an apparatus for dripping liquid into a blood vessel.

**drive** (drives, driving, drove, driven) *verb* 1 to travel in a vehicle or make it go. *My brother drives a tractor.* 2 to take somebody in a car. *I'll drive the children home.* 3 to force to go. *She drives all the customers away.* 4 to make somebody do something. *His illness has driven him to drink.* 5 to direct force into or on to something. *To drive a nail into the wall. The engine is driven by steam.* **driver** *noun.*

**drive** *noun* 1 a journey in a car or bus. 2 a private road to a house or garage. 3 energy and enthusiasm. *People with a lot of drive are often very successful.* 4 the act of hitting a ball or the force with which it is hit, especially in golf or cricket. 5 a planned effort by a group for a particular purpose. *We are having a sales drive.*

The drive to our house sweeps through the gates and up to the front door.

**GRAMMAR NOTE**

*Be careful to use 'drank' and 'drunk' correctly. 'Drank' is the past tense of 'drink'. 'He drank the whole can in one go.' 'Drunk' is the past participle and goes with have. 'I've drunk my tea.' A person who is drunk has had too much alcohol.*

**drizzle** *noun* light rain. **drizzle** *verb.*

**drone** *noun* 1 a male bee. 2 a low humming sound. **drone** *verb* 1 to make a low humming sound. 2 to talk in a low, boring voice. *He droned on and on.*

**drool** *verb* 1 If you drool over something, you are very exited and show foolish pleasure in looking at it. 2 to dribble.

**droop** *verb* to bend or hang down. *The flowers were drooping after the heavy rain.*

**drop** *noun* 1 a small spot of liquid, a small amount. *Drops of rain.* 2 a fall. *A drop in temperature. A drop of 100 metres.*

**drop** (drops, dropping, dropped) *verb* 1 to fall. *Water dropped into the bucket.* 2 to let fall. *I dropped my spoon on the floor.* 3 to become less. *Prices have dropped.* 4 to let somebody get out of the car. *Could you drop me at the station?* 5 to stop doing something or meeting somebody. *He's dropped his girlfriend for someone else.* 6 to not select somebody for a team. *The goalkeeper let the ball into the net too many times and was dropped for the next match.* **drop in** to visit somebody without warning. **drop out** to stop taking part in something or doing something. *She dropped out of the race.*

The girl dropped the ball to see how high it would bounce.

**drove** past tense of drive.

**drown** *verb* 1 to die under water by not being able to breathe. *Hundreds drowned in the* Titanic *disaster.* 2 to cover something with water or make something very wet. *The peaches were drowned in brandy.* 3 to make a sound impossible to hear by making more noise. *Her voice was drowned by the children's shouting.*

**drowsy** *adjective* sleepy. **drowsiness** *noun.*

**drug** *noun* 1 a medicine. 2 a substance that affects your mind and feelings and is addictive. *Most drugs are illegal, except for nicotine and alcohol.* **drug** (drugs, drugging, drugged) *verb.* When you drug somebody, you give them a drug to make them unconscious.

**drug addict** *noun* somebody addicted to drugs, who cannot stop taking them.

**drugstore** *noun* a shop where you can buy medicines and other goods. You can also have drinks and snacks in a drugstore.

**drum** *noun* 1 a musical instrument made of a hollow round frame with a skin stretched tightly over it. *To beat the drum.* 2 a round container for liquids. *A large drum full of oil.* **drum** (drums, drumming, drummed) *verb* 1 to play a drum. 2 to tap. *He drummed his fingers on the table.* **drummer** *noun.*

Bongo drums are fun to play.

**drumstick** *noun* a stick for beating a drum.

**drunk** *adjective* having had too much alcohol. *He drank too much beer and got extremely drunk.* **drunk** *noun* a person who often gets drunk.

**dry** (drier, driest) *adjective* 1 not wet. Without water. *The washing is dry.* 2 not rainy. *It was a dry day.* 3 uninteresting, boring. *He's a dry old stick.* 4 without butter. *Dry toast.* 5 witty. *She has a dry sense of humour.*

**dry** (dries, drying, dried) *verb* to make or become dry.

**dry-clean** *verb* to clean clothes with chemicals, without using water.

**dry-cleaner's** *noun* a shop where clothes are taken to be dry-cleaned.

**DID YOU KNOW?**

*There are two main types of duck: dabbers and divers. Dabbers feed on the surface of the water, and divers swim under the water to get food. The Aylesbury duck was bred originally in the town in Buckinghamshire, but a Bombay duck isn't a duck at all – it's a kind of dried fish!*

**dual** *adjective* having two parts or two functions. *The driving instructor's car had dual controls.*

**Dublin** *noun* the capital of Ireland.

**duck** *noun* a water-bird with a wide beak.

**duck** *verb* 1 to bend down quickly, to avoid being seen or hit. *When he saw the policeman, he ducked behind a wall.* 2 to dip under water. *My horrible brother ducked me in the swimming pool.* **duck out of** to avoid doing something.

**duel** *noun* a fight with guns or swords between two people in order to settle a quarrel. **duel** *verb* to fight a duel. **duellist** *noun.*

The fencing champion challenged his friend to a duel.

**duet** *noun* 1 a performance by two singers or musicians. 2 a piece of music for two singers or players. *A piano duet.*

**dug** past tense of dig.

**dull** *adjective* 1 not bright, clear or shining. *A dull colour. The weather was dull.* 2 slow in understanding, stupid. *Some of his pupils are rather dull.* 3 uninteresting, boring. *A dull lesson.* 4 not sharp. *He felt a dull pain. It made a dull sound.* **dullness** *noun.*

**dumb** (say dum) *adjective* 1 unable to speak. 2 unwilling to speak, silent. *He remained dumb throughout the trial.* 3 stupid. *You aren't really that dumb.*

**dump** *noun* 1 a place where rubbish is left. 2 an unpleasant, dull and dirty place. *I couldn't live in such a dump.*

There is all sorts of rubbish at the dump, including old furniture and carpets.

**dump** *verb* 1 to get rid of something unwanted. *People shouldn't dump dangerous chemicals at sea.* 2 to leave or put something down carelessly. *She dumped her things in the hall.*

**dune** *noun* a sand hill on a seashore or in the desert piled up by the wind.

**dung** *noun* solid waste matter from the bowels of large animals, especially cattle.

**dungeon** *noun* (say **dun**-jun) a dark underground prison cell in a castle.

The prisoner was thrown into the filthy dungeon without food or water.

**duplicate** *adjective* exactly the same. *Duplicate keys.* **duplicate** *noun* something that is exactly the same as something else; an exact copy. *Luckily I had a duplicate of the missing photograph.* **duplicate** *verb* to make or be a duplicate.

**during** *preposition* 1 throughout, something that happens continuously within a period. *We never go to the cinema during the week.* 2 at some point within a period. *He rang twice during the morning.*

**Dushanbe** *noun* the capital of Tajikistan.

**dusk** *noun* the time when it is not completely dark, just before nightfall.

**dust** *noun* tiny specks of earth, sand or dirt that look like dry powder. *There is a lot of dust on the books.* **dust** *verb* 1 to wipe away dust. *She dusts her room every day.* 2 to cover with dust or fine powder. *To dust a cake with icing sugar.*

**duster** *noun* a cloth for dusting.

**dusty** (dustier, dustiest) *adjective* 1 covered with dust. 2 like dust. *A dusty brown.*

**Dutch** *noun* the language spoken in Holland. **Dutch** *adjective*. *Dutch people.* **go Dutch** to share expenses. *We always go Dutch when I go out with my boyfriend.* **Dutch courage** so-called courage that comes from being drunk.

Windmills are a major feature of the Dutch landscape. The wind blows fiercely across the flat land and its power used to be harnessed to grind the corn into flour.

**WORD HISTORY**

*'Duvet' comes from an Old French word for down, a bird's soft feathers that are used inside the quilt. A duvet is also called a continental quilt.*

**duty** (duties) *noun* 1 something a person must do because they think it right. *It's my duty to look after my sick uncle.* 2 a task, something you have to do as part of your job. *He told me what my duties would be.* 3 a tax on certain goods. *A duty on cigarettes.* **on duty** at work. *The doctor is on duty tonight.* **off duty** not at work.

**duvet** *noun* (say **doo**-vay) a thick soft quilt used as a bed covering.

**dwarf** (dwarfs or dwarves) *noun* a very small person, animal or plant. **dwarf** *verb* to make something seem very small by comparison. *The new office block dwarfs the other buildings.*

**dwell** (dwells, dwelling, dwelt) *verb* to live. *Strange creatures dwell in the forest.* **dwell on** to think or talk about something for a long time. *It's no good dwelling on the past.*

**dwelling** *noun* a place to live in.

High in the mountains of South America, people make their dwellings from reeds.

**dwindle** (dwindles, dwindling, dwindled) *verb* to get gradually smaller or fewer. *Numbers are dwindling.*

**dye** (dyes, dyeing, dyed) *verb* to colour something, especially hair or cloth, by soaking it in a coloured liquid. *I want to dye my hair red.* **dye** *noun* the substance used for dyeing things.

**dynamo** *noun* a machine that turns mechanical power into electricity.

**dynasty** (dynasties) *noun* (say **din**-a-stee) a line of rulers of a country who all belong to the same family. *The Tudor dynasty.*

**dyslexia** *noun* (say dis-**leks**-ee-a) great difficulty with reading and spelling. **dyslexic** *adjective*.

# Ee

**each** *adjective, pronoun* 1 every person or thing in a group. *Each student.* 2 for one. *The tickets are £10 each.* **each other** one another. *They loved each other.*

**eager** *adjective* wanting to do something very much, keen. **eagerly** *adverb.*

**eagle** *noun* a large meat-eating bird, or bird of prey, with very good eyesight.

**ear** *noun* the organ of hearing. You have two ears, one on either side of your head. **all ears** listening with great interest. *Tell us what she did, we're all ears.* **play it by ear** to act from moment to moment, without making plans in advance.

Cochlea

Eardrum

Sound waves travel down the ear canal to the eardrum. The ear is also the body's organ of balance.

**ear** *noun* the part at the top of a cereal plant that contains the seeds. *Ears of corn stood in a vase on the altar.*

**early** (earlier, earliest) *adjective, adverb* 1 before the expected time. *The train was 10 minutes early.* 2 happening near the beginning. *Early last week.*

**earn** *verb* 1 to get money in return for working. 2 to get something, especially praise, because you deserve it. *That will earn him our respect.* **earnings** *plural noun.*

**earnest** *adjective* very serious. **in earnest** very seriously.

**earring** *noun* a piece of jewellery worn on the ear.

**earth** *noun* 1 the planet we live on. *The spacecraft has returned to Earth.* 2 the soil in which plants thrive and grow. 3 the ground. 4 a wire that passes from electrical equipment to the ground and makes the equipment safe. 5 the hole that a fox lives in.

Here the Earth, with clouds above it, is seen from space.

**SPELLING NOTE**

*The planet we live on can be spelt with or without a capital 'e' ('Earth' or 'earth'). When you use it together with the names of other planets, such as Mars and Venus, write 'Earth'.*

**earth** *verb* to connect a piece of electrical equipment to the ground.

**earthquake** *noun* a sudden violent shaking of the Earth's surface.

**earthworm** *noun* a long thin worm that lives under the ground.

**earwig** *noun* a crawling insect.

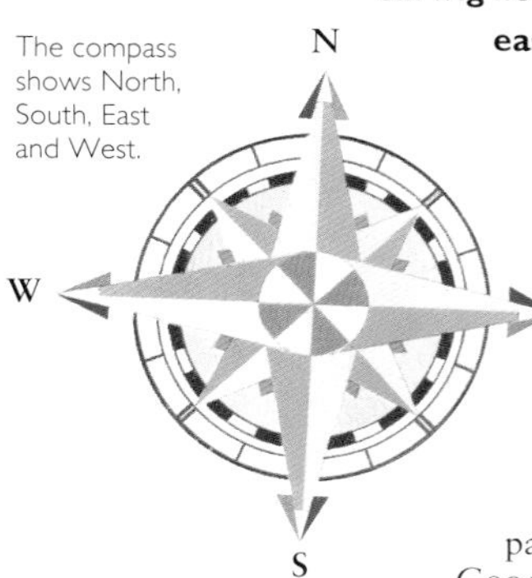


The compass shows North, South, East and West.

**easily** *adverb* 1 without difficulty or very likely. *I'll easily finish my essay by tonight.* 2 without doubt. *I'm easily the fastest runner in the class.*

**east** or **East** *adjective, adverb* to or in the direction in which the Sun rises (the opposite of west). *An east wind.* **east** *noun* 1 *The Sun rises in the east.* 2 the eastern part of a country or continent. *Good news from the east.*

**Easter** *noun* a religious festival when Christians remember the death and resurrection of Christ.

**easterly** *adjective* towards or in the east. *We walked in an easterly direction.*

**eastern** *adjective* in or from the east. *A small village in eastern Russia.*

**easy** (easier, easiest) *adjective, adverb* 1 not difficult, not needing much effort. *It was easy to persuade him to come.* 2 without any problems. *She has an easy life.* **take it/things easy** to relax and not do or work too much. **go easy on something** to avoid using too much of it.

**easy-going** *adjective* not easily worried or upset. *My parents are very easy-going, they don't mind what I do.*

**eat** (eats, eating, ate, eaten) *verb* 1 to put food in your mouth and swallow it. 2 to have a meal. 3 to damage or destroy, especially by chemical action. *The acid has eaten a hole in the metal.* **eat in** to have a meal at home. **eat out** to have a meal in a restaurant. **eat up** to finish a meal.

**eavesdrop** (eavesdrops, eavesdropping, eavesdropped) *verb* to listen secretly to somebody else's conversation.

**ebb** *verb* 1 to flow back from the land to the sea. 2 to become weaker or grow less. *Her strength is ebbing.* **ebb** *noun* 1 *The ebb and flow of the tides.* 2 a low mood. *He felt at a very low ebb.*

**ebony** *noun* a hard black wood. **ebony** *adjective. Ebony skin.*

**eccentric** (say ek-sen-trik) *adjective* behaving strangely, having odd habits. **eccentric** *noun* an eccentric person. **eccentricity** *noun.*

**echo** (echoes) *noun* a sound that is heard again as it is sent back from a wall or inside a cave. **echo** (echoes, echoing, echoed) *verb* 1 to make an echo. *Our footsteps echoed in the tunnel.* 2 to repeat somebody else's words or actions. *His views echoed those of his elder sister.*

**eclipse** *noun* the disappearance of the Sun's or Moon's light when the Moon or the Earth is in the way. *A total eclipse of the Sun.* **eclipse** *verb* to do or be much better than somebody or something. *His paintings eclipsed all the other exhibits.*

This solar eclipse was photographed on 16 February 1980, over Africa.

**ecology** *noun* the pattern of relationships between plants, animals and people to each other and their surroundings. **ecologist** *noun.* **ecological** *adjective.*

**economic** *adjective* 1 relating to economics. 2 making a profit. *It's not economic to run buses to the village.*

**economical** *adjective* using money, time or goods carefully, not wasteful. *He's very economical with the stationery, if nothing else.* **economically** *adverb.*

**economics** *noun* the science of the production and distribution of wealth.

**economy** (economies) *noun* 1 the system by which a country spends its money and organizes its industry and trade. 2 the careful spending of money or use of goods in order to save money.

**ecosystem** *noun* a system relating all the plants, animals and people in an area to their surroundings.

**ecstasy** (say **ek**-stuh-see) *noun* a feeling of extreme joy and happiness. **ecstatic** *adjective.* **ecstatically** *adverb.*

**Ecuador** *noun* a country in South America.

**edge** *noun* 1 the thin cutting part of a knife or another cutting tool. 2 the place or line where something stops and something else begins. The side of something. *The edge of the cliff.* **on edge** nervous.

The Galapagos Islands in the Pacific Ocean belong to Ecuador, a country on the west coast of South America.

**SPELLING NOTE**

*The noun 'effect' goes with the verb 'affect'. 'It had no effect on me; it didn't affect me.' The verb 'effect' has a different meaning, to make happen.*

**edge** *verb* 1 to form the edge of something or put an edge on something. *The lawn was edged with flowers.* 2 to move slowly and carefully. *He edged towards me.*

**edible** *adjective* fit to be eaten, eatable.

**edifice** (say **ed**-if-iss) *noun* a large building.

**Edinburgh** *noun* the capital of Scotland.

**edit** *verb* 1 to plan and work on a newspaper, magazine or book. *This manuscript needed a lot of editing.* 2 to choose, arrange and put parts of a film or recording together.

**edition** *noun* 1 the form in which a book or magazine is printed. *A paperback edition.* 2 the number of copies of a book or magazine printed. *The first edition has already sold out.*

**editor** *noun* 1 a person who edits a book, magazine or newspaper. 2 the person who is in charge of a newspaper.

**educate** *verb* to teach or train somebody. **education** *noun.*

**eel** *noun* a long thin fish that looks like a snake.

The young of the eel is called an elver.

**effect** *noun* 1 a condition caused by something, a result. *He could feel the effects of the drink.* 2 an impression produced on the mind. *Sound effects are very important in a film.* **effect** *verb* to produce or make something happen. *The changes in the law will be effected soon.* **in effect** really. *In effect the reply told her nothing.* **take effect** to start happening.

**effective** *adjective* 1 impressive. 2 producing the result you set out to achieve. *Petrol can be an effective stain remover.* 3 actual or real. *She took effective control.* **to become effective** to come into force. *The new opening hours become effective on Tuesday.* **effectiveness** *noun.* **effectively** *adverb.*

**efficient** *adjective* working well without wasting time or effort. *He's very efficient at his job.* **efficiency** *noun.*

**effort** *noun* trying hard to do something, or the result of it. *I make an effort to be polite.*

**egg** *noun* 1 an oval object laid by female birds, fishes and reptiles which contains new life. 2 a hen's egg used as food. 3 a female reproductive cell in humans, animals and plants. The scientific term for a human egg is an ovum.

**e.g.** *abbreviation* for example. *In certain countries, e.g. Italy, France and Holland.*

**Egypt** *noun* a country in Africa.

**Eid** (say eed) *noun* a Muslim festival celebrating the end of the fast of Ramadan (Eid ul-Fitr), or the end of a journey to Mecca (Eid ul-Adha).

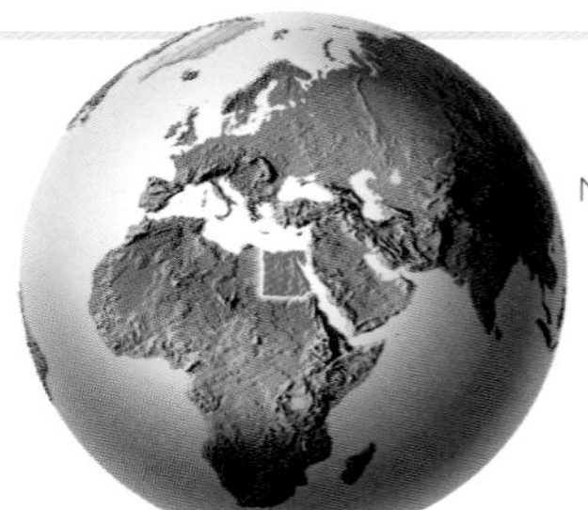

Egypt lies on the Mediterranean Sea in North Africa.

**either** *adjective, pronoun* 1 one or the other of two. *Both computers work, you can use either.* 2 one and also the other, both. *'Which do you prefer?' 'I don't like either.'* **either** *adverb* also (used in negative statements). *I don't like cats and I don't like dogs either.* **either** *conjunction* the first of two or more possibilities. *I'll either write or ring you when I feel better.*

**eject** *verb* 1 to throw somebody out of a place. *They were forcibly ejected from the stadium.* 2 to push out with force. *The machine ejected the coins.*

**El Salvador** *noun* a country in Central America.

**elaborate** (say i-**lab**-uh-rut) *adjective* full of detail with a number of complicated parts. *The curtains had an elaborate pattern of flowers.* **elaborate** (say i-**lab**-uh-rate) *verb* When you elaborate on something, you describe or explain it in detail.

**elapse** *verb* (of time) to pass by. *Three months have elapsed since the wedding.*

**elastic** *adjective* able to stretch and go back to its original shape. *An elastic band.* **elasticity** *noun.*

**elastic** *noun* material that stretches.

**elbow** *noun* the joint where the arm bends.

Joints, such as the elbow joint, are cushioned by soft, squashy cartilage, which is more flexible than bone.

**elder** *noun* a tree with white flowers and red or black berries.

**elder** *adjective* older. *My elder sister.* **elder** *noun* 1 the older of two people. 2 an older person. *We should respect our elders.*

**elect** *verb* 1 to choose by voting. *A new government was elected.* 2 to decide to do something. *They elected to stay.*

**election** *noun* voting to choose a person or party to hold an official position. *She stood for parliament in the general election.*

### DID YOU KNOW

*An element is one of more than 100 substances that consist of atoms of the same type. Everything in the Universe, whether living or non-living, is made up of combinations of chemical elements. For example, water combines the elements hydrogen and oxygen.*

**electric** *adjective* 1 producing or produced by electricity. *An electric toaster.* 2 very exciting. *The atmosphere at the concert was simply electric.*

**electrical** *adjective* relating to electricity. *An electrical fault.*

**electrician** *noun* a person whose job is to fit and repair electrical equipment.

**electricity** *noun* a form of energy that is used for heating and lighting or for driving machines. Electricity is produced by generators or batteries.

**electrode** *noun* the point where an electric current enters or leaves a battery.

**electron** *noun* a tiny particle of matter with a negative electric charge.

**electronic** *adjective* produced or worked by electrons, usually using microchips. *Electronic music.* **electronics** *noun.*

**elegant** *adjective* showing good taste in design and style. Graceful and pleasing. *An elegant new dress.* **elegance** *noun.*

**element** *noun* 1 a single part that combines with others to make a whole. *Listening is an important element of her job.* 2 an amount of something. *There is an element of truth in what she said.* 3 the heating part of an electrical appliance. 4 the most important parts or the basics of a subject. *The elements of mathematics.* 5 in science, an element is a substance that consists of only one type of atom. Gold and oxygen are elements. 6 a suitable surrounding. *He was in his element talking about films.* **the elements** the weather, especially wind and rain.

**elementary** *adjective* easy, simple. *I took an elementary course.*

**elephant** *noun* the largest living land animal, with a trunk and tusks.

The elephant uses its trunk for taking food from high in the trees. It can also smell, drink and shower with its trunk.

**elevator** *noun* a lift.

**eligible** *adjective* 1 entitled to be chosen. *You are eligible for a grant.* 2 desirable or suitable. *An eligible bachelor.*

**elite** (say ay-**leet**) *noun* the most important or powerful group of people in a community. *He was hoping to join the elite.*

**elm** *noun* a tree with broad leaves.

E

**eloquent** *adjective* able to make good speeches that persuade and influence others. **eloquence** *noun.*

**else** *adverb* 1 besides, in addition, other. *What else can I do?* 2 otherwise. *You must pay the fine, or else you'll lose your membership card.*

**elusive** *adjective* difficult to catch or find. *Success proved elusive.*

**e-mail** *noun* electronic mail. *I'll send it to you by e-mail.*

**emancipate** *verb* to free somebody from things that are holding them back. **emancipated** *adjective. Today's women are much more emancipated than their grandmothers.* **emancipation** *noun.*

**embankment** *noun* a wall of stones or earth to hold back a river or carry a road or railway.

**embark** *verb* to go on board a ship or plane. **embark on** to start. *She embarked on a new life.*

**embarrass** *verb* to make somebody feel awkward or self-conscious. *The questions embarrassed me so much that I blushed.* **embarrassment** *noun.*

**embroider** *verb* to sew a design on cloth. *She embroidered the tablecloth with pink flowers.* **embroidery** *noun.*

**embryo** (say **em**-bree-oh) *noun* an unborn baby or animal as it starts to grow in its mother's womb. **embryonic** *adjective* undeveloped.

This sequence of pictures shows the development of the embryo in the womb.

**emerald** *noun* 1 a green precious stone. 2 a clear green colour.

**emergency** (emergencies) *noun* an unexpected dangerous event that needs immediate action. *Ring 999 in an emergency.*

**emigrate** *verb* to leave your own country to live in another country. **emigration** *noun.* **emigrant** *noun.*

**eminent** *adjective* an eminent person is somebody famous and admired.

**DID YOU KNOW?**

*An e-mail address is made of a group of letters, numbers and dots, with no spaces in between any of them, such as info@bbc.co.uk for the information department of the BBC. E-mail users sometimes call the ordinary postal system 'snail mail', because they think it is so slow.*

Emmeline Pankhurst led the campaign to emancipate women. She was arrested and imprisoned several times.

**SPELLING NOTE**

*When they start their journey from their original country, people are called emigrants. At the end of the journey, when they arrive in their new country, they are called immigrants.*

**emotion** *noun* a strong feeling. Love and jealousy are emotions. *She was overcome with emotion.* **emotional** *adjective.*

**emotive** *adjective* causing emotion. *It was a very emotive issue.*

**emperor** *noun* the ruler of an empire. If the ruler is a woman, she is called an empress.

**emphasize** *verb* to give special importance to something. *He emphasized that he wanted to be on his own.* **emphasis** *noun.*

**empire** *noun* 1 a country or group of countries controlled by one person. *The former British Empire.* 2 a large group of firms or shops controlled by one person. *She has built up a huge empire.*

**employ** *verb* 1 to pay somebody to do work for you. *The firm employs 20 people.* 2 to make use of something or somebody. *He employed all his charm to win her over.*

**employee** *noun* a person who is paid to work for somebody else.

**employer** *noun* a person who employs people. *The workers were in dispute with their employer.*

**employment** *noun* 1 having a paid job. Employing or being employed. *I have never been out of employment.* 2 a person's regular job.

**empty** (emptier, emptiest) *adjective* 1 with nothing or nobody in it. 2 with no meaning. *They were empty promises.* **empty** *noun. The milkman collects the empties.* **empty** (empties, emptying, emptied) *verb* to make empty. **emptiness** *noun.* **emptily** *adverb.*

**emu** *noun* a large Australian bird, like an ostrich.

The emu can run very fast but it cannot fly.

**enable** *verb* to make somebody able to do something or give somebody the means to do something.

**enamel** *noun* 1 a shiny substance that is put on to metal, glass or pottery to decorate and protect it. 2 the outer covering of a tooth. **enamel** *adjective. Enamel paint.*

**enchant** *verb* 1 When you enchant somebody, you charm and delight them. 2 to put somebody or something under a magic spell. **enchanted** *adjective* magic. *An enchanted forest.*

**enclose** *verb* 1 to put a wall or fence around something to shut it in. 2 to put something with a letter or a parcel. *I'm enclosing a photograph.* **enclosure** *noun.*

**encounter** *verb* 1 to meet unexpectedly. 2 to be faced with something bad, especially danger or prejudice. *We encountered many difficulties.* **encounter** *noun.*

**encourage** *verb* 1 to give courage or hope to somebody. *I encouraged her to take up painting.* 2 to support or help develop. *Don't encourage his laziness.* **encouragement** *noun.* **encouraging** *adjective. Encouraging news from the hospital.*

**end** *noun* 1 the point or place where something stops, the last part of something. *At the end of the street.* 2 finish. *It was the end of our friendship.* 3 a small piece left. *There were lots of cigarette ends in the ashtray.* 4 death. *His was a cruel end.* 5 purpose. *He is doing this for his own selfish ends.* **in the end** finally. **make ends meet** to have just enough money to live on. **end** *verb* to finish. *How did the play end?*

**endanger** *verb* to cause danger to. *Smoking seriously endangers your health.*

**endeavour** (say in-**dev**-uh) *verb* to try. **endeavour** *noun.*

**endurance** *noun* the ability to endure or bear something. *Henry very much admired the soldiers' endurance.*

The 20,000 men who survived the 9,700 km Long March in China in 1934–35 performed an astonishing feat of endurance. 80,000 men died on the journey.

**endure** *verb* 1 to put up with, to bear, especially pain or suffering. *She was forced to endure great hardship.* 2 to last. *His love for me will endure for ever.*

**enemy** (enemies) *noun* 1 somebody who hates or wants to hurt another person. When two people hate each other, they are enemies. 2 a country or army that is at war with another. *The enemy attacked at night.*

**energetic** *adjective* full of energy.

**energy** *noun* 1 the strength and ability to do a lot. 2 the effort put into work. *She concentrated all her energy on her job.* 3 the power that works and drives machines.

**engage** *verb* 1 to employ. If you are engaged in something, you are doing it or working on it. 2 to attract somebody's attention. 3 to fit into or lock together parts of a machine. *To engage the clutch.*

**DID YOU KNOW?**

*English is an official language in 57 countries of the world. But more people speak Mandarin Chinese in China and Hindi in India as their first language. After Mandarin, Hindi and English, the next most common language is Spanish.*

**engaged** *adjective* 1 having agreed to marry. 2 occupied or in use. *This number seems to be constantly engaged.*

**engagement** *noun* 1 an agreement to marry. *She called off their engagement.* 2 the period of time during which two people are engaged. 3 an arrangement to meet somebody or do something. *A dinner engagement is something I look forward to.*

**engaging** *adjective* attractive, interesting.

**engine** *noun* 1 a machine that produces power which makes a vehicle move. 2 a machine that pulls a railway train, also called a locomotive.

This is a car engine with four cylinders.

**engineer** *noun* 1 a person who designs machines, roads and bridges. 2 a person who repairs machines or electrical devices. 3 a person in control of an engine or engines, especially on a ship.

**engineer** *verb* to plan or cause something to happen. *He engineered an interview with the top boss.*

**England** *noun* a country that is part of the United Kingdom.

England is part of the British Isles. It is separated from the mainland of Europe by the English Channel.

**English** *noun* 1 the people of England. 2 the language spoken in Great Britain, America, Canada, Australia and elsewhere. **English** *adjective. English customs and traditions.*

**enjoy** *verb* to get pleasure from something. **enjoyment** *noun.*

**enlarge** *verb* to make or get bigger. *The house was enlarged by the previous owners.* **enlargement** *noun. I'd like an enlargement of this photograph.*

**enormous** *adjective* very big.

**enough** *adverb* having the right amount or to the right degree. *He's not old enough to understand.* **enough** *adjective* as much or as many as necessary. *Have we got enough time for a cup of coffee?* **enough** *pronoun. Not enough is known about the universe.*

**enquire,** enquirer, enquiry. See inquire, inquirer, inquiry.

**enrol** (enrols, enrolling, enrolled) *verb* to become a member, especially on a course. *I have enrolled at the local college.*

**ensure** *verb* to make certain (of). *This medicine will ensure a good night's sleep.*

**enter** *verb* 1 to come in or go into. *He entered the room.* 2 to become a member, especially of a university or profession. 3 to write down in a book or type into a computer. *He entered the amount in the cash book.* 4 to take part in a competition.

**entertain** *verb* 1 to give food and drink to guests at your home. 2 to amuse and interest. *He entertained us with stories about his trip around the world.* 3 to think about. *I didn't even entertain the idea.*

**entertainer** *noun* a person whose job it is to entertain, especially a comedian or singer. *Frank Sinatra was a great entertainer.*

**entertainment** *noun* 1 the act of being entertained or being entertaining. *He told stories for the children's entertainment.* 2 a performance at the theatre or cinema.

**enthusiasm** *noun* a strong feeling of interest, liking and excitement. *She was full of enthusiasm.* **enthusiast** *noun. He's a fitness enthusiast.* **enthusiastic** *adjective.*

**entire** *adjective* whole. *They spent the entire evening arguing.* **entirely** *adverb.*

**entrance** *noun* 1 a way into a place, for example a door or gate. 2 the arrival in a room. *She made a dramatic entrance.* 3 the right to go into a place. *He was refused entrance.*

**entry** (entries) *noun* 1 coming or going in. 2 the right to enter. *No entry.* 3 something entered in a list or book. *A dictionary entry.*

The main entrance to Mycenae in ancient Greece was through the Lion Gate.

**envelop** (say in-**vel**-up) *verb* to cover or surround completely. *The hills were enveloped in mist.*

**envelope** (say **en**-vuh-lope) *noun* a paper cover for a letter.

**envious** *adjective* feeling envy. *He was envious of his successful brother.*

**environment** *noun* the surroundings and conditions in which people, animals and plants live. **environmental** *adjective. Environmental pollution.* **environmentalist** *noun. Environmentalists are protesting about the new bypass.*

**SPELLING NOTE**

*Don't confuse 'ensure' and 'insure'. To ensure is to make certain, which is quite a different meaning from to insure.*

**WORD HISTORY**

*Early in its ancient Greek history, 'enthusiastic' meant 'possessed by a god'. In old English 'enthusiasm' was used to mean great religious emotion.*

**DID YOU KNOW?**

*In huge amounts of geological time, epochs make up a period, and periods make up an era.*

**envy** (envies, envying, envied) *verb* wishing you had something that somebody else has. *I envied her her beauty.* **envy** *noun* a feeling of resentment towards somebody who has something that you would like. *His car was the envy of all his friends.*

**epic** *noun* 1 a long poem about heroes and heroic deeds. 2 a historic, grand book or film. **epic** *adjective. An epic adventure.*

**epidemic** *noun* a large number of cases of an infectious disease in one area at the same time. *A flu epidemic has been forecast.*

**episode** *noun* 1 one separate and important event. *That holiday was one of the funniest episodes in my life.* 2 one of several parts of a radio or TV series.

**epoch** (say **ee**-pok) *noun* a period of time in history or life. *A new epoch in the history of space travel.*

**epoch-making** *adjective* very important, remarkable. *An epoch-making discovery.*

**equal** *adjective* the same amount, size or degree. *Women demand equal rights and opportunities.* **equal to something** having enough strength and courage for something. *Will he be equal to running the business on his own?* **equally** *adverb.*

The scales are equally balanced.

**equal** *noun* a person or thing with the same qualities as another. *The two brothers are always treated as equals.*

**equal** *verb* 1 to be the same as another one in amount, size or value. *His salary doesn't equal mine.* 2 to be as good or do as well as somebody else. *With this win, they have equalled the record.*

**equality** *noun* being equal, having the same rights and opportunities.

**equate** *verb* to consider two things or people to be equal. *It is impossible to equate his novels with his films.*

**equator** *noun* an imaginary circle around the middle of the Earth.

The Earth is at its hottest at the equator.

E

**Equatorial Guinea** *noun* a country in Africa.

The flag of Equatorial Guinea has vertical red, yellow and green stripes.

**equestrian** *adjective* to do with horses and horse-riding. *An equestrian event.*

**equinox** *noun* the time of the year when day and night are equally long, about 20 March and 22 September.

**equip** *verb* to supply with what is needed. *The gym is fully equipped with weights and exercise machines.*

**equipment** *noun* things needed for certain activities. *Office equipment, climbing equipment, cleaning equipment.*

**equivalent** *adjective* same, equal in value or meaning. *That sum of money is almost equivalent to a day's work.* **equivalent** *noun.*

**era** *noun* a period of time that starts from a particular point. *The Christian era.*

**eradicate** *verb* to get rid of something or destroy it completely. *We are determined to eradicate crime.*

**erase** *verb* 1 to rub out. 2 to wipe out a recording. *I erased the tape by mistake.*

**eraser** *noun* a rubber used to erase marks or writing, usually on paper.

**erect** *adjective* upright. *He stood erect.*

**erect** *verb* to build or set up. *They erected a statue in the town.* **erection** *noun.*

**Eritrea** *noun* a country in Africa.

**err** (say er) *verb* to make a mistake or do something wrong. *It is better to err on the side of mercy.*

**errand** *noun* a short journey that you make to get something, especially buy things, or to deliver a message. *Could you do a few errands for me in town?*

**error** *noun* a mistake.

**erupt** *verb* 1 to explode and spurt out lava. *The volcano erupted.* 2 to break out or happen suddenly. *Violence erupted after the football match.* **eruption** *noun.*

**escalate** *verb* to increase by stages. *The violence soon escalated.*

**escalator** *noun* a moving staircase that goes up or down.

**escape** *verb* 1 to get away from a person or place, to get out. *Three prisoners escaped last night.* 2 to avoid, especially something unpleasant. *They escaped the accident unhurt. To escape punishment.* **escape** *noun. They had planned the escape for weeks.*

**GRAMMAR NOTE**

*You can use the word 'to' with the adjective 'equivalent'. 'That's equivalent to £10.' With 'equivalent' as a noun, use the word 'of'. 'That's the equivalent of £10.'*

**especially** *adverb* specially, in particular. *I love chocolate, especially milk chocolate.*

**espionage** *noun* spying.

**essential** *adjective* 1 absolutely necessary. *A knowledge of languages is essential for foreign correspondents.* 2 most important. *I only read the essential books on the reading list.* **essential** *noun. Just tell me the bare essentials.*

**establish** *verb* 1 to set up, especially a new government or business. 2 to place or settle yourself or somebody else. *Once he has established himself in the firm, he'll make progress very quickly.* 3 to find out or make certain. *We must establish the truth first.*

**estate** *noun* 1 a large piece of land in the country owned by one person. 2 an area of land with houses or factories on it. *A housing estate.* 3 everything, including money and property, that a person leaves when they die.

When a volcano erupts, it may hurl rocks and ash into the air, and lava may flow down slopes.

**estate agent** *noun* a person or a business that sells and lets property for others.

**Estonia** *noun* a Baltic country in Europe.

**estuary** (estuaries) (say ess-tew-uh-ree) *noun* the wide mouth of a river where it flows into the sea.

**etc.** *abbreviation* et cetera (Latin for 'and other things'), and so on.

**eternal** *adjective* lasting for ever.

**Ethiopia** *noun* a country in Africa.

**ethnic** *adjective* relating to people's race or culture. *Ethnic minorities must have the same rights as everybody else.*

**etymology** (etymologies) *noun* (say et-im-ol-uh-jee) 1 the history and source of a word. 2 the study of the origins and meanings of words. **etymological** *adjective.*

**EU** *abbreviation* European Union.

The flag of the European Union has a circle of 12 gold stars on a blue background.

**DID YOU KNOW?**

*The European Union (EU) began in 1957 as the European Economic Community, when it was made up of six countries: Belgium, France, Italy, Luxembourg, the Netherlands and West Germany. Now the EU has nine more countries as members. They include the United Kingdom, Spain and Sweden.*

**Europe** *noun* one of the Earth's seven continents.

**European** *adjective* coming from or relating to Europe. *A common European currency.*

**evacuate** *verb* to leave a place or move people out of a place, especially because of a crisis. *You must evacuate the building immediately. Thousands were evacuated after the earthquake.* **evacuation** *noun.*

During World War II, many children were evacuated from cities to the country, where they would be safe from bombing.

**evade** *verb* to avoid a person or thing. *He cleverly evaded the question of money.* **evasion** *noun. He was fined for tax evasion.*

**evaporate** *verb* 1 to change from a liquid into a gas called water vapour. *Water evaporates in the heat of the Sun.* 2 to disappear. *My hopes evaporated.* **evaporation** *noun.*

**even** *adjective* 1 flat, smooth. *The floor is not very even.* 2 regular, unchanging. *Indoor plants do best in an even temperature.* 3 equal, especially when talking about things that can be measured. *An even distribution of wealth. We both won a game, now we're even.* 4 Even numbers are numbers that can be divided by two. *Four and 26 are even numbers.* **evenly** *adverb.* **evenness** *noun.*

**even** *adverb* 1 used to stress a word or statement. *Even the teacher was surprised how difficult the exam was.* 2 used before a comparison, meaning still. *He is even taller than his father.* **even so** nevertheless. *She says she doesn't get on with her parents, but even so, she doesn't want to leave home.* **even though** despite the fact that. *Even though she's upset, she won't say anything.* **even out** to make or become even. *Things even themselves out in the end.*

**evening** *noun* the end of the day, before nightfall. *We usually go to the cinema on Saturday evening.*

**event** *noun* 1 something that happens, especially something unusual or important. 2 one of the races or other sporting activities in a competition. **in any event** whatever happens.

Russian astronaut Yuri Gagarin was the first man in space. It was a great event in the history of space exploration.

**eventual** *adjective* happening at last. *He deserved his eventual success.*

**ever** *adverb* 1 at any time. *Getting a computer was the best thing I ever did.* 2 all the time. *They lived happily ever after.* 3 (used for stress) very. *I had ever such a nice letter from him.* **ever since** since the time. *Ever since I've known him, he has never been late.*

**evergreen** *adjective* having green leaves all the year round. *Evergreen trees.*

**every** *adjective* 1 each one. *Every word she says is true.* 2 happening at regular intervals. *Every time I ask her she refuses.* 3 all possible. *He has every reason to be unhappy.* **every now and then** sometimes. *I see my parents every now and then.*

**everybody** *pronoun* each person or all people. *Everybody wants to come to Marianne's birthday party.*

**everyone** *pronoun* everybody.

**everything** *pronoun* each thing or all things. *Money isn't everything.*

**everywhere** *adverb* in, at or to every place. *I've looked everywhere for it.*

**evidence** *noun* proof, something that makes a matter or statement clear. *The thieves destroyed the evidence by burning their clothes.* **give evidence** to tell what is known about somebody or something in a court of law.

**evil** *adjective* very bad, wicked, usually causing harm. *He's an evil man.* **evil** *noun. The difference between good and evil.*

**evolution** *noun* the change and development that takes place over a long period of time, during which animals and plants evolve. **evolutionary** *adjective.*

**WORD BUILDING**

*In words such as 'excavate' the prefix 'ex–' means 'out'. In Latin, 'excavare' means to hollow out, from 'cavus', meaning a hollow or a cave.*

As early people evolved, they gradually became less like apes and more like humans.

**evolve** *verb* to develop gradually.

**ewe** (rhymes with 'boo') *noun* a female sheep. *Ewe's milk.*

**ex-** *prefix* former, no longer the thing the noun refers to. *An ex-minister is no longer a minister. My ex-wife has married again.*

**exaggerate** *verb* to say that something is bigger, better or worse than it really is. *You can't believe his stories, he always exaggerates.* **exaggeration** *noun.*

**examine** *verb* 1 to test somebody's knowledge. 2 to look at a person or thing carefully. *The doctor examined the patient.* **examination** *noun.*

**example** *noun* 1 something that shows how a rule works or what others of the same kind are like. *The penguin is an example of a flightless bird.* 2 a person or thing worth copying. *Her courage is an example to us all.* **for example** *Some birds can't fly – penguins, for example.*

**exasperate** *verb* to annoy or make angry. *Her stupidity is extremely exasperating.* **exasperation** *noun.*

**excavate** *verb* to dig out. *Archaeologists are excavating an ancient Roman site.* **excavation** *noun.*

**exceed** *verb* to be greater than something. *The whole cost of the journey must not exceed £100.*

**excel** (excels, excelling, excelled) *verb* to be extremely good. *He excels at maths.*

**excellent** *adjective* extremely good. *He's an excellent tennis player.*

**except** *preposition* not including. *The film's all right, except that it's too long.* **except** *verb* to leave out. *No one can be excepted.*

**exception** *noun* somebody or something that does not follow the general rule. *The exception proves the rule.*

**exceptional** *adjective* 1 very unusual. *Only in exceptional circumstances.* 2 unusually or extremely good. *Her results were quite exceptional.*

**excess** (excesses) *noun* more than is needed, too much of something. *She cleans the house to excess.* **excess** *adjective. You will have to pay an excess fare.*

**exchange** *verb* to get something else for something. *I exchanged my pounds for pesetas. We exchanged addresses.* **exchangeable** *adjective.*

The penpals exchanged addresses and started a regular correspondence.

**exchange** *noun* 1 getting something else for something. *They gave us a bottle of wine in exchange for some bread.* 2 changing places with somebody. *We went on an exchange to France.*

The emperor penguin is an example of a bird that cannot fly. The penguin has waterproof feathers and a thick layer of fat to keep out the cold of Antarctica.

E

**excite** *verb* to arouse strong feelings. *We were very excited when we got tickets for the concert.* **exciting** *adjective. An exciting adventure.* **excitable** *adjective. He is very nervous and excitable.* **excitement** *noun.*

**exclaim** *verb* to shout out with strong feeling. *'No!' he exclaimed. 'You are never to go there again.'* **exclamation** *noun.*

**exclamation mark** *noun* the punctuation mark (!) which shows an exclamation.

**exclude** *verb* to keep or leave somebody or something out. *If you are not a member, you will be excluded from the meeting.* **exclusion** *noun.*

**exclusive** *adjective* 1 excluding many people and so catering for just a few. *An exclusive club.* 2 not appearing anywhere else. *The newspaper has an exclusive interview with the American film star.*

The exclusive interview was the scoop of the year. It was printed on the front page.

**excursion** *noun* a short journey. *We went on an excursion to the country.*

**excuse** (say iks-**kewz**) *verb* 1 to forgive. You excuse a person for doing something wrong or inconvenient. *Please excuse me for being late.* 2 to free somebody from a duty. *He asked to be excused from rugby training because of injury.* **excuse me** used as an apology or when asking for something or interrupting somebody.

**excuse** *noun* (say iks-**kewss**) the reason given or an explanation for something that has been done. *That's no excuse.*

**execute** *verb* 1 to kill somebody as a punishment for a crime. *The murderer was executed.* 2 to perform or carry out something, especially a plan or an order. *This task is not easy to execute.* **execution** *noun.* **executioner** *noun.*

A large crowd gathered to witness the execution of Charles I.

**GRAMMAR NOTE**

*An exclamation mark (!) is used at the end of sentences that express a strong command ('Shut up! Put it down!') or surprise (What an extraordinary idea!). It is also used for warnings (Look out!) and after interjections (Ouch!).*

**executive** *noun* a senior person with authority in a business.

**executor** *noun* somebody appointed to carry out a person's instructions in their will. *Her son was the executor of her will.*

**exercise** *noun* 1 movements done to keep healthy or train for a particular sport. *Cycling and swimming are good forms of exercise. Gymnastic exercises.* 2 a short piece of work, especially a set of questions for practice at school. *A grammar exercise.*

**exercise** *verb* 1 to do exercises to become fit and healthy. *I try to exercise every day.* 2 If a problem exercises your mind, you think a lot about it.

Some people exercise every day to keep fit.

**exert** *verb* to use power or influence in order to achieve something. If you exert yourself, you make an effort. **exertion** *noun.*

**exhaust** *verb* 1 to tire out. *I'm exhausted.* 2 to use up completely. *Our food supplies were soon exhausted.* **exhausting** *adjective.*

**exhaust** *noun* 1 the waste gas produced by an engine. 2 the pipe through which waste gas escapes, also called an exhaust pipe.

**exhaustion** *noun* the state of being tired out. *Physical and mental exhaustion set in after we had worked all day at a boring job.*

**exhaustive** *adjective* thorough, comprehensive. *An exhaustive search.*

**exhibit** *verb* 1 to show in public in a museum or a gallery. *The gallery exhibited the artist's latest paintings.* 2 to show your feelings to other people. *His manner exhibited signs of distress.*

**exhibit** *noun* something exhibited in a museum or gallery. *Please do not touch the exhibits.*

**exhibition** *noun* a collection of things shown in a public place.

**exile** *noun* 1 a person who has been forced to leave his country, usually for political reasons. 2 having to live away from your own country. *He died alone and in exile.* **exile** *verb.*

**exist** *verb* 1 to be real. *Do you think ghosts really exist?* 2 to stay alive. *She exists on love alone.* **existence** *noun.*

**exit** *noun* 1 a way out. *Where's the exit?* 2 leaving a room or the stage. *She made a quick exit.* **exit** *verb* to leave.

**exorcize** *verb* to get rid of an evil spirit. *They had special rituals to exorcize ghosts.* **exorcism** *noun.* **exorcist** *noun.*

**exotic** *adjective* unusual and interesting. *There are many exotic flowers in the botanical gardens.*

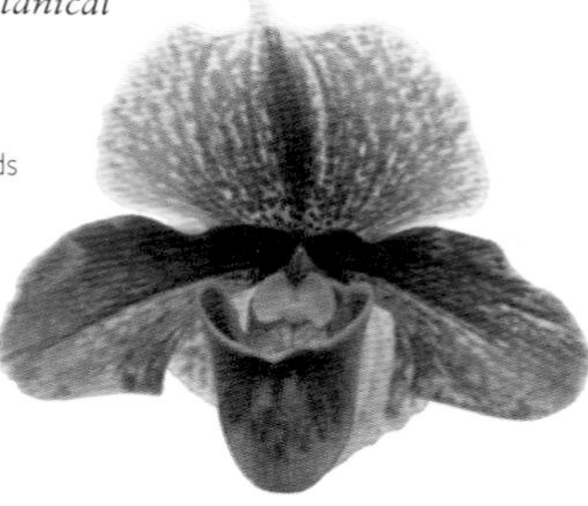

The orchid is a very exotic flower. Orchids grow wild in tropical countries.

**expand** *verb* to become larger. *Scientists say the universe is expanding.* **expansion** *noun.*

**expand** *verb* When you expand on something, you tell a story in more detail.

**expect** *verb* 1 to think that something will happen. *I never expected to win the race. She expects them to make their own beds.* 2 to believe that somebody will come. *We are expecting them at five o'clock.* **expectation** *noun. The holiday didn't come up to our expectations.*

**expel** (expels, expelling, expelled) *verb* 1 to send somebody away, usually for doing wrong. *He was expelled from school for severe misbehaviour.* 2 to force out. *When you breathe out, air is expelled from your lungs.*

**expend** *verb* to spend or use up. *She expended a lot of energy.*

**expenditure** *noun* the spending of money or effort.

**expense** *noun* spending money. If you spare no expense, you don't worry about the cost of something. *I've had a lot of expenses during this past month.*

**expensive** *adjective* costing a lot of money. *He drives an expensive car.* **expensively** *adverb. Expensively dressed.*

**experience** *noun* 1 knowledge or skill gained from doing or seeing things. *Most shops only employ people with sales experience.* 2 an event that has happened to you. *Riding a camel is a strange and wonderful experience.* **experience** *verb* to have something happen to you. *She has experienced great sadness in her life.*

**DID YOU KNOW?**

*Exports are sent to and sold in another country, while imports are bought in and sent from another country.*

**experiment** *noun* a test made in order to learn or prove something. *A scientific experiment.* **experiment** *verb* to try things out and make experiments. *We know that it's dangerous to experiment with drugs.* **experimental** *adjective.*

In this experiment, a tin is left on the grass for a few days. Starved of light, the grass under the tin turns yellow.

**explain** *verb* 1 to make something clear so it can be understood. *He explained how to use the computer.* 2 to give a reason for something. *That explains his strange behaviour.* **explanation** *noun.*

**explode** *verb* 1 to blow up, especially of a bomb. 2 to burst out suddenly or show violent feelings. *She exploded with anger.* **explosion** *noun.* **explosive** *adjective. Explosive materials.*

**exploit** (say **eks**-ploit) *noun* a brave or adventurous deed.

**exploit** (say iks-**ploit**) *verb* 1 to use or develop, especially a country's natural resources. *Exploiting the country's diamond wealth.* 2 to use unfairly and selfishly for your own profit. *The poor have always been exploited.* **exploitation** *noun.*

**explore** *verb* 1 to travel to places in order to find out what they are like. 2 to examine something and learn about it. *Have you definitely explored all the possibilities?* **exploration** *noun.*

**explorer** *noun* somebody who explores. *An Arctic explorer.*

**export** *verb* to send goods to another country for sale. **export** *noun* 1 exporting goods. *The export of ivory has been banned.* 2 exported goods. Exports are products sold in another country. *Exports are up this year.*

Sir Walter Raleigh first brought tobacco and potatoes from South America to Britain. Now tobacco is one of South America's main exports.

E

**expulsion** *noun* expelling or being expelled. *The football hooligans faced expulsion.*

**extend** *verb* 1 to stretch out or make bigger. *They extended the garden.* 2 to offer. *They extended a warm welcome to the delegation of foreign visitors.*

**extension** *noun* 1 an extra period of time. *I should have handed my essay in today, but the teacher gave me an extension.* 2 something added on, especially a room or building. *The new extension to the school will house the library.* 3 an additional telephone connected to the same line. *I'll take the call on the extension in my office.*

**extensive** *adjective* covering a large area or amount. *There was extensive damage to the building from the bomb blast.*

**exterior** *noun* the outside of something. **exterior** *adjective. The exterior walls are gradually crumbling away.*

**exterminate** *verb* to destroy or kill. *Many tribes have been exterminated.* **extermination** *noun.* **exterminator** *noun.*

**extinct** *adjective* 1 not existing any more. *Dinosaurs have been extinct for millions of years.* 2 no longer active. *An extinct volcano.*

Extinct animals such as dinosaurs can be studied from their fossilized remains.

**extra** *adjective, adverb* more than usual, additional. *She says the vitamin tablets give her extra strength.*

**extract** (say iks-**trakt**) *verb* 1 to pull or take something out. *The dentist had to extract two teeth.* 2 to obtain, against a person's will. *They used force to extract information.*

**extract** (say **eks**-trakt) *noun* 1 a small part taken from a book or film. *They printed extracts from the new book in the newspaper.* 2 something that has been extracted. *Meat extract.*

**extraordinary** *adjective* 1 very strange or unusual. *It was an extraordinary sight.* 2 unusually great. *She has an extraordinary musical talent.*

**extravagance** *noun* 1 spending more money than is reasonable or you can afford. 2 something that is very expensive. *A sports car is a real extravagance.* **extravagant** *adjective. She has extravagant tastes.*

**exuberant** *adjective* full of energy and cheerfulness. *They greeted us noisily with lots of exuberant shouting and waving.* **exuberance** *noun.*

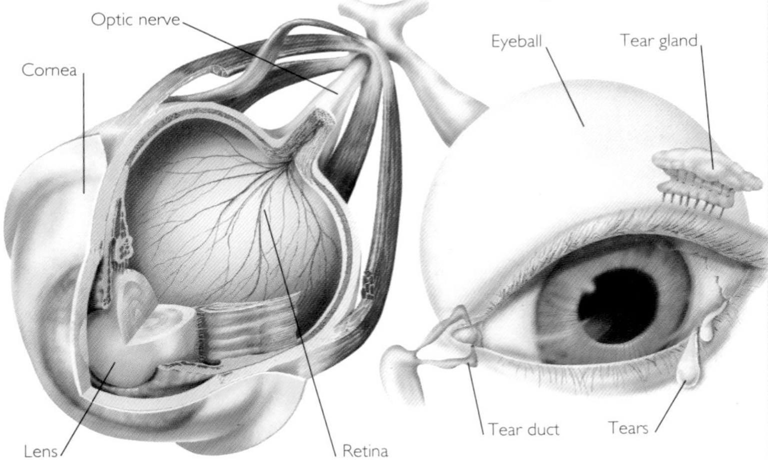


You see something when light bounces off it and enters your eyes.

**eye** *noun* 1 one of two organs in the face to see with. *We close our eyes when we go to sleep.* 2 the power of seeing. *To have sharp eyes.* 3 the hole in a needle through which the thread passes. 4 a dark spot on a vegetable, such as a potato, from which a new plant grows. **eye** *verb* to watch or look at closely. *He eyed her jealously.* **keep an eye on** to watch somebody or something. *Please keep an eye on the house while we're away.*

**eyeball** *noun* the whole of the eye, formed like a ball, including the part concealed behind the eyelids.

**eyebrow** *noun* the line of hairs growing above the eyes.

**eyelash** *noun* one of the hairs that grow on the edge of your upper and lower eyelids.

**eyelid** *noun* either of the two pieces of covering skin that move down when you close your eyes or blink.

**eyesight** *noun* the power to see. *He wears glasses because he has poor eyesight.*

**eyewitness** *noun* a person who has seen an accident or a crime happen and can describe it. *Will eyewitnesses to the accident please contact the police.*

**eyrie** (rhymes with 'weary') *noun* an eagle's nest. *The eagle builds its eyrie of large twigs.*

**WORD BUILDING**

*The prefix 'extra–' comes from the Latin for outside or beyond. So something that is extraordinary is 'outside the usual order'.*

An eagle builds its eyrie way up in the mountains. The parent birds use the nest every year, and each year they make it a bit bigger.

# Ff

**fable** *noun* a short story, usually one with animals, that teaches a lesson about behaviour or truth.

**fabric** *noun* 1 cloth. 2 the structure of a building or the system of a society.

**face** *noun* 1 the front part of the head. 2 a look or expression on the face. *A sad face.* 3 the front, upper side or surface of something. *The north face of the mountain.* **face to face** looking straight at each other.

**face** *verb* 1 to have or turn the front towards a certain direction. *Our house faces the park.* 2 to be brave enough to deal with something unpleasant or dangerous. *I can't face the truth.* 3 to cover a surface, such as a wall, with a layer of different material.

**facsimile** (say fak-**sim**-il-ee) *noun* an exact copy or reproduction.

**fact** *noun* something that is true or has actually happened. **in fact** really.

**factor** *noun* 1 one of the things that influences an event and brings about a result. *Money was a very important factor in the decision.* 2 a number by which a larger number can be divided. *2 and 4 are factors of 8.*

**factory** (factories) *noun* a large building where goods are made, usually by machines.

Smoke from factories pollutes the atmosphere.

**factual** *adjective* based on facts. *She gave a factual account of events.*

**faculty** *noun* 1 any of the powers of the mind or body, such as speech or understanding. *After the accident her faculties were impaired.* 2 a large department in a university.

**fade** *verb* 1 to become less strong or clear. *The colours have faded in the sunshine.* 2 to disappear gradually.

**Fahrenheit** *adjective* measuring temperature on a scale where water freezes at 32° and boils at 212°.

**DID YOU KNOW?**

*The most famous collection of fables was supposedly written by a Greek slave over 2,500 years ago. The writer's name was Aesop.*

**WORD HISTORY**

*The word 'fairy' comes from the French 'faie' and the Latin 'fata', which means 'the Fates'. These were three goddesses who controlled people's lives.*

**WORD HISTORY**

*The Fahrenheit scale was named after its inventor, the German scientist Daniel Gabriel Fahrenheit (1686–1736).*

**fail** *verb* 1 to try to do something and not succeed. *All my plans failed.* 2 not to do or remember something. *You failed to warn me that she doesn't like dogs.* 3 not to produce the expected result or work as expected. *The brakes failed.* 4 If a teacher fails you, she grades you as not having passed a test. **failed** *adjective* unsuccessful.

**failing** *noun* a weakness or fault.

**failure** *noun* 1 lack of success, failing to do something. *After many failures, he has succeeded at last.* 2 an unsuccessful person.

**faint** *adjective* weak, not clear. *The writing was very faint.*

**faint** *verb* to lose consciousness suddenly. *He faints at the sight of blood.*

**fair** *noun* 1 a festival with roundabouts, shows and other amusements. 2 a market or exhibition where goods are displayed and sold. *A trade fair.*

**fair** *adjective* 1 honest and just. 2 pale or light in colour. 3 fine, especially when talking about the weather. 4 fairly good. *After living in France for a year, he has a fair knowledge of French.* **fairness** *noun.*

**fairground** *noun* the place where a fair is held. *Fairground rides.*

We had fun at the fairground.

**fairly** *adverb* 1 quite, to some extent. *This restaurant is fairly cheap.* 2 in a fair way. *The election was conducted fairly.*

**fairy** (fairies) *noun* a small imaginary person with magical powers.

**fairy tale** *noun* a story about fairies and other creatures with magical powers.

**faith** *noun* 1 a strong belief or trust. 2 a particular religion. *The Christian faith.*

**faithful** *adjective* trustworthy and loyal. **faithfully** *adverb.*

**fake** *noun* a person or thing that is not what it is supposed to be or looks like. *The painting is a fake.* **fake** *verb* 1 to make something look better or more valuable in order to deceive people. 2 to pretend. *He faked a stomach ache to get off school.*

**falcon** *noun* a bird of prey that can be trained to hunt other birds and animals. **falconry** *noun.*

F

**fall** (falls, falling, fell, fallen) *verb* 1 to come or go down, to drop to a lower place. *A brick fell on his head.* 2 to become lower. *The temperature fell.* 3 to happen. *Silence fell.* 4 to become or pass into another state. *I have fallen in love.* 5 to die in battle. **fall apart** to break into pieces. **fall behind** to not produce something on time, especially money. *He's fallen behind with the rent.* **fall for** 1 If you fall for somebody, you are attracted to them. 2 to be deceived by. *I don't fall for his tricks.* **fall out** to quarrel. **fall through** to fail. *The plan fell through.*

The spectacular Iguaçu Falls are a string of 275 waterfalls on the border between Argentina and Brazil.

**fall** *noun* 1 a drop from a higher to a lower place. 2 getting lower or less. 3 a waterfall. *Niagara Falls.* 4 (US) autumn, the season between summer and winter.

**false** *adjective* 1 not true, wrong. *She gave a false address to the police.* 2 not natural, artificial. *False teeth.*

**falsehood** *noun* 1 something not true, a lie. 2 telling lies.

**fame** *noun* being famous. *Her fame soon spread throughout the country.*

**familiar** *adjective* 1 well known. 2 knowing something well. *Are you familiar with this play?* 3 very friendly.

**family** *noun* 1 parents and their children, grandparents and other relations. 2 a group of related things, especially animals or plants. *Lions belong to the cat family.*

**famine** *noun* a severe lack of food in a region. *There is a terrible famine in Africa.*

**famous** *adjective* well known by many people. *A famous actor.*

**fan** *noun* something that moves the air to make you or a room cooler.

**fan** (fans, fanning, fanned) *verb* to make the air move.

**fan** *noun* an admirer or supporter. *Dean is a football fan.*

In summer, a fan is essential in a hot office.

**fancy** (fancies, fancying, fancied) *verb* 1 to want to do or have something. *Do you fancy a game of tennis?* 2 to imagine. *He fancies himself as a dancer.* **fancy** (fancies) *noun* 1 an imagined or unlikely idea. 2 a liking. *I have taken a fancy to that restaurant.* **fanciful** *adjective.*

**GRAMMAR NOTE**

*When talking about distance you can use 'farther' or 'further', and 'farthest' or 'furthest'. But when talking about time, you can only use 'further/furthest'. 'Remain here until further notice.'*

**fancy** *adjective* brightly coloured and decorated. *Fancy dress.*

**fang** *noun* a long sharp tooth.

**fantasy** (fantasies) *noun* something imagined, a situation that you think about. *His mind is crammed full of fantasies.* **fantastic** *adjective.*

**far** (farther/further, farthest/furthest) *adverb* 1 at or to a great distance. *I live not far from here.* 2 much. *That's far too expensive.* **far** *adjective* distant, a long way off.

**far-fetched** *adjective* unlikely or impossible, especially an idea or example. *His story was too far-fetched for us to believe.*

**far-reaching** *adjective* having wide influence or effect over a long period of time. *Far-reaching reforms.*

**farce** *noun* 1 a play in which lots of silly things happen. 2 an event that is treated too lightly and becomes ridiculous. *The election was a farce as the winner had already been decided on.* **farcical** *adjective.*

**fare** *noun* 1 the money paid by passengers for a journey. 2 food and drink.

The farmer is at work in the tractor, baling the hay.

**fare** *verb* to get along. If you fare badly, you are unsuccessful or treated badly.

**farm** *noun* 1 a place where crops are grown and animals are kept. 2 a farmhouse. **farm** *verb* to grow crops or raise animals.

**farmer** *noun* a person who owns or works on a farm. *My ambition is to be a farmer.*

**farther** *adjective, adverb* at or to a more distant point. *I'm too tired, I can't walk any farther up the mountain.*

**farthest** *adjective, adverb* at or to a most distant point.

**fascinate** *verb* to attract and be very interesting. *He has always been fascinated by space travel.* **fascination** *noun.* **fascinating** *adjective.*

**fashion** *noun* 1 the style of clothes or the way of doing something at a particular time. *Short skirts are back in fashion this autumn.* 2 a way of doing something. *She walks in a strange fashion.* **fashionable** *adjective.* **fashionably** *adverb.*

**fast** *adjective* 1 quick. *A fast car.* 2 firmly fixed. *Wash the shirt separately, the colours aren't fast.* 3 showing a time that is later than the real time. *My watch is fast.* **fast food** hot food that is cooked and served quickly after ordering.

**fast** *adverb* 1 quickly. *He was driving too fast.* 2 fully. *She was fast asleep.*

**fast** *verb* to eat no food. *Lent is a time of fasting.* **fast** *noun.*

**fasten** *verb* 1 to fix one thing to another. 2 to close or lock. *Fasten your seatbelts.* **fastener** *noun.* **fastening** *noun.*

**fat** *noun* 1 the greasy part of human flesh or animal meat. *Fat under the skin keeps us warm.* 2 oil or grease used for cooking.

**fat** (fatter, fattest) *adjective* 1 Fat people have a lot of flesh on their body. *He is fat because he eats too much.* 2 thick or large. *A fat book.* **fatness** *noun.*

**fatal** *adjective* bringing or ending in death. *A fatal accident.* **fatally** *adverb.*

**fate** *noun* 1 the power that is believed to control events. *Fate was against us.* 2 what will happen or has happened to somebody. *It was her fate.*

**father** *noun* a male parent. *Your father and mother are your parents.*

**father-in-law** *noun* the father of your wife or husband.

**fatigue** *noun* 1 a feeling of great tiredness. 2 weakness in metals caused by stress.

**fault** *noun* 1 something wrong, a mistake or imperfection. *An electrical fault.* 2 a bad point about a person or thing. *He's always finding fault with me.* 3 a crack in the surface of the earth. *Earthquakes usually occur along faults.* **fault** *verb* to find fault with something or somebody. *His attitude can't be faulted.* **faulty** *adjective.*

Earthquakes occur along faults.

**fauna** *noun* all the wild animals living in a region. *She was studying the flora and fauna of the Alps.*

**favour** *noun* 1 a liking of somebody or something. *He is trying to win her favour.* 2 If you are in favour of something, you like the idea of it. If somebody is in favour, he is liked. If he is out of favour, he is not liked. 3 a kind act. *Could you do me a favour and take me to the station?* **favour** *verb* 1 to like or support, especially a plan or an idea. *The government favours free school meals.* 2 to be kinder to one person than another. *The teacher tends to favour the girls.*

**AMAZING FACT**

'Phobia' means 'fear of'. There is a state called 'phobophobia' which means 'fear of fear'.

Some people have an irrational fear of spiders.

**WORD HISTORY**

*The phrase 'a feather in your cap' comes from a Native American custom. Indian braves were given a feather for their headdress for every warrior they killed in battle.*

**WORD HISTORY**

*Fauna was the name of a Roman goddess of the countryside. She was the sister of Faunus, who was associated with the Greek god Pan.*

**favourable** *adjective* good, approving. *The teacher gave her a favourable report.*

**favourite** *adjective* liked more than all others. *What is your favourite TV programme?* **favourite** *noun* 1 a person or thing preferred over others. *This book is my favourite.* 2 in sport, the competitor expected to win.

**favouritism** *noun* being unfairly kinder to one person than another. *It's not fair if teachers show favouritism.*

**fear** *noun* 1 an unpleasant feeling that something dangerous or painful might happen. *She has a fear of flying.* 2 danger. *There is no fear of failure.* **fear** *verb* to be afraid or worry about something or somebody. *They feared for their lives.* **for fear of** because of worry about something. *I didn't ring the bell last night for fear of disturbing you.* **never fear** there is no danger of that.

**fearful** *adjective* 1 causing fear or being afraid. *A fearful storm.* 2 bad, terrible, great. *Your room is always in a fearful mess.*

**fearless** *adjective* without fear, not afraid. *She was fearless in the face of danger.* **fearlessly** *adverb.*

**fearsome** *adjective* terrible or frightening. *The monster was a fearsome sight.*

**feasible** *adjective* possible, that can be done. *Is it feasible to rebuild the bridge?*

**feast** *noun* 1 a large and very good meal. *A wedding feast.* 2 a religious festival. **feast** *verb* to eat and drink very well.

**feat** *noun* a courageous or skilful action that is difficult to do.

**feather** *noun* one of the many soft, light things that cover a bird's body. **as light as a feather** very light. **a feather in your cap** an achievement that you can be proud of.

**feature** *noun* 1 an important part. *Sand is a feature of the desert.* 2 an important part of your face. *Your eyes, mouth and nose make up your features.* 3 an article in a newspaper or a special programme on radio or television.

**feature** *verb* to be an important part of something. *The film features an unknown but very beautiful actress.*

**February** *noun* the second month of the year. February has 28 days, but in leap years it has 29.

**fed** past tense of feed.

**federation** *noun* a united group of states with one government.

**fee** *noun* a sum of money paid for services. *The agency charges a fee for arranging holidays abroad.*

**feeble** *adjective* weak, having very little power. *He made rather a feeble attempt.* **feebly** *adverb.*

**feed** (feeds, feeding, fed) *verb* 1 to give food to. *Don't forget to feed the cat.* 2 to eat. *Horses feed on hay.* 3 to put something in. *All the data has been fed into the computer.* **feed** *noun* food for animals.

**feedback** *noun* comments about something that you have done, so that possible changes can be made. *Most shops welcome feedback from their customers.*

**feel** (feels, feeling, felt) *verb* 1 to touch something with your fingers or hold it. *Just feel the quality of the fabric.* 2 to be a certain sensation – wet, dry, soft or sticky, for example. *My clothes feel damp.* 3 to be aware of a mood or to know that something is happening to your body. *I'm not feeling well.* 4 to think something or have an opinion. *I feel strongly that the action is wrong.* 5 to search, usually with your hands, feet or a stick. *He felt in his pockets for money.* **feel** *noun. I like the feel of silk.* **feel like** to want. *I feel like a swim.*

**feeler** *noun* the long, thin part on the front of an insect's head with which it touches things. **put out feelers** to suggest something in order to find out what others think or want to do.

Feelers

An insect uses its feelers to help it find its way about.

**feeling** *noun* 1 the power to feel things. *I'm so cold, I've lost all feeling in my hands.* 2 an emotion or physical sensation. *An itchy feeling.* If you have a feeling for somebody or something, you like them. 3 what you think, an idea. *I have a feeling that he'll do very well in the exams.* 4 sympathy and understanding. *He read the poem with great feeling.*

**feet** plural of foot. **fall on one's feet** to have good luck. *He's fallen right on his feet with that new job.*

**feint** (say faynt) *noun* a pretend attack, especially in fencing or boxing. **feint** *verb.*

**feline** (say fee-line) *adjective* like a cat.

**fell** past tense of fall.

**felt** past tense of feel.

**female** *adjective* 1 referring to a woman or girl. *Male and female workers.* 2 A female animal or plant can have babies, lay eggs or produce fruit. *A bitch is a female dog.* **female** *noun* a female person or animal.

**WORD HISTORY**

*'Fence' is a shortened form of the word 'defence', which makes sense both for the wooden barrier and the sport of sword-fighting.*

**AMAZING FACT**

Fencing was once a form of sword practice and a preparation for fighting in duels. Now it is an Olympic sport.

**feminine** *adjective* 1 with the qualities of a woman. *She designs very feminine clothes.* 2 in grammar, referring to words that are classed as female. *French nouns are either masculine or feminine.* **femininity** *noun.*

**feminist** *noun* a person who believes that women should have the same rights and opportunities as men. **feminism** *noun.*

**fence** *noun* a barrier made of wood or wire round an area or used to divide two areas of land. **fence** *verb* 1 to build a fence round an area or along something. *We fenced in the garden to keep the cows out.* 2 to fight with a long thin sword as a sport. **fencing** *noun.*

**ferment** (say fer-**ment**) *verb* to change chemically; to turn liquid into an alcoholic drink by the action of yeast, for example. **fermentation** *noun.*

**fern** *noun* a plant with green, feathery leaves and no flowers.

**ferocious** *adjective* fierce, savage. *A ferocious dog guards the entrance to the house.* **ferocity** *noun.*

**ferret** *noun* a small animal with a pointed nose. Ferrets are used for catching rats and rabbits. **ferret out** *verb* to search for something or find out information.

**ferry** (ferries) *noun* a boat that goes across a river or other narrow channel of water carrying people and cars. **ferry** (ferries, ferrying, ferried) *verb* to transport people or goods. *She ferried the children to and from school every day.*

**fertile** *adjective* 1 land or soil is fertile when plants grow well in it. *Silt from the river makes the land very fertile.* 2 able to produce babies or seeds. 3 full of ideas. *My brother has a very fertile imagination.* **fertility** *noun.*

**fertilize** *verb* 1 to put pollen into a plant or sperm into an egg to make them grow. 2 When you fertilize the soil you add things to it to make it more fertile. **fertilization** *noun.*

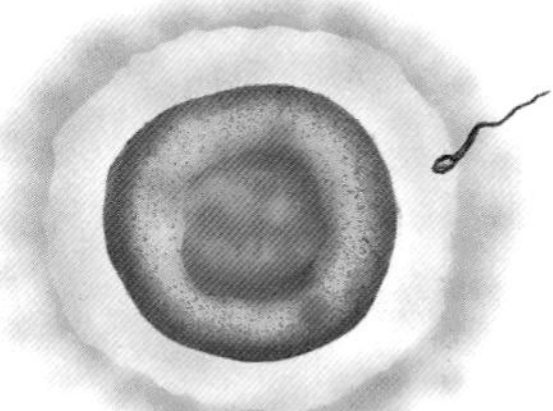

A sperm swims towards an egg. In a moment, fertilization will occur.

**fertilizer** *noun* a natural substance or chemical added to soil to make it more fertile. *Organic fertilizers are best.*

**fester** *verb* 1 to become infected, especially of a wound or cut. 2 to poison the mind, causing bitterness over a period of time. *Hatred still festers between the brothers.*

**festival** *noun* 1 a day or time for public celebration which is usually a holiday. *Christmas is a Christian festival.* 2 a number of events like a concert, ballet or other entertainment at a stated time in a place.

**festive** *adjective* joyful and suitable for a festival. *It was Christmas and we were all in a very festive mood.* **festivity** *noun*.

At New Year the Chinese celebrate by dressing up as a dragon and parading through the streets.

**fetch** *verb* 1 to get and bring back. *We must fetch a doctor.* 2 to be sold for a certain price. *These old books might well fetch a lot of money.*

**fetching** *adjective* attractive.

**fetlock** *noun* the back part of a horse's leg near the foot.

**feud** *noun* (say fewd) a long-lasting quarrel, especially between families.

**feudal** *adjective* (say **few**-dal) relating to a method practised in the Middle Ages in which people were given land in exchange for fighting and working for the owner.

**fever** *noun* 1 a body temperature that is higher than usual, because of illness. 2 an illness that causes a high body temperature. 3 great excitement. *There was a fever of anticipation in the hall.* **feverish** *adjective*.

**few** *adjective*, *pronoun* not many, a small number. *A few went home early.* **fewer than** not as many as. *Fewer than ten students passed the exam.*

**fiancé** *noun* (say fee-**ahn**-say) a man engaged to be married. *She introduced her friends to her fiancé.* **fiancée** *noun* (say fee-**ahn**-say) a woman engaged to be married.

**fiasco** *noun* (say fee-**ass**-koh) an absurd failure. *Everything went wrong and the holiday was a complete fiasco.*

**fibre** *noun* 1 a very thin thread, especially one used to make cloth or rope. 2 parts of plants or seeds which the body cannot digest. Brown bread and beans are high in fibre. 3 a thin piece of flesh, like thread, in the body. *Muscles are made of fibres.* **fibrous** *adjective*.

These are artificial fibres seen under the microscope.

**GRAMMAR NOTE**

*'Fewer' is the comparative form of 'few' and is the right word to use with plural nouns to mean 'not as many'. 'There were fewer people in the shop today.' Use 'less' with singular nouns. 'We had less time today.'*

The Earth's magnetic field is called the magnetosphere.

**fickle** *adjective*. Fickle people always change their mind. They are not loyal in love or friendship. **fickleness** *noun*.

**fiction** *noun* writing or stories about something that is not true. *Is the report I read in the paper fact or fiction?* **fictional** *adjective*.

**fictitious** *adjective* imaginary, invented. *He gave the police a fictitious name.*

**fiddle** *noun* 1 a violin. *He gave us a tune on the fiddle.* 2 a dishonest action, a swindle. **as fit as a fiddle** in very good health.

**fiddle** *verb* 1 to play the violin. 2 to get or change something, especially a bill or an account, dishonestly. *He fiddled the figures.* 3 to touch or move things around with your fingers. *Stop fiddling with the matches.* **play second fiddle** to be less important. *He gets fed up playing second fiddle to his brother.* **fiddler** *noun*.

**fidget** *verb* to move around restlessly and never sit still. *Some children fidget a lot.* **fidget** *noun*.

**field** *noun* 1 a piece of land with grass or crops growing on it. 2 an area of grass marked out for a game. *A football field.* 3 a battlefield. 4 a piece of land where oil, coal, gold or other things might be found. 5 a subject, an area of study or activity. *She is an expert in the field of medical research.* 6 an area of space where something is strong. *A magnetic field.* Your field of vision is the whole area you can see.

**field** *verb* 1 to catch the ball in cricket, baseball or other games. 2 to be on the side whose turn it is to bowl rather than bat in cricket or other games. 3 to play players or a team. *Our school fields three rugby teams.*

**fierce** *adjective* 1 angry and violent. 2 very strong. *In the fierce heat.*

F

**fiery** *adjective* flaming, like fire. *He has a fiery temper.*

**fig** *noun* a soft fruit full of seeds that grows on trees in hot countries. **I don't give a fig** I don't care at all.

Figs ripened in the Sun are one of the most delicious of all fruits.

**fight** (fights, fighting, fought) *verb* 1 to use your hands, weapons or words against another in order to try and win. When people fight, they try to hurt each other. 2 to try to overcome or stop something. *We must fight crime.* When you fight for something, you try to get or keep it. 3 to quarrel. **fight** *noun* 1 the act of fighting somebody, using hands or weapons. 2 a struggle to overcome something. *The fight against poverty.*

**fighter** *noun* 1 a person who fights. 2 a fast military aircraft.

**figure** *noun* 1 a sign that stands for a number. 1, 3 and 9 are figures. 2 an amount, how much money something costs. *A huge figure.* 3 a diagram or drawing, usually in a book. 4 the shape of the body. *She's got a very good figure.* 5 the shape of a person or an animal in a picture or carved in wood or stone. *A wooden figure of an African tribesman.* 6 a person. *He was a great figure in the world of pop music.* **figure of speech** a word or an expression used to produce an impression, making your meaning stronger. 'As pretty as a picture' is a figure of speech.

**figure** *verb* 1 to take part in something. *He doesn't figure much in the article.* 2 to believe, imagine or work out. *I figure they'll make him captain.*

**Fiji** *noun* a country of many islands in the Pacific Ocean.

The flag of Fiji has the Union Jack and a crest against a turquoise blue background.

**file** *noun* a tool with a rough surface for smoothing, cutting or shaping things. *A nail file.* **file** *verb* to smooth, shape or cut with a file. *The woman sat filing her nails.*

**file** *noun* 1 a holder for keeping papers and documents in order. 2 a set of papers kept in a file. 3 information stored in a computer. 4 a line of people or things one behind the other. **file** *verb* 1 to put papers or documents in a file. 2 When you file an application, you apply for something officially. 3 to walk one after another. *The class filed into the room.*

**fill** *verb* 1 to make or become full. 2 to block up. *She pulled the nails out of the wall and filled the holes.*

**DID YOU KNOW?**

*There are 176 different kinds of bird in the finch family. They are found in most regions of the world except Australia, and range in size from 10 to 27 cm long. The finch family includes chaffinches, canaries and crossbills.*

**fillet** *noun* a piece of fish or meat without any bone. **fillet** *verb* to remove the bones from meat or fish.

**filling** *noun* something used to fill something. *I went to the dentist and had two new fillings.*

**film** *noun* 1 moving pictures taken with a film camera which can be seen in the cinema or on television. 2 a roll of thin plastic that is put in a camera for taking photographs or shooting a film. 3 a thin layer. *A film of dust.* **film** *verb* 1 to make a film. 2 to take moving pictures with a film camera.

John took his film to the chemist's to be developed.

**filter** *noun* 1 a device through which liquids are passed to make them clean. 2 a piece of glass or plastic used on a camera lens to hold back light.

**filter** *verb* 1 to pass through a filter. *It's a good idea to filter drinking water.* 2 to pass or move slowly, especially of people, traffic or ideas. *Light filtered through the curtains.*

**filth** *noun* a disgusting amount of dirt. **filthy** *adjective*. *Your bedroom looks filthy.*

**fin** *noun* 1 a wing-like part that a fish uses in swimming. 2 something shaped like a fish's fin, such as a swimmer's flipper or the surface of a car or plane.

**final** *adjective* last, at the end. *The final word on the page.* **final** *noun* the last match in a competition or the last examination. *They are in the Cup Final.* **finalist** *noun*.

**finally** *adverb* 1 lastly or at last. *Finally, I'd like to thank the headmaster.* 2 after a long time. *I finally found out where he lives.*

**finance** *noun* the control and management of money. **finances** *plural noun* money, especially of a business. *How are the firm's finances?* **finance** *verb* to provide money for something. *Who is financing the trip?*

**finch** *noun* a small songbird.

**find** (finds, finding, found) *verb* 1 to get or see somebody or something by searching or by chance. 2 to learn by working, experimenting or by experience. *Doctors are hoping to find a cure for Aids.* **find** *noun* something found.

**fine** *adjective* 1 excellent. *We had a fine time on Sunday.* 2 dry, bright and sunny. *In fine weather.* 3 very thin. *Fine hair.* **fine** *adverb* very well. *That suits me fine.* **cut it fine** to just make it on time.

**fine** *noun* a sum of money to be paid as punishment. *I had to pay a parking fine.* **fine** *verb* to make somebody pay a fine.

**finger** *noun* 1 one of the parts of the hand. You have five fingers on your hand. 2 a thin piece of something. *Fish fingers.* **finger** *verb* to touch with your fingers.

**fingernail** *noun* the hard flat piece at the end of your finger.

**fingerprint** *noun* the mark made by the lines on the skin of the finger. *The thieves left no fingerprints.*

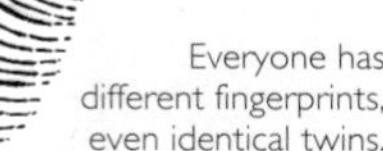

Everyone has different fingerprints, even identical twins.

**finish** *verb* to reach the end or bring to the end.

**finish** (finishes) *noun* 1 the end or last part of something. *The finish of a race.* 2 the coating, especially of painted or polished articles.

**Finland** *noun* a Scandinavian country in Europe.

**Finnish** *noun* the language spoken by the Finns.

The capital of Finland is Helsinki.

**Finnish** *adjective. A Finnish lake.*

**fir** *noun* an evergreen tree with leaves that look like needles. The seeds are formed in cones. *A plantation of firs.*

**fire** *noun* 1 burning with flames. *The house is on fire.* If you set fire to something, you light it in order to burn it. 2 burning coal or wood or an apparatus using gas or electricity for heating or cooking. 3 the shooting of guns. *The enemy opened fire.* **catch fire** to begin to burn.

**fire** *verb* 1 to shoot a gun or propel bullets, missiles or arrows. 2 to let off other things. *He fired lots of questions at us.* 3 to bake pottery. *Clay pots are fired in a kiln.* 4 to dismiss somebody from a job. *He was fired for misconduct.* 5 to excite. *His speech fired our enthusiasm.*

**firearm** *noun* a gun.

**fire engine** *noun* a large vehicle that carries firefighters and equipment for putting out fires. *The fire engine raced towards the fire.*

**firefighter** *noun* a person who puts out fires. *The firefighter was awarded a medal.*

**fireplace** *noun* a place in a room for a fire.

**fireproof** *adjective* fireproof things cannot be damaged by fire or heat.

**firework** *noun* an object filled with chemical powder that makes sparks and noises when lit.

**DID YOU KNOW?**

*Finnish is one of two official languages in Finland. The other is Swedish. An English word borrowed from Finnish is 'sauna'. Finland joined the European Union in 1995.*

**AMAZING FACT**

A fish's fins are used primarily for steering and balance. Most fish propel themselves by beating their tail from side to side.

**firm** *adjective* 1 hard, not changing shape when pressed. *Firm muscles.* 2 steady, not shaking or moving. *Keep a firm grip on it.* 3 strong and sure, not likely to change. *We need a firm decision.*

**firm** *noun* a business or organization. *He works for a computer firm.*

**first** *adjective, adverb* before all others or everything else. *He came first in the race.* **at first** in the beginning. *They didn't like each other at first.* **first** *noun* the first thing, person or event. *I was the first to know.*

**first aid** *noun* emergency treatment given to an injured person, usually before a doctor arrives. *She went on a first aid course.*

**first name** *noun* your given or Christian name. *My first name is Jane.*

**first-rate** *adjective* excellent. *A first-rate performance.*

**fish** (fish or fishes) *noun* an animal that lives and breathes in water. Fish use their fins and tail to swim.

**fish** *verb* 1 to try and catch fish. *We went fishing on holiday.* 2 to try to get something, especially information or compliments. *She is fishing for praise.* 3 to pull something out.

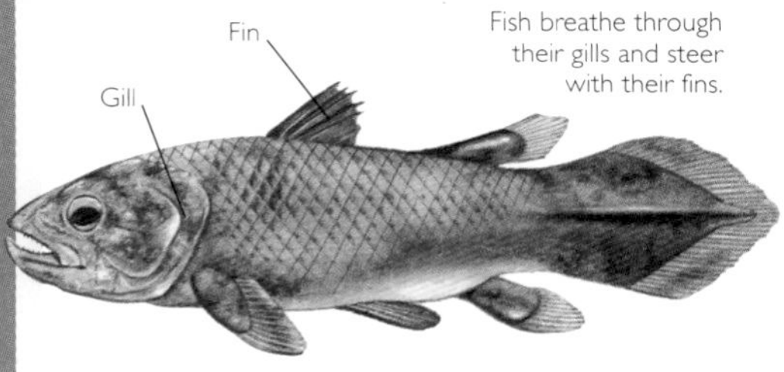


Fish breathe through their gills and steer with their fins.

**fisherman** *noun* a man who catches fish, usually for a living.

**fist** *noun* a hand with the fingers tightly closed. *In boxing you fight with your fists.*

**fit** (fitter, fittest) *adjective* 1 right or good enough. *The meal was fit for a king.* 2 healthy. *She goes jogging every day to keep fit.* **fitness** *noun.*

**fit** (fits, fitting, fitted) *verb* 1 to be the right size or shape. *The shoes don't fit, they're too small.* 2 to make clothes the right size and shape for somebody. *He had a suit fitted.* 3 to put into place. *We had a new lock fitted on the door.* 4 to be or make suitable. *The description fits her well.* **fit in** 1 to feel comfortable among a group of people. 2 to find time to do something. *We'll fit in an extra lesson before the exam.*

**fit** *noun* 1 the way something fits. 2 a sudden attack of an illness or loss of consciousness. *A coughing fit.* 3 an outburst. *He hit him in a fit of anger.* **have someone in fits** to make someone laugh uncontrollably.

F

**fix** *verb* 1 to make something firm, to attach it. 2 to decide or arrange. *We have fixed the date for our holiday.* 3 to repair. *He managed to fix the bike.* 4 to treat colours or a photographic film with chemicals to protect them from light. 5 to prepare or cook, especially food or a drink. *I'll fix myself dinner.* **fix up** to arrange.

**fix** *noun* 1 something arranged, especially by deception. *The election was a fix.* 2 an injection of illegal drugs. **in a fix** in a difficult situation.

**fixture** *noun* 1 built-in furniture or equipment that is fixed to a house or flat and left behind when you move. *The bath and lights are fixtures.* 2 a match or other competition that has been arranged to take place on a particular date. *All the football matches are in the fixture list.*

**fizzy** *adjective* bubbling. *A fizzy drink.*

**fjord** *noun* (say fee-ord) a long narrow inlet of sea between steep cliffs, especially in Norway. *Norwegian fjords.*

The fjords of Norway were created by glaciers during the Ice Age.

**flabby** *adjective* too soft, fat. *He's a bit flabby around the waist.*

**flag** *noun* a piece of cloth with a design on it, which is used as a signal or sign of something, especially a country.

**WORD HISTORY**

*'A flash in the pan' referred originally to a flash in the lock-pan of an old gun called a musket. Sometimes it only flashed instead of lighting the charge and firing when the trigger was pulled.*

**flamingo** (flamingos or flamingoes) *noun* a tropical water bird with long legs and pink feathers. *Flamingo pink.*

Flamingoes, with their soft pink feathers, are among the world's most beautiful birds.

**flammable** *adjective* likely to catch fire or burn easily. Flammable is the same as inflammable. The opposite of flammable is non-flammable.

**flank** *noun* the side of something, especially an animal. **flank** *verb* to be placed on one or both sides. *The actress was flanked by two tall men in dinner suits.*

**flap** (flaps, flapping, flapped) *verb* 1 to move up and down or from side to side. *The bird flapped its wings and took off.* 2 to panic or become anxious.

**flap** *noun* 1 a piece of material or flat part of something that covers an opening. *A cap with ear flaps.* 2 the sound of flapping. 3 a state of anxiety or panic. *I got into a terrible flap when I couldn't find my purse.*

**flare** *noun* 1 a sudden bright flame or light. 2 a device producing a bright light that is used as a signal. **flare** *verb* to burn with a bright flame for a short time. **flare up** to show sudden anger.

**flared** *adjective* shaped so as to get wider towards the bottom. *Flared trousers.*

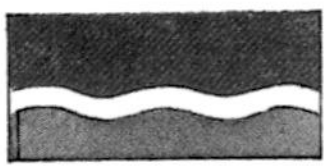

Each country is represented by its own flag.

**flag** (flags. flagging, flagged) *verb* 1 to become weak. *My interest is flagging.* 2 to signal with a flag. **flag down** to wave, especially at a car, to make it stop.

**flagstone** *noun* a stone slab used for paving.

**flair** *noun* instinctive talent. *She has a real flair for fashion.*

**flake** *noun* 1 a small, thin piece of something. *Flakes of paint.* 2 a piece of falling snow. **flake** *verb* to come off in flakes. *The paint is starting to flake.*

**flame** *noun* a portion of fire or burning gas. *The car burst into flames.* **in flames** burning.

**AMAZING FACT**

Signal flags for sending messages at sea include a flag for each letter of the alphabet and the numbers 1–10.

**flash** (flashes) *noun* 1 a sudden bright light. *Flashes of lightning.* 2 a sudden idea or display of wit. *She had a flash of inspiration.* 3 a device producing a sudden bright light for taking photographs in the dark. 4 a short news report. **flash in the pan** a sudden short-lived success. **in a flash** quickly. *The ambulance was there in a flash.*

**flash** *verb* 1 to shine brightly once or several times. *Lights flashed across the sky.* 2 to suddenly think of something. *It flashed through my mind that he was lying.* 3 to move very fast or appear suddenly. *Cars flashed past me.* 4 When you flash a look at somebody, you look at them very quickly.

F

**flashback** *noun* a scene in a film or story that shows events that happened in the past.

**flat** (flatter, flattest) *adjective* 1 not curved, smooth with no bumps. 2 spread out. *Lie down flat on the ground.* 3 dull or boring. *Everything seems very flat since our holiday.* 4 not deep or high. *She is wearing flat shoes.* 5 complete or absolute. *A flat refusal.* 6 A flat tyre has no air in it. A flat drink is not fizzy. A flat battery no longer produces electricity. **flat** *adverb* 1 exactly. *He arrived in five minutes flat.* 2 If something falls flat, it is unsuccessful. **flat out** 1 at top speed. 2 using all your energy. *I'm working flat out.*

AMAZING FACT

Flint was used by Stone Age people to make tools and weapons.

The farmlands of Arizona, USA are flat and featureless.

**flat** *noun* a set of rooms on one floor of a building. *A rented flat.*

**flatten** *verb* to make or become flat.

**flatter** *verb* 1 to say that a person or thing is better, more important or beautiful than they really are. 2 to show somebody or something as better then they really are. *The picture flatters her.* **flattery** *noun.*

**flavour** *noun* the taste of something. **flavour** *verb* to give a taste to something. *Flavour it with vanilla.* **flavouring** *noun.*

**flaw** *noun* something that makes a person or thing imperfect, something wrong. **flawed** *adjective.*

**flea** *noun* a small jumping insect that bites and sucks blood from people and animals.

**fledgling** *noun* a young bird.

**flee** (flees, fleeing, fled) *verb* to run away from something or somewhere. *We had to flee the country.*

**fleece** *noun* the woolly covering of sheep.

**fleece** *verb* to trick a person out of their money. *We were fleeced in the market.*

**fleet** *noun* a group of ships, planes or other vehicles belonging to one country or company. *A fleet of taxis.*

**flesh** *noun* 1 the soft substance that includes fat and muscle between the bones and the skin of people and animals. 2 the soft part of fruit and vegetables. **fleshy** *adjective.* **in the flesh** in real life. *He doesn't look so tall in the flesh.* **flesh out** to give more details.

DID YOU KNOW?

*There are about 1,600 different kinds of fleas around the world. Some are tiny, and the largest is 8 mm long. One of the best jumpers is the cat flea, which is known to have reached a height of 34 cm in a single jump.*

**flew** past tense of fly.

**flex** *verb* to bend or stretch, especially a muscle, leg or arm. *He flexed his muscles.*

**flex** (flexes) *noun* a long flexible covered wire for electricity.

**flexible** *adjective* 1 easily bent. 2 easily changed to suit new conditions, or adaptable. *I prefer flexible working hours.* **flexibility** *noun.*

**flicker** *verb* 1 to burn or shine unsteadily. 2 to move lightly or jerkily. *His eyelids flickered.* **flicker** *noun.*

**flight** *noun* 1 flying. 2 a plane journey. 3 a set of stairs. 4 the act of running away and escaping. 5 a group of birds flying together. *A flight of geese.*

**flimsy** (flimsier, flimsiest) *adjective* thin or light and easily damaged. **flimsily** *adverb. The wardrobe is very flimsily built.* **flimsiness** *noun.*

**fling** (flings, flinging, flung) *verb* 1 to throw quickly or carelessly. *She flung a few clothes in a case and left.* 2 to move quickly and violently. *She flung her head back angrily.*

**fling** *noun* 1 throwing something quickly. 2 a short, wild time of fun and enjoyment. 3 a dance.

**flint** *noun* 1 a hard grey stone. 2 a small piece of flint or hard metal that can be struck to produce sparks and light things.

Flints were shaped by Stone Age people and used as tools.

**flip** (flips, flipping, flipped) *verb* 1 to turn something over quickly. 2 to move something into a different position or send it spinning in the air with a quick push or light hit. *She flipped open her diary and searched for the appointment.* **flip** *noun.*

**flippant** *adjective* not serious, especially when trying to be amusing. *She made some very flippant remarks.* **flippancy** *noun.*

**flipper** *noun* 1 the flat limb of some sea animals used for swimming. 2 Flippers are attachments you can wear on your feet to help you swim more quickly.

**flirt** *verb* to behave in a playful way as if you were attracted to somebody. *She flirts with all the boys.* **flirt** *noun* somebody who flirts a lot. **flirtatious** *adjective.*

**float** *verb* 1 to stay or move in a liquid or in the air. *We floated down the river.* 2 to move aimlessly about. *She floats from one job to another without ever settling down.*

**float** *noun* 1 a light object, such as a cork, that is used to help somebody or something float. 2 a lorry on which special shows of people and things travel through the streets in a festival procession. 3 a sum of money kept, especially by shopkeepers, for giving change or paying small bills.

**floating voter** *noun* somebody who does not always vote for the same party.

**flock** *noun* a group of sheep, goats or birds. **flock** *verb* to gather or move in large crowds. *People flocked to the fair.*

**floe** *noun* (rhymes with glow) a sheet of floating ice. *Ice floes.*

**flog** (flogs, flogging, flogged) *verb* 1 to beat a person or an animal, especially with a whip or rod. 2 (slang) to sell. *He flogged us his old car and bought a new one.* **flogging** *noun.*

**flood** *noun* 1 a large amount of water in a place that is usually dry. *The village was almost destroyed by the flood.* 2 a large amount. *A flood of complaints.* **flood** *verb* 1 to cover with a flood. 2 to arrive in large amounts. *Calls flooded in.*

The flood washed away the houses and made the people homeless.

**floor** *noun* 1 the surface, especially of a room, that you walk on. 2 all the rooms that are on the same level in a building. *Our flat is on the second floor.* 3 The ground at the bottom of the sea, a cave or a valley.

**floor** *verb* 1 to knock down. *The punch floored him.* 2 to confuse. *His question completely floored me.*

**flop** (flops, flopping, flopped) *verb* 1 to sit or lie down suddenly and heavily. 2 to fail or be unsuccessful. *The play flopped.* **flop** *noun* 1 a flopping movement or sound. 2 a total failure.

**floppy** *adjective* not firm, hanging loosely. *They wore floppy hats.*

**floppy disk** *noun* a disk that can be put into a computer to transfer information, also called a diskette.

**WORD HISTORY**

*An ice floe comes from the Norwegian word 'flo', which originally meant a layer. Other Norwegian words are 'fjord' and 'ski'.*

**DID YOU KNOW?**

*To the British, the first floor of a building is the one above the ground floor. To Americans this is the second floor, because they call the ground floor the first floor.*

**flora** *noun* all the plants growing in a region. *Flora and fauna.*

Mountain flora, such as edelweiss and mountain avens, grow well in the poor rocky soil above the tree-line.

**florist** *noun* a person or shop that sells flowers. *The florist's art is arranging flowers.*

**flour** *noun* a powder made from ground grain, especially wheat, used to make bread and cakes. **floury** *adjective.*

**flourish** (flourishes, flourishing, flourished) *verb* 1 to grow healthily. 2 to be well and successful. *The shop is flourishing, we are going to expand.* 3 to wave something about for people to notice it. *He rushed into the room flourishing a cheque.* **flourish** *noun.*

**flow** *verb* 1 to move along smoothly. *The conversation soon began to flow really well.* 2 to hang down loosely, especially of clothing or hair. **flow** *noun.*

**flower** *noun* 1 the coloured or white part of a plant which produces seeds and fruit. 2 the flower and its stem. **flower** *verb* to produce flowers. *Daffodils flower in spring.*

**flown** past tense of fly.

**flu** *noun* short for influenza, an illness in which you may have a cold, a temperature and aching muscles.

**fluent** *adjective* able to speak and write a language easily. *She speaks fluent French.* **fluently** *adverb.* **fluency** *noun.*

**fluff** *noun* 1 soft bits from woolly material. 2 soft newly grown hair on young animals.

**fluff** *verb* 1 to shake or push something to make it seem larger and lighter. *The bird fluffed out its feathers.* 2 to do something badly or unsuccessfully. *She fluffed her test.*

**fluffy** *adjective* like or covered with fluff.

**fluid** *noun* a substance that can flow, such as a liquid or a gas.

F

**fluid** *adjective* 1 able to flow, not solid. 2 not fixed, likely to change. *Her ideas were totally fluid.* 3 smooth and graceful. *The dancer's fluid movements.*

**fluke** *noun* an unexpected piece of accidental good luck. *He won the match, but only by a fluke.* **fluke** *verb.*

**flung** past tense of fling.

**flush** *verb* 1 to become red, to blush. 2 to clean something with a sudden flow of water. *Don't forget to flush the lavatory every time you use it.* **flush** *noun.*

**fluster** *verb* to make somebody nervous and confused. *I got flustered when they all started asking me questions.*

**flute** *noun* a musical instrument shaped like a long tube with holes.

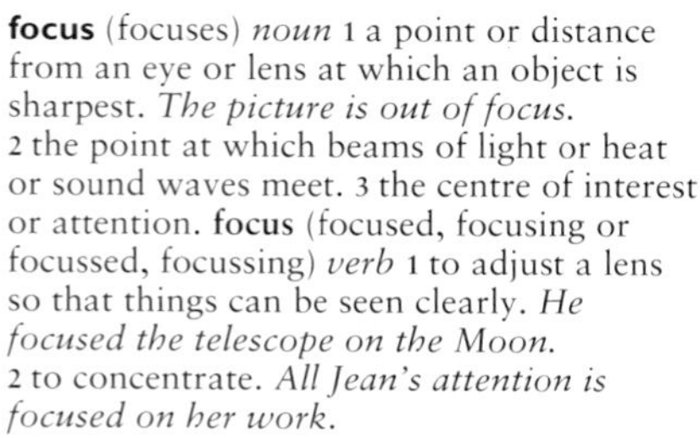

The flute is a woodwind instrument.

**flutter** *verb* 1 to move quickly and irregularly, up and down or from side to side. *The flags fluttered prettily in the wind.* 2 to move through the air with small quick movements. *Ticker tape fluttered down.*

**flutter** *noun* 1 a fluttering movement. 2 a feeling of panic or excitement. *He was in a flutter because of moving house.*

**fly** (flies, flying, flew, flown) *verb* 1 to move through the air like a bird or plane. 2 to control a plane or transport passengers in a plane. *A helicopter flew the injured to the nearest hospital.* 3 to make something fly. *To fly a kite.* 4 to move at speed or pass quickly. *Time flies when you enjoy your work.* 5 to move or wave about. *Flags were flying.* **send somebody flying** to hit a person so they fall over. **fly at somebody** to attack a person suddenly and violently.

**fly** (flies) *noun* 1 a small flying insect. 2 (usually in the plural, flies) the front opening on trousers.

Flies often carry germs and can spread disease.

**foal** *noun* a young horse.

**foam** *noun* 1 a mass of small white air bubbles, especially on top of a liquid. 2 rubber with plastic air bubbles inside, used for making mattresses and cushion stuffing, also called foam rubber.

**WORD HISTORY**

*'Focus' comes from the Latin for hearth, or fireplace. This was the central point of a Roman home, and all members of every Roman household worshipped the goddess Vesta at the hearth. The round temple of Vesta, in Rome, was thought to represent the original hearth of the king of the city.*

**focus** (focuses) *noun* 1 a point or distance from an eye or lens at which an object is sharpest. *The picture is out of focus.* 2 the point at which beams of light or heat or sound waves meet. 3 the centre of interest or attention. **focus** (focused, focusing or focussed, focussing) *verb* 1 to adjust a lens so that things can be seen clearly. *He focused the telescope on the Moon.* 2 to concentrate. *All Jean's attention is focused on her work.*

**fodder** *noun* food for farm animals.

**foe** *noun* an enemy.

**foetus** (foetuses) *noun* (say **fee**-tus) a developing embryo, especially a baby inside its mother.

**fog** *noun* very thick mist.

**foggy** *adjective* thick with fog. **I haven't got the foggiest.** I have no idea at all.

**foil** *noun* 1 metal sheet as thin as paper, especially for wrapping up food. 2 somebody or something that makes another person or thing look better. *Richard acted as a foil for his friend.*

**foil** *noun* a long thin sword with a covered point used in the sport of fencing.

**foil** *verb* to stop somebody from carrying out a plan. *The police managed to foil the robbers after hearing of their plan.*

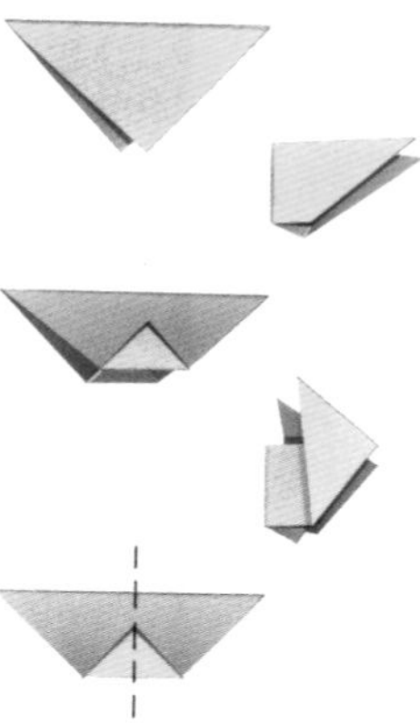

Origami is the Japanese art of folding paper to make models.

**fold** *verb* 1 to turn back a part of something, especially paper or cloth, and cover it with another part. When you fold something, you make it into a smaller shape. 2 to bring together or cross, especially your arms or hands. *The old woman folded her hands and prayed.* 3 to bend back or close up furniture or equipment. **fold** *noun* a line where something is folded, a crease. **fold up** 1 to make something into a smaller shape. 2 to fail. *The business has folded up.*

**fold** *noun* a fenced-in area for sheep.

**-fold** *suffix* meaning 'by the number of times stated', showing that something has a particular number of parts or kinds. 'Fivefold' means five times. *My problem is twofold. I don't have any money or time.*

**folder** *noun* a folded piece of cardboard for keeping papers in.

F

**foliage** *noun* leaves of plants and trees.

Autumn foliage is a beautiful sight, with the leaves turning red and gold.

**folk** (folk or folks) *noun* people.

**follow** *verb* 1 to come or go after, to move behind in the same direction. 2 to go in the same direction. *I followed the route on the map.* 3 to come next on a list. *Tuesday follows Monday.* 4 to do what somebody says or suggests. *I followed his advice.* 5 to take an interest in something. *He follows his local football team.* 6 to understand. *I couldn't follow his line of thought.* 7 to be true or logical. *It doesn't follow that because you don't like school, you don't have to go.* **follower** *noun.* **following** *adjective.* **following** *noun. She has a large following of fans.*

**fond** *adjective* 1 To be fond of somebody or something means liking them. *She is very fond of children.* 2 loving and kind. *His fond parents.* 3 foolishly hopeful. *Fond hopes.* **fondly** *adverb.*

**fondle** *verb* to stroke gently.

**font** *noun* a typeface, such as you choose on a computer.

**font** *noun* a stone water basin in a church that is used for baptisms.

**food** *noun* something that is eaten by people or animals, or taken in by plants to help them to grow and live.

All sorts of food was spread on the ground for a wonderful picnic.

**food chain** *noun* a series of animals in a community, in which each member feeds on another in the chain. Humans are at the top of the food chain.

**fool** *noun* 1 a silly person who acts stupidly. If you make a fool of somebody, you make them look stupid. 2 a clown. 3 a pudding made of cream and crushed fruit. *Gooseberry fool.* **fool** *verb* 1 to trick somebody. *She fooled me into thinking it was her car.* 2 to behave in a silly way. *Please stop fooling about.* **foolish** *adjective* unwise or stupid.

**WORD HISTORY**

*The word 'fool' has a very interesting history. It comes originally from the Latin 'follis', which means bellows – a bag that blows air. It could be that people thought fools were full of hot air and spoke nonsense, or that their heads were full of air, in other words empty.*

**foolproof** *adjective* Something that is easy to use and cannot go wrong is foolproof. *My plan is absolutely foolproof.*

**foot** (feet) *noun* 1 the part at the end of the leg below the ankle that people and animals stand on. 2 the lowest part or the bottom end. *At the foot of the hill.* 3 a measurement of length (*abbreviation* ft, equal to 12 inches or 30·5 centimetres). **on foot** walking. *What's the quickest way on foot?* **fall on your feet** to be lucky. **have cold feet** to be nervous. **stand on your own two feet** to be financially independent. **have one foot in the grave** to be very old. **put your foot in it** to say the wrong thing or make a mistake.

**football** *noun* 1 a game played by two teams of eleven players who kick a ball and try to score goals. 2 the ball used in this game. **footballer** *noun.*

**footnote** *noun* a note at the bottom of a page. *This book has too many footnotes.*

**footprint** *noun* a mark made by a foot.

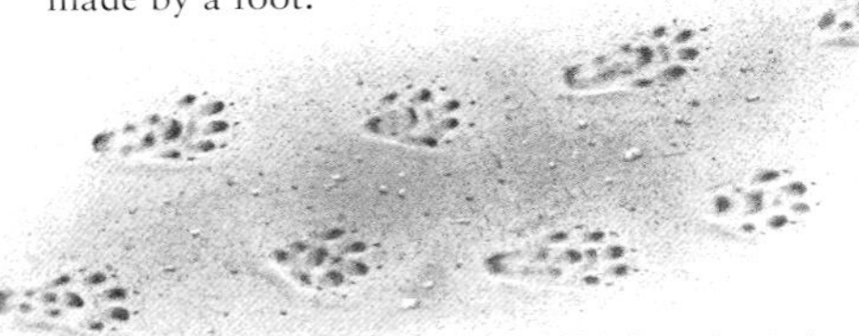

The footprints led us to the animal's lair.

**for** *preposition* 1 to show that something is intended to be given to or aimed towards somebody. *This huge present is for you.* 2 towards, in order to reach. *This train is for London.* 3 for the purpose of. *The computer is for my office.* 4 in order to have, get or do something. *I'm doing it for your own good.* 5 to show distance, time or price. *For the first time.* 6 in favour of. *How many people are for a strike and how many are against it?* 7 because of something. *I was told off for being late.* 8 as being or meaning. *She looked so old I took her for your grandmother.* 9 with reference to something surprising. *She looks amazingly young for her age.* 10 being suitable. *The right person for the job.* **for ever** always.

**forbid** (forbids, forbidding, forbade, forbidden) *verb* to order somebody not to do something. *I forbid you to go out.*

**force** *noun* 1 power or strength. *He had to use force to open the door.* 2 a power that produces changes of movement in a body. *The force of gravity.* 3 a person, thing, belief, influence or idea that causes changes. *The forces of good and evil.* 4 an organized group of police or soldiers. *The police force.* **in force** in large numbers. **join forces** to combine efforts.

F

**force** *verb* 1 to make somebody do something, although they are unwilling. *He forced the children to tidy their room.* 2 to use force to do or get something. *I had to force the lock to get in.* **forced** *adjective. A forced smile.*

**ford** *noun* a shallow place where you can cross a river. *The ford was liable to flood.*

After heavy rains, the road was impassable at the ford.

**forecast** *noun* a statement that tells you what is likely to happen. *The weather forecast was good.* **forecast** (forecasts, forecasting, forecast) *verb.*

**forehand** *noun* a stroke played in tennis with the palm turned forward. The opposite of forehand is backhand.

**forehead** *noun* (say **for**-hed) the part of the face above the eyebrows and below where your hair grows.

**foreign** *adjective* 1 belonging to a country that is not your own. *Foreign languages.* 2 not natural or belonging. *She is such an honest person, lying is foreign to her.*

**foreigner** *noun* a person from another country. *Foreigners are always welcome.*

**foresee** (forsees, forseeing, foresaw) *verb* to know what is going to happen in the future. *I forsee trouble.* **foresight** *noun.*

**forest** *noun* a large area of land covered with trees. *A pine forest.*

The forest is a mysterious place where many small animals live.

**forever** *adverb* continually. *He was forever complaining about his mother-in-law.*

**foreword** *noun* an introduction to a book.

**forfeit** *verb* (say **for**-fit) to lose something because you have done something wrong or broken a rule. *If you don't pay the bill within two weeks, you forfeit your discount.* **forfeit** *noun* 1 something lost, a price to be paid. 2 something you have to do when you lose in games. *She lost the round and was made to pay a forfeit.*

**SPELLING NOTE**

*The foreword that sometimes acts as the introduction to a book is spelt differently from 'forward' (meaning to or towards the front). A foreword is often written by a person other than the book's author.*

**AMAZING FACT**

Forests in the United States cover over 700 million acres. The US Government owns and manages about a third of this land.

**forge** *verb* 1 to copy things, especially banknotes, paintings or documents, in order to deceive people. 2 to shape something by heating and hammering it. *The blacksmith forged an iron staircase and a fire grate.* 3 to form or create something, especially links or a friendship. **forger** *noun.*

**forge** *noun* a place where metal is heated and shaped. *Horseshoes are made in a forge.*

**forgery** *noun* 1 a crime of forging things like banknotes. 2 something forged. *The painting was discovered to be a forgery.*

**forget** (forgets, forgetting, forgot, forgotten) *verb* 1 to not remember. 2 to stop thinking about. *Let's forget about the money you owe me.* **forget yourself** to behave thoughtlessly, to lose your temper. *When she kept on complaining, he forgot himself and shouted at her.*

**forgive** (forgives, forgiving, forgave, forgiven) *verb* to say or feel that you are no longer angry with somebody about something. *He still hasn't forgiven his sister for forgetting his birthday.* **forgivable** *adjective. A forgivable error.* **forgiveness** *noun. He begged for forgiveness.*

**fork** *noun* 1 an instrument with prongs at the end of a handle for eating food. 2 a large tool with prongs for digging the garden. 3 a point, especially in the road, which divides into two parts in the shape of a Y. **fork** *verb* 1 to lift, dig or move with a fork. 2 to divide in a Y-shape. *Turn right where the road forks.* **fork out** to pay out money, usually unwillingly.

**fork-lift truck** *noun* a truck with a platform at the front for lifting, lowering and moving heavy goods.

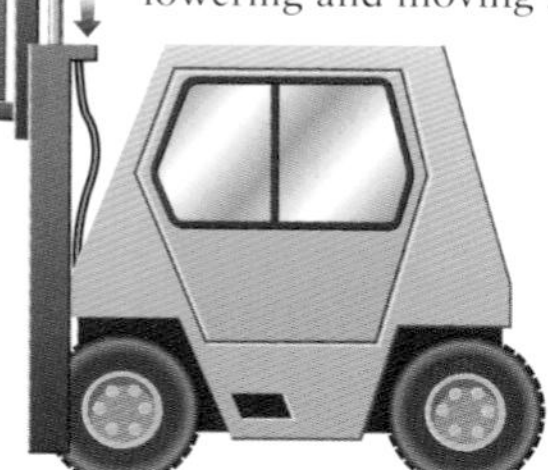

A fork-lift truck works by hydraulics.

**form** *noun* 1 the shape or appearance of something or somebody. *A pencil sharpener in the form of a crocodile.* 2 a particular kind or a particular way of behaving. *Ice and snow are forms of water. It's bad form to whisper.* 3 a piece of paper with questions to be answered and filled in. 4 a class in school. 5 a way in which a word may be spoken, written or spelt. *The irregular forms of verbs are listed in this dictionary.* **on form** fit, performing well. **off form** not fit.

**form** *verb* 1 to take shape, develop or come into existence. 2 to shape or create something. *He can hardly form a sentence.*

**formal** *adjective* correct, according to accepted rules or customs. *I'm expecting a formal apology from my boss.* **formally** *adverb. We dressed formally for the dance.* **formality** (formalities) *noun.*

**format** *noun* the shape and size of something, or the way it is presented. *I like the format of this book.*

**former** *adjective* 1 of an earlier period. *Her former husband has married again, to a very wealthy woman.* 2 the first of two people or things just mentioned. *Extra trains and buses are needed. The former will be more expensive.* (The second of two things just mentioned is called the latter.)

**formerly** *adverb* in earlier times.

**formidable** *adjective* very difficult to overcome. *They faced some formidable problems in their first year of marriage.*

**formula** (formulae) *noun* 1 a group of letters, signs or numbers that make up a rule. *The chemical formula for water is $H_2O$.* 2 a list of substances or directions for making or achieving something. *My formula for success is plenty of sleep.* 3 a set of words or behaviour used regularly for a particular occasion. *They changed the formula of the meetings.* 4 a plan, or suggestions worked out to deal with a problem.

**forsake** (forsakes, forsaking, forsook, forsaken) *verb* to leave. *He has forsaken his wife and children.*

**fort** *noun* a strong building used as a military base. **hold the fort** to look after things while somebody is away.

**fortify** (fortifies, fortifying, fortified) *verb* 1 to strengthen a place against attack. 2 to eat or drink something to make you stronger. **fortification** *noun.*

**fortnight** *noun* a period of two weeks. *A fortnight's holiday.* **fortnightly** *adverb.*

**fortress** (fortresses) *noun* a castle or other strong building that is difficult to attack.

The fortress came under heavy cannon fire and was eventually engulfed in flames.

**AMAZING FACT**

Most fossils are found in places that were once under or near seas.

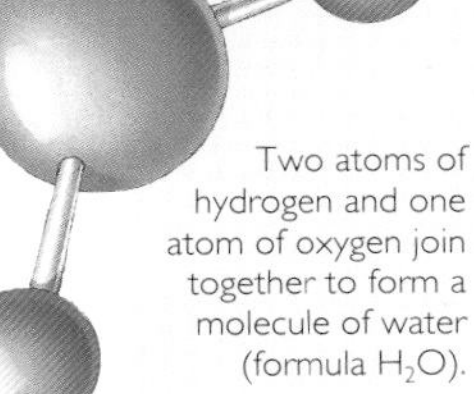

Two atoms of hydrogen and one atom of oxygen join together to form a molecule of water (formula $H_2O$).

**WORD HISTORY**

*'Fortnight' is a shortened form of the Old English words 'feowertiene niht', which meant 'fourteen nights' or two weeks.*

**fortuitous** *adjective* by chance, especially by lucky chance, accidental.

**fortunate** *adjective* lucky. **fortunately** *adverb. Fortunately he didn't notice that I was very late.*

**fortune** *noun* 1 (good) luck. 2 fate, what will happen in the future. *The old woman told him his fortune.* 3 a large amount of money. *She earns a fortune in advertising.*

**forward** *adjective, adverb* 1 to or towards the front, towards the future. *A step forward.* 2 advanced or early in development. *The boy is very forward for his age.* 3 to be sure or eager in an unpleasant way. *She is too forward for my liking.* **forward** *noun* an attacking player in the front line of a team, especially in football, hockey and rugby.

**forward** *verb* to send on a letter, parcel or information. *Please forward letters to my new address in Spain.*

**forwards** *adverb* to or towards the front or future. *Let's move forwards.*

**fossil** *noun* the remains of an animal or a plant that lived long ago and has hardened into rock. *A fossil of a dinosaur tooth.* **fossilize** *verb.*

This fossil was once an ammonite, a creature like a squid.

**foster** *verb* 1 to bring up a child as if you were her/his father or mother. 2 to help something grow or develop. *France is fostering good relations with Germany.*

**fought** past tense of fight.

**foul** *adjective* 1 dirty, having a disgusting taste or smell. 2 very bad, unpleasant or angry. *She's got a foul temper.* **foul play** unfair play, actions against the rules. **foul** *noun* an action against the rules in sport. **foul** *verb* 1 to dirty. 2 to commit a foul against another player.

**found** past tense of find.

**found** *verb* 1 to establish or give money to start something. *The school was founded by monks.* 2 to base on. *Her success was founded on hard work.*

**foundation** *noun* 1 concrete and stonework that support the walls of a building or other structure, often in the plural, foundations. 2 the things that beliefs and ideas are based on. **be without foundation** to be untrue.

**founder** *verb* 1 to fill with water and sink. *The ship foundered on the rocks.* 2 to fail or collapse. *The company foundered and eventually went bankrupt.*

**fountain** *noun* an apparatus, often hidden in a stone figure or bowl, that pumps a stream of water up into the air.

The sound of the water splashing in the fountain was like music to his ears.

**fox** *noun* a wild animal that looks like a dog with a long bushy tail.

**foxglove** *noun* a tall straight plant that has flowers shaped like the fingers of a glove.

**foyer** *noun* (say **foy**-ay) the entrance hall in a theatre, cinema or hotel.

**fraction** *noun* 1 a small part or bit. *For a fraction of a second.* 2 a number that is not a whole number, a part of a whole number. $^1/_2$ and $^1/_3$ are fractions.

**fracture** *noun* a crack or break, especially in a bone. **fracture** *verb.*

**fragile** *adjective* easy to break or easily damaged. **fragility** *noun.*

**fragment** *noun* 1 a small piece that has broken off. *She dropped the vase and it broke into a million fragments.* 2 a small piece or part of something, especially an unfinished work of art.

**fragrance** *noun* a sweet or pleasant smell. **fragrant** *adjective.*

**frame** *noun* 1 the border into which something like a picture or window is fitted. 2 the main structure that forms the support for something. *A bicycle frame.* 3 the part that holds the lenses of a pair of glasses in place. 4 the shape or body of a person or animal. *Years of hardship had weakened his powerful frame.* 5 one of a number of small photographs that make up a film. **frame of mind** the mood somebody is in at a particular time. **frame** *verb* 1 to put a frame on or around. 2 to give shape to or express in a particular language, especially words or a plan. 3 to make an innocent person seem guilty and look as if they had committed a crime. *He was framed and sent to prison, but he didn't commit the crime.*

The mirror had an elegant gold frame.

**DID YOU KNOW?**

*The word 'fraction' comes from the Latin for break, referring to a whole number broken up into little parts. $^1/_2$ is called a vulgar fraction ('vulgar' meaning common), and 0·5 is called a decimal fraction.*

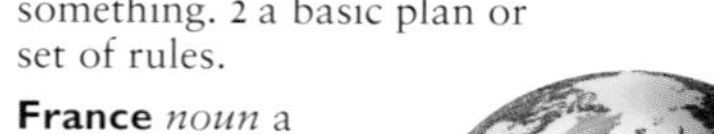

**framework** *noun* 1 a supporting frame for something. 2 a basic plan or set of rules.

**France** *noun* a country in western Europe.

France is famous for the excellent food and wine enjoyed in homes across the land.

**frank** *adjective* honest and direct. The open way in which you say what you think. *I will be frank with you, I don't think he'll pass the exam.* **frankly** *adverb.* **frankness** *noun.*

**frank** *verb* to stamp a letter or parcel to show that postage has been paid.

**frantic** *adjective* wild and desperate; extremely anxious. *He was frantic with worry.* **frantically** *adverb.*

**fraud** *noun* 1 a swindle, a crime of getting money by trickery. 2 a person who pretends to be something he is not, a swindler. **fraudulent** *adjective.*

**freak** *noun* 1 an unusual or very strange person, animal, thing or happening. *That was a pure freak, it will never happen again.* 2 a person who takes a fanatical interest in something. *A football freak.* **freak** *adjective. A freak storm.* **freakish** *adjective.*

**freckle** *noun* a small brown spot on the skin, caused by the Sun. **freckly** *adjective.*

The freckles on her face always appear in early summer.

**free** (freer, freest) *adjective, adverb* 1 able to do what you want, go where you want, not shut up, be held in prison or controlled by anybody. *He set the prisoners free.* 2 without payment, costing nothing. *Entrance to the museum is free.* 3 not fixed on to anything. *The free end of the sail has been torn in the storm.* 4 not busy. *Are you free on Wednesday?* 5 not being used. *Is this seat free?* 6 without obstruction or anything being in the way. *A free flow of water.* **have a free hand** to be able to do things, without having to ask others for permission. **free with** If you are free with something, you are generous and ready to help. **freely** *adverb.* **free** (frees, freeing, freed) *verb* to set free. **freedom** *noun.*

**Freetown** *noun* the capital of Sierra Leone.

**freeze** (freezes, freezing, froze, frozen) *verb* 1 to harden into ice or become covered with ice. 2 to preserve food by making it very cold and storing it below freezing point. 3 to be extremely cold. *I'm absolutely freezing.* 4 to stop moving and stand completely still. *The boy froze at the sight of the snake.* 5 to fix prices or wages for a certain time so they cannot be increased. **freeze** *noun.*

The trees look beautiful when they freeze. They are covered with frost and snow.

**freezer** *noun* a refrigerator in which food can be frozen, because the temperature inside it is below freezing-point.

**freezing-point** *noun* the temperature at which water freezes into ice. Freezing-point is 0° Celsius.

**freight** *noun* (say frayt) 1 the transport or transportation of goods by lorries, ships, trains or planes. 2 goods. **freight** *verb.*

**French** *noun* 1 the people of France. 2 the language of France. **French** *adjective. The French flag is red, white and blue.*

**French fries** *plural noun* thin pieces of potato fried in oil, chips.

**frequent** *adjective* (say **freek**-wunt) happening often. *My brother is a frequent visitor, he comes every day.* **frequently** *adverb.* **frequency** *noun.*

**frequent** (say frik-**went**) *verb* to be or go somewhere often.

**fresh** *adjective* 1 newly made, picked, grown or arrived. Not old or stale, tinned or cooked. *I prefer fresh fruit to tinned.* 2 cool, refreshing and unused. *She put fresh sheets on the bed.* 3 new. *Let's make a fresh start.* 4 Fresh water is not salty. **freshly** *adverb. Freshly caught fish.* **freshness** *noun.*

**friction** *noun* 1 the rubbing of one thing against another. *Oil is used in machines to stop friction.* 2 disagreement and quarrels. *There is always friction between them.*

**Friday** *noun* the sixth day of the week, following Thursday.

Sarah made an appointment to see the dentist on Friday.

**fridge** *noun* a refrigerator.

**fried** past tense of fry.

**DID YOU KNOW?**

*Frogs, toads and newts belong to a group of animals called amphibians. They spend part of their lives on land, but always go back to water when it is time to lay their eggs. Most frogs lay between 1,000 and 20,000 eggs.*

**friend** *noun* 1 a person you know and like. 2 a helpful person or an object that you know well and like using. **make friends** to become somebody's friend. **be friends** If you are friends with somebody, you like spending time together.

**friendly** *adjective* acting as a friend. *A friendly gesture.* **friendship** *noun.*

**frighten** *verb* to fill with fear. *The big dog frightened the little girl.* **fright** *noun.*

**frill** *noun* 1 a pleated strip of paper or cloth attached to something as a decoration. *A frill on a dress.* 2 an unnecessary extra. **frilly** *adjective. A frilly lampshade.*

**fringe** *noun* 1 hair cut to hang in a straight line over the forehead. 2 a decorative border of many threads hanging down loosely, especially on shawls and rugs. 3 the part furthest from the centre, the edge of something. *They live on the fringes of London.* **fringed** *adjective.*

**frisk** *verb* 1 to run and jump about playfully, especially children or animals. 2 to search somebody with your hands for hidden weapons or goods. *The police frisked the man and found a gun on him.* **frisky** *adjective. A frisky little dog.*

**frivolous** *adjective* 1 not serious, light-heartedly looking for pleasure. *Clubbing is a frivolous way of spending your time.* 2 amusing, not important.

**frock** *noun* a dress.

**frog** *noun* a jumping animal, usually brownish-green, that lives in water and on land. Frogs croak.

Frogs develop from tadpoles.

**from** *preposition* 1 showing a starting point in time, place or number. *We took the train from London to Cardiff.* 2 showing who gave or sent something. *He got the money from the bank.* 3 showing what something is made of, what it is based on or where you might find it. *It was cut from cardboard.* 4 out of the possession of, showing separation. *He took the doll from his little sister.* 5 judging by. *From the noise they are making, it must be a party.* 6 showing difference or change. *I can't tell one from the other.* 7 because of, showing the reason for something. *In Africa people are suffering terribly from the famine.*

F

**front** *noun* 1 the side that is normally seen and faces forward. *The front of the house.* 2 the part that is ahead of others. *He went to the front of the queue.* 3 a road along the seashore. *We walked along the front.* 4 the place where two armies are fighting in war. 5 a line of separation where masses of cold air meet masses of warm air. *A cold front.* **in front** ahead of others. **in front of** facing somebody or something. *He spends too much time in front of the television.*

**frontier** *noun* the border where one country meets another country.

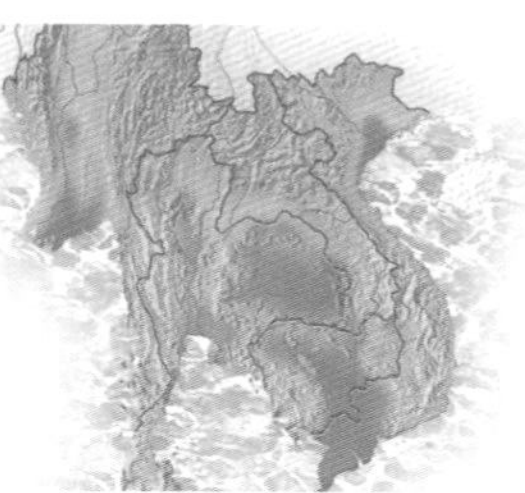

The frontiers were clearly marked on the map.

**frost** *noun* 1 weather at a temperature below freezing-point. *Unfortunately, the frost has killed our new plants.* 2 a thin layer of powdery ice crystals that form on the ground when there is a frost. **frost** *verb* 1 to become covered with frost. 2 to cover with sugar, especially a cake.

**froth** *noun* small white bubbles on liquid that look like foam. **frothy** *adjective.*

**frown** *verb* to move your eyebrows towards each other and wrinkle your forehead because you are annoyed or worried. **frown** *noun. He frowned with disapproval.*

**froze** past tense of freeze.

**frugal** *adjective* 1 careful with money or food, not wasteful. 2 small and costing little. *A frugal meal.* **frugally** *adverb.*

**fruit** (fruits or fruit) *noun* 1 Fruit grows on trees and bushes, contains seeds and is used for food. *Apples, oranges and strawberries are all kinds of fruit.* 2 good or bad results of something. *Now you can enjoy the fruits of your hard work.* **fruity** *adjective.*

Fresh fruit forms an important part of a healthy diet.

**fruitful** *adjective* producing good results. *We had a fruitful meeting.*

**AMAZING FACT**

Fruits are actually the seed-cases that a plant uses to protect and distribute its seeds.

Many fruits are distributed by the animals that eat them but some fruits scatter their seeds when the are ripe.

**GRAMMAR NOTE**

*When 'full' is used as a suffix at the end of a word, it is usually spelt '–ful': 'beautiful', 'useful', 'fruitful', etc. This also applies if the suffix is used to mean 'the amount needed to fill': e.g.'bucketful', 'handful' etc.*

**frustrate** *verb* 1 to stop you from doing what you would like to do or to stop plans from being carried out. *Our plans for a picnic were frustrated by bad weather.* 2 to make you feel disappointed and angry. *It's frustrating not to be able to see you when I want to.* **frustration** *noun.*

**fry** (fries, frying, fried) *verb* to cook something in hot fat, usually in a frying pan.

**fudge** *noun* a soft brown sweet made with butter, sugar and milk.

**fudge** *verb* to avoid taking firm action or making a clear decision. *The government have fudged the issue.*

**fuel** *noun* something that is burnt to produce heat, especially coal and oil. **fuel** (fuels, fuelling, fuelled) *verb* 1 to supply something with fuel or take in fuel. 2 to make a situation worse or cause an argument. *His anger was fuelled by a tremendous jealousy of his brother.*

**fugitive** *noun* (say few-jit-iv) somebody who is running away from something. *A fugitive from justice.*

**fulcrum** *noun* the point on which a bar (called a lever) is fixed or is supported in lifting something.

The weights are perfectly balanced at the fulcrum.

**fulfil** (fulfils, fulfilling, fulfilled) *verb* 1 to do what was promised, to carry out what is required. *He didn't fulfil his promises.* 2 to make true or come true. **fulfilment** *noun.*

**full** *adjective* 1 completely filled, holding as much or as many as possible. 2 containing a large number of people or things. *He is always full of ideas.* 3 complete, with nothing missing. *She wrote down her full name and address.* 4 as much or great as possible. *He drove at full speed.* 5 rounded. *She has a full figure.* 6 wide and loosely fitting. *A full skirt.* **full of something** to be talking about something with great enthusiasm. **in full** not leaving out anything. *She told me the story in full.* **full up** with no space left. **fully** *adverb.* **fullness** *noun.*

**full stop** *noun* a dot (.) which is put at the end of a sentence as a punctuation mark.

**fumble** *verb* to handle or search for something clumsily. *He fumbled in his pocket for his keys.*

**fun** *noun* amusement, something enjoyable. **make fun of** to tease or laugh at somebody in an unkind way.

**Funafuti** *noun* the capital of Tuvalu.

**function** *noun* 1 a special duty or purpose. What somebody or something is there to do. *One of the chairman's functions is to conduct meetings.* 2 an important party or event. *We were invited to a function at the embassy.* 3 an activity a computer can carry out. **function** *verb* to be in action or work.

**fundamental** *adjective* very important or basic. **fundamentally** *adverb.*

**funeral** *noun* the ceremony of burying or cremating a dead person.

**fungus** (fungi, say **fung**-guy) *noun* a plant-like organism without flowers, leaves or green colouring. Mushrooms, toadstools and mould are all fungi.

Bracket fungus grow on the trunk of a tree.

**funnel** *noun* 1 a chimney on a steamship or steam engine for letting out smoke. 2 an object with a wide round top and a tube at the bottom used for pouring liquids and powders into a container with a narrow opening. **funnel** *verb* to move as if through a funnel. *Crowds funnelled through the gateway and into the square.*

**funny** (funnier, funniest) *adjective* 1 amusing, making you laugh. 2 strange or unusual. *The car is making a funny noise.*

**fur** *noun* 1 the thick hair that covers the bodies of many animals. 2 the fur-covered skin used for making clothes, especially fur coats. *The fur traders sold mink and beaver furs.* 3 a coat made from real fur or fabric that looks like fur.

**furnace** *noun* a container with a very hot fire, used for burning things, melting metal, making glass or producing steam in a factory. *A burning fiery furnace.*

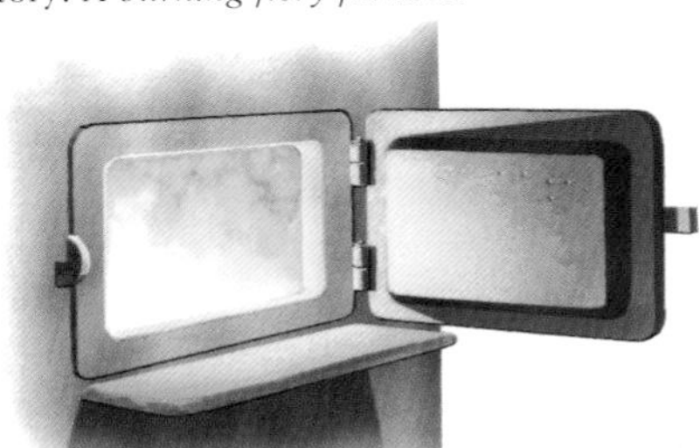

The heat was white hot inside the furnace.

**DID YOU KNOW?**

*There are about 50,000 different kinds of fungi. They are different from green plants because they cannot make their own food. They get their food mainly from decaying plants, and sometimes from living plants or animals.*

**furnish** *verb* 1 to put furniture in a place. *The flat is not furnished.* 2 to supply what is necessary. *Luckily we were furnished with a dictionary for the translation.*

**furniture** *noun* movable things like tables, chairs and beds that are put in a room or needed in a place.

**furry** *adjective* like or covered with fur. *The little boy likes furry toys.*

**further** *adjective, adverb* 1 at or to a more distant point or greater degree. *We can't walk any further.* 2 more or additional. *He works in further education.* **further** *verb* to help to be successful. *We will do everything to further peace.*

**furtive** *adjective* done secretly, hoping not to be seen. *The thief gave a furtive glance at my handbag.* **furtively** *adverb.*

**fury** *noun* great anger, rage. **furious** *adjective. I am furious that you are late.*

**fuse** *noun* 1 a short thin piece of wire, e.g. in an electric plug, that acts as a safety device by melting if too much electricity is passed through it. *The lights went out when a fuse blew.* 2 a tube or cord on a bomb or firework used for setting it off. **fuse** *verb* 1 to stop working because a fuse has melted. *Suddenly all the lights in the house fused.* 2 to melt in great heat or become joined by melting. *The wires have fused together.*

**fuselage** (say **few**-zuh-lahzh) *noun* the main body of an aircraft.

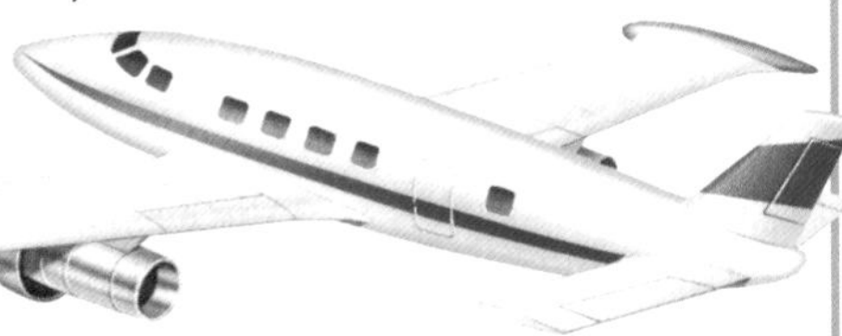

The fuselage of an aircraft can be used for transporting passengers or freight.

**fuss** (fusses) *noun* unnecessary excitement or anger, especially about unimportant things. *Don't make such a fuss.* **make a fuss of somebody** to pay a lot of attention to a person. **fuss** *verb* to behave in an unnecessarily excited or anxious way. **fussy** (fussier, fussiest) *adjective.*

**futile** (say **few**-tile) *adjective* of no use, not successful. *It's futile to argue with me because I know I'm right.* **futility** *noun.*

**future** *noun* the time or events that come after the present, the things that will happen. *We all wish you a very happy future.* **in future** from now on. **future** *adjective. What are your future plans?*

**fuzz** *noun* 1 something fluffy and soft, especially from wool. 2 short curly hair. 3 *slang* the police. **fuzzy** (fuzzier, fuzziest) *adjective* 1 not clear in shape, blurred. *Some of the photographs were very fuzzy.* 2 soft and curly. *Fuzzy hair.*

# Gg

**gabble** *verb* to speak so quickly that people cannot understand you.

**gable** *noun* the triangular outside end of a house between two sloping roofs. **gabled** *adjective. Gabled houses.*

**Gabon** *noun* a country in Africa.

**Gaborone** *noun* the capital of Botswana.

**gadget** *noun* a small, useful instrument or tool for a particular job. *This gadget is called a garlic press.*

**gag** (gags, gagging, gagged) *verb* 1 to put something over or into somebody's mouth to stop them speaking. **gag** *noun.* 2 to retch or feel like being sick.

**gag** *noun* a joke.

**gain** *verb* 1 to win, earn or obtain something. 2 to increase. *He's gained half a stone.* **gain** *noun* 1 a profit. 2 an increase.

**gala** *noun* a special public event or entertainment.

**galaxy** *noun* a huge group of stars and planets. The Milky Way is a galaxy.

**gale** *noun* a very strong, violent wind. *A force-10 gale.*

**gallant** *adjective* 1 brave. *A gallant knight.* 2 honourable and polite.

**galleon** *noun* a large Spanish sailing ship of the 16th century. *A galleon in full sail.*

**gallery** *noun* 1 a building or long room for displaying paintings and other works of art. 2 the highest floor of seats in a theatre.

**galley** (galleys) *noun* 1 the kitchen on a ship or aircraft. 2 a single-decked ship of ancient times that was driven by both sails and oars.

**gallop** *noun* the fastest pace of a horse.

**gallon** *noun* a measure for liquids. There are eight pints or 4.5 litres in a gallon. (US 3.8 litres.)

**gallop** *verb. We galloped across the moor.*

**gallows** *singular and plural noun* a wooden structure on which criminals used to be hanged. *The gallows on the hill.*

**galore** *adverb* in large numbers or amount, in plenty. *The library has got books galore.*

**WORD HISTORY**

*Like the letter C, the shape of the letter G comes from an ancient Egyptian symbol for a boomerang or throwing stick. The Romans used it for two sounds – C and G. They later added a stroke to the C (G) and used the new letter for the G sound and the old letter for the K sound.*

Galaxies are classified according to their shapes. This one is a spiral galaxy.

**AMAZING FACT**

Our galaxy, the Milky Way, is one of many. The other galaxies are moving away from us. The farther away a galaxy is, the faster it is moving. The most distant galaxies are receding at almost the speed of light.

**galvanized** *verb* 1 to cover a metal with zinc to protect it from rusting. 2 to shock into doing something. *The threat of flooding galvanized the men into action.* **galvanized** *adjective. A galvanized dustbin.*

**Gambia** *noun* a country in Africa.

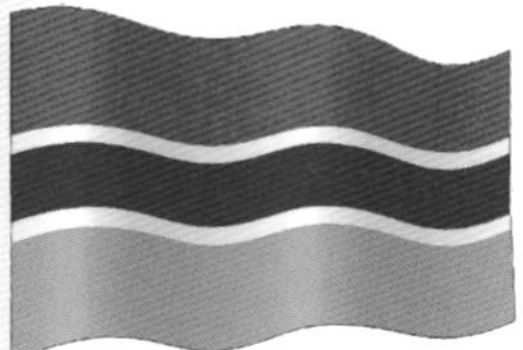

The flag of Gambia has red, blue and green stripes, divided by narrow white stripes.

**gamble** *verb* to risk something, particularly money, for possible gain, especially on the result of a game or race. *He's gambled away all his family fortune on cards.* **gamble** *noun.* **gambler** *noun.*

**game** *noun* 1 an activity or contest with rules. Football, baseball, chess and bridge are all different kinds of game. **games** athletic competitions. *The Olympic Games take place every four years.* 2 wild animals and birds that are hunted for food and as a sport.

Farmers breed game birds because they bring in a lot of money in the shooting season.

**game** *adjective* brave and willing to try something.

**gamekeeper** *noun* a person who looks after game animals and birds.

**gander** *noun* a male goose.

**gang** *noun* a group of people who regularly go about and do things together.

**gangster** *noun* one of a gang of criminals.

**gangway** *noun* 1 a gangplank or movable bridge for passengers between a ship and the shore. 2 a space between rows of seats in an aeroplane, train or cinema, etc.

**gaol** *noun* (also spelt jail) a prison.

**gap** *noun* an opening or empty space.

**gape** *verb* 1 to stare with your mouth wide open, usually in surprise. 2 to be wide open. *A gaping hole in the ground.*

**garage** *noun* 1 a place where cars and other motor vehicles are kept. 2 a place that sells petrol or where cars can be repaired.

**garbage** *noun* (especially North American) kitchen rubbish.

**garden** *noun* land, usually near a house, where flowers and vegetables are grown. **gardener** *noun.* **gardening** *noun.*

G

**gargle** *verb* to wash your throat with a medicated liquid without swallowing it and then to spit it out.

**gargoyle** *noun* a grotesque carving on a building of a human or animal head forming part of a gutter.

This gargoyle comes from an Oxford college.

**garish** *adjective* (say **gair**-ish) over-coloured and too bright, gaudy.

**garlic** *noun* a strong-tasting bulb like an onion that is used in cooking to add flavour to food.

**garment** *noun* a piece of clothing such as a jacket or skirt.

**garnish** *verb* to decorate food. *He garnished the vegetables with sprigs of parsley.*

**garret** *noun* a small room in the attic of a house. *The poet lived in a garret.*

**garter** *noun* a band of cloth or elastic at the top of a sock or stocking to hold it up.

**gas** (gases) *noun* 1 any of many substances like air that are neither liquid nor solid. Oxygen and nitrogen are gases. 2 the kind of gas we use as a fuel in our homes for heating and cooking. 3 (in US, short for gasoline) petrol.

**gash** *noun* a deep, long cut, a slash. **gash** *verb. She gashed her knee on the rock.*

**gasoline** see gas.

**gasp** *verb* to breathe quickly and noisily through your mouth because you have been running etc. or because you are ill. **gasp** *noun. A gasp of surprise.*

**gastric** *adjective* relating to or belonging to the stomach. *A gastric ulcer.*

**gate** *noun* 1 a kind of outside door or barrier across an opening in a fence, hedge or wall. 2 the number of people who pay to see a sporting event.

**gatecrash** *verb* to go to a party when you have not been invited. **gatecrasher** *noun.*

**gateway** (gateways) *noun* 1 an opening with a gate. 2 an opportunity or an opening to something. *The gateway to stardom.*

**gather** *verb* 1 to come together as a group, to bring together. *A crowd gathered in the square.* 2 to pick. *He gathered nuts and blackberries.* 3 to understand or find out something. *We gather you're going away.*

**gathering** *noun* a meeting or coming together of people for some purpose.

**gaucho** *noun* a cowboy of South America.

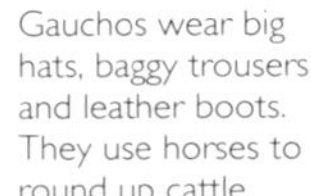

Gauchos wear big hats, baggy trousers and leather boots. They use horses to round up cattle.

**AMAZING FACT**

Birthstones are gemstones that symbolize the month of a person's birth.

Do you know what yours is?

January – garnet
February – amethyst
March – aquamarine
April – diamond
May – emerald
June – pearl
July – ruby
August – peridot
September – saphire
October – opal
November – topaz
December – turquoise

**gaudy** (gaudier, gaudiest) *adjective* (say **gaw**-dee) Something that is gaudy is too brightly coloured and showy.

**gauge** *noun* (rhymes with cage) an instrument for measuring. *A fuel gauge.* **gauge** *verb. She tried to gauge (measure or estimate) the depth of the pond.*

**gaunt** *adjective* very thin, bony and haggard. *His gaunt face.*

**gauntlet** *noun* a long, thick glove with special protection for the wrist, worn by motorcyclists etc. **take up the gauntlet** take up a challenge.

**gauze** *noun* a thin net-like cloth often used with bandages.

**gave** past tense of give.

**gay** *adjective* 1 homosexual. **gay** *noun. A club for gays.* 2 bright and cheerful. *Gay colours.* **gaiety** *noun.* **gaily** *adverb.*

**gaze** *verb* to look steadily at something or somebody for a long time. **gaze** *noun.*

**gazelle** *noun* a small, graceful antelope of Africa and Asia.

**gazetteer** *noun* a geographical dictionary that lists and describes places.

**gear** *noun* a wheel with teeth around the edge which can work with other gears in a machine. Gears in a car or on a bicycle send power to the wheels.

**gear** *noun* clothes or equipment needed for a special purpose. *Climbing gear.*

**geese** plural of goose.

**gelding** *noun* a castrated (neutered) horse.

**gem** *noun* a precious stone that has been cut. Diamonds, emeralds and rubies are kinds of gems.

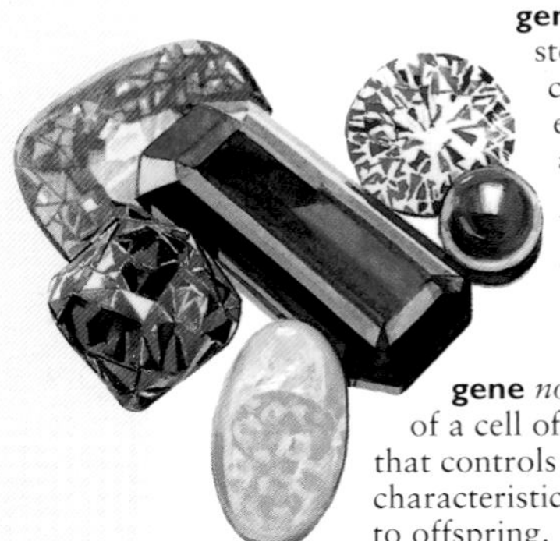

The empress built up a huge collection of beautiful gems.

**gene** *noun* one of the parts of a cell of all living things that controls and passes on characteristics from parents to offspring.

**general** *noun* a very senior officer in the army. *General Custer.*

**general** *adjective* 1 concerning several or most people or things. *General knowledge.* 2 not in detail but in broad outline. *A general description.* **in general** mainly, usually. *In general, I prefer cats to people.*

**generate** *verb* 1 to produce electricity. *Electricity is generated in power stations.* 2 to bring into being, to cause. *The Viking exhibition generated a great deal of interest.*

G

**generation** *noun* all the people now living who were born at about the same time. The period of time between generations (about 25 years). *The beat generation.*

**generator** *noun* a machine that generates (produces) electricity.

**generous** *adjective* A generous person is kind and helpful and gives freely of their time and money. **generosity** *noun.*

**genetic** *adjective* concerning the genes or inherited through the genes. *He was suffering from a genetic disorder.*

**genitals** *plural noun* the sexual organs.

**genius** *noun* (say **jee-nee-us**) an exceptionally clever and creative person.

**gentile** *noun* a person who is not Jewish. **gentile** *adjective.*

**gentle** *adjective* 1 a gentle person is quiet, kind and thinks of others. 2 not rough or violent. 3 not extreme. **gentleness** *noun.* **gently** *adverb.*

**genuflect** *verb* to bend a knee, especially in church as a sign of reverence. **genuflexion** *noun. Genuflexion shows humility.*

**genuine** *adjective* real and not fake or untrue. *A genuine need for help.*

**genus** (genera) *noun* a group of similar plants or animals but containing different species or kinds. Foxes and hyenas are two species of the dog genus.

**geography** *noun* the study of the Earth, its natural features, its people, resources, weather etc. *World geography.* **geographer** *noun.* **geographic** *adjective.*

**geology** *noun* the study of the Earth's rocks and layers of soil. **geological** *adjective.* **geologist** *noun.*

**geometry** *noun* a branch of mathematics concerned with the study of angles, lines, shapes and solids. **geometric** *adjective.*

**Georgetown** *noun* the capital of Guyana.

**Georgia** *noun* a country in Southwest Asia.

**geranium** *noun* a plant with clusters of pink, red or white flowers.

**gerbil** *noun* a small desert rodent with long back legs, often kept as a pet.

**WORD HISTORY**

*Some words borrowed from German are 'angst' ('anxiety'), 'kaput' ('broken'), 'kindergarten', 'kitsch' ('in bad taste'), 'spanner', 'waltz' and 'zinc'.*

Once the seeds had germinated they began to grow very quickly.

**AMAZING FACT**

Old Faithful, in Yellowstone National Park in the northwestern United States, is a famous geyser. It is called Old Faithful because it erupts at the same time every day. Yellowstone became the world's first national park in 1872.

Rocks were Carl's passion. He had wanted to study geology since childhood.

The steam from the geyser seemed to rise for miles into the sky.

**geriatric** *adjective* relating to or concerning old people. *A geriatric ward in the hospital.*

**germ** *noun* a microscopic living thing that can cause diseases.

**German** *noun* 1 a person who comes from Germany. 2 the language spoken in Germany, Austria and parts of Switzerland. **German** *adjective. German music.*

**German Shepherd dog** another name for an alsatian.

**Germany** *noun* a country in central Europe.

**germinate** *verb* when seeds germinate, they begin to sprout.

**gesture** *noun* 1 a movement of the hand or head intended to mean something. *She wrung her hands in a gesture of despair.* 2 an action that expresses feelings. *He invited them to supper as a friendly gesture.*

**get** (gets, getting, got) *verb* 1 to obtain. *I must get a new book from the library.* 2 to receive. *I got a lot of presents at Christmas.* 3 to bring. *Can you get me a glass of lemonade?* 4 to become. *You'll get wet if you stand in the rain.* 5 to prepare. *Dad got the supper.* 6 to catch an illness. *I hope you don't get my cold.* 7 to cause to happen. *You must get your watch repaired.* 8 to own something. *Have you got a dog?* 9 to understand. *I don't get the joke.* 10 to ask somebody to do something. *We got the builders to move the bricks.* 11 to arrive. *We got home at midnight.* **get about** 1 *How do these stories get about?* 2 *He's over 90 but still manages to get about.* **get ahead** *She got ahead through hard work.* **get along with** *He's friendly and gets along with everybody.* **get at** 1 *The truth is difficult to get at.* 2 *Why are you always getting at me?* **get by** *He gets by on his small pension.* **get down to** *She's getting down to some serious work.* **get off** 1 *Don't get off the train until it has stopped.* 2 *She got off with a small fine.* **get on** 1 *How are you getting on with you homework?* 2 *She's over 80, so she's getting on a bit.* **get on to** *Get on to (contact) the press immediately.* **get over** *He's got over his illness.* **get up to** *He's always getting up to mischief.*

**geyser** *noun* a natural spring from which hot water and steam erupt, often at regular intervals.

**Ghana** *noun* a country in Africa.

G

**ghastly** *adjective* very unpleasant, horrible. *A ghastly accident.* **ghastliness** *noun.*

**ghost** *noun* the spirit or shape of a dead person that some people believe walks about at night. **ghostly** adjective.

**giant** *noun* in fairy stories, a huge and often frightening and cruel man. **giant** *adjective. A giant marrow.*

**gibberish** *noun* speech that makes no sense at all. *Don't talk gibberish.*

**gibbon** *noun* an ape with very long arms.

**giddy** (giddier, giddiest) *adjective* feeling dizzy, light-headed and about to fall over. **giddiness** *noun.*

**gift** *noun* 1 something that you give somebody, a present. 2 a talent. *He has a gift for languages.* **gifted** *adjective.*

**gig** *noun* a public performance of pop music or jazz. *A gig in the park.*

**gigantic** *adjective* (say jie-**gan**-tik) of giant size, enormous.

**giggle** *noun* a silly, nervous laugh. **giggle** *verb. Granny giggled into her soup.*

**gill** *noun* an organ on each side of a fish through which it breathes.

**gimmick** *noun* something clever or unusual that is done to attract attention, especially to advertise something. **gimmicky** *adjective.*

**gin** *noun* a colourless alcoholic drink.

**ginger** *noun* 1 a hot spice made from the root of a tropical plant used to flavour food or drinks such as ginger ale and gingerbeer. 2 an orange-brown colour. **ginger** *adjective. Ginger hair.*

**gingerbread** *noun* a sweet biscuit or cake flavoured with ginger.

**gingerly** *adjective, adverb* carefully and timidly. *Gingerly, he peeled off the label.*

**giraffe** *noun* an African animal with long legs and a very long neck. It has yellow fur with brown patches as camouflage.

**girder** *noun* a long metal beam used as a support in buildings, bridges etc.

**girl** *noun* a female child. **girlish** *adjective.*

**girlfriend** *noun* 1 a boy or man's usual and regular female friend. 2 the female friend of a woman. 3 the partner of a lesbian woman.

**gist** *noun* the rough outline or main points of something. *He gave us the gist of the story while we were on the way there.*

**AMAZING FACT**

Nearly two million years ago, North America was almost completely covered by huge ice sheets. The ice melted, forming rivers and river valleys. The Great Lakes were also formed from ice that melted. Glaciers have given us some of our most dramatic and beautiful scenery.

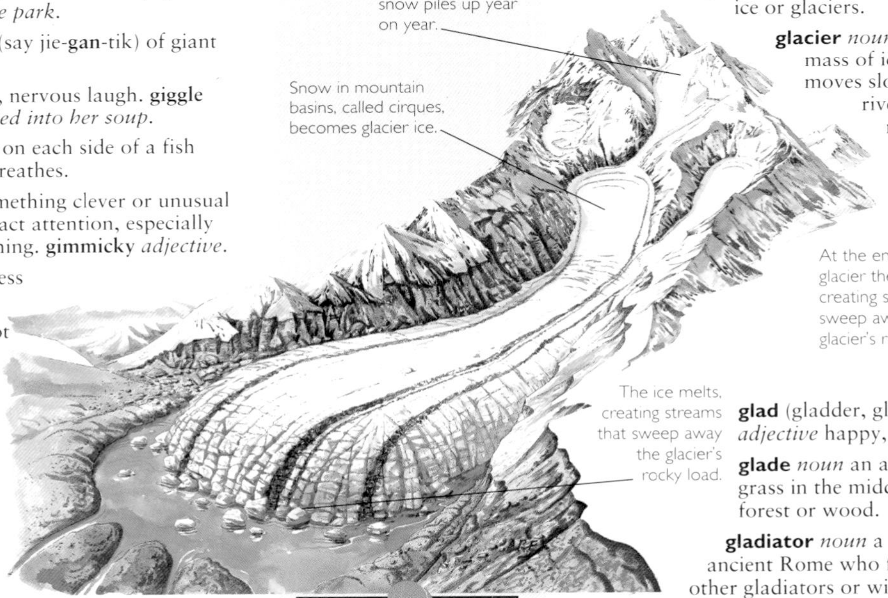

**WORD HISTORY**

*Until the 17th century giraffes were called 'cameleopards' because of their camel-like necks and leopard-like spots.*

**give** (gives, giving, gave, given) *verb* 1 to hand something over to somebody. 2 to bend or collapse. *The fence gave under her great weight.* 3 to organize or present something. *They are giving a concert tonight.* 4 to do something suddenly. *Pat gave a sigh of relief.* **give away** *I'm giving away all my money.* **give back** *Jack gave back the tapes he'd borrowed.* **give in** 1 *They gave in their guns to the police.* 2 *He won't give in (succumb) to your threats.* 3 *You don't know the answer, so why don't you give in (admit defeat)?* **give off** 1 *The bonfire is giving off a lot of smoke.* **give out** 1 *She gave out (distributed) the prizes.* 2 *The engine has finally given out (broken).* **give up** 1 *We gave up (renounced) the idea of moving away.* 2 *Mum has given up (stopped) smoking.*

**glacial** *adjective* 1 concerning ice or glaciers.

**glacier** *noun* a huge mass of ice that moves slowly like a river down a mountain valley.

**glad** (gladder, gladdest) *adjective* happy, pleased.

**glade** *noun* an area of open grass in the middle of a forest or wood.

**gladiator** *noun* a warrior in ancient Rome who fought other gladiators or wild animals for the entertainment of spectators.

**glamorous** *adjective* exciting and charming. *She has got a glamorous job in the fashion business.* **glamour** *noun.*

**glance** *verb* 1 to look at something for a moment. *She glanced at her watch.* **glance** *noun.* 2 to hit and then bounce off something at an angle. *The ball glanced off the bat and smashed the window.*

**gland** *noun* an organ in the body that produces substances for the body to use or that removes unwanted substances. *Sweat glands.* **glandular** *adjective. Glandular fever.*

**glare** *verb* 1 to look at somebody fiercely and angrily. 2 to shine with strong, dazzling light. **glare** *noun.*

G

**glaring** *adjective* 1 very bright. *Glaring headlights.* 2 obvious. *Glaring gaps in your general knowledge.*

**glass** *noun* 1 a hard, brittle and usually transparent material used in making window panes, bottles, mirrors, etc. 2 a container made of this material, for drinking. 3 a mirror. **glassy** *adjective.*

**glasses** *plural noun* a pair of lenses in a metal or plastic frame that people with poor eyesight wear over their eyes to help them see better, also called spectacles.

He needed glasses for reading and watching television.

**glaze** *verb* 1 to fit glass into something. *He glazed the windows.* **glazier** *noun.* 2 to cover something with a coating of shiny material called glaze.

**gleam** *verb* to shine softly. *The furniture is gleaming.* **gleam** *noun.*

**glen** *noun* a Scottish word for a long narrow valley. *The lochs and glens.*

**glide** *verb* 1 to move smoothly and silently. 2 to fly smoothly.

**glider** *noun* a small aircraft without an engine that floats on air currents.

**glimmer** *verb* to flicker or to shine very faintly. **glimmer** *noun. A glimmer of hope.*

**glisten** *verb* to shine or gleam, especially of a wet or polished surface.

**glitter** *verb* to sparkle. *The glittering lights of the city.* **glitter** *noun.*

**global** *adjective* relating to the whole world. *Global issues.*

**globe** *noun* a ball-shaped object with a map of the Earth on it.

Sheila kept a globe on her desk to remind her of her travels around the world.

**AMAZING FACT**

Glass has been used to correct weak eyesight since the 1300s, although eyeglasses did not became common until the 1500s.

In 1760, Benjamin Franklin invented the bifocal lens.

**DID YOU KNOW?**

*The 'g' in most words beginning with 'gn' was once pronounced. We have dropped the 'g' sound in words like 'gnarled', 'gnash' and 'gnat' but kept the spelling.*

The gnomes invited the fairies and elves to a tea party under their toadstool.

**gloom** *noun* 1 near-darkness, dimness. 2 sadness and a feeling of depression. **gloomy** *adjective. A gloomy cave.*

**glorious** *adjective* 1 magnificent, causing great happiness. *A glorious holiday.* 2 worthy of glory or praise. *A glorious victory was won by the Persians.*

**glory** *noun* 1 great fame, praise. 2 splendour. *The glory of the mountains.* **glory** *verb. They gloried in their achievements.*

**glossy** *adjective* shiny and smooth. *A glossy magazine.* **gloss** *noun.*

**glove** *noun* a covering for your hand with parts for each finger and thumb.

**glow** *verb* to give out a warm, steady light without flames. **glow** *noun.*

**glow-worm** *noun* an insect that gives out a greenish glow from its tail.

Katharine saw the glow-worms in the Botanical Gardens at Munich.

**glucose** *noun* a natural sugar found in plants. *Glucose is good for athletes.*

**glue** *noun* a thick, sticky substance used for sticking things together. **glue** *verb. Sue glued the handle on to the cup.*

**glum** (glummer, glummest) *adjective* gloomy and sad, depressed.

**glut** *noun* a much greater supply of something than is needed. *A glut of fruit.*

**glutton** *noun* a person who always eats too much. **gluttony** *adjective.*

**GMT** *abbreviation* for Greenwich Mean Time.

**gnarled** *adjective* (say narld) twisted and full of lumpy knots. *A gnarled old oak.*

**gnash** *verb* (say nash) to grind or strike your teeth together with anger or pain.

**gnat** *noun* (say nat) any of many small, mosquito-like insects that bite. *A swarm of gnats.*

**gnaw** *verb* (say naw) to chew on something hard for a long time. *A dog gnaws a bone if it's hungry.*

**gnome** *noun* (say nowm) a little old man in fairy stories who lives under the ground.

**gnu** *noun* (say new) an African ox-like antelope, also known as a wildebeest.

G

**go** (goes, going, went, gone) *verb* 1 to move away from or to somewhere, to travel. 2 to visit. 3 to leave. 4 to disappear. *My tools have gone.* 5 to do something. *I'm going to mow the lawn.* 6 to become. *This fruit is going bad.* 7 to work correctly. *The car won't go.* 8 to fit or have a place somewhere. *The knives go in that drawer.* 9 to lead somewhere. *The road goes to the sea.* 10 to make a certain sound. *Cats go 'miaow'.* **go about** *There's a bug going about.* **go ahead** *Despite the weather, we decided to go ahead with the game.* **go back** *We're going back home to Ireland.* **go in for** *George is going in for the competition.* **go off** 1 *The bomb went off with a bang.* 2 *The milk tastes sour, it must have gone off.* 3 *I don't eat hamburgers any more, I've gone right off them.* **go on** *She keeps going on about how clever she is.* **go with** *Does this tie go with (look good with) this shirt?*

**goal** *noun* 1 the space or net between two posts that players have to kick or hit a ball into in games like hockey and football. 2 A goal is something you hope to achieve, an ambition.

**goat** *noun* a farm animal with short hair and horns.

The milk of goats is recommended to anyone suffering from allergies.

**gobble** *verb* to eat quickly, noisily and greedily. *Peter gobbled up his Big Mac.*

**gobsmacked** *adjective* (slang) stunned and shocked. *I was gobsmacked by the result.*

**god** *noun* any one of many supernatural beings that were thought to control the world. *The gods lived on Mt Olympus.*

**God** *noun* the creator of the universe in Christianity, Islam and Judaism.

**godparent** *noun* a godfather or godmother who at a child's baptism promises to help their godchild be brought up as a Christian.

**goggles** *plural noun* special glasses that fit tightly around the eyes to protect them from dirt, water, etc.

**go-kart** *noun* a small racing car.

**gold** *noun* a very valuable yellow metal that is found in rocks and streams, used for making jewellery. **gold** *adjective*.

**golden** *adjective* made of gold or of the colour of gold. **golden wedding** *noun* the 50th anniversary of a wedding.

**AMAZING FACT**

Some golf courses in desert areas are all sand, the 'greens' are not green at all!

**SPELLING NOTE**

*Try not to confuse 'goal' with 'gaol', which means 'prison'.*

The gondola made its way down the narrow canal.

**SPELLING NOTE**

*Take care not to confuse 'gorilla' ('ape') with 'guerrilla' ('a soldier who fights by surprise attacks'). And notice one 'r' and two 'l's in 'gorilla' and two 'r's and two 'l's in 'guerrilla'.*

Rich seams of gold run underground in South Africa.

**goldfish** *noun* a small orange fish related to carp. *Lots of goldfish in our pond.*

**golf** *noun* an outdoor game in which players use long-handled sticks called golf clubs to hit a small ball from one hole to another around a large grassy area called a golf course. **golfer** *noun*.

**gondola** *noun* a long narrow boat with high pointed ends used on the canals of Venice. **gondolier** *noun* a person who operates a gondola. *The gondolier earned lots of tips.*

**gone** past participle of go.

**good** (better, best) *adjective* 1 of a high quality or standard. 2 kind and helpful. 3 able to do something well. 4 obedient and behaving well. 5 health-giving. 6 enjoyable. **goodness** *noun*. **good-looking** *adjective*.

**goodbye** *interjection* what we say when we leave somebody.

**Good Friday** *noun* the Friday before Easter when Jesus was crucified.

**goods** *plural noun* things that can be bought and sold or that are carried on trains and lorries.

**gooey** *adjective* (slang) sticky. *A gooey pudding.* **gooeyness** *noun*.

**goose** (geese) *noun* a water bird with webbed feet, similar to a large duck. It makes a loud, honking sound. **wild goose chase** a useless journey. **cook someone's goose** to ruin somebody's chances.

**gooseberry** *noun* the small, round green fruit of the gooseberry bush.

**goosepimple** *noun* (also goosebump and gooseflesh) tiny bumps on the skin caused by cold or fear.

**gorilla** *noun* the largest and strongest of the apes. It lives in Africa.

**gorge** *noun* a deep valley with steep sides.

**gorge** *verb* to eat your fill greedily.

**gorgeous** *adjective* 1 very pleasant. 2 beautiful.

G

**gosling** *noun* a young goose.

**gospel** *noun* one of the first four books of the New Testament which describe the life and teachings of Jesus.

**gossip** *noun* talking about other people's personal affairs and saying things that are sometimes untrue. **gossip** *verb*.

**got** past tense of get.

**govern** *verb* to manage or be in charge of a country or organization and make laws and rules for it.

**government** *noun* a group of people who govern or rule a country.

**governor** *noun* 1 a person elected to manage or govern a state in the US. 2 a person who controls an organization. *A school governor.*

**gown** *noun* 1 a long, formal dress worn by a woman. 2 a long, flowing robe worn by such people as lawyers, judges and lecturers.

**GP** *abbreviation* General Practitioner, a family doctor who is not a specialist and who works in the community rather than in a hospital.

**grab** (grabs, grabbing, grabbed) *verb* to take or seize something suddenly and roughly, to snatch. **grab** *noun*. *The mugger made a grab for the old woman's handbag.* **how does it grab you?** What do you think about it?

**grace** *noun* 1 a beautiful and easy way of moving. **graceful** *adjective*. 2 the love and favour of God. 3 a short prayer of thanks said before and after meals.

According to a very old tradition, a judge still wears a wig and gown.

**gracious** *adjective* pleasant and polite. *A gracious smile.*

**grade** *noun* 1 a scale that sorts people or things according to quality, rank, size, etc. *Vegetables of the highest grade.* 2 marks given in an exam. 3 (US) a class of a particular level or year. *He's in the fourth grade.* **grade** *verb*. *The eggs were graded according to size.*

**gradient** *noun* the measure of how steep a slope is. *That hill has a gradient of one in seven. It rises one metre for every seven.*

**gradual** *adjective* changing or happening slowly. *A gradual improvement.*

**graduate** *noun* a person who has finished a course of studies and taken a university degree. **graduate** *verb*.

**graffiti** *plural noun* (say gra-**fee**-tee) drawings and writing scribbled on buildings, trains, etc.

**DID YOU KNOW?**

*Words that include 'ph' (pronounced 'f') as part of the spelling come from the Greek, as in 'graphic' and 'photograph'.*

Grain can be ground into flour for making into pasta or bread.

**grain** *noun* 1 the seed of cereal plants like maize, rice and wheat. 2 tiny bits of something. *Grains of salt, sand and sugar.* 3 the pattern of lines made by the fibres in wood.

**gram** *noun* a metric unit of weight. There are 1000 grams in a kilogram.

**grammar** *noun* the rules of a language and how the words are put together properly.

**grand** *adjective* 1 large, important and magnificent. *Blenheim Palace is very grand.* 2 very pleasant. *We had a grand time at the theme park.*

**grandchild, granddaughter, grandson** the child of a person's son or daughter.

**grandparent, grandfather, grandmother** the parent of one of a person's parents.

**grandstand** *noun* a covered area at a sports ground with rows of raised seats.

**granite** *noun* (say **gran**-it) a very hard rock used in building.

**granny** *noun* grandmother.

**grant** *verb* to agree to, to give something. *The government granted the island independence.* **take something for granted** to feel sure something will happen without checking or without appreciating it.

**grant** *noun* a sum of money given for a particular purpose. *A university grant.*

**grape** *noun* a small, round green or purple fruit that grows in bunches on a bush called a grapevine. Wine is made from grapes.

**grapefruit** (grapefruit or grapefruits) *noun* a round fruit like a big orange but with a yellow skin.

**graph** *noun* (rhymes with half) a diagram or chart that shows how numbers, amounts etc. compare or are related.

The graph showed how sales figures had risen dramatically.

**graphic** *adjective* 1 clear and vivid. *A graphic account of the murder.* 2 relating to painting and drawing. *The graphic arts.*

**graphics** *plural noun* pictures and patterns.

**grasp** *verb* 1 to hold something tightly, to seize. 2 to understand. **grasp** *noun. Get a good grasp on the rope.*

**grass** *noun* a plant with long, thin, green leaves that grows in fields. **grassy** *adjective.*

**grasshopper** *noun* a small jumping insect with long back legs. It makes a chirping sound by rubbing its wings together.

**grate** *noun* a metal frame in a fireplace, for holding the burning fuel.

**grate** *verb* 1 to rub or shred into little pieces against a tool with a rough surface called a grater. 2 to make an unpleasant, scraping sound by rubbing something.

**grateful** *adjective* pleased and wanting to thank somebody, thankful.

**gratitude** *noun* a feeling of being grateful, thankfulness. *Helen was full of gratitude.*

**grave** *adjective* very serious or important. *A grave illness.*

**grave** *noun* a hole in the ground in which to bury a corpse. **gravestone** a carved stone slab placed over a person's grave. **graveyard** a place where people are buried.

**gravel** *noun* small stones used to cover paths and roads.

**gravity** *noun* 1 seriousness. 2 the natural force that draws things to the Earth so that they stay there and do not float away.

The Earth's pull of gravity holds satellites and rockets in orbit around the planet.

**gravy** *noun* hot sauce made from the juices of cooked meat.

**graze** *verb* 1 when animals graze, they eat grass as it grows. 2 to scrape your skin by rubbing it against something rough.

**grease** *noun* a thick, oily substance. **greasy** *adjective.*

**great** *adjective* 1 big or heavy. 2 important, famous or clever. *A great composer.* 3 Very good. *It's great to be here.* **greatness** *noun.*

**Great Britain** *noun* the main island and small islands of England, Scotland and Wales.

**great-grandparents, great-grandfather great-grandmother** the grandparents of somebody's father or mother.

**AMAZING FACT**

Grasshoppers can jump up to 20 times the length of their own bodies. Because they eat leaves and the shoots of young plants, they can become a pest to farmers. Locusts can travel great distances when they swarm and may do serious damage to large areas.

**AMAZING FACT**

Not all greenhouse gases are produced by burning fossil fuels such as gasoline and coal. Large amounts of methane are produced by termites and cattle digesting cellulose.

**Greece** *noun* a country in Southeast Europe.

The flag of Greece is blue and white with a cross in the corner.

**greed** (greedier, greediest) *adjective* a selfish wish to have more of something than you need. **greedy** *adjective.*

**Greek** *noun* 1 a person who comes from Greece. 2 the language spoken in Greece. **Greek** *adjective. Greek civilization.*

**green** *noun* 1 the colour of grass. 2 an open piece of grassy ground for use by everybody. **green** *adjective* 1 *A green light means 'go'.* 2 *They are interested in such green issues as protecting the environment.* 3 young and without much experience.

**greenhouse** *noun* a building made of glass used for growing plants. **greenhouse effect** the effect of the atmosphere around the Earth warming up because gases such as methane and carbon dioxide are trapped in the atmosphere and become heated by the Sun.

A greenhouse is the ideal place for growing pot plants as well as vegetables.

**greet** *verb* to meet and welcome somebody in a friendly way. **greeting** *noun.*

**Grenada** *noun* a country in the West Indies.

**grew** past tense of grow.

**grey** *noun* a colour that is a mixture of black and white. *Rain clouds are grey.*

**greyhound** *noun* a slim breed of dog that can run very fast and is used in racing.

**grid** *noun* 1 a pattern of squares formed by straight lines crossing each other at right angles. 2 a network of cables carrying electricity.

**grief** *noun* (rhymes with leaf) great sorrow or sadness, especially after a death or misfortune. **grieve** *verb. He is grieving for his dead wife.*

**grievance** *noun* a reason to complain or be angry about something.

**grievous** *adjective* very serious or harmful. *A grievous injury.*

**grill** *noun* a part of a cooker where food is cooked under or above direct heat. **grill** *verb. They grilled sausages for breakfast.*

G

**grim** (grimmer, grimmest) *adjective* 1 stern and unsmiling. *A grim look of disapproval.* 2 unpleasant. *Grim news.*

**grime** *noun* dirt rubbed deeply into a surface. **grimy** *adjective.*

**grin** *noun* a broad, cheerful smile. **grin** (grins, grinning, grinned) *verb.* **grin and bear it** to put up with something unpleasant without complaint.

**grind** (grinds, grinding, ground) *verb* to crush something into very small pieces. *The coffee beans have just been ground.* **grind to a halt** slowly to come to a complete stop.

**grip** (grips, gripping, gripped) *verb* 1 to hold something very firmly, to grasp. **grip** *noun.* 2 to hold somebody's complete attention. *She was gripped by the news of his death.*

**grit** *noun* tiny pieces of stone. **grit** *verb. The council grit the roads in icy weather for safety.* **gritty** *adjective.*

**groan** *noun* a long, deep sound showing pain or unhappiness. **groan** *verb.*

**groceries** *plural noun* things such as flour, tea, jam and sugar that you buy from a grocer's shop or from a supermarket.

**groin** *noun* the place where the top of your legs meet.

**groom** *verb* to clean and brush an animal, particularly a horse. **groom** *noun* 1 a person who looks after horses. 2 a man who is about to get married, a bridegroom.

**groove** *noun* a long, narrow cut into the surface of something.

**grope** *verb* to feel your way or search with your hands for something you cannot see.

**grotesque** *adjective* (say grow-**tesk**) weird and unnatural.

**ground** *noun* 1 the solid surface of the Earth. The floor. 2 a sports field. **gain ground** to make progress. **break new ground** to do something new or for the first time.

**ground** past tense of grind.

**grounded** *adjective* If an aircraft is grounded it is unable to fly.

**grounds** *plural noun* 1 the land around a large building. *The school grounds.* 2 reasons. *What grounds have you for believing her?* 3 the little bits that fall to the bottom of a drink like coffee.

**group** *noun* a number of people, animals or things that are in one place or that belong together in some way. A family group. *Lions, tigers and leopards belong to the same group of animals.* **group** *verb.*

A tadpole will soon grow into a frog.

**AMAZING FACT**

The largest North American frog, the bullfrog is very slow to mature. Although the eggs hatch in only about five or six days, it may take from two to five years for the tadpoles to grow into adult bullfrogs.

Dorian cut a groove in the wood with his chisel.

**SPELLING NOTE**

*Note the 'u' in words like 'guarantee' and 'guard'. Before 'i' and 'e' the 'g' is usually soft, as in 'gem' and 'ginger'. Inserting 'u' makes the 'g' hard' as in 'guest' and 'guide'.*

**grovel** (grovels, grovelling, grovelled) *verb* to behave in an over-humble and respectful way to somebody because you think they are important.

**grow** (grows, growing, grew, grown) *verb* 1 to become larger and taller, to develop. 2 to plant in the ground. *We are growing vegetables this year.* 2 to become. *He's growing stronger every day.* **grow up** to become an adult. **grow out of** *She'll grow out of biting her nails.*

**growl** *verb* to make a deep, low and angry sound. *The dog growled when I tried to take her bone.*

**growth** *noun* 1 growing, developing. *The population growth.* 2 a lump growing in a part of person's body.

**grown-up** *noun* an adult. **grown-up** *adjective. He has a grown-up son.*

**grub** *noun* 1 the larva or worm-like creature that will grow into an insect. 2 (slang) food.

One day the grub would turn into a beautiful moth.

**grubby** (grubbier, grubbiest) *adjective* dirty. *Wash your grubby hands.*

**grudge** *noun* a long-lasting feeling of dislike or resentment towards somebody because they harmed you in the past.

**gruelling** *adjective* very tiring, severe. *A long, gruelling journey.*

**gruesome** *adjective* revolting and shocking. *A gruesome murder.*

**gruff** *adjective* unfriendly and rough. *A gruff voice.*

**grumble** *verb* to mutter and complain in a bad-tempered way. *He's always grumbling about the noise.*

**grumpy** (grumpier, grumpiest) *adjective* irritable and bad-tempered. **grumpiness** *noun. Gary's grumpiness got them down.*

**grunt** *verb* to make a short, gruff sound like a pig. **grunt** *noun.*

**guarantee** *noun* 1 a promise by a manufacturer etc that something is of a certain quality and that it will be repaired or replaced if it goes wrong within a certain time. *The computer has a year's guarantee.* 2 a promise that something will definitely happen. *There's no guarantee that we'll win the match.* **guarantee** *verb.*

**guard** *verb* to watch over and protect somebody or something. *Police officers guarded the palace.*

**guard** *noun* 1 a person or group etc. that guards. *A guard dog.* 2 some device or thing that guards or protects. *A fire guard.* 3 a person in charge of a train (US brakeman). **on guard** prepared to defend and protect. **off guard** unprepared.

**guarded** *adjective* 1 protected. 2 cautious and careful not to say too much. *A guarded reply.*

**Guatemala** *noun* a country in Central America.

**Guatemala City** *noun* the capital of Guatemala.

**guess** *verb* 1 to say what you think is the answer without having enough information to know whether it is really correct. *Joe guessed the weight of the cake.* 2 to think. *I guess I'd better be going.* **guess** *noun*. *My guess is that she is older than she looks.* **guesswork** making guesses or the result of guesses. *He cooked the cake by guesswork.*

**guest** *noun* 1 a person who has been invited to stay for a short time in somebody's house, a visitor. *Be my guest!* 2 a person staying in an hotel.

**guide** *noun* somebody who leads or shows the way; a person who helps or advises. *A guide showed us around the magnificent cathedral.* **guide** *verb*.

**guidebook** *noun* a book containing information for visitors to a place.

**guide dog** *noun* a dog that has been trained to help a blind person.

**guideline** *noun* advice or rules on how something should be done.

**guillotine** *noun* (say **gill**-uh-teen) a machine used in France to cut off people's heads (behead). It consists of a blade that slides down between two posts.

**guilt** *noun* 1 the miserable feeling you have when you know you have done something wrong. 2 the fact that you have done something wrong.

**guilty** *adjective* 1 having done something wrong or committed a crime. *She was guilty of shop-lifting.* 2 the feeling of guilt or shame.

**Guinea** *noun* a country in Africa.

**Guinea-Bissau** *noun* a country in Africa.

Guinea pigs make ideal pets.

**AMAZING FACT**

Guinea pigs are rodents, not pigs, and they are originally from Peru, not Guinea.

The tame Guinea pigs that we keep as pets are actually decendents of the cavy, an animal that lives in the Andes mountains.

Some Guinea pigs have very long coats. They may be white, black, gray or brown.

**SPELLING NOTE**

*The guillotine was first used during the French Revolution (1789–95) and is named after its inventor, Dr Joseph Guillotin.*

Marie Antoinette, Queen of France, lost her head on the guillotine.

**guinea pig** *noun* 1 a furry, tail-less South American rodent, often kept as a pet. 2 somebody used in a scientific experiment.

**guitar** *noun* a musical instrument with six strings that you pluck with your fingers or with a plectrum. **guitarist** *noun*.

**Gujurati** *noun* the language spoken in the state of Gujurat in western India.

**gulf** *noun* a bay or large area of the sea almost surrounded by land.

**gull** *noun* a large sea bird (seagull) with grey and white feathers and webbed feet.

**gum** *noun* 1 the firm pink flesh in your mouth that holds your teeth. 2 glue or sticky liquid for sticking things together. **gum** *verb*. 3 chewing-gum.

**gun** *noun* a weapon that shoots bullets through a metal tube. **gunfire** the repeated firing of guns.

**gunpowder** *noun* a powder that explodes easily. Gunpowder is used in fireworks.

**gush** *verb* When a liquid such as water gushes, it flows out suddenly and in large quantities. **gush** *noun*.

**gust** *noun* a strong and sudden rush of wind. **gusty** *adjective*.

**guts** *plural noun* 1 the intestines. 2 bravery.

**gutter** *noun* a channel for rainwater to flow along, fixed to the edge of a roof or built along a street.

**Guyana** *noun* a country in South America.

**gym** short for gymnasium and gymnastics.

**gymnasium** *noun* a room or building with special equipment for doing physical exercises. *Sarah goes to the gymnasium at least once a week.*

**gymnast** *noun* a person who is trained in gymnastics.

**gymnastics** *noun* highly skilled physical exercises using equipment such as bars, ropes and jumping horses.

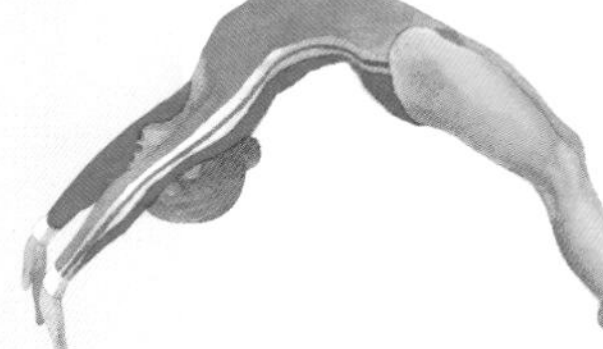

Gymnastics is one of the most respected events at the Olympic Games.

**gypsy** *noun* a member of a dark-haired race of people who travel from place to place, usually in caravans. *The gypsies danced and played music by the camp fire.*

# Hh

**habit** *noun* 1 something that you do regularly, usually without thinking about it. A custom. *She has an annoying habit of twisting her hair.* **habitual** *adjective*. 2 the loose clothes worn by a monk or nun.

**habitat** *noun* the place where an animal or plant naturally lives or grows.

**hack** *verb* 1 to cut something, roughly, with repeated blows. *He hacked his way through the undergrowth.* 2 to ride a horse in open countryside. 3 to get information from a computer system illegally. **hacker** *noun*.

**haddock** *noun* an edible sea fish, related to cod. *Smoked haddock with poached egg.*

**hag** *noun* an offensive word meaning ugly old woman.

**haggard** *adjective* looking thin, ill and tired. *Worry has made her look terribly haggard.*

**haggle** *verb* to argue over the price of something, to bargain.

**hail** *noun* frozen rain. **hail** *verb*. **hailstone** *noun* a frozen raindrop.

**hail** *verb* to call out or wave to get attention. *She hailed a taxi.*

**hair** *noun* 1 a fine thread that grows on the skin of people and animals. 2 the soft mass of these threads covering a person's head. *Harry has fair hair.* **let your hair down** to behave in a very relaxed way. **keep your hair on** to stay calm and not get excited. **split hairs** to argue about unimportant details.

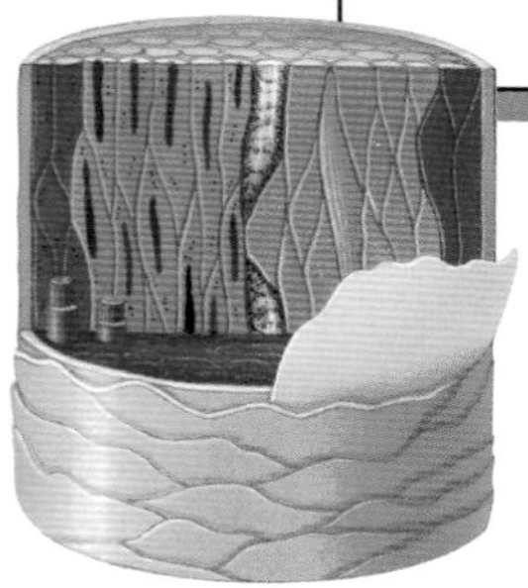

This section through a hair shaft shows how layers of keratin (a protein) make up the outer coating or cuticle. Inside, more keratin makes up the cortex and the inner layer, or medulla.

**haircut** *noun* the act of cutting somebody's hair. The style in which the hair has been cut.

**hairdresser** *noun* a person who cuts and arranges (styles) hair.

**hair-raising** *adjective* terrifying.

**hairy** (hairier, hairiest) *adjective* 1 covered in hair. 2 (slang) exciting and risky. *A hairy ride on the roller-coaster.*

**Haiti** (say **hay**-tee) *noun* a country in the West Indies, the western part of the island of Hispaniola.

**halal** *noun* meat from animals that have been killed according to Islam's religious laws. *A halal butcher.*

**WORD HISTORY**

*The shape of the letter H comes from the ancient Egyptian symbol for a twist of rope. In the Greek alphabet it has an 'ee' sound. The Romans gave it its present 'h' sound.*

**SPELLING NOTE**

*Hallowe'en comes from All Hallows Eve, the eve of All Saints' Day, 31 October. 'Hallow' is an Old English word for saint.*

**half** (halves) *noun* one of two equal parts. *Half an apple.* **half** *adverb* partly, not completely. *The meat is still half-frozen.* **half** *adjective A half bottle of wine.* **half-hearted** *adjective* not very keen or enthusiastic. *A half-hearted effort.*

Jackie likes prawn cocktail made with half an avocado.

**half-time** *noun* a short break between two halves of a game such as football or hockey.

**halfmast** *noun* the position half-way down a pole at which a flag is flown as a sign that somebody important has died.

**hall** *noun* 1 a room or passageway at the entrance to a house. 2 a large room or building for public meetings, concerts etc.

**Halloween** *noun* the evening of 31 October, the day before All Saints' Day when some people believe that ghosts and witches roam about.

**hallucinate** *verb* to hear or see things that are not really there. **hallucination** *noun*.

**halt** *verb* to come or bring to a stop. *The train halted at the station.* **halt** *noun*.

**halve** *verb* 1 to divide or cut something into two equal parts. 2 to reduce by half.

**ham** *noun* 1 salted meat from a pig's back leg. 2 (slang) an actor who is not very good and who overacts.

**hamburger** *noun* a bread roll containing a round cake of chopped beef.

**hamlet** *noun* a small village (in Britain), usually without a church.

**hammer** *noun* a tool with a long handle and a heavy head used mainly for hitting (hammering) nails into things. **hammer** *verb*.

**hammock** *noun* a swinging bed made of strong cloth or rope that is hung up at the ends between two supports.

Andy lazed all day in the hammock.

**hamper** *noun* a large basket with a lid, for carrying things. *A picnic hamper.*

**hamper** *verb* to prevent or make something difficult to do, to hinder. *Her tight jacket hampered her movements.*

**hamster** *noun* a small, furry, tail-less rodent that can store food in its cheeks. Hamsters are often kept as pets.

Lola's hamster won first prize in the show.

**hand** *noun* 1 the part of your body at the end of your arm and below your wrist with four fingers and a thumb. 2 a pointer on a clock. *My watch has an hour hand, a minute hand and a second hand.* 3 help. *Can you give me a hand, please?* 4 a worker. *A farm hand.* 5 the cards a player holds in his or her hand in a card game. *I had a winning hand.* 6 The measure of the height of horses and ponies (equal to 10 centimetres). **hand** *verb* to give. *She handed me the letter.* **at first hand** directly and not through other people. **in hand** being dealt with, under control. **hand out** to give out, share. **on hand** ready and available. **out of hand** out of control.

**handbag** *noun* a small bag usually carried by women for money and personal belongings (US purse).

**handbook** *noun* a book with instructions or useful facts about something.

**handcuffs** *plural noun* a pair of metal rings joined by a chain and locked around a prisoner's wrists to stop them escaping. **handcuff** *verb*.

**handicap** *noun* 1 a disadvantage or something that makes it difficult to do what you want to do. *His lack of experience was a handicap.* 2 a disability of the body or mind. *Being deaf can be a terrible handicap.*

**handicraft** *noun* work such as pottery or weaving that needs skilful use of the hands.

**handkerchief** *noun* (say **hang**-ker-cheef) a small piece of cloth or tissue used for blowing and wiping your nose.

**handle** *noun* the part of an object that you can hold it by or make it work by. *Turn the handle to open the door.* **handle** *verb* 1 to hold, touch or move something with your hands. 2 to deal with or control. *Grooms handle horses.*

**handlebars** *plural noun* the bar with a handle at each end at the front of a bicycle or motorbike that the rider holds and steers with. *Hold on to the handlebars.*

**WORD HISTORY**

*'Handsome' once meant 'easy to handle'. The meaning then changed to 'pleasant' and then to the present meaning of 'pleasant to look at, noble, gracious and generous.'*

**SPELLING NOTE**

*Try not to confuse 'hangar' with an 'a' and 'hanger' with an 'e'.*

**AMAZING FACT**

'Hangman' is a game that you can play to improve your spelling. Play with a friend. Take turns. Think of a word. Put a blank – for each letter of the word on a piece of paper. The other person guesses a letter. If the word contains that letter, write it in the correct blank. If not, draw one part of the 'hangman'. There are 10 parts.

**handsome** *adjective* attractive, good-looking. *A handsome man.*

**handy** (handier, handiest) *adjective* 1 nearby and easy to reach. *There's a handy shop round the corner.* 2 useful and easy to use. *Penknives are handy tools.* 3 skilful in the use of tools. *He's handy around the house.*

**hang** (hangs, hanging, hung) *verb* 1 to attach something by its top part so that the lower part is free. *She hung her coat on a hook.* 2 to swing loosely. *The dog's tongue is hanging out of its mouth.* 3 **hang** (hangs, hanging, hanged) to kill somebody by putting a rope around their neck and letting them drop from a support. **hang about** to wait about a place with nothing to do. **hang back** to be unwilling to do something. **hang on** 1 to hold tightly. 2 to wait. *Hang on a minute, wait for me!*

**hangar** *noun* a large building where aircraft are kept. *Aircraft hangar.*

**hanger** *noun* something on which to hang clothes to be stored in a cupboard.

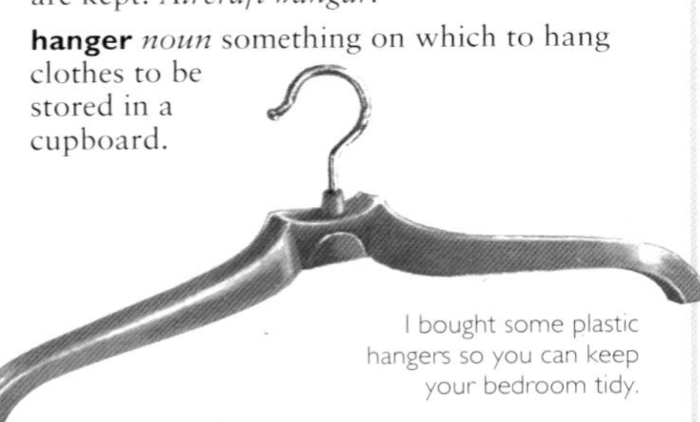

I bought some plastic hangers so you can keep your bedroom tidy.

**hang-glider** *noun* a kite-like glider to which you are strapped and can then fly from the top of cliffs etc. in the sport of hang-gliding.

**hanker** *verb* to want something very badly, to long for. *She is hankering after a ride in the helicopter.*

**Hanoi** *noun* the capital of Vietnam.

**Hanukkah** *noun* the Jewish festival of lights, which is held in December.

**haphazard** *adjective* unplanned, happening by accident. *A haphazard arrangement.*

**happen** *verb* 1 to take place. *What happened next in the story?* 2 to occur by chance. *I just happened to see him.*

**happening** *noun* an event. *Great happenings in history.*

The space walk was the greatest happening of his life.

**happy** (happier, happiest) *adjective* 1 the feeling of being pleased and cheerful. 2 willing. *I'd be happy to go instead of you.* **happiness** *noun.* **happily** *adverb.*

**Harare** *noun* the capital of Zimbabwe.

**harass** *verb* to annoy or bother somebody repeatedly. **harassment** *noun.* **harassed** *adjective. Sarah feels very harrassed today.*

**harbour** *noun* a place where ships stop to load or unload cargoes and where they can shelter. A port.

**hard** *adjective* 1 solid and difficult to shape or break, not soft. *Concrete becomes hard when it sets.* 2 difficult. *A hard jigsaw.* 3 severe and tough. *Hard discipline.* **hard** *adverb* with great energy or effort. *Work hard, play hard.* **hardness** *noun.*

**hardback** *noun* a book with a long-lasting, stiff cover.

**harden** *verb* to make or to become hard and stiff. *The concrete hardened.*

**hard-copy** *noun* a printed copy of information created on a computer, also called a printout.

**hard-disc** *noun* a device inside a computer that holds a large amount of data.

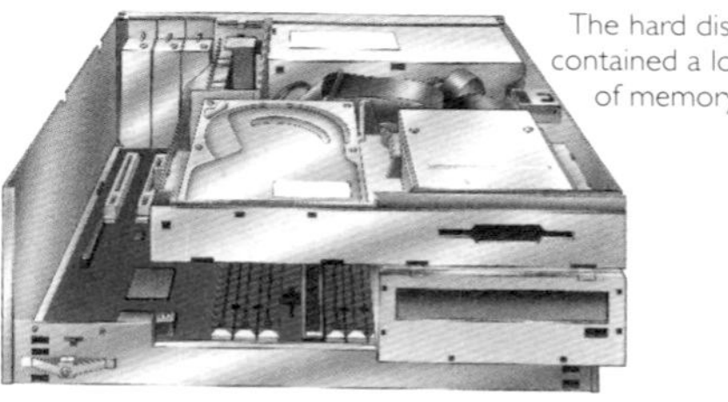

The hard disc contained a lot of memory.

**hardly** *adverb* almost but not completely, scarcely. *He was so tired he could hardly keep his eyes open.*

**hardship** *noun* causing suffering or difficulty. *He suffered great hardship.*

**hardware** *noun* 1 all the pieces of machinery that make up a computer, e.g. the printer and VDU. 2 tools and equipment used in the home, ironmongery.

**hardy** *adjective* strong, robust and able to endure severe conditions. *Hardy plants.*

**hare** *noun* an animal like a large rabbit.

**harm** *verb* to hurt or damage somebody or something. **harm** *noun.*

**harmful** *adjective* bad for you. *Too much sugar is harmful to your teeth.*

**harmless** *adjective* safe and not dangerous or harmful. *A harmless insect.*

**harmony** *noun* 1 musical notes played at the same time and which sound pleasant. 2 agreement and cooperation. **harmonious** *adjective.* **harmonize** *verb.*

The harp is a favourite instrument in Wales.

**SPELLING NOTE**

*Note the one 'r' and two 's's in 'harass'. But remember that 'embarrass' has two 'r's'.*

**AMAZING FACT**

Some animals have special words for the young, for males, for females, a group of the animal and for the place the animals live.

For example, a young hare is called a leveret, a male hare is a buck, a female is a doe. A group of hares is called a drove and the home of a hare is a form. These specialized words probably developed during the Middle Ages, when hunting was a main source of food.

**harness** *noun* the leather straps fastened to a horse to control it. The bridle, reins and saddle are parts of the harness. **harness** *verb.*

**harp** *noun* a musical instrument that you play by plucking its strings. **harpist** *noun.*

**harpoon** *noun* a spear with a rope attached that is used to hunt whales. **harpoon** *verb.*

**harpsichord** *noun* a keyboard instrument similar to a piano with strings that are plucked.

**harsh** *adjective* 1 stern, unkind and severe. *Harsh treatment.* 2 rough and unpleasant. *A harsh sound.*

**harvest** *noun* the time when grain and other crops are cut and gathered. *Harvest is the busiest time of the year for the farming community.* **harvest** *verb.*

**hassle** *noun* a bother or a cause of trouble. *It's too much hassle to go by bus.* **hassle** *verb* (slang) to pester or bother somebody. *Stop hassling me!*

**haste** *noun* a hurry. *She was late and left in great haste.* **hasten** *verb. He hastened home.*

**hasty** (hastier, hastiest) *adjective* done quickly, and sometimes too quickly and without care. *A hasty decision.*

**hat** *noun* a covering for the head, usually with a brim. *A hat keeps your head warm.* **talk though your hat** to talk nonsense.

Hats can be decorated with feathers, bows and coloured bands.

**hatch** *noun* a movable covering for a hole in a floor, wall or ceiling etc. *An escape hatch on an aeroplane.* **hatchback car** a car with a door at the back that opens upwards.

**hatch** *verb* 1 An egg hatches when it breaks open and a chick or reptile comes out. 2 to plan. *What scheme are you hatching?*

**hate** *verb* to dislike somebody or something very much, to loathe. **hate, hatred** *noun.*

**hateful** *adjective* causing hatred, unpleasant. *What a hateful person he is.*

**haul** *verb* to pull or drag something heavy with a lot of effort.

**haunt** *verb* If a ghost haunts a place, it visits it regularly. **haunted** *adjective.*

**Havana** *noun* the capital of Cuba.

H

**have** (has, having, had) *verb* 1 to own. *She has 20 pairs of shoes.* 2 to experience or enjoy something. *Let's have a party.* 3 to be forced to do something. *I have to go home today.* 4 to receive. *I had a lot of cards on my birthday.*

**havoc** *noun* great damage, chaos.

**hawk** *noun* a bird of prey with good eyesight and sharp talons.

**hay** *noun* grass that has been cut and dried for feeding to animals. **make hay while the sun shines** to do things while you have the opportunity to.

**hayfever** *noun* an illness like a bad cold caused by an allergy or bad reaction to breathing in the pollen of grasses or flowers.

**hazard** *noun* a risk or something that can cause harm. *That loose step is a hazard.*

**hazel** *noun* 1 a small tree on which hazelnuts grow. 2 a yellowish-brown colour. *Hazel eyes glow with a special warmth.*

**hazy** (hazier, haziest) *adjective* 1 misty. *A hazy day.* **haze** *noun.* 2 not clear, confused. *I have only a hazy idea of how to get there.*

**head** *noun* 1 the top part of your body above your neck, containing your face, hair and skull. 2 the leader or person in charge of something. *The head of department.* 3 the front or upper part of something. *The head of a letter.* **heads** the side of a coin showing somebody's head. **head** *verb* 1 to move in a direction. *They headed for the beach.* 2 to be in charge of. *She heads the news team.*

**headache** *noun* 1 a pain in your head. 2 a problem.

**headland** *noun* a piece of land jutting out into the sea.

**headlight** *noun* one of the strong lights at the front of a motor vehicle.

**headline** *noun* 1 heading or words printed in large, bold print at the head of a story in a newspaper. 2 **headlines** the main items of news. *The news headlines in brief.*

**headquarters** *noun* the main place from which a business or organization is controlled. *The headquarters of the bank.*

**headway** *noun* progress. *He's making some headway in Japanese.*

**heal** *verb* to make or become better or healthy again. *Physician, heal thyself.*

AMAZING FACT

A group of hawks is called a cast of hawks.

The hawk is a fearsome predator.

GRAMMAR NOTE

*'To hear' means to receive sounds through your ears, and 'to listen' means to pay attention to what you hear.*

AMAZING FACT

Headlines are short and contain only the most important information in a news story. They are supposed to get your attention and be easy to read. Space is often limited, too, so headlines are rarely complete sentences. Next time you read a newspaper, look at the language of headlines – not only is the grammar different, certain words are more common in headlines than in any other form of writing.

**health** *noun* the condition of your body and how well or ill it is.

**healthy** (healthier, healthiest) *adjective* 1 well and not suffering from any illness or injury, fit. 2 something that is good for you. *Healthy exercise.* **healthily** *adverb.*

**heap** *noun* 1 an untidy pile or mass of things. *A heap of dirty dishes.* 2 **heaps** a large amount. *There's heaps of time before the train goes.* **heap** *verb. She heaped the rubbish in the corner.*

Dad left a heap of dirty dishes in the sink.

**hear** *verb* 1 to receive or pick up sound with our ears, to listen to. 2 to receive information. *We hear you are going away.*

**hearing** *noun* One of the body's five senses is the ability to hear.

**hearing-aid** *noun* a small device that makes sounds louder and which people with poor hearing wear in or behind their ears to help them hear better.

**hearse** *noun* a vehicle for carrying a coffin to a cemetery etc.

**heart** *noun* 1 the organ inside your chest that pumps blood around your body. 2 the main or most important part. *The heart of the matter.* 3 courage and enthusiasm. *She put her heart into the job.* 4 **hearts** one of the four suits in a pack of playing cards.

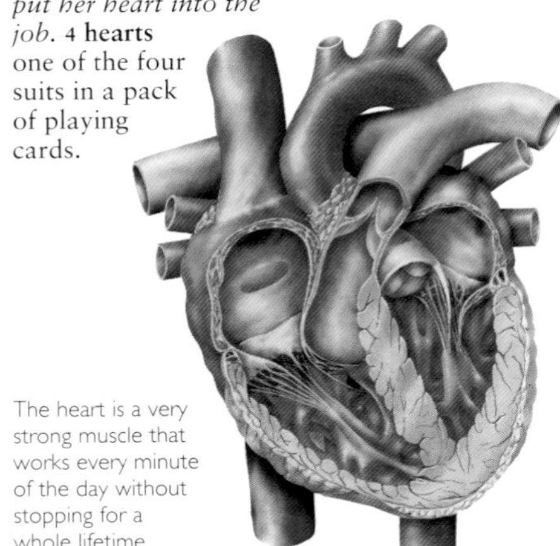

The heart is a very strong muscle that works every minute of the day without stopping for a whole lifetime

**heart-attack** *noun* a serious condition when the heart suddenly does not work properly and may even stop, causing death.

**heart-breaking** *adjective* causing great sadness. *I am so sorry to hear your heart-breaking news.*

**heartbroken** *adjective. She was heartbroken when her budgie died.*

H

**heart-felt** *adjective* very sincere. *My heart-felt thanks to all concerned.*

**heartless** *adjective* cruel and pitiless. **heartlessness** *noun.*

**hearth** *noun* the floor of a fireplace.

**hearty** (heartier, heartiest) *adjective* 1 enthusiastic and friendly. *They gave us a hearty welcome.* 2 strong, big and healthy. *A hearty meal was enjoyed by all.*

**heat** *adjective* 1 the hotness or warmth of something. *The heat of the fire.* 2 one of a number of races in a competition, the winners of which go forward into the next trial. **heat** *verb* to make something hot. *The fire heated the room.* **heated** *adjective.*

**heath** *noun* a wild and open area of land covered with grass and shrubs.

**heather** *noun* an evergreen shrub with pink, purple or white flowers that grows on moors and heaths.

Heather is the national flower of Scotland.

**heave** *verb* to lift, move or throw something using a lot of effort.

**heaven** *noun* a place of great happiness and the home of God, where good people are said to go when they die.

**heavy** (heavier, heaviest) *adjective* 1 having great weight and hard to lift. *A heavy suitcase.* 2 great amount or force. *Heavy rain fell in sheets.* 3 (slang) serious, boring and complicated. *She gets heavy when she talks about her work.* **heaviness** *noun.* **heavily** *adverb.*

**Hebrew** *noun* the original language of Judaism.

**hecta e** *noun* a measure of an area of land, equal to 10,000 square metres.

**hectic** *adjective* very busy and full of exciting activity. *A hectic day.*

**hedge** *noun* a fence around a field or garden made of closely planted shrubs or small trees. **hedge** *verb* 1 to surround land with a hedge. 2 to avoid giving a straight answer. *She hedged around the subject.*

**hedgehog** *noun* a small animal covered in needle-like prickles. Hedgehogs come out at night. They roll up into a ball if frightened.

Hedgehogs can get quite tame if you feed them on bread and milk.

**SPELLING NOTE**

*A word with the same sound as 'heel' is 'heal'.*

**DID YOU KNOW?**

*'Heir' is one of a small number of words beginning with 'h' in which the 'h' is not pronounced. Others are 'hour', 'honour' and 'honest'.*

**hedgerow** *noun* a row or line of bushes forming a hedge around a field or along a country road.

**heel** *noun* 1 the back part of your foot. 2 the part of sock, shoe etc. that covers or supports the heel. *She's wearing shoes with very high heels.*

**heifer** *noun* (say **heff**-er) a young cow that has not yet had a calf.

**height** *noun* 1 how high something is from top to bottom. *The height of the room is nearly three metres.* 2 the highest, best or most important point or part of something. *The height of fashion.*

**heighten** *verb* to make something higher or become greater. *Their excitement heightened as they approached the park.*

**heir** *noun* (say air) an heir is a person who will have (inherit) the money, title etc. of somebody when they die.

**heiress** *noun* (say **air**-ess) a female heir.

**heirloom** *noun* a special or valuable object that is passed down in a family from one generation to the next.

**held** past and past participle of hold.

**helicopter** *noun* an aircraft with a large, fast-turning blade (rotor) on top, which acts as both a propeller and wings.

**helium** *noun* a colourless gas that is lighter than air and does not burn. It is used to fill balloons and airships.

**hell** *noun* a place where some people believe the devil lives and where wicked people go to be punished after they die.

**hello** *interjection* a word we use to attract somebody's attention or to greet somebody. *'Hello! Can you help me?'*

**helm** *noun* a ship's steering wheel, a tiller.

**helmet** *noun* a strong, hard covering to protect the head.

He wore the splendid golden helmet when he went on parade.

**help** *verb* 1 to do something that is needed or useful for somebody else, to assist. *'Can you help me move this sofa, please?'* 2 **can't help** unable to prevent or control. *She can't help sneezing.* **help** *noun.* **helper** *noun.*

**helpful** *adjective* useful and willing to help. *That was helpful advice.*

**helping** *noun* a share or amount of food put on your plate. *A big helping of pudding.*

**helpless** *adjective* not able to take care of yourself. *Babies are quite helpless.*

**Helsinki** *noun* the capital of Finland.

**hem** *noun* the edge of a piece of cloth that is folded over and sewn. **hem** (hems, hemming, hemmed) *verb. She hemmed her skirt.* **hem in** to surround closely and prevent from escaping.

**hemisphere** *noun* 1 the shape of half a sphere. 2 one half of the Earth. *Europe is in the northern hemisphere.*

**hen** *noun* a female chicken, especially one kept for its eggs. 2 any female bird. *A hen pheasant.*

The brown hen lays an egg for my breakfast every day.

**hence** *adverb* 1 therefore, for this reason. *There's been no rain, hence it's very dry.* 2 from now on. *From this day hence.*

**herald** *verb* 1 to say that something is going to happen. 2 to be a sign that something is going to happen. *Dark clouds herald storms.*

**heraldry** *noun* the study of coats-of-arms and family histories.

**herb** *noun* a plant used to add flavour in cooking or for making medicines. **herbal** *adjective. Herbal remedies.*

**herbivore** *noun* an animal that eats only plants. Horses and cattle are herbivores. **herbivorous** *adjective.*

**herd** *noun* a group of animals of one kind that graze and live together. *A herd of cows.* **herd** *verb* to crowd together.

**here** *adverb* at or to this place. *Come here immediately!*

**hereafter** *adverb* in the future, after this time. *Hereafter, things will be different.*

**heretic** *noun* (say **hair**-it-ik) a person who supports an opinion (usually religious or political) that is against the official view or what most people generally accept. **heretical** *adjective.* **heresy** *noun.*

**heritage** *noun* traditions, buildings etc. that are passed from one generation to the next.

**hermit** *noun* somebody who chooses to live alone and away from people, usually for religious reasons.

**AMAZING FACT**

Herons use their long beaks to grasp their prey rather than to spear it.

Florence Nightingale was a heroine to all the men she nursed.

**AMAZING FACT**

Animals hibernate during the cold, winter months when food is scarce. They eat as much as they can before finding a safe place to curl up for the winter. Hibernation isn't the same as sleeping, though. Sleeping takes more energy than hibernation. To conserve energy, the breathing and heartbeat of a hibernating animal slows down so much that they may appear to be almost dead.

**hero** (heroes) *noun* 1 a man or boy admired for having done something brave or especially good. **heroism** *noun.* **heroic** *adjective. Heroic deeds are related in many myths and fairytales.* 2 the most important male character in a book, film or play.

**heroin** *noun* a very strong drug that some people become addicted to.

**heroine** *noun* a woman or girl admired for having done something brave or especially good. **heroism** *noun.* **heroic** *adjective.* 2 the most important female character in a book, film or play.

**heron** *noun* a bird with long legs and a long thin beak that lives near ponds or rivers.

**hesitate** *verb* to pause or to stop doing something for a short time because you are uncertain, undecided or worried. **hesitation** *noun. He agreed to help without any hesitation.* **hesitant** *adjective.*

**heterosexual** *adjective* sexually attracted to people of the opposite sex. Most people are heterosexual. **heterosexuality** *noun.*

**hew** (hews, hewing, hewed, hewn or hewed) *verb* to cut with an axe.

**hexagon** *noun* a shape with six equal sides. **hexagonal** *adjective.*

A hexagon is a shape with six equal sides.

**hibernate** *verb* when animals hibernate, they spend the winter in a deep sleep. Bears, hedgehogs and tortoises all hibernate. **hibernation** *noun.*

**hiccough** *noun* (say **hik**-up) a sudden, repeated sound in your throat which people sometimes make after eating or drinking.

**hide** (hiding, hid, hidden) *verb* 1 to go to a place where you cannot be seen. *She hid in the attic.* 2 to put something in a place where people will not see it. *She hid the presents in a cupboard.*

H

**hide** *noun* the skin of an animal used for making leather.

**hideous** *adjective* very ugly, unpleasant. *A hideous smell wafted up out of the drain.*

**hieroglyphics** *plural noun* (say **hy**-er-uh-glif-iks) the ancient Egyptian system of writing that uses pictures to represent words and sounds.

**high** *adjective* 1 a long way above the ground. 2 the distance from the top to the bottom of something. *The door is two metres high.* 3 greater than normal. *The police car drove at a high speed.* 4 not deep or low. *Children have high voices.* 5 important or above others in rank.

**highlands** *plural noun* a hilly region, especially the Highlands of northern Scotland.

In the Highlands of Scotland you can see lochs, mountains and castles.

**highlight** *noun* the most interesting part of something. *Seeing the game park was the highlight of the visit.* **highlight** *verb* 1 to draw attention to something. *He highlighted the importance of good spelling when he spoke to the class.* 2 to use a coloured pen to mark important parts of a document.

**high-pitched** *adjective* shrill and high in sound. *A high-pitched wail.*

**high-rise** *adjective* High-rise buildings are very tall.

High-rise buildings lined the waterfront.

**highly-strung** *adjective* sensitive and nervous. *The horse is very highly-strung.*

**high tech** *noun* high technology. The use of advanced computers, electronics etc.

**high tide** *noun* the time when the sea reaches its highest level.

**highway** *noun* a main road.

**WORD HISTORY**

*'Hieroglyphics' comes from two Greek words, 'hieros', 'sacred or priestly' and 'glyphe', 'carving' or 'writing'. The Greeks believed that only the Egyptian priests understood and used this system of writing.*

**SPELLING NOTE**

*The word 'hippopotamus' comes from two Greek words and means 'river horse'. Hippos are in fact more closely related to pigs than horses.*

**highwayman** (highwaymen) *noun* in the past, a robber on horseback who stopped travellers at gunpoint.

**hijack** *verb* to take control of an aircraft, car etc. by force and make it go somewhere. **hijack** *noun. The hijack ended in disaster.*

**hijacker** *noun* a person who hijacks.

**hike** *verb* to go on a long walk. *I hiked all over Wales.* **hike** *noun.* **hiker** *noun.*

**hilarious** *adjective* very funny in a noisy way. **hilarity** *noun.*

**hill** *noun* an area of ground that is higher than the ground around it. **hilly** *adjective. Hilly countryside.*

**hilt** *noun* the handle of a sword or dagger. **up to the hilt** completely. *I support my team right up to the hilt.*

**hinder** *verb* to get in the way and so make things difficult for somebody, to prevent and delay. **hindrance** *noun.*

**Hindu** *noun* (say hin-**doo**) a follower of Hinduism, an Indian religion which has many gods and teaches that people will return to Earth in a different form after death. **Hindu** *adjective.*

**Hindustani** *noun* a dialect of the language Hindi, and one of the main languages of India. *Fluent Hindustani.*

**hinge** *noun* a moving metal joint on which such things as doors, gates, windows and lids to boxes can swing when opened.

**hint** *verb* to mention something without actually saying it. *Jack hinted that it was time to go by looking at his watch.* **hint** *noun* 1 a suggestion or clue. 2 helpful advice. *Gardening hints.*

**hip** *noun* one of the two joints on either side of your body between the top of your legs and your waist.

**hippopotamus** (hippopotamuses) *noun* a very large African animal with short legs and thick skin that lives in or near lakes and rivers. It is often called a hippo for short.

A hippopotamus was bathing in the water hole, enjoying wallowing in the mud.

**hire** *verb* to pay money to employ somebody or use something for a short time. *She hired two men to mend the roof.*

**hiss** *verb* to make a long S sound to show anger or disapproval. **hiss** *verb. The audience hissed at the actors.*

**historian** *noun* a person who studies and writes about history.

**historic** *adjective* famous or important in the past. *Historic houses.*

The Parthenon is a historic building in Athens.

**SPELLING NOTE**

*Try to distinguish between 'historic', meaning 'famous' or 'important in history'; and 'historical', meaning 'having actually happened in history' or 'concerned with history'. 'Hitler is a historical person.'*

**historical** *adjective* concerned with events and people in history. *Was Hamlet a historical person?*

**history** *noun* 1 the study of the people and events of the past. 2 a description of the past. *A history of Wales.*

**hit** (hits, hitting, hit) *verb* to strike with a blow, to touch something violently. *She hit the ball with a bat.* **hit** *noun* 1 a blow. *A hit on the nose.* 2 a great success.

**hitch-hike** *verb* to travel by getting free rides from passing vehicles by holding up your thumb.

**HIV** short for human immunodeficiency virus, a virus that weakens a person's resistance to diseases and may lead to Aids.

**hive** *noun* bee-hive, a box-like structure for keeping bees in.

The bees buzzed round the hive, busy making honey.

**hoard** *noun* a secret store of money, treasure, food etc. **hoard** *verb. Squirrels hoard nuts for the winter.* **hoarder** *noun.*

**hoarding** *noun* a large board or temporary wooden fence covered in advertisements.

**hoarse** *adjective* a rough, low voice caused by a sore throat or by shouting too much.

**SPELLING NOTE**

*Another word that sounds like 'hoarse' is 'horse'.*

**hoax** *noun* a practical joke, a trick or deception. *We had to evacuate the building, but the bomb scare was a hoax.* **hoax** *verb.*

**hobble** *verb* to limp or walk with difficulty. *He twisted his ankle and hobbled about in pain for more than a month.*

**hobby** *noun* an activity such as model-making that you enjoy doing in your spare time. *His hobby is collecting stamps.*

**hockey** *noun* an outdoor game played with curved sticks and a ball by two teams of 11 players who try to score goals.

**hoe** *noun* a garden tool with a long handle and a short blade, used for weeding.

**hog** *noun* a male pig that has been neutered.

**hog** (hogs, hogging, hogged) *verb* to be very selfish and, for example, take much more of something than you can use.

**Hogmanay** *noun* New Year's Eve in Scotland. *A glorious Hogmanay.*

**hoist** *verb* to raise or lift up something, usually with ropes or a special machine. *The soldiers hoisted the flag.*

**hold** (holds, holding, held) *verb* 1 to carry something in your hand or mouth, to grasp. 2 to contain a certain amount. *The bottle holds a pint of milk.* 3 to arrange or carry on. *They held a dance in the hall.* 4 to have in control or in your possession. *Who holds the land speed record?* 5 to support or to keep something steady. *The pillars hold up the roof.* **hold off** to stay away. *I hope the rain holds off for the match.* **hold on** 1 to continue holding something. 2 to wait. *Hold on a minute.* **hold up** 1 to delay or hinder. *The roadworks held us up for an hour.* 2 to stop and rob somebody with threats. *She was held up at gunpoint.*

**hold** *noun* a place in a ship or aircraft where cargo is kept.

**hole** *noun* an opening or gap in something, a hollow space. *There's a hole in my sock. She hit the golf ball into the hole.*

**holiday** *noun* a day or a longer period of time away from school or work when you can enjoy doing what you want. *We're going to Mexico for our summer holidays.*

**hollow** *adjective* not solid, having an empty space inside. *Bottles and pipes are hollow.* **hollow** *noun* 1 a hole. 2 a small valley.

**holly** *noun* an evergreen tree with shiny, spiky leaves and sometimes red berries in winter.

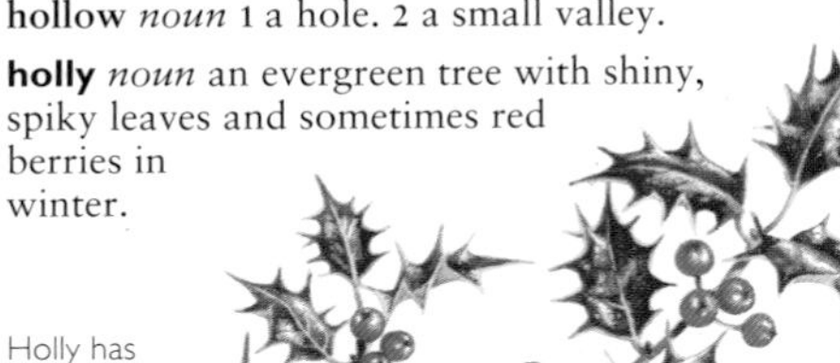

Holly has beautiful red berries that the birds eat in winter.

**hologram** *noun* a photograph created by laser beams that appears to be three-dimensional (seeming to have width, depth and height).

**holy** *noun* relating to or belonging to God or a religion. Churches and temples are holy places. **holiness** *noun.*

**home** *noun* the place where you usually live or where you were brought up. **feel at home** to feel relaxed with somebody or something.

**homeless** *adjective, noun* without a place to live in. *How can we help the homeless?* **homelessness** *noun.*

**homely** *adjective* 1 pleasantly plain and simple. 2 (US) ugly.

**homesick** *adjective* unhappy and lonely because you are away from your family and home. *I was homesick for America.*

**homework** *noun* work that teachers give their pupils to do at home.

**homicide** *noun* (say **hom**-uh-side) the killing of a human being.

**homosexual** *adjective, noun* sexually attracted to somebody of the same sex, gay. **homosexuality** *noun.*

**Honduras** *noun* a country in Central America.

The flag of Honduras is blue and white striped. Five blue stars decorate the central white stripe.

**honest** *adjective* (say **on**-est) an honest person is somebody who always tells the truth and whom you can trust. **honesty** *noun. Honesty is always the best policy.*

**honey** *noun* (rhymes with bunny) the sweet, sticky food made by bees from the nectar of flowers. *Toast and honey for tea.*

**honeycomb** *noun* rows of six-sided wax containers made by bees to store their honey and eggs.

**honeymoon** *noun* a holiday spent together by two people who have just married.

**honeysuckle** *noun* a climbing shrub with sweet-smelling flowers.

He fetched the honeycomb out of the hive and it was dripping with honey.

**Honiara** *noun* the capital of the Solomon Islands.

**honour** *noun* (say **on**-ur) 1 to give great respect to somebody. *He was honoured by everybody for his great achievements.* 2 to praise and reward somebody publicly. 3 to keep an agreement. **honour** *noun* good reputation. **honourable** *adjective. She behaved in an honourable way and told the absolute truth.*

**AMAZING FACT**

Animals that have hooves are divided into two major groups: animals with an even number of claws or 'toes' such as sheep, goats and camels; and those with an odd number such as horses and zebras.

**WORD HISTORY**

*'Hooligan' comes from the name of an unruly Irish family that lived in southeast London in the 19th century.*

**AMAZING FACT**

Be careful when writing 'horde' (a crowd) and 'hoarde' (a secret store of something). They sound the same but are spelled differently.

**hood** *noun* 1 a part of a coat that you can pull up to cover your head and neck. 2 a soft roof for a car or pram that you can fold back. 3 (US) the bonnet of a car.

**hoodwink** *verb* to trick somebody. *He was hoodwinked into paying a lot of money for a worthless clock.*

**hoof** (hooves or hoofs) *noun* the hard covering on the feet of some animals such as horses, cows and sheep.

**hook** *noun* 1 a bent piece of metal or plastic for hanging things on. *Hang your raincoat on the hook to dry.* 2 a bent piece of metal for catching fish. **by hook or by crook** by any means possible. **get off the hook** to get out of a difficult situation.

For fly-fishing, anglers use hooks decorated with colourful feathers.

**hooked** *adjective* 1 shaped like a hook. *A hooked nose.* 2 (slang) fascinated by or addicted to. *He's hooked on bird watching.*

**hooligan** *noun* a violent, noisy person who gets into trouble and breaks things. **hooliganism** *noun.*

**hoop** *noun* a large ring made of metal or wood. At the circus we saw an acrobat jump through a hoop of fire.

**hoot** *verb* to make a sound like the horn of a car or the long 'oo' cry of an owl. *We hooted with laughter.* **hoot** *noun. We heard the hoot of the owl.*

**hop** (hops, hopping, hopped) *verb* 1 to jump on one foot. 2 (of animals) to make short jumps. *The rabbit hopped across the lawn and disappeared under the fence.*

**hop** *noun* a climbing plant used to flavour beer. *Hops grow well in the county of Kent.*

**hope** *verb* to want something to happen and be expecting it to happen. *I hope you will win first prize.* **hope** *noun* a feeling that something you want will happen. *She has no hope of passing her exams.*

**hopeful** *adjective* feeling confident and full of hope. **hopefulness** *noun.*

**hopefully** *adverb* if all goes well. *Hopefully I'll be home tomorrow.*

**hopeless** *adjective* 1 without hope. 2 very bad, useless. *He's hopeless at drawing, but very good at maths.*

**horde** *noun* a large crowd. *Hordes of tourists swarmed into the piazza.*

H

**horizon** *noun* the line in the distance where the sky and land or sea seem to meet.

The Sun dropped behind the horizon, leaving a golden path across the sea.

**horizontal** *adjective* lying flat to the ground in line with the horizon, going from side to side and not up and down.

**hormone** *noun* a chemical substance produced in your body and that controls particular functions of the body. Some hormones, for example, control growth and others control digestion.

**horn** *noun* 1 one of the hard, bony growths on the heads of certain animals such as cows and goats. 2 a brass musical instrument that you play by blowing into it. 3 a device on a vehicle that makes a loud, warning sound. *The driver sounded her horn, but it was too late.*

**horoscope** *noun* a forecast of somebody's future, based on the position of the stars at the time of that person's birth.

**AMAZING FACT**

A horse's height is measured in hands, not feet. A hand is equal to ten centimetres.

**horse-chestnut** *noun* a large tree that has clusters of white flowers in the spring and shiny brown nuts called conkers in autumn.

**horse-play** *noun* rough and noisy play by children. *Too much horse-play!*

**horseshoe** *noun* a curved piece of iron nailed to a horse's hoof to protect it.

**horticulture** *noun* the science of gardening and the growing of fruit, flowers and vegetables. **horticultural** *adjective*.

**hose** *noun* a long rubber or plastic tube that water can go through. Firefighters use hoses for putting out fires.

**hospice** *noun* a hospital where people who are suffering from incurable diseases are looked after by doctors and nurses.

**hospitable** *adjective* friendly and generous to guests and strangers. *A most hospitable welcome.* **hospitality** *noun*.

**hospital** *noun* a place where people who are ill or injured are treated and looked after.

**host** *noun* 1 a person who invites guests and looks after them. 2 a person who introduces guest performers on a TV or radio show. 3 a very large number. *We now have a whole host of problems.*

**hostage** *noun* a person who is held prisoner by people who will not release her or him until their demands have been carried out.

**hostel** *noun* a place where people such as students or hitch-hikers can stay cheaply.

**hostile** *adjective* behaving in an unfriendly way. *The president was met by a hostile group of pensioners.*

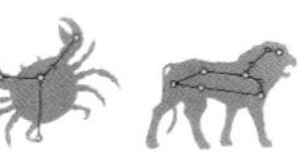

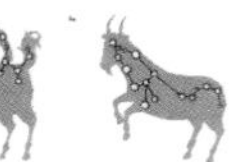
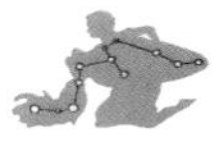

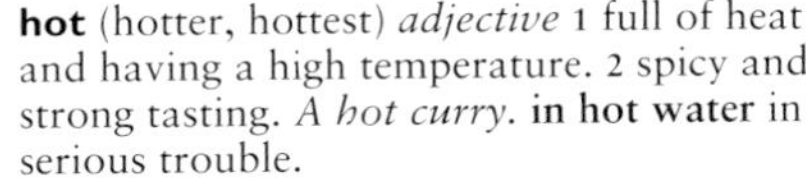

When you want to read your horoscope, you have to look up your sign of the zodiac in the newspaper.

**horrible** *adjective* terrible, very unpleasant. *What a horrible noise!*

**horrid** *adjective* horrible, unkind or hateful. *What a horrid person she is.*

**horrify** (horrifies, horrifying, horrified) *verb* to shock or fill with great horror and disgust. *I was horrified to hear about the earthquake in Armenia.*

**horror** *noun* a feeling of shock or fear. *He watched the snake slide towards him with horror.*

**horse** *noun* 1 a big four-legged animal with hooves, a long mane and a tail that can be used for riding or for pulling things like carts or ploughs. 2 a piece of equipment in a gym used for jumping over and doing exercises.

The horse's coat glowed from so much grooming.

**hot** (hotter, hottest) *adjective* 1 full of heat and having a high temperature. 2 spicy and strong tasting. *A hot curry.* **in hot water** in serious trouble.

**hot dog** *noun* a thin, hot sausage in a bread roll, a frankfurter. *Hot dogs with mustard and tomato ketchup.*

We ate delicious hot dogs at the fair.

**hotel** *noun* a building with many bedrooms where people pay to stay and have meals.

**hound** *noun* a breed of dog that is used for hunting and racing. Foxhounds, deerhounds and bloodhounds are all different kinds of hound. **hound** *verb* to follow or harass somebody. *The princess was hounded by photographers wherever she went.*

**hour** *noun* a period of time consisting of 60 minutes. There are 24 hours in a day. **hourly** *adjective, adverb. The hourly rate for the job is not very impressive.*

**house** *noun* 1 a building where people live. 2 a building used for a particular purpose. *The White House.* **house** *verb* to provide a place for somebody to live.

A cross-section through this house shows all the rooms from cellar to attic.

**household** *noun* all the people who live together in one house.

**householder** *noun* the person who owns a house.

**househusband** *noun* a man who normally looks after the house for the family.

**housekeeper** *noun* a person who is paid to look after a house.

**housewife** *noun* a woman who normally looks after the house for the family.

**housework** *noun* cleaning, washing and cooking and other work that has to be done in a house.

**hovel** *noun* a small, filthy and broken house or hut. *The hermit lived in a hovel.*

**hover** *verb* 1 to remain in the air over one spot without moving. 2 to linger or to stay near one place.

**hovercraft** *noun* a boat that can fly over sea or land, lifted up on a cushion of air.

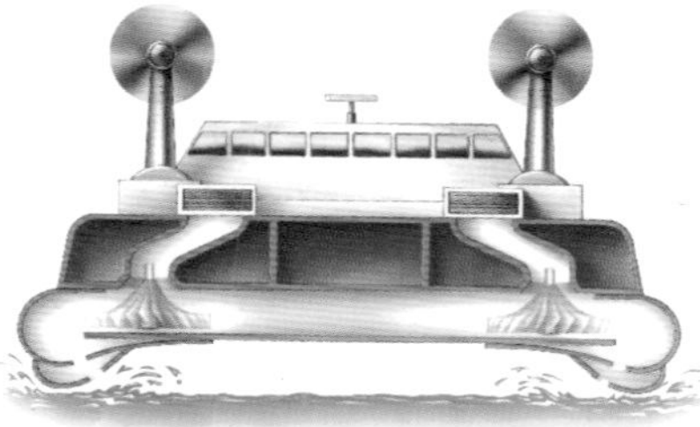

The hovercraft runs between Calais and Dover.

**howl** *verb* to make a long cry like an animal makes when it is in pain. **howl** *noun.*

**howler** *noun* a ridiculously funny mistake of fact. *A real howler in your essay.*

**HQ** *abbreviation* Headquarters.

**hub** *noun* the centre part of a wheel.

**AMAZING FACT**

'Hug' probably comes from an old Norse word that meant 'to console'.

**SPELLING NOTE**

*Some howlers!*
*1 The practice of having only one wife is called monotony. 2 She's at her wick's end. 3 Calm down - don't get so historical. 4 Russia uses the acrylic alphabet.*

**huddle** *verb* to crowd closely together. *They huddled under the tree to shelter from the rain.* **huddle** *noun.*

**hue** *noun* a colour or shade of colour.

**hug** (hugs, hugging, hugged) *verb* to put your arms around somebody and hold them tightly. **hug** *noun. He gave his cousin a big hug to welcome him home.*

**huge** *adjective* very big, enormous.

**hull** *noun* the body or frame of a ship.

**hum** (hums, humming, hummed) *verb* 1 to sing a tune with your mouth shut. 2 to make the low, continuous sound of an insect. **hum** *noun. The hum of the traffic.*

**human** *noun* human being. A man, woman or child. **human** *adjective* having natural and understandable feelings. *It's only human to cry when you are upset.*

**humane** *adjective* kind and gentle, not cruel. *Humane treatment of animals.*

**humanity** *noun* 1 all people. 2 being kind and humane.

**humble** *adjective* modest and not vain or self-important. *He's very clever, but in spite of his achievements, he's modest too.*

**humid** *adjective* damp and sometimes warm. *Humid weather.* **humidity** *noun.*

**humiliate** *verb* to make somebody feel ashamed or appear stupid to other people. **humiliation** *noun.*

**hummingbird** *noun* a very small, brightly coloured bird with a long slender beak. It hovers over flowers, beating its wings so fast that they make a humming sound.

The hummingbird sucked nectar from the flower.

**humorous** *adjective* funny. *A very humorous book.*

**humour** *noun* 1 what makes people laugh or smile. 2 a mood. *Is she in a good humour today?* **sense of humour** the ability to see what is funny and to laugh at it.

**hump** *noun* a small, round lump. A camel has a hump on its back.

**hunch** *verb* to lean forward with your shoulders raised and your head bent down.

**hunch** *noun* a feeling about something but not based on facts. *I had a hunch you would be on this train.*

**hung** past tense of hang.

**Hungarian** *noun* 1 a person who comes from Hungary. 2 the language spoken in Hungary. **Hungarian** *adjective. Hungarian dances.*

**Hungary** *noun* a country in eastern Europe.

The Hungarian flag has red, white and green stripes.

**hunger** *noun* a strong wish or need to eat. **hunger** *verb. She hungered for fame and fortune.*

**hungry** (hungrier, hungriest) *adjective* feeling hunger or the need for food. *The hungry dog hurried to eat all its supper.* **hungrily** *adverb.*

**hunk** *noun* a large piece or slice of something. *A hunk of bread.*

**hunt** *verb* 1 to look for and chase wild animals and then kill them for food or sport. 2 to search carefully for something. *I hunted everywhere for her phone number.* **hunt** *noun.*

Australian aborigines hunt with spears and boomerangs.

**hurdle** *noun* 1 a small fence a runner jumps over in a race called hurdling. 2 a difficulty or problem to be overcome.

**hurl** *verb* to throw something with force as far as you can.

**hurricane** *noun* a violent storm with strong winds. *The hurricane tore off the roof.*

**hurry** (hurries, hurrying, hurried) *verb* to move quickly or do something as fast as you can. **hurry** *noun. Why are you in such a hurry, when we have all day to spare?*

**hurt** *verb* 1 to cause pain or harm to a person or an animal. *I didn't mean to hurt you.* 2 to feel pain. My bruised knee hurts.

**husband** *noun* a husband is the man that a woman has married.

**hush** *interjection* Be quiet! **hush** *noun* a sudden silence. *A hush fell over the concert hall and the music began.*

**hush-hush** *adjective* secret and in confidence. *A hush-hush story.*

**husk** *noun* the outer covering of some fruits and cereals. *Don't eat the husk.*

**husky** *adjective* (of a voice) low and rough.

**husky** *noun* a strong dog used to pull sledges in Arctic regions.

**AMAZING FACT**

Hyenas have very powerful jaws that they use to crush the bones of their prey. The spotted hyena has the most powerful jaws of any mammal.

**WORD HISTORY**

*'Husband' comes from an Old Norse word meaning 'master of a household'. It was generally applied to all men who were masters of a household whether married or single.*

**hut** *noun* a small house or temporary shelter, usually made of wood.

**hutch** *noun* a wooden cage for pet rabbits or other small animals.

**hybrid** *noun* a plant or animal produced from two different kinds (species) of plant or animal. A mule is a hybrid of a horse and a donkey. **hybrid** *adjective. A hybrid rose.*

**hydrant** *noun* an outdoor water tap to which a hose can be attached to supply water for fires or other emergencies.

**hydroelectricity** *noun* electricity produced by using water power, at a dam or a waterfall, for example.

**hydrofoil** *noun* a fast, light boat that skims over the surface of water on fin-like foils attached to its hull.

**hydrogen** *noun* hydrogen is the lightest of all gases and the simplest of all chemical elements. It combines with oxygen to make water.

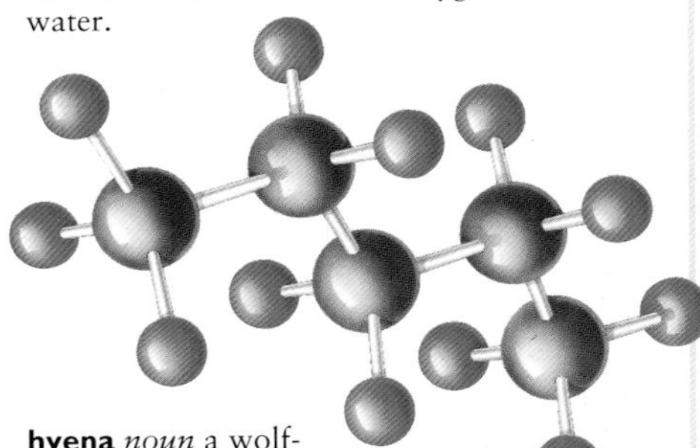

Hydrogen is the most abundant element in the whole universe.

**hyena** *noun* a wolf-like wild animal from India and Africa that hunts in packs and lives off the flesh of dead animals. The howl of a hyena is like hysterical laughter.

**hygiene** *noun* (say **hy**-jeen) the science and practice of cleanliness and good health. **hygienic** *adjective.*

**hymn** *noun* (say him) a religious song of praise. *We sang hymns in church.*

**hype** *noun* exaggerated and excessive publicity about something in order to sell it.

**hyphen** *noun* a mark ( - ) used in writing to join two parts of a divided word at the end of a line or to join two words to make a new word. *Stage-coach, self-defence, record-player.*

**hypocrite** *noun* a person who pretends to have feelings, good qualities or beliefs which he or she does not really have.

**hypodermic needle** *noun* a thin, hollow needle that is used to inject drugs into a vein. *Never re-use a hypodermic needle.*

**hysteria** *noun* uncontrollable excitement or distress. *She had a fit of hysteria.*

**hysterical** *adjective* extremely emotional and uncontrollably excited.

**hysterics** *plural noun* a fit of hysteria.

I

# Ii

**ice** *noun* water that has frozen hard.

**ice** *verb* to spread icing sugar on a cake.

**ice-age** *noun* a time long ago when large areas of the Earth were covered with ice.

**iceberg** *noun* a huge lump of ice floating in the sea. Most of an iceberg is hidden under the surface of the sea. **the tip of the iceberg** only a small part of a problem.

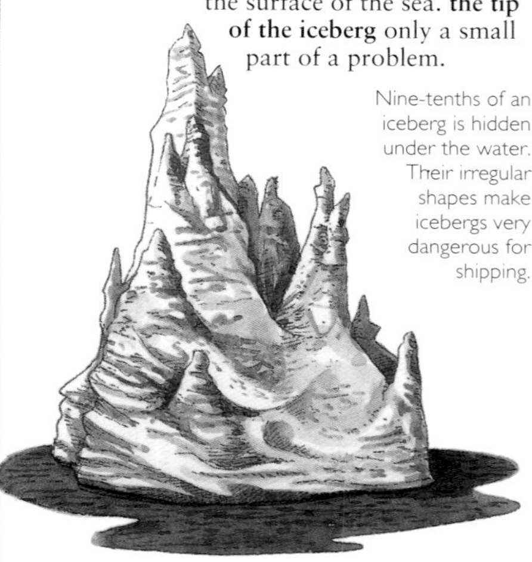

Nine-tenths of an iceberg is hidden under the water. Their irregular shapes make icebergs very dangerous for shipping.

**ice-cream** *noun* a smooth, sweet frozen food usually made with milk or cream.

**ice cube** *noun* a small block of ice used to cool drinks.

**ice hockey** a game played on ice by two teams in which the skaters try to score goals by hitting a rubber puck (ball) with a long stick. *Canada won the ice hockey match.*

**Iceland** *noun* a Scandinavian country in Europe.

The flag of Iceland shows a red on white cross, on a blue ground.

**ice skate** *noun* a boot with a metal blade on the bottom for sliding smoothly over the ice. **ice skate** *verb* to move on ice wearing ice skates.

**icicle** *noun* a long, pointed stick of ice formed by water freezing as it drops.

**WORD HISTORY**

*The shape of the letter I comes from an ancient Egyptian symbol of a hand. The Romans gave the letter its present shape.*

**SPELLING NOTE**

*Try not to confuse 'idle', a lazy person, with 'idol', a god.*

**icing** *noun* a mixture of sugar and water that is spread on cakes to decorate them.

**icon** *noun* 1 a picture of Jesus Christ or a saint painted on wood seen in many Greek or Russian Christian (orthodox) churches. 2 a small picture on a computer screen representing a program and which can be selected by clicking the mouse.

**icy** (icier, iciest) *adjective* 1 very cold. *Icy weather.* 2 covered in ice. *Icy roads.*

**idea** *noun* 1 a thought or picture in your mind. 2 a plan. *She had the idea of becoming a vet.* 3 purpose. *The idea of the game is to score as many goals as possible.*

**ideal** *adjective* perfect or very suitable. *He's an ideal father.* **ideal** *noun* the best possible person, thing, situation or example.

**identical** *adjective* exactly the same in every way. *Identical twins.*

**identify** (identifies, identifying, identified) *verb* to recognize somebody or something and be able to name them. *The police identified the body.* **identification** *noun.*

**identity** *noun* a person's distinguishing characteristics that make them individual.

**idiom** *noun* an expression or special way of saying something in which the words have a meaning different from what they appear to have. 'To drop off' means to fall asleep; and 'heads will roll' means that some people will get into trouble.

**idiot** *noun* a very stupid person. **idiotic** *adjective. What an idiotic idea.*

**idle** *adjective* 1 lazy and work-shy. **idleness** *noun.* 2 not working. *During the strike the machines were left idle.* 3 worthless or not really meant. *Idle threats.*

**idol** *noun* 1 something, such as a statue, that is worshipped as a god. 2 a famous person who is greatly admired. *A pop idol.*

This statue of Zeus, the Greek king of the gods, was probably worshipped as an idol.

**igloo** *noun* a house made out of blocks of snow and ice in the shape of a dome by the Inuits of the Arctic region.

**ignite** *verb* to set fire to or to catch fire.

**ignition** *noun* a device in a motor vehicle that starts the engine working by igniting the fuel. *Turn the key to start the ignition.*

**ignorant** *adjective* knowing very little about something, badly educated. *He's ignorant about computers.* **ignorance** *noun.*

**ignore** *verb* to take no notice of somebody or something, to disregard. *She totally ignored me when I asked her a question.*

**il-** *prefix* used before many words beginning with l to indicate against or negation. *illiterate* (not literate or able to read), *illegal* (against the law).

**ill** (worse, worst) *adjective* 1 not in good health, unwell. **illness** *noun.* 2 bad or harmful. *The ill effects of smoking.* **ill at ease** feeling unhappy and uncomfortable with other people. **ill disposed** unfriendly. **ill-founded** without good reasons. *Ill-founded suspicions.* **ill-timed** happening at a bad time. **ill-treat** to treat cruelly.

**illegal** *adjective* not allowed by the law. *It is illegal to drive at over 70 mph.*

**illegible** *adjective* handwriting that is so poor that it is difficult or impossible to read.

**illiterate** *adjective* unable to read or write. **illiteracy** *noun.*

**illogical** *adjective* not obeying logic and therefore not making sense.

**illness** *noun* a disease such as flu or measles that makes people unwell.

**illuminate** *verb* 1 to light up or shine a light on something. *The castle is illuminated at night.* **illuminations** *plural noun. The streets are decorated with Christmas illuminations.* **illuminating** *adjective. An illuminating idea.* 2 to decorate a book such as a Bible with gold and coloured letters and pictures. **illumination** *noun.*

In the Middle Ages, monks spent a lot of time copying texts and illuminating the manuscripts with coloured painting.

Sometimes when people have been travelling for a long time in the desert, they see a mirage. This is an illusion, perhaps brought about by exhaustion, and also the sand in the air seen though a heat haze. This mirage is of a camel at an oasis, something that desert travellers would dearly love to see.

**DID YOU KNOW?**

*The word 'illustrate' had the same meaning as 'illuminate' – to throw light upon. The word had nothing to do with pictures until the 17th century.*

**illusion** *noun* a false idea or image of something that is really not there. *An optical illusion.*

**im-** *prefix* like in- , used before certain words beginning with b, m and p and meaning against, negation or without. *immeasurable* (too great to be measured). *immature* (not mature).

**image** *noun* 1 a picture or statue. 2 any picture in a book, film, or on television. 3 your reflection in a mirror. 4 a picture of something in your mind. 5 a very close likeness. *He is the image of his twin brother.* 6 a person's image is the general opinion that others have of them.

**imagery** *noun* the descriptive words used by writers to create pictures in the minds of readers. *Beautiful imagery.*

**imaginary** *noun* not real but existing only in the mind. Goblins and elves are imaginary creatures.

This imaginary creature is a goblin. He lives underneath the toadstool.

**imagination** *noun* 1 the ability to create pictures in the mind. *Use your imagination and write a story about space travel.* 2 the ability to create new ideas.

**imaginative** *adjective* having a lot of imagination. *Imaginative ideas.*

**imagine** *verb* 1 to have a picture of something in your mind. *Can you imagine life without cars?* 2 to think you see or hear things that are not really there. *You're just imagining there's a ghost under your bed.*

**imitate** *verb* to copy or behave like somebody or something. *She can imitate her mother's voice perfectly.* **imitation** *noun. He does a good imitation of a dog barking.*

**immature** *adjective* 1 not fully grown or developed, unripe. 2 behaving childishly and not like an adult. **immaturity** *noun.*

**immediately** *adverb* at once and without delay. **immediately** *conjunction* as soon as. *I knew I'd get on with her immediately I met her.* **immediate** *adjective*.

**immense** *adjective* very big. *The Sahara is an immense desert in North Africa.* **immensity** *noun*.

**immerse** *verb* to put something into a liquid until it is completely covered. **immerse yourself in** to give all your attention to something.

Pat immersed the dirty plate in the soapy water and began to wash up.

**immigrant** *noun* somebody who immigrates to and comes to settle in a country. **immigration** *noun*.

**immigrate** *verb* to come to live and settle in a country. *They immigrated quite recently.*

**imminent** *adjective* Something that is imminent is expected to happen very soon. *The forecast says that snow is imminent.*

**immobile** *adjective* not moving or able to move. **immobility** *noun*. **immobilize** *verb* to make immobile and unable to move. *All traffic has been immobilized by the snow.*

**immoral** *adjective* behaving in a way that is considered wrong. **immorality** *noun*.

**immortal** *adjective* never dying but living and lasting for ever.

**immune** *adjective* protected against a disease and so unable to catch it. **immunity** *noun*. **immunize** *verb* to give somebody an injection so that they cannot catch a disease.

**imp** *noun* a mischievous little creature in fairy stories.

The mischievous imp was exhausted after all the damage he had done in the shoe shop.

**impact** *noun* 1 the force of one object colliding with another. 2 the strong effect or impresssion that something has. *Computers have had a great impact on the way we learn, both at home and at school.*

**AMAZING FACT**

The impala is an extremely fast animal, speed is its main defence. It can also leap as far as ten metres, which it does to escape predators, but also, it seems, because it just enjoys leaping!

**SPELLING NOTE**

*Try not to confuse 'immigrate' (to come from another country) with 'emigrate' (to go to another country).*

**impala** *noun* a small African antelope that lives in great herds.

The impala is a graceful creature that lives in herds in the South African veld.

**impartial** *adjective* fair and not favouring one person or side more than another. **impartiality** *noun*.

**impassable** *noun* not able to be passed through or across. *Heavy snowstorms made the mountain roads impassable.*

**impatient** *adjective* unwilling to wait and easily annoyed. **impatience** *noun*.

**impede** *verb* to get in the way of somebody or something and so slow down progress.

**impenetrable** *adjective* 1 impossible to get through. *An impenetrable forest.* 2 impossible to understand. *He posed us an impenetrable problem.*

**imperfect** *adjective* 1 not perfect and having some fault. **imperfection** *noun*. 2 a verb tense indicating a repeated or incomplete action in the past. *She was sitting in a chair.*

**imperial** *adjective* 1 of or having to do with an empire or an emperor or empress. 2 The imperial system is a traditional non-metric British system of weights and measures using inches, feet, yards and miles, ounces pounds and hundredweight, and pints and gallons.

**impersonal** *adjective* unfriendly and showing no personal feelings or warmth. *Her manner was cold and impersonal.*

**impersonate** *verb* to pretend to be somebody else by copying their behaviour. **impersonation** *noun*.

**impertinent** *adjective* rude and impudent, especially to somebody in authority.

**impetuous** *adjective* an impetuous person acts suddenly and without thinking first.

**implement** *noun* a tool or instrument. *Garden implements.*

The gardening tools were useful implements.

I

**imply** (implies, implying, implied) *verb* to suggest or hint at something without actually saying it directly. *By questioning everything he said, she implied that he was lying.* **implication** *noun.*

**impolite** *adjective* rude and bad-mannered.

**import** *verb* (say im-**port**) to buy goods from another country to sell in your own country. **import** *noun* (say **im**-port). *One of our main imports is cloth.* The opposite of import is export.

Coffee beans are imported to Europe from South America and Africa.

**important** *adjective* 1 of great interest and which matters a lot. *Your birthday is an important day for you.* 2 having influence and power. *An important writer.*

**imposing** *adjective* large and making a great impression. *An imposing palace.*

**impossible** *adjective* not possible, something that cannot be done or happen.

**impostor** *noun* someone who pretends to be somebody else in order to deceive and get things they want.

**impracticable** *adjective* not possible to use or put into practice. *An impracticable idea.*

**impractical** *adjective* not useful and lacking common sense. *He's quite impractical and couldn't boil an egg.*

**impress** *verb* to cause somebody's admiration or respect. *I was impressed by his knowledge.* **impressive** *adjective.*

**impression** *noun* 1 the way something appears to you and the effect it has on you. *His kindness made a great impression on us.* 2 a vague idea or belief. *I have the impression I've been here before.* 3 a mark made by something pressing on to a surface. *Our cats, Onion and Plumage, left the impressions of their paws in the wet concrete.* 4. an impersonation or attempt at copying how somebody talks and behaves, usually in order to entertain people.

The cat left the impression of her feet in the wet concrete.

**impressionable** *adjective* very easily influenced or impressed by others. *Some young people are very impressionable.*

**WORD BUILDER**

*You can make many words negative by adding the prefix 'in–' to certain words, as in 'incurable', 'informal'. It is often only necessary to look up the definition of a word to discover its negative meaning.*

**AMAZING FACT**

The system of weights and measures used in the United States is called the English system and is based on the system that was used in Britain until it was officially replaced by the metric system. In 1975, Congress passed the Metric Conversion Act, which called for a voluntary changeover to metric.

**imprison** *verb* to put somebody in prison. **imprisonment** *noun. His punishment was imprisonment.*

**improve** *verb* to become better or to make something better. *Her health is improving.* **improvement** *noun.*

**improvise** *verb* 1 to do something as you go along without planning or rehearsing beforehand. *She had lost her notes and had to improvise the speech.* 2 to make something quickly with whatever materials are available. *We improvised a table from cardboard boxes.* **improvisation** *noun.*

**impudent** *noun* rude and showing no respect, insolent. **impudence** *noun.*

**in-** *prefix* meaning 'not' when added to the beginning of certain words. *inadequate* (not adequate), *inactive* (not active), *inconsistent* (not consistent).

**inarticulate** *adjective* unable to express yourself well when speaking.

**inaudible** *adjective* not loud enough to be heard clearly **inaudibility** *noun.*

**inborn** *adjective* natural and present in a person or animal from birth. *Birds have an inborn ability to build nests.*

Birds have an inborn capacity to build nests.

**incapable** *adjective* unable to do things expected of you. *She's incapable of getting to school on time.*

**incentive** *noun* something that encourages you to do something. *He was promised a bike as an incentive to work hard.*

**incessant** *noun* going on and on and never stopping. *The incessant noise of the traffic.*

**inch** *noun* a measurement of length, equal to 2.55 centimetres. There are 12 inches in a foot. **inch by inch** very slowly.

**incident** *noun* a single event or happening.

**incidentally** *adverb* by the way. *Incidentally, I haven't eaten all day, so I'm ravenously hungry.*

**incinerator** *noun* a container for burning rubbish. *Please put all these papers straight in the incinerator.*

**incision** *noun* a cut into a patient's body made by a surgeon during an operation.

**incite** *verb* to stir up and encourage people to do something, usually bad and violent. *The leader incited the crowd to riot, and the troops retalliated with tear gas and batons.*

I

**inclination** *noun* a tendency or slight preference to do something. *My inclination is to take the right-hand turning.*

**incline** *verb* 1 to lean or slope towards something, to bend. 2 to have a tendency or preference for doing something. *He's inclined to be a bit slow in the morning.* **incline** *noun* a slope.

**include** *verb* to consider or count something as a part of a whole or a group of other things. **inclusion** *noun.*

**including** *preposition* forming part of a larger group. *Everybody went on holiday, including our dog and cat.*

**inclusive** *adjective* including everything. *The price is inclusive of tax.*

**incoherent** *adjective* speaking in a rambling way that is not easy to follow or understand. **incoherence** *noun.*

**income** *noun* the money a person regularly earns. *She has an income of £30,000 a year.* **income tax** a tax that is charged on a person's income.

**incompetent** *adjective* lacking the ability to do a job well. **incompetence** *noun.*

**incomplete** *adjective* unfinished, not complete. *An incomplete set of encyclopedias was delivered to the school.*

When Jane left the room, the puzzle was still incomplete.

**incongruous** *adjective* strange and out of place. *A skyscraper would look incongruous in a small village.*

**inconsiderate** *noun* thoughtless and not considering the feelings of others.

**inconspicuous** *adjective* small and not easily noticeable.

**incorporate** *verb* to include something and make a part of the whole. *The sports wing incorporates a gym and a swimming pool.*

**incorrect** *adjective* wrong. *The man always seemed to give the incorrect answer.*

**increase** *verb* (say in-**krees**) to make bigger or to become bigger. **increase** *noun* (**in**-krees) *A sharp increase in prices.*

A microscope gives an increased ability to examine the structure of a leaf.

**AMAZING FACT**

The prefixes 'il-', 'im-', 'in-' and 'ir-' are all used to form the negative of various words (illogical, improbable, indigestible, irresponsible), but they are not interchangeable. Check the spelling in your dictionary if you're not sure which prefix to use.

**DID YOU KNOW?**

*'Bungalow', 'khaki', 'polo', 'jungle' and 'shampoo' are all words that come from India.*

**incredible** *adjective* 1 difficult or impossible to believe. *An incredible adventure story.* 2 amazing, very good. *An incredible film.*

**incriminate** *verb* to show that somebody is guilty of a crime.

**incubator** *noun* 1 a container in which premature and weak babies are kept alive and safe until they are strong. 2 a heated container for keeping eggs warm until the chicks hatch. **incubate** *verb* to keep eggs warm until they hatch.

Stephanie put the eggs in the incubator to hatch.

**incurable** *adjective* not able to be cured or made better. *An incurable disease.*

**indecent** *adjective* shockingly rude and offensive. **indecency** *noun.*

**indefinite** *adjective* vague, not fixed or limited. *He's gone away to Outer Mongolia for an indefinite time.* **indefinite article** the adjectives 'a' and 'an'.

**independent** *adjective* free, not controlled by or needing help from others. *Most colonies have become independent.* **independence** *noun.*

**index** *noun* a section at the end of some books giving an alphabetical list and page number of all the subjects mentioned in the book. *The index in this book is very useful.*

**India** *noun* a country in South Asia.

India is the seventh largest country in the world and has the second largest number of people.

**Indian** *noun* 1 a person who comes from India. 2 a Native American. **Indian** *adjective. An Indian temple.*

**indicate** *verb* 1 to show or point out something. *He indicated on the map where the village is.* 2 to be a sign of. *Dark clouds indicate rain.* 3 to show which way you are turning, to signal. *Indicate left.* **indication** *noun. He gave no indication of his plight.*

**indicator** *noun* a flashing light on a motor vehicle that shows other drivers which way you are going to turn.

**indifferent** *adjective* 1 having no feelings and not caring. *She is indifferent to what people think of her.* 2 not very good. *An indifferent meal.* **indifference** *noun*.

**indigestion** *noun* pain you get in your stomach when you have eaten too much and have difficulty in digesting your food. **indigestible** *adjective*.

**indirect** *adjective* not direct or straightforward. *An indirect route.*

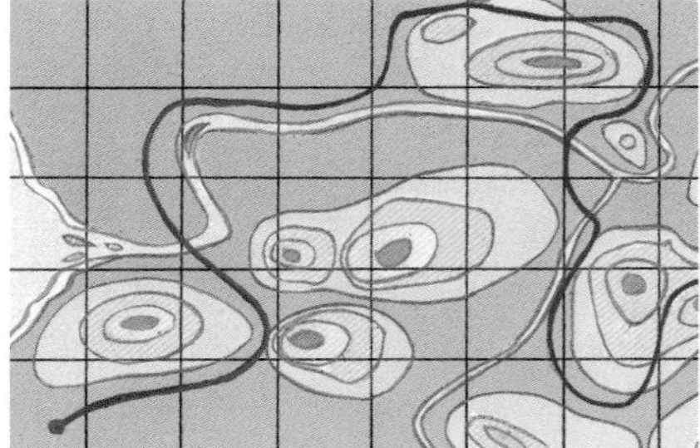

Because of the mountainous landscape, the road had to take an indirect route across country.

**individual** *adjective* 1 relating to one person or thing and not to a group. *She has individual tennis coaching from the champion.* 2 having an unusual quality or way of behaving. *He has an individual way of walking.* **individual** *noun* a single person. **individually** *adjective* separately.

**individuality** *noun* a quality that makes a person or thing different and stand out from others. *Striking for its individuality.*

**Indonesia** *noun* a country in Southeast Asia, made up of Sumatra, Java and many other islands.

**indulge** *verb* 1 If you indulge in something you take great pleasure in it, even if it is bad for you. 2 To indulge somebody is to let them have or do what they want, to spoil them. **indulgence** *noun*. **indulgent** *adjective*. *Indulgent grandparents.*

**industrial** *adjective* concerning industry and factories. *The industrial regions of Italy.* **Industrial Revolution** the name given to the widespread use of machines in factories during the 18th and 19th centuries, particularly in Britain.

**industrialist** *noun* a person who owns an industry.

**industrious** *adjective* hardworking.

**industry** *noun* 1 work and the making of things in factories. 2 a particular business or branch of industry. *The car industry.* 3 hard work.

**inefficient** *adjective* not working well and wasting time or energy.

**AMAZING FACT**

'Infantry' refers to soldiers who fight on foot, 'cavalry' used to refer to soldiers who fought on horseback but now it is more likely to mean soldiers who fight from vehicles.

**GRAMMAR NOTE**

*Indirect speech is reported speech and not the exact words of the speaker. 'He said he was happy to be home,' is indirect speech. 'I am happy to be home,' is direct speech.*

During the Industrial Revolution, many factories and railways were built.

**inert** *adjective* without power and unable to move. **inertia** *noun* lack of energy.

**inevitable** *adjective* sure to happen or impossible to stop. **inevitability** *noun*.

**infamous** *adjective* well known or famous for being bad. *An infamous thief.*

**infant** *noun* a very young child. **infancy** *noun* the time of being an infant.

**infantry** *noun* soldiers who fight on foot.

Soldiers in the infantry have to be very fit, because they march long distances carrying heavy equipment.

**infatuated** *adjective* to have such a strong love for somebody that you cannot think sensibly about them. **infatuation** *noun*.

**infect** *verb* to fill with germs or to pass on a disease to somebody. *He infected the whole class with his cold.*

**infection** *noun* a disease caused by germs. *She has an eye infection.*

**infectious** *adjective* something, particularly a disease, that can spread easily from one person to another. *Infectious laughter.*

**inferior** *adjective* not so good or important in rank or quality. The opposite of inferior is superior. *An inferior bottle of wine.*

**inferiority complex** Somebody who has an inferiority complex always thinks that he or she is less important or less good than others.

**infertile** *adjective* 1 unable to produce babies. 2 Infertile land is of such poor quality that crops will not grow.

**infested** *adjective* full of pests such as insects or rats. *The house was infested with a plague of fleas.*

**infinite** *adjective* endless and without limits, so great that it cannot be measured or imagined. *I loved him for his infinite kindness towards animals.* **infinity** *noun.*

**infinitive** *adjective* the basic form of a verb, having 'to' in front of it. *To go, to dream, to plan, to talk, to visit.*

**inflammable** *adjective* catching fire easily.

**inflate** *verb* to make something expand by filling it with air or gas. *They inflated the balloons with a pump.*

Jim inflated the raft on which he hoped to shoot the rapids.

**SPELLING NOTE**

*The opposite word for 'inflate' is 'deflate', and the opposite word for 'inhale' is 'exhale'.*

**inflation** *noun* a rise in prices.

**inflexible** *adjective* unable to bend or change in any way. *Inflexible rules.*

**inflict** *verb* to make somebody suffer pain or something unpleasant.

**influence** *noun* 1 the power you have to make somebody do something or cause something to happen. 2 a person who has such power. *His uncle was a great influence on his decision to become an actor.* **influence** *verb.* **influential** *adjective.*

**influenza or flu** *noun* an infectious disease that gives you headache, fever and aching muscles. *I was in bed for a week with flu.*

**AMAZING FACT**

Influenza is a very common disease and is not normally serious. But in 1918–19, a flu epidemic killed about 20 million people around the world.

**inform** *verb* to tell somebody about something. *Please keep me informed.*

**informal** *adjective* 1 friendly and relaxed, not following rules. *Informal clothes.* 2 used in ordinary conversation or writing. 'Bangers and mash' is an informal way of saying 'sausages and mashed potatoes'. **informality** *noun.*

**information** *noun* all the facts or knowledge about something. *Can you give me any information about the crash?*

**information technology** the use of computers to store, arrange and send out information.

**informative** *adjective* giving useful or helpful facts. *An informative programme about endangered animals.*

**ingenious** *adjective* clever and imaginative. *An ingenious invention.* **ingenuity** *noun.*

**ingot** *noun* a lump of metal, usually in the shape of a brick. *The Queen was presented with a gold ingot.*

Ingots are pieces of cast metal moulded into a form useful for transport and storage.

**ingredient** *noun* any one of a number of things that go into a mixture from which something is made, particularly in cooking. *Flour, eggs and milk are ingredients of the batter used for making pancakes.*

**inhabit** *verb* to live in a place. *The island is not inhabited.*

**inhabitant** *noun* the people or animals that live in a place or country. *The inhabitants of the mental asylum were treated kindly.*

**inhale** *verb* to breathe in. *She inhaled deeply the fresh sea air.*

**inhaler** *noun* a container that people who suffer from diseases such as asthma use to breathe in medicine. *The doctor gave him an inhaler to ease his breathing.*

**inherit** *verb* 1 to receive something such as money or property from somebody who has died. *She inherited the house from her aunt.* 2 to have the same qualities or characteristics as your parents or ancestors. *He has inherited his father's bad temper!* **inheritance** *noun.*

**inhuman** *adjective* cruel, showing no kindness or pity. **inhumanity** *noun.*

**initial** *noun* (say in-**ish**-ul) the first letter of a word or name. *Robin Ashe's initials are R.A.* **initial** *adjective* first or at the beginning. *My initial reaction is good.*

**initiative** *noun* the ability to do things on your own and to lead the way. *Marcus showed a lot of initiative and got the job done in extra quick time.*

**inject** *verb* to use a hollow needle to put liquid medicine into somebody's body. **injection** *noun. Billy didn't like having injections at the dentist's.*

The doctor used a syringe to inject the patient.

**injure** *verb* to hurt or damage a part of a person's or an animal's body. *She injured her arm when she fell.* **injury** *noun.*

**ink** *noun* a coloured liquid used for writing with a pen or for printing.

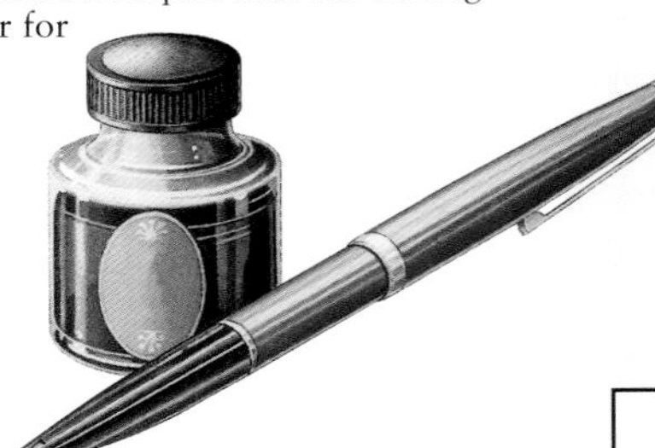

Margaret prefers to write with a fountain pen and blue or black ink.

**inkling** *noun* a slight idea, a hint. *She had no inkling I'd be coming.*

**inland** *adjective* away from the sea and towards the middle of a country.

**inn** *noun* a small hotel or pub, usually in the country.

**inner** *adjective* on the inside and near the middle. *The inner tube of a bicycle tyre.*

**innocent** *adjective* 1 without blame or guilt. *The prisoner was innocent.* 2 harmless. *Innocent fun.* **innocence** *noun.*

**innovation** *noun* something that is completely new. A new invention or way of doing things. *Computers were a major innovation in schools and businesses.*

**innumerable** *adjective* too many to be counted. *Innumerable stars in the sky.*

On a clear night, you can see innumerable stars in the sky.

**inoculate** *verb* to protect somebody from a disease by injecting them with a weak form of the disease. **inoculation** *noun.*

**input** *noun* information that you put into a computer. **input** *verb.*

**inquest** *noun* an official inquiry to find out why somebody suddenly died.

**inquire** *verb* to ask questions to find out about something. *Madge inquired about the times of trains.*

**inquiry** *noun* 1 a question. 2 a detailed and official investigation. *There was an inquiry into the cause of the fire.*

**inquisitive** *noun* eager to find out about things, always asking questions.

**SPELLING NOTE**

*Note that 'inoculate' has only one 'n' and one 'l'. Also note that 'inquire' and 'inquiry' can be spelled 'enquire', 'enquiry'.*

**AMAZING FACT**

Edward Jenner first inoculated a person in 1796. He injected a boy with cowpox as a vaccine against smallpox.

**insanitary** *adjective* unclean and likely to harm people's health by causing disease.

**inscribe** *verb* to write or carve words on to the hard surface of something.

**inscription** *noun* words written or carved on something.

**insect** *noun* a small animal with six legs, no backbone, and usually with wings. An insect has three parts to its body. Beetles, butterflies and flies are insects.

Butterflies are some of the world's most beautiful insects.

**insecticide** *noun* a poison that is used to kill insects that are pests.

**insert** *verb* to put something inside something else.

**inside** *noun* the interior and centre part of something, near the middle. *The inside of my mouth is sore.* **inside** *preposition. The owl lives with its young family inside the hollow tree.* **inside** *adverb. Come inside a minute.* **inside out** the inside of a piece of clothing turned to the outside. The opposite of inside is outside.

**insight** *noun* having a clear understanding of something. *An insight into his behaviour.*

**insincere** *adjective* not honest and pretending to have feelings about something. *He said he liked me but I knew he was insincere.*

**insipid** *adjective* without taste, dull. *An insipid cup of tea.*

**insist** *verb* to demand and be very firm in asking or doing something. *He insisted on buying me an ice cream.* **insistent** *adjective.*

**insolent** *adjective* rude and insulting. *Insolent behaviour.* **insolence** *noun.*

**insoluble** *adjective* 1 If something is insoluble, it will not dissolve. 2 A problem that is insoluble cannot be solved.

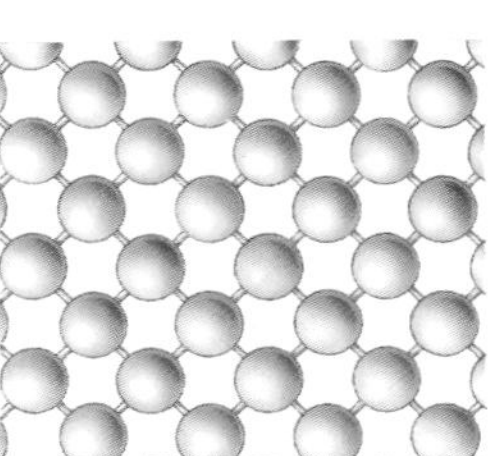

The molecules of an insoluble solid are joined together in a regular pattern.

**insomnia** *noun* sleeplessness or difficulty in going to sleep.

I

**inspect** *verb* to look at every part of something very carefully, to check. **inspection** *noun*.

**inspire** *verb* to influence somebody and encourage them to feel confident and enthusiastic about what they are doing. *The teacher inspired me to practise harder.* **inspiration** *noun*. **inspiring** *adjective*.

**install** *verb* 1 to put something in a place ready to be used. *He installed a new cooker.* 2 to give somebody an important position. *She was ceremonially installed as mayor.*

**instalment** *noun* 1 one of the parts into which something is divided. An episode. *An instalment of the story was read every evening on the radio.* 2 one of a series of regular payments for something.

**instant** *noun* a very short time. *He paused for an instant.* **instant** *adjective* 1 happening straight away. *An instant success.* 2 able to be prepared very quickly. *Instant soup.*

It's very convenient to have a cup of instant soup at lunchtime.

**instead** *adverb* in place of something or somebody. *Can I have milk instead of cream in my coffee?*

**instinct** *noun* behaviour that is natural and does not have to be thought about or learnt. *Birds build their nests by instinct.* **instinctive** *adjective*. *Instinctive behaviour.*

**institute** *noun* an organization that is established for a particular purpose. *A medical research institute.* **institute** *verb* to start something. *To institute reforms.*

**institution** *noun* 1 a large or important organization. *Hospitals, prisons, universities and other institutions.* 2 an established custom, habit or tradition. *Putting up decorations at Christmas is an institution.*

**instruct** *verb* 1 to teach or tell somebody how to do something. 2 to tell somebody what to do. *The teacher instructed the boys to wait until the bell rang.* **instruction** *noun*.

**instructions** *plural noun* directions or words that tell you how to do something. *Read the instructions carefully before connecting the computer.*

**instructive** *adjective* giving helpful information. *An instructive talk.*

**AMAZING FACT**

'Inspire' comes from a word that originally meant 'breathe in'.

**SPELLING NOTE**

*Try not to confuse 'intense', meaning 'extreme' or 'very strong', as in 'intense heat' with 'intensive', meaning 'thorough' or 'concentrated', as in 'intensive language course'.*

**instructor** *noun* a person who instructs you to do something. *A driving instructor.*

**instrument** *noun* 1 a device or tool you use to help you with your work. *Scientific instruments.* 2 A musical instrument is an object such as a piano or a guitar that you play to make music.

**insulate** *verb* to cover something with a material that will not let heat or electricity escape from it. *Electric wires are insulated with rubber or plastic.* **insulation** *noun*.

Safety demands that electric wires should be fully insulated.

**insult** *verb* (say in-**sult**) to upset somebody by saying something rude to them or behaving in a bad way. **insult** *noun* (say **in**-sult). *It was an insult to my intelligence.*

**insurance** *noun* small sums of money (premiums) you pay regularly to an organization (an insurance company) that agrees to protect you and give you a large amount of money to replace something of yours that has been stolen or damaged, or to pay medical bills if you injure yourself or become ill etc.

**intact** *adjective* not damaged, complete and not changed. *My feelings for her remain intact, despite the way she has behaved.*

**intake** *noun* 1 the number of people taken in. *A high intake of students.* 2 the process of taking something in. *The news was greeted by a sharp intake of breath.*

**integrate** *verb* 1 to combine people, often of different races, into one community. 2 to fit different parts together. **integration** *noun*.

**integrity** *noun* complete honesty and trustworthiness. *A woman of integrity.*

**intelligent** *adjective* clever and able to learn and understand things quickly and easily. **intelligence** *noun*.

Chimpanzees are intelligent creatures that can be taught many human skills.

**intend** *verb* to plan or have in mind to do something. *She intends to visit her sister.*

**intense** *adjective* 1 very strong or great. *Intense cold.* 2 very serious and with strong feelings. *He gets very intense about his work.* **intensity** *noun.*

**intensive** *adjective* 1 very thorough. *Intensive investigations.* 2 concentrated. *The patient is in intensive care.*

**intention** *noun* what you intend or plan to do. *Please state your intentions clearly.*

**intentional** *adjective* intended or done on purpose. *Intentional damage.*

**inter-** *prefix* among or between. *Interplanetary travel.*

**interact** *verb* to have an effect on one another. *All the chemicals in this experiment interact with one another.*

**interaction** *noun* the action or influence of people or things on one another.

**interactive** *adjective* (in computers) the exchange of information between a computer and the user.

**intercept** *verb* to stop somebody or something that is moving from one place to another. *He intercepted the ball with a fine catch.*

The player cleverly intercepted the ball and passed it back to her own team.

**interest** *verb* to want to learn or find out more about something. **interest** *noun* 1 *He has a great interest in geology.* 2 extra money you pay to a bank etc. for money you have borrowed.

**interested** *adjective* wanting to find out or learn more about something.

**interesting** *adjective* If something is interesting you want to find out more about it. *Archaeology is a very interesting subject.*

**interface** *noun* in computing, a connection that allows two pieces of equipment to be operated together.

**interfere** *verb* to meddle or take part in something that has nothing to do with you. **interference** *noun.*

**interior** *noun* the inside part of something. **interior** *adjective. Interior design.*

**interjection** *noun* a word or phrase used to express surprise, pain etc. *'Ouch! It hurts.'*

The plan of the new house showed internal features, such as the staircase.

**AMAZING FACT**

Be careful not to confuse the two prefixes 'inter-' meaning 'between' and 'intra-' meaning 'within'. Think of the Internet, a system of connected computers around the world, and 'intranet' which is a system of connected computers, usually within a company.

**DID YOU KNOW?**

*'Interfere' was once used about horses and referred to when a horse struck its fetlock with the hoof of the opposite foot. It then came to mean 'to collide' and later 'to intervene'.*

**internal** *adjective* relating to the inside of something or somebody. *The internal organs of the body.*

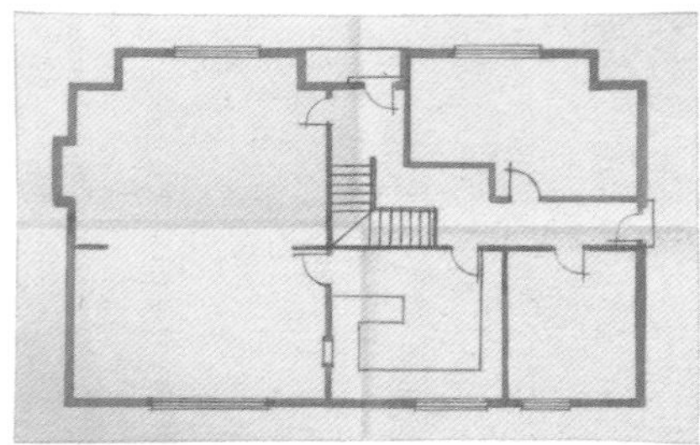

**international** *adjective* concerning several nations or countries. *An international peace-keeping force flew into the country.*

**interpret** *verb* 1 to translate or put the words of one language into another. 2 to decide or explain what something means. *He interpreted her nod as meaning 'yes'.* **interpretation** *noun.*

**interpreter** *noun* a person who translates from one language into another.

**interrupt** *verb* 1 to stop somebody while they are talking or doing something. *I'm reading, so don't interrupt me.* 2 to disturb or stop something happening for a short time. *Thunder interrupted the lesson.* **interruption** *noun.*

**interval** *noun* 1 a period of time between two dates or events. 2 a short break in a play or concert. **at intervals** happening sometimes but not regularly.

**intervene** *verb* to become involved in or join in something such as a quarrel in order to stop it happening. **intervention** *noun.*

**intervening** *adjective* the time between two events. *The intervening years.*

**interview** *noun* a meeting at which a person is asked questions to see if he or she is suitable for a job. A meeting at which things are discussed. **interview** *verb. He was interviewed for the job.*

**intestines** *plural noun* the long tube that food passes through after it has left our stomach.

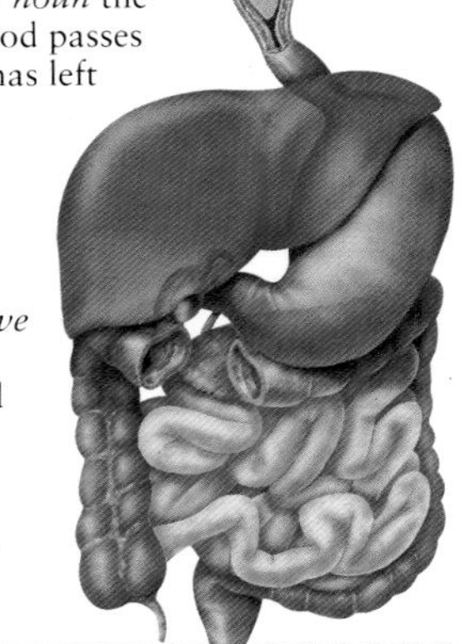

The intestines are coiled inside the abdomen.

**intimate** *adjective* (say **in**-tim-at) 1 very friendly and close. *Intimate relations.* 2 personal and private. *Intimate details.*

I

**intimidate** *verb* to frighten somebody violently to make them do something you want, to threaten. **intimidation** *noun*.

**intolerant** *adjective* unable to put up with people with ideas or beliefs that are different from yours. **intolerance** *noun*.

**intoxicated** *adjective* having drunk too much alcohol. *Peter was intoxicated.*

**intrepid** *adjective* brave and bold, without fear. *Intrepid astronauts.*

**intricate** *adjective* complicated and hard to follow, detailed. *An intricate pattern.*

The silk scarf was designed with an intricate pattern in gorgeous colours.

**intrigue** *noun* (say **in**-treeg) a scheme or plot. *Intrigue was rife in the office.*

**intrigue** *verb* (say in-**treeg**) to interest or fascinate somebody. *Animal behaviour has always intrigued him.*

**introduce** *verb* 1 to bring people together for the first time and make them known to one another. 2 to bring in something or use it for the first time. *The company introduced a new computer.*

**introduction** *noun* 1 the act of introducing somebody or something. 2 a piece of writing at the beginning of a book telling you what it is about. 3 a first experience of something. *An introduction to swimming.*

The introduction to the book told how fruits are formed.

**intrude** *verb* to enter somewhere or join in something when you are not wanted or have not been invited. To disturb. **intrusion** *noun*. **intrusive** *adjective*.

**intruder** *noun* somebody who intrudes or breaks in, such as a burglar.

**intuition** *noun* a feeling or understanding about something that you do not have to think about but cannot explain in a logical way. *His intuition told him that something was very badly wrong.*

**WORD HISTORY**

*'Intoxicate' comes from the Latin word 'toxicum', meaning 'poison'.*

**DID YOU KNOW?**

*'Invent' originally had the sense of 'to discover something that already exists'. Only much later did it acquire the meaning of 'to think up or create something entirely new'.*

**inundate** *verb* 1 to flood. 2 to receive so much of something that you cannot cope with it, to overwhelm. *She was inundated with job offers.* **inundation** *noun*.

**invade** to send troops into another country or place to fight the people living there and to take control of it. **invasion** *noun*.

**invalid** *noun* (say **in**-val-id) a person who is ill or disabled.

**invalid** *adjective* (say in-**val**-id) something that is not legal and so cannot be used. *Your ticket is out of date and therefore invalid.*

**invaluable** *adjective* very valuable or priceless, very useful. *Learning to ride a bike is an invaluable experience.*

**invent** *verb* 1 to make something or think of something for the first time. *Who invented the computer?* 2 to make something up that is not true. *She invented an excuse so as not to go to the dentist.*

**invention** *noun* something that has been invented. *A terrific new invention.*

**inventive** *adjective* able to think up new ideas, original. *Peter is very inventive.*

**inventor** *noun* a person who invents things.

**invertebrate** *noun* any animal without a backbone such as an insect, slug or worm.

The common garden worm is an invertebrate.

**inverted commas** *plural noun* the marks (') and (') used in writing to show what somebody has said. *'Hello,' he whispered.*

**investigate** *verb* to try to find out all the facts about something, to examine carefully. *The police are investigating the boy's disappearance.* **investigation** *noun*.

**invisible** *adjective* something that cannot be seen. *Air is invisible.*

**invitation** *noun* written or spoken words asking you to come to something such as a party. *I've lost your kind invitation.*

**invite** *verb* to ask somebody to come to something or to go somewhere. *He asked me to stay for the Easter holidays.*

**inviting** *adjective* tempting or attractive. *An inviting warm fire.*

**invoice** *noun* a document asking for payment for goods that have been sent or for work that has been done.

**involve** *verb* 1 to be necessary as a part of a job. *The job involves a lot of letter writing.* 2 to be interested in and concerned with. *I don't want to be involved with your problems.* **involvement** *noun*.

**IQ** *abbreviation* intelligence quotient, a way of measuring a person's intelligence by asking special questions.

**Iran** *noun* a country in Southwest Asia.

**Iranian** *noun* a person who comes from Iran. **Iranian** *adjective*. *Iranian oil wells.*

**Iraq** *noun* a country in Southwest Asia.

Iraq is an Arab state at the top of the Persian Gulf. Its economy is built on reserves of oil.

**irate** *adjective* (say eye-rate) angry and complaining. *She wrote an irate letter to the council.*

**Ireland** *noun* a country in Northwest Europe.

**iris** *noun* 1 a tall garden flower. 2 the coloured part of your eye.

**Irish** *adjective* connected to or relating to Ireland and its people (the Irish). *Irish eyes are smiling.*

**iron** *noun* 1 a heavy grey metal that is one of the chemical elements. 2 a heavy electrical tool that heats up and which you use to smooth creases from clothes. **ironing** *noun*. *Have you got any ironing to do?*

**irony** *noun* the use of words to say the very opposite of what they mean. *'That was clever of you to smash my best plate!'* **ironic** *adjective*. *An ironic chain of events.*

**irregular** *adjective* 1 not regular or usual. *He works irregular hours, so I never know when he'll be home.* 2 not even or smooth.

**irrigate** *verb* to supply water for crops on dry land by means of ditches, pipes, canals etc. **irrigation** *noun*.

An irrigation channel brought water to the parched fields.

**irritable** *adjective* easily annoyed, in a bad mood. *Father was in an irritable mood.*

**irritate** *verb* 1 to make somebody annoyed, cross and impatient. 2 to make your skin feel sore or itchy. **irritation** *noun*.

**Islam** *noun* a religion that Muslims follow. It is based on the teachings of the prophet Muhammad. **Islamic** *adjective*.

**AMAZING FACT**

Be careful when you are writing 'it's' (a contraction of either 'it is' or 'it has') and 'its' (which means 'a characteristic of or something that belongs to it').

In 'it's' the apostrophe takes the place of the letters that are left out. for example, 'It's a nice day for a picnic.'

'Its' doesn't have an apostrophe: 'A robin built its nest in a tree in our back yard.'

**Islamabad** *noun* the capital of Pakistan.

**island** *noun* a piece of land surrounded by water. *She is buried on an island in the lake.*

**isle** *noun* an island, usually used as part of its name. *Isle of Skye.*

**isobar** *noun* a line on a weather map that connects places with the same or equal atmospheric pressure.

**isolate** *verb* to place something apart from others and by itself, to separate. *She had to be isolated because she had an infectious disease.* **isolation** *noun*.

**Israel** *noun* a country in Southwest Asia.

The flag of Israel features the star of David on a white ground bordered with blue stripes.

**issue** *noun* 1 an edition of a newspaper or magazine brought out at a particular time. *Today's issue has the latest news.* 2 something that is given out, a supply. 3 a problem or an important topic for discussion. *The issue of bullying.* **issue** *verb* to supply with. *The hikers were issued with special boots.* **take issue with** to disagree.

**isthmus** *noun* a narrow strip of land that joins two larger pieces of land.

**IT** *abbreviation* information technology, the use of computers to store and retrieve information.

**Italian** *noun* 1 a person who comes from Italy. 2 the language spoken in Italy. **Italian** *adjective*. *Italian opera.*

**Italy** *noun* a country in southern Europe.

**itch** *noun* an uncomfortable, tingling feeling on your skin that makes you want to scratch yourself. **itch** (itches, itching, itched) *verb*. *The mosquito bite itches.*

**item** *noun* a single thing on a list or in a group of other things. *An item of news.*

**ivory** *noun* the hard, smooth white material that the tusks of elephants and some other animals are made of.

**Ivory Coast** *noun* a country in Africa.

**ivy** *noun* a climbing evergreen plant with shiny, pointed leaves.

Holly and ivy are traditional Christmas decoration plants. Bringing green leaves indoors in midwinter looks forward to springtime.

# Jj

**jab** (jabs, jabbing, jabbed) *verb* to hit or stab with something pointed. **jab** *noun* an injection. *A flu jab.*

**jack** *noun* 1 a tool for lifting something heavy such as a car off the ground. 2 a picture playing card with a value between the ten and the queen. A jack is sometimes called a knave.

**jackal** *noun* a wild animal of the dog family that feeds off the dead bodies of other animals. Jackals come from Asia and Africa.

**jackass** *noun* a male donkey.

**jacket** *noun* 1 a short coat that covers the top half of your body. 2 a covering for something. *A book jacket.*

**jackknife** *verb* when the trailer of an articulated lorry suddenly bends round towards the cab. *The lorry jackknifed on the black ice.*

**jackpot** *noun* the biggest prize to be won in a game or a lottery.

**jacuzzi** *noun* a bath with underwater jets that make the water swirl.

**jade** *noun* a precious green stone used in making jewellery.

**jaded** *adjective* bored and tired and lacking in enthusiasm.

**jagged** *adjective* with many sharp, rough and uneven points. *Jagged rocks.*

**jaguar** *noun* a South American wild cat with yellow and black spots like a leopard.

The jaguar turned and growled as it heard us approach.

**jail** *noun* another spelling for gaol, a prison where people are kept as a punishment for committing a crime.

**Jakarta** *noun* the capital of Indonesia.

**jam** *noun* 1 a sweet, sticky food made by boiling fruit and sugar together 2 a lot of vehicles or people crowded so closely together that they cannot move easily. *A traffic jam.* **in a jam** in a difficult situation.

**SPELLING NOTE**

*The letter J developed from the letter I during the Middle Ages and was used to show an I at the beginning of a word. Later it became a symbol for the consonant J as in 'jewel' and 'jolly'.*

**jam** (jams, jamming, jammed) *verb* 1 to get stuck or to make something get stuck so that it cannot move. *The door has jammed and I can't open it.* 2 to fill and press things tightly in a place. *Kevin jammed the bag into the boot of the car.* **jam-packed** packed very tightly.

The Jamaican flag has a diagonal yellow cross bisecting a green and black ground.

**Jamaica** *noun* a country in the West Indies.

**Jamaican** *noun* a person who comes from Jamaica. **Jamaican** *adjective. Jamaican sugar.*

**jangle** *verb* to make a ringing noise like pieces of metal banging together. *The bracelets jangled as she threw up her arms.*

**January** *noun* the first month of the year. January has 31 days.

**Japan** *noun* a country in East Asia.

**Japanese** *noun* 1 somebody who comes from Japan. 2 the language spoken in Japan. **Japanese** *adjective. Japanese gardens.*

Sumo wrestling is a very popular sport among the Japanese.

**jar** *noun* a glass container with a lid for storing food such as jam.

**jar** (jars, jarring, jarred) *verb* 1 to make an irritating noise that has an unpleasant effect on people. *The loud music jarred her nerves.* 2 to jolt or give a sudden shock.

**jargon** *noun* the special technical language used by a particular group of people. *Computer jargon.*

**jaunt** *noun* a trip or short journey made for pleasure. *A jaunt to the seaside.*

The javelin is one of the events in the Olympic Games.

**jaunty** *adjective* cheerful and carefree. *A jaunty walk.* **jauntiness** *noun.*

**javelin** *noun* a short, light spear thrown by hand, usually in athletic sports.

**jaw** *noun* one of two large bones in your mouth that hold your teeth. Your jaws move up and down when your speak and eat.

**jazz** *noun* a type of music with a very strong rhythm. Jazz was first played by the Black people of America.

J

**jealous** *adjective* unhappy because you want what somebody else has. **jealousy** *noun. Jealousy poisons the mind.*

**jeans** *noun* trousers made from a strong cotton material called denim.

**jeer** *verb* to make fun of somebody in a rude, loud and unkind way, to mock.

**jelly** *noun* a clear, soft, sweet food flavoured with fruit juice. Jellies wobble. They are made from a substance called gelatine.

**jellyfish** *noun* a sea animal without a backbone (invertebrate) that looks like an umbrella made of jelly. Jellyfish have tentacles that can sting.

Because of their transparent bodies, it is sometimes hard to spot jellyfish floating in the sea.

**jeopardy** *noun* (say jep-ur-dee) If somebody or something is in jeopardy they are in danger or somehow threatened.

**jerk** *verb* to move or pull something suddenly and quickly. **jerk** *noun.*

**jersey** (jerseys) *noun* a kind of knitted shirt or pullover with sleeves, a sweater.

**Jerusalem** *noun* the capital of Israel.

**jest** *noun* a joke or something said or done for fun. **in jest** as a joke.

**jester** an entertainer at a royal court during the Middle Ages.

The jesters danced and sang for the entertainment of the court.

**jet** *noun* 1 a strong stream of liquid or gas forced under pressure. *The fountain threw up jets of water.* 2 an aircraft that is driven forward by a strong jet of air forced out of the back of the engine (a jet engine).

**jet-lag** *noun* great tiredness and a feeling of confusion that some people suffer after a long plane journey.

**jetty** *noun* a pier or landing stage where boats can moor and unload.

**SPELLING NOTE**

*'Jewellery' is one of several words that are spelled differently in American English. The American spelling is 'jewelry'.*

**WORD HISTORY**

*The name 'jeans' comes from the name of the material they are made from: 'jenes' or 'geanes', the French names for the city of Genova where the cloth was first made.*

**Jew** *noun* 1 a person of the Hebrew race described in the Old Testament of the Bible. 2 a person who follows the religion of Judaism. **Jewish** *adjective.*

**jewel** *noun* a beautiful and precious stone such as a ruby or emerald.

**jewellery** *noun* rings, bracelets, necklaces and other ornaments that people wear.

This gold necklace is part of a collection of jewellery that dates from the Bronze Age.

**jiffy** *noun* a very short time. *I'll be back in a jiffy to make the tea.*

**jig** *noun* a lively folk dance. **jig** *verb.*

**jigsaw** *noun* a puzzle made up of pieces of cardboard or wood cut in different shapes that you fit together to form a picture.

**jingle** *noun* 1 the ringing sound made by small bells or keys knocking together. **jingle** *verb. She jingled the coins in her purse.* 2 a simple but catchy tune or song used in radio and TV adverts.

**jinx** *noun* something that is thought to bring bad luck. *There is a jinx on this job.*

**job** *noun* 1 the work that somebody does regularly to earn money. 2 a task or a particular piece of work that has to be done. **just the job** exactly what is required. **job centre** a place where people can go to find out about jobs that are available. **job lot** an assortment of things that you buy together.

**jockey** (jockeys) *noun* a person whose job it is to ride horses in races.

The jockey urged the horse on to win the race.

**jodhpurs** *plural noun* (say **jod**-purz) close-fitting trousers that you wear for riding a horse. *Jodhpurs and riding boots.*

**jog** (jogs, jogging, jogged) *verb* 1 to run at a slow steady pace for exercise. 2 to push or shake something gently. *She jogged my arm and I upset the jug.* **jog somebody's memory** to make somebody remember something.

**join** *verb* 1 to fasten, tie or somehow connect things together. **join** *noun.* 2 to become a member of a club or organization. 3 to unite or come together. **join in** take part in. *They all joined in the fun.* **join up** to become a member of the armed forces.

J

**joint** *noun* 1 a place where two things join and are fixed. 2 a place where two bones in your body are joined together, such as your elbow or knee. **joint** *adjective* shared by two or more people. *I can't take all the credit, it was a joint effort.*

The joints found in the human body are, from left to right, ball and socket, pivot, saddle and hinge.

**joke** *noun* something that you say or do that makes people laugh. **joke** *verb*. **beyond a joke** not at all funny but very serious.

**joker** *noun* 1 somebody who tells jokes. 2 an extra card in a pack of playing cards which in certain games may have any value.

**jolly** (jollier, jolliest) *adjective* happy, cheerful and full of fun.

**jolt** *verb* to move suddenly and roughly, to jerk. *The train jolted to a halt.*

**Jordan** *noun* a country in the Middle East.

The flag of Jordan has a red triangle with a white star on a black, white and green background.

**Jordanian** *noun* a person who comes from Jordan. **Jordanian** *adjective*. *Jordanian oil.*

**jostle** *verb* to shove or push and bump into people roughly.

**jot** (jots, jotting, jotted) *verb* to write down something quickly and briefly. *He jotted down a list of things he wanted.*

**journal** *noun* (say **jer**-nul) 1 a diary or daily record of things you have done etc. 2 a magazine, especially one that deals with a particular subject. *The Nursing Journal.*

**journalese** *noun* (say jer-nul-**eez**) a style of careless and far-fetched writing used in some newspapers and magazines.

**journalism** *noun* (say **jer**-nul-izum) the job of gathering news and writing articles for newspapers and magazines.

**journalist** *noun* (say **jer**-nul-ist) a person who writes or edits articles for a newspaper or magazine.

**journey** ( journeys) *noun* (say **jer**-nee) the act of travelling from one place to another, a trip. **journey** *verb*.

**joust** *noun* (say **jow**-st) a sporting fight in the Middle Ages between two knights on horses, using long spears. **joust** *verb*.

**WORD HISTORY**

*'Jubilee' comes from a Hebrew word 'yobel', meaning a ram's horn. The ram's horn was blown to proclaim a year of celebration, especially a celebration held every 50 years.*

**joy** *noun* 1 a feeling of great happiness. 2 success or luck. The opposite of joy is sorrow.

**joyride** *noun* a ride in a stolen car, to experience danger. **joyrider** *noun*.

**jubilee** *noun* a celebration to commemorate an important event. **silver jubilee** a celebration of a 25th anniversary. **golden jubilee** a celebration of a 50th anniversary. **diamond jubilee** a celebration of a 60th anniversary.

**Judaism** *noun* the religion of the Jewish people. *He converted to Judaism.*

**judge** *noun* 1 a person who hears cases in a court of law and decides how a guilty person should be punished. 2 a person who decides who is the winner of a competition. 3 a person who forms an opinion about something. *She's a good judge of character.* **judgement** *noun*.

**judo** *noun* a Japanese sport of self-defence in which two people wrestle, using special movements, and try to throw each other to the ground.

**jug** *noun* a container with a handle and a lip part for pouring liquids.

**juggle** *verb* to keep throwing and catching a number of objects, such as balls, in the air without dropping them. *We learned to juggle at camp last summer. I'm pretty good at it now.* **juggler** *noun*.

**juice** *noun* (rhymes with loose) the liquid you can squeeze from fruit and vegetables. **juicy** *adjective*. *Mavis bit into a juicy orange.* **juiciness** *noun*.

**juke-box** *noun* a machine that plays music you select when you put coins into it.

Jousting only takes place in pageants and fairs these days.

**July** *noun* the seventh month of the year. July has 31 days.

**jumble** *verb* to mix things up so that they are an untidy mess. *She jumbled up the pieces of the jigsaw puzzle.* **jumble** *noun* a messy and mixed collection of things. ***The floor of my closet is a jumble of clothes and shoes.***

**jumbo** *adjective* very large. **jumbo jet** a large passenger plane, a 747.

The jumbo jet took off with the 350 passengers aboard.

**jump** *verb* 1 to leap or throw your body up into the air. 2 to go over something by leaping. **jump** *noun* something you jump over. *The horse is coming to the last jump.* **jump at** to accept enthusiastically. *He jumped at the chance to go riding.*

**jumper** *noun* a dress without sleeves that you usually wear a blouse under.

**jumpy** (jumpier, jumpiest) *adjective* nervous. *My mistake made me feel jumpy.*

**junction** *noun* a place where railroad lines or roads join or cross over.

**June** *noun* the sixth month of the year. June has 30 days.

**jungle** *noun* a dense forest in a tropical country. *I spent a year exploring the jungle.*

The toucan, the monkey and the chameleon are all creatures of the jungle.

**WORD HISTORY**

*The name 'July' comes from the Latin word for this month. The month was named by the Romans in honor of the general and statesman Julius Caesar.*

**junior** *adjective* 1 of lower rank or importance. *A junior executive.* 2 of or for younger people. *A junior dictionary.*

**junk** *noun* 1 things that are old and useless or worthless. 2 a Chinese sailing boat with a flat bottom.

Traditional junks can still be seen in modern Hong Kong harbor.

**junk food** *noun* food that is not good for you but may be quick and easy to prepare.

**junkie** *noun* a drug addict.

**junk mail** *noun* leaflets and advertisements that are sent to you in the mail and which you do not want.

**junk shop** *noun* a place that sells second-hand clothes etc.

**jury** *noun* a group of people who are chosen to hear a case in a court of law and decide whether an accused person is guilty or not.

**just** *adjective* fair and right, honest. *A just decision was eventually reached.*

**just** *adverb* 1 not long ago. *She just went home.* 2 only. *Just a minute!* 3 exactly. *This is just the right color.* 4 almost not. *There is just enough to eat.*

**justice** *noun* 1 treatment that is just, fair and right. 2 a country's system of laws and how they are operated by the law courts. 3 a judge. *A justice of the peace.*

**justify** (justifies, justifying, justified) *verb* to defend or to prove that something is just and fair. *How can you justify hitting the child?* **justification** *noun.*

**jut** (juts, jutting, jutted) *verb* to stick out farther than other things around it, to project *The balcony juts out from the side of the house.*

**jute** *noun* a fiber used to make rope and coarse cloth for sacks etc.

**juvenile** *adjective* 1 concerning young people. 2 childish and silly. *Juvenile behavior is inappropriate here.*

K

# Kk

**Kabul** *noun* the capital of Afghanistan.

**kaleidoscope** *noun* a tube that you turn as you look through it to see changing patterns of colour made by mirrors and pieces of glass fitted at one end of it.

**Kampala** *noun* the capital of Uganda.

**kangaroo** *noun* a large Australian animal with strong back legs for jumping. The female has a pouch on her stomach in which she carries her baby, called a joey. Kangaroos belong to a group of pouched animals called marsupials.

A kangaroo with her baby in her pouch is a familiar sight to travellers in Australia.

**karaoke** *noun* (say ka-ree-**ok**-kee) a kind of entertainment from Japan in which people sing pop songs to recorded music and follow the words of the song on a screen.

**karate** *noun* a self-defence sport originating from Japan in which two people fight one another using special kicks and blows.

**Kathmandu** *noun* the capital of Nepal.

**kayak** *noun* (say **kye**-ak) a canoe covered in canvas, originally used by the Inuit people.

**Kazakhstan** *noun* a country in West Asia.

Kazakhstan exports oil, metals, chemicals, grain and wool.

**kebab** *noun* small pieces of meat or vegetable cooked on a skewer. *A chicken kebab.*

**WORD HISTORY**

*The shape of the letter K comes from the ancient Egyptian symbol for an open hand. Its sound comes from 'kaph', a Semitic word for an open palm of a hand.*

**AMAZING FACT**

Kangaroos, wallabies oppossums and other marsupials begin carrying their babies in their pouches before they are fully developed. The baby may stay inside its mother for only 11 days, it continues to develop in the pouch.

**keel** *noun* the long piece of steel that lies along the bottom of a ship's frame.

**keen** *adjective* 1 eager and interested. 2 sensitive and sharp. *A keen sense of smell.* 3 clever and quick. *A keen wit.*

**keep** (keeps, keeping, kept) *verb* 1 to have something and not to give it to anybody. 2 to look after something for somebody. *Can you keep my place for me please?* 3 to remain. *Please keep still!* 4 to remain fresh or in a good condition. *Will this meat keep till Sunday?* 5 to look after and feed. *Mary keeps goats.* **keep** *noun* the food and money etc. a person needs to live. *He earns his keep by gardening.* **keep away** stay away. **keep down** *The food disagrees with her and she can't keep it down.* **keep on** to continue. **keep to** *Keep to the footpath all the way.* **keep up** *Keep up with your studies.*

**keep** *noun* the main tower in a castle.

**keeper** *noun* a person whose job it is to look after animals in a zoo or who is responsible for the objects in a museum.

**keg** *noun* a small barrel.

**kelp** *noun* a kind of seaweed used as a fertilizer. *Sea otters eat kelp.*

**kennel** *noun* 1 a small shelter or hut for keeping a dog in. 2 **kennels** a place where dogs are bred or where dogs can be looked after when their owners are away.

**Kenya** *noun* a country in Africa.

**kept** past tense of keep.

**kerb** *noun* the line of stones along the edge of a pavement. *Don't trip up the kerb.*

**kernel** *noun* the edible middle part of a nut, inside the shell.

**kestrel** *noun* a small falcon. Kestrels kill and eat small animals.

Kestrels are becoming more common in urban areas of Britain.

**ketchup** *noun* a thick sauce, usually made from tomatoes.

**kettle** *noun* a container for boiling water in. Kettles have a lid, a handle and a narrow spout for pouring.

**key** *noun* 1 a shaped metal object that you turn to open a lock or to start an engine. 2 the buttons on typewriters and computers or the black and white bars on a piano or organ that you press with your fingers. 3 the answers to a problem or mystery. *The key to the crime.* 4 a set of musical notes in a scale based on one note. **key** *adjective* important. *A key witness.*

**keyboard** *noun* 1 the set of keys on a computer, piano etc. that you press when you use them. 2 an electronic musical instrument. *A keyboard player.*

This diagram shows what is inside the keyboard of your computer.

**keyhole** *noun* a hole in a lock where you put the key.

**keystone** *noun* the stone in the centre of an arch. It holds the other stones in the arch in place. *A marble keystone.*

**kg** *abbreviation* kilogram.

**khaki** *noun* (say **kah**-key) a yellowish-brown colour. *Soldiers wear khaki.*

**Khartoum** *noun* the capital of Sudan.

**kick** *verb* 1 to hit somebody or something with your foot. 2 to move your legs about with force. **kick** *noun* 1 *The pony gave Peter a nasty kick.* 2 a thrill. *She gets a kick out of pop music.* **kick-off** the kick of a ball that starts a match. **kick out** to get rid of.

**kid** *noun* 1 a young goat. 2 a child.

**kid** *verb* to tease somebody by pretending that something is true. *It's not broken. I was just kidding.*

**kidnap** (kidnaps, kidnapping, kidnapped) *verb* to capture somebody and keep them prisoner until you get what you demand, e.g. money. **kidnapper** *noun.*

**kidney** (kidneys) *noun* Your kidneys are organs in your body that keep your blood clean by removing waste products and passing them out in the form of urine.

**Kiev** *noun* the capital of Ukraine.

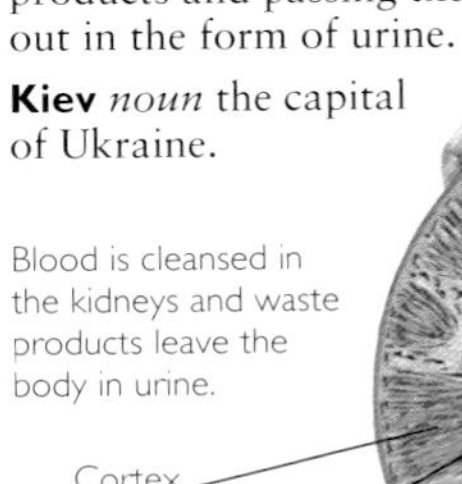


Blood is cleansed in the kidneys and waste products leave the body in urine.

**WORD BUILDER**

*'Kilo' is a Greek word meaning a thousand. So a kilogram is a thousand grams, a kilowatt is a thousand watts and kilobyte is a thousand bytes.*

**AMAZING FACT**

'Kindergarden' comes from the German words 'kind' (child) and 'garten' (garden) – so its orignal meaning was 'children's garden'.

**Kigali** *noun* the capital of Rwanda.

**kill** *verb* to end the life of a person or animal, to destroy something. **kill** *noun* 1 the act of killing. 2 the animal killed. *The tiger stood over its kill.*

**killer** *noun* a person or animal that kills.

**kiln** *noun* a very hot oven for baking pottery and bricks to make them hard.

Pottery is baked in a kiln.

**kilogram** or **kilogramme** *noun* a measure of weight equal to 1,000 grams. Also called a kilo. *A kilo of sugar.*

**kilometre** *noun* a measure of length equal to 1,000 metres.

**kilt** *noun* a knee-length pleated skirt made from tartan cloth, traditionally worn by Scottish men.

**kimono** *noun* a long loose robe with wide sleeves, traditionally worn by Japanese women.

The Japanese wear traditional dress to perform kabuki, their national dance theatre.

**kin** *noun* (old-fashioned) your family and relations. **next of kin** your closest relation.

**kind** *adjective* helpful and friendly to people, gentle. *It was kind of you to visit me in hospital.* **kindness** *noun.*

**kind** *noun* a group of things that are similar. A type or sort of something. *What kind of dog is this?* **kind of** something like. *An igloo is a kind of a house built of ice.*

**kindle** *verb* to set light to and start something burning.

**kindergarten** *noun* a small school for very young children.

**king** *noun* 1 a male ruler of a country. Kings are not elected but inherit their position by succeeding the previous ruler. 2 a playing card with a picture of a king on it. 3 a chesspiece. When the king is taken the game is lost.

King Henry VIII of England had six wives. He divorced two wives and had two others executed. One wife died a natural death and his last wife survived him.

**kingdom** *noun* 1 a country that is ruled by a king or queen. 2 a division of the natural world. *The animal kingdom.*

**kingfisher** *noun* a bird with bright blue and brown feathers and a dagger-like beak that it uses to catch fish from lakes and rivers.

**Kingston** *noun* the capital of Jamaica.

**Kingstown** *noun* the capital of St Vincent and the Grenadines.

**Kinshasa** *noun* the capital of the Democratic Republic of the Congo (formerly Zaire).

**kiosk** *noun* (say **kee**-osk) a small hut-like shop on the street where you can buy things like newspapers and sweets.

**Kiribati** *noun* a country of many islands in the Pacific Ocean.

**kiss** *verb* to touch somebody with your lips as a sign of love or friendship. **kiss** *noun. He gave me a kiss.*

**kiss of life** a way of helping somebody to breathe again after an accident by blowing air into their lungs.

**kit** *noun* 1 the clothes and equipment you need to do something. *Cricket kit.* 2 all the things you need to make something. *A model ship kit.*

David got his tennis kit ready for the match.

**SPELLING NOTE**

*'K' is not pronounced when it comes before 'n' at the beginning of a word, as in 'knave', 'knee', 'knot' and 'knuckle'.*

**AMAZING FACT**

'Knickers' were originally called 'knickerbockers' after the pretended author of Washington Irving's 'History of New York', 1809.

**kitchen** *noun* a room in a house that is used for preparing and cooking food.

**kite** *noun* 1 a toy that you fly in the wind. It consists of a light frame covered in paper or cloth on the end of a long piece of string. 2 a bird of prey belonging to the hawk family.

**kitten** *noun* a very young cat. **kittenish** *adjective* behaving like a kitten, playful.

**kitty** *noun* a sum of money put in by several people for everybody in the group to use.

**kiwi** *noun* (say **kee**-wee) a New Zealand bird that cannot fly.

The kiwi is the national bird of New Zealand.

**km** *abbreviation* kilometre.

**knack** *noun* the ability to do something difficult with ease and skill.

**knave** *noun* 1 a picture playing card with a value between the ten and the queen. A knave is often called a jack. *The knave of hearts.* 2 a dishonest person.

**knead** *verb* to squeeze and stretch dough with your hands before baking.

**knee** *noun* the joint in the middle of your leg where it bends.

**kneecap** *noun* the movable bone in front of your knee.

The kneecap is also called the patella.

**kneel** *verb* to bend your knees and go down on them. *They knelt to pray for forgiveness.*

**knew** the past tense of know.

**knickers** *plural noun* underpants worn by women and girls.

**knife** (knives) *noun* a metal tool with a handle and a sharp blade that you use for cutting. **knife** *verb* to stab with a knife.

**knight** *noun* 1 in the Middle Ages a soldier who fought on horseback for his king or lord. 2 a man who has been given the title 'Sir' by the monarch. *Sir Andrew Marvell.* 3 a chesspiece with a horse's head.

The noble knight was training a falcon to hunt for him.

**knit** (knits, knitting, knitted) *verb* 1 to make clothes by looping wool together with two long needles. 2 to join closely. *The broken bones will soon knit together.*

**knob** *noun* a round handle on a door or drawer. *Knobs and knockers.*

**knock** *verb* 1 to hit or strike something hard. *Is there somebody knocking at the door?* 2 to hit something so that it falls. *Sue knocked her mug off her desk.* **knock** *noun*. **knock out** to hit somebody so hard they become unconscious.

**knocker** *noun* a hinged metal ring, knob or hammer on a door that you use for knocking. *He banged the door knocker.*

**knot** *noun* 1 a join or fastening made by tying pieces of string, rope or cloth together. 2 a hard, dark part in wood where a branch joined the tree. 3 a measure of speed for ships. 1 knot is about 1.85 kph.

**knot** (knots, knotting, knotted) *verb* to fasten something by tying its ends into a knot. *Fishermen's knots.*

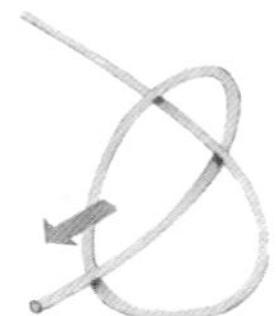

These diagrams show how to tie a simple knot, for example in your shoelaces. Many more complicated knots are used by fishermen on their nets.

**know** (knows, knowing, knew, known) *verb* to have learnt something or to have information about something and to have it in your mind. *Do you know French?* 2 to remember or to recognize somebody or something. *I know Sharon very well.*

**WORD HISTORY**

*The word 'knight' comes from an Old English word 'cniht', meaning a boy servant or warrior.*

**DID YOU KNOW**

*The lord of a manor provided horses and armour for his knights. In time it became a great honour to be a knight, and knights formed an important part of the feudal system of the Middle Ages.*

**knowing** *adjective* showing that you know something secret. *He knew she was lying and gave her a knowing look.*

**knowledge** *noun* the things that you know and understand, things that you learn by study. *A good knowledge of French.*

**knowledgeable** *adjective* clever and well-informed about a subject.

**know-all** *noun* somebody who thinks they know a great deal about everything.

**know-how** *noun* practical knowledge and ability. *I admire your know-how.*

**knuckle** *noun* the bones at the joint of a finger. *Knuckles swollen with arthritis.*

**koala** *noun* an Australian animal that looks like a small bear. Koalas live in eucalyptus trees and feed on their leaves.

Koala bears sleep for 22 out of every 24 hours.

**kookaburra** *noun* an Australian bird of the kingfisher family that makes a loud laughing noise. *The kookaburra has a strange laugh.*

**Koran** or **Qu'ran** *noun* the holy book of Islam, the religion of the Muslims.

**kosher** *adjective* (say **koh**-shur) food that has been prepared in accordance with the laws of the Jewish religion.

**kph** *abbreviation* kilometres per hour.

**Kuala Lumpur** *noun* the capital of Malaysia.

**Kuwait City** *noun* the capital of Kuwait.

**Kuwait** *noun* a country in Southwest Asia.

Kuwait is a country that has grown rich because of its vast reserves of oil.

**Kyrgyzstan** *noun* a country in central Asia.

# Ll

**lab** *noun* a laboratory.

**label** *noun* a piece of paper, cloth or plastic that is attached to something and that gives information about it. **label** (labels, labelling, labelled) *verb* to put a label on something.

**laboratory** *noun* a room or building where scientists work.

**laborious** *adjective* difficult and needing a lot of hard work or effort. *Digging is a laborious job.*

**labour** *noun* 1 hard, physical work. 2 workers considered as a group. 3 the pain a woman feels when giving birth. 4 **Labour Party** one of the three main political parties in Great Britain. **labour** *verb* to work hard. **labourer** *noun* an unskilled worker.

**labyrinth** *noun* a maze.

Trying to find your way out of a labyrinth can be a nightmarish experience.

**lace** *noun* 1 a delicate material made of fine threads woven into a pretty pattern with holes in it. 2 a long, thin cord that is threaded through holes and used, for example, to tie up a shoe or a boot. **lace** *verb. Lace up your trainers tightly.*

**lack** *verb* to be without something that is needed or wanted. *She lacks the intelligence to be a good teacher.* **lack** *noun.*

**lacquer** *noun* (say **lack**-ur) a varnish or glossy paint.

**lad** *noun* a boy or young man.

**ladder** *noun* 1 two long wooden or metal poles with cross-pieces called rungs used for climbing up or down. A set of steps. 2 a tear in a pair of tights or stockings.

**ladle** *noun* a large, deep spoon with a long handle used for lifting out liquids such as soup. *A generous ladle of soup.*

### WORD HISTORY

*The shape of the letter L comes from the ancient Egyptian symbol for a shepherd's crook. Its sound comes from 'lamed', a Semitic word for a shepherd's crook. The Greeks called the letter 'lambda'.*

### SPELLING NOTE

*A word that sounds like 'lain' is 'lane'. Try not to confuse the two.*

### AMAZING FACT

Labyrinths are created by carefully planting hedges in an intricate pattern. When the plants are fully grown, they are taller than a person and so you cannot see which path to take. If you succeed in finding your way to the middle of the puzzle, there is usually a reward – a beautiful fountain or a peaceful place to sit.

**lady** *noun* 1 a woman, especially one with very good manners. 2 the title of a noblewoman. *Sir John and Lady Brown.* **ladylike** *adjective. Ladylike behaviour.*

**ladybird** *noun* (US ladybug) a small round flying beetle, usually with black spots on red wings. Ladybirds eat aphids and other harmful plant pests.

Ladybirds are the gardener's friend because they eat aphids (greenfly).

**lag** (lags, lagging, lagged) *verb* to move or develop more slowly than others and so be unable to keep up. *Catch up! You're lagging behind everybody else.* **time lag** the time that passes between one event and another.

**lager** *noun* a kind of beer that is light in colour. **lager lout** a young man who behaves rudely and violently when he has drunk too much alcohol.

**lagoon** *noun* a seawater lake separated from the sea by sandbanks or rocks.

**laid** past tense of lay.

**laid-back** *adjective* (slang) relaxed and unworried. *A laid-back kind of guy.*

**lain** past participle of lie.

**lair** *noun* a den or hidden place where a wild animal sleeps.

**lake** *noun* a large area of fresh water with land all around it.

**lamb** *noun* 1 a young sheep. 2 the meat of a young sheep. *Roast lamb and mint sauce.* **lamb** *verb* to give birth (to lambs).

**lame** *adjective* 1 unable to walk properly because of an injured leg. *The pony is lame and walks with a limp.* **lameness** *noun.* 2 weak and not good enough. *A lame excuse.* **lame duck** a person or company that cannot manage without help.

**lamp** *noun* a device that gives light by burning electricity, gas, oil or a candle. **lamp-post** *noun* a tall post holding a street lamp. **lampshade** *noun* a cover placed over a lamp to soften its light.

**lance** *noun* a long spear once used by knights on horseback.

The knights charged at each other, their lances poised to strike.

**land** *noun* 1 all the dry surface of the Earth that is above the sea. 2 the ground used for farming, gardening, building etc. 3 a country or nation. **land** *verb* 1 to arrive on land from a ship. 2 to bring an aircraft down to the ground. *The plane landed at noon.* 3 to get into trouble. *He landed up in prison.*

**landing** *noun* 1 a level area at the top of a flight of stairs. 2 bringing into ground or shore. *An emergency landing.*

**landlady, landlord** *noun* 1 a person who rents a house or flat to somebody. 2 a person who runs a public house.

**landmark** *noun* some building or object that you can see clearly from a distance. *The church spire is a clear landmark.*

The American presidents carved in the rock at Mount Rushmore in South Dakota are an instantly recognizable landmark.

**landscape** *noun* a wide view or all that you can see from one place.

**lane** *noun* 1 a narrow country road. 2 one of the strips on a motorway that is wide enough for a single line of traffic. 3 a strip of track or water for a runner or swimmer.

**language** *noun* 1 all the words that we use to talk or write to one another. Human speech. 2 the system of words used in one or more countries. *Spanish is the language spoken in Spain and in most of South America.* 3 any other system of communicating. *Sign language.*

**lanky** *adjective* tall and thin.

**lantern** *noun* a container, often with glass sides, for holding a candle or oil lamp.

**Laos** *noun* a country in Southeast Asia.

The flag of Laos shows red and blue stripes and a white circle.

**lap** *noun* 1 the top, flat part of your legs when you are sitting down. 2 one journey around a race track.

**lap** (laps, lapping, lapped) *verb* An animal laps up water by flicking it into its mouth with its tongue.

**DID YOU KNOW?**

*'Laser' is an acronym for 'light amplification by stimulated emission of radiation'.*

**WORD HISTORY**

*'Larva' is a Latin word meaning 'mask' or 'ghost'. Because the larva of an insect looks so different from the actual insect it was thought to mask or be the ghost of the fully developed insect.*

**La Paz** *noun* the seat of government of Bolivia.

**lapel** *noun* the part below the collar of a jacket that folds back on the chest.

**lapse** *noun* 1 a small careless mistake. 2 a period of time that has passed.

**laptop** *noun* a small portable computer that you can use on your lap.

**lard** *noun* fat from pigs, used in cooking.

**large** *adjective* big in size, amount etc., not small. **largeness** *noun.* **at large** free after escaping. *The zoo's lion is still at large.*

**largely** *adverb* mostly.

**lark** *noun* a small brown bird that flies high in the sky and sings beautifully.

**larva** (larvae) *noun* an insect at its first stage of development after coming out of the egg and before becoming a pupa. A grub. A larva looks like a worm.

**laser** *noun* a device that produces a very narrow and powerful beam of light, used for cutting in surgery.

Precision cutting can be carried out with a laser.

**lash** *verb* 1 to hit violently, as with a whip. *The waves lashed against the rocks.* 2 to make rapid movements like a whip. *The cat lashed its tail in anger.* **lash** *noun* 1 a whip. 2 one of the small hairs growing around the eye (eyelash).

**lass** *noun* a girl or young woman.

**lasso** *noun* (say lass-oo) a long rope with a loop or noose at one end, used to catch cattle and horses. **lasso** *verb.*

**last** *adjective* 1 coming after all the others. *The last horse in the race.* 2 the only one remaining. *The last slice of cake.* 3 most recent, just past. *Last night.* 4 previous or one before this one. *Her last job.*

**last** *verb* 1 to continue. *The concert lasted four hours.* 2 to remain in good condition for some time. *These shoes are already worn out – they haven't lasted long.*

**late** *adjective, adverb* 1 not early but after the usual or expected time. *She was an hour late for her appointment, but she always arrives late.* 2 near the end of a period of time. *They arrived home late in the evening.* 3 previous, recently dead. *The late queen.* **lateness** *noun.* **lately** *adverb* recently.

**later** *adverb* after some time.

**lateral** *adjective* concerned with the side, sideways. *Lateral movement.*

**lathe** *noun* a machine that holds and turns wood or metal while it is being shaped with a cutting tool.

**lather** *noun* the bubbles or foam you get when you mix soap or detergent in warm water. *This soap makes a good lather.*

**Latin** *noun* the language spoken by the ancient Romans.

**latitude** *noun* a position or distance measured in degrees on a map north or south of the equator.

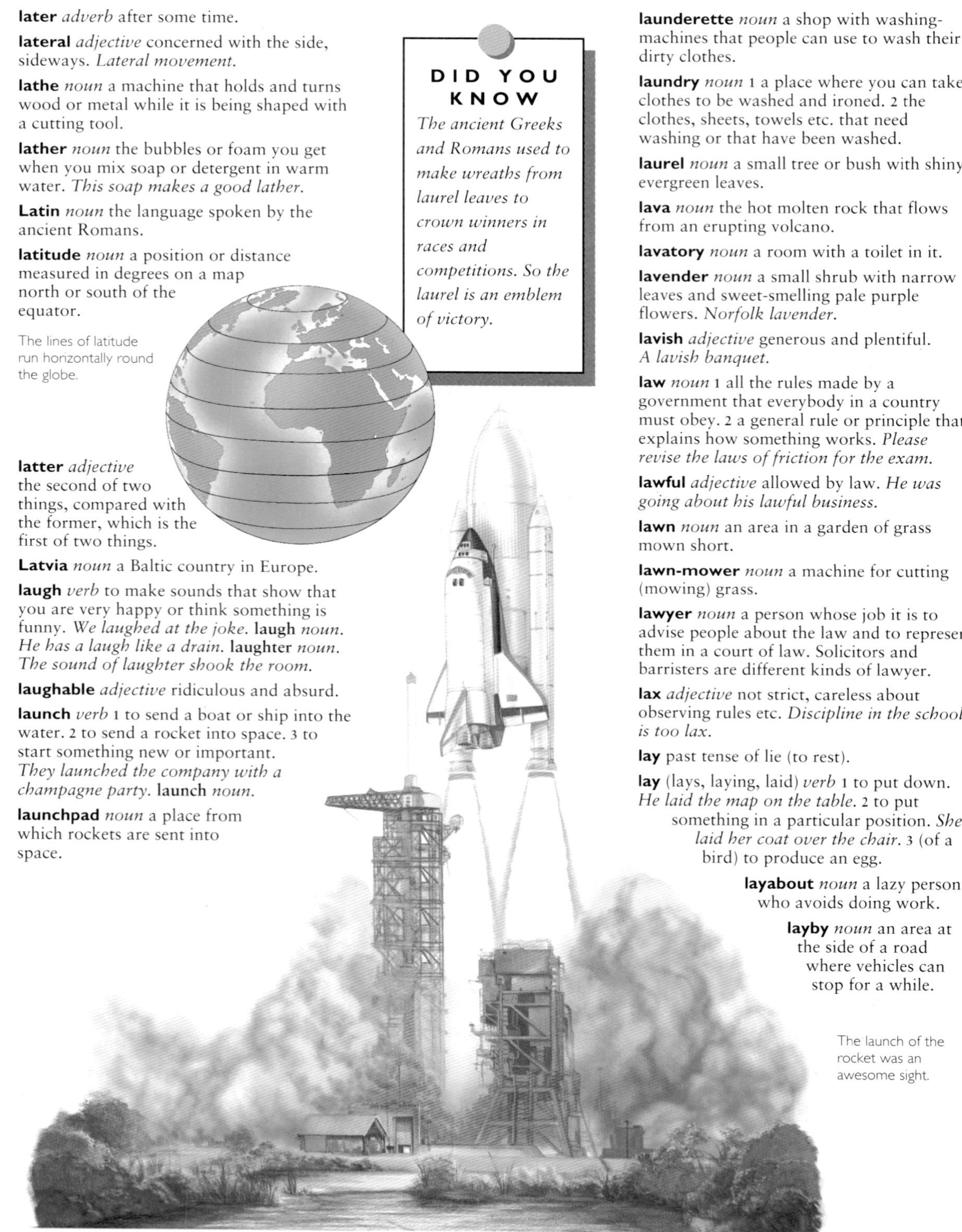

The lines of latitude run horizontally round the globe.

**latter** *adjective* the second of two things, compared with the former, which is the first of two things.

**Latvia** *noun* a Baltic country in Europe.

**laugh** *verb* to make sounds that show that you are very happy or think something is funny. *We laughed at the joke.* **laugh** *noun. He has a laugh like a drain.* **laughter** *noun. The sound of laughter shook the room.*

**laughable** *adjective* ridiculous and absurd.

**launch** *verb* 1 to send a boat or ship into the water. 2 to send a rocket into space. 3 to start something new or important. *They launched the company with a champagne party.* **launch** *noun.*

**launchpad** *noun* a place from which rockets are sent into space.

**DID YOU KNOW**

*The ancient Greeks and Romans used to make wreaths from laurel leaves to crown winners in races and competitions. So the laurel is an emblem of victory.*

**launderette** *noun* a shop with washing-machines that people can use to wash their dirty clothes.

**laundry** *noun* 1 a place where you can take clothes to be washed and ironed. 2 the clothes, sheets, towels etc. that need washing or that have been washed.

**laurel** *noun* a small tree or bush with shiny evergreen leaves.

**lava** *noun* the hot molten rock that flows from an erupting volcano.

**lavatory** *noun* a room with a toilet in it.

**lavender** *noun* a small shrub with narrow leaves and sweet-smelling pale purple flowers. *Norfolk lavender.*

**lavish** *adjective* generous and plentiful. *A lavish banquet.*

**law** *noun* 1 all the rules made by a government that everybody in a country must obey. 2 a general rule or principle that explains how something works. *Please revise the laws of friction for the exam.*

**lawful** *adjective* allowed by law. *He was going about his lawful business.*

**lawn** *noun* an area in a garden of grass mown short.

**lawn-mower** *noun* a machine for cutting (mowing) grass.

**lawyer** *noun* a person whose job it is to advise people about the law and to represent them in a court of law. Solicitors and barristers are different kinds of lawyer.

**lax** *adjective* not strict, careless about observing rules etc. *Discipline in the school is too lax.*

**lay** past tense of lie (to rest).

**lay** (lays, laying, laid) *verb* 1 to put down. *He laid the map on the table.* 2 to put something in a particular position. *She laid her coat over the chair.* 3 (of a bird) to produce an egg.

**layabout** *noun* a lazy person who avoids doing work.

**layby** *noun* an area at the side of a road where vehicles can stop for a while.

The launch of the rocket was an awesome sight.

**layout** *noun* 1 the way text and pictures are arranged on a page. 2 the way things are arranged on a plan. *The layout of the new supermarket.*

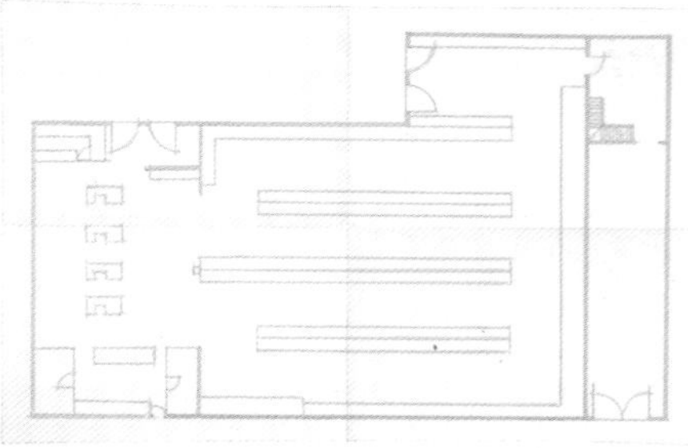

The managers studied the architect's plan for the layout of the new supermarket.

**layer** *noun* a thickness of something that lies between two other pieces of it or on top. *The cake was covered with a layer of icing.*

**lazy** (lazier, laziest) *adjective* not liking work, effort or exercise. *Cats are lazy and sleep a lot.* **laziness** *noun.* **lazily** *adverb.*

**lead** *noun* (rhymes with bed) 1 a soft, grey metal. 2 the substance in the middle of a pencil that makes a mark.

**lead** (leads, leading, led) *verb* (rhymes with need) 1 to go in front and show the way, to take in a certain direction. *He led me out of the maze.* 2 to be in the first place. *The grey horse was leading for most of the race.* 3 to be in charge of other people. *The captain led her team bravely.* 4 to live a certain way of life. *Our dog leads a happy life.* **lead** *noun* 1 the front position. *The grey horse is in the lead.* 2 a strap you attach to a dog's collar to lead or control it. 3 a cable that carries electricity. 4 a piece of information or a clue that helps you to solve a crime etc.

**leader** *noun* somebody who leads or who goes first, a person in charge of a group.

**leaf** (leaves) *noun* 1 one of the flat, usually green, parts of a plant that grows from a stem or twig. 2 a page of a book.

The green leaves of summer provided a dappled shade for the picnickers.

**leaflet** *noun* a usually folded sheet of paper with information etc. printed on it. *The politician pushed the leaflet through the widow's letter box.*

**AMAZING FACT**

In green plants, leaves make food to nourish the plant. This process is called photosynthesis. The chlorophyll in the leaf uses a combination of carbon dioxide, water and light to make sugar. It then passes the sugar to the rest of the plant through tubes.

**SPELLING NOTE**

*Do not confuse the past tense of 'lie' to rest ('I lay in bed thinking') with the verb 'lay' meaning 'put down'. ('When you've finished reading, lay the book on the table.')*

**leak** *noun* a hole in a container or pipe through which liquid or gas can escape. **leak** *verb* 1 (of a gas or liquid) to escape through a hole or crack. *This pipe is leaking.* 2 to give away secret information.

**lean** *adjective* having little or no fat. *Lean meat.* **leanness** *noun.*

**lean** (leans, leaning, leaned or leant) *verb* 1 to bend towards something. *Tom leant out of the window and waved to his friends.* 2 to rest against something for support. *Lean the ladder against the wall.*

**leap** (leaps, leaping, leapt or leaped) *verb* to jump up high or to jump over something. **leap** *noun.* **leap year** every fourth year in which February has 29 days instead of 28. Leap years have 366 days instead of 365.

**learn** (learns, learning, learnt or learned) *verb* to find out about something or how to do something. *Joe's learning French.*

**learned** *adjective* A learned person knows a lot. *A learned monk.*

**learning** *noun* having a great deal of knowledge. *His learning is phenomenal.*

**lease** *noun* an agreement between the owner of a property and a person renting it for a stated period of time. *They signed a 20-year lease on the house.*

**leash** *noun* a lead attached to a dog's collar so that you can take it for walks.

**least** *adjective* smallest or less than all the others. *This is the least expensive bike.* **at least** the minimum, but likely to be more. *It will cost at least £50.*

**leather** *noun* the skin of animals used to make such things as shoes, handbags and belts. **leathery** *adjective* tough like leather.

Tom was given a leather executive briefcase for his birthday.

**leave** *verb* 1 to go away from somewhere. The opposite of leave is arrive. 2 to let something remain where it is. *She left her clothes all over the floor.* 3 to forget about something by not taking it with you. *I left my coat indoors.* 4 what remains after the main part has been used or taken away. *Seven from eight leaves one.* 5 to pass on something to somebody after you die. *My uncle left me his gold watch.* **leave out** not to include or forget to put in.

**leave** *noun* 1 a holiday or time away from a job. 2 permission to do something.

**leaves** plural of leaf. *In autumn the leaves turn red and gold before they fall.*

**Lebanon** *noun* a country in Southwest Asia.

The flag of Lebanon has red and white stripes and a central symbol in green and gold.

**lecture** *noun* 1 a formal talk about a particular subject given to a class or audience. 2 a scolding or telling off. *The teacher gave him a lecture on how to behave.* **lecture** *verb.*

**led** past tense of lead. *The dog led the children out of danger.*

**ledge** *noun* a shelf-like space on a cliff, rock or wall. *The bird nested on the ledge.*

**leek** *noun* a long white vegetable with green leaves at one end. It tastes like an onion.

**leer** *verb* to look and smile at somebody in an evil way. *The old man gave her a leer.*

**leeward** *adjective* on the sheltered side, turned away from the wind.

**left** past tense of leave.

**left** *noun* You are reading these words from left to right. **left** *adjective. Close your left eye.*

**left-overs** *plural noun* food that has not been eaten after a meal. *I like eating left-overs.*

**left-wing** *adjective* in politics supporting socialism and big social changes. The opposite of left-wing is right-wing.

**leg** *noun* 1 one of the parts of the body that animals and humans use for walking, running and standing on. 2 one of the parts that support a chair or other piece of furniture. **pull somebody's leg** to tease or make a fool of somebody by trying to make them believe something that is not true.

**legal** *adjective* 1 allowed by the law. *Cock-fighting is no longer legal.* 2 concerned with the law. *The legal system.* The opposite of legal is illegal.

**legend** *noun* an old, well-known story that may or may not be true. *The legend of King Arthur.* **legendary** *adjective.*

**legible** *adjective* clear enough to be read easily. *The writing is very faded but it is just legible.* **legibility** *noun.*

Lemons grow in sunny countries around the Mediterranean Sea.

**DID YOU KNOW?**

*Native American legends are stories that explain things like how the sun and moon were created and where fire comes from.*

Janet put her left leg forward and marched off, swinging her left arm high in the air.

**legion** *noun* a large division of the ancient Roman army (from three to six thousand soldiers).

**legitimate** *adjective* allowed by the law, lawful. **legitimacy** *noun.*

**leisure** *noun* free time when you can do what you like and you do not have to work. **leisurely** *adjective. A leisurely life is the life for me.*

**lemon** *noun* a bright yellow, oval citrus fruit with a sour-tasting juice.

**lemonade** *noun* a sweet, and sometimes fizzy, drink with a lemon flavour.

**lend** (lends, lending, lent) *verb* to let somebody have something for a short time, before they give it back to you. *It was raining so I lent him my umbrella.* The opposite of lend is borrow.

**length** *noun* 1 how far it is from one end of something to the other horizontally. *A length of cloth.* 2 how long something lasts. *We were surprised at the length of her prison sentence.*

**lengthen** *verb* to make or become longer.

**lengthy** (lengthier, lengthiest) *adjective* long, lasting a long time.

**lenient** *adjective* not severe or strict. *A really lenient teacher.* **lenience** *noun.*

**lens** *noun* 1 a piece of curved glass or plastic used in a camera, a pair of glasses etc. that bends light and makes it go where it is needed. 2 a part of the eye that focuses light on to the retina.

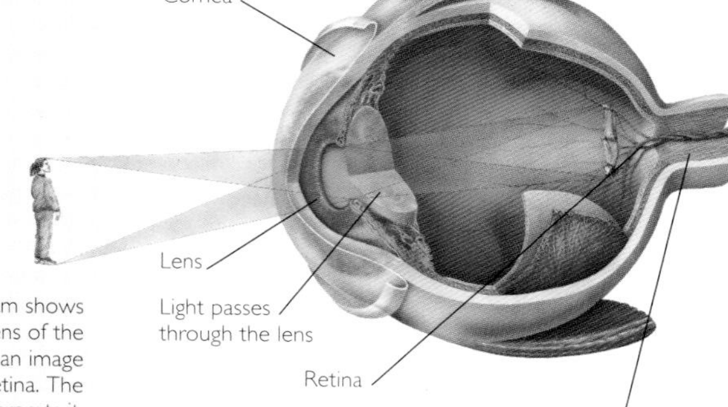


This diagram shows how the lens of the eye reverses an image on to the retina. The brain then interprets it, so that we see things the right way up.

**Lent** *noun* in the Christian Church a period of 40 days fasting and penance before Easter. *Sarah gave up chocolate for Lent.*

**lent** the past tense of lend.

**leopard** (say **lep**-urd) *noun* a large wild, spotted cat of Africa and Asia.

There is a saying: 'A leopard never changes its spots.' It means that you can't expect people to change their habits.

**leper** *noun* a person who has leprosy.

**leprosy** *noun* a disease of the skin and nerves which can lead to fingers and toes dropping off.

**lesbian** *noun* a woman who is attracted to other women, a gay woman.

**Lesotho** *noun* a country in Africa.

**-less** *suffix* without. *Colourless, smokeless.*

**less** (lesser, least) *adjective* not so much. *Please make less noise.* **less** *adverb. You should eat less and sleep more.* **less** *preposition* minus. *Six less four equals two.*

**lessen** *verb* to make or become smaller in size, importance etc.

**lesson** *noun* 1 a period of time when you are taught something by a teacher. 2 an experience that is a warning or example. *His accident was a lesson to him to be more careful in the future.*

**let** *verb* 1 to allow. *He let me borrow his bike.* 2 to allow somebody to rent a house and use it if they pay money. **let's** to suggest something. *Let's go swimming.* **let off** 1 to set light to a firework or to fire a gun. 2 to allow somebody to go without punishing them. **letdown** disappointment. *The film was a big letdown.* **let go** to set free.

**lethal** *adjective* able to cause death, deadly. *A lethal weapon.*

**letter** *noun* 1 one of the signs we use to write words. 2 a written message we send to somebody by post.

Jamie wrote a letter to his cousins thanking them for the birthday present.

**lettuce** *noun* a plant with large green leaves that we eat in salads.

**leukemia** *noun* (say loo-**kee**-mee-uh) a serious cancer-like disease in which the blood produces too many white cells.

**level** *adjective* smooth and horizontal, not sloping. *A level surface.* **level** *adverb* equal or at the same height or distance.

**lever** *noun* 1 a strong bar that you use to lift something heavy by placing one end under the object and pushing down on the other end. 2 a long handle that you use to work a machine.

**GRAMMAR NOTE**

*'Fewer' is the comparative of 'few', and means 'a smaller number of'. 'Less' is the comparative of 'little', and means 'a smaller quantity or amount'. 'Fewer' is followed by a plural noun, as in: 'There were fewer than 100 women in the hall.' 'Less' is followed by a singular noun or a noun describing an amount, as in: 'Put less milk in my tea, please.'*

**AMAZING FACT**

Lichens are very simple plants. They don't have any true leaves, roots or flowers. They grow very slowly and are an ancient form of life. A small, hand-sized patch of lichen on a rock could be hundreds of years old.

**liable** *adjective* 1 legally responsible for something. *You are liable for damaging the machine.* 2 likely to. *In winter the lake is liable to freeze.*

**liar** *noun* a person who tells lies.

**liberal** *adjective* generous and tolerant. *A liberal attitude.*

**Liberal Democrat** *noun* one of three main political parties in Great Britain.

**liberate** *verb* to set somebody or an animal free. **liberation** *noun.*

**Liberia** *noun* a country in Africa.

**liberty** *noun* freedom from control, slavery etc. **take liberties** to behave rudely and without respect.

The Statue of Liberty in New York Harbor was a present to the US from the people of France.

**librarian** *noun* a person who is in charge of or who works in a library.

**library** (libraries) *noun* a room or building where a lot of books, records etc. are kept, usually for people to borrow.

**Libreville** *noun* the capital of Gabon.

**Libya** *noun* a country in Africa.

**Libyan** *noun* a person who comes from Libya. **Libyan** *adjective. The Libyan coast.*

**lichen** *noun* (say **litch**-in or **lie**-kin) a flat, green or yellowish plant that grows in patches on rocks and tree trunks.

When you see lichen growing on rocks, trees or buildings, it is a sign of relatively pure air.

**lick** *verb* 1 to touch something with your tongue. *The dog licked my hand.* 2 (informal) to defeat or overcome. *He is determined to lick the problem.* **lick** *noun.*

L

**lid** *noun* 1 a cover for a box, jar, pot etc. that you can remove or lift up. 2 the eyelid, the piece of skin that covers the eye.

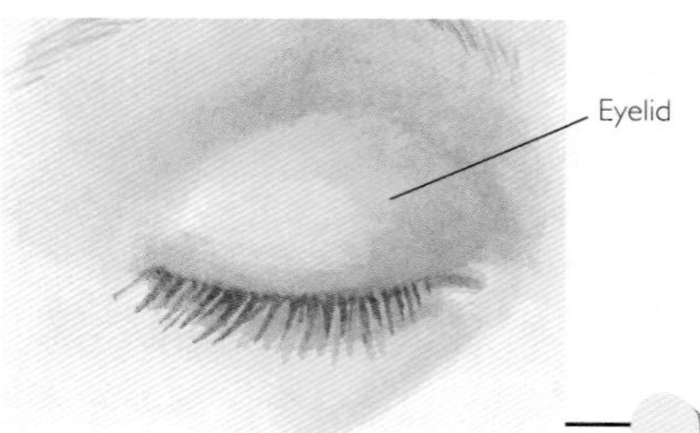

The eyelid shields the eye from light and protects it against dust flying in the air.

**lie** (lies, lying, lied) *verb* to say something that you know is untrue. *She lied to the police about the theft.* **lie** *noun. It is dishonest to tell lies.*

**lie** (lies, lying, lay, lain) *verb* 1 to rest your body in a flat position. *She felt ill so she lay on the sofa.* 2 to remain. *The snow lay on the ground for weeks.* 3 to be located in a certain place. *The village lies 10 kilometres north of Newtown.*

**Liechtenstein** *noun* a country in central Europe.

**life** *noun* 1 the time between a person's or an animal's birth and death when they are alive. 2 the ability of plants and animals to grow and develop, unlike such things as rocks, metals etc. 3 a way of living. *She leads a very exciting life.* 4 liveliness. *He is full of life.* **take somebody's life** to kill somebody

**lifebelt** *noun* a ring or belt that floats and which a person holds on to or wears to prevent them sinking or drowning.

**lifeboat** *noun* a boat that rescues people who are shipwrecked or in danger at sea.

The lifeboat set out to rescue the holidaymakers who had capsized their dinghy.

**lifeguard** *noun* a person who has been trained to help rescue swimmers in danger.

**lifejacket** *noun* an inflatable jacket that keeps you afloat in the water.

**lifeless** *adjective* 1 dead. *Her lifeless body.* 2 uninteresting. *Lifeless acting.*

**lifelike** *adjective* looking like a real person or animal. *A lifelike painting.*

**lifestyle** *noun* the way people live their lives, where they live and what their interests are.

**SPELLING NOTE**

*Try not to confuse 'lightning' in 'thunder and lightning' ( no 'e') with the present participle of 'lighten' (with an 'e') meaning 'to become brighter'.*

**lift** *verb* 1 to pick something up and raise it to a higher place. *He lifted the child on to his knee.* 2 to rise. *The plane lifted into the air.* **lift** *noun* 1 a container for carrying people or goods up or down between floors inside a building (US elevator). 2 a short ride in somebody's car, lorry etc.

**lift-off** *noun* the launching of a rocket.

**light** (lights, lighting, lit or lighted) *verb* 1 to make something start burning. *Let's light the candles.* 2 to give light to a place. **light** *noun* 1 what makes us able to see things, not dark. *The Sun gives us light.* 2 something that gives out light. **light** *adjective* 1 (of colour) pale and not strong. *Light blue.* 2 full of bright light. *A light room.*

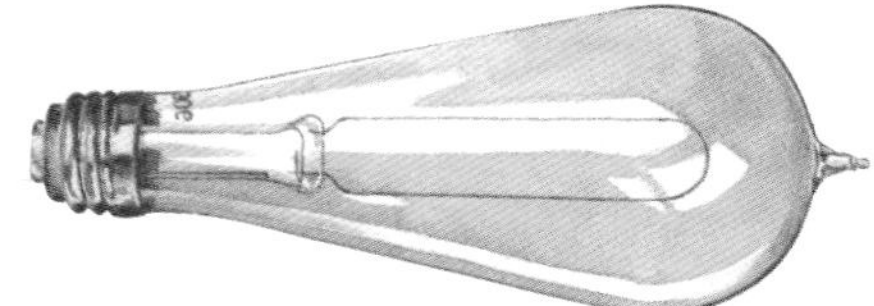
The electric current flows through a thin coil of wire called a filament to light up the bulb.

**light** *adjective* 1 weighing little, not heavy. *As light as a feather.* 2 gentle or small in amount. *We ate a light meal.* 3 not too serious. *Light music on the radio.*

**lighten** *verb* 1 to become brighter or less dark. 2 to make something less heavy.

**lighter** *noun* a device for lighting cigarettes or a fire etc.

**light-hearted** *adjective* cheerful and without a care.

**light year** *noun* the distance in space that light travels in a year.

**lighthouse** *noun* a tower-like building by the sea that sends out a very bright flashing light to guide ships or warn them off dangerous rocks.

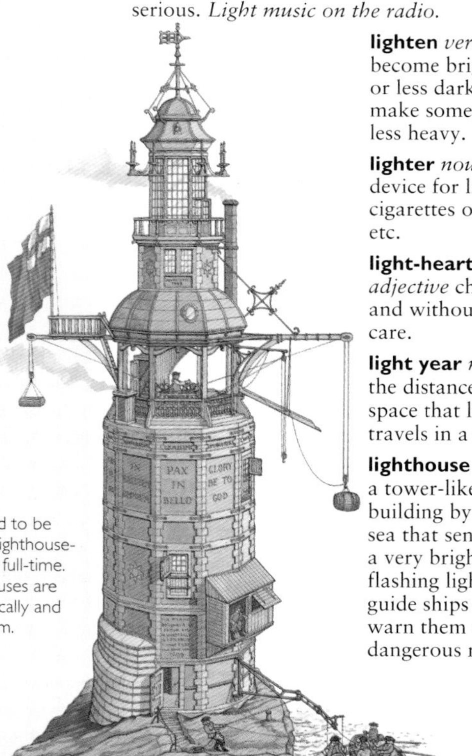

All lighthouses used to be manned, with the lighthouse-keeper living there full-time. Nowadays, lighthouses are operated automatically and no one lives in them.

**lighting** *noun* artificial lights such as candles and electric light.

**lightning** *noun* a bright flash of electricity that lights up the sky during a thunderstorm. *Thunder and lightning.*

**like** *verb* 1 to be fond of and to find somebody pleasant. 2 to enjoy something.

**like** *preposition* 1 nearly the same as or similar to, resembling. *He looks like his dad.* 2 in the same way as. *He roared like a lion.* 3 typical of or in the character of. *It's not like Laura to be early.* 4 for example, such as. *Indoor games like chess and snooker are my favourites.*

**likely** (likelier, likeliest) *adverb* probable and expected to happen. *I think it's likely to rain, if not today, then tomorrow.*

**likeness** *noun* a resemblance. *There's a great likeness between the brothers.*

**lilac** *noun* a small tree or shrub with sweet-smelling purple or white flowers.

**Lilongwe** *noun* the capital of Malawi.

**lily** (lilies) *noun* a plant that grows from a bulb with white, yellow or red flowers.

**Lima** *noun* the capital of Peru.

**limb** *noun* an arm or a leg or the wing of a bird.

**lime** *noun* 1 an oval, green citrus fruit similar to a lemon. 2 a substance obtained from limestone and used in making cement.

**limerick** *noun* a humorous poem in five lines. *An Irish limerick.*

**limestone** *noun* a kind of rock from which lime is obtained for making cement.

Stalactites and stalagmites form in limestone caves. Stalactites hang from the ceiling and stalagmites grow from the floor.

**limit** *noun* 1 a boundary or some point beyond which you should not go. *A 70 mph speed limit.* **limit** *verb* to prevent going beyond a certain limit or point, to restrict. *She limits herself to one small bar of chocolate a day.*

**limp** *adjective* drooping, soft and floppy. *A limp handshake.*

**limp** *verb* to walk with difficulty and unevenly because you have an injury to your leg or foot. **limp** *noun.*

**AMAZING FACT**

A group of lions is called a pride. This term probably dates from the Middle Ages and arose because lions look majestic and proud.

A female lion is called a lioness. In fact, the lioness does most of the hunting and feeds the cubs and the rest of the pride.

Waterlilies thrive in ponds. Their large waxy flowers and leaves float on the surface of the water.

**DID YOU KNOW**

*This is a limerick:*
*'There was a young lady of Wilts,*
*Who walked up to Scotland on stilts;*
*When they said it is shocking*
*To show so much stocking,*
*She answered,*
*"Then what about kilts?'"*

**line** *noun* 1 a long, thin mark on a surface. *She tried to draw straight lines on the paper.* 2 a group of people, things or words in a row. *Count the lines on this page.* 3 a rope, string etc. with a special purpose. *A washing line.* 4 a system of buses, trains or aircraft that travel regularly. 5 **lines** the words that actors have to say. **line** *verb. Great crowds lined the streets.*

**line** *verb* to sew material inside something. *I am going to line the jacket with blue silk.*

**linen** *noun* a strong cloth made from the fibres of the flax plant and used for sheets, tablecloths etc.

**liner** *noun* a large passenger ship or aircraft.

**linger** *verb* to dawdle, wait around, seeming unwilling to leave.

**lining** *noun* a layer of material to line the inside of something. *Most jackets have a lining, and in some, it's quilted, for warmth.*

**linguist** *noun* a person who studies foreign languages and is good at learning and speaking them.

**link** *noun* 1 a ring or loop in a chain. 2 a connection between two things. *The Eurotunnel is a link between England and France.* **link** *verb* to join up. *They linked arms.*

The links in a chain are extremely strong.

**lion** *noun* a large wild cat with light brown fur that lives in Africa and Asia. The male has a thick mane. Lions live in family groups called prides.

**lioness** *noun* a female lion.

The lioness was proudly guarding her cubs.

**lip** *noun* Your lips are the soft edges of your mouth. *Luscious lips.*

**lip-read** *verb* (of a deaf person) to understand what somebody is saying by looking carefully at their lips while they are speaking. *Sally learned to lip-read.*

**liquefy** (liquefies, liquefying, liquefied) *verb* to make or become liquid.

**liquid** *noun* any substance that flows, such as water. Any substance that is not a gas or a solid. **liquid** *adjective*. **liquidize** *verb* to crush food like fruit and vegetables into a liquid in a liquidizer. **liquidizer** (*noun*).

**Lisbon** *noun* the capital of Portugal.

**lisp** *verb*, *noun* a speech problem in which the 's' sounds like a 'th'.

**list** *noun* a series of names or things written down one under the other. *A list of the club's members.* **list** *verb* to write things down on a list.

**list** *verb* (of a ship) to lean over to one side.

**listen** *verb* to pay attention to what you hear. **listener** *noun*.

**lit** past tense of light.

**literally** *adverb* exactly as the words state. *He literally knocked me flying.*

**literate** *adjective* able to read and write.

**literature** *noun* 1 novels, plays and poetry that are especially good. 2 printed material on a particular subject. *Is there any literature about this washing machine?*

**Lithuania** *noun* a Baltic country in Europe.

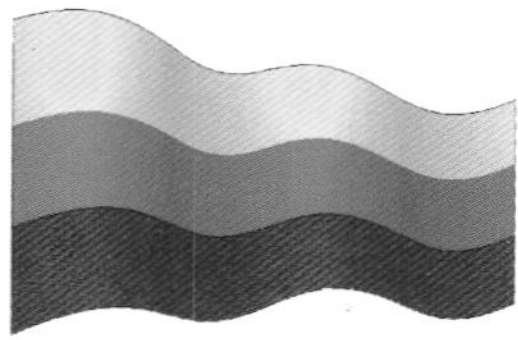

The flag of Lithuania has three stripes, yellow, green and red.

**litre** *noun* a measure of liquids equal to 1,000 millilitres.

**litter** *noun* rubbish such as paper and bottles left lying around.

**litter** *noun* all the animals born to the same mother at the same time.

**little** *adjective* 1 small in size or quantity. 2 not much. *There's very little time left.*

**live** *verb* (rhymes with give) 1 to be alive, to have life. Plants and animals live. 2 to continue to stay alive. *The tortoise lived for 50 years.* 3 to have your home in some place. *My gran lives in Jersey.*

**live** *adjective* (rhymes with dive) 1 not dead, but living. *There was a live rabbit under the bed.* 2 full of electricity. *This wire is live.* 3 a performance on radio or television that is happening as you listen or watch.

**SPELLING NOTE**

*Try not to confuse 'liquefy' or 'liquify', meaning 'to make something liquid' with 'liquidize', meaning 'to crush fruit etc. in a blender'.*

Mum left the shopping list behind when she went to the supermarket.

**AMAZING FACT**

In order to survive, lizards have evolved in some very bizarre ways. Some lizards have adapted to their surroundings by becoming snake-like; their legs have become tiny, but movable flaps. The komodo dragon, which may grow to ten feet long, has well-developed limbs and is a good climber and swimmer.

**livelihood** *noun* the way a person earns money to live. *He earns a good livelihood from doing up old houses and selling them.*

**lively** *adjective* full of energy. *He has a very lively mind and is interesting company.*

**liver** *noun* 1 a large and important organ in your body that helps to clean your blood and helps to process food. 2 this organ from an animal used as food.

**lives** plural of life. *Do cats really have nine lives, as it is thought?*

**livestock** *noun* animals kept on a farm. *John keeps cattle and other livestock.*

**living** *adjective* alive not dead. **living** *noun* how a person earns money to live. *What do you do for a living?*

**lizard** *noun* a small reptile with a long scaly body, four legs and a tail. Most lizards live in warm countries.

This lizard has a ruff around its neck that scares off its enemies.

**Ljubljana** *noun* the capital of Slovenia.

**llama** *noun* a South American animal similar to a camel, but without a hump. *Llamas make good sheep guards, and one llama can guard over 100 animals.*

**load** *noun* something heavy that is carried. An amount of something to be carried. *A load of wood.* **load** *verb* 1 to put a load on to something that will carry it. *He loaded the wood on to the lorry.* 2 to put bullets in a gun, a film into a camera or data into a computer. **loads of** a lot of something.

**loaf** (loaves) *noun* a large piece of bread baked in a shape. *A farmhouse loaf.*

**loan** *noun* something that somebody lends you, usually money.

**loathe** *verb* (rhymes with clothe) to hate or to dislike something very much.

**lob** (lobs, lobbing, lobbed) *verb* 1 to hit or throw something slowly or high in the air. 2 (in cricket) to bowl underhand. **lob** *noun*.

**lobby** *noun* an entrance hall in a theatre, hotel etc. *I met him for drinks in the lobby of the hotel.*

**lobe** *noun* the soft part of the ear that hangs down. *Her ear lobes were pierced several times, and she wore many earrings.*

**lobster** *noun* a shellfish or sea animal with a long body covered in a hard shell. It has eight legs and two large claws in front. Lobsters can be eaten.

Lobsters turn pink when boiled.

**AMAZING FACT**

When a lobster is in danger, it curls its tail under its body, pushing the animal backwards and helping it to escape.

**local** *adjective* belonging to or affecting a particular area or place. *The local newspaper carried daily reports of our campaign.* **locally** *adverb.*

**locality** *noun* an area. *This is a very well-to-do locality.*

**locate** *verb* 1 to find the exact position of. *Joe located the source of the river on the map.* 2 to be situated in a particular place. *The supermarket is located out of town, for the convenience of shoppers.*

**loch** *noun* a Scottish word for lake. *Loch Lomond is so beautiful in spring.*

**lock** *noun* 1 a device that fastens a door or lid and that you open and shut with a key. **lock** *verb* to fasten with a lock and key. 2 a section of a canal or river between gates that can be opened and shut to raise or lower ships by altering the level of the water. *The barge went through the lock.*

**locust** *noun* a large kind of grasshopper that travels in huge swarms and destroys crops. *A plague of locusts.*

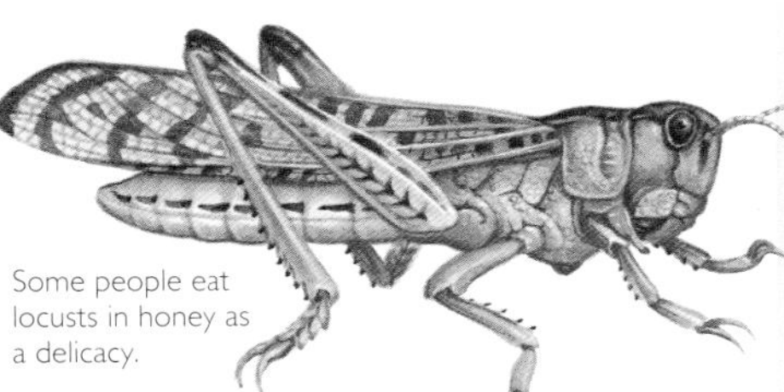

Some people eat locusts in honey as a delicacy.

**lodge** *noun* 1 a small house, usually at the gates leading to a large house. 2 a beaver's home. **lodge** *verb* 1 to live in rented rooms (lodgings). 2 to become firmly fixed in.

**lodger** *noun* somebody who pays to live in a room in another person's house.

**loft** *noun* a room or space under the roof of a building. *I put the junk in the loft, rather than throw it away.*

**log** *noun* 1 a length of wood that has been cut from a branch of a felled tree. 2 a written record of the journey of a ship or aircraft. *The log book.*

**SPELLING NOTE**

*Some -logies*
*anthropology (the study of mankind)*
*astrology (the stars)*
*chronology (dates)*
*cosmology (universe)*
*dendrology (trees)*
*etymology (word origins)*
*meteorology (weather)*
*ornithology (birds)*
*pathology (diseases)*
*vexillology (flags)*

**logic** *noun* the science of careful and correct reasoning. *I rely on logic, not imagination.*

**logical** *adjective* 1 following the rules of logic. 2 sensible and reasonable.

**logo** *noun* a symbol or lettering that represents a company or organization, an emblem or trademark. *The diaries were printed with the company's logo.*

**-logy** *suffix* the study of some subject. *Geology, anthropology, biology.*

**loiter** *verb* to stand around somewhere with nothing to do. *The woman loitering near that car looks suspicious.*

**Lomé** *noun* the capital of Togo.

**London** *noun* the capital of England and the United Kingdom.

**lonely** (lonelier, loneliest) *adjective* 1 unhappy at being alone. 2 far away and not often visited. *A lonely island off the north coast of Scotland.*

**long** *adjective* 1 measuring far from one end to the other. The opposite of long is short. *The longest bridge in the world is in Japan.* 2 taking a lot of time. *It's a long journey from London to Beijing.* 3 a certain amount of distance or time. *An hour-long flight.* **no longer** not any more.

**long** *verb* to want something very much. *She longed to go home.* **longing** *noun.* **longingly** *adverb. He looked longingly at the shiny bike.*

**longitude** *noun* the position of a place measured as a distance in degrees east or west of a line on a map that runs through Greenwich near London from the North and South Poles.

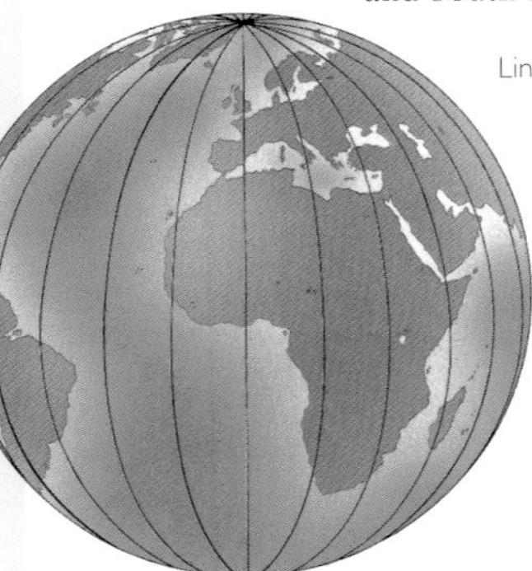

Lines of longitude run vertically around the globe.

**loo** *noun* a lavatory.

**look** *verb* 1 to move your eyes to see something. 2 to seem or appear to be so. *Dick looks happy today.* **look after** to take care of somebody or something. **look for** to search. *Betty is looking for her trainers.* **look forward to** to wait for something eagerly. **look into** to investigate. **look out** Be careful! **look up to** to admire.

L

**loom** *noun* a machine for weaving thread into cloth.

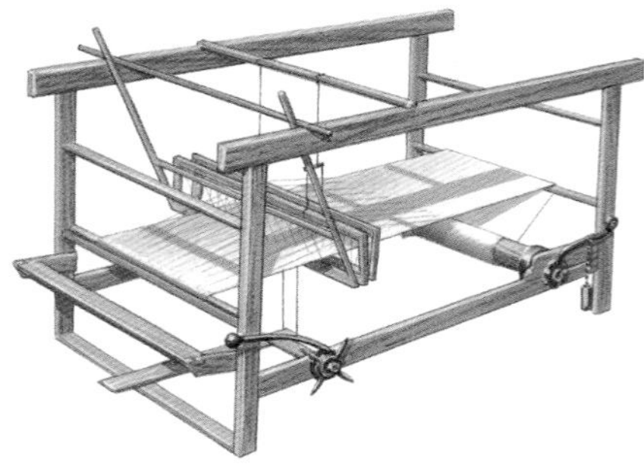

Many different kinds of fabrics can be woven on a loom.

**loop** *noun* a circular shape made in a rope or piece of string. **loop** *verb*. *He looped the rope around the post.*

**loose** *adjective* 1 not held firmly in place. *My loose tooth fell out.* 2 not attached or fastened. *The ponies were loose in the paddock all day.* 3 (of clothes) not fitting tightly, too big.

**loosen** *verb* to make or become loose. *His tie was too tight so he loosened it.*

**loot** *noun* goods and money that have been stolen. **loot** *verb*. *During the riots people looted shops and houses.*

**lord** *noun* 1 the title of a nobleman, bishop or male judge. 2 **Lord** the name given to God and Jesus. 3 **Lords** short for House of Lords, the unelected upper house in the British parliament. **lordly** *adjective*. *Lordly behaviour doesn't suit you.*

**lorry** (lorries) *noun* a big motor vehicle that carries heavy goods by road, a truck.

**SPELLING NOTE**

*Try not to confuse 'loose', meaning 'set free', 'undo', and 'loosen', meaning 'to make less tight'.*

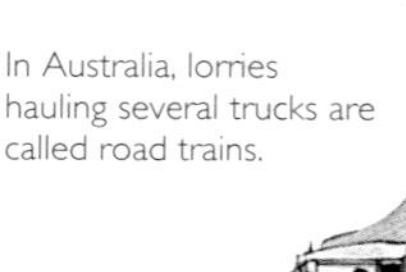

In Australia, lorries hauling several trucks are called road trains.

**lose** (loses, losing, lost) *verb* 1 If you lose something, you do not have it any more and cannot find it. 2 to fail to win. *They lost the match.* 3 to go astray. *We lost our way.*

**loser** *noun* somebody who seems never to be successful. *I always back the loser.*

**loss** *noun* something that has been lost and that you no longer have. *She was very upset by the loss of her precious bracelet.*

**lost** past tense of lose.

**lot** *noun* 1 large amount or number. *What a lot of presents!* 2 **lots** *Put lots of jam on the bread.* 3 an article in an auction. **the lot** everything. *You can take the lot.*

**lotion** *noun* a liquid or cream that you put on your skin to clean, soften or protect it. *Suntan lotion.*

**lottery** *noun* a way of making money by selling a lot of tickets to try to win prizes.

**loud** *adjective* 1 making a large amount of sound, not quiet. 2 unpleasantly bright and colourful. *He was wearing a loud purple shirt.* **loudness** *noun*.

**loudspeaker** *noun* a piece of equipment in a radio, televison or stereo system etc. that turns electrical waves into sound. A device for making sounds louder.

When a sound signal from the amplifier of a loudspeaker passes through the metal coil, it makes the cone vibrate, producing sound.

**lounge** *noun* a sitting room with comfortable chairs where you can relax. **lounge** *verb* to sit around in a lazy way doing nothing.

**love** *verb* to like somebody very much and want to be with them all the time. **lovable** *adjective* easy to love. **lover** *noun*.

**lovely** (lovelier, loveliest) *adjective* 1 beautiful to look at, listen to or touch. 2 very pleasant.

**loving** *adjective* showing love. *She gave him a loving smile.*

**low** *adjective* 1 not high but near the ground. 2 not loud. *He talked in a low voice so nobody could hear.* **the Low Countries** the Netherlands and Belgium.

**low** *verb* to moo or make a noise like a cow.

**lower** *verb* to move or let something down. *The soldiers lowered the flag.* The opposite of lower is raise.

**loyal** *adjective* always faithful and true to your friends. **loyalty** *noun*.

**Luanda** *noun* the capital of Angola.

**lubricate** *verb* to put oil or grease on parts of a machine so that they move easily and smoothly. **lubrication** *noun*.

**lucid** *noun* 1 easy to understand. *A lucid explanation.* 2 clear, not confused. *Despite the accident his mind was lucid.*

**luck** *noun* 1 something that happens to you by chance and that you have not planned or cannot control. *Winning a lottery is pure luck.* 2 something good but unexpected that happens to you. *Wish me luck!*

**lucky** (luckier, luckiest) *adjective* 1 something lucky happens by chance. *She was lucky to win the lottery.* 2 bringing good luck. *A lucky charm.*

**ludicrous** *adjective* (say **loo**-dee-kruss) very silly, absurd. *You look ludicrous in those clothes.*

**luggage** *noun* the suitcases and bags that travellers take with them.

**lukewarm** *adjective* 1 A liquid that is lukewarm is only just warm. 2 not enthusiastic. *The film received only lukewarm praise.*

We had so much luggage that we had to pay excess charges.

**lull** *noun* a short period of quiet when little is happening. *There was a lull in the traffic noise.*

**lull** *verb* to soothe and make somebody relaxed and calm. *The gentle music lulled her to sleep.*

**lullaby** *noun* a gentle song that helps a child go to sleep. *Mum sang the baby a lullaby.*

**lumber** *noun* rough timber.

Jake looked in the lumber pile for a piece of wood he could make into a chair leg.

**lumber** *verb* to walk slowly in a heavy, clumsy way. **lumber with** to give somebody something they do not want. *Lizzie was lumbered with mowing the lawn.*

**lumberjack** *noun* in North America, a person who cuts down and saws up trees.

**lump** *noun* 1 a bump or swelling. *Luke has a lump on his knee.* 2 a small solid piece of something without shape. *A lump of clay.*

**DID YOU KNOW?**

*The formal word for the midday meal, 'luncheon', is really a long form of the original but less formal word 'lunch'.*

**AMAZING FACT**

The lynx has a much shorter tail than most of the other 'big cats'. It is a nocturnal animal that lives on rodents and young deer.

**lunar** *adjective* concerned with the Moon. *A lunar journey.* **lunar month** the time it takes for the Moon to orbit the Earth – 29 days.

**lunatic** *noun* somebody who is foolish or insane. **lunatic** *adjective*. *A lunatic idea.*

**lunch** *noun* a meal eaten in the middle of the day. **lunch** *verb*.

**lung** *noun* one of two organs inside your chest that you use for breathing. The lungs take in oxygen from the air and give out carbon dioxide.

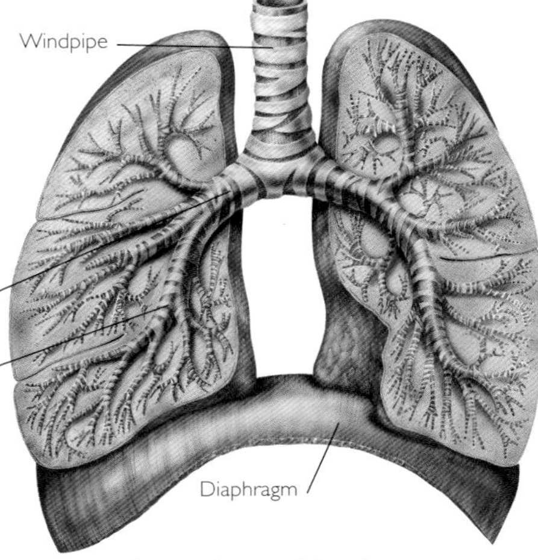


The lungs are the organs of breathing.

**lunge** *verb* to make a sudden thrust forward. *She lunged at the dog with a stick.* **lunge** *noun*.

**lure** *verb* to attract and tempt, to lead astray. *They were lured by the bright lights of the fair.* **lure** *noun*.

**lurk** *verb* to wait around out of sight with a dishonest purpose, to prowl. *There is somebody lurking under the trees.*

**Lusaka** *noun* the capital of Zambia.

**lush** *adjective* growing thickly and healthily, fertile. *Lush vegetation.*

**lust** *noun* a very strong desire. *A lust for fame got him nowhere.*

**lute** *noun* an old-fashioned stringed musical instrument in the shape of half a pear.

**Luxembourg** *noun* a country in Northwestern Europe, and its capital city.

**luxury** *noun* 1 something expensive that is very nice to have but that you do not really need. 2 great comfort and having a lot of expensive luxuries. *She grew up in luxury.* **luxurious** *adjective*. *A luxurious house.*

**lynx** *noun* a wild cat with a short tail and tufts of hair in its ears.

**lyre** *noun* a musical instrument like a small harp. *A gentle tune on the lyre.*

**lyrics** *plural noun* the words of a popular song. *I really like these lyrics.*

M

# Mm

**macabre** *adjective* strangely frightening and gruesome. *A macabre film.*

**macaroni** *noun* tube-shaped pasta.

**Macedonia** *noun* a country in Southeast Europe. *Macedonian wine.*

**machine** *noun* a piece of equipment with moving parts that uses electricity or an engine to do a job or make work easier.

**machinery** *noun* 1 the parts of a machine. 2 machines. 3 an organized system of doing something. *The machinery of local government runs very slowly.*

**macho** *adjective* (say **match**-oh) (of a man) aggressively and exaggeratedly masculine. Strong and virile.

**mackintosh** *noun* a raincoat that keeps the water out.

**mad** (madder, maddest) *adjective* 1 mentally ill, insane. 2 wildly foolish, not sensible. *What a mad idea to run across a busy road.* 3 very angry. **madness** *noun.*

**Madagascar** *noun* a country in the Indian Ocean off East Africa.

**madam** *noun* a formal and polite way of addressing a woman without using her name. *Can I help you, madam?*

**madden** *verb* to make somebody angry. *It maddens me when you bite your nails.*

**made** past tense of make.

**Madrid** *noun* the capital of Spain.

**magazine** *noun* a publication with a paper cover that comes out usually every week or month and which contains articles, photographs, stories etc.

**maggot** *noun* the larva or grub of the house-fly. Maggots look like small worms.

Maggots are used to catch fish.

**magic** *noun* 1 in stories, a strange power that makes wonderful or impossible things happen. 2 clever tricks that look as though they happen by magic. *She pulled a pigeon out of the hat by magic.*

**magical** *adjective* 1 produced by magic. 2 strange and exciting. *A magical evening was had by all.*

**magician** *noun* (say maj-**ish**-un) a person who can do tricks or magic.

When the paperclips come within the magnet's magnetic field, they become magnetized too, and so attract other paperclips.

**WORD HISTORY**

*The shape of the letter M comes from an Ancient Egyptian symbol for water. Its sound comes from 'mem', a Semitic word meaning 'water'.*

**AMAZING FACT**

The forerunner of the mainframe computer, and all the personal computers that we use today, was actually a tabulating and adding machine designed in 1837 by Charles Babbage. His machine was only partially built and was never completed. In fact, the records of his work were lost for 100 years.

**magistrate** *noun* a person who acts as a judge in a court of law that deals with less serious offences.

**magnet** *noun* a piece of metal that has the power to attract or make iron or steel move towards it. **magnetic** *adjective. A magnetic compass.* **magnetism** *noun.* **magnetize** *verb.*

**magnificent** *adjective* beautiful and very impressive. *A magnificent castle stood on the hill.* **magnificence** *noun.*

**magnify** (magnifies, magnifying, magnified) *verb* to make something seem larger than it really is by looking at it through a magnifying glass or microscope. *Astronomers use telescopes to magnify the stars.*

**magnifying glass** *noun* a special lens with a handle that makes objects look bigger than they really are.

**mahogany** *noun* a very hard, reddish-brown wood used in making furniture. *A mahogany table.*

**maid** *noun* a female servant.

**maiden** *noun* (old-fashioned) an unmarried young woman. **maiden name** a woman's surname before she marries. **maiden voyage** a ship's first voyage.

The maiden waited shyly for her knight to arrive.

**mail** *noun* 1 letters and parcels sent by post. **mail** *verb* (mainly US) to send by post. 2 a kind of armour made from small metal rings.

**maim** *verb* to injure somebody so badly that they are disabled for life.

**main** *adjective* the most important. *The main shopping area is near our house.*

**mainframe** *noun* a big, powerful computer that can be used by several people at once.

**mainland** *noun* the principal and largest mass of land without its islands.

**mains** *plural noun* the chief cable or pipes that carry electricity, gas, or water to a street. *They repaired the burst mains.*

**maintain** *verb* 1 to keep in good condition. *The council maintains the grass verges.* 2 to support and look after. 3 to state as true or as a belief. *She maintains that she is always right.* 4 to continue. *The pupils have maintained high standards.*

**maize** *noun* a tall plant that produces cobs of sweetcorn, a cereal with large seeds.

Maize is used as cattle fodder.

**majesty** *noun* 1 impressive greatness, splendour. *The majesty of the mountains.* 2 **Your Majesty** the title people use when speaking to a king or queen. **majestic** *adjective.*

**major** *adjective* important, main. *The new government made major changes.* **major** *noun* an officer in the army above a captain.

**majority** *noun* 1 more than half of a total. *The majority of people watch television every day.* 2 the number of votes by which somebody wins an election.

**Majuro** *noun* the capital of the Marshall Islands.

**make** (makes, making, made) *verb* 1 to put things together to produce something new, to create or build. 2 to prepare. 3 to cause or force something to happen. *The aeroplane made a forced landing.* 4 to add up or produce. *Three and six make nine.* 5 to earn or gain. *How much money does a waiter make?* **make** *noun* the maker's name or brand. *What make of car is this?* **make somebody's day** to make somebody feel happy all day long.

**make do** *verb* to use something to replace what you really want. *You'll have to make do with this old saucepan.*

**make-up** *noun* special coloured creams and powders (cosmetics) that women and actors put on their faces.

The actress kept her make-up on her dressing table.

**make up** *verb* 1 to invent. *Make up a story about a monster.* 2 to become friends again after quarrelling. 3 to put on make-up.

**WORD HISTORY**

*'Malaria' comes from two Italian words, 'mal aria', meaning 'bad air'. People once thought the disease was caused by breathing the 'bad air' of marshy places.*

**AMAZING FACT**

Mammals were the last major animal group to appear on Earth. During the period that dinosaurs lived, the only existing mammals were small rodents that looked like shrews.

**make-believe** *verb* to pretend and imagine things. *Let's make-believe we are cowboys.*

**makeshift** *adjective* temporary and only meant to last until something better can be used. *Makeshift accommodation.*

**mal-** *prefix* bad or ill. *Malformed, malfunction, malnutrition.*

**Malabo** *noun* the capital of Equatorial Guinea.

**malaria** *noun* a tropical disease that is carried from person to person by the bite of a female mosquito.

**Malawi** *noun* a country in Africa.

**Malaysia** *noun* a country in Southeast Asia.

The Malaysian flag is red and white striped with a yellow Moon and Sun on a square blue ground.

**Malaysian** *noun* a person who comes from Malaysia. **Malaysian** *adjective. Malaysian rubber plantations.*

**Maldives** *plural noun* a country of many islands in the Indian Ocean.

**Malé** *noun* the capital of the Maldives.

**male** *noun, adjective* a human or animal belonging to the sex that does not produce babies or eggs. Boys and men are males. *A male horse is called a stallion.* The opposite of male is female.

**Mali** *noun* a country in Africa.

**malicious** *adjective* (say mal-**ish**-uss) unkind and wishing to see others hurt or unhappy, spiteful. *She has a very malicious tongue.* **malice** *noun.*

**mall** *noun* (mainly US) a shopping centre.

**mallard** *noun* a kind of wild duck.

**mallet** *noun* a large wooden hammer.

**malnutrition** *noun* illness caused by eating too little food or the wrong kind of food.

**malt** *noun* dried barley that is used to make beer and whisky.

**Malta** *noun* a country in southern Europe.

**Maltese** *noun* 1 a person who comes from Malta. 2 the language of Malta. **Maltese** *adjective. The Maltese Cross.*

**maltreat** *verb* to treat a person or animal roughly or unkindly. *We should never maltreat our pets.*

**mammal** *noun* any animal of which the female feeds her young with milk from her own body. Humans, elephants and whales are mammals.

**mammoth** *noun* a kind of large hairy elephant that lived thousands of years ago during the Ice Age. Mammoths are now extinct.

Animals such as mammoths adapted to the Ice Age by growing thick woolly coats.

**man** *noun* 1 a fully grown male human. 2 humans in general. *When did man first appear on Earth?* **mankind** *noun*. *A giant step for mankind.*

**manage** *verb* 1 to control or be in charge of something. *Lucy manages the production department.* 2 to be able to do something, especially something difficult or awkward, to succeed. *She managed to solve the crossword.* **manager** *noun*. **management** *noun*. *Bad management.*

**Managua** *noun* the capital of Nicaragua.

**Manama** *noun* the capital of Bahrain.

**mane** *noun* the long thick hair on the neck of a horse or male lion.

**manger** *noun* a long narrow container in a barn or stable from which cattle and horses feed.

The baby Jesus was wrapped in swaddling clothes and laid in a manger.

**mangle** *verb* to damage something by crushing and twisting it out of shape.

**manhood** *noun* the state or condition of being a man.

**mania** *noun* a strong desire or enthusiasm for something. *He has a mania for motorbikes.*

**maniac** *noun* 1 a person suffering from a mental illness that makes them behave violently. 2 (informal) an over-enthusiastic person. *She drives like a maniac.*

**Manila** *noun* the capital of the Philippines.

**mankind** *noun* all people in general.

**manner** *noun* 1 the way in which something is done. *Let's do this in a professional manner.* 2 the way a person behaves or talks. *She has a very friendly manner.* 3 **manners** polite behaviour.

**AMAZING FACT**

The word 'marathon' comes from a long distance run made by a messenger from Marathon, Greece, to Athens in 490 BC to report a Greek victory in the battle at Marathon.

**DID YOU KNOW**

*Some people object that the use of 'man', as in 'the origins of man' for people in general is sexist. You can get round the problem by using words such as 'person', 'people', or 'human'.*

**manoeuvre** *noun* (say man-**oo**-ver) a skilful or difficult movement or clever trick.

**manor** *noun* a large, important house in the country with land around it.

**mansion** *noun* a large, impressive house.

**manslaughter** *noun* killing somebody through carelessness but not with the intention of doing so.

**mantelpiece** *noun* a shelf above a fireplace.

**manual** *noun* a book with instructions on how to use or work something. **manual** *adjective* worked with the hands. *Manual controls, manual labour.*

**manufacture** *verb* to make things in large quantities by machine in a factory.

**manure** *noun* dung or animal waste used as a fertilizer to help produce better crops.

**manuscript** *noun* a handwritten or typed copy of a book etc. before it is printed.

**Manx** *adjective* relating to the Isle of Man. *Manx cats do not have tails.*

**many** *adjective*, *pronoun* a large number of people or things.

**Maori** (Maori or Maoris) *noun* (say **mow**-ree) the original people who lived in New Zealand.

**map** *noun* a drawing of an area, country etc. showing things like mountains, rivers, roads and towns. *A map of Treasure Island.*

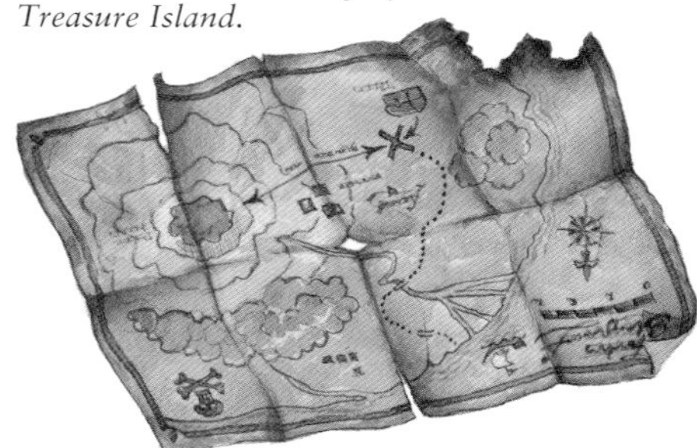

The map showed exactly where the treasure had been buried.

**maple** *noun* a tree with large leaves with five points. The maple leaf is the national emblem of Canada.

**Maputo** *noun* the capital of Mozambique.

**marathon** *noun* a race in which people run 26 miles (42 km).

**marble** *noun* 1 a very hard stone that can be polished to show its pattern or colour. 2 a small coloured glass ball used in children's games. *A game of marbles.*

**march** *verb* to walk with regular steps and arm movements in time with one another, like soldiers. **march** *noun* 1 a piece of music with a regular beat suitable for marching to. 2 a boundary. *The Welsh marches.*

**March** *noun* the third month of the year. March has 31 days.

**mare** *noun* a fully grown female horse. The opposite of a mare is a stallion.

**margarine** *noun* a soft yellow butter-like fat made mainly from vegetable oils.

**margin** *noun* the blank space or gap down the sides of a page.

**marigold** *noun* a plant of the daisy family with large orange or yellow flowers.

**marine** *adjective* to do with the sea. *Whales are marine mammals.* **marine** *noun* a soldier who serves at sea on board ship.

A school party visited the museum of marine life, where they saw many different sea creatures swimming in huge tanks.

**mark** *noun* 1 a stain or scratch on something. *There's a dirty mark on my shirt.* 2 a special sign on something. 3 a number or sign on a piece of schoolwork to show how good it is. *She got full marks, ten out of ten.* **mark** *verb*.

**market** *noun* a place where things are sold, usually from stalls in the open.

**marmalade** *noun* a jam made from oranges or some other citrus fruit and usually eaten at breakfast. *Orange marmalade.*

**maroon** *noun*, *adjective* dark reddish-brown. *Maroon socks.*

**maroon** *verb* to abandon or leave somebody alone in an isolated place such as a desert island.

**marquee** *noun* a very large tent used for summer parties, circuses etc.

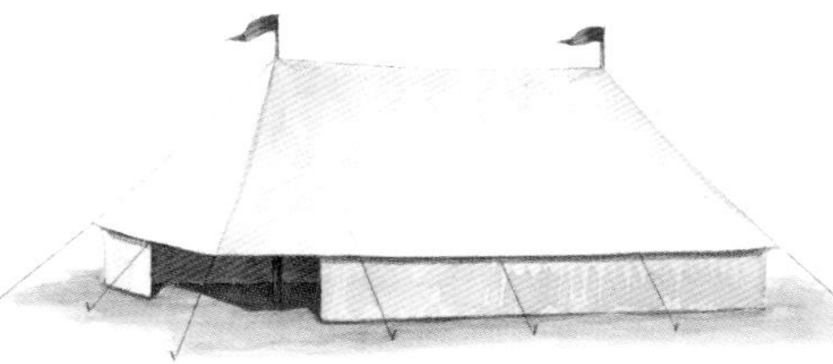

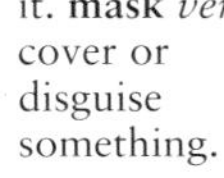

She hired a marquee and gave a big party when her daughter got married.

**marriage** *noun* 1 a wedding ceremony. 2 the state of being married. *My sister got married last year.*

**marrow** *noun* 1 a long, large green vegetable like a huge cucumber. 2 a soft substance containing blood vessels in the hollow parts of bones.

**marry** (marries, marrying, married) *verb* 1 to take somebody as your husband or wife. *My uncle married an American.* 2 to carry out the ceremony of marriage.

**WORD HISTORY**

*'Marmalade' is from a Portuguese word 'marmelada', named after the quince ('marmelo' in Portuguese), from which fruit the preserve was originally made.*

**AMAZING FACT**

Newly-born marsupials are very small and have not finished developing when they crawl into their mother's pouch. The babies drink their mothers' milk inside the pouch and grow strong.

**marsh** *noun* an area of low-lying land that is always wet, a bog. *The house was always damp because it was so near the marsh.*

**Marshall Islands** *plural noun* a country of many islands in the Pacific Ocean.

**marshmallow** *noun* a soft jelly-like sweet. *Toasted marshmallows for tea.*

**marsupial** *noun* an animal the female of which carries her young in a pouch on her stomach. Kangaroos are marsupials.

**martial** *adjective* to do with wars, battles, fighting, soldiers etc. *The band played marches and other kinds of martial music.* **martial arts** systems of self-defence such as karate, kendo and judo that come from China and Japan.

**Martian** *noun* an imaginary person from the planet Mars.

**martin** *noun* a bird with a forked tail similar to a swallow.

**martyr** *noun* somebody who chooses to suffer or be killed rather than give up their beliefs. **martyrdom** *noun*.

**marvel** (marvels, marvelling, marvelled) *verb* to be astonished or surprised. *I always marvel at how clever sheepdogs are.* **marvel** *noun*. *A computer is an electronic marvel.*

**marvellous** *adjective* excellent, very good.

**mascara** *noun* a colouring substance used on eyelashes to make them look longer or thicker. *Black mascara.*

**mascot** *noun* an animal or thing that people think brings good luck. *The team's mascot is a rabbit.*

**masculine** *adjective* concerned with men or typical of men, manly. **masculinity** *noun*. The opposite of masculine is feminine.

**Maseru** *noun* the capital of Lesotho.

**mask** *noun* a covering worn over the face to hide, disguise or protect it. **mask** *verb* to cover or disguise something.

This gold mask was found in Greece by the archaeologist Heinrich Schliemann. He believed it to be the death mask of King Agamemnon of Troy.

**mason** *noun* a person who makes or builds things from stone.

**masonry** *noun* stonework.

M

**mass** *noun* 1 a large number or quantity. *The plant was covered in a mass of flowers.* 2 a large shapeless lump of something. 3 **the masses** the ordinary people. **mass** *verb* to gather into a group or mass. *The crowd massed on to the pitch.* **mass-media** ways of communicating through such things as newspapers, radio and television, from which most people get their news and information. **mass-produced** made by machines in great quantities.

**mass** *noun* the celebration of the Holy Communion service in Roman Catholic and some other Christian churches.

**massacre** *noun* (say mass-uh-ker) the brutal killing of a large number of people. **massacre** *verb*. *The troops stormed the castle and massacred all the prisoners.*

**massage** *verb* to rub and knead parts of a person's body to get rid of pain or stiffness and to help them relax. **massage** *noun*.

**massive** *adjective* huge in size and heavy. *A massive rock blocked the road.*

**mast** *noun* a pole that holds a flag or supports a ship's sails.

Tom the cabin boy climbed to the top of the mast and searched the horizon for sight of land.

**master** *noun* 1 a male teacher. 2 the male owner of an animal. *The dog obeys its master.* 3 a man who controls other people. *He is master in his own house.* 4 a person who is very skilled at something. **master** *verb* 1 to learn something and become skilled in it. *She mastered Japanese in six months.* 2 to control. *He mastered his fear of flying and took off for the States.*

**masterly** *adjective* showing skill. *A truly masterly performance.*

**masterpiece** *noun* an outstandingly skilful work of art.

**mastery** *noun* 1 having complete control of something. *Mastery over his phobia.* 2 skill. *Mastery of the piano.*

**mat** *noun* 1 a small piece of material for covering a part of a floor. *Please wipe your feet on the mat.* 2 a small piece of material placed on a table to protect it from hot or wet plates, cups etc.

**match** *verb* to be like or equal to something, to go well together. *These two socks don't match.* **match** *noun* 1 an equal to. *At exams, she's no match for her sister.* 2 a game between two teams. *A tennis match between two champion players.*

**AMAZING FACT**

Matter is anything – gas, solid or liquid – that takes up space. And nearly all matter can exist in all three of these forms. You may or may not be able to see and touch matter in all three forms, however.

The building materials stood waiting for Colin to arrive, but he was busy on another job.

**GRAMMAR NOTE**

*Try not to confuse 'masterful', meaning 'showing authority' or 'overbearing' with 'masterly', which means 'showing skill'.*

**match** *noun* a thin piece of wood with one end tipped with a material that ignites when you rub it against something rough.

**mate** *verb* (of animals) to come together to breed in order to produce offspring. **mate** *noun* 1 one of the two animals brought together to breed. 2 a friend. *My best mate.*

**material** *noun* 1 a substance from which you can make other things. *Wood, glass, bricks and cement are some of the materials used in building houses.* 2 cloth for making clothes from.

**maternal** *adjective* relating to a mother or mothers, motherly. *Maternal feelings.* The opposite of maternal is paternal.

**maternity** *adjective* relating to a mother-to-be or birth. *A maternity ward.*

**mathematics** *plural noun* the study of the science of numbers, measurements, quantities and shapes. **mathematical** *adjective*. *I was given an extremely tricky mathematical problem.* **mathematician** *noun* an expert in mathematics.

**maths** *abbreviation* for mathematics.

**matrimony** *noun* marriage or the state of being married. **matrimonial** *adjective*.

**matron** *noun* 1 (old-fashioned) a senior nurse in charge of a hospital. 2 a person in a school responsible for the health of the children. *Matron bandaged his knee.*

**matter** *verb* to be important. *You can go or stay – it doesn't matter.*

**matter** *noun* 1 the substance or material from which all things are made. Matter can be a solid, a gas or a liquid. 2 a subject of interest. *Financial matters.* 3 a problem. *What's the matter with you today?*

**mattress** *noun* the thick oblong padding you put on a bed to lie on.

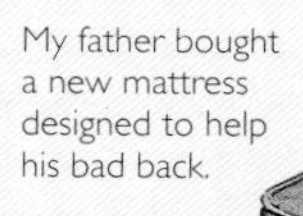

My father bought a new mattress designed to help his bad back.

**mature** *adjective* 1 fully developed and adult, grown up. 2 ripe. **mature** *verb. Puppies mature into dogs.*

**maul** *verb* to injure somebody badly by attacking or handling them savagely.

**Mauritania** *noun* a country in Africa.

**Mauritius** *noun* a country in the Indian Ocean off East Africa.

**mauve** *noun, adjective* pale purple colour.

**maxim** *noun* a general rule or wise piece of advice. *'Look before you leap' is an old maxim, and a wise one.*

**maximum** *noun* the greatest number or amount possible. *The box holds 50 matches at the maximum.* **maximum** *adjective. 70 mph is the maximum speed on motorways.* The opposite of maximum is minimum.

**May** *noun* the fifth month of the year. May has 31 days.

**maybe** *adverb* perhaps, possibly. *Maybe we'll see you later.*

**mayhem** *noun* general chaos.

**mayor** *noun* a person in charge of the council or government of a town or city.

**maze** *noun* a system of complicated paths or lines to follow and which is difficult to find your way through.

The children got lost in the maze.

**Mbabane** *noun* the capital of Swaziland.

**meadow** *noun* a grassy field where animals can graze. *A meadow full of buttercups.*

**meal** *noun* the food that people eat at a particular time. Breakfast, lunch, tea and dinner are all meals.

**mean** *adjective* unwilling to give, not generous or kind. **meanness** *noun.*

**mean** (means, meaning, meant) *verb* 1 to intend or plan to do something. *I meant to telephone, but I forgot.* 2 to intend to show or express. *Red means danger.* **mean well** to intend to be helpful. *She is very slow, but she means well.* **by all means** certainly.

**meaning** *noun* 1 what something means. *Dictionaries tell us the meaning of words.* 2 the importance, purpose or intention of something. *What is the meaning of poetry?*

**GRAMMAR NOTE**

*'May' or 'might'? 'Might' is the past of 'may'. Both express possibility. 'It may snow tonight.' 'I thought you might have come yesterday.'*

**AMAZING FACT**

The ancient Egyptians had a system of measurements that was based on the human body. The smallest unit, based on the hand, was a digit. Four digits made a palm. The distance between the little finger and thumb of an outstretched hand was called a span. A cubit was equal to 2 spans, 7 palms or the distance from fingertips to elbow.

**meaningful** *adjective* full of significance, important. *A meaningful debate.*

**meaningless** *adjective* without any purpose. *His life seems meaningless.*

**means** *plural noun* 1 a method or way of doing something. *The prisoner found some means of escape.* 2 wealth. *A woman of substantial means.*

**meantime** *noun* the time between two things happening. *I'm going to the shop, and in the meantime you can lay the table.*

**meanwhile** *adverb* at the same time as. *The rain fell. Meanwhile, Megan slept.*

**measles** *noun* a mainly children's infectious disease causing a fever and a rash of small red spots on the skin.

**measure** *verb* to find out or to show how long, tall, wide or heavy something is. *Ian measured the length of his desk.* **measure** *noun* 1 a unit of measure. A metre is a measure of length. 2 an action or law. *The government took measures to reduce crime.*

Jane took a ruler to measure the space exactly.

**measurement** *noun* how much something measures. *What are the measurements of the room?*

**meat** *noun* the flesh of animals or birds that we eat.

**mechanic** *noun* a person who understands machines and is skilled at making and mending them.

**mechanical** *adjective* 1 relating to machinery. 2 worked by machines. *A funny mechanical mouse.* 3 automatic and done without thought.

**mechanism** *noun* the system of the working parts of a machine.

**medal** *noun* a flat round piece of metal or plastic similar to a large coin with words or a symbol on it, which is given as a reward.

Henry was awarded a medal for his achievements in athletics.

**meddle** *verb* to interfere in things when you have not been asked. **meddlesome** *adjective. He's turned into a meddlesome old man.*

**media** see mass-media.

**medical** *adjective* concerning doctors and their work in preventing and treating disease. **medical** *noun* a complete examination of your body by a doctor.

**medicine** *noun* 1 the tablets and liquid substances you swallow to try to treat and cure an illness. *The medicine tasted horrible.* 2 the science of treating illnesses.

**medieval** *adjective* relating to the Middle Ages, a period in European history that lasted between about AD 1100 and 1450.

**meditate** *verb* to think about something quietly and deeply. **meditation** *noun*.

**meek** *adjective* timid and patient and sometimes too obedient.

**meet** (meets, meeting, met) *verb* 1 to come face to face with somebody or something. 2 to come together by plan. *Shall we meet in the club this evening?* 3 to join or come together from different places. *The place where two rivers meet is called a confluence.*

**meeting** *noun* a time and place planned for people to come together to discuss or contest something.

**mega-** *prefix* very big. *Megawatt.*

**megabyte** *noun* a unit of memory in a computer (about a million bytes).

**megalith** *noun* a very large stone put up in prehistoric times.

The megalith marked an ancient burial ground.

**melancholy** *noun, adjective* very sad or gloomy. *A melancholy tale.*

**mellow** *adjective* 1 (of fruit) sweet and juicy. 2 (of light) soft and golden. 3 (of people) older but pleasanter. **mellow** *verb*. *She has mellowed with age.*

**melodious** *adjective* nice to listen to. *A beautifully melodious voice.*

**melody** (melodies) *noun* a sweet, pleasing tune. *I played a lovely melody on the flute.*

**melon** *noun* a large round juicy fruit with a green or yellow skin and lots of seeds inside.

**melt** *verb* to change from a solid to a liquid by heating. *The ice-cream melted in the Sun.*

**member** *noun* somebody or something that belongs to a group, team, club, family etc. **membership** *noun*.

**memorable** *adjective* worth remembering, famous, easy to remember. *A memorable day at the fair.*

**memorize** *verb* to learn something so well that you can remember it word for word. *Actors have to memorize their lines.*

**memory** *noun* 1 the ability to remember things. *He has a good memory for telephone numbers.* 2 things that you can remember about the distant past. *Childhood memories.* 3 the part of a computer that stores and retrieves information.

Janice mended the rip in her skirt by sewing it up with a needle and thread.

**SPELLING NOTE**

*In British English we 'meet people'. The British may also 'meet with' opposition, disapproval or an accident. Americans 'meet with' people as well as with accidents etc.*

**AMAZING FACT**

Because Mercury is so close to the Sun, it has a very short year. A year on Mercury is only 88 Earth days.

Mercury is also the name of a planet, the planet nearest to the Sun.

**men** *noun* the plural of man.

**menace** *noun* somebody or something that is a threat or danger and may cause damage. *Black ice is a menace to drivers.*

**mend** *verb* to repair or to make something that is broken useful again. *When is somebody coming round to mend the washing machine?*

**menstruation** *noun* blood that comes from a woman's womb about once a month. A period. **menstruate** *verb*.

**mental** *adjective* relating to the mind, done in the head. *Mental arithmetic.*

**mention** *verb* to make a casual or brief remark about something. *I think she did mention you would be away.* **mention** *noun*.

**menu** (menus) *noun* 1 a list of the dishes you can choose from in a restaurant. 2 a list of choices displayed on a computer screen.

**MEP** *abbreviation* Member of the European Parliament.

**merchandise** *noun* goods for sale.

**merchant** *noun* a person who buys and sells large quantities of goods of a particular kind. *A coffee merchant.* **merchant navy** a nation's ships that carry goods.

**merciful** *adjective* willing to forgive somebody and not punish them.

**merciless** *adjective* cruel and showing no pity, ruthless.

**mercury** *noun* a silvery metal that is usually liquid. Mercury is used in thermometers.

**mercy** *noun* ready to show kindness and forgiveness to somebody who has done something wrong.

**merely** *adverb* simply, only. *She merely laughed when I fell down.* **mere** *adjective*. *Lucy is a mere child.*

**merge** *verb* to combine or blend together. *The two firms decided to merge.* **merger** *noun*.

**merry** (merrier, merriest) *adjective* 1 cheerful and happy. *Have a merry Christmas.* 2 (informal) very slightly drunk.

M

**mesmerize** *verb* to be so fascinated by something that you can think of nothing else. To be hypnotized.

**mess** *noun* untidy with things lying everywhere, a confused muddle. *What a mess your desk is!* **messy** *adjective.*

**message** *noun* information sent from one person or group to another. *Are there any telephone messages for me?*

**met** past tense of meet.

**metal** *noun* a hard material that goes soft and can be bent when heated. Metals are usually shiny and conduct heat well. Copper, gold, iron and silver are all metals.

**metamorphosis** *noun* the complete change in form that some animals go through as they develop. *The metamorphosis of a tadpole into a frog.*

**metaphor** *noun* an expression in which something or somebody is described as though they were something else. *She has green fingers and he has a heart of gold.*

**meteor** *noun* a large piece of metal or rock that travels through space and normally burns up if it enters Earth's atmosphere.

The meteor shower was spectacular, with up to six shooting stars lighting up the sky at once.

**meteorite** *noun* a meteor that has fallen to Earth from space.

**meteorology** *noun* the scientific study of the atmosphere and weather. **meteorologist** *noun* a person who forecasts the weather.

**meter** *noun* an instrument that measures how much electricity, gas, water etc. has been used. *He came to read the meter.*

**method** *noun* a certain way of doing something, a system. *There are several methods for making coffee.*

**methodical** *adjective* in an orderly, well-organized way, according to plan.

**metre** *noun* a measure of length equal to 1,000 millimetres. **metric** *adjective* to do with the metre or metric system. **metric system** a system of weighing and measuring based on 10 and multiples of 10. Kilograms, litres and metres are all metric measures.

**metropolis** *noun* a very large city.

**Mexican** *noun* a person who comes from Mexico. **Mexican** *adjective. A Mexican hat.*

**Mexico City** *noun* the capital of Mexico.

**DID YOU KNOW**

*You can mix metaphors in a really confusing way. Can you unravel these? 'She took the bull by the tail.' 'You can't teach an old dog to suck eggs.'*

**SPELLING NOTE**

*Try not to confuse 'meter', a measuring instrument, and 'metre', a measure of length. In American English both words are spelled 'meter'.*

There are 12 hours between midnight and midday, so the hands of the clock move once around its face in that time.

**Mexico** *noun* a country in North America.

In Mexico 90 per cent of the population belongs to the Roman Catholic Church.

**mice** plural of mouse.

**micro-** *prefix* very small. *Microchip, microfilm, microsecond.*

**microbe** *noun* a living thing that is so tiny that it can be seen only through a microscope. *Swarming with microbes.*

**microchip** or **silicon chip** *noun* a tiny piece of silicon with electronic circuits printed on it, used in computers and other electronic equipment. *The microchip industry.*

**Micronesia** *noun* a country of many islands in the Pacific Ocean.

**microphone** *noun* an electrical instrument that is used to help record sound, or to make sounds louder than they really are.

**microscope** *noun* an instrument with lenses that makes tiny objects look much larger. *We looked at the ant under the microscope.*

**microscopic** *adjective* so tiny that it cannot be seen except through a microscope.

**microwave** *noun* an oven that cooks food very quickly by using energy in very short waves (electronic microwaves).

**midday** *noun* the middle of the day, 12 noon.

**middle** *noun, adjective* the part of something that is half-way or the same distance from its ends or its sides. *A cherry has a stone in the middle.* **middle age** the time of a person's life between about the ages of 40 and 60. **Middle Ages** a period in European history between about 1100 and 1450. **Middle East** an area at the eastern end of the Mediterranean Sea and including Egypt and Iran.

**midge** *noun* a tiny gnat-like insect that bites.

**midget** *noun* an exceptionally short person.

**midnight** *noun* 12 o'clock in the middle of the night. **midnight** *adjective. A midnight feast.*

**midwife** *noun* a person whose job it is to help women at the birth of their babies.

**migraine** *noun* (say **mee**-grane) a very severe, throbbing headache that makes you feel sick.

**migration** *noun* the movement from one place to another to live. **migrate** *verb*. *Swallows migrate every autumn.* **migratory** *adjective*. **migrant** *noun* 1 a person who is moving or migrating from one country to another. 2 a bird that migrates each year.

**mild** *adjective* 1 gentle. *She has a mild nature.* 2 not too bad or severe. *A mild fever.* 3 (of weather) rather warm. *A mild winter.* 4 (of food or drink) not strong or too spicy. *A mild curry.*

**mildew** *noun* a greyish fungus that grows on plants or decaying matter.

**mile** *noun* a measure of distance equal to 1,760 yards or 1.6 km. **to be miles away** to daydream. *I was miles away when you rang.*

**militant** *adjective* aggressive and ready to fight, very active in support of a cause.

**military** *adjective* relating to armed forces and warfare. *In some countries, all young men have to do military service.*

Military life was hard during the war.

**milk** *noun* 1 the white liquid that female mammals make in their bodies to feed their young. 2 the milk of cows and goats used as food for humans and to make such things as cheese and butter. **milk** *verb* to take milk from a cow. **milky** *adjective*. **milk-tooth** one of the first, temporary teeth in young mammals. Milk teeth fall out and are replaced by teeth that should last you the rest of your life.

**mill** *noun* 1 a building with machinery for grinding grain into flour. 2 a factory. *A steel mill.* 3 a small grinding tool. *A pepper mill.*

**millennium** (millennia) *noun* a period of a thousand years.

**milligram** *noun* a very small measure of weight. There are 1,000 milligrams in a kilogram.

**millilitre** *noun* a very small liquid measure. There are 1,000 millilitres in a litre.

**millipede** *noun* a small worm-like creature with many pairs of legs.

**WORD HISTORY**

*'Mile' comes from a Latin word for a thousand (as do 'millennium', 'milligram', 'millipede', etc). A mile was a Roman unit of length – 'mille passuum', or a thousand paces.*

**mime** *noun* a kind of acting without words in which the actors use gestures and facial expressions. **mime** *verb*.

**mimic** (mimics, mimicking, mimicked) *verb* to imitate somebody's actions or speech, usually to amuse people. **mimic** *noun*. *He's a good mimic.*

**minaret** *noun* a tall tower near a mosque from the top of which the muezzin calls people to prayer.

A muezzin, a holy man, calls Muslims to prayer from the minaret on a mosque.

**mince** *verb* to chop food into tiny pieces. **mince** *noun* meat that has been minced or ground into small pieces.

**mincemeat** *noun* finely chopped dried fruit and spices, used in making mincepies.

**mind** *noun* the part of you that thinks, feels, learns, understands and remembers. *He has a very fine mind.* Your intelligence. **make up your mind** to decide.

**mind** *verb* 1 to care about or feel unhappy about something. *Do you mind if I turn on the TV?* 2 to look after something. *She is minding the baby for me.* 3 Be careful. *Mind your head on that door!*

**mindless** *adjective* stupid and unthinking.

**mine** *noun* 1 an underground place where people dig to obtain such things as gold or diamonds. 2 a bomb buried under the ground or in the sea. *The car was blown up by a mine.* **mine** *verb*. **minefield** *noun* an area covered with buried explosive mines.

**miner** *noun* a person who works down a mine. *The miners went on strike.*

**mineral** *noun* a natural substance such as coal, gold and salt, which is mined from the earth. **mineral** *adjective* of or containing minerals. *Mineral water.*

This beautiful blue-green mineral is Mexican selenite.

**mingle** *verb* to mix with or blend. *The police mingled with the crowd.*

**mini-** *prefix* smaller or shorter than normal.

**miniature** *adjective* very small. *A miniature railway.* **miniature** *noun* a small version of something much larger, such as a painting.

M

**minim** *noun* a musical note equal to the time value of two crotchets.

**minimize** *verb* 1 to make something seem unimportant. *She tried to minimize the problem.* 2 to make as small as possible.

**minimum** *noun* the smallest amount or number of something you can have. *You need a minimum of ten people for the trip.* **minimum** *adjective. The minimum cost will be £10.* The opposite of minimum is maximum.

**mining** *noun* the process or industry of extracting minerals from the earth. *The coal-mining industry.*

**minister** *noun* 1 a member of the clergy who holds services in a Protestant church. 2 the head of a government department. *The Minister of Health.*

**ministry** *noun* 1 the work of a clergyman. 2 a government department. *The Ministry of Agriculture.*

**minnow** *noun* a tiny fish found in lakes and rivers. *He caught only minnows.*

A shoal of minnows flashed past as the children watched from the bridge.

**minor** *adjective* small, unimportant, not serious. *A minor accident.* The opposite of minor is major. **minor** *noun* a young person who is under the age of 18.

**minority** *noun* 1 the smaller of two groups of people or things. *Only a minority voted against.* 2 a small number of people of one race, culture or religion living among a much larger group of people of a different race, culture or religion. The opposite of minority is majority.

**Minsk** *noun* the capital of Belarus.

**mint** *noun* 1 a plant whose leaves are used as a flavouring. 2 a place where coins are made.

**minus** *noun* a mathematical term or symbol (–) meaning subtraction or taking away. *Seven minus five equals two, or 7–5 = 2.*

**minute** *noun* (**min**-it) a period of time consisting of 60 seconds. There are 60 minutes in an hour.

**minute** (**my**-newt) *adjective* 1 very small, tiny. *A minute speck of soot.* 2 very detailed. *A minute examination.*

**miracle** *noun* an amazing and unexpected happening for which there is no explanation. *His escape from the blazing car was a miracle.* **miraculous** *adjective.*

**WORD BUILDING**

*The prefix 'mini-' (a shortening of 'miniature') has become a very useful word builder, producing such new words as: 'minibreak' (short holiday), 'minibus', 'minicab' and 'minicomputer'.*

**AMAZING FACT**

Dividing the day into 24 hours, the hour into 60 minutes, and the minute into 60 seconds is an ancient system of time measurement but it did not come into general use until about AD 1600.

Today, not all cultures measure the day in the same way, though. In Kenya, for example, seconds, minutes and hours are the same but the day is split into two halves – from dawn until sunset, then sunset to sunrise. The two halves are more or less equal because the country is on the Equator.

**mirage** *noun* something that you imagine you see but that is not really there, an optical illusion. *The travellers saw a mirage of an oasis in the desert.*

**mirror** *noun* a piece of special glass, metal or plastic that reflects light and whatever is in front of it.

Mum kept a mirror on her dressing table for checking her make-up.

**mis-** *prefix* wrongly. *Misbehave, misjudge.*

**misbehave** *verb* to behave badly. **misbehaviour** *noun.*

**miscellaneous** *adjective* a mixture or assortment of various things.

**mischief** *noun* annoying but harmless behaviour. **mischievous** *adjective. A mischievous child.*

**miser** *noun* a very mean person who likes to hoard money but who will not spend it. **miserly** *adjective.*

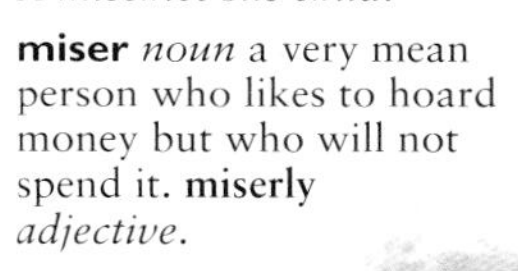

The miser spent a lot of time alone, enjoying counting his money.

**misery** *noun* 1 a feeling of great unhappiness, wretchedness. 2 (informal) a person who is always complaining. *She's a real misery.* **miserable** *adjective. Jane is miserable because she can't go to the concert with her friends.*

**misfit** *noun* somebody who does not belong to a group because they are in some way strange or different.

**misfortune** *noun* bad luck.

**mishap** *noun* an unfortunate accident.

**mislay** (mislays, mislaying, mislaid) *verb* to lose something for a short time because you have forgotten where you put it. *I seem to have mislaid my glasses.*

**mislead** *verb* to give somebody a false idea by making them believe something that is untrue. To deceive or give wrong information. **misleading** *adjective. This newspaper article is very misleading.*

M

**miss** *verb* 1 to fail to do something such as hitting or catching. *Peter threw me a ball but I missed it.* 2 to fail to be somewhere at the right time. *Matt missed the train by a minute.* 3 to be sad because somebody is no longer with you. *She missed her friend when he was sent abroad.*

**Miss** *noun* a polite title often put before the name of a girl or unmarried woman.

**missile** *noun* a weapon that is sent through the air and which explodes when it hits its target. *The missile hit the ammunition store.*

**missing** *adjective* 1 lost. *A missing dog.* 2 absent. *Two men are missing from the team.*

**mission** *noun* 2 an important job that somebody is sent somewhere to do. *The astronauts were sent on a mission to Mars.* 2 important work that somebody thinks they should do. *Her mission in life was to help the poor.*

Their mission to the Moon was a milestone in the history of humankind.

**missionary** *noun* somebody who is sent to another country to tell the people about a religion. *The missionaries were eaten by tigers, or so the local people said.*

**mist** *noun* a low cloud of damp air that is difficult to see through.

**mistake** *noun* something that is wrong or incorrect, an error. *Can you see a spelling misstake?*

**mistake** (mistakes, mistaking, mistook) *verb* 1 to misunderstand or to make an error about something. *She mistook my instructions and went the wrong way.* 2 to confuse one person or thing for another. *I mistook you for your brother.*

**mistaken** *adjective* wrong and not correctly understood. *He has the mistaken belief that the Sun spins around the Earth.*

**misty** *adjective. Misty autumn mornings.*

**mistreat** *verb* to treat in a bad, cruel or unfair way. **mistreatment** *noun.*

**misunderstand** (misunderstands, misunderstanding, misunderstood) *verb* not to understand the meaning of something correctly, to get the wrong idea.

**misunderstanding** *noun* 1 a wrong or false idea about the meaning of something. *There must be some misunderstanding.* 2 a quarrel or disagreement.

**AMAZING FACT**

Since the 1970s, many women, whether married or unmarried, prefer to use the title 'Ms' instead of 'Miss' or 'Mrs'.

**WORD HISTORY**

*Mob comes from the Latin words 'mobile vulgus'. 'Vulgus' means 'masses' or 'crowd' and 'mobile' means 'moveable', 'fickle' or 'easily swayed'.*

**SPELLING NOTE**

*'Moccasin' is often misspelled. Note that it has two 'c's and only a single 's'.*

**mitten** *noun* a kind of glove that either leaves the tips of the fingers bare or that has one part for the thumb and one part for four fingers.

**mix** *verb* to combine or put different things together. **mixture** *noun. A cake mixture.* **mix-up** *noun* a confusion or muddle. *There's some mix-up in the dates.*

**mixer** *noun* a machine that you use to mix things together. *A cement mixer.*

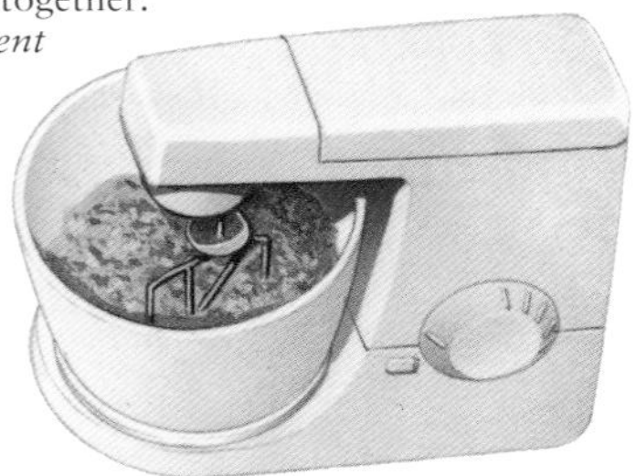

Stephen put the ingredients for the crumble topping in the food mixer.

**mnemonic** *noun* (say nem-**on**-ik) an aid, such as a rhyme, to help us remember facts.

**moan** *verb* 1 to make a low, unhappy sound because you are in pain or sad. 2 to grumble and complain. *He's always moaning about the weather.* **moan** *noun. A moan of grief.*

**moat** *noun* a deep, wide ditch, usually filled with water, around a castle. Moats helped to protect castles from attack.

**mob** *noun* a noisy, and often violent, crowd of angry people. **mob** *verb* to crowd around. *The fans mobbed the pop star.*

**mobile** *adjective* able to be moved about easily and quickly. *A mobile home.*

Mobile phones have become extremely popular in a very short time.

**mobile phone** *noun* a portable telephone that fits easily into a pocket or handbag. Often shortened to mobile.

**moccasin** *noun* a soft leather shoe without a heel. Moccasins were first worn by Native Americans.

**mock** *verb* to make fun of somebody, often by copying them in a cruel and unpleasant way. *She mocked the way he stuttered.* **mock** *adjective* not real, imitation. *Mock diamonds.* **mockery** *noun.*

**model** *noun* 1 a small, to-scale copy of something. *A model of a castle.* 2 a good example. *He is a model of good behaviour.* 3 a person whose job is to wear new clothes to show them off to people before they buy them. 4 a person who poses for an artist or photographer. 5 a style or particular version of a product. *This computer is the latest model.* **model** *verb.*

**modem** *noun* an electronic device that sends information between one computer and another by telephone.

**moderate** *adjective* 1 not extreme, neither too big nor too small. *He eats a moderate amount of food.* 2 average or fairly good. *She had quite moderate marks for her exam.*

**modern** *adjective* happening now, new and not old-fashioned. *Modern technology.*

**modest** *adjective* 1 quiet and not boastful. 2 not extreme or very large, moderate. *Her needs are very modest.*

**Mogadishu** *noun* the capital of Somalia.

**moist** *adjective* a little wet, damp. **moisten** *verb* to make or become slightly wet or damp. *He moistened his lips.*

**moisture** *noun* dampness. Tiny drops of water such as steam.

**Moldova** *noun* a country in eastern Europe.

The flag of Moldova has blue, yellow and red stripes with an eagle and crest in the centre.

**mole** *noun* a small brown spot that is slightly raised on the skin.

**mole** *noun* a small, dark grey, furry animal that digs tunnels under the ground with its strong front paws. Moles leave behind piles of earth called molehills.

**molecule** *noun* the smallest amount of a substance that can exist on its own. A molecule of water is made up of two atoms of hydrogen and one atom of oxygen.

**mollusc** *noun* any animal with a soft body and no backbone such as a snail, slug or octopus.

A garden snail is a mollusc. It is like a slug with a shell on its back.

**molten** *adjective* turned to liquid and melted. *Molten silver.*

**moment** *noun* a very short period of time. *Wait a moment.* **momentary** *adjective*. *A momentary pause.* **at the moment** now.

**momentum** *noun* the force gained by an object as it moves. *The sledge gained momentum as it travelled downhill.*

**Monaco** *noun* a country in southern Europe.

**monarch** *noun* (say **mon**-ark) a king or queen. **monarchy** *noun*.

**AMAZING FACT**

There are about 70,000 different types of molluscs. They range in size from a few millimetres to the giant squid, which may grow to be twelve metres.

Monkeys are extremely intelligent animals. Some types are becoming endangered due to hunting or destruction of habitat.

**WORD BUILDER**

*The prefix 'mono' is a useful word builder, as in: 'monoplane' (an aeroplane with one set of wings), 'monorail' (a railway with carriages hanging from one rail), and 'monosyllable' ( a word with one syllable).*

**monastery** *noun* a group of buildings in which a community of monks lives and works, an abbey. **monastic** *adjective*.

**money** *noun* the coins and banknotes we use to buy things.

**Mongolia** *noun* a country in central Asia.

**mongoose** (mongooses) *noun* a small African or Asian animal with a long body that kills poisonous snakes.

**mongrel** *noun* a dog that is a mixture of different breeds. *Many mongrels make very good pets.*

**monitor** *noun* 1 a pupil at school who has been given special duties or responsibilities. 2 a computer screen. 3 an instrument, usually with a screen, that keeps a check on something and records any changes.

**monk** *noun* a member of a religious community of men who live, pray and work together in a building called a monastery.

**monkey** *noun* an animal with long arms and a long tail that climbs trees. Monkeys are primates and belong to the same group as apes and people. **monkey business** some mischievous or illegal activity. **monkey with** play the fool with.

**mono-** *prefix* one or alone. *Monorail.*

**monopoly** *noun* having sole control of the manufacture or supply of a product or service. **monopolize** *verb* to control something completely.

**monotonous** *adjective* dull, boring and lacking any variety. *She has a monotonous voice.* **monotony** *noun*.

**Monrovia** *noun* the capital of Liberia.

**monsoon** *noun* a strong prevailing wind around the Indian Ocean that changes directions in winter and summer. The summer monsoon brings heavy rainfall.

**monster** *noun* 1 a huge, terrifying but imaginary creature. 2 a cruel, wicked person. **monster** *adjective* very big or strange. **monstrous** *adjective* horrible and shocking. *A monstrous crime.*

This monster is the sort of creature that inhabits nightmares.

**Monte Carlo** *noun* the capital of Monaco.

**Montevideo** *noun* the capital of Uruguay.

**month** *noun* a period of time and one of the twelve divisions of the year. **monthly** *adjective* happening once a month or every month. *A monthly magazine.* **calendar month** one of the twelve divisions of the year. From 1 March to 31 March is a calendar month. **lunar month** a period of about 29 days, the time it takes the Moon to orbit the Earth.

**monument** *noun* 1 an old and important building, statue etc. *Ancient monuments.* 2 a building or statue erected so that people will remember an important person or event. **monumental** *adjective.*

**mood** *noun* the way you feel or your state of mind at a particular time. *Winning the match put him in a good mood.* **moody** *adjective* bad-tempered or liable to change mood quickly for no apparent reason. **moodiness** *noun.*

**moon** *noun* 1 a natural satellite or small planet that orbits a larger planet. 2 **the Moon** the natural satellite that orbits the Earth once every four weeks (lunar month). The Moon is our closest neighbour in space.

As the Moon waxes and wanes, it passes through various phases.

**moonlight** *noun* the light from the Sun reflected by the Moon.

**moor** *noun* a large area of open land usually covered with heather.

**moor** *verb* to tie up a boat so that it cannot drift away. **moorings** *noun.*

**moose** (plural moose) *noun* a large brown deer found in the forests of North America. The male has huge, flattened antlers.

The moose uses its antlers to fight off rivals for a mate.

**mop** *noun* an implement with soft material such as a sponge attached to a long handle, used for cleaning floors and dishes. **mop** (mops, mopping, mopped) *verb* to wipe with a mop or cloth. *He mopped his brow in the midday heat.*

**WORD HISTORY**

*'Mosquito' comes from a Portuguese word that means 'little fly', originally from the Latin 'musca', 'fly'.*

**AMAZING FACT**

'Moose' is a Native American word. Moose and elk are completely different animals – in the US and Canada, that is.

In Europe, the moose is actually called an 'elk', which is an old German name.

**mope** *verb* to feel sad and sorry for yourself.

**moral** *adjective* relating to good behaviour and what is right and wrong. *Euthanasia is a moral question.* **moral** *noun* a lesson or point made in a story about what is right and wrong. **morals** *plural noun* standards of behaviour and beliefs in right and wrong.

**morale** *noun* (say mor-**al**) the spirit of hope, confidence and enthusiasm among members of a group or team. *After its win, the team's morale is very high.*

**more** *adjective, pronoun* bigger in number, size or amount. *She has more marbles than me.* **more** *adverb. Can you say it once more?*

**morgue** *noun* a mortuary or place where corpses are kept until they are buried or cremated.

**Moroccan** *noun* a person who comes from Morocco. **Moroccan** *adjective. A Moroccan mosque.*

**Morocco** *noun* a country in Africa.

Morocco, in northern Africa, is a Muslim country with many mosques.

**Moroni** *noun* the capital of Comoros.

**morning** *noun* the part of the day before midday, from sunrise to noon.

**morsel** *noun* a very small piece of food.

**mortal** *adjective* 1 incapable of living for ever. All living things are mortal. 2 causing death. *A mortal illness.* **mortal** *noun* a human being.

**mortgage** *noun* (say **more**-gage) a loan of money from a building society or bank that you use to buy a house. **mortgage** *verb* to transfer the ownership of your house or property to a bank or building society in return for money they lend you.

**mortuary** *noun* a place where dead bodies are kept before they are buried or cremated.

**mosaic** *noun* (say moh-**zay**-ik) a picture or design made from small pieces of coloured glass or stone set in concrete.

Tiles from Turkey are often patterned with intensely coloured mosaic designs.

**Moscow** *noun* the capital of Russia.

**Moslem** another spelling for Muslim.

**mosque** *noun* a building in which Muslims worship. *They prayed in the mosque.*

**mosquito** *noun* (say moss-**kee**-toe) a small flying insect that bites animals and people and sucks their blood. Some mosquitoes transmit the disease malaria.

**moss** (mosses) *noun* a small green plant that forms a soft covering on stones in damp places. **mossy** *adjective.*

**most** *noun, adjective* the largest in size, number or amount. *Most apples are green or red.* **most** *adverb. The most intelligent boy in the class.*

**mostly** *adverb* generally, mainly. *What you are saying is mostly nonsense.*

**motel** *noun* a hotel that caters specially for motorists and their vehicles.

**moth** *noun* an insect like a butterfly that is usually seen flying at night.

The peppered moth camouflages itself against the bark of trees.

**mother** *noun* a female parent, the woman who gave birth to you. **mother** *verb* to look after like a mother. **motherly** *adjective.* **motherhood** *noun. Motherhood was her greatest joy.*

**mother-in-law** *noun* the mother of a person's husband or wife.

**motion** *noun* movement, the action of moving. *The motion of the coach sent him to sleep.* **motion** *verb* to signal or make a movement, usually with the hand. *She motioned him to sit down.*

**motion picture** *noun* a cinema film.

**motionless** *adjective* not moving.

**motive** *noun* a reason that causes somebody to do something. *What was the motive for the crime?*

**motor** *noun* an engine in a machine that uses fuel to make it work or move. **motor** *adjective* having to do with engines and vehicles. *A motor show.*

**motorcycle** *noun* a heavy two-wheeled vehicle with an engine.

**motorist** *noun* a person who drives a motor car. *A tax on motorists.*

**motorway** *noun* a long wide road with several lanes for traffic to travel quickly over long distances.

**mottled** *adjective* marked with patches of different colour.

**DID YOU KNOW**

*'Motel' is a good example of a hybrid or blend word. It is a blend of 'motor car' and 'hotel'. Other examples are 'brunch' ('breakfast' and 'lunch') and 'smog' ('smoke' and 'fog').*

**AMAZING FACT**

'The Jazz Singer', starring Al Jolson, was the first 'talkie' – a motion picture that had sound.

**motto** *noun* a phrase that sums up what is important to a group or a guiding principle to good behaviour. *'Think before you speak' is a good motto.*

**mould** *verb* to model or to make something into a shape with your hands. *She moulded the clay into a vase.* **mould** *noun* a container into which a liquid is poured, which takes the shape of the container when it sets. *A jelly mould in the shape of a rabbit.*

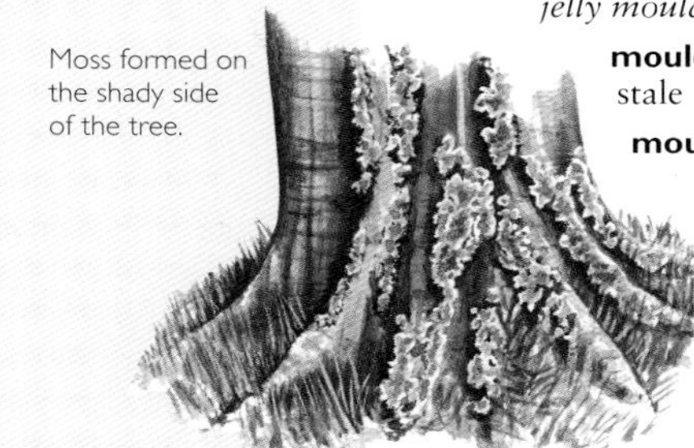

Moss formed on the shady side of the tree.

**mould** *noun* a fungus found on stale food or damp things.

**moult** *verb* (of a bird) to lose feathers or (of an animal) to shed hair. *Our dog moults every spring.*

**mound** *noun* a small hill, a pile or heap. *A burial mound.*

**mount** *verb* 1 to climb on the back of a horse, pony etc. 2 to increase. *The cost of building is mounting.* 3 to fix something somewhere, for example in a frame so as to display it.

**mount** *noun* a mountain, usually as part of the name of a mountain. *Mount Everest.*

**mountain** *noun* a very high and usually steep hill. *Climb every mountain.*

**mourn** *verb* to feel great sadness because somebody has died, to grieve. **mourning** *noun. They mourned their lost loved ones.*

**mouse** (mice) *noun* 1 a small grey furry animal with a long tail and sharp teeth. Mice are rodents. 2 a small device on your desk that you move on the surface with your hand to control the position of the cursor on a computer screen.

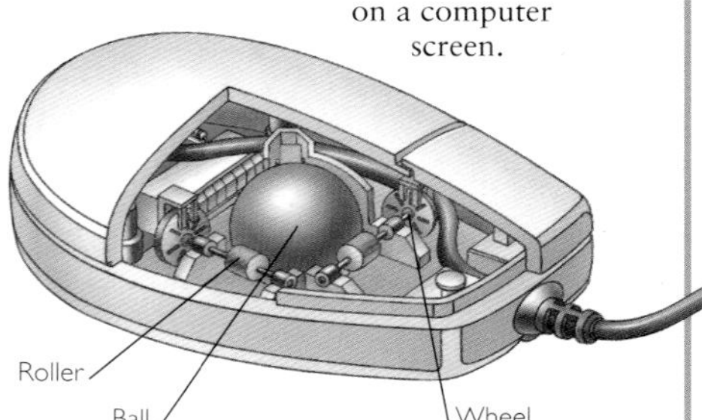


The mouse on a computer moves the cursor on the screen.

**moustache** *noun* hair growing above a man's top lip.

**mouth** *noun* 1 the part of your face that opens when you speak and into which you put food. 2 the place where a river flows out to sea. 3 the entrance to a cave etc.

**mouthful** (mouthfuls) *noun* the amount you put in your mouth at one time.

**mouth-organ** *noun* a small musical instrument that you play by moving it along your lips while blowing and sucking.

M

**mouthpiece** *noun* the part of a musical instrument, pipe etc. that you put in your mouth.

**movable** *adjective* able to be moved. *The hands of a clock are movable.*

**move** *verb* 1 to go from one position or place to another. *Don't move, I want to take your photograph.* 2 to change your home. *We moved into a new house.* 3 to make you feel something deeply. *He was moved to pity by the sad film.*

**movement** *noun* 1 the act of moving. *She made a sudden movement.* 2 a group of people working together for a common cause. *The animal rights movement.* 3 a section into which some pieces of classical music are divided. *Most symphonies have a slow movement.*

**movie** *noun* a film in the cinema, a motion picture. *Let's go to the movies.*

**moving** *adjective* touching or moving the feelings. *It was a moving film about orphans.*

**mow** (mows, mowing, mowed, mown) *verb* (rhymes with go) to cut grass or hay with a machine called a **mower** or **lawnmower** *noun*. *Sid mowed the front lawn.*

**Mozambique** *noun* a country in Africa.

Mozambique lies on the east coast of Africa opposite the island of Madagascar.

**MP** *abbreviation* Member of Parliament.

**mph** *abbreviation* miles per hour.

**Mr** *abbreviation* mister (say **mist**-er) a polite title put before a man's name.

**Mrs** *abbreviation* mistress (say **miss**-iz) a polite title put before the name of a married woman. *Mrs Jones.*

**Ms** (say miz) a title that some people put before the name of woman, which does not show whether she is married or single.

**much** *adjective*, *adverb*, *pronoun* a large amount, a lot. *Did you drink much?*

**muck** *noun* dirt, filth. **muck about** *verb* (slang) to behave in a silly way and waste time. *Pay attention and stop mucking about.* **muck in** *verb* (slang) to join in with other people. **muck out** *verb* to clean stables. **muck up** *verb* (slang) to spoil. *He mucked up our plans.*

**mud** *noun* soft, wet earth. **muddy** *adjective*. *Take off your muddy boots.*

AMAZING FACT

In Ancient Egypt, it was not only humans who were mummified. Cats were also preserved.

WORD HISTORY

*'Mummy' was originally an Arabic word 'mumiya' meaning 'an embalmed body'. 'Mum' was the Arabic word for the wax used in the process of preserving the corpse.*

Mummies were stored in beautifully painted and decorated caskets.

**muddle** *noun* a thoroughly confused mess, a jumble. **muddle** *verb* 1 to mix things up in a confused way. 2 to confuse somebody or be confused. *You muddle me with all these complicated questions.*

**mudguard** *noun* a shield above a wheel on a vehicle that stops water and mud being splashed about.

**muesli** *noun* a food of mixed crushed cereals, nuts and dried fruit that people usually eat for breakfast.

**muezzin** *noun* a person who calls Muslims to prayer, usually from a minaret.

**mug** *noun* a tall cup with straight sides that you use without a saucer. *A mug of cocoa.*

**mug** (mugs, mugging, mugged) *verb* to attack and rob somebody in the street. *Jane was mugged outside her flat.* **mugger** *noun*.

**mule** *noun* an animal that is the offspring of a male donkey and a female horse or pony. *The mule carried us up the mountain.*

**multi-** *prefix* many. *Multi-coloured.*

**multi-media** *adjective* involving the use of a mixture of different media such as TV, radio, video etc.

**multiple** *adjective* involving more than one, many. *She suffered multiple injuries in the accident.* **multiple** *noun* any number that can be divided exactly by another number. 20, 30 and 40 are multiples of 2, 5 and 10.

**multiply** (multiplies, multiplying, multiplied) *verb* to increase a number by adding the number to itself a given number of times. Three plus three plus three make nine or 3 x 3 = 9. **multiplication** *noun*. The opposite of multiply is divide.

**multitude** *noun* a crowd, a large number of things. *I've a multitude of things to do.*

**mumble** *verb* to speak in a low, indistinct voice that is not easy to understand.

**mummy** *noun* a word for mother.

**mummy** (mummies) *noun* a dead body that has been preserved from decay by being rubbed with special oils and wrapped in cloths, especially in ancient Egypt.

**mumps** *noun* a painful infectious disease that makes your neck and the sides of your face swell.

**munch** *verb* to chew something in a noisy way. *The horse munched a crisp apple.*

**mural** *noun* a picture painted on a wall.

**murder** *verb* to kill somebody on purpose. **murder** *noun. The police are investigating three murders.* **murderous** *adjective.*

**murderer** *noun* a person who commits a murder. *The murderer was jailed for life.*

**Muscat** *noun* the capital of Oman.

**muscle** *noun* a part inside your body that stretches and relaxes to make different parts of your body move. *Tennis players need to have strong arm muscles.*

Thin tissue

Bundles of fibres

Each fibre is made of hundreds of strands called fibrils.

Muscles work in pairs. As one contracts or tightens, the other relaxes.

Muscle fibres are so small that 1 sq cm would contain a million of them.

**AMAZING FACT**

The oldest musical instrument is something called a 'bull-roarer' that was made from a piece of bone with a cord attached to it.

**muse** *verb* to think deeply about something.

**museum** *noun* (say meeyou-zee-um) a place where interesting or rare objects are kept on display for people to look at.

**mushroom** *noun* a fungus that looks like an umbrella. Some you can eat, but others are poisonous.

**music** *noun* 1 the pleasing mixture and pattern of sounds made by somebody singing or by musical instruments. 2 the written or printed signs and notes that represent musical sounds.

**musical** *adjective* 1 relating to music. *Musical instruments.* 2 good at making or understanding music. *She is very musical.* **musical** *noun* a play or film in which singing and dancing form an important part.

**musician** *noun* a composer of music, a person who plays a musical instrument well.

**musket** *noun* an oldfashioned kind of gun with a long barrel.

**Muslim** or **Moslem** *noun* a person who believes in Islam, the religion founded by the prophet Mohammed. **Muslim** *adjective.*

**mussel** *noun* a small shellfish with two black shells.

**must** verb that strengthens other verbs 1 to need to, to have to. *I must go to bed now.* 2 to be obliged to. *You must obey the rules.* 3 to be definitely or likely. *You must be happy to have won.*

**mustard** *noun* a hot-tasting yellow paste made from the seeds of the mustard plant and used to flavour food.

This is what mustard seeds look like under the microscope.

**SPELLING NOTE**

*Scholars and most Muslims prefer the spelling 'Muslim' to 'Moslem', although 'Moslem' is more widespread.*

**mute** *adjective* 1 unable to speak. 2 silent, speechless. *They stared at one another in mute amazement.*

**mutilate** *verb* to damage somebody or something, usually by cutting off a part of it. *A mutilated body.*

**mutiny** *noun* a rebellion by sailors or soldiers against officers in charge. **mutiny** *verb.* **mutinous** *adjective. Mutinous troops.* **mutineer** *noun. The mutineers took over the ship and threw the captain overboard.*

**mutter** *verb* to speak in a very low angry voice that cannot be heard properly, to grumble. *Please don't mutter into your beard because I can't hear you.*

**mutual** *adjective* 1 shared by two or more people. In common. *We have mutual friends.* 2 done equally one to another. *Mutual respect.*

**muzzle** *noun* 1 the nose and mouth of an animal such as a dog or wolf. 2 straps put over an animal's muzzle to prevent it biting. *The dog wore a muzzle after it had bitten the postman.* 3 the open end of a gun.

**Myanmar** *noun* a country in Southeast Asia, formerly called Burma.

**mystery** *noun* 1 something strange that has happened and which you cannot explain or understand, puzzling. *It's a complete mystery how he disappeared.* 2 a secret. **mysterious** *adjective. A mysterious castle.*

**myth** *noun* 1 an imaginary story from the distant past, usually about gods and heroes and how the world began. 2 a belief that is imagined and untrue. *It's a myth that spinach builds your muscles.* **mythical** *adjective. A mythical dragon got married to the princess in the fairytale.*

**mythology** *noun* a collection of myths. *Norse mythology.*

Greek mythology tells of the legend of the minotaur, a monster half-human and half-bull. The minotaur lived inside a maze and was eventually killed by the hero Theseus.

N

# Nn

**nag** (nags, nagging, nagged) *verb* to annoy somebody by constantly complaining or trying to persuade them to do something. *Mum's always nagging me to tidy my room.* **nag** *noun*.

**nail** *noun* 1 the hard covering that protects the ends of your fingers and toes (fingernails, toenails). 2 a thin piece of metal with one end pointed and the other end flat that can be used for fastening pieces of wood etc. together. *She hammered a nail into the wall.* **nail** *verb*. *He nailed a notice on the door.*

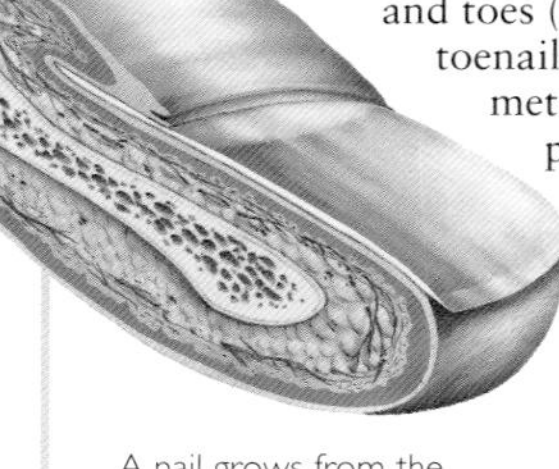

A nail grows from the cuticle under the skin.

**Nairobi** *noun* the capital of Kenya.

**naked** *adjective* with no clothes on, uncovered. **nakedness** *noun*.

**name** *noun* 1 a word by which a person, animal or place is known or called. *My cat's name is Archie.* 2 a reputation. *The bank has a very good name.* **name** *verb*. *They named their baby Billy.* **name after** to give somebody or something the same name as somebody else. *The city of Adelaide in Australia is named after Queen Adelaide.*

**namesake** *noun* somebody with the same name as you.

**Namibia** *noun* a country in Africa.

**nanny** *noun* a person who is trained to look after young children in their own home.

**nanny goat** *noun* a female goat.

**nap** *noun* a short sleep.

**nape** *noun* the back of your neck.

**napkin** *noun* a square piece of cloth or paper that you put on your lap to protect your clothes or to wipe your hands or lips during a meal.

These are two deserts in Namibia, the Namib and the Kalahari.

**WORD HISTORY**

*The shape of the letter N comes from an ancient Egyptian symbol for a snake. The sound comes from 'nun', a Semitic word for 'fish'. The Greeks called the letter 'nu'.*

**AMAZING FACT**

The world's first national park, Yellowstone National Park in the western US, was established in 1872. There are 50 national parks in the US, the largest being Wranell-S. Elias in Alaska. There are 32 national parks in Canada.

**nappy** *noun* a piece of thick, soft paper or cloth that is put around a baby's bottom (US diaper).

**narrate** *verb* to tell a story or relate an account of something.

**narrative** *noun* a story or account of things that have happened.

**narrator** *noun* a person who tells a story or explains what is happening.

**narrow** *adjective* thin and not measuring very much from one side to the other. *The door is too narrow for the piano to go through.* **narrow** *verb*. *The road narrowed as we climbed the hill.* The opposite of narrow is wide.

**narrow-minded** *adjective* unwilling to understand or even consider ideas that are new or different.

**nasal** *adjective* relating to the nose. *The nasal passages.*

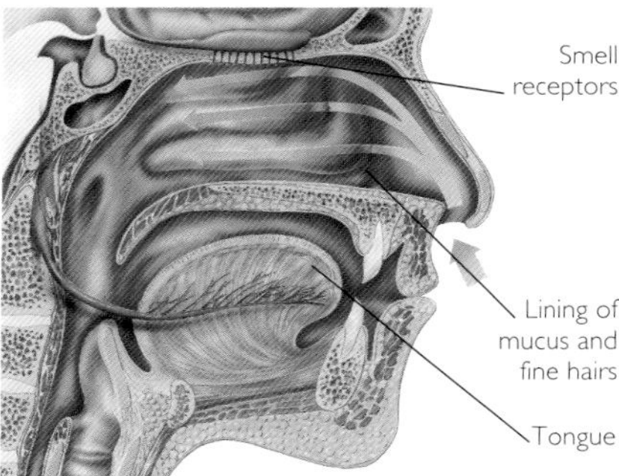


Air is inhaled through the nasal passages, where it is warmed before it is taken into the chest.

**Nassau** *noun* the capital of the Bahamas.

**nasty** (nastier, nastiest) *adjective* 1 unpleasant. *A nasty smell.* 2 unkind. 3 serious. *A nasty accident.*

**nation** *noun* a country with all the people who live there under one government and often sharing the same language, customs etc. *The nations of the world.*

**national** *adjective* belonging to a nation. *National dress.* **national anthem** a country's official hymn or song. **national park** an area of countryside under the care and ownership of the nation.

**nationalism** *noun* great pride in the culture, history and success of your own country.

**nationalist** *noun* 1 person who is very proud of their country. 2 a person who wants their country to be independent. *Scottish nationalist.*

**nationality** *noun* belonging to a particular nation. *He is of Russian nationality.*

**nationalize** *verb* to put a privately owned company under state control. **nationalization** *noun*. The opposite of nationalize is privatize.

N

**native** *noun* 1 one of the first inhabitants of a country. *Native American.* 2 a person who was born in a particular place. *She's a native of Glasgow.* **native** *adjective. What is your native language?*

**Native American** *noun* a member of the original race of people who lived in North America (often incorrectly called American Indians).

**nativity** *noun* the birth of Jesus Christ.

**natter** *verb* to talk busily about this and that, to chatter. **natter** *noun. They had a good natter about old times.*

**natural** *adjective* 1 relating to or concerned with nature. *Earthquakes are natural disasters.* 2 made by nature and not by humans. *The natural beauty of the mountains.* 3 ordinary and not surprising. *It's natural to laugh if you are amused.*

Native Americans lived in conical tents called tipis.

**naturalist** *noun* somebody who studies wildlife. *A naturalist in the field.*

**nature** *noun* (say **nay**-chur) 1 everything in the world around us not made by people, such as plants, animals, oceans, mountains etc. 2 characteristics that make up what a person or animal is really like. Personality. *He has a forgiving nature.*

**naughty** (naughtier, naughtiest) *adjective* badly behaved, mischievous. **naughtiness** *noun.* **naughtily** *adverb.*

**nautical** *adjective* relating to ships, sailing and the sea. *A nautical map.*

**naval** *adjective* relating to the navy or ships of war. *The battle of Trafalgar was fought at sea – it was a naval battle.*

**navel** *noun* the small round hollow in your stomach where your umbilical cord was attached when you were born.

**navigate** *verb* to steer a ship or to pilot an aircraft in the right direction with the help of maps and special instruments. **navigation** *noun.*

**navigator** *noun* somebody who navigates or directs the movement of a ship or aircraft.

**navy** *noun* the warships and sailors that help defend a country at sea.

**navy blue** *noun, adjective* very dark blue.

The compass, sextant and map are three tools of navigation.

**AMAZING FACT**

Native Americans came to the Americas from Asia via Siberia and Alaska about 30,000 years ago. Tribes settled in various places and developed distinct languages and cultures. Many states retain their Native American names: Wisconsin means 'grassy place', Ohio is 'fine river' and Michigan means 'great water'.

**N'Djamena** *noun* the capital of Chad.

**n.b.** *abbreviation* Latin words 'nota bene', meaning 'note well'.

**near** *preposition, adjective, adverb* 1 not far away, close to. *We live near the station.* 2 closely related. **near** *verb. As the boat neared the rocks it slowed down.*

**nearby** *adjective* not far away. *We stayed in a nearby village.*

**nearly** *adverb* almost but not quite. *He's nearly as tall as his father.*

**neat** *adjective* 1 very clean and tidy. *A neat pile of clothes.* 2 well done. *She has extremely neat handwriting.*

**necessary** *adjective* what must be done or is needed, essential and very important. *The climb is dangerous so please take all necessary precautions.*

**neck** *noun* the narrow part of a person or animal that joins the head to the body.

**necklace** *noun* a piece of jewellery that you wear around your neck.

**nectar** *noun* sweet juice that bees collect from flowers to make honey.

**nectarine** *noun* a fruit similar to a peach but with a smooth skin.

**need** *verb* 1 to want something that is a necessity. *We all need air to live.* 2 to have to do something. *I need to go to the vet.* **need** *noun. There's no need for you to hurry.*

**needle** *noun* 1 a thin piece of steel with a sharp point at one end and a hole (or eye) for thread at the other end that is used for sewing. 2 a long thin pointed stick made of plastic or steel that is used for knitting. 3 an instrument with a long thin part used for giving injections. 4 a moving pointer on a meter. 5 the narrow pointed leaf of a coniferous tree.

**needless** *adjective* unnecessary. *Needless worry is quite destructive.*

**needlework** *noun* sewing and embroidery.

**negative** *adjective* 1 meaning 'no'. 'I will not come' and 'I'll never go' are negative answers. 2 a number less than zero. The opposite of negative is positive. **negative** *noun* 1 a photographic film showing dark areas as light and light areas as dark, used to make prints. 2 (in electricity) the opposite charge to positive.

**neglect** *verb* to fail to look after or give enough attention to. *The garden is overgrown because he neglected to weed it.* **neglect** *noun. The house fell into neglect.*

**negotiate** *verb* to discuss something in order to come to an understanding or agreement, to bargain. **negotiation** *noun. The dispute was settled by negotiation.*

N

**neigh** *noun* the sound that a horse makes. **neigh** *verb. The horse neighed happily.*

**neighbour** *noun* (say **nay**-bor) somebody who lives near or next door to you.

**neighbourhood** *noun* the area surrounding where you live.

**neighbouring** *adjective* next to one another. *Italy and France are neighbouring countries.*

**neighbourly** *adjective* friendly and helpful like a good neighbour.

**neither** *adjective, pronoun* not either, not one and not the other. *Neither answer is right.* **neither** *conjunction. I neither like him nor dislike him.*

**neon** *noun* a chemical gas. Neon is sometimes used in glass tubes to make them glow orange-red when electricity is passed through (neon light).

**Nepal** *noun* a Himalayan country in South Asia.

**nephew** *noun* the son of your brother or sister. *My nephew Tim.*

**nerve** *noun* 1 a long thin fibre in your body that carries messages and feelings between your brain and body so that your body can feel and move. 2 calm bravery. *You need a lot of nerve to be a paraglider.*

Nerves carry information and instructions to and from the brain and from one part of the brain to another.

**nervous** *adjective* 1 relating to the nerves. *The nervous system.* 2 timid and easily frightened. *A nervous horse.* **nervousness** *noun.*

**nest** *noun* a home built by birds, some insects and some animals in which to lay eggs, give birth and raise their young. **nest** *verb. Swallows are nesting in the stable.*

**nestle** *verb* to curl up close together as if in a nest. *They nestled together in the hay.*

**net** *noun* 1 a material made of knotted string or rope with a regular pattern of holes between the threads. 2 net material used as a fishing net, tennis net, hairnet etc.

**netball** *noun* a game in which two teams of seven players try to score goals by throwing a ball through a high net at each end of a court. *May was captain of the netball team.*

**Netherlands** *noun* a country in northwestern Europe, sometimes called Holland.

The flag of the Netherlands has horizontal red, white and blue stripes.

**GRAMMAR NOTE**

*'Neither' is always followed by a singular verb, as in 'neither Jim nor Jane is clever' (not 'are clever'). And remember that you should always use 'neither... nor', as in 'neither you nor I' and never 'neither you or I'.*

**AMAZING FACT**

Most species of newts lay 200–400 eggs at a time but some, such as the rough-skinned newt of North America, lay just one egg at a time.

**nettle** *noun* (or stinging nettle) a wild plant with leaves covered with hairs that sting you if you touch them.

**network** *noun* 1 a widespread organization. *The telecommunications network.* 2 an arrangement looking like a pattern of criss-crossing lines. *A network of underground tunnels.* 3 a system of linked computers that share a storage system.

**neuter** *adjective* (say **new**-ter) neither male nor female, with no sexual organs or with the sexual organs removed.

**neutral** *noun* 1 not taking sides or having strong feelings for or against in, for example, a disagreement or war. *A neutral country.* 2 (of colours ) not too strong. *Grey is a neutral colour.*

**neutron** *noun* one of the particles that make up the nucleus of an atom but carry no electrical charge.

**never** *adverb* not ever, at no time in the past or in the future. *I will never let you go.*

**new** *adjective* 1 just made, built, bought, not used, fresh. *I had a new bike for my birthday.* 2 not known, seen or done before. *A new way of doing things.* 3 different, changed. *We have a new science teacher.* The opposite of new is old.

**New Delhi** *noun* the capital of India.

**news** *noun* information about events that have recently happened.

**newsagent** *noun* a shop that sells newspapers, magazines etc.

**newspaper** *noun* printed sheets of folded paper containing news reports, articles, photographs, advertisements etc. and published daily or weekly.

**newt** *noun* an animal with short legs and a long tail that lives on land but lays its eggs in water. Newts are amphibians.

Newts are commonly found in ponds and damp places.

**New Year** *noun* the beginning of a year, starting on 1 January.

**New Zealand** *noun* a country in Australasia.

**New Zealander** *noun* a person who comes from New Zealand. **New Zealand** *adjective. New Zealand lamb.*

**next** *adjective* 1 the nearest. *She lives in the next house but one.* 2 the one immediately after. *I'll catch the next train.* **next** *adverb. What happens next?*

N

**Niamey** *noun* the capital of Niger.

**nib** *noun* the point at the end of a pen that touches the paper as you write.

**nibble** *verb* to eat something by biting very small bits of it.

**Nicaragua** *noun* a country in Central America.

**nice** *adjective* pleasant and kind. *What a nice girl she is.*

**nickel** *noun* 1 a silver-coloured metal that is mixed with other metals to make coins. 2 (US) a 5 cent coin.

**nickname** *noun* a special name that people call you instead of your real name.

**Nicosia** *noun* the capital of Cyprus.

**niece** *noun* the daughter of your brother or sister. *I love my niece very dearly.*

**Niger** *noun* a country in Africa.

**Nigeria** *noun* a country in Africa.

**Nigerian** *noun* a person who comes from Nigeria. **Nigerian** *adjective*. *Nigerian gold mines are very productive.*

**night** *noun* the time when it is dark, between sunset and sunrise. The opposite of night is day.

At night time you can see the Moon shining and the stars twinkling in the sky.

**nightfall** *noun* the end of the day and the beginning of the night.

**nightingale** *noun* a small brown bird whose beautiful singing is often heard at night.

**nightly** *adjective*, *adverb* taking place at night or every night. *The news is broadcast nightly at 9 o'clock.*

**nightmare** *noun* 1 a terrifying dream. 2 a frightening experience or situation. *Trying to shelter from the gunfire was a nightmare.*

**nil** *noun* nothing. 0. *The team won the match by three goals to nil.*

**nimble** *adjective* able to move quickly and easily, active.

**nip** (nip, nipping, nipped) *verb* 1 to give a small sharp bite, to pinch. *The dog nipped the postwoman on the ankle.* 2 to move quickly and for a short time. *I'll just nip out and buy a paper.*

**nipple** *noun* the small part that sticks out on each of a person's breasts and from which a baby sucks milk from its mother.

**nitrogen** *noun* a colourless, tasteless gas that makes up over three-quarters of the Earth's atmosphere and the air we breathe.

**WORD BUILDER**

*The sense of a word with the prefix 'non-' is usually easy to work out, if the meaning of the main or root word is clear. Here are examples: 'non-alcoholic', 'non-believer', 'non-existent', 'non-fiction' and 'non-stop'.*

The first inhabitants of America were nomads who walked there from Siberia.

**AMAZING FACT**

There are still many nomadic peoples in Africa and Asia such as the Bedouin tribes of North Africa and the Middle East and the Maasai of Kenya.

**noble** *adjective* 1 aristocratic, important and of high social rank. *The Bourbons are a noble French family.* 2 honest and of a good and generous nature. **nobility** *noun*. **nobleman, noblewoman** *noun*.

**nobody** *pronoun* not one person. *There's nobody at home.* **nobody** *noun* an unimportant person. *She's a nobody.*

**nocturnal** *adjective* concerned with or active during the night. *Nocturnal animals.*

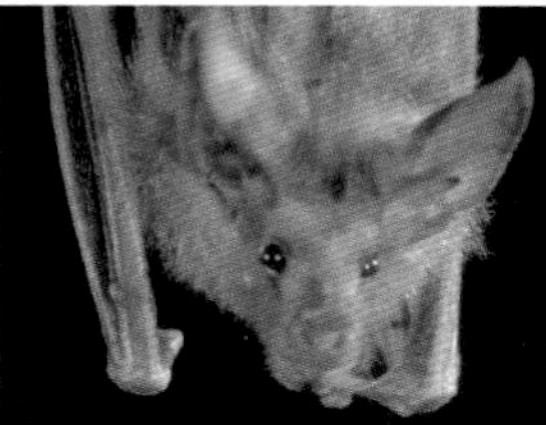

Bats are nocturnal creatures.

**nod** (nods, nodding, nodded) *verb* to bend your head up and down, perhaps as a sign of agreement or to say yes. **nod off** to half fall asleep by letting your head droop.

**noise** *noun* sound, usually one that is harsh, loud and unwanted. *Cats make a terrible yowling noise.* **noisily** *adverb*. The opposite of noise is silence.

**noisy** (noisier, nosiest) *adjective* making a lot of unpleasant noise, full of noise. *Noisy streets.*

**nomad** *noun* a member of a group of people without a permanent home who wander from place to place with their herds looking for pasture. **nomadic** *adjective*. *A nomadic way of life.*

**nominate** *verb* to propose that somebody would be the right person to do a job and should be a candidate in an election. To put forward somebody's name. *I nominate Tom Jones, the famous singer, as president of the club.* **nomination** *noun*.

**non-** *prefix* not, without. *Non-alcoholic drink is recommended for drivers.*

**none** *pronoun* not one, not any. *You've eaten all the biscuits and there are none left!*

**nonfiction** *noun* books about real events rather than novels, poetry, plays etc.

**nonsense** *noun* 1 foolish words that are meaningless. *You're talking utter nonsense.* 2 silly behaviour. *I'll stand no nonsense.*

**nonstop** *adjective* going on without stopping. *A nonstop flight to San Francisco.*

**noodles** *plural noun* long thin pieces of pasta used in soups etc.

**noon** *noun* midday, 12 o'clock in the middle of the day.

**noose** *noun* a loop in a rope that tightens as one end of the rope is pulled.

**nor** *conjunction* and not (used with neither). *I like neither spinach nor cabbage.*

**normal** *adjective* ordinary, as expected, usual. *She's a perfectly normal child.* **normality** *noun.*

**north** *noun* If you face the direction of the Sun as it rises in the morning, north is on your left. The opposite of north is south.

The magnetic needle of a compass always points to the north.

**North America** *noun* one of the Earth's seven continents.

**North Korea** *noun* a country in East Asia, officially called the Democratic People's Republic of Korea.

**northern** *adjective* in the north or of the north. *The lakes of northern Italy are beautiful in spring.*

**Northern Ireland** *noun* a country that is part of the United Kingdom.

**North Pole** *noun* the most northerly point on Earth. The north end of the Earth's axis.

**northward** *adjective*, *adverb* towards the north. *The troops marched northward.*

**Norway** *noun* a Scandinavian country in Europe.

**Norwegian** *noun* 1 a person who comes from Norway. 2 the language spoken in Norway. **Norwegian** *adjective. Norwegian fjords were created by glaciers.*

**nose** *noun* the part sticking out in the middle of your face that you use for breathing and smelling. **pay through the nose** pay too much.

**nostalgia** *noun* a feeling of sadness for the past and the happy times you had.

**nostril** *noun* one of the two holes at the end of your nose.

**notable** *adjective* famous or important. *Notable French cheeses.*

**notch** *noun* a small cut in the shape of a V.

**note** *verb* 1 to write something down as a reminder. *He noted down my telephone number.* 2 to call attention to something, to notice. *Note how long the leaves are.*

**GRAMMAR NOTE**

*Where you put 'not' can change the meaning of a sentence. 'He is trying not to win,' is different from 'He is not trying to win.'*

**SPELLING NOTE**

*'Nought' or 'naught'? 'Naught' means 'nothing', as in the phrase: 'It came to naught.' 'Nought' is used for the figure 0 or zero.*

**note** *noun* 1 a short letter. *A thank-you note.* 2 a few words you write down as a reminder of something. *He made a note of my address.* 3 a banknote or piece of paper money. *A £20 note.* 4 a single musical sound or a symbol representing the sound.

These notes, composed long ago, are the beginning of a popular piece of music.

**notebook** *noun* a small book in which to write notes. *He scribbled in his notebook.*

**noted** *adjective* well-known.

**nothing** *pronoun* no thing, not any thing. *She says she has nothing to wear!*

**notice** *noun* 1 a written message or announcement that is put in a public place so everybody can read it. *The notice on the wall says: Private.* 2 attention. *Pay no notice to what he says.* 3 warning. *The water may be cut off without notice.* **hand in your notice** to tell your employer that you intend to leave your job.

**notice** *verb* to become aware of, to see or hear. *She noticed a big crack in the wall.*

**noticeable** *adjective* easily seen or noticed. *There's been a noticeable improvement in your handwriting.*

**noticeboard** *noun* a piece wood or cork etc. to which notices can be attached, usually with drawing pins.

We always pin our holiday postcards to the noticeboard.

**notify** (notifies, notifying, notified) *verb* to tell somebody formally about something. *You should notify the post office when you move.* **notification** *noun. We had official notification to move.*

**notion** *noun* a general idea or vague belief. *I have a notion that he's gone to India.*

**notorious** *adjective* well known for being bad or unpleasant, infamous.

**Nouakchott** *noun* the capital of Mauritania.

**nought** *noun* (say nawt) the figure 0.

**novel** *noun* a long written story about imaginary people and events.

**novel** *adjective* new but different and original. *A novel design.*

**novelty** *noun* something new, unusual and different. *Gifts and novelties.*

**November** *noun* the eleventh month of the year. November has 30 days.

**novice** *noun* 1 a beginner without any experience. 2 a person who is training to be a monk or nun.

**now** *adverb* 1 the present time. *I am busy now.* 2 immediately and with no delay. *Do it right now, please!*

**nowadays** *adverb* at this present time. *Few people wear hats nowadays.*

**nozzle** *noun* the narrow part at the end of a pipe, tube or hose through which a gas, liquid or powder is forced out.

**nuclear** *adjective* to do with the nucleus, especially that of an atom, and the power created by splitting its nucleus. *Nuclear energy, nuclear missile, nuclear reactor.*

**nucleus** (nuclei) *noun* the central part or core of something such as an atom or a living cell.

The nucleus is found at the centre of an atom. Negatively charged electrons whirl around it.

**nude** *adjective* naked, not wearing clothes. **nude** *noun* a person not wearing clothes. **nudity** *noun.*

**nudge** *verb* to gently poke or push somebody with your elbow.

**nugget** *noun* a rough lump of precious metal. *A gold nugget.*

**nuisance** *noun* somebody or something that is annoying. *It's a nuisance I forgot to bring the tapes.*

**numb** *adjective* unable to feel anything. *My fingers are numb with cold.*

**Nuku'alofa** *noun* the capital of Tonga.

**number** *noun* 1 a word or numeral we use for counting. One, two, three. 1, 2,3. 2 a quantity or amount. *She has a large number of CDs.* **number** *verb* 1 count. *The flock numbered 500 sheep.* 2 to put a number on. *The pages are numbered.*

**numeral** *noun* a symbol or group of symbols you use to write a number. 5, 10, 12 are Arabic numerals and V, X, X11 and C are Roman numerals.

**numerate** *adjective* able to understand numbers and do calculations. **numeracy** *noun. Literacy and numeracy.*

**AMAZING FACT**

November comes from a Latin word meaning 'ninth' because it was the ninth month of the Roman calendar.

**AMAZING FACT**

The system of writing numbers that we now use, Arabic numerals, actually originated in India. Most Arabian countries use completely different symbols to represent numbers.

**numerical** *adjective* concerning numbers. *Numerical order.*

**numerous** *adjective* many. *He made numerous visits to the hospital.* The opposite of numerous is few.

**numismatics** *plural noun* the study of coins and medals.

**nun** *noun* a member of a religious community of women who live, pray and work together in a building called a convent or an abbey.

**nurse** *noun* a person who has been trained to look after ill, injured or old people, especially in hospital. **nurse** *verb. Ned nursed his dad when he was ill.*

**nursery** *noun* 1 a place where young children can go to play during the day while their parents are away. 2 a child's bedroom and playroom in a home. 3 a place where plants are grown to be sold.

**nursery rhyme** *noun* a short, simple poem that children like to recite.

**nut** *noun* 1 a fruit with a hard shell and a soft, seed (nut) inside that you can eat. *Brazil nut, hazelnut, walnut.* 2 a piece of metal with a hole through it for screwing on to a bolt. Nuts and bolts are used for holding pieces of metal etc. together. **do your nut** (slang) suddenly to become very angry. *She absolutely did her nut when I broke the mirror.*

**nutcracker** *noun* an instrument for cracking the shells of nuts.

**nutritious** *noun* nourishing and good for you as food. *We try to serve three nutritious meals every day.*

Nutritious foods include fruit, vegetables, wholemeal bread, fish, cheese and eggs.

**nutty** *adjective* 1 tasting of nuts or filled with nuts. *A nutty fruitcake.* 2 (slang) foolish. *I think she's as nutty as a fruitcake.*

**nylon** *noun* a strong artificial fibre made of chemicals used in making clothes, ropes, brushes etc. *Nylon stockings.*

# Oo

oak *noun* a large deciduous tree with hard wood. The nut of an oak tree is called an acorn. *Mighty oaks from small acorns.*

**OAP** short for old age pensioner, an old person who receives a pension.

**oar** *noun* a long pole with a flat part at the end (the blade), used for rowing a boat.

**oasis** (oases) *noun* an area in a desert where there is water and where plants grow. *At last we arrived at the oasis, where we ate dates and drank mint tea.*

**oath** *noun* a serious promise to tell the truth, be faithful etc. *I swore an oath on the Bible to tell the truth.*

**oatmeal** *noun* oats that have been ground to make porridge etc.

**oats** *plural noun* a type of cereal grain, used as food. *Porridge oats.*

Porridge is a favourite breakfast food in Scotland, where oats grow well.

**obedient** *adjective* obeying, willing to do what you are told to do. *The children were brought up to be very obedient.*

**obese** *adjective* (say oh-**beez**) very fat. **obesity** *noun.*

**obey** *verb* to do what somebody asks or tells you to do. *A sheepdog always obeys commands.* **obedience** *noun.*

**obituary** *noun* an announcement of somebody's death, usually in a newspaper and with a short account of the person's life and achievements.

**object** *noun* (say **ob**-ject) 1 a non-living thing that you can see and touch. 2 the purpose or thing you are trying to achieve, aim. *The object of the meeting is to choose a new team.* 3 in grammar, the person or thing towards which the action of a verb is directed. 'Flower' is the object in the sentence 'John picked a flower.'

**WORD HISTORY**

*The shape of the letter O comes from an ancient Egyptian symbol for the eye. Its sound comes from 'ayin', a Semitic word for the eye. The Greeks called it 'omicron'.*

**object** *verb* (say ob-**ject**) to say that you dislike or disapprove of something. *He objected to the woman's rude behaviour.*

**objectionable** *adjective* disagreeable. *What an objectionable man!*

**objective** *noun* the aim or goal you are trying to achieve. **objective** *adjective* based on facts and not influenced by feelings, opinions or prejudice. *She wrote a completely objective report on the causes of the famine in the Sudan.*

**obligation** *noun* something that you have to do, a duty. **obligatory** *adjective. Answering these questions is obligatory.*

**oblige** *verb* 1 to make somebody do something, to force or compel. *She was obliged to leave the room.* 2 to help or do a favour for somebody. *Please oblige me by closing the door.*

**obliging** *adjective* willing to help others. *A very obliging young man gave me his seat.*

**oblique** *adjective* 1 sloping. 2 indirect. *The question seemed rather oblique to me.*

**obliterate** *verb* to destroy something completely. *Bombs obliterated the town.*

Fireman worked among the rubble of the town that had been all but obliterated by the bombing.

**oblong** *noun* a shape with four sides with two parallel long sides and two parallel short sides.

**obnoxious** *adjective* very unpleasant. *An obnoxious smell wafted out of the school dustbins.*

**oboe** *noun* a woodwind instrument.

Ann clapped loudly when the oboe solo ended.

**obscene** *adjective* (say ob-**seen**) indecent and sexually offensive. *I will not tolerate obscene behaviour.* **obscenity** *noun.*

**obscure** *adjective* 1 not well known. *An obscure book by Dickens.* 2 not clear or easy to see or understand. *An obscure problem.* **obscurity** *noun.* **obscure** *verb. The pillar obscured my view of the stage.*

**AMAZING FACT**

'Obscure' comes from a Latin word meaning 'dark'.

O

**observatory** *noun* a building with large telescopes for observing the stars, planets and the skies.

From my observatory I can watch the night sky and record my sightings of the planets.

**observe** *verb* 1 to watch somebody or something carefully. 2 to see and notice something. 3 to obey something such as a law or custom. *Jews observe the festival of Hanukka in December.* 4 to remark. *Tim observed that the post was late.* **observant** *adjective* quick at observing things. **observation** *noun.*

**obsolete** *adjective* out of date and no longer used. *This computer is obsolete.*

**obstacle** *noun* something that blocks the way and makes it difficult for you to do something. A hindrance.

**obstinate** *adjective* refusing to obey or do what somebody wants, stubborn. *An obstinate child.* **obstinacy** *noun.*

**obtain** *verb* to get something by buying, taking, being given etc. **obtainable** *adjective. Tickets are obtainable in the foyer.*

**obtuse angle** *noun* an angle between 90 and 180 degrees. An obtuse angle is greater than a right angle.

An obtuse angle is bigger than a right angle.

**obverse** *noun* the side of a coin showing the head or principal design. The opposite of obverse (heads) is reverse (tails).

**obvious** *adjective* easy to see and understand, clear. *It's obvious to me that she's broken her finger.*

**occasion** *noun* a particular time when something happens. *Weddings and birthdays are important occasions.*

**SPELLING NOTE**

*'Occurred', 'occurrence' and 'occurring' are frequently misspelled. Note the 'cc', the 'rr' and the '–ence' (not '–ance').*

**occasional** *adjective* happening sometimes but not regularly.

**occupation** *noun* 1 the work a person does for a living, a job. 2 a hobby or something you like doing in your spare time. 3 the invasion and taking control of a town or country by an army. *The German occupation of France during World War II.*

**occupy** (occupies, occupying, occupied) *verb* 1 to live in. *Who occupies the house next door?* 2 to keep busy. 3 to invade and capture an enemy town, country etc. **occupant, occupier** *noun.*

**occur** (occurs, occurring, occurred) *verb* to happen. *Thunder storms occur mainly in summer.* **occur to** to suddenly think about something. **occurrence** *noun.*

**ocean** *noun* any of the great masses of salt water that surround the continents.

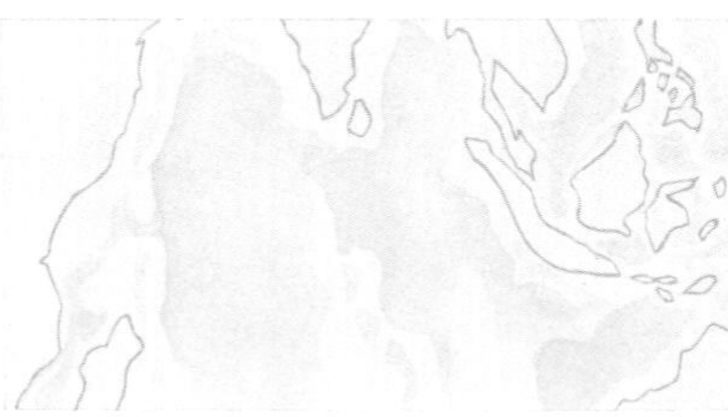

Some of the world's earliest sea journeys took place across the Pacific Ocean.

**o'clock** *adverb* 'of the clock', an expression we use when telling the time.

**octagon** *noun* a flat shape with eight sides. **octagonal** *adjective.*

**octave** *noun* in music, the eight notes of any scale.

**October** *noun* the tenth month of the year. October has 31 days.

**octopus** (octopuses) *noun* a sea creature with a round body and eight tentacles.

The octopus is one of the Greeks' favourite foods. It can be fried gently in olive oil until tender, and served with tomatoes and garlic.

**odd** *adjective* 1 strange, not ordinary. 2 of numbers, not even and not divisible by two. Three, five and 37 are odd numbers. 3 one of a pair and not matching. *An odd sock.* 4 different. *Odd jobs.* 5 **odds** chances or probability of something happening (especially in gambling). **odd one out** the one that is different.

**ode** *noun* a poem, often addressed to somebody or to something.

**odious** *adjective* very unpleasant.

**AMAZING FACT**

The main defence of the octopus is its ability to squirt a cloud of ink around itself so that it can escape unseen.

O

**odour** *noun* a strong smell, often an unpleasant one.

**odourless** *adjective* without smell.

**offend** *verb* 1 to upset a person's feelings. 2 to do wrong or commit a crime. **offence** *noun. Drink-driving is a serious offence.* **offensive** *adjective. Offensive behaviour.*

**offhand** *adjective* 1 unthinking and casual, rude. *An offhand manner.* 2 impromptu and without preparation. *I can't tell you the answer offhand.*

**offer** *verb* 1 to say that you are willing to do something. 2 to ask somebody if they would like something. To hold out. *She offered him a glass of juice.* 3 to say how much you are willing to give for something. *Harry offered her £100 for the clock.* **offer** *noun.*

**office** *noun* 1 a place where people work and where a business is carried on. Offices usually contain desks, telephones, computers etc. 2 an important position. *The office of mayor.*

The new office was ready for the company secretary to move into.

**officer** *noun* a senior person in the armed forces or police who is in charge of other people. *Promoted to the rank of officer.*

**official** *adjective* coming from or done by people in authority. *An official inquiry.* **official** *noun* a person with a position of authority. *Government officials.*

**offspring** *noun* the children or young of humans and animals.

**often** *adverb* frequently, again and again. *We often go swimming in the evening.*

**ogre** *noun* a frightening and cruel giant in fairy stories.

**oil** *noun* different kinds of smooth, thick liquids that do not mix with water and which burn easily. You can use oil as a fuel for heating and cooking and for making machines run smoothly. **oil** *verb.*

**ointment** *noun* a cream that you put on your skin to heal cuts and scratches.

**OK** or **okay** *adjective, adverb* all right.

**old** *adjective* 1 having lived, existed, or lasted for a long time. 2 having lived for a certain amount of time. *Owen is 11 years old.* 3 belonging to an earlier time. *My old geography teacher.* 4 worn out and no longer new. *Old clothes.* The opposite of old is new.

**AMAZING FACT**

The first Olympic Games were held at Olympia in Greece in 776BC. The modern Olympic Games began in 1896.

**SPELLING NOTE**

*Try not to confuse 'official', meaning 'authorized' with 'officious', meaning 'meddling' or 'bossy'. So we can talk about 'the official opening of a library' and 'an officious librarian'.*

**old-fashioned** *adjective* out of date, belonging to the past.

**olive** *noun* a small black or green oval fruit that can be crushed to produce olive oil used in cooking. Olive trees grow in Mediterranean countries.

**Olympic Games** *plural noun* international competitions in sports held in a different country every four years.

**Oman** *noun* a country in Southwest Asia.

Oman lies on the Arabian Sea and exports fish as well as petroleum.

**omelette** *noun* a food made by beating eggs together and frying them, often with a savoury filling.

**omen** *noun* a sign or warning of good or evil in the future. *Some people believe that putting shoes on a table is a bad omen.*

**ominous** *adjective* suggesting that something bad is about to happen, threatening. *Those dark clouds look very ominous to me.*

**omit** (omits, omitting, omitted) *verb* 1 to leave something out. *Your name has been omitted from the list.* 2 to fail to do something. *She omitted some important details.* **omission** *noun.*

**omnivore** *noun* an animal that eats both plants and flesh. **omnivorous** *adjective.*

**once** *adverb* 1 at one time in the past. 2 happening one time only. *She comes here once a day.* **once** *conjunction* when. *Once you understand it, you'll never forget it.*

**onion** *noun* a strong-tasting, rounded bulb eaten as a vegetable.

When Aunt Julia cuts up onions, she always cries.

**on-line** *adjective* a service etc. with a direct connection to and interaction with a computer. *On-line shopping will soon be a reality for many homes.*

**onlooker** *noun* somebody watching something happen without taking part, a spectator. *The onlookers cheered.*

**only** *adverb* 1 no more than. *It'll only take me a minute to get ready.* 2 just. *She only wants to play for an hour.* **only** *adjective* no others of the same kind. *This is the only watch I have.* **only** *conjunction* but. *I'd love to come, only I can't.* **only child** a child with no brothers or sisters.

**ooze** *verb* to flow slowly through a narrow opening. *Mud oozed under the door.*

**opaque** *adjective* If something is opaque, you cannot see through it and it does not let light through.

**open** *adjective* 1 not shut so people or things can go through, not covered. 2 ready for business. *The shop is open.* 3 honest. *She was very open about her doubts.* **open** *verb* 1 to make open or no longer shut, to become open and no longer shut. *Omar opened the door and let in the cat.* 2 to begin. *The story opens during the Civil War.*

**opening** *noun* 1 a space. *An opening in the fence.* 2 the beginning of something. *The official opening of the library is next week.* 3 an opportunity. *An opening into the music business would be a dream come true.*

**opera** *noun* a play with music in which the words are sung. **operatic** *adjective*.

**GRAMMAR NOTE**

*Be sure to place 'only' in the right place in a sentence to express exactly what you mean. 'He drinks beer only on Saturday' is not the same as 'He only drinks beer on Saturday' or 'Only he drinks beer on Saturday.'*

Joan was an overnight success at the opera.

**operate** *verb* 1 to make something work. *Can you operate this machine?* 2 to cut a part of somebody's body to heal a disease or repair an injury. *The surgeon had to operate on Dick's broken leg.* **operation** *noun*.

**opinion** *noun* what you think or believe about something. *What is your opinion of the Scottish team?*

**opinionated** *adjective* stubbornly believing that your opinions are right.

**opossum** *noun* a small tree-dwelling American marsupial.

The opossum has strong feet and claws for climbing trees.

**AMAZING FACT**

The opposum is North America's only marsupial. It climbs trees and uses its tail to hold on.

When opposums are in danger, they pretend to be dead. When someone acts as though they have been hurt but haven't, we say they are 'playing possum'.

**opponent** *noun* somebody who is against you in a contest or fight etc. *Sam outwitted his opponents in the debate.*

Audrey was the chess champion, but she found Steven a formidable opponent.

**opportunity** *noun* a good time to do something. *Now is your opportunity to learn German.*

**oppose** *verb* to be against and try to prevent something. *The village opposed the building of a motorway.* **opposition** *noun*.

**opposite** *noun* something that is completely different in every way from another thing. Happy is the opposite of sad. **opposite** *adjective* 1 different. *They drove in opposite directions.* 2 facing, on the other side. *They stood on opposite sides of the street.*

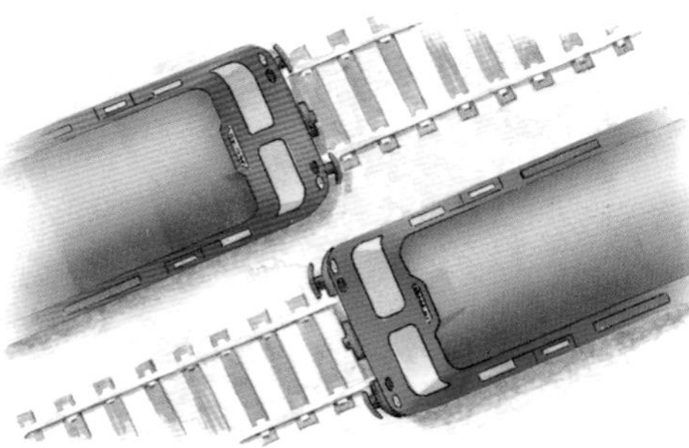

The trains were travelling in opposite directions.

**oppress** *verb* to govern or treat people harshly and unjustly. **oppression** *noun*. *Albania suffered years of oppression.* **oppressor** *noun*.

**opt** *verb* to choose. *We opted to go skiing.* **option** *noun*. *I have two options, to go or to stay.* **opt out** to decide not to take part.

**optical** *adjective* relating to the eyes and eyesight. *An optical illusion.*

**optician** *noun* a person who sells glasses and who is trained to test people's eyesight.

**optimism** *noun* the belief that only the best will happen and all will end successfully. **optimist** *noun*. *She is always the cheerful optimist.* **optimistic** *adjective*. The opposite of optimistic is pessimistic.

**optional** *adjective* not compulsory, that you can choose or not choose.

**oral** *adjective* relating to the mouth. *Oral hygiene.* 2 spoken not written. *An oral test.*

**orang-utan** *noun* a large Indonesian ape with shaggy reddish fur and long arms.

**orange** *noun* 1 a round juicy fruit with a reddish-yellow skin (peel). 2 the colour of this fruit. **orange** *adjective*.

**orator** *noun* a skilled public speaker.

**orbit** *noun* an imaginary path followed by an object such as a spacecraft or planet as it moves around a planet or star. **orbit** *verb*. *The Moon orbits Earth once a month*.

**orchard** *noun* a piece of land on which a lot of fruit trees are grown.

AMAZING FACT

The word 'orang-utan' comes from a Malaysian word meaning 'wild man' or 'man of the forest'.

**organ** *noun* a part inside the body that does a particular job. The heart, kidneys, liver and lungs are organs.

**organ** *noun* a musical instrument with a keyboard and pipes of different length through which air is pumped to produce sounds. *Rousing chords from the organ*.

**organic** *adjective* grown without using chemicals or pesticides. *Organic farming*.

**organism** *noun* any living animal or plant.

We used to love helping with the apple-picking in Grandma's orchard.

**orchestra** *noun* (say **or**-kess-trah) a large group of people who perform music together, playing different instruments. **orchestral** *adjective*.

**orchid** *noun* (say **or**-kid) one of many varieties of plant that usually has brightly coloured, strangely shaped flowers.

**ordeal** *noun* a difficult, unpleasant or dangerous experience.

**order** *noun* 1 a command given by somebody in control telling people what to do. *The officer gave his orders*. 2 a sequence or a way things are arranged. *Alphabetical order*. 3 neatly arranged, tidy. *He put his papers in order*. **order** *verb* 1 to tell somebody firmly to do something. 2 (in a restaurant) to ask for something to be brought to you, to ask for something to be obtained. *We ordered pie and chips*. **out of order** not working, broken.

**ordinary** *adjective* not special or interesting. Usual. *A very ordinary sort of guy*.

**ore** *noun* rock or earth containing metal that can be extracted.

Copper, a reddish-gold metal, is extracted from copper ore.

WORD HISTORY

*The orchestra in ancient Greek theatres was a 'dancing place', where dancers and musicians performed in an area between the stage and the audience. Much later the musicians who played there themselves became known as the orchestra.*

**organization** *noun* 1 a group of people working together, a club, business etc. 2 the act of organizing something so it runs smoothly. *The organization of the timetable*.

**organize** *verb* 1 to plan and prepare something in an orderly way. *Wendy organized a party for her brother's birthday*. 2 to put things in order. **organizer** *noun*.

**oriental** *adjective* relating to countries of the Far East such as China, India and Japan.

**origami** *noun* the Japanese art of folding paper into beautiful shapes.

Kylie made a beautiful origami swan.

**origin** *noun* 1 the start or source of something and why it began. *What is the origin of Halloween?* 2 ancestry or where somebody or something came from. *She's of Jamaican origin*.

**original** *adjective* 1 the first of its kind to exist or to be made. *The original palace was burned down*. 2 not an imitation. *Original paintings*. 3 different and imaginative. *An original design*.

**originate** *verb* to start to exist, to have origins. *Cricket originated in England.*

**ornament** *noun* a small, pretty object that you wear or put on a shelf or table as a decoration. *Ornaments for a Christmas tree.* **ornamental** *adjective. Ornamental gardens.*

One of Marcia's favourite ornaments was the ginger jar Fred had brought back from his travels in China.

**ornithology** *noun* the scientific study of birds. **ornithologist** *noun.*

**orphan** *noun* a child whose parents are both dead. *Orphans of the war.*

**orphanage** *noun* a place where orphans are looked after. *Romanian orphanages.*

**orthodontist** *noun* a dentist who specializes in straightening and adjusting irregular or crooked teeth.

**orthodox** *adjective* what is accepted and generally thought to be right by most people. Believing in traditional ideas. *She has very orthodox views.* **orthodoxy** *noun.*

**oscillate** *noun* to swing backwards and forwards like a pendulum. **oscillation** *noun.*

**Oslo** *noun* the capital of Norway.

**ostrich** *noun* a very large bird with long legs and a long neck. Ostriches can run very fast but cannot fly. They come from Africa.

Ostriches are now being farmed in Britain for their meat, which tastes a little like venison.

**other** *adjective* 1 different, not the same as. *The other way is shorter.* 2 opposite. *On the other side of the road.* **other** (others) *pronoun* the rest, more. *Jim's here, but where are the others?*

**otherwise** *conjunction* or else. *Eat your food, otherwise it will get cold.* 2 except for that. *It was cold, otherwise we had a good time.* **otherwise** *adverb* differently. *He's naughty and cannot behave otherwise.*

**ought** *verb* must, should.

**Ottawa** *noun* the capital of Canada.

**WORD HISTORY**

*'Ounce' comes from the Latin word 'uncia', which means a twelfth part of a pound weight. (The Roman pound consisted of 12 ounces).*

**AMAZING FACT**

The ostrich is the world's largest living bird. It cannot fly but is the fastest creature on two legs and is capable of running 45 mph. Ostrich eggs are the largest laid by any bird – one is equivalent to about 40 hen's eggs.

**otter** *noun* a small animal with brown fur that lives near rivers and eats fish. Otters have webbed feet to help them swim.

**Ouagadougou** *noun* the capital of Burkina Faso.

**ounce** *noun* a measure of weight equal to 28.3 grammes. There are 16 ounces to a pound. *An ounce of tobacco.*

**out-** *prefix* 1 surpassing, more. *Outclassed.* 2 external, outside. *Outhouse.* 3 longer, beyond. *Outlive.*

**outback** *noun* the huge unpopulated inland areas of Australia.

We travelled into the outback and lived rough for several weeks.

**outbreak** *noun* a sudden appearance or start of something. *An outbreak of flu.*

**outcome** *noun* the result. *What's the outcome of the competition?*

**outdoor** *adjective* in the open air. *Outdoor activities.* **outdoors** *adverb, noun. In summer we eat outdoors.* The opposite of outdoors is indoors.

**outer space** *noun* everything beyond the Earth's atmosphere. The universe.

This is a spiral galaxy way beyond planet Earth in outer space.

**outfit** *noun* a set of clothes, especially for a particular occasion. *Masie wanted a new outfit for the wedding.*

**outgrow** (outgrows, outgrowing, outgrew, outgrown) *verb* to grow too large or too old for something. *He has outgrown his shoes.*

**outing** *noun* a day-trip or short journey somewhere for pleasure. *They went on a works outing to the seaside once a year.*

**outlaw** *noun* a criminal who has not been caught and is hiding. **outlaw** *verb* to make something illegal.

O

**outline** *noun* 1 a line around the edge of something that shows its shape. *Mike drew the outline of the building.* 2 the main points rather than a detailed description of something. *An outline of the play's plot.* **outline** *verb. She outlined her plans.*

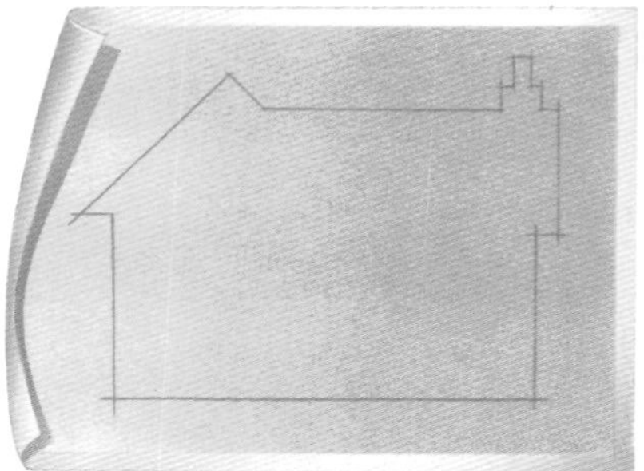

Carl drew the outline of his house on a piece of paper to show the architect.

**outlook** *noun* 1 a view. *A room with a fine outlook.* 2 a person's general attitude or way of looking at things. *Jennie has a cheerful outlook on life.* 3 what is likely to happen. *The weather outlook is fine.*

**output** *noun* 1 the amount of something produced in a factory, by a person etc. 2 data produced by a computer.

**outrage** *noun* a feeling of anger about a shocking or violent act. **outrageous** *adjective* shocking. *Outrageous behaviour.*

**outright** *adjective* complete, absolute. *She's the outright winner.* **outright** *adverb* instantly. *I told him the bad news outright.*

**outset** *noun* the beginning. *I knew from the outset she'd win.*

**outside** *noun* the exterior or outer part of something, the surface of something farthest from the middle. **outside** *adjective, adverb, preposition. The outside lane of the motorway.* The opposite of outside is inside.

We were warm and snug sitting by the fire, but outside it was raining.

**outskirts** *plural noun* the parts around the outer edges of a town.

**outspoken** *adjective* saying clearly and strongly what you think even if you offend people. *An outspoken critic of the system.*

**outstanding** *adjective* 1 excellent. *An outstanding performance.* 2 not paid. *An outstanding bill.*

**AMAZING FACT**

The saying 'Out of the frying pan and into the fire', meaning to go from a bad situation to a worse one, was originally 'To go from the smoke to the fire' in Greek.

**WORD BUILDER**

*Dozens of new words have been made (and can be made) with the prefix 'over–'. Here are a few: 'over-anxious', 'over-boil', 'over-charge', 'overcook', 'overeat', 'overload' and 'over-optimistic'.*

**outwit** (outwits, outwitting, outwitted) *verb* to be too clever for somebody.

**oval** *noun* egg-shaped. **oval** *adjective. Rugby balls are oval.*

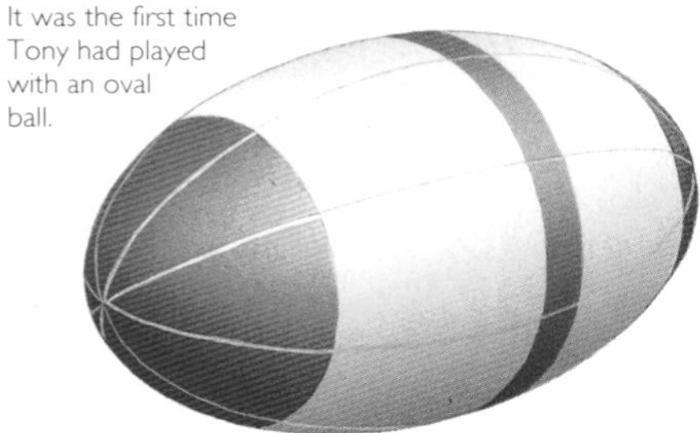

It was the first time Tony had played with an oval ball.

**oven** *noun* the box-like part of a cooker in which you roast or bake food.

**over** *preposition* 1 above, higher. *She hung the picture over her bed.* 2 across. *The dog jumped over the stream.* 3 more than. *She's got over a dozen pairs of shoes.* 4 on top of. *He laid blankets over the bed.*

**over** *adverb* 1 ended. *The ordeal is over.* 2 down from being upright. *I fell over.* 3 upside down. *Flip the pancake over.* 4 not used, remaining. *Any tea left over?* **over and over again** many, many times.

**over-** *prefix* 1 excessive. *Overconfident.* 2 above, in a higher position. *Overlord.* 3 movement or position above. *Overhang.* 4 extra. *Overcoat.*

**overalls** *plural noun* a one-piece garment that you wear over your ordinary clothes to keep them clean when doing a messy job.

**overboard** *adverb* over a ship's side and into the water. *He jumped overboard to rescue the child.* **go overboard** to become too enthusiastic about something.

**overcast** *adjective* (of the sky) cloudy and dark. *The sky was overcast and it looked very much like rain.*

**overcome** (overcomes, overcoming, overcame, overcome) *verb* 1 to conquer or defeat, to get the better of. *She has overcome her fear of flying.* 2 to be affected by very strong emotions. *He was overcome with sadness when he heard the news.*

**overdue** *adjective* behind time, late. *The plane is overdue.*

**overflow** *verb* to spill or run over the edges of a container. *The river overflowed its banks and flooded the meadow.*

**overhaul** *verb* to examine something carefully to see if it needs repairing. **overhaul** *noun. She gave her bike a thorough overhaul.*

**overhead** *adjective, adverb* above you. *An overhead railway.*

**overheads** *plural noun* all the regular costs involved in running a business such as lighting, heating, insurance and advertising.

**overhear** (overhears, overhearing, overheard) *verb* to hear accidentally what people are saying when they do not know you are listening.

**overlap** (overlaps, overlapping, overlapped) *verb* to partly cover or lie across something else. *Roof tiles overlap.*

David fixed on the roof tiles so they overlapped and no rain could get inside.

**overlook** *verb* 1 to fail to see or do something, to not notice. *You have overlooked how much it will cost!* 2 to forgive and not punish somebody. *I'll overlook your mistake.* 3 to have a view above something. *Your rooms are at the front of the hotel and overlook the sea.*

**overrated** *adjective* not so good as most people say. *An overrated film.*

**overrun** (overruns, overrunning, overran) *verb* 1 to spread over; to swarm. *The kitchen was overrun with cockroaches.* 2 to go beyond the time allowed. *The TV programme overran by ten minutes.*

**overseas** *adjective*, *adverb* abroad, across the sea. *Overseas visitors.*

**overtake** (overtakes, overtaking, overtook, overtaken) *verb* to pass another moving person or vehicle. *He overtook the tractor.*

The rivals were running neck and neck, but then Ayrton overtook as they began the last lap.

**overthrow** (overthrows, overthrowing, overthrew, overthrown) *verb* to defeat or cause something to fall. *The French revolution overthrew the monarchy.* **overthrow** *noun*.

**overtime** *noun* extra time spent working outside normal working hours.

**overture** *noun* a short piece of music at the start of a ballet etc. that sets the mood.

**AMAZING FACT**

There are over 500 different species of owl. Most owls live in trees but some species actually live in burrows in the ground.

**WORD HISTORY**

*'Ozone' comes from the Greek word for 'to smell', 'ozein'. The name was first given to the gas by the German chemist C.F. Schönbein in 1840 because of its extraordinary smell.*

**overturn** *verb* to fall over or cause something to fall over so that it is upside down. *The lorry crashed and overturned.*

**overwhelm** *verb* 1 to defeat completely, to crush. 2 to cover completely. *The waves overwhelmed the boat and the twins bailed out frantically.* 3 to put too great a load on. *Paul was overwhelmed with work.*

**owe** *verb* to have to pay or give something to somebody, especially money that you have borrowed. *I owe you £6 for the tickets.*

**owl** *noun* a bird of prey with a flat face and large eyes that hunts for small animals such as mice at night. *A wise old owl.*

Owls often nest in hollow trees. They fly slowly and almost silently, very close to the ground, so they can spot their prey in the dark without being heard.

**own** *verb* to have something that belongs to you, to possess. *Who owns this skateboard?* **own** *adjective* belonging only to you. *Meg has her own computer.* **owner** *noun*. **on your own** by yourself and without help, alone. *He cooked the meal all on his own.*

**ox** (oxen) *noun* a bull that is used in some countries for pulling carts, ploughs etc.

**oxygen** *noun* a colourless, tasteless gas that makes up about a fifth of the Earth's atmosphere. All life on Earth needs oxygen to live. *Astronauts need to take a supply of oxygen with them into outer space.*

**oyster** *noun* an edible sea creature that lives inside two shells (a bivalve). Some oysters produce a pearl inside their shell. *David loves oysters and all other shellfish.*

**ozone** *noun* a gas that is a form of oxygen with three atoms instead of two.

**ozone-friendly** *adjective* not harmful to the layer of ozone around the Earth. *An ozone-friendly aerosol.*

**ozone layer** *noun* a layer or belt of ozone high in the atmosphere that protects the Earth by absorbing harmful rays from the Sun. *The ozone layer is becoming depleted, and as a result, many more people who don't wear protective cream in the sun are contracting skin cancer.*

# Pp

**pace** *noun* 1 walking or running speed, or the speed at which something happens. *Work at your own pace.* 2 a single step when walking or running. *She took three paces forwards.* **keep pace with** to go forward at the same rate. *He kept pace with the latest developments.* **pace** *verb* 1 to walk with regular steps. 2 to set the speed, especially for a runner in a race.

**pacemaker** *noun* 1 a person who sets the speed that others in a race try to keep up with. 2 a machine that is used to keep a weak heart beating.

**pacifist** *noun* a person who believes that all wars are wrong and who refuses to fight.

**pacify** (pacifies, pacifying, pacified) *verb* to make calm or quiet.

**pack** *verb* 1 to put things into a box, bag or case for carrying, storing or moving them. 2 to crowd together, to fit into a space. *The cinema was packed with children.* 3 When you pack something in something, you wrap it up to protect it. *The bowl was packed in newspaper.* **pack in** 1 to stop doing something. *She's packed her job in.* 2 to do a lot of things in a short time. *We packed in a lot of sightseeing.* **pack off** to send somebody away. **send somebody packing** to make somebody leave, especially a person you don't want to be with. **pack up** 1 to pack your belongings. 2 to finish work. *What time do you pack up?* 3 to stop working. *The computer has packed up.*

Jane wrapped the china in newspaper and packed it carefully in the box.

**pack** *noun* 1 a number of things wrapped or tied together for carrying. *He carried food in a pack on his back.* 2 a group of wild animals, especially wolves or dogs. 3 a group of unpleasant people or a number of bad things. *A pack of lies.* 4 a group of Cub Scouts or Brownies. 5 a complete set of cards. 6 a packet of things. *Alan bought a pack of cigarettes.*

**WORD HISTORY**

*The shape of the letter P comes from the ancient Egyptian symbol for mouse. The sound comes from 'P', a Semitic word for mouse.*

**DID YOU KNOW**

*An artificial pacemaker that helps to keep a person's heart beating is operated by a tiny battery. It replaces a small section of the natural heart muscle, which we also call the pacemaker, that regulates our heartbeat.*

**package** *noun* 1 a number of things packed together, a parcel. 2 an offer that includes a number of things. **package** *verb. Juice is packaged in cartons.*

**package holiday** *noun* a complete holiday at a fixed price, including travel, accommodation and food. *We went on a package holiday to Spain.*

**packet** *noun* a small parcel.

**pact** *noun* an agreement. *The two countries signed a trading pact.*

**pad** *noun* 1 anything filled with soft material used to protect, clean or stuff something. *Skaters wear knee pads.* 2 a number of sheets of paper fixed together at the top or the side that can be torn out. *A writing pad.* 3 the place where a helicopter or rocket takes off. 4 the soft part of an animal's paw. 5 a room, especially in a flat. *We went back to his pad to watch TV.* **pad** (pads, padding, padded) *verb* to put a pad in or on something. *The jacket has padded shoulders.*

John wore protective pads on his knees and elbows while rollerblading.

**padding** *noun* soft material on or inside something to make it soft.

**paddle** *noun* a short pole with a flat blade on one or both ends for moving a small boat in water. **paddle** *verb* 1 to move a boat through water. *They paddled really hard in their canoes.* 2 to walk about barefoot in shallow water.

**paddock** *noun* a field near a house or stables where horses are kept.

**paddy field** *noun* a field where rice is grown. *The paddy fields of China.*

**padlock** *noun* a lock that can be put on and taken off, for use on a door, box or locker. **padlock** *verb. He padlocked the shed.*

**paediatrician** (say pee-dee-uh-**tri**-shun) *noun* a doctor who specializes in children's illnesses. **paediatric** *adjective.*

**pagan** (say **pay**-gun) *adjective, noun* not believing in the main religions of the world.

**page** *noun* a piece of paper in a book, newspaper or magazine.

**page** *noun* 1 a servant, usually a boy, dressed in a uniform who works in a hotel. 2 a boy who attends a bride at a wedding.

**page** *verb* to call the name of a person, especially in a hotel or hospital. *Can you page Mr Smith?*

**pageant** *noun* 1 a show, usually outdoors, about the history of a place and its people. 2 a ceremony with a procession of people in costume. **pageantry** *noun.*

**pager** *noun* a radio device with a bleeper to alert somebody or pass a message.

**pagoda** *noun* a temple, especially Buddhist or Hindu, shaped like a tower.

Many of the pagodas of southeast Asia have beautiful gilded roofs.

**paid** *verb* past tense of pay.

**pail** *noun* a bucket. *A pail of milk.*

**pain** *noun* 1 an unpleasant feeling of hurt when you are injured or ill. 2 a feeling of unhappiness when something upsetting happens. **pain** *verb. It pains me to see you unhappy.* **take pains** to make an effort. *She takes great pains with her homework.* **a pain in the neck** an annoying person. **painful** *adjective.* **painless** *adjective* not causing pain. *A painless operation.*

**painkiller** *noun* medicine that lessens or stops pain.

**painstaking** *noun* careful and thorough. *A painstaking investigation.*

**paint** *noun* 1 a coloured liquid or other substance that can be put on a surface. 2 **paints** a set of tubes or cakes of paint, usually in a box, for painting pictures. **paint** *verb* 1 to put paint on something. *He painted the chair black.* 2 to make a picture with paint.

Hannah knocked over the tin of paint, and it spilled all over the floor.

**painter** *noun* 1 a person whose job is painting and decorating houses or rooms. 2 a person who paints artistic pictures. *A portrait painter.*

**painting** *noun* a painted picture.

**pair** *noun* 1 two things, usually used together. *A pair of shoes.* 2 two people. 3 an object made up of two parts. *A pair of scissors.* **pair** *verb* to form a pair.

**WORD HISTORY**

*The first palace was on the Palatium, the Palatine hill in Rome, where the house of the Roman emperor was situated. The Palatine was one of the seven hills on which ancient Rome was built.*

**AMAZING FACT**

Pandas' natural habitat are the forests of Eastern Asia. There are two types of panda. The red panda is about the size of a house cat and has a bushy tail. The giant panda looks like a black and white bear. They aren't bears, though, their closest relatives are raccoons!

**Pakistan** *noun* a country in South Asia.

**palace** *noun* a large house which is the home of a king or queen or other important person. **palatial** *adjective* like a palace.

**palate** *noun* 1 the top of the mouth. 2 a person's sense of taste.

**pale** *adjective* 1 having little colour. You look pale when your face is almost white or lighter than usual. *She went pale when she heard the bad news.* 2 light, not bright in colour. *In the pale light of dawn.*

**palette** *noun* a board, with a hole for the thumb, on which an artist mixes colours.

**Palikir** *noun* the capital of Micronesia.

**palindrome** *noun* a word or phrase that reads the same backwards or forwards. 'Deed' is a palindrome.

**palisade** *noun* a fence made of pointed iron or wooden poles.

**pallid** *adjective* unhealthily pale.

**palm** *noun* the inner part of the hand between the fingers and the wrist. **palm** *verb* to steal something by picking it up and hiding it in your palm. **palm off** to trick someone into buying or taking something.

**palm** *noun* a tree that grows in hot countries with large leaves at the top and no branches. *Swaying coconut palms.*

**pampas** *noun* treeless grassy plains in South America. *Herding cattle on the pampas.*

**pamper** *verb* to treat too kindly or do too much for somebody.

**pamphlet** *noun* a small booklet that gives information about something.

**pan** *noun* 1 a metal container with a handle for cooking. 2 the bowl of a lavatory.

**Panama** *noun* a country in central America.

**Panama City** *noun* the capital of Panama.

The flag of Panama has red, blue and white squares and blue and red stars.

**pancake** *noun* a thin flat cake made of flour, eggs and milk (called batter) and fried on both sides.

**Pancake Day** *noun* Shrove Tuesday, when people traditionally eat pancakes.

**pancreas** *noun* a gland near the stomach that produces chemicals to help digestion.

**panda** *noun* a large bear-like animal with black and white fur that lives in Chinese bamboo forests. Also called a giant panda.

P

**pane** *noun* a piece of glass in a window.

**panel** *noun* 1 a flat piece of wood or other material that is part of a door or larger object. 2 a group of people chosen to discuss or decide something. *An advisory panel.* 3 a piece of material different in colour or fabric that is put in a dress. **panelled** *adjective. A panelled room.* **panelling** *noun.*

**pang** *noun* a sudden strong feeling. *A pang of sadness.*

**panic** *noun* a sudden uncontrollable fear. *She got into a panic when she lost her bag.* **panic** (panics, panicking, panicked) *verb* to suddenly become afraid and do things without thinking carefully.

**panic-stricken** *adjective* afraid, filled with terror. *The panic-stricken burglar fled.*

**panorama** *noun* a complete view of a wide area. *A panorama of fields spread below.*

**pansy** (pansies) *noun* a small garden flower.

The name 'pansy' came originally from the French word for thought, 'pensée'.

**pant** *verb* to breathe quickly with your mouth open, usually after running or when you're hot. *The dog panted.*

**panther** *noun* a wild animal of the cat family, usually black.

**panties** *noun* underpants worn by girls.

**pantomime** *noun* a funny musical play for children that is based on a fairy-tale and usually shown at Christmas.

**pantry** (pantries) *noun* a small room in a house, where food is kept.

**pants** *plural noun* 1 underpants. 2 (especially US) trousers.

**papacy** (say **pay**-puh-see) *noun* the power of the Pope or the position of Pope.

**papal** (say **pay**-pul) *adjective* to do with the Pope. *A papal decree.*

**paparazzi** *plural noun* photographers who follow famous people to take pictures.

**paper** *noun* 1 material made in thin sheets from wood or cloth for writing, printing or drawing on or for wrapping and covering things. 2 a newspaper. 3 part of a written examination with questions that have to be answered. 4 **papers** documents showing who a person or thing is. **paper** *verb* to put wallpaper on a wall. *We want to paper the sitting room.* **paper over something** to hide faults by pretending things are going well.

**SPELLING NOTE**

*Note that the words to do with the Pope, 'papacy' and 'papal', are spelt with an 'a' (not 'popacy' or 'popal'!). The origin of all the words is the Latin 'papa', meaning bishop, from the Greek 'papas', meaning father.*

**paperback** *noun* a book with a soft cover.

**papoose** *noun* a bag on a frame for carrying a baby on a person's back.

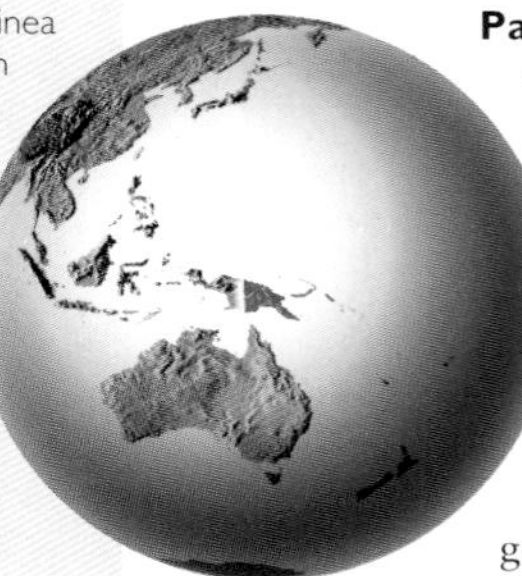

Papua New Guinea has a population of four million people.

**Papua New Guinea** *noun* a country in Australasia, forming part of the island of New Guinea.

**par** *noun* 1 an average or normal amount, degree or condition. When something is on a par with something else, both are equally good or equally bad. 2 in golf, the number of strokes an average player should take on one hole.

**parable** *noun* a simple story with a moral point. *Parables from the bible.*

**parachute** *noun* a device attached to a person or thing to make them fall slowly when dropped from a plane. **parachutist** *noun.*

There was a wonderful parachute display at the airfield.

**parade** *noun* 1 a procession or gathering of people or things for the purpose of being looked at or to celebrate a special event. *A fashion parade.* 2 soldiers marching together for inspection or for a ceremony. 3 a public square, or a row of shops. **parade** *verb* 1 to march in procession in order to be looked at by other people. *The winners paraded triumphantly around the stadium.* 2 to show something off in order to impress.

**paradise** *noun* 1 heaven, a place of perfect happiness. 2 in the Bible, the Garden of Eden, home of Adam and Eve.

**paradox** (paradoxes) *noun* 1 a statement that seems wrong or impossible, but has some truth in it. 2 two facts or ideas that are opposite to what is generally believed to be true. **paradoxical** *adjective.*

**paraffin** *noun* a kind of oil used for heating or lighting. *A paraffin lamp.*

**paragliding** *noun* a sport involving cross-country gliding using a parachute shaped like wings.

**paragraph** *noun* a section of a piece of writing consisting of a number of sentences on a subject. A paragraph starts on a new line. *Please write two paragraphs.*

**Paraguay** *noun* a country in South America.

**parakeet** *noun* a small parrot.

**parallel** *adjective* lines that are at the same distance from each other are parallel. *The road runs parallel to the railway.*

**parallel** *noun* 1 a line parallel to another. 2 something similar to something else, or a comparison that shows likeness. *She is without parallel.*

**parallelogram** *noun* a four-sided figure with opposite sides parallel.

**paralyse** *verb* 1 to make some or all of the body's muscles unfeeling and unable to move. *A stroke paralysed his left arm.* 2 to make somebody or something unable to act, move or work properly. *Paralysed with fear.* **paralysis** *noun.*

**Paramaribo** *noun* the capital of Suriname.

**parapet** *noun* a low wall at the edge of a bridge or roof.

**paraplegic** *noun* (say par-uh-**plee**-jick) a person whose lower body, including both legs, is paralysed. **paraplegic** *adjective.* **paraplegia** *noun.*

**parasite** *noun* a plant or animal that lives on or in another and gets food from it. **parasitic** *adjective.*

Ticks are parastites that live on sheep. They can also infest humans, dogs and cats.

**parasol** *noun* an umbrella used as a sunshade. *A dainty parasol.*

**parcel** *noun* something wrapped up so it can be sent by post or carried. **parcel** (parcels, parcelling, parcelled) *verb.* **parcel up** to make into a parcel.

**parchment** *noun* a kind of thick yellowish paper. In ancient times parchment was made from the skin of sheep or goats and used for writing on.

**pardon** *noun* forgiveness. *I beg your pardon.* **pardon** *verb* to forgive or excuse a person. **pardonable** *adjective.*

**parent** *noun* Your parents are your father and mother. **parental** (say puh-**rent**-ul) *adjective. Parental care.*

**parenthesis** (parentheses) *noun* (say puh-**ren**-thi-sis) 1 a sentence or a phrase inserted in a sentence, usually in brackets. 2 a bracket.

**Paris** *noun* the capital of France.

**DID YOU KNOW?**

*The term 'parrot-fashion' came about because people sometimes teach parrots to 'talk', or repeat the sounds they make. Today, many people feel it is wrong to keep birds in cages. In the wild, parrots have a harsh, screaming voice. They use their short, hooked bill to open nuts and feed on fruits and seeds.*

**AMAZING FACT**

There are both animal and plant parasites.

Animal parasites such as fleas and ticks, live on birds and mammals and suck blood.

Plant parasites, such as fungus, take nourishment from plants by twining around or growing into the host.

Mistletoe, traditionally used as a decoration at Christmas time, is a parasite that lives off trees.

**parish** (parishes) *noun* a village or town that has its own church. *The vicar of this parish.* **parishioner** *noun.*

**park** *noun* 1 a public garden or place, usually in a town, for people to walk in. 2 the large private garden of a country house. *The duke went riding in the park.*

**park** *verb* to leave a car or other vehicle somewhere for a time. *I parked the car in the car park.*

**parliament** *noun* an institution made up of a group of people who are elected and make a country's laws. **parliamentary** *adjective.*

**parlour** *noun* (old-fashioned) a sitting room. *The piano is in the parlour.*

**parody** (parodies) *noun* a piece of writing or music that makes fun of somebody else's style by copying it.

**parrot** *noun* a tropical bird with bright feathers and a hooked beak.

Conservationists are working to stop the illegal export of parrots from their native homes. Many parrots die in transit.

**parrot-fashion** *adjective* mechanical, without understanding. *She repeated everything parrot-fashion.*

**parsley** *noun* a plant with green leaves, used to add taste to food.

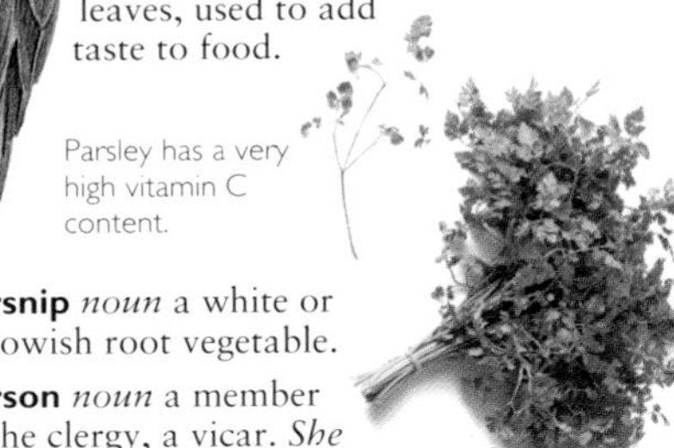

Parsley has a very high vitamin C content.

**parsnip** *noun* a white or yellowish root vegetable.

**parson** *noun* a member of the clergy, a vicar. *She took tea with the parson every Tuesday afternoon.*

**part** *noun* 1 any piece or portion of a whole, anything that belongs to something bigger. *The afternoon is the best part of the day.* 2 an important piece of a machine or other apparatus. *You can order spare parts for the bike.* 3 a share or duty in doing something. *He never takes part in games.* 4 a person's role in a play or film. *She played the part of the witch.* 5 any of several equal amounts in something. *This mixture is two parts milk and one part cream.* **take something in good part** to show that you are not offended by something. **play a part in** to have an important effect on what happens.

P

**part** *verb* to separate or divide, to leave each other. *Let's part as friends.* **part with** to give away. *I won't part with my dog.*

**partial** *adjective* 1 not complete. *A partial success.* 2 supporting one person or side, more than the other, especially in a way that is unfair. 3 liking something very much. *I'm very partial to chocolate.* **partiality** *noun.*

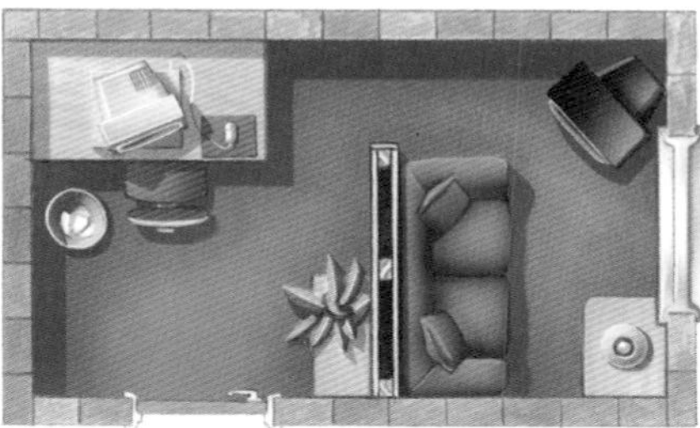

Ann was so partial to television, that she had a tv set and a sofa in her office.

**participate** *verb* to take part in something or have a share in an event. **participation** *noun. Your participation is appreciated.*

**particle** *noun* a very small piece or amount. *Food particles.*

**particular** *adjective* 1 relating to one and not any other. *This particular car is faster than the others.* 2 special. *She takes particular care to please her parents.* 3 difficult to please. *She is very particular about her food.* **particularly** *adverb.*

**particular** *noun* 1 a detail. *He is right in every particular.* 2 **particulars** facts or details, especially about events. *Fill in your particulars.* **in particular** especially.

**parting** *noun* the line on the head where the hair is parted.

**partition** *noun* 1 a thin wall that divides a room. 2 division into two or more parts. **partition** *verb* to divide into two or more parts. *A partition divides these rooms.*

**partner** *noun* one of two people who do things together or share the same activity. *My tennis partner.* **partner** *verb.* **partnership** *noun.*

Her tennis partner was very good at volleying.

**part of speech** *noun* one of the classes of words in grammar. Nouns, verbs and adjectives are parts of speech.

**partridge** *noun* a bird with brown feathers. Partridges are shot for sport and food.

**GRAMMAR NOTE**

*Try to avoid using the passive form of verbs. The active form is more direct and easier to understand. For example: 'Pencils are to be found in the drawer' is not as good as: 'You will find pencils in the drawer.'*

**DID YOU KNOW?**

*The common or grey partridge ranges across Europe and western Asia. It was also introduced to North America. Partridges eat mainly plant food such as seeds and young shoots.*

**part-time** *adjective, adverb* during a part of a day or week. *She works part-time.* The opposite of part-time is full-time.

**party** (parties) *noun* 1 a gathering of people who come together to enjoy themselves. *We gave a birthday party for my sister.* 2 a political organization. *The Labour Party.* 3 a group of people who work or travel together. *A party of tourists.* 4 a person who is taking part in a lawsuit. *The guilty party has to pay the costs.* **be party to** to be responsible for something. *I was party to the decision.* **party** *verb* to go to parties.

**pass** (passes, passing, passed) *verb* 1 to move past something or somebody. 2 to get or go through or between. *No one is allowed to pass this line.* 3 to go by, or spend time. *Three months passed before she heard from him.* 4 to give something to another person. *Can you pass me the jam?* 5 to do well and be successful, especially in an exam. *She passed her driving test.* 6 to accept or agree, especially a law. *The law was passed by Parliament.* 7 in sport to kick, throw or hit, especially a ball, to somebody in your team. **pass on** to tell something to another person. **pass out** to faint.

**pass** (passes) *noun* 1 a way between two mountains. 2 a successful result in an exam or test. 3 kicking, throwing or hitting a ball to somebody in your team. 4 a document or ticket that allows you to do something, especially go into a place. **make a pass** to try to make somebody of the opposite sex interested in you, usually in an unwelcome approach. *The boss made a pass at me.*

**passenger** *noun* a person who is driven in a car or is travelling by public transport.

The passenger enjoyed a comfortable ride.

**passer-by** (passers-by) *noun* a person who happens to pass a place. *A few passers-by saw the accident.*

**passion** *noun* a very strong attraction or strong feeling about somebody or something. *She has developed a passion for painting.* **passionate** *adjective.*

**passive** *adjective* 1 not active, showing no feeling or interest in what is said or done to you. 2 in grammar, a form of a verb when it describes what happens or will happen to somebody or something. 'The car was driven by me' is passive. 'I drove the car' is active. **passive** *noun.*

**Passover** *noun* a Jewish festival in memory of the freeing of the Jews from Egypt.

**passport** *noun* an official document that has to be shown when entering or leaving a country.

Michael renewed his passport so that he could go abroad on holiday.

**password** *noun* a secret word or phrase that you have to know to show that you are a friend or to gain access to something.

**past** *adjective* 1 referring to the time before now. *During the past hours.* The verbs 'went', 'called' and 'wrote' are in the past tense. **past** *adverb, preposition* 1 up to and beyond a point. *The bus drove past.* 2 after. *It's ten past four.* **be past it** to be no longer able to do things, because you are too old. **past** *noun* the time before the present.

**pasta** *noun* an Italian food made of a mixture of flour, eggs and water. Spaghetti, macaroni and noodles are all forms of pasta. *Pasta with parmesan cheese.*

Pasta may be coloured with spinach, tomato or beetroot.

**paste** *noun* 1 a soft mixture used for sticking things together. 2 food, especially fish or meat, made into a soft mixture that can be spread on bread. 3 hard shiny glass used for making imitation jewellery. **paste** *verb* to stick something using paste. *I spent all day pasting cuttings into my scrap-book.*

**pastel** *noun* 1 a coloured crayon. 2 a picture drawn with coloured crayons. *He loves working in pastels.* 3 a light colour.

**pasteurize** *verb* to remove bacteria from milk by heating and then cooling it.

**pastry** (pastries) *noun* 1 a mixture of flour, fat and water rolled out and baked in the oven. 2 something made of pastry.

**pasture** *noun* land covered with grass, suitable for grazing animals such as cattle or sheep. *Lush pasture.*

**SPELLING NOTE**

*Take care not to confuse 'past' with 'passed'. 'Past' is an adjective, adverb or preposition, as in: 'We walked past the school.' 'Passed' is the past tense of the verb to pass, as in: 'A week passed before we received the letter.' 'Past' can also be a noun: 'That's all in the past.'*

**AMAZING FACT**

Italian words for pasta, such as spaghetti, macaroni, linguini and tagliatelli, are all plural forms. The plurals end in 'i'.

This is also true of other Italian plural nouns such as graffiti and paparazzi.

**pasty** (say **pay**-stee) (pastier, pastiest) *adjective* looking pale and unhealthy.

**pasty** (say **pas**-tee) (pasties) *noun* a small pie made of folded pastry filled with meat, fish, fruit or vegetables.

**pat** (pats, patting, patted) *verb* to tap lightly with your fingers on something flat. *He patted the dog.* **pat** *noun* 1 a friendly pat. 2 a light sound. 3 a small piece of butter or something else soft. **pat on the back** praise for doing well. **know something off pat** to be prepared for something and have a ready answer. *He had the answer off pat.*

**patch** (patches) *noun* 1 a small piece of material to put over a hole or damaged place. *She put a patch on her jeans.* 2 a pad worn to protect an eye that has been hurt. 3 a small piece of ground. *A vegetable patch.* 4 a small area of something or a part that is different from the space around it. *Patches of fog.* **A bad patch** is a period of bad luck. **patchy** *adjective.* **not a patch on** not nearly as good. **patch** *verb* to put a patch on something. **patch up** 1 to repair something roughly. 2 to end a quarrel. *They tried to patch things up, but it hasn't worked out.*

Aunt Mary kindly sewed a patch on my trousers.

**patent** *noun* the official right given to an inventor to make or sell their invention and stop others from copying it. **patent** *verb* to get a patent for an invention. **patent** *adjective* 1 protected by a patent. 2 obvious. *It was a patent lie.* **patent leather** leather that has a shiny surface.

**paternal** *adjective* like or relating to a father. *Paternal feelings.*

**path** *noun* 1 a strip of ground for people to walk on or made by people walking over it. *We followed the path through the woods.* 2 a line along which somebody or something moves. *The path to success.*

**pathetic** *adjective* sad, weak or helpless. *What a pathetic joke!* **pathetically** *adverb.*

**patient** *adjective* able to wait calmly without getting annoyed. *Please be patient, I'll be as quick as I can.* **patience** *noun.*

**patient** *noun* a person who has medical treatment from a doctor or hospital.

**patio** *noun* a paved area next to a house.

**patriot** *noun* a person who loves and supports his or her country. **patriotic** *adjective.* **patriotism** *noun.*

**patrol** (patrols, patrolling, patrolled) *verb* to go at regular times over an area or a building to make sure that there is no trouble. *Soldiers patrolled the border.* **patrol** *noun* 1 the time of patrolling. *A soldier on patrol.* 2 a person, group of soldiers or vehicles patrolling an area.

**patron** (say **pay**-trun) 1 somebody important who gives money to or takes an interest in a person, especially an artist. 2 a person who uses a shop regularly.

**patronize** *verb* 1 to act towards others in a superior way, as if more important. *She has no right to patronize me.* 2 to support and give money to artists.

**patron saint** *noun* the protecting saint of a person or place. Saint Christopher is the patron saint of travellers.

**patter** *verb* to make light tapping sounds. **patter** *noun* 1 a number of quick, light tapping sounds. *The patter of children's little feet.* 2 the fast talk of a salesperson or an entertainer.

**pattern** *noun* 1 an arrangement of lines, shapes or colours, especially a design that is repeated. 2 a particular way in which something is done or happens. *A behaviour pattern.* 3 The shape of something to be copied. *A dress pattern.*

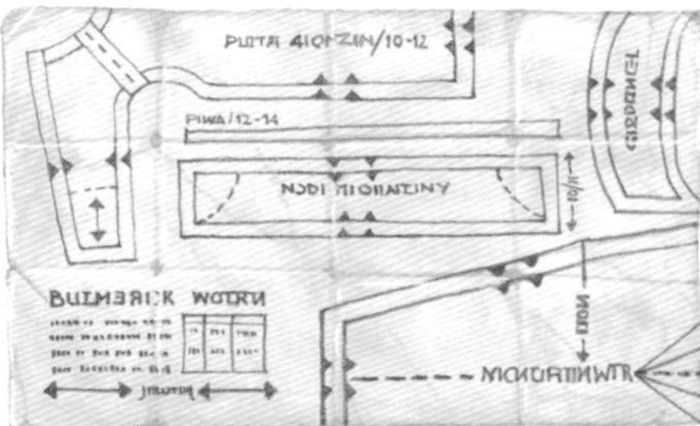

Carrie spread out the dress pattern to see how much material she would need.

**pauper** *noun* a very poor person.

**pause** *noun* 1 a moment of silence. 2 a break from doing something. **pause** *verb* to stop for a short while.

**pave** *verb* to put flat stones or bricks on a path or an area. **pave the way** to make something more likely to happen. *Their meeting paved the way to an agreement.*

**pavement** *noun* a path at the side of the street for people to walk on.

**pavilion** *noun* 1 a building next to a sports field for the use of players and spectators. 2 an ornamental building used for dances, concerts or exhibitions.

**paw** *noun* an animal's foot. **paw** *verb* to feel or touch with a hand or foot.

**pawn** *noun* 1 the smallest and least valuable playing piece in chess. 2 an unimportant person used by others to their own advantage. *He was a pawn in their game.*

**DID YOU KNOW?**

*Most groups of people and occupations have their own patron saint, and some have more than one. Here are some: athletes, St Sebastian; comedians, St Vitus; grocers, St Michael; librarians, St Jerome; scientists, St Albert the Great; students, St Thomas Aquinas and St Catherine of Alexandria.*

**pawn** *verb* to leave something, especially valuable articles, with a pawnbroker as a security for money borrowed. *He pawned his guitar to buy some food.*

**pawnbroker** *noun* a person who lends money to people in exchange for articles which they leave as security.

**pay** (pays, paying, paid) *verb* 1 to give money for goods bought or work done. *I paid five pounds for his old bike.* 2 to settle a bill or debt. *I'll pay!* 3 to give somebody an advantage, to be worth the trouble or cost. *It doesn't pay to cheat.* 4 to give or say something to a person, especially in certain phrases. *He paid her a compliment.* **pay back** to give back the money that you owe. **pay somebody back** to make somebody suffer for what they did to you. **pay up** to pay fully, to give all the money you owe. **pay** *noun* money received for work.

**payee** *noun* a person to whom money is paid or should be paid.

**payment** *noun* 1 paying money or being paid. *When can we expect payment?* 2 an amount of money paid to somebody.

**PC** *abbreviation* 1 personal computer. 2 police constable. 3 politically correct.

**PE** *abbreviation* physical education, especially sports at school.

**pea** *noun* the small round green seed growing inside a pod, eaten as a vegetable.

**peace** *noun* 1 a time when there is no war between countries, no trouble, quarrelling or fighting among people. 2 calm and quietness. *Leave us in peace.* **make peace** to end a quarrel. **peaceful** *adjective.*

**peach** *noun* a round juicy fruit with soft yellowish-red skin and a large stone.

**peacock** *noun* a large male bird with long colourful tail feathers that it can spread out like a fan.

**peahen** *noun* a large brownish bird, the female of the peacock.

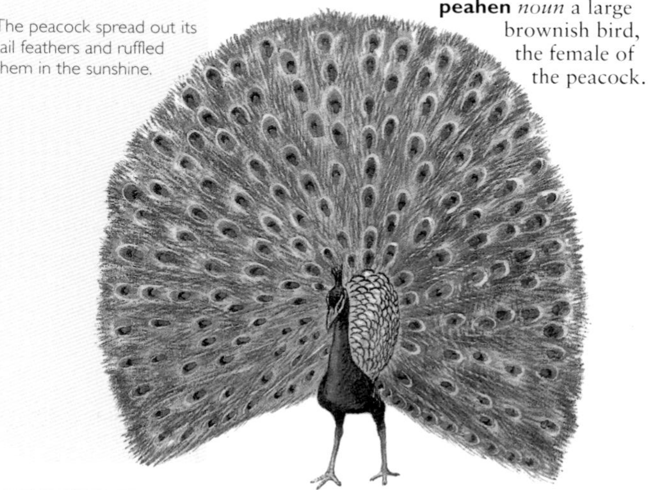

The peacock spread out its tail feathers and ruffled them in the sunshine.

P

**peak** *noun* 1 the pointed top of a mountain. 2 the front part of a cap, that sticks out to shade your eyes. 3 the highest level or most successful part of something. *She has reached the peak of her career.* **peak** *verb* to reach its highest point or level of success.

**peanut** *noun* a small round nut that grows under the ground.

**peanut butter** *noun* roasted peanuts crushed into a paste and eaten as a spread on bread.

**pear** *noun* the hard, juicy fruit of the pear tree. *Pear and apple crumble.*

**pearl** *noun* 1 a hard, round, shiny white object that grows inside the shell of an oyster and is a valuable jewel. *A pearl necklace.* 2 something that looks like a pearl or is a copy of a pearl. **pearly** *adjective*.

They found a pearl inside the oyster.

**peasant** *noun* a person who works on a farm or owns a small piece of land.

**peat** *noun* rotted plant material found under the ground. Peat is used for burning instead of coal or to improve soil and make plants grow better.

**pebble** *noun* a smooth round stone.

**pebbledash** *noun* cement with lots of small pebbles in it which is used for covering the outside walls of a house.

**peck** *verb* 1 to hit, tap or bite with the beak. *The bird pecked a hole in the apple.* 2 to kiss quickly and lightly. **peck** *noun* 1 a quick hit or tap with the beak. 2 a quick kiss. *She gave him a peck on the cheek.*

**peculiar** *adjective* 1 strange, unusual, often in an unpleasant way. *He gave me a peculiar look.* 2 belonging or relating to a particular thing or person only. *The accent is peculiar to the people in this valley.* **peculiarity** *noun*.

**pedal** *noun* a bar which is pushed or pressed with the foot to make a bicycle move or work a car or machine. **pedal** (pedals, pedalling, pedalled) *verb* to work something by using pedals. *He had to pedal hard to get up the hill.*

**pedant** *noun* a person who is very strict about unimportant rules and pays too much attention to detail. **pedantic** *adjective*.

**pedestal** *noun* the base on which a statue or pillar stands.

**DID YOU KNOW?**

*Peanuts are also called groundnuts or earthnuts. They come originally from tropical South America, but now most of the world's peanuts are grown in Africa and Asia. There are usually two peanuts in a pod.*

**WORD HISTORY**

*A pedant was originally simply a teacher. The word comes from the Italian 'pedante', meaning teacher, perhaps from the Latin paedagogus, who was originally a slave who looked after his master's son, including taking him to school.*

**pedestrian** *noun* a person walking, especially in a town. **pedestrian** *adjective* 1 for people walking. *A pedestrian crossing.* 2 dull, uninspired. *A very pedestrian speech.*

**pedigree** *noun* a list showing the families from which a person or animal has come, especially to show the quality of an animal. *A dog with a fine pedigree.* **pedigree** *adjective*. *A pedigree cat.*

The pedigree dalmatian was in perfect condition and won first prize at the show.

**peek** *noun* a quick look. **peek** *verb*. *He peeked round the corner.*

**peel** *noun* the skin of oranges, apples, potatoes and other fruit and vegetables. **peel** *verb* 1 to take the skin off fruit and vegetables. 2 to come off in layers, strips or flakes. *The paint is peeling.*

**peep** *verb* 1 to look quickly, often secretly. 2 to look through an opening. 3 to begin to show. *The ticket peeped out of his pocket.* *noun* 1 a quick look. 2 a high, weak sound.

**peer** *verb* to look very hard or closely, usually because something is difficult to see.

**peer** *noun* 1 a member of the nobility. A duke or a baron is a peer. 2 a person who is the same age or has the same rank.

**peer group** *noun* a group of people of the same age.

**peevish** *adjective* bad-tempered.

**peg** *noun* 1 a piece of wood, metal or plastic used to fasten things or to attach washing to a line. *A tent peg.* 2 a hook or knob for hanging things on. **peg** (pegs, pegging, pegged) *verb* 1 to fix with pegs. 2 to keep prices or wages unchanged.

**pelican** *noun* a large water bird with a long beak and a pouch for storing fish.

Pelicans can be seen on Lake Galilee in Israel.

**pellet** *noun* a small ball of metal, paper or other material.

P

**pelmet** *noun* a piece of wood or material that hides a curtain rod.

**pelvis** *noun* the round bony frame with the hip bones at the lower end of the spine.

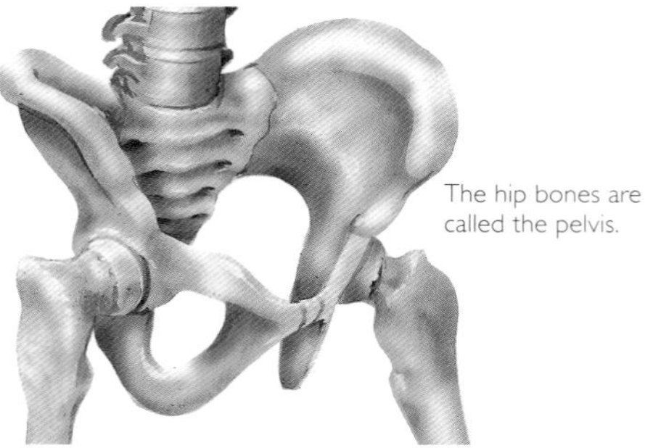

The hip bones are called the pelvis.

**pen** *noun* an instrument for writing with ink. *A fountain pen.*

**pen** *noun* a small place, an enclosure, for farm animals or pets. **pen** (pens, penning, penned) *verb* to shut into a small place. *The chickens were penned in for the night.*

**penal** (say **peen**-ul) *adjective* connected with the punishment of criminals. *Penal laws.*

**penalize** *verb* to punish.

**penalty** *noun* 1 punishment. 2 a point or a chance to score a goal, especially in football, rugby or hockey, because an opponent has committed a foul.

**pence** *plural* of penny.

**pencil** *noun* a wooden instrument for writing or drawing, with a thin stick of lead or coloured material inside it. **pencil** (pencils, pencilling, pencilled) *verb* to write or draw with a pencil.

**pendulum** *noun* a weight hanging from a rod so it can swing from side to side. Some old clocks have a pendulum.

The pendulum on a grandfather clock is what makes the comforting 'tick-tock' sound.

**penetrate** *verb* to force or manage to find a way into something. *A strange smell penetrated the room.* **penetration** *noun.* **penetrating** *adjective. Penetrating questions.*

**penfriend** *noun* a friend, especially somebody from a foreign country, who you write letters to and receive letters from.

**penguin** *noun* a black and white bird that lives in the Antarctic and cannot fly.

**penicillin** *noun* an antibiotic used in medicine to destroy bacteria.

**peninsula** *noun* a piece of land that is almost surrounded by water. *Italy is a peninsula.* **peninsular** *adjective.*

**GRAMMAR NOTE**

*The plural 'pence' is used for a sum of money, and 'pennies' for separate coins. The expressions 'to spend a penny' and 'the penny has dropped' both refer to the old, large penny coin that was in use before 1971. Public lavatories used to have a coin slot for a penny to open the door, so you had to spend a penny to go to the loo.*

**AMAZING FACT**

Penguins are flightless birds, but they are extremely good swimmers and divers.

**penis** (penises) *noun* the part of the body a man or male animal uses for urinating and for reproducing.

**penknife** *noun* a small knife with a blade that folds into the handle.

**pen-name** *noun* the name a writer uses in books instead of his or her own name. A pseudonym. *She writes under a pen-name.*

**penniless** *adjective* having no money, very poor. *Penniless orphans.*

**penny** (pennies or pence) *noun* a British coin worth one hundredth of a pound. **spend a penny** to go to the toilet. **the penny has dropped** something has finally been understood.

**pension** *noun* a sum of money paid regularly by the government or a firm to a retired or disabled person.

**pensioner** *noun* somebody who gets a pension, a retired person.

**pentathlon** *noun* an athletic competition made up of five different events.

**penthouse** *noun* a flat or apartment on the roof or top floor of a tall building

**people** *plural noun* 1 two or more persons. *Only three people came.* 2 all the men, women and children of a particular place, class or group. *Young people.*

**pepper** *noun* 1 a hot-tasting powder made from peppercorns and used for making food spicy. 2 a hollow green, red or yellow vegetable.

Peppercorns are spread out in the sun to dry before they are used to flavour food.

**peppermint** *noun* 1 a mint grown for its strong flavouring. 2 a sweet that tastes of peppermint.

**per** *preposition* for each. *Ten kilometres per hour.* **per annum** for each year. *She earns £20,000 per annum.* **per cent** in each hundred. *Ten per cent (10%).*

**perceive** *verb* to notice or see something.

**percentage** *noun* an amount stated as part of a whole or as a share of one hundred parts. *A large percentage of students pass their exams every year.*

**perception** *noun* the ability to notice, an understanding.

**perceptive** *adjective* quick to notice and understand. *A very perceptive guess.*

P

**perch** *noun* 1 a branch or other place a bird rests on. 2 a high position taken up by a person. **perch** *verb* to be on something high. *The house perched on top of the cliff.*

**percussion** *noun* 1 the striking together of two hard things. 2 musical instruments that are hit together, especially drums and cymbals.

It is Jamie's ambition to play the cymbals. They are his favourite percussion instrument.

**perennial** *adjective* lasting for a long time or for many years. **perennial** *noun* a plant that lives for many years.

**perfect** *adjective* 1 excellent, without fault. 2 complete. *A perfect stranger.* **perfectly** *adverb. I feel perfectly at home here.*

**perform** *verb* 1 to do something, especially something difficult. 2 to act in a play or do something in front of an audience. **performer** *noun.*

**performance** *noun* 1 doing something in front of an audience. *Samantha went to the first performance of the new play.* 2 an action performed.

**perfume** *noun* 1 a fragrant liquid people put on to smell nice. 2 a nice smell.

**perhaps** *adverb* it may be, possibly. *Perhaps we'll win the game.*

**perimeter** *noun* the border or outer edge around something. *We walked all round the perimeter of the grounds.*

The perimeter of the pitch was marked with a white line.

**period** *noun* 1 a length or portion of time. *For a short period. Sunny periods.* 2 a woman's monthly flow of blood. **period** *adjective* made at an earlier time in history. *The hotel was full of period furniture, including original four-poster beds.*

**periodic** *adjective* happening at regular intervals. *Periodic amazement.*

**DID YOU KNOW**

*Periscopes are sometimes used at sporting events or other occasions where there are crowds, so that people can see over the heads of others. They work by reflecting the light across mirrors.*

**DID YOU KNOW?**

*In American English, a period is a full stop, such as appears at the end of a sentence. Sometimes the word is used at the end of a spoken sentence, meaning 'and that's all there is to it.'*

**periodical** *noun* a magazine that comes out at regular intervals, for example monthly. **periodical** *adjective.*

**periscope** *noun* a tube with mirrors and lenses through which somebody in a submarine can see things above the water.

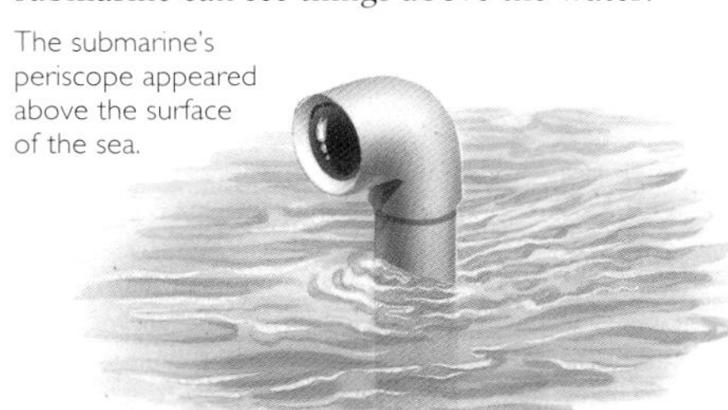

The submarine's periscope appeared above the surface of the sea.

**perish** *verb* 1 to die or become destroyed. 2 to rot or fall to pieces. *Soft fruit perishes quickly.* **perishable** *adjective.*

**perk** *noun* an advantage.

**perk up** *verb* to become or make somebody more cheerful. *She perked up after tea.*

**permanent** *adjective* lasting for ever, not expected to change. *My permanent address.* **permanently** *adverb.*

**permissible** *adjective* allowed by the rules.

**permission** *noun* the right to do something, the act of allowing something. *The teacher gave us permission to leave early.*

**permissive** *adjective* allowing too much personal freedom.

**permit** (say per-**mit**) (permits, permitting, permitted) *verb* to allow or make something possible. **permit** (say **per**-mit) *noun* an official document stating that somebody is allowed to do something or go somewhere.

**perpendicular** *adjective* pointing straight up. *Perpendicular lines.*

**perpetrate** *verb* to be guilty of something, to do something wrong. **perpetrator** *noun. We caught the perpetrator of the crime.*

**perpetual** *adjective* never ending or changing. *The perpetual noise of the traffic.* **perpetually** *adverb.*

**perpetuate** *verb* to preserve from being forgotten. *Let us perpetuate his memory.*

**persecute** *verb* to continually treat a person or group of people cruelly, especially because of their beliefs. **persecution** *noun.*

**persevere** *verb* to go on doing something and not give up. **perseverance** *noun. His perseverance won him the match.*

**persist** *verb* 1 to continue in spite of warning. *If he persists in breaking the rules, he will be expelled.* 2 to continue to exist. *If your headaches persist, take these tablets.* **persistent** *adjective.* **persistently** *adverb.* **persistence** *noun.*

P

**person** *noun* 1 a human being. *It's too much work for one person.* 2 in grammar, any of the three forms of pronouns or verbs that show who is speaking. **in person** bodily. *I can't come in person, but I'll send my brother to collect the prize.*

**personal** *adjective* 1 belonging, concerning or done by a particular person. *I want your personal opinion.* 2 concerning a person's private life. *There's no need to be personal.* **personally** *adverb. Don't take it personally.*

**personal computer** *noun* a computer used by a single person, especially at home.

**personality** (personalities) *noun* 1 the character or nature of a person. *He has a weak personality.* 2 a famous person. *A well-known television personality.*

**personal stereo** *noun* a small cassette player or radio with headphones.

**personnel** *noun* the people employed in a business. *The personnel are very friendly.*

**perspective** *noun* 1 the art of drawing so that things in the background look further away than things in the foreground. *The house is in perspective.* 2 a particular way of thinking about something. *What happened put everything in perspective.*

The line of the trees in this photograph show perspective.

**perspire** *verb* to sweat. **perspiration** *noun.*

**persuade** *verb* to make somebody do or believe something. *We persuaded him to buy a new bike.* **persuasion** *noun.* **persuasive** *adjective. A persuasive salesman.*

**perturb** *verb* to worry. *The news about the accident perturbed him greatly.*

**Peru** *noun* a country in South America.

**Peruvian** *adjective* of Peru. *Peruvian people speak Spanish.* **Peruvian** *noun.*

**perverse** *adjective* continuing to do something wrong or in a different way from what is wanted. *How perverse of you to like exams.* **perversely** *adverb.* **perversity** *noun.*

**pervert** (say **per**-vert) *noun* a person whose behaviour, especially sexual behaviour, is not normal or is disgusting. **pervert** (say puh-**vert**) *verb* to turn away from what is right or what it used to be. *He perverted the course of justice.* **perversion** *noun.*

**pessimism** *noun* thinking that whatever happens will be bad. **pessimist** *noun.* **pessimistic** *adjective.*

**AMAZING FACT**

Ancient Egyptians believed that all pharaohs were the same god incarnated in the shape of different men. Pharaohs were supposed to be the absolute rulers of the country, but the priests and noblemen actually ran things.

This lily has pink petals.

**GRAMMAR NOTE**

*'Phenomena' is sometimes used mistakenly as a singular. Remember that 'phenomena' is the plural of 'phenomenon'. 'The growth in popularity of mobile phones is a remarkable phenomenon.'*

**pester** *verb* to annoy somebody continually, especially by asking questions or wanting something.

**pet** *noun* 1 an animal kept in the home as a companion. *Cats are my favourite pets.* 2 a person who is a favourite. *The teacher's pet.* **pet** (pets, petting, petted) *verb* to treat or touch with special love.

**petal** *noun* one of the bright coloured parts that form a flower.

**petrify** (petrifies, petrifying, petrified) *verb* 1 to make somebody extremely frightened. *The strange noises petrified him.* 2 to turn into stone. *A petrified forest.*

**petrol** *noun* a liquid made from oil and used as a fuel for engines.

**petty** (pettier, pettiest) *adjective* unimportant. *Petty squabbles.*

**pew** *noun* a long wooden bench in a church. *He sat on the pew and prayed.*

**phantom** *noun* a ghost.

**pharaoh** (say **fair**-oh) *noun* a king of ancient Egypt.

Tutankhamun was one of the most famous pharaohs of ancient Egypt.

**pharmacy** (pharmacies) *noun* 1 a shop where medicines are sold. 2 the making or giving out of medicine. **pharmacist** *noun.*

**phase** *noun* a stage of development. **phase** *verb* to happen or make something happen in stages. *We can phase payment over three years, if it would make it easier for you.*

**pheasant** *noun* a long-tailed bird that is hunted for food. *A pheasant shoot.*

**phenomenal** *adjective* unusual, amazing. *He's got phenomenal strength for his age.*

**phenomenon** (phenomena) *noun* an unusual fact, event or thing. *Summer snow is an almost unknown phenomenon.*

**philately** (say fil-**at**-il-ee) *noun* stamp-collecting. **philatelist** *noun.*

**-phile** *suffix* indicating a person or thing that has a liking for something. *Francophiles like France and everything French.*

**Philippines** *noun* a country of many islands in Southeast Asia.

The flag of the Philippines is blue, red and white with a design of the Sun and stars.

**philistine** (say **fil**-ist-ine) *noun* a person who does not like or want to understand art and beautiful things.

**philology** *noun* the study of the development of language. **philologist** *noun.*

**philosopher** *noun* a person who studies or teaches philosophy.

**philosophy** *noun* 1 the study of the meaning of life and how people should live. 2 the ideas and beliefs that a philosopher has, or your own rules for living your life. *The philosophy of the ancient Greeks.* **philosophical** *adjective.*

**Phnom Penh** *noun* the capital of Cambodia.

**phobia** (say foh-bee-uh) *noun* a great fear of something. *He's got a phobia about spiders.*

**phone** *noun* a telephone. **on the phone** speaking to somebody by phone. **phone** *verb* to telephone. *Please phone home.*

Old-fashioned phones had a dial instead of push-buttons.

**phone-in** *noun* a programme on radio or television in which people ring up and take part. *I took part in a phone-in about pets.*

**photo** *noun* a photograph.

**photocopier** *noun* a machine that can quickly copy documents and other papers by photographing them.

**photocopy** (photocopies) *noun* a photographic copy of a document or page made by a photocopier. **photocopy** (photocopies, photocopying, photocopied) *verb. Can you photocopy this page?*

**photogenic** *adjective* looking nice in photographs. *She is very photogenic, and will probably be a model when she is old enough to work.*

**WORD HISTORY**

*The original Philistines were driven from Egypt about 1200 BC and settled in Canaan. The region took the name Palestine from the new settlers.*

**AMAZING FACT**

There are many different types of phobia. Most of them are named after the Greek word for the thing that is feared. 'zoophobia' is fear of animals; 'acrophobia' is fear of heights; 'entomophobia' is fear of insects; 'nyctophobia' is fear of night; and 'ophidiophobia' is fear of snakes.

**photograph** *noun* a picture made with a camera and a film sensitive to light. **photograph** *verb* to use a camera to take a photograph. **photography** *noun.* **photographic** *adjective.*

**photographer** *noun* somebody who takes photographs. *A wedding photographer.*

The photographer told the guests to smile for the camera.

**photosynthesis** *noun* the process by which green plants make food in their leaves, using the Sun's energy, carbon dioxide and water.

**phrase** *noun* a group of words used together, that form part of a sentence. 'In the park' is a phrase in 'We went for a walk in the park.' **phrase** *verb* to express something in words. *A well-phrased letter.*

**physical** *adjective* 1 connected with a person's body, not their mind. *Physical exercise.* 2 of things that can be touched and seen. *The physical world.* 3 connected with physics. **physically** *adverb.*

**physician** *noun* a doctor.

**physics** (say **fiz**-iks) *noun* the study of forces such as heat, light, sound, electricity and gravity. *She's good at physics and maths.*

**physiotherapy** (say **fiz**-ee-o-the-ruh-pee) *noun* treatment by means of exercise, massage, light and heat. **physiotherapist** *noun. The injured player was treated by the physiotherapist.*

**physique** (say fiz-**eek**) *noun* the shape and size of a person's body, especially a man's.

**piano** *noun* a large musical instrument that is played by the pianist's fingers pressing down on black and white keys. **pianist** *noun.*

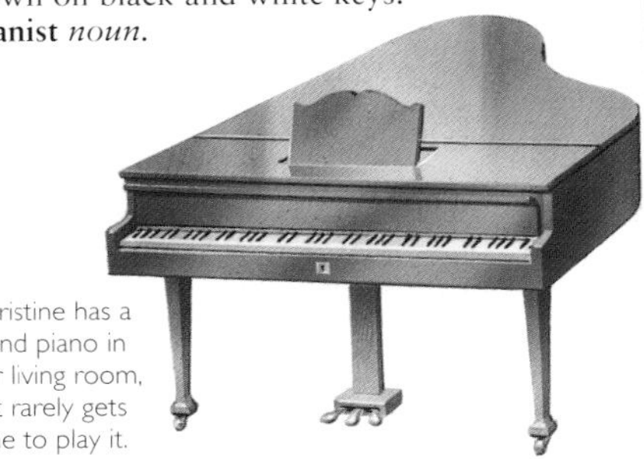

Christine has a grand piano in her living room, but rarely gets time to play it.

**piccolo** *noun* a small flute that plays high notes. *A piccolo solo.*

**pick** *verb* 1 to pull or break off part of a plant, especially a flower or fruit. *We picked some strawberries.* 2 to choose carefully. *He always picks the best.* 3 to remove unwanted things or pull bits off something. *Don't pick your nose.* 4 to take up. *Birds picking at the grain.* **pick a lock** to open a lock without a key. **pick a quarrel** to want to have a quarrel with somebody. **pick somebody's pocket** to steal from somebody. **pick holes in** to find weak points in something. **pick up** 1 to lift or take up. 2 to collect. *I can pick the children up from school.* 3 to take somebody as a passenger. *They picked up a hitch-hiker.* 4 to get better. *His health is picking up.* 5 to get to know somebody. *He picked up a girl at the party.* 6 to learn or hear something. *I picked up some Italian on holiday in Tuscany.*

**pick** *noun* 1 choice. *Take your pick.* 2 the best of many. *The pick of the bunch.*

**pick** *noun* 1 a pickaxe. 2 a plectrum.

**pickaxe** *noun* a pointed tool with a long handle used for breaking up rocks or hard ground.

A geologist needs a pickaxe to get samples of rocks for analysis.

**DID YOU KNOW**

*Wild pigs, or boars, were probably first kept by people in Asia about 5,000 years ago. They were used for clearing vegetation and for their meat, which we now call pork and bacon.*

**pickle** *noun* vegetables or fruit preserved in water, salt and vinegar. **pickle** *verb* to preserve food in water, salt and vinegar. **be in a pickle** to be in a difficult situation.

**pickpocket** *noun* a thief who steals things from people's pockets.

**picnic** *noun* a meal eaten out of doors, at the beach or in a field. **picnic** (picnics, picnicking, picnicked) *verb* to have a picnic. **picnicker** *noun*.

The picnic hamper was packed full of good things to eat and drink.

**pictorial** *adjective* with pictures.

**picture** *noun* 1 a painting, drawing or photograph of somebody or something. 2 a film at the cinema or on television. 3 an idea or impression. *She had quite a different picture of the house in her mind.* 4 a perfect example or a description of an event. *The baby is a picture of health.* **go to the pictures** to go to the cinema to see a film. **get the picture** to understand a situation somebody is telling you about. **put somebody in the picture** to tell somebody about a situation they need to know about. **picture** *verb* to imagine something.

**picturesque** *adjective* attractive and interesting. *A picturesque mountain village.*

**pie** *noun* a pastry case filled with meat, fish, vegetables or fruit, usually baked in a dish.

**piece** *noun* 1 a part or bit of something. *A piece of cake.* 2 one single thing, object or example. *A piece of paper.* 3 something written or composed, especially an article or a play. *A piece of music.* 4 a counter or any object used when playing a board game. *A chess piece.* 5 a coin. *A 50-pence piece.* **piece together** to make something by putting pieces together. *We tried to piece together the facts.*

**pier** *noun* 1 a bridge-like structure built out into the sea, used as a landing-stage or for people to walk along. 2 a pillar for supporting a bridge or roof.

**pierce** *verb* to make a hole with something sharp or pointed. *She had her ears pierced.* **piercing** *adjective* sharp in an unpleasant way. *A piercing scream.*

**pig** *noun* 1 a pink or black fat animal with a snout, usually kept on farms for its meat. 2 a dirty or greedy person.

Pigs are extremely intelligent creatures. More farmers are now rearing pigs outside, instead of confining them in sties and sheds.

**pigeon** *noun* a grey bird with a fat body.

**pigeon-hole** *noun* a small open box or one of many compartments on a wall for papers and messages. *He left the letter in my pigeon-hole, so I could collect it later.*

**piglet** *noun* a young pig.

**pigment** *noun* a substance that gives a particular colour to things. *The red pigment of blood.* **pigmentation** *noun*.

**pigsty** (pigsties) *noun* 1 a hut for pigs. 2 a dirty room or home.

**pile** *noun* 1 a number of things lying on top of each other. 2 a large quantity of things or amount of money. **pile** *verb* to put things in or on a pile. **pile in** to come or get into a place in a large group. **pile out** to leave a place in a large group.

Graham was taking a pile of newspapers to the recycling bank.

**pile** *noun* a heavy wooden, metal or stone post that is hammered into the ground as a support for a bridge or building. *A pile-driving machine.*

**pilfer** *verb* to steal small things. *She used to pilfer from my purse.* **pilferage** *noun.*

**pilgrim** *noun* somebody who travels to a holy place for religious reasons.

**pilgrimage** *noun* a journey made by pilgrims to visit a holy place.

They set off on a pilgrimage across the desert.

**pill** *noun* 1 a tablet of medicine. 2 a tablet taken by women, so they do not become pregnant. *She is on the pill.*

**pillar** *noun* 1 a tall upright stone or wooden post that supports a building. 2 something that looks like a pillar. *A pillar of smoke.* 3 an important member of a group of people. *He's a pillar of society.*

**pillow** *noun* a cushion for resting your head on, especially in bed.

**pillowcase** *noun* a cover for a pillow.

**pilot** *noun* 1 a person trained to fly an aircraft. 2 a person who steers a ship in and out of port. **pilot** *verb* 1 to act as a pilot of an aircraft or a ship. 2 to guide carefully. *He piloted me through the crowd.*

**pilot** *noun* a test to find out if something will work. *The TV producers are making a pilot of the series.*

**pimple** *noun* a small spot on the skin. **pimply** *adjective. A pimply complexion.*

**WORD HISTORY**

*The pineapple probably got its name because the fruit looks like a large pine cone. It is thought that pineapples originated in Brazil. Christopher Columbus and his crew were probably the first Europeans to taste the fruit.*

**DID YOU KNOW?**

*An imperial, or British, pint is equal to 0.565 litres. A US pint is slightly less, being equivalent to 0.551 litres.*

**pin** *noun* 1 a metal needle with a sharp point and a round head for fastening pieces of cloth or paper together. 2 a short pointed piece of metal or wood for fixing or marking something. **pins and needles** a prickly feeling in your hands or legs. **pin** (pins, pinning, pinned) *verb* 1 to fasten with a pin or pins. *She pinned a flower to her dress.* 2 to hold or keep in a particular position, to make unable to move. *She was pinned under the wrecked car.* 3 to fix. *I'm pinning all my hopes on getting the job.*

**pincers** *plural noun* 1 an instrument used for gripping things or pulling things out. 2 the claws of a crab or lobster.

**pinch** *verb* 1 to squeeze somebody's skin using your thumb and first finger. *It hurt when he pinched my arm.* 2 to be too tight. *My shoes are too small, they pinch.* 3 to steal. *Don't pinch my sweets.* **pinch** (pinches) *noun* 1 an amount that can be held between thumb and first finger. *A pinch of salt.* 2 a squeeze, usually a painful one. 3 suffering or stress, especially caused by not having enough money to buy things. *We are feeling the pinch, now I have lost my job.* **at a pinch** if absolutely necessary.

**pine** *noun* an evergreen tree with leaves that look like needles.

**pine** *verb* to become weak and sad because of wanting something very much. *The dog is pining for his master.*

The seeds of the pine tree are inside the pine cone.

**pineapple** *noun* a large tropical fruit with spiny leaves, a thick skin and sweet, yellow juicy flesh.

**pink** *adjective* pale red. You can mix pink by adding a lot of white to red.

**pinpoint** *verb* to find or discover exactly what or where something is. *Can you pinpoint the problem?*

**pint** *noun* a measure for liquids. *A pint of beer and a plate of fish and chips, please.*

**pioneer** *noun* the first person to go to a place or do or study something new. **pioneer** *verb* to help to develop something. *He pioneered the solar car.*

**pious** *adjective* very religious.

**pip** *noun* 1 a small fruit seed. *The pips of an apple.* 2 a short, high sound, especially as a time signal on the telephone or radio. **pip** (pips, pipping, pipped) *verb* to just beat somebody in a competition.

**pipe** *noun* 1 a long hollow metal or plastic tube through which water or gas can flow. 2 an object used for smoking tobacco. 3 a tube-like musical instrument, played by blowing. **pipe** *verb* 1 to carry liquid or gas through a pipe. 2 to send music or other sound through a loudspeaker. 3 to play music on a pipe. 4 to add a strip of decoration (called piping). 5 to pipe icing on a cake. **pipe down** to be quiet.

**pipeline** *noun* pipes, often underground, for carrying oil, water or gas a long way. **in the pipeline** being planned or on the way. *Plans for a shorter school day are in the pipeline.*

**piranha** *noun* a small, fierce, meat-eating fish from South America.

Piranhas have sharp teeth.

**pirate** *noun* 1 a sailor who attacks and robs other ships. 2 somebody who copies or broadcasts somebody else's work, like books, video tapes or cassettes, without permission. *Pirate radio stations do not pay for the music they play.* **pirate** *verb* to copy or broadcast somebody else's work without permission. **piracy** *noun.*

**pit** *noun* 1 a deep hole. 2 a coal mine. 3 (usually plural, pits) a place at the side of the racing track where racing cars are repaired and refuelled. *The Ferrari came into the pits.* **pit** (pits, pitting, pitted) *verb* to make a hole in something. *The road was pitted with holes.* **pit against somebody** to set or match a person against another in a competition. *We were pitted against the darts champions.*

**pitch** (pitches) *noun* 1 a ground marked out and used for playing certain games. *A cricket pitch.* 2 the highness or lowness of a sound. *Her voice dropped to a lower pitch.* 3 the degree or strength of something. *A pitch of excitement.* **pitch** *verb* 1 to set up, especially a tent or camp. 2 to throw or fling something. 3 to fall suddenly or heavily. *I tripped and pitched forward.* 4 to give a particular feeling to something, to set a level. *Her stories are pitched so that even the youngest children can easily understand them.* **pitch in** to join in an activity, to get working or eating.

**pitch-dark** *adjective* very dark.

**AMAZING FACT**

Piranhas are not large fish, measuring not more than about 12 inches in length, but they travel in very large schools. Despite their bloodthirsty reputation, carnivorous piranhas feed mainly on fish, seeds and fruit.

Pizzas are often topped with tomatoes, anchovies and olives.

**DID YOU KNOW?**

*There were many pirates, or buccaneers, around the Caribbean Sea in the second half of the 17th century. The word pirate comes from the Greek 'peirates', meaning 'an attacker'.*

**pitfall** *noun* an unexpected difficulty.

**pith** *noun* 1 the white substance under the peel of oranges, lemons and other citrus fruit. 2 the soft white substance in the stems of certain plants and trees.

A little of the white pith can be seen on the inside of this strip of lemon peel.

**pitiful** *adjective* sad and weak, making you feel pity. *A pitiful story.*

**pitiless** *adjective* showing no feeling or pity. *The boss is pitiless, he makes us pay for every error.*

**pity** *noun* 1 feeling sorry for somebody who is suffering or unhappy. *Don't help me out of pity.* 2 a state of disappointment. *It's a pity you can't come to the party tonight.* **take pity on** to feel sorry for somebody and help them. **pity** (pities, pitying, pitied) *verb* to feel sorry for somebody.

**pivot** *noun* 1 a point or pin on which something turns. 2 the most important thing, which everything depends on. **pivot** *verb* to turn round as if on a pivot. **pivotal** *adjective. His mother has a pivotal influence on him.*

**pizza** *noun* a round piece of bread dough baked with a mixture of tomatoes, cheese and other food on top.

**placard** *noun* a large poster or notice. *The demonstrators carried placards with slogans on them.*

**place** *noun* 1 a particular position where something belongs or should be. *I put the books back in their place.* 2 any point like a building, an area, a country, a town or a village. *This is the place where we used to live.* 3 a seat. *He saved me a place.* 4 a house or home. *Come round to my place after school.* 5 a particular point in a story or book or part of it. *I lost my place because my bookmark fell out.* 6 a position in a group, race or competition. *First place.* 7 somebody's role in relation to other people or things. *It's not my place to tell him off.* 8 a job, a position in a team, a school or at a university. *He got a place in the team.* 9 a point in a series of things, especially in an explanation. *In the first place I don't want to come, and in the second place I haven't been invited.* **all over the place** everywhere. **in place** in the proper position, suitable. **out of place** not in the proper position, unsuitable. **in place of** instead of. **take place** to happen. *When did the party take place?*

P

**place** *verb* 1 to put something in a particular place. 2 to say that somebody has achieved a particular position or put somebody in a particular position. *This places him in a difficult position.* 3 When you place an order, you order goods from a firm.

**placid** *adjective* calm, not easily made angry or upset. *She has a placid nature.*

**plague** *noun* 1 a dangerous illness that spreads quickly and kills many people. 2 a large number of unpleasant things. *A plague of rats.* **plague** (plagues, plaguing, plagued) *verb* to annoy or trouble all the time. *The child plagued me with questions.*

The procession of people prayed to be spared from the plague.

**plaice** (plaice) *noun* (say place) a flat sea-fish used for food.

**plaid** *noun* (say plad) a cloth with a tartan pattern. *A plaid shirt.*

**plain** *adjective* 1 simple, not decorated, patterned or flavoured. Not complicated. *I prefer plain food.* 2 easy to see, hear or understand. *It was plain he didn't like her.* 3 honest and open, especially about feelings or opinions. 4 not beautiful or handsome. **plainly** *adverb*. **plainness** *noun*.

**plain** *noun* a large flat area of land.

**plait** (say plat) *verb* to twist three or more strands, especially hair or rope, under and over one another into one thick length. **plait** *noun* a length of hair or rope that has been plaited. *She wears her hair in plaits.*

**plan** *noun* 1 an outline or drawing showing all the parts of something. *We were looking at the plans for the new house.* 2 an arrangement for carrying out something that is to be done or used in the future. *We have made plans for our holiday.* 3 a map of a town or district. **plan** (plans, planning, planned) *verb* to make a plan for something.

**plane** *noun* 1 an aeroplane. 2 a flat surface. 3 a tool with a sharp blade for making wood smooth by shaving small pieces off its surface. **plane** *verb* to smooth wood with a plane. *Peter planed down all the doors.*

**plane** *noun* a tall tree with big leaves.

**DID YOU KNOW?**

*Nine planets orbit the Sun. From nearest the Sun: Mercury, Venus, Earth, Mars, Jupiter, Saturn, Uranus, Neptune and Pluto.*

**AMAZING FACT**

The nursery rhyme, 'Ring-a-ring-a-rosy' originates from the time of the plague in the 1300s when herbs and fragrant flowers were thought be protection against the disease.

**WORD HISTORY**

*Plaster of Paris was first made from gypsum in the Montmartre district of Paris in the 15th century. It is called the same in French: 'plâtre de Paris'.*

**planet** *noun* any of the large bodies in space that travel around the Sun, such as Earth, Venus and Mars. **planetary** *adjective*.

The planet Uranus spins at a tilt.

**plank** *noun* a long, usually heavy, flat piece of wood. *Two men carried the plank.*

**plankton** *noun* tiny plants and animals that live in water and are food for many fish.

**plant** *noun* 1 a living thing that grows in the earth and has leaves and roots. Plants need water and light. 2 large machinery used in industry. 3 a factory. 4 a thing, especially stolen goods, hidden on somebody to make that person look guilty. *The drugs were a plant by the police.* **plant** *verb* 1 to put something in the ground to grow. 2 to fix firmly or place in a position. *She planted herself in the chair next to mine.* 3 to hide something or somebody secretly in order to wrongly accuse an innocent person. *He planted the stolen bike in his friend's garage.*

**plantation** *noun* 1 a large piece of land, especially in hot countries, on which crops like tea, sugar or cotton are grown. 2 a large group of trees planted especially for wood.

Slaves were forced to worked on the plantation, harvesting the sugar cane.

**plaque** (say plak) *noun* 1 a flat metal or stone plate fixed to a wall in memory of a famous person or event. 2 a substance that forms on teeth and gums and in which bacteria can live.

**plaster** *noun* 1 a mixture of lime, water and sand which hardens when dry and is used for covering walls and ceilings. 2 a piece of sticky material used to cover a wound. 3 a white paste (called plaster of Paris) that dries quickly and is used for making moulds or for casts around broken bones. *His arm was in plaster for five weeks.* **plaster** *verb* 1 to cover with plaster. 2 to cover something thickly, usually too thickly. *They plastered stickers all over the window.*

**plastic** *noun* a manmade material that can easily be formed into various shapes. Plastic is light and does not break easily. **plastic** *adjective* made of plastic.

P

**plastic surgery** *noun* an operation to repair and replace damaged skin or injured and deformed parts of the body.

**plate** *noun* 1 a flat dish from which food is eaten or served. *A dinner plate.* 2 a flat sheet of metal, glass or other hard material. 3 a small piece of metal with a person's name on, usually beside the front door of an office or a house. 4 metal articles, dishes, bowls and cutlery with a thin covering of gold or silver. 5 a picture or photograph usually printed on special paper in a book. 6 a piece of plastic with false teeth on, shaped to fit inside a person's mouth. **plate** *verb* to cover metal objects with a thin layer of gold, silver or tin. *The spoons are silver plated.*

**plateau** (plateaux) *noun* (say **platt**-oh, **platt**-ohz) a flat area of land high above sea-level.

The high plateau was lit up with brilliant reds and purples in the setting sun.

**platform** *noun* 1 a flat raised structure, often made of wood, which people stand on when they make speeches or give a performance. 2 the area next to the railway line in a train station where people wait for or get off a train. *The train to Dover leaves from platform 5.* 3 a statement of what a political party will do if they are elected.

**platinum** *noun* a very valuable metal used for making jewellery.

**platypus** (platypuses) *noun* an Australian animal with a beak like a duck.

The platypus has a beak for feeding underwater and strong webbed feet for digging.

**play** *verb* 1 to take part in a sport, a game or other pleasant amusement. 2 to make music with a musical instrument, perform a musical work or operate a tape-recorder or cassette player. *She plays CDs all the time.* 3 to act in a play or film. *He played a king in the school play.* 4 to behave in a certain way. *She played it very cool when offered the job.* **play along** to pretend to agree with somebody. **play up** 1 to not work properly. *The car is playing up again, it keeps stalling.* 2 to be naughty or annoying. *The children always play up when I look after them.*

**DID YOU KNOW**

*The modern pack of playing cards is based on the French pack of 52 cards, which itself came from tarot cards, which were once used for games but are now used for fortune-telling.*

**AMAZING FACT**

The platypus is considered a primitive mammal because it lays eggs and retains some repitilian characteristics.

Because of its extremely odd appearance, when the first specimen arrived at London's Natural History Museum 200 years ago, it was thought to be a hoax.

**play** *noun* 1 a story performed in a theatre, on TV or on the radio. A piece of writing to be performed. *He has written a new play.* 2 playing. *Children learn through play.* **in/out of play** when the ball is/is not in a position where it is allowed to be played by the rules of the game. **come into play** to begin to be used. *The new rules are coming into play from Wednesday.*

**player** *noun* a person who plays a game.

**playground** *noun* a place where children can play. *Skipping in the playground.*

**playing card** *noun* one of a set of cards used to play games. *We always take a pack of playing cards on holiday.*

**plc, PLC** *abbreviation* public limited company. The shares of a plc can be bought by the public.

**plea** *noun* 1 a strong request. *A plea for help.* 2 an excuse. *A plea of insanity.* 3 a statement made by the accused in court stating whether they are guilty or not guilty.

**plead** *verb* 1 to make a strong request. *He pleaded with the teacher to give him another chance.* 2 to state in court whether one is guilty or not guilty. 3 to offer an excuse.

**pleasant** *adjective* nice, enjoyable. *We spent a pleasant day together.* A pleasant person is friendly and polite. **pleasantness** *noun.*

**please** *verb* 1 used when politely asking somebody to do something or asking for something. *Please don't touch.* 2 to give satisfaction, make a somebody happy. *He always tries to please his parents.* **please yourself** to do what you want. **as you please** as you think best. *I'll do as I please.*

**pleasure** *noun* 1 a feeling of satisfaction, happiness and enjoyment. 2 something that is enjoyable and pleases you.

**pleat** *noun* a flattened fold in cloth. **pleat** *verb* to make folds. **pleated** *adjective. A pleated skirt.*

The skirt had a kick pleat in the back of it.

**plectrum** *noun* a small piece of plastic or wood, held in the hand and used for playing the guitar.

**pledge** *noun* 1 a serious promise or agreement. *He made a pledge of loyalty to the queen and to his country.* 2 something given as a sign of friendship or love. 3 an object given in return for money until that money is repaid. **pledge** *verb* 1 to make a serious promise. *She pledged never to leave home again.* 2 to make a serious promise to give something. *The firm pledged £1,000 to cancer research.*

**plenty** *pronoun, noun* enough, as much or more than is needed. *We've got plenty of time before the next train.* **plenty** *adverb* quite. *It's plenty big enough for three.*

**pliers** *plural noun* a gripping tool for holding or pulling out things. *He used a pair of pliers to pull out the nail.*

**plight** *noun* a difficult situation.

**plod** (plods, plodding, plodded) *verb* 1 to walk slowly with a heavy step. 2 to work slowly and without much interest.

**plot** *noun* 1 a small piece of ground. *A vegetable plot.* 2 a secret plan. *The police uncovered a plot to shoot the president.* 3 the story in a film or novel. *The director changed the plot.* **plot** (plots, plotting, plotted) *verb* 1 to make a secret plan. 2 to mark the position or course, especially of a ship or plane, on a map.

**plough** *noun* (say plow) a farming tool with sharp blades for turning the soil over before seeds are planted. **plough** *verb* to turn over the soil with a plough. To plough a field. **plough through** to make your way through, usually with difficulty. *He ploughed through all the books on the reading list.* **plough back** to put money back into a business. *The firm ploughed back last year's profits.*

Martin used a pair of pliers to pull out all the nails.

**GRAMMAR NOTE**

*The plural of most English nouns is formed by adding an s at the end. But there are exceptions. Nouns ending in '–y' usually change to '–ies': 'sty', 'sties'. Some nouns that end in '–o' change to '–oes': 'hero', 'heroes'; but 'photo', 'photos'. Some nouns ending in '–f' change to '–ves': 'half', 'halves'; but 'roof', 'roofs'. Some nouns have irregular plurals, and these are given in their entries.*

**plum** *noun* 1 a soft juicy fruit with a stone in the middle. 2 a dark reddish-blue colour. 3 something very good. *He's got a plum job in the new company.*

**plumber** *noun* a person whose job is to fit and repair water pipes. **plumbing** *noun*.

**plump** *adjective* slightly fat, round. **plumpness** *noun*.

**plunder** *verb* to rob, especially in a war. *The soldiers plundered the town.* **plunder** *noun*. **plunderer** *noun*.

**plunge** *verb* 1 to suddenly fall or jump downwards or forwards. *He plunged into the water.* 2 to push quickly and forcefully. *The murderer plunged the knife into his victim's back.* 3 to fall steeply. *Prices have plunged to rock bottom.* **plunge** *noun* a dive. **take the plunge** to decide to do something risky or difficult.

**plural** *noun* a word that expresses more than one. *Cats is the plural of cat.* **plural** *adjective. Pliers is a plural noun.*

**plus** *preposition* 1 showing that one number is added to another, often written as a plus sign (+). Three plus three, or 3 + 3. 2 with the addition of. *She lost her job plus the company car.* **plus** *noun* 1 a plus sign (+). 2 an advantage. *Knowing lots of languages is a definite plus.*

**plutocrat** *noun* a person who is powerful because he or she is very rich.

**pluck** *verb* 1 to pull feathers off. *The cook plucked a chicken.* 2 to pull out, especially something unwanted. *She plucks her eyebrows.* 3 to pick a flower or fruit. 4 to pull and let go the strings of a stringed instrument. **pluck up courage** to overcome fear to do something. **pluck** *noun* courage.

**plug** *noun* 1 a plastic object with metal pins that fit into a socket to connect wires to the electricity supply. 2 a piece of rubber, wood or other material to block up a hole. *She pulled the plug out of the bath to let the water out.* 3 a piece of publicity praising a product. *His new song got a plug on TV.* **plug** (plugs, plugging, plugged) *verb* 1 to block up a hole. 2 to advertise something by frequently mentioning it.

The man in front drives the team of oxen that pull the plough, while the man behind steadies it and keeps the furrow straight.

**AMAZING FACT**

'p.m.' is an abbreviation of a Latin phrase – 'p' stands for 'post' meaning after and 'm' stands for 'meridiem' meaning noon or midday.

**ply** *noun* 1 a thickness of wood or cloth. Three-ply wood has three layers. 2 a thickness of wool, thread or rope measured in strands.

**ply** (plies, plying, plied) *verb* 1 to go regularly from one place to another. *The ferry plies between Dover and Calais.* 2 to use a tool or weapon. 3 to keep a person supplied, especially with food or questions. 4 to do a particular kind of work regularly. *They plied their trade by night.*

**p.m.** *abbreviation* written after a number and used to show the time after midday. *Shops close at 5.00 p.m.*

**pneumatic** *adjective* worked or filled with compressed air. *A pneumatic drill.*

**pneumonia** *noun* an illness with inflammation of one or both lungs.

**poach** *verb* to cook an egg, fish or fruit in boiling water or other liquid, sometimes in a special pan. *Poached plums.*

**poach** *verb* 1 to catch or shoot animals, fish or birds without permission from somebody else's land. *He was caught poaching rabbits.* 2 to take or use unfairly somebody else's ideas or belongings. *The football club has poached our best players.* **poacher** *noun.*

**pocket** *noun* 1 a small bag-shaped part of an article of clothing. *He put his hands in his pockets.* 2 a small area. *A pocket of cloud.* **to be out of pocket** to have no money or less money than you should have. **pocket** *verb* 1 to put something into a pocket. 2 to steal something. **pocket** *adjective* small enough to fit into a pocket. *A pocket calculator.*

Andrew took his pocket calculator everywhere.

**poem** *noun* a piece of writing with short lines that often rhyme.

**poet** *noun* a person who writes poems. **poetic** *adjective.* **poetry** *noun* poems. *A book of poetry.*

**pogrom** *noun* a planned killing often for racial or religious reasons.

**point** *noun* 1 a sharp end. *The point of a pencil.* 2 a small dot. *A decimal point.* 3 something that shows an important idea, particular fact or a position from which something is seen. *The point is, he can't act.* 4 a particular place or time. *At that point in the journey I just wanted to go to sleep.* 5 a mark on a scale. *The boiling-point of water.* 6 a score in some games or competitions. *They beat us by three points.* 7 a detail or quality of something or somebody. *He has his good points.* 8 a purpose, use. *There is no point in tidying up before the party.* 9 an electrical socket. *A power point.* 10 (usually plural, points) a junction of railway tracks for changing a train from one line to another. **up to a point** to a certain degree. *I like him up to a point.* **beside the point** of little importance. **come to the point** to give the necessary facts. **point of view** a way of looking at something.

**WORD HISTORY**

*Long ago market traders would try to trick customers by putting a cat in a bag and claiming that it was a pig. Those who failed to check properly would buy 'a pig in a poke' – actually a cat! The 'poke' came from Old French for 'pouch', or 'bag'.*

Poland is famous for its shipyards and its sausages.

**point** *verb* 1 to direct or aim. *He pointed the water pistol at his friend.* 2 to show a direction or where something is, especially by holding out a finger. *The sign pointed in the other direction.* 3 to show that something is likely to happen. *Everything points to a war.* 4 to fill in the spaces between the bricks with cement. **point out** to draw attention to something. *She pointed out a mistake.*

He pointed out the castle on the horizon, our distant destination.

**point-blank** *adjective, adverb* 1 aimed or said very directly or rudely. *She told him point-blank that she didn't like him.* 2 from a very close distance. *At point-blank range.*

**pointed** *adjective* 1 with a point at one end. 2 said or done in an unfriendly, critical way. *The teacher made a few pointed comments about homework being handed in late.*

**pointless** *adjective* with no purpose. *A pointless question.*

**poison** *noun* a substance that harms or kills animals or plants. **poison** *verb* 1 to put poison in or on something. To kill with poison. *The air is being poisoned by car fumes.* 2 to spoil something or influence somebody in a harmful way. *He poisoned her mind against her friend.* **poisonous** *adjective. A poisonous snake.*

**poke** *verb* 1 to push or jab, usually with something sharp. *She poked him in the ribs.* 2 to stick out or push through. *She poked her head through the door.* **poke** *noun.* **poke about** to search. *He was poking about in the house.* **poke fun at** to make jokes against, have a laugh at. **buy a pig in a poke** to buy something without seeing it and find afterwards that it is useless.

**poky** (pokier, pokiest) *adjective* too small. *A poky room.*

**Poland** *noun* a country in central Europe.

**polar** *adjective* near the North or South Pole.

**polar bear** *noun* a white bear that lives near the North Pole.

**pole** *noun* a long, round, usually thin stick or post. *One of the tent poles is missing.*

**pole** *noun* 1 either of the two ends of the earth's axis. The point as far north as the North Pole or as far south as the South Pole. 2 either of the ends of a magnet. 3 either of the two points of an electric battery. *The positive pole, the negative pole.* **be poles apart** to have completely different opinions on a subject.

**police** *noun* the men and women whose job and duty is to catch criminals and protect people and property. **police** *verb* to keep order by using the police. *Football matches are heavily policed.*

**police force** *noun* an organized group of police. *The West Midlands police force.*

**policeman** *noun* a male member of a police force. *The policemen flagged him down.*

**police officer** *noun* a male or female member of a police force.

**policewoman** *noun* a female member of a police force.

**policy** (policies) *noun* a plan of action or statement of aims. *One of our policies is to reduce classroom sizes.*

**policy** *noun* a document that shows the agreement made with an insurance company. *A life insurance policy.* **policyholder** *noun.*

**polish** *verb* to make things smooth and shiny by rubbing. **polish off** to finish quickly, especially food or work. **polish up** to make something better, improve it. *I must polish up my French.* **polish** *noun* 1 a substance, like wax, for polishing. 2 a shining surface. 3 elegance and good behaviour. *Samantha has real polish.*

**Polish** *noun* the language spoken in Poland. **Polish** *adjective. Polish sausages.*

**polite** *adjective* having good manners. **politely** *adverb. The children thanked their grandmother politely.* **politeness** *noun.*

**political** *adjective* concerning the government of a country. *A political party.*

**politics** *noun* the ways in which a country is governed, political affairs. **politician** *noun.*

**polka** *noun* a dance for couples or the music to which it is danced.

**poll** *noun* (say pole) 1 voting in an election. 2 a questioning of people chosen by chance to find out the general opinion about something, an opinion poll. **poll** *verb* 1 to receive a stated number of votes at an election. 2 to vote at an election.

**pollen** *noun* a fine yellow powder on the male part of the flower that fertilizes other flowers to produce seeds. Bees carry pollen from one flower to another.

The hummingbird gets pollen on its beak as it sucks nectar from the flower.

**WORD HISTORY**

*The polka is a 19th-century Bohemian dance with three steps and a hop. The name comes from the Czech 'pulka', meaning 'half-step'.*

**DID YOU KNOW?**

*Poodles were once used as hunting and retrieving dogs. The breed originated in Germany during the 1500s. The name comes from the German Pudel(hund), from 'pudeln', meaning 'to splash'; the dogs were clearly once used as retrievers in water.*

**pollinate** *verb* to fertilize with pollen. **pollination** *noun.*

**pollute** *verb* to make dirty and dangerous to live in or use. *Many of our rivers have been polluted.*

**pollution** *noun* 1 polluting the water, air or atmosphere. 2 substances that pollute. *There's too much pollution on our beaches.*

**poly-** *prefix* many. Polyatomic means having many atoms.

**polygon** *noun* a shape with many sides.

This is an irregular polygon.

**polymath** *noun* somebody who has knowledge in many fields of learning.

**polythene** *noun* a very light plastic material for making plastic bags and packaging.

**polyunsaturated** *adjective* containing fats that are healthier and more easily digested. Polyunsaturated margarine is made from vegetable fats.

**pompous** *adjective* full of self-importance. **pomposity** *noun.*

**pond** *noun* a very small lake.

**ponder** *verb* to think deeply and carefully.

**ponderous** *adjective* 1 slow and clumsy. *His movements were very ponderous.* 2 dull and serious. *He speaks in a ponderous way.* **ponderously** *adverb.*

**pony** (ponies) *noun* a small horse.

Sophie had always wanted a white pony of her own.

**poodle** *noun* a dog with curly hair.

**pool** *noun* 1 a small amount of water or other liquid. *A pool of blood spread across the floor.* 2 a swimming pool.

**pool** *noun* 1 an amount of money used by gamblers. 2 a common supply of workers or goods that can be shared by a number of people. *Our firm has a pool car that we all use.* 3 an American billiard game. **pool** *verb* to share. *We pooled our money and rented a villa in Spain for the summer.*

P

**poor** *adjective* 1 having very little money. 2 not good, of low quality or small in quantity. *She's in poor health.* 3 needing help or sympathy. *The poor little boy was crying.* **poorly** *adverb* badly. *Most foreign workers are poorly paid.* **poorly** *adjective* unwell. *She's been poorly for weeks.*

**pop** *adjective* popular. *A pop singer.* **pop** *noun* popular music.

**pop** *noun* 1 a short explosive sound. *The cork came out with a pop.* 2 a fizzy drink. **pop** *verb* 1 to make a bursting sound. *The balloon went pop.* 2 If you pop something somewhere, you put it there quickly. *She popped a sweet in the child's mouth.* 3 to go quickly. *Could you pop into the shop?* **pop out** 1 to quickly go out. *I'm just popping out for a coffee.* 2 If something pops out of something, it suddenly comes out. *Her eyes almost popped out when she saw that she had the winning numbers.* **pop over** to make a short visit. **pop up** to spring up or to appear unexpectedly.

**popcorn** *noun* grains of maize heated until they burst open and look like little balls.

Popcorn is a favourite cinema snack in Britain and America.

**pope** *noun* the head of the Roman Catholic Church.

**poppy** (poppies) *noun* a plant with big flowers.

Poppies grow on the fields of Flanders, in Belgium, where so many soldiers fell during World War I.

**popular** *adjective* 1 liked, enjoyed or admired by many people. *Katie is a very popular name.* 2 of or for the general public. *The popular press pays too much attention to gossip.* **popularity** *noun.*

**WORD HISTORY**

*'Porcupine' comes from the Latin words 'porcus' ('pig') and 'spina' (thorn); it is a thorny or spiny pig. The porpoise is a 'porcus/piscis' ('pig fish'); you could say it has a piglike snout!*

If attacked, the porcupine runs backwards at its enemy, driving in its sharp spines.

**AMAZING FACT**

Porcupines usually give birth to a single offspring after a gestation period of seven months. The baby is well-developed at birth, with fur, open eyes and soft quills that harden in about an hour. It is able to climb trees and eat solid food just a few hours after it is born.

**populate** *verb* to live in, inhabit. *We live in a heavily populated area.*

**population** *noun* the people living in a place, especially a country or town. *The population of India is expanding rapidly.*

**porcelain** *noun* a hard shiny material, used for making cups, plates and other articles, which is produced by baking clay. China.

**porch** *noun* a roofed entrance to a building.

**porcupine** *noun* a small animal with long prickles over its back and sides.

**pork** *noun* meat from pigs.

**porpoise** *noun* a large sea animal similar to a dolphin.

**porridge** *noun* soft food made from oats cooked in water and milk.

**port** 1 a harbour where goods are loaded and unloaded. 2 a town with a harbour. 3 the left side of a ship when you are facing towards the front of it.

**port** *noun* a strong sweet red Portuguese wine. *Fine ruby port.*

**portable** *adjective* able to be carried. *A portable television.*

**Port-au-Prince** *noun* the capital of Haiti.

**portcullis** *noun* a framework of pointed bars above the entrance in old castles that could be lowered as a protection against attack. *Let down the portcullis!*

**porter** *noun* 1 a person who is employed in a building like a hotel or hospital to stand at the entrance and open doors. 2 a person employed to carry people's luggage at a railway station, an airport or in a hotel.

**Port Louis** *noun* the capital of Mauritius.

**Port Moresby** *noun* the capital of Papua New Guinea.

**Port of Spain** *noun* the capital of Trinidad and Tobago.

**Porto Novo** *noun* the capital of Benin.

**portrait** *noun* a painted picture, drawing or photograph of somebody.

P

**portray** *verb* 1 to make a picture of somebody or something. 2 to describe in words. 3 to play the part of a character in a film or play.

**Portugal** *noun* a country in Southwest Europe.

**Portuguese** *noun* the language spoken in Portugal and Brazil. Portuguese *adjective. The Portuguese flag.*

**Port Vila** *noun* the capital of Vanuatu.

**pose** 1 a particular position in or for a photograph or painting. *He sat in an unnatural pose.* 2 a way of behaving in order to impress or deceive people. **pose** *verb* 1 to sit or stand in a pose for a photograph or painting. 2 to behave in a way to impress other people or be admired by them. *I hate the way she is always posing at parties.* 3 to pretend. *The spy was posing as a car mechanic.* 4 to bring into being, to cause. *Lack of money is posing too many problems.* **poser** *noun.*

**position** *noun* 1 the place where something is or stands. *The house is in a sunny position.* 2 the way of sitting or standing. *He slept in an uncomfortable position.* 3 a situation or condition. *You've put me in an awkward position.* 4 a job. 5 a particular place in a group. 6 an opinion. **position** *verb* to put somebody or something into position. *I positioned the table by the door.*

**positive** *adjective* 1 sure, certain, having no doubt about something. *I am positive that I have seen you before.* 2 practical, helpful. *Let me give you some positive advice.* 3 agreeing, saying yes. *I got a positive reply to my request.* 4 real, noticeable. *It was a positive delight to see the children playing so happily together.* 5 greater than zero. *A positive number.* The positive sign is +. 6 If a medical test is positive, it shows that something, usually a disease, is present. **positively** *adverb* 1 definitely, really being the case. 2 without doubt. *The food was positively horrible.*

**possess** *verb* 1 to have or own. *I wish he possessed some of his brother's charm.* 2 to influence somebody's behaviour or thinking. *What possessed you to drive so fast?*

**GRAMMAR NOTE**

*You make the possessive form of a singular noun by adding apostrophe 's' at the end: 'my father's book'. Plural nouns have 's' apostrophe at the end: 'my parents' house'.*

The Japanese woman adopted a traditional pose for her photograph.

**WORD BUILDING**

*The usual opposite of 'post–' is 'pre–', or sometimes 'ante–': 'post-war' and 'pre-war'; ' post-natal' and 'ante-natal'.*

Our friends sent a postcard from the seaside.

**AMAZING FACT**

In the 1880s a New England post office received a letter with the following address:

John
Hill
Mass.

He realised that it was to John Underhill, Andover, Massachusetts.

**possession** *noun* 1 ownership, possessing. *How did the paper come into your possession?* 2 the things you possess or own. *He left all his possessions to his best friend.*

**possessive** *adjective* 1 wanting to keep things for yourself. *My brother is very possessive about his bike.* 2 in grammar, a possessive word shows ownership. 'My' and 'their' are possessive adjectives. **possessiveness** *noun.*

**possible** *adjective* able to happen, be done or that may be true. *Please come as soon as possible.* **possibility** *noun.* **possibly** *adverb.*

**post** *noun* 1 an upright bar of wood, metal or concrete fixed into the ground, especially as a support. *A lamp post.* 2 the starting or finishing point in a race. 3 a job. 4 a special place on duty, especially on guard. *The soldiers had to stay at their posts.*

**post** *noun* 1 the service of collecting, sorting and delivering of letters and parcels. *The cheque is in the post.* 2 the letters and parcels that are delivered. **post** *verb* 1 to put a letter or parcel into a postbox or take it to the post office for collection. 2 to send somebody to a particular place to work or to place soldiers on duty or guard. *Guards were posted around the building.* **postal** *adjective. Postal charges have gone up for the third time this year.* **keep somebody posted** to keep somebody informed.

**post-** *prefix* later than. *A post-war building.*

**postcard** *noun* a card for sending a message without an envelope.

**postcode** *noun* a group of letters and figures added to an address to help the post office sort mail.

**poster** *noun* a large picture or notice that is stuck to a wall or noticeboard.

**posthumous** *adjective* printed or happening after a person's death. **posthumously** *adverb. Posthumously awarded a medal.*

**post-mortem** *noun* an examination of a dead body to find the cause of death.

**post office** *noun* the place that deals with the post and postal business.

**postpone** *verb* to fix a later date or move to a later time. *The match was postponed because of rain.* **postponement** *noun.*

P

**pot** *noun* a round container for cooking or keeping things in. **go to pot** to be ruined, especially from lack of care. **take pot luck** to take whatever is offered or available. **pot** (pots, potting, potted) *verb* 1 to put into a pot, especially food for preserving or plants. 2 to hit a ball into one of the pockets in snooker or pool.

**potato** *noun* a round vegetable with brown or red skin that grows underground.

**potential** *adjective* capable of happening or being used. Not yet developed, but able to come into existence. *This film is a potential success.* **potential** *noun. The boy shows lots of potential.* **potentially** *adverb.*

**potholing** *noun* the sport of exploring underground caves. **pothole** *noun.* **potholer** *noun. The potholer called for help.*

**pottery** *noun* 1 pots, plates and other objects that are made from clay and then baked in an oven. 2 a place where pottery is made. **potter** *noun.*

Classical Greek pottery is often decorated with designs of red and black showing scenes of life in ancient Greece.

**potty** *noun* a pot used by little children as a toilet. *The baby is being potty-trained.*

**pouch** (pouches) *noun* a small bag or anything shaped like a bag.

**poultry** *noun* farm birds like chickens and ducks that are kept for eggs and meat.

**pounce** *verb* to leap or swoop down quickly, especially in order to get something. *The cat pounced on the mouse as it crept out from behind the cupboard.*

**pound** *noun* 1 a unit of weight equal to 454 grams or 16 ounces. 2 a unit of money, used in Britain. One pound is divided into a hundred pence. *I earned fifteen pounds (£15) today.*

**pound** *noun* a place where stray animals and illegally parked cars are taken and kept until collected by the owner.

**pound** *verb* 1 to hit something loudly and repeatedly. *I can feel my heart pounding.* 2 to crush into a powder or paste.

**WORD HISTORY**

*There are various explanations of where the expression 'to go to pot' comes from. It might have referred originally to putting old used items into a pot, or waste bin; or it might have meant putting food into a pot for stewing; it could even have referred to putting a cremated person's ashes into an urn.*

**DID YOU KNOW?**

*Potatoes first grew in the Andes Mountains of South America. Spanish and Portuguese conquerors took them back to their countries in the 16th century, and Sir Walter Raleigh introduced them to England around 1585.*

**pour** *verb* 1 to flow or make liquid or another substance flow. *He poured me a drink.* 2 to rain. *It's been pouring all day.* 3 to come or go quickly and in large amounts. *Fan mail has been pouring in.* **pour out** to tell freely and with feeling, especially a story or your troubles. *She poured out all her worries.*

**poverty** *noun* the state of being very poor. *They live in poverty.*

**powder** *noun* any substance that has been crushed or rubbed to dust. *Washing powder.* **powder** *verb* to put powder on. *She powdered her nose.* **powdered** *adjective* in the form of powder. *Powdered milk.* **powdery** *adjective* like powder.

**power** *noun* 1 the ability to do something or have a certain effect. *He did everything in his power to help.* 2 force, physical strength. *The power of the waves threw the boat on to the beach.* 3 energy, the force that makes things work. *Electric power.* 4 authority, the right to do something. *The power of the press.* 5 a person or organization that has great influence. *America is a world power.* **in power** having the right to govern. **powerful** *adjective.* **powerless** *adjective* without energy or influence.

Nuclear power stations generate energy.

**practicable** *adjective* that can be done.

**practical** *adjective* 1 good at doing or making things. Clever at dealing with difficulties, sensible. 2 useful, convenient, good for a particular purpose. *A plastic tablecloth is very practical, you can just wipe it clean.* 3 concerned with action and practice, rather than just ideas. A practical lesson is a lesson in which you make things or do experiments. *She didn't get the job because she had no practical experience.* **practicality** *noun.*

**practical joke** *noun* a funny trick played on a person.

**practically** *adverb* 1 in a practical way. 2 almost. *He practically walked into her.*

**practice** *noun* 1 something done regularly or as an exercise. *We have football practice twice a week.* 2 doing something, knowledge of a skill. *In practice this arrangement will never work.* 3 the business of a doctor or lawyer. **out of practice** no longer very good, because of lack of practice.

P

**practise** *verb* 1 to do something often in order to be good or get better at it. *I'm practising this piece on my guitar for the concert.* 2 to take part in an activity, do something actively. *People are allowed to practise any religion in this country.* 3 to work as a doctor or lawyer.

The team practised every day before the big match.

**pragmatic** *adjective* dealing with things in a practical way, a way which is best under the actual conditions. **pragmatist** *noun*.

**Prague** *noun* the capital of the Czech Republic.

**Praia** *noun* the capital of Cape Verde.

**prairie** *noun* flat grassland in North America. *Wheat prairies.*

The pioneers travelled across the prairies of the US.

**praise** *verb* to say that somebody or something is very good. *He praised her courage.* **praise** *noun* words that praise somebody or something.

**prattle** *noun* meaningless childish talk. **prattle** *verb*. *She prattled on about the clothes she wants to buy.*

**prawn** *noun* a small shellfish like a shrimp.

**pray** *verb* to speak to God. *She prayed that God would give her strength.*

**prayer** *noun* 1 the activity of praying. 2 the words used in praying. A set form of words used during service. 3 a strong hope. *My prayers were answered when he asked me out for a meal.*

**praying mantis** *noun* an insect.

**pre-** *prefix* before a particular time. *A pre-war building.*

**preach** (preaches, preaching, preached) *verb* to give a talk, especially a moral or religious talk. **preacher** *noun*.

**precaution** *noun* something done in order to avoid a possible known danger or trouble. **precautionary** *adjective*. *We took precautionary measures and put up a fence.*

**AMAZING FACT**

If you add a word or part of a word (called a prefix) to the beginning of a root word, you can form a new word. The word 'prefix' itself comes from 'pre–' ('before') and 'fix' ('fasten').

**GRAMMAR NOTE**

*If you add a word or part of a word (called a prefix) to the beginning of a root word, you can form a new word. The word 'prefix' itself comes from 'pre–' '('before') and 'fix'('fasten').*

**precede** *verb* to come or go in front.

**precinct** (say **pree**-sinkt) *noun* 1 a specially built shopping area, in which cars are not allowed. 2 the area around a cathedral or university, often enclosed by walls.

**precious** *adjective* 1 very valuable. 2 much loved by somebody. *My dolls are very precious to me.* **precious little** very little.

**precipice** *noun* a very steep side of a rock, mountain or cliff. **precipitous** *adjective*. *A precipitous mountain path.*

Karen got ready to abseil down the precipice.

**precipitation** *noun* 1 being too hurried, unwise haste. 2 the amount of rain or snow that falls. **precipitate** *verb*.

**precise** *adjective* exact, clear. *He gave a precise description of the accident.* **precision** *noun*. **precisely** *adverb*. *At precisely that moment he appeared at the door.*

**precocious** (say prik-**oh**-shus) *adjective* seeming older, having developed earlier than is normal in mind or body. *He is a precocious little boy, he talks like an adult.*

**predecessor** (say **pree**-dis-ess-er) *noun* somebody who has had a job before another person, or something that was used before something else. *The new headmaster is much better than his predecessor.*

**predict** *verb* to say what will or might happen, to forecast. **prediction** *noun*. *My prediction is that the idea will be very successful.* **predictable** *adjective*. *A predictable mistake.*

**prefabricated** *adjective* made in parts in a factory. *Prefabricated buildings are fitted together on site.* **prefabricate** *verb*.

**preface** *noun* an introduction to a book or speech. *The preface is by a famous writer.*

**prefer** (prefers, preferring, preferred) *verb* to like one person or thing better than another. *I prefer coffee to tea.* **preference** *noun*. *What is your preference?*

**prefix** (prefixes) *noun* a word or group of letters in front of a word to make a new word. The prefix 'un-' before 'load' makes the word 'unload'.

P

**pregnant** *adjective* When a woman or female animal is pregnant, a baby develops inside her body. **pregnancy** *noun.*

**prehistoric** *adjective* of the time before history was written down. *Dinosaurs were prehistoric animals.*

Scientists think that prehistoric animals such as the dinosaur were wiped out when the Earth suffered a dramatic climate change, killing the vegetation on which they fed.

**prejudice** *noun* an unfair opinion or dislike of somebody or something, not based on knowledge or experience. *They were accused of racial prejudice and brought to trial.* **prejudiced** *adjective.*

**premature** *adjective* done or happening earlier than usual or expected. *A premature baby may need to be put in an incubator.*

**premiere** *noun* the first showing or performance of a film or play.

**premises** *plural noun* a building and its grounds. *Residential premises.*

**preoccupied** *adjective* thinking a lot about something and therefore not giving attention to other matters. *She is so preoccupied with plans for her wedding that she can't work.* **preoccupation** *noun.*

**prepare** *verb* to get or make ready. **prepared** *adjective* 1 got ready in advance. 2 willing. *I'm not prepared to help you.*

**preposition** *noun* in grammar, a word or group of words used with a noun or pronoun to show its connection with another word such as place, position or time. In 'the woman on the stage', 'on' is a preposition.

**prescribe** *verb* 1 to advise what medicine or treatment a patient should have. *The doctor prescribed a cough mixture.* 2 to state what must be done. **prescription** *noun. I get the drugs on prescription.*

**DID YOU KNOW**

*The youngest ever President of the United States was the 26th president, Theodore Roosevelt (1858–1919), who was 42 when he entered office; he was president from 1901 to 1909.*

**present** *noun* (say **pre**-zunt) something given, a gift. *Christmas presents.* **present** *verb* (say pree-**zent**) 1 to give something formally, especially something like a prize. *They presented her with a bouquet of flowers.* 2 to introduce somebody to an important person or introduce a television or radio programme. *Professor Bird presented the documentary.* 3 to put on a play or show. 4 to offer, show or be the cause of. *He loves sailing because it presents such a challenge.* **presentation** *noun.*

She was thrilled when she saw her present.

**present** *noun* (say **pre**-zunt) the time that is taking place now or the things that are happening at the moment. *Try to live in the present, not the past.* **at present** now.

**present** *adjective* (say **pre**-zunt) 1 there, in this or that place. *Is a doctor present?* 2 existing now. *The present government.* 3 being talked or written about now. *We'll make an exception in the present case.* **presence** *noun. I don't talk about it in her presence.* **presently** *adverb.*

**president** *noun* 1 the leader of a country. *The president of the United States.* 2 a person who has a high position in an organization such as a club, a college or a company. *The president of our golf club.* **presidency** *noun.* **presidential** *adjective.*

Nelson Mandela cast a vote for the ANC in South Africa's first free election. He became the first black president of his nation.

**press** *verb* 1 to push hard against something or push one thing against another. *You have to press harder to make it work.* 2 to squeeze or flatten. To press flowers in a book. 3 to iron. *Can you press my trousers?* 4 to persuade somebody to do something or make demands. *She's always pressing us to stay longer.* **press on** to go on doing something. **pressed for** If you are pressed for time, you are in a hurry. If you are pressed for money, you do not have enough money at the moment. *I am pressed for time and money.*

**press** (presses) *noun* 1 the action of pushing against something. *At the press of a button.* 2 a device or machine for pressing. *A flower press.* 3 newspapers, magazines and journalists. *He was interviewed by the press.* 4 a business for printing and making books and magazines. 5 a machine for printing books and magazines. *A printing press.*

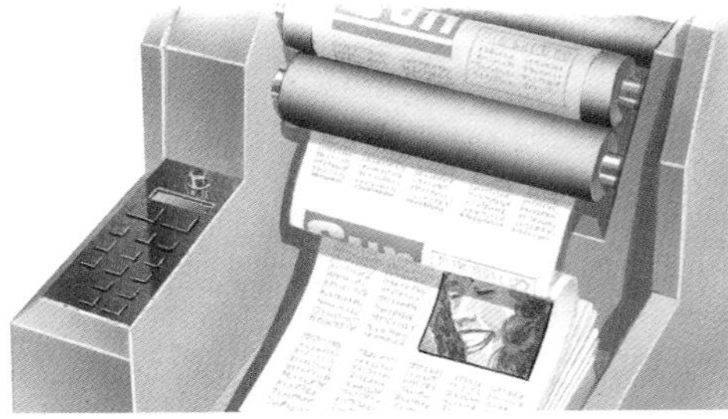

The newspapers rolled off the printing presses.

**press conference** *noun* an interview with journalists. *He held a press conference.*

**pressure** *noun* 1 the action of pressing. 2 the force with which something presses. *The water pressure is very low.* 3 a feeling of being forced to do something, a strain. *She was under pressure to do well at school.* **put pressure on somebody** to force somebody to do something. *They put pressure on her to leave the country.* **pressure** *verb* to forcefully make somebody do something. *They pressured me into going to university.* **pressurize** *verb.*

**presume** *verb* to think that something is the case or true. *An accused person is presumed innocent until proved guilty.* **presumption** *noun.*

**pretend** *verb* to act in a way as if something is true or real, although in fact it is not, either as a game or to deceive people. *He's snoring, pretending to be asleep.* **pretence** *noun. He doesn't really like the job, it's all a pretence.*

**Pretoria** *noun* the seat of government of South Africa.

**pretty** (prettier, prettiest) *adjective* nice, attractive. *A pretty girl.* **prettily** *adverb.* **prettiness** *noun.*

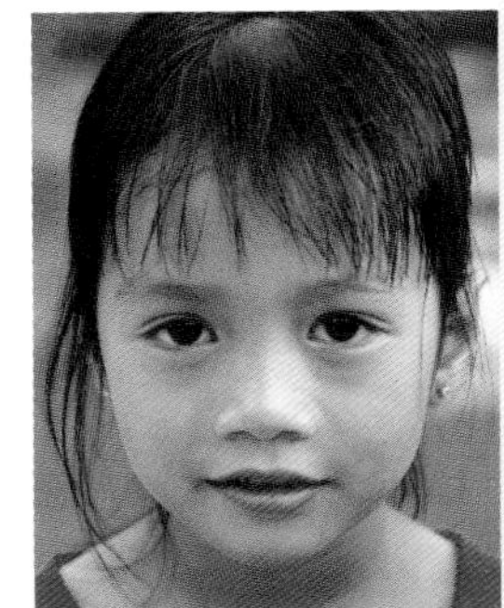

She's a pretty girl with pierced ears.

**pretty** *adverb* quite or rather. *It was pretty hot.* **pretty much** very nearly, almost.

We went up into the mountains to observe the birds of prey.

**GRAMMAR NOTE**

*You can pressure or pressurize someone into doing something: 'My father pressured (or pressurized) me into taking the exam again.'*

**DID YOU KNOW?**

*The South African city of Pretoria was founded in 1855 and named after the Afrikaner leader Andries Pretorius (1799–1853). Today it is the administrative capital of South Africa.*

**prevailing** *adjective* most common or general, especially of a custom or belief. *The prevailing wind is a westerly.*

**prevent** *verb* 1 to stop somebody from doing something. 2 to make sure something does not happen. *How can we prevent war?* **prevention** *noun. Crime prevention.* **preventive** *adjective. Preventive medicine.*

**previous** *adjective* happening or being earlier in time or before the one you are talking about. *In my previous job.* **previously** *adverb. They previously lived in Germany.*

**prey** (say pray) *noun* 1 an animal that is hunted and eaten by other animals. *The lion pounced on its prey.* 2 a helpless person, a victim. **bird of prey** a bird that hunts and eats animals or other birds. **prey on** *verb* 1 to hunt for food. 2 to attack and steal from people. 3 to trouble you greatly, to make you worry about something. *The journey is preying on my mind.*

**price** *noun* 1 an amount of money for which something is bought or sold. *We have to fix a price.* 2 what you must do in order to get what you want. *He paid the price of becoming rich and famous.* **price** *verb* 1 to fix the price of something. 2 to mark goods in a shop with a price. *I've priced the jam at £2.00 a pot.*

**priceless** *adjective* worth a lot of money, very valuable. *A priceless painting.*

**prick** *verb* 1 to make a small hole in something. *I pricked my finger with a needle.* 2 to hurt somebody with a pin or something sharp, or feel a sharp pain on the skin. *The thorns pricked me.* **prick** *noun* 1 a small hole. 2 a sharp pain.

**prickle** *noun* 1 a small sharp point that sticks out from a plant or an animal. *The prickles of a cactus.* 2 a feeling that something is pricking you. **prickle** *verb* to have or give a pricking feeling. *Wool makes my skin prickle.* **prickly** *adjective. Prickly holly leaves.*

**pride** *noun* 1 a feeling of delight and pleasure in what you or people you know have done. *She showed him her certificate with pride.* 2 something that makes you feel proud. *The children are her pride and joy.* 3 too high an opinion of yourself, especially because of wealth or position. 4 self-respect. *He swallowed his pride and said sorry.* **pride yourself on** to be proud of. *She prides herself on never having missed a lesson.*

P

**priest** *noun* 1 a member of the Christian clergy, a clergyman. 2 a specially trained person who performs religious ceremonies. **priestess** *noun.*

**prim** (primmer, primmest) *adjective* very correct and easily shocked by anything rude.

**primary** *adjective* extremely important, main. *A peace agreement is our primary aim.* **primarily** *adverb.*

**primary colour** *noun* The primary colours are red, yellow and blue. All other colours can made up by mixing them in different ways.

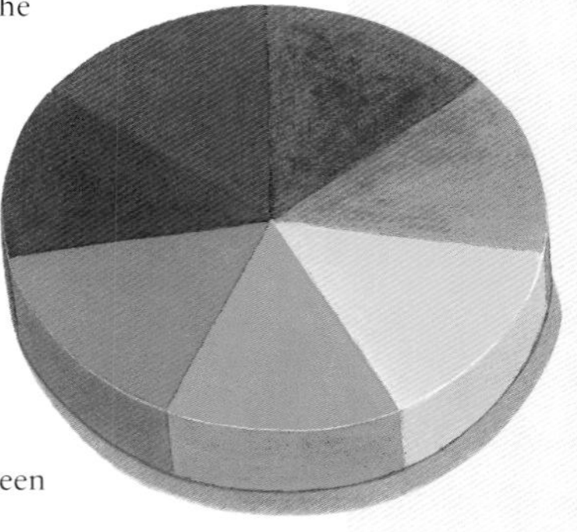

Primary colours can be mixed to form all the other colours of the spectrum.

**primary school** *noun* a school for children between 5 and 11 years old.

**prime** *adjective* 1 most important. *Computers are of prime importance in all businesses, hospitals and schools.* 2 of the very best quality, best. *Early evening is the prime time for advertising on television.* **prime minister** the head of a government. **prime number** a number that can be divided only by itself and the number 1. 3, 7 and 11 are prime numbers.

**prime** *noun* the best or most successful stage of something. *He is past his prime.*

**prime** *verb* 1 to give somebody information beforehand so that they are prepared, especially for difficulties. *She had primed him before the interview, so he could answer all the questions.* 2 to cover a surface, especially wood, with a coat of paint or oil to prepare it for painting. 3 to get a machine ready for use.

**primitive** *adjective* 1 belonging to a society of people who lived at an earlier time. *Primitive man made tools from sharp stone and animal bones.* 2 simple or old-fashioned. *This cottage is too primitive for me, it has no central heating.*

**primrose** *noun* a wild plant that has pale yellow flowers.

**prince** *noun* a man or boy in a royal family, especially the son of a king or queen.

**princess** *noun* 1 a woman or girl in a royal family, especially the daughter of a king or queen. 2 the wife of a prince.

**principal** *adjective* most important.

**principal** *noun* 1 the head of a school or college. 2 money lent or put into a business on which interest is paid.

**AMAZING FACT**

An easy way to remember how to spell 'principal' is to think of the principal as your pal or friend!.

**SPELLING NOTE**

*As an adjective, 'principal' is spelt '–pal'. As a noun, 'principal' is the spelling for the head of a school or an amount of money. A 'principle' (with '–ple') is a rule.*

**principle** *noun* 1 a general rule about how something should be done or how it works. *The principles of grammar.* 2 a rule for behaviour. *It was against his principles.* **in principle** in general. *In principle I agree with you.* **on principle** because of your personal beliefs. *I'm against war on principle.*

**print** *verb* 1 to produce words or pictures on paper with a machine or shapes covered with ink. To make books, magazines and pictures in this way. *How many copies of this dictionary were printed?* 2 to write words without joining the letters, usually in capitals. *Please print your name and then sign here.* 3 to press a mark on to a surface or make a pattern on cloth. *The pattern has been printed on to the scarf by hand.* 4 to make a photograph from a negative film. **print** *noun* 1 the printed letters and numbers on a page. *The print is too small to read without glasses.* 2 a mark made on a surface showing the shape of the thing pressed on it. *The tyres left prints in the sand.* 3 a printed picture, photograph or pattern. **in print** 1 printed in a book, magazine or newspaper. *Don't believe everything you see in print.* 2 If a book is in print, it is still available and can be bought. **printing** *noun.*

We followed the tyre prints and discovered the stolen car.

**printer** *noun* 1 a person or firm that prints books, newspapers and other printed material. 2 a machine connected to a computer that prints out what you have written or any other information.

**print-out** *noun* information from a computer printed on a piece of paper.

**prior** *preposition, adjective* earlier or more important than something else. *They had already decided prior to the event.*

**prior** *noun* a monk who is the head of a religious house, called a priory.

**priority** *noun* something considered more important than other things. *We must do that as a priority.*

**prism** (say **priz**-um) *noun* 1 a solid shape with a flat base and parallel upright edges. 2 a three-sided block, usually made of glass, that breaks up light into the colours of the rainbow.

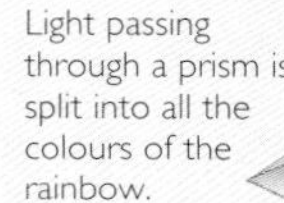

Light passing through a prism is split into all the colours of the rainbow.

**prison** *noun* a building where criminals are kept locked up as a punishment. *The thief was sent to prison for three years.*

The prison had tall gates with a window to check a visitor's identity.

**prisoner** *noun* a person kept in prison as a punishment. 2 a person or animal who has been captured and is kept locked up.

**privacy** *noun* being private, away from others and able to do things without other people seeing you.

**private** *adjective* 1 for one person or a small group of people, not public, not shared with others, personal. *A house with a private swimming pool.* 2 secret or kept secret. *He has some private information about the president.* 3 personal, rather than to do with work or business. *He never talks about his private life at work.* 4 quiet, sheltered. Somebody who is a private person is shy and does not like to share their feelings with other people. 5 independent, not owned by the state. *Private hospitals and private schools are not paid for by the government.* **in private** without other people listening or hearing, away from others. *Could we have a talk in private?*

**privileged** *adjective* having an advantage that most other people do not have. *She came from a privileged background.* **privilege** *noun. It was a privilege to be able to work with such a famous director.*

**prize** *noun* something of value given to the winner of a game, competition or particular good work. **prize** *verb* to value highly. *Italian tomatoes are prized for their taste.*

The first prize for excellence at school went to Jennifer Jones.

**pro** *noun* a professional. *He turned pro when he was just eighteen.*

**pro-** *prefix* for somebody or something, in favour of. *He is very pro-Italian.* **pro and con** for and against.

**AMAZING FACT**

It is best not to begin a sentence with the 'probably' . For example, 'Probably I will spend Easter at home.' is not correct. It should read 'I will probably spend Easter at home.'

**WORD HISTORY**

*Originally a privilege was a 'law affecting an individual', from the Latin 'privilegium'. This word itself came from two other Latin words: 'privus', meaning 'private', and 'legis', meaning 'law'.*

**probably** *adverb* very likely. *I'll probably see you tomorrow.* **probable** *adjective. He is the probable winner.*

**probation** *noun* 1 a period of time during which somebody's abilities at work are tested before they are finally given the job. 2 a system of letting a criminal go free if he behaves well. Somebody on probation is supervised by an official, a probation officer, for a period of time.

**probe** *noun* 1 a long thin metal instrument used by doctors to search inside the body. 2 an object used for exploring space. **probe** *verb* to search or explore.

**problem** *noun* something difficult, a question for which an answer is needed. **problematic, problematical** *adjective.*

**proboscis** (say pro-**boss**-iss) *noun* 1 the long part of an insect's mouth. 2 an elephant's trunk.

The elephant's trunk is technically called a proboscis.

**procedure** *noun* a way of doing something, especially in a correct way.

**proceed** *verb* 1 to continue with an action, often after stopping. 2 to go forward in a particular direction.

**proceedings** *plural noun* 1 a series of happenings. 2 a lawsuit.

**process** (processes) *noun* (say **proh**-sess) 1 a series of actions for doing or achieving something. *Packing the car was a slow process.* 2 a series of things that happen naturally. *Chemical processes.* 3 an action in law. **process** *verb* 1 to treat food and other materials using a particular process. *To process (develop) a film.* 2 to produce information by putting it through a process. *It will take a week for us to process the applications.*

**procession** *noun* a group of people or vehicles moving forward, following each other. *A funeral procession.*

**proclaim** *verb* to make officially known. **proclamation** *noun.*

**prod** (prods, prodding, prodded) *verb* 1 to push with your finger or something pointed. 2 to get or remind somebody to act. *You have to prod him into action.* **prod** *noun.*

**prodigal** *adjective* wasteful, especially of money. *The prodigal son.*

**produce** *verb* 1 to make, grow or create. *The Sun produces heat.* 2 to show, bring out to be seen. *He produced a ticket to prove he had paid.* 3 to cause to happen. *Good soil will produce good vegetables.* 4 to organize a film, play, record or programme. *The film was directed and produced by the same person.* **produce** *noun* things produced, especially things grown. **producer** *noun.*

**product** *noun* 1 something produced, especially something manufactured. *Cleaning products.* 2 the result of thought or conditions. 3 in maths, the number obtained by multiplying two or more numbers.

**production** *noun* 1 the process of producing, making or growing things in large quantities. 2 something produced, a play, opera or show.

**productive** *adjective* producing a lot of things, especially in large amounts. *We had a very productive meeting.*

**profession** *noun* a job that needs special training. *Teaching always has been a poorly paid profession.*

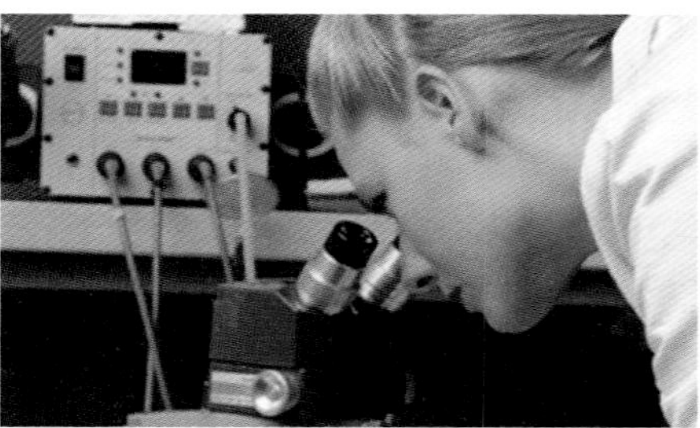

Science is a serious profession.

**professional** *adjective* 1 of a particular profession. 2 doing work as a proper job for payment. *You can earn a lot of money as a professional footballer.* 3 showing the skill of a professional, competent. **professional** *noun. He is a true professional.* **professionally** *adverb.*

**program** *noun* a set of instructions for a computer to carry out. **program** (programs, programming, programmed) *verb. Can you program a computer to answers questions?* **programmer** *noun.*

**programme** *noun* 1 a fixed plan of events, activities or a list of duties. *What is on the programme today?* 2 a booklet or list that gives information about what you have come to see or take part in. *A theatre programme.* 3 a performance, talk or show on radio or television. *A new music programme.* **programme** *verb. The central heating is programmed to come on at six.*

The theatre programme explained the history of the production.

**DID YOU KNOW?**

*A prodigal son is a wasteful person who changes his ways, and the expression is sometimes also used just to mean a returned wanderer. This comes from a parable in the Bible.*

**AMAZING FACT**

Computer programs use a system of numbers called the 'binary system'. Instead of using the numbers 0–9, as we do, the binary system uses only 0 and 1.

**progress** (say **pro**-gress) *noun* 1 forward movement, the process of gradually getting nearer to something. *We made slow progress up the hill.* 2 development or improvement. *You are making good progress in your work.* **in progress** happening now. *When we arrived, the game was already in progress.* **progress** *verb* (say pro-**gress**) to make progress.

**progressive** *adjective* 1 moving forward or happening gradually over a period of time. *The progressive closure of the coal industry.* 2 having modern ideas how things should be done. *Most progressive schools are against wearing uniform.*

**prohibit** *verb* to say that something must not be done, to ban. **prohibition** *noun.*

**project** *noun* (say **pro**-jekt) 1 a plan. 2 a study of a subject by a student. *Our class is doing a project on pop music.* **project** *verb* (say pruh-**jekt**) 1 to stick out above a surface or edge. 2 to make a light or picture from a film appear on a surface. *The pictures were projected on to a screen.* 3 to throw or send through the air with force. *Missiles were projected into space.* 4 to plan. *The minister's projected visit to Spain has been cancelled.* **projection** *noun.*

**projector** *noun* a machine for showing films or slides on a screen or wall.

We bought a projector so we could see our holiday slides.

**prolong** *verb* to make longer or make something last longer. *Let's not prolong this ludicrous argument.*

**prominent** *adjective* 1 important, well known. *The Ritz is full of prominent people.* 2 standing out, noticeable. *Her bottom is unfortunately the most prominent part of her body.* **prominently** *adverb.* **prominence** *noun.*

**promise** *noun* 1 a statement that you make to somebody to say that you will do or give them something. *She always keeps her promises.* 2 expectation or hope of success. *The singer shows great promise.* **promise** *verb. He promised to buy her a new bike.*

**promising** *adjective* likely to be successful.

**promote** *verb* 1 to give somebody a more important job or higher rank. 2 to bring to notice, especially to increase sales or somebody's popularity. *The firm is promoting a new shampoo on television.* **promotion** *noun.* **promoter** *noun.*

**prompt** *adjective* without delay, punctual. A prompt reply. **promptly** *adverb*. *He arrived promptly at 9 o'clock.*

**prompt** *verb* 1 to make you decide to do something. *Poor results prompted the manager to change the team.* 2 to remind an actor or speaker of the next words when they have been forgotten.

**prone** *adjective* lying face downwards. **be prone to** be likely to do or have something. *He is prone to bad moods.*

**prong** *noun* a spike of a fork.

The fork has three prongs.

**pronoun** *noun* in grammar, a word that is used in place of a noun that has already been or will be mentioned. He, she, it, hers, them are pronouns.

**pronounce** *verb* 1 to make the sound of a letter or word. In the word 'gnaw' the 'g' is not pronounced. 2 to declare formally. He was pronounced dead. **pronunciation** *noun*. *His French pronunciation is very good.*

**proof** *noun* 1 a thing or fact that shows that something is true. *He has no proof that the car belongs to him.* 2 a trial copy of something printed, made for checking before other copies are printed.

**proof** *suffix* showing that something cannot be damaged or gives protection against something harmful. *A waterproof jacket. A foolproof tin-opener.*

**prop** *noun* 1 a support used to keep something up. 2 (usually plural, props) the furniture and other objects used in a play or film. **prop** (props, propping, propped) *verb* to support or keep in position by putting something under or against. *She propped the door open with a shoe.* **prop somebody up** to help and give support to somebody.

The plastic knife was often used as a prop during theatre productions.

**propaganda** *noun* information, often false information, given to influence people. *The extremists put out a lot of propaganda.*

**DID YOU KNOW?**

*Propellers work by thrusting a vehicle forwards. A ship's propeller is connected to a shaft, which is turned by the engine. As it turns, the propeller pushes water backwards, and this thrusts the ship forwards.*

**SPELLING NOTE**

*Note that the noun from 'pronounce' is spelt 'pronunciation': the middle part is spelt – and pronounced! 'Nun' rather than 'noun'.*

**propel** (propels, propelling, propelled) *verb* to push or drive forward.

**propeller** *noun* blades fixed to a bar which spin round and make an aircraft or ship go.

**proper** *adjective* 1 suitable, correct, right for the situation. *Everything was in its proper place.* 2 respectable. *Proper behaviour.* 3 great, real. *I felt a proper fool.* **properly** *adverb*. *She doesn't eat properly, all she has for lunch is bag of crisps.*

**prophecy** (prophecies) *noun* telling something that will happen in the future.

**prophet** *noun* 1 a person who is believed to be chosen by God to teach a religion to the people. *Muslims are followers of the Prophet Muhammad.* 2 somebody who makes prophecies.

A prophet is often a person who has spent a great deal of time alone among nature, asking difficult questions about religion and existence.

**proposal** *noun* 1 a plan or suggestion. 2 an offer of marriage.

**propose** *verb* 1 to suggest an idea or plan. 2 to ask somebody to marry you. *Tom proposed to Emma.*

**prosecute** *verb* to accuse somebody of a crime and try and prove it in a court of law. *He was prosecuted for burglary.* **prosecution** *noun* 1 the action of prosecuting somebody. 2 the lawyers who try to prove that the accused person is guilty.

**prospect** (say **pross**-pekt) *noun* 1 a possibility or hope. *What are the prospects of getting a job?* 2 a wide view.

**prospect** (say pruh-**spekt**) *verb* to search in the ground, especially for gold, silver or oil. **prospector** *noun*.

**prosper** *verb* to be successful or rich.

**prosperity** *noun* success and riches. **prosperous** *adjective*.

**prostitute** *noun* a person who offers sex for payment. **prostitution** *noun*.

**prostrate** *adjective* lying face downwards flat on the ground.

**protect** *verb* to keep safe from harm, danger or enemies. *Vitamin C helps protect against flu.* **protection** *noun*. *As a protection against the cold.* **protector** *noun*.

P

**protective** *adjective* 1 giving protection. 2 wishing to protect. *She is very protective towards her children.*

**protein** *noun* a body-building substance found in all living things. Protein is in foods such as meat, eggs, beans and milk.

**protest** (say **pro**-test) *noun* an act of saying or showing that you do not agree with something. *There were many protests against experiments on animals.* **protest** (say pruh-**test**) *verb* 1 *The workers protested against poor conditions.* 2 to state firmly. *He protested his innocence.* **protester** *noun.*

**protestant** *noun* a member of the Christian church which separated from the Catholic church in the sixteenth century.

**proton** *noun* a very small piece of matter, an atomic particle, that has a positive electric charge.

**prototype** *noun* the first model of something, from which others have been developed or are copied.

Mark sketched the prototype of the new car.

**proud** *adjective* 1 feeling pleased about something good that you or somebody else has done. *The Queen's visit was a proud day for the hospital.* 2 having self-respect or having too high an opinion of yourself. *She is too proud to say sorry.* **proudly** *adverb. She proudly showed us her son's medal.*

**prove** *verb* 1 to show that something is true. *Can you prove that all the doors were locked?* 2 to turn out or to be found to be as expected. *He proved to be a bad loser.*

**proverb** *noun* a short well-known saying, usually giving a general truth. 'Too many cooks spoil the broth' is a proverb. **proverbial** *adjective. The proverbial ill wind blows no one any good.*

**provide** *verb* 1 to give things that are needed or useful. *The hostel provides bed and breakfast.* 2 to state arrangements or make special arrangements that must be fulfilled. **provider** *noun.*

**provided, providing** *conjunction* on the condition that. *I'll lend you some money provided you promise to pay me back.*

**AMAZING FACT**

Canada is divided into ten provinces and two national territories: The Yukon Territory and the Northwest Territories

**DID YOU KNOW?**

*There are many proverbs to do with words. 'Actions speak louder than words.' 'Least said, soonest mended.' 'Easier said than done.' 'The pen is mightier than the sword.'*

**province** 1 a part of a country, a state. *Newfoundland is a province of Canada.* 2 (usually plural, the provinces) all the country outside the capital. 3 special knowledge or learning somebody has or is responsible for. *I'm in computing, but games consoles are outside my province.* **provincial** *adjective.*

Ottawa is the capital of Canada. It is in the province of Ontario.

**provoke** *verb* 1 to make somebody angry, usually on purpose. *That dog bites if provoked.* 2 to cause or force an action. *The boy's rudeness provoked a fight.* **provoking** *adjective* annoying. **provocation** *noun.* **provocative** *adjective.*

**prow** *noun* the front part of a boat.

**prowess** *noun* great ability or skill.

**prowl** *verb* to move about quietly, trying not to be seen or heard. **prowl** *noun.* An animal on the prowl is looking for food. **prowler** *noun.*

**prune** *noun* a dried plum.

Prunes are delicious with cream or custard.

**prune** *verb* to cut off or shorten branches of a tree or bush.

**psalm** *noun* (say sahm) a religious song from the Bible. The Book of Psalms is part of the Old Testament.

**pseudonym** *noun* a false name used by a writer. *He writes rather bad novels under the pseudonym John Smith.*

**psychiatry** *noun* (say sigh-**kie**-uh-tree) the study and treatment of mental illness. **psychiatric** (say sigh-key-**ah**-trik) *adjective.* **psychiatrist** *noun.*

**psychology** *noun* the study of the human mind and how it works. **psychological** *adjective. Psychological problems.* **psychologist** *noun.*

**pub** *noun* a public house, a building where people drink alcohol.

**puberty** *noun* (say **pew**-buh-tee) the time in a young person's life when they physically develop into an adult.

P

**pubic** *adjective* (say **pew**-bic) relating to the area around the sexual organs.

**public** *adjective* belonging to, for, connected with or known by everyone. Not private. *Public transport.* **public** *noun* all the people. *The castle is open to the public.* **in public** with other people there. *People sometimes say different things in public from what they say in private.*

**public school** *noun* a private school that charges fees.

**publish** *verb* 1 to have books, magazines, newspapers and other material printed and sold. *Her first book was published last spring.* 2 to make known to the public. *They published news of her death the day she died.* **publisher** *noun.*

**pudding** *noun* 1 a sweet food made with flour, fat, eggs and other ingredients. *I love vanilla pudding.* 2 the sweet dish in a meal, usually eaten at the end of a meal.

**puddle** *noun* a small pool of liquid, especially rainwater on the ground.

**puerile** (say **pew**-er-I'll) *adjective* childish.

**puffin** *noun* a sea-bird with a brightly coloured beak.

Puffins feed on fish from the sea.

**pull** *verb* 1 to use force to make something come towards or after you. *He pulled the chair up to the table.* 2 to drive, move a vehicle. *The car pulled out of the entrance.* 3 to attract interest or support. *Their concerts always pull big crowds.* 4 to injure. *He pulled a muscle in the race.* **pull a face** to make a strange or funny face. **pull apart** to separate by using force. **pull down** 1 to make something lower. *Pull the blind down if the sun bothers you.* 2 to destroy a building, usually to build a new one. **pull in** 1 to drive a car somewhere and stop. *We pulled in at the petrol station.* 2 to arrive at a station. *The train from London has just pulled in.* **pull off** 1 to take clothes off quickly. *He pulled off his boots.* 2 to succeed in a difficult situation. *He managed to pull the trick off.* **pull out** 1 to take something out. *The dentist pulled out a tooth.* 2 to move or drive out of a place. *The train pulled out of the station.* 3 When you pull out of an agreement, you get out of it. **pull through** to recover from a serious illness or accident. *She was very ill, but fortunately she pulled through.* **pull yourself together** to control your feelings and behave in a sensible way.

A pulley is an essential mechanism on any crane.

**AMAZING FACT**

In humans, pulse rates between 50 and 85 beats per minute are considered normal. Generally, the normal rate for men is about 72 beats per minute, for women the normal range is 76–80 beats. Children's pulse rates are faster.

You can take your own pulse by gently gripping your wrist with the fingertips of your other hand. Use a watch to count the number of beats per minute. Try taking your pulse after various activites.

**WORD HISTORY**

*You might think that the name of the drink 'punch' came from its power or zing. In fact, it has nothing to do with this. The origin is the Sanskrit word 'panca', meaning five. The number refers to the five ingredients that traditionally went into punch: wine, water, sugar, spice and fruit juice.*

**pulley** *noun* a wheel over which a rope or chain is moved, used for lifting heavy things.

**pulp** *noun* 1 the soft inner part of a fruit or vegetable. 2 a soft mass of other material. *Wood pulp.* 3 cheap books and magazines. **pulp** *verb* to crush.

**pulpit** *noun* a small platform for the preacher in a church.

**pulse** *noun* 1 the regular beating of blood as it is pumped through the body by the heart. You can feel your pulse when you touch your wrists. 2 the regular beat or throbbing of music. **pulse** *verb* to beat or shake with strong, regular movements.

**pulverize** *verb* 1 to crush into or become fine powder. 2 to destroy. *The town was pulverized by shelling.*

**puma** (say **pew**-muh) *noun* a large brown wild cat of western America, also called a cougar or mountain lion.

The puma pricked up her ears to hear a rustling in the grass.

**pump** *noun* a machine with a tube for forcing liquid, air or gas into or out of something. *A petrol pump.* **pump** *verb* 1 to force liquid or air into or from something with a pump. *Her heart was pumping fast. I must pump up my tyres.* 2 to get information, usually by asking questions. *He pumped me about my new job.* 3 to force something into somebody or something. *They have pumped a lot of money into the business.*

**pumpkin** *noun* a large round fruit with a hard orange skin. People hollow out pumpkins to make lanterns at Halloween.

**pun** *noun* an amusing use of words that have the same sound but different meanings.

**punch** *verb* 1 to hit hard with a fist. *He punched him in the stomach.* 2 to make a hole in something. **punch** (punches) *noun* 1 a hit with a fist. *The boxer had to take a lot of punches.* 2 a tool for making holes, especially in paper or leather. 3 a drink made of wine and fruit juice.

**punchline** *noun* the last few words in a joke that make it funny.

**punctual** *adjective* doing things at the right or fixed time. *He is always punctual, never even a minute late.* **punctually** *adverb.*

**punctuate** *verb* 1 to put full stops, commas and other punctuation marks in text. 2 to interrupt from time to time, especially a speech. **punctuation** *noun.*

**puncture** *noun* a small hole made by a sharp object, especially in a tyre. **puncture** *verb* to make or get a puncture. *A nail in the road must have punctured my tyre.*

Peter drove into the bonfire and punctured his tyre on a nail.

**punish** *verb* to make somebody suffer because they have done something wrong. **punishment** *noun.* **punishable** *adjective. In some countries murder is still punishable by the death penalty.*

**Punjabi** *noun* the language of the Punjab, an area in north-western India and Pakistan. **Punjabi** *adjective. The Punjabi people.*

**punt** *noun* a flat-bottomed boat pushed along by a pole. **punt** *verb* to travel in a punt. *Let's go punting on the river.*

**punt** *verb* to kick a ball by dropping it from the hands on to the foot. **punt** *noun.*

**punter** *noun* 1 a person who bets money, especially on horse races. 2 (slang) a customer. *It's what the punters want.*

**pupa** (pupae) *noun* (say **pew**-puh) an insect in a covering between the time when it creeps and the time when it flies.

The pupa was waiting to hatch out into a fully-fledged insect.

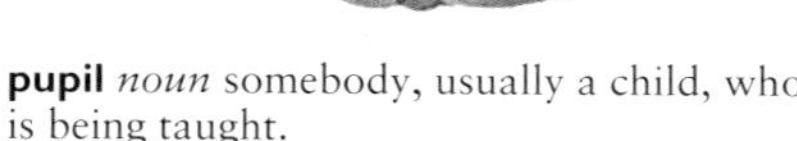

**pupil** *noun* somebody, usually a child, who is being taught.

**pupil** *noun* the small, round black opening in the middle of the coloured part of the eye. *Her pupils dilated.*

**puppet** *noun* 1 a doll you can move by pulling strings that are fixed to it, or by putting your hand inside its body (called a glove puppet). 2 somebody whose actions are controlled by others. *He is the politicians' puppet.*

**AMAZING FACT**

Puppies are blind when they are born. Their vision improves as they mature but even when they are fully grown, they are near-sighted and don't see things in colour, just shades of gray.

**WORD HISTORY**

*What's the connection between somebody being taught and the middle of the eye? They are both called 'pupils', but why? They actually come from the same Latin words, 'pupillus' or 'pupilla', meaning little boy or girl. A pupil in school is a boy or girl. The word came to refer to the eye because of the tiny reflection you get of yourself when you look closely into someone else's eye – you see a tiny boy or girl!*

**puppy** (puppies) *noun* a young dog.

The puppies looked identical.

**purchase** *verb* to buy. **purchase** *noun* 1 something bought. *Most of her purchases were clothes.* 2 buying. *Do you remember the date of purchase?* 3 a firm hold for pulling or stopping something from slipping. *His hands lost their purchase and he fell into the precipice.*

**pure** *adjective* 1 not mixed with anything else, clean and clear. 2 complete, total. *The hotel is pure luxury.* **purity** *noun.*

**purge** *verb* to get rid of unwanted people or feelings. *I'll purge this town of crime.*

**purple** *adjective, noun* reddish-blue.

**purpose** *noun* 1 a plan, a reason for doing something. *What is the purpose of this machine?* 2 a feeling of having an aim, willpower. *Teaching has given her a sense of purpose.* **on purpose** intentionally, not by accident. *She bumped into him on purpose.*

**purr** *verb* to make a low sound like a cat when it is pleased. **purr** *noun.*

**purse** *noun* a small bag for money.

**purse** *verb* to draw your lips together into a rounded shape. *She pursed her lips in distaste at the horrible smell.*

**pus** *noun* (say puhss) a thick yellowish liquid that comes out of an infected wound or other part of the body.

**push** *verb* 1 to press using force in order to make something or somebody move away or to a different position. *He pushed the window up.* 2 to make your way through something by using force. *Don't push in front of me.* 3 to force somebody to do something or force something on people. *The advertisers are pushing a new drink.* 4 to try to sell something illegal. *To push drugs.* **push ahead** to carry out. *We are pushing ahead with the new building.* **push for** to try to get. **push in** to come into a queue in front of other people. **push off** to go away. **push on** to continue to travel or work. **push** (pushes) *noun* 1 the action of pushing. 2 drive or energy. **to get the push** to be dismissed from your job. **to give somebody the push** to end a relationship. *Her boyfriend gave her the push last week.* **at a push** if really necessary, if forced. *I can finish the essay by next week at a push.*

**pushy** *adjective* unpleasantly keen to get things done so as to make yourself noticed.

**pussyfoot** *verb* to act very cautiously.

**put** (puts, putting, put) *verb* 1 to move, place, lay or fix something or somebody in a certain place or position. *Put your bike in the garage.* 2 to cause something or somebody to be in a particular state. *The news put her in a good mood.* 3 to express something in words or write something down. *She put it rather cleverly.* 4 to give money for something, or time or energy to something. *They only put £100 into the business.* **put across** to describe or explain something to somebody. **put away** to put something into a place where it is usually kept. If somebody is put away, they are sent to prison. **put something off** not to do something until later. **put somebody off** 1 to not see somebody until later than planned. 2 to make somebody dislike something or lose interest. *The smell puts me off fish.* **put on** 1 to make a light or piece of equipment work. *To put a CD on.* 2 *He put on his clothes.* 3 to pretend to be something or behave in an unnatural way. *She only puts on that shy voice.* 4 to add more to something. *She has put on weight.* **put out** 1 to stop a candle or fire from burning, to stop a light shining. 2 to make something known. *They put out a warning.* 3 to place things that are needed somewhere ready to be used. *I put out a clean shirt for you.* 4 to annoy or upset. *I was put out when everybody laughed at me.* **put up** 1 to build. *We put up a new fence.* 2 to give somebody a place to sleep. *We can put up your friends.* 3 to raise or unfold. *She put up her hand.* 4 to fix. *To put up a poster.* 5 to provide. *Who is putting up the money for the event?* 6 to increase. *Petrol prices have been put up.* **put up to** If you put somebody up to something, you tell them to do something foolish. **put up with** to accept something or somebody unpleasant, to suffer without complaining. *She puts up with a lot of trouble to keep her job.*

**AMAZING FACT**

Making your own crossword puzzles is a good way to practice spelling and helps you remember the meaning of words. Make a grid on a sheet of paper. Start with a longish word either across or down the page. Then add words to it, using a letter from the original word. Write short definitions as clues.

**WORD HISTORY**

*The word 'pyjamas' originally referred to just the trousers. The word comes from the Persian 'pay' and 'jama', meaning leg clothing.*

**putrid** (say **pew**-trid) *adjective* rotting and smelling bad. *Putrid vegetation.*

**putty** *noun* a soft paste used to fix glass into window frames or fill holes.

**puzzle** *noun* 1 a game or toy. *A jigsaw puzzle.* 2 a difficult question, problem or something that is hard to understand. *Why she wants to go there is a puzzle to me.* **puzzle** (puzzles, puzzling, puzzled) *verb* to make somebody feel confused because they do not understand. **puzzle out** to think hard to try and find an answer. **puzzle over** to think hard about something confusing. **puzzlement** *noun.*

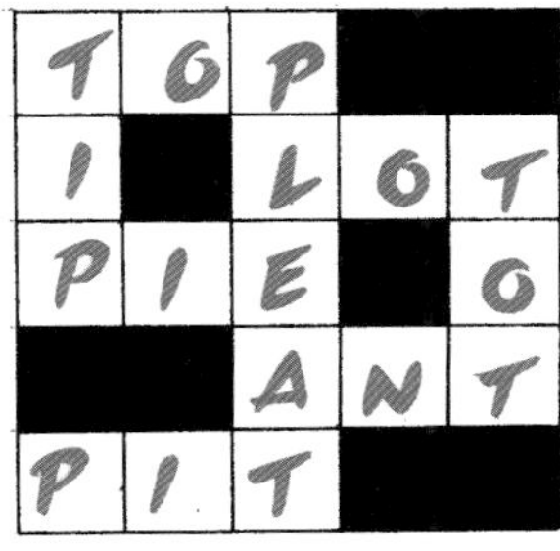


Muriel is addicted to crossword puzzles.

**pyjamas** *plural noun* a loose top and trousers worn for sleeping in.

**pylon** *noun* a tall metal structure used for holding wires that carry electricity over long distances. *Electricity pylons.*

**Pyongyang** *noun* the capital of North Korea.

**pyramid** *noun* 1 a shape with a flat base and three or four sloping sides that come to a point at the top. 2 an ancient Egyptian stone building over the tombs of the kings and queens of Egypt in a pyramid shape.

The ancient Egyptians buried their dead on the west bank of the Nile, where the Sun sets, and built their homes on the east bank, where it rises.

**pyrotechnics** *noun* 1 the art of making fireworks. 2 a fireworks display.

**python** *noun* a large snake that kills by winding its body round animals and squeezing them.

Qq

**Qatar** *noun* a country in Southwest Asia.

**quack** *verb* to make the harsh sound that a duck makes. **quack** *noun*.

**quadrangle** *noun* 1 a four-sided shape. 2 a four-sided area or courtyard with buildings all around it.

**quadrant** *noun* 1 a quarter of a circle. 2 an instrument for measuring vertical angles.

**quadri-** *prefix* four.

**quadrilateral** *noun* a flat shape with four straight sides.

**quadruped** *noun* any animal with four legs.

**quadruple** *verb* to multiply by four. *My wages have quadrupled in the last ten years.* **quadruple** *noun*.

**quadruplet** *noun* one of four babies born at the same time to the same mother (quad for short). *The quadruplets were doing fine.*

**quagmire** *noun* a very soft, marshy area of land. *I got bogged down in a quagmire.*

**quail** *verb* to show fear by trembling.

**quail** *noun* a small, plump bird related to the partridge, often shot as game.

Quail eggs are very popular as starters.

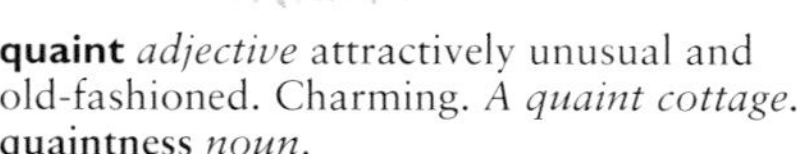

**quaint** *adjective* attractively unusual and old-fashioned. Charming. *A quaint cottage.* **quaintness** *noun*.

**quake** *verb* to shake, to tremble. *Quentin quaked with fear at the sight of the ghost.*

**qualification** *noun* your skills or the training you have had that make you suitable to do a certain job.

**qualify** (qualifies, qualifying, qualified) *verb* 1 to be suitable for a job, especially by passing a test or exam to reach a certain standard. *Karen has qualified as a vet.* 2 to obtain enough points to go on to the next part of a competition etc. 3 to limit. To make a remark less strong. *He qualified his remark that all his pupils are lazy and said only some are lazy.*

**WORD HISTORY**

*The shape of the letter Q comes from an ancient Egyptian symbol for monkey. The sound probably came from 'qoph', a Semitic word for monkey. The Greeks called it 'koppa'.*

**AMAZING FACT**

Qatar is an 'emirate' or nation that is ruled by a monarch called an 'emir'. Oil was discovered in Qatar in the 1940s.

**AMAZING FACT**

The biggest quarry in the world is in Utah. It is the Bingham Copper Mine. It is approximately 770 metres deep.

**quality** *noun* 1 how good or bad something is. *The sound quality is very poor.* 2 what somebody or something is like. Good characteristics. *His best quality is his cheerfulness.*

**qualm** *noun* (sounds like harm) a feeling of unease or doubt.

**quandary** *noun* uncertainty. *I'm in a quandary – should I go or should I stay?*

**quantity** *noun* an amount or number of things. *A large quantity of fodder.* **in quantity** in large amounts.

**quantum leap** *noun* a dramatic advance. *A quantum leap in space research.*

**quarantine** *noun* a period when a person or an animal that may be carrying a disease is kept away from others to prevent the disease from spreading.

**quarrel** (quarrels, quarrelling, quarrelled) *verb* to have an angry argument or disagreement with somebody. To stop being friendly. **quarrel** *noun*. **quarrelsome** *adjective*. *Quarrelsome children.*

**quarry** *noun* 1 a place where sand or stone is dug out of the ground for building etc. **quarry** *verb*. 2 an animal that is being hunted. Prey.

**quart** *noun* a measure of liquid equal to 2 pints or .95 litres.

**quarter** *noun* 1 one of four equal parts into which something can be divided. A fourth. 2 three months. 3 (in Canada and USA) a 25-cent coin. 4 a district of a city. *The Chinese quarter.* 5 **quarters** a place to stay. *Officers' living quarters.* **quarterly** *adjective* happening every three months. *A quarterly magazine.*

The green square is a quarter of the size of the mauve square.

**quartet** *noun* 1 a group of four singers or players. 2 a piece of music written for four musicians.

**quartz** *noun* a crystal-like mineral used in electronic equipment.

**quasi-** *prefix* almost or seeming to be. *Quasi-official, quasi-scientific.*

**quaver** *verb* to speak in a trembling voice because of fear or nervousness. **quaver** *noun*. *There was a quaver in her voice.*

**quaver** *noun* a note in music equal in length to a quarter of a minim or half a crotchet.

**quay** *noun* (say key) a place in a harbour for boats to load and unload.

The fishing boats bobbed on the water by the quay.

**queasy** (queasier, queasiest) *adjective* a feeling that you are going to be sick. **queasiness** *noun*.

**queen** *noun* 1 a female ruler of a country or the wife of a king. A monarch. Queens are not elected but either inherit their position by succeeding the previous ruler or marry a king. 2 a playing card with the picture of a queen on it. 3 a chesspiece that can move in any direction. **queen mother** the widowed mother of a reigning king or queen.

**queer** *adjective* strange, unusual.

**quell** *verb* to prevent by squashing. *The police quelled the riots.*

**quench** *verb* 1 to drink enough to satisfy your thirst. 2 to put out a fire.

**query** *noun* a question, a doubt. **query** (queries, querying, queries) *verb*.

**quest** *noun* a thorough search.

**question** *noun* 1 what you ask when you want to find out about something. 2 a problem. *The question of finance.* **question** *verb. The police questioned her for hours.*

**question mark** *noun* a punctuation mark (?) that is put at the end of a question.

**questionnaire** *noun* a list of questions to be answered by a number of people as part of a report etc.

**queue** *noun* (sounds like cue) a waiting line of people or vehicles. **queue** *verb. People are queuing to get into the stadium.*

**quibble** *noun* a small, unimportant point not really worth arguing about. *Don't quibble!*

**quiche** *noun* (say **key**-sh) a pastry tart with a filling of beaten egg, cheese, ham etc.

**quick** *adjective* 1 moving rapidly, fast. 2 done in a short time. *A quick and tasty snack.* 3 fast to understand, lively. *A quick brain.* **quickness** *noun*.

**quicksand** *noun* dangerously wet sand into which you can sink if you walk on it.

**quicksilver** *noun* the liquid metal mercury.

The people queued up to cast their votes in the general election.

**GRAMMAR NOTE**

*Take care how you use 'quite', because this little word can mean 'very' or 'rather'. 'This cake is quite good' could mean fairly good but not very good. But there is no doubt about 'This cake is quite excellent'. So it might be quite a good idea to avoid using 'quite', if it's going to cause offence.*

**quid** *noun* (slang) a pound in British money (£1). *Can you lend me a quid?*

**quiet** *adjective* 1 without much noise. Silent. 2 calm or without movement. *A quiet life in the country.* **quietness** *noun*.

**quill** *noun* 1 one of the sharp spines on a hedgehog or porcupine. 2 a long, strong feather used as a pen.

**quilt** *noun* a light bed covering filled with warm soft material.

**quintet** *noun* 1 a group of five singers or players. 2 a piece of music written for five musicians. *A string quintet.*

The quintet played some lively music at the dance.

**quintuplet** *noun* one of five babies born at the same time to the same mother (quin for short). *The quintuplets were a surprise.*

**quip** *noun* a witty and often cutting remark.

**quit** (quits, quitting, quitted or quit) *verb* 1 to give up or stop doing something. *She quit smoking.* 2 to go away.

**quite** *adverb* 1 totally. *I'm quite sure you are right.* 2 to some extent, rather. *It was quite a good meal.*

**Quito** *noun* the capital of Ecuador.

**quiver** *verb* to shake slightly but quickly. *Her lip quivered and she started to cry.*

**quiver** *noun* a long container for arrows.

**quiz** *noun* a game in which people are asked questions to test their knowledge. *Sue got all the answers right and won the quiz.*

**quota** *noun* a share of something.

**quotation** *noun* a person's words repeated exactly by somebody else, a passage from a play or book for example.

**quotation marks** *plural noun* the punctuation marks (') or ("") used before and after words somebody has said or to highlight words. *'What did you say?' she asked. 'Nothing,' I replied.*

**quote** *verb* 1 to repeat words that were first said or spoken by somebody else. *He quoted some lines from Shakespeare.* 2 to give a price. *The shop quoted me a price for mending my bike.*

**Qu'ran** another spelling for Koran.

# Rr

**Rabat** *noun* the capital of Morocco.

**rabbi** *noun* a Jewish religious leader and teacher. *The rabbi prayed in the synagogue.*

**rabbit** *noun* a small furry animal with long ears that lives in a hole (called a burrow) in the ground.

**rabble** *noun* a crowd of noisy people.

**rabies** *noun* a disease passed on by a bite that makes people and animals go mad and die. *He was bitten by a fox and got rabies.*

**raccoon** *noun* a small furry animal from North America with a long tail.

**race** *noun* a competition to see who is the fastest. **race** *verb* 1 to take part in a race. *I'll race you to the end of the road and back again.* 2 to go very quickly.

As they came round the bend into the last lap of the race, Nigel moved into the lead.

**race** *noun* a group of people with the same ancestors and history, or a division of people with a type of body or colour of skin. The human race. Race relations are the relationships between people of different races who live in the same country.

**racial** *adjective* relating to people's race. **racially** *adverb. Racially different.*

**racist** *noun* a person who does not like people from other races because he thinks his own race is the best. **racist** *adjective. Racist remarks.* **racism** *noun.*

**rack** *noun* 1 a framework with bars, pegs or shelves for holding things or hanging things on. *A plate rack.* 2 a shelf for luggage in a train or bus. 3 an instrument used in the Middle Ages for torturing people by stretching them. **rack** *verb* to hurt a lot. *He left his family for another woman and was racked with guilt.* **rack your brain** to try hard to think of something.

**racket** *noun* a bat with strings across it for playing tennis, squash or badminton.

**SPELLING NOTE**

*Be careful about the difference between the adjectives 'racial', which refers to race, and 'racist', which refers to racism and so is offensive.*

**SPELLING NOTE**

*The word 'radar' is an acronym, which means that is made up of the initial letters of other words. It comes from 'radio detection' and 'ranging'. The system was developed during the 1930s.*

**racket** *noun* 1 a loud noise. 2 a dishonest way of making money, a swindle.

**racoon** *noun* see raccoon.

**radar** *noun* a way of finding the position or speed of objects that cannot be seen by using radio signals that show on a screen. *The plane was last seen on radar.*

**radiant** *adjective* 1 sending out light or heat. *The radiant Sun.* 2 looking very happy. *She looked radiant on her wedding day.*

**radiate** *verb* to send out light, heat or happiness. **radiation** *noun. Exposure to radiation can cause serious illness and even death.* **radiate from** to spread out from a central point in many directions.

**radiator** *noun* 1 an apparatus, usually connected to a central heating system, used for heating buildings. 2 a device that keeps a car's engine cool.

**radio** (radios) *noun* 1 a method of sending or receiving sound through the air by means of electrical waves. 2 a piece of equipment, a radio set, for listening to radio programmes. 3 broadcasting of programmes. *She works in radio.* **radio** *verb. The ship radioed for help.*

**radioactive** *adjective* Something is radioactive if it has atoms that break up and send out radiation in the form of rays that can be harmful to living things. *After the reactor accident there was radioactive dust in the air.* **radioactivity** *noun.*

**radish** *noun* a small red vegetable that is eaten raw.

**radius** *noun* 1 the distance, a straight line, from the centre of a circle to its outside edge. A circle's radius is half its diameter. 2 the distance from a particular central point where something happens or exists. *All citizens living within a three-mile radius of the town centre are allowed free bus travel.*

The radius of the circle is shown by the green line from the centre to the circumference.

**raft** *noun* 1 logs tied together and used as a boat. 2 an inflatable rubber boat. *The raft saved Jane's life.*

**rag** *noun* 1 a small, usually torn piece of cloth. 2 a badly written newspaper. 3 a student carnival held to raise money for charity. **rag** (rags, ragging, ragged) *verb* to make fun of, tease.

**rage** *noun* 1 a strong uncontrollable anger. 2 the latest fashion. *Snowboarding is all the rage.* **rage** *verb* 1 to be very angry. 2 to be very violent. *The storm raged all night.*

R

**raid** *noun* 1 a sudden attack on an enemy. 2 an unexpected visit by the police. **raid** *verb* to make a raid. *The police raided the minister's office.* **raider** *noun.*

**rail** *noun* 1 a fixed bar to hang things on or hold on to, or forming part of a fence. *Put the towel on the rail.* 2 one of a pair of metal bars that a train runs on. **by rail** in a train.

**railing** *noun* (usually plural, railings) a fence made from metal bars. *The child got his head stuck in the railings.*

**railway** *noun* 1 the track or route between two places on which trains run. 2 a system of rail transport and the organization operating that system.

**rain** *noun* drops of water that fall from clouds. **rain** *verb* 1 to fall as rain. *It's raining.* 2 to fall like rain. *Tears rained down her cheeks.*

**rainbow** *noun* an arch of colours that you can sometimes see in the sky when the Sun shines through rain.

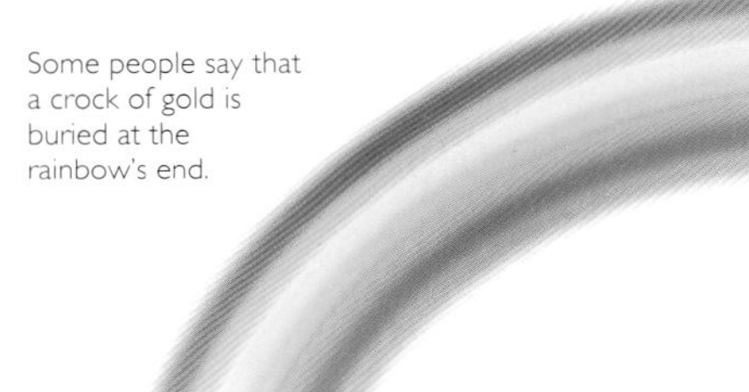

Some people say that a crock of gold is buried at the rainbow's end.

**raincoat** *noun* a waterproof coat that is worn in the rain. *Put on your raincoat, because it's pouring down outside.*

**rainfall** *noun* the amount of rain that falls in a place in a certain time. *The Atacama Desert in Chile has the lowest rainfall of any place on Earth.*

**rainforest** *noun* a tropical forest with tall trees in which it rains a lot.

**DID YOU KNOW?**

*Because the Islamic calendar is based on the Moon, Ramadan falls at different times of the year. Muslims celebrate Ramadan as the month during which the prophet Muhammad received the first of the revelations that make up the Koran, the holy book of Islam. Fasting during Ramadan is one of the chief duties of a Muslim. It is also a time for other religious activities, and nights are often devoted to special prayers and readings from the Koran.*

**raise** *verb* 1 to move to a higher position. *Raise the flag.* 2 to increase in amount or level. *To raise prices.* 3 to manage to get something together. *The school raised £100 for charity.* 4 to bring up a child, breed animals. 5 to bring up for discussion or attention. *I'm sorry to have to raise the question of money.* 6 to make appear. *It raised doubts in my mind.* **raise** *noun* an increase in salary. *They offered me a raise if I would stay in my job, but I didn't accept.*

**rake** *noun* a gardening tool with a row of metal teeth attached to a long handle. **rake** *verb* to collect or make smooth with a rake. *He raked the leaves into a pile.* **rake up** 1 to collect. 2 to talk about something unpleasant that should be forgotten. *She kept raking up the past until it drove him out of his mind with guilt.*

**rally** (rallies) *noun* 1 a large public meeting in support of something. *A peace rally.* 2 a car or cycling competition. 3 a series of shots players exchange in tennis or badminton. **rally** (rallies, rallying, rallied) *verb* 1 to come together in support of something. *My friends rallied round and helped me when I was ill.* 2 to become stronger again, recover.

**ram** *noun* a male sheep. *The ram with the curly horns can be quite aggressive.*

**ram** *noun* a device for pushing something. **ram** (rams, ramming, rammed) *verb* to push with great force. *He rammed the post hard into the ground.*

**RAM** *abbreviation* random-access memory. The amount of memory in a computer that is available and stored directly.

**Ramadan** *noun* the ninth month of the Muslim year, when no food or drink may be taken between sunrise and sunset. *They sat in the market place waiting for the Sun to go down, so they could eat a bowl of soup.*

**ramble** *noun* a long walk, often in the country. **ramble** *verb* 1 to go for a ramble. 2 to talk or write in a confused way. *My grandmother often rambles and says strange things.* **rambler** *noun.* **ramble on** to talk for a long time without sticking to the subject.

The world's rainforests are home to many species of plants and animals that may hold the key to health cures of the future.

R

**ramp** *noun* a slope used instead of a step or stairs. *She pushed his wheelchair up the ramp so fast that he nearly fell out of it.*

**rampart** *noun* a wide bank of earth built to protect a fort or city.

**ramshackle** *adjective* badly made and needing repair. *A ramshackle old shed.*

**ran** *verb* past tense of run.

**ranch** (ranches) *noun* a cattle-farm in North or South America. **rancher** *noun.*

Jeff herded the cattle on his uncle's ranch.

**rancid** *adjective* tasting or smelling unpleasant, especially fatty food. *The smell of rancid butter makes me feel sick.*

**random** *adjective* made or done without any plan. *A random selection of CDs.* **at random** without any plan or pattern. *He asked us questions at random.*

**rang** *verb* past tense of ring.

**range** *noun* 1 a connected series of hills or mountains. 2 the distance at which you can see or hear or that a gun can shoot. *Within range, out of range.* 3 a number of different things of the same kind. *We sell a wide range of gardening tools.* 4 the limits that can be measured between two points, the distance between which things vary. *The age range is from 20 to 30.* 5 grassy land in North America for grazing or hunting. 6 an area for shooting practice. 7 a large stove for cooking. **range** *verb* 1 to reach from one limit to another, to vary within limits. *Sizes range from small to extra large.* 2 to place or arrange. 3 to wander.

The distant mountain range was covered in snow.

**ranger** *noun* somebody who looks after a park or forest. *A forest ranger.*

**Rangoon** *noun* the capital of Myanmar.

**rank** *noun* 1 a position or grade in an organization. *He holds the rank of general.* 2 a line of people or things. *A taxi rank.* **rank** *verb* to put or be in a position on a scale. *I rank him as one of the best of the new breed of American writers.*

**DID YOU KNOW?**

*The city of Rangoon is also sometimes called Yangon. And the country of which it is capital has the official name Myanmar, but is often called by its old name of Burma. Rangoon became the capital in 1886, and was badly damaged in World War II when it was occupied by the Japanese. A famous golden temple in Rangoon, called the Shwe Dagon Pagoda, is Myanmar's holiest Buddhist shrine.*

**ransack** *verb* 1 to search a place thoroughly, usually leaving it in a mess. *The police ransacked the building in their search for clues.* 2 to search and rob a place.

**ransom** *noun* a sum of money that has to be paid to free a kidnapped person. **hold to ransom** to keep somebody as a prisoner until money is paid for them to be set free. **ransom** *verb* to set somebody free in exchange for a ransom.

**rap** *noun* 1 the sound of a quick hit or knock against something. 2 blame or punishment. *I'm always taking the rap.* 3 rhymes with a backing of rock music. **rap** *verb* 1 to hit something quickly and lightly. *He rapped him on the knuckles.* 2 to speak in rhymes with a rock music backing.

**rape** *verb* to perfoem intercourse against someone's will. **rape** *noun.* **rapist** *noun.*

**rapid** *adjective* quick. **rapidly** *adverb. The town is growing rapidly.*

**rapier** *noun* a thin, light sword.

**rare** *adjective* 1 uncommon, not often found or happening. *A rare plant.* 2 lightly cooked. *I like my steak rare.* **rarely** *adverb* not often. *We rarely go to the cinema.* **rarity** *noun.*

Pandas are now quite rare, because the clearance of bamboo forests has deprived them of their major food source.

**rash** *adjective* acting foolishly without thinking first. *Don't make rash promises.* **rashly** *adverb.* **rashness** *noun.*

**rash** (rashes) *noun* an outbreak of small red spots on the skin, caused by an illness or allergy. *An itchy heat rash.*

**rasher** *noun* a slice of bacon.

**raspberry** (raspberries) *noun* a small soft red fruit that grows on bushes.

**rat** *noun* 1 an animal with a long tail that looks like a large mouse. 2 a nasty, untrustworthy person.

Rats are rodents that can carry disease in the wild, though some people love them as pets.

**rate** *noun* 1 speed. *We were travelling at a steady rate.* 2 an amount, value, cost or speed measured by comparing it to some other amount. *The unemployment rate.* 3 a charge. *Postage rates are rising.* **at any rate** in any case. **at this rate** if things go on in the same way as now. *He'll never find a job at this rate.* **rate** *verb* to consider, to put a value on something. *How do you rate my chances of passing the test?*

**rather** *adverb* 1 to a slight extent or to a large extent. *It's rather cold today.* 2 more willingly, in preference. *I would rather not say.* 3 more exactly. *I went to bed late last night – or rather, early this morning.* 4 to a greater degree. *I'm looking for something practical rather than fashionable.*

**ratio** (say **ray**-shee-oh) *noun* the relationship between two numbers or amounts which shows how much greater one is than the other. If there are ten applicants for every five jobs, the ratio of applicants to jobs is two to one.

**ration** *noun* a fixed amount allowed to one person. *I've eaten my ration of chocolate for this week.* **ration** *verb* 1 to limit somebody to a ration. 2 to limit something. *During the hot weather water was rationed.*

**rational** *adjective* 1 sensible. *There must be a rational explanation.* 2 able to think, make decisions and judgements. *She's usually a very rational person.* **rationally** *adverb.* **rationality** *noun.*

**rat-race** *noun* a competitive struggle for success or power.

**rattle** *noun* 1 short, sharp sounds. 2 a baby's toy that makes a rattling sound. **rattle** *verb* 1 to make short, sharp sounds. *The windows rattled in the wind.* 2 to make somebody nervous. *She gets rattled if you ask her too many questions.* **rattle off** to say something quickly without thinking. *She rattled off the answers automatically.* **rattle on** to continue to talk quickly and without thinking.

**rattlesnake** *noun* a poisonous American snake that makes a rattling noise with its tail. *He was bitten by a rattlesnake.*

A number of hard rings at the end of the rattlesnake's tail make a rattling noise when shaken together.

**raucous** (say **raw**-kus) *adjective* loud and unpleasant, especially of voices. *There was a lot of raucous shouting.*

**rave** *verb* 1 to talk wildly and in an uncontrolled way. *He had a high temperature and was raving all night.* 2 to talk or write enthusiastically about something. **rave** *noun.*

**rave-up** *noun* a wild party.

**WORD HISTORY**

*The adjective 'ravenous' has nothing to do with the bird called a raven. 'Ravenous' comes from Latin and old French words meaning 'on the prowl for prey', presumably because the prowling person or animal is very hungry.*

**SPELLING NOTE**

*The prefix 're–' is usually spelt with a hyphen before a word that begins with an 'e', such as 're-enact', or if it could be confused with another word (to re-form means to form again, to reform is to make or become better).*

**raven** *noun* a large black bird. **raven** *adjective* glossy black. *Raven hair.*

**ravenous** *adjective* very hungry.

**ravine** *noun* a very deep, narrow valley.

**raw** *adjective* 1 not cooked. 2 in the natural state, not treated. *Raw materials.* 3 untrained, new to the job. 4 without skin. *Her fingers were rubbed raw.* 5 cold and wet, especially of weather. **rawness** *noun.*

**raw deal** *noun* unfair treatment.

**ray** *noun* 1 a beam of heat, light or energy. *The rays of the Sun.* 2 a small amount. *A ray of hope.* 3 one of a number of lines radiating out from the centre of something.

**razor** *noun* an instrument used for shaving hair from the skin.

**re-** *prefix* again. *He remarried last year.*

**reach** *verb* 1 to arrive at, to get to. *When did the news reach you?* 2 to stretch out a hand to get or touch something. *Can you reach the tin on the top shelf?* **reach** (reaches) *noun* 1 the distance that you can reach. *Put the bottle out of her reach.* 2 the length of an arm. *Sebastian has a very long reach.* 3 a straight stretch of a river between two bends.

She reached up to the top of the cupboard where she hid the children's presents.

**react** *verb* to behave in a particular way because of something, to behave differently as a result. *How did your boss react when he heard about the strike?* **reaction** *noun.* 1 an effect produced by an earlier action. 2 a change in one chemical substance caused by another. *A chemical reaction.*

**reactionary** *adjective* against changes in society. **reactionary** *noun.*

**reactor** *noun* a machine used to produce nuclear energy.

**read** (reads, reading, read) *verb* (say red) 1 to look at and understand or say out loud something written or printed. *He plays lots of instruments, but he can't read music.* 2 to judge how somebody feels. *I can read her mind.* 3 to say. *The sign reads 'Exit'.* 4 to show, register. *The thermometer reads 35 degrees.* 5 to study. *He is reading English at Oxford.* **read up** to find out about something by reading about it. **readable** *adjective* interesting and easy to read. **reader** *noun.* **reading** *noun. Children learn reading and writing at school.*

**ready** (readier, readiest) *adjective* 1 prepared, able to be used or do something. *Lunch is ready.* 2 willing to do something. *She's always ready to help.* 3 about to do something. *She was ready to cry.* 4 quick and prepared. *My sister always has a ready answer.* 5 easily reached. *Have your tickets ready.* **readiness** *noun.*

**real** *adjective* actually existing, not imaginary or artificial. *Real pearls.*

**realistic** *adjective* 1 practical, based on actual facts. *Their prices are realistic.* 2 like people or things in real life. *A realistic painting.* **realism** *noun.*

It was not very realistic of Malcolm to want a sportscar when he had a family of five.

**reality** (realities) *noun* something real, the truth. *He tries to escape reality by going to the cinema.* **in reality** in actual fact.

**realize** *verb* 1 to understand, to become aware of something. *I never realized that she was your mother.* 2 to make a hope or plan happen. *He realized his dreams of becoming an actor.* 3 to get money by selling something. **realization** *noun.*

**really** *adverb* 1 truly, without doubt. *It's really hot today.* 2 used for showing interest, doubt or surprise. *'I saw a film all about Batman yesterday.' 'Really?'*

**realm** *noun* (say relm) 1 a kingdom. 2 an area of thought or knowledge. *Fairies exist only in the realm of fantasy.*

**reap** *verb* 1 to cut down and gather. *We reaped the harvest.* 2 to gain as a result of something done. *One day she'll reap the benefit of all that hard work.*

The summer was very hot that year and everyone reaped a good harvest.

**rear** *noun* the back part. *We were at the rear of the queue when it happened.* **rear** *adjective. The rear wheel.*

**rear** *verb* 1 to bring up a child or animal. 2 to lift up, or rise upright on its back legs. *The snake suddenly reared its head.*

**AMAZING FACT**

The saying, 'You reap what you sow' means that you get what you deserve in life. If you 'sow' or plant goodness by doing kind things, you will 'reap' benefits.

**SPELLING NOTE**

*Note the spelling of 'receipt', 'receive' and 'receiver': it's 'ei', not 'ie'. An easy way to remember this is the saying 'I before E except after C,' but there are exceptions to the rule, such as 'weird'.*

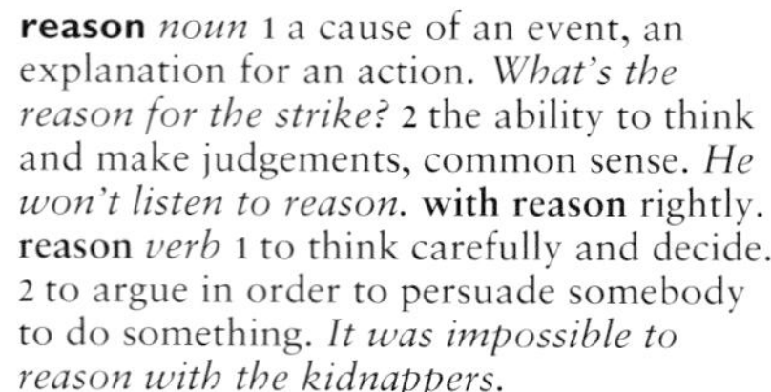

**reason** *noun* 1 a cause of an event, an explanation for an action. *What's the reason for the strike?* 2 the ability to think and make judgements, common sense. *He won't listen to reason.* **with reason** rightly. **reason** *verb* 1 to think carefully and decide. 2 to argue in order to persuade somebody to do something. *It was impossible to reason with the kidnappers.*

**reasonable** *adjective* 1 sensible. 2 fair, not too much. *An extremely reasonable price.* **reasonably** *adverb.*

**rebel** (rebels, rebelling, rebelled) *verb* (say rib-**el**) to fight or protest against anybody in power. *They rebelled against the government.* **rebel** *noun* (say **reb**-ul) somebody who rebels. *The rebels stormed the castle and killed the king.* **rebellious** *adjective.* **rebellion** *noun* fighting or opposition to anybody in power.

**rebuke** *verb* to give somebody a short telling off. *His boss rebuked him for not wearing a tie.* **rebuke** *noun.*

**recall** *verb* 1 to remember. 2 to ask somebody to come back. **recall** *noun.*

**recede** *verb* 1 to move back or further away. *His hair is receding and he will soon go completely bald.* 2 to become less clear.

As we took off in the helicopter, our home receded into the distance.

**receipt** *noun* (say ris-**eet**) 1 a piece of paper that states that money or goods have been received. *I will need a receipt for the payment.* 2 the act of receiving. *He rang the school on receipt of the letter.*

**receive** *verb* 1 to get or take something given or sent to you. *The news was received with horror.* 2 to suffer. *She received nasty injuries to the spine.* 3 to welcome a visitor. *We were very well received.*

**receiver** *noun* 1 the part of a telephone you speak into. *Pick up the receiver and dial this number.* 2 a person who receives something, especially stolen goods. 3 the part of a radio or television set that receives broadcasts. 4 a person officially appointed to take charge of a bankrupt business.

The satellite beamed the television programme to a receiver near Michael's home.

**recent** *adjective* having happened only a short time ago. *A recent discovery.* **recently** *adverb. I was at college until recently.*

**reception** *noun* 1 the way somebody or something is received, a welcome. *His new book got a very good reception.* 2 an office or place in a hotel or large organization where appointments, reservations and enquiries can be made. *She left her keys at reception when she went upstairs.* 3 a formal party. 4 the quality of receiving sounds or pictures from radio or television.

**recess** (recesses) *noun* 1 a period of time when work or business is stopped. *The judge announced a recess.* 2 a space in the wall of a room. *Let's put shelves in the recess.* 3 a hidden part that is difficult to reach. *The recesses of the mind.*

**recession** *noun* 1 a decline in wealth and economic success. *The government is doing its best to avoid recession.* 2 receding.

**recipe** *noun* instructions on how to make a particular dish, or something else. *It was a recipe for disaster to use Paul as designer.*

The recipe for winter vegetable soup called for lots of carrots and onions.

**recital** *noun* 1 a musical performance. *A piano recital.* 2 a detailed account.

**recite** *verb* to say something learned out loud. *She recited the poem in class.*

**reckless** *adjective* not caring about danger.

**reckon** *verb* 1 to consider. *It's reckoned to be one of his best books.* 2 to guess, feel confident. *I reckon he's a liar.* 3 to add up. *The rent is reckoned from the first of July.*

**reclaim** *verb* 1 to get something back that was taken away from you. 2 to make land ready for use again. *To reclaim land from the sea for agricultural use.*

**recline** *verb* to lean or lie back.

**recognizable** *adjective* easy to identify or recognize. *An easily recognizable style.*

**recognize** *verb* 1 to know what something is or who somebody is. 2 to be willing to agree, to see clearly. *The importance of his work has now been recognized.* 3 to accept as real, welcome or lawful. *The new government was not recognized by the people.* **recognition** *noun.*

**WORD BUILDING**

*The nouns 'reception' and 'receipt' both come from the verb to 'receive'. The reception in a hotel is a place where people are received, and guests are also received at the formal party called a reception (such as a wedding reception).*

**WORD HISTORY**

*'Reckless' seems an odd word, because there is no 'reck' or 'reckful'. There used to be a verb 'reck', however, which meant to pay attention or take account. This has now gone out of use.*

**DID YOU KNOW?**

*A square is a rectangle with four equal sides. A rectangle that is not a square can also be called an oblong.*

**recollect** *verb* to remember.

**recommend** *verb* to say that somebody or something would be good or useful for a particular job. *I can recommend a good carpenter.* **recommendation** *noun.*

**record** *noun* (say **rek**-ord) 1 information, especially facts, either written down or stored on a computer. *She keeps a record of how much she spends.* 2 a disc on which sound, especially music, is stored. 3 the best yet done, especially in sport, or the most amazing achievement. *He broke the world record for 400 metres.* 4 facts known about the past or somebody's past life. *This aircraft has a good safety record.* **for the record** to be reported. **off the record** not to be written down or made known. **record** *verb* (say rik-**ord**) 1 to put something down in writing or on a computer. 2 to store sound or television pictures on disc or tape. *We recorded the programme, so we can watch it tomorrow.* **recording** *noun.*

The recording came out on CD as well as on tape.

**recover** *verb* 1 to become well again. *She is recovering from a very serious illness.* 2 to get something back after it is lost or taken away. **recovery** *noun.*

**recruit** *noun* a new member of an army, group or society. **recruit** *verb* to get new members. *Lots of people were recruited to put up tents in the field.*

**rectangle** *noun* a shape with four straight sides and four right angles. **rectangular** *adjective. A rectangular dish.*

**recuperate** *verb* to get better and become strong again after an illness.

**recur** (recurs, recurring, recurred) *verb* to happen again, either once or many times. **recurrence** *noun. A recurrence of illness.*

**recycle** *verb* to treat things that have already been used so that they can be used again. *To recycle newspapers and bottles.* **recyclable** *adjective. Some aluminium drinks cans are recyclable.*

R

**red** *noun* the colour of blood. **red** *adjective. Red wine.* **see red** to become very angry. **in the red** to have spent more money than is in your bank account. **red herring** something that takes people's attention away from what is important.

**redundant** *adjective* no longer needed because there is no work or something is no longer used. *The workers were all made redundant when the firm closed down.* **redundancy** *noun.*

**refectory** (refectories) *noun* the dining hall in a monastery or university.

The monks ate every day in the refectory.

**refer** (refers, referring, referred) *verb* 1 to speak about or mention. 2 to go to for information. *We were not allowed to refer to a dictionary in the exam.* 3 to send somebody or something, especially a problem, to somebody else for action. *He was referred to a specialist.*

**reference** *noun* 1 mentioning something. *There were a number of references to the trial in the paper.* 2 referring to somebody or something for information. A note that tells you where information can be found. *I use my computer for quick reference.* 3 a statement, usually a letter, about a person's character. *His old headmaster gave him a good reference.* **with reference to** regarding.

**reference book** *noun* a book for looking things up in. *Dictionaries, encyclopedias and other reference books.*

**referendum** *noun* a vote in which all the people in a country or area can decide on a particular political question.

**refine** *verb* 1 to make substances pure by taking out unwanted substances. *Refined sugar.* 2 to make more cultured. *Refined behaviour can sometimes be unfriendly.*

**refinery** (refineries) *noun* a factory where substances such as oil or sugar are refined.

**reflection** *noun* 1 the sending back of light, heat or sound from a surface. 2 an image of something in a mirror or shiny surface. *She looked at her reflection in the lake.* 3 a deep thought. *Reflections on old age.* 4 Something that makes a bad impression. *Hooliganism is a sad reflection on football.* 5 being the result of something. *His meanness is a reflection of his upbringing.* **on reflection** after thinking about something. **reflect** *verb.*

**WORD HISTORY**

*A red herring was originally a specially prepared fish with a very strong smell. The dried smoked herring was used to train hunting dogs. It was pulled along the ground in front of the hounds to draw them away from the foxes' trail.*

**WORD BUILDING**

*A refugee is really a person who is seeking refuge. Both words come originally from the Latin for 'to flee'.*

**WORD HISTORY**

*'Regatta' is an Italian word that comes originally from the Venetian dialect. A famous regatta is still held on the canals of Venice every September.*

**reform** *verb* to make or become better. *He reformed completely after giving up drink.* **reform** *noun Prison reforms.*

**refrain** *verb* to hold yourself back from doing something. *I refrained from having another drink in case I was sick.*

**refrain** *noun* part of a song that is repeated at the end of each verse.

**refreshing** *adjective* 1 pleasing and interesting, different from what you are used to. *It was refreshing to meet such helpful people.* 2 giving strength. *A most refreshing sleep.* **refresh** *verb.*

**refreshments** *plural noun* light food or drink. *Refreshments are served.*

**refrigerator** *noun* a large box or cupboard in which food and drinks are kept cool.

**refuge** *noun* a place that gives shelter and protection from trouble or danger. *The explorers found a refuge from the cold.*

**refugee** *noun* a person who has been forced to leave home, usually his or her country, because of war or disaster. *Refugees poured across the border after the earthquake.*

The refugees had walked many miles looking for shelter, taking it in turns to carry their baby.

**refuse** *verb* (say ri-**fewz**) to say 'no' to something, to not do or accept something. *She refused my offer of help.* **refusal** *noun.*

**refuse** *noun* (say **ref**-yooss) waste material, rubbish. *There is a weekly refuse collection.*

**regal** *adjective* (say **ree**-gul) suitable for a king or queen, splendid.

**regatta** *noun* a meeting for boat races.

**region** *noun* a large area, especially of land. *Forest regions.* **in the region of** about.

**register** *noun* 1 a list of things or names. *A register of births, deaths and marriages is kept in the register office.* 2 the range of a voice or musical instrument. **register** *verb* 1 to list something in a register. 2 to show on a scale, record. *The thermometer registered 35 degrees.* 3 to make something clear, usually a feeling or an opinion. *Her face registered fear.* 4 to send a letter or parcel by registered post. *To register a letter you have to pay extra, but it's worth it.*

**regret** (regrets, regretting, regretted) *verb* to feel sorry about something you have done or not done. *She regretted her mistakes all her life.* **regret** *noun.* **regrettable** *adjective.* **regretful** *adjective.*

R

**regular** *adjective* 1 happening, coming or doing something again and again at certain times. *Regular meals.* 2 evenly arranged or shaped, not varying. *Regular, white, shining teeth.* 3 normal, standard or proper. *That's not the regular procedure.* 4 A regular verb is a verb that follows the common pattern. The verb 'write' is not a regular verb. **regularly** *adverb.* **regularity** *noun.*

**rehearse** *verb* to practise something, especially a play, speech or music, before a performance. **rehearsal** *noun.*

**reign** *verb* (say rain) 1 to rule a country as a king or queen. 2 to exist. *Silence reigned.* **reign** *noun. During the reign of Queen Elizabeth.*

The coin was issued to commemorate the long reign of the king and queen.

**rein** *noun* a strap for guiding a horse. *Don't let go of the reins!*

**reindeer** (reindeer) *noun* a deer with large antlers that lives in the coldest parts of the world. *The people of Lapland herd reindeer.*

**reinforce** *verb* to make stronger. *Reinforced concrete is strengthened with metal bars.* **reinforcement** *noun.*

**reject** *verb* 1 to not accept a person or thing. *The machine rejects bent coins.* 2 to throw away or send back as not good enough. *The oranges were rotten and had to be rejected.* **rejection** *noun.*

**rejoice** *verb* to feel or show great happiness. *Rejoice and be merry!*

**relapse** *verb* to fall back into a worse state, to return to a previous condition, usually after having been better. **relapse** *noun.*

**relate** *verb* 1 to see or show a connection, to compare one thing with another. *It is difficult to relate these two results.* 2 to tell a story. 3 to get on with. *He cannot relate to children, not even his own.*

**relation** *noun* 1 a member of your family. 2 a connection. *There is no relation between her health and her results at school.* **relations** the dealings between people or groups. *Business relations with Germany.*

All the relations gathered together for the naming ceremony of the youngest family member.

**AMAZING FACT**

The English language has relatively few words for relatives compared to other languages. Many languages have different words for male and female cousins. Others have different terms for paternal or maternal aunts, uncles, or grandparents.

**AMAZING FACT**

The reindeer is the only deer in which both sexes have antlers.

**relationship** *noun* 1 how people and things are connected. *The relationship between light and heat.* 2 a family connection. *What is your brother's relationship to her?* 3 a friendship or the way people or groups behave towards each other. *She has never had a lasting relationship.*

**relative** *noun* a person who is related to another, a relation. *My aunt is my only living relative.*

**relative** *adjective* 1 compared to each other or to something else. 2 connected with. **relatively** *adverb. Relatively well off.*

**relax** *verb* 1 to become less stiff, tight or strict. *He relaxed his grip.* 2 to be more calm and rest. *After work I like to relax.*

**relay** *noun* 1 a relay race. 2 a fresh group taking over from a tired one. *We worked all through the night in relays.* 3 a piece of equipment that receives messages by telephone, television or radio and passes them on to another place. **relay** *verb* to pass on a message or broadcast.

**relay race** *noun* a team race in which each member runs part of the whole distance.

Clive handed the baton to Mark, who ran the next leg of the relay race.

**release** *verb* 1 to set free. *He was released from prison.* 2 to let your grip go. 3 to allow to be shown or published. *His new single will be released on Monday and shoot to the top of the charts.* **release** *noun* 1 being released or something released. 2 a new film, record or piece of news that has come out. 3 a handle, button or other device that can be pressed to unfasten something.

**relent** *verb* to become less stern. *She relented after hearing the explanation.*

**relentless** *adjective* without pity.

**relic** *noun* 1 something that was used or made a long time ago. 2 something that belonged to a saint and is usually kept in a church. *This bone is a relic of Saint James.*

**relief** *noun* 1 a lessening or ending of pain, worry or boredom. *The medicine gave relief.* 2 help for people in trouble, especially food, money and clothes. *Famine relief.* 3 a person or group taking over a duty for another. *We went on relief buses during the train strike.*

R

**relieve** *verb* 1 to lessen pain, trouble or boredom. 2 to take over a duty from somebody else. *To relieve the guard.* **relieve of** to rob somebody of something.

**religion** *noun* a belief in god or many gods. **religious** *adjective. A religious text.*

**reluctant** *adjective* unwilling. **reluctantly** *adverb. He reluctantly agreed to help.*

**rely** (relies, relying, relied) *verb* to depend on something happening or trust somebody or something. *She has always relied on her parents for help.* **reliance** *noun.*

**remain** *verb* 1 to be left behind after other parts have gone. *Two of the guests remained.* 2 to continue to be the same, to stay unchanged. *He remained silent.* **it remains to be seen** we will know later on.

**remainder** *noun* the rest, the part that is left over. *She paid £10 and promised to give me the remainder next week.*

**remains** *plural noun* 1 parts that are left after everything else has gone. *They found some remains of Greek pottery.* 2 a dead body. *The prince's remains were buried in the family vault.*

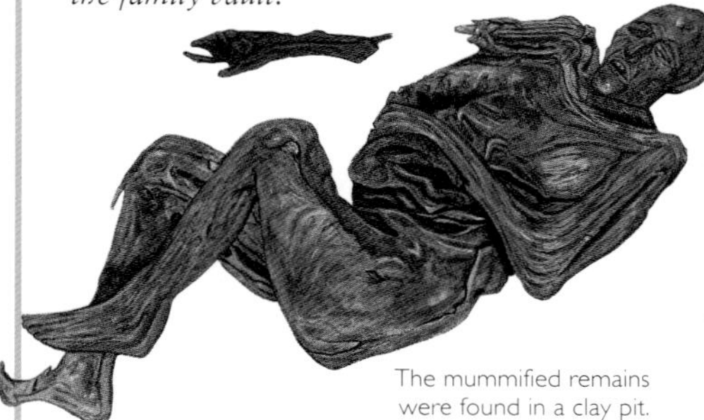

The mummified remains were found in a clay pit.

**remark** *noun* something said. *He made some embarrassing remarks about her new hairstyle.* **remark** *verb.*

**remarkable** *adjective* worth speaking about, impressive. **remarkably** *adverb. She did remarkably well in the exam.*

**remember** *verb* 1 to keep in the mind. *I'll always remember the first time we met.* 2 to call back into mind, especially after having forgotten it for a while. **remembrance** *noun.*

**remind** *verb* to tell or make somebody remember something. *She reminds me of my mother.* **reminder** *noun.*

**remnant** *noun* 1 a small part of something left over. *We ate up the remnants of the meal.* 2 a small piece of material.

**remorse** *noun* a feeling of guilt about something you have done wrong. **remorseful** *adjective. Gary felt very remorseful.*

**remove** *verb* to take something away, off or out. *How can I remove this stain?* **removal** *noun. The removal of the furniture.*

**SPELLING NOTE**

*Note the spelling of relieve. It has 'i' before 'e' and not 'e' before 'i'.*

**WORD HISTORY**

*Rent comes from the Latin word 'reddere', 'to give', so it means something given or paid.*

**AMAZING FACT**

The saying 'Opposites attract' refers to people who have different personalities, rather than magnets, which is where the saying comes from.

**renew** *verb* 1 to replace something old with something new of the same kind. *Passports have to be renewed every ten years.* 2 to begin or make again. *After meeting up again we renewed our friendship.* 3 to put new strength into something, to make as good as new again. **renewal** *noun.*

**renown** *noun* fame, being well known for something good. *A writer of extremely high renown.* **renowned** *adjective.*

**rent** *noun* the amount of money paid for the use of something, especially a flat or house that belongs to somebody else. **rent** *verb. I rent my flat and my television set.* **rent out** to allow something to be used in return for rent.

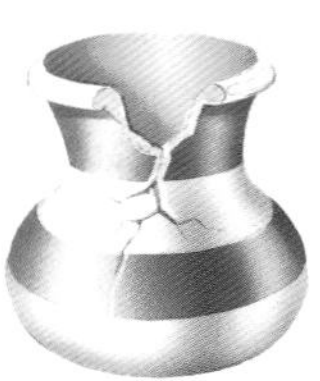

**repair** *verb* to mend or put something right that has broken or gone wrong. **repair** *noun. I left the car in the garage for repairs.*

The vase was impossible to repair, because a big chunk had been knocked out of it and lost.

**repay** (repays, repaying, repaid) *verb* to give back, especially money. *He repaid her kindness with insults.* **repayment** *noun.*

**repeat** *verb* to say or do the same thing again. **repeat** *noun. They show too many repeats on television.*

**repel** (repels, repelling, repelled) *verb* 1 to drive back. *The army repelled the attack.* 2 to find something horrible or disgusting. *The sight of blood repels him.* **repellent** *adjective, noun. An insect repellent.*

We used powerful magnets in the scientific experiment.

**replace** *verb* to put something back in its place or take the place of somebody or something else. *She broke one of my best cups but replaced it next day with a new one.*

**replica** *noun* a copy, especially of a painting. *This is only a cheap replica of the original statue in the British Museum.*

**reply** (replies) *noun* something said or written as an answer to somebody. *I rang Jane's doorbell, but there was no reply.* **in reply** as an answer. **reply** (replies, replying, replied) *verb* to give an answer.

R

**report** *verb* 1 to tell or give information about something. *They reported the accident to the police.* 2 to make a complaint against somebody. *The teacher reported the boy to the headmaster.* 3 to let somebody know that you are there. *We have to report to the manager every morning.* **report** *noun* 1 a written or spoken account of an event. 2 a written account of how well or badly a pupil has done during the school term. 3 the sound of an explosion.

**reporter** *noun* somebody who writes or broadcasts news reports.

**represent** *verb* 1 to be a picture, sign or example of something. To show or mean. *Love is often represented by a heart.* 2 to act for another person, especially as a lawyer or leader of a group. *We chose Gregory to represent the class at the school meeting.* **representation** *noun.*

**representative** *noun* somebody chosen to represent others. *Travel representatives welcome and help holidaymakers.* **representative** *adjective* being an example of what others are like. *This painting is representative of the artist's work.*

**repress** *verb* to hold back or control. *Steve could hardly repress a grin.* **repression** *noun.*

**reprieve** *noun* an order to delay or cancel the punishment of a prisoner, especially one who was to die. *She won a last-minute reprieve.* **reprieve** *verb. The prisoner was reprieved and set free at last.*

**reprimand** *verb* to tell somebody officially that they should not have done a particular thing. **reprimand** *noun. The superintendent gave him a severe reprimand.*

**reproduce** *verb* 1 to make a copy of something. To cause something to be seen or heard again. *This painting has been reproduced in many books.* 2 to produce young. *Dinosaurs reproduced by laying eggs.* **reproduction** *noun.*

**reptile** *noun* an animal with scaly skin whose blood changes temperature according to the temperature around it. Snakes, lizards and crocodiles are all reptiles.

**republic** *noun* a country with an elected president at the head, rather than a king or queen. **republican** *noun.*

**DID YOU KNOW?**

*Reptiles are cold-blooded, which means that they need lots of sunshine to warm them up. Reptiles live in all warm parts of the world, and they usually lay eggs which are soft and leathery. Dinosaurs were reptiles, though some scientists think that they may have been warm-blooded creatures. The word reptile comes from the Latin repere, 'to crawl': reptiles are 'crawling animals'.*

**AMAZING FACT**

The first republics in history were Ancient Greece and Ancient Rome. They were considered republics even though many of the people were slaves.

**repugnant** *adjective* horrible and disgusting. *A repugnant smell.*

**repulsive** *adjective* horrible. *Some people find eating snails repulsive.* **repulsion** *noun.*

**reputation** *noun* people's opinion of how good somebody or something is. If you live up to your reputation, you behave in the way people expect you to.

**request** *noun* asking for something or the thing asked for. *My next request is an early song by Mozart with words by Schiller.* **request** *verb* to ask politely.

**require** *verb* 1 to need. 2 to demand, make somebody do something. *Students are required to bring their own dictionaries.* **requirement** *noun.*

**rescue** *verb* to save from danger, to set free. *The fireman rescued the child from the burning house.* **rescue** *noun.* **rescuer** *noun.*

**research** (researches) *noun* a study of a subject to find out facts and information. **research** *verb. He is researching the feeding habits of monkeys.* **researcher** *noun.*

**resemble** *verb* to be like or similar. *She resembles her younger sister – they have the same nose.* **resemblance** *noun.*

**reservation** *noun* 1 an arrangement to keep something for somebody for later use. *Holiday reservations.* 2 doubt in your mind. *I've got reservations about this plan.* 3 a piece of land kept for a special purpose.

**reserve** *verb* to keep or order something for somebody. *We reserved two rooms in the hotel.* **reserve** *noun* 1 something kept for later use. *Reserves of food.* 2 an extra player who may replace another player before or during a game. 3 a piece of land for a special purpose. *A nature reserve.* 4 not showing your feelings. **reserved** *adjective. She is very reserved, which is why I don't like her.*

**reservoir** (say rez-uh-vwar) *noun* a place where water is stored.

In summer they used to go sailing on the reservoir.

**resident** *noun* a person who lives in a particular place. *Parking is for residents only.* **resident** *adjective. The resident doctor.*

R

**resign** *verb* to give up your job or post. *He disagreed with the committee and resigned.* **resign yourself** to accept and put up with something without complaint. *She resigned herself to a very boring evening at the office dinner.* **resignation** *noun.*

**resist** *verb* to fight back against something or not allow yourself to do something. *I can't resist another piece of cake.* **resistance** *noun.* **resistant** *adjective.*

**resolution** *noun* 1 being firm. 2 something you make up your mind to do. *My New Year's resolution is to give up smoking.* 3 a decision taken at a meeting by a vote. 4 solving problems.

**resolve** *verb* 1 to decide. *She resolved to work harder.* 2 to solve a problem or clear up a difficulty.

**resort** *noun* a holiday place. *Davos is a famous skiing resort.*

The twins visited a resort in the mountains that was famous for its good skiing facilities.

**resort** *verb* to turn to, especially something bad. *When he lost his money he resorted to crime and broke into the office safe.*

**resourceful** *adjective* clever at finding ways of doing things.

**resources** *plural noun* possessions such as wealth or goods. *Oil is one of the country's main resources.*

**respect** *noun* 1 a high opinion or admiration of somebody. *She has great respect for his work.* 2 If you show respect to somebody, you are polite. 3 a detail or particular point. *She's like her mother in every respect.* **with respect to** relating to. *With respect to your order, please find the invoice enclosed.* **respect** *verb.*

**respond** *verb* to reply or react to something. **response** *noun.* *He made no response to the question.*

**responsibility** (responsibilities) *noun* 1 the duty of having to deal with something and making decisions. Being responsible. *If you borrow my bike, it's your responsibility to lock it up properly.* 2 a duty, something for which you are responsible. *Parents have a lot of responsibilities.*

**WORD HISTORY**

*'Restaurant' is a French word, meaning the same as in English. It comes from the French 'restaurer', which means to rebuild, restore, or bring back to health.*

**DID YOU KNOW?**

*Someone who runs a restaurant is properly called a 'restaurateur' (without the 'n'); this is sometimes misspelt with the 'n', like restaurant.*

The result was a resounding win for the team from Athens.

**responsible** *adjective* 1 having the duty of looking after somebody or something, having to take the blame if things go wrong. *She is responsible for keeping her room tidy.* 2 trustworthy. **be responsible for** to be the cause of. *Who is responsible for the damage?* **responsibly** *adverb.*

**rest** *noun* 1 not doing anything active. Quiet or sleep. 2 a support. **rest** *verb* 1 to take or have a rest. *She never rests for a second.* 2 to support or be supported. *Now rest your head on your knees.* **rest assured** to be certain. **restful** *adjective.* **restless** *adjective.*

Alan rested in bed after a day at the zoo.

**rest** *noun* the part that is left, the others. *Take what you want and throw the rest away or give it to charity.*

**restaurant** *noun* a place where you can buy and eat meals.

**restore** *verb* 1 to give back, especially something stolen or lost. 2 to put or bring back as before. *The old church has been restored.* **restoration** *noun.*

**restrain** *verb* to hold back from doing something, to control. *I had to restrain myself from hitting him.* **restraint** *noun.*

**restrict** *verb* to keep within a limit. *She restricts herself to two cups of coffee a day.* **restriction** *noun.*

**result** *noun* 1 something that happens because of an event or activity. An effect. *You get good results with this washing powder.* 2 the final score of a game, competition or race. *The football results.* 3 the answer to a sum. *Each time I add up the figures I get a different result.* **result** *verb* to happen as an effect.

**resume** *verb* to begin again. *Talks resumed yesterday.* **resumption** *noun.*

**résumé** *noun* a summary.

R

**resurrect** *verb* to bring back into use. *I resurrected the old piano.* **resurrection** *noun. The resurrection of some old ideas.*

**resuscitate** *verb* to revive a person so they become conscious again. **resuscitation** *noun.*

**retail** *verb* to sell goods. *The camera retails at £50.* **retail** *noun* selling goods to the public. **retailer** *noun.*

**retain** *verb* to keep or continue to have. *If you don't play football it's very difficult to retain an interest in the World Cup.*

**retina** *noun* the area at the back of the eye that is sensitive to light. *A damaged retina.*

**retire** *verb* 1 to give up work, especially when you are old. *My father retired at 60.* 2 to leave a place or room. 3 to go to bed. **retirement** *noun.*

Grandfather was very much enjoying his retirement.

**retreat** *verb* to go away or move back, especially when forced to do so. *After a three-day battle the enemy retreated.* **retreat** *noun* 1 the act of retreating. 2 a quiet, restful place. *A weekend retreat in the country.*

**return** *verb* 1 to come or go back. *He returned from holiday yesterday.* 2 to give, put or send back. *She returned the book I lent her.* **return** *noun* 1 the act of returning or returning something. 2 a return ticket. 3 profit on an investment of money. **in return** in exchange. *I gave him my stamp collection in return for a computer game.*

**reunion** *noun* a meeting of old friends or family members who have not seen each other for some time. *At the school reunion, Clarrie met up with a lot of her old friends.*

**reveal** *verb* 1 to uncover something so it can be seen. *Her dress revealed a tattoo on her shoulder.* 2 to make known. *To reveal a secret.* **revelation** *noun.*

**revenge** *noun* hurting in return for having been hurt. *In revenge for her betrayal he refused to return her posessions.* **revenge** *verb.*

**revenue** *noun* the money that an organization receives from people, especially money paid as tax to the government.

**reverse** *adjective* opposite in position or order. *The reverse side of the material has lines through it.*

**AMAZING FACT**

Palindromes are words, phrases, sentences or even longer pieces of text that read the same when you reverse them. 'Dad' 'mom' 'noon' and 'peep' are short ones. 'Was it a car or a cat I saw?' is longer but still works in reverse.

Marie reversed the green car neatly into the parking space.

**WORD HISTORY**

*'Retina' comes from the Latin 'rete', meaning 'net'. Perhaps early doctors saw it as a sort of net at the back of the eye that caught light. If so, they were right in a way. The retina actually contains light-sensitive cells that send signals along the optic nerve to the brain. There are two kinds of cells: rods are sensitive to light and dark, and cones are more sensitive to colour.*

The people won a massive victory in the French Revolution.

**reverse** *noun* 1 the exact opposite. *She always does the reverse from what you expect.* 2 the back. 3 a gear in which you drive a car backwards. **in reverse** in the opposite way from what usually happens. **reverse** *verb* 1 to go backwards. *She reversed the car into the parking space.* 2 to change to the opposite or change round. *Roles are often reversed, with men looking after children and women going out to work.* **reverse the charges** to make a phone call for which the receiver pays. **reversal** *noun.*

**review** *noun* 1 a critical opinion in a newspaper, magazine or on radio or television about a book, film, concert or play. *He writes film reviews.* 2 an inspection or examination. *Hospital practices have been under review.* **review** *verb.*

**revise** *verb* 1 to study facts already learnt, especially for an exam. 2 to change or correct something. *He's been so helpful I'll have to revise my opinion of him.* **revision** *noun. I still have a lot of revision to do.*

**revive** *verb* to come back to life or strength again. To bring back. *A warm drink will soon revive me.* **revival** *noun.*

**revolt** *verb* 1 to fight against something. *The army revolted against the dictator.* 2 to be disgusted. **revolting** *adjective. A revolting banana skin was in the wastepaper bin.*

**revolt** *noun* a fight to change a system.

**revolution** *noun* 1 a rebellion, especially one overthrowing a political system. 2 complete change in ways of doing things or methods. *The green revolution.* 3 one complete turn of a wheel. **revolutionary** *adjective.* **revolutionize** *verb. Computers have revolutionized office work.*

**revolve** *verb* to turn or keep turning round.

**revolver** *noun* a small gun that does not have to be reloaded after each shot.

R

**reward** *noun* 1 something given in return for something good or useful you have done. 2 an amount of money given to somebody who helps the police. **reward** *verb. The boy was rewarded for his bravery with a medal.*

**rewarding** *adjective* giving you satisfaction. *Teaching can be a rewarding job.*

**Reykjavik** *noun* the capital of Iceland.

**rheumatism** (say **roo**-muh-tizum) *noun* an illness that makes joints or muscles stiff and painful. **rheumatic** *adjective.*

**rhino** (rhinos) *noun* a rhinoceros.

**rhinoceros** (rhinoceroses) *noun* a large animal from Africa or Asia with one or two horns on its nose.

The rhinoceros is endangered because poachers value its horn.

**rhyme** *noun* 1 a similar sound at the ends of words or lines in poetry, as in 'say' and 'day' and 'school' and 'fool'. 2 a word that rhymes with another. 3 a short piece of writing with rhymes. **rhyme** *verb.*

**ribbon** *noun* 1 a long strip of material for tying things together or used as a decoration. *She tied her hair with a red ribbon.* 2 a narrow strip of inked material that is put into a typewriter. *A typewriter ribbon.*

**rice** *noun* white or brown grains that are cooked and eaten.

The rice terraces at Luzon in the Philippines were carved out of the rock thousands of years ago.

**rich** *adjective* 1 having a lot of money or possessions. *A country rich in oil.* 2 containing a lot of goodness or quality of sound or colour. *Rich soil is good for growing things.* 3 containing a lot of cream, oil, sugar or eggs. *Rich food.* 4 expensive, luxurious. **riches** *plural noun.* **richly** *adverb.* **richness** *noun.*

**rickety** *adjective* not made strongly, likely to break. *The old chairs were very rickety.*

**riddle** *noun* a difficult question to which you must guess the answer.

**DID YOU KNOW?**

*Rhymes can be either masculine or feminine. A masculine rhyme is one in which the two words have the same sounds in their final stressed syllables, such as 'betray' and 'delay'. In a feminine rhyme, the words' same sounds are in stressed syllables before other unstressed syllables, such 'joviality' and 'morality', or 'stocking' and 'shocking'.*

**AMAZING FACT**

The word 'rhinoceros' comes from the Greek word for nose – rhino. When people have plastic surgery on their nose, it is called 'rhinoplasty'.

**riddle** *verb* to make holes in somebody or something, to make full of holes. *He riddled the target with bullets.* **riddled with** full of. *Your essay is riddled with mistakes.*

**ride** (rides, riding, rode, ridden) *verb* 1 to sit on a horse, bicycle or motorbike and go along on it. 2 to travel in a car, bus or train. 3 to float on something. *The boat rode the waves.* **rider** *noun.* **ride up** to move up the body. *I hate it when my vest rides up under my dress.* **ride** *noun* a journey on an animal, a bike or in a vehicle. **take for a ride** to cheat somebody.

**ridiculous** *adjective* silly. *She wore a ridiculous hat to the wedding.*

**rifle** *noun* a gun with a long barrel, fired from the shoulder.

**rifle** *verb* to search through and possibly steal things. *Thieves rifled through every drawer and cupboard.*

**rig** *noun* 1 a large structure that is used for drilling for oil or gas. *An oil rig.* 2 the way a ship's sails and masts are arranged. **rig** (rigs, rigging, rigged) *verb* 1 to fit out a ship with ropes and sails. 2 to arrange an event dishonestly in order to get the results that are wanted. *The race was obviously rigged.* **rig up** to put something together quickly out of materials that are handy. *The scouts rigged up a shelter for the night.*

Oil rigs are lit up at night to warn ships of their presence.

**Riga** *noun* the capital of Latvia.

**rigging** *noun* the ropes and sails of a ship.

**right** *adjective* 1 of or belonging to the right-hand side. *In Italy cars drive on the right.* 2 correct, true. *Is that the right time?* 3 morally good, just. *Giving her the money back was the right thing to do.* 4 most suitable or healthy. *She is the right person for the job.* **right** *adverb* 1 towards the right-hand side. 2 directly, straight. *He stood right in front of me.* 3 properly, correctly. 4 immediately. *Right now.* 5 expressing agreement. *Right, I'll see you tomorrow afternoon.* **right angle** an angle of 90 degrees. **right-wing** not wanting political change, conservative.

R

**right** *noun* 1 the right-hand side, part or direction. *Keep to the right.* 2 a political party or group of people with conservative views. 3 morally good actions. *The difference between right and wrong.* 4 something you are allowed to do or have, a claim. *I know my rights.* **right of way** a right to go before other vehicles. **right** *verb* 1 to make something return to its usual position. *The boat righted itself.* 2 to make something right. *To right a wrong.*

**rigid** *adjective* 1 stiff, not bending. 2 strict. *The army has rigid discipline.*

**rim** *noun* the edge of a cup, plate, wheel or other round object.

**rind** *noun* the tough outer skin of fruit, cheese or bacon. *Orange rind.*

Orange rind is finely chopped and added to marmalade.

**ring** *noun* 1 a circle or something the shape of a circle. *Smoke rings.* 2 a small circle of metal worn on the finger. *A wedding ring.* 3 a space with seats around it where a circus performs or a boxing or wrestling match takes place. 4 a group of people who are doing something illegal. **ring** *verb* to put a ring around something. *The teacher ringed all the mistakes in red pen.*

**ring** (rings, rang, ringing, rung) *verb* 1 to make or cause the sound of a bell. *The telephone is ringing.* 2 to telephone. *She rang her mother.* 3 to be filled with sound. *It was so loud, my ears were ringing.* **ring true/false** to sound true or untrue. **ring** *noun* 1 the action or sound of ringing. 2 a telephone call. *I'll give you a ring either tomorrow or the day after.*

**rink** *noun* a place for skating.

For her birthday, Jemma took her friends ice-skating at the local rink.

**rinse** *verb* to wash something with clean water and without soap. She rinsed the plates. **rinse** *noun* 1 rinsing with clean water. 2 a special liquid for colouring the hair.

**SPELLING NOTE**

*Riddles were originally clever puzzles that people had to solve. They occur in many myths and legends, with gods and rulers 'talking in riddles'. In recent times they have tended to be more like jokes, such as those you find in Christmas crackers.*

**WORD HISTORY**

*A rival was originally a person using the same stream as another, from the Latin 'rivus', meaning stream. Perhaps in places where there was a water shortage, the two rivals competed with each other for use of the stream. Strangely, the word river is thought to come from the Latin 'ripa', meaning bank.*

**riot** *noun* violent or noisy behaviour by a number of people, usually in a public place. **riot** *verb* to take part in a riot.

**rip** (rips, ripping, ripped) *verb* 1 to tear quickly. *She ripped her skirt on the barbed wire.* 2 to remove quickly. *He ripped the letter out of her hand.* **rip** *noun.* **rip off** to cheat by asking for too much money.

**rip-off** *noun* a fraud or swindle.

**ripe** *adjective* 1 ready to be picked and eaten. 2 ready, fit for something. *The country is ripe for change.* **ripen** *verb. The bananas will soon ripen.*

**ripple** *noun* a small wave or small waves. *Ripples on the pond.* **ripple** *verb* to make ripples or move in ripples.

I threw a stone in the pond and watched the ripples grow.

**rise** (rises, rising, rose, risen) *verb* 1 to go up, get higher. *The water is rising.* 2 to come up. *The Sun rises in the east.* 3 to get up from a lying, sitting or kneeling position, to get out of bed. *He rises early.* 4 to get stronger. *The child's voice rose to a scream.* 5 to come up to the surface. 6 to show above the surroundings as a tall shape. *The tower rose above the rooftops.* **rise from the dead** to come back to life. **rise up** to fight against somebody in power. *The people rose up against the dictator.* **rise** *noun* 1 a small hill or upward slope. 2 an increase, such as an increase in wages. A rise in prices or the temperature. 3 the act of growing more powerful. *The rise and fall of the Roman Empire.* **give rise to** to lead to, especially something bad.

**risk** *noun* a danger of something bad happening. A chance of a loss. *There's a risk of showers.* **risk** *verb* to take a chance. *I don't want to risk losing my place in the queue.* **risky** *adjective. Gambling is a risky business, but Peter enjoys it.*

**ritual** *noun* a series of actions that people regularly carry out in certain situations. *Religious rituals.*

**rival** *noun* somebody who competes with you. **rival** *verb* to be as good as somebody or something else. *Nobody else's cooking can rival his mother's.* **rivalry** *noun. A great rivalry between two brothers caused big problems for the family.*

**river** *noun* a large stream of fresh water. *The River Thames winds its way through London and out towards the east.*

**rivet** *noun* a short nail with a flat head used for holding pieces of metal together. **rivet** *verb* 1 to fasten with rivets. 2 to attract or hold somebody's attention. *She watched the film, riveted to the screen.* **riveting** *adjective. He gave a riveting performance.*

**Riyadh** *noun* the capital of Saudi Arabia.

**road** *noun* 1 a specially made way between places for traffic to travel on. 2 a method or way. *The road to success is often very bumpy.* **on the road** travelling.

**roam** *verb* to wander about.

**roar** *noun* a loud, deep noise like the sound a lion makes. *The roar of traffic.* **roar** *verb* 1 to make a loud, deep sound like a lion or thunder. 2 to say or shout something loudly. *She roared with laughter.* **a roaring success** something very successful. **to do a roaring trade** to sell a lot of something.

**roast** *verb* 1 to cook meat or vegetables in the oven or over a hot fire. 2 to get very hot. *I've been roasting in the Sun all day.* **roast** *noun.* **roast** *adjective* roasted. *Roast meat.*

**rob** (robs, robbing, robbed) *verb* 1 to take what belongs to somebody else, usually by force. *The thieves robbed the safe.* 2 to take away. *She was robbed of a real opportunity.* **robber** *noun.* **robbery** *noun.*

**robe** *noun* a long loose piece of clothing.

**robin** *noun* a small bird with a red breast.

**robot** *noun* a machine programmed to do things automatically. Some robots look and act like a person. *Cars are put together by robots in factories.* **robotic** *adjective.*

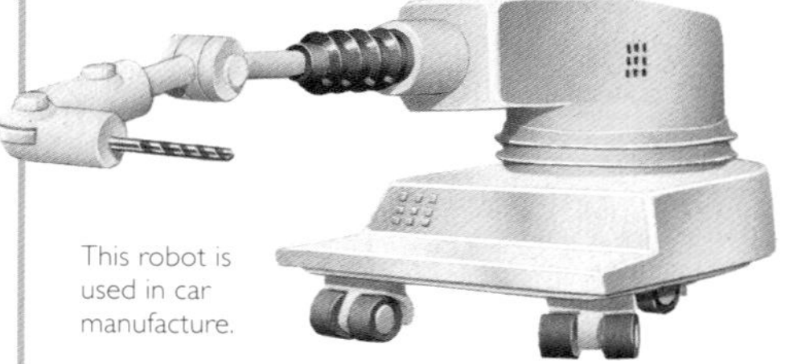

This robot is used in car manufacture.

**robust** *adjective* strong. *A robust wine.*

**rock** *noun* 1 the hard stony part that is part of the earth's crust. 2 a large stone that sticks up above the ground or out of the sea. *We climbed up a rock and then jumped off it.* 3 a hard stick of sweet stuff, usually sold at the seaside. **rocky** *adjective.*

**rock** *verb* 1 to move backwards and forwards or from side to side. *She rocked the baby in her arms.* 2 to shock or shake. *The news of his death rocked the world.* **rock** *noun* 1 a rocking movement. 2 music with a strong beat, rock music.

**rock-bottom** *adjective* at the lowest point. *Everything was sold at rock-bottom prices.*

**AMAZING FACT**

Rodeos are still held in the US and Canada. The Stampede in Calgary, Alberta is the most important in Canada. One of the most important events in the US is in Oklahoma City – The National Finals.

**SPELLING NOTE**

*Be careful about the spellings of 'roll' and 'role'. A roll is something that is rolled up, including the round shape of bread. The actor's part or somebody's position is spelt 'role', as in 'role-play' or 'role model'. This word comes from French, and is sometimes still spelt in the French way with a circumflex accent, 'rôle'.*

**AMAZING FACT**

Roller skates were first invented in Belgium in about 1760 by Joseph Merlin who is said to have skated into a ballroom playing the violin.

**rocket** *noun* 1 a machine in the shape of a long tube that flies by burning gases and is used to send up missiles or spacecraft. 2 a kind of firework. **give somebody a rocket** to tell somebody off. **rocket** *verb* to move up quickly. *The song rocketed to Number One in the charts.*

**rocking-chair** *noun* a chair in which you can rock backwards and forwards.

The rocking chair stood by the fire in Grandma's house.

**rod** *noun* 1 a long thin stick. 2 a stick with a line for fishing.

**rode** *verb* past tense of ride.

**rodent** *noun* an animal that has sharp front teeth for gnawing. Rats, mice and squirrels are all rodents.

**rodeo** (rodeos) *noun* (say **roh**-dee-oh) a show at which cowboys ride wild horses and catch cattle with ropes.

**rogue** *noun* a dishonest person.

**role** *noun* 1 an actor's part in a play, film or musical. 2 somebody's position in a particular situation. *She didn't like the role of leader, but accepted it gracefully.*

**role-play** *noun* an exercise in which people play the part of a character.

**roll** *verb* 1 to move along turning over and over. 2 to make something into the shape of a ball or tube. *Can you roll cigarettes?* 3 to move along on wheels or as if on wheels. *The years rolled by.* 4 to make flat by pressing. *To roll pastry.* 5 to make a deep sound. *Thunder rolled.* 6 to move from side to side. *Drunks rolled down the street.* **roll over** to face the other way by turning over. **roll up** 1 to roll something into a tube or ball. 2 to arrive. *His friends rolled up at midnight.* **roll** *noun* 1 something rolled into a tube. 2 bread in a round shape for one person. 3 a rolling movement. 4 a rolling sound. 5 an official list of people's names. *The electoral roll.*

**rollerblades** *plural noun* boots fitted with small wheels in a line for roller-skating. **rollerblading** *noun.*

**roller-skate** *verb* to move over a surface wearing roller-skates. **roller-skate** *noun* a shoe fitted with four small wheels. **roller-skating** *noun.*

**ROM** *abbreviation* read-only memory. ROM is the memory a computer uses which cannot be changed.

R

**Roman Catholic** *noun* a member of the Roman Catholic Church, which has the Pope at its head. Roman Catholics believe in the Christian religion. **Roman Catholic** *adjective*.

**Romania** *noun* a country in eastern Europe.

**Romanian** *noun* 1 the language of Romania. 2 a person who comes from Romania. **Romanian** *adjective*. *The Romanian flag.*

The Romanian flag has blue, yellow and red vertical stripes.

**romantic** *adjective* having feelings about love and beauty, seeing things in an unreal way. Romantic novels and films are about love and usually have a happy ending. **romantic** *noun*. **romantically** *adverb*. **romance** *noun*.

**Rome** *noun* the capital of Italy.

**roof** *noun* 1 the covering on top of a building, tent, car or bus. 2 the upper part of the inside of the mouth.

**rook** *noun* 1 a black crow. 2 a chess piece, also called a castle.

**rook** *verb* to get money from somebody by cheating. *I was rooked!*

**room** *noun* 1 a part in a house or other building that has its own walls, floor, ceiling and door. 2 space. **roomy** *adjective* spacious.

**rooster** *noun* a cockerel.

**root** *noun* 1 the part of a plant that grows under the ground. 2 the part of a tooth or hair beneath the skin. 3 the cause or basis of something. *The root of the problem.* 4 in mathematics, a number in relation to the number it makes when multiplied by itself. *The square root of 9 is 3.*

**root** *verb* 1 to grow roots. *Ivy roots very quickly.* 2 to search through things. *Pigs root around for food.* **rooted to the spot** unable to move.

The tree's roots spread far down into the earth and draw moisture up the trunk and into the branches and leaves.

**SPELLING NOTE**

*You might think that the plant rosemary was named after two women, Rose and Mary. In fact in old English it use to be called 'rosmarine', and it came from the Latin 'ros marinus', which meant 'sea dew'. As the word changed, people probably thought that it had to do with the plant 'rose' and the Virgin Mary.*

**AMAZING FACT**

Helicopters are the slowest aircraft. Because of their rotor, they are able to hover in the air. Planes, on the other hand, have to fly at a certain speed of they or they will crash.

Leonardo da Vinci (1452-1519) first had the idea of a helicopter – he sketched one and may even have built a model.

**rope** *noun* a strong thick string. **know the ropes** to know how something should be done. **rope** *verb* tie together with a rope. **rope in** to persuade somebody to help you with an activity. **rope off** to separate an area with ropes, usually to keep people away from it. *The accident area was roped off.*

**rose** *noun* 1 a sweet-smelling flower with a thorny stem that grows on a bush. 2 a pink colour. 3 a nozzle with little holes in it that is fitted at the end of a pipe or watering can for watering the garden.

**rose** *verb* past tense of rise.

**Roseau** *noun* the capital of Dominica.

**rosemary** *noun* a bush with evergreen leaves that are used in cooking.

**Rosh Hashanah** *noun* a festival marking the Jewish New Year.

**rot** (rots, rotting, rotted) *verb* to go bad, to decay. *The apples were rotting in the box.* rot *noun* 1 rotting. 2 nonsense. *He talks a load of rot.* **rotten** *adjective*. 1 *Rotten apples.* 2 bad, unpleasant.

**rota** *noun* (say **roh**-tuh) a list of people who take turns doing a particular job.

**rotate** *verb* 1 to move round a fixed point. *A wheel rotates.* 2 to take turns or come round in regular order. *We rotate the babysitting.* **rotation** *noun*. *The Earth's rotation is a mystery to me.*

The Earth rotates on its axis as it moves around the Sun.

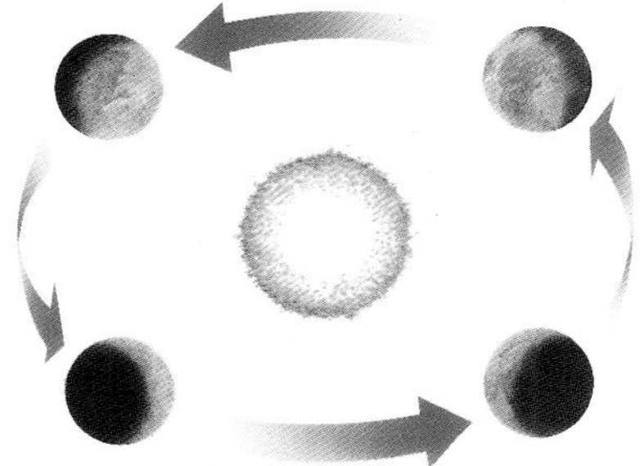

**rotor** *noun* a part of a machine that rotates, especially the rotating blades of a helicopter.

**rouble** *noun* Russian money.

**rough** *adjective* 1 uneven, not smooth or polished. *Rough skin.* 2 not calm, gentle or polite, using force. *Rough manners.* 3 not exact, without detail. *A rough description.* **roughly** *adverb*. **roughness** *noun*.

**rough** *verb* to make something untidy. If you rough somebody up, you hit them. **rough it** to live in an uncomfortable way. *Students usually don't mind roughing it for a while on their first trips abroad.* **rough out** to make a quick drawing or plan of something. **rough** *noun* 1 the long grass on a golf course. 2 a rough person. 3 a piece of writing or a drawing without much detail, not finished.

R

**round** *adjective* 1 shaped like a circle or ball. 2 complete. *A round dozen.* 3 going and returning. *A round trip.* **roundness** *noun.* **in round figures** not exactly, but to the nearest 10, 100, 1000, etc.

The meeting was held at a round table, where all the participants were equal.

**round** *adverb* 1 in a circle. 2 from one to another, all over the place. *Hand the books round.* 3 to your home. *They invited us round.* 4 facing the other way. *Round the corner.* **round about** 1 about. 2 very near a place.

**round** *preposition* 1 in a circle. 2 on all the sides of. 3 in every direction or everywhere. 4 in the neighbourhood. **round the clock** all the time. *Paul made us work round the clock.*

**round** *noun* 1 something round. 2 a regular journey to a number of houses. *A paper round.* 3 a slice of bread or a sandwich made with two slices of bread. 4 a share given out to everyone. *This round of drinks is on me!* 5 one stage in a game or a competition. *Our team is through to the next round.* 6 a bullet or bullets from a gun. 7 in golf, playing all the holes once.

**roundabout** *noun* 1 a place where a number of roads meet and cars drive in a circle. 2 a merry-go-round.

**roundabout** *adjective* not in the shortest or most direct way. *He told us in a roundabout way that he was leaving.*

**rout** *verb* to defeat heavily. **rout** *noun.*

**route** *noun* (say root) the way you take to get to a place.

**routine** *noun* (say roo-**teen**) the usual way of doing things. *Getting up late upsets my routine.* **routine** *adjective. A routine job.*

**rove** *verb* to roam.

**row** *noun* (rhymes with go) a line of people or things. *A row of houses.*

**row** *verb* (rhymes with go) to move a boat through the water with oars. **rower** *noun.* **rowing** *noun.*

**row** *noun* (rhymes with now) 1 a noisy quarrel. 2 a loud noise.

**rowdy** (rowdier, rowdiest) *adjective* rough and noisy. *The twins are too rowdy.*

Rubies are gemstones valued for their beautiful red colour.

**SPELLING NOTE**

*In British English, people often use 'round' when there's the idea of going in a curve: 'It's just round the corner.' For a more general area, they more often use 'around': 'Do you live around here?' To mean approximately, you should only use around: 'I'll see you around eight.'*

**rowing boat** *noun* a small boat with oars.

**royal** *adjective* belonging to or connected with a king or queen. **royally** *adjective.* **royalty** (royalties) *noun* 1 people of the royal family. 2 part of the price of a book that is paid to the writer for each copy sold.

**rub** (rubs, rubbing, rubbed) *verb* to move something backwards and forwards or round and round against something else. *Rub some cream on it to make it better.* **rub out** to remove something, especially pencil marks, with a rubber.

**rubber** *noun* 1 an elastic substance that keeps out water, made from the juice of some tropical trees. *Rubber gloves.* 2 a small piece of rubber used for rubbing out pencil marks, an eraser. **rubbery** *adjective.*

**rubbish** *noun* 1 unwanted things to be thrown away. 2 nonsense, foolish talk. *Switch that rubbish off!*

**rubble** *noun* broken stones or bricks. *Fill the hole with rubble.*

**ruby** (rubies) *noun* a red precious stone. **ruby** *adjective. Ruby port.*

**rudder** *noun* a piece of metal or wood at the back of a boat or plane, used for steering.

**rude** *adjective* 1 impolite. *It's rude to laugh.* 2 vulgar. *Rude jokes.* 3 unexpected and unpleasant. *A rude awakening.* 4 very simple and roughly made. *A rude shelter.* **rudeness** *noun. Her rudeness is appalling.*

**rug** *noun* 1 a mat, smaller than a carpet. 2 a thick blanket.

**rugby** *noun* a game similar to football but played with an oval ball that can be handled. *Tim loves playing rugby.*

**rugged** *adjective* 1 craggy and rocky. *A rugged landscape.* 2 rough and strong. *A rugged face.*

**ruin** *noun* 1 destruction. *Drink will be the ruin of her.* 2 the state of no longer having any money. *My business is facing ruin.* 3 part or parts of a building still standing after the rest has been destroyed. *The ruins of a castle.* **ruin** *verb* 1 to destroy or harm. 2 to lose all your money.

The castle ruins provided a fascinating introduction to the archaeology lesson.

**rule** *noun* 1 an order or a law that says what is allowed or not allowed. Instructions on how things are to be done. *The rules of grammar.* 2 power to govern or control. *Under British rule.* **as a rule** usually. **rule** *verb* 1 to govern or control. 2 to decide. *The judge ruled that he must pay a fine.* 3 to make a straight line with a ruler. *Ruled paper.* **rule out** to decide that something is impossible.

**ruler** *noun* 1 a person who rules. 2 a long, flat piece of wood, metal or plastic with straight edges that are marked with centimetres, used for measuring things or drawing straight lines.

**rum** *noun* an alcoholic drink made from sugar cane. *Rum and blackcurrant.*

**rumble** *verb* to make a low rolling sound. *My stomach is rumbling.* **rumble** *noun.*

**rumour** *noun* talk, especially false information, spread from one person to another. **rumour** *verb* to say as a rumour.

**rump** *noun* the back part (buttocks) of an animal. *Rump steak.*

**run** (runs, running, ran, run) *verb* 1 to move quickly on your legs. 2 to take part in a race. *He runs for the school.* 3 to go, travel or drive somebody somewhere. *The bus runs every hour.* 4 to flow. *Shall I run you a bath?* 5 to move quickly. *A strange thought ran through her mind.* 6 to work, operate. *He left the car running.* 7 to organize, control or own. *He runs a shop.* 8 to stretch or continue. *The road runs through the forest.* 9 to continue to go on for a period of time. *The play ran for a week.* **run away** to leave suddenly. **run behind** to be late ending or starting. **run into** 1 to hit a person or thing while driving. 2 to happen to meet or come across. *She ran into an old friend.* **run out** to have used up everything and have nothing left. *We ran out of money.* **run over** to knock somebody or something down when driving. *He ran over his neighbour.*

**rung** *noun* a bar in a ladder. *My foot was on the bottom rung when I fell off the ladder and broke my arm.*

**rung** *verb* past tense of ring.

**runner** *noun* 1 a person who runs, especially in a race. 2 a thin wooden or metal strip on which something slides or moves. *The runners of a sledge.* 3 a messenger. 4 a long strip of carpet.

Anna was a good runner who trained every day.

**DID YOU KNOW?**

*From 1922 to 1991 Russia was part of the USSR (Union of Soviet Socialist Republics) or Soviet Union, which was the biggest country in the world. When the Soviet Union broke up into separate republics, the Russian Federation, or Russia, remained the world's largest country. Its area covers more than 17 million square kilometres, much larger than the continent of Europe.*

**DID YOU KNOW?**

*Rugby, or rugby football, was first played at Rugby School in Warwickshire, which is where the name comes from.*

**runner bean** *noun* a climbing bean, the pods of which are used as food.

**runner-up** *noun* somebody who finishes second in a race or competition.

**runway** *noun* the long strip of hard surface on which planes take off and land.

**rural** *adjective* of or like the countryside, far away from the city.

**rush** *verb* 1 to hurry, act quickly. *Don't rush me, I have to think about it.* 2 to move quickly. *He was rushed to hospital.* 3 to get through, over or into something by pressing forward. **rush** (rushes) *noun* 1 hurry or hurried activity. 2 a sudden interest or demand for something. *A rush for tickets.*

**rush hour** *noun* the busy part of the day when most people are travelling to or from work.

**Russia** *noun* a country in eastern Europe and Asia.

Russia is a vast country that spans eight time zones.

**Russian** *noun* 1 the language of Russia. 2 a person who comes from Russia. **Russian** *adjective. A Russian church.*

**rust** *noun* a reddish-brown substance formed on iron when it becomes damp. **rust** *verb. The bike will rust if you leave it out in the rain.* **rusty** *adjective.*

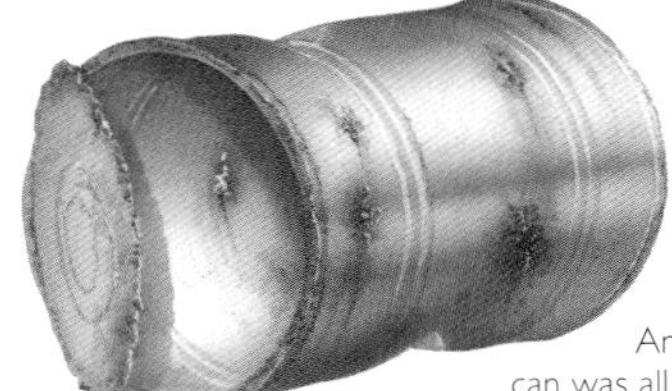

An old rusty can was all that Tom caught when he went fishing.

**rustic** *adjective* connected with the country, rough and simple. *Rustic furniture.*

**rut** *noun* 1 a deep, narrow track made in the ground by wheels. 2 a fixed way of thinking or doing things which is difficult to get out of. *The only way to get out of this rut is to leave home and start a new life.*

**ruthless** *adjective* showing no pity, cruel. *You have to be ruthless in business.* **ruthlessness** *noun.*

**Rwanda** *noun* a country in Africa.

**rye** *noun* a grass grown in cold countries, and the grain of that plant which is used for making flour. *Rye bread.*

S

# Ss

**sabbath** *noun* a weekly day of rest, Saturday for Jews, Sunday for Christians.

**sabotage** *noun* secretly carried-out damage, usually to machines or buildings as a protest, to weaken an enemy or ruin a plan. **sabotage** *verb. The railway lines had been sabotaged by enemy troops.*

**sachet** *noun* (say **sash**-ay) a small closed plastic or paper bag for holding something. *A sachet of shampoo.*

**sack** *noun* a large bag made of strong material. *A sack of potatoes.*

**sack** *noun* taking away somebody's job. *He got the sack for being late.* **sack** *verb.*

**sacred** (say **say**-krid) *adjective* connected with religion, holy.

**sacrifice** *noun* 1 giving something to a god as an offering. 2 giving up something you like or value for the good of something else. **sacrifice** *verb* to offer or give up something as a sacrifice. *He sacrificed his job to look after his sick parents.* **sacrificial** *adjective. A sacrificial lamb.*

**sad** (sadder, saddest) *adjective* unhappy, showing or causing sorrow. **sadly** *adverb.* **sadness** *noun. Tears of great sadness.*

**saddle** *noun* a seat on a horse or bicycle for a rider to sit on. **saddle** *verb* to put a saddle on a horse or other animal.

**safe** *adjective* out of danger or free from risk or harm. *Have a safe journey.* **safely** *adverb. They arrived home safely.*

**safe** *noun* a strong box or cupboard with special locks for keeping money or valuable things in. *Put your jewels in the safe.*

Marcia kept her jewels locked in the hotel's safe.

**safeguard** *noun* a protection against something unwanted. *She eats a lot of fruit as a safeguard against catching colds and flu.* **safeguard** *verb* to protect.

**DID YOU KNOW?**

*S, the 19th letter in the English alphabet, was the 21st letter in the ancient Hebrew and Phoenician alphabets, in which it was called shin.*

**DID YOU KNOW?**

*The original sagas were long stories of heroic achievement in the Old Norse language. The best sagas were written down in Iceland in the 12th and 13th centuries.*

**WORD HISTORY**

*Both 'salad' and 'salary' come originally from the Latin word for salt, 'sal'. 'Salad' simply meant 'salted', since that way your vegetables tasted better. A Roman soldier's pay was his salarium, or salt money, which enabled him to buy salt to improve the flavour of his food.*

**safety** *noun* being safe, freedom from danger or harm.

**safety belt** *noun* 1 a strap attached to the seat in a car or plane worn by travellers. 2 a belt for fastening to something solid worn by somebody working high up or in a dangerous position.

**safety pin** *noun* a metal pin for fastening things together.

**sag** (sags, sagging, sagged) *verb* to hang down loosely or in the middle, usually because of weight. **sag** *noun.*

**saga** *noun* (say **sah**-guh) a long story. *A family saga is my favourite entertainment.*

**sage** *noun* a plant used as a herb.

**sage** *adjective* wise. **sage** *noun* a wise person. *Three sages came on camels.*

**said** *verb* past tense of say.

**sail** *noun* 1 a large piece of cloth attached to the mast of a ship to catch the wind and make the ship move. **set sail** to leave a port. 2 the blade of a windmill. **sail** *verb* 1 to travel across the water, to be able to control a sailing boat. 2 to move quickly and easily. *She sailed through the exam.* 3 to begin a voyage. *Our ship sails tomorrow.*

Jonanthan took a course in navigation so he could sail long distances across the sea.

**sailboard** *noun* the board used for windsurfing. *He bought a new sailboard.*

**sailing boat** *noun* a boat driven by sails.

**sailor** *noun* 1 somebody who can sail a boat. 2 a member of a navy, somebody who works on a ship.

**saint** *noun* a holy person or a very kind and patient person. **saintly** *adjective.*

**sake** *noun* for the sake of somebody or something, for the good of somebody or for the purpose of something. *For heaven's sake, stop arguing with each other.*

**salad** *noun* 1 a mixture of uncooked vegetables, such as lettuce, cucumber and tomatoes, eaten cold.

**salad dressing** *noun* a sauce for putting on salads. *Salad dressing with garlic and herbs.*

**salary** (salaries) *noun* fixed pay, usually monthly, earned by somebody for work.

**sale** *noun* 1 the selling of goods for money. 2 a special time when goods are sold in shops at lower prices. **on sale** if something is on sale, it can be bought in the shops. **for sale** offered to be sold. *The house is for sale.*

**saliva** *noun* the watery liquid that naturally forms in the mouth.

**salmon** (salmon) *noun* (say **sam**-un) a large fish with pink flesh eaten as food.

Salmon swim upstream in spring to spawn.

**salt** *noun* a white substance found in seawater, used for making food taste better or for preserving it. Salt crystals. **rub salt into somebody's wounds** to make somebody's pain even worse. **salt** *verb* to put salt in or on food. **salty** *adjective.*

**salute** *verb* 1 to greet somebody. Soldiers salute by raising their right hand to their forehead. 2 to show respect or admiration. *We salute the enormous efforts you have made.* **salute** *noun. A salute to freedom.*

**salvage** *verb* to save from something that has been destroyed, so it can be used again. **salvage** *noun.*

**salvation** *noun* 1 being saved from sin, the saving of the soul, especially in the Christian religion. 2 something that stops loss or damage.

**same** *adjective* 1 not different, exactly alike. *She wore the same dress as me.* 2 not changed. *She still does the same job for him.* 3 a particular one or one already mentioned. *I saw a flash and at the same moment the car crashed into a tree.* **same** *adverb* in the same way. *I don't feel the same about him now.* **sameness** *noun.*

**sample** *noun* a small quantity that shows what something or what the rest is like. *A free sample of washing powder.* **sample** *verb* to test a part of something.

Diane took samples of curtain material home to try them against her walls.

**WORD HISTORY**

*The sandwich is named after the 4th Earl of Sandwich, John Montagu (1718–92), who was so addicted to gambling that he never wanted to leave the gaming table. So when the Earl needed something to eat, a servant would bring him some cold beef, which he liked to have between two slices of bread. This snack soon came to be known as a sandwich.*

**SPELLING NOTE**

*Santa Claus is the legendary Saint Nicholas, the patron saint of children. Nicholas was a bishop who lived in Asia Minor, present-day Turkey, over 1600 years ago. Stories about Nicholas giving gold to poor children led to the legend of Father Christmas bringing gifts to all children.*

**San'a** *noun* the capital of Yemen.

**sanction** *noun* 1 permission given to do something. 2 actions taken by countries against a country that is breaking international laws. A punishment ordered when a law or rule is broken. *The sanctions included a total trade ban.* **sanction** *verb* to allow something to be done. *The minister sanctioned the sale of the pictures.*

**sanctuary** (sanctuaries) *noun* 1 a holy place, especially in a church or temple. 2 a place of safety. 3 a place where animals or birds are protected. *A bird sanctuary.*

**sand** *noun* a mass of finely crushed stones as on beaches and in deserts. **sandy** *adjective* 1 full of sand. *A sandy beach.* 2 yellowish-red. *Sandy hair.*

**sand** *verb* to smooth or clean a surface by rubbing sandpaper over it.

**sandal** *noun* a shoe with straps over the foot, worn in summer.

**sandpaper** *noun* paper with sand stuck to it, used for smoothing surfaces. **sandpaper** *verb. Please sandpaper the woodwork.*

**sandwich** *noun* two slices of bread with a filling between. **sandwich** *verb* to put something between two others. *The bag was sandwiched between two big suitcases.*

Trudy packed the sandwiches for the picnic.

**sane** *adjective* 1 able to think normally, not mentally ill or mad. 2 sensible. **sanity** *noun.*

**sang** *verb* past tense of sing.

**sanitary** *adjective* 1 concerning the treatment of waste for the protection of public health. *In the Middle Age, sanitary conditions were very poor.* 2 clean, free from dirt or infection.

**San José** *noun* the capital of Costa Rica.

**sank** *verb* past tense of sink.

**San Marino** *noun* a country in southern Europe. Its capital is also called San Marino.

**San Salvador** *noun* the capital of El Salvador.

**Santa Claus** *noun* another name for Father Christmas. Small children are told that Santa Claus comes in a sleigh to bring presents to them at Christmas.

**Santiago** *noun* the capital of Chile.

**Santo Domingo** *noun* the capital of the Dominican Republic.

**São Tomé** *noun* the capital of São Tomé and Príncipe.

**São Tomé and Príncipe** *noun* a country in the Gulf of Guinea off West Africa.

**sap** *noun* the watery liquid in plants and trees. *The sap rises in the spring.*

**sap** (saps, sapping, sapped) *verb* to weaken somebody's strength or confidence, especially over a period of time.

**sapling** *noun* a young tree.

**sapphire** *noun* a bright blue precious stone.

**Sarajevo** *noun* the capital of Bosnia-Herzegovina.

**sarcasm** *noun* amusing, often hurtful things said to mock or upset somebody's feelings, usually by saying the opposite of what is really thought. **sarcastic** *adjective*. *Your sarcastic tone of voice.* **sarcastically** *adverb*.

**sardine** *noun* a small seafish. *A tin of sardines is a delicacy.*

**sari** (saris) *noun* a long piece of material wrapped around the body, usually worn by Indian women.

Madhur wore a red silk sari embroidered with gold thread.

**sat** *verb* past tense of sit.

**Satan** *noun* the devil, an evil power. **satanic** *adjective*. *Satanic powers.*

**satellite** *noun* 1 a heavenly body like a small planet, or a man-made object like a spacecraft, moving around a larger planet. The Moon is a satellite of the Earth. *A weather satellite was sent into space.* 2 a person or country taking orders from another more powerful one.

**satellite dish** *noun* a dish-shaped aerial for receiving signals from a space satellite.

**satin** *noun* a shiny cloth, usually made from silk. *Kate dressed up in satin pantaloons.*

**satire** *noun* amusing writing used to show how foolish or bad people or their ideas are.

**satisfy** (satisfies, satisfying, satisfied) *verb* 1 to give enough of what is wanted to make somebody pleased. *Nothing satisfies her, she is always complaining.* 2 to be enough or good enough for what is needed. *One bowl of soup is not enough to satisfy my hunger.* 3 to make somebody free from doubt, to convince. *When I had satisfied myself that everybody had gone, I locked the door.* **satisfaction** *noun*. **satisfactory** *adjective* good enough. **satisfying** *adjective* pleasing.

**AMAZING FACT**

'Saturday' comes from Old English and originally meant 'the day of Saturn', referring to the planet Saturn.

**WORD HISTORY**

*Both 'sardine' and 'satin' come from place names. The small fish were originally caught off the coast of the Italian island of Sardinia, and they have been called sardines since the 15th century. The silky fabric called satin comes originally from China. The Arabs called the fabric 'zaytuni', which was their name for the Chinese port of Qingjiang.*

**saturate** *verb* 1 to make very wet. 2 to fill completely so that no more can be held. *The handkerchief was saturated with perfume.* **saturation** *noun*.

**Saturday** *noun* the seventh and last day of the week. Saturday comes after Friday and before Sunday.

**saucepan** *noun* a metal cooking pot with a lid and a handle.

**saucer** *noun* a small dish on which a cup stands. *A cup and saucer.*

**Saudi** *noun* a person from Saudi Arabia. **Saudi** *adjective*. *A Saudi prince.*

**Saudi Arabia** *noun* a country in Southwest Asia.

Saudi Arabia is one of the world's richest countries, due to its vast reserves of oil.

**sauna** *noun* 1 a hot steam bath. 2 a room or place where you have a sauna.

**saunter** *verb* to walk in a slow, casual way.

**sausage** *noun* chopped-up meat in a thin casing that looks like a tube. *He had sausage, egg and chips for breakfast.*

**savage** *adjective* wild, uncontrollable or cruel. *The boy was bitten by a savage dog and had to go to hospital to have stitches.* **savagely** *adverb*. **savage** *noun* a cruel, wild or primitive person.

**savannah** *noun* a grassy plain with few trees. *The African savannah.*

**save** *verb* 1 to make somebody or something free from danger. *He saved my life.* 2 to keep something, especially money, for later use. *He has saved enough to buy a new bike.* 3 to make something unnecessary for somebody, so they don't have to do it. *Using a computer saves time.* 4 to stop a player from scoring. **save** *noun*.

**savings** *plural noun* money saved, especially in a bank. *My savings are under the bed.*

**saw** *verb* past tense of see.

**saw** *noun* a tool with a blade with sharp teeth along one edge for cutting wood or metal. *He gave me the saw to cut the wood into lengths.*

Arnold took the saw from the shed and prepared to cut the dead branch from the tree.

**say** (says, saying, said) *verb* 1 to speak words, using your voice to express something. 2 to give an opinion or thought in words or writing. *He said how nice everybody was to him on his trip to India.* **say** *noun* the power of acting or deciding. *She had no say in the matter.* **have your say** to have a chance to say what you think.

**saying** *noun* a sentence people often say that makes a wise statement.

**scab** *noun* 1 a dry crust, mainly of dried blood, which forms over a cut or wound. 2 somebody who does not join a trade union or a strike.

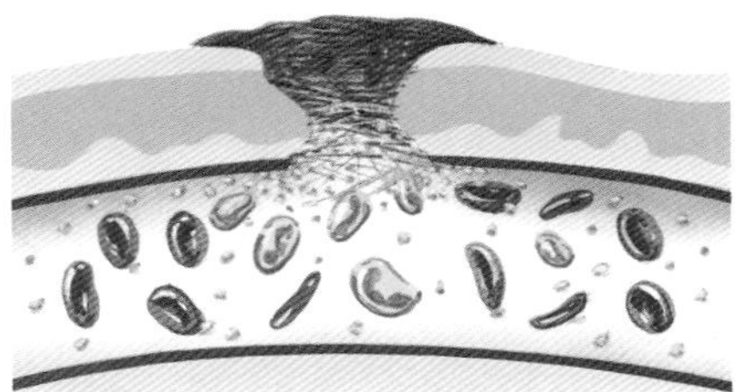

The blood clot dries in the air to form a hard crust called a scab.

**scaffolding** *noun* a framework of metal poles and boards put up round a building for workers to stand on while building or repairing a house.

**scald** *verb* 1 to burn yourself with hot liquid or steam. 2 to clean pans or instruments with boiling water or steam. **scald** *noun* a skin burn from hot liquid or steam. **scalding** *adjective*. *Scalding hot water.*

**scale** *noun* 1 a small, flat piece of hard skin that covers the skin of fish and reptiles. 2 a hard layer that forms at the bottom of a kettle, in pipes or on teeth. **scale** *verb* 1 to remove the scales, especially from fish. 2 to remove from a surface in thin pieces.

**scale** *noun* 1 a set of numbers, marks or degrees for measuring. *A ruler with a metric scale.* 2 a set of numbers comparing measurements on a map or model with the measurements in the real world. *The model is to scale.* 3 a size or importance in relation to other things. *The party is going to be on a grand scale.* 4 a set of musical notes arranged in order going upward or downward. *She practises the scales on the piano every day.* **scale** *verb* 1 to climb up. *The thief scaled the wall.* 2 to make a copy of something according to a certain scale. **scale down** to make something smaller in size or amount than it used to be.

**scales** *plural noun* a weighing machine. *Bathroom scales.*

**scalp** *noun* 1 the skin under the hair on the head. 2 a piece of skin and hair that was taken as a mark of victory when somebody was scalped. **scalp** *verb* to cut the scalp off a dead enemy.

**DID YOU KNOW?**

*Sayings are often clichés or proverbs, and people sometimes use the expression 'as the saying goes' to go with them: 'The left hand didn't know what the right hand was doing, as the saying goes.'*

**scamper** *verb* to run quickly with small, short steps. *Ned scampered up the tree.*

**scan** (scans, scanning, scanned) *verb* 1 to look closely and carefully, to examine. *Mother scanned our faces to see if anything was wrong.* 2 to look at something quickly without reading it properly or to search through information, especially on a computer. 3 to use special equipment to examine a person or pass an electronic beam over an area in search of something. 4 to count the pattern of beats in each line of poetry. **scan** *noun*.

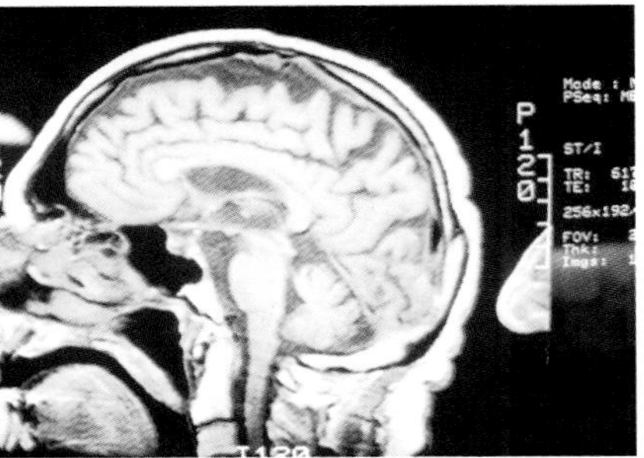

A scan can detect tumours growing inside the brain.

**scandal** *noun* 1 careless talk, gossip that shocks. *The tabloid newspapers love a bit of scandal.* 2 action that shocks or makes people angry. **scandalous** *adjective*.

**Scandinavia** *noun* a region covering the countries of northern Europe – Denmark, Finland, Iceland, Norway and Sweden.

The Little Mermaid sits on a rock on the harbour at Copenhagen, Denmark. She is Scandinavia's best-loved sculpture.

**DID YOU KNOW?**

*Some Native Americans scalped their enemies, and the scalp was considered to be a war trophy. This trophy was a symbol of triumph, and in modern American English the verb 'scalp' is used to mean to defeat.*

**Scandinavian** *noun* a person from Scandinavia. **Scandinavian** *adjective*. *Scandinavian languages.*

**scanner** *noun* 1 a device for putting pictures into a computer. 2 a machine used in hospitals for examining a person by moving a beam of light or X-rays over them.

**scanty** (scantier, scantiest) *adjective* very small, hardly big enough. **scantily** *adverb*. *Helen and Sarah were scantily dressed.*

**scar** *noun* a mark on the skin which is left after a wound or burn has healed. **scar** (scars, scarring, scarred) *verb* to mark with a scar or scars.

**scarce** *adjective* not enough compared with what is wanted, difficult to find. *Fruit is scarce in winter.* **scarcity** *noun*. *There is a scarcity of good humour in the office.*

**scarcely** *adverb* hardly, only just.

S

**scare** *noun* a sudden fear, alarm. **scare** *verb* to frighten or make you frightened, to become afraid. *I'm scared of the dark.* **scare away** to frighten somebody so that they go away. **scary** *adjective.*

**scarecrow** *noun* a figure dressed in old clothes that is put up in a field to frighten birds away.

The scarecrow was dressed in the farmer's old clothes.

**scarf** (scarves) *noun* a piece of cloth worn around the neck or head.

**scarlet** *adjective, noun* bright red.

**scarper** *verb* to run away.

**scatter** *verb* to throw or go in different directions. *He scattered his toys about and made a terrible mess.*

**scatty** (scattier, scattiest) *adjective* being a little mad or forgetful.

**scavenge** *verb* to look among rubbish for food or other things. *The old man scavenges in dustbins for food.* **scavenger** *noun* 1 somebody who scavenges. 2 a bird or animal that feeds on waste and decaying flesh.

**scene** *noun* 1 one of the parts of a play, film or book. 2 the background for a play. *There were only three scene changes.* 3 the place where an event or action happens or an area of activity. *The scene of the crime.* 4 a showing of anger. *He made a scene in the restaurant when I arrived late.* 5 a view. *She paints mountain scenes.* **behind the scenes** secretly. **set the scene** to prepare in order to understand what is going to happen next.

**scenery** (sceneries) *noun* 1 the landscape and everything natural around you. *When we reached the mountains, the scenery suddenly changed for the better.* 2 things used on a theatre stage, like the furniture and painted backgrounds.

Nick and Daphne like walking in the mountains because the air is clear and the scenery is breathtaking.

**WORD HISTORY**

*The word 'sceptic' comes from the Greek 'skepsis', meaning speculation. The original Sceptics were ancient Greek philosophers who thought it was impossible to know things definitely. This philosophy began with Pyrrhon of Elis (c. 365–c.270* BC*), who was influenced by some of the thinkers he met on his travels to India.*

**scent** *noun* 1 a pleasant smell. *The scent of violets.* 2 a liquid perfume you put on your skin to smell nice. 3 a smell left by an animal that other animals can follow. **scent** *verb* 1 to smell. *The dog scented a fox.* 2 to feel that something is going to happen, to detect. *I scent trouble.* 3 to put scent on something or fill with scent. *The air was scented with flowers and full of the buzz of insects.*

**sceptic** (say **skep**-tik) *noun* somebody who does not believe things. **sceptical** *adjective I'm sceptical about our chances of winning.*

**schedule** (say **shed**-yool) *noun* a plan that gives a list of events and times for doing things. **on schedule** on time. **behind schedule** not on time. **schedule** *verb* to put into a plan or timetable. *A scheduled flight to Paris.*

**scheme** *noun* a plan of action or an arrangement. *I like your colour scheme better than your furniture.* **scheme** *verb* to make clever, secret plans. **schemer** *noun.*

**scholar** *noun* 1 a person who studies an academic subject and knows a lot about it. 2 a pupil or student who receives money (a bursary or scholarship) to study at a school or university.

**school** *noun* 1 a place for teaching children. 2 the time when teaching is done and you are at school. 3 all the teachers and pupils in a school. 4 a place for the study of a particular subject, especially a college or university department. 5 a group of people who think the same or have the same methods of work. 6 a group of dolphins or fish. **school** *verb* to train. **schooling** *noun.*

**science** *noun* the study of nature, natural things and the testing of natural laws. If you study science you might do chemistry, physics or biology. Psychology is a social science. **scientific** *adjective. Microscopes and thermometers are scientific instruments.*

**scientist** *noun* somebody who studies science or works in one of the sciences.

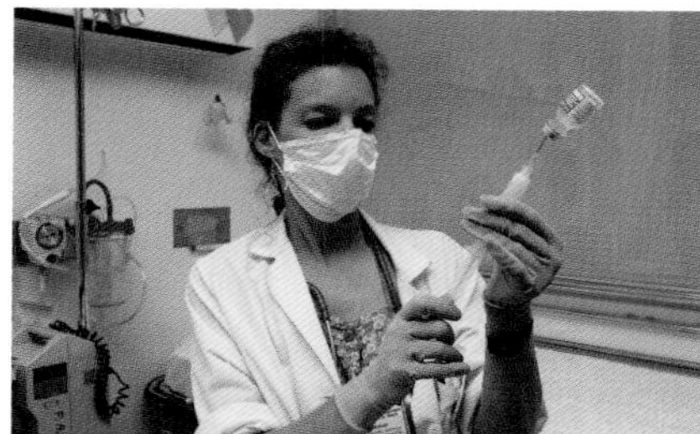

Jane trained as a scientist, then got a job as a lab technician.

**scissors** *plural noun* a tool with two sharp blades for cutting.

**scoff** *verb* 1 to speak in a mocking way about somebody or something. 2 to eat food quickly and greedily. *Who scoffed the cake?*

**scold** *verb* to tell somebody off, to speak angrily. *She scolded the children.*

**scone** *noun* (say skon rhyming with on, or skohn rhyming with bone) a small flat cake usually eaten with butter.

**scoop** *noun* 1 a deep round spoon for dishing out soft food such as ice-cream. 2 a shovel-shaped spoon for picking up grain, flour or sugar. *A measuring scoop.* 3 the amount a scoop holds. 4 an exciting news story reported by a newspaper before any other newspapers. 5 a successful piece of business, usually a large profit made from acting faster than others. **scoop** *verb* 1 to lift something or make a hole as if with a scoop. *She scooped out a hole in the sand.* 2 to pick something up with a scoop or spoon. *I scooped out some ice-cream.*

**scooter** *noun* 1 a kind of small motorbike. 2 a child's vehicle with a long handle and two small wheels attached to a board.

Scooters were very popular in the 1970s with Mods, while Rockers preferred motorbikes.

**scope** *noun* 1 an opportunity, a chance for action. *I wish there was more scope for doing your own mixing in music lessons.* 2 a range, a whole area of action.

**scorch** *verb* to burn something so it goes slightly brown. *The grass was scorched by the hot Sun.* **scorching** *adjective* very hot.

**score** *noun* 1 the number of points, goals or runs made in a game. 2 a written copy of a piece of music for the performers, showing what each one has to play. 3 a piece of music for a film or play. 4 twenty. *Two score and ten is 50.* When you get scores of something, you get a large number. *Scores of complaints.* 5 a reason or point. *He won't let us down, you can trust him on that score.* **score** *verb* 1 to win points in a game or competition, to get a goal, try or run in sport. 2 to keep a record of scores. 3 to gain or win success or an advantage. *She is only interested in scoring over her sister at parties.* 4 to mark or cut lines with a sharp instrument. *Score the card to make it easier to fold.* 5 to write out a musical score. **scorer** *noun. The scorer of most goals gets a medal and a certificate.*

**scorn** *noun* the feeling that somebody or something is worthless, contempt. **scorn** *verb* to show scorn. *She admires the rich and scorns the poor.* **scornful** *adjective. She is scornful about boys.* **scornfully** *adverb.*

**AMAZING FACT**

Scorpions belong to the same family as spiders because they have eight legs. They are very ancient creatures.

**DID YOU KNOW?**

*The first language of Scotland was Gaelic, which was introduced by Celts from Ireland about 1400 years ago. This became the native tongue of the Highlands and Islands of northern and western Scotland. English was introduced into these areas when it started being used in schools in the mid-18th century, but Gaelic is still spoken in the region today.*

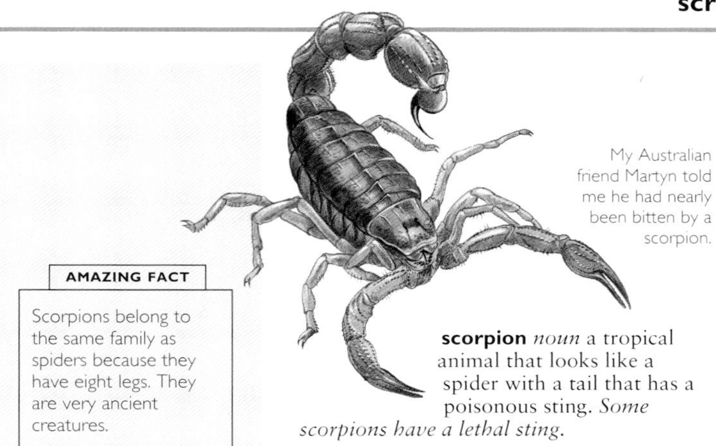

My Australian friend Martyn told me he had nearly been bitten by a scorpion.

**scorpion** *noun* a tropical animal that looks like a spider with a tail that has a poisonous sting. *Some scorpions have a lethal sting.*

**Scot** *noun* a person who comes from Scotland. *Most Scots like whisky.*

**Scotland** *noun* a country that is part of the United Kingdom.

**Scots** *noun* a dialect of the English language spoken in Scotland. **Scots** *adjective. A Scots writer from Glasgow.*

**Scottish** *adjective* from or belonging to Scotland. *The Scottish team.*

**scour** *verb* to clean something by rubbing it with rough material. *She scoured the pans.*

**scour** *verb* to search everywhere. *She scoured the papers for information.*

**scout** *noun* 1 somebody sent out to get information or look for talented sportsmen. 2 a member of the Scout Association. **scout** *verb* to go about looking for somebody or something. *We scouted around for a good hotel, but without any luck.*

**scowl** *noun* an angry expression on the face. **scowl** *verb* to frown to show anger. *He didn't say anything, he just scowled at me.*

**scrap** *noun* 1 a small piece, especially something unwanted or a small amount. *A scrap of paper.* Scraps are pieces of food that are usually thrown away. 2 waste material, especially metal. *Scrap metal.* **scrap** (scraps, scrapping, scrapped) *verb* to throw something unwanted away or cancel a plan or an idea.

After the accident, Gerry's car was a write-off and he had to send it for scrap.

S

**scrap heap** *noun* a pile of waste, unwanted things and ideas. *That plan might as well go on the scrap heap, it'll never work.*

**scrape** *verb* 1 to remove something by pulling or pushing a knife or other object over it. *He scraped the mud from his boots.* 2 to make something clean or smooth by pulling a knife or something rough over it. *She scraped the carrots before boiling them.* 3 to rub roughly or damage by rubbing. *He scraped his knee.* 4 to get or pass something with difficulty. *She scraped through the exam.* **scrape a living** to get just enough food or money to stay alive. **scrape** *noun* 1 a scraping movement or sound. 2 damage or hurt caused by scraping. 3 a difficult position, usually caused by yourself. *She got into a scrape for not doing her homework.*

**scraper** *noun* a tool for scraping.

**scratch** *verb* 1 to rub, cut or mark with something sharp or rough. *The cat scratched me.* 2 to rub the skin to stop itching. 3 to withdraw from a race or competition before it starts. **scratch** *noun* 1 a mark, cut or injury made by scratching. 2 the action or sound of scratching. *The dog likes a good scratch.* **scratchy** *adjective.* **start from scratch** to start from the beginning. **be up to scratch** to be good enough.

**scrawl** *verb* to write untidily. *He scrawled a message on the pad.* **scrawl** *noun.*

**scrawny** (scrawnier, scrawniest) *adjective* thin and bony. *A scrawny pigeon.*

**scream** *noun* 1 a loud cry or noise, usually because of pain or fear. *I could hear screams of laughter.* 2 somebody or something very funny. *You'd like her, she's a scream.* **scream** *verb* to make a scream.

**screen** *noun* 1 a flat surface on which television pictures, films or photographs are shown. *A computer screen.* 2 an upright frame, usually made to fold, used to divide a room or other area. 3 something that gives protection or hides. **screen** *verb* 1 to shelter, hide, protect or divide something or somebody. *The trees screened her from view.* 2 to show a film on television or in the cinema. 3 to examine or look carefully at somebody's ability or health. *She was screened for cancer.* **screen off** to make part of a room into a separate area.

If you stare at the screen on your computer all day, you may risk eyestrain or headaches.

I bought Basil a set of screwdrivers to thank him for plumbing in my washing machine.

A scroll is like a book on one long sheet of paper. The reader unrolls and rolls it as he or she reads.

**WORD HISTORY**

*'Scuba' comes from the first letters of the words 'self-contained underwater breathing apparatus'.*

**AMAZING FACT**

Word meaning changes as our lifestyles change. For example, the meaning of 'scroll' has changed since computers have become such an important part of our lives. It still has the original meaning of a roll of paper but it also means to move up or down a screen to view more information.

**screw** *noun* 1 a metal pin with spiral grooves round it used for fastening or holding things together. 2 a turning movement or something that twists like a screw. *He gave it another screw to make sure it was tight.* 3 a propeller on a ship or plane. 4 slang for a prison warder.

**screwdriver** *noun* a tool for turning screws.

**scribble** *verb* 1 to write quickly and untidily. 2 to make meaningless marks or rough drawings. **scribble** *noun. I can't read her scribble.*

**script** *noun* 1 a written form of a play, film or talk. *He writes scripts for television programmes.* 2 handwriting. 3 a particular system of writing. *Arabic script.*

**scripture** *noun* sacred writing.

**scroll** *noun* 1 a long roll of paper or other material with writing on it. 2 a spiral design.

**scrotum** (say **skroh**-tum) *noun* the bag of skin that holds the testicles.

**scrounge** *verb* to get something, usually money or food, by asking for it without paying or working for it. **scrounger** *noun.*

**scrub** (scrubs, scrubbing, scrubbed) *verb* 1 to clean by rubbing hard, usually with a brush. *She scrubbed the floor.* 2 to cancel. *The match was scrubbed.* **scrub** *noun.*

**scrub** *noun* low-growing bushes and trees or land covered with them.

**scruffy** (scruffier, scruffiest) *adjective* dirty and untidy. **scruffiness** *noun.*

**scrum**, **scrummage** *noun* 1 a group of rugby players from both teams pushing against each other to get the ball. 2 a crowd pushing against each other.

**scuba** *noun* a container of air under pressure which a diver carries on his back and uses for breathing while swimming under water.

**scuba-diving** *noun* swimming underwater using a scuba.

**sculpt** *verb* to carve or model shapes in clay, wood or metal. **sculpture** *noun* the art of making shapes in wood, clay or metal or the shape made in this way. **sculptor** *noun* an artist who makes sculptures.

**scum** *noun* 1 a covering of dirt on top of water or other liquid. 2 worthless people.

**scurf** *noun* bits of dry, dead skin in the hair.

**scurvy** *noun* a disease caused by not eating enough fruit and vegetables with vitamin C.

**scythe** *noun* a tool with a long curving blade on a long handle for cutting grass.

**sea** *noun* 1 salty water that covers most of the Earth's surface. 2 a particular area of the sea surrounded by land. *The North Sea.* 3 a large number. *A sea of daffodils.* **by the sea** at the seaside. **at sea** 1 on the sea. 2 confused. *She was completely at sea.*

**seagull** *noun* a seabird.

Seagulls eat worms on land and fish at sea.

**sea horse** *noun* a very small upright fish with a head that looks like a horse.

**seal** *noun* a large sea-animal without legs but big flippers that eats fish and lives both on land and in the sea.

**seal** *noun* 1 something fixed to a letter or container that must be broken before opening. *The seal on the packet was damaged.* 2 a piece of wax or lead stamped with a design or fixed to documents to show that they are official. 3 the metal tool with the design or a small decorative sticker for sealing a letter or document. 4 something made to close an opening to stop gas, air or liquid getting out. **seal** *verb* 1 to close something tightly. *To seal an envelope.* 2 to put a seal on something. 3 to stop something up or close an opening. *He sealed the cracks with mud.* 4 to make something certain. *We sealed the agreement by shaking hands.* **seal off** to close tightly to stop somebody or something from getting in or out. *The police sealed off the street around the accident.*

**sea level** *noun* the height of the sea halfway between high and low tide, used for measuring height on land and depth at sea. *1,000 metres above sea level.*

**sea lion** *noun* a kind of large seal.

**seam** *noun* 1 a line of stitches that joins two pieces of cloth together or a line where two edges meet. 2 a long layer of coal or another mineral in the ground.

**SPELLING NOTE**

*When it is used with names, 'sea' is written with a capital 's': 'the North Sea'. The biggest sea in the world is the South China Sea, which is part of the Pacific Ocean. The next three biggest are the Caribbean Sea, the Mediterranean Sea and the Bering Sea.*

**AMAZING FACT**

Seahorses swim by moving a fin located in the middle of their backs. They are strange, delicate-looking creatures – and their behaviour is unusual, too. The males, not the females, take care of the eggs until they hatch by keeping them in a pouch on their belly.

**search** *verb* 1 to look carefully through a place to try to find something. *She searched for her purse.* 2 to examine somebody's clothing for something hidden. *They were searched by the police.* **search** *noun.*

**seasick** *adjective* feeling sick when travelling in a ship. **seasickness** *noun.*

**seaside** *noun* a place at the edge of the sea, especially one where people go for their holiday. *Let's take a trip to the seaside.*

The children loved their holidays by the seaside.

**season** *noun* 1 one of four periods of time each year. The four seasons are spring, summer, autumn and winter. 2 the time of year when something usually happens. *The football season.* **in season** available and ready for eating. *Peaches are in season.* **out of season** 1 not available. 2 not busy. *We usually go to Venice out of season, when it is easy to find a cheap hotel.*

As the seasons change, so the leaves bud, open, flourish, dry and eventually drop.

**season** *verb* 1 to add salt, pepper or other spices to food to give it a special taste. 2 to leave wood to dry so it can be used. **seasoning** *noun* salt, pepper and spices used to season food.

**season ticket** *noun* a ticket that can be used whenever you like during a fixed period of time.

**seat** *noun* 1 a place for sitting on or the part you sit on. *I prefer to sit in the back seat.* 2 a place an official member holds. *A seat on the committee.* 3 a place where something is. *London is the seat of government.* **take a back seat** to leave decisions to others. **seat** *verb* 1 to have enough seats for. *The stadium seats 50,000 people.* 2 to sit down.

**seat belt** *noun* a belt fixed to the seat of a car or plane which you fasten around you for safety. *Fasten your seat belts ready for take-off, please.*

**seaweed** *noun* a plant that grows in the sea.

S

**seaworthy** *adjective* in good condition and fit for a sea voyage. **seaworthiness** *noun*.

**second** *adjective* 1 next in order after the first. *February is the second month of the year.* 2 another or extra. *Many families have a second car.* **second** *adverb*.

**second** *noun* 1 a length of time. There are 60 seconds in a minute. 2 a very short time, a moment. *Wait a second.* 3 a person or thing that is second. *I was the second to arrive.* 4 a thing that is not the best. Seconds are goods that are sold cheaply, usually because they are of less good quality. **second** *verb* to help or speak in support of somebody. *I seconded her proposal.*

**second-hand** *adjective* owned by somebody else before. *We bought a second-hand car.*

**second-rate** *adjective* of poor quality.

**secret** *adjective* 1 not told or shown to anybody else, not known by everybody. *We made a secret plan to leave before midnight.* **secret** *noun* something secret. **secrecy** *noun* the habit of keeping secrets. **secretive** *adjective*. *Secretive whisperings.*

Philip confided his most secret thoughts to his diary.

**secretary** (secretaries) *noun* 1 somebody whose job it is to deal with letters, telephone calls and arranging meetings and other business affairs. 2 a government minister. *The Secretary of State for Wales.*

**sect** *noun* a small group of people who have the same religious or political beliefs.

**section** *noun* 1 a part of something larger. *Picture books go in the children's section.* 2 one of a number of equal parts that can be put together. 3 a cross-section. *This a section through an apple.* **sectional** *adjective*.

**secular** *adjective* not religious.

**secure** *adjective* 1 safe, well protected against danger. *Secure locks and windows.* 2 firmly fixed or certain not to be lost. *She has a secure job.* 3 not worried, happy. *Small children need to feel secure with their parents.* **secure** *verb* 1 to make something safe from harm or attack. 2 to get, usually after having made an effort. *We managed to secure two tickets for the concert.* 3 to fix firmly in position. *The shelf was secured to the wall.* **securely** *adverb*. **security** *noun*.

**AMAZING FACT**

The difference between 'to see' and 'to look' is attention, like the difference between 'hear' and 'listen'. In other words, you can see something, then decide to pay attention and look at it.

**WORD HISTORY**

*The word 'secret' comes from the Latin 'secretus', meaning 'separate' or 'hidden'. 'Secretary' comes from the same source, because it originally referred to a person who was entrusted with a secret.*

**AMAZING FACT**

Plants use a variety of methods to scatter or spread their seeds. Some seeds, such as those from the maple tree, have wings that carry them on the wind. Others, like the acorns produced by oak trees, are stored or eaten by animals. Some seeds have tiny hooks that stick to the fur of animals, allowing them to 'hitch a ride'.

**sedative** *noun* a drug that calms you or helps you go to sleep.

**sediment** *noun* solid material that sinks to the bottom of a liquid.

David dredged the sediment from the bottom of the pond and tipped it into a heap.

**seduce** *verb* to tempt or persuade somebody to do something they might not normally do. *The sales seduced me into buying myself new clothes.* **seductive** *adjective*. **seduction** *noun*.

**see** (sees, seeing, saw, seen) *verb* 1 to use your eyes, to look at something. 2 to visit or meet. *He has to see the doctor.* 3 to understand. *I can see what you mean.* 4 to watch a film or play. 5 to make sure something is done. *I'll see that dinner is ready.* 6 to imagine or tell what might happen. *I can't see him giving the money back.* 7 to go with somebody, to accompany. *Can you see her home?* 8 to learn something, usually by reading about it. *I see that your team has been promoted.* **see you!** goodbye! **see about** to make arrangements for something to be done. *My brother will see about the tent.* **we'll see about that** perhaps. **see off** to go to the airport or station with somebody who is going on a trip to say goodbye. **see through** 1 to see the truth about somebody or something, not to be fooled. *He made all sorts of promises, but I saw through him.* 2 to support or help until the end. *He earned enough money in one week to see him through the whole summer.* **see to** to take care of, to deal with something.

**seed** *noun* 1 the small hard part of a plant from which a new plant grows. 2 one of the players named as the best before the start of a competition. *The top seeds don't play against each other in the early rounds.* **seed** *verb* 1 to plant or grow seeds. 2 to place players, especially tennis players, in order of likelihood of winning.

When a seed germinates, it sends up a shoot and sends down a root. It needs water, warmth and light to do this.

**seedling** *noun* a young plant raised from seed. *The seedlings are in the greenhouse.*

**seedy** (seedier, seediest) *adjective* looking poor, run-down or uncared for. *He lives in a seedy part of town.*

**seek** (seeks, seeking, sought) *verb* to search for, to try to get or find.

**seem** *verb* to appear to be, to give the impression of being something. *It seemed a good idea at the time.* **seemingly** *adverb.*

**seen** *verb* past tense of see.

**seep** *verb* to flow slowly through a small opening. *The water seeped slowly away.*

**see-saw** *noun* a plank balanced in the middle for children to sit on at each end, so that when one end goes down the other goes up. **see-saw** *verb* to move backwards and forwards or up and down. *Prices see-sawed up and down all year.*

**seethe** *verb* 1 to be very angry, excited, or upset about something. *She was seething with rage.* 2 to bubble as if boiling.

**segment** *noun* a part marked or cut off from other parts. *An orange segment.*

Annette divided the orange into segments and offered one to each of the triplets.

**segregate** *verb* to put somebody or something apart from the rest. *It is wrong to segregate people by the colour of their skin.* **segregation** *noun. Religious segregation causes wars.*

**seismic** *adjective* of earthquakes or sudden shakings of the ground. *There is a lot of seismic activity in the area.*

**seismology** *noun* the study of earthquakes. **seismologist** *noun.*

**seize** *verb* 1 to take hold of suddenly and forcefully or to take control of. *Panic seized us.* 2 to take by force, to arrest or capture somebody. *The goods were seized by the police.* 3 to take and use something, especially a chance or an idea. **seize up** to become unable to move. *My back seized up after the tennis match.*

**seldom** *adverb* not often.

**select** *verb* to choose somebody or something. **selection** *noun.*

**self** (selves) *noun* somebody's personality or nature. *She is her old self again.*

**self-** *prefix* done by or to yourself.

**AMAZING FACT**

Seismographs show how strong the tremors of an earthquake are. A weight is suspended from a spring, the weight holds a tracer which moves up and down, 'drawing' the strength of the tremor on a drum.

**DID YOU KNOW?**

*One of the most famous seismologists was Charles Francis Richter (1900–85). In 1935 he devised the Richter scale, which is still used to measure the strength of earthquakes. Richter's system measured the strength of seismic waves.*

**self-centred** *adjective* interested only in yourself. *A very self-centred child.*

**self-confidence** *noun* a feeling of power or confidence to do things successfully. **self-confident** *adjective.*

**self-conscious** *adjective* embarrassed and nervous because you know or think people are looking at you. *I'm too self-conscious to be a good actor.*

**self-contained** *adjective* complete in itself. *A beautiful self-contained flat.*

**self-control** *noun* control over your feelings. **self-controlled** *adjective. He is very self-controlled and never loses his temper.*

**self-defence** *noun* the use or skill of defending yourself.

James always excelled himself in his self-defence class.

**self-employed** *adjective* working for yourself and not for an employer. **self-employment** *noun.*

**self-explanatory** *adjective* clear and needing no explanation.

**self-important** *adjective* having a high opinion of yourself. **self-importance** *noun.*

**self-respect** *noun* a feeling of pride in your own ability and respect for yourself.

**self-sacrifice** *noun* giving up what you want, so others can have it.

**self-satisfied** *adjective* very pleased with yourself. **self-satisfaction** *noun.*

**self-service** *adjective* a system in shops, restaurants or petrol stations where you serve yourself and pay a cashier.

Luke and Hannah enjoyed choosing their own food at the self-service restaurant.

**self-sufficient** *adjective* able to make or produce everything that is needed without outside help. A self-sufficient country does not have to buy goods from other countries. **self-sufficiency** *noun. Rod and Hazel decided to try self-sufficiency and bought a farm in Wales.*

S

**selfish** *adjective* thinking mainly of yourself and what you want. **selfishness** *noun*. **selfishly** *adverb*.

**sell** (sells, selling, sold) *verb* to give something in exchange for money. **sell out** 1 to sell everything so there is nothing left. *They have sold out of sunglasses.* 2 to agree secretly to work for the other side, to betray. **sell up** to sell everything you have. *I'll sell up and leave.* **seller** *noun*.

Dave and Janice sold meat at the market every Thursday.

**semen** *noun* (say **seem**-un) the fluid produced by the male sex organs that carries sperm for fertilizing.

**semi-** *prefix* half or partly. *A semi-detached house is my mother's dream.*

**semicircle** *noun* one half of a circle. **semicircular** *adjective*.

**semicolon** *noun* a punctuation mark (;) used in writing that separates different parts of a sentence.

**senate** *noun* 1 the upper house or council in the government of some countries, for example in the USA, France and Australia. 2 the highest council of state in ancient Rome.

**senator** *noun* a member of a senate.

**send** (sends, sending, sent) *verb* 1 to make somebody or something go or be taken somewhere. 2 to make something move quickly in a direction. *The explosion sent glass flying everywhere.* 3 to cause somebody to feel in a particular way. *The noise is sending me crazy.* **send for** to ask somebody to come or order something. *They sent for an ambulance.* **send up** 1 to make something go up. *The coffee shortage has sent the prices up.* 2 to make fun of by imitating something or somebody.

**Senegal** *noun* a country in Africa.

The flag of Senegal has green, yellow and red strips, with a star in the centre.

**senile** *adjective* mentally confused because of old age. **senility** *noun*.

**senior** *adjective* 1 older in age. 2 higher in rank. 3 A senior citizen is an old-age pensioner. **seniority** *noun*.

**GRAMMAR NOTE**

*A semicolon can be used along with commas to separate items in a list in a logical way: 'You will need knives, forks and spoons; cups and saucers; and plates, bowls and glasses.'*

**SPELLING NOTE**

*Both ancient and modern senates are usually spelt with a capital 's'. In the USA, the Senate and the House of Representatives together make up Congress.*

**WORD HISTORY**

*A sentence was originally a 'way of thinking', and came from the Latin 'sententia', meaning 'opinion'.*

**sensation** *noun* 1 a feeling, especially of heat or pain. 2 a state of excitement. *The new film created a sensation.* 3 a general feeling in the mind that cannot be described. *It gave me a strange sensation to see the house I lived in as a child.*

**sensational** *adjective* exciting or shocking.

**sense** *noun* 1 any of the five senses, the ability to see, hear, smell, touch and taste. 2 the ability to make good judgements, be sensible. *He should have shown a little more sense.* 3 a meaning or explanation. *This word has many senses.* 4 an awareness of something. *She has a great sense of humour!* **make sense** to have a clear meaning. **make sense of** to understand. *Can you make sense of his letter?* **sense** *verb* to become aware of something. *He sensed danger.*

During the mating season a warthog's sense of smell becomes highly developed.

**sensibility** *noun* sensitiveness.

**sensible** *adjective* able to make good decisions, wise. *It was not very sensible to set off without a map.*

**sensitive** *adjective* 1 easily hurt in your feelings or offended. 2 quick to feel the effect of something, easily affected by something. *My eyes are very sensitive to bright light.* 3 being aware of other people's feelings or problems. 4 measuring exactly or showing very small changes. *A very sensitive pair of scales.* **sensitivity** *noun*.

**sensual** *adjective* enjoyable or giving pleasure to your body. *Eating and drinking were sensual pleasures in ancient Rome.* **sensuality** *noun*.

**sent** *verb* past tense of send.

**sentence** *noun* 1 a group of words that form a statement, question or command. When you write a sentence, you start with a capital letter and end with a full stop. 2 a punishment for a criminal who is found guilty in court. *He received the death sentence.* **sentence** *verb* to give a punishment to somebody in court.

**sentiment** *noun* 1 an opinion or judgement based on your feelings or thoughts. *We did not agree with the headmaster's sentiments.* 2 a tender feeling like love, happiness or sadness or memories of the past.

**sentimental** *adjective* having or showing romantic feelings, usually not reasonable or practical ones. Sentimental songs are about love, sadness or childhood memories. *She keeps her old teddy for sentimental reasons.* **sentimentality** *noun*.

**sentry** (sentries) *noun* a soldier keeping watch. *The sentry fell asleep on duty.*

**Seoul** *noun* the capital of South Korea.

**sepal** *noun* any of the leaves forming the calyx of a bud.

**separate** (say **sep**-rut) *adjective* 1 divided, not joined to anything, not shared with another. *She cut it into two separate parts.* 2 different. *He gave her three separate reasons for not going.*

**separate** (say **sep**-uh-rate) *verb* 1 to keep apart, to be or become divided. *A wall separates our gardens.* 2 to stop living together. *My parents separated when I was eight.* **separation** *noun* 1 separating or being separated. 2 a time of being or living apart.

**September** *noun* the ninth month of the year. September has 30 days.

**septic** *adjective* infected with poison. *The wound has turned septic.*

**sepulchre** *noun* a tomb. *The king was buried in a sepulchre.*

**sequel** *noun* 1 a book or film that continues the story of an earlier one. 2 an event or situation that follows something else that happened before.

**sequence** *noun* 1 a number of things that come one after another. 2 the order in which things are arranged. *Don't mix up the tickets, they have to be kept in sequence.* 3 a part of a film when something particular happens. *In the opening sequence the hero changes into a monster.*

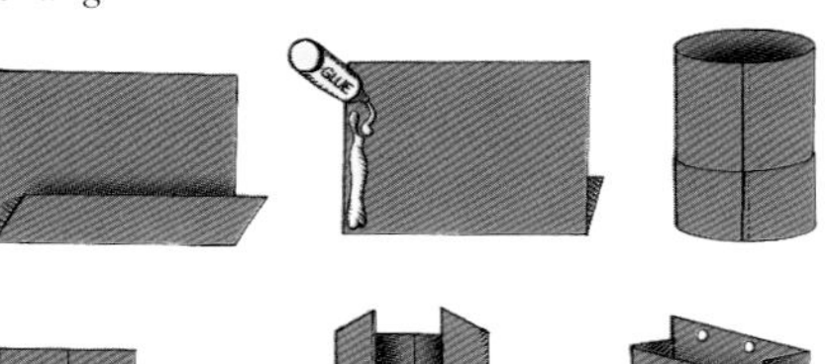

This sequence of diagrams shows step-by-step instructions for making a bag.

A sentry in traditional costume stands on duty outside the Vatican in Rome.

**DID YOU KNOW?**

*Seoul has been an important settlement since the 11th century. During the Korean War (1950–53) the city was badly damaged and changed hands four times. The city now has a population of more than 10 million.*

**serene** *adjective* calm and peaceful.

**sergeant** (say **sar**-junt) *noun* 1 an officer in the army or air force who ranks above corporal. 2 an officer in the police force who ranks below inspector.

**serial** *noun* a story with a number of separate parts. **serialize** *verb*. *The book has been serialized on television.*

**series** (series) *noun* a number of things coming one after another or in order. *A series of books on outer space.*

**serious** *adjective* 1 thoughtful, not cheerful, joking or funny. If something is serious, it is important and has to be thought about carefully. 2 not slight, causing worry. *A serious illness.* **seriously** *adverb*. **seriousness** *noun*.

**sermon** *noun* 1 a speech given in church. 2 a lecture or telling-off.

**serpent** *noun* a snake.

A serpent is a symbol of temptation.

**servant** *noun* somebody who works for another person, usually in their house.

**serve** *verb* 1 to work for somebody, an organization or your country. 2 to provide with something necessary or be suitable for something. *That old raincoat has served me well.* 3 to help customers in a shop or restaurant. *A very nice waitress served us.* 4 to give or offer food to people. *Strawberries are usually served with cream.* 5 to spend a time in prison. *He has already served three years of his sentence.* 6 to begin a game of tennis by hitting the ball. **it serves you right** it is your own fault. **serve** *noun* serving, as in tennis. *He has a good serve.* **server** *noun*.

**service** *noun* 1 something that helps people or provides what the public need. *The train service is poor.* 2 a job done for somebody. *You might need the services of a lawyer.* 3 the serving of customers in a shop or restaurant. *The food is good, but the service is slow.* 4 the repairing of cars and other machines. *I took the car in for a service.* 5 a set of plates and dishes. *A tea service.* 6 a religious ceremony. *Morning service.* 7 serving in tennis. **service** *verb* to check or repair a car or other machine. *Peter made a lovely job of servicing my car.*

**session** *noun* 1 a formal meeting of an organization. *The court is in session.* 2 a meeting or a time used for an activity. *A recording session.*

**set** (sets, setting, set) *verb* 1 to put or place in a position. *The story is set in the mountains.* 2 to fix something. *He set a price for the house.* 3 to cause somebody or something to be in a condition. *They set the house on fire.* 4 to prepare something for use or to start doing something. *To set the table.* 5 to go hard. *Wait for the glue to set.* 6 to give yourself or somebody work or a task. *The teacher set the questions for the exam.* 7 to go down. *The Sun was setting.* **set about** to start doing something. *He doesn't know how to set about getting a job.* **set back** 1 to place something at a distance behind something. *The house is set back from the road.* 2 to delay or make late. *The rain has set back the final.* 3 to cost somebody a lot of money. *How much did the car set you back?* **set off** 1 to begin a journey. 2 to make something begin or happen. *Don't set her off crying.* 3 to cause an explosion. *He set off the rocket.* **set out** 1 to present or make something known. *He set out the rules.* 2 to start a journey. **set to** to begin to do something. **set up** 1 to place in position. *We still have to set up the telescope.* 2 to arrange. *He set up a meeting.* 3 to start, establish. *They set up a new school in the village.*

**set** *noun* 1 a group of people or things that go together. *A set of screwdrivers.* 2 a radio or TV receiver. 3 the place where a play or film is acted. 4 a group of six or more games that make up part of a tennis match.

The chess set was carved out of black and white wood.

**setback** *noun* something that makes your position less good than it was before.

**settee** *noun* a sofa. *The children hid behind the settee when something frightening came on the television.*

**setting** *noun* 1 the surrounding or place in which something is or happens. *A dark forest is the perfect setting for a fairy tale.* 2 the positions in which the controls of a machine are set. *The dishwasher has three settings – hot, cold and economy.*

**settle** *verb* 1 to decide or fix something. *They have finally settled their quarrel.* 2 to become quiet or make calm, to rest. *The medicine will settle your stomach.* 3 to stay in a place or job, to stop being restless. *He travelled the world and finally settled in Canada.* 4 to sink in liquid or come down and cover something. *The snow is settling.* 5 to pay a bill or money owed. **settle down** 1 to become quiet or calm. 2 to start living a quiet life. *He got married and settled down.* 3 to sit down and concentrate on something.

**GRAMMAR NOTE**

*Watch out for sexism in your writing. Many people now object to the use of 'he' and 'his' when what is really meant is 'he or she' and 'his or hers'. One way round this is to use 'they' or 'their': 'If a student is unsure how to register, they should ask their tutor.' You can also easily avoid male-sounding words, for example by using 'the human race' or 'humans' for 'mankind', etc.*

**AMAZING FACT**

After Daniel Boone blazed the Wilderness Road in 1775, thousands of settlers headed west, beyond the Appalachian Mountains. They, in turn, pushed the Native Americans farther west. Most settlers were not prepared for life in the wilderness and many did not survive.

**settlement** *noun* 1 a place people have gone to and built homes in, setting up a community. *There was a settlement near the river.* 2 an agreement or decision between two sides. 3 payment of a debt.

The settlement was made up of conical houses with roofs of straw.

**settler** *noun* a person who goes to live in a new country.

**sever** *verb* to break or cut. *He severed all links with his family.*

**several** *adjective*, *pronoun* some things or people, usually a fairly small number, not many more than two.

**sew** (sews, sewing, sewed, sewn) *verb* (say soe) to join pieces of material together or make or mend clothing with a needle and thread or a sewing-machine.

**sewage** (say **soo**-ij) *noun* waste material from houses people live and work in which flows through sewers.

**sewer** (say **soo**-uh) *noun* a large pipe under the ground that carries sewage away.

**sewing machine** *noun* a machine for sewing things.

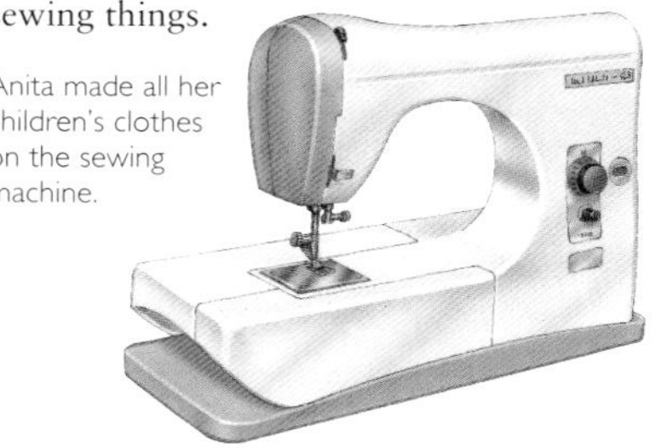

Anita made all her children's clothes on the sewing machine.

**sex** (sexes) *noun* 1 the condition of being either male or female, gender. *It is difficult to tell what sex the bird is.* 2 the two groups, male and female, into which people and animals are divided. *The opposite sex.* 3 sexual activity by which people and animals produce young and all the activities connected with this act. **sexy** *adjective.*

**sexism** *noun* the belief that one sex is not as good as the other, especially that women are less able than men.

**sexist** *adjective* showing sexism. *It's simply sexist to say that women are bad drivers.* **sexist** *noun.*

**sexual** *adjective* 1 being male or female. *The sexual differences between boys and girls.* 2 connected with sex as male and female activity and the wish for it. 3 connected with the process by which people and animals produce young. *Sexual intercourse.* **sexually** *adverb.* **sexuality** *noun.*

**Seychelles** *noun* a country in the Indian Ocean off West Africa.

The Seychelles has a flag of unfurling colours, blue, orange, red, white and green.

**shade** *noun* 1 darkness under or next to an object, made when something blocks out the Sun. *We sat in the shade of a tree.* 2 Something that keeps out light. *The lamp needs a new shade.* 3 the different forms of a colour. How light or dark a colour is. *Many shades of blue.* 4 a little bit. *There was a shade of fear in his voice.* 5. a slight difference. *A word with many shades of meaning.* **shade** *verb* 1 to protect something from bright light. *He shaded his eyes with his hand.* 2 to make part of a drawing darker. *She shaded in the background with a pencil.*

**shadow** *noun* 1 a dark shape on a surface made when something stands between a light and the surface. *I saw his shadow on the wall.* 2 a dark area. *She has shadows under her eyes.* 3 a darkness in a place due to no light reaching it. *The valley is in shadow.* 4 a form not as real as it used to be. *She is just a shadow of her former self.* 5 a little bit. *A shadow of doubt.* **shadow** *verb* 1 to follow somebody secretly. *The detective shadowed the man on his journey through the town.* 2 to make a shadow on something.

**shady** (shadier, shadiest) *adjective* 1 giving shade. 2 dishonest. *Shady dealings.*

**shaft** *noun* 1 a long thin pole or handle. *The shaft of an arrow.* 2 a beam of light coming through an opening. 3 a deep, narrow hole.

**shaggy** (shaggier, shaggiest) *adjective* untidy and rough hair or fur. *A shaggy beard.*

**shake** (shakes, shaking, shook, shaken) *verb* 1 to move quickly backwards and forwards or up and down. *He shook the pears from the tree.* 2 to shock or upset. *She was shaken by the bad news.* 3 to tremble. *They were shaking with laughter.* **shake hands** to hold somebody's right hand when meeting or saying goodbye to them. **shake your head** to move your head from side to side to say 'no'. **shake** *noun* 1 the action of shaking. 2 a drink. *Milk shake.* **shaky** (shakier, shakiest) *adjective* weak, not very good or unsafe. **shakiness** *noun.*

The shallow part of the river provided an easy crossing for the buffalo.

### WORD HISTORY

*The word 'shambles', which is plural but usually treated as if it were singular, comes from the Old English 'sceamul', which meant a stall or stool. Stalls were used by butchers to set out their meat for sale, and the word 'shamble' came to mean a slaughterhouse. Presumably the stalls must often have been scattered about a room or street, leading to the modern meaning of a shambles.*

These building blocks are made of many different shapes.

**shallot** *noun* a small onion.

**shallow** *adjective* 1 not deep. *A shallow river.* 2 not showing much thought, not very serious. *She lives a shallow life.*

**sham** *noun* something false pretending to be real. *Her friendliness is just a sham.* **sham** (shams, shamming, shammed) *verb. She shammed interest.* **sham** *adjective.*

**shamble** *verb* to walk dragging your feet.

**shambles** *plural noun* a place or scene of disorder, a mess. *After the party the whole house was a shambles.*

**shame** *noun* 1 a feeling of guilt or embarrassment. *He had a deep sense of shame after the incident.* 2 feeling sorry about something. *It's a shame you can't come.* **shame** *verb* to feel shame or make somebody feel ashamed. **shameful** *adjective.*

**shampoo** *noun* 1 a special liquid for washing hair. 2 a liquid for cleaning a car or carpet. **shampoo** *verb* to wash or clean with shampoo. *Please shampoo your hair.*

**shape** *noun* 1 the outer form of something, an outline. *A square and a circle are shapes.* 2 condition. *She looks in good shape.* **take shape** to develop. **shape** *verb* 1 to make something into a particular shape. *The cake was shaped like a heart.* 2 to develop in a particular way. *Being bullied at school shaped her whole life.*

**share** *noun* 1 a part belonging, given or done by a person. *He does his share of the washing-up.* 2 one of the equal parts into which the ownership of a company is divided. *He owns shares in British Telecom.* **share** *verb* 1 to have or use something with others. *She shares a flat.* 2 to give a portion of something to others, to divide. *They shared the money between them.*

S

**shark** *noun* a large fish with sharp teeth.

Contrary to popular belief, most sharks will not attack humans.

**sharp** *adjective* 1 with a fine cutting edge or point. *A sharp knife.* 2 clear to see. *A sharp outline.* 3 quick in thinking, seeing or hearing, quickly aware of things. 4 having a quick change in direction or steep and sudden. *A sharp bend.* 5 severe and sudden, firm. *A sharp frost.* 6 sudden and loud. *A sharp cry of pain.* 7 sour, fresh in taste. *Gooseberries are too sharp for me, even with sugar sprinkled over them.* 8 a sharp note in music is higher than the normal pitch. **sharply** *adverb.* **sharpness** *noun.*

**sharp** *adverb* 1 immediately. *Turn sharp left at the church.* 2 exactly, punctually. *We arrived at 3 o'clock sharp.*

**shatter** *verb* 1 to suddenly break into small pieces. *A stone shattered the windscreen.* 2 to destroy or upset. *My hopes were shattered.* If you are shattered after a hard day, you are very tired.

**shave** *verb* 1 to cut hair off the skin with a razor. 2 to cut or scrape thin pieces off something. *You'll have to shave some wood off the bottom to make the door shut.* **shave** *noun.* He needs a good shave. **a close shave** a near accident or disaster. **shaver** *noun.*

**shawl** *noun* a piece of material worn around the head or shoulders or wrapped around a baby. *Wrap the baby warmly in the shawl.*

**shear** (shears, shearing, sheared, shorn) *verb* to cut off hair or wool from sheep.

David could shear sheep faster than anyone else in the county.

**DID YOU KNOW?**

*The Arabic word 'sheikh' is a term of respect and courtesy, dating from pre-Islamic times, that means 'old man'.*

**WORD BUILDING**

*The word 'shepherd' is a contraction, or shortening, of the words 'sheep herd', meaning a person who herds sheep.*

**shears** *plural noun* a tool that looks like a large pair of scissors for cutting hedges and long grass. *Shears for shearing sheep.*

**shed** *noun* a small building for storing things. *A bike shed.*

**shed** (sheds, shedding, shed) *verb* 1 to flow out or let something fall. *She shed many tears.* 2 to get rid of or give off. *Snakes shed their skin as they grow.*

**sheep** (sheep) *noun* a farm animal with thick woolly fur. *A flock of sheep.*

**sheepish** *adjective* embarrassed, usually because you have done something silly. *He gave her a sheepish look.*

**sheet** *noun* 1 a large piece of cloth, usually cotton, put on a bed. 2 a piece of paper. 3 a large, flat, thin piece of glass, metal or wood. 4 a wide stretch of something thin. *A sheet of ice.*

**sheikh** (say shake) *noun* an Arab chief or prince. *The sheikh gave the queen a ruby.*

**shelf** (shelves) *noun* 1 a flat board fixed against a wall or in a cupboard for putting things on. 2 a piece of rock on a mountain that sticks out like a shelf.

**shell** *noun* 1 the hard outer covering of an animal, egg, fruit, nut or seed. 2 the walls of a building or ship. 3 a metal case filled with explosive for firing from a large gun. **shell** *verb* 1 to take something out of a shell. *She was shelling peas.* 2 to fire explosive shells. *The town was shelled during the attack.*

Karen made a beautiful collection of shells from the beach.

**shelter** *noun* 1 something that gives protection, usually a small building or covered place. *A bus shelter.* 2 protection or being kept safe. *We took shelter under a tree.* **shelter** *verb* 1 to protect somebody or something from harm. *They sheltered an escaped prisoner.* 2 to take shelter.

**shepherd** *noun* a person who looks after sheep. *The shepherds watched their flocks.*

**shield** *noun* 1 a large piece of metal, wood or leather which soldiers used to carry to protect their body. 2 a badge shaped like a shield. 3 a protection, or protective cover. *Sun lotion acts as a shield against the Sun.* **shield** *verb* to protect.

**shift** *verb* to move from one place to another, to change direction. *She shifted in her seat.* **shift** *noun* 1 a change of position or direction. *A shift in the wind.* 2 the time for which a worker or a group of workers works. *A late shift.* 3 a straight dress.

S

**shifty** (shiftier, shiftiest) *adjective* dishonest, not to be trusted.

**shilling** *noun* 1 a British coin used until 1971 which was worth 12 old pence. 2 an amount of money in some other countries.

**shimmer** *verb* to shine with a soft light.

**shin** *noun* the front of the leg between the knee and the ankle.

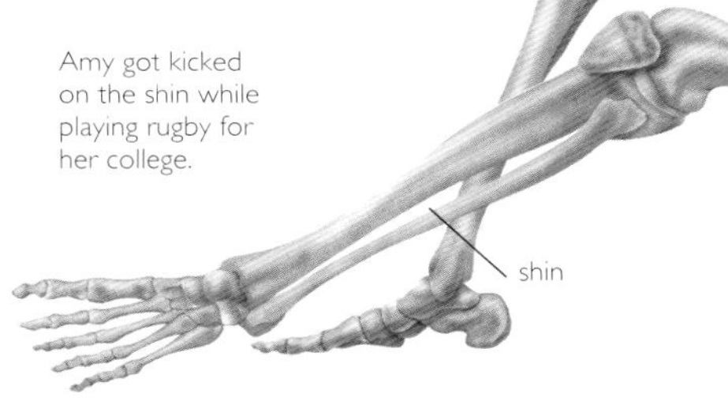


Amy got kicked on the shin while playing rugby for her college.

**shine** *verb* to polish, make bright by rubbing. **shine** *noun* polishing.

**shine** (shines, shining, shone) *verb* 1 to give off light, to be bright. *The Sun is shining.* 2 to direct light at something. *Can you shine the torch on the wall?* 3 to be excellent. *He is good at most sports, but he really shines at tennis.* **shine** *noun* a brightness or polish.

**shiny** (shinier, shiniest) *adjective* looking bright or polished.

**ship** *noun* a large boat for carrying people or goods.

**ship** (ships, shipping, shipped) *verb* to take or send goods by ship.

**shipshape** *adjective* neat and tidy.

**shipwreck** *noun* 1 the loss of a ship at sea. 2 a ship that has been wrecked. **shipwreck** *verb* to lose a ship at sea. *They were shipwrecked on a desert island.*

**DID YOU KNOW?**

*There were 20 old shillings in a pound, and 21 shillings made up a sum called a guinea. An old shilling was worth 5 of today's pence.*

**WORD HISTORY**

*The verb 'to shirk' probably comes originally from the German noun 'Schurke', meaning rogue or scoundrel. 'Only a scoundrel shirks the washing-up!'*

Terrifying high seas resulted in a shipwreck in which all crew and passengers were drowned.

**shipyard** *noun* a place where ships are built.

**shire** *noun* a county.

**shirk** *verb* to try to get out of doing a job. *He is always shirking the washing-up.*

**shirt** *noun* a piece of clothing for the top half of the body, worn with trousers or a skirt. *He was wearing a satin shirt.*

**shiver** *verb* to tremble, especially with cold or fear. **shiver** *noun*. **shivery** *adjective*. *She has a temperature and feels shivery.*

**shoal** *noun* a group of fish swimming together. *A shoal of fish among the reef.*

**shock** *noun* 1 a strong unpleasant feeling of surprise or fear. *It was a shock to hear that he had died.* 2 a movement from something being hit, an explosion or a crash. *We could feel the shock of the bridge crashing.* 3 the effects of electricity passing through the body, an electric shock. *I got a shock when I touched the wire.* **shock** *verb* to surprise or upset somebody, to make somebody feel shocked. *I was shocked by his rudeness.*

**shocking** *adjective* very bad or wrong. *A shocking waste of money.*

**shoddy** (shoddier, shoddiest) *adjective* badly made or done. *Katie produced truly shoddy work.* **shoddiness** *noun*.

**shoe** *noun* 1 a covering you wear on your feet, usually made of leather with a hard sole. 2 a horseshoe. **shoe** *verb* to fix a horseshoe on to a horse's hooves.

**shoelace** *noun* a strip of material like a piece of string for tying up shoes.

**shone** *verb* past tense of shine.

**shoo** *verb* to make somebody, usually an animal, go away by saying 'shoo' and waving your arms.

**shook** *verb* past tense of shake.

**shoot** (shoots, shooting, shot) *verb* 1 to fire a gun or an arrow. 2 to kill or injure somebody by shooting. 3 to kick or throw a ball at a goal. 4 to move or send quickly in a direction, to move over or through something. *The pain shot up his arm.* 5 to put out new growth or shoots from a stem. 6 to photograph a scene in a film. *The film was shot in London.* **shoot** *noun* 1 a young growth of a plant. 2 shooting of a film or still photographs for an advertisement or book. 3 a group of people hunting animals or birds for sport.

**shop** *noun* a building or room in a building where goods are sold. **shop** (shops, shopping, shopped) *verb* to buy things in a shop. **shopper** *noun*. **shopping** *noun*. *Did you do the shopping?*

**shoplifter** *noun* somebody who steals things from shops. **shoplifting** *noun*.

**shore** *noun* the land along the edge of a sea or lake. *Let's go down to the sea shore.*

**short** *adjective* 1 not long, little in distance or length. Having or taking only a little time. If somebody is short, he is not tall. 2 not enough of something. *We are a bit short of money.* 3 rude, usually because you are angry or impatient with somebody. If somebody has a short temper, they get angry easily. 4 Short pastry is made with a lot of fat and is very crumbly. **for short/short for** abbreviated. *My name is William, Will' for short.* **shortness** *noun*. **short** *adverb* suddenly. *He stopped short at the edge of the cliff.* **short** *noun* 1 a strong alcoholic drink. 2 a short film.

**shortage** *noun* lack of something, not having enough. *There is a terrible food shortage in Sudan.*

**shortcoming** *noun* a fault or defect.

**shorten** *verb* to make or become short.

**shorthand** *noun* a way of writing that uses special signs or shorter forms for words and phrases, so something can be written down as fast as somebody is saying it.

**shortly** *adverb* 1 soon, in a little time. 2 in a few words. 3 in a cross way, not politely.

**shorts** *plural noun* short trousers.

**short-sighted** *adjective* not able to see things far away properly. *My brother has to wear glasses because he is short-sighted.*

**shot** *verb* past tense of shoot.

**shoulder** *noun* the two parts of the body between the neck and the top of the arms. *He put the rucksack over his shoulder.* **shoulder** *verb* 1 to take on something, especially a problem or responsibility. 2 to push with the shoulder. *He shouldered his way through the crowd.*

**shout** *noun* a loud call or cry. **shout** *verb* to cry or call loudly.

**shove** *verb* to push roughly. **shove** *noun*.

**shovel** *noun* a tool like a spade for lifting and moving coal, sand, earth, snow and other things. **shovel** (shovels, shovelling, shovelled) *verb* 1 to move, lift and work with a shovel. *He shovelled a path through the snow.* 2 to push a lot of something quickly into a place. *Don't shovel the food into your mouth like that.*

**AMAZING FACT**

A West German man, Hans-Gunter Winkler, has won a record number of show-jumping events. He has the Men's World Championship twice, the European Championship and has won five Olympic gold medals.

There was a wonderful show of tulips in the park that spring.

**AMAZING FACT**

The phrase, 'a parting shot', which means to say or do something as you leave, was originally 'a Parthian shot'.

The Parthians were an ancient kingdom in Western Asia. As the Parthian troops retreated, they customarily fired a final shot at the enemy.

Dean used the shovel to move the huge mound of stones outside the window.

**show** (shows, showing, showed, shown) *verb* 1 to allow or offer to be seen. 2 to be seen easily, to be noticeable. *Any marks show on white.* 3 to demonstrate, or make somebody understand something. *He showed me how to use the computer.* 4 to point to a mark or number. 5 to guide. *The waitress showed us to our seats.* 6 to prove or make something clear. *Her marks show that it was worth revising for the exam.* 7 to act towards somebody in a certain way. *He shows no pity for the homeless.* **show off** to show something to impress people. **show up** 1 to arrive at a place. *Only a few people showed up at the party.* 2 to be seen clearly, be noticeable. **show** *noun* 1 a public showing, a collection of things to be looked at. *The Chelsea Flower Show.* 2 a performance in a theatre, on television or in a club. 3 a way of behaving. If something is for show, it is only done to make a good impression. **on show** to be seen by the public. *His paintings are on show at the gallery.* **showy** *adjective* too noticeable, gaudy. *The bride's aunt wore a showy hat.*

**show business** *noun* the business of entertainment. If you are in show business, you work in television, films or the theatre.

**shower** *noun* 1 a short rainfall. 2 a fall of many small things arriving at the same time. *She was covered in a shower of blossom.* 3 a device, usually in the bathroom, for washing yourself that sprays water on your body. 4 a wash under a shower. *I have a shower every day.* **showery** *adjective*. *It's been showery all day.* **shower** *verb* 1 to fall in a shower. 2 to have a shower.

Peter had a relaxing shower after work.

**showjumping** *noun* the sport of riding a horse over fences and barriers.

**shown** *verb* past tense of show.

**shred** *noun* 1 a small piece torn or cut off something. 2 a very small amount. *There is not a shred of truth in what he says.* **shred** (shreds, shredding, shredded) *verb* to cut or tear into shreds.

**shrewd** *adjective* having common sense, clever. *She is a very shrewd businesswoman.*

**shriek** *noun* a sudden loud, wild cry. *A shriek of laughter.* **shriek** *verb.*

**shrill** *adjective* high-sounding and painful to the ear. *A shrill voice.*

**shrimp** *noun* a small shellfish with a long legs and a tail like a fan.

**shrine** *noun* a holy place where people pray. *They left offerings at the shrine.*

The Temple of Angkor Wat become a Buddhist shrine in the 1500s.

**WORD HISTORY**

*The word 'shrewd' used to have a much more negative meaning than it does today. At first it meant 'wicked' or 'cruel'. Then it came to mean 'strict' or 'harsh', before taking on a sly slant.*

**shrink** (shrinks, shrinking, shrank, shrunk) *verb* 1 to become smaller in size. *The sweater has shrunk in the wash.* 2 to move back, usually in fear. 3 to avoid doing something because it is not pleasant. **shrinkage** *noun.*

**shrivel** (shrivels, shrivelling, shrivelled) *verb* to become dry and wrinkled.

**shrub** *noun* a small bush.

**shrug** (shrugs, shrugging, shrugged) *verb* to raise your shoulders to show that you don't know or don't care. **shrug** *noun.*

**shudder** *verb* to tremble with fear, cold or horror. **shudder** *noun.*

**shuffle** *verb* 1 to walk by dragging your feet. 2 to mix up the order of a pack of playing cards before beginning a game. **shuffle** *noun.*

The magician shuffled the pack of cards, and ended with the whole suite in the right order.

**WORD HISTORY**

*The original Siamese twins, Chang and Eng (1811–74), were joined at the hip. They were called Siamese because they were born in Siam, which is now called Thailand. Since that time many pairs of Siamese twins have been successfully separated.*

**shun** (shuns, shunning, shunned) *verb* to avoid. *I was hurt when he shunned me.*

**shut** (shuts, shutting, shut) *verb* 1 to move into a covered, blocked or folded-together position, to close. 2 to close for a period of time or stop business. **shut down** to stop business or work. *The factory has shut down.* **shut in** to leave or lock in a room. *He shut himself in his room to work.* **shut up** 1 to make a place safe before leaving. 2 to stop talking or stop somebody from talking.

**shutter** *noun* 1 a cover fitted on the outside of a window that can be opened or shut to keep out the light. *Please close the shutters.* 2 the part in a camera that opens to let in light when a photograph is taken.

The light is regulated by the shutter. It travels through the lens and on to the film inside the camera.

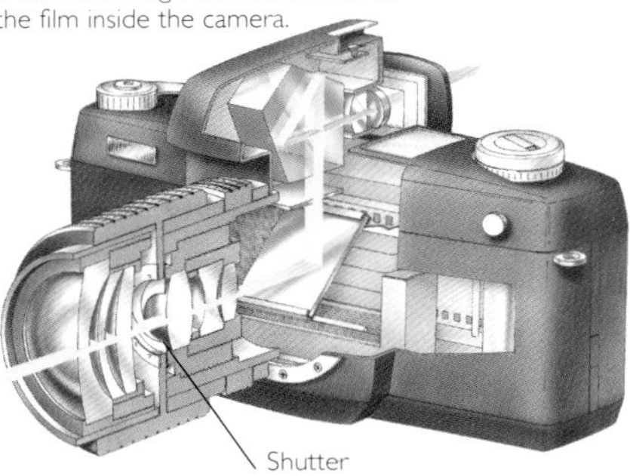


**shuttle** *noun* 1 a train, bus or aircraft that makes regular journeys between two places. *There is a shuttle service between the sports ground and the college in the centre of town.* 2 a pointed instrument used in weaving by which a thread is carried between other threads. 3 a spacecraft used to make a number of journeys into outer space, a space shuttle. **shuttle** *verb* to move or send backwards and forwards.

**shy** *adjective* nervous and uncomfortable when with others. *He is too shy to speak up.* **shyly** *adverb.* **shyness** *noun.*

**shy** (shies, shying, shied) *verb* to move away suddenly. *The horse shied at the sound of the police siren.*

**Siamese twins** *plural noun* twins who are born with their bodies joined together. *The Siamese twins were successfully separated and grew up happily.*

**sibling** *noun* a brother or sister.

**sick** *adjective* 1 ill, not well. 2 likely to vomit or throw up food. *Going on a boat always makes me feel sick.* 3 angry or fed up. *I'm sick of washing-up.* 4 making fun of misfortune or illness. *He told some sick jokes.* **sickly** *adjective.*

**sickness** *noun* 1 illness or bad health. 2 a disease. 3 feeling sick, vomiting.

S

**side** *noun* 1 a surface of something that is not the top or the bottom. 2 one of the two surfaces of something flat. *Please write on both sides of the paper.* 3 the two halves of an area which could be divided by a line in the middle, the right or the left part of your body, or a place next to somebody or something. *I've got a pain in my left side.* 4 an edge or border. *Our friends live on the other side of town.* 5 an upright surface of a building or mountain. 6 a particular position in a discussion, or a group which holds a particular position. *Which side is he on?* 7 a team. **on the side** as a sideline. *She sells flowers on the side.* **side by side** next to one another. **to be on the safe side** to be careful and prepared in case something happens. **side** *verb* to take somebody's side. *My mother always sides with my brother.*

**side effect** *noun* an effect in addition to the intended one. *This drug can have extremely unpleasant side effects.*

**siege** *noun* an operation, usually by an army, surrounding a place to force it to give in by stopping food reaching the people in it. *The town was under siege for months.*

The siege went on and on until the defences inside the castle collapsed.

**Sierra Leone** *noun* a country in Africa.

**siesta** (say see-**est**-uh) *noun* a rest or sleep in the afternoon.

**sieve** (say siv) *noun* a tool, mainly used in the kitchen, made of wire or plastic net on a metal ring for liquid or soft parts to pass through and large lumps to be left in the net. **sieve** *verb* to put something through a sieve. *Sieve the flour before baking a cake.*

**sift** *verb* 1 to put something through a sieve. 2 to examine something carefully. *He sifted through his papers to find the letter.*

**sigh** *verb* to let out a deep breath with a sound as a sign of tiredness, sadness or gladness. **sigh** *noun* the act or sound of sighing. *She breathed a sigh of relief when the job finally came to an end.*

**DID YOU KNOW?**

*The longest known siege was that of the Russian city of Leningrad (now called St Petersburg) by the German army during World War II. The siege lasted for 880 days, from August 1941 to January 1944.*

The sign of a cross and skull signals danger.

**WORD HISTORY**

*The Spanish word 'siesta' comes from the Latin 'sexta', meaning 'sixth hour'. This must refer to the time at which people originally had their siesta.*

**sight** *noun* 1 the ability to see. 2 the act of seeing something or something seen or worth seeing. *We went to see the sights of Florence.* 3 something that looks very bad or laughable to look at. *Her hair looks a real sight.* 4 the distance within which things can be seen. *She doesn't let the children out of her sight.* 5 a part of a telescope or gun you look through to help you aim. **in sight** likely to happen very soon. *A cure is in sight.* **catch sight of** to see for a moment. **know somebody by sight** to recognize somebody without ever having spoken to them or knowing their name. **sight** *verb* to see something for the first time by coming near. *After a month at sea they sighted land.*

**sightseer** *noun* a tourist visiting interesting places. **sightsee** *verb*. **sightseeing** *noun*.

**sign** *noun* 1 a mark or shape that has a particular meaning. *A dove is a sign of peace.* 2 a movement of the body showing a particular meaning. *Putting your finger to your lips is a sign to be quiet.* 3 a board or notice that gives a warning or piece of information. *A road sign.* 4 something that shows that something exists or is happening. *A temperature is the first sign of flu.* **sign** *verb* 1 to make a movement as a sign to somebody. 2 to write your name on a document or form as a sign of agreement. *We signed the contract.*

**sign language** *noun* a way of talking, usually to deaf people, by using hand movements.

**signal** *noun* 1 a sound or action that warns, gives a message or causes something else to happen. *Smoke signals.* 2 a piece of equipment, usually with coloured lights, beside a railway which tells drivers if they should stop. 3 a sound or picture sent by radio or TV. **signal** (signals, signalling, signalled) *verb* 1 to make a signal to somebody. 2 to make something known by using a signal. *He signalled right, but went left.* 3 to be a sign of something.

The signal told them to stop because the red light was flashing.

**signature** *noun* a person's name written by himself or herself, usually at the end of a letter or document.

**significant** *adjective* meaningful or important. *Significant others.*

S

**Sikh** (say seek) *noun* a member of an Indian religious group.

**silence** *noun* 1 the absence of sound, extreme quietness. 2 not speaking, making a noise, answering questions or mentioning a particular thing. **silence** *verb* to stop somebody or something from speaking or making a noise.

**silent** *adjective* not speaking, totally quiet.

The church stood out in dramatic silhouette against the night sky.

**silhouette** (say sil-oo-**ett**) *noun* 1 an outline of a dark shape against a light background. 2 an outline drawing filled in with black or cut out of black paper. **silhouette** *verb. The church was sharply silhouetted against the sky.*

**silk** *noun* a soft, fine cloth made from the fine thread produced by silkworms. *A luxurious silk scarf.*

**silkworm** *noun* a type of caterpillar that produces a silk covering for its body (cocoon) which is used to make silk.

**sill** *noun* a flat shelf at the bottom of a window. *A plant pot on the window sill.*

**silly** (sillier, silliest) *adjective* foolish. *It was such a silly question.*

**silt** *noun* fine sand or mud that is carried along by a river. **silt up** to fill or become blocked with silt.

**silver** *noun* 1 a valuable soft metal used for making ornaments, jewellery and coins. 2 the colour of silver. 3 coins and things made from silver, especially cutlery and dishes. *She always polishes her silver so it sparkles.* 4 a silver medal, given as the second prize. **silver** *adjective* 1 made of silver. 2 like the colour of silver. *Silver paint.*

**silver wedding** *noun* the 25th anniversary of a wedding.

**simile** (say **sim**-il-ee) *noun* a comparison of one thing with another, being similar to somebody or something else.

**simmer** *verb* to cook very gently, just below boiling point. *Simmer the rice for ten minutes, then stir in the beans.*

**simper** *verb* to smile in a silly way. **simper** *noun. I can't stand the way she simpers when the boss asks her to do something.*

**WORD HISTORY**

*The word 'silhouette' was named after Etienne de Silhouette (1709–67), a finance minister of France, but we are not sure why. Silhouette proposed taxing rich people very heavily, and it could be that this is why his name was applied to a thin, minimal drawing. Or perhaps it was simply that Silhouette himself drew such outlines as a hobby.*

**GRAMMAR NOTE**

*In a simile two things are compared in order to point out a feature they share. A simile contains the words 'as' or 'like'. For example: 'as blind as a bat'.*

**simple** *adjective* 1 easy to understand or do, not difficult. *Give me a simple explanation of how it works.* 2 uncomplicated, without much decoration. Ordinary or plain. *Simple food tastes best.* 3 with nothing added. *The simple truth is, she is hopeless at playing the guitar.* 4 without much intelligence or easily fooled. *He's a bit simple.* **simplicity** *noun.*

**simplify** (simplifies, simplifying, simplified) *verb* to make something easy to understand. **simplification** *noun.*

**sin** *noun* 1 the breaking of a religious law or something that should not be done. *Stealing is a sin.* **sin** (sins, sinning, sinned) *verb* to break a religious law or do something that is believed to be very bad. **sinner** *noun.*

**since** *conjunction, preposition, adverb* 1 from that time until now. *I haven't seen her since she left school.* 2 during or at a time after a particular time or event in the past. *He used to play tennis regularly, but has since given up.* 3 because, used to state a reason for doing or not doing something. *Since you say you are too tired, we won't go for a walk along the beach.*

**sincere** *adjective* honest, not false. **sincerely** *adverb. I sincerely hope that they will believe what he tells them.* 'Yours sincerely' is written at the end of a letter before your signature. **sincerity** *noun.*

**sing** (sings, singing, sang, sung) *verb* to make musical sounds with the voice, usually by saying words that fit a tune. *Can you hear the birds singing?* 2 to make a buzzing or ringing sound. **singer** *noun.*

**Singapore** *noun* a city and country in Southeast Asia.

The flag of Singapore has a red stripe with a white Moon and stars, and a white stripe beneath.

**singe** (say sinj) *verb* to burn slightly.

**single** *adjective* 1 only one, not more. 2 not married. 3 for or by one person. *She booked a single room at the hotel.* 4 considered by itself, separate. *He repeated every single word I said.* **single ticket** a ticket for a journey from one place to another but not back again. **singly** *adverb.* **single** *noun* 1 a small record with one song on each side. 2 a single person or thing. 3 a single ticket.

**single-handed** *adjective* without help.

**singular** *noun* a word that expresses one person or thing. **singular** *adjective.*

**sinister** *adjective* evil or harmful. *The empty house was a sinister place.*

**sink** *noun* a basin with taps in the kitchen, especially for washing dishes.

S

**sink** (sinks, sinking, sank, sunk) *verb* 1 to go down below the surface of water. *The ship sank to the bottom of the sea.* 2 to go or fall down. *She sank to the ground.* 3 to get smaller or less. *Prices are sinking.* 4 to become weaker. *His voice sank to a whisper.* 5 to become depressed. *Her heart sank.* 6 to put money or work into something. *My brother has sunk all his savings into a new car.* 7 to make something hard or sharp go deeply into something. *She sank her teeth into the apple.* **sink in** to be or become understood. *I hope my warning has really sunk in.*

**sinus** *noun* a space in the bones of the face just behind the nose. If you have a cold, your sinuses often get blocked.

**sip** *verb* to drink taking in small mouthfuls at a time. **sip** *noun. She took a sip of tea.*

**sir** *noun* 1 You say 'sir' when you speak politely to a man. It is mainly used by children to a teacher, or by staff in shops or restaurants. 2 a title given to a knight or baronet. 3 used at the beginning of a formal letter to a man. *Dear Sir.*

**siren** *noun* 1 a device that makes a long, loud warning sound. Police cars and fire engines have sirens. 2 a dangerously beautiful woman.

**WORD HISTORY**

*In Greek mythology, the beautiful Sirens sang such wonderful melodies that sailors passing their rocky island were lured to shipwreck and death. Odysseus ordered his men to plug their ears with beeswax so that they could not hear the Sirens' songs and to tie him to the ship's mast so that he could not swim ashore to them.*

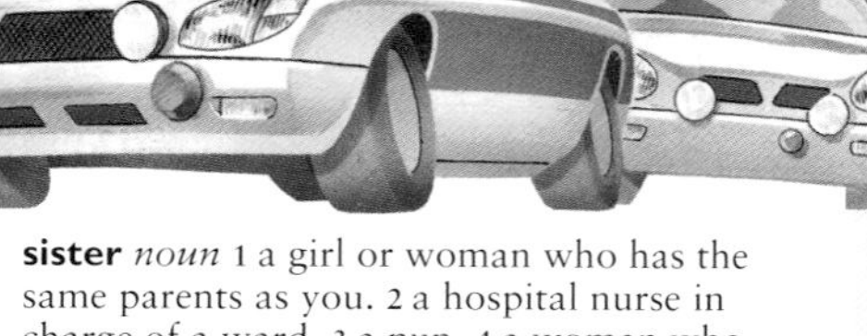

The police cars went into the chase, sirens blaring.

**sister** *noun* 1 a girl or woman who has the same parents as you. 2 a hospital nurse in charge of a ward. 3 a nun. 4 a woman who stands up for women's rights and feels very close to other women. **sisterly** *adjective.*

**sister-in-law** (sisters-in-law) *noun* the sister of a person's husband or wife.

**sit** (sits, sitting, sat) *verb* 1 to be in a position with the upper body upright and the bottom resting on something. 2 to rest on a surface, especially when talking about a bird or animal. *The bird was sitting on a branch.* 3 to take an exam. *We are sitting the exam at the end of term.* 4 to be a member of a committee or of a law court or parliament. To meet and work together. *He sits on the school board.* 5 to be in a place. **sit about** to do nothing for a long time. **sit back** to relax and not do anything while things are happening. **sit tight** to stay in the same place or situation without taking any action. *Sit tight and wait until it's over.*

**site** *noun* a place where something was or is happening. *A building site.*

**situation** *noun* 1 what is happening in a particular place at a particular time or the things that are happening to you. *The situation in Africa looks very bad.* 2 a job. 3 the surroundings of a place. *Our house is in a beautiful situation.*

**size** *noun* 1 how big or small something is. *The dog had eyes the size of saucers.* 2 a set of measurements, especially for clothes and shoes. *What size does he take?* **size** *verb* to arrange people or things according to their size. **size up** to form an opinion of a person or thing, to decide how to act after thinking about a situation. *It took me a little while to size up the situation.*

**sizzle** *verb* to make a crackling or hissing sound like the sound made when you fry food. *The bacon sizzled in the pan.*

**skate** *noun* a boot with a steel blade (ice-skate) or wheels (roller-skate) attached to the sole for skating. **skate** *verb* to move about on ice wearing ice-skates (or on a hard surface wearing roller-skates). *We skated across the frozen lake.*

**skate** *noun* a large, flat seafish.

**skateboard** *noun* a board with small wheels at each end for people to ride on for fun. **skateboarding** *noun.*

**skeleton** *noun* 1 the framework of bones in a human or animal body. 2 something forming a framework or an outline. *The metal skeleton of the building was erected.* **a skeleton in the cupboard** something of which you are afraid or ashamed.

**skeleton key** *noun* a master key that opens a number of different locks.

**sketch** (sketches) *noun* 1 a quickly made drawing. *He made a sketch of the castle.* 2 a short description of something. 3 a short, funny piece of writing or acting. **sketch** *verb* 1 to draw something quickly. 2 to give a short description of something with few details. **sketchy** *adjective. A sketchy plan.*

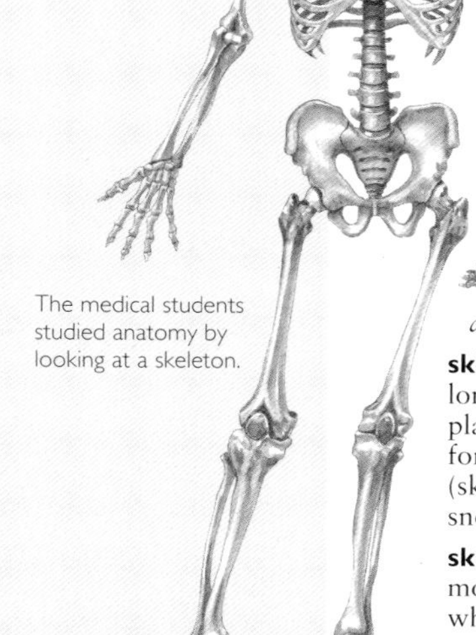

The medical students studied anatomy by looking at a skeleton.

**ski** *noun* one of a pair of long flat pieces of wood, metal or plastic that are fastened to a ski boot for skiing on the snow. **ski** (skis, skiing, skied) *verb* to move on snow wearing skis. **skier** *noun.*

**skid** (skids, skidding, skidded) *verb* to move sideways out of control on wheels. *The car skidded on the icy road.* **skid** *noun.*

**skill** *noun* the knowledge or ability to do something well. **skilful** *adjective*. *She is a very skilful painter.* **skilfully** *adverb*. **skilled** *adjective*. *A skilled job.*

**skim** (skims, skimming, skimmed) *verb* 1 to remove cream or other unwanted things from the surface of a liquid. *Skimmed milk.* 2 to read something quickly. *He skimmed the newspaper.* 3 to move quickly along or just above something. *The plane skimmed the treetops, then crashed.*

**skin** *noun* 1 the outer covering of the body. *Fur coats are made from animal skins.* 2 the outer covering of some fruit and vegetables. *He slipped on a banana skin and broke his ankle.* 3 a thin layer that forms on liquid, especially when it gets cool. *I hate skin on milk.* **skin** (skins, skinning, skinned) *verb* to take the skin off something.

This cross-section through the skin shows how hairs grow and sweat pores reach the surface.

**skinny** (skinnier, skinniest) *adjective* very thin. *A skinny little boy.*

**skint** *adjective* having no money. *I'm skint, can you lend me a fiver?*

**skip** (skips, skipping, skipped) *verb* 1 to jump or hop along lightly. *The children skipped around the garden.* 2 to jump up and down over a rope (skipping rope). 3 to leave something out in order to go on to another subject. *I read the book but skipped the boring bits.* 4 to miss out something you usually do. *I skipped lunch.* **skip** *noun*.

**skip** *noun* a builder's large metal container for taking away old bricks and rubbish.

**skipper** *noun* a captain.

**skirt** *noun* a piece of clothing for women or girls that hangs down from the waist. **skirt** *verb* 1 to go around the edge of something. *The old road skirts the village.* 2 to avoid dealing with something. *She tried to skirt the issue because she was embarrassed.*

**Skopje** *noun* the capital of Macedonia.

**AMAZING FACT**

The World's first skyscraper was built in Chicago in 1884 by William Le Baron Jenney.

**GRAMMAR NOTE**

*Many slang words and expressions that work well in spoken English are not effective when written down. Try to use more formal expressions in a serious piece of writing.*

**skull** *noun* the bones of the head that enclose the brain.

**skunk** *noun* a small North American black and white animal that gives out a nasty smell if it is frightened.

**sky** (skies) *noun* the space above the Earth that you see when you are outside and look up. *You can see the Moon in the sky.*

**skyscraper** *noun* a very tall building.

Skyscrapers were originally built so that many people could live in a small area.

**slab** *noun* a thick flat piece. *A slab of cake.*

**slack** *adjective* 1 not pulled tight, especially a rope or wire. 2 not firm, weak. *The rules are very slack.* 3 not busy or working hard. *Business is slack.* **slackness** *noun*. **slack** *verb* to not work enough, to be lazy. **slacker** *noun*. *My brother is a lazy slacker.*

**slam** (slams, slamming, slammed) *verb* 1 to shut loudly. *Don't slam the door!* 2 to push or put down quickly and with force. *He slammed on the brakes.*

**slander** *noun* an untrue spoken statement about somebody which damages a person's reputation. **slander** *verb* to harm somebody by making a false statement.

**slang** *noun* words and expressions used in informal conversation. Dosh, dough and bread are all slang for money.

**slap** (slaps, slapping, slapped) *verb* 1 to hit somebody or something with the palm of your hand. *She slapped his face.* 2 to put roughly or carelessly. *He slapped paint on the walls.* 3 to put down with force. *He slapped the book on the table.* **slap** *noun*.

**slapdash** *adjective* careless.

**slate** *noun* 1 a dark grey rock that splits easily into thin layers. 2 a piece of slate used for covering roofs. 3 a small board made of slate which was used for writing on with chalk. **slate** *verb* 1 to cover a roof with slates. 2 to criticize severely or attack. *The papers slated his new film.*

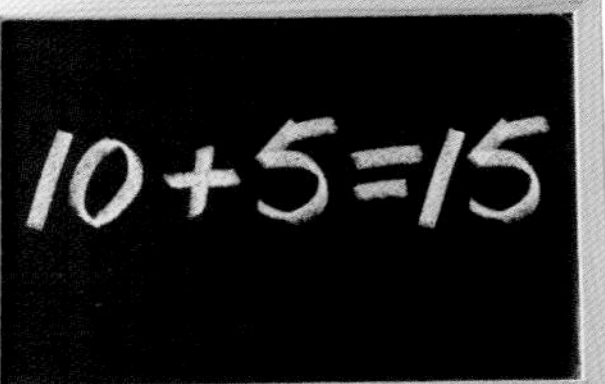


The teacher wrote a sum on the slate.

**slaughter** *verb* 1 to kill animals for food. 2 to kill cruelly, especially many people. **slaughter** *noun*.

**slave** *noun* somebody who is owned by another and has to work for that person without getting paid. **slave** *verb* to work very hard, like a slave. *I slaved away cleaning the house all Sunday*. **slavery** *noun*.

**slay** (slays, slaying, slew, slain) *verb* to kill.

**sleazy** (sleazier, sleaziest) *adjective* dirty and poor-looking. **sleaze** *noun*. **sleaziness** *noun*.

**sled, sledge** *noun* a vehicle for sliding across snow and ice on metal blades. **sledge** *verb* to go on a sledge.

**sleek** *adjective* smooth and shiny, especially hair or fur. *A sleek fat cat*.

**sleep** *noun* a rest state of the body when the eyes are closed and the mind is not conscious, a period of sleep. *Most people need about eight hours sleep*. **sleep** (sleeps, sleeping, slept) *verb* to be asleep, to have a sleep. **sleepy** *adjective*. **sleepiness** *noun*.

**sleeper** *noun* 1 a person who sleeps. *I'm a very light sleeper, so any noise will wake me*. 2 one of a row of heavy beams supporting a railway track. 3 a bed on a train. *I booked the sleeper to Rome*.

**sleeping bag** *noun* a warm bag made of thick material in which you can sleep, usually when camping.

Arthur wanted to sleep under the stars, but he didn't realize that his sleeping bag would get damp in the dew.

**sleet** *noun* a mixture of rain and snow, frozen rain. **sleet** *verb*. *It's sleeting*.

**sleeve** *noun* 1 the part of a piece of clothing that covers the arm. 2 a stiff envelope for a record or a stiff case for a book.

**slender** *adjective* thin, slim.

**sleuth** (say slooth) *noun* a detective.

**slice** *noun* 1 a thin piece cut from something. 2 a part or share of something. **slice** *verb* 1 to cut into slices. 2 to cut off a slice. 3 to cut through something.

**slick** *adjective* 1 well-made and good-looking, but not meaningful. *The show was too slick*. 2 clever, but not honest. *A slick salesman*. 3 quick and smooth.

**slick** *noun* a thin sheet of oil floating on water. *The oil slick spoiled Sarah's swim*.

**DID YOU KNOW?**

*Slaves have existed in most countries throughout history. The American Civil War (1861–65) was fought between the northern and southern states partly over the issue of slavery. Abraham Lincoln declared slaves free in 1863, and two years later slavery was officially abolished throughout the United States.*

**AMAZING FACT**

Newborn babies sleep most of the time – about 18–20 hours every day.

**slide** (slides, sliding, slid) *verb* 1 to move smoothly over or on something. *She slid the door open*. 2 to move quietly and quickly, usually in order to go unnoticed. **slide** *noun* 1 the action of sliding. 2 a structure with a slope for sliding down, usually for children in a playground. 3 a small piece of film in a frame that you can look at on a screen or through a viewer to see it bigger. *Our holiday slides*. 4 a glass plate on which something is put to be looked at under a microscope. 5 a small fastener to keep hair in place, a hair slide.

She examined the object under the slide.

**slight** *adjective* 1 small and thin. 2 small and not important. *A slight headache*. **slightly** *adverb*. **slightness** *noun*.

**slight** *verb* to treat somebody without respect. **slight** *noun*.

**slim** (slimmer, slimmest) *adjective* 1 thin, not fat. 2 small. *There is still a slim chance of getting tickets for the concert*.

**slime** *noun* thick, sticky liquid, usually unpleasant. *The snail left a trail of slime*. **slimy** *adjective*. **sliminess** *noun*.

**sling** *noun* 1 a piece of material tied round the neck to support a broken arm. 2 a loop or an object made of ropes and straps for carrying or lifting things. *She carries her baby in a sling*. 3 a strap for throwing stones, like a catapult. **sling** (slings, slinging, slung) *verb* 1 to throw carelessly. *He slung his bag in the ditch*. 2 to throw with force. *They were slinging stones*. 3 to attach or hold in a sling.

A broken arm supported in a sling helps the healing process

**slip** (slips, slipping, slipped) *verb* 1 to slide and almost fall because you have lost your balance. 2 to move, go or put something quickly and smoothly, especially without being noticed. *The girl slipped out of the room*. 3 to put on or take off, especially clothes. 4 to get away, escape or be forgotten. *His birthday slipped my mind*. 5 to get worse or fall in quality. **slip up** to make a mistake. **slip** *noun* 1 the act of slipping. 2 a slight mistake. 3 a small piece of paper. 4 a piece of clothing without sleeves that women wear under a dress. 5 a pillowcase. **give somebody the slip** to escape from somebody.

**slipper** *noun* a soft shoe worn indoors.

**slippery** *adjective* difficult to hold or stand on because of being wet or very smooth.

**slipshod** *adjective* careless.

**slip-up** *noun* a slight mistake.

**slit** *noun* a narrow cut or opening. **slit** (slits, slitting, slit) *verb* to cut or make a slit in.

**slog** (slogs, slogging, slogged) *verb* 1 to do hard dull work without stopping, or to make a long, tiring journey. 2 to hit hard, especially a ball. **slog** *noun*. **slogger** *noun*.

**slogan** *noun* a short phrase that is easy to remember, mainly used to advertise something. *A catchy slogan.*

**slope** *noun* 1 a piece of ground that goes up or down. 2 a slanting line or direction. **slope** *verb* to have a slope or to lean to the right or the left. **slope off** to go off quietly, usually in order to avoid work.

As Craig skiied down the slope, he heard the rumblings of an avalanche behind him.

**slot** *noun* a slit, groove or channel. **slot** *verb* to put into a slot.

**slot machine** *noun* a machine from which you can buy things by putting coins in a slot. Some slot machines are for gambling.

**slouch** *verb* to move with shoulders and head drooping down. **slouch** *noun*.

**Slovakia** *noun* a country in eastern Europe.

The flag of Slovakia has white, blue and red stripes, and a crest.

**Slovenia** *noun* a country in Southeast Europe.

**slovenly** *adjective* careless and untidy. *Your room is a slovenly mess.*

**slow** *adjective* 1 taking a long time or too long, not quick. 2 showing a time that is earlier than the correct time. *My watch is five minutes slow.* 3 not able to understand things quickly, not very active. **slow** *verb* to make or become slower. **slowly** *adverb*. **slowness** *noun*.

**slow motion** *noun* movement that is much slower than in real life, especially as shown in a film or on television. *They showed the goal again in slow motion.*

**AMAZING FACT**

The slug belongs to the same family as the snail, gastropods. The main difference between the two animals is that snails have shells while slugs usually do not.

**DID YOU KNOW?**

*Slovakia was part of Hungary until 1918, when it became part of Czechoslovakia. It has been an independent republic since 1993.*

**GRAMMAR NOTE**

*People often use 'slow' as an adverb in spoken English: 'Drive/eat slower.' In formal writing, it is better to use 'slowly' as the correct adverb: 'Drive/eat more slowly.'*

**slug** *noun* a small slow-moving animal like a snail without a shell.

**sluggish** *adjective* slow-moving.

**slum** *noun* an area of a town that is poor, with dirty streets and bad living conditions.

**slumber** *noun* sleep. **slumber** *verb*.

**slur** (slurs, slurring, slurred) *verb* 1 to say words unclearly so they are difficult to understand. 2 to say unfair or bad things. **slur** *noun* 1 a slurring way of speaking. 2 unfair or bad remarks that could damage a person's reputation. *His words were a slur on my character.*

**sly** (slyer, slyest, or slier, sliest are also used) *adjective* cunning and not honest, keeping things secret. *A sly fox tricked the red hen.* **on the sly** secretly.

**smack** *verb* 1 to hit with the hand. 2 to open and close your lips noisily. 3 to put, throw or hit something so it makes a loud noise. **smack** *noun*. **smack** *adverb*. *He drove smack into the wall and killed his passenger.*

**smack** *noun* a particular taste. *A smack of lemon.* **smack** *verb* to have a trace of. *She smacks of money.*

**smack** *noun* a sailing boat used for fishing.

**small** *adjective* not big, little in size, weight or importance. **smallness** *noun*.

**small change** *noun* coins.

**small-minded** *adjective* thinking in a small way, unwilling to change your mind or listen to others. The opposite of small-minded is open-minded.

**small talk** *noun* conversation about unimportant things. *I loathe small talk.*

**smart** *adjective* 1 neat and elegant looking. 2 clever. 3 stylish and fashionable. 4 sharp and quick. *We walked at a smart pace.* **smartly** *adverb*. **smartness** *noun*.

**smart** *verb* 1 to feel a stinging pain. *My eyes are smarting.* 2 to feel upset, especially about something unkind said or done to you.

**smash** (smashes) *noun* 1 the action or sound of something breaking to pieces. 2 a car crash. 3 a very successful show or film, a smash hit. 4 a disaster in business. 5 a hard stroke, especially in tennis. **smash** *verb* 1 to break noisily into many pieces. 2 to go, drive, hit or throw with great force. *The car smashed into a tree.* 3 to destroy or ruin.

Alison accidentally smashed the pot beyond repair.

**smashing** *adjective* great, excellent.

**smell** *noun* 1 the ability the nose has to smell things. *Dogs have a strong sense of smell.* 2 something in things that has an effect on the nose, something you can smell. *A smell of gas.* 3 smelling something. *Have a smell of this cheese!* **smell** (smells, smelling, smelt) *verb* 1 to use your nose to discover a smell. 2 to have or give out a smell. If you say something smells, it has a bad smell. 3 to have a feeling or notice. *She smelt trouble.* **smelly** *adjective*.

**smile** *noun* an expression on the face with the corners of the mouth turned up that shows happiness or friendliness. **smile** *verb* to give a smile.

Phyllis smiled for the photographer.

**smirk** *noun* an unpleasant smile. **smirk** *verb* to give a smirk.

**smoke** *noun* 1 gas and small bits of solid material that are seen in the air when something burns. *Smoke from the chimney.* 2 smoking a cigarette or pipe. *He likes a smoke.* **smoke** *verb* 1 to give out smoke. *The volcano is smoking.* 2 to have a cigarette, cigar or pipe in your mouth and suck in the smoke and blow it out again. 3 the habit of smoking. *Do you smoke?* 4 to preserve meat or fish by hanging it in smoke. **smoky** *adjective*. **smoker** *noun*.

**smooth** *adjective* 1 having an even surface without lumps or holes, not rough. 2 calm and comfortable without sudden bumps. *A smooth ride.* 3 free from lumps, evenly mixed. 4 very polite, almost too pleasant. *I don't trust Gary, he's really too smooth.* 5 pleasant tasting, not sour or bitter. 6 not harsh. *A smooth voice.* **smooth** *verb* to make smooth. **smooth something over** to make a difficulty seem less serious.

**smother** *verb* 1 to die from not having enough air, or to kill by covering somebody's mouth so they cannot breathe. 2 to put a fire out by covering it with something. *He smothered the flames with a blanket.* 3 to cover thickly. *The cake was smothered in cream.* 4 to control or hold something back. *She tried to smother a yawn, but he saw she was bored.*

**smoulder** *verb* 1 to burn slowly without a flame. 2 to have strong feelings without showing them. *She smouldered with hatred.*

**smudge** *noun* a dirty mark, usually made by rubbing something. **smudge** *verb* to make a smudge on something or become messy.

The smugglers lured a boat on to the rocks with flashing lights by night. The next day, after the ship was wrecked, they brought the treasure ashore.

**DID YOU KNOW?**

*There are more than 80,000 different species of snails, widely distributed on land, in the sea and in fresh water. Most land snails have two pairs of tentacles, usually with eyes at the tips of the longer ones. Most water-snails have one pair of tentacles, with eyes at the base.*

The snake coiled round and hissed dangerously.

**AMAZING FACT**

Most snakes hatch from eggs, although there are some species that give birth to live young.

Some snakes are very tiny while others, such as the python and anaconda, grow to lengths of up to ten metres.

**smug** *adjective* being too pleased with yourself and what you can do. *He had a smug look on his face when he got his prize.*

**smuggle** *verb* to take something secretly into a country or place. *It is against the law to smuggle drugs.* **smuggler** *noun*. **smuggling** *noun*. *Smuggling is illegal.*

**snack** *noun* a small, quick meal, especially one eaten between main meals. **snack** *verb*.

**snag** *noun* 1 a problem or difficulty. 2 a sharp part that sticks out and may catch you in passing. **snag** *verb* to get caught on and tear. *I snagged my tights.*

**snail** *noun* a small animal with a slimy body and a shell on its back. **at a snail's pace** very slowly. *Mum walks at a snail's pace.*

**snake** *noun* a long thin reptile with no legs and a fork-shaped tongue. Some snakes are poisonous. *A snake slithered out of the tree.*

**snap** *noun* 1 the action or sound of snapping. *The trap closed with a snap.* 2 a photograph taken quickly, a snapshot. 3 a small biscuit. *Ginger snaps.* 4 a card game in which players shout 'snap' when they see two of the same cards laid down together. **snap** (snaps, snapping, snapped) *verb* 1 to break with a sharp cracking noise. *His patience finally snapped.* 2 to make a sharp sound like something breaking. 3 to bite or catch something with the teeth. *The dog snapped at her ankle.* 4 to say something quickly and in an angry way. 5 to move or shut quickly into a position with a sharp sound. 6 to take a photograph. *She snapped us at the beach.* **snap at** to take or get something quickly. *We snapped at the chance of spending a week in the sun.* **snap up** to buy something quickly because it is a bargain. *Kate snapped it up in the sales.*

**snap** *adjective* done immediately. *A snap decision may sometimes be regretted.*

**snare** *noun* a trap for catching birds or small animals. **snare** *verb. He snared a rabbit and ate it for his dinner.*

**snarl** *verb* to growl angrily or speak in an angry voice. **snarl** *noun.*

**snarl** *noun* a tangle in wool or a tangled-up situation. *Traffic snarls.*

**sneak** *verb* 1 to move quietly and secretly, trying not to be seen or heard. 2 to take something somewhere secretly. *He sneaked his pet mouse into school.* 3 to tell tales. *He sneaked on his best friend to the teacher.*

**sneak** *noun* a person who tells others secretly that somebody else had done something bad, a tell-tale. **sneaky** *adjective.* **sneakily** *adverb.*

**sneaker** *noun* a sports shoe with a rubber sole, a trainer.

**sneeze** *noun* a sudden outburst of air through the nose and mouth. **sneeze** *verb. I felt a tickle in my nose and had to sneeze.*

**snide** *adjective* intending to hurt your feelings by being nasty, especially in a pretended funny way, about something that is important to you. *She made some snide remarks about my friends.*

**sniff** *verb* 1 to make a sound by breathing in air through your nose. 2 to smell something. *The dog sniffed the ground.* **sniff** *noun.* **sniffer** *noun. A glue sniffer.*

**snigger** *verb* to laugh quietly and in a disrespectful way, especially at something rude. **snigger** *noun.*

**snip** (snips, snipping, snipped) *verb* to cut with scissors or shears in short quick cuts. *She snipped at my hair.*

**snip** *noun.* 1 an act of snipping. 2 a bargain. *I had to buy it, it was a real snip.*

**snivel** (snivels, snivelling, snivelled) *verb* to speak or cry in a sniffing and whining way.

**snob** *noun* somebody who admires people with money, power and of a higher social class. **snobbish** *adjective.* **snobbery** *noun.*

**snooker** *noun* a game played on a special table in which you hit a white ball with a long stick (cue) and get points each time you knock a coloured ball into a pocket at the side of the table.

**snooze** *noun* a short sleep. **snooze** *verb.*

**snore** *verb* to breathe noisily while asleep. *Peter claims not to snore, but he makes a funny sawing noise while asleep.* **snore** *noun. Richard gave out a loud snore.*

**snorkel** *noun* a tube through which you can breathe when you swim under water. **snorkelling** *noun. Gudrun went snorkelling at the Great Barrier Reef.*

**DID YOU KNOW?**

*British army officers invented the game of snooker in India in 1875. They developed it as an alternative to billiards.*

**WORD HISTORY**

*'Snorkel' comes from the German 'Schnorchel', which was originally a dialect word meaning 'nose' or 'mouth'.*

**snort** *verb* to make a rough noise by breathing out through the nose. **snort** *noun.*

**snout** *noun* an animal's long nose. *A pig's snout is ideal for rootling in the ground.*

Each snowflake has an individual pattern never to be repeated.

**snow** *noun* frozen white bits of water (flakes) that fall from the sky in cold weather and cover the ground. **snow** *verb.*

**snowball** *noun* snow pressed into a hard ball, for throwing at friends.

**snowflake** *noun* a tiny and unique piece of snow.

**snowman** *noun* a shape of a person made of snow. *The children built a snowman.*

**snug** *adjective* 1 cosy, warm and comfortable. *I love being snug in bed, especially when there's a storm.* 2 fitting very closely or tightly. **snugly** *adverb.*

**snuggle** *verb* to move into a comfortable position, especially close to another person. *The little boy snuggled up to his mother.*

**so** *adverb* 1 very, to such an extent. *He is so clever.* 2 in this or that way. *He was wrong and she told him so.* 3 also. *My brother has blue eyes and so has my sister.* 4 when agreeing with something that has been said. *'I didn't manage to tidy up my room.' 'So I see.'* **so** *conjunction* that is why, for that reason. *I missed the bus, so I was late.* **so far** up to now. **or so** about that number. *We've been here for a week or so.* **and so on/forth** and other things like this. *They brought their pens, paints, and so on.* **so long!** goodbye! **so as to** in order to. *She asked us to come, so as to get to know us.* **so what?** I don't care, it's not important.

**soak** *verb* to make or become completely wet. *We were completely soaked.* **soak up** to take in liquid. **soak** *noun.*

The car splashed through a puddle and completely soaked Elizabeth, who was just jumping out of the way.

**so-and-so** *noun* 1 a certain somebody or something that doesn't need to be specified. *She told me to do so-and-so.* 2 a rude or annoying person. *The headmaster is a real old so-and-so.*

S

**soap** *noun* 1 a product used with water for washing and cleaning. *A bar of soap.* 2 a soap opera. **soap** *verb.*

**soap opera** *noun* a light television or radio serial, usually about the daily life of a group of people. *An Australian soap opera.*

**soar** *verb* 1 to fly or go up in the air. 2 to rise, increase quickly. *Prices are soaring.*

The eagle soared through the mountain air, watching out for prey.

**sob** (sobs, sobbing, sobbed) *verb* to cry in gasps. *Linda sobbed all night.* **sob** *noun.*

**sober** *adjective* 1 not drunk. 2 serious and thoughtful, not silly. 3 dull, not bright. *Sober colours.* **soberly** *adverb.* **sober up** to stop being drunk.

**soccer** *noun* association football.

**social** *adjective* 1 liking to be with other people, friendly. *We met for a fabulous social evening.* 2 of somebody's position in society or of relations between people. *Social workers are supposed to help people.* 3 living together by nature. *Social animals live in groups.* **socially** *adverb.*

**socialism** *noun* a political system in which business and industry are controlled by the government with every person getting an equal share of the state's money. **socialist** *noun, adjective.*

**society** (societies) *noun* 1 a large group of people in a country who have a particular way of life. *In ancient Greek society women did not have an important role.* 2 a group of people with the same interests. *The film society.*

**sock** *noun* a piece of clothing that covers your foot. *A pair of socks.*

**sock** *verb* (slang) to punch.

**socket** *noun* 1 a device usually in a wall into which you put a plug to make an electrical connection. 2 a hollow opening into which something fits.

**sofa** *noun* a soft seat with a back for two or three people to sit on. *I bought a really comfortable sofa.*

**Sofia** *noun* the capital of Bulgaria.

**WORD HISTORY**

*The term soap opera came about when they were first broadcast on radio during the 1930s. Their main sponsors were soap manufacturers.*

**DID YOU KNOW?**

*The solar system contains the Sun, 9 planets, about 50 moons or satellites, more than 1,000 comets, and thousands of smaller bodies known as asteroids and meteoroids.*

**soft** *adjective* 1 not hard, firm. *A soft bed.* 2 smooth to the touch, not rough. *Babies have soft skin.* 3 gentle, not loud or bright. Calm. *Her soft voice.* 4 kind and caring. *A soft heart.* **softly** *adverb.* **softness** *noun.*

**soft drink** *noun* a drink that is not alcoholic. *Lemonade is a soft drink.*

**soften** *verb* 1 to make or become soft. 2 to become kinder. 3 to make something less terrible or strong. *He tried to soften the shock by telling some amusing stories.*

**software** *noun* programs for computers.

**soggy** (soggier, soggiest) *adjective* unpleasantly wet and heavy. *The ground was very soggy.*

**soil** *noun* the earth on which plants and trees grow. *The soil here is very sandy.*

**soil** *verb* to make or become dirty.

**solar** *adjective* of or from the Sun. If you heat a building with solar power, you make use of the power of the Sun.

**solar system** *noun* the Sun and all the planets going around it.

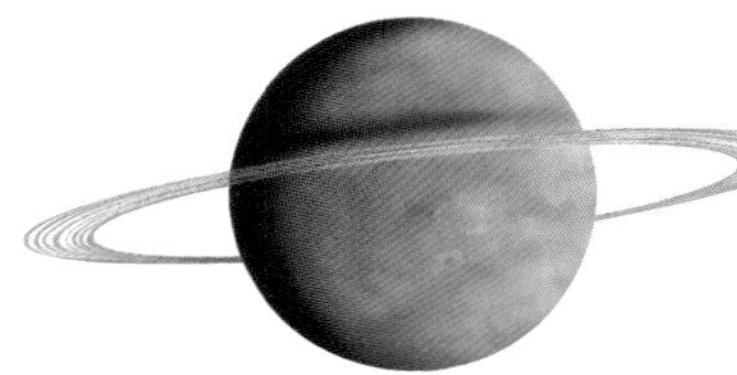

**sold** *verb* past tense of sell.

**soldier** *noun* a member of an army.

**sole** *noun* 1 the bottom of the foot, especially the part you walk or stand on. 2 the flat bottom part of a shoe. 3 a flat fish. **sole** *verb* to put a sole on a shoe.

**sole** *adjective* being or belonging to only one. *He is the sole survivor.* **solely** *adverb* only. *She acted solely for herself.*

**solemn** *adjective* 1 serious, not cheerful. 2 formal, in a sincere way. *He made a solemn promise.* **solemnly** *adverb.*

**solicitor** *noun* a lawyer who gives legal advice to his clients and prepares legal documents. *A solicitor in criminal law.*

**solid** *adjective* 1 filled up inside, not hollow, with no spaces or gaps. *Solid gold.* 2 not liquid or gas, having a shape. *When milk freezes it turns solid.* 3 of good quality, strong and not flimsy, reliable. *A solid house.* 4 showing complete agreement. 5 continuous, without a break. *I slept for six solid hours.* **solidly** *adverb.* **solidity** *noun.*

**solid** *noun* 1 something that is solid. *The baby is on solids now.* 2 a solid figure in geometry with length, width and height.

**solitary** *adjective* 1 alone, without a companion. *A solitary walk.* 2 spending a lot of time alone, lonely. *Bears are solitary animals.* 3 single. *I can't think of a solitary reason for moving.*

**solo** *noun* a piece or passage performed by one person alone. **solo** *adjective.* **solo** *adverb. He flew solo for the first time.*

**soloist** *noun* a person who plays a piece of music or sings a song alone. **solo** *noun.*

**Solomon Islands** *noun* a country of many islands in the Pacific Ocean.

**solution** *noun* 1 an answer to a question or problem. 2 a liquid in which something has been dissolved. *Bathe the cut knee in a solution of salt and water.*

**solve** *verb* to find the answer to a problem or puzzle. *Try and solve this riddle.*

**Somalia** *noun* a country in Africa.

**sombre** *adjective* dark and gloomy, or serious and sad. *Sombre music filled the chapel at Tracy's funeral.*

**some** *adjective* 1 a small number or amount, a few. 2 somebody or something that is not named. *Some guy asked me the way to town.* 3 a fairly large number or amount. *She had been dead for some years before we knew about it.* 4 about. *The river is some 10 m deep.* **some** *pronoun* a certain amount, number or part of something. *Some wore red, others pink.*

**somebody, someone** *pronoun* some person, but not a particular person. *Somebody/someone told me that you were moving house, and now I know it's true.*

**somersault** *noun* a jump or move in which you bring your legs over your head. **somersault** *verb. He somersaulted on the grass for glee.*

**something** *pronoun* a thing that is unknown, some thing. *May I have something to drink?* **something like** rather like or about. *She got something like £50 for her old bike.* **something to do with** connected with. *The party is something to do with her birthday.*

**sometime** *adverb* at one point in time. *I'll see her sometime next week.*

**sometimes** *adverb* from time to time, not always. *She sometimes walks to school.*

**somewhere** *adverb* in or to a place, but not a known one. *She lives somewhere in Kent.*

**DID YOU KNOW?**

*The first European to visit the Solomon Islands was a Spaniard, Alvaro de Mendana de Neyra, in 1568. Mendana believed that the islands might be the source of King Solomon's gold for the Temple in Jerusalem, which is how they got their name.*

**son** *noun* the male child of a man or woman. *Their son is called Peter.*

**son-in-law** (sons-in-law) *noun* a daughter's husband. *Their son-in-law is a solicitor.*

**song** *noun* 1 a piece of music with words for singing. 2 singing. 3 the sound of a bird. **song and dance** a great fuss about nothing. **for a song** very cheaply.

**sonic** *adjective* of the speed of sound or sound waves. *A sonic boom.*

**sonnet** *noun* a poem with 14 lines.

**soon** *adverb* 1 in a very short time from now. 2 early. *The sooner the better.* **as soon as** 1 quickly. *As soon as possible.* 2 at the moment when. *As soon as I get paid.* **as soon** readily or willingly. *I'd just as soon go home.* **sooner or later** at some time, certainly. *Sooner or later she'll discover the terrible truth about Paula.*

**soot** *noun* black powder left from burning or carried in the air in smoke. *The chimney is blocked with soot.* **sooty** *adjective.*

**soothe** *verb* to make less angry or less painful. **soothing** *adjective. A soothing medicine will do your throat good.*

**sophisticated** *adjective* 1 used to fashionable and elegant ways, not simple. 2 complicated, with many parts. *A highly sophisticated machine.* **sophistication** *noun.*

**soppy** *adjective* foolishly sentimental.

**sorcerer** *noun* a man who does magic with the help of evil spirits. *The sorcerer's apprentice.* **sorceress** *noun.* **sorcery** *noun.*

The sorcerer consulted a magic book to find the right spell.

**sore** *adjective* 1 painful or aching. *A sore throat.* 2 upset or angry. *She is still feeling sore about not being invited.* 3 serious, causing worry. *In sore need.* A sore point is something you do not want to talk about because it upsets you. **soreness** *noun.*

S

**sore** *noun* 1 a painful place on the body where the skin is infected. 2 a painful memory or subject.

**sorry** (sorrier, sorriest) *adjective* 1 feeling sadness or pity for somebody, expressing regret. *I'm sorry your dog died.* 2 feeling disappointed with yourself for doing or not having done something, usually said as an apology. *I'm sorry I laughed.* 3 used as a polite way to say that you did not hear or that you do not agree with something. *Sorry, what was the name?* 4 in a bad way, not good. *The house is in a sorry state.*

**sort** *noun* 1 a particular group of people or things that are the same in certain ways, a kind or type. *I don't like this sort of music.* 2 a person. *He is not the complaining sort.* **out of sorts** slightly ill or annoyed. **sort of** a little, in some way. *Her hair is sort of blond.*

**sort** *verb* to put things in order or arrange in groups according to their kind. *I spent all day sorting my books.* **sort out** to tidy, deal with or put in order. *She tried to sort out their quarrel, but they remained enemies.*

**soul** *noun* 1 the part of a person that is believed to live on after the body has died. 2 a person's thoughts and feelings. *That man has no soul, he is hard and unfeeling.* 3 anybody. *She didn't know a soul at the party.* 4 a style of pop music.

**soulless** *adjective* 1 without feeling or care for others. 2 dull.

**sound** *noun* 1 something you hear or that can be heard. When you turn the sound down on a television, you make it less loud. 2 an idea or impression from something read or heard. *I don't like the sound of your plans.* **sound** *verb* 1 to make a sound or cause something to make a sound. *The siren sounded a warning.* 2 to say what noise something makes or is. *The rustling of the leaves sounded ghostly.* 3 to seem. *She sounds happy.* **sound out** to find out what somebody thinks or will do.

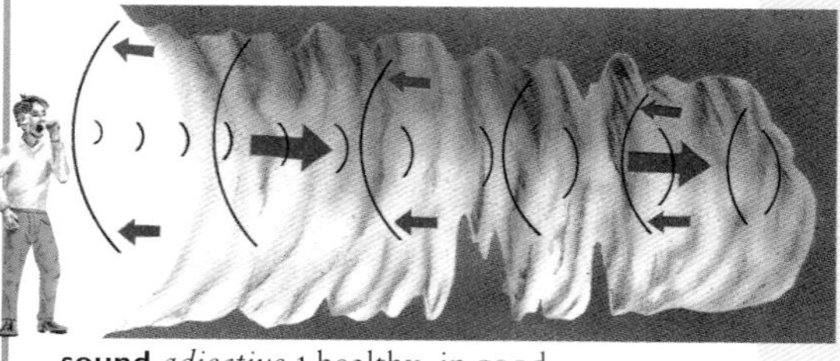

This is how an echo forms in a cave. Sound waves travel to the end wall, then bounce back. The bounce is the echo.

**sound** *adjective* 1 healthy, in good condition. 2 reliable and sensible. *Sound advice.* 3 deep or strong. **soundly** *adverb*. *Our team was soundly beaten in the first five minutes.* **sound asleep** deeply asleep.

**soundproof** *adjective* able to stop all sound from getting in or out. *A soundproof room.*

**soundtrack** *noun* speech and music that go with a film. *I have the soundtrack on CD.*

**soup** *noun* a liquid food you drink or eat with a spoon. *A nourishing soup.*

**sour** *adjective* 1 tasting sharp. *Lemons are sour.* 2 not fresh, gone bad. *The milk is sour.* 3 bad-tempered, unfriendly. *She gave me a sour look.* **sour** *verb* to become unpleasant or less friendly.

**source** *noun* a place where something starts. *The source of the river is in the hills.*

**south** *noun* the direction of one of the four main points of the compass. South is to the right of a person facing the rising Sun. **south** *adjective*, *adverb* towards, from or in the south. *The south wind is warm.*

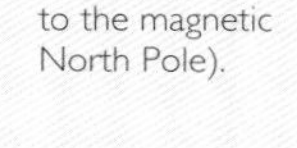

South on the compass is opposite to north (opposite to the magnetic North Pole).

**South Africa** *noun* a country in Africa.

**South America** *noun* one of the Earth's seven continents.

**South Korea** *noun* a country in East Asia, officially called the Republic of Korea.

**southerly** (say **suth**-uh-lee) *adjective* in or towards the south. *We drove in a southerly direction until we came to the coast.*

**souvenir** (say soo-vun-**eer**) *noun* something you buy or keep to remind you of a holiday or another event. *A souvenir of Blackpool.*

**sovereign** (say **sov**-rin) *noun* 1 a king or queen who rules a country. 2 an old British gold coin. **sovereign** *adjective* 1 independent, not under the control of another country. 2 having the highest power in a country.

**sow** (sows, sowing, sowed, sown) *verb* (rhymes with go) to plant seeds into the ground that will grow into plants.

**sow** *noun* (rhymes with cow) a female pig.

**soya** *noun* a plant that can be made into flour, oil, butter or other food.

**soya bean** *noun* the seed of soya.

**spa** *noun* a place with a spring of mineral water where people come to cure illnesses.

**space** *noun* 1 an empty area in a place. *The desk takes up too much space.* 2 the whole area outside the Earth where the stars and other planets move. 3 an empty area or gap in something. *A parking space.* 4 a period of time. *Within the space of a month.* **space** *verb* to arrange things with gaps between them.

**spacecraft** *noun* a vehicle for travelling in space. *The spacecraft was in orbit.*

**AMAZING FACT**

We can taste whether food is sour, salty, sweet or bitter because we have tastebuds that are sensitive to those tastes. All tastebuds are located on the tongue. The tastebuds for sour foods are located at the back of the tongue.

**SPELLING NOTE**

*Note the different spellings of 'sow' and 'sew', which are both pronounced in the same way (rhyming with 'go').*

S

**space shuttle** *noun* a reusable spacecraft that can travel into space and back a number of times. *The space shuttle travelled to Mir.*

**spacesuit** *noun* a suit for wearing in space with its own air supply.

**spade** *noun* a tool with a blade and a handle for digging.

**spade** *noun* a playing card with a picture of a black heart-shaped leaf with a short stem. *The ace of spades.*

**spaghetti** *noun* long, thin sticks of pasta that you boil before eating.

**Spain** *noun* a country in Southwest Europe.

**span** *noun* 1 a period in time from beginning to end, or the length of time over which something exists. *During a ten-year span at the factory he was never late.* 2 the length of something from one end to the other. *The wing span of a glider.* 3 the distance from the tip of the thumb to the tip of the little finger when the hand is spread. 4 the part between two supports of an arch or a bridge. **span** (spans, spanning, spanned) *verb* 1 to last for a length of time or reach across. 2 to form an arch or bridge over.

**Spanish** *noun* 1 the language spoken in Spain, Mexico and other South American countries. 2 the people of Spain. **Spanish** *adjective*. *Spanish flamenco dancing.*

**spank** *verb* to smack on the bottom.

**spanner** *noun* a tool for holding and turning nuts and bolts.

**spare** *adjective* 1 kept for use when needed. *She left a spare key with her neighbour.* 2 free or not being used. *Have you got any spare cash?* 3 thin. *A spare figure.* **go spare** to become very angry. **spare** *noun* a spare part for a machine or engine.

**spare** *verb* 1 not to harm or kill somebody or something, to keep from harming. *Take all I have but spare the children.* 2 to find enough money or time to give to somebody or for a purpose. *Can you spare me a minute?* 3 to keep from using or spending. *No expense was spared.* **enough to spare** more than enough.

**sparing** *adjective* using or giving very little.

**spark** *noun* 1 a small bit of burning material that flies up from a fire. 2 a flash of light produced by electricity. 3 a small bit. *A spark of interest.* **spark** *verb* to give out sparks. **spark off** to lead to or be the cause of something. *The discussion sparked off a bitter quarrel between the two families.*

**DID YOU KNOW?**

*The first American space shuttle was called Columbia, and its first blast-off was from Kennedy Space Center in Florida in 1981.*

Spain is a favourite holiday destination for many Europeans. Tourism is one of its major industries.

**WORD HISTORY**

*Different pasta shapes have different Italian names. Spaghetti are 'little strings', which are thicker than vermicelli ('little worms') and thinner than macaroni (originally from the Greek for 'food made from barley').*

**AMAZING FACT**

The Space Age officially began in 1957, with the launch of the Sputnik, a Soviet satellite that carried a radio transmitter. The first manned space flight was in 1961.

**sparkle** *verb* 1 to shine with a lot of small flashes of light. 2 to bubble. *Sparkling wine.* 3 to be lively, bright and witty.

**sparrow** *noun* a small brown bird.

**sparse** *adjective* small in number or amount, not crowded. *His sparse white hair.* **sparsely** *adverb*. *Sparsely populated.*

**spawn** *noun* the eggs of fish, frogs and some other water animals. **spawn** *verb* 1 to lay spawn. 2 to produce something, especially in large numbers. *The latest fashion show has spawned new ideas.*

Our pond was full of frogspawn. We waited eagerly for the tadpoles to hatch.

**speak** (speaks, speaking, spoke, spoken) *verb* 1 to say things using your voice, to talk. 2 to know and be able to talk a language. *She speaks French.* 3 to give a speech. *He spoke for an hour.* **speak out** to speak freely about something, especially in favour or against it. **speak up** to speak more loudly.

**speaker** *noun* 1 somebody making a speech. 2 somebody who speaks a language. *English speakers.* 3 a piece of equipment on a radio or cassette player through which the sound comes, a loudspeaker.

**spear** *noun* a weapon with a long pole and sharp point for throwing or stabbing. **spear** *verb* to make a hole in or catch with a spear or something pointed. *She speared the meat with a fork and stuffed it in her mouth.*

Spears are used for hunting animals for meat.

**special** *adjective* 1 not usual, better or more important than others. *I'm doing it as a special favour.* 2 for a particular person or thing. *Astronauts wear special suits in space.* **specially** *adverb* 1 more than usual, in a special way. *He was specially nice to me.* 2 for a special purpose. *A school specially for deaf students.*

**specialist** *noun* a person who has special skills or knowledge in a particular subject, an expert. *A heart specialist is a doctor who treats heart diseases.*

**speciality** (specialities) *noun* 1 a particular work or study. *Her speciality is French.* 2 fine or best product. *The chef's soup is the speciality of the house.*

**specialize** *verb* to study one subject or know about one thing so you are an expert in it. *His father specializes in racing bikes.*

**species** (species) *noun* (say **spee**-sheez) a group of animals or plants that are of the same kind and are the same in all important ways. *This species has become very rare.*

**specify** (specifies, specifying, specified) *verb* to describe or name something exactly. **specification** *noun. Please give me the exact specifications for the project.*

**specimen** *noun* 1 a typical thing or example. 2 one piece or a small amount of something that shows what the whole is like. *The doctor took a specimen of blood.*

**speck** *noun* a small spot.

**spectacle** *noun* 1 a big show or public performance. 2 a strange or silly sight. *Don't make a spectacle of yourself.*

**spectacles** *plural noun* a pair of glasses.

**spectacular** *adjective* grand, impressive. *A spectacular view of the mountains.*

**spectator** *noun* a person who watches something, especially sport.

**spectrum** (spectra) *noun* 1 the band of colours as seen in the rainbow. 2 a range of different kinds of things, ideas or opinions.

The spectrum contains all the colours of the rainbow.

**speech** (speeches) *noun* 1 the act or power of speaking. 2 words spoken to a group of people, a talk. *The minister made a speech.*

**speed** *noun* 1 how quickly something moves, travels or happens. *I was amazed at the speed of his serve.* 2 fastness or swiftness. **at speed** fast. **speed** (speeds, speeding, sped) *verb* 1 to go quickly. *He sped past us.* 2 to go too fast. *He was stopped by the police for speeding.* **speed up** (speeded up) to make something go or happen faster.

**speed limit** *noun* the fastest speed you are allowed to drive by law.

**spell** *noun* 1 a period of time. *It rained for a short spell.* 2 a quick period of activity or illness. *A spell in prison.*

**spell** *noun* words or an attraction that are supposed to have magical powers. *The witch cast a spell on him.*

**spell** (spells, spelling, spelt) *verb* 1 to put letters of the alphabet in the right order to make a word or words. *Her name is spelt R-o-s-y.* 2 to mean. *Her silence usually spells trouble.* **speller** *noun.*

**DID YOU KNOW?**

*In Greek legend the Sphinx was a winged monster with the body of a lion and the head of a woman. She asked travellers a riddle. Those who could not answer were killed. Oedipus got the right answer and the Sphinx then killed herself.*

**WORD HISTORY**

*The word 'spider' comes from the Old English 'spinnan' ('to spin'), referring to the spider's web. Spiders look like insects, but actually belong to a group called arachnids, which take their name from the mythological character Arachne, a peasant girl who had great weaving skills.*

**spelling** *noun* the way a word or words are spelt. *American spelling.*

**spend** (spends, spending, spent) *verb* 1 to give money to pay for something. 2 to pass or use up time. *I spent all day reading.* **spender** *noun. A big spender.*

**sperm** (sperm or sperms) *noun* the male cell that fertilizes a female egg to produce new life. *Sperm look like tadpoles swimming.*

**sphere** *noun* 1 a round shape like a ball. 2 a particular area of interest or activity. *The sphere of politics.* **spherical** *adjective.*

**sphinx** (sphinxes) *noun* an ancient Egyptian stone statue with the body of a lion and a man's head. *The sphinx asked me a riddle.*

The Sphinx stands at Giza, near the Nile in Egypt.

**spice** *noun* powder or seeds from a plant used to give a taste to food. **spicy** *adjective.*

**spider** *noun* a small creature with eight legs that spins webs in which it catches other insects. **spidery** *adjective* long and thin. *Spidery handwriting.*

A tarantula is a spider that has hairs on its body and legs which contain an irritant.

**spike** *noun* 1 a long pointed piece of metal. *The spikes on the fence.* 2 a piece of metal with a sharp point fixed to the bottom of some shoes, especially running shoes. **spike** *verb* 1 to put spikes in or on something. 2 to catch or pierce with a spike.

**spill** (spills, spilling, spilt or spilled) *verb* 1 to pour out, especially over the edge of a container. *I spilt some milk.* 2 to come out in large numbers. *People spilled out of the stadium.* **spill** *noun.*

**spin** (spins, spinning, spun) *verb* 1 to make thread by twisting together fibres. 2 When spiders spin, they make a web out of thread from their bodies. 3 to turn around fast or make something go round and round. *My head is spinning.* **spin a yarn** to tell a story. **spin out** to make something last longer. **spin** *noun* 1 the movement of going round and round. 2 a short ride in a car or other vehicle. *A spin in the country would be very pleasant on a sunny afternoon.*

**spinach** *noun* a vegetable with large green leaves. *Spinach is good for you.*

**spindly** (spindlier, spindliest) *adjective* long, thin and weak-looking. *Spindly legs.*

**spine** *noun* 1 the row of bones down the middle of your back, the backbone. 2 a sharp point like a thorn on an animal's body or on a plant. 3 the stiff back part of a book to which the pages and covers are fastened. The title of the book is usually printed on the spine.

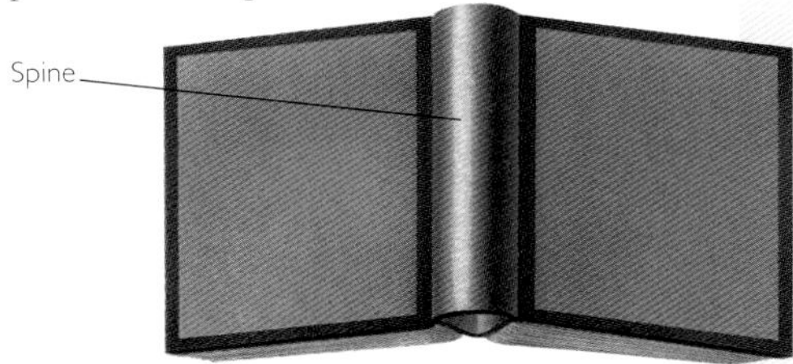


When you are making a photocopy, please don't break the spine of my book.

**spire** *noun* the pointed part on top of a church or tower. *Dreaming spires.*

**spirit** *noun* 1 a person's mind, the part that is connected with thoughts and feelings. *She was in good spirits.* 2 a supernatural being, a ghost. 3 liveliness and energy, effort shown. *He keeps the team spirit going.* 4 what something really means, not what it actually says. *Making her pay for her food would be against the spirit of our agreement.* 5 a strong alcoholic drink. Whisky and brandy are spirits. **spirit** *verb* If you spirit somebody or something away, you take them quickly and secretly to another place.

**spit** (spits, spitting, spat) *verb* 1 to force liquid out of your mouth. *She coughed and spat blood.* 2 to rain lightly. **spit out** 1 *She ate a grape and spat out the pips.* 2 to say something quickly and angrily. *She spat out his name.* **spit** *noun* the watery liquid that is produced in the mouth, saliva. **spitting image** an exact likeness. *She is the spitting image of her mother.*

**spit** *noun* 1 a thin, pointed metal rod for cooking meat over a fire. 2 a point of land sticking out into the sea.

Barry roasted the meat for the barbecue on a spit.

**spite** *noun* a wish to hurt or annoy somebody. *She said it out of spite.* **spite** *verb*. **in spite of** despite.

**AMAZING FACT**

Spiders need air to breathe but there is one spider, the Water Spider, that actually lives underwater. It builds a living space underwater, then carries air down to fill it.

**WORD HISTORY**

*The term 'spitting image 'was originally 'spit and image', from the phrase 'the very spit of', which meant the exact likeness. Perhaps this was because everyone's spit looks exactly the same?*

**spiteful** *adjective* being nasty about people you do not like. *A spiteful remark.*

**splash** *verb* 1 to hit water or throw liquid about so it flies up in drops and makes a noise. If you splash somebody, you make them wet. *We splashed through the waves.* 2 to fall or hit in small noisy drops. *Rain splashed on the window.* 3 to throw liquid on something. *He splashed his face with water.* **splash** (splashes) *noun* 1 the sound made when something hits water. 2 a small amount of liquid that has been spilt. *There is a splash of paint on your skirt.* 3 a bright colour or effect. *A yellow dress with a splash of red.*

**splendid** *adjective* 1 beautiful and impressive to look at. 2 great.

**splendour** *noun* impressive beauty. *The utter splendour of the throne room.*

**splinter** *noun* a small, sharp piece of wood or other hard material that has broken off a bigger piece. *I'm trying to get this glass splinter out of my finger.* **splinter** *verb* to break into splinters.

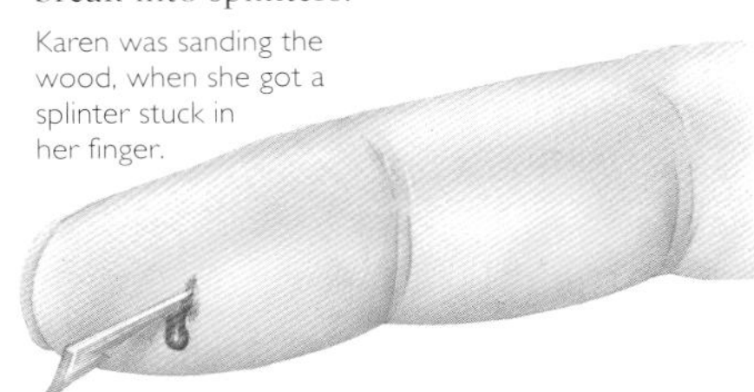

Karen was sanding the wood, when she got a splinter stuck in her finger.

**split** (splits, splitting, split) *verb* 1 to break, tear or crack. *This wood splits easily.* 2 to divide into parts or share. *The children were split into groups.* **split the difference** to agree on a price which is halfway between the two amounts. **split up** to separate. *We split up and went separate ways.* **split** *noun* 1 a cut or break made by splitting. 2 the splitting or dividing of something. 3 a division between different things. 4 a dish made from cut-up fruit and ice-cream. *A banana split.*

**spoil** (spoils, spoiling, spoiled or spoilt) *verb* 1 to ruin or damage something so it is no longer any good. *The rain spoilt our holiday.* 2 to harm somebody so they become very selfish by giving them everything they want. *Some parents spoil their children.* 3 to treat very well or too well. *I spoilt myself with an ice-cream.* **spoils** *plural noun* stolen goods, especially those taken in war.

**spoilsport** *noun* somebody who stops others from having fun and wants to spoil their enjoyment of things.

**spoke** *verb* past tense of speak.

**spoke** *noun* each of the bars or wire rods that go from the rim of a wheel to the centre. *Bicycle spokes.*

**sponge** *noun* 1 a small sea animal with a body full of holes. 2 a piece of the body of the sea animal or soft rubber or plastic with holes in for washing or padding things. 3 a soft cake. **spongy** *adjective*. **sponge** *verb* 1 to wash or wipe with a sponge. 2 to live by getting money or things free from people without giving anything in return. *He sponges off his friends.* **sponger** *noun*.

**sponsor** *noun* a person or business who gives money or help to a person, team or event, usually in return for advertising a product. **sponsor** *verb* to be a sponsor for somebody or something. *We are sponsoring the school football team.*

**spook** *noun* a ghost. **spooky** *adjective*. *A spooky old house.*

The spooky old house on the hill was always lit up at night, though no one had lived there for years.

**spool** *noun* a round holder or roll for winding something on. *A spool of thread.*

**spoon** *noun* an object with a long handle and a shallow bowl used for eating or stirring food. **spoon** *verb* to lift or take with a spoon. *She spooned soup into bowls.*

**spoonerism** *noun* an exchange of the first letters of a pair of words, usually with a funny result. 'You have hissed the mystery lesson,' is a spoonerism.

**spoonful** *noun* the amount a spoon can hold. *Two spoonfuls of sugar.*

**sport** *noun* 1 an activity, competition or game, usually done outdoors. 2 somebody who is kind, cheerful and does not mind losing or being teased. *He is a very good sport.* **sport** *verb* to have or wear something. *He was sporting a bright blue tie.*

**spot** *noun* 1 a small round mark or a dirty mark. *A blue dress with red spots.* 2 a lump or pimple on the skin. *Don't squeeze your spots.* 3 a particular place. *This is the spot where the accident happened.* 4 a small amount. *A spot of trouble.* 5 a drop. *Spots of rain.* **on the spot** 1 at once. *He was dismissed on the spot.* 2 If you put somebody on the spot, you make them give an answer or make a decision. **in a tight spot** in a little difficulty. **spot on** exactly right. *Your guess turned out to be spot on.* **spot** (spots, spotting, spotted) *verb* 1 to notice, pick out. *Can you spot the mistake?* 2 to rain lightly. 3 to mark with spots. **spotted** *adjective*. *A spotted scarf.* **spotty** *adjective*. *A spotty face.*

**DID YOU KNOW?**

*There are about 10,000 known species of sponges, and they are found in seas all over the world. But there are only about 20 species of freshwater sponges.*

**WORD HISTORY**

*William Archibald Spooner (1844–1930), an eccentric clergyman and Oxford don, became famous for his silly slips of the tongue. These became known as 'spoonerisms'. He would say, for example, 'a well-boiled icicle', when he meant 'a well-oiled bicycle'.*

**spotless** *adjective* very clean.

**spout** *noun* 1 the tube or pipe-like opening for pouring liquid from a kettle, jug or pot. 2 a stream of liquid going upwards with great force. **spout** *verb* 1 to stream out with great force. 2 to say a lot in a boring way. *He spouted boring facts all evening.*

Grandma hated teapots with a chipped spout.

**sprain** *verb* to damage a joint by twisting or bending it. *He sprained his ankle jumping off the cliff.* **sprain** *noun*.

**sprawl** *verb* 1 to sit or lie with your arms and legs spread out. *He sprawled on the sofa.* 2 to spread over a large area. *The town sprawls across the valley.*

**spray** *verb* to scatter small drops of liquid on or over something. *She sprayed the room with air freshener.* **spray** *noun* 1 small drops of liquid sent through the air, either blown by the wind or from a special container. *Sea spray.* 2 a special container with liquid in it for spraying. *Hair spray.*

**spray** *noun* a number of flowers or leaves on a stem or branch.

We ordered a spray of spring flowers to be sent to Sally's bedside.

**spread** (spreads, spreading, spread) *verb* 1 to open something out so that all of it can be seen, to stretch out. *The bird spread its wings and flew away.* 2 to cover a large area or time. *The rainforest spreads for thousands of kilometres.* 3 to cover something with something. 4 to make or become more widely known or have a wide effect. *The fire spread to the next village and engulfed the huts in flames.* 5 to share or divide evenly. *We spread the work over a period of three years.* **spread** *noun* 1 the act or action of spreading. *The spread of Aids is increasing, especially in Africa.* 2 the distance or time of spreading. 3 a big meal with lots of food and drink. *Claire put on a magnificent spread for the wedding.* 4 a soft food, paste that can be spread with a knife. *Cheese spread.* 5 a number of things, ideas or interests.

**spring** *noun* 1 the season of the year between winter and summer. 2 a coil of wire that goes back to its normal shape after it is pressed. *One of the springs in the mattress has gone.* 3 a place where water comes up from the ground. *A mountain spring.* 4 being able to stretch and go back to a normal shape. *There is no spring in the sofa.* **spring** (springs, springing, sprang, sprung) *verb* 1 to move quickly and suddenly. 2 to come into being, appear or be the result of. *Her unhappiness springs from her wish to be famous.* 3 to make something happen or known suddenly and unexpectedly. *We sprang a surprise birthday party on him.*

**sprinkle** *verb* to scatter small drops or tiny pieces on something. *They sprinkled sand on the icy path.*

**sprint** *verb* to run at full speed for a short distance. sprint *noun* 1 running very fast. *He made a sprint for the bus.* 2 a short race. **sprinter** *noun.*

**sprout** *noun* 1 a new growth on a plant. 2 a vegetable like a small cabbage. *Brussels sprouts.* **sprout** *verb* to grow or come out.

**spruce** *adjective* very neat, clean and smart looking. **spruce** *verb* to make yourself look neat. *He spruced himself up to meet his girlfriend's parents.*

**spruce** *noun* a kind of evergreen tree.

The Norwegians sent a spruce tree to London, where it was put up in Trafalgar Square at Christmas.

**spud** *noun* (slang) potato.

**spun** *verb* past tense of spin.

**spurn** *verb* to refuse with anger or pride. *He spurned her offer of help.*

**spurt** *verb* 1 to flow out suddenly, to gush out. *Blood spurted from the wound.* 2 to run faster, increase speed suddenly. *She spurted towards the finishing line.* spurt *noun* 1 a sudden spurting. 2 a sudden increase of effort or speed.

**spy** (spies) *noun* somebody who finds out secret information about other people or countries. **spy** (spies, spying, spied) *verb* 1 to work as a spy to get information. 2 to watch secretly. *He spies on his neighbours.* 3 to notice. *I spied a sweet in your bag.*

**squabble** *verb* to quarrel about something unimportant. **squabble** *noun. I hope you have made it up after your squabble.*

**DID YOU KNOW?**

*There are about 50 different species of spruce, widely distributed in the forests of the cooler northern regions of the world, especially in China. They also grow as far south as the mountains of Mexico, southern Europe and the Himalayas.*

**AMAZING FACT**

Early settlers are responsible for the word 'squash'. When they began to arrive in the 17th centrury, they had trouble pronouncing Native American words. One of them was 'asquatasquash' which they shortened to 'squash'.

The farmer grew his best crops of squash in years.

**squalid** *adjective* dirty and untidy. **squalor** *noun. She lives in squalor.*

**squander** *verb* to spend money or time foolishly and wastefully. *She squandered her youth and now she regrets it.*

A square has four equal sides.

**square** *adjective* 1 having the shape of a square with four equal sides and four right angles. 2 forming a right angle. 3 fair, honest. *He wasn't square with me.* 4 even in points, equal or settled. *I've paid up and now we are square.* 5 having an area equal to that of a square with sides of the length stated or being the length from a corner in both directions. *The room has an area of 3 square metres.* **a square meal** a good meal that fills you. **a square number** any number that is the square of another number. 4 is a square number (4 = 2 x 2). **square root** a number that equals another number when it is multiplied by itself. 2 is the square root of 4 (2 x 2 = 4).

**square** *noun* 1 a shape with four sides that are all the same length and four corners at right angles. 2 a place surrounded by buildings that is the shape of a square. *Nelson's Column is in Trafalgar Square.* 3 a number equal to another number when it is multiplied by itself. 16 is the square of 4. (16 = 4 x 4). **square** *verb* 1 to make something square, give a square shape to something, or mark squares on something. 2 to multiply a number by itself. 6 squared is 36. 3 to pay or settle something. *He has to square his account first.* 4 to match or fit a particular explanation or situation. *His story does not square with the facts.*

**squash** (squashes) *noun* 1 a game played with rackets and a small rubber ball that is hit against the walls of an indoor court. 2 a fruit drink. *Orange squash.* 3 a crowd of people in a small place. 4 a vegetable similar to a pumpkin. **squash** *verb* 1 to press something so it goes into a flat shape, to crush. *The grapes got squashed at the bottom of the bag.* 2 to press into a small place. *We all squashed on to the bus.*

**squat** (squats, squatting, squatted) *verb* 1 to sit on your heels, to crouch. 2 to live in an empty building without being allowed to or paying rent. **squat** *noun. We lived in a squat for a year.* **squatter** *noun.*

S

**squat** *adjective* short and fat.

**squeak** *verb* to make a short, very high, loud sound. *Mice squeak.* **squeak** *noun.* **squeaky** *adjective. Squeaky floorboards.*

**squeal** *verb* 1 to make a long, very high sound or cry. 2 to report a criminal to the police. **squeal** *noun. A squeal of brakes.*

**squeamish** *adjective* easily upset or made sick, especially if something looks unpleasant. *She is very squeamish and can't stand the sight of blood.*

**squeeze** *verb* 1 to press from two sides. *He squeezed his finger in the door.* 2 to press to get liquid out of something. *To squeeze an orange.* 3 to manage to get through or into something. *She squeezed herself into her jeans.* **squeeze** *noun.*

**squid** *noun* a sea creature with a long soft body, eight arms and two long tentacles.

The Greeks love to eat squid cut into rings and deep-fried in batter.

**squint** *verb* 1 to look with your eyes almost closed. *She squinted in the bright sunlight.* 2 to have eyes that look in different directions. **squint** *noun* a condition in which the eyes look in two different directions.

**squirrel** *noun* a small furry animal with a long bushy tail that climbs trees and eats nuts. *Squirrels love acorns.*

**squirt** *verb* to force or come out in a thin stream of liquid. *She squirted the water pistol at me.* **squirt** *noun.*

**Sri Lanka** *noun* a country in South Asia, formerly called Ceylon.

**St** *abbreviation* 1 street. 2 saint.

**St George's** *noun* the capital of Grenada.

**St John's** *noun* the capital of Antigua and Barbuda.

**St Kitts and Nevis** *noun* a country in the West Indies.

**St Lucia** *noun* a country in the West Indies.

**St Vincent and the Grenadines** *noun* a country in the West Indies.

**stab** (stabs, stabbing, stabbed) *verb* to strike or pierce with something pointed. *The thief stabbed the policeman with a knife.* **stab** *noun* 1 the act of stabbing. 2 a wound made by something pointed. 3 a sudden painful feeling. *A stab of guilt.* 4 If you have a stab at something, you try something and hope to be successful. *I had a stab at the exam questions, but I didn't do very well.*

**SPELLING NOTE**

*Most people use 'stadiums' as the plural of the sports ground, but 'stadia' can also be used. Most of the original Latin words ending in '–um' have '–a' as their plural.*

**DID YOU KNOW?**

*Sri Lanka is an island in the Indian Ocean off the southern tip of India. It had a highly developed civilization as early as the 5th century* BC.

**stable** *noun* a building in which horses are kept. *There are two horses in the stable.*

**stable** *adjective* firmly fixed in a position, not likely to fall or change. *A stable relationship.* **stability** *noun.*

**stadium** (stadiums or stadia) *noun* a sports ground. *A football stadium.*

Every seat in the stadium was booked for the big match.

**staff** *noun* 1 the people who work for an organization, for example an office or a shop. 2 a strong stick. **staff** *verb* to provide workers, supply with staff. *The restaurant is staffed with excellent cooks.*

**stag** *noun* a male deer.

**stage** *noun* 1 a period, point or part in a development or journey. *We divided the journey into three easy stages.* 2 the platform on which plays and musicals are performed. 3 acting in theatres. *A stage production.* If you are on stage, you are acting. **stage** *verb* 1 to put on a play or perform a show. 2 to organize. *The students staged a protest.*

**stagger** *verb* 1 to walk or move unsteadily. *The drunk staggered across the street.* 2 to surprise. *I was staggered that he had left the country.* 3 to arrange things so that they do not happen at the same time. *We staggered our holidays, so that someone was always there to mind the shop.*

**stain** *noun* 1 a mark that is difficult to remove. 2 a liquid used for darkening or staining wood. 3 a mark of shame or guilt. **stain** *verb* 1 to make a stain on something. *The peach juice has stained my fingers.* 2 to colour with a special liquid. *We stained the chairs red.*

**stained glass** *noun* glass made up of pieces of different colours fitted together and used for windows and other objects.

The village fair raised hundreds of pounds towards a new stained glass window for the church.

**stainless steel** *noun* metal made from steel that does not rust or stain.

**stair** *noun* one of a number of steps. The stairs are a set of steps which go from one floor to another.

**staircase** *noun* a set of stairs inside a house.

**stalactite** *noun* a downward-pointing spike of limestone hanging like an icicle from a cave roof.

**stalagmite** *noun* an upward-pointing spike of limestone standing like a pillar on the floor of a cave.

**stale** *adjective* not fresh. **staleness** *noun.*

**stalemate** *noun* a situation in which neither side can win. *We had reached stalemate in our discussions.*

**stalk** *noun* a stem of a plant or fruit.

**stalk** *verb* 1 to walk in a stiff, angry or proud way. 2 to follow an animal or person quietly in order to hunt or catch them. **stalker** *noun.*

**stall** *noun* 1 a table or small shop in a market where things are sold. 2 a place for an animal in a barn or stable. *Cattle in their stalls.* 3 the stalls are the seats on the ground floor in front of the stage in a theatre. **stall** *verb* to stop suddenly or make an engine stop. *The car stalled.*

**stall** *verb* to not give a clear answer or not do something in order to get more time, to delay. *I'll try and stall them for a while.*

**stallion** *noun* a male horse, especially kept for breeding. *A beautiful white stallion.*

**stamen** *noun* the male part of a flower that produces pollen.

**stamina** *noun* the strength of body or mental energy needed to do tiring things for a long time.

**stammer** *verb* to repeat sounds of the same word when speaking, to speak with pauses. **stammer** *noun.*

**stamp** *noun* 1 a small piece of gummed paper with a design on it that is stuck on an envelope before posting to show that postage has been paid. 2 a small pad with a design or letters on one side which is pressed on to a surface. 3 the mark made by using a stamp. *An official stamp on a document.* 4 a mark or sign typical for something. *His songs bear the stamp of youth.* **stamp** *verb* 1 to lift your foot and put it down hard on the ground. *The little boy stamped his foot and cried.* 2 to walk noisily and with heavy footsteps. 3 to put a postage stamp on a letter or parcel. 4 to press a design or letters on something.

**SPELLING NOTE**

*'Stalactite' comes from an ancient Greek word for 'dripping', and 'stalagmite' from the Greek 'stalagma', 'drop'. Both types of rock formation are formed by dripping, trickling water containing dissolved limestone.*

**AMAZING FACT**

Stamp collecting is also called 'philately' and the person who collects stamps is known as a 'philatelist'.

Paul collected lots of different stamps and stuck them in an album.

**stand** (stands, standing, stood) *verb* 1 to be on your feet in an upright position. 2 to put or be in an upright position. 3 to remain or stay the same. *My invitation still stands.* 4 to put up with or endure. *I can't stand him.* 5 to be a candidate in an election. *He is standing for parliament.* 6 to pay for. *Let me stand you a drink.* **stand between** to be an obstacle. *Only one more election stands between me and a place in parliament.* **it stands to reason** it makes sense or is likely to happen. *It stands to reason she'll fail the exam if she never does any work.* **stand by** to be ready to help or take action. *Ambulances were standing by at the match.* **stand for** 1 to represent or mean. *BT stands for British Telecom.* 2 to put up with, to allow. *She doesn't stand for any nonsense.* **stand out** 1 to be easily seen and clear. *Red stands out well.* 2 to be outstanding. *He stands out as a real artist.* **stand up** 1 to get up. 2 to be accepted as true. *His story won't stand up in court.* 3 to defend. *You must learn to stand up for yourself.* 4 If you stand somebody up, you don't meet them as arranged. **stand up to** 1 to resist attack. 2 to stay in good condition. *The carpet stood up to constant use.*

**stand** *noun* 1 a piece of furniture for putting things on or in. *An umbrella stand.* 2 a stall or small shop for selling things. *A flower stand.* 3 a position against or in favour. *She took a stand against animal experiments.* 4 a position for sitting or standing in a stadium, from where people can watch a game or other event. *We had seats in the stand.*

**standard** *adjective* 1 of the usual or accepted kind. *The standard rules of good behaviour.* 2 most widely used or best of its kind. *The standard book on grammar.*

**standard** *noun* 1 how good something is. *The standard of spelling is very high.* 2 something used for measuring or judging the quality of something. *Different countries use different standards.* 3 a stand or upright base for holding something. *A standard lamp.* 4 a flag of an important person or family. *The royal standard.*

**stanza** *noun* a verse of poetry.

**staple** *adjective* regular or main. *Rice is the staple food of India.*

Potatoes were the staple food in Ireland.

**staple** *noun* 1 a small piece of wire used for holding pieces of paper together. Staples are pushed through the paper with a stapler. 2 a U-shaped nail. **staple** *verb* to fasten papers together with a stapler. **stapler** *noun*.

**star** *noun* 1 a large ball of burning gas in space, a heavenly body. 2 a shape, an object or a mark with points sticking out round it. If a hotel has five stars, it means that it is extremely good. 3 a famous actor, sports player or performer. *A pop star*. **star** (stars, starring, starred) *verb* 1 to have an important part in a play or film. 2 to mark with a star shape. **starry** *adjective*.

**starch** (starches) *noun* 1 a white substance in food. There is starch in bread, rice and pasta. 2 a white substance for stiffening clothes, especially clothes made of cotton. **starch** *verb* to stiffen with starch.

**stare** *verb* to look at somebody or something hard or for a long time. *Don't stare at me, it makes me blush*.

**starfish** (starfish or starfishes) *noun* a sea animal with five arms that has a star shape.

**starling** *noun* a small, dark speckled bird.

**start** *verb* 1 to come into being or to begin, especially something you were not doing before. *She started laughing*. 2 to take place, to begin. *His music started a new craze*. 3 to set out on a journey. *She started as a secretary*. 4 to jerk or move suddenly, usually because you are surprised or frightened. *A sudden noise makes me start*. **start** *noun* 1 the place of starting, the beginning of an activity. *Let's make an early start*. 2 a sudden uncontrolled movement. *She woke up with a start*. 3 an advantage or an amount of time somebody has over somebody else. *We had an hour's start*. **make a fresh start** to start again from the beginning.

**startle** *verb* to make somebody jump or be surprised. *The noise startled him*.

**starve** *verb* 1 to suffer or die from not having any food to eat. To make somebody die from hunger. *Thousands starved to death during the drought*. 2 to be very hungry. *When's lunch, I'm starving*. 3 When you are starved of something, you lack that particular thing and need it very much. *The children were starved of love*. **starvation** *noun*. **starving** *adjective*.

**state** *noun* 1 a condition which somebody or something is in. *His state of health*. 2 the government of a country or a country. *Italy is a European state*. 3 part of a large country. *The state of Texas*.

### DID YOU KNOW?

*An ancient Greek scientist called Thales discovered static electricity over 2,500 years ago, when he rubbed a piece of amber with a cloth.*

Starfish cling to the rocks with suckers under their arms.

### SPELLING NOTE

*Be careful not to mix up the spelling of the adjective 'stationary' (not moving) and the noun 'stationery' (writing materials). Both come from the Latin for 'standing', which came to refer to a shopkeeper as opposed to a 'moving' pedlar.*

**state** *verb* to express something in words, especially in a formal way. *The police stated that no charges had been laid*.

There are 52 states in the USA.

**statement** *noun* 1 something you state, facts and information given in a written or spoken declaration. *I don't believe the minister's statement*. 2 a printed document showing amounts of money paid in, taken out or owed, usually sent out by your bank. *I get a monthly bank statement*.

**static** *adjective* not moving or changing.

**static electricity** *noun* electricity that builds up or is present in certain things like your hair or nylon.

**station** *noun* 1 a place where trains or buses stop for people to get on and off. *Where is the railway station?* 2 a building for a particular service. *A police station*. 3 a company that sends out radio or television programmes. *The new radio station plays club dance music all day*. **station** *verb* to put people or things in a certain place for a particular purpose.

**stationary** *adjective* not moving. *The bus was stationary when the accident happened*.

**stationery** *noun* materials for writing, such as paper, envelopes, pens and pencils.

Jennifer was in charge of the office stationery cupboard.

**statistics** *plural noun* information shown in numbers that can be compared. *The statistics seem to show that examination results have been getting better every year*. **statistical** *adjective*.

**statue** *noun* a model of a person or animal in stone, wood or metal. *The statue of the Venus de Milo has no arms*.

S

**stay** *verb* 1 to remain in the same place or condition. *The weather stayed fine.* 2 to live at a place as a visitor. *She is staying with her brother in London.* 3 to last out. *The horse stayed the course.* **stay put** to remain in one place. **stay on** to remain in a place or for an extra spell of time. *He stayed on as headmaster.* **stay up** to go to bed after your normal bed time.

**stay** *noun* 1 a short time spent somewhere. 2 a delay or postponement. *The judge ordered a stay of execution.*

**steady** (steadier, steadiest) *adjective* 1 not moving, firm. *He is not very steady on his legs.* 2 not changing, regular. *She has now found a steady job.*

**steak** *noun* a thick slice of meat (especially beef) or fish.

**steal** (steals, stealing, stole, stolen) *verb* 1 to take something that belongs to somebody else without any right. *He stole some money.* 2 to move quietly and secretly. *She stole out of the room.*

**steam** *noun* 1 the hot mist that is produced when water is boiled. *The steam from a boiling kettle.* 2 the power from steam used to drive machines. *A steam engine.* 3 energy. If you run out of steam, you have no more energy. **steam** *verb* 1 to give out steam. 2 to cook in steam, not water. *Do you want to steam the fish?* 3 to travel by steam power. *The ship steamed out of the harbour.*

The glorious days of the steam train are long gone, and rail travel is now less exciting but much cleaner.

**steel** *noun* a very strong hard metal used for making knives and tools.

**steep** *adjective* 1 rising or falling sharply. *A steep slope.* 2 expensive. *£100 for his old bike is a bit steep.*

**steeple** *noun* a tall pointed church tower.

**steeplechase** *noun* a race across country with hedges, fences and ditches.

**steer** *verb* 1 to control a car, boat or ship so it goes in the direction you want it to go. 2 to guide. *He steered me towards the door.*

**steering wheel** *noun* the wheel in a car or lorry that the driver holds and turns to steer with. *He gripped the steering wheel.*

**AMAZING FACT**

Steam fills 1700 times as much space as the water that it has been boiled from. If you compress steam into a small container, it pushes against the sides. If there is a place or thing that the steam can move, such as a piston, the steam will force the piston outward. When the steam cools, it turns back into water, takes less space, and the piston returns to its original position. Early steam engines used this principle to power pumps to pump water out of mines.

**WORD HISTORY**

*The steeplechase gets its name from early races when a local church with a tall steeple was used as a landmark, probably the finish. Steeplechase races using horses can be traced back to 18th-century fox hunting.*

**stem** *noun* 1 the long central part of a plant above the ground. 2 the thin part of a plant that has leaves or flowers on it. 3 the thin part of a wine glass or bowl that looks like a stem. **stem** (stems, stemming, stemmed) *verb* to stop something flowing or spreading. *The nurse tried to stem the flow of blood.* **stem from** to have as its origin, to come from. *Her fear of dogs stems from being bitten as a child.*

She cut the stem of the flower near the base and put it in water.

Stem

**stench** (stenches) *noun* a very nasty smell.

**stencil** *noun* a piece of paper, metal or plastic with a design or letters cut out of it, used for making designs or letters on something. **stencil** (stencils, stencilling, stencilled) *verb*.

**step** *noun* 1 the movement made when lifting a foot and putting it down in a different place. *He takes very big steps.* 2 the sound made when walking. *She could hear steps coming towards her.* 3 a short distance. *The beach is just a few steps from the house.* 4 a flat surface on which you put your foot when you walk up or down, a stair. *Mind the step!* 5 one of a series of actions that are done to get a certain result, or one of a series of stages. *What is the next step?* 6 a movement of the feet in dancing. If you are in step, you are moving your feet forward at the same time as your partner or others walking. If you are out of step, you are not in agreement with the others. **step by step** doing one thing at the time, slowly. **take steps to do something** to get a result. **watch your step!** be careful! **step** (steps, stepping, stepped) *verb* to walk. *She stepped into the house.* **step in** to become involved in order to help. *Her mother stepped in and sorted out her problems.* **step up** to increase in size or speed. *We must step up production.*

Father climbed up the step ladder to paint the ceiling.

S

**stepchild** (stepchildren) *noun* a child of a husband's or wife's earlier marriage. **stepbrother** *noun*. **stepsister** *noun*.

**stepfather** *noun* your stepfather is the man who has married your mother after your real father has died or your parents have divorced. **stepmother** *noun*.

**steppe** *noun* a large area of grassland without trees, especially in Russia.

**stereo** *adjective* stereophonic, giving out sound or sound coming from two different places. *Stereo equipment*. **stereo** *noun* 1 a stereo sound or recording. 2 a stereo record/CD player.

**stereotype** *noun* a fixed idea or typical example of somebody or something. *He is small and thin and does not fit the stereotype of a boxer*. **stereotype** *verb*.

**stern** *adjective* strict. **sternly** *adverb*. *He looked at her sternly*.

**stern** *noun* the back end of a ship.

**stethoscope** *noun* a medical instrument that a doctor uses to listen to somebody's heartbeat. *The stethoscope felt cold*.

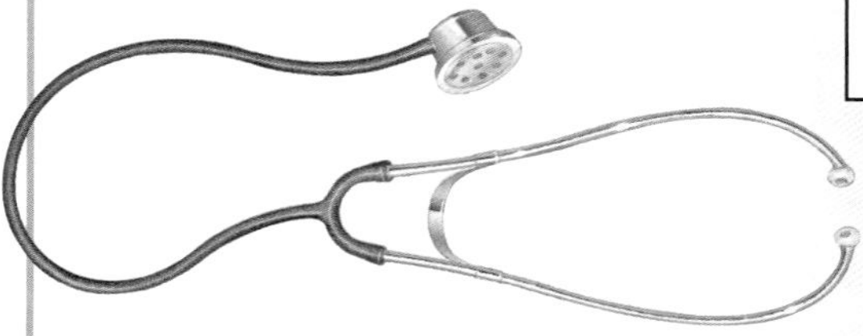

Dr Smith listened to Peggy's heart through his stethoscope.

**stew** *verb* to cook slowly in liquid. **stew** *noun* a meal with meat and vegetables cooked in liquid.

**stick** *noun* 1 a long thin piece of wood, a branch broken from a tree. 2 a piece of wood specially made for leaning on when walking. *A walking stick*. 3 any long thin piece of something. *A stick of celery*. **get the wrong end of the stick** to misunderstand something. **stick** (sticks, sticking, stuck) *verb* 1 to push something pointed into something. *She stuck a pin into the noticeboard*. 2 to fix one thing to another thing with glue or another sticky substance. *Don't forget to stick a stamp on the envelope*. 3 to become fixed, unable to move. *My zip sticks*. 4 to not give up, to keep on doing something. *How can you stick having to get up so early every morning?* 5 to stay. *We must stick together*. 6 to put. *Stick your bags in the corner*. **stick at** to continue to work hard at something. *If she sticks at the job, she'll do well*. **stick to** 1 If you stick to somebody, you are loyal to that person and support him. 2 If you stick to something, you refuse to change. *We are sticking to our plan*. **sticky** *adjective*. *A sticky bun*. **stickiness** *noun*.

**WORD HISTORY**

*The prefix 'step–', as in 'stepbrother', 'stepchild', etc. comes from the Old English word 'steop', meaning an orphan or a child whose parent has died.*

**DID YOU KNOW?**

*The Russian steppes are bordered by forests to the north and by desert to the south. The climate is too cold in winter and too hot and dry in summer for trees to survive. But the steppe grasses have long roots that can tap water from deep under the ground.*

**stiff** *adjective* 1 not bending or moving easily. *Stiff cardboard*. 2 firm, not runny. *Beat the cream until it is stiff*. 3 not friendly, formal. *The new teacher is very stiff with the children*. 4 difficult. *A stiff test*. 5 strong. *A stiff drink*. **stiffness** *noun*.

**stile** *noun* a step used to climb over a fence or gate. *Let me help you over the stile*.

We crossed the stile and walked towards the distant hills.

**still** *adjective* 1 not moving. 2 silent. 3 not fizzy. *Still water*. **still** *adverb* 1 up to now or up to that moment. *Is he still waiting?* 2 even. *More amazing still, she never spoke again*. 3 nevertheless, in spite of what has been said. *The children were very naughty – still, she shouldn't have hit them*. 4 even so. *He is not the most brilliant footballer, but he still deserves a place in the team*.

**still** *noun* 1 quietness with no activity. *In the still of the night*. 2 a still photograph taken from a cinema film. 3 an apparatus for making alcoholic spirits.

**stimulate** *verb* to make more active or interested in something. *Sunlight stimulates growth*. **stimulation** *noun*.

**sting** *noun* 1 the sharp pointed part of some insects such as bees, or on some plants such as nettles, that can prick and hurt. 2 a sharp pain or wound caused by a sting. **sting** (stings, stinging, stung) *verb* 1 to prick with a sting. 2 to feel a strong pain or to feel hurt. *His eyes were stinging from the smoke*. 3 to take too much money from somebody. *They stung us for ten pounds*.

**stink** *noun* 1 a nasty smell. 2 a big fuss, usually made by complaining. **stink** (stinks, stinking, stank or stunk) *verb* 1 to smell very badly. *The changing rooms stink of old socks*. 2 to be very unpleasant or bad. *The plan stinks*.

The skunk was responsible for the terrible stink.

S

**stir** (stirs, stirring, stirred) *verb* 1 to mix something by moving it around with a spoon. 2 to move. *She is fast asleep and hasn't stirred.* 3 to excite or be touched by something. *The news stirred him into action.* 4 to cause trouble between others, especially by telling stories. *She loves stirring.* **stir** *noun* 1 the action of stirring. 2 excitement, shock. *The discovery caused quite a stir.*

**stir-fry** (stir-fries, stir-frying, stir-fried) *verb* to cook small pieces of meat and vegetables quickly by stirring them in a wok or frying pan. **stir-fry** *noun.*

**stirrup** *noun* a metal loop on a horse's saddle for the rider's foot.

**stock** *noun* 1 the supply of goods or other things to be sold or used. *A large stock of food.* 2 a group of farm animals used for breeding or kept for their meat. 3 your ancestors or original family, or a type of animal or plant. *Many Americans are of European stock.* 4 a liquid made from vegetables or meat used in cooking. *Vegetable stock cubes.* 5 shares in the ownership of a business company. 6 a garden flower with a sweet smell. **take stock** to think about something before deciding what to do next. **stock** *verb* 1 to keep goods in stock. 2 to fill or supply a place with food or other thing.

**stock exchange** *noun* a place where shares are bought and sold.

Many people called 'dealers' work at the stock exchange. Their job is to buy and sell shares.

**Stockholm** *noun* the capital of Sweden.

**stodgy** (stodgier, stodgiest) *adjective* 1 heavy, sticky and filling, especially food. *Stodgy rice.* 2 dull and uninteresting.

**stole** *verb* past tense of steal.

**stole** *noun* a long piece of material worn around the shoulders.

**stomach** *noun* 1 an organ in the body where food is digested. 2 the front part of the body below the waist. *He is doing exercises to get rid of his big stomach.* **stomach** *verb* to put up with, usually something unpleasant. *How can you stomach his nonsense?*

**DID YOU KNOW?**

*The famous London stock exchange, in the City of London, was founded in 1773. It replaced coffee-houses, where financial dealings had previously been made. The New York stock exchange is situated on Wall Street, in the financial district of New York.*

**AMAZING FACT**

The human stomach is a large, muscular bag that has openings at both ends.

The stomach of a human baby is about the size of a chicken egg, while an adult's stomach can hold about one litre or one quart.

**stone** *noun* 1 very hard material found in the ground, rock. 2 a small piece of rock. *He threw a stone at the window.* 3 a jewel. *A precious stone.* 4 the hard seed in the middle of some fruit such as cherries or peaches. 5 a measure of weight (1 stone = 14 pounds or 6.35 kilograms). **stone** *verb* 1 to throw stones at somebody. *They stoned the traitor to death.* 2 to take the stones out of fruit. **stony** *adjective.*

**stone** *prefix* completely. *He is stone-deaf.*

**stoned** *adjective* under the influence of drugs. *Angela gets stoned every night.*

**stood** *verb* past tense of stand.

Bill sat on the stool to play the guitar.

**stool** *noun* a seat with legs but without arms or a back. *A milking stool.*

**stoop** *verb* 1 to stand or walk with your shoulders bent forward. 2 to lower or allow yourself to do something. *I wouldn't stoop to thanking that woman.* **stoop** *noun.*

**stop** (stops, stopping, stopped) *verb* 1 to come to an end or put an end to an activity or movement. To finish moving, to not continue working. *My watch has stopped.* 2 to prevent somebody from doing something or something from happening. *How can I stop him smoking?* 3 to stay, especially for a short visit. *She stopped for a chat.* 4 to fill a hole, to close. 5 to block. 6 to prevent money from being paid. *She stopped the cheque.* **stop** *noun* 1 the moment something stops, a pause, an end. 2 a place where buses stop. 3 a dot or mark of punctuation, especially a full stop. 4 a knob or lever that changes the level of the notes (pitch) and controls the pipes on an organ.

**stopwatch** *noun* a watch that can be started and stopped and is used for timing things such as races.

**storage** *noun* the keeping of things in a special place. *We put our furniture in storage when we went abroad.*

**store** *noun* 1 a supply of something that is kept for later use. 2 a shop, especially a larger one. **in store** 1 kept ready for later use. 2 about to happen. *There are lots of adventures in store for you.* **store** *verb* to keep things until they are needed. *The wood is stored in the shed.*

**storey** *noun* a floor of a building. *A block of flats with six storeys.*

**stork** *noun* a tall bird with a long beak and long legs. *A stork nesting on a chimney pot.*

**storm** *noun* 1 a very strong wind, usually with rain, thunder or snow. 2 an excited or angry show of feeling. *A storm of protest.* **storm** *verb* 1 to attack or force your way into a place. *The soldiers stormed the stronghold.* 2 to show anger by moving about or shouting loudly and angrily. *He stormed out of the room.* **stormy** *adjective.*

**story** (stories) *noun* 1 a description of real or made-up events. 2 a lie. *He is always telling stories.*

**stout** *adjective* 1 thick and strong. *Stout climbing boots.* 2 rather fat. *He is short and stout.* 3 firm. *A stout supporter of the club.*

**stout** *noun* strong, dark beer.

**stove** *noun* a device for heating a room or cooking on. *A hot stove.*

**straddle** *verb* to sit or stand across something, with one leg on each side. *To straddle a horse.*

**straggle** *verb* 1 to grow in an untidy way. *Ivy straggled over the wall.* 2 to move forward slowly behind others. **straggler** *noun.* **straggly** *adjective. Straggly hair.*

**straight** *adjective* 1 going in the same direction, not bent or curved. *Straight hair.* 2 upright. *The picture is not straight.* 3 tidy. 4 honest. *A straight answer.* If you keep a straight face, you look serious and try not to laugh. **straight** *adverb* 1 in a straight line. 2 directly, without stopping. *Go straight home.* **straight away** immediately. **go straight** to leave a life of crime and live an honest life.

**straightaway** *adverb* immediately.

**straighten** *verb* to make something straight or become straight.

**straightforward** *adjective* 1 easy to understand or do. *The instructions are quite straightforward.* 2 honest. *He is a very straightforward person.*

**strain** *verb* 1 to stretch tightly, usually by pulling. 2 to make a great effort. *She strained her ears to hear.* 3 to damage a part of your body. *I've strained a muscle.* 4 to pour something through a strainer to remove liquid. *He strained the peas.* **strain** *noun* 1 the condition or force of being stretched. *The cable broke under the strain.* 2 a state of worry or tension. Something that tests you or uses up strength. *Looking after children is a great strain.* 3 an injury to a muscle. 4 a tune. *The strains of a song wafted up to where she sat on the deck.*

We use a tea strainer because we don't like leaves floating in our tea.

The stove roared indoors, keeping us warm while the wind rattled at the windows.

**DID YOU KNOW?**

*The layer of atmosphere just above the Earth's surface, where we live, is called the troposphere; then comes the stratosphere; then the mesosphere, thermosphere, and finally the exosphere.*

The plane took off and climbed steeply until it reached the stratosphere.

**strain** *noun* 1 a type of plant or animal. *A new strain of beans.* 2 a quality that develops, or a characteristic. *There has always been a strain of madness in my family, unfortunately.*

**strainer** *noun* an instrument for straining solids from liquids.

**strange** *adjective* unusual or surprising, not known or seen before. **strangely** *adverb. Strangely, it seems that she did not leave at her usual time.*

**stranger** *noun* 1 somebody you don't know. 2 somebody who is in a place he doesn't know. *I'm a stranger in this town.*

**strangle** *verb* to kill by pressing on the throat. **strangulation** *noun..*

**strap** *noun* a strip of leather or other material used for fastening. **strap** (straps, strapping, strapped) *verb* to fasten with a strap or straps. *He strapped the child into the car seat.* **be strapped for** to be short of. *I'm a bit strapped for cash at the moment.*

**strategy** (strategies) *noun* 1 a particular plan to achieve something. *He worked out a clever strategy to get more money.* 2 the planning of the movements of armies in war. *A military strategy.*

**stratosphere** *noun* the outer part of the air which surrounds the earth, between about 10 and 50 km above the earth's surface.

**straw** *noun* 1 dried stalks of grain. 2 a thin tube of paper or plastic used for drinking through. *Drinking straws.* **the last straw** the last or latest in a row of unpleasant events. *After a terrible day at the office, losing my purse was the last straw.*

**strawberry** (strawberries) *noun* a soft and juicy red fruit.

**stray** *verb* 1 to wander away from somewhere you are supposed to be. 2 to move away from a subject, to not concentrate. *During the lesson his thoughts strayed to football.* **stray** *adjective* without a home or not in its usual place. *Stray animals need loving homes.*

**streak** *noun* 1 a long stripe or mark that is different from what is around it. *He has a few grey streaks in his hair.* 2 a quality of character, a trace. *That boy has a streak of cruelty.* **streak** *verb* 1 to move very quickly. 2 to mark with streaks. 3 to run in a public place with no clothes on. **streaker** *noun*. *At half time a streaker ran on to the pitch.*

**stream** *noun* 1 a flow of water smaller than a river. 2 a flow of people or things. *A long stream of cars.* **stream** *verb* 1 to flow. *Tears streamed down her face.* 2 to move like a stream or float in the air. *The sun streamed in through the window.*

**streamer** *noun* a long ribbon or strip of coloured paper.

Streamers hung from the ceiling at David's party.

**streamlined** *adjective* smooth and regular in shape, able to move easily through air or water. Racing cars and powerboats are streamlined. **streamline** *verb*.

**street** *noun* a road with buildings along the side in a town or village. *The street where I live.* **streets apart** very different.

**streetwise** *adjective* used to the ways of modern city life. *If you're not streetwise in New York, you'll get mugged or ripped off.*

**strength** *noun* 1 the quality of being strong. *Superman has enough strength to lift a lorry.* 2 something that gives power. *Translation is her biggest strength.*

**strengthen** *verb* to make or become stronger. *Please strengthen your resolve.*

**strenuous** *adjective* using or needing great effort. *I had a very strenuous day at work.*

**stress** (stresses) *noun* 1 worries caused by difficulties in life. *She has been under a lot of stress because of her father's illness.* 2 saying a word or part of a word more strongly than another. In the word 'bookshop', the stress is put on 'book'. 3 the force of weight or pressure on something. *The heavy traffic puts stress on the bridge.* **stress** *verb* to give importance to something. *He stressed the need for peace.* **stressful** *adjective*.

**DID YOU KNOW?**

*Strawberries belong to the rose family of plants. Wild strawberry plants, bearing tiny fruits, have been picked for food since ancient times. They started to be grown as garden plants in 13th-century France.*

**WORD BUILDING**

*Words that are spelt the same can have a different stress to make different meanings. In this dictionary, stress in punctuation is marked by bold letters.*

**stretch** *verb* 1 to become wider or longer. If you pull a rubber band it stretches. 2 to spread out or extend over a distance or period of time. *The forest stretches from the mountains to the sea.* 3 to straighten your body to full length. To push out your arms to reach something. 4 to reach, be long enough. 5 If a job stretches you, you have to work very hard at it. **stretch** (stretches) *noun* 1 stretching or being stretched. *The cat got up and had a good stretch.* 2 an area of land or water, or a period of time. *He was given a long stretch in prison.* **stretchy** *adjective*. *Stretchy material.*

**stretcher** *noun* a long piece of cloth between two poles, or something similar, on which a sick or injured person can be carried lying down. *The injured player was carried off on a stretcher.*

The patient was put on a stretcher and taken by ambulance to the hospital.

**strict** *adjective* 1 firm, making people do what you want. *Our teacher is very strict about punctuality.* 2 exact, complete. *The strict truth.* **strictness** *noun*.

**stride** (strides, striding, strode, stridden) *verb* to walk with long steps. *She strode across the lawn to meet him.* **stride** *noun* 1 a long step in walking. 2 If you make great strides, you do much better.

**strife** *noun* trouble between people.

**strike** (strikes, striking, struck) *verb* 1 to hit somebody or something. *He was struck by lightning.* 2 to stop working for a time, usually to get more money or because you are angry about something. 3 to suddenly happen or come to mind. *It struck me that we should have visited him.* 4 to sound. *The clock struck eight.* 5 to find something in a place. *They struck oil in the desert.* 6 to seem. *She strikes me as very intelligent.* 7 If you are struck by something, you are very impressed by it. *He was struck by her beauty.* 8 to light or produce a flame. *He struck a match.* **strike lucky** to have good luck. **strike off** to cross somebody's name off an official list. *The doctor has been struck off for negligence.* **strike up** 1 to begin a friendship. 2 to begin to play music. **strike** *noun* 1 a time when no work is done. *The train drivers are on strike.* 2 a hit. 3 an air attack. 4 finding oil or gold. **striker** *noun*.

S

**string** *noun* 1 a thin piece of cord for tying things. 2 nylon or wire in a guitar or other stringed instrument for making sounds. The strings are the stringed instruments in an orchestra. 3 a line or number of things. *A string of accidents.* **string** (strings, stringing, strung) *verb* 1 to put a string or strings on something. *To string a tennis racket.* 2 to thread on a string or hang something on a string. *Flags were strung across the street.* **highly strung** somebody who is easily excited or hurt in feelings.

**strip** (strips, stripping, stripped) *verb* 1 to take a covering off something. *We stripped the paint off the wood.* 2 to undress. *He stripped off his shirt.* 3 to take somebody's belongings away from them. *He was stripped of his rights.* **strip** *noun* 1 a long narrow piece of material or land. 2 a comic strip. **stripper** *noun.*

**stripe** *noun* 1 a long line of colour among other colours. 2 a band of cloth sewn on to a soldier's or policeman's uniform to show his rank. **stripy** *adjective.* **striped** *adjective.*

The stripes on her uniform indicated a high rank.

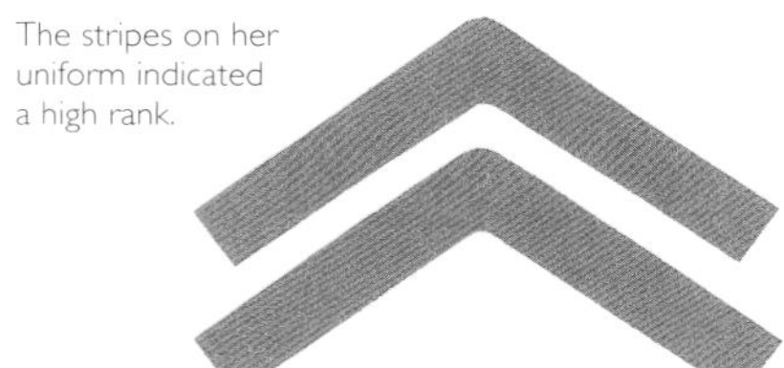

**strobe lighting** *noun* a light that goes on and off very quickly.

**stroke** *noun* 1 a hit or blow. *He cut off the giant's head with a single stroke of his sword.* 2 a movement or action with your arms, especially in sports like golf or tennis. *She swims with strong strokes.* 3 a line made by the movement of a pen or brush. *Brush strokes.* 4 the sound made by a clock striking. *He arrived on the stroke of three.* 5 a sudden illness that often makes people unable to move parts of their body. **a stroke of luck** being very lucky.

**stroke** *verb* to move your hand slowly and gently over something. *She stroked the dear old cat.* **stroke** *noun.*

**stroll** *verb* to walk slowly and in a relaxed way. **stroll** *noun. A stroll in the park.*

**strong** *adjective* 1 having great power, especially of the body. *He is very strong and can lift heavy weights.* 2 feeling confident and sure, not easily frightened or upset. *She has a very strong imagination.* 3 not easily broken. 4 having a great effect or taste, not weak. *A strong smell of gas.* 5 having a certain number of people. *Our club is a hundred strong.* **strongly** *adverb.* **strong** *adverb. She is old but still going strong.*

**AMAZING FACT**

Not all guitars have the same number of strings. The Spanish guitar and most types of electric guitar have six strings. The bass guitar has four strings. Some musicians play a twelve-string guitar which is tuned in six pairs.

The Taj Mahal is one of the world's most beautiful structures.

**DID YOU KNOW?**

*Strobe lighting is often used in clubs and discos, to flash in time with the beat of the music. The word 'strobe' comes from the Greek 'strobos', meaning 'whirling'. The stroboscope was perfected in 1931 by the American scientist Harold Edgerton.*

The studs around Mike's watch make it look very sporty.

**stronghold** *noun* 1 a fortified place. 2 a place where many people do or believe the same. *This southern town is a stronghold of Conservatism.*

**struck** *verb* past tense of strike.

**structure** *noun* 1 an arrangement of parts, something built. *The bridge is an interesting structure.* 2 the way in which parts are put together or in which something is made. *The structure of a sentence.* **structure** *verb* to arrange or organize. **structural** *adjective.*

**struggle** *noun* a hard fight. **struggle** *verb* 1 to twist, kick and fight to get free. *She struggled against her attacker.* 2 to make a great effort, fight hard to do something difficult. *He struggles with his homework.*

**strum** (strums, strumming, strummed) *verb* to play the guitar by moving your fingers up and down the strings.

**strut** (struts, strutting, strutted) *verb* to walk in a proud way, usually with your head held high and chest out.

**stub** (stubs, stubbing, stubbed) *verb* to hurt your toe by hitting it against something.

**stub** *noun* 1 a short end left when something has been used. *The stub of a pencil.* 2 the part of a cheque or ticket that you keep.

**stubble** *noun* short stiff pieces of something growing, especially a short beard after shaving or corn stalks after harvest.

**stubborn** *adjective* having a strong will. If you are stubborn, you do what you want.

**stuck** *verb* past tense of stick.

**stud** *noun* 1 a small piece of metal like a nail with a large head used as a decoration. *A belt with silver studs.* 2 a kind of fastener, used instead of a button, usually two parts that are pressed together. **stud** (studs, studding, studded) *verb* to decorate with studs. *A watch studded with diamonds.*

**stud** *noun* 1 horses kept for breeding. 2 the place where horses are kept for breeding.

**student** *noun* somebody who is studying or training, especially at a college or university.

**studio** *noun* 1 a room where a painter or photographer works. 2 a room where film, radio or television programmes are made.

**study** (studies, studying, studied) *verb* 1 to spend time learning about a particular subject. 2 to look at something carefully. *He studied her face for a long time.* **study** (studies) *noun* 1 the activity of studying a subject. 2 a subject you study or a piece of writing on a subject. *He made a study of Greek philosophy.* 3 a drawing or painting planned as part of a larger picture. *A study of a rose.* 4 a room used for reading, writing and studying.

**stuff** *noun* 1 things or personal things. *Take your stuff up into your room.* 2 material of which something is made. *Try this, it's good stuff for a cold.* **stuff** *verb* 1 to fill something. *She stuffed the cushion with feathers.* 2 to push something quickly and carelessly somewhere. *He stuffed the card in his pocket.* 3 to eat a lot. *I stuffed myself with biscuits.*

**stuffing** *noun* 1 material used to fill something. 2 cut-up food put into meat or vegetables. *Turkey with chestnut stuffing.*

**stumble** *verb* 1 to trip and almost fall over. 2 to stop or make a mistake while reading or speaking. *He stumbled over a difficult word because he was dyslexic.*

**stun** (stuns, stunned, stunning) *verb* 1 to make somebody unconscious by hitting them on the head. 2 to shock. *He was stunned by the news of her death.*

**stung** *verb* past tense of sting.

**stunning** *adjective* brilliant, beautiful.

**stunt** *noun* a dangerous and risky act that somebody does in a film or in order to draw attention. *Most actors don't do their own stunts, they hire a stuntman.*

**stuntman** *noun* somebody who does stunts in a film so the actor does not have to take any risks.

We went into the sty to see Beryl's new litter of pigs.

**WORD HISTORY**

*The word 'style' comes from the Latin 'stilus', meaning a pen. It came to have the wider meaning of 'the manner of writing with a pen', which gave rise to the present senses of style.*

The stuffing was poking out of the teddy bear's foot.

The stuntman drove up the ramp and flew over the roofs of several cars.

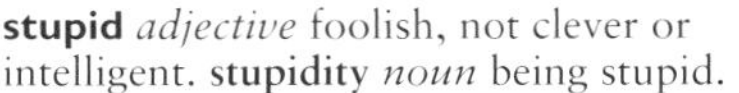

**stupid** *adjective* foolish, not clever or intelligent. **stupidity** *noun* being stupid.

**sturdy** (sturdier, sturdiest) *adjective* strong, not easily broken. *A sturdy chair.* **sturdily** *adverb. Sturdily built.* **sturdiness** *noun.*

**stutter** *verb* to find it difficult to say the first sound of a word, to stammer. **stutter** *noun. He stuttered because he was nervous.*

**sty** (sties) *noun* a place where pigs are kept.

**sty** or **stye** (sties or styes) *noun* a red swelling on the edge of the eyelid.

**style** *noun* 1 a kind or sort. *This is a new style of house.* 2 the way something is written, spoken or performed. *The essay was written in an interesting style.* 3 a superior quality or elegance. *They live in grand style.* 4 a kind of fashion or design. *The latest styles in shoes.* 5 part of a flower involved in pollination. **style** *verb* to design or make in a particular style. **stylish** *adjective* showing superior quality, elegant, fashionable. *Stylish clothes.*

**sub-** *prefix* 1 below, under. *Submarine.* 2 subordinate, secondary. *Subsection.*

**subconscious** *adjective* of thoughts and feelings which you are not completely conscious or aware of. **subconsciously** *adverb.* **subconscious** *noun.*

**subdue** (subdues, subduing, subdued) *verb* 1 to overcome or bring under control. *He managed to subdue his emotions.* 2 to soften. *The restaurant had subdued lighting.*

**subject** (say sub-djikt) *noun* 1 somebody or something being talked or written about. 2 something studied. 3 in grammar, the word or phrase that does the action of a verb. In the sentence 'The flower is red,' 'flower' is the subject. 4 a member of a nation. *The Queen wished a Happy Christmas to all her subjects.* **change the subject** to talk about something different.

S

**subject** (say **sub**-djikt) *adjective* 1 having to follow or obey something. *We are all subject to the laws of the land.* 2 liable or prone to. *She is subject to colds.* 3 dependent on. *The plan is subject to approval.*

**subject** (say sub-**djekt**) *verb* 1 to make somebody experience something. *They subjected him to torture.* 2 to bring under control. **subjection** *noun.*

**subjective** *adjective* depending on your own taste and opinions.

**sublime** *adjective* grand or extreme. *I think Mozart was a sublime genius.*

**submarine** *noun* a ship that can travel under water. **submarine** *adjective. A submarine cable.*

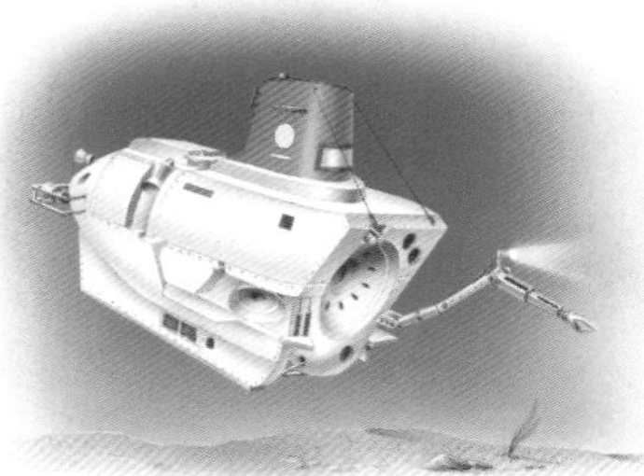

The submarine travelled into the ocean's depths.

**submit** (submits, submitting, submitted) *verb* 1 to give way. *They had to submit to defeat.* 2 to put forward for consideration. *She submitted her plans to the committee.* **submission** *noun.*

**subscribe** *verb* 1 to pay regularly for something. *He subscribes to several magazines.* 2 to agree. *I don't subscribe to that theory.* **subscriber** *noun.* **subscription** *noun. Please pay your subscription.*

**subside** *verb* 1 to sink lower. *The floods finally subsided.* 2 to become less strong. *Her fear subsided.* **subsidence** *noun.*

**substance** *noun* 1 matter. *Chemical substances.* 2 the main part. *The panel agreed with the substance of the report, but queried some details.*

**substitute** *noun* a person or thing that takes the place of another. *They put on a substitute in the second half and he scored a goal.* **substitute** *verb* to use in place of another. **substitution** *noun.*

**subtle** (say **sut**-ul) *adjective* 1 small and hard to grasp. *A subtle difference between the two.* 2 delicate. *A very subtle taste.* 3 clever. *A subtle argument.* **subtlety** *noun.*

**subtract** *verb* to take away, deduct. *Subtract 5 from 8.* **subtraction** *noun.*

**suburb** *noun* a housing district at the edge of a town. **suburban** *adjective.* **suburbia** *noun* the suburbs. *They live in suburbia.*

**subway** *noun* an underground passage.

**AMAZING FACT**

The first submarine was probably one made of wood and leather in England in 1620. But the first successful submarine was built in 1770. Both of these early attempts were operated by hand.

**SPELLING NOTE**

*'Suède' is French for Sweden. Gloves made from soft Swedish leather were very popular in France. When the English took them up in the 19th century, they abbreviated 'gants de Suède' ('Swedish gloves') into 'suede'.*

**succeed** *verb* 1 to do well. *The plan was good and succeeded.* 2 to come next. *Who will succeed the present chancellor?*

**success** *noun* 1 doing well, achieving an aim. 2 somebody or something that does well. *The play is a real success in the West End.* **successful** *adjective.*

**succession** *noun* 1 a series of people or things. *They met with a succession of defeats.* 2 following in order. 3 coming next, especially to the throne. **in succession** one after another.

**succulent** *adjective* 1 juicy. *A succulent steak.* 2 fleshy. *Succulent plants.*

**such** *adjective* 1 of this kind. *Such people are to be avoided.* 2 so great. *I had such a fright!* **such-and-such** particular but not specified. *He promises to come at such-and-such a time but is always late.* **such as** of the same kind as. *Big cats such as tigers and lions.* **suchlike** of such a kind. *Ghosts and ghouls and suchlike.*

**suck** *verb* 1 to take liquid into the mouth by using your lip and tongue muscles. *She sucked the juice from an orange.* 2 to squeeze something in your mouth. *He still sucks his thumb.* 3 to pull. *The boat was sucked into the whirlpool.* **suck up to** to flatter somebody to gain their favour. *He's always sucking up to the teachers.*

**sucker** *noun* 1 something that sticks to a surface by suction. 2 a person who is easily deceived. *He thinks I am a sucker.*

**Sucre** *noun* the legal capital of Bolivia.

**Sudan** *noun* a country in Africa.

Sudan has the biggest sugar factory in Africa, and the third largest in the world.

**Sudanese** *noun* the people of Sudan. **Sudanese** *adjective. His second wife is Sudanese.*

**sudden** *adjective* happening unexpectedly or without warning. *A sudden storm broke and lightning flashed.* **all of a sudden** suddenly. **suddenly** *adverb.*

**suds** *plural noun* froth on soapy water.

**sue** (sues, suing, sued) *verb* (say soo) to take legal action against somebody. *He sued his employer for damages.*

**suede** *noun* (say swade) soft leather with a velvety surface. *Blue suede shoes.*

**suffer** *verb* 1 to feel or experience something bad. *Before the operation he was suffering badly.* 2 to put up with. *He does not suffer fools gladly.* **sufferer** *noun.* **suffering** *noun.*

**sufficient** *adjective* enough. **sufficiently** *adverb*. **sufficiency** *noun*.

**suffix** *noun* letters added to the end of a word to make another word. In the word 'forgetful', 'ful' is a suffix.

**suffocate** *verb* 1 to make it difficult or impossible for somebody to breathe. *The fumes almost suffocated her.* 2 to suffer or die because you can't breathe. **suffocation** *noun*. *Auntie died of suffocation.*

**sugar** *noun* a sweet food obtained from the juices of various plants, especially sugar cane and sugar beet. **sugar** *verb* to sweeten, especially with sugar. **sugary** *adjective*.

Sugar can come from either sugarcane or sugarbeet. This is a field of sugarbeet.

**suggest** *verb* 1 to put forward as a possibility. *She suggested a different plan.* 2 to bring into the mind. *The colour white suggests peace.*

**suggestion** *noun* 1 a plan or idea. 2 an act of suggesting. 3 a small amount. *A slight suggestion of an accent.* 4 putting beliefs into somebody's mind.

**suicide** *noun* 1 killing yourself deliberately. *He committed suicide.* 2 somebody who commits suicide. **suicidal** *adjective*.

**suit** *noun* 1 matching jacket and trousers for men, or jacket and skirt for women. 2 special clothes, such as a spacesuit or swimsuit. 3 one of the four sets of cards in a pack (hearts, clubs, diamonds or spades). 4 a lawsuit.

**suit** *verb* 1 to go well with, or look good on. *That jacket suits you.* 2 to be suitable or convenient. *Friday doesn't suit me at all.* 3 to adapt. *He suited his style to the audience.* **suit yourself** to do as you want to.

**suitable** *adjective* right for the purpose, appropriate. *Make sure you wear suitable clothes.* **suitability** *noun*.

**suitcase** *noun* a case used to hold clothes and other things when travelling. *I packed my suitcase and drove to the airport.*

**sulk** *verb* to be in a bad mood and show this by being silent. *She hated the party and sulked all evening.* **sulk** *noun*. **sulky** *adjective*. *A sulky pout.*

**sullen** *adjective* 1 silent and bad-tempered. *She gave me sullen looks.* 2 dark and gloomy. *A sullen sky.* **sullenness** *noun*.

**GRAMMAR NOTE**

*If you add a word or part of a word (called a suffix) to the end of a root word, you can form a new word.*

**DID YOU KNOW?**

*The expression 'to suffer fools gladly' comes from the Bible: 'For ye suffer fools gladly, seeing ye yourselves are wise.' (2 Corinthians 11:19).*

**AMAZING FACT**

Although the Sun appears to be small when we look at it from the Earth, it is actually a million times bigger than the Earth.

**sultan** *noun* a Muslim ruler.

**sultana** *noun* 1 a seedless raisin. 2 the mother, wife or daughter of a sultan.

**sum** *noun* 1 a total. The sum of 4 and 3 is 7. 2 a problem in arithmetic. 3 an amount of money. **sum** *verb* to find a total. **sum up** 1 to summarize, especially at the end of a talk. *The judge summed up at the end of the hearing.* 2 to form a judgement. *He summed her up very quickly.*

**summarize** *verb* to make a summary of. *He summarized the agreement in a few words.* **summarizer** *noun*.

**summary** *noun* a short account giving the main points. *A quick summary of events.*

**summary** *adjective* 1 brief. 2 without delay or mercy. *Summary justice.*

**summer** *noun* the warm season between spring and autumn. **summery** *adjective*.

**summit** *noun* 1 the top of a mountain. 2 the highest point. *He was at the summit of his career.* 3 a meeting between heads of government. *The prime minister attended a summit meeting.*

**summon** *verb* 1 to call to appear. *He was summoned to court as a witness.* 2 to call upon. *She summoned him to help her.* **summon up** to build up, gather. *He summoned up all his energy.* **summons** *noun* an official order to appear in a law court.

**Sun** *noun* 1 the star which the Earth travels around and from which it receives light and warmth. *It's dangerous to look directly at the Sun.* 2 light and warmth from the Sun. She loves sitting in the sun. **sun** (suns, sunning, sunned) *verb* to be in the Sun. *The cat was sunning itself on the terrace.*

The surface of the Sun is a phenomenal 6,000 degrees Centigrade and would melt absolutely anything.

**sunburn** *noun* reddening of the skin caused by too much sun. **sunburn** *verb* to suffer from sunburn. *She was badly sunburnt.*

**Sunday** *noun* the first day of the week, after Saturday and before Monday.

**sundial** *noun* an instrument that shows the time by a shadow on a dial.

**sunflower** *noun* a very tall plant with a large round flower.

**sung** *verb* past tense of sing.

**sunglasses** *plural noun* dark glasses that protect the eyes from strong sunlight.

**sunk** *verb* past tense of sink.

**sunlight** *noun* light from the Sun.

**sunny** (sunnier, sunniest) *adjective* 1 bright with sunlight. *A sunny room.* 2 cheerful. *She gave me a sunny smile.*

**sunrise** *noun* the rising of the Sun at dawn.

We danced all night and breakfasted at sunrise.

**sunset** *noun* the setting of the sun.

**sunshine** *noun* light from the Sun. *We sat in the sunshine and did our knitting.*

**suntan** *noun* browning of the skin from exposure to the sun. **suntan** *verb.*

**super** *adjective* exceptional, brilliant.

**super-** *prefix* 1 above or beyond. *Superstructure.* 2 extra large or good. *Supertankers are the biggest ships.*

**superb** *adjective* excellent. *A superb wine.*

**superficial** *adjective* not very deep. *A superficial wound.* **superficiality** *noun.*

**superfluous** *adjective* more than enough.

**superintend** *verb* to supervise and inspect. **superintendent** *noun.*

**superior** *adjective* 1 in a higher position. *A superior officer.* 2 better than average. *Superior quality.* **superior** *noun. She is my superior.* **superiority** *noun.*

**superlative** *adjective* 1 of the highest quality. 2 in grammar, the highest degree of an adjective. Bravest is the superlative form of brave. **superlative** *noun.*

**supermarket** *noun* a large self-service store that sells food and other goods. *We buy all our groceries from the supermarket.*

Penny looked at the sundial and saw that it was already half past two.

**GRAMMAR NOTE**

*The superlatives of short words add '–est' on to the end: 'oldest', 'youngest', 'tallest'. Longer words use 'most' in front: 'most beautiful', 'most cowardly'. Don't use '–est' and 'most' with the same word.*

The bridge was supported by a metal framework on concrete pillars.

**AMAZING FACT**

Superstitions vary from culture to culture. In the US, black cats are considered bad luck, but in the UK, good luck cards often have a black cat on them! Black cats crossing your path are supposed to be bad luck in both places.

**supernatural** *adjective* magical or mystical. *He thought there were supernatural forces at work.* **supernatural** *noun.*

**supersede** (say soup-uh-**seed**) *verb* to take the place of somebody or something.

**supersonic** *adjective* faster than the speed of sound. *Concorde is a supersonic aircraft.*

**superstition** *noun* a personal belief in the special effects of something. Most superstitions are not based on scientific fact. **superstitious** *adjective. He is very superstitious and won't walk under ladders.*

**supervise** *verb* to oversee actions or work. *The foreman's job is to supervise the workers.* **supervision** *noun.* **supervisor** *noun.* **supervisory** *adjective.*

**supper** *noun* an evening meal, especially a light one. *A supper of crackers and cheese.*

**supple** *adjective* easily bent, flexible. *Athletes have to be supple.* **suppleness** *noun.*

**supplement** *noun* 1 an added part. *She takes vitamin supplements to add to her diet.* 2 a separate section, especially a colour magazine. *The Sunday supplement.* 3 an extra charge. **supplementary** *adjective.*

**supply** *verb* to provide something that is needed. **supply** (supplies) *noun* 1 providing what is needed. 2 a stock. *A large supply of tyres.* 3 (plural supplies) provisions and equipment. *The explorers took enough supplies for three months.* **in short supply** scarce. **supplier** *noun.*

**supply teacher** *noun* a teacher who acts as a substitute for another teacher for a time.

**support** *verb* 1 to carry the weight of something. *This wall supports the whole house.* 2 to provide with things needed. *He has a family to support.* 3 show the truth of something. *The evidence supports her statement.* 4 to speak in favour. *Most speakers supported the resolution.* 5 to be a fan of. *She supports Manchester United.* **support** *noun.* **supporter** *noun.*

**suppose** *verb* to assume or think. *I suppose they'll come back.* **be supposed to** to be expected or required to do something. *You were supposed to be there by nine.*

**suppress** *verb* 1 to prevent from being seen or known. *She tried to suppress a yawn.* 2 to put out of your mind. *She tried to suppress her fear.* **suppression** *noun.*

**supreme** *adjective* highest in rank, most important. *The case went to the supreme court.* **supremacy** *noun.*

**surcharge** *noun* an extra charge. **surcharge** *verb. The travel company added a surcharge to my holiday bill.*

**sure** *adjective* 1 convinced. *I'm sure he's telling the truth.* 2 certain. *She is sure to go.* 3 reliable, definite. *A sure way to find out.* **sure** *adverb* certainly. **for sure** without doubt. **sure enough** certainly. **be sure** not fail to do something. *Be sure to lock up before you leave.*

**surely** *adverb* 1 certainly. *Slowly but surely.* 2 according to reason. *Surely that can't be right?* 3 safely. *The goat picked its way surely up the cliff.*

**surf** *noun* foam made by the sea breaking near the shore. **surf** *verb* to ride the surf on a board. **surfing** *noun*. **surfer** *noun*.

Hal thought Bondi Beach in Australia the very best place to surf.

**surface** *noun* 1 the outside of a solid body. *We have to dust every surface.* 2 the top of a liquid or of the ground. *The diver swam to the surface.* 3 outward appearance. *On the surface everything was quiet.* **surface** *verb* 1 to make a surface. *They surfaced the road.* 2 to rise to the surface. *The submarine surfaced slowly.* 3 to come to light. *The missing papers have suddenly surfaced.*

**surgeon** *noun* a doctor who performs medical operations.

**surgery** *noun* 1 medical treatment involving an operation. 2 the place where a doctor or dentist treats patients. 3 the time when a doctor or dentist treat patients. 4 the place where a politician or lawyer gives advice. *My MP holds a surgery every Thursday.*

**surgical** *adjective* relating to medical surgery. *Surgical instruments.*

**Suriname** *noun* a country in South America.

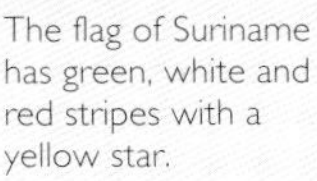

The flag of Suriname has green, white and red stripes with a yellow star.

**surly** *adjective* bad-tempered and unfriendly. *He had a surly look about him.*

**WORD HISTORY**

*The word 'surly' has changed its meaning over the years. It originally meant 'sir-like', in the sense of lordly or masterful, and was spelt 'sirly'. This changed to meaning haughty (misusing a lordly position perhaps), then fell to the present meaning of bad-tempered and unfriendly.*

**surname** *noun* a family name. *Jones is a surname.*

**surplus** *noun* an extra amount left over when requirements have been met. **surplus** *adjective*. *These items are surplus to government requirements.*

**surprise** *noun* an unexpected event. *Promotion came as a surprise to her.* **surprise** *verb* 1 to catch by surprise. 2 to shock. *I'm surprised at you!* 3 to take by surprise. *He surprised her taking a chocolate bar.* **surprising** *adjective*. **surprisingly** *adverb*.

**surrender** *verb* 1 to give up. *The army surrendered after the heavy defeat.* 2 to hand over. *They surrendered control of affairs.* **surrender** *noun*.

**surround** *verb* to be all around or enclose. *Trees surround the house.* **surround** *noun* an area or border surrounding something.

**surroundings** *plural noun* things around somebody or something. *She quickly got used to her new surroundings.*

**survey** *verb* (say ser-**vay**) 1 to take a general look. *He surveyed the situation.* 2 to examine the condition of something. *They had the house surveyed.* **survey** *noun* (say **ser**-vay) 1 a general view. *The book gave a historical survey.* 2 an examination of property. 3 a report or plan of an examination of property. **surveyor** *noun*.

**survive** *verb* 1 to continue to live or exist. *They were lucky to survive the earthquake.* 2 to live longer than someone. *He was survived by his wife and two children.* **survival** *noun*. **survivor** *noun*.

**suspect** *verb* (say suh-**spekt**) 1 to be inclined to believe. *The police suspect murder.* 2 to doubt somebody's innocence. *They suspect him of drug-dealing.* **suspect** *noun* (say **suh**-spekt) a suspected person. **suspect** *adjective* (say **suh**-spekt) not to be trusted.

**suspend** *verb* 1 to hang up. 2 to put off. *The match was suspended due to bad weather.* 3 to keep away from school. *They were suspended for bad behaviour.*

**suspense** *noun* anxious or exciting uncertainty. *The film was full of suspense.* **keep in suspense** to make somebody wait for important information. *Don't keep me in suspense – have I passed?*

The suspense was incredible as Tracey leaped from one trapeze to the other.

**suspension** *noun* 1 the act of suspending or being suspended. 2 springs and other devices that support a vehicle on its axles and give a comfortable ride.

**suspension bridge** *noun* a bridge with a roadway suspended from cables.

**suspicion** *noun* 1 feeling inclined to believe or doubt something. *His suspicions were confirmed when she was arrested.* 2 a slight trace. *A suspicion of anger in his voice.* **above suspicion** too good to be suspected. **under suspicion** suspected. **suspicious** *adjective*. *Suspicious circumstances.*

S

**Suva** *noun* the capital of Fiji.

**swagger** *verb* to walk or behave in an arrogant way. *The dictator swaggered into the room.* **swagger** *noun.*

**swallow** *verb* 1 to cause to pass down the throat. *Chew your food well before you swallow it.* 2 to accept something too easily. *I made up an excuse and he swallowed it.* 3 to overcome. *He swallowed his pride and apologized.* **swallow** *noun.*

**swallow** *noun* an insect-eating bird with a forked tail. *Swallows on the telegraph wires.*

The swallow flew swiftly through the air.

**swam** *verb* past tense of swim.

**swamp** *noun* waterlogged land, a bog or marsh. **swamp** *verb* to overwhelm, flood. *The radio station was swamped with letters of complaint.* **swampy** *adjective.*

**swan** *noun* a large, white waterbird with a long neck. *Black swans are unusual.*

**swan** *verb* to move aimlessly. *They swanned about the town all day.*

**swap** *verb* to exchange one thing for another. *He swapped his football for a cricket bat.* **swap** *noun.*

**swat** (swats, swatting, swatted) *verb* to hit with a sharp blow. *He swatted the fly with a newspaper, but missed.*

**sway** *verb* 1 to lean in one direction and then another. *The drunk swayed up the road.* 2 to be uncertain. 3 to control or rule over. *He swayed the crowd with his speech.* **sway** *noun* 1 a swaying motion. 2 influence or rule. *Common sense held sway.*

**Swaziland** *noun* a country in Africa.

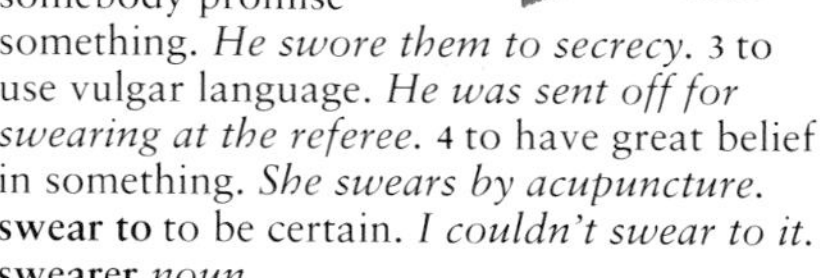

The flag of Swaziland has spears and shields against a striped blue, yellow and red background.

**swear** (swears, swore, sworn) *verb* 1 to promise something faithfully. *He swore that he would never return.* 2 to make somebody promise something. *He swore them to secrecy.* 3 to use vulgar language. *He was sent off for swearing at the referee.* 4 to have great belief in something. *She swears by acupuncture.* **swear to** to be certain. *I couldn't swear to it.* **swearer** *noun.*

**sweat** *noun* 1 moisture that is given off by the body through the skin. 2 hard effort. *Moving all that furniture was a real sweat.* **sweat** *verb* to give off sweat, to perspire. **sweat it out** put up with a difficulty to the end. **sweaty** (sweatier, sweatiest) *adjective.*

**AMAZING FACT**

European swallows migrate all the way from their nesting grounds in England, across Europe to the Mediterranean and then to Southern Africa.

**AMAZING FACT**

Swans are one of the heaviest flying birds in the world. An adult swan might weigh as much as 35 pounds. To take off, a swan runs as fast as it can across the surface of a lake and beats its wings.

**sweater** *noun* a jersey or pullover.

**swede** *noun* a yellow kind of turnip.

**Sweden** *noun* a Scandinavian country in Europe.

**Swedish** *noun* 1 the language spoken in Sweden. 2 the people of Sweden. **Swedish** *adjective. The Swedish national anthem.*

**sweep** (sweeps, sweeping, swept) *verb* 1 to clean dust or dirt with a brush. *He swept the floor.* 2 to remove quickly. *The floods swept away the bridge.* 3 to go quickly. *She swept out of the room.* 4 to cover quickly. *The trend swept the country.* **sweep** *noun* 1 an act of sweeping. 2 a chimney sweep. 3 a sweepstake, a kind of lottery. **sweeper** *noun.*

**sweeping** *adjective* wide-ranging. *They made sweeping changes to the rules.*

**sweet** *adjective* 1 tasting sugary, not bitter. 2 very pleasant. *Sweet memories.* 3 charming. *A sweet little girl.* **sweet** *noun* 1 a small piece of sweet food, made with sugar or chocolate. 2 a pudding, dessert. **sweetness** *noun.* **sweeten** *verb.*

Tom has a sweet tooth and enjoys cakes, milkshakes and fruit.

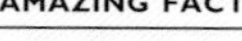

**sweet pea** *noun* a climbing plant with sweet-smelling flowers.

**swell** (swells, swelled, swollen) *verb* to grow larger, to expand. *He swelled with pride.* **swell** *noun* 1 the process of swelling. 2 the rise and fall of the sea's surface.

**swelling** *noun* a part of the body that has swollen. *There was a swelling on his neck.*

**sweltering** *adjective* uncomfortably hot.

**swept** *verb* past tense of sweep.

**swerve** *verb* to change direction suddenly. **swerve** *noun. She swerved to avoid the car.*

**swift** *adjective* quick. *A swift response.* **swiftly** *adverb.* **swiftness** *noun.*

**swift** *noun* a small bird with long wings, similar to a swallow.

**swill** *verb* to pour water over. *She swilled out the dirty basin.* **swill** *noun* 1 swilling. *Give it a good swill.* 2 sloppy food for pigs.

**swim** (swims, swimming, swam, swum) *verb* 1 to move through the water. 2 to cover by swimming. *We swam two lengths of the pool.* 3 to float on the surface. 4 to feel dizzy. *My head was swimming.* **swim** *noun. We went for a quick swim.* **swimmer** *noun.* **swimming pool** *noun* an indoor or outdoor pool for swimming.

**swindle** *verb* to cheat a person. *He swindled her out of her savings.* **swindle** *noun.* **swindler** *noun. A notorious swindler.*

S

**swing** (swings, swinging, swung) *verb* 1 to move to and fro or in a curve. *The door swung open.* 2 to change from one opinion or mood to another. *Popular opinion is swinging away from the government.* **swing** *noun* 1 a swinging movement. 2 a seat hanging from ropes or chains, for swinging on. 3 the amount by which opinions change from one side to another. *A big swing against the Tories.* 4 a kind of jazz music. **in full swing** fully active. *A party in full swing.*

**swirl** (say swurl) *verb* to move round quickly in circles. **swirl** *noun.* **swirly** *adjective. Swirly patterns on her dress.*

**Swiss** *noun* the people of Switzerland. **Swiss** *adjective. A Swiss watch.*

**switch** *noun* 1 a device for turning something on and off. 2 a change. **switch** *verb* 1 to turn on or off. *Don't forget to switch off the lights.* 2 to change. *They switched seats.*

**Switzerland** *noun* a country in southern Europe.

**swivel** (swivels, swivelling, swivelled) *verb* to turn round. *I swivelled in amazement.*

**swoop** *verb* to come down with a rush. *The eagle swooped on its prey.* **swoop** *noun.*

**sword** *noun* (say sord) a weapon with a long metal blade and a handle.

**swordfish** *noun* a large seafish with a long upper jaw that looks like a sword.

A swordfish has a razor-sharp upper jaw that looks like a sword.

**swum** *verb* past tense of swim.

**swung** *verb* past tense of swing.

**syllable** *noun* a part of a word with one sound. 'Dog' has one syllable, 'tiger' and 'giraffe' have two syllables, and 'gorilla' has three syllables.

**syllabus** *noun* the programme or outline of a course of study. *The chemistry syllabus.*

**symbol** *noun* a mark or sign used to represent something. *The dove is a universal symbol of peace.* **symbolic** *adjective.* **symbolically** *adverb.*

**symbolize** *verb* to be a symbol.

**symmetrical** *adjective* able to be divided into two halves that are exactly the same. A butterfly shape is symmetrical. **symmetry** *noun. Beautiful symmetry.*

**sympathy** *noun* 1 the understanding and sharing of another person's feelings or opinions. *My sympathies are with the miners.* 2 feeling pity and sadness for somebody. **sympathetic** *adjective.*

**DID YOU KNOW?**

*There is no language called Swiss. In fact, Switzerland has four official languages, German, French, Italian and Romansch.*

**WORD HISTORY**

*The word 'syntax' comes from the Greek 'suntaxis', meaning 'arranging together'. The way we arrange words together grammatically is called syntax.*

**symphony** *noun* a long piece of music for an orchestra, usually in three or four parts (called movements). **symphonic** *adjective.*

**symptom** *noun* 1 a sign that an illness exists. *He has all the symptoms of pneumonia.* 2 a sign of something. *These are symptoms of social unrest.* **symptomatic** *adjective. Headaches may be symptomatic of many different illnesses.*

**synagogue** (say sin-uh-gog) *noun* the building where Jewish people worship.

Every Friday night they went to the synagogue to pray.

**synonym** (say sin-uh-nim) *noun* a word that means the same or nearly the same as another. 'Small' and 'little' are synonyms. **synonymous** (say sin-**on**-im-us) *adjective.* 'Shut' is synonymous with 'close'.

**syntax** (say **sin**-tax) *noun* in grammar, the way words are arranged to form sentences.

**synthesizer** *noun* an electronic musical instrument with a keyboard that can make a wide range of different sounds.

**synthetic** *adjective* artificially made, not natural. *Nylon is a synthetic material.*

**Syria** *noun* a country in Southwest Asia.

**Syrian** *noun* the people of Syria. **Syrian** *adjective. Her husband is Syrian.*

**syringe** *noun* a device for injecting liquids into the body, also called a hypodermic needle. **syringe** *verb. I had my ears syringed.*

The syringe was filled with plasma.

**syrup** *noun* a thick sweet liquid. *Valerie loved syrup sandwiches when she was a child.* **syrupy** *adjective. A syrupy drink contains lots of sugar.*

**system** *noun* 1 a group of connected parts that work together as a whole. *A new computer system was set up in the office.* 2 an organized set of methods. *A good system of government.* **get something out of your system** get rid of something. **systematic** *adjective. He took a systematic approach to the problem.*

T

# Tt

**tab** *noun* a small piece of paper or metal attached to something that you can hold or pull. *Pull the tab to open the carton.*

**table** *noun* 1 a piece of furniture with a flat top supported by one or more legs. 2 a list of facts or figures, especially arranged in columns. **multiplication tables** a list of numbers multiplied. **tablecloth** a cloth for covering a table. **tablespoon** a large spoon used for serving food. **tablespoonful** the amount that a tablespoon can hold.

**tablet** *noun* 1 a small, usually round, solid piece of medicine that you swallow, a pill. 2 a small flat piece of soap.

**table tennis** *noun* a game for two or four people who use small bats to hit a small ball over a net on a large table.

**tabloid** *noun* a small-sized newspaper with lots of photographs and short news stories.

**taboo** *noun* something that is forbidden or generally disapproved of by custom or tradition. *Cannibalism is a taboo among most people.* **taboo** *adjective.*

**tack** *noun* 1 a short, sharp nail with a large flat head. 2 the saddle, reins, bridle etc. needed to ride a horse, saddlery.

**tack** *verb* 1 to use tacks or small nails to fasten something. 2 to sew something roughly with long stitches before sewing it neatly. 3 to sail into the wind on a sideways or zigzag course.

Sophie kept the tack clean and tidy in the tack room at the stables.

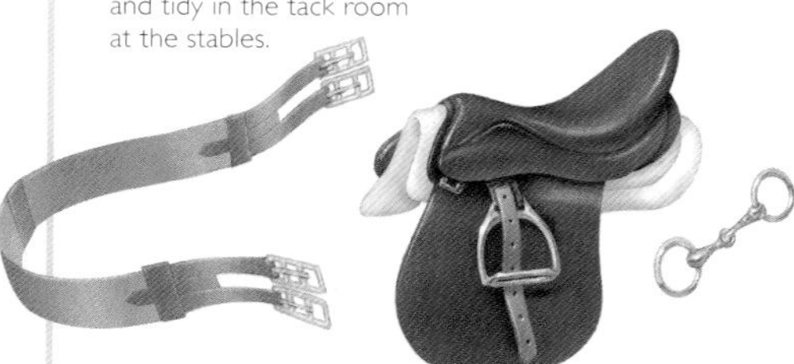

**tackle** *verb* 1 to try to deal with a problem or difficulty. 2 to try to get a ball from another player or bring a player to the ground in games such as football and rugby. **tackle** *noun. He made a brilliant tackle.*

**tackle** *noun* all the things you need for doing something. *Fishing tackle.*

**tacky** *adjective* 1 sticky. *The paint is still tacky.* 2 (slang) vulgar, in bad taste.

**DID YOU KNOW?**

*The shape of the letter 'T' comes from an ancient Egyptian symbol for ticking things off on a list. It looked like an 'X'. Its sound comes from 'taw', a Semitic word for a mark. The Greeks moved the crossbar to the top and called the letter 'tau'.*

Tajikistan used to be part of the Soviet Union, but gained independence in 1991.

**WORD HISTORY**

*'Tabloid' was originally the trademark of a medicine produced in tablet form. The word was then applied to anything produced in a concentrated form, and soon to newspapers that report in a condensed and lively style.*

**tact** *noun* skill in not upsetting people, especially when a situation is difficult. **tactful** *adjective.* **tactless** *adjective.*

**tactics** *plural noun* the way of organizing or planning things to the best advantage so as to win a game, battle etc. or to achieve what you want. **tactical** *adjective.*

**tadpole** *noun* a tiny black creature with a long tail that lives in water and that will grow into a frog, toad or newt.

**tag** *noun* 1 a small paper, cloth or plastic label. *I sewed a name tag on to his pyjamas.* 2 a children's chasing game.

**tail** *noun* 1 the long part that sticks out of the back of an animal, bird or fish. 2 a part that sticks out at the back of something. *The tail of an aircraft.* 3 **tails** the side of the coin that does not have a head (heads and tails). **tail** *verb* to follow closely.

**tailback** *noun* a long queue of traffic.

**tailor** *noun* a person whose business is to make clothes, especially men's suits.

**Taipei** *noun* the capital of Taiwan.

**Taiwan** *noun* a country in East Asia.

**Tajikistan** *noun* a country in central Asia.

**take** (takes, taking, took, taken) *verb* 1 to reach out for something and to hold or grasp it. 2 to move or lead to another place. *He took the dishes to the sink.* 3 to remove. *Who has taken my ruler?* 4 to perform an action, to do. *I'm going to take a bath.* 5 to photograph. *She took my picture.* 6 to swallow. *Take three tablets a day.* 7 to accept. *Take my advice.* 8 to need or require. *It takes half an hour to get to the airport.* 9 to travel by. *Take the bus.* 10 seize or capture. *The troops took the town.* 11 to choose. *Take which one you like.* **take after** to look or behave like. *He takes after his father.* **take away** 1 to subtract. 2 to remove. **take down** 1 to remove something that is hanging. *They took down the decorations.* 2 to write down. *He took down some notes.* **take in** 1 to deceive. *She took me in with her sad story.* 2 to understand. *I didn't take in all you said.* **take off** 1 to remove clothes. 2 (of an aircraft) to leave the ground. 3 to imitate somebody in an unkind way. **take on** 1 to start to employ somebody. 2 to challenge somebody. **take out** 1 to remove from a place. 2 to invite somebody somewhere. **take over** to take control of. **take place** to happen. *Our wedding took place under the stars.* **takeaway** *noun* a restaurant where you buy cooked food to eat somewhere else.

**talc** (talcum powder) *noun* a soft, scented powder that you sprinkle on your body after a bath.

**tale** *noun* 1 a story. *A fairy tale.* 2 an untrue or gossipy story, a lie.

**talent** *noun* great skill or natural ability to do something really well.

**talk** *verb* to speak, to use words to express feelings ideas etc., to discuss. **talk** *noun* 1 a conversation. 2 a short, informal lecture. **talk down** to to speak to somebody condescendingly as if to a child. **talking to** a telling-off or reprimand.

**talkative** *adjective* fond of talking a lot. *Are girls more talkative than boys?*

**tall** *adjective* high or of more than average height. *He's a tall man.* 2 having a certain height. Henry is 2 metres tall. **tall story** a story that is hard to believe.

**Tallinn** *noun* the capital of Estonia.

**talon** *noun* a hooked claw of a bird of prey.

**tambourine** *noun* a small drum with metal discs around the edge that you shake or tap with your fingers.

The gypsies danced around the camp fire banging and shaking their tambourines.

**tame** *adjective*. A tame animal or bird is not wild and is not afraid of human beings. **tame** *verb*.

**tamper** *verb* to interfere or meddle with something without permission. *She tampered with the lock and now it's broken.*

**tampon** *noun* a plug of soft material such as cotton wool. *A sanitary tampon.*

**tan** *noun* 1 light brown. 2 (suntan) light brown skin caused by its being exposed to the Sun. **tan** *verb*.

**tandem** *noun* a bicycle with two seats, one behind the other.

**tandoori** *noun* an Indian way of cooking food in a clay oven.

**tangerine** *noun* a fruit like a small orange with a loose skin.

**tangle** *verb* to make things such as wires or string into a twisted and confused muddle. **tangle** *noun*. *A tangle of wool.*

**tank** *noun* 1 a large container for storing a liquid or gas. 2 a heavy armoured military vehicle armed with guns.

**WORD HISTORY**

*The word 'tank' was coined during World War I as a secret code name for the newly invented armoured military vehicle. The name was kept when the vehicles eventually went into battle.*

**WORD HISTORY**

*Tangerines are named after the Moroccan port of Tangier, from where the fruit was originally imported to Europe.*

**tanker** *noun* a large ship or lorry used for carrying liquids such as oil.

**tantrum** *noun* a sudden attack of bad temper. *Brian threw a tantrum at school.*

**Tanzania** *noun* a country in Africa.

**Tanzanian** *noun* a person who comes from Tanzania. **Tanzanian** *adjective*. *Tanzanian lakes and mountains.*

**Taoiseach** *noun* ( Say tee-shak) the prime minister of the Republic of Ireland.

**tap** *noun* a device that you turn on or off to control the flow of a liquid or gas (US faucet). *Turn off the taps – the bath is overflowing!*

Jemima was very thirsty, but the tap had a notice on it saying that the water was not fit for drinking.

**tap** (taps, tapping, tapped) *verb* 1 to knock gently but repeatedly. *A twig tapped against the window.* 2 to fit a device so that you can take water, information etc. *Her phone was tapped because she was a spy.*

**tape** *noun* 1 a strip of cloth, paper, plastic etc. used to tie up parcels. *Sticky tape.* 2 a long strip of magnetic material on which sound and pictures can be recorded, usually in a plastic box or cassette.

**tape** *verb* to record sound on an audio tape or images on a video tape.

**tape measure** *noun* a metal or cloth strip marked in centimetres or inches for measuring. *Lend me your tape measure?*

**tape recorder** *noun* an instrument for recording sound on tape and for playing back sound. **tape-record** *verb*.

**taper** *verb* to become narrower towards the end. *Church spires taper.*

**tapestry** *noun* a heavy cloth with pictures or designs woven into it and which is hung on a wall. *She wove a beautiful tapestry.*

The tanks went into action and blocked the bridge.

T

**tapir** *noun* an animal with a long snout that looks a bit like a pig.

**tar** *noun* a thick, black sticky substance that is made from wood and coal. **tar** (tars, tarring, tarred) *verb. He tarred the roof to make it waterproof.*

**tarantula** *noun* a large, hairy poisonous spider. *There was a tarantula in the bath.*

**Tarawa** *noun* the capital of Kiribati.

**target** *noun* 1 a mark that you aim at and try to hit. *He shot an arrow at the target.* 2 aim or purpose that you are trying to achieve. *Production targets.*

**tariff** *noun* 1 a list of prices, especially for hotel rooms and meals. 2 a tax to be paid on exports and imports.

**tarmac** *noun* a mixture of tar and crushed stones, used to make road surfaces.

**tarragon** *noun* a plant whose leaves are used to flavour food.

**tart** *noun* a pastry case with no crust on top, usually with a sweet filling. *A jam tart.* **tart** *adjective* sharp or sour to taste.

**tartan** *noun* a Scottish woollen cloth with a pattern of different coloured squares.

**Tashkent** *noun* the capital of Uzbekistan.

**task** *noun* a job or piece of work that must be done, a duty. *An onerous task.*

**taste** *noun* 1 the sense by which you can tell the flavour of food and drink. 2 the particular flavour of food. Food can be sweet, sour, salty or bitter. 3 the ability to know what is beautiful or good. **tasteful** *adjective.* **taste** *verb.*

There are about 10,000 microscopic taste buds sunk in the surface of the tongue.

**tasteless** *adjective* 1 without flavour. 2 unattractive and showing poor taste. *Tasteless furniture.*

**tasty** *adjective* having a pleasant taste.

**tattoo** *noun* 1 a permanent coloured pattern on somebody's skin. 2 a military display of music, marching etc. usually held at night.

**taught** past tense of teach.

**taunt** *verb* to tease somebody and say hurtful things in order to make them angry. **taunt** *noun. She taunted him about the size of his nose, which really was enormous.*

**taut** *adjective* stretched or pulled tight so that it is firm. **tauten** *verb.*

**AMAZING FACT**

Tapirs live mainly in forests and eat vegetation such as leaves, buds and fruit. They are nocturnal creatures and most species are very shy.

**WORD HISTORY**

*Our word 'tea' comes from 'tíe', the word used in Amoy Chinese. The Dutch borrowed the word and renamed it 'thee'. It was then absorbed into other European languages e.g. 'tea' (English) and 'te' (Italian).*

**tautology** *noun* the use of a word that repeats the meaning of a word that has already been used. 'A four-sided square, 'free gifts' and 'a new innovation' are all examples of tautology.

**tavern** *noun* an old-fashioned word for an inn or public house.

**tawny** *noun* a light, brownish-yellow colour. **tawny** *adjective.*

**tax** (taxes) *noun* an amount of money that people and businesses have to pay to the government to help pay for public services. **tax** *verb. The government taxes our income far too much.* **taxation** *noun.*

**taxi** (taxis) *noun* a car with a driver that you can hire to take you on short journeys. *We took a taxi to the station.*

**taxi** (taxies, taxiing, taxied) *verb* of an aircraft, to travel along the runway before takeoff or after landing.

**Tbilisi** *noun* the capital of Georgia.

**tea** *noun* 1 a drink made by pouring hot water on the dried leaves of a tea plant. 2 a light meal eaten in the afternoon or a main meal eaten in the evening.

Tea bushes grow in China, India and Sri Lanka. The leaves are picked and dried before being exported.

**teach** (teaches, teaching, taught) *verb* 1 to tell somebody about a subject and to help them learn about it, to educate. 2 to show somebody how to do something. *Jane taught me how to skate.*

**teacher** *noun* a person who teaches, especially at a school.

The teacher pointed with her stick to a sum on the blackboard and asked if anyone knew the answer.

**team** *noun* a group of people who work together or who play on the same side in a game. *Our team won the match.*

**tear** *noun* (rhymes with near) one of the drops of salty liquid that comes from your eyes when you cry. **tearful** *adjective.*

T

**tear** (tears, tearing, tore, torn) *verb* (rhymes with fair) 1 to pull something apart, to rip. 2 to make a hole in something. *Tina tore her skirt on a nail.* 3 to pull something violently. *Vic tore the paper off the wall.* **tear** *noun.* 4 to move quickly. *The dog tore across the field and leaped over the fence.*

**tease** *verb* to annoy somebody by making fun of them for your own amusement.

**teaspoon** *noun* a small spoon. **teaspoonful** the amount that a teaspoon can hold.

**teat** *noun* 1 the nipple or soft pointed part on a female mammal through which her babies suck milk. 2 a piece of rubber or plastic on a feeding bottle through which a baby can suck milk etc.

**technical** *adjective* 1 concerned with science and machines and how they work. *Technical experts.* 2 concerned with a particular specialized subject. *Technical jargon is very boring.*

**technique** *noun* (say tek-**neek**) a special way of doing something skilfully.

**technology** *noun* the study of technical ideas and the practical use of science in industry. **technological** *adjective.*

**teddy-bear** (**teddy**) *noun* a soft toy bear.

**tedious** *adjective* boring because it is dull and long.

**teenager** *noun* a person between the ages of 13 and 19. **teenage** *adjective.*

**teeth** *plural* of tooth.

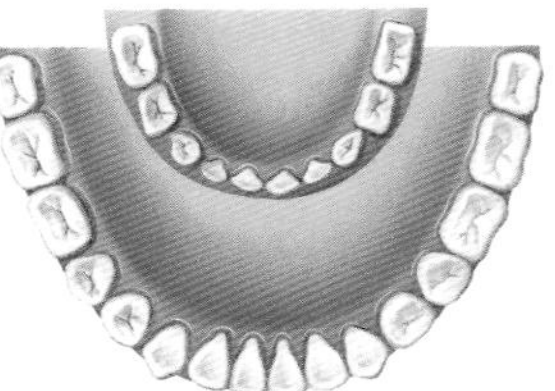

Each person has two natural sets of teeth during their life. The first 20 are called milk teeth, the second 32 are adult teeth.

**teetotaler** *noun* somebody who never drinks alcohol. **teetotal** *adjective. Many Muslims are teetotal.*

**Tegucigalpa** *noun* the capital of Honduras.

**Tehran** *noun* the capital of Iran.

**telecommunications** *plural noun* the technology of sending information over long distances by radio, telephone, television, etc.

**telephone** *noun* an instrument that uses electrical current travelling along wires, or radio waves, to allow you to speak to somebody over long distances. **telephone** or **phone** *verb. Please phone me tonight.*

AMAZING FACT

The first television set, made by John Baird, was made of old cans, bike parts, lenses and string.

Television signals are picked up by the receiver's TV aerial, demodulated and amplified to work the picture tube and loudspeaker of the TV set.

**DID YOU KNOW?**

*Teddy bear is named after 'Teddy' the pet name of Theodore Roosevelt, the US president (1858–1919), who was well known as a bear hunter.*

This is Pashupatinath temple near Kathmandu in Nepal. Hindu's are taken here to be cremated on the funeral pyres next to the Bagmati River.

AMAZING FACT

In 1876, Alexander Graham Bell spoke his first words over a telephone when he called out to his assistant to come and help him – he had spilled acid on his leg!

**telescope** *noun* a tube-shape instrument with lenses that you look through with one eye to make distant objects appear bigger and nearer.

**television** *noun* a box-shaped instrument that receives programmes that have been broadcast and shows them on a screen as moving pictures with sound.

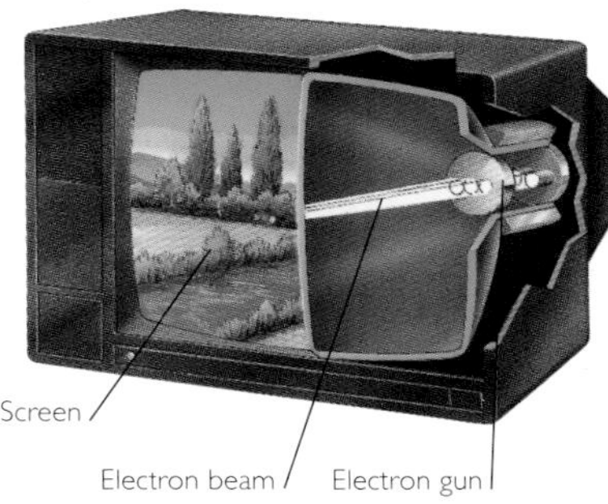


**telex** *noun* a system of sending written messages by means of teleprinters.

**tell** (tells, telling, told) *verb* 1 to pass on information etc. by speaking. 2 to know or recognize. *Can you tell what this is?* 3 to order. *Terry told us to be there on time.* **tell off** to scold. **telling-off** *noun.*

**telling** *adjective* meaningful and striking. *A telling argument.*

**temper** *noun* the mood you are in, how you feel. *Is she in a good temper?* **lose your temper** to become angry.

**temperament** *noun* your personality or the way you usually feel and behave. *She has a very calm temperament.*

**temperamental** *adjective* liable to sudden changes of mood, excitable.

**temperature** *noun* 1 a measure of how hot something is. *The temperature has dropped to below freezing.* 2 a fever. *Take your temperature with this thermometer.*

**tempest** *noun* a violent storm with strong winds. **tempestuous** *adjective. A tempestuous sea.*

**temple** *noun* 1 a building in which people of some religions worship. 2 the flat part on either side of your head between your ear and forehead.

**tempo** (tempi) *noun* the speed at which music is played.

**tempt** *verb* to try to persuade somebody to want to do something they would not normally do, to entice. *He tried to tempt me to cheat in the exam.* **temptation** *noun.*

**tempting** *adjective* attractive. *It's very tempting to skip classes and go swimming.*

**tenant** *noun* a person who rents from somebody the place he or she lives in.

**tend** *verb* to happen often or usually, to be inclined to. *It tends to be cold at night.* tendency *noun. A tendency to eat too much.*

**tend** *verb* to look after a person or animal.

**tender** *adjective* 1 sore to touch, painful. *The bruise feels very tender.* 2 easy to chew, not tough. *Tender meat.* 3 loving and gentle, kind. *A tender kiss.* 4 delicate. *Tender seedlings.* **tenderness** *noun.*

**tendon** *noun* a strong cord-like tissue joining muscles to bones.

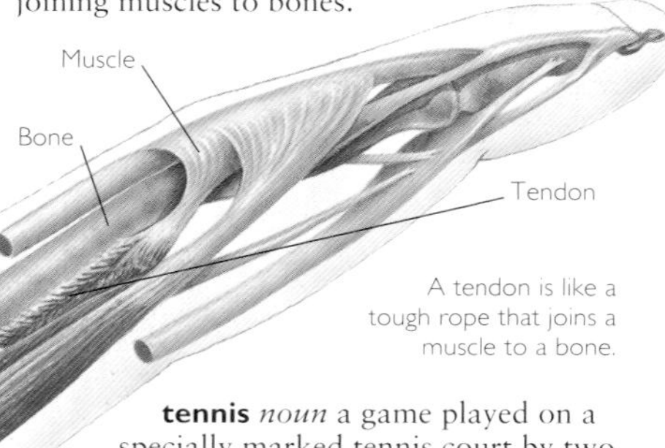


A tendon is like a tough rope that joins a muscle to a bone.

**tennis** *noun* a game played on a specially marked tennis court by two or four people using rackets to hit a ball to each other over a net.

**tenor** *adjective, noun* the highest normal singing voice for a man.

**tense** *adjective* 1 showing excitement, stress or nervousness. 2 stiff and tightly stretched, taut. **tension** *noun.* **tense** *verb. She tensed her muscles for the fight.*

**tense** *noun* a form of a verb that shows when something happens (present tense), happened (past tense) or will happen (future tense).

**tent** *noun* a shelter made from a waterproof material such as canvas or nylon stretched and supported over poles and held down by ropes.

**tentacle** *noun* one of the long, snake-like limbs of animals such as octopuses and squid.

A squid has eight tentacles.

**SPELLING NOTE**

*The plural of some English words of Latin origin can be variable. For example, the plural of 'terminus' is usually 'termini' (but it can be 'terminuses').*

**WORD HISTORY**

*'Tennis' comes from a French word 'tenez' meaning 'hold' or 'take', which a player called out to his opponent to attract their attention.*

**tepee** *noun* a cone-shaped tent made of animal skins or tree bark, first used by Native Americans.

**tepid** *adjective* only slightly warm.

**term** *noun* 1 a length of time. *The school term.* 2 a word or name for something. *ROM is a computer term.* **terms** plural *noun* agreed conditions. *Terms of employment.* **term** *verb* to name. **to be on good terms with somebody** to get on with or to like somebody.

**terminal** *noun* 1 a building where people begin or end a journey. *Planes for Australia depart from terminal four.* 2 a computer monitor linked to a network. **terminal** *adjective* (of an illness) incurable and liable to cause death.

**terminate** *verb* to stop, to come to an end.

**terminus** *noun* a station at the end of a railway line or bus route.

**terrace** *noun* 1 a row of houses joined together as a single block. 2 a level area cut out of sloping ground. 3 a paved area next to a building where people can sit.

**terrapin** *noun* a small turtle from North America. Terrapins live in fresh water.

A terrapin can sometimes be kept in an aquarium as a pet.

**terrestrial** *adjective* 1 relating to the Earth rather than to space. *Terrestrial television.* 2 living on land and not in the air or in water. *Terrestrial animals.*

**terrible** *adjective* 1 dreadful, causing fear or hardship. 2 bad. *A terrible film.*

**terrier** *noun* one of several breeds of small dogs. *A fox terrier yaps a lot.*

**terrific** *adjective.* 1 very good, wonderful. 2 very great, causing terror. *A terrific bang.*

**terrify** (terrifies, terrifying, terrified) *verb* to make somebody very frightened. *My dog is terrified of thunder.*

**territory** *noun* 1 an area of land, especially land controlled by the government of a country. 2 an area of land where an animal lives and which it will fight to defend.

**terror** *noun* great fear.

**terrorism** *noun* the use of violence and threats to obtain demands. **terrorist** *noun. Terrorists planted bombs along the route.*

**test** *verb* to try out something, to check to see if something works. *An eye test.* **test** *noun* 1 a set of questions or actions that a person has to answer or perform to find out how much they know or can do. **test tube** *noun* a thin glass container that is closed at one end, used in laboratories to do tests.

**tether** *verb* to tie an animal by a rope to a post so that it cannot move far or escape. **tether** *noun*. **at the end of your tether** to run out of patience.

**testicle** *noun* one of two small ball-like glands in a man's scrotum .

**text** *noun* the printed words in a book or newspaper. *The text was rather dull.*

**textbook** *noun* a book containing basic information about a particular subject.

**textile** *noun* woven cloth. **textile** *adjective*. *The textile industry.*

Tartan is a textile that is woven in Scotland.

**texture** *noun* the way something feels when you touch it, e.g. rough or smooth.

**Thai** *noun* a person who comes from Thailand. **Thai** *adjective*. *Thai silk.*

**Thailand** *noun* a country in Southeast Asia.

**thank** *verb* to tell somebody how pleased you are for something they have given you or done for you. **thanks** *noun* a word we use to say how pleased we are for what somebody has done for us.

**thankful** *adjective* feeling glad or grateful.

**Thanksgiving** *noun* a holiday celebrated in the United States on the fourth Thursday in November. Many people eat turkey on this day and give thanks for what they have.

**thatch** (thatches) *noun* layers of reeds or straw used in roofs.

Thatched houses need to be insured for lots of money because of the risk of fire.

**AMAZING FACT**

The earliest theatres were in Greece. The theatre at Delphi was so skillfully built that people at the back of the theatre could hear every spoken word.

**WORD HISTORY**

*'Thesaurus' was originally a Greek word meaning 'treasury' and has been used since the 19th century to describe a treasury of information and knowledge or a treasury of words.*

**thaw** *verb* to change from being frozen solid to a liquid through warming, to melt. *The ice on the pond is thawing.*

**theatre** *noun* 1 a building where you go to see plays performed. 2 a room in a hospital where surgeons perform operations. **theatrical** *adjective* connected with plays or acting. *A theatrical family.*

**theft** *noun* stealing.

**theme** *noun* 1 the principal subject. *The theme of the book is poverty.* 2 (in music) the main melody.

**theme park** *noun* a park with different activities and attractions all based on one particular subject or idea.

**theme song** *noun* a tune that is often repeated in a film or musical.

**theology** *noun* the study of God and religion. **theologian** *noun* a person who studies theology. **theological** *adjective*.

**theory** *noun* 1 an unproved idea put forward to explain something. 2 the rules and principles of a subject rather than the actual practice. *In theory it should work – in practice it doesn't seem to!*

**therapeutic** *adjective* being good for the health and the treatment of illnesses.

**therapy** *noun* a treatment for an illness without the use of surgery or drugs. **therapist** *noun*. *I need a therapist.*

**therm** *noun* a measurement of heat.

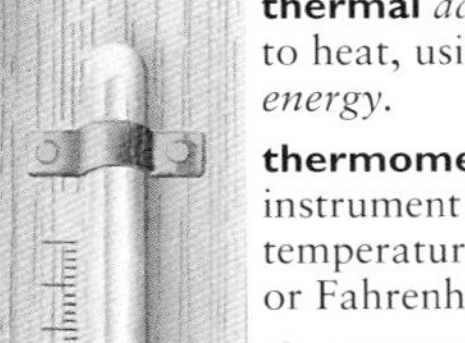

It is very useful to hang a thermometer in the greenhouse.

**thermal** *adjective* relating to heat, using heat. *Thermal energy.*

**thermometer** *noun* an instrument for measuring temperature in degrees Celsius or Fahrenheit.

**thermostat** *noun* a device that automatically switches off radiators, irons etc. when the temperature is hot enough.

**thesaurus** (thesauruses) *noun* a book that lists together words with similar meanings. In my thesaurus the words 'glow', 'gleam', 'glitter', 'sparkle' and 'flash' are listed under the headword 'shine'.

**thick** *adjective* 1 measuring a long way between two sides. Wide, not thin or slender. 2 measuring a certain amount between two sides. *The wood block is 5 cm thick.* 3 dense and closely packed. *Thick, blond hair.* 4 fatty and not flowing freely. *Thick cream.* 5 (slang) stupid. **thickness** *noun*. **thicken** *verb*. The opposite of thick is thin.

**thief** (thieves) *noun* a person who steals things. *The thief ran off with my money.*

**thigh** *noun* (rhymes with high) the top part of your leg above your knee.

**thimble** *noun* a small metal or plastic covering for the tip of your finger to prevent you pricking it when sewing.

**Thimphu** *noun* the capital of Bhutan.

**thin** (thinner, thinnest) *adjective* 1 measuring a short distance between two sides. Narrow, not thick. The opposite is thick. 2 having very little fat on your body, slender. The opposite is fat.

**thing** *noun* 1 an unnamed object that you see or touch. 2 **things** belongings. *Have you packed your things for our holiday?* **it's a good thing** it's lucky. *It's a good thing you arrived on time.*

**think** (thinks, thinking, thought) *verb* 1 to use your mind. 2 to believe, to have an opinion or idea. 3 to remember. 4 to plan or intend. *We're thinking of learning karate.* 5 to admire. *I think a lot of you.* **think up** to invent. **think twice about something** to consider very carefully whether to do something or not.

**third** *adjective* the next after the second. *You're the third person to ask me that.* **third** *noun* one of three equal parts that make up a whole. **third rate** *adjective* of poor quality. **third world** the poorer countries of the world that are slowly developing, many of them in Asia and Africa.

**thirst** *noun* 1 feeling the need to drink. 2 a strong wish for something. *a thirst for adventure.* **thirsty** *adjective.*

**thistle** *noun* a prickly wild plant with purple flowers.

**thorax** *noun* 1 the middle section of an insect's body, carrying the wings and legs. 2 the chest of a human.

**thorn** *noun* a sharp point on the stem of a plant such as a rose.

Thorax

Abdomen

Sting

All insects have a thorax and an abdomen.

**thorough** *adjective* (say thur-uh) 1 done well and carefully. *A thorough search.* 2 complete. *A thorough shambles.* **thoroughness** *noun. He was famed for his thoroughness.*

**AMAZING FACT**

Some people believe that we can communicate by thought alone. This is called 'telepathy'.

**DID YOU KNOW?**

*You can avoid ambiguity by the correct placing of a hyphen. Where would you put a hyphen in these sentences? 'There are 20 odd pupils in the class.' 'She has nine inch long feet'.*

**thoroughfare** *noun* a main road or street.

**thought** past tense of think. **thought** *noun* an idea, something that you think. *Have you any thoughts about what we should do?*

**thoughtful** *adjective* 1 thinking quietly and carefully. 2 considerate and thinking about others. *It was very thoughtful of you to buy me flowers.*

**thoughtless** *adjective* inconsiderate and not thinking about other people's feelings.

**thread** *noun* a long thin piece of twisted cotton, silk etc. used for sewing or weaving. **thread** *verb* to put thread through a hole (eye) of needle to sew.

She matched the thread with the colour of her dress.

**threadbare** *adjective* (of clothes) worn thin.

**threat** *noun* 1 a warning that something unpleasant may happen. 2 a possible cause of future harm, a danger. *A threat of drought hung over the country.*

**threaten** *verb* to warn that you may do something unpleasant or harm somebody. *Mat threatened to hit me.*

**three-dimensional** *adjective* having depth as well as height and width, solid.

**thresh** *verb* to beat grain from stalks of corn. *We threshed the grain at harvest.*

**threw** past tense of throw.

**thrifty** (thriftier, thriftiest) *adjective* not wasteful, careful about spending money etc. **thrift** *noun.*

**thrill** *noun* a feeling of great excitement and enjoyment. **thrill** *verb. She was thrilled to be chosen.*

They all screamed because the rollercoaster ride was such a thrill.

T

**thriller** *noun* a book, play or film with an exciting story about crime and detection.

**thrilling** *adjective* very exciting.

**thrive** *verb* to be healthy and successful. *A thriving business.*

**throat** *noun* the front part of your neck. The tube from inside your mouth that takes food and drink to your stomach and air to your lungs. *He has a sore throat.*

**throb** (throbs, throbbing, throbbed) *verb* to beat strongly and rapidly. *My heart throbbed with terror.*

**throne** *noun* a special seat for a king or queen. *The king sat on the throne.*

**through** *preposition, adverb* (say throo) 1 from one side to the other. *The train went through the tunnel.* 2 among or between. *We walked through the crowd.* 3 by means of, because of. *We bought it through the catalogue, but it's not very nice.*

**throughout** *preposition* 1 in all parts. *Throughout the world.* 2 from the beginning to the end, during. *Throughout the night.*

**throw** (throws, throwing, threw, thrown) *verb* to make something go through the air, to hurl or fling. Tracy threw the ball. **throw away** to get rid of something you do not want. **throw together** to put something together quickly. **throw up** (slang) to be sick, to vomit.

**thrush** *noun* a small brown bird with a speckled breast that sings beautifully.

The thrush cocked its head then pounced on a worm.

**thrust** *verb* to push suddenly and with force, to shove. *Doug thrust the clothes into the bag.* **thrust** *noun.*

**thud** *noun* a low, dull sound made, for example, by something heavy hitting the ground. **thud** *verb.*

**thumb** *noun* the short, thick finger at the side of your hand. **thumb a lift** to hitch-hike. **thumbs down** showing that you do not approve. **thumbs up** showing that you approve. *Our plan got the thumbs up.*

**thump** *noun* the dull heavy sound made by punching somebody.

**thunder** *noun* the rumbling noise you hear after a flash of lightning. **thunder** *verb* to make the dull, continuous noise of thunder.

The princess wore her most beautiful tiara to the ball.

**AMAZING FACT**

In the tropics thunderstorms may occur on as many as 200 days a year.

A tidal wave is sometimes called a tsunami. It can cause enormous damage and great loss of life.

**DID YOU KNOW?**

*The word 'tide' originally meant 'time'. The meaning of the modern word came about because of the rising and falling of the sea at regular times of the day.*

**thunderstorm** *noun* a storm with thunder, lightning and heavy rain.

**thunderstruck** *adjective* amazed.

**thwart** *verb* to hinder somebody doing what they planned. *He thwarted my plan.*

**thyme** *noun* a herb, a plant whose leaves are used for flavouring food.

**tiara** *noun* a small, jewelled crown worn by women. *A golden tiara.*

**tick** *noun* 1 a small mark (✓) used to show that something is correct or to mark in a list. 2 a small, regular sound. *The tick of a clock.* 3 a very short time. *I'll be back in a tick.* **tick** *verb. She ticked off the names on her list as the pupils entered the class.*

**ticket** *noun* a small printed piece of paper that shows that you have paid for something such as a train or bus fare or for a seat in a cinema or theatre etc. Traffic wardens give a ticket to a driver who has committed a parking offence.

**tickle** *verb* to touch somebody very lightly in a place that makes them laugh or giggle. *He tickled the baby's tummy.* **tickle** *noun.*

**ticklish** *adjective* easily tickled.

**tidal wave** *noun* an exceptionally huge wave caused by an earthquake.

**tide** *noun* the regular rising and falling movement of the sea as it comes into the land and goes away from the land. Tides are caused by the pull of the Moon and Sun on the Earth. **tidal** *adjective.*

**tidy** (tidier, tidiest) *adjective* 1 neat and with everything in its proper place. 2 (slang) quite big. *A tidy sum of money.* **tidy** *verb.* **tidiness** *noun. Tidiness is a great virtue.*

**tie** *noun* a narrow piece of cloth that is worn around the neck under a shirt collar and knotted at the throat.

**tie** (ties, tying, tied) *verb* 1 to fasten something with rope, string etc. *She tied her shoelaces.* 2 to score an equal number of points in a contest. *They tied for second place.* **tie** *noun. The score was a tie.*

**tier** (rhymes with near) *noun* two or more layers, two or more raised rows of seats etc. one above the other.

**tiger** *noun* a large wild cat from Asia that has an orange coat with black stripes.

The pattern of stripes on a tiger's skin is unique. No two tigers have quite the same pattern.

**tight** *adjective* 1 very closely fitting. *These jeans are too tight.* 2 firmly fixed so that it will not move. *The lid is so tight I can't open the jar.* 3 fully and firmly stretched. *Tight violin strings.* 4 having little room to spare. *A tight timetable is very hard to work to.*

**tightrope** *noun* a tightly stretched rope along which acrobats walk.

**tights** *plural noun* a piece of clothing made of very thin material that fits tightly over your feet, legs and hips and worn mainly by women. *Linda wears purple striped tights.*

**tile** *noun* a flat piece of hard material used for covering floors, roofs and walls. **tile** *verb. Dad tiled the bathroom.*

Tiles can be used to decorate many rooms in the house.

**till** *conjunction, preposition* until, up to a certain time. *Wait till I get home.*

**till** *noun* a box or container for money in a shop. *Sam stole money from the till.*

**till** *verb* to plough and cultivate land.

**tilt** *verb* to slope or lean so that one side is higher than the other.

**SPELLING NOTE**

*'Tinsel' comes from a French word, 'étinceller', which means sparkle.*

**SPELLING NOTE**

*Both 'till' and 'until' are interchangeable, meaning 'up to the time that' or 'as far as'. For example: 'I will stay until you get back.' And: 'Go straight ahead till you come to a roundabout.'*

**timber** *noun* wood ready for building or making furniture etc.

**time** *noun* 1 the passing of years, months, weeks, days, hours etc. 2 a particular moment. *What time does the train go?* 3 how long something takes or a period in which you do something. **time** *verb* to measure how long something takes. **from time to time** occasionally. **in time** in step with the music. **once upon a time** some time long ago. **on time** not late.

**times** *preposition* multiplied by. *Four times four are 16.*

**timetable** *noun* a list showing the times of classes at school or the times when trains, planes etc. depart and arrive.

**timid** *adjective* lacking courage and easily frightened, shy. **timidity** *noun.*

**tin** *noun* 1 a soft, silvery-white metal. usually mixed with other metals or forming a coat on other metals. 2 a tin-coated metal container for storing food etc., a can.

It's best to open a tin of paint by levering off the lid with a screwdriver.

**tinge** *noun* a slight colouring. *White paint with a tinge of blue.*

**tingle** *verb* to have a slight stinging or tickling feeling. **tingle** *noun.*

**tinker** *verb* to fiddle with or make small changes to something with the idea of repairing or improving it.

**tinkle** *noun* a ringing sound like a small bell. **tinkle** *verb.*

**tinsel** *noun* strips of glittering material used for decorations.

**tint** *noun* a light, delicate shade of a colour. **tinted** *adjective. Tinted glasses.*

**tiny** (tinier, tiniest) *adjective* very small. *A tiny insect fell into his beer.*

**tip** *noun* 1 the end of something long and thin. *The tip of your nose.* 2 a small gift of money you give, for example, to a waiter or taxi driver. 3 a place for dumping rubbish. 4 a useful piece of advice. *He gave me a few tips on how to draw faces.*

**tip** (tips, tipping, tipped) *verb* 1 to knock over something so that the contents spill out, to empty. *He tipped over the milk bottle.* 2 to give somebody a small gift of money for helping you.

T

**tipsy** *adjective* very slightly drunk.

**tiptoe** *verb* to walk on your toes so that you make very little noise.

Simon walked on tiptoe so as not to wake his parents.

**Tirana** *noun* the capital of Albania.

**tire** *verb* to become tired or to make somebody tired and weary. 2 to become bored with something. **tired** *adjective*.

**tiresome** *adjective* irritating, annoying.

**tissue** *noun* 1 the cells that make up a particular part of an animal or plant. *Leaf tissue.* 2 **tissue paper** very soft, thin paper used for wiping, wrapping etc. Paper handkerchiefs are often called tissues.

**tit** *noun* any of a variety of small European birds. *The tits were nesting in an old kettle.*

**titbit** *noun* a small piece of particularly tasty food (US tidbid).

**title** *noun* 1 the name of a book, film, piece of music etc. 2 a word like Dr, Mrs, Sir put before a person's name to show rank etc.

**titter** *verb* to laugh in a silly, nervous way, to giggle. **titter** *noun*.

**toad** *noun* an amphibian like a frog with a rough, warty skin. Toads live mainly on land.

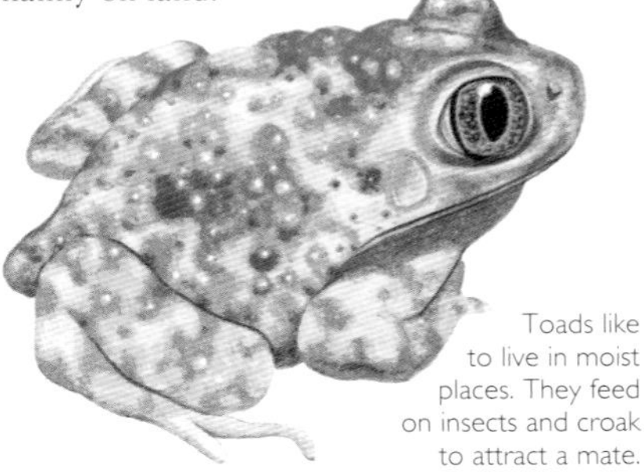

Toads like to live in moist places. They feed on insects and croak to attract a mate.

**toadstool** *noun* an umbrella-shaped fungus similar to a mushroom, but nearly always poisonous. *The fairy under the toadstool.*

**toast** *noun* a slice of bread that has been heated under a grill until it has turned crisp and brown. *Toast and marmalade.*

**toast** *verb* to hold up your glass and wish for the success or happiness of somebody. **toast** *noun*. *We drank a toast to the bride.*

**AMAZING FACT**

Tokyo is one of the biggest cities in the world. Many people work there, but most of them live outside of the city. Some people have to spend over 4 hours a day travelling to and from work.

**WORD HISTORY**

*'Tyre' (or 'tire' in the old or US spelling) comes from the word 'attire' (clothing), because it was thought of as the clothing of a wheel. And the fitting of tyres to wheels was once known as shoeing.*

**tobacco** *noun* the cut and dried leaves of the tobacco plant which people smoke as cigars and cigarettes or in pipes.

**toboggan** *noun* a small sledge without runners. **toboggan** *verb*.

**today** *adverb, noun* 1 this very day. 2 the present time, nowadays. *People travel more by plane today than they used to.*

**toddler** *noun* a child who is just learning to walk. *Toddlers are a real handful.*

**toe** *noun* 1 one of the five parts at the end of your foot. 2 the front part of a shoe, sock etc. that fits over your toes. **on your toes** ready and alert. **toe the line** to do as you are told. *Imran expected his staff to toe the line.*

**toffee** *noun* a sticky sweet made from sugar and butter. *Toffee and pear crumble.*

**toga** *noun* a loose flowing garment worn by men in ancient Rome.

**together** *adverb* 1 with another. *She stuck the two pieces together.* 2 at the same time as another. *They arrived home together.*

**Togo** *noun* a country in Africa.

The flag of Togo has a ground of yellow and green stripes and a white star on a red square.

**toilet** *noun* a room with a bowl called a toilet for getting rid of waste from the body.

**token** *noun* 1 a piece of printed plastic or paper that can be used instead of money for buying things. *A book token.* 2 a small sign or symbol of something. *A token of love.*

**Tokyo** *noun* the capital of Japan.

**told** past tense of tell.

**tolerate** *verb* to put up with or allow something to happen, to endure. *How can you tolerate living in such a mess!* **tolerable** *adjective*. **tolerance** *noun*. **tolerant** *adjective*.

**tomahawk** *noun* a war hatchet once used by Native Americans.

**tomato** (tomatoes) *noun* a round, sweet fruit eaten raw in salads and much used in cooking. *Tomato ketchup.*

**tomb** *noun* a place where a body is buried. A grave. **tombstone** a stone with writing on it marking where a person is buried.

**tomorrow** *adverb, noun* 1 the day after today. 2 the future. *Tomorrow's children.*

**ton** *noun* a unit of weight equal to 1,016 kg. *This dictionary weighs a ton!*

**tone** *noun* 1 the quality of a sound or the way something is said. *The piano has a mellow tone.* 2 a shade of colour. 3 muscle tone. **tone** *verb*.

T

**Tonga** *noun* a country of many islands in the Pacific Ocean.

**tongue** *noun* the long, soft pink thing that moves about inside your mouth and that helps you taste things and talk. **tongue-twister** something that is difficult to say.

Different parts of the tongue are sensitive to different tastes.

Bitter tastes

Sour tastes

Salty tastes

Sweet tastes

**tonic** *noun* a medicine or something else that makes you feel better or stronger.

**tonight** *adverb*, *noun* this night of this day.

**tonne** *noun* a unit of weight equal to 1,000 kg. *Tonnes of cargo.*

**tonsils** *plural noun* two soft lumps of flesh at the back of your throat. They may swell and become sore in an illness called tonsilitis.

**too** *adverb* 1 as well, also. *I can sing too.* 2 more than enough or than is needed. *There are too many knives in this drawer.*

**took** past tense of take.

**tool** *noun* a hand-held instrument or implement such as a hammer or drill that you use to do a particular job.

**tooth** (teeth) *noun* 1 one of the hard white bony parts inside your mouth that you use for biting and chewing. 2 one of the pointed parts of a comb or saw.

**toothache** *noun* severe pain in a tooth.

**toothbrush** *noun* a brush for cleaning teeth.

**top** *noun* 1 the highest part of something; the summit. *The top of the mountain.* 2 a covering, a lid. *Put the top back on the toothpaste.* 3 a piece of clothing that a woman or a girl wears on the upper part of her body. 4 a cone-shaped toy that spins on a point. **top** *adjective* the highest or best. *A top football player.* The opposite of top is bottom. **top** (tops, topping, topped) *verb*. **top dog** *noun* a leader or winner. **top heavy** *adjective* heavier at the top than at the bottom and so likely to topple over. **top secret** information that is very secret.

**TONGUE TWISTER**

*A tutor who tooted the flute*
*Tried to tutor two tooters to flute*
*Said the two to the tutor:*
*Is it harder to toot, or*
*To tutor two tooters to toot?*

**SPELLING NOTE**

*Try not to confuse 'to', 'too', and 'two'. 'Two days is too long to wait. Do you think so too?'*

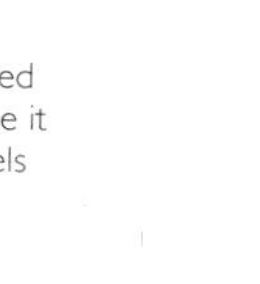

A tooth is coated in enamel. Inside it are blood vessels and nerves.

**AMAZING FACT**

Tornados or 'twisters' can reach speeds of up to 300 miles per hour.

**topaz** *noun* a semi-precious stone of varying colours.

**topic** *noun* a subject to talk about or write about. *A fascinating topic.*

**topical** *adjective* relating to important or interesting things happening now.

**topography** *noun* the study and description of the landscape's features such as the position of its mountains, roads, towns etc.

**topple** *verb* to overbalance and fall because it is too heavy at the top.

**topsy-turvy** *adjective* upside-down and in a state of confusion.

**Torah** *noun* a scroll used in synagogues on which are written the first five books of the Old Testament – Genesis, Exodus, Leviticus, Numbers and Deuteronomy known as the Pentateuch.

**torch** *noun* 1 a light with an electric battery that you can carry around with you (US flashlight). 2 a pole with burning material at one end that gives light.

**tore** past tense of tear.

**torment** *verb* (say tor-**ment**) to tease and be deliberately cruel to somebody or an animal. **torment** *noun* (say **tor**-ment).

**tornado** (tornadoes) *noun* a violent storm with strong winds that spin at high speeds causing great damage.

The whole village was devastated by the tornado and many lives were lost.

T

**torrent** *noun* 1 a violent rushing stream. 2 a flood or heavy downpour of rain. **torrential** *adjective*. *Torrential rain.*

**torso** (torsos) *noun* the main part of a body but excluding the head and limbs.

**tortoise** *noun* (say **tor**-tuss) a slow-moving land reptile with a hard shell.

The tortoise lost its race against the hare.

**torture** *verb* to make somebody suffer extremely cruel physical or mental pain, often to force them to confess something. **torture** *noun*. *He was cruelly tortured.*

**toss** *verb* 1 to throw something carelessly into the air. 2 to move up and down and from side to side. *The boat tossed on the sea.* 3 to spin a coin to see whether heads or tails faces upwards.

**total** *noun* the amount when everything is added together. **total** *adjective* complete. *A total success.*

**totem pole** *noun* a large pole carved or painted with traditional symbols of Native American families.

Magical creatures are carved on this totem pole. It was made by skilled craftsmen in Northwest America (present-day Canada).

**totter** *verb* to walk in an unsteady way.

**toucan** *noun* a brightly coloured South American bird with a huge beak.

**touch** *verb* 1 to feel something with your hand or with some other part of your body. 2 to come into contact and be so close to something that there is no space in between. 3 to move the feelings. *I was touched by your kind letter.* **touch** *noun* one of the five senses, the ability to feel. **in touch** in communication. **out of touch** not in communication.

**touching** *adjective* causing a deep feeling of pity, sorrow etc. *A touching love story.*

**touchline** *noun* the line around the edge of a football pitch etc.

**touchy** *adjective* easily offended or annoyed. *Beth seemed very touchy.*

**WORD HISTORY**

*'Toupee' comes from the French word 'toupe', meaning a tuft of hair.*

**DID YOU KNOW?**

*American spelling was simplified by the lexicographer Noah Webster. One of his reforms was to drop the 's' in words like backward(s), westward(s) and toward(s). Words that may be spelled '–ize' or '–ise' are always '–ize' in American English.*

**tough** *adjective* (say tuff) 1 strong and very hard to damage or break. 2 able to put up with hardships or difficulties. *Arctic explorers need to be tough.* 3 difficult. *A tough exam.* 4 hard to chew. *Tough meat.* 5 strict. *The government is tough on crime.* **toughen** *verb*. **toughness** *noun*.

**toupee** *noun* a false piece of hair worn to cover a bald part of the head.

**tour** *noun* 1 a journey on which you visit many different places. 2 a short trip around one place. **tour** *verb*.

**tourist** *noun* a person who visits different places for pleasure.

**tournament** *noun* a sports competition or contest in which the skills of the players are tested.

**tousled** *adjective* (of hair) untidy.

**tow** *verb* to pull or drag something behind. *The tractor towed the car out of the mud.*

**towards** *preposition* 1 in the direction of *Towards the beach.* 2 regarding. *My feelings towards you.* 3 as a contribution. *Everyone gave £2 towards the cost.*

**towel** *noun* a piece of thick, absorbent cloth or paper for drying things.

**tower** *noun* a tall, narrow building or part of building. **tower** *verb* to rise very high. *The chimney towered over the factory.* **towering** *adjective*.

Paris's most famous landmark is the tower designed by Gustave Eiffel.

**town** *noun* a place with a lot of houses and other buildings such as schools, shops, factories and offices.

**towpath** *noun* a path along the side of canal. *Let's walk along the towpath.*

**toxic** *adjective* poisonous. *Toxic waste.*

**toy** *noun* a thing for a child to play with. **toy** *verb* to play with or consider something not too seriously. *Ted toyed with the idea of becoming a policeman.*

**trace** *verb* 1 to copy a design etc. by placing a thin piece of half-transparent paper over it and drawing over the lines of the design etc. 2 to search and find where somebody is. *The police traced her to a hotel in Crewe.* **trace** *noun* a small mark or amount.

**track** *noun* 1 a series of marks left on the ground by an animal, person or vehicle. 2 a path. 3 a railway line. 4 a course for horses, runners, cars etc. 5 one of the pieces of music on a CD or tape recording. **off the beaten track** remote and not near a made-up road. **keep (or lose) track of** to know where somebody is, what is going on etc.

**tract** *noun* 1 a wide area of land. *Huge tracts of desert.* 2 a leaflet.

**tractor** *noun* a strong vehicle used on farms to pull ploughs and other machinery.

Tractor cabs are air-conditioned for comfort in the heat of the summer.

**trade** *noun* 1 the business of buying and selling goods. 2 an occupation or job that requires a special skill, a craft. *Paul's a farrier by trade.* **trade** *verb* to buy and sell, to exchange.

**trade union** *noun* a group of workers in the same job who join together to represent common interests on such things as working conditions and wages to their employers.

**tradition** *noun* customs, beliefs and habits that people hand down from one generation to another. **traditional** *adjective. A very traditional folk song.*

**traffic** *noun* vehicles travelling along the road at the same time.

**traffic jam** *noun* a long queue of traffic that has come to a standstill.

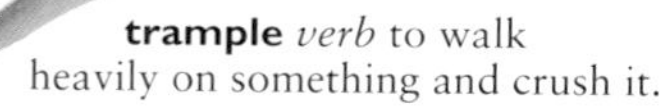

It is very frustrating to get stuck in a traffic jam behind a broken-down lorry.

**traffic warden** *noun* a person whose main job is to control where cars are parked.

**tragedy** *noun* 1 a very sad event, a terrible disaster. 2 a play about sad events and with an unhappy ending. **tragic** *adjective. Two children were killed in the tragic accident.*

**trail** *noun* 1 marks left behind by a person or animal as they move through a place. *A trail of footprints in the snow.* 2 a track or narrow path through the countryside.

**WORD HISTORY**

*A tram was originally a sledge or truck that was pulled along. The word was then used for the wooden or iron track along which the tram was pulled. The later passenger vehicles were called tramcars – 'trams' for short.*

**trail** *verb* 1 to follow a trail of somebody or something. *I am on your trail.* 2 to drag or be dragged along the ground.

**trailer** *noun* 1 a vehicle for carrying things that is towed by a car or lorry. *The car pulled a yacht on a trailer.* 2 an advertisement for a film that shows short extracts from it.

**train** *noun* 1 a railway engine with a set of carriages or trucks. 2 a series of ideas or events. *You broke my train of thought.*

**train** *verb* 1 to learn the skills you need to do something. 2 to teach an animal or person how to do something. 3 to practise and exercise for a sport.

**trainer** *noun* a person who trains or teaches somebody or an animal to compete in a sport. *A horse trainer.*

**trainers** *plural noun* shoes with soft, thick soles worn by runners and other sports people. *Trainers are really expensive.*

**traitor** *noun* a person who is disloyal and betrays friends or country.

**tram** *noun* a large vehicle like a bus but which runs on rails in the road and is driven by electricity (US streetcar).

**tramp** *verb* to walk a long way slowly and steadily. **tramp** *noun* a person without a home who travels from place to place on foot.

**trample** *verb* to walk heavily on something and crush it.

**tranquil** *adjective* (say **tran**-kwill) calm and quiet. **tranquillity** *noun. The tranquillity of a monastery.*

**tranquilizer** *noun* a medicine that is given to somebody to make them feel calm and peaceful. **tranquilize** *verb.*

**trans-** *prefix* across or beyond. *Transatlantic telephone calls.*

**transfer** (transfers, transferring, transferred) *verb* (say tranz-**fur**) to move somebody or something from one place to another. *She transferred her affection to another man.*

**transfer** *noun* (say **tranz**-fur) 1 the act of moving a person or thing from one place to another. 2 a design or picture on a small piece of paper that can be transferred and stuck to another surface by rubbing or heating. *A transfer of a teddy bear.*

**transform** *verb* to make a complete change in form or nature. *We transformed the shed into a bathroom.* **transformation** *noun.*

**transfusion** *noun* injecting blood into a person who has lost a lot of blood in an accident. *He needed a blood transfusion.*

**transistor** *noun* 1 an electronic device that controls the flow of electricity in radios and television sets. 2 a small portable radio that uses a transistor.

**translate** *verb* to change words from one language into another. **translator** *noun.* **translation** *noun.*

**transmit** (transmits, transmitting, transmitted) *verb* 1 to pass something on from one place or person to another. *How are diseases transmitted?* 2 to send out a radio or television programme over the air. **transmission** *noun.*

**transparency** *noun* a photograph that lets light through so that you can project it on to a screen.

**transparent** *adjective* able to be seen through. *Clear water is transparent.*

The cocktail glass is transparent, and so is the drink. You can see the olive on the stick inside it.

**transplant** *verb* 1 to move a plant growing in one place to another place. 2 to perform a surgical operation to put a part of one person's body into the body of another person. **transplant** *noun. A heart transplant.*

**transport** *noun* cars, buses, trains and planes or any other way of travelling.

**transport** *verb* to carry people or goods from one place to another.

**trap** *noun* a device for catching birds and animals. **trap** *verb* 1 to catch an animal using a trap. 2 to catch a person by a trick. *They trapped her into admitting guilt.*

**trapeze** *noun* a bar hanging from two ropes used by acrobats and gymnasts to swing from and perform skilful movements.

**trash** *noun* anything to be thrown away.

**DID YOU KNOW?**

*'Treble' and 'triple' are interchangeable in the sense of 'three times as much'. But 'treble' is usually preferred when meaning 'three times as great', as in 'treble the amount', and 'triple' is preferred when meaning 'consisting of three parts', as in 'triple bypass'.*

**AMAZING FACT**

The first successful human heart transplant operation was performed in South Africa by Dr Cristiaan Barnard in 1967.

**travel** (travels, travelling, travelled) *verb* to journey or move from one place to another. *Sound travels fast.* **travel** *noun. Air travel.*

**traveller** *noun* 1 a person who travels regularly. 2 a person who travels from place to place in a mobile home or van.

**trawl** *verb* to fish with a wide net called a trawl. *Rod trawled the deep ocean for fish.*

**trawler** *noun* a fishing boat that pulls a large net called a trawl behind it.

**tray** *noun* a flat object with a rim around the edge for carrying things such as food and drinks.

**treachery** *noun* disloyalty, the betrayal of people who trust you. **treacherous** *adjective* 1 disloyal. 2 dangerous. *Treacherous rocks.*

**treacle** *noun* a thick, sticky syrup made from syrup. *Treacle tart.*

**tread** (treading, trod, trodden) *verb* to walk or to put your foot down on something, to trample. *She trod on the cat's tail!* **tread** *noun* 1 the top part of a ladder or stairs you put your foot on. 2 the raised pattern of ridges on a car tyre or on the sole of a shoe.

**treason** *noun* the betrayal of your country, especially by giving away secrets to the enemy in wartime. **treasonable** *adjective. A treasonable crime.*

**treasure** *noun* 1 a store of gold, jewels and other precious things. 2 a precious object such as a painting. **treasure** *verb* to value something very much or to look after something because it is important to you.

The treasure Sally found in the attic consisted of beautiful jewels and valuable gold coins.

**treasurer** *noun* a person who looks after the money of a club etc.

**treat** *verb* 1 to behave towards somebody in a particular way. *She treats me like a servant.* 2 to give medical care to a person or animal. *The doctor is treating her for eczema.* **treatment** *noun.* **treat** *noun* a special gift such as an outing or a meal.

**treaty** *noun* a formal agreement between two or more countries. *An arms treaty.*

**treble** *adjective, adverb* three times as much, as many or as big. **treble** *verb. He has trebled his income.*

T

**treble** *noun* a boy with a high singing voice.

**tree** *noun* a tall plant that has a long, thick wooden stem called a trunk and branches and leaves. *Many trees in the forest.*

Trees are the lungs of the world, as they take in carbon dioxide and give out oxygen.

AMAZING FACT

Trees are the largest of all plants. Some grow to over 100 metres high.

**trek** *noun* a long journey, usually on foot and in a remote area. **trek** *verb.*

**trellis** *noun* a fence or framework of wooden strips for plants to climb up.

**tremble** *verb* to shake all over because you are frightened, cold or excited.

**tremendous** *adjective* 1 very big. *A tremendous crowd.* 2 very good. *We had a tremendous time.*

**trench** *noun* a long, thin ditch or channel dug in the earth. *Trench warfare.*

**trend** *noun* the general direction in which things seem to be changing and becoming different. *A trend for smaller families.* **set a trend** to start a fashion.

**trespass** *verb* to go on somebody's land without their permission. **tresspasser** *noun.*

**tri-** *prefix* meaning three or three times. *Tricycle, triangle, trilogy, tripod, tripartite.*

**trial** *noun* 1 the period of time when a prisoner is in a law court and when the lawyers, jury and judge try to decide whether or not he or she has done wrong and is guilty. 2 a test of something to see how well it works.

**triangle** *noun* 1 a flat shape with three straight sides and three corners. 2 a triangular musical instrument that makes a bell-like sound when you hit it. **triangular** *adjective.*

A triangle has three sides.

DID YOU KNOW?

*English spelling does not allow triples of the same letter, so where a compound word contains three of the same letters consecutively a hyphen is inserted, as in bell-like, cross-section, Inverness-shire.*

**tribe** *noun* a group of families descended from the same ancestors who live together and who have the same traditions, language etc. **tribal** *adjective. Tribal chief.*

The Masai people of Kenya are a tribe of cattle herders. They wear bright cloth and beaded collars.

**tributary** *noun* a stream that flows into a river or another stream.

**trick** *noun* 1 something you do to cheat somebody or to make a fool of somebody. 2 some clever or skilful thing that you have learned to do to entertain people. *Card tricks.* 3 a practical joke. **trick** *verb* to deceive or make a fool of somebody.

**trickle** *verb* to flow slowly like a very small stream. *Tears trickled down his cheeks.* **trickle** *noun. A trickle of water.*

**tricky** *adjective* difficult to deal with. *A tricky situation.*

**tricolour** *noun* a flag with three bands of different colours such as the French and Irish flags.

**tricycle** *noun* a cycle with three wheels.

**tried** past tense of try.

**trifle** *noun* 1 a sweet made of sponge cake and fruit covered in jelly, custard and cream. 2 something that is of no importance. **trifling** *adjective.*

**trigger** *noun* the small lever you pull with a finger to fire a gun.

**trilogy** *noun* a group of three novels, plays, operas etc. that go together and make a related series by having the same people or themes in common.

**trim** (trims, trimming, trimmed) *verb* 1 to cut the edges or ends off something to make it neat, to clip. *He trimmed her hair.* 2 to decorate a piece of clothing. *She trimmed the hat with flowers.* **trim** *adjective* having a good shape. *He has a trim figure.*

**Trinidad and Tobago** *noun* a country in the West Indies.

The flag of Trinidad and Tobago has a diagonal black and white stripe on a red ground.

**trinity** *noun* 1 a group of three. 2 the Trinity in Christianity, the Father, the Son and the Holy Spirit as one God.

**trio** *noun* a group of three singers or players, a piece of music written for three musicians. *A string trio.*

**trip** (trips, tripping, tripped) *verb* 1 to catch your foot in something and stumble or fall over. 2 to move with quick, light steps. *She tripped along the path as happy as could be.* **trip up** to make a mistake.

**trip** *noun* 1 a short return journey or visit. *A trip to Paris.* 2 (slang) a dream-like experience caused by drugs.

**tripe** *noun* 1 the stomach lining of such animals as cows and pigs which is cooked and eaten. 2 worthless nonsense. *Don't talk such tripe.*

**triple** *adjective* three times as great or many. 2 consisting of three parts. **triple** *verb. The tree has tripled in height in one month.*

**triplet** *noun* one of three babies born at the same time to the same mother.

**tripod** *noun* (say **try**-pod) a three-legged support for a camera etc.

**Tripoli** *noun* the capital of Libya.

**triumph** *noun* (say **try**-umf) a great success or achievement, a victory. **triumph** *verb. He triumphed over evil.* **triumphant** *adjective.*

**trivial** *adjective* of very little importance. *A trivial problem.*

**troll** *noun* an ugly, mischievous creature in fairy tales from Scandinavia.

Trolls are favourite storybook creatures for children in Norway, Sweden and Denmark.

**trolley** *noun* a small cart or a large basket on wheels for carrying things. *A supermarket trolley.*

**trombone** *noun* a large, brass musical instrument that you blow through and move a slide to change the note.

**WORD HISTORY**

*'Truant' once meant a beggar. In the 16th century it took on the meaning of a pupil absent without leave from school. It originally comes from a Welsh word 'truan', meaning 'wretched'.*

**AMAZING FACT**

Trinidad and Tobago is one country made up of two islands in the West Indies.

**troops** *plural noun* a group of soldiers. **troop** *verb* to move together as a crowd. *The fans trooped into the stadium.*

**trophy** *noun* (say **trow**-fee) an award or prize such as a silver cup given to somebody who wins a game or competition.

**tropic** *noun* 1 one of the two lines of latitude running around the Earth at about 23 degrees north and south of the equator and known as the Tropic of Cancer and the Tropic of Capricorn. 2 **tropics** *plural noun* the very warm regions between the Tropic of Cancer and the Tropic of Capricorn. **tropical** *noun. Tropical rain forests.*

This tropical rainforest can be found in the equatorial region of South America.

**trot** *noun* one of the four paces of a horse, between a walk and a canter. **trot** (trots, trotting, trotted) *verb* 1 of a horse, to run but not to canter or to gallop. 2 of humans, to move quickly. *Trot along now.*

**trouble** *noun* a difficult, unpleasant or worrying situation, a problem. **trouble** *verb* 1 to cause worry, concern or distress. 2 to make an effort to do something, to bother. *She didn't trouble to ask if she could help.*

**troublesome** *adjective* causing problems or worries, annoying. *A troublesome wasp.*

**trough** *noun* 1 a long, narrow container for food and water for animals. 2 in weather forecasting, an area of low pressure between areas of high pressure.

**trousers** *plural noun* a piece of clothing covering your body from your waist to your ankles with a separate part for each leg.

**trout** (trout) *noun* a silvery-brown freshwater fish of the salmon family that can be eaten. *Trout with almonds.*

**trowel** *noun* 1 a small spade-like hand tool with a short handle used for garden work. 2 a flat hand tool used by builders to spread plaster etc. *Lay it on with a trowel.*

**truant** *noun* a pupil who stays away from school without permission or a good excuse.

**truce** *noun* a short period when two sides in a war etc. agree to stop fighting.

**truck** *noun* a motor vehicle that can carry heavy loads, a lorry. An open railway wagon. *A truck full of coal.*

**trudge** *verb* to walk slowly with tired, heavy steps. **trudge** *noun.*

**true** *noun* 1 what really happened. 2 not invented or guessed at but real and accurate. 3 loyal and trustworthy. *A true friend.*

**trumpet** *noun* a brass musical instrument that makes high sounds when you blow into it.

**trunk** *noun* 1 the long stem of a tree from which the branches grow. 2 a large container with a hinged lid and a handle for carrying or storing things such as clothes. 3 the main part of your body but not including your limbs, neck and head, the torso. 4 an elephant's long nose. 5 (US) the boot of a car.

**trunks** *plural noun* shorts worn by men and boys for swimming.

**trust** *verb* to believe that somebody is honest, reliable and truthful and that they will do nothing to harm you, to depend on. **trustworthy** *adjective*. **trustworthiness** *noun*.

**truth** *noun* what is real, accurate and correct, what has actually happened. *Are you telling me the truth?* **truthful** *adjective*. **truthfulness** *noun*.

**try** (tries, trying, tried) *verb* 1 to attempt to do something. *I don't think I can do it but I'll try.* 2 to test something by using it to see what it is like. *Try this ice-cream and see if you like it.* 3 to judge somebody in a court of law. **try** *noun* 1 an attempt. 2 in rugby, a way of scoring by putting the ball down on the ground over the opponents' goal line. **trying** *adjective* exhausting and irritating. *A trying child.*

**tsar** *noun* (say zar) in former times, a Russian king or emperor. His wife was called a tsarina. Also spelt czar, czarina.

**T-shirt** a kind of shirt or vest with short sleeves and no collar.

**tub** *noun* a round, wide and usually open container.

**tuba** *noun* a large brass musical instrument that makes deep sounds when you blow into it.

**tubby** *adjective* short, round and rather fat.

**tube** *noun* 1 a long, hollow metal, plastic or rubber cylinder, a pipe. 2 a long container. *A tube of toothpaste.* 3 London's underground railway. **tubular** *adjective*.

**tuber** *noun* the roundish swollen part of the underground stem of some plants. Potatoes are tubers.

**tuck** *verb* to fold under or push the loose end of something into a place to make it look tidy. *He tucked his shirt into his trousers.* **tuck in** *verb* to eat with great enjoyment. *Bunter tucked into the cake.*

**tuft** *noun* a bunch or clump of hair, feathers, grass etc.

**WORD HISTORY**

*'Tsar' is sometimes spelled 'Czar'. It is a Russian word derived from the Latin, 'Caesar'. The German equivalent is 'kaiser'.*

**WORD HISTORY**

*'Turban' comes from the Portuguese 'turbante', which in turn comes from a Persian word for this headdress.*

My dad played oom-pah music on the tuba.

**tug or tugboat** *noun* a small powerful boat that tows ships in and out of port.

**tug o' war** *noun* a contest between two teams who pull on opposite ends of a long rope to test their strength.

The best event at the village fete was the tug o' war.

**tulip** *noun* a plant with brightly coloured flowers that grows from a bulb in the spring. *The tulips of Amsterdam.*

**tumble** *verb* to fall down suddenly or to fall and roll over. *Tim tumbled down the stairs.*

**tumbler** *noun* a drinking glass.

**tummy** *noun* (slang) the stomach.

**tumour** *noun* a lump or growth on the body made of diseased or abnormal cells.

**tuna** *noun* a large sea fish, used for food.

**tundra** *noun* the vast treeless plains of the Arctic that remain frozen all year.

**tune** *noun* a sequence of musical notes in a pattern that is pleasant to listen to and often easy to remember. **tune** *verb* 1 to adjust a musical instrument so that it plays the correct notes. 2 to adjust a radio so that it receives the programme you want. **tuneful** *adjective*. **change your tune** to change the way you think.

**tunic** *noun* 1 a tight-fitting jacket, often worn as part of a uniform. 2 a loose, sleeveless garment without a collar.

**Tunis** *noun* the capital of Tunisia.

**Tunisia** *noun* a country in Africa.

**Tunisian** *noun* a person who comes from Tunisia. **Tunisian** *adjective*. *The Tunisian coast is extremely beautiful.*

**tunnel** *noun* a long underground passage for a railway etc. **tunnel** (tunnels, tunnelling, tunnelled) *verb* to dig a tunnel.

**turban** *noun* a headdress worn by Muslim and Sikh men consisting of a long piece of cloth wound around the head.

**turbine** *noun* an engine that works by water, steam, or hot air etc. pushing round the curved blades on a wheel.

Wind turbines produce a clean, renewable source of electricity.

**turbojet** *noun* an aircraft driven by a turbine.

**turf** *noun* 1 short, thick grass. 2 a piece of earth with grass growing from it, cut from the ground.

**turkey** *noun* a large bird that is reared for its meat.

**Turkey** *noun* a country partly in Europe and mostly in Asia.

Turkey is famous for its richly patterned carpets.

**Turkish** *noun* 1 a person who comes from Turkey. 2 the language of Turkey. **Turkish** *adjective. Turkish architecture.*

**Turkmenistan** *noun* a country in West Asia.

**turmoil** *noun* a state of great confusion and unrest.

**turn** *verb* 1 to go around or move around a central point, to revolve or twist. *Turn the handle.* 2 to move and change direction. *He turned to look at me.* 3 to move so as to make the topside become the bottom side. *He turned the mattress.* 4 to change or to become different. *The frog turned into a prince.* 5 to adjust a switch, tap etc. *Turn the lights off.* **turn** *noun.* **do somebody a good turn** to help somebody. **turn down** 1 to refuse. 2 to make quieter. **turn up** 1 to arrive. 2 to make louder. *Please turn up the sound.*

**turnip** *noun* a round, white root vegetable.

**turnstile** *noun* a revolving gate that lets people walk through one at a time.

**turquoise** *noun* a greenish-blue semi-precious stone. The colour of the stone.

**turret** *noun* a small tower on a castle or the side of a building.

**turtle** *noun* a large reptile covered with a shell like a tortoise that lives in the sea.

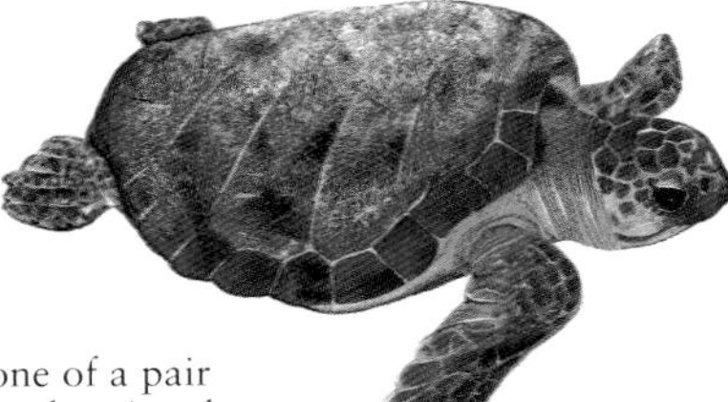

Turtles swim ashore to lay their eggs in the sand on the beach.

**tusk** *noun* one of a pair of long, curved, pointed teeth that sticks out of the mouth of elephants, walruses and wild boar.

**tutor** *noun* a teacher who gives classes to one person at a time or to very small groups of people. *My maths tutor is very clever.*

**tutu** *noun* the very short, stiff skirt worn by female ballet dancers.

**Tuvalu** *noun* a country of islands in the Pacific Ocean.

**TV** *abbreviation* television.

**DID YOU KNOW?**

*Many of our clichés rely on twinning words as in 'leaps and bounds', 'fast and furious', 'pick and choose', 'slow but sure' and 'nice and easy'.*

**AMAZING FACT**

The female turtle buries her eggs in the sand. When the eggs of the turtle hatch, the hatchlings have to dig their way up to the surface.

**tweed** *noun* a strong woollen cloth, often made of several colours.

**tweezers** *plural noun* a small tool with two prongs for lifting things or for pulling out hairs etc., pincers.

**twice** *adverb* two times.

**twiddle** *verb* to turn something round and round in a purposeless way. *He kept twiddling with the radio knobs.* **twiddle your thumbs** to have nothing to do.

**twig** *noun* a thin, tiny branch of a tree.

**twilight** *noun* the time of day when it is getting dark, between sunset and night.

**twin** *noun* one of two babies born at the same time to the same mother.

**twine** *noun* very strong string made by twisting threads together.

**twinge** *noun* a sudden, short pain. *A twinge of rheumatism.*

**twinkle** *verb* to sparkle with little unsteady flashes of light. *Stars twinkle in the sky.* **twinkle** *noun. He has a twinkle in his eye!*

**twirl** *verb* to turn or spin something quickly round and round.

**twist** *verb* 1 to turn. *To open the box you must twist the knob.* 2 wind something around something else. *She twisted her hair around her finger.* 4 to bend and turn in different directions. *The road twisted around the mountain.* 4 to bend something so as to damage it. *She twisted her wrist.* **twist** *noun.* **round the twist** mad.

**tycoon** *noun* a rich, powerful business person or industrialist. *A newspaper tycoon.*

Sabon

'Sabon' is the name of the type used in this book.

**type** *noun* 1 the different designs of letters used in printing. 2 a kind or sort. *Apples and pears are two types of fruit.*

**type** *verb* to write something by pressing the keys of a typewriter or computer.

**typewriter** *noun* a machine with keys that you press to print letters and figures on a piece of paper.

**typhoid** *noun* (say **tie**-foid) a very dangerous infectious disease in which the intestines become inflamed.

**typhoon** *noun* (say tie-**foon**) a tropical storm with violent winds.

**typical** *adjective* 1 the most usual or characteristic of its kind. *A typical Tudor house.* 2 what you would expect. *It's typical of you to be late, I'm afraid.*

**tyrant** *noun* a cruel, unjust and unkind ruler. **tyranny** *noun.* **tyrannical** *adjective. A tyrannical dictator.*

**tyre** *noun* the thick ring of rubber usually filled with air around the wheel of a vehicle.

U

# Uu

**udder** *noun* the bag-like part of a cow, sheep etc. that hangs down between its back legs and from which milk is taken.

**UFO** *abbreviation* unidentified flying object. *Ted likes films about UFOs.*

**Uganda** *noun* a country in Africa.

**Ugandan** *noun* a person who comes from Uganda. **Ugandan** *adjective. Ugandan exports include avocado pears.*

**ugly** (uglier, ugliest) *adjective* unattractive and not beautiful to look at. **ugliness** *noun.*

**UHF** *abbreviation* ultra high frequency.

**Ukraine** *noun* a country in eastern Europe.

**Ukrainian** *noun* a person who comes from the Ukraine. **Ukrainian** *adjective. Ukrainian wheat is an important export.*

**Ulan Bator** *noun* the capital of Mongolia.

**ulcer** *noun* (say **ull**-sur) an open sore on the body usually with a flow of pus.

**ultimate** *adjective* final, last. *Our ultimate wish is to win.*

**ultimatum** *noun* a final offer or warning.

**ultra-** *prefix* beyond. *Ultra high frequency.*

**ultraviolet light** *noun* light that is beyond the visible spectrum at its violet end and which causes your skin to tan.

**umbilical cord** *noun* the tube that connects the body of a mother and child until the child is born.

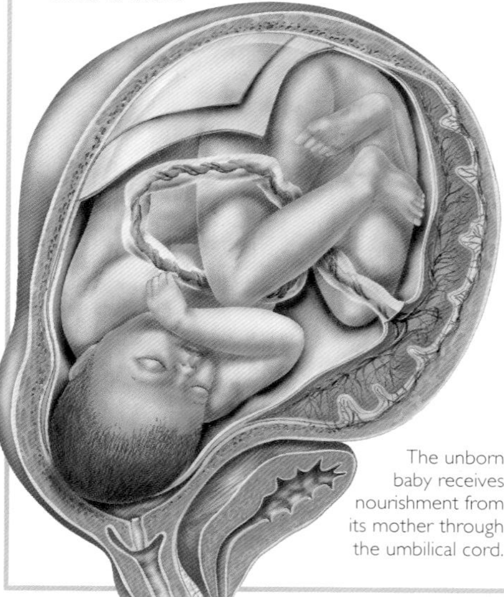

The unborn baby receives nourishment from its mother through the umbilical cord.

**DID YOU KNOW?**

*The shape of the letters U, V and W comes from a Semitic letter called 'waw', which was symbolised as a tenthook. The Romans used V for both U and V sounds. In the Middle Ages scholars began using U for the vowel sound and V for the consonant sound.*

**WORD BUILDER**

*Here are some words with the 'un–' prefix. You can easily work out the meaning if you look up the root word: 'unable', 'unaffected', 'unaided', 'unarmed', 'unbearable'.*

**umbrella** *noun* something that you hold over your head to keep you dry when it rains. The umbrella's frame is covered with a round piece of material and joined to a long handle. An umbrella folds up when you are not using it.

**umpire** *noun* a person who watches a game and makes sure that the rules are followed.

**UN** *abbreviation* United Nations.

The flag of the United Nations is a symbol of world peace and harmony.

**un-** *prefix* 1 not, opposite. *Uncomfortable.* 2 the opposite of an action. *Unfasten.*

**unaccustomed** *adjective* not used to doing something. *He is unaccustomed to work.*

**unanimous** *adjective* (say you-**nan**-im-us) of the same opinion, agreed by everybody. *A unanimous decision.* **unanimity** *noun.*

**unassuming** *adjective* modest and not showing off. *An unassuming young man.*

**unaware** *adjective* not knowing that something exists or is happening.

**unbalanced** *adjective* 1 lacking balance, unfair. *An unbalanced account of what happened.* 2 slightly mad. *She became rather unbalanced after the accident.*

**unbecoming** *adjective* not suitable.

**unbiased** *adjective* not favouring one side or the other, fair. *An unbiased opinion.*

**uncanny** *adjective* strange, weird and unnatural. *An uncanny silence.*

**uncle** *noun* the brother of your mother or your father or the husband of your aunt.

**unconscious** *adjective* 1 not conscious, in a kind of sleep and not knowing what is happening. 2 not being aware of something. *I was unconscious of the difficulties you were in until yesterday.*

**uncooperative** *adjective* making no attempt to help or do things for others.

**uncouth** *adjective* coarse and rough in behaviour and speech, rude.

**undaunted** *adjective* not discouraged or put off doing something despite setbacks and difficulties. *Her grandmother's criticism left her undaunted.*

U

**undeniable** *adjective* so certainly true that you cannot disagree.

**under-** *prefix* 1 below, beneath. *Underground.* 2 less than or not enough. *Underdeveloped.* 3 lower in rank. *Undersecretary, understudy.*

**undercarriage** *noun* the landing gear of an aircraft, including the wheels.

**undercover** *adjective* secret. *Undercover activities were common during the war.*

**underdog** *noun* in a game or contest, an unfortunate person or team that is unlikely to win. *I always want the underdog to win.*

**undergo** (undergoes, undergoing, underwent, undergone) *verb* to experience, endure or suffer something. *The town has undergone many changes in recent years.*

**undergraduate** *noun* a person studying for a first degree at a university.

**underground** *adjective* 1 beneath the ground or surface of the Earth. *Underground passages.* 2 acting in secret. *An underground group.* **underground** *noun* a railway that runs through tunnels under the ground (US subway).

**WORD BUILDER**

*Here are some words with the 'under–' prefix. You can easily work out what they mean: 'underclothes', 'undercook', 'underemployed', 'underfeed'.*

**understanding** *noun* 1 having a knowledge of something and knowing what it means or how it works, intelligence. *He has no understanding of machinery.* 2 sympathy and knowledge of a person. *There's a deep understanding between them.* 3 an agreement. *Perhaps we could come to an understanding about who does what.* **understanding** *adjective* tolerant and kind.

**understudy** *noun* an actor who learns the lines of the actor who usually plays a part and who takes over that part in an emergency. *The understudy was a great hit.*

**undertake** (undertakes, undertaking, undertook, undertaken) *verb* to agree or promise to do something and to be responsible for it. **undertaking** *noun.*

**undertaker** *noun* a person whose job it is to prepare dead bodies for burial or cremation and arrange funerals.

**underwear** *noun* clothes that you wear under your other clothes next to your skin. Knickers and vests are underwear.

**underworld** *noun* 1 all the criminals and their activities in a city. 2 the place in myths where the spirits of dead people go.

Moles spend most of their time underground. Because they are used to living in the darkness, their eyesight is very poor.

**undergrowth** *noun* bushes and plants that grow near the ground under trees in woods and forests. *He hid in the undergrowth.*

**underhand** *adjective* secret and dishonest, deceitful. *An underhand plot.*

**underline** *verb* 1 to draw a line under words to make them stand out. 2 to stress the importance of something *The accident underlines the need to be more careful.*

**undermine** *verb* to weaken or slowly destroy something. *The cold, damp climate is undermining her health.*

**understand** (understands, understanding, understood) *verb* 1 to know what something means, how it works or why it happens. 2 to know somebody or something well. *I quite understand what you feel.* 3 to believe something to be true because you have been told. *I understand that you got married in secret.*

**undo** (undoes, undoing, undid, undone) *verb* 1 to unfasten, untie, unwrap something that was fixed or tied. *She undid her shoelaces.* 2 to do away with or reverse something that has been done. *Try to undo the damage your remarks have done.*

Marcus undid his shoelaces, took off his shoes and put on his slippers.

**undoubted** *adjective* accepted as true, certain. *An undoubted success.*

**undress** *verb* to take your clothes off.

**undue** *adjective* excessive, more than necessary. *Undue noise.*

**undying** *adjective* never dying or fading. *They swore undying love.*

**unearth** *verb* to dig up or find something after searching for it, to discover. *He unearthed some old photos in a trunk.*

**unearthly** *adjective* 1 strange and terrifying, like nothing on Earth. *An unearthly sound of howling.* 2 absurdly unreasonable. *She telephoned at some unearthly hour.*

**uneasy** *adjective* anxious, not settled. *I feel uneasy around dogs.* **uneasiness** *noun*.

**uneven** *adjective*. 1 not smooth or flat. 2 not equally matched, one-sided. *An uneven contest.* 3 (of a number) odd and leaving a remainder of one when divided by two. Five is an uneven number.

**unfailing** *adjective* never failing or weakening, continuous, endless. *You have my unfailing sympathy.*

**unfeeling** *adjective* severe and hard-hearted.

**unfit** *adjective* 1 unhealthy, in poor physical condition. 2 unsuitable and not good enough. *This food is unfit to eat.*

**unfold** *verb* 1 to spread out by opening. *He unfolded the blanket.* 2 to reveal or gradually to make something clear. *The story unfolded gradually.*

**unfurl** *verb* to unroll, spread out and display something that has been wrapped up. *The soldier unfurled the flag.*

**unforeseen** *adjective* not expected. *Due to unforeseen circumstances, I cannot come.*

**unfounded** *adjective* not based on fact. *Unfounded rumours.*

**ungainly** *adjective* clumsy and ungraceful.

**unicorn** *noun* an animal in stories that looks like a white horse with a long, spiralled horn on its forehead.

Legend says that if a maiden falls asleep with the head of a unicorn in her lap, she will dream of the man she is to marry.

**SPELLING NOTE**

*Try not to confuse 'uninterested' meaning 'not interested' with 'disinterested' meaning 'not favouring one side and being fair to both'.*

The track through the hills was very uneven, making our journey uncomfortable.

**GRAMMAR NOTE**

*You cannot say something is 'very unique' or 'rather unique' because 'unique' means 'the only one, so either it's unique or it's not!*

**uniform** *noun* special distinctive clothes worn by members of a particular group or organization. Nurses, firefighters and soldiers wear uniforms. **uniform** *adjective* not changing, always the same. *The concrete blocks are of uniform size and colour.*

**unify** *verb* to make several things come together to form a whole to share a common purpose. *The various Italian states unified to make modern Italy.*

**unintelligible** *adjective* very difficult to understand. *Your writing is unintelligible.*

**uninterested** *adjective* showing no interest or enthusiasm. *I told him about the match but he seemed quite uninterested.*

**union** *noun* 1 A trade union is an organized group of workers who discuss with managers any problems affecting all the workers. 2 the act of joining things together, something united.

**unique** *adjective* (say yoo-**neek**) 1 being the only one of its kind and different from anybody or anything else. *His style of painting is unique.* 2 very unusual. **uniqueness** *noun*.

**unisex** *adjective* designed for or capable of being used by both men and women. *A unisex hairdresser.*

**unison** *noun* **in unison** all together.

**unit** *noun* 1 a single, complete thing that is part of a whole. 2 a group working together. *The physiotherapy unit.* 3 an amount that is used as a standard weight or measurement. *A litre is a unit of liquid measurement.*

**unite** *verb* to join together to form one thing or to do something together, to combine. **unity** *noun*.

**United Arab Emirates** *noun* a country in Southwest Asia.

**United Kingdom** *noun* a country in Northwest Europe, made up of England, Scotland, Wales and Northern Ireland.

**United States of America** *noun* a country in North America.

Alaska (top left on the map) belongs to the United States of America.

**universal** *adjective* relating to and including everybody and everything.

**universe** *noun* (say **yoo**-ni-verse) the whole of everything that exists, including the Earth, Sun, Moon, planets and all the stars in space. *The end of the universe.*

**university** *noun* a place of higher education where people go after they have left school to study for a degree or do research.

**unkempt** *adjective* untidy and not well looked after. *An unkempt beard.*

**unleaded** *adjective* (of petrol) containing no lead. *This car runs on unleaded petrol.*

**unless** *conjunction* if not. Except when. *I will go unless you stop talking.*

**unlucky** *adjective* 1 having bad luck and with bad things happening to you. 2 causing bad luck. *Some people believe it is unlucky to walk under ladders.*

**unmistakable** *adjective* distinct and not possible to be mistaken for somebody or something else. His handwriting is quite unmistakable. *An unmistakable style.*

**UNO** *abbreviation* United Nations Organization.

**unravel** (unravels, unravelling, unravelled) *verb* to undo knots or untie woven, knitted or tangled threads. 2 to solve a mystery or difficult problem.

The cat unravelled my knitting. I had to roll the wool back up into a ball.

**unreasonable** *adjective* 1 not sensible. *An unreasonable fear of spiders.* 2 too much, excessive. *Unreasonable demands.*

**unreliable** *adjective* not to be trusted or depended on. *Dad's old car is unreliable.*

**unrest** *noun* 1 discontent. 2 restlessness. Disturbance and riots. *There was great unrest among the workers.*

**unruly** *adjective* badly behaved, hard to control or rule. *An unruly child.*

**unscathed** *adjective* not harmed or damaged. *The horses escaped the stable fire unscathed and lived to see another day.*

**unscrupulous** *adjective* not caring whether something is right or wrong, having no principles. *An unscrupulous employer.*

**unseemly** *adjective* not suitable for the time and place. *Her laughter at the funeral was really quite unseemly.*

**unsettle** *verb* to make or become unstable and anxious, to disturb. *Thunder unsettles our dogs and cats.*

**AMAZING FACT**

The United Nations, or UN, was founded in 1945 after the Second World War to encourage world peace.

**GRAMMAR NOTE**

*We use 'an' instead of 'a' before words that start with a vowel* **sound.** *So say and write 'a uniform' or 'a used car' but say or write 'an unusual vase' or 'an umbrella'.*

**unsightly** *adjective* unpleasant to look at, ugly. *An unsightly building blocks the view.*

**unsound** *adjective* 1 not in a good condition, unhealthy. *The upstairs floors are unsound.* 2 not based on fact. *I thought her theory was very unsound.*

**unstable** *adjective* 1 liable to change suddenly. *She's very moody and unstable.* 2 not steady, wobbly. *The table is unsteady.*

**unsuitable** *adjective* not right or fitting for a particular purpose. *Slippers are unsuitable for playing football.*

**untidy** (untidier, untidiest) *adjective* messy and with nothing in its proper place. *Adrian's office is always untidy!*

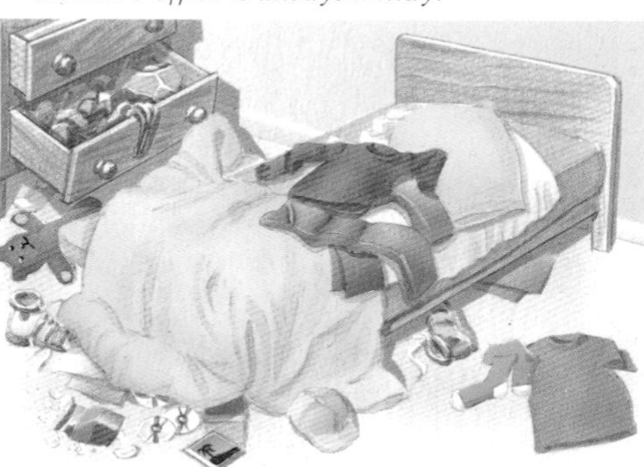

Shelby left her bedroom in an untidy mess.

**untie** (unties, untying, untied) *verb* to undo or loosen the knots of something that was tied. *She untied the bows in her hair.*

**until** *conjunction, preposition* up to the time of or when. *She stayed up until long past midnight to welcome in the New Year.*

**untold** *adjective* too much or too many to calculate. *Locusts do untold damage to some crops.*

**unusual** *adjective* strange, rare and unexpected. *An unusual necklace.*

This very unusual vase will create lots of interest at the antiques fair.

**unwelcome** *adjective* not wanted. *An unwelcome visitor.*

**unwieldy** *noun* bulky, clumsy and difficult to hold, manage or move.

U

**unwitting** *adjective* 1 not knowing and not intended. *An unwitting error.*

**unworthy** *adjective* not deserving. *Such a ridiculous story is unworthy of attention.* 2 out of character and below standards expected. *It's unworthy of you to tell lies.*

**unwrap** (unwraps, unwrapping, unwrapped) *verb* to remove the covering or wrapping off something such as a parcel, to

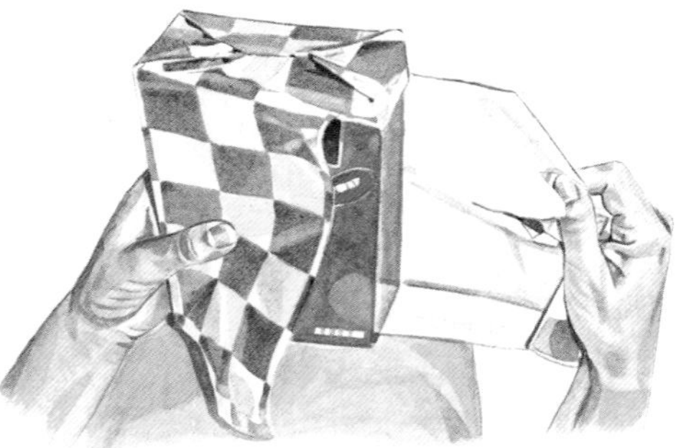

Simon unwrapped the parcel and was astonished to find a box of pasta inside.

**up** *adverb, preposition* 1 to a higher level, amount etc. *Jack went up the hill.* 2 to a sitting or standing position. *Please stand up.* 3 completely, so that it is finished. *She ate up her crusts.* 4 out of bed. *She gets up early.* 5 along. *I was walking up the road.* 6 into pieces. *He tore up the letter.* **ups and downs** good times and bad times. **up and coming** on the way to being successful.

**upbeat** *adjective* happy and ever hopeful.

**upbringing** *noun* the way that a child is brought up and told how to behave.

**update** *verb* to add all the latest information and make more modern. *The files are constantly updated.*

**upheaval** *noun* a great change causing a lot of worry. *Moving is a huge upheaval.*

**uphill** *adverb* going up a slope or hill. *We walked uphill.* The opposite is downhill. **uphill** *adjective* difficult and needing a lot of effort. *An uphill struggle to survive.*

Adam cycled slowly uphill, thinking of the chocolate he would eat when he reached the top.

**GRAMMAR NOTE**

*'Upon' and 'on' are synonymous and interchangeable. 'He threw himself upon the bed.' 'She walked on a tightrope.' 'Upon' is slightly more formal, and in speaking 'on' is usually preferred.*

**AMAZING FACT**

The word 'urchin' comes from an ancient word meaning hedgehog.

**uphold** (upholds, upholding, upheld) *verb* to give support to or defend an action or cause. *The umpire upheld the referee's decision, and was booed.*

**upholstery** *noun* the springs, padding, covering and cushions of chairs and sofas. *Leather upholstery.* **upholster** *verb.*

**upkeep** *noun* the cost of keeping something in a good condition. *What's the upkeep of your car?*

**upon** *preposition* on, on top of.

**upper** *adjective* above, in a higher position. the upper part of your body.

**upright** *adjective, adverb* 1 in a vertical position. *Upright posts.* 2 good and honest. *An upright person.*

**uprising** *noun* a rebellion or revolt against people in authority.

**uproar** *noun* noisy and angry or excited confusion, a disturbance.

**uproot** *verb* to pull a plant out of the ground by its roots.

**upset** (upsets, upsetting, upset) *verb* 1 to overturn or knock something over by accident. *The cat upset the milk jug.* 2 to make somebody feel worried or unhappy. *You've upset your mother by being so rude.* **upset** *noun* 1 a minor illness. *A tummy upset.* 2 a sudden change. *The bad weather has caused an upset to our plans.*

**upside-down** *adjective* 1 with the top facing down and the bottom facing up. 2 utter disorder. *She turned the house upside-down looking for her watch.*

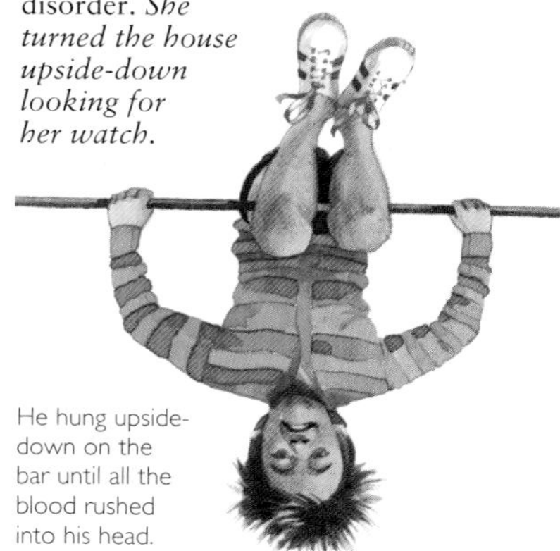

He hung upside-down on the bar until all the blood rushed into his head.

**upstairs** *adjective, adverb* situated on or going to a higher floor. *He walked upstairs.* The opposite is downstairs.

**uptight** *adjective* 1 (slang) nervous, angry, irritated. 2 (US) prim and conventional.

**up-to-date** *adjective* modern, containing all the very latest information etc. *An up-to-date map.* The opposite is out-of-date.

**urchin** *noun* a poor, shabbily dressed, mischievous child.

**Urdu** *noun* one of the official languages of Pakistan, also widely spoken in India.

**urge** *verb* to encourage and try to make somebody do something, to plead. *He urged her to try a little harder.* **urge** *noun* a strong desire to do something, an impulse. *She had a sudden urge to go for a walk.*

**urgent** *adjective* very important and needing to be dealt with at once. *An urgent phone call.* **urgency** *noun.*

**urine** *noun* the clear, yellowish fluid waste passed from the bodies of animals and humans from the bladder. **urinate** *verb* to pass urine from the body.

**urn** *noun* 1 an ornamental vase or a container for a dead person's ashes. 2 a large container for holding hot drinks. *A tea urn.*

**Uruguay** *noun* a country in South America.

Uruguay is famous for its pampas grasslands, its fine herds of beef cattle and the cowboys called gauchos.

**Uruguayan** *noun* a person from Uruguay. **Uruguayan** *adjective. Uruguayan pasturelands.*

**USA** *abbreviation* United States of America.

**usage** *noun* 1 a way of using, treatment. *The video has been damaged through rough usage.* 2 the usual or customary way of doing or saying things. *American usage is to say 'hood' for 'bonnet', 'billfold' for 'wallet', and 'windshield' for' windscreen'.*

**use** *verb* (say **yoo-zz**) 1 to make something do a job. *She used scissors to cut the cloth.* 2 to consume or take. *Don't use all the hot water.* **use** *noun* (rhymes with juice) 1 the act of using or being in use. *The photocopier is in constant use.* 2 the purpose for using something. *This tool has many uses.*

**used** *adjective* not new, already owned by somebody. *It is sometimes possible to find a real bargain at used car sales, especially if you understand engines and can repair them.*

Roy did not trust the used car salesman.

**AMAZING FACT**

When the United States of America was formed, a vote was taken to decide what the official language of the US would be. English won, but only by one vote. Otherwise, the US would have been a German-speaking country.

"These whisks are my favourite cooking utensils," cried Mary.

**WORD HISTORY**

*'Utopia' comes from a Latin word for 'no place' and was the title of a book by Sir Thomas More (1477–1536) describing an ideal land where everything is shared by everyone and where everyone is educated.*

**used to** *verb* 1 accustomed to. *He isn't used to so much exercise.* 2 something that once happened often or that was once true. *We used to swim every afternoon.*

**useful** *adjective* helpful, having a purpose. *Useful tips on removing stains.* **usefulness** *noun. Gary's usefulness was very limited.*

**useless** *adjective* 1 of little or no help, having no effect. *It's useless asking him the way .* 2 (slang) very bad. *I'm useless at maths.* **uselessness** *noun.*

**user** *noun* a person who uses something. *A rehabilitation centre for drug users.*

**user-friendly** *adjective* designed to be easy to use and understand. *A user-friendly video-recorder.*

**usual** *adjective* happening often or most of the time, normal and everyday. *She arrived home at her usual time.* **usually** *adverb. We usually go shopping on Friday.*

**utensil** *noun* a tool or container, especially one used everyday in the home. *Cooking utensils.*

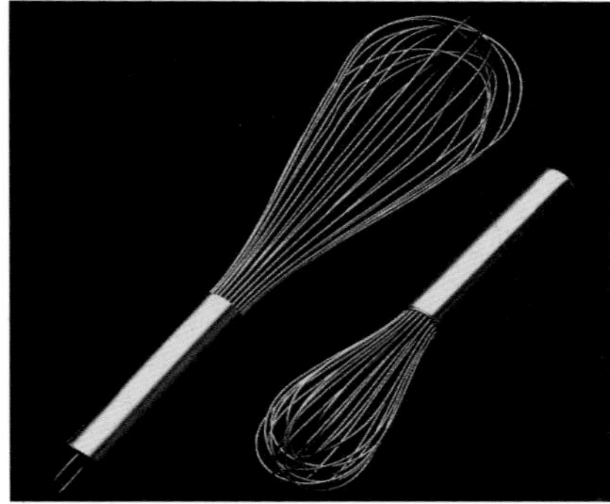

**uterus** *noun* the womb in which a baby develops. *The uterus was our first home.*

**utmost** *adjective* 1 the greatest possible. *It's a matter of the utmost importance.* 2 farthest. *The utmost ends of the Earth.*

**utopia** *noun* an imaginary place where everything is perfect, a paradise. **utopian** *adjective. Sarah leads a utopian existence.*

**utter** *verb* to speak or make a sound with your mouth. *He uttered a squeal of delight.*

**utterly** *adverb* completely. *An utterly stupid thing to do.* **utter** *adjective. An utter idiot.*

**U-turn** *noun* 1 a U-shaped turn that a vehicle makes to go back the way it came. 2 a reversal of plans.

**Uzbekistan** *noun* a country in West Asia.

Uzbekistan was a member of the Soviet Union. It became independent in 1991.

V

# Vv

**vacant** *adjective* empty, unoccupied and not in use. *The bathroom is vacant.* **vacancy** *noun* a job that is available. *Are there any vacancies in the factory?* **vacate** *verb. The room should be vacated by 11 a.m.*

**vacation** *noun* 1 a holiday between terms at college or university. 2 (US) a holiday.

**vaccinate** *verb* (say **vak**-sin-ate) to inject somebody to protect them from a disease such as measles. **vaccination** *noun.*

**vaccine** *noun* (say **vak**-seen) a medicine made from the germs of a disease injected into people to protect them from the disease.

**vacuum** *noun* space that is quite empty with all gases removed. **vacuum** *verb* to clean with a vacuum-cleaner.

**vacuum-cleaner** *noun* an electrical machine that sucks up dust from carpets etc.

The first ever vacuum-cleaner was designed to blow the dust away rather than to suck it up.

**Vaduz** *noun* the capital of Liechtenstein.

**vagina** *noun* a passage in a woman's body that leads to the womb.

**vague** *noun* (say vayg) not clear or definite. *I could just see a vague shape in the twilight, but I couldn't identify who it was.*

**vain** *adjective* 1 too interested in your appearance or what you can do, too proud. 2 useless or unsuccessful, meaningless. *A vain attempt.* **in vain** without success.

**valentine** *noun* 1 a card you send to somebody you love on 14 February – Saint Valentine's Day. 2 the person to whom you send the card. *You are my valentine.*

**valiant** *adjective* brave.

**valid** *adjective* acceptable, legally acceptable. *A valid ticket.* **validity** *noun.*

### WORD HISTORY

*The shape of the letter V – as well as U and W – comes from a Semitic letter called 'waw', which was symbolized as a tenthook. The Romans used V for both V and U sounds. In the Middle Ages scholars began using U for the vowel sound and V for the consonant sound.*

### WORD HISTORY

*Vandals were Germanic people who invaded Gaul, Spain and Rome in the fourth and fifth centuries, destroying beautiful cities, churches and palaces as they went. Any destructive people became known as vandals after the word was first used during the French Revolution.*

**Valletta** *noun* the capital of Malta.

**valley** (valleys) *noun* low land between hills, usually with a river flowing through it.

**valuable** *adjective* 1 precious and worth a lot of money. **valuables** *plural noun.* 2 useful, helpful. *Valuable advice.*

**value** *noun* 1 the amount of money that something is worth or that it can be sold for, price. *What is the value of this diamond?* 2 the importance or usefulness of somebody or something. **value** *verb. I greatly value your friendship.*

**valve** *noun* a device on a tube, pipe etc. that controls the flow of a gas or liquid. You pump air into a tyre through a valve.

**vampire** *noun* in stories, a corpse that leaves its grave at night to suck people's blood.

The best way to protect yourself against a vampire is to carry a cross or some garlic.

**van** *noun* a small enclosed lorry for carrying goods. *The van delivered the new sofa.*

**vandal** *noun* a person who deliberately and for no good reason smashes and ruins things. **vandalize** *verb.* **vandalism** *noun.*

**vane** *noun* **weather vane** a pointer that moves with the direction of the wind and so shows which way the wind is blowing.

**vanilla** *noun* a sweet flavouring for ice cream, cakes etc. made from the pod of a tropical kind of orchid.

**vanish** *verb* to disappear, to become invisible. *The bus vanished into the mist.*

**vanity** *noun* being too proud of what you look like or of what you can do. Conceit.

**Vanuatu** *noun* a country of islands in the Pacific Ocean.

Eighty islands make up the Pacific nation of Vanuatu. Some are coral islands with reefs and brilliant blue lagoons.

**vapour** *noun* a gas produced by heating a liquid or solid form of the substance. Steam is water vapour.

**variable** *adjective* changing or varying a lot, not stable. *The weather has been variable.*

**variation** *noun* 1 varying. 2 something that has changed. 3 differences.

**varied** *adjective* different kinds of.

**variety** *noun* a collection or number of different things or kinds. *There are many varieties of sheep.*

Anthony had a variety of gold and silver coins in his collection.

**various** *adjective* of different sorts, several. *Victor had various jobs after he left school.*

**varnish** *noun* a shiny, transparent liquid that you paint on to wood to protect it and to make it look glossy.

**vary** (varies, varying, varied) *verb* 1 to alter, to change constantly. *The weather varies from day to day.* 2 to make different. *I try to vary the menu from one day to the next.*

**vase** *noun* an ornamental container or jar for flowers.

**vast** *adjective* very wide, immense. *The vast rainforests of the Amazon.*

**VAT** *abbreviation* value-added tax.

**vat** *noun* a large container or tub for storing liquid. *A vat of wine.*

**Vatican City** *noun* an independent city and state within the city of Rome, Italy.

**vault** *noun* 1 a room below a church. A strong underground room in which to store valuable things. 2 an arched roof.

Down in the vaults the air was very cold and damp.

**vault** *verb* to jump over something using a pole. **vault** *noun*.

**DID YOU KNOW?**

*The word 'veal' comes from the French word for calf, 'veau'. After the Norman Conquest (1066) the French word for some animals was used for the name of the meat, so we get beef (from the French 'boeuf'), pork (from 'porc'), mutton (from 'mouton') and veal.*

**AMAZING FACT**

Vatican City is the world's smallest independent country. It is tiny, about the size of a small farm, and stands on a hill in northwest Rome. Only about 750 people live there, yet it has its own flag, railroad and radio station and issues its own stamps.

**VCR** *abbreviation* video cassette recorder.

**VDU** *abbreviation* visual display unit.

**veal** *noun* the meat of a calf used as food.

**veer** *verb* to turn suddenly and change direction, to swerve.

**vegan** *noun* a vegetarian who does not use or eat any animal products.

**vegetable** *noun* a plant that is grown to be eaten. Carrots and peas are vegetables. **vegetable** *adjective*. *Vegetable curry.*

Henry brought in the vegetables that he had grown in his allotment.

**vegetarian** *noun* somebody who does not eat meat, only vegetables and sometimes dairy foods and fish.

**vegetation** *noun* plant life. *Rainforests have lush vegetation.*

**vehicle** *noun* a machine such as a car, bus or lorry that transports people and goods from one place to another on land.

**veil** *noun* a very fine piece of material worn by some women to cover their face or head.

**vein** *noun* (rhymes with pain) 1 one of the tubes inside your body through which blood flows back to your heart. 2 one of the fine lines on a leaf or insect wing.

**velocity** *noun* speed, particularly speed at which something travels in one direction.

**velvet** *noun* a material with a soft thick pile. *The cat sat on a velvet cushion.*

**Venezuela** *noun* a country in South America.

**Venezuelan** *noun* a person who comes from Venezuela. **Venezuelan** *adjective*. *Venezuelan oil wells.*

**venison** *noun* the meat from deer, used as food. *Vension was served at the banquet.*

**venom** *noun* poison produced by some snakes and spiders. **venomous** *adjective*.

**ventilate** *verb* to let fresh air move freely through a place. *A well-ventilated bathroom.* **ventilation** *noun*.

**ventriloquist** *noun* a person who entertains by making their voice seem to come not from their mouth but from a dummy or from another place.

**venture** *verb* to risk doing something. *'Nothing ventured, nothing gained.'* **venture** *noun. A risky business venture.*

**verandah** *noun* a platform around the outside of a house, usually with a roof.

**verb** *noun* a word or words in a sentence that describes what somebody or something is doing etc. In the sentence 'The dog is eating its bone,' 'is eating' is the verb.

**verbose** *adjective* using too many words. 'At this point in time' is a verbose way of saying 'now'.

**verdict** *noun* the decision of the judge and jury at the end of a trial in a law court saying whether the accused is guilty or not guilty. *The jury returned a verdict of guilty.*

**verge** *noun* the grassy strip of ground along the edge of a road or path. **verge** *verb. His behaviour verges on rudeness.*

**verify** (verifies, verifying, verified) *verb* to prove by showing the truth of something.

**vermin** *noun* any animal, bird or insect that can transmit a disease or that damages food crops. Pests.

The old house was infested with vermin.

**verse** *noun* 1 a part of a poem consisting of a group of lines. 2 poetry and having rhythm and sometimes rhyme.

**version** *noun* 1 one form or a changed type of something. *A new version of the Bible.* 2 one person's description. *Mary gave her version of the accident.*

**versus** *preposition* a Latin word meaning against, often shortened to v. *Swansea versus Cardiff. Sheffield v. Nottingham.*

**vertebra** (vertebrae) *noun* any one of the bones that make up the spine.

**vertebrate** *noun* any animal with a backbone. *Humans are vertebrates.*

**vertical** *adjective* upright, straight up. *The telegraph posts should be vertical.* The opposite is horizontal.

**vessel** *noun* 1 a ship or boat. 2 a container for liquids. *A drinking vessel.*

**WORD HISTORY**

*The ancient Greeks believed that ventriloquism was the work of demons and thought the voice came from the abdomen. The word comes from the Latin 'venter' (belly) and 'loqui' meaning 'to speak'.*

**WORD HISTORY**

*'Vermin' comes from a Latin word meaning 'worm'. It was later used to describe any unwanted animals.*

**AMAZING FACT**

There are seven main groups of vertebrates: mammals, birds, reptiles, amphibians, fish, sharks, skates and, the simplest group, lampreys.

**vet** or **veterinary surgeon** *noun* a person who is trained to treat sick animals, an animal doctor.

**veto** *noun* the ability not to allow something to happen. **veto** *verb. The general vetoed the decision.*

**vex** (vexes, vexing, vexed) *verb* to annoy or worry somebody.

**via** *preposition* (say **vye**-ah) by way of. *We fly to Tehran via Rome.*

**viable** *adjective* likely to be successful, workable. *Building a bridge across the Atlantic is simply not viable.*

**viaduct** *noun* (say **vye**-a-dukt) a long, arched bridge that carries a road or railway across a valley.

The train travelled across the viaduct.

**vibrate** *verb* to shake to and fro rapidly. *The windows vibrate when lorries whizz past.* **vibration** *noun.*

**vicar** *noun* a clergyman in charge of a parish in the Anglican Church.

**vicarage** *noun* the house where a vicar lives.

**vice** *noun* very bad, immoral or criminal behaviour. A bad habit.

**vice** *noun* a device that grips things firmly while you are working on them.

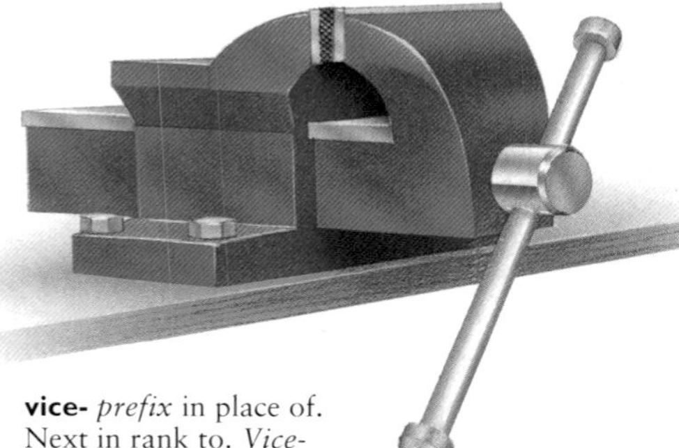

Paul had a new vice clamped to his work bench.

**vice-** *prefix* in place of. Next in rank to. *Vice-president.*

**vice-versa** *adverb* the same is true either way or the other way round. *When he wants to eat, she doesn't want to eat and vice versa.*

**vicinity** *noun* (say viss-**in**-it-ee) the surrounding or nearby area.

**vicious** *adjective* violent, cruel.

**victim** *noun* a person who has been attacked, injured, robbed or killed.

**victimize** *verb* to deliberately choose somebody to treat unfairly or cruelly.

**victor** *noun* the winner in a competition, battle etc. *The victor was given a medal.*

**Victoria** *noun* the capital of Seychelles.

**victory** *noun* success in a battle, contest etc. A win. **victorious** *adjective.*

**video** *noun* 1 a machine (video cassette recorder) that records television programmes so that you can watch them at another time. 2 a tape (videotape contained within a videocassette) used to record a television programme.

**vie** (vies, vying, vied) *verb* to compete.

**Vienna** *noun* the capital of Austria.

**Vientiane** *noun* the capital of Laos.

**Vietnam** *noun* a country in Southeast Asia.

**Vietnamese** *noun* a person who comes from Vietnam. **Vietnamese** *adjective. Vietnamese ricefields.*

**vigorous** *adjective* physically energetic, enthusiastic, strong. *A vigorous walk in the Black Forest.* **vigour** *noun.*

**Vikings** *plural noun* seafarers from Scandinavia who invaded many parts of Europe between the 8th and 11th centuries. **Viking** *adjective. Viking hordes.*

The Vikings sailed for thousands of kilometres across the icy northern oceans in small wooden boats that were completely open to the elements. They leaped from their boats and rushed up the beach to make a surprise attack.

**SPELLING NOTE**

*'Vigorous' is often misspelled. Notice how the 'u' of 'vigour' is dropped before the suffix '–ous' in vigorous. Also take care not to spell 'villain' as 'villian'.*

**vile** *adjective* disgusting and very unpleasant, horrible. *A vile smell.*

**villa** *noun* a detached house with a garden in the suburbs. In Roman times a villa was a country house.

**village** *noun* a small group of houses, often with a church, school, shop and pub.

**villain** *noun* 1 a person who breaks the law on purpose. 2 a wicked person, especially in a film, novel etc. *The villain of the story was a cruel king.* **villainy** *noun.*

**Vilnius** *noun* the capital of Lithuania.

**vine** *noun* a climbing plant on which grapes grow. *A vine clambered up the terrace.*

**vinegar** *noun* a sharp-tasting liquid made from wine or malt and used to flavour food.

**vineyard** *noun* (say **vin**-yard) a place where grapes are grown for making wine.

We drank a full-bodied red wine that came from the south end of the vineyard.

**vintage** *adjective* (of wine) 1 a very good example of a particular year. 2 (of cars) made between 1919 and 1930. 3 of high and enduring quality.

V

**viola** *noun* a stringed musical instrument that is slightly larger than a violin and with a lower sound. *The beautiful mellow sound of the viola reached my ears.*

Rachel played the viola in the youth orchestra.

**violent** *adjective* 1 using a lot of physical force to frighten, hurt or even kill. 2 sudden, strong and rough. *A violent storm blew up over the dark Sargasso Sea.* **violence** *noun. I don't like violence on television or in films.*

**violet** *noun* 1 a small plant with purplish flowers and a sweet smell. *Come, buy my lovely violets!* 2 the purplish colour of a violet. **violet** *adjective.*

**violin** *noun* a musical instrument with four strings stretched across a wooden frame. *Hilary was learning to play the violin.*

**viper** *noun* a European poisonous snake, an adder. *Ian was bitten by a viper.*

**virgin** *noun* a person who has never had sexual intercourse. *Queen Elizabeth I remained a virgin.* **virginity** *noun.*

**virtual** *adjective* 1 in practice, but not in name. *His wife was the virtual prime minister.* 2 almost but not completely; not actually said. *The virtual collapse of law and order.* **virtual reality** an impression of a real environment in which you can interact, created by a computer.

**virtue** *noun* a particular good quality, goodness. Kindness and honesty are virtues.

**virus** *noun* 1 a microscopically tiny organism or living thing, smaller than bacteria, that can carry or cause disease. *A flu virus.* 2 a computer program that can damage or destroy data in a computer.

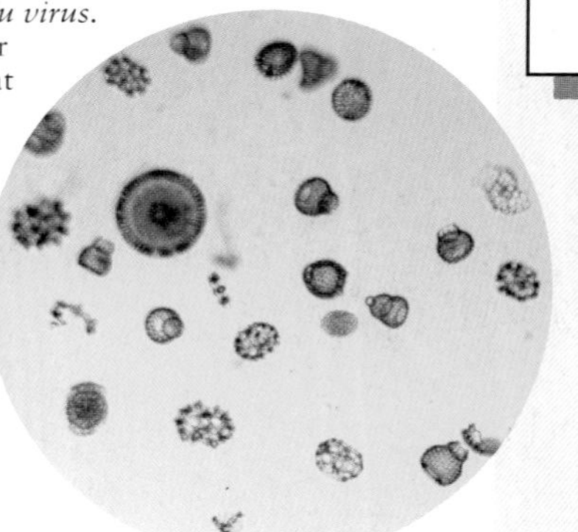

We looked at the virus under the microscope.

**AMAZING FACT**

New computer viruses are developed every day. A virus might send just a harmless joke or a cryptic message to your screen – or it could do serious damage.

**WORD HISTORY**

*The word 'vitamin' is taken from the Latin word 'vita' meaning 'life' and the chemical 'amine'. The word was invented by the chemist Casimir Funk in 1913.*

**viscount** *noun* (say vie-count) the title of a nobleman. *We invited the viscount and the viscountess to luncheon, but unfortunately, they had a prior engagement.*

**viscountess** *noun* (say vie-count-ess) the wife of a viscount. *The viscountess wore blue at her sister's wedding.*

**visible** *adjective* capable of being seen. *From the top of a bus the whole street is visible.* **visibility** *noun* how clearly you can see. *On foggy days visibility is poor.*

**vision** *noun* 1 sight, your ability to see. 2 what you can see or imagine in a dream. 3 great power of imagination and ability to plan. *His vision is that everybody should own their own home.*

**visit** *verb* 1 to go to see somebody or a place. 2 to stay somewhere for a short time. **visit** *noun.* **visitor** *noun.*

**visual** *adjective* relating to seeing and sight. *Computers display information on a visual display unit.*

**visualize** *verb* to form a picture in your mind, to imagine. *Can you visualize the awful situation Jane put me into?*

**vital** *adjective* essential to life, very important. *Air and water are vital to all living creatures.*

**vitality** *adjective* full of life and energy.

**vitamin** *noun* any one of several substances in food that we need to stay healthy. *Terry takes a vitamin supplement with her morning coffee.*

**vivid** *adjective* bright and clear. *Vivid colours are the ones I like best.*

**vivisection** *noun* the use of living animals in scientific experiments.

**vixen** *noun* a female fox. The male is called a dog. The young are called cubs.

The vixen went on the prowl at night, looking for food to feed her cubs.

**viz** *adverb* namely.

**vocabulary** *noun* all the words somebody knows in a language. *His vocabulary in Spanish is about 1,000 words.*

**vocal** *adjective* 1 relating to the voice. *Vocal cords.* 2 speaking out freely and loudly. *He is very vocal about his beliefs.*

**vocation** *noun* a calling or very strong feeling that you want to do a particular job. *Dan had a vocation to become a priest.* 2 a profession or occupation, a career.

**vodka** *noun* a colourless, strong alcoholic drink. *Penny likes vodka and tomato juice.*

**vogue** *noun* a fashion.

**voice** *noun* the sound produced by your vocal cords when you speak or sing, the power to speak.

**void** *noun* emptiness, a huge space with nothing in it. **void** *adjective* having no legal effect. *Null and void.*

**volcano** (volcanoes) *noun* a mountain with a crater (hole) on top through which molten lava from below the Earth's crust erupts from time to time. **volcanic** *adjective.*

**WORD HISTORY**

*'Vodka' is a Russian word meaning 'little water'. Other Russian words that have come into the English language include 'steppe', 'tundra' and 'samovar'.*

**AMAZING FACT**

Volcanoes have caused enormous damage throughout history. One of the most famous of volcanoes, Vesuvius, destroyed the city of Pompeii in AD 79.

**volume** *noun* 1 the amount of space that something takes up or contains. *The volume of water in the lake.* 2 one of a set of books. *A 20-volume encyclopedia.* 3 the loudness of sound. *Turn up the volume so I can hear.*

**voluntary** *adjective* done willingly and not because you have been forced. *She made a voluntary statement.* 2 done without payment. *She does voluntary work for charity.* **volunteer** *noun.*

**vomit** *verb* to bring food back from your stomach through your mouth, to be sick.

**vote** *verb* to choose from a group the person or thing you prefer by raising your hand or marking a piece of paper. **vote** *noun. Each candidate got three votes.*

**vow** *verb* to make a very serious promise, to pledge. *He vowed to improve conditions for all the householders in the street.* **vow** *noun.*

**vowel** *noun* a letter that is not a consonant – a,e,i,o and u and sometimes y.

**voyage** *noun* a long sea journey.

**vulgar** *adjective* rude, offensive, coarse. **vulgarity** *noun. The teacher put a stop to vulgarity in the playground.*

**vulnerable** *adjective* easily harmed because unprotected, weak. *Old people are particularly vulnerable during the cold winter months.* **vulnerability** *noun.*

**vulture** *noun* a large bird of prey that feeds mostly on carrion (dead animals). *The vulture swooped out of the sky and landed on the sheep's carcass.*

When a volcano erupts, igneous rocks are formed from magma, which may solidify beneath or on the Earth's surface. Magma reaches the surface through vents, which are holes in the ground.

**wad** *noun* a thick lump of soft material, a tight bundle or pile of paper. *A wad of banknotes was thrust into my hand.*

**waddle** *verb* to walk in a clumsy way with short steps like a duck.

**wade** *verb* to walk through water or mud. To move slowly and with difficulty.

**wafer** *noun* a very thin crisp biscuit.

**waffle** *noun* a light crisp cake made of batter with a pattern of little squares on it. Waffles are very popular in North America.

**waffle** *verb* to speak or write eloquently and at great length without saying anything important. **waffle** *noun. What a lot of waffle you talk!*

**wag** (wags, wagging, wagged) *verb* to move quickly from side to side or up and down. *The cat wagged its tail in anger.*

**wage** (wages, waging, waged) *verb* to begin and carry on something for a period of time. *The police are waging war on car theft.*

**wages** *plural noun* the money you earn for the work you do.

**wagon** *noun* 1 a four-wheeled cart pulled by a horse. 2 an open railway truck for carrying freight. *Twenty wagons carrying coal.*

**DID YOU KNOW**

*The shape of the letter W – as well as U and V - developed from a Semitic letter called 'waw' which was symbolized as a tenthook. The Romans used V for both V and U sounds. In the Middle Ages scholars began using U for the vowel sound and they doubled the U to make W and called the new letter double U.*

The wagons rolled westwards across America. The weary people were in search of a dream.

**wail** *noun* a long, sad cry. **wail** *verb. The wind wailed in the trees.*

**waist** *noun* the narrow, middle part of your body above your hips.

**waistcoat** *noun* a close-fitting jacket without sleeves, usually worn under another jacket (US vest).

**wait** *verb* to stay where you are until something happens or someone arrives, to pause. *We waited 15 minutes for the bus.*

**waiter** *noun* a man or a woman (also waitress) who brings food and drinks to you in a restaurant.

**wake** (waking, woke, woken) *verb* 1 to stop being asleep. 2 to rouse somebody from sleep. **wake** *noun* (especially in Ireland) a group of people who stay with a dead body to mourn on the night before it is buried.

**Wales** *noun* a country that is part of the United Kingdom.

**walk** *verb* to move along on your feet. **walk** *noun. A walk in the hills.* **walker** *noun.* **walk off with** to take something without asking. **walk-over** an easy victory in a competition.

**wall** *noun* a structure made of bricks or stones surrounding a piece of land. The side of a building or room. **walled** *adjective. A walled garden.* **up the wall** crazy. *The noise is sending me up the wall.*

**wallaby** *noun* a small kind of kangaroo.

Wallabies are marsupials. The female wallaby carries her baby in a pouch.

**wallet** *noun* a small, folding case or purse for keeping money and credit cards.

**wallflower** *noun* 1 a sweet-smelling plant with red or orange flowers. 2 somebody who nobody ever seems to want to dance with.

**wallow** *verb* 1 to roll and splash about in water or mud. 2 to enjoy something to excess. *She wallowed in everybody's praise.*

**walnut** *noun* the edible nut of the walnut tree. Walnut wood is used for furniture.

**walrus** *noun* a large sea animal similar to a seal with two long tusks.

**waltz** *noun* a graceful dance for two people with three beats to a bar.

**wan** *adjective* pale and tired-looking.

**wand** *noun* a stick that magicians and fairies use to perform magic.

**wander** *verb* to move slowly from one place to another without going in any particular direction, to roam. **wanderer** *noun.*

**wane** *verb* to become smaller, to lose power. *The Moon is waning tonight.* The opposite is to wax.

**want** *verb* 1 to desire something or to wish to do something. *I want to go home.* 2 to need. *The dogs want feeding.*

**war** *noun* 1 armed fighting between countries or groups of people. A long period of fighting. 2 a struggle or campaign. *The war against poverty.*

Shortly after the tanks landed on the beach, the soldiers charged ahead to fight the war.

**ward** *noun* 1 a room in a hospital with beds where patients are treated. 2 a ward of court is a child who is under the protection of a court or an adult guardian. 3 a part into which a town is divided for voting.

**-ward, -wards** *suffix* in the particular direction of. *Homewards, southward.*

**warden** *noun* somebody who is in charge of a college, hostel etc., a guard. *Tom wants to be a traffic warden when he grows up.*

**warder** *noun* a prison guard.

**wardrobe** *noun* a cupboard in which to hang your clothes.

**warehouse** *noun* a building for storing goods that are to be sold.

The farmer used his barn as a warehouse for the fertilizers he was selling.

**warfare** *noun* the state of fighting wars.

**warlike** *adjective* hostile and prepared for war. *The soldiers had a warlike manner.*

**warm** *adjective* 1 slightly hot but not too hot. 2 friendly and enthusiastic. *A warm smile.* **warm** *verb. Can you warm the plates?* **warmth** *noun. The warmth of the Sun is doing my old bones a lot of good.*

**warn** *verb* 1 to tell somebody about a possible danger in the future. 2 to advise. *He warned me to go carefully.* **warning** *noun* a notice or statement that warns.

**DID YOU KNOW?**

*The 'DC' in Washington DC stands for District of Columbia. The city of Washington covers the entire District. The site was chosen by George Washington in 1790 and planned by the French engineer Pierre L'Enfant.*

**warp** *verb* to become twisted or misshapen through damp or heat. *The heat of the fire has warped the table.*

**warren** *noun* a network of underground burrows or passages in which rabbits live.

**warrior** *noun* a great fighting soldier.

**Warsaw** *noun* the capital of Poland.

**warship** *noun* a ship armed with guns for use in war.

**wart** *noun* a hard lump on your skin. **warty** *adjective. He has warty hands.*

**was** past tense of be.

**wash** *verb* 1 to clean with water, soap etc. *Wash your hands.* 2 to flow over or against something. 3 to carry away by flowing water. *The rain washed the mud away.*

**washing** *noun* clothes that need washing or that have been washed.

The washing blew madly on the line and was dry in no time in the warm sunshine.

**washing-machine** *noun* a machine that washes clothes.

**washing-up** *noun* the plates, knives and forks etc. that you wash after a meal. **wash up** *verb. I'll wash up, you dry.*

**Washington DC** *noun* the capital of the United States of America.

**wasp** *noun* a yellow and black striped insect that can sting.

**waste** *noun* 1 things that you throw away because they are broken, worn or you do not need them any more, rubbish. 2 not using things in a careful way. *It's a waste to throw away food.* **waste** *verb* to use more of something than you need or to throw something away that could be used. **waste** *adjective. Waste paper.*

**wasteful** *adjective* extravagant, using more than is needed. **wastefulness** *noun.*

**wastepaper basket** *noun* a basket or container for paper rubbish.

**watch** *verb* 1 to look at for some time. *Watch how I do this.* 2 to notice and be careful about something. *Watch how you cross the road.* 3 to keep guard or take care of somebody or something. *Watch the soup doesn't boil over.* **watchdog** *noun* a dog that guards property **watch out!** be careful.

W

**watch** *noun* a small clock that you usually wear on your wrist.

**watchful** *adjective* always noticing what is happening, alert. **watchfulness** *noun*.

**water** *noun* a clear liquid that falls as rain and that all living things drink to survive. Water is found in oceans, rivers and lakes. Water is made of two gases – oxygen and hydrogen. **water** *verb* 1 to pour water on. 2 to produce tears in the eyes or saliva in the mouth. 3 to dilute.

**watercolour** *noun* a painting done with watercolours, paints you mix with water.

**waterfall** *noun* water from a stream or river flowing down over a cliff or big rock to the ground below.

**water-lily** *noun* a plant with flat, floating leaves that grows in water.

**watermill** *noun* a mill – a tall building for grinding grain – with machinery powered by water. *The watermill on the River Floss.*

The wheel on the mill is turned by the running water. The energy is used to turn stones inside the mill to grind corn into flour.

**water-polo** *noun* a ball game played in a swimming pool by two teams of seven players. *Water-polo is a sport of the rich.*

**waterproof** *adjective* not letting water through. *A waterproof coat.*

**water-skiing** *noun* a sport of skimming over the water on skis, towed by a rope attached to a motorboat.

**watertight** *adjective* closed so tightly that water cannot get through.

**watery** *adjective* full of water or containing too much water. *Watery soup.*

**watt** *noun* a unit of electricity.

**wave** *noun* 1 a moving curved line or ridge on the surface of water, especially the sea. 2 a curl or curved piece of hair. 3 the vibrating way in which energy such as heat, light, sound and radio travels. 4 the act of moving your hand up and down to attract attention, say goodbye etc.

**wave** *verb* 1 to move your hand up and down to say 'hello' or 'goodbye'. 2 to move something quickly to and fro, to flutter. *The flag waves in the wind.*

**wavelength** *noun* 1 the size of a radio wave to transmit a programme. 2 the distance between electrical, radio or sound waves.

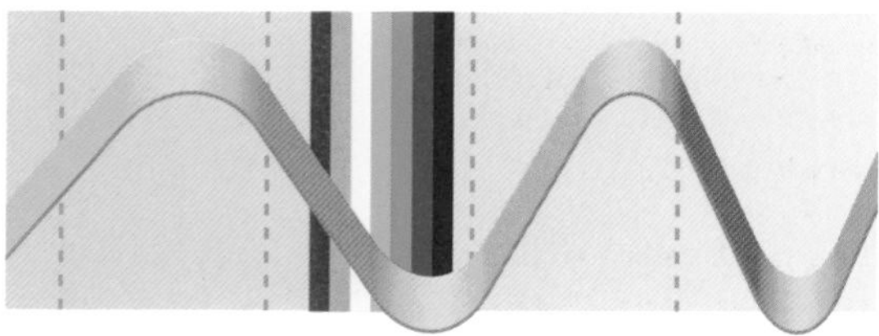

All the different colours of light have different wavelengths. The longest waves we can see are red.

**HANDY HINT**

Remember the order of the colours of the spectrum – red, orange, yellow, green, blue, indigo, violet – by using a mnemonic (a word or sentence made up of the first letter of each word.)

'Richard of York gave battle in vain.' or 'Roy G. Biv'.

**WORD HISTORY**

*Watt, the unit of electricity, is named after James Watt, a Scottish inventor who developed the steam engine.*

**wax** *noun* 1 a solid substance made from fat or oil that becomes soft and sticky when you heat it. Wax is used to make things like candles and furniture polish. 2 a similar substance produced by bees (beeswax). 3 a wax-like substance found in your ears.

**wax** *verb* to grow bigger. *The Moon waxes and then it wanes (grows smaller).*

**way** (ways) *noun* 1 an opening, a passage. *Don't block the way.* 2 a road or path that you should follow, a route. *Is this the way home?* 3 a direction. *Look the other way.* 4 a distance that you travel. *It's a long way to your aunty Lou's.* 5 a state or condition. *He's in a bad way.* 6 means or method of doing something. *Is this the right way to mix paints?* 7 manner. *In a clumsy way.* 8 **ways** customs. The typical behaviour of somebody. **by the way** incidentally. **in the way** blocking the place you want to go.

**-ways** *suffix* in the direction of. *Widthways.*

**weak** *adjective* having little strength or power, easily broken. **weakness** *noun*.

**weaken** *verb* to make or become weak.

**wealth** *noun* 1 a lot of money and possessions, great riches. 2 a large amount. *A wealth of detail.* **wealthy** *adjective* rich.

**weapon** *noun* some device such as a gun, dagger or sword with which to fight.

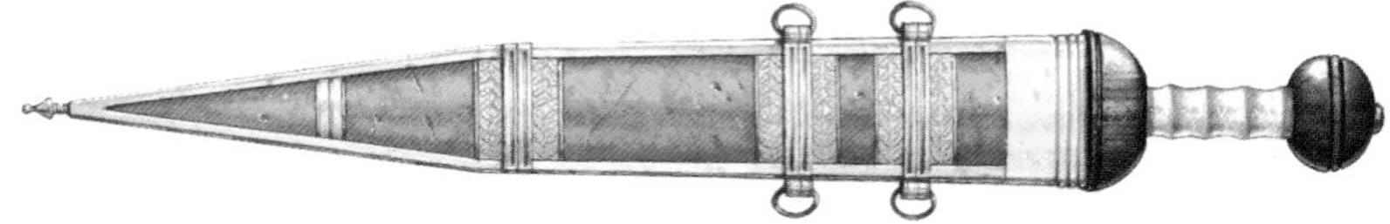

The magnificent dagger in its scabbard was one of the prize weapons in the museum's collection.

**HANDY HINT**

Be careful when you write words that sound the same, like 'wear' and 'where'.

**wear** (wears, wearing, wore, worn) *verb* 1 to be dressed in, to have on your body. *Do you wear glasses?* 2 to become damaged through use. *I wore a hole in the knee.* **wear** *noun*. *Men's wear.* **wear down** to weaken a person's resistance. *She wore him down with her nagging.* **wear off** to fade away or to become less. *The pain is wearing off.* **wear out** 1 to become damaged and useless. 2 to feel tired.

**wearing** *adjective* tiring, exhausting.

**weary** (wearier, weariest) *adjective* very tired. *You must be weary after your long journey.* **weariness** *noun*.

**weather** *noun* the condition of the atmosphere at a particular time or place. Whether it is warm, cold, windy or rainy.

**weathercock** *noun* a weathervane shaped like a cockerel.

**weather forecast** *noun* a report on what the weather is expected to be like in the near future. *The weather forecast is good.*

**weathervane** *noun* a pointer that moves with the wind and so shows which way the wind is blowing.

**weave** (weaves, weaving, woven, woven) *verb* 1 to make cloth by using a machine called a loom that passes threads over and under other threads. 2 to make baskets etc. by plaiting cane etc. 3 (past tense weaved) to move in and out between people or things. *He weaved through the traffic on his bike.*

**web** *noun* **cobweb** a fine sticky net of threads spun by a spider to catch insects.

**webbed** *adjective* having the toes joined by pieces of skin. *Ducks and geese have webbed feet to help them swim better.*

Dewdrops glistened on the spider's web that morning.

**wedding** *noun* the marriage service.

**we'd** *abbreviation* we had.

**wedge** *noun* 1 a piece of wood that is thick at one end and thin and pointed at the other, used to stop things such as doors from moving. 2 something in the shape of a wedge. *A wedge of cheese.* **wedge** *verb*. *She wedged the door open.*

**wee** *adjective* very small.

**weed** *noun* a wild plant that grows where it is not wanted. **weed** *verb* to remove weeds.

**weedy** *adjective* 1 full of weeds. 2 weak and thin. *A weedy person.*

**week** *noun* a period of time from Monday to the following Sunday. There are seven days in a week and 52 weeks in a year. **weekly** *noun*. *A weekly magazine.*

**weekend** *noun* Saturday and Sunday.

**weep** (weeps, weeping, wept) *verb* to cry. *She wept when she read the sad story.*

**SPELLING NOTE**

*Avoid misspelling these words, which sound similar: 'weather' and 'whether'; 'weave' and 'we've'; 'we'd' and 'weed'; 'week' and 'weak'; 'weigh' and 'way'; 'weight' and 'wait'.*

**WORD BUILDING**

*Here are some words with the prefix 'well–': 'well-advised'; 'well-balanced'; 'well-behaved'; 'well-bred'; 'well-built'; 'well-earned'; 'well-educated'; 'well-fed'; 'well-groomed'; 'well-informed' and 'well-intentioned'.*

**weigh** *verb* 1 to place something on scales to find out how heavy it is. 2 to have a certain weight. *Dave weighs more than he used to.*

**weight** *noun* 1 how heavy somebody or something is. 2 a unit of weight or a piece of metal of a certain weight.

There were two sets of weights, one to weigh cooking ingredients, the other for heavier things.

**weird** *adjective* very strange, unusual.

**welcome** *verb* to greet somebody in a way that shows that you are very pleased to see them. **welcome** *noun, interjection*. *Welcome home!* **welcoming** *adjective*.

**weld** *verb* to join two pieces of metal together by melting the ends and pressing and hammering them together. **welder** *noun*.

**welfare** *noun* 1 A person's welfare is their general wellbeing, health, happiness and prosperity. 2 money or help a person in need gets from the state.

**well** *noun* a very deep hole in the ground from which you can get water or oil from far beneath the Earth.

**well** *adjective* in good health, in good order. *I'm very well thank you.* **well** *adverb* 1 in a good or correct way. *Wendy plays tennis well.* 2 thoroughly. *I washed the car very well.* 3 also. *Two packets of crisps and a bar of chocolate as well.* **well** *interjection*. *Well, I hope you had a nice time.*

**we'll** *abbreviation* we shall or we will.

**Wellington** *noun* the capital of New Zealand.

**wellingtons or wellington boots** *plural noun* rubber or plastic boots up to your knees that keep your feet and legs dry.

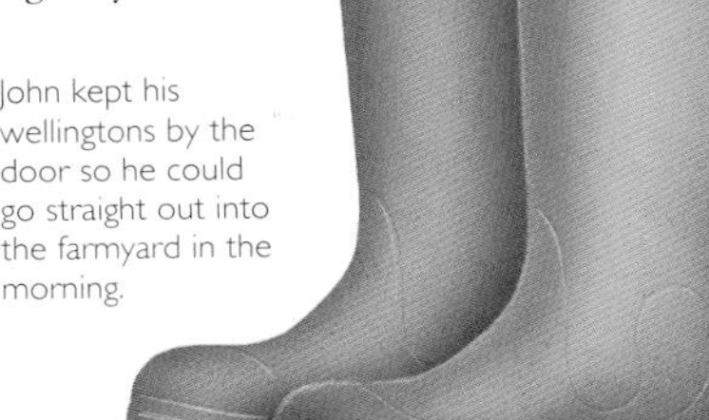

John kept his wellingtons by the door so he could go straight out into the farmyard in the morning.

W

**well-off** *adjective* wealthy. *We are well-off.*

**Welsh** *noun* the language of Wales. **the Welsh** the people of Wales. **Welsh** *adjective*. *Welsh sheep are very hardy.*

**went** past tense of go.

**wept** past tense of weep.

**were** past tense of be.

**we're** short for we are.

**weren't** short for were not.

**werewolf** *noun* in stories and folklore, a man who sometimes turns into a wolf, usually at full moon.

David gave a charming smile, and we suddenly realized that he had turned into a werewolf.

**west** *noun* the direction in which the Sun sets. The opposite direction is east. **west** *adjective, adverb*. *They travelled west.*

**western** *adjective* relating to the west, of the west. *Western Europe.* **western** *noun* a book or film about life in the 19th century in the western USA and involving gunfights and cowboys.

**Western Samoa** *noun* a country of islands in the Pacific Ocean.

**West Indian** *noun* a person from the West Indies. **West Indian** *adjective*. *A West Indian cricketer won the man of the match award.*

**West Indies** *plural noun* a series of islands that separate the Caribbean Sea from the Atlantic Ocean.

**wet** (wetter, wettest) *adjective* covered with or full of water or some other liquid. 2 rainy. *The weekend was very wet.* **wet** (wets, wetting, wet or wetted) *verb* to make something wet. The opposite is dry.

**we've** short for we have.

**whale** *noun* a very large sea mammal that looks like a fish. Whales need air to breathe.

Whales feed on tiny sea creatures called krill, which they sieve through the baleen, plates of fringed material growing from the upper jaw.

**AMAZING FACT**

The biggest animal that has ever lived is the blue whale. It may grow to more than 30 metres in length and weighs about 160 tons when fully grown. Blue whales have been hunted by whalers over the years and are now very rare.

**SPELLING NOTE**

*The following words sound similar and should not be confused: 'we're' and 'weir' (a small dam across a river), 'we've' and 'weave', 'whale' and 'wail' (a long, sad cry), 'wheel' and 'we'll', 'where' and 'ware', 'whine' and 'wine'.*

**wharf** (wharfs or wharves) *noun* platform or landing place where ships dock to be loaded or unloaded.

**wheat** *noun* a cereal crop from whose grain flour is made.

Wheat is the world's second largest crop after rice.

**wheel** *noun* a circular object or disc that rotates around an axle and that is used to move a vehicle or help make machinery work. **wheel** *verb*. *She wheeled the trolley down the aisle.*

**wheelbarrow** *noun* a small handcart with one wheel at the front and two legs and two handles at the back.

**wheelchair** *noun* a chair with large wheels for somebody who cannot walk easily.

**when** *adverb, conjunction* 1 at what time. *When does the bus arrive?* 2 at the time that. *When I get home I change my clothes.*

**whenever** *adverb, conjunction* when, at every time, at any time. *Come whenever you like, as long as you bring me a present.*

**where** *adverb* 1 in what place. *Where's the dog?* 2 to what place. *Where did you go at the weekend?* 3 from what place. *Where did you find those shoes?* **where** *conjunction* at or in what place. *He went over to the window where there was more light.*

**whiff** *noun* a sudden, slight scent of something. *A whiff of honeysuckle.*

**whim** *noun* a sudden, and often silly, desire or thought. *On a sudden whim, Richard bought two tickets for Paris and gave one to the delighted Sarah.*

**whimper** *verb* to make a quiet, crying noise because of pain. **whimper** *noun*. *The puppy gave a frightened whimper.*

**whine** *verb* to keep moaning and complaining in a miserable, irritating voice.

**whinge** *verb* to grumble and complain all the time. **whinger** *noun*. *Steve was a real whinger, but no one took any notice of him.*

**whip** *noun* a strip of leather or a cord attached to a stick, used for hitting animals. **whip** (whips, whipping, whipped) *verb* 1 to hit with a whip. 2 to whisk or beat eggs etc. until they are stiff. 3 to move very quickly. *The actress whipped off her clothes.*

**whirl** *verb* to move round and round quickly. **whirl** *noun. A whirl of activity.*

**whirlpool** *noun* a current of water that turns round and round rapidly.

Janet stared mesmerised into the whirlpool, hoping she would not be sucked in.

**whirlwind** *noun* a strong wind that spins as it travels over land and sea.

**whisk** *noun* a kitchen implement made of wire for beating air into eggs, cream etc. **whisk** verb. *The chef whisked the sauce.*

**whisker** *noun* 1 a long, stiff hair growing around the mouth of an animal such as a cat or dog. 2 hair growing on a man's face.

**whisky** *noun* an alcoholic drink made from barley, rye or other grains *Whisky and water.* (Ireland and USA whiskey).

**whisper** *verb* to speak very quietly using only your breath without vibrating your vocal cords. **whisper** *noun.*

**whistle** *noun* 1 the shrill noise you can make when you blow through your lips. 2 a device you blow to make a sound like a whistle. **whistle** *verb. He whistled a happy tune.*

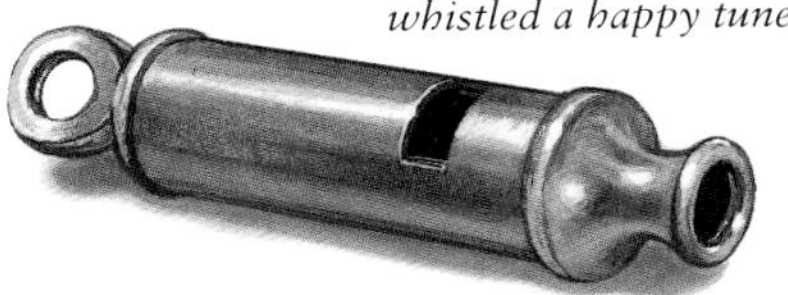

**white** *noun* 1 the colour of milk or new snow. 2 the liquid in an egg around the yoke. 3 (often White) a person belonging to a race with light-coloured skin. **white** *adjective.* **whiten** *verb.* **white lie** a small lie told in order to avoid hurting somebody's feelings. *It was just a little white lie.*

**whizz** (whizzes, whizzing, whizzed) *verb* to move very quickly with a rushing noise. *The racing cars whizzed past.*

**whizz kid** *noun* a very clever and successful young person. *Dean is a real whizz kid.*

**WHO** *abbreviation* World Health Organization.

**GRAMMAR NOTE**

*Try not to confuse 'who's' and 'whose'. 'Who's' is an abbreviation of 'who has' or 'who is', as in 'Who's eaten all the cake?' 'Whose' means 'of whom' or 'of which', as in 'The man whose mother is a singer.' It also means 'of whom' in questions, as in 'Whose book is this?'*

**WORD HISTORY**

*'Whisky' comes from Gaelic words meaning 'water of life'. Gaelic is the original language of Scotland.*

"Stop, thief!" cried Granddad, and he blew his whistle, racing after the burglar.

**AMAZING FACT**

Words like WHO are acronyms, words made up of the first letter of each of the words in a title. Other acronyms are NATO, North Atlantic Treaty Organization and SCUBA, self-contained underwater breathing apparatus.

**whole** *adjective* the complete and total amount of something. *She ate a whole box of chocolates.* **whole** *noun. Two halves make a whole.*

**wholesale** *noun* 1 the sale of goods in large quantities or amounts by a wholesaler to shops (retailers) who then sell to the public. 2 on a big scale. *Wholesale slaughter.*

**wholesome** *adjective* good for you. *Wholesome soup.*

**whooping cough** *noun* an infectious disease that makes you cough a lot and make a terrible noise as you breathe in.

**who's** short for who is.

**why** *adverb* for what reason.

**wick** *noun* the twisted thread in a candle or oil lamp which you light.

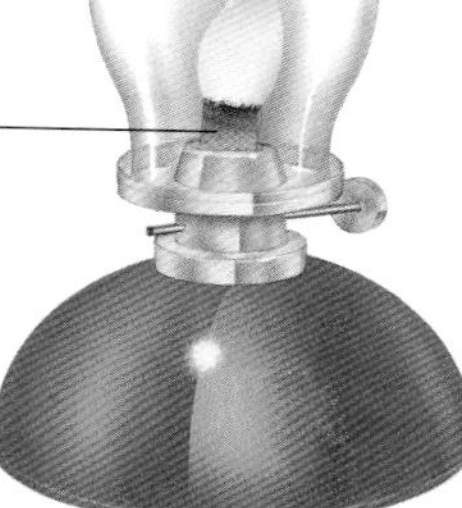


Matty turned up the wick and the lamp flared in the window, calling the children home.

**wicked** *noun* very bad, evil and cruel. **wickedness** *noun.*

**wicket** *noun* three stumps with two bails on top at which the ball is bowled in cricket.

**wide** *adjective* 1 measuring a long way from one side to the other, broad. *Motorways are very wide roads.* 2 measuring a certain distance. *10 m wide.* 3 including a large area or variety. *Wide experience.* The opposite of wide is narrow.

**widespread** *adjective* happening over a wide area or among many people. *Widespread flooding.*

**widow** *noun* a woman whose husband has died. *The widow sobbed beside the grave.*

**widower** *noun* a man whose wife has died.

**width** *noun* how much something measures from one side to the other. *What is the width of the door?*

**wield** *verb* 1 to hold and use with the hands. *He wielded an axe.* 2 to exercise power. *Dictators wield complete power.*

**wife** (wives) *noun* the woman that a man marries. *The sultan had 20 wives.*

**wig** *noun* a false covering of hair that fits on a bald head or over somebody's own hair.

**wigwam** *noun* a dome-shaped tent made from animal skins by Native Americans.

**wild** *adjective* 1 natural and not cultivated or tamed by people. *A wild flower.* 2 uncontrolled, angry. *A wild night.*

**wilderness** *noun* a wild, uncultivated area where nobody lives. A desert.

**wildlife** *noun* wild animals and plants in their natural habitats.

**will** *noun* 1 an ability to make firm decisions, determination. *A will to win.* 2 what somebody wants. *The will of the people.* 3 a written document listing who is to have your belongings and money after your death. *I burned my will.*

**willing** *adjective* happy to do whatever is needed. **willingness** *noun*. *Eva always shows a great willingness to help.*

**willow** *noun* a tree with long thin, hanging branches that grows near water.

The weeping willow is a graceful tree to plant beside a pond.

**willowy** *adjective* tall and graceful like a willow tree. *A willowy young girl.*

**wilt** *verb* to become weak and droop and shrivel like a plant without water.

**wily** (wilier, wiliest) *adjective* cunning and full of artful tricks.

**wimp** *noun* a man who is weak, feeble and lacking courage. *Poor Rob is a real wimp.*

**win** (wins, winning, won) *verb* 1 to come first in a contest. 2 to obtain something through luck. *He won the lottery.* **win** *noun.*

**wince** *verb* to jerk and make your face look twisted because of pain or fear.

**winch** *noun* a machine with a rope around a turning part for lifting things.

**wind** (winds, winding, wound) *verb* (rhymes with kind) 1 to bend and twist. 2 to roll or wrap around. 3 to tighten a clock spring. **wind up** 1 to end in a place or situation. 2 to tease. *Stop winding me up.*

**wind** *noun* (rhymes with pinned) 1 a strong moving current of air. **windy** *adjective*. *A windy day.* 2 gases in the stomach that make you feel uncomfortable.

**winded** *adjective* out of breath through heavy exercise.

**Windhoek** *noun* the capital of Namibia.

**DID YOU KNOW?**

*The American's use different words for many parts of a motor car (automobile). Besides 'windshield' (for 'windscreen') they say 'fenders' ('bumpers'), 'gear shift' ('gear lever') 'hood' ('bonnet') and 'muffler' ('silencer').*

**AMAZING FACT**

In Greek mythology, Icarus tried to escape imprisonment by fastening wings made of wax and feathers to his shoulders. Icarus flew so close to the Sun that the wax melted and he fell to his death.

**wind instrument** *noun* a musical instrument that you play by blowing into it. *Clarinets, flutes and trombones are wind instruments.*

**windmill** *noun* a mill – a tall building for pumping water, grinding grain etc. – with machines powered by wind blowing a set of arm-like sails.

Some windmills are still working, others have been turned into museums or homes.

**window** *noun* a hole covered with glass in a wall or roof of a building that lets in light and air.

**windpipe** *noun* a tube leading from your mouth to your lungs that carries air to your lungs. *A fishbone got stuck in her windpipe.*

**windscreen** *noun* the window at the front of a car, lorry etc. (US windshield).

**windsurf** *verb* to ride over waves on a special board with a sail. **windsurfer** *noun.*

**wine** *noun* an alcoholic drink made from grapes or sometimes other plants.

**wing** *noun* 1 one of the parts of a bird, bat or insect used for flying. 2 one of the parts sticking out of the side of an aircraft that it uses for flying. 3 one of the parts covering a wheel of a car. 4 a part of a building that stands out from the main part. *The east wing.* 5 a side of a stage hidden from the audience. 6 the right or left edge of the pitch in games such as hockey, rugby and soccer.

Birds evolved the power of flight millions of years ago. Humans have tried and failed to fly, like birds, with wings.

**wingspan** *noun* the length across the wings of a bird, insect or aeroplane.

**wink** *verb* 1 to open and close one eye quickly. 2 (of light) to flash on and off. **wink** *noun. He gave me a wink to show that he was only joking.*

**winner** *noun* a person, animal or vehicle that wins a race, contest etc.

**winning** *adjective* charming. *Will has a winning smile, but he doesn't fool me!*

**winnings** *plural noun* money that has been won. *She frittered all her winnings away.*

**winter** *noun* the season of the year between autumn and spring. **wintry** *adjective.*

**wipe** *verb* to rub something with your hand or a cloth in order to clean or dry it. **wiper** *noun* a windscreen wiper.

**wire** *noun* a thin length of metal that can easily be twisted, used especially to carry electricity and for fencing. **wire** *verb* to put in wires to carry electricity. *The house was wired last year.* **wire** *adjective. Wire fencing.*

**wireless** *noun* an old-fashioned word for radio. *Let's listen to the wireless tonight.*

**wisdom** *noun* being wise and having great understanding and judgement. **wisdom tooth** *noun* a tooth that sometimes grows at the back of your jaw after the other teeth have stopped growing.

**wise** *adjective* sensible and having a great understanding and experience of something, knowing the right action or decision.

**-wise** *suffix* 1 acting like somebody or something. In the direction of. *Clockwise.* 2 with reference to something. *Health-wise, I'm fine, and so is your dear father.*

**wish** *verb* 1 to want or to desire something. 2 to say that you hope something will happen. *I wish you well.* **wish** *noun* a strong desire for something. *A wish to travel.*

**wishbone** *noun* the V-shaped bone in the breast of birds.

**wit** *noun* 1 common sense, the ability to think clearly. 2 skill in saying things in a clever and funny way. 3 a clever and amusing person. *He's a great wit.* **witty** *adjective. What a witty writer!* **at your wits' end** not knowing how to solve a serious and worrying problem.

**-witted** *suffix* having a particular kind of ability. *Quick-witted.*

**witch** *noun* a woman in fairy stories who can perform magic.

**witchcraft** *noun* magic used by witches.

The witch said a magic spell over the toad and turned it into a prince.

**AMAZING FACT**

Radio broadcasting, from a 'wireless' began in 1920. The system for naming radio stations, or assigning call letters, in the US is based on which side of the Mississippi River the station is based. Stations to the east of the Mississippi start with the letter 'K' like KROC, stations west of the Mississippi begin with the letter 'W'.

**SPELLING NOTE**

*Are you a pronunciation wizard? Try these: 'bough', 'cough', 'enough', 'plough', 'hiccough', 'through', 'though', 'thought', 'thorough'.*

**AMAZING FACT**

The Salem Witchcraft Trials took place in Salem, Massachusettes in 1692. As a result of the trials, nineteen people were hanged for witchcraft.

**witchdoctor** *noun* a person who is believed to have magic powers to cure illnesses.

**withdraw** (withdraws, withdrawing, withdrew, withdrawn) *verb* 1 to take back or take away, to remove. *She withdrew £100 from her bank account.* 2 to go away from. *After the war the troops withdrew.* **withdrawal** *noun.* **withdrawn** *adjective.* 1 remote. 2 unable to communicate. *She's unhappy and withdrawn.*

**wither** *verb* to dry up, droop and die, to shrivel. *Flowers wither without water.*

Sue forgot to put fresh water in the vase and the flowers began to wither.

**within** *preposition* inside, not beyond. *They were within a mile of home.*

**withhold** (withhold, withholding, withheld) *verb* to hold on to and refuse to give something, to keep back. *He withheld the evidence from the court.*

**without** *preposition* not having, in the absence of. *He made it without any help.*

**witness** *noun* a person who has seen something important happen and so can describe what happened to others, especially to the police or in a law court. **witness** *verb.*

**wives** the plural of wife.

**wizard** *noun* 1 a man in fairy stories who can perform magic. 2 an expert at something. *A computer wizard.*

**wobble** *verb* to move in an unsteady way from side to side, to shake a little. **wobbly** *adjective. A wobbly jelly.*

**woe** *noun* great sorrow, misery. **woeful** *adjective. A woeful look.*

**woke** past tense of wake.

**wolf** (wolves) *noun* a wild animal of the dog family that hunts in a packs. **wolf** *verb* to eat greedily.

The wolf howled because it was hungry.

**woman** (women) *noun* a grown-up female human. *A truly beautiful woman.*

**womb** *noun* a part inside a woman or any female mammal where her young develop before being born.

**wombat** *noun* a small burrowing Australian marsupial related to the koala.

In Australia, there are signs by the road telling you to beware of wombats.

**won** past tense of win.

**wonder** *verb* 1 to ask yourself something, to want to know about. *I wonder what day it is.* 2 to be surprised or astounded. **wonder** *noun* 1 a feeling of surprise and amazement. 2 something so impressive that it causes a feeling of amazement.

**wonderful** *adjective* 1 very pleasing, excellent. *What a wonderful day.* 2 marvellous and very impressive. *Computer technology is a wonderful achievement.*

**wonky** *adjective* unsteady and liable to collapse. *This chair is a bit wonky.*

**wood** *noun* the substance that trees are made of. Furniture is usually made of wood and so is paper. 2 a place where there are a lot trees growing closely together. **woody** *adjective. Woody carrots.*

**wooded** *adjective* covered with trees. *A wooded mountainside.*

**wooden** *adjective* made of wood.

**woodpecker** *noun* one of a family of tree-climbing birds that have a strong pointed beak for drilling holes in trees to find insects to eat.

**woodwind** *noun* a group of musical instruments that you play by blowing through a mouthpiece and into a hollow tube. *The flute and clarinet are woodwind instruments.*

**woodwork** *noun* (the making of) things made of wood.

**woodworm** *noun* the larva of a beetle that makes holes in wood by feeding on it.

**wool** *noun* the thick hair of sheep and goats used for knitting and making cloth, the yarn made from wool.

**AMAZING FACT**

Wombats and other marsupials such as wallabies, opposums and kangaroos, carry their young in a pouch on their stomach where they continue their development. Australia has only marsupial mammals.

**SPELLING NOTE**

*Try not to confuse 'wander' and 'wonder'. 'Wander' means 'to move about without trying to reach anywhere in particular'. 'Wonder' means 'something exciting, strange or marvellous'. As a verb it can also mean 'to think about' or 'to feel surprise'.*

The clarinet is Helen's favourite woodwind instrument.

**AMAZING FACT**

Not all woodwind instruments are made of wood. Saxophones and most flutes are made of metal, while recorders are sometimes made of plastic.

**woolly** *adjective* made of wool. *A woolly hat keeps his head warm in winter.*

**word** *noun* a group of letters that mean something. We speak or write words to communicate. **give your word** to promise. **keep your word** to keep your promise. **in a word** to sum up. **word for word** each word exactly as said or written. **have words with** to quarrel.

**word processor** *noun* a computer with a keyboard and screen that is used to type letters, write articles, store information etc.

**wore** past tense of wear.

**work** *noun* 1 the job that somebody does to earn money. 2 the energy you use to do or make something. *Hard work.* 3 something you have made or done. *Works of art.* **work** *verb* 1 to do a job. 2 to use effort to do work. 3 to operate or make something go. *Can you work this machine?* **work out** to calculate and solve. *Work out a problem.* **have your work cut out** to have a difficult task to do.

**workable** *adjective* able to be done successfully. *A workable plan.*

**worker** *noun* somebody who works or who does a particular job. *Factory workers.*

**works** *plural noun* 1 the working parts of a machine. 2 a factory.

**workshop** *noun* a place where things are made or repaired.

**world** *noun* 1 the universe and space with all the stars and planets. 2 the Earth and everything on it. 3 all the things concerned with a particular subject or activity. *The world of music.* **the New World** America.

When seen from outer space, our world seems extremely fragile. On the brightly illuminated globe, we can see not only continents and oceans, but also the devastation we have caused to the world's rainforests.

**worldly** *adjective* interested only in money and things of the world.

**worm** *noun* a small, long, thin creature without legs that lives in the soil.

**worn** past tense of wear.

**worn-out** *adjective* 1 too old and no longer in a good condition. 2 exhausted. *You must be worn-out after running so far.*

**worry** (worries, worrying, worried) *verb* 1 to be upset and and uneasy and think something bad may happen. *She worried about leaving her dog alone all day.* 2 to trouble somebody. *Stop worrying me with your silly questions!*

**worse** *adjective* less good or well. More bad but not as bad as worst. *The weather was bad yesterday but it's worse today.*

**worship** (worships, worshipping, worshipped) *verb* 1 to pray to and give praise to God or gods, to take part in a religious ceremony. **worshipper** *noun*. 2 to love somebody very much.

**worst** *adjective, adverb* least good or well, most bad. Worst is the opposite of best.

**worth** *noun, adjective* 1 the value of something or somebody. 2 good or useful. *This job is worth doing well.*

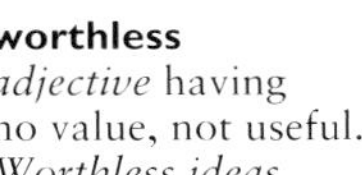

The jewels fetched twice as much at the auction as Mary thought they were worth.

**worthless** *adjective* having no value, not useful. *Worthless ideas.* **worthlessness** *noun*.

**worthwhile** *adjective* useful and important enough to spend time on. *A worthwhile scheme is always a pleasure for the committee to consider.*

**worthy** *adjective* good and deserving respect. **worthiness** *noun*.

**wound** (rhymes with sound) past tense of wind.

**wound** *noun* (say **woon**-d) an injury or bad cut, especially one caused by a knife or gun etc. **wound** *verb*. *The soldier was badly wounded in the battle.*

**wove, woven** past tense and past participle of weave.

**WPC** *abbreviation* woman police constable.

**wrap** (wraps,wrapping, wrapped) *verb* to put a cover around or to fold paper, cloth etc. around. *We wrapped up Dad's present.*

**wrapping** *noun* paper or other material put around something to cover or protect it.

**wreath** *noun* flowers and leaves arranged in a circle and tied together.

**wreck** *verb* to destroy or ruin something completely so that it is unusable. *Vandals wrecked the bus shelter.*

**AMAZING FACT**

The opposite of 'worthless' is 'valuable' (meaning that it has worth) or 'priceless' (meaning so valuable that it is impossible to attach a price to it). Something may be priceless to us, not because it is worth a lot of money, but because it is something that cannot be replaced or has sentimental value.

**SPELLING NOTE**

*Words that sound similar and should not be confused are: 'wrap' and 'rap', 'wring' and 'ring', 'write', 'right' and 'rite', and 'wrung' and 'rung'.*

**wreckage** *noun* all the pieces that remain after something has been wrecked. *We cleared up the wreckage after the flood.*

An international team of aid workers helped clear up the wreckage after the flood.

**wren** *noun* a very small brown bird with an upward-pointing tail.

**wrench** *verb* to tug or twist something with violence. *He wrenched off the lid.* **wrench** *noun* a tool used for gripping and twisting things such as nuts and bolts.

**wrestle** *verb* 1 to get hold of somebody and try to throw them to the ground, especially in a sport called wrestling. 2 to struggle. *I'm wrestling with my feelings.* **wrestler** *noun* somebody who wrestles as a sport.

**wretched** *adjective* 1 sad and very unhappy. 2 poor quality or unpleasant. *This wretched machine won't work.*

**wriggle** *verb* to twist and turn about. *Stop wriggling in your chair.*

**wring** (wrings, wringing, wrung) *verb* to force water out of a wet cloth by squeezing it. *He wrung out the wet dish cloth.*

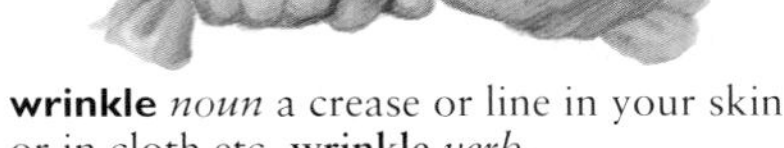

He wrung out the flannel and laid it on the side of the bath.

**wrinkle** *noun* a crease or line in your skin or in cloth etc. **wrinkle** *verb*.

**wrist** *noun* the joint connecting your arm to your hand. *A limp wrist.*

**write** (writes, writing, wrote, written) *verb* 1 to form words, especially with a pen or pencil on paper. 2 to compose a book, piece of music etc. **writer** *noun* a person who writes books etc., usually to earn money.

**writing** *noun* 1 anything that has been written. Literature, poems etc. 2 handwriting *He has neat writing.*

**wrong** *adjective* 1 incorrect. The opposite is right. 2 bad and immoral. *It's wrong to lie.*

**wrung** past tense of wring.

**wry** *adjective* 1 twisted, bent. *A wry smile.* 2 slightly mocking. *A wry remark.*

**WYSIWYG** *abbreviation* what you see (on the screen) is what you get (when printed).

X
Y
Z

**xenophobia** *noun* a hatred of all foreigners.

**Xmas** *noun* a short informal spelling for Christmas. *Merry Xmas.*

**X-ray** *noun* 1 a kind of ray that can pass through solid things. 2 a photograph using x-rays of a part of the inside of your body. This enables doctors to see if anything is broken or diseased.

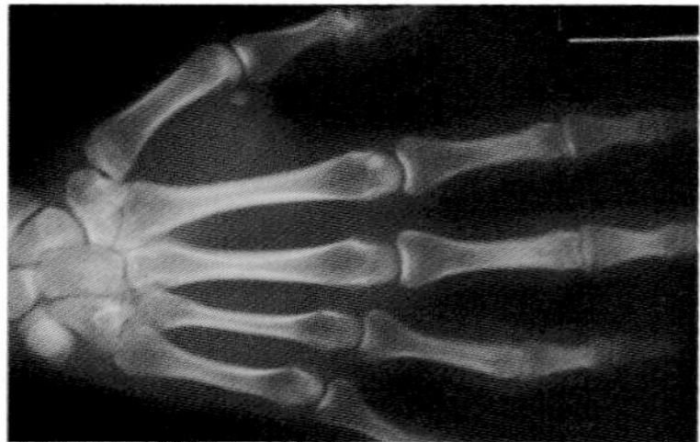

This X-ray of a human hand shows that no bones are broken.

**xylophone** *noun* a musical instrument with wooden bars that you hit with small hammers to make notes.

**yacht** *noun* a sailing boat or a small motor-driven used for cruising or for racing.

**yak** *noun* a long-haired ox from Tibet and the Himalayas.

**yam** *noun* a tropical vegetable similar to a potato. *Yams are delicious in stews.*

**Yamoussoukro** *noun* the capital of the Ivory Coast.

**yank** *verb* to pull something suddenly and violently. **yank** *noun.*

**Yaoundé** *noun* the capital of Cameroon.

**yap** *noun* the short high-pitched bark of a small dog. **yap** (yaps, yapping, yapped) *verb. Their terrier yapped at the postman.*

**yard** *noun* 1 a measure of length equal to 3 feet or 0.91 metres. 2 an enclosed area next to a building and sometimes used for a particular purpose. *A timber yard.* 3 (US) a garden next to a house.

**WORD HISTORY**

*The shape of the letter X comes from an ancient Egyptian symbol for a fish. The Semites called it 'samekh', their word for a fish. The Greeks used the symbol for the sound 'ch'.*

**AMAZING FACT**

The whole of a yeast plant is just one cell and very tiny. As a fungus, it cannot produce its own food. Instead, it lives on sugar. Yeast turns sugar into alcohol (in wine and beer making) and carbon dioxide (in bread baking). The process is called fermentation.

**WORD HISTORY**

*The shape of the letter Y – like the letters U, V and W developed from the Semitic word 'waw', meaning 'tenthook'. The Greeks called the letter Upsilon.*

**yarn** *noun* 1 wool or cotton spun into thread for sewing, knitting etc. 2 a long and often untrue story.

**yasmak** *noun* a veil worn by some Muslim women to cover all or part of their face.

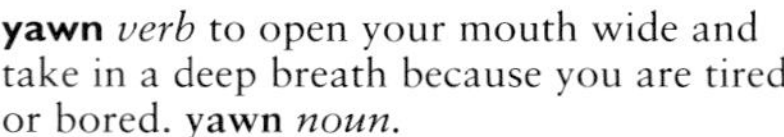

Muslim women often wear a yasmak in public.

**yawn** *verb* to open your mouth wide and take in a deep breath because you are tired or bored. **yawn** *noun.*

**year** *noun* 1 the time it takes the Earth to travel once around the Sun – 365 days or 12 months or 52 weeks. 2 the period of time between 1 January and 31 December. **leap year** *noun* a year having 366 days, occurring every four years. In leap years February has 29 days.

**yearly** *adjective* 1 taking place once a year. 2 during or lasting a single year. *A yearly membership fee.* **yearly** *adverb.*

**yeast** *noun* a kind of fungus used in making bread rise and in brewing beer.

**yell** *noun* a loud shrill shout. **yell** *verb. He yelled above the noise of the traffic.*

**yellow** *noun* the colour of ripe bananas and lemons. **yellow** *adjective. Yellow roses.*

**yelp** *noun* a sudden, sharp sound of pain or excitement. **yelp** *verb. The dog yelped when I stood on its tail.*

**Yemen** *noun* a country in Southwest Asia.

The main exports of Yemen are petroleum products, cotton and fish.

**yen** *noun* the main Japanese unit of money.

**Yerevan** *noun* the capital of Armenia.

**yesterday** *noun, adverb* the day before today. *Today is Monday, yesterday was Sunday.*

**yew** *noun* an evergreen tree with dark, needle-like leaves.

**yield** *verb* 1 to surrender, to give up and admit defeat. *He yielded under pressure.* 2 to produce. *How much wheat does this field yield?* **yield** *noun.*

**yoga** *noun* an Hindu system of meditation and self-control involving exercises to exercise and relax the body and the mind.

**yogurt** *noun* a thick, liquid food made from soured milk. *Greek yogurt.*

**yoke** *noun* a bar with two pieces that fit around the necks of a pair of oxen to keep them together so they can pull a plough etc. yoke *verb.*

**yolk** *noun* (rhymes with oak) the yellow part in the middle of an egg.

The yolk of an egg is its most nutritious part.

**Yom Kippur** *noun* a Jewish holy day at the start of the Jewish New Year in mid-September. It is a time of fasting and prayer.

**yonder** *adjective, adverb* (old-fashioned) over there. *The bench is under yonder tree.*

**young** *adjective* not old, having lived or existed for only a short time. **young** *plural noun* the offspring of animals. *The young of cows are called calves.*

**youngster** *noun* a young person.

**youth** *noun* 1 the time when a person is young. *He was a gymnast in his youth.* 2 a young man. 3 young people in general.

**youthful** *adjective* 1 young. 2 having the qualities of being young, relating to the young. *Youthful enthusiasm.*

**yo-yo** *noun* a toy made of two joined discs that you make run up and down a string that you hold.

**Yugoslavia** *noun* a country in Europe, made up of Serbia and Montenegro.

**yule** *noun* Christmas.

**AMAZING FACT**

A zebra's stripes make them stand out in a zoo, but in their natural habitat, the grasslands of Africa, the stripes act as camouflage and help conceal them from predators.

**DID YOU KNOW?**

*The 12 signs of the zodiac are: Aries, Gemini, Taurus, Cancer, Leo, Virgo, Libra, Scorpio, Sagittarius, Capricorn, Aquarius and Pisces.*

# Zz

**Zagreb** *noun* the capital of Croatia.

**Zambia** *noun* a country in Africa.

**Zambian** *noun* a person who comes from Zambia. **Zambian** *adjective. Zambian copper mines.*

**zany** *adjective* funny in an odd kind of way. zanily *adverb.*

**zap** (zaps, zapping, zapped) *verb* 1 to strike or attack something suddenly in, for example, a computer game. 2 to keep changing quickly from one section of a tape, video, TV program etc.

**WORD HISTORY**

*The shape of the letter Z developed from an ancient Egyptian symbol for an arrow. The Semites gave it the name 'zayin', their word for an arrow. The Greeks called it 'zeta'.*

**zeal** *noun* enthusiasm, determined eagerness. *Religious zeal.*

**zebra** *noun* an African animal like a horse with black and white stripes on its body. **zebra crossing** a crossing place on a road marked with broad black and white stripes where traffic must stop for pedestrians.

**zenith** *noun* 1 the sky directly overhead. 2 the highest point, the peak or summit.

**zero** (zeros) *noun* nought, the name of the figure 0.

**zest** *noun* 1 enthusiasm, great enjoyment. *A zest for living.* 2 the outer peel of a lemon or orange.

**zigzag** *noun* a line that sharply bends one way then another like the letter Z. **zigzag** *verb. The path zigzagged up the hillside.*

**Zimbabwe** *noun* a country in Africa.

**Zimbabwean** *noun* a person who comes from Zimbabwe. **Zimbabwean** *adjective. Zimbabwean lakes.*

**zinc** *noun* a hard white metal used in alloys.

**zip or zipper** *noun* a long narrow fastener with two rows of teeth that can be made to lock and unlock by sliding a tab up or down. *His zip got stuck.*

**zither** *noun* a ancient musical instrument with strings that are plucked.

**zodiac** *noun* (say **zoh**-dee-ak) a band in the sky through which the Sun, Moon and planets move and which astrologers divide into twelve sections each with its own symbol or sign and name.

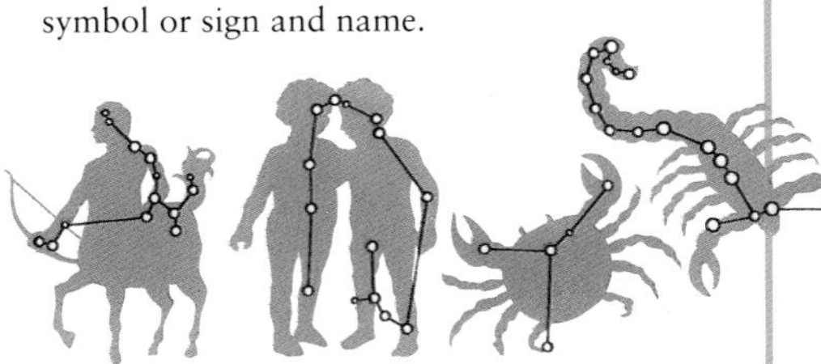

On the right are some of the signs of the zodiac as seen in the sky: Sagittarius, Gemini, Cancer and Scorpio.

**zombie** *noun* 1 in stories, a dead body that is brought back to life. 2 a person who does not seem to be aware of what is going on and does things without seeming to think.

**zone** *noun* an area that is made separate for some special purpose. *A no-parking zone.*

**zoo** *noun* a place where wild animals are kept for people to look at and study.

**zoology** *noun* (say zoo-**ol**-ogee) the scientific study of animals. **zoological** *adjective.* **zoologist** *noun.*

**zoom** *verb* 1 to move very quickly. 2 to focus a camera quickly from long distance to close up. **zoom lens** a camera lens that can be made to focus quickly on close-up things then far-away things.

## What's wrong?

Try to correct the mistakes in these sentences.

1 Was you angry with me?

2 The cat is eating it's supper.

3 Im to busy to see you.

4 He drunk all the milk.

5 He dances good.

6 You could of said you wasn't coming.

7 Lie the book on the desk.

8 The cacti needs watering.

9 This is the widower of the late Mrs Jones.

10 Calm down and don't get so historical.

Answers 1 were 2 its 3 I'm 4 drank 5 well 6 have 7 lay 8 need 9 no late 10 hysterical.

## Guess my definition

In this game you read out the definition of a word and ask your friends to say what the headword is. For example 'a soft yellow food made from cream and milk'. The answer is butter.

## Matching sounds

Try to match the words that sound the same: beat him thyme cymbal steal knight meddle bear see two symbol steel beet bare time night sea medal.

## Hidden words

Take a long word like 'drawing' or 'measurement' and see how many other words you can find in it. 'Drawing' contains draw, raw, win, wing, in.

## Odd ones out

Which are the odd ones out in these groups:

Cod, trout, whale, herring, shark.

Car, lorry, van, aeroplane, motorbike.

Orange, apple, lamb, plum, cherry.

## Backword

The word 'evil' becomes 'live' if you spell it backwards. Can you think of any other words that do this?

## Code words

This code hides a simple sentence. All you have to do is read down the first column and then up the last column to find the message 'Thanks for the presents'.

**TENS**
**HURT**
**AVON**
**NINE**
**KISS**
**SIDE**
**FOUR**
**OLOP**
**RISE**
**TOSH**

## In alphabetical order

Put these words in their correct alphabetical order:

Crown, cruise, crane, crow.

Live, lamb, loose, letter, likely.

Dragon, donkey, dust, dinosaur, deaf.

## Sounds right

Think of a phrase or sentence using these words:

Roar, croak, neigh, bellow.

Crash, clang, bang, thud.

## Kinds of

A crow is a kind of ?

A violin is a kind of ?

A beetle is a kind of ?

An apple is a kind of ?

## Sets

Think of a single word for each of these sets of words:

Aluminium, brass, bronze, iron, zinc.

Plaice, cod, herring, trout.

Chair, sofa, bed, table.

## Scrambled words

See if you can make new words from these words, e.g. the eyes – they see.

Angered, astronomers, evil, funeral, nameless, night, nuclear, orchestra, organ.

(Answers: enraged, moon-starers, veil, real fun, maleness/lameness, thing, unclear, groan.)

## Changed

Take two words of the same length and link these two words together by putting in other words, each different from the next word by one changed letter. Here, for example, is how you could change 'head' into 'tail': HEAD HEAL TEAL TELL TALL TAIL.

## Guess words

Open the dictionary at any page with a friend and read out the first and last word on that page. Your friend must try to guess other words on that page.

## Chain words

A game to play with several people. Using the last two letters of the previous word make another word, e.g. reserve vest street etiquette telescope pedal alone negligent entire and so on.

## Months of the year

January was named after Janus, the Roman god of doors.

February comes from the Latin for a religious festival.

March is named after the Roman god of war. This was originally the first month of the year.

April comes from the Latin for 'to open' and refers to buds opening.

May is named after the Roman earth goddess, Maia.

June was named after Juno, the queen of the Roman gods.

July was named after Julius Caesar.

August was named after the emperor Augustus Caesar.

September was once the seventh month (after 'septem', Latin for seven).

October was the eighth month (after 'octem', Latin for eight).

November was the ninth month (after 'novem', Latin for nine).

December was the tenth month (after 'decem', Latin for ten).

# Some general spelling rules

(But always remember there are lots of exceptions to most rules!)

## Nouns

To make a noun plural you normally add 's' – road roads, cake cakes.

But if the noun ends in -ch, -s, -ss, -sh or -x you add -es –

Ass asses, church churches, bush bushes, bus buses, mix mixes.

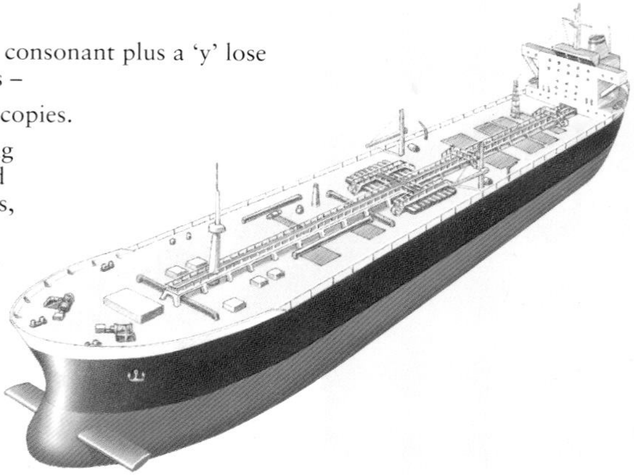

Nouns ending in a consonant plus a 'y' lose the 'y' and add -ies –

Baby babies, copy copies.

Many nouns ending in 'o' generally add -es – Cargo cargoes, hero heroes.

Plurals that do not follow these rules are shown in the dictionary –

child children, mouse mice.

Some nouns that are always plural in form:

Scissors, shears, oats, clothes, pyjamas, trousers, measles, spectacles.

Some very irregular plurals:

Man men, mouse mice, woman women, goose geese, mouse mice, foot feet, tooth teeth, ox oxen.

Some nouns that are both singular and plural in form:

Fish, sheep, deer.

## Adverbs

Adverbs are usually formed by adding -ly to the adjective – Odd oddly, amazing amazingly, quick quickly.

But if the adjective ends in -ll, just add -y –

Dull dully.

If the adjective ends in -le, drop the -le and add -ly –

Simple simply.

If the adjective ends in -ic, add ally –

Historic historically.

(A notable exception is public publicly.)

Adverbs that do not follow these rules will be found in the dictionary.

## Adjectives

To most adjectives of one syllable you normally add -er to make a comparative –

Near nearer, fast faster – Anne can run faster than her sister.

And you add -est to make a superlative –

Nearest, fastest – Andy is the fastest runner in his class.

If the adjective ends in -e just add 'r' or 'st' –

Simple simpler simplest.

With some short adjectives ending with a consonant the consonant is doubled –

Red redder reddest.

With adjectives of more than two syllables use 'more' and 'most' for the comparative and superlative –

Careful, more careful, most careful. He's the most careful person I know.

Adjectives that do not follow these rules will be show in the dictionary, for example –

Bad worse worst, good better best.

## Verbs

To make the present participle, past tense and past participle to most regular verbs you add -ing, or -ed or -d –

Talk talking talked, pray praying prayed.

If the verb ends in 'e', the 'e' is dropped and -ing, or -ed are added –

Tame taming tamed.

The final consonant is doubled when a short word ends in a consonant –

Chat chatting chatted, slam slamming slammed.

## I before E

'I before e except after c' is a good general rule, but only applies if the 'ie' in the word is pronounced like an 'ee'. So it is 'ie' in words such as field, believe and siege, and 'e' in words such as ceiling and receipt.

Some exceptions are: either, neither (which can be pronounced 'ee'), seize, weird, protein, and certain names such as Keith and Neil.

Words like eight, deign, reign and neighbour are spelled with 'ei' because they are not pronounced 'ee'.

## Apostrophies

The possessive form of a noun is shown by writing ''s' at the end –

The boy's book.

The children's house.

Charles's bike.

When a noun is plural with the ending 's', add an apostrophe alone –

The girls' mother.

## Each other or one another

Use 'each other' for two –

The two boys helped each other.

Use 'one another' for more than two.

All the children helped one another.

## Double negative

'I never said nothing' is incorrect if what you want to say is 'I never said anything'. But it is correct if what you want to say is 'At no time did I ever say nothing'.

Aa Bb Cc

Gg Hh Ii Jj

Nn Oo Pp

Uu Vv Ww

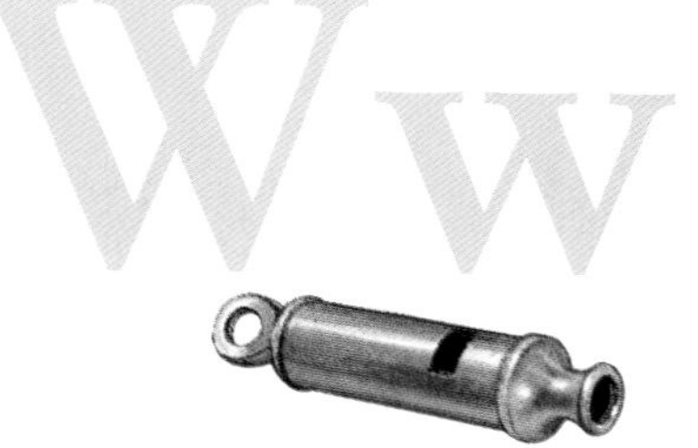

Dd Ee Ff

Kk Ll Mm

Qq Rr Ss Tt

Xx Yy Zz

# Acknowledgements

The publishers would like to thank the following artists who have contributed to this book:

The Maltings Partnership
Andrew Clark
Julie Banyard
Gill Platt
Sally Launder
Wayne Ford
Guy Smith
Mike Saunders

All photographs supplied by Miles Kelly Archives.

KU-081-041

**10** = Distance in miles
10 = Distance in kilometers

| | NEW YORK CITY | WASHINGTON, DC | CHICAGO | MIAMI | NEW ORLEANS | DALLAS | DENVER | SEATTLE | SAN FRANCISCO |
|---|---|---|---|---|---|---|---|---|---|
| WASHINGTON, DC | **233** 375 | | | | | | | | |
| CHICAGO | **779** 1253 | **688** 1107 | | | | | | | |
| MIAMI | **1286** 2069 | **1050** 1689 | **1371** 2206 | | | | | | |
| NEW ORLEANS | **1300** 2092 | **1073** 1726 | **922** 1483 | **856** 1377 | | | | | |
| DALLAS | **1541** 2479 | **1315** 2116 | **921** 1482 | **1349** 2171 | **515** 829 | | | | |
| DENVER | **1793** 2885 | **1669** 2685 | **994** 1599 | **2079** 3345 | **1390** 2237 | **878** 1413 | | | |
| SEATTLE | **2816** 4531 | **2725** 4385 | **2030** 3266 | **3329** 5356 | **2690** 4328 | **2178** 3504 | **1306** 2101 | | |
| SAN FRANCISCO | **2873** 4623 | **2782** 4476 | **2106** 3389 | **3106** 4998 | **2272** 3656 | **1729** 2782 | **1248** 2008 | **801** 1289 | |
| LOS ANGELES | **2763** 4444 | **2640** 4248 | **1989** 3200 | **2736** 4402 | **1902** 3060 | **1445** 2325 | **998** 1606 | **1131** 1820 | **38** 61 |

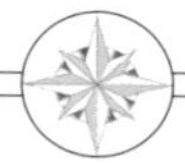

EYEWITNESS TRAVEL GUIDES

# USA

EYEWITNESS TRAVEL GUIDES
USA
DK

LONDON, NEW YORK,
MELBOURNE, MUNICH AND DELHI
www.dk.com

MANAGING EDITOR Aruna Ghose
ART EDITOR Benu Joshi
PROJECT EDITOR Vandana Mohindra
EDITORS Kajori Aikat, Rimli Borooah, Nandini Mehta, Manjari Rathi
DESIGNERS Pallavi Narain, Supriya Sahai, Priyanka Thakur
SENIOR CARTOGRAPHER Uma Bhattacharya
CARTOGRAPHER Alok Pathak
PICTURE RESEARCHER Taiyaba Khatoon
ADDITIONAL PICTURE RESEARCH Kiran K. Mohan
DTP COORDINATOR Shailesh Sharma
DTP DESIGNER Vinod Harish
US EDITOR Mary Sutherland

MAIN CONTRIBUTORS
Andrew Hempstead, Jamie Jensen, Joanne Miller, Eric Peterson, Kevin Roe, Kap Stann

MAIN PHOTOGRAPHERS
Andy Holligan, Jon Spaull, Peter Wilson

MAIN ILLUSTRATORS
Arun P, Gautam Trivedi

Reproduced by Colourscan (Singapore)
Printed and bound by South China Printing Co. Ltd. (China)

First published in Great Britain in 2004
by Dorling Kindersley Limited
80 Strand, London WC2R 0RL

**Reprinted with revisions 2006**

Copyright © 2004, 2006 Dorling Kindersley Limited, London
A Penguin Company

ALL RIGHTS RESERVED. NO PART OF THIS PUBLICATION MAY BE REPRODUCED, STORED IN A RETRIEVAL SYSTEM, OR TRANSMITTED IN ANY FORM OR BY ANY MEANS, ELECTRONIC, MECHANICAL, PHOTOCOPYING, RECORDING OR OTHERWISE WITHOUT THE PRIOR WRITTEN PERMISSION OF THE COPYRIGHT OWNER.

A CIP CATALOGUE RECORD IS AVAILABLE FROM THE BRITISH LIBRARY.

ISBN 1-40531-195-9
ISBN 978-1-40531-195-3

FLOORS ARE REFERRED TO THROUGHOUT IN ACCORDANCE WITH AMERICAN USAGE; IE THE "FIRST FLOOR" IS THE FLOOR AT GROUND LEVEL.

**The information in every Eyewitness Travel Guide is checked regularly.**
Every effort has been made to ensure that this book is as up-to-date as possible at the time of going to press. Some details, however, such as telephone numbers, opening hours, prices, gallery hanging arrangements and travel information are liable to change. The publishers cannot accept responsibility for any consequences arising from the use of this book, nor for any material on third party websites, and cannot guarantee that any website address in this book will be a suitable source of travel information. We value the views and suggestions of our readers very highly. Please write to: Publisher, DK Eyewitness Travel Guides, Dorling Kindersley, 80 Strand, London WC2R 0RL, Great Britain.

**Statuary, Grand Central Terminal, New York City**

# CONTENTS



◁ **Utah's Bryce Canyon, with its series of deep amphitheaters filled with flame-colored rock formations**

Nighttime view of the US Capitol in Washington, DC



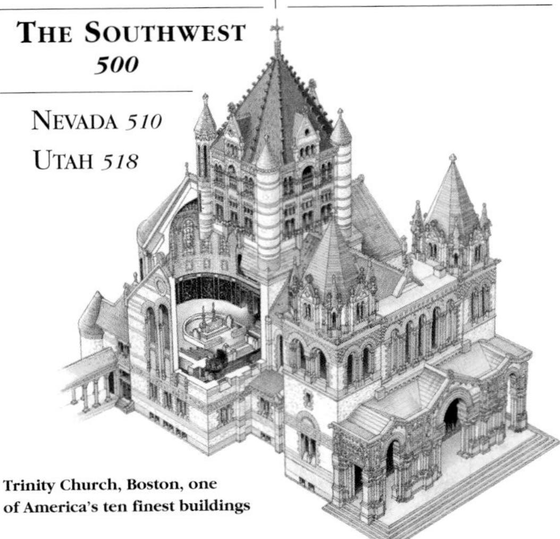

Trinity Church, Boston, one of America's ten finest buildings

# How to Use this Guide

This Dorling Kindersley travel guide helps you to get the most from your visit to the United States. *Visiting the USA* maps the country and gives tips on practical considerations and travel. *USA at a Glance* gives an overview of some of the main attractions and a brief history. The book is divided into 14 regional sections, each covering from one to seven states. The chapter on each region starts with a historical portrait and a map of the area. The main sightseeing section then follows, with maps of the major cities. For each region there is a section of practical and travel information, followed by listings of recommended hotels and restaurants.

**USA Map**
The colored areas shown on the map on the inside front cover indicate the 14 regional chapters in this guide.

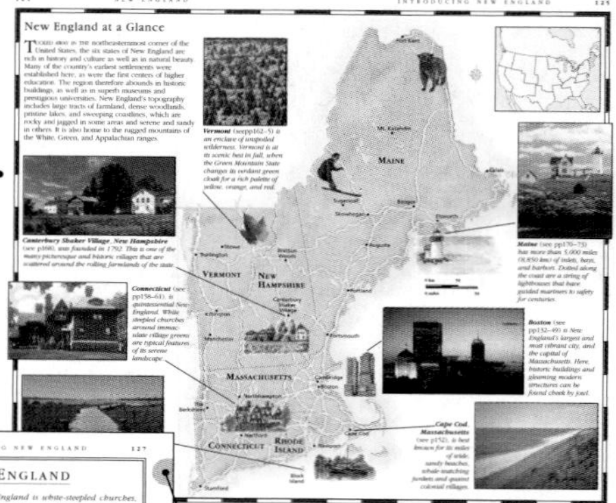


**1 At a Glance**
*The map here highlights the different states in each section as well as the most interesting cities, towns, and regions.*

**Each region chapter** has color-coded thumb tabs.

**2 Introduction to a Region**
*This section gives the reader an insight into the region's geography, historical background, politics, and the character of the people. A chart lists the key dates and events in the region's history.*

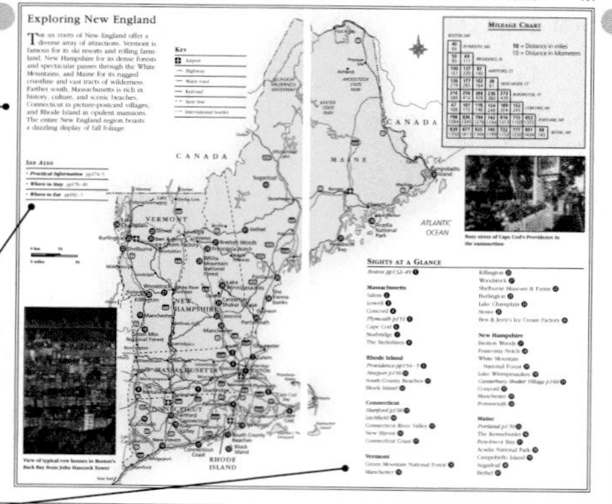


**3 Regional Map**
*For easy reference, sights in each region are numbered and plotted on a map. The black bullet numbers (eg. ❸) also indicate the order in which the sights are covered in the chapter.*

**For each region** there is an index of the practical and listings pages at the end of the chapter.

**Sights at a Glance** lists the numbered sights in sequential order.

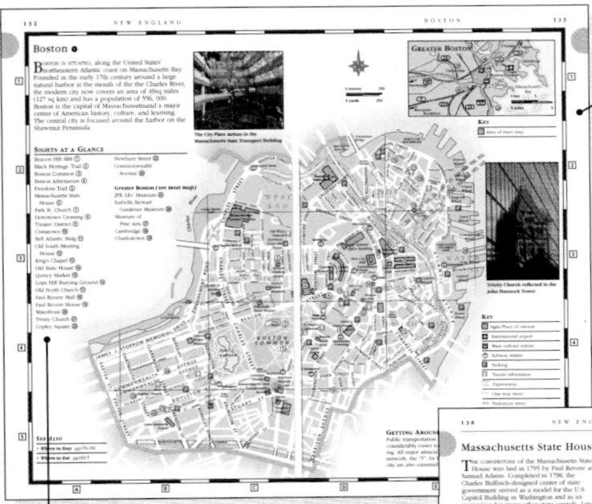

## 4 City Map

*This plots individual sights within the most important cities. The sights within a city such as Boston are indicated with clear bullet numbers (eg. ③), in contrast to the black bullets used on the regional maps.*

**Visitors' Checklist** gives all the practical information needed to plan your visit.

**Sights at a Glance** lists the numbered sights within the city.

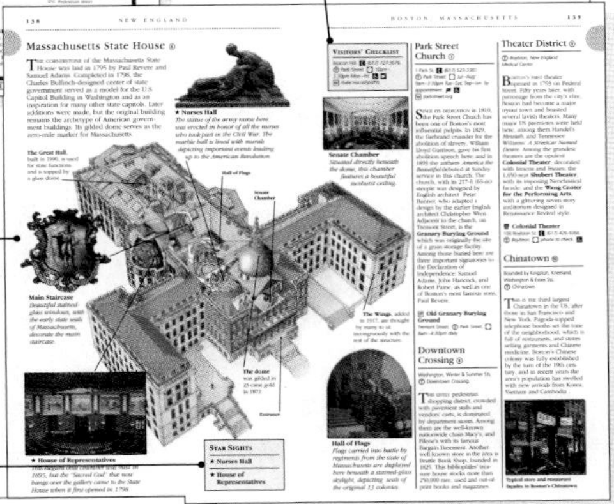

## 5 Major Sights

*Historic buildings are dissected to reveal their interiors, while museums and galleries have color-coded floor plans to help you find the most important exhibits.*

**Stars indicate** the features that no visitor should miss.

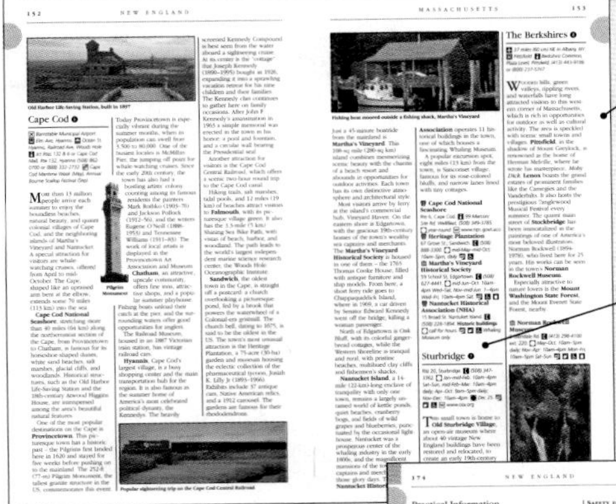

## 6 Detailed Information

*Cities, towns, and other sights are described individually. Their entries appear in the same order as the numbering on the regional map at the beginning of the section.*

**Each entry** begins with essential practical information, including the address and telephone number of the local tourist information office. Opening times are given for major sights and museums.

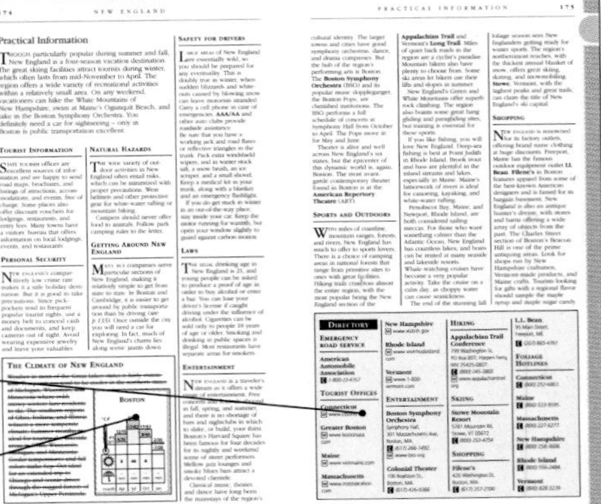

## 7 Practical Information

*This section covers subjects such as travel, security, shopping, and entertainment. Some cities, such as New York, are covered separately.*

**Directory boxes** give contact information for the services and venues mentioned in the text.

**Climate charts** are also provided for each region.

GUSTAFSON'S
MOTEL
RESTAURANT
SELF SERVE
ITS LIKE MONEY IN THE TANK

# Visiting the USA

# Putting the USA on the Map

SPREADING OVER 3,000 miles (4,800 km) east to west between the Atlantic and Pacific Oceans, the United States covers the heart of the North American continent and has a population of 285 million people. Bordered by Mexico to the south and Canada to the north, it extends for over 1,500 miles (2,414 km), covering an area of more than 3.5 million sq miles (9 million sq km), and includes climates from the tropics to the Arctic Circle. The US is divided into 48 states. These, together with the two states, Alaska in the extreme northwest, and the islands of Hawai'i in the Pacific Ocean, comprise the 50 United States of America. The national capital is Washington, DC, a small federal district located between the states of Maryland and Virginia.

◁ **Gustafson's Motel in Brevort in Michigan's Upper Peninsula**

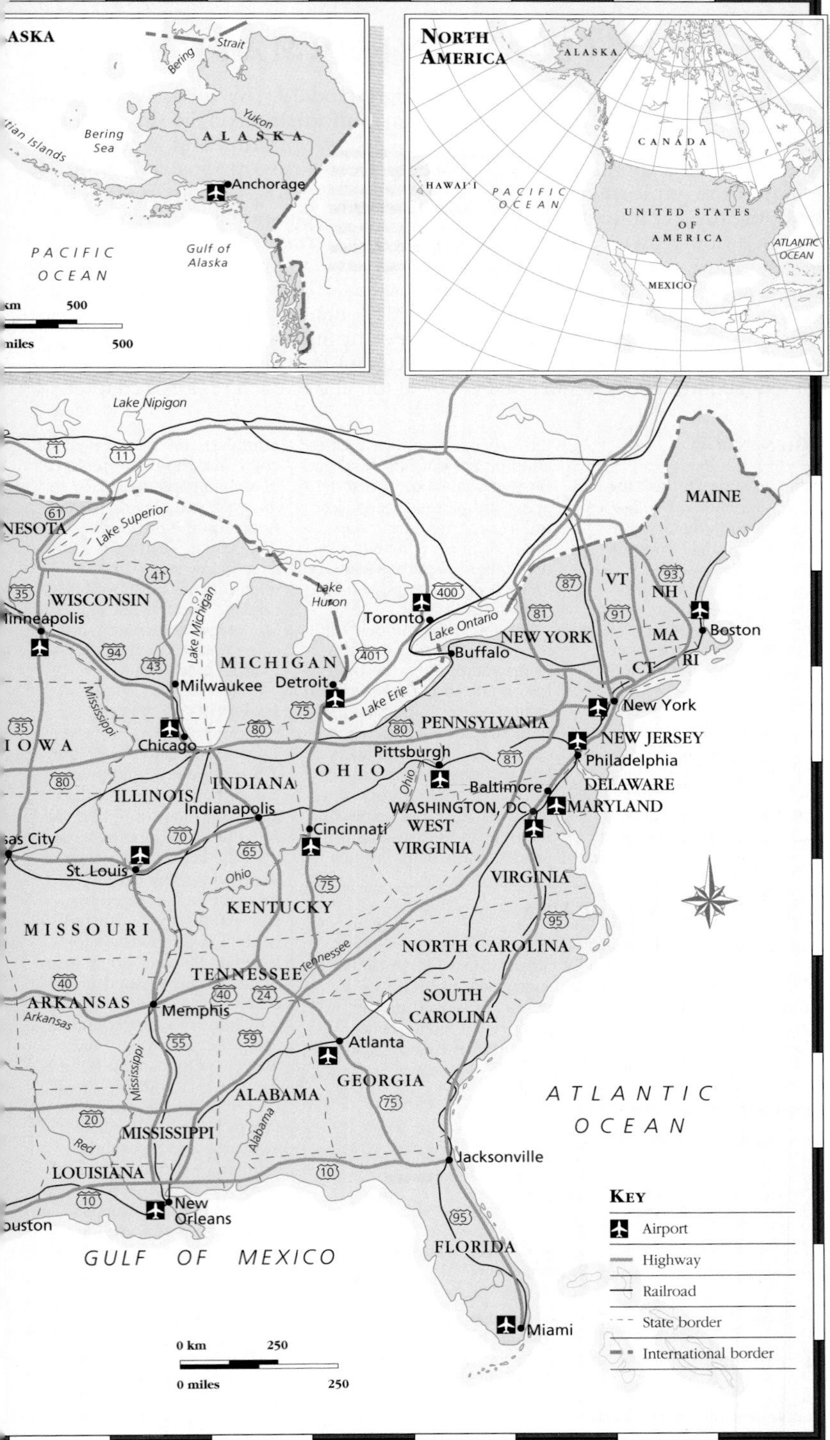
ASKA
Bering Strait
Yukon
Bering Sea
ALASKA
Anchorage
PACIFIC OCEAN
Gulf of Alaska
km 500
miles 500
NORTH AMERICA
ALASKA
CANADA
HAWAI'I
PACIFIC OCEAN
UNITED STATES OF AMERICA
ATLANTIC OCEAN
MEXICO
Lake Nipigon
Lake Superior
Lake Michigan
Lake Huron
Lake Ontario
Lake Erie
MAINE
WISCONSIN
MICHIGAN
NEW YORK
VT
NH
MA
CT
RI
Toronto
Buffalo
Boston
Milwaukee
Detroit
New York
PENNSYLVANIA
NEW JERSEY
Philadelphia
DELAWARE
Chicago
IOWA
Pittsburgh
OHIO
INDIANA
ILLINOIS
Indianapolis
Baltimore
WASHINGTON, DC
MARYLAND
Cincinnati
WEST VIRGINIA
St. Louis
VIRGINIA
KENTUCKY
MISSOURI
NORTH CAROLINA
TENNESSEE
ARKANSAS
Memphis
SOUTH CAROLINA
Atlanta
GEORGIA
ALABAMA
MISSISSIPPI
LOUISIANA
New Orleans
Jacksonville
FLORIDA
Miami
ATLANTIC OCEAN
GULF OF MEXICO
KEY
Airport
Highway
Railroad
State border
International border
0 km 250
0 miles 250

# Practical Information

Millions of visitors travel to the US from around the world every year, and millions of Americans also spend their leisure time exploring and enjoying their country. The nation's richly diverse history, culture, art, and landscape, as well as its tradition of hospitality and service, makes traveling in the US both enjoyable and stress-free. In all parts of the country, tourist facilities are generally of a very high standard. This section gives some basic information on the various transportation and accommodation options available. It deals with issues such as passport and visa formalities, travel insurance, banking, communications, and health care. This section covers the country as a whole, but more specific information is provided in subsequent *Practical Information* sections at the end of each regional chapter.

Flag of the United States of America

## When to Go

The best time to visit the US depends on a visitor's interests and itinerary. It is important to time your visit carefully, because the country's geography and weather patterns vary greatly from region to region, even at the same time of the year. Summer is generally the warmest and most popular time to travel, especially to the northern areas. Summer in the southern parts, especially in the deserts of the Southwest, can be unbearably hot, while in New England they are generally cool and pleasant. All over the country, the summer months are when children are out of school and on vacation, so most resort areas and national parks are full to capacity during these times. Summer is also the time when numerous outdoor cultural events, fairs, and festivals take place.

Spring can be the best time to visit the Rockies and the Deep South; the crowds are fewer, and discounts are often available. April and May in particular are ideal times to experience the wildflowers and gardens of the southern US. Fall is another good time to travel, since the leaves on the trees in the mountain forests, particularly in the northeast, are at their peak of color, and the high humidity of summer has decreased to more pleasant levels. Winter brings on the greatest diversity of weather, ranging from heavy snows in the winter sports capitals of New England and the Rocky Mountains, to tropical sunshine on the beaches of Florida and Hawai'i.

## Passport & Visas

All travelers to the US are required to hold a valid passport, regardless of their age. Passports should be valid for at least six months longer than the last date you expect to remain in the country. Visas are not required for citizens of Canada, Australia, or the UK if the visit is for less than 90 days. Some form of government-issued photo ID, though, is required.

Citizens of many countries may take part in the "visa waiver" plan, using a Form I-94, which is available on all US-bound flights. However, due to increased security measures and constantly changing international conditions, it is wise to confirm visa requirements with the US embassy before traveling. Check with a travel agent for the latest requirements.

Travelers interested in studying, working, or staying for a longer period than the stated 90 days should request special visas from the nearest US embassy. If you are in the United States and need to extend your stay, you should

## The Climate of the USA

Given the sheer vastness of its size, the United States is characterized by a diversity of climates. In addition to the many regional variations, the country also experiences dramatically shifting weather patterns, produced mostly by the Pacific westerlies that sweep across the entire continent. The *Practical Information* section for each region contains a panel like the one below.

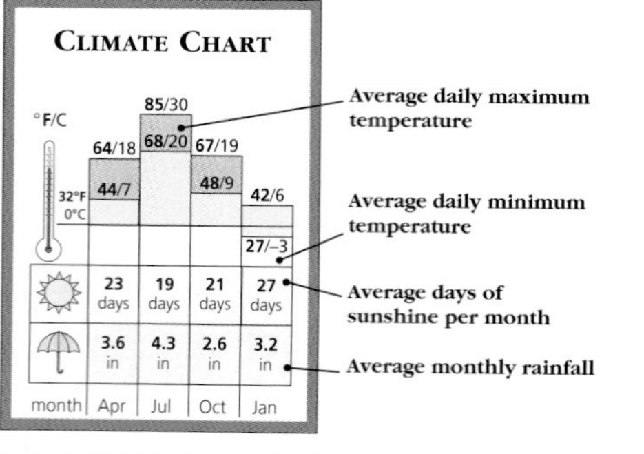

contact the nearest office of the **Bureau of Citizenship and Immigration Services** *(see p17)* in the US, and apply for an extension. Failure to request an extension may result in a fine or deportation.

### Customs Allowances & Duty-Free

All visitors to the US are required to complete a Customs Declaration before entering the country. On this form, which is available from airlines and customs officials upon arrival, you must state the value of any goods being brought into the US, and you may be charged duty on especially valuable items. Travelers are allowed to bring small quantities of tobacco and alcohol along with them, but certain goods are forbidden. These include meat products, plants or seeds, Cuban cigars, and ancient cultural artifacts. When you leave the US, make sure that you are aware of the duty-free allowances for tobacco products (200 cigarettes for each person over 18 years old), and for alcoholic beverages (0.2 gallons or one liter of spirits for each person over 21). No meat products, plants, seeds, fruits, or firearms may be taken out of the US.

### Planning the Trip

Since the country is so large and diverse, it is essential to plan ahead in order to make the most of your time in the United States. Following a logical, efficient itinerary, and allowing enough time to get between places to enjoy them are two of the most important concerns. Also, bear in mind that the US is divided into six time zones *(see p20)*. All of the states and major cities offer a variety of information which can be ordered in advance over the telephone or accessed via web sites. A particularly useful web site is **www.SeeAmerica.org**. Local bookstores are also a valuable source of travel information, as are municipal libraries, travel agencies, and local and regional tourism bureaus across the country.

### Public Holidays

**New Year's Day** (Jan 1)
**Martin Luther King Jr. Day** (3rd Mon in Jan)
**Presidents' Day** (3rd Mon in Feb)
**Memorial Day** (last weekend in May)
**Independence Day** (Jul 4)
**Labor Day** (1st Mon in Sep)
**Columbus Day** (Oct 2 weekend)
**Veterans' Day** (Nov 11)
**Thanksgiving** (4th Thu in Nov)
**Christmas Day** (Dec 25)

### Children

Children are welcomed everywhere, and an amazing number of attractions exist primarily for the enjoyment of young people. From amusement parks and aquariums to national parks and children's museums, their enjoyment is catered to all over the United States.

Most restaurants have special children's menus, with simple foods, smaller portions, and lower prices. For a small charge, most lodgings will provide an extra bed or crib *(see p19)*, and many hotels or motels have adjoining or connecting rooms available especially for families. The main exceptions to kid-friendly status are most bed-and-breakfast accommodations, certain gourmet restaurants in the larger cities, as well as those deluxe resorts that focus on providing relaxing escapes or luxurious spa-like pampering to their guests. Restaurants and lodgings that welcome children are marked in the chapter-by-chapter listings.

### Senior Citizens

Older travelers, or "seniors," make up a fairly large proportion of the traveling public, and most hotels and other establishments offer discounts and special services to attract them. Visitors over the age of 50 can contact the **American Association of Retired Persons** or AARP *(see p17)* to request a membership, which costs about $13 per year. ElderHostel and a few other organizations cater to seniors who enjoy traveling both in and outside the US.

### Conversion Chart

**US Standard to Metric**
1 inch = 2.54 centimeters
1 foot = 30 centimeters
1 mile = 1.6 kilometers
1 ounce = 28 grams
1 pound = 454 grams
1 US pint = 0.5 liter
1 US quart = 0.947 liter
1 US gallon = 3.8 liters

**Metric to US Standard**
1 centimeter = 0.4 inch
1 meter = 3 feet 3 inches
1 kilometer = 0.6 miles
1 gram = 0.04 ounce
1 kilogram = 2.2 pounds
1 liter = 1.1 US quarts

### Disabled Travelers

Disabled travelers will find traveling easy in the US, because the country has initiatives aimed at providing "barrier-free" access throughout. The Americans with Disabilities Act (ADA) requires most public buildings, including museums, hotels, and restaurants, to make their services and facilities accessible to all people, including those in wheelchairs. However, it is mostly only the newer hotels that have handicap-accessible bathrooms *(see p19)*. Two of the many organizations in the country that will help disabled visitors plan and enjoy their trips are **The Guided Tour Inc** (215-782-1370/ www.guidedtour.com) and **Care Vacations** (780-986-6404/www.carevacations.com). Hotels that offer facilities for disabled tourists are marked in the "Where to Stay" listings at the end of each regional section. For restaurants that offer similar facilities, look at the restaurant listings for the wheelchair access symbol.

# Communications & Banking

ANY BANK IN THE US can accept transfer of funds from foreign banks. Many travelers already use credit cards or "automated teller" (ATM) cash/debit cards, so getting money from a bank or ATM should be relatively simple. It's best to buy traveler's checks in US dollar amounts before entering the country in order to avoid delays and extra charges. The country offers excellent telephone and mail services; cell phones and public Internet cafés have made keeping in touch easier and less expensive than ever, and most hotels also offer Internet hookups.

## Telephones

MANY COMPANIES offer telephone services in the US at varying rates. Most public pay phones accept coins, but calls can also be charged to a credit card. Local calls cost between 25 and 50 cents, with additional charges for longer calls. Some hotels offer guests free local calls, but some levy hefty charges per call, so check ahead. Making international calls is very expensive. Consider using a calling card with discounted rates, as they allow you to charge calls to your home number, while others deduct charges from a prepaid account. Some foreign cell phones work in the US, but the charges can be high. Many car rental companies also rent cell phones for customers.

### Reaching the Right Number

- The international code for the US is 1.
- For long distance calls within the US or to Canada: dial 1, the 3-digit area code, and the 7-digit local number.
- For local calls: dial the 7-digit local number.
- International direct-dial call: dial **011** followed by country code (UK: **44**; Australia: **61**; New Zealand: **64**; South Africa: **27**) then the city or area code (omit the first 0) and then the local number.
- International call via the operator: dial **01**, followed by country code, then city code (without the first 0), and then the local number.
- For operator assistance: dial **0**.
- An **800, 888, 877**, or **866** prefix indicates a free call.
- Directory inquiries: dial **411**.
- **For emergencies: dial 911.**

## Postal Services

POST OFFICES ARE open from 9am to 5pm (weekdays) with some open on Saturday mornings. Postcards and letters can be dropped into big blue mailboxes on street corners. Domestic mail should include the five-digit zip code. Rates for international mail vary, so buy stamps from a local post office. To receive mail, General Delivery service is available, whereby letters are held for you at a specific post office for 30 days. Mail forwarding services also exist for a fee.

## Internet Access

LOCAL LIBRARIES, shopping malls, hotels, and university hangouts are perhaps the least expensive and easiest places to access the Internet. Most library computers will let you send e-mail and surf the web. Many large cities have designated stores that offer Internet access for a small fee.

## Banking

BANKS CAN BE FOUND in all US cities and towns, and many have service centers in supermarkets and malls. Other financial institutions such as savings-and-loans and credit unions also offer banking services. Traveler's checks can be cashed as long as you have your passport. Banks also give cash advances against credit cards, but card companies charge a high fee for this service. Most banks will not exchange foreign currency. Banking hours are 9am to 4pm, weekdays, but some banks remain open till 6pm on Fridays, and some open on Saturday mornings as well.

### Directory

#### Financial Services

**Thomas Cook Currency Services**
(415) 362-3452.

**Thomas Cook Refund Assistance**
(800) 223-7373.

**American Express Travel Service**
(415) 536-2600.

**American Express Helpline**
(800) 221-7282.

**Cirrus**
(800) 424-7787.

**Plus**
(800) 843-7587.

## Automated Teller Machines

ALMOST ALL BANKS have 24-hour ATMs, as do most train stations, airports, and malls. ATMs are connected to a number of bank-card networks and can dispense cash from accounts held in other states or countries. The primary US bank-card networks are **Plus**, **Cirrus**, **Star**, and **Interlink**. Be sure that your bank permits international cash withdrawals, and that your card and personal identification number (PIN) are compatible with US machines. Many ATMs charge a fee of $1 to $2.50 per transaction. Exchange rates for ATM transactions, however, are better than those for traveler's checks or foreign currency.

## Credit Cards

THE MOST commonly accepted credit cards are VISA, MasterCard, American Express, Japanese Credit Bureau (JCB),

Discover, and Diners Club (DC). Credit cards can be used in hotels, restaurants, stores, and to pay for such services as medical care or car rental. Having a credit card will make your stay much easier, and the exchange rates on cards are often better than those for traveler's checks or currency.

## Traveler's Checks

The most widely accepted traveler's checks are those issued by American Express and Thomas Cook in US dollars. It is easier to pay for purchases with traveler's checks and get cash as change, than go to the trouble of cashing the checks at a bank. Buy checks in a variety of denominations, with $10, $20, and $50 bills. It can be difficult to cash $100 bills except at a bank. Foreign currency checks are not accepted, and out-of-state checks are difficult to cash. Contact **Thomas Cook Refund Assistance** or **American Express Helpline** for lost, stolen, or destroyed traveler's checks.

## Foreign Exchange

Try to change your money into US denominations before traveling to the US. You may find it difficult to exchange foreign currency except in international airport terminals in major cities. The main foreign exchange companies in the US are American Express and Thomas Cook. If you are in the need of ready cash, you can always visit a duty-free shop and buy something so that you can cash a traveler's check.

**10-cent coin (a dime)**

**5-cent coin (a nickel)**

**1-dollar coin**

**25-cent coin (a quarter)**

**Coins**

*American coins come in 2-dollar, 1-dollar, and 50-, 25-, 10-, 5-, and 1-cent pieces. 1-cent pieces are popularly called pennies, 5-cent are nickels, 10-cent are dimes, and 25-cent pieces are quarters.*

**Bank Notes**

*Units of currency are dollars and cents; 100 cents make a dollar. Notes (bills) come in $1, $5, $10, $20, $50, and $100s. All bills are green, so it is important to check the amount carefully. The only exception is the new $20 bill (not shown), which has other colors.*

# Health & Security

THE UNITED STATES DOES NOT have a national health service, and health care, though excellent, is operated for the most part by the private sector, making it extremely expensive. Medical travel insurance is highly recommended in order to defer some of the costs related to an accident or sudden illness. In terms of safety, some of the larger urban areas have a higher crime rate than rural locations, so a few basic precautions are necessary for a trouble-free visit. Be sure to check with friends or hotel staff about which parts of town are best avoided.

## PERSONAL SAFETY

WHILE MOST places on the tourist trail are reasonably safe to travel, visitors should nonetheless take safety precautions to avoid being a victim of crime. Generally speaking, most crimes occur in neighborhoods or areas not frequented by travelers. It is always a good idea to steer clear of neighborhoods that are off the beaten track. Avoid wearing expensive jewelry, carry only small amounts of cash, wear a money belt under clothing, and always carry cameras or camcorders securely.

## MONEY

CARRY ONLY small amounts of cash, and keep credit cards in a money belt rather than a backpack or trouser pocket. The safest way of carrying money is in the form of traveler's checks, which allow you to keep your hard cash to a minimum. Always use ATM machines during the day or on busy, well-lit streets.

## HOTEL SAFETY

THEFT FROM HOTEL rooms is uncommon, but it's best not to leave valuables out when you leave the room. Consider placing them, and any large amounts of cash, in the hotel safe, a service that is usually free of charge. While in your room, use the deadbolt lock for additional safety, and take time to familiarize yourself with the nearest emergency exits and fire escape routes. Never allow strangers into your hotel room or give them details of where you are staying.

## SECURITY IN YOUR CAR

A RENTAL CAR CAN serve as a convenient place to store your new purchases. However, it is also a magnet for criminals, especially in parking areas at major sites or hiking trails. Always lock your car when you leave it, and place suitcases and valuables in the trunk. Expensive items such as cameras left out in the open or in an unlocked car are easy targets for smash-and-grab thieves. Use hotel parking garages for overnight.

## KEEPING VALUABLES & DOCUMENTS SAFE

BEFORE YOU leave home, make photocopies of important documents such as passport and visa, and bring one copy with you and leave another in a safe place or with a friend. Do the same for the serial numbers of your traveler's checks and credit cards, in the event they are stolen or lost. All important documents and wallet should be kept in a money belt.

## OUTDOOR SAFETY

PARTICIPATING IN outdoor recreational activities can entail certain risks, which can be minimized by taking proper precautions. For activities such as mountain biking, rock-climbing, white-water river-rafting, or motorcycling, wearing helmets and other protective devices are essential. Always wear a life-jacket when canoeing or sailing. Desert and high altitude travelers should wear hats and sunscreen, and drink plenty of water to avoid dehydration. In desert areas, be sure to take a first-aid kit, extra gasoline, and a tool kit for your vehicle, and always carry a cell phone.

Hikers should always be prepared for sudden weather changes, especially at higher elevations. Stay on marked trails, and if camping or hiking alone, it's best to notify someone of your plans, destination, and estimated time of arrival. Many trails have sign-in sheets where you mark the start and completion of your hike or campout. In forested areas, hikers should wear bright-colored clothes and avoid off-trail forests and fields during hunting season.

## INSECTS & ANIMALS

OUTDOOR enthusiasts should be wary of dangerous animals in wilderness areas. Be especially careful in bear country, as attacks have become more frequent. A wise precaution is never to feed animals, or interfere with any wildlife. Insect stings and bites are an annoyance but are not usually life-threatening. Black flies, mosquitos, and deer flies are a nuisance, so be sure to carry insect repellant. Also, carry a snakebite or first aid kit if going into snake country. If bitten by a snake or scorpion, seek medical help immediately.

Try to avoid contact with allergenic plants such as poison ivy or poison oak. In the wild drinking water should always be treated or boiled to combat water-borne bacteria.

## SAFETY IN WATER

IF POSSIBLE, surfers and ocean swimmers should stay in areas with lifeguards on duty. If you are not used to dangerous currents, avoid unguarded beaches. Whether or not you are an experienced swimmer, pay attention to the lifeguards and the overall condition of the lake or ocean water. Never swim alone, and watch out for surfers, waterskiers, motorboats, and jet skis. Keep an especially close eye on children at all times.

## Preventing Forest Fires

While hiking in wilderness areas, be very careful lighting campfires. Since firewood is scarce, and forest fires start very quickly, always check whether campfires are allowed where you are camping. Make sure to extinguish all fires carefully and completely. A fire that still smokes is not out.

## Reporting Lost & Stolen Property

Although the chances of recovering lost or stolen property are very slim, it is a good idea to report all missing items (including your car) to the police. Most public transportation companies, such as taxi firms, buses, subways, and airlines, operate Lost and Found departments, which can be reached by phoning their general access number. It is useful to have a record of your valuables' serial numbers and a receipt of purchase. Be sure to ask for a copy of the police report for your insurance claim. For lost or stolen credit cards or traveler's checks, contact **American Express** *(see also p15)*.

## Police

Most law enforcement in the US is handled at the state and local government level. State troopers and the State Highway Patrol deal with traffic accidents and offenses outside city boundaries. County police and sheriffs patrol rural areas, small towns, and villages.

Law enforcement officers carry handguns and other weapons, and should always be treated with respect and courtesy. The officers are usually friendly, helpful, and interested in your safety. In the wake of the recent terrorist threat, National Transportation Security Administration officials are stationed in all US airports, train stations, bus terminals, and large, crowded venues. They provide passenger screening, crowd control, and other services.

On federal lands, including national parks and forests, park rangers are there to protect the visitors. Wilderness areas are, for the most part, free of crime.

## Legal Assistance

Travelers from outside the US who are in need of legal assistance should contact their nearest consulate or the embassy in Washington, DC. If arrested, you have the right to remain silent, to have legal counsel, and to make at least one phone call. The police will provide you with any necessary phone numbers, and should treat you with respect and courtesy.

## Insurance & Medical Treatment

Comprehensive travel insurance is highly recommended to anyone intending to visit the US. Any emergency medical or dental care can be very expensive, so having proof of insurance coverage is essential to help defray some of the costs related to an unscheduled hospital visit. Bring a back-up prescription if you take any medication.

A good insurance policy will also pay for the replacement of stolen or damaged property. If you need to cancel or change your travel plans, many policies will refund your costs.

## Emergencies

If you need emergency help from fire, police, or medical services dial 911. The call is free from any public phone, and emergency phone boxes are located along major highways and Interstates. All US medical facilities will provide emergency care to injured people, regardless of means. The **Travelers' Aid Society** specializes in giving assistance to those travelers who find themselves stranded or in need of emergency help.

## Directory

### Emergencies

**All Emergencies**
*911 for police, fire or medical emergency.*

**Travelers' Aid Society**
*(800) 327-2700.*
www.travelersaid.org

### Hospitals & Medical Facilities

*411 for directory assistance.*

### Lost/Stolen Credit Cards & Traveler's Checks

**American Express**
*(800) 528-4800 (credit cards).*
*(800) 221-7282 (checks).*
www.americanexpress.com

**Mastercard**
*(800) 826-2181.*
www.mastercard.com

**VISA**
*(800) 336-8472.*
www.visa.com

### Embassies

**Australia**
www.austemb.org

**Canada**
www.canadianembassy.org

**New Zealand**
www.nzembassy.com

**South Africa**
www.saembassy.org

**United Kingdom**
www.britainusa.com

**US Embassy**
www.travel.state.gov

**Bureau of Citizenship & Immigration Services**
www.bcis.gov

### Senior Citizens

**American Association of Retired Persons**
601 E St NW
Washington D.C., 20049
*(888) 687-2277.*
www.aarp.org

# Accommodations

THE US OFFERS A WIDE VARIETY of accommodations to suit all tastes and budgets. At the high end of the comfort scale, visitors can choose from luxury hotels and resorts, found in most major cities. Country inns and bed-and-breakfasts (B&Bs), usually located in large, refurbished historic houses, offer a more personal and hospitable atmosphere. If you're traveling on a budget, there are thousands of convenient inexpensive motels all along the highways. Generally, hotels, motels, and inns offer impeccably clean surroundings. For those who wish to experience the country's wide open spaces, there are more than enough campgrounds in parks and forests.

## Hotels & Resorts

THERE IS NO better place to experience the comfort of the US than to stay in one of the country's many chain hotels, such as the **Hilton**, **Marriott**, and **Renaissance**. Historic and ultramodern hotels and resorts are usually located in downtown areas, at the heart of the city. The best hotels, in major cities, often have the finest restaurants and pleasant cocktail bars. These hotels offer a full range of guest services, including swimming pools and health clubs, and their concierge can provide shopping and tourist information, as well as preferential seating at restaurants and theaters.

There are also a number of classic older hotels located in traditional vacation spots, notably the early 20th-century rustic lodges found in state and national parks. Some of the national parks' famous hotels, such as Yellowstone's Old Faithful Inn (*see p602*), are also located in unforgettably scenic locations. Most large resort hotels focus on relaxation and offer spa facilities or access to golf courses, tennis, and other outdoor activities.

An alternative to the large chain or resort hotels are the growing boutique hotels. These small, unique places all have their own personalities and stress service over amenities. These hotels are often quite expensive, so always ask for rates. For a complete listing of accommodations, see Where to Stay in each regional section.

## Business Travelers

MANY DOWNTOWN hotels cater mainly to business people, and some offer special "club-level" accommodations with extra-large rooms for long stays or occasional meetings. These club-level suites often provide breakfast, snacks, and evening cocktails, and on weekends they are great for the whole family.

## Motels

MOST OVERNIGHT accommodations are provided by motels. Generally located along the main highways, they offer parking for your car right next to your room. Motels usually have fewer amenities than hotels, but they are less expensive and often include swimming pools and children's play areas as well as a restaurant. Motel rooms usually have one large or two smaller beds, a bathroom, a TV, and a phone.

Many motels are run as part of national franchises, but many of the more pleasant ones are locally owned. Some of the most popular chain motels include **Motel 6**, **Howard Johnson**, **Fairfield Inn**, **Holiday Inn**, and the well-known **Best Western**.

## Bed-and-Breakfast & Historic Inns

MOST HISTORIC INNS offer a much more luxurious experience. Generally located in beautifully restored historic homes or mansions, they are often decorated with heirlooms and antiques. B&Bs, on the other hand, offer a wider choice, from rooms in private homes, where you may have to share a bathroom, to luxurious private accomodations that differ from historic inns in name only.

Most inns and B&Bs rent rooms on a nightly basis, though some offer discounts for week-long stays. Most are run as full-time businesses by professional staff. B&Bs also offer a fully cooked breakfast, often served communally so guests can get to know each other. Breakfasts are usually fairly lavish, multi-course affairs, with eggs, pancakes, and pastries. Some B&Bs, especially in rural areas near popular tourist areas, may also serve gourmet dinners with regional specialties with advance notice.

## Hostels

FOR SOLO TRAVELERS, one of the best ways to meet others and save money is to take advantage of the clean hostels run by **Hostelling International (HI)**, the American affiliate of the International Youth Hostels Association (IYHA). Hostels can be found in the centers of most major cities and near popular destinations. They offer inexpensive beds in dormitory-style shared rooms, segregated by sex, and many also have a few private rooms for couples or families. Some hostels are housed in unique buildings, such as lighthouses or renovated army barracks.

All hostels have kitchen facilities, bathrooms, and common rooms. HI Hostels have several rules, including no alcohol and sometimes a curfew, and guests are expected to bring their own bed linen. HI Hostels are open to travelers of all ages, although nonmembers are asked to pay a nominal surcharge in addition to nightly rates, which can run between $15 and $20. In many urban areas, there are also a number of privately run hostels that offer basic rooms or dormitory beds. Check the listings in the Yellow Pages.

### CAMPGROUNDS

MOST LOCAL, state, and national parks, national forests, and other public lands provide parking and a single or double campsite for tents, along with a picnic table, a campfire pit, toilet facilities, and sometimes hot showers. Some are fancier, with electrical and water "hook-ups" for self-contained recreational vehicles (RVs). Overnight fees vary with location, facilities, and season but generally run from $8 to $20 a night. Many campgrounds accept advance reservations, but some operate on a "first-come, first-served" basis. **Campgrounds Woodalls** and **Trailer Life** carry listings of campsites.

Privately operated campgrounds, such as those run by **Kampgrounds of America** (KOA) offer several features, including game rooms, swimming pools, and small grocery stores. Some also feature log cabins, suitable for families with children. The most popular campgrounds fill up early during vacation weekends and in the summer. It is also a good idea to set up camp well before sunset. Overnight camping in highway rest areas or along public roads is not only illegal but dangerous as well.

### RUSTIC OR BASIC ACCOMMODATIONS

THERE ARE several very basic "walk-in" primitive campgrounds in forest areas, used primarily by backpackers. These are generally free, but check with park rangers about wilderness permits and other regulations you might need. Vast portions of the West have such areas, managed by US government departments such as the **National Park Service**, the **US Forest Service**, and the **Bureau of Land Management** *(see p37)*.

### PRICES

ROOM RATES for overnight accommodations vary tremendously, from under $20 a night for a campground or hostel, to well over $500 a night in a deluxe downtown hotel. Most places quote the rate per room, but in some places, such as Las Vegas and New England, rates are often quoted per person, should two people share one room.

Room rates at all levels of comfort vary with demand. It is, therefore, worthwhile to ask for discounts, especially on the weekends in urban areas, weekdays in rural areas, or almost anywhere in the off-season, depending on the region.

### RESERVATIONS

MAKING ADVANCE reservations can also secure lower rates. Short-notice discounts are also offered, often through advertisements in local newspapers. Many hotels offer package deals in conjunction with a special event, such as theater or concert tickets with overnight accommodations.

Most lodgings will request a credit card number when you make a reservation. If you choose to cancel, you may be charged for a night's stay, depending on the time. For example, if you don't cancel by 6pm or earlier, you may be charged for one night. At the most popular places in peak season, many hotels and resorts may insist on a two-night minimum stay.

Most of the large lodging companies operate toll-free telephone lines for reservations, which can be useful if you are heading to a new city. These lines give up-to-date information about room rates, availability, and are also a good way to compare prices. Most companies publish free directories of all their properties, with maps and full details of rates and facilities.

### CHILDREN

MOST HOTELS welcome children and provide extra supplies, such as cots, for families. Babysitting services may also be available. In some family-oriented spots, hotels offer activities for kids and other fun programs. Children from the ages of 12 to 16, sometimes up to 18, can stay free of charge in their parents' room. Rooms often have sofas that unfold into beds; or extra beds may be set up for an additional fee. For more information see p13.

### DISABLED TRAVELERS

THE US LAW requires that all businesses provide facilities for the disabled *(see p13)*. However, lodgings do their best to accommodate all customers. If you have specific needs, give advance notice. Most places have wheelchair accessibility, wide doorways, handicap-accessible bathrooms, and support bars near toilets and showers.

## DIRECTORY

### HOTELS

**Hilton**
(800) 445-8667.
www.hilton.com

**Marriott**
(800) 228-9290.
www.marriott.com

**Renaissance**
(800) 468-3571.
www.renaissancehotels.com

### MOTELS

**Holiday Inn**
(800) 465-4329.
www.ichotelsgroup.com

**Howard Johnson**
(800) 654-2000.
www.hojo.com

**Motel 6**
(800) 466-8356.
www.motel6.com

### HOSTELS

**Hostelling International**
(301) 495-1240.
www.hiusa.org

### CAMPGROUNDS

**Campgrounds Woodalls**
www.woodalls.com

**Kampgrounds of America**
www.koa.com

**Trailer Life**
www.tldirectory.com

# Travel by Air

THE UNITED STATES IS A NATION on the move, with a huge number of airlines that fly both within the country and all around the world. While international travel is offered by US airlines as well as by hundreds of airlines in other countries, domestic travel is limited to airlines based in the United States. Because the country is so enormous, and recent competition has reduced prices considerably, air travel has become an integral part of life. Today, most long-distance and medium-distance domestic travel is by plane.

## FLYING TO THE US

MOST LARGE foreign cities have several daily flights to a number of US cities, especially pimary gateways to the East Coast, the West Coast, and throughout the Midwest. The main East Coast cities include New York, Boston, Washington, DC, Atlanta, and Miami; Chicago, St. Louis, Houston, Dallas, and Denver serve as main cities in the central region; and the West Coast is served by Los Angeles, San Francisco, and Seattle.

Most international flights from Europe travel across the Atlantic to New York, Washington, DC, Miami, Boston, and Chicago, taking roughly seven hours. Flights from Asia arrive at the West Coast airports, often stopping in Hawai'i on the way. These flights, as well as flights from Australia, take between 11 and 12 hours.

## KEEPING COSTS DOWN

AIR FARES FLUCTUATE in the US depending on the season, sometimes doubling during the peak holiday periods, especially in summer, and around Thanksgiving and Christmas. Fares are usually less expensive between February and March, when round-trip transatlantic flights can cost significantly less. You often get a better deal, too, by flying mid-week.

The least expensive fares are the APEX (Advance Purchase Excursion) tickets for scheduled airlines. These must be bought 21 days in advance and are valid for a seven- to 30-day period. However, any changes that need to be made can cost an additional fee. Some airlines also offer cheaper fares if you limit your stay to a certain period of time. Senior citizens and children may also receive discounts on certain flights.

These tickets are not always available, though. Another option is the short-term Internet fares advertised by airlines if there are any available seats. These are valid within a few days of the announcement (fares may be announced on a Wednesday for traveling that weekend and returning the next weekend).

## ARRIVAL AT THE AIRPORT

ALL INTERNATIONAL visitors must go through customs and immigration when they arrive in the US *(see p13)*. All major airports have multilingual information booths to answer your questions and give details on transportation into the city.

Most international airports are well connected to the nearest city either by public transportation or the vast array of rental car facilities. Many rentals supply shuttle buses to car pick-up points, usually located just outside the airport. Major airlines are connected to countless domestic airline services, and all have facilities for disabled passengers. Still, it is a good idea to prearrange any necessary services through your airline or agent.

## SECURITY

AFTER THE September 11, 2001 terrorist attacks, airport authorities tightened their pre-flight security checks (especially for domestic flights). International visitors should expect to be frisked thoroughly and have their hand luggage examined. Items such as battery cells, scissors, nail files, knitting needles, and sharp objects are prohibited. Signs throughout the Customs areas explain which items are prohibited in checked luggage. New plans are in place for

## TIME ZONES ACROSS THE UNITED STATES

The United States covers six different times zones – the "Lower 48" states are divided into Eastern, Central, Mountain, and Pacific time, while Alaska and Hawai'i have their own zones. The zones are divided into one-hour increments. For instance, when it is 8pm in New York, it is 7pm in Chicago, 6pm in Denver, 5pm in Los Angeles, 4pm in Anchorage, and 3pm in Honolulu.

Eastern Time is five hours behind Greenwich Mean Time, and Hawai'i is 11 hours behind Greenwich Mean Time. With a few variations, the United States observes Daylight Savings Time between spring and fall.

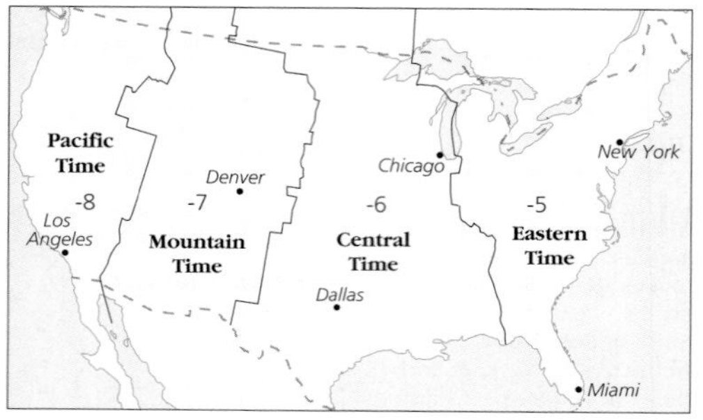

visitors with visas to be photographed and fingerprinted on arrival, for details to be checked against a national security database. In light of increased security, expect a long wait to check in.

## Flying Within the United States

Visitors interested in seeing the entire country may want to take advantage of domestic flights. These are operated by more than a dozen different major airlines, many of which fly internationally as well. An extensive domestic flight network serves most cities, making it easy to fly within the US.

The major US airlines operate what is known as a "hub-and-spoke" network, meaning that long-distance flights travel between regional airports, from where shorter flights continue on to your desired destination. Most **Delta Airlines** flights converge on their hub in Atlanta; **United Airlines** flights converge in Chicago and Denver; while **American Airlines** usually flies first to Dallas.

## Booking a Domestic Flight

For foreign visitors the easiest way to book a domestic flight is to have it agree with your itinerary. This way you have to buy only one set of tickets and often get a better deal. Another money-saving option is to take advantage of "Visit USA" (VUSA) coupons, which are good for numerous domestic flights (between three and ten flights), for a pre-paid fee. However, these coupons must be bought before you arrive and can be redeemed only with the same airline on which you flew internationally.

The Internet and the deregulation of the airline industry have made planning trips and purchasing tickets much easier. The best prices now are on airlines' websites.

## Domestic Airlines

Most international airlines have formed alliances with domestic flights, for instance, **British Airways** is partnered with American Airlines, and **Lufthansa** with United Airlines, making flight networks effectively interlinked. Beside the major international US airlines, there are a large number of domestic airlines that offer inexpensive flights. The most popular of these is **Southwest Airlines**, a "no-frills" carrier that connects to and from smaller airports rather than from major ones. These airlines are a less expensive and reliable means of travel. They offer basic snacks, and do not transfer to or from other carriers, which can make connecting flights a hassle, but the fares are low, and there are fewer restrictions.

## Directory

### Airline Carriers

**American Airlines**
*(800) 433-7300.*
www.aa.com

**British Airways**
*(800) 247-9297.*
www.britishairways.com

**Continental**
*(800) 231-0856.*
www.continental.com

**Delta Airlines**
*(800) 241-4141.*
www.delta.com

**United Airlines**
*(800) 241-6522.*
www.united.com

## Fly-Drive

Many airlines, in addition to travel companies and agents, offer fly-drive packages for tourists, which combine air fares and car rentals. These deals are well worth considering, since they give you flexibility and usually save you more money than if you were to book plane and car travel separately.

| Airport | Information | Distance from City | Taxi Fare to City | Average Travel Time |
|---|---|---|---|---|
| Chicago (O'Hare) | (800) 832-6352 | 17 miles (27 km) from downtown | $35–40 to downtown | Road: 30 mins to downtown |
| Dallas–Fort Worth (International) | (972) 574-8888 | 18 miles (29 km) from Dallas | $38 to downtown Dallas | Road: 25 mins to downtown Dallas |
| Los Angeles (LAX) | (310) 646-5252 | 15 miles (24 km) from downtown | $27 to downtown | Road: 30 mins to downtown |
| Miami (International) | (305) 876-7000 | 10 miles (16 km) from Miami Beach | $24 to Miami Beach | Road: 20 mins to Miami Beach |
| New York City (JFK) | (718) 244-4444 | 15 miles (24 km) from Manhattan | $40 to downtown Manhattan | Road: 1 hr to downtown Manhattan |
| San Francisco (SFO) | (650) 821-8211 | 14 miles (22 km) from downtown | $35 to downtown | Road: 25 mins to downtown |
| Seattle (Sea-Tac) | (206) 431-4444 | 14 miles (22 km) from downtown | $30 to downtown | Road: 25 mins to downtown |
| Washington, DC (Dulles International) | (703) 572-2700 | 26 miles (42 km) from downtown | $44–50 to downtown | Road: 40 mins to downtown |

# Travel by Road

AWAY FROM MAJOR CITIES, where traffic can be frustrating, driving in the United States is a delightful experience. Driving is a favorite American pastime, and to see the country in all its glory, you have to drive a car. Major roads and most highways are rarely crowded, and drivers are generally courteous and safe. Gasoline in the US is inexpensive, and car rental rates are also reasonable. You can get by without a car in a few larger towns, and in cities like New York, Boston, or San Francisco you will probably be better off without one. However, in most of the country, if you want to explore the wide open spaces of the western US, you will need a car since public transportation there is limited.

## Types of Road

THE US HAS AN excellent network of roads, with over 4 million miles (6 million km) of paved roads open to the public. For long distance travelers, the fastest and most convenient part of the US highway system is the Interstate Highway, a high-speed, limited-access highway. Some have between six and 12 lanes running both directions, while rural areas generally have two or three lanes.

Stretching all across the country in an east-to-west and north-to-south grid, Interstate Highways are abbreviated on signs with a capital "I," followed by a number. The main Interstates start with I-5 on the West Coast and end with I-95, the busy main route along the East Coast. Transcontinental Interstates run east-to-west and range from I-10 between Florida and California to I-90 between Boston and Seattle.

In and around cities, a complicated system of ring roads, link roads, and spur roads are also part of the Interstate system. These roads are often better known by name than number, for instance I-405 in Southern California is referred to as the "San Diego Freeway."

Most Interstates are free, but some states charge tolls. These sections, known as "turnpikes," have the same numbers as sections without toll booths.

Before the Interstate Highway System came into use, the primary long-distance highways were federal ones. Today, these are the main routes in rural areas and are officially signed as "US" and a number, ranging from US-1 along the East Coast to US-101 along the West Coast.

## Rules of the Road

- All traffic drives on the right.
- All distances are measured in miles.
- Seat belts are compulsory, and children under the age of 4 are required to have special car seats.
- At traffic signals, green lights mean you can proceed safely; amber lights mean prepare to stop; and red lights mean stop. A flashing red light means stop before proceeding; and a flashing yellow light means proceed with caution.
- At a red octagonal stop sign, traffic must come to a complete halt before proceeding. When two or more cars reach a stop sign simultaneously from different sides of the intersection, drivers must yield to traffic on the right.
- A yellow triangular yield sign directs you to give way to other traffic.
- In towns and cities, roads are usually divided by a painted center line (usually white). Smaller streets may have no dividing line.
- On all roads, a double yellow line means do not pass or cross the lines.
- Some roads have a central lane, protected by painted single lines; this is a designated turning area for making left-hand turns.
- "U" turns are legal only where posted.
- On multi-lane highways, the fastest traffic travels in the left-hand lanes; slower traffic occupies the right-hand lane.
- Cargo-carrying heavy trucks generally stay in the slow lane. Keep your distance from these vehicles, because they have poor visibility and enormous weight and size.
- On multi-lane highways traffic can pass only on the left-hand side. On smaller roads safe passing places are indicated with a broken yellow line on your side of the double yellow line.
- Speed limits vary from state to state, but range from 25mph (40 km/h) in residential areas to 65–75mph (105–120 km/h) on highways.
- There is a minimum speed of 45mph (72 km/h) on highways and Interstate Highways. Farm traffic and pedestrians are not permitted on Interstates.
- Parking is allowed on most streets, subject to posted rules, but any restrictions are posted at the site. Park only in the direction of travel. If you receive a ticket, pay it immediately or it will be charged (with a penalty) to the rental car company, who will collect it from your credit card.
- Visitors should be aware of regional exceptions to the standard US driving laws. Some of these are pointed out in the "Practical Information" section of each chapter.
- Most foreign licenses are valid, but if your license is not in English, or does not have a photo ID, you must get an International Driver's License.
- Drunk driving is a serious offense and can result in a heavy fine or jail term.

Lined by neon-lit motels, and other classic landmarks of roadside America, these roads are slower but more enjoyable, and along with many other state and country roads, provide the country's most scenic routes (*see pp40–41*).

Road names vary from state to state. In the northeast, for example, highways are called "routes" while in Texas, roads are labeled "FM," farm to market or "RM," ranch to market.

### Tips for Renting a Car

Most rental cars are relatively new and low on mileage, and rates are as low as $150 a week. The best rates are generally offered for cars rented for full week time periods, and for returning cars to the same location they were rented from. A more economical option is the fly-drive (*see p21*).

Small economy or subcompact cars have the lowest rates. Many companies also offer upgrades to larger or more luxurious vehicles for very modest rates. Most rental cars have automatic transmissions, power steering, and air conditioning, but you should confirm this in advance. Also, check for any pre-existing damage to the car and note this on your contract.

To rent a car, you must be at least 25 years old, have a valid driving license, a clean driving record, and a major credit card. The car company will "authorize" an amount ranging between $250–1,000, to assure payment and return of the vehicle. Depending on your existing car insurance policy, you may want to accept the "damage waiver" and liability insurance that the rental company will offer you, and this will add $10–20 per day to the rental cost.

### Driveaways

An inexpensive option for a long-distance road trip is a driveaway car. Driveaways let you take a private car to a predetermined place in a specified amount of time. Most driveaways are offered to private members, but some ads may appear in magazines or newspapers.

Flexiblity is essential for a driveaway deal since the destination is beyond your control. You have to choose an efficient route and average about 400 miles (644 km) a day. However, since you have to pay only for the gas, the price is quite good. To use a driveaway car, you must have a clean driving record, and most companies require a minimum deposit to cover the insurance deductible.

One of the biggest driveaway companies, **Auto Driveaway**, has offices all over the US. Other firms are listed in phone books under "Automobile Transporters."

### RV Rentals

Recreational vehicles (RVs) or mobile homes, are great for families or groups, as they are equipped with beds, kitchens, and bathroom facilities. Costs run between $900–1,400 for seven nights plus a per-mile charge, but lodging is free and you have some flexibility, despite the vehicles' slow, stocky designs. Although rental RVs are usually older, conditions are similar to those for cars.

It is illegal in most places to pull over to the side of the road and camp. Many chain retail outlets, notably Wal-Mart, allow one night's free stay in their parking lots, with approval of the manager or front desk. Even with an RV, it costs about $20 a night to park in a campground (*see p19*). For more details contact **Recreational Vehicle Association of America** or **Cruise America**.

### Insurance

It is extremely important that you have adequate insurance if you plan on driving around in the US. Rental agencies generally include insurance in the cost, but if you bring a car into the country, you must make absolutely sure that you are adequately covered by car and life insurance.

## Directory

### Car Rental Agencies

**Alamo**
T *(800) 354-2322.*
W www.alamo.com

**Avis**
T *(800) 331-1212.*
W www.avis.com

**Budget**
T *(800) 527-0700.*
W www.budget.com

**Hertz**
T *(800) 654-3131.*
W www.hertz.com

### Driveaways

**Custom Auto Delivery**
T *(800) 647-7992.*
W www.driveaway.com

### RV Rentals

**Cruise America**
T *(800) 327-7778.*
W www.cruiseamerica.com

**Recreational Vehicle Association of America**
T *(888) 467-8464.*
W www.gorving.com

### Road Conditions Information

**American Automobile Association (AAA)**
T *(800) 222-4357.*

### Gas Stations

Except in the most remote areas, gas stations are easy to find and conveniently located. Many stations require advance payment, either by cash or credit/debit card. Most gas stations also have attached convenience stores, where you can buy food, beverages, and newspapers.

### Rest Areas

Conveniently located immediately adjacent to Interstates and major highways, rest areas are easily accessible and provide restrooms, telephones, picnic tables, dog-walking areas, and sometimes free coffee. Some even allow overnight stays, but be wary of strangers. It is a good idea to take a rest when driving long distances.

# Travel by Motorcycle or Bike

For visitors with time on their hands as well as a sense of adventure, touring the United States by motorcycle or bicycle can be a rewarding experience. Ride the open road with a Harley-Davidson, or mountain bike throughout the beautiful and peaceful American wilderness for the adventure of a lifetime. Good planning, familiarizing yourself with the rules and regulations, and using the right equipment can make this an enjoyable way of seeing the country.

## Motorcycles

Fans of Marlon Brando's famous movie *The Wild One* (1954) or the Jack Nicholson's classic *Easy Rider* (1969) may dream of exploring the United States on a motorcycle. Today, there are several motorcycle rental companies, especially in bike-friendly areas, where licensed riders drive classic motorcycles such as Harley-Davidsons or BMWs.

An American motorcycle license or an International Driving Permit for motorcycles is necessary. Also, the law in most states requires that you wear a helmet.

## Motorcycle Rentals & Tours

Renting is expensive, since the rates and liability insurance can add up to well over $100 a day. Moreover, you have to pay extra for collision insurance. Most companies allow short-term rentals in a single location, but larger firms such as **Eagle Rider** have branches or affiliates all over the country. If you plan to stay for a longer period, it might be less expensive to buy a bike for a few months, then resell it.

For long-distance motorcycle trips, Eagle Rider offers guided tours along selected routes. **Blue Sky Motorcycle Tours** also offers a wide range of tours.

Riders may be interested in taking part in one of the many motorcycle rallies, when thousands of riders get together for annual gatherings held in places like Daytona Beach, Florida (early March); Laconia, New Hampshire (mid June); or Sturgis, South Dakota (August).

## Bicycles

Bicycles are another great way to see the country. Unlike motorcycles, bicycles can be brought on most airplanes as luggage. Check the requirements first with your airline – many carriers require that you disassemble and pack the bike into a special box, which is available in most good bike shops.

In a great many cities, there are extensive networks of bike paths, which are often separated from car traffic. In some larger cities, bikes can be strapped onto the outside of local buses or carried on the subway.

For serious long-distance biking, it's important to equip yourself with a good bike, tools and spares, maps, and preferably a helmet. Cyclists must obey all traffic laws and should be careful to lock up their bikes and gear.

In the US, bikes are not as common as they are in many other countries. Car and truck drivers are not used to sharing the road with bikes, which can make cycling hazardous. Be aware of RV drivers in particular, because it is easy for them to misjudge the sizes of their vehicles. Bikes are prohibited on restricted-access highways and freeways.

## Bicycle Rentals & Tours

Bikes are available for rent in all major US cities for around $25 a day, or you can buy used bikes from flea markets or garage sales. Notices of second-hand sales appear in newspaper ads or hostel notices. Look in the Yellow Pages for local bike rental companies.

**Backroads** organizes a variety of guided bike tours, following some of the most spectacular scenic routes, with overnight stays in country inns or national park campsites. If interested in long-distance cycling, be sure to contact the **Adventure Cycling Association**, which has developed a network of bike-friendly routes following quieter and more scenic federal and state highways.

## Recreational Biking

In country areas, many bike paths have been reclaimed from unused railroad lines. Known as "rail trails," these are some of the best long-distance bicycling and walking routes in the country, often running alongside rivers and having moderate grades. In addition, there are miles and miles of country roads everywhere you go. Areas such as California's Wine Country and New England's river valleys are among the most popular.

The more athletic or daredevil travelers may also want to try off-road mountain biking, which is encouraged in many recreational areas such as downhill ski resorts in summer.

## Directory

### Motorcycle Rentals & Tours

**Eagle Rider Motorcycles**
(888) 900-9901.
www.eaglerider.com

**Blue Sky Motorcycle Tours**
(866) 971-5501.
www.blueskymotorcyclerentals.com

### Bicycle Tours

**Backroads**
(800) 462-2848.
www.backroads.com

**Adventure Cycling Association**
150 E Pine St, Missoula, MT 59802. (406) 721-1776.
www.adventurecycling.org

# Travel by Bus or Train

ALTHOUGH MORE TIME-CONSUMING than flying, you can enjoy long-distance bus and train trips that let you see the beauty of the US. Greyhound – the major long-distance buses – offers clean, modern travel conditions with on-board movies and restroom facilities. Amtrak trains are spacious and comfortable. Amtrak provides restaurant cars, observation cars, and great social atmospheres. If you want to meet fellow travelers, buses and trains are the transportation options for you.

## TRAVELING BY BUS

THE NATION-WIDE carrier **Greyhound Lines** serves all the major cities that airlines do, plus many smaller towns along the way, but the travel times are much longer. On long journeys, be sure to take something to eat and drink as meals are determined by where the bus stops.

Buses are also a good option for urban or suburban transportation, but because service can be limited in rural areas, you should plan your route carefully when visiting the countryside. Greyhound buses also provide links with major airports as well as Amtrak services.

## TICKETS & RESERVATIONS

MANY BUS stations are located in low-rent parts of town, so it is usually a good idea to take a taxi home from the station at night.

Ask about discounts and special fares on Greyhound and other carriers. Most major bus lines offer discounts for children under 12, students, and senior citizens (with proper ID), as well as unlimited travel within a set period. Tickets can be bought on the same day of travel, although fares are much less expensive if they are bought in advance. For advance tickets, contact Greyhound directly or ask a travel agent.

International visitors should know that Greyhound tickets are cheaper if bought from an agent outside the US. If you plan to interrupt your trip to explore on your own, or tour the US on an extended trip, there may be a travel package just for you.

## BUS TOURS

IN MOST STATES, bus companies offer short package trips in deluxe air-conditioned buses that tour major attractions. These guided tours provide a comfortable way of seeing the sights, without having to worry about time schedules, admission tickets, and opening hours.

For passengers with more time to spare, you may want to try certain bus companies, such as **Green Tortoise**, that offer leisurely trips between major cities. Passengers on these buses can take breaks to camp out, prepare meals, and explore the countryside. Unlike other buses, there are foam mattresses for sleeping. These tours are not for everyone, nevertheless they can provide an enjoyable, relaxed, and memorable tour of the country.

## TRAVELING BY TRAIN

THE USE OF RAILROADS in the US is dwindling. Still, there is a small and enjoyable network of long-distance passenger train routes, operated by **Amtrak**, the national rail system. In spite of its limited network and sometimes inconvenient schedules, a scenic train ride can be a unforgettable experience.

## TRAIN TICKETS & RESERVATIONS

TO MAKE THE most of an Amtrak trip, consider paying the extra money to get a sleeping compartment, which costs around $150 a night on a twin-sharing basis. Meal service is included in the price.

Amtrak travel is an especially good value for international visitors, who can take advantage of a number of rail tickets that give 15 or 30 days of train travel for a fee of $350–500, depending on the dates and regions of travel.

## HISTORIC RAILROADS

MANY PIONEER railroads that braved the Wild West frontier are now back in business as tourist attractions, running short trips (often under coal-fired steam) through some spectacular scenery. Many trains, running along narrow-gauge tracks, were constructed by mining or logging companies over a century ago.

Among the most popular railroads are the **Durango and Silverton Narrow Gauge** in southwestern Colorado (*see p591*), the **Cumbres and Toltec** line in New Mexico, and the **Grand Canyon Railroad** in Williams, Arizona, which goes to the rim of the Grand Canyon.

## DIRECTORY

### LONG-DISTANCE BUSES

**Greyhound Lines**
☎ *(800) 231-2222 (24 hrs).*
W www.greyhound.com

### BUS TOURS

**Green Tortoise**
☎ *(415) 956-7500.*
W www.greentortoise.com

### RAILROADS

**Amtrak**
☎ *(800) 872-7245.*
W www.amtrak.com

**Durango & Silverton Narrow Gauge**
☎ *(970) 247-2733.*
W www.durangotrain.com

**Cumbres & Toltec Railroad**
☎ *(505) 756-2151.*
W www.cumbrestoltec.com

**Grand Canyon Railroad**
☎ *(800) 843-8724.*
W www.thetrain.com

# USA at a Glance

# USA Through the Year

THE SIZE AND SCOPE of the United States means that at almost any time of year you can find the right weather to suit any activity. In the middle of winter, for example, while skiers are enjoying the deep snows of the Rockies and New England, sun-seekers flock to Florida or the Arizona deserts. Both the weather and the calendar of events heat up in the summer with a proliferation of county fairs, arts and music festivals, and other events, many celebrating the nation's diverse history and culture. October and November are prime time for harvest festivals, especially near Thanksgiving. The year ends with a variety of religious holidays, including Christmas, Hannukah, Ramadan, and the African-American celebration Kwanzaa, while the college and professional football seasons climax with a series of New Year's Day championship games and the Super Bowl finale.

**Jazz Festival musician, New Orleans**

## Spring

SPRING INSPIRES a definite sense of renewal all over the country. Wildflowers carpet the deserts, the magnolias and cherry trees burst into bloom, and melting snows fill streams and waterfalls to their annual peak. Among the events that celebrate the season, the most symbolic are the first games of the baseball season, which begins in April.

### March

**Lahaina Whalefest** *(early Mar)*, Lahaina, HI. Lectures, dives, and whale-watching activities celebrate the humpback whale that winters off the Hawaiian coast.

**Bike Week** *(early Mar)*, Daytona, FL. Motorcycle racers and enthusiasts congregate in one of the US's largest gatherings of bikers.

**St. Patrick's Day Parade** *(Sun nearest Mar 17)*, Boston, MA; New York City, NY; Chicago, IL; San Francisco, CA. Parades celebrating Irish heritage are held in these major cities. Towns such as Butte, MT, and Savannah, GA, also hold parties.

**South by Southwest Festival** *(mid-Mar)*, Austin, TX. An independent pop-music festival.

**Academy Awards** *(mid-Mar)*, Hollywood, CA. The movie industry honors its stars with golden Oscars.

**Natchez Pilgrimage** *(early Mar–early Apr)* Natchez, MS. A month-long celebration of Old South culture and antebellum architecture *(see p30)*.

### April

**Easter** *(date varies)*. This spring holiday is a study in contrasts. Early morning outdoor "Easter Sunrise" services are held all over the country, while in New York City, outrageously dressed characters join in the Easter Parade down Fifth Avenue. At this time, college kids flock to warm climes in Florida, Texas, and California for their annual "Spring Break."

**National Cherry Blossom Festival** *(early Apr)*, Washington, DC. A number of events celebrate the blossoming of hundreds of the city's famous cherry trees.

**Patriot's Day** *(Mon nearest Apr 18)*, Lexington and Concord, MA. Early morning re-enactments of the first battles of the American Revolution are followed by the country's most famous race, the Boston Marathon.

### May

**Cinco de Mayo** *(May 5)*. Celebrations of Mexican culture featuring folk dancing and mariachi music, take place all over the US to mark the anniversary of the Battle of Puebla.

**Kentucky Derby** *(first Sat in May)*, Louisville, KY. The country's biggest horse race and the start of the "Triple Crown" championship takes place at the end of a two-week-long public party.

**Wright Plus** *(mid- or late May)*, Chicago, IL. You can tour architect Frank Lloyd Wright's buildings and residences during this annual housewalk at Oak Park.

**Spoleto Festival USA** *(late May-early Jun)*, Charleston, SC. The largest arts festival in the United States.

**Jockeys at Churchill Downs for the Kentucky Derby, Louisville**

◁ **Silhouettes of tall saguaro cacti, unique to the Sonoran Desert, Arizona**

**Indianapolis 500** *(Sun before Memorial Day)*, Indianapolis, IN. The most famous auto race in the US draws over 100,000 fans.
**Kinetic Sculpture Race** *(Memorial Day weekend)*, Arcata, CA. Northern California's good-natured culture is evident at this three-day event, in which human-powered sculptures are raced over land and sea.

Independence Day fireworks light up the sky in Houston, Texas

## Summer

The Memorial Day holiday, at the end of May, marks the unofficial beginning of summertime. This is prime vacation and travel time for students and families. It is also a good time to enjoy music festivals, usually held in idyllic rural locations. The weather is hot and frequently humid, with afternoon storms in much of the country.

The flamboyant Lesbian and Gay Pride Parade, New York City

## June

**Harvard-Yale Regatta** *(early Jun)*, New London, CT. This series of collegiate rowing races offers visitors a chance to observe the Ivy League elite at play.
**B.B. King Homecoming Festival** *(late May/early June)*, Indianola, MS. One of the oldest and most popular of the many Deep South summer blues festivals.
**Red Earth Native American Festival** *(first weekend)*, Oklahoma City, OK. One the largest gatherings of Native American dancers and musicians is held at what was the last vestige of "Indian Territory."
**Lesbian and Gay Pride Day** *(Sun in late Jun)*, New York City, NY; San Francisco, California. Major parades and festivities fill the streets of both these cities.

## July

**Independence Day** *(Jul 4)*, Bristol, RI; Boston, MA; Independence, MO; Stone Mountain near Atlanta, GA. Although the entire country celebrates the Fourth of July with parades and fireworks displays, these cities put on particularly good shows.
**Taste of Chicago**, *(first week in Jul)*, Chicago, IL. The city's best food and music can be experienced at an open-air party, held on the Lake Michigan waterfront.
**Ernest Hemingway Days** *(mid-Jul)*, Key West, FL. The city where the famous writer lived offers a week of theatrical productions, short story contests, and a Hemingway look-alike competition.
**Tanglewood Music Festival** *(Jul–Aug)*, Lenox, MA. The Boston Symphony and Boston Pops give outdoor concerts in a beautiful Berkshire Mountains estate.

## August

**Hawaiian International Billfish Tournament** *(first week in Aug)*, Kailua-Kona, HI. This international fishing tournament draws people in search of record-sized marlin.
**Sunflower River Blues Festival** *(early-Aug)*, Clarksdale, MS. One of the country's most enjoyable blues festivals takes place in the home of the blues, the Mississippi Delta.
**Elvis International Tribute Week** *(mid-Aug)*, Memphis, TN. Also called "Deathweek," a series of events are held to celebrate the life and times of Elvis Presley, leading up to the anniversary of his death on August 16.
**Alaska State Fair** *(mid-Aug)*, Palmer, AK. This fair is especially famous for its super-sized vegetables, with pumpkins and cabbages grown to world-record sizes due to the state's 24-hour summer sunshine.
**Newport Jazz Festival** *(mid-Aug)*, Newport, RI. Sponsored by electronics firm JVC, this popular festival draws the very best jazz musicians from all over the country and the world.
**US Open Tennis Championships** *(Aug–Sep)*, New York City, NY. Professional tennis players from the world over compete in this Grand Slam tournament.

Opening ceremony of the 2002 US Open Tennis Championships

**The famous fiery colors of New England's fall foliage**

## Fall

During fall in New England, the leaves of the hardwood trees turn stunning shades of red and gold, drawing appreciative tourists from all over the country. In the West, wine-growing regions celebrate the annual harvest, and in the Great Lakes and Midwest, beer lovers join the Oktoberfest celebrations in the nation's many German enclaves. The approach of winter and the start of the Christmas shopping season is kicked off by the nationally televised Macy's Thanksgiving Day parade down Broadway in New York City.

### September

**Mississippi Delta Blues and Heritage Festival** *(mid-Sep)*, Greenville, MS. A blues and African-American culture festival in the heart of the Mississippi Delta.
**Miss America Pageant** *(mid-Sep)*, Atlantic City, NJ. The nation's oldest beauty contest, held in the seaside resort of Atlantic City.
**Festivals Acadiens** *(late Sep)*, Lafayette, LA. Over 100,000 people flock to this Cajun Country capital to enjoy the unique sights, sounds, and tastes of Louisiana life.
**Northeast Kingdom Fall Foliage Festival** *(mid-Sep–early Oct)*, VT. Celebrating the change of seasons, as well as the brilliantly colored fall foliage, several tours and events are held in small towns all over northern Vermont.
**Major League Baseball Championships** *(Sep–Oct)*. The nation's top professional teams face off, with the winners competing in October's World Series.

### October

**Texas State Fair** *(late-Sep–early Oct)*, Dallas, TX. One of the country's largest state fairs, with a focus on Texas.
**King Biscuit Blues Festival** *(early Oct)*, Helena, AR. Once sponsored by the King Biscuit flour company, the small Mississippi River town of Helena has been celebrating the blues since the 1920s.
**Ironman Triathlon** *(Sat nearest to full moon)*, Kailua-Kona, HI. More than 1,000 of the world's fittest athletes take part in a highly challenging series of trials, combining a 2.4-mile (3.8-km) swim, a 112-mile (180-km) bike ride, and a 26-mile (42-km) marathon run.

**Giant cowboy balloon at the Texas State Fair in Dallas**

**American Royal Rodeo** *(date varies, mid-Oct to early Nov)*, Kansas City, MO. One of the country's largest and most prominent professional rodeo competitions.
**Columbus Day Parade** *(second Mon in Oct)*, San Francisco, CA. Columbus Avenue, winding through the city's Italian-American North Beach district, comes alive with a parade celebrating the achievements of the Italian-born explorer Christopher Columbus. Several other such parades are held throughout the country.
**Fall Pilgrimage** *(mid-Oct)*, Natchez, MS *(see p28)*. A three-week-long series of events celebrate antebellum architecture and culture.
**Oktoberfest** *(late Oct)*. Modeled on the famous one in Munich, beer-flavored festivals are held in German neighborhoods of most large cities in the US, as well as small German towns like New Braunfels TX, Hermann MO, and Leavenworth, WA.
**Haunted Happenings** *(late Oct)*, Salem, MA. Leading up to Halloween, the historic home of the Salem Witch Trials stages a series of supernatural-themed events and activities.
**Halloween** *(Oct 31)*. While children dress up in scary costumes and beg for candy, many adults flock to raucous public parties in places like Key West, FL, and New York's Greenwich Village.

### November

**Dia de los Muertos (Day of the Dead)** *(Nov 1)*, San Francisco, CA. Festivities in San Francisco's Mission District highlight this Catholic festival, when the souls of the dead are said to visit the living. Similar festivities take place in Mexican neighborhoods across the country.
**Thanksgiving** *(last Thu in Nov)*. Celebrating the survival of the pilgrims who landed at Plymouth, MA, in 1620, this holiday sees

Turkey Float in Macy's Thanksgiving Day Parade, New York City

families coming together from all over the country to share in a massive meal of roast turkey, stuffing, cranberry sauce, and pumpkin pie. Many restaurants serve special Thanksgiving meals, and an old-fashioned celebration of the festival is held at Plimoth Plantation.
**Macy's Thanksgiving Day Parade** *(Thanksgiving Day)*, New York City, NY. Giant inflatable figures march down New York's Broadway to celebrate Thanksgiving and the start of the Christmas holiday season.

## Winter

Perhaps best known for the shopping mania that leads up to Christmas, winter in American cities is a time of twinkling lights, ringing cash registers, and occasional snowstorms. Department stores along New York's Fifth Avenue, Chicago's State Street, and other shopping districts attract shoppers with exuberant displays in their store windows. Many ski resorts stage special winter activities, such as sleigh rides and visits from Santa Claus. Winter is also the best time to watch the gray whale migration along the Pacific Ocean, or to observe the humpback whales on the way to their winter breeding grounds in Hawai'i. February also sees a number of public parades and parties, which range from the Chinese New Year celebrations to the wild fun and festivity of Mardi Gras in New Orleans.

### December

**Triple Crown of Surfing** *(late Nov to mid-Dec)*, North Shore O'ahu, HI. The world's most prestigious surfing competition usually spans three weeks, waves and weather permitting.
**Boston Tea Party Reenactment** *(mid-Dec)*, Boston, MA. Costumed performers and interpreters bring to life the famous Boston Tea Party, a protest that played an important role in precipitating the famous American Revolution.
**New Year's Eve** *(Dec 31)*, New York City, NY. The country's foremost New Year celebration starts with the countdown in New York's Times Square, which is televised live across Eastern US and repeated (on tape) for viewers elsewhere in the country. Major New Year's Eve parties occur in most major cities, with great public celebrations in Las Vegas and San Francisco.

### January

**New Year's Day** *(Jan 1)*. A variety of parades and lively festivities are held all around the country; these are very often connected with a championship college football game such as the well-known Orange Bowl in Miami, the Cotton Bowl in Dallas, the Sugar Bowl in New Orleans, and the Rose Bowl in Pasadena, CA.
**Martin Luther King Jr. Day** *(Mon nearest Jan 15)*. Events are held around the country to honor the birth and life of the Civil Rights leader.
**Mud Week** *(mid-Jan)*, San Antonio, TX. While workers drain the water to clear out downtown's River Walk, musicians and artists have fun in the mud.
**Cowboy Poetry Festival** *(late Jan)*, Elko, NV. Cowboys come to this town to tell tales, quote their very own poems, and sing songs about the heroic American West.

### February

**Groundhog Day** *(Feb 2)*, Punxsutawney, PA. The star of this festival is a small rodent who forecasts the beginning of spring.
**Mardi Gras** *(date varies, mid-Feb)*, New Orleans, LA. Colorful parades, lavish parties, and masked balls are held. Many smaller cities hold similar celebrations.

Lion dance during Chinese New Year, Chinatown, San Francisco

**Chinese New Year** *(date varies, late Jan to mid-Feb)*, San Francisco, CA. To celebrate Chinese New Year, colorful parades are held here, in New York City, and several other cities.
**Iditarod Trail Sled Dog Race** *(late Feb–early Mar)*, Anchorage, AK. This test of endurance takes packs of dogs and their drivers two grueling weeks.

# Climate of the USA

Much of the US enjoys temperate weather, but the country is so vast that many regions experience climatic extremes. Alaska has the harshest winter, while the warmest temperatures are in Hawai'i and Florida. Even within the "Lower 48" states, the weather varies tremendously, from the heavy snows of the Rocky Mountains to the intense heat of Death Valley in the California desert. Beside the four main seasons, the US also sees some unusual weather, including destructive tornadoes that may form in spring and summer across the Great Plains; thunderstorms that burst over the South during summer; and powerful hurricanes that strike coastal areas in the Southeast in autumn.

**Subarctic (Alaska)**
*Though temperatures drop well below freezing for most of the year, the warm summers are extended by the non-stop daylight of the "midnight sun."*

**Temperate (California)**
*The West Coast's mild climate is much like that of the Mediterranean regions, with mild winters and long, sunny summers.*

**Tropical (Hawai'i)**
*This island paradise is warm and pleasant year-round. Significant rain falls in winter, usually on the northeastern or windward coasts.*

**Arid (Southwest)**
*The hot, dry climate of the Southwestern desert draws millions of visitors. Winter snows can fall at higher elevations, but sunshine is guaranteed throughout the year.*

**Cool Temperate (New England)**
*Bright, sunny days followed by frosty nights cause the most intense color in New England's famous autumn foliage. The region experiences warm summers and cold winters with high snowfalls in certain areas.*

**Cool Continental (Great Lakes)**
*The Great Lakes states are famous for their frigid winters, when the region receives the country's heaviest snowfall.*

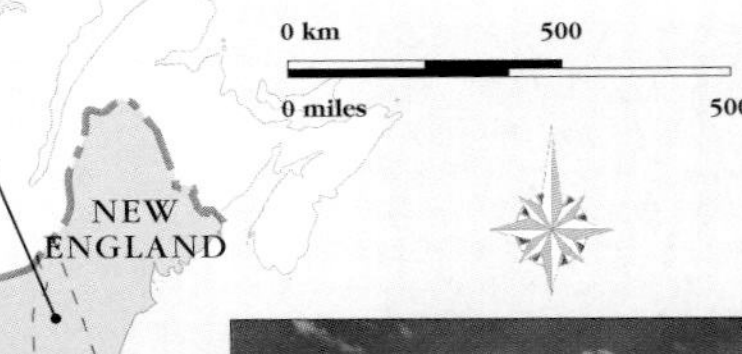

**Cool Temperate (Great Plains)**
*Chilled by arctic winds in winter, and hit by fierce tornadoes in spring, the Midwest states usually enjoy long, hot summers.*

**Warm Tropical (Florida)**
*The sultry climate of Florida and the Gulf of Mexico is usually warm and frequently very humid. Hurricanes can hit the coast between June and late November, making December to April the most popular time to visit the region.*

# National Parks

For many visitors, the highlight of a visit to the US is to experience the country's sublime scenery and abundant wildlife. Some 80 million acres (32 milion hectares) of pristine splendor have been preserved as national parks, found in 49 of the 50 states. From Acadia National Park on the rugged coast of Maine to the deserts of Death Valley in California, the parks encompass a variety of terrain, as well as the habitats of several endangered species. Most have a full range of facilities, including delightful rustic lodges, and offer a variety of outdoor activities.

***Yellowstone National Park*** (see pp584–5) *in Wyoming is the country's first and oldest national park. Highlights include geysers and the country's largest bison herd.*

**Grand Teton National Park's** *(see p583)* peaks make it one of Wyoming's top sights.

**Badlands National Park** *(see p444)*, South Dakota's most important park, combines craggy sandstone formations with mixed grass prairie.

Olympic NP
North Cascades NP
Mt. Rainier NP
Glacier NP
THE PACIFIC NORTHWEST
THE ROCKIES
Crater Lake NP
Yellowstone NP
Grand Teton NP
Badlands NP
Redwood NP
CALIFORNIA
Lassen Volcanic NP
Rocky Mountain NP
Great Basin NP
THE GREAT PLAI…
Yosemite NP
Bryce Canyon NP
Arches NP
Kings Canyon NP
Mesa Verde NP
Death Valley NP
Grand Canyon NP
Sequoia NP
Petrified Forest NP
THE SOUTH-WEST
Joshua Tree NP
Saguaro NP
Carlsbad Caverns NP
TEXA…
Guadalupe Mountains NP
Big Bend NP

***Olympic National Park*** (see p620), *a UNESCO biosphere reserve, preserves Washington's lush forests.*

**Death Valley National Park** *(see pp684–5)* in California's Mojave Desert, is one of the world's hottest places.

**Mesa Verde National Park's** *(see p596)* great cliff dwellings offer glimpses of Colorado's early inhabitants.

***Yosemite National Park*** (see p718), *a wilderness of forests, meadows, and granite rocks, is California's prime destination.*

***Grand Canyon National Park*** (see pp536–9), *perhaps the most-visited park in both Arizona and the US, is an awe-inspiring spectacle of magnificent rock formations.*

***Voyageurs National Park*** (see p421), *an area of staggering natural beauty, was named after French-Canadian fur trappers. Although most visitors traverse the park's network of lakes and streams by boat, there are numerous biking trails as well.*

**Caribou in Denali National Park, Alaska**

## Alaska

Kobuk Valley NP
Gates of the Arctic NP
Denali NP *(see pp742–3)*
Wrangell St. Elias NP
Lake Clark NP
Glacier Bay NP
Katmai NP
Kenai Fjords NP *(see p739)*

## Hawai'i

Haleakalā NP
Hawai'i Volcanoes NP *(see pp752)*

**Great Smoky Mountains National Park** *(see p262)*, in Tennessee and North Carolina, supports an incredible diversity of plant life.

***Acadia National Park*** (see p172), *a wild, unspoiled island paradise in Maine, is crisscrossed by biking trails that offer breathtaking coastal views. Its main attraction, however, is the scenic 27-mile (43-km) Loop Road.*

***Everglades National Park*** (see p321) *covers a vast expanse of low-lying wetlands at the southern tip of Florida. This unique ecosystem is characterized by tree islands or hammocks that support a fantastic variety of flora and fauna. Alligators are the park's best-known and most-feared residents.*

# Exploring the National Parks

A National Park ranger

IT'S NO EXAGGERATION to claim that one could spend a lifetime exploring the sprawling expanses of national parks such as the Grand Canyon or Yosemite. Most people visit parks simply because they happen to be near one, or to see specific sights such as the geysers of Yellowstone. To make their trip more worthwhile and enjoyable, visitors should restrict the number of parks they intend to visit, and instead explore a couple of the most appealing ones at leisure. Plan for a minimum of one full day per park.

## Background

THE WORLD'S first national park was established in 1872 to protect the geothermal wonders and wild creatures of Yellowstone, on the crest of the Rocky Mountains. In the years since, a staggering 375 places of scenic or historical interest in the US have been given federal protection, including 56 parks in the National Park system.

America's national parks offer visitors some of the most unforgettable wilderness experiences anywhere in the world, from stunning glacial lakes and lush forests to arid expanses of desert.

In addition to the most prominent parks, the **National Park Service**, a unit of the US Department of the Interior, also manages national historic sites (such as Independence Hall in Philadelphia, Pennsylvania) and national memorials (such as Mount Rushmore in South Dakota).

## Planning your Visit

THE NATIONAL parks draw millions of visitors each year. In fact, the immensely popular Great Smoky Mountains National Park sees over 10 million visitors, while more than 3 million people visit comparatively remote parks such as Yellowstone and Yosemite. To avoid the crowds, aim to visit the parks outside the peak summer season (June–August), when they are full to capacity.

While the most popular parks are the jewels in the crown of US public lands, there are many quieter parks where you can enjoy nature without the crowds. Also try to take advantage of the many well-maintained trails to enable you to get away from the crowds and the traffic, and to really enjoy the parks at close range.

## Passports, Fees & Permits

TO HELP MAINTAIN their facilities, most parks charge admission fees, valid for seven days, which range from nominal amounts ($1–5) at the smaller sites to upwards of $20 at prime attractions. Some parks don't charge a fee but do collect charges for specific activities.

If planning to visit more than two or three parks, visitors should consider purchasing a **National Parks Pass**. Valid for one year, these cost approximately $50, and give admission to the bearer and all

## Top National Parks

Listed below, are some of the most popular national parks in the United States (in alphabetical order), including the top parks featured on the previous pages. This chart depicts the various types of landscape and geological formations that are found within each park.

| | Volcanic/Geothermal | Mountainous | Glaciers | Climatic Extremes | Dramatic Erosion | Coral Reefs & Islands | Coastal Marshlands |
|---|---|---|---|---|---|---|---|
| **Acadia NP, ME** *(see p172)* | | | ● | | | | |
| **Arches NP, UT** *(see pp520–21)* | | | | | ● | | |
| **Badlands NP, SD** *(see p444)* | | | | | ● | | |
| **Biscayne NP, FL** *(see p322)* | | | | | | ● | |
| **Bryce Canyon NP, UT** *(see pp526–7)* | | | | | ● | | |
| **Canyonlands NP, UT** *(see p522)* | | | | | ● | | |
| **Death Valley NP, CA** *(see pp684–5)* | | | | ● | | | |
| **Denali NP, AK** *(see pp742–3)* | | ● | | | | | |
| **Everglades NP, FL** *(see p321)* | | | | | | | ● |
| **Glacier NP, MT** *(see p579)* | | | ● | | | | |
| **Glen Canyon & Lake Powell, AZ** *(see p523)* | | | | | ● | | |
| **Grand Canyon NP, AZ** *(see p536–9)* | | | | | ● | | |
| **Grand Teton NP, WY** *(see p583)* | | ● | | | | | |
| **Great Smoky Mts. NP, TN, NC** *(see p262)* | | ● | | | | | |
| **Hawai'i Volcanoes NP, HI** *(see p752)* | ● | | | | | | |
| **Mesa Verde NP, CO** *(see p596)* | | | | ● | | | |
| **Mount Rainer NP, WA** *(see pp626–7)* | ● | | | | | | |
| **Olympic NP, WA** *(see p620)* | | | | ● | | | |
| **Rocky Mountain NP, CO** *(see p591)* | | ● | | | | | |
| **Sequoia & Kings Canyon NP, CA** *(see p719)* | | | | ● | | | |
| **Shenandoah NP, VA** *(see p219)* | | ● | | | | | |
| **Voyageurs NP, MN** *(see p421)* | | | ● | | | | |
| **Yellowstone NP, WY** *(see pp584–5)* | ● | | | | | | |
| **Yosemite NP, CA** *(see p718)* | | | ● | | | | |
| **Zion NP, UT** *(see p525)* | | | | | ● | | |

**Visitors overlooking Thunder Hole, Acadia National Park, Maine**

visitors traveling in the same private vehicle. In parks where a per person fee is charged, the pass admits the pass holder, his or her spouse, and their children. This pass can be bought at any park entrance, or even in advance via credit card payment. US citizens or permanent residents over the age of 62 are eligible for the **Golden Age Passport** (for a one-time $10 fee), a lifetime entrance pass to national parks, monuments, historic sites, recreation areas, and wildlife refuges. It admits the pass holder and accompanying passengers in a private vehicle (if there is a per vehicle fee). It also provides a 50 percent discount on federal fees charged for various facilities and must be obtained in person from a federal area, such as a national park or monument.

**Wildlife warning sign**

If visitors expect to see many national forests, recreation areas, or Bureau of Land Management lands, they may opt to pay an additional $15 and purchase a **Golden Eagle Pass**, which covers the fees for all US federal lands. For citizens or permanent residents who are disabled or blind, the **Golden Access Passport** is a lifetime pass for national parks, monuments, historic sites, recreation areas, and wildlife refuges.

## Types of Accomodation

Visitor facilities vary from park to park. Some provide very basic amenities, while others, especially the popular ones, have deluxe hotels close by. It is advisable to make reservations for overnight accommodation well in advance. Some parks make reservations on a first-come-first-served basis only, so the sooner you arrive at your destination, the better.

Most parks have campsites for both tents and RVs but these are often "unserviced," with no RV hookups for electricity, water, or sewage. Campsites usually cost about $20 a night. The US Forest Service and **Bureau of Land Management** (BLM) campsites are less expensive and more readily available.

### Directory

**National Park Services**
W www.nps.gov
W www.americanpark network.com

**National Park Campground Reservations**
T *(800) 365-2267*
W http://reservations.nps.gov

**National Parks Pass**
T *(888) GO-PARKS*
W www.nationalparks.org

**US Forest Service**
T *(202) 205-8333.*
W www.fs.fed.us

**Bureau of Land Management**
T *(202) 452-5125.*
W www.blm.gov

### Practical Tips for Visiting the Parks

- Wear appropriate clothing – sturdy boots, a protective hat, plus waterproof or warm clothing, depending on the conditions.
- Carry drinking water, a pair of binoculars, a first-aid kit, sun screen, and insect repellant.
- Do not litter. Use the litter bins provided, or carry your waste out of the park.
- Do not play loud music or blow car horns within park limits, as this disturbs everyone.
- Do not interfere, provoke, or try to feed any wildlife.
- Hunting is prohibited and visitors found in violation will face heavy penalties.
- Do not approach bears or other wild animals; they can be extremely dangerous.
- Talk softly when on park trails to improve your chances of spotting wildlife.
- Do not wander off on your own, and do not venture off marked park trails; it is not only hazardous if you encounter dangerous animals but is also easy to get lost in the wilderness.
- Be sure to tell a friend or fellow traveler your itinerary; in case you don't return on time they can inform the park ranger.
- Observe and obey all signs throughout the individual park regarding speed limits, food, animals, water, and all other safety precautions. Following these rules and regulations will enhance your enjoyment of the park and keep both you and the wildlife safe.

# Great American Cities

One of the main attractions of visiting the US is the chance of enjoying its many great cities. They vary from Colonial-era, pedestrian-friendly places such as Boston, with its distinctly European ambience, to the frenzied modern metropolis of Los Angeles, where no one walks, except to and from the car. In between, there is a wide range of cities, each with its own history and culture. Washington, DC, the capital, is known for its political focus and national galleries; Miami offers a spicy taste of Latin America; New Orleans is packed with multicultural music, food, and fun; and New York and Chicago are famous for their architecture and exciting nightlife. On the West Coast, San Francisco and Seattle have picturesque settings and vibrant arts scenes. All in all, cities here have something for everyone.

***Seattle*** (see pp616–19) *has risen from the ashes of the Great Fire of 1889 to become a prosperous city of gleaming skyscrapers, upscale shops, and sophisticated hotels.*

***San Francisco's*** (see pp694–711) *many hills, ocean views, and rich ethnic mix give it a distinctive character, in keeping with its status as the West Coast's cultural capital.*

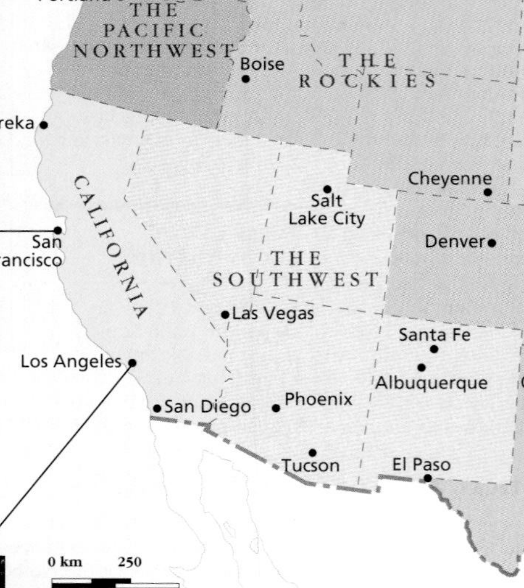

**Dallas** *(see pp478–9)* in many ways is synomous with the wealth of Texan oil fields and cattle. Today, it is both the state's financial and entertainment center.

***Los Angeles*** (see pp658–77) *is often associated with movies, the glamor of Hollywood, the luxury of residential Beverly Hills, and the excitement of Sunset Boulevard. Yet, this vibrant city is also home to some of the country's finest museums and galleries as well as the most popular beaches along the Pacific Ocean.*

***Chicago*** (see pp386–97), *located on the southwestern edge of Lake Michigan, is famous throughout the world for its magnificent, innovative architecture. New building techniques were perfected here, and it was here too that architects, such as Frank Llyod Wright and others, created masterpieces of modern design.*

***Boston*** (see pp132–49) *is justly proud of its past. While its Colonial heritage is reflected in its buildings, the city also includes numerous important sites directly related to America's fight for freedom.*

**Philadelphia** *(see pp98–105)*, where the Declaration of Independence was signed on July 4, 1776, is the birthplace of America. Today, this "City of Brotherly Love" is one of the country's most popular destinations.

NEW ENGLAND
neapolis
Buffalo
NYC & MID-ATLANTIC REGION
Boston
Milwaukee
Detroit
New York
Chicago
Philadelphia
THE GREAT LAKES
Baltimore
Indianapolis
Cincinnati
DC & THE CAPITAL REGION
WASHINGTON, DC
sas City
St. Louis
Richmond
Nashville
Charlotte
Memphis
THE SOUTHEAST
Atlanta
Charleston
THE DEEP SOUTH
Savannah
Mobile
Jacksonville
New Orleans
uston
FLORIDA
Miami

***New York*** (see pp64–89), *the "Big Apple," is one of the world's great cities. One aspect of its character lies in its striking modern architecture. Others revolve around its many outstanding museums, its ethnic neighborhoods, and the choice of entertainment.*

**New Orleans** *(see pp344–53)* is a fun city of bars, restaurants, and the always lively Mardi Gras celebrations.

**Miami's** *(see pp290–99)* focus of action concentrates on South Beach, with its Art Deco hotels and trendy shops.

***Washington, DC*** (see pp196–211), *the nation's capital, is an impressive city of classical architecture and grand, tree-lined avenues. Beside its political focus, the city also has a cultural heart, with museums located along the Mall.*

# Best Scenic Routes

One of the great pleasures of traveling in the US is the chance to explore its many scenic highways and byways. From quiet rural lanes to breathtaking coastal drives, they offer glimpses of the land's abundant natural beauty, and provide an opportunity to get to know its many inviting small towns. Many of the best-known routes are also historic and follow in the footsteps of the pioneer wagon trains, the Pony Express, or along trails taken by Civil War soldiers. For additional information on scenic routes, visit www.byways.org.

***Going-to-the-Sun Road*** (see p579) *cuts across Glacier National Park, following the steep Rocky Mountain cliffs. The route offers breathtaking mountain views.*

**Historic Columbia River Highway** *(see p632)* offers incomparable views of Oregon's diverse landscape, including Mount Hood's snowcapped summit. It also passes several waterfalls and lush orchards.

***Pacific Coast Highway*** *(Highway 1) was named California's first scenic highway in 1966. One of the world's most stunning drives, its most beautiful stretch is through Big Sur.*

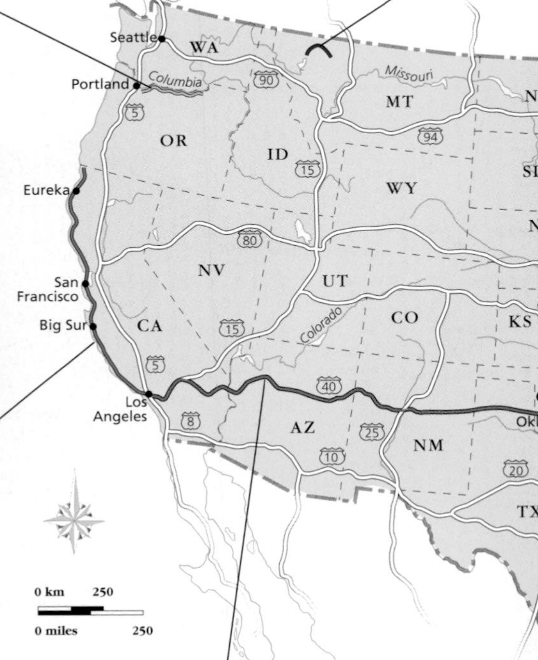

***Route 66*** (see p461), *from Chicago to Los Angeles, is perhaps America's best-loved highway. Much of the original route remains intact, offering a nostalgic cruise across the country's heartland.*

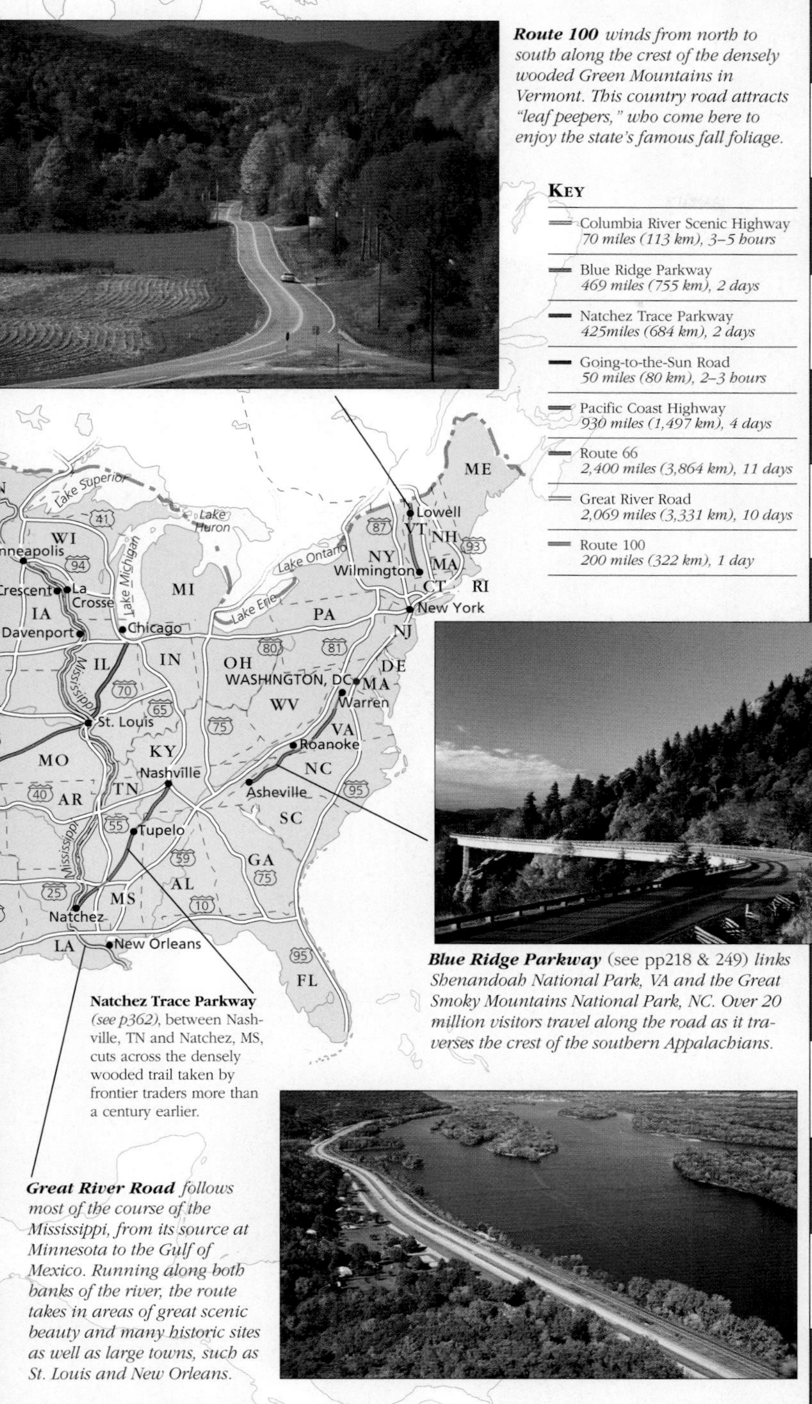


***Route 100*** *winds from north to south along the crest of the densely wooded Green Mountains in Vermont. This country road attracts "leaf peepers," who come here to enjoy the state's famous fall foliage.*

**KEY**

- Columbia River Scenic Highway *70 miles (113 km), 3–5 hours*
- Blue Ridge Parkway *469 miles (755 km), 2 days*
- Natchez Trace Parkway *425miles (684 km), 2 days*
- Going-to-the-Sun Road *50 miles (80 km), 2–3 hours*
- Pacific Coast Highway *930 miles (1,497 km), 4 days*
- Route 66 *2,400 miles (3,864 km), 11 days*
- Great River Road *2,069 miles (3,331 km), 10 days*
- Route 100 *200 miles (322 km), 1 day*

***Blue Ridge Parkway*** (see pp218 & 249) *links Shenandoah National Park, VA and the Great Smoky Mountains National Park, NC. Over 20 million visitors travel along the road as it traverses the crest of the southern Appalachians.*

**Natchez Trace Parkway** *(see p362)*, between Nashville, TN and Natchez, MS, cuts across the densely wooded trail taken by frontier traders more than a century earlier.

***Great River Road*** *follows most of the course of the Mississippi, from its source at Minnesota to the Gulf of Mexico. Running along both banks of the river, the route takes in areas of great scenic beauty and many historic sites as well as large towns, such as St. Louis and New Orleans.*

# History of the USA

MAN FIRST ENTERED NORTH AMERICA *from Siberia some 13,000 and 30,000 years ago, migrating over the Bering Strait land bridge to Alaska. As the ice receded, they moved south into the rich gamelands of the Great Plains. Isolated from Eurasia by melting ice and rising sea levels, those early settlers were mainly hunter-gatherers, as agricultural life evolved sporadically.*

During this period of isolation, unique ecological, genetic, and social patterns emerged that proved disastrously fragile when confronted by the first Europeans in the late 15th century.

### Early European Explorers

European exploration began in earnest when improvements in shipping made the longer voyages of Columbus (1492) and Cabot (1497) viable. Early explorers were astonished by the quantity of natural resources they encountered here. Fur-bearing animals such as beavers were quickly exploited for their pelts. Once Europeans began to investigate further, they were able to draw heavily on the indigenous peoples' detailed knowledge, and use their pre-existing trails to explore the continent. An early map of 1507 displays the name "America," taken from one of the New World's early explorers, Amerigo Vespucci.

### Competing Colonies

The long rivalry between Spain, France, and Great Britain continued with the discovery of the New World in 1492. Spain founded the first successful North American colonies, in Florida in 1565 and New Mexico in 1598, combining commercial and religious interests. France's first permanent settlement was at Quebec (1608), while the Dutch set up a trading post (1624) at the mouth of the Hudson River. However, it was the English who gained control, with colonies in Virginia (1607), New England (1620), and Pennsylvania (1681). Many early colonists died of disease and malnutrition. Virginia eventually became the most lucrative New World colony, thanks to the production of tobacco. By 1700, these English colonies' population was 250,000, excluding Native Americans, while only some 1,000 non-Natives lived in Spanish or French regions.

**Christopher Columbus sets foot in the New World on October 12, 1492**

◁ **George Washington before Yorktown, painted by Rembrandt Peale between 1824 and 1825**

John Trumbull's 1786 painting of the Battle of Bunker Hill

### The American Revolution

The 18th century was a period of significant change throughout the world, and this was especially true in the New World. Colonists expanded their domain, displacing or killing the native tribes through a combination of land purchases, warfare, and disease. In the southern colonies of Virginia and Carolina, where the lack of available land discouraged new immigrants, African slaves were imported in great numbers, reaching a total of 150,000, 40 percent of the population, by 1750.

The American Revolution began swiftly, and transformed the face of the world in a few short years. The removal of a potential French threat, following Britain's conquest of Canada in the Seven Years' War, led to American complaints about British abuse, epitomized by the phrase "No Taxation without Representation." In 1770, British troops opened fire on a group of unruly workers, killing five in what became known as the Boston Massacre. In 1773, some colonial merchants disguised as Indians dumped a boatload of tea into Boston Harbor, to protest Britain's monopoly of the tea trade.

War broke out in April 1775, when British "Redcoats" marched on the town of Concord in an attempt to seize a stockpile of weapons from the American "Minutemen." As the British fought their way back to Boston, more than 75 Redcoats and over 90 Americans were killed. The British occupied New York City and Philadelphia, while the ill-equipped Americans struggled through a harsh winter. The war moved south, and frontier fighters under Daniel Boone and George Rogers Clark captured British outposts in Kentucky and Illinois. The Americans eventually succeeded, largely due to French support, and the war officially ended in 1783.

#### Key Dates in History

**1763** The Seven Years' War ends, France surrenders its Great Lakes lands to Great Britain

**1773** Boston Tea Party

**April 19, 1775** The Revolutionary War begins

**1776** The Declaration of Independence is adopted in Philadelphia

**1783** Treaty of Paris puts an end to the Revolutionary War

**1790** A 100-mile square on the Maryland/Virginia border, Washington, the District of Columbia, is set aside as the new capital

**1793** Samuel Slater's water-powered mill at Pawtucket, Rhode Island, brings the Industrial Revolution to the US

**1803** Ohio is the first of the Northwest Territories to become a state

**1803** The Louisiana Purchase

**1814** Francis Scott Key composes "The Star-Spangled Banner"

**1824** The Bureau of Indian Affairs, a division of the US War Department, is formed to handle relations with Indian tribes

**1832** Resisting attempts to remove his people from their traditional homelands, Chief Black Hawk leads a militant band of 1,000 Fox-Sauk Indians but is destroyed by the US Army

Patriots disguised as Indians dumping tea into Boston Harbor, Boston Tea Party

**George Washingtion holding a copy of the US Constitution, surrounded by Founding Fathers, 1787**

### Birth of a Nation

By 1783, the newly formed United States of America had a draft constitution and a border that extended as far west as the Mississippi River. The new Constitution was officially adopted in 1788, and in 1791 the ten amendments of the "Bill of Rights" were added, enumerating each citizen's freedom of speech, press, religion, and public assembly. In 1800, the capital moved from Philadelphia to the newly created city of Washington, DC, which by now had a population of 3,200 people.

### Manifest Destiny

America expanded greatly in its early years, first opening the "Northwest Territory" lands along the Great Lakes in 1787. The Louisiana Purchase of 1803 added a huge area of western lands formerly controlled by France. This rapid expansion created the need to survey the new territories. Lewis and Clark's famed cross-continental expedition between 1803 and 1806, was funded by Congress at the express request of President Thomas Jefferson.

The first test of strength for this new independent country came in 1812, when the US found itself caught in the middle of an ongoing war between France and Great Britain. Though both countries agreed to stop interfering with American ships, US forces attacked British interests in Canada, and in retaliation the British burned the Capitol and White House in Washington, DC. Ironically, the war was ended by a peace treaty that was signed two weeks before its biggest skirmish – the Battle of New Orleans – took place in January 1815.

After the War of 1812, the US abandoned hopes of annexing Canada, and so began its great push westward. Settlers poured into the Great Plains, Oregon, and eventually the northern periphery of the Republic of Mexico, including Texas and California. The Santa Fe Trail, open for trade by 1823, brought New Mexico under US influence. By 1850, there was an extensive communications network. Steamboat traffic dominated the rivers, augmented by canals and cross-country railroads.

The consolidation of western lands encouraged millions of pioneers to migrate west and forge new lives for themselves. By the mid-19th century, people had grown accustomed to the idea that the country would stretch undivided across the continent, from ocean to ocean. This idea, in the words of populist journalist John L. O'Sullivan, was the country's "Manifest Destiny." Orderly settlement was made possible by the official survey and division of these lands into rectangular sections, each one square mile in area. Overland trails were opened leading west to the gold fields of California, which itself became a state in 1850. By 1860, more than half the population lived west of the Appalachian Mountains, compared to less than 10 percent in 1800.

An 1891 illustration depicting Indians fighting US soldiers

### Territorial Conflict

Although involved in conflicts with Britain over Canada, the US managed to resolve these issues peacefully. However, this was not so with Mexico, who feared US territorial ambitions, especially after President Andrew Jackson offered to purchase Texas. The crisis accelerated after Texas declared independence from Mexico in 1835. Turning a blind eye to Native American tribes (and the legal ownership of much of the land by Spain), the United States took over Texas in 1845, a move that set off war with Mexico. This war in turn led to the US confiscation of California and much of the Southwest. In 1848, Mexico yielded nearly half of its territory; the cession of the northern Oregon territory by Britain in 1846, and James Gadsden's 1853 purchase of 30,000 square miles in the Southwest completed the westward expansion. Thus, in less than 50 years, the country had more than tripled in size.

### Key Dates in History

**1838** US Government forcibly expels native Cherokee Indians westward along the "Trail of Tears"

**1846–1848** Mexican War. US acquires Arizona, California, Utah, Nevada, and New Mexico

**1859** Abolitionist John Brown raids the Federal Armory at Harpers Ferry

**1861** Confederates attack Fort Sumter in South Carolina

**1861** The Battle of Bull Run (Manassas), the first major land battle of the Civil War

**Jan 1, 1863** President Abraham Lincoln issues the Emancipation Proclamation, freeing slaves in areas controlled by the Confederate army

**July, 1863** Union forces defeat General Robert E. Lee and the Confederacy at Gettysburg

**April 9, 1865** Robert E. Lee surrenders to Union General Ulysses Grant at Appomattox Court House, Virginia

**April 14, 1865** President Lincoln assassinated by a Confederate sympathizer, John Wilkes Booth, in Washington, DC

**Dec 18, 1865** The 13th amendment to the US Constitution is adopted, effectively putting an end to slavery in the US

**1870** African-Americans granted full citizenship

### The Destruction of the Indians

Since the 1500s, diseases such as small pox and syphilis had wiped out almost 90 percent of some tribes. As European settlement increased, forced relocation of tribes became frequent. It reached its peak with the forced march of most of the Cherokee Nation from the southeast to Oklahoma along the "Trail of Tears." As Europeans spread westward, tribes were forced onto reservations, often the poorest and most desolate lands, where many remain even today.

The building of the transcontinental railroads in the late 19th century opened the West to hunters who eventually killed millions of buffalo. Within a few hundred years, North America's indigenous cultures had been destroyed or marginalized by Europeans, who transformed the continent into a world economic, industrial, and political power.

### Civil War

Between independence in 1783 and 1860, two very different societies developed within the US. In the North, there emerged an industrialized society, committed to liberal banking and credit systems, and protective tariffs, whereas the South was a less populous, agrarian society opposed to the sale of public land in the Midwest, high duties, and restrictions on slavery.

The causes of the Civil War are still up for debate. Though slavery was clearly the divisive issue, the war was not fought to free the slaves. Instead, the battle lines were drawn over the question of extending slavery into the newly forming western states. The South, resisting the federal government's growing power, wanted each new state to decide this question independently. The northern states wanted to keep slavery within its current limits, in part to protect their own manual labor. The federal government left the decision to the new states, and riots between pro- and anti-slave campaigners raged across the west. In 1856, pro-slave guerillas burned the city of Lawrence, and 200 people were killed in retaliation. Three years later, 22 abolitionists led by John Brown attacked the Federal Armory at Harpers Ferry, Virginia, hoping to incite a slave rebellion. Instead, he and his forces were killed, but his efforts further polarized the already divided nation. By 1860, the country was composed of 18 "free states" – mainly in the North, and 15 "slave states" – mainly in the South. When Abraham Lincoln was elected president in 1860, South Carolina seceded from the Union, followed by six other southern states, which joined together to form the Confederate States of America.

The first shots of the Civil War were fired in April, 1861, when the Confederates attacked Fort Sumter in South Carolina. President Lincoln mobilized US soldiers to quell the rebellion, and soon four other slaveholding states, including Virginia, seceded from the Union. Richmond became the new Confederate capital, and Virginia provided most of the Confederate military leadership. Four slave states remained in the Union, and the western counties of Virginia separated to form West Virginia, which joined the Union in 1863.

The Confederates won the first major land battle at Manassas, Virginia, in July 1861, and for the next two years battles raged across Virginia and Maryland. With their defeat at Gettysburg in 1863, the Confederates were finally turned back. In the same year, Union forces gained control of the Mississippi River. Union forces destroyed Atlanta in 1864 and marched across Georgia, cutting off supply lines and virtually encircling the remaining Confederate army. By April 1865, the Civil War was over.

The destruction caused by the war was immense. Nearly three million soldiers (some 10 percent of the total population at the time) fought in the war, and 620,000 of them died. Entire cities lay in ruins, and it would be years before the nation recovered from the ravages of war.

**Confederate forces occupy Fort Sumter, South Carolina, on April 15, 1861**

### THE WILD WEST

The end of the 19th century was a time of radical change across the country. The conquered South and the newly freed slaves suffered the ravages of the Reconstruction, while in the West, Native Americans saw their lands taken away and their lifestyles destroyed. Their culture's death knell was sounded in 1862, when the Homestead Act granted 160 acres of land to any white settler, freed slave, or single woman. The Army battled Indian tribes across the Great Plains in the 1870s and 1880s, and Indian resistance in the Southwest desert came to an end with the surrender of Apache chief Geronimo in 1886.

**Buffalo Bill's Wild West poster, 1900**

In the East and Midwest, massive mills and factories replaced local producers, as the population shifted from self-sufficient farms to the chaotic city life. In a relatively brief period, the pace of life was altered by the growth of railroads, the telegraph, the telephone, the airplane, and the automobile. Railroads brought the once-distant West within reach of eastern markets, and the frontier towns that appeared along the railroads were often lawless places. During this post-Civil War period, the US became an international power, buying Alaska from Russia in 1867, then taking over Hawai'i in 1893, the Philippines in 1899, and Panama in 1903.

### KEY DATES IN HISTORY

**1867** Russia sells Alaska for $7.2 million

**1869** First transcontinental railroad is completed when the Union Pacific and Central Pacific meet at Promontory, Utah

**1876** The Battle of Little Big Horn, Montana

**1876** The US Supreme Court legalizes "separate but equal" facilities for whites and non-whites, sanctioning racial segregation

**1884** New York and Boston telephone link

**1886** The Statue of Liberty erected in New York

**1898** USS *Maine* explodes in Havana, sparking Spanish-American War

**1915** The Lincoln Highway from New York City to San Francisco is the first transcontinental highway

**1915** The "Great Migration" of African-Americans to northern cities begins

**April 6, 1917** US declares war on Germany

**1925** Fundamentalist Christians ban the teaching of the theory of evolution in many states

**1929** The US stock market crash

**1934** Benny Goodman's orchestra popularizes "Swing" jazz

**1939** The first regular commercial TV broadcasts begins

### IMMIGRATION, URBANIZATION, & INDUSTRIALIZATION

While stories of the Wild West captivated people's imagination, the most significant development was the increasing importance of industrialization. The rapid demographic shift from small towns and farms to big cities and factories was inevitable. This change was made possible in part by waves of immigration that doubled the population in a few decades.

In the 1880s, over six million immigrants arrived, and by the first decade of the 20th century a million people were arriving every year. By World War I, the population reached 100 million, 15 percent of whom were foreign born. The majority settled in East Coast cities, and for the first time in US history the population was predominantly urban.

The consolidation of the population was mirrored by a consolidation in industry and business. By 1882, John D. Rockefeller's Standard Oil Company had a monopoly in the petroleum industry, followed by other effective monopolies, legally organized as "trusts," in tobacco products, banking, and steel. These corporations' abuse of monopoly power was exposed by such writers as Upton Sinclair and Frank Norris. Political movements too resisted the rise of corporations, finding an ally in "trust-busting" President Theodore Roosevelt, who also made significant steps toward protecting the natural environment from the ravages of unrestrained industrial development.

**Cartoon of Uncle Sam welcoming immigrants into the "US Ark of Refuge"**

The early 20th century also saw the growth of labor unions, which staged successful and sometimes violent strikes to improve pay and conditions, and helped protect children from working in factories.

### Boom & Bust

Involvement in World War I confirmed America's position as a world power, drawing the nation away from its long-cherished isolationism. But, after the war, soldiers returned home from Europe to severe unrest, with labor strikes and race riots. This economic depression caused enormous suffering and changed the domestic role of the government forever.

The 1920s, known as the "Jazz Age," saw an explosion of artistic creativity, especially in popular music. Architectural and engineering landmarks were constructed, and the rising popularity of the automobile encouraged the building of the first transcontinental highways, which linked the nation and gave rise to the first suburbs.

This creativity coincided with Prohibition, when the sale of alcohol was made illegal. Ironically, it was Prohibition itself that led to the freewheeling, drug-and alcohol-fuelled lifestyles of the Roaring Twenties.

**Duke Ellington, celebrated icon of the Jazz Age**

### The Great Depression & the "New Deal"

The Wall Street Crash of 1929 shattered millions of dreams and left many Americans destitute. Farmers and black people in cities and rural areas were particularly hard hit, as banks withdrew funding. Unemployment and the gross domestic product dropped to half of what it was in the 1920s. Extended drought and sustained winds caused such destruction that the Great Plains was dubbed the "Dust Bowl," forcing some 200,000 Great Plains farmers to migrate west to California.

The Republican government, which had promoted the boom and was blamed for the crash, was rejected by the electorate, leading to the 1932 election of Democrat Franklin Delano Roosevelt. In his first 100 days in office, Roosevelt established federal government relief programs (the "New Deal") to revitalize the economy, provide jobs, and aid those who were hurt by the economic downtown. Roosevelt also set up regulatory bodies to help prevent economic turmoil in the future. Although millions of dollars of federal funding were spent on relief, 20 percent of Americans still continued to be unemployed in 1939.

**The battleships USS *West Virginia* and *Tennessee* burning after the Japanese attack on Pearl Harbor**

### The Cold War

The Japanese attack on Pearl Harbor in 1941 and the subsequent US entry into World War II marked the beginning of America's new role in international politics. With the onset of the Cold War, the numerous US military bases, established during World War II, gained renewed importance. The Cold War also encouraged alliances with other nations. America's powerful influence, and investment overseas was seen as a way to bind other nations to the capitalist sphere. The Marshall Plan of 1948 provided $13 billion to aid reconstruction of postwar western Europe and reduce Communist influence.

Economic and social developments were often overshadowed by the specter of nuclear war. The Korean War was the first of many fought to stop the spread of Communism. Fear on the domestic front inspired years of anti-Communist "Witch Trials," such as those conducted by Senator Joseph McCarthy. Cold War fears also led to numerous military operations around the world, including the takeover of Guatemala in 1954, an ill-fated invasion of Cuba in 1961, and the Vietnam War of the 1960s and 1970s, the longest and most costly of attempts to contain the perceived Communist threat.

After Vietnam, the US retreated from an active international role. The Soviet invasion of Afghanistan in 1979 revived the Cold War for another decade. With the collapse of the Soviet Union in 1991, the United States became the world's only superpower.

### Key Dates in History

**Dec 7, 1941** Japanese attack on Pearl Harbor

**1945** The UN established in San Francisco

**Aug 14, 1945** After US bombing of Hiroshima and Nagasaki, Japan surrenders, ending WW II

**1950** The Korean War begins

**1961** Alan Shepard is the first American in outer space; the Soviets erect the Berlin Wall

**1962** Naval blockade against Soviet missile bases in Cuba

**1963** Assassination of John F. Kennedy, Dallas

**1968** Martin Luther King Jr. assassinated

**1969** Neil Armstrong walks on the moon

**1970** The Environmental Protection Agency (EPA) is established

**1973** Energy crisis

**1974** Richard Nixon resigns after Watergate

**1988** The Indian Gaming Regulatory Act opens up tribal lands to legalized gambling

**1989** Fall of Berlin Wall; end of Cold War

**1990–1** The Gulf War

**Sept 11, 2001** Terrorist attacks on NYC & DC

**2003** Space shutte *Columbia* explodes, killing all on board

**2003** George W. Bush declares war on Iraq

### Postwar Prosperity

Unlike much of the rest of the world, this was one of the most prosperous periods in US history. The economy, stimulated by mobilization of industry during World War II, and the arms race with the Soviet Union were key factors in creating unprecedented affluence. As manufacturing switched to a peacetime mode, consumer durables flowed into the marketplace, generating a flourishing service sector. America's position at the hub of the international trading system gave her access to crucial

**Vietnam veterans marching toward the Democratic National Convention, Miami Beach**

foreign markets. Home ownership was brought within reach of middle-class Americans, thanks to government supports and mass-production construction techniques. Most adults owned a car, and consumer products, such as refrigerators, washers, dryers, and dishwashers, multiplied within the home.

### Civil Rights Movement

As black Americans migrated from the rural south to urban centers in the 1940s and 1950s, whites abandoned city life for the suburbs, taking their tax dollars with them. The financial crisis was made worse by the decline of traditional industries, and many cities during the 1960s and 1970s suffered as well. Housing deteriorated, roads went unrepaired, and poverty, crime, and racial tension were common features of many urban areas. Poverty was not confined to the inner cities; people in rural areas in the Deep South and the Appalachians were some of the most deprived in the country.

The new postwar opportunities were denied to many African-Americans, particularly in the still-segregated South. Aided by a 1954 Supreme Court judgment that ruled segregation unconstitutional, African Americans fought for an end to discrimination. In 1955, a bus boycott in Montgomery, Alabama, forced the company to end segregation. The success inspired similar protests throughout the South. In 1964 and 1965, Congress passed legislation banning racial discrimination.

The 1960s also saw a rise in political consciousness among other groups; protests against the Vietnam War grew in number, as did the movement for women's rights. In the 1970s, the women's movement narrowly failed to achieve an end to sexual discrimination. During the AIDS crisis of the late 1980s, homosexuality became an increasingly accepted aspect of life, with gay and lesbian couples earning greater legal protections.

### The Modern Era

The postwar boom ended in the early 1970s, with the Vietnam War and the energy crisis producing prolonged

**Reverend Martin Luther King Jr. delivering a sermon at the Ebenezer Baptist Church, Atlanta**

inflation and recession. Europe and Japan challenged American economic domination. American firms tried to secure access to valuable raw materials, most importantly oil in the Middle East, and companies found ways to exploit cheap foreign labor by establishing factories overseas, which in turn threatened jobs at home.

In the 1980s, computers and other digital devices began to change the way Americans communicated. The Internet opened new ways of working and generated large amounts of wealth. By the turn of the millennium, the Internet-fuelled boom went bust, causing a stock market collapse, and the economy fell into recession for the first time in a decade. The controversial appointment of George W. Bush dominated the news and showed that the American public was deeply divided over crucial issues.

The terrorist attacks on New York and Washington, DC in September 2001, instigated President Bush to launch a war against terrorism. This resulted in a war against the Taliban in Afghanistan in 2002 and another one to oust Saddam Hussain in Iraq in 2003. Despite these setbacks, the US still embodies the ideas of freedom and indomitable optimism.

# The American Presidents

THE PRESIDENTS OF THE United States have come from all walks of life; at least two were born in a log cabin – Abraham Lincoln and Andrew Jackson. Others, such as Franklin D. Roosevelt and John F. Kennedy, came from privileged backgrounds. Millard Fillmore attended a one-room schoolroom, and Jimmy Carter raised peanuts. Many, including Ulysses S. Grant and Dwight D. Eisenhower, were military men, who won public popularity for their great achievements in battle.

**George Washington** (1789–97) was a Revolutionary War general. He was unanimously chosen to be the first president of the United States.

**James Madison** (1809–17), known as the Father of the Constitution, was co-author of the Federalist Papers.

**W.H. Harrison** (1841)

**James K. Polk** (1845–49)

**Zachary Taylor** (1849–50)

**Millard Fillmore** (1850–53)

**Franklin Pierce** (1853–57)

**Andrew Johnson** (1865–69)

**Rutherford B. Hayes** (1877–81)

**Chester A. Arthur** (1881–85)

**Benjamin Har** (188

1775 1800 1825 1850 1875

1775 1800 1825 1850 1875

**John Adams** (1797–1801), a lawyer and historian, was the first president to live in the White House.

**Thomas Jefferson** (1801–1809), architect, inventor, landscape designer, diplomat, and historian, was the quintessential Renaissance man.

**James Monroe** (1817–25)

**John Quincy Adams** (1825–29)

**Andrew Jackson** (1829–37) defeated the British at the Battle of New Orleans in the War of 1812.

**Martin Van Buren** (1837-41)

**John Tyler** (1841–45)

**James Buchanan** (1857–61)

**Abraham Lincoln** (1861–65) won the epithet, the Great Emancipator, for his role in the abolition of slavery. He led the Union through the Civil War.

**Ulysses S. Grant** (1869–77)

**James A. Garfield** (1881)

**Grov Clevela** (1885–

**illiam**
**cKinley**
897–1901)

**Woodrow Wilson** (1913–21) led the country through World War I and paved the way for the League of Nations.

**Harry S. Truman** (1945–53) made the decision to drop the atomic bombs on Hiroshima and Nagasaki in 1945.

**KEY TO TIMELINE**

- Federalist
- Democratic Republican
- Whig
- Republican
- Democrat

**John F. Kennedy** (1961–63) was one of the most popular presidents. He sent the first astronaut into space, started the Peace Corps, and created the Arms Control and Disarmament Agency. His assassination rocked the nation.

**Richard Nixon** (1969–74) opened up China and sent the first men to the moon. He resigned after the Watergate scandal.

**Franklin D. Roosevelt** (1933–45) started the "New Deal", a reform and relief program, during the Great Depression. He was elected to four terms.

**Jimmy Carter** (1977–81), who brokered the peace accord between Israel and Egypt, won the 2002 Nobel Peace prize.

**George Bush** (1989–93)

**George W. Bush** (2001– )

**1900** **1925** **1950** **1975** **2000**

**1900** **1925** **1950** **1975** **2000**

**Dwight D. Eisenhower** (1953–61)

**William H. Taft** (1909–13)

**Herbert Hoover** (1929–33)

**Gerald Ford** (1974–77)

**Calvin Coolidge** (1923–29)

**Warren Harding** (1921–23)

**William J. Clinton's** (1993–2001) two-term presidency saw unprecedented prosperity.

**Lyndon B. Johnson** (1963–69) escalated the Vietnam conflict, resulting in widespread protests.

**Ronald Reagan** (1981–89), a one-time movie actor and popular president, cut taxes, increased military spending, and reduced government programs.

**Theodore Roosevelt** (1901–9) created many national parks and oversaw the construction of the Panama Canal.

**ver**
**veland**
93–97)

## THE ROLE OF THE FIRST LADY

**First Lady & Senator Hillary Clinton in New York, 1999**

In the 19th century, the First Lady acted primarily as hostess and "behind-the-scenes" adviser. Dolley Madison was known as the "Toast of Washington." Later, when Eleanor Roosevelt held her own press conferences, the role of First Lady changed greatly. Jackie Kennedy gave unprecedented support to the arts, Rosalynn Carter attended Cabinet meetings, Nancy Reagan told the world to "Just Say No" to drugs, Barbara Bush promoted literacy, and Hillary Clinton ran her own political campaign.

# NYC & THE MID-ATLANTIC REGION

# NYC & the Mid-Atlantic Region at a Glance

THE THREE-STATE REGION surrounding New York City is one of the most fascinating areas in the US. New Jersey, the region's smallest but most densely populated state, extends between New York and Philadelphia. To its west, the idyllic pastoral landscape of Pennsylvania stretches almost all the way to the Great Lakes, with towns, green farm valleys, and the rolling folds of the Allegheney Mountains. Farther north, New York State has cities, towns, and rural hamlets spreading between the Hudson River Valley and Niagara Falls. Of the two main cities, New York City is a vibrant, cosmopolitan city and the financial capital of the world, while Philadelphia is more historic, in keeping with its status as the capital of Colonial America.

***Niagara Falls*** (see p95), *located on the border between Canada and the US, is one of New York State's prime attractions, drawing more than 10 million visitors a year.*

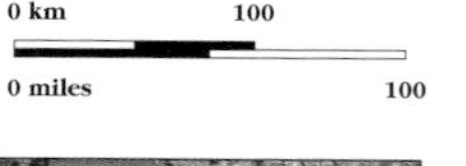

***Pittsburgh*** (see p108), *in Pennsylvania, has rebuilt itself from the ashes of an industrial past to become one of the country's most attractive cities. The Andy Warhol Museum and the Carnegie Institute are popular tourist attractions here.*

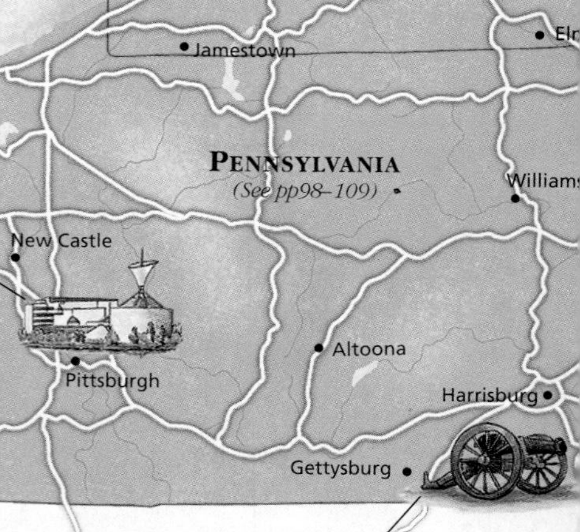

***Gettysburg*** (see p106) *is one of Pennsylvania's most significant historic sites. In July 1863, this peaceful town was the scene of a devastating Civil War battle. It was here, four months later, that President Abraham Lincoln delivered his moving Gettysburg Address.*

◁ **A view of New York City's glittering skyscrapers as seen from Brooklyn Bridge**

***New York State*** (see p90–95) *offers a diversity of landscapes, from the beauty of the Hudson Valley, to the craggy Adirondack Mountains and the lush wine country of the Finger Lakes. Other highlights include Albany, the state capital, and the awesome Niagara Falls.*

**LOCATOR MAP**

***New York City*** (see pp64–89), *with its world-class museums and wide variety of shopping, dining, and entertainment options, is one of the most frequently visited cities in the United States. Its most distinctive sight, however, is the Statue of Liberty, the symbol of freedom for millions who have now made this city their home.*

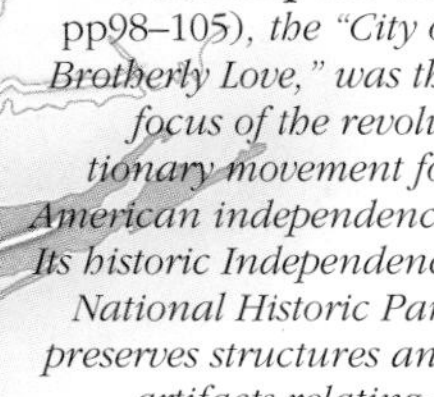

***Philadelphia*** (see pp98–105), *the "City of Brotherly Love," was the focus of the revolutionary movement for American independence. Its historic Independence National Historic Park preserves structures and artifacts relating to those stirring times.*

***Cape May*** (see p97), *at the southern tip of New Jersey, is a Victorian-period resort that draws many visitors. The state's other attractions include the opulent casinos of Atlantic City and the picturesque wilds of the Delaware Gap.*

# NEW YORK CITY & THE MID-ATLANTIC REGION

THE TRI-STATE REGION AROUND NEW YORK CITY *truly embodies American diversity and dynamism. The vitality of New York City and Philadelphia is balanced by a surprisingly calm, almost pastoral hinterland. The Mid-Atlantic landscape is spectacular and ranges from dramatic mountain scenery, superb river valleys, and forests, interspersed with rolling farmlands.*

New York City, or the "Big Apple," dominates northeastern US, and to a large extent controls the country's economy and culture. It is, without exaggeration, one of the world's great cities, and it is hard to imagine visiting the region without spending some time here. Philadelphia, the other major city, was the nation's leading city during Colonial times, and its wealth of history offers unforgettable insights into early American ideals.

Fascinating as these cities are, the broader region around them paints a much fuller picture of the nation. New Jersey, despite its reputation for heavy industry and sprawling suburbia, has much to offer, from the Victorian-era coastal resort of Cape May to Ivy League Princeton University. Pennsylvania, to the west, juxtaposes peaceful scenes of rural farmland in the "Pennsylvania Dutch" country where Amish and Mennonite communities still speak German (Deutsch), with the industrial cities of Pittsburg and Reading. Farther north, the state of New York has majestic mountains, picturesque lakes, and the scenic Hudson River Valley.

## HISTORY

The Mid-Atlantic Region's natural wealth supported some of early America's most powerful and accomplished Native peoples. The first main groups were the Algonquian tribes, including the Lenni Lenape who lived in what is now New Jersey and Pennsylvania. In the early 16th century, the Algonquian Indians were ousted by incoming tribes of Iroquois Indians. Settling in the Finger Lakes area in central New York State, the

**Amish farmers harvesting corn in Lancaster County, Pennsylvania**

◁ **Swirling mists surround the Niagara Falls, New York State's most famous natural wonder**

Iroquois, one of North America's most socially sophisticated tribes, formed a powerful alliance among their five constituent tribes – the Senecas, Cayugas, Oneidas, Mohawks, and Onondagas.

Around this time, the first Europeans were making efforts to forge trade relations. Although Giovanni da Verrazano visited New York as early as 1524, it was not until 1609, when the Dutch West India Company sent Henry Hudson to explore the river that now bears his name, that the first settlements were established. In the same year, a French explorer, Samuel de Champlain, laid claim to northeastern New York State, having ventured there by way of Quebec.

Giovanni da Verrazano

In 1624 the Dutch founded the region's first colony, Fort Orange, at present-day Albany, began another at New Amsterdam (later New York) the following year, and later expanded to make footholds in New Jersey and

### Key Dates in History

**1524** Italian sailor Giovanni da Verrazano sails into New York harbor

**1609** Henry Hudson explores and maps the Hudson River and New Jersey shore

**1624** The Dutch establish Fort Orange

**1664** England takes over New Netherland. The city of New Amsterdam is renamed New York

**1731** Benjamin Franklin establishes the nation's first public library in Philadelphia

**1776** The Declaration of Independence is adopted in Philadelphia

**1825** The 363-mile (588-km) Erie Canal opens

**1863** Union forces defeat Robert E. Lee and the Confederacy at Gettysburg

**1929** Stock Market crash triggers the Great Depression

**1933** New York Governor Franklin Delano Roosevelt is elected president

**1978** Gambling legalized in Atlantic City

**1987** Stock Market crash

**1994** Rudolph Giuliani becomes mayor of New York City

**2001** World Trade Center (WTC) destroyed in terrorist attack

**2004** Cornerstone laid for new tower at WTC site

**Detail from Benjamin West's monumental *Penn's Treaty with the Indians*, circa 1770**

Pennsylvania. Relations between the Dutch and the Indians were mutually beneficial, in that the Dutch supplied guns and other metal products to the Indians, who paid for them with valuable beaver and other pelts. However, contact with foreigners led to the spread of diseases, including smallpox and measles, which soon decimated Native populations.

From the 1660s onward, as England wrestled for power in the New World, upstate New York evolved into a battleground for distant European wars. To consolidate their control over trans-Atlantic trade, the English first acquired the Dutch colonies and established a new one of their own – Pennsylvania. This colony, which developed on land granted by King Charles II to wealthy Quaker William Penn in 1680, thrived, thanks to fertile soil, a healthy climate, and a group of comparatively wealthy and industrious colonists. Its capital, Philadelphia, flourished and became the key center of the nascent movement for American independence.

### Independence & Industry

Throughout the first half of the 18th century, the English and their American colonists fought a series of frontier battles against the French and their Indian allies. The cost of these wars in loss of life and property was high, and to pay for them the English crown raised a series of taxes, many of which were especially onerous for the merchants of New York and Philadelphia. In 1774, and again in 1776, delegates to Philadelphia's Continental Congress debated the issues and eventually declared independence from

England. Soon after, the English military occupied New York and Philadelphia and held them until the end of the Revolutionary War in 1783.

Perhaps the most significant early battle took place in the summer of 1777 at Saratoga Springs, where patriots defeated the English under General John Burgoyne. Although this success earned the Americans the vital support of France, the revolutionary forces, organized into the Continental Army under George Washington, still suffered tremendous hardships. More than 3,000 soldiers died of disease at Valley Forge, outside Philadelphia, in the winter of 1777–78. After the British abandoned their American colonies in 1783, New York City served as the capital of the new nation until 1790, followed by Philadelphia from 1790 to 1800.

War memorial in Congress Park, Saratoga Springs

Although the battle for independence was fought and won by farmers and tradesmen, the following century saw the region emerge as a major industrial powerhouse. The Erie Canal was cut across upstate New York between 1817 and 1825, and Pennsylvania became the nation's biggest producer of coal and steel. Railroads crisscrossed the region by the mid-19th century, and it was this industrial might that enabled the North to withstand the divisive Civil War. The region sent more than 600,000 men to fight for the Union, but the main battle fought here was in July 1863, at the small town of Gettysburg in southeastern Pennsylvania. Known as the "high tide" of the war, this battle was the northern limit of Confederate success, the only time southern forces crossed the Mason-Dixon Line, the Pennsylvania–Maryland border that marked the divide between free and slave states.

### People & Culture

For nearly a century after the Civil War, the mines, mills, and factories of New York, New Jersey, and Pennsylvania attracted a huge influx of European immigrants. Between 1880 and 1910, some 12 million immigrants passed through New York City's port. During the World War years more people, including African Americans from the Deep South, came here to work in the several arms-related factories. Today, as much as one-third of the present population counts itself as ethnic minorities, and in many cities these "minorities" often comprise a large majority of the residents. Thus some neighborhoods are identified by their ethnic makeup – Chinatown or Little Italy in New York City, the Italian Market in South Philadelphia, or the Polish areas of Pittsburgh's South Side.

San Gennaro Festival in Manhattan's Little Italy

Years of labor strife, and many economic upheavals led to many industries closing down in the 1960s and 70s. New York City, the financial center of world capitalism, flirted with bankruptcy in the 1970s.

Today, however, things are different. "Heritage tourism" of battlefields, former industrial sites, historic canals, and railroads is a significant business, drawing almost as many millions of visitors as the natural wonders of Niagara Falls.

# Exploring New York City & the Mid-Atlantic Region

THE TWO MAJOR CITIES OF New York and Philadelphia naturally dominate travel in the Mid-Atlantic Region. However, the region's other attractions include the exclusive summer retreats of the Hamptons, the collegian environs of Princeton, and industrial Pittsburg, today a vibrant cultural center. Equally attractive are its scenic wonders, ranging from the broad beaches of New Jersey and the tranquil beauty of Pennsylvannia's Amish Country to the wilderness of New York State's Adirondacks. A car is essential to explore the region's vast interior. All roads tend to lead through both New York City and Philadelphia, especially the New Jersey Turnpike (I-95), the main north–south artery. Heading west from the coast, the two main roads are I-80 across Pennsylvania and I-90, the New York Thruway. Many state and country roads connect the rural areas, while the major cities have good Amtrak and commuter train services.

**Taughannock Falls surrounded by trees in fall foliage, Taughannock Falls State Park**

## SIGHTS AT A GLANCE

***SEE ALSO***

- ***Practical Information*** pp110–11
- ***Where to Stay*** pp112–17
- ***Where to Eat*** pp118–21

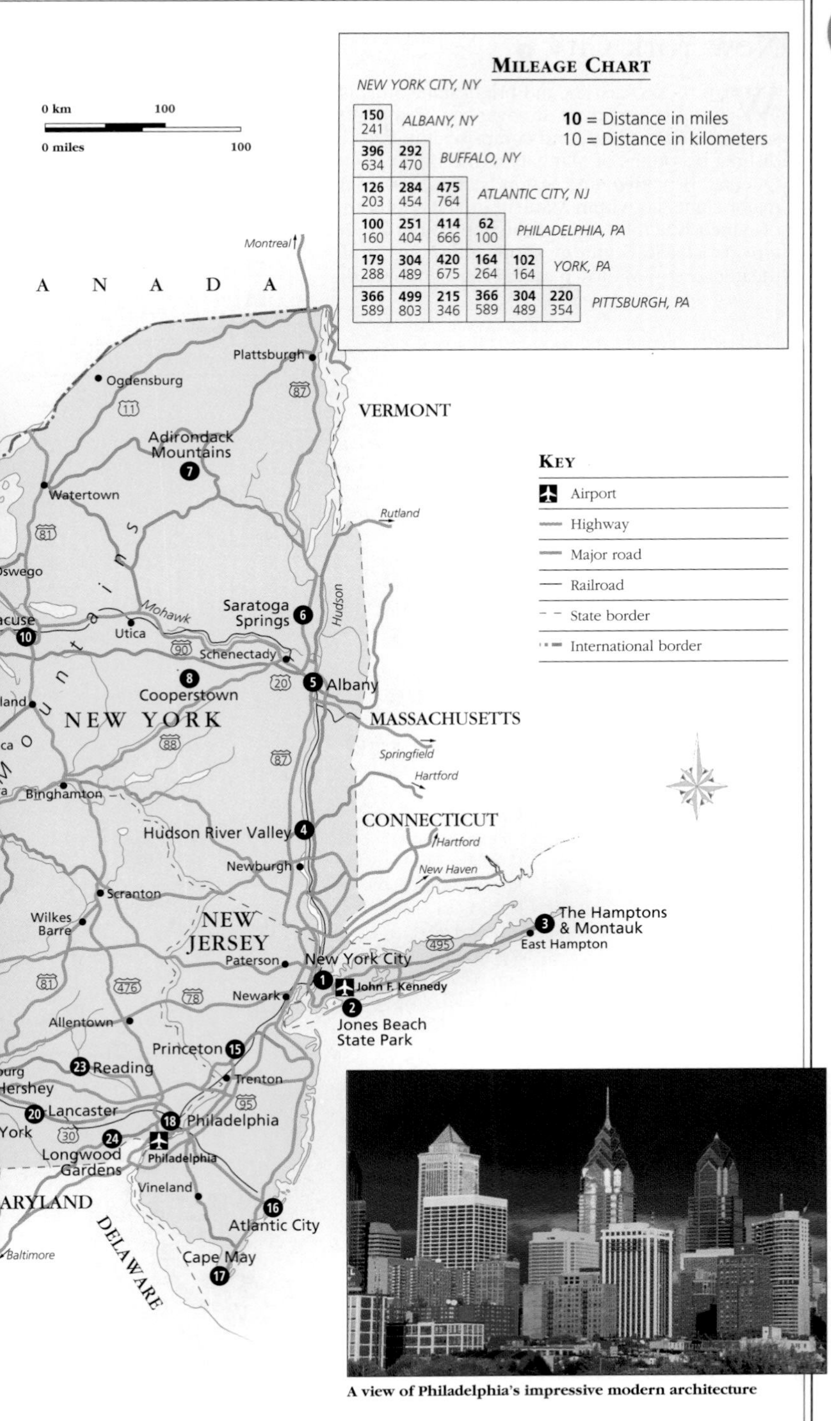

**Mileage Chart**

10 = Distance in miles
10 = Distance in kilometers

| | NEW YORK CITY, NY | ALBANY, NY | BUFFALO, NY | ATLANTIC CITY, NJ | PHILADELPHIA, PA | YORK, PA |
|---|---|---|---|---|---|---|
| ALBANY, NY | **150** 241 | | | | | |
| BUFFALO, NY | **396** 634 | **292** 470 | | | | |
| ATLANTIC CITY, NJ | **126** 203 | **284** 454 | **475** 764 | | | |
| PHILADELPHIA, PA | **100** 160 | **251** 404 | **414** 666 | **62** 100 | | |
| YORK, PA | **179** 288 | **304** 489 | **420** 675 | **164** 264 | **102** 164 | |
| PITTSBURGH, PA | **366** 589 | **499** 803 | **215** 346 | **366** 589 | **304** 489 | **220** 354 |



A view of Philadelphia's impressive modern architecture

# New York City ❶

With its skyscrapers and bright lights, this is a city of superlatives. It covers an area of 301 sq miles (780 sq km), and comprises the five distinct boroughs of Manhattan, the Bronx, Queens, Brooklyn, and Staten Island. Most of the major sights lie within Manhattan, the southern tip of which was the target of the September 11, 2001 terrorist attack. Glittering shops, museums, and theaters are in Midtown and along Central Park.

### Key to Street Finder

- Place of interest
- Airport
- Ferry terminal
- Subway station
- Main railroad station
- Bus terminal
- Tourist information
- Church
- Synagogue
- Highway

### Sights at a Glance

Wall Street ①
World Trade Center Site ②
Battery Park City ③
Statue of Liberty ④
Ellis Island ⑤
South Street Seaport ⑥
*Brooklyn Bridge p68* ⑦
Civic Center ⑧
Eldridge Street Synagogue ⑨
Chinatown ⑩
Little Italy ⑪
TriBeCa ⑫
SoHo Historic District ⑬
Washington Square ⑭
Greenwich Village ⑮
East Village ⑯
Union Square ⑰
Flatiron Building ⑱
Madison Square ⑲
*Empire State Building p73* ⑳
Herald Square ㉑
Times Square ㉒
The New York Public Library ㉓
Morgan Library ㉔
Grand Central Terminal ㉕
United Nations ㉖
Rockefeller Center ㉗
*St. Patrick's Cathedral p77* ㉘
Museum of Modern Art ㉙
Fifth Avenue ㉚
*A Tour of Central Park pp78–9* ㉛
Whitney Museum of American Art ㉜
Frick Collection ㉝
Metropolitan Museum of Art ㉞
*The Solomon R. Guggenheim Museum p82* ㉟
American Museum of Natural History ㊱
Lincoln Center ㊲

**Greater New York**
***(see inset map)***

Columbia University ㊳
Riverside Church ㊴
St. Nicholas Historic District ㊵
Studio Museum in Harlem ㊶
*The Cloisters p86* ㊷
The Bronx ㊸
Brooklyn ㊹

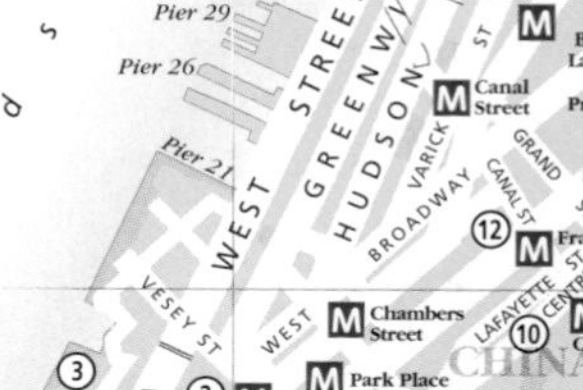

## Getting Around

With over 6,000 miles (9,600 km) of streets, walking around New York can be very strenuous. The city's taxis are convenient, except during rush hour. Other options are buses or the subway; the public transportation system is safe and an excellent way to get around the city.

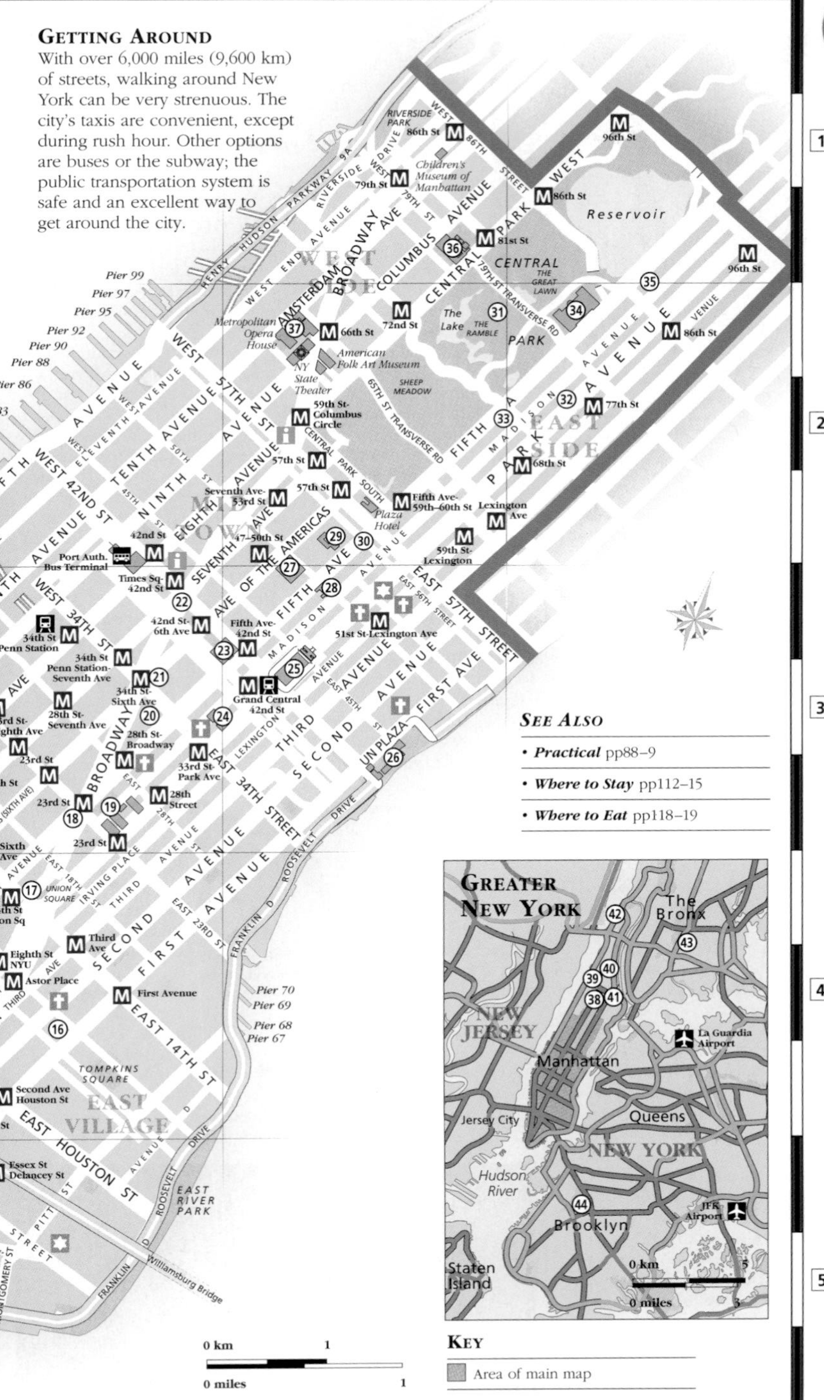


### See Also


- ***Practical*** pp88–9
- ***Where to Stay*** pp112–15
- ***Where to Eat*** pp118–19

Trinity Church at the foot of Wall Street

## Wall Street ①

**Map** B5. *2, 3, 4, 5 to Wall St, N, R to Rector St. M1, M6, M15.*

NAMED FOR THE wall that kept enemies and warring Indians out of Manhattan, Wall Street is now the heart of the city's financial district. One of the prominent sites here is the **Federal Reserve Bank** on Liberty Street. Inspired by the Italian Renaissance, this is a government bank for banks, where US currency is issued. Five-stories below ground is a large storehouse for international gold. Each nation's hoard is stored in its own compartment within the subterranean vault, guarded by 90-ton doors.

Farther away is the **Federal Hall National Monument**, where a bronze statue of George Washington on the steps marks the site where the nation's first president took his oath of office in 1789 *(see p61)*. The present imposing structure (under renovation until 2007) was built between 1834 and 1842 as the US Custom House, and is one of the finest Classical designs in the city.

At the head of Wall Street is **Trinity Church**. Built in 1846, this square-towered Episcopal church is the third one on this site in one of America's oldest Anglican parishes, founded in 1697. Designed by Richard Upjohn, it was one of the grandest churches of its day, marking the beginning of the best period of Gothic Revival architecture in America. The sculpted brass doors were inspired by Ghiberti's *Doors of Paradise* in Florence. Its 280-ft (85-m) steeple was New York's tallest structure until the 1860s. Many famous New Yorkers are buried here.

The hub of the world's financial markets, the **New York Stock Exchange** (NYSE) is housed in a 17-story building built in 1903. Initially, trading in stocks and shares took place haphazardly in the area, but 24 brokers signed an agreement in 1792 to deal only with one another. This formed the basis of the NYSE. Membership is strictly limited. In 1817, a "seat" cost $25; today it costs more than two million dollars, and a rigorous test of suitability is required. The NYSE has weathered slumps ("bear markets") and booms ("bull markets") and has seen advances in technology, from tickertape to microchip, turn a local market into a global one.

Bronze bull, symbol of Wall Street, near Custom House

**Trinity Church**
Broadway at Wall St. *(212) 602-0872. 7am–6pm Mon–Fri; 8am–4pm Sat, 7am–4pm Sun. 9am, 11:15am Sun.* **Concerts** *1pm Mon & Thu.* www.trinitywallstreet.org

**New York Stock Exchange**
20 Broad St. *(212) 656-3000. 9:30am–4pm Mon–Fri (last adm: 3:30pm). public hols.* ***Video displays.*** www.nyse.com

## World Trade Center Site ②

**Map** B5. Viewing wall on Church St. *Chambers St, Rector St.* www.wtcsitememorial.org

IMMORTALIZED BY countless filmmakers and photographers, the twin towers of the World Trade Center dominated the Manhattan skyline for 27 years, until the September 2001 terrorist attack. The enormous weight of each building was supported by an inner wire cage, which melted from the heat of the fire caused by the two aircraft that were flown into the towers. These towers were part of a buildings complex consisting of six office blocks and a hotel, connected by a vast underground concourse lined with shops and restaurants. A bridge linked the complex to the World Financial Center, which survived the attack. The "Ground Zero" perimeter continues to shrink as buildings around the site are reoccupied. Things are moving quickly – the new design for the site has been approved, and the cornerstone for the new tower was laid on July 4, 2004. In addition to rebuilding part of the 16 acre (6.5 ha) site as business and office space, a memorial to the thousands who died here is also planned.

Battery Park City's World Financial Center from the Hudson River

## Battery Park City ③

**Map** B5. *1, 9 to Rector St.* www.batteryparkcity.org **World Financial Center** West St. *(212) 945-0505.* *1, 2, A, C, & J, M, Z to Chambers St; 4, 5, 6 to Brooklyn Bridge/City Hall Station; E to WTC Station; N, R to City Hall.* www.worldfinancialcenter.com

NEW YORK'S newest neighborhood is an ambitious development on 92 reclaimed acres (37 ha) along the Hudson River. This huge commercial and residential complex can house more than 25,000 people, at an estimated cost of $4 billion. A 2-mile (3-km) esplanade offers grand Statue of Liberty views.

The most visible part is the **World Financial Center**. A model of urban design by Cesar Pelli & Associates, this development is a vital part of the revival of Lower Manhattan, and its damage in the World Trade Center attack was attended to as a matter of urgency. Some of the world's most important financial companies are housed here. At the heart of the complex lies the dazzling Winter Garden (re-opened September 2002), a vast glass-and-steel public space often used for concerts and arts events. It is flanked by restaurants and shops, and opens onto a lively piazza and marina on the Hudson River.

Among the new attractions is the Skyscraper Museum, located at the Ritz-Carlton hotel.

## Statue of Liberty ④

**Map** A5. Liberty Island. *(212) 363-3200.* *1, 9, N, R to S Ferry, 4, 5 to Bowling Green.* *M6, M15 to S Ferry, then Circle Line–Statue of Liberty Ferry from the Battery every 30–45 mins, 9:15am–3:30pm summer (winter hours vary).* *(212) 269-5755.* *Jul–Aug: 9am–6pm daily; Sep–Jun: 9:30am–5pm daily.* *Dec 25. Ferry fare includes entry to Ellis & Liberty Is.* *elevator to observation deck only.* www.statueoflibertyferry.com

THE FIGURE presiding over New York harbor, titled "Liberty Enlightening the World," has been the symbol of freedom for millions since

**Statue of Liberty, an enduring symbol of New York**

her inauguration by President Grover Cleveland in 1886. A gift from the French to the American people to mark the US centennial in 1876, the statue was the brainchild of sculptor Frédéric-Auguste Bartholdi. In Emma Lazarus's poem, which is engraved on the base, Lady Liberty says: "Give me your tired, your poor, / Your huddled masses yearning to breathe free."

The 305-ft (93-m) high statue stands on a pedestal set within the walls of an old army fort. In one hand Liberty holds the new torch, with a 24-carat gold-leaf flame, while in the other is a book inscribed July 4, 1776, in Latin. The rays of her crown represent the seven seas and seven continents. The flight of 354 steps (22 stories) that took visitors right up to the crown, has been closed indefinitely since the September 11 terrorist attack.

After a $100 million restoration in time for its bicentennial, the statue was unveiled on July 3, 1986. The spectacular $2 million fireworks display to celebrate the occasion was the largest public party in the city.

## Ellis Island ⑤

**Map** A5. *(212) 363-3200.* *4, 5 to Bowling Green; 1, 9, N, R to Whitehall/South Ferry, then Circle Line/Statue of Liberty Ferry from the Battery.* **Departures** *every 30 mins 8:30am–3:30pm summer (winter hours vary).* *(212) 269-5755.* *Jul–Aug: 9am–6pm daily; Sep–Jun: 9:30am–5pm daily.* *Dec 25.* *entry inc Ellis and Liberty Is.* www.ellisisland.org; www.statueoflibertyferry.com

MORE THAN HALF of America's population can trace its roots to Ellis Island, which served as the country's immigration depot from 1892 until 1954. Nearly 17 million people passed through its gates and dispersed across the country in the greatest wave of immigration the world has ever known. First- and second-class passengers were processed on board, but steerage passengers were ferried from arrival vessels and taken to the crowded island for medical and legal examinations. Immigrants with contagious diseases could be sent back. Ellis Island lay in ruins until 1990, when a $189 million project by the Statue of Liberty–Ellis Island Foundation, Inc., renewed the buildings.

Centered on the Great Hall or Registry Room, the site today houses the three-story **Ellis Island Immigration Museum** with permanent exhibits. Much of its story is told with photos and the voices of immigrants, and an electronic database traces ancestors. Outside, the American Immigrant Wall of Honor is the largest wall of names in the world. No other place explains so well the "melting pot" that formed the character of the nation.

**A view of the main building, Ellis Island**

## South Street Seaport ⑥

**Map** C5. Fulton St. (212) 732-7678. *Fulton St.* *10am– 7pm Mon–Sat, 11am–6pm Sun.* ***Concerts.*** www.southstseaport.com
**South Street Seaport Museum** 12 Fulton St. *(212) 748-8600.* *Apr–Oct: 10am–5pm daily; Nov–Mar: 10am–5pm Fri–Sun.* *Tue; Jan 1, Thanksg., Dec 25.* ***Exhibits, films.*** www.southstreetseaportmuseum.org

Called the "street of sails" in the 19th-century, the heart of New York's port has now been imaginatively restored as a tourist center. Glitzy stores and restaurants sit harmoniously beside seafaring craft, historic buildings, and museum exhibits, with spectacular views of Brooklyn Bridge and the East River from the cobblestone streets. The historic ships docked here range from the little tugboat *W.O. Decker* to the grand four-masted bark *Peking*, the second-largest sailing ship in existence. Mini-trips on the schooner *Pioneer* are a great way to see the river.

**The Ambrose lightship at a South Street Seaport pier on the East River**

The **Fulton Fish Market** has been here since 1821. Once sold fresh from the boat, the fish now arrive in refrigerated trucks. The market is open only in the early morning. **South Street Seaport Museum** covers the 12 blocks of what was America's leading port. In addition to the six historic ships, it has more than 10,000 artifacts, artworks, and documents from the 19th- and early 20th-century maritime world. **Schermerhorn Row**, on Fulton and South Streets, was built as warehouses in 1813. The Row has been restored and now houses a visitor center, shops, restaurants, and an ice-skating rink.

A Frank Gehry-designed Guggenheim Museum being built here will add to South Street Seaport's attractions.

## Brooklyn Bridge ⑦

**Map** C5. *J, M, Z to Chambers St, 4, 5, 6 to Brooklyn Bridge–City Hall (Manhattan side); A, C to High St, Brooklyn Bridge (Brooklyn side).* *M9, M15, M22, M103.*

An engineering wonder when it was built in 1883, the Brooklyn Bridge linked Manhattan and Brooklyn, then two separate cities. At that time it was the world's largest suspension bridge and the first to be constructed of steel. The German-born engineer John A. Roebling conceived of a bridge spanning the East River while ice-bound on a ferry to Brooklyn. The bridge took 16 years to build, required 600 workers, and claimed over 20 lives, including Roebling's. Most died of caisson disease (known as "the bends") after coming up from the underwater excavation chambers. From the pedestrian walkway there are fabulous views of the city towers, seen through the artistic cablework.

**Brooklyn Bridge, the first ever steel suspension bridge**

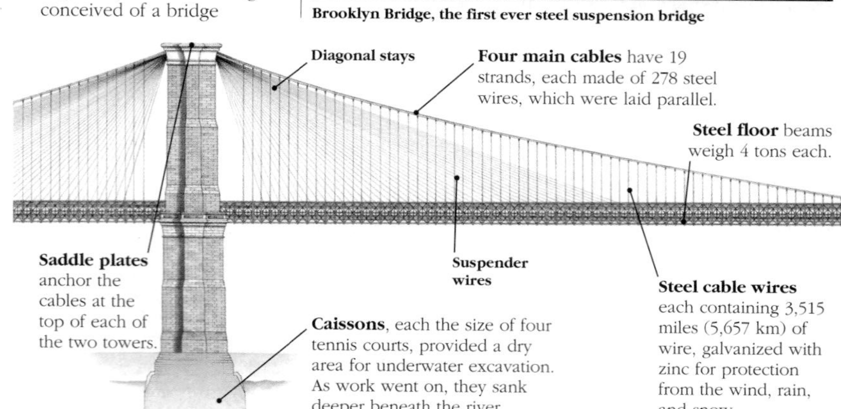

City Hall's imposing early 19th-century façade

## Civic Center ⑧

**Map** C5. M *7th Ave/Broadway 2 & 3 to Park Pl; 8th Ave A, C, & E to Chambers St; N, R to City Hall.* **Woolworth Building** 233 Broadway. M *City Hall.* *office hours.* **City Hall** City Hall Park. (212) 788-6865. M *Brooklyn Br–City Hall.* *for prearranged tours only.* **Municipal Building** 1 Center St. M *Brooklyn Br–City Hall.*

MANHATTAN'S busy Civic Center is the hub of the city, state, and federal government court systems and the city's police department. The 1926 New York County Courthouse is adjacent to the 31-story pyramid-topped 1933 US Courthouse. The Tweed Courthouse, constructed by the infamous Boss Tweed, a corrupt politician, is being restored to house the Museum of the City of New York.

The monumental buildings here include the 1913 Gothic **Woolworth Building**, headquarters of Five-and-Dime mogul Frank W. Woolworth. Designed by architect Cass Gilbert, it was the city's tallest building until 1930 and set the standard for future skyscrapers. In contrast is the historic **City Hall**, the seat of government since 1812. This Georgian building with French Renaissance influences is considered one of the finest examples of early 19th-century American architecture. The City Hall Park was New York's village green 250 years ago. To its northeast, the **Municipal Building** is a wedding-cake fantasy of towers and spires, topped by the statue *Civic Fame*.

## Eldridge Street Synagogue ⑨

**Map** C5. 12 Eldridge St. *(212) 219-0888.* M *E Broadway.* *11am–4pm Sun.* *Fri at sundown, Sat 10am onward.* *11:30am & 2:30pm Tue, Thu, & by appt.* W www.eldridgestreet.org

THIS MOORISH-STYLE house of worship was the first large temple built in the US by Jewish immigrants from Eastern Europe, from where 80 percent of American Jews came. At the turn of the century, it was the most flamboyant temple in the neighborhood, and as many as 1,000 people attended services here. As congregants left the area, attendance waned and the temple closed in the 1950s.

Three decades later a group of citizens raised funds to restore the magnificent sanctuary. The synagogue is now a National Historic Landmark.

## Chinatown ⑩

**Map** C5. Streets around Mott St. M *Canal St.*
**Eastern States Buddhist Temple** 64b Mott St. *9am–6pm daily.*

NEW YORK'S LARGEST and most colorful ethnic neighborhood is Chinatown. In the early 20th century this was primarily a male community, made up of immigrant workers. Wages were sent to families back in China who were prevented from joining them by strict immigration laws. Today, more than 200,000 Chinese Americans live here. The shops and sidewalks overflow with exotic foods and herbs, and gifts ranging from backscratchers to fine antiques. Most people, however, visit Chinatown to eat in one of the more than 200 restaurants or shop for Asian delicacies.

Other sights here include the **Eastern States Buddhist Temple**, with its incense-scented interior and more than 100 golden Buddhas; and tiny, crooked Doyers Street, called "Bloody Angle," reminiscent of the Tong wars between the 1920s and 40s. The Tongs were social clubs or rival criminal fraternities who gave the old locale its dangerous reputation.

## Little Italy ⑪

**Map** C4. Streets around Mulberry St. M *Canal St.* W www.littleitalynyc.com

THE LOWER EAST SIDE'S other ethnic neighborhood is Little Italy, home to southern Italian immigrants in the late 19th century. The immigrants preserved their language, customs, and food, making Mulberry Street lively with the colors, flavors, and atmosphere of Italy. Today, although Little Italy has shrunk to a few blocks, the 10-day Feast of San Gennaro in September draws crowds of joyful celebrants. Also on Mulberry Street is **Old St. Patrick's Cathedral**. It became a local parish church when the cathedral moved uptown *(see p77)*.

NoLita, north of Little Italy, is filled with boutiques, and the city's fashionable flock here for the coolest small labels.

Little Italy, once home to thousands of immigrants

## TriBeCa ⑫

**Map** C4. S of Houston St, N of Chambers St, & W of Lafayette St to Hudson River. **M** *Prince St, Spring St, Canal St, Franklin St, Chambers St.*

UNTIL RECENTLY, the area named for its geographic shape – TRIangle BElow CAnal – consisted mostly of abandoned warehouses. Then Robert de Niro set up his TriBeCa Film Center in a converted coffee warehouse, and TriBeCa became the center of the city's movie industry. Known as Hollywood East, many screenings and events take place here. This is now one of New York's hottest neighborhoods, with stylish restaurants, art galleries, and big loft spaces occupied by celebrity residents.

## SoHo Historic District ⑬

**Map** C4. S of Houston St. **Greene Street** **M** *Canal St.*

THE LARGEST concentration of cast-iron architecture in the world survives in SoHo (south of Houston), a former industrial district. Its heart is Greene Street; 50 cast-iron buildings are stretched out over a five-block area. The finest are those at 72–76, the "King" and 28 –30, the "Queen." A 19th-century American innovation, cast iron was cheaper than either stone or brick and allowed decorative elements to be prefabricated in foundries from molds and used as building façades.

The **Singer Building** on Broadway was built by Ernest Flagg in 1904, at a time when steel-framed brick and terra-cotta were replacing cast iron. This ornate 12-story building, adorned with wrought-iron balconies and graceful arches painted in striking dark green, was an office and warehouse for the Singer sewing machine company. The original Singer name is cast in iron above the entrance to the store on Prince Street.

Nearby was the **Museum for African Art**. One of only two American museums devoted to African art, these galleries were ingeniously designed by architect Maya Lin, creator of Washington's Vietnam Veterans Memorial *(see p205)*. But the museum is now on the move and has taken temporary residence at 36–01 43rd Avenue, Long Island City (two blocks from the 33rd Street stop on the #7 subway line). Its final resting place will be at the top of Museum Mile on Fifth Avenue sometime in 2007. Meanwhile, the high-caliber changing shows continue, and the museum remains a pre-eminent organizer of exhibitions and publisher of books devoted exclusively to historical and contemporary African art. Besides museums, galleries, and cast-iron architecture, SoHo's streets are lined with trendy cafés, shops, and chic designer boutiques. It is also the city's favorite Sunday brunch-and-browse neighborhood.

The "Queen," SoHo Historic District

### 🏛 Museum for African Art

Temporary location: 36–01 43rd Ave, Long Island City. ☎ *(718) 784-7700.* 🕐 *10am–5pm Mon, Thu, Fri, 11am–6pm Sat–Sun.* ● *Tue–Wed.* 🎫 *(free on Sun).* 🛍 **W** www.africanart.org

Window on the corner of West 4th Street and Washington Square

## Washington Square ⑭

Greenwich Vil. **Map** C4. **M** *W 4th St.*

NOW ONE of the city's most vibrant open spaces, Washington Square was once a marshland that was filled to form a park. Stanford White's magnificent marble arch, completed in 1895, replaced a wooden version that marked the centenary of George Washington's inauguration. In 1916, a group of artists led by John Sloan and Marcel Duchamp broke in, climbed atop the arch, and declared the "free and independent republic of Washington Square, the state of New Bohemia." Decades later, Bob Dylan sang his first folk songs near the fountain in the small park's center.

## Greenwich Village ⑮

**Map** C4. N of Houston St & S of 14th St. **M** *W 4th St-Washington Square, Christopher St-Sheridan Square, 8th St.*

SIMPLY KNOWN as "the Village," this crazy-quilt pattern of streets is a natural enclave that has been a bohemian haven and home to many celebrated writers, artists, and jazz musicians. Later, it became a popular gay district, and the spirited gay Halloween Parade held here is a fantastic event. The Village comes alive at night, when cafés, theaters, and clubs beckon at every turn. A stroll through its narrow old-fashioned lanes reveal charming row houses, hidden alleys, and leafy courtyards. The 15 Italianate row houses, lining the north side of **St. Luke's Place**, date from the 1850s. Poet Marianne Moore lived here, and Theodore Dreiser wrote his *An American Tragedy* at No. 16.

The heart of the Village is **Sheridan Square**, where seven streets meet in such a maze that early guidebooks called it "the mousetrap." The Stonewall Inn, a gay bar on Christopher Street, was where a riot took place against police harassment on June 27, 1969. It was a landmark moral victory for the budding Gay Rights Movement. Stonewall Inn still stands, but is no longer a bar.

**Jefferson Market Courthouse**, "Old Jeff," is perhaps the Village's most treasured landmark. It was built as a courthouse in 1877 and voted the fifth most beautiful building in America. After remaining empty for over 20 years, it was restored and turned into a public library in 1967. Opposite is Patchin Place, a small pocket of 19th-century houses where playwright Eugene O'Neill, and poets e e cummings and John Masefield once lived.

**Jefferson Market Courthouse**
425 Ave of the Americas. *(212) 243-4334.* *noon–8pm Mon & Wed, 10am–6pm Tue, noon–6pm Thu, 1–6pm Fri, 10am–5pm Sat.* *public hols.* www.nypl.org

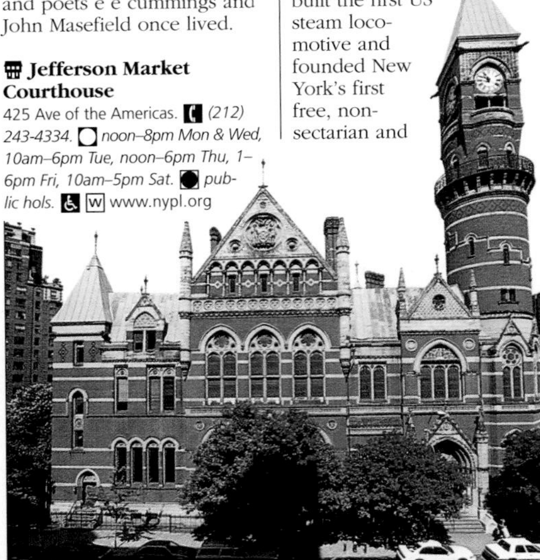
**Pointed tower of "Old Jeff," Greenwich Village**

**Original furnishings in East Village's Merchant's House Museum**

## East Village ⑯

**Map** D4. 14th St to Houston St. *Astor Place.*

PROMINENT New Yorkers, such as Peter Stuyvesant, the Astors, and the Vanderbilts, lived in this fomer Dutch enclave until 1900, when they moved uptown. Thereafter, it was home to German, Jewish, Irish, and Ukrainian immigrants. In the 1960s the East Village became a haven for hippies, and this is the place where punk rock was born.

The six-story **Cooper Union** was set up in 1859 by Peter Cooper, a wealthy industrialist who built the first US steam locomotive and founded New York's first free, non-sectarian and coeducational college. Its Great Hall was inaugurated in 1859 by Mark Twain, and Abraham Lincoln delivered his "Right Makes Might" speech there in 1860. Cooper Union still provides free education.

The 1832 **Merchant's House Museum**, a remarkable Greek Revival brick town house, is a time capsule of a vanished way of life. It was bought by Seabury Tredwell, a wealthy merchant, and remained in the family until 1933. It still has its original fixtures and displays authentic Federal, American Empire, and Victorian furniture.

One of New York's oldest churches, the 1799 **St. Mark's-in-the-Bowery** is located on East 10th Street. Governor Peter Stuyvesant and his descendants are buried here.

The English-style **Tompkin Square** was the site of America's first organized labor demonstration in 1874, the main gathering place during the neighborhood's hippie era and, in 1991, an arena for violent riots when the police tried to evict the homeless who had occupied the grounds. A small statue of a boy and a girl looking at a steamboat commemorates the more than 1,000 local residents who died in the *General Slocum* steamer disaster on June 15, 1904.

**Merchant's House Museum**
29 E 4th St. *(212) 777-1089.* *noon–5pm Thu–Mon & by appt.* *(no flashes).* www.merchantshouse.com

## Union Square ⑰

**Map** D4. **M** *14th St-Union Square.* **Greenmarket** *Mon, Wed, Fri, Sat.*

Opened in 1839, this park was once the hangout for drug dealers and soapbox orators. Today, renovations have transformed it into a flourishing section of Manhattan. A greenmarket fills the square where more than 200 farmers from all over New York State sell fresh produce four times a week, drawing patrons from all over the city. Herbs and berries, miniature vegetables, fresh flowers and home-baked pastries, honey, and newly woven yarns are all available at this bountiful market.

## Flatiron Building ⑱

**Map** D3. 175 5th Ave. **M** *23rd St.* *office hours.*

This unusual building, its shape conforming to a triangular plot of land, has intrigued New Yorkers since it was built by Chicago architect David Burnham in 1902. One of the first buildings to use a steel frame, it heralded the era of the skyscrapers.

It soon became known as the Flatiron for its triangular shape, but some called it "Burnham's folly," predicting that the winds created by the building's shape would knock it down. It has, however, withstood the test of time.

The stretch of Fifth Avenue to the south of the building was once rather run down, but has come to life with chic shops such as Emporio Armani and Paul Smith, giving the area new cachet and a new name, "the Flatiron District."

**Flatiron Building, New York's most famous early skyscraper**

**Appellate Court, said to be the world's busiest courthouse, Madison Square**

## Madison Square ⑲

**Map** D3. **M** *23rd St.*

Quiet Madison Square opened in 1847 at the center of a fashionable residential district where politican Theodore Roosevelt and writer Edith Wharton were born. It was bordered by the elegant Fifth Avenue Hotel, the Madison Square Theater, and Stanford White's Madison Square Garden. The torch-bearing arm of the Statue of Liberty was exhibited here in 1884. Newly landscaped, this statue-filled park borders some of the city's hottest restaurants. Area residents stroll and walk their dogs at all hours.

Just off Madison Square is the spectacular **New York Life Insurance Company** building, designed in 1928 by Cass Gilbert of Woolworth Building fame *(see p69)*. The building has Gilbert's trademark pyramid-shaped tower, modeled on the Giralda in Seville. Its interior is adorned with hanging lamps, bronze doors and paneling, and a grand staircase leading to a subway station.

Opposite is the **Appellate Division of the Supreme Court of the State of New York**, a small marble palace designed by James Brown Lord in 1900. Considered to be the busiest courthouse in the world, appeals relating to civil and criminal cases for New York and the Bronx are heard here. During the week, the public can admire the fine interior, designed by the Herter brothers, including the courtroom when it is not in session. Displays in the lobby often feature some of the court's more famous and infamous cases. Among the celebrities whose appeals were settled here are Babe Ruth, Charlie Chaplin, Fred Astaire, Harry Houdini, Theodore Dreiser, and Edgar Allan Poe.

On the east side of Madison Square is the 54-story **Metropolitan Life Tower**. Built in 1909, this was the world's tallest building at that time, an appropriate corporate symbol for the largest insurance company in the world. The huge four-sided clock has minute hands said to weigh 1,000 lb (454 kg) each. A series of historical murals by N.C. Wyeth, the famed illustrator of such classics as *Robin Hood*, *Treasure Island*, and *Robinson Crusoe* (and the father of painter Andrew Wyeth), are now on display in the lobby.

**Appellate Division of the Supreme Court of the State of New York**

E 25th St at Madison Ave. *9am–5pm Mon–Fri.* *public hols.*

## Empire State Building ⑳

**Map** D3. 350 5th Ave. *(212) 736-3100.* *B, D, F, N, Q, R, 1, 2, 3, 9 to 34th St; 6 to 33rd St.* *Q32, M1–M5, M16, M34.* **86th-floor Observatory** *9:30am–last adm: 11:15pm; 11am–7pm Jan 1; 9am–5pm Dec 24; 11am–7pm Dec 25.* www.esbnyc.com

THE EMPIRE State Building is New York's tallest and most impressive skyscraper. Construction began in March 1930 not long after the stock market crash, and by the time it opened in 1931, space was so difficult to rent that it was nicknamed "the Empty State Building." Only the immediate popularity of the observatories saved the building from bankruptcy – to date, they have attracted more than 120 million visitors – but the building soon became a symbol of the city the world over. It only took 410 days to build this 102-story limestone and brick skyscraper, with an average of four and a half stories added every week. The 102nd floor has been closed to the public for several years. Each February, the annual Empire State Run-Up is held, when 150 runners race up the 1,576 steps from the lobby to the 86th floor (known for its outdoor observation decks), in 10 minutes.

**102nd-floor observatory**

**The building** was planned to be 86 stories high, but a 150 ft (46 m) mooring mast for zeppelins was added. The mast, now 204 ft (62 m), transmits TV and radio to the city and four states.

**Colored floodlighting** of the top 30 floors marks special and seasonal events.

**High-speed** elevators travel at up to 1,200 ft (366 m) a minute.

**The framework** is made from 60,000 tons of steel and was built in 23 weeks.

**Aluminum panels** were used instead of stone around the 6,500 windows. The steel trim masks rough edges on the facing.

**Ten million bricks** were used to line the entire building.

**Sandwich space** between the floors houses the wiring, pipes and cables.

**Fifth Avenue Entrance Lobby, Empire State Building**

**Macy's 34th Street entrance**

## Herald Square ㉑

**Map** D3. 6th Ave. *34th St-Penn Station.*

NAMED AFTER the New York *Herald,* which had its offices here from 1893 to 1921, the square was the hub of the rowdy, mid-19th century theater district known as the Tenderloin District. Theaters, dance halls, hotels, and restaurants kept the area humming with life until reformers clamped down on sleaze in the 1890s. The ornamental clock, on an island where Broadway meets 6th Avenue, is all that survives of the Herald Building.

Herald Square became a mecca for shoppers after the Manhattan Opera House was razed in 1901 to make way for **Macy's**. The "world's largest store" began modestly. It was founded by former whaler Rowland Hussey Macy in 1857; the red star logo was from his tattoo, a souvenir of his sailing days. The store was sold in 1888 and moved to its present premises in 1902. The 34th Street façade still has its original clock, canopy, and lettering.

Macy's sponsors New York's famous Thanksgiving Day parade *(see p31)* and the Fourth of July fireworks. Its annual Spring Flower Show draws thousands of visitors.

**Macy's**
151 W 34th St. *(212) 695-4400.* *10am–8:30pm Mon–Sat; 11am–7pm Sun.* *public hols.* www.macys.com

## Times Square ㉒

**Map** D3. *42nd St-Times Square.* *1560 Broadway (46th St), 8am–8pm daily.* *noon Fri.* www.timessquarenyc.org

NAMED FOR THE New York Times Tower, Times Square is the city's most famous intersection. Although the *New York Times* has moved from its original headquarters at the square's southern end, the crystal ball still drops at midnight on New Year's Eve, as it has since the building opened with fanfare in 1906.

Since 1899, when Oscar Hammerstein built the Victoria and Republic theaters, this has also been the heart of the city's theater district. The district's transformation in the 1990s led to the renovation of many theaters, such as the New Victory and the New Amsterdam. Their new productions, as well as the area's bars and restaurants, attract theatergoers each evening.

Old-world Broadway glamor rubs shoulders with modern entertainment in Times Square *(see p88)*. MTV has its studios here, and E Walk is a vast entertainment and retail complex. Exciting new buildings, such as the Bertlesmann building and the fashionably minimalist Condé Nast offices, sit alongside the classic establishments, such as Sardi's, the Paramount Hotel, and the Baroque Lyceum Theater.

**The New York Public Library's Main Reading Room**

## The New York Public Library ㉓

**Map** E3. 5th Ave & 42nd St. *(212) 869-8089.* *42nd St-Grand Central.* *Tue–Sun; hours vary.* *public hols.* ***Lectures, workshops, readings.*** www.nypl.org

ARCHITECTS Carrère and Hastings won the coveted job of designing New York's main public library in 1897. The white marble Beaux Arts edifice they designed fulfilled the library's first director's vision of a light, quiet, airy place, where millions of books could be stored and yet be available to readers as promptly as possible. Built on the site of the former Croton Reservoir, it opened in 1911 to immediate acclaim, despite having cost the city $9 million. The architects' genius is best seen in the newly renovated Main Reading Room, a vast paneled space as majestic as a cathedral, extending almost two city blocks. Below it are 88 miles (140 km) of shelves, holding over seven million volumes. It takes only minutes for the staff or a computerized dumbwaiter to supply any book. The Periodicals Room holds 10,000 current periodicals from 128 countries. On its walls are murals by Richard Haas, honoring New York's great publishing houses. The original library combined the collections of John Jacob Astor and James Lenox. Its collections today range from Thomas Jefferson's handwritten copy of the Declaration of Independence to T.S. Eliot's typed copy of "The Waste Land." More than 1,000 queries are answered daily, using the vast database of the CATNYP and LEO computer catalogs.

This library is the hub of a network of 82 branches, with nearly seven million users. Other well-known branches include the New York Public Library for the Performing Arts at the Lincoln Center *(see p83)* and the Schomburg Center in Harlem.

### MIDTOWN MANHATTAN

**Elevator door at the Chrysler Building**

Midtown Manhattan's skyline is graced with some of the city's most spectacular towers and spires – from the familiar beauty of the Empire State Building's Art Deco pinnacle to the dramatic wedge shape of Citigroup's modern headquarters. As the shoreline progresses uptown, so the architecture becomes more varied; the United Nations complex dominates a long stretch, and then Beekman Place begins a strand of exclusive residential enclaves that offer the rich and famous some seclusion.

**United Nations**, founded in 1945, has its impressive headquaters on an 18-acre (7-ha) site on the East River *(see p76)*.

**Empire State Building** *(see p73)*

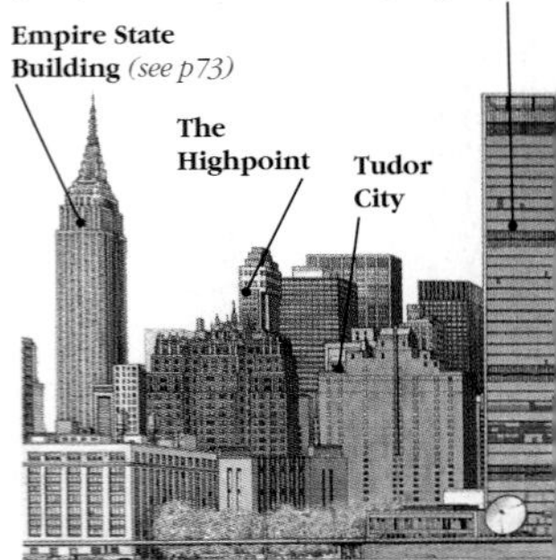

**The skylit Garden Court, Morgan Library**

## Morgan Library ㉔

**Map** E3. 29 E 36th St. *(212) 685-0610.* *closed for refurbishment until spring 2006.* www.morganlibrary.org

THIS MAGNIFICENT palazzo-style building was designed in 1902 to house the private collection of banker Pierpont Morgan (1837–1913), one of the great collectors of his time. Established in 1924 as a public institution by Morgan's son, J.P. Morgan Jr, it has a splendid collection of rare manuscripts, prints, books, and bindings. However, because of an expansion program, the Morgan Library is currently closed and is reopening in spring 2006.

The complex includes the original library and J.P. Morgan Jr.'s home. Pierpont Morgan's opulent study and his original library contain some of his favorite paintings, objets d'art, and priceless acquisitions. Prominent among the exhibits are one of the 11 surviving copies of the Gutenburg Bible (1455), printed on vellum, and six surviving leaves of the score for Mozart's Horn Concerto in E-flat Major, written in different colored inks.

The Garden Court, a three-story skylit garden area, links the library with the house. Exhibits are changed regularly to provide access to some of the world's most significant cultural artifacts.

## Grand Central Terminal ㉕

**Map** E3. E 42nd St at Park Ave. *(212) 532-4900.* *4, 5, 6, 7, S to Grand Central.* *M101–104, M42.* *5:30–1:30am daily.* *Wed 12:30pm (free), call (212) 935-3960 & Fri 12:30pm (free), call (212) 697-1245.* ***Baggage check; lost & found.*** www.grandcentralterminal.com

ONE OF THE world's great train terminals, this outstanding Beaux Arts building is New York's most visited, with 500,000 people passing through it daily. The present building, dating from 1913, is resplendent after its recent restoration. Its glory is the main concourse, dominated by three great arched windows that fill the space with natural light. The high vaulted ceiling of this vast pedestrian area is decorated with twinkling constellations. The information booth here is surmounted by a wonderful four-faced clock. The Grand Staircase, styled after the staircase in Paris' Opera House, is a reminder of the glamorous days of early rail travel. Adjacent to the main concourse is the Vanderbilt Hall, named after Cornelius Vanderbilt, the railroad magnate who opened the station in 1871.

Today, Grand Central is no longer limited to the city's commuters. It has become an attraction in its own right, with a museum, over 40 shops, and an extensive food court, including the famed Oyster Bar *(see p118)*. This New York classic with a vaulted ceiling of yellow Guastavino tiles, has a huge dining concourse and specializes in seafood.

**A fine clock on the Grand Central Terminal building**

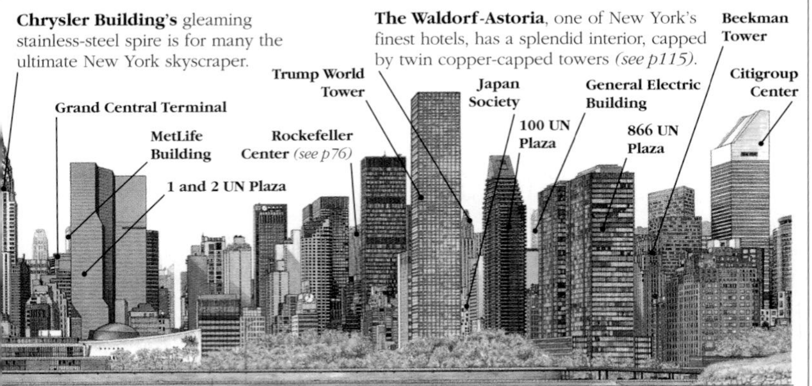

**The UN Buildings seen from the garden**

## United Nations ㉖

**Map** E3. 1st Ave at 46th St. *(212) 963-8687.* M *4, 5, 6, 7 to 42nd St-Grand Central Station.* *M15, M27, M42, M50, M104.* *Mar–Dec: 9:30am–4:45pm daily; Jan–Feb: Mon–Fri only.* *Jan 1, Presidents' Day, Thanksgiving, Dec 25, (limited schedule during year-end hols).* *for tours.* *in 20 languages.* ***Lectures, films.*** W www.un.org

When New York was chosen as the UN headquarters, philanthropist and multimillionaire John D. Rockefeller Jr. donated $8.5 million for the purchase of the East River site. This complex was the creation of American architect Wallace Harrison and a team of international consultants.

The United Nations was formed near the end of World War II to preserve world peace, promote self-determination, and to aid economic and social well-being around the globe. Currently 189 members meet regularly each year from mid-September to mid-December in the General Assembly, the closest thing to a world parliament.

The most powerful body is the Security Council, housed in the Conference Building. Here, delegates and their assistants meet around the horseshoe-shaped table to confer on issues related to international peace and security. In 1988, the UN was awarded the Nobel Peace Prize. The Trusteeship Council and the Economic and Social Council are in the same building.

The UN is an international zone and has its own stamps and post office. Daily guided tours show visitors the various council chambers and General Assembly hall.

## Rockefeller Center ㉗

**Map** E3. 630 5th Ave between 49th & 52nd Sts. *(212) 332-6868.* M *47th-50th Sts.* W www.rockefellercenter.com

A city within a city, and a National Historic Landmark, this urban wonder is the world's largest privately owned complex. Begun in the 1930s, it was built on a site leased by John D. Rockefeller Jr. for a new opera house he had planned. When the 1929 Depression scuttled the plans, Rockefeller, stuck with a long-term lease, went ahead with his own development. This was the first commercial project to integrate gardens, dining, and shopping with office space. The number of buildings has now grown to 19, though the newer structures do not match the Art Deco elegance of the original 14. The center's Channel Gardens, named after the English Channel because they separate the French and British buildings, change with the calendar.

The centerpiece of the center is the 70-story G.E. Building, headquarters of NBC studios. Backstage tours of the network's studios are a popular attraction. The TV show *Today* can also be viewed live every weekday morning from the sidewalk in front of the studio. Another attraction is the 1932 Radio City Music Hall. Once a movie palace, it now hosts dazzling events, including the annual Christmas and Easter shows. Its renovation in 1999 brought back the glitter and sparkle of the original interior. The center also houses a skating rink, and over 100 works of art, including a major mural in each building.

**A view of Rockefeller Center**

### Works of Art at the UN

The UN Building has acquired numerous works of art and reproductions by major artists; many have been gifts from member nations. Most of them have either a peace or international friendship theme. The legend on Norman Rockwell's *The Golden Rule* reads "Do unto others as you would have them do unto you." Marc Chagall designed a large stained-glass window as a memorial to former Secretary General Dag Hammarskjöld, who was accidentally killed while on a peace mission in 1961. A Henry Moore sculpture, *Reclining Figure: Hand* (1979), graces the grounds. There are many other sculptures and paintings by the artists of many nations.

***Reclining Figure: Hand* (1979), a gift from the Henry Moore Foundation**

The Great Bronze Doors in Saint Patrick's Church

## Saint Patrick's Cathedral ㉘

**Map** E3. 5th Ave & 50th St. *(212) 753-2261.* *6 to 51st St; E, F to Fifth Ave.* *M1, M2, M3, M4, M27, M50.* *7:30am–8:30pm daily.* *frequent Mon–Sat; 7, 8, 9, 10:15am & noon, 1, 4, 5:30pm Sun.* ***Concerts & lectures.***

NEW YORK's finest Gothic Revival building was designed by James Renwick Jr. and completed in 1878. This is also the largest Catholic cathedral in the United States and seats more than 2,500 people every Sunday. When Archbishop John Hughes decided to build a cathedral here in 1850, many criticized his choice of a site so far from the city's center at the time. Today his foresight has given the church one of the best locations in midtown Manhattan.

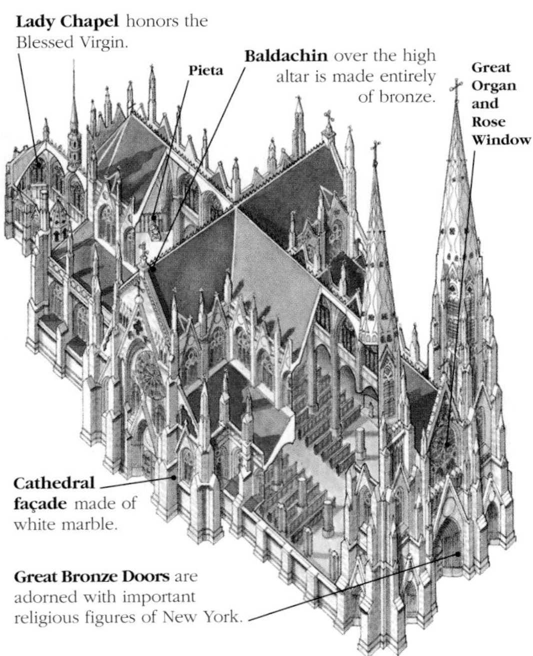


## Museum of Modern Art ㉙

**Map** E2. 11 W 53rd St. *(212) 708-9400.* *5th Ave–53rd St.* *M1, M2, M3, M4, M27, M50.* *10:30am–5:30pm Wed–Mon, 10:30am–8pm Fri.* *Tue, Dec 25.* *groups.* www.moma.org

ONE OF THE world's most comprehensive collections of modern art is on view at the Museum of Modern Art (MoMA). Founded in 1929, it set the standard for other museums of its kind. It was also the first art museum to include utilitarian objects in its collection, from ball bearings and silicon chips to household appliances.

Following a $650 million expansion project, MoMA re-opened in 2004. The renovated building provides gallery space over six floors, almost twice that of the old museum. Expanses of glass allow abundant natural light into the building. MoMA's collection includes some 150,000 works of art, ranging from Impressionist classics to an unrivaled collection of modern and contemporary art, including paintings, sculptures, prints, drawings, photographs and graphic designs. Some of the highlights of the collection include well-known works, such as Picasso's *Les Demoiselles d'Avigon* (1907), Van Gogh's *Starry Night* (1889), and Monet's *Water Lillies* (c.1920).

## Fifth Avenue ㉚

**Map** E2. *5th Ave–59th St.*

FROM ITS inception in the early 1800s, Fifth Avenue has been the territory of New York's rich and famous. Then, it was lined with palatial mansions built by the Astors, Vanderbilts, Belmonts, and Goulds, giving it the sobriquet Millionaires' Row. But as retail and commercial ventures set up outlets here in the 1900s, society moved farther north.

Today, the heart of New York's best-known avenue extends from the Empire State Building *(see p73)* to the Grand Army Plaza, presided over by the 1907 Plaza Hotel. Along this stretch are a range of famous stores symbolizing wealth and social standing, which have made Fifth Avenue synonymous with luxury goods.

The Cartier store, at 52nd Street, is housed in a 1905 Beaux Arts mansion, originally the home of banker Morton F. Plant, who supposedly traded it for a perfectly matched string of pearls. Other well-known jewelry and accessory stores include Tiffany's, made famous by Truman Capote's 1958 *Breakfast at Tiffany's*, Harry Winston, and Henri Bendel. Among the high-quality department stores are Saks Fifth Avenue, Bergdorf Goodman, and the wonderful F.A.O. Schwarz toy store.

# A Tour of Central Park ㉛

NEW YORK'S "BACKYARD," an 843-acre (340-ha) swath of green, provides recreation and beauty for residents and visitors. Designed by Frederick Law Olmsted and Calvert Vaux in 1858, the park took 16 years to create and involved the planting of over 500,000 trees and shrubs. A short walking tour from 59th to 79th Streets takes in some of Central Park's most picturesque features, from the dense wooded Ramble to the open formal spaces of Bethesda Terrace.

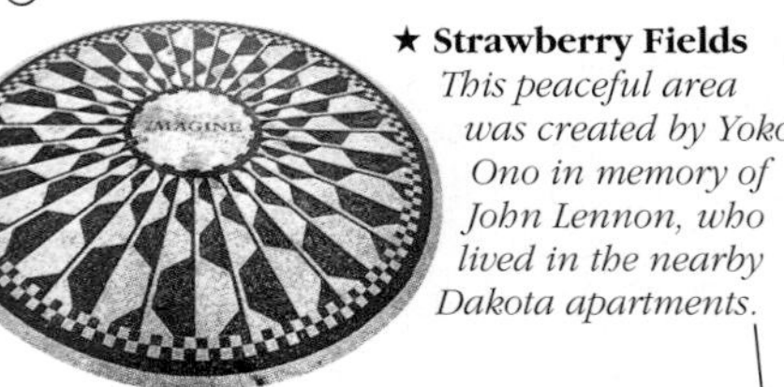


**★ Strawberry Fields**
*This peaceful area was created by Yoko Ono in memory of John Lennon, who lived in the nearby Dakota apartments.*

**★ Bethesda Fountain**
*The richly ornamented formal terrace overlooks the Lake and the wooded shores of the Ramble.*

**Wollman Rink**
*was restored by tycoon Donald Trump in the 1980s for future generations of skaters.*

**Wildlife Conservation Center** has three climate zones that are home to over 130 species of animals.

**The Pond**

**Plaza Hotel**

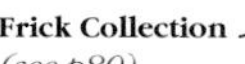

**Frick Collection**
*(see p80)*

**★ The Dairy**
*This Victorian Gothic building houses the visitor center. Make it your first stop and pick up a calendar of park events.*

**Hans Christian Andersen's Statue**
*A favorite Central Park landmark for children, this is a popular site for storytelling in summer.*

**Bow Bridge**
*This cast-iron bridge links the Ramble with Cherry Hill by a graceful arch, 60 ft (18 m) above the Lake.*

**LOCATOR MAP**
*See Map pp64–5*

**San Remo Apartments**
*This is one of the five twin-towered apartments on Central Park West, famed for their grace and architectural detail.*

**Alice in Wonderland** is immortalized in bronze at the northern end of Conservatory Water, along with the Cheshire Cat, the Mad Hatter, and the Dormouse.

**STAR SIGHTS**

- ★ **Belvedere Castle**
- ★ **Bethesda Fountain**
- ★ **Conservatory Water**
- ★ **Strawberry Fields**
- ★ **The Dairy**

**The Dakota Apartment Building**

**American Museum of Natural History** *(see p83)*

**Metropolitan Museum** *(see p80)*

**Obelisk**

**Reservoir**

**Guggenheim Museum** *(see p82)*

**The Ramble** is a wooded area of 37 acres (15 ha), crisscrossed by paths and streams. It is a paradise for bird-watchers – over 250 species have been spotted in the park, which is on the Atlantic migration flyway.

**★ Belvedere Castle**
*From the terraces there are unequaled views of the city and surrounding park. Within the stone walls is the Central Park Learning Center.*

**★ Conservatory Water**
*From March to November, this is the scene of model boat races each Saturday. Many of the tiny craft are stored in the boathouse that adjoins the Lake.*

## Whitney Museum of American Art ㉜

**Map** F2. 945 Madison Ave. *(212) 570-3600, (800) WHITNEY.* *6 to 77th St.* *M1, M2, M3, M4, 30, 72.* *11am–6pm Wed–Thu, Sat–Sun, 1–9pm Fri.* *public hols.* *(by donation 6–9pm Fri).* ***Lectures, film/video presentations.*** www.whitney.org

AN ENTIRE RANGE of 20th- and 21st-century American art is showcased in the Whitney Museum. Sculptor Gertrude Vanderbilt Whitney founded the museum in 1930 after the Metropolitan Museum of Art rejected her personal collection of works by living artists, such as George Bellows and Edward Hopper. Initially, the museum was set up behind Whitney's studio in Greenwich Village *(see pp70–71)* and moved to its present inverted pyramid building designed by Marcel Breuer in 1966. A midtown branch is now housed in the Philip Morris Building. The Leonard and Evelyn Lauder galleries on the fifth floor have permanent collections, showing works by Calder, O'Keeffe, and Hopper. Changing exhibitions occupy the lobby, and the second, third, and fourth floors. Highlights include Alexander Calder's fanciful sculpture *Circus* (1926–31), and works by Edward Hopper, whose *Early Sunday Morning* (1930) depicts the emptiness of American city life. Other artists represented here include Roy Lichtenstein. The Whitney Biennial takes place in even-numbered years and is the most significant survey of new trends in American art.

**James Whistler's second portrait of *Lady Meux* (1881), Frick Collection**

**The grand entrance of the Metropolitan Museum of Art**

## Frick Collection ㉝

**Map** F2. 1 E 70th St. *(212) 288-0700.* *6 to 68th St.* *M1, M2, M3, M4, 30, M72, M79.* *10am–6pm Tue–Sat, 1–6pm Sun.* *most public hols.* *(children under 10 not admitted).* ***Concerts, lectures, film & video.*** www.frick.org

THE PRICELESS art collection of steel magnate Henry Clay Frick (1849–1919) is exhibited in a residential setting amid the furnishings of his opulent mansion, providing a rare glimpse of how the extremely wealthy lived in New York's gilded age. Frick intended the collection to be a memorial to himself and bequeathed the entire house to the nation on his death.

The collection includes a suberb display of Old Master paintings, French furniture, and Limoges enamel. Of special interest is the skylit West Gallery offering oils by Hals, Rembrandt, and Vermeer, whose *Officer and the Laughing Girl* (1655–60) is a fine example of the Dutch painter's use of light and shadow. The Oval Room features Whistler, while the Library and Dining Room are devoted to English works. In the Living Hall are works by Titian, Bellini, and Holbein.

## Metropolitan Museum of Art ㉞

**Map** F2. 1000 Fifth Ave. *(212) 535-7710.* *4, 5, 6 to 86th St.* *M1, M2, M3, M4.* *9:30am–5:15pm Sun & Tue–Thu, 9:30am–8:45pm Fri, Sat.* *Jan 1, Thanksgiving, Dec 25.* ***Concerts, lectures, film & video presentations.*** www.metmuseum.org

ONE OF THE world's great museums, the Metropolitan houses treasures that span 5,000 years of culture from all over the world. Founded in 1870 by a group of artists and philanthropists who visualized an American art institution to rival those of Europe, it began with three private European collections and 174 paintings. Today, its holdings number over two million, and the original 1880 Gothic Revival building by Calvert Vaux and Jacob Wrey has been expanded many times. Recent additions are inviting courts with huge windows overlooking Central Park, and the breathtaking **Byzantine Galleries**, located under the Grand Staircase.

Most of the collections are housed on the two main floors. On the first floor are the **Costume Institute**, and part of the **Robert Lehman Collection**. This extraordinary private collection, acquired in 1969, includes Old Masters, Dutch, Spanish, and French artists, Post-Impressionists, and Fauvists, as well as ceramics and furniture. The state-of-the-art Costume Institute covers fashion trends from the 17th century to the present day. On view are Napoleonic and Victorian ballgowns, Elsa

*Cypresses* (1889), painting by Vincent Van Gogh

Schiaparelli's shocking pink evening dresses, creations by Worth and Quant, and the costumes of the Ballets Russes.

The second floor includes the **American Wing**, European Sculpture and Decorative Arts, **Egyptian Art**, and the **Michael C. Rockefeller Wing**. Built by Nelson Rockefeller in memory of his son, who lost his life on an art-finding expedition in New Guinea, the wing showcases a superb collection of over 1,600 primitive artworks from Africa, the islands of the Pacific, and the Americas. Among the African works are outstanding ivory and bronze sculptures from the royal kingdom of Benin (Nigeria). Also on view are pre-Columbian gold, ceramics, and stonework from Mexico and Central and South America. The American Wing has one of the world's finest collections of American paintings, including several by Edward Hopper. Prize exhibits include Gilbert Stuart's first portrait of George Washington, John Singer Sargent's notorious portrait of *Madame X*, and the monumental *Washington Crossing the Delaware* by Emanuel Leutze. There are also period rooms, including one designed by Frank Lloyd Wright, and Tiffany glass.

The Metropolitan has one of the largest collections of Egyptian art outside Cairo. Objects range from the fragmented jasper lips of a 15th-century BC queen to the massive Temple of Dendur. Many of the objects were discovered during museum-sponsored expeditions during the early 20th century.

The **Lila Wallace Wing** holds the museum's growing contemporary art collection. Some great works include Picasso's portrait of *Gertrude Stein* (1905) and Jackson Pollock's *Autumn Rhythm*.

The heart of the museum, however, is its awe-inspiring collection of 3,000 **European Paintings**. Its highlights are masterpieces by Dutch and Flemish painters, specifically Brueghel's *The Harvesters* (1551) and Rembrandt's *Self Portrait* (1660), painted when he was 54. Among the finest Impressionist and Post-Impressionist paintings is *Cypresses* (1889), painted by Vincent Van Gogh the year before he died.

The third floor has a comprehensive collection of **Asian Art**, featuring textiles, sculpture, and ceramics from China, Japan, Korea, Southeast Asia, and India. The full-size Ming-style Chinese scholar's garden in the Astor Court was built by craftspeople from Souzhou. The **Cantor Roof Garden** has superb annual shows of 20th-century sculpture, displayed against the dramatic backdrop of the city's skyline. Guests can also visit the museum shops, located on the main floor and mezzanine.

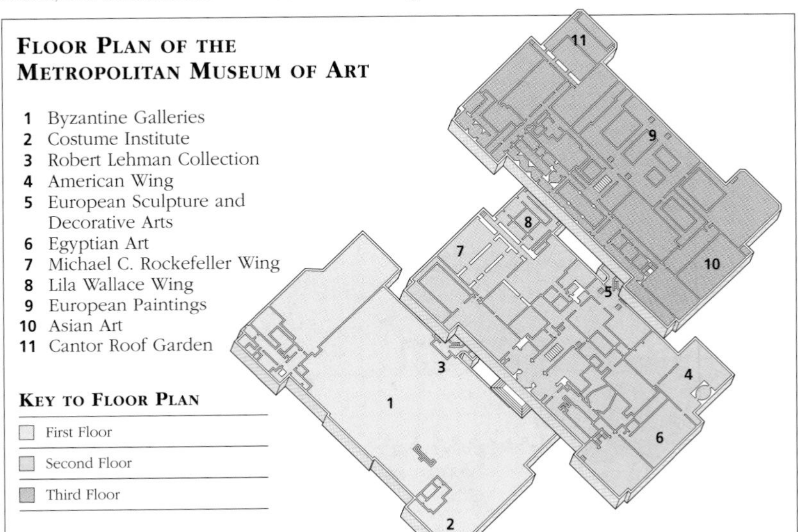

## The Solomon R. Guggenheim Museum ㉟

1071 5th Ave at 89th St. *(212) 423-3500.* *4, 5, 6 to 86th St.* *M1, M2, M3, M4.* *10am–5:45pm Sat–Wed, 10am–8pm Fri.* *Jan 1, Dec 25.* ***Concerts, lectures, performing art series.*** www.guggenheim.org

One of the world's finest collections of modern and contemporary art is housed in a building that is considered one of the great architectural achievements of the 20th century. The only New York building to be designed by the celebrated American architect Frank Lloyd Wright *(see p396)*, it was completed after his death in 1959. Its shell-like façade is a New York landmark, while the interior is dominated by a spiral ramp that curves down and inward from the dome, passing works by major 19th- and 20th-century artists.

Over the years, Solomon Guggenheim's core collection of Abstract art has been added to by donations of several important collections. The museum now owns a large body of work by famous artists such as Kandinsky, and major holdings of Brancusi, Calder, Klee, Chagall, Miró, Léger, Mondrian, Picasso, Oldenberg, and Rauschenberg.

Not all of the permanent collection is on display at any one time. Only a small portion is on view as the main gallery, the Great Rotunda, usually features special exhibitions. The Small Rotunda shows some of the museum's famous Impressionist and Post-Impressionist holdings. The new Tower galleries feature exhibitions of work from the permanent collection and contemporary pieces. A fifth-floor sculpture terrace overlooks the scenic Central Park.

**Cézanne's *Man With Arms Crossed* (1895-1900), Guggenheim Museum**

Two important acquisitions of the museum are the Justin Thannhauser collection and more than a 100 photographs from the Robert Mapplethorpe Foundation.

Guggenheim SoHo, a downtown site, closed down recently in 2002 but a new Guggenheim, designed by Frank Gehry, is to be built near the South Street Seaport *(see p68)*. This museum will house the postwar collection and have two theaters.

### The Solomon R. Guggenheim Museum

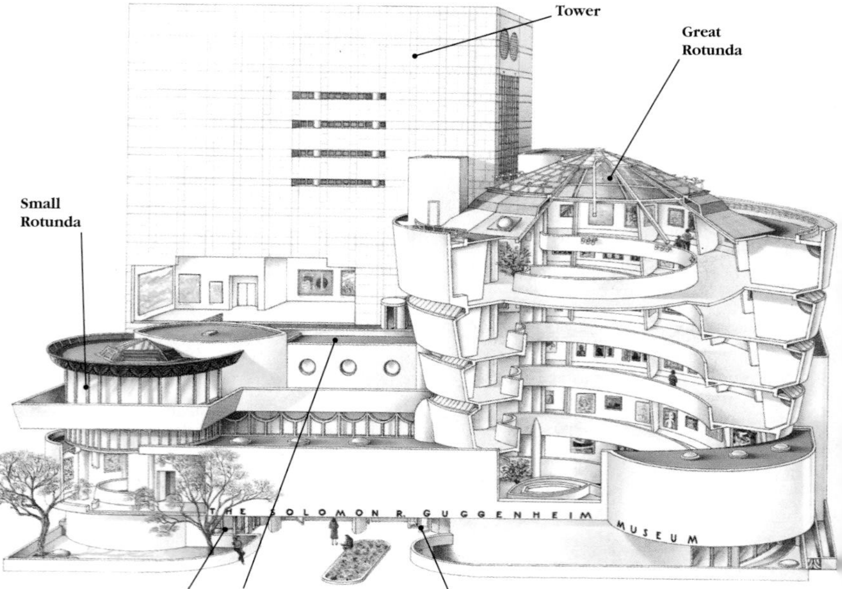

## American Museum of Natural History ㊱

Central Park West at 79th St. (212) 769-5100. B, C to 81st St. M7, M10, M11, M79. 10am–5.45pm daily. Donation. **Rose Center** until 8:45pm Fri. www.amnh.org

This is one of the largest natural history museums in the world, attracting more than 4.5 million visitors each year. Since the original building opened in 1877, the complex has grown to cover four city blocks, and today holds more than 30 million specimens and artifacts. The most popular areas are the dinosaurs, and the newly renovated Milstein Family Hall of Ocean Life.

Enter at Central Park West onto the second floor to view the Barosaurus exhibit, African, Asian, Central and South American peoples, and animals. First floor exhibits include ocean life, meteors, minerals and gems, and the Hall of Biodiversity. North American Indians, birds, and reptiles occupy the third floor. Dinosaurs, fossil fishes, and early mammals are on the fourth floor.

The new **Rose Center** for Earth and Space has as its centerpiece the Hayden Planetarium. The planetarium contains a technologically advanced Space Theater, the famous Cosmic Pathway, and a Big Bang Theater.

**Barosaurus, American Museum of Natural History**

**The Lincoln Center for the Performing Arts complex**

## Lincoln Center ㊲

Broadway between W 62nd & W 65th Sts. 1,9 to 66th St. M5, 7, 10, 11, 66, 104.

A giant cultural complex, built in the 1950s, Lincoln Center was conceived when both the Metropolitan Opera House and the New York Philharmonic needed homes. At that time, the notion of a single complex where different performing arts could exist side by side, was considered both daring and risky. Today, the Lincoln Center draws audiences of over five million each year.

The **Lincoln Center for the Performing Arts** was born in May 1959, when President Eisenhower traveled to New York to turn a shovelful of earth, composer Leonard Bernstein lifted his baton, and the New York Philharmonic and the Juilliard Choir broke into the *Hallelujah Chorus*. The center soon covered 15 acres (6 ha) on the site of the slums that had once been the setting for Bernstein's classic musical *West Side Story*.

Lincoln Center includes the **New York State Theater**, home to the highly acclaimed New York City Ballet and the New York City Opera, a troupe devoted to presenting opera at popular prices; and the **Metropolitan Opera House**, the focal point of the plaza. This fine building has five great arched windows, which offer views of the opulent foyer and two radiant murals by Marc Chagall. All the greats have sung here, including Maria Callas, Jessye Norman, and Luciano Pavarotti. The other two significant institutions here are the Lincoln Center Theater and Avery Fisher Hall, home to the New York Philharmonic, America's oldest orchestra (scheduled to return to Carnegie Hall in 2006). The best way to see the complex is by guided tour.

Although the **American Folk Art Museum** is now housed in a dramatic state-of-the-art building on West 53rd Street, the museum continues to operate the **Eva and Morris Feld Gallery** at the Lincoln Center. The gallery provides additional exhibition space for the museum, for displaying artwork from the museum's permanent collection, such as quilts, carvings, and paintings. The museum itself is well worth a visit to see its extensive collection of folk art.

The **Hotel des Artistes**, nearby, was built in 1918 as working artists' studios. Interesting residents have included Alexander Woollcott, Isadora Duncan, Noël Coward, Rudolf Valentino, and Norman Rockwell. The Café des Artistes is well known for its misty, romantic Howard Chandler Christy murals and fine cuisine.

**Lincoln Center for the Performing Arts**
(212) 546-2656. (212) 875-5350. www.lincolncenter.org

**American Folk Art Museum**
45 West 53rd Street. (212) 265-1040. 10:30am–5:30pm Wed– Thu & Sat–Sun; 10:30am-7:30pm Fri. www.folkartmuseum.org

**Eva and Morris Feld Gallery**
2 Lincoln Square. (212) 977-7170. 11am–7:30pm Tue–Sun; 11am–6pm Mon. www.folkartmuseum.org

# Greater New York

THOUGH OFFICIALLY PART of New York City, upper Manhattan and the boroughs outside Manhattan are very different in feel and spirit. Away from the bustle of the inner city, they are residential and do not have the famous skyscrapers of New York. The difference is evident even in the way residents describe a trip to Manhattan as "going into the city." Yet these areas feature such attractions as Columbia University, the city's largest zoo, botanical gardens, museums, churches, beaches, and huge sports arenas.

**View across Columbia University's quadrangle toward Butler Library**

## Columbia University ㊳

**Map** F4. Main entrance at W 116th St & Broadway. *(212) 854-1754.* *116th St-Columbia University (lines 1, 2).* www.columbia.edu

ONE OF America's oldest and finest universities, Columbia was founded as King's College under a charter granted by King George II of Great Britain, in 1754. Originally situated in lower Manhattan, the present campus was built in Morningside Heights. Architects McKim, Mead & White, who designed its first buildings around a central quadrangle, placed the university on a terrace, serenely above street level. A Classical, columned building, the **Low Library**, dominates the quadrangle. Daniel Chester French's statue *Alma Mater,* in front of it, became familiar as the backdrop to the 1968 anti-Vietnam War student demonstrations. The building now houses offices, and the rotunda is used for a variety of academic and ceremonial purposes. Its books were moved to Butler Library, across the quadrangle, in 1932. To the right, the 1904 **St. Paul's Chapel** is known for its fine woodwork and vaulted interior. The whole chapel is bathed in light from above, and has fine acoustics.

Columbia, part of the Ivy League, is noted for its law, medicine, and journalism schools. Founded in 1912 by publisher Joseph Pulitzer, the School of Journalism is the home of the Pulitzer Prize awarded for the best in letters and music. Columbia's distinguished faculty and alumni, past and present, include over 50 Nobel laureates. Famous alumni include Isaac Asimov, J.D. Salinger, and James Cagney.

Visitors to the campus can stroll along the central quadrangle, where jeans-clad future leaders of America meet and mingle between classes. Across from the campus are the cafés where students engage in lengthy philosophical arguments, debate in the topics of the day, or simply unwind.

Also across the campus to the east on Amsterdam Avenue lies the **Cathedral of St. John the Divine**. Begun in 1892 and only two-thirds finished, with its 600 ft (180 m) long and 146 ft (45 m) wide interior, this Neo-Gothic cathedral, with its hand-carved gargoyles, is slated to be the largest in the world. Medieval construction methods, such as stone on stone with supporting buttresses, continue to be used to complete the structure, which is also a venue for theater, music, and avant-garde art.

**St. Paul's Chapel**
Columbia University. *(212) 854-1487 concert info.* *116th St-Columbia Univv.* *10am–11pm Mon–Sat (term time), 10am–4pm (breaks).* *Sun.*

**Cathedral of St. John the Divine**
Amsterdam Ave at W 112th St. *(212) 316-7540.* *1, 2 to Cathedral Pkwy (110th St).* *M4, M5, M7, M11, M104.* *7am–6pm daily.* *Vespers 7pm Sun. Donations.* ***Concerts, plays, lectures, exhibitions, gardens.*** www.stjohndivine.org

## Riverside Church ㊴

**Map** F4. 490 Riverside Dr at 122nd St. *(212) 870-6700.* *116th St-Columbia Univ.* *10:30am–5pm Tue–Sun.* *10:45am Sun.* *with prior permission.* **Carillon Bell Concerts** *(212) 870-6784. noon, 3pm Sun.* **Theater** *(212) 864-2929.* www.theriversidechurchny.org

THE DESIGN OF Riverside Church was inspired by the cathedral at Chartres in France. This Gothic church with a 21-story steel frame was lavishly funded by John D. Rockefeller Jr, in 1930.

The Laura Spelman Rockefeller Memorial Carillon (in honor of Rockefeller's mother) is the largest in the world, with 74 bells. The 20-ton Bourdon, or hour bell, is the largest and heaviest tuned carillon bell ever cast. The organ, with its 22,000 pipes, is among the world's largest. The second gallery features a figure by Jacob Epstein, *Christ in Majesty,* cast in plaster and covered in gold leaf. Another Epstein

**Carved stonework at the Cathedral of St. John the Divine**

The 21-story Riverside Church, from the north

statue, *Madonna and Child*, stands in the court next to the cloister. The screen panels honor eight men and women including Socrates, Michelangelo, Florence Nightingale, and Booker T. Washington, whose lives exemplified the teachings of Christ.

For quiet reflection, enter the small, secluded Christ Chapel, patterned after an 11th-century Romanesque church in France. Visitors can take the elevator to the 20th floor and then walk the 140 steps to the top of the 392-ft (120-m) bell tower for a fine panorama of Upper Manhattan from the windy observation deck. There is no access to the bell tower during carillon concerts.

## St. Nicholas Historic District ⑩

**Map** F4. 202–250 W 138th & W 139th St. **M** *135th St (B, C).*

A STARTLING CONTRAST to the run-down surroundings, the two blocks here, known as the King Model Houses, were built in 1891 when Harlem was considered a neighborhood for New York's gentry. They still comprise one of the city's most distinctive examples of row townhouses. A distinct feature of these houses is the provision of a central service alley that can be accessed from the avenue ends and at different points along the block. The alley serves a very useful feature in concealing garbage cans and service deliveries.

The developer, David King, chose three leading architects, who succeeded in blending their different styles to create a harmonious whole. The most famous of these was the firm of McKim, Mead & White, who were responsible for the northernmost row of solid brick Renaissance palaces. Their homes featured ground floor entrances rather than the typical New York brownstone stoops. The parlor floors have ornate wrought-iron balconies below, as well as carved decorative medallions above their windows.

The Georgian buildings designed by Price and Luce are built of buff brick with white stone trim. James Brown Lord's Georgian-style buildings feel much closer to Victorian, with outstanding red-brick façades and brownstone foundations.

Over the years, many distinguished professional and civic leaders made their homes here. Among them were celebrated musicians W.C. Handy and Eubie Blake, and one of the founders of the American Negro Theater, Abram Hill. He collaborated in the production of a play set in the historic district and called it "On Striver's Row," a name by which the district is now commonly known.

## Studio Museum in Harlem ⑪

**Map** F4. 144 W 125th St. *(212) 864-4500.* **M** *125th St (2, 3).* *noon–6pm Wed, Thu, noon–8pm Fri, 10am–6pm Sat, Sun.* *Jan 1, Thanksgiving, Dec 25.* ***Donation*** ***Lectures, children's programs, films.*** www.studiomuseum.org

THE MUSEUM WAS founded in 1967 in a loft on upper Fifth Avenue with the mission of becoming the premier center for the collection and exhibition of the art and artifacts of African Americans.

The present premises, a five-story building on Harlem's main commercial street, was donated to the museum by the New York Bank for Savings in 1979. There are galleries on two levels for changing exhibitions featuring artists and cultural themes, and three galleries are devoted to the permanent collection of works by major black artists, such as Romare Bearden and Elizabeth Catlett.

The photographic archives comprise one of the most complete records in existence of Harlem in its heyday. From the main floor a side door opens onto a small sculpture garden. In addition to its excellent exhibitions, the museum also maintains a national artist-in-residence program and offers regular lectures, children's programs, and film festivals. A range of books and African crafts are available in the small shop.

Exhibition space at the Studio Museum in Harlem

## The Cloisters ㊷

**Map** F4. Fort Tryon Park. *(212) 923-3700.* *A to 190th St (exit via elevator).* *M4.* *Mar–Oct: 9:30am–5:15pm Tue–Sun; Nov–Feb: 9:30am–4:45pm Tue–Sun.* *Jan 1, Thanksg., Dec 25.* *donations. No videos.* *book in advance.* ***Concerts.*** www.metmuseum. org

**Vaulted ceiling of the Pontaut Chapter House at the Cloisters**

THIS WORLD-FAMOUS branch of the Metropolitan Museum *(see pp80–81)*, devoted to medieval art, resides in a building that incorporates medieval cloisters, chapels, and halls. The museum, organized in chronological order, starts with the Romanesque period (AD 1000) and moves to the Gothic (1150 to 1520). It is noted for its exquisite illuminated manuscripts, stained glass, metalwork, enamels, ivories, and beautifully preserved tapestries. Perhaps the most interesting exhibits in the Cloisters are the gardens, planted according to horticultural information found in medieval treatises and poetry. Early music concerts are performed regularly here and are extremely popular. Call in advance for tickets.

**Intricate floral ornamentation** can be found on the capitals of the Saint-Guilhem Cloister.

**Pontaut Chapter House**

**Unicorn Tapestries** featured on the upper floor were woven in Brussels around 1500 and depict the quest and capture of the mythical unicorn.

**Romanesque Hall**

**Upper floor**

**The 12th-century** Cuxa Cloister features Romanesque architectural detail and motifs.

**The Campin Room** is the location of the *Annunciation* Triptych by Robert Campin, a magnificent example of early Flemish painting.

**Lower floor**

**Main entrance**

**Bonnefont Cloister**

**Trie Cloister**

**The Treasury** houses several exquisite Gothic illuminated manuscripts and folios, such as *Les Belles Heures*, the book of hours, commissioned by Jean, Duc de Berry.

**Jungle World, a climate-controlled tropical rainforest at the Bronx Zoo**

## The Bronx ㊸

**Map** F4. M *161st St (Yankee Std); 2, 5 to Tremont Ave (Bronx Zoo); 4, D to Bedford Park Blvd (NY Bot. Garden).*

ONCE A PROSPEROUS suburb with a famous Grand Concourse lined with apartment buildings for the wealthy, parts of the Bronx have now become a symbol of urban decay. However, visitors still frequent the area to escape the overwhelming city concrete for some beauty and quiet, while New Yorkers flock to the 1923 **Yankee Stadium**, home of the New York Yankees baseball team. Don't miss a sidetrip to one of the city's wealthiest and most beautiful parts – Riverdale – located between W 242 and Broadway.

But the most outstanding attraction of the Bronx is the **Bronx Zoo**. Opened in 1899, this is the largest urban zoo in the US, home to some 7,166 animals of 531 species, living in realistic representations of their natural habitats. The Park is a leader in the perpetuation of endangered species, such as the Indian rhinoceros and the snow leopard. Its 265 acres (107 ha) of woods, streams, and parklands include a children's zoo, camel safaris, a seasonal Skyfari cable car, and a shuttle train that takes visitors around the sprawling park.

Across the road from the Zoo's main entrance, visitors can experience 250 acres (101 ha) of beauty and hands-on enjoyment at the **New York Botanical Garden**. One of the oldest and largest botanical gardens in the world, it has 48 specialty gardens and plant collections, 50 acres (20 ha) of virgin forest, and a vast Children's Adventure Garden. The Enid A. Haupt conservatory with 11 interconnected glass galleries has been wonderfully restored as "A World of Plants," with misty tropical rainforests and dramatic deserts.

### Bronx Zoo

Fordham Rd /Bronx River Pkwy. *(718) 367-1010.* *Nov–Mar: 10am–4:30pm daily; Apr–Oct: 10am–5pm daily (5:30pm Sat & Sun).* *(free Wed & 10am–noon Sat).* ***Children's zoo.*** W www.wcs.org

## Brooklyn ㊹

**Map** F5. M *Prospect Pk (Brooklyn Bot. Gardens); 2, 3 to Eastern Pkwy (Brooklyn Mus); Kingston (Brooklyn Children's Mus); Stillwell Ave (Coney Is).*

ONE OF THE most ethnically diverse boroughs in New York, Brooklyn, if it were a separate city, would be the country's fourth largest. Many entertainment greats, such as Mel Brooks, Phil Silvers, Woody Allen, and Neil Simon, celebrate their birthplace with great affection and humor. . Among the diverse neighborhoods are the historic residential districts of Park Slope and Brooklyn Heights, beautiful tree-lined enclaves that offer a wonderful stroll past Victorian houses and cafés. An oval gateway in the Grand Army Plaza, designed by Frederick Law Olmsted and Calvert Vaux, leads to the lush, green Prospect Park.

The adjacent **Brooklyn Botanic Gardens** feature a traditional Elizabethan-style "knot" herb garden, one of the largest bonsai and rose collections in the country, and some rare rainforest trees.

To its southeast, lies the 1897 **Brooklyn Museum of Art**, designed by McKim, Mead & White. Though only one-fifth completed, the museum is one of the most impressive cultural institutions in the US, with a permanent collection of some 1.5 million objects, housed in a grand five-story structure spanning 560,000 sq ft (41,805 sq m). Highlights include African, Oceanic, and New World art; a collection of classic Egyptian and ancient Middle Eastern artifacts, and some works of American and European contemporary art.

To the north on Brooklyn Avenue lies the imaginative **Brooklyn Children's Museum**, the world's first designed especially for young people. Programs and displays are based on a remarkable collection of 20,000 cultural artifacts and natural history specimens, live plants and animals, and interactive exhibits, all designed to satisfy the curiosity of young minds.

Brooklyn poet Walt Whitman composed many of his works on the borough's farthest point, **Coney Island**. It was billed as the "World's Largest Playground" in the 1920s, with its combination of hair-raising rides and lovely beaches. Today, Coney Island is a bit run down but holds historical memorabilia. A short trip to the New York Aquarium is a must.

**Ibis Coffin (332–330 BC) in gold leaf and silver, Brooklyn Museum of Art**

### Brooklyn Museum of Art

200 Eastern Pkwy, Brooklyn. *(718) 638-5000.* *10am–5pm Wed–Fri, 11am–6pm Sat, 11am–11pm first Sat in month, 11am–6pm Sun.* *Jan 1, Thanksgiving, Dec 25. Donation expected.* ***Concerts, lectures.*** W www.brooklynmuseum.org

# New York City Practical Information

Visitors to New York are treated very much the same as anyone else. While you may not be given special treatment, as long as you follow a few guidelines on personal security you'll be able to explore the city as freely as any native New Yorker. Buses and subway trains are reliable and inexpensive. Beside, the wide range of prices offered by the many hotels, restaurants, and entertainment venues means your New York trip can be both fun and affordable.

## Tourist Information

Advice on any aspect of life in New York City is available from the **New York Convention and Visitors' Bureau (NYC & Co.)**. Their 24-hour touch-tone phone service offers help outside office hours. Brochures and information kiosks are also found at the walk-in office of the **Times Square Visitors Bureau**.

## Personal Security

Though New York is rated among the safest large US cities with around-the-clock foot, horse, bike, and car patrols by the police in tourist areas, it is always good to be cautious. Avoid certain areas, such as Chinatown and Lower East Side after dark. At night, if you can't afford a taxi, try to travel with a group. Walk as if you know where you're going. Avoid making eye contact and getting into confrontations with down-and-outs. If someone asks you for money, do not get drawn into conversation. Always keep change handy for phone calls or bus fares; carry your Metrocard in your pocket. Never carry too much cash, and lock your valuables in the hotel safe. Do not allow anyone except hotel or airport personnel to carry your luggage.

Public toilets in bus stations should be avoided. It is best to find a hotel or store if you want to use a restroom. Since parks are also often used for drug dealing, they are safest when there is a crowd for a rally or concert. If you want to go for a jog, avoid lonely areas and pathways, and follow a map of safe routes.

## Getting Around

New York's rush hours extend from 8 to 10am, 11:30am to 1:30pm and 4:30 to 6:30pm, Mon–Fri. During these times, every form of public transportation is crowded, and the streets are much harder to navigate on foot.

Buses are a comfortable way to get around, but they often tend to be slow. Subways are quick, reliable, and inexpensive, and make stops throughout central Manhattan. The vast system extends over 233 miles (375 km) and most routes operate throughout the year. You can buy a Metrocard for subway and bus fares. Cards come in $5 to $80 amounts depending on the number of trips you intend to take. Taxis are best for door-to-door service, but can be held up in traffic jams. You should hail only yellow taxis, as they are the only ones with licences. Accepting a ride from anyone else can be dangerous. If their roof numbers are lit up, they are available.

Heavy traffic and expensive rentals make driving in New York a frustrating experience. The speed limit is 30 mph (48 km/h) – which is hard to exceed due to traffic. Parking in Manhattan is difficult and costly. Many hotels include parking charges in their room rates. New York's tow-away crews are active, and one-third of cars towed suffer damage. If you cannot find your car at its parking place, first call the traffic department's tow-away office. For specific details call the **Department of Transportation**. If you receive a parking ticket, you have seven days to pay the hefty fine. If the car is not at the pound, report it to the police.

## Etiquette

It is illegal to smoke in *any* public place or building in New York. Bars all over the city also ban smoking.

Tipping for service is part of New York life. In general, 10 to 15 percent of your bill is sufficient, though 20 percent for outstanding service is always appreciated.

## Entertainment

New York City is a non-stop entertainment extravaganza, every day, all year round. Whatever your taste, you can be sure the city will satisfy it on both a grand and an intimate scale.

New York is famous for its extravagant musicals and its ferocious critics. The Times Square area hosts the "power productions" of Broadway – the big, highly publicized dramas, musicals, and revivals starring many Hollywood luminaries in sure-fire money earners, in theaters such as the **Ambassador** and the **Lyceum** (1903), the oldest theater still in operation. Off-Broadway and Off-Off-Broadway stages such as **Actors' Playhouse**, host experimental shows, ranging from the well-appointed to the improvised, in lofts, churches, or even outside at the open-air **Delacorte Theater** in Central Park.

The city is also a great center of traditional ballet and modern dance. The New York City Ballet, founded by the legendary choreographer George Balanchine, performs in the **New York State Theater**. The **Dance Theater of Harlem** is world famous for its modern, and ethnic productions.

There's every imaginable form of music in New York, from international stadium rock to the sounds of the 1960s, from Dixieland jazz or country blues, soul, and world music to street musicians. The city's music scene changes at a dizzying pace, with many new arrivals, so there's no way to predict what you may find when you arrive. The top performers such as Elton John, Bruce Springsteen, and the Stones perform in the huge arenas at **Shea Stadium** and **Madison Square Garden**. The **Knitting Factory** has live jazz and new music. The **Limelight** is a good bet for the latest sounds and newest groups.

New York's nightlife and club scene is legendary. Whatever your preference – noisy disco, stand-up comedy, or the soothing melodies of a Harry Connick Jr. – you'll be amazed at the choice. New Yorkers thrive on dancing. Dance floors available all over the city range from the ever-popular **SOB's** – for jungle, reggae, soul, jazz, and salsa – to huge basketball-court-sized places, such as **Roseland**. The historic **Copacabana** alternates live bands with a popular disco.

The city is also a film buff's paradise. Apart from new US releases, which show months in advance of other countries, many classic and foreign films are screened in this hotbed for new and innovative talent.

New Yorkers are sports crazy, and there are activities to suit every taste. Visitors can choose from health clubs and horseback riding to playing tennis or jogging. Spectator sports are provided by professional baseball (**Yankee Stadium**), ice hockey and basketball (**Madison Square Garden**), and football (Giants Stadium), while for tennis fans there is the US Open and Virginia Slims tournaments.

## Shopping

NEW YORK IS the consumer capital of the world: a shopper's paradise, with dazzling displays and a staggering variety of goods for sale. Everything is available here, from high fashion to rare books, state-of-the-art electronics, and an array of exotic food. Keep in mind that the city's sales tax is a hefty 8.625%.

Known as the fashion capital of America, New York boasts such names as **Polo/Ralph Lauren** and **Calvin Klein**. There are fashion stores such as **Brooks Brothers** (menswear) and **Ann Taylor** (women's wear), and shops of international names such as **Yves St. Laurent** and **Giorgio Armani**. Manhattan is also known for its world-class jewelry shops including **Cartier** and **Tiffany's**. The city is a bargain hunter's dream, with huge discounts on anything from household goods to designer clothes.

As the publishing capital of the US, New York has the country's best bookstores. Don't miss the **Barnes & Noble** stores, the **Strand** for rare and used books, and **Shakespeare & Co**.

Dozens of tiny shops around the city specialize in unusual merchandise, from butterflies and bones to toy firefighting equipment and occult potions. Don't miss a trip to the legendary **FAO Schwarz** for toys of all kinds. Some of New York's best souvenirs can be found in the city's many museum shops, including the **Museum of Arts & Design** and the **American Museum of Natural History**.

## Directory

### Tourist Offices

**NYC & Co.**
W www.nycvisit.com
W www.ci.nyc.ny.us

**Times Square Visitors' Bureau**
W www.timessquarenyc.org

### Transportation

**Department of Transportation**
Staten Island Ferry, S Ferry.
*(212) 487-5761 or 66.*

### Bars & Clubs

**Copacabana**
560 W 34th St.
*(212) 582-2672.*

**Roseland**
239 W 52nd St.
*(212) 247-0200.*

**SOB's**
204 Varick St.
*(212) 243-4940.*

### Entertainment

**Actors' Playhouse**
100 Seventh Ave S.
*(212) 463-0060.*

**Ambassador**
219 W 49th St.
*(212) 239-6200.*

**Dance Theater of Harlem**
466 W 152nd St.
*(212) 690-2800.*

**Delacorte Theater**
Central Park, 81st St.
*(212) 549-8750 (summer time only).*

**Knitting Factory**
74 Leonard St, New York City.
*(212) 219-3132.*

**Limelight**
660 6th Ave
*(212) 807-7780.*

**Lyceum**
149 W 45th St, New York City.
*(212) 239-6200.*

**Madison Sq. Garden**
7th Ave at 33rd St.
*(212) 465-6741.*
W www.thegarden.com

**New York State Theater**
Lincoln Center, Broadway at 65th St.
*(212) 870-5570.*

**Yankee Stadium**
River Ave at 161st St, Bronx.
*(718) 293-4300.*

### Shopping

**American Museum of Natural History**
W 79th St, Central Park W.
*(212) 769-5100.*

**Ann Taylor**
645 Madison Ave.
*(212) 832-2010.*

**Barnes & Noble**
105 5th Ave.
*(212) 807-0099.*

**Brooks Brothers**
346 Madison Ave.
*(212) 682-8800.*

**Cartier**
653 5th Ave.
*(212) 753-0111.*

**FAO Schwarz**
767 5th Ave.
*(212) 644-9400.*

**Giorgio Armani**
760 Madison Ave.
*(212) 988-9191.*

**Museum of Arts & Design**
40 W 53rd St.
*(212) 956-3535.*

**Polo/Ralph Lauren**
Madison Ave at 72nd St.
*(212) 606-2100.*

**Strand Book Store**
828 Broadway.
*(212) 473-1452.*

**Tiffany & Co**
5th Ave at 57th St.
*(212) 755-8000.*

**Yves St. Laurent Rive Gauche**
859 Madison Ave.
*(212) 517-7400.*

# New York State

STRETCHING NORTH FOR OVER 200 miles (322 km) to the Canadian border, and 400 miles (644 km) west to the Great Lakes, the "Empire State" is a world away from New York City. Due east of Manhattan, Long Island is the largest island adjoining the continental US, with miles and miles of suburbs, farmland, and beaches jutting out into the Atlantic Ocean. To the north, the Hudson River is an area of opulent mansions and small towns. The state capital, Albany, marks the start of the vast Upstate area, comprising the Adirondacks, rural farmland, and vibrant cities.

## Jones Beach State Park ❷

Wantagh. *Long Island Railroad from Penn Station to Jones Beach. Operates Jun–Labor Day, (718) 217-5477.* *(516) 785-1600.*
*Jun–Labor Day: sunrise–midnight.*
www.visitjonesbeach.com

LOCATED ON Long Island, Jones Beach State Park is only 33 miles (53 km) from Midtown Manhattan. A popular destination since it was created in 1929, this barrier island resort features more than 2,400 acres (972 ha) of parkland, beaches, and a wide variety of outdoor and cultural activities.

The park's oceanside beaches are complemented by a stillwater bayside beach and several swimming, diving, and wading pools, and surf facilities. The park's other recreational options include golf courses, restaurants, fishing docks, and a 2-mile (3-km) boardwalk.

The 11,200-seat **Jones Beach Theater** is a popular venue for rock and pop concerts in summer. Another landmark, the 200-ft (61-m), brick-and-stone structure, the **Jones Beach Tower**, is modeled on the campanile of St. Mark's Cathedral in Venice.

## The Hamptons & Montauk ❸

*15,000.*
*(877) 386-6654.*
www.hamptonstravelguide.com

AT RIVERHEAD, Long Island splits into two peninsulas – the mostly pastoral North Fork and the more urban South Fork. Most of South Fork's beaches and cultural attractions are concentrated in the expensive and trendy summer retreats of The Hamptons and Montauk.

Most New Yorkers tend to associate The Hamptons (from west to east, Westhampton Beach, Hampton Bays, Southampton, Bridgehampton, East Hampton, and Amagansett) exclusively with its many celebrity residents. However, the area also has a rich historical heritage. In the 19th-century whaling community of Sag Harbor, to the north of Bridgehampton, the **Old Custom House**, built in 1789, commemorates the town's post-Revolutionary War heyday as one of the first official ports of entry into the young US. On the Village Green in East Hampton, the **Home Sweet Home Museum** houses a variety of early Colonial, rough-shingled structures, including a classic saltbox house built in 1750, and the still-operational Old Hook Mill, constructed in 1806.

The easternmost Long Island community, Montauk is a busy summer resort, serving as a jumping-off point for the area's nature trails and beaches. Other activities are golf, horseback riding, and fishing. Montauk State Park contains the **Montauk Point Lighthouse**, commissioned by George Washington in 1792. Still in operation, the octagonal stone structure is an important landmark for oceangoing vessels.

**The octagonal Montauk Point Lighthouse, completed in 1796**

**One of the many swimming pools at Jones Beach State Park**

### Custom House

Main St. & Garden Sq, Sag Harbor.
*(631) 692-4664.* *Jul–Aug: 10am–5pm daily; Memorial Day–Jun & Labor Day–Oct: 10am–5pm Sat–Sun.* *public hols.*
www.splia.org/museum_custom.html

### Home Sweet Home Museum

14 James Lane, East Hampton.
*(631) 324-0713.* *May–Sep: 10am–4pm Mon–Sat, 2–4pm Sun; Oct–Nov: 2–4pm Fri–Sun.*
*public hols.*
www.easthampton.com/homesweethome

# Hudson River Valley ❹

3 Neptune Rd, Poughkeepsie. (845) 463-4000. www.dutchesstourism.com

FROM ITS SOURCE high in the Adirondack Mountains, the Hudson courses past bustling riverport towns and the dramatic Catskill and Taconic mountain ranges for nearly 315 miles (507 km) to its mouth at New York harbor. Strikingly beautiful and strategically located, the valley has played a pivotal role in North American military, economic, and cultural history.

Settled by the Dutch in the 1620s *(see p43)*, it was soon dotted with trading posts that grew up around the thriving fur trade with local Iroquois tribes. The area's Dutch heritage survives in names of places such as Catskill, Kinderhook, and Claverack, as well as in the early 19th-century fictional writings of Washington Irving (1783–1859), whose tales of *Rip Van Winkle* and *The Legend of Sleepy Hollow* made him America's first internationally recognized author. Irving's modest but whimsically eclectic Hudson River home, **Sunnyside**, is now a tourist attraction.

The Hudson's economic and transportation advantages also made it a key strategic objective of both British and American forces during the Revolutionary War, resulting in many pitched battles. Fort Putnam, one of the forts built along the river in 1778 to defend the colonies from British attacks, has been restored and is now part of the **United States Military Academy** at West Point. Established in 1802, the academy has trained the nation's leading military officers, including opposing Civil War generals Ulysses S. Grant and Robert E. Lee, and World War II commanders Douglas MacArthur and Dwight D. Eisenhower. The Military Academy Museum provides a comprehensive introduction to a tour of the fortress-like grounds.

The imposing exterior of the lavishly furnished Vanderbilt Mansion

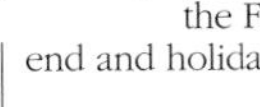

Statue of George Washington at the US Military Academy

In the 19th century, many of New York's emerging elite constructed seasonal retreats along the Hudson. The largest of these is the **Vanderbilt Mansion** in Hyde Park. Completed in 1899, this Italian-Renaissance style palace was built by the architecture firm of McKim, Mead & White, for railroad baron Frederick W. Vanderbilt. The magnificent home offers a spectacular view of the river, and is laden with French furniture, art, tapestries, and architectural details taken from a Parisian château once occupied by Napoleon. An older and less ostentatious mansion is Springwood, the home of Franklin D. Roosevelt (FDR), America's 32nd president *(see p49)*. Roosevelt was born here in 1882, and it was used as a summer White House during his 1933–45 term. The house is now part of the **Home of Franklin D. Roosevelt National Historic Site**, which also includes an extensive museum and library detailing Roosevelt's leadership during the Great Depression and World War II. Both FDR and Eleanor are buried here. The nearby Eleanor Roosevelt National Historic Site preserves Val-Kill, the First Lady's weekend and holiday cottage retreat.

Sunnyside, Washington Irving's home

### Sunnyside

W Sunnyside Lane, off Rte 9, Tarrytown. *(914) 591-8763. Apr– Oct: 10am–5pm Wed–Mon; Nov–Dec: 10am–4pm Wed–Mon; Mar: 10am–4pm Sat–Sun. Thanksg., Dec 25.* www.hudsonvalley.org

### US Military Academy

W Sunnyside Lane, Rte 9 W, West Point. *(845) 938-2638. by tour only. Mon–Sat: 9:45am–3:30pm every half hr, photo IDs required; Dec–Feb: only 2 tours per day. (for tours only). Jan 1, Thanksg., Dec 25.* www.usma.edu

### Home of Franklin D. Roosevelt National Historic Site

4097 Albany Post Rd, Rte 9, Hyde Park. *(845) 229-9115. 9am–5pm daily.* www.nps.gov/hofr **Library & Museum** *(800) 337-8474.* **Museum** *May–Oct: 9am–6pm; Nov–Apr: 9am–5pm. Jan 1, Thanksg., Dec 25.* **Library** *8:45am–5pm Mon–Fri.* www.fdrlibrary.marist.edu

**New York State Capitol in Albany, a blend of architectural styles**

## Albany 5

*101,000.* 
*25 Quackenbush Square, (518) 434-1217.* www.albany.org

ALBANY HAS BEEN a central force in New York State since 1614, when the explorer Henry Hudson *(see p60)* established a fur-trading post, Fort Orange, at the northernmost navigable point on the Hudson River. When the British took over the settlement in 1664, they changed its name to Albany. In 1797 Albany was selected as the New York State capital, and the town's political future was secured. The city expanded dramatically in the 1830s with the completion of the Erie Canal, which linked the Hudson River to the Great Lakes. When canal traffic declined in the 1850s, Albany retained its commercial dominance, rapidly evolving into a New York Central railroad terminus and manufacturing center.

While transportation and industry are still important components of the local economy, government is the main concern in today's Albany. The majestic **New York State Capitol**, built over 30 years and completed in 1898, occupies a central location near the city's downtown. The massive stone building is a curious amalgam of Italian and French Renaissance and Romanesque, replete with ornamented stairways, soaring arches, and an ornate Senate chamber embellished with red granite, yellow and pink marble, stained glass, onyx, and mahogany.

The **New York State Museum** chronicles the state's rich heritage, beginning with its first Native American occupants and incorporating the stories of New York's many immigrants, early settlers, and business elite. A reconstructed Iroquois longhouse and a restored 1940s subway car from New York City's legendary A-train are among the many highlights here.

### New York State Capitol

Empire State Plaza. *(518) 474-2418.* *tours at 10am, noon, 2pm, 3pm Mon–Fri, 11am, 1pm, 3pm Sat–Sun.* *Jan 1, Easter, Thanksgiving, Dec 25, public hols.*

### New York State Museum

Empire State Plaza. *(518) 474-5877.* *9:30am–5pm daily.* *Jan 1, Thanksgiving, Dec 25.*

**Sprawling Saratoga National Historical Park**

## Saratoga Springs 6

*25,000.* 297 Broadway, *(518) 587-3241.* www.saratoga.org

THIS TOWN has been known for its horseracing, gambling, and high society since it emerged as a resort in the 19th century. The therapeutic waters from the town springs at **Saratoga Spa State Park** sparked an annual influx of wealthy tourists seeking relief from various ailments. Other more enjoyable distractions were offered by the lavish casinos and horseracing facilities. One of Saratoga's original gambling establishments, the elegant Canfield Casino, is now part of **Congress Park**. The gabled grandstand of the Saratoga Race Track, built during the Civil War, is still in use, attracting large crowds during the racing season in August. For a glimpse of the area's more tempestuous Revolutionary War past, **Saratoga National Historical Park**, 15 miles (24 km) southeast, was the site of the 1777 Battle of Saratoga. Here, American commander Horatio Gates led Colonial forces to a decisive victory over 9,000 British regulars, Hessians, and Native Americans commanded by General John Burgoyne. The victory ensured American control of the Hudson River shipping corridor, and prompted the French King Louis XVI to send troops to the colonists' aid later that year.

**Saratoga Race Track**

### Saratoga Spa State Park

I-87, exit 13N. *(518) 584-2535.* *8am–sunset daily.* www.saratogaspastatepark.org

### Saratoga National Historical Park

Rte 4, 8 miles (13 km) S of Schuylerville. *(518) 664-9821.* *9am–5pm daily.* *Jan 1, Thanksgiving, Dec 25.* www.nps.gov/sara

**The tranquil waters of Otsego Lake, Cooperstown**

## Adirondack Mountains 7

216 Main St, Lake Placid
*(518) 523-2445.*

Spanning almost one-fourth of the state, the Adirondack Mountains encompass various ecosystems and hundreds of lakes and rivers, with only 1,100 miles (1,770 km) of road. Rugged peaks such as the 5,344-ft (1,629-m) Mount Marcy are some of the scenic highlights. Two visitor centers serve as gateways to **Adirondack Park** and provide information about the conservation movement that led to the park's creation in 1894 as part of the nation's first forest preserve.

The picturesque village of **Lake Placid** straddles Mirror Lake and Lake Placid in the north-central section of the park. Home to the 1932 and 1980 Winter Olympic Games, it is both a summer resort and winter sports training and competitive center.

### Baseball

"America's Pastime," the country's first nationwide spectator sport, evolved from the British games of cricket and rounders, as well as town ball, a New England variant. The first recorded amateur game took place in 1845 in New York City. Since the 1870s, when professional play matured, baseball has seen many superstars such as Babe Ruth, Ty Cobb, and Ted Williams.

**Babe Ruth**

### Adirondack Park

1 mile N of Rte 86/Rte 30,& 14 miles (22km) E of Long Lake, Rte 28N.
*(518) 327-3000.* *9am–5pm daily.* *Thanksgiving, Dec 25.*

## Cooperstown 8

*2,200.* *31 Chestnut St.*
*(607) 547-9983.*

Overlooking Otsego Lake, this neat little village is the legendary birthplace of baseball and home of the **National Baseball Hall of Fame**. This engaging shrine and museum pays homage to baseball greats from the last 150 years, with a colorful array of gear, uniforms, audio-video features, and special exhibits. Founded in 1786, Cooperstown also has a superb collection of Native American artifacts, folk art, and Hudson River School paintings in the **Fenimore Art Museum**. The adjacent Farmer's Museum features exhibits on 19th-century rural life. Glimmerglass Opera, on the shores of Lake Ostego, is nationally renowned.

### National Baseball Hall of Fame

25 Main St. *(888) 425-5633.*
*Memorial Day–Labor Day: 9am–9pm daily; Labor Day–Memorial Day: 9am–5pm daily.* *Jan 1, Thanksgiving, Dec 25.*
www.baseballhalloffame.org

## Finger Lakes 9

*904 E Shore Dr, Ithaca.* *(607) 272-1313.*
www.visitithaca.com

According to the Iroquois tribes of west-central New York, the Finger Lakes were created when the Great Spirit placed his hand on the region, leaving behind a series of slender lakes. Seneca Lake is the deepest of these water bodies, at 630 ft (192 m), while Cayuga Lake is the longest, stretching 40 miles (64 km) between the lively town of **Ithaca** – containing the picturesque Cornell University campus – and historic **Seneca Falls**.

Downtown Ithaca, which has a diverse array of art galleries, bookstores, and excellent restaurants, is a pleasant place to start a tour of the Finger Lakes region. **Taughannock Falls State Park**, north of Ithaca, is a wooded oasis, with the 215-ft (65-m) falls tumbling gracefully into a cool, green pool, where swimming is permitted in season. At the top of Cayuga Lake, the quiet Seneca Falls is the spot where 19th-century feminists Elizabeth Cady Stanton and Susan B. Anthony held the first American women's rights convention in 1848, laying the foundation for the Suffrage Movement some 70 years later.

### Taughannock Falls State Park

10 miles (16 km) N of Ithaca, Rte 89. *(607) 387-6739.*
*8am–sunset daily.*
www.nysparks.state.ny.us/parks

**Taughannock Falls State Park in the Finger Lakes region**

## Syracuse ⑩

163,900. 572 S Salina St, (315) 470-1910. www.visitsyracuse.org

LIKE MANY UPSTATE New York cities, Syracuse prospered after the arrival of the Erie Canal in the 1820s. The informative **Erie Canal Museum**, housed in a restored canal-side building just east of downtown, has a full-size canal boat replica and a multimedia overview of the canal's important role in the city's history. The downtown Armory Square historic and entertainment district preserves many brick and cast-iron commercial and warehouse buildings from Syracuse's late 19th-century boom period, as well as the 3,000-seat **Landmark Theatre**, built in 1928.

A downtown surprise is the **Everson Museum of Arts**, which houses a remarkable collection that ranges from Ming dynasty porcelains to works by American painters from Gilbert Stuart to Jackson Pollock. The museum building is the first designed by architect I.M. Pei.

**Erie Canal Museum**
318 Erie Blvd E. *(315) 471-0593.* *10am–5pm daily.* *public hols.* www.eriecanalmuseum.org

**Everson Museum of Arts**
401 Harrison St. *(315) 474-6064.* *noon–5pm Tue–Fri, 10am–5pm Sat, noon–5pm Sun.* www.everson.org

**Old lithograph showing the inauguration of Erie Canal**

**The Kodak Company's office building in Rochester**

## Rochester ⑪

231,600. 45 East Ave, (800) 677-7282. www.visitrochester.com

THIS LOVELY CITY, with its abundant parkland and fine museums, evolved out of an industrial past, rooted in the milling industries that developed around the Genesee River's High Falls. The Center for High Falls includes a pedestrian bridge with scenic views of the still-roaring falls, an art gallery, a local history display, and a tour of an 1816 factory that lies three stories below street level. The city's top cultural attractions are the **Strong Museum's** vast collection of Americana, which features a restored 1956 working diner, and the **George Eastman House**, where the eccentric founder of the city's Eastman Kodak Company lived until his death in 1932. The George Eastman House is now the superb International Museum of Photography. It contains massive still, film, and video holdings, and cameras and books on photography.

**Strong Museum**
1 Manhattan Square. *(585) 263-2702.* *10am–5pm Mon–Thu & Sat, 10pm–8pm Fri, noon–5pm Sun.* *Jan 1, Thanksgiving, Dec 25.* www.strongmuseum.org

**George Eastman House**
900 East Ave. *(585) 271-3361.* *10am–5pm Tue–Sat (to 8pm Thu), 1–5pm Sun.* *Mon, Jan 1, Thanksgiving, Dec 25.* www.eastman.org

## Chautauqua ⑫

4,600. *Chautauqua Institution, Chautauqua, (800) 836-2787.*

A SECLUDED community located on Chautauqua Lake in western New York State, this town doubles in population in summer, when its Victorian cottages and tree-lined streets are crowded with people attending the town's famous **Chautauqua Institution**. Founded in 1874 as an instructional center for Methodist Sunday-school teachers, it spawned the Chautauqua Movement, sponsoring correspondence courses and lecture tours in an effort to make the liberal arts more accessible. The town is now one of the nation's premier venues for theater, classical music, and opera. The shady, open-air amphitheater on the timeless Chautauqua campus holds lectures, performances, and religious services from late June to late August.

**Renoir's *Little Blue Nude*, Albright-Knox Art Gallery, Buffalo**

## Buffalo ⑬

328,100. 617 Main St, (800) 283-3256. www.buffalocvb.org

BURNED BY THE British during the War of 1812, the fortunes of the frontier outpost of Buffalo revived some 13 years later, when it became the western terminus of the Erie Canal. This secured its economic future as the gateway to the prosperous Great Lakes trade.

**Buffalo's skyline on a sunny morning from the city harbor**

The **Buffalo and Erie County Historical Society** is housed in what was originally the New York State Pavilion, the only building to survive from the 1901 Pan-American Exposition. Its numerous exhibits focus on the town's rich ethnic and industrial heritage.

The nearby **Albright-Knox Art Gallery** overlooks bucolic Delaware Park, designed by Frederick Law Olmsted *(see p78)*. On display are works by Picasso and de Kooning, and a large collection of North American paintings by Jackson Pollock, Frida Kahlo, and others. Also worth a stop is the Jell-O Museum, on Main Street, containing displays and trivia relating to "America's favorite dessert."

**Albright-Knox Art Gallery**
Elmwood Ave, Off Rte 198. (716) 882-8700. *10am–5pm Tue–Thu, 10am–10pm Fri, 10am–5pm Sat–Sun.* *Jan 1, Thanksgiving, Dec 25.* www.albrightknox.org

## Niagara Falls 14

*61,800.*
*Prospect St, (716) 282-8992.*
www.niagara-usa.com

Louis Hennepin, the French priest who was one of the first Europeans to gaze upon Niagara Falls in 1678, wrote that "the Universe does not afford its parallel." Even today the three Niagara Falls waterfalls, which plunge nearly 200 ft (61 m) into a rocky gorge, are as awe-inspiring as they were over 300 years ago. Despite the rampant development on both the US and Canadian sides of the Niagara River (which separates the Canadian province of Ontario from New York State), the spectacle still provides enough drama, mist, and romance to lure more than 10 million tourists a year to view this natural wonder.

Visitors on the American side often start their exploration with a visit to **Niagara Falls State Park**, where the 240-ft (73-m) Prospect Point Observation Tower provides a scenic overview of the falls. For a closer exploration, there are a number of paid excursions, such as the **Cave of the Winds** elevator ride to the base of the falls, and the **Maid of the Mist** boat ride, which departs from Prospect Park and passes directly in front of the falls and into the river's Horseshoe Basin, for a view of the more dramatic Canadian Falls.

The pedestrian-friendly Rainbow Bridge provides quick passage from downtown Niagara Falls to the Canadian side, where most of the area's commercial attractions are located. At night, the falls are dramatically illuminated by electricity generated by the **Niagara Power Project**. Its visitor center traces the development of hydroelectricity in the area and features an operating model of a hydropower turbine.

**Niagara Falls State Park**
Prospect St. *(716) 278-1796.* *sunrise–sunset daily.* www.niagarafallsstatepark.com
**Cave of the Winds** Goat Island. *(716) 278-1730.* *mid-May–Labor Day: 9am–10pm Sun–Thu, 9am–11pm Fri–Sat; post Labor Day–Oct: 9am–8:30pm Sun–Thu, 9am–10pm Fri–Sat.* **Maid of the Mist Ride** Prospect Park. *(716) 284-8897.* *timings vary depending on season. Check at office for details.*

**The majestic Niagara Falls, one of the most dramatic spectacles the country offers**

# New Jersey

DESPITE THE INDUSTRIAL IMAGE earned by New Jersey's manufacturing and railroad towns such as Newark and Hoboken, the "Garden State" really does live up to its moniker. Outside the urban, industrial corridor that lies across the Hudson River from New York City and extends all the way into Philadelphia, New Jersey is a gentle country of green and orderly small towns, dairy farms, rolling hills, pine forests, and miles and miles of white sandy beaches along the Atlantic Ocean.

**Strolling on the peaceful campus of Princeton University**

## Princeton ⓯

*12,000.*
*Princeton Chamber of Commerce, 216 Rockingham Row, Princeton Forrestal Village, (609) 520-1776.*
www.visitprinceton.org

THE CENTRAL New Jersey village of Princeton witnessed considerable activity during the Revolutionary War period, changing hands between British forces under General Charles Cornwallis and the Continental Army, led by General George Washington. The once-sleepy agricultural village is now a pleasant tree-lined town, combining sophisticated shops, lodgings, and a variety of restaurants, with one of America's most prestigious universities.

The center of Princeton's shopping and dining area is Nassau Street. Located here is Bainbridge House, built in 1766, which now accommodates **The Historical Society of Princeton**. The Society offers local history exhibits and free walking tours, highlighting the town's fine 18th-century architecture. The popular Palmer Square, on Nassau Street, is home to Nassau Inn, Princetown's premier hotel since 1756.

The College of New Jersey, one of the 14 original Colonial colleges, moved to Princeton in 1756 and was renamed **Princeton University** in 1896. Nassau Hall, a landmark building on campus, was the site of the initial meeting of the New Jersey State Legislature in 1776. Renowned physicist Albert Einstein spent his final years here at the Institute for Advanced Study.

**Princeton's tiger mascot**

Today, the campus covers 1,600 acres (647 ha), and the university enrolls 6,000 students annually. The grounds include sculptures by Picasso, Henry Moore, Louise Nevelson, and Alexander Calder. The Art Museum in McCormick Hall displays paintings and sculptures that range from ancient pre-Columbian, Asian, and African art to modern works.

The University Chapel is one of the world's largest – of special interest are the Gothic architecture, stained-glass windows, and the superb 16th-century French pulpit and lectern. About 30 gargoyles in different styles decorate buildings on the campus, including the Firestone Library, Princeton's central research facility. Inside the Library, the Cotsen Children's Library features a small museum focused on the works of C.S. Lewis, Lewis Carroll, and E.B. White.

### Princeton University Visitors' Center

Welcome Desk, First Campus Center.
*(609) 258-1766. Guided tours: 10am–3:30pm Sat, 1:30–3:30pm Sun.*
*mid-Dec–early Jan, public hols.*
www.princeton.edu

## Atlantic City ⓰

*38,000. Greater Atlantic City Convention & Visitors Bureau, 2314 Pacific Ave, (609) 449-7130.* www.atlanticcitynj.com

CALLED THE "Queen of the Coast" by generations of beachgoers, Atlantic City has been a favored vacation spot since the mid-1800s. The first casino opened on the boardwalk in 1978, and since then the town has become one of the most popular destinations on the eastern seaboard.

All gambling – euphemistically referred to as "gaming"– takes place in the large, ostentatious, casino-hotels that lie within a block of the

**Tourists in a rolling chair on the boardwalk at Atlantic City**

Lucy, the Margate Elephant, near Atlantic City

boardwalk and beach. Although the casinos are justly famous for their night-life, families will find plenty of other entertainment during the day. Atlantic City's boardwalk, lined with shops and amusement arcades, is always busy with people enjoying a stroll at any time of day or night. Another way to see the boardwalk is in a "**Rolling Chair**," a rickshaw-like wicker chair on wheels that seats up to three people. Beyond the boardwalk, white-sand beaches beckon sunbathers and swimmers.

Atlantic City also hosts the prestigious Miss America Pageant, which has been held here since 1928. In nearby Margate City, **Lucy, the Margate Elephant** stands tall in celebration of American marketing ingenuity. Built by a real estate developer in 1881 to draw prospects to his holdings, "Lucy" has served as a residence and a tavern over the years. Today, guided tours take visitors into the 90-ton (90,000-kg) structure that has become instantly recognizable as part of the Jersey Shore and Atlantic City.

### Rolling Chair

Atlantic City Famous Rolling Chair Co, 1605 Boardwalk. *(609) 347-7148.*

### Lucy, the Margate Elephant

9200 Atlantic Ave, Margate City. *(609) 823-6473. mid-Jun–Labor Day: 10am–8pm Mon–Sat, 10am-5pm Sun; Apr–mid-Jun & after Labor Day–last weekend in Oct: 10am–5pm weekends; Nov–Dec: hours vary.*

## Cape May 17

*4,400.* *Cape May Welcome Center, Lafayette & Elmira Sts, Cape May, (609) 884-9562.* www.capemaychamber.com

First explored by Cornelius Mey for the Dutch West India Company in 1621, Cape May is one of the oldest seashore resorts on the Atlantic Coast. Visited by a number of US presidents including James Buchanan, Ulysses S. Grant, Benjamin Harrison, and Franklin Pierce, it was popular with socialites from New York and Philadelphia during the late 1800s. Since then, this resort at the southernmost point of New Jersey, has continued to enjoy a fine reputation among beach lovers. A small boardwalk and sandy beach afford a lovely view of sunrise over the Atlantic Ocean.

Today, the area is characterized by the great Victorian building boom that took place in the 19th century. The central district is made up of so-called "cottages," two- and three-story buildings intended as summer homes for large families. They have been built in styles popular at the turn of the 20th century, ranging from lacy Queen Anne to Italianate. Most of the historic homes have been lovingly restored to period condition, and some are open to the public. Many others have been converted into B&B (bed-and-breakfast) lodgings. The town offers several tours of the Victorian homes, including a special trolley tour.

The **Historic Cold Spring Village** is a living history museum consisting of 25 authentically restored buildings set on a 20-acre (8-ha) site. Costumed interpreters portray 19th-century lifestyles that would have been common in a southern New Jersey rural community. Trades and crafts such as pottery making, book binding, and blacksmithing are also demonstrated.

Nearby, the **Cape May County Park and Zoo** is home to 170 species of animals; some, such as Brazilian golden lion tamarins, are rare or endangered species. The park also features a 35-acre (14-ha) African savanna habitat accessed by an 800-ft (244-m) long boardwalk.

### Historic Cold Spring Village

720 US 9, Cape May. *(609) 898-2300. mid-Jun–Labor Day: 10am–4:30pm Tue–Sun; after Labor Day–Sep 30 & Memorial Day–mid-Jun: 10am–4:30pm Sat–Sun.*

One of Cape May's charming bed & breakfast lodgings

# Philadelphia ⑱

PENNSYLVANIA'S LARGEST CITY, Philadelphia or the "City of Brotherly Love," is also the birthplace of the nation. In 1776, representatives from the 13 British colonies signed the Declaration of Independence here, and the city served as an early capital of the fledgling United States. Since its founding by English Quaker William Penn in the late 17th century, Philadelphia's port on the Delaware River has welcomed thousands of immigrants from all over the world. Their labor strengthened the expanding city through two centuries of industrial growth, wars, and economic reversals. Even today, the city's neighborhoods and restaurants reflect this ethnic mix. Philadelphia's rich history, world-class art collections, special-interest museums, fine restaurants and hotels, and the nation's largest landscaped public park combine to make the city one of America's most popular destinations.

**William Penn's statue on Philadelphia City Hall**

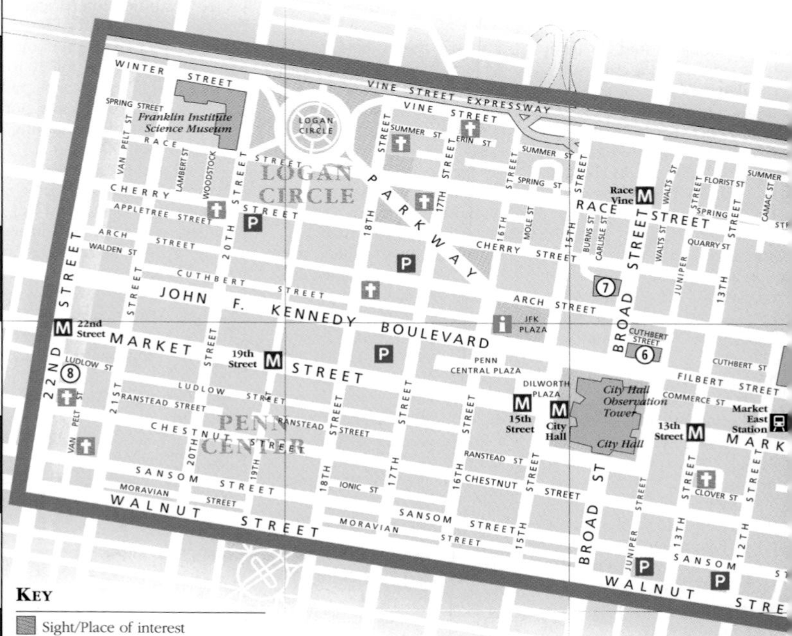

**KEY**

- Sight/Place of interest
- Metro station
- Train station
- Bus station
- Tourist information
- Parking
- Church
- Expressway

### GETTING AROUND

Philadelphia's excellent local transit system, SEPTA, operates buses throughout Greater Philadelphia in addition to two subway lines: the Market-Frankford line (east–west, under Market St) and the Broadway Street line (north–south). Purple-painted, tourist-oriented "Philly Phlash" shuttles travel in a loop through downtown to all major attractions. Taxis are plentiful and moderately priced.

## SIGHTS AT A GLANCE

Independence Hall ①
Second Bank of the United States ②
US Mint ③
Independence Seaport Museum ④
Reading Terminal Market ⑤
Masonic Temple ⑥
Pennsylvania Academy of Fine Arts ⑦
College of Physicians of Philadelphia/ Mutter Museum ⑧

**Greater Philadelphia *(see inset map)***
Eastern State Penitentiary ⑨
Philadelphia Zoo ⑩
Fairmount Park ⑪
Philadelphia Museum of Art ⑫
The Barnes Foundation ⑬

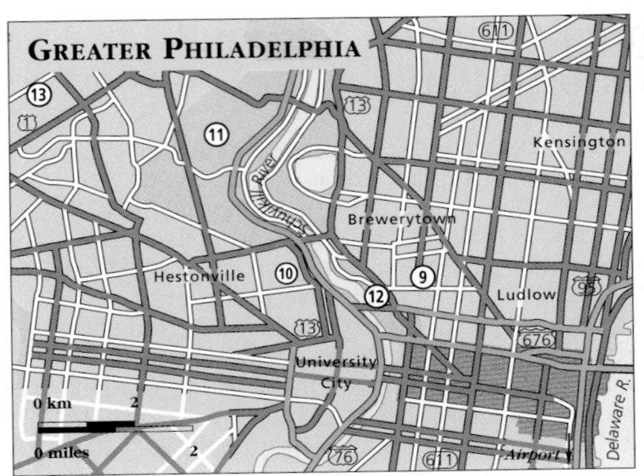


**KEY**

Area of main map

***SEE ALSO***

- ***Where to Stay*** p117
- ***Where to Eat*** p121

0 meters 250
0 yards 250

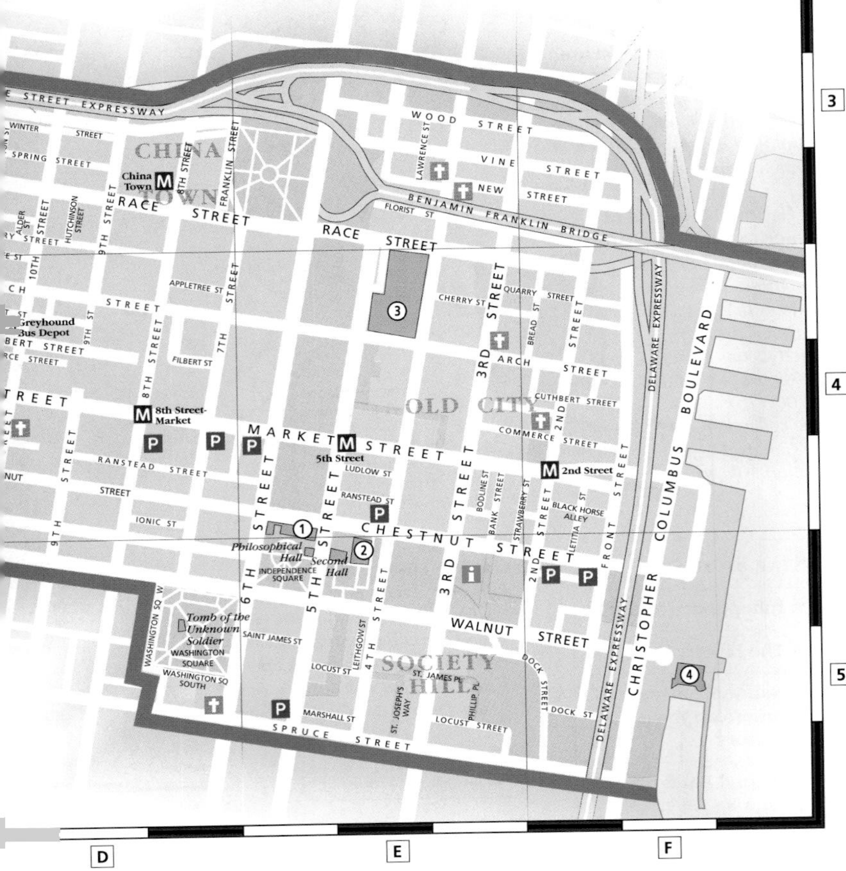

EXPRESSWAY
WINTER STREET
SPRING STREET
CHINA TOWN
China Town
RACE STREET
8TH STREET
FRANKLIN STREET
WOOD STREET
VINE STREET
NEW STREET
LAWRENCE ST
BENJAMIN FRANKLIN BRIDGE
FLORIST ST
ALDER ST
HUTCHINSON STREET
10TH
9TH STREET
APPLETREE ST
7TH STREET
CHERRY ST
QUARRY STREET
BREAD ST
3RD STREET
Greyhound Bus Depot
FILBERT ST
ARCH STREET
DELAWARE EXPRESSWAY
BOULEVARD
8th Street-Market
OLD CITY
CUTHBERT STREET
COMMERCE STREET
MARKET STREET
5th Street
2nd Street
RANSTEAD STREET
LUDLOW ST
RANSTEAD ST
BODINE ST
BANK STREET
STRAWBERRY ST
BLACK HORSE ALLEY
IONIC ST
CHESTNUT STREET
LETITIA ST
FRONT STREET
COLUMBUS
Philosophical Hall
Second Bank
INDEPENDENCE SQUARE
6TH STREET
5TH STREET
4TH STREET
2ND STREET
WASHINGTON SQ W
Tomb of the Unknown Soldier
WASHINGTON SQUARE
WASHINGTON SQ SOUTH
SAINT JAMES ST
WALNUT STREET
LEITHGOW ST
SOCIETY HILL
ST. JAMES PL
DOCK STREET
CHRISTOPHER
LOCUST ST
ST. JOSEPH'S WAY
PHILLIP PL
DOCK ST
MARSHALL ST
LOCUST STREET
SPRUCE STREET

1 2 3 4 5
D E F

# Independence National Historic Park

KNOWN LOCALLY AS Independence Mall, this 45-acre (18-ha) urban park encompasses several well-preserved 18th-century structures associated with the American Revolution. The Declaration of Independence that heralded the birth of a new nation was signed in this historic area. Dominated by the tall brick tower of Independence Hall, the park includes the oldest street in Philadelphia, the US Mint, and several special-interest museums exploring Philadelphia's Colonial and seafaring past as well as its ethnic heritage. Around 20 of the buildings are now open to the public.

**Plaque commemorating Independence Hall**

**African American Museum**
*Inspirational stories of Philadelphia's famous African-American citizens are displayed alongside exhibits of contemporary works.*

**★ National Museum of American Jewish History**
*This unique museum celebrates the history of Jews in America through artifacts such as this Torah scroll and ark (mid-1700s) from the collection of Congregation Mikveh Israel.*

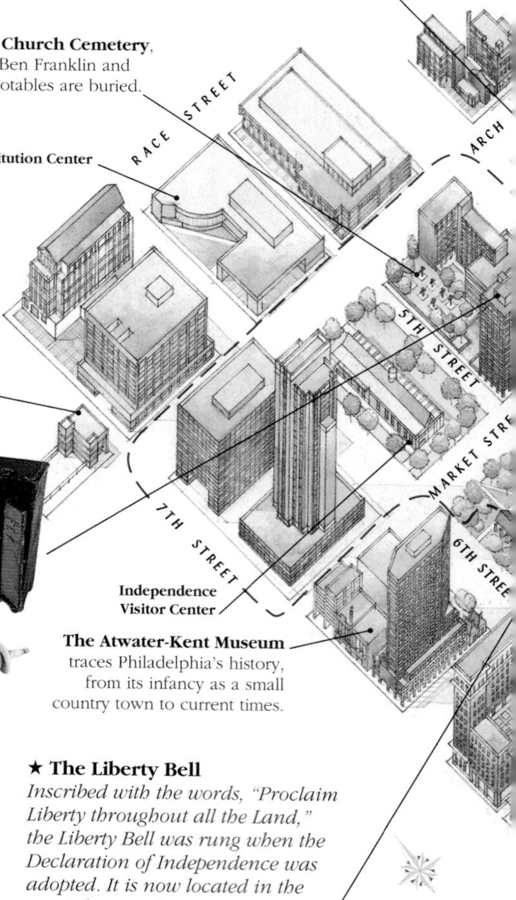

**Arch St. Friends Meeting House**

**Christ Church Cemetery**, where Ben Franklin and other notables are buried.

**Constitution Center**

RACE STREET

ARCH

5TH STREET

MARKET STREET

7TH STREET

6TH STREET

**Independence Visitor Center**

**The Atwater-Kent Museum** traces Philadelphia's history, from its infancy as a small country town to current times.

**★ The Liberty Bell**
*Inscribed with the words, "Proclaim Liberty throughout all the Land," the Liberty Bell was rung when the Declaration of Independence was adopted. It is now located in the new Liberty Bell Center* (see p102).

**STAR SIGHTS**

- ★ **Independence Hall**
- ★ **The Liberty Bell**
- ★ **National Museum of American Jewish History**
- ★ **Second Bank of the US**

**KEY**

– – – Suggested route

0 meter 200

0 yards 200

**Elfreth's Alley**
*The city's oldest residential street is lined with 18th-century houses, many of which are now shops.*

### Visitors' Checklist

6th & Market Sts, (800) 537-7676. 8:30am–5pm daily. **Independence Hall, Liberty Bell** 9am–5pm daily. **National Museum of American Jewish History** (215) 923-3811. 10am–5pm Mon–Thu, 10am–3pm Fri, noon–5pm Sun. Sat, Jewish hols. www.nmjh.org **Second Bank of the US** 9am–5pm daily. **African American Museum** (215) 574-0380. 10am–5pm Tue–Sat, noon–5pm Sun.

**Betsy Ross House**, a restored 18th-century home, is a memorial to Betsy Ross, who is credited with stitching the first American flag.

**Christ Church**

**City Tavern** was the venue of frequent debates during Colonial times. It still serves food and drink today.

**Franklin Court**
*Benjamin Franklin lived and worked in these buildings, which include the B. Free Franklin post office and museum.*

**18th Century Garden**, created by the Pennsylvania Horticultural Society (1827), was the first of its kind in the US.

**★ Second Bank of the US**
*An extensive collection of portraits of luminaries involved in the military, diplomatic, and political events of 1776 is on display at this Grecian style building* (see p102). ②

**Washington Square Park**

**★ Independence Hall**
*The centerpiece of the park, this World Heritage Site was the place where the Declaration of Independence was signed on July 4, 1776* (see p102). ①

## Independence Hall ①

Chestnut St between 5th & 6th Sts. *(800) 967-2283 for timed tickets in Mar–Dec.* Philly Phlash. *9am–5pm daily, longer hours in summer.* www.nps.gov/inde

Just west of the Delaware River, this unadorned brick building is the most important structure in the Independence Hall National Park. Previously designated the State House of Pennsylvania, it is the site of the drafting of the Declaration of Independence, the document that declared America's freedom from the British Empire.

Independence Hall, completed in 1748, was designed by master carpenter Edmund Woolley and lawyer Andrew Hamilton. The chambers of the meeting rooms are furnished simply, as they were during the late 1700s. Today, park personnel re-create history by pointing out the Windsor-style chairs from which Colonial leaders debated the contents of the Declaration. Although the Continental Congress rejected two passages in the first draft – an ill-tempered reference to the English people, and a bitter denunciation of the slave trade – the document was adopted without significant change and approved by Congress on July 4, 1776. The US Constitution was drafted in the same room in 1787.

The large, brass **Liberty Bell** that once hung in the tower has now been placed in the new Liberty Bell Center near Independence Hall. In 1846, a small crack developed and the bell could no longer be sounded. However, it remains the best-known symbol of the Colonial struggle for self-governance. The center incorporates displays that highlight Liberty Bell's importance to the story of America's independence.

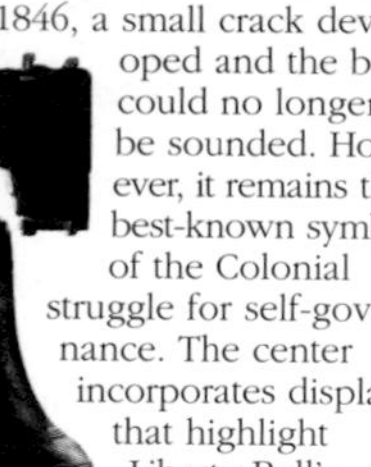

**The Liberty Bell on display near Independence Hall**

## Second Bank of the United States ②

420 Chestnut St. *(215) 965-2305.* *call for times.* www.nps.gov/inde

Built between the years 1819 and 1824, this is one of America's finest examples of Greek Revival architecture. Once a repository that provided credit for federal government and private businesses, it now houses a collection of late 18th- and early 19th-century portraits. On view are 185 paintings of Colonial and federal leaders, military officers, explorers, and scientists.

Many of the portraits are by Charles Willson Peale (1741–1827), his brother James, and their respective sons and daughters, who together form America's most distinguished family of artists. After the Revolutionary War, Peale began collecting portraits, and today, 94 of his original paintings, including likenesses of the American founding fathers George Washington and Alexander Hamilton, and the Continental Army's French ally, the Marquis de Lafayette, are on display along with the portraiture of other artists.

**Aerial view of Independence Hall**

## US Mint ③

5th & Arch Sts. *(215) 408-0114.* *for group tours, available on a limited basis by prior arrangement only.*

The Philadelphia mint, the oldest in the US, makes most of the coins that Americans use every day, and also produces gold bullion coins and national medals. The first US coins, minted in 1793, were copper pennies and half pennies intended solely for local commerce in the colonies. Today, 24 hours a day, five days a week, hundreds of machines and operators in a room the size of a football field blank, anneal, count, and bag millions of dollars worth of quarters, dimes, and pennies. Commemorative coins and numismatic collectables are available in the gift shop, opened on a limited basis.

## Independence Seaport Museum ④

211 S Columbus Blvd. *(215) 925-5439.* Philly Phlash. *Market-Frankford line.* *10am–5pm daily.* *Jan 1, Thnksg., Dec 25.* www.phillyseaport.org

Quartered in a stunning modern building on the waterfront, this 100,000-sq-ft (9,290-sq-m) museum's mandate is to preserve US maritime history and traditions, with special focus on the Chesapeake Bay, and the Delaware River and its tributaries. Displays combine art and artifacts with hands-on computer games, large-scale models, and audio-visuals. The Ben Franklin Bridge, which connects Pennsylvania with New Jersey, is re-created in the museum as a three-and-a-half story replica that straddles a working model of the Delaware River.

Other highlights include "Divers of the Deep," featuring underwater technology through the ages, and "Workshop on the Water," an active boat shop and gallery where visitors can watch boat building in progress as artisans craft traditional wooden 19th-century boats. The World War II submarine USS *Becuna*, commissioned in 1943, and the USS *Olympia*, Admiral George Dewey's flagship in the Battle of Manila (1898), are berthed next to the museum.

**Coffee shop in Philadelphia's Reading Terminal Market**

## Reading Terminal Market ⑤

12th & Filbert Sts. *(215) 922-2317.* *Philly Phlash, SPREE bus.* *8am–6pm Mon–Sat.* *Jan 1, Dec 25.* www.readingterminalmarket.org

THIS MARKET was created underneath a train shed after two farmers' markets were leveled to make space for a new terminal in 1892. So modern was the market that people came from as far as the New Jersey shore to buy fresh Lancaster County produce. Reading Terminal Market declined over the years and was nearly destroyed in the 1970s. Today, however, it has been revitalized, and fishmongers, butchers, bakers, florists, and greengrocers vie for space with quick-breakfast stands run by modestly dressed Amish women, and purveyors of Greek specialties.

**Equestrian statue in the Masonic Temple courtyard**

## Masonic Temple ⑥

1 N Broad St. *(215) 988-1917.* *Philly Phlash.* *tours at 11am, 2pm, 3pm Tue–Fri; 10am, 11am Sat.* *Jul–Aug: Sat, Jan 1, Easter, Thnksg., Dec 25.* www.pagrandlodge.org

AN ARCHITECTURAL jewel dedicated in 1873 as the Grand Lodge of Free and Accepted Masons of Pennsylvania, this remarkable building contains a number of meeting halls in various decorative styles. Among them, the Oriental Hall's (1896) coloring and ornamentation has been copied from the Alhambra in Granada, Spain, the Renaissance Hall (1908) follows an Italian Renaissance motif, while the Egyptian Hall (1889) takes its inspiration from the Temples of Luxor, Karnak, and Philae. High arches, pinnacles, and spires form the Gothic Hall, and the cross-and-crown emblem of Sir Knights – "Under this sign you will conquer" – hangs over a replica of the Archbishop's throne in Canterbury Cathedral. The halls, still in use, were created to honor the building trades, and much of the stone and tilework are imperceptibly faux finished – an attestation to the skill of the men who made them. President George Washington wore his Masonic apron when he laid the cornerstone of the Capitol building in Washington, DC. The apron is on display, along with other Masonic rarities, in the museum on the first floor.

## Pennsylvania Academy of Fine Arts ⑦

118 N Broad S at Cherry St. *(215) 972-7600.* *Philly Phlash.* *10am–5pm Tue–Sat, 11am–5pm Sun.* *public hols.* www.pafa.org

THE COLLECTION of this museum and school, founded in 1805, spans the history of American painting. Galleries display works by some of the art world's best-known denizens. One of them, the classical stylist Benjamin West (1738–1820), a Quaker from Philadelphia, helped organize the British Royal Academy in 1768, and four years later was named Historical Painter to the King. Impressionist and former Academy of Fine Arts student, Mary Cassatt (1824–1926), and modern abstractionist Richard Diebenkorn (1922–93) among others, share wall space. This distinctive building, with its ornate arched foyer, is considered one of the finest examples of Victorian-Gothic architecture in America.

***The Foxhunt* by Winslow Homer, Pennsylvania Academy of Fine Arts**

**The well-lit display of medical curiosities at Mutter Museum**

## College of Physicians of Philadelphia/ Mutter Museum ⑧

19 S 22nd St. *(215) 563-3737.* *17, 21.* *10am–5pm daily.* *Jan 1, Thanksgiving, Dec 25.* www.collphyphil.org

FOUNDED IN 1787 for the "advancement of the science of medicine," the still-active college is a major source of health information. This is provided by the institute's C. Everett Koop Community Health Information Center, through the library, videotapes, and searchable computer system.

Mutter Museum, on the first floor of one of the buildings, is a fascinating collection of preserved specimens, skeletal constructions, and wax figures. These were originally used for educational purposes in the mid-19th century, when diseases and genetic defects were identifiable only by their physical manifestations. Some afflictions are quite grotesque, and may not be suitable for small children or those who have a tendency toward queasiness.

The museum also contains medical instruments, exhibits on the history of medicine over the last 100 years, a re-creation of an early 20th-century doctor's office, and a medicinal plant garden. Special exhibits on medical phenomena, such as Siamese (conjoined) Twins, are an additional feature.

## Eastern State Penitentiary ⑨

Fairmount Ave at 22nd St. *(215) 236-3300.* *33.* *April–Nov: 10am–5pm Wed–Sun.* *Dec–Mar.* www.easternstate.org

NAMED THE "HOUSE" by inmates and guards, the Eastern State Penitentiary, established in 1829, was a revolutionary concept in criminal justice. Prior to this, criminals were thrown together in despicable conditions and punished by physical brutality. The Philadelphia Quakers proposed an alternative – a place where a criminal could be alone to ponder and become penitent for his actions. During incarceration, with sentences seldom less than five years in length, prisoners literally never heard or saw another human being for the entire duration of their stay. The prison had a single entrance and 30-ft (9-m) high boundary walls. Each solitary cell had a private outdoor exercise yard contained by a 10-ft (3-m) wall. Eastern State's many "guests" included bootlegger and crime lord Al Capone. The prison was officially closed in 1971, but prison tours continue to draw many visitors today.

**Long corridor inside the Eastern State Penitentiary**

## Philadelphia Zoo ⑩

3400 W Girard Ave. *(215) 243-1100.* *Philly Phlash.* *9:30am–4pm daily.* *Jan1. Jun 9, Thnksg., Dec 24, 25 & 31.* www.philadelphiazoo.org

THIS ZOO, THE OLDEST in America, was founded in 1859. Set within verdant grounds, interspersed with statuary, the zoo is home to over 2,000 animals, including rare species such as naked mole rats and bamboo-eating lemurs. A walk-through giant otter habitat shows the animals at their playful best. The big cats – lions, clouded leopards, tigers (including rare white tigers), and jaguars – are kept in near-natural habitats or inside the Carnivora House, in weather-protected cages that provide close-up views. Other features are an open bird-house with uncaged finches and hummingbirds, a reptile house, where alligators bask in a tropical paradise, and a 3-acre (1-ha) reserve for 11 primate species, including the nation's only blue-eyed lemurs. The new zoo balloon takes passengers aloft for a panoramic view of the city.

## Fairmount Park ⑪

*John F. Kennedy Blvd & N 16th St, (215) 683-0200.* *Philly Phlash Market-Frankford line.* *daily.*

DESIGNED BY Frederick Law Olmsted (1822–1903), America's pre-eminent land-scape architect, Fairmount Park is an 8,900-acre (3,601-ha) greenway. It encompasses seven historic manor houses decorated in period style, dozens of sculptures, a horti-

**Downtown Philadelphia rising above Fairmount Park**

cultural center, and Japanese house and gardens among other features. A waterworks, innovative in 1840, was designed and built to pump water from the Schuylkill River, which divides the park into east and west. The grounds are interspered with roads, hiking, biking, and bridle trails. Visitors can also rent rowboats and canoes.

A handful of rowing clubs occupy Victorian boathouses along the river. The boathouses are turreted, gabled, and decorated with coats-of-arms. At night, when viewed from the West Fairmount Park shore, the houses are outlined with tiny lights and reflect magically on the river.

In 1894, wealthy manufacturer Richard Smith donated Smith Playground to the children of Philadelphia in memory of his son. Among the attractions are muscle-powered merry-go-rounds, a giant slide, and a renovated mansion and playhouse. Also in Fairmount Park is the 99-acre (40-ha) **Laurel Hill Cemetery**. This vast "park within a park" is dotted with obelisks, statuary, and classic Greek mausoleums. It was such a popular picnic and walking area during the late Victorian period that admission was by ticket only.

## Philadelphia Museum of Art ⑫

26th St & Benjamin Franklin Pkwy. *(215) 763-8100.* *Philly Phlash, 38.* *10am–5pm Tue–Thu, 10am–8:45pm Fri, 10am–5pm Sat–Sun.* *Mon, legal hols.* www.philamuseum.org

THIS MUSEUM ATTRACTS major exhibitions to supplement its superlative permanent collection ranging from 15th-century illuminated manuscripts to modern sculpture by Constantin Brancusi. The full-scale medieval cloister courtyard and fountain on the second floor is a favorite, as are the French Gothic chapel and a pillared temple from Madurai, India. Scattered throughout the museum are computerized stations with information on the exhibits. A collection of Pennsylvania Dutch and American decorative arts adjoins galleries that feature paintings by American artists.

**Medieval diptych, Philadelphia Museum of Art**

## The Barnes Foundation ⑬

300 N Latch's Lane, Merion. *(610) 667-0290.* *17, 33.* *reservation only: Sep–June: 9:30am–5pm Fri–Sun; July–Aug: 9:30am–5pm Wed–Fri.* *public hols.* www.barnesfoundation.org

ESTABLISHED IN the year 1922 to share the private collection of pharmaceutical magnate Albert C. Barnes with "people of all socio-economic levels," this museum has one of the world's premier displays of French modern and Post-Impressionist paintings. Among the more than 800 works on view, there are 180 by August Renoir, 69 by Paul Cézanne, 60 by Henri Matisse, and more by Picasso, Seurat, Modigliani, Van Gogh, Rousseau, and almost every other noteworthy artist of that era. Other exhibits include ancient Greek and Egyptian art, medieval manuscripts, African sculpture, American furniture, ceramics, and handwrought ironwork. The art is displayed to highlight artistic affinities between diverse works. For instance, the Barnes Collection is displayed in accordance with Dr. Barnes' unique specifications – paintings, sculpture, and craft pieces are grouped into 96 distinct ensembles, without labels and with very little regard to chronology.

**The glittering silhouettes of Victorian boathouses along Schuylkill River, Fairmount Park**

# Pennsylvania

**P**ENNSYLVANIA HAS IT ALL – American history, beautiful scenery, varied recreation, lodging, and dining, ranging from the refined to the simple. Of its two main cities, Philadelphia *(see pp98–105)*, the birthplace of America, is a complex, stunning city, while Pittsburgh re-created itself from a grimy, industrial center to a sparkling gem on the forks of the Ohio River. Most of the state, however, is rural and bucolic, a green patchwork of dairy and produce farms, embroidered with forests and waterways, trim fields and small towns.

Memorial at Gettysburg National Military Park

## Gettysburg 19

7,000. 102 Carlisle St, (800) 337-5015. www.gettysburgcvb.org

**A** PIVOTAL CONFRONTATION of the Civil War *(see p47)* took place near the small farming community of Gettysburg in early July 1863. Nearly 100,000 Union soldiers gathered here to confront some 75,000 invading Confederates led by Robert E. Lee. After three days of fighting, a staggering 50,000 soldiers lay dead or wounded, and the Confederates were turned back.

Though the war raged for another two years, Gettysburg was recognized as a turning point. To commemorate the site, a burial ground was purchased, and President Lincoln dedicated the **Gettysburg National Cemetery** with his now-famous three-minute-long speech, the Gettysburg Address. Several impressive monuments, honoring heroism on both sides, have been placed throughout the fields and forests of the battlefield, now the **Gettysburg National Military Park**. The Cyclorama, a giant circular mural painted in 1884, dramatizes a crucial battle scene – Picket's Charge, where over 6,000 Confederate soldiers were killed or wounded.

**Gettysburg National Military Park**
*(717) 334-1124. Sep–May: 8am–5pm daily; Jun–Aug: 8am–6pm daily.* www.nps.gov/gett

## Lancaster 20

*55,600. 501 Greenfield Rd, Lancaster, (800) 723-8824.* www.padutch.com

**T**HIS MARKET TOWN at the heart of the Pennsylvania Dutch Country *(see p59)* is surrounded by almost 5,000 small farms. The region is famous for the German-immigrant "Old Order Amish" Christians, who live and work without modern conveniences like electricity. The **Landis Valley Museum's** large outdoor collection focuses on the state's German rural heritage. Among the exhibits are a crossroads village and an adjoining farmstead with traditional breeds of animals and heirloom plants. Visitors can see demonstrations of skills such as sheep-shearing.

**Ephrata Cloister**, northeast of town in the village of Ephrata, is a collection of medieval-style buildings, founded in 1732. It was home to one of America's earliest communal societies, semi-monastics who practiced an austere lifestyle emphasizing spirituality, and the artistic use of music and the written word. In 1745, the colony set up one of the country's earliest printing presses. This tradition continues today; Ephrata is the home of the world-famous Rodale Press.

**Landis Valley Museum**
2451 Kissel Hill Rd. *(717) 569-0401. 9am–5pm Mon–Sat, noon–5pm Sun.* www.landisvalleymuseum.org

## Hershey 21

*7,400. 1255A Harrisburg Pike, Harrisburg, (800) 995-0969.* www.hersheycaptialregion.com

**T**HIS FACTORY town, now a popular tourist destination, revolves around chocolate, so much so that even its streetlights are shaped like silver-foil-wrapped Hershey Kisses. The town's main attraction is **Chocolate World**, which features a 15-minute ride through a series of animated tableaux revealing Hershey's chocolate-making process. A free sample awaits at the end of the tour, while a series of shops sell souvenirs and every Hershey product made. Nearby is **Hershey Park**, a 90-acre (36-ha) amusement park. Hershey Park offers 80

"Sisters House" and "Meeting House" in Ephrata Cloister

rides including five water slides, four roller coasters, and one of the finest Philadelphia Toboggan Company four-row carousels in existence today.

**Chocolate World**
SR 743 & US 422, Hershey. *(717) 534-4900.* *9am–5pm daily, hours may vary so call for details.* www.hersheyschocolateworld.com

## York ㉒

*42,200.* *1425 Eden Rd, York, (717) 852-9675.* www.yorkpa.org

THE FIRST Pennsylvania settlement west of the Susquehanna River, York was laid out in 1741. At that time, its inhabitants were mainly tavernkeepers and craftspeople, catering to pioneers heading west. Since then, manufacturing has become the prime economic force. York's many covered public markets include the 1888 **Central Market**, the best place in town for local fresh produce, flowers, meats, baked goods, and inexpensive restaurants.

**Last checks at the Harley-Davidson Vehicle Operations Plant in York**

East of historic York, at the **Harley-Davidson Vehicle Operations Plant**, giant presses form steel sheets into fenders while gleaming motorcycles fly overhead. The plant is noisy, colorful, and easily the size of two football fields. A small museum shows Harley-Davidson's history from its days as a motorized bike company in 1903 to the present.

**Harley-Davidson Final Assembly Plant**
1425 Eden Rd. *(717) 848-1177.* *reservation only: 8am–4pm Mon–Fri.* *hourly 9am–2pm Mon–Fri.* www.harley-davidson.com

**A lush greenhouse in Longwood Gardens**

## Reading ㉓

*78,400.* *352 Penn St, Reading, (800) 443-6610.* www.readingberkspa.com

ONCE A CENTER of industry, Reading has reinvented itself as a discount-outlet capital, with clusters of buildings housing more than 80 name-brand stores from Brooks Brothers to Mikasa and Wedgewood. The **Reading Pagoda**, on the town's outskirts, is modeled after a Shogun dynasty castle that was built as part of an early 1900s resort. Today, cherry trees encircle the building, and there are walking trails throughout the adjacent park.

North of town, the **Mary Merritt Doll Museum** has over 1,500 dolls ranging in age and origin from 7th-century Egypt to 20th-century America. Also featured are dozens of mechanical dolls that blow kisses or dance.

**Mary Merritt Doll Museum**
843 Ben Franklin Hwy, (US 422), Douglassville. *(610) 385-3809.* *10am–4:30pm Mon, Wed–Sat; 1–5pm Sun.* *Tue.*

## Longwood Gardens ㉔

US 1, Kennett Square. *(610) 388-1000.* *9am–5pm daily; longer hrs in summer & at Christmas.* www.longwoodgardens.org

PIERRE DU PONT, millionaire financier and industrialist, acquired the 1,000-acre (405-ha) Longwood Gardens in the beautiful, wooded Brandywine Valley in 1906. His aim was to preserve the property's unusual trees, and to provide a place of entertainment for his family and friends.

Over 11,000 varieties of plants including spectacular year-round seasonal displays, whimsical topiaries, and a children's garden are open to the public. The massive main greenhouse and conservatory are engineering marvels that shelter an array of exotics. But the real star of Longwood are the fabulous fountains whose choreographed eruptions rise above the treetops and are highlighted at night by colored lights, creating dazzling displays that are often the backdrop for musical events.

### HARLEY-DAVIDSON

What began as a tinkering project for 21-year-old William Harley and 20-year-old Arthur Davidson, grew into a company that has dominated racing since 1914. After World War I, the first American entered Germany astride a Harley-Davidson. In 1956, Elvis Presley posed on a model KH. Today, Harley Owners Group (HOG) has more than 900,000 members.

**15th Anniversary Fat Boy**

Pittsburgh's Golden Triangle, with its downtown skyscrapers

## Pittsburgh ㉕

369,900. 425 6th Ave, 30th Floor, (800) 359-0758. www.visitpittsburgh.com

LOCATED AT THE point where the Allegheny and Monongahela rivers come together to form the Ohio River, Pittsburgh is an American success story. It grew from a frontier outpost to become an industrial giant, home to the huge mills of the US Steel conglomerate as well as the food-processing company Heinz and the Westinghouse electric company. From the Civil War through World War II, Pittsburgh was a thriving metropolis, but in the 1950s and 60s its fortunes faded. Today, the city has rebuilt itself to become one of the most livable urban areas in the country.

Endowed by steel magnate Andrew Carnegie, the **Carnegie Institute's Museum of Art** offers a brilliantly lit suite of galleries with collections ranging from ancient Egyptian sculpture to Impressionist, Post-Impressionist, and modern American art by Roy Lichtenstein and Alexander Calder. The Hall of Sculpture is a two-storied columned hall that replicates the interior of the Temple of Athena in Athens. It is adorned with casts from the Greek classical era. Next door, the Hall of Architecture is filled with reproductions of some of the best examples of classical, medieval, and Renaissance architectural details. The Carnegie Museum of Natural History, in the same complex, opens out on a central gallery and relies on filtered natural light as a part of its architectural charm. Exhibits change from time to time, but most of the displays in this museum consist of dioramas that feature taxidermy specimens.

At the **Carnegie Science Center** on Allegheny Avenue, the idea is to make science accessible through play. More than 40,000 sq ft (3,716 sq m) of the 186,000-sq-ft (17,280-sq-m) center is devoted to numerous interactive exhibits. The Miniature Railroad and Village displays the rich historical, architectural, and cultural heritage of western Pennsylvania. In the four-story Rangos Omnimax® Theater – one of 13 in the country – audience members recline while images are projected onto a 79-ft (24-m) domed ceiling.

Hall of Sculpture at Carnegie Institute's Museum of Art, Pittsburgh

The 42-story **Cathedral of Learning** houses the University of Pittsburgh's Nationality Classrooms, which seek to reflect the different ethnic groups that contribute to the city's heritage. Started in the 1930s, each of the 26 rooms, the last of which were completed in 2000, has authentic decor and furnishings depicting a unique time and place from 5th-century BC Greece to 16th-century Poland.

In the city's north side, the tile-clad exterior of the **Andy Warhol Museum** reflects the workaday character of the neighborhood. Appearances are deceptive here, and this former warehouse conceals a brightly illuminated, ultramodern interior. The museum celebrates the Pittsburgh-born founder of American Pop Art, Andy Warhol (1928–87) through selections of works from its archives. These include paintings, and video and film clips. Works of related artists are also on display.

Students relaxing at Pittsburgh University

Located 5 miles (8 km) southeast of Pittsburgh is **Kennywood Amusement Park**. It was built in 1905 as a Luna Park, a popular name for amusement parks that showcased the new electric light bulb. The park offers thrill rides, a stunt show, and a 1926 carousel made by the Dentzel Company – premier hand-carvers of carousel animals.

**The Carnegie Institute**
4,400 Forbes Ave. *(412) 622-3131.* *Jul–Aug: 10am–5pm Mon–Sat; noon–5pm Sun; Sep–Jun: 10am–5pm Tue–Sat; noon–5pm Sun.* www.cmoa.org

**Andy Warhol Museum**
117 Sandusky St. *(412) 237-8300.* *10am–5pm Tue–Thu, Sat–Sun 10am–10pm Fri.* *Mon.*

## Laurel Highlands 26

120 E Main St Ligonier, (800) 333-5661. www.laurelhighlands.org

To the south of Pittsburgh, ridges gather together, valleys become canyons, and mountain laurel covers the slopes, giving the region its name. The splendid 1,700-ft (518-m) deep Youghiogheny Gorge cuts through the scenic Laurel Ridge Mountains, where an area of nearly 19,000 acres (7,689 ha) forms the **Ohiopyle State Park**. The park includes more than 28 miles (45 km) of the Youghiogheny River. Whitewater rafting is popular here, as are hiking, jogging, biking, and cross-country skiing on the 43-mile (69-km) Youghiogheny River Trail.

**Fallingwater**, an architectural tour de force by renowned architect Frank Lloyd Wright, lies north of the park. Built in 1936, the house reflects Wright's interest in structures that were an integral part of the landscape.

**Laurel Ridge State Park** stretches from the village of Ohiopyle in the west to the Conemaugh River in the east. The 70-mile (113-km) long Laurel Highlands Hiking Trail is open all year round. The Johnstown Flood Museum chronicles the Conemaugh River disaster that killed more than 2,000 people and destroyed Johnstown in 1889.

**Ohiopyle State Park**
*7 Sheridan St, Ohiopyle. (724) 329-8591. daily.*

### The Amish

All Amish trace their roots to the Swiss Anabaptist ("New Birth") movement of 1525, an offshoot of the Protestant Reformation, whose creed rejected the formality of established churches. Today's Old Order Amish are the most conservative of the sect, disdaining any device that would connect them to the larger world, including electricity, phones, and cars. Conspicuous because of their plain, dark attire – with white prayer caps for the women and straw hats for the men – and their horse-and-buggy mode of transportation, the Amish in America are little changed from their 17th-century ancestors who came seeking religious freedom.

**Amish buggy on a rural highway**

**Fallingwater**
*SR 381, Mill Run. (724) 329-8501. mid-Mar–mid-Nov: 10am–4pm Tue–Sun; Dec–mid-Jan: 10am–4pm Sat–Sun. mid-Jan–mid-Mar, Jan 1, Easter, Thanksgiving, Dec 25.* www.paconserve.org

## Western Amish Country 27

229 S Jefferson St, New Castle, (888) 284-7599.

The scenic territory around the town of New Castle, 56 miles (145 km) from Pittsburgh, is a hand-stitched quilt of agricultural acreage, parks. and villages. Like the residents of the Pennsylvania Dutch Country near Lancaster *(see p106)*, a large population of Old Order Amish and Mennonites have plowed and planted farms in the Enon Valley, near New Castle. **Montgomery Locks and Dam**, completed in 1936, is one of 20 huge locks and dams on the Ohio River from Pittsburgh to Cairo, Illinois. The dam creates a pool more than 18 miles (29 km) long for recreational and commercial use. **McConnell's Mill State Park** follows the path of Slippery Rock Creek and contains a former water-driven gristmill, now a museum. The untamed beauty of Slippery Rock Gorge is very popular with rock climbers and rappellers. **Moraine State Park**, which is about 5 miles (8 km) east of McConnell's Park, is a small paradise reborn from an industrial wasteland where underground and strip mining flourished until the 1950s. Mines were then sealed, gas and oil wells plugged, and the 3,225-acre (1,305-ha) Lake Arthur was constructed.

**McConnell's Mill State Park**
*Portersville. (724) 368-8091. sunrise–sunset daily.*

**The Youghiogheny River looping through Ohiopyle State Park, Laurel Highlands**

## Practical Information

SUCCESSFUL TRAVELING AROUND New York, New Jersey, and Pennsylvania benefits from advance planning, simply because there is so much to see and do in such a concentrated area. The major cities are packed with attractions, hotels, and restaurants, while the expansive and diverse areas in between often double as resort areas, catering to city-dwellers in need of a change of pace. Depending upon the time, you can explore significant historical sights, appreciate stunning scenery, take in a local celebration, or simply relax along the coast.

### TOURIST INFORMATION

NEW YORK, New Jersey, and Pennsylvania each publishes a wide variety of informative, richly illustrated travel guides. All of this information can be ordered by telephone or accessed via web sites, and further information is available from the multitude of local and regional tourism bureaus across the three states. The wealth of available information covers climate, transportation, attractions, accommodations, restaurants, recreation, festivals, regional history, and much more.

### NATURAL HAZARDS

THUNDERSTORMS occur frequently across the Mid-Atlantic Region. A basic precaution that visitors should take if they find themselves in the middle of a sudden storm, is to never stand under a tree, as they are perfect targets for lightning strikes. Also, there is danger of the tree toppling due to strong winds. Western New York State and Pennsylvania experience extreme winter conditions; the Adirondacks face severe winter storms and sub-zero temperatures, while sudden heavy snowfalls often cause chaos in New York City. Visitors should listen for weather warnings and broadcasts on the radio and TV.

### GETTING AROUND

UNLIKE MUCH OF the US, the Mid-Atlantic is a region where you can get around without a car. Some of the most modern, and fast **Amtrak** train services in the US link New York and Washington, DC with Philadelphia, bringing the two cities within an hour of each other. Other lines run across Pennsylvania, up the Hudson Valley between New York City and Albany then across to Buffalo and Niagara Falls, and between Philadelphia and Atlantic City. Seat belts are required for drivers and front seat passengers in the entire Mid-Atlantic Region. Most states also require seat belts for back seat passengers, and child seats are required for all automobile occupants age four and under. Speed limits vary but are usually 70 to 75 mph (113 to 121 km/h) on Interstate Highways outside of densely populated urban areas, weather permitting. Talking on a cell phone while driving is dangerous and against the law.

### EVENTS & FESTIVALS

NEW YORK CITY and the Mid-Atlantic states stage a diverse range of annual community, regional, and national festivals. One of the nation's most unusual annual events takes place in central Pennsylvania on February 2, when a chubby rodent named "Punxsutawney Phil" wakes up from his winter hibernation on **Groundhog Day**. "Phil" forecasts the advent of spring, which in US folklore is related to whether he can see his shadow. In March, as an expression of New York City's strong Irish heritage, the city politicians and other characters march through the city as part of a boisterous **St. Patrick's Day** celebration. Summer brings a deluge of outdoor events, and fireworks, bands, and street festivals are the norm for community celebrations of the July 4 Independence Day holiday. County and state fairs crop up in the Mid-Atlantic countryside in July and August, as do music festivals like the **Glimmerglass Opera Festival** in Cooperstown. The "Miss America" pageant takes place toward the end of summer every year in Atlantic City, and the Christmas shopping season kicks off with the annual extravaganza of massive inflatable figures in the **Macy's Thanksgiving Day** parade in New York City.

### SPORTS

WITH HIGH-QUALITY professional teams in every major sport, the New York and Mid-Atlantic Region is a

### THE CLIMATE OF THE MID-ATLANTIC REGION

Weather across the vast Mid-Atlantic Region can be as varied as the scenery. New York's Adirondack Mountains are famed for the extremities of climate, while in Long Island and the coastal areas of New Jersey, the climate is milder. Western New York and Pennsylvania see some of the nation's heaviest snowfalls in winter. By late spring, the snows melt and the foliage returns to the gardens. Summer brings warm weather and high humidity, and thunderstorms that can put a sudden end to a pleasant day. Late summer and fall have comparatively stable weather.

**NEW YORK CITY**

| month | Apr | Jul | Oct | Jan |
|---|---|---|---|---|
| °F/C (high) | 59/15 | 79/26 | 69/20 | 37/3 |
| °F/C (low) | 43/6 | 63/17 | 49/9 | 26/–3 |
| sunshine | 17 days | 20 days | 19 days | 16 days |
| rainfall | 3.8 in | 4 in | 3 in | 3 in |

32°F 0°C

great place to watch some of the world's greatest athletes perform. The cities here host a wide array of professional and amateur sports teams, with major pro baseball, football, and basketball franchises operating in New Jersey, New York City, Philadelphia, and Pittsburgh. Another extremely popular spectator sport is ice hockey.

There are also many "minor league" teams in smaller cities, and hundreds of high-quality sports teams fielded by the various public and private universities across the region.

The baseball season is from April to September, football from September through January, and basketball from winter through mid-Spring.

However, an extremely popular sports event is the **US Open Tennis Championships**, held annually outside New York City in August. Horseracing's **Belmont Stakes** in early June is the last leg of the "Triple Crown" championship, while throughout the months of July and August racing continues at historic Saratoga Springs. Participant sports are also prominent, with the New York Marathon in November being one of the more popular events.

## Outdoor Activities

New York State is also home to one of the country's prime winter sports resorts – Lake Placid in the Adirondack Mountains, where the 1932 and 1980 Winter Olympics were held. There are also ski areas in the Pocono Mountains of Pennsylvania and New Jersey, as well as Camelback Mountain and Hidden Valley in Western Pennsylvania, and Hunter Mountain and Catamount in Catskills, in New York State. For the best skiing, however, the most avid skiers head to the resorts of Vermont and New Hampshire.

## Entertainment

The world capital of the entertainment industry, New York City is a showcase for just about any form of performance. A quick read of the many local newspapers, like the *New York Times* or the *Village Voice*, and magazines such as *Time Out New York* and the *New Yorker* will point you toward hundreds of events and activities. **Lincoln Center** is home to many ballet, opera, and orchestral performances, as is legendary **Carnegie Hall**. The region's other large cities, Philadelphia, Pittsburgh, and Newark, also host numerous cultural and entertainment events. The newest venue is the **New Jersey Performing Arts Center** in Newark.

## Shopping

New York City can be called one of the world's greatest marketplaces, and it is safe to say that if you cannot buy a certain thing here, it probably does not exist at all. Everything ranging from fashionable boutiques to cut-price computers can be found in Manhattan, and some neighborhoods of New York City cater especially to the interest of shoppers and bargain hunters. Don't miss a trip to at least one of the city's exceptional department stores, such as **Macy's**, **Bloomingdale's**, **Saks Fifth Avenue**, or **Barney's**.

## Directory

### Tourist Information

**New Jersey**
C *(800) 847-4865.*
W www.visitnj.org

**New York City**
C *(212) 484-1200.*
W www.nycvisit.com

**New York State**
C *(518) 474-4116.*
W www.iloveny.com

**Pennsylvania**
C *(800) 847-4872.*
W www.experiencepa.com

### Festivals

**Bach Festival**
Bethlehem, Pennsylvania.
C *(610) 866-4382.*

**Glimmerglass Opera Festival**
Cooperstown, New York.
C *(607) 547-2255.*
W www.glimmerglass.org

**NJ Performing Arts Center**
Newark, NJ.
C *(888) 466-5722.*
W www.njpac.org

### Baseball

**New York Mets**
C *(718) 507-8499.*
W www.newyorkmets.mlb.com

**New York Yankees**
C *(718) 293-4300.*
W www.yankees.com

**Philadelphia Phillies**
C *215) 463-1000.*
W www.phillies.com

### Basketball

**New York Knicks**
C *(212) 465-6000.*

**Philadelphia 76ers**
C *(215) 339-7600.*

### Football

**Buffalo Bills**
C *(716) 649-0015.*
W www.buffalobills.com

**New York Giants**
C *(201) 935-8222.*
W www.giants.com

**Pittsburgh Steelers**
C *(412) 323-1200.*
W www.steelers.com

### Other Sports

**Belmont Stakes**
C *(718) 641-4700.*
W www.nyra.com/belmont

**Skiing**
W www.goski.com

### Entertainment

**Carnegie Hall**
C *(212) 247-7800.*
W www.carnegiehall.org

**Lincoln Center**
C *(212) 875-5030.*
W www.lincolncenter.org

### Shopping

**Barney's**
660 Madison Ave NYC.
C *(212) 826-8900.*

**Bloomingdale's**
Lexington & 59th St NYC.
C *(212) 705-2000.*

**Macy's**
Broadway & 34th NYC.
C *(212) 695-4400.*

# Where to Stay

NEW YORK CITY AND THE MID-ATLANTIC REGION offers something for everyone in terms of accommodation. In New York City, the top hotels are not quite as expensive as those in Paris or London, but the best news for travelers is the increase in budget hotels. Other budget options are furnished apartments and studios and bed and breakfast in private homes.

## NEW YORK CITY

**EAST VILLAGE:** *St. Mark's Hotel* $
2 St. Mark's Place. (212) 674-0100. FAX (212) 420-0854.
W www.stmarkshotel.qpg.com
In a city where ancient carpets and dingy walls are the norm in budget hotels, this bright and clean hotel offers welcome relief. Oak-and-marble hallways lead to sparse but neat rooms with small bathrooms. Shop-lined St. Mark's Place features a constant parade of tattooed youth, so don't expect quiet.

**EAST VILLAGE:** *Union Square Inn* $$
209 E 14th St. (212) 614-0500. FAX (212) 614-0512.
W www.unionsquareinn.com
Here's a wonderful find for discerning travelers who want standard comforts at a reasonable price. Rooms are small but have high-quality mattresses and brand-new bathrooms. A basic breakfast is included.

**GARMENT DISTRICT:** *Americana Inn* $
69 W 38th St. (212) 840-6700. FAX (212) 840-1830.
W www.theamericaninn.com
Linoleum floors lend an institutional feel, but otherwise this is a winner in the budget-basic price category. Rooms have private sinks and bright, spotless baths. The location is central, and the friendly, professional service is of a higher caliber than most in this price range.

**GARMENT DISTRICT:** *Hotel Chelsea* $$
222 W 23rd St. (212) 243-3700. FAX (212) 675-5531.
W www.hotelchelsea.com
This legendary artists' haven has housed famous names from Sarah Bernhardt to Dylan Thomas and Sid Vicious. Good for short-term visitors with a bohemian spirit. Rooms are large and eccentrically outfitted.

**GARMENT DISTRICT:** *Holiday Inn/Martinique on Broadway* $$$
49 W 32nd St. (212) 736-3800. FAX (212) 277-2702.
W www.holiday-inn.com
This fine branch of the reliable Holiday Inn chain is housed in a landmark French-Renaissance building. Rooms are chain standard once you move past the marble lobby. The Little Korea location offers affordable Asian dining at all hours. Rates are high, so ask for discounts.

**GREENWICH VILLAGE:** *Abingdon Guest House* $$
13 Eighth Ave. (212) 243-5384. FAX (212) 807-7473.
W www.abingdonguesthouse.com
This lovely guest house is located in the brownstone-lined, boutique-dotted West Village, one of the city's most charming neighborhoods. Each artfully decorated room is outfitted with first-rate comforts.

**GREENWICH VILLAGE:** *Washington Square Hotel* $$
103 Waverly Place. (212) 777-9515. FAX (212) 979-8373.
W www.wshotel.com
Facing Washington Square Park in the heart of New York University territory, this hotel offers small but recently refurbished rooms. Rates are a bit high, but the location is great for bar-hoppers and live-music fans.

**GRAMERCY & THE FLATIRON DISTRICT:** *Gershwin Hotel* $$
7 E 27th St. (212) 545-8000. FAX (212) 684-5546.
W www.gershwinhotel.com
An original Andy Warhol Campbell's Soup Can hanging in the lobby sets the tone for this pop-art-inspired hotel. Rooms are bright and stylishly decorated and range from bunk beds to suites. The hotel is excellent value for money considering its location – it's just steps away from the Empire State Building and plenty of good restaurants.

| Hotel | Credit Cards | Number of Rooms | Recommended Restaurant | Children's Facilities | Garden or Terrace |
|---|---|---|---|---|---|
| St. Mark's Hotel | ■ | 70 | | | |
| Union Square Inn | ■ | 40 | | | |
| Americana Inn | ■ | 50 | | | |
| Hotel Chelsea | ■ | 400 | ■ | | |
| Holiday Inn/Martinique on Broadway | ■ | 532 | ■ | | |
| Abingdon Guest House | ■ | 9 | | | |
| Washington Square Hotel | ■ | 170 | ■ | | |
| Gershwin Hotel | ■ | 150 | ■ | ● | |

**Price categories** for a standard double room per night, inclusive of breakfast, service charges, and any additional taxes:

- $ under $100
- $$ $100–$150
- $$$ $150–$200
- $$$$ $200–$250
- $$$$$ over $250

**CREDIT CARDS**
Major credit cards accepted.

**NUMBER OF ROOMS**
Number of rooms in the hotel.

**RECOMMENDED RESTAURANT**
Good restaurant within the hotel.

**CHILDREN'S FACILITIES**
Hotel has various facilities for young children.

**GARDEN OR TERRACE**
Hotel has a garden, courtyard, or terrace.

| Hotel | Credit Cards | Number of Rooms | Recommended Restaurant | Children's Facilities | Garden or Terrace |
|---|---|---|---|---|---|
| **GRAMERCY & THE FLATIRON DISTRICT:** *Hotel Giraffe* $$$$<br>365 Park Ave S. *(212) 685-7700.* FAX *(212) 685-7771.*<br>W www.hotelgiraffe.com<br>The Flatiron District's finest hotel brims with inspired elegance – rich textiles and custom furnishings. Amenities include CD players and granite bathrooms; deluxe rooms have French doors on to a Juliet balcony. Complimentary breakfast, plus a stylish Euro-Asian fusion restaurant. | ■ | 73 | ■ | | |
| **LOWER EAST SIDE:** *Off SoHo Suites Hotel* $<br>11 Rivington St. *(212) 979-9808.* FAX *(212) 979-9801.*<br>W www.offsoho.com<br>It used to be that this budget hotel was in no-man's-land – but hip downtown has expanded so much as to practically embrace it. Decor is nonexistent and beds are a bit too firm, but rooms are well tended. Deluxe suites have fully outfitted kitchens and baths, while economy suites share facilities. | ■ | 38 | ■ | | |
| **LOWER MANHATTAN:** *Holiday Inn Wall Street* $$$<br>15 Gold St. *(212) 232-7800.* FAX *(212) 269-9569.*<br>W www.holiday–inn.com<br>Wall Street's most technologically mature hotel was designed with business travelers in mind. Standard features include a desk and personal computer with CD/DVD drive, fax/copier/printer, ergonomic chair, and portable phones. Good buffet breakfast. | ■ | 138 | ■ | | |
| **LOWER MANHATTAN:** *Ritz Carlton Battery Park* $$$$<br>2 West St. *(212) 344-0800.* FAX *(212) 344-3801.*<br>W www.ritzcarlton<br>Telescopes in the elegantly modern rooms offer spectacular close-up views of the Statue of Liberty and the harbor. Kids are well looked after, with a toy menu, and a teddy bear in bed at turndown. The kids' food menu even has peanut butter and jelly sandwiches. | ■ | 298 | ■ | ● | |
| **LOWER MIDTOWN:** *Clarion Hotel Fifth Avenue* $$$<br>3 E 40th St. *(212) 683-5890.* FAX *(212) 787-3447.*<br>W www.hotelchoice.com<br>This freshly renovated chain hotel offers excellent value in a pricey neighborhood. Rooms are outfitted in comfort with a hint of smart Art Deco style. The location, near New York Public Library and Grand Central Terminal, is convenient for the Theater District. | ■ | 189 | ■ | | |
| **LOWER MIDTOWN:** *Kitano* $$$$$<br>66 Park Ave. *(212) 885-7000.* FAX *(212) 885-7100.*<br>W www.kitano.com, www.summithotels.com<br>This elegant Japanese-owned hotel is a sea of tranquility in the bustle, chaos, and excitement of the city. Hotel rooms are elegantly appointed havens of restful Japanese luxury. The Kaiseki cuisine in the restaurant is exceptional, and the service is flawless. | ■ | 149 | ■ | | |
| **MORNINGSIDE HEIGHTS & HARLEM:** *Sugar Hill International House* $<br>722 St Nicholas Ave. *(212) 926-7030.*<br>W www.sugarhillhostel.com<br>This quiet, well-run, all-nonsmoking hostel offers two-dozen dorm beds to shoestring travelers. Bunks fill spacious rooms; a few double rooms are available to early arrivals. Security is good, the neighborhood is quiet, there is a common kitchen, and the kind owners are happy to offer advice. | ■ | 25 | | | |
| **MORNINGSIDE HEIGHTS & HARLEM:** *Morningside Inn Hotel* $$<br>235 W 107th St. *(212) 864-9234.* FAX *(212) 864-9155.*<br>W www.morningsideinn–ny.com<br>This hotel is best for students and single travelers – try to score a deluxe room if you want a private bath and air conditioning. Budget rooms share a bathroom and a kitchen, but all rooms are clean and well cared for. | ■ | 96 | | | |

For key to symbols see back flap

**Price categories** for a standard double room per night, inclusive of breakfast, service charges, and any additional taxes:

- $ under $100
- $$ $100–$150
- $$$ $150–$200
- $$$$ $200–$250
- $$$$$ over $250

**Credit Cards**
Major credit cards accepted.

**Number of Rooms**
Number of rooms in the hotel.

**Recommended Restaurant**
Good restaurant within the hotel.

**Children's Facilities**
Hotel has various facilities for young children.

**Garden or Terrace**
Hotel has a garden, courtyard, or terrace.

**SoHo & TriBeCa:** *Cosmopolitan Hotel – Tribeca* $
95 W Broadway. (212) 566-1900. FAX (212) 566-6909.
W www.cosmohotel.com
In the heart of hip TriBeCa is one of Manhattan's best budget hotels. Rooms are petite but well maintained and pleasantly furnished; the bathrooms are tiny but pristine. The location is super-convenient, and a wealth of first-rate restaurants are within walking distance. Highly recommended.

**SoHo & TriBeCa:** *60 Thompson* $$$$
60 Thompson St. (212) 431-0400. FAX (212) 431-0200.
W www.60thompson.com
Despite its chic modernist lines, this smallish newcomer boasts a warm and surprisingly domestic ambience. Done in a soothing celadon-and-mahogany palette, rooms are plush and well equipped with DVD and CD players, Internet access, and marble baths. Location is first rate.

**Theater District:** *Big Apple Hostel* $
119 W 45th St. (212) 302-2603. FAX (212) 302-2605.
W www.bigapplehostel.com
New York's best hostel caters to a world of young travelers with super-clean accommodations and a prime location. Most beds are in dormitories, but a few private doubles are available. Everything is newer and nicer than at most hostels. Book well in advance.

**Theater District:** *Algonquin* $$$
59 W 44th St. (212) 840-6800. FAX (212) 944-1419.
W www.algonquinhotel.com
This restored legend, home to Dorothy Parker's literary "Round Table" of the 1920s, is one of Midtown's most evocative hotels. Rooms are small but comfortable; the literary-themed suites make a worthy splurge. The Oak Room offers star-quality cabaret.

**Theater District:** *Ritz-Carlton* $$$$$
50 Central Park S. (212) 308-9100. FAX (212) 207-8831.
W www.ritzcarlton.com
This reliable luxury chain's first Midtown hotel opened in 2002. Expect all of the classic Ritz-Carlton hallmarks, which blend traditional stylings and premier comforts: state-of-the-art technology, a full-service spa, and staff who never say "no."

**Upper East Side:** *Surrey Hotel* $$$$
20 E 76th St. (212) 288-3700. FAX (212) 628-1549.
W www.mesuite.com
Experience the high life for less at this lovely all-suite hotel. The Old World suites are spacious and pleasing from tip to toe; each one has a fully equipped kitchen. In-suite dining, from Cafe Boulud, one of New York's finest restaurants, is reason enough to stay.

**Upper East Side:** *Franklin* $$$$$
164 E 87th St. (212) 369-1000. FAX (212) 369-8000.
W www.franklinhotel.com
Rooms may be tiny at this modern hotel, but they are elegant and well-appointed, with romantic beds, VCRs and the like. Limited space make it the choice for short-term travelers, or for those who pack light. Check for discount rates and packages on their website.

**Upper Midtown:** *Kimberly Hotel* $$$
145 E 50th St. (212) 755-0400. FAX (212) 486-6915.
W www.kimberlyhotel.com
This low-profile hotel boasts mostly apartment-style one- and two-bedroom suites featuring home comforts, such as a full-size kitchen, dining area, and large, well-appointed rooms. Excellent for families and long-term business travelers. Check for discounts and packages.

| Hotel | Credit Cards | Number of Rooms | Recommended Restaurant | Children's Facilities | Garden or Terrace |
|---|---|---|---|---|---|
| Cosmopolitan Hotel – Tribeca | ■ | 105 | | | |
| 60 Thompson | ■ | 100 | ■ | | |
| Big Apple Hostel | ■ | 39 | | | |
| Algonquin | ■ | 174 | ■ | | |
| Ritz-Carlton | ■ | 287 | ■ | | |
| Surrey Hotel | ■ | 130 | ■ | | |
| Franklin | ■ | 48 | ■ | | |
| Kimberly Hotel | ■ | 185 | ■ | | |

**UPPER MIDTOWN:** *Waldorf-Astoria/Waldorf Towers* $$$$
301 Park Ave. (212) 355-3000. FAX (212) 872-7272.
W www.hilton.com
This New York legend is as great as ever. Rates are very reasonable in the main hotel, considering the glamorous air, extra-large rooms, and first-class dining and amenities. The exclusive Waldorf Towers has 24-hour butler service and a solid reputation for discretion.

1242

**UPPER WEST SIDE:** *Jazz on the Park* $
36 W 106th St, New York. (212) 932-1600. FAX (212) 932-1700.
W www.jazzonthepark.com
This funky, artsy hostel brings a downtown vibe to the Upper West Side. A coffeehouse with live music most evenings lends a party atmosphere. Dorm rooms are hostel-basic, and bathrooms are decent. Expect a young, energetic, and international crowd. Continental breakfast is a value-added touch.

220

**UPPER WEST SIDE:** *Trump International Hotel & Tower* $$$$$
1 Central Park West, New York. (212) 299-1000. FAX (212) 299-1150.
W www.trumpintl.com
Housed in a freestanding tower overlooking Central Park, this hotel is one of the city's finest. Smartly designed rooms are softened with soothing Tuscan hues; floor-to-ceiling windows offer great views. Each guest is assigned a personal concierge, making service unparalleled.

167

## NEW YORK STATE

**ALBANY:** *Mansion Hill Inn* $$$
115 Philip St. (518) 465-2038, (888) 299-0455. FAX (518) 434-2313.
W www.mansionhill.com
This downtown inn, located near the Governor's Mansion and housed in an 1860s private home, has been fully modernized but still holds considerable charm.

8

**BUFFALO:** *Best Western Inn On The Avenue* $$
510 Delaware Ave. (716) 886-8333. FAX (716) 884-3070.
W www.bestwesternnewyork.com
This medium-sized mid-range hotel is conveniently located in the lively "Allentown" neighborhood downtown, with easy access to parks, museums, and other attractions.

61

**COLD SPRING (HUDSON RIVER VALLEY):** *Hudson House Inn* $$$
2 Main St. (845) 265-9355.
W www.hudsonhouseinn.com
Set on the banks of the Hudson River, looking across to Storm King Mountain and the US Military Academy at West Point, this inn has been in business since the 1830s and is rich in period charm.

13

**COOPERSTOWN:** *Otesaga Hotel* $$$$$
60 Lake St. (607) 547-9931. FAX (607) 547-9675.
W www.otesaga.com
Recently restored to its 1909 splendor, this well-located downtown hotel is intimate and luxuriously appointed. Facilities include a swimming pool and a full-service gym. It is closed in winter.

136

**ITHACA:** *Buttermilk Falls Inn* $$
110 E Buttermilk Falls Rd. (607) 272-6767. FAX (607) 273-3947.
W www.buttermilkfallsinn.com
Located near the foot of a waterfall, adjacent to a 750-acre (304-ha) state park, this B&B inn dates back to the 1820s.

5

**LAKE PLACID:** *Mirror Lake Inn* $$$$$
5 Mirror Lake Dr. (518) 523-2544. FAX (518) 523-2871.
W www.mirrorlakeinn.com
A lakefront landmark, rebuilt after a 1988 fire, this large old-fashioned hotel has a wide variety of luxurious rooms, as well as a full range of restaurants and activities, including a private beach and an ice-skating rink.

128

**MONTAUK:** *Shepherds Neck Inn* $$
90 Second House Rd. (631) 668-2105. FAX (631) 668-0171.
W www.shepherdsneckinn.com
Set on 8 acres (3.2 ha), complete with tennis courts, a swimming pool, and an award-winning restaurant, this inn has a welcoming, easy-going feel.

86

**Price categories** for a standard double room per night, inclusive of breakfast, service charges, and any additional taxes:

- $ under $100
- $$ $100–$150
- $$$ $150–$200
- $$$$ $200–$250
- $$$$$ over $250

**Credit Cards**
Major credit cards accepted.

**Number of Rooms**
Number of rooms in the hotel.

**Recommended Restaurant**
Good restaurant within the hotel.

**Children's Facilities**
Hotel has various facilities for young children.

**Garden or Terrace**
Hotel has a garden, courtyard, or terrace.

**Niagara Falls:** *Comfort Inn The Pointe* $$

1 Prospect Pointe. *(716) 284-6835.* FAX *(716) 284-5177.*
W www.comfortinn.com

This inn is located in a historic building just 1,200 ft (366 m) from Niagara Falls, so close you can feel the mist and hear the rumbling (though you cannot actually see the falls). True to its name, the inn offers comfortable accommodations at a good price.

| Credit Cards | Number of Rooms | Recommended Restaurant | Children's Facilities | Garden or Terrace |
|---|---|---|---|---|
| ■ | 120 | | ● | |

**Rhinebeck:** *Beekman Arms* $$

4 Mill Street. *(845) 876-7077.* FAX *(845) 876-7077.*
W www.beekmanarms.com

In business since 1766, this is one of the oldest inns in America, having hosted everyone from George Washington to Franklin Roosevelt. Rooms in the original inn are somewhat small but comfortable. Larger rooms are available in adjacent buildings.

| Credit Cards | Number of Rooms | Recommended Restaurant | Children's Facilities | Garden or Terrace |
|---|---|---|---|---|
| ■ | 73 | ■ | ● | ■ |

**Rochester:** *Clarion Riverside Hotel* $$

120 E Main St. *(585) 546-6400, (800) 223-9330.* FAX *(585) 546-3908.*
W www.clarionriversidehotel.com

This is a very large, business-oriented downtown hotel, located right on the river across from the convention center. Four Points Sheraton offers all modern amenities at reasonable rates. Among the facilities provided are a full-service gym and swimming pool.

| Credit Cards | Number of Rooms | Recommended Restaurant | Children's Facilities | Garden or Terrace |
|---|---|---|---|---|
| ■ | 466 | ■ | | |

**Saratoga Springs:** *Adelphi Hotel* $$$

365 Broadway. *(518) 587-4688.* FAX *(518) 587-0851.*
W www.adelphihotel.com

Located right in the center of town, this historic hotel has been renovated with extravagant furnishings. Each room is decorated in a unique version of late Victorian excess, and the hand-painted murals in the opulent lobby have to be seen to be believed.

| Credit Cards | Number of Rooms | Recommended Restaurant | Children's Facilities | Garden or Terrace |
|---|---|---|---|---|
| ■ | 35 | | | ■ |

**Skaneateles (Finger Lakes):** *Hobbit Hollow Farm* $$$

3061 W Lake Rd. *(315) 685-2791.* FAX *(315) 685-3426.*
W www.hobbithollow.com

Set on more than 300 acres (121 ha) of rolling fields overlooking Skaneateles Lake, this pleasant bread-and-breakfast inn offers a relaxing respite in the heart of the Finger Lakes. Each of the rooms is furnished with antiques and has a luxurious private bath.

| Credit Cards | Number of Rooms | Recommended Restaurant | Children's Facilities | Garden or Terrace |
|---|---|---|---|---|
| ■ | 5 | | | ■ |

## New Jersey

**Atlantic City:** *Atlantic City Hilton* $$$

Boston Ave and The Boardwalk. *(609) 347-7111.* FAX *(609) 340-4858.*
W www.hiltonac.com

This hotel has a day spa, massage, and a swimming pool that has views of the Atlantic Ocean. Most of the rooms have views too, but guests might be more interested in the casino in the hotel than the view. Choice of several restaurants and evening entertainment in either the bar or the theater.

| Credit Cards | Number of Rooms | Recommended Restaurant | Children's Facilities | Garden or Terrace |
|---|---|---|---|---|
| ■ | 800 | ■ | | |

**Atlantic City:** *Bally's Park Place Hotel* $$$

Boardwalk and Park Place. *(609) 340-2000, (800) 225--5977.*
FAX *(609) 340-4713.* W www.ballys.com

One of the few remnants of historic Atlantic City, the 1860s-era Dennis Hotel has been restored as part of this mega-resort complex, which also includes a modern 37-story tower. Fans of the board game Monopoly will know that the hotel stands on the city's most valuable corner.

| Credit Cards | Number of Rooms | Recommended Restaurant | Children's Facilities | Garden or Terrace |
|---|---|---|---|---|
| ■ | 1270 | ■ | ● | ■ |

| Hotel | | Rooms | | | |
|---|---|---|---|---|---|
| **CAPE MAY:** *Chalfonte Hotel* $$$<br>301 Howard St. (609) 884-8409. FAX (609) 884-4588.<br>W www.chalfonte.com<br>Like a living-history museum, this white-washed Victorian-era hotel offers old-fashioned charms like rocking chairs on the wrap-around front porch. Rooms have no TVs or phones, but the hotel is just two blocks from the beach, and guests are invited to enjoy family-style communal meals. P | ■ | 66 | ■ | ● | ■ |
| **CAPE MAY:** *Queen's Hotel* $$$<br>601 Columbia Ave. (609) 884-1613.<br>W www.queenshotel.com<br>Built in the 1870s and fully restored in 1995, this mansard-roofed Victorian inn is located in the heart of historic Cape May, just a block from the beach. Rooms have antique furnishings, and free bicycles are available. TV P | ■ | 11 | | | ■ |
| **PENNSYLVANIA** | | | | | |
| **BIRD IN HAND:** *Village Inn and Suites* $$<br>2695 Old Philadelphia Pike. (717) 768-1535, (800) 914-2473.<br>FAX (717) 768-1117. W www.bird-in-hand.com/villageinn<br>Located in the heart of this picturesque, if oddly-named Pennsylvania Dutch country village, this 1734 inn now welcomes travelers with all modern comforts and conveniences. Great service and facilities. TV P | ■ | 24 | | | ■ |
| **LITITZ:** *General Sutter Inn* $$<br>14 E Main St. (717) 626-2115. FAX (717) 626-0992.<br>W www.generalsutterinn.com<br>Dating from 1764, this is the oldest inn in Pennsylvania and has retained its stately period architecture and its position at the center of a very quaint Pennsylvania Dutch country hamlet. Facilities include a good restaurant and a lively bar. TV P | ■ | 15 | ■ | | ■ |
| **PHILADELPHIA:** *Comfort Inn* $$<br>100 N Chris. Columbus Blvd. (215) 627-7900. FAX (215) 238-0809.<br>W www.choicehotels.com<br>This budget-priced high-rise hotel has no frills but a great location, near Penn's Landing and the historic Independence Hall. Rooms are sparse but clean and comfortable, and all have large private baths. TV P | ■ | 185 | | | |
| **PHILADELPHIA:** *Penn's View Hotel* $$$<br>14 N Front St. (215) 922-7600. FAX (215) 922-7642. W www.pennsviewhotel.com<br>Overlooking the Delaware River from the heart of historic Philadelphia, this small full-service hotel has well-appointed rooms and a welcoming, European-style ambience. TV | ■ | 52 | ■ | | |
| **PHILADELPHIA:** *Radisson Plaza Warwick* $$$<br>1701 Locust St. (215) 735-6000. FAX (215) 789-6105.<br>W www.radisson.com<br>Located downtown in lovely Rittenhouse Square, this historic hotel is the grand dame of Philadelphia. Excellent service, and all the usual amenities make it great for the business traveler. TV P | ■ | 545 | ■ | | |
| **PHILADELPHIA:** *Loews Philadelphia* $$$$<br>1200 Market Street. (215) 627-1200.<br>W www.loewshotels.com/philadelphia<br>Housed in the PSFS building, a 1932 landmark of modernist architecture at the heart of Philadelphia's Center City, this ultra-stylish luxury hotel opened in 2002 and has set a new standard for comfort and service. TV P | ■ | 581 | ■ | ● | ■ |
| **PITTSBURGH:** *Omni William Penn* $$$<br>530 William Penn Place. (412) 281-7100. FAX (412) 553-5252.<br>W www.omnihotels.com<br>Located in the heart of the downtown business district, this landmark hotel offers a sumptuous lobby, spacious, comfortable rooms, and a full-service gym. Very popular, so book early. TV P | ■ | 595 | ■ | ● | ■ |
| **PITTSBURGH:** *The Priory* $$$<br>614 Pressley St. (412) 231-3338. FAX (412) 231-4838.<br>W www.thepriory.com<br>One of the city's nicest places to stay, this chaming B&B inn has been brought back to life after its original incarnation as a rooming house for traveling Benedictine monks. Guests today can enjoy complimentary afternoon glasses of wine in the central courtyard. TV P | ■ | 25 | | | ■ |

For key to symbols see back flap

# Where to Eat

A VARIED DINING EXPERIENCE IS OFFERED across much of the Mid-Atlantic Region. New York City, especially, has more than 25,000 restaurants catering to every taste. Here, "in" places and cuisine change with great regularity, while some favorite places remain popular. In the listings below, opening times are indicated by a "B" for breakfast, "L" for lunch, and "D" for dinner.

## NEW YORK CITY

**EAST VILLAGE:** *Great Jones Café* $

54 Great Jones St. *(212) 674-9304.*

Cajun food lovers come to this hole-in-the-wall NoHo neighborhood café for spicy gumbo made with andouille sausage, jambalaya, corn-meal fried catfish, and other delicious New Orleans fare. *D.*

**GREENWICH VILLAGE:** *Babbo* $$$$$

110 Waverly Pl. *(212) 777-0303.*

The setting in a century-old duplex Greenwich Village townhouse, with its grand stairway and skylight, and the inventive, rustic Italian country fare of notable chef Mario Batali, make this one of the most popular Italian restaurants in the city; reserve well in advance. *D.*

**GRAMERCY & THE FLATIRON DISTRICT:** *Union Square Café* $$$$

21 East 16th St. *(212) 243-4020.*

Restaurant entrepreneur Danny Meyer's first venue has been one of New York's most popular since 1985, loved for delicious fare served in friendly surroundings. Chef Michael Romano's new takes on American standards include the freshest ingredients from the neighboring Union Square Greenmarket. *Mon–Sat L, D.*

**LOWER EAST SIDE:** *Grand Sichuan* $

125 Canal St. *(212) 625-9212.*

For those who favor the spicy seasonings of China's Szechwan province, this is a Chinatown find, a no-frills storefront with authentic specialties of the region at reasonable prices. Its reputation has spawned two uptown siblings at 229 Ninth Avenue and 745 Ninth Avenue. *L, D.*

**LOWER EAST SIDE:** *Il Palazzo* $$

151 Mulberry St. *(212) 343-7000.*

One of the better choices on Mulberry Street: cozy, candlelit, and non-touristy. The menu includes all the Italian favorites, including tempting pastries. The serene garden with a fountain out back is a summer delight. *L, D.*

**LOWER MANHATTAN:** *Battery Gardens* $$$

Battery Park, opposite 17 State St. *(212) 809-5508.*

A great location at the tip of the Battery with wall-to-wall harbor views makes this a popular choice. Sit on the terrace in summer while you dine on primarily seafood with Italian and Asian twists. *L, D.* ● *Sun D.*

**LOWER MANHATTAN:** *14 Wall Street Restaurant* $$$$

14 Wall St. *(212) 233-2780.*

Once J.P. Morgan's private dining room, this penthouse with wonderful views is a Wall Street expense-account favorite. The room with high ceilings, dark wood trim, and vintage French posters is a handsome setting for fine French cuisine. The service is impeccable. *L, Mon–Fri D.*

**LOWER MIDTOWN:** *Grand Central Oyster Bar* $$$

Grand Central Station, lower level, 42nd St & Lexington Ave. *(212) 490-6650.*

A New York classic beneath a vaulted ceiling of Guastavino tiles, this big, noisy, restaurant features the freshest of seafood, from simple preparations, which are not too pricey, to a menu with over with a dozen kinds of oysters. The atmosphere is casual, so leave the fur coats at home and bring your appetite. *L, D.* ● *Sun.*

**MORNINGSIDE HEIGHTS & HARLEM:** *Sylvia's* $$

328 Lenox Ave. *(212) 996-0660.*

A New York tradition since 1962, Sylvia's serves good ol' soul food in a kitschy dining room, sometimes with live music. It gets busy with students and locals enjoying the inexpensive menu of staples such as fried chicken, collard greens, and black-eyed pees. *B (Mon–Sat), L, D, Sun brunch.*

| Restaurant | Credit Cards | Outdoor Tables | Vegetarian | Good Wine List | Children's Facilities |
|---|---|---|---|---|---|
| Great Jones Café | | | ■ | | |
| Babbo | ■ | | | ● | |
| Union Square Café | ■ | | ■ | ● | ■ |
| Grand Sichuan | ■ | | | | |
| Il Palazzo | ■ | ● | ■ | | ■ |
| Battery Gardens | ■ | ● | | | ■ |
| 14 Wall Street Restaurant | ■ | | | | |
| Grand Central Oyster Bar | ■ | | | ● | ■ |
| Sylvia's | ■ | | | | ■ |

**Price categories** include a three-course meal for one, a glass of house wine, and all unavoidable extra charges such as sales tax and service.
$ under $20
$$ $20–30
$$$ $30–45
$$$$ $45–60
$$$$$ over $60

**CREDIT CARDS**
Major credit cards accepted.

**OUTDOOR TABLES**
Garden, courtyard, or terrace with outside tables.

**VEGETARIAN**
A good selection of vegetarian dishes available.

**GOOD WINE LIST**
Extensive list of good wines, both domestic and imported.

**CHILDREN'S FACILITIES**
Small portions and/or high chairs available on request.

| Restaurant | Price | Credit Cards | Outdoor Tables | Vegetarian | Good Wine List | Children's Facilities |
|---|---|---|---|---|---|---|
| **SOHO & TRIBECA:** *Lupa*<br>170 Thomson St. *(212) 982-5089.*<br>Much less expensive than his Babbo, Chef Mario Batali's rustic, candle-lit Roman trattoria serves elegant fare at affordable prices: appetizers like heavenly prosciutto with figs, and pastas such as squid ink tagliarini with spicy calamari. You may have to wait for a seat, but you won't be sorry you came. *L, D.* | $$$ | ■ | | ■ | | ■ |
| **SOHO & TRIBECA:** *Kittichai*<br>60 Thompson St. *(212) 219-2000.*<br>A modern Thai restaurant in a beautifully designed space in the Thompson hotel *(see p114)*. The menu offers an interesting selection of "Thai tapas," such as scallop and caviar ceviche, plus traditional entrées such as soup, curry and seafood dishes. Jacket and tie required. *B, L, D, Dim Sum (Sat–Sun).* | $$$$ | ■ | | ■ | | |
| **THEATER DISTRICT:** *Virgil's Real BBQ*<br>152 West 44th St. *(212) 921-9494.*<br>This big, boisterous restaurant offers a tour of barbecue styles throughout the South, from Memphis to Carolina to Texas, 10 different platters of beef, pork, or chicken with a variety of sauces. Sides are flaky buttermilk biscuits with honey-butter and collard greens. *L, D.* | $ | ■ | | | | ■ |
| **THEATER DISTRICT:** *Le Bernardin*<br>155 West 51st St. *(212) 554-1515.*<br>Seafood doesn't come any better than at this luxurious French restaurant lauded for revolutionizing the way fish is served in New York. It is considered one of America's best restaurants, and Chef Eric Lipert seems to have no critics. Perfection has its price, but the meal will be memorable. *Mon-Fri L, Mon–Sun D.* | $$$$$ | ■ | | | ● | ■ |
| **UPPER EAST SIDE:** *Shanghai Pavilion*<br>1378 Third Ave. *(212) 585-3388.*<br>Authentic Shanghai cuisine is served here. The menu is vast, with plenty of options at reasonable prices making it good value in this neighborhood. The service is friendly, and there is also great dim sum, noodle dishes, and specialties such as velvet sea bass and lobster. *L, D.* | $$ | ■ | | | | ■ |
| **UPPER EAST SIDE:** *Orsay*<br>1057 Lexington Ave. *(212) 517-6400.*<br>An authentic style French café with an upscale atmosphere. It's so popular that it gets noisy in the evenings. Still, the crowds come to try exotic creations such as the margarita tartare or crispy duck leg with garlic beignet. There's also a separate bar menu for late-night eating. *L, D.* | $$$$ | ■ | | | ● | |
| **UPPER MIDTOWN :** *Dawat*<br>210 East 58th St. *(212) 355-7555.*<br>One of the more attractive Indian dining places in the city, Dawat features recipes inspired by Madhur Jaffrey, a noted Indian cookbook author. It is known for signature dishes such as salmon rubbed in coriander chutney and steamed in a banana leaf. *Mon–Sat L, D.* | $$$ | ■ | | ■ | | ■ |
| **UPPER WEST SIDE:** *Pasha*<br>70 West St. *(212) 579-8751.*<br>A serene and stylish Turkish restaurant with friendly service. The lamb dumpling appetisers are delicious, as are the various dips, in particular the smoky *Patlican Salatasi* – mashed eggplant with garlic, olive oil and lemon. *D.* | $$$ | ■ | | | | |
| **UPPER WEST SIDE:** *Picholine*<br>West 64th St. *(212) 724-8585.*<br>For fine dining in the Lincoln Center area, the top choice is Terrance Brennan's elegant Mediterranean restaurant, where the chef's blending of subtle flavors transforms every dish. The cheese course is famous – be sure to save room. *Sat L, D.* | $$$$$ | ■ | | | | |

**Price categories** include a three-course meal for one, a glass of house wine, and all unavoidable extra charges such as sales tax and service.
($) under $20
($)($) $20–30
($)($)($) $30–45
($)($)($)($) $45–60
($)($)($)($)($) over $60

**CREDIT CARDS**
Major credit cards accepted.

**OUTDOOR TABLES**
Garden, courtyard, or terrace with outside tables.

**VEGETARIAN**
A good selection of vegetarian dishes available.

**GOOD WINE LIST**
Extensive list of good wines, both domestic and imported.

**CHILDREN'S FACILITIES**
Small portions and/or high chairs available on request.

## NEW YORK STATE

**ALBANY:** *Jack's Oyster House* ($)($)($)
4244 State St. *(518) 465-8854.*
A popular haunt with state legislators and lobbyists, this lively restaurant specializes in seafood. *L, D.*

**AMAGANSETT:** *Lobster Roll* ($)($)
1980 Montauk Highway. *(631) 267-3740.*
Known locally as "Lunch," thanks to the huge sign that looms over the shack-like building, this informal beachfront café serves all kinds of fresh seafood and great fruit pies. *L, D.* ● *mid-Oct–May.*

**BUFFALO:** *Roycroft Inn* ($)($)($)($)
40 S Grove St. *(716) 652-5552.*
If you want to appreciate the life and times of Buffalo at its turn-of-the-20th-century peak, enjoy a meal at this cozy restaurant, housed in a landmark Arts and Crafts-style hotel. *L, D.*

**COOPERSTOWN:** *Doubleday Café* ($)($)
93 Main St. *(607) 547-5468.*
Catering to the many baseball fans making a pilgrimage to the nearby Hall of Fame, with walls covered in baseball memorabilia, this family-friendly restaurant serves hearty American fare like soups and burgers. *B, L, D.* ● *Thanksgiving, Dec 25.*

**HYDE PARK:** *American Bounty* ($)($)($)
433 Albany Post Rd. *(845) 471-6608.*
Located in the massive Culinary Institute of America (CIA), and operated by student chefs, this nationally famous restaurant is one of the best places to eat in the Hudson River Valley area. *L, D.* ● *Sun, Mon, late Jul.*

**ITHACA:** *Moosewood* ($)($)
215 N Cayuga St. *(607) 273-9610.*
One of the earliest and most influential natural-food restaurants in the country, this cooperatively owned and warmly decorated vegetarian café has excellent food and an easy-going ambience. The wine list is excellent. *L, D.* ● *Sun L.*

**MILLBROOK (HUSDSON RIVER VALLEY):** *Millbrook Diner* ($)
Franklin Ave. *(845) 677-5319.*
Set at the center of a quaint Hudson River Valley village, this classic 1950s O'Mahony stainless-steel diner serves up excellent breakfasts and other meals to a wide range of locals and visitors. *B, L, D.*

**MONTAUK:** *Gosman's Dock* ($)($)($)
West Lake Dr. *(631) 668-5330.*
Overlooking the harbor, this large and very popular restaurant has been serving fresh fish for over 50 years. The restaurant also features a well-stocked bar. *L, D.*

**SHARON SPRINGS:** *American Hotel* ($)($)($)
192 Main St. *(518) 284-2105.*
Located in the middle of a sleepy former spa town and inside a recently restored hotel that dates back to the mid-1840s, this stylish little restaurant offers urban sophistication in a relaxing setting. *L (Sat–Sun), D.* ● *Nov–Mar: Mon–Tue.*

**SKANEATELES (FINGER LAKES):** *Doug's Fish Fry* ($)
8 Jordan St. *(315) 685-3288.*
This Finger Lakes eatery offers truly delicious fresh fried fish, served up in an unpretentious setting that has hardly changed for 40-odd years. *L, D.* ● *Jan 1–15, major hols.*

| | Credit Cards | Outdoor Tables | Vegetarian | Good Wine List | Children's Facilities |
|---|---|---|---|---|---|
| Albany: Jack's Oyster House | ■ | | ■ | ● | ■ |
| Amagansett: Lobster Roll | ■ | ● | ■ | | ■ |
| Buffalo: Roycroft Inn | ■ | ● | ■ | ● | ■ |
| Cooperstown: Doubleday Café | ■ | | ■ | | |
| Hyde Park: American Bounty | ■ | | ■ | ● | |
| Ithaca: Moosewood | ■ | ● | ■ | ● | ■ |
| Millbrook: Millbrook Diner | ■ | | ■ | ● | ■ |
| Montauk: Gosman's Dock | ■ | ● | ■ | ● | ■ |
| Sharon Springs: American Hotel | ■ | ● | ■ | ● | |
| Skaneateles: Doug's Fish Fry | ■ | ● | ■ | | ■ |

## NEW JERSEY

**ATLANTIC CITY:** *Dock's Oyster House* $$$
2405 Atlantic Ave. *(609) 345-0092.*
One of the oldest in the state, this restaurant, decorated in wood and stained glass, has been run by the same family since 1897. *D.*

**CAPE MAY:** *Mad Batter* $$$
19 Jackson St. *(609) 884-5970.*
For an unforgettable breakfast, lunch, or dinner, head to this energetic café, housed in a Victorian-era B&B inn. Generous portions are served in a casual setting by a friendly staff. *B, L, D.* *Jan.*

## PENNSYLVANIA

**EPHRATA:** *Doneckers Restaurant* $$$
333 N State St. *(717) 738-9501.*
This stylish country French restaurant located in the heart of the Pennsylvania Dutch Country, has an excellent wine list which includes 500 different wines, and also has a less formal bistro. *L, D.* *Wed, Sun.*

**GETTYSBURG:** *Dobbins House* $$$
89 Steinwehr Ave. *(717) 334-2100.*
Located in an old house that dates from 1776, this history-rich restaurant serves old-fashioned hearty dishes like roast duck and a cherry-stuffed pork tenderloin. *L, D.*

**MOUNT JOY:** *Groff's Farm* $$$
650 Pinkerton Rd. *(717) 653-2048.*
For a taste of Pennsylvania Dutch Country cooking, plan to visit this popular, family-style restaurant, where you can serve yourself as much as you like of the well-prepared roasted meats, plentiful vegetables, and heart-stopping desserts. A la carte is also available. *Fri–Sat D.*

**PHILADELPHIA:** *Reading Terminal Market* $
1200 Arch St. *(215) 922-2317.*
Inside this historic downtown market, over 80 different stands sell all kinds of lunch food from around the world, including Chinese, Japanese, Greek, Middle Eastern, and Pennsylvania Dutch. Open since 1892, the Reading Terminal Market now sits at the entrance to the city's convention center. *L.* *Sun.*

**PHILADELPHIA:** *Jim's Steaks* $
400 South St. *(215) 928-1911.*
To sample the sandwich that's named for the city, the "Philly Cheesesteak," come to this unique Art Deco stand, which has been serving up these sliced steak and melted cheese concoctions for over 60 years. The original branch is still open at 431 N 62nd Street. *L, D.*

**PHILADELPHIA:** *City Tavern* $$$
138 S 2nd St. *(215) 413-1443.*
Part of the Independence National Historical Park, this is a faithful re-creation of the city's most popular meeting place in the days leading up to the American Revolution. *L, D.*

**PHILADELPHIA:** *Striped Bass* $$$$$
1500 Walnut St. *(215) 732-4444.*
The high ceilings and marble pillars of the main dining room set the tone for one of the city's best restaurants, which features modern variations on traditional fish dishes. Start the evening with fresh oysters at the adjacent bar. *L (Sun only), D.*

**PHILADELPHIA:** *Susanna Foo* $$$$
1512 Walnut Street. *(215) 545-2666.*
French culinary techniques meet fresh American produce in these wonderfully inventive versions of traditional Chinese dishes. *L (Mon–Fri), D.*

**PITTSBURGH:** *Primanti Brothers* $
46 18th St. *(412) 263-2142.*
A blue-collar institution in this hard-working city, this is the first of many locations around Pittsburgh serving excellent "cheesesteaks" and other sandwiches, 24 hours a day. *B, L, D.*

For key to symbols see back flap

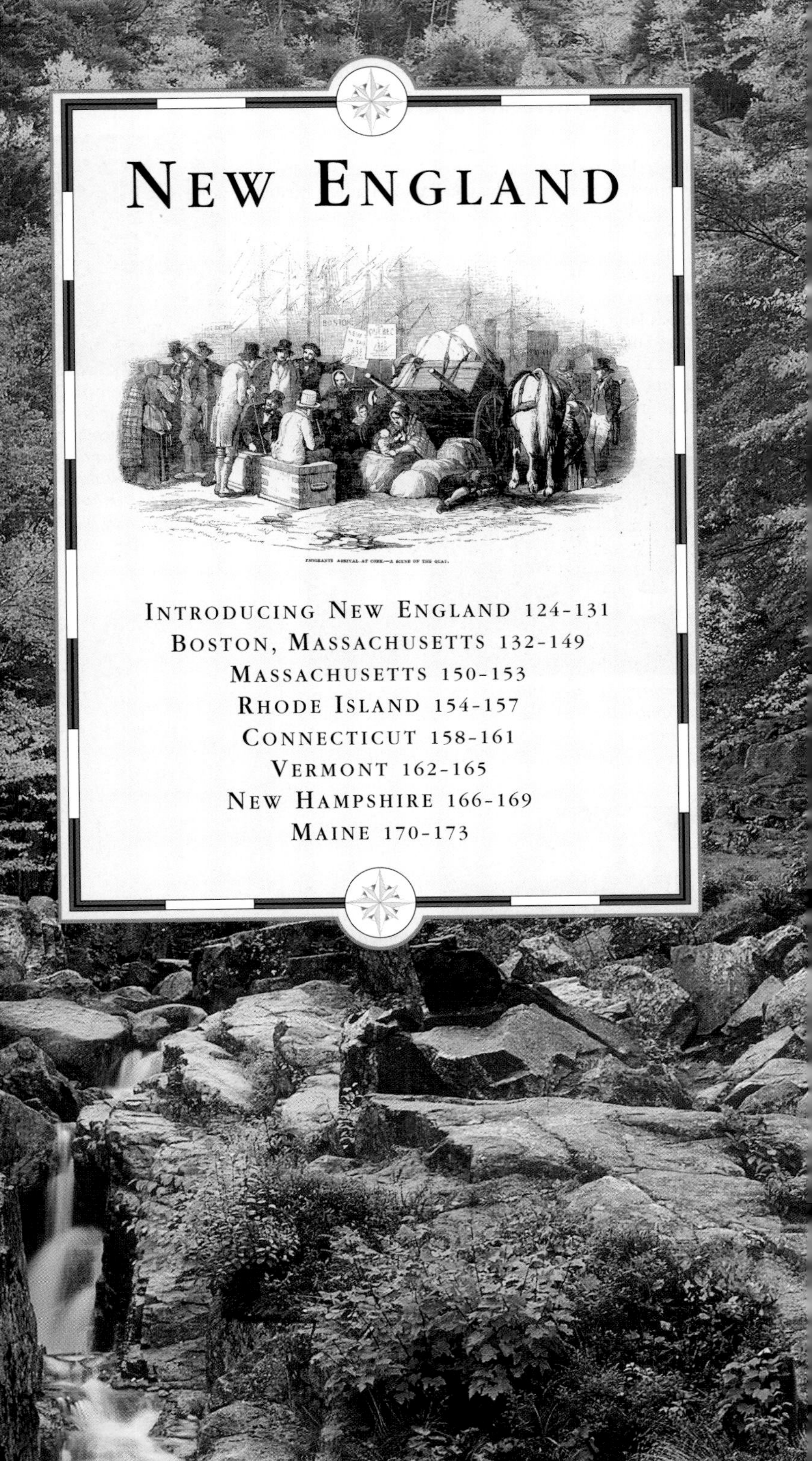


# NEW ENGLAND

# New England at a Glance

TUCKED AWAY IN THE northeasternmost corner of the United States, the six states of New England are rich in history and culture as well as in natural beauty. Many of the country's earliest settlements were established here, as were the first centers of higher education. The region therefore abounds in historic buildings, as well as in superb museums and prestigious universities. New England's topography includes large tracts of farmland, dense woodlands, pristine lakes, and sweeping coastlines, which are rocky and jagged in some areas and serene and sandy in others. It is also home to the rugged peaks of the White, Green, and Appalachian Mountains.

***Vermont*** (see pp162–5) *is an enclave of unspoiled wilderness. Vermont is at its scenic best in fall, when the Green Mountain State changes its verdant green cloak for a rich palette of yellow, orange, and red.*

***Canterbury Shaker Village*** (see p168) *located in New Hampshire, was founded in 1792. This is one of the many picturesque historic villages that are scattered around the rolling farmlands of the state.*

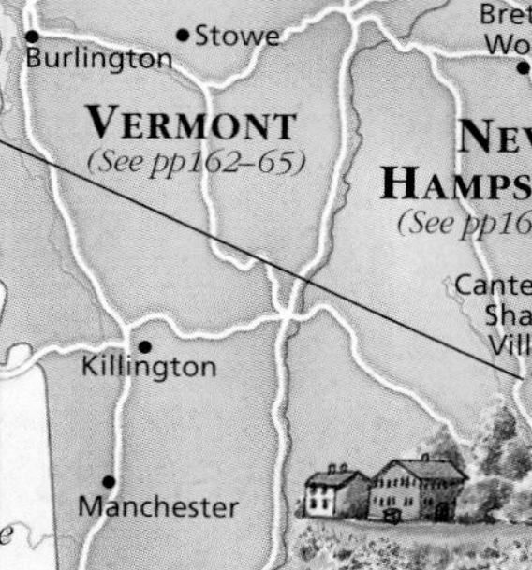

***Connecticut*** (see pp158–61) *is quintessential New England. Steepled churches around immaculate village greens are typical features of its serene landscape.*

***Block Island*** (see p157) *in Rhode Island is one of the many tranquil havens situated along the pristine shoreline of this tiny state. Great Salt Pond has three marinas and is an excellent spot for kayaking and fishing.*

◁ **Silver Cascades, Crawford Notch State Park, New Hampshire, in the autumn**

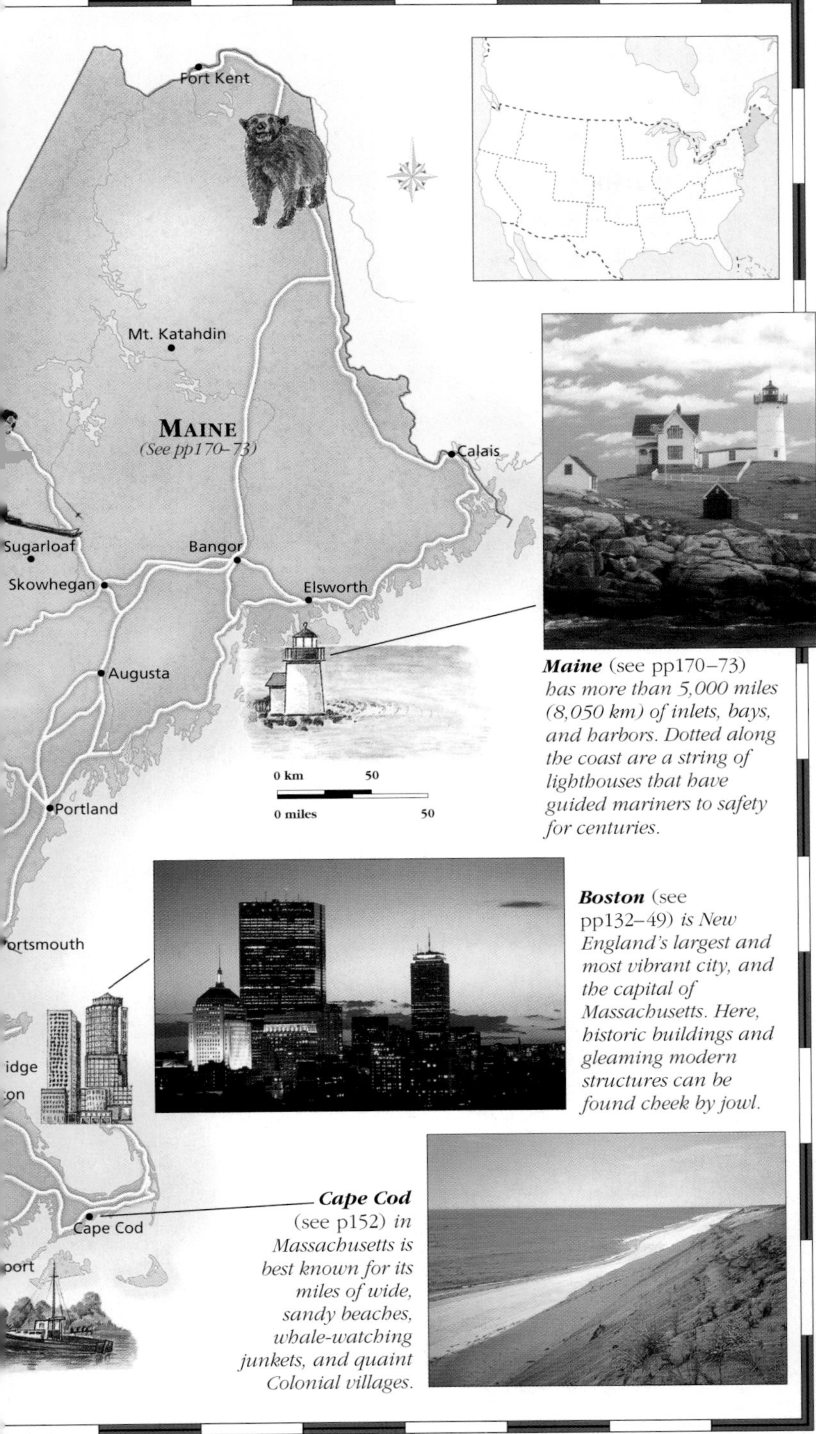


***Maine*** (see pp170–73) *has more than 5,000 miles (8,050 km) of inlets, bays, and harbors. Dotted along the coast are a string of lighthouses that have guided mariners to safety for centuries.*

***Boston*** (see pp132–49) *is New England's largest and most vibrant city, and the capital of Massachusetts. Here, historic buildings and gleaming modern structures can be found cheek by jowl.*

***Cape Cod*** (see p152) *in Massachusetts is best known for its miles of wide, sandy beaches, whale-watching junkets, and quaint Colonial villages.*

# New England

*For many people, New England is white-steepled churches, craggy coastlines, historic villages, and timeless landscapes of tranquil farmlands and country roads, with the sophisticated city of Boston as its cultural and commercial hub. Many also regard it as the cradle of American civilization, for New England's early history is the history of the United States itself.*

From the beginning, the region has been shaped by both geography and climate. Early explorers charted its coastline, and communities soon sprang up by the coast, where goods and people could be ferried more easily from the Old World to the New. Early commerce depended heavily on the ocean, from shipping and whaling to fishing and boat-building.

The harsh, unpredictable climate, poor soil, hilly terrain, and dense virgin forests also helped shape the character of its people. To survive in this area required toughness, ingenuity, and a spirit of independence – all traits that became ingrained in the New England psyche. The slogan "Live free or die" on New Hampshire license plates is a reminder that the same spirit lives on. Indeed, New England today is as much a state of mind as it is a physical space. Despite this, New England is also home to the opulence of Newport, Rhode Island, the beautiful surburban communities of Connecticut, and the self-assured sophistication of Boston.

### History

New England's historical connections are far richer than any other area in America, for it was here that much of the drama of forming a new country was played out. In 1614, the English explorer John Smith sailed along the coast of Massachusetts, named it New England, and declared that it was the best place to set up a new colony. On December 26, 1620, a group of 102 Puritans, who had left England to escape religious persecution, landed at Plymouth Rock after a grueling 66-day voyage on the *Mayflower* and established one of America's first permanent English settlements. Soon,

**Stonington, a scenic town on Deer Isle, Penobscot Bay, Maine**

◁ **Craggy Bass Harbor Head, a picturesque spot in Acadia National Park, Maine** large settlements had also grown up in Boston, Rhode Island, Connecticut, New Hampshire, and Maine.

As the colonists became more prosperous and self-sufficient, their resentment of British control and British taxes increased. The turning point came with the "Boston Tea Party" in 1773, when three British ships arrived at Boston Harbor laden with tea. About 60 local leaders, disguised as Indians, boarded the ships and dumped 342 tea chests, valued at £18,000, into the harbor as an act of defiance against an oppressive regime.

***Minute Man* statue in Concord**

Meanwhile, locals had begun stockpiling arms in the countryside. In 1775, when British soldiers were sent to Concord to destroy these caches, American patriots (known as "Minutemen" for their ability to muster at a moment's notice) repelled them at Concord and nearby Lexington. They had been tipped off by a dramatic "midnight" horseback ride from Boston by Paul Revere. The American Revolution had begun, with the first major battle at Bunker Hill in Boston on June 17, 1775. The Declaration of Independence, signed by Colonial leaders in Philadephia on July 4, 1776, announced the birth of a new nation.

In the 19th century, New England's maritime trade grew more lucrative, as ships plied between the region's harbors and the West Indies, Europe, and the Far East. The whaling industry reached its zenith at this time, and cotton and wool manufacturing also flourished.

New England's role in 19th-century America was not merely one of economic powerhouse. It was the cultural heart of the nation as well. Boston was the center of a strong protest against slavery. Instigated by a newspaper called *The Liberator*, the so-called abolitionist movement set up what came to be known as the Underground Railroad which provided escape routes for fleeing slaves.

## Key Dates in History

**1614** John Smith explores the Northeast coast
**1620** The Pilgrims land at Plymouth
**1630** Group of Puritans settle in Boston
**1636** Harvard, America's first college, founded
**1692** Salem witch trials begin
**1770** British soldiers kill 5 in Boston Massacre
**1773** New taxes spur Boston Tea Party
**1774** British close Boston Harbor
**1775** Battles at Concord and Lexington mark beginning of Revolutionary War
**1776** Continental Congress ratifies Declaration of Independence
**1783** Treaty of Paris ends Revolutionary War
**1820** Maine breaks away from Massachusetts and becomes 20th state
**1831** Abolitionist William Lloyd Garrison publishes first edition of anti-slavery newspaper
**1851** Herman Melville publishes *Moby Dick*
**1884** Mark Twain publishes *The Adventures of Huckleberry Finn*
**1897** Country's first subway opens in Boston
**1961** John F. Kennedy becomes president
**1999** John F. Kennedy Jr. dies in plane crash off Martha's Vineyard
**2004** Boston hosts Democratic National Convention

## People & Culture

New England has continued to play an important role in the life of the nation. It was this region that produced the first flowering of American culture, with influential 19th-century literary giants such as Henry David Thoreau, Herman Melville, Nathaniel Hawthorne, and Mark Twain. All these writers won international recognition and acclaim. The literary tradition still lives on in New England, led by such outstanding

**Harvard University's Widener Library, the third largest library in the United States**

**The New England shoreline, a haven for water sports**

contemporary talents as John Updike, Saul Bellow, and Stephen King, who are all residents of this region. The beauty and majesty of the landscape, which inspired some of America's best-known creative spirits, such as the poet Robert Frost and the painters Norman Rockwell and Grandma Moses, still continues to exert its charm on contemporary artists, such as Sabra Field and photographer Nanocole.

In 1636, Harvard College was founded in Boston, making it the birthplace of higher education in America. Today, the region's concentration of educational institutions, including famous Ivy League universities such as Yale, and Brown, is a magnet for some of America's best and brightest.

By the mid-19th century, New England's population, which had earlier been quite homogenous, changed dramatically as waves of Irish immigrants arrived, driven from their homeland by the potato famines in the 1840s. Immigrants from Italy, Portugal, and Eastern Europe also arrived, flocking to the textile mills which had boomed in New England just after the Industrial Revolution. They have left a lasting impact on the region's social life and politics, many of them ascending to the top of New England's social hierarchy – a fact that became evident to the country with the election of the Boston-born Democrat John F. Kennedy (1917–63) in 1960 as the very first Roman Catholic president of America. Nevertheless, even today there is a special cachet in New England's society for people known as "Boston Brahmins" popularly called WASPS (White Anglo-Saxon Protestants) – descendants of the earliest British settlers.

**National Monument of Forefathers, Plymouth**

While industrialization and urbanization have left their stamp on the region, New England's stunning physical beauty still remains. The craggy coastline of Maine, the beautiful beaches located in Cape Cod, the picturesque Vermont villages, the magnificent mountains and forests of New Hampshire, and the places of historic interest found across the region attract thousands of visitors. In recent years, the growth of hi-tech industries in the area has brought a new dynamism and prosperity to New England. This seems fitting, since it was the area's natural beauty that convinced the early settlers of New England's viable future.

# Exploring New England

THE SIX STATES of New England offer a diverse array of attractions. Vermont is famous for its ski resorts and rolling farmland, New Hampshire for its dense forests and spectacular passes through the White Mountains, and Maine for its rugged coastline and vast tracts of wilderness. Farther south, Massachusetts is rich in history, culture, and scenic beaches, Connecticut in picture-postcard villages, and Rhode Island in opulent mansions. The entire New England region boasts a dazzling display of fall foliage.

***See Also***


- ***Practical Information*** pp174–5
- ***Where to Stay*** pp176–81
- ***Where to Eat*** pp182–5


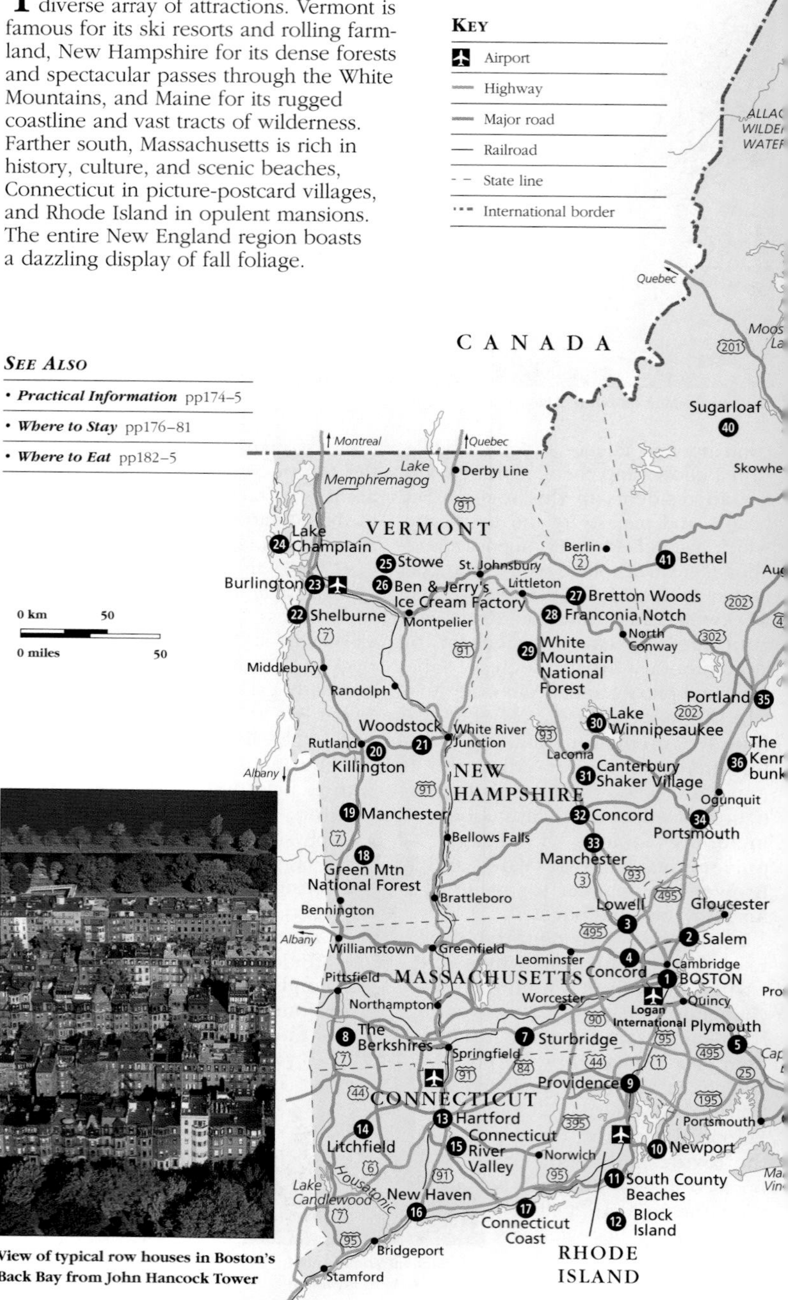


View of typical row houses in Boston's Back Bay from John Hancock Tower

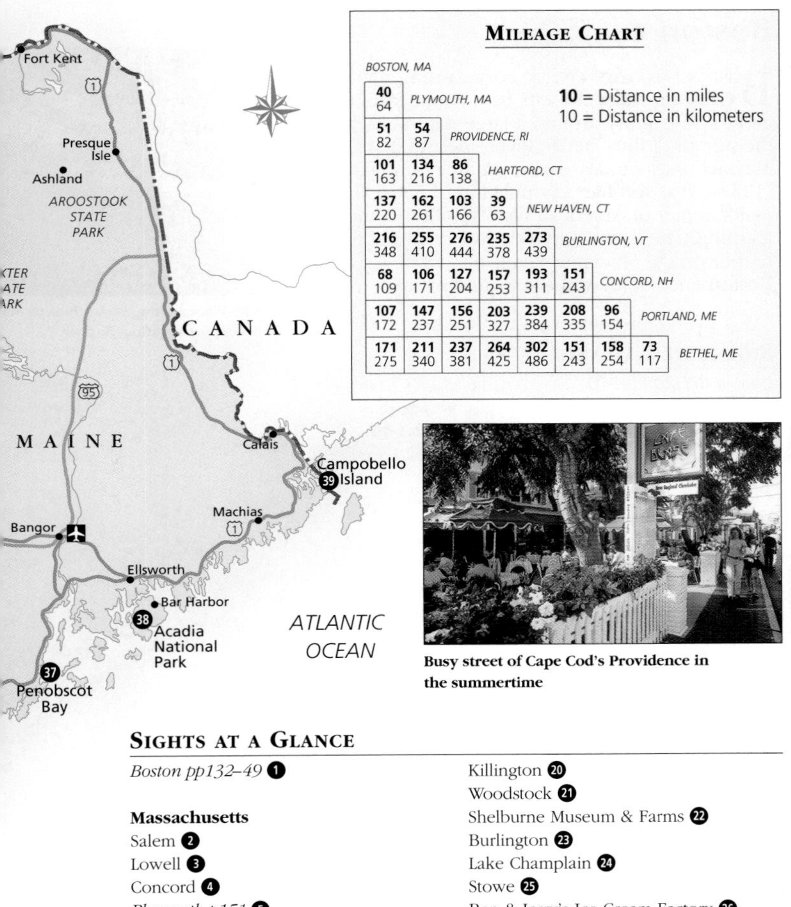


**MILEAGE CHART**

**10** = Distance in miles
10 = Distance in kilometers

| | BOSTON, MA | PLYMOUTH, MA | PROVIDENCE, RI | HARTFORD, CT | NEW HAVEN, CT | BURLINGTON, VT | CONCORD, NH | PORTLAND, ME |
|---|---|---|---|---|---|---|---|---|
| PLYMOUTH, MA | **40** 64 | | | | | | | |
| PROVIDENCE, RI | **51** 82 | **54** 87 | | | | | | |
| HARTFORD, CT | **101** 163 | **134** 216 | **86** 138 | | | | | |
| NEW HAVEN, CT | **137** 220 | **162** 261 | **103** 166 | **39** 63 | | | | |
| BURLINGTON, VT | **216** 348 | **255** 410 | **276** 444 | **235** 378 | **273** 439 | | | |
| CONCORD, NH | **68** 109 | **106** 171 | **127** 204 | **157** 253 | **193** 311 | **151** 243 | | |
| PORTLAND, ME | **107** 172 | **147** 237 | **156** 251 | **203** 327 | **239** 384 | **208** 335 | **96** 154 | |
| BETHEL, ME | **171** 275 | **211** 340 | **237** 381 | **264** 425 | **302** 486 | **151** 243 | **158** 254 | **73** 117 |

**Busy street of Cape Cod's Providence in the summertime**

## Sights at a Glance

*Boston pp132–49* ❶

**Massachusetts**
Salem ❷
Lowell ❸
Concord ❹
*Plymouth p151* ❺
Cape Cod ❻
Sturbridge ❼
The Berkshires ❽

**Rhode Island**
*Providence pp154–5* ❾
*Newport p156* ❿
South County Beaches ⓫
Block Island ⓬

**Connecticut**
*Hartford p158* ⓭
Litchfield ⓮
Connecticut River Valley ⓯
New Haven ⓰
Connecticut Coast ⓱

**Vermont**
Green Mountain National Forest ⓲
Manchester ⓳
Killington ⓴
Woodstock 21
Shelburne Museum & Farms 22
Burlington 23
Lake Champlain 24
Stowe 25
Ben & Jerry's Ice Cream Factory 26

**New Hampshire**
Bretton Woods 27
Franconia Notch 28
White Mountain National Forest 29
Lake Winnipesaukee 30
*Canterbury Shaker Village p168* 31
Concord 32
Manchester 33
Portsmouth 34

**Maine**
*Portland p170* 35
The Kennebunks 36
Penobscot Bay 37
Acadia National Park 38
Campobello Island 39
Sugarloaf 40
Bethel 41

# Boston 1

BOSTON IS LOCATED ON THE northeastern Atlantic Coast on Massachusetts Bay. Founded in the early 17th century around a large natural harbor at the mouth of the Charles River, the capital of Massachussetts today covers an area of 49 sq miles (127 sq km) and has a population of 556,000. It is a major center of American history, culture, and learning. The central city is focused around the harbor on the Shawmut Peninsula, while Greater Boston encompasses the surrounding area.

**City Place atrium, Massachusetts State Transport Building, Boston**

## SIGHTS AT A GLANCE

*Beacon Hill pp134–5* (1)
Black Heritage Trail (2)
Boston Common & Public Garden (3)
Boston Athenaeum (4)
*The Freedom Trail pp136–7* (5)
*Massachusetts State House pp138–9* (6)
Park Street Church (7)
Downtown Crossing (8)
Theater District (9)
Chinatown (10)
Verizon Building (11)
Old South Meeting House (12)
King's Chapel & Burying Ground (13)
*Old State House p141* (14)
Quincy Market (15)
Copp's Hill Burying Ground (16)
Old North Church (17)
Paul Revere Mall (18)
Paul Revere House (19)
Waterfront (20)
*Trinity Church p144* (21)
Copley Square (22)
Newbury Street (23)
Commonwealth Avenue (24)

**Greater Boston**
***(see inset map)***
John F. Kennedy Library & Museum (25)
Isabella Stewart Gardner Museum (26)
Museum of Fine Arts (27)
Cambridge (28)
Charlestown (29)

### SEE ALSO


- ***Where to Stay*** pp176–8
- ***Where to Eat*** pp182–3

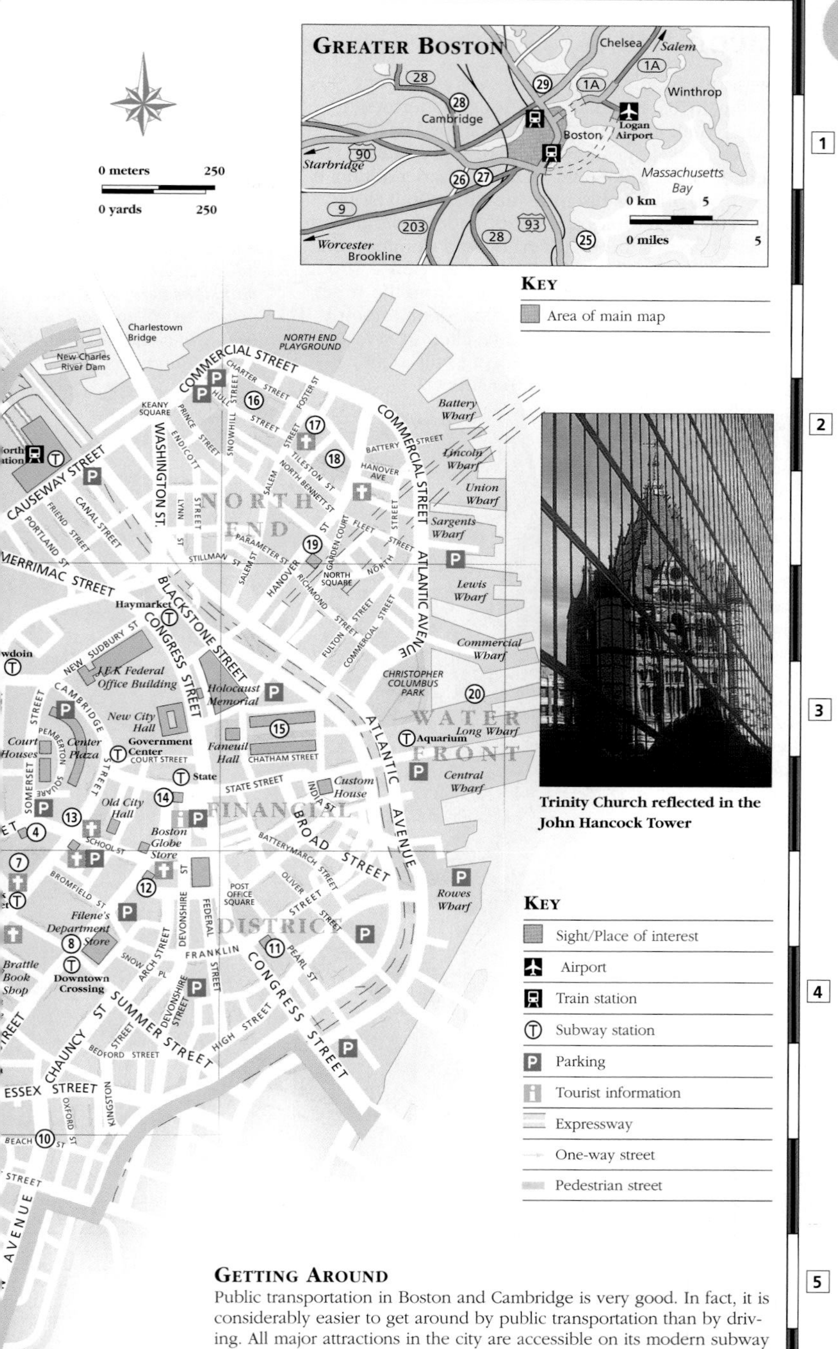


Trinity Church reflected in the John Hancock Tower

## GETTING AROUND

Public transportation in Boston and Cambridge is very good. In fact, it is considerably easier to get around by public transportation than by driving. All major attractions in the city are accessible on its modern subway network, the T, or by bus or taxi. The historic central sections of the city are also extremely easy to navigate on foot.

# Beacon Hill ①

THE SOUTH SLOPE OF BEACON HILL WAS, from the 1790s to the 1870s, Boston's most sought-after neighborhood, until its wealthy elite decamped to the more exclusive Back Bay. Many of the district's houses were designed by the influential architect Charles Bulfinch (1763–1844) and his disciples, and the south slope evolved as a textbook example of Federal architecture. The finest houses are either on Boston Common or perched on top of the hill, offering fine views. Though the earlier houses were set well back from the street, the economic depression of 1807–12 resulted in row houses being built right out to the street.

**Beacon Street**
*The fine Federal-style mansions here, some with ornate reliefs, overlook the beautiful green expanse of Boston Common.*

**Louisburg Square**
*The crowning glory of the Beacon Hill district, this square was developed in the 1830s. Today, it is still Boston's most desirable address.*

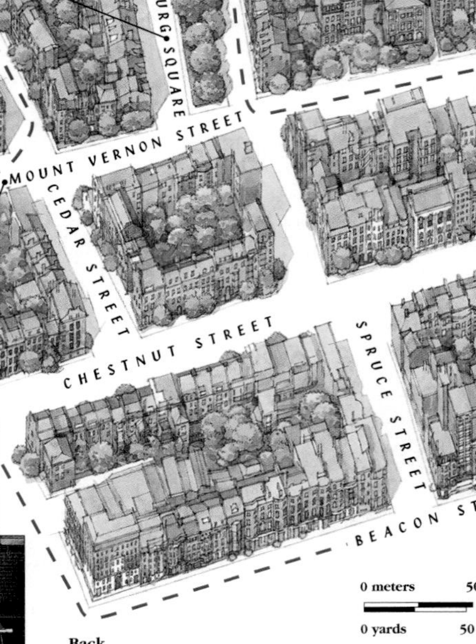


**Charles Street Meeting House** was built in the early 19th century to house a congregation of Baptists.

**Mount Vernon Street**, with its gracious mansions, was described by novelist Henry James in the 1890s as "the most civilized street in America."

**Back Bay and South End**

**★ Charles Street**
*This elegant street is lined with antique stores, fine restaurants, and gourmet groceries. At its top end are two groups of striking Greek Revival row houses.*

**KEY**

- - - Suggested route

**STAR SIGHTS**

**★ Charles Street**

**★ Nichols House Museum**

★ **Nichols House Museum**
*This small museum offers an insight into the life and times of Beacon Hill resident Rose Nichols, who lived here from 1885 to 1960.*

**Hepzibah Swan Houses**
*Bulfinch designed these three elegant houses for the daughters of a wealthy Beacon Hill proprietress.*

## Black Heritage Trail ②

**Map** C3. *tours by National Park Service Rangers, (617) 742-5415.*

In the first US census in 1790, Massachusetts was the only state to record no slaves. During the 1800s, Boston's large free African-American community lived principally on the north slope of Beacon Hill and in the adjacent West End. Free walking tours of several key sites associated with this community, linked by the Black Heritage Trail, are led by the National Park Service Rangers departing from the Robert Gould Shaw Memorial on Boston Common. The sights include safe houses for escaped slaves, the **Museum of Afro American History**, and the country's oldest black church. Dedicated in 1806, the building's simple interior once rang with the passionate oratory of abolitionists Frederick Douglass and William Lloyd Garrison, who founded the New England Anti-Slavery Society in 1832.

**Museum of Afro American History**
46 Joy St. *(617) 725-0022.* *10am–4pm Mon–Sat; Jun–Aug: also 10am–4pm Sun.* *public hols.*
www.afroammuseum.org

## Boston Common & Public Garden ③

**Map** C4. Park St, Boylston St, Arlington. *24 hrs.* **Visitor Center** *146 Tremont St, (617) 426-3115.* *8:30am–5pm Mon–Fri, 9am–5pm Sat–Sun.* www.bostonusa.com

The city's most beautiful green space, the 48-acre (19-ha) Boston Common was established in 1634. For two centuries it served as a common pasture, gallows site, and a military camp and drill ground. By the 19th century, it had become a center for open-air civic activity and remains so to this day. At the northeastern edge of the Common is the **Robert Shaw Memorial**, with a magnificent relief depicting the first free black regiment in the Union Army during the Civil War, and their white colonel, Robert Shaw. In the southeastern corner is the Central Burying Ground, dating from 1756, with graves of British and American casualties from the historic Battle of Bunker Hill in 1775 *(see p149)*.

Southwest of the Common is the more formal 24-acre (10-ha) Public Garden, designed in English style in 1869. Amid its beautifully tended lawns and flowerbeds is a superb bronze equestrian statue of George Washington. A path leads from the statue to a serene lagoon, spanned by the miniature, ornamental Lagoon Bridge. Visitors can explore the lagoon on the delightful Swan Boats.

**Bronze statue of George Washington in the Public Garden**

## Boston Athenaeum ④

**Map** D3. 10 Beacon St. *(617) 227-0270.* *Park St.* *9am–8pm Mon, 9am–5:30pm Tue–Fri; Sep–May: 9am–4pm Sat.*
www.bostonathenaeum.org

Housed in an elegant Palladian-style building, this library's treasures include George Washington's personal library and the theological library given by King William III of England to the King's Chapel *(see p140)*. The Athenaeum's collection, first organized in 1807, originally included many fine paintings. These were later donated to the Museum of Fine Arts *(see p146)* when that was set up.

# The Freedom Trail ⑤

BOSTON HAS MORE SITES directly related to the American Revolution than any other city. The most important of these sites, as well as some associated with the city's history, have been linked together as "The Freedom Trail." This 2.5-mile (4-km) walking route, marked in red on the sidewalks, starts at Boston Common, weaves through the central city and Old Boston, and ends at Bunker Hill in Charlestown.

**Faneuil Hall, popularly known as the "Cradle of Liberty"**

## Central City

The Freedom Trail starts at the Visitor Information Center on Boston Common ① *(see pp135)*. This is where angry colonials rallied against their British masters and where the British forces were encamped during the 1775–76 military occupation. Political speakers still expound from their soapboxes here. Walking toward the northwest corner of the Common provides a wonderful view of the Massachusetts State House ② *(see pp138–9),* located on Beacon Street. It was built as the new center of state governance after the Revolution. Along Park Street, at the end of the Common, is Park Street Church ③ *(see p139),* built in 1810 and a bulwark of the anti-slavery movement. Adjacent to it, the Granary Burying Ground ④, is the final resting place of patriots John Hancock and Paul Revere. Continuing along Tremont Street you will come to King's Chapel and Burying Ground ⑤ *(see p140).* The tiny cemetery is Boston's oldest, while King's Chapel was the principal Anglican church in Puritan Boston. The box pew on the right, just inside the front entrance, was reserved for condemned prisoners to hear their last sermons before going to the gallows on Boston Common.

**Steeple of Park Street Church**

## Heart of Old Boston

Head back along Tremont Street and turn down School Street, where a hopscotch-like mosaic embedded in the sidewalk marks the site of the First Public School ⑥, established in 1635. At the bottom of the street is the Old Corner Bookstore ⑦, a landmark which is more associated with Boston's literary flowering than with the Revolution. To its south on Washington Street is the Old South Meeting House ⑧ *(see p140),* a graceful, white-spired brick church, modeled on Sir Christopher Wren's English country churches. A few blocks along, the Old State House ⑨ *(see p141)* presides over the head of State Street. The Colonial government building, it also served as the first state legislature, and the merchants' exchange in the basement was where Boston's Colonial shipping fortunes were made. The square in front of the Old State House is the Boston Massacre Site ⑩, where British soldiers opened fire on a taunting mob in 1770, killing five. Follow State Street down to Congress Street and turn left to reach Faneuil Hall ⑪ with its distinctive grasshopper weathervane. Though built primarily as Boston's first central marketplace, it was also known as "Cradle of Liberty." The red stripe of the Freedom Trail points the way to the North End and the Paul Revere House ⑫. This is Boston's oldest house, home to the man known for his "midnight ride" *(see p142).*

## The North End

Following the Freedom Trail through the North End, allow time to try some of the Italian cafés and bakeries along

Hanover Street. Cross through the Paul Revere Mall to reach Old North Church ⑬ *(see p142)*, whose spire is instantly visible over the shoulder of the equestrian statue of Paul Revere. In 1775, two lanterns hung in the belfry signaled the advance of British troops on Lexington and Concord. The crest of Copp's Hill lies close by on Hull Street. Some of Boston's earliest gallows were here, and people would gather below to watch the hangings of heretics and pirates. Much of the hilltop is covered by Copp's Hill Burying Ground ⑭, established in 1660 *(see p142)*.

**Charlestown**

Cross the iron bridge over the Charles River, which links the North End in Boston with City Square in Charlestown, and turn right, following the Freedom Trail along Water Street to the Charlestown Navy Yard ⑮. Berthed alongside Pier 1 is the USS *Constitution (see p149)*. In the War of 1812, she earned the nickname "Old Ironsides" for the resilience of her live oak hull against cannon fire. The granite obelisk that towers above the Charlestown waterfront is Bunker Hill Monument ⑯ *(see p149)*.

**KEY**

•••• Walk route

Ⓣ Subway station

Tourist information

HARVARD STREET
JEFFERSON STREET
MAIN STREET
WINTHROP STREET
WARREN STREET
CHELSEA STREET
WATER STREET
CHARLESTOWN STREET
COMMERCIAL STREET
PRINCE STREET
SNOWHILL STREET

0 meters 250

0 yards 250

This landmark commemorates the battle of June 17, 1775, which ended with a costly victory for British forces. British losses were heavy, and the battle would presage future success for the Colonial forces. As a monument to the first large-scale battle of the Revolution, the obelisk, based on those of ancient Egypt, remains a prototype for others across the US.

**WALK**

- Boston Common ①
- Massachusetts State House ②
- Park Street Church ③
- Granary Burying Ground ④
- King's Chapel & Burying Ground ⑤
- First Public School ⑥
- Old Corner Bookstore ⑦
- Old South Meeting House ⑧
- Old State House ⑨
- Boston Massacre Site ⑩
- Faneuil Hall ⑪
- Paul Revere House ⑫
- Old North Church ⑬
- Copp's Hill Burying Ground ⑭
- Charlestown Navy Yard & the USS *Constitution* ⑮
- Bunker Hill Monument ⑯

**TIPS FOR WALKERS**

**Map** C4. ***Starting point:*** *Boston Common. Maps available at Boston Common Visitor Center.*
***Length:*** *2.5 miles (4 km).*
***Getting there:*** *Park Street Station (Ⓣ Green and Red lines) to start. State (Orange and Blue lines) and Haymarket (Orange and Green lines). Ⓣ stations can be found on route. Visitors should follow red stripe on sidewalk for the full route.*

**View of Bunker Hill Monument from Charlestown harbor**

# Massachusetts State House ⑥

The cornerstone of the Massachusetts State House was laid in 1795 by Paul Revere and Samuel Adams. Completed in 1798, the Charles Bulfinch-designed center of state government served as a model for the US Capitol building in Washington and as an inspiration for many other state capitols. Later additions were made, but the original building remains the archetype of American government buildings. Its gilded dome serves as the zero-mile marker for Massachusetts.

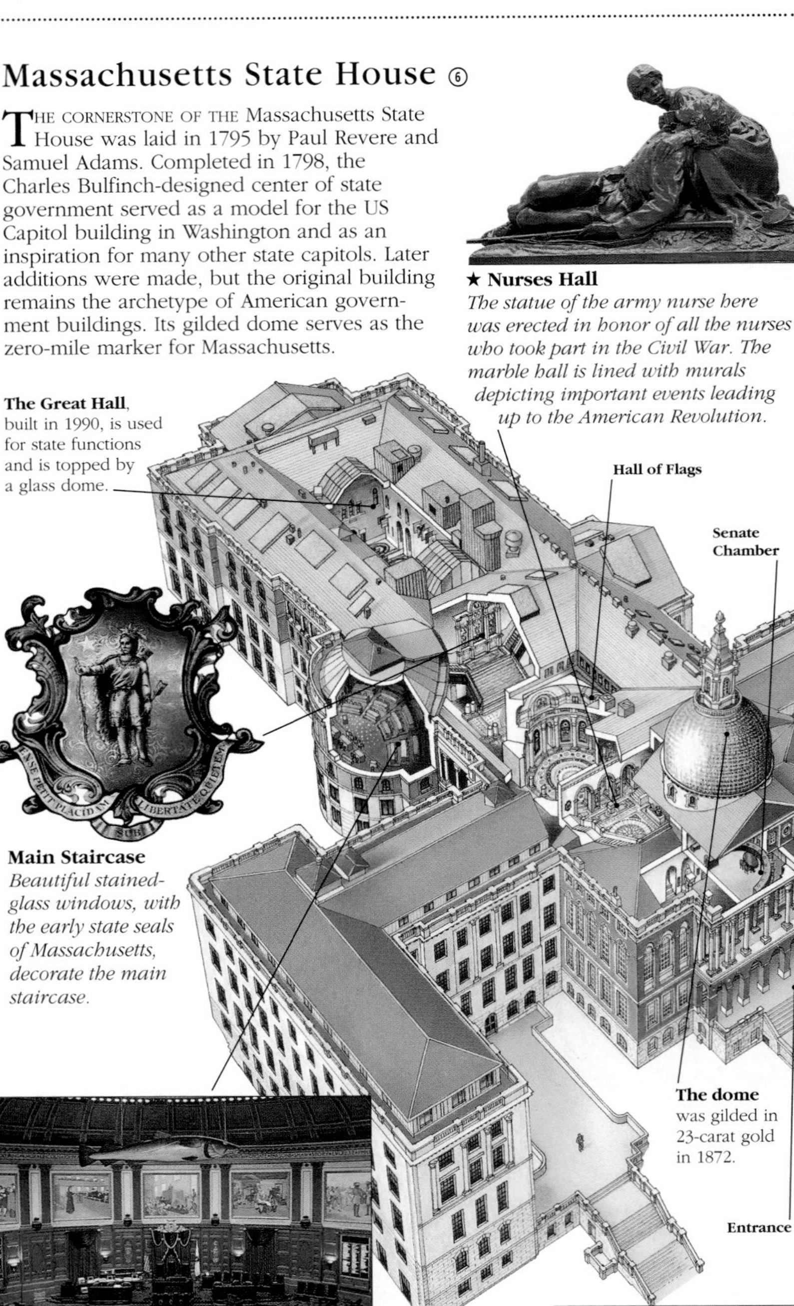

**★ Nurses Hall**
*The statue of the army nurse here was erected in honor of all the nurses who took part in the Civil War. The marble hall is lined with murals depicting important events leading up to the American Revolution.*

**The Great Hall**, built in 1990, is used for state functions and is topped by a glass dome.

**Hall of Flags**

**Senate Chamber**

**Main Staircase**
*Beautiful stained-glass windows, with the early state seals of Massachusetts, decorate the main staircase.*

**The dome** was gilded in 23-carat gold in 1872.

**Entrance**

**★ House of Representatives**
*This elegant oval chamber was built in 1895, but the "Sacred Cod" that now hangs over the gallery came to the State House when it first opened in 1798.*

**Star Sights**

- **★ House of Representatives**
- **★ Nurses Hall**

**VISITORS' CHECKLIST**

**Map** D3. Beacon Hill. *(617) 727-3676.* Park Street. *10am–3.30pm Mon–Fri.* www.sec.state.ma.us/trs

**Senate Chamber**
*Situated directly beneath the dome, this chamber features a beautiful sunburst ceiling.*

**The Wings**, added in 1917, are thought by many to sit incongruously with the rest of the structure.

**Hall of Flags**
*Flags carried into battle by regiments from the state of Massachusetts are displayed here beneath a stained-glass skylight, depicting seals of the original 13 colonies.*

## Park Street Church ⑦

**Map** D4.1 Park St. *(617) 523-3383.* *Park St.* *Jul–Aug: 9am–3:30pm Tue–Sat; Sep–Jun: by appointment.* www.parkstreet.org

SINCE ITS DEDICATION in 1810, the Park Street Church has been one of Boston's most influential pulpits. In 1829, the firebrand crusader for the abolition of slavery, William Lloyd Garrison, gave his first abolition speech here; and in 1893 the anthem *America the Beautiful* debuted at Sunday service in this church. The church, with its 217-ft (65-m) steeple was designed by the English architect Peter Banner, who actually adapted a design by the earlier English architect, Christopher Wren.

Adjacent to the church, on Tremont Street, is the mid-17th century **Granary Burying Ground**, which was once the site of a grain storage facility. Among those buried in this historic cemetery are three important signatories to the Declaration of Independence – Samuel Adams, John Hancock, and Robert Paine, as well as one of the city's most famous sons, the patriot Paul Revere.

**Old Granary Burying Ground**
Tremont St. *9am–5pm daily.*

## Downtown Crossing ⑧

**Map** D4. Washington, Winter, & Summer Sts. *Downtown Crossing.*

THIS LIVELY pedestrian shopping district, crowded with sidewalk stalls and vendors' carts, is dominated by department stores. Among them are the well-known nationwide chain Macy's, and Filene's with its famous Bargain Basement. Another well-known store in the area is Brattle Book Shop, founded in 1825. This bibliophiles' treasure house stocks more than 250,000 rare, used, and out-of-print books and magazines.

## Theater District ⑨

**Map** C4. *Boylston, New England Medical Center.*

BOSTON'S FIRST theater opened in 1793 on Federal Street. Fifty years later, with patronage from the city's elite, Boston had become a major tryout town and boasted several lavish theaters. Many major US premieres were held here, among them Handel's *Messiah*, and Tennessee Williams' *A Streetcar Named Desire*. Among the grandest theaters are the opulent **Colonial Theater**, decorated with frescos and friezes; the 1,650-seat **Shubert Theater**, with its imposing Neo-Classical façade; and the **Wang Center for the Performing Arts**, with a glittering seven-story auditorium.

**Colonial Theater**
106 Boylston St. *(617) 423-4008.* *phone to check.* www.broadwayinboston.com

## Chinatown ⑩

**Map** D5. Bounded by Kingston, Kneeland, Washington, & Essex Sts. *Chinatown.*

THIS IS THE third largest Chinatown in the US, after those in San Francisco and New York. Pagoda-topped telephone booths set the tone of the neighborhood, which is full of restaurants, and stores selling garments and Chinese medicine. Boston's Chinese colony was fully established by the turn of the 19th century, and in recent years the area's population has swelled with new arrivals from Korea, Vietnam, and Cambodia.

**Typical store and restaurant façades in Boston's Chinatown**

***Telephone Men and Women at Work*, Verizon Building**

## Verizon Building ⑪

**Map** E4.185 Franklin St. *(617) 743-4747.* Ⓣ *State, Aquarium.* **Museum** *24 hours daily.*

THIS IMPRESSIVE Art Deco building, dating to 1947, is renowned for the monumental 160-ft- (49-m-) long mural in its lobby, *Telephone Men and Women at Work*. This remarkable work of art, created by Dean Cornwell, is peopled with 197 life-size figures. At the street level is a small museum which re-creates Alexander Graham Bell's laboratory, where he invented the telephone. A native of Scotland, Bell (1847–1922) moved to Boston in 1871 to teach speech to the deaf, but in his spare time worked on an apparatus for transmitting sound by electric current. The first demonstration of the "telephone" took place in Boston in May 1876. On the building's northern side is the Post Office Square.

## Old South Meeting House ⑫

**Map** D4. 310 Washington St. *(617) 482-6439.* Ⓣ *Park St, State, Government Center.* *Apr–Oct: 9:30am–5pm daily; Nov–Mar: 10am–4pm daily.* www.oldsouthmeetinghouse.org

BUILT FOR Puritan religious services in 1729, this edifice, with a tall octagonal steeple, had Colonial Boston's biggest capacity for town meetings. From 1765 on, it became the venue for large and vociferous crowds, led by a group of merchants called "the Sons of Liberty" to gather in protest against British taxation and the hated Stamp Act. During a protest rally on December 16, 1773, the fiery speechmaker Samuel Adams flashed the signal that led to the Boston Tea Party *(see p143)* at Griffin's Wharf several hours later. The British retaliated by turning Old South into an officers' tavern and a stable for army horses. Today, the Meeting House holds lectures, concerts, and a multimedia show, which relives those raucous days. The shop sells the ubiquitous tins of "Boston Tea Party" tea.

**Alexander Graham Bell**

## King's Chapel & Burying Ground ⑬

**Map** D3. 58 Tremont St. *(617) 523-1749.* Ⓣ *Park St, State, Government Center.* *late May–mid-Nov: 9am–4pm Mon, Thu, Fri, Sat; mid-Nov–late May: 9am–4pm Sat.* **Music Recitals** *Tue & Sun.* www.kings-chapel.org

THE FIRST CHAPEL on this site was built in 1689, but when the Governor of New England decided that a larger church was needed, the present granite edifice was begun in 1749. It was constructed around the original wooden chapel, which was then dismantled and heaved out of the windows of its replacement. High ceilings and open arches enhance the sense of spaciousness and light inside the chapel. Its other notable features include a pulpit shaped like a wine glass, dating to 1717, and a huge bell that was re-cast by the foundry of Revolutionary hero Paul Revere *(see p142)*.

The cemetery adjacent to the chapel is Boston's oldest. Among those buried here is Elizabeth Pain, the inspiration for the adultress Hester Prynne in Nathaniel Hawthorne's famous moralistic novel, *The Scarlet Letter*.

**The simply decorated interior of King's Chapel on Tremont Street**

## Old State House ⑭

**Map** D3. Washington & State Sts. (617) 720-1713. Ⓣ State. 9am–5pm daily. www.bostonhistory.org

Now dwarfed by the towers of the Financial District, the Old State House was the seat of the British Colonial government between 1713 and 1776. The royal lion and unicorn still decorate each corner of its eastern façade. After independence, the Massachusetts legislature took possession of the building, and it has had many uses since, including a produce market, Masonic Lodge, and Boston City Hall. Its wine cellars now function as a subway station, and the building houses two floors of historic memorabilia of the Bostonian Society.

**Old State House amid the skyscrapers of the Financial District**

In 1776, the Declaration of Independence was read from the balcony on the East Façade. A circle of cobblestones below the balcony marks the site of the Boston Massacre. On March 5, 1770, an unruly mob of colonists taunted British guardsmen with insults, rocks, and snowballs. The soldiers opened fire, killing five colonists. After the Boston Tea Party, this was one of the most inflammatory events leading up to the American Revolution *(see p44)*.

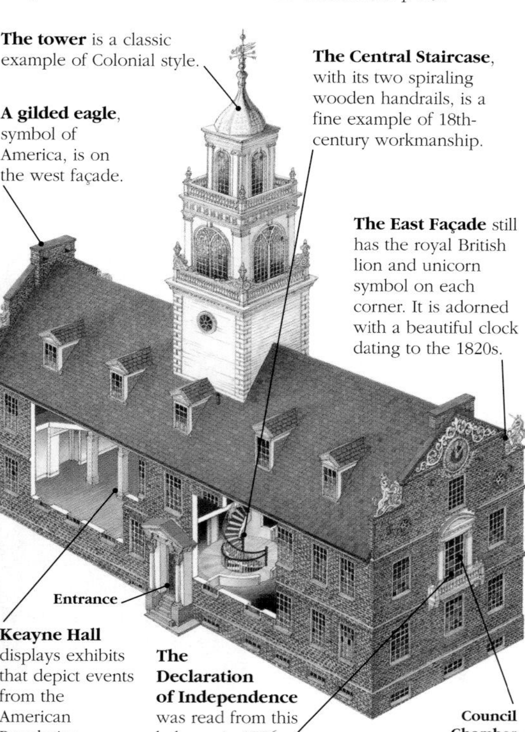

**Greek Revival Custom House tower, one of Boston's most striking sights**

## Quincy Market ⑮

**Map** E3. Between Chatham & Clinton Sts. *(617) 523-1300.* Ⓣ *Government Center, State.* *10am–9pm Mon–Sat, noon–6pm Sun.* www.faneuilhallmarketplace.com

This immensely popular shopping and dining complex attracts nearly 14 million people every year. It was developed from the old buildings of the city's meat, fish, and produce markets, which were beautifully restored in the 1970s. The 535-ft- (163-m-) long Greek Revival-style colonnaded hall is now filled with fast-food stands, and a comedy nightclub is located in the spectacular central rotunda. Completing the ensemble are the twin North and South Market buildings, refurbished to house boutiques, restaurants, and business offices.

A short distance southeast of Quincy Market is the **Custom House** with its Greek Revival tower. When first completed in 1847 this building had a skylit dome. The 495-ft (150m) tower with a four-sided clock was built in 1915 and for much of the 20th century was Boston's only skyscraper. There is a museum of maritime history in the rotunda.

**Custom House**
3 McKinley Square. *(617) 310-6300.* **Museum** *8am–11pm daily.* www.marriott.com/vacationclub

Slate tombstones of Boston's early settlers, Copp's Hill Burying Ground

## Copp's Hill Burying Ground ⑯

**Map** E2. Entrances at Charter & Hull Sts. Ⓣ *Government Center, N Station.* *8am–5pm daily.*

EXISTING SINCE 1659, this is Boston's second oldest cemetery, after the one by King's Chapel *(see p140)*. Among those buried here are Robert Newton, the sexton who hung Paul Revere's signal lanterns in the belfry of the Old North Church, influential Colonial period Puritan ministers, as well as hundreds of black slaves and freedmen.

During the British occupation of Boston, King George lll's troops were said to have used the slate headstones for target practice, and pockmarks from their musket balls are still visible. Copp's Hill Terrace, directly across Charter Street, is the site where, in 1919, a 2.3 million-gallon tank of molasses exploded, drowning 21 people in a huge, syrupy tidal wave.

## Old North Church ⑰

**Map** E2.193 Salem St. *(617) 523-6676.* Ⓣ *Haymarket, Aquarium, N Station.* *9am–5pm daily.* *9am, 11am & 4pm Sun (also 5pm Jul–Aug).* *Jun–Aug: "Behind the Scenes Tour."* www.oldnorth.com

OFFICIALLY NAMED Christ Episcopal Church, the Old North Church, which dates from 1723, is Boston's oldest surviving religious edifice. It is built of brick in the Georgian style, similar to that of St. Andrew's-by-the-Wardrobe in Blackfriars, London, designed by Sir Christopher Wren. The church was made famous on April 18, 1775, when sexton Robert Newman, aiding Paul Revere, hung a pair of lanterns in the belfry. These were to warn the patriots in Charlestown of the westward departure of British troops, on their way to engage the revolutionaries.

An imposing marble bust of George Washington, dating from 1815, adorns the church interior, which has unusual high-sided box pews. These were designed to enclose footwarmers, which were filled with hot coals or bricks during wintry weather. The tower contains the first set of church bells made in North America, cast in 1745. The top of the bell tower offers panoramic views of the beautiful city.

## Paul Revere Mall ⑱

**Map** E2. Hanover St. Ⓣ *Haymarket, Aquarium.*

THIS BRICK-PAVED plaza, between Hanover and Unity Streets, provides a precious stretch of open space in the crowded neighborhood of the North End, populated largely by people of Italian descent. Laid out in 1933, its focal point is an equestrian statue of Paul Revere (1735–1818). Benches, a fountain, and twin rows of linden trees give the space, much used by local people, a distinctly European feel. South of the Mall is busy Hanover Street, which is lined with Italian eateries.

## Paul Revere House ⑲

**Map** E2.19 N Square. *(617) 523-2338.* Ⓣ *Haymarket, Aquarium.* *mid-Apr–Oct: 9:30am–5:15pm daily; Nov–mid-Apr: 9:30am–4:15pm daily.* www.paulreverehouse.org

BOSTON'S OLDEST surviving clapboard frame house is historically significant, for it was here in 1775 that Paul Revere began his legendary horseback ride to warn his compatriots in Lexington *(see p149)* of the impending arrival of British troops. This historic event was later immortalized by Henry Wadsworth Longfellow *(see p148)* in his epic poem which begins, "Listen, my children, and you shall hear of the midnight ride of Paul Revere."

A versatile gold- and silversmith, and maker of church bells and cannons, Revere lived here from 1770 to 1800. Small leaded casement windows, an overhanging upper story, and nail-studded front door make the house a fine example of 18th-century Early American architecture. Three rooms in the house contain artifacts and furniture made in Revere's workshop. In the courtyard is a large bronze bell cast by Revere, who is known to have made nearly 200 church bells.

Paul Revere House, where Paul Revere began his midnight ride

## Waterfront ⑳

**Map** E3. Atlantic Ave. **New England Aquarium** Central Wharf. *(617) 973-5200.* *Aquarium.* *Sep–Jun: 9am–5pm Mon–Fri, 9am–6pm Sat & Sun; Jul–Aug: 9am–6pm Mon–Thu, 9am–7pm Fri–Sun.* www.neaq.org
**Boston Tea Party Ship** Congress St Bridge. *(617) 338-1773.* *South Station.* *Jun–Sep: 9am–6pm daily; Oct–May: 9am–5pm daily.* www.historictours.com/boston
**Children's Museum** 300 Congress St. *(617) 426-8855.* *S Station.* *mid-Jun–Aug: 10am–5pm Sat–Thu, 10am–9pm Fri; Sep–mid-Jun: 10am–5pm Tue–Sun.* www.bostonkids.org

Boston's waterfront is one of the city's most fascinating areas. Fringed by wharves and warehouses – a reminder of the city's past as a key trading port – its attractions include a famous aquarium and two fine museums.

One of the largest wharves is **Long Wharf**, established in 1710. Once extending 2,000 ft (610 m) into Boston Harbor and lined with shops and warehouses, it provided secure mooring for the largest ships of the time.

Harbor Walk connects Long Wharf with other adjacent wharves, dating from the early 1800s. Most of them have now been converted to fashionable harborside apartments. **Rowes Wharf**, to the south of the waterfront is a particularly fine example of such revitalization. This modern red-brick development, with opulent condominiums and offices, features a large archway that links the city to the harbor.

The waterfront's prime attraction is the **New England Aquarium**, which dominates Central Wharf. Designed in 1969, the aquarium's core encloses a vast four-story ocean tank, which houses a Caribbean coral reef and contains a wide array of marine creatures such as sharks, moray eels, barracudas, and sea turtles, as well as exotic, brightly colored tropical fish. A curving walkway runs around the outside of the tank from the top to the bottom, and provides different viewpoints of the interior at many levels.

**Exotic fish, New England Aquarium**

A particularly popular section of the aquarium is the Penguin Pool, which runs around the base of the ocean tank, while a recently added west wing has an outdoor tank with a lively colony of harbor seals. In 2001, the Simons IMAX® Theater was opened on the wharf, which presents changing programs of 3-D films on a giant screen. A highlight of the aquarium's programs are the boat trips from Boston Harbor, which take visitors to the whale feeding grounds far offshore. The aquarium also has a gift shop and a café with a beautiful view of the harbor.

Griffin's Wharf, where the Boston Tea Party took place on December 16, 1773, was buried beneath landfill many years ago. But a short distance south of the original site, on Fort Point Channel, the **Boston Tea Party Ship** is anchored. The ship is a Danish-built sailing brig, *Beaver II*, which resembles one of the three original British East India Company ships involved in the Tea Party protest *(see p44)*. Today, modern-day patriots toss imitation bales of tea overboard, re-creating one of the acts of defiance that prompted the British to put the Massachusetts Bay Colony under martial law. A museum on an adjacent pier displays ship models and Tea Party memorabilia.

Overlooking Fort Point Channel is a rejuvenated 19th-century wool warehouse that houses the **Children's Museum**, one of the best in the country. Its many attractions and interactive exhibits include a two-story maze, and a hands-on recyling area with barrels of materials for children to use in self-instructive creative projects. They can also weave fabrics on looms or act in kidstage plays. An international flavor is added by a visit to the silk merchant's house, transplanted from Kyoto in Japan.

**View down Long Wharf toward the waterfront and Custom House**

# Trinity Church ㉑

**Bas-relief in Chancel**

ROUTINELY VOTED ONE OF America's ten finest buildings, this masterpiece by Henry Hobson Richardson dates from 1877. The church is a beautiful granite and sandstone Romanesque structure, standing on wooden piles driven through mud into bedrock, surmounted by granite pyramids. John LaFarge designed the interior, while some of the windows were designed by Edward Burne-Jones and executed by William Morris.

**VISITORS' CHECKLIST**

**Map** B5. Copley Sq. *(617) 536-0944.* Ⓣ *Copley.* *daily.* *9am, 11:15am, & 6pm Sun.* **Concerts** *Sep–Jun: noon Fri.* *11am, 1pm, 2pm Mon–Sat.* www.trinitychurchboston.org

**The Chancel**
*Seven beautiful windows here show the life of Christ.*

**★ North Transept Windows**
*Designed by Burne-Jones and executed by William Morris, the three stained-glass windows above the choir relate the story of Christmas.*

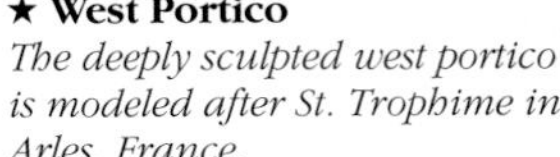

**★ West Portico**
*The deeply sculpted west portico is modeled after St. Trophime in Arles, France.*

**STAR SIGHTS**

- ★ North Transept Windows
- ★ West Portico

**View over Back Bay and Charles River from the John Hancock Tower**

## Copley Square ㉒

**Map** B5. Ⓣ *Copley.*

NAMED AFTER the famous painter John Singleton Copley *(see p147)*, Copley Square was a marsh until 1870 and took on its present form only in the late 20th century. Today, this inviting plaza is an open space of trees and fountains, and a hive of civic activity with weekly farmers' markets and concerts in summer. It is surrounded by some of Boston's most striking architecture.

The **John Hancock Tower**, constructed in 1975, anchors the southeastern side of the Square. The tallest building in New England, the 740-ft (226-m) tower's mirrored façade reflects the beautiful Trinity Church and the original (1947) Hancock Building. Unfortunately, the observatory on the 60th floor has been closed following the events of September 11, 2001.

West of the Hancock Tower, across Copley Square, is the Italian palazzo-style **Boston Public Library**, built in 1887–95. A marvel of fine wood and marble, the library has huge bronze doors, and murals by John Singer Sargent in a third-floor gallery. The vast Bates Hall on the second floor of this library is notable for its soaring barrel-vaulted ceiling. Close by, on the corner of Boylston and Dartmouth Streets, is the fabulous Italian Gothic-style **New Old South Church**, built in 1874–75.

**John Hancock Tower**
200 Clarendon St. ● *to the public.*

**Boston Public Library**
Copley Square. ☎ *(617) 536-5400.* ○ *Apr–Sep & Oct–May: 9am–9pm Mon–Thu, 9am–5pm Fri–Sat; Oct–May: 1–5pm Sun.* ● *public hols.* W www.bpl.org

## Newbury Street ㉓

**Map** B5. Ⓣ *Arlington, Copley, Hynes Convention Center/ ICA.*

NEWBURY STREET is a Boston synonym for "stylish." Lined with high-fashion outlets, art galleries, and chic restaurants, this is a great place for people-watching. Churches provide vestiges of a more decorous era. Most notable is the **Church of the Covenant**, which contains the world's largest collection of Louis Comfort Tiffany stained-glass windows and an elaborate Tiffany lantern. At the corner of Newbury and Dartmouth Streets lies the striking Newbury Street Mural, which depicts 72 eminent Bostonians.

**Church of the Covenant**
67 Newbury St. ☎ *(617) 266-7480.* ○ *10am Sun.* W churchofthecovenant.org

## Commonwealth Avenue ㉔

**Map** B4. Ⓣ *Arlington, Copley, Hynes Convention Center/ ICA.*

ENVISIONED AS Boston's Champs Elysees, this avenue, 200-ft (61-m) wide, is lined with beautiful townhouses. In the second half of the 19th century, it became an arena for America's leading domestic architects, and a walk along it is like flicking through a catalog of architectural styles. One of the few grand buildings open to the public is the **Boston Center for Adult Education**. Built in 1912, it has a ballroom modeled on the Petit Trianon in Versailles, France.

The Romanesque-style **First Baptist Church**, on the corner of Commonwealth Avenue and Clarendon Street, is one of the most distinctive buildings of the city skyline. Completed in 1872, its free-standing square bell tower, modeled on Italian campaniles, is topped with a decorative frieze by Bartholdi, the sculptor who created the Statue of Liberty. The faces in the frieze, which depict the sacraments, are likenesses of prominent Bostonians of the time, among them Henry Wadsworth Longfellow and Ralph Waldo Emerson.

**Boston Center for Adult Education**
5 Commonwealth Ave. ☎ *(617) 267-4430.* ○ *9am–7pm Mon–Thu, 9am–5pm Fri.* ● *Sat–Sun, May 11.* *for courses.* W www.bcae.org

**First Baptist Church**
110 Commonwealth Ave. ☎ *(617) 267-3148.* ○ *for Sun worship.*

# Greater Boston

SOUTHWEST OF CENTRAL BOSTON, what were once the marshlands of the Fenway now house two superb art museums – the Museum of Fine Arts and the Isabella Stewart Gardner Museum. West of the city, across the Charles River, is the college town of Cambridge, dominated by Harvard University. To its east is historic Charlestown, which forms a major part of Boston's Freedom Trail *(see pp136–7)*.

**The dramatic structure of the John F. Kennedy Library and Museum**

## John F. Kennedy Library & Museum ㉕

Columbia Point, Dorchester. (617) 514-1600. *JFK/ U Mass.* *9am–5pm daily.* *Jan 1, Thanksgiving, Dec 25.*
www.jfklibrary.org

HOUSED IN A dramatic white concrete and black glass building designed by architect I.M. Pei, this museum chronicles the 1,000 days of the Kennedy presidency. The combination of video and film footage, papers, and memorabilia evoke the euphoria of "Camelot" as well as the numb horror of the assassination with an immediacy that is uncommon in historical museums. Some of the key chambers in the White House, including the Oval Room, are re-created here.

The house at 83 Beals Street in Brookline, where the late president was born in 1917, is now the **John F. Kennedy National Historic Site**. The Kennedy family moved to a larger house in 1921; in 1966 they repurchased this house, furnished it with their belongings circa 1917, and turned it into a memorial.

## Isabella Stewart Gardner Museum ㉖

280 The Fenway. *(617) 566-1401.* *MFA.* *11am–5pm Tue–Sun.* *Jan 1, Thanksgiving, Dec 25.* *call for concert schedule.*
www.gardnermuseum.org

THIS VENETIAN-STYLE palazzo houses a remarkable collection of over 2,500 works of art, including Old Masters and Italian Renaissance pieces. Advised by art scholar Bernard Berenson, the wealthy and strong-willed Isabella Stewart Gardner began collecting art in the late 19th century. Among the works she acquired were masterpieces by Titian, Rembrandt, and Matisse as well as by the American painters James McNeill Whistler and John Singer Sargent. The paintings, sculptures, and tapestries are displayed on three levels around the stunning skylit central courtyard.

Unfortunately, in 1990, 13 of these priceless works were stolen, including a rare Rembrandt seascape, *Storm on the Sea of Galilee*, then conservatively valued in the region of $200 million.

## Museum of Fine Arts ㉗

Avenue of the Arts, 465 Huntington Ave. *(617) 267-9300.* *MFA.* *10am–4:45pm Sat–Tue, 10am–9:45pm Wed–Fri.* *Jan 1, 3rd Mon in Apr, Jul 4, Thanksgiving, Dec 25.* **Lectures, concerts, & films.**
www.mfa.org

THE LARGEST ART museum in New England, and one of the five largest in the US, the Museum of Fine Arts

**Central courtyard of the *palazzo*-style Isabella Stewart Gardner Museum**

**Japanese Temple Room, Museum of Fine Arts**

(MFA) has a permanent collection of approximately 400,000 objects, ranging from Egyptian artifacts to modern American paintings. Though founded in 1876, the MFA's present Classical-style building dates from 1909, with a west wing designed by I.M. Pei added in 1981. American decorative arts and paintings are on the first floor, and European art is on the second floor, while Classical, Far Eastern, and Egyptian artifacts can be seen on both floors of the museum.

The Museum of Fine Art's excellent collection of ancient **Egyptian and Nubian Art** is unparalleled outside of Africa and derives primarily from the MFA-Harvard University excavations along the Nile, which began in 1905. It also includes a wonderful collection of mummies that is located on the first floor. The adjacent gallery of Ancient Near Eastern Art exhibits Babylonian, Assyrian, and Sumerian reliefs. On the second floor are several monumental sculptures of Nubian kings, dating from the 7th to 6th centuries BC.

**Egyptian Mummies**

The MFA boasts one of America's top holdings of **Classical Art** as well. Among the highlights of this collection are Greek figured vases, carved Etruscan sarcophagi, and Roman portrait busts. Also on display are a series of wall panel paintings unearthed in Pompeii in 1901.

The collections of **Asian Art** are said to be the most extensive under one roof anywhere in the world. They include Indian sculpture and narrative paintings, and exhibitions of Islamic miniature paintings that keep changing.

A beautiful stairway with carved lions leads to the Chinese and Japanese galleries on the second floor. Outstanding exhibits here include scroll and screen paintings. A highlight of the museum is the serene **Japanese Temple Room**, on the first floor, which is known for its exquisite examples of Buddhist art.

The **European Art** collections date from the 16th to the 20th centuries and begin with Dutch paintings, including several portraits by Rembrandt. The Koch Gallery, with its magnificent wooden coffered ceiling, displays masterpieces by El Greco, Titian, and Rubens.

Boston's 19th-century collectors enriched the MFA with wonderful French art: the museum features several paintings by Pierre François Millet as well as by 19th-century French artists such as Edouard Manet, Pierre-August Renoir, and Edgar Degas. It also has several paintings by Van Gogh, and holds the most important Monet collection outside of Paris. One of the most popular galleries displays *La Japonaise* by Monet and *Dance at Bougival* by Renoir. Examples of European decorative arts include medieval frescoes, 18th-century French silver, and tableware, ceramics, and glass from the 17th to the early 20th centuries.

The **American Painting Galleries** on the first floor begin with portraits by the Boston artist John Singleton Copley, perhaps America's most talented 18th-century painter. Farther on are lush society portraits by John Singer Sargent, who also embellished the museum's domed rotunda with fine murals. The large and airy Lane Gallery exhibits the works of 20th-century American masters such as Stuart Davis, Jackson Pollock, and Georgia O'Keeffe.

The exhibits in the superb **American Decorative Arts** galleries include silver tea services made by Paul Revere *(see p142)*; 18th-century Boston-style desks, chests, and tall clocks; and reconstructed rooms from a 19th-century mansion, which evoke the well-to-do lifestyle of the Federal era. There is also a gallery of ship models and outstanding examples of contemporary crafts.

In addition to these major collections, the Museum of Fine Arts also has important holdings in the multifarious arts of Africa, Oceania, and the ancient Americas, and collections of musical instruments and manuscripts.

**John Singer Sargent's murals on the domed rotunda, MFA**

The simple interior of Christ Church in Cambridge

## Cambridge ㉘

Ⓣ *Harvard.* 🚌 *1, 69.* ℹ **Harvard Square Information Booth** *(617) 497-1630,* **Cambridge Office of Tourism** *(800) 862-5678.* *Sun.* *River Festival (late Jun).* W www.harvard.edu, www.cambridge-usa.org

THOUGH PART OF the Greater Boston metropolitan area, Cambridge is a town in its own right, dominated by two world-famous universities, the **Massachusetts Institute of Technology** (MIT) and **Harvard**. It also has a number of sights associated with the American Revolution.

Among them is the historic house on Brattle Street, now known as the **Longfellow National Historic Site**. Built by Colonial-era merchants loyal to the British Crown during the Revolution, it was seized by American revolutionaries, and served as George Washington's headquarters during the Siege of Boston. From 1843 until his death in 1888 it was also the home of the famous poet Henry Wadsworth Longfellow, who wrote his most famous poems, including *The Song of Hiawatha*, here.

**Harvard Square** is the area's main shopping and entertainment district, full of cafés, inexpensive restaurants, trendy boutiques, and street performers. Harvard's large student population is much in evidence here, adding to the square's lively character.

**Cambridge Common**, north of Harvard Square, was set aside as a common pasture and military drill ground in the 1630s. It has served as a center for social, religious, and political activity ever since. The Common was used as an army encampment from 1775 to 1776, and a stone here marks the spot where George Washington took command of the Continental Army on July 3, 1775, beneath the Washington Elm. Today, its tree-shaded lawns and playgrounds are popular with families and students.

**Christ Church**, a short distance south of the Common, was designed in 1761 by Peter Harrison, the architect of Boston's King's Chapel *(see p140)*. In 1775, it served as a barracks for Continental Army troops, who melted down the organ pipes to cast musket balls. The church was restored for services on New Year's Eve, 1775, when George Washington and his wife were among the worshipers.

The 135-acre (55-ha) campus of the Massachusetts Institute of Technology (MIT), one of the world's leading universities in engineering and the sciences, stretches along the Charles River. Among the masterpieces of modern architecture that dot its campus are Eero Saarinen's Kresge Auditorium and Kresge Chapel, and the Wiesner Building designed by I.M. Pei, which houses a noted collection of avant-garde art in the List Visual Art Center. Art and Science are blended in the MIT Museum, with exhibits such as Harold Edgerton's stroboscopic flash photographs and the latest holographic art.

An altogether more old-world atmosphere prevails at the campus of Harvard University, with its red-brick, ivy-covered walls. Founded in 1636, Harvard is the oldest university in the US and one of the world's most prestigious centers of learning. At the heart of the campus, which encompasses more than 400 buildings, is the leafy **Old Harvard Yard**, dotted with student dormitories. Its focal point is the statue of its most famous benefactor, the cleric John Harvard. Adjacent to the statue is the imposing Widener Library which, with over 3 million volumes, is the third largest in the US. Another impressive building in the Yard is the Memorial Church, built in 1931, whose steeple is modeled on that of the Old North Church *(see p142)*. Standing out amid Harvard's Georgian-style buildings is the Carpenter Center for Visual Arts, designed by the avant-garde French architect Le Corbusier.

A major draw for visitors to Harvard are its five outstanding museums. The **Fogg Art Museum** focuses on masterpieces of European art from the late Middle Ages to the present. Its galleries are organized around a beautiful central courtyard, modeled on

Students strolling through Harvard Yard

a 16th-century church in Montepulciano, Italy. The ground floor galleries and the two-story Warburg Hall display pre-Renaissance Italian art, including massive altarpieces, as well as 17th- and 18th-century Dutch, Flemish, English, and American art. Among the latter are unfinished studies made by John Singleton Copley *(see p147)*. On the second level are pre-Raphaelite paintings and works by John Singer Sargent.

The highlight of the Fogg Museum is its Maurice Wertheim Collection of Impressionist and Post-Impressionist art, also on the second level, with paintings by Renoir, Manet, and Degas. An adjacent gallery has modern American works, such as the minimalist paintings of Frank Stella.

The adjoining **Busch-Reisinger Museum**, entered through the second level of the Fogg Museum, displays the work of 20th-century masters such as Wassily Kandinsky, Paul Klee, and Oskar Kokoschka.

The **Peabody Museum of Archaeology and Ethnology** has impressive collections of Egyptian, North American Indian, and Central American artifacts as well as objects from the South Pacific Islands. Outstanding exhibits include totem carvings by Pacific Northwest tribes, Navajo weavings, and casts of objects unearthed at Chichen Itza in Mexico.

The highlight of the **Harvard Museum of Natural History** is its collection of "glass flowers" – 3,000 botanically correct, exquisite models of 850 plant species in handblown glass, created between 1887 and 1936 by father and son artisans Leopold and Rudolph Blaschka. Don't miss the collections of gems and minerals; the wild animals exhibits are extraordinary.

The **Sackler Museum**, housed in a striking modern building, holds a rich collection of ancient Greek and Roman, Asian, Indian, and Near Eastern art. These include Buddhist and Hindu

**Chinese statues from the Sackler Museum's collection**

sculptures, Islamic art, and Chinese bronzes, jades, ceramics, and stone statues. The latter are thought to be among the finest works of Chinese art in the West.

**Fogg Art & Busch-Reisinger Museums**
32 Quincy St. *(617) 495-9400.* *10am–5pm Mon–Sat, 1–5pm Sun.* *public hols.*
www.artmuseums.harvard.edu

**Peabody Museum of Archaeology & Ethnology**
11 Divinity St. *(617) 496-1027.* *9am–5pm daily.* *Jan 1, Jul 4, Thanksgiving, Dec 25.*
www.peabody.harvard.edu

**Harvard Museum of Natural History**
26 Oxford St. *(617) 495-3045.* *9am–5pm daily.* *Jul 4, Thanksgiving, Dec 25.*
www.hmnh.harvard.edu

## Charlestown ㉙

*Community College.* *93.* *from Long Wharf.* *Wed.* *Jun 24.*

Historic Charlestown, its picturesque streets lined with Colonial houses, is the site of the infamous battle of Bunker Hill, which took place on June 17, 1775. This was the Revolution's first pitched battle between British and Colonial troops, and though the latter lost, they made a courageous stand, inflicting huge losses on the much larger British force. The **Bunker Hill Monument**, a 221-ft (67-m) granite obelisk, dedicated in 1843, commemorates this event. The Washington Monument was erected in 1885 *(see p204)* and the top is reached by 294 steps where there are spectacular views of Boston Harbor. In mid-2006 there will be limited or no access during renovations, but the exhibits will remain open. At the **Bunker Hill Pavilion**, next to Charlestown Navy Yard, a lively multimedia presentation re-enacts this battle. The show consists of color slides projected on 14 screens, audio effects, and life-sized figures.

**Charlestown Navy Yard**, established in 1800, is the home of America's most famous warship, the USS *Constitution*. Built in 1797, and nicknamed "Old Ironsides" *(see p137)*, she is the oldest commissioned warship afloat and a veteran of 42 victorious battles at sea. Thoroughly overhauled for the 1997 bicentennial, she is taken out into the harbor on July 4 each year for an annual turnaround that reverses her position at the Navy Yard pier, to insure equal weathering on both sides.

**Environs:** The Colonial town of **Lexington**, 16 miles (26 km) northwest of Boston, is the site of the first bloody skirmish between armed colonists, called Minutemen, and British troops. This battle, on April 19, 1775, acted as a catalyst for the Revolutionary War *(see p44)*. The Lexington Battle Green, with its Minute Man statue, is the focal point of the town. Three historic buildings associated with the battle and maintained by the local Historical Society are open to visitors.

**Granite obelisk of the Bunker Hill Monument in Charlestown**

# Massachusetts

Of all the New England states, Massachusetts may have the most diverse mix of natural and man-made attractions. Scenic seascapes and picturesque villages beckon along the eastern seaboard and Cape Cod. Venturing inland, visitors will find historic towns where America's early architecture has been well preserved. In the west, green mountains and valleys, and rich culture characterize the Berkshire Hills.

## Salem ❷

*38,000. From Boston's Long Wharf. 2 New Liberty St, (978) 740-1650. Haunted Halloween (Oct). www.salem.org*

This coastal town, founded in 1626, is best known for the infamous witch trials of 1692, which resulted in the execution of 20 innocent people. A chilling, multi-media re-enactment of the witch-hunt and subsequent trials can be seen at the **Salem Witch Museum**.

In the 18th and 19th centuries, Salem was one of New England's busiest ports, its harbor filled with ships carrying treasures from around the globe. The **Peabody Essex Museum** contains some of the world's deepest holdings of Asian art and artifacts. Many of the museum's exhibits, such as jewelry, porcelain figures, costumes, and scrimshaw objects, were brought back from distant shores by Salem's sea captains. The town's historic waterfront has been preserved as the **Salem Maritime National Historic** Site. It maintains three restored 18th-century wharves and a reconstructed East Indiaman sailing ship built in 1797, the *Friendship*, which is moored at the dock.

### Peabody Essex Museum

East India Sq. *(800) 745-4054.*
*10am–5pm daily.*

**Environs:** Marblehead, just 4 miles (6 km) from Salem, is a picturesque and historic seaport village. Its hilly twisting lanes are lined with historic buildings, mansions, and cottages, most notable of which are Abbot Hall and the Jeremiah Lee Mansion.

## Lowell ❸

*103,000. 9 Central St, Ste 201, (978) 459-6150.*

Lowell has the distinction of being the country's first industrial city. In the early 19th century, the first cloth mill equipped with a power loom opened here, and the town soon had a number of giant mill complexes. But after the Great Depression *(see p49)* the mills closed down, leaving Lowell a ghost town. Since 1978, many of Lowell's downtown buildings have been restored, and two of its museums trace the history of the town's textile industry. Lowell is also home to the **New England Quilt Museum**, which has a varied collection of displays of beautiful antique as well as contemporary quilts.

### Salem Witch Trials

**Early accused: Rebecca Nurse**

In 1692, Salem was swept by a wave of hysteria in which 200 citizens were accused of practicing witchcraft. In all, 150 people were jailed and 19 were hanged as witches, while another man was crushed to death with stones. No one was safe: two dogs were executed on the gallows for being witches. Not surprisingly, when the governor's wife became a suspect, the trials came to an abrupt and officially sanctioned end.

**Concord's Old Manse, home to 19th-century literary giants**

## Concord ❹

*17,750. 58 Main St, (978) 369-3120. Battle of Concord Re-enactment (Apr). www.concordmachamber.org*

This peaceful, prosperous town has an eventful past. It was here that the Battle of Concord took place on April 19, 1775 which, together with the battle at nearby Lexington *(see p149)*, signaled the beginning of the Revolutionary War. The 900-acre (400-ha) **Minute Man National Historic Park** preserves the site of the battle, where a group of ordinary citizens and colonist farmers, known as Minutemen *(see p44)*, fought against British troops, driving them back from the park's North Bridge and chasing them back to Boston.

In the 19th century, Concord blossomed into the literary heart and soul of the country, with many writers establishing homes here. Both Ralph Waldo Emerson and Nathaniel Hawthorne lived briefly in **The Old Manse**; Emerson lived for nearly 50 years, until his death in 1882, at **Emerson House**, where his furniture, books, and memorabilia are on display.

Also in Concord is **Walden Pond**, immortalized in the writings of the essayist Henry David Thoreau (1817–62). In his influential work, *Walden; or Life in the Woods*, Thoreau called for a return to simplicity in everyday life and a respect for nature. Walden is widely considered to be the birthplace of the conservaionist movement. The pond nd its surrounding 333 acres 135 ha) of undeveloped voodland are ideal for walks, wimming, and fishing.

**Walden Pond State Reservation**
15 Walden St. (978) 369-3254.
call for hours.

## Plymouth 5

52,000. to Provincetown seasonal). 130 Water St, (508) 747-7533, (800) USA-1620.
www.visit-plymouth.com

THE SHIP *Mayflower*, with 102 Pilgrims aboard, sailed nto Plymouth Harbor in 1620 nd established the first permanent European settlement n New England. Today the own bustles with visitors exploring the sites of America's earliest days, including **Plimoth Plantation**. Plymouth tself is a popular seaside esort, with a 3.5-mile (6-km) beach, offering harbor cruises nd fishing excursions. In the all, the surrounding bogs turn ruby red as the annual cranberry harvest gets underway.

***Mayflower II*, replica of the original Pilgrim ship, in Plymouth**

Most of the historic sights can be accessed on foot by the Pilgrim Path that stretches along the waterfront and downtown areas. A sightseeing trolley also connects points of interest. At the Harbor is **Plymouth Rock**, a boulder marking the spot where the Pilgrims are said to have first stepped ashore. Moored by it is the *Mayflower II*, a replica of the 17th-century sailing ship that carried the Pilgrims over from England. Many of those who survived the brutal crossing on this small, cramped ship succumbed to illness and malnutrition during their first winter in Plymouth. They are buried across the street on **Coles Hill**, where there is a statue of the Indian chief Massasoit, who became an ally of the survivors. There is a panoramic view of the harbor from here.

The **Pilgrim Hall Museum**, opened in 1824 has the largest existing collection of Pilgrim-era furniture, armor, and decorative arts. There are also several historic homes, including **Spooner House**. Built in 1749 and occupied by one family until 1954, the house and its contents were left to the Plymouth Antiquarian Society as a museum.

**Plimoth Plantation**
Rte 3A. 137 Warren Ave, (508) 746-1622. Apr–Nov: 9am–5pm daily. limited access to certain parts of site; wheelchairs available on request. www.plimoth.org

### Plimoth Plantation

Encircled by a palisade, Plimoth Plantation is a painstakingly accurate re-creation of the Pilgrims' 1627 village, complete with rudimentary thatched dwellings and livestock. Costumed interpreters, portraying personages from the original colony, enhance the period atmosphere.

**Storehouse**
*Provisions were stored here, along with furs and other goods to be shipped to England.*

**Hopkins House**
*Stephen Hopkins' wife gave birth to their son Oceanus on the Mayflower.*

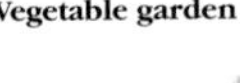

**Vegetable garden**

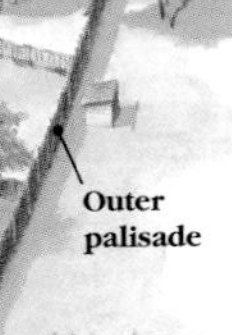

**Outer palisade**

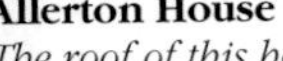

**Allerton House**
*The roof of this house is thatched with the long-lasting, virtually waterproof local reeds.*

**The Cow Shed** is enclosed by a paddock.

Cape Cod's Old Harbor Life-Saving Station, built in 1897

## Cape Cod 6

*Elm Ave, Hyannis.* *Ocean St, Hyannis; Railroad Ave, Woods Hole.* *Jct Rtes 132 & 6, Rte 25, Hyannis, (508) 862-0700, (888) 332-2732.* *Cape Cod Maritime Week (May), Annual Bourne Scallop Festival (Sep).*

More than 13 million people arrive each summer to enjoy the boundless beaches, natural beauty, and quaint Colonial villages of Cape Cod, and the neighboring islands of Martha's Vineyard and Nantucket. A special attraction for visitors are whale-watching cruises, offered from April to mid-October. The Cape, shaped like an upraised arm bent at the elbow, extends some 70 miles (113 km) into the sea.

**Cape Cod National Seashore**, stretching more than 40 miles (64 km) along the northernmost section of the Cape, from Provincetown to Chatham, is famous for its horseshoe-shaped dunes, white sand beaches, salt marshes, glacial cliffs, and woodlands. Historical structures, such as the **Old Harbor Life-Saving Station** and the 18th-century Atwood Higgins House, are interspersed among the area's beautiful natural features.

One of the most popular destinations on the Cape is **Provincetown**. This picturesque town has a historic past – the Pilgrims first landed here in 1620 and stayed for five weeks before pushing on to the mainland. The 252-ft (77-m) **Pilgrim Monument**, the tallest granite structure in the US, commemorates this event. Today, Provincetown is especially vibrant during the summer months, when its population can swell from 3,500 to 80,000. One of the busiest locales is McMillan Wharf, the jumping off point for whale-watching cruises. Since the early 20th century, the town has also had a bustling artists' colony, counting among its famous residents the painters Mark Rothko and Jackson Pollock, and the writers Eugene O'Neill and Tennessee Williams. The work of local artists is also displayed in the Provincetown Art Association and Museum.

Pilgrim Monument

**Chatham**, an attractive, upscale community, offers fine inns, attractive shops, and a popular summer playhouse. Fishing boats stop and unload their catch at the pier, and the surrounding waters offer good opportunities for enthusiastic anglers. The Railroad Museum, housed in an 1887 Victorian train station, has photos, memorabilia, and vintage railroad cars.

**Hyannis**, the largest village in Cape Cod, is a busy shopping center and the main transportation hub for the region. It is also famous as the summer home of the country's most celebrated political dynasty, the Kennedys. The heavily screened Kennedy compound is best seen from the water aboard a sightseeing cruise. At its center is the "cottage" that multi-millionaire Joseph Kennedy (1888–1969) bought in 1926, expanding it into a sprawling vacation retreat for his nine children and their families. The Kennedy clan continues to gather here on family occasions. After John F Kennedy's assassination in 1963, a simple memorial was erected in the town in his honor: a pool and fountain, and a circular wall bearing Kennedy's profile.

One of Hyannis' most popular forms of transportation is the **Cape Cod Central Railroad**, which offers a scenic two-hour round trip to the Cape Cod canal.

Hiking trails, salt marshes, tidal pools, and 12 miles (19 km) of beaches attract visitors to **Falmouth**, with its picturesque village green. It also has the 3.3-mile (5-km) Shining Sea Bike Path, with vistas of beach, harbor, and woodland. The path leads to the world's largest independent marine science research center, the Woods Hole Oceanographic Institute.

**Sandwich**, the oldest town in the Cape, is straight off a postcard: a church overlooking a picturesque pond, fed by a brook that powers the waterwheel of a Colonial-era gristmill. The church bell, dating to 1675, is said to be the oldest in the US. The town's most unusual attraction is **Heritage Museums & Gardens**, a 75-acre (30-ha) garden and museum housing the eclectic collection of the pharmaceutical tycoon, Josiah K. Lilly Jr. (1893–1966). Exhibits include 37 antique cars, Native American relics, and a 1912 carousel. The gardens are famous for their lovely rhododendrons.

Just a 45-minute boatride away from the mainland lies

Popular sightseeing trip on the Cape Cod Central Railroad

Fishing boat moored outside a fishing shack, Martha's Vineyard

**Martha's Vineyard**. This 108-sq mile (280-sq km) island combines mesmerizing scenic beauty with the charms of a beach resort and abounds in opportunities for outdoor activities. Each town has its own distinctive atmosphere and architectural style.

Most visitors arrive by ferry at the island's commercial hub, Vineyard Haven. On the eastern shore is Edgartown, with the gracious 19th-century homes of the town's wealthy sea captains and merchants. The **Martha's Vineyard Historical Society** is housed in one of them – the Thomas Cooke House (c.1730), filled with antique furniture and ship models. From here, a short ferry ride goes to Chappaquiddick Island, where in 1969, a car driven by Senator Edward Kennedy went off the bridge, killing a woman passenger.

North of Edgartown is Oak Bluff, with its gingerbread cottages, while the Western Shoreline is tranquil and rural with pristine beaches.

**Nantucket Island**, a 14-mile (22-km) long enclave of tranquility with only one town, remains a largely untamed world of kettle ponds, quiet beaches, cranberry bogs, and fields of wild grapes and blueberries, punctuated by occasional houses. Nantucket was a prosperous center of the whaling industry in the early 1800s, and the mansions of sea captains and merchants reflect those glory days. The **Nantucket Historical Association** (NHA) operates 11 historical buildings in the town, one of which houses a fascinating Whaling Museum. A popular spot, 8 miles (13 km) from town, is Siasconset village, famous for its rose-colored bluffs and lanes with tiny cottages.

**Cape Cod National Seashore**
Rte 6, Cape Cod. *Salt Pond Visitor Center, Rte 6, Eastham, (508) 255-3421. year-round.*
www.nps.gov/caco

**Heritage Museums & Gardens**
67 Grove St, Sandwich. *(508) 888-3300. May–Oct: 9am–6pm daily, Nov–mid-May: call for hours.*

**Martha's Vineyard Historical Society**
59 School St, Edgartown. *(508) 627-4441. mid-Jun–Sep: 10am–5pm Tue–Sat; Oct–mid-Jun: 1–4pm Wed–Fri, 10am–4pm Sat; Jan–Feb:10am–4pm Sat.*

**Nantucket Historical Association (NHA)**
15 Broad St, Nantucket Island.
*(508) 228-1894.* **Historic buildings** *call for hours.*
*Whaling Museum only.*

## Sturbridge 7

**Old Sturbridge Village** Rte 20, Sturbridge. *(508) 347-3362.*
*Apr–Oct: 9:30am–5pm daily; Jan–mid-Feb: 9:30am–4pm Sat–Sun; mid-Feb–Mar: 9:30am–4pm Tue–Sun.*
*Dec 25.*

This small town is home to **Old Sturbridge Village**, an open-air museum in the form of an early 19th-century village. At the heart of the museum are about 40 vintage buildings that have been restored and relocated from all over New England. They include the Federal-style Towne House, a meeting-house, a tavern, and a store, with authentic period settings.

## The Berkshires 8

*Pittsfield.* *Berkshire Common Plaza, Pittsfield, (413) 443-9186, (800) 237-5747.*
www.berkshire.org

Wooded hills, green valleys, rippling rivers, and waterfalls have long attracted visitors to this western corner of Massachusetts, which is rich in opportunities for outdoor as well as cultural activity. The area is speckled with scenic small towns and villages. **Pittsfield**, in the shadow of Mount Greylock, is famous as the home of Herman Melville (1819–91), where he wrote his masterpiece, *Moby Dick*. **Lenox** has the grand estates of prominent families such as the Carnegies. It also hosts the prestigious Tanglewood Musical Festival every summer. The main street of **Stockbridge** has been immortalized in the paintings of one of America's most beloved illustrators, Norman Rockwell (1894–1978), who lived here for 25 years. His works can be seen in the town's **Norman Rockwell Museum**.

Especially attractive to nature lovers is the **Mount Washington State Forest**, and the Mount Everett State Forest, nearby.

**Norman Rockwell Museum**
Rte 183. *(413) 298-4100 ext 220.*
*May–Oct: 10am–5pm daily; Nov–Apr: 10am–4pm Mon–Fri, 10am–5pm Sat–Sun. Jan 1, Thanksgiving, Dec 25.* www.nrm.org

Bash Bish Falls, Mount Washington State Forest in the Berkshires

# Rhode Island

THE SMALLEST STATE IN AMERICA, Rhode Island is not an island at all but has a shoreline dotted with lovely islets and beaches. Although known as the Ocean State, half of Rhode Island is woodland, ideal for nature walks and camping. The state's two major cities are Providence, the lively capital, and Newport, which has some of New England's most opulent mansions.

**Stately buildings along Benefit Street's Mile of History in Providence**

## Providence 9

*174,000. Providence Station, 100 Gaspee St. 1 Bonanza Way. Point St (to Newport). 1 W Exchange St, (401) 274-1636 or (800) 233-1636. Festival of Historic Houses (Jun–Dec); International Film Festival (Aug).* www.goprovidence.com

PERCHED ON seven hills on the banks of Narragansett Bay, Providence is an interesting blend of the historic and the modern. It started life as a farming community, established in 1636 by the clergyman Roger Williams, who was driven from the Massacusetts Bay colony for his outspoken beliefs on religious freedom. It soon became a flourishing seaport, and then evolved into a hub of industry in the 19th century, with immigrants from Europe pouring in to work in its textile mills.

Providence is bisected by the Providence River. On its west bank is the downtown district, revitalized by recent renewal projects, which have restored old buildings, constructed new malls and markets, and developed the waterfront. To the east is tthe campus of Brown University and several historic streets. The most outstanding of these is **Benefit Street's Mile of History**. This lovely tree-lined street has more than 100 houses ranging in style from Colonial and Federal to Greek Revival and Victorian. Its architectural gems include the **Providence Athenaeum**, a Greek Revival-style library, whose collection dates back to 1753, to the First Unitarian Church. Its 2,500-lb (1,350-kg) bell was one of the largest cast by Paul Revere's foundry. Also on Benefit Street is the Rhode Island School of Design's **RISD Museum of Art**, whose comprehensive collection ranges from Ancient Egyptian to contemporary American art. A short distance to the north, on Main Street, is the **First Baptist Church in America**. Built in 1774–75, it has an intricately carved wooden interior and a Waterford crystal chandelier.

Founded in 1764, **Brown University** is the seventh-oldest college in the US and one of the prestigious Ivy League schools. Its beautiful campus, a rich blend of Gothic and Beaux Arts styles, is worth exploring. Notable buildings here include the John Hay Library with its collection of memorabilia relating to President Abraham Lincoln, the John Carter Brown Library with a fascinating collection of Americana, and the List Art Center, a striking building designed by Philip Johnson, which features classical and contemporary art.

**John Brown House**, a Georgian mansion, built in 1786 for a wealthy merchant and shipowner, has been impeccably restored. Its interior is decorated with ornate plaster ornamented ceilings, a grand staircase with twisted balusters, and wallpapers from France. Its 12 rooms are a repository for some of the finest furniture and antiques of that period. Nearby, another house with fine 18th-century furnishings is the 1707 **Governor Stephen Hopkins House**.

One of the newest and brightest additions to downtown Providence is **Waterplace Park and Riverwalk**, a 4-acre (1.6-ha) walkway located at the junction of three rivers – the Moshassock, Providence, and Woonasquatucket. Visitors can also stroll along the park's cobblestone paths, float under

**Roger Williams Park and Zoo, a highlight of downtown Providence**

footbridges in canoes or gondolas, and enjoy free concerts at the amphitheater during the summer season.

Another successful downtown renewal project is **The Arcade**, an 1828 Greek Revival building that covers an entire block in the city's old financial district. The first indoor shopping mall in the US, this massive three-story stone complex with its high Ionic granite columns, has a skylight extending the entire length of the building, providing light even on rainy days. Restored in 1980, this lively marketplace contains specialty shops, clothing boutiques, and several restaurants.

Downtown Providence is dominated by the imposing **Rhode Island State House** constructed in 1904. Its magnificent white marble dome is topped by a bronze statue called Independent Man, a symbol of Rhode Island's free spirit. Among the displays inside are the original state charter of 1663 and a full-length portrait of President George Washington by Gilbert Stuart.

The city's largest green space is the **Roger Williams Park and Zoo**. Once farmland, this 422-acre (171-ha) park now holds gardens, greenhouses, and ponds, a lake with paddleboats and rowboats, as well as jogging and cycling tracks and a tennis center. Children especially love the carousel rides and train, the planetarium, and the Museum of Natural History. The highlight of the park, however, is the zoo, which has more than 900 animals, including mammals such as zebras, giraffes, and cheetahs. An underwater window allows visitors to look at the penguins and polar bears as they cavort playfully in the water.

**Rhode Island State House with its marble dome**

**RISD Museum of Art**
224 Benefit St. *(401) 454-6500.*
*10am–5pm Tue–Sun, 10am–9pm third Thu of month.* *public hols.*

**John Brown House**
52 Power St. *(401) 273-7507.*
*Jan–Feb: 10am–5pm Fri & Sat, noon–4pm Sun; Mar–Dec: 10am–5pm Tue–Sat, noon–4pm Sun.* *Mon & public hols.*

**Rhode Island State House**
82 Smith St. *(401) 222-2357.*
*8:30am–4:30pm Mon–Fri.*
*public hols.* *self-guided, others by appt.*

## Downtown Providence

Benefit Street's Mile of History ①
Providence Athenaeum ②
RISD Museum of Art ③
First Baptist Church in America ④
Brown University ⑤
John Brown House ⑥
Governor Stephen Hopkins House ⑦
Waterplace Park and Riverwalk ⑧
The Arcade ⑨
Rhode Island State House ⑩

**Key**

Interstate
Highway
Train station
Railroad
Tourist information
Parking

*To Roger Williams Park and Zoo*

0 meters 300
0 yards 300

Scores of yachts in the harbor at Newport

## Newport ⑩

28,000. Gateway Center, 23 America's Cup Ave. Perrotti Park (to Providence). 23 America's Cup Ave, (401) 849-8048. Newport Tennis Week (Jul), JVC Jazz Festival (Aug). www.gonewport.com

A CENTER OF trade, culture, wealth, and military activity for more than 300 years, Newport is a true sight-seeing mecca. The town's main attractions are its mansions, most of them located on Bellevue Avenue on the southeastern side of the city. Built between 1748 and 1902, when the rich and famous flocked here each summer to beat New York's heat, these summer "cottage" retreats of the country's wealthiest families, such as the Vanderbilts and the Astors, are some of America's grandest private homes. Modeled on European palaces and decorated with the finest artworks, the mansions were used for only 10 weeks of the year. **The Breakers** is one of the finest examples.

Newport is also home to the oldest synagogue in USA. Built in 1763 by Sephardic Jews who had fled Spain and Portugal in search of religious tolerance, the **Touro Synagogue** is an outstanding example of 18th-century architecture. It is located just east of Washington Square where a number of historic Colonial buildings have been preserved. Among them is the fascinating Museum of Newport History, housed in the Brick Market, which was the center of commerce in Colonial times. Also on the Square is the White Horse Tavern *(see p184)*, which claims to be the oldest continuously operating tavern in America; it was granted its liquor license in 1673.

Apart from its mansions and historic sites, Newport also has numerous outdoor attractions. South of

### The Breakers

The architecture and ostentation of the Gilded Age of the late 1800s reached its pinnacle with The Breakers, the summer home of the railroad magnate Cornelius Vanderbilt II (1843–99). Completed in 1895, the four-story, 70-room limestone mansion was modeled after 16th-century palaces in Turin and Genoa. Its interior is adorned with marble, stained glass, gilt, and crystal.

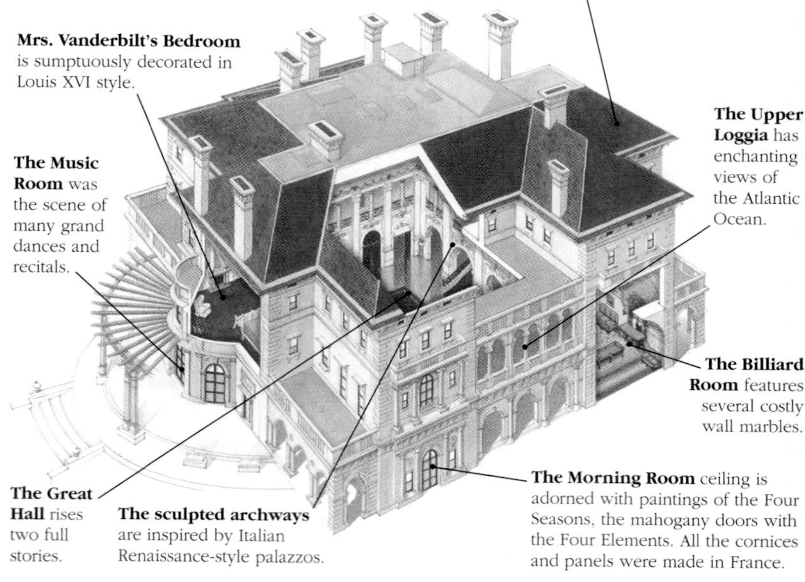

**The Dining Room,** a two-story room, has a stunning arched ceiling and two huge crystal chandeliers.

**Mrs. Vanderbilt's Bedroom** is sumptuously decorated in Louis XVI style.

**The Upper Loggia** has enchanting views of the Atlantic Ocean.

**The Music Room** was the scene of many grand dances and recitals.

**The Billiard Room** features several costly wall marbles.

**The Morning Room** ceiling is adorned with paintings of the Four Seasons, the mahogany doors with the Four Elements. All the cornices and panels were made in France.

**The Great Hall** rises two full stories.

**The sculpted archways** are inspired by Italian Renaissance-style palazzos.

**The breathtaking Cliff Walk, popular with visitors in Newport**

Washington Square is **Fort Adams State Park**, with Fort Adams, built in 1853, as its centerpiece. No longer in use as a garrison, the fort is surrounded with facilities for swimming and other sports. Each year, Newport's famous Jazz Festival is held here. The park also has the Museum of Yachting, as well as a collection of luxury yachts.

Another popular site is the 3.5-mile (5.5-km) long **Cliff Walk**, southwest of downtown. The trail, along the city's ragged cliffs, offers some fine views of the Gilded-Age mansions and has been designated a National Recreation Trail in 1975. The Forty Steps, each named for someone lost at sea, lead to the ocean.

**The Breakers**
Ochre Point Ave. *(401) 847-1000.*
*mid-Apr–Oct: 10am–5pm daily. Call for winter hours.*
*Thanksgiving, Dec 24 & 25.*
*every 15 minutes.*
www.newportmansions.org

**Touro Synagogue**
85 Touro St. *(401) 847-4794.*
*call for times.* *every half hour.*
*Shabbat & all Jewish hols.*

**Fort Adams State Park**
Harrison Ave. *(401) 847-2400.*
*sunrise to sunset daily.* **Museum of Yachting** *(401) 847-1018.*
*mid-May–Oct: 10am–4pm daily; Nov–mid-May: by appt.*

## South County Beaches ⓫

**Narragansett** *36 Ocean Rd, (401) 783-7121.*
**Charlestown** *4945 Old Post Rd, (401) 364-3878.*

Southwest of Newport, between **Narragansett** and Watch Hill, are some 100 miles (161 km) of pristine white sand beaches and a series of tidal salt ponds. The ponds are big lures for bird-watchers hoping to study the egrets, sandpipers, and herons that swim and wade in the salty marshes. Many of the beaches are free to the public, except for parking fees. **Scarborough State Beach** is excellent for bodysurfing and surfboarding, while the sheltered, cove-protected **Roger Wheeler Memorial Beach** is a favorite for families. **East Matunuck State Beach** is popular with surfers on windy days. The beautiful sandy stretch of **Charlestown Town Beach** has a boat ramp with access to the coastal ponds of the Ninigret National Wildlife Refuge.

Farther west along the coast is **Misquamicut State Beach**. The largest beach in the state, it has gentle surf and an old-time amusement park with rides and many diversions for children.

## Block Island ⓬

*Point Judith. Ferries carry cars by advance reservations, (401) 783-4613.*

Lying just 13 miles (21 km) off the coast, Block Island is a great destination for outdoor enthusiasts who enjoy such activities as swimming, fishing, sailing, bird-watching, canoeing, and horseback riding. Some 30 miles (48 km) of natural trails entice hikers and cyclists to experience the island's natural beauty.

The village of **Old Harbor** is the island's main hub of activity. Victorian houses, hotels, and shops line the streets, and anglers can charter boats to fish for striped bass, bluefish, flounder, and cod. South of the village are the dramatic 200-ft (61-m) high red clay cliffs of **Mohegan Bluffs**, and the Southeast Lighthouse, which was once the most powerful in New England.

A favorite with hikers is **Rodman's Hollow Natural Area**. This glacial depression, well marked with nature trails, is a refuge for hawks and white-tailed deer.

On Block Island's northwestern coast is **Great Salt Pond**, which is completely protected from the ocean. It is an excellent spot for kayaking and fishing. Nearby New Harbor is the island's prime marina and boating center. **Clayhead**, on the island's northeastern coast, offers wonderful views of the Atlantic Ocean, and is the starting point for a nature trail that goes all the way north to **Settler's Rock**. A plaque here honors the 16 Englishmen who landed here in 1661. The rock is at the edge of Sachem Pond, a favorite for swimming and kayaking. An 18-mile (29-km) driving tour of Block Island is a comfortable way to take in all these sites.

**Plaque to early English pioneers, Settlers Rock, Block Island**

**The dramatic red clay cliffs at Mohegan Bluffs, Block Island**

# Connecticut

ALTHOUGH compact enough to cross in a few hours, Connecticut has treasures that entice visitors to stay for days. Along its magnificent shoreline are beaches, marinas, and the remarkable maritime museum at Mystic Seaport. Inland, the Connecticut River Valley and the Litchfield Hills are dotted with scenic and historic villages. Hartford, the bustling capital, and New Haven, home of Yale University, are its main cities.

## Hartford ⓭

*139,000. 1 Union Place. 31 Pratt St, 4th floor, (860) 244-8181, (800) 793-4480. Mark Twain Days (summer). www.enjoyhartford.com*

FOUNDED IN 1636 by a group of English settlers from the Massachusetts Bay Colony, Hartford's golden age was in the 19th century when it became a flourishing center of the insurance industry. It also became a vibrant cultural center, thanks to resident authors such as Mark Twain. In recent years, an ambitious revitalization program has breathed new life into the city.

Dominating the cityscape is the gleaming gold-leaf dome of the **State Capitol**, a Victorian-Gothic building perched on a hilltop. Many of Hartford's attractions are accessible on foot from here. The Capitol overlooks the 40-acre (16-ha) **Bushnell Park**, the creation of Hartford native Frederick Law Olmsted (1822–1903), who also laid out New York's Central Park. There are 100 varieties of trees, and a 1914 carousel with 48 hand-carved horses.

The 1796 **Old State House**, designed by Charles Bulfinch *(see p134)*, is the country's oldest Capitol building. With its grand center hall and staircase, and ornate cupola, it is a superb example of Federal architecture. Nearby, the **Center Church** has five stained-glass windows designed by the US artist Louis Comfort Tiffany (1848–1933). To its south is the **Wadsworth Atheneum**, the oldest continuously operating public art museum in the country. Its collection includes Renaissance, Baroque, and Impressionist art, as well as works by American artists.

West of downtown is the **Mark Twain House**, a picturesque Gothic-style masterpiece with peaked gables, expansive upper balconies, and towering turrets. Legend has it that Twain (1835–1910), once a riverboat captain, designed the house to give it the appearance of one of his beloved Mississippi

**The Connecticut State Capitol, overlooking Bushnell Park**

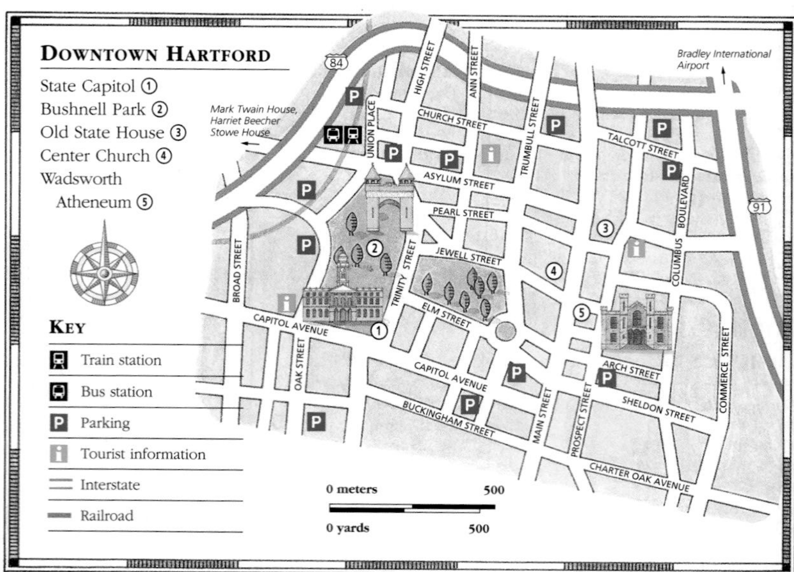

The Billiard Room, Mark Twain House, Hartford

steamboats. Of special interest are the library with its ornate wooden fireplace mantel; the tranquil Billiard Room where Twain wrote some of his best known works, including *The Adventures of Tom Sawyer*; and the Master Bedroom with its beautifully carved bed. A new visitor center illuminates Twain's life and work.

Next door is the **Harriet Beecher Stowe House**, where the famous author of the anti-slavery novel, *Uncle Tom's Cabin* (1852), lived until her death in 1896. The house is adorned with gingerbread ornamentation typical of late 19th-century Victorian design, while the elegance of its interior displays Harriet's less well-known talent as a decorator.

**Mark Twain House**

351 Farmington Ave.
*(860) 247-0998 ext 26.*
*9:30am–5:30am daily; 9:30am–8pm 1st Thu of the month.*
*Jan 1, Easter Sun, Thanksgiving, Dec 24 & 25.* *obligatory.*
*1st floor only.*
www.marktwain.org

## Litchfield ⑭

*8,850.* *Litchfield Hills Visitors' Bureau, PO Box 968, (860) 567-4506.*

THIS PICTURESQUE and historic town is at the center of the Litchfield Hills region in northwestern Connecticut, which many people consider the most scenic part of the state. Anchored by the Housatonic River, the bucolic landscape of lovely woods, valleys, lakes, and wildlife offers great opportunities for sports such as canoeing, kayaking, whitewater rafting, tubing, fly-fishing, and hiking. In fall, the brilliant foliage along the region's roads entrances sightseers. Litchfield's many historic houses include the 1784 **Tapping Reeve House** and Law School, the country's first law school. On the outskirts of the town, on Route 202, **Mount Tom State Park** has trails leading to the 1,325-ft (404-m) summit. The lake is ideal for scuba diving, swimming, boating, and fishing.

## Connecticut River Valley ⑮

**Windsor** *27,800.* *Hartford, (860) 244-8181.* **Old Lyme** *6,800.* *470 Bank St, New London, (860) 444-2206, (800) 863-6469.*

THE CONNECTICUT River Valley is dotted with picture postcard-perfect little towns and villages. **Windsor**, settled in the early 1630s by Pilgrims from Plymouth *(see p151)* has a number of historic houses, open to visitors, such as the 1758 John & Sarah Strong House with its fine furnishings. Nearby is the Palisado Green, where nervous settlers built a walled stockade in their 1637 war with the Pequot Indians.

**Wethersfield**, settled in 1634, stands as a primer of American architecture from the 18th to the 20th centuries. Especially worth visiting is the Webb-Deane-Stevens Museum, which is a trio of dwellings that depict the lifestyles of three different 18th-century Americans – a diplomat, a wealthy merchant, and a leather tanner.

The **Dinosaur State Park**, farther south, preserves some 500 prehistoric dinosaur tracks beneath a geodesic dome. It also has a display of a life-sized model of an 8-ft (2-m) tall Dilophosaurus.

Just outside the town of East Hadham is the bizarre and ostentatious **Gillette Castle**, built in 1919 by the actor William Gillette. This 24-room granite mansion is built like a medieval castle, complete with battlements and turrets, and is rife with oddities such as Gillette's homemade trick locks and furniture set on wheels and tracks.

Picturesque Old Lyme boasts several 18th- and 19th-century houses built for sea captains. It is also renowned for the **Florence Griswold Museum**, housed in an 1817 mansion. Paintings by some of America's leading artists, such as Childe Hassam and Clark Voorhees, adorn the walls of this museum, together with superb works by other artists who lived in art patron Florence Griswold's house and painted on its wall panels to repay her generosity.

**Wethersfield**

*Greater Hartford Tourism District, 31 Pratt St, Hartford, (860) 244-8181, (800) 793-4480.*
www.enjoyhartford.com

**Gillette Castle**

67 River Rd off Rte 82, Hadlyme. *(860) 526-2336.* *late May–Columbus Day 10am–5pm daily.*

**Florence Griswold Museum**

96 Lyme St, Old Lyme. *(860) 434-5542.* *until summer 2006.* *Jan–Apr: 1–5pm Wed–Sun; May–Dec: 10am–5pm Tue–Sat, 1–5pm Sun.*
www.flogris.org

***The Harpist*** **by Alphonse Jongers at the Florence Griswold Museum**

# New Haven ⓰

123, 626. 1 Long Wharf Dr, (203) 777-8550. www.cityofnewhaven.com **Yale University** Dwight Hall, (203) 432-2300. International Festival of Arts and Ideas (Jun). www. yale.edu

FOUNDED IN 1638, New Haven is located on the coast, where three rivers flow into Long Island Sound. Although this has helped make it a major manufacturing center, the city is better known as the home of **Yale University**, one of the world's most prestigious institutions of higher learning. Its alumni include no less than four American presidents, including the Bushes Sr. and Jr, and Bill Clinton. Yale, founded in 1701, has made New Haven a leading center for education, research, and technology, and has enriched its cultural life as well.

The main area of the town is the 16-acre (6-ha) **New Haven Green**, serving as the setting for many of New Haven's activities and festivals. Three beautiful early 19th-century churches are located on the Green, of which the **First Church of Christ** has a Tiffany stained-glass window, regarded as a masterpiece of American Georgian style.

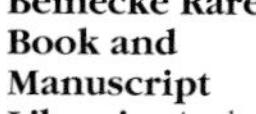

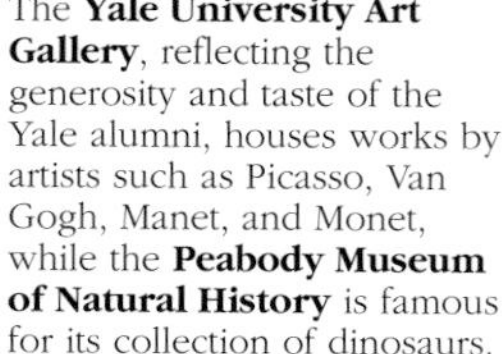

Tiffany stained-glass window, First Church of Christ

Much of the core of downtown New Haven is covered by the Yale University campus, dotted with Georgian and Neo-Gothic buildings, as well as modern structures designed by Eero Saarinen and Philip Johnson. Major landmarks on the campus are the beautiful Gothic-style Memorial Quadrangle and the Harkness Tower, whose carillon rings out at intervals through the day.

Yale's outstanding museums are a prime attraction for visitors. The **Yale Center for British Art**, whose collection was donated by the philanthropist Paul Mellon (1907–99), has the largest collection of British art outside the UK and includes paintings by Gainsborough, Hogarth, and Turner. The treasures of the **Beinecke Rare Book and Manuscript Libraries** include one of the world's few remaining Gutenberg Bibles. The **Yale University Art Gallery**, reflecting the generosity and taste of the Yale alumni, houses works by artists such as Picasso, Van Gogh, Manet, and Monet, while the **Peabody Museum of Natural History** is famous for its collection of dinosaurs.

A must for the musically inclined is the **Yale Collection of Musical Instruments**. Its stunning exhibits consist of violins and harpsichords dating back centuries. These historical instruments are still played at concerts held here today.

Entrance to the Peabody Museum of Natural History, Yale University

The most popular park in New Haven is the 84-acre (34-ha) Lighthouse Point Park on Long Island Sound. It has nature trails, a picnic grove, a bird sanctuary, as well as a 1840 lighthouse.

**Yale Center for British Art**
1080 Chapel St. (203) 432-2800. 10am–5pm Tue–Sat, noon–5pm Sun. public hols.

**Beinecke Rare Book & Manuscript Libraries**
121 Wall St. (203) 432-0600. 8:30am–5pm Mon–Fri, 10am–5pm Sat. Sat in Aug & public hols.

**Yale University Art Gallery**
1111 Chapel St. (203) 432-0600. 10am–5pm Tue–Sat (upto 8pm on Thu), 1–6pm Sun. public hols.

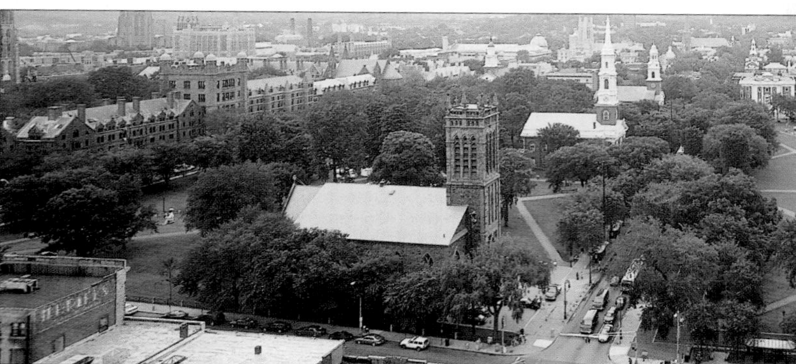

Church spires around New Haven Green, the focal point of the town

The *Charles W. Morgan*, the last wooden whaling ship, in Mystic Seaport

## Connecticut Coast ⓱

**Mystic** 2,600. 28 Cottrell St, (860) 572-9578. **Madison** 16,000. 22 Scotland Ave, (203) 245-7394. **Stamford** Fairfield County. 117, 083. (203) 977-6600.

CONNECTICUT'S magnificent 105-mile (170-km) long shoreline, is scalloped by coves, inlets, and harbors, dotted with beaches, marinas, and state parks. Historic towns and villages also lie along the coast.

One the most popular tourist destinations along the Connecticut Coast is **Mystic Seaport**. This authentic 18th- and 19th-century seafaring village, where nearly every home sports a nautical motif, also has the world's largest maritime museum. Mystic's main attraction is its preservation shipyard and its fleet of antique ships, including the *Charles W. Morgan*, the last wooden whaling ship in the world, built in 1841. Another highlight is the Mystic River Scale Model, with more than 250 detailed buildings. The impressive Mystic Aquarium has a huge gallery of penguins, stingrays, and sharks, while seals and sea lions can be seen cavorting in the outdoor Seal Island.

A short distance west of Mystic Seaport is **New London**. This historic town was torched by British forces during the American Revolution, but remarkably, many of the houses survived. Among them is the Joshua Hempsted House, built in 1678, which is insulated with seaweed. By the 19th century New London had recovered to become a prosperous center of the whaling industry – the row of colonnaded Greek Revival mansions on Whale Oil Row attest to the affluence of that era.

The resort town of **Madison**, full of antique stores and boutiques, also has several historic homes open for viewing. Among the fascinating artifacts on display at the **Deacon John Grave House** is the family bookkeeping ledger, with entries from 1678 to 1895. Also in Madison is **Hammonasset Beach State Park**, the largest shoreline park in the state, with a 2-mile (3-km) long beach that attracts swimmers, sailors, sunbathers, and divers. Neighboring **Guilford** has a Tudor Gothic-style granite fort. This three-story stronghold, built in 1640 by a group of Puritans settlers to protect themselves against attacks by the local Indians, is the oldest stone dwelling of its kind in New England.

From Guilford's Stony Creek Dock, travelers can cruise to the **Thimble Islands** aboard tour boats that operate in the area, watching seals or taking in the glorious fall colors. Many of the 365 islands are little more than large boulders, but some privately owned islands have small communities. Legend has it that the privateer Captain Kidd (1645–1701) hid plundered treasure on Money Island while being pursued by the British fleet.

The Thimbles, home to seals, whales, and colorful legends

**Coastal Fairfield County**, in the southernmost corner of the state, has attractions for every taste. The shoreline is dusted with beaches offering a variety of summer recreation opportunities, while naturalists are drawn to its nature preserves and zoo. The area also has numerous art galleries and museums.

**Bridgeport** is home to the Beardsley Zoo, the Barnum Museum (named after the circus impresario P.T. Barnum who was the town's mayor), and the Discovery Museum.

The charming town of **Westport** on the banks of the Saugatuck River has the Sherwood Island State Park. **Norwalk** has historic buildings, shops, and cafés along its waterfront, as well as a Maritime Aquarium. **New Canaan**, set in a landscape of woods, streams, and rolling fields, is spectacular in fall. **Stamford** has a unique First Presbyterian Church, shaped like a fish, and a lively downtown area.

**Greenwich**, blessed with a stunning coastline, is home to an art colony, the Bush-Holley Historic Site. A 44-mile (71-km) drive through Fairfield County gives a good overview of the Connecticut coast.

**Mystic Seaport**

75 Greenmanville Ave (Rte 7). (860) 572-5315. **Ships & exhibits** *Apr– Oct: 9am–5pm; Nov–Mar: 10am–4pm.* **Grounds** *9am–6pm daily.* *Dec 25.*
www.mysticseaport.com

**Deacon John Grave House**

Madison, 581 Boston Post Rd. *(203) 245-4798.* *May–Sep: 1–4pm Wed–Sat.*

**Hammonasset Beach State Park**

I-95, exit 62. **Park** *(203) 245-2785.* *8am–dusk daily.*
**Campground reservations** *(877) 668-2267.*

# Vermont

VERMONT'S VARIED ATTRACTIONS are scattered throughout the state. Historic villages and the natural splendors of the Green Mountain National Forest grace the south, while in the northwest Lake Champlain provides a backdrop for the lively college town of Burlington. Famous ski resorts such as Stowe are perched amid the mountains that run the length of the state. In fall, Vermont's display of leaf colors is spectacular.

**Woodward Reservoir in the Green Mountain National Forest**

## Green Mountain National Forest 18

*Forest Supervisor, Green Mountain National Forest, 231 N Main St, Rutland. (802) 747-6700.*

THIS HUGE SPINE of greenery and mountains runs for 350,000 acres (142,850 ha) – almost the entire length of Vermont – along two-thirds of the Green Mountain Range. The mountains, many of them over 4,000 ft (1,200 m) high, have some of the best ski centers in the US, including Sugarbush and Mount Snow.

The National Forest is divided into northern and southern sectors, and encompasses six wilderness areas, many of them with no roads, electricity, or clearly marked trails. Less primitive areas of the forest, however, have picnic sites, camping grounds, and more than 500 miles (805 km) of hiking paths, including the famous Long and Appalachian Trails. The area's lakes, rivers, and reservoirs offer excellent boating and fishing, and there are designated paths for horseback riders as well as bikers.

In the southwest corner of the Green Mountain National Forest is **Bennington**, Vermont's third-largest city. An important manufacturing center, Bennington is also home to the small but prestigious Bennington College. Three 19th-century wooden covered bridges (just off Route 67) herald the approach to the town, which was established in 1749. A few decades later, Ethan Allen arrived on the scene to lead the Green Mountain Boys, a citizen's militia that scored several decisive victories against British forces during the Revolutionary War.

The town's most prominent landmark is the 306-ft (93-m) high **Bennington Battle Monument**, a granite obelisk commemorating a 1777 battle, when Colonial forces defeated the British. The monument looms over the Old Bennington Historic District, which has a village green ringed by Federal-style brick buildings. The 1806 First Congregational Church is particularly striking, with its vaulted plaster and wood ceilings. Next to the church is the Old Burying Ground where one of America's most loved poets, Robert Frost, is buried.

**The 1891 Bennington Battle Monument**

A major attraction for visitors is the **Bennington Museum and Grandma Moses Gallery**. Apart from an impressive collection of Americana, the museum houses several paintings by famed folk artist Anna Mary "Grandma" Moses, who lived in the Bennington area. A farmer's wife with no formal art training, Grandma Moses (1860–1961) started painting landscapes as a hobby when she was in her mid-70s. "Discovered" by critics in 1940, her distinctive primitive paintings soon won international renown.

**Bennington Museum & Grandma Moses Gallery**

75 Main St. *(802) 447-1571. 10am–5pm Tue–Thu. Jan 1, Thanksgiving, Dec 25.* www.benningtonmuseum.com

## Manchester 19

*3,860. Suite 1, 5046 Main St, (802) 362-2100.*

THIS SCENIC TOWN, ringed by mountains, is a favorite destination for both shoppers and skiers. Manchester Village and Manchester Center are major outlet centers in New England, offering brand-name goods in their designer outlets and factory stores. Visitors also enjoy following the Equinox Skyline Drive, with its panoramic views from the crest of Mount Equinox.

The town has two major ski areas – **Stratton**, with more than 90 trails and a hillside ski village with shops and restaurants, and **Bromley**, a busy, family-oriented ski area.

Manchester has been a vacation resort since the 19th century, and its gracious mansions evoke that era. One of the most elegant is **Hildene**, a 24-room Georgian manor built by Robert Todd Lincoln, son of President Abraham Lincoln. Among its notable features are a 1,000-pipe Aeolian organ and an impeccable formal garden.

**Hildene**

Rte 7A. *(802) 362-1788. mid-May–Oct: 9:30am–4pm daily. every 30 mins.* www.hildene.org

## Killington ⓴

1,000. Rte 4, West Killington, (802) 422-3333 or (800) 621-6867.

Sporty types who like outdoor adventure and a lively social life head for this year-round resort. Killington operates the largest ski center in the eastern United States, with 200 runs for alpine skiing and snowboarding spread across seven peaks, including nearby Pico Mountain. It also has superb cross-country ski centers at Mountain Top Inn and Mountain Meadows.

Killington itself is the second highest peak in Vermont, at 4,240 ft (1,295 m). The ski season here lasts eight months, longer than anywhere else in Vermont.

In summer as well as fall a gondola ferries visitors up to the peaks from where, on clear day, there are breathtaking views of five states and distant Canada.

## Woodstock ㉑

1,000. 18 Central St, (802) 457-3555, (888) 496-6378.

Even in Vermont, where historic, picturesque villages are commonplace, Woodstock stands out. Founded in 1761, the town is an enclave of renovated brick and clapboard Georgian houses, many of them beautifully restored, thanks to the generosity of philanthropists such as the Rockefeller family, and the railroad magnate Frederick Billings (1823–90), who also financed the planting of 10,000 trees here. **Billings Farm and Museum** is still a working entity. The 1890 farmhouse has been restored, and visitors can attend seasonal events such as apple-cider pressing in the fall and plowing competitions in the spring. The museum's exhibits include vintage farm implements, butter churns, and ice cutters.

Woodstock is also home to the **Vermont Raptor Center**, a reserve where injured birds such as owls, falcons, eagles, and other birds of prey are cared for until they can be returned to the wild. The center also offers summer day camps for children.

**Billings Farm & Museum**
River Rd. (802) 457-2355.
May–Oct: 10am–5pm daily. Call for winter hours.

**Vermont Raptor Center**
Church Hill Rd. (802) 457-2779.
10am–4pm daily.

**Environs:** Six miles (10 km) east of town is the stunningly beautiful **Quechee Gorge**. The best view of the chasm is on Route 4, which crosses the gorge via a steel bridge. A short hiking trail leads from the parking lot on the east side to the Ottauquechee River that flows below.

The SS *Ticonderoga*, in Shelburne Museum

## Shelburne Museum & Farms ㉒

Rte 7, 7 miles (11 km) S of Burlington. (802) 985-3346. Apr–mid May: 1–4pm daily (selected buildings only); mid-May–mid-Oct: 10am–5pm daily. mid-Oct–Mar, Thanksgiving, Dec 25. www.shelburnemuseum.org

Established in 1947 by collector Electra Webb, Shelburne Museum's 37 historic structures and their contents constitute one of America's finest museums. Its eclectic collection, which celebrates three centuries of American ingenuity, includes folk art, antique tools, and circus memorabilia, along with scrimshaw, Native American artifacts, and paintings by artists such as Winslow Homer and Grandma Moses.

Among the relocated or replicated historic buildings on view are a horseshoe-shaped **Circus Building**, housing a 500-ft (152-m) long miniature circus parade, an 1890 **Railroad Station**, and an 1871 Lake Champlain lighthouse. Visitors can explore the SS *Ticonderoga*, a former Lake Champlain steamship, which was rescued from the scrap heap by Webb in 1950. The visitor center is located in the 1901 Round Barn, which also features changing exhibits.

Shelburne is home to a historic 1,400-acre (566-ha) estate, Shelburne Farms, with its beautiful green rolling pastures and woodlands. There are tours of the dairy, and there are also special areas where children can pet and play with the animals.

One of the many beautiful homes in the village of Woodstock

**First Unitarian Church, Burlington**

## Burlington ㉓

40,700. 345 Pine St. King St Dock. Suite 100, 60 Main St, (802) 863-3489, (877) 686-5253. *Discover Jazz Festival (Jun).* www.vermont.org

VERMONT'S LARGEST city, Burlington is one of the most popular tourist destinations in the state. Half of the population of this lively town is made up of students from the University of Vermont and the city's four colleges. Rich in interesting shops and restaurants as well as grand old mansions and historic landmarks, Burlington is also Vermont's center of commerce and industry. It is scenically located on the shores of Lake Champlain.

The center of Burlington is compact and easy to explore on foot. It includes the historic district, at the core of which is the four-block section known as the **Church Street Marketplace**. The neighborhood has been converted into a pedestrian mall, complete with trendy boutiques, patio restaurants, and crafts shops. Many of them are housed in Queen Anne-style buildings from the late 1800s. The historical attractions in this neighborhood include the 1861 **First Unitarian Church**, the oldest house of worship in Burlington, and the **City Hall**, which marks the southern boundary of the marketplace. This graceful building, built of local brick, marble, and granite, dates to 1928. The City Hall Park is a popular outdoor concert venue, and in summer street performers and musicians add color and action to the area.

On the waterfront is **Battery Park**, the site of a battle between US soldiers and the British Royal Navy in 1812. Today, the park is a peaceful place, from where there are lovely views of Burlington Bay and the backdrop of the Adirondack Mountains on the other side of Lake Champlain. South of the park is the **Burlington Boat House**; here a three-decker cruise ship, *Spirit of Ethan Allen III*, takes visitors on a 90-minute trip, which gives a good historical overview, as the captain narrates tales of the Revolutionary War.

The **Robert Hull Fleming Museum**, on the campus of the University of Vermont, is on a hillside overlooking the city. The artifacts in this elegant 1931 Colonial Revival building range from ancient Mesopotamian objects to European paintings and sculptures and Native American crafts.

**Robert Hull Fleming Museum**

61 Colchester Ave. *(802) 656-0750.* *May–mid-Sep: noon–4pm Tue–Fri; mid-Sep–May: 9am–5pm Tue–Fri; year-round: 1–5pm Sat–Sun.* *public hols.*

## Lake Champlain ㉔

Vermont-New York border from Whitehall to Alburg. *60 Main St, Burlington, (802) 863-3489, (877) 686-5253.*

SOMETIMES CALLED the sixth Great Lake because of its size, Lake Champlain is 120 miles (190 km) long, 12 miles (19 km) wide, and has 500 miles (800 km) of shoreline. Said to be the home of "Champ," a water serpent that could be a distant cousin of the Loch Ness monster, the lake is sprinkled with about 70 islands. At the northern end of the lake is **Isle La Motte**, which has a statue of Samuel de Champlain, the French explorer who discovered and explored much of the surrounding region. On nearby **Grand Isle** is America's oldest log cabin (1783). The lake has its western shore in New York State, and scenic hour-long ferry rides run between Burlington and Port Kent, New York.

**Statue in Burlington's Battery Park**

Some of Lake Champlain's treasures are underwater, preserved in a marine park

**Sailing and boating, popular on beautiful Lake Champlain**

where scuba divers can explore shipwrecks resting on sandbars and at the bottom of this clear-water lake.

The **Lake Champlain Maritime Museum** at Basin Harbor gives a complete overview of the region's marine history through fascinating displays of ship models, old divers' suits, and photographs of vintage Lake Champlain steamers.

**Lake Champlain Maritime Museum**
4472 Basin Harbor Rd, Vergennes. *(802) 475-2022. May–mid-Oct: 10am–5pm.* www.lcmm.org

## Stowe 25

*3,500. 51 Main St, (802) 253-7321, (800) 247-8693.* www.gostowe.com

THIS MOUNTAIN-RINGED village is the skiing capital of New England and draws hordes of visitors in winter. Mountain Road begins in the village and is lined with chalets, motels, restaurants, and pubs; it leads to the area's highest peak, **Mount Mansfield** (4,393 ft/1,339 m).

In summer, too, there are plenty of outdoor activities on offer. Visitors can hike, rock-climb, fish, canoe, bike, or inline skate along the paved, meandering 5.5-mile (8.5-km) **Stowe Recreational Path**, which winds from the village church across the West Branch River, then through green woodlands.

Stowe's other claim to fame is as the home of the musical Von Trapp family, who were the inspiration behind the 1965 movie *The Sound of Music*. After their daring escape from Austria during World War II, they chose Stowe as their new home. Their **Trapp Family Lodge** is set in a 2,700-acre (1,092-ha) estate. This giant wooden chalet is now one of the most popular hotels in the area *(see p180)*.

The Austrian-style Trapp Family Lodge in Stowe

## Ben & Jerry's Ice Cream Factory 26

Rte 100, Waterbury. *(802) 244-5641, (866) BJTOURS. Jun: 9am–5pm daily; Jul–Aug: 9am–8pm daily; Sep–Oct: 9am–6pm daily; Nov–May: 10am–5pm daily.*

ALTHOUGH Ben Cohen and Jerry Greenfield hail from Long Island, New York, they have done more than any other "flatlanders" to put Vermont's dairy industry on the map. In 1977, these childhood friends paid $5 for a correspondence course on making ice cream, and soon parlayed their knowledge into what became an enormously successful ice-cream franchise.

No longer privately owned, the factory uses the richest dairy products to produce their ice cream and frozen yogurt. The Ben & Jerry trademark is the black and white Holstein cow, which embellishes everything on sale in the gift shop.

Tours of the factory start every 15 minutes and run for 30 minutes. Visitors learn all there is to know about making ice cream. They are given a bird's-eye view of the factory floor, and at the end of the tour they get a chance to sample the products and sometimes taste new flavors.

Ben & Jerry's bus, gaily decorated with dairy cows

### Skiing in New England

A ski-lift in Vermont, one of the best skiing areas of the US

In New England, topnotch slopes and cross-country ski trails are never far away. The best skiing is concentrated in the three northern states. Vermont has the most high-quality peaks, and the world-famous resorts of Killington and Stowe. Two great trails in Vermont for skiers and snowshoers are the Catamount Trail and the Trapp Family Lodge Ski Center. New Hampshire's White Mountains have some of the best downhill, alpine, and cross-country ski trails in the Northeast. In Maine, Sugarloaf/USA and Sunday River are considered the best hills in the state. Downhill ski trails are rated by a standard code: Easier=green circle; More difficult=blue square; Most Difficult=black diamond; and Expert=double diamond. Equipment, and lessons for all levels are available at all the resorts.

# New Hampshire

NEW HAMPSHIRE'S NATURAL BEAUTY is evident all over the state. The northern part is rippled by the tall peaks of the White Mountain Range and the spectacular chasm of Franconia Notch. Ponds and lakes, such as the pristine Lake Winnipesaukee, dot central New Hampshire. The main cities – historic Concord and lively Portsmouth, with its scenic Atlantic coastline – nestle amid the tranquil farmlands of the south.

**The striking exterior of the Mount Washington Hotel & Resort**

## Bretton Woods 27

550. (800) 346-3687. www.visitwhitemountains.com

THIS TINY ENCLAVE in the Mount Washington Valley has an unusual claim to fame. In 1944, with the need for currency stability after the economic upheavals of World War II, it hosted the United Nations conference that led to the establishment of the International Monetary Fund and, later, the World Bank. The setting for this historic meeting was the magnificent Spanish Renaissance-style **Mount Washington Hotel and Resort** *(see p180)*. Opened in 1902, the hotel's sparkling white exterior and crimson roof stand out in contrast to Mount Washington, looming behind it. The hotel has entertained several distinguished guests, including the British Prime Minister Winston Churchill, and three US presidents. Surrounded by 17,300 acres (7,000 ha) of parkland, its facilities include a 27-hole golf course. Nearby, Bretton Woods ski area offers alpine skiing and 62 miles (100 km) of cross-country trails.

**Mount Washington Hotel & Resort**
Rte 302, Bretton Woods. *(603) 278-1000, (800) 258-0330.*

**ENVIRONS:** Dominating the Mount Washington Valley is the 6,288-ft (1,917-m) peak of **Mount Washington**, the highest in the northeastern United States. The peak has the dubious distinction of having the worst weather in the world, and in April 1934 clocked the highest wind ever recorded on earth: 230 mph (370 kph). On clear days, however, there are panoramic views from the top. There are hiking trails and an auto road to the summit, but the most exciting way up is by the **Mount Washington Cog Railroad**. This steam-powered train chugs the 3.5-mile (5.6-km) route to the top along a heart-stoppingly steep track. Some of the best alpine skiing is in Tuckerman Ravine on Mount Washington.

## Franconia Notch 28

I-93, Franconia Notch Pkwy. *(603) 823-8800.* **Park** *daily.* **Flume Gorge Visitor Center** *(603) 745-8391.* *May–Oct: 9am–5pm daily.* *for Flume Gorge, Visitor Center, & campsites.* www.flumegorge.com

THIS SPECTACULAR mountain pass, carved between the Kinsman and Franconia ranges, and designated as the Franconia Notch State Park, has some of the state's most stunning natural wonders. Foremost among them was the **Old Man of the Mountain**, a rocky outcrop on the side of a cliff that resembled a man's profile until the nose and forehead crashed down in May 2003. Other attractions compensate for the loss. The trout-filled **Profile Lake** reflects the brilliant colors of fall foliage on the slopes of **Cannon Mountain**. A boardwalk and stairways lead visitors through the **Flume Gorge**, a narrow, chasm whose granite walls tower more than 90 ft (27 m) above the boardwalk, while an aerial tramway speeds

### FALL FOLIAGE IN NEW ENGLAND

Thousands of visitors head for New England in the fall, to gaze in wonder at the annual changing of leaf colors. The color change is not just a capricious act of Nature. As daylight hours diminish, the leaves of deciduous trees stop producing the green pigment chlorophyll, and other pigments hidden behind the chlorophyll's color now burst into view. More pigments are produced by sugars that remain trapped in the leaves. The result is a riotous display of shades of yellow, orange, crimson, and maroon. The peak period for "leaf-peeping" varies from early October in northern New England to late October in the southern section, but this can differ, depending on the weather *(see Fall Foliage Hotlines, p175)*.

**Glorious colors lighting up the New England landscape in fall**

**Narrow Flume Gorge in Franconia Notch State Park**

passengers to the 4,180-ft (1254-m) summit of Cannon Mountain in just 8 minutes.

Robert Frost (1874–1963), one of America's best-loved poets, settled in the Franconia Notch region in 1915. The majestic setting inspired him to pen many of his greatest works here, including the famous poem *Stopping By Woods on a Snowy Evening*.

## White Mountain National Forest ㉙

*719 N Main St, Laconia, (603) 528-8721.*
**Camping** *(877) 444-6777. Call for availability & reservations.*

NEW HAMPSHIRE'S most beautiful wilderness area, the White Mountain National Forest, sprawls over 770,000 acres (311,600 ha). The area has an abundance of wildlife, including a large population of moose, which can often be seen from the road.

Outdoor activities offered in this region range from bird-watching and rock-climbing to skiing and kayaking. But even less sporty travelers will revel in the spectacular scenery visible from their car – valleys flanked by tall pine forests, waterfalls that tumble over rocky outcrops, and more than 20 summits that soar to over 4,000 ft (1,200 m). An especially scenic stretch of road is the 100-mile (161-km) long **White Mountains Trail** that loops across Mount Washington Valley through Crawford Notch and Franconia Notch. In autumn, brilliant fall foliage colors transform the rugged countryside into a palette of flaming red maples, golden birch, and maroon northern red oaks, interspersed with evergreens.

Another popular route is the **Kancamagus Highway**, touted by many as the most beautiful road in New England. This 34-mile (55-km) road, which runs through the White Mountain National Forest between Lincoln and Conway, offers exceptional vistas as it climbs 3,000 ft (914 m) through the Kancamagus Pass. The road descends into the Saco Valley and joins up with the trout-filled Swift River. There is easy access for fishermen from the highway to the river, and there are campgrounds and picnic areas along the entire length of the highway. Well-marked trails allow drivers to stretch their legs amid the beautiful scenery – a popular one is the short loop that leads to the lovely Sabbaday Falls.

**Kancamagus Hwy**
Rte 112 between Lincoln & Conway.
*Saco District Ranger Station, 33 Kancamagus Hwy, (603) 447-5448.*

**ENVIRONS:** Close to the White Mountains is the **Lincoln/ Woodstock** region, whose main attraction is **Clark's Trading Post**. This curious combination of circus acts, amusement park rides, and museums makes a welcome change for children after a leaf-peeping drive. Lincoln is a base camp for both backwoods adventurers and stick-to-the-road sightseers. Nearby **Loon Mountain** is one of the state's premier ski resorts. In summer, it offers activities such as nature walks, tours of caves, mountain biking, and horseback riding.

**Loon Mountain**
E of I-93, near Lincoln. *(603) 745-6281, (800) 229-5666.*

## Lake Winnipesaukee ㉚

*Lakes Region Association, (800) 605-2537.*
www.winnipesaukee.com

WITH A SHORELINE that meanders for 240 miles (386 km), and a surface area of 72 sq miles (187 sq km), this stunning lake has New Hampshire's largest stretch of waterfront. Ringed by mountains and scattered with 274 islands, Lake Winnispesaukee has sheltered bays, harbors, and resort towns around its shores. The largest and prettiest of these is **Wolfeboro**. Leaving from Weirs Beach, the M/S *Mount Washington* offers the best scenic cruise in all New England. To its north is upscale **Meredith**, with lovely lakeside homes.

North of Meredith is pristine **Squam Lake**, ideal for boating and fishing, where the movie *On Golden Pond* (1981) was filmed. The town of **Center Sandwich** is on Winnipesaukee's north shore. Surrounded by woodland, it is a favorite destination during fall foliage season. On the eastern shore, the Castle in the Clouds mansion crowns the crest of a hill that rises some 750 ft (229 m) above the lake. A 70-mile (113-km) drive around Lake Winnipesaukee takes in all these sights.

**Along the Kancamagus Highway, White Mountain National Forest**

## Canterbury Shaker Village 31

288 Shaker Rd, Canterbury. *(603) 783-9511, (866) 783-9511.* *May–Oct: 10am–5pm daily; Apr & Nov–Dec: 10am–4pm Sat & Sun.* www.shakers.org

FOUNDED IN 1792, this village was occupied by Shakers for 200 years. The Shakers were a sect that broke away from the Quakers, who fled to America to escape religious persecution in Britain in the mid-18th century. Their belief in celibacy and strict separation from the rest of the world eventually led to their demise. The 690-acre (280-ha) site, which has several buildings open to visitors, is punctuated by millponds, nature trails, and traditional gardens. Skilled artisans can be seen re-creating Shaker crafts, known for their simple lines and beautiful workmanship.

**Picturesque buildings at Canterbury Shaker Village**

**The belfry** contains a bell made by the Revolutionary War hero Paul Revere.

**Dormer rooms** were used for summer sleeping and as clothes cupboards.

**Brethren's Retiring Room**

**The Sisters' Retiring Room** was where women had their separate sleeping quarters, each equipped with plain furniture.

**The Dining Room** could hold as many as 60 Shakers per sitting.

**The Old Library and Museum** contains 1,500 Shaker books and documents, and a museum of Shaker artifacts.

## Concord 32

*37,500.* *40 Commercial St, (603) 224-2508.*

NEW HAMPSHIRE'S capital is a quiet little town, dominated by its impressive **State House**. Built in 1819 from granite and marble, it is one of the oldest state houses in America. Another landmark is the giant glass pyramid of the **Christa McAuliffe Planetarium**. A Concord schoolteacher, McAuliffe (1948–86) was tragically killed when the *Challenger* Space Shuttle *(see p302)*, launched by NASA on January 28, 1986, exploded and crashed 73 seconds after lift-off. The astronomy and space exploration exhibits in the planetarium also include multi-media shows such as "Destination Mars."

**Christa McAuliffe Planetarium**

2 Institute Dr. *(603) 271-7827.* *10am–2pm Mon–Wed, 10am–5pm Thu–Sat, noon–5pm Sun.* *weekend after Labor Day*

## Manchester 33

*105,250.* *889 Elm St, (603) 666-6600.* *(603) 622-7531.*

ONCE A MAJOR center of the textile industry, with its mills powered by waterpower from the Merrimack River, today Manchester is famous as the home of New Hampshire's premier art museum, the **Currier Gallery of Art**. Its collection includes works by such European masters as John Constable, Claude Monet, and Henri Matisse. The west wing houses the works of 20th-century American painters such as Andrew Wyeth (b.1917) and Georgia O'Keeffe (1887– 1986).

**Painting in the Currier Gallery of Art in Manchester**

**Portsmouth's Market Street, a favorite with tourists**

Also part of the museum is the Zimmerman House. The single-story home with its elegant exterior was built in 1950 by the pioneering American architect Frank Lloyd Wright. In 2006, the Currier will be closed for renovations, but Zimmerman house will be open.

The only indoor mall in the state is the Mall of New Hampshire in Manchester.

**Currier Gallery of Art**
201 Myrtle Way. (603) 669-6144.
*11am–5pm Mon, Wed, Fri, & Sun, 11am–8pm Thu, 10am–5pm Sat.*
www.currier.org

## Portsmouth 34

*26,000. 10 Ladd St.*
*500 Market St or Market Sq, (603) 436-1118. mid-May–Oct: 8:30am–1pm daily. Market Square Day (Jun), Prescott Park Arts Festival (Jul–Aug daily).*
www.portsmouthchamber.org

GIRDED BY THE Piscataqua River and North and South Mill ponds, Portsmouth is a historic town, compact enough to be explored on foot. Established in 1623, it became a prosperous hub of maritime commerce by the 18th century. It was also a hotbed of revolutionary fervor, and the place where the Colonial naval hero John Paul Jones (1747–92) took command of the warship *Ranger*. During the American Revolution, Jones led several raids along the British coast, for which he was awarded a gold medal by Congress.

A number of Portsmouth's historic buildings, many of which have been turned into boutiques and restaurants, are in the downtown core, especially along **Market Street**. Historic houses and gardens can also be found along the **Portsmouth Harbor Trail**, a walking tour of the Historic District. Especially worth visiting is the elegant 1763 Moffatt-Ladd House on Market Street, one of the earliest examples of the Federal style of architecture. The Wentworth-Gardner House on Mechanic Street, is regarded as one of the finest examples of Georgian architecture in the country. Both houses have beautiful interiors with period furnishings.

A popular destination in summer is Water Country, which has a huge wave pool, a pirate ship, and a man-made lagoon. Interactive exhibits are the highlight of the **Children's Museum of Portsmouth**, where children can fly in the replica of a space shuttle or command a submarine. Visitors can explore the real thing at Albacore Park where a sleek submarine, the USS *Albacore*, is on display. When it was built in 1953, it was the fastest underwater vessel of its kind.

Portsmouth's most popular attraction is **Strawbery Banke**, a 10-acre (4-ha) site near the waterfront located at the very spot at which Portsmouth was founded. This outdoor museum, which can be explored on foot or in authentic horse-drawn carriages, contains more than 40 buildings that depict life from 1695 to 1955. Many buildings are set amid gardens cultivated according to their eras, from early pioneer herb gardens to formal Victorian flower beds. The houses open to the public are furnished in period style and contain interesting collections of decorative arts and ceramics.

The **Jones House**, a 1790 structure, displays artifacts excavated at the site. The elegant 1760s Chase House is furnished with sumptuous pieces from several periods, while the Sherburne House, built in 1695, now serves as an exhibit on 17th-century house design and construction. In the Dinsmore Shop, built in 1800, visitors can watch a cooper making barrels and casks in the traditional way.

Strawbery Banke also has a Colonial Revival Garden, the Aldrich Garden, planted with flowers mentioned in the poetry of Portsmouth native Thomas Bailey Aldrich.

**Children's Museum of Portsmouth**
280 Marcy St. (603) 436-3853.
*mid-Jun–Sep: 10am–5pm Mon–Sat, 1–5pm Sun; Oct–mid-Jun: 10am– 5pm Tue–Sat, 1–5pm Sun.*

**Strawbery Banke**
Marcy St. (603) 433-1100.
*check for hours. limited access to some buildings.*
www.strawberybanke.org

**Inside lavishly furnished Chase House, Strawbery Banke, in Portsmouth**

# Maine

THE LARGEST STATE in New England, Maine is truly the Great Outdoors. Its most popular attractions are found along the spectacular coastline, beginning in the southeast with its largest and liveliest city, Portland, and the resort towns of the Kennebunks. Farther north, yachts and windjammers ply the waters of Penobscot Bay, while Acadia National Park stands as Maine's coastal jewel. World-class skiing, hiking, and boating opportunities are found inland, at Bethel and Sugarloaf.

## Portland 35

*65,000. 950 Congress St. Commercial & Franklin Sts. 245 Commercial St, (877) 833-1374. Wed & Sat. Old Port Festival (Jun 4), Victorian Holiday (Nov 24–Dec 23).* www.visitportland.com

THIS HISTORIC city has a beautiful location on the crest of a peninsula, with expansive views of Casco Bay and the Calendar Islands. Once a flourishing port, Portland was devastated by no less than four major fires, the last one in 1866. Nevertheless, the city still has a number of sturdy stone Victorian buildings, testifying to its prosperous past.

The West End has fine mansions and a splendid promenade overlooking the water. Portland's liveliest area, however, is around the Old Port, near the harbor. This restored neighborhood's narrow streets are filled with shops, restaurants, and art galleries. Dominating the area is the regal **United States Customs House**, with its gilded ceilings, marble staircases, and chandeliers. It was built after the Civil War (1861–65). From the docks, ships offer cruises to the Calendar Islands, harbor tours, and deep-sea fishing trips.

West of the Old Port, the **Portland Museum of Art**, displays works by the area's most famous artist, Winslow Homer (1836–1910), as well as by European masters such as Gauguin and Picasso. The **Children's Museum of Maine** has three floors of interactive exhibits to keep youngsters amused. The **Maine Narrow Gauge Railroad Co. & Museum** displays vintage locomotives and offers scenic trips along the waterfront.

Several of Portland's fine historic houses are open to visitors. They include the **Wadsworth-Longfellow House** (1785) where poet Henry Wadsworth Longfellow grew up; and the Victoria Mansion with its painted trompe l'oeil walls. Portland's signature landmark is the Portland Head Light at Fort Williams Park. First illuminated in 1791, the lighthouse is surrounded by beach and picnic areas, and the keeper's house is now a museum.

**Children's Museum banner**

### Portland Museum of Art

7 Congress Sq. *(207) 775-6148. mid-Oct–early May: 10am–5pm Tue, Wed, Sat, & Sun, 10am–9pm Thu & Fri; late May–mid-Oct: 10am–5pm Mon. Oct–May: Mon.*

### Children's Museum of Maine

142 Free St. *(207) 828-1234. year-round: 10am–5pm Tue–Sat, noon–5pm Sun; May–Sep: 10am–5pm Mon. public hols.*

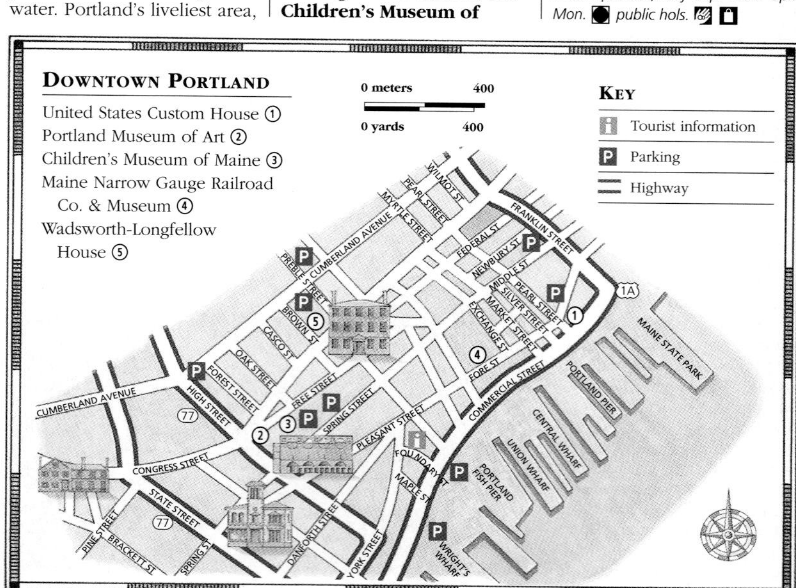

## The Kennebunks 36

17 Western Ave, Kennebunk, (207) 967-0857.
www.visitthekennebunks.com

First a thriving shipbuilding center and port, then a summer retreat for the rich, the Kennebunks are made up of two villages, Kennebunk and Kennebunkport.

Kennebunkport's historic village is graced by several Federal and Greek Revival structures, and the striking 1824 **South Congregational Church**, with its soaring white steeple. History of a different sort can be found at the **Seashore Trolley Museum**, where some 200 antique streetcars are housed, including one called "Desire." Tours of the countryside are offered on one of the restored trolleys. The scenic drive along Route 9 offers views of surf along rocky Cape Arundel. At **Cape Porpoise**, travelers can sample lobster pulled fresh from the Atlantic. Kennebunk is famous for its beaches, notably **Kennebunk Beach**, and for one of the most romantic houses in New England, the 1826 **Wedding Cake House**. According to local lore, George Bourne was unexpectedly called to sea before his marriage. Although a very hastily arranged wedding took place, there was no time to bake the traditional wedding cake. So the shipbuilder vowed to his bride that on his return he would remodel their home to look like a wedding cake. Today the ornate latticework offers proof that Bourne was a man of his word. Interesting architectural walking tours of Kennebunk's historic area are offered by the **Brick Store Museum**, housed in four restored 19th-century buildings.

**Seashore Trolley Museum**
195 Log Cabin Rd, Kennebunkport.
(207) 967-2800. *call for times.*
www.trolleymuseum.org

**Brick Store Museum**
117 Main St, Kennebunk. *(207) 985-4802.* *May–Dec: 10am–4:30pm Tue–Fri, 10am–1pm Sat.*
*Sun, public hols.*
www.brickstoremuseum.org

**Boats on the waters of Penobscot Bay's Stonington village, Deer Isle**

## Penobscot Bay 37

**Rockland** *1 Harbor Pk, (207) 596-0376.* **Camden** *Commercial St, Public Landing, (207) 236-4404.* **Searsport** *Main & Steamboat, (207) 548-6510.* **Castine** *Emerson Hall, Court St, (207) 326-4502.* **Deer Isle** *Rte 15 at Eggemoggin Rd, (207) 348-6124.*

Penobscot Bay is picture-book Maine, with hills sloping down into the ocean, wave-pounded cliffs, sheltered harbors bobbing with boats, and lobster traps piled on the docks. Penobscot Bay is also famous for its islands, which can be visited on boat tours from the mainland.

Penobscot Bay's commercial center is the fishing town of **Rockland**, whose biggest event is the lobster festival on the first full weekend of August. A prime attraction is the Farnsworth Art Museum, displaying the works of leading American painters such as Edward Hopper and Andrew Wyeth.

A favorite destination for tourists is **Camden**, with its spired churches, elegant homes, and shops along the waterfront. A short distance from the village is Camden Hills State Park, which offers breathtaking views of the bay from the summit of Mount Battie. Standing on this point, the poet Edna St. Vincent Millay (1892–1950) was inspired to write her first volume of poetry. Nearby **Searsport** is regarded as the antiques capital of Maine and has large and busy fleamarkets on weekends in the summer.

**Sailboats moored in Penobscot Bay's Camden Harbor**

The more remote eastern shore leads to serene, perfectly preserved villages such as **Castine** and Blue Hill. In Castine is the historic Fort George, built by the British in 1799, and witness to the American Navy's worst defeat during the Revolutionary War. Blue Hill is a living postcard, surrounded by fields of blueberries, and with many of its clapboard buildings listed on the National Historic Register.

**Deer Isle**, reached from the mainland via a graceful suspension bridge, is actually a series of small islands linked by causeways. Island highlights include the scenic towns of Stonington and Deer Isle. From Stonington, it is an 8-mile (13-km) boat ride to the thickly wooded Isle au Haut, much of which belongs to Acadia National Park *(see p172)*. Another unspoiled haven is Monhegan Island with its dramatic cliffs and hiking trails. North Haven Island is a summer colony, covered with meadows of wildflowers. Vinalhaven, with its granite shoreline and inland moors, is a perfect place for a swim or a hike.

Bass Harbor Head, which exemplifies Maine's rock-bound shoreline

## Acadia National Park 38

Hulls Cove Visitor Center, off Rte 3 in Hulls Cove, (207) 288-3338. mid-Apr–Oct: daily. Bangor-Bar Harbor. at Hulls Cove. www.nps.gov/acad

An unspoiled paradise, heavily visited in summer, the 35,000-acre (14,164-ha) Acadia National Park covers much of Mount Desert Island, off the southeast Maine coast.

The park's main attraction is the scenic Loop Road, a 27-mile (43-km) drive that climbs and dips with the pink granite mountains of the east coast of the island and takes in its main sights. Among these is the 1,527-ft (465-m) high **Cadillac Mountain**, the highest point on the Atlantic Coast. Hiking trails and an auto road lead to spectacular panoramas at the summit. The road continues south to the idyllic **Sand Beach**, but the icy water discourages many swimmers. Farther south there is a unique natural phenomenon known locally as **Thunder Hole** – when the tide rises during heavy winds, air trapped in this crevice is compressed and then expelled with a resounding boom. The Loop Road continues inland, swinging past Jordan Pond, Bubble Pond, and Eagle Lake.

On the southern shore of the park is the quaint village of **Bass Harbor Head**, where an 1858 lighthouse is perched on the rocky coastline, offering magnificent views of the ocean. The park is home to numerous animals, including woodchucks, white-tailed deer, and red foxes. Visitors who want a closer, more intimate look at the park's flora and fauna can do so on foot, bike, or horseback along the 45 miles (72 km) of old broken-stone carriage roads, which wind through the park.

Cutting through the center of Mount Desert Island is **Somes Sound**, a finger-shaped natural fjord that juts 5 miles (8 km) inland. It separates the quiet village of Southwest Harbor from Northeast Harbor, which is the center of Mount Desert Island's social scene, with its upscale shops and handsome mansions. Southwest Harbor is home to the **Mount Desert Oceanarium**, which features 20 tanks teeming with live coastal sea animals.

The elegant resort town of **Bar Harbor** is a lively tourist center and a good base from which to explore the Acadia National Park. More than 5,000,000 visitors each year pass through Bar Harbor on their way to the wilds of park Located on Mount Desert Island's northeastern shore, it was the 19th century summer haven for some of America's richest people, including the Astors and the Vanderbilts. In 1947, a fire destroyed a third of the town's lavish homes, thus ending its reign as a high-society enclave. The town's attractions include the **Criterion Theater**, an Art Deco gem that shows both popular and art films, and the **Abbe Museum**, which celebrates Maine's Native American heritage with displays of tools, crafts, art, artifacts, and archaeology. The Wild Gardens of Acadia, with some 300 species of local plants, are located next to the museum.

**Bar Harbor Oceanarium**, situated 8.5 miles (14 km) northwest of the town, is the place to see harbor seals, explore a salt marsh on Thomas Bay Marsh Walk, or visit the Maine Lobster Museum and take in demonstrations of lobstering.

**Acadia Zoo** in Trenton, lying across the bridge from Mount Desert Island, is home to some 45 species of animals, including reindeer, wolves, monkeys, and moose

### Bar Harbor

*93 Cottage St, (207) 288-5103.*

Cadillac Mountain, the highest point on the Atlantic coast, with striking panoramas at the summit

Roosevelt Cottage, built in 1897, on Campobello Island

## Campobello Island 39

**Roosevelt Campobello International Park** (506) 752-2922. 10am–6pm daily. every 15 mins. www.fdr.net

LOCATED ON Campobello Island is the **Roosevelt Campobello International Park**, established in 1964 as a memorial to President Franklin D. Roosevelt *(see p49)*. The island's main settlement of Welshpool was where the future president spent most of his summers until 1921, when he contracted polio. Despite his disability, Roosevelt was elected to four terms, leading the US through the Great Depression and World War II.

The highlight of the 2,800-acre (1,333-ha) park – which actually lies in Canada and is the only international park in the world – is **Roosevelt Cottage**. Built in 1897, this sprawling, 34-room wood-frame summer home displays mementos that had belonged to President F.D. Roosevelt.

At the island's southern tip is **Liberty Point**, where a pair of observation decks perched on the rugged cliffs offer far-ranging views of the Atlantic.

A short distance inland from here is **Lower Duck Pond Bog**, a prime habitat for the great blue heron, killdeer, and the American black duck.

On the island's western shore is **Mulholland Point**, with an 1885 lighthouse and a picnic site offering views of the FDR Memorial Bridge. Other good picnic sites are at Raccoon Beach located on the eastern shore.

## Sugarloaf 40

*(207) 237-2000, (800) 843-5623.*

MAINE'S HIGHEST ski mountain, Sugarloaf is the center of this touristy village packed with hotels, restaurants, and condominiums. Downhill skiers, in particular, are attracted to **Sugarloaf/USA** ski center with its more than 100 trails and a vertical drop of 2,800 ft (870 m). The center also offers cross-country skiing, ice skating, and snowshoeing.

In summer, the emphasis shifts to the resort's 18-hole golf course, boating on the lakes and rivers, and hiking in the nearby Carrabassett Valley. The resort is also famous for its network of more than 50 miles (80 km) of mountain biking trails, through flat as well as steep and challenging terrain.

**Sugarloaf/USA**
Carrabassett Valley. *(207) 237-2000, (800) 843-5623.* *8:30am–3:50pm daily.* *in lodge.*

## Bethel 41

*2,500.* *30 Cross St; (207) 824-2282, (800) 442-5826.* www.bethelmaine.com

A PICTURESQUE historic district, a major ski resort, and proximity to the White Mountains give Bethel year-round appeal. First settled in 1796, the town was a farming and lumbering center until the coming of the railroad in 1851 made it a popular resort. The line-up of classic clapboard mansions on the town green include the Federal-style **Moses Mason House** (c.1813), restored and furnished with period pieces.

There are scenic drives in all directions, taking in unspoiled Colonial hamlets such as Waterford to the south, and beautiful mountain terrain to the north. **Sunday River Ski Resort**, 6 miles (10 km) north of town in Newry, has more than 100 ski trails. **Grafton Notch State Park** has spectacular scenery along its drives and hiking trails. The park's special spots include waterfalls and sweeping views of the scenic surroundings from Table Rock and Old Speck Mountain.

**Moses Mason House**
10–14 Broad St. *(207) 824-2908.* *Jul–early Sep: 1–4pm Tue–Sun; year round: by appt.*

**Sunday River Ski Resort**
Off Rte 2 in Newry. *(207) 824-3000, (800) 5432-SKI.* *9am–4pm Mon–Fri, 8am–4pm Sat–Sun.*

**Grafton Notch State Park**
Rte 26 NW of Newry. *(207) 824-2912.* *mid-May–mid-Oct.*

Screw Auger Falls in Grafton Notch State Park, Bethel

# Practical Information

ALTHOUGH PARTICULARLY POPULAR during summer and fall, New England is a four-season vacation destination. The superb skiing facilities attract tourists during winter, which often lasts from mid-November to April. The region offers a wide variety of recreational activities within a relatively small area. On any weekend, vacationers can hike the White Mountains of New Hampshire, swim at Maine's Ogunquit Beach, and take in the Boston Symphony Orchestra. Outside of Boston, where public transportation is excellent, you definitely need a car for sightseeing.

## Tourist Information

STATE TOURSIM offices are great sources of information and are happy to send road maps, brochures, and listings of attractions, accommodations, and events, free of charge. Some places also offer discount vouchers for lodgings, restaurants, and entry fees. Many towns have a visitors' bureau that offers information on local lodgings, events, and restaurants.

## Personal Security

NEW ENGLAND'S comparitively low crime rate makes it a safe holiday destination. But it is good to take precautions. Since pickpockets tend to frequent popular tourist sights, use a money belt for cash and documents and keep cameras out of sight. Avoid wearing expensive jewelry and leave your valuables in the hotel safe.

## Natural Hazards

THE VARIETY of outdoor activities in New England often entail risks, which can be minimized with proper precautions. Always be prepared for sudden changes in the weather, especially in higher elevations. Wear protective gear for adventure sports and never try to interfere with wildlife.

## Getting Around

MANY BUS companies serve particular sections of New England, making it relatively simple to get from state to state. In Boston and Cambridge, it is easier to get around by public transportation than by driving. Once outside the city you will need a car. In fact, much of New England's charm lies along scenic jaunts down the coast and driving tours during the fall-foliage season.

## The Climate of New England

New England's weather can vary greatly from year to year. Generally, the short spring is cloudy and wet, with rainy skies and melting snow. Summer can be unpredictable, but is generally dry – July and August are usually the sunniest months. Bright fall days out among the colorful foliage are spectacular – the peak fall-foliage period usually lasts from mid-September to late October. Snow usually starts in December; the temperature can dip to 0° F (–18° C) or lower in winter. In general, it is warmer along the coast and in the southern section of New England.

### Boston

| month | Apr | Jul | Oct | Jan |
|---|---|---|---|---|
| °F/C (high) | 55/12 | 80/27 | 63/17 | 36/2 |
| °F/C (low) | 39/4 | 63/17 | 46/8 | 20/–7 |
| sunshine | 17 days | 20 days | 19 days | 16 days |
| rainfall | 3.5 in | 2.8 in | 3.3 in | 3.6 in |

32°F / 0°C

Several books list the best driving tours of the region. **Yankee** magazine, for instance, offers a complete itinerary of recommended routes, historic stops, and places to eat and stay.

## Safety for Drivers

LARGE AREAS of New England are wild, so be prepared for any eventuality. This is doubly true in winter, when sudden blizzards and whiteouts caused by blowing snow can leave motorists stranded. In winter, stock salt, a snow brush, an ice scraper, and a small shovel. If you do get stuck in an out-of-the-way place, stay inside your car. Keep the motor running for warmth, but open your window slightly to prevent carbon monoxide buildup. **American Automobile Association (AAA)** and other auto clubs provide roadside assistance.

## Laws

THE LEGAL drinking age in New England is 21, and young people can be asked to produce a proof of age in order to buy alcohol or enter a bar. You can lose your driver's license if caught driving under the influence of alcohol. Cigarettes can be sold only to people 18 years of age or older. Smoking and drinking in public spaces is illegal. Most restaurants have separate areas for smokers.

## Sports & Outdoor Activities

WITH MILES OF coastline, mountain ranges, forests, and rivers, the region has much to offer to sports lovers. The choice of camping areas in national forests range from primitive sites to ones with various facilities. Hiking trails crisscross almost the entire region, with the most popular being the New England section of the Appalachian Trail and Vermont's Long Trail. The **Appalachian Trail Conference** runs various information and education programs on the Appalachian

Trail. Miles of quiet back roads in the region are a cyclist's paradise. Mountain bikers also have plenty to choose from. Some ski areas let bikers use their lifts and slopes in summer.

New England's Green and White Mountains offer superb rock climbing, hang gliding, and paragliding sites.

Anglers will love New England. Deep-sea fishing is best at Point Judith in Rhode Island. Brook trout and bass are plentiful in the inland streams and lakes, especially in Maine. The state's latticework of rivers is ideal for canoeing, kayaking, and whitewater rafting.

Penobscot Bay, Maine, and Newport, Rhode Island, are both considered sailing meccas. For those who want something calmer than the Atlantic Ocean, New England has countless lakes, and boats can be rented at many seaside and lakeside resorts. Whale-watching cruises have become a very popular activity. Take the cruise on a calm day, as choppy water can cause seasickness.

The region's northernmost reaches, with a thick annual blanket of snow, offer great skiing, skating, and snowmobiling opportunities. Stowe, located in Vermont, can claim the title of New England's ski capital. The world-famous **Stowe Mountain Resort** offers excellent trails for skiers of all levels.

## Entertainment

New England is a traveler's dream as it offers a wide range of entertainment. Free concerts and festivals abound in fall, spring, and summer, and there is no shortage of bars and nightclubs in which to slake, or build, your thirst. Boston's Harvard Square has been famous for four decades for its nightly and weekend scene of street performers. Mellow jazz lounges and smoky blues bars attract a devoted clientele.

Classical music, theater, and dance have long been the mainstays of the region's cultural identity. The larger towns and cities have good symphony orchestras, dance, and drama companies. But the hub of the region's performing arts is Boston. The **Boston Symphony Orchestra (BSO)** and its popular music doppleganger, the Boston Pops, are the city's cherished institutions. The BSO performs a full schedule of concerts at Symphony Hall from October to April. The Pops move in for performances in May and June.

Theater is alive and well across New England's six states, but the epicenter of this dynamic world is, again, Boston. The most avant-garde contemporary theater found in Boston is at the **American Repertory Theater (ART)**.

## Shopping

New England's well-known factory outlets offer brand name clothing at huge discounts. Freeport, Maine has the famous outdoor equipment outlet **L.L. Bean**. **Filene's** in Boston features apparel from some of the best-known American designers and is famed for its bargain basement. The region is an antique hunter's dream, with stores and barns offering a wide array of objects from the past. The Charles Street section of Boston's Beacon Hill is one of the prime antiquing areas. Look for shops run by New Hampshire craftsmen, Vermont-made products, and Maine crafts. Tourists looking for gifts with a regional flavor should sample the maple syrup and maple sugar candy.

## Directory

### Tourist Offices

**Connecticut**
W www.ctbond.org

**Greater Boston**
W www.bostonusa.com

**Maine**
W www.visitmaine.com

**Massachusetts**
W www.massvacation.com

**New Hampshire**
W www.visitnh.gov

**Rhode Island**
W www.visitrhodeisland.com

**Vermont**
W www.1-800-vermont.com

### Fall Foliage Hotlines

**Connecticut**
*(800) 252-6863.*

**Maine**
*(800) 777-0317.*

**Massachusetts**
*(800) 227-6277.*

**New Hampshire**
*(800) 258-3608.*

**Rhode Island**
*(800) 556-2484.*

**Vermont**
*(800) 837-6668.*

### Road Emergency

**American Automobile Assn. (AAA)**
*(800) 222-4357.*

### Hiking

**Appalachian Trail Conference**
799 Washington St, PO Box 807, Harpers Ferry, WV 25425-0807.
*(304) 535-6331.*
W www.appalachiantrail.org

### Skiing

**Stowe Mountain Resort**
5781 Mountain Rd, Stowe, VT 05672.
*(800) 253-4754.*
W www.stowe.com

### Entertainment

**American Repertory Theater**
64 Brattle St,. Cambridge, MA.
*(617) 547-8300.*

**Boston Symphony Orchestra**
301 Massachusetts Ave, Boston, MA.
*(617) 266-1492.*

### Shopping

**Filene's**
426 Washington St, Boston, MA.
*(617) 357-2100.*

**L.L. Bean**
95 Main Street, Freeport, ME.
*(800) 552-3268.*

# Where to Stay

The incredibly varied accomodations of the New England states are tailored to suit all tastes and budgets. Rustic country inns and B&Bs are plentiful, offering travelers quaint facilities and a more personal touch. Hotels are listed by area and then by price category, with symbols highlighting some of the amenities that may influence your choice of where to stay.

| Boston, Massachusetts | Credit Cards | Number of Rooms (Suites) | Recommended Restaurant | Children's Facilities | Garden or Terrace |
|---|---|---|---|---|---|
| **Beacon Hill & the Theater District:** *John Jeffries House* \$\$<br>14 David G. Mugar Way. (617) 367-1866. FAX (617) 742-0313.<br>W www.johnjeffrieshouse.com<br>Rooms are Victorian in style, and while some are tiny, the two-room suites are a bargain. Most of the rooms have kitchenettes. Breakfast is not included. | ■ | 46 (23) | | | ■ |
| **Beacon Hill & the Theater District:** *Boston Tremont Hotel* \$\$\$<br>275 Tremont St. (617) 426-1400. FAX (617) 482-6730.<br>W www.marriott.com<br>The refurbished lobby of this imposing 1925 brick and stone building is decorated with pillars and carved granite. Rooms are simple but have more flair than those in a standard chain hotel. | ■ | 322 | ■ | ● | |
| **Beacon Hill & the Theater District:** *Boston Park Plaza* \$\$\$\$<br>64 Arlington St. (800) 225-2008, (617) 426-2000. FAX (617) 654-1916.<br>W www.bostonparkplaza.com<br>Opened in 1927, this grand luxury hotel is classically Bostonian. Elegantly appointed, the spacious rooms also have many modern amenities, such as voice mail and dataports. | ■ | 950 (22) | ■ | ● | |
| **Beacon Hill & the Theater District:** *Holiday Inn* \$\$\$\$<br>5 Blossom St. (800) 465-4329, (617) 742-7630. FAX (617) 482-7630.<br>W www.sixcontinentshotel.com<br>A modern 15-story, business-class chain hotel. On the north side of Beacon Hill near Massachusetts General Hospital, a short walk from the Government Center. | ■ | 303 (2) | | ● | |
| **Beacon Hill & the Theater District:** *Beacon Hill Hotel* \$\$\$\$\$<br>19 Charles St. (888) 959-2442. FAX (617) 723-7575.<br>A renovated brick townhouse that blends the charm of Beacon Hill with modern amenities such as flat-screen TV and Internet access. Rooms overlook bustling Charles Street. | ■ | 13 | ■ | | ■ |
| **Beacon Hill & the Theater District:** *Charles Street Inn* \$\$\$\$\$<br>94 Charles St. (877) 772-8900, (617) 314-8900. FAX (617) 371-0009.<br>W www.charlesstreetinn.com<br>Deluxe boutique hotel in a 1860s townhouse. The Charles Street Inn has sumptuous antiques-filled rooms with fireplaces, whirlpool tubs, and Internet access. | ■ | 9 | | | |
| **Beacon Hill & the Theater District:** *Four Seasons* \$\$\$\$\$<br>200 Boylston St. (800) 332-3442, (617) 338-4400. FAX (617) 423-0154.<br>W www.fourseasons.com<br>The ultimate in service and luxury, and ranked among the top hotels in the city. It has grand reception rooms and sumptuous bedrooms, many overlooking the Public Garden. | ■ | 274 (66) | ■ | ● | |
| **Old Boston & the Financial District:** *Shawmut Inn* \$\$<br>280 Friend St. (800) 350-7784, (617) 720-5544. FAX (617) 723-7784.<br>W www.shawmutinn.com<br>Simply furnished rooms, all with kitchenettes, in a former state office building across the street from North Station. A fine budget choice; suites are a bargain for families. | ■ | 65 (11) | ■ | ● | |
| **Old Boston & the Financial District:** *Harborside Inn* \$\$\$<br>185 State St. (888) 723-7565, (617) 723-7500. FAX (617) 670-6015.<br>W www.hagopianhotels.com<br>The small guest rooms in this old mercantile warehouse have exposed brick walls, period furniture, and wooden floors with Oriental rugs. Located just steps away from Faneuil Hall Marketplace and the Freedom Trail. | ■ | 54 (2) | | | |

**Price categories** for a standard double room per night, inclusive of breakfast, service charges, and any additional taxes:

($) under $100
($)($) $100–$150
($)($)($) $150–$200
($)($)($)($) $200–$250
($)($)($)($)($) over $250

**CREDIT CARDS**
Major credit cards accepted.

**NUMBER OF ROOMS**
Number of rooms in the hotel (suites shown in parentheses).

**RECOMMENDED RESTAURANT**
Good restaurant within the hotel.

**CHILDREN'S FACILITIES**
Hotel has various facilities for young children.

**GARDEN OR TERRACE**
Hotel has a garden, courtyard, or terrace.

| Hotel | Credit Cards | Number of Rooms (Suites) | Recommended Restaurant | Children's Facilities | Garden or Terrace |
|---|---|---|---|---|---|
| **OLD BOSTON & THE FINANCIAL DISTRICT:** *Omni Parker House* ($)($)($)($)<br>60 School St. *(800) 843-6664, (617) 227-8600.* FAX *(617) 742-5729.*<br>W www.omnihotels.com<br>Home of the Parker House Roll and Boston Cream Pie, the traditional, comfortable Omni Parker House has been open and running since 1855. | ■ | 551 (21) | ■ | ● | |
| **OLD BOSTON & THE FINANCIAL DISTRICT:** *Fifteen Beacon* ($)($)($)($)($)<br>15 Beacon St. *(877) 982-3226, (617) 670-1500.* FAX *(617) 670-2525.*<br>W www.xvbeacon.com<br>Coolly opulent boutique hotel in a former office building. Chic rooms all have a high-style mix of traditional and contemporary furnishings, with facilities including CD players and fax machines. | ■ | 61 (2) | ■ | ● | |
| **OLD BOSTON & THE FINANCIAL DISTRICT:** *Langham Boston* ($)($)($)($)($)<br>250 Franklin St. *(800) 543-4300, (617) 451-1900.* FAX *(617) 423-2844.*<br>W www.langhamhotels.com<br>This deluxe hotel in the heart of the Financial District often offers affordable weekend getaway packages. | ■ | 326 (26) | ■ | ● | |
| **NORTH END & THE WATERFRONT:** *Seaport Hotel* ($)($)($)($)<br>One Seaport Lane. *(877) 732-7678, (617) 385-4000.* FAX *(617) 385-4001.*<br>W www.seaporthotel.com<br>A modern, towering business hotel next to the World Trade Center, every room has an Internet hookup, plus in-room conferencing facilities. Weekend specials are attractive. | ■ | 426 (24) | ■ | ● | |
| **BACK BAY & SOUTH END:** *Beacon Street Guesthouse* ($)($)<br>463 Beacon St. *(617) 536-1302.* FAX *(617) 247-8876.* W www.463beacon.com<br>The stately five-story Beacon Street Guesthouse is good value for money. Rooms vary, but some have fireplaces and other original features, plus microwaves and refrigerators; most have a private bath. Breakfast not included. | ■ | 20 | | | |
| **BACK BAY & SOUTH END:** *The College Club* ($)($)<br>44 Commonwealth Ave. *(617) 536-9510.* FAX *(617) 247-8537.*<br>W www.thecollegeclubofboston.com<br>A hidden gem and excellent value, this Victorian town house near the Public Garden is also home to a private club. The College Club rents six lovely double rooms, and five more austere singles that share bathrooms. | ■ | 13 | | | |
| **BACK BAY & SOUTH END:** *Newbury Guesthouse* ($)($)($)<br>261 Newbury St. *(800) 437-7668, (617) 437-7666.* FAX *(617) 262-4243.*<br>W www.hagopianhotels.com<br>In Boston's chic shopping neighborhood, this brownstone guesthouse caters to people from all walks of life – business people and fashionable vacationers. Tasteful rooms are furnished with Victorian-style reproductions. | ■ | 32 | | | ■ |
| **BACK BAY & SOUTH END:** *Eliot Suite Hotel* ($)($)($)($)($)<br>370 Commonwealth Ave. *(800) 443-5468, (617) 267-1607.* FAX *(617) 536-9114.*<br>W www.eliothotel.com<br>Graciously furnished, all-suite hotel, built in 1925. Rooms have separate sitting rooms, plus business amenities. Home of fine French-American restaurant Clio. | ■ | 95 (95) | ■ | ● | |
| **BACK BAY & SOUTH END:** *The Lenox* ($)($)($)($)($)<br>61 Exeter St. *(800) 225-7676, (617) 536-5300.* FAX *(617) 267-1237.*<br>W www.lenoxhotel.com<br>This highly regarded and recently refurbished 100-year-old hotel has sumptuously appointed rooms with all manner of luxuries. It is also home to the excellent Azure restaurant. | ■ | 212 (12) | ■ | ● | |

For key to symbols see back flap

**Price categories** for a standard double room per night, inclusive of breakfast, service charges, and any additional taxes:

($) under $100
($)($) $100–$150
($)($)($) $150–$200
($)($)($)($) $200–$250
($)($)($)($)($) over $250

**CREDIT CARDS**
Major credit cards accepted.

**NUMBER OF ROOMS**
Number of rooms in the hotel (suites shown in parentheses).

**RECOMMENDED RESTAURANT**
Good restaurant within the hotel.

**CHILDREN'S FACILITIES**
Hotel has various facilities for young children.

**GARDEN OR TERRACE**
Hotel has a garden, courtyard, or terrace.

| Hotel | Price | Credit Cards | Number of Rooms (Suites) | Recommended Restaurant | Children's Facilities | Garden or Terrace |
|---|---|---|---|---|---|---|
| **GREATER BOSTON:** *Constitution Inn*<br>150 Second Ave, Charlestown. *(617) 241-8400.* FAX *(617) 241-2856.*<br>W www.constitutioninn.com<br>An economy inn run by the armed services, most rooms have two twin beds; although several have queen-sized ones. | ($)($) | ■ | 149 (2) | | | |
| **GREATER BOSTON:** *Harvard Square Hotel*<br>110 Mt. Auburn St, Cambridge. *(800) 458-5886, (617) 864-5200.*<br>FAX *(617) 864-2409.* W www.harvardsquarehotel.com<br>Its location is the best feature of this refurbished hotel in the heart of Harvard Square. The rooms are basic but comfortable. | ($)($) | ■ | 73 | | ● | |
| **GREATER BOSTON:** *Hotel@M.I.T. – University Park*<br>20 Sidney St, Cambridge. *(800) 222-8733, (617) 577-0200.*<br>FAX *(617) 494-8366.* W www.hotelatmit.com<br>This contemporary hotel, owned by the Massachusetts Institute of Technology, is filled with state-of-the-art technology such as ergonomically designed furniture, in-room Internet access, and phones with voice mail. | ($)($)($)($) | ■ | 210 (28) | | ● | ■ |
| **GREATER BOSTON:** *Irving House*<br>24 Irving St, Cambridge. *(877) 547-4600, (617) 547-4600.*<br>FAX *(617) 576-2814.* W www.irvinghouse.com<br>This wooden-framed Victorian house inn has simple rooms (some are rather small), and an attractive terrace. Some of the rooms share baths. | ($)($)($)($) | ■ | 44 | | ● | ■ |
| **MASSACHUSETTS** | | | | | | |
| **CONCORD:** *Colonial Inn*<br>48 Monument Sq. *(800) 370-9200, (978) 369-9200.* FAX *(978) 371-1533.*<br>@ colonial@concordscolonialinn.com W www.concordscolonialinn.com<br>This historic place was built in 1716 and has been operating as a hotel since 1889. Beautiful Colonial-style rooms are ornately furnished with period furniture. | ($)($)($)($) | ■ | 56 (7) | ■ | ● | |
| **NANTUCKET:** *The Nesbitt Inn*<br>21 Broad St. *(508) 228-0156.*<br>Located right in town, this Victorian B&B is operated by the exceptionally friendly hosts, Mr. and Mrs. Nesbitt, and is decorated with antiques and Oriental carpets. *Mar 1–mid-Dec.* | ($)($) | ■ | 12 | | ● | ■ |
| **PLYMOUTH:** *John Carver Inn*<br>25 Summer St. *(800) 274-1620, (508) 746-7100.* FAX *(508) 746-8299.*<br>W www.johncarverinn.com<br>Just a ten-minute stroll from the Waterfront attractions, the John Carver epitomizes Colonial-Revival style but combined with modern facilities such as a fitness center and large pool. | ($)($)($) | ■ | 85 (6) | | ● | |
| **PROVINCETOWN:** *The Beaconlight Guesthouse*<br>12 Winthrop St. *(800) 696-9603.* FAX *(508) 487-9603.*<br>W www.beaconlightguesthouse.com<br>A romantic B&B in a sprawling beach house (built around 1900). The Beaconlight Guesthouse is located in a quiet but convenient location for downtown. Children are not allowed. | ($)($)($) | ■ | 10 | | | ■ |
| **SALEM:** *Hawthorne Hotel*<br>18 Washington Sq W. *(800) SAY-STAY, (978) 744-4080.*<br>FAX *(978) 745-9842.* @ info@hawthornehotel.com<br>W www.hawthornehotel.com<br>This upscale Federal-style hotel located in downtown Salem combines tasteful decoration with modern amenities. | ($)($)($) | ■ | 89 (6) | ■ | ● | |

## RHODE ISLAND

**BLOCK ISLAND:** *1661 Inn and Hotel Manisses* $$$
Spring St. (800) 626-4773, (401) 466-2421. FAX (401) 466-3162.
W www.blockislandresorts.com
This historic inn, animal farm, and Victorian hotel is a perfect base from which to explore Block Island. No air-conditioning. *mid-Oct–Mar.*

■ | 26 | ■ | ● | ■

**CHARLESTOWN:** *General Stanton Inn* $$$
4115A Old Post Rd, Rte 1A. (401) 364-8888. FAX (401) 364-3333.
One of the oldest continuously run inns in North America, it retains some of the old atmosphere, with fireplaces and brick ovens.

■ | 15 (4) | ■ | | ■

**NEWPORT:** *Beech Tree Inn* $$$$
34 Rhode Island Ave. (800) 748-6565, (401) 847-9794. FAX (401) 847-6824.
W www.beechtreeinn.com
This Victorian home boasts rooms with fireplaces and jacuzzis. It is noted for "the biggest breakfast in Newport."

■ | 8 (2) | | | ■

**NEWPORT:** *Castle Hill Inn and Resort* $$$$$
590 Ocean Dr. (888) 466-1355, (401) 849-3800. FAX (401) 849-3838.
W www.castlehillinn.com
This resort with a private beach includes several houses. The restaurant has repeatedly won the *Wine Spectator* Award of Excellence. Limited availability for children under 12.

■ | 25 (2) | ■ | | ■

**PROVIDENCE:** *C.C. Ledbetter B&B* $$
326 Benefit St. (401) 351-4699. FAX (401) 351-4699.
@ info@providence-inn.com W www.providence-inn.com
Located opposite John Brown House, a block from Brown University. The C.C. Ledbetter B&B has charming rooms with traditional handmade quilts.

■ | 10 | | | ■

**PROVIDENCE:** *The Westin Providence* $$$$
One West Exchange St. (800) WESTIN1, (401) 598-8000.
FAX (401) 598-8200. W www.westinprovidence.com
Four-time Pinnacle Award winner. The Agora restaurant was named Best in Hotel Dining by the *Food Network* in 2000. Connected to Providence Place Mall and the Rhode Island Convention Center, the Westin Providence makes a good base for exploring the surroundings.

■ | 364 (19) | ■ | ● |

## CONNECTICUT

**HARTFORD:** *Goodwin Hotel* $$$
One Haynes St. (888) 212-8380, (860) 246-7500.
FAX (860) 247-4576. W www.goodwinhotel.com
The historic Goodwin Hotel serves guests with poise and style, but without pretension. The restaurant has been voted Best Hotel Dining by *Connecticut Magazine* for 10 years running.

■ | 124 (11) | ■ | ● |

**LITCHFIELD:** *Litchfield Inn* $$$
432 Bantam Rd. (800) 499-3444, (860) 567-4503. FAX (860) 567-5358.
@ litchfieldinn@compuserve.com W www.litchfieldinnct.com
A quaint country inn located just west of Litchfield. Features a gigantic chandelier, delicately carved main staircase, and four working fireplaces. Eight luxurious theme rooms.

■ | 32 | ■ | ● | ■

**MYSTIC:** *Seaport Motor Inn* $$
Coogan Blvd. (877) 523-0993, (860) 536-2621. FAX (860) 536-4493.
Overlooking Olde Mistick Village and the Mystic Aquarium. The Seaport Motor Inn offers intimate dining steps away at Jamm's Restaurant and adjoining Captain's Lounge. Close to all the major attractions, including beaches and the USS *Nautilus*.

■ | 118 | | ● |

**MYSTIC:** *Steamboat Inn* $$$$
73 Steamboat Wharf. (860) 536-8300. FAX (860) 536-9528.
@ sbwharf@aol.com
Spacious rooms are named after famous Mystic ships from the schooner days. All the rooms in this quaint Steamboat Inn have whirlpool baths and antique furnishings. Magnificent views of the river and the dock.

■ | 10 (4) | | ● |

For key to symbols see back flap

**Price categories** for a standard double room per night, inclusive of breakfast, service charges, and any additional taxes:

- $ under $100
- $$ $100–$150
- $$$ $150–$200
- $$$$ $200–$250
- $$$$$ over $250

**CREDIT CARDS**
Major credit cards accepted.

**NUMBER OF ROOMS**
Number of rooms in the hotel (suites shown in parentheses).

**RECOMMENDED RESTAURANT**
Good restaurant within the hotel.

**CHILDREN'S FACILITIES**
Hotel has various facilities for young children.

**GARDEN OR TERRACE**
Hotel has a garden, courtyard, or terrace.

## VERMONT

**BURLINGTON:** *Wyndham Hotel* $$$
60 Battery St. *(800) 996-3426, (802) 658-6500.* FAX *(802) 658-4659.*
W www.radisson.com/burlingtonvt
Burlington's most upscale hotel, the Radisson is situated right in the heart of the downtown area. The best rooms have breathtaking views of Lake Champlain.

| Credit Cards | Number of Rooms (Suites) | Recommended Restaurant | Children's Facilities | Garden or Terrace |
|---|---|---|---|---|
| ■ | 256 (8) | ■ | | |

**KILLINGTON:** *Mountain Meadows Lodge* $$$$
285 Thundering Brook Rd. *(800) 370-4567, (802) 775-1010.*
@ havefun@mtnmeadowslodge.com W www.mtmeadowslodge.com
Vermont's only mountain lodge set on both a lake and the famous Appalachian Trail, it is perfect for outdoor types. It features excellent family services. *Apr–mid-May.*

| Credit Cards | Number of Rooms (Suites) | Recommended Restaurant | Children's Facilities | Garden or Terrace |
|---|---|---|---|---|
| ■ | 20 (1) | ■ | ● | ■ |

**MANCHESTER:** *The Equinox Resort* $$$$$
3567 Main St. *(802) 362-4747.* FAX *(802) 362-1595.*
@ reservations@equinoxresort.com W www.equinoxresort.com
This historic 18th-century resort has stunning public spaces and spacious, country-style rooms. The resort also offers outdoor activities such as golf, falconry, fishing, and off-road driving.

| Credit Cards | Number of Rooms (Suites) | Recommended Restaurant | Children's Facilities | Garden or Terrace |
|---|---|---|---|---|
| ■ | 172 (17) | ■ | ● | ■ |

**RICHMOND:** *The Richmond Victorian Inn* $$$
191 East Main St. *(888) 242-3362, (802) 434-4410.* FAX *(802) 434-4411.*
@ innkeeper@richmondvictorianinn.com W www.richmondvictorianinn.com
Located in the foothills of the Green Mountains, this inexpensive inn's six guest rooms are furnished in a country Victorian style with antiques. No televisions or air-conditioning in rooms. Children over 12.

| Credit Cards | Number of Rooms (Suites) | Recommended Restaurant | Children's Facilities | Garden or Terrace |
|---|---|---|---|---|
| ■ | 6 (1) | | | ■ |

**SHELBURNE:** *Inn at Shelburne Farms* $$$$
1611 Harbor Rd. *(802) 985-8498.* FAX *(802) 985-8123.*
W www.shelburnefarms.org
Built in 1897 on a bluff overlooking Lake Champlain, the inn is situated on a 1,400-acre (400-ha) property, landscaped by Frederick Law Olmsted. *mid-Oct–mid-May.*

| Credit Cards | Number of Rooms (Suites) | Recommended Restaurant | Children's Facilities | Garden or Terrace |
|---|---|---|---|---|
| ■ | 24 | ■ | ● | ■ |

**STOWE:** *Wood Chip Inn* $$
Mountain Rd. *(800) 676-9181, (802) 253-9080.* FAX *(802) 253-7873.*
@ wdchipinn@aol.com W www.gostowe.com/members/woodchip
Charming and economical, the inn offers homemade breads and soups in the fall and winter, and afternoon refreshments in the summer.

| Credit Cards | Number of Rooms (Suites) | Recommended Restaurant | Children's Facilities | Garden or Terrace |
|---|---|---|---|---|
| ■ | 9 | | | ■ |

**STOWE:** *Trapp Family Lodge* $$$$$
700 Trapp Hill Rd. *(800) 826-7000, (802) 253-8511.* FAX *(802) 253-5740.*
@ info@trappfamily.com W www.trappfamily.com
World-famous 116-room resort on 2,700-acre (1.092-ha) property. Along with large Austrian-style main lodge, the resort features 100 guesthouses and exquisite cuisine.

| Credit Cards | Number of Rooms (Suites) | Recommended Restaurant | Children's Facilities | Garden or Terrace |
|---|---|---|---|---|
| ■ | 116 (18) | ■ | ● | ■ |

## NEW HAMPSHIRE

**BRETTON WOODS:** *The Mount Washington Hotel & Resort* $$$$$
Rte 302. *(800) 258-0330, (603) 278-1000.* FAX *(603) 278-8838.*
@ hotelinfo@mtwashington.com W www.mtwashington.com
Since 1902, this elegant resort has offered quality service in a beautiful setting.

| Credit Cards | Number of Rooms (Suites) | Recommended Restaurant | Children's Facilities | Garden or Terrace |
|---|---|---|---|---|
| ■ | 191 (6) | ■ | ● | ■ |

**CONCORD:** *The Centennial Inn* $$
96 Pleasant St. *(800) 360-4839, (603) 225-7102.* FAX *(603) 225-5031.*
@ centennialinn@totalnetnh.net W www.someplacesdifferent.com
Housed in a restored 1876 Victorian mansion, this centrally located inn provides well-furnished rooms and suites.

| Credit Cards | Number of Rooms (Suites) | Recommended Restaurant | Children's Facilities | Garden or Terrace |
|---|---|---|---|---|
| ■ | 32 (5) | ■ | ● | |

**FRANCONIA:** *The Franconia Inn* $$$
1300 Easton Rd. (800) 473-5299, (603) 823-5542. FAX (603) 823-8078.
@ info@franconiainn.com W www.franconiainn.com
The Franconia Inn is a cozy historic lodging, surrounded by stunningly beautiful scenery. This place has enough sports and activities to keep outdoor enthusiasts satisfied year round. No air-conditioning in any of the rooms. Television in common room. ● *Apr–mid-May.*

| ■ | 34 (2) | ■ | ● | ■ |
|---|---|---|---|---|

**MANCHESTER:** *The Highlander Inn* $$
2 Highlander Way. (800) 548-9248, (603) 625-6426. FAX (603) 625-6466.
W www.highlanderinn.com
A popular resort for Bostonians since the late 19th century. Its proximity to the airport is a great convenience for both business and pleasure travelers.

| ■ | 88 (10) | ■ | ● | ■ |
|---|---|---|---|---|

**MEREDITH:** *Meredith Inn B&B* $$
2 Waukewan St. (603) 279-0000. FAX (603) 279-4017.
@ inn1897@meredithinn.com W www.meredithinn.com
A restored Victorian home refurbished with all the modern amenities. Great for fitness enthusiasts – convenient for Lake Winnipesaukee activities – it is walking distance to the beach on Lake Waukewan. Six rooms have air-conditioning.

| ■ | 8 | | | |
|---|---|---|---|---|

**PORTSMOUTH:** *The Inn at Christian Shore* $$
335 Maplewood Ave. (603) 431-6770. FAX (603) 431-7743.
W www.portsmouthnh.com/christianshore
The Inn at Christian Shore is a well-preserved late 1800s home furnished with the unlikely mix of antiques, African art, and contemporary paintings. The gourmet breakfasts are delicious and offer vast choice. No children are allowed.

| ■ | 5 | | | |
|---|---|---|---|---|

**PORTSMOUTH:** *Sheraton Harborside Portsmouth* $$$
250 Market St. (603) 431-2300. FAX (603) 433-5649.
@ info@sheratonportsmouth.com W www.sheratonportsmouth.com
A modern hotel in the historic waterfront district. Close to waterfront restaurants and shops. Rates vary.

| ■ | 200 (19) | ■ | ● | |
|---|---|---|---|---|

## MAINE

**BAR HARBOR:** *Mira Monte Inn and Suites* $$$
69 Mount Desert St. (800) 553-5109, (207) 288-4263.
FAX (207) 288-3115. @ mburns@miramonte.com W www.miramonte.com
Constructed in 1864, this is one of only two B&Bs in town owned by Bar Harbor natives. All rooms of the Mira Monte Inn and Suites have the comfort of air-conditioning.

| ■ | 16 (3) | | | ■ |
|---|---|---|---|---|

**BETHEL:** *Bethel Inn and Country Club* $$$$
On the Common. (800) 654-0125, (207) 824-2175.
FAX (207) 824-2233. @ info@bethelinn.com W www.bethelinn.com
A premier Maine resort, the property has its own championship golf course and a tennis court. Price includes free golf and dinner, except for townhouse guests.

| ■ | 140 (12) | ■ | ● | ■ |
|---|---|---|---|---|

**OGUNQUIT:** *The Cliff House* $$$$
Shore Rd. (207) 361-1000. FAX (207) 361-2122.
@ info@cliffhouse@maine.com W www.cliffhousemaine.com
Oceanside resort with full floor devoted to recreation. It also has a spa. Cliff house trolley takes guests to spots of interest in the area in July and August. ● *mid-Dec–Mar.*

| ■ | 194 (2) | ■ | ● | ■ |
|---|---|---|---|---|

**PORTLAND:** *Inn at St. John* $$
939 Congress. (800) 636-9127, (207) 773-6481. FAX (207) 756-7629.
@ theinn@maine.rr.com W www.innatstjohn.com
Century-old inn just minutes from Portland's Old Port, Waterfront, and Arts districts. The Inn at St. John has rooms that are tastefully decorated, and all are air-conditioned. Some rooms share baths.

| ■ | 40 | | ● | |
|---|---|---|---|---|

**PORTLAND:** *Portland Regency Hotel* $$$$
20 Milk St. (800) 727-3436, (207) 774-4200. FAX (207) 775-2150.
@ public@the regency.com W www.theregency.com
Situated in the heart of the Old Port district, the Portland Regency Hotel is Portland's premiere hotel. An added bonus in this hotel – fitness center is free for guests.

| ■ | 95 (8) | ■ | ● | |
|---|---|---|---|---|

For key to symbols see back flap

# Where to Eat

New England's cuisine is a melting pot of different cultures – the English, Irish, and the Italians have each brought their own cuisines as well as adopted native ingredients. The chart below highlights some of the factors that may influence your choice of where to eat. Opening times of restaurants are indicated by a "B" for breakfast, "L" for lunch, and "D" for dinner.

## Boston, Massachusetts

**Back Bay & South End:** *Men Tei Noodle House* $
66 Hereford St. (617) 425-0066.
Osaka-style *udon* noodles and an array of great snack foods and entrées for the low-budget visitor. Efficient staff and a mixed, lively clientele make this restaurant well worth a visit. No wine. *L, D.*

**Back Bay & South End:** *Tapeo* $$$
266 Newbury St. (617) 267-4799.
A wonderfully earthy tapas bar right in the middle of pretentious Newbury Street. Regulars are really devoted to the sangria and the tiny dishes, though there is a full menu if you so prefer. *L, D.*

**Back Bay & South End:** *Aujourd'Hui* $$$$$
200 Boylston St (Four Seasons Hotel). (617) 351-2037.
One of the best dining experiences in Boston, the contemporary cuisine is complemented by a lovely ambience and a view of the Public Garden. There is also an alternative healthy cuisine menu. *B, L, D.*

**Back Bay & South End:** *Tremont 647* $$$$
647 Tremont St. (617) 266-4600.
Pushing the boundaries of new and old American food alike, this youthful and unpretentious restaurant enjoys innovation, and it succeeds. Try the sea bass on jasmine rice or the spice-rubbed steak. Sundays' Pajama Brunch is a must, if solely for the cinnamon rolls. *D, Sun Brunch.*

**Beacon Hill & Theater District:** *Legal Seafoods* $$$$
26 Park Square. (617) 426-4444.
This popular restaurant has many locations throughout the city, all serving the freshest and the best prepared seafood available. Try their raw bar for oysters, then one of their superb entrées, which are delicious. *L, D.*

**Beacon Hill & Theater District:** *Locke-Ober* $$$$$
3 Winter Place. (617) 542-1340.
New owners have rejuvenated one of America's most legendary restaurants, founded in 1875. Inventive twists enliven European and American classics. Reservations essential. *L, D.* ● *Sun.*

**Greater Boston:** *Mr. Bartley's Burger Cottage* $
1246 Massachusetts Ave, Cambridge. (617) 354-6559.
A glorious profusion and variety of hamburgers and truly wonderful sweet potato fries to try out in an overwhelmingly chaotic atmosphere. *L, D.* ● *Sun.*

**Greater Boston:** *Harvest* $$$$
44 Brattle St, Cambridge. (617) 868-2255.
A favoured haunt of university professors. Modern American cuisine bursting with fresh flavors and local produce. Reservations suggested. *L, D, Sun Brunch.*

**Greater Boston:** *Olives* $$$$$
10 City Square, Charlestown. (617) 242-1999.
Mediterranean-influenced cuisine by local celebrity chef Todd English, served in a bistro-like setting. Perpetually crowded, they do not accept reservations. Dress well to minimize your wait. ● *Sun.*

**North End & the Waterfront:** *La Famiglia Giorgio* $$
112 Salem St. (617) 367-6711.
Huge portions of well-prepared pasta are the order of the day here, and La Famiglia is always ready to help you choose. It's a bargain – you will leave full and happy. *L, D.*

| Restaurant | Credit Cards | Outdoor Tables | Vegetarian | Good Wine List | Late Opening |
|---|---|---|---|---|---|
| Men Tei Noodle House | | | ■ | | |
| Tapeo | ■ | ● | ■ | ● | |
| Aujourd'Hui | ■ | | ■ | ● | |
| Tremont 647 | ■ | ● | ■ | ● | |
| Legal Seafoods | ■ | | ■ | ● | ■ |
| Locke-Ober | ■ | | | ● | |
| Mr. Bartley's Burger Cottage | | ● | ■ | | |
| Harvest | ■ | ● | ■ | ● | |
| Olives | ■ | ● | ■ | ● | |
| La Famiglia Giorgio | ■ | | ■ | | |

**Price categories** include a three-course meal for one, a glass of house wine, and all unavoidable extra charges such as sales tax and service.
$ under $20
$$ $20–30
$$$ $30–45
$$$$ $45–60
$$$$$ over $60

**CREDIT CARDS**
Major credit cards accepted.
**OUTDOOR TABLES**
Garden, courtyard, or terrace with outside tables.
**VEGETARIAN**
A good selection of vegetarian dishes available.
**GOOD WINE LIST**
Extensive list of good wines, both domestic and imported.
**LATE OPENING**
Full menu or light meals served after 11pm.

**NORTH END & THE WATERFRONT:** *Pomodoro* $$
319 Hanover St. *(617) 367-4348.*
Crowded, raucous, and aromatic, the small storefront housing Pomodoro brims with patrons at all hours. It is popular for its real Italian dishes, which are always well prepared. Try the monkfish and saffron risotto, which are absolutely delicious. *L, D.*

**NORTH END & THE WATERFRONT:** *Barking Crab* $$$
88 Sleeper St. *(617) 426-2722.*
Boston's classic shoreside seafood joint, facing the city from across Fort Point Channel. Lobster, steamers, clamrolls, and chowder, served along with paper napkins. *L, D, Sun Brunch (winter only).*

**NORTH END & THE WATERFRONT:** *Rudi's* $$$
30 Rowes Wharf (Boston Harbor Hotel). *(617) 330-7656.*
Large delicatessen, where patrons order portions from the serving counter, and seat themselves at café tables. Rudi's also sells pastries and gourmet food gifts. No wine. *B, L, D.*

**NORTH END & THE WATERFRONT:** *Terramia* $$$$
98 Salem St. *(617) 523-3112.*
Boisterous and mixed clientele line up every night to dine on the trademark gnocchi, prepared daily, as well as on the sublime lobster fritters. Casual, friendly service, and setting. *D.*

**OLD BOSTON & THE FINANCIAL DISTRICT:** *Durgin-Park* $$$
340 North Market St (Faneuil Hall Marketplace). *(617) 227-2038.*
A Boston institution, serving all the New England standards that no one else seems to cook anymore – Indian pudding, baked beans, and baked scrod, all of which are dished up by a sharp-tongued staff. *L, D.*

## MASSACHUSETTS

**CAPE COD:** *Oysterman's Grill & Fish Market* $$$
975 Rte 6, Wellfleet. *(508) 349-3825.*
Seafood restaurant specializes in clams and oysters and other fish and shellfish. The sesame-seared local tuna is a must-have. *L, D.*
*mid-Oct–April.*

**CAPE COD:** *Chillingsworth* $$$$$
2449 Main St (Rte 6A), Brewster. *(508) 896-3640.*
Fine dining served in a 300-year-old house. This place exudes charm, has seamless service, and an elegant French prix-fixe menu. The casual fare available in the Bistro is quite delicious. *L, D, Sun Brunch.*
*Mon; Dec–mid-May.*

**CONCORD:** *Aigo Bistro* $$$$
84 Thoreau St. *(978) 371-1333.*
Exotic food consisting of superlative Mediterranean and Provençal cuisine. Fine service is the other given in this sophisticated restaurant located upstairs in Concord depot. *D.* *Sun, Mon.*

**MARTHA'S VINEYARD:** *Black Dog Tavern* $$$
Beach St Extension, Vineyard Haven. *(508) 693-9223.*
Facing the harbor, this place is a hit with patrons for the little neck clams, grilled bluefish sandwiches, and other fresh seafood. *B, L, D, Sun Brunch.*

**PLYMOUTH:** *Lobster Hut* $$$
25 Town Wharf. *(508) 746-2270.*
Fried clams, fish & chips, and clam chowder are particularly delicious. Huge portions of seafood are notable at this self-serve waterfront spot. *L, D.* *Jan.*

| Restaurant | Credit Cards | Outdoor Tables | Vegetarian | Good Wine List | Late Opening |
|---|---|---|---|---|---|
| Pomodoro | | | ■ | | |
| Barking Crab | ■ | ● | ■ | ● | |
| Rudi's | ■ | ● | ■ | | |
| Terramia | ■ | | ■ | ● | |
| Durgin-Park | ■ | ● | ■ | ● | |
| Oysterman's Grill & Fish Market | ■ | ● | ■ | | |
| Chillingsworth | ■ | ● | ■ | ● | |
| Aigo Bistro | ■ | | ■ | ● | |
| Black Dog Tavern | ■ | | ■ | | |
| Lobster Hut | ■ | ● | | | |

For key to symbols see back flap

**Price categories** include a three-course meal for one, a glass of house wine, and all unavoidable extra charges such as sales tax and service.
$ under $20
$$ $20–30
$$$ $30–45
$$$$ $45–60
$$$$$ over $60

**CREDIT CARDS**
Major credit cards accepted.

**OUTDOOR TABLES**
Garden, courtyard, or terrace with outside tables.

**VEGETARIAN**
A good selection of vegetarian dishes available.

**GOOD WINE LIST**
Extensive list of good wines, both domestic and imported.

**LATE OPENING**
Full menu or light meals served after 11pm.

**SALEM:** *Lyceum Bar & Grill* $$$$
43 Church St. *(978) 745-7665.*
In this historic building, where Alexander Graham Bell gave the first phone demo in 1877, you'll find a good assortment of New American and grilled dishes. *L (except Sat), D, Sun Brunch.*

**STURBRIDGE:** *Publick House* $$$$
295 Main St. *(508) 347-3313.*
In the Sturbridge spirit, this atmospheric 1771 Colonial house with open hearths features Americana, such as lobster pie and prime rib. *B, L, D.*

## RHODE ISLAND

**BLOCK ISLAND:** *Finn's Seafood Restaurant* $$
Water St. *(401) 466-2473.*
Its location facing the harbor makes ferry-watching a cinch. The upstairs deck of this popular seafood restaurant looks over the water. Lobster, steamed mussels, clam rolls, and broiled swordfish are all tasty. *L, D.*
*mid-Oct–mid-May.*

**NEWPORT:** *The Black Pearl* $$$
Bannister's Wharf. *(401) 846-5264.*
Justifiably famous for its clam chowder, this landmark blends classic French fare in the sedate Commodore Room with casual dining in the tavern and bar. Try the apple-raisin bread pudding. *L, D.* *mid-Jan–mid-Feb.*

**NEWPORT:** *White Horse Tavern* $$$$
26 Marlborough St. *(401) 849-3600.*
The oldest operating tavern in America, with low-beamed ceilings, hearth fires, Colonial bric-a-brac, and candlelit dining rooms. Good American food with modern touches. *L (except Mon–Tue), D, Sun Brunch.*

**PROVIDENCE:** *L'Epicureo* $$$$
311 Westminster St. *(401) 521-3333.*
The widely acclaimed Federal Hill Trattoria has been reborn. A superb wine list mates with impeccable northern Italian cuisine at this elegant establishment. *D.*

**PROVIDENCE:** *Al Forno* $$$$$
577 S Main St. *(401) 273-9760.*
Wood-fire grilled meats, pizzas from stone floor pizza ovens, and baked pasta dishes are signatures of this popular, informal, no-reservations-taken place. The chef-owners keep inventing new and fabulous dishes using fresh, local ingredients. *D.* *Sun–Mon.*

## CONNECTICUT

**HARTFORD:** *Max Downtown* $$$$$
City Place, 185 Asylum St. *(860) 522-2530.*
Smart, modern, bustling, this favorite-with-locals downtown spot features excellent Modern American dishes. *Mon–Fri L, D.*

**LITCHFIELD:** *West Street Grill* $$$$
43 West St. *(860) 567-3885.*
The area's most popular gathering place for big-name New Yorkers who weekend in the vicinity offers pace-setting food in a comfortably casual setting. *L, D.* *Mon–Tue in winter.*

**MYSTIC:** *Mystic Pizza* $
56 W Main St. *(860) 536-3700.*
Immortalized by Julia Roberts' movie, this pizza-and-pasta parlor is a "must-stop" for most Mystic visitors. *L, D.*

| | CREDIT CARDS | OUTDOOR TABLES | VEGETARIAN | GOOD WINE LIST | LATE OPENING |
|---|---|---|---|---|---|
| Lyceum Bar & Grill | ■ | | ■ | | |
| Publick House | ■ | | ■ | ● | |
| Finn's Seafood Restaurant | ■ | ● | | | |
| The Black Pearl | ■ | ● | ■ | ● | |
| White Horse Tavern | ■ | | | ● | |
| L'Epicureo | ■ | ● | | ● | |
| Al Forno | ■ | ● | ■ | ● | |
| Max Downtown | ■ | | ■ | ● | ■ |
| West Street Grill | ■ | ● | ■ | ● | |
| Mystic Pizza | ■ | | ■ | | |

**NEW HAVEN:** *Union League Café* $$$$$
1032 Chapel St. (203) 562-4299.
This historic building plays second fiddle to superb French food, well prepared. The Union League Café is also known for its impeccable service. *L, D.* *Sun.*

**NEW HAVEN:** *Zinc* $$$$$
964 Chapel St. (203) 624-0507.
Stunning minimalist decor suits the vibrant food, a stylish blend of New American with Asian influences, producing unique results. *Tue–Sat L, D.*

## VERMONT

**BURLINGTON:** *India House Restaurant* $$
207 Colchester Ave. (802) 862-7800.
Specializing in traditional North Indian food, with both vegetarian and non-vegetarian choices, the India House offers authentic tandoori cooking. Good choice of beers. *L, D.*

**MANCHESTER CENTER:** *Up For Breakfast* $
4935 Main St. (802) 362-4204.
Delicious, nutritious breakfasts, with many varieties of eggs, pancakes, French toast, waffles, fruit plates, and tofu "eggs vegetarian." Choice of coffees, including a maple latte, fresh-squeezed orange or grapefruit juice, or a champagne-and-OJ mimosa. Full champagne menu. *B.*

**STOWE:** *Maxwell's at Top Notch* $$$$$
4000 Mountain Rd. (800) 451-8686, (802) 253-8585.
The fine dining option at the Top Notch at Stowe Resort and Spa, Maxwell's serves gourmet American cuisine with many health-conscious options, specializing in game and prime aged meats. This is an elegant room with beautiful views from large windows. It has received the Award of Excellence from *Wine Spectator. B, D.*

## NEW HAMPSHIRE

**CONCORD:** *Cat'n Fiddle* $$$
118 Manchester St. (603) 228-8911.
This 26-year-old family business is a Concord institution. The traditional American fare includes prime rib, steak, seafood, a huge salad bar, and shish kebabs. The restaurant has a casual setting. Reservations are required on weekends. *L, D.*

**PORTSMOUTH:** *The Blue Mermaid World Grill* $$$
409 The Hill. (603) 427-2583.
A wonderful selection of internationally flavored dishes that include spiced pork, marinated lamb, and a great choice of seafoods prepared on a wood-burning grill. Beverage list has 12 different margaritas, tropical coolers, martinis, and a good wine list. *L, D, Sun Brunch.*

**PORTSMOUTH:** *The Oar House* $$$$
55 Ceres St. (603) 436-4025.
A museum restaurant in a restored 1803 waterfront warehouse. Both the decor and the mainly seafood menu of the Oar House reflect Portsmouth's maritime heritage. Reservations recommended. *L, D, Sun Brunch.*

## MAINE

**KENNEBUNKPORT:** *The Clam Shack* $
2 Western St. (207) 967-3321.
This take-out stand is the quintessential seaside experience. The menu consists of some of the best fast-food seafood you'll find in New England, including fried and steamed clams, scallops, and a truly remarkable lobster roll. Known for its fresh-cut onion rings. *L, D.* *mid-Oct–mid-May.*

**PORTLAND:** *Back Bay Grill* $$$$
65 Portland St. (207) 772-8833.
The Back Bay Grill has a seasonal menu and offers elegant food in a modern setting. A *Wine Spectator* Award of Excellence winner, this restaurant has an enormous selection of wine and is also known for its superb desserts. *D.* *Sun.*

For key to symbols see back flap

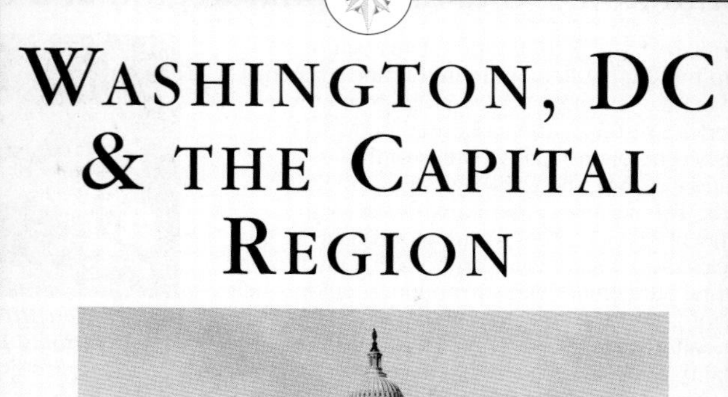

# Washington, DC & the Capital Region

# Washington, DC & the Capital Region at a Glance

Washington, DC and the four states that make up the Capital Region lie in the northeastern United States. This area played an important role in America's history – the earliest colonies were established here, and many battles of the Revolutionary War and Civil War were fought on its fields. The region is, therefore, dotted with magnificent historic sites. Washington is one of America's most visited cities and offers a great range of cultural attractions. The surrounding region's rich variety of landscapes includes Virginia's lush, rolling countryside, West Virginia's rugged mountains, Maryland's picturesque bays and harbors, and Delaware's parks, beaches, and opulent country mansions.

***New River Gorge National River*** (see p220), *in West Virginia, runs through dense forests. The dramatic gorge is a perfect white-water rafting destination.*

***Blue Ridge Parkway*** (see p218), *stretching 215 miles (346 km) through Virginia, winds its way along the crest of the Appalachian Mountains all the way to North Carolina. This lovely route is at its best during spring and fall.*

◁ **A dramatic nighttime view of the United States Capitol, one of the world's best-known symbols of democracy**

***Baltimore*** (see p222) *epitomizes the rich maritime heritage of Maryland. This pleasant port city's redeveloped waterfront features several shops and restaurants, as well as the stunning National Aquarium.*

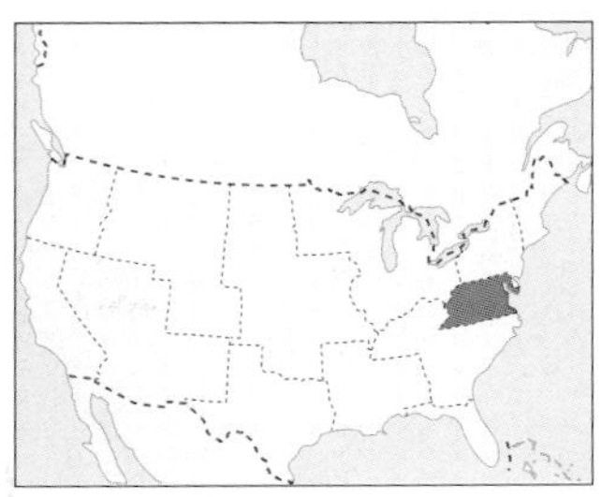

**LOCATOR MAP**

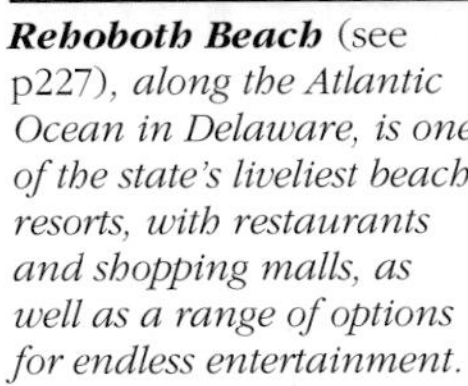

***Rehoboth Beach*** (see p227), *along the Atlantic Ocean in Delaware, is one of the state's liveliest beach resorts, with restaurants and shopping malls, as well as a range of options for endless entertainment.*

***Washington, DC*** (see pp196–211), *the nation's imposing capital, is dominated by the White House, the president's official residence since the 1820s. Millions of visitors take the guided tour of this elegantly decorated mansion, the city's signature landmark.*

# WASHINGTON, DC & THE CAPITAL REGION

CENTER OF GOVERNMENT *for the world's most powerful nation, Washington, DC is a stately, Neo-Classical city, with grand avenues and monumental public buildings that reflect the pride and ambitions that course through the corridors of power. Its surrounding region preserves important places where the young nation evolved from a Colonial outpost to an independent country.*

Located midway along the Atlantic Coast, the nation's capital lies at the heart of the East Coast. This was also the heart of the Colonial landscape where the country began, and where many of its most significant events occurred. Besides its rich tapestry of historical events, this region also has one of the country's most beautiful and varied landscapes. Just 30 miles (48 km) east from the White House is Chesapeake Bay, the country's largest and most productive estuary, while to the west are the lush Appalachian hardwood forests. This wide variety of topography and scenery is paralleled by an equally wide range of social and economic situations; the area in and around the nation's capital is home to some of the wealthiest as well as the most deprived citizens in the United States.

## HISTORY

The first Europeans to this area were a small band of Spanish explorers and Jesuit priests who tried unsuccessfully to set up a colony around Chesapeake Bay in 1570. They were followed by the English, who in honor of the "Virgin Queen" Elizabeth I, named the entire region between Spanish Florida and French Canada, "Virginia." But, it was not until 1607, under the reign of James I, that Virginia's first successful English settlement, Jamestown, was founded a few miles up the James River on Chesapeake Bay. Despite the initial hardships, the colonists' prospects improved after they learned to cultivate tobacco and corn. By the 1630s, Virginia had become the world's leading producer of tobacco.

Jamestown's eventual success led to the establishment of the Catholic

**Natural chimney formations in the Shenandoah Valley at Front Royal, Virginia**

◁ **Attractive Colonial townhouses, a typical feature of Georgetown, Washington, DC**

**Nighttime view of Lincoln Memorial and Washington Monument with the US Capitol in the distance**

colony of Maryland, named in honor of King James's wife, Queen Mary. Governed by Lord Baltimore, the colony attracted Catholics from England as well as Puritan and Quaker settlers from Virginia. Every year, thousands of English immigrants came to the new colonies in search of opportunities impossible back home. By the mid-1660s, both Virginia and Maryland had evolved into England's most profitable New World colonies. In 1664, the English took control of Delaware, founded and settled by the Dutch and the Swedish in the early 1600s. West Virginia, however, did not separate from Virginia until the Civil War.

By the 1670s, a simulataneous rise in taxes and a swift drop in tobacco prices caused widespread suffering and a short-lived rebellion. The situation stabilized in the early 1700s, when some of the tobacco farmers began to reap great fortunes. Much of their success was based on the shift from servant labor to that of African slaves, whose numbers grew from a few hundred in 1650 to over 150,000 in 1750, when blacks made up nearly half the total population.

### Key Dates in History

**1607** Establishment of the private English colony of Jamestown in Virginia

**1624** Virginia becomes a royal colony

**1632** King Charles I establishes Maryland

**1664** Delaware comes under British rule

**1699** Williamsburg becomes Virginia's capital

**1774** Virginia's Peyton Randolph leads the first Continental Congress to discuss freedom

**1775–81** The Revolutionary War

**1791** George Washington obtains land for the capital city

**1830** The Baltimore and Ohio Railroad (B&O) is the nation's first long-distance railroad

**1846** The Smithsonian Institution is established

**1865** Confederate General Robert E. Lee surrenders to the Union at Appomattox

**1932** During the Great Depression, a "Bonus Army" of WWI veterans camp around the Capitol to plead for government aid

**1935** US Supreme Court building is completed

**1963** Martin Luther King Jr. delivers his "I have a Dream" speech before Lincoln Memorial

**1989** L. Douglas Wilder is elected governor of Virginia, the first black to hold such high office

**1999** Impeachment, trial, and acquittal of President Clinton

**Sept 11, 2001** Terrorist attack on the Pentagon

### Independence & Civil War

Frustration over British rule eventually led to calls for independence. Although the Revolutionary War ended at Yorktown, Virginia, in 1781, it was only after the Treaty of Paris that American independence became a reality. Virginia, by far the largest and wealthiest of the American colonies, provided many of the "Founding Fathers," including George Washington, the military leader and first president; Thomas Jefferson, author of the Declaration of Independence and third president; and James Madison, author of the Constitution and two-term president.

In 1791, Washington, empowered by a Congressional act, selected the site for the nation's capital on land incorporated from Maryland and Virginia, a choice determined by its location midway between north and south. This independent federal territory, termed the District of Columbia (DC) was merged with the city of Washington in 1878. When the government moved to Washington in 1800, the US Capitol and the president's home (later renamed the "White House") were still under construction. Both were burned by the British during the War of 1812.

Nothing has been more divisive in the region's history than the issue of slavery. Many residents were slaveholders; others became ardent abolitionists. As racial tensions escalated, war between the North and the South became inevitable. Over the course of the four-year Civil War (1861–65), many significant battles, including General Robert E. Lee's surrender at Appomattox Court House, took place here. The area was also home to the rival capitals – Washington, DC and Richmond, Virginia.

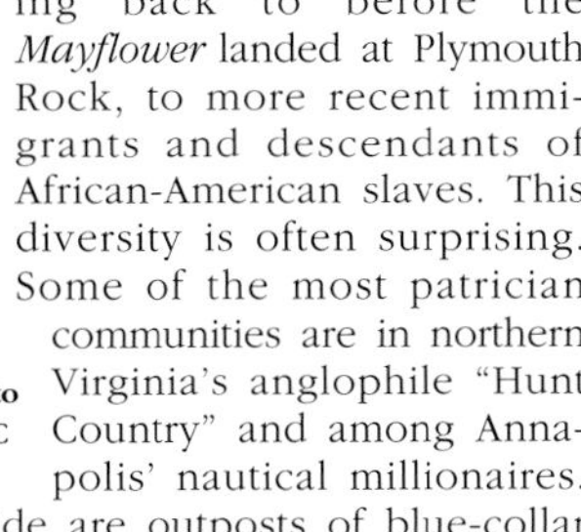

**Cycling, a pleasant way to explore Washington, DC**

Between the 1880s and the 1930s, Washington, DC evolved into the grand city intended by its planners nearly a century before. Wide avenues were opened up, tawdry railroads were removed from the National Mall, and many grand buildings were constructed to house the expanding bureaucracy. Even so, it wasn't until the mid-1900s, with the advent of air conditioning, that the capital became a year-round, world-class city.

**Lee's surrender at Appomattox Court House**

### People & Culture

Washington and the surrounding area reflect less stereotypical aspects of contemporary US. Its residents range from "blue-bloods" with roots reaching back to before the *Mayflower* landed at Plymouth Rock, to more recent immigrants and descendants of African-American slaves. This diversity is often surprising. Some of the most patrician communities are in northern Virginia's anglophile "Hunt Country" and among Annapolis' nautical millionaires. Alongside are outposts of blue-collar industry, and many anachronistic communities, such as the Chesapeake's traditional fisherman ("watermen") villages and the proud holdouts of Appalachian mountain culture, still visible in West Virginia.

Washington itself offers very revealing images of class and character, with its many poor, minority neighborhoods seemingly a world away from the wealthy, mainly white enclave of Georgetown. Even more expressive are the anonymous postwar middle-class suburbs that lie on both sides of the busy "Beltway" surrounding the capital.

From these diverse social strata have emerged many remarkable people. Francis Scott Key composed the national anthem "The Star-Spangled Banner" in Baltimore, while Thurgood Marshall championed Civil Rights as an activist and later as a Supreme Court Justice. Writers include the poet and horror-story creator Edgar Allen Poe, the scholar, editor, and journalist H.L. Mencken, and contemporary novelist Anne Tyler. Singers include Patsy Cline and Ella Fitzgerald, from Virginia, and Baltimore's Billie Holliday and DC native Duke Ellington who made jazz and swing the nation's soundtrack.

# Exploring Washington, DC & the Capital Region

WASHINGTON, DC, the nation's capital, with its magnificent monuments, superb museums, and cosmopolitan flavor, is a favorite destination for tourists. Within easy reach of the capital, the four states of Virginia, West Virginia, Maryland, and Delaware are equally rewarding to explore, offering a varied area of mountains, plains, beaches, and historic towns. Among the region's most popular attractions are the Colonial town of Williamsburg, the scenic splendours of the Shenandoah Valley and the Blue Ridge Parkway, and the unspoiled wilderness of West Virginia. The port city of Baltimore and the tranquil beaches of Delaware also draw many visitors.

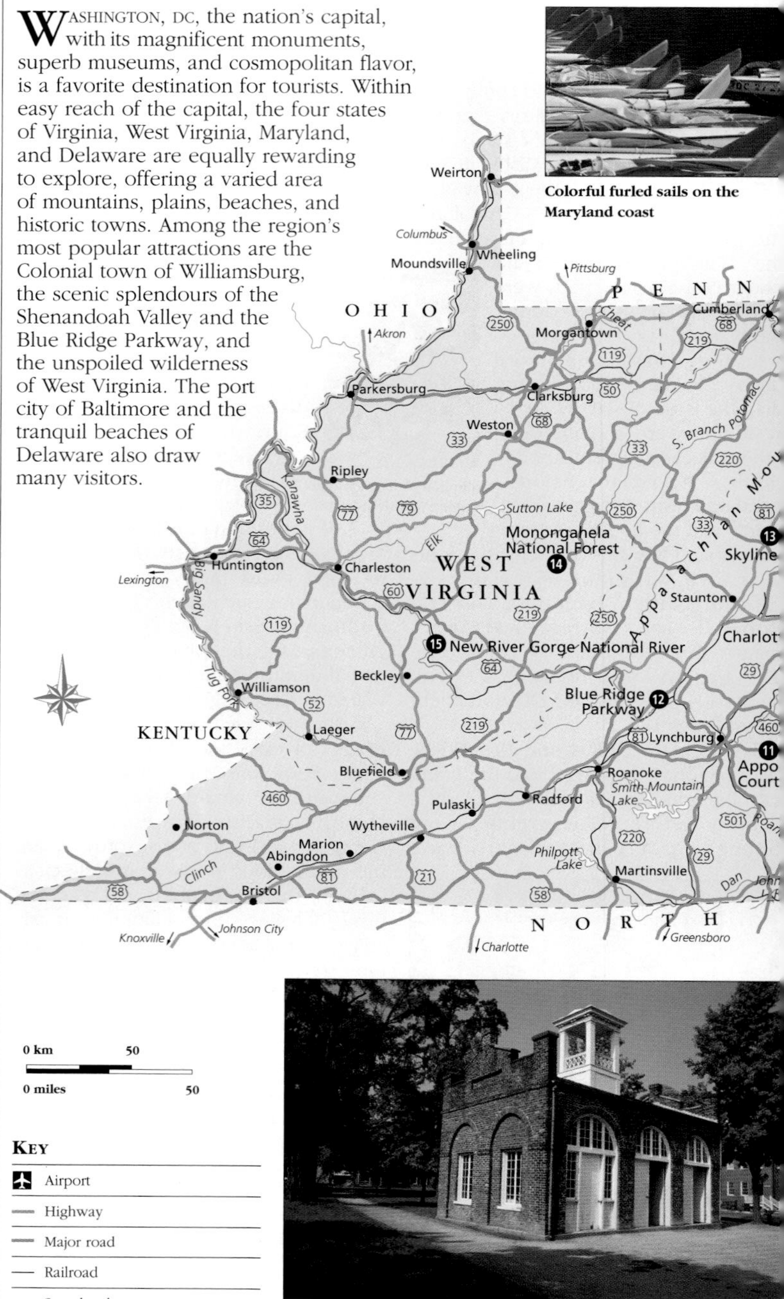


Colorful furled sails on the Maryland coast

John Brown's Fort, Harpers Ferry National Park in West Virginia

0 km 50

0 miles 50

**KEY**

- Airport
- Highway
- Major road
- Railroad
- State border

**SEE ALSO**


- ***Practical Information*** pp228–9
- ***Where to Stay*** pp230–33
- ***Where to Eat*** pp234–7

**The interior of the Oval Office in the White House, Washington, DC**

**MILEAGE CHART**

**10** = Distance in miles
10 = Distance in kilometers

| | WASHINGTON, DC | ALEXANDRIA, VA | RICHMOND, VA | HARPERS FERRY, WV | BALTIMORE, MD | ANNAPOLIS, MD | WILMINGTON, DE |
|---|---|---|---|---|---|---|---|
| ALEXANDRIA, VA | **7** 11 | | | | | | |
| RICHMOND, VA | **107** 172 | **104** 167 | | | | | |
| HARPERS FERRY, WV | **68** 109 | **72** 116 | **166** 267 | | | | |
| BALTIMORE, MD | **46** 74 | **46** 74 | **154** 248 | **67** 108 | | | |
| ANNAPOLIS, MD | **34** 55 | **40** 64 | **142** 228 | **89** 143 | **31** 50 | | |
| WILMINGTON, DE | **109** 175 | **115** 185 | **223** 359 | **141** 227 | **70** 113 | **98** 158 | |
| NEW CASTLE, DE | **108** 174 | **121** 195 | **223** 359 | **140** 225 | **69** 111 | **97** 156 | **6** 10 |

## SIGHTS AT A GLANCE

*Washington, DC pp196–211* 1

**Virginia**
Alexandria 2
*Mount Vernon pp212–13* 3
Fredericksburg 4
*Colonial Williamsburg pp214–15* 5
Jamestown & Yorktown 6
Norfolk 7
Richmond 8
Chincoteague 9
*Charlottesville p217* 10
Appomattox Court House 11
Blue Ridge Parkway 12
*Skyline Drive p219* 13

**West Virginia**
Monongahela National Forest 14
New River Gorge National River 15
Harpers Ferry 16

**Maryland**
Antietam National Battlefield 17
Frederick 18
Baltimore 19
Annapolis 20
North Bay 21
St. Michaels 22
Easton 23
Crisfield 24
Salisbury 25
Ocean City 26

**Delaware**
Wilmington 27
Winterthur 28
Hagley Museum/ Eleutherian Mills 29
Nemours Mansion & Gardens 30
New Castle 31
Lewes 32
Rehoboth Beach 33

# Washington, DC ❶

WASHINGTON, DC COVERS an area of 61 sq miles (158 sq km) and has a population of about 600,000. As the capital of the US and the seat of federal government, it is rich in grand monuments. It also has a vibrant cultural life, with superb museums, most of them free, and an array of entertainments. The city is made up of four quadrants, with the US Capitol at the central point. The northwest quadrant contains most of the tourist sights, with other sights and places of interest located round the Capitol and south of the Mall, in the southwest quadrant.

**Tourists checking their routes at a tourist information kiosk**

## GETTING AROUND

Washington's excellent public transportation system is more convenient than driving a car. Traffic is generally heavy, and parking spaces are limited. All the major tourist attractions in the city are accessible on foot, or by Metrorail, Metrobus, or taxi.

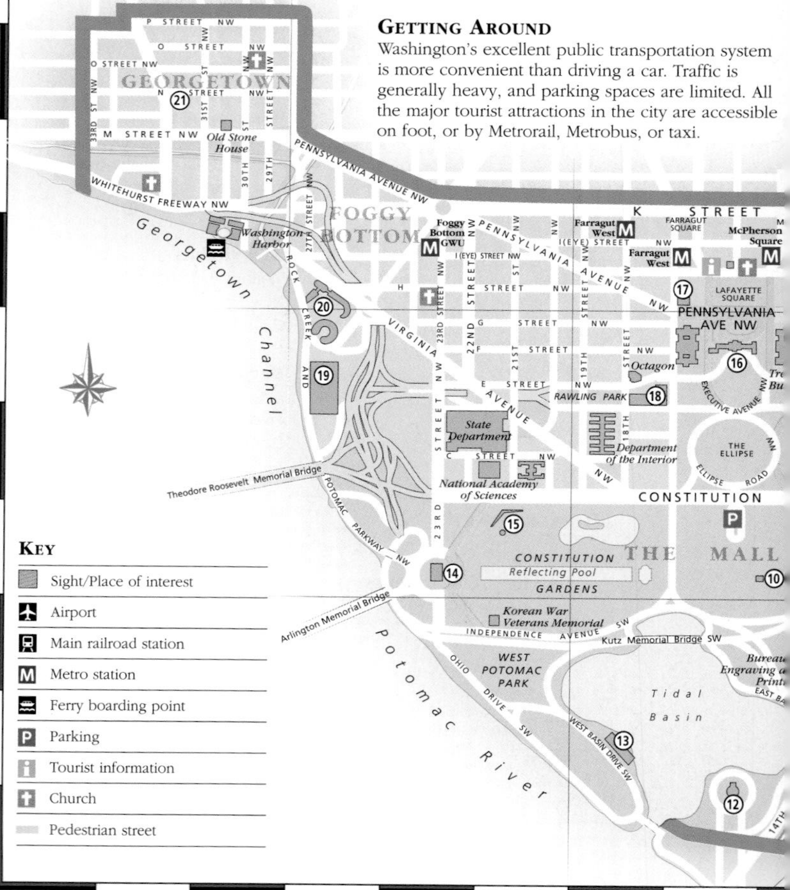

**KEY**

- Sight/Place of interest
- Airport
- Main railroad station
- Metro station
- Ferry boarding point
- Parking
- Tourist information
- Church
- Pedestrian street

## Sights at a Glance

United States Capitol pp198–9 ①
Library of Congress ②
US Supreme Court ③
National Air & Space Museum ④
National Gallery of Art ⑤
National Museum of Natural History ⑥
National Museum of African Art ⑦
National Museum of American History ⑧
Smithsonian American Art Museum & National Portrait Gallery ⑨
Washington Monument ⑩
United States Holocaust Memorial Museum ⑪
Jefferson Memorial ⑫
Franklin D. Roosevelt Memorial ⑬
Lincoln Memorial ⑭
Vietnam Veterans Memorial ⑮
*The White House pp206–207* ⑯
Renwick Gallery ⑰
Corcoran Gallery of Art ⑱
The Kennedy Center ⑲
Watergate Complex ⑳
Georgetown ㉑

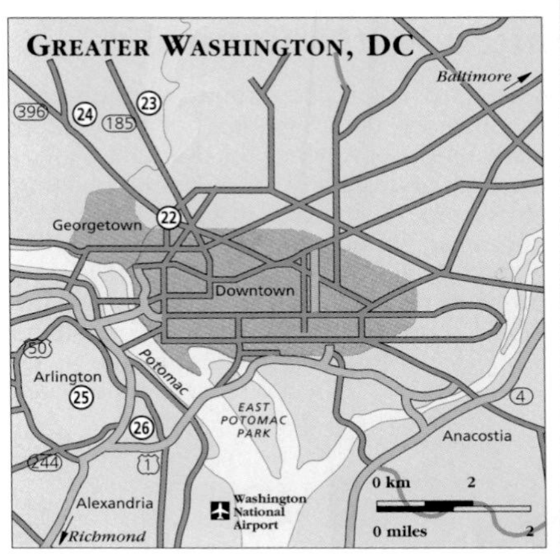

**Key**

Area of main map

**Greater Washington, DC**
***(see inset map)***
Phillips Collection ㉒
National Zoological Park ㉓
Washington National Cathedral ㉔
Arlington National Cemetery ㉕
The Pentagon ㉖

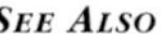

***See Also***

- ***Where to Stay*** pp230–2
- ***Where to Eat*** pp234–6

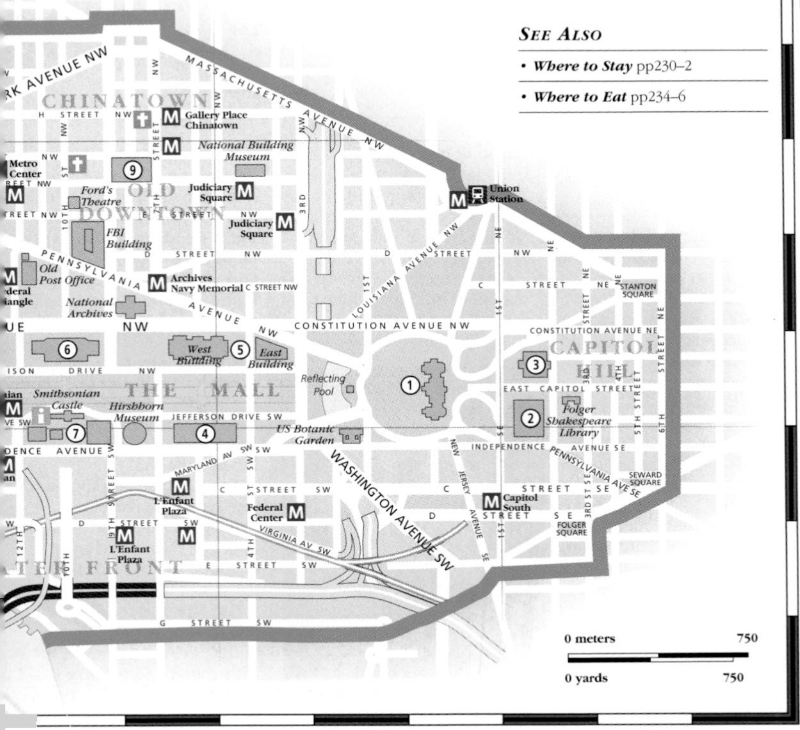

# United States Capitol ①

One of the world's best known symbols of democracy, the US Capitol has been the legislative heart of America for over 200 years. The cornerstone of this grand Neo-Classical building was laid by George Washington in 1793, and by 1800 it was occupied, though unfinished. The British burned the Capitol in the War of 1812, and in 1815 work began on its restoration. Many architectural and artistic features, such as Constantino Brumidi's murals and the Statue of Freedom, were added later.

**★ The Rotunda**
*Completed in 1824, the 180-ft (55-m) Rotunda is capped by* Apotheosis of Washington, *a fresco by Brumidi.*

**US Capitol**
*The Capitol also marks the center of Washington, DC. The city's four quadrants radiate out from the middle of the building.*

**The House Chambers**

**★ National Statuary Hall**
*The statues of two prominent citizens from each state stand in this hall.*

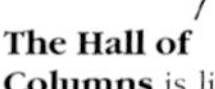

**The Hall of Columns** is lined with statues of notable Americans.

## Library of Congress ②

**Map** F4. 10 1st St, SE. *(202) 707-5000.* *(202) 707-8000.* *Capitol S.* *32, 34, 36, 96.* *10am–5:30pm Mon–Sat.* *federal hols.* *For access to reading rooms, visitors must have a user card. The website or information desk can explain how this can be obtained.* www.loc.gov

The Library of Congress holds the largest collection of books, manuscripts, microfilms, maps, and music in the world. First established in the US Capitol in 1800, the library was destroyed when the Capitol was burned in 1814. Thomas Jefferson then offered his personal collection as a replacement, and from this seed the collection continued to grow. Since 1897, it has been housed in a grand Italian Renaissance-style main building, now known as the Thomas Jefferson Building. In front of it is a fountain with a striking bronze statue of the Roman sea god, Neptune.

One of the highlights of this marvel of art and architecture is the **Great Hall** with its splendid marble arches and columns, grand staircases, bronze statues, rich murals, and stained-glass skylights.

**The Great Hall, with its splendid marble arches and columns**

Equally impressive is the **Main Reading Room**, where eight huge marble columns, and 10-ft (3-m) high female figures, personifying aspects of human endeavor, dwarf the reading desks. The domed ceiling soars to a height of 160 ft (49 m). There are 10 other reading rooms in the Jefferson Building, notably the African and Asian Reading Rooms.

The staircase landing near the Visitors' Gallery, overlooking the Main Reading Room, is dominated by a beautiful marble mosaic figure of Minerva.

The Library's treasures include one of only three perfect vellum copies of the 15th-century Gutenberg Bible, the first book printed using movable metal type.

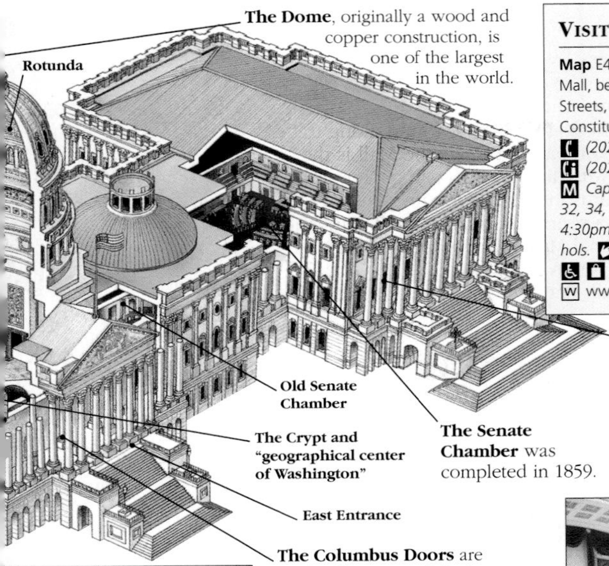

Rotunda

**The Dome**, originally a wood and copper construction, is one of the largest in the world.

**Old Senate Chamber**

**The Crypt and "geographical center of Washington"**

**The Senate Chamber** was completed in 1859.

**The Brumidi Corridors** are lined with frescoes, bronzeworks, and paintings by the Italian artist Constantino Brumidi (1805–80).

**East Entrance**

**The Columbus Doors** are made of bronze and depict Christopher Columbus' life and explorations.

### VISITORS' CHECKLIST

**Map** E4. Independence Mall, between 1st & 3rd Streets, & Independence & Constitution Aves. *(202) 224-3121.* *(202) 225-6827.* *Capitol S, Union Station.* *32, 34, 36, 96.* *9am–4:30pm Mon–Sat.* *federal hols.* *except Sun.* www.aoc.gov

### STAR FEATURES

★ **National Statuary Hall**

★ **Old Senate Chamber**

★ **The Rotunda**

**★ Old Senate Chamber**

*This sumptuous chamber was occupied by the Senate until 1859, and then by the Supreme Court for 75 years. It is now used mainly as museum space.*

## US Supreme Court ③

**Map** F4. 1st St between E Capitol St & Maryland Ave NE. *(202) 479-3000.* *Capitol S.* *9am–4:30pm Mon–Fri.* *federal hols.* ***Lectures.*** www.supremecourtus.gov

THE JUDICIAL BRANCH of the US government and the highest court in the land, the Supreme Court is the last stop in the disposition of the nation's legal disputes and issues of constitutionality. Groundbreaking cases settled here include *Brown v. Board of Education*, which abolished racial segregation in schools, and *Miranda v. Arizona*, which declared that crime suspects were entitled to a lawyer before they were interrogated.

As recently as 1929, the Supreme Court was still meeting in various sections of the US Capitol. Then, at Chief Justice William Howard Taft's urging, Congress authorized a separate building to be constructed. The result was a magnificent Corinthian edifice designed by Cass Gilbert that opened in 1935. Allegorical sculptures depicting the Contemplation of Justice and the Guardian of the Law stand beside the steps.

**The impressive Neo-Classical façade of the US Supreme Court**

The Great Hall that leads to the courtroom is an expanse of marble, lined with columns and the busts of former chief justices. The elegant court chamber itself has a coffered plaster ceiling decorated with gold leaf, and a frieze running around the walls that depicts both real and allegorical legal figures. The exhibit hall has displays on legal systems from around the world and an array of international judges' robes.

Visitors may watch the court in session Monday to Wednesday from October through April. Admission is on a first-come, first-served basis. When the court is not in session, public lectures on the Supreme Court are held every hour in the Courtroom.

# The Mall

THIS BOULEVARD, BETWEEN THE Capitol and the Washington Monument, stretches for 1 mile (1.6 km) and is the city's cultural heart; the many great museums of the Smithsonian Institution can be found along this green strip. At the northeast corner of the Mall is the National Gallery of Art. Directly opposite is one of the most popular museums in the world – the National Air & Space Museum – a soaring construction of glass and steel. Both the National Museum of American History and the National Museum of Natural History, on the north side of the Mall, draw huge numbers of visitors.

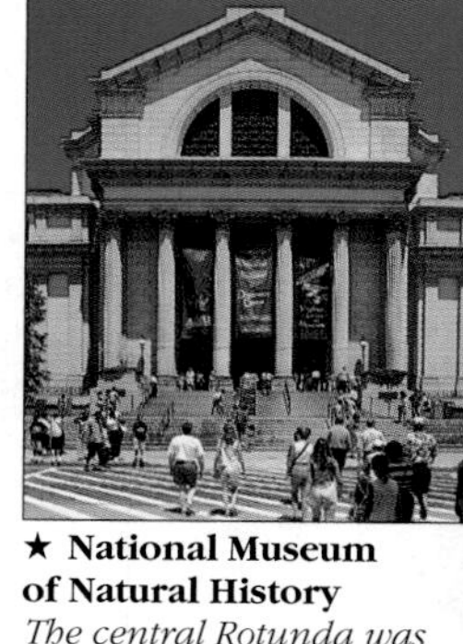

**★ National Museum of Natural History**
*The central Rotunda was designed in the Neo-Classical style and opened to the public in 1910* ⑥

**★ National Museum of American History**
*From George Washington's uniform to this 1940s Tucker Torpedo, US history is documented here* ⑧

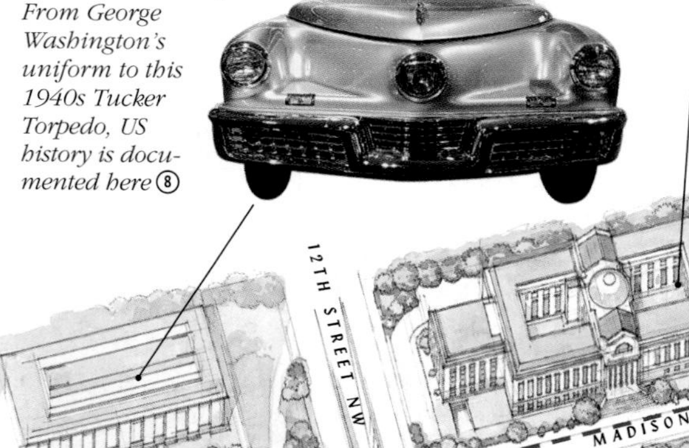


**Smithsonian Castle**, with its elegant Victorian façade, is the main information center for all Smithsonian activities.

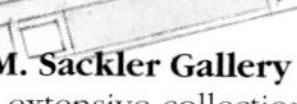


**National Museum of African Art**
*Founded in 1965 and located underground, this museum houses a comprehensive collection of ancient and modern African art* ⑦

**Freer Gallery of Art** displays masterpieces of American and Asian art.

**Arthur M. Sackler Gallery** holds an extensive collection of Asian art, which was donated to the nation by New Yorker Arthur Sackler.

**Arts & Industries Building**, a masterpiece of Victorian architecture, was built to contain exhibits from the Centennial Exposition in Philadelphia.

0 meters 100
0 yards 100

**★ National Gallery of Art**
*This gallery's fine collection of art treasures, such as* The Alba Madonna *(c.1510) by Raphael, chronicle the history of art from the Middle Ages to the 20th century* ⑤

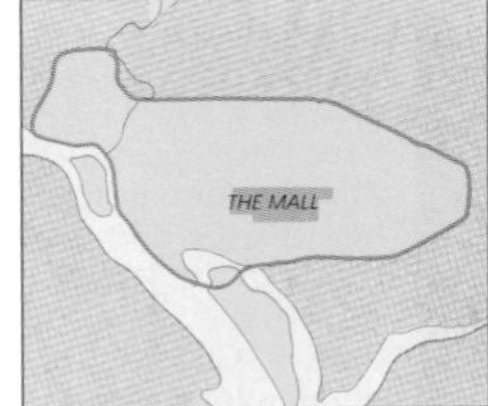


**Locator Map**
*See Map pp196–97*

**Key**

— — — Suggested route

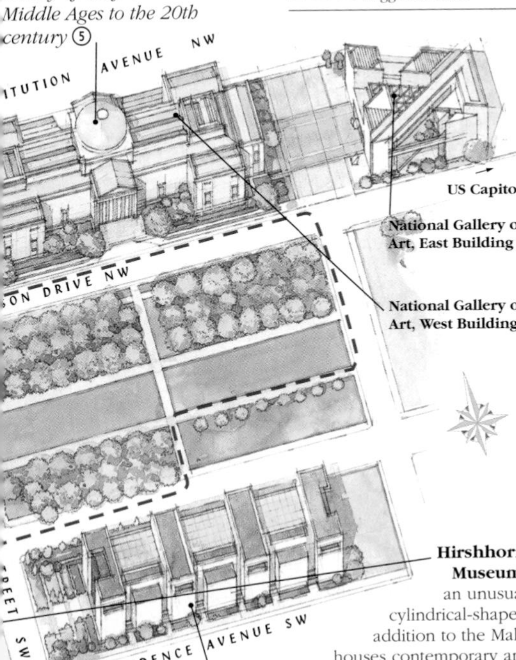


**Hirshhorn Museum**, an unusual cylindrical-shaped addition to the Mall, houses contemporary art. Only a small selection of the 18,000 works it holds is on display at any one time.

**★ National Air & Space Museum**
*The clean, modern design of the National Air & Space Museum echoes the technological marvels on display inside* ④

**Star Sights**

- ★ **National Air & Space Museum**
- ★ **National Gallery of Art**
- ★ **National Museum of American History**
- ★ **National Museum of Natural History**

## National Air & Space Museum ④

**Map** D5. 601 Independence Ave, SW. (202) 633-1000. *Smithsonian.* *32, 34, 36, 52.* *10am–5:30pm daily.* *Dec 25.* *10:15am, 1pm.* www.nasm.si.edu

Opened on America's Bicentennial on July 1, 1976, the Air & Space Museum is today the most visited site in Washington. The museum's entrance leads into the lofty **Milestones of Flight** gallery, which displays many of the firsts in air and space travel. These include the 1903 Wright *Flyer*, the first powered, heavier-than-air machine to achieve controlled, sustained flight, built by the Wright Brothers; the *Spirit of St. Louis*, in which Charles Lindbergh made the first transatlantic solo flight in 1927; and the *Apollo 11* Command Module, which carried astronauts Buzz Aldrin, Neil Armstrong, and Michael Collins on their historic mission to the moon in 1969. Another gallery that attracts crowds is the **Space Hall**, where exhibits include space suits, a working model of the *Columbia* Space Shuttle, and the Skylab, an orbiting workshop for three-person crews.

An eye-catching exhibit in the **Developments in Flight** gallery is the red Lockheed Vega in which Amelia Earhart became the first woman to make a solo transatlantic flight in 1932. The very popular **World War II Aviation** gallery displays fighter aircrafts from the American, British, German, and Japanese air forces.

**Milestones of Flight gallery in the National Air & Space Museum**

The façade of the National Gallery of Art

## National Gallery of Art ⑤

**Map** E4. **West Building** Constitution Ave between 4th & 7th Sts, NW. **East Building** 4th St between Madison Drive & Constitution Ave, NW. *(202) 737-4215. Archives/Navy Memorial, Judiciary Square, Smithsonian. 32, 34, 36, 70. 10am–5pm Mon–Sat, 11am–6pm Sun. Jan 1, Dec 25. call (202) 842-6690. call (202) 842-6176.* www.nga.gov

One of Washington, DC's top attractions, this superb museum was established when American financier Andrew Mellon bequeathed his collection of European art to form the basis of a National Gallery of Art. Spurred on by his example, other collectors left their art to the proposed museum.

Of the two main buildings, the stately Neo-Classical-style West Building, opened in 1941, features European art from the 13th to the 19th centuries. The modern East Building, completed in 1978, features 20th-century art. An underground concourse, with a cafeteria and shops, joins the two buildings.

Matching wings flank a central rotunda in the **West Building**. West of the rotunda are the galleries displaying Italian, Dutch, Flemish, and Spanish art. The Italian paintings include works by Giotto, Botticelli, Raphael and Leonardo da Vinci; and other masterpieces on display include works by Rembrandt, Van Dyck, Rubens, Goya, El Greco, and Velasquez. The sculpture galleries here display decorative arts from the Middle Ages to the 20th century. Galleries east of the rotunda house an outstanding collection of French Impressionist and Post-Impressionist art. Among its highlights are Monet's *Woman with a Parasol,* Degas' *Four Dancers*, and Toulouse-Lautrec's *Quadrille at the Moulin Rouge*. Portraits by John Singer Sargent and James McNeill Whistler are among the gallery's important collection of American paintings. Adjacent to the West Building is a Sculpture Garden, which is transformed into an ice skating rink in winter.

The huge **East Building** is designed to accommodate large pieces of modern art. Centered in its courtyard is a giant red, blue, and black mobile by Alexander Calder, completed in 1976. Near the entrance is a sculpture by Henry Moore; the atrium displays a 1977 tapestry by Joan Miró.

## National Museum of Natural History ⑥

**Map** D4. Constitution Ave & 10th St, NW. *(202) 633-1000 (recorded message after museum hours). Smithsonian. 32, 34, 36. 10am–5:30pm daily. Dec 25. 10:30am & 1:30pm Mon–Fri.* www.nmnh.si.edu

Established in 1910, this vast museum's collection of 120 million artifacts includes samples from the world's diverse cultures, as well as fossils and living creatures from land and sea. The museum's entrance leads into the lofty Rotunda, where visitors are greeted by the impressive sight of a massive African Bush elephant. To the right of the Rotunda is one of the most popular areas of the museum, the newly renovated **Dinosaur Hall**, featuring dinosaur skeletons and eggs, and Ice Age mammals, such as the woolly mammoth. Also on the ground floor are galleries displaying objects from Native American, Asian, and Pacific cultures; don't miss the huge Easter Island stone statues. To the left of the Rotunda is an IMAX® Theater and the Discovery Room, where visitors can handle objects such as crocodile heads and elephant tusks.

On the second floor is the **Gems and Minerals** collection, whose highlight is the 45.52-carat Hope Diamond. The largest deep blue diamond in the world and famed for its stunning color and clarity, it once belonged to Louis XVI of France. Also on the second floor is the highly popular **Insect Zoo**, with its giant hissing cockroaches and large leaf-cutter ant colony.

Dinosaur skeleton in the National Museum of Natural History

## National Museum of African Art ⑦

**Map** D5. 950 Independence Ave, SW. *(202) 357-4600. Smithsonian. 10am–5:30pm daily. Dec 25.* www.si.edu/nmafa

This quiet museum is missed by many visitors, perhaps because much of its exhibition space is underground. The small entrance pavilion at the ground level leads to three subterranean floors where the exhibits are displayed. The 7,000-piece permanent collection includes both modern and ancient art from Africa, although the majority of pieces date from the 19th and 20th centuries. Traditional African bronzes, ceramics, and pottery are on display, as are stunning ivory and gold objects, brightly colored *kente* textiles from Ghana, and photographs.

## National Museum of American History ⑧

**Map** D4. 14th St & Constitution Ave. *(202) 633-1000 (recorded message outside opening hours). Smithsonian–Federal Triangle. 32, 34, 36. 10am–5:30pm daily. Dec 25.* www.americanhistory.si.edu

THIS THREE-STORY museum is a collection of artifacts from America's past. The highlight of the first-floor galleries is the 100-year-old Headsville Post Office from West Virginia, which was dismantled and reassembled here in its entirety in 1971 and is still a working post office. Another popular exhibit on this floor is a *Model T* Ford, an engineering landmark that heralded the beginning of the motor age. Visitors can eat at the **Palm Court**, which has a 1900 candy store and an early 20th-century ice-cream parlor.

Dominating the East Wing of the second floor is the **First Ladies** exhibit, which includes First Ladies' gowns worn to the presidents' inaugural balls. Jackie Kennedy's and Nancy Reagan's haute couture gowns are on display here along with Rosalynn Carter's "off the rack" one. Also on the second floor are the largest single exhibit, **America on the Move**, which offers a look at modes of transport from 1876 to the present. It also includes the Star-Spangled Banner that flew over Fort McHenry in 1814 and inspired the Francis Scott Key poem that later became the US national anthem.

Another big draw on the second floor is the **Hands-On Science Room**, where everything can be touched by hand. Visitors can investigate the conservation of the Star-Spangled Banner, unravel some of the mysteries of DNA, or measure radioactive hot

**Ford's *Model T*, in the National Museum of American History**

spots. On the third floor, the **American Presidency** displays objects that represent the lives and offices of the presidency in 11 themed sections. American popular culture exhibits include the ruby slippers worn by Judy Garland in *The Wizard of Oz*.

## Smithsonian American Art Museum & National Portrait Gallery ⑨

**Map** D4. **Smithsonian American Art Museum** 8th & G Sts NW. *(202) 638-1000.* www.americanart.si.edu
**National Portrait Gallery** 8th & F Sts NW. *(202) 633-1000. Gallery Place–Chinatown.* www.npg.si.edu

NOWHERE IN Washington is the city's penchant to copy Greek and Roman architecture more obvious than in the former US Patent Office building, now the home of the Smithsonian American Art Museum and the National Portrait Gallery. The Patent Office was converted into the twin museums in 1968, and was recently renovated. The art museum contains a wealth of works by American artists, reflecting the history and culture of the country. The highlight of the American folk art collection is an amazing piece of visionary art called *Throne of the Third Heaven of the Nations' Millenium* (c.1950–64), created out of light bulbs, silver and gold foil, and old furniture by a Washington janitor by the name of James Hampton. Among the 19th- and early 20th-century works, the Western landscapes by Thomas Moran stand out. Especially dramatic is his *Cliffs of the Upper Colorado River*, painted in 1882, which captures the vastness of the American West. Another outstanding work from this period is *Achelous and Hercules* by Thomas Hart Benton (1889–1975). In this mythical analogy of early American life, Hercules symbolizes man taming the wild and then enjoying the fruits of his labor. Works by Modernists Jasper Johns, Andy Warhol, and Robert Rauschenberg are among the other treasures of this museum.

The National Portrait Gallery is America's family album, featuring paintings, sculptures, etchings, and photographs of thousands of famous Americans. Assembled here are such diverse works as Gilbert Stuart's famous portrait of George Washington (which features on the one-dollar bill), busts of Dr. Martin Luther King Jr. and the poet T.S. Eliot, and some recently acquired photographs of actress Marilyn Monroe.

***George Washington* by Gilbert Stuart**

## Washington Monument ⑩

**Map** C4. Independence Ave at 17th St, SW. *(202) 426-6841.* *Smithsonian.* *13, 52.* *early Sep–early Apr: 9am–4:45pm; early Apr–early Sep: 9am–11:30pm.* *Dec 25.* ***Interpretive talks.*** www.nps.gov/wamo

CONSTRUCTED from 36,000 pieces of marble and granite, the 555-ft (170-m) tall Washington Monument is one of the capital's most recognizable landmarks, clearly visible from almost all over the city. Conceived of as a tribute to the first president of the US, its construction began in 1848, but stopped in 1858 when funds ran out. The building work resumed in 1876 after public interest in the project revived – a slight change in the color of the stone indicates the point at which construction stopped and then began again. The original design included a circular colonnade around the monument, but lack of funds prevented its construction.

Recently renovated and cleaned to a gleaming white, the monument has a capstone weighing 3,300 pounds (2,000 kg). It is topped by an aluminum pyramid, and surrounded by 50 flagpoles. Inside the monument are 192 commemorative stones, donated by individuals, states, societies, and nations. There are stunning views across the city from the top.

**Washington Monument, which dominates the city skyline**

**The soaring Hall of Witness in the US Holocaust Memorial Museum**

## United States Holocaust Memorial Museum ⑪

**Map** C5. 100 Raoul Wallenberg Place, SW. *(202) 488-0400.* *Smithsonian.* *13 (Pentagon shuttle).* *mid-Jun–Mar: 10am–5:30pm daily; Apr–mid-Jun: 10am–5:30pm daily (to 8pm Tue & Thu).* *Dec 25 & Yom Kippur. Time pass required for permanent exhibit. Advance passes: (800) 400-9373.* www.ushmm.org

OPENED IN 1993, the US Holocaust Memorial Museum bears witness to the systematic persecution and annihilation in Europe of six million Jews and others deemed undesirable by the Third Reich. The museum is meant to be experienced, not just seen. Within the exhibition space, which ranges from the intentionally claustrophobic to the soaringly majestic, are thousands of photographs and artifacts, 53 video monitors, and 30 interactive stations that contain graphic and emotionally disturbing images of violence, forcing visitors to confront the horror of the Holocaust.

Starting from the top, the fourth floor documents the early years of the Nazi regime, with exhibits exposing their ruthless persecution of Jews. The third floor exhibits are devoted to the "Final Solution," the killing of six million "undesirable" people. Artifacts include a box car that carried prisoners to concentration camps.

On the second floor is the **Hall of Remembrance**, which houses an eternal flame that pays homage to the victims of the Holocaust. The soaring central atrium on the first floor, the **Hall of Witness** features temporary exhibits. On the same floor is a poignant exhibit called **Daniel's Story**, aimed at children. It tells the story of the Holocaust from the point of view of an eight-year-old Jewish boy living in 1930s Germany.

At the Concourse Level is the **Children's Tile Wall**. Over 3,000 tiles, painted by children, constitute this moving memorial to the one-and-a-half million children murdered in the Holocaust.

## Jefferson Memorial ⑫

**Map** C5. S bank of the Tidal Basin. *(202) 426-6841.* *Smithsonian.* *8am–midnight.* *Dec 25.* ***Interpretive talks.*** www.nps.gov/thje

WHEN THIS Neo-Classical-style memorial to the third US president, Thomas Jefferson (1743–1826), was completed in 1943, critics gave it the derisive nickname "Jefferson's Muffin." It was dismissed as far too "feminine" for so bold and influential a man who had played a significant part in drafting the Declaration of Independence in 1776. The dome of this round, colonnaded building covers a majestic 19-ft (6-m) statue of Jefferson. The statue was originally cast in plaster since metal was rationed when the building was dedicated in 1943. It was recast in bronze after the end of World War II, and the plaster version is now in the basement of the building. Etched on the walls are Jefferson's words from the Declaration of Independence. Legend says that the architects

**Majestic statue of Jefferson**

**The colonnaded domed Jefferson Memorial, housing the bronze statue**

are said to have purposely misquoted and mispelled these words (they claimed because of lack of space).

Jefferson Memorial stands on the banks of the scenic **Tidal Basin**, built in 1897 to catch the overflow from the Potomac River. In the 1920s, hundreds of Japanese cherry trees were planted along its shores, and the sight of the trees in bloom is one of the most photographed in the city. Peak blooming time is for two weeks, between mid-March and mid-April. Rental paddle-boats are available at the Tidal Basin.

## Franklin D. Roosevelt Memorial ⑬

**Map** C5. W Basin Dr, SW. *(202) 426-6841.* M *Smithsonian.* *13.* *8am–midnight daily.* *Dec 25.* ***Interpretive programs & talks.*** W www.nps.gov/fdrm

THE MEMORIAL to President Franklin D. Roosevelt, opened in 1997, is a mammoth park of four granite open-air rooms, one for each of Roosevelt's terms *(see p49)*. The first room has the visitor center, and a bas-relief of Roosevelt's first inaugural parade. In the second room is a sculpture titled *Hunger*, recalling the hard times of the Great Depression. A controversial statue of Roosevelt in the third room of this open air park shows the disabled president sitting in a wheelchair hidden by his Navy cape.

Dramatic waterfalls cascade into a series of pools in the fourth room, which also has a statue of Roosevelt's wife, Eleanor, and a relief of his funeral cortege carved into the granite wall. The water symbolizes the peace that Roosevelt was so eager to achieve before his death.

## Lincoln Memorial ⑭

**Map** B4. Constitution Ave, between French & Bacon Drs. *(202) 426-6841.* M *Smithsonian.* *8am–midnight daily.* *on request.* W www.nps.gov/linc

THE LINCOLN MEMORIAL is one of Washington's most awe-inspiring sights, with the seated figure of President Abraham Lincoln in his Neo-Classical "temple," looming over a reflecting pool.

The site chosen for the monument was a swamp, and before building could begin in 1914 it had to be drained. Concrete piers were poured for the foundation so that the building could be anchored in bedrock. As the memorial neared completion, architect Henry Bacon realized that the statue of Lincoln would be dwarfed inside the huge edifice. The original 10-ft (3-m) statue by Daniel Chester French was doubled in size and carved from 28 blocks of white marble. Engraved on the wall are the words of Lincoln's famous Gettysburg Address *(see p106)*.

In 1963, the memorial was the site of a mammoth gathering of 200,000 people in support of Civil Rights, where Dr. Martin Luther King Jr. made his historic "I have a Dream" speech. A direct result of this speech was the passing by Congress of Civil Rights legislation in 1964.

## Vietnam Veterans Memorial ⑮

**Map** B4. 21st St & Constitution Ave, NW. *(202) 426-6841.* M *Smithsonian.* *8am–midnight daily.* *on request.* W www.nps.gov/vive

POWERFUL IN ITS symbolism and dramatic in its simplicity, this memorial was designed by Maya Lin, then a 21-year-old student at Yale University, whose design was selected from 1,421 entries. Dedicated in 1982, it consists of two triangular black walls, set into the earth at an angle of 125 degrees, one end pointing to the Lincoln Memorial and the other to the Washington Monument. The walls are inscribed with the names of the Americans who died in the Vietnam War, in chronological order from 1959 to 1975. The site is covered by tokens of remembrance placed by veterans and their families – poems, pictures, toys, and flowers – making this one of the most moving memorials on the Mall. A more conventional memorial was added in 1984 – a statue of three soldiers.

**The Lincoln Memorial, one of Washington's most visited monuments**

# The White House ⑯

THE OFFICIAL RESIDENCE OF the president, the White House was designed by Irish-born architect James Hoban. Known as the Executive Mansion, it was first occupied in 1800 by President John Adams. Burned by the British in 1814, the partially rebuilt edifice was reoccupied in 1817. In 1901, President Theodore Roosevelt renamed the building the White House and ordered the West Wing to be built. The East Wing was added in 1942, completing the building as it is today. Beautifully decorated with period furniture, valuable antiques, and paintings, the White House attracts more than a million and a half visitors every year.

**The White House**
*The official residence of the US president for 200 years, the White House façade is familiar to millions of people around the world.*

**★ State Dining Room**
*Able to seat as many as 140 people, the State Dining Room was enlarged in 1902. A portrait of President Abraham Lincoln, by George P.A. Healy, hangs above the mantel.*

**The West Terrace** leads to the West Wing and the Oval Office, the president's official office.

**★ Red Room**
*One of four reception rooms, the Red Room is furnished in red in the Empire Style (1810–30). The fabrics were woven in the US from French designs.*

**The stonework** has been painted over and over to maintain the building's white façade.

**STAR ROOMS**

- ★ **Red Room**
- ★ **State Dining Room**
- ★ **Vermeil Room**

**Lincoln Bedroom**
*President Lincoln used this room as his Cabinet Room, then turned it into a bedroom, furnishing it with Lincoln-era decor. Today it is used as a guest room.*

### Visitors' Checklist

**Map** C4. 1600 Pennsylvania Ave, NW. *10–11am Tue–Sat only for groups with Congressional or embassy appointments. Contact Visitor Center for information.* *federal hols & official functions.* *obligatory.* www.nps.gov **White House Visitor Center** 1450 Pennsylvania Ave, NW. *(202) 208-1631.* *Federal Triangle.* *7:30am–4pm daily.* *Jan 1, Thanksgiving, Dec 25.* www.nps.gov/whho

**The East Terrace** leads to the East Wing.

**The East Room** is used for large gatherings, such as dances and concerts.

**Treaty Room**

**The Green Room** was first used as a guest room before Thomas Jefferson turned it into a dining room.

**★ Vermeil Room**
*This yellow room houses seven paintings of First Ladies, including this portrait of Eleanor Roosevelt by Douglas Chandor.*

**Blue Room**

**Diplomatic Reception**
*This room is used to welcome friends and ambassadors. It is elegantly furnished in the Federal Period style (1790–1820).*

### The White House Visitor Center

The Visitor Center has interesting exhibits about the history of the White House as well as royal gifts on display. There are also seasonal lectures by famous speakers on aspects of history in and out of the White House. The center has a monthly Living History program with actors portraying historic figures. The gift shop carries an extensive range, including the annual White House Christmas ornament. Tours of the president's official residence in the White House are extremely limited at this time. Guided tours can be booked only by special arrangement through a member of Congress or an embassy.

**Façade of the Visitor Center**

**The magnificent Renwick Gallery, a fine example of French Empire style**

## Renwick Gallery ⑰

**Map** C4. Pennsylvania Ave at 17th St, NW. *(202) 633-1000.* *Farragut W.* *10am–5:30pm daily.* *Dec 25.* *noon Mon–Fri.* www.americanart.si.edu

THIS MAGNIFICENT red-brick building was designed by James Renwick in 1859. It originally housed the art collection of William Wilson Corcoran until it was moved to the current Corcoran Gallery of Art in 1897.

After efforts by First Lady Jacqueline Kennedy saved the building from destruction, it was bought by the Smithsonian. Refurbished and renamed, the Renwick Gallery opened in 1972. It is dedicated primarily to 20th-century American crafts and houses some impressive exhibits in every material including clay, glass, and metal. *Gamefish* (1988) by Larry Fuente is a stunning example of mixed media art.

## Corcoran Gallery of Art ⑱

**Map** C4. 500 17th St, NW. *(202) 639-1700.* *Farragut W, Farragut N.* *10am–5pm Mon–Wed, 10am–9pm Thu (except Thanksgiving).* *Dec 25, Jan 1.* www.corcoran.edu

A TREASURE TROVE of fine art, this privately funded collection was founded by William Wilson Corcoran, a banker. His collection soon outgrew its original home in the Renwick Gallery and moved to this massive edifice in 1897. Many of the European works were added in 1925 by art collector and US Senator William A. Clark. The gallery's masterpieces now include 16th-century paintings by Titian, 17th-century works by Rembrandt, and 19th-century Impressionist paintings by Monet and Renoir. It also has the largest collection of paintings by Jean-Baptist Camille Corot outside France, and fine examples of African-American art. Paintings from the 20th century include works by Picasso, John Singer Sargent, and de Kooning. Every Sunday, a gospel brunch takes place in the beautiful atrium, with live music.

**Lion Statue, guarding the Corcoran Gallery**

## The Kennedy Center ⑲

**Map** B4. New Hampshire Ave & Rock Creek Pkwy, NW. *(202) 467-4600, (800) 444-1324.* *Foggy Bottom.* *80.* *10am–9pm daily; 10am–9pm Mon–Sat, noon–9pm Sun & hols (box office).* *10am–5pm Mon–Fri, 10am–1pm Sat–Sun (call 416-8340).* www.kennedy-center.org

IN 1958, President Eisenhower signed an act to begin fund-raising for a national cultural center that would attract the world's best opera, music, and dance companies to the US capital. His successor, John F. Kennedy, was also an ardent supporter and fund-raiser for this project but he was assassinated before the completion of the center, which was named in his honor.

Designed by Edward Durrell Stone, the center opened in 1971. The **Grand Foyer**, adorned with a remarkable bronze bust of Kennedy by sculptor Robert Berks, stretches 630 ft (192 m) and provides an impressive entrance to the three main theaters of this vast arts complex. In front of the foyer is the **JFK Terrace**, which runs the length of the center and offers glorious views of the Potomac River.

Of the three huge theaters, the **Eisenhower Theater**, with a bronze bust of Eisenhower, is at one end of the foyer. At the other end is the **Concert Hall**, which seats 2,450 people and is the home of the National Symphony Orchestra. Between them is the sumptuous **Opera House**, hung with an enormous crystal chandelier, and with seating for 2,300 people. The Opera House is flanked by the **Hall of States**, with the flags of each of the 50 American states, and the **Hall of Nations**, with the flags of every country with which the US has diplomatic relations.

**The impressive Grand Foyer of the Kennedy Center**

## Watergate Complex ⑳

**Map** B3. Virginia Ave between Rock Creek Pkwy & New Hampshire Ave, NW. **M** *Foggy Bottom-GWU.* ♿

LOCATED NEXT to the Kennedy Center on the banks of the Potomac, the four rounded buildings that make up the Watergate Complex were completed in 1971 and designed to contain apartments, offices, and shops. The Watergate soon became one of Washington's most desirable addresses. In 1972, however, the complex found itself at the center of international news. Burglars, linked to President Nixon, broke into the offices of the Democratic Party headquarters in the complex to bug the telephones there, sparking off a major political scandal. Investigations by *Washington Post* reporters Bob Woodward and Carl Bernstein uncovered the extent of the president's involvement through incriminating tapes and proven bribery. This led to an impeachment hearing, but before Mr. Nixon could be impeached, he resigned. Vice-President Gerald Ford succeeded him.

## Georgetown ㉑

**Map** A3. **Old Stone House** 3051 M St, NW. ☎ *(202) 426-6851.* ◯ *phone ahead.* 🚌 *30, 32, 34, 36, 38.* ♿ W www.nps.gov/olst **Georgetown University** 37th & O Sts, NW. ☎ *(202) 687-0100.* ◯ *varies.* *call 687-3600 for details.* ♿ W www.georgetown.edu **Dumbarton Oaks** 1703 32nd St, NW. ☎ *(202) 339-6401.* ♿ *house only.* W www.doaks.org

GEORGETOWN developed well before Washington, DC. Native Americans had a settlement here, and by the mid-18th century Georgetown had a substantial population of immigrants from Scotland. With the construction of Washington Harbor and the Chesapeake and Ohio Canal in 1828, it soon grew into a wealthy port.

**The picturesque Old Stone House in Georgetown, built in 1765**

Today one of Washington, DC's most attractive neighborhoods, Georgetown is lined with elegant townhouses, many of them converted into upscale bars, restaurants, and boutiques. The two main business streets of the area are Wisconsin Avenue and M Street. On the latter is the historic **Old Stone House** (built in 1765), which may be the only building in Washington that predates the American Revolution. N Street, lined with historic buildings, has an array of 18th-century Federal-style mansions, as well as some fine Victorian townhouses. The 1794 Thomas **Beall House** (number 3017), is where Jackie Kennedy lived for a year after JFK's death.

More Federal houses can be seen lining the banks of the **Chesapeake and Ohio Canal**, which was built in 1828 and runs for 184 miles (296 km) from Georgetown to Cumberland, Maryland. The canal, with its ingenious transportation system of locks, aqueducts, and tunnels, fell out of use with the arrival of the railroad in the 19th century. It is now a protected national park, offering many recreational facilities. Park rangers in period costume guide tours of the canal in mule-drawn barges, and boating is also popular, especially between Georgetown and Violette's Lock – the first 22 miles (35 km) of the canal. The tow-path along the canal is ideal for walks and bike rides.

**The Riggs National Bank, on Wisconsin Avenue in Georgetown**

A major center of activity in this district is **Georgetown University**, founded in 1789. Among the historic buildings on its campus is the Gothic-inspired Healy Building, topped by a fanciful spiral.

Sprawling over 22 acres (9 ha) of land in Georgetown is the historic **Dumbarton Oaks** estate. Its superbly landscaped gardens surround a grand Federal-style brick mansion, which houses a priceless art collection assembled by pharmaceutical heirs Robert and Mildred Bliss.

The historic Dumbarton Oaks Conference, attended by President Franklin Roosevelt and British Prime Minister Winston Churchill, was held in the music room of this house in 1944, laying the groundwork for the establishment of the United Nations.

The Blisses donated the house to Harvard University, and it now houses a library, research institution, and museum, the highlight of which is its superb collection of Byzantine art. A new wing of the house, designed by Philip Johnson, houses pre-Columbian masks, gold jewelry from Central America, frescoes, and Aztec carvings.

**Auguste Renoir's masterpiece, *The Luncheon of the Boating Party* (1881)**

## Phillips Collection ㉒

1600 21st St at Q St, NW. (202) 387-2151. Dupont Circle. 10am–5pm Tue–Wed & Fri–Sat, 10am–8:30pm Thu, noon–5pm Sun. Mon, Jan 1, Jul 4, Thanksg., Dec 25. 2pm Wed & Sat. www.phillipscollection.org

This is one of the finest collections of Impressionist art in the world, and the first museum in the US devoted to modern art of the 19th and 20th centuries. Housed in the beautiful 1897 Georgian Revival mansion of the collection's founders, Marjorie and Duncan Phillips, this museum has a more intimate and personal ambience than the larger Smithsonian art museums.

Among the wonderful selection of Impressionist and Post-Impressionist works on display are *Dancers at the Barre* by Degas, *Self-Portrait* by Cezanne, *Entrance to the Public Gardens at Arles* by Van Gogh, and Renoir's masterpiece, *The Luncheon of the Boating Party* (1881).

Other great paintings in the collection include El Greco's *The Repentant Saint Peter* (1600), *The Blue Room* (1901) by Picasso, Piet Mondrian's *Composition No III* (1921–25), and *Ochre on Red* (1954) by Mark Rothko.

The museum hosts a number of special events, such as gallery talks, film retrospectives, and live jazz concerts. Especially popular are its Sunday afternoon concerts, staged in the Music Room, with performances by classical artists of world renown. These popular concerts are free to anyone who has purchased a ticket for the gallery on that day.

## National Zoological Park ㉓

3001 Connecticut Ave, NW. (202) 673-4800. Cleveland Park, Woodley Park-Zoo. Apr–Oct: 10am–6pm daily (buildings), 6am–8pm daily (grounds); Oct–Apr: 10am–4:30pm daily (buildings), 6am–6pm daily (grounds). Dec 25. call (202) 673-4671. www.natzoo.si.edu/

Located in a sprawling 163-acre (66-ha) park designed by Frederick Law Olmsted (the landscape designer of New York's Central Park), the National Zoo was established in 1887. Since 1964 it has been part of the Smithsonian Institution, which has developed it as a dynamic "biopark" where animals are studied in environments that replicate their natural habitats.

**The Komodo dragon, a rare lizard in the National Zoological Park**

The zoo's most famous residents are a pair of giant pandas, Mei Xiang and Tian Tian, who can be seen playing and roaming around the large trees, pools, and air-conditioned outdoor grottos in the **Giant Panda Exhibit**.

Equally popular with visitors is the **Great Ape House**, which houses lowland gorillas, each weighing around 400 lbs (180 kg), and arboreal orangutans.

The **Reptile Discovery Center** features the rare Komodo dragons, lizards that can grow up to a length of 10 ft (3 m) and weigh up to 200 lbs (90 kg).

In **Amazonia**, which re-creates the lush green Amazonian habitat, visitors can see poison arrow frogs and giant catfish, while the **Prairie Exhibit** houses prairie dogs and bisons.

Other rare creatures include the endangered Golden Lion Tamarins and red wolves.

## Washington National Cathedral ㉔

Massachusetts & Wisconsin Aves, NW. (202) 537-6200. (202) 364-6616. 32, 34, 36. 10am–5:30pm Mon–Sat, 12:30–4pm Sun. group reservations call 537-6207. noon Mon–Sat, hourly 8am–11am & 4pm & 6:30pm Sun, 5:30pm Mon–Fri, 4pm Sat & Sun. www.nationalcathedral.org/

The building of the Church of St. Peter and St. Paul (its official name) was financed entirely by donations. It is the world's sixth largest cathedral, measuring 518 ft (158 m) in length and 301 ft (95 m) from grade to the top of the central tower. It uses building techniques of the Gothic style of architecture, evident in the pointed arches, rib vaulting, stained-glass windows, and exterior flying buttresses. Inside, sculpture, needlework, wrought iron, and wood carving depict the nation's history and biblical scenes.

Above the west entrance is a splendid relief of *The*

**Gothic-style architecture of the Washington National Cathedral**

*Creation* by Frederick Hart, which depicts mankind being formed from chaos. The pinnacles on the Cathedral towers are decorated with leaf-shaped ornaments. Above the south entrance is an exquisite stained-glass **Rose Window**, while in the nave another stained-glass window commemorates the *Apollo 11* space flight and contains a sliver of moon rock. The **High Altar** has carvings of 110 figures surrounding the central statue of Christ. The floor in front of the altar has stone from Mount Sinai. By the **Children's Chapel**, built to the scale of a six-year-old, is a statue of Jesus as a boy.

***The Creation*, National Cathedral**

## Arlington National Cemetery ㉕

Arlington, VA. *(703) 697-9486.* M *Arlington National Cemetery.* *Oct–Mar: 8am–5pm daily; Apr–Sep: 8am–6:30pm daily.* *Dec 25.*

A SEA OF simple headstones covers Arlington National Cemetery, marking the graves of around 280,000 American servicemen killed in the nation's major conflicts – from the Revolution to the September 11 terrorist attack. The focus of the cemetery, which sprawls over 624 acres (252 ha) of a hillside, is the **Tomb of the Unknowns**, honoring the thousands whose bodies were never found or identified. Its four vaults are for soldiers from World Wars I and II, Korea, and Vietnam. Each vault held one unidentified soldier until recently, when the Vietnam soldier was identified by DNA analysis and reburied in his hometown. Near it is the **Memorial Amphitheater**, which has hosted many state funerals, and where annual services are held on Memorial Day.

North of the Tomb of the Unknowns, an eternal flame burns at the **Grave of John F. Kennedy**, lit by his wife Jacqueline on the day of his funeral in December 1963. She and their son John Jr. are buried next to the late president, as is his brother Robert F. Kennedy. Close to the Kennedy graves is the imposing **Tomb of Pierre L'Enfant**, the French architect responsible for planning the city of Washington. The cemetery also houses poignant memorials to the victims of the Lockerbie air crash and the *Challenger* Space Shuttle, which exploded seconds after take-off in January 1986.

The grand Georgian-Revival mansion at the top of the hill, above the Kennedy graves, is **Arlington House**, which was the home of the Confederate general Robert E. Lee (1807–70). When Lee left his home in 1861 to lead Virginia's armed forces during the Civil War, the Union confiscated the estate for a military cemetery. The house, now a memorial to the general, is open to visitors.

## The Pentagon ㉖

1000 Defense Pentagon, Hwy 1-395, Arlington, VA. *(703) 695-1776.* M *Pentagon.* *tours by appointment only. For details call the above number.* W www.defenselink.mil

THE WORLD'S largest office building, the Pentagon is almost a city in itself. This enormous edifice houses 23,000 people who work for the US Department of Defense, which includes the Army, Navy, and Airforce, and 14 other defense agencies. Despite its enormous size – it has 17.5 miles (28 km) of corridors, and the entire US Capitol could fit into one of its five wedge-shaped sections – the building's efficient design ensures that it takes no more than seven minutes to walk between any two points in the Pentagon. Designed by army engineers, it is built from sand and gravel dredged from the Potomac and molded into concrete. The building was started in September 1941, and completed in January 1943 at a cost of $83 million.

The headquarters of the US military establishment and the ultimate symbol of America's military might, the Pentagon was one of the targets of terrorists who flew a hijacked American Airlines plane into one side of the building on September 11, 2001, killing 189 people. It has now been completely restored.

**Uniform rows of headstones in Arlington National Cemetery**

# Virginia

THERE IS ENOUGH HISTORY and natural beauty in Virginia to satisfy the most avid sightseer. Mount Vernon, the perfectly preserved home of President George Washington, is close to Washington, DC. In eastern Virginia is the old capital, Williamsburg, a living museum of the Colonial era. To its west, the Skyline Drive reveals the spectacular beauty of the Shenandoah National Park and the Blue Ridge Mountains. The state capital, Richmond, retains a charming Old South aura.

## Alexandria ❷

*119,000.* *Union Station, 110 Callahan St.* *King Street.* *Ramsay House Visitor Center, 221 King St (703) 838-4200.* www.funside.com

OLD TOWN Alexandria has kept a special historical flavor, dating back to its incorporation in 1749. Accessible by Metro from Washington, Alexandria is still a busy port, with its lively Market Square. Its tree-lined streets are filled with elegant, historic buildings, among them the 1753 **Carlyle House**, a Georgian Palladian mansion on Fairfax Street. A guided tour of the house, now beautifully restored, provides fascinating details about 18th-century everday life. On the same street is the **Stabler Leadbeater Apothecary Shop**, established in 1792. When it closed in 1933, the doors were locked with all its contents intact. Now reopened as a museum, the shop's 8,000 original objects include huge mortars and pestles, and jars of herbal remedies.

**Façade of the elegant Carlyle House, built in 1752, Alexandria**

The **Boyhood Home of Robert E. Lee**, a Federal townhouse where General Lee *(see 193)* lived from the age of 11 until he went to the West Point Military Academy, is currently a private residence and not open to the public. The **Lee-Fendall House Museum** nearby is rich with artifacts from the Revolution to the 1930s Labor Movement. To its south is the 1773 **Christ Church**, a Georgian edifice where George Washington's pew is still preserved with his nameplate, as is that of Robert E. Lee.

On Union Street is the **Torpedo Factory Art Center**, displaying the work

## Mount Vernon ❸

THIS COUNTRY ESTATE on the Potomac River was George Washington's home for 45 years. The house is furnished as it would have been during Washington's presidency (1789–97), and the 500-acre (202-ha) grounds still retain aspects of the original farm, such as the flower and vegetable gardens, the sheep paddock, and quarters for the slaves who worked the plantation.

**The Upper Garden**
*The plants in this colorful garden replicate those grown in Washington's time.*

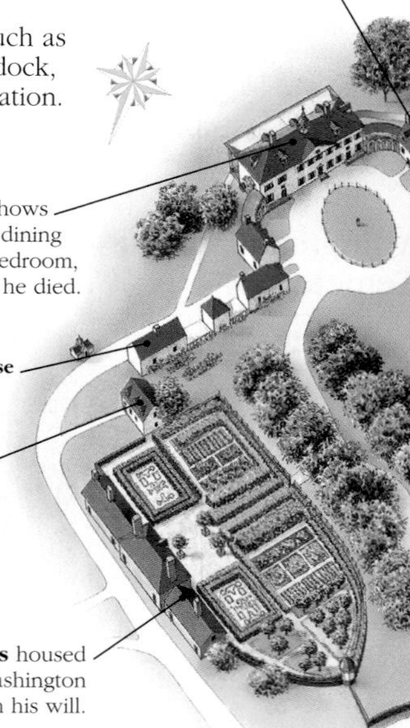

**The Kitchen**, set slightly apart from the main house, has been completely restored.

**The Mansion Tour** shows visitors the study and dining room, Washington's bedroom, and the bed in which he died.

**Overseer's House**

**The Museum** displays belongings of George and Martha Washington.

**The Slave Quarters** housed the estate's slaves. Washington freed all his slaves in his will.

of local artists and craftsmen. From the nearby waterfront, there are boat tours on the Potomac River.

The **Farmers Market** in the center of town dates back to 1749, and George Washington regularly sent produce from his farm at Mount Vernon to be sold here. Today, shoppers can find fresh vegetables and fruit, flowers, baked goods, preserves, and local crafts.

**Carlyle House**

121 N Fairfax St. *(703) 549-2997.* *10am–5pm Tue–Sat, noon–5pm Sun; Nov–Mar: last tour 4pm.* *Mon, Jan 1, Thanksgiving, Dec 25.*

**Lee-Fendall House Museum**

614 Oronoco St. *(703) 548-1789.* *10am–4pm Tue–Sat, 1–4pm Sun.* *Dec 25–Jan 31 (except 3rd Sun, Lee's birthday celebration).*

**Torpedo Factory Art Center**

105 N Union St. *(703) 838-4565.* *10am–5pm daily.* *Jan 1, Easter, Jul 4, Thanksgiving, Dec 25.* www.torpedofactory.org

**The elegant dining room at Kenmore House, Fredericksburg**

## Fredericksburg ❹

*22,600.* 706 Caroline St, *(800) 678-4748.* *9am–5pm daily (Memorial Day & Labor Day until 7pm).* *Dec 25.* www.fredericksburgva.net

FREDERICKSBURG'S attractions are its historic downtown district and four Civil War battlefields, including those at Chancellorsville and The Wilderness. The Rising Sun Tavern and Hugh Mercer Apothecary Shop in the old downtown offer living history accounts of life in a town that began as a 50-acre (20-ha) port on the Rappahannock River. **Kenmore Plantation and Gardens**, also in the heart of town, has beautiful rooms and gardens. The town's visitor center offers horse-and-carriage or trolley tours. The battlefields evoke the Union's long push toward Richmond during the Civil War *(see p46)*.

**Kenmore Plantation & Gardens**

1201 Washington Ave. *(540) 373-3381.* *Jan–Feb: 11am–5pm Sat; Mar–May: 11am–5pm daily; Jun–Sep: 10am–5pm daily; Oct-Dec: 11am–5pm daily.* *Thanksgiving, Dec 24–25, 31.* www.kenmore.org

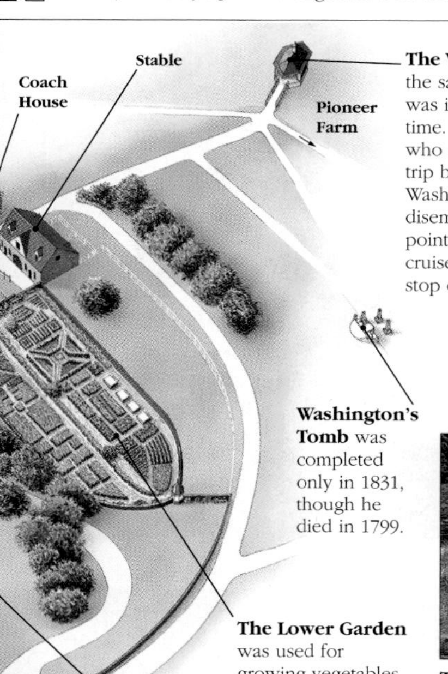


**The Wharf** is on the same site as it was in Washington's time. Today, visitors who come on day-trip boats from Washington, DC, disembark at this point. Potomac cruise boats also stop off here.

**Washington's Tomb** was completed only in 1831, though he died in 1799.

**The Lower Garden** was used for growing vegetables and berries.

**The Bowling Green** was added to the estate by Washington.

**VISITORS' CHECKLIST**

S end of George Washington Memorial Pkwy, Fairfax County, VA. *(703) 780-2000.* *Yellow line to Huntington Station.* *Fairfax Connector bus 101 to Mount Vernon: call (703) 339-7200.* ***Tour bus services & boat cruises available.*** *Apr–Aug: 8am–5pm daily; Sep–Mar: 9am–4pm daily* *first floor.* www.mountvernon.org

**The Pioneer Farm**

*This exhibit demonstrates farming techniques pioneered by Washington. There is also a replica of his unique 16-sided treading barn, created using authentic tools.*

# Colonial Williamsburg ❺

Colonial couple

As Virginia's capital from 1699 to 1780, Williamsburg was the hub of the loyal British colony. After 1780 the town went into decline. Then in 1926, John D. Rockefeller embarked on a massive restoration project. Today, in the midst of the modern-day city, the 18th-century city has been re-created. People in colonial dress portray the lifestyle of the original townspeople; blacksmiths, silversmiths, cabinet makers, and bakers show off their skills; and horse-drawn carriages pass through the streets, providing visitors with a fascinating insight into America's past.

**Courthouse**
*Built in 1770–71 this was the home of the county court for more than 150 years.*

**★ Governor's Palace**
*Originally built in 1720 by Governor Alexander Spotswood, the palace has been reconstructed in its full pre-Revolution glory.*

**Nursery**
*Costumed living-history interpreters work the land in Colonial Williamsburg using replica tools and the same techniques as the original settlers.*

0 meters 200

0 yards 200

**Star Sights**

**★ Capitol**

**★ Governor's Palace**

**★ Robertson's Windmill**

**★ Robertson's Windmill**
*The windmill has daily demonstrations of the settlers' crafts, such as basket-making and barrel-making. The cart was a traditional means of transporting materials.*

**Print Office**
*This store stocks authentic 18th-century foods, including wine, Virginia ham, and peanuts.*

**VISITORS' CHECKLIST**

421 N Boundary St.
(757) 253-0192, (800) 368-6511.
www.colonialwilliamsburg.com
www.visitwilliamsburg.com

**Milliner**
*Owned by Margaret Hunter, the milliner shop stocked a wide range of items. Imported clothes for women and children, jewelry, and toys could all be bought here.*

**Raleigh Tavern**
*The Raleigh was once an important center for social, political, and commercial gatherings. The building burned in 1859, but this reproduction evokes the original spirit.*

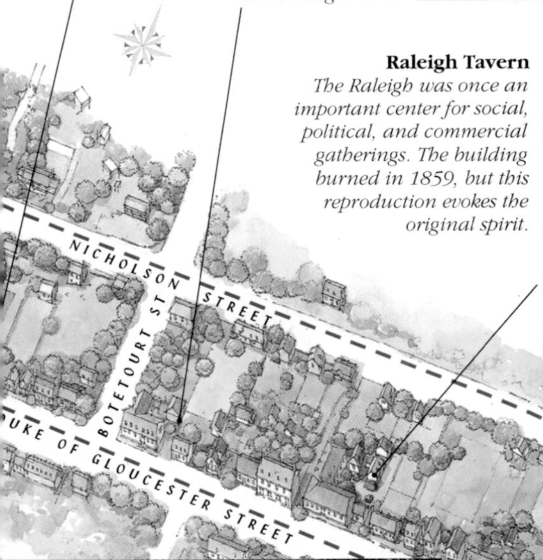

**★ Capitol**
*This is a 1945 reconstruction of the original 1705 building. The government resided in the West Wing, while the General Court was in the East Wing.*

**KEY**

- - - Suggested route

**Jamestown Settlement, a re-creation of Colonial James Fort**

## Jamestown & Yorktown ❻

*York County Public Information Office, (757) 890-3300.*

JAMESTOWN, established in 1607 on the banks of the James River, was the first permanent English settlement in the US. One of the early settlers was John Rolfe, who married Pocahontas, daughter of the Indian chief, Powhatan. But the colony didn't last long – disease, famine, and attacks by Algonquin Indians caused heavy loss of life and in 1699, the colony was abandoned.

Present-day Jamestown Island contains 1,500 acres (607 ha) of marshland and forest. Close to the ruins of the colony, the **Jamestown Settlement** is a re-creation of the original colony, complete with costumed interpreters and replicas of James Fort, an Indian village, and the ships that brought the first successful colonists to Virginia.

On the opposite side of the peninsula, 15 miles (24 km) away, Yorktown was the site of the decisive battle of the American Revolution in 1781. Battlefield tours at **Colonial National Historical Park** explain the siege at Yorktown, which ended with the surrender of the British forces.

**Jamestown Settlement**
*(757) 253-4838, (888) 593-4682.*
*9am–5pm daily. Jan 1, Dec 25.*
www.historyisfun.org

**Colonial National Historical Park**
*(757) 898-3400, (757) 229-1733.*
*9am–5pm daily. Dec 25.*
www.nps.gov/colo

## Norfolk ❼

*262,000. 232 E Main St, (800) 368-3097, (757) 664-6620.* www.norfolkcvb.com

A HISTORIC Colonial port, located at the point where Chesapeake Bay meets the Atlantic Ocean, Norfolk is a busy maritime center with the world's largest naval base. The city's logo – a mermaid – is the theme of sculptures and emblems all over Norfolk. The downtown waterfront centers on the massive battleship USS *Wisconsin*, a part of the new **Nauticus, The National Maritime Center**. The center offers multimedia presentations about naval battles, ships, and deep-sea creatures.

Another top attraction is the **Chrysler Museum of Art**, which displays the eclectic personal collection of automobile tycoon Walter Chrysler Jr. The works of art include paintings by Velasquez, Rubens, Degas, Renoir, and modern masters such as Roy Lichtenstein.

Neighboring Virginia Beach is the site of the 18th-century lighthouse at Cape Henry, where the English first landed in 1607. The waterfront is also home to the Virginia Marine Science Museum.

**Nauticus, The National Maritime Center**
*(757) 664-1000. Apr–Aug: 10am–6pm daily; Sep–Mar: 10am–5pm Tue–Sat, noon–5pm Sun. Thanksgiving, Dec 24 & 25, Jan 1.*
www.nauticus.org

## Richmond ❽

*198,300. 405 N Third St, (804) 783-7450.* www.richmondva.org

THE OLD capital of the Confederacy *(see p47)*, Richmond still retains an aura of Old South gentility. Bronze statues of Civil War generals and other heroes line Monument Avenue, while Victorian mansions and brownstones testify to this area's postwar prosperity.

Civil War artifacts, including General Robert E. Lee's coat and sword, are among the exhibits at the **Museum of the Confederacy**. Next door, the White House of the Confederacy is a treasure of the Victorian age.

The graceful Neo-Classical **State Capitol** dominating downtown houses a lifesize sculpture of George Washington by Jean Antoine Houdon. To its west is the serene **Hollywood Cemetery**, the resting place of presidents John Tyler and James Monroe, as well as of 18,000 Confederate soldiers who are buried under a communal pyramid. Palmer Chapel offers superb views of James River and Belle Isle. Farther uptown are two fine museums, the fascinating **Science Museum of Virginia** and the **Virginia Museum of Fine Arts**, which has collections ranging from ancient Egyptian, Indian, and Himalayan art to French Impressionist and modern American masterpieces. The museum's highlight, however, is the priceless Pratt Collection of Imperial Russian Art, which includes five fabulous jeweled Easter eggs made for the Tsar by the jeweler Peter Carl Fabergé.

**Statue of Robert E. Lee in Richmond**

**Virginia Museum of Fine Arts**
200 North Blvd. *(804) 340-1400. 11am–5pm Wed–Sun. Mon–Tue, Jan 1, Jul 4, Thanksg., Dec 25. only exhibitions.*
www.vmfa.state.va.us

## Chincoteague 9

3,500. 6733 Maddox Blvd, (757) 336-6161.

THE MAIN tourist attraction on Virginia's sparsely developed Eastern Shore, Chincoteague draws fishermen, bird-watchers, and beachcombers. The town itself is primarily a service center, with hotels, motels, and restaurants catering to visitors bound for the **Chincoteague National Wildlife Refuge**, which protects a number of offshore islands, as well as coastal marshlands and a 10-mile (16-km) stretch of Atlantic Ocean beachfront.

A driving tour loops for over 3 miles (4.8 km) through the wildlife preserve, but the best way to see some of the numerous egrets, snow geese, herons, falcons, and other birds found here is by walking or paddling in a canoe.

**Chincoteague National Wildlife Refuge**
(757) 336-6122. 6am–6pm daily. limited.

## Charlottesville 10

40,700. Rte 20 S, (434) 977-1783, (877) 386-1102. www.charlottesvilletourism.org

CHARLOTTESVILLE was Thomas Jefferson's hometown. It is dominated by the University of Virginia, which he founded and designed, and also by his home, **Monticello**.

It took Jefferson 40 years to complete Monticello, which he began building in 1769. It is now one of the most celebrated houses in the country. The entrance hall doubled as a private museum, and the library held a collection of around 6,700 books.

The 5,000-acre (2,023-ha) grounds include a large terraced vegetable garden where Jefferson grew and experimented with varieties. The remains of the slaves' quarters still stand; nearly 200 slaves worked the estate's plantations, and recent evidence suggests that one of them, Sally Hemmings, bore Jefferson's child.

The obelisk over Jefferson's grave in the family cemetery lauds him as "Father of the University of Virginia." The university's Neo-Classical buildings and grounds are open to visitors. Vineyards and wineries surround Charlottesville. Michie Tavern *(see p237)*, joined to the Virginia Wine Museum, has been restored to its 18th-century appearance and serves typical Southern cuisine.

**The obelisk over Jefferson's grave**

Montpelier, on a 2,500-acre (1,012-ha) site, 25 miles (40 km) to the north, was the home of the fourth president, James Madison.

**Monticello**
Route 53, 3 miles (4.8 km) SE of Charlottesville. (434) 984-9822. *Mar–Oct: 8am–5pm; Nov–Feb: 9am–4:30pm.* Dec 25. www.monticello.org

**MONTICELLO, CHARLOTTESVILLE**

*Situated in the leafy foothills of the Blue Ridge Mountains, this Palladian masterpiece was built between 1769 and 1809 by Thomas Jefferson.*

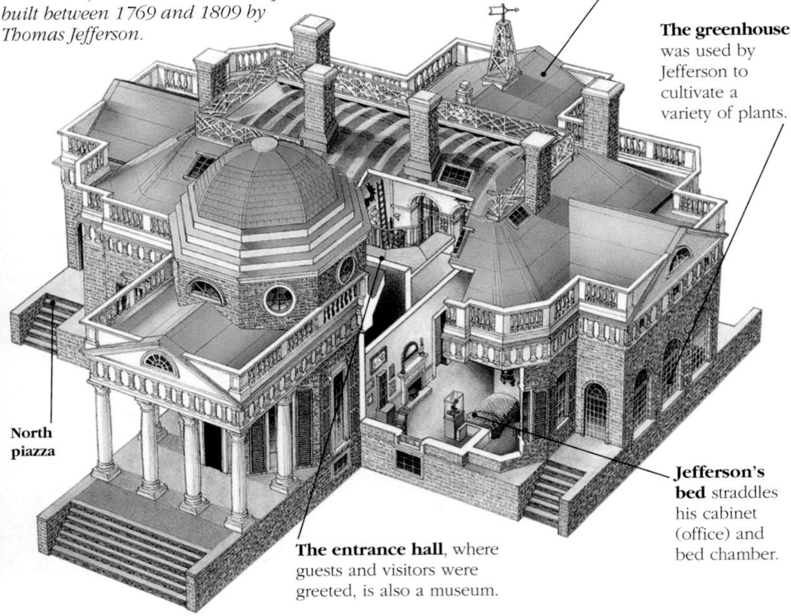

**East portico**

**The greenhouse** was used by Jefferson to cultivate a variety of plants.

**North piazza**

**The entrance hall**, where guests and visitors were greeted, is also a museum.

**Jefferson's bed** straddles his cabinet (office) and bed chamber.

A reconstructed building, Appomattox Court House

## Appomattox Court House ⓫

(434) 352-2621. 8:30am–5pm daily. Jan 1, Thanksgiving, Dec 25.

THIS NATIONAL historic park, located 3 miles (4.8 km) northeast of the town of Appomattox, re-creates the spot where Confederate General Robert E. Lee surrendered to US General Ulysses S. Grant to signal the end of the Civil War *(see p193)*. Today, markers trace the sites of the last skirmishes of the war, and 27 reconstructed and restored buildings replicate the scene where, on April 9, 1865, the two leaders and their armies put an end to that long and destructive war. In the last months of fighting, General Grant had successfully captured the Confederate stronghold at Petersburg, while General Sherman's "March to the Sea" across Georgia surrounded Confederate forces from the South. With the fall of the Confederate capital at Richmond on April 2, General Lee realized that victory was impossible. The terms of surrender were more than generous, since Union leaders hoped to ease reconciliation between the warring sides. When the rebel Confederates laid down their arms, the Northern soldiers saluted their opponents, instead of jeering.

Much of the original setting was destroyed in battle or later dismantled by souvenir hunters. Most of what stands here today was reconstructed by the National Park Service in the 1940s.

## Blue Ridge Parkway ⓬

(828) 298-0398.
www.nps.gov/blri

STRETCHING for 469 miles (755 km) along the crest of the Appalachian Mountains, the Blue Ridge Parkway *(see p41)* extends from the southern border of Shenandoah National Park all the way to North Carolina, ending finally at Great Smoky Mountains National Park *(see p262)*. Created as a public works project during the "New Deal" era in the depths of the 1930s Great Depression, the scenic route was begun in 1935 but was not completed until 1987. Mileposts along the way, measured from north to south, help travelers discover the points of interest along the route. Some of the highlights along the 216-mile (348-km) portion of the Blue Ridge Parkway in Virginia include a crossing of the James River at milepost 63 and the lakefront lodge in the Peaks of Otter section near milepost 86. The historic **Mabry Mill** at milepost 176 was in use as a backwoods sawmill and blacksmith shop until 1935.

This parkway passes through Asheville, North Carolina, and Roanoke, Virginia, and is primarily rural and scenic, with no advertising or commercial traffic allowed. Open all year, the peak travel season is fall.

The picturesque Mabry Mill at milepost 176 of the Blue Ridge Parkway

## Skyline Drive ⓭

SKYLINE DRIVE RUNS along the backbone of the Shenandoah National Park's Blue Ridge Mountains. Originally farmland, the government designated the area a national park in 1926. Deer, wild turkey, bears, and bobcats inhabit the park, and wildflowers, azaleas, and mountain laurel are abundant. The park's many hiking trails and its 75 viewpoints offer stunning natural scenery.

North entrance station

**Whiteoak Canyon ②**
The Whiteoak Canyon Trail passes six waterfalls on its route.

**Pinnacles Overlook ①**
The view of Old Rag Mountain with its outcroppings of granite is spectacular.

**Bearfence Mountain ⑤**
Although it is a bit of a climb up this mountain, partly on rock scramble, it is not too difficult, and the reward is a breathtaking 360-degree view of the surrounding landscape.

**Big Meadows ③**
Close to the visitor center, this meadow has been kept in its centuries-old state. It was probably kept clear by fires lit by Indians or by lightning strikes. Herds of deer can easily be seen here.

**Rapidan Camp ④**
At the end of Mill Prong Trail, this 164-acre (66-ha) resort was President Hoover's weekend retreat until 1932, when he donated it to the park.

**Lewis Mountain ⑥**
This heavily wooded mountain features quaint cabins, campground, picnic area, camp store, laundry, and showers for campers and hikers on the Appalachian Trail.

**KEY**

- – – Walk route
- Lookout point
- Road

0 km 10

0 miles 10

### TIPS FOR DRIVERS

***Starting points:*** *North at Front Royal, central at Thornton Gap or Swift Run Gap, south at Rockfish Gap.*
***Length:*** *105 miles (168 km), duration of 4–8 hrs depending on the number of stops.*
***When to go:*** *Mid-October for fall leaf colors; spring and summer for wildflowers.*
***What it costs:*** *Toll charge of $10 per car (valid for 7 days).*

**Fall in Shenandoah National Park**

# West Virginia

SET ENTIRELY WITHIN THE Appalachian Mountains, this "Mountain State" remains largely forested, despite centuries of aggressive lumbering and mining. The state was part of Virginia until the Civil War, and its early European pioneers were less wealthy and generally very different from the genteel planters of eastern Virginia. As talk of secession grew, western Virginia aligned with the Union. Four years after abolitionist John Brown raided a federal arsenal in Harpers Ferry in a failed attempt to inspire a slave rebellion in 1859, West Virginia was declared a separate state. Today it is known for its woodworking, quilting, and basketry crafts, and traditional Appalachian music and dancing.

**Blackwater Falls State Park, in Monongahela National Forest**

## Monongahela National Forest ⓮

*200 Sycamore St, Elkins. (304) 636-1800. 8am–4:45pm Mon–Fri.*

THE EASTERN HALF of the state lies deep within the Allegheny Mountains, a part of the longer Appalachian Range. Much of this rugged terrain is protected as the vast Monongahela National Forest, which encompasses five federally designated wilderness areas and serves as the headwaters for six major river systems. Its landscapes of rhododendron, black cherry, highland bogs, blueberry thickets, and exposed rocks are the habitat for black bear, white-tailed deer, bobcat, otter, mink, and many other species. The forest's trails attracts hikers, horseback riders, and mountain bikers, while in winter, the area is popular for downhill and cross-country skiing.

The small town of **Elkins**, the headquarters of the national forest, makes a convenient base to explore the area. The town's Augusta Heritage Center hosts residential summer programs on traditional folklife and folk arts, as well as bluegrass and old-time mountain music dances and concerts.

Northeast of Elkins, an 8-mile (13-km) stretch of the 124-mile (200-km) Allegheny Trail links two state parks – **Canaan Valley Resort State Park**, a downhill ski resort, and **Blackwater Falls State Park**, a good place for backcountry ski touring. Both parks have restaurants and provide facilities for lodging and camping. Farther south, Snowshoe Mountain Resort is the state's largest downhill resort in winter and a mountain biking center from spring to fall (rentals and guided trips are available). The nearby **Cass Scenic Railroad State Park** organizes vintage steam train rides across the mountaintops for panoramic views. Fall foliage rides are the most popular.

Southeast of Elkins, the **Spruce Knob–Seneca Rocks National Recreation Area** draws rockclimbers up the sandstone strata of Seneca Rocks, an hour's drive away. The 75-mile (121-km) Greenbrier River Trail, running parallel to the Virginia border, from White Sulphur Springs in the south all the way to the Cass Scenic Railroad State Park in the north, is a converted "rails-to-trails" rail bed route, which is quite popular for bicycle tours.

**Spruce Knob-Seneca Rocks National Rec. Area**
*(304) 567-2827. May–Oct: 9am–4:30pm daily; Nov–Apr: 9am–4:30 pm Sat–Sun.*

**Cass Scenic Railroad**
Route 66/Main St, Cass. *(304) 456-4300. May–Sep.*

## New River Gorge National River ⓯

**Canyon Rim Visitor Center** US Hwy 19, Lansing. *(304) 574-2115.*
*9am–5pm daily.*
*Jan 1, Thanksgiving, Dec 25.*
www.nps.gov/neri

THE NEW RIVER courses through a deep gorge in the southeastern corner of the state, drawing rafters for some of the most exciting whitewater adventures in eastern US. The National Park Service, located between Fayetteville and Hinton, oversees a stretch that falls 750 ft (225 m) within 50 miles (80 km), with a compact set of

**Rock Climber above New River Gorge National River**

**Overlook at Hawk's Nest State Park, New River Gorge National River**

Class V rapids. The modern Canyon Rim Visitor Center and gorge bridge provide easy access to panoramic overlooks and rim hiking trails. The visitor center also distributes comprehensive lists of local rafting outfitters, while the nearby **Hawk's Nest State Park** offers modest lodge rooms and operates an aerial tram down to the river for boat rides during summer. The former mining town of Fayetteville is also a popular base for rafters and outfitters, while the old industrial town of Hinton holds a grittier appeal and is easily accessible to visitors via Amtrak.

**Hawk's Nest State Park**
Hwy 60, Ansted. (304) 658-5212.
**Tram Rides, Boat Rides** *Call for seasonal operating days and hours.*

## Harpers Ferry ⑯

300. *NPS Visitor Center, (304) 535-6298.*

Nestled at the confluence of the Potomac and Shenandoah Rivers, where West Virginia meets Virginia and Maryland, is the tiny town of Harpers Ferry. Named after Robert Harper, the Philadelphia builder who constructed a ferry here in 1761, most of the historic downtown area is today the **Harpers Ferry National Historic Park**. It was here in 1859, that Maryland abolitionist John Brown led an ill-fated raid on the federal arsenal. Although his attempt failed, this event ignited the Civil War two years later.

The town looks just as it did in the 19th century, with small clapboard storefronts clinging to steep hillsides that slope down to the rushing rivers. Several historic buildings, including John Brown's Fort and the arsenal, are open to visitors.

The famous Appalachian Trail *(see p174)*, which runs through town, has its headquarters at the **Appalachian Trail Conservancy**. The Trail is a 2,000-mile (3,220-km) footpath that stretches along the spine of the Appalachian Mountains from Georgia to Maine. With an Amtrak train station in the heart of downtown, Harpers Ferry is just an hour's ride from Washington, DC, making this remote region accessible for visitors without a car.

**Appalachian Trail Conservancy**
799 Washington St. (304) 535-6331. *9am–5pm Mon–Fri, 9am–4pm Sat–Sun.* *Nov–Mar.*

**Aerial view of Harpers Ferry, located at the confluence of the Potomac and Shenandoah Rivers**

# Maryland

MARYLAND HAS AN ABUNDANCE of both natural attractions and historical sites. The rolling farmlands around Antietam in western Maryland are rich in Civil War heritage. Water-related tourism is a mainstay of southern Maryland's Chesapeake Bay, the longest inland shoreline in the US, which attracts sailors, fishermen, and seafood lovers who can indulge in the delicious local specialty – soft-shell blue crabs. The Eastern Shore on the Delmarva Peninsula, dotted with picturesque villages, is also graced by the wild beauty of Assateague and Chincoteague Islands.

## Antietam National Battlefield 17

Rte 65, 10 miles (16 km) S of Hagerstown. *(301) 432-5124.* *Jun–Aug: 8:30am–6pm daily; Sep–May: 8:30am–5pm.* *Jan 1, Thanksgiving, Dec 25.* www.nps.gov/anti

ONE OF THE worst battles of the Civil War was waged here on September 17, 1862, culminating in 23,000 casualties among the Confederate as well as the Union armies.

An observation tower offers a panoramic view of this historic battlefield. Antietam Creek runs peacefully under the Burnside Bridge, where the fighting was severe and much blood was spilled. The whole site has a haunted atmosphere even today. Although the battle did not end in a decisive victory, the horrendous bloodshed at Antietam inspired President Lincoln to issue the Emancipation Proclamation. The visitor center movie recreating the battle should not be missed.

## Frederick 18

*50,000.* *19 E Church St, (301) 228-2888.* *9am–5pm daily.* www.fredericktourism.org

FREDERICK'S HISTORIC center, dating back to the mid-18th century, was renovated in the 1970s and is now a popular tourist attraction.

This charming town is a major antique center and home to hundreds of antique dealers. Its shops, galleries, and eateries are all in 18th- and 19th-century settings, and several historic houses in the town, beautifully restored and furnished with period artifacts, are open to visitors. Francis Scott Key, author of "The Star Spangled Banner," is buried in Mt. Olivet Cemetery. Tourist information is available at the visitor center, which also conducts popular walking tours during the weekends.

## Baltimore 19

*675,500.* *Inner Harbor West Wall, (410) 837-4636, (800) 282-6632.* www.baltimore.org

THERE IS MUCH to do and see in this pleasant port city of restaurants, antiques, arts, boats, and monuments. A good place to start is the Inner Harbor, the city's redeveloped waterfront, with its harborside complex of shops and restaurants. The centerpiece, and one of Baltimore's most popular attractions, is the stunning **National Aquarium**, whose collection includes many exhibits. The National Aquarium also offers a seal pool, and a delightful dolphin show.

The Harbor is also home to the **Maryland Science Center**, where "do touch" is the rule. It features a number of interactive exhibits, and the Planetarium and IMAX® Theater thrill visitors with images of earth and space.

The **American Visionary Art Museum**, also on the Inner Harbor, houses a collection of extraordinary works by self-taught artists whose materials range from matchsticks to faux pearls. Uptown is the **Baltimore Museum of Art**, with its famous collection of modern art, including works by Matisse, Picasso, Degas, and Van Gogh. It also has a large collection of pieces by Andy Warhol and two sculpture

**The eye-catching architecture of the National Aquarium, Baltimore**

gardens featuring works by Rodin and Calder.

Also impressive is the **Walters Art Gallery** on the elegant Mount Vernon Square, lined with Colonial brick townhouses. The gallery's collection includes Greek and Roman classical art, Southeast Asian and Chinese artifacts, Byzantine silver, pre-Columbian carvings, and jeweled objects by Fabergé. There are also paintings by Rubens, Monet, Manet, and the Victorian artist Alma-Tadema, whose beautiful *Sappho and Alcaeus* (1881) should not be missed.

The lively neighborhood of Little Italy is also definitely worth a visit, not only for its knockout Italian restaurants but also for the games of bocce (Italian lawn bowling), played around Pratt or Stiles Street on warm evenings.

**National Aquarium**
501 E Pratt St, Pier 3. (410) 576-3800. *Mar–Jun & Sep–Oct: 9am–5pm daily (to 8pm Fri); Jul–Aug: 9am–7:30pm Sun–Thu, 9am–9:30pm Fri–Sat.* *Thnksg., Dec 24, 25.* www.aqua.org

**Maryland Science Center**
601 Light St. *(410) 685-5225.* *10am–5pm Mon–Fri, 10am–6pm Sat, noon–6pm Sun.* *Thnksg., Dec 25.* www.mdsci.org

**Baltimore Museum of Art**
N Charles St & 31st St. *(410) 396-7100.* *11am–5pm Wed–Fri, 11am– 6pm Sat–Sun.* *Mon, Tue, Jan 1, Jul 4, Thanksgiving, Dec 25.* *free on Thu.*

**Walters Art Museum**
600 N Charles St. *(410) 547-9000.* *10am–5pm Wed–Sun, 10am–8pm 1st Thu of month.* *Dec 24, 25, Jan 1, Jul 4, Thnksg.* *Sat, Sun.*

## Annapolis ⓴

*33,300.* *Annapolis & Anne Arundel County Visitors Bureau, 26 West St, (410) 280-0445.* *9am–5pm daily.* www.visit-annapolis.org

THE CAPITAL of Maryland, Annapolis, is regarded as the jewel of Chesapeake Bay. It is defined by the nautical character that comes with the 17 miles (27 km) of shoreline and the longtime presence of the **United States Naval Academy**. A walk down Main Street leads past the 200-year-old Maryland Inn, shops, and wonderful seafood restaurants that serve local fish, to the City Dock lined with boats. It is then a short walk to the 150-year-old US Naval Academy. Inside the visitor center is the *Freedom* 7 Space Capsule that carried the first American, Alan Shepard, into space. The US Naval Academy Museum in Preble Hall is also worth visiting, especially to see the gallery of detailed ship models.

**The beautiful formal gardens of the William Paca House, in Annapolis**

The **Maryland State House**, completed in 1779, is the oldest state capitol in continuous use. Its Old Senate Chamber is where the Continental Congress (delegates from each of the American colonies) met when Annapolis was briefly the capital of the United States in 1783–84. It was also here that the Treaty of Paris was ratified in 1784, formally ending the Revolutionary War.

Annapolis teems with Colonial-era buildings, most of them still in use. The 1765 **William Paca House**, home of Governor Paca who signed the Declaration of Independence, is a fine Georgian house with an enchanting garden, both of which have recently been lovingly restored. Another restored mansion worth visiting is the magnificent red brick **Hammond Harwood House**, which boasts exceptionally fine woodcarving. Built in 1774, this masterpiece of Georgian design, a short walk west of the State House on Maryland Avenue, was named after the Hammond and Harwood families. Worth exploring are the Cornhill and Duke of Gloucester Streets, examples of the city's historic residential streets. Many tours are on offer in Annapolis, including bus, boat, and walking tours. It is particularly enjoyable for tourists to view the city from the water by sightseeing boat, schooner, or kayak.

**Tiffany window in the Naval Academy, Annapolis**

**US Naval Academy**
Corner of King George, E of Randall St. *(410) 263-6933.* *9am–5pm daily.* *Jan 1, Thanksgiving, Dec 25.*

**Maryland State House**
State Circle. *(410) 974-3400.* *9am–5pm (call ahead).* *Dec 25.* *11am & 3pm.*

**William Paca House**
186 Prince George St. *(410) 263-5553.* *Mar–Dec: 10am–5pm Mon–Sat, noon–5pm Sun; Jan–Feb: weekends only.* *Thanksgiving, Dec 24, 25.*

## North Bay 21

121 N Union St, Ste. B, Havre de Grace, (800) 597-2649.

At the northern end of Chesapeake Bay, the lovely town of Havre de Grace is home to the Concord Point Lighthouse. Popular with artists and photographers, the lighthouse has been in continuous operation since the mid-1800s. The **Havre de Grace Decoy Museum** exhibits a fine collection of working decoys and chronicles how the craft evolved from a purely practical wildfowl lure into a highly sophisticated form of American folk art.

Across the bay to the east, the lush forests of **Elk Neck State Park** cover the tip of a peninsula crowned by Turkey Point Lighthouse, one of the bay's oldest. The park offers a sandy beach for swimming, boat rentals, miniature golf, and hiking trails.

Northeast of the park across the Elk River is Chesapeake City, where rooftops appear much as they did 100 years ago when the village grew to service the Chesapeake and Delaware Canal. Today, the village is a "boutique town," with fine shops and restaurants. The **C and D Canal Museum** is housed in the canal's original pumphouse. Working models of canal locks, the original steam power plant, and a giant water wheel are on display.

**Havre de Grace Decoy Museum**
215 Giles St. (410) 939-3739. 11am–4pm daily. public hols.

**Elk Neck State Park**
End of Route 272. (410) 287-5333.

**C&D Canal Museum**
End of 2nd St. (410) 885-5621. 8am–4pm Mon–Sat. Sun, hols.

## St. Michaels 22

1,900. (800) 808-7622.
www.stmichaelsmd.org

St. Michaels, founded in 1677, was once a haven for ship builders, privateers, and blockade-runners. Today, the town is a destination for pleasure boaters and yachts flying international colors. B&Bs, a variety of shops, and good restaurants abound.

**Chesapeake Bay Maritime Museum** is one of Maryland's top cultural attractions. The museum features interactive exhibits on boat building, historic boats, decoys, and various other aspects of Chesapeake Bay life. Several vessels unique to the area are anchored on the property, and the **Hooper Strait Lighthouse**, a fully restored 1879 screwpile wooden structure, is open for exploration.

**Chesapeake Bay Maritime Museum**
Navy Point at Mill St. (410) 745-2916. 9am–5pm (until 6pm in summer, 4pm in winter).
www.cbmm.org

The bay in Blackwater National Wildlife Refuge, Easton

## Easton 23

9,400. (410) 770-8000.
www.eastonmd.org

A handsome little town, Easton is an interesting combination of unique shops and historic homes. A restored 1820s schoolhouse serves as the premises of the **Academy of the Arts**. Although the emphasis is on Eastern Shore artists, the gallery's permanent collection includes works by famous artists such as James Whistler and Grant Wood.

Once a farm used by muskrat trappers for the fur trade, **Blackwater National Wildlife Refuge** was established in 1933 to provide sanctuary for migrating waterfowl. Geese number 35,000 and ducks exceed 15,000 at the peak of the fall migration. The best time to observe migratory birds is from October through March; however, many song-

Hooper Strait Lighthouse at Chesapeake Bay silhouetted by a pink and violet sunset

birds, reptiles, and mammals can be seen all year round. Blackwater is a haven for endangered species, including the peregrine falcon.

**Academy of the Arts**
106 South St. *(410) 822-0455.* *10am–4pm Mon–Sat, 10am–9pm Wed.* www.art-academy.org

**Blackwater National Wildlife Refuge**
2145 Key Wallace Dr, Cambridge. *(410) 228-2677.* *8am–4pm Mon–Fri, 9am–5pm Sat–Sun.*

## Crisfield 24

*2,900.* *906 W Main St, Crisfield, (800) 782-3913.*

THIS BUSY commercial seafood port supports a bustling sportfishing industry. From Mid-May through October, the fish are running. The **Governor J. Millard Tawes Historical Museum** is named after a resident who became Maryland's 54th governor. The museum has displays on local history and marine life. It also offers walking tours through a boatyard and a seafood processing plant as well as trolley tours through historic Crisfield to the Ward Brothers Waterfowl carving workshop and the crab-processing shanties of Jenkins Creek.

**Captain John Smith (1580-1631)**

**Governor J. Millard Tawes Historical Museum**
3 Ninth St, Somers Cove Marina. *(410) 968-2501.* *9am–5pm Mon–Sat.* *Sun, week of Christmas, week after Christmas.*

**ENVIRONS:** Accessible only by boat, **Smith Island**, 10 miles (16 km) to the west, was chartered in 1608 by Captain John Smith, founder of the Jamestown settlement *(see p191)*. Ewell, at the north end of the island, is where most of the island's population resides. Some claim that the distinctive local speech is reminiscent of the Elizabethan/Cornwall dialect brought here in the 1770s.

**Ferris wheel at Trimper's Rides, Ocean City**

## Salisbury 25

*29,000.* *8480 Ocean Hwy, (800) 332-8687.*

THE LARGEST CITY on the Eastern Shore, Salisbury is known for its fine antique shops. It developed as a mill community in 1732 and soon became the principal crossroads of the southern Delmarva Peninsula. Salisbury's **Ward Museum of Wildfowl Art** contains the world's premier collection of wildfowl art. Here, wood is carved and painted to resemble wild birds in natural settings. The museum looks at the history of the art, from antique working decoys to contemporary carvings. **Pemberton Historical Park** is the site of Pemberton Hall, built in 1741 for Isaac Handy, a British Army colonel. The grounds are threaded by self-guided nature trails, and the manor house contains a small museum maintained by the local historical society.

**Ward Museum of Wildfowl Art**
909 S Schumaker Dr. *(410) 742-4988.* *10am–5pm Mon–Sat, noon–5pm Sun.*

**A specialist duck decoy maker at work in Crisfield**

## Ocean City 26

*5,100.* *4001 Coastal Hwy, (410) 289-2800.*

SOFT BEIGE SAND extends endlessly along the Ocean City peninsula, fronted by miles of hotels. In summer, brightly colored umbrellas provide shade, while at night, the beach boardwalk that stretches from the inlet north past 27th Street is lively with strolling couples, singles, and families.

At the inlet, on the southern border of Ocean City, the **Ocean City Life-Saving Museum**, housed in a decommissioned 1891 Life-saving Station, relates the history of Ocean City and the US Life-saving Service.

North on the broadwalk, **Trimper's Rides** began operating in 1902 with a steam-powered 45-animal carousel. Today, Trimper's includes a 1905 Herschel-Spellman merry-go-round glittering with jewels and fantasy animals, Ferris wheels, bumper rides, mechanized fortune-tellers, and a host of other entertainments.

Ocean City also has many miniature golf courses: visitors can play beneath plaster polar bears, bask in the tropics, or putt around rubber sharks.

**Ocean City Life-Saving Museum**
Boardwalk at the Inlet. *(410) 289-4991.* *May & Oct: 11am–4pm daily; Jun–Sep: 11am–10pm daily; Nov–Apr: 11am–4pm Sat–Sun.* www.ocmuseum.org

**Trimper's Rides**
Baltimore & 1st St on the boardwalk. *(410) 289-8617.* *mid-May–mid-Sep: 1pm–midnight Mon–Fri, noon–midnight Sat–Sun; mid-Sep–mid-May: limited hours.*

# Delaware

Although Delaware is the country's second-smallest state, larger only than tiny Rhode Island, its importance in industry, banking, and technology far exceeds its size. This is mainly due to the laissez faire tax and corporation laws that have attracted several large companies to base their headquarters here. Along with a significant history, stately country homes, and some of the nation's best museums, Delaware's 2,000 square miles (500,000 ha) also boasts more than 20 miles (32 km) of sandy beaches along the Atlantic Ocean.

**Detail from *Washington Crossing the Delaware,* Delaware Art Museum**

## Wilmington 27

71,500. 
100 W 10th St, (800) 489-6664.
www.visitwilmingtonde.com

This former Swedish colony is home to one of the country's finest art museums, the **Delaware Art Museum**. Its outstanding collections contain works by American illustrators such as Howard Pyle, and his students N.C. Wyeth and Maxfield Parrish. There are also paintings and sculpture by other 19th- and 20th-century American artists such as Winslow Homer. The galleries feature paintings and decorative arts from the English pre-Raphaelite movement, led by Dante Gabriel Rossetti. The romantic works, second only to those of Victoria and Albert Museum, were bequeathed to the museum in 1935 by the wealthy Wilmington industrialist Samuel Bancroft Jr.

**Delaware Art Museum**
2301 Kentmere Parkway.
*(302) 571-9590.* *10am–4pm Tue–Sat (until 8pm Wed), noon–4pm Sun.* *Mon.*
www.delart.org

## Winterthur 28

SR 52. *(302) 448-3883, (800) 448-3883.* *10am–5pm Tue–Sun.*
*Thanksgiving, Dec 25.*
www.winterthur.org

Originally the home of Evelina du Pont and James Biderman, Winterthur was named after the Biderman ancestral home in Switzerland. Henry Francis du Pont inherited the house in 1927. Du Pont was one of the many post-World War I collectors, whose nationalistic sentiments caused them to take a fresh look at American decorative objects. His collection of American furniture is one of the most important assemblages of early American decorative arts in the world.

Winterthur showcases the du Pont family's fascination with American decorative arts and horticulture. The surrounding 982-acre (397-ha) grounds are landscaped beautifully, with miles of surfaced paths and scenic woodland trails. The part of the museum open to the public consists of two buildings, 175 period rooms, and two floors of exhibition galleries.

## Hagley Museum/ Eleutherian Mills 29

Rte 141. *(302) 658-2400.*
*mid-Mar–Dec: 9:30am–4:30pm daily; Jan–mid-Mar: 9:30am–1:30pm Mon–Fri, 9:30am–4:30pm Sat–Sun.*
*Thanksgiving, Dec 25.*
www.hagley.org

Picturesquely located on the banks of the Brandywine River, Hagley Yard is the origin of the du Pont fortune in America. Its serene setting is visible in spring when the river banks are ablaze with purple and pink rhododendrons and azaleas.

Eleuthere du Pont acquired the property and established a black powder (explosives) factory here in 1884. Factory buildings, storehouses, drying tables, and the workers' village are open to the public. Facing the river are the Eagle Roll Mill's "mixing rooms," with their 5-ft (1.5-m) thick walls, where powder explosions – 299 blowouts in 20 years – did the least damage. Hagley Museum, at the entryway to the property, explores the history of the sites with exhibits and dioramas.

The modest du Pont family home, **Eleutherian Mills**, dates from 1803. It overlooks the powder works at the far end of the property and contains many original furnishings. This large property is verdant with a variety of native plants, shrubs, and trees.

**Boxcar exhibit at Hagley, on the banks of the Brandywine River**

**The elegant French-style Nemours Mansion, built by Alfred I. du Pont**

## Nemours Mansion and Gardens ㉚

1600 Rockland Rd.
*(302) 651-6912. closed for renovations until May 2007. Check website for details.*
www.nemoursmansion.org

BUILT BY Alfred I. du Pont in 1909-1910, this Louis XVI-style château is named after the north-central French town that Pierre Samuel du Pont de Nemours, his great-great-grandfather, represented as a member of the French Estates General in 1789. The mansion's 102 rooms are opulently decorated with Oriental rugs, tapestries, and paintings dating from the 15th century. The 300-acre (12-ha) gardens are landscaped in the classic French style.

## New Castle ㉛

*4,800. 220 Delaware St, (302) 322-9801.*
www.visitnewcastle.com

DELAWARE'S FORMER capital is today a well-preserved historic site, with restaurants, shops, and residential areas. The **New Castle Courthouse** displays artifacts that illuminate the town's multinational origins; Sweden, Holland, and Britain all have claimed New Castle as their own. Several historic homes lie a short stroll from each other. One, the **Amstel House**, was the home of Governor Van Dyke. The town's most elegant dwelling place in 1738, its most famous guest was George Washington.

### New Castle Courthouse

211 Delaware St. *(302) 323-4453. 10am–3:30pm Tue–Sat, 1:30–4:30pm Sun. Mon, public hols.*

## Lewes ㉜

*3,000. 120 Kings Hwy, (302) 645-8073.*

THE SITE OF Zwaanendael ("Valley of the Swans"), Delaware's original Dutch settlement in 1631, Lewes is a quiet town with a small beach, sophisticated restaurants, residences, and shops. The **Zwaanendael Museum**, built in 1931, is a striking replica of the Town Hall of Hoorn, home of most of the settlers. Its exhibits elaborate on the first encampment as well as the area's other historical aspects.

In 1682, the British Crown granted the colony of Delaware to Englishman William Penn *(see p98)* who established one of the nation's first public lands by setting aside Cape Henlopen for the citizens of Lewes. Besides a bay and ocean beaches, **Cape Henlopen State Park** contains Gordon's Pond Wildlife Area and the Great Dune, which rises 80 ft (24 m) above sea level. The park's varied habitats are home to many birds, reptiles, and mammals, including threatened shorebirds. Attractions include hiking trails, interpretive displays, a pier, camping, and swimming.

### Zwaanendael Museum

Kings Hwy & Savannah Rd. *(302) 645-1148. 10am–4:30pm Tue–Sat, 1:30–4:30pm Sun. Mon, hols.*

### Cape Henlopen State Park

42 Cape Henlopen Dr.
*(302) 645-8983.*

## Rehoboth Beach ㉝

*1,200. 501 Rehoboth Ave, (302) 227-2233.*
*www.beach-fun.com*

REHOBOTH BEACH WAS originally a Methodist summer camp. A commercial strip of restaurants and shops stretches along Rehoboth Avenue, meeting sand beaches at Funland on the boardwalk. The Outlets, between Lewes and Rehoboth Beach, feature every major outlet store, taking advantage of the fact that there is no sales tax in Delaware.

Three miles (5 km) south of the beach, the 2,700-acre (1093-ha) **Delaware Seashore State Park** covers the strip of land between the Atlantic Ocean and Rehoboth Bay. **Millsboro**, west of Reheboth Bay, is home to the Nanticoke tribe. In mid-September, the tribe holds a public pow-wow to preserve their heritage and explain their beliefs.

South of the park, the 89-ft (27-m) Fenwick Island Lighthouse marks the Delaware-Maryland border. Built in 1852, it was decommissioned during World War II.

### Delaware Seashore State Park

Inlet 850. *(302) 227-2800.*
*Mar 1–Nov 30.*

**A Nanticoke Indian at the annual pow-wow, Rehoboth Beach**

# Practical Information

WASHINGTON, DC AND THE CAPITAL REGION is very rich in museums, cultural events, and entertainment, as well as in scenic sites and outdoor activities around its seashores, rivers, and mountains. This region offers excellent amenities for the large numbers of tourists that it attracts. Spring and fall are the best times to visit, as the summers are hot and humid in much of the region, and the winters cold and damp. However, summer sees the largest number of visitors, so it is best to make reservations for this time of year.

## Tourist Information

THE CAPITAL REGION is well-equipped to cater to visitors' needs. Visitor information desks at airports and within cities will provide guides and maps, information on guided tours, events, and festivals. Major hotels also have guest services desks. The Smithsonian **Dial-a-Museum** line is a useful resource for finding out about special events in DC's museums. State tourism bureaus are other reliable sources of comprehensive information.

## Personal Security

IN RECENT YEARS, Washington has made great efforts to clean up its streets and bring down crime. If you stick to the tourist areas and avoid outlying neighborhoods, you should not run into any trouble. When visiting sights off the beaten track, stay alert and study your map properly before you set off. If you plan to hike alone, always carry a cell phone, and inform someone in advance about your itinerary.

## Getting Around

TRAVEL WITHIN DC and the Capital Region is easy. Washington has a comprehensive public transportation system, and all major attractions in the capital are accessible on foot, or by **Metrorail**, **Metrobus**, or taxi. If you decide to drive in DC, be prepared for traffic jams and unexpected route changes. Avoid driving at night if you are unfamiliar with the area.

Several DC-based tour companies offer tours that include Mount Vernon, Williamsburg, and Monticello in Virginia. Baltimore and Annapolis, Maryland's major cities, are connected to DC by rail and bus. Car rental is widely available, but often expensive. Both **Amtrak** trains and **Greyhound** buses are cheaper alternatives, but your choice of destination may be more limited. To explore many of the scenic parts of the Capital Region, it is best to travel by car. Visitors should avoid shortcuts and stay on well-traveled roads.

## Etiquette

SMOKING IS prohibited in many buildings, restaurants, and stores in the region. Cigarettes can only be purchased by those over 18 years old; proof of age may be required. The legal age for drinking alcohol in Washington is 21, and you may need a photo identification (ID) as proof of your age in order to purchase alcohol and be allowed into bars. It is illegal to drink alcohol in public parks or to carry an open container of alcohol in your car while driving. Penalties for driving under the influence of alcohol are quite severe, and may even include a jail sentence.

## Outdoor Activities

MARYLAND'S Chesapeake Bay and Eastern Shore offer wonderful opportunities for boating, sailing, and fishing. For outdoor enthusiasts, other highlights of the Capital Region include hiking the **Appalachian Trail** in Virginia and West Virginia, whitewater rafting in West Virginia, and cycling along the picturesque Chesapeake and Ohio Canal Towpath, which runs all the way from Washington to Maryland. There is also a beautiful 16-mile (26-km) biking trail from Washington to Mount Vernon. Delaware's Rehoboth Beach and Seashore State Park are a magnet for those in search of sea and sand.

Among spectator sports, the **Washington Redskins** (football) and the **Baltimore Orioles** (baseball) are hot tickets. If tickets have sold out, it is fun to watch the game along with other enthusiasts at a sports bar.

## The Climate of DC & Capital Region

The Capital Region's climate varies greatly. In winter, temperatures can plummet below freezing. During this time, Virginia's Appalachian Mountains are covered with snow, attracting skiers and snowboarders. Summers can be very hot and humid, with almost continuous sunshine. Summer is also the season for the heaviest rainfall, especially between May and August, when the rain comes as a welcome break from the humidity. The rains taper off in September and October, when the weather is pleasantly mild. The region is at its best in spring and fall.

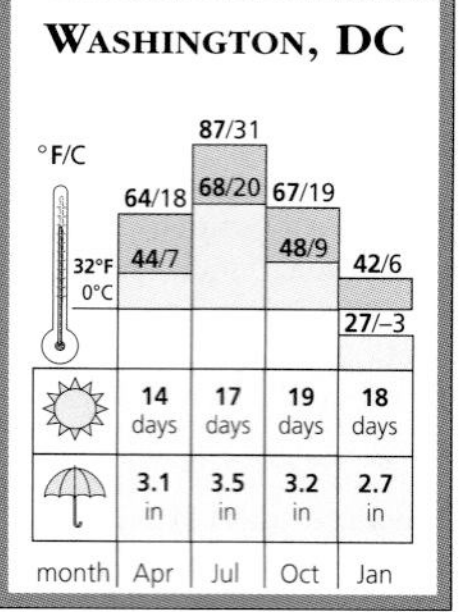

## Entertainment

Visitors to this region will never be at a loss for entertainment or cultural events. There are more free activities in DC than in any other American city. The weekend section of Friday's edition of the *Washington Post*, provides listings of free concerts, gallery talks, films, book signings, poetry readings, plays, and concerts.

The **Kennedy Center** in Washington is home to the **Washington Opera Company** and the **National Symphony Orchestra**, two of the capital's crown jewels. It offers a magnificent dance and ballet season as well, featuring the world's finest companies, including the Bolshoi, the American Ballet Theater, and the Dance Theater of Harlem. The center also hosts touring theater companies and many top jazz performers. Other good jazz and blues venues are **Blues Alley** in Georgetown, the **Merriweather Post Pavilion** in Columbia, Maryland, and the **Nissan Pavilion** in Manassas, Virginia.

Film classics and film premieres are shown at the Kennedy Center's American Film Institute and documentaries at the Library of Congress. Many of the capital's museums have regular series of film shows, lectures, and concerts.

Washington holds many seasonal cultural events. In June, there are nightly performances by the **Shakespeare Theatre Free for All** at the Carter Barron Amphitheater. Independence Day celebrations are spectacular along the Mall, with fireworks from the steps of the US Capitol. Labor Day Weekend in September is marked by a free concert by the National Symphony Orchestra on the lawns of Capitol Hill. Tours of the White House are limited at present. Check at the White House Visitor Center for the latest information.

## Shopping

Washington, DC as well as Maryland and Virginia are famous for their antique stores. Frederick, Maryland, has the **Emporium at Creekside Antiques**, which houses over 100 antique shops. A great place to shop are the museum shops in DC, which stock an incredibly wide range of products, from African textiles and artwork reproductions to contemporary American crafts. Popular department stores are **Hecht's** in DC and **Nordstrom** in Arlington, Virginia. There are large malls in the Virginia and Maryland suburbs, and at Fashion Center in Pentagon City. Discount hunters should head for the 230 outlets at Potomac Mills, situated 30 miles (48 km) south of DC on I-95, or to Rehoboth Beach in Delaware, with its huge concentration of outlet stores.

Many shops in the Washington, DC area are closed on federal holidays.

## Directory

### Tourist Information

**Delaware**
99 King's Hwy, Dover, DE 19901.
T *(302) 739-4271.* W www.visitdelaware.net

**Dial-a-Museum**
1000 Jefferson Dr, SW Washington, DC.
T *(202) 357-2020.*

**Maryland**
217 E Redwood St, Baltimore, MD 21202.
T *(800) 634-7386.* W www.visitmaryland.org

**Virginia**
901 E Byrd St, Richmond, VA 23219.
T *(800) 847-4882.*
W www.virginia.org

**Washington, DC**
901 Seventh St NW, Suite 400, Washington, DC 20001.
T *(202) 789-7000.*
W www.washington.org

**West Virginia**
T *(800)-225-5982.*
W www.callwva.com

### Travel

**Amtrak**
T *(800) 872-7245.*
W www.amtrak.com

**Greyhound**
T *(800) 229-9424.*
W www.greyhound.com

**Metrorail & Metrobus**
600 Fifth St, NW, Washington, DC 20001.
T *(202) 637-7000, (202) 638-3780.*
W www.wmata.com

### Sports & Outdoor Activities

**Baltimore Orioles**
Oriole Park at Camden Yards, 333 W Camden St, Baltimore, MD 21201.
T *(888) 848-2473.*
W www.theorioles.com

**Washington Redskins**
FedExField 1600, FedEx Way, Landover, MD 20785.
T *(301) 276-6050 (ticket office), (301) 276-6000, (301) 276-6800, (703) 726-7000.*
W www.redskins.com

### Entertainment

**Blues Alley**
1073 Wisconsin Ave, NW.
T *(202) 337-4141.*

**Kennedy Center**
New Hampshire Ave & Rock Creek Pkwy, NW.
T *(202) 467-4600.*
W www.kennedy center. org

**Merriweather Post Pavilion**
Columbia, MD.
T *(301) 445-SEAT, (703) 218-6500, (800) 955-5566.*

**National Symphony Orchestra**
T *(202) 467-4600.*

**Nissan Pavilion**
7800 Cellar Door Dr, Haymarket, VA.
T *(703 )754-6400.*

**Shakespeare Theatre Free for All**
Carter Barron Amphitheater, 16th St & Colorado Ave, NW.
T *(202) 334-4790.*
W www. shakespeare theatre.org

### Shopping

**Emporium at Creekside Antiques**
112 E Patrick St, Frederick, MD.
T *(301) 662-7099.*

**Hecht's Department Store**
12th & G St, NW.
T *(202) 628-6661.*

# Where to Stay

Washington offers a wide range of accomodations. For a relaxing holiday, you may want to choose a hotel with all the amenities: pool, health club, deluxe restaurant, and room service, though cheaper options are also available. The hotels in Washington, DC tend to be expensive, but there are bargains to be had, especially during the off season and on weekends.

## Washington, DC

| Hotel | Credit Cards | Number of Rooms (Suites) | Recommended Restaurant | Children's Facilities | Garden or Terrace |
|---|---|---|---|---|---|
| **Capitol Hill:** *Bull Moose Bed-and-Breakfast on Capitol Hill* $$<br>101 5th St, NE (at A St). *(202) 547-1050, (800) 261-2768.* FAX *(202) 548-9741.*<br>W www.BullMoose-B-and-B.com<br>This historic B&B, five blocks from the Capitol, has original oak woodwork and turreted bedrooms. | ■ | 9 (1) | | | |
| **Capitol Hill:** *Holiday Inn on the Hill* $$$$<br>415 New Jersey Ave, NW (between D St & E St). *(202) 638-1616, (800) 638-1116.* FAX *(202) 638-0707.* W www.holiday-inn.com/was-onthehill<br>A good choice for both business travelers and families. During the summer there is a play area for children called the Discovery Zone. | ■ | 343 (9) | ■ | ● | ■ |
| **Capitol Hill:** *Hyatt Regency Washington* $$$$<br>400 New Jersey Ave, NW (at D St). *(202) 737-1234, (800) 233-1234.* FAX *(202) 942-1512.* W www.washingtonregency.hyatt.com<br>Entrance to the Hyatt is through a superbly elegant plant-filled atrium. Children under 18 stay for free. | ■ | 834 (32) | ■ | ● | |
| **Capitol Hill:** *Phoenix Park Hotel* $$$$<br>520 N Capitol St, NW (at F St and N Capitol). *(202) 638-6900, (800) 824-5419.* FAX *(202) 393-3236.* W www.phoenixparkhotel.com<br>The rooms here are furnished in an 18th-century Irish Manor style. Three of the suites have spiral staircases, three have balconies. Irish entertainers perform nightly in the pub. | ■ | 149 (9) | ■ | ● | |
| **The Mall:** *Loews L'Enfant Plaza Hotel* $$$$<br>480 L'Enfant Plaza, SW. *(202) 484-1000, (800) 235-6397.* FAX *(202) 646-5060.*<br>W www.loewshotels.com<br>Named after Pierre L'Enfant, architect of the original city plans, this luxury three-star hotel is one of the top properties in DC. Many of the rooms have spectacular views of the city. | ■ | 370 (21) | ■ | ● | ■ |
| **Old Downtown:** *Washington International Youth Hostel* $<br>1009 11th St, NW (at K St, NW). *(202) 737-2333.* FAX *(202) 737-1508.*<br>W www.hiwashingtondc.org<br>Very inexpensive accommodation for the thrifty young traveler, the dormitory rooms hold up to 12 people. | ■ | 270 | | | |
| **Old Downtown:** *Hotel Harrington* $$<br>436 11th St, NW (at E St NW). *(202) 628-8140.* FAX *(202) 347-3924.*<br>W www.hotel-harrington.com<br>The Harrington is clean and comfortable. Popular with tourists and students, the central location and low prices offset the rather threadbare decor. | ■ | 250 | | ● | |
| **Old Downtown:** *Willard Inter-Continental Hotel* $$$$$<br>1401 Pennsylvania Ave, NW (at 14th St). *(202) 628-9100, (800) 327-0200.* FAX *(202) 637-7390.* W www.washington.interconti.com<br>This famous hotel offers rooms with marble bathrooms. The public areas feature chandeliers and mosaic floors. 24 | ■ | 340 (40) | ■ | | |
| **White House & Foggy Bottom:** *Doubletree Guest Suites* $$$<br>801 New Hampshire Ave (at H St NW). *(202) 785-2000, (800) 222-8733.* FAX *(202) 785-9485.* W www.doubletree.com<br>A full kitchen, pull-out beds, and two televisions per suite make this a good choice for families. The staff is friendly and efficient. | ■ | (105) | | ● | |
| **White House & Foggy Bottom:** *Hotel Lombardy* $$$<br>2019 Penn. Ave, NW (at I St, NW). *(202) 828-2600, (800) 424-5486.* FAX *(202) 872-0503.*<br>W www.hotellombardy.com<br>A European-style boutique hotel with two restaurants in the building and an accommodating multilingual staff. | ■ | 130 (30) | ■ | | |

**Price categories** for a standard double room per night, inclusive of breakfast, service charges, and any additional taxes:

- $ under $100
- $$ $100–$150
- $$$ $150–$200
- $$$$ $200–$250
- $$$$$ over $250

**CREDIT CARDS**
Major credit cards accepted.

**NUMBER OF ROOMS**
Number of rooms in the hotel (suites shown in parentheses).

**RECOMMENDED RESTAURANT**
Good restaurant within the hotel.

**CHILDREN'S FACILITIES**
Hotel has various facilities for young children.

**GARDEN OR TERRACE**
Hotel has a garden, courtyard, or terrace.

| Hotel | Credit Cards | Number of Rooms (Suites) | Recommended Restaurant | Children's Facilities | Garden or Terrace |
|---|---|---|---|---|---|
| **WHITE HOUSE & FOGGY BOTTOM:** *Lincoln Suites Downtown* $$$$<br>1823 L St, NW (between 18th St & 19th St). Tel *(202) 223-4320, (800) 424-2970.* FAX *(202) 223-8546.* W www.lincolnhotels.com<br>All rooms in this modern, boutique hotel are large studio apartments with full-size kitchens. Continental breakfast is included. | ■ | (99) | ■ | | |
| **WHITE HOUSE & FOGGY BOTTOM:** *Wyndham City Center* $$$$<br>1143 New Hampshire Ave (between 22nd St & M St). Tel *(202) 775-0800.* FAX *(202) 331-9491.* W www.wyndham.com<br>The Wyndham City Center is in a very good location for the busy tourist, close to all amenities and main sights. | ■ | 337 (15) | ■ | | |
| **WHITE HOUSE & FOGGY BOTTOM:** *Hay-Adams Hotel* $$$$$<br>800 16th St, NW (at H St). Tel *(202) 638-6600, (800) 424-5054.* FAX *(202) 638-2716.* W www.hayadams.com<br>Italian Renaissance-style property located directly across from the White House. Rooms have antiques and ornamental ceilings. | ■ | (143) | ■ | | |
| **WHITE HOUSE & FOGGY BOTTOM:** *St. Regis Washington* $$$$$<br>923 16th St, NW (at K St). Tel *(202) 638-2626, (800) 562-5661.* FAX *(202) 638-4231.* W www.stregis.com<br>A luxury hotel with more character than some of the chain hotels. Dinner in the restaurant makes for a romantic evening. | ■ | 181 (14) | ■ | | |
| **GEORGETOWN:** *The Georgetown Inn* $$$$<br>1310 Wisconsin Ave, NW (between N St & O St). Tel *(202) 333-8900, (800) 368-5922.* FAX *(202) 333-8308.* W www.georgetowninn.com<br>A small, boutique hotel built in the style of historic Georgetown. The large rooms have Colonial-style decor and luxurious bathrooms. | ■ | 86 (10) | ■ | | |
| **GEORGETOWN:** *The Latham Hotel* $$$$<br>3000 M St, NW (at 30th St). Tel *(202) 726-5000, (800) 368-5922.* FAX *(202) 337-4250.*<br>A European-style boutique hotel with four poolside bungalows and an excellent French restaurant. | ■ | 143 (9) | ■ | | ■ |
| **GEORGETOWN:** *Four Seasons Hotel* $$$$$<br>2800 Pennsylvania Ave, NW (between M St NW and Rock Creek & Potomac Parkway NW). Tel *(202) 342-0444, (800) 332-2443.* FAX *(202) 944-2076.* W www.fourseasons.com<br>A modern exterior belies the old-world elegance of this luxurious hotel, which prides itself on excellent service. | ■ | 257 (55) | ■ | ● | ■ |
| **FARTHER AFIELD:** *Brickskeller Inn* $$<br>1523 22nd St, NW (between P St & Q St NW). Tel *(202) 293-1885.* FAX *(202) 293-0996.* W www.thebrickskeller.com<br>An old, quaint hotel with an old-fashioned elevator dating from 1950. The restaurant offers over 1,000 kinds of beer from all around the world. | ■ | 40 | ■ | | |
| **FARTHER AFIELD:** *The Taft Bridge Inn* $$$<br>2007 Wyoming Ave, NW (at 20th St). Tel *(202) 387-2007.* W www.taftbridgeinn.com<br>This Georgian-style mansion is within walking distance of Adams-Morgan. Some rooms have a shared bathroom. Breakfast is included. | ■ | 12 | | | ■ |
| **FARTHER AFIELD:** *Hotel Madera* $$$$<br>1310 New Hampshire Ave, NW (at 13th St). Tel *(202) 296-7600, (800) 368-5691.* FAX *(202) 293-2476.* W www.hotelmadera.com<br>A small, simple boutique hotel in a great location near DuPont Circle and the White House. Some suites have kitchenettes. | ■ | (82) | ■ | | ■ |
| **FARTHER AFIELD:** *Westin Embassy Row* $$$$<br>2100 Massachusetts Ave, NW (at 21st St). Tel *(202) 293-2100.* FAX *(202) 293-0641.* W www.westin.com This stylish hotel is elegantly furnished. It's ideally located close to Dupont Circle and the Phillips Collection *(see p210).* | ■ | 206 | ■ | ● | |

For key to symbols see back flap

**Price categories** for a standard double room per night, inclusive of breakfast, service charges, and any additional taxes:

- $ under $100
- $$ $100–$150
- $$$ $150–$200
- $$$$ $200–$250
- $$$$$ over $250

**CREDIT CARDS** Major credit cards accepted.

**NUMBER OF ROOMS** Number of rooms in the hotel (suites shown in parentheses).

**RECOMMENDED RESTAURANT** Good restaurant within the hotel.

**CHILDREN'S FACILITIES** Hotel has various facilities for young children.

**GARDEN OR TERRACE** Hotel has a garden, courtyard, or terrace.

| Hotel | Credit Cards | Number of Rooms (Suites) | Recommended Restaurant | Children's Facilities | Garden or Terrace |
|---|---|---|---|---|---|
| **FARTHER AFIELD:** *Swann House* $$$$<br>1808 New Hampshire Ave, NW (between S St & Swann St). *(202) 265-7677.* FAX *(202) 265-6755.* W www.swannhouse.com<br>This B&B, in a Romanesque-style house built in 1883, is within walking distance of Du Pont Circle. | ■ | 9 (4) | | | ■ |
| **FARTHER AFIELD:** *Jefferson Hotel* $$$$$<br>1200 16th St, NW (at M St). *(202) 347-2200, (800) 235-6397.* FAX *(202) 331-7982.* W www.loewshotels.com<br>Built in 1923, this hotel is part of the America Hotel Historic Association. The rooms are decorated in Federal-style elegance, with antiques and original art. Service is outstanding. | ■ | 100 (35) | ■ | | |
| **FARTHER AFIELD:** *Madison Hotel* $$$$$<br>1177 15th St, NW (at M St). *(202) 862-1600, (800) 424-8577.* FAX *(202) 785-1255.* W www.themadisondchotel.net<br>The lobby of this hotel is filled with beautiful antiques, including a Louis XVI commode. Though modern on the outside, the hotel specializes in old-world luxury and meticulous service. | ■ | 311 (32) | ■ | | |
| **FARTHER AFIELD:** *Renaissance Mayflower* $$$$$<br>1127 Connecticut Ave, NW (at Desales St). *(202) 347-3000, (800) 468-3571.* FAX *(202) 776-9182.* W www.renaissancehotels.com<br>The Mayflower was built in 1925 and is on the National Register of Historic Places. | ■ | 660 (80) | | | ■ |
| **MARYLAND** | | | | | |
| **BALTIMORE:** *Ann Street Bed-and-Breakfast* $$<br>804 South Ann St. *(410) 342-5883.*<br>Originally two 18th-century townhouses, this B&B offers an authentic Colonial atmosphere with open fires and antique furniture. | | 3 (1) | | | |
| **BALTIMORE:** *Renaissance Harborplace Hotel* $$$$<br>202 E Pratt St (between South St & S Calvert St). *(410) 547-1200, (800) 535-1201.* FAX *(410) 539-5780.* W www.renaissancehotels.com<br>Many rooms in this hotel have a view of the harbor. The staff is attentive, and the restaurant serves excellent seafood. | ■ | 622 (30) | ■ | | |
| **BALTIMORE:** *Peabody Court, A Clarion Hotel* $$$$$<br>612 Cathedral St (between W Centre St & W Monument St). *(410) 727-7101, (800) 292-5500.* FAX *(410) 789-3312.* W www.peabodycourthotel.com<br>A small boutique hotel offering excellent service and located close to the Walters Art Gallery. | ■ | 104 (1) | ■ | | |
| **BERLIN:** *Merry Sherwood Plantation* $$$<br>8909 Worcester Hwy (nr Assateague). *(410) 641-2112, (800) 660-0358.* W www.merrysherwood.com<br>This inn is a restored 1850s Italianate Revival-style mansion, set on 21 acres (8.5 ha). The rooms have working fireplaces and Victorian-style furniture. | ■ | 8 (1) | | | ■ |
| **EASTON:** *Tidewater Inn* $$<br>101 East Dover St (near Chesapeake Bay). *(410) 822-1300, (800) 237-8775.* FAX *(410) 820-8847.* W www.tidewaterinn.com<br>A charming, historic inn furnished with antiques. The restaurant serves all types of food but the crab cakes are the specialty. | ■ | 114 (18) | ■ | | |
| **TILGHMAN ISLAND:** *Chesapeake Wood Duck Inn* $$$$<br>Gibsontown Rd, at Dogwood Harbor. *(410) 886-2070, (800) 956-2070.* FAX *(413) 677-7526.* W www.woodduckinn.com An award-winning, waterfront B&B offering great hospitality and innovative cuisine (dinner is available for guests). Recently received 3-diamond AAA and three-star Mobil awards. | ■ | 6 (1) | | | |

## VIRGINIA

| Hotel | | | | | |
|---|---|---|---|---|---|
| **ALEXANDRIA:** *Holiday Inn Select Old Town* $$$$<br>480 King St (at S Pitt St). (703) 838-8000, (800) 465-4329. FAX (703) 684-6508.<br>www.hiselect.com<br>A huge, old-fashioned lobby greets guests at this hotel. The refurbished rooms are Victorian in style. | ■ | 227 (2) | ● | | ■ |
| **CHARLOTTESVILLE:** *The Boar's Head Inn* $$$$<br>Route 250 West. (434) 296-2181, (800) 476-1988. FAX (434) 972-6024.<br>www.boarsheadinn.com<br>A luxurious inn, with two lakes on the grounds. Facilities include an 18-hole golf course, tennis, fishing, biking, and a spa. | ■ | 160 (11) | ■ | ● | |
| **COLONIAL WILLIAMSBURG:** *Colonial Houses* $$$$<br>136 East Francis St. (757) 229-1000. www.colonialwilliamsburg.com<br>Restored 18th-century houses with traditional furnishings and up-to-date facilities. You can rent one of the 28 independent houses or a room in a house. The facilities of the nearby Williamsburg Inn are also available. | ■ | 26 | | | |
| **COLONIAL WILLIAMSBURG:** *The Williamsburg Inn* $$$$$<br>136 East Francis St. (757) 229-1000. www.colonialwilliamsburg.com<br>This famous hotel offers all the luxuries of a modern hotel in a Regency-style setting. The Regency Room provides fine dining, and afternoon tea is served in the Terrace Room. Golf, croquet, and tennis are also available. | ■ | 68 | ■ | ● | |
| **FREDERICKSBURG:** *Kenmore Inn* $$$<br>1200 Princess Anne St. (540) 371-7622. FAX (540) 371-5480.<br>A historic inn with rooms decorated in either Victorian or Colonial style. It has two dining facilities – formal dining upstairs, and a pub downstairs. | ■ | 9 (1) | ■ | | |
| **LURAY:** *Skyland Resort* $<br>PO Box 727, Luray, VA 22835 (Skyline Drive). (540) 999-2211, (800) 999-4714. FAX (540) 999-2231. www.visitshenandoah.com<br>The Skyland Resort is on the highest point of a mountain, and most rooms have a view of the valley below. ● Dec–early Mar. | ■ | 171 (6) | ■ | | |
| **RICHMOND:** *The Berkeley Hotel* $$$$<br>1200 E Cary St. (804) 780-1300. www.berkeleyhotel.com<br>A warm welcome is given at this gracious hotel, with its lavish, traditional furnishings. Situated in the heart of downtown Richmond. | ■ | 55 (1) | ■ | ● | |

## WEST VIRGINIA

| Hotel | | | | | |
|---|---|---|---|---|---|
| **CHARLES TOWN:** *The Washington House Inn* $$<br>216 S George St. (304) 725-7923, (800) 297-6957.<br>www.washingtonhouseinnwv.com<br>This historic three-story brick mansion is located near Harpers Ferry and Blue Ridge Mountains. Open all year. | ■ | 7 | ■ | ● | |
| **ELKINS:** *Tunnel Mountain B&B* $<br>Route 1, Box 59-1. (304) 636-1684, (888) 211-9123.<br>This three-story stone house is spread across 5 acres (2 ha), at the edge of the Monongahela National Forest. No kids under 12 permitted. | | 3 | | | ■ |

## DELAWARE

| Hotel | | | | | |
|---|---|---|---|---|---|
| **LEWES:** *Sleep Inn & Suites* $$<br>1595 Hwy 1. (302) 645-6464, (800) 424-6423. www.choicehotels.com<br>Fairly close to Rehoboth Beach and the plethora of tax-free outlets in the area, this inn offers a free Continental breakfast, and free coffee and juice all day. | ■ | 81 | | | |
| **NEW CASTLE:** *The Jerry House* $$<br>130 Delaware St. (302) 322-2505. www.jerryhouse.com<br>This elegant 1860s townhouse is in the heart of New Castle's historic district, and features tastefully appointed rooms and a mini-museum that highlights Delaware history. | ■ | 5 | | | |
| **WILMINGTON:** *Hotel DuPont* $$$$<br>11th St & Market. (302) 594-3100, (800) 441-9019.<br>www.hoteldupont.com<br>Delaware's only four-star hotel provides easy access to Longwood Gardens and Delaware Art Museum. There are two superb restaurants. | ■ | 217 | ■ | | ■ |

For key to symbols see back flap

# Where to Eat

An eclectic choice of food is on offer across Washington. There are many traditional restaurants that serve classic American dishes, while DC's cosmopolitan population is reflected in the vast number of Ethiopian, Vietnamese, and Italian restaurants. The opening times of some restaurants are indicated by a "B" for breakfast, "L" for lunch, and "D" for dinner.

## Washington, DC

**Capitol Hill:** *America* — $
Union Station, 50 Massachusetts Ave, NE. *(202) 682-9555.*
The 200-item menu, including all the American classics, is sure to please everybody and makes the choice both easy and inexpensive.

**Capitol Hill:** *Market Lunch* — $
Eastern Market, 225 7th St, SE (at C St). *(202) 547-8444.*
Authentic regional food, such as crab cakes and crab sandwiches, are offered here. The cafeteria-style breakfast and lunch are casual but delicious. Expect a long wait on Saturday and Sunday mornings. *Mon.*

**Capitol Hill:** *Tunnicliff's* — $
222 7th St, SE (opposite Eastern Market). *(202) 544-5680.*
The old wooden interior attracts a casual and diverse crowd. The cuisine is American pub-type food.

**Georgetown:** *Café Divan* — $
1834 Wisconsin Ave, NW (north of S St). *(202) 338-1747.*
There's a small take-out area as well as a dining room for a leisurely meal. Specialties include lamb, chicken, seafood, and pides (Turkish pizza with a thin crust). The mezze platter makes a reasonable lunch.

**Georgetown:** *Café La Ruche* — $
1039 31st St NW (between K St & C&O Canal). *(202) 965-2684.*
A typical Parisian bistro with a comfortable atmosphere that is great for chatting with friends. There is a wide range of dishes available, including rainbow trout, crab cakes, mussels niçoise, and soups and salads.

**Georgetown:** *Zed's Ethiopian Cuisine* — $
1201 28th St, NW. *(202) 333-4710.*
An Ethiopian restaurant, popular with vegetarians, Zed's is known for its traditional Ethiopian fare – *wats* (red pepper sauces), *alechas* (stews), and *injera* (bread).

**Georgetown:** *Martin's Tavern* — $$
1264 Wisconsin Ave, NW (at N St). *(202) 333-7370.*
Martin's is the oldest family-owned restaurant in DC, and one of the most charming locations for American pub food.

**Georgetown:** *Old Glory All American Barbecue* — $$
3139 M St, NW (between Wisconsin Ave & 31st St). *(202) 337-3406.*
This homey restaurant serves traditional and much-loved American fare, such as spare ribs, hickory-smoked chicken, wood-fried shrimp, and apple crisps.

**Georgetown:** *Sequoia* — $$
Washington Harbor, 3000 K St, NW. *(202) 944-4200.*
A trendy restaurant that combines American cuisine with fabulous views of the Potomac and Virginia skyline.

**Georgetown:** *Citronelle* — $$$$$
Latham Hotel, 3000 M St, NW (at 30th St). *(202) 625-2150.*
This excellent restaurant serves wonderful food including a variety of sophisticated and exotic French dishes, such as pastry "cigars" stuffed with wild mushrooms, as well as seafood such as potato-crusted halibut.

**Greater Washington:** *Ben's Chili Bowl* — $
1213 U St, NW (between 12th & 13th Sts). *(202) 667-0909.*
A favorite for anyone who loves a good, high-calorie meal. The chili dogs are known nationally. Ben's Chili Bowl also happens to be Bill Cosby's favorite haunt when he visits DC.

| Restaurant | Credit Cards | Outdoor Tables | Vegetarian | Good Wine List | Late Opening |
|---|---|---|---|---|---|
| America | ■ | ● | ■ | ● | |
| Market Lunch | | ● | | | |
| Tunnicliff's | ■ | ● | ■ | | ■ |
| Café Divan | ■ | | ■ | | |
| Café La Ruche | ■ | ● | ■ | ● | |
| Zed's Ethiopian Cuisine | ■ | ● | ■ | ● | |
| Martin's Tavern | ■ | ● | ■ | ● | ■ |
| Old Glory All American Barbecue | ■ | ● | ■ | | ■ |
| Sequoia | ■ | ● | ■ | ● | ■ |
| Citronelle | ■ | | ■ | ● | |
| Ben's Chili Bowl | | | ■ | | ■ |

**Price categories** include a three-course meal for one, a glass of house wine and all unavoidable extra charges such as sales tax and service.
$ under \$20
$$ \$20–30
$$$ \$30–45
$$$$ \$45–60
$$$$$ over \$60

**CREDIT CARDS**
Major credit cards accepted.
**OUTDOOR TABLES**
Garden, courtyard, or terrace with outside tables.
**VEGETARIAN**
A good selection of vegetarian dishes available.
**GOOD WINE LIST**
Extensive list of good wines, both domestic and imported.
**LATE OPENING**
Full menu or light meals served after 11pm.

| Restaurant | Price | Credit Cards | Outdoor Tables | Vegetarian | Good Wine List | Late Opening |
|---|---|---|---|---|---|---|
| **REATER WASHINGTON:** *City Lights of China*<br>731 Connecticut Ave, NW (between R & S Sts). *(202) 265-6688.*<br>lany people attest that the crowds and waiting in line are worth it. he City Lights of China serves inexpensive and delicious Chinese food. elivery is available too. | $ | ■ | | ■ | | |
| **REATER WASHINGTON:** *Kramerbooks & Afterwords Café*<br>517 Connecticut Ave, NW (between Dupont Circle & Q St). *(202) 387-1462.*<br>his café serves salads, pasta, as well as exotic Asian-influenced egetarian dishes. Kramerbooks and Afterwards Café is open 24 hours n weekends. | $ | ■ | ● | ■ | ● | ■ |
| **REATER WASHINGTON:** *Georgetown Seafood Grill*<br>200 19th St, NW (between M & N Sts). *(202) 530-4430.*<br>ligh-quality seafood at a moderate price – the crab cakes are said to be ie best in town. The service is quick and friendly. P | $$ | ■ | ● | ■ | ● | |
| **GREATER WASHINGTON:** *La Tomate*<br>701 Connecticut Ave NW (between R & S Sts). *(202) 667-5505.*<br>his Italian restaurant's prime location near Du Pont Circle makes a summer favorite with the locals for outdoor eating. P | $$ | ■ | ● | ■ | ● | |
| **REATER WASHINGTON:** *Pesce*<br>016 P St, NW (between 20th & 21st Sts). *(202) 466-3474.*<br>he French and Italian menu changes daily but always includes delicious eafood and a fabulous wine list. Great food at a reasonable price. | $$ | ■ | | | ● | |
| **REATER WASHINGTON:** *Nora's*<br>132 Florida Ave, NW. *(202) 462-5143.* W www.noras.com<br>ne of the stalwarts of Washington dining, this restaurant features varied menu of contemporary American cuisine and organic igredients. P | $$$ | ■ | | ■ | ● | |
| **LD DOWNTOWN:** *Full Kee*<br>09 H St, NW (between 5th & 6th Sts). *(202) 371-2233.*<br>he Cantonese noodles and dumplings are excellent. A great place to rab a cheap meal before an MCI Center event. | $ | | | ■ | | |
| **LD DOWNTOWN:** *Hard Rock Café*<br>99 E St, NW (at 10th St). *(202) 737-7625.*<br>l the American classics are available, including a variety of burgers, indwiches, and salads. Videos, music, and memorabilia make the two floors f this restaurant an exciting, but rather hectic, tourist experience. | $ | ■ | | ■ | | |
| **LD DOWNTOWN:** *Bistro Bis*<br>5 E St, NW (between N Capitol & New Jersey). *(202) 661-2700.*<br>rench food with a distinctly American twist, served in a beautiful, cozy ining area. The duck confit and salmon Provençal are recommended. | $$ | ■ | ● | ■ | ● | |
| **LD DOWNTOWN:** *Old Ebbitt Grill*<br>75 15th St, NW (between Pennsylvania Ave & G St). *(202) 347-4801.*<br>xpect this upbeat American grill to be packed with both locals and urists – anyone who likes a great meal. Old Ebbitt Grill offers a chance sample the DC scene as well as quality seafood, pasta, and steaks. | $$ | ■ | | ■ | ● | ■ |
| **HE MALL:** *Cascade Café*<br>ational Gallery of Art, Concourse Level, Constitution Ave, NW (between 4th 7th Sts). *(202) 216-5966.*<br>ne of the better options for hungry museum-goers, Cascade Café ffers fast and convenient buffet-style food, including salads and great esserts. | $ | ■ | | ■ | | |

For key to symbols see back flap

**Price categories** include a three-course meal for one, a glass of house wine and all unavoidable extra charges such as sales tax and service.
($) under $20
($)($) $20–30
($)($)($) $30–45
($)($)($)($) $45–60
($)($)($)($)($) over $60

**Credit Cards**
Major credit cards accepted.

**Outdoor Tables**
Garden, courtyard, or terrace with outside tables.

**Vegetarian**
A good selection of vegetarian dishes available.

**Good Wine List**
Extensive list of good wines, both domestic and imported.

**Late Opening**
Full menu or light meals served after 11pm.

**The Mall:** *Flight Line Café* ($)
National Air & Space Museum, Independence Ave (between 4th & 7th Sts). *(202) 357-2700.*
The only restaurant in the museum, it offers a range of hamburgers, pizzas, and sandwiches.

**The Mall:** *The Palm Court Ice Cream Parlor and Café* ($)
National Museum of American History, Constitution Ave, NW (between 12th & 14th Sts). *(202) 357-2700.*
A typical American selection of cuisine is offered, but this is a bit more expensive than some of the other Mall eateries.

**White House & Foggy Bottom:** *Aroma* ($)
1919 I St, NW (between 19th & 20th Sts). *(202) 833-4700.*
This North Indian restaurant is one of the best-kept secrets in Washington. It is casual yet elegant, and the food is excellent.

**White House & Foggy Bottom:** *Bombay Club* ($)
815 Connecticut Ave, NW (between H & I Sts). *(202) 659-3727.*
Exotic Indian food in a Colonial setting. The attentive service and exclusive clientele provide a glimpse of upper-crust Washington.

**White House & Foggy Bottom:** *Hors D'Oeuvrerie* ($)
Kennedy Center. *(202) 416-8560.*
The Kennedy Center location for light fare, such as salads and wraps. Open after the last show, it is an ideal place to grab a cocktail.

**White House & Foggy Bottom:** *Galileo* ($)($)
1110 21st St, NW (between L & M Sts). *(202) 293-7191.*
The most talked-about Italian restaurant in DC, Galileo is famous for its innovative and elaborate dishes, such as homemade pastas, risottos, and game dishes, as well as its fine selection of wines.

**White House & Foggy Bottom:** *Georgia Brown's* ($)($)
950 15th St, NW (between I & K Sts). *(202) 393-4499.*
Anyone who craves Carolina shrimp, grits (fried, coarse grain), or fried green tomatoes should come here. Southern cooking with style in an inviting but hectic atmosphere.

**White House & Foggy Bottom:** *Kinkead's* ($)($)
Red Lion Row, 2000 Pennsylvania Ave, NW (bet. 20th & 21st Sts). *(202) 296-7700.*
A fantastic seafood restaurant without the price inflation that can come with a big name. Bob Kinkead's creations, such as the pepita-crusted salmon, are wonderfully complemented by the fine wine list.

## Maryland

**Annapolis:** *Middletown Tavern Oyster Bar & Restaurant* ($)($)
2 Market Space. *(410) 263-3323.*
Located across the street from the harbor, this outdoor restaurant is a perfect spot to soak up the view. The oysters come with beer; also on the menu are crab cakes, seafood, and pasta dishes.

**Baltimore:** *Obrycki's Crab House* ($)($)
1727 E Pratt St. *(410) 732-6399.*
A seasonal restaurant that offers superb seafood dining. A favorite of the house is the hard-shell steamed crabs. *Dec–Mar.*

**Chesapeake Bay:** *The Crab Claw* ($)($)
304 Mill St at Navy Point, St. Michaels. *(410) 745-2900.*
A seasonal restaurant located right on the harbor, with spectacular views. The fresh seafood dishes are the specialty of the house.
*Dec–Feb.*

| Restaurant | Credit Cards | Outdoor Tables | Vegetarian | Good Wine List | Late Opening |
|---|---|---|---|---|---|
| Flight Line Café | ■ | | | | |
| The Palm Court Ice Cream Parlor and Café | ■ | | | | |
| Aroma | ■ | | ■ | | |
| Bombay Club | ■ | ● | ■ | ● | |
| Hors D'Oeuvrerie | ■ | | ■ | ● | ■ |
| Galileo | ■ | ● | ■ | ● | |
| Georgia Brown's | ■ | | ■ | ● | |
| Kinkead's | ■ | ● | ■ | ● | |
| Middletown Tavern Oyster Bar & Restaurant | ■ | ● | ■ | ● | ■ |
| Obrycki's Crab House | ■ | | ■ | ● | ■ |
| The Crab Claw | | ● | ■ | ● | |

**REDERICK:** *The Red Horse Steak House* $$

96 W Patrick St. (301) 663-3030.

local institution, famous for the prime ribs, humongous steaks, and fresh rout. An excellent wine list. *Mon–Fri L, Mon–Sat D, Sun buffet 4pm–9pm.*

**CEAN CITY:** *Phillips Crab House* $

1st St & Philadelphia Ave. (410) 289-6821.

Vhat's a visit to the Eastern Shore without a visit to Phillips. Fresh crab in arious guises, oysters, clams, and anything fishy. The famous seafood uffet opens daily at 3:30pm. *mid-Mar–Oct: daily.*

## VIRGINIA

**LEXANDRIA:** *Gadsby's Tavern* $$

38 N Royal St, at Cameron St. (703) 548-1288.

Iere the waiters are in Colonial costume, and the decor is in the style of ate 1700s. The menu includes duck, venison, seafood, and pies.

**HARLOTTESVILLE:** *Michie Tavern* $

83 Thomas Jefferson Parkway. (434) 977-1234. www.michietavern.com

asual dining with a Colonial touch – serving staff dress in Colonial utfits, and the decor is on the rustic side. The traditional Southern fried hicken is outstanding. *L.*

**OLONIAL WILLIAMSBURG:** *Chowning's Tavern* $

09 Duke of Gloucester St (at Queen St). 1-800-HISTORY.

his restaurant is a step back into the 18th century. Lunches include full-are cafeteria style dishes such as Brunswick stew and ribs; dinners are ight. Gambols (18th-century entertainment) take place nightly.

**OLONIAL WILLIAMSBURG:** *The Trellis* $$

03 Duke of Gloucester St. (757) 229-8610.

egional cuisine which concentrates on fresh food – the menu changes very season. Located in the heart of the historic district, it offers an xtensive wine list with more than 20 wines from Virginia.

**ICHMOND:** *Southern Culture* $

229 W Main St. (804) 355-6939.

his restaurant serves a variety of regional Southern food, ranging from irginia chicken to seafood from the Gulf of Mexico. *Mon.*

**KYLINE DRIVE:** *Inn at Little Washington* $$$$$

89 Main St, Little Washington. (540) 675-3800.

his five-star and five-diamond restaurant offers regional, eclectic merican cuisine. The 90-minute drive might be discouraging, but the nviting country house makes it worthwhile.

## WEST VIRGINIA

**LKINS:** *Cheat River Inn* $$

lkins, WV (304) 636-6265. www.cheatriverlodge.com

iverside dining, prime beef and rainbow trout specialties. Ideal for in iking and camping in the Monogahela National Forest. *Mon.*

**EW RIVER GORGE:** *Hawk's Nest Restaurant* $

JS Route 60, Ansted, WV, in the Hawk's Nest State Park. (304) 658-4444.

reat views of the New River Gorge. This family resturant is popular for s good home cooking, fine wines, and domestic beers. *B, L, D.*

*7 days: 7am–7:45pm, Sun: deli bar.* *Dec 25.*

## DELAWARE

**EW CASTLE:** *Jessop's Tavern* $$

14 Delaware St. (302) 322-6111.

Jnique, Colonial decor and tavern fare. Home cooking, authentic with arly American entrees and appetizers. Not commercial at all but a real tmospheric treat. Nice wooden tables, excellent food. Reservations ecommended. *L, D.*

**EHOBOTH BEACH:** *The Back Porch Café* $$$

9 Rehoboth Avenue. (302) 227-3674.

ocated in an old beach house, this café specializes in seafood, with a ig wine list and live music on weekends. *Jun–Sep: L, D daily; May & Oct: ri–Sun.* *Nov–Apr.*

For key to symbols see back flap

# THE SOUTHEAST

# The Southeast at a Glance

Although the five Southeast states – North and South Carolina, Kentucky, Tennessee, and Georgia – share a common history and culture, they are quite distinct from one another. The region covers three different topographical areas. To the east, the low-lying coastal plains along the Atlantic include the historic cities of Savannah, Georgia, and Charleston, South Carolina, bordered by pristine beaches. The central Blue Ridge and Appalachian Mountains hold acres and acres of stunningly scenic wilderness, while in the inland foothills, linked to the Gulf of Mexico by the Mississippi and other broad rivers, are cities such as Louisville, Kentucky, and Tennessee's twin music capitals, Nashville and Memphis. Atlanta is the main commercial center.

***Lexington*** (see p270) *is Kentucky's main horse-bre[...] ing center. Visitors are allo[...] access to most of the stud farms surrounding the city*

***Nashville*** (see pp264–5) *is Tennessee's state capital as well as the nation's country music capital. The town's revitalized downtown, with its lively restaurants, cafés, and nightclubs, is the center of action, day and night.*

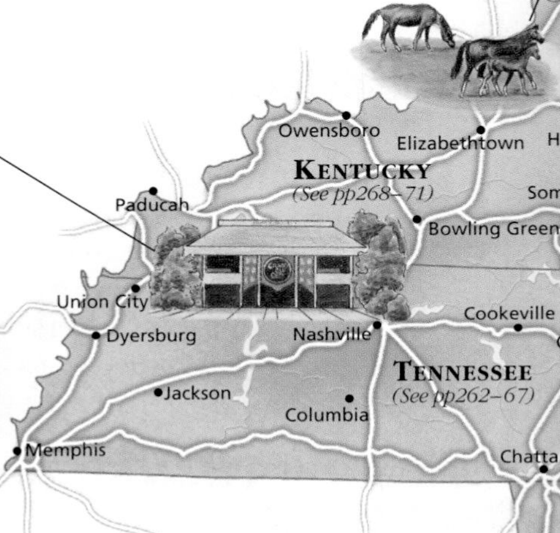

***Atlanta*** (see pp260–61), *Georgia's capital, is the place where Coca-Cola was born in the 1880s. Since then, the drink has become an international favorite. The hard-hitting TV news channel, CNN, is also based in Atlanta.*

◁ **Acres of farmlands stretching across southwestern Georgia**

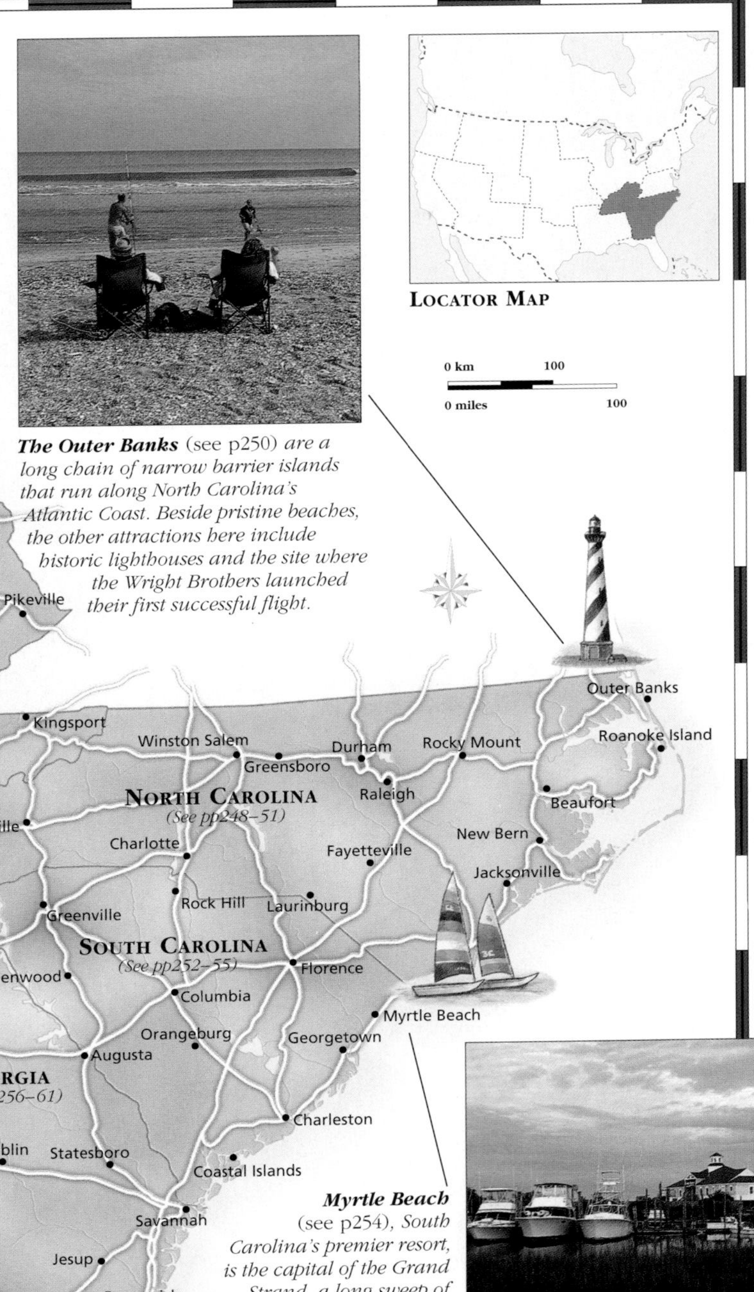


***The Outer Banks*** (see p250) *are a long chain of narrow barrier islands that run along North Carolina's Atlantic Coast. Beside pristine beaches, the other attractions here include historic lighthouses and the site where the Wright Brothers launched their first successful flight.*

***Myrtle Beach*** (see p254), *South Carolina's premier resort, is the capital of the Grand Strand, a long sweep of Atlantic coastline. The beach and its environs offer a wide variety of seaside amusements.*

# THE SOUTHEAST

ONE OF THE COUNTRY'S *most fascinating regions, the Southeast is home to two of America's most beautiful cities – Charleston and Savannah – as well as some of its most pristine beaches and expanses of primeval forests. Culturally, the region is famous for its vibrant musical traditons, as both country-western and the blues originated in Nashville and Memphis.*

The Southeast's cities reflect the region's proud cultural heritage. Celebrated for their beauty and sophistication, Charleston and Savannah are urban gems, with lushly landscaped parks and gracious homes. Both actively preserve their stately architecture as well as support a fine range of hotels, restaurants, and cultural institutions. Other cities vary greatly. The quiet college town of Durham, North Carolina, rated the "most educated city in America," stands in direct contrast to burgeoning commercial centers such as Atlanta, Georgia, the economic capital of the "New South." Equally engaging are Nashville, the capital of country-western music, and Memphis, the birthplace of the blues.

The region's natural landscape is as memorable. Nearly a thousand miles of Atlantic coastline are formed by a long series of offshore barrier islands, ranging from Cape Hatteras to Cumberland Island on the Florida border. Just inland, and linked to the ocean by several broad rivers, is the heartland of the Colonial-era plantation country. Farther inland are the farmlands of North Carolina, the primary US producer of tobacco products, and the rolling bluegrass fields of Kentucky's verdant Horse Country. At the center lies unforgettable mountain scenery.

### HISTORY

Long before the arrival of the first Europeans, the region was home to a highly developed Native American culture, known as the Moundbuilders. Evidence of their large cities can be seen at Georgia's Ocmulgee National Monument. Later Indians, especially the Cherokee who lived in western North Carolina and northern Georgia,

**Kentucky Derby, the annual horse-racing event held in Louisville's Churchill Downs**

◁ **Colorful, patriotic roofline, South Carolina**

**Exhibits in the Civil War Museum, Bardstown, Kentucky**

were among North America's most civilized tribes. Other tribes included the Creek, Tuscarora, Yamasee, and Catawba, but by the early 1800s, most of the Indians had been decimated by war and disease, or driven westward. Apart from a prominent Cherokee community in the far western corner of North Carolina, very few Indians survive in the region today.

In the early 1500s, explorers from Florida's Spanish colonies ventured here, lured by Indians' tales of great wealth. The Spanish were followed by the French and then the English. But it was only in 1670, under Charles II, that the first successful colony, called Carolina, was established near what is today Charleston. Carolina's first settlers came from the congested English colony of Barbados, and it was their agricultural expertise that made the land-owning "planters" the wealthiest in the American colonies. Their wealth, however, was based on slave labor, and thousands of Africans were imported to clear the swamps, dig canals, and harvest the crops. Along the coast where the main crops, rice and indigo, were grown, the white colonists were a small minority, outnumbered four to one by the workers whose labor they exploited.

The great fortunes made in Carolina inspired the creation in 1732 of another colony, Georgia, located to the south. In many ways Georgia was a novel colony, funded by the government rather than private interests and founded with social, rather than commercial, intentions. For the first time in the Americas, slavery was banned, as was drinking alcohol and the presence of lawyers. The new colony, however, faltered and came under the control of Carolina, which introduced the slave-holding practices.

In December 1860, the state of South Carolina declared itself independent from the rest of the country. Though Georgia followed soon after, the other Southeast states remained with the Union. It was only after South Carolina forces attacked the fortress at Fort Sumter near Charleston, on April 12, 1861, did Tennessee and North Carolina join the rebel cause. Ironically, only Kentucky, the birthplace of President Abraham Lincoln and Confederate President Jefferson Davis, remained divided – a true border state.

The impact of the four-year Civil War lasted for another 100 years, as the struggle against the iniquities of slavery gained momentum as the Civil Rights Movement. While primarily a grassroots

## KEY DATES IN HISTORY

**1587** Sir Walter Raleigh sponsors the establishment of an ill-fated colony at Roanoke in present-day North Carolina

**1670** The first permanent English settlement in the Carolina colony is established at Charleston

**1729** Carolina divided into North and South

**1763** The Anglo-Spanish treaty fixes the Mississippi River as the western extent of the Southeast colonies

**1792** Kentucky becomes the 15th US state

**1795** The University of North Carolina, the country's first state-sponsored university, opens at Chapel Hill

**1838** The government forcibly expels the Cherokees westward on the "Trail of Tears"

**1861** Confederates attack on Fort Sumter

**1864** General Sherman spares Savannah at the end of his notorious "March to the Sea"

**1903** The Ohio-based Wright Brothers make the first successful powered airplane flight at Kitty Hawk, North Carolina

**1976** Georgia Governor Jimmy Carter elected 39th president of the United States

**1996** Atlanta hosts the centennial Olympics

**2002** Jimmy Carter wins the Nobel Peace Prize

Grave of Dr. Martin Luther King Jr. in Atlanta, a pilgrimage site for people from all over the world

campaign, many of the battles were led by Atlanta-born Baptist minister Martin Luther King Jr, who practiced the use of nonviolent direct action to win equality for black people. Though Dr. King was assassinated while participating in a strike by black sanitation workers in Memphis in 1968, the movement for Civil Rights eventually saw his colleague Andrew Young elected to Congress from Georgia. Young was later elected mayor of Atlanta in 1981.

### Society, Culture, & the Arts

The Southeast has been, and continues to be, a major contributor to American culture. Atlanta gave the world Coca-Cola and CNN, while Kentucky, particularly Colonel Sanders and his Kentucky Fried Chicken, spread the craze for fast food. Kentucky is also well known all over the world for its production of high-quality bourbon whiskey and high-speed horses.

Important though the region's cities are, they are also the conduit through which the outside world reaches into their hinterlands. Nashville's country music, for example, is deeply rooted in Appalachian folkways, while the blues and rock 'n' roll of Memphis emerge from the different ethnic and historical cultures of the broad Mississippi Delta. A roll call of the artists born and bred here spans all musical genres – the Everly Brothers, Bill Monroe, and Loretta Lynn are from Kentucky; John Coltrane, Doc Watson, Thelonius Monk, and Nina Simone hail from North Carolina; the Allman Brothers, James Brown, Otis Redding, and Gladys Knight came from Georgia; while Tennessee can take credit for Chet Atkins, Tina Turner, and Carl Perkins, and its favorite adopted son, Elvis Presley (1935–77).

This is also true of literature, which witnessed the creativity of such diverse writers as Alice Walker, Thomas Wolfe, Carson McCullers, and James Agee, and characters and settings such as "God's Little Acre" and "Catfish Row" from George Gershwin's opera *Porgy & Bess.* Music, literature, and the arts still dominate Southeastern culture, and numerous events and festivals are celebrated all over the region.

### Tourism

The Appalachain Mountains and their local constituents, the Blue Ridge and Great Smoky Mountains, offer miles of spectacular scenery in near-pristine condition. Much of the mountain landscape is now preserved in a series of local, state, and national parks, and forests. The Great Smoky Mountains National Park, in particular, is one of the country's most popular, drawing millions of visitors each year. Other attractions include the beach resorts that proliferate along the Outer Banks in North Carolina, and Louisville's Kentucky Derby, reputed to be the biggest racing event in the country.

Local band performing in one of the many clubs in downtown Nashville, Tennessee

# Exploring the Southeast

DESPITE THE SOUTHEAST'S diverse landscape and topography, the region is compact enough to tour in about a week. The coastal cities of Charleston and Savannah, as well as the inland metropolises of Atlanta, Nashville, and Memphis, are well linked by road and short-haul airline flights. The broad crest of mountains that rise up at the center include such prime attractions as the scenic Blue Ridge Parkway and the Great Smoky Mountains National Park. Among the region's other highlights are Georgia's beautiful Golden Isles and Kentucky's spectacular mountain landscapes and bluegrass pasturelands, famous for their thoroughbred horse farms.

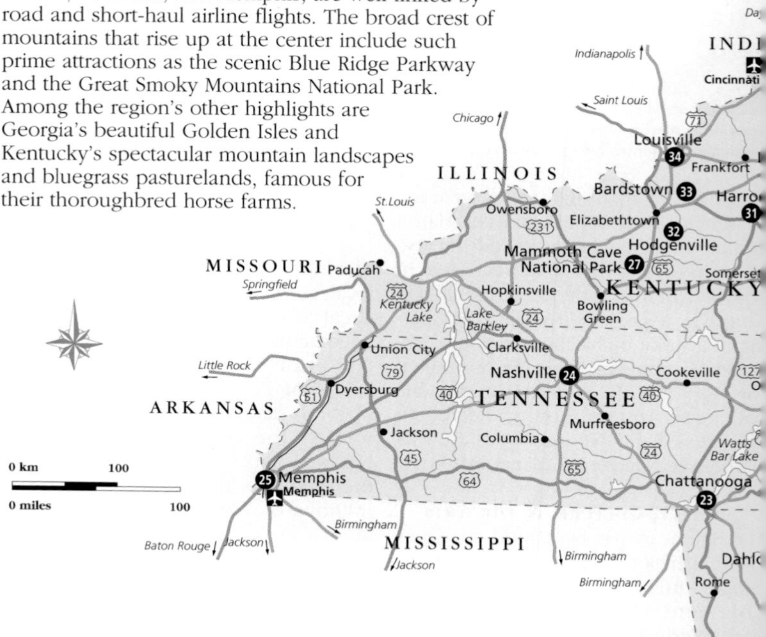

## SIGHTS AT A GLANCE

**Key**

- Airport
- Highway
- Major road
- Railroad
- State border

## Mileage Chart

10 = Distance in miles
10 = Distance in kilometers

| | Atlanta, GA | Savannah, GA | Asheville, NC | Charleston, SC | Nashville, TN | Memphis, TN | Lexington, KY |
|---|---|---|---|---|---|---|---|
| Savannah, GA | 248 / 399 | | | | | | |
| Asheville, NC | 207 / 333 | 310 / 499 | | | | | |
| Charleston, SC | 324 / 522 | 115 / 185 | 268 / 432 | | | | |
| Nashville, TN | 250 / 402 | 497 / 800 | 294 / 473 | 551 / 887 | | | |
| Memphis, TN | 460 / 740 | 711 / 1143 | 506 / 814 | 787 / 1266 | 213 / 343 | | |
| Lexington, KY | 379 / 609 | 583 / 938 | 283 / 455 | 540 / 869 | 213 / 343 | 423 / 681 | |
| Louisville, KY | 422 / 678 | 658 / 1058 | 358 / 576 | 616 / 991 | 175 / 281 | 385 / 619 | 79 / 127 |

### *See Also*


- ***Practical Information*** pp272–3
- ***Where to Stay*** pp274–7
- ***Where to Eat*** pp278–81

**View of smoky mist from Clingman's Dome, Great Smoky Mountains National Park**

# North Carolina

THE SITE OF THE FIRST English outpost in America in 1585, North Carolina became the 12th of the original 13 states in 1789 – it was also one of the country's 13 original colonies. While the population is increasingly based in cities, much of the state remains covered with fields of tobacco, a crop whose politics are the source of local and national debate. Still, the sight of green fields dotted with plank-wood, tin-roofed drying sheds continues to conjure up a classic image of North Carolina. Though tobacco-growing dominates the state's center, the east is lined by miles of pristine Atlantic Ocean beachfront, and the western mountains are among the most majestic found east of the Rockies.

**Façade of North Carolina Museum of History, Raleigh**

## Research Triangle Region ❶

1,188,000. Durham Convention and Visitors' Bureau, 101 E Morgan St, Durham, (919) 687-0288, (800) 446-8604.

THE STATE CAPITAL of Raleigh forms a regional triangle with the two major university towns of Durham and Chapel Hill. This region is the state's intellectual center, and has spawned the high-technology Research Triangle Park, a corporate campus located between the three cities.

Primarily a business region and gateway, the Triangle provides various urban conveniences and offers some interesting sights. Quiet downtown Raleigh includes a handful of modern state museums located across from the 1840 Greek Revival State Capitol, including the Sports Hall of Fame, the Museum of Natural Sciences, and the **North Carolina Museum of History**. The latter is well known for a Civil War exhibit describing the state's divided loyalties. A Civil Rights exhibit is also due to open here in 2004. A few miles north toward the airport, the **North Carolina Museum of Art** holds three floors of statuary and paintings. Among these is the 16th-century *Madonna and Child in a Landscape* by the artist Lucas Cranach the Elder, which had been stolen by the Nazis. When this was discovered, the museum returned the painting to its original owner, who in turn, has now loaned it back to the museum.

Of the two university towns, the smaller Chapel Hill, with its wooded **University of North Carolina (UNC)** campus, Morehead Planetarium, art museum, and genteel Carolina Inn with its aristocratic clientele, is by far the quainter of the two. Downtown Durham, wedged between the three-part **Duke University** campus, is home to the Durham Bulls minor-league baseball team. It also hosts the annual September Blues Festival. A major landmark on the West Campus is the superb Neo-Gothic Duke Chapel. Alumni and students of the two universities enjoy the lively rivalry between their respective sports teams – the Duke's Blue Devils and UNC's Tar Heels.

**North Carolina Museum of History**
5 E Edenton St, Raleigh. (919) 80 7900. 9am–5pm Tue–Sat, 1–5pm Sun. Mon.

**North Carolina Museum of Art**
2110 Blue Ridge Rd, Raleigh. (919) 839-6262. 9am–5pm Wed–Sat (to 9pm Fri), 10am–5pm Sun.
www.ncartmuseum.org

**UNC Visitor Center**
250 E Franklin St, Chapel Hill. (919) 962-1630. 9am–5pm Mon– Fri. Sat–Sun, public hols.

## Winston-Salem ❷

186,000. 200 Brookstown Ave 27101, (336) 777-3796.
www.visitwinstonsalem.com

NORTH CAROLINA'S close ties with the tobacco industry are evident in the fact that two major US cigarette brands have been named after this twin city. Moravian immigrants first settled here in 1766. Their descendants celebrate their roots at **Old Salem**, an interesting restoration of a Colonial village, where guides dressed in period costume demonstrate traditional crafts in the church, bakery, tavern, homes, and gardens. They also relate the story of this Protestant sect's journey from Moravia to this region. Gift shops throughout the village offer such Moravian wares as handmade lace and pewter ornaments. The complex is set invitingly on a hill and is compact enough to be covered in an hour or two.

Adjacent to the village is the **Museum of Early Southern Decorative Arts**. Guides take

**Actors dressed in period costume, Old Salem Colonial village**

panoramic view of lush vegetation and mountains from the Blue Ridge Parkway

isitors through 24 rooms xhibiting antebellum ırnishings and artifacts from cross the region. A children's nuseum is downstairs.

**Old Salem**
00 Old Salem Rd. (336) 721-7300. 9am–5pm Mon–Sat, 12:30–5pm un. Easter, Thnksg., Dec 24, 25. museum. www.oldsalem.org

## 3lue Ridge Parkway ❸

(828) 298-0398.
www.nps.gov/blri

A SCENIC two-lane highway, the Blue Ridge Parkway (*see pp40–41*) runs 469 miles (755 km) south from Virginia along the Blue Ridge Mountain ridge-line. Its most scenic stretches lie in North Carolina, where the road meanders for 250 miles (402 km) past peaks, waterfalls, and the towering, 6,684-ft (2,037-m) Mount Mitchell.

The National Park Service's most popular destination with over 23 million visitors every year, the route has a maximum speed limit of 45 mph (72 km/h), which is strictly enforced. It is most scenic during spring and fall. Some sections close in winter. There are ample opportunities to detour to nearby trails and mountain towns such as Boone and Blowing Rock.

The parkway ends at the entrance to **Great Smoky Mountains National Park**, north of Cherokee *(see p262)*. Here, at the reservation of the Eastern Band of Cherokee Indians, a museum relates the history of the Cherokee people, focusing on the forcible removal of the tribe in 1838 to Oklahoma on the "Trail of Tears." The town of Cherokee itself has a large Indian-run gambling casino.

## Asheville ❹

69,000.
151 Haywood St, (828) 258-6101.
www.ashevillechamber.org

PERCHED ON TOP of a hill, this town's commercial district retains many buildings from its boom years as an early 20th century resort. Downtown Asheville continues to evoke the period of local author, Thomas Wolfe (1900–38), who wrote about his hometown in *Look Homeward Angel*. Today the modest "Dixieland" boardinghouse described in the novel is preserved as the **Thomas Wolfe State Historic Site**. Asheville is said to be among the healthiest towns in the country, with many health-food stores, cafés, bookstores, bluegrass clubs, and music shops, patronized by a nonconformist crowd who hark back to the 1960s. It is probably better known for its 250-room, art-studded, **Biltmore Estate** to the south of town. This French Renaissance-style mansion holds a collection of 18th- and 19th-century art and sculpture, and also has the distinction of being the largest residence in America. Beside the main Neo-Classical house, the splendid estate also has a winery, a deluxe inn *(see p274)*, and sprawling gardens designed by Frederick Law Olmsted, who also designed New York's Central Park. Visitors should expect long lines, as the estate attracts huge crowds, making it among the country's most visited house tours, along with the White House and Elvis Presley's "Graceland" *(see p267)*. Whether or not one visits Biltmore, however, Asheville makes a great base for exploring the surrounding mountain region.

Biltmore Estate in Asheville, one of the most visited house tours in America

**Thomas Wolfe State Historic Site**
52 N Market St. (828) 253-8304. 9am–5pm Tue–Sat, 1–5pm Sun. Nov–Mar: Mon.

**Biltmore Estate**
Biltmore Ave (Hwy 25). (828) 225-1333. 8:30am–5pm daily. public hols.

Cape Hatteras National Seashore, protecting the Outer Banks' northern coast

## Outer Banks 5

32,000. 1 Visitors Center Rd, Manteo, (800) 446-6262, (252) 473-2138. www.outerbanks.org

NORTH CAROLINA'S Atlantic coastline is made up of a long chain of narrow barrier islands known as the Outer Banks. Most of the northern coast is protected as part of the **Cape Hatteras National Seashore**, where long stretches of pristine beach, dune, and marsh shelter wild ponies, sea turtles, and many varieties of waterbirds. Offshore, two jet streams that meet in a fury stir up the wild currents, storms, and hurricanes that have earned North Carolina's coast its reputation as "the Graveyard of the Atlantic." The coastline's many historic lighthouses, life-saving stations, and pirate lore are as important a part of the Outer Banks' maritime heritage as is its seafood industry.

In the early 20th century, bridges built from the mainland brought in the tourist trade, and now hotels and resort-home developments line the northernmost coast from Corolla all the way to Nags Head. In addition to the sun, surf, and sand, this tourist region offers many historic attractions and family amusements, in the town of **Kill Devil Hills**. The "First in Flight" slogan found on coins and the state's license plates commemorates the Wright Brothers' first historic flight, which took place here. The **Wright Brothers National Memorial** stands at the very site where Orville and Wilbur Wright launched *Flyer*, the first successful experiment in powered flight in 1903. Exhibits here go beyond aviation history to applaud the contributions of dreamers, inventors, and adventurers.

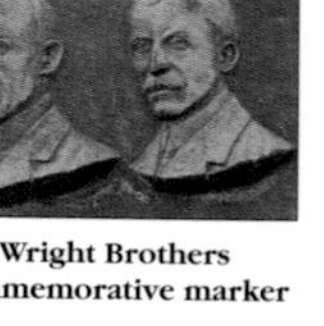

Wright Brothers commemorative marker

A few minutes drive south at **Jockey Ridge State Park**, hang-gliders participate in a modern version of the Wright Brothers' adventures, while "sandboarders" ride the largest sand dune on the East Coast. "Sandboarding," or running headfirst down the sheer 110-ft (34-m) high sand wall, is a revered local tradition. The dune is also a great spot to watch the sunset. Fewer people venture to the inland side of the island, where a slow kayak ride through the tidal marsh, or a walk through the scenic maritime forest at **Nags Head Woods Preserve**, hold a quieter appeal. Peculiar to barrier islands, these maritime forests, on the rough Atlantic Coast, are lined with banks of sturdy live oaks that protect the lush vegetation from the onslaughts of the water and wind. Follow the signs to the preserve west off Hwy 158 close to the Wright Brothers Memorial.

The drive along the National Seashore is one of the country's most scenic routes, with many opportunities to visit lighthouses and walk along dune and marsh boardwalks. Among the dozens of lighthouses, the 1847 Bodie Island Lighthouse is the only one still in operation. A free ferryride transports cars and passengers between **Hatteras Island** and **Ocracoke Island**. Hatteras's distinctive black-and-white spiral **Cape Hatteras Lighthouse**, built in 1870, is the tallest brick lighthouse in the world at 193 ft (59 m). The scenic village of Ocracoke has a good selection of inns, restaurants, and shops, which makes this remote port an inviting destination for an overnight stay. Visitors can connect with toll mainland ferries (reservations recommended) from here.

**Wright Brothers National Memorial**
US Hwy 158, milepost 8, Kill Devil Hills. *(252) 441-7430.* *9am–5pm daily.* *Dec 25.*

**Nags Head Woods Preserve**
701 W Ocean Acres Dr, Kill Devil Hills. *(252) 441-2525.* *dawn–dusk daily.*

**Cape Hatteras Lighthouse**
Hatteras Is, off Hwy 12, 1 mile (1.6 km) SE of Buxton. *(252) 995-4474.* *9am–5pm daily.* *Dec 25.*

**Ocracoke Island**
Ocracoke Car Ferry to Cedar Island or Swan Quarter. *(800) 293-3779 for fares & schedules (subject to change).*

Cape Hatteras Lighthouse, the world's tallest brick lighthouse

The landscaped Elizabethan Gardens on Roanoke Island

## Roanoke Island ❻

*1 Visitors Center Rd, Manteo, (800) 446-6262, (252) 473-2138.* www.outerbanks.org

A MARSH ISLAND lying between the Outer Banks and the mainland, Roanoke Island was the site of the first English settlement in North America. The first expedition to these shores, sponsored by by Sir Walter Raleigh, was in 1584. In 1587, another ship carrying more than 100 colonists disembarked at the island to create a permanent settlement. But when the next group arrived three years later, all the earlier colonists, including the first English women and children to land in the present-day US, had vanished without a trace. Today, the **Fort Raleigh National Historic Site**, the adjacent **Elizabethan Gardens**, an outdoor drama, and the nearby theme park with a replica of a 16th-century sailing ship as its centerpiece, all relate the mysterious story of this legendary "Lost Colony."

At the northern tip of the island, Fort Raleigh preserves the ruins of the colony's original disembarkation point, and ranger-led tours reveal what little is known about it. The Elizabethan Gardens are ideal for a walk through landscaped paths and lawns. A short drive south, at the port of Manteo, the **Roanoke Island Festival Park** tells the story of the first ship of explorers through tours aboard a re-creation of the *Elizabeth II*, with costumed guides. There is also a museum that relates both the Native and European history of the region.

**Fort Raleigh National Historic Site**
US Hwy 64/264, Manteo. *(252) 473-5772. 9am–5pm daily. Dec 25. Elizabethan Gardens only.* www.nps.gov/fora

**Roanoke Island Festival Park**
Port of Manteo. *(252) 475-1506. 10am–4pm or 6pm daily (seasonal, call & check). Jan 1, Thanksgiving, Dec 24–25.*

## Beaufort ❼

*4,000. (252) 726-8148 (Morehead City).*

BEAUFORT'S considerable charms lie in its historic B&B inns, seafood markets, and restaurants. The highlight of this coastal resort's small attractive waterfront is the **North Carolina Maritime Museum**, which interprets the boating, fishing, and pirate history of this coastline. A swashbuckling robot of Edward "Blackbeard" Teach, a notorious pirate who was captured and killed off the Outer Banks in November of 1718, welcomes visitors in the shell room. A popular event is the family-oriented, educational Pirate Day, which is dedicated to pirate lore and has costumes, flag flying, and treasure hunts. Other activities include boat-building and net-making classes, kayaking excursions, and other events. At the docks, private ferries take passengers out to the deserted sands of Lookout Island, preserved from development as the **Cape Lookout National Seashore**. The ecology of Lookout Island is similar to Cape Hatteras, with virgin beaches, marshland, and dunes, all rich in birdlife, but the limited access makes it more remote and less visited. The town at the island's northern tip was abandoned by its last two residents in the 1970s.

**North Carolina Maritime Museum**
315 Front St. *(252) 728-7317. 9am–5pm Mon–Fri, 10am–5pm Sat, 1–5pm Sun. Jan 1, Thanksgiving, Dec 25.* www.ah.dcr.state.nc.us/ sections/ maritime/

**Cape Lookout National Seashore**
3601 Bridge St, Morehead City. *(252) 728-2250.* www.nps.gov/calo

The waterfront at Salt Marsh and Newport River, Beaufort

# South Carolina

After separating from its sibling North Carolina in 1729, the South Carolina colony spread Upcountry, where Welsh, Irish, and Scottish immigrants established small owner-operated farms, in sharp contrast to the Low-country gentry. By the 1860s, however, the differences between the two had subsided and a unified South Carolina became the first Southern state to declare independence from the Union. Soon after, the first shot of the American Civil War was fired at Fort Sumter. Today, the state's "glory days" of resistance and revolution are re-created at plantations, museums, and monuments. Many visitors, however, head straight for the miles of beaches.

## Charleston 8

*100,000. 375 Meeting St, (843) 853-8000. Spoleto Festival (late May–early Jun).* www.charlestoncvb.com

One of the South's most beautiful cities and South Carolina's first capital, Charleston is situated on the tip of a peninsula between the Ashley and Cooper Rivers. Named after King Charles II of England, the city was founded in 1670 and soon became a wealthy colony of tobacco, rice, and indigo plantations. The first shot of the Civil War was fired just off the city's harbor, where people gathered to watch the Confederate seige of Fort Sumter. Today, Charleston retains much of its original period architecture and is a popular destination for antebellum house-and-garden tours, horse-and-carriage rides, fine Southern cuisine, and plantation retreats.

### Charleston Historic District

**Edmondston-Alston House** 21 E Battery. *(843) 722-7171. 10am–4:30pm Tue–Sat, 1:30–4:30pm Sun–Mon. Thanksg., Dec 25.*
**Gibbes Museum of Art** 135 Meeting St. *(843) 722-2706. 10am–5pm Tue–Sat, 1–5pm Sun.*

The historic district's beautifully preserved architecture evokes the city's Colonial and early American past. The civic and religious buildings here range from styles as varied as Colonial and Georgian, Greek and Gothic Revival, to Italianate and Victorian. Among the highlights are distinctive Charlestonian residences, set perpendicular to the street with grand piazzas running along their lengths. The only high structures are the towering church steeples. Horse-and-carriage rides through tree-lined streets provide a graceful overview.

**The charming 1772 Heyward-Washington House**

A trip south from Old City Market to the Battery takes in many highlights along Church Street, including the old magazine, the Gothic French Huguenot Church, and the **Heyward-Washington House**. This 1772 house was built by rice planter Daniel Heyward as a town house for his son and has a splendid collection of Charleston-made furniture. A half-block detour to the east on Chalmers leads to the Old Slave Mart, once one of the busiest in the American colonies. At the Battery, the **Edmondston-Alston House** features two floors of an opulent 1825 mansion overlooking the harbor. White Point Gardens Park lies to the south, while in the north, Waterfront Park, with its walk-through fountain, stands across from the popular restaurant row. Visitors can explore the cobblestone alleyways in search of hidden gardens, gargoyles, and harbor views.

To the west of Waterfront Park, the **Gibbes Museum of Art** reveals local history through landscape paintings and portraits of famous South Carolinians from the 18th century to the present day.

### South Carolina Aquarium

100 Aquarium Wharf. *(843) 577-3474. 9am–5pm Mon–Sat, noon–5pm Sun. public hols.*

Picturesquely set overlooking the harbor, Charleston's newest attraction provides an excellent introduction to the indigenous creatures found within the state's aquatic habitats. These range from Appalachian rivers and blackwater swamps, to salt marshes and coral reefs. An IMAX® Theater lies adjacent.

### Fort Sumter Visitor Center

340 Concord St. *(843) 883-3123. 8:30am–5:30pm daily. Jan 1, Dec 25. boat tours.*

An embarkation point for boat tours to Fort Sumter, the visitor center relates the story of the American Civil War's first battle. The fort, which stands

**Civil War cannon lying preserved at Fort Sumter**

on an island at the entrance to Charleston harbor, was controlled by Union troops. In April 1861, the Confederate army besieged the fort. When Union troops tried to bring in supplies, the Confederates, who had occupied nearby Fort Johnson, unleashed a 34-hour bombardment. Union forces finally surrendered on April 14, 1861, and the fort remained under Confederate control until 1865. Ironically, General Beauregard, the Confederate leader, was a student of the defending Union commander, Major Robert Anderson, at the US Military Academy at West Point, New York *(see p91)*. Fort Sumter has been preserved unchanged since the end of the war. It is a National Monument and has long been a symbol of Southern independence and pride.

### Charleston Museum

360 Meeting St. *(843) 722-2996.* *9am–5pm Mon–Sat, 1–5pm Sun.* *public hols.* www.charlestonmuseum.org

This museum presents a comprehensive overview of the city's history from pre-Colonial days. Its most distinctive exhibits are in the Native American and Natural History galleries; the former has dugout canoes and costumed mannequins, and the latter has a number of mounted skeletons of prehistoric animals such as the Cretaceous dinosaur *Thescelosaurus neglectus*.

**Flowers in bloom at Audubon Swamp Gardens, Magnolia Plantation**

### Ashley River Plantations

**Middleton Place** 3550 Ashley River Rd. *(843) 556-6020.* *9am–5pm daily.* *Dec 25.* **Drayton Hall** 3380 Ashley River Rd. *(843) 769-2600.* *9:30am–3pm or 4pm (seasonal).* *Jan 1, 1st week Feb, Thanksgiving, Dec 24–25, Dec 31.* **Magnolia Plantation** Rte 4/Hwy 61. *(843) 571-1266.* *8am–5:30pm daily.*

Within a short drive upriver, three house tours provide a glimpse of Charleston-style country living. Of them, the grandest is **Middleton Place**, with its 1755 mansion located on a bluff overlooking America's oldest landscaped gardens. Closeby, **Drayton Hall** is one of the country's finest examples of Colonial architecture. Built in 1738, the Georgian Palladian mansion has been preserved in its original condition without electricity or plumbing. A daily program on African-American heritage is held here.

**Magnolia Plantation** has a more modest house, with a petting zoo and a motorized train ride around the property. Prized attractions are the acres of riverfront formal gardens with charming pathways that lead through a profusion of flowers, and **Audubon Swamp Gardens**, a lush tupelo-and-cypress sanctuary.

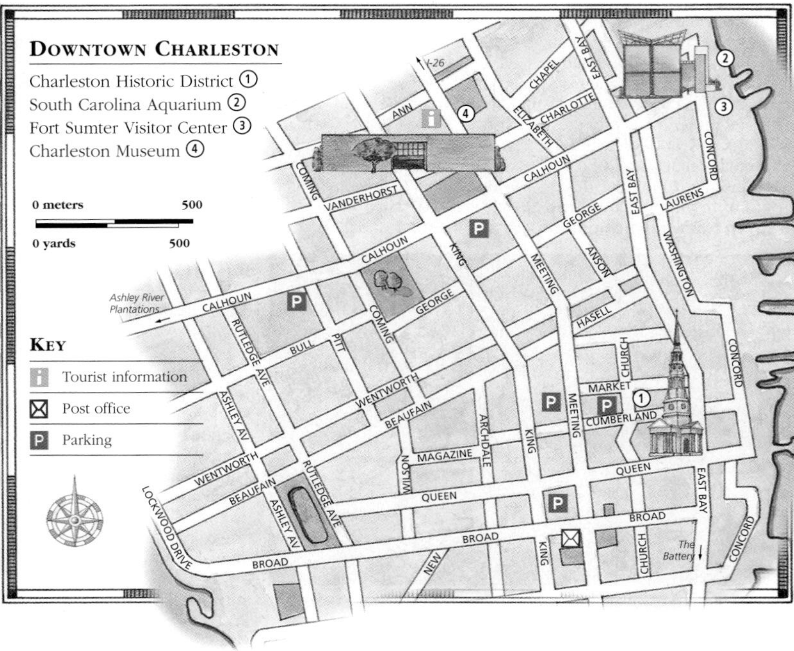

**DOWNTOWN CHARLESTON**

Charleston Historic District ①
South Carolina Aquarium ②
Fort Sumter Visitor Center ③
Charleston Museum ④

0 meters 500
0 yards 500

**KEY**

Tourist information
Post office
Parking

## Columbia 9

116,000. 900 Assembly St, (803) 545-0000. www.columbiacvb.com

Situated at the fall line of the Congaree River – the area that marked the limit of inland navigation – this city was declared the state capital over Charleston in 1786. Although General William T. Sherman destroyed most of Columbia during the Civil War, the **State House** managed to survive intact. Today, six bronze stars mark the spots where Union cannonballs hit the 1855 copper-domed building, located in the center of the quiet downtown on Gervais Street.

On the banks of the river, the **South Carolina State Museum** is housed in an artfully recycled textile mill built in 1894. Informative exhibits on the state's natural, cultural, and industrial history are displayed on three spacious floors. The adjacent **South Carolina Confederate Relic Room and Museum** maintains a huge collection of artifacts that trace the military history of South Carolina's participation in US wars from the Civil War onward, as well as an exhibit on the history and sometimes controversial meanings of the Confederate flag. While Southern traditionalists proclaim the flag a symbol of regional pride, many others see it as a symbol of white supremacy that should be abolished. A 20-minute drive south of town, the **Congaree Swamp National Monument** offers visitors a close-up look of the biodiversity found within a cypress swamp ecosystem. The swamp is at its best from late fall to early spring.

**A view of the Grand Strand on Myrtle Beach**

**South Carolina State Museum**
301 Gervais St. *(803) 898-4921. 10am–5pm Tue–Sat, 1–5pm Sun. Mon, Easter, Thanksg., Dec 25.* www.museum.state.sc.us

**South Carolina Confederate Relic Room & Museum**
301 Gervais St. *(803) 737-8095. 10am–5pm Tue–Sat. public hols.* www.state.sc.us/crr

## Myrtle Beach 10

*23,000. 1200 N Oak St, (843) 626-7444.* www.myrtlebeachinfo.com

This popular beach is the center of the "Grand Strand," a long sweep of the Atlantic coastline south of the North Carolina border, which is dominated by hotels, golf courses, amusement parks, and arcades. Its heyday was in the 1950s, when as a Spring Break destination, college students from many cold northeastern campuses descended on this beach town for a weeklong party. "The Shag," South Carolina's official state dance, was invented here and caused a craze all over the country. The elite crowd vacations at exclusive resort communities, but everyone ventures to the nearby fishing village of **Murrell's Inlet** for seafood.

South of Myrtle Beach two attractions make a worthwhile detour. On the inland side of the coastal Hwy 17, 16 miles (26 km) south of the beach, is **Brookgreen Gardens**, landscaped around 550 works of statuary by 250 artists. Oceanside, **Huntington Beach State Park** offers access to an undeveloped beach and salt-marsh boardwalk, as well as an art studio that once belonged to Anna Huntington, the sculptor who created Brookgreen Gardens in the 1930s.

**Brookgreen Gardens**
US Hwy 17. *(843) 235-6000. 9:30am–5pm daily. mid-Nov–Mar: Mon; Dec 25.*

## Georgetown 11

*10,000. 1001 Front St, (843) 546-8436.*

Set along the banks of the Sampit River, Georgetown was the center of the state's lucrative rice trade, producing almost half the rice grown in the US in the 1840s. Downtown's **Rice Museum**, housed in the 1842 Old Market building, explains how the rice industry influenced almost every facet of life here. The museum's new maritime

**Civil War arms on display at the South Carolina State Museum, Columbia**

gallery features examples of historic local watercraft. The museum leads out to a waterfront park where a wooden boardwalk makes an attractive marsh-side promenade.

The commercial district is reminiscent of a Southern small town in the early-to-mid-1900s, a quiet contrast to the Grand Strand or the bustle of Charleston. About 15 miles (24 km) south of Georgetown, **Hampton Plantation State Park** is an unfurnished 1750 Georgian house undergoing restoration. Visitors can get an inside look at the preservation process through several cutaway displays that reveal the "before, during, and after" stages of restoration.

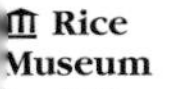

Hampton Plantation State Park, Georgetown

**Rice Museum**
Front & Screven Sts. (843) 546-7423. 10am–4:30pm Mon–Sat. public hols. www.ricemuseum.com

**Hampton Plantation State Park**
US Hwy 17. (843) 546-9361. *Memorial Day–Labor Day: 9am–5pm daily (grounds), 11am–4pm daily (house); Labor Day–Memorial Day: 9am–6pm Thu–Mon (grounds), 1–4pm Thu–Mon (house).* house.

## Coastal Islands ⓬

*Hilton Head Island Chamber of Commerce, William Hilton Pkwy (Hwy 278), (843) 785-3673.* www.hiltonheadisland.org

EXTENDING FROM Georgetown south to beyond Savannah in Georgia, the remote islands of the Lowcountry are a semi-tropical region with a rich natural and cultural history. Shifting sand dunes, dense maritime forests of live oak draped with Spanish moss and muscadine vines, and numerous lagoons and marshes harbor a mix of wildlife such as sea turtles, bobcats, alligators, ospreys, and dolphins.

The area's unique African-American history evolved around the common heritage of slaves, brought here from the rice-growing regions of West Africa, to cultivate this crop along the tidal creeks. Isolated on these islands, the Lowcountry Africans were able to perpetuate their cultural traditions over the generations. Today, their "Gullah" heritage remains distinct in the local language, music, cuisine, and folkways.

To the east of Beaufort, two islands preserve the natural and cultural history. Both are accessible by car via Hwy 21, which offers a panoramic view of the Port Royal Sound marsh landscape.

On St. Helena Island, the renowned **Penn Center** is a touchstone of Gullah culture. A former school established in 1862 by Pennsylvanian abolitionists during the Civil War, the center has a distinguished history from the Civil Rights era. National leaders such as Martin Luther King and groups such as the Southern Christian Leadership Conference met here to advance the Civil Rights Movement. A modest museum located in the old schoolhouse relates numerous events from the center's past through photographs and other displays. The center also sponsors storytelling programs and an annual festival that celebrates Gullah culture.

Canoeing at the Hilton Head Island Resort, Coastal Islands

Beyond St. Helena, **Hunting Island State Park** on Hunting Island preserves a natural barrier island environment. Its highlights include a pleasant, uncrowded beach, a coastside campground, and a 19th-century lighthouse.

**Hilton Head Island**, named after the English sea captain William Hilton who explored the island in 1664, is South Carolina's premier beach resort. It is dominated by several deluxe resort complexes, including the Westin Resort, Hyatt Regency, Crowne Plaza, Disney, and of course, the Hilton, providing golf, tennis, and spa facilities. Among the other recreational opportunities are horseback riding, fishing, boating, sailing, and a variety of other water sports.

**Penn Center**
Martin Luther King Dr, St. Helena. *(843) 838-2432. 11am–4pm Mon–Sat. public hols.*

**Hunting Island State Park**
Hwy 21. *(843) 838-2011. Apr–Oct: 6am–9pm daily; Nov–Mar: 6am–6pm daily.*

A view of the Port Royal Sound marshland at dusk, Coastal Islands

# Georgia

THE LAST OF THE 13 original colonies, Georgia was founded by a British general, James Oglethorpe, to stop Spanish expansion up from Florida. While the state initially banned slavery, economic pressures from competing slaveholding colonies led to its introduction. As a result, it grew wealthy from slave labor on rice, indigo, and cotton plantations. Georgia was devastated during the Civil War, when General Sherman's "March to the Sea" set ablaze a swath of land across the state. Led by pragmatic Atlanta *(see pp260–61)*, Georgia was able to overcome the many hardships of its troubled past, and was well positioned to benefit from the economic boom in the late 20th century.

**A colorful Halloween display on River Street, Savannah**

## Savannah ⓭

*251,000.* *Martin Luther King Jr. Blvd, (912) 944-0460.* www.savannahvisit.com

LABELED THE "most beautiful city in America" by the Paris newspaper *Le Monde*, the lushly landscaped parks and gracious homes of Savannah have earned it a reputation for scenic beauty and sophistication. It was established in 1733 on the banks of the Savannah River, 16 miles (26 km) from the Atlantic Ocean. Its founder, James Oglethorpe, laid out a town grid dotted with small squares designed to deter invaders. Today, even after the turmoil of the Revolution and Civil War, his design remains intact, with the squares now serving as scenic parks filled with statues and fountains. The city has one of the largest, and perhaps most beautiful, urban historic districts in the US, which now thrives as the city's downtown commercial center. Horse-and-carriage tours provide an introduction to historic Savannah, though walking around is the best way to explore the area.

**River Street** is one of the city's central entertainment districts, lined with seafood restaurants, raucous taverns, and souvenir shops housed in old warehouses constructed of ballast-stones. Water taxis shuttle passengers to the modern Convention Center across the river on Hutchinson Island. Uphill, **Factors Walk** is a stately promenade on top of the bluff. A few blocks in from the river, **City Market** is another lively arts and entertainment district, housed in historic buildings.

Historic house museums throughout Savannah shed light on the city's history, architecture, and culture. Many homes and religious centers are open to tours year-round. Of these, the **Davenport House** on Columbia Square is considered one of the country's finest examples of Federal-style architecture, while nearby, the **Owens-Thomas House** on Oglethorpe Square is among the finest Regency buildings, built by English architect William Jay in 1816. Other houses can be seen on the popular **Tour of Homes and Gardens**, held in spring.

A handful of museums also highlight different aspects of the city's history. The **Telfair Academy of Arts**, at the center of the historic district, displays a fine collection of Impressionist paintings and decorative arts within an 1818 Regency-style mansion. At the western edge of the district, the **Ships of the Sea Maritime Museum** holds ship models of all shapes and sizes within the palatial 1819 Scarborough House. Located just beyond the historic district, the **Ralph Mark Gilbert Civil Rights Museum** has exhibits relating to the city's history. In-depth African-American heritage tours also start at the museum.

Many more attractions await in the surrounding Lowcountry – the marsh-laden coastal region of Georgia and South Carolina *(see p255)*. A drive out on Hwy 80, east of the **Tybee Island** beach resort (18 miles/29 km east of downtown), passes the **Bonaventure Cemetery**, where singer Johnny Mercer and writer Conrad Aitken are buried. Also located en route is the behemoth brick **Fort Pulaski National Monument**, which rises like a medieval fortress from the vast expanses of cordgrass at the mouth of the Savannah River.

### Davenport House

324 E State St. *(912) 236-8097.* *10am–4pm daily.* *Jan 1, Mar 17, Jul 4, Thanksgiving, Dec 25.*

**Fort Pulaski National Monument, Savannah**

**Jekyll Island Club Hotel, one of many historic buildings on the Golden Isles**

## Golden Isles ⓮

*68,000 (Glynn County).* *4 Glynn Ave, (912) 265-0620.* www.bgicvb.com

THE SPANISH called the barrier islands off Georgia's southern coast "the Golden Isles" – possibly after lost treasure or the golden hue of the marshlands in fall – a term that tourism promoters were happy to revive. While they are primarily beach resorts, the islands retain a number of historic sights. **Fort Frederica National Monument**, located on St. Simons, along a scenic stretch of the Frederica River that lies adjacent to Christchurch, holds the ruins of a fortified village built by James Oglethorpe in 1736. Another significant site is the quiet expanse of marsh off Demere Road, south of Fort Frederica, where the Battle of Bloody Marsh was fought in 1742. This decisive battle between English and Spanish forces determined which Colonial power would control this part of the American continent. Near the island's southern tip, Neptune Park in downtown St. Simons has the historic 1872 **St. Simons Lighthouse**, where visitors can climb to the top. Lying across Bloody Marsh from St. Simons, Sea Island is home to the luxurious Cloister Hotel. At the turn of the 20th century, **Jekyll Island** was the exclusive preserve of the nation's premier industrialists, such as the Vanderbilts, Goodyears, and Rockefellers. With the advent of World War II, however, this vulnerable coastal island was deemed unsafe and the families moved elsewhere. Today, the island's historic district comprises the "cottages," as the millionaires' mansions were known, and the elegant Jekyll Island Club. The cottages have been restored and are now open as museums or inns. Among these are the 1892 Indian Mound Cottage, which passed into the hands of William Rockefeller in 1904, and Crane Cottage, which is now part of the **Jekyll Island Club Hotel** *(see p276)* and features a fine restaurant. Other highlights are a former stable, now a small museum, and Faith Chapel, with its Tiffany windows. The historic Jekyll River Wharf, next to the Jekyll Island Club Hotel, has a popular seafood restaurant serving raw seafood, mainly fresh oysters. On the ocean side, a selection of franchise motels and restaurants offer family lodging and dining. There is also a campground located at the island's northern tip near "Boneyard Beach," where sun-bleached driftwood gives the beach its name.

**St. Simons Lighthouse**

### Fort Frederica National Monument

Frederica Rd, St. Simons Island. *(912) 638-3639.* *8am–5pm.* *Dec 25.* www.nps.gov/fofr

## Okefenokee Swamp National Wildlife Refuge ⓯

Hwy 121, Folkston. *(912) 496-7836.* *sunrise–5:30pm (7:30pm in summer).* *Dec 25.* *exhibits.*

IN THE REMOTE southeastern corner of the state, the Okefenokee Swamp is an exotic, primeval landscape of blackwater and cypress that harbors alligators, softshell turtles, otters, and all kinds of birdlife. The Seminole Indian name "Okefenokee," loosely translated as "trembling earth," characterizes the peat moss hammocks that bubble up from the water as a natural part of swamp ecology. Boat tours provide a close-up view at three sections of the swamp, including the **Okefenokee Swamp Park** near Waycross, and the wildlife refuge headquarters at **Folkston**, which provides details about overnight paddling trips into the swamp. Fargo, near the swamp's western entrance, is the nearest town to the **Stephen C. Foster State Park**, 18 miles (29 km) to the northeast. This section is perched on a peninsula in the deep recesses of the swamp. Camping facilities and cabins are available here.

### Okefenokee Swamp Park

Hwy 177, Waycross. *(912) 283-0583.* *9am–5:30pm daily.* *Thanksg., Dec 25.* *exhibits only.*

**Suwanee Canal Recreation Area, Okefenokee Swamp Refuge**

## Americus 16

*18,000. Windsor Hotel Visitor Center, 123 W Lamar St, (229) 928-6059.*

Off the beaten track in south Georgia, the tidy county seat of Americus lies in a region of diverse attractions. The **Habitat for Humanity**, a worldwide organization offering "self-build" housing for the poor, has its headquarters downtown. In 2003 it opened its Global Village and Discovery Centre, which includes an international marketplace and up to 40 examples of habitat homes built around the world, including Papua New Guinea, Botswana, Ghana, and others.

Located 10 miles (16 km) north of town, Andersonville is the **National Prisoner of War (POW) Museum**. This marks a spot that was a notorious prisoner-of-war camp during the Civil War, which later became a veterans' cemetery. Almost 13,000 of the camp's inmates died from the terrible living conditions. Housed in a structure built to resemble a concentration camp, the museum's disturbing exhibits commemorate American POWs in conflicts from the Civil War through Vietnam to the Gulf and Iraqi Wars.

The local high school in Plains, 10 miles (16 km) west of Americus, is part of the **Jimmy Carter National Historic Site**. It was here that a teacher predicted that her student would become president. Carter proved her right, and the school is now dedicated to the life of the Plains-area peanut farmer's son who became the 39th president in 1976, in the wake of Nixon's resignation *(see p209)*. The former president, recipient of the Nobel Peace Prize in 2002, lives here and teaches Sunday school at the Maranatha Baptist Church when he is in town. An excursion train runs from Cordele in the east through Plains up to Carter's boyhood farm in Archery.

**Headstones at the Andersonville cemetery near Americus**

**Habitat for Humanity**
121 Habitat St at W Lamar St. *(229) 924-6935. 8am–3pm Mon–Fri, 10am–1pm Sat. Sun.*

## Macon 17

*107,000. 200 Cherry St, (478) 743-3401.* www.maconga.org

Founded on the south bank of the Ocmulgee River in 1823, Mason was laid out in a grid of avenues, which still exist in its historic district downtown. Uphill from here is one of the city's highlights, the Intown Historic District. This area has some of the city's most beautiful homes, a few of which are open to the public. The 1855 **Hay House Museum**, built in the Italian Renaissance style, features period characteristics such as trompe l'oeil marble, a ballroom, and hidden passages. The 1842 House Inn is also located here. Guided architectural tours begin at the visitor center.

The city also has a vibrant musical history and was home to such greats as Little Richard, Otis Redding, and the Allman Brothers. The **Georgia Music Hall of Fame**, located in the historic district, provides an overview of the state's contribution to rhythm-and-blues, rock 'n' roll, gospel, country, and other genres. The nearby **Sports Hall of Fame** celebrates Georgia's athletes, such as Hank Aaron and Ty Cobb. Across the river from downtown, the **Ocmulgee National Monument** marks a historic mound complex built around 1100 as the capital of the Creek Confederacy.

**Exterior of the Italianate Hay House Museum, Macon**

**Hay House Museum**
934 Georgia Ave. *(478) 742-8155. 10am–4:30pm Mon–Sat, 1–4:30pm Sun. public hols.*

## Athens 18

*80,000. 280 E Dougherty St, (706) 353-1820.*

Home to the **University of Georgia** (UGA), Athens is well known as the state's intellectual and literary center. It has also gained repute as the originator of alternative music. Local bands such as REM, the B-52s, and Widespread Panic have made it big, and the 40-Watt Club on West Washington Street and the annual Athfest in June continue the tradition. The city is largely deserted in summer, while in fall it overflows with Georgia Bulldog fans for the home football games. The visitor center provides details about house and garden tours, such as the 1856 structure that now houses the Lyndon House Arts Center and the Founders Memorial Garden in North Campus. The university visitor center directs guests to the art museum, with its 19th- and 20th-century paintings and sculpture, and gives details on sports events and performances on campus.

**UGA bulldog mascot**

View from the Amicalola Falls, Amicalola State Park

## Dahlonega ⓳

13 S Park St, (706) 864-3711.
www.dahlonega.org

THE LEGENDARY Blue Ridge Mountain range extends across the state's northeastern corner. With abundant waterfalls and flowering forests, the region is well known for its cultural heritage of outstanding folk arts such as quiltmaking, woodworking, and bluegrass music. The discovery of gold in the main town of Dahlonega in 1828 precipitated the nation's first gold rush, two decades before California's famous "Forty-Niners." The state's **Gold Museum**, housed in the 1836 courthouse in the center of Dahlonega's attractive town square, displays mining equipment, nuggets, and mining lore. The town also offers gold-panning and gold-mine tours as well as a complete set of coins minted in the US Mint that operated here from 1838 to 1861.

### Gold Museum

1 Public Square.
*(706) 864-2257. 9am–5pm Mon–Sat, 10am–5pm Sun. Jan 1, Thanksgiving, Dec 25.*
www.georgiastateparks.org

**ENVIRONS:** About 18 miles (29 km) from Dahlonega, the **Amicalola Falls State Park** is the gateway to the southern terminus of the 2,144-mile (3,450-km) Appalachian Trail, a hiking route that leads from the top of Springer Mountain in Georgia all the way north to Mount Katahdin, deep in Maine. Less ambitious hikers can head to the park's new Len Foote Hike Inn, which offers ecologically sensitive, comfortably rustic overnight accommodations. The park also features a mountain-top lodge, restaurant, campground, and the Amicalola Falls. East of Dahlonega, along Hwy 441 at the Georgia–South Carolina border, the federally designated "Wild and Scenic" Chatooga River is considered one of the most daring rivers to navigate in eastern US. The book and the film *Deliverance* were based on this region (though the locals don't appreciate being reminded of this notoriety). Visible from high above the river, the Tallulah Gorge features a suspension bridge.

### Amicalola Falls State Park & Lodge

Hwy 52. *(706) 265-8888. 8am–10pm daily. Jan 1, Thanksgiving, Dec 25.*

## Stone Mountain Park ⓴

US Hwy 78. *(770) 498-5600. 6am–midnight (hours vary so call ahead). Dec 24–25. partial.*
www.stonemountainpark.com

THE CENTERPIECE of this popular park, located about a 30-minute drive east of downtown Atlanta, is a bas-relief carved into the side of a massive granite mountain. The sculpture depicts three Confederate heroes – Jefferson Davis, president of the Confederacy, and generals Robert E. Lee and Stonewall Jackson. Its creator, Gutzon Borglum, began work here in 1924 and later sculpted the faces of four American presidents at Mount Rushmore *(see p447)*.

A sky-lift takes visitors up to the summit, and the walk down affords a close-up view of the unusual "monadnock" habitat – it harbors many species of plants that are more commonly associated with the desert than the humid Southeast. The huge lawn, lying between the granite wall and Stone Mountain Park Inn, is the location of various events such as the summer laser light shows and the annual Fourth of July fireworks. Other attractions include an antebellum village, an ice rink, and paddlewheel riverboat rides around the lake. A number of lodging and dining options are also available here.

The centerpiece bas-relief sculpture at Stone Mountain Park

## Atlanta 21

*400,000. Underground Atlanta, (404) 521-6600.* www.atlanta.net

FOUNDED AS A terminus for two railroad routes in 1837, Atlanta's importance as a transportation hub made it a Union target during the Civil War. After a 75-day siege, General William T. Sherman broke the Confederate defenses and set most of the town ablaze, a history recounted romantically in Margaret Mitchell's *Gone With the Wind.* Today, the city claims to be the "Capital of the New South" and has since been considered more brash and faster paced than its Southern neighbors.

**Exploring Atlanta**

This cosmopolitan city is home to many industrial giants including Coca-Cola. Its entrepreneurial spirit led to an economic boom that lasted two decades, capped by a successful bid to host the Olympics in 1996. One of the city's landmarks, the **Centennial Olympic Park** downtown, commemorates this event. Yet another is **Turner Field**, where the former boxer Muhammad Ali famously lit the Olympic torch in the stadium. Downtown's attractions, Underground Atlanta, World of Coca-Cola, and the Martin Luther King Jr. Historic Site, are all within a mile of these Olympic landmarks. A short Metro ride north leads to the city's exceptional High Museum in midtown. East of midtown lie the residential neighborhoods of Virginia Highlands and Little Five Points, with their superb specialty restaurants.

### World of Coca-Cola

55 Martin Luther King Jr. Blvd SW. *(404) 676-5151. 9am–5pm Mon–Sat, noon–6pm Sun.*

The World of Coca-Cola redefines the factory tour with three floors of dazzling print ads and TV commercials, covering the history of this international beverage company, launched in the 1880s. The admission fee includes all the free Coke one can drink.

**The Centennial Olympic Park in downtown Atlanta**

### Underground Atlanta

Alabama St at Peachtree. *(404) 523-2311. 10am–9pm Mon–Sat, noon–6pm Sun.*

In the heart of downtown across from the Five Points light railway station, Underground Atlanta is made up of the subterranean streets that were encased under bridges built to bypass the rail yards. Abandoned for decades, the hidden town was reinvented in the 1970s as an underground shopping mall, topped with an above-ground visitor center.

### CNN Studio

Marietta St at Techwood Dr. *(404) 827-2300. 9am–5pm daily. with advance notice.*

A 45-minute guided tour of CNN Studio takes visitors through the inner workings of the world's first 24-hour news station, located in a 14-story atrium hotel building. Book in advance for the tour. The lobby gift shop sells merchandise ranging from Atlanta Braves paraphernalia to videos of Desert Storm coverage.

### Martin Luther King Jr. National Historic Site

450 Auburn Ave. *(404) 331-5190. 9am–5pm or 6pm. Dec 25.*

Situated in a long reflecting pool beside an eternal flame, the crypt of the Nobel Peace Prize-winner Dr. Martin Luther King Jr. is a pilgrimage site for people from all over the world. The pool lies within the complex of the Center for Nonviolent Social Change, which has a gallery displaying portraits and memorabilia. Also located nearby is the original Ebenezer Baptist Church, where Martin Luther King Jr, his father, and grandfather presided. The Martin Luther King birthplace is down the street to the east, while the National Park Service Visitor Center, housing portraits and exhibits that relate the area's role in the Civil Rights Movement, is right across the street.

This district preserves the heart of the **Sweet Auburn** neighborhood, which was the center of African-American life in the early 1900s.

**Margaret Mitchell**

### Margaret Mitchell House and Museum

990 Peachtree St. *(404) 249-7015. 9:30am–5pm daily. Jan 1, Thanksgiving, Dec 24–25.*

Margaret Mitchell (1900–1949) wrote her magnum opus *Gone With the Wind* here in a basement apartment she affectionately called "the Dump." The three-story Tudor Revival house has had a dramatic history. It was abandoned, threatened by urban renewal, and then torched several times by

**The reflecting pool, eternal flame, and crypt of Dr. Martin Luther King Jr.**

High Museum, the art museum of Atlanta

arsonists, once on the eve of the Olympics opening. Various exhibits tell the story of the Georgia-born writer and reveal the extent of house's restoration. Mementos from the famous film, such as Scarlett O'Hara's bonnet, are also on display.

### High Museum

280 Peachtree St NE. *(404) 733-444.* *10am–5pm Tue–Sat, noon–pm Sun.* *public hols.*

One of the country's best museums, the High Museum lies in the city's premier arts district and is housed behind a colorful Alexander Calder sculpture in a strikingly modern Richard Meier structure. Its extensive permanent collection careens from regional folk art and 19th-century American art to 18th-century Asian ceramics and sub-Saharan artifacts. Among the museum's packed calendar of events are blockbuster traveling exhibits, art films, make-art events, and lectures. A satellite gallery located in downtown Atlanta, at Peachtree and John Wesley Dobbs Avenue, is devoted to folk art and photography.

### Atlanta History Center

130 W Paces Ferry Rd. *(404) 814-4000.* *10am–5:30pm Mon–Sat, noon–5:30pm Sun.*

The center contains a museum and two historic houses. The museum is built in the style of a massive railroad depot. Exhibits such as **Fact or Myth?** shed light on antebellum life and the city's African-American community.

Contrasting examples of rural and urban life are presented in the two houses. The Tullie Smith Farm, with its livestock and traditional crafts demonstrations, is a typical mid-1800s farmhouse, while the elegant 1928 Swan House has a grand interior staircase and swan motifs throughout.

### Fernbank Natural History Museum

767 Clifton Rd NE. *(404) 929-6300.* *10am–5pm Mon–Sat, noon–5pm Sun.* *Thanksg., Dec 25.*

This museum is housed in a striking modern building centered around a skylit four-story atrium. It has natural history exhibits ranging from plate tectonics to bubble science. Of local interest is its coverage of Georgia's diverse ecosystems, including the Appalachian forest, the coastal plain, and a particular favorite, the exotic Okefenokee Swamp habitat *(see p257)*. The museum's IMAX® Theater features frequent "IMAX® and Martinis" nights, and there is also an on-site café. A number of in-town nature trails weave through the forest outside.

### Jimmy Carter Library & Museum

441 Freedom Pkwy. *(404) 865-7100.* *9am–4:45pm Mon–Sat, noon–4:45pm Sun.* *Jan 1, Thanksgiving, Dec 25.*

Located on a lushly landscaped hilltop site, the library highlights the humanitarian successes of President Carter's administration *(see p258)*. These include the Camp David accords, Panama Canal treaties, and human-rights and energy policies.

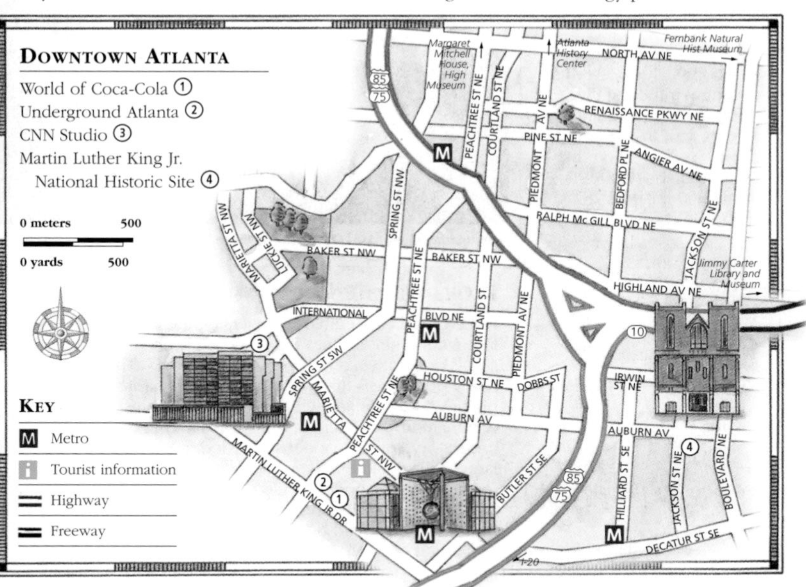

# Tennessee

TENNESSEE IS MADE UP OF THREE distinct regions. Memphis anchors the western lowlands along the Mississippi River; Nashville, the state capital, heads the central plateau; and the east is dominated by the Appalachian Mountains, with Knoxville as its urban base. With the Cumberland and Tennessee Rivers feeding into the Ohio, then into the Mississippi, the state was well positioned to prosper from the steamboat trade, and later, the railroads. During the Civil War, Chattanooga was the scene of battles, while Memphis and Nashville were occupied by Union forces. Today, Tennessee is known for its tremendous contribution to American roots music, from bluegrass, country, gospel, and blues, to rockabilly, rock 'n' roll, and soul.

**Visitors at a preserved log cabin, Cades Cove**

## Great Smoky Mountains National Park ㉒

*US Hwy 441, Gatlinburg, (865) 436- 1200.* *daily.* 
www.nps.gov/grsm

THE "SMOKIES," which earn their name from the smoke-like haze that clings to the ridge, hold some of the highest peaks in eastern US and support a diversity of plant life. With more than 10 million visitors each year, this is one of the country's most-visited parks. Established as a national park in 1934, half of it is in Tennessee and the other half in North Carolina. The Tennessee entrance is through Gatlinburg and Hwy 441, which bisects this sprawling park along the Newfound Gap Road and meets up with the Blue Ridge Parkway *(see p249)* on the North Carolina side.

Of the 800 miles (1,287 km) of trails, the most popular is the **Appalachian Trail**, which straddles the state border through the park. Trails to the park's many scenic waterfalls are also popular. The hike to **Mount LeConte** offers panoramic views, and there is even a hike-in lodge that provides rustic overnight accommodations, for which reservations are required. The 6,643-ft (2,025-m) tall **Clingman's Dome**, the state's highest peak, has an observation tower that offers fine views of the surrounding landscape. At the western end of the Great Smoky Mountains National Park, **Cades Cove** still preserves the historic farm buildings that were erected back in the 1820s. These include structures such as log cabins, barns, and a still operating gristmill. Bicycling, horseback riding, fishing, and whitewater rafting are some of the popular activities available to adventurous tourists in this beautiful park and its surrounding region.

**Spectacular view from Clingman's Dome**

**Sugar Maple** **Magnolia** **Mountain Laurel** **Rhododendron**

### FLORA OF THE GREAT SMOKY MOUNTAINS

Famed for its incredible biodiversity, the Great Smoky Mountains shelter more than 1,500 species of flowering plants, including some 143 species of trees. The mountains' hardwood forests are made up of sugar maples, yellow birches, and poplars, while its spruce-fir forests are dominated by coniferous red spruce and Frasier fir. The understory consists of dense rhododendron and mountain laurel. Closely interwoven with Appalachian culture, the forest produces honeysuckle vines for basketry and various hardwoods for whittling and musical instruments, in addition to offering wild berries and fruits, medicinal plants (including ginseng), and harboring wild game.

## Chattanooga ㉓

153,000. 
2 Broad St, (423) 756-8687.
www.chattanoogafun.com

LOCATED ON THE banks of the Tennessee River along the Georgia border, Chattanooga is surrounded by several high landmasses – the plateaus of Lookout Mountain, Signal Mountain, and Missionary Ridge. Founded as a ferry landing by the Cherokee Indian Chief John Ross in 1815, Chattanooga was later occupied by white settlers after the Cherokees were forced out from here along the tragic "Trail of Tears" to Oklahoma in 1838 *(see p46)*. The railroad leading to Atlanta provided a natural target for the Union Army during the Civil War, and several battles were fought on this dramatic terrain.

Downtown Chattanooga is today a revitalized center surrounding the original site of the ferry landing known as Ross's Landing. Within this compact area are many of the city's most popular attractions such as the Chattanooga Regional History Museum, which covers the area's local history – Native American, Civil War, and cultural; the **Tennessee Aquarium**; the attractive Riverwalk promenade; and the pedestrian-only Walnut Street Bridge that spans the river to Coolidge Park and Carousel. At the Tennessee Aquarium, visitors can trace the journey of a single drop of water from its origins in the Smoky Mountains through rivers, reservoirs, and deltas, then out into the Gulf of Mexico. Over 9,000 species of fish, amphibians, reptiles, mammals, and birds illustrate the state's varied habitats and ecosystems. An IMAX® Theater lies adjacent.

**Former Chickamauga battlefield, with cannons, statuary, and memorials**

A short drive south of downtown on East Brow Road, the homespun **Battles for Chattanooga Electric Map** was originally known as "Confederama." It tells the story of local Civil War battles with 5,000 miniature soldiers and a series of tiny lights on large boards which are used to represent the advancing Confederate and Union troops.

At the foot of Lookout Mountain, the station at St. Elmo Avenue is the start point for the mile-long **Lookout Mountain Incline Railway**. The train climbs a gradient of 72.7 percent up the side of Lookout Mountain for panoramic views. It was built in the 1890s to bring tourists up to the hotels that were once located on top. The **Chickamauga and Chattanooga National Military Park** of Point Park is a three-block walk away. The other section of the military park is the Chickamauga battlefield near Fort Oglethorpe across the border in northwest Georgia. The site at Point Park commemorates all the brave Confederate and Union soldiers who fought on the precipitous slopes of this steep plateau in the Battle Above the Clouds in 1863. This battle took place after Union forces were able to reverse an earlier Confederate victory and planted the US flag on the top of Lookout Mountain.

**Lookout Mountain Incline Railway**

At **Ruby Falls**, 3 miles (5 km) away, visitors descend by elevator to the floor of a cave, then walk past stalactites and stalagmites to the 145-ft (44-m) waterfall. A light show transforms the lovely natural surroundings of the falls into a somewhat gaudy display.

On the Georgia side of Lookout Mountain, **Rock City Gardens** has natural limestone rock formations beautified by the Enchanted Trail, a Lover's Leap, and little gnomes peering out from the crevices.

**The Tennessee Aquarium, Chattanooga**

**Tennessee Aquarium**
1 Broad St. (423) 265-0695.
10am–6pm daily. Thnksg., Dec 25. www.tnaqua.org

**Chickamauga & Chattanooga National Military Park**
110 Point Park Rd. (423) 821-7786. 8am–8pm daily. Dec 25.
www.nps.gov/chch

**Ruby Falls**
(423) 821-2544.
www.rubyfalls.com

## Nashville ㉔

507,000. Broadway at Fifth St, (615) 259-4747. www.nashvillecvb.com

BEST KNOWN TODAY as the capital of country music, Nashville is a friendly and fun place to visit. Its musical history dates to 1927, when a radio broadcaster changing from music from the Grand Opera to the more popular Barn Dance show, introduced the upcoming selection as the "Grand Ole Opry." A musical legend was thus born and has flourished ever since. The city, however, has more to it than just music. It was founded as Fort Nashborough on the banks of the Cumberland River in 1779 and was named the state capital of Tennessee in 1843. It is also the financial center of the region and home to Vanderbilt University, one of the country's most prestigious institutions.

### Exploring Nashville

Nashville's vibrant downtown area is anchored by the new Country Music Hall of Fame. Most of the city's major attractions are within comfortable walking distance, such as the imposing State Capitol at the top of the hill, the historic and beautifully renovated Ryman Auditorium on Fifth Avenue, and the scenic riverfront with its reconstructed fort – a replica of the original outpost. Plenty of restaurants, cafés, and nightclubs lie in the surrounding area, locally known as "the District."

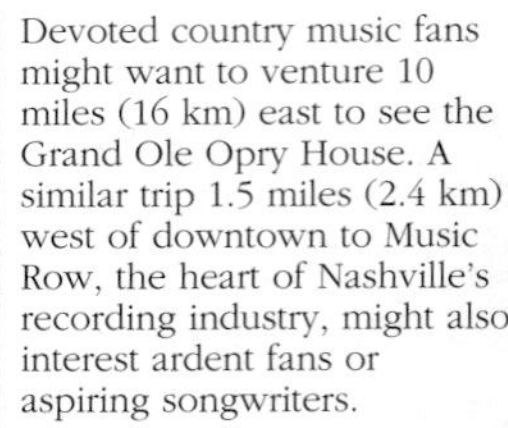

Devoted country music fans might want to venture 10 miles (16 km) east to see the Grand Ole Opry House. A similar trip 1.5 miles (2.4 km) west of downtown to Music Row, the heart of Nashville's recording industry, might also interest ardent fans or aspiring songwriters.

### Country Music Hall of Fame & Museum

*222 Fifth Ave S. (615) 416-2001. 10am–6pm daily. Jan 1, Thanksgiving, Dec 25.* www.countrymusichalloffame.com

"Spreading the gospel of country music," the Country Music Hall of Fame honors scores of such outstanding musicians as Patsy Cline, Merle Haggard, and Hank Williams in a huge rotunda at a grand new downtown location. In keeping with its exhibits, the building itself has been specially designed to resemble the black and white keys of a giant piano. Inside there is a beloved collection of vintage guitars, costumes, string ties, cowboy boots, well-known lyrics composed on bar napkins, and the celebrated golden Elvis Cadillac. A country music primer explains the academic distinctions between the subgenres of bluegrass, Cajun, honky-tonk, and rockabilly.

**Legendary Hank Williams**

### Ryman Auditorium

*116 Fifth Ave N. (615) 458-8700. 9am–4pm. Thanksgiving, Dec 25.* www.ryman.com

This landmark auditorium is still an evocative setting for live performances. The Grand Ole Opry was broadcast from here for 31 years, from 1943 to 1974, when it moved to the new Opry House. Daytime tours of the Mother Church of Country Music are available, but the best way to see the 2,000-seat theater is by taking in a show; performers from B.B. King to the Dixie Chicks and Sheryl Crow are typical of the diverse all-star lineup. Within a few blocks o[f] Ryman Auditorium, the modern Nashville Convention Center, Gaylord Entertainmen[t] Center, and nightclubs also feature all kinds of music – country, bluegrass, and blues.

**View of Nashville's colorful riverfront**

**Façade of the Ryman Auditorium, a Nashville landmark**

### Frist Center

*919 Broadway. (615) 244-3340. 10am–5:30pm Mon–Sat (until 8pm Thu), 1–5pm Sun. Jan 1, Thanksgiving, Dec 25.*

Downtown's 1934 Art Deco post office has been beautifully restored to house the city's premier arts center. Established in 2001, it has no permanent collection, but displays a wide selection of traveling exhibitions instead.

### Tennessee State Museum

*Fifth Ave btwn Union & Deaderick. (615) 741-2692. 10am–5pm Tue–Sat, 1–5pm Sun. public hols.*

Although the main focus of this museum is the Civil War, it also covers other aspects of the state's past. Starting with a dugout canoe, exhibits showcase local Native American history, early pioneer life, slavery, the Civil Rights Movement, the river trade, and the Natchez Trace route. There is also a large collection of 19th-century decorative arts, such as European and American antique furnishings. Biographical exhibits shed light on heroes of the state such as President Andrew Jackson and the 19th-century explorer Davy Crockett.

### Grand Ole Opry House

xterior of the Grand Ole Opry House in Nashville

### Grand Ole Opry House

804 Opryland Dr. (615) 889-060. 7:30pm Fri, 6:30pm & :30pm Sat. Sun–Thu.
ocated 10 miles (16 km) east f downtown in a gulch of )pry-themed development alled Music Valley, the 4,400-eat modern Opry House ontinues the "world's longest unning radio show" beyond s 75th year. The Who's Who f country music grace the tage of this legendary institu-ion (live broadcast on 650 VSM-AM). The nearby Grand )le Opry Museum tells the )pry story with wax figurines. car museum, the Opry mall, nd the fabulous Opryland Iotel are part of the complex.

### Belle Meade Plantation

5025 Harding Rd. (615) 356-0501. 9am–5pm Mon–Sat, 11am–5pm Sun. Jan 1, Thanksgiving, Dec 25. partial.
A 20-minute drive southwest of downtown, Belle Meade is among the state's best-preserved antebellum estates. The 1853 Greek Revival mansion was once the centerpiece of a 5,300 acre (2144.8 ha) plantation and has been restored to its former splendor. Guides in period costume offer tours of the mansion and outbuildings, including an 1832 slave cabin. A Sunday summer concert series features live performances on the spacious grounds.

### The Hermitage

4580 Rachel's Lane. (615) 889-2941. 9am–5pm daily. 3rd week in Jan, Thanksg., Dec 25.
The home of Tennessee's foremost political and military hero, Andrew Jackson, this estate is a 20-minute drive east of downtown. After distinguishing himself as a military leader in the War of 1812, Jackson became the state's single Congressional representative before Tennessee gained statehood. He was elected the seventh president of the United States in 1828 and re-elected in 1832, serving two terms. Most of the contents of the house remain intact from Jackson's time. This famous president and his wife are buried in the garden.

### Natchez Trace Parkway

Originally a series of Indian trails, the Natchez Trace Parkway, which links Nashville with Natchez in Mississippi, is today a national historic parkway *(see p362)*. Its northern terminus lies 15 miles (24 km) southwest of town. Here, the contour of the Trace is more rolling and deeply forested than farther down in Mississippi.

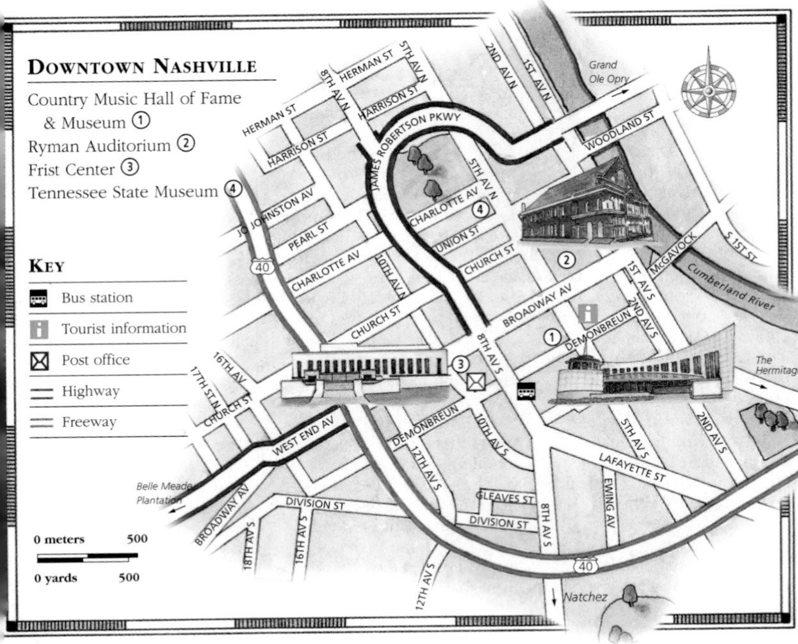

**DOWNTOWN NASHVILLE**

Country Music Hall of Fame & Museum ①
Ryman Auditorium ②
Frist Center ③
Tennessee State Museum ④

**KEY**

Bus station
Tourist information
Post office
Highway
Freeway

0 meters 500
0 yards 500

A neon B.B. King's Blues Club sign on Beale Street

## Memphis 25

*650,000. 119 N Riverside Dr, (901) 543-5333.* www.memphistravel.com

MEMPHIS SITS ON the banks of the Mississippi River at Tennessee's southwestern corner, where it meets the states of Arkansas and Mississippi. The city is most closely associated with two very different American icons – Civil Rights leader Dr. Martin Luther King Jr, and the singer Elvis Presley.

Since the early 20th century, Memphis has been synonymous with music. As the birthplace of rock 'n' roll, which originated from blues *(see p361)*, the city celebrates this legacy in its many nightclubs and saloons, and out on the streets. Even its festivals revolve around music. Highlights include Elvis's birthday on January 8; "Memphis in May," a month-long series of concerts and cookouts (Memphis is also famous for its barbecue); the W.C. Handy Awards, the blues answer to the Grammys, also in May; Elvis Week or "Tribute Week" around August 16; and the Music and Heritage Festival on Labor Day weekend.

### Beale Street

A thriving commercial center for the city's African-American community, Beale Street's heyday was in the first half of the 20th century. After a period of decline, this historic street has now been resurrected as the heart of a vibrant entertainment district, rivaling New Orleans' Bourbon Street *(see p350)* in popularity. Restaurants, nightclubs, saloons, and shops line a four-block stretch. Many statues also punctuate the strip on either side. There is one of Elvis Presley across from Elvis Presley's Memphis Nightclub, which was established after his death, and one of W.C. Handy stands at the entrance to a plaza where many outdoor festivals take place. A block away, a tiny white shotgun shack that was Handy's home is now a museum to the man who has often been called the "Father of the Blues." At the center of the strip stands the **A. Schwab's Dry Goods Store** at 163 Beale. This shop has been open here since 1876. Many nights Beale Street is closed to traffic, and people come to listen to live music emanating from every door. A short walk from Beale Street, **AutoZone Park** is the new red and green stadium of the Memphis Redbirds baseball franchise. It lies across from the landmark Peabody Hotel at 149 Union Street, where the famous ducks march twice a day to and from the lobby to the fountain where they can be seen frolicking all day *(see p277)*.

B.B. King, Rock-N-Soul Museum

### National Civil Rights Museum

450 Mulberry St. *(901) 521-969*
*9am–5pm Mon–Sat, 1–5pm Sun.*
*Tue.*
www.civilrightsmuseum.org

The museum was once the Lorraine Motel, where Dr. Martin Luther King Jr. was tragically assassinated on April 4, 1968. Room 306 is preserved a it was on the day of his killin and a memorial wreath rests outside the window. Across th street, the assasination scene is recreated in the bathroom from which James Earl Ray apparently fired his fatal shot

### Memphis Rock-N-Soul Museum

Fedex Forum, 200 3rd St. *(901) 205-2533.* *10am–6pm daily.* *Dec 25.*

The intersection between history and race, and its expression in song, is explained wit outstanding musical accompaniment at this museum. It i located opposite the Gibson Guitar factory, which offers a fascinating tour. The exhibit i sponsored by the Smithsonian Institute and examines the blues and country roots of rock 'n' roll with a fascinating movie, and displays of old instruments as well as vintage jukeboxes, elaborate stage costumes, and profiles of artists. A digital audio tour features more than six hours of fabulous music. Music fans may want to travel 10 minute south to the Stax Museum of American Soul Music, opened in 2003 in the old Stax Records recording studio.

### Mud Island

Via Front & Main Sts. *(901) 576-7241.* *10am–5pm Tue–Sun.* *Mon.* www.mudisland.on

Reached via monorail, Mud Island holds a museum that tells the story of the Mississippi River with artifacts such as an 1870 steamboat replica. The museum also has many Native American exhibits. The most engaging exhibit in the museum however, is located outside where water courses through a replica of the Mississippi for a five-block-long stretch, ending at a swimming pool shaped like the Gulf of Mexico.

vis Presley's grave in his lavish Graceland estate

**Center for Southern ɔlklore**

9 S Main St. (901) 525-3655. *11am–7pm Mon–Fri.* *Thanks- ving, Dec 25.* *hourly.* *shows.* www.southernfolklore.com

touchstone for all that is ıthentically Southern, the ɛnter offers a great café, folk t gallery, gift shop, and a age for shows ranging from g bands to puppetry, with enty of blues, soul, folk, ɔck, and gospel in between. also sponsors the acclaimed usic and Heritage Festival.

**Sun Studio**

)6 Union Ave. *(901) 521-0664.* *10am–6pm daily.* *anksgiving, Dec 25.* www.sunstudio.com

ımous musicians from all ver the world come to ɛcord in the legendary studio ıat launched the careers of Elvis, B.B. King, Johnny Cash, Jerry Lee Lewis, Roy Orbison, and others. Founded in 1954 by Sam Philips, the studio's exhibits include Elvis's original drum set and microphone. Souvenir items with the familiar yellow rooster logo are on sale, and visitors can also make their own souvenir recordings.

**Graceland**

3734 Elvis Presley Blvd. *(901) 332-3322.* *9am–5pm Mon–Sat, 10am–4pm Sun.* *Jan 1, Thanksgiving, Dec 25.* www.elvis.com

A 10-minute drive from downtown, Graceland attracts more than 700,000 visitors each year to the estate that Elvis Presley bought as a 22-year-old superstar and called his home until his death in 1977. Starting at the grand visitor complex, guests are taken by van through the metal gates up the drive to the house to view the front rooms, famous Jungle Room den, gallery, racquetball court, and Memorial Gardens, where he is buried. The tour is self-guided. Across the street, additional admission charges are needed to see Elvis's car collection, his two airplanes, and a **Sincerely Elvis** exhibit with home movies and personal effects. The rows of unofficial souvenir shops along **Elvis Presley Boulevard** offer some bizarre but entertaining items, such as Elvis-emblazoned nail clippers, shot glasses, and beach towels.

**Full Gospel Tabernacle Church**

787 Hale Rd. *(901) 396-9192.* *11am Sun.* *donation.*

The Reverend Al Green left a successful recording career in the 1970s (his hits included songs such as "Tired of Being Alone") to pursue his calling. He often presides over Sunday services at his church in Southside Memphis, not far from Graceland. Visitors to the electric gospel service should show respect by wearing decent attire, donating a little, and staying for the entire service.

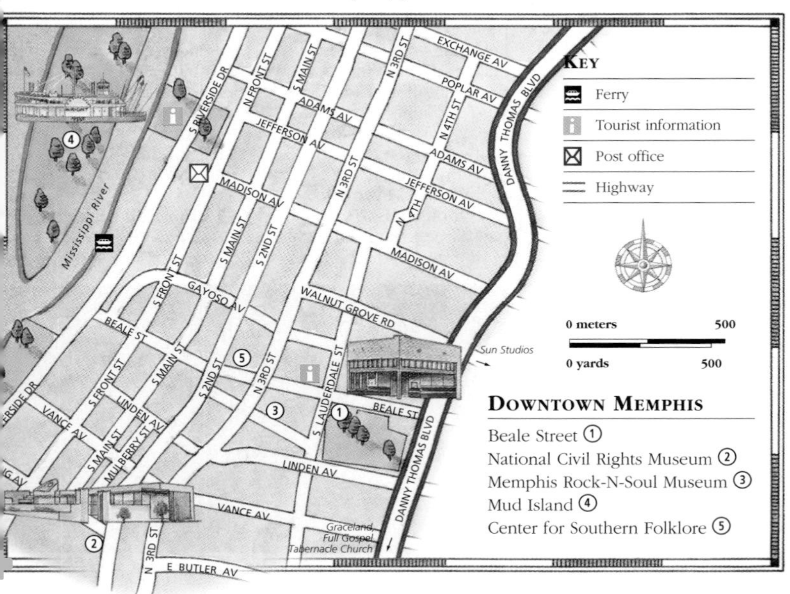


**DOWNTOWN MEMPHIS**

Beale Street ①
National Civil Rights Museum ②
Memphis Rock-N-Soul Museum ③
Mud Island ④
Center for Southern Folklore ⑤

# Kentucky

WITH ITS APPALACHIAN MOUNTAIN landscapes and rolling rural pasturelands, where horses run on acres and acres of bluegrass, Kentucky is easily one of the most picturesque states in the country. The lands west of the mountains were once inhabited by Indian tribes who strenuously opposed the encroachment of white settlers. Today, Kentucky is widely known for its horses, and many thoroughbred stud farms are centered around Lexington. One of the most prestigious horse races, the Kentucky Derby, takes place in Louisville. This state is also famous for its downhome style of country music, and Hwy 23 along its eastern border has been designated the Country Music Highway.

**A cannon at Fort McCook, Cumberland Gap National Historic Park**

## Cumberland Gap National Historic Park ㉖

US Hwy 25 E, Middlesboro. *(606) 248-2817.* *8am–5pm daily.* *Jan 1, Thanksgiving, Dec 25.*

SITUATED IN THE southeastern corner where Kentucky meets the states of Virginia and Tennessee, the Cumberland Gap is a natural pass through the Cumberland Mountains, once used by migrating deer and bison. It was first explored by Dr. Thomas Walker in 1750 on behalf of a land company. Some five years later, the legendary fur trapper and explorer Daniel Boone ran his Wilderness Road through the Gap, thus opening the way for some 200,000 pioneers to establish homesteads in the interior wilderness.

This rugged area is thickly forested, and many sights, such as the Sand Cave sandstone overhang and White Rocks sandstone outcrop, are accessible only by hiking trails. The hardwood and softwood forests shelter wild turkeys, white-tailed deer, and many varieties of songbirds.

The Gap was also a strategic point in the Civil War. It was held alternately by Confederate and Union forces, and the fortifications can still be seen throughout the park. Today, a four-lane Interstate Highway and a railroad tunnel run through the Gap. A drive up to **Pinnacle Overlook** leads to a short trail for a view of three states, most dramatic during fall.

## Mammoth Cave National Park ㉗

I-65 exit 53. *(270) 758-2180.* *Mar–Oct: 8am–6pm daily, Nov–Feb: 8am–5pm.* *Dec 25.*

HALFWAY BETWEEN Louisville *(see p271)* and Nashville *(see p264)*, this park offers guided tours of one of the largest cave systems known, formed by underground river that left a dramatic landscape of stalactites and stalagmites. Guests are free to choose fro[m] tours with names such as "Historic" or "Wild Cave Tour" (helmets provided). Accordin[g] to experts, evidence suggests that the cave had been inhab ited as far back as 4,000 years ago. The Green River runs its course above Mammoth Cave an area that is crisscrossed by several hiking trails.

## Berea ㉘

*9,000.* *(800) 598-5263.* *Berea Crafts Festival (Jul).*

HOME TO BEREA College, a liberal arts school dedicated to educating disadvantaged Appalachian youth, Berea is known as a highlands crafts center. Typical crafts include woodworking, pottery, and textiles. The town hosts the Kentucky Guild of Artists Fai[r], the Craftmen's Fair, as well as the Berea Crafts Festival. Year-round, there are public tours of artisans' studios, such as **Churchill Weavers**, founded in 1922.

**Churchill Weavers**
100 Churchill Dr. *(859) 986-312[4].* *9am–4pm Mon–Fri.* *Dec 25.*

**The path leading into the interior of Mammoth Cave**

iew of dense forest foliage from the Zilpo Road National Scenic Byway, Daniel Boone National Forest

## )aniel Boone Vational Forest ㉙

700 Bypass Rd, Winchester. (859) 745-3100. *8am–4:30pm aily. Jan 1, Thanksg., Dec 25.*

NAMED AFTER the legendary pioneer and fur trapper )avid Boone, who lived in .entucky, this National Forest rotects some of the most ramatic scenery in Kentucky. 'he dense forest provides helter to over 35 endangered pecies, including red-cockad-d woodpeckers, big-eared ats, and bald eagles. The **heltowee Trace National Recreation Trail** runs the ntire 260-mile (418-km) ength of the forest, from Aorehead near the Ohio order in the north to Pickett tate Rustic Park in Tenessee. Also near Morehead, **Cave Run Lake** is popular for oating, and the **Zilpo Road National Scenic Byway** offers a good chance to see the forest's rich variety of wildlife on a short drive. The central area east of Stanton features the **Natural Bridge State Resort Park**, a naturally occuring archway surrounded by rugged terrain, and the picturesque **Red River Gorge**, both of which offer great hiking, canoeing, and whitewater rafting opportunities. At the southern end, **Cumberland Falls State Resort Park** offers lodging, camping, and swimming.

### Cumberland Falls State Resort Park

7351 Hwy 90, Corbin. *(606) 528-4121. daily.*

**ENVIRONS:** Visitors to the southern portion of the park might want to detour to **Corbin**, off I-75, 50 miles (80 km) north of the state's southern border with Tennessee. Corbin is notable as the original home of Kentucky Fried Chicken, where Colonel Harland Sanders first served the special recipe that went on to become a global franchise. The kitchen where the famous herbs and spices were first put together is on display, along with vintage advertisements and KFC artifacts.

**Chairlifts carrying visitors up to the Natural Bridge**

## COUNTRY & BLUEGRASS MUSIC

**Country singer Billy Ray Cyrus in concert**

As the Mississippi Delta is to blues music, so the stretch of eastern Kentucky (along with West Virginia) is home to the greatest proportion of country music artists in America. British, Irish, and Scottish immigrants brought Elizabethan ballads, rhythms, and instruments to the area, which they then forged into a distinctly American style known as "country." It was characterized by fast fiddling, occasional yodeling, and laments on the hardscrabble life of the American Southeast. Hwy 23, which runs from Ashland to Pikeville along the state's eastern border, has been dubbed the "Country Music Highway" to commemorate the vast number of artists who come from here. Along its length, the route passes by the hometowns of Billy Ray Cyrus, the Judds, Loretta Lynn, Patty Loveless, and Dwight Yoakum.

Kentucky's vast bluegrass pasturelands defined a particular style of country music known as "bluegrass." This evolved from the musical style played in the late 1940s by Bill Monroe and his Bluegrass Boys. The name "bluegrass" stuck, and this acoustic folk style remains popular in the region today. Traditional bluegrass instruments include the fiddle, guitar, mandolin, five-string banjo, and bass and dobro guitars.

Thoroughbred race horses grazing in pastures near Lexington

## Lexington 30

226,000. 301 E Vine St, (859) 233-7299. www.visitlex.com

KENTUCKY'S second largest city, Lexington is also the capital of the state's bucolic horse country. The surrounding bluegrass-covered countryside is lined with hundreds of throroughbred stud farms, where many Kentucky Derby winners are bred, reared, and trained. Most farms are open to visitors, who are welcome either on their own with advance reservations or as part of an organized tour. The visitor center supplies lists of farms and tour operators.

About 6 miles (9.6 km) north of town lies the **Kentucky Horse Park**, a state-operated working farm that serves as an equestrian theme park. Here, visitors can watch live shows, ride ponies, sign up for escorted trail rides, take carriage tours, and go swimming and camping. The park's **International Museum of the Horse** is a monument to the role of the horse in the development of human history. The adjacent **Saddlebred Museum** is named for, and focuses on, America's first registered horse breed. Outside, the Man o' War Memorial marks the grave of the beloved thoroughbred who won several acclaimed races. In town, the 1803 **Mary Todd Lincoln House** preserves the girlhood home of Abraham Lincoln's wife.

**Kentucky Horse Park**
4089 Iron Works Pkwy. (859) 233-4303. mid-Mar–Oct: 9am–5pm daily. Nov–mid-Mar: Mon–Tue. www.kyhorsepark.com

## Harrodsburg 31

7,400. 124 S Main St, (859) 734-2364.

A LARGE NUMBER of Shaker families from New England relocated in and around Harrodsburg in 1805 and established a farming community renowned for its handicrafts. It grew to a sizeable population of around 500 in 1830 and then, in part due to the Shaker belief in celibacy, it grew less cohesive and became scattered by 1910. The area's premier attraction is the **Shaker Village of Pleasant Hill**, America's finest, largest, and most completely restored Shaker community and living history museum. The architecture and furnishings at the village reflect the spare, utilitarian style that typifies the Shaker values. Artisans demonstrate crafts such as woodworking and weaving. Lodging, dining, and riverboat rides are also available.

**Shaker Village of Pleasant Hill**
3501 Lexington Rd. (859) 734-5411. 10am–5pm daily. Dec 24–25. partial.

Barrel making in the Shaker Village of Pleasant Hill, Harrodsburg

## Hodgenville 32

2,700. 72 Lincoln Square, (270) 358-3411.

HODGENVILLE IS the base for the **Abraham Lincoln Birthplace National Historic Site**, located 3 miles (5 km) to its south. The site commemorates the 16th US president's Kentucky roots by preserving his childhood home. Here, 56 steps representing the years of Lincoln's life lead up to a granite-and-marble Memorial Building built around a 19th-century log cabin, where the resident was born. The site lso encompasses a large portion of the original Lincoln family farmland.

**Abraham Lincoln Birthplace National Historic Site**
2120 Bardstown Rd (Hwy 31 E). (270) 358-3137. *8am–4:45pm or 6:45pm (seasonal). Jan 1, Thnksg., Dec 25.* www.nps.gov/abli

**The Hodgenville log cabin in which Abraham Lincoln was born**

## Bardstown 33

*6,800. 107 E Stephen Foster Ave, (502) 348-4877.* www.visitbardstown.com

The self-proclaimed "Bourbon Capital of the World," Bardstown is surrounded by the state's largest whiskey distilleries, which have earned Kentucky its legendary reputation as the whiskey-making center of the US. (Bourbon is made from corn, malt, and rye, and is aged in charred white oak barrels.) The most popular distillery, James Beam, known in countless country songs as "Jim Beam," lies 14 miles (22.5 km) west of Bardstown, while a 20-mile (32-km) drive south leads to the famed Maker's Mark distillery, Kentucky's oldest distillery operating in the same site. However, Bardstown's most popular attraction is **My Old Kentucky Home State Park.** Here, guides lead visitors through the historic mansion that, according to legend, inspired composer Stephen Foster to write "My Old Kentucky Home," the state's beloved anthem. The park also hosts outdoor musicals.

**Stephen Foster statue, My Old Kentucky Home State Park, Bardstown**

**My Old Kentucky Home State Park**
US Hwy 150. *(502) 348-3502. Sep–May: 9am–4:45pm; Jun–Aug: 8:30am–6:15pm. Jan 1, Thanksgiving, Dec 24–31.*

## Louisville 34

*269,000. 30 Market St, (502) 584-2121.*

Founded at the falls of the Ohio River in 1788, Louisville (pronounced "Loo-avul") is home to one of the world's most famous horse races, the Kentucky Derby. What Mardi Gras is to New Orleans, or the Masters Tournament is to Augusta, the Derby is to Louisville – it is the event around which all local calendars revolve. Since it first began in 1875, three-year-old horses have run the track at Churchill Downs on the first Saturday in May. Kentucky's high society turns out in spring finery for this social event of the year, with hats and seersucker suits constituting battle uniform. Mint juleps, the Southern concoction of bourbon, ice, sugar, and fresh mint are the unofficial beverage of choice. "My Old Kentucky Home" plays while the horses are led onto the track for an event that lasts less than two minutes. Winners take home the coveted trophy, decorated with lucky silver horseshoes in a "U" shape "so that the luck doesn't spill out." The adjacent **Kentucky Derby Museum** showcases horse-racing history and offers "backside track tours" through the Churchill Downs track. A couple of blocks from the historic district on the waterfront, the **Louisville Slugger Museum** produces the worldclass baseball bat in a factory marked by a landmark 120-ft (36-m) high bat.

**Gigantic baseball bat outside the Louisville Slugger Museum**

The **J.B. Speed Art Museum** on South 3rd Street displays a large collection of Renaissance paintings and sculpture. At the Riverfront Plaza on the banks of the Ohio River at Main and Fourth Streets, several paddlewheelers tour the area, and a fountain periodically shoots water 375 ft (114.3 m) into the air. The surrounding historic district's old warehouses have been recast as cafés, galleries, and shops.

Located 2 miles (3.2 km) northeast of downtown, Cave Hill Cemetery is one of the largest and most beautiful in the US. Many Louisvillians go visit the grounds just to feed the ducks, or take in the landscaped lawns. Thirty miles (48.2 km) southwest of Louisville, the exterior of the federal gold bullion repository at **Fort Knox** can be seen.

**Kentucky Derby Museum**
704 Central Ave. *(502) 637-1111. 8am–5pm Mon–Sat, noon–5pm Sun. Breeder's cupdays, first Fri–Sat in May, Thanksgiving, Dec 25.* www.derbymuseum.org

**Louisville Slugger Museum**
800 W Main St. *(502) 588-7228. 9am–5pm Mon–Sat, Apr–Nov: 1–5pm Sun.* www.sluggermuseum.org

# Practical Information

SUCCESSFUL TRAVELING AROUND the Southeast requires a great deal of advance planning, as there is so much to see and do in the vast area. With miles of sandy beaches, picturesque historic cities such as Charleston, the stunning rugged wilderness of the Blue Ridge and Appalachian Mountains, and rolling hills and valleys of the foothills, the Southeast truly has it all. In addition to myriad natural wonders, the region also offers burgeoning commercial centers such as Atlanta, and engaging cultural towns including Memphis, the birthplace of the blues, and Nashville, the commercial and cultural capital of "country-western" music, arts, and entertainment.

## Tourist Information

EACH OF THE five Southeast states, North Carolina, South Carolina, Kentucky, Tennessee, and Georgia, publishes travel information that can be ordered by phone or via web sites. State "Welcome Centers" located along most major highways greet visitors as soon as they enter each of the Southeast states. Open between 8am and 5pm daily, these centers offer free road maps and a full range of tourist information, covering climate, transportation, attractions, and accommodations. More information is available from a multitude of tourism bureaus across the five states.

## Natural Hazards

THE END OF SUMMER in the Southeast can be very pleasant, but this is also the main hurricane season, and potentially one of the most troubling times for visitors. Hurricane season stretches from August to the end of the year, but since storms form in the Atlantic Ocean near the Equator, emergency alert systems usually give at least a day or two warning before strong winds and heavy rains arrive.

Watch out for tornadoes and thunderstorms in late spring and summer, especially in the south, where they strike suddenly and create flash floods. If a tornado watch or warning is issued, take cover straight away.

## Getting Around

LIKE MUCH OF THE US, the Southeast is a region where it can be hard to get around without a car. **Greyhound** buses do serve some larger towns and cities, and visitors can also take **Amtrak** trains to travel around the Southeast. Nevertheless, driving is the best way to get around the region, as public transportation can be limited. Seat belts are required for drivers and front seat passengers in all of the five states. Most states also require seat belts for back seat passengers, and child seats are required for all automobile occupants aged 4 and under. Speed limits vary, but are usually 70 to 75 mph (112 to 120 km/h) on Interstate Highways outside of densely populated urban areas, weather permitting.

## Etiquette

COMPARED TO THE rest of the country, Southerners are largely a teatotalling lot. Many of them are Baptists, a religion that frowns on the consumption of alcohol. "Dry" counties can still be found in some rural areas, particularly in the mountains where alcohol cannot be legally served or sold to the public. But exceptions to this tradition are legendary. Makers of "moonshine" a 100-proof home-made whisky typically distilled from corn, gained an outlaw reputation in the days of the Prohibition for evading federal agents by hiding stills deep in the woods and working them by cover of darkness – hence the name "moonshine".

Drinking mint juleps on the day of the Kentucky Derby in Louisville is such a revered local custom that girls start collecting the traditional sterling silver "julep cups" as young as 12 years of age.

## Festivals

THE SOUTHEAST states stage a diverse range of annual community, regional, and national festivals. In February, cultural sites all over the Southeast, especially the Martin Luther King Jr. Center for Non-Violent Social Change in Atlanta, celebrate the **Black History Month** with various special programs. In March, Savannah, Georgia, hosts a lively **St. Patrick's Day** celebration, when thousands come together to drink beer, dance, sing, and celebrate

## The Climate of the Southeast

The region's states have a mild climate with temperatures rarely dipping below freezing in winter, though summer in the low-lying areas can be very hot. Spring sees azaleas and other blossom in the region's famous gardens. Summer, with its sunny days and warm water along sandy beaches, is the most popular time for travel. The end of summer is the primary hurricane season. In inland areas, leaves change color on mountain hardwood trees in October. In winter, snow can fall across all parts of the region.

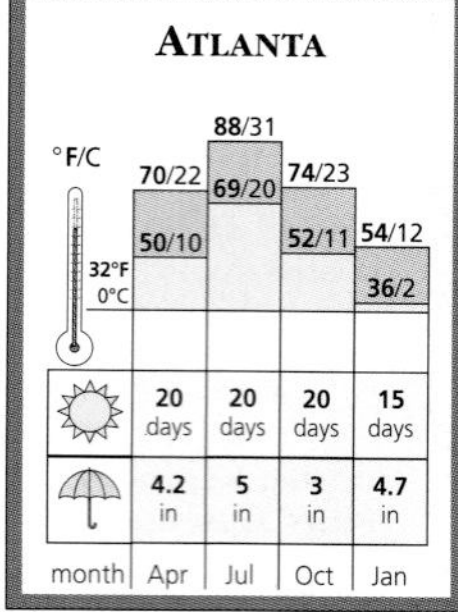

al or imagined Irishness. arch and April are also ideal onths for enjoying house-d-garden tours and the ossoms of the Southeast's any fruit trees, celebrated events like the **Cherry ossom Festival** of Macon, eorgia, where visitors can e more than 200,000 trees ie the city streets.

Throughout May, one of e country's largest music id arts festivals takes place historic Charleston, South arolina, as part of the **poleto Festival USA**.

Summer brings a deluge outdoor events. Bands, eworks, and street festivals e the norm for community elebrations of the July 4 dependence Day holiday. ne of the largest fireworks splays in the US is staged Stone Mountain, outside tlanta. Numerous county nd state fairs crop up around is time, as do music festivals ich as **Old Time Fiddlers' mboree** in Smithville, ennessee. The end of immer brings **Elvis Week** Memphis, Tennessee, cele-rating the life and times of lvis Presley with a week-ong festival around the nniversary of his death n August 16.

A highlight of autumn is the **ennessee Fall Home-coming**, an Appalachian-themed crafts, and culture festival that takes place annually at the Museum of Appalachia. At the end of the year, an old-fashioned Christmas is re-created at the living history village of Old Salem, outside Winston-Salem in North Carolina.

## Sports & Outdoor Activities

The cities of the Southeast host a wide array of professional and amateur sports teams, and there are many minor league teams in smaller cities. Especially in basketball and football, hundreds of high-quality and passionately supported sports teams are fielded by public and private colleges and universities. Atlanta has major league teams in all four main American spectator sports, baseball, football, hockey, and basketball, but professional NFL football is also played in Charlotte, North Carolina, and Nashville, Tennessee. At the minor league level, Memphis has an enormous new downtown stadium for their Class AAA baseball team, the Redbirds; Nashville, Charlotte, and Louisville also have high-quality Class AAA baseball teams. Baseball season runs from April to September, football from September through January, and basketball from winter through mid-spring.

In other sports, the **Kentucky Derby** in early May draws hundreds of thousands of horse-racing fans from all over the world. Golf fans flock to Augusta, Georgia to watch the Masters tournament in April. **NASCAR** stock car races are the region's most popular attractions, drawing more than 200,000 people to weekly races at Atlanta, Bristol, Concord, Rockingham, and Darlington.

Numerous state parks provide opportunities for camping, boating, fishing, and hiking. The coastal states of the Southeast are known to excel in beach activities.

## Entertainment

The birthplace of the blues, rock 'n' roll, and country-western music, the Southeast is a great place to enjoy live music. Hundreds of events take place all over the region almost every night. Besides the various nightclubs hosting talented musicians, the major entertainment venues of the region include the legendary **Grand Old Opry** in Nashville and **B.B. King's Blues Club** in Memphis.

## Directory

### Tourist Offices

**Georgia**
(800) 847-4842.
www.georgia.onmymind.org

**Kentucky**
(800) 225-8747.
www.kentuckytourism.com

**North Carolina**
(800) 847-4862.
www.visitnc.com

**South Carolina**
(800) 872-3505.
www. discoversouthcarolina. com

**Tennessee**
((800) 462-8366.
www.tnvacation.com

### Travel

**Amtrak**
(800) 872-7245.
www.amtrak.com

**Greyhound**
(800) 231-2222.

### Parks & Outdoor Information

**Georgia**
205 SE Butler St, Atlanta.
(800) 864-7275.
www.gastateparks.org

**Kentucky**
2200 Capital Plaza Tower, Frankfort.
(800) 255-7275.
www.kystateparks. com

**North Carolina**
1615 Mail Service Center, Raleigh.
(919) 733-4181.
www.ncsparks.net

**South Carolina**
1205 Pendleton St, Columbia.
(803) 734-0159.
www. southcarolinaparks. com

**Tennessee**
401 Church St, Nashville.
(615) 532-0001, (800) 421-6683.
www.tnstateparks.com

**Kentucky Derby**
(800) 928-3378.
www.kdf.org

**NASCAR**
www.nascar.com

**Atlanta Falcons**
(404) 223-8000.
www.atlantafalcons.com

**Carolina Panthers**
(704) 358-7000.
www.panthers.com

**Tennessee Titans**
(615) 565-4000.
www.titansonline.com

### Entertainment

**B.B. King's Blues Club**
143 Beale St, Memphis, Tennessee.
(901) 524-5464.

**Grand Old Opry**
Nashville, Tennessee.
(615) 889-3060.

# Where to Stay

One of the best ways to sample Southern hospitality is to stay in one of Southeast's many distinctive hotels. Larger cities such as Atlanta offer the widest range of lodging choices, while hideaways can readily be found along the Atlantic shore. National chains, spread throughout the region, offer affordable rooms, designed to be most convenient for motorists.

## North Carolina

**Asheville:** *Inn on Biltmore Estate* $$$
1 Antler Hill Rd. (828) 225-1660, (800) 858-4130. FAX (828) 274-6396.
W www.biltmore.com
This seven-story hotel provides luxurious accommodations within the vast Biltmore Estate, with access to nature trails, a winery, restaurants, and the art-filled house museum.

**Beaufort:** *Beaufort Inn* $$
101 Ann St. (252) 728-2600, (800) 726-0321. FAX (252) 728-1864.
W www.beaufort-inn.com
Overlooking Gallants Channel, the inn makes a good base to explore the compact waterfront area of this quaint coastal town.

**Chapel Hill:** *Carolina Inn* $$$$
211 Pittsboro St. (919) 933-2001. FAX (919) 962-3400.
W www.carolinainn.com
Adjacent to the bucolic University of North Carolina, this genteel historic inn offers a refined faculty club atmosphere.

**Durham:** *Durham Marriot at the Civic Center* $$$
201 Foster St. (919) 768-6000. FAX (919) 768-6037. W www.marriott.com
This eight-story hotel opens onto a fountain plaza next to the Civic Center, near the historic Brightleaf Square district.

**Manteo:** *Tranquil House Inn* $$$
405 Queen Elizabeth St. (252) 473-1404. FAX (252) 473-1526.
W www.tranquilinn.com
This inn is set against the marsh overlooking the sails of the re-created ship *Elizabeth II*, part of a popular theme park.

**Nags Head:** *First Colony Inn* $$$
6720 Virginia Dare Trail. (252) 441-2343. FAX 252-441-9234.
W www.firstcolonyinn.com
Right on the beach, this three-story wooden inn offers a homier alternative to the high-rise hotels lining the shore.

**Ocracoke:** *Beach House B&B* $$
1111 Irving Garrish Hwy. (252) 928-1411. W www.ocracokebeachhouse.com
Located next on the outer banks of Ocracoke Island, this beach-style cottage with its white picket fence dates back to 1918. Inside, amongst the antiques, you'll find air-conditioning and a modern kitchen.

**Raleigh:** *Days Inn* $
3901 S. Wilmington St. (919) 772-8900. FAX (919) 772-1536.
W www.daysinn.com
A no-frills and affordable lodging on the capitol side of the Raleigh-Durham-Chapel Hill Research Triangle region.

| Hotel | Credit Cards | Number of Rooms | Recommended Restaurant | Children's Facilities | Garden or Terrace |
|---|---|---|---|---|---|
| Asheville: Inn on Biltmore Estate | ■ | 213 | ■ | | ■ |
| Beaufort: Beaufort Inn | ■ | 44 | | | |
| Chapel Hill: Carolina Inn | ■ | 184 | ■ | | ■ |
| Durham: Durham Marriot at the Civic Center | ■ | 184 | ■ | | ■ |
| Manteo: Tranquil House Inn | ■ | 25 | ■ | | ■ |
| Nags Head: First Colony Inn | ■ | 26 | | | ■ |
| Ocracoke: Beach House B&B | ■ | 4 | | | ■ |
| Raleigh: Days Inn | ■ | 103 | | | |

## South Carolina

**Charleston:** *Days Inn Historic District* $$$
155 Meeting St. (843) 722-8411. FAX (843) 723-5361.
W www.daysinn.com
Within an inviting two-story courtyard motel, this inn provides extremely affordable lodging in the heart of the historic district.

**Charleston:** *Charleston Place* $$$$$
205 Meeting St. (843) 722-4900. FAX (843) 722-4074.
W www.charlestonplacehotel.com
Conveniently located, near shops, restaurants and tourist sites, this hotel is elegantly furnished. Facilities include boutique shops, restaurant and a full service spa and health club.

| Hotel | Credit Cards | Number of Rooms | Recommended Restaurant | Children's Facilities | Garden or Terrace |
|---|---|---|---|---|---|
| Charleston: Days Inn Historic District | ■ | 124 | | | |
| Charleston: Charleston Place | ■ | 441 | ■ | | |

**Price categories** for a standard double room per night, inclusive of breakfast, service charges, and any additional taxes:

- $ under $100
- $$ $100–$150
- $$$ $150–$200
- $$$$ $200–$250
- $$$$$ over $250

**CREDIT CARDS**
Major credit cards accepted.

**NUMBER OF ROOMS**
Number of rooms in the hotel.

**RECOMMENDED RESTAURANT**
Good restaurant within the hotel.

**CHILDREN'S FACILITIES**
Hotel has various facilities for young children.

**GARDEN OR TERRACE**
Hotel has a garden, courtyard, or terrace.

| Hotel | Credit Cards | Number of Rooms | Recommended Restaurant | Children's Facilities | Garden or Terrace |
|---|---|---|---|---|---|
| **CHARLESTON:** *The Inn at Middleton Place* $$$<br>4300 Ashley River Rd. (843) 556-0500. FAX (843) 556-5673.<br>W www.middletonplace.org/inn<br>This striking blond-wood-and-glass inn provides a refined retreat on the bluffs of the Ashley River. Horseback riding and nature walks are among the amenities, and room rates include breakfast. | ■ | 54 | ■ | | ■ |
| **COLUMBIA:** *Columbia Marriott* $$<br>1200 Hampton St. (803) 771-7000. FAX (803) 254-8307<br>W www.marriott.com/caemh<br>On Main Street, the capital's premier hotel offers 15 stories of comfortable rooms across the street from the art museum. | ■ | 303 | ■ | | ■ |
| **HILTON HEAD:** *Disney's Hilton Head Island Resort* $$$<br>22 Harbourside Lane. (843) 341-4100. FAX (843) 341-4130.<br>W www.dvcmagic.com<br>This all-American family resort features a four-story luxury hotel, complete with a waterslide pool, fishing, and a huge array of fun children's activities. Room rates increase dramatically in summer. | ■ | 123 | ■ | ● | ■ |
| **MYRTLE BEACH:** *Breakers* $$<br>2701 N Ocean Blvd. (843) 626-5000, (800) 845-0688. FAX (843) 626-5001.<br>W www.breakers.com<br>Typical of the high-rise hotels that line the Grand Strand, this 19-story beachfront resort offers an exercise room, a restaurant, and a lounge in the heart of the action. | ■ | 141 | ■ | ● | ■ |
| **MYRTLE BEACH:** *Hilton Myrtle Beach Resort* $$$<br>10000 Beach Club Dr. (843) 449-5000. FAX (843) 497-0295.<br>W www.hilton.com<br>Offering a stretch of the Grand Strand Atlantic coastline, far removed from the congestion of Myrtle Beach proper, this resort offers pools, restaurants, and an 18-hole golf course. | ■ | 385 | ■ | | ■ |
| **GEORGIA** | | | | | |
| **AMERICUS:** *Windsor Hotel* $$<br>125 W Lamar St. (229) 924-1555, (888)-297-9567.<br>FAX (229) 924-1555.<br>This rambling Victorian hotel covers an entire city block and comes as a surprise in this rural region. Rooms are plain, despite the hotel's Moorish architecture, three-story atrium, and refined dining room. | ■ | 53 | ■ | | |
| **AMICALOLA FALLS:** *Amicalola Falls State Park Lodge* $$<br>Hwy 52. (706) 265-8888.<br>W www.gastateparks.org<br>This modern lodge, with spacious rooms and 14 cabins, overlooks a Blue Ridge Mountain panorama, surrounded by scenic trails. A restaurant offers hearty country meals, ideal after a day on the trails. | ■ | 57 | | ● | |
| **ATLANTA:** *Quality Inn Fairlie Poplar* $<br>89 Luckie St. (404) 524-7991. FAX (404) 524-0672.<br>W www.qualityinnatlanta.com<br>This modest, affordable hotel is wonderfully situated in the re-emerging Fairlie-Poplar district downtown. Restaurants, cafes, nightclubs, and the CNN Center are all within a few blocks. | ■ | 75 | | | |
| **ATLANTA:** *Four Seasons Hotel* $$$$$<br>75 14th St. (404) 881-9898, 800-332-3442. FAX (404) 873-4692.<br>W www.fourseasons.com<br>Atlanta's hottest new hotel, furnished with all conceivable modern amenities, is known for its impeccable service and the acclaimed Park 75 restaurant. | ■ | 244 | ■ | | ■ |

For key to symbols see back flap

**Price categories** for a standard double room per night, inclusive of breakfast, service charges, and any additional taxes:

$ under \$100
$$ \$100–\$150
$$$ \$150–\$200
$$$$ \$200–\$250
$$$$$ over \$250

**CREDIT CARDS**
Major credit cards accepted:

**NUMBER OF ROOMS**
Number of rooms in the hotel.

**RECOMMENDED RESTAURANT**
Good restaurant within the hotel.

**CHILDREN'S FACILITIES**
Hotel has various facilities for young children.

**GARDEN OR TERRACE**
Hotel has a garden, courtyard, or terrace.

| Hotel | Credit Cards | Number of Rooms | Recommended Restaurant | Children's Facilities | Garden or Terrace |
|---|---|---|---|---|---|
| **ATLANTA:** *Westin Buckhead* \$\$\$\$\$<br>3391 Peachtree Rd, NE. *(404) 365-0065.* FAX *(404) 365-8787.*<br>W www.westin.com/buckhead<br>Overlooking Lenox Mall in the heart of upper Buckhead, the 22-story Westin has striking modern architecture stocked with contemporary artwork and Biedermeier-style furnishings. | ■ | 365 | ■ | | ■ |
| **DAHLONEGA:** *Smith House* \$<br>84 S Chestatee St. *(706) 867-7000, (800) 852-9577.* FAX *(706) 864-7564.*<br>W www.smithhouse.com<br>This 1804 inn was built atop a gold mine, famed as the center of Georgia's 1830's gold rush. Today, the site includes a modern hotel annex. Modest rooms in the original house are the most evocative and comfortable, and only a short walk to the lively town square. | ■ | 18 | ■ | | |
| **JEKYLL ISLAND:** *Jekyll Island Club Hotel* \$\$\$<br>371 Riverview Dr. *(912) 635-2600, (800) 535-9547.* FAX *(912) 635-2818.*<br>W www.jekyllclub.com<br>This historic club was the center of a wealthy vacation community that occupied the island at the turn of the 20th century. It is set in the historic district by the marsh. | ■ | 157 | ■ | ● | ■ |
| **MACON:** *1842 Inn* \$\$\$\$\$<br>353 College St. *(478) 741-1842.* FAX *(478) 741-1842.*<br>W www.1842inn.com<br>Offering an amiable setting, this historic inn is ideal for venturing into the state's heartland. The main house is wonderful, and a more modern annex is set across a delightful central courtyard. | ■ | 19 | | | ■ |
| **SAVANNAH:** *River Street Inn* \$\$\$<br>124 E Bay St. *(912) 234-6400, (800) 253-4229.* FAX *(912) 234-1478.*<br>W www.riverstreetinn.com<br>Carved out of a 1853 warehouse, this three-story inn offers small, well-appointed rooms, ideally located for waterfront nightlife. | ■ | 86 | | | |
| **SAVANNAH:** *Kehoe House* \$\$\$\$\$<br>123 Habersham St. *(912) 232-1020.* FAX *(912) 231-0208.*<br>W www.williamkehoehouse.com<br>Modeled on a European boutique hotel, the refined Kehoe House sits in a square at a quiet corner of the historic district. | ■ | 14 | | | |
| **ST. SIMONS:** *King & Prince Hotel* \$\$\$<br>201 Arnold Rd. *(912) 638-3631, (800) 342-0212.* FAX *(912) 628-7699.*<br>W www.kingandprince.com<br>Anchoring the East Beach, this rambling beachfront hotel expands from its central building, with an indoor-outdoor pool, dining room, and tavern, to outlying condos, townhouses, and adjacent facilities for this attractive, approachable full-scale resort. | ■ | 129 | ■ | ● | ■ |
| **TENNESSEE** | | | | | |
| **CHATTANOOGA:** *Chattanooga Choo Choo Holiday Inn* \$\$<br>1400 Market St. *(423) 266-5000.* FAX *(423) 265-4635.*<br>W www.choochoo.com<br>Forty-eight rail cars named for the legendary song "Chattanooga Choo-Choo" provide the setting for this chain motel resort, where arcades, fish ponds, and gardens keep families entertained. | ■ | 360 | ■ | ● | ■ |
| **CHATTANOOGA:** *Read House* \$\$<br>827 Broad St. *(423) 266-4121.* FAX *(423) 267-6193.*<br>W www.readhousehotel.com<br>This venerable historic hotel features a 10-story tower, with each floor decorated with illustrations of Civil War battles. | ■ | 136 | ■ | | ■ |

**GREAT SMOKIES:** *Mt. Leconte Lodge* $$$
250 Apple Valley Rd Seiverville 37862. (865) 429-5704.
www.leconte-lodge.com
This rustic and extremely popular mountain lodge, open in spring and summer only, provides group lodges and individual cabins for 50 guests. No electricity, no telephones or TV, and accessible only to hikers able to make the 5.5-mile (9-km) hike to the lodge. *late Mar–mid-Nov.*

**GATLINBURG:** *Buckhorn Inn* $$
2140 Tudor Mountain Rd. (865) 436-4668.
www.Buckhorninn.com
Overlooking Mount LeConte about a mile outside the national park, the Buckhorn Inn provides well-appointed rooms in a classic mountain lodge and cottages. Walk-in stone fireplaces, piano, and rocking chairs on the porch are important facets of the inn's relaxing atmosphere.

**MEMPHIS:** *Elvis Presley's Heartbreak Hotel* $$
3677 Elvis Presley Blvd. (901) 332-1000. FAX (901) 332-2107.
www.elvis.com
The 1950s rooms and continuously looping Elvis movies here make the Heartbreak Hotel the best place to indulge in the full kitschy appeal of a pilgrimage to Graceland.

**MEMPHIS:** *Peabody Hotel* $$$$
149 Union Ave. (901) 529-4000. FAX (901) 529-3600.
www.peabodymemphis.com
One of the most distinguished hotels in the South, the historic Peabody is also one of the quirkiest. A legion of ducks descend daily from their penthouse lair to cavort in the lobby fountain.

**NASHVILLE:** *Union Station Hotel* $$$
1001 Broadway. (615) 726-1001. FAX (615) 248-3554.
www.wyndham.com
In a stunningly vast old train depot resembling a Gothic cathedral, Union Station Hotel offers deluxe lodging and dining downtown, a short cab ride from the lively waterfront district.

**NASHVILLE:** *Gaylord Opryland Resort & Convention Center* $$$$$
2800 Opryland Dr. (615) 889-1000. FAX (615) 871-7741.
www.gaylordopryland.com
The phenomenal Opryland Hotel more closely resembles a giant lunar biosphere than any earthy hotel, with breathtaking acreage of gardens, waterfalls, cafés, shops, and amusements. Even if you're not staying overnight, it has to be seen to be believed.

## KENTUCKY

**LEXINGTON:** *Gratz Park Inn* $$$
120 W 2nd St. (859) 231-1777. FAX (859) 233-7593.
www.gratzparkinn.com
Intimate, historic hotel, the Gratz Park Inn features antiques in every room, exemplary service, and a horse-drawn carriage to take visitors around town.

**LEXINGTON:** *Hyatt Regency* $$$
401 W High St. (859) 253-1234. FAX (859) 233-7974.
www.hyatt.com
This comfortable, modern high-rise hotel is ideally located in the heart of the city.

**LOUISVILLE:** *Galt House* $$
140 N 4th St. (502) 589-5200, (800) 626-1814. FAX (502) 589-3444.
www.galthouse.com
This modern hotel, with an 18-story interior atrium is located right on the river. Amazing views can be seen from most rooms and the revolving rooftop restaurant and cocktail bar.

**LOUISVILLE:** *Seelbach Hilton Hotel* $$$
500 4th Ave. (502) 585-3200. FAX (502) 585-9239.
www.seelbachhilton.com
Opulent hotel, with gold-plated everything and murals in the two-story lobby depicting scenes from Kentucky history. Built in 1905, and impeccably maintained ever since, the hotel is now part of the Hilton chain.

| Hotel | | | | | |
|---|---|---|---|---|---|
| Mt. Leconte Lodge | ■ | | | | |
| Buckhorn Inn | ■ | 9 | ■ | | ■ |
| Elvis Presley's Heartbreak Hotel | ■ | 128 | | | |
| Peabody Hotel | ■ | 468 | ■ | ● | |
| Union Station Hotel | ■ | 124 | ■ | | ■ |
| Gaylord Opryland Resort & Convention Center | ■ | 2,881 | ■ | ● | ■ |
| Gratz Park Inn | ■ | 44 | ■ | | ■ |
| Hyatt Regency | ■ | 365 | ■ | | ■ |
| Galt House | ■ | 650 | ■ | | |
| Seelbach Hilton Hotel | ■ | 321 | ■ | | |

For key to symbols see back flap

# Where to Eat

TRADITIONAL SOUTHERN FOOD is affordable across the region. A typical country meal includes meat, bread, and two or three vegetables, washed down by sweet iced tea, and topped off by banana pudding. Innovators are now creating new dishes with local ingredients. In the listings below, opening times are indicated by a "B" for breakfast, "L" for lunch, and "D" for dinner.

## NORTH CAROLINA

**ASHEVILLE:** *Tupelo Honey* $$

12 College St. *(828) 255-4863.*

The New South cuisine at Tupelo Honey offers a lighter take on such regional specialties as fried green tomatoes, cheese grits, pimento cheese, chips, and catfish, though the banana pudding is strictly traditional. Open late, till 3am some nights. *B, L, D.* *Mon, Jan 1, Thanksgiving, Dec 25.*

**ASHEVILLE:** *Zambra* $$$

85 W Walnut St. *(828) 232-1060.*

This restaurant is famed for its exotic gypsy cuisine, including salmon herb roll with polenta, succotash, and curry coconut mojo sauce, and for its colorful interior and Moorish style. *L (summer only), D.* *Sun, Mon.*

**BEAUFORT:** *Clawson's 1905 Restaurant & Pub* $$$

425 Front St. *(252) 728-2133.*

Within a 1905 grocery store building, Clawson's offers ribs, steaks, and seafood in a setting surrounded by historic photos, displays, and memorabilia. *L.* *Sun, Labor Day–Memorial Day.*

**CHAPEL HILL:** *Mama Dip's* $$$

408 W Rosemary St. *(919) 942-5837.*

Mama Dip's has been serving up such regional favorites as fried chicken, cornbread, and peach cobbler for over 25 years. This restaurant has a casual atmosphere. *B, L, D.* *public hols.*

**DURHAM:** *Magnolia Grill* $$$$

1002 9th St. *(919) 286-3609.*

Named by *Gourmet* magazine as one of America's 50 Best Restaurants, Magnolia is noted for Chef Ben Barker and his wife Karen, a pastry chef known for her outstanding dessert repertory. *D.* *Sun, Mon, public hols.*

**MANTEO:** *1587 Restaurant* $$$$

405 Queen Elizabeth St. *(252) 473-1587.*

Set within the Tranquil House Inn, 1587 makes the most of its beautiful setting along the small Manteo waterfront and a special-occasion menu of seafood, steaks, and vegetarian entrées. *D.* *Dec 25.*

**NAGS HEAD:** *Sam & Omies* $$$

Milepost 16.5, 7228 Virginia Dave Trail. *(252) 441-7366.*

Sam and Omies has been a popular local hangout for inexpensive but well-prepared family fare for more than 50 years. *B, L, D.* *mid-Dec–Mar.*

**OCRACOKE:** *Howard's Pub* $$$

SR 12 ,1 mile from ferry. *(252) 928-4441.*

Ocracoke's only year-round restaurant, Howard's Pub offers a raw bar, burgers, and pizza in a casual tavern setting. *Sun.*

## SOUTH CAROLINA

**BEAUFORT:** *Beaufort Inn Dining Room* $$$$

809 Port Republic St. *(843) 521-9000.*

New Southern cuisine is served in this historic building downtown in the interesting town of Beaufort; tuna and rack of lamb are among the favorite entrées. *D.* *Dec 24–25.*

**CHARLESTON:** *Blossom Cafe* $$$

171 E Bay St. *(843) 722-9200.*

A sister restaurant to Magnolia's, Blossom next door features a Tuscan-inspired menu and design, along with flowing fountains and greenery on its spacious sheltered patio. *L, D, Sun brunch.* *public hols.*

| Restaurant | Credit Cards | Outdoor Tables | Vegetarian | Good Wine List | Children's Facilities |
|---|---|---|---|---|---|
| Asheville: Tupelo Honey | ■ | ● | ■ | ● | ■ |
| Asheville: Zambra | ■ | | ■ | ● | |
| Beaufort: Clawson's 1905 Restaurant & Pub | ■ | | | | |
| Chapel Hill: Mama Dip's | ■ | ● | ■ | | |
| Durham: Magnolia Grill | ■ | | ■ | ● | |
| Manteo: 1587 Restaurant | ■ | | ■ | ● | |
| Nags Head: Sam & Omies | ■ | | | | |
| Ocracoke: Howard's Pub | ■ | ● | ■ | | ■ |
| Beaufort: Beaufort Inn Dining Room | ■ | ● | ■ | ● | |
| Charleston: Blossom Cafe | ■ | ● | ■ | ● | |

**Price categories** include a three-course meal for one, a glass of house wine, and all unavoidable extra charges such as sales tax and service.
($) under $20
($)($) $20–30
($)($)($) $30–45
($)($)($)($) $45–60
($)($)($)($)($) over $60

**CREDIT CARDS**
Major credit cards accepted.

**OUTDOOR TABLES**
Garden, courtyard, or terrace with outdoor tables.

**VEGETARIAN**
A good selection of vegetarian dishes available.

**GOOD WINE LIST**
Extensive list of good wines, both domestic and imported.

**CHILDREN'S FACILITIES**
Small portions and/or high chairs available on request.

**CHARLESTON:** *Magnolia's* ($)($)($)($)
185 E Bay St. *(843) 577-7771.*
In a restaurant row on the waterfront, Magnolia's offers contemporary American cuisine, with such regional specialties as crisp and creamy shrimp-and-grits. The casually elegant setting of the place is banked by light wood walls filled with modern artwork. *L, D.* ● *public hols.*

**CHARLESTON:** *Middleton Place Restaurant* ($)($)($)($)
4300 Ashley River Rd. *(843) 556-6020.*
Within the 1933 guest house on the Middleton Place plantation, the restaurant serves such Low Country plantation fare as okra gumbo, she-crab soup, and Hoppin' John in a comfortably elegant setting overlooking the old rice-mill pond. *L, Tue–Sun D.* ● *public hols.*

**CHARLESTON:** *McCrady's* ($)($)($)($)($)
2 Unity Alley. *(843) 577-0025.*
From its obscure little alleyway entrance, McCrady's opens into a spacious set of modern rooms, which includes a wine bar. At McCrady's, they serve French-influenced American cuisine to a sophisticated crowd. *D.* ● *public hols.*

**COLUMBIA:** *Maurice's Piggie Park BBQ* ($)
1600 Charleston Hwy. *(803) 796-0220.*
The famous Piggie Park draws truckers, RV campers, and barbecue aficionados from across the region to its big spread devoted to the almighty pig. *L, D.* ● *Thanksgiving, Dec 25.*

**COLUMBIA:** *Al's Upstairs Italian Restaurant* ($)($)($)
304 Meeting St. *(803) 794-7404.*
Seafood, steak, Italian specialties, and such regional items as Oysters Rockefeller are served in this upscale, second-story restaurant downtown. *D.* ● *Sun, Thanksgiving, Dec 25.*

**HILTON HEAD:** *Charlie's L'Etoile Verte* ($)($)($)($)
1000 Plantation Center. *(843) 785-9277.*
This French bistro is noted for its fish, shellfish, and lamb specialties, along with Cobb salad and homemade desserts, all served in a French country decor. *L, D.* ● *Sun, Mon, public hols.*

**MURRELLS INLET:** *Oliver's Lodge* ($)($)($)($)
4204 Hwy 17. *(843) 651-2963.*
The oldest restaurant in Murrells Inlet, Oliver's has been serving fresh seafood here since 1910. Right on the waterfront, the restaurant offers a view of the fishing fleet. *D.*

## GEORGIA

**ATHENS:** *Last Resort Grill* ($)($)($)
174 W. Clayton St. *(706) 549-0810.*
This popular grill in a downtown storefront serves Southern cuisine with Southwestern influences. The salmon-and-grits plate and praline chicken are among the most requested specialties. *L, D.* ● *Sun, public hols.*

**ATLANTA:** *Harvest* ($)($)($)
853 N Highland Ave NE. *(404) 876-8244.*
Harvest offers light takes on regional cuisine emphasizing fresh vegetables, fish, and pecan-encrusted fare. *L (except Sat), D.* ● *public hols.*

**ATLANTA:** *Mid City Cuisine* ($)($)($)
Near Pershing Point. *(404) 888-8700.*
In a first floor office building, this restaurant serves fresh organic vegetables, homemade pastas, seafood, and meats. *B, L, D.* ● *Jan 1, Thanksgiving, Dec 25.*

| Restaurant | Credit Cards | Outdoor Tables | Vegetarian | Good Wine List | Children's Facilities |
|---|---|---|---|---|---|
| Magnolia's | ■ | | ■ | ● | |
| Middleton Place Restaurant | ■ | | | ● | |
| McCrady's | ■ | | | ● | |
| Maurice's Piggie Park BBQ | ■ | ● | | | ■ |
| Al's Upstairs Italian Restaurant | ■ | | ■ | | |
| Charlie's L'Etoile Verte | ■ | | | ● | |
| Oliver's Lodge | ■ | ● | ■ | | ■ |
| Last Resort Grill | ■ | ● | ■ | ● | |
| Harvest | ■ | | ■ | ● | |
| Mid City Cuisine | ■ | ● | ■ | ● | ■ |

For key to symbols see back flap

**Price categories** include a three-course meal for one, a glass of house wine, and all unavoidable extra charges such as sales tax and service.
Ⓢ under $20
ⓈⓈ $20–30
ⓈⓈⓈ $30–45
ⓈⓈⓈⓈ $45–60
ⓈⓈⓈⓈⓈ over $60

**CREDIT CARDS**
Major credit cards accepted.

**OUTDOOR TABLES**
Garden, courtyard, or terrace with outdoor tables.

**VEGETARIAN**
A good selection of vegetarian dishes available.

**GOOD WINE LIST**
Extensive list of good wines, both domestic and imported.

**CHILDREN'S FACILITIES**
Small portions and/or high chairs available on request.

| Restaurant | Credit Cards | Outdoor Tables | Vegetarian | Good Wine List | Children's Facilities |
|---|---|---|---|---|---|
| **ATLANTA:** *Atlanta Grill* ⓈⓈⓈⓈ<br>181 Peachtree St NE. *(404) 221-6550.*<br>This always-open, elegant restaurant offers balcony seating above Peachtree Street to watch bustling Atlanta go by. *B, L, D.* | ■ | ● | ■ | ● | ■ |
| **ATLANTA:** *Food Studio* ⓈⓈⓈⓈ<br>887 W Marietta St NW. *(404) 815-6677.*<br>Squirreled away in the King Plow Arts Center, Food Studio is the city's most radical restaurant, serving complex fusion dishes in a recycled factory space. *D.* ● *Jan 1, Thanksgiving, Memorial Day, Labor Day, Dec 25.* | ■ | ● | ■ | ● | |
| **ATLANTA:** *Seeger's* ⓈⓈⓈⓈⓈ<br>111 W Paces Ferry Rd. *(404) 846-9779.*<br>Internationally recognized as one of the best restaurants in the South, Seeger's offers an eclectic European-influenced menu – prix fixe daily specialties served in a minimalist setting. *D.* ● *Sun, public hols.* | ■ | ● | ■ | ● | |
| **DAHLONEGA:** *Rick's* ⓈⓈⓈ<br>47 S Park St. *(706) 864-9422.*<br>Set invitingly in a comfortable clapboard house, a short walk up from the main square, Rick's offers a wide range of entrées from crawfish risotto to meatloaf and burgers. The wine lists offers 200 wines. *L, D, Sun brunch.* ● *Easter, Thanksgiving, Dec 25.* | ■ | ● | ■ | ● | ■ |
| **MACON:** *Len Berg's* Ⓢ<br>Old Post Office Alley. *(478) 742-9255.*<br>Tucked away in an alley downtown, Len Berg's has been serving traditional Southern lunch plates since 1908. *L.* ● *Sun, public hols.* | | | | | |
| **SAVANNAH:** *Mrs. Wilkes' Boarding House* Ⓢ<br>107 W Jones St. *(912) 232-5997.*<br>In the ground floor of a Savannah row house, Mrs. Wilkes has been serving Southern specialties, family-style, for generations. *L.* ● *Sun, public hols.* | | | ■ | | |
| **SAVANNAH:** *Elizabeth on 37th* ⓈⓈⓈⓈ<br>105 E 37th St. *(912) 236-5547.*<br>Namesake Chef Elizabeth Terry pioneered nouvelle Southern cuisine in this old house in the Victorian district. *D.* ● *Sun, public hols.* | ■ | | ■ | ● | |
| **SAVANNAH:** *Il Pasticcio* ⓈⓈⓈⓈ<br>2 E Broughton St. *(912) 231-8888.*<br>This sophisticated restaurant offers Italian dishes in a smart storefront on the Broughton Street corridor. *D.* ● *Thanksgiving, Dec 24–25.* | ■ | | ■ | ● | |
| **ST. SIMON'S:** *Crabdaddy's* ⓈⓈⓈ<br>1217 Ocean Blvd. *(912) 634-1120.*<br>A crab shack for the polo set, this casual family restaurant serves seafood plates and a variety of other dishes. *D.* ● *public hols.* | ■ | | | ● | ■ |

## TENNESSEE

| Restaurant | Credit Cards | Outdoor Tables | Vegetarian | Good Wine List | Children's Facilities |
|---|---|---|---|---|---|
| **CHATTANOOGA:** *Dinner on the Diner* ⓈⓈⓈⓈ<br>1400 Market St. *(423) 266-5000 or (800) 872-2529.*<br>In the dining car that is one of 48 train cars constituting the Chattanooga Choo Choo of musical legend, this diner serves family-friendly options that highlight the setting over the cuisine. *D.* ● *Sun, Mon, public hols.* | ■ | | | | |
| **CHATTANOOGA:** *212 Market Restaurant* ⓈⓈⓈⓈ<br>212 Market St. *(423) 265-1212.*<br>Fresh seafood, steak, and homemade bread are the specialties of this appealing restaurant conveniently located right across from the Tennessee Aquarium. *L, D.* ● *Jan 1, Thanksgiving, Dec 25.* | ■ | ● | ■ | ● | ■ |

For key to symbols see back flap

ɜATLINBURG: *Buckhorn Inn* $$$
!140 Tudor Mountain Rd. (865-436-4668.
'ind the finest meals in the area at this fixed price country inn. The daily special might be mountain trout, beef tenderloin, or a mixed grill. Make 'eservations early in the day. *D.*

ᴍEMPHIS: *The Cupboard* $
400 Union St. *(901) 276-8015.*
ᴍodestly set in an aging strip mall off the busy connector in midtown, The Cupboard offers traditional meat-and-three dishes, including such avorites as dried catfish and meatloaf. *B, L, D (except Sat–Sun).*

ᴍEMPHIS: *Rendezvous* $$$
ɔ2 S 2nd St. *(901) 523-2746.*
'his landmark alleyway restaurant offers popular spice-rubbed dry rib ɔarbecue in a tavern setting decorated with memorabilia, a short block rom the Peabody Hotel. *L, D.* *Sun, Mon.*

ᴍEMPHIS: *Automatic Slim's Tonga Club* $$$$
33 S 2nd St. *901) 525-7948.*
ᴧt the exotically arty Automatic Slim's downtown, the Southwest meets he Caribbean in such dishes as the pork loin with adobo dry rub served over with a exotic mole sauce. There's live music on Friday nights. *, D.* *Sun, public hols.*

ɴASHVILLE: *Monell's* $$
235 Sixth Ave N. *(615) 248-4747.*
ɿuch traditional favorites as pork chops, Cajun catfish, corn pudding, and pple strudel are served here. (Call and confirm which meals will be erved on which days). *L, D, Sun brunch.* *Thanksgiving, Dec 25.*

ɴASHVILLE: *Zanzibar* $$$
12 S Main St. *(901) 543-9646.*
n the arts district south of Beale Street, an artist and gallery owner operates this eclectic bistro for Post-Modern fare accompanied by live jazz Thursday and Friday nights. *B, L, D.* *Sun–Tue, public hols.*

ɴASHVILLE: *F. Scott's* $$$$
!210 Crestmoor Rd. *(615) 269-5861.*
t's worth the 15-minute drive south of downtown to F. Scott's, where the nenu changes every few days. Visitors can also stop for drinks in the azz bar that features live music nightly. *D.* *public hols.*

ɴASHVILLE: *Mad Platter* $$$$
239 Sixth Ave N. *(615) 242-2563.*
ɴorth of the Farmers' Market, the Mad Platter offers gourmet cuisine, and he quiet Germantown neighborhood is a nice alternative to the bustling vaterfront district of lower Broad. *L, D.* *Mon, public hols.*

## KENTUCKY

.EXINGTON: *Ala Lucie* $$$$
59 N Limestone. *(859) 252-5277.*
ᴧn offbeat blend of Continental and new American is available at this elegant and romantic dining spot. Try the crab cake taco with avacado. *(except Sat), D.* *Sun.*

.EXINGTON: *Nadine's* $$$$
'735 Harrodsburg Rd. *(859) 223-0797.*
ɿettle down into an overstuffed chair and enjoy one of the famous ocktails, while contemplating the eclectic menu of European, Asian, and raditional American dishes. *L, D.*

OUISVILLE: *Mazzoni's Oyster Café* $$
804 Taylorsville Rd. *(502) 451-4436.*
n business for over a century, this informal café specializes in oysters hat come freshly shucked, cooked in stews, or rolled up in cornmeal atter and fried. The menu includes many fish dishes. *L, D.* *Sun.*

.OUISVILLE: *Lilly's* $$$$$
147 Bardstown Rd. *(502) 451-0447.*
ntimate dining rooms, draped in green and deep purple decor, showcase ɔcal seasonal produce in dishes like country ham with morel mushrooms or rabbit stuffed with lamb sausage. *L, D.* *Sun, Mon.*

A lush, swampy forest in the Everglades, Florida ▷

# FLORIDA

MARLIN
1200

# FLORIDA

*FOR THE MAJORITY OF FLORIDA'S 40 million-plus annual visitors, the typical travel poster images of Florida – sun, sea, sand, and Mickey Mouse – are reason enough to jump on the next plane. The Sunshine State deserves its reputation as the perfect family vacation spot, but Florida is much richer in its culture, landscape, and character than its stereotypical image suggests.*

Both climatically and culturally, Florida is a state divided – a bridge between temperate North America and tropical Latin America and the Caribbean. In the north, roads are lined with stately live oak trees and people speak with a southern drawl, while, in the south, shade from the subtropical sun is cast by palm trees, and the inhabitants of Miami are as likely to speak Spanish as English.

For most visitors, Florida's prime attractions lie along the coasts, where the beaches are varied and abundant enough to satisfy every visitor. However, great rewards await those who want to explore farther. The lush forests and rolling hills of the north provide some of the loveliest countryside in the state. Equally exciting are the so-called "wild areas," such as the Everglades, which harbor an extraordinary diversity of plant and animal life, and where alligators and snakes are living reminders of the inhospitable place that Florida was not much more than 100 years ago.

### HISTORY

At first glance, Florida appears to be a state without history. Yet behind its modern veneer lies a long and rich past, molded by different nationalities and cultures. Until the 16th century, Florida supported a large indigenous population, whose complex political and religious systems demonstrated a high degree of social organization. However, colonization soon decimated the Indians through warfare and disease. In 1513, the Spanish explorer Juan Ponce de León discovered Florida and named it after Pascua Florida, the Feast of the Flowers

**Deerfield Beach, a quiet coastal resort within easy reach of Boca Raton**

**◁ The Marlin Hotel in Miami's South Beach, a classic establishment illuminated in colorful neon**

(Easter). For almost 200 years several Spanish conquistadors attempted unsuccessfully to search for gold and colonize the region. Their primary concern was Florida's strategic position. The Gulf Stream carried Spanish galleons laden with gold and treasure from the New World colonies past Florida's coast on their journey back across the Atlantic, and it was thus vital that "La Florida" not fall into enemy hands.

**Henry Flagler, 1830–1913**

Initially the French troubled the Spanish, but the real threat to their control came in 1742 when English colonists from Georgia defeated them and finally acquired Florida about 20 years later. Though Florida was returned to Spain in 1783, numerous boundary disputes followed. It was only after Andrew Jackson, the ambitious US general, captured Pensacola that the official US occupation took place in 1821. During this period, the plantation system was firmly established in north Florida. The principal cash crop was cotton, for which intensive slave labor was required to work in the fields.

### Key Dates in History

**1513** Ponce de León discovers "La Florida"

**1563** Pedro Menéndez de Avilés founds St. Augustine after defeating the French

**1763** Britain acquires Florida

**1783** Britain returns Florida to the Spanish

**1785–1821** Spanish-American border disputes

**1821** Florida becomes part of the US; Andrew Jackson becomes the first American governor

**1835–42** Second Seminole War

**1845** Florida becomes the 27th state

**1852** Harriet Beecher Stowe publishes the anti-slavery epic, *Uncle Tom's Cabin*

**1853** Third Seminole War begins

**1886** Henry Flagler starts construction of the Florida East Coast Railway

**1958** *Explorer I* is launched after NASA chooses Cape Canaveral as the site of its space program

**1959** Over 300,000 Cubans flee to Florida

**1980** 125,00 Cubans arrive in the Mariel boatlift

**1992** Hurricane Andrew devastates south Florida

**2000** George W. Bush appointed president after the Florida election debacle

**2003** Space Shuttle *Columbia* explodes on re-entry and *Spirit*, a rover, heads for Mars

American attempts to subdue the Seminole Indians and take over their land led to over 65 years of conflict. When the Third Seminole War ended in 1858, the Indians retreated to the Everglades, where they still live. Soon after came the Civil War, by the end of which, in 1865, Florida was in ruins. But the state recovered rapidly. Railroad barons, such as Henry Flagler and Henry Plant, built a network of railroads and opulent hotels, which attracted wealthy visitors from the north. Tourism flourished in the early 20th century, and by 1950 it had become Florida's top industry. The launch of the NASA space program at Cape Canaveral in the 1950s also helped boost the state's prosperity.

### Society & Culture

The state "where everyone is from somewhere else," Florida has always been a cultural hodgepodge. The earliest inhabitants were the Seminole Indians and the early pioneers of the 1800s, the Cracker farmers, named perhaps from the cracking of their cattle whips or the cracking of corn to make grits. However, both groups are rarely encountered along the affluent, heavily populated coast.

Americans have poured into this land of opportunity since World War II; the twentieth most populous state in the US in 1950, Florida is now ranked fourth. The largest single group to move south has been the retirees, for whom Florida's climate, lifestyle of leisure, and low tax rates, hold great appeal after a life of hard work. While

**Space shuttle *Discovery* lifts off from the Kennedy Space Center, Cape Canaveral**

Iural inside the US Federal Courthouse, Miami

uper-rich communities like Palm Beach fit the conservative and staid nage that some people still have of lorida, the reality is very different. An icreasing number of the new arrivals re young people for whom Florida s a land of opportunity, a place o enjoy the good life. Today, ie younger generation has elped turn Miami's South Beach into one of the ountry's trendiest resorts.

From 1959 on, there has lso been massive immigration rom Latin America; Dade County in particular has a huge Iispanic community. This ethnic iversity is today celebrated in an ndless cycle of exuberant festivals, music, and local food.

Beach buggie, Daytona Beach

### ECONOMICS & TOURISM

conomically, Florida is not in bad hape compared with the rest of the ountry. For most of its history, its main ource of revenue has been agriculture – itrus fruits, vegetables, sugar, and cattle, which was originally introuced by the Spanish olonists. In fact, Florida roduces over 70 percent f the citrus fruits conumed in the United States oday, while Kissimmee is nown as the "cow capital" f the state. High-tech ndustry is significant as vell, and the proximity of Iiami to Latin America and ie Caribbean has made it ie natural route for trade vith the region. This proxnity has also contributed to the state's flourishing cruise industry. Florida's warm climate has also generated high-profile moneyspinners, such as car racing, and the Daytona International Speedway attracts thousands of visitors every year. Spring baseball training also draws teams and lots of fans south, while the fashion trade brings models by the dozen and plenty of glamour to Miami.

It is tourism, however, that fills the state's coffers. The Walt Disney World Resort may appear to dominate the industry, but Florida makes the most of all its assets. Its superb beaches and the promise of winter sunshine have lured millions of vacationers through the years. Beside beaches and theme parks, there are natural habitats, state-of-the-art musems, and towns, such as St. Augustine and Pensacola, that still retain their Spanish Colonial ambience.

Conservation is a major issue in Florida today. After decades of intense urban development, Floridians have finally learned the importance of preserving their rich and varied natural heritage. Great swathes of the natural landscape have already disappeared beneath factories, condos, and cabbage fields, but those involved in industry and agriculture are acting more responsibly, and water use is now strictly monitored. Florida's natural treasures, from its freshwater swamps and hardwood forests to its last remaining panthers, are now protected for posterity.

A vibrant mural in Key West's Bahama Village

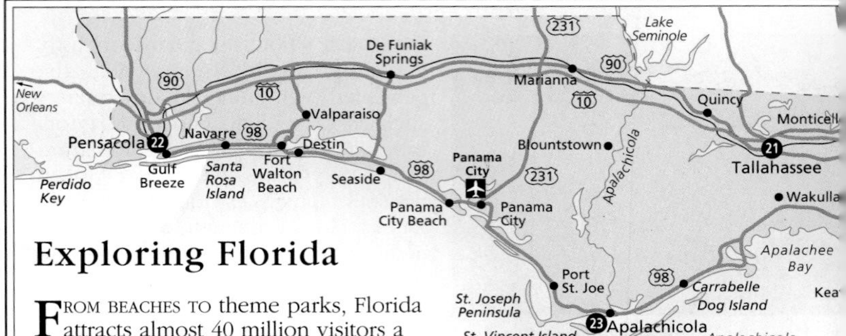


# Exploring Florida

FROM BEACHES TO theme parks, Florida attracts almost 40 million visitors a year. The principal attractions are Miami and Orlando, but there are other exciting destinations as well, such as St. Augustine and Pensacola, established by Spanish colonialists in the 16th century. For nature lovers, the Everglades is a thrilling experience, while the Keys offer a choice of activities, such as fishing, diving, and snorkeling. An extensive road network links the main towns, so traveling by car in Florida is both quick and enjoyable.

Art Deco motif, popular in Miami

## Sights at a Glance

*Miami pp290–99* 1

**The Gold & Treasure Coasts**
- Fort Lauderdale 2
- Boca Raton 3
- Loxahatchee National Wildlife Refuge 4
- Palm Beach 5

**Orlando & the Space Coast**
- Cocoa Beach 6
- Kennedy Space Center 7
- Canaveral National Seashore & Merritt Island 8
- *Walt Disney World® Resort pp304–307* 9
- *Universal Orlando pp308–309* 10
- *SeaWorld Orlando & Discovery Cove pp310–11* 11
- Orlando 12
- Winter Park 13
- International Drive 14
- Kissimmee 15
- Disney Wilderness Preserve 16

**The Northeast**
- Daytona Beach 17
- St. Augustine 18
- Fernandina Beach 19
- Ocala National Forest 20

**The Panhandle**
- Tallahassee 21
- Pensacola 22
- Apalachicola 23

**The Gulf Coast**
- Tampa 24
- St. Petersburg 25
- *Sarasota p319* 26
- Lee Island Coast 27

**The Everglades & the Keys**
- Big Cypress Swamp 28
- Everglades National Park 29
- Biscayne National Park 30
- The Keys 31
- Key West 32

**Key**
- Airport
- Cruise port
- Highway
- Major road
- Railroad

## Mileage Chart

**10** = Distance in miles
10 = Distance in kilometers

| | Miami | Palm Beach | Orlando | St. Augustine | Tallahassee | Pensacola | Tampa | St. Petersburg | Sarasota |
|---|---|---|---|---|---|---|---|---|---|
| Palm Beach | **70** / 113 | | | | | | | | |
| Orlando | **237** / 381 | **171** / 275 | | | | | | | |
| St. Augustine | **314** / 505 | **247** / 398 | **107** / 172 | | | | | | |
| Tallahassee | **504** / 811 | **438** / 705 | **257** / 414 | **205** / 330 | | | | | |
| Pensacola | **707** / 1138 | **642** / 1033 | **450** / 724 | **399** / 642 | **197** / 317 | | | | |
| Tampa | **279** / 449 | **200** / 322 | **84** / 135 | **190** / 306 | **274** / 441 | **468** / 753 | | | |
| St. Petersburg | **262** / 422 | **228** / 367 | **106** / 171 | **212** / 341 | **299** / 481 | **490** / 789 | **24** / 39 | | |
| Sarasota | **230** / 370 | **195** / 314 | **131** / 211 | **236** / 380 | **333** / 536 | **520** / 837 | **60** / 97 | **35** / 56 | |
| Key West | **161** / 259 | **233** / 375 | **394** / 634 | **478** / 769 | **641** / 1032 | **873** / 1405 | **426** / 686 | **410** / 660 | **376** / 605 |

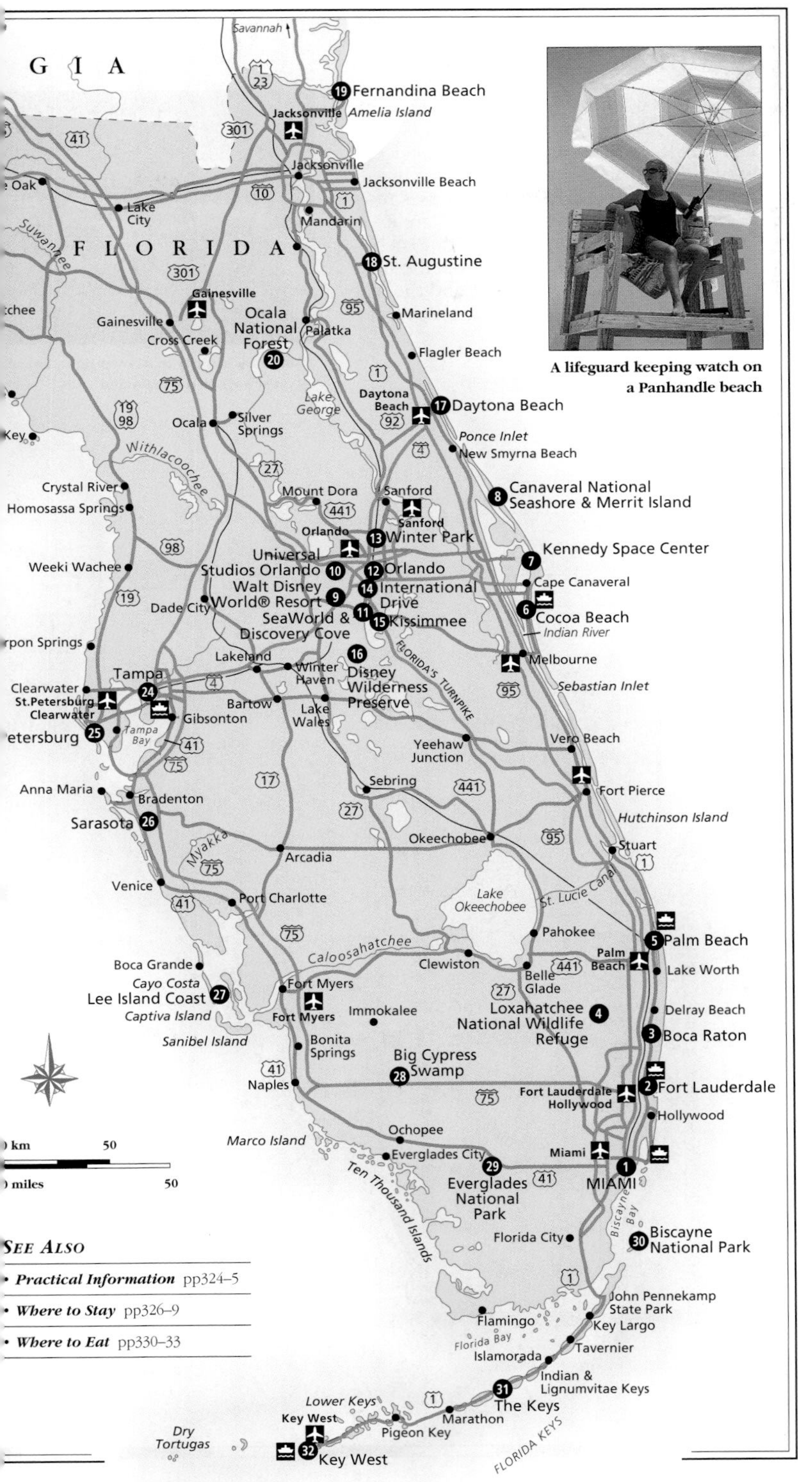


A lifeguard keeping watch on a Panhandle beach

*SEE ALSO*

- ***Practical Information*** pp324–5
- ***Where to Stay*** pp326–9
- ***Where to Eat*** pp330–33

# Miami ❶

A SMALL TRADING POST a century ago, Miami, or Greater Miami, now covers 2,000 sq miles (5,180 sq km) and has a population of two million. The metropolis incorporates many districts and cities and comprises most of Dade County. Miami's top sights are its beaches, especially fun-filled South Beach. Other sights include Little Havana, the heart of the city's Cuban population, and the leafy suburbs of Coral Gables and Coconut Grove.

**Miami Beach, a city in its own right, linked by causeways to the mainland**

### KEY

- Sight/Place of interest
- Beach area
- Airport
- Metrorail station
- Boat boarding point
- Parking
- Tourist information
- Expressway

## ETTING AROUND

ublic transportation in Miami is run by the Miami-Dade ransit Agency, which operates the buses, the Metrorail ommuter rail network, and downtown's elevated etromover. However, the best way to get around by car, while taxis are recommended at night.

### SEE ALSO


- ***Where to Stay*** p326
- ***Where to Eat*** p330


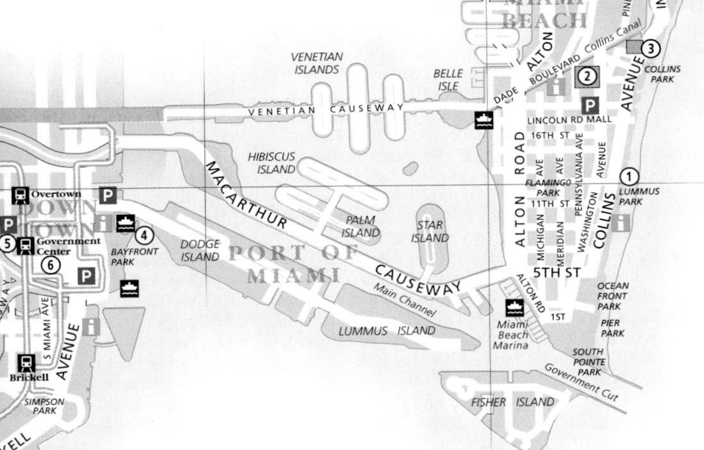


## SIGHTS AT A GLANCE

South Beach ①
Holocaust Memorial ②
Bass Museum of Art ③
Biscayne Bay Boat Trips ④
Miami-Dade Cultural Center ⑤
Downtown ⑥
Little Havana ⑦
Coral Gables ⑧
Biltmore Hotel ⑨
Venetian Pool ⑩
Coconut Grove Village ⑪
*Vizcaya p297* ⑫

**Greater Miami**
***(see inset map)***
North Beaches ⑬
*Ancient Spanish Monastery p298* ⑭
Key Biscayne ⑮
Fairchild Tropical Garden ⑯
Miami Metrozoo ⑰
Wings Over Miami ⑱

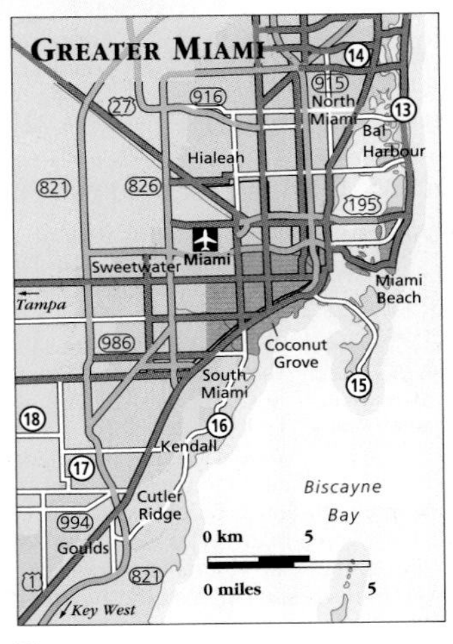


**KEY**

Area of main map

Lifeguard hut in South Beach to match buildings on Ocean Drive

## South Beach ①

**Map** F2. 🚌 *M, S, C, H, G, L, F, M, Night Owl, Airport Owl.* ℹ *1001, Ocean Drive, (305) 672-2014.* W www.mdpl.org

This trendy district, also known as SoBe, extends from 6th to 23rd Streets between Lenox Avenue and Ocean Drive. A hedonistic playground, enlivened by an endless parade of fashion models, body builders, and drag queens, SoBe is also home to the world's largest concentration of well-preserved Art Deco buildings.

The 800-odd buildings along Ocean Drive were, in fact, modest hotels built in the 1930s by architects, the most famous of whom was Henry Hohauser, who used inexpensive materials to create an impression of stylishness. The present use of bright colors, known as Deco Dazzle, was introduced in the 1980s by designer Leonard Horowitz.

**Collins and Washington Avenues**, too, have their share of Art Deco buildings, such as the classic Marlin Hotel at 1200 Collins Avenue, one of the finest representations of Streamline Moderne. Farther north is the luxury Delano Hotel *(see p326)*, with its striking non-Deco interior of billowing white drapes and original Gaudi and Dali furniture. Other buildings of interest are the 1920s Mediterranean Revival Old City Hall and the austere Miami Beach Post Office on Washington Avenue. Inside the Post Office is a mural showing the arrival of Juan Ponce de León, the Spanish conquistador who discovered Florida in 1513. Also on Washington Avenue is the Wolfsonian Museum–FIU, built in the 1920s, which has an excellent collection of fine and decorative arts.

Between Washington and Drexel Avenues is **Española Way**, a small, pretty enclave of Mediterranean Revival buildings, where ornate arches, capitals, and balconies adorn salmon-colored, stuccoed frontages. Built from 1922–25, this street is said to be the inspiration for Addison Mizner's Worth Avenue in Palm Beach *(see p301)*. Off-beat art galleries and boutiques line this leafy street, and on weekends craft booths are set up here.

The pedestrian **Lincoln Road Mall** is Miami's up-and-coming cultural corner, dominated by the ArtCenter South Florida. Established in 1984, the ArtCenter has three exhibition areas and a dozen studios that double as work-in-progress and selling space, as well as independent galleries. The galleries are usually open in the evenings when the mall comes alive as theater-goers frequent the restored Art Deco Lincoln and Colony theaters. After a heavy dose of modern art, the stylish restaurants and cafés, such as Van Dyke at 846, along Lincoln Road, offer respite.

**The Beach**, extending for 10 miles (16 km) up the coast, evolved into a spec-

### Ocean Drive: Deco Style

Deco detail, South Beach

The splendid array of buildings, on Ocean Drive, illustrates Miami's unique interpretation of the Art Deco style, popular all over the world in the 1920s and 30s. Florida's version, often called Tropical Deco, uses motifs such as flamingos, sunbursts, and jaunty nautical features, appropriate to South Beach's seaside location. Three main styles exist: traditional Art Deco, futuristic Streamline Moderne, and Mediterranean Revival, inspired by French, Italian, and Spanish architecture. A spirited preservation campaign, led by Barbara Capitman in the 1970s, made this area the first 20th-century district in the country's National Register of Historic Places.

**A flamingo** is etched into glass doors in the Beacon's lobby.

***Beacon*** *(1936)*
*A contemporary color scheme, an example of Horowitz's Deco Dazzle, brightens the abstract decoration above the ground floor windows.*

acular winter playground ıfter the bridge connecting he island with the mainland vas built in 1913. Much of he sand flanking the beach was imported several decades ıgo, and it continues to be eplenished to counter coastal erosion. The vast stretches of sand are still impressive and draw large crowds of people.

The beach constantly changes atmosphere. Surfers predominate up to 5th Street. The vast beach beyond is an extension of SoBe's lively persona, with colorful lifeguard huts and posing bathers. Alongside runs Lummus Park, where Yiddish is spoken by the mainly Jewish population. Around 21st Street, the clientele is predominately gay.

The stretch, north of 23rd Street, is sometimes known as **Central Miami Beach**. The most eye-catching sight here is the impressive Fontainebleau Hotel (pronounced "Fountain-blue" locally). Completed in 1954, this curvaceous structure was architect Morris Lapidus' (1903–2001) interpretation of a modern French château. With its dated grandeur, pool, and waterfall, the hotel was the ideal setting for the 1960s James Bond film classic, *Goldfinger*.

## Holocaust Memorial ②

**Map** F2.1933–45 Meridian Ave. (305) 538-1663. A, FM, G, L, W. 9am–9pm daily. www.holocaustmmb.org

MIAMI BEACH HAS one of the largest populations of Holocaust survivors in the world, hence the great appropriateness of Kenneth Treister's gut-wrenching memorial, finished in 1990. The centerpiece is an enormous bronze arm and hand stretching skyward, representing the final grasp of a dying person. It is stamped with a number from Auschwitz and covered with more than 100 life-size bronze statues of men, women, and children in the throes of the most unbearable grief. Titled *The Sculpture of Love and Anguish*, this is one of the most powerful contemporary sculptures in Florida today. Around the central plaza is a tunnel lined with the names of Europe's concentration camps, a graphic pictorial history of the Holocaust, and a granite wall inscribed with the names of thousands of victims who perished.

**The Holocaust Memorial**

***Coronation of the Virgin* (c.1492) by Domenico Ghirlandaio**

## Bass Museum of Art ③

**Map** F2. 2121 Park Ave. (305) 673-7530. M, S, C, H, G, L. 10am–5pm Tue–Sat (until 9pm 2nd Thu of month), 1–5pm Sun. public hols. (free 2nd Thu of month) www.bassmuseum.org

THIS MAYAN-influenced, 1930s Deco building has a good collection of European paintings, sculpture, and textiles donated in 1964 by the philanthropists John and Johanna Bass. The collection, dating from the 15th to 17th centuries, includes Renaissance works, paintings from the northern European schools, featuring paintings by Rubens, and huge 16th-century Flemish tapestries. The permanent galleries have more than 2,800 pieces on display.

**Terra-cotta tiles**

**A veranda** is a prerequisite for most Ocean Drive hotels.

***Adrian*** *(1934)*
*Its Mediterranean inspiration and subdued colors make the Adrian stand out from other buildings.*

**The corners** of the building are beautifully rounded.

**The terrazzo floor** in the bar is a mix of stone chips and mortar – an inexpensive version of marble that brought style at minimal cost.

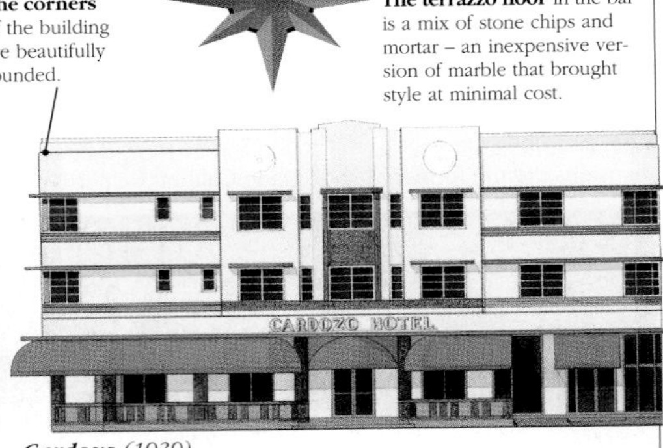


***Cardozo*** *(1939)*
*A late Henry Hohauser work and Barbara Capitman's favorite, this Streamline gem replaces traditional Art Deco details with curved sides and aerodynamic racing stripes.*

## Biscayne Bay Boat Trips ④

**Map** D3. Bayside Marketplace. *College/Bayside.* *16, 3, C, 95, BM, S, FM, Night Owl.* **Island Queen Cruises and Gondola Tours** *(305) 379-5119.* **Floridian Cruises** *(305) 445-8456.* **Duck Tours** *(786) 276-8300.*

A LEISURELY WAY to view the sprinkling of exclusive private island communities around Biscayne Bay is to take one of the many cruises from **Bayside Marketplace**. Tours, such as "Estates of the Rich and Famous" run by Island Queen Cruises, leave regularly and last about 90 minutes.

Biscayne Bay tour boat sign

Tours begin by sailing past Dodge and Lummus islands, where the world's busiest cruise port is situated. This port, which contributes an annual income of more than $5 billion to the local economy, handles more than three million cruise passengers a year.

Near the eastern end of MacArthur Causeway is the US Coastguard's fleet of high-speed craft. Opposite lies the unbridged Fisher Island, separated from South Beach by Government Cut, a water channel dredged in 1905. A restricted beach for African Americans in the 1920s, this is now, ironically, a highly exclusive residential enclave, with homes rarely costing less than $500,000. The tour continues north around the man-made Star, Palm, and Hibiscus islands, where real estate lots were sometimes sold "by the gallon." Among the lavish mansions are the former homes of Frank Sinatra and Al Capone, as well as the present abodes of celebrities such as Gloria Estefan and Julio Iglesias.

Other boat trips include nighttime cruises, deep-sea fishing excursions, and even gondola rides. Duck Tours take place on an amphibious vehicle that departs several times a day from South Beach, just off Lincoln Road. The tour takes in points of interest in South Beach and heads into Miami before "splashing" into Biscayne Bay for a closer look at the homes of the rich and famous on Star Island.

Bayside Marketplace is a fun complex with several shops, bars, and restaurants, including the Hard Rock Café, complete with a guitar erupting from its roof. **Bayfront Park** is nearby. At its center is the Torch of Friendship, commemorating John F. Kennedy, surrounded by the coats of arms of Central and South American countries; a plaque from the city's exiled Cuban community thanks the US for allowing them to settle here.

One of the lavish mansions seen during a Biscayne Bay boat tour

## Miami-Dade Cultural Center ⑤

**Map** D3. 101 West Flagler St. *Government Center.* *All buses to Miami Ave.* **Historical Museum of Southern Florida** *(305) 375-1492.* *10am–5pm Mon–Wed & Fri–Sat, noon–5pm Sun.* **Miami Art Museum of Dade County** *Tue–Sun.* **Main Public Library** *daily.*

DESIGNED BY THE celebrated American architect Philip Johnson in 1982, the Miami-Dade Cultural Center is a large complex, with a Mediterranean-style central courtyard and fountains. It includes an art gallery, museum, and library. Of these, the most interesting is the Historical Museum of Southern Florida, which concentrates on pre-1945 Miami. Besides displays on the Spanish colonization and Seminole culture there is a fascinating collection of old photographs. These bring to life Miami's early history, from the hardships endured by the early pioneers to the fun-filled Roaring Twenties. The Miami Art Museum of Dade County, across the plaza, has a limited permanent collection and many short-term exhibitions, mainly on post-1945 American art.

Metro-Dade Cultural Center, in downtown Miami

## Downtown ⑥

**Map** D3. *various stations.* **US Federal Courthouse** 301 N Miami Ave. *(305) 523-5100.* *Arena/State Plaza.* *8am–5pm Mon–Fri.* *public hols.*

WHEN THE development of Miami took off with the arrival of the Florida East Coast Railway in 1896, the early city focused on one square mile (2.5 km) on the banks of the Miami River. Today, this is the site of present downtown and the hub of the city's financial district. Its futuristic skyscrapers are a monument to the banking boom of the 1980s, when the city emerged as a major financial and trade center. The raised track of the Metromover, a driverless shuttle launched in 1986, provides a swift but good overview of the area.

Among the most striking high-rises here are the Wachovia Financial Center

View of downtown Miami's skyline from the MacArthur Causeway

and the Bank of America Tower, constructed in 1983, and famous for its changing nighttime illuminations. Older structures include the Alfred I. DuPont Building (1938), home of the Florida National Bank, and the Ingraham Building (1927), a Neo-Classical/ Renaissance Revival work.

The **US Federal Courthouse**, completed in 1931, is an imposing Neo-Classical building, with a pleasant, very Mediterranean courtyard. It has hosted a number of high-profile trials, including that of Manuel Noriega, the former Panamanian president, in 1990. Its main attraction, however, is the mural on the second floor. Designed by Denman Fink *(see p296)*, it depicts Miami's transformation from a wilderness into a modern city. Entry is often restricted, especially during high-profile cases.

Miami's oldest Catholic parish, **Gesu Church**, built in 1925, is located on Northeast 2nd Street. It is noted for its fine stained-glass windows, which were made in Munich, Germany. The **Freedom Tower**, on Biscayne Boulevard, is loosely modeled on the Giralda in Seville. At first home to the now-defunct *Miami News*, it became the reception center for Cuban exiles in the 1960s. It now stands empty. Macy's (formerly Burdines, founded in 1898) is on Flagler Street.

## Little Havana ⑦

**Map** C3. *8 from Downtown, 17, 12, 6.* **El Credito Cigar Factory** 1106 SW 8th St *(305) 858-4162.* *8am–6pm Mon–Fri, 8am–4pm Sat.*

As its name suggests, the 3.5 sq miles (9 sq km) area comprising Little Havana has been the surrogate homeland of Cuban immigrants since the 1960s. The atmosphere here, especially on the streets, is vibrant and reflects the Cuban way of life. Spanish is spoken everywhere, while a salsa beat emanates from every other shop, and *bodegas* (canteens) sell Cuban specialties. The main commercial thoroughfare and sentimental heart is **Calle Ocho** (Southwest 8th Street), with its liveliest stretch between 11th and 17th Avenues.

Freedom Tower (1925)

The small but authentic **El Crédito Cigar Factory**, near the corner of Calle Ocho and 11th Avenue, sells boxes of a wide range of cigars. The factory, set up in Havana in 1907, moved to Miami only in 1968. Cigar rollers can be seen at work here. The leaves are grown in the Dominican Republic, reputedly from Cuban tobacco seeds, the world's best.

The district's nationalistic focal point, **Cuban Memorial Boulevard**, as Southwest 13th Avenue is known, is dotted with memorials in honor of Cuban heroes. The most prominent is the Brigade 2506 Memorial's eternal flame commemorating the disastrous Bay of Pigs invasion in 1961. Every April 17, people gather here to remember the Cubans who died in the attempt to overthrow Fidel Castro's regime. Beyond are other memorials to heroes who fought against Cuba's Spanish colonialists in the 1880s. At intervals, too, along Calle Ocho between 12th and 17th Avenues, are stars on the pavement honoring more recent Latin celebrities such as Julio Iglesias and Gloria Estefan in Little Havana's version of Hollywood's Walk of Fame.

Salsa music album covers

North of Calle Ocho, at West Flagler Street and Southwest 17th Avenue, the Plaza de la Cubanidad has a map of Cuba sculpted in bronze. There's a flourish of banners advertising the headquarters of Alpha 66, Miami's most hard-line anti-Castro group.

Also in this district are the tiny Máximo Gómez Park, or Domino Park, and Woodlawn Cemetery. The Versailles restaurant, nearby, is the Cuban community's cultural and culinary bastion.

A Cuban mural in Little Havana, symbolizing nostalgia for the homeland

## Coral Gables ⑧

**Map** A4. **Lowe Art Museum** *(305) 284-3535.* *Metrorail (University).* *52, 56, 72.* *10am–5pm Tue–Sat, noon–5pm Sun, noon–7pm Thu.* *major public hols.* **Miracle Mile** *Metrorail (Douglas Rd), then bus J or 40, 42, 24 from downtown.*

Aptly named the City Beautiful, Coral Gables is a separate city within Greater Miami. In the 1920s, George Merrick planned this aesthetic wonderland with Denman Fink as artistic advisor, Frank Button as landscaper, and Phineas Paist as architectural director. Regulations guarantee that new buildings follow the same part-Italian, part-Spanish style advocated by Merrick. Major landmarks here include the Spanish Baroque **Coral Gables Congregational Church**, the district's first church, the Spanish Renaissance Coral Gables City Hall, and the **Lowe Art Museum**, located in the University of Miami's campus.

Its main shopping street was named **Miracle Mile** (the walk along one side and down the other being the mile in question) by a developer in 1940. The Colonnade Hotel was built in 1926 by Merrick as the headquarters for his real estate business. Nearby, at Salzedo Street and Aragon Avenue, is the Old Police Station Building, built in 1939.

**Coral Gables Congregational Church**

**South view of the Biltmore Hotel, Coral Gables' most famous landmark**

## Biltmore Hotel ⑨

**Map** A4. 1200 Anastasia Ave. *(305) 445-1926.* *Metrorail (S Miami) then bus 72.* *Sun free.* www.biltmorehotel.com

During its heyday in the 1920s, this hotel *(see p.326)* hosted figures such as Al Capone, Judy Garland, and the Duke and Duchess of Windsor. During World War II, it served as a military hospital and remained a veterans' hospital until 1968. After a $55-million restoration in 1986, it went bankrupt in 1990 but reopened two years later. The Biltmore's most striking feature is a 315-ft (96-m) near replica of Seville Cathedral's La Giralda, also the model for Miami's Freedom Tower *(see p295)*. Inside is a grand lobby, lined with Herculean pillars. The Biltmore has the largest hotel swimming pool in the US, where its famous instructor, Johnny Weismuller – known for his role as Tarzan – set a world record in the 1930s.

## Venetian Pool ⑩

**Map** A4. 2701 De Soto Blvd. *(305) 460-5356.* *Metrorail (S Miami) then bus 72.* *mid-Jun–mid-Aug: 11am–7:30pm Mon–Fri; Apr–May & Sep–Oct: 11am–5:30pm; Nov–Mar: 10am– 4:30pm; all year: 10am–4:30pm Sat & Sun.* *Mon Sep–May, Jan 1, Thanksgiving, Dec 24–25.* www.venetianpool.com

Perhaps the most beautiful swimming pool in the world, the Venetian Pool was ingeniously fashioned from a coral rock quarry in 1923 by Denman Fink and Phineas Paist. Pink stucco towers and vine-covered loggias, candy-cane Venetian poles, a cobblestone bridge, fountains, waterfalls, and numerous caves surround crystal-clear, spring-fed waters, which are great for swimming. The pool was once one of the most fashionable social spots in Coral Gables – in the lobby are a series of photographs of beauty pageants staged here during the 1920s. This beautiful public swimming pool is definitely worth a visit, for a swim or just a look.

**Venetian Pool, ingeniously created in the 1920s out of an old coral rock quarry**

## oconut Grove illage ⑪

lap B4. Metrorail (Coconut rove). 42 from Coral Gables, 48 om downtown, 6, 27, 22.

MIAMI'S OLDEST community, Coconut Grove was a abled hippy hangout in the 960s. Today, "the village," as is simply known, is famous or its cafés and restaurants, specially at night or on veekends. This is also the ity's most relaxed shopping rea with many boutiques nd two malls – the outdoor CocoWalk, and the stylish Streets of Mayfair. In contrast are the food stalls of the colorful farmers' market, held every Saturday at McDonald Street and Grand Avenue.

On Grand Avenue, too, are the simple homes of the local Bahamian community, descendants of the Wreckers *(see p323)*, who lived here from the mid-1800s. The exuberant Goombay Festival, a party with a parade, great food, and Caribbean music, is held here every June.

In a shady, affluent neighborhood south along Main Highway, is the **Barnacle**, home of Ralph Monroe, a Renaissance man who made his living from ship building and wrecking. At 3400 Devon Road is the picturesque **Plymouth Congregational Church**, built in 1916.

**Coconut Grove Village, a lively area of shops, cafés, and bars**

## Vizcaya ⑫

lap C4. 3251 S Miami Ave. (305) 250-9133. Metrorail (Vizcaya). 48. 9:30am–5pm, gardens till 5:30pm (last adm: 4:30pm) daily. Dec 25. limited. www.vizcayamuseum.org

FLORIDA'S GRANDEST residence was completed in 1916 as the winter retreat for millionaire industrialist James Deering. His vision was to replicate a 16th-century Italian estate, but one that had been altered by succeeding generations. As a result, Vizcaya and its opulent rooms come in a blend of styles from Renaissance to Neo-Classical, furnished with the fruits of Deering's shopping sprees around Europe. The formal gardens, a rarity in Florida, beautifully combine Italian and French garden features with tropical foliage. They are dotted with sculptures and quaint buildings, including a Japanese tea house.

**Statue of Pulcinella**

Deering would always ask of his architect: "Must we be so grand?" fearing that Vizcaya would be too costly to support. After Deering's death in 1925, it proved to be so until it was bought by Dade County in 1952. The house and gardens were opened to public thereafter.

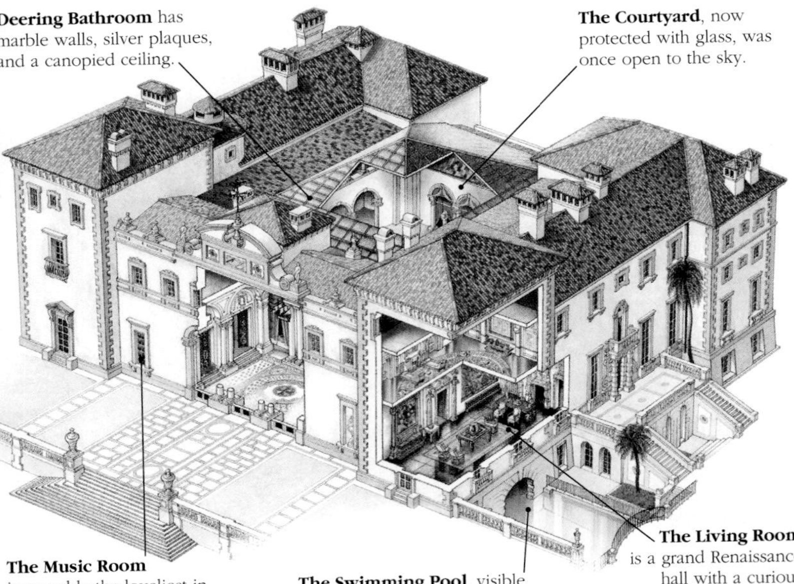

## Greater Miami

THE AREAS NORTH OF MIAMI BEACH and downtown and south of Coral Gables are seldom very scenic, but they are still well worth exploring for the great beaches and family amusements. Many of the area's primary attractions, such as zoos, gardens, and citrus orchards, were badly damaged by Hurricane Andrew, the country's costliest-ever natural disaster, which devastated southern Florida in 1992. Most sights have reopened, although restoration work continues in many cases.

**Beach at Haulover Park, under the protective eye of a lifeguard**

## North Beaches ⑬

**Map** F4. Collins Ave. *K, S, or T from South Beach or downtown.*

THE BARRIER ISLANDS to the north along Collins Avenue are occupied mainly by posh residential areas and inexpensive resorts, popular with package tours. A quiet strip of sand between 79th and 87th Streets separates Miami Beach from **Surfside**, a simple community popular with French Canadians. At 96th Street Surfside merges with **Bal Harbour**, a stylish enclave known for its flashy hotels and one of Miami's swankiest malls, Bal Harbour Shops. To the north is the pleasant **Haulover Park**, with a marina on the creek side and dune-backed sands facing the ocean.

## Ancient Spanish Monastery ⑭

**Map** F4. 16711 W Dixie Hwy, N Miami Beach. *(305) 945-1462.* *H from South Beach, 3 from downtown.* *9am–5pm Mon-Fri, 10am–5pm Sat, 1:30 –5pm Sun.* *public hols, may close Sat or Sun for special events.* www.spanishmonastery.org

THESE MONASTERY cloisters have an unusual history. Built in Spain between 1133 and 1141, they were bought in 1925 by newspaper tycoon William Randolph Hearst *(see p688)*, who had their 35,000 stones packed into crates. An outbreak of foot-and-mouth disease led to the crates being opened (to check the packing straw), and the stones were repacked incorrectly. Once in New York, they remained there until 1952, when it was decided to piece together "the world's largest and most expensive jigsaw puzzle." The cloisters resemble the original, but there is still a pile of unidentified stones in a corner of the gardens.

**Chapterhouse**

**The Chapel**, at one time the dining hall, is still used for worship.

**Statue of Alphonso VII, patron of the monastery**

**The cloister entrance** is a carved, early Gothic arch.

**The bell outside the chapel door**

**The quiet gardens** are a popular spot for wedding photos.

The tranquil, palm-fringed lakes of the Fairchild Tropical Garden

## Key Biscayne ⑮

**Map** F5. 7 miles (11 km) SE of downtown. *B.* **Bill Baggs Cape Florida State Park** *(305) 361-5811.* *daily.* www.floridastateparks.org

THE VIEW OF downtown from Rickenbacker Causeway, connecting the mainland to Virginia Key and Key Biscayne, is one of Miami's best. Views aside, this has some of the city's top beaches. The most impressive is at Crandon Park in the upper half of the Key, which is 3 miles (5 km) long and enormously wide, with palm trees and picnic areas. At the southern end, the **Bill Baggs Cape Florida State Park** has a shorter beach joined to more picnic areas by boardwalks across the dunes.

## Fairchild Tropical Garden ⑯

**Map** F5.10901 Old Cutler Rd. *(305) 667-1651.* *65 from Coconut Grove.* *9:30am–4:30pm daily.* *Dec 25.* www.fairchildgarden.org **Mattheson Hammock Park** *(305) 665-5475.* *6am–sunset daily.*

ESTABLISHED IN 1938, this beautiful tropical garden is also a major botanical research institution. One of world's largest collections of palm trees (550 of the 2,500 known species) stands around a series of man-made lakes. The garden also has an impressive array of cycads – relatives of palms and ferns that bear unusual giant red cones – as well as countless other trees and plants, including a comical-looking sausage tree.

Guides on the 40-minute tram tours describe how plants are used in the manufacture of medicines and perfumes (the flowers of the ylang-ylang tree, for example, are used in Chanel No. 5). The waterfront **Mattheson Hammock Park** is next door to the Fairchild Tropical Garden. Its highlight is the Atoll Pool, an artificial saltwater swimming pool circled by sand and palm trees alongside Biscayne Bay.

Palms in Fairchild Tropical Garden

## Miami Metrozoo ⑰

**Map** E5. 12400 SW 152nd St, Miami. *(305) 251-0400.* *Metrorail (Dadeland North) then Zoo Bus.* *9:30am–5:30pm daily.* www.miamimetrozoo.com

THIS ENORMOUS ZOO is considered one of the country's best. Animals are kept in spacious landscaped habitats, separated from humans by moats. Highlights include lowland gorillas, Malayan sun bears, and white tigers. The Petting Zoo is a favorite with kids, and the Wildlife Show demonstrates the agility of the big cats. Take the 20-minute ride on the monorail for an overview, and then visit what you like; or take the monorail to Station 4 and then walk back.

## Wings Over Miami ⑱

**Map** E5.14710 SW 128th St, adjacent to Tamiami Airport. *(305) 233-5197.* *10am–5pm Thu–Sat.* *public hols.* www.wingsovermiami.com

THIS MUSEUM is dedicated to the preservation of old aircraft. Its hangars contain a superb collection of finely preserved examples of aircraft that are still in operation. These include a 1943 AT6D Texan "Old Timer," a Douglas B-23 Dragon, and a British Provost Jet, as well as a wide range of other fascinating exhibits such as a machine-gun turret.

All these planes take to the sky during the Memorial Day weekend celebration. While in February, they are joined by B-17 and B-24 bombers in the Wings of Freedom event.

White tiger in front of a mock Khmer temple at Miami Metrozoo

## Fort Lauderdale ❷

150,000. 1850 Eller Dr, Ste 303, (954) 765-4466.

PROCLAIMED the "Yachting Capital of the World," Fort Lauderdale's character is defined by its waterways, which branch from the New River. The area around the mouth of the river is known as the **Isles**. This is the city's prime neighborhood, with sweeping mansions lying behind lush foliage and luxurious yachts moored in the waterways.

Millions of visitors head for the barrier islands lying along the coast between the beaches and the Intracoastal Waterway. The waterway crosses **Port Everglades**, the world's second largest cruise port after Miami. Riverboat cruises and water taxis are also available.

**Las Olas Boulevard**, the city's busiest street, is lined with eateries and boutiques. The fine **Museum of Art**, also located here, is best known for its works by the CoBrA artists, a group of 20th-century Expressionist painters from Copenhagen, Brussels, and Amsterdam.

Water taxi on the New River, Fort Lauderdale

Downtown is the city's business and cultural center. **Riverwalk**, a 1.5-mile (2.4-km) stretch along the New River's north bank, links most of the city's historical and cultural landmarks; it starts at **Stranaham House** (1901), which originally served as a trading post, post office, and bank. **Old Fort Lauderdale** runs along Southwest 2nd Avenue and has a few early 1900s buildings, such as the Old Fort Lauderdale Museum of History. The city has the liveliest beaches on the Gold Coast, especially toward the end of Las Olas Boulevard, where skaters cruise past bars and shops. To the west is Sawgrass Mills, Florida's largest mall, with its own indoor theme park, Wannado City.

Peach-pink Mizner Park, one of Boca Raton's shopping malls

## Boca Raton ❸

80,000. 1555 Palm Beach Lakes Blvd, (561) 233-3000.

AFFLUENT BOCA RATON was originally a sleepy pineapple-growing settlement that architect Addison Mizner (1872–1933) envisaged as the "greatest resort in the world." The nucleus of his vision was the ultra-luxurious Cloister Inn, finished in 1926, with his trademark Spanish details. The hotel is now part of the exclusive **Boca Raton Resort and Club** *(see p326)*. Weekly tours for non-residents are arranged by the Boca Raton Historical Society, based at the Mizner-designed Town Hall.

Just opposite is the open-air **Mizner Park**, perhaps the most impressive of Boca Raton's dazzling malls. Located in a spectacular setting within Mizner Park is the **Boca Raton Museum of Art**. This museum contains 44,000 sq ft (4,088 sq m) of space for world-class exhibitions and an impressive display of contemporary art.

The verdant and historic **Old Floresta** district, a mile (1.6 km) west of the Town Hall, has 29 Mediterranean-style houses built by Mizner.

Boca Raton's long, undeveloped beach is reached via beachside parks, such as **Red Reef Park**, which also has the informative **Gumbo Limbo Nature Center**. The most northerly of the parks, **Spanish River Park** is also the most attractive, with pleasant picnic areas shaded by pines and palm trees. It also has a lovely lagoon on the Intracoastal Waterway, next to an observation tower.

**Boca Raton Museum of Art**
501 Plaza Real, Mizner Park.
(561) 392-2500. *Tue–Sun.*
*public hols.*
www.bocamuseum.org

## Loxahatchee National Wildlife Refuge ❹

10216 Lee Rd. *(561) 734-8303.*
*Delray Beach.* **Refuge** *daily.* *Dec 25.*
**Visitor Center** *Nov–Apr: daily; May–Oct: Wed–Sun.* *Dec 25.*

THE NORTHERNMOST part of the Everglades *(see p321)*, this 221-sq mile (572-sq km) refuge is known for its superb wildlife. The best time to visit is in winter, when migrating birds arrive here from the

Cyclists and skaters enjoying the beachfront in Fort Lauderdale

ı alleyway along Worth Avenue, Palm Beach's most exclusive street

›rth. The visitor center, off ›ute 441, has a display that ‹plains the Everglades' eco- gy, and there are also two ıils. The Cypress Swamp ›ardwalk is lined with wax yrtle trees; the longer Marsh ail is a bird-watcher's para- se, with ibis, herons, and ıhingas. Visitors can also •ot turtles and alligators. ıose with canoes can ‹plore the 5.5-mile (9-km) noe trail, and there are also ımerous nature walks.

## alm Beach ❺

10,000. 45 coanut Row, (561) 655-3282.

SSENTIALLY A winter resort for the rich and famous, ılm Beach was created at the d of the 19th century by the lroad baron Henry Flagler. the 1920s Addison Mizner ilt luxurious Spanish-style ınsions for its residents, a nd that established its ique look and influenced ıure architectural styles.

Palm Beach's major sights can be viewed in the area between Cocoanut Row and South County Road. Of these, the **Flagler Museum** (formerly Whitehall), Flagler's 55-room winter residence, has a grand marble entrance hall, an Italian Renaissance library, and a Louis XV ballroom. Flagler's private railroad car is on display on the South Lawn.

To the south, the **Society of the Four Arts**, founded in 1936, has two libraries, an exhibition space, and an auditorium for concerts and films. Other interesting buildings include the Town Hall, built in 1926, the Mizner Memorial Park, and **The Breakers**, a mammoth Italian Renaissance structure and Palm Beach's grandest hotel *(see p327)*.

The epitome of Palm Beach's opulent lifestyle, however, is **Worth Avenue**. Stretching across four blocks from Lake Worth to the Atlantic Ocean, this is the town's best known thoroughfare. It first became fashionable with the construction of the Everglades Club in 1918, a collaborative effort between Mizner and his patron, Paris Singer, heir to the sewing machine fortune. Today, Worth Avenue boasts a spectacular mix of glitzy fashion boutiques, art galleries, and shops.

Picturesque alleyways, reminiscent of the backstreets of Spanish villages, connect with Worth Avenue. These interlinking pedestrian alleys, created by Mizner, are a riot of arches, twisting flights of stairs, cascading bougainvillea, and courtyards. The Esplanade, an open-air mall, is at the eastern end.

The multimillion-dollar mansions of Palm Beach are located in the suburbs. Some were built by Mizner and his imitators in the 1920s, but since then hundreds of other houses have proliferated in styles from Neo-Classical to Art Deco. The most easily visible are on a ridge along South Ocean Boulevard, nicknamed "Mansion Row." The most elaborate residence, Mar-a-Lago (# 1100), is now a top-end private club owned by millionaire Donald Trump.

### Flagler Museum

Cocoanut Row & Whitehall Way. (561) 655-2833. 10am–5pm Tue–Sat, noon–5pm Sun. Jan 1, Thnksg., Dec 25. limited. www.flaglermuseum.us

Flagler Museum at Palm Beach, formerly Henry Flagler's winter home

## Cocoa Beach ❻

*14,000. Merritt Island. 400 Fortenberry Rd, (321) 459-2200.*

THIS LARGE, no-frills resort calls itself the East Coast's surfing capital. Surfing festivals set the tone, along with win-your-weight-in-beer competitions. Motels, restaurants, and gift and souvenir shops characterize the main street. The dazzling **Ron Jon Surf Shop** has surf boards galore (for sale and rent) and a huge T-shirt collection. In front of its flashing towers are sculptures of sports figures.

## Kennedy Space Center ❼

Off Rte 405, 6 miles (9.6 km) E of Titusville. *(321) 449-4444. Titusville. 9am–7pm daily. Dec 25. The center occasionally closes for operational requirements; always call ahead. wheelchairs available at Information Central. (321) 867-4636 for schedule of launches.* www.kennedyspacecenter.com

WHEN Cape Canaveral was chosen as the site for NASA's (National Aeronautics and Space Administration) space program in the 1960s, the area came to be known as the Space Coast. The Kennedy Space Center on Merritt Island is the only place in the Western Hemisphere where shuttles carrying humans are launched into space. It was also the site of the historic launch of *Apollo 11* in July 1969, when President John F. Kennedy's dream of landing a man on the moon was realized. The **Visitor Complex**, built in

**Rockets on display at the Cape Canaveral Air Station**

1967 for astronauts and their families to view space center operations, is a 131-sq mile (340-sq km) facility that includes many attractions. Its highlight, the Galaxy Center, has two **IMAX® Theaters**, which show films on space exploration on screens that are five floors high. Footage from the shuttle missions offer breathtaking views of Earth from space. West of the entrance, the **Rocket Garden** is where visitors can walk through a group of rockets, each representing different stages in space history. **Robot Scouts**, located to the east of Rocket Garden, reveals the latest planetary explorer robots, while **Exploration in the New Millennium** shows visitors what the future holds for space exploration; guests can even touch a piece of a Mars meteorite. The **Astronaut Encounter** in the same building is where visitors can meet real astronauts.

Guests can also climb aboard **Explorer** – a life-size replica of the Space Shuttle, a Shuttle Plaza in the northeastern corner of the Complex. The **Launch Statu Center** alongside, has displays of genuine flight hardware and rocket boosters, as well as exhibits that re-create the shuttle's re-launch, liftoff, and flight procedures. Shuttle were the ingenious alternativ to the very expensive, single-use crafts, used in the Apollo missions. Designed in the lat 1970s, these re-usable spacecraft are now the backbone of the space program. Close by, the **Astronaut Memoria** honors the astronauts, from the *Apollo 1* to the Space Shuttle *Columbia* missions, who died in the service of space missions.

Close to the entrance of the Complex, an all-glass rotunda leads to **Early Space Exploration**, which showcases key figures from the early days of rocketry. In the **Mercury Mission Control Room**, visitors view the actual consoles from which the first eight manned missions were

**A life-size replica of the space shuttle *Explorer*, Kennedy Space Cente**

### TIMELINE OF SPACE EXPLORATION

**1958** First American satellite, the *Explorer 1*, is launched (Jan 31)

**1961** On May 5, Alan Shepherd becomes the first American in space. Kennedy commits nation to moon landing

**1962** John Glenn orbits the earth in *Mercury* spacecraft

**1969** Neil Armstrong and Buzz Aldrin *(Apollo 11)* walk on the moon (Jul 24)

**1975** American *Apollo* and Russian *Soyuz* vehicles dock in orbit (Jul 17)

**1981** *Columbia* is the first shuttle in space (Apr 12)

**1986** The *Challenger* explodes, killing its crew (Jan 28)

**1990** The Hubble telescope is launched (Apr 24)

**1996** *Mars Pathfinder* sent to gather data from the surface of Mars

**2001** Dennis Tito pays $20 million to spen one week on board an International Space Center

**2003** Space Shuttle *Columbia* breaks up upon re-ent into the atm sphere (Feb

1950 | 1960 | 1970 | 1980 | 1990 | 2000

aunch pads seen on Kennedy Space Center Tours

ıonitored. Footage and ıterviews with some of ıe personnel are the high- ghts. Next are displays of ɔme of the authentic ſercury and Gemini space- ·aft, which help create some ands-on excitement of early ɔace exploration.

The Center also offers a ·umber of interesting tours. he **Kennedy Space Center KSC) Bus Tour** leaves fre- ·uently from the Visitor omplex and offers an overall ·ur of two major facilities. isitors enter secured areas, ·here guides explain the ·ner workings of each facility. ·ach tour can take between ·o and six hours, as visitors ·n take their time to explore ·ch site.

At the tour's first stop – the **C 39 Observation Gantry** – ıe can get a bird's-eye view the launch pads from the ·-ft (18-m) observation tower. ·ck on the ground, a film ·d several exhibits tell the ɔry of a shuttle launch. The ·cond facility to visit is the **pollo/Saturn V Center**, ·aturing an actual 363-ft (110- ) Saturn V moon rocket, ·ed by the Apollo missions. ·sitors can watch the launch *Apollo 8*, the first manned ·ssion to the moon, in the ·ing Room Theater, followed a film at the Lunar Theater, ·hich shows footage of the ɔon landing. This is also the ·ly place in the world where ·ests can dine next to a ·nuine moon rock, at the ɔon Rock Café. There are ·o special-interest tours – **pe Canaveral: Then & ·w Tour**, a historic tour of the Mercury, Gemini, and Apollo launch pads; and the **NASA Up Close Tour**, an insider's view of the entire space shuttle program. This tour stops at the **International Space Station Center**, where visitors can peer inside the facility where each space station is readied for launch. Special tours to see actual shuttle launches can be arranged by booking at the Visitor Complex. However, missions have been postponed since the *Columbia* disintegrated in 2003; launches will resume at a rate of eight per year once all safety issues have been resolved. Outside the center, prime viewing sites are in Titusville and Cocoa Beach.

**Environs:** The **US Astronaut Hall of Fame** at Titusville, 9 miles (14 km) west of KSC, offers exciting opportunities to try out weightlessness and ride flight simulators with G-forces.

## Canaveral National Seashore & Merritt Island ❽

Titusville.
www.nps.gov/cana

These adjacent preserves on the Space Coast share an astounding variety of fauna and a range of habitats including estuaries and hardwood hammocks. Visitors can often see alligators and the endangered manatee, but the highlight is the rich birdlife.

The **Canaveral National Seashore** has a pristine 24-mile (39-km) stretch of beach. Apollo Beach at the northern end, and Playalinda Beach to the south are fine for sunbathing, but swimming can be hazardous, and there are no lifeguards. The top of Turtle Mound offers splendid views of Mosquito Lagoon (aptly named, so bring repellent in spring and summer).

Route 402 to Playalinda Beach has views of the Kennedy Space Center's launch pads. It also crosses **Merritt Island National Wildlife Refuge**, which covers an area of 220 sq miles (570 sq km). Much of the refuge lies within the Space Center and is out of bounds. Winter is the best season to visit. To view the local wildlife, follow the Black Point Wildlife Drive, which has the 5-mile (8-km) Cruickshank Trail. Be sure to pick up the informative leaflet at the drive's entrance. The Visitors' Information Center has displays on the habitats and wildlife in the refuge. One mile (1.6 km) farther east, the Oak Hammock and Palm Hammock trails have short boardwalks across the marshland for bird-watchers.

**Canaveral National Seashore**
Rte A1A, 20 miles (32 km) N of Titusville or Rte 402, 10 miles (16 km) E of Titusville. *(321) 267-1110.* *daily.* *for shuttle launches.*

**Merritt Island National Wildlife Refuge**
Rte 406, 4 miles (6.5 km) E of Titusville. *(321) 861-0667.* *daily.* *for shuttle launches.*

### Space Coast Bird Life

The Space Coast is a bird-watcher's paradise. Its magnificent and abundant birdlife is best viewed early in the morning or shortly before dusk. Between November and March, in particular, the marshes and lagoons teem with migratory ducks and waders, as up to 100,000 birds arrive from colder northern climates. Royal terns, white ibis, black skimmers, brown pelicans, and sandhill cranes are some of the birds that are frequently seen.

Brown pelican

# Walt Disney World® Resort ❾

WALT DISNEY WORLD, covering 43 sq miles (69 sq km), is the largest entertainment complex on earth. The main draw is its theme parks: Magic Kingdom, Epcot, Disney-MGM Studios, and Animal Kingdom. A self-sufficient vacation spot, the Resort supplies everything from hotels to golf courses, and each year brings a new wonder – Disney's Animal Kingdom is the biggest new attraction. Peerless in its imagination and attention to detail, the Resort is also a hermetic bubble cocooned from the real world. Everything runs like clockwork, and nothing shatters its illusions of fantasy. Unless you're a confirmed cynic, Walt Disney World Resort will amaze you.

## When to Visit

THE BUSIEST TIMES of the year are Christmas and Easter, June to August, and the last week in February. At these times, the parks approach capacity – some 90,000 people in the Magic Kingdom alone. Even so, all the rides operate and the parks remain open for much longer. During the off-season, 10,000 visitors a day might visit the Magic Kingdom, and certain attractions may be closed for maintenance. The weather is also a factor – in July and August, hot and humid afternoons are regularly punctuated by thunderstorms. Between October and March, the temperatures and humidity are much more comfortable and permit a more energetic schedule.

## Length of Visit

WALT DISNEY WORLD offers at least a week of entertainment. To enjoy it to the full, give Magic Kingdom and Epcot two days each, and a day each for Disney-MGM Studios and Animal Kingdom. Keep three nights to see the splendid fireworks displays of Fantasmic!, Fantasy in the Sky, and IllumiNations.

## Getting Around

AN EXTENSIVE transportation system handles an average of 200,000 guests each day. Even if you stay outside Walt Disney World Resort, many nearby hotels offer free shuttle services to and from the theme parks. Check when you make your reservation.

## Walt Disney Resort

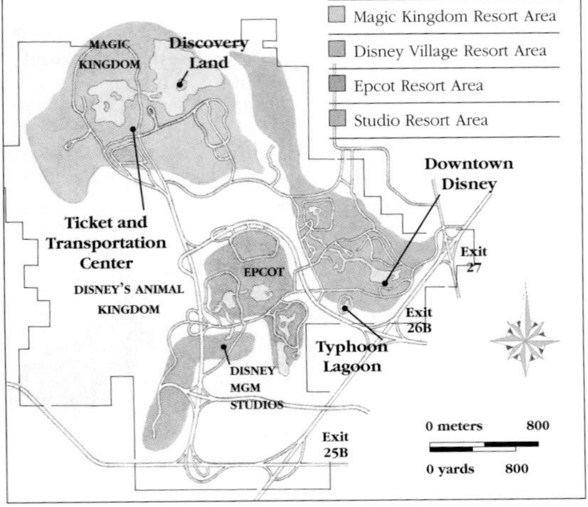

**Key**

- Magic Kingdom Resort Area
- Disney Village Resort Area
- Epcot Resort Area
- Studio Resort Area

Magic Kingdom
Discovery Land
Ticket and Transportation Center
Disney's Animal Kingdom
Epcot
Disney MGM Studios
Typhoon Lagoon
Downtown Disney
Exit 27
Exit 26B
Exit 25B
0 meters 800
0 yards 800

## Useful Numbers

**General information**
(407) 824-4321.

**Accommodation information/reservations**
(407) 934-7639.

**Dining reservations**
(407) 939-3463.
www.disney.go.com

The transport hub of Walt Disney World is the **Ticket and Transportation Center** (TTC). Connecting it to the Magic Kingdom are two monorail services. A third monorail links the TTC to Epcot. Ferries run from the TTC to the Magic Kingdom. They also connect the Magic Kingdom and Epcot with resorts in their areas. Buses link everything in Walt Disne World, including direct links to Magic Kingdom. Residents and pass holders can use the entire transportation system for free, while one-day tickets allow holders to use the ferries and monorails between the TTC and Magic Kingdom

## Disabled Travelers

WHEELCHAIRS CAN be borrowed at the park entrance, and special bypass entrances allow disabled guests to board rides withou waiting in line. Staff, howeve are not allowed to assist wit lifting for safety reasons.

## Very Young Children

PARENTS WITH pre-school ag kids can make use of the unique system known as "switching off," where they can enjoy various rides and attractions one at a time wh the other parent stays with the child, without having to line up twice.

The Resort can be exhausting, so it is a good idea to rent a stroller from any park entrance. Take frequent breaks from the excitement and the heat by building in time for snacks or naps.

If you've come with youn kids you should focus main on the Magic Kingdom.

### AFETY

THE RESORT'S first-rate security force means problems 'e dealt with promptly. Cast embers are trained to watch it for unaccompanied ildren and escort them to st children centers.

### ARKING

VISITORS TO THE Magic Kingdom must park at the TTC id use public transportation; )cot and Disney-MGM udios have their own parkg lots. Parking is free for isney Resort residents; oths must pay, but only once a y regardless of how many nes they move their vehicle.

### DVANTAGES OF STAYING THE RESORT

ODGING IN THE resorts and in Walt Disney World Swan d Dolphin (operated indendently but Disneyesque in every other respect) are of a very high standard. However, even the lowest-priced places are more expensive than many hotels outside Walt Disney World.

However, a few practical reasons to stay there are:

- Proximity to parks and free use of Disney's transportation.
- Early entry privileges into the parks (up to 90 minutes). Check in advance with each park for details.
- Guaranteed admission to the theme parks even when the parks are otherwise full.
- The possibility of dining with your favorite Disney character in your hotel.
- The delivery of shopping purchases made anywhere within the Resort.
- Note that the hotels close to the Marketplace (which are not run by Disney) offer few of the above mentioned privileges. For information on hotel listings see page 327.

### RESORT DINING

VISITORS SHOULD make reservations in advance for any full-service restaurant in Walt Disney World Resort, especially in the theme parks and above all in Epcot. Whether or not you are staying at one of the resorts, reservations for dining can be made 60 days in advance. Some tables are held for same-day reservations, so make your reservation as early in the morning as possible. For restaurant details, see page 331.

### MEETING MICKEY

FOR MANY YOUNGSTERS, meeting the Disney characters is the high point of their visit. Apart from seeing them in the parks, you can also meet them in numerous restaurants (usually at breakfast). Each park and many resorts also offer "character dining," but you must book ahead.

## INFORMATION

### TICKETS & TYPES OF PASSES

YOU CAN BUY one-day, onepark tickets, but if you're staying for over three days consider the following:

**Park Hopper Pass:** entitles one-day entry to each park on any four or five days.

**All-in-One Hopper Pass:** offers unlimited access to theme parks, water parks, and Pleasure Island on any five, six, or seven days.

**Length of Stay Pass:** this useful pass is exclusively for Resort hotel guests; unlimited entry to theme parks, Pleasure Island, water parks, and Sports complex. Prices depend on length of stay.

**Annual Pass and Premium Annual Pass:** non-Disney guests visiting for over ten days should consider these, which cost little more than a -day park hopper. Child pricing applies to ages 3–9.

**FastPass** allows one to reserve time at 19 popular attractions rather than wait in line. Passes are available at Disney stores, the airport, and the Tourist Information Center on I-Drive *(see p313).*

### BUSIEST DAYS

EACH OF THE theme parks is busiest on certain days:

**Magic Kingdom:** Monday, Thursday, and Saturday.

**Epcot:** Tuesday, Friday, and Saturday.

**Disney-MGM Studios:** Wednesday and Sunday.

### OPENING HOURS

WHEN THE theme parks are busiest, opening hours are the longest: 9am to 10/11pm or midnight. In less busy periods, hours are 9am to 6/7/8pm. The parks open early for pass holders and guests at any of the Resort hotels. Call to check details.

### THE IDEAL SCHEDULE

TO AVOID THE worst of the crowds and heat, arrive early and visit the popular attractions first. Take a break in the afternoon, when it is hot and parks are busy, and return in the evening to see parades and fireworks.

### TOP TIPS

LINES ARE shortest at the start and end of the day, and during parade and meal times. The wait for a show, however, is rarely longer than the show itself.

- Parks fill rapidly after the first hour of opening. Until then, you can often just walk onto rides for which there will be a line later.
- After a thunderstorm, the water parks are often almost empty, even at the busiest times of the year.
- Information regarding timings of shows, parades, and rides, and tips such as the waiting times at various attractions, are usually available at each park. Check at notice boards, Information Centers, and Guest Services.
- During parades, other attractions are quiet.
- Wear a comfortable pair of shoes, as the parks entail a lot of walking.
- There is very little shade, so be sure to wear a hat.

## Magic Kingdom

MAGIC KINGDOM is the essential Disney theme park. Disney characters fill its cheerful acres, and seven lands evoke different themes.

It is best to head straight for **Space Mountain**, a superb coaster in Tomorrowland. It shoots around in stygian blackness against projections of asteroids and galaxies, creating superb effects of space travel. **Stitch's Great Escape** is a ride based on the film Lilo and Stitch, who is a crazy, uncontrollable space alien who manages to cause mayhem even out in space. Another popular attraction, **The Timekeeper**, is a 360-degree Circle-Vision screen show, which takes visitors on a whirling trip through time. **Buzz Lightyear's Space Ranger Spin** is a fabulous journey in a two-seater car. It is fitted with laser cannons and a control, so you can shoot at targets with a laser beam.

Fantasyland, dominated by Cinderella's Castle, forms the core of the Magic Kingdom. **The Many Adventures of Winnie the Pooh** uses the latest technology, lighting, and sound effects to create an enchanting experience, while **Peter Pan's Flight** combines the feeling of flying with the delight of perfectly matched music and movement.

**The Haunted Mansion** in Liberty Square leads visitors through a spook-ridden mansion and graveyard.

Set in the Wild West, Frontierland offers a journey on a runaway train known as **Big Thunder Mountain Railroad**. The fun **Country Bear Jamboree** is an Audio-Animatronics® animal show, and **Splash Mountain** is an exciting flume ride, which ends with a big drop.

Adventureland is a fusion of Africa and the Caribbean. **The Jungle Cruise** goes past an animatronically animated setting of Africa. Another voyage, **Pirates of the Caribbean**, leads you into underground prisons and past 16th-century galleons.

Main Street USA is famous for the **SpectroMagic Parade**, a shimmering fantasy of music, live action, and illuminated floats. In peak season, it takes place at 7pm and again at 9pm. The afternoon parade is best viewed from Frontierland. The evening parade also features **Wishes Nighttime Spectacular** – an extravaganza of fireworks and music. Mickey's ToonTown Fair (with numerous attractions for children), is the best place to watch the show.

## Eating & Drinking

The typical fare at **Magic Kingdom** is fast food. However, try the Liberty Tree Tavern or Crystal Palace for quieter dining. Cinderella's Royal Table in the castle has a regal ambience, and Aunt Polly's is great for sandwiches.

The dining at **Epcot** is superb, particularly **World Showcase**, where reservations are required. Recommended are: **Mexico:** the San Angel Inn serves interesting but pricey Mexican cuisine. **Italy:** L'Originale Alfredo di Roma has elegant fare. **Japan:** you can eat communally, either in the Mitsukoshi Teppan Dining Rooms or at the bar of Mitsukoshi Tempura Kiku for sushi and tempura. **France:** the upscale Bistro de Paris (dinner only); Les Chefs de France, an exclusive restaurant with *haute cuisine*; and the terraced Le Cellier Steakhouse for steaks, and crêpes.

At **Disney-MGM Studios**, you can soak up the atmosphere at three of the full-service restaurants. The costly Hollywood Brown Derby replicates Hollywood's Original Brown Derby, where the stars met in the 1930s. Children prefer the Sci-Fi Dine-In Theater Restaurant, where you sit in mini-Cadillacs and watch old sci-fi films. For dining without a reservation, try Hollywood & Vine, which serves pasta, salads, seafood, ribs, and steaks.

## Epcot

EPCOT, AN ACRONYM for the Experimental Prototype Community of Tomorrow, was Disney's dream of a tec nologically advanced comm nity that represented a utopian vision of the future.

The enormous 250-acre (1 ha) park is divided into two halves: **Future World** with a emphasis on entertainment and education; and **World Showcase**, which represent the art, culture, and culinary skills of different countries around the globe. Boats cros the World Showcase Lagoon frequently and are a convenient method of getting here

The unmistakable seven-and-a-half-thousand-ton glo of **Spaceship Earth** is the focal point of Future World. takes visitors past superbly crafted tableaux and Animatronics® scenes portraying future possibilities in techno logy. Since most people visi here first, there are long lin in the mornings, so it is bes seen in the afternoon.

**Test Track**, one of Epcot's top rides, places visitors in a simulator that moves on trac at high speeds. You test a pro type sports car at over 66 mp (106 km/h) on a raised roadway. Try to visit this ride first in the morning. The popula **Mission: SPACE** uses state-the-art technology to simula a ride to Mars in a rocket. T may cause motion sickness.

**The Imagination Pavilio** is best known for the hilarious "Honey, I Shrunk the Audience," which integrates Disney's unique 3-D film te nology with special effects.

The **Wonders of Life** pav ion deals with the human body. **Body Wars**, Epcot's first simulator thrill ride, take a miniaturized version of you on an adventure inside the human body, while **Cranium Command** is an Animatronics® show about the human brain.

**The Living Seas** offers Se Base Alpha, where visitors journey to the "bottom of th ocean" past sharks and dolphins, and watch the sea lif through transparent walls.

'orld Showcase has architec-
ıral showpieces of 11 differ-
ıt countries, with replicas of
.mous buildings. Each pavil-
·n is staffed by people from
.e country it represents, sell-
.g ethnic products and food.
ıe best live shows are the
:robats at China and the
ving Statues at Italy. High-
ghts include **Reflections of
hina** – a Circle-Vision film
ı China's ancient sites;
**aelstrom** in Norway – an
:citing trip through fjords;
ıd **Impressions de France**
a film offering a whirlwind
ur of France. Do not miss
**lumiNations**, a *son-et-lum-
re* show with lasers, fire-
ıd waterworks. It is staged
:ar closing time around
orld Showcase Lagoon.

## ISNEY-MGM STUDIOS

ISNEY-MGM STUDIOS opened in 1989, both as a theme
.rk and as a working film
d TV studio. It combines
ɔ-notch shows and rides,
sed on Disney and Metro-
ɔldwyn-Mayer films (to
ıich Disney bought the
:hts), with entertaining tours
ıt allow visitors to glimpse
: magic of filmmaking in the
ɔrking section of the Studios.
At Hollywood Boulevard, Art
·co styled buildings vie with
eplica of Mann's Chinese
eater. The best shops are
:ated here: Celebrity 5 & 10
s a range of affordable
ɔvie souvenirs, such as
pper boards and Oscars®,
d the pricey Sid Cahuenga's
ıe-Of-A-Kind stocks rare film
:morabilia such as auto-
ıphed photos and famous
:ors' clothes. **The Great
ɔvie Ride** carries visitors
st enormous movie sets,
ıere scenes from films are
created using live action.
Sunset Boulevard is an evo-
ion of the famous Holly-
ɔod street in the 1940s. Re-
ated theaters and storefronts
dominated by the Holly-
ɔod Tower Hotel. This light-
ıg-ravaged hotel is the spot
Orlando's scariest ride –
**e Twilight Zone Tower of
rror** – in which you are
ıpped into an elevator for a
yage inspired by the 1950s
TV show *The Twilight Zone*™. Its high point is the ghastly 13-story plunge that everyone knows will come, repeated no fewer than seven times. The **Rock 'n Roller Coaster Starring Aerosmith** accelerates to 60mph (96 km/h) in 2.8 seconds in the dark, and pulls 5G in the first corkscrew.

Animation Courtyard gives visitors a glimpse behind the scenes during the creation of Disney's Audio-Animatronics®. The **Magic of Disney-Animation** is a guided visit with a Disney artist, while **Playhouse Disney-Live on Stage!** features a collection of Disney Channel characters singing and dancing.

At Mickey Avenue, the entertaining **Disney-MGM Studios Backlot Tour** has a tram ride that takes visitors for a peek at the camera, wardrobe, and lighting departments. It ends in Catastrophe Canyon, in the midst of a flood and explosions. The walking tour demonstrates how special effects are used: battles at sea are re-created using models in a water tank.

New York Street is a clever re-creation of the Big Apple. Its highlight is the spectacular **Jim Henson's Muppet™ Vision 3-D**, a slapstick 3-D movie starring the Muppets. Trombones, cars, and rocks launch themselves at you out of the screen – so realistic that children often grasp the air expecting to touch something. Audio-Animatronics® characters and special effects, such as a cannon blowing holes in the walls of the theater, provide the fourth dimension.

Echo Lake offers the sensational **Star Tours** ride, based on the *Star Wars* films. The spaceship – a flight simulator akin to those used to train astronauts, has to cope with a fierce intergalactic battle.

At 5pm, the park holds a parade based on one of Disney's animated films. The evening show, **Fantasmic!** is the finest of its kind in Florida. It combines music, lasers, animation, and over a hundred actors and dancers. Although it seats 10,000 people, you still need to arrive two hours early to get a good seat.

## ANIMAL KINGDOM

THIS PARK HAS both real and mythical beasts, spread over seven different "lands."

At Discovery Island, the **It's Tough to be a Bug** show is a superb 3-D presentation. Camp Minnie-Mickey is where visitors meet Disney characters. The **Festival of the Lion King** show here is superb.

Africa offers the fabulous **Kilimanjaro Safaris**, where you see hippos, rhinos, lions, and elephants roaming freely.

Asia features gibbons, birds, and tigers in a re-creation of Indian ruins. Tapirs and Komodo dragons are found on the **Maharaja Jungle Trek**, the climax of which are the magnificent Bengal tigers that roam the ruins. Dinoland USA has the wild **DINOSAUR** ride, where a motion simulator bucks and weaves, trying to ensnare and avoid dinosaurs. Two new rides, **Primeval Whirl** and **Tricera Top Spin**, attempt to spin visitors dizzy.

## THE REST OF WALT DISNEY WORLD® RESORT

WALT DISNEY WORLD offers much more than just its theme parks. There are 22 resorts *(see p327)*, two water parks, a campground, nearly 300 restaurants, a host of nightclubs, a shopping village, and half a dozen golf courses.

Of the waterparks, **Blizzard Beach**, a reconstructed Alpine ski resort, claims to have the tallest freefall slide in the world. At **Fort Wilderness Resort and Campground**, activities include horseback riding, fishing, and biking. Jet skiing, rental boats, and fishing gear are also available at the **Marketplace** and at all lakeside resorts. After-dark entertainment revolves around three distinct areas in Downtown Disney: **Pleasure Island** has a range of clubs and discos; The Marketplace is an outdoor mall with lots of shops – The World of Disney sells mountains of merchandise; and **Disney's West Side** has jazz and blues clubs, and the famous Cirque du Soleil.

# Universal Orlando ⑩

ONCE A SINGLE MOVIE PARK, Universal Orlando now boasts two theme parks, an entertainment complex, and the first of its many planned hotels. Together, Universal Studios Florida, Islands of Adventure, and Universal CityWalk present a formidable reason to spend time away from Walt Disney World. The parking lot feeds into Universal CityWalk where there is a series of moving walkways to a fork leading to the two separate parks.

**Universal's globe, the logo for the new combined complex of parks**

## Tackling the Parks

THE BUSIEST SEASONS are during Christmas and Easter. During the off-season, check with Guest Services for special deals on tickets. Arrive early to combat the long lines for rides (the gates open an hour before opening time). Arrive 15 minutes early for shows to ensure a seat. Children may find most rides too intense but there are some child-friendly attractions: ET Adventure, the Woody Woodpecker Coaster, A Day in the Park with Barney, the Nickelodeon Studios, Jurassic Park Islands, and the Seuss Landing Island.

## Eating & Shopping

There are plenty of options for dining. The Hard Rock Café is the largest in the world. Lombard's Seafood Grill specializes in fish dishes, while Universal Studios Classic Monsters Café serves Californian and Italian cuisine, and has a great buffet. Most rides and attractions have their own stores. In Hitchcock's 3-D Theater, one can buy a Bates Motel Soap, while Universal Studio Store has everything from fake Oscars to oven mitts with the Universal logo.

## Universal Studios Florida

THE ENTRANCE IS known as Front Lot, as it is built to look like the front lot of a 1940s Hollywood film studio. Actors in costumes wander the streets playing characters from *Ghostbusters, Frankenstein*, and legends such as Marilyn Monroe and the Marx Brothers. The shooting schedule posted near the turnstiles has details of shows that are being filmed. Tickets for these are available at the booth located near Guest Services.

A new example of the increasing number of 3-D plus one attractions, **Shrek 4-D** allows visitors to experience 3-D film special effects. At **Nickelodeon Studios** kids can experience **Game Lab**, an interactive show with whacky games and stunts based on the programs and shows on this TV network. Children will definitely enjoy the Slime Geyser outside, which erupts in a shower of green slime every ten minutes or so.

The New York area has more than 60 façades, some of which replicate real buildings, others reproduce famous movie settings. There are cut-outs of the Guggenheim Museum and the New York Public Library, as well as Macy's department store, and Louie's Italian Restaurant, scene of a shootout in the original *Godfather* movie. The park's newest ride is the **Revenge of the Mummy – The Ride**. This high-speed rollercoaster propels you though Egyptian passageways and includes frighteningly lifelike robotics. The other ride here is **Twister...Ride It Out**, which pits visitors against a simulated tornado, and lets them experience the terrifying power of the elements standing inside 20 ft (6 m) of the five floor high funnel of winds.

In the section known as Hollywood, sets of Hollywood Boulevard and Rodeo Drive pay tribute to Hollywood's golden age, from the 1920s to the 50s – with the famous Mocambo nightclub, the luxurious Beverly Wilshire Hotel and top beauty salon, Max Factor. There is even a replica of the Hollywood Walk of Fame, with the names of stars embedded in the ground.

Hollywood's most popular attraction is **Terminator 2: 3-D**, a ride that uses superb robotics and the latest 3-D technology to catapult the audience into the action alongside the star of the *Terminator* films, Arnold Schwarzenegger.

The **Universal Horror Make-Up Show** offers a behind-the-scenes look at scary make-up effects.

One of the park's most thrilling rides, **Back to the Future – The Ride** is located

**Universal Studios' Terminator 2: 3-D, a state-of-the-art attraction**

.e thrilling river ride in Jurassic Park
ver Adventure, Jurassic Park Island

World Expo. During the zzying journey in a time-aveling car, visitors plunge er lava, skim ice fields, and oop into the mouth of an ormous dinosaur. In the credibly addictive **Men In ack – Alien Attack**, visitors n Will Smith in a simulator, ttling aliens with lasers and nnons. In Woody oodpecker's Kid Zone, the chanting **ET Adventure** is sed on Steven Spielberg's 82 film. Guests soar off to "s home planet on a flying cycle, gliding over a inkling cityscape, before iving at a world inhabited ET look-alikes.

The San Francisco section's g draw is **Earthquake – e Big One**, which demon-ates how earthquakes are nulated. Visitors ride a oway train, set in the movie *rthquake*, and contend th a tremor of 8.3 on the chter scale, a tidal wave, d a train collision. Amity, other half of this section, s the blood-chilling **Jaws** e, where a giant great ite shark lunges at the at, tearing through the ter at terrifying speed.

## IE ISLANDS OF VENTURE

ONE OF THE world's most technologically advanced me parks, Islands of Adven-e demands a day's visit of own. The first island visi-s encounter is the Marvel per Hero Island where the me draws from the Marvel Comics' Super Hero stable of characters. The **Incredible Hulk Coaster**, probably Florida's best, is a green leviathan that accelerates you to over 40 mph (64 km/h) in two seconds before turning upside down at 110 ft (33.5 m) above the ground. The **Amazing Adventures of Spider-man**, shows a stunning integration of 3-D technology with motion simulation. Toon Lagoon Island, where cartoons transmute into reality, hosts two wet rides, and the riotous **Toon Lagoon Beach Bash**. Popeye and Bluto star in many rides.

Jurassic Park Island boasts the **Jurassic Park River Adventure**, a cruise where visitors encounter friendly dinosaurs before being diverted due to a raptor breakout. The **Pteranodon Flyers** ride flies pairs of riders over the island on an 80-second trip, while the **Discovery Center** is an interactive natural history exhibit where guests can view the results of mixing DNA from various species, including themselves.

The Lost Continent Island is an island of myth and legend. **The Flying Unicorn** is a pleasant introduction to roller coasting for young children. However, for coaster addicts, **Duelling Dragons** is the ride of choice. Two coasters – Fire and Ice, battle to see who will arrive back first. Stage shows include the Eighth Voyage of Sinbad, and Poseidon's Fury, with a myriad special effects.

### VISITORS' CHECKLIST

1000 Universal Studios Plaza, exits 29 or 30B on I-4. *(407) 363-8000.* *21, 37, 40 from Orlando.* *9am–6pm daily; extended evening hours in summer & on public hols.*
www.universalorlando.com

Seuss Landing Island, based on the popular Dr. Seuss children's books, the creation of Theodor Seuss Geisel, caters to children. The **Cat in the Hat** ride serves as an introduction to the characters. There are also a host of innovative rides that captivate younger children.

## UNIVERSAL CITYWALK

INSPIRED BY MANY of popular culture's innovators such as Bob Marley and Motown, Universal CityWalk is a 30-acre (12-ha) entertainment complex of restaurants, nightclubs, and cinemas. Open between 11am and 2am, its dazzling array of restaurants range from Emeril's (a top TV chef) to the nostalgic Motown Café, and the famous Hard Rock Café. A restaurant known as "Bob Marley – A Tribute to Freedom," is an exact replica of this famous musician's home. Among the many nightclubs are CityJazz and The Groove Dance Club where visitors can watch live musical performances. The complex also has stores and movies, and its stages host concerts, art festivals, and celebrity appearances. A lagoon provides a picturesque setting to sip a cool drink or take a moonlight stroll.

The Hard Rock Café and music venue, Universal CityWalk

# SeaWorld Orlando & Discovery Cove ⓫

In scale and sophistication, SeaWorld is one of the world's most impressive marine-life adventure parks. Established in 1973 to promote its educational, research, and conservation programs, the park abounds in fun as well as entertainment. SeaWorld's answer to the Disney mouse is Shamu the killer whale, and the Shamu Adventure Show tops the bill. Next to SeaWorld is Discovery Cove, a new, all-inclusive park, where guests can swim with rays, dolphins, and other fascinating sea creatures.

**Dolphin Cove, where everyone can touch and feed the dolphins**

## Exploring SeaWorld

SeaWorld is less crowded than Orlando's other theme parks. Most of the presentations are either walk-through exhibits or stadium shows. Arriving 15 minutes early guarantees a good seat. Show timings overlap, so guests cannot leave a show just in time for another. However, it is possible to get a seat in the Clyde and Seamore (Sea Lion and Otter) show by leaving the Shamu Stadium while the performers are taking their bows. The best time to see shows such as Wild Arctic and Shark Encounter is while visitors are busy watching the stadium events. Young children enjoy meeting the actors in furry suits who play the parts of Shamu and Crew – guests can normally find them near SeaWorld's exit around closing time. The 400-ft (122-m) Sky Tower ride offers a superb overview of the park. For more information, go to Guest Relations near the exit gate.

### Top Tips

- *SeaWorld allows guests to feed many of the animals, but it restricts both the type and the amount of food, which must be purchased from them. If this is something you would like to do, check with guest services as soon as you enter the park for feeding times and food availablility.*
- *Build your schedule around the four main types of presentations: Shamu Killer Whale, Atlantis Water Ski, Sea Lion and Otter, and Whale and Dolphin shows.*
- *Bring a waterproof plastic bag for your camera as, especially during the Shamu and Dolphin shows, people sitting in the first 12 rows often get splashed by salt water.*
- *Journey to Atlantis is guaranteed to get you wet, so reserve this for the hottest part of the day.*
- *SeaWorld's gentle pace means that visiting after 3pm is a less crowded experience.*

## Exhibits & Rides

Three meticulously landscaped habitats are incorporated in **Key West at SeaWorld**. Dolphin Cove, a wave pool in the style of a Caribbean beach, offers underwater viewing of bottlenose dolphins and the chance to pet and feed them. Visitors can also touch one of the 200-odd rays at Stingray Lagoon, while Turtle Point is home to rescued loggerhead, hawksbill, and green sea turtles, which are too injured to survive in the wild.

**Pacific Point Preserve** recreates the rugged north Pacific Coast in the form of a large, rocky pool. One can watch harbor seals, South American fur seals, and noisy California sea lions basking on the rocks or gliding effortlessly through the water.

Most of the other wildlife at SeaWorld is viewed through glass. **Manatees: The Last Generation?** offers a splendid underwater view of these irresistibly appealing herbivores *(see p319)*.

In the fabulous **Penguin Encounter**, a moving walkway leads past a frozen landscape where a large colony of penguins demonstrate their comical waddling and elegant swimming. The gawky puffins are also a delight to watch.

Billed as the world's largest collection of dangerous sea creatures, **Shark Encounter** is very popular. Moray eels, barracuda, and pufferfish are the tantalizing appetizers before a main course of sharks, whose toothy grins are a short distance away, as visitors walk through a glass tunnel inside their aquarium.

**Shamu, the park's official mascot**

**Shamu: Close Up!** next to the **Shamu Stadium**, is a research and breeding facility study killer whale behavior – ten whales have been born here so far.

**Wild Arctic** is a thrilling, hi-tech ride that simulates a helicopter flight through blizzards and avalanches. Visitors arrive at Base Station Wild Arctic, created around an old expedition ship, and encounter polar bears, harbor seals, walruses, and beluga whales.

SeaWorld's new **Journey to Atlantis**, a water coaster with a mythological twist, and **Kraken**, a winner of the annual Orlando roller-coaster competition, are hot tickets.

## Shows & Tours

The excitement of seeing a killer whale erupt out of the water carrying one of the SeaWorld trainers on its nose hard to overstate. In the ırk's number one show, **he Shamu Adventure**, unts such as this are ıpplemented by a giant deo screen, oviding close-ups the action. There e five orcas, hich take turns to erform, as well as baby killer hale. The show so features the ller whales per- rming an amazing "under- ater ballet."

**Key West Dolphin Fest** is other remarkable show, ısed on the speed and ility of bottlenose dolphins d false killer whales. ıring the show, the ammals play with their ainers and interact with embers of the audience. owever, the show's highlight the dolphins' synchronized ıps over a rope.

The **Clyde and Seamore ıke Pirate Island** show, ld in the Sea Lion and Otter adium, features two sea ns (Clyde and Seamore), ers, and a walrus in a vashbuckling adventure of st loot, pirate ships, and larity on the high seas.

The Nautilis Theater hosts **dyssea**, a 30-minute eathtaking show based on n-traditional circus acts. ere are great visual effects d amazing acrobatic feats mbined with dramatic ısic and imaginative stumes. The overall effect ıkes this show one of the ost popular at SeaWorld.

Another show, **Pets Ahoy**, ıtures talented cats, birds, gs, and pigs, all of whom ve been rescued from imal shelters. **Shamu cks America**, held at the amu Stadium, features the aWorld trainers and killer ıales in a nighttime rock 'n' l show, complete with enching salt-water waves d dazzling theatrical effects. her exhibits include **amu's Happy Harbor**, a ıy area for smaller children, **lphin Nursery** for new lphin moms and their lves, and **Caribbean Tide- ol**, which encourages close examination of tropical fish, starfish, sea anemones, and other underwater denizens.

Cuddly versions of SeaWorld stars

The **Hubbs–SeaWorld Research Institute** runs a number of nonprofit "Research, Rescue and Rehabilitation" projects. It has helped thousands of manatees, dolphins, and whales in difficulty – nursing and operating on them. Those that recover fully are released into the wild. Several tours such as The Sharks! tour, offer a glimpse of this work. If interested, inquire at Guest Relations. The **Adventure Express Tour** offers exclusive guided park tours, reserved seats, feeding opportunities, and back door access to rides. **Mistify**, the laser-fireworks show held nightly at the Waterfront, constitutes a stunning finale to the day.

## Discovery Cove

Just across the road from SeaWorld, Discovery Cove is a quiet revolution in Florida's theme parks. With a capacity of only 1,000 guests a day (the car park is limited to only 500 cars), it offers some unforgettable experiences, the most vaunted of which is an opportunity to swim with Atlantic bottlenose dolphins.

Discovery Cove has been conceived as a private island. Its five main areas are set within beautifully landscaped grounds with waterfalls, pools, and niches connected by beaches. **Coral Reef** abounds with grottos and a shipwreck, and offers the opportunity to swim alongside threateningly large sharks, separated from visitors by a transparent plexi-glass wall. At the **Aviary**, guests can feed birds, while **Ray Lagoon** offers the chance to snorkel above rays, some of which grow up to a length of 5 ft (1.5 m). The **Dolphin Lagoon** has a 15-minute orientation session, followed by 30 minutes of wading and swimming with these highly intelligent mammals.

It's a good idea to split your party into two for the dolphin experience, to be able to take each other's photographs. Do not bring any sunscreen, as the park has its own "fish friendly" one, the only brand permitted. If you decide not to visit the Dolphin Lagoon, the price of the visit is less. The package price (no child reductions) includes the dolphin experience (children under six cannot participate), all equipment, a free snorkel, a meal, and seven days admission to SeaWorld or Busch Gardens, Tampa Bay. Despite the price, the park is very popular, and it is better to book well in advance.

**A performing killer whale, one of the star attractions at SeaWorld Orlando**

### Visitors' Checklist

7007 SeaWorld Drive, intersection of I-4 & Bee Line Expressway. *(407) 351-3600.*
*8, 42 from Orlando.*
*minimum hours 9am–7pm daily (until 11pm in summer).*
www.seaworld.com

Downtown Orlando, dominated by the SunTrust Center

## Orlando 12

*200,000.* *8723 International Dr, (407) 425-1234.* www.orlandoinfo.com

ORLANDO WAS JUST a sleepy provincial town until the 1950s. However, its proximity to Cape Canaveral and the theme parks soon transformed it into a burgeoning business center. Downtown, with its glass-sided high-rises, comes to life only at night, when both visitors and locals flock to the many bars and restaurants around Orange Avenue, the town's main street.

During the day, the area around **Lake Eola**, east of Orange Avenue, offers views of the wooden homes of the town's earliest settlers. The residential districts north of downtown have many parks and museums, including the serenely beautiful Harry P. Leu Gardens and **Loch Haven Park**, which houses a trio of museums. The most highly regarded of these is the **Orlando Museum of Art**. Its collections include pre-Columbian artifacts with figurines from Peru, African art, and American paintings from the 19th and 20th centuries. The park is also home to the John and Rita Lowndes Shakespeare Center, which includes the 350-seat Margeson Theater and smaller Goldman Theater. The Center holds the Orlando-UCF Shakespeare Festival.

The **Maitland Art Center**, on Packwood Avenue in the leafy suburb of Maitland, occupies studios designed in the 1930s by artist André Smith as a winter retreat for fellow artists. Set around courtyards and gardens, the buildings show a profusion of Mayan and Aztec motifs. The studios are still used, and exhibitions of contemporary American crafts are held often here.

North of Lake Eola is the town's newest attraction, the **Orlando Science Center**. Covering 207,000 sq feet (19,200 sq m) of floor space, the center's aim is to offer a stimulating environment for experimental science learning. It thus provides a huge range of exciting state-of-the-art interactive exhibits. Among its attractions are the Dr. Philips CineDome, which also functions as a planetarium, its dinosaur fossils collection, and the ShowBiz Science exhibit, which reveals some of the tricks and special effects used in movies.

### Loch Haven Park

N Mills Ave at Rollins St.

**Orlando Museum of Art** *(407) 896-4231.* *Tue–Sun.* *public hols.* www.omart.org

### Orlando Science Center

777 East Princeton St.

*(407) 514-2000.* *9am–5pm Tue–Thu, 9am–9pm Fri–Sat, noon–5pm Sun.* www.osc.org

## Winter Park 13

*25,000.* *150 N New York Ave, (407) 644-8281.* **Scenic Boat Tour** *(407) 644-4056.* www.scenicboattours.com

GREATER ORLANDO'S most refined neighborhood took off in the 1880s, when wealthy northerners came south and began to build winter retreats here. The **Charles Hosmer Morse Museum of American Art** probably has the finest collection of works by Art Nouveau craftsman, Louis Comfort Tiffany. There are superb examples of his jewelry, lamps, and many of his windows, including the *The Four Seasons* (1899). To the south of Winter Park is **Rollins College**, dotted with 1930s Spanish-style buildings. The finest is the **Knowles Memorial Chapel**, whose main entrance has a relief of a meeting between the Seminole Indians and the Spanish conquistadors. The college's **Cornell Fine Arts Museum's** impressive collection of Italian Renaissance paintings is the oldest in Florida. The **Scenic Boat Tour** explores the nearby lakes and canals.

Tiffany's *Four Seasons* window, Winter Park

### Charles Hosmer Morse Museum of American Art

445 Park Ave N. *(407) 645-5311.* *Tue–Sun.* *public hols.* www.morsemuseum.org

Main entrance of Knowles Memorial Chapel, Winter Park

ıe sinking home of Ripley's Believe It or Not!, International Drive

## ıternational )rive 14

Orlando. Orlando. Visitor Center, 8723 International ive, (407) 363-5872.

A STONE'S THROW from Walt Disney World, "I Drive" a 3-mile (5-km) ribbon of otels, shops, and theaters. s most popular attraction is **Vet'n Wild**, known for its g-thrill rides. The Storm nd Mach 5 feature terrifying escents down near-vertical ides, and there is also the atery Kid's Playground. Filled with fantastic objects, usions, and film footage of range feats, **Ripley's Believe or Not!** was created by the merican cartoonist, Robert ipley. It is housed in a building that appears to be falling to one of Florida's sinkoles, which occur due to the rosion of the limestone bedock. **Titanic – The Exhiition** displays artifacts, ıovie memorabilia, and reeations of the ship's rooms nd grand staircase. Two locks from the mall is rlando's **Official Visitor ıformation Center**, which as coupons for many attracons, such as discounts on dmission and bargain meals.

## ıissimmee 15

41,000. 1925 E o Bronson Memorial Hwy, (407) 47-5000. www.floridakiss.com

MEANING "Heaven's Place" in the language of the alusa Indians, Kissimmee is aid to be the cow capital f Florida. In the early 20th entury, cows freely roamed ıe streets of this cattle oom town. Today, the only livestock visitors are likely to encounter are those that appear in the rodeos at **Silver Spur Arena**. Held every February and July, this is the state's oldest and wildest rodeo. Other less extravagant rodeos are held every Friday night at the **Kissimmee Sports Arena**.

Most visitors headed for Walt Disney World often stop at Kissimmee, drawn by the many inexpensive motels, strung along the busy, traffic-ridden US 192. For those who want to linger, Kissimmee's Old Town is a re-created pedestrian street of early 20th-century buildings with several eccentric shops offering psychic readings and tattoos. Near the airport, the **Flying Tigers Warbird Restoration Museum** is another enjoyable experience. Old and damaged World War II aircraft are brought here for restoration. The museum provides guided tours of the hanger, where visitors can learn more about the finer points of airplane reconstruction. For a fee, visitors can even take a spin in a T-6 Navy Trainer.

**Flying Tigers Warbird Restoration Museum**
231 N Hoagland Blvd. *(407) 933-1942.* *daily.* *Dec 25.* www.warbirdmuseum.com

## Disney Wilderness Preserve 16

**Road map** E3. 2700 Scrub Jay Trail, 12 miles (18 km) SW of Kissimmee. *(407) 935-0002.* *Kissimmee.* *Kissimmee.* *9am–5pm daily.* *Sat–Sun Jun-Sep.* *Sun 1:30pm Oct–May.* www.nature.org

ORLANDO'S BEST wilderness preserve is a haven for native plants and animals, and also for people wanting to get away from the crowds. Unlike other Disney attractions, there are no thrill rides on these 12,000 acres (18.75 sq miles), but there is still plenty to do. There is an off-road buggy tour on Sundays, and three hiking trails that lead to Lake Russell. The interpretive trail is 0.8-mile (1.2-km) long and visitors can learn about nature along the way. The longer trails are mostly unshaded, so bring sunscreen, a hat, plenty of water, and insect repellent.

Lake Russell, one of many lakes at the Disney Wilderness Preserve

## Daytona Beach 17

*64,000. 126 E Orange Ave, (386) 255-0415.* W www.daytonabeach.com

THIS RESORT IS famous for its 23-mile (37-km) beach, lined with a wall of hotels. The old-fashioned boardwalk offers concerts in the bandstand, arcades, and go-karts. During the April Spring Break, nearly 200,000 college students descend on the beach for this ritual party.

This is also one of the few beaches in Florida where cars are allowed on the sands, a hangover from the days when motor enthusiasts, such as Louis Chevrolet and Henry Ford, raced on the beaches. The **Daytona International Speedway** nearby draws huge crowds, especially during the Speedweek in February and the Motorcycle Weeks in March and October *(see p28)*.

Across the Halifax River downtown, the **Halifax Historical Society Museum** occupies a 1910 bank building and displays local history. To the west, the **Museum of Arts and Sciences** has exhibits from 1640 to 1920. **Gamble Place**, run by the museum, is a hunting lodge built in 1907 for James N. Gamble, of Procter & Gamble fame. Museum tours include the Snow White House, built for Gamble's grandchildren.

**Museum of Arts & Sciences**
1040 Museum Blvd. *(386) 255-0285. daily. public hols.*

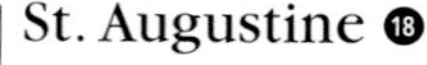

## St. Augustine 18

*16,000. 100 Malaga St, (904) 829-6401. 10 Castillo Dr, (904) 825-1000. Arts & Crafts Spring Festival (Apr).* W www.visitoldcity.com

AMERICA'S OLDEST continuously occupied European settlement was founded by the Spanish colonist Pedro Menéndez de Avilés on the feast day of St. Augustine in 1565. Today, this town has many attractions for the modern tourist, not least its 43 miles (69 km) of beaches and the fact that it is within easy reach of several golf courses and marinas. St. Augustine burned down in 1702 but was soon rebuilt in the lee of the **Castillo de San Marcos**. This mighty fortress is the largest and most complete Spanish fort in the US. Constructed of coquina, a sedimentary limestone formed by seashells and corals that could withstand the impact of cannonballs, this is a superb example of 17th-century military architecture.

The historic heart of St. Augustine is compact and easy to explore on foot. Horsedrawn carriage tours are popular and depart from Avenida Menendez, north of the Bridge of Lions, which was built across Matanzas Bay in 1926. The 18th-century City Gate is the entrance to the **Old Town**. Its focus is the pedestrian St. George Street, lined with attractive stone buildings. Some of the main attractions here are the **Spanish Quarter Village**, a museum that recreates an 18th-century garrison town, and **Peña-Peck House**, a fine First Spanish Period home dating to the 1740s. The **Oldest Wooden Schoolhouse**, buil from cypress and red cedar wood in the mid-1700s, is also located on this street. The heart of the Spanish settlement is **Plaza de la Constitution**, a leafy square flanked by Government House Museum and the grand Basilica Cathedral.

***Cleopatra* (c.1890) by Romanelli, Lightner Museum**

The splendid **Flagler College** started out as the Ponce de Leon Hotel, built by Henry Flagler *(see p286)* in 1883, a year after he honeymooned in St. Augustine. Its gilded and stuccoed cupola has symbolic motifs representing Spain an Florida, notably the golden mask of the Timucuan Indian su god and the lamb – symbol of Spanish knighthood. The other resort Flagler built here are the Cor doba and Alcazar Hotels. Th latter, a three-floor Hispano-Moorish structure, is now the **Lightner Museum**, devoted to the country's Gilded Age. Its exhibits include glass works by Louis Tiffany, and its Grand Ballroom houses a eclectic exhibit of "American Castle" furniture. The lovely **Ximenez-Fatio House** is now a museum run by the National Society of Colonial Dames. It seeks to re-create the genteel boarding house that it was in the 1830s, whe invalids and adventurers first visited Florida in order to escape from the harsh northern winters.

**Castillo de San Marcos**
1 S Castillo Dr. *(904) 829-6506. 8:45am–4:45pm daily. Dec 25. limited. call for detail*
W www.nps.gov/casa

**Lightner Museum**
75 King St. *(904) 824-2874. daily. Dec 25.*
W www.lightnermuseum.org

**Cars cruising the hard-packed sands of Daytona Beach**

ernandina's Beech Street Grill with Chinese Chippendale motifs

## ·ernandina ʒeach 19

10,000. Jacksonville.
Jacksonville. 961687 Gateway 'vd Ste 101 G, (904) 261-3248.

THE TOWN OF Fernandina Beach on Amelia Island, ıst across the St. Mary's River ·om Georgia, was famous as pirates' den until the early 800s. Its harbor attracted a ıotley crew of foreign adven- ırers, whose various alle- iances earned the island its ɔubriquet, the "Isle of Eight lags." Today, Fernandina is ·etter known as a charming 'ictorian resort and Florida's ·rimary source of sweet ·tlantic white shrimp: more ıan 2 million pounds 900,000 kilos) are harvested ·y shrimping fleets each year.

Occupying a large section ·f the town's **Historic District**, the Silk Stocking )istrict was named after the 'fluence of its original resi- ents. Sea captains and timber ·arons built homes here in a ariety of styles. Queen Anne ouses with turrets jostle with raceful Italianate residences nd fine Chinese Chippendale tructures, such as the **Beech treet Grill**. The weathered ·uildings on Centre Street ·nce housed chandleries and ·aval stores. Antique shops nd gift shops have now eplaced them; the 1878 'alace Saloon, however, still erves a wicked Pirate's 'unch at the mahogany bar dorned with hand-carved aryatids. Farther south, the **Amelia Island Museum of History** occupies the former jail and offers twice daily, 90-minute guided history tours recounting the island's turbulent past – from the time of its first Indian inhabitants to the early 1900s.

The **Fort Clinch State Park**, at the island's northern tip, has trails, beaches, and campsites, as well as a 19th-century fort built in 1847. Park rangers now dress in Civil War uniforms and perform 19th-century war re-enactments one weekend a month.

**Amelia Island Museum of History**
233 S 3rd St. *(904) 261-7378.* *Mon–Sat.* *public hols.* *limited.* *compulsory, two tours daily.*

## Ocala National Forest 20

*daily.* *campgrounds & swimming areas.* **Visitor Center** 3199 NE Co Rd. *(352) 236-0288.* **Juniper Springs Canoe Rental** *(352) 625-2808.*

BETWEEN OCALA and the St. John's River, the world's largest sand pine forest covers 366,000 acres (148,000 ha) and is crisscrossed by rivers and hiking trails. One of the last refuges of the endangered Florida black bear, it is also home to animals such as deer and otter, and a variety of birds such as bald eagles, barred owls, wild turkey, and several wading birds. Hiking trails vary from boardwalks and short loop trails to the 66-mile (106-km) stretch of the National Scenic Trail. Bass-fishing is popular, and there are swimming holes and campgrounds at the recreation areas of Salt Springs and Alexander Springs.

Canoe rental is widely available; the 7-mile (11-km) canoe run down Juniper Creek from the **Juniper Springs Recreation Area** is one of the finest in Florida. The Salt Springs trail is especially good for bird-watching. There are guides at the main visitor center on the forest's western fringe or at the centers at Salt Springs and Lake Dorr, on Route 19.

**ENVIRONS: Silver Springs**, on the western border of Ocala National Forest, 29 miles (46 km) west of the Juniper Springs Recreation Area, is the world's largest artesian spring and Florida's oldest tourist attraction. Its famous glass-bottomed boat tours have been running since 1878. Jeep safaris and "Jungle Cruises" also travel through the Florida outback, where the early Tarzan movies starring Johnny Weismuller were filmed. Wild Waters, next to the springs, is a lively water park. The quieter **Silver River State Park**, 2 miles (3 km) southeast, has a lovely walking trail through a hardwood hammock and cypress swamp, leading to a swimming hole in a bend of the crystal clear river.

**Silver River State Park**
1425 NE 58th Ave, Ocala. *(352) 236-7148.* *daily.*

Juniper Springs, Ocala National Forest

## Tallahassee 21

137,000. 918 Railroad Ave, (800) 872-7245. 106 E Jefferson, (850) 413-9200. *Springtime Tallahassee (Mar–Apr).*

ENCIRCLED BY rolling hills, Florida's dignified state capital is gracious and uncompromisingly Southern. Tallahassee grew dramatically during the plantation era, and the elegant town houses built in the 1800s can still be seen around Park Avenue and Calhoun Street. The Chamber of Commerce, on Duval Street, is housed in the city's oldest building, a 1830 Classical-Revival mansion, known as "The Columns."

The **Old Capitol Building** in downtown Tallahasse has been beautifully restored to its 1902 state, with a pristine white dome and striped awnings. Once inside, guests can visit the Supreme Court chamber and the Senate. The high-rise **New Capitol Building** behind it offers a fabulous view of the city. The **Museum of Florida History** situated on Bronough Street, covers about 12,000 years of the region's history.

**The Old and the New Capitol Buildings, Tallahassee**

**ENVIRONS:** During the 1820s and 30s, the area around Tallahassee was Florida's most important cotton-growing region. A tour along the canopied roads of the old **Cotton Trail** takes visitors past former cotton plantations and cattle pastures. The **Goodwood Museum and Gardens** retains its lovely 1830s mansion; Bradley's Country Store, set up in 1927, still serves their famous homemade sausages. Located 15 miles (24 km) south of Tallahassee, **Wakulla Springs State Park** has one of the world's largest freshwater springs, which pumps 700,000 gal (2.6 million liters) of water a minute into a large pool. Here, visitors can swim or snorkel in its clear waters or ride in a glass-bottomed boat. Boat trips on the Wakulla River are the best way to see alligators and wading birds. The elegant Wakulla Springs Lodge was built in the 1930s.

**Wakulla Springs State Park**

550 Wakulla Park Dr, Wakulla Springs. (850) 224-5950. daily. www.floridastateparks.org

## Pensacola 22

294,000. 980 E Heinburg St, (850) 433-4966. (850) 476-4800. 1401 E Gregory St, (850) 434-1234. *Fiesta of Five Flags (Jun).* www.visitpensacola.com

FLORIDA'S EARLIEST Spanish settlement, Pensacola was established by Don Tristan de Luna, who sailed into Pensacola Bay in 1559. The city features diverse architectural

## The Beaches of the Panhandle

LYING BETWEEN Perdido Key and Panama City Beach are some of Florida's most beautiful beaches. The brilliant sand, consisting mainly of quartz, is washed down from the Appalachian Mountains. One can choose between quiet, pristine beaches and more lively resorts, with ample opportunities for water sports. The main season is April–July.

**Perdido Key** ①
Florida's most westerly shores on Perdido Key are inaccessible by car and quieter than most.

**Quietwater Beach** ②
On Santa Rosa Island, it's not the Panhandle's finest but is an easy hop from Pensacola.

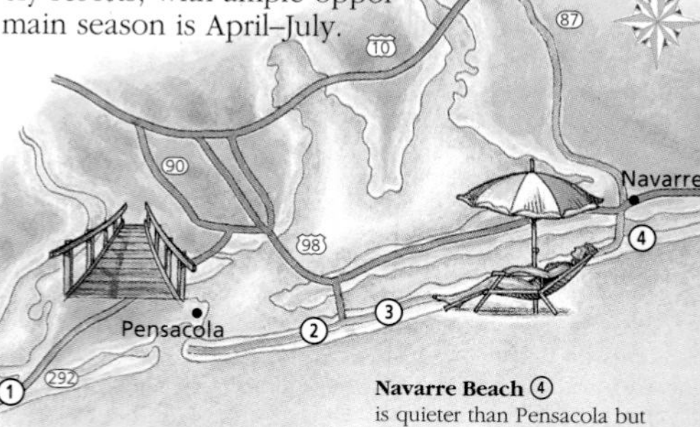


**Pensacola Beach** ③
has miles of pristine sand and a string of shops, hotels, and bars. Large crowds gather here on weekends to sunbathe and swim.

**Navarre Beach** ④
is quieter than Pensacola but nevertheless has good facilities, water sports, and a pier for fishing.

tyles, from Colonial cottages o elegant Classical-Revival iomes. Pensacola was wiped ɔut by a hurricane two years fter it was established, but it vas soon rebuilt, and over he next 300 years the city vas occupied by the Spanish, rench, English, and the Americans. The 1800s were a ɔeriod of prosperity ushered n by the timber boom, and nuch of today's downtown lates from this time.

Pensacola's oldest quarter, he **Historic Pensacola Village**, has a number of nuseums and houses, built by wealthy pioneers and raders. There are daily tours rom Tivoli House on Zaragoza Street. Forming a backdrop to the Museum of Commerce is a cleverly constructed Victorian streetscape, complete with a printer's workshop, a saddlery, and an old-time music store. Florida's earliest church, the Old Christ Church (1832), stands in the eafy Seville Square shaded by oaks and magnolia trees.

The **TT Wentworth, Jr., Florida State Museum**, set in a Spanish Renaissance Revival building, has an eclectic collection that includes oddities such as a shrunken head from pre-Columbian times and old Coca-Cola bottles.

Farther north, the **North Hill Preservation District** has 19th- and 20th-century houses, built on the sites of British and Spanish forts. Even today, cannonballs are found in local gardens. A very striking home is the McCreary House on North Baylen Street. A Queen Anne home built in 1900, it has a gabled roof and tower. Lying between the two districts, **Palafox Street** is the city's commercial hub.

**TT Wentworth, Jr., Florida State Museum**
330 S Jefferson St. *(850) 595-5985.* *Mon–Fri.* *public hols.* www.historicpensacola.org

**Guides in 19th-century costume in the Historic Pensacola Village**

## Apalachicola ㉓

*3,000.* *Tallahassee.* *122 Commerce St, (850) 653-9419.* www.apalachicolabay.org

A RIVERSIDE CUSTOMS station established in 1823, Apalachicola's first 100 years were its finest. It flourished first with the cotton trade, and later with the lumber boom. Today, pines and hardwoods still stand in the **Apalachicola National Forest**. The area offers hiking trails, canoeing opportunities, and campsites. Oystering in the Apalachicola River began in the 1920s. Oyster boats still pull up at the dockside, and Water Street has many places where fresh oysters are available.

A walking map of the old town, available at the Chamber of Commerce, takes in buildings from the cotton era, such as the 1838 Greek Revival Raney House. The **John Gorrie State Museum** houses a model of Gorrie's patent ice-making machine. Designed to cool yellow fever patients, the doctor's 1851 invention was the vanguard of modern refrigeration and air conditioning.

**Fort Walton Beach** ⑤ A relaxed resort, ideal for family holidays. It is also one of the best beaches for water sports.

**Panama City Beach** ⑨ Condos and amusement parks line buzzing Panama City Beach, the Panhandle's biggest resort. Water sports facilities are excellent here.

Valparaiso
Choctawhatchee Bay
Seaside
Panama City

**Santa Rosa Beach** ⑦, an undeveloped beach, is backed by dunes and marshlands teeming with birds and other wildlife.

**Destin** ⑥ attracts bathers, water sports fans, and deep-sea fishing enthusiasts to its splendid beach.

**Grayton** ⑧ has boardwalks across the dunes, which lead to one of the finest beaches in the country.

**St. Andrews** ⑩ has a superb beach that, unlike Panama City Beach, is well protected against developers.

**The high-rise skyline of downtown Tampa on the Gulf Coast**

## Tampa ㉔

300,000. 601 Nebraska Ave, (800) 872-7245. 610 Polk St, (800) 231-2222. Channelside Dr, (800) 741-2297. 615 Channelside Dr, (813) 223-1111. Gasparilla Festival (Feb). www.visittampabay.com

Situated at the mouth of the Hillsborough River, Tampa is one of Florida's fastest-growing cities. A perfect harbor, Tampa Bay was a magnet to the Spanish, who arrived here in 1539. However, the city's greatest period of prosperity was in the 1800s, when railroad baron Henry Plant extended his railroad here and made it an important center for trade.

Tampa's downtown area is centered around the partly pedestrian Franklin Street, which has the historic Tampa Theater. To its southeast, on North Ashley Drive, is the **Tampa Museum of Art**. This museum's exhibits range from Greek, Roman, and Etruscan antiquities to 20th-century American art.

The luxurious Tampa Bay Hotel, which houses the **Henry B. Plant Museum**, is the city's premier landmark, its Moorish minarets visible from all over the city. Plant commissioned the building in 1891, and its construction alone cost $3 million. Currently a part of the University of Tampa, the south wing has been preserved as a museum. Its splendidly furnished interior retains the original Wedgwood china, Venetian mirrors, and 18th-century French furniture.

The **Florida Aquarium** is on Channelside Drive. It displays a variety of sea creatures such as seabirds, otters, and baby alligators living in tanks that replicate their natural habitats.

Located 3 miles (5 km) east of downtown, **Ybor City** was created by Spaniard Don Vicente Martinez Ybor, when he moved his cigar business from Key West to Tampa in the late 1800s. About 20,000 migrant workers settled here, and the legacy of the cigar boom is still visible on 7th Avenue, with its Spanish tiles and wrought-iron balconies. Today, the area is known for its lively shops, clubs, and restaurants, including the Columbia Restaurant, Florida's oldest establishment.

Northeast of downtown, the **Museum of Science and Industry** features various exhibits including an IMAX® Cinema. The GTE Challenger Learning Center, a living memorial to the Space Shuttle *Challenger*, has simulators and a mission control room.

**Greek vase, Tampa Museum of Art**

Nearby is Tampa's biggest attraction – **Busch Gardens**. This theme park incorporates an unusual zoo that re-creates colonial-era Africa. The zoo supports over 2,600 animals, with giraffes and zebras roaming freely over the "Serengeti Plain." Lions and other African animals can be seen on a unique Edge of Africa safari ride.

### Busch Gardens

Busch Blvd, Tampa. (813) 987-5082. 9:30am–6pm daily, extended hours for summer & hols. www.buschgardens.com

## St. Petersburg ㉕

265,000. 180 9th St North, (727) 898-1496. 100 2nd Ave N, (727) 821-4715. Festival of the States. www.stpete.com

Established in 1875, "St. Pete," as it is often called, was originally a retired person's mecca. Times have changed however, and extensive renovations have rejuvenated the downtown waterfront area.

The city's claim to fame is the prestigious **Salvador Dali Museum**, which has the largest private collection of the Spanish artist's work in the world, worth more than $350 million. It was opened in 1982, 40 years after the Ohio businessman Reynolds Morse first met Dali and began collecting his works. There are 95 oil paintings, 100 watercolors and drawings, 1,300 graphics, sculptures, and other objects. Spanning the years 1914–70, they range from Dali's early figurative paintings to his first experiments in Surrealism, as well as those mature, large-scale paintings described as his "masterworks."

The city's best-known landmark is **The Pier**, which has a string of shops and restaurants. Close by, the **St. Petersburg Museum of History** focuses on the city's history and has exhibits ranging from mastodon bones and native pottery to a replica of the sea plane that made the world's first flight with a paying passenger in 1914.

The modern Palladian-style **Museum of Fine Arts**, near the bay, is famous for its wide-ranging collection of European, American, and Asian works. Supreme among the French Impressionist paintings are *A Corner of the Woods* (1877) by Cézanne and Monet's classic *Parliament, Effect of Fog, London* (1904).

### Salvador Dali Museum

1000 3rd St S. (727) 823-3767. 4, 32, trolley from The Pier. 9:30am–5:30pm Mon–Sat (8pm Thu), noon–5:30pm Sun. Thanksgiving, Dec 25. www.salvadordalimuseum.org

South Lido Park Beach on Lido Key, one Sarasota's off-shore islands

**Environs:** The Gulf Coast's much advertised "361 days of sunshine a year," lures tourists from all over the world to the beaches between St. Petersburg and Clearwater. Known as the Holiday Isles or the Suncoast, the strip encompasses 28 miles (45 km) of barrier island beaches. St. Pete Beach is the busiest, with excellent water sports facilities; the **Fort de Soto Park** beaches have been ranked among the top 10 in the US. Florida's famous sea cows, or manatees, found all along in the coastal waters, are gentle herbivorous giants that grow to a length of 10 ft (3 m). Once plentiful, today only about 2,500 survive.

## Sarasota ㉖

*60,000. 575 N Washington Blvd, (941) 955-5735; Amtrak bus, (800) 872-7245. 655 N Tamiami Trail, (941) 957-1877. Circus Festival (Jan).* W www.sarasotafl.org

Known as Florida's cultural center, Sarasota's affluence is often credited to the millionaire circus owner, John Ringling, who invested much of his fortune, estimated at $200 million, in the area. His legacy is best seen at his house and in his splendid collection of European art, Sarasota's biggest attraction. The **Ringling Museum Complex** comprises the Museum of Art, a colorful Circus Museum, and the Ca' d'Zan – Ringling's winter residence overlooking Sarasota Bay. Ringling had a particular love for Italy, and his fine collection of Italian Baroque paintings are the cornerstone of his collection. The highlight of the Museum of Art is the Rubens Gallery. Also noteworthy are the Astor Rooms, displaying the lavish 19th-century interiors of a New York mansion.

Sarasota has an attractive waterfront setting, and numerous artists and writers have settled here. The restored storefronts in the downtown area around Palm Avenue and Main Street house antique shops, bars, and restaurants.

The nearby barrier islands – Longboat Key, Lido Key, and Siesta Key – have great beaches and excellent tourist accommodations. **South Lido Park Beach** on Lido Key has a lovely woodland trail. The broad **Siesta Key Beach** is always lively, while Turtle Beach is quieter and has the only campsite on these Keys. Longboat Key is well known for its golf courses. Most of the beaches offer excellent water sports facilities.

### Ringling Museum Complex: Ca' d'Zan

The Ca' d'Zan (House of John), modeled after a Venetian palace with Renaissance and Baroque features, is set off by a 200-ft (60-m) marble terrace. Its opulence epitomizes the life of the American super-rich of the early 20th-century.

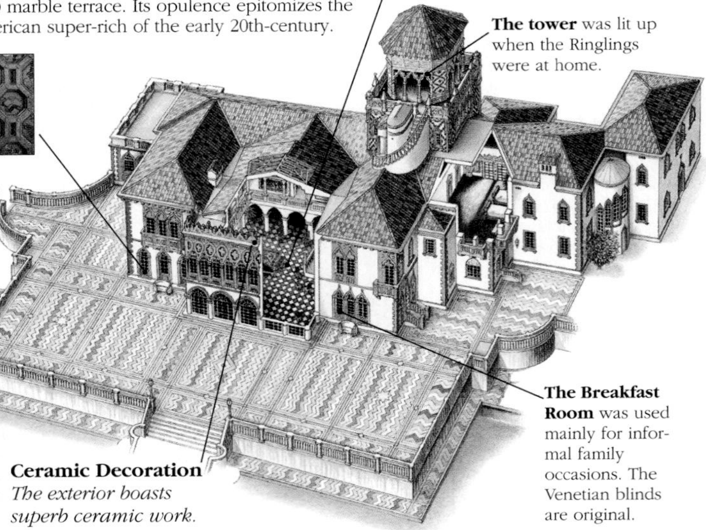

**The court**, with its marble floors and onyx columns, was the living room and the focal point of the house.

**The tower** was lit up when the Ringlings were at home.

**Ballroom**
*The ballroom has a splendid ceiling painting,* Dancers of the Nations.

**The Breakfast Room** was used mainly for informal family occasions. The Venetian blinds are original.

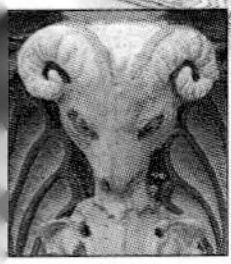

**Ceramic Decoration**
*The exterior boasts superb ceramic work.*

Beachfront cottages on Sanibel Island, Lee Island Coast

## Lee Island Coast 27

2275 Cleveland Ave, Fort Myers, (800) 231-2222. 1159 Causeway Rd, Sanibel, (239) 472-1080. **Boat Services** Tropic Star (239) 283-0015; Captiva Cruises (239) 472-5300; North Captiva Island Club Resort (239) 395-1001.

THIS COASTLINE OFFERS an irresistible combination of sandy beaches, beautiful sunsets, and exotic wildlife. Of the two most popular islands, **Sanibel** has manicured gardens and rows of shops and restaurants along Periwinkle Way, the town's hub. Most of the beaches with public access are along Gulf Drive, the best being Turner and Bowman's beaches.

The **Sanibel Captiva Conservation Foundation** on Sanibel-Captiva Road, protects a chunk of the island's wetland. It has 4 miles (6 km) of boardwalk trails and an observation tower, which is a vantage point for viewing birds. The **JN "Ding" Darling National Wildlife Refuge** occupies two-thirds of Sanibel. Its wildlife includes raccoons, alligators, and birds such as roseate spoonbills, bald eagles, and ospreys. The popular scenic "Wildlife Drive" can be covered by bike or car. Paths and canoe trails are lined with red mangrove and sea grape. Canoes and fishing boats are available for rent.

**Captiva Island**, the other popular island, is less developed. However, visitors can enjoy the ambience of the old-fashioned South Seas Plantation Resort with its busy marina, which is the starting point for boat trips to Cayo Costa Island – a beautiful, untouched barrier island.

Both islands are best known for their shells, and visitors soon get drawn into the shell-collecting culture. Other less developed islands lie close by and can be explored by boat.

**JN "Ding" Darling National Wildlife Refuge**
Mile Marker 2, Sanibel Captiva Rd. (239) 472-1100. Sat–Thu. public hols.

**ENVIRONS: Fort Myers**, about 25 miles (40 km) east of the Lee Island Coast, is an old-fashioned city that was put on the map in the 1880s by one of America's most famous inventors, Thomas Alva Edison (1847–1931). The Edison Winter Home is Fort Myers' most enduring attraction. Edison built his estate in 1886, and the house, laboratory, and botanical gardens are much as he left them. The laboratory contains his original equipment and is still lit by carbon filament light bulbs, which have been in constant use since Edison invented them. The museum displays personal items, phonographs, and a 1916 Model T car that was given to Edison by Henry Ford, his great friend. Next door, the Ford Winter Home has a few early Ford cars on display.

Original equipment in Thomas Edison's laboratory, Fort Myers

The Fort Myers Historical Museum, on Peck Street, is housed in the former railroad station. Interesting exhibits include a model of Fort Myers in the 1900s, and a P-39 bomber that crashed in the 1940s. To the south of the city are a handful of lively beaches

## Big Cypress Swamp 28

**Big Cypress National Preserve** (239) 695-1201. daily. Dec 25. **Fakahatchee Strand Preserve State Park** (239) 695-4593. daily. **Audubon of Florida's Corkscrew Swamp Sanctuary** (239) 348-9151. daily.

HOME TO SEVERAL hundred plants and animals including the endangered Florida panther, this vast, wetland basin features islands of slash pine, prairies, and hardwood hammocks. A third of the swamp is covered by cypress trees growing in long, narrow forests or "strands." The Tamiami Trail (US 41) stretches from Tampa to Miami and cuts directly through the swamp.

**Big Cypress National Preserve** is the swamp's largest protected area. Visitors can stop at the Oasis Visitor Center for information and enjoy the views from US 41. The **Fakahatchee Strand Preserve State Park** lies to the west. The few remaining specimens of old growth cypresses, some of which are 600 years old, are found at Big Cypress Bend. The country's largest cluster of royal palms are also found here. Route 846 leads to **Audubon of Florida's Corkscrew Swamp Sanctuary**, with its old-growth cypresses. It is famous for its birds and is a winter nesting area for endangered wood storks.

## verglades 'ational Park ㉙

daily. all centers open Dec– r: daily; check for rest of year. **nest F. Coe Visitor Center** )5) 242-7700. 8am–4:30pm all ır. **Gulf Coast Visitor Center** erglades City) (239) 695-3311; at tours & canoe rental (239) 695- 91. **Shark Valley Information nter** (305) 221-8776; tram ırs & cycle rental (305) 221-8455. **yal Palm Visitor Center** (305) 2-7700. **Flamingo Visitor Center** (239) 695-2945. For canoe, bicycle ıtal & boat tours, call (239) 695- 01. most boardwalks are acces- le. (800) 365-2267 to book. www.nps.gov/ever

OVERING 1.4 million acres (566,580 ha), the Ever- ıdes National Park makes only a fifth of the world- mous Everglades – low ng wetlands formed from e overspill of Lake Okee- obee. The unique land- ape consists of a vast panse of sawgrass prairie, oken by tree islands, mmocks, and meandering annels. A paradise for ildlife, the park has a wide nge of fauna, including 400 ecies of birds.

The main entrance lies 10 iles (16 km) west of Florida ty. Inside are walking trails, ost of them elevated board- alks; some are suitable for cycles. Boats and canoes n be rented. The best time visit is during winter. South the main entrance lies the formative Royal Palm Visitor enter and two boardwalk ails. The popular **Anhinga rail** attracts wildlife in the y winter months, and its oen site is excellent for otographs. Alligators con- egate at the "gator hole" (a ond that is hollowed out by ligators in the dry season to ach the water below) at the ead of the trail, and a wide nge of fauna, including deer, ccoons, and the splendid ıhinga bird, can be spotted. lose by, the **Gumbo Limbo rail** offers the best chance to xplore a tropical hardwood ammock but is ridden with osquitos. Watch for the etty bromeliads, non-parasitic members of the pineapple family that grow on other plants, and the trail's namesake, the gumbo-limbo tree with its red bark.

A short distance to the west, **Long Key Pine's** campsite is beautifully situated and is one of the main reasons that people stop here. Several shady trails lead off from it: do not stray from the paths as the limestone bed-rock has "solution holes" created by rain, which are deep and difficult to spot.

**Shark Valley** lies north of Long Key Pine, near the park boundary. The area is best visited by taking a tram tour or a bicycle along the 15-mile (25-km) loop road. A 60-ft (18-m) tower at its end offers great views. The valley is home to the Seminole Indians, who settled here in the 19th-century after being driven into the Everglades by land-hungry Europeans *(see p286)*.

The elevated **Pa-hay-okee Overlook** lies northwest of Long Key Pine. The expanse of sawgrass prairie seen from here is typical of the Everglades landscape. The view from the observation tower is worth the climb: tree islands break the horizon, and a multitude of birds, such as hawks, roseate spoonbills, great blue herons, and snail kites, can be easily spotted.

The **Mahogany Hammock Trail** leads through one of the park's largest hammocks, and it has a variety of fauna and flora. Trails such as West Lake Trail and Snake Bight Trail lie between Mahogany Hammock and **Flamingo** on Florida Bay and are especially rich in birdlife. Flamingo has the park's only hotel and also offers a wide choice of activities such as hiking, fishing, boating, and wildlife viewing. An overnight stay at the campsite is a must, especially for bird-watching. The bays around Flamingo have manatees *(see p319)*, as well as the rare, endangered American crocodile. The Flamingo Visitor Center has information about ranger-led activities: talks, slideshows, and walks through the swamp. Canoeing is the best way to explore the watery trails around Flamingo. These range from short trips to a week-long adventure of the remote Wilderness Waterway, leading past Whitewater Bay along the park's western coast. Northwest of Flamingo, the park's western entrance is marked by the island of Chokoloskee.

**Park ranger**

Today, the Everglades are under threat. Irrigation canals have disrupted the flow of water from Lake Okeechobee, which could prove disastrous for this delicate ecosystem.

Visitors should follow a few, simple safety tips. Bring insect repellent and protection against the sun. Follow park rules and respect all wildlife. Note that some shrubs and trees are poisonous, as are some caterpillars, spiders, and snakes. Do not wander off the pathways, and drive slowly because animals often venture onto the road.

**Boardwalk through swamps in the Everglades National Park**

# Biscayne National Park 30

9700 SW 328th St, Convoy Point. Miami. (305) 230-7275. daily. Dec 25. limited. **Boat Tours** (305) 230-1100. www.nps.gov/bisc

DENSE MANGROVE swamp protects the shoreline of Biscayne National Park, which incorporates the northernmost islands of the Florida Keys. Its waters hold the park's greatest draw – a living coral reef with myriad forms and over 200 types of tropical fish. The barrier islands are unoccupied, so the coral here is healthier and the water even clearer than in the more popular parks farther south. Activities include glass-bottomed boat tours, snorkeling, and diving – all arranged by the visitor center.

# The Keys 31

Miami.

RUNNING SOUTHWEST off the tip of the Florida peninsula are the Keys, a chain of fossilized coral islands protected by North America's only coral reef. Visitors flock to the resorts here to enjoy several activities ranging from fishing to snorkeling.

From the 1500s, the Keys lured a succession of settlers, pirates, and "wreckers." Its development, however, took off in the early 1900s, when rail baron Henry Flagler *(see p286)* constructed the Overseas Railroad across the Keys. It has since been replaced by the magnificent Overseas Highway, which ends at Key West.

**Bahia Honda's beautiful beach, the finest in the Florida Keys**

The largest island in the Upper Keys is **Key Largo**, named "long island" by Spanish explorers. One of its highlights is the *African Queen*, the boat used in the eponymous 1951 film, which makes short pleasure trips. The island's greatest draws, however, are the diving and snorkeling opportunities just offshore in the **John Pennekamp Coral Reef State Park**. The park has a visitor center, swimming areas, and woodland trails, but it is best known for its fabulous underwater reaches, which provide a glimpse of the extraordinary forms of coral reef life.

**Islamorada**, south of Key Largo, declares itself as the "Sport Fishing Capital of the World." Encompassing seven islands, it is known for its outstanding big game fishing. The Whale Harbor Marina on Upper Matecumbe Key bristles with impressive deep sea charter craft, used to catch blue-water fish. Fishing boats, based here, offer half-day trips, even if visitors are not expert anglers.

**Gold ornament from a treasure ship**

Long Key Bridge marks the beginning of the Middle Keys. The **Dolphin Research Center**, a nonprofit concern on Grassy Key, conducts the delightful "Dolphin Encounter," where one can swim with these endearing marine mammals. It is also a rest home for sick and injured dolphins.

The heavily developed **Marathon Key** is the main center of the Middle Keys. Its primary appeal lies in fertile fishing grounds, and enthusiasts can choose from a range of angling techniques, including spear-fishing and line-fishing. Crane Point Hammock has 64 acres (26 ha) of tropical forest and mangroves, and several trails, while the **Museum of Natural History of the Florida Keys** explains the islands' history, geology, and ecology.

The Lower Keys are more rugged and less developed than the Upper and Middle Keys. The vegetation is more wooded and supports a different flora and fauna. The most striking change, however, is in the slow and languid pace of life.

After crossing the Seven Mile Bridge, visitors can head for the **Bahia Honda State Park**, which has the finest beach in the Keys. Brilliant

## FISHING IN THE FLORIDA KEYS

**Deep-sea fishing from a sports boat**

Islamorada, Marathon, and Key West are the area's major fishing centers, and small marinas throughout the region offer boats for rent. There are options to suit most budgets and abilities, and one can book places on fishing party boats or hire guides. Deep-sea fishing, an exhilarating option, appeals to the Hemingway spirit of the angler, while backcountry fishing calls for stealth and cunning. The numerous bait and tackle shops rent out gear and sell licenses.

hite sand is backed by opical forest, with unusual ecies of trees, such as silver alm and yellow satinwood. anoes, kayaks, and water orts gear are available to nt. The adjacent **Looe Key ational Marine Sanctuary** a spectacular dive location, ith abundant marine life.

The second largest island, **g Pine Key** is the Lower eys' main residential com-unity and the best place to e the diminutive Key deer. he turning near MM 30 leads the **Blue Hole**, a flooded uarry whose viewing plat-orm is ideal for watching the eer and other wildlife.

**ey Largo**
*MM 106, (305) 451-1414, (800) 2-1088.* www.fla-key.com

**John Pennekamp Coral eef State Park**
M 102.5. *(305) 451-1202.* *daily.* *limited.*

## Key West 32

*28,000.* *402 Wall (305) 294-2587.*

THE SOUTHERNMOST settle-ment in the US, Key West a magnet for people who ant to leave the rest of merica behind. In the 16th entury, it became a haven r pirates and "wreckers." Wrecking," or the salvage of ipwrecks on the Keys' coral ef, was the business that rst made Key West rich. soon became Florida's ealthiest city, and its oppor-tunistic lifestyle attracted a stream of settlers from the Americas, the Caribbean, and Europe; their legacy is visible in the island's unique archi-tecture and cuisine. An influx of writers and a large gay community in recent years have added to Key West's cultural cocktail.

Most of the sights are within a few blocks of **Duval Street**, the main axis of Old Key West. Bylanes, such as Fleming Street, have many fine 19th-century wooden buildings, which contrast with the simple homes erected to house Cuban cigar-workers.

The **Wreckers' Museum** on Duval Street was originally the home of the wreck cap-tain Francis B. Watlington. Built in 1829, its design displays some eccentric maritime influences, such as a hatch used for ventilation in the roof. It is stuffed with nautical bric-a-brac. Farther down, the **San Carlos Institute**, founded in 1871, is a Cuban heritage center. The garden of **Heritage House Museum**, on Caroline Street, has the Robert Frost cottage, named after the famous American poet who fre-quently stayed here. At the northern edge of the Old Town is **Mallory Square**, which comes to life at sunset, when a variety of performing artists amuse the crowds.

The **Bahama Village** on the western fringe of the Old Town is named after Key West's earliest settlers. It has a lively Caribbean flavor with a number of brightly painted clapboard buildings.

A prime attraction is the Spanish-colonial style **Hemingway Home**, where novelist Ernest Hemingway lived from 1931 to 1940. The room where he penned several of his most famous works, such as *To Have and Have Not* (the only book set in Key West), is above the carriage house. His library, travel mementos, and memo-rabilia, such as the cigar-maker's chair on which he sat and wrote, are on display.

The **Mel Fisher Maritime Museum** on Green Street, displays fabulous shipwreck treasures such as coins, jewels, and crucifixes. These were salvaged by the late Mel Fisher, who discov-ered the wrecks of the Spanish galleons *Nuestra Señora de Atocha* and *Santa Margarita*, about 40 miles (64 km) west of Key West, in 1985. Inside were 47 tons of gold and silver bars, and 70 lbs (32 kg) of raw emeralds that sank with the galleons in 1622.

**Diver's helmet, Mel Fisher Museum**

The **Conch Train** and **the Old Town Trolley Tour** are convenient options for exploring the town.

**Hemingway Home**
907 Whitehead St. *(305) 294-1136.* *daily.* *limited.*
www.hemingwayhome.com

### FLORIDA'S CORAL REEF

North America's only live coral reef extends 200 miles (320 km) along the length of the Keys, from Miami to the Dry Tortugas. A complex and delicate ecosystem, it protects these islands from oceanic storms. Coral reefs are created over thousands of years by tiny marine organisms known as polyps and are home to a multitude of plants and sea creatures, including 500 species of fish.

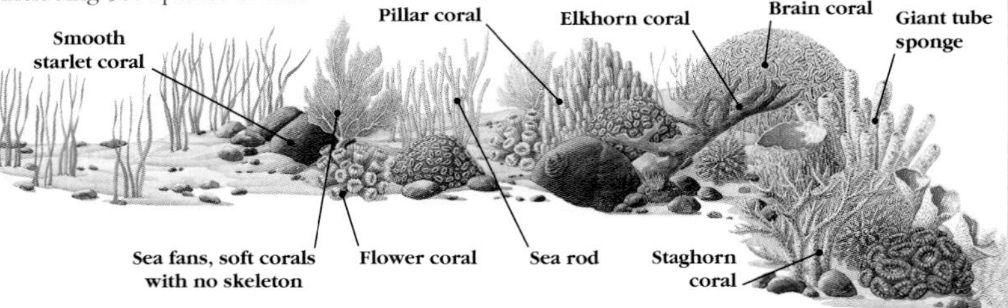

# Practical Information

WITH OVER 40 MILLION VISITORS a year, Florida is very well geared for catering to tourists' needs. It is the ultimate family vacation destination. A strong emphasis is placed on entertaining children, and the superb facilities available, make traveling with youngsters a real pleasure. Given its warm climate, Florida is a winter destination for many Americans. The peak season runs from December to April, when the beaches and other attractions are at their busiest. Anyone visiting Walt Disney World or other theme parks should be prepared for long lines during the peak season.

## TOURIST INFORMATION

MOST LARGE CITIES in Florida have a Convention and Visitor's Bureau (CVB), offering a huge array of brochures. Most hotels also have a brochure rack or free "WHERE" magazines that list museums, entertainment, shopping, and dining. To get information before you leave home, call or write for a vacation pack, issued by the Florida Tourism group.

## SECURITY & HEALTH

THOUGH CRIMES against tourists have fallen since the 1990s, it is best to be take precautions in urban areas, especially in Miami. Avoid deserted neighborhoods at night. Carry as little money as possible, and leave valuables at home or check them at the hotel reception desk (it is best not to leave valuables in your hotel room). If attacked, hand over your wallet at once, and do not try to resist. In case of a serious illness or accident, hospitals provide good treatment. Minor ailments can be treated at the 24-hour walk-in clinics. Medical care is expensive, so be sure your insurance documents are up-to-date. In an emergency dial 911, or you can contact **Metro-Dade Police Information**.

## NATURAL HAZARDS

HURRICANES ARE infrequent but devastating when they do occur. If a storm is imminent follow the announcements on local television and radio. The **National Hurricane Center** in Miami gives details on impending hurricanes. On beaches, keep an eye on children as riptides are a danger in some places.

The worst climatic hazard is the sun. Use sunscreen, wear hats, and drink plenty of fluids to avoid dehydration.

Alligators are a thrilling sight in the Everglades but they ca and do kill, so treat them wi respect. Look out for spiders scorpions, and venomous snakes native to Florida. It is best not to touch unfamiliar vegetation. Wear insect repellent when visiting parks and nature preserves.

## DRIVING IN FLORIDA

DRIVING IN FLORIDA is a delight because of its excellent road network, inexpensive gasoline, and affordable car rentals. The fastest routes are the six-lane Interstate Highways, referred to as I-10, I-75, and so on. Be warned that local drivers change lanes frequently on expressways, so stick to the right and be alert near exits. Speed limits can vary within a few miles, from 55–70 mph (90–105 km/h) on highways, to 20–30 mph (32–48 km/h) in residential areas, and 15 mph (24 km/h) near schools Speed limits are rigorously enforced, and fines can be as much as $150.

In the event of a serious breakdown, call the emergency number on the rental agreement and the agency will provide a new vehicle. The **American Automobile Association (AAA)** also has its own breakdown service and will assist its members.

Miami has had a bad reputation for crimes against motorists, but be careful in other areas as well. Avoid driving in unfamiliar territory after dark. If you have to refe to a map, stop only when yo are in a well-lit area. Ignore any attempt by anyone to stop you from driving.

## ETIQUETTE

DRESS IN FLORIDA is mostly casual, but it is illegal fo women to go topless on beaches, except in a few places, such as Miami's Soutl Beach. Drinking alcohol on beaches and in other public places is illegal, as is smoking in buses, trains, taxis, and in most public buildings. All restaurants and cafés are no-smoking in Florida.

## THE CLIMATE OF FLORIDA

With its warm climate, Florida is a year-round destination. Its climatic divide between the temperate north and the subtropical south means that the state has two distinct tourist seaons. In south Florida (including Orlando), the busiest time is when tourists come to enjoy the mild winters. Here the summers can be uncomfortably hot. In the north, the Panhandle attracts most visitors in the summer. Despite this difference, the Sunshine State by and large lives up to its reputation of clear, blue skies and a pleasant climate.

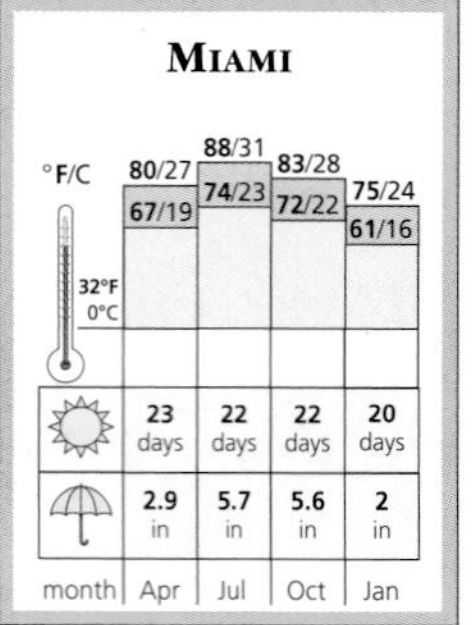

## Sports & Outdoor Activities

Florida's climate makes the state a top destination for all sports enthusiasts, from golfers and tennis players to canoeists and deep-sea divers. The best sources of information on outdoor activities are the **Florida Sports Foundation** and the **Department of Environmental Protection (DEP)**.

Water sports of all kinds are well represented, with wonderful beaches on both the Atlantic and Gulf coasts. Most resorts offer the full range from windsurfing to jetskiing. Water-skiing can also be enjoyed on lakes and inland waterways. The state provides ample opportunities for canoeing as well, with the Wilderness Waterway in the Everglades National Park being a favorite run.

Florida has superb diving and snorkeling sports. The country's only living coral reef skirts the state's southeast coast, stretching the length of the Keys. Excellent guided snorkeling trips are available to view the coast's coral and fish. For information on diving, contact the **Keys Association of Dive Operators**.

Fishing off the pier is popular at coastal spots, but the state is best known for its sport fishing. Deep-sea fishing boats can be chartered at seaside resorts; the biggest fleets are in the Panhandle and the Keys. Many rivers and parks offer freshwater fishing. The **Florida Game and Fresh Water Fish Commission** provides details on lcations and licensing costs.

Outdoor adventure tours to wilder areas, such as the Everglades, are organized by some companies, including **Build a Field Trip**.

## Entertainment

Whether your preference is for a Broadway drama, a lavish Las Vegas-style floorshow, or a small cruise, Florida has something for everyone. **Walt Disney World® Resort**, **Universal Orlando** and other attractions offer the best in family entertainment, with theme parks galore to thrill children during the day and dinner shows at night. Here, meals are served, generally themed to the show you are watching. Water parks, throughout Florida, are also big draws.

Lavish road shows are the highest-quality productions in Florida. The state has its own theater groups, orchestras, and opera companies, such as the the **Symphony of the Americas** and the **Florida Grand Opera**. Some of the best places to dance are clubs offering live and varied music. Nightclubs require an ID to prove that you are over 18.

Florida is the world's leading departure point for cruises to the Caribbean. You can also go on mini-cruises, for a day or just an evening, for around $40. Evening cruises usually entail dinner and dancing; casino cruises, operating out of Miami and Port Everglades, are the new rage. Fort Lauderdale and St. Petersburg also have popular tour boats.

## Shopping

Shopping is also a very popular pastime in Florida, with Miami attracting many overseas shoppers. Although the state has some very upscale stores, often clustered in shopping districts such as the exclusive Worth Avenue on Palm Beach, it is best known for its discount stores. If searching for gifts or souvenirs, the theme parks and seaside tourist centers offer a vast choice. Florida is also famed for its citrus fruit, which you can buy fresh or preserved as colorful candies and jellies. Other buys include seashells, Seminole crafts, Latin music, and hand-rolled cigars.

## Directory

### Tourist Information

(888) 735-2872.
www.visitflorida.com

### Emergency Numbers

**All Emergencies**
*911 to alert police, fire, or medical services.*

**Miami-Dade Police Information**
*(305) 595-6263.*

**National Hurricane Center**
*(305) 229-4470, recorded message with hurricane details.*

**American Automobile Assn. (AAA)**
*(407) 444-7000.*

**AAA General Breakdown Assistance**
*(800) 222-4357.*
*NOTE: Rentals also provide 24-hour assistance.*

### Sports

**Department of Environmental Protection (DEP)**
3900 Commonwealth Blvd, Tallahassee, FL 32399.
*(850) 245-2052.*

**Florida Sports Foundation**
Tallahassee, FL 32308.
*(850) 488-8347.*
www.flasports.com

### Backcountry Pursuits

**Build a Field Trip**
Fort Lauderdale, FL 33308.
*(954) 772-7800.*

### Fishing

**Florida Fish & Wildlife Conservation Commission**
*(850) 488-4676.*
*(888) 347-4356 (fishing licenses).*
www.state.fl.us/fwc

### Diving & Snorkeling

**Keys Association of Dive Operators (KADO)**
www.divekeys.com

### Entertainment

**Florida Grand Opera**
1200 Coral Way, Miami.
*(305) 854-7890.*

**Symphony of the Americas**
199 N Ocean Blvd, Pompano Beach.
*(954) 545-0088.*

**Universal Orlando**
*(407) 363-8000.*
www.universalorlando.com

**Walt Disney World® Resort**
*(407) 934-7639 (for reservations).*
www.disneyworld.com

# Where to Stay

FLORIDA HAS A HUGE VARIETY of places to stay suitable for all budgets and tastes – from rustic wooden cabins with minimal facilities to luxurious resort hotels that cater to their guests' every need. In between, visitors can choose from ordinary hotels, more charming B&Bs, convenient motels, or fully equipped apartments.

## MIAMI

**MIAMI BEACH:** *Clay Hotel & International Hostel* $$
1438 Washington Ave, FL 33139. *(305) 534-2988.* FAX *(305) 673-0346.*
Booking is essential for this youth hostel, in a lovely Spanish Revival building. Unbeatably cheap for such a prime location. ***Beds:*** *220.*

**MIAMI BEACH:** *Brigham Gardens* $$$
1411 Collins Ave, FL 33139. *(305) 531-1331.* FAX *(305) 534-0341.*
W www.brighamgardens.com
Two 1930s buildings and a gorgeous garden. The rooms are decorated with a Deco mix of color and art. ***Rooms:*** *23.*

**MIAMI BEACH:** *Delano* $$$$$
1685 Collins Ave, FL 33139. *(305) 672-2000.* FAX *(305) 532-0099.*
W www.morganshotelgroup.com SoBe's best hotel – where staff dress in white to match the gorgeous, if stark, rooms. 24 P ***Rooms:*** *195.*

**MIAMI BEACH:** *Fontainebleau Hilton Resort* $$$$$
4441 Collins Ave, FL 33140. *(305) 538-2000.* FAX *(305) 673-5351.* W www.hilton.com
Miami Beach's most prestigious resort has every amenity imaginable, from children's activities to the famous Tropigala floor show. 24 P ***Rooms:*** *920.*

**DOWNTOWN:** *Courtyard By Marriott* $$$
200 SE 2nd Ave, FL 33131. *(305) 374-3000.* W www.marriott.com/miadt
This mid-priced hotel offers good value for money. Recently renovated, it is well located in the heart of downtown. P ***Rooms:*** *238.*

**CORAL GABLES:** *The Biltmore Hotel* $$$$$
1200 Anastasia Ave, FL 33134. *(305) 445-1926.* FAX *(305) 913-3159.*
W www.biltmorehotel.com
Rich in history (Al Capone gambled here in the 1920s), the grande dame of Miami's hotels will pamper you with every modern amenity in opulent, antique-filled suites. 24 P ***Rooms:*** *280.*

**COCONUT GROVE:** *Wyndham Grand Bay* $$$$$
2669 S Bayshore Drive, FL 33133. *(800) 327-2788, (305) 858-9600.*
FAX *(305) 859-2026.* W www.wyndham.com
Among the world's finest hotels, with crystal chandeliers, designer furnishings, and original art. Pavarotti's suite can be rented when he's not in residence. P ***Rooms:*** *177.*

**GREATER MIAMI:** *Ritz Carlton* $$$$$
455 Grand Bay Drive, Key Biscayne, FL 33149. *(305) 365-4500.*
FAX *(305) 365-4501.* W www.ritzcarlton.com/keybiscayne
With a Colonial-styled decor inspired by the West Indies, this hotel has all the amenities you would expect from what is possibly the finest hotel in Florida. 24 P ***Rooms:*** *402.*

## THE GOLD & TREASURE COASTS

**BOCA RATON:** *Boca Raton Resort & Club* $$$$$
501 E Camino Real, FL 33431. *(561) 395-3000.* FAX *(561) 447-3183.*
W www.bocaresort.com
The most chic and pretentious place in town, this Spanish-style hotel offers rooms in a choice of décor. 24 P ***Rooms:*** *1,056.*

**FORT LAUDERDALE:** *Westin Diplomat Resort & Spa* $$$$
3555 South Ocean Drive, Hollywood, FL 33019. *(954) 602-6000.* FAX *(954) 602-8275.*
W www.diplomatresort.com Located right on the beach in Hollywood, just outside Fort Lauderdale. There are great restaurants, ocean views, a spa, golf, tennis and, of course, an enormous pool. 24 P ***Rooms:*** *900.*

| Hotel | Credit Cards | Children's Facilities | Swimming Pool | Good Restaurant | Kitchen Facilities |
|---|---|---|---|---|---|
| Clay Hotel & International Hostel | ■ | | | | |
| Brigham Gardens | ■ | | | | ■ |
| Delano | ■ | ● | ■ | ● | |
| Fontainebleau Hilton Resort | ■ | ● | ■ | ● | |
| Courtyard By Marriott | ■ | | ■ | | |
| The Biltmore Hotel | ■ | ● | ■ | ● | |
| Wyndham Grand Bay | ■ | ● | ■ | ● | |
| Ritz Carlton | ■ | ● | ■ | ● | |
| Boca Raton Resort & Club | ■ | ● | ■ | ● | ■ |
| Westin Diplomat Resort & Spa | ■ | ● | ■ | ● | |

**Price categories** for a standard double room per night in high season, including tax and service charges:
- $ under $60
- $$ $60-$100
- $$$ $100-$150
- $$$$ $150-$200
- $$$$$ over $200

**CREDIT CARDS**
Major credit cards accepted.
**CHILDREN'S FACILITIES**
Cribs, high chairs, and other facilities for young children.
**SWIMMING POOL**
The hotel has a swimming pool for use by residents.
**GOOD RESTAURANT**
Good restaurant, normally also accessible to nonresidents.
**KITCHEN FACILITIES**
The hotel has some rooms equipped with cooking and other kitchen facilities, usually known as "efficiencies."

| Hotel | Credit Cards | Children's Facilities | Swimming Pool | Good Restaurant | Kitchen Facilities |
|---|---|---|---|---|---|
| **PALM BEACH:** *Plaza Inn* $$$$$<br>215 Brazilian Ave, FL 33480. *(561) 832-8666.* FAX *(561) 835-8776.*<br>W www.plazainnpalmbeach.com<br>This Deco gem has four-poster beds, hand-crocheted spreads, and cooked-to-order breakfasts. ***Rooms:*** *50.* | ■ | ● | ■ | | |
| **PALM BEACH:** *The Breakers* $$$$$<br>1 South County Rd, FL 33480. *(561) 655-6611.* FAX *(561) 655-8403.*<br>W www.thebreakers.com<br>Sumptuous and classy, this "Italian palace" is Palm Beach's finest hotel. It offers excellent children's facilities. 24 P ***Rooms:*** *569.* | ■ | ● | ■ | ● | |
| **ORLANDO & THE SPACE COAST** | | | | | |
| **CAPE CANAVERAL:** *Radisson Resort at the Port* $$$<br>8701 Astronaut Blvd, FL 32920. *(321) 784-0000.* FAX *(321) 784-3737.*<br>W www.radisson.com<br>Ceiling fans and wicker give this resort a Caribbean feel. Ten minutes' drive from the Kennedy Space Center. ***Rooms:*** *285.* | ■ | ● | ■ | ● | |
| **COCOA BEACH:** *Inn at Cocoa Beach* $$$$<br>4300 Ocean Beach Blvd, FL 32931. *(321) 799-3460.* FAX *(321) 784-8632.*<br>W www.theinnatcocoabeach.com<br>Patios and balconies give ocean views at this B&B. The decor ranges from modern to traditional. ***Rooms:*** *50.* | ■ | | ■ | | |
| **DOWNTOWN ORLANDO:** *The Courtyard at Lake Lucerne* $$$<br>211 N Lucerne Circle E, FL 32801. *(407) 648-5188.* FAX *(407) 246-1368.*<br>W www.orlandohistoricinn.com<br>This well-run B&B in a quiet garden beside Lake Lucerne comprises four historic houses. ***Rooms:*** *30.* | ■ | | | | ■ |
| **DOWNTOWN ORLANDO:** *Radisson Plaza Hotel Orlando* $$$<br>60 S Ivanhoe Blvd, FL 32804. *(407) 425-4455.* FAX *(407) 425-7440.*<br>W www.radissonorlando.com<br>Located near the entrance to Universal Orlando *(see p308)*, it also has good facilities for business travelers. ***Rooms:*** *250.* | ■ | | ■ | ● | |
| **INTERNATIONAL DRIVE:** *The I Drive Inn* $$$<br>6323 International Drive, FL 32819. *(407) 351-4430.* FAX *(407) 345-0742.*<br>Close to Walt Disney World, the Inn is geared to children. They stay and eat for free and enjoy a special "comedy zone." ***Rooms:*** *218.* | ■ | ● | ■ | | ■ |
| **WALT DISNEY WORLD:** *Seralago Hotel & Suites* $$$<br>5678 W Irlo Bronson Hwy, FL 34746. *(407) 396-4488.* FAX *(407) 396-1296.*<br>Children rule here – there is even a kids' check-in desk. Clowns make up rooms and lead activities at a nearby children's camp. ***Rooms:*** *614.* | ■ | ● | ■ | | ■ |
| **WALT DISNEY WORLD:** *Disney's Caribbean Beach Resort* $$$$<br>900 Cayman Way, FL 32830. *(407) 934-3400.* FAX *(407) 934-3288.*<br>Five cheerful "villages" with attractive rooms are situated around a lake where water birds congregate. ***Rooms:*** *2,112.* | ■ | ● | ■ | | |
| **WALT DISNEY WORLD:** *Disney's Beach Club Resort* $$$$$<br>1800 Epcot Resorts Blvd, FL 32830. *(407) 934-8000.* FAX *(407) 934-3850.*<br>Echoing the style of New England's grand hotels of the 1870s, this lavish resort has exquisite rooms, and one of the best restaurants in the area. P ***Rooms:*** *621.* | ■ | ● | ■ | ● | |
| **WALT DISNEY WORLD:** *Disney's Wilderness Lodge* $$$$$<br>901 Timberline Drive, FL 32830. *(407) 824-3200.* FAX *(407) 824-3232.*<br>Wind down at this isolated but romantic "mountain retreat" with wooden floors and crackling fires. P ***Rooms:*** *728.* | ■ | ● | ■ | ● | |

**Price categories** for a standard double room per night in high season, including tax and service charges:
$ under $60
$$ $60-$100
$$$ $100-$150
$$$$ $150-$200
$$$$$ over $200

**CREDIT CARDS**
Major credit cards accepted.
**CHILDREN'S FACILITIES**
Cribs, high chairs, and other facilities for young children.
**SWIMMING POOL**
The hotel has a swimming pool for use by residents.
**GOOD RESTAURANT**
Good restaurant, normally also accessible to nonresidents.
**KITCHEN FACILITIES**
The hotel has some rooms equipped with cooking and other kitchen facilities, usually known as "efficiencies."

**WALT DISNEY WORLD:** *Disney's Yacht Club Resort* $$$$$
1700 Epcot Resorts Blvd, FL 32830. *(407) 934-7000.* FAX *(407) 934-3450.*
Styled like a posh Cape Cod yacht club, with brass fittings and charts on the walls, this lavish resort shares its wide range of facilities with the adjacent Beach Club. 24 P ***Rooms:** 630.*

**WALT DISNEY WORLD:** *Walt Disney World Dolphin* $$$$$
1500 Epcot Resorts Blvd, FL 32830. *(407) 934-4000.* FAX *(407) 934-4888.*
Close to Epcot and architecturally arresting, the urbane Dolphin caters to a business crowd. 24 P ***Rooms:** 1,510.*

## THE NORTHEAST

**DAYTONA BEACH:** *Inn on the Beach* $$
1615 S Atlantic Ave, FL 32118. *(386) 255-0921.* FAX *(386) 255-3849.*
This budget oceanfront hotel has spacious efficiencies, a sundeck, and both full-sized and kids' swimming pools. ***Rooms:** 195.*

**FERNANDINA BEACH:** *Amelia Island Plantation* $$$$$
3000 First Coast Hwy, FL 32034. *(904) 261-6161.* FAX *(904) 277-5159.*
W www.AIPFL.com At the southern end of Amelia Island surrounded by live oak trees and huge dunes, this golf resort has spacious rooms, condos, and villas. 24 P ***Rooms:** 680.*

**FERNANDINA BEACH:** *Amelia Island Williams House* $$$$$
103 S 9th St, FL 32034. *(904) 277-2328.* FAX *(904) 321-1325.*
Rated one of the South's best B&Bs, this 1856 mansion has exquisite rooms with clawfoot baths. Priceless antiques range from 16th-century Japanese prints to a carpet owned by Napoleon. ***Rooms:** 8.*

**ST. AUGUSTINE:** *Casa De Suenos* $$$$
20 Cordova St, FL 32084. *(800) 824-0804.* W www.casadesuenos.com
This re-converted home is located in the heart of Old Town and is in walking distance to shops and restaurants. Beautifully furnished, there's a hot breakfast in the morning and a social hour every afternoon. P ***Rooms:** 5.*

## THE PANHANDLE

**APALACHICOLA:** *Coombs House Inn* $$$$
80 6th St, FL 32320. *(850) 653-9199.* FAX *(850) 653-2785.*
W www.coombshouseinn.com
In two 1900s clapboard homes, this B&B offers lovely antiques and full, sumptuous breakfasts. The inn also provides rental bikes for exploring the surroundings. ***Rooms:** 19.*

**FORT WALTON BEACH:** *The Four Points Hotel* $$$$
1325 Miracle Strip Parkway, FL 32548. *(850) 243-8116.* FAX *(850) 244-3064.*
W www.sheraton4pts.com
The Four Points Hotel has large, brightly decorated rooms, many with views of the Gulf. Some rooms are right on the beach. ***Rooms:** 216.*

**PANAMA CITY BEACH:** *Edgewater Beach Resort* $$$$$
11212 Front Beach Rd, FL 32407. *(800) 874-8686.* FAX *(850) 235-6899.*
W www.edgewaterbeachresort.com This lavish seaside resort offers condos with one, two, or three bedrooms. The resort is particularly known for its extensive recreational facilities. 24 ***Rooms:** 520.*

**PENSACOLA BEACH:** *Hilton Garden Inn* $$$$$
12 Via Luna Drive, FL 32561. *(850) 916-2999.* FAX *(850) 934-0891.*
W www.hiltongardeninn.com
Right on the beach with rooms overlooking the Gulf, the hilton is also located close to water sports, shopping and nightlife. ***Rooms:** 181.*

| Hotel | Credit Cards | Children's Facilities | Swimming Pool | Good Restaurant | Kitchen Facilities |
|---|---|---|---|---|---|
| Disney's Yacht Club Resort | ■ | ● | ■ | ● | |
| Walt Disney World Dolphin | ■ | ● | ■ | ● | ■ |
| Inn on the Beach | ■ | ● | ■ | ● | ■ |
| Amelia Island Plantation | ■ | ● | ■ | ● | ■ |
| Amelia Island Williams House | ■ | | | | |
| Casa De Suenos | ■ | | | | |
| Coombs House Inn | ■ | ● | | | ■ |
| The Four Points Hotel | ■ | | ■ | ● | ■ |
| Edgewater Beach Resort | ■ | ● | ■ | ● | ■ |
| Hilton Garden Inn | ■ | ● | ■ | ● | |

**ALLAHASSEE:** *Radisson Hotel* $$$$
5 N Monroe St, FL 32301. (850) 224-6000. FAX (850) 222-0335.
www.radisson.com This elegant, cheerful hotel provides complimentary ·port transportation to the downtown area. **Rooms:** 119.

**ALLAHASSEE:** *Ramada Inn North* $$$
00 N Monroe St, FL 32303. (850) 386-1027. FAX (850) 224-0472.
] www.ramada.com Just a short drive from downtown, this efficiently run ›tel provides spacious and comfortable rooms. **Rooms:** 200.

## THE GULF COAST

**ORT MYERS:** *Ramada Inn* $$$$
00 Edwards Drive, FL 33901. (800) 833-1620. FAX (239) 337-1530.
www.ramada.com
ıis fancy high-rise has fine views of the yacht basin and river. ›wntown sights are just a short walk away. **Rooms:** 419.

**. PETERSBURG:** *Inn at the Bay Bed & Breakfast* $$$
6 4th Ave NE, FL 33701. (888) 873-2122. W www.innatthebay.com
ıis romantic inn, with period furnishings and whirpool spas in almost ery room, also offers high-speed internet access. **Rooms:** 12.

**. PETERSBURG:** *Renaissance Vinoy Resort & Golf Club* $$$$$
1 5th Ave NE, FL 33701. (727) 894-1000. FAX (727) 822-2785.
www.renaissancehotels.com Dating from 1925, this elegantly restored ·tel offers lovely bay views. Most downtown attractions are within ılking distance. **Rooms:** 360.

**NIBEL ISLAND:** *Sanibel Harbor Resort & Spa* $$$$$
260 Harbour Point Drive, FL 33957. (239) 466-4000, (800) 767-7777.
www.sanibel-resort.com
ıis world-class resort is one of the best in the area. Choose from a ıge of accommodation – suites, condos or hotel rooms. The restaurant outstanding. 24 **Rooms:** 400.

**RASOTA:** *Best Western Golden Host Resort* $$$
75 N Tamiami Trail, FL 34234. (941) 355-5141. FAX (941) 355-9286.
.e resort is set in lovely tropical grounds, close to local attractions and e beach. Breakfast is included. **Rooms:** 80.

**MPA:** *Days Inn Airport Stadium* $$$
22 N Dale Mabry Hwy, FL 33607. (813) 877-6181. FAX (813) 875-6171.
cated between downtown and the airport, this motel offers mfortable rooms. Breakfast is included. **Rooms:** 296.

**MPA:** *Wyndham Harbour Island Hotel* $$$$$
5 S Harbour Island Blvd, FL 33602. (813) 229-5000. FAX (813) 229-5322.
ı an island overlooking the river mouth, this exclusive hotel is linked to ›wntown Tampa by the Peoplemover. **Rooms:** 300.

## THE EVERGLADES & THE KEYS

**EY LARGO:** *Kona Kai Resort & Gallery* $$$$$
802 Overseas Hwy, FL 33037. (305) 852-7200. FAX (305) 852-4629.
cluded with its own beachfront. It also has a superb collection of ›dern European art. **Rooms:** 12.

**EY WEST:** *Key West Youth Hostel* $
8 South St, FL 33040. (305) 296-5719. FAX (305) 296-0672.
www.keywesthostel.com At this simple but well-maintained hostel, the smopolitan backpacking crowd have the use of pool tables. Rental cycles are available to explore the area. **Beds:** 92.

**EY WEST:** *Wicker Guesthouse* $$$$
3 Duval St, FL 33040. (305) 296-4275. W www.wickerhousekw.com
is is a friendly complex of new as well as restored houses in the historic trict and has a wide range of rooms and spacious suites. **Rooms:** 18.

**EY WEST:** *Curry Mansion Inn* $$$$$
1 Caroline St, FL 33040. (305) 294-5349. FAX (305) 294-4093.
www.currymansion.com
is historic house, just off Duval Street, is also a museum. Most rooms : in a lovely annex and very comfortable. **Rooms:** 28.

# Where to Eat

The joy of Florida is the abundant fresh produce, from tropical fruit to seafood, which all restaurants use to great effect. Restaurants cater to every palate and budget, from the trendy establishments in Miami to simpler places in the interior, where food tends to be more homey. In the listings below, "L" indicates lunch and "D" stands for dinner.

## Miami

**Miami Beach:** *Nexxt* $$$
700 Lincoln Rd. (305) 532-6643.
An encyclopedic menu, an eclectic mix, and outside tables in this cafeteria-style eatery make this spot your best bet for a quick, cheap meal.

**Miami Beach:** *Joe's Stone Crab* $$$$
11 Washington Ave. (305) 673-0365.
This Miami institution is a must. There's lobster, shrimp, and fish as well as the signature stone crab claws. No reservations are required. *Mon L, May–Oct.*

**Miami Beach:** *The Forge* $$$$$
432 41st St. (305) 538-8533.
Celebrities abound at this Miami Beach landmark. Its glitzy decor has opulent American cuisine to match. *L.*

**Miami Beach:** *Tuscan Steak* $$$$$
433 Washington Ave. (305) 534-2233.
One of Miami Beach's best. A flashy crowd goes for the giant antipasto, the T-bone with garlic puree, and the pricey drinks.

**Downtown:** *Big Fish* $$$$
55 SW Miami Ave. (305) 373-1770.
An unassuming seafood restaurant on the shore of the Miami River. It offers a great view of the skyline and some of the freshest fish in town.

**Little Havana:** *Casa Juancho* $$$$
2436 SW 8th St. (305) 642-2452.
Deservedly famous for its superlative Spanish cuisine, this restaurant is very popular with Miami's Hispanic community. The decor evokes rural Spain, and troubadors entertain in the evenings.

**Coral Gables:** *Christy's* $$$$
3101 Ponce de Leon Blvd. (305) 446-1400.
A very popular steak house featuring succulent beef and seafood in a club-like setting. A tasty Caesar salad accompanies each entrée. *Sat–Sun L.*

**Coconut Grove:** *Señor Frog's* $$$
3480 Main Hwy. (305) 448-0999.
Expect traditional food at this Mexican eatery, where only fresh produce is used. Try the sizzling fajitas and stuffed enchiladas, or one of the unusual savory chocolate *mole* dishes.

**Greater Miami:** *Chef Allen's* $$$$$
19088 NE 29th Ave, North Miami Beach. (305) 935-2900.
Sleek and chic, this Miami landmark is known for its high quality, daring New Florida cuisine. The activity in the kitchen, framed by a huge picture window, is fascinating. *L, Super Bowl.*

| Restaurant | Credit Cards | Children's Facilities | Early Bird Specials | Good Regional Cuisine | Bar |
|---|---|---|---|---|---|
| Nexxt | ■ | | | | ■ |
| Joe's Stone Crab | ■ | ● | | ● | ■ |
| The Forge | ■ | | | ● | ■ |
| Tuscan Steak | ■ | | | | ■ |
| Big Fish | ■ | | | | ■ |
| Casa Juancho | ■ | ● | | | ■ |
| Christy's | ■ | | | | ■ |
| Señor Frog's | ■ | ● | | | ■ |
| Chef Allen's | ■ | | | ● | ■ |

## The Gold & Treasure Coasts

**Boca Raton:** *La Vieille Maison* $$$$$
770 E Palmetto Park Rd. (561) 391-6701.
Built by architect Addison Mizner, this home is now an intimate five-star French restaurant. The restaurant makes a perfect setting for romantic dinners.

**Fort Lauderdale:** *Le Café de Paris* $$$
715 E Las Olas Blvd. (954) 467-2900.
This French-style bistro has been in business for 30 years. Consistently good food and reasonable prices make it a firm favorite with locals. The *escargot* is excellent, and complete dinners are good value. *L, D.*

| Restaurant | Credit Cards | Children's Facilities | Early Bird Specials | Good Regional Cuisine | Bar |
|---|---|---|---|---|---|
| La Vieille Maison | ■ | | | ● | ■ |
| Le Café de Paris | ■ | ● | | | ■ |

rice categories include a
ree-course meal for one, a
ass of house wine, and all
navoidable extra charges such
s sales tax and service.
$ under $20
$$ $20–30
$$$ $30–45
$$$$ $45–60
$$$$$ over $60

**CREDIT CARDS**
Major credit cards accepted.

**CHILDREN'S FACILITIES**
Small portions and high chairs available, and there may also be a special children's menu.

**EARLY BIRD SPECIALS**
Meals offered at a discounted price if you eat early.

**GOOD REGIONAL CUISINE**
Florida specialties, such as seafood or dishes with Hispanic or Caribbean influence.

| Restaurant | Price | Credit Cards | Children's Facilities | Early Bird Specials | Good Regional Cuisine | Bar |
|---|---|---|---|---|---|---|
| **LM BEACH:** *Chuck & Harold's*<br>7 Royal Poinciana Way. (561) 659-1440.<br>e porch tables are the best for celebrity-spotting while you enjoy dishes ch as conch chowder or one of the blackboard specials. P | $$$$ | ■ | ● | ■ | ● | ■ |
| **LM BEACH:** *L'Escalier*<br>eakers Hotel, 1 S County Rd. (561) 655-6611.<br>r a truly memorable experience, try the refined setting of this restaurant d the lavish New Florida cuisine served here. P | $$$$$ | ■ | ● | | ● | ■ |

## ORLANDO & THE SPACE COAST

| Restaurant | Price | Credit Cards | Children's Facilities | Early Bird Specials | Good Regional Cuisine | Bar |
|---|---|---|---|---|---|---|
| **OCOA BEACH:** *The Mango Tree Restaurant*<br>3 N Atlantic Ave. (321) 799-0513.<br>is gourmet restaurant serves local dishes, with seafood as a specialty. uated just yards from the Atlantic Ocean, there is a tropical garden with aterfowl, Japanese carp, and lush foliage. ● *Mon.* V | $$$$$ | ■ | ● | | ● | ■ |
| **OWNTOWN ORLANDO:** *O'Boys Barb-Q*<br>4 W Colonial Dr, 32804. (407) 425-6269.<br>ocal favorite with simple decor and stunning slow-smoked barbeque isine. They have great all-you-can-eat specials in the evenings. *Sun.* | $$ | ■ | ● | | | ■ |
| **OWNTOWN ORLANDO:** *Le Coq au Vin*<br>00 S Orange Ave. (407) 851-6980.<br>elcoming surroundings and consistently fine rustic French cuisine are a aw at this popular restaurant. ● *Mon, Sat–Sun L, most public hols.* | $$$ | ■ | | | | |
| **TERNATIONAL DRIVE:** *The Crab House*<br>91 International Dr. (407) 352-6140.<br>oose from no less than nine crab dishes at this informal restaurant. The afood salad bar is loaded with freshly shucked oysters, shrimp, marinated issels, and crawfish, and other seafood dishes. | $$$$ | ■ | ● | | ● | ■ |
| **SSIMMEE:** *Pacino's Italian Ristorante*<br>95 W Hwy 192. (407) 396-8022.<br>arbroiled food is the focus of this comfortable and friendly family staurant. If you prefer, there's a free delivery service to any nearby tel. | $$$ | ■ | ● | | | ■ |
| **ALT DISNEY WORLD:** *Whispering Canyon Café*<br>sney Wilderness Lodge. (407) 939-3463.<br>ap on your six-guns and settle in for an all-you-can-eat campfire cookout ffet in a Wild West setting. Also open for frontier-style breakfasts. P V | $$$ | ■ | ● | | | ■ |
| **ALT DISNEY WORLD:** *California Grill*<br>sney's Contemporary Resort. (407) 939-3463.<br>stylish restaurant with good views and an open-plan kitchen, serving eative West Coast fare. Try the excellent smoked salmon pizza, and pork d polenta. P | $$$$ | ■ | ● | | | ■ |
| **ALT DISNEY WORLD:** *Narcoossee's*<br>sney's Grand Floridian Resort. (407) 824-1400.<br>is restaurant in an octagonal chalet alongside the Seven Seas lagoon ves delicious meat. It is also famed for its superlative fish dishes served th fresh vegetables. ● *L.* P | $$$$$ | ■ | ● | | | ■ |
| **ALT DISNEY WORLD:** *Victoria & Albert's*<br>sney's Grand Floridian Resort. (407) 824-1089.<br>servations are a must at this lavish restaurant. The six-course, fixed-price enu is superlative, and you're waited on by a butler and a maid. Ask for chef's table, the most exclusive one in the house. ● *L.* P V | $$$$$ | ■ | | | ● | |

For key to symbols see back flap

**Price categories** include a three-course meal for one, a glass of house wine, and all unavoidable extra charges such as sales tax and service.
$ under $20
$$ $20–30
$$$ $30–45
$$$$ $45–60
$$$$$ over $60

**Credit Cards**
Major credit cards accepted.

**Children's Facilities**
Small portions and high chairs available, and there may also be a special children's menu.

**Early Bird Specials**
Meals offered at a discounted price if you eat early.

**Good Regional Cuisine**
Florida specialties, such as seafood or dishes with Hispanic or Caribbean influence.

## The Northeast

**Daytona Beach:** *Aunt Catfish's* $$$
4009 Halifax Dr. *(386) 767-4768.*
This popular eatery on the Intracoastal Waterway is famed for its fried catfish, crab cakes, and clam strips. Also open for Sunday brunch.

**Fernandina Beach:** *Florida House Inn* $$
20–22 S 3rd St. *(904) 261-3300.*
At this lovely gingerbread house (Florida's oldest surviving hotel), diners sit at long trestle tables laden with generous servings of good American home cooking. Always "all-you-can-eat"! *Sun, Mon D; Dec 24 D.*

**St. Augustine:** *Raintree* $$$$
102 San Marco Ave. *(904) 824-7211.*
Occupying one of the street's remaining historic buildings, Raintree is renowned for its award-winning food. Round off a meal of superb seafood or traditional meat dishes with a crêpe at the dessert bar. *L, Dec 25.*

## The Panhandle

**Apalachicola:** *Seafood Grill & Steakhouse* $$$
100 Market St. *(850) 653-9510.*
Located downtown, this friendly grill features a good range of meals. Tuck into the "world's largest" fried fish sandwich, the area's famous oysters, and pick one of the 30 or more beers offered. *public hols.*

**Destin:** *Marina Café* $$$$
404 E Hwy 98. *(850) 837-7960.*
A jewel on the Emerald Coast, this restaurant combines excellent service, a spectacular location, and creative, internationally inspired cuisine. Early diners benefit from two-for-one dinners. *L, Dec 25, Jan.*

**Fort Walton Beach:** *Staff's Seafood Restaurant* $$$
24 Miracle Strip Pkwy. *(850) 243-3482.*
Opened in 1913, Staff's has been famed for its fine local recipes ever since. The menu combines fish and seafood dishes with some brilliantly prepared steak, roast beef, and pork dishes. *L, public hols, Super Bowl.*

**Panama City Beach:** *The Treasure Ship* $$$$
3605 S Thomas Dr. *(850) 234-8881.*
Housed in a replica of a 16th-century galleon, this three-level restaurant combines welcoming surroundings of open-air decks and water views with well-prepared fresh seafood. The grilled tuna, salmon, and mahi steaks are house specialties. *Nov–Feb.*

**Pensacola:** *McGuire's Irish Pub* $$$
600 E Gregory St. *(850) 433-6789.*
A visit to Pensacola isn't complete without a stop at McGuire's,where huge portions of steak, pasta, pizza, and pub fare are served. Wash it down with one of their home-brewed beers. *Thanksgiving, Dec 25.* V

**Tallahassee:** *Andrew's Capitol Bar & Grille* $$$$
228 South Adams St. *(850) 222-3444.*
This goumet restaurant is one of three at this address; here the set menu is excellent, and the flavor is Mediterranean dishes. Service is attentive. *Sun.*

**Tallahassee:** *Chez Pierre* $$$
1215 Thomasville Rd. *(850) 222-0936.*
Southern hospitality, reasonable rates, and excellent French food make this bistro a local favorite. Chez Pierre is also famed for its desserts, especially delicious pastries. *Sun, Dec 25, Jan 1.*

| Restaurant | Credit Cards | Children's Facilities | Early Bird Specials | Good Regional Cuisine |
|---|---|---|---|---|
| Aunt Catfish's | ■ | ● | ■ | ● |
| Florida House Inn | ■ | | | |
| Raintree | ■ | ● | ■ | ● |
| Seafood Grill & Steakhouse | ■ | ● | | ● |
| Marina Café | ■ | ● | ■ | ● |
| Staff's Seafood Restaurant | ■ | ● | | ● |
| The Treasure Ship | ■ | ● | ■ | ● |
| McGuire's Irish Pub | ■ | ● | | ● |
| Andrew's Capitol Bar & Grille | ■ | ● | | |
| Chez Pierre | ■ | ● | | |

## THE GULF COAST

**ORT MYERS:** *The Veranda* $$$$
22 2nd St. *(239) 332-2065.*
is charming restaurant housed in a 1902 building offers original culinary eations like artichoke fritters stuffed with blue crab. The décor is Deep uth and the service attentive. *Sat L, Sun, public hols.*

**. PETERSBURG:** *Fourth Street Shrimp Store* $$
06 4th St . *(727) 822-0325.*
fun place with fresh shrimp, low prices and casual dining. Seafood mes straight out of the cooker. *L, D.*

**. PETE BEACH:** *Hurricane Seafood Restaurant* $$$
7 Gulf Way. *(727) 360-9558.*
t right on the beach, this restaurant prides itself on its crab cakes and sh Florida grouper, which comes blackened, grilled, broiled, or in a ndwich. The cocktail deck is especially popular at sunset.

**NIBEL ISLAND:** *Windows On The Water* $$$$
ndial Beach Resort, 1451 Middle Gulf Drive. *(239) 395-6014.*
a beautiful location overlooking the Gulf of Mexico, this rather egant restaurant features delicious Floribbean cuisine.

**RASOTA:** *Michael's On East* $$$$
12 East Ave S. *(941) 366-0007.*
ne of Sarasota's premier restaurants, Michael's has innovative regional isine and a large selection of microbrewed beers. *Sat & Sun L.*

**RASOTA:** *Café L'Europe* $$$$$
1 Armands Circle. *(941) 388-4415.*
cated on exclusive St Armands Circle, this restaurant provides a romantic tting for some elegant dining. Jacket and tie are preferred. *L, D.*

**MPA:** *Lauro Ristorante Italiano* $$$$
15 Henderson Blvd. *(813) 281-2100.*
is restaurant offers delicious traditional Italian food in pleasant surroundgs. Good service, moderate prices. *Sat–Sun L.*

**MPA:** *Mis en Place* $$$$
2 W Kennedy Blvd. *(813) 254-5373.*
e innovative menu of this busy bistro changes daily but never fails to ease. Locals love this place, so reserve ahead. *Sat L, Mon, Sun.*

**MPA:** *Bern's Steak House* $$$$$
08 S Howard Ave. *(813) 251-2421.*
must for meat lovers, Bern's has made steak cuisine a fine art. Each order prepared to your specifications, and accompanied by organic vegetables. is very popular and reservations are essential. *L, Dec 25.*

## THE EVERGLADES & THE KEYS

**LAMORADA:** *Atlantic's Edge* $$$$
M 82, Overseas Hwy. *(305) 517-4411.*
ere's a spacious wooden deck here with great ocean views, but this place better known for its locally caught seafood. Steaks are also on offer, and ere is a healthy spa menu, too. *D, Sun brunch (winter only).*

**EY LARGO:** *The Fish House Restaurant and Seafood Market* $$$$
M 102.4, Overseas Hwy. *(305) 451-4665.*
looks like a shack, but this is the place locals depend on for the freshest h and conch salad. No frills, just good seafood.

**EY WEST:** *Blue Heaven* $$$$
9 Thomas St. *(305) 296-8666.*
oused in a wonderful old Key West building, this friendly restaurant fers delicious seafood in a laid-back atmosphere. The seating at painted ooden tables is basic. *Thanksgiving, Dec 25.*

**EY WEST:** *Pier House Resort* $$$$
er House Resort, 1 Duval St. *(305) 296-4600.*
is exclusive waterfront restaurant, one of the best in the Keys, rves fancy Florida cuisine such as lobster with marinated plantain. sure to reserve an outside table for the best sunset views. *Mon–Sat L.*

For key to symbols see back flap

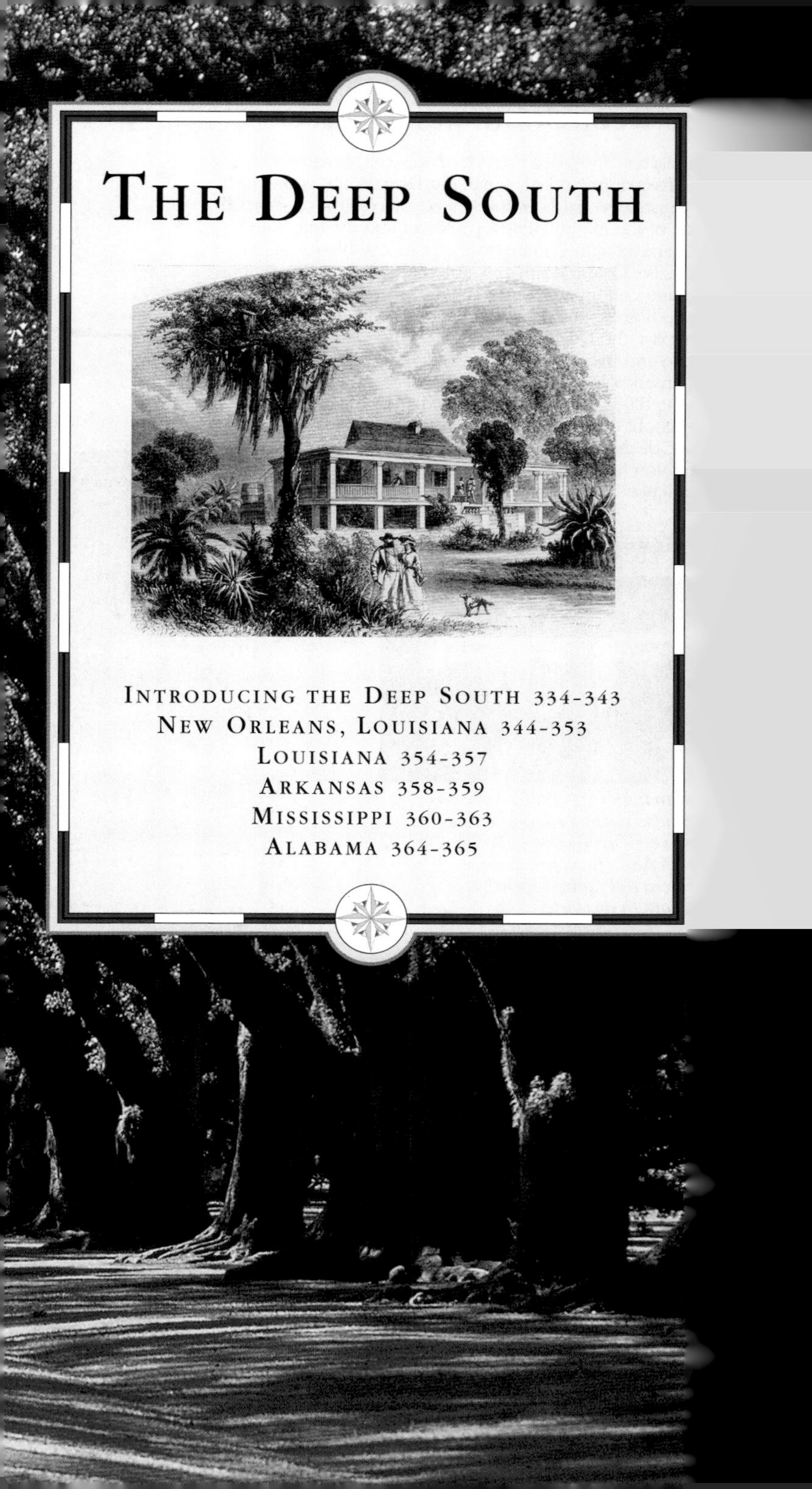

# The Deep South

# The Deep South at a Glance

COMPRISING THE FOUR STATES OF Louisiana, Arkansas, Mississippi, and Alabama, the Deep South is one of the most distinctive parts of the United States. From the broad plains of the mighty Mississippi River and the bayous of Louisiana's Cajun Country to the hardscrabble forests of Arkansas's Ozark Mountains, the region is both geographically and culturally diverse. While opulent mansions, antebellum homes, and Civil Rights Movement sights are aspects of its past, the Deep South's special charms rest with the people and their natural appreciation of the good things in life. America's two most beloved musical creations – jazz and the blues – were born here, a legacy that is celebrated throughout the region, particularly in New Orleans. This city's universal reputation for nonstop fun is best experienced during Mardi Gras.

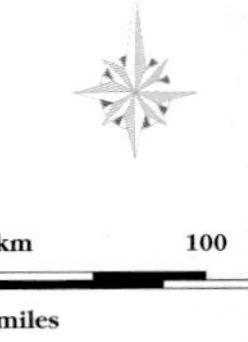

***Hot Springs*** (see p358), *Arkansas, is home to the historic Bathhouse Row, where the Buckstaff Bathhouse still offers spa facilities. Former president Bill Clinton spent his youth in this city.*

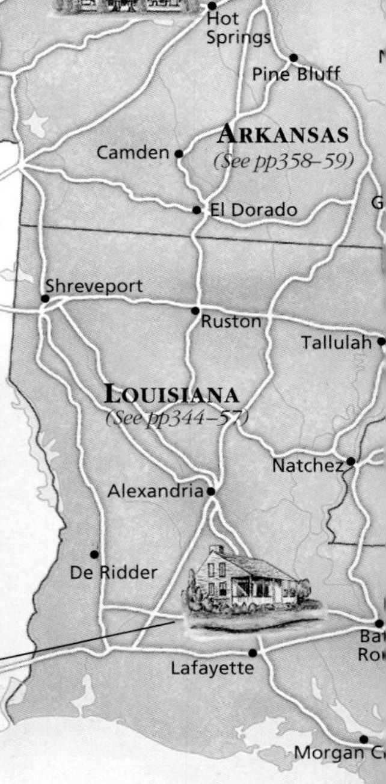

***Lafayette*** (see p356) *is the heart of Louisiana's Cajun Country, where the descendants of French Canadian immigrants still preserve their language and culture. Much of this local culture can be found in restaurants and nightclubs, at the city's museums and historic parks, as well as out in the surrounding swamps.*

◁ **Two rows of magnificent oak trees lining the drive to Oak Alley, a Lower Mississippi plantation**

***elma** (see p364) is one of the many towns in labama that played a significant role during the 'ivil Rights Movement in the 1950s and 60s. An nportant sight here is the National Voting Rights Museum, which tells the story of the successful Selma-to-Montogomery March led by Dr. Martin Luther King Jr. in 1965.*

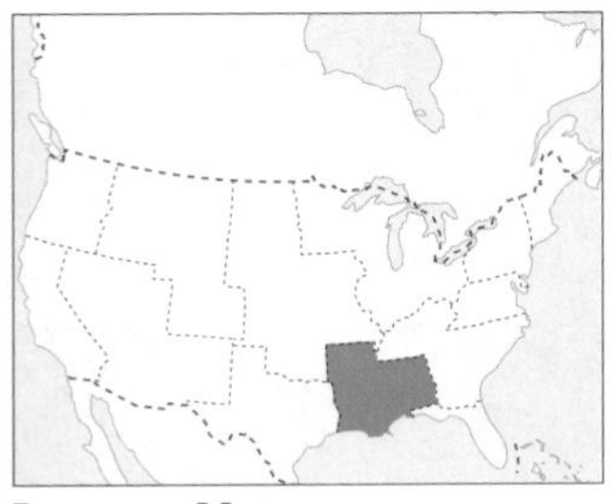

**LOCATOR MAP**

***The Gulf Coast** (see p363) has traditionally been dominated by the seafood industry. But over the last decade, lavish Las Vegas-style casinos have proliferated along the coast, offering a choice of cuisines as well as different types of entertainment.*

***New Orleans** (see pp344–53), the region's cultural capital, is characterized by Colonial architecture, lively bars, and the annual Mardi Gras festivities.*

ROYAL
CAFE
BALCONY
DINING

# THE DEEP SOUTH

WITH ITS WARM, SEMITROPICAL CLIMATE *and easy-going temperament, the Deep South is perhaps the most culturally diverse region of the United States. Multiethnic and all-embracing in a friendly, hospitable way, the region offers visitors an unforgettable introduction to Southern charm, as embodied by the pleasure-seeking lifestyle of New Orleans.*

Some 14 million people live in the Deep South, in a region covering about 200,000 sq miles (517,998 sq km), which is similar in size and population density to neighboring Texas. While the four states share a natural appreciation for the good things in life, they are otherwise quite different. Louisiana epitomizes French Catholic culture, whereas Mississippi and Alabama were the heart of the Confederacy during the Civil War. Arkansas differs in its rugged landscape matched by its people's pride in the state's mountain heritage. Most residents of the primarily rural Deep South have family roots reaching deep into history, and a rare continuity exists between past and present.

The rich bottomlands that line the meandering path of the Mississippi River across parts of Mississippi, Arkansas, and Louisiana once yielded the world's largest crops of cotton, and it was here that some of the greatest early American fortunes were made. However, the industry's labor-intensive demands were based on the iniquities of slavery, which has haunted the economy and culture of the Deep South for two centuries.

## HISTORY

Some of the region's earliest known inhabitants were the city-based agricultural communities of the Mississippian culture, whose members cultivated extensive fields of corn, beans, and squash, and constructed elaborate mounds for their religious and political rituals. The 3,700-year-old effigy mounds at Poverty Point in northeastern Louisiana, one of North America's oldest, largest, and most significant archaeological remains, dates from this period.

**The steamboat *Natchez* leaving Mississippi River port**

**Royal Café, a popular Cajun-Creole restaurant in the French Quarter, New Orleans**

Dennis Malone Carter's painting, *The Battle of New Orleans*

When Spanish conquistador Hernando de Soto and his troops first encountered the Mississippian cities, they soon decimated the people and their culture. Thereafter, other more dispersed Indian groups rose to power, most notably the Chickasaw, Choctaw, Quapaw, Creek, and Cherokee tribes. The Creek Indians of central and northern Alabama were perhaps the most successful, numbering some 15,000 at their peak. In the early 1700s, European colonists supported tl Creeks, and supplied the with guns and ammunitio in exchange for their he in vanquishing the oth tribes. A century later, tl Creeks themselves we under assault, and by 18 they had been forced give up their vast and fert territory to the incomir Americans. The story most other Deep Sou Indians is similar, endi tragically in the 1830 when they were moved to dista Oklahoma. A few, including tl Choctaw tribe in central Mississippi, st live on their ancestral lands.

While English-speaking America dominate the past and present, tl French and Spanish carried out mu of the early exploration and settleme Louisiana and Arkansas were und nominal French control until 180 while Alabama and Mississippi we part of the Spanish colony of We Florida until 1814. Boundaries ar allegiances varied until the US too control, through the Louisiana Purcha of 1803, and by the multiple battles wi England, Spain, and their Indian allies

With the defeat of the British at tl Battle of New Orleans in January 181 the Deep South entered an era unprecedented growth and prosperit New Orleans became the fourth-large US city and the nation's second-busie port. Steamboats plied the Mississip River, as chronicled by writer Ma Twain (1835–1910), himself a form steamboat captain.

By the mid-1800s, wealthy individua from the Carolinas, in particular, intr duced the slave-owning, cotto growing plantation culture that wou reap huge fortunes and lead inexorab toward the Civil War. Mississippi, th second state to secede from the U provided the rebel Confederacy with i president, Jefferson Davis, whi Montgomery, Alabama, served as i first capital. The fall of Vicksburg i 1863 effectively ended Confedera control of the Mississippi, and after tl war much of the region lay in ruins.

## Key Dates in History

**1539** Hernando de Soto leads the first European expedition to the Deep South

**1699** Fort de Maurepas, near present-day Biloxi, Mississippi, becomes capital of France's Louisiana colony

**1723** Louisiana's capital moved to New Orleans

**1803** Louisiana Territory purchased from Napoleonic France (the Louisiana Purchase)

**1814** Creek and Chickasaw Indians are forced to relinquish their territorial claims

**1812** Louisiana becomes a state

**1817** Mississippi becomes a state

**1819** Alabama becomes a state

**1836** Arkansas becomes a state

**1863** US forces take control of Vicksburg to end Confederate access to the Mississippi River

**1935** Populist Louisiana Governor Huey "Kingfish" Long assassinated in Baton Rogue

**1955** Montgomery Bus Boycott

**1962** African-American student James Meredith becomes the first nonwhite person to attend classes at the University of Mississippi

**1992** Former Arkansas Governor Bill Clinton is elected 42nd president of the United States

**2005** Hurricane Katrina hits the southern US, destroying towns and cities and killing thousands of people in New Orleans and the Gulf Coast

ıe post-Civil War economic and social asteland gave rise to a doctrine of hite supremacy and racist violence at plagued the region the following ntury. It wasn't until the 1950s and )s, when the dramatic confrontations ' the Civil Rights Movement, such as ose at Selma, Alabama, in 1965, egan to change things for the better.

### People & the Economy

ıe Deep South is remembered for its ften troubled history as well as its eople's resolute and indomitable spirit cope with the problems of the past. espite a large exodus of African mericans to northern US cities after e Civil War, descendants of slaves still rm a large percentage of the population, and the slow but steady process f overcoming racial segregation has ansformed the region. Today, African mericans are legally entitled to equal eatment, although in reality there mains a distinct gap in opportunities etween whites and nonwhites.

Another distinctive component is ouisiana's Cajuns, who live in the atery region north and west of New rleans. A third very different culture found in the densely forested ountains of Arkansas and northern labama. Long denigrated as "hillillies" like their figurative cousins ı Tennessee, Kentucky, and West irginia, these mountain people have a ercely protected independence and elf-reliance. Hunting and fishing, both or recreation and sustenance, many till practice traditional crafts and erform the so-called "bluegrass" music erived from the folk music of their cottish and Irish forebears.

As the cotton-based economy of lantation and Reconstruction days has isappeared, little has emerged to take s place. Thanks to inexpensive mports, the region's once-thriving extile industry has all but disappeared. xcept for the steel mills of Birmingam, Alabama, the corridor of petrohemical factories along the Mississippi ı Louisiana, or the gambling centers in he Mississippi Delta and along the Gulf of Mexico, the Deep South still uffers from a major lack of industry and employment opportunities. Success stories include Dillard's department stores and the world-dominating retail might of Wal-Mart, both of which started and still have their corporate headquarters in Arkansas. In contrast, one of the region's economic darlings of the 1990s, the Mississippi-based telecommunications company, WorldCom, crashed into bankruptcy in 2002.

### Culture & Arts

If culture and the arts were the most valuable market commodities, the Deep South would be the wealthiest region in the country. The region has been instrumental in creating some of the world's most popular forms of musical, literary, and culinary expression. Jazz, for example, grew from the bubbling melting pot of Creole culture that was New Orleans after the Civil War, while the blues and its offspring rock 'n' roll, emerged from the slave songs of the Mississippi Delta. Writers such as Tennessee Williams and William Faulkner, and novels like Harper Lee's classic *To Kill a Mockingbird*, helped earn the Deep South a place in world literature, while the melange of Cajun, Creole, "Soul Food," and barbecue make it a delicious place to travel.

**Statue of William Faulkner in the courthouse square in downtown Oxford, Mississippi**

# Exploring the Deep South

STRETCHING FROM THE GULF COAST to the Appalachians in the north and the Great Plains in the west, the Deep South region sprawls across some 200,000 sq miles (517,998 sq km). Although large in area, the population is sparse and the transportation facilities limited. As elsewhere in the US, a car is the best way to get around. New Orleans, has the region's major airport, while smaller airports serve other cities. In 2005, Hurricane Katrina destroyed towns and cities in Mississippi, Alabama, and Louisiana *(see p366)*. Please check for the latest information before you travel.

**KEY**

- Airport
- Highway
- Major road
- Railroad
- State border

## SIGHTS AT A GLANCE



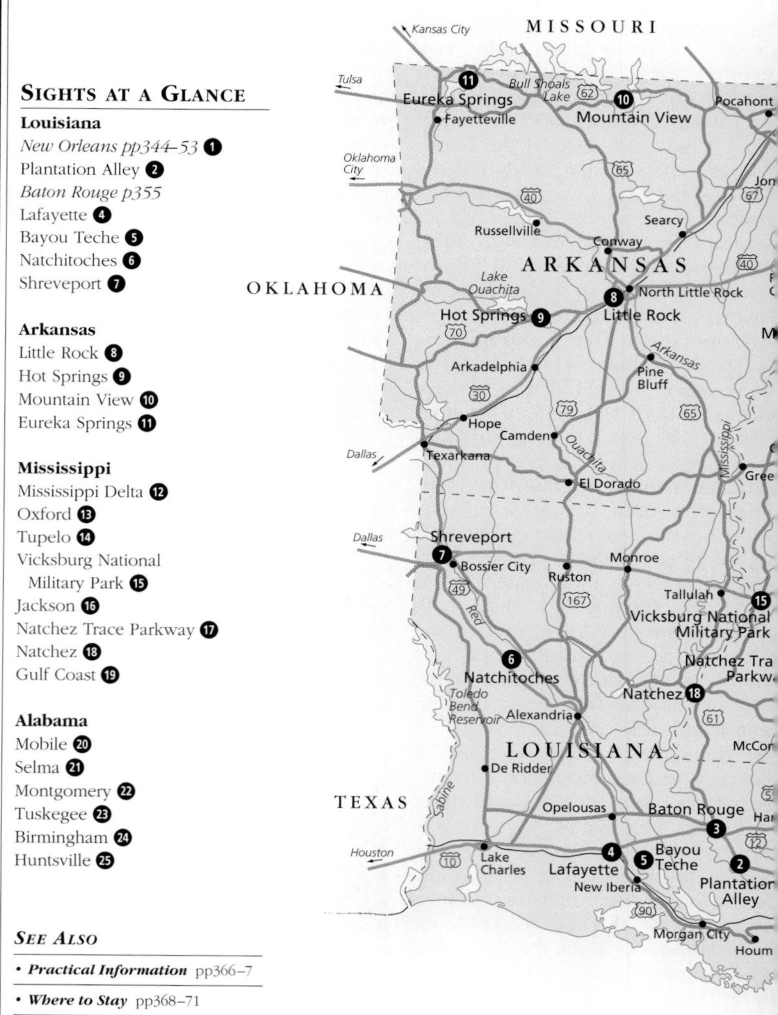


**SEE ALSO**


- ***Practical Information*** pp366–7
- ***Where to Stay*** pp368–71
- ***Where to Eat*** pp372–5

A traditional sternwheeler riverboat cruising the Mississippi River

## Mileage Chart

**10** = Distance in miles
10 = Distance in kilometers

| NEW ORLEANS, LA | | | | | | |
|---|---|---|---|---|---|---|
| **80** 129 | BATON ROUGE, LA | | | | | |
| **529** 851 | **480** 772 | LITTLE ROCK, AR | | | | |
| **345** 555 | **333** 536 | **221** 356 | OXFORD, MS | | | |
| **185** 298 | **173** 278 | **344** 553 | **174** 280 | JACKSON, MS | | |
| **144** 232 | **199** 320 | **573** 922 | **402** 647 | **189** 304 | MOBILE, AL | |
| **343** 552 | **399** 642 | **377** 607 | **187** 301 | **238** 382 | **258** 415 | BIRMINGHAM, AL |

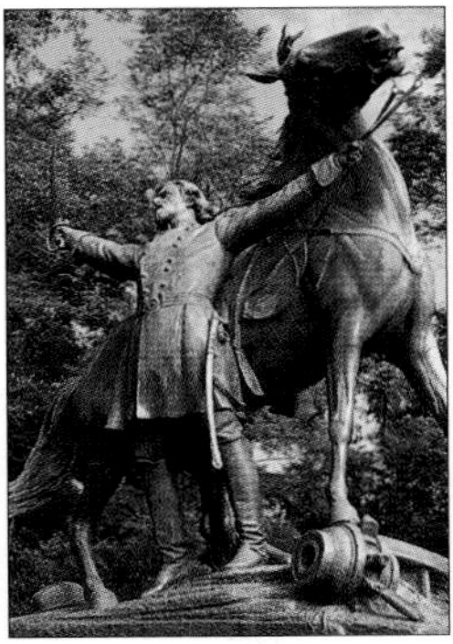

Statue of General Tilghman, Vicksburg National Military Park

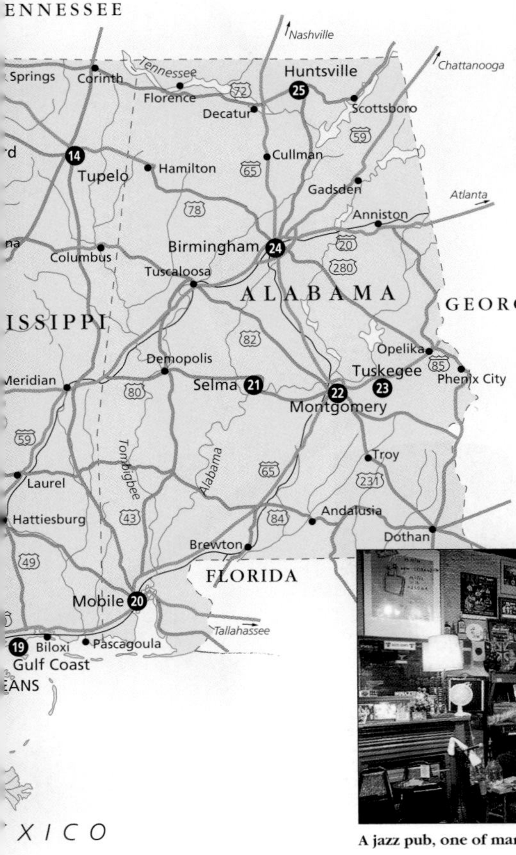

ENNESSEE
Nashville
Chattanooga
Tennessee
Springs
Corinth
Huntsville
Florence
Decatur
Scottsboro
Cullman
Tupelo
Hamilton
Gadsden
Atlanta
Anniston
Birmingham
Columbus
Tuscaloosa
ALABAMA
GEORGIA
ISSIPPI
Opelika
Demopolis
Tuskegee
Phenix City
Meridian
Selma
Montgomery
Troy
Laurel
Tombigbee
Alabama
Hattiesburg
Andalusia
Dothan
Brewton
FLORIDA
Mobile
Tallahassee
Biloxi
Pascagoula
Gulf Coast
EANS
XICO
0 km 100
0 miles 100

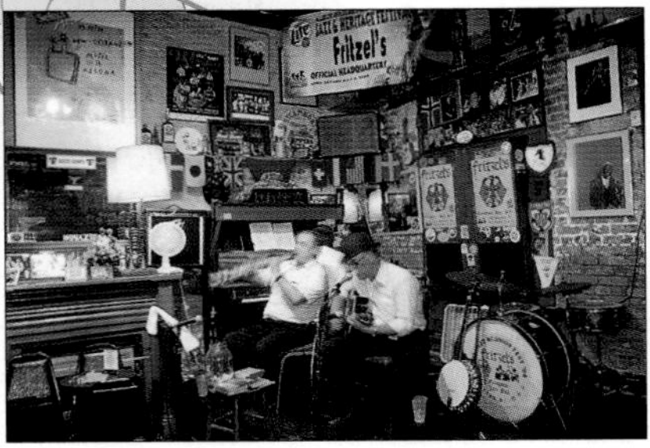

A jazz pub, one of many in New Orleans

# New Orleans ❶

Diners at the popular Acme Oyster House

LOCATED IN SOUTHEAST LOUISIANA, New Orleans lies between Lake Pontchartrain and a bend in the Mississippi. It covers an area of 199 sq miles (516 sq km) and has a population of nearly 500,000 residents. The city's topmost tourist destination is the French Quarter, where the cultural heritage of its Colonial past is ever present. The legendary Royal and Bourbon Streets are located here, as are Creole-style cottages, lively bars, and markets offering local specialties. Beyond this lie the Central Business District centered along the waterfront, the verdant Garden District, and the area around City Park.

## SIGHTS AT A GLANCE

Old US Mint ①
Old Ursuline Convent ②
French Market ③
Café du Monde ④
Jackson Square ⑤
St. Louis Cathedral, Cabildo, & Presbytère ⑥
Washington Artillery Park and Moonwalk ⑦
St. Louis Cemetery #1 ⑧
Hermann-Grima Historic House ⑨
Bourbon Street ⑩
Royal Street ⑪
Steamboat Natchez ⑫
Custom House & Insectarium ⑬
Aquarium of the Americas ⑭
Ferry to Algiers & Mardi Gras World ⑮
Riverwalk Marketplace ⑯

**Greater New Orleans**
***(see inset map)***
Garden District ⑰
City Park ⑱

Royal Street and its well-known LaBranche buildings

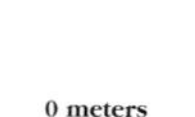

## Getting Around

Although most of the city's popular tourist sights in and near the French Quarter are easily accessible on foot, New Orleans also has a useful public transportation system. Bus routes cover the city, and no visitor should miss a chance to travel on the St. Charles Avenue Streetcar, the oldest streetcar in the nation. Riverboats also provide a pleasant way to see the sights along the basin of the Mississippi River. Taxis are affordable and convenient, and are recommended for trips after dark.

Neo-Classical façade of the Old US Mint

## Old US Mint ①

**Map** E2. 400 Esplanade Ave. *(504) 568-6968.* *Riverfront.* *3, 55.* *9am–5pm Tue–Sun.* *public hols.* www.sm.crt.state.la.us/mintex.htm

This Greek Revival building, built in 1835 by William Strickland, functioned as a mint until 1909, turning out a variety of coinage, including Confederate and Mexican currency. It then became a federal prison and was later used by the Coast Guard. In the late 1970s, it was taken over by the state and converted into a museum to house the **New Orleans Jazz Collection**. The exhibit tells the story of jazz *(see p349)* through a collection of original musical instruments, vintage photographs, and historic documents. Among the instruments displayed are the ebony clarinet George Lewis played on to record "Burgundy Street Blues," and the cornet Louis Armstrong learned to play on. At the entrance are a series of photographs of early bands and musicians, as well as a steamboat scale model.

The building also houses the **History of the Old US Mint Exhibition**, which displays gold and silver coins formerly minted here. The carefully restored façade is embellished with some of the city's most beautiful wrought-iron balconies and railings.

Photograph, New Orleans Jazz Collection

## Old Ursuline Convent ②

**Map** E2. 1100 Chartres St. *(504) 529-3040.* *Riverfront.* *3, 55.* *10am–4pm Tue–Fri, 11am–4pm Sat–Sun (guided tours only).*

The oldest building in the Mississippi Valley, the Old Ursuline Convent was built in 1752, some 25 years after the Ursuline Sisters first arrived in New Orleans. With its steep-pitched roof punctuated by a row of dormers and tall chimneys, it is a typical French Colonial structure and one of the few to remain from that period. In the 1820s, the nuns moved to new quarters, and the convent became the first official residence for the bishops and archbishops of New Orleans, and the home of the archdiocesan archives. Later, it became part of a parish.

The current chapel, now known as Our Lady of Victory, was consecrated in 1845. Inside, visitors can admire the splendid pine-an[d] cypress ceiling, two superb Bavarian stained-glass windows, and a window depicting the Battle of New Orleans, beneath an image o[f] Our Lady of Prompt Succor. The nuns' old kitchen and laundry is now the rectory.

A formal French garden containing a handsome iron gazebo lies in front of the building. It is accessed via the porter's lodge.

Old Ursuline Convent, dating from 1752

## French Market ③

**Map** E2. N Peters St, from St. Ann t[o] Barracks St. *Riverfront.* *3, 5, 48.* *Shops: 9am–7pm daily; Farmers Market: 24 hours daily.* www.frenchmarket.org

A New Orleans institution since 1791, this area served as a trading place for Native Americans much before European settlement. Officially the French Market [i]s five blocks between St. Ann and Barracks Streets, beginning roughly at Café du Monde and ending at the Ol[d] Mint museum. In daily use, the term "French Market" usually denotes the open air markets from St. Philip to Barracks, which stock many New Orleans specialties. The Farmers Market (beginning a[t] Ursulines Street) is a shadow of its former vigorous self but even today shoppers can find fresh Louisiana produce here. Strawberries in the spring and the pecans in the fall are especially prized.

The majority of the space is now given over to the **Flea Market** – all kinds of items, ranging from jewelry and pottery to African arts and crafts, can be bought at the stalls and tables around the French Market buildings. The Flea Market stands on the site of the notorious neighborhood around Gallatin Street, which was once inhabited by criminals, prostitutes, and visiting sailors.

## ;afé du Monde ④

łap E2. 1039 Decatur. (504) 37-0833. Riverfront. 3, 5, 55. ] 24 hours daily. ] www.cafedumonde.com

EVERYONE WHO visits New Orleans stops here for a late of sugar-dusted *beignets* ;quare French donuts) accom-anied by plain *café au lait* or ɪe famous chicory-flavored ersion. These are the only ems offered at this 100-year ld coffee house, where visi-ɔrs can relax at a table under ɪe arcade and listen to the :reet musicians, or simply ratch people as they go by.

During the mid-19th century ɪere were 500 similar coffee ouses in the French Quarter. ;offee was one of the city's ɪost important commodities, nd the coffee trade helped ɪe economy recover after the ;ivil War, when New Orleans ied with New York City to ontrol coffee imports. ;hicory-flavored coffee was onceived during the Civil Var, when the root was used ɔ stretch the coffee supply.

'aking a break at Café du Monde ʋith coffee and *beignets*

## ackson Square ⑤

ʌlap E2. Riverfront. 3, 5, 55.

ONCE LITTLE MORE than a muddy field called the 'lace d' Armes where troops vere drilled, criminals were ɔlaced in the stocks, and :xecutions were carried out, his square lies in the heart ɔf the French Quarter. It vas renamed in honor of ;eneral Andrew Jackson *(see p265)* who defeated the 3ritish at the Battle of New )rleans in 1815.

**Jazz band playing in Jackson Square**

The gardens and pathways, as they exist today, were laid out in 1848, when the beau-tification of the square took place under the patronage of Baroness Micaela Pontalba, then one of the city's most colorful personalities. Under her auspices, the Pelanne brothers designed the hand-some wrought-iron fence that encloses the square. At the center stands a statue of General Jackson astride a rearing horse, sculpted by Clark Mills for $30,000. The inscription "The Union must and shall be preserved," on the plinth was added by Union General Benjamin "Beast" Butler, when he occupied the city during the Civil War.

Today, the square is a lively meeting place, where artists exhibit their works and jazz musicians entertain visitors throughout the week.

A developer like her philanthropist father Don Andreés Almonester y Rojas *(see p348)*, the baroness also commis-sioned the **Pontalba Buildings**, flanking the uptown and downtown sides of Jackson Square. Built at a cost of over $300,000, they were considered the best and the largest apartments of their kind at that time. These elegant apartment buildings are based on plans the baroness brought back from Paris after she separated from her husband. The design of the initials A and P (for Almonester and Pontalba) in the cast-iron railings of the balconies and galleries is attributed to one of the baroness's sons, an artist.

The **1850 House**, in the lower Pontalba building, displays opulent decorations that re-create the middle-class lifestyles of the antebellum era. Opposite Jackson Square is Le Petit Théâtre du Vieux Carré, established in 1916 by a small group of actors called the Drawing Room Players. Behind it, at 632 St. Peter Street, is the apartment where Tennessee Williams wrote his famous play *A Streetcar Named Desire*.

**1850 House**
523 St. Ann St. *(504) 568-6968.*
*9am–5pm Tue–Sun.* *public hols.*
W www.lsm.crt.state.la.us

### NEW ORLEANS IRONWORK

The shadows cast by New Orleans ironwork add a roman-tic touch to the city. Wrought iron, which came first, was fashioned by hand into beautiful shapes by German, Irish, and African-American artisans. Cast iron, on the other hand, was poured into wooden molds and allowed to set. As a result, the latter has a somewhat solid, fixed appearance, unlike wrought iron, which is handmade and has a more fluid aspect. Both kinds of ironwork can be seen throughout the city, particularly in the French Quarter and the Garden District, where balconies, fences, window grilles, and gates are adorned with decorative motifs such as abstracts, cherubs, fruit, flowers, and animals.

**Ironwork on the Pontalba Buildings**

St. Louis Cathedral

## St. Louis Cathedral, Cabildo, & Presbytère ⑥

**Map** D2. Jackson Square. *(504) 525-9585 (St. Louis Cathedral), (504) 568-6968 (Cabildo & Presbytère).* *St. Charles Ave, Canal.* *3, 5, 55, 81.* *9am–5pm daily (St. Louis Cathedral); 9am–5pm Tue–Sun (Cabildo & Presbytère).* *Cabildo & Presbytère.* *St. Louis Cathedral, regular services throughout the day.*
www.saintlouiscathedral.org

This complex of buildings comprises the cathedral, Cabildo, and Presbytère. St. Louis Cathedral stands on the site of two earlier churches that were destroyed. The current building, begun in 1789, was dedicated as a cathedral in 1794. Inside are superb murals and a carved-wood Baroque main altar.

The Cabildo, designed by Guilberto Guillemard, was built and financed in 1795 by Don Andrés Almonester y Rojas. It served as a capitol for the legislative assembly of the Spanish Colonial government and subsequently as the City Hall. From 1853 to 1911 it housed the state Supreme Court. The Louisiana Purchase *(see p340)* was signed in the Sala Capitular in 1803.

The Casa Curial, or Presbytère, was built between 1794 and 1813, and used as a courthouse until 1911. It now houses the Mardi Gras Museum, featuring colorful objects and memorabilia.

## Washington Artillery Park and Moonwalk ⑦

**Map** E2. Decatur St, between St Ann & St Peter sts. *3, 5, 55.* *Riverfront.*

Washington Artillery Park faces Jackson Square from Decatur Street. Inside the park is an austere concrete amphitheater with a central staircase leading to the Moonwalk. This community boardwalk was named after former New Orleans Mayor Maurice "Moon" Landrieu, who approved the construction of flood walls that made the riverfront area accessible to the public.

The park was built in 1976 and was once used as a military training ground, but today the amphitheater and Moonwalk are favored by street performers. Crowds often gather to enjoy performances by musicians, including guitarists, clarinettists, saxophonists, trombonists, and steel drummers, who play with an open case at their feet to collect donations.

The breeze along the waterfront can provide a welcome break from the humidity of the city, and it's also the perfect vantage point from which to see the river, Jackson Square, and the surrounding area. Stone steps lead down to where you can dangle your feet in the water, but don't attempt to stand in it, as the current is deceptively powerful.

## St. Louis Cemetery #1 ⑧

**Map** D2. Basin St between St. Louis & Conti. *(504) 596-3050.* *46, 48, 52, 57.* *9am–3pm Mon–Sat, 9am–noon Sun.*

The city's oldest surviving cemetery was established in 1789. This fascinating place, with its rows of mausoleums, is the resting place of many legendary local residents. The most famous of all is probably Marie Laveau. Crowds visit her tomb, marking it with an "X" (symbolically requesting that she grant a particular wish). By 1829, St. Louis Cemetery #1 was filled, mostly with victims of yellow fever, and the nearby **St. Louis Cemetery #2** was established as an extension. Many of the city's 19th-century Creole aristocracy are buried here in ornate mausoleums.

Statue of an angel, St. Louis Cemetery #1

However, the cemeteries should not be visited alone, as they are in secluded areas where muggers and pickpockets operate. It is advisable for visitors to join guided tours, given by the **Save Our Cemeteries** organization and by **New Orleans Tours, Inc.** Both provide plenty of excellent local information.

**New Orleans Tour Inc.**
*(888) 486-8687.*
www.bigeasy.com
**Save Our Cemeteries**
*(888) 721-7493.*

### Voodoo Worship

Portrait of Marie Laveau

Voodoo arrived in New Orleans from Africa, via the Caribbean, where it originated as a form of ancestor worship among the West African tribes, who were brought to North America as slaves. During the slave uprising in Saint Dominigue in 1793, many of the planters from Haiti fled to New Orleans, bringing their slaves (and voodoo) with them. Marie Laveau (c.1794–1881), the voodoo queen, used Catholic elements such as prayer, incense, and saints in her rituals, which she opened to the public for an admission fee. The voodoo calendar's high point was the celebration she held along Bayou St. John on St. John's Eve.

# New Orleans Jazz

JAZZ IS AMERICA'S original contribution to world culture. It evolved slowly and almost imperceptibly from a number of sources – from the music played at balls, parades, dances, and funerals, and New Orleans' unique blend of cultures. Its musical inspirations included African work chants and spirituals, as well as European and American folk influences – the entire mélange of music that was played in 19th-century New Orleans.

**Blue Lu Barker**

***Trumpeter Oscar "Papa" Celestin***, *the founder of the Tuxedo Brass Band in 1911, also composed "Down by the Riverside."*

***Kid Ory's trombone***, *which he played while performing with King Oliver and others, is displayed at the Old US Mint.*

**STORYVILLE JAZZ SALON**

The 38-block area bounded by Iberville, Basin, Robertson, and St. Louis Streets, was the city's legal red-light district from 1897 to 1917. Known as Storyville, many early jazz artists, including Jelly Roll Morton, King Oliver, and Edward "Kid" Ory, entertained at the bordellos, playing behind screens.

***Riverboat Jazz Bands*** *came into being after Storyville was closed down in 1917. New Orleans' best musicians either performed on boats or migrated to northern cities. Pianist Fate Marable's band included Louis Armstrong, who played the cornet.*

***Congo Square*** *was where slaves gathered every Sunday to celebrate their one day off by playing music and dancing.*

***Louis Armstrong***, *the internationally famous jazz trumpeter, began singing on the streets of New Orleans. He played with Kid Ory before leaving the city in 1923 to join King Oliver's band in Chicago.*

**Master bedroom at the Hermann-Grima Historic House**

## Hermann-Grima Historic House ⑨

**Map** D3. 820 St. Louis St. *(504) 525-5661.* *3.* *10am–3:30pm Mon–Fri.* *public hols.* www.hgghh.org

THIS GABLED BRICK house is one of the French Quarter's few examples of American Creole-style architecture. It was built in 1831 by William Brand for Samuel Hermann, a German-Jewish merchant who lost his fortune in 1837 and sold the house to Judge Felix Grima. It features a central doorway with a fanlight and marble steps; another window with a fanlight graces the second floor. Inside, the floors and doors are made of cypress. The three-story service quarters are in a building off the parterre behind the house. They contain a kitchen with a rare four-burner wood-fired stove with a beehive oven.

## Bourbon Street ⑩

**Map** D3. *3, 55, 89.*

TODAY BOURBON Street, rather than Basin Street, is synonymous with sin. This legendary street, named after the French royal family of Bourbon, is lined with bars that offer vats of such lethal concoctions as Brain Freeze, Nuclear Kamikaze, and Sex on the Bayou, most often to the accompaniment of blasting rock or blues. Other places offer everything from peep shows, topless dancers, and strip joints, to drag shows and gay action. During Mardi Gras, the sidewalks and overhanging balconies are jammed with crowds and drinking revelers.

Some of the most famous establishments near this lively street include **Pat O'Brien's** (St. Peter Street), which is well-known for its rum-based "Hurricane" cocktail, **Preservation Hall** (St. Peter Street), a top-quality jazz venue, and **Arnaud's** (Bienville Street), a restaurant that is a true Ne Orleans classic. Galatoire's, close to Arnaud's, is another premier New Orleans restaurant *(see p373)*. **Lafitte's Blacksmith Shop**, at 941 Bourbon Street, is considere one of the finest bars in New Orleans. Constructed sometime before 1772, it is a goo example of the brick-betwee posts French-style building, i which soft local bricks are supported by cypress timber and protected by plaster. Inside, several small fireplace warm the place on cool evenings, and there is also a small patio containing a sculpture of Adam and Eve, created by an artist as payment for his bar bill.

**Fire fountain at Pat O'Brien's, near Bourbon Street**

Despite its name, there is n concrete evidence that the pirate brothers, Jean and Pierre Lafitte, operated a smithy here as a front for their smuggling activities. They were also prominent slave traffickers, selling "black ivory" to Louisiana's prominent slave-holding families. The brothers earne local gratitude by warning the Americans of the planne British attack on New Orlea in 1815, and they fought bravely in the ensuing battle

Just up from Lafitte's is the oldest gay bar in the country **Lafitte's in Exile**. It is so called because, until the earl 1950s, gays frequented the o Lafitte's; when the bar change hands, its new owner refuse to renew the lease, and its gay patrons established their new quarters here. It has remained a popular alternativ ever since.

### A VIEW OF ROYAL STREET

The pride of the French Quarter, Royal Street is lined with beautiful buildings that have been carefully restored. Today, they are occupied by elegant stores and restaurants.

***Brennan's (#417)*** *Built around 1802 for a Spanish merchant, this building became a bank, and then a restaurant in 1954. Its balcony seal is made of cast iron.*

***Antoine Peychaud's Pharmacy (#437)*** *An antique shop offering a range of fine objects is now housed in the pharmacy where the cocktail was born.*

**Louisiana State Bank (#403)**

**Moss Antiques**

[La]fitte's Blacksmith Shop, Bourbon Street

## [R]oyal Street ⑪

[M]ap D3. St. Charles Ave. [...] 3, 5, 55, 81, 82.

ANTIQUE SHOPS filled with beautiful, often French, [o]bjects line Royal Street, [u]ndoubtedly the most fetch[in]g street in the French [Q]uarter. In the early colony, [th]is was the city's financial [c]enter and its main and most [fa]shionable street. Today, [m]any of the antique stores [o]ccupy handsome landmarks. [T]heir merchandise includes [cr]ystal chandeliers, massive [in]laid armoires, and ormolu [fu]rnishings – treasures [a]ssociated with an opulent [S]outhern lifestyle.

The **Historic New Orleans [C]ollection**, born of one [c]ouple's interest in the Battle [o]f New Orleans (1815), is [h]oused in a complex of [h]ouses built for Jean François [M]erieult and his wife in 1792. [T]he collectors were General [a]nd Mrs. L. Kemper Williams, [w]ho lived in the residence at [th]e rear of the courtyard from [th]e 1940s to the 60s.

The museum's 10 galleries [d]isplay historical artifacts, [ra]nging from maps and paintings to furnishings and decorative objects. The Empire Gallery displays tables, chests, and sofas, alongside portraits of such native New Orleanians as Madame Auguste de Gas, mother of artist Edgar Degas. The museum's other galleries include the Plantation Gallery, the Louisiana Purchase Gallery, the Victorian Gallery, and the Spanish Colonial Gallery.

Farther away are **Gallier House Museum**, an attractive 19th-century residence that combines Creole and American architectural elements, and the lovely **Lalaurie House**, associated with ghosts. Also on Royal Street is **Rumors**, a gift shop that sells Mardi Gras souvenirs all year long – masks, beads, krewe costumes, and posters are all available for sale here.

### Historic New Orleans Collection

533 Royal St. (504) 523-4662. 10am–4:30pm Tue–Sat.

Artifacts from the Historic New Orleans Collection on Royal Street

Steamboat *Natchez*, offering regular two-hour cruises

## Steamboat Natchez ⑫

**Map** E3. Woldenberg Riverfront park wharf. (504) 586-8777, (800) 233-2628. Riverfront. 45, 87. *Harbor Jazz Cruises: 11:30am & 2:30pm daily; Dinner Jazz Cruise: 7pm daily.*
www.steamboatnatchez.com

A REMINDER OF THE old days of river travel, the Steamboat *Natchez* is typical of the steamboats that traveled the length of the Mississippi, taking three to five days to get from Louisville, Kentucky *(see p271)*, to New Orleans. The boatmen, notorious brawlers in search of women and liquor at the end of a trip, established New Orleans' reputation as the "City of Sin." In their heyday, from 1830 to 1860, some 30 steamboats lined up at the levee. The era ended by the close of the 19th century as railroads and highways replaced them. Today, daily cruises offer visitors a glimpse into a forgotten lifestyle.

***[S]t. Anthony's Garden***
*[T]his beautiful garden stands at [th]e back of St. Louis Cathedral. [It]s serenity hides the fact that it [w]as a staging ground for duels [in] the 18th century.*

***The LaBranche Buildings (#700)***
*Embellished with fine oak-leaf ironwork, these buildings were constructed in 1835 for sugar planter Jean Baptiste LaBranche.*

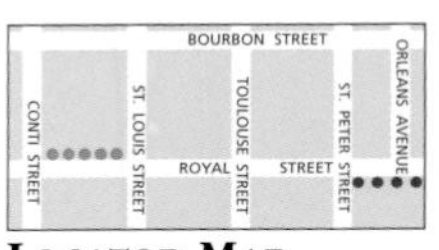


**LOCATOR MAP**

## Custom House & Insectarium ⑬

**Map** D3. 423 Canal St. 3. *Canal.* *daily.* *some public hols.*
www.audoboninstitute.org

PERHAPS THE MOST important Federal-style structure in the South, this Quincy granite building took 33 years (from 1848 to 1881) to complete. Inside, the Marble Hall is a dramatic space under a ground-glass ceiling supported by 14 marble columns.

The Insectarium on the ground floor is devoted to the 900,000 or so known species of insects. There's an interactive theater experience and cooking shows, as well as live insects, gigantic animatronic bugs, and lots of butterflies.

## Aquarium of the Americas ⑭

**Map** E3. Canal St at Mississippi River. *(504) 581-4629.* *Riverfront.* *3, 5, 55, 57.* *9:30am–7pm Fri–Sat, 9:30am–6pm Sun (9:30am–7pm daily in summer).* *Dec 25 & Mardi Gras.*

FOCUSING ON the waters around New Orleans, from the Mississippi and the swamps to the Gulf of Mexico and the Caribbean, this complex features some 560 species of marine life. Highlights include a tank containing a Caribbean reef, and a replica of an oil rig. Other tanks contain species that illustrate everything there is to know about life beneath the ocean, including how fish communicate and how they camouflage themselves. The complex also includes The Entergy IMAX® Theater. Daily riverboat cruises can also be taken from here.

**Under the sea at the Aquarium of the Americas**

**Entrance to the Riverwalk Marketplace**

## Ferry to Algiers & Mardi Gras World ⑮

**Map** E4. Take the ferry at the end of Canal St. In Algiers take the shuttle. *Riverfront.* *55, 57.* *9am–4:30pm daily.* **Blaine Kern's Mardi Gras World** 233 Newton St, Algiers. *(504) 361-7821.* *9:30am–5pm daily.*
www.mardigrasworld.com

A FERRY TAKES visitors across the Mississippi to Algiers and the fascinating Blaine Kern's Mardi Gras World. Blaine Kern is often called "Mr. Mardi Gras" because many of the massive floats are constructed here in his warehouse.

The tour begins with coffee and the traditional King Cake. A short film shows the floats and the stages of their production, from the original drawings and molds to the end result. Visitors can try on some of the flamboyant costumes worn by Krewe members in past parades. Visitors can also wander through the warehouses and view huge decorative figures made of fiberglass or Styrofoam overlaid with papier-mâché. The cost of making the floats is usually borne by each Krewe and can range from anywhere between $300 and $3,000.

## Riverwalk Marketplace ⑯

**Map** E4. 1 Poydras St. *(504) 522-1555.* *Riverfront.* *3, 55, 57, 65.*
www.riverwalkmarketplace.com

THIS MASSIVE riverside shopping mall, designed by the same company that developed Boston's Faneuil Hall *(see p136)*, contains more than 140 stores, most of which are brand-name favorites such as Eddie Bauer Banana Republic, and the Museum Company. The top floor is devoted to a food court, while a highlight of the ground floor is the Creole Delicacies Gourmet Shop, which offers a two-hour course in cooking. In addition to plentiful shopping opportunities, the mall has an outdoor walkway that runs along the Mississippi River, giving visitors one of the best views of the river and river traffic in the city. International and other cruise ships dock alongside the marketplace, the most notable being those operated by the Delta Queen Steamboat Company, which was established in 1890. Several information plaques attached to railings along the walkway describe everything from the types of boats plying the river to the seagulls that drift up from the Gulf of Mexico.

The **Spanish Plaza**, near the entrance, has a fountain in the center. Surrounding it is a circular mosaic bench, depicting the coats of arms of the city's Spanish immigrants.

t. Charles Avenue Streetcar, New Orleans landmark

## ɜarden District ⑰

etween Jackson & Louisiana Aves, St. Charles Ave & Magazine St. *St. Charles.* *11, 14, 27.*

WHEN THE Americans arrived in New Orleans fter the Louisiana Purchase ı 1803, they settled upriver om the French Quarter. This rea is referred to as the ɜarden District because of ıe lush gardens planted with ıagnolia, camellia, azalea, nd jasmine. A residential eighborhood, it is filled with ırge mansions built by vealthy city planters and ıerchants. Some of the grand esidences here are the Robinon House and Colonel Short's 'illa, which has a handsome ast-iron cornstalk fence.

A romantic New Orleans xperience is to take a ride on ıe slow-moving **St. Charles venue Streetcar**. The last f the sort that featured in ennessee Williams' *A Streetar Named Desire*, it travels .5 miles (10.5 km) from Canal treet to Carrollton Avenue. long the way it passes many ımous landmarks. The most prominent are Lee Circle with its memorial to Confederate general Robert E. Lee, the Gothic Revival Christ Church, Touro Synagogue, the Latter Public Library, and Loyola and Tulane Universities.

Just off St. Charles Avenue is one of the loveliest urban parks in the country. The 340-acre (137-ha) Audubon Park was originally the sugar plantation of Jean Etienne Boré, who developed the commercially successful sugar granulation process. It was also the location of the 1884 World Exposition. The **Audubon Zoo** occupies 58 acres (23 ha) of the park's grounds. Beautifully landscaped, the zoo opened in 1938 but was completely redesigned in the 1980s. Today, the animals live in open paddocks that replicate their natural habitats. The Louisana Swamp, where white alligators bask along the banks or float in the muddy lagoon, is one of the most engaging exhibits. Don't miss the flamingo gardens or the lush Jaguar Jungle.

Evocative statue in the City Park's New Orleans Botanical Gardens

## City Park ⑱

*45, 46, 48, 87, 90.* **New Orleans Museum of Art** *(504) 488-2631.* *10am–5pm Tue–Sun.* *public hols.* www.noma.org

THE FIFTH LARGEST urban park in the US, the 1,500-acre (607-ha) City Park is a New Orleans institution, where visitors can relax and enjoy the semitropical Louisiana weather. The **New Orleans Botanical Gardens** and the prestigious **New Orleans Museum of Art** share this space with moss-draped live oaks, lagoons for boating and fishing, and the championship Bayou Oaks Golf Course.

Housed in an impressive Beaux Arts building, the museum has an astonishingly varied collection. Originally the Delgado Museum of Art, it was founded in 1910 when Isaac Delgado, a millionaire bachelor, donated the original $150,000 to construct an art museum in City Park. In 1971 it was renamed the New Orleans Museum of Art in deference to some of its later benefactors. Prize exhibits include a Faberge egg (1896) and Picasso's *Woman in an Armchair* (1960). The New Orleans Botanical Garden was created in the 1930s. Then, it was primarily a rose garden, but today there are also spring and perennial gardens, featuring camellias, azaleas, and magnolias, as well as tropical plants and trees. Several statues by Mexican artist Enrique Alferez stand among the live oaks and other flora.

Colorful costume for the Mardi Gras parade

### Mardi Gras

Culminating on the day before Ash Wednesday – Mardi Gras – the Carnival festivities in New Orleans are celebrated with lavish masked balls, presented by groups of citizens known as "Krewes." Although most balls are private, many Krewes also put on parades, with ornate costumes and colorful floats. Many Carnival traditions began with the Krewe of Rex. The symbolic purple, green, and gold colors used for masks, banners, and other decorations are derived from the original costume worn by Rex, the King of Mardi Gras, in the 1872 parade. The tradition of throwing souvenir doubloons (coins), beads, and dolls from the floats to the crowds began in 1881.

# Louisiana

Old Plantation water pump

RENOWNED FOR ITS exotic landscape of bayous and swamps, antebellum plantation homes, jazz, and fine food, Louisiana is a state richly steeped in history and tradition. Its predominant French heritage is the legacy of the French settlers who named the colony for Louis XIV. Both France and Spain colonized Louisiana before the United States finally acquired the territory through the Louisiana Purchase of 1803. Louisiana became a state in 1812 and in the following decades played a strategic role in the Civil War and the painful struggle for Civil Rights. Today, the state preserves both its Colonial history as well as its distinct Creole and Cajun heritage. Highlights include the beautiful plantations along the Mississippi and the cultural delights of Cajun Country.

## Plantation Alley ❷

Hwy 18 from New Orleans, which joins Hwy 1. *New Orleans Convention & Visitors' Bureau, (800) 672-6124; the bureau maintains a list of tour operators.*

BEFORE THE CIVIL WAR, the Mississippi River was lined with plantations producing first indigo, then cotton, rice, and sugar. At the time, this was one of the nation's wealthiest regions and home to two-thirds of America's millionaires. Of the 350 opulent estates that once flourished here, around 40 remain. Of these about a dozen are open to the public on a stretch of the Great River Road *(see pp40–41)* between New Orleans and Baton Rouge, known as "Plantation Alley."

Today, large neighboring petrochemical plants have replaced sugar cane and cotton as the mainstay of the riverside economy. High levees, reinforced by the Army Corps of Engineers after the flood of 1927, block the river from the road. The tradition since the 1880s has been to light bonfires atop them each Christmas Eve, to illuminate the way for Santa Claus.

**Oak Alley Plantation** in Vacherie, is 40 miles (64 km) west from New Orleans airport. An arcade of 28 arching live oaks, planted some 300 years ago, leads to this striking 1839 house. The picture of the Greek Revival mansion down the long arcade seems the archetypal Hollywood image. Both the recently refurbished house and garden have been used as a location for several movies, including *Interview with the Vampire* (1994). The mansion offers five B&B cottages for overnight stay. To its east, **Laura Plantation** has an 1805 Creole house constructed of cypress, designed by Senegalese builders. The plantation slaves are thought to be the source of various Senegalese folk tales, including the famous *Br'er Rabbit* stories translated into English by Joel Chandler Harris.

A 15-minute drive from New Orleans, **Destrehan Plantation**, built in 1787, is the oldest documented plantation home in the Lower Mississippi Valley. The French Colonial-style home features demonstrations of indigo dyeing and other crafts like bousillage construction, a method using a mixture of clay and Spanish moss. San Francisco Plantation, near Garyville, is a 40-minute drive away from New Orleans. Built in 1856, under centuries old spreading live oak trees, this galleried home in the Creole open-suite style is listed as a National Historic Landmark. Viewed from some vantage points, the design of the house resembles that of a riverboat.

Closest to Baton Rouge and the area's largest plantation home, the palatial 1860 **Nottoway Mansion** occupies an area of 53,000 sq ft (4,924 sq m), and comprises 65 rooms, 165 doors, and 200 windows. Completed in 1859, its largest room happens to be the Grand White Ballroom where the owner, John Hampden Randolph, celebrated his daughters' weddings.

In addition to guided house tours, several plantations now operate restaurants and comfortable B&B inns. The region is best explored by car, although there are many bus tours available.

**The Grand White Ballroom, Nottoway Mansion, in Plantation Alley**

**Oak Alley Plantation**
3645 Hwy 18 Vacherie. *(225) 265-2151.* *9am–5pm daily.* *Jan 1, Thanksgiving, Dec 25.*

**Laura Plantation**
2247 Hwy 18. *(225) 265-7690.* *9am–5pm daily.* *Jan 1, Mardi Gras, Easter, Thanksg., Dec 25.*

**Destrehan Plantation**
13034 River Road, Destrehan. *(985) 764-9315.* *9am–4pm daily.* *public hols.*

**Nottoway Mansion**
White Castle. *(225) 545-2730.* *9am–5pm daily.* *Dec 25.*

ɔuisiana Old State Capitol, Baton Rouge

## ɜaton Rouge ❸

ɜ 470,000. ✈ 🚌 1253 Florida vd, (225) 383-3811. ℹ 730 North vd, (800) 527-6843. Greater ɜton Rouge State Fair (mid-Oct). W www.visitbatonrouge.com

ESTABLISHED BY THE French in 1699 to control access to ɪe Mississippi, Baton Rouge 'Red Stick") was named for ɪe spikes hung with bloody sh heads that marked the oundary between two Native merican territories. The apital of Louisiana since 849, this city is a favored ɔurist destination.

North of downtown, the **tate Capitol** was built in 932 under the tireless irection of ex-governor and S Senator Huey Long (1893–1935), who persuaded legislators to approve the $5 million construction budget. Ironically, Long was assassinated in the building in 1935. This 34-story structure, the country's tallest capitol, offers superb city views from its 27th-floor observation deck. To the south, the autocratic senator's penchant for lavish buildings is further reflected in the **Old Governor's Mansion**, built in 1930 and modeled on the White House. Today, this restored Greek Revival structure displays such memorabilia of past governors as Jimmie Davis's guitar and Huey Long's pajamas. The ornate 1849 Gothic Revival **Louisiana Old State Capitol**, to the southwest, holds interactive exhibits on the state's tumultuous political history. Outside, an observation plaza overlooks the river, where the massive World War II-era destroyer, USS *Kidd*, offers public tours. Farther south, visitors can get a feel of the antebellum era firsthand at the 1791 **Magnolia Mound Plantation**, a 16-acre (6-ha) French-Creole style home and working plantation.

A short, 10-minute drive southwest from downtown leads to the attractive, tree-shaded **Louisiana State University** campus and the **LSU Rural Life Museum**, maintained by the university. Unlike the grand plantation restorations, this museum, with its simple artifacts, reveals how the common owner-operated farming families lived in the 19th century. On view are a grist mill, cockfighting spurs, and pirogues (shallow canoes used to ply the bayous).

Statue in the new State Capitol

**Louisiana Old State Capitol**
100 N Blvd. (225) 342-0500. 10am–4pm Tue–Sat, noon–4pm Sun. Mon, public hols.

**LSU Rural Life Museum**
I-10 exit 160, at 4650 Essen Ln. (225) 765-2437. 8:30am–5pm daily. Jan 1, Easter, Thanksgiving, Dec 24–25.
W www.rurallife.lsu.edu

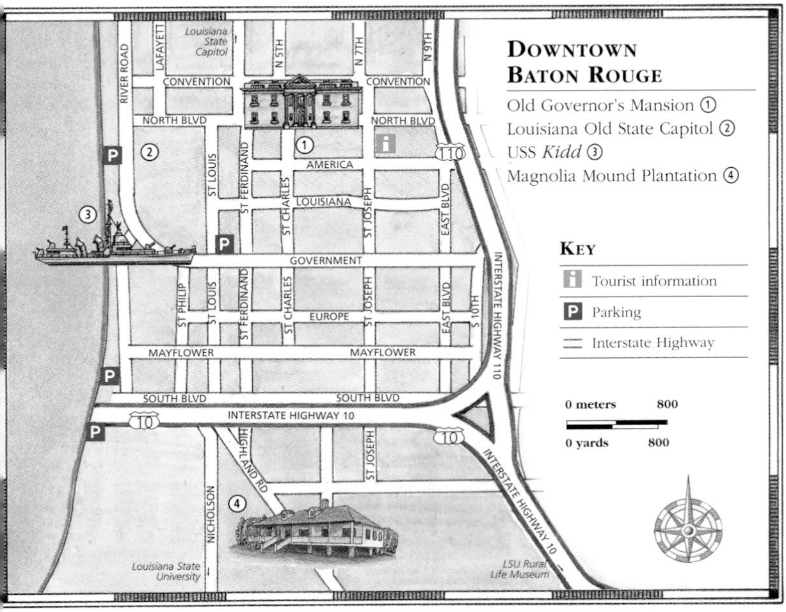

**DOWNTOWN BATON ROUGE**

Old Governor's Mansion ①
Louisiana Old State Capitol ②
USS *Kidd* ③
Magnolia Mound Plantation ④

**KEY**

Tourist information
Parking
Interstate Highway

0 meters 800
0 yards 800

Louisiana State Capitol
RIVER ROAD
LAFAYETTE
N 5TH
N 7TH
N 9TH
CONVENTION
NORTH BLVD
AMERICA
LOUISIANA
GOVERNMENT
EUROPE
MAYFLOWER
SOUTH BLVD
INTERSTATE HIGHWAY 10
INTERSTATE HIGHWAY 110
ST LOUIS
ST FERDINAND
ST CHARLES
ST JOSEPH
EAST BLVD
ST PHILIP
S 10TH
HIGHLAND RD
NICHOLSON
Louisiana State University
LSU Rural Life Museum

Cathedral of St. John the Baptist, Lafayette

## Lafayette ❹

115,000. 1400 NW Evangeline Thruway, (337) 232-3808. www.lafayettetravel.com

THE UNOFFICIAL "Capital of French Louisiana" is an entertaining introduction to the world of bayous, alligators, superb cuisine, and lilting Cajun accents. When the first Acadians arrived here in 1765, they settled along the bayous and prairies west of New Orleans, working as farmers to make a living from the swamps and marshes.

Lafayette evolved from a small settlement, set up in the 1821 around a church, now the towering **Cathedral of St. John the Baptist**, near the Vermilion River. Today, the town is the heart of Cajun Country, distinguished by its unique cultural heritage.

Lafayette's living history museum, **Vermilionville** (the original name of the town), evokes 19th-century Acadiana with its characteristic French-influenced architecture. The buildings here are constructed of bousillage *(see p354)*, and have high-pitched roofs. Both Vermilionville and nearby **Jean Lafitte National Historical Park Acadian Cultural Center** feature exhibits as well as demonstrations on the skills needed to survive in 18th- and 19th-century Louisiana. These include the netmaking that was vital for a life dependent on harvesting food from the bayou, and woodcraft that built plows and the shallow-draft wooden pirogue. The National Park Service, which operates the Jean Lafitte National Historic Park, also maintains other Acadian cultural centers in the wetlands region in Thibodaux (100 miles/160 km to the southeast), and in the prairie region in Eunice that lies about 30 miles (48 km) to the northwest.

**Vermilionville**
300 Fisher Rd. *(337) 233-4077.* *10am–4pm Tue–Sun.* *Mon, Jan 1, Martin Luther King Jr. Day, Thanksgiving, Dec 24, 25, & 31.* www.vermillionville.org

**Jean Lafitte National Historical Park Acadian Cultural Center**
501 Fisher Rd. *(337) 232-0789.* *8am–5pm daily.* *Dec 25.*

## Bayou Teche ❺

Hwy 31 runs from Breaux Bridge to New Iberia. *2513 Hwy 14, (337) 365-1540.* www.iberiatravel.com

BAYOU TECHE (pronounced "Tesh") meanders north-to-south alongside a scenic route between Lafayette and the Atchafalaya Swamp. Stretching between Breaux Bridge and New Iberia, the 25-mile (40-km) length of Hwy 31, with its lush vegetation and beautiful moss-draped oaks, offers a true flavor of the region.

In downtown **Breaux Bridge**, a tiny drawbridge over Bayou Teche proclaims the town "the Crawfish Capital of the World." The town also hosts the annual Crawfish Festival in May. At **Lake Martin**, the Nature Conservancy's Cypress Island Preserve offers an opportunit to see swamp wildlife from a hiking trail and boat tours. The preserve has the world's largest white ibis rookery.

Farther south, in **St. Martinville**, the famous Evangeline Oak marks the spot where Evangeline and her lover Gabriel were supposed to be reunited. Both their tragic tal and the Acadian saga are narrated in *Evangeline*, Henr Wadsworth Longfellow's 184 poem. Nearby, St. Martin de Tours Church dates back to the town's founding in 1765. An adjacent museum display carnival costumes.

Just outside town, the evocative **Longfellow-Evangeline State Historic Site** offers tours of an 18th-century sugar plantation house. Bayou Teche flows through the town of **New Iberia**, famous for its grand plantation home – the 1834 Shadows-on-the-Teche, whic is now a museum.

A detour to Avery Island leads to the **McIlhenny Tabasco Company**, a popul stop for gourmands where a guide presents information

Shadows-on-the-Teche plantation house in New Iberia, Bayou Teche

he Fort St. Jean Baptiste reconstruction in Natchitoches

bout the company's history nd manufacturing. The djacent **Jungle Gardens** s a natural swamp, which ou can also take a tour of.

**Longfellow-Evangeline tate Commemorative Area**
200 N Main St, St. Martinville. (337) 394-3754. *9am–5pm daily.* *Jan 1, Thanksgiving, Dec 25.*
www.ohwy.com/la/l/lonevasa

**McIlhenny Tabasco ompany**
very Island. *(337) 365-8173.* *am–4pm daily.* *public hols.*

## Natchitoches 6

*17,000.* *781 Front St, 318) 352-8072, (800) 259-1714.*
www.natchitoches.net

THE OLDEST permanent settlement in Louisiana, Natchitoches ("Nack-a-tish") was founded on the banks of he Cane River by the French n 1714. The town's compact 3-block riverfront district etains much of its 18th-entury Creole architecture, with elaborate ironwork and piral staircases. South of owntown, **Fort St. Jean Baptiste** re-creates the 1732 rontier outpost designed to eter Spanish expansion astward from Texas.

The surrounding Cane River Country has several plantation ouse tours. Of these, **Melrose Plantation** was visited by uch writers as John Steinbeck nd William Faulkner. The **Bayou Folk Museum** takes isitors into the house of the amed author Kate Chopin, whose daring 19th-century ovel, *The Awakening*, lthough initially banned, was ater widely acclaimed.

**Melrose Plantation**
LA 119. *(318) 379-0055.* *noon–4pm daily.* *public hols.*

**Bayou Folk Museum**
LA 1, Cloutierville. *(318) 379-2233.* *10am–5pm Mon–Sat, 1–5pm Sun.* *public hols.*

## Shreveport 7

*393,000.* *629 Spring St, (318) 222-9391.*
www.shreveport-bossier.org

SITUATED NEAR the Texas border, Shreveport was founded on the Red River in 1839. Agriculture and river transport trade were mainstays of the local economy until the turn of the 20th century, when the discovery of oil made the city a boom town. Shreveport declined after the oil industry moved offshore. Today, however, the town is rapidly changing and has a friendly atmosphere with a number of cultural activities. The **Louisiana State Museum** illustrates the state's history through murals and exhibits, while the annual Louisiana State Fair, held here in late October or early November, attracts more than 300,000 visitors.

**ENVIRONS:** About 165 miles (265 km) from Shreveport in the far northeastern corner of Louisiana state is one of the most significant archaeological sites located in the eastern part of the country. **Poverty Point National Monument** *(see p339)* outside Epps retains the religious mounds built by the early civilization that flourished in the Lower Mississippi basin around 600 BC. Visitors can get here through Hwy 577.

**Poverty Point National Monument**
Hwy 577. *(888) 926-5492.* *9am–5pm daily.* *Jan 1, Thanksgiving, Dec 25.*

Exterior of Louisiana State Museum in Shreveport

### THE ACADIANS – CAJUN COUNTRY

The Acadians, or "Cajuns," were originally French immigrants who had founded a colony in Nova Scotia, Canada, in 1604, naming it l'Acadie after the legendary Greek paradise, Arcadia. Exiled by the British in 1755, they finally settled along the isolated bayous of Louisiana, where they developed a rich French-influenced culture, deeply rooted in its music and cuisine. Acadian culture is best seen in the region's many festivals. Of these the Courir de Mardi Gras, literally "the race," is a distinctly Cajun version of the Mardi Gras *(see p353)*. Colorfully dressed and masked horseback riders ride from house to house, ostensibly collecting ingredients for a community gumbo. They then triumphantly parade through the town, before gathering together for food, drink, music, and frivolity. "Acadiana" is a 22-parish region comprising the wetlands area near New Orleans, the prairies north of Lafayette, and the remote southwestern coast.

Acadian dress

# Arkansas

APTLY KNOWN AS THE "Natural State," Arkansas abounds in mountains, valleys, dense woodlands, and fertile plains. Its two mountain ranges, the Ozark and the Ouachita, are separated by the Arkansas River, which flows through the state capital, Little Rock. The birthplace of former president Bill Clinton, the state actively promotes sights associated with him, including his birthplace, Hope, his boyhood home in Hot Springs, and Little Rock, where he served as governor and waged his campaign for presidency. This former frontier state remains largely wild even today, with vast areas of natural beauty, famous for adventure sports.

**Display in the Central High Museum, Little Rock**

## Little Rock 8

183,133. 615 E Capitol Ave, (501) 370-3290. www.littlerock.com

FOUNDED ON the Arkansas River, near a boulder for which it is named, Little Rock was another modest-sized Southern state capital until native son Bill Clinton was elected 42nd US president in 1993. As a result, executive attention has helped revitalize the city. A new center for much activity is Little Rock River Market District, lined with lively clubs, restaurants, cafés, and shops. Adjacent to the district is the new William J. Clinton Presidential Center. The **Old State House State History Museum**, just west of Main Street, is where Clinton celebrated his presidential victories in 1992 and 1996. The 1833 Greek Revival structure features state history exhibits.

In 1957, the contentious desegregation of Little Rock Central High School catapulted the city to the forefront of the national struggle for Civil Rights. Despite the Supreme Court ban, the governor refused to integrate the school, forcing President Eisenhower to send in the 101st Airborne Division to protect the "Little Rock Nine" (the first nine black students) as they entered the school amid the protests of local segregationists. Today, Central High School is a national historic site and the only operating school to be thus designated. **Central High Museum and Visitor Center** documents this story.

**Central High Museum & Visitor Center**
2125 W 14th St. *(501) 374-1957.* *9am–4:30pm Mon–Sat, 1–4:30pm Sun.* *Jan 1, Thnksg., Dec 25.*

**Old State House State History Museum**
300 W Markham St. *(501) 324-9685.* *9am–5pm Mon–Sat, 1–5pm Sun.* *Jan 1, Thanksg., Dec 25.*

## Hot Springs 9

*35,750.* *629 Central Ave, (501) 321-2277.*

IN ITS HEYDAY in the early 20th century, this was a popular resort for people seeking restorative cures from the thermal springs flowing from the southwestern slope of Hot Springs Mountain. The area became the first US federal reserve park in 1832 and a national park in 1921. The original "Bathhouse Row" is now a National Historic

**Exterior of the Spanish-style Fordyce Bathhouse, the visitor center for Hot Springs National Park**

ndmark District within **Hot** **rings National Park**. The sitor center is housed in the ulent Spanish Renaissance-yle 1915 Fordyce Bathhouse. nly the **Buckstaff Bath-ouse** today remains in oper-on, offering spa facilities. otels, such as the Arlington esort Hotel *(see p370)*, also fer full bathing facilities.

At the Row's south end, the y visitor center distributes aps to sights associated with esident Clinton, who spent s childhood in the city. Hot rings High School, where inton graduated in 1964, is w an apartment building th a "cultural campus" that s exhibits from Clinton's enage years. Visitors can also ur sights such as Clinton's urch and his favorite burger nt. A scenic drive to the mmit of Hot Springs Moun-n leads to an observation wer offering panoramic ews of the Ouachita Moun-ns, the city, and the forests d lakes that surround it.

**Hot Springs National rk**
9 Central Ave. *(501) 624-2701.*
*9am–5pm daily.* *Jan 1, anksgiving, Dec 25.*

**Buckstaff Bathhouse**
9 Central Ave, Bathhouse Row.
*(501) 623-2308.* *7am–noon on–Sat, 1:30–3pm Mon–Fri.* *1, Jul 4, Thanksg., Dec 25.*

## ountain View 10

*2,876.* *107 N Peabody, 38) 679-2859.*

NESTLING DEEP in the hills and valleys of the mote Ozark Mountains, the cluded hamlet of Mountain ew is a haven for outdoor thusiasts. A short drive to e north is the **Ozark Folk enter State Park**. The park lebrates the Ozark Moun-in region's cultural heritage th living history exhibits, afts demonstrations, festivals, d traditional music perfor-ances held at the state park eater. It also offers hiking ils, a lodge open year und, a lively restaurant, and swimming pool. The nearby Vild and Scenic" **Buffalo** **National River** is highly popular for float fishing and canoeing; many local outfitters organize guided canoe trips of the river. The National Forest Service maintains several campgrounds in the area.

**Steeply inclined streets of the Victorian commercial area, Eureka Springs**

**Ozark Folk Center State Park**
1032 Park Ave. *(870) 269-3851.*
*check for times.*
www.ozarkfolkcenter.com

**ENVIRONS:** About 15 miles (24 km) northwest of Mountain View, via Hwy 14, lie **Blanchard Springs Caverns**, which feature an extensive collection of limestone cave formations and an underground stream open for public tours. The ever-changing crystalline formations in these "living" caves are the result of minerals deposited by dripping water. Exploring the magnificent caves can be difficult because of the damp air and cramped conditions. However, both the two main routes, the half-mile (1-km) Dripstone Trail as well as the 1.2-mile (2-km) Discovery Trail, offer an unforgettable experience of life underground. A visitor center features exhibits and videos that describe the caves and their long process of creation.

**Christ of the Ozarks, Eureka Springs**

**Blanchard Springs Caverns**
off Hwy 14. *(870) 757-2211.*
*mid-Apr–Oct: 9am–5pm daily; Oct–Apr: 9:30am–4pm Wed–Sun.*
*Jan 1, Thanksgiving, Dec 25.*

## Eureka Springs 11

*2,278.* *137 W Van Buren, (479) 253-8737, (888) 387-3520.*
www.eurekasprings.org

THE WORLD'S second-largest statue of Jesus, the seven-story-high "**Christ of the Ozarks**," towers above the former resort town of Eureka Springs. After nearly a century of decline, the town has benefited by its development as an artists' community, as a romantic getaway, and by the establishment of country music performances in the style of Nashville's Grand Ole Opry *(see p264)* held at the Hoe-Down and Pine Mountain Jamboree. For almost 30 years running, the Great Passion Play has been performed at the **Sacred Arts Center**. This outdoor drama depicts the days leading up to the death of Jesus Christ.

The religious tone of the town is perpetuated in the **Bible Museum** with its collection of more than 6,000 Bible editions in 625 languages. Eureka Springs Historic Gardens and a scenic railroad are the town's other attractions. Many visitors also tour the well-preserved Victorian buildings and savor the magic of the town's forested mountain setting.

**Sacred Arts Center**
935 Passion Play Rd.
*(800) 882-7529.* *Apr–Oct: call for times.*

# Mississippi

THE BIRTHPLACE OF Tennessee Williams, Elvis Presley, B.B. King, and Oprah Winfrey, Mississippi is a complex state best known for blues music, antebellum plantation homes, and a lamentable Civil Rights history. The endless horizon of cotton fields, most often associated with Mississippi, can be found in the northwest Delta region, while in the northeastern corner is the hardscrabble hill area around Tupelo. The state capital, Jackson, sits in the central plain and is the urban center of this largely rural state. Today, Mississippi offers such contrasting diversions as glittering Las Vegas-style casinos, excellent Vietnamese seafood restaurants, and ferry rides to deserted beaches.

## Mississippi Delta ⓬

*20,000 (Clarksdale).* *Greenwood.* *1540 DeSoto Ave, Hwy 49, Clarksdale, (662) 627-7337.*

THE MISSISSIPPI DELTA, a vast, alluvial basin, cleared of its once-thick forests, and blanketed with cotton fields, is the birthplace of blues music. The **Delta Blues Museum** in downtown Clarksdale is the touchstone for music lovers from around the world. Located in a renovated 1920's freight depot, this museum is a virtual repository of blues music, with personal belongings, photographs, instruments, and videos of such resident legends as Robert Johnson, Howlin' Wolf, and Muddy Waters. Exhibits include the wooden "Muddywood" guitar created by Z.Z. Top with planks from the original House of Blues, the birthplace of Muddy Waters. The Sunflower River Blues and Gospel Festival is held outside the museum each August. The Delta's creative legacy extends beyond music. The annual Tennessee Williams festival celebrates the work of the famous playwright who spent his childhood in Clarksdale.

About 55 miles (88 km) south of Clarksdale, the **Cottonlandia Museum** in Greenwood documents the history of the Delta with a special emphasis on cotton, the industry that fueled the culture and economy of the region. A 24-mile (38-km) drive south brings visitors to Greenville, the largest town in the Delta. The visitor center of this major riverport occupies a riverboat docked at the foot of the bridge. The Mississippi Delta Blues Festival is held in town every September. Other sights include the tiny museum in Leland honoring Jim Henson, the creator of the Muppets; Belzoni, said to be the "Catfish capital of the World," located in the county that has the most farm-raised catfish; and Indianola, the hometown of B.B. King.

Catfish farm sign

**Delta Blues Museum**
1 Blues Alley, Clarksdale. *(662) 627-6820.* *Mar–Oct: 9am–5pm Mon–Sat; Nov–Feb: 10am–5pm Mon–Sat.* *Jan 1, Jul 4, Thnksg., Dec 25.* www.deltabluesmuseum.org

**Cottonlandia Museum**
1608 Hwy 82 W. *(662) 453-0925.* *9am–5pm Mon–Fri, 2–5pm Sat–Sun.* *major public hols.* www.cottonlandia.org

Ventress Hall, University of Mississippi campus, Oxford

## Oxford ⓭

*13,000.* *(662) 234-4680.* www.touroxfordms.com

HOME TO THE stately 1848 University of Mississippi fondly known as "Ole Miss," the appealing college town Oxford is the state's intellectual and cultural center. The local literary landmark is the secluded 1844 **Rowan Oak**, home of William Faulkner, one of the most influential writers of the time and pioneer of the Southern Gothic literature movement. The pl outline of *A Fable*, the book the Nobel Prize-winning author was working on at hi death, can be seen inscribed on the walls. A Faulkner statue stands in downtown's classic courthouse square, surrounded by sophisticated galleries, restaurants, cafés, and live music venues.

The University of Mississippi campus houses the **University Museums**. I addition to classical Greek and Roman antiquities, the

One of the many riverboat casinos in the Mississippi Delta

djacent museums hold a nall but dynamic collection f Southern folk art.

**Rowan Oak**
d Taylor Rd. *(662) 234-3284.* *10am–4pm Tue–Sat, 1–4pm Sun.* *some public & university hols.*

**University Museums**
niversity Ave at Fifth St. *(662) 915-7073.* *10am–30pm Tue–Sat, 1–4 pm Sun.* *some public & university hols.*

## upelo 14

*35,000.* *399 E Main St, (662) 41-6521.* www.tupelo.net

AN HOUR'S DRIVE west from Oxford, Tupelo is the irthplace of Elvis Presley, ne of the world's most nduring cultural icons. Here, a modest, two-room hotgun shack on the eastern inge of town, the King of ock 'n' roll was born in 935, along with his stillborn vin Jesse. Elvis lived in upelo until age 13, when the mily was forced by financial onstraints to move to emphis *(see p266)*. Today e **Elvis Presley Birthplace**, efurbished to look as it id in 1935, is a pilgrimage te for Elvis fans the world ver. An adjacent museum olds a unique private ollection of Elvis memora-ilia. A chapel, which verlooks the birthplace, atures Elvis' own bible.

The new Tupelo Auto-obile Museum, the first of its kind in the state, displays more than 100 restored cars and includes a replica of a vintage garage.

Tupelo offers all the basic necessities for lodging and dining, and serves as a pit stop for the famous Natchez Trace Parkway *(see p362)*.

atue of young Elvis at Tupelo, is birthplace

**Elvis Presley Birthplace**
306 Elvis Presley Dr. *(662) 841-1245.* *9am–5pm Mon–Sat, 1–5pm Sun.* *Thanksgiving, Dec 25.* www.elvispresleybirthplace.com

**Grave markers in Vicksburg National Military Park**

## Vicksburg National Military Park 15

3201 Clay St. *(601) 636-0583.* *8am–5pm daily.* *Dec 25.* www.nps.gov/vick

THE VICKSBURG National Military Park, established in 1899, commemorates one of the most tragic sieges in Civil War history *(see p47)*. Its strategic location, high on the bluffs overlooking the Mississippi River, made Vicksburg the target of Union forces, which wanted to gain control of the vital river corridor and cut the Confederacy in half. On March 29, 1863, the Union Army surrounded the city. After a 47-day siege, the Confederates surrendered on July 4, 1863, giving the North undisputed control of the river and sounding the death knell of the Confederacy. The impact of defeat was so severe that Vicksburg's citizens refused to recognize the Fourth of July holiday until the mid-20th century. The campaign's story is retold in statuary headstones, earthworks, and artifacts at the park. Guided tours bring the landscape to life, where re-enactments of the Civil War are held from June through August.

### Blues Music

The sound at the root of all contemporary popular music heard around the world springs from the large, flat, alluvial basin called the Mississippi Delta. Here African rhythms, work chants, and spirituals evolved into a distinctive style of music known as the blues. When Alabama musician W.C. Handy came through the Delta in 1903, he declared it "the weirdest music I ever heard," and carried the sound up to Memphis, where he recorded the Memphis Blues. Along with the Great Migration of African Americans from the rural South to the industrial North in the early 1900s, the blues reached Chicago, where such famous artists as Muddy Waters electrifed the sound. Rock 'n' roll is said to be born from this sound.

**Muddy Waters figure in Delta Blues Museum**

Old gas station at the Mississippi Agriculture and Forestry Museum

## Jackson ⓰

202,000. 921 S President St, (601) 960-1891.

FOUNDED on a bluff above the Pearl River, Mississippi's capital city was named after popular national hero General Andrew Jackson *(see p265)*. During the Civil War, the city was torched on three separate occasions by Union General William Tecumseh Sherman, earning it the nickname "Chimneyville." The few buildings that survive are treasured landmarks today. Of these, the old 1839 Capitol, now the **Old Capital Museum of Mississippi History**, presents an overview of the state's Civil Rights history, juxtaposing stark black-and-white video footage of violent clashes between the police and protesters, with plainspoken commentary. Upstairs, the museum features revolving exhibits on such topics as author Eudora Welty, a Jackson resident, or "Pride of the Fleet" about the battleship USS *Mississippi*. A small, 20th-century room elaborates on the impact of the cotton and lumber industries on the state's economy, ecology, and society. Yet, the city itself is the best historical exhibit. With its railroad trestles, smoky coffee shops, and franchise-free main street, downtown Jackson appears like a movie set from the 1950s. The **Mississippi State Capitol**, built in 1903, resembles the US Capitol in Washington, DC, and houses the legislative, judicial, and executive branches of the state government. Jackson is also home to the **Mississippi Agriculture and Forestry Museum**, a very appealing family attraction that celebrates the state's rural heritage. Among its exhibits are an 1850s homestead, complete with livestock and gardens, and a 1930s small-town Main Street with a general store selling penny candy. The Chimneyville Crafts Gallery, a handicraft store on the grounds, displays and sells folk arts, including Choctaw crafts. The expansive site also has a lively cafeteria and produce stand. The adjacent Sports Hall of Fame honors the state's beloved athletes and college teams with enjoyable interactive exhibits.

Other sights in Jackson include the local zoo, Mynelle Gardens, the Mississippi Museum of Natural Science, and the Mississippi Museum of Art, which displays the state's largest art collection. All these attractions, plus the city's growing reputation as a blues venue, make Jackson a pleasant stop for visitors coming through the Natchez Trace Parkway.

**Old Capital Museum of Mississippi History**
Old Capitol, 100 S State St. *(601) 576-6920.* *daily.* *public hols.*

**Mississippi Agriculture & Forestry Museum**
1150 Lakeland Dr. *(800) 844-8687.* *9am–5pm Mon–Sat.* *Sun, Jan 1, Thnksg., Dec 25.*

Natchez Parkway sign

## Natchez Trace Parkway ⓱

**Visitor Center** Mount Locust. *(662) 680-4027.* *8am–5pm daily.* www.nps.gov/natr

ESTABLISHED AS a national historic parkway in 1938, this 450-mile (724-km) highway linking Natchez with Nashville, Tennessee *(see p264–5)*, was originally an animal trail. Later, it evolved into a footpath and played a vital role in the development of the country's midsection b linking the Ohio River Valley and the Gulf of Mexico. Pioneers used the route to transport their crops and produce downriver by barge to Natchez, where they sold both their goods and barges for scrap lumber, and then returned north on foot.

Today, the Natchez Trace Parkway *(see pp40–41)* is a scenic, year-round destination. No commercial traffic is perm ted in this haven for hikers, motorists, and cyclists, and the speed limit is a leisurely 50 mph (80 km/h).

The parkway preserves several historical sites, such a **Emerald Mound**. Situated near Natchez, it dates from AD 1400 and is the second largest Native American ceremonial mound in the countr A detour west, along Hwy 552, leads to the "**Ruins of**

Natchez Trace Parkway, a histori wooded trail

/indsor," where a ghostly et of 23 towering Corinthian olumns serves as a poignant eminder of a mansion that urned down in 1890. The **Iount Locust** visitor center, ocated 15 miles (24 km) ortheast of Natchez in a estored 1783 inn, distributes aaps detailing various sights long the route.

## Natchez 18

*20,000.* *640 S Canal t, (601) 442-5880.*

BEST KNOWN for its fine antebellum architecture, Jatchez is an attractive little own on the bluffs above Aississippi River. Many of its istoric buildings lie within asy walking distance of the ompact downtown district. ome of these gems include he oldest house in town, the 798 **House on Ellicott's Hill**; the stately and palatial **tanton Hall** (1857); the nfinished **Longwood** (1860), vhose construction was nterrupted by the Civil War; nd **Rosalie**, an 1829 brick nansion atop the bluff that erved as Union headquarters luring the Civil War.

Many house museums are open all year, but many more can be seen during the **Natchez Pilgrimage** held in March, April, October, and November *(see p28)*. A short drive east of downtown is **Melrose Plantation**, the US's most intact antebellum estate. Maintained by the National Park Service, it displays African-American history in slave quarters alongside the 1845 Greek Revival mansion. At the south end of town, a mile (1.6 km) off Hwy 61, is the Grand Village of the Natchez Indians, with Indian mounds, replicas of huts, nature trails, and a museum.

**House on Ellicott's Hill**
Jefferson & Canal Sts. *(601) 442-2011.* *9am–4:30pm daily.* *Dec 25.*

**Natchez Pilgrimage Tour**
*(601) 446-6631, (800) 647-6742.*

Longwood, the octagonal, domed house, in Natchez

## Gulf Coast 19

*124,000 (Biloxi & Gulfport).* *942 Beach Dr, Gulfport, (228) 896-6699.* www.gulfcoast.org

LINGERING French influences and a maritime heritage combine to make the scenic Gulf of Mexico coastline unlike the rest of Mississippi. In 1699, two Québcois brothers, Pierre le Moyne, Sieur d'Iberville, and Jean Baptiste le Moyne, Sieur de Bienville, reached what is now Ocean Springs, to set up France's first permanent settlement in the South. In 1704, the French government sponsored the transport of 20 young women as prospective brides for the male colonists. Armed with their trousseaux in state-issued suitcases or "cassettes," the "cassette girls" were housed on Ship Island.

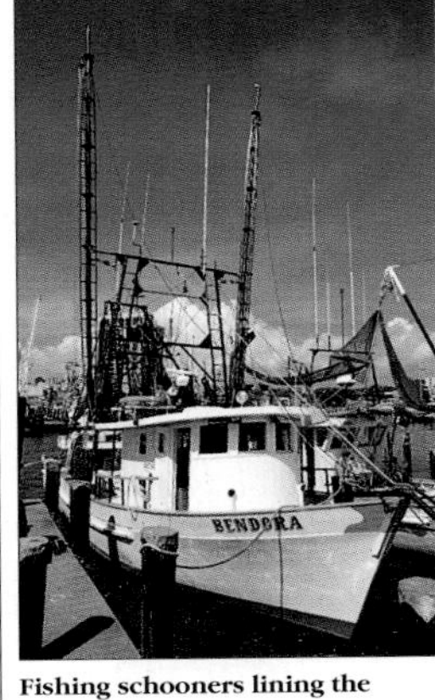


Fishing schooners lining the waterfront on the Gulf Coast

After the Americans gained control of the coast, they built **Fort Massachusetts** in the mid-1800s on Ship Island. During the Civil War, the Union used the fort to house POWs, including a troop of African-American Confederates from Louisiana.

In August 1965, Hurricane Camille, one of the worst storms to hit mainland US, split Ship Island into two – West Ship and East Ship (although it is still referred to locally in the singular). Today, both are part of the **Gulf Islands National Seashore**. A ferry transports passengers to the beach and for tours of the historic fort. Boating is a popular recreation – visitors can take boat and kayak trips to deserted islands, or fishing charters on traditional shrimp boats. The **Maritime and Seafood Industry Museum**, at Point Cadet in Biloxi, holds elaborate displays on the industry that dominated the local economy until gambling was legalized in the 1990s. Now, huge Vegas-style casinos line the coast.

**Gulf Islands National Seashore**
3500 Park Rd, Ocean Springs. *(228) 875-9057.* www.nps.gov/guis

**Maritime & Seafood Industry Museum**
115 1st St. *(228) 435-6320.* *8:30am–4:30pm daily; Labor Day–Jun: 8:30am–4:30pm Mon–Sat.* *Jan 1, Thanksg., Dec 25.* www.maritimemuseum.org

# Alabama

ALABAMA SLOPES FROM THE Cumberland Plateau in the northeast, across forested ridges and fertile plains to the Gulf of Mexico at Mobile Bay. The first European presence was established by the French along the coast in the early 1700s. During the next 100 years, settlement increased as overland immigrants from Tennessee and Georgia moved here, ousting the Choctaw, Cherokee, and Creek Indians from their ancestral lands. With progress, cotton fed the port of Mobile, and the steel industry drove Birmingham's economy. Today, the state is known for its diverse landscape, its antebellum architecture, and, most importantly, its Civil Rights history.

**Reconstructed Fort Conde, Mobile**

## Mobile 20

*201,200.* *1 S Water St, (251) 208-2000.*

THIS BEAUTIFUL port city was founded as a French colony in 1702. Later it served as a strategic Confederate port until the final days of the Civil War. Today, the city retains both its French and Southern flavor and is best known for its **Mardi Gras Cottage Museum**, which includes memorabilia dating from the early 1800s.

At the head of Mobile Bay is **Fort Conde**, a partially reconstructed fort built by the French. Moored nearby is the World War II battleship, USS *Alabama*. A scenic loop drive around the bay leads to two other historic forts, Fort Morgan to the east, and Fort Gaines on Dauphin Island. Both are havens for birdlife.

**Fort Conde**
150 Royal St. *(251) 208-7304.*
*8am–5pm daily.* *public hols, Mardi Gras.*

## Selma 21

*19,500.* *912 Selma Ave, (334) 875-7241.*

SITUATED ON a bluff high above the Alabama River, this city was the site of one the most notorious scenes in Civil Rights history. On March 7, 1965, a day that became known as "Bloody Sunday," 600 Civil Rights protesters heading toward Montgomery, the capital, violently clashed with the police at Edmund Pettus Bridge. A few weeks later, however, Dr. Martin Luther King Jr. led a successful march to the State Capitol steps. The **National Voting Rights Museum** encapsulates the story, and an annual re-enactment pays tribute to the event.

**Display inside the Voting Rights Museum in Selma**

Before the Civil Rights era, Selma's place in history was assured as the "Arsenal of the Confederacy." It produced weapons, cannons, and ironclad ships. Much of the city was destroyed during the war, but the townscape along the river remained intact. The city's 1891 cherry-red train depot holds exhibits on all aspects of local history.

**National Voting Rights Museum**
1012 Water Ave. *(334) 418-0800.*
*9am–5pm Mon–Fri, 10am–3pm Sat.* www.voterights.org

## Montgomery 22

*220,000.* *300 Water St, (334) 262-0013.*

ALABAMA'S CAPITAL city since 1846, Montgomery was also the Confederacy's first capital during the Civil War. In 1861, Jefferson Davis was sworn in as the Confederate president on the steps of the Greek Revival State Capitol. Across the street, the **First White House of the Confederacy** is now a museum related to those times.

The city also played a pivotal role during the Civil Rights Movement. The segregation of the city's transportation system led to an act of defiance by Rosa Parks, when she refused to surrender her bus seat to a white man. In 1956, the young Dr. Martin Luther King Jr. supported the year-long Montgomery Bus Boycott, which ultimately brought about the desegregation of the city's public transportation system. Its success was significant as it not only strengthened the movement, but also saw the rise of King as the campaign's leader. The city's landmark **Civil Rights Memorial**, designed by Vietnam Veterans Memorial artist Maya Lin

**ontgomery's Civil Rights Memorial Fountain**

*ee p205)*, honors 40 martyrs ho sacrificed their lives in e fight for racial equality. Montgomery is also associ- ed with two major figures of )th-century arts. Local girl elda Fitzgerald and her ısband, writer F. Scott ızgerald, lived here in 1931, hile he was writing *Tender the Night*. Their house is ›w a museum. In 1958, ›untry singer Hank Williams ayed his final concert in e city three days before s death. Williams is buried Oakwood Cemetery, ıd a statue of the singer ınds downtown.

**First White House of the ›nfederacy**
4 Washington Ave. *(334) 242- 61.* *8am–4:30pm Mon–Fri. Sat–Sun, state hols.*

## 'uskegee ㉓

*11,534.* *121 Main St, 34) 727-6619.*

ORMER SLAVE Booker T. Washington founded the ıskegee Normal and Indus- al Institute here in 1881 to ıprove educational opportu- :ies for African Americans. ıe school evolved into **Tuskegee University**, best known for agriculturist George Washington Carver's innovations that revolutionized agricultural growth in the region. The "Tuskegee Airmen," the group of African American pilots who distinguished themselves in World War II, also graduated from the institute, now part of the Tuskegee Institute National Historic Site.

## Birmingham ㉔

*245,600.* *2200 9th Ave N, (205) 458-8000.*

THE LARGEST city in Alabama, Birmingham was once the region's foremost producer of steel. Celebrating the city's industrial past is **Sloss Furnaces National Historic Landmark**, a museum housed in an old steel mill, and a 55-ft (17-m) high iron statue of Vulcan, the Roman god of fire, on the summit of Red Mountain, the source of the iron ore. Today, the city's attractions are typical of a modern Southern city – antebellum houses, botanical gardens, and the acclaimed **Birmingham Museum of Art**, with its fine collection of Wedgwood. Yet, the most moving landmarks are those that relate to the city's African-American history. These can be seen within walking distance of the central downtown district's visitor center, where maps as well as guided neighborhood tours are available.

The **Birmingham Civil Rights Institute** uses vintage film footage to explain the city's Civil Rights Movement. Among the exhibits is the door of the cell in which Dr. Martin Luther King Jr. wrote his famous "Letter from a Birmingham Jail," arguing that individuals have the right to disobey unjust laws. Down the street, the restored Sixteenth Street Baptist Church stands as a memorial to four black girls killed by a Ku Klux Klan bomb in 1963. To its southeast, in the historic **Carver Theatre**, the Alabama Jazz Hall of Fame hosts live music performances and celebrates the achievements of such artists as Dinah Washington, Nat King Cole, W.C. Handy, and Duke Ellington. At the north end of town, the **Alabama Sports Hall of Fame** honors beloved native African-American athletes such as Joe Louis and Jesse Owens.

**Dr. Martin Luther King Jr.**

**Birmingham Civil Rights Institute**
520 16th St N. *(205) 328-9696.* *10am–5pm Tue–Sat, 1–5pm Sun.* *public hols.* *(Sun free).*

## Huntsville ㉕

*160,000.* *500 Church St, (256) 533-5723.*

SET IN A curving valley in northern Alabama, the cotton market town of Huntsville developed into a space and military research and development, and manufacturing center after World War II. Home to the NASA-Marshall Space Flight Center, the city's main attraction is the US Space and Rocket Center and the mission control tours. Exhibits include Apollo capsules and a life-size space shuttle. A camp here also teaches children about space exploration.

**orge Washington Carver Museum, Tuskegee University**

# Practical Information

ADVANCE PLANNING IS NECESSARY for a successful tour around the Deep South, simply because there is so much to see and do. New Orleans, the region's largest city, is packed with entertainment and music venues, clubs, hotels, and restaurants, while many small towns and the expansive and diverse areas between them often double as low-key resort areas, catering to city-dwellers in need of a change of pace. Depending upon the time, visitors can explore significant historical sights, appreciate stunning scenery, gaze at the well-manicured gardens of former plantation homes, take in a local celebration, or simply relax alongside a lazy river.

## TOURIST INFORMATION

EACH OF THE Deep South states publishes a wide variety of informative travel guides, which may be ordered by telephone or accessed via web sites. As soon as visitors enter Louisiana, Mississippi, Alabama, or Arkansas, they may check in one of a dozen official "Welcome Centers" along major highways. Staffed by helpful volunteers and open from 8am to 5pm daily, these centers offer free road maps and a full range of tourist information. Such information is also available from the multitude of local and regional tourism bureaus across all four states.

## NATURAL HAZARDS

THE DEEP SOUTH is prone to hurricanes and occasional tornadoes from early June to November each year. In August 2005, Hurricane Katrina hit the Gulf Coast, destroying New Orleans and coastal towns and killing thousands of people. If planning a visit, visitors should follow the storm forecasts for the Gulf and Caribbean. The **National Hurricane Center** in Miami provides information on impending hurricanes. When a Hurricane Warning is posted in the area you are visiting, either cancel your trip or evacuate the area. Follow the broadcasts about emergency procedures on radio and television.

The biggest hazard is the sun. Use high-factor sunscreen and wear a hat. Also, drink plenty of fluids to avoid getting dehydrated. Biting and stinging insects, especially mosquitoes, are a nuisance between April and November, so remember to carry insect repellent.

## GETTING AROUND

LIKE MUCH OF the US, the Deep South is a region where it can be difficult to get around without a car. Seat belts are mandatory for drivers and front-seat passen-gers in all Deep South states. Most states also require seat belts for back-seat passenger All automobile occupants under the age of four require child safety seats.

Public transportation options are limited. **Grey-hound** buses only serve some larger towns and cities, while **Amtrak** runs two train routes – north–south across the Mississippi Delta betwee Memphis and New Orleans, and east–west, connecting New Orleans with Mobile an Birmingham. However, an unusual way to get around the Deep South is to board a replica Mississippi riverboat. The **Delta Queen Steamboa Company** offers tours along "Old Muddy," from New Orleans up to Baton Rouge, Natchez and other cities.

## THE CLIMATE OF THE DEEP SOUTH

The climate across this region does not vary much from state to state, although sea-sonal differences are distinct. Winter is rather wet, while the summer heat and humidity can be sweltering. By Septem-ber the weather is fine again, though late summer storms or hurricanes can put a damper on travel. Spring and autumn are the ideal times to plan an extended trip. Spring flowers, such as magnolia blossoms, set the tone for the early months of the year.

**NEW ORLEANS**

| month | Apr | Jul | Oct | Jan |
|---|---|---|---|---|
| °F/C (high) | 77/25 | 90/32 | 79/26 | 62/17 |
| °F/C (low) | 61/16 | 76/24 | 64/18 | 47/8 |
| sunshine | 14 days | 19 days | 18 days | 20 days |
| rainfall | 4.5 in | 6.1 in | 3 in | 5 in |

32°F 0°C

## ETIQUETTE

THE OLD-WORLD traditions of the Deep South hospi-tality and courtesy, especially toward women, are legendar Addressing people politely, with a "sir" or "ma'am" will b much appreciated, and will help social interaction.

Check for non-smoking signs as smoking is prohibite in most public buildings, including stores and restau-rants. Although the laws for drinking alcohol vary from state to state, the legal age is 21. Only in New Orleans is i permissible to drink on the streets, though only in plasti containers called "go cups."

## FESTIVALS

THE DEEP SOUTH states stage a diverse range of annual community, regional, and national festivals. The nation's biggest party, and one of the world's most colorful and lively annual events, is the 10-day long series of celebrations leading up to **Mardi Gras**, French fc "Fat Tuesday." The carnival parades, music, drinking, an dancing are at their liveliest New Orleans, though smalle but no less energetic celebra tions are also held in several her Deep South towns, cluding Mobile, Alabama.

Spring is a fine time to be Mississippi, especially if ɔu can time your trip to ɲjoy the *"Gone With the 'ind"*-like re-creations of the **ıtchez Pilgrimage**, a onth-long celebration of the ıtebellum "Old South." any of the city's historic ɔmes are open to the public, ıd several pageants and ɜrformances take place.

Summer brings a profusion outdoor events, and fireɔrks, bands, and street stivals are the norm for ɔmmunity celebrations of e July 4 Independence Day ɔliday. Numerous county ıd state fairs take place in e countryside in July and ıgust, as do a number of usic festivals such as the **B. King Homecoming ɛstival** in Indianola ississippi, the first of many ues-themed festivals that ke place in and around the ississippi Delta. Later in the ımmer comes the grand **ississippi Delta Blues and eritage Festival**, held in ɛptember in Greenville, ississippi. In October, the storic homes of Natchez ıd Vicksburg are again ɔened to the public during e **Fall Pilgrimage**. During is time, lucky visitors may mple freshly-made, sugary ɛalines, sold by vendors.

## SPORTS & OUTDOOR ACTIVITIES

THE TOWNS AND cities of the Deep South are not large enough to support top-tier professional sports teams, but they field dozens of minor league teams and hundreds of high-quality sports teams of various public and private colleges and universities. New Orleans has the New Orleans Hornets basketball team and the New Orleans Saints football team, which plays in the **Superdome**, one of the world's largest indoor sports arenas. The main events of the college sporting seasons are football and basketball games between regional rivals, including Louisiana State University Tigers, the University of Alabama's Crimson Tide, and the Rebels of the University of Mississippi. Baseball season runs from April to September, football from September through January, and basketball from winter through mid-spring.

Although both fishing and boating are also prominent, fishing is by far the more popular of the two sports. Lake fishing for bass or crappie is available in many state parks, while Arkansas streams offer trout fishing. Deep-sea fishing for grouper, tarpon, or snapper, or by net for the shrimp, can be arranged from Gulf of Mexico ports such as Biloxi, Mississippi, Mobile, Alabama, or Grand Isle, Louisiana. Visitors should check with the various state fish and game departments to see which permits are required.

## ENTERTAINMENT

THE BIRTHPLACE of jazz and a melting pot of American music, New Orleans is a showcase for all types of performances. Local newspapers such as the *Times-Picayune* or the weekly *New Orleans Magazine* carry detailed listings of the events and activities. A major venue for music in New Orleans is the historic **Preservation Hall**, where traditonal "Dixieland" jazz may be heard most nights. A huge range of nightclubs in the tourist-dominated French Quarter as well as in the uptown area offer live musical entertainment. For traditional Cajun music, head to Lafayette and the roadhouse restaurant, **Prejean's**, the most reliable of the music venues in the region.

Many other cities also host popular musical events. Blues festivals take place all over Mississippi and Arkansas during summer. A wonderful place to listen to the blues is **Ground Zero Blues Club**, in Clarksdale, Mississippi.

## DIRECTORY

### TOURIST OFFICES

**Alabama**
(800) 252-2262.
www.touralabama.org

**Arkansas**
(800) 628-8725.
www.arkansas.com

**Louisiana**
(800) 994-8626.
www.louisianatravel.com

**Mississippi**
(866) 733-6477.
www.visitmississippi.org

### NATURAL HAZARDS

**National Hurricane Center, Miami**
(305) 229-4470.
www.nhc.noaa.gov

### TRAVEL

**Amtrak**
(800) 872-7245.
www.amtrak.com

**Greyhound**
(800) 231-2222.
www.greyhound.com

### RIVER CRUISES

**Delta Queen Steamboat Co.**
Robin St Wharf, 1380 Port of New Orleans Place.
(800) 543-1949.

### FESTIVALS

**Mardi Gras, New Orleans**
(800) 672-6124.
www.neworleansonline.com

**B.B. King Homecoming Festival**
(662) 887-4454.

### SPORTS

**Superdome**
(504) 587-3663.
www.superdome.com

### DEPARTMENTS OF FISH & GAME

**Arkansas**
(501) 223-6300.

**Alabama**
(334) 242-3465.

**Louisiana**
(225) 765-2800.

**Mississippi**
(601) 432-2400.

### ENTERTAINMENT

**Preservation Hall**
(504) 522-2841.
www.preservationhall.com

**Prejean's**
(337) 896-3247.
www.prejeans.com

**Ground Zero Blues Club**
(662) 621-9009.
www.groundzerobluesclub.com

# Where to Stay

In the Deep South region, New Orleans has the greatest selection and variety of accommodations, with many historic and architecturally distinctive properties. Beyond New Orleans, the bayou country around Lafayette and the Mississippi town of Natchez also offer historic lodgings. Casino hotels along the Mississippi River and Gulf Coast generally offer low room rates.

## Louisiana

**Baton Rouge:** *Courtyard Acadian Center* $$$
2421 S Acadian Thruway. *(225) 924-6400, (800) 321-2211.* FAX *(225) 923-3041.*
www.marriott.com/btrch
Close to downtown Baton Rouge, this chain motel is comfortable, convenient, and hosts many business travelers.

**Baton Rouge:** *Holiday Inn Select* $$$
4728 Constitution Ave. *(225) 925-2244, (800) 678-4065.* FAX *(225) 930-0140.*
www.ichotelsgroup.com
A comfortable hotel conveniently located near Louisiana State University, casinos, and the Government Center.

**Bayou Teche, New Iberia:** *Comfort Suites New Iberia* $$
2817 Hwy 14. *(337) 367-0855.* FAX *(337) 367-0845.*
www.comfortsuites.com
Conveniently close to Jefferson Island, Avery Island, and Jungle Gardens, this hotel offers large, comfortable suites.

**Bayou Teche, St. Martinville:** *Bienvenue House* $$$
421 N Main St. *(337) 394-9100.*
www.bienvenuehouse.com
In one of the loveliest towns in South Louisiana, this antebellum house has porch swings, gardens, and Foti's is just across the square for some of the best food in Louisiana.

**Lafayette:** *Courtyard Lafayette Airport* $$
214 E Kaliste Saloom Rd. *(337) 232-5005, (800) 321-2211.* FAX *(337) 231-0049.*
www.courtyard.com/LFTCYI
Close to Acadian Mall, restaurants, the university, and dance halls, the Courtyard offers spacious rooms.

**Lafayette:** *Bois des Chenes B&B Inn* $$$
338 N Sterling St. *(337) 233-7816.* FAX *(337) 233-7816.*
www.bbgetaways.com
This former 1820s sugar and cattle plantation has suites with antique furniture and ambience galore. The owner will arrange trips through the Atchafalaya Swamp for nature lovers. Reservations essential.

**Natchitoches:** *Comfort Inn* $$
5362 Hwy 6 at I-49. *(318) 352-7500, (800) 228-5150.* FAX *(318) 352-7500.*
www.comfortinn.com
This chain motel offers furnished rooms, complete with microwave ovens and refrigerators, and a free Continental breakfast.

**New Orleans (French Quarter):** *St. Louis Hotel* $$$
730 Bienville St. *(504) 581-7300, (888) 508-3980.* FAX *(504) 524-8925.*
www.stlouishotel.com
This small, centrally located hotel, has all the amenities. The elegant, Louis XVI restaurant is one of the best in the city.

**New Orleans (French Quarter):** *Cornstalk Hotel* $$$$
915 Royal St. *(504) 523-1515.* FAX *(504) 522-5558.*
www.cornstalk.com
A great place to stay in Victorian splendor and comfort. The second-floor gallery is perfect for morning coffee and people-watching.

**New Orleans (French Quarter):** *Hotel St. Pierre* $$$$
911 Burgundy St. *(504) 524-4401, (800) 225-4040.* FAX *(504) 593-9425.*
www.frenchquarterinns.com
A lovely hotel with French-style cottages, it serves Continental-style breakfast in the Louis Armstrong Room.

| Hotel | Credit Cards | Number of Rooms | Recommended Restaurant | Children's Facilities | Garden or Terrace |
|---|---|---|---|---|---|
| Courtyard Acadian Center | ■ | 149 | ■ | | ■ |
| Holiday Inn Select | ■ | 294 | ■ | | |
| Comfort Suites New Iberia | ■ | 78 | | | |
| Bienvenue House | ■ | 4 | | | ■ |
| Courtyard Lafayette Airport | ■ | 90 | ■ | | ■ |
| Bois des Chenes B&B Inn | ■ | 5 | | | ■ |
| Comfort Inn | ■ | 59 | ■ | | |
| St. Louis Hotel | ■ | 81 | ■ | ● | |
| Cornstalk Hotel | ■ | 14 | | | |
| Hotel St. Pierre | ■ | 74 | | | |

?rice categories for a standard
louble room per night, inclusive
of breakfast, service charges,
and any additional taxes:

($) under $100
($)($) $100–$150
($)($)($) $150–$200
($)($)($)($) $200–$250
($)($)($)($)($) over $250

**Credit Cards**
Major credit cards accepted.

**Number of Rooms**
Number of rooms in the hotel.

**Recommended Restaurant**
Good restaurant within the hotel.

**Children's Facilities**
Hotel has various facilities for young children.

**Garden or Terrace**
Hotel has a garden, courtyard, or terrace.

| | Credit Cards | Number of Rooms | Recommended Restaurant | Children's Facilities | Garden or Terrace |
|---|---|---|---|---|---|
| **ew Orleans (French Quarter):** *Le Richelieu* ($)($)($)($)<br>234 Chartres St. (504) 529-2492, (800) 535-9653. FAX (504) 524-8179.<br>www.lerichelieuhotel.com<br>he luxurious guest rooms and deluxe suites in this hotel are decorated traditional style. | ■ | 86 | ■ | | ■ |
| **ew Orleans (French Quarter):** *Monteleone Hotel* ($)($)($)($)($)<br>4 Royal St. (504) 523-3341, (800) 535-9595. FAX (504) 528-1019.<br>www.hotelmonteleone.com<br>his is the oldest, largest, and most charming hotel in New Orleans. The arousel Bar in the lobby is world famous. | ■ | 597 | ■ | | ■ |
| **ew Orleans (French Quarter):** *Ritz Carlton Hotel* ($)($)($)($)($)<br>21 Canal St. (504) 524-1331, (800) 241-3333. FAX (504) 524-7675.<br>www.ritzcarlton.com<br>his luxurious hotel, housed in two of Crescent City's restored landmarks, e Maison Blanche and the Kress Building, preserves many of the riginal late 19th century design elements. | ■ | 452 | ■ | ● | ■ |
| **ew Orleans (French Quarter):** *Royal Sonesta* ($)($)($)($)($)<br>)0 Bourbon St. (504) 586-0300, (800) 766-3782. FAX (504) 586-0335.<br>www.royalsonestano.com<br>ink marble and beveled glass doors highlight the lobby of this timelessly egant, luxurious, and expensive hotel. | ■ | 500 | ■ | ● | ■ |
| **ew Orleans (Central Business District):** *Lafayette Hotel* ($)($)($)<br>)0 St. Charles Ave. (504) 524-4441, (888) 211-3447. FAX (504) 523-7327.<br>www.thelafayettehotel.com<br>his charming hotel with marble baths and wrought-iron balconies, makes a ood getaway from the noise of the Quarter. | ■ | 44 | ■ | | |
| **ew Orleans (Central Business District):** *Le Pavillon Hotel* ($)($)($)($)<br>33 Poydras St. (504) 581-3111, (800) 535-9095. FAX (504) 529-4415.<br>www.lepavillon.com<br>his 1907 hotel has the most spectacular lobby in New Orleans. Reason-bly priced, it offers upscale amenities. | ■ | 226 | ■ | ● | |
| **ew Orleans (Central Business District):** *Fairmont Hotel* ($)($)($)($)($)<br>23 Baronne St. (504) 529-7111, (800) 441-1414. FAX (504) 529-4764.<br>www.fairmont.com<br>)nce the famous Roosevelt Hotel, the Sazerac Bar and extravagant lobby ill speak of the 1930s at this hotel. Every conceivable luxury is offered ere, including in-room computer hook-ups. | ■ | 700 | ■ | ● | |
| **ew Orleans (Central Business District):** *Windsor Court Hotel* ($)($)($)($)($)<br>00 Gravier St. (504) 523-6000, (800) 262-2662. FAX (504) 596-4513.<br>www.windsorcourthotel.com<br>his may be the best hotel in New Orleans in terms of service and menities. The corridors in the lobby level hold original Renaissance and aroque art. | ■ | 324 | ■ | | |
| **ew Orleans (Garden District):** *Hampton Inn* ($)($)($)<br>626 St. Charles Ave. (504) 899-9990, (800) 426-7866. FAX (504) 899-9908.<br>www.hamptoninn.com<br>his Garden District chain hotel is located right on the St. Charles Avenue reetcar line. The rooms strike a balance between the elegance of old lew Orleans and the comfort of modern facilities. | ■ | 100 | | ● | |
| **ew Orleans (Garden District):** *1891 Castle Inn* ($)($)($)($)<br>539 4th St. (504) 897-0540, (866) 569-8700. FAX (504) 895-2231.<br>www.castleinnofneworleans.com The rooms in this large, converted house oast ornate mirrors and carved wooden furniture, including some fantastic our-poster beds. | ■ | 9 | | | |

For key to symbols see back flap

**Price categories** for a standard double room per night, inclusive of breakfast, service charges, and any additional taxes:

$ under $100
$$ $100–$150
$$$ $150–$200
$$$$ $200–$250
$$$$$ over $250

**CREDIT CARDS**
Major credit cards accepted:

**NUMBER OF ROOMS**
Number of rooms in the hotel.

**RECOMMENDED RESTAURANT**
Good restaurant within the hotel.

**CHILDREN'S FACILITIES**
Hotel has various facilities for young children.

**GARDEN OR TERRACE**
Hotel has a garden, courtyard, or terrace.

## ARKANSAS

**EUREKA SPRINGS:** *Crescent Hotel & Spa* $$$
75 Prospect Ave. (479) 253-9766, (888) 342-9766. FAX (479) 253-5296.
W www.crescent-hotel.com
One of the "Historic Hotels of America," this luxurious hotel offers a full-service spa and swimming pool among its many deluxe amenities.

**HOT SPRINGS:** *Arlington Resort Hotel* $$
239 Central Ave. (501) 623-7771, (800) 643-1502. FAX (501) 623-2243.
W www.arlingtonhotel.com
Guests have been coming to the Arlington Hotel and Spa since 1907 to partake of its healing waters. It is the only spa on historic Bathhouse Row that offers overnight accommodations.

**LITTLE ROCK:** *Comfort Inn* $$
300 Markham Center Dr. (501) 227-0120, (877) 550-7666. FAX (501) 227-0120.
W www.choicehotels.com
Four miles from downtown, this reliable chain motel is convenient for drivers who prefer to skirt the downtown area.

**LITTLE ROCK:** *Capital Hotel* $$$$
111 Markham St. (501) 374-7474, (800) 766-7666. FAX (501) 370-7091.
W www.thecapitalhotel.com
The elegant Capital Hotel was built in the 19th century and features two restaurants, including the acclaimed Ashleys.

**MOUNTAIN VIEW:** *Ozark Folk Center Dry Creek Lodge* $$
1032 Park Ave. (870) 269-3871. FAX (870) 269-2909.
W www.ozarkfolkcenter@arkansas.com
The State Park Service operates this modern lodge at the engaging Ozark Folk Center, where there is a restaurant and a truckload of amusing family activities.

## MISSISSIPPI

**BILOXI:** *Grand Casino Biloxi Hotel* $$
265 Beach Blvd. (228) 436-2946. FAX (228) 435-8901.
W www.caesars.com
The Grand Casino mimics Vegas style with accommodations that are large, bright, and stimulating, yet affordable. It is right on the scenic inlet, and the local museum is across the street.

**CLARKSDALE:** *Best Western* $$
710 State St. (601) 627-9292. FAX (601) 624-4763.
W www.bestwestern.com
This motor lodge, offering the fanciest accommodations in Clarkesdale, is relatively new and slightly more upscale than others. It serves complimentary Continental breakfast to guests.

**JACKSON:** *Best Value Inn & Suites* $$
5035 I-55 N. (601) 982-1011.
This no-frills motel, right off the Interstate might be all that Natchez Trace through-travelers are looking for. The attached restaurant offers excellent fare.

**JACKSON:** *Edison Walthall Hotel* $$
225 E Capitol St. (601) 948-6161, (800) 932-6161. FAX (601) 948-0088.
W www.edisonwalthallhotel.com
This institution is where Mississippi powerbrokers have gathered for generations to conduct the business of state. Rooms are more modest and motel-like, unlike the fancy lobby.

| Hotel | Credit Cards | Number of Rooms | Recommended Restaurant | Children's Facilities | Garden or Terrace |
|---|---|---|---|---|---|
| Crescent Hotel & Spa | ■ | 72 | ■ | | ■ |
| Arlington Resort Hotel | ■ | 481 | ■ | ● | |
| Comfort Inn | ■ | 70 | | | |
| Capital Hotel | ■ | 126 | ■ | | |
| Ozark Folk Center Dry Creek Lodge | ■ | 60 | ■ | ● | ■ |
| Grand Casino Biloxi Hotel | ■ | 1000 | ■ | ● | ■ |
| Best Western | ■ | 93 | ■ | | |
| Best Value Inn & Suites | ■ | 133 | ■ | | |
| Edison Walthall Hotel | ■ | 208 | ■ | | |

**[N]ATCHEZ:** *Natchez Eola Hotel* $$$
[1]10 N Pearl St. (601) 445-6000, (866) 445-3652. FAX (601) 446-5310.
[W] www.natchezeola.com
[A] downtown hotel since 1927, the restored Natchez Eola is within easy [w]alking distance of several museums, attractions, restaurants, shops, and [th]e riverfront. Carriage tours start outside.

■ | 131 | ■ | | ■

**[N]ATCHEZ:** *Monmouth Plantation Inn* $$$$
[3]6 Melrose Ave. (601) 442-5852, (800) 828-4531. FAX (601) 446-7762.
[W] www.monmouthplantation.com
[R]ated among the country's top romantic hotels, Monmouth sits on a hill [o]utside town near the Natchez Trace. The luxurious antebellum inn is [fu]rnished with antiques, and breakfast is provided.

■ | 30 | ■ | | ■

**[O]XFORD:** *Downtown Oxford Inn and Suites* $$
[4]00 N Lamar Blvd. (662) 234-3031, (800) 606-1497. FAX (662) 234-2834.
[W] www.downtownoxfordinnandsuites.com
[L]ocated in a quiet residential area, this motel is a minute away from [r]estaurants, shops, and nightclubs, and a 15-minute walk from the [U]niversity of Mississippi and Faulkner's Rowan Oak house museum.

■ | 100 | ■ | |

**[O]XFORD:** *Oliver Britt House Inn* $$
[5]12 Van Buren Ave. (662) 234-8043. FAX (662) 236-2816.
[W] www.travelguides.com
[T]his modest guest house is centrally located between the town square [a]nd the university. Reasonably priced for the area, the rooms are quiet [a]nd comfortable.

■ | 5 | | |

## ALABAMA

**[B]IRMINGHAM:** *Pickwick Hotel* $$$
[1]023 S 20th St. (205) 933-9555, (800) 255-7304. FAX (205) 933-6918.
[W] www.pickwickhotel.com
[T]his small 1920s building, which retains its Art Deco styling, is within [w]alking distance of some of the best restaurants, clubs, and shops. [C]ontinental breakfast and nightly wine and cheese are served in the [l]obby pub.

■ | 63 | | |

**[B]IRMINGHAM:** *Tutwiler Wyndham Hotel* $$$
[2]021 Park Place N. (205) 322-2100. FAX (205) 325-1198.
[W] www.wyndham.com
[B]irmingham's 1913 grande dame hotel, the Tutwiler offers spacious, [e]legant rooms near downtown attractions. Includes a pleasant bar and [r]estaurant.

■ | 147 | ■ | ● |

**[H]UNTSVILLE:** *Huntsville Marriott* $$$
[5] Tranquility Base. (256) 830-2222. FAX (256) 895-9528.
[W] www.marriott.com
[A] popular choice, adjacent to the US Space Center, the Huntsville [M]arriott offers attractive and comfortable rooms and suites, furnished [w]ith all sorts of amenities.

■ | 290 | ■ | ● |

**[M]OBILE:** *Radisson Admiral Semmes Hotel* $$$
[2]51 Government St. (251) 432-8000, (800) 333-3333. FAX (251) 405-5942.
[W] www.radisson.com
[B]uilt in the 1940s, this historic hotel offers free Continental breakfast with [it]s spacious rooms. Guests can also use its well-equipped gym and [s]wimming pool.

■ | 170 | ■ | |

**[M]ONTGOMERY:** *Guest House Inn and Suites* $$
[1]20 Madison Ave. (334) 264-2231, (800) 214-8378. FAX (334) 263-3179.
[W] www.guesthouseinternational.com
[A] few blocks from the Capitol and Old Alabama Town, the spacious [r]ooms of this elegant, well-located hotel open onto an attractive atrium. [T]he restaurant serves excellent meals.

■ | 172 | ■ | | ■

**[S]ELMA:** *St. James Hotel* $$
[1]200 Water Ave. (334) 872-3234. FAX (334) 872-0332.
[W] www.stjameshotelselma.com
[T]he St. James began operating in the steamboat era, accommodating [p]assengers en route up the Alabama River. The lovely historic hotel [r]etains its original grill work and many architectural flourishes. It also has [a] restaurant and a few shops.

■ | 42 | ■ | | ■

For key to symbols see back flap

# Where to Eat

THE ENTIRE DEEP SOUTH REGION IS known for its outstanding and distinctive cuisine. Chefs in New Orleans enjoy the same celebrity status as film stars do in Los Angeles. Creole and Cajun delicacies make the most of fresh local seafood. Opening times for restaurants are indicated by a "B" for breakfast, "L" for lunch, and "D" for dinner.

## LOUISIANA

**BATON ROUGE:** *Don's Seafood & Steak House* $$$
6823 Airline Hwy. *(225) 357-0601.*
This institution since 1934 has dishes prepared with the freshest seafood and meats. *L, D.* *Thanksg., Dec 25.*

**BATON ROUGE:** *Juban's* $$$
3739 Perkins Rd. *(225) 346-8422.*
With progressive Creole cuisine, this restaurant has a charming courtyard bar. *L, D.* *Sun, public hols.*

**BAYOU TECHE, ST. MARTINVILLE:** *Foti's Oyster Bar/Restaurant* $
108 S Main St. *(337) 394-3058.*
No frills, but this is where you will find the very best fried seafood, boiled crawfish, and raw or fried oysters. Try the fresh-brewed Cajun coffee. *L, D.* *public hols.*

**BAYOU TECHE, NEW IBERIA:** *Clementine's* $$$
113 E Main St. *(337) 560-1007.*
Classic south Louisiana cooking offering seafood, salad bar, and a wide selection of cocktails. *L, D.* *public hols.* *Fri & Sat.*

**LAFAYETTE:** *Café Vermilionville* $$$
1304 W Pinhook Rd. *(337) 237-0100.*
Housed in a 19th-century Acadian inn, this elegant restaurant offers French and Cajun seafood dishes. The soft-shelled crabs, snapper Acadian, and the andouille gumbo are superb. *L, D.* *Sun, Dec 25.*

**LAFAYETTE:** *Prejean's* $$$
3480 US Hwy 167 N. *(337) 896-3247.*
A favorite with locals, this restaurant offers great Cajun rack of elk and American buffalo au poivre, along with an authentic atmosphere and live Cajun music. B, *L, D.* *public hols.*

**NACHITOCHES:** *The Landing* $$
530 Front St. *(318) 352-1579.*
The Landing serves some of the city's best seafood, including crawfish etouffée and blackened alligator, in an elegant setting in the historic district. *L, D.* *Mon, Thanksgiving, Dec 25.*

**NEW ORLEANS (FRENCH QUARTER):** *Acme Oyster House* $
724 Iberville St. *(504) 522-5973.*
Although there are mixed opinions about the look of the place, most maintain that the lack of decor is part of its charm, and it is still one of the best places in town for raw oysters and crawfish.

**NEW ORLEANS (FRENCH QUARTER):** *Café du Monde* $
800 Decatur St. *(504) 587-0833.*
Sit and watch the world go by from this historic 24-hour open-air coffee shop, offering mouth-watering *beignets* and *café au lait* *(see p347).*

**NEW ORLEANS (FRENCH QUARTER):** *Johnny's Po-Boy* $
511 St. Louis St. *(504) 524-8129.*
This po'boy shop is one of the better ones in the French Quarter – the roast beef is especially good in a very messy way. If it's crowded, order takeout and have a picnic down by the river. *L.*

**NEW ORLEANS (FRENCH QUARTER):** *Antoine's* $$
713 St. Louis St. *(504) 581-4422.*
Antoine's offers over 130 dishes on its vintage French-Creole menu. Although it is a bit faded, the classic elegance and excellent cuisine never go out of style. *L, D.* *Sun.*

| Restaurant | Credit Cards | Outdoor Tables | Vegetarian | Good Wine List | Regional Cuisine |
|---|---|---|---|---|---|
| Don's Seafood & Steak House | ■ | | | ● | ■ |
| Juban's | ■ | ● | | | ■ |
| Foti's Oyster Bar/Restaurant | ■ | | | | ■ |
| Clementine's | ■ | | | ● | ■ |
| Café Vermilionville | ■ | | | ● | ■ |
| Prejean's | ■ | ● | | | ■ |
| The Landing | ■ | ● | ■ | | ■ |
| Acme Oyster House | ■ | | | | ■ |
| Café du Monde | | ● | | | |
| Johnny's Po-Boy | | | | | ■ |
| Antoine's | ■ | | ■ | ● | ■ |

Price categories include a hree-course meal for one, a glass of house wine, and all inavoidable extra charges such is sales tax and service.
$ under $20
$$ $20–30
$$$ $30–45
$$$$ $45–60
$$$$$ over $60

**CREDIT CARDS**
Major credit cards accepted.

**OUTDOOR TABLES**
Garden, courtyard, or terrace with outside tables.

**VEGETARIAN**
A good selection of vegetarian dishes available.

**GOOD WINE LIST**
Extensive list of good wines, both domestic and imported.

**REGIONAL CUISINE**
A good selection of regional specialties available.

| Restaurant | Credit Cards | Outdoor Tables | Vegetarian | Good Wine List | Regional Cuisine |
|---|---|---|---|---|---|
| **EW ORLEANS (FRENCH QUARTER):** *Arnaud's* $$$<br>3 Bienville St. *(504) 523-5433.*<br>he lovely atmosphere makes this elegant 19th-century French Quarter assic one of the great old New Orleans restaurants. The famous shrimp moulade alone is worth the trip. *L Sun–Fri, D.* | ■ | | ■ | ● | ■ |
| **EW ORLEANS (FRENCH QUARTER):** *Bayona* $$$<br>30 Dauphine St. *(504) 525-4455.*<br>New World" is the label Chef Susan Spicer applies to her cooking style. naginative dishes are served in an early 19th-century Creole cottage on is quiet French Quarter street. *L Mon–Fri, D.* ● *Sun.* | ■ | ● | ■ | ● | ■ |
| **EW ORLEANS (FRENCH QUARTER):** *Bacco* $$$$<br>0 Chartres St *(504) 522-2426.*<br>local favorite, the stylish Bacco serves delicious wood-fired pizza and very kind of seafood. *L, D.* | ■ | | ■ | ● | |
| **EW ORLEANS (FRENCH QUARTER):** *Galatoire's* $$$$<br>9 Bourbon St. *(504) 525-2021.*<br>his restaurant epitomizes the old-style French-Creole bistro. A lengthy enu filled with standard-setting sauces, glistening brass chandeliers, entwood chairs, and white tablecloths add to its timeless atmosphere. *D.* ● *Mon.* | ■ | | ■ | ● | ■ |
| **EW ORLEANS (FRENCH QUARTER):** *K-Paul's Louisiana Kitchen* $$$$<br>6 Chartres St. *(504) 524-7394.*<br>hef Paul Prudhomme started the Cajun craze in this rustic café. Its ventive gumbos and fresh seafood are mouthwatering. Prices are steep dinner but moderate at lunch. *L Thu–Sat, D Mon–Sat.* ● *Sun.* | ■ | | ■ | ● | ■ |
| **EW ORLEANS (MARIGNY):** *Siam Café* $<br>35 Esplanade Ave *(504) 949-1750.*<br>urrounded by the sights, sounds, and aromas of Thailand, Siam offers uthentic Thai food, from vegetarian dishes to such specialties as angkok beef in oyster sauce. *L, D.* | ■ | | ■ | | |
| **EW ORLEANS (MARIGNY):** *Feelings Café* $$<br>00 Chartres St. *(504) 945-2222.*<br>way from the bustle of the Quarter, with a beautiful piano and intimate, omantic atmosphere, this café offers updated renditions of Creole vorites such as chicken Clemenceau. *L Fri, D, Sun brunch.* *Fri & Sat.* | ■ | ● | | | ■ |
| **EW ORLEANS (CENTRAL BUSINESS DISTRICT):** *Mother's* $<br>1 Poydras St. *(504) 523-9656.*<br>nce 1938 locals have lined up for great po' boys, red beans and rice, and am biscuits. Service is cafeteria-style, and you can't beat the prices. B, *L, D.* | ■ | | | | ■ |
| **EW ORLEANS (CENTRAL BUSINESS DISTRICT):** *Herbsaint* $$$<br>1 St. Charles St. *(504) 524-4114.*<br>he Louisiana-inspired French cooking in this chic restaurant produces ver-changing gumbo, prime steak, and gorgeous desserts. A must for ny visiting gourmand. *L Mon–Fri, D Mon–Sat.* ● *Sun.* | ■ | | | ● | ■ |
| **EW ORLEANS (CENTRAL BUSINESS DISTRICT):** *Palace Café* $$$<br>5 Canal St. *(504) 523-1661.*<br>olorfully crafted from a building that was once the city's oldest music store, e Palace offers imaginative contemporary Creole dishes like crab cakes and bbit ravioli in piquant sauce. There's a jazz brunch on weekends. *L, D.* | ■ | | | ● | ■ |
| **EW ORLEANS (CENTRAL BUSINESS DISTRICT):** *Emeril's* $$$$<br>0 Tchoupitoulas St. *(504) 528-9393.*<br>hef Emeril Lagasse's fantastic contemporary Louisiana cuisine makes this vant-garde restaurant a special treat. *L Mon–Sat, D.* | ■ | | ■ | ● | ■ |

For key to symbols see back flap

**Price categories** include a three-course meal for one, a glass of house wine, and all unavoidable extra charges such as sales tax and service.
$ under $20
$$ $20–30
$$$ $30–45
$$$$ $45–60
$$$$$ over $60

**CREDIT CARDS**
Major credit cards accepted.
**OUTDOOR TABLES**
Garden, courtyard, or terrace with outside tables.
**VEGETARIAN**
A good selection of vegetarian dishes available.
**GOOD WINE LIST**
Extensive list of good wines, both domestic and imported.
**REGIONAL CUISINE**
A good selection of regional specialties available.

| Restaurant | Credit Cards | Outdoor Tables | Vegetarian | Good Wine List | Regional Cuisine |
|---|---|---|---|---|---|
| **NEW ORLEANS (GARDEN DISTRICT):** *Commander's Palace* $$$$<br>1403 Washington Ave. *(504) 899-8221.*<br>No restaurant captures New Orleans' gastronomic heritage and celebratory spirit as well as this one in a stately Garden District mansion. This restaurant is considered to be one of the best in the US.<br>*L, D.* | ■ | ● | ■ | ● | ■ |
| **NEW ORLEANS (UPTOWN):** *Jamila's Café* $$<br>7808 Maple St. *(504) 866-4366.*<br>A romantic restaurant in the university area, where you can coo over the couscous and other North African dishes. Among the better ethnic restaurants in New Orleans. *L, D.* ● *Mon.* | ■ | | ■ | | |
| **NEW ORLEANS (UPTOWN):** *Brigtsen's* $$$<br>723 Dante St. *(504) 861-7610.*<br>The ever-changing menus at Brigtsen's add up to some of the best Creole/Cajun cooking you will find anywhere in the US. Lucky are the customers who can get one of the two tables in an enclosed sunroom out front. *D.* ● *Sun, Mon.* | ■ | | | ● | ■ |
| **NEW ORLEANS (MIDCITY):** *Mandina's* $$<br>3800 Canal Street. *(504) 482-9179.*<br>This classic Creole seafood restaurant with an old-fashion bar offers large portions of good food, especially great oyster and shrimp po' boys and tasty trout *amandine*. *L, D.* | | | | | ■ |
| **ARKANSAS** | | | | | |
| **EUREKA SPRINGS:** *The Balcony Restaurant* $$<br>12 Spring St. *(479) 253-7837.*<br>This restaurant offers casual dining overlooking the city's historic Spring Street and Basin Park shopping district. The menu is eclectic, including traditional American and Mexican dishes. *L, D.* | ■ | ● | ■ | | |
| **HOT SPRINGS:** *McClard's BBQ* $<br>505 Albert Pike. *(501) 623-9665.*<br>www.mcclards.com<br>A local Bill Clinton landmark, McClard's has been in business since 1928 and is considered Arkansas's premier house of barbecue.<br>*L, D.* ● *Sun–Mon, Thanksgiving, Dec 15–Jan 15, one week in August.* | | | | | ■ |
| **HOT SPRINGS:** *Belle Arti Ristorante* $$$<br>719 Central Ave. *(501) 624-7474.*<br>Excellent Italian cuisine with friendly service. Full selection of veal, seafood, pasta and chicken selections, including Pollo alla Cacciatora, chicken with mushrooms, peppers, onions and fresh tomatoes. *L, D.* ● *Jan 1, Dec 25.* | ■ | | ■ | ● | |
| **LITTLE ROCK:** *Doe's Eat Place* $$<br>1023 W Markham St. *(501) 376-1195.*<br>Occupying a worn corner storefront at the fringe of downtown, this landmark dive is a favorite with capital politicos. Doe's serves tamales, and "pillowy" sirloin steaks up to six pounds. *L Mon–Fri, D.* ● *Sun.* | ■ | | | | ■ |
| **LITTLE ROCK:** *Ashley's* $$$<br>111 W Markham St. *(501) 374-7474.*<br>Within the Capital Hotel, Ashley's is widely considered the best restaurant in town, specializing in steaks and seafood. *L, D.* ● *Sun.* | ■ | | | ● | ■ |
| **MOUNTAIN VIEW:** *Bar None Bar-B-Q* $<br>1613 E Main St. *(870) 269-2200.*<br>The family-friendly restaurant specializes in dishes such as dry-rubbed ribs and hickory BBQ, as well as a variety of steaks. There's a drive-through facility or you can eat on the patio. *L, D.* ● *Sun, Mon, public hols.* | | ● | | | ■ |

## MISSISSIPPI

**LARKSDALE:** *Madidi* $$
54 Delta Ave. *(662) 627-7770.*
o-owned by actor and local resident Morgan Freeman, this restaurant ffers French-influenced cuisine, such as herb-encrusted rack of lamb, in restored brick storefront downtown. *D.* *Sun, Mon.*

**ULFPORT/BILOXI:** *Mary Mahoney's Old French House* $$
16 Rue Magnolia. *(228) 374-0163.*
you can tear yourself away from the casino buffets, Mary Mahoney's ffers Southern hospitality and traditional dishes in a historic 1737 house ppointed in period decor. *L, D.* *Sun, Dec 24–25.*

**ACKSON:** *Julep Restaurant & Bar* $$$
55 North at Northside Dr, Highland Village. *(601) 362-1411.*
ll the southern favorites with a delightful difference. Regional "fusion" iisine, with tasty combinations of traditional and unusual ingredients. The ienu includes low-carb and vegetarian selections. *L, D.* *Sun D.*

**ATCHEZ:** *Cock of the Walk* $$
00 N. Broadway. *(601) 446-8920.*
his restaurant offers a crowd-pleasing, wide menu selection in an old train ation at the top of the bluff above the Mississippi River. *L Sun, D.*

**ATCHEZ:** *Monmouth Plantation Inn* $$$
5 Melrose Ave. *(601) 442-5852, (800) 828-4531.*
onmouth offers plantation fare in a richly appointed antebellum iansion, and also provides overnight accommodations. *D.*

**XFORD:** *Bottletree Bakery* $
23 Van Buren Ave. *(662) 236-5000.*
nis welcoming town bakery offers European-style breads and pastries, ecialty coffees, and light lunches in a folk-arty, laid-back café nvironment. *B, L.* *Mon.*

**XFORD:** *City Grocery* $$
52 Courthouse Square. *(662) 232-8080.*
nis hardwood-floored, exposed-brick restaurant is famous for its gnature shrimp-and-grits. *L, D.* *Sun, major hols.*

## ALABAMA

**IRMINGHAM METRO AREA, BESSEMER:** *Bob Sykes Bar-B-Que* $
724 N 9th Ave. *(205) 426-1400.*
short drive from Birmingham on I-20 W, Bob Sykes is a culinary landmark erving delicious barbecue. *L, D.* *Sun, Thanksgiving, Dec 25, Jan 1.*

**IRMINGHAM:** *Bombay Café* $$
339 7th Ave S. *(205) 322-1930.*
ombay Café offers seafood, lamb, and children's dishes in the former 020s Arondale Theater downtown. *L Mon–Fri, D.* *Sun, public hols.*

**UNTSVILLE:** *Little Paul's Gibson Barbeque* $
15 Madison St. *(256) 536-7227.*
earty plates of barbeque ribs, chicken, beef and pork, and be sure to y the fried catfish, coleslaw and the hush puppies. *B, L, D.* *Sun D.*

**OBILE:** *The Pillars Restaurant* $$$
757 Government St. *(251) 471-3411.*
an elegantly appointed Victorian mansion, The Pillars offers Italian asta and a Continental menu, including fresh Gulf seafoods, Angus beef, omemade breads, and tempting desserts. *D.* *Sun, public hols.*

**ONTGOMERY:** *Vintage Year* $$
05 Cloverdale Rd. *(334) 264-8463.*
ne of the best spots in town for a nice dinner, it offers a wide range of ntrées, including chicken and seafood. *D.* *Sun, Mon, public hols.*

**ELMA:** *Major Grumble's* $$
300 Water Ave. *(334) 872-2006.*
et at the bluff above the Alabama River, Major Grumble's serves harbroiled chicken, steaks, and seafood in a former cotton warehouse ating from 1850. *L Tue–Sat, D.* *Sun, public hols.*

For key to symbols see back flap

# THE GREAT LAKES

# The Great Lakes at a Glance

Spreading between the Colonial-era landscapes of the East Coast and the wide open spaces of the Wild West, this region stakes a strong claim to being the most "American" part of the US. Home to more than one in five Americans, the Great Lakes is energetic and surprisingly varied. With its bustling big cities and sleepy small towns, idyllic rural scenes and sublime waterfront wilderness, industrial might and broad swaths of pristine natural beauty, the attractions here are as varied as the six states of Illinois, Ohio, Michigan, Indiana, Wisconsin, and Minnesota that form the center of America's heartland.

0 km 100
0 miles 100

Crookston
Grand Rapids
Apostle Islan
MINNESOTA
(See pp416–21)
Willmar
Minneapolis-St.Paul
Rochester
La Cross
WIS
(See p
Ro
ILL
(See p
Ca

***Voyageurs National Park*** (see p421) *in Minnesota covers endless stretches of watery wilderness near the Canadian border. The park, with its lakes, bogs, and islands, is now a prime outdoor destination.*

***Wisconsin's*** (see pp412–15) *natural wonders attract hikers, bikers, and campers who explore the state's glacial moraines, lakes, and valleys through well-marked trails.*

***Springfield*** (see p399) *is the capital of Illinois, a state characterized by vast expanses of rich, flat farmland. Abraham Lincoln, who lived here for 31 years (1830–61), delivered his famous "House Divided" speech in 1858 at the Old State Capitol.*

◁ **Aerial view of Chicago's magnificent high-rises, towering above Lake Shore Drive**

***hicago** (see pp386–97), the region's largest 'ty, is located on the southwestern edge of Lake 'ichigan. One of the world's most celebrated enters of architectural innovation, the city has ttracted many of North America's most influen- al architects. The most significant of these 'as Frank Lloyd Wright.*

**Locator Map**

***Detroit** (see p408–409), still known as the Motor City, is also Michigan's main city and commerical center. Downtown's Hart Plaza, at the riverfront, is the site of the city's lively summer festivals.*

***Ohio** (see pp404–407) is a curious combination of a rural and heavily industrial state. It also contains some of the earliest examples of Native American cultures, such as the symbolic earthen Serpent Mound.*

***Indianapolis'** (see p402) Monument Circle is the dominant feature of downtown. The city's many excellent museums adds to its status as Indiana's state capital.*

# THE GREAT LAKES

*SURROUNDING THE WORLD'S largest bodies of fresh water, the Great Lakes region is a land of epic proportions. From the towering skyscrapers of Chicago, Illinois, and the factories of Detroit, Michigan, to the seemingly endless plains of Indiana, the bountiful pastures of Wisconsin, and Minnesota's watery wilderness, this is one of the most exciting destinations in the country.*

Spreading west from the original American colonies to beyond the Mississippi River, the Great Lakes region formed the first frontier of the early United States. The lakes themselves – Ontario, Erie, Huron, Michigan, and Superior – were a conduit for trade and exploration, and a key to the region's development. Plentiful harvests from the fertile soils, lumber from the forests, and ore from the region's mines all came together to support the growth of such cities as Chicago, Cleveland, Detroit, and Minneapolis. From the mid-19th century on, immigrants from all over the country and around the world came here to work on farms and in factories, thus establishing the diverse cultures and traditions that still flavor Great Lakes life. While industry and agriculture have given way to the service economy, the region's history and heritage have now become important tourist attractions, enhancing the natural beauty of its many lakes, rivers, forests, and mountains.

## HISTORY

Long before the United States was founded, the region surrounding the Great Lakes was home to some of the most developed and powerful Native American cultures. Evidence of one of the most significant archaeological remnants in North America can be found in southern Ohio and Illinois, where the enigmatic Moundbuilder culture constructed the largest cities north of Mexico. Of these, the most

**A 1920s photograph showing parked automobiles at Detroit's Cadillac Square**

**Stacked icicle formations in the Sawtooth Mountain Range along Lake Superior's northern shore, Minnesota**

impressive is at Cahokia. Farther north, spanning the international border between the US and Canada – which runs right through the center of the Great Lakes – Native Americans were grouped together into many distinct though related tribes. The Huron and Ojibwe in the north, and the Fox, Shawnee, and Menominee in the south and west had developed intricate trade and cultural relationships. However, after some 100 years of European contact, large Native populations had been decimated through disease and internecine warfare.

**Replica of Christopher Columbus's ship *Santa Maria* in Columbus, Ohio**

Initially, early European exploration of this part of the New World was dominated by the French. Traveling from their colony at Quebec, the first French explorers were rapidly followed by fur trading "voyageurs" who bartered tools and weapons for beaver pelts. At the same time, French Jesuit missionaries began establish commerci military, and religio outposts at Sault Sain Marie in 1668 and Detroit in 1701. Until t mid-1700s, religion a the fur trade remain the main points contact between India and Europeans.

The pace of settleme accelerated after the e of the Seven Years W in Europe in 1763, a the Americans a British acquired territorial control of region. Within a few decades Oh Indiana, and Illinois had changed fr isolated frontier territories to stat Following the completion of the E Canal in 1825, and improved tra portation on the lakes, settlers w able to reach the previously dist lands of Michigan and Wisconsin. 1858, Minnesota became the last of Great Lakes states to join the nation.

### Key Dates in History

**1620** Etienne Brule is the first European to explore present-day Michigan and Wisconsin

**1673** Jesuit missionary Jacques Marquette and explorer Louis Jolliet cross the northern Great Lakes and descend the Mississippi River

**1750** The population of Detroit, the only large Great Lakes settlement, numbers 600

**1763** France surrenders its Great Lakes territorial claims to Great Britain

**1783** The US acquires the region from Britain, forms the Northwest Territory

**1803** Ohio is the first to become a state

**1903** Henry Ford establishes the Ford Motor Company in Detroit

**1936** A factory strike leads General Motors to accept the United Auto Workers union as the sole bargaining agent for its workers

**1968** Chicago police attack anti-Vietnam War protestors at the Democratic National Convention

**1995** Heat wave kills more than 500 people in Chicago

**2000** Former World Wrestling Federation champion Jesse "The Body" Ventura is elected Governor of Minnesota

**2003** Ohio celebrates its bicentennial

### Immigrants & Industry

The opening up of the Great Lak region to settlement coincided wit major influx of immigrants. From 1840s on, immigration increas tenfold as more than 200,000 peo mostly Irish and Germans fleeing potato famine and political unr respectively, came to America ev

**Historical Museum, Winona on the Mississippi**

ear. Many settled in ethnic enclaves in ıpidly growing cities such as Chicago, etroit, Cincinnati, and Cleveland, here some three-quarters of residents ere either foreign-born or first-eneration Americans.

Large numbers of other immigrants et up wheat and dairy farms on ecently cleared forests, or found work ı other resource-based industries. opper mining in Michigan's Upper eninsula, for example, produced more ıan 75 percent of the nation's supplies etween 1850 and 1900. With a total ılue of nearly $10 billion, this mining oom was 10 times more lucrative than ıe legendary California Gold Rush of 349. Another major industry was food rocessing. Meat-packing, which was oncentrated on the huge stockyards of hicago and Minneapolis, relied on the ilroads to transport millions of cattle ıd pigs from across the Midwest. The reat Lakes also came to dominate rain processing, and some of the ation's largest companies, including ıe world-famous Kellogg's and eneral Mills, are still based here.

The early 20th century witnessed the rgest and most enduring industrial oom, mainly because of the mutually ependent growth of the steel and utomobile industries, both largely ased in the Great Lakes region. earborn and Detroit, headquarters of ord Motor Company as well as other naller companies that evolved into the ant General Motors, emerged as the Motor City." Despite competition from ther countries, the Great Lakes automobile industry flourished and in turn supported a network of other industries, such as the iron mines in Minnesota, steel mills in Indiana, and rubber plants in Ohio.

### Politics & Culture

The success of the industries may have reaped huge fortunes for its owners, but the workers' conditions were often dire. This exploitation led to a number of violent battles, particularly around Chicago, such as the riots in Haymarket Square in 1886 and the bitter strike against the Pullman Palace Car company in 1894. The growth of unions gave workers some semblance of political power, which in turn supported a number of left-leaning social movements. The Great Lakes in general, and Minnesota and Wisconsin in particular, were early strongholds of the Populist and Progressive movements, which in the early 1900s proposed such now-accepted innovations as the eight-hour workday and graduated rates of income tax.

This social awareness also influenced art and literature. One of the region's most famous works of art, Diego Rivera's massive mural on the walls of the Detroit Institute of Art, depicts workers struggling under the demands of industrialization. The region's great literary works include Hamlin Garland's depictions of life on the Wisconsin frontier, Sherwood Anderson's *Winesburg, Ohio*, the vivid exposés of Sinclair Lewis, and the stories of St. Paul native F. Scott Fitzgerald.

**view of Detroit's gleaming skyscrapers, including the Renaissance Center, from across the Detroit River**

# Exploring the Great Lakes


**SEE ALSO**

- ***Practical Information*** pp422–
- ***Where to Stay*** pp424–7
- ***Where to Eat*** pp428–31


ENCOMPASSING LARGE CITIES as well as endless stretches of pastoral farmland and places of natural beauty, the Great Lakes covers a vast area that is best explored by car. While the major towns and cities are linked by both Interstate Highways and Amtrak trains, public transportation is otherwise limited, particularly across the lakes themselves. Chicago is the region's largest and most cosmopolitan city; other cities include Indianapolis, Detroit, Cleveland, Cincinnati, Milwaukee, and Minnesota's twin cities of Minneapolis & St. Paul.

Visitors near Old Mission Lighthouse, Lake Michigan Shore, Michigan

## SIGHTS AT A GLANCE

**Illinois**
*Chicago pp386–97* ❶
Rockford ❷
Galena ❸
Springfield ❹
Southern Illinois ❺

**Indiana**
New Harmony ❻
Bloomington ❼
Indiana Dunes National Lakeshore ❽
South Bend ❾
Shipshewana ❿
Fort Wayne ⓫
Indianapolis ⓬
Columbus ⓭
Ohio River Valley ⓮

**Ohio**
Cincinnati ⓯
Dayton ⓰
Serpent Mound ⓱
Hopewell Culture National Historic Park ⓲
Columbus ⓳
Berlin ⓴
Cleveland 21
Lake Erie Islands 22
Sandusky 23
Toledo 24

**Michigan**
*Detroit pp408–409* 25
Ann Arbor 26
Lansing 27
Grand Rapids 28
Lake Michigan Shore 29
Mackinac Island 30
Upper Peninsula 31

**Wisconsin**
Milwaukee 32
Door County 33
Wisconsin Dells 34
Baraboo 35
Madison 36
Spring Green 37
La Crosse 38
Apostle Islands 39

**Minnesota**
*Minneapolis & St. Paul pp416–17* 40
Mississippi River Towns 41
Rochester 42
Pipestone National Monument 43
Brainerd Lakes Area 44
Duluth 45
Iron Range 46
Boundary Waters Canoe Area Wilderness 47
Voyageurs National Park 48

Ottumwa
St.Josep
Columb
MISSC
Springfi

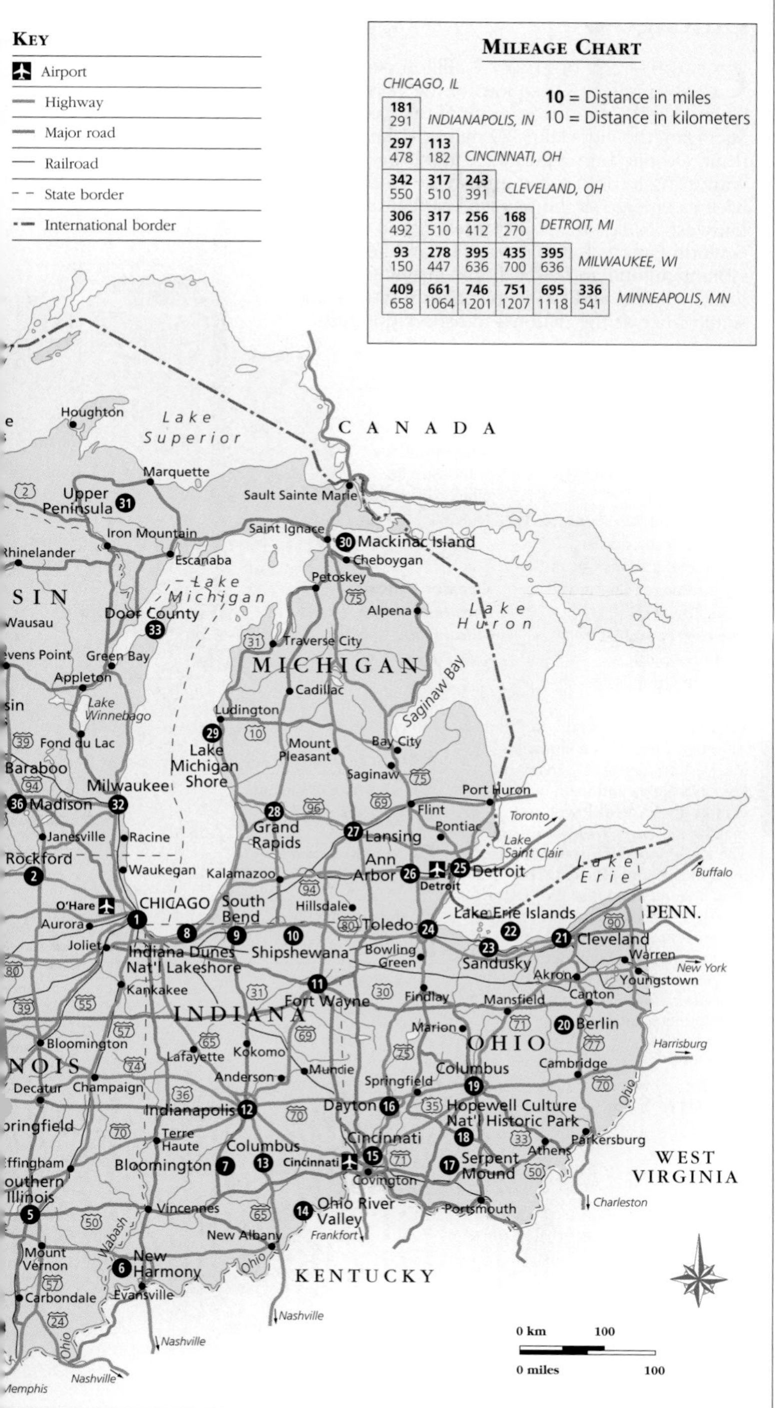


**MILEAGE CHART**

| | CHICAGO, IL | INDIANAPOLIS, IN | CINCINNATI, OH | CLEVELAND, OH | DETROIT, MI | MILWAUKEE, WI |
|---|---|---|---|---|---|---|
| INDIANAPOLIS, IN | 181 / 291 | | | | | |
| CINCINNATI, OH | 297 / 478 | 113 / 182 | | | | |
| CLEVELAND, OH | 342 / 550 | 317 / 510 | 243 / 391 | | | |
| DETROIT, MI | 306 / 492 | 317 / 510 | 256 / 412 | 168 / 270 | | |
| MILWAUKEE, WI | 93 / 150 | 278 / 447 | 395 / 636 | 435 / 700 | 395 / 636 | |
| MINNEAPOLIS, MN | 409 / 658 | 661 / 1064 | 746 / 1201 | 751 / 1207 | 695 / 1118 | 336 / 541 |

# Chicago ❶

CHICAGO, A CITY OF ALMOST 3 million people, covers 228 sq miles (591 sq km) of the US's Midwest. Situated at the southwest edge of the vast Lake Michigan, the city claims 29 miles (47 km) of lakefront. Despite burning to the ground in 1871 and witnessing terrible social unrest, the city soon rebuilt itself to emerge as the financial capital of the Midwest. Today, this third largest city in the US is world famous for its innovative architecture, its vibrant cultural and educational institutions, and for its colorful and turbulent political history and significance as the national transportation hub.

## Sights at a Glance

Chicago Historical Society ①
Newberry Library ②
Magnificent Mile ③
John Hancock Center ④
Navy Pier ⑤
Chicago Children's Museum ⑥
Museum of Broadcast Communications ⑦
Art Institute of Chicago ⑧
Sears Tower ⑨
*The Loop pp390–91* ⑩
South Loop ⑪
Museum Campus ⑫

**South Side**
***(see inset map)***
Museum of Science & Industry ⑬
University of Chicago ⑭
DuSable Museum of African American History ⑮

**Greater Chicago**
***(see inset map)***
Lincoln Park Zoo ⑯
*Oak Park pp396–7* ⑰

## Getting Around

Although Chicago is a sprawling Midwestern metropolis, many of the city's sights and main cultural centers are located downtown, making the city a walker's dream. The city's public transportation is inexpensive and efficient. The train system, known as the "L" for elevated, is the easiest way to get around. Buses crisscross the city, but the system is complicated and best left to regular commuters. Taxis are affordable, convenient, and readily available.

### Key

- Sight/Place of interest
- Airport
- Metro train station
- CTA train station
- Tourist information
- Parking
- Railroad line
- Expressway

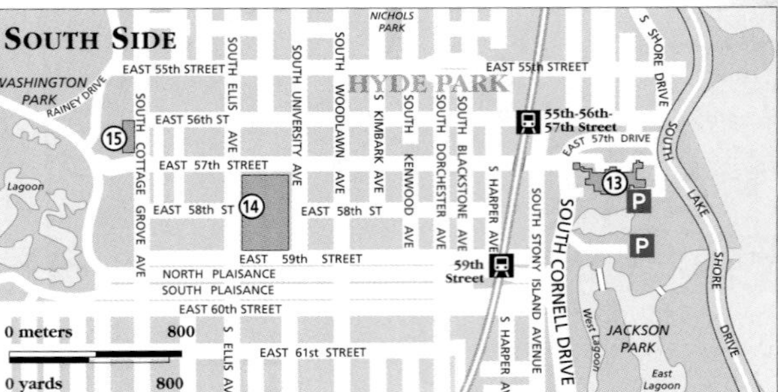

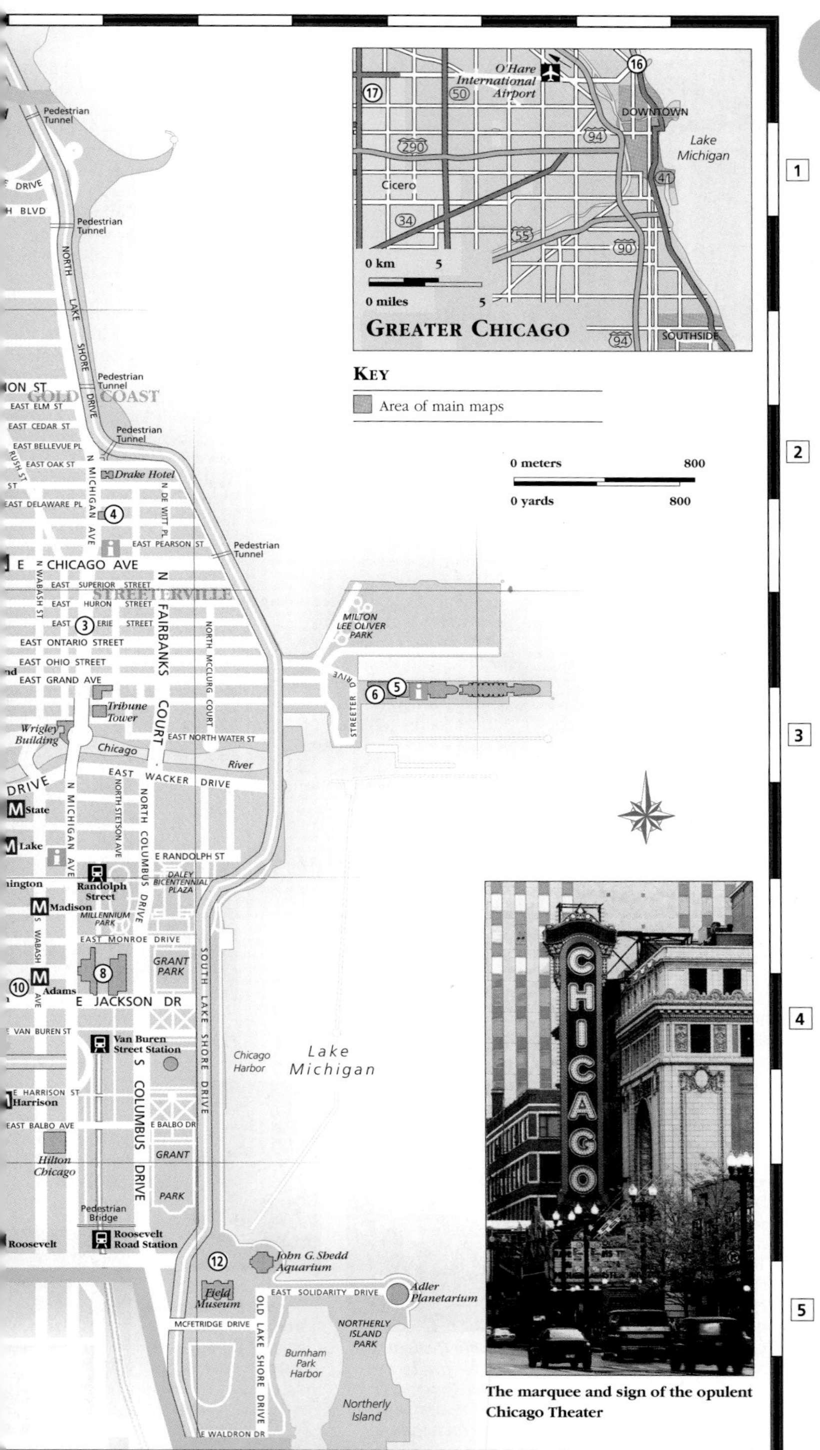


The marquee and sign of the opulent Chicago Theater

**Original Neo-Georgian entrance to the Chicago Historical Society**

## Chicago Historical Society ①

**Map** D1. 1601 N Clark St. *(312) 642-4600.* *Clark/Division then bus 22, 36.* *11, 151, 156.* *9:30am–4:30pm Mon–Sat; noon–5pm Sun.* *Jan 1, Thanksg., Dec 25.* *(free Mon).* *(call for times).* ***Concerts, lectures.*** www.chicagohistory.org

The city's oldest cultural institution, the 1856 Chicago Historical Society is a major museum and research center, with a library open for public research. It traces the history of Chicago and Illinois, from its first explorers through the development of the city to the major events in modern-day Chicago. Miniature dioramas depict great events such as the the Great Fire of 1871, the Chicago River during the Civil War, and the bustling LaSalle Street in the mid-1860s.

The American Wing holds one of only 23 copies of the Declaration of Independence, and a 1789 copy of the American Constitution, first printed in a Philadelphia newspaper. The building itself is fascinating with its two faces – the original 1932 Neo-Georgian structure, and a 1988 addition with a three-story, glass-and-steel atrium entrance.

## Newberry Library ②

**Map** D2. 60 W Walton St. *(312) 943-9090.* *Chicago (red line).* *hours for lobby, book rooms, & exhibits vary. Call ahead.* *public hols.* *3pm Thu; 10:30am Sat.* ***Exhibits, lectures, concerts.***

Founded in 1887 by banker Walter Newberry, this independent research library for the humanities was designed by Henry Ives Cobb, master architect of the Richardsonian Romanesque style.

The superb collection includes cartography, Native American history, Renaissance studies, geneology, and such rarities as first editions of Milton's *Paradise Regained,* the King James Version of the Bible, and a 1481 edition of Dante's *Divine Comedy.*

## Magnificent Mile ③

Michigan Ave, between E Walton Pl & E Kinzie St.

The Magnificent Mile, a stretch of Michigan Avenue north of the Chicago River, is the city's most fashionable street. Almost completely destroyed in the 1871 fire, the street grew int Chicago's premier shopping district after the opening of the Michigan Avenue Bridge in 1920. Exclusive shops lin the wide boulevard, while modern retail outlets and skyscrapers rub shoulders with historic buildings.

To the north lies the Goth Revival-style **Fourth Presbyterian Church**. Its exposed buttresses, stone spire, and recessed main wi dow reflect the influences o medieval European churche

To its right are two histori castellated structures, the **Water Tower** and the **Pumping Station**, among t few buildings that survived the 1871 fire. The tower, ori inally housing a standpipe, now home to a photography gallery and a theater. The station still fulfills its origina purpose of pumping water and houses a Visitor

**Open-air skywalk topping the John Hancock Center**

### Architecture in Chicago

Chicago is world famous as a center of architectural innovation, a city where architects have pushed the boundaries of creativity. This reputation had its beginnings in the tragic fire of 1871. Working on a blank slate, architects rose to the challenge of reshaping a devastated city. It was in Chicago that the world's first skyscraper was built, and here that Frank Lloyd Wright developed his Prairie School of architecture.

***Gothic Revival** style, represented by the Water Tower, drew from medieval European architecture.*

***Italianate design** sty was inspired by Renais sance palaces and vill of northern Italy. The elegant Drake Hotel exemplifies this style.*

***Richardsonian Romanesque** style – typified by rough-cut stone, round arches, and recessed windows – can be seen in the Newberry Library.*

ormation Center (163 E arson St) and café. Across street, **Water Tower Place** ntains eight floors of upscale utiques and restaurants. her "vertical shopping malls" the street include Chicago ice and Westfield North idge. **Hershey's Chicago** is arby and well-stocked, and s sugar-free versions of its ost popular products.

n the south, the Gothic-style **ibune Tower**, office of the *icago Tribune*, holds rock gments from world-famous es, such as St. Peter's Basilica Rome, the Forbidden City in ijing, and even a 3.3-billion-ar-old piece of moon rock nbedded in its exterior walls.

At the southern end of the eet is the two-part **Wrigley iilding**. This white terra-tta structure, one of iicago's most beloved, atures a giant four-sided ock and a quiet courtyard, nich is open to the public.

## ohn Hancock Center ④

**ap** D2. 875 N Michigan Ave. **servatory** *(312) 751-3681.* *Chicago (red line).* *9am–11pm ily.* *to observatory (children der 5 free).*

FFECTIONATELY called "Big John" by Chicagoans, the 0-story, cross-braced steel hn Hancock Center stands it in the Chicago skyline. ie tapering obelisk tower's ajor attraction is the ancock Observatory on the 94th floor. Here, 1,127 ft (344 m) above the Magnificent Mile, an open-air (screened) skywalk offers spectacular views of the city. The elevator ride to the top at 20 miles (32 km) is one of the fastest in the US.

Designed by architect Bruce Graham of Skidmore Owings and Merrill and engineer Fazlur R. Khan, the center houses offices, condominiums, and shops in 2.8 million sq ft (0.26 million sq m) of space. The ground-level plaza has a fountain and cafés.

## Navy Pier ⑤

**Map** D2. 600 E Grand Ave. *(800) 595-7437.* *29, 56, 65, 66, 120, 121, 124.* *10am; closing times vary by day & season.* *Thanksgiving, Dec 25.* ***Lake cruises.*** www.navypier.com

NAVY PIER is a bustling recreational and cultural center. Designed by Charles S. Frost, the 3,000-ft (915-m) long and 400-ft (120-m) wide pier was the largest in the world when built in 1916. Over 20,000 timber piles were used in its construction.

**The giant Ferris wheel, Navy Pier Park**

Originally a municipal wharf, the pier was used for naval training during World War II. After a four-year renovation, Navy Pier opened in its present incarnation in 1995. Navy Pier Park has a 150-ft (45-m) Ferris wheel, an old-fashioned carousel, an outdoor amphitheater, ice skating, miniature golf, and an IMAX® 3D Theater. The Smith Museum features stained glass.

## Chicago Children's Museum ⑥

**Map** E3. 700 E Grand Ave. *(312) 527-1000.* *29, 56, 65, 66.* *10am–5pm Tue–Sun; Memorial Day–Labor Day.* *Thanksg., Dec 25.* *(free 5–8pm Thu).* ***Special activities daily.*** www.chichildrensmuseum.org

CHICAGO Children's Museum, focusing on activating the intellectual and creative potential of children ages 1 to 12, is an activity center for the whole family. All exhibits are hands-on: kids can build a fort, climb three levels of rope rigging on a schooner, make a flying machine, or channel water with dams and locks. The Dinosaur Expedition is where children can dig for bones in an excavation pit, or simply slide, climb, and jump around.

***ueen Anne** style, ice a popular design r Chicago residences, exemplified by row ouses in Crilly Court.*

***Chicago School**, developed here, led to an ngineering and aesthetic revolution with commercial skyscrapers like the Reliance building.*

***Neo-Classical** style has classical Greco-Roman elements, as seen in the Chicago Cultural Center.*

***International Style** stresses severe geometry and large expanses of glass. Sears Tower is a fine example.*

***Post-Modern** architecture, an eclectic style without strict rules, is seen in the Harold Washington Library Center.*

## Museum of Broadcast Communications ⑦

**Map** D3. State & Kinzie. *(312) 245-8200.* Washington *(red line). Open mid-2006. Call for details* www.museum.tv

Founded in 1987 and housed in brand new premises at State and Kinzie, this museum is one of the only three broadcast museums in the US. Permanent displays and special exhibitions examine popular culture through the sights and sounds of TV and radio. A TV studio offers visitors the opportunity to anchor the "news" and take home a souvenir videotape.

The Sportscaster Café shows replays of famous moments in sports history, and the Radio Hall of Fame features taped voices, such as Jack Benny and Bing Crosby from radio's golden age. The museum's collection of media icons include Charlie McCarthy, Garfield Goose, and Dirty Dragon. Exhibits also include vintage and contemporary TV sets and radios, as well as "the camera that changed America," the one used to televise the Kennedy/Nixon debate (1960) that marked a turning point in the relationship between TV and politics. In the museum's research center guests can, for a fee, hear from a collection of over 50,000 hours of radio programming, or view thousands of TV broadcasts and commercials. A gift shop sells postcards, books, and broadcast memorabilia.

**"His Master's Voice" dog and early NBC microphone**

**The Neo-Classical façade of the Art Institute of Chicago**

## The Art Institute o Chicago ⑧

**Map** D4.111 S Michigan Ave. *(312) 443-3600.* *Adams.* *3, 6 7, 126, 145, 147.* *Van Buren St.* *10:30am–4:30pm Mon, Wed–Fr 10:30am–8pm Tue; 10am–5pm Sat, noon–5pm Sun.* *Thanksg., Dec 2* *(children under 6 free; free Tue; separate adm to some exhibits).* *via Columbus Dr entrance.* *at Monroe St.* ***Exhibits, lectures films.*** www.artic.edu

The extensive collections at the Art Institute of Chicago represent nearly 5,000 years of creativity through paintings, sculptures textiles, photographs, cultura objects, and decorative arti-

## The Loop ⑩

The loop gets its name from the elevated track system that circles the center of downtown. Screeching trains and a steady stream of people add to its bustle. In the canyon vistas, through the historic buildings and modern edifices, you can catch glimpses of the bridges spanning the Chicago River. The renovation of warehouses and historic theaters is helping to enliven the Loop at night.

**Marquette Building,** an early skyscraper (1895), was designed by William Holabird and Martin Roche, central Chicago School figures and architects of more than 80 buildings in the Loop.

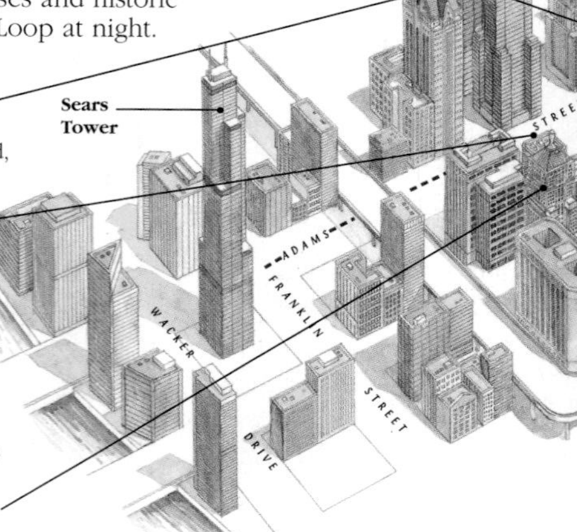


**190 South LaSalle Street** (1987), designed by Philip Johnson, has a white-marble lobby with a gold-leafed, vaulted ceiling.

**The Rookery,** designed by Burnham and Root in 1888, typifies the Richardsonian Romansque style.

**Chicago Board of Trade** occupies a 45-story Art Deco building, a statue of Ceres atop its roof. The frenetic action inside can be observed from a viewers' gallery.

ts from around the world. unded by civic leaders and patrons in 1879 as The icago Academy of Fine ts, the museum became e Art Institute of Chicago in 82. Outgrowing two homes wealthy patrons donated eir art collections, it finally tled in this Neo-Classical ucture. Today, the complex mbines modern additions in e original structure made by epley, Rutan, and Coolidge. The museum's holdings an from 3rd millennium BC yptian and Chinese artifacts modern and contemporary nerican and European art. ough best known for its orld famous Impressionist d Post-Impressionist collec- n with such masterpieces Paul Cézanne's *The Basket Apples* (c.1895), Henri de ulouse-Lautrec's *At the oulin Rouge* (1895), and aude Monet's six versions a wheat field, the museum presents almost every major tistic movement of the 19th d 20th centuries. Particu- ly strong are examples of bism, Surrealism, and erman Expressionism. The 35,000-strong exquisite ian collection is also note-worthy for its Japanese wood-block prints, and Indian and Chinese historic artifacts.

## Sears Tower ⑨

**Map** C4. 233 S Wacker Dr. *(312) 875-9696.* *Quincy.* *May–Sep: 10am–10pm daily; Oct–Apr: 10am–8pm daily; last adm 30 min before closing.* www.thesearstower.com; www.theskydeck.com

At a height of 1,450 ft (442 m) the Sears Tower is one of the world's tallest buildings. Boasting the highest occupied floor and the highest height to the rooftop, it was designed by Bruce Graham, of Skidmore Owings and Merrill, and engineer Fazlur Khan. Over 110 concrete caissons, anchored in bedrock, support the tower's 222,500 tons.

Today, the tower contains 3.5 million sq ft (0.3 million sq m) of office space, more than 100 elevators, and almost enough telephone cable to circle the Earth twice. The elevator to the glass-enclosed 103rd-floor Skydeck travels at 1,600 ft (490 m) per minute, and offers stunning views.

**View of the Sears Tower and Skydeck, looking northeast**

Nearby, the 12-story **Rookery** building, the world's tallest when it opened in 1888, is one of the city's most photographed edifices. Its dark red-brick façade with terra-cotta trim gives way to a two-tiered court, remodeled in 1907 by Frank Lloyd Wright, who covered the iron columns and staircases with white marble, inlaid with gold leaf.

**The Rookery**
209 S LaSalle St. *(312) 553-6150.* *9am–8pm Mon–Fri; 9am–3pm Sat.* *public hols.*

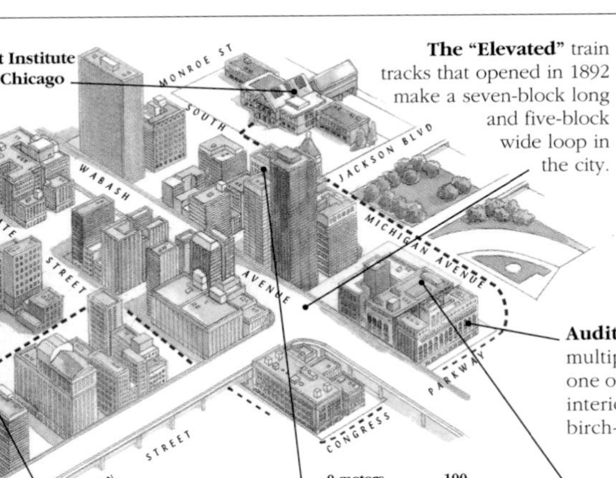


**The "Elevated"** train tracks that opened in 1892 make a seven-block long and five-block wide loop in the city.

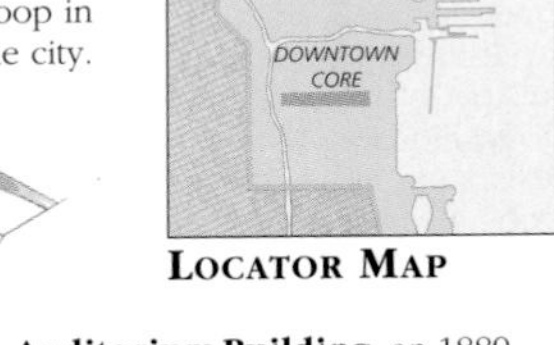


**Locator Map**

**Auditorium Building**, an 1889 multipurpose skyscraper, features one of Adler and Sullivan's best interiors in its seventh-floor, birch-paneled recital hall.

**Monadnock Building's** north half is the tallest building ever constructed entirely of masonry.

**Fine Arts Building**, designed by Solon S. Beman in 1885, was originally a wagon carriage showroom. It once also housed Frank Lloyd Wright's studio.

**Santa Fe Center,** a classic Chicago School building, with an elegant two-story atrium, houses the Chicago Architecture Foundation.

**ederal Center** is a three-uilding office complex lesigned around a central plaza y Ludwig Mies van der Rohe.

**Key**

- - - Suggested route

Rowe Building, Printing House Row District

## South Loop ⑪

**Map** D4. *Harrison, Roosevelt.* *via State St & Dearborn St buses (near South Side: Michigan Ave bus 3).*

Located a short walk south of the downtown core, the South Loop has changed dramatically in recent decades, from a run-down industrial district to a residential and retail neighborhood. The South Loop developed as an industrial area in the late 1800s, but after World War II, manufacturers left and the area declined. In the 1970s, with the conversion of the district's derelict warehouses to fashionable lofts, businesses sprang up as Chicagoans took advantage of the area's proximity to downtown.

This transformation is most evident in the two blocks of the **Printing House Row Historic District**, which in the 1890s had earned Chicago the title of the printing capital of the US. By the 1970s, with the closing of the nearby Dearborn Station, manufacturers withdrew and the area fell into decline. Many of the massive buildings erected for the printing trade remain today. Their conversion into stylish condominiums and office lofts has led to the revitalization of the neighborhood and an influx of commercial activity. The Second Franklin Building has ornamental tilework illustrating the history of printing over its entranceway, while the Rowe Building houses a bookstore specializing in local authors and travel literature. The adjacent Richardsonian Romansque-style **Dearborn Station Galleria**, Chicago's oldest surviving passenger train station building, has also been converted into a shopping mall. Its square clock tower is a landmark.

Dominating the South Loop, on South Street, is the world's largest public library building, the **Chicago Public Library, Harold Washington Library Center**, holding close to 2 million books and periodicals on its 90 miles (145 km) of shelving. This Post-Modern giant pays tribute to many of Chicago's historic buildings, through its varied architectural features. Artwork is displayed throughout the building, including work by Cheyenne artist Heap of Birds. The library also showcases exhibits relating to Chicago's history.

To the east, the **Museum of Contemporary Photography** focuses on American photography produced since 1945, with selections from its 5,000-strong collection and temporary exhibitions. Next to it, the **Spertus Museum** is Chicago's Jewish Museum. Found on the first two floors of Spertus Institute of Jewish Studies, it invites visitors to learn about the Jewish experience through a series of thought-provoking exhibitions and programs on Jewish history, religion, art, and culture, over the centuries and today. Often these exhibitions draw from Spertus' own world-class collection of art and artifac including ritual objects, textiles and jewelry.

A computer in the Zell Holocaust Memorial lists th names of people lost in the Holocaust by Chicago famil – it takes a full day to read list – and an exhibition on 2nd floor is geared to teach young people about it.

On the lower level, the ARTiFACT Center, has a 32-f (10-m) long interactive dig s where you can learn about ancient Middle East while unearthing replicas of real artifacts. The Asher Library, the fifth floor, is the largest public Jewish library in the central US, with over 100,00 books and 1,000 Jewish film on video and DVD. A new facility is due to open in 200

A short walk east leads to **South Michigan Avenue**, one of Chicago's finest street Featuring a spectacular row historic buildings, it is an exc lent place to window sho and admire the varied architectural styles for which the city is famous. Farther alon the street lies the opulent Hilton Chicag Decorated in French Renaissance style, this 2 story hotel – with 3,000 rooms, a rooftop golf course, and a 1,200-seat theater – was the largest the world when it open in 1927. Across the street Buddy Guy's Legends presents bi names and local blues acts. Owner and blues legend Buddy Guy is ofte there himself.

Judaic art showcased in the Spertus Museum

**Chicago Public Library, Harold Washington Librar Center**
400 S State St. *(312) 747-4300.* *Library.* *9am–7pm Mon–Thu, 9am–5pm Fri–Sat, 1–5pm Sun.* *public hols.* *call (312) 747-4136.* ***Exhibits, lecture films.*** www.chipublib.org

**Spertus Museum**
618 S Michigan Ave. *(312) 322-1747.* *Harrison.* *10am–5pm Sun–Wed, 10am–7pm Thu, 10am–3pm Fri.* *Sat, public & Jewish ho* *(free Fri).* ***Concerts, lectures, films.*** www.spertus.e

## ⁄Iuseum Campus ⑫

ſlap E5. S Lake Shore Dr. *Roosevelt then free trolley.* 12, 46. *Roosevelt then free trolley.*

THE MUSEUM CAMPUS is a vast lakefront park connecting ıree world-famous natural cience museums, thus ›roviding educational and ecreational opportunities for ll. This 57-acre (23-ha) xtension of Burnham Park vas created by the reloca- .on of Lake Shore )rive in 1996.

Located in the outhwest part of the .ısh green campus is ıe Daniel Burnham- lesigned Neo-Classical tructure housing the 'ield Museum. This ;reat natural history nuseum holds an ·ncyclopedic collection ›f zoological, geo- ɔgical, and anthropological ›bjects from around the vorld. Founded in 1894 (with unding from Marshall Field) ɔ house objects from the 1893 Vorld's Columbian Exposition, ıe museum now holds over ?0 million objects.

Particular strengths of the nuseum include such dino- aur fossils as "Sue" – the nost complete *Tyran- ıosaurus rex* skeleton ever ound, Native Indian and \ncient Egyptian artifacts, and :xtensive displays on mam- nals and birds.

The newly renovated Hall ›f Jades displays more than ;00 artifacts from Neolithic imes to the Bronze Age and Chinese Dynasties. The high- ight is a 300 lb (136 kg) jar rom the palace of Emperor Quanlong. The Underground \dventure is also great – it's a subterranean exhibit where visitors can walk through worm tunnels, meet giant bugs, and feel reduced to insect size.

ʼhe monumental Neo-Classical :ntrance to Field Museum

Xochpilli, Aztec God of Flowers, Field Museum

A short walk northeast along terraced gardens leads to the **John G. Shedd Aquarium**, housing nearly 8,000 saltwater and freshwater animals, representing 650 species of fish, birds, reptiles, amphibians, invertebrates, and mammals. Named for its benefactor, a prominent Chicago businessman, the aquarium opened in 1930 in a Neo-Classical building. The Oceanarium has a magnificent curved wall of glass facing Lake Michigan, whose water flows into its tank. This marine-mammal pavilion showcases beluga whales and dolphins. The aquarium's exhibits can be viewed from many viewpoints, some under water.

Farther east, the Museum Campus houses the **Adler Planetarium and Astronomy Museum** featuring one of the world's finest astronomical collections, with artifacts dating as far back as 12th-century Persia. It also has the world's first virtual-reality theater. Spectacular sky shows complement displays on navigation and space exploration. State-of-the-art technology enables visitors to explore exhibits hands-on. Funded by businessman Max Adler, this 12-sided, Art Deco structure was designed by Ernest Grunsfeld in 1930 and is now a historical landmark.

**Beluga whale at the Oceanarium in the John G. Shedd Aquarium**

**Field Museum**
1400 S Lake Shore Dr. *(312) 922-9410.* *9am–5pm daily.* *Jan 1, Dec 25.* *(free Sep–Feb: Mon–Tue).* *via west entrance.* *11am, 1pm.* ***Lectures, films, events.*** www.fieldmuseum.org

**John G. Shedd Aquarium**
1200 S Lake Shore Dr. *(312) 939-2438.* *Memorial Day–Labor Day: 9am–6pm daily (Jun–Aug: 9am–10pm Thu, Oceanarium 9am–8pm Thu); Labor Day–Memorial Day: 9am–5pm Mon–Fri; 9am–6pm Sat, Sun, public hols.* *Jan 1, Dec 25.* *(free Sep– Feb: Mon & Tue; except special exhibits).* ***Lectures.*** www.shedd.org

**Adler Planetarium & Astronomy Museum**
1300 S Lake Shore Dr. *(312) 922-7827.* *9:30am–4:30pm daily (5–10pm 1st Fri of each month).* *Thanksgiving, Dec 25.* *(free Sep–Feb: Mon & Tue, but separate adm to theaters still applies).* ***Lectures, films, light shows.*** www.adlerplanetarium.org

### OLD MONEY

**Potter Palmer**

Chicago has a beautiful sound because Chicago means money – so the late actress Ruth Gordon reputedly said. By the beginning of the 20th century the city was home to 200 millionaires. One of the most prominent was dry-goods merchant and real-estate mogul Potter Palmer who, with his socialite wife Bertha Honoré, had an enormous impact on the city's cultural and economic life. In 1882, Palmer built an opulent home at North Lake Shore Drive. Perhaps no feature of the mansion epitomized the family's wealth as much as the doors: there were no outside handles, as the doors were always opened from inside, by servants. Department-store owner Marshall Field was less ostentatious. Although he rode in a carriage to work, he stopped short of his store to walk the last few blocks so people would not see his mode of transport. Likewise, he asked the architect of his $2-million, 25-room mansion not to include any frills.

View of the Museum of Science and Industry from across Columbia Basin

## Museum of Science & Industry ⑬

**Map** B5. 57th St & S Lake Shore Dr. *(773) 684-1414, (800) 468-6674.* *Garfield then eastbound bus 55.* *1, 6, 10.* *55th-56th-57th St, 59th St.* *9:30am–4pm Mon–Fri, 9:30am–5:30pm Sat, Sun, public hols.* *Dec 25.* *(free Jan–Feb, mid-Aug–mid-Dec: Mon & Tue; Jun: 1st Mon & Tue).* ***Films.*** www.msichicago.org

The museum of Science and Industry celebrates scientific and technological accomplishments, with an emphasis on achievements of the 20th and 21st centuries. With its collection of over 800 exhibits and 2,000 interactive displays, the museum makes the exploration of science and technology an accesssible experience.

Though best known for its exhibits on space exploration and transportation, the 350,000 sq ft (32,500 sq m) of exhibition space in the museum has more than enough to keep visitors of all ages engaged for a full day.

The **Henry Crown Space Center** features the Apollo 8 Command Module, the first manned spacecraft to circle the moon, in 1968, a replica of NASA's Apollo Lunar Module Trainer, and a 6.5-oz (185-gm) piece of moon rock. A 20-minute movie simulates the experience of blasting off in a space shuttle, complete with shaking seats, allowing viewers to feel like astronauts, if only briefly.

The transportation section features outstanding examples of transport from train and plane to automobile. In **All Aboard the Silver Streak** visitors can climb aboard a record-breaking 1930s train that revolutionized industrial design. One of the most popular exhibits, **Take Flight** explores the inner workings of a 727 jetliner, cantilevered to the museum's balcony, and simulates a seven-minute San Francisco-to-Chicago flight.

Visitors can walk through a 16-ft (5-m) tall replica of the human heart, seeing it from the perspective of a blood cell, and calculate the number of times their heart has beaten since birth, or look inside the human body in a detailed exhibit on anatomy. **AIDS: The War Within** is the world's first permanent museum exhibit on AIDS and HIV. It explores the nine stages of the AIDS virus and the efforts of scientists to control it.

A few exhibits fall outside the museum's defined focus but prove to be enduring crowd pleasers, such as **Circus**. Roland Weber, a railroad worker, spent 33 years carving and casting the 22,000 figures that come to life in this tiny, animated circus.

### From Plaster to Stone

Originally built as the Palace of Fine Arts for the 1893 World's Fair, this structure later became the first home of the Field Museum of Natural History. Based on Classical Revival style, this plaster-clad building was designed by Charles B. Atwood. After the Field Museum moved out, the building sat in a state of disrepair until the mid-1920s, when Julius Rosenwald, chairman of Sears Roebuck and Co., campaigned to save it, launching a million-dollar reconstruction program. Exterior plaster was replaced with 28,000 tons of limestone and marble in an 11-year renovation. The Museum of Science and Industry opened in 1933, in time for the Century of Progress World's Exposition.

The original building during the 1893 World's Columbian Exposition

## University of Chicago ⑭

**Map** A5. Bounded by 56th & 59th Sts, Ellis & Woodlawn Aves. *Garfield (green line) then bus 55.* *59th.*

The university of Chicago, was founded in 1890 with the endowment of John D. Rockefeller, on land donated by Marshall Field *(see p393)*. Today, this outstanding private university has the greatest number of Nobel laureates among faculty, alumni, and researchers of any US university. It is particularly lauded in

The Rockefeller Memorial Chapel, University of Chicago

ne Robie House, a masterpiece of the Prairie School of architecture

ie fields of economics and ıysics. Henry Ives Cobb esigned 18 of the university's mestone buildings and devel-ped its cloistered quadrangle lan (along the lines of Cam-ridge and Oxford), before ie Boston firm Shepley utan and Coolidge took ver as the main architects ı 1901. Now the campus atures designs from more ıan 70 architects.

The north entrance ouses the ornamental obb Gate, a gargoyled eremonial gateway onated by Henry Cobb ı 1900. Across the reet, the Regenstein ibrary holds rare book nd manuscript collec-ons, along with millions f other volumes.

Situated at the northern nd of the campus is the ght-filled, intimate **Smart luseum of Art**. Named fter its benefactors, avid and Alfred Smart, ie museum holds nore than 8,000 bjects, including ntiquities and Old laster prints, Asian aintings, calligraphies, and eramics, spanning five enturies of Western and astern civilizations. The nuseum's café, with tall vindows overlooking the ranquil sculpture garden, is a reat spot for a quiet lunch. Outside the museum, sculptor Ienry Moore's *Nuclear Energy*, marks the spot vhere, in 1942, a team of cientists led by Enrico Fermi ıshered in the atomic age with the first controlled nuclear reaction.

In the southeast of the vast campus lies the **Oriental Institute Museum**, the exhibition arm of the university's Oriental Institute, whose scholars have excavated in virtually every region of the Near East since 1919. Highlights of the museum's collections include a rare reconstruction of an Assyrian palace (c.721–705 BC) and a 17-ft (5-m) sculpture of King Tutankhamen, the tallest ancient Egyptian statue in the Western Hemisphere (c.1334–25 BC). Opposite the museum, the massive Gothic-style **Rockefeller Memorial Chapel**, topped with a 207-ft (63-m) carillon tower, is the tallest building on campus. John D. Rockefeller had requested that this limestone-and-brick structure representing religion be the university's most dominant feature. Two blocks north lies Frank Lloyd Wright's world-famous **Robie House** (1908–1910). Designed for Frederick Robie, a bicycle and motorbike manufacturer, the home is one of Wright's last Prairie School houses: Wright left both his family and his Oak Park practice during its three-year construction. The exterior design of the house perfectly captures the prairie landscape of flat, open fields. The roof's sweeping planes embody the house's aesthetic of bold rectilinear simplicity. Steel beams support the overhanging roof. Also bold but simple, the interior is furnished with Wright-designed furniture. The house is an organic whole, underscored by the harmonious interplay between the exterior and interior and is admired by architects worldwide.

**Statue of King Tutankhamen, Oriental Institute Museum**

**Oriental Institute Museum**
1155 E 58th St. *(773) 702-9514.* *10am–4pm Tue & Thu–Sat, 10am–8:30pm Wed, noon–4pm Sun.* *public hols.* ***Special events.***

**Robie House**
5757 S Woodlawn Ave. *(773) 834-1847.* *daily.* *Jan 1, Thanksgiving, Dec 25.* *(children under 7 free).* *mandatory: 11am, 1pm, 3pm Mon–Fri; every 30 min between 11am–3:30pm on weekends.*
www.wrightplus.org

## DuSable Museum of African American History ⑮

**Map** A5. 740 E 56th Pl. *(773) 947-0600.* *Garfield (green line) then bus 55.* *4, 10.* *10am–5pm Mon– Sat, noon–5pm Sun & public hols.* *Jan 1, Thanksgiving, Dec 25.* *(children under 6 free; free on Sun).* *book in advance.* ***Lectures, films.***

FOUNDED in 1961 to preserve and interpret the diverse historical experiences and achievements of African Americans, the DuSable Museum highlights the accomplishments of the ordinary and extraordinary alike.

The museum's permanent exhibit, **Songs of My People**, brings together diverse images by Black photojournalists of African-American lives. Other exhibits include memorabilia from the life and political career of Chicago's first Black mayor, Harold Washington, and **Distorted Images: Made in USA?**, an exhibit focusing on contrived and demeaning images of African Americans. **Africa Speaks** presents handcrafted functional art from Africa, and fascinating ritual masks from closed West African societies.

# Greater Chicago

VISITORS EAGER TO DISCOVER more of Chicago will not be disappointed by the rich mix of historical sights, recreational activities, and picturesque suburbs that the city's outlying areas have to offer. For lovers of architecture, Oak Park is a must-see for its Frank Lloyd Wright designs. Other Chicago neighborhoods, such as Wicker Park and Lakeview are ideal day-trip destinations. The vast expanse of Lincoln Park offers a respite from the bustle of the city in its lush gardens, flowering plants, and a zoo, famed for its naturalistic animal habitats.

**Frank Lloyd Wright's Home and Studio, Oak Park**

**A lowland gorilla at the zoo's Regenstein Center for African Apes**

## Lincoln Park Zoo ⑯

2200 N Cannon Dr. *(312) 742-2000.* *Clark/Division.* *22, 36, 135, 136, 145, 146, 147, 151.* *8am–6pm daily (May–Sep: 8am–7pm Sat, Sun & hols).* *on N Cannon Dr.* **Workshops** *(312) 742-2053.* **Special events** *(312) 742-2000.* www.lpzoo.com

LOCATED IN THE heart of Lincoln Park, this zoo is easily accessible from downtown. Established in 1868 with the gift of two swans from New York's Central Park, Lincoln Park Zoo is the country's oldest free public zoo. Today, more than 1,000 mammals, reptiles, and birds from around the world live here in realistic habitats. A world leader in wildlife conservation, the zoo shelters such animals as the threatened Grevy's zebra from Africa and the endangered Bactrian camel from Mongolia, as well as rare gazelles, deer, antelopes, and alpacas in its 11 outdoor habitats. A 1912 historic building houses rare cats, including Siberian tigers. The zoo's large collection of lowland gorillas bears testimony to a successful breeding program. A working farm with cows, horses, pigs, and chickens, is popular with kids for the daily milking and horse-grooming demonstrations.

Lincoln Park, Chicago's largest, offers walking and biking paths that wind along paddle-boating ponds, lagoons, and sandy beaches.

## Oak Park ⑰

Bounded by North Ave, Roosevelt Rd Austin Blvd, & Harlem Ave. *(708) 848-1500.* *Oak Park (green line); Harlem/Lake (green line).* *Oak Par (Union Pacific/ West line).* **Visitor Center** 158 N Forest Ave. *10am–3pm Mon–Fri, 11am–3:30pm Sat–Sun* *Jan 1, Thanksg., Dec 25.* **Frank Lloyd Wright Preservation Trust** 931 Chicago Ave. *(708) 848-1976.* www.wrightplus.org

FRANK LLOYD Wright moved to Oak Park in 1889, at the age of 22. During the next 20 years here, he created many groundbreaking buildings as his legendary Prairie School style evolved. This tranquil community is now home to 25 Wright buildings – the largest grouping of his work anywhere. The best place to feast on Wright's achievement is the superbly restored **Frank Lloyd Wright Home and Studio**, designed by

**Pink flamingos in the Waterfowl Lagoon at Lincoln Park Zoo**

ity Temple, Frank Lloyd Wright's "little jewel," Oak Park

right in 1889. This was also
ıere he developed his
fluential architectural style.
Nearby are two private
mes that reveal Wright's
rsatility. The 1902 **Arthur
eurtley House** is typically
airie style, with its row of
ndows spanning the low
ofline, and a simple but
egant entrance arch. The
95 **Moore-Dugal House**
ross the street, is a hybrid
styles, rich with Tudor
vival and Gothic elements.
At the southern end of Oak
rk is the masterful **Pleasant
ome**, a 30-room Prairie-
yle mansion designed in
97 by George W. Maher.
ıe house holds extraordi-
ry art glass – designed panels of leaded glass. It also includes intricate woodwork, and decorative motifs, and a display on the area's history.

Wright was especially proud of **Unity Temple**, his design for the Unitarian Universalist Congregation. He called this church one of his most important designs, his first expression of an "entirely new architecture." It was built between 1906 and 1908, using a then-unusual technique of poured reinforced concrete, in part because of a budget of only $45,000. Unity Temple is a masterpiece of powerful simplicity wedded with functional ornamentation.

Oak Park is also famous as the birthplace of the famed American writer Ernest Hemingway (1899–1960), who lived here until the age of 20. Although Hemingway *(see p323)* rejected the conservative mindset of this Chicago suburb saying it was full of "wide lawns and narrow minds," Oak Park continues to pride itself on its literary association. The **Ernest Hemingway Birthplace**, a grand Victorian home decorated with turn-of-the-20th-century furnishings, has displays on this Nobel Prize-winner's life. The **Ernest Hemingway Museum**, features several artifacts from Hemingway's early life, including a childhood diary.

**The Victorian house in which Ernest Hemingway was born**

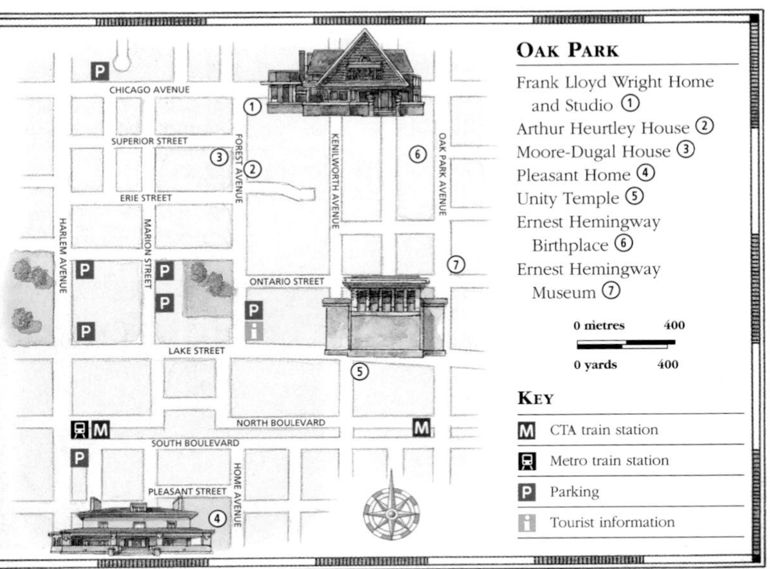

# Illinois

EXCEPT FOR THE DENSELY populated area around Chicago *(see pp386–97)*, Illinois is a predominantly rural state. Large expanses of rich, flat farmland are dotted with the occasional small agricultural community or county seat. Known as the "Land of Lincoln," most of the sites related to the president are concentrated in Springfield, the heart of the state. Some rather unusual and picturesque scenery can be found in the hilly "Driftless Region" along the Mississippi in the northwest, and in the rugged "Illinois Ozarks" in the southeast.

**Statue of Sac hero Black Hawk, southwest of Rockford**

## Rockford ❷

*150,000.* *102 N Main St, (800) 521-0849.* www.gorockford.com

DUBBED THE Forest City in the late 1800s, Rockford today has beautiful public and private gardens and miles of parkland along the Rock River, which bisects the city. Of its two most-visited gardens, the **Klehm Arboretum and Botanic Garden** contains 150 acres (61 ha) of plants. The other, the **Sinnissippi Gardens**, runs south along the Rock River's east bank. Its features include an aviary, lagoon, and recreation path. The path offers views of downtown's historic buildings, including the restored Coronado Theater, a gilded 1927 Moorish movie palace.

On the town's east side, the **Midway Village and Museum Center** is both a living history center and local history museum. Exhibits tell the story of ethnic groups who flocked to the city's factories. The grounds have been turned into a 19th-century village, with restored buildings from the area.

The growth of Rockford followed the tragic 1830s Blackhawk War between the Sac Indians of northern Illinois and the US Army, determined to displace the tribes from their farmlands. After the Sacs lost, they were relocated to Iowa. A stone statue of the Sac warrior Chief Blackhawk is located 27 miles (43 km) southwest of Rockford.

**Klehm Arboretum & Botanic Garden**
2701 Clifton Ave. *(888) 419-0782.* *9am–4pm daily; Memorial Day–Labor Day: 9am–8pm daily.* www.klehm.org

**Sinnissippi Gardens**
1300 N 2nd St. *(815) 987-8858.* *9am–4pm daily.* *Thanksgiving, Dec 24, 25, 31, Jan 1.* www.rockfordparks.org/sinnissi

## Galena ❸

*3,600.* *720 Park Ave, (815) 777-3557.* www.galena.org

PERCHED ON a bluff overlooking the Galena River near its confluence with the Mississippi, this immaculately preserved town is a relaxing tourist destination with 19th-century homes, historical landmarks, and antique shops. Its status as the shipping center for the region's many lead mines made Galena the busiest Mississippi River Valley port between St. Louis and St. Paul in the 1840s.

The town's population peaked at 15,000 during the Civil War, when the elite erected many magnificent homes in a wide variety of ornate styles.

Many of Galena's historic homes are now open to visitors. **The Belvedere Mansion**, built in 1857 by a local steamboat owner, is a 22-room Italianate structure with a varied collection of period furnishings and some quaint recent additions, including the draperies from the *Gone with the Wind* movie set. Civil War general and US president Ulysses S. Grant lived quietly in Galena between the signature events of his military career and time in the White House. His small, Federal-style 1860 home contains many of Grant's original possessions and furnishings.

**The Galena/Jo Daviess County History Museum** chronicles Galena's lead mining and Civil War shipping days. **Vinegar Hill Lead Mine**, 6 miles (10 km) north of town, provides regular 30-minute tours of the 19th-century mine.

**The Belvedere Mansion**
1008 Park Ave.
*(815) 777-0747.* *May 20–last weekend in Oct: 11am–4pm.*

**Galena/Jo Daviess County History Museum**
211 S Bench St.
*(815) 777-9129.*
*9am–4:30pm daily.*
*Jan 1, Easter, Thanksgiving, Dec 24, 25, 31.*
www.galenahistorymuseum.org

**A view of Galena with its historic landmarks**

**zy Dog Drive-in, a popular Route 66 café**

## pringfield ❹

111,000. ✈ 🚉 🚌
109 N 7th St, (800) 545-7300.
www.visit–springfieldillinois.com

HE STATE CAPITAL since 1837, Springfield gained fame the adopted hometown of th US president, Abraham ncoln, who lived here for years before assuming e presidency in 1861. The ur-block **Lincoln Home ational Historic Site** is pedestrian-only historic strict, with restored 19th-ntury homes, gaslights, d wooden sidewalks sur-unding the neat frame ouse where Lincoln and his ife, Mary, lived for 16 years. An on-site visitor center ovides details about the y's other Lincoln-related tractions, including his law fice, tomb, and the 1853 **ld State Capitol**. It was re that he delivered his mous 1858 "House Divided" eech, outlining the sec-onal differences that would on plunge the nation into e Civil War. Lincoln's litical career began in 1834, hen he was elected to the inois General Assembly hile working as postmaster the nearby community of ew Salem, now a living story museum.

The town's other attraction the elegant **Dana-Thomas ouse**, a 1904 Prairie-style ome designed by Frank oyd Wright *(see p396)*. It ntains much of Wright's iginal white oak furniture, ght fixtures, art-glass doors, indows, and light panels. any Wright experts consider is to be the best-preserved the houses designed by e famous architect.

Springfield is also rich in Route 66 lore *(see pp40–41)*. The old road follows a clearly marked path through the city, leading to the southside **Cozy Dog Drive-in**, a legendary Route 66 eatery, which claims to have invented the corndog. The café's Route 66 Museum and its trademark "cozy dogs," still available at rock-bottom prices, make it a popular tourist destination.

### Lincoln Home National Historic Site

426 S 7th St. ☎ *(217) 492-4241.*
◯ *8:30 am–5pm daily.* ● *Jan 1, Thanksgiving, Dec 25.* ♿
W www.nps.gov/liho

### Old State Capitol

5th & Adams Sts, Springfield.
☎ *(217) 785-7960.* ◯ *Apr–Labor Day: 9am–5pm daily; Nov–Feb: 9am–4pm Tue–Sat; call for hours at other times.* ● *public hols.* ♿
W www.state.il.us/HPA/hs/Capitol

## Southern Illinois ❺

🚌 ℹ *501 W DeYoung St, Marion, (618) 998-9397.*
W www.adventureillinois.com

IN SOUTHERN Illinois, flat farmlands give way to rolling hills and forests along the Mississippi and Ohio Rivers. This terrain provided strategic vantage points from which Native Americans and, later, French traders and missionaries could monitor river traffic.

Near the confluence of the Mississippi, Missouri, and Illinois Rivers (90 miles/145 km southwest of Springfield) are the remains of the largest prehistoric Native American city north of Mexico. The **Cahokia Mounds State Historic and World Heritage Site** contains more than 100 earthen mounds dating from 1050–1250, when 15,000 people of the Mississippian culture are estimated to have occupied the city. The flat-topped Monks Mound covers 14 acres (6 ha) and rises, in four terraces, to a height of 100 ft (30 m), providing sweeping views of the nearby river valleys and the Gateway Arch *(see p454)*, about 12 miles (19 km) away in downtown St. Louis. The site's interpretive center recounts the fascinating story of these mounds, which were mysteriously abandoned by around 1500.

Further evidence of Native American habitation is abundant in the rugged, unglaciated "Illinois Ozarks," or "Little Egypt" region, where the Ohio River separates the state from Kentucky. The forested ridges and hollows of the sprawling **Shawnee National Forest** can be viewed most dramatically at the Garden of the Gods, a rocky outcropping marked by sandstone towers, boulders, and strangely shaped rocks.

### Cahokia Mounds State Historic Site

30 Ramey Dr, Collinsville. ☎ *(618) 346-5160.* ◯ *8am–sunset daily.*
**Visitor Center** ◯ *9am–5pm Wed–Sun.* ● *public hols.* ♿
W www.cahokiamounds.com

**Grass-covered mounds in the Cahokia Mounds State Historic Site**

# Indiana

UNLIKE THE OTHER STATES of the Great Lakes region, Indiana has only a short, 45-mile (72-km) stretch of shoreline along Lake Michigan. As a result, the state's history has centered on its extensive river systems – the Maumee/Wabash in the north, and the Ohio in the south – and the development of the railroads and highways that linked Indiana to key Midwestern and Eastern markets. Indiana today is an engaging place to explore by car, especially along its hilly Ohio River backroads and Amish-country scenic lanes.

## New Harmony 6

*800. Atheneum, North & Arthur Sts, (800) 231-2168.*
www.newharmony.org

AMERICA'S TWO most successful utopian communities flourished in this neat village on the eastern banks of the Wabash River. The first, the Harmonie Society, was founded by a Pennsylvania-based German Lutheran separatist group in 1814. The sect followed a doctrine of perfectionism and celibacy in anticipation of the second coming of Christ, focusing on the development of profitable agricultural and manufacturing enterprises.

In 1825, the Harmonists returned to Pennsylvania, after selling the town and the surrounding lands to Scottish textile magnate Robert Owen. The latter, too, sought to create an ideal society based on free education and the abolition of social classes and personal property ownership. The colony failed after two years, but Owen's sons, David and Robert, pursued their father's ideas and later established the Smithsonian Institution in Washington, DC.

The tree-lined town is now a State Historic Site with 25 well-preserved Harmonist buildings, an inn, and many beautiful manicured gardens. These include the reconstructed Labyrinth, a maze-like set of hedges arranged in concentric circles around a stone temple that stands at the center.

**Historic New Harmony**
410 Main St. *(812) 682-4488. Mar–Dec daily, call for times.*

**Monroe County Courthouse, Bloomington, a Beaux Arts building**

## Bloomington 7

*70,000. 2855 N Walnut St, (800) 800-0037.*
www.visitbloomington.com

SURROUNDED BY rugged limestone outcrops, this city is home to the leafy Indiana University campus. Quarrying of the limestone deposits fueled Bloomington's 19th-century growth, the results of which can still be seen in the city's magnificent public buildings. A prime example is the 1906 Beaux Arts **Monroe County Courthouse**, at the center of the Courthouse Square Historic District located downtown.

On the campus are a variety of historic buildings and outdoor spaces. The 1941 Auditorium displays 20 panels of Thomas Hart Benton's controversial 1933 mural, *The Social and Industrial History of Indiana*, which ironically relates several key events of the state's history. The **Indiana University Art Center** was designed by architect I.M. Pei. It includes works by Henri Matisse, Claude Monet, Auguste Rodin, and Andy Warhol, as well as Picasso's 1934 *L'Atelier (The Studio)* and Stuart Davis's 1938 *Swing Landscape*, a mural inspired by the 1920s jazz age.

**Indiana University Art Center**
1133 7th St. *(812) 855-5445. 10am–5pm Tue–Sat, noon–5pm Sun. public hols.*
www.artmuseum.iu.edu

## Indiana Dunes National Lakeshore 8

*Dorothy Buell Memorial Visitor Center, cnr Kemil Rd & Hwy 12. (219) 926-7561. Jun–Aug: 8am–6pm daily; Sep–May: 8am–5pm daily. Jan 1, Thanksgiving, Dec 25.*
www.nps.gov/indu

ONE OF THE nation's most diverse groups of ecosystems is contained within the 15,000-acre (6,070-ha) Indiana Dunes National Lakeshore. Only a 30-minute drive from downtown Chicago, this stunning refuge is located along the 25-mile (40-km) stretch of the Lake Michigan shore. Its ecosystems include bogs, swamps, marshes, glacial moraines, prairies, forests, oak savannas, and dunes linked by scenic roads and a network of hiking and biking trails. Home to a dizzying variety of native plant

**Deer at the Indiana Dunes National Lakeshore**

pecies, the park is also :nown as a bird-watcher's ›aradise as herons, cardinals, :ingfishers, and towhees are :equently spotted here.

## ›outh Bend 9

107,789. 401 Colfax Ave, (800) 828-7881.
www.exploresouthbend.org

SOUTH BEND is widely known today as the home of ıe Roman Catholic **Univer-ity of Notre Dame**. The 0,800-student institution vas established in 1842 by ather Edward Sorin, a priest :om the Congregation of ıe Holy Cross.

While religion is still nportant, the students and ountless alumni are equally assionate about the Notre )ame "Fighting Irish" football eam, one of the most suc-essful in college football istory. In fact, one of the ıost famous sculptures at the rt-filled campus is a large ıural of Christ known as *The Vord of Life* that students call Touchdown Jesus."

The **College Football Hall f Fame** relates the history of ıch legends as coaches :nute Rockne and Ara arseghian, and play-rs George Gipp, aul Hornung, and oe Montana. xtensive displays re enlivened by a layful exhibit on heerleaders, bands, nd mascots. A 360-egree theater literally urrounds visitors with s range of historical film and ideo highlights.

South of downtown, the **tudebaker National Museum** contains the horse-rawn carriages and early utomobiles manufactured y the town's now-defunct tudebaker corporation. The ollection includes the arriage in which President incoln rode to Ford's Theatre ıe night he was assassinated ı Washington, DC, and a 909 backward-forward utomobile that shuttled US enators between their offices nd the Capitol.

"Touchdown Jesus" mural at Notre Dame, South Bend

### College Football Hall of Fame

111 S St Joseph. (800) 440-3263. 10am–5pm. Jan 1, Thanksgiving, Dec 24, 25.
www.collegefootball.org

## Shipshewana 10

525. 440 1/2 S Van Buren St, (800) 254-8090.
www.backroads.org

THIS SMALL VILLAGE, nestled in the rolling farmlands of northeastern Indiana, has one of the world's largest Amish communities *(see p109)*. The town's **Menno-Hof Mennonite Anabaptist Interpretive Center** provides a detailed background on the European Anabaptist movement, which gave rise to the Mennonite, Hutterite, and Amish sects. Religious persecution in the 19th century led to the large-scale immigration of Anabaptists to the US and Canada. Exhibits at the center re-create this dark period. The town also has the Midwest's largest open-air flea market.

Amish horse-drawn carriage

Local Amish farmers, with their distinctive black hats, white shirts, and black suits, riding horse-drawn buggies, are frequent sights in Shipshewana and the surrounding villages of Bristol, Elkhart, Goshen, Middlebury, Nappanee, and Wakarusa. Tourists come to the villages in search of furniture, dairy, baked goods, and quilts.

### Menno-Hof Mennonite Anabaptist Interpretive Center

510 S Van Buren St. (260) 768-4117. Apr–Dec: 10am–5pm Mon–Sat, noon–4pm Tue–Fri; Jan–Mar: 10am– 5pm Sat. Jan 1, Thanksgiving, Dec 25.
www.mennohof.org

## Fort Wayne 11

230,000. 1021 S Calhoun St, (800) 767-7752.
www.visitfortwayne.com

FORT WAYNE'S location at the confluence of the St. Mary's, St. Joseph, and Maumee Rivers made it a strategic site for the Native Americans, French fur traders, British armies, and American settlers who sought to control the access to the Great Lakes. The city's prosperity during the railroad era is exemplified in the fascinating downtown Allen County Courthouse, constructed in 1902.

Although Abraham Lincoln had no personal connection with Fort Wayne, the city boasts one of the nation's finest collections of Lincoln memorabilia. Besides displays on the president's life and achievements, the **Lincoln Museum** has over 300 documents, including the Emancipation Proclamation.

### Lincoln Museum

200 E Berry St. (260) 455-3864. 10am–5pm Tue–Sat, 1–5pm Sun. Mon, Jan 1, Easter, Thanksgiving, Dec 25.
www.thelincolnmuseum.org

A view of the Allen County Courthouse in Fort Wayne

**A view of the architecture of modern Indianapolis**

## Indianapolis ⓬

*860, 500. 201 S Capitol Ave, (800) 958-4639.* www.indy.org

KNOWN AS "The Crossroads of America," Indianapolis is much more than a transportation hub where multiple railroads and Interstate Highways intersect. The city's many parks and monuments, and vibrant in-town neighborhoods make it one of the region's most surprising and satisfying destinations.

Selected as the state capital in 1820, Indianapolis was laid out on the banks of the shallow White River, with a network of wide boulevards radiating outward from the central **Monument Circle**. Today, this is downtown's main gathering point, dominated by the towering 1901 Beaux Arts obelisk, the Soldiers' and Sailors' Monument.

The city's first-rate museums and lively arts and theater scenes are complemented by an active interest in sports. Every Memorial Day, the world's largest, single-day sporting event – the Indianapolis 500 auto race – fills the **Indianapolis Motor Speedway** with nearly 400,000 fans. Built in 1909 as a 2.5-mile (4-km) test track for the city's then-burgeoning automotive industry, the speedway played host to the first Indy 500 in 1911. The race was the brainchild of Indianapolis auto parts manufacturer Carl Fisher, who later gained fame as the tireless promoter of the Lincoln Hwy (now US 30), the nation's first transcontinental highway, from New York to San Francisco. The track's Hall of Fame displays more than 75 racing cars and other Indy 500 memorabilia, in addition to examples of the Stutz, Cole, Marmon, National, and Duesenberg automobiles built in the city before the industry centralized in Detroit. Visitors can also take a guided test drive around the famous track.

The five-story **Children's Museum of Indianapolis**, which opened in 1976, has been consistently rated as one of the country's best. The museum's 10 galleries and over 100,000 artifacts are displayed in a manner that encourages hands-on, interactive exploration of the sciences, history, world cultures, and the arts. Among the many highlights here are an authentic Indy 500 race car, a restored carousel, and a dinosaur discovery exhibit, where children work along side practicing paleontologists to excavate ancient fossils.

The **Indiana State Museum** relocated in early 2002 to a brand-new facility west of downtown in White River State Park, a 250-acre (101-ha) urban oasis. The spacious new building is constructed of locally sourced materials, including Indiana limestone, sandstone, brick, steel, extruded aluminum, and glass. Focusing on Indiana's natural and cultural history, the museum displays extensive exhibits on sports and the early days of radio in this predominantly rural state.

**Display in the Indianapolis Motor Speedway Hall of Fame**

**Lockerbie Square District**, northeast of downtown, is the city's oldest surviving 19th-century immigrant neighborhood. Immortalized in the poetry of resident James Whitcomb Riley (1849–1916), the square has attracted recent attention for the dogged efforts to preserve its modest workers' cottages and restore its cobblestone streets and period street lights. Riley's 1872 brick Italianate home is now a museum, displaying many of the writer's books, furniture, and personal items.

Situated on the grounds of the Oldfields estate of local pharmaceutical pioneer, J.K. Lilly Jr, 5 miles (8 km) north of downtown, the **Indianapolis Museum of Art** houses a wide-ranging collection of American, European, Asian, and African art. Among the museum's more acclaimed holdings are Winslow Homer's *The Boat Builders*, Edward Hopper's *Hotel Lobby*, Georgia O'Keeffe's *Jimson Weed*, and many of Paul Gauguin's works from his 1886 visit to the French artists' colony of Pont-Aven.

The restored Oldfields-Lilly house and superb gardens, designed by Percival Gallagher of the famed Olmsted Brothers landscape architecture firm, have been carefully restored to their original 1920s grandeur. The house and gardens are open for tours.

The **Eiteljorg Museum of American Indians and Western Art**, west of downtown, has one of the most impressive collections of Native American and Western American art in the US.

:orge Carlson's *The Greeting* 989) outside Eiteljorg Museum

:tablished in 1989 by Harri- ›n Eiteljorg, a successful dianapolis businessman and t collector, the museum is ›used in a Southwest- spired adobe building, in :ference to Eiteljorg's large ›llection of works from the ırly 20th-century Taos Soci- y of Artists *(see p544)*, who corporated Native American, 'estern American, and His- ınic themes into their work. On view are paintings by ıch celebrated artists as eorgia O'Keeffe, Frederic :mington, and Charles M. ıssell, whose *Indians rossing the Plains* is a mous depiction of vanishing ative American culture on e late 19th-century Great ains. Many Native American tifacts are also displayed.

**Indianapolis Motor peedway**
ıll of Fame, 4790 W 16th St. *(317) 492-6784.* *9am–5pm ily.* *Dec 25.*
www.brickyard.com

**Indianapolis Museum f Art**
›00 Michigan Rd. *(317) 923-1331.* *10am–5pm Tue–Sat (until 8:30pm u), noon–5pm Sun.* *Jan 1, anksgiving, Dec 25.* *(Lilly House free Thu).* www.ima-art.org

**Eiteljorg Museum of merican Indians & 'estern Art**
›0 W Washington St. *(317) 636-9378.* *Sep–Jun: )am–5pm Tue–Sat, noon–5pm Sun; emorial Day–Labor Day: 10am–5pm on–Sat, noon–5pm Sun.* *Jan 1, anksgiving, Dec 24, 25.*
www.eiteljorg.org

## Columbus ⓭

*39,000.* *506 5th St, (800) 468-6564.* www.columbus.in.us

ONE OF THE world's most concentrated collections of modern architecture can be found in this small southern Indiana city. From 1942 on, after the completion of architect Eliel Saarinen's **First Christian Church**, Columbus garnered international attention for the more than 60 churches, schools, banks, and commercial and public buildings constructed here. Today, the city's commitment to high-quality design has resulted in Columbus being ranked sixth on the American Institute of Architects list of cities marked by innovation in architecture and design.

A philanthropic foundation endowed by the city's largest employer, Cummins Engine, attracted some of the world's most distinguished architects. Among those who left their stamp on the city environment are Robert Trent Jones, Richard Meier, Robert Venturi, Alexander Girard, and I.M. Pei, whose 1969 Cleo Rodgers Memorial Library is at 536 5th Street. The **Columbus Architecture Tours** allow visitors to view catch a glimpse of these architectural delights.

**Columbus Architecture Tours**
506 5th St. *(800) 468-6564.* *Mar–Nov 30: daily.* *Dec–Feb.* *call for tour times.*

## Ohio River Valley ⓮

*601 W First St, (800) 559-2956.* www.visitmadison.org

FROM INDIANA'S eastern border with Ohio, Routes 56 and 156 follow the serpentine Ohio River for nearly 80 miles (129 km) as it winds lazily through the river towns of Rising Sun, Patriot, Florence, and Vevey. These highways are the best way to explore both the river valley and the southern hill country.

The antebellum river port of **Madison**, 90 miles (145 km) southeast of Indianapolis, is one of the best-preserved towns on the river. Many of its residential and commercial buildings have benefited from a generous grant from the National Trust for Historic Preservation. The town's architectural charms include the Greek Revival **Lanier Mansion**, built in 1844 for railroad magnate James Lanier, and the Shrewsbury-Windle House, an 1849 riverboat entrepreneur's home featuring an elegant, free-standing circular staircase. Downtown is the restored 19th-century office of progressive frontier physician Dr. William D. Hutchings.

**Lanier Mansion State Historic Site**
511 W 1st St Madison. *(812) 265-3526.* *Apr–Dec: 9am–5pm Tue–Sat, 1–5pm Sun; Jan–Mar: group tours by appointment only.* *public hols, except Memorial Day, Jul 4, Labor Day.*

**Exterior of Eliel Saarinen's First Christian Church (1942), Columbus**

# Ohio

OHIO IS A STUDY IN CONTRASTS. As one of the nation's largest agricultural producers, the state is dotted with picturesque farmland, small towns steeped in history, and more recently settled Amish areas where horse-drawn buggies and barns are a thing of the present. Ohio also contains several of the country's most urbanized industrial centers along the Ohio River – the state's southern and eastern border – and in port cities that lie along the shores of Lake Erie.

**Art Deco façade of the Union Terminal, Cincinnati**

## Cincinnati ⓯

*331, 285. 511 Walnut St, (800) 246-2987.*
www.cincyusa.com

BUILT ON A series of steep hills overlooking the Ohio River, Cincinnati was once called "Porkopolis" for its rank slaughterhouses and belching factories. Later, its winding side streets and stunning views from the hilltop Mount Adams neighborhood inspired British prime minister Winston Churchill to call it "the most beautiful of America's inland cities." The city is today a vibrant corporate center with a revitalized riverfront entertainment and parks district.

Cincinnati's location at the intersection of the Erie Canal and the Miami and Ohio Rivers, and its strategic perch on the border of the slave-holding South and the industrializing North made it a heterogeneous cultural and commercial crossroads. Many prominent locals, including writer Harriet Beecher Stowe, whose home is now a state historic site, strongly supported the anti-slavery movement. The recently opened (summer 2004) **National Underground Railroad Freedom Center**, focuses on the city's one-time heroic past.

Cincinnati's most celebrated landmark is the 1867 stone and steel suspension bridge, built by Brooklyn Bridge engineer John A. Roebling to link this city with Covington, Kentucky, across the Ohio River. Another landmark is the vaulting 1933 Art Deco **Union Terminal**, west of downtown. The refurbished terminal now houses a complex of superb museums such as the Cincinnati History Museum and its re-creation of the 1850s waterfront, which is complete with a paddlewheeler.

On the eastern part of town, the **Cincinnati Art Museum** overlooks Eden Park. The museum's extensive collections include Roman, Greek, Egyptian, Asian, and African artifacts. Among its exhibits of contemporary art is a specially commissioned portrait by Andy Warhol of the controversial Cincinnati Reds baseball great, Pete Rose.

**The Cincinnati Art Museum**
953 Eden Park Dr. *(513) 721-5204.* *11am–5pm Tue–Sat, 5–9pm Wed, 11am–5pm Sun.* *Thanksgiving, Dec 25.*
www.cincinnatiartmuseum.org

## Dayton ⓰

*201,134. 1 Chamber Plaza, Suite A, (800) 221-8235.*
www.daytoncvb.com

THIS PLEASANT city on the Great Miami River is known as the "Birthplace of Aviation." It was here that aviation pioneers, Wilbur an Orville Wright *(see p250)*, carried out much of their research and experimentatio which led to their successful flight in 1903 in Kitty Hawk, North Carolina. Five miles northeast lies the new Dayto Aviation Heritage Center at the spot where the brothers tested their second and third aircraft in 1904 and 1905. Th **Carillon Historical Park** contains the Wright *Flyer III* aircraft – the first capable of executing a turn. Over 300 aircraft and missiles from the post-Wright aviation era are also displayed at the **United States Air Force Museum** that lies nearby.

Overlooking the Great Miami River, the Italian Renaissance-style **Dayton Ar Institute** features a large collection of European and American paintings, such as Claude Monet's *Waterlilies* an Edward Hopper's *High Noon*.

**Carillon Historical Park**
1000 Carillon Blvd. *(937) 293-2841.* *Apr–Oct: 9:30am–5pm Tue–Sat, noon–5pm Sun & public ho*
www.carillonpark.org

**Dayton Art Institute**
456 Belmonte Park N. *(800) 296-4426.* *10am–4pm daily, 10am–8 pm Thu.*
www.daytonartinstitute.org

**Italian Renaissance-style Dayton Art Institute, Dayton**

ıe 1,348-ft (411-m) Serpent Mound

## erpent Mound 17

350 Rte 73, Peebles. (800) 752-757. **Museum** *Apr–May: 10am–m Sat–Sun; May–Labor Day: 10am–m Wed–Sun.* **Grounds** *year und.* *Jan 1, Thnksg., Dec 25.*

THE LARGEST serpent-shaped effigy mound in the US, e 1,348-ft (411-m) long erpent Mound overlooks rush Creek in the Ohio River alley. Although its exact age unknown, research suggests at the mound was con-ructed between 800 BC and D 400 by the ancient Adena eople, Ohio's earliest farming ative American community.

The 5-ft (1.5-m) high, 20-ft -m) wide mound appears represent an uncoiling erpent, with a tightly coiled il at one end and a mouth-ke opening, swallowing an val-shaped egg, at the other. n on-site museum describes e mound's history and s protection under an 388 law, the first in the S to safeguard important cheological sites.

## lopewell Culture lational Historic 'ark 18

5062 Rte 104, Chillocothe. (740) 74-1125. *8:30am–5pm daily.* *Jan 1, Thanksgiving, Dec 25.* www.nps.gov/hocu

OCATED IN THE Scioto River Valley, this 120-acre (48-ha) ark preserves 23 Native merican burial mounds built y the Hopewell people who ved here from 200 BC to AD 00. The Hopewell culture, hich emerged from the dena culture, covers a broad network of beliefs and practices among different Native groups spread over eastern US. As characteristic of the culture, the mounds are arranged in geometric shapes, ringed by an earthen wall.

A visitor center provides an in-depth look at the social and economic life of the long-vanished Hopewell peoples, based on the archeological work conducted here.

## Columbus 19

*632,900.* *90 N High St, (614) 221-6623, (800) 354-2657.* www.experiencecolumbus.org

OHIO'S CAPITAL since 1816, Columbus has grown from a sleepy, swampy lowland site on the east bank of the Scioto River to become a bustling cultural, political, and economic center. Today, the city supports a thriving arts scene, with a superb symphony and ballet, in addition to revitalized historic neighborhoods and entertainment districts. Downtown's central feature is the Greek-Revival style **Ohio Statehouse**. Built between 1839 and 1861, the structure is surmounted by a unique drum-shaped cupola marked by a 29-ft (9-m) wide skylight.

The **Ohio Historical Center** is the best place to begin the exploration of Columbus. Its interactive displays trace Ohio's evolution from an 18th century frontier outpost to its current urban and industrial status. Permanent exhibits detail the origin of the city's fine public architecture and parklands, dating from its 1890s fascination with the City Beautiful Movement.

The **Franklin Park Conservatory and Botanical Garden**, built in 1895, has a bonsai and sculpture garden. It also has indoor simulations of exotic climates, and a Pacific Island water garden.

Sculpture in Franklin Park Conservatory and Botanical Garden

**Ohio Historical Center**
1982 Velma Ave. *(614) 297-2300.* *9am–5pm Tue–Sat, noon–5pm Sun; call for special Dec hours.* *Jan 1, Thanksgiving, Dec 25.*

**Franklin Park Conservatory & Botanical Garden**
1777 E Broad St. *(614) 645-8733.* *10am–5pm Tue–Sun (until 8pm Wed).* *Jan 1, Thanksgiving, Dec 25.*

## Berlin 20

*3,100.* *35 N Monroe St, Millersburg, (330) 674-3975.*

MUCH OF Ohio's large Amish population is concentrated in Holmes County in the north-central part of the state, about 90 miles (145 km) northeast of Columbus. Lying just outside Berlin village, **Schrock's Amish Farm** provides a good overview of the reclusive Amish, who have maintained their simplified 19th-century way of life. The farm has a multimedia visitor center and offers a tour of a working farm, complete with freshly baked goods and buggy rides.

Amish quilt patterns on display

Visitors are requested to drive carefully along the rural backroads and busier thoroughfares, out of respect for the dark-attired Amish farmers and their slow-moving, horse-drawn carriages.

**Schrock's Amish Farm**
4363 SR 39. *(330) 893-2951.* *Apr–Oct: 10am–5pm Mon–Fri, 10am–6pm Sat.*

View of the Cleveland skyline from The Flats, the city's nightlife zone

## Cleveland ㉑

505,600.
Terminal Tower, Suite 3100, 50 Public Square, (800) 321-1001.
www.travelcleveland.com

HARD-WORKING Cleveland has re-invented itself and is now a role model for other Great Lakes cities seeking to revitalize their urban cores while celebrating their industrial pasts. Founded in 1796 by speculator Moses Cleaveland, the city evolved from a frontier town into a bustling commercial port in 1832, when the Ohio and Erie Canal linked Cleveland to the Ohio River.

Cleveland's steel industry was born after the Civil War, when railroads linked the city with Minnesota's Iron Range and the coalfields of western Pennsylvania. The industry thrived in the early 1900s, catering to the Detroit automobile industry's demand for easily transported steel. After World War II, however, the city's fortunes faded as industries moved away, leaving behind vast polluted landscapes and scores of unemployed workers.

Cleveland's "Rust Belt" image is today a thing of the past. The city now encompasses 19,000 acres (7,689 ha) of pristine parkland, while its downtown riverfront industrial zone is a bustling entertainment district, **The Flats**.

A signature feature since 1927, the 52-story Beaux Arts **Terminal Tower**, was designed as a "city within a city." It made maximum use of vertical space, squeezing an office building, railroad station, and hotel into its confines. The 42nd-floor observation deck offers grand views of the city and, on a clear day, one can see the Canadian shoreline.

The 1995 **Rock and Roll Hall of Fame and Museum** on the Lake Erie waterfront in downtown, put Cleveland at center stage of the nation's entertainment scene. The massive 150,000-sq-ft (13,935-sq-m) I.M. Pei-designed Hall traces the development of the musical genre, beginning with its roots in the Mississippi Delta blues *(see pp360–61)* and Appalachian string bands. On display are memorabilia ranging from Chuck Berry's Gibson electric guitar to a Cub Scout shirt worn by Jim Morrison. To its west, the **Great Lakes Science Center** uses interactive exhibits to stimulate public interest in the fragile ecosystem of the Great Lakes region.

Cleveland's principal cultural attractions lie about 4 miles (6 km) east of downtown, around University Circle. Surrounding this expanse of parkland near th Case Western Reserve University campus are a seri of early 20th-century buildings that now contain severa fine museums. Among them is the **Cleveland Museum o Art**, with its superb collectio of ancient Egyptian relics an pre-Columbian artifacts. Its European painting collection includes such masterpieces a Renoir's *Mother and Child* and Van Gogh's *Landscape with Wheelbarrow*. Facing th museum, the city's popular **Botanical Garden** features 4 acres (1.6 ha) of outdoor gardens, as well as a Japane garden and a peace garden.

**Rock and Roll Hall of Fame & Museum**
1 Key Plaza. *(216) 515-1945.*
*10am–5:30pm daily, 10am–9pm Wed; also 10am–9pm Sat (Memorial Day–Labor Day only).*
*Thanksgiving, Dec 25.*
www.rockhall.com

**Cleveland Museum of Art**
11150 East Blvd.
*(216) 421-7340.*
*10am–5pm Tue–Sun (until 9pm Wed & Fri).* *Mon, Jan 1, Jul 4, Thanksgiving, Dec 25.*
www.clevelandart.org

**ENVIRONS:** Located 25 miles (40 km) west of Cleveland, **Oberlin** is home to Oberlin College, one of the first to admit African-American and female students. The Allen Memorial Art Museum on campus displays American, Asian, and European art.

The steel manufacturing center **Canton** 60 miles (96 km) south of Cleveland, is famed for the Pro Football Hall of Fame.

The Rock and Roll Hall of Fame and Museum in downtown Cleveland

:rry's Victory Memorial at Put-in-
ıy, Lake Erie Islands

## ,ake Erie Islands 22

i 770 SE Catawba Rd, Port
inton, (800) 441-1271.
] www.lake-erie.com

OCATED JUST offshore from
the Marblehead Peninsula
:parating Sandusky Bay
om Lake Erie, the Lake Erie
lands are a prime summer
ourist destination. The
lands include the bucolic,
eaceful Kelleys Island and
e rowdier South Bass
land, with the village of
ut-in-Bay as its lively
ghtlife center.

Home of the Erie, Ottawa,
nd Huron Indian tribes until
e 19th century, the Lake
rie Islands rose to national
rominence during the War
f 1812. On September 10,
813, US Navy Commodore
)liver Hazard Perry defeated
ıe more heavily fortified
ritish fleet in the pivotal
attle of Lake Erie, fought
ff South Bass Island. A new
isitor center and a 352-ft
107-m) granite column at
ut-in-Bay, **Perry's Victory
nd International Peace
lemorial**, commemorates
is victory and his famous
ıessage to US General
Villiam Henry Harrison:
We have met the enemy
nd they are ours."

**Kelleys Island State Park**
as the fascinating Glacial
;rooves, a series of deep
mestone grooves caused by
ıe movement of a heavy
lacial wall. These grooves
ave been protected from
uarrying since 1923.

Short ferry rides from
earby Sandusky, Port
linton, and Marblehead are
vailable. The Marblehead
ighthouse, built in 1821, is a
opular regional icon.

**Perry's Victory & International Peace Memorial**
93 Delaware Ave, Put-in-Bay, S Bass Island.
*(419) 285-2184.*
*mid-Apr–Oct: 10am–5pm daily; by appointment rest of year.*
www.nps.gov/pevi

**Kelleys Island State Park**
Kelleys Island.
*(419) 797-4530.*
*Apr–Nov: sunrise–sunset.*
www.ohiostateparks.org

## Sandusky 23

*29,800. 4424 Milan Rd, Sandusky, (800) 255-3743.*
www.visitohio.com

SANDUSKY WAS once one of the Great Lakes' largest coal-shipping ports. Today, its ferry terminal provides easy access to many of the Lake Erie Islands. The city is, however, best known for the 364-acre (147-ha) **Cedar Point Amusement Park**, one of the busiest summer tourist spots in the Midwest. The park claims to have the world's largest collection of roller coasters, ranging from rickety old wooden ones to the high-speed Magnum, Millennium Force, and Top Thrill Dragster. Cedar Point also includes a water park, the children-centered Camp Snoopy, an ice show, and a sandy Lake Erie beach.

**Cedar Point Amusement Park**
One Cedar Point Dr. *(800) 237-8386.* *early May–Labor Day: 10am–sunset daily; Labor Day–end of Oct: 10am–sunset Sat–Sun.*
www.cedarpoint.com

## Toledo 24

*332,900. 401 Jefferson Ave, (800) 243-4667.*
www.toledoohionow.com

ONE OF THE world's leading glass manufacturing centers and the third busiest Great Lakes port, Toledo occupies a Maumee River site steeped in history. The 1794 Battle of Fallen Timbers that took place nearby opened northwestern Ohio and Indiana to white settlement. The area was also a strategic one during the War of 1812. The reconstructed Fort Meigs, about 10 miles (16 km) south of Toledo in Perrysburg, commemorates the stockade that withstood two British and Native American sieges in 1813.

Today, the city is famed for the **Toledo Museum of Art**, a Neo-Classical marble structure in the historic Old West End founded by local glass tycoon Edward Drummond Libbey. In addition to Egyptian, Greek, Roman, and medieval exhibits, the museum features one of the world's largest collections of ornamental glass. Some of the best pieces are an oversized punch bowl crafted by Libbey's firm, and *Vitrano*, a colorful 1969 glass sculpture by Dominick Labino. Adjoining the main gallery is a sand castle-like structure by architect Frank Gehry. The building is now used for fine art classes at the School of Art and Design.

**Toledo Museum of Art**
2445 Monroe St. *(419) 255-8000.*
*10am–4pm Tue–Sat, 10am–10pm Fri, 11am–5pm Sun.* *Mon, Jan 1, Jul 4, Thnksg., Dec 25.*
www.toledomuseum.org

A roller-coaster ride at Cedar Point Amusement Park, Sandusky

# Michigan

THIS INLAND STATE HAS A rich maritime history. Michigan's principal land mass, the so-called Lower Peninsula, is a mitten-shaped area surrounded by the four Great Lakes – Michigan, Superior, Huron, and Erie. This landmass contains the largest cities, including Detroit, and accounts for most of Michigan's industry and population. In the 19th century, the Lower Peninsula, with its wind-blown dunes and rolling cherry orchards, was a prime destination. The rugged Upper Peninsula to the northwest only became part of the state in 1834. More recently, the Upper Peninsula's fine scenic views have also made it a popular tourist getaway.

**Crowds enjoying the annual jazz festival in Detroit's Hart Plaza**

## Detroit ㉕

*951,270.*
*211 W Fort St, (800) 338-7648.*
www.visitdetroit.com

KNOWN TODAY AS the "Motor City," Detroit (meaning "the Strait" in French) was founded in 1701 by the French fur trader Antoine de la Mothe Cadillac. The city has since evolved from a shipbuilding center into a leading manufacturer of railroad equipment, cars, and bicycles. Its massive industrial growth, however, took place after Henry Ford began manufacturing automobiles in Detroit in 1896. By the 1920s, most American automobile manufacturers – Ford, General Motors, Pontiac, and Chrysler – had moved their headquarters and production facilities to the city.

The automobile industry still dominates Detroit. A confusing web of highways fan out from the city's revitalized downtown. The city's present focal point is the huge riverfront **Renaissance Center**, General Motors' current headquarters. Nearby, **Hart Plaza** hosts summer riverfront festivals, including the Ford Detroit International Jazz Festival. Directly across, the 25-ft (8-m) Big Fist outdoor sculpture on Woodward Avenue, is a tribute to the local African-American boxer Joe Louis, known as "The Brown Bomber." East of downtown is the lively Greek neighborhood and restaurant district centered on Monroe Avenue. Northwest of downtown is the former General Motors Building, designed by Albert Kahn in 1922.

### Charles H. Wright Museum of African American History

315 E Warren Ave. *(313) 494- 5800.* *9:30am–5pm Tue–Sat, 1–5pm Sun.* *Mon, public hols.*
www.maah–detroit.org

Built in 1997, this center commemorates the contributions made by Detroit's large African-American population to the city's commercial and cultural progress. It depicts the Middle Passage of enslaved Africans across the Atlantic, the Underground Railroad, the Civil Rights Movement, and other milestones in African-American history. There is an exciting program of changing exhibit as well as some that are long term. One of these, aimed at very young children, is called "A is for Africa" and has 26 interactive stations and a three-dimensional "dictionary

### The Detroit Institute of Arts

5200 Woodward Ave, Detroit Cultural Center. *(313) 833-7900* *10am–4pm Wed–Thu, 10am–9pm Fri, 10am–5pm Sat–Sun* *Mon, Tue, public hols.*
www.dia.org

The museum's centerpiece is a monumental 27-panel mur by Mexico City artist Diego Rivera. His controversial *Detroit Industry* depicts the automobile manufacturing process in a stark way, reflec ing the artist's Leftist views c the relationship between management and labor.

The museum's outstanding collections range from pre-Columbian, Native American and African art to 17th-century Dutch and Flemish paintings. It has a large selection of 19th-century American paintings.

### Detroit Historical Museum

**Detroit Historical Museums & Society** 5401 Woodward Ave. *(313) 833-1805.* *9:30am–5p Tue–Fri, 10am–5pm Sat, 11am–5pm Sun.* *public hols.*
www.detroithistorical.org

The recently renovated "Streets of Old Detroit" display as well as a permanent exhibit on Detroit's automotive heritage are the main features of this museun Located in the Detroit Cultural Corridor near

***Nymph and Eros*, The Detroit Institute of Ar**

ayne State University, this
ıseum is also the base of
e Detroit Historical Society,
ıich operates a series of
es across the city.
The society's **Historic Fort
ayne and Tuskegee
rmen Museum**, along the
etroit River on the city's
uthwest side, incorporates
any of the surviving build-
gs from Fort Wayne, the last
litary bastion to defend the
y. The society also operates
e **Dossin Great Lakes
useum** in Belle Isle Park in
e Detroit River. The focus
re is the maritime history
the Great Lakes.

**Motown Historical
useum**

48 W Grand Blvd. *(313) 875-
64.* *10am–6pm Tue–Sat.
Sun, Mon, public hols.*
www.motownmuseum.org

ıring the early 1960s, the
otown record label revolu-
nized American popular
usic with its trademark
Iotown Sound," which is a
elodic blend of pop, soul,
d rhythm and blues. The
eative genius of label
under Berry Gordy Jr. and
s stable of talented artists
ch as Marvin Gaye, Smokey Robinson, Stevie Wonder, the Temptations, and Diana Ross and the Supremes are honored in this museum, housed in the original brick building where hit records such as "Heard It Through the Grapevine" and "Baby Love" were produced. The renovated building, called Hitsville USA by Gordy, has a good display of a wide range of old photographs, instruments, and recording equipment, including the original "Studio A" where the classic sounds were first created. Displays narrate the story of Motown as the singlemost successful independent African-American-controlled record label in the history of the country. Today this label is owned by the PolyGram Corporation.

**Exterior of Henry Ford Museum in Dearborn, a suburb of Detroit**

**Environs:** The suburb of Dearborn, 8 miles (13 km) west of Detroit, is home to **The Henry Ford Museum and Greenfield Village**, one of the nation's most impressive collections of Americana. Within the complex is the Henry Ford Museum, which displays a range of vintage cars. The open-air Greenfield Village, on the other hand, exhibits Ford's eclectic collection of historical artifacts. These include diverse objects: a cot used by George Washington during the Revolutionary War; the chair in which Abraham Lincoln was shot; inventor Thomas Edison's laboratory; and the Dayton home and bicycle shop of aviation pioneers Orville and Wilbur Wright.

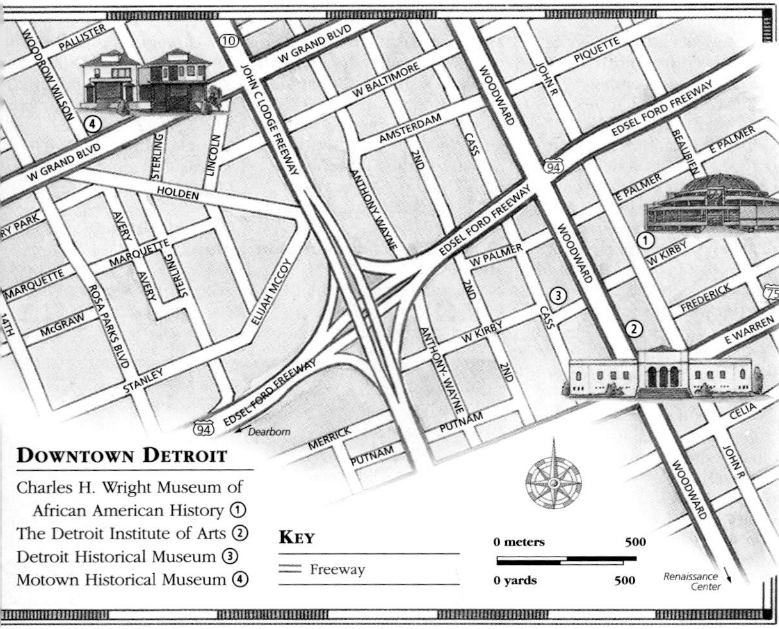

**Downtown Detroit**

Charles H. Wright Museum of African American History ①
The Detroit Institute of Arts ②
Detroit Historical Museum ③
Motown Historical Museum ④

**Key**

Freeway

0 meters 500
0 yards 500

University of Michigan campus, Ann Arbor

## Ann Arbor 26

114, 000.
120 W Huron St, (800) 888-9487.
www.annarbor.org

A PICTURESQUE, midsized city, with a vibrant pedestrian-friendly downtown, Ann Arbor is a bastion of laid-back liberalism and environmental activism on the western fringe of conservative Detroit. The city's independent streak springs from the professors and students affiliated with the **University of Michigan**, the city's largest employer.

Music, film, and art festivals are a year-round tradition. One of the nation's largest outdoor art fairs is held in the city. This annual July event attracts more than 1,000 artists and 500,000 art fans and dealers. Ann Arbor is also home to many new and used bookstores, including **Border's Books**, a global chain that began in 1973. Its downtown Liberty Street store is still the city's focal point.

The 2,800-acre (1,133-ha) Gothic central campus of the University of Michigan straddles Washtenaw Avenue, southeast of downtown. The **Kelsey Museum of Archaeology**, on the main campus, houses a variety of Greek, Roman, Egyptian, and Near Eastern artifacts from university-sponsored excavations over the past century.

## Lansing 27

119,128.
1223 Turner St, (888) 252-6746.
www.lansing.org

A GOVERNMENT and industrial center, this city benefits from its proximity to the Michigan State University in adjacent East Lansing. Selected as the state capital in 1847, the subsequent arrival of railroads in 1871 and the completion of the downtown statehouse in 1879 fueled the city's growth. The **Michigan Historical Museum** recounts the construction of the Second Renaissance Revival-style State Capitol and traces the state's history from the prehistoric era to the present through various interactive exhibits.

Exhibit from the Olds Museum

Lansing's status as a major automotive manufacturing center is linked to the business founded by Ransom E. Olds, who began building prototype vehicles here in 1885. He later produced the Curved Dash Olds, considered by many to have been the world's first mass-produced automobile. The **R.E. Olds Transportation Museum** has the distinction of showcasing an original 1901 Curved Dash Olds Runabout and a variety of classic Oldsmobiles from the 1930s and 1940s. General Motors now owns the Oldsmobile brand, and produces over 400,000 vehicles every year.

**R.E. Olds Transportation Museum**
240 Museum Dr. *(517) 372-0422.*
*10am–5pm Tue–Sat; Apr–Oct: daily. public hols.*

## Grand Rapids 28

*197,800.* *171 Monroe Ave, Suite 700, (877) 847-4847.* www.visitgrandrapids.or

GRAND RAPIDS owes its reputation as a major furniture manufacturing center to the Grand River th flows through the heart of tl city. The water-powered lumber mills that were set u along its banks in the 19th century formed the foundation for the growth of fine furniture makers such as Herman Miller and Steelcase

East of downtown is the fashionable **Heritage Hill Neighborhood**, where several of the city's industria moguls once lived. Now a historic district, this area has many Tudor, Victorian, Italianate, and Spanish-style mansions. The stately 1895 **Voigt House Victorian Museum**, with its grand period furnishings, is now a museum, and the 1909 **Meyer May House** is one of Frank Lloyd Wrigh last Prairie-style family home

Also in town is the **Gerald R. Ford Museum**. It traces the career of the 38th president, who grew up in Granc Rapids, where his father ran a paint and varnish compan The museum includes a hol graphic tour of the White House and a replica of the Oval Office.

**Voigt House Victorian Museum**
115 College Ave SE. *(616) 456-4600.* *11am–3pm Tue, 1–3pm 2nd & 4th Sun of month.*
www.grmuseum.org/voigt

Frank Lloyd Wright's 1909 Meyer May House in Grand Rapids

kers at Sleeping Bear Dunes
keshore, Lake Michigan Shore

## ake Michigan hore 29

950 28th St SE, Grand
pids, (800) 442-2084.
www.wmta.org

MAJOR tourist destination since wealthy Chicagoans st came here in the late 00s, Lake Michigan Shore is ed with sandy beaches, th-century resorts, working rts, and more than 25 enic lighthouses. The resort wn of South Haven makes ideal base to explore the ore. One of its many attrac-ns is the town's excellent **ichigan Maritime useum** narrates the history fishing, shipping, and ship-ilding on the Great Lakes.

Located 200 miles (322 km) the north on US 31, **Sleep-g Bear Dunes National keshore** incorporates any ecosystems and its gnature sand dunes, which wer some 460 ft (140 m) ove the lakefront beaches d an inland lake. The rk's ghost forest of sand-ried trees can be explored rough hiking trails or 7-mile (11-km) drive.

The busy resort of **Traverse ty**, 25 miles (40 km) north Sleeping Bear Dunes, is a nvenient base to visit the cturesque Old Mission ninsula. A short trip toward e north along Route 37 ovides beautiful views of een rolling hills, cherry chards, and the lake. At its stands the Old Mission int Lighthouse, built in 70. The white wooden structure sits exactly on the 45th parallel, which is halfway between the Equator and the North Pole.

**Sleeping Bear Dunes National Lakeshore**
9922 Front St, Empire. *(231) 326-5154.* *Park: year-round. Visitor Center: Jun–Sep: 9am–6pm daily; Oct–May: 9am–4pm daily.* *Jan 1, Thanksgiving, Dec 25.*
www.nps.gov/slbe

**Michigan Maritime Museum**
260 Dyckman Ave, South Haven.
*(800) 747-3810.* *Memorial Day–Labor Day:10am–5pm Mon–Sat, noon –5pm Sun.* *Tue, Sep–May.*

## Mackinac Island 30

*500.* *Main St, (800) 454 5227.*
www.mackinacisland.org

THE LIMESTONE OUTCROP of Mackinac Island, covering 6 sq miles (16 sq km), sits in the middle of the Straits of Mackinac, separating the Lower and Upper Peninsulas. Ferries that depart regularly from Mackinaw City and St. Ignace on the mainland are the only way to reach the island, where no cars are permitted. The principal landmark here is the 1887 **Grand Hotel** *(see p425)*, a classic Gilded Age summer resort that has the world's longest front porch at 660 ft (201 m). Fort Mackinac, over-looking the harbor, is in the **Mackinac Island State Park**. This restored fort commem-orates the island's 18th-century past as a French, British, and American military outpost through a variety of demonstrations as well as multimedia shows.

## Upper Peninsula 31

*Iron Mountain, (906) 774-5190.* www.uptravel.com
**Soo Locks Boat Tours** Dock #1, 1157 E Portage Ave, Sault Ste. Marie.
*(800) 432-6301.* *May 12–Oct 15; call for tour schedule.*
www.soolocks.com

THE SPARSELY populated wilderness of the 384-mile (618-km) wide Upper Peninsula is dotted with old lumber, mining, and fishing towns, and some of Michigan's most striking natural attractions. Also called the "UP," this region was first explored by 17th-century French adventurers, one of whom, Etienne Brule, estab-lished Michigan's oldest community, **Sault Sainte Marie**, on its northeastern tip.

One of its most popular attractions, **Pictured Rocks National Lakeshore**, stretches along Lake Superior. Although accessible by car from Hwy 28, this 40-mile (64-km) stretch of beaches and bluffs can be viewed more dramatically on guided cruis-es, departing from Munising.

For more rugged scenery, head west to **Porcupine Mountains Wilderness State Park** along Lake Superior. It is known for its old-growth forests, lakes, rivers, and a 90-mile (145-km) network of hiking trails.

Canon at the British Landing, Mackinac Island State Park

# Wisconsin

MOST AMERICANS ASSOCIATE Wisconsin either with cheese – because of its advertised nickname of "America's Dairyland" – or with beer, from Milwaukee's many historic breweries. While both images are accurate, this predominantly agricultural state is also famed as the Midwest's premier vacation destination. Wisconsin's recreational jewels range from the gorgeous Apostle Islands on its northern Lake Superior coast to 85 carefully maintained state parks that allow hikers and bikers to explore glacial moraines, rugged lakeside cliffs, broad rivers, dense forests, and lush green valleys.

**Façade of the 1892 Pabst Mansion in Milwaukee**

## Milwaukee 32

*590,500.* *101 W Wisconsin Ave, (800) 554-1448.* *Summerfest.* W www.milwaukee.org

LIKE CHICAGO, its more famous neighbor 90 miles (145 km) to the south, this manufacturing and brewing center grew up on a swampy Lake Michigan marshland. Treaties signed with local Indian tribes opened the area to white settlement in the 1830s. The city's strong German ambience dates to the arrival of "Forty-Eighters," the revolutionaries who fled Germany after an aborted attempt to overthrow the monarchy in 1848. By the 1870s, Milwaukee had as many as six daily German-language newspapers.

Pabst, Blatz, Schlitz, and Miller were the beers that "made Milwaukee famous." This tradition took such strong root in the city that even the local baseball team came to be called the Brewers. Milwaukee's wealthy beer barons were active philanthropists, investing in the arts, architecture, and social causes. The city's spectacular Lake Michigan shoreline hosts a long schedule of festivals, the most popular being Summerfest, an 11-day culinary and musical extravaganza that takes place in late June and early July.

The **Milwaukee County Historical Society** is located in the heart of downtown. Housed in a stately Beaux Arts bank building, the institution provides an excellent introduction to the city's economic, political, and social history. Its permanent displays explore the impact of the German immigrants on Milwaukee's active socialist movement, while revolving exhibits take a look at the city's multicultural heritage.

To its southwest, the 150,000-square-ft (13,935-m) **Milwaukee Public Museum** is part science museum, part local and cultural history center. Its interactive, child-targeted science holdings include the world's largest dinosaur skull and a glass-enclosed tropical butterfly garden. Here, visitors can walk amid more than 300 free-flying moths and butterflies. The museum's pre-Columbian and Native American exhibits paint a vivid and honest portrait of the culture and fate of the continent's Native Americans while the "Streets of Old Milwaukee" provides a fascinating glimpse of this metropolitan melting pot.

Captain Frederick Pabst, a successful Milwaukee brewe amassed a fortune with his popular Pabst Blue Label be brand and real estate investments. The cornerstone of his empire, the 1892 Flemish Renaissance Revival-style **Pabst Mansion**, lies at the west end of the city's grand Wisconsin Avenue. At that time the 37-room palace was considered one of the world's most technologically sophisticated houses, as it was equipped with full electrical service, a heating system, and nine bathrooms Much of the original ornate woodwork, furniture, and artwork has been restored by a historical trust that purchased the home in 1978

Located in the city's Histor Third Ward warehouse district, south of downtown, th **William F. Eisner Museum of Advertising and Design** critically assesses the impact of advertising on culture and society. It is one of the few museums in the country dedicated to this subject. Revolving exhibits focus on

**Spectacular new entrance of the Milwaukee Art Museum**

pics as diverse as the arketing of US presidents, e use of sports heroes to arket beers, and the legndary Burma-Shave adversing campaigns. The preursor to billboards on merica's earliest highways, e signs for one of the orld's first brushless shaving eams were often humorous ngles placed at intervals ong the road. Each revealed ne line of a four-part rhyme, hile the fifth and final sign oncluded with the simple gline "Burma Shave."

Eastward, the lakefront **ilwaukee Art Museum** was stablished in 1888 and holds 20,000-piece collection, novated galleries, and assive new reception hall, esigned by Spanish architect antiago Calatrava. This pavilon has a grand, winglike inshade to complement the useum's windswept setting. s signature collections are s Frank Lloyd Wright decotive arts holdings and the odern and contemporary lleries, which include Mark othko's *Green, Red, Blue* nd Picasso's *The Cock of the beration*. The recently dded Asian and African art ugment the museum's ready existing collection f Haitian folk art.

The Miller Brewing Comany, the only major brewer ill in operation in the city, is the town's western edge. his firm, which produces the p-selling Miller beers, pened in 1855, hen immigrant rewer Frederick iller purchased e floundering ank Road Brewry. Today, it is e second-largest rewer in the US, ter the St. Louisased Anheuser-Busch *(see 455)*. The **Miller Brewing ompany Tour** takes visitors n a tour of its brewery and e nearby Caves Museum, here beer was naturally ooled deep inside Milwauee's bluffs. Complimentary iller beverages, including ater and sodas for children nder legal drinking age, are ffered at the end of the tour.

**Sign of the Miller Brewing Company**

Milwaukee's other major sight is the Annunciation Greek Orthodox Church, one of Frank Lloyd Wright's last commissions. Designed in 1956, it was opened in 1961, two years after Wright's death.

**William F. Eisner Museum of Advertising & Design**
208 N Water St. *(414) 847-3290.* *11am–5pm Wed–Fri, (until 8pm Thu), noon–5pm Sat, 1–5pm Sun.* www.eisnermuseum.org

**Milwaukee Art Museum**
700 N Art Museum Dr. *(414) 224-3200.* *10am–5pm daily, (until 8pm Thu).* www.mam.org

**Miller Brewing Company Tour**
4251 W State St. *(414) 224-3220.* *10am–5pm Mon–Sat; call (414) 931-2337 for free guided tours Mon–Sat.* *Sun, public hols.* www.millerbrewing.com

## Door County 33

*1015 Green Bay Rd, Sturgeon Bay, (920) 743-4456.* www.doorcounty.com

Stretching like the spout of a teapot, between Green Bay and Lake Michigan, the Door Peninsula is a rugged New England-like expanse of rolling hills, lakeside cliffs, and pretty port villages. The county comprises the northern two-thirds of the peninsula and derives its name from the French-Canadian voyageurs' sobriquet for the treacherous shipping channel off the peninsula's northern point – Porte des Morts, or "Death's Door." The area's fishing and shipping heritage is on display at the **Door County Maritime Museum**, in downtown Sturgeon Bay, the county's largest port and southernmost city. A few miles north is **The Farm**, a traditional Wisconsin dairy farm and petting zoo, replete with an array of animals – cows, goats, pigs, chickens, horses, and barn cats.

**A view of Eagle Bluff Lighthouse, Door County**

The peninsula's 250-mile (402-km) shoreline is lined with more than a dozen county parks and five magnificent state parks. The largest of these is the 3,776-acre (1,528-ha) **Peninsula State Park**, between the picturesque communities of Fish Creek and Ephraim on the northwestern coast. After traversing the park's miles of hiking and biking trails and visiting the restored Eagle Bluff Lighthouse, visitors can take in a performance by the Peninsula Players, the nation's oldest resident summer stock theater company.

**Washington Island**, 6 miles (10 km) across the Porte des Morts Straits to the northeast of Newport State Park, can be reached, year-round, via a short ferry ride. The island was home to the Potawatomi Indians until a hardy group of Icelandic immigrants arrived in the 19th century. The latter's descendants continue to farm the island's fertile soil and to welcome day-trippers who come in search of peace, quiet, and splendid lake views.

**Door County Maritime Museum**
120 N Madison Ave, Sturgeon Bay. *(920) 743-5958.* *Memorial Day–Labor Day: 9am–6pm daily; 10am–5pm daily other times of year.* *some public hols.* www.dcmm.org

**Peninsula State Park**
9462 Shore Rd, Fish Creek. *(920) 868-3258.* *6am–11pm daily.* www.dnr.state.wi.us

**Guided boat tour along the Wisconsin River**

## Wisconsin Dells 34

*4,000.* *701 Superior St, (800) 223-3557.* www.wisdells.com

WISCONSIN DELLS has one of the most spectacular locations along the Wisconsin River as it winds through an awe-inspiring, 15-mile (24-km) stretch of deep sandstone canyons. The area's natural beauty and a variety of attractions, such as miniature golf, and amusement and water parks, make it a prime summer vacation destination. Among the highlights are the guided **Dells Boat Tours**, which offer excursions past the storied cliffs through the Upper and Lower Dells.

The region owes much of its popularity to photographer H.H. Bennett, whose late-19th-century photographs of the Wisconsin River's rugged landscapes became famous throughout America. The Wisconsin Historical Society operates the **H.H. Bennett Studio and History Center**, displaying examples of Bennett's portrait and landscape photography.

**Dells Boat Tours**
Upper & Lower Dells Docks.
*(608) 254-8555.* *Apr–Oct: 9am–6pm daily.*
www.dellsboats.com

**H.H. Bennett Studio & History Center**
215 Broadway, Wisconsin Dells.
*(608) 253-3523.* *May–Sep: 10am–5pm daily; Sep 15–Oct 31: 10am–5pm Sat–Sun.*
www.wisconsinhistory.org/sites/bennett

## Baraboo 35

*9,200.* *600 W Chestnut St, (800) 227-2266.* www.baraboo.com

THIS TINY TOWN was the winter base of the Ringling Brothers Circus *(see p319)* from 1884 until 1918. Thereafter, the troupe merged with its popular rival Barnum and Bailey to create the Ringling Brothers, Barnum and Bailey Circus, the largest in the United States. The **Circus World Museum**, located on the original Ringling wintering grounds, celebrates the town's heritage with live performances, music, parades, calliope concerts, and demonstrations from the early 20th century heyday of the traveling circus. The museum also contains one of the world's largest collections of carved and painted circus wagons.

**Circus World Museum, Baraboo**

**Circus World Museum**
550 Water St. *(866) 693-1500.* *mid-May–Aug: 9am–6pm; Sep–mid-May: 10am–4pm.* *Jan 1, Easter, Thanksgiving, Dec 24–25, 31.*
www.circusworldmuseum.com

## Madison 36

*210,000.* *615 E Washington Ave, (800) 373-6376.*
www.visitmadison.com

NESTLED ON a narrow isthmus of land between Lake Mendota and Lake Monona, Madison is one of the country's most attractively situated capital cities. Established as the territorial capital in 1836, it became the state capital and home of the lakeside University of Wisconsin campus when Wisconsin achieved statehood, in 1848.

The majestic, 200-ft (60-m) dome of the **Wisconsin State Capitol** rises above the city's beautiful downtown. Among its key interior features are a rotunda encircled by marble Corinthian columns and an exquisite four-panel, glass mosaic symbolizing the themes of liberty and justice.

Madison is considered one of the nation's best places to live and work. The University of Wisconsin and the city's liberal political leanings have drawn scores of artists, environmentalists, and health food devotees to the area. As a result, downtown features a variety of bookshops, galleries, and restaurants that are vegetarian-friendly. A network of biking and walking trails provides access to the shimmering lakes around the city of Madison.

The **Monona Terrace Community and Convention Center**, completed in 1997 from plans proposed by Frank Lloyd Wright *(see p396)*, has a tranquil rooftop garden that provides great views of downtown and Lake Monona. It includes a memorial to soul singer Otis Redding, who died in a plane crash on the lake in 1967.

**Monona Terrace Community & Convention Center**
2 blocks E of Capitol Square.
*(608) 261-4000.* *8am–5pm daily.* *1 pm daily.*
www.mononaterrace.com

**Wisconsin State Capitol**
2 E Main St. *(608) 266-0382.* *8am–6pm Mon–Fri, 8am–4pm Sat–Sun.* *9am, 10am, 11am, 1pm, 2pm, 3pm Mon–Sat; 1pm, 2pm, 3pm Sun.*

**Majestic dome of the Wisconsin State Capitol, Madison**

liesin, architect Frank Lloyd Wright's sprawling estate in Spring Green

## pring Green 37

1,300. 150 E Jefferson St, )0) 588-2042.
] www.springgreen.com

HIS HANDSOME farming community lies just north the Wisconsin River, sur- unded by undulating hills. 1911, architect Frank Lloyd right, who spent his child- od in nearby Richland Cen- r, built **Taliesin** ("Shining ow" in Welsh) on a bluff erlooking the river. The )0-acre (240-ha) estate was right's home until his death 1959 and included a school here his disciples were structed in his Prairie-style esign philosophy. Today, the aliesin Fellowship runs the hool and an architectural m on the grounds. Guided urs lead visitors through right's eclectic home and ardens. About 9 miles (14 km) orth of Spring Green is the **ouse on the Rock**. This rawling resort complex has home built on top of a 60-ft 8-m) chimney rock. The ouse, built in the 1940s by ccentric architect Alex Jordan, the focal point for a rambling useum exhibiting Jordan's ast collection of Americana.

**Taliesin**
507 County Rd C, Spring Green.
(608) 588-7900. May–Oct: am–6pm daily.

**House on the Rock**
754 Hwy 23. (608) 935-3639.
mid-Mar–Memorial Day: 9am–4pm aily; Memorial Day–Labor Day: 9am– om daily; Labor Day–Oct: 9am–4pm aily; Nov–Dec: 9am–4pm Thu–Mon. Jan–mid-Mar, Thnksg., Dec 25.
www.houseontherock.com

## La Crosse 38

51,000. 410 Veterans Memorial Dr, (800) 658-9424. www.explorelacrosse.com

FOUNDED AS A trading post in 1842, La Crosse emerged as a key railroad junction after the Civil War. The city's well-preserved downtown district, and tree-lined neighborhoods around the University of Wisconsin-La Crosse campus, add to its charm. It also makes a fine base for exploring the Mississippi River towns along the Great River Road Scenic Byway *(see p41)* as it passes through the state.

East of downtown, **Grandad Bluff**, 600 ft (180 m) above the city, offers superb views of La Crosse and the Mississippi River Valley. Two restored paddlewheel steamboats offer great views of the river. A good alternative may be **Perrot State Park**, 30 miles (48 km) north of La Crosse. In Trempeleau, south of the park entrance, stands the Trempeleau Hotel *(see p427)*, the town's only building to have survived a fire that took place in 1888.

Grandad Bluff, an observation point east of downtown La Crosse

## Apostle Islands 39

*Ashland.* *Ashland County (800) 284-9484, Bayfield County (800) 472-6338.* www.travelbayfieldcounty.com; www.visitashland.com

OFF THE STATE'S northeastern Lake Superior coast lie a group of 22 islands, the remains of retreating glaciers from the last Ice Age. They were named the Apostle Islands by 17th-century French missionaries, who incorrectly assumed that the archipelago included only 12 islands. Today, 21 islands form part of the **Apostle Islands National Lakeshore**. The old-growth forests here provide the habitat for resident bald eagles and black bears, while vast stretches of sand beaches with sea caves, carved by the wind and lake into craggy, brownstone cliffs, make the Apostle Islands a popular destination for those interested in eco-tourism.

Sailor mannequins for sale at Bayfield

A local cruise service from **Bayfield**, on the mainland, ferries visitors to the islands, many of which hold historic lighthouses, such as the 1881 Sand Island Light Station, with its octagonal tower built from locally quarried sandstone. The 22-chain archipelago also offers the area's best sea kayaking. Various outfitters in Bayfield rent kayaks and provide guided charter tours.

**Apostle Islands National Lakeshore**
415 Washington Ave, Bayfield. (715) 779-3397. 8am–4:30pm Mon–Fri; summer: 8am–9:30pm daily.
www.nps.gov/apis

# Minnesota

MINNESOTA HAS BEEN seductively nicknamed "The Land of 10,000 Lakes." While beautiful lakes have added to the state's appeal as an affordable outdoors destination, it was the meandering rivers that actually shaped Minnesota's history as an important trading and agricultural hub. Many of these rivers, streams, and lakes have now been preserved and offer a rare solitude and natural splendor in vast stretches of its watery wilderness.

## Minneapolis & St. Paul 40

**Minneapolis** *368,400.* *215 Marquette Ave, (800) 445-7412.* www.minneapolis.org
**St. Paul** *287,150.* *175 W Kellogg Blvd, (800) 627-6101.* www.visitstpaul.com

THE TWIN CITIES, separated by the Mississippi, are a study in contrasts. Flamboyant Minneapolis, with its modern skyscrapers, is an urbane, commercial center where most of the state's corporate headquarters, museums, and high-end retail stores are located. St. Paul, the state capital, is more sedate, but has a colorful history, well-preserved downtown, and some architectural and cultural attractions.

**Exploring Minneapolis**
Downtown revolves around the pedestrian **Nicolett Mall**, which hosts various cultural events, including the Minnesota Orchestra's annual summer MusicFest. The **Uptown** neighborhood, on the southwest, revolves around the Chain of Lakes, with its network of biking and jogging trails. The country's largest enclosed shopping mall, the **Mall of America**, is in the southern suburb of Bloomington.

### Walker Art Center

1750 Hennepin Ave. *(612) 375-7622.* *11am–5pm Tue–Sun (until 9pm Thu & Fri).* *public hols.* www.walkerart.org
The performing, visual, and media arts are the focus of the exhibits at the Twin Cities' most complete contemporary art resource. Among the highlights of the Walker's permanent and revolving exhibits are the minimalist work of sculptor Donald Judd, including the restored 1971 *Untitled,* a group of six, large-scale aluminium cubes, and painter Edward Hopper's *Office at Night* (1940). The Center also presents dance, theatrical, performance art, and musical productions, and also conducts community outreach programs.

***Spoonbridge and Cherry*** **at the Walker Art Center**

### Minneapolis Institute of Arts

2400 3rd Ave S. *(612) 870-3131* *10am–5pm Tue–Sat (until 9pm Thu), 11am–5pm Sun.* *Jul 4, Thanksg., Dec 25.* www.artsmia.org
Established in 1915, this is one of the region's largest and most highly regarded museums. Its traditional collection includes a wide range of Greek and Roman statuary, Italian and Dutch Renaissance paintings, as well as American works by John Singleton Copley, Benjamin West, Georgia O'Keeffe, and regionalist Grant Wood.

The **Ulrich Architecture and Design Gallery** houses an astonishing collection of Prairie School furniture, architectural fragments, art-glass windows, and silver.

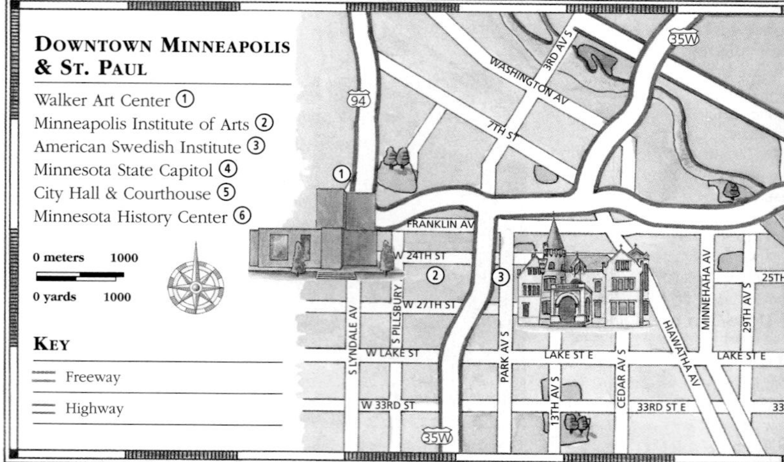

**American Swedish stitute**

)0 Park Ave. *(612) 871-4907.* *›n–4pm Tue–Sat (until 8pm Wed, 5pm Sun.* *public hols.*

www.americanswedishinst.org

›used in a grand 1907 ›manesque mansion, this stitute chronicles the ntributions of Swedish-nericans to the state's story and culture. Guided ırs of the house, built by vedish newspaper publisher van Turnblad, allow sitors to view his collection Swedish-American *kelugnar* (porcelain tile ›ves), woodcarvings, xtiles, and immigration ifacts. A revolving exhibit ces the journey of Swedes the Twin Cities and plores the popular culture early 20th-century Swedish-nerican districts.

**xploring St. Paul**

›unded in 1841 on the site Pig's Eye, the notorious ench-Canadian trading post, Paul flourished as the ısiest river port on the pper Mississippi. By the late th century, the new state pital had emerged as a rail-ad hub, powered by the ›mpletion of the railroad tween St. Paul and Seattle 1893. The stately Roman-que, Queen Anne, and cobean mansions along **ımmit Avenue** date from ›se prosperous days.

Downtown centers on the Art Deco City Hall and Courthouse on Kellogg Boulevard and St. Peter Street. The popular Minnesota Public Radio program, *A Prairie Home Companion*, is recorded live on many Saturday evenings at the **Fitzgerald Theater**, a beautifully restored 1910 vaudeville and movie palace at Exchange and Wabasha Streets. The city also hosts the Minnesota State Fair in late August and early September.

**Minnesota State Capitol**

75 Constitution Ave. *(651) 296-2881.* *9am–5pm Mon–Fri, 10am–4pm Sat, 1–4pm Sun.* *Jan 1, Mar 31, Nov 23, Dec 25.*

Designed by Cass Gilbert, architect of the US Supreme Court *(see p199)*, the Minnesota State Capitol is a monumental domed Beaux Arts structure. It features the sculpture, *Progress of the State*, a group of gold-leafed copper and steel statues in the front.

**The sculpture *Progress of the State*, Minnesota State Capitol**

**City Hall & Courthouse**

15 W Kellogg Blvd. *(651) 266-8500.* *8am–4:30pm Mon–Fri.*

This Art Deco masterpiece, painstakingly restored from 1990 to 1993, is built of Indiana limestone and black Wisconsin granite. Its three-story base steps back to the central tower, making the structure appear to soar above the surrounding downtown. No detail was spared in the building's construction, with every light fixture, elevator door, railing, mailbox, door handle, and lock specially crafted in the ornate style of Art Deco.

**Minnesota History Center**

345 W Kellogg Blvd. *(800) 657-3773.* *10am–8pm Tue, 10am–5pm Wed–Sat, noon–5pm Sun.* *public hols.*

A treasure trove of interactive exhibits that chronicles the state's 19th century history is housed in this granite and limestone building. Exhibits such as a huge boxcar, giant grain elevator, lifelike meat-packing plant, and a replica of a 1930s dairy farm – complete with two full-size model cows with milking instructions – help visitors relive history from the point of view of a farmer or factory worker. The center's pop culture highlight, **Sounds Good to Me: Music in Minnesota**, showcases the music that originated here.

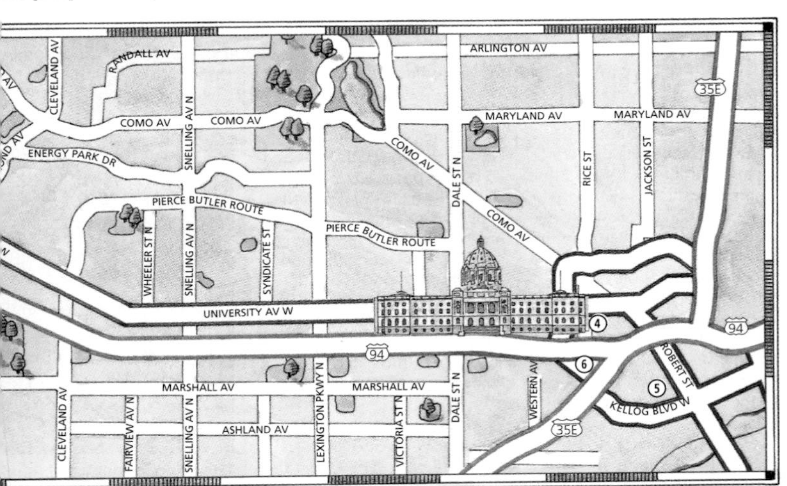

View of the Mississippi River from the Great River Bluffs State Park, southeast of the river town Winona

## Mississippi River Towns 41

(651) 385-5934.
www.redwing.org

THE MISSISSIPPI RIVER courses 572 miles (921 km) through Minnesota. It originates in the north-central part of the state and continues until its confluence with the St. Croix River near Hastings. South of the confluence, it widens and picks up speed, rushing through deep, fog-laden valleys along the Minnesota-Wisconsin border. The Great River Road Scenic Byway *(see p41)*, or US 61, hugs the river's west bank, revealing breathtaking views of attractive towns and parks.

The 19th-century town of **Red Wing** was built on the site of a Dakota Sioux farming village. Today, the town is known primarily as the headquarters of the Red Wing Shoe Company, the popular work boot manufacturer, established in 1905. A downtown museum showcases its manufacturing process. The restored 1904 Sheldon Theater presents a musical history of the city.

About 10 miles (16 km) southeast of Red Wing is **Frontenac State Park**, one of the premier bird-watching sites along the river, where over 260 species pause on their journeys north and south every year. Bald eagles and warblers flock to the diverse habitats of Lake Pepin, the widest stretch of the river.

Picturesque **Winona**, 65 miles (105 km) southeast of Red Wing, is located on an island in the river. It prospered in the 19th century as a steamboat refueling stop, mill town, and wheat-shipping depot.

The beautiful **Great River Bluffs State Park**, about 20 miles (32 km) southeast of Winona, occupies one of the river's most scenic stretches. The park features half-dome bluffs and sheer rock cliffs.

## Rochester 42

*90,000.*
*Centerpiece-Galleria 111 S Broadway St 301, (800) 634-8277.*
www.visitrochestermn.com

THE PRIMARY attraction in this southeastern Minnesota city is the **Mayo Clinic**, founded by the physician brothers Will and Charles Mayo in the early 1900s. They initiated the first collaborative medical practice, integrating the findings of a group of medical specialists to more effectively diagnose and treat serious illnesses. With an 18,000-strong staff, the clinic now treats over 240,000 patients.

**Mayo Clinic**

200 1st St SW. *(507) 284-2511.* *tours at 10am Mon & Fri, 1:30pm Tue & Thu.* www.mayoclinic.org

## Pipestone National Monument 43

*4,600.* *117 8th Ave SE, (507) 825-3316.*
www.nps.gov/pipe

PIPESTONE SITS in the state's southwestern corner. The name derives from Dakota Sioux Indians who lived here for generations, quarrying the region's soft red quartzite to craft elegant ceremonial pipes. The stone catlinite has been named in honor of artist George Catlin, who depicted this place in his 1838 masterpiece, *Pipestone Quarry*.

Indian craftsmen continue the tradition in the remains of the quarries. The pipes are then sold at the adjoining Upper Midwest Indian Cultural Center.

Visitors negotiating a trail through Pipestone's quarries

## rainerd Lakes rea 44

65,000. 124 N 6th St, ainerd, (800) 450-2838.
www.explorebrainerdlakes.com

OUNDED BY the Northern Pacific Railroad in 1871, the oper Mississippi River city of ainerd was carved out of a nse forest, felled to meet the mands of the state's lumber om. The area's heritage as hard-working railroad and mber town is personified in e flannel-shirted, bearded aracter of Paul Bunyan, the ythical Herculean Minnesota oodsman, and his massive t, Babe, the Blue Ox. His me seems to appear at ery turn; the Paul Bunyan ail bike route, and Paul inyan Scenic Byway back-ads auto tour are the more steful examples.

**Crow Wing State Park**, cated 9 miles (14 km) south Brainerd, offers canoe urs of the placid Crow ing and Mississippi ver waters.

Brainerd is also e gateway to orth-central innesota's lake gion, where the ate's trademark dge-resorts ere first developed on the ores of more than 500 fresh-ater lakes. **Mille Lacs Lake**, ) miles (64 km) southeast Brainerd, is bordered by eautiful state parks and the ille Lacs Band of Ojibwe bal reservation. The Min-esota Historical Society ollaborated with the tribe develop the Mille Lacs dian Museum, on the lake's uthwest shore.

Babe, the Blue Ox

ille Lacs Lake, Minnesota's second largest lake, southeast of Brainerd

The restored railroad Depot, the centerpiece of downtown Duluth

## Duluth 45

87,000. 100 Lake Place Dr, (800) 438-5884.

MINNESOTA'S THIRD largest city, Duluth is one of the Midwest's most enjoyable destinations. Clinging to the sides of the 800-ft (240-m) high granite slopes that ring its lively downtown, this city successfully juxtaposes numerous nature preserves with operating industries, which fuel its bustling port. Its most striking feature is the **Aerial Lift Bridge**, a huge steel structure linking the mainland to the mouth of the Duluth harbor with a 385-ft (115-m) span. The bridge can raise at the rate of 138 ft (41 m) a minute to allow hulking freighters to pass into the harbor. One of these massive ships, the docked 610-ft (186-m) SS *William A. Irwin*, is now a museum.

The **Great Lakes Aquarium and Freshwater Discovery Center**, the country's only "all-freshwater" aquarium, provides a close-up view of the bridge in action. In Canal Park, next to the bridge, the **Lake Superior Maritime Visitor Center** details the shipping history of the Upper Great Lakes. It also relates the US Army Corps of Engineers' feat of constructing the Aerial Lift Bridge in 1930.

The centerpiece of the redbrick-paved streets of Duluth's attractive downtown is the 1892 **Depot**, or **St. Louis County Heritage and Arts Center**. The restored brownstone railroad depot houses four superb museums, including the Duluth Art Institute, Duluth Children's Museum, and Lake Superior Railroad Museum. Depot Square, a re-creation of early 20th-century Duluth, features the waiting room where US immigration officials processed many of the state's Scandinavian and German immigrants.

The **North Shore Scenic Railroad** offers sightseeing trips from the depot in period trains. The excursions head north along the shore of Lake Superior, yielding spectacular views of waterfalls and cliffs plunging down to the shoreline. Motorists can also experience this magical trip on the North Shore Scenic Drive, a section of old Hwy 61 that runs along the lakeshore from Duluth all the way to the Canadian border.

### The Depot/St. Louis County Heritage & Arts Center

506 W Michigan St. *(888) 733-5833.* *Jun–Sep: 9:30am–6pm daily; Oct–May: 10am–5pm Mon–Sat, 1–5pm Sun.*
www.duluthdepot.org

A view of Mesabi, one of the three ranges that comprise the Iron Range

## Iron Range 46

*10–2nd Ave W, Chisholm, (800) 422-0806.*

When iron ore was discovered in northeastern Minnesota in the 1880s, waves of immigrant workers came to boomtowns that grew up along three ranges – the Vermilion, Mesabi, and Cuyana. These ranges collectively came to be known as the Iron Range district. By the 1960s, the mines' productivity diminished and many were shut down, decimating local communities and leaving behind empty mining pits. But in the past two decades, a growing tourist interest in the mining era has revitalized the Iron Range district.

About 225 miles (362 km) north of Minneapolis, the **Soudan Underground Mine** is Minnesota's oldest and deepest iron mine. It opened in 1884, closed in 1962, and is now part of a 1,300-acre (520-ha) state park. Visitors can go a half-mile (1 km) underground into the heart of the mine that also holds an operating atomic physics lab.

Statue outside Ironworld

The Iron Range city of Chisholm, 45 miles (72 km) southwest of Soudan, is home to the **Ironworld Discovery Center**. The center presents a glitzier, theme-park version of the Iron Range story with living history interpreters and trolley rides. Its highlight is the Minnesota CCC History Museum, commemorating the achievements of the state's Civilian Conservation Corps, a Depression-era program that put 84,000 young men to work on soil and forest conservation projects.

**Soudan Underground Mine**
1379 Stuntz Bay Rd, Soudan. *(218) 753-2245. Jun–Sep: 10am–4pm.*

**Ironworld Discovery Center**
Hwy 169 W, Chisholm. *(800) 372-6437. May–Sep: 9:30am–5pm.* www.ironworld.com

## Boundary Waters Canoe Area Wilderness 47

*1600 E Sheridan St, Ely, (800) 777-7281.* www.ely.org

The largest wilderness preserve east of the Rocky Mountains, the Boundary Waters Canoe Area Wilderness stretches for almost 200 miles (322 km) along the Canadian border in the state's northeastern corner. One of country's most unspoiled natural regions, this vast area attracts adventurers seeking an escape from civilization. The region is also one of the world's largest canoeing and fishing destinations, with more than 1,200 miles (1,932 km) of canoe routes which snake through 1,000 streams and lakes in the dense Superior National Forest.

To preserve the area's unique appeal, there is a limit on the number of campers as well as restrictions on the use of motorized watercraft. The area has no roads, and campers have to carry their equipment from lake to lake via portage methods perfected by the Ojibwe Indians. Still, visitors throng to the area either to canoe in water teeming with northern pike or to spot rare Canadian lynx or wolverine.

Most camping parties begin their exploration at Ely, 240 miles (386 km) north of Minneapolis. One of the park's far-western entry points, Ely has more canoe-trip outfitters per capita than any other town in the world. It also has the **Dorothy Molter Museum**, a memorial to the wilderness area's last human resident, who ran a resort here and died in 1986. The **International Wolf Center** in town promotes the survival of the region's once-threatened wolf population through interactive exhibits and close views of the resident gray and Arctic wolf.

Visitors can also take the 63-mile (101-km) Gunflint Trail, a scenic auto road into the northeastern corner of the Boundary Waters area. Motorists are encouraged to fill up the tank, pack food and water, and drive carefully to avoid moose.

**Dorothy Molter Museum**
2002 E Sheridan St. *(218) 365-4451. Memorial Day–Labor Day: 10am–5:30pm Mon–Sat, noon–5:30pm Sun; May: weekends.* www.rootbeerlady.com

**International Wolf Center**
1396 Hwy 169 Ely. *(218) 365-4695. May–Oct: 9am–5pm daily; Nov–May first week: 9am–5pm Sat & Sun.* www.wolf.org

Kayakers on Moose Lake, near Ely, Boundary Waters Wilderness

# 'oyageurs National 'ark 48

3131 Highway 53, International lls, (218) 283-9821.
www.nps.gov/voya

Pelicans on one of the numerous lakes of Voyageurs National Park

THE WATERY Rainy Lake borderlands west of ıperior National Forest ɔntain the old Voyageur ighway, an old network of kes, streams, and portage ɔutes used by Native mericans and French-anadian trappers to move ırs from the Minnesota and orthern Ontario forests cross the Great akes to Montreal. he route was taken ver by the British fter the French and ndian War, and xtended as far west s the Canadian rovince of Alberta. Today, 218,000 cres (87,200 ha) of ıis largely empty anadian Shield ilderness are preserved in ıe Voyageurs National Park, water-based park with 30 kes and countless bogs, wamps, beaver ponds, and lands – habitat of large packs f Eastern timber wolves. Rainy Lake, the finest fishing ıke in the park, abounds in alleye, pike, and bass. The ainy Lake Visitor Center, near nternational Falls, 295 miles (475 km) north of Minneapolis and 160 miles (258 km) west of Duluth, is one of three staffed access points to the park and the only one open year-round. The center features interactive exhibits concerning the fur trade and provides information about naturalist-guided tours. Although most vistors traverse the park's vast area using boat (motorized watercrafts are permitted here) and canoe, hikers can take advantage of a network of hiking trails, including a self-guided trek to Locater Lake and the Cruiser Lake Trail. This trail is the only means of exploring the roadless Kabetogama Peninsula. Shorter guided tours are available at the park visitor centers.

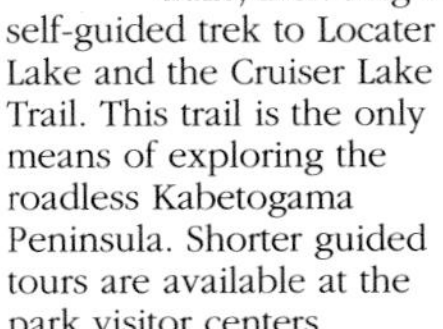
Lithograph of a fur trapper's cabin

For those people keen on boating, the border city of International Falls is the home base for stocking up on supplies or arranging a boat or canoe rental. The town's Boise Paper Solutions houses what the company claims to be the "largest, fastest paper machine in the world." In winter, the Voyageurs National Park offers opportunities for snowmobiling, ice fishing, and cross-country skiing.

### WOLVES

Voyageurs National Park is one of the largest wolf sanctuaries in the US. The animals that roam here are gray wolves, one of three species of wolves in the world. Wolves live in packs, dominated by two adult parents, their offspring of the past 2–3 years, and several unrelated members. Contrary to folklore, wolves tend to shy away from humans.

Gray Wolf

erial view of the many islets in wild, spectacular Voyageurs National Park

# Practical Information

TRAVELING AROUND THE GREAT LAKES states requires a lot of planning, since there is so much to see and do in such a wide area. From the towering skyscrapers of bustling big cities such as Chicago to the idyllic pastures of Wisconsin, the attractions here are as varied as the six states that form the Great Lakes region. With its rolling hills, endless farmlands, and sublime waterfront wilderness, America's heartland abounds in pristine wonders that offer a wide choice of outdoor pursuits.

## Tourist Information

EACH OF THE Great Lakes states houses a state Welcome Center that offers a full range of tourist information, as well as clean restrooms and free coffee. Most airports have information desks stocked with free brochures and maps. All the larger cities and many smaller towns have Convention & Visitors' Bureaus or Chambers of Commerce, with free directories of attractions, accommodations, and events.

## Natural Hazards

WINTERS IN the northern parts of Michigan, Minnesota, and Wisconsin can be very cold, with blizzards and snowstorms. Visitors should dress warmly and pack a small snow shovel, gloves, and a hat when traversing this region between November and April. Ice and snow can make driving extremely treacherous.

## Getting Around

MOST MAJOR CITIES in the region have public bus systems, which provide limited service around town for a reasonable fare. Light rail, subway, and commuter train services only run in Chicago and Cleveland. A new public rail transit system is under construction in the Twin Cities, serving Minneapolis, St. Paul, and the surrounding metro area. It should open in 2004.

However, driving is the best way to get around this region. Seat belts are a must for drivers, front seat passengers, and back seat passengers. Child seats are mandatory for occupants aged four and under. Helmets are compulsory for motorcyclists under the age of 18 in all of the Great Lakes states, except Illinois, which has no restrictions regarding helmet usage. Speed limits vary, but are usually 70–75 mph (113–121 km/hour) on Interstate Highways outside urban areas.

## The Climate of the Great Lakes

Weather in most of the Great Lakes states is fairly consistent. Temperatures tend to be cooler in the northern states of Michigan, Wisconsin, and Minnesota where cold, snowy winters lure residents to ski. The southern regions of Ohio, Indiana, and Illinois witness a more temperate climate. Summer months are ideal for touring the lakeside areas in Ohio, Wisconsin, Michigan, and Minnesota. Cooler temperatures and fall colors make Sep–Oct ideal for an extended trip to Chicago and scenic drives through the rugged forests of Michigan's Upper Peninsula.

**Chicago**

| °F/C | Apr | Jul | Oct | Jan |
|---|---|---|---|---|
| High | 59/15 | 86/30 | 65/18 | 33/1 |
| Low | 40/4 | 66/19 | 46/8 | 19/–7 |
| Sunshine | 15 days | 20 days | 17 days | 14 days |
| Rainfall | 3.6 in | 3.6 in | 2.6 in | 1.7 in |

32°F 0°C

## Etiquette

RESIDENTS OF the Great Lakes are friendly and polite – especially in Minnesota, where the phrase "you bet," epitomizes the helpful attitude of the state's hearty residents. Visitors to the Amish communities in Indiana and Ohio will be impressed by the shy, reserved manner of the traditional Amish inhabitants, whose simple, black outfits and horse-driven buggies are common sights on the roads.

## Festivals

THE GREAT LAKES states stage a diverse range of annual, community, regional, state, and cultural festivals. As an expression of Chicago's strong Irish heritage, the city actually dyes the Chicago River green as part of its boisterous **St. Patrick's Day Parade**. The Mexican-American population residing in the region celebrates **Cinco de Mayo** (early May) festivals in many of the Great Lakes cities; it is celebrated in a big way especially in Chicago. Summer brings a deluge of outdoor events, starting on Memorial Day weekend with the Indianapolis 500 auto race. Fireworks and street festivals are the norm for various county and state fairs that cro up in July and August. The Minnesota State Fair (August), held in St. Paul is one of the largest summer events, along with the immensely popular Milwaukee **Summerfest**.

## Sports

THE GREAT LAKES region harbors a wide array of professional and amateur sports teams, with major pro baseball, football, and basket ball franchises operating in nearly all of the major cities. The onset of spring signals the beginning of the baseball season, with fans flocking to historic **Wrigley Field**, home of the Chicago Cubs. Ohio boasts some of the region's best minor league parks in Toledo, Akron, and Dayton. This region also loves its ɔotball. The gregarious fans f the Chicago Bears and leveland Browns pro teams o head-to-head with the Visconsin "Cheeseheads," ho strip to the waist in the eezing cold to cheer on the reen Bay Packers. The egion's universities compete ı the **Big Ten** conference at draws over 100,000 fans. Winter brings basketball nd hockey to the frozen egion, with four NHL hockey ams, and many minor ague teams active in arenas cross the region.

## OUTDOOR ACTIVITIES

RELATIVELY SHORT summers and long winters do not eter Great Lakes residents om enjoying the outdoors. n the contrary, the region's imate seems to encourage a ore passionate pursuit of creational activities, with ountain biking and cycling nthusiasts thronging paths nd trails from April through arly November. Northern innesota and Wisconsin are vorite canoe and kayak estinations, while sail and otorboats are omnipresent n all of the Great Lakes roughout summer. Many shing enthusiasts look forard to ice fishing in winter. Skiing and snowmobiling are also extremely popular outdoor winter pursuits in the region.

Some of the region's best outdoors outfitters are located at Ely, entrance to the Boundary Waters Area Canoe Wilderness, and in Bayfield, gateway to the Apostle Islands National Lakeshore. For a list of outfitters in these locations, contact the **Ely Chamber of Commerce** or the **Bayfield Chamber**.

## ENTERTAINMENT

MOST OF THE region's most famous live music and theatrical venues are in Chicago. **Buddy Guy's Legends** and the **Kingston Mines** are the best places to hear authentic electric Chicago blues. The **House of Blues** hosts a wide range of blues and alternative rock acts. Comedy fans flock to Chicago's **Second City**, training ground for many *Saturday Night Live* cast members, and to St. Paul's **Fitzgerald Theater**, home base for Minnesota humorist Garrison Keillor's long-running *A Prairie Home Companion* comedy and radio program. The summertime **Big Top Chautauqua**, situated near the Apostle Islands, holds similar, old-time comic and musical shows. Visitors can also check out rides at the region's largest amusement parks: **Cedar Point** in Sandusky and **Paramount Kings Island** in Cincinnati.

## SHOPPING

THE REGION'S premier retail destination is Chicago's "Magnificent Mile." This dense stretch of Michigan Avenue north of the Chicago River holds some the nation's premier specialty shops, augmenting the classic **Marshall Field's** department store on State Street in the heart of the Loop. Another popular shopping destination is the pedestrian **Nicolett Mall** in Minneapolis. This pleasantly designed downtown district is far removed from the Twin Cities' busiest retail attraction, the 500-store **Mall of America**, the country's largest indoor shopping mall. Tourists can also travel to the Amish communities in northern Indiana. **Shipshewana** has a busy flea market, where quilts, rugs, and baked goods can be bought at fairly reasonable prices.

## DIRECTORY

### TOURIST OFFICES

**Illinois**
(800) 226-6632.
www.enjoyillinois.com

**Indiana**
(888) 365-6946.
www.enjoyindiana.com

**Michigan**
(888) 784-7328.
www.michigan.org

**Minnesota**
(800) 657-3700, 511.
www.exploreminnesota.com

**Ohio**
(800) 282-5393.
www.ohiotourism.com

**Wisconsin**
(800) 432-8747.
www.travelwisconsin.com

### SPORTS & OUTDOOR ACTIVITIES

**Bayfield Chamber of Commerce**
(800) 472-6338.

**Ely Chamber of Commerce**
(800) 777-7281.

**Wrigley Field**
(773) 404-2827.

### ENTERTAINMENT

**Big Top Chautauqua**
Ski Hill Rd.
(888) 244-8368.

**Buddy Guy's Legends**
754 S Wabash.
(312) 427-0333.

**Cedar Point**
1 Cedar Point Dr.
(419) 627-2350.

**House of Blues**
329 N Dearborn St.
(312) 923-2000.

**Kingston Mines**
2548 N Halsted St.
(773) 477-4646.

**Paramount Kings Island**
5688 Kings Island Dr.
(800) 288-0808.

**Second City**
1616 N Wells.
(877) 778-4707.

### SHOPPING

**Magnificent Mile**
(312) 642-3570.
www.themagnificentmile.com

**Mall of America**
(952) 883-8800.
www.mallofamerica.com

**Marshall Field's**
(312) 781-1000. www.marshallfields.com

**Nicolett Mall**
(800) 445-7412.
www.minneapolis.org

**Shipshewana Flea Market**
(260) 768-4129.
www.tradingplaceamerica.com

# Where to Stay

Most great lakes cities offer a range of chain hotels and motels to visitors. While larger centers such as Chicago, St. Paul, Cincinnati, and Indianapolis have historic boutique hotels and bed-and-breakfast inns, the remote northwoods areas of Minnesota, Wisconsin, and Michigan's Upper Peninsula harbor a choice of relaxing lakeside lodge and cabin resorts.

## Illinois

**Chicago:** *Days Inn Lincoln Park North* $$
644 W Diversey Pkwy, Lincoln Park. (773) 525-7010, (888) 576-3297. FAX (773) 525-6998.
W www.lpndaysinn.com
This winner of the Days Inn Chairman's Award for consistent quality has been recently remodeled.

**Chicago:** *Hotel Burnham* $$$
1 W Washington St. (312) 782-1111, (877) 294-9712. FAX (312) 782-0899.
W www.burnhamhotel.com
Originally designed by Daniel Burnham in 1895, the remodeled steel-and-glass Reliance Building is just minutes away from the theater district. This Kimpton hotel is pet-friendly.

**Chicago:** *House of Blues Hotel* $$$
333 N Dearborn St. (312) 245-0333, (877) 569-3742. FAX (312) 923-2444.
W www.loewshotels.com
The creatively furnished rooms of this musically themed, River North hotel, sport stereo systems and an in-room blues CD collection.

**Chicago:** *Renaissance Chicago Hotel* $$$
1 W Wacker Dr. (312) 372-7200, (800) 228-9290. FAX (312) 795-3474.
W www.renaissancehotels.com
Friendly service and richly appointed rooms overlooking the river. The fee for Club Level, which includes complimentary breakfast and evening hors d'oeuvres, is well worth the fare.

**Chicago:** *Tremont Hotel* $$$
100 E Chestnut St. (312) 751-1900, (800) 621-8133. FAX (312) 751-8691.
W www.tremontchicago.com Located just off Michigan Avenue, this European-style hotel offers cozy, comfortable lodgings. The lobby, with its carved-wood ceiling, has an English-country atmosphere.

**Chicago:** *Ritz-Carlton Chicago* $$$$
160 E Pearson St. (312) 266-1000, (800) 621-6906. FAX (312) 266-1194.
W www.fourseasons.com
Located above Water Tower Place, the Ritz-Carlton (owned by the Four Seasons chain) provides unparalleled service.

**Chicago:** *The Silversmith* $$$$
10 S Wabash Ave. (312) 372-7696, (800) 227-6963. FAX (312) 372-7320.
W www.crowneplaza.com/silversmith
This Arts-and-Crafts-style hotel, housed in a historic building, has pleasant rooms with high windows and ceilings.

**Chicago:** *The Drake* $$$$$
140 E Walton St. (312) 787-2200, (800) 553-7253. FAX (312) 787-2549.
W www.hilton.com
This ornate, 1920 Gold Coast classic offers great views of Lake Michigan and the intimate Coq d'Or piano bar.

**Galena:** *DeSoto House Hotel* $$$
230 S Main St. (815) 777-0090. FAX (815) 777-9529.
W www.desotohouse.com
Built in 1855, this smartly renovated period hotel provides easy access to the Galena Historic District's shops and restaurants.

**Oak Park:** *Carleton of Oak Park Hotel* $$
1110 Pleasant St, Oak Park. (708) 848-5000, (888) 227-5386. FAX (708) 848-0537.
W www.carletonhotel.com
The hotel offers pleasant accommodations just minutes away from specialty shops and boutiques.

| Hotel | Credit Cards | Number of Rooms | Recommended Restaurant | Children's Facilities | Garden or Terrace |
|---|---|---|---|---|---|
| Days Inn Lincoln Park North | ■ | 133 | | ● | |
| Hotel Burnham | ■ | 122 | ■ | ● | |
| House of Blues Hotel | ■ | 360 | ■ | ● | |
| Renaissance Chicago Hotel | ■ | 553 | ■ | ● | |
| Tremont Hotel | ■ | 130 | | ● | |
| Ritz-Carlton Chicago | ■ | 435 | ■ | ● | |
| The Silversmith | ■ | 143 | ■ | ● | |
| The Drake | ■ | 537 | ■ | ● | |
| DeSoto House Hotel | ■ | 55 | ■ | | |
| Carleton of Oak Park Hotel | ■ | 154 | ■ | ● | |

rice categories for a standard
ouble room per night, inclusive
f breakfast, service charges,
nd any additional taxes:

$ under $100
$$ $100–$150
$$$ $150–$200
$$$$ $200–$250
$$$$$ over $250

**CREDIT CARDS** Major credit cards accepted.
**NUMBER OF ROOMS** Number of rooms in the hotel.
**RECOMMENDED RESTAURANT** Good restaurant within the hotel.
**CHILDREN'S FACILITIES** Hotel has various facilities for young children.
**GARDEN OR TERRACE** Hotel has a garden, courtyard, or terrace.

| Hotel | Credit Cards | Number of Rooms | Recommended Restaurant | Children's Facilities | Garden or Terrace |
|---|---|---|---|---|---|
| **INDIANA** | | | | | |
| **OLUMBUS:** *The Columbus Inn Bed & Breakfast* $$$ <br> 5 5th St. ((812) 378-4289. FAX (812) 378-4289. <br> www.thecolumbusinn.com <br> is 1895 Romanesque-style inn was built as the Columbus City Hall. Its novated rooms and downtown location make it a favorite for tourists eking architecturally significant accommodations. | ■ | 34 | ■ | | |
| **DIANAPOLIS:** *The Canterbury Hotel* $$$$ <br> 3 S Illinois St. (317) 634-3000, (800) 538-8186. FAX (317) 685-2519. <br> www.canterburyhotel.com <br> is European-style boutique hotel offers fine service and plush quarters a beautifully restored downtown building. | ■ | 99 | ■ | | |
| **ADISON:** *Hillside Inn* $$ <br> 1 E Main St. (812) 265-3221. FAX (812) 265-2453. <br> www.hillsidemadison.com <br> fering panoramic views of the Ohio River and downtown historic strict, this newly renovated property was the site of the 1958 film *Some me Running*, starring Frank Sinatra, Dean Martin, and Shirley acLaine. | ■ | 30 | | | ■ |
| **EW HARMONY:** *The New Harmony Inn* $ <br> 4 North St. (812) 682-4491, (800) 782-8605. FAX (812) 682-3423. <br> www.newharmonyinn.com <br> ilt in the simple Harmonist style, The New Harmony Inn has a storative ambience, complete with an enclosed swimming pool. | ■ | 90 | ■ | | ■ |
| **MICHIGAN** | | | | | |
| **ETROIT:** *The Atheneum Suite Hotel* $$$$ <br> 00 Brush Ave. (313) 962-2323, (800) 772-2323. FAX (313) 962-2424. <br> www.atheneumsuites.com <br> owntown Detroit's only all-suite luxury hotel provides convenient cess to the Renaissance Center office complex. | ■ | 174 | ■ | | |
| **RAND RAPIDS:** *Amway Grand Plaza Hotel* $$$ <br> 7 Monroe Ave NW. (616) 774-2000, (800) 253-3590. FAX (616) 458-6641. <br> www.amwaygrand.com <br> signed in 1913 by the architects of New York's Grand Central Terminal, s hotel features a gold-leafed lobby ceiling. | ■ | 682 | ■ | | |
| **ACKINAC ISLAND:** *The Grand Hotel* $$$$$ <br> Grand Ave. (906) 847-3331, (800) 334-7263. FAX (906) 847-3259. <br> www.grandhotel.com <br> ine summer resort, this 1887 hotel provides picturesque lake views, d guest rooms filled with elegant antiques. | ■ | 381 | ■ | ● | ■ |
| **UTH HAVEN:** *Carriage House at the Harbor Bed & Breakfast* $$$ <br> 3 Woodman St. (269) 639-2161. FAX (269) 639-2308. <br> www.carriagehouseharbor.com <br> ll-appointed accommodations and scenic Lake Michigan views are the demark of this inn, housed in a Victorian mansion. | ■ | 11 | ■ | | ■ |
| **AVERSE CITY:** *Bayshore Resort* $ <br> 3 E Front St. (231) 935-4400, (800) 634-4401. FAX (231) 935-0262. <br> www.bayshore-resort.com <br> is smoke-free, Victorian-style beachside resort offers sweeping views West Grand Traverse Bay, as well as on-site sailboat, parasail, and jet-rentals. | ■ | 120 | | ● | ■ |

**Price categories** for a standard double room per night, inclusive of breakfast, service charges, and any additional taxes:

$ under $100
$$ $100–$150
$$$ $150–$200
$$$$ $200–$250
$$$$$ over $250

**CREDIT CARDS**
Major credit cards accepted.

**NUMBER OF ROOMS**
Number of rooms in the hotel.

**RECOMMENDED RESTAURANT**
Good restaurant within the hotel.

**CHILDREN'S FACILITIES**
Hotel has various facilities for young children.

**GARDEN OR TERRACE**
Hotel has a garden, courtyard, or terrace.

## MINNESOTA

| Hotel | Credit Cards | Number of Rooms | Recommended Restaurant | Children's Facilities | Garden or Terrace |
|---|---|---|---|---|---|
| **DULUTH:** *Fitger's Inn* $$$<br>600 E Superior St. *(218) 722-8826, (800) 726-2982.* FAX *(218) 722-8826.*<br>W www.fitgers.com<br>Breathtaking Lake Superior views and graciously appointed rooms are among the many charms of this downtown hotel, located in a restored 1880s brewery building. | ■ | 62 | ■ | | |
| **ELY:** *Grand Ely Lodge Resort and Conference Center* $$$<br>400 N Pioneer Rd. *(218) 365-6565.* FAX *(218) 365-2840.*<br>W www.grandelylodge.com<br>This commodious, northwoods lodge is perched on the shores of the secluded Shagawa Lake. Guests can explore the surrounding wilderness on foot, by bike, or by boat. | ■ | 61 | ■ | ● | ■ |
| **ELY:** *Burntside Lodge* $$$<br>2755 Burntside Lodge Rd. *(218) 365-3894.* FAX *(218) 365-3459.*<br>W www.burntside.com<br>This serene resort located at the water's edge on the spring-fed Burntside Lake, features sandy beaches, a Finnish sauna, and an excellent restaurant. | ■ | 21 | ■ | ● | ■ |
| **GRAND MARAIS:** *Gunflint Lodge* $$$$<br>143 S Gunflint Lake. *(218) 388-2294, (800) 328-3325.* FAX *(218) 388-9429.*<br>W www.gunflint.com<br>This Lake Superior lodge features lakeside cabins with fireplace, saunas and hot tubs, and provides guided fishing tours, nature hikes, and horseback rides through the Boundary Waters region. | ■ | 27 | ■ | ● | ■ |
| **LAKE KABETOGAMA (VOYAGEURS NATIONAL PARK):** *Kettle Falls Hotel* $<br>10502 Gamma Rd. *(218) 875-2070.*<br>W www.kettlefallshotel.com<br>Constructed by a timber baron in 1910, this remote lakeside inn can only be reached by boat or float plane, with free shuttle boats departing daily from nearby towns. | ■ | 12 | ■ | | ■ |
| **MINNEAPOLIS:** *Marquette Hotel* $$$<br>710 Marquette Ave. *(612) 333-4545, (800) 328-4782.* FAX *(612) 288-2188.*<br>W www.marquettehotel.com<br>This boutique-style, downtown hotel is conveniently located near Nicolett Mall's many shops and restaurants. | ■ | 281 | ■ | | ■ |
| **MINNEAPOLIS:** *Minneapolis Grand Hotel* $$$$$<br>615 2nd Ave S. *(612) 288-8888, (866) 843-4726.* FAX *(612) 373-0407.*<br>W www.grandhotelminneapolis.com<br>Every room is unique in this upscale, downtown hotel, which also features an exceptional two-story fitness center and spa. | ■ | 140 | ■ | | |
| **RED WING:** *St. James Hotel* $$$$<br>406 Main St. *(800) 252-1875.* FAX *(651) 388-5226.*<br>W www.st-james-hotel.com<br>Each guest room is named after a different Mississippi River steamboat in this elegant 1875 hotel, which offers spectacular Sunday-brunch river views from the top-floor Summit Room. | ■ | 61 | ■ | | ■ |
| **ST. PAUL:** *St. Paul Hotel* $$$$$<br>350 Market St. *(651) 292-9292.* FAX *(651) 228-9506.*<br>W www.stpaulhotel.com<br>From the lobby's Gustav Klimt paintings to the plushly furnished guest rooms, this stately 1910 Italian Renaissance hotel is a destination unto itself in downtown St. Paul. | ■ | 254 | ■ | | |

| | | | | | |
|---|---|---|---|---|---|
| **OHIO** | | | | | |
| **INCINNATI:** *The Cincinnatian Hotel* $$$$<br>)1 Vine St. (513) 381-3000, (800) 876-2100. FAX (513) 651-0256.<br>] www.cincinnatianhotel.com<br>rtfully renovated and attired, this hotel has been consistently ranked as<br>e city's premier luxury hotel. | ■ | 146 | ■ | | |
| **LEVELAND:** *Renaissance Cleveland Hotel* $$$<br>Public Sq. (216) 696-5600, (888) 236-2427. FAX (216) 696-0432.<br>] www.renaissancehotels.com<br>nis historic, upscale downtown hotel is connected via an indoor<br>alkway to The Avenue shops and Jacobs Field, home of the Cleveland<br>dians baseball team. | ■ | 441 | ■ | | ■ |
| **OLUMBUS:** *The Lofts Hotel* $$$$<br>E Nationwide Blvd. (614) 461-2663, (800) 735-6387. FAX (614) 461-2630.<br>] www.55lofts.com<br>nis 1882 commercial building, now offers loft-style guest rooms with<br>xurious beds and high-speed Internet access. | ■ | 44 | | | |
| **OLEDO:** *Mansion View Inn* $$<br>35 Collingwood Ave. (419) 244-5676. FAX (419) 244-9268.<br>] www.bbhost.com/mansionview<br>nis elegant, 11,000-sq-ft (1,022-sq-m) Victorian mansion offers cozy suites<br>ithin walking distance of the Toledo Museum of Art. | ■ | 4 | | | ■ |
| **WISCONSIN** | | | | | |
| **AYFIELD:** *Old Rittenhouse Inn* $$$<br>1 Rittenhouse Ave. (715) 779-5111, (800) 779 2129. FAX (715) 779-5887.<br>] www.rittenhouseinn.com<br>nis Lake Superior inn holds a superb restaurant and rooms with fireplaces<br>two Victorian-style homes and a guest cottage. | ■ | 23 | ■ | | ■ |
| **ADISON:** *Mansion Hill Inn* $$$<br>4 N Pinckney St. (608) 255-3999, (800) 798-9070. FAX (608) 255-2217.<br>] www.mansionhillinn.com<br>erched on a ridge along Lake Mendota, this elegant inn was built in<br>57 as a private residence. The lush grounds include a Victorian garden<br>ith a beautiful fountain. | ■ | 11 | ■ | | ■ |
| **ILWAUKEE:** *Hotel Metro* $$$$<br>1 E Mason St. (414) 272-1937, (877) 638-7620. FAX (414) 223-1158.<br>] www.hotelmetro.com<br>ilwaukee's only historic boutique hotel features enormous guest suites<br>d one of the city's liveliest lounges. | ■ | 64 | ■ | | |
| **ILWAUKEE:** *Pfister Hotel* $$$$$<br>4 E Wisconsin Ave. (414) 273-8222, (800) 558-8222. FAX (414) 273-5025.<br>www.pfister-hotel.com<br>is grand downtown hotel was built in 1893 by a successful Milwaukee<br>erchant. Renovated to its original opulence, the Pfister offers excellent<br>rvice and luxurious accomodations. | ■ | 307 | ■ | | |
| **STER BAY:** *Country House Resort* $$$<br>5 N Highland Rd. (920) 854-4551, (800) 424-0041. FAX (920) 854-9809.<br>www.country-house.com<br>nis cedar-framed, native stone 1907 building overlooks the Green Bay<br>oreline, just south of the peaceful village of Sister Bay. The plush<br>enthouse suite includes a fireplace and whirlpool. | ■ | 46 | | ● | ■ |
| **URGEON BAY:** *Glidden Lodge Beach Resort* $$$$<br>76 Glidden Dr. (920) 746-3900, (888) 281-1127. FAX (920) 746-3905.<br>www.gliddenlodge.com<br>ery condominium unit in this secluded, upscale, and trendsetting resort<br>s a well-appointed kitchen, private patio, and sweeping views of Lake<br>chigan. | ■ | 31 | ■ | | ■ |
| **REMPELEAU:** *Trempeleau Hotel* $<br>0 Main St. (608) 534-6898. FAX (608) 534-6054.<br>www.trempeleauhotel.com<br>is laid-back 1871 inn features a vegetarian-friendly restaurant and<br>mfortable rooms with views of the Mississippi River. | ■ | 11 | ■ | | ■ |

For key to symbols see back flap

# Where to Eat

Although family-style dining establishments are legion in all the Great Lakes states, nearly every sizable community contains a variety of fine-dining alternatives to the traditional meat-and-potatoes Midwestern fare. Very few Great Lakes restaurants require formal dining attire. Opening times are indicated by a "B" for breakfast, "L" for lunch, and "D" for dinner.

## Illinois

**Chicago:** *Ed Debevic's* $
640 N Wells St, Chicago. *(312) 664-1707.*
The menu, from meatloaf to milkshakes, is painted on the wall outside, Inside, a disc jockey spins 1950s tunes while costumed wait staff sing, dance, and dish out sassy attitude with the fries. *B Sat–Sun, L, D.*

**Chicago:** *Heaven on Seven* $
Garland Building, 111 N Wabash Ave (7th Fl). *(312) 263-6443.*
A spicy tingle in your mouth on your first bite is an indication that you're in for real Cajun cooking here. That, and the 1,165 bottles of hot sauces on the wall. The gumbo is truly heavenly. *B, L, D on 3rd Fri of the month. Sun.*

**Chicago:** *Star of Siam* $
11 E Illinois St. *(312) 670-0100.*
This sunny, open-concept River North Thai restaurant features spicy curries and Phad Thai – with many vegetarian options – in a contemporary, stylish setting. *L, D.*

**Chicago:** *Carson's "The Place for Ribs"* $$
612 N Wells St. *(312) 280-9200.*
Famous nationwide for its ribs, Carson's also offers outstanding Greek chicken, and pork chops. Seating is ample and comfortable, and the service excellent. *L, D.*

**Chicago:** *La Cantina Enoteca* $$
71 W Monroe St. *(312) 332-7005.*
This cozy spot is the first in a trilogy of Italian restaurants at this location known as Italian Village. The kitchen specializes in fresh seafood and hearty traditional Italian dishes. Not wheelchair accessible. *L, D. Sun, Mon D.*

**Chicago:** *The Berghoff* $$
17 W Adams St. *(312) 427-3170.* W www.berghoff.com
A Loop institution since 1898, this former corner saloon dishes out hearty portions of German favorites such as bratwurst, schnitzel, and sauerkraut, washed down with The Berghoff's house beer. *L, D. Sun.*

**Chicago:** *North Pond* $$$
2610 N Cannon Dr, Lincoln Park. *(773) 477-5845.*
Both the regional American cuisine inspired by local produce, and the decor, reflect the philosophy of the Arts and Crafts movement – simplicity and respect for quality craftsmanship. Excellent weekend brunch. *Mon.*

**Chicago:** *Topolobampo* $$$$
445 N Clark St. *(312) 661-1434.*
Some of the most innovative Mexican food is served at Topolobampo, one of the country's most highly ranked restaurants and its casual Frontera Grill sister restaurant. The restaurant offers various facilties for young children. *L, D. Sun, Mon; Sun–Wed in winter.*

**Galena:** *Perry Street Brasserie* $$$$
124 N Commerce St. *(815) 777-3773.*
Organically grown ingredients, international cuisine, and rich desserts are the hallmarks of this historic brasserie. The chocolate desserts are strongly recommended. *D. Sun, Mon.*

**Rockford:** *Paragon on State* $$$
205 W State St. *(815) 963-1660.*
A hip, sophisticated interior augments some of the state's finest gourmet cuisine, along with an impressive wine list in this bustling downtown establishment. *L Tue–Fri, D Tue–Sat. Sun, Mon.*

| Restaurant | Credit Cards | Outdoor Tables | Vegetarian | Good Wine List |
|---|---|---|---|---|
| Ed Debevic's | ■ | | ■ | |
| Heaven on Seven | | | ■ | |
| Star of Siam | ■ | | ■ | |
| Carson's "The Place for Ribs" | ■ | | | ● |
| La Cantina Enoteca | ■ | | ■ | ● |
| The Berghoff | ■ | | ■ | ● |
| North Pond | ■ | ● | | |
| Topolobampo | ■ | ● | ■ | ● |
| Perry Street Brasserie | ■ | | ■ | ● |
| Paragon on State | ■ | ● | ■ | ● |

rice categories include a
iree-course meal for one, a
lass of house wine, and all
navoidable extra charges such
s sales tax and service:
$) under $20
$$ $20–30
$$$ $30–45
$$$$ $45–60
$$$$$ over $60

**CREDIT CARDS**
Major credit cards accepted.

**OUTDOOR TABLES**
Garden, courtyard, or terrace with outside tables.

**VEGETARIAN**
A good selection of vegetarian dishes available.

**GOOD WINE LIST**
Extensive list of good wines, both domestic and imported.

**CHILDREN'S FACILITIES**
Various facilities for young children.

| | Price | Credit Cards | Outdoor Tables | Vegetarian | Good Wine List | Children's Facilities |
|---|---|---|---|---|---|---|
| **INDIANA** | | | | | | |
| **LOOMINGTON:** *Michael's Uptown Café*<br>2 E Kirkwood Ave. *(812) 339-0900.*<br>nis downtown bistro serves a dizzying array of Cuban, Creole, and ijun creations alongside adventurous continental fare. The persimmon idding is a house specialty. *B, L, D.* | $$ | ■ | ● | ■ | ● | ■ |
| **LOOMINGTON:** *Scholar's Inn Gourmet Café & Wine Bar*<br>7 N College Ave. *(812) 332-1892.*<br>19th-century brick mansion houses one of the state's top restaurants, fering award-winning steak, poultry, seafood, and vegetarian entrées. ie cuisine is immaculately matched by an excellent wine list. *L, D.*<br>*Mon.* | $$$ | ■ | ● | ■ | ● | ■ |
| **RT WAYNE:** *Park Place Grill*<br>0 E Main St. *(260) 420-7275.*<br>iown for its casually elegant atmosphere and choice of fine steaks, e Park Place Grill also features a wide variety of fresh seafood dishes, cluding filet of escalore and Thai-blackened mahi. *L, D.* ● *Sun.* | $$$ | ■ | | ■ | ● | |
| **DIANAPOLIS:** *Dunaway's Palazzo Ossigeno*<br>1 S East St. *(317) 638-7663.*<br>cated in the historic Indiana Oxygen building, Dunaway's features a eside dining room and a summer-only rooftop view. The superb crab kes, risotto-encrusted salmon, and roasted pork loin are highly commended. *L Mon–Fri, D.* ● *Sun.* | $$$$ | ■ | ● | ■ | ● | |
| **DIANAPOLIS:** *St. Elmo Steak House*<br>7 S Illinois St. *(800) 637-1811.* www.stelmos.com<br>iis New York-style steakhouse has been an Indianapolis fixture since 02. Its 20,000-bottle wine cellar and photo gallery of celebrity visitors hance a selection of succulent steaks, chops, seafood, and chicken. *D.* | $$$$ | ■ | | ■ | ● | |
| **UTH BEND:** *LaSalle Grill*<br>5 W Colfax Ave. *(574) 288-1155. (800) 382-9323.*<br>iis bustling urban establishment specializes in grilled steaks, seafood, mb, and pork chops, served in a comfortable dining room in an historic wntown office building. *D.* ● *Sun.* | $$$$ | ■ | | ■ | ● | |
| **MICHIGAN** | | | | | | |
| **NN ARBOR:** *The Earle*<br>1 W Washington St. *(734) 994-0211.*<br>esh French and Italian cuisine has made this romantic bistro Ann bor's premier downtown dining establishment. A piano bar and live eekend jazz combos complement the exquisite cuisine. *D.*<br>*May–Sep: Sun.* | $$$$ | ■ | | ■ | ● | |
| **ETROIT:** *Cyprus Taverna*<br>9 Monroe Ave. *(313) 961-1550.*<br>cozy atmosphere and a rich range of gourmet Greek dishes – including ftedakia lamb and beef meatball appetizer – have made this one of eektown's most popular restaurants. The exotic entrées on the menu e equally matched by some excellent wines. *L, D.* | $$$ | ■ | | ■ | ● | ■ |
| **ARMINGTON HILLS:** *Tribute*<br>425 W 12 Mile Rd. *(248) 848-9393.*<br>ne of *Gourmet* magazine's top 50 US restaurants, the Tribute achieves innovative synthesis of European and regional American cuisine in a old, colorful dining space. *D.* ● *Sun, Mon.* | $$$$$ | ■ | | ■ | ● | |

For key to symbols see back flap

**Price categories** include a three-course meal for one, a glass of house wine, and all unavoidable extra charges such as sales tax and service:
$ under $20
$$ $20–30
$$$ $30–45
$$$$ $45–60
$$$$$ over $60

**CREDIT CARDS**
Major credit cards accepted.

**OUTDOOR TABLES**
Garden, courtyard, or terrace with outside tables.

**VEGETARIAN**
A good selection of vegetarian dishes available.

**GOOD WINE LIST**
Extensive list of good wines, both domestic and imported.

**CHILDREN'S FACILITIES**
Various facilities for young children.

| | Price | Credit Cards | Outdoor Tables | Vegetarian | Good Wine List | Children's Facilities |
|---|---|---|---|---|---|---|
| **GRAND RAPIDS:** *The Sierra Room*<br>25 Ionia SW. (616) 459-1764.<br>A fusion of Asian, American, French, and Southwestern ingredients make eating at the downtown Sierra Room, one of western Michigan's most sophisticated dining experiences. *D.*<br>● *Sun.* | $$$ | ■ | | ■ | ● | ■ |
| **MARQUETTE:** *Vierling Restaurant and Brewery*<br>119 S Front St. (906) 228-3533.<br>This renovated 1883 saloon now houses a festive brewpub, featuring an ample selection of microbrewed beers alongside regional specialties such as Lake Superior whitefish, served in the traditional, Cajun, or picatta style. *L, D.* ● *Sun.* | $$ | ■ | | ■ | ● | |
| **MINNESOTA** | | | | | | |
| **DULUTH:** *Bennett's on the Lake*<br>600 E Superior St. (218) 722-2829.<br>Located in the historic Fitger's Brewery building overlooking Lake Superior, this romantic hideaway's specialties include honey-drizzled, pan-fried lake trout and a seared Isle Royale whitefish. The wine list is excellent. *B, L, D.* | $$$ | ■ | | ■ | ● | ■ |
| **ELY:** *The Dining Room at Blue Heron*<br>827 Kawishiwi Trail. (218) 365-4720.<br>Tucked away in an intimate B&B of the same name, the Blue Heron features such unique creations as pecan-crusted walleye, Korean bulgogi beef, and Honduran Mayan pork medallions.<br>*D.* ● *Mon, Tue.* | $$$ | ■ | | ■ | ● | |
| **MINNEAPOLIS:** *Nye's Polonaise Room*<br>112 E Hennepin Ave. (612) 379-2021.<br>A lively piano bar and even livelier polka band provide the perfect backdrop for this no-nonsense, Polish supper club's hearty pierogi, cabbage rolls, sausage, and sauerkraut.<br>*L, D.* ● *Sun L.* | $$ | ■ | | ■ | ● | ■ |
| **MINNEAPOLIS:** *Goodfellow's*<br>40 S 7th St. (612) 332-4800.<br>Tender cuts of beef, spicy Southwestern chicken, and a delicate mushroom ravioli are among the signature dishes at this elegant, downtown Minneapolis favorite.<br>*L, D.* ● *Sun.* | $$$$ | ■ | | ■ | ● | ■ |
| **ROCHESTER:** *Broadstreet Café & Bar*<br>300 1st Avenue NW. (507) 281-2451.<br>Housed in a renovated historic warehouse, this luxurious and spacious bistro specializes in French and American *haute* cuisine.<br>*L, D Sat–Sun.* | $$$ | ■ | | ■ | ● | ■ |
| **ST. PAUL:** *Mickey's Dining Car*<br>36 W 7th St. (651) 222-5633.<br>Built in 1937, this classic streamlined diner serves some of the Twin Cities' best breakfast food, burgers and milkshakes, alongside its time-tested mulligan stew.<br>*L, D.* | $ | ■ | | | | |
| **ST. PAUL:** *Pazzaluna Urban Trattoria and Bar*<br>360 St Peter St. (651) 223-7000.<br>Hand-painted tiles, plush seating and marble floors set the mood for this trendy, downtown St. Paul restaurant's superb antipasto, shiitake ravioli, and gourmet pizzas.<br>*D.* ● *Sun, Mon.* | $$$$ | ■ | | ■ | ● | |

## OHIO

**INCINNATI:** *The Celestial* $$$
71 Celestial St. *(513) 241-4455.*
stunning hilltop view, cozy fireplace, and sophisticated jazz combo eate the perfect mood for this Mount Adams establishment's French-fluenced cuisine and excellent wine list. *D.* *Sun.*

**LEVELAND:** *Blue Point Grille* $$$
0 W St Clair. *(216) 875-7827.*
1 elegant Warehouse District space houses one of Cleveland's most novative seafood restaurants. Honduran tilapia and sea bass with red rry coconut sauce augment the more traditional grouper, swordfish, d salmon offerings. *L Mon–Fri, D Sat–Sun.* *Sun.*

**LEVELAND:** *Il Circo Zibibbo* $$$
00 W 9th St. *(216) 575-0699.*
and-blown glass, intimate lighting, and a colorful decor combine with likely combinations of Italian ingredients for one of Cleveland's more emorable downtown dining experiences. *D.*

**OLUMBUS:** *Alana's* $$$
33 N High St. *(614) 294-6783.*
menu that changes daily, and a multiple-course "degustation" menu are nong the many unexpected delights at this remarkable University strict find. Some dishes are vegan. *D.* *Sun, Mon.*

**OLEDO:** *Tony Packo's Café* $
02 Front St. *(419) 691-6054.*
ade famous by M.A.S.H. TV star Jamie Farr, Tony Packo's serves spicy ungarian hot dogs, with live Dixieland jazz on weekends. Don't miss e gallery of celebrity-autographed buns. *L, D.*

## WISCONSIN

**ADISON:** *Café Continental* $$$
8 King St. *(608) 251-4880.*
timate lighting, textured walls, and a funky zinc bar complete the risian atmosphere of this downtown favorite, known locally for its stas, gourmet pizzas, and continental cuisine. *L, D.*

**ADISON:** *Quivey's Grove* $$$
61 Nesbitt Rd. *(608) 273-4900.*
ocated in a renovated 1855 stable structure, Quivey's Grove specializes comfort food – perch, trout, meatloaf, portobella mushrooms – epared with fresh, native Wisconsin ingredients and served with gional beers and wines. *L, D.* *Sun.*

**ILWAUKEE:** *Coquette Café* $$
6 N Milwaukee Ave. *(414) 291-2655.* www.coquettecafe.com
oused in a former bank, this delightful Third Ward bistro's French and editerranean offerings include a crisp Alsatian pizza, sweet potato occhi, and fennel-puréed potatoes. *L Sun–Fri, D.* *Sun.*

**ILWAUKEE:** *Mader's Restaurant* $$$
37 N Old World Third St. *(414) 271-3377.* www.maders.com
is landmark downtown restaurant serves German fare such as pork ank and schnitzel, as well as steaks, seafood, and a special children's enu. Housed in a 1913 brick building, it includes an art gallery and ore featuring art prints, beer steins, and Lladró figurines. *L, D.*

**STER BAY:** *Sister Bay Café* $$
1 N Bayshore Dr. *(920) 854-2429.*
is friendly, unassuming café dishes out hearty doses of traditional vedish cuisine in a casual, small town setting. Don't miss the chilled eatballs or the Rodgrod Med Flode pudding for dessert. High chairs or ecial items for children can be requested. *B, L, D.*

**RING GREEN:** *Spring Green General Store* $
7 S Albany St. *(608) 588-7070.*
oused in a converted cheese warehouse, this spunky café features me-style health food and ethnic cuisine, as well as an adjoining store lling gourmet groceries and natural products. The restaurant offers od facilities for young children. *B, L.*

For key to symbols see back flap

# The Great Plains

# The Great Plains at a Glance

Centering on the midway longitude, the 100th meridian – which divides the United States roughly into East and West – this region is the essence of Middle America. Stretching from Canada to Texas, and sloping gradually from the foot of the Rocky Mountains to the floodplain of the Mississippi River, the Great Plains covers seven states, from North and South Dakota across Iowa, Nebraska, Missouri, Kansas, and Oklahoma. This largely rural and agricultural region is a place of small towns, wide open spaces, and distant horizons. Museums, historic sights, and entertainment options can be found in cities such as Tulsa, St. Louis, Kansas City, and Oklahoma City.

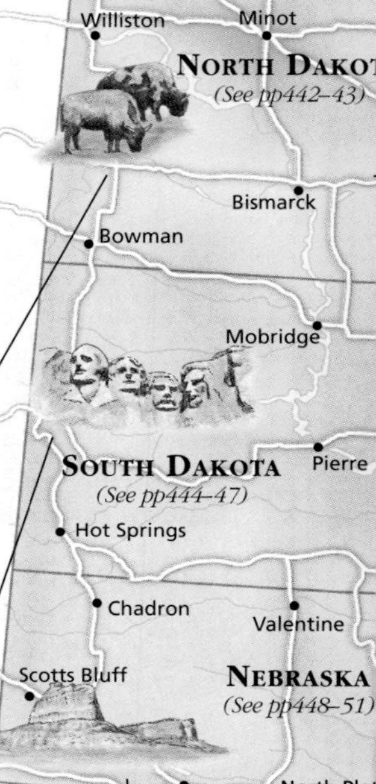

***Theodore Roosevelt National Park*** (see p443), *in North Dakota, was created in 1947 as a memorial in the president's honor. Today, herds of buffalo can frequently be seen roaming the park's stark but beautiful badlands.*

***Black Hills*** (see pp446–7), *South Dakota's main attraction, has six Native American reservations, as well as Mount Rushmore, with its giant, sculpted heads of four US presidents.*

***Scotts Bluff*** (see p450) *is a major landmark on the Nebraska portion of the Oregon Trail. Vast, grassy expanses of open range still contain reminders of 19th-century overland routes, along which pioneer settlers traveled westward. The Oregon Trail from Independence, Missouri, followed the North Platte River as it headed northwest across the Rocky Mountains.*

◁ **Endless expanse of cornfields, a common sight in rural Iowa**

***Des Moines*** (see p452) *is the state capital of Iowa, one of the country's largest agricultural producers, with a rich stock of hard-working farming communities. Iowa's green river valleys and lush cornfields encapsulate an idyllic image of a nearly vanished rural America.*

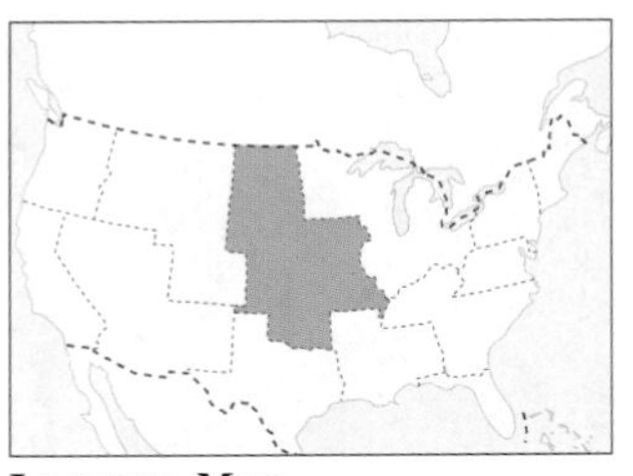

**LOCATOR MAP**

***St. Louis*** (see pp454–5) *is one of Missouri's largest and most cosmopolitan cities. Its location on the route leading west made St. Louis an active commercial and cultural crossroads, a role symbolized by the Gateway Arch.*

0 km 100

0 miles 100

Springfield

Poplar Bluff

***Wichita*** (see p459), *Kansas, was once a cattle drive destination, where cowboys stopped to let off steam. The town's colorful past is displayed at the Old Cowtown Museum. Dodge City is the state's other Old West town.*

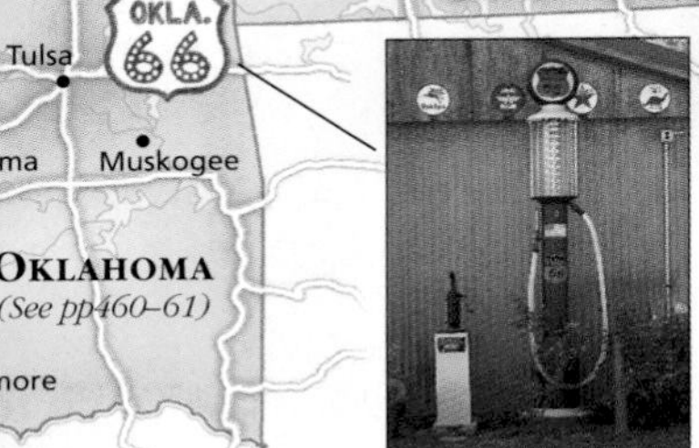


***Oklahoma*** (see pp460–61) *boasts more miles of the original Old Route 66 highway than any other state. This historic road, famous as the "mother road" in John Steinbeck's* The Grapes of Wrath, *has also been celebrated in blues and jazz. Old gas pumps, signboards, and other exhibits can be seen at some Route 66 museums, especially in Clinton.*

# THE GREAT PLAINS

FROM AN AIRPLANE, *the Great Plains looks like a repeated pattern of rectangular fields and arrow-straight highways, prompting urban Americans to dub it "fly-over country." This predominately rural and agricultural region, which stretches clear across the center of the country, embodies the all-American ideals of independence and hard-working self-sufficiency.*

The Great Plains are deeply rooted, both literally and figuratively, at the center of the American psyche. Though city-dwellers on both the East and West coasts may deride the region's general lack of sophistication, its residents' obvious pride in traditional values and old-fashioned lifestyles explains why this area is still the ideal location for all that is essentially American.

In fiction and film, the region has spawned such all-American creations as Mark Twain's *Huckleberry Finn*, Dorothy in *The Wizard of Oz*, the pioneer family of *Little House on the Prairie*, and the homespun sentimentality of *Field of Dreams* and *The Bridges of Madison County*.

Its rural reaches, with their vast expanses of fertile farmlands, form the basis of the Great Plains identity. Larger cities, such as Tulsa, St. Louis, Kansas City, and Oklahoma City, hold the bulk of the population as well as the museums, historic sights, and a wide range of hotels and resturants. Visitors can get a better sense of the region's culture by spending some time in bucolic, smaller towns.

### HISTORY

Throughout the 17th and 18th centuries, French traders and fur trappers explored the region, coming into contact with the diverse Native American tribes who lived here. These tribes varied from the sedentary, agriculture-based cultures of the Caddo and Mandan people to the Pawnee, Osage, and Comanche Indians, whose livelihoods depended on hunting migratory herds of bison (or buffalo). As Europeans settled along the East Coast, other tribes relocated westward to the Great Plains. The most tragic mass migration to this region took place in 1838, when the

**Herd of bison roaming the grasslands of Custer State Park, South Dakota**

◁ **Eroded sandstone forms at Theodore Roosevelt National Park, North Dakota**

**Lewis and Clark expedition mural at the Lewis & Clark Interpretive Center, Washburn, North Dakota**

Cherokee Nation was forced to relinquish all lands east of the Mississippi River. In exchange, they were granted land for "as long as the grass grows and the waters run," in what was then known as Indian Territory (present-day Oklahoma). More than 4,000 people died from hunger, disease, and exposure on the long journey, dubbed the "Trail of Tears from North Carolina to Oklahom Native American influence on th region is hard to quantify, but i heritage survives in numerous plac names, including those of each state Iowa, Missouri, Oklahoma, Kansa Nebraska, and the Dakotas.

Among the first Americans to explo the Great Plains were the legendar Lewis and Clark, whose expedition t the Pacific Ocean and back took almo three years, from 1803 to 1806. Remark able as their journey was, the late expedition of the German Prince Ma imilian made perhaps the mo enduring contribution to the region lore. Maximilian's journals, as well a artist Karl Bodmer's drawings an paintings of Indians, were published i Germany in 1838, and finally put th Great Plains on the international map.

Both expeditions embarked from S Louis, the region's oldest city founde as a distant French fur-trading fronti outpost. By the mid-19th century Kansas City had joined St. Louis as a outpost for pioneers crossing the Gre Plains on the legendary Santa Fe California, and Oregon Trails.

After the Civil War, a series of trans continental railroads followed many c the same routes, cutting down on trave time and transportation costs. Th railroads, however, sliced across th migration routes for the bison herds

## Key Dates in History

**1738-43** French fur trader Pierre Gaultier du Varennes, Sieur de la Verendrye, explores the northern Great Plains

**1764** St. Louis established

**1803** The US buys much of the region from France as part of the Louisiana Purchase

**1833** German artist Karl Bodmer documents Native American lifestyles

**1882** "Buffalo Bill" stages the world's first rodeo in North Platte, Nebraska

**1890** Massacre of 300 Sioux Indians by the US Army at Wounded Knee on Pine Ridge Reservation, South Dakota

**1907** Hollywood actor John Wayne is born in Winterset, Iowa

**1930-37** Extended drought and sustained winds create the Dust Bowl

**1941** Mount Rushmore completed

**1993** Disastrous springtime floods in Iowa and across the Great Plains

**1995** The Federal Building in downtown Oklahoma City is destroyed by a truck bomb

**2000** White supremacist Timothy McVeigh is executed for his role in the Oklahoma City bombing

hose numbers dwindled from millions near extinction. As the railroads ›ened up the land, the Indians were rced onto reservations, while home-:ading settlers took their place. These mily-run farms, growing wheat, corn, ttle, and pigs, are still emblematic of e region, though many farms are now ›erated on an industrial scale by ›sentee landlords. The high point of ;riculture was the World War I era, hen farm prices were high and mech-ıization had yet to replace horse-'awn plows and other labor-intensive ethods. The economic low point ıme soon afterward, when a sudden ›stwar drop in prices and a decade of :ought turned the region into the )ust Bowl," forcing some 200,000 rmers and their families to move west › California, a saga movingly ›cumented in John Steinbeck's *he Grapes of Wrath.*

### Geology & Climate

he land is what defines life in ıe Great Plains. Some 500 ıillion years ago, a deep inland :a laid the foundation of layers f sedimentary rock, with their ch array of ancient fossils as well as ıe fossil fuels that industries rely on ›day. Above this solid rock, a series of :e Age glaciers, scraping their way ›uth from Canada, deposited the ulverized soil that makes the eastern alf of the Great Plains – and Iowa in articular – some of the world's most :rtile farmland. Exceptions to the /pically horizontal landscape are ›und at its fringes. The rugged Ozark lountains lie in southern Missouri and )klahoma, while in western South )akota, the densely forested, gold-earing granite peaks of the Black Hills :se high above the eroded sandstone f Badlands National Park.

While the underlying geology may ıake for uneventful scenery, the limate is anything but mild. The Great 'lains experiences some of the nation's ıost extreme weather, particularly its ıerce tornados. These powerful wind-torms form with little warning in late pring and are most frequent along the Tornado Alley," which runs through eastern Kansas and Oklahoma. The region also frequently suffers from flood-inducing rains and thunder-storms, scorching summer heat and humidity, and frigid winter blizzards.

Prairie dog, Badlands

### People & Culture

The Great Plains is, by and large, conservative, with patriotism and religion the dominating cultural values. Yet it also is a region of varied cultural and political traditions. In the 19th century, Kansas was one of the prime anti-slavery battlegrounds, but at the turn of the 21st century the state insisted that biblical ideas of creationism be taught in school science classes.

Ethnically, however, the population is surprisingly diverse. Many of the original immigrants were lured here from similar terrain in Europe, notably the steppes of eastern Europe, by promises of land ownership. A significant number were adherents of nonconformist religions, such as the Mennonites who came from German-speaking regions of Russia to settle in central Kansas and the Dakotas. Their past explains the presence of the many German-style pastry shops in what may seem like quintessentially American small towns.

Native Americans also play an increasingly visible role in the region's identity, thanks both to burgeoning casinos operated by the various tribes and to a growing respect for their culture and heritage. Oklahoma, for example, has one of the country's largest Native American populations, numbering nearly 10 percent of the state's 3 million inhabitants.

Pine Ridge Indian Reservation in South Dakota

# Exploring the Great Plains

THE GREAT PLAINS DRAWS VISITORS in search of a taste of wholesome America. Its singular attraction is the countryside with its wide-open, seemingly endless spaces, where visitors can travel for miles without seeing more than a few railroad tracks, a set of power lines, or perhaps an occasional windmill or grain elevator. For those who want to explore farther, the Great Plains' highlights include the magnificent, sculpted monument of Mount Rushmore, the eerie landscape of Badlands National Park, and historic frontier outposts such as St. Louis and Kansas City, two of the region's largest cities. A car is essential to make the most of a visit to the Great Plains.

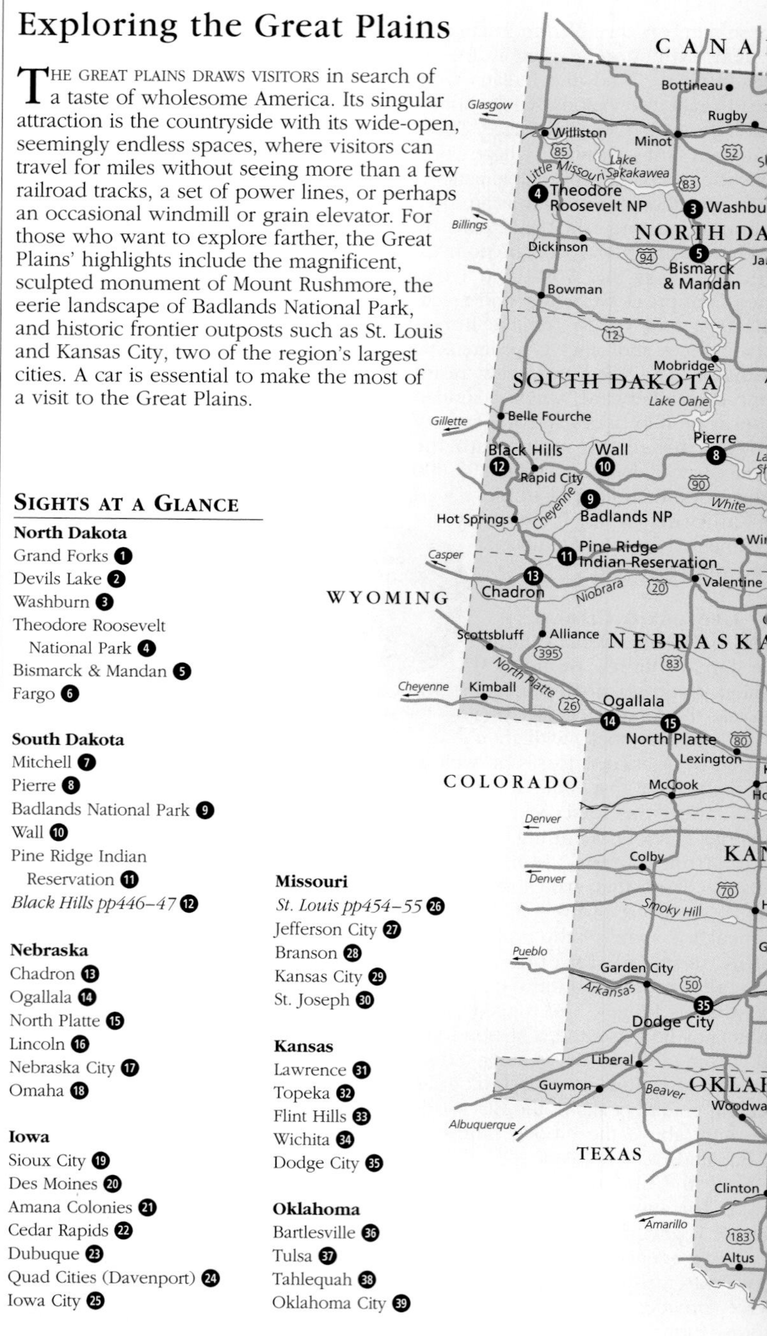


## SIGHTS AT A GLANCE

**North Dakota**
Grand Forks 1
Devils Lake 2
Washburn 3
Theodore Roosevelt National Park 4
Bismarck & Mandan 5
Fargo 6

**South Dakota**
Mitchell 7
Pierre 8
Badlands National Park 9
Wall 10
Pine Ridge Indian Reservation 11
*Black Hills pp446–47* 12

**Nebraska**
Chadron 13
Ogallala 14
North Platte 15
Lincoln 16
Nebraska City 17
Omaha 18

**Iowa**
Sioux City 19
Des Moines 20
Amana Colonies 21
Cedar Rapids 22
Dubuque 23
Quad Cities (Davenport) 24
Iowa City 25

**Missouri**
*St. Louis pp454–55* 26
Jefferson City 27
Branson 28
Kansas City 29
St. Joseph 30

**Kansas**
Lawrence 31
Topeka 32
Flint Hills 33
Wichita 34
Dodge City 35

**Oklahoma**
Bartlesville 36
Tulsa 37
Tahlequah 38
Oklahoma City 39

**MILEAGE CHART**

**10** = Distance in miles
10 = Distance in kilometers

| | BISMARCK, ND | RAPID CITY, SD | OMAHA, NE | DES MOINES, IA | ST. LOUIS, MO | KANSAS CITY, MO | WICHITA, KS |
|---|---|---|---|---|---|---|---|
| RAPID CITY, SD | **350** 563 | | | | | | |
| OMAHA, NE | **607** 977 | **524** 843 | | | | | |
| DES MOINES, IA | **667** 1073 | **624** 1004 | **135** 217 | | | | |
| ST. LOUIS, MO | **1039** 1672 | **953** 1534 | **434** 698 | **434** 698 | | | |
| KANSAS CITY, MO | **786** 1265 | **702** 1130 | **183** 295 | **194** 312 | **247** 397 | | |
| WICHITA, KS | **1034** 1664 | **952** 1532 | **385** 620 | **393** 632 | **444** 715 | **203** 327 | |
| OKLAHOMA CITY, OK | **1123** 1807 | **1040** 1674 | **519** 835 | **546** 879 | **500** 805 | **349** 562 | **161** 259 |

**Rolling wheat plains near Washburn, South Dakota**

***SEE ALSO***


- ***Practical Information*** pp462–3
- ***Where to Stay*** pp464–7
- ***Where to Eat*** pp468–71

# North Dakota

**Fort Lincoln State Park**

A STATE OF UNEXPECTED VARIETY, North Dakota's vast blue skies, tiny farming communities, and endless wheat fields along its eastern half can lull visitors into a state of quiet contemplation. Toward the west, North Dakota's drier, more rugged Missouri Plateau contains the stark badlands of Theodore Roosevelt National Park and more than a dozen historic sites visited by Lewis and Clark *(see p570)* on their 1803–06 expedition up the Missouri River. The explorers spent 146 days in North Dakota on their outbound and return journeys. Vast tracts of undeveloped areas along the river north of the pleasant capital city of Bismarck still look much like they did in the early 19th century.

## Grand Forks ❶

*49,400.* *4251 Gateway Dr, (800) 866-4566.*
www.visitgrandforks.com

LOCATED AT THE junction of the Red and Red Lake Rivers, the city attracted international attention in 1997, when the Red River flooded downtown, destroying many historic structures and inflicting huge damage. Massive clean-up, water control, and reconstruction efforts have helped Grand Forks overcome much of the flood's disastrous effects.

The **Empire Arts Center**, housed in the restored 1919 Empire Theatre, is now downtown's vibrant performing arts center. The University of North Dakota campus, 2 miles (3 km) west of downtown, is home to the **North Dakota Museum of Art**, with its good collection of contemporary art.

**Empire Arts Center**
415 Demers Ave. *(701) 746-5500.*
*call for times.*
www.empireartscenter.org

## Devils Lake ❷

*7,800.* *208 Hwy 2 W, (800) 233-8048.*
www.devilslakend.com

THE PRIMARY recreational attraction in northeastern North Dakota is the 120,000-acre (48,600-ha) glacial Devils Lake, 90 miles (150 km) west of Grand Forks. With miles of shoreline and no natural outlet, the lake is an excellent spot for fishing and boating. Many of the area's residents, however, face an uncertain future, as the lake's ever-rising waters have forced them to relocate their homes.

**Fort Totten State Historic Site**, 14 miles (22 km) to the south, is one of the best-preserved United States Army bases from the post-Civil War era. The restored buildings around the parade ground contain period furniture.

**Fort Totten State Historic Site**
Rte 57. *(701) 766-4441.*
*8am–5pm daily.* www.state.nd.us/hist/totten/totten

## Washburn ❸

*1,500.*
*(701) 462-3660.*
www.washburnnd.com

THE KEY ATTRACTION in the area surrounding this sleepy Missouri River town is the **Lewis and Clark Interpretive Center**. A stunning view of the Missouri River Valley greets visitors, who can also don buffalo robes, listen to Native American music, and view exhibits tracing the river's shifting course over the past 200 years.

The newly constructed museum is an ideal starting point for a tour of the sites associated with Lewis and Clark's historic expedition. About 2 miles (3 km) north of the visitor center is the reconstructed **Fort Mandan**. It was near here that Lewis and Clark's 44-man Corps of Discovery wintered between 1804 and 1805.

The **Knife River Indian Village National Historic Site**, 20 miles (32 km) west of Washburn, contains the remains of the largest village of the interrelated Mandan, Hidatsa, and Arikara tribes. Among these are a restored 50ft x 12-ft (15m x 12-m) earth lodge. The French trapper Charbonneau, and his Native American wife, Sacagawea, joined the Lewis and Clark expedition near this spot in 1804.

**Lewis & Clark Interpretive Center**
US 83 & Rte 200A.
*(877) 462-8535.*
*Jun–Sep: 9am–7pm; Oct–May: 9am–5pm.*
www.fortmandan.com

**The reconstructed, high-stockaded façade of Fort Mandan, near Washburn**

ıe Painted Canyon, Theodore Roosevelt National Park

## 'heodore Roosevelt Iational Park ❹

ədora. (701) 623-4466.
] 8am–4:30pm daily. Jan 1,
anksgiving, Dec 25.
] www.nps.gov/thro

THE TINY WESTERN North Dakota town of Medora is .e gateway to the Theodore ɔosevelt National Park and ıe remote, beautiful North akota badlands. The bill ıat created this park as a ıemorial to Roosevelt was gned on April 25, 1947, by resident Truman. On Nov- mber 10, 1978, the area was ·ven national park status by ırtue of another bill signed y President Carter.

The Theodore Roosevelt ational Park is a sprawling ne, covering over 70,000 cres (28,328 ha) of land. It is ·vided into two pockets – the orth and South Units – about ) miles (112 km) apart. The utte-studded South Unit has ıe phantasmagoric **Painted anyon** and can be explored n horseback or seen from an verlook from a 36-mile (58- m) self-guided auto tour. The orth Unit features a ramatic, oxbow bend in the ittle Missouri River. Its ıoonlike landscape is dotted vith mushroom-shaped stone ɔrmations and windswept rasslands. Unlike the much- isited South Unit, this pocket es in very isolated country. Iowever, a 14-mile (22-km) uto route through this ıgged landscape provides ccess to a nature trail and umerous scenic overlooks.

## Bismarck & Mandan ❺

*65,000.* *1600 Burnt Boat Dr, Bismarck, (800) 767-3555.*
www.bismarckmandancvb.com

RIVERBOAT TRAFFIC, railroads, and the government were instrumental in the devel- opment of the state capital of Bismarck, founded in 1872 on the east bank of the Missouri River. The 19-story, Art Deco **North Dakota State Capitol** dominates the city's leafy, low-slung skyline. Known as the "Skyscraper of the Prairies," the 1933 structure is visible for miles in every direction, mainly because of its location on top of a small rise north of downtown. The **North Dakota Heritage Center**, abutting the Capitol, provides a fascinating intro- duction to the state's Native American heritage and terri- torial settlement. It also traces the story of the Capitol's design and construction.

The shipping and ware- housing center of Mandan lies just across the Missouri. To the south of downtown is **Fort Abraham Lincoln State Park**, which contains On-a- Slant Indian Village, the excavated remains of a 17th- century Mandan Native American community, and several other reconstructed buildings. The fort was the last base for reckless George Armstrong Custer, who led the 7th Calvary from here to their disastrous defeat at the Battle of Little Bighorn *(see p581)* in 1876.

**North Dakota Heritage Center**
Capitol Mall, Bismarck. *(701) 328-2666.* *8am–5pm Mon–Fri, 9am–5pm Sat, 11am–5pm Sun.*

**Fort Abraham Lincoln State Park**
4480 Fort Lincoln Rd. *(701) 663-9571.* *May 1–Memorial Day: 9am–5pm daily; Memorial Day–Labor Day: 9am–7pm; Labor Day–Sep 30: 9am–5pm.*

## Fargo ❻

*90,600.*
*2001 44th St S, (800) 235-7654.*
www.fargomoorhead.org

A GRAIN PROCESSING center, Fargo lies directly across the Red River from its sister city, Moorhead, Minnesota. Fargo's historic downtown includes the renovated 1926 **Fargo Theatre**, an Art Moderne structure that still presents art and period films as well as live performances. Southwest of the theater is the superb **Plains Art Museum**, housed in a restored 1904 International Harvester Company ware- house. This museum has the state's largest public art collection, with works by the region's Native American and folk artists. The **Roger Maris Baseball Museum**, in the West Acres Shopping Center, celebrates the achievements of Fargo's most famous native son, who hit 61 home runs in 1961, setting a record for most home runs in a season.

**Fargo Theatre**
314 Broadway. *(701) 239-8385.*
*call for schedule.*

**Exterior of the historic Fargo Theatre, Fargo**

# South Dakota

Pine Ridge Reservation

RIVERS, HILLS, BUTTES, rolling prairies, and badlands are South Dakota's defining geographical features. The Missouri River bisects the state from north to south, with the corn and soybean fields of the flatter eastern plains giving way to shortgrass prairie and rocky badlands as one heads west on the state's main east–west corridor, I-90. Culturally, the state is dominated by the heritage of the Dakota, Lakota, and Nakota Sioux tribes, who roamed and hunted the buffalo-rich area until they were moved onto reservations in the late 1800s. Over 60,000 Native Americans still reside here.

## Mitchell 7

*14,500. 601 N Main St, (866) 273-2676.* www.cornpalace.com

LOCATED IN THE fertile James River Valley, Mitchell is the state's corn, grain, and cattle center. The city's claim to fame is the well-known **Corn Palace**, a Moorish auditorium that was built in 1921 to house the city's Corn Belt Exposition. Colorful domes, minarets, and kiosks are the only permanent design features on the ever-changing façade of the palace. Every year, local artists use more than 3,000 bushels of corn and grasses to create new murals, which depict agricultural scenes from South Dakota. This tradition dates back to 1892, when the Corn Real Estate Association constructed the first palace to showcase the area's crops, in an endeavor to lure settlers.

**Corn Palace**
*Memorial Day–Aug 30: 8am–9pm daily; Apr–May & Sep–Oct: 8am–5pm daily; Nov–Mar: 8am–5pm Mon–Fri.*

Mural at the Corn Palace, Mitchell

## Pierre 8

*14,000. 800 W Dakota Ave, (800) 962-2034.* www.pierrechamber.com

THE SECOND smallest capital in the US, Pierre lies in the Missouri River Valley, and forms a leafy oasis in the shortgrass, largely treeless plains of central South Dakota. The 1910 **South Dakota State Capitol** has a grand marble staircase and overlooks a lake visited each spring and fall by thousands of migratory birds. In 2004, Pierre hosted a bicentennial commemoration of the famed Lewis and Clark expedition.

The excellent **South Dakota Cultural Heritage Center** is built into the side of a Missouri River bluff, covered with shortgrass prairie. Its exhibits trace the history of South Dakota's Sioux tribes and also provide information on the diverse ethnic backgrounds of the state's homesteading white settlers. On display is a lead plate that was buried in a nearby river bluff in 1743 by the French-sponsored Verendrye expedition to mark the site as French territory. The **Verendrye Museum**, across the river in Fort Pierre, focuses on French trading and exploration activities.

Exterior of the South Dakota State Capitol in Pierre

**South Dakota State Capitol**
500 E Capitol Ave. *(605) 773-3765. 8am–10pm daily.*

**South Dakota Cultural Heritage Center**
900 Governors Dr. *(605) 773-3458. 9am–4:30pm Mon–Fri, 1–4:30pm Sat–Sun. Jan 1, Thanksgiving, Dec 25.*

## Badlands National Park 9

*Ben Reifel Visitor Center, Rte 240 S of I-90 exit 131. (605) 433-5361. Jun–Aug: 7am–8pm; Sep–Oct: 8am–6pm; Nov–May: 9am–4pm.* www.nps.gov/badl

THE EERIE desolation of Badlands National Park is an awe-inspiring sight for travelers unprepared for such a stark, rugged landscape after miles of gentle, rolling South Dakota prairie. Formed over 14 million years ago from silt and sediment washing down from the Black Hills *(see pp446–7)*, the badlands were sculpted into their present craggy form by harsh sun and powerful winds.

Some of the region's most dramatically eroded buttes, pinnacles, and spires are contained in this 244,000-acre (98,744-ha) park. The **Ben Reifel Visitor Center** is the gateway to several self-guided hiking tours and the 30-mile (48-km) Badlands Loop Road (Route 240). The scenic drive follows the northern rim of the 450-ft (137-m) high Badlands Wall escarpment and leads to several overlooks and trails that provide breath-taking vistas of the eroded

ew of the eroded gullies from Changing Scenes Overlook in Badlands National Park

llies below. The road loops ck north to I-90 near **Sage reek Wilderness Area**, here golden eagles, hawks, d various songbirds gather a vast expanse of steep asslands, festooned each mmer with wildflowers. e park-managed buffalo rd can be seen grazing on ge stretches of prairie.

all Drug Store, a shopping and tertainment complex

## Vall ⑩

800. 🚌 ℹ 501 Main St, 88) 852-9255.
] www.wall-badlands.com

WALL HAS DONE a thriving tourist trade since 1936, hen local pharmacist Ted ustead put up signs along e highway offering free ice ater. This primitive roadside lvertising tactic soon grew to a statewide slew of billoards, which still line I-90 all e way across South Dakota. ustead's small-town pharacy, **Wall Drug**, is now a rawling Wild West opping and entertainment mplex. Along with Western d Native American souvenirs are interactive exhibits of cowboys, homesteaders, gunfighters, and medicine-show hucksters.

The sprawling **Buffalo Gap National Grasslands** lies south, west, and east of Wall. Its visitor center describes the ecological and cultural history of the grasslands. Various exhibits outline the various habitats and illustrate the astonishing biodiversity of the shortgrass, mixed-grass, and tallgrass prairies, which once covered most of the region.

**Wall Drug**
510 Main St. ☎ *(605) 279-2175.*
🕐 *6:30am–6pm daily (extended summer hours).*
W www.walldrug.com

**Buffalo Gap National Grasslands**
ℹ *708 Main St, (605) 279-2125.*
🕐 *Memorial–Labor Day: 8am–4:30pm daily; Labor Day–Memorial Day: 8am–4:30pm Mon–Fri.* ♿

## Pine Ridge Indian Reservation ⑪

ℹ *Oglala Sioux Tribe, Pine Ridge, (605) 867-6075.*

HOME TO THE Oglala Sioux tribe, the Pine Ridge Reservation is the nation's second-largest Native American reservation. The reservation lands abut the South Dakota–Nebraska border and extend west into the badlands region. The Oglala and their chief, Red Cloud, were relocated here in 1876. On December 29, 1890, the US Army's 7th Cavalry massacred about 300 Lakota men, women, and children at **Wounded Knee**. This was the last in a series of misunderstandings concerning the ceremonial Ghost Dance, which the tribe believed would reunite them with their ancestors, bring the buffalo back, and help them regain their lost lands. A lone stone monument, about 10 miles (16 km) east of the village of Pine Ridge, marks the site.

The **Red Cloud Heritage Center**, on the Red Cloud Indian School campus near Pine Ridge, contains the gravesite of Chief Red Cloud. It also displays a range of Native American artifacts.

**Red Cloud Heritage Center**
4.5 miles (7 km) N of Pine Ridge Village on Hwy 18. ☎ *(605) 867-5491.* 🕐 *8am–5pm Mon–Fri.* ● *public hols.* ♿
W www.redcloudschool.org

The Red Cloud Heritage Center at the Pine Ridge Indian Reservation

# Black Hills ⓬

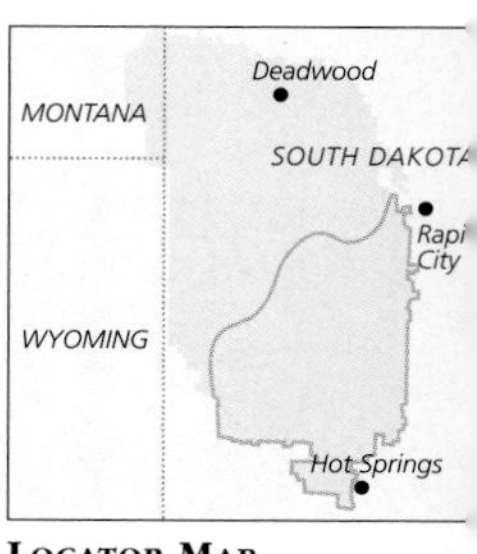


**Locator Map**

☐ *Black Hills* ☐ *Area illustrated*

KNOWN TO THE LAKOTA SIOUX as Paha Sapa, these majestic hills were a mysterious, sacred place where Native Americans would retreat to seek guidance from the Great Spirit. In 1874, George Armstrong Custer's *(see p581)* expedition discovered evidence of gold deposits in the thickly forested, oddly shaped granite hills. A series of misleading treaties followed, forcing the Sioux to relinquish their land, as miners, speculators, and settlers rushed into these once-sacred hills to stake their claims. Today, the Black Hills harbor some of the state's most visited attractions, particularly Mount Rushmore National Memorial. The 125-mile x 65-mile (201-km x 105-km) area is linked by US 385 and US 16, which meanders from Rapid City, the main center in the area, to Wyoming.

**Crazy Horse Memorial**
*When complete, the statue of the great Sioux warrior, Crazy Horse, will be the world's largest sculpture. At present only the nine-story high face has been finished.*

**Jewel Cave National Monument**
*The underground attractions in the third-longest cave in the world are more varied than those at Wind Cave. Tough spelunking (cave exploring) tours allow participants into some of the more astounding areas. A simpler paved route offers a broad overview.*

**Deadwood**
*The restored downtown re-creates Deadwood's past as a wild, lawless gold mining town. Gunfighter Wild Bill Hickock was shot here in 1876, and Calamity Jane also left her mark here. Today, visitors try their luck in the historic gaming halls.*

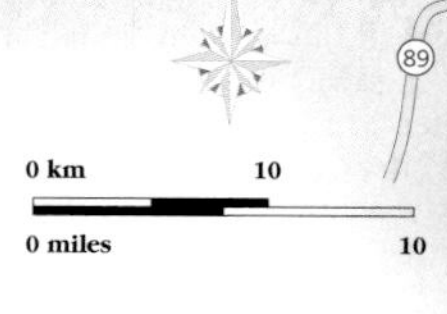


**Key**

- Custer State Park boundary
- Wind Cave NP boundary
- Major road

**ount Rushmore National Memorial**

*American icon since its completion in 1941, the giant, ulpted heads of presidents George Washington, Thomas ferson, Abraham Lincoln, and Theodore Roosevelt took years to create. Sculptor Gutzon Borglum's studio, tools, and models are preserved on site.*

**Custer State Park**

*This 73,000-acre (29,542 ha) park is one of the region's most pristine natural habitats, with towering rock formations such as the Needles Eye, a spire rising 30–40 ft (9–12 m) high.*

**Wind Cave National Park**

*This park contains the world's sixth-longest limestone cavern, its underground labyrinth studded with strange, popcorn-like formations. Guided tours include a historical candlelight tour, and the Natural Entrance tour.*

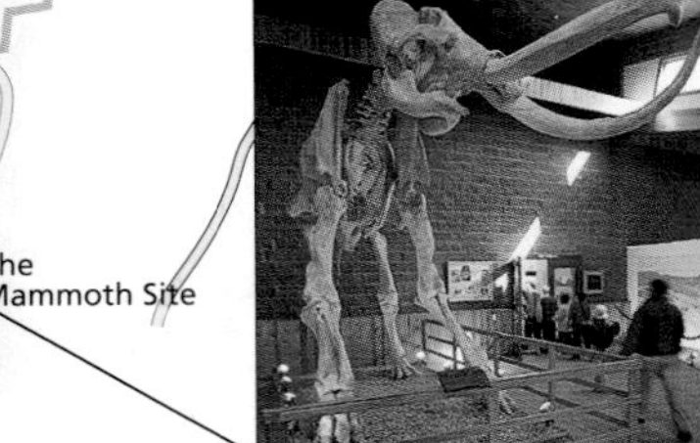

**The Mammoth Site**

*Discovered in 1974, this site displays the world's largest concentration of Columbian mammoth fossils. Originially a spring-fed sinkhole where animals were trapped and preserved, only 30 percent of the 26,000-year-old site has been explored so far.*

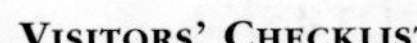

**VISITORS' CHECKLIST**

*Rapid City.* *Rapid City.* *Black Hills Visitor Information Center, Exit 61 off I-90, Rapid City, (605) 355-3700.* www.blackhillsbadlands.com

**Mount Rushmore National Memorial** *(605) 574-2523.* *call for timings.* www.nps.gov/moru

**Crazy Horse Memorial** *(605) 673-4681.* *call for timings.* www.crazyhorsememorial.org

**Custer State Park** *(605) 255-4515.* *call for timings.* www.custerstatepark.info

**Wind Cave National Park** *(605) 745-4600.* *call for timings.* www.nps.gov/wica

**Jewel Cave National Monument** *(605) 673-2288.* *call for timings.* *Jan 1, Thanksgiving, Dec 25.* *Visitor center only.* www.nps.gov/ jeca

**The Mammoth Site** *(605) 745-6017.* *call for timings.* www.mammothsite.com

**Deadwood** *(800) 999-1876.* *call for timings.* www.deadwood.org

# Nebraska

Indian tepee, Chadron

NEBRASKA'S VAST, grassy expanses of open range, and ruts from old overland routes, epitomize the geography and history of the Great Plains. The modern I-80 freeway stretches westward in the shadow of the wide Platte River Valley, the historic Oregon, Mormon, and Pony Express Trails, and the original Lincoln Hwy (now US 30). Farther north, the sparsely settled central Nebraska Sandhills contain some of the nation's largest expanses of unbroken, mixed-grass prairie, while the Panhandle in the northwest is studded with rocky outcrops and jagged canyons. The state's two largest cities, Omaha and Lincoln, are in the southeast.

## Chadron ⓭

*5,600.* *706 W 3rd St, (800) 603-2937.* www.chadron.com

CHADRON IS THE ideal base to tour the Pine Ridge and Sandhills regions as well as explore aspects of the state's fascinating past. About 3 miles (5 km) east of town is the **Museum of the Fur Trade**. Built on the grounds of an 1833–49 American Fur Company post, the museum traces the history of the complex North American fur trade and its effect on Native American communities. One of its main features is a reconstructed trading post built into the sides of a low hill.

The area's key historical attraction is **Fort Robinson State Park**, just west of Crawford, which itself is 23 miles (37 km) west of Chadron. The park occupies the parade grounds, barracks, and officers' quarters of the US Army's Fort Robinson. The fort was built in 1874 to protect the nearby Red Cloud Indian Agency, where Sioux chief Red Cloud and his followers moved to before being relocated at Pine Ridge *(see p445)*. In 1877, the great Oglala Sioux chief, Crazy Horse *(see p446)*, and 900 of his tribe surrendered and set up camp outside of the fort. In a series of tragic events, Crazy Horse was killed while federal troops attempted to imprison him. A restored blockhouse commemorates the site where he fell.

The excellent Fort Robinson Museum details the fort's other lives as an experimental cattle ranch and a training ground for the army's World War II canine corps. The fort's restored quarters provide accommodation for visitors, while horseback trails lead through the surrounding lonesome buttes and grassy plains. The park also harbors a large herd of longhorn cattle and more than 400 bison.

**Chadron State Park**, 8 miles (13 km) south of Chadron, is a quieter, more scenic alternative, with ample campgrounds and cabin facilities. Hiking and biking trails from the park crisscross the spine of the 230-mile (370-km) long Pine Ridge escarpment. Hikers and mountain bikers seeking more challening routes can follow the 25-mile (40-km) Pine Ridge Trail, a steep, meandering route through patches of meadows and thick stands ‹ ponderosa pine. The trail is part of the Pine Ridge National Recreation Area, a craggy portion of the vast Nebraska National Forest, which runs along the brow of the escarpment, south of US 20, between Chadron and Crawford.

Restored officers' quarters in Fort Robinson State Park, Chadron

**Fort Robinson State Pa**
US 20, 3 miles (5 km) W of Crawfo
*(308) 665-2900.* *daily.*
www.stateparks.com/fort_robinsc

Martin Bay in Lake McConaughy State Recreation Area, near Ogall

## Ogallala ⓮

*5,100.* *204 E A St, (800) 658-4390.* www.visitogallala.co

LOCATED ON THE South Platt River near the junction c I-80, US 26, and Route 92, Ogallala is the gateway to th Panhandle part of the Oregc Trail tour *(see p450)*. The cit gained a rowdy reputation a the "Gomorrah of the Plains soon after its founding in 1867, when the arrival of the railroad drew herds of cattle and hordes of Texas cowboys. Most modern visitors now come seeking camping, boating, hunting, and fishing supplies for their exploratior of **Lake McConaughy State Recreation Area**, about 9 miles (14 km), to the north.

A refreshing oasis in the middle of the dry Panhandle

ains, Lake McConaughy is e state's largest reservoir. ıown locally as "Big Mac," cool waters are a prime eeding ground for rainbow ɔut, catfish, walleye, and hite bass. The north shore is ıed with fine sand beaches, hile the marshes, wood-ıds, and grasslands on the ke's western end attract a ıde variety of waterfowl. ons, ducks, mergansers, ıd western grebes frequent g Mac, making it one of the hest birding spots in the eat Plains region.

**Lake McConaughy State ecreation Area**
75 Hwy 61 N. *(308) 284-8800.* *Memorial Day–Labor Day: 8am–m daily. Visitor center only.* www.ngpc.state.ne.us

## orth Platte 15

*25,000.* *219 S Dewey, 0) 955-4528.* www.visitnorthplatte.com

NOW ONE OF the country's major railroad centers, ɔrth Platte was the late-19th-ntury home of the famed illiam "Buffalo Bill" Cody *(ee p582)*. The comfortable nch house he built on the ıtskirts of town was the ıse of operations for his ıveling Wild West show ıtil 1902, when he founded ɔdy in Wyoming. Cody's ɔme is now part of the **ıffalo Bill Ranch State istorical Park** that includes horse barn and log cabin ɔm one of his previous nches. The nearby **Lincoln ɔunty Historical Museum** hibits a replica of the mous North Platte Canteen, which served countless pots of coffee and quantities of snacks to the military troops who passed through the town during World War II.

**Buffalo Bill Ranch State Historical Park**
2921 Scouts Rest Ranch Rd. *(308) 535-8035.* *Apr–Memorial Day: 10am–4pm Mon–Fri; Memorial – Labor Day: 9am–5pm daily; Labor Day–Oct: 10am–4pm Mon–Fri.* *Oct–Apr.* www.ngpc.state.ne.us

**Lincoln County Historical Museum**
2403 Buffalo Bill Ave. *(308) 534-5640.* *Jun–Labor Day: 9am–8pm Mon–Sat, 1–8pm Sun; Labor Day–Sep 30: 9am–5pm Mon–Sat, 1–5pm Sun.* www.npcanteen.tripod.com/canteen/lchm.html

**Cody's house in North Platte's Buffalo Bill Ranch State Historical Park**

**colorful billboard in a parking lot welcoming visitors to North Platte**

## Lincoln 16

*235,000.* *201 N 7th St, (402) 434-5348.* www.lincoln.org

STATE CAPITAL and Nebraska's second-largest city, Lincoln is also home to the University of Nebraska, whose Cornhuskers football team is so popular that it has sold out every home game at the 77,000-seat Memorial Stadium since 1962. The city's principal landmark, however, is the 400-ft (120-m) Indiana limestone tower of the **Nebraska State Capitol**. Completed in 1932, the "Tower of the Plains" is surmounted by a bronze statue of a man sowing grain and visible for miles around. Intricate murals and ornate ceilings adorn the interior. The building houses the nation's only unicameral legislature, a vestige of cost-saving measures introduced by the state during the Great Depression of the 1930s.

The state's political history is related alongside its rich Native American heritage in the excellent **Museum of Nebraska History**, located on 15th and P Streets. The **University of Nebraska State Museum**, in the downtown campus, has a wide-ranging collection of elephant fossils and Native American artifacts. In the nearby historic Haymarket District, several 19th-century warehouses have been converted into bars, restaurants, and shops.

**Bronze statue surmounting the Nebraska State Capitol in Lincoln**

**Museum of Nebraska History**
15th & P Sts. (402) 471-4754. *9:30am–4:30pm Mon–Fri, 1–4:30pm Sat & Sun.* *public hols.* www.nebraskahistory.org

**University of Nebraska State Museum**
Morrill Hall, 14th & Vine Sts. *(402) 472-2642.* *9:30am–4:30pm Mon–Sat, 1:30–4:30pm Sun.* *Jan 1, Thanksgiving, Dec 25.* www.museum.unl.edu

# The Oregon Trail

FOUNDED BY TRADER William Sublette in 1830, this formidable 2,000-mile (3,200-km) trail was the main wagon route between Independence, Missouri *(see p457)* in the east and Oregon to the west. The original route curved northwest after crossing the Missouri River near present-day Kansas City, passing through northeastern Kansas and southeastern Nebraska on the way to the Platte River. Between 1841 and 1866, a staggering 500,000 settlers bound for the fertile farmlands of Oregon and the goldfields of northern California passed through Nebraska, following the northern banks of the Platte, past a string of army forts to Ogallala. As the trail veered northwest, away from the flat landscape of the Platte River Valley and up into the craggy Panhandle plateau along the North Platte River, pioneers were awestruck by the massive rock formations that signaled the Rockies to the west.

**Trail marker, North Platte**

**THE OREGON TRAIL IN NEBRASKA**
More than 428 miles (689 km) of the original Oregon Trail passed through the flat grasslands of Nebraska before it turned northwestards. Today, most of the old routes are easily accessible, with historic markers guiding travelers on I-80, along the Platte River, or Route 92 and US 26, which follows the trail's northwestern ascent of the North Platte. This undated illustration by William H. Jackson depicts the first covered wagon caravan, led by Smith-Jackson-Sublette, consisting of ten wagons drawn by five mules each, heading for Wind River Valley near present-day Lander in Wyoming.

**LOCATOR MAP**
*The Oregon Trail*

***Chimney Rock**, east of the town of Scottsbluff, rises 500 ft (152 m) above the mixed-grass plains. This was one of the more frequently noted sights in travelers' diaries and sketchbooks.*

***Scotts Bluff National Monument** has a well-staffed visitor center, which runs various interpretive and living history programs. These include an excellent overview of the Oregon Trail history as well as exhibits on the Mormon Trail. Visitors can hike to the summit of the 800-ft (244-m) sandstone outcropping and walk along still-visible Oregon Trail ruts.*

ɪrton's mansion at Arbor Lodge State Historical Park, Nebraska City

## 'ebraska City 17

7,200. 806 1st Ave, (800) 4-9113. www.nebraskacity.com

EDATE, TREE-LINED Nebraska City's origins were as a wdy Missouri River way ıtion, where families and venturers bound for the ·egon Trail mingled with ppers, traders, and river-ıat employees. Today, the y is best known as the ·thplace of Arbor Day, tablished by Nebraska ılitician and newspaper itor Julius Sterling Morton 332–1902). When he was cretary of Agriculture under esident Grover Cleveland, ɔrton introduced a resolu-ın to make April 10 a state ıliday to encourage farmers Nebraska to plant trees as otection from high plains nds and soil erosion. Later, e date was changed to April , Morton's birthday. Arbor ıy is still commemorated roughout the United States, :hough the date varies ɔm state to state.

The city is also well known the home of **Arbor Day ırm**, a 260-acre (105-ha) perimental farm, confer-ıce center, and forestry search center. Scenic hiking ıils and guided tours offer sual explorations of the :m's apple orchards, wind-eak arboretum, and a newable energy plant.

The **Arbor Lodge State istorical Park** contains ɔrton's Georgian Revival ansion, greenhouse, and ounds. The park includes urs of the formal Italian ırden and 52-room mansion, ımpleted in 1902, and a carriage house with a stagecoach once driven by Wild West impresario Buffalo Bill *(see p582)*.

### Arbor Day Farm

100 Arbor Ave. *(402) 873-9347.* *9am–5pm Mon–Sat, noon–5pm Sun.* *Jan 1, Thanksgiving, Dec 25.* www.adflcc.com

## Omaha 18

*335,700.* *1001 Farnam St, Ste 200, (402) 444-4660.* www.visitomaha.com

OMAHA EVOLVED from a rough-and-tumble Missouri River town and outfitting post into a major railroad terminus with the construction of the transcontinental railroad in 1868 *(see p571)*. The restored Old Market warehouse district just south of downtown preserves the city's historical roots. Its old commercial buildings and cobblestone streets are now home to some of the region's best restaurants, bookstores, and antique shops. A few blocks south, the city's landmark 1931 Art Deco Union Station has been refurbished and converted into the **Durham Western Heritage Museum**. This splendid local history museum features displays on Omaha's railroad and transportation heritage.

Just west of downtown is the pink marble **Joslyn Art Museum**, a Smithsonian affiliate and the crown jewel of Omaha's cultural attractions. The museum features 19th and 20th century European and American art. It also is a treasure trove of Western American art, with paintings, sculpture, and photographs by George Catlin, Frederic Remington, George Caleb Bingham, and Edward S. Curtis. The centerpiece of its Western collection are the watercolors and prints by Swiss artist Karl Bodmer *(see p438)*, who documented life on the upper Plains when he traveled across North America with German naturalist, Prince Maximilian of Wied, in 1833.

North of downtown, the **Great Plains Black History Museum** relates the rarely told story of African-American migration and settlement on the Great Plains, beginning with the Exoduster group of freed slaves that left Reconstruction-ravaged Tennessee in the 1870s to homestead in Kansas. The **Mormon Trail Center**, about 5 miles (8 km) to the north, commemorates the 1846-48 migration of Mormons from the Midwest to Utah *(see p519)*. Located on the pioneers' late-19th-century Winter Quarters campsite, an informative visitor center provides background on the religious persecution that led to the migration. It also displays a reconstructed Mormon Trail handcart and wagon.

### Durham Western Heritage Museum

801 S 10th St. *(402) 444-5071.* *10am–5pm Tue–Sat, 1–5pm Sun.* www.dwhm.org

### Joslyn Art Museum

2200 Dodge St. *(402) 342-3300.* *10am–4pm Tue–Sat, noon–4pm Sun.* www.josyln.org

Art Deco façade of Omaha's Durham Western Heritage Museum

# Iowa

STRETCHING FROM THE Mississippi on its eastern border to the Missouri River on the west, Iowa offers seemingly endless vistas of rolling hills, lush cornfields, old-fashioned barns, and clapboard, country churches. It is one of the nation's largest agricultural producers, with a rich stock of tidy, hard-working farming communities. These are the images that make the state a perfect setting for Hollywood movies seeking to capture a nearly vanished rural America. Iowa also has a handful of lively cities, including the state capital Des Moines, with its excellent art and history museums.

## Sioux City 19

*85,000.* *801 4th St, (800) 593-2228.* www.siouxcitytourism.com

A BUSY RAILROAD center and Missouri River port, Sioux City sits on the northern cusp of Iowa's green, shaggy Loess Hills. This unique ecosystem is comprehensively explained at the **Dorothy Pecaut Nature Center** in Stone State Park, about 3 miles (5 km) north of the city. The northern tip of the 200-mile (320-km) Loess Hills Scenic Byway, which traverses the hills, can be accessed from the park. The park also has one of the state's few surviving stands of tallgrass prairie and a network of bike and hiking trails.

Just south of downtown, the **Floyd Monument** standing on a loess bluff marks the 1804 burial of Sargent Charles Floyd, who was a member of Lewis and Clark's *(see p570)* Corps of Discovery. Floyd was the first and only member to die on the transcontinental journey of the three-year long expedition. The city's newest attraction, the **Lewis & Clark Interpretative Center**, opened along the riverfront in September 2002.

**Floyd Monument**

**Dorothy Pecaut Nature Center**
4500 Sioux River Rd. *(712) 258-0838.* *9am–5pm Tue–Sat, 1–5pm Sun.* *public hols.*

## Des Moines 20

*199,005.* *405 6th Ave, (800) 451-2625.* www.seedesmoines.com

THE STATE CAPITAL draws its name from French voyageurs who explored the Raccoon and Des Moines River Valleys, calling the latter *La Rivière des Moinesk*, "River of the Monks." The city is now an important agricultural and entertainment center and home of the massive Iowa State Fair, which lures more than a million visitors every August.

Dominating the area east of downtown is the gold-leafed central dome of the **Iowa State Capitol**. Nearby is the **Iowa Historical Building**, with its displays on the state's Native American, geological, and cultural history. West of the Capitol, the Eliel Saarinen-designed **Des Moines Art Center** exhibits an impressive collection of paintings by Henri Matisse, Jasper Johns, Andy Warhol, and Georgia O'Keeffe. The center's modern sculpture gallery was designed by I.M. Pei.

**Des Moines Art Center**
4700 Grand Ave. *(515) 277-4405.* *11am–4pm Tue–Sat, 11am–9pm Thu, noon– 4pm Sun.* www.desmoinesartcenter.org

**ENVIRONS:** Winterset, located about 35 miles (56 km) to the south, is the attractive seat of **Madison County** and birthplace of Hollywood Western star John Wayne. The four-room house where the actor grew up is a much-visited museum today. The local Chamber of Commerce provides a map of the five covered bridges that inspired author Robert Waller's famous 1992 novel, *The Bridges of Madison County.*

**A typical family home in the Amana Colonies**

## Amana Colonies 2

*39 38th Ave, Amana, (800) 579-2294.* www.amanacolonies.com

THE SEVEN Amana Colonies along the Iowa River were settled in the 1850s by the Inspirationists, a mainly German religious sect. The colonists prospered, building a profitable woolen mill and a series of communal kitchens, shops, and factories. In 1932, residents voted to end their communal lifestyle setting up a profit-sharing society instead.

One of the community businesses has since evolved into the Amana appliance manufacturer, while the 185 Amana Woolen Mill is the state's only woolen mill still in operation. The **Museums of the Amana Heritage Society** commemorate the success of the colonies' enterprises and its unique history in five separate museums.

**Museums of the Amana Heritage Society**
*(319) 622-3567.* *May–Oct: 10am–5pm Mon–Sat, noon–5pm S* www.amanaheritage.org

## edar Rapids ㉒

108,800. 119 1st Ave (800) 735-5557.
www.cedar-rapids.com

HIS TOWN'S downtown straddles the Cedar River. e Iowa artist Grant Wood ed in Cedar Rapids for ıch of his adult life and veloped a Regionalist style at celebrated the people d landscapes of his home ıte. The **Cedar Rapids useum of Art** has one of e country's largest collection Wood's paintings, including e well-known *Young Corn*. The recently renovated story Center details the ea's early history, while the **tional Czech and Slovak useum** celebrates the city's ge Czechoslovak immigrant pulation. Czech Village, a rridor along 16th Avenue V, is still lined with shops lling kolaches, babovkas, d other Czech delicacies.

## ubuque ㉓

57,500. 300 Main St, 0) 798-8844.
www.dubuquechamber.com

OWA'S OLDEST CITY was established in 1788 by a ench voyageur, Julian ıbuque. During the 19th ntury, the city's noveau he constructed luxurious mes atop the bluffs ringing e city. These citizens rode and from downtown, 189 ft 7 m) below, via the **Fenelon

**View of Dubuque from the Fenelon Place Elevator**

Place Elevator**, an incline railway that is a major tourist attraction today.

The city's main attraction is the **Mississippi River Museum**, a riverfront complex with exhibits on the mighty river's history and ecology. A series of aquariums replicate the habitat and ecosystem of the country's different rivers.

## Quad Cities (Davenport) ㉔

102,000. 2021 River Dr, Moline, Il, (800) 747-7800.
www.visitquadcities.com

DAVENPORT IS ONE of the four Mississippi River communities that comprise the sprawling 400,000-person "Quad Cities" area on both sides of the Iowa and Illinois border. It is the only city not blocked off from the river by flood control walls. The excellent **Figge Art Museum** west of downtown has one of the better collections of early-20th-century American Regionalist paintings. It displays works by Missouri's Thomas Hart Benton and Kansas-born John Steuart Curry, as well as the only painted self-portrait of Grant Wood. The **Putnam Museum** charts the early history of the Mississippi River Valley and includes an aquarium. Its newest addition is the IMAX® Theater at the Putnam.

**Figge Art Museum**
225 W 2nd St.
(563) 326-7804.
11am–5pm Tue–Sun.
Mon, public hols.
www.figgeartmuseum.org

## Iowa City ㉕

62,220. 900 1st Ave, Coralville, (800) 283-6592.
www.iowacitycoralville.org

EASYGOING Iowa City is home to the 1,900-acre (769-ha) University of Iowa campus and the school's noteworthy American Writers' Workshop. The town served as the territorial and state capital until 1857 and the Old Capitol, now the **Old Capitol Museum**, is on campus.

About 10 miles (16 km) east of Iowa City is the **Herbert Hoover National Historic Site**. The president's boyhood cottage has been restored, along with a number of buildings constructed by the local Quaker community.

**ats sailing below a bridge that spans the mighty Mississippi River, Davenport**

# Missouri

THE MISSOURI RIVER AND THE I-70 Interstate Highway bisect the state of Missouri, linking its two largest cities – St. Louis and Kansas City – and providing quick access to the centrally located state capital of Jefferson City. In the southwestern corner of Missouri, the rugged Ozark Mountain region is veined with beautiful streams and rivers, making the area a popular camping and canoeing destination.

**Gateway Arch, symbol of the city of St. Louis**

## St. Louis 26

*348,189.* 308 *Washington Ave, (314) 241-1764.* www.explorestlouis.com

LOCATED JUST south of the point where the Missouri empties into the Mississippi River, St. Louis has been one of the country's most active crossroads. Founded by a French fur trader in 1764, this frontier city became a part of the US as a result of the Louisiana Purchase in 1803. It soon established itself as the "Gateway to the West," as steamboats chugged up the Missouri River into territories opened up by the Lewis and Clark expedition.

### Gateway Arch-Jefferson National Expansion Memorial

Memorial Dr & Market St. *(314) 655-1600.* *9am–6pm daily.* *Jan 1, Thanksgiving, Dec 25.* **Old Courthouse** 11 N 4th St. *(314) 655-1700.* *8am–4:30pm daily.* *Jan 1, Thanksgiving, Dec 25.* www.nps.gov/jeff **Museum of Westward Expansion** *(314) 655-1600.* *Jun–Sep: 8am–10pm; Oct–May: 9am–6pm.* www.stlouisarch.com

Completed in 1965 on the site of fur trader Pierre Laclede's original 1764 settlement, Eero Saarinen's 630-ft (192-m) tall **Gateway Arch** symbolizes the city's role as a commercial and cultural gateway between the settled eastern US and the wide-open lands to the west. The excellent **Museum of Westward Expansion** at the base of the arch features several detailed exhibits on the 1803–1806 expedition by the explorers Lewis and Clark *(see p570)* and other 19th-century expeditions. The museum also includes two movie theaters. Elevator-like tram rides transport visitors to the top of the arch, where picturesque views of the surrounding city and Illinois farmlands make the cramped quarters well worth the one-hour round trip.

**Scott trial plaque in the Old Courthouse**

The stately, domed **Old Courthouse** (1839–62) is one of the oldest buildings in the city of St. Louis. This Greek Revival structure was the site of two of the initial trials in the landmark Dred Scott case, which resulted in an 1857 decision by the US Supreme Court stating that African Americans were not citizens of the country and had no rights under the laws of the US. The decision overturned an earlier suit by Scott, an African-American slave who had returned to St. Louis with his owners after nine years in free states, to win his freedom. It also deepened the sectional and racial differences that finally erupted in the American Civil War that lasted for four years (from 1861 to 1865) and went on to claim many thousands of lives.

A museum that stands within the Old Courthouse recounts the events of the famous Dred Scott trial for the benefit of visitors and depicts what life must have been like for ordinary people living in 18th-century St. Louis under the yoke of French and Spanish rule.

### Laclede's Landing

Morgan St & Lucas St between I-70 & the Mississippi River. *(314) 241-5875.* *area open year-round; individual restaurant and club hours vary.* www.lacledeslanding.org

This vibrant restaurant and entertainment district consists of several blocks of restored 19th-century cotton, tobacco, and food warehouses that lie along the riverfront. The popular restaurants and blues clubs are known to attract large crowds, especially during the annual Big Muddy Blues Festival during the Labor Day weekend. The tall, six-story, cast-iron Raeder Place Building located on 719-727 N 1st Street), was built in 1873 and is one of the best-preserved warehouses in St. Louis. The 1874 Eads Bridge defines the Landing's southern boundary.

**Raeder Building in Laclede's Landing area**

**Forest Park**

**Louis Art Museum** 1 Fine Arts
(314) 721-0072. 10am–
m Tue–Thu & Sat–Sun, 10am–9pm
Jan 1, Thanksgiving, Dec 25.
www.slam.org

**issouri History Museum** Jefferson
emorial Bldg. (314) 746-4599.
10am–6pm Wed–Mon, 10pm–
m Tue. www.mohistory.org

esigned in 1876 by German-ained landscape architect aximilian Kern, this 1,300-re (526-ha) park is one of e nation's largest urban een spaces. The 1904 orld's Fair, known officially the Louisiana Purchase xposition, was held on the ounds, drawing nearly 20 illion visitors. After the fair, early all the grand Beaux ts structures designed by ass Gilbert were demol-hed. The only exception, e Palace of Fine Arts, is w home to the **St. Louis rt Museum**. Its sweeping llection of American art cludes paintings by issourians George Caleb ngham and Thomas Hart enton, and artists Georgia 'Keeffe, Winslow Homer, d Andy Warhol. The **issouri History Museum** s on the site of the main trance to the 1904 fair. The eaux Arts building houses pressive exhibits depicting the multicultural history of St. Louis. Its holdings include an original Louisiana Purchase transfer document, a replica of aviator Charles Lindberg's 1927 *Spirit of St. Louis* airplane (re-opening in May 2004), and extensive displays on the World's Fair. An interactive arts gallery explores the city's rich musical history.

**Brick exterior of Anheuser-Busch Brewery**

**Anheuser-Busch Brewery**

1127 Pestalozzi St. *(314) 577-2626. Jun–Aug: 9am–5pm Mon–Sat, 11:30am–5pm Sun; Sep–May: 9am–4pm Mon–Sat, 11:30am–4pm Sun.*
www.budweisertours.com

The world's largest brewery, Anheuser-Busch, was founded in 1860 by entrepreneurial German immigrants. Its famous trademark Budweiser lager brand is still very popular. The complex contains many of the company's 19th-century brick structures. Tours include a visit to the famous Clydesdale horse stables.

**Missouri Botanical Garden**

4344 Shaw Blvd. *(800) 642-8842, (314) 577-9400. 9am–5pm Sun–Tue & Thu–Fri, 7am–7pm Wed & Sat. Dec 25.*
www.mobot.org

This garden was created in 1859 by a wealthy St. Louis businessman on the grounds of his estate. The grounds contain an English garden, a Japanese garden, as well as a scented garden for the visually impaired. The geodesic domed Climatron® has exotic birds and over 1,200 species of tropical plants, including banana trees, orchids, and epiphytes.

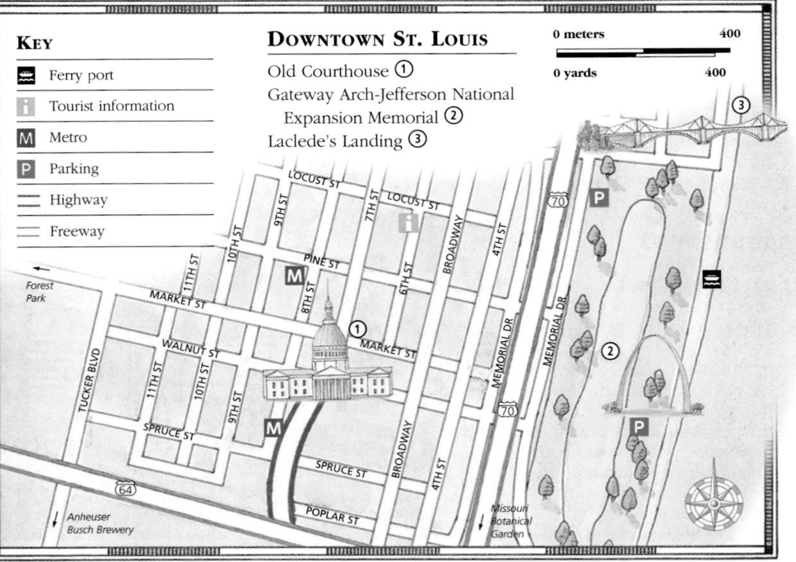

The Classic Revival Missouri State Capitol, Jefferson City

## Jefferson City 27

*40,000.* *213 Adams St, (800) 769-4183.* www.visitjeffersoncity.com

SOON AFTER ITS founding as the state capital in 1821, Jefferson City grew into a busy Missouri River port. The **Jefferson Landing State Historic Site** preserves many structures from its original waterfront, including the 1839 Lohman Building. The Classic Revival **Missouri State Capitol**, completed in 1924, now houses the Missouri State Museum and a mural by Thomas Hart Benton. His bold 1935 *A Social History of the State of the Missouri* was criticized by Missouri's conservative power brokers for its stark depiction of the state's widespread poverty and seamier underclass.

### Jefferson Landing State Historic Site

*(573) 751-2854.* *10am–4pm Tue–Sat.* *Jan 1, Thnksg., Dec 25.*

## Branson 28

*6,000.* *269 State Hwy 248, (800) 214-3661.* www.explorebranson.com

THIS SLEEPY Ozark Mountain resort was radically transformed over the past 40 years, thanks to the phenomenal success of several family-oriented tourist attractions. A musical pageant revolving around the Ozarks-based novel, *The Shepherd of the Hills*, was one of the area's first big hits. It is still staged every night in a picturesque, outdoor arena attached to a working, mountain farm.

**The Silver Dollar City** amusement park features high-tech roller coasters and water rides in a 19th-century Ozark pioneer setting, about 9 miles (14 km) west of town. The area's biggest draws are Branson's nightly music programs, presented at more than 30 alcohol-free performance venues crowded together on the "The Strip" (Route 76 W).

### Shepherd of the Hills Homestead

5586 W Hwy 76, 2 miles W of Branson. *(800) 653-6288.* *May–Oct: 9am–4pm.* www.oldmatt.com

## Kansas City 29

*435,100.* *1100 Main St, (800) 767-7700.* www.visitkc.com

A DELIGHTFUL study in contrasts, Kansas City is rife with imagery associated with the Wild West. This vibrant city now contains beautifully landscaped parks and boulevards, sophisticated museums, fine public architecture, and high-end urban retail districts.

On the bluffs overlooking the Missouri River, just north of downtown, the **City Market** sits on the site of the town's original Westport Landing business district. The riverfront's 19th-century brick and cast-iron warehouses were converted into loft apartments and restaurants i the 1970s. Today, the 1930s City Market building houses an eclectic collection of shops, farmers' markets, reta outlets, and the Arabia Steamboat Museum, which displays artifacts salvaged from a 1856 wreck.

Northeast of the City Market, the **Kansas City Museum** is housed in a 50-room mansion in one of the city's most exclusive 19th-century neighborhoods. Its collections trace the city's evolution from a fur trading post into a powerful railroa and agricultural center. Exhibits include a replica of fur trader François Choteau' original 1821 Westport Landing post and a 1910 corner drugstore with a working soda fountain.

The newly minted "**Cross-roads District**" refers to the area stretching south of downtown to Penn Valley Park and Crown Center, roughly bounded on the eas and west by Main Street and Broadway. The city's two most prominent architectura landmarks, **Union Station** and **Liberty Memorial** are located here. The magnifice Beaux Arts Union Station, built in 1914, was one of the country's busiest and most glamorous railroad terminals It rose to national prominen in 1933 when outlaw Pretty Boy Floyd gunned down an accomplice and several polic officers in what became known as the Union Station Massacre. Renovated after years of neglect, the station

Kansas City skyline with Union Station in the foreground

rawling lawn of the Nelson-Atkins Art Museum, Kansas City

ɔw a local history museum, ildren's science museum, ıd restaurant complex. The recently restored 217-ft 6-m) Liberty Memorial ˈerlooks the old train depot ı the grassy bluffs of Penn ılley Park. It houses the ıtion's only World War I ıuseum. The "Torch of ɔerty" observation tower fers a sweeping view of the y. To its south, the **Hall-ark Visitors Center** esents the history of allmark, the well-known eeting card company.

Southeast of ɔwntown, the **ßth & Vine eritage istrict** com-emorates the y's rich rican-nerican heritage. the 1930s, all-ght jazz clubs showcased e innovative riffs of local ısicians such as Count ısie, Lester Young, and ıarlie Parker. This was ınsas City's heyday, when ıder the free-wheeling ıle" of Tom Pendergast, a cal concrete contractor, it as known as a "wide-open" wn that stayed awake all ght. Refurbished to form the ıckdrop for Robert Altman's ˈ96 film *Kansas City*, the strict's premier attractions clude the **American Jazz useum**, which re-creates e city's swinging jazz era, ıd the **Negro Leagues aseball Museum**, which ɔnors talented African-nerican baseball players ho toiled in low-paid ɔscurity for all-black teams the US, Canada, and Latin America. In 1945, Kansas City Monarchs shortstop Jackie Robinson broke the color barrier by signing with the all-white Brooklyn Dodgers in the National League.

Once an outfitting post for travelers on the Santa Fe and Oregon Trails, the village of **Westport** became part of Kansas City in 1899. In the retail district along Westport Road, shops and restaurants now occupy some of the city's oldest buildings, such as Kelly's Westport Inn, an 1837 tavern. Several blocks south of Westport, the **Country Club Plaza**, the nation's first planned suburban shopping district, was designed in 1922. To its east, the **Nelson-Atkins Art Museum** has a stellar collection of paintings by Missouri's George Caleb Bingham and Thomas Hart Benton. The outdoor sculpture garden features 13 exclusive works by British artist Henry Moore.

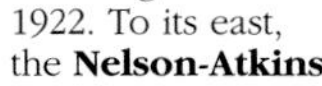

Mural at the American Jazz Museum

**American Jazz Museum**
1616 E 18th St. (816) 474-8463. *9am–6pm Tue–Sat, noon–6pm Sun.* *public hols.* www.americanjazzmuseum.com

**Nelson-Atkins Art Museum**
45th St & Oak St. *(816) 751-1278.* *10am–4pm Tue–Fri, 10am–5pm Sat, noon–5pm Sun.* *public hols.* www.nelson-atkins.org

**Kansas City Museum**
3218 Gladstone Blvd. *(816) 483-8300.* *9:30am–6pm Mon–Sat, noon–4:30pm Sun.* *Jan 1, Thanksgiving, Dec 25.*

**Environs:** The suburb of **Independence**, 15 miles (24 km) east of downtown Kansas City, has one of the country's best westward expansion museums, the National Frontier Trails Center. It was also the home of Harry S. Truman, 33rd US president. His simple downtown home is now a national historic site.

## St. Joseph 30

*72,000.* *109 S 4th St, (800) 785-0360.* www.stjomo.com

Like many Missouri River communities, St. Joseph grew from a fur trading post into a wagon train outfitting center. Its position as the nation's westernmost railroad terminal instigated local entrepreneurs to launch the Pony Express in the mid-1800s. This service sought to deliver mail from St. Joseph to Sacramento – a 1,966-mile (3,214-km) trip – in less than 10 days. Informative displays in the **Pony Express Museum** relate the story of this short-lived enterprise, while the Patee House Museum preserves an 1858 hotel that served as the headquarters of the Express. On its grounds is the house where the notorious Missouri outlaw, Jesse James, was killed by one of his former gang members in 1882.

**Pony Express Museum**
914 Penn St. *(800) 530-5930.* *9am–5pm Mon–Sat, 1–5pm Sun.* *Jan 1, Thanksg., Dec 24–25 & 31.* www.ponyexpress.org

Bronze statue of a Pony Express rider, St. Joseph

# Kansas

FOR MOST AMERICANS, Kansas conjures up images of rolling wheat fields, flatlands, sunflowers, and scenes from the 1939 film *The Wizard of Oz*. The real Kansas, however, is infinitely more interesting, both historically and geographically. Reminders of the state's turbulent 19th-century history as an Indian resettlement territory, anti-slavery battleground, and cattle drive destination can be seen frequently as one traverses the principal Interstate Highways, I-70 and I-35, and the meandering backroads. Kansas is also home to two of the country's few remaining stands of unbroken, tallgrass prairie, preserved in the undulating Flint Hills, just south of the lovely Kansas State University town of Manhattan.

**Entrance to the Kansas Natural History Museum, Lawrence**

## Lawrence 31

*65,600.* *734 Vermont Ave, (888) 529-5267.*
www.visitlawrence.com

FOUNDED BY New England abolitionists in 1854, Lawrence's strong "free state" leanings made it a target for Missouri's pro-slavery "border ruffians," only 40 miles (64 km) to the east. The attractive, downtown retail district is lined with 19th-century stone and brick commercial buildings, reminders of the city's massive reconstruction drive after a destructive 1863 raid led by Confederate guerrilla William Quantrill.

A restored 1889 railroad depot houses the **Lawrence Visitor Information Center**, which relates key episodes in the city's history and provides information about the University of Kansas campus, just southwest of downtown. Situated astride a hill, known locally as Mount Oread, the campus includes the **Kansas Natural History Museum** and the **Spencer Museum of Art**. Its broad sampling of American and contemporary art makes this is one of the finest university art museums in the United States.

**Spencer Museum of Art**
1301 Mississippi St. *(785) 864-4710.* *10am–5pm Tue–Sat (until 9pm Thu), noon–5pm Sun.* *public hols.* www.spencerart.ku.edu

## Topeka 32

*125,000.* *1275 SW Topeka Blvd, (800) 235-1030.*
www.topekacvb.org

A QUIET GOVERNMENT center, Topeka's most significant historical attraction is Kansas Regionalist painter John Steuart Curry's mural in the **Kansas State Capitol**. His mural, *The Settlement of Kansas*, depicts abolitionist John Brown in a dramatic confrontation with pro-slavery forces that threatened to make Kansas a slave state in the 1850s. More background on this tense period and the state's settlement can be found at the superb **Kansas History Center**, to the city's west.

**Kansas History Center**
6425 SW 6th Ave.
*(785) 272-8681.*
*9am–5pm Tue–Sat, 1–5pm Sun.*
*public hols.*
www.kshs.org

## Flint Hills 33

*Manhattan CVB, 501 Poyntz Ave, (800) 759-0134.*
www.manhattancvb.org

THE SHAGGY, rolling Flint Hills are among Kansas' most spectacular natural features. The best way to explore the area is to drive along the scenic 85-mile (13 km) stretch of Route 177, running south from the university town of **Manhattan**, across I-70, and down to Cassody at I-35. About 6 mil (10 km) southeast of Manhattan is **Konza Prairie**, the country's largest remaini parcel of virgin tallgrass prairie. The 8,600-acre (3,48 ha) preserve contains a varie of spectacular hiking trails th wind up and down the chert studded hills, providing awe-inspiring views of the surrounding landscape.

Route 177 intersects US 56 at **Council Grove** (40 miles, 64 km south of Manhattan). The town takes its name fro a huge oak tree, the Council Oak, which commemorates the spot where the Kansa an Osage tribes agreed to allow the old Santa Fe Trail to pass through their ancestral lands The **Kaw Mission School**, now a state historic site, was set up by the Methodists fro 1851 to 1854 in an attempt t "westernize" male children from the Kaw (also known a Kansa or Kanza) tribe. This experiment did not succeed. The site now displays artifac from the Mission school.

**The red-roofed Chase County Courthouse, Cottonwood Falls, Flint Hills**

…kers at the Tallgrass Prairie National Preserve, Flint Hills

…e **Tallgrass Prairie** …tional Preserve, 20 miles …2 km) south of Council …ove, protects what remains …an 11,000-acre (4451-ha) …h-century cattle ranch. A …ing trail leads visitors …m the ranch's …cond Empire main …use through large …nds of native prairie. …e ranching commu…y of **Cottonwood** …**lls**, located about 3 …les (5 km) south on …ute 177, contains …other impressive …cond Empire struc…e. Built in 1873, the …l-roofed, limestone …**ase County Court**…**use** is the oldest …l in use in Kansas.

**Konza Prairie**
…Dowell Creek Rd. (785) 587-…41. *sunrise-sunset daily.*
www.naturalkansas.org

**Tallgrass Prairie** …**tional Preserve**
…y 177, 2 miles (3 km) N of …ong City. *(620) 273-8494.*
*9am–4pm daily.*
www.parktrust.org

## …ichita 34

*304,000. 100 S …in St, (800) 288-9424.*
www.visitwichita.com

Wichita developed in 1865 as a lawless railhead …wn, where cowboys driving …ttle north from Texas on the …isholm Trail *(see p481)* …ould stop to let off steam in …e city's rowdy saloons and …othels. Those early cattle …nds would not recognize …day's Wichita, which has …own into a busy aircraft manufacturing and oil refining center. The town's colorful past is recreated at the **Old Cowtown Museum**. The original jail and period houses, as well as stores and saloons from surrounding rural communities are on display here. To its southeast is the **Mid-America All-Indian Center**, which depicts the 19th-century Great Plains lifestyles of the Kiowa, Cheyenne, and Lakota tribes. The main feature in this center is a reconstructed village featuring a winter lodge built of local materials such as grasses and wood.

Artifact, Indian Center Museum, Wichita

**Old Cowtown Museum**
1871 Sim Park Dr. *(316) 264-0671.*
*Apr–Oct: 10am–5pm Mon–Sat, noon–5pm Sun.*
www.old-cowtown.org

**Mid-America All-Indian Center**
650 N Seneca St.
*(316) 262-5221. 10am–5pm Tue–Sat, Apr– Dec: 1–5pm Sun.*
*public hols.*
www.theindiancenter.com

## Dodge City 35

*21,100. 400 W Wyatt Earp Blvd, (800) 653-9378.*
www.visitdodgecity.org

The Wild West's two most colorful characters, lawmen Wyatt Earp and Bat Masterson, earned their tough reputations in Dodge City during its brief but boisterous heyday. Between 1872 and 1884, the town flourished as a High Plains buffalo-hunting, cattle-driving, and railroad center. The **Boot Hill Museum** re-creates the infamous Front Street strip of saloons and burlesque houses that earned Dodge City the sobriquet of "Hell on the Plains." On the museum grounds is Boot Hill cemetery, where many gunfight victims were buried.

Before hordes of cowboys and gun-toting buffalo hunters came to town, Dodge City was just another stop on the Santa Fe Trail. Ruts from the old wagon trail can still be seen 9 miles (14 km) west of Dodge City along US 50 and at the **Fort Larned National Historic Site**, 55 miles (88 km) east of Dodge City. The site contains several restored original sandstone structures from the US Army fort that protected travelers along the Santa Fe Trail from 1859 to 1878.

**Boot Hill Museum**
Front St & 5th Sts. *(620) 227-8188. Jun–Aug: 8am–8pm daily, Sep–May: 9am–5pm Mon-Fri, 1–5pm Sun. Jan 1, Thanksgiving, Dec 25.*
www.boothill.org

Fort Larned National Historic Site, east of Dodge City

# Oklahoma

**Delaware tribe mask**

Bordered by six states, Oklahoma is a cultural, geographical, and historical crossroads, where jagged mountain ranges and High Plains mesas merge with forests, flatland wheat fields, and vast grassy ranges. The state has the nation's largest Native American population – more than 250,000 people representing 67 tribes – as a result of forced 19th-century migrations to the region, then known as the Indian Territory. Several "land runs" between 1889 and 1895 brought a huge influx of white and African-American settlers to this area, which joined the US in 1907 after oil was discovered.

***Praying Hands* at Oral Roberts University, Tulsa**

## Bartlesville 36

*34,300.* *201 SW Keeler, (800) 364-8708.* www.bartlesville.com

The state's first commercial oil well was drilled here in 1897, kicking off a large-scale oil boom. A replica of the original well, the Nellie Johnstone #1, now stands as a memorial in a downtown park. Today, the city's largest employer is still the Conoco-Phillips company, founded in 1917 as Phillips Petroleum, by two speculators from Iowa.

**Environs:** Frank Phillips's extensive 3,600-acre (1456-ha) rural estate, **Woolaroc Ranch**, is located 12 miles (19 km) southwest of Bartlesville. The picturesque ranch includes a superb Western art collection, the Native American Heritage Center, and a wildlife preserve. About 45 miles (72 km) northwest of Bartlesville (by way of Pawhuska) is the Nature Conservancy's **Tallgrass Prairie Preserve**. In this vast expanse of rolling prairie, a herd of bison graze among stands of big bluestem grasses, coneflowers, and blazing star wildflowers.

### Woolaroc Ranch

Rte 123, 12 miles (19 km) SW of Bartlesville. *(918) 336-0307.* *Jun–Sep: 10am–5pm daily; Oct–May: 10am–5pm Tue–Sun.* *Thanksgiving, Dec 25.* www.woolaroc.org

## Tulsa 37

*367,300.* *Williams Center Tower 2, 2 W 7th St, (800) 558-3311.* www.visittulsa.com

Originally a railroad town, Tulsa prospered after the discovery of oil in 1901. Fortunes were made literally overnight, leading to the construction of Art Deco commercial buildings, roads, and bridges across the Arkansas River. Although Tulsa is still a major oil center, it also contains numerous man-made lakes, parks, and Arkansas River bike trails. Its top attraction is the **Thomas Gilcrease Institute**, a comprehensive art museum founded by a wealthy local oilman. Its collection includes a wide range of Native and Western American paintings by such well known artists as George Catlin and Frederic Remington. The city's most popular roadside sight is the Prayer Tower Visitor Center at Tulsa's **Oral Roberts University**. The 200-ft (60-m) glass and steel tower includes an 80-ft (24-m) pair of hands folded in prayer.

### Thomas Gilcrease Institute

1400 N Gilcrease Museum Rd, off US 64. *(918) 596-2700.* *10am–4pm Tue–Sun.* *Mon & Dec 25.* www.gilcrease.org

## Tahlequah 38

*10,400.* *123 E Delaware (800) 456-4860.* www.okchamber.com

The capital of the Cherokee Nation, Tahlequah lies in the eastern Oklahoma Ozark Mountain foothills, the tribe's home since 1839. The city preserves several late 19th-century buildings, including the prison and the Cherokee National Capitol Building.

Of primary interest here is the **Cherokee Heritage Center**. Its attractions include a village dating from the 1875–90 Indian Territory era and a re-creation of a 17th-century settlement from the tribe's ancestral lands in the

**Carriage on display at Woolaroc Ranch Museum, near Bartlesville**

**rth lodges in the Cherokee Heritage Center, Tahlequah**

ɔpalachian Mountains. :hibits at the Cherokee ıtional Museum chronicle e tribe's forced march along e "Trail of Tears" from ɔrth Carolina to Oklahoma the 1830s *(see p438)*. This ıgic event is also dramatized 'ery year in June.

**' Cherokee Heritage :nter**
. 62, 3 miles (5 km) S of Tahlequah. *(888) 999-6007.* *10am–5pm ɔn–Sat, 1–5pm Sun.* *public ls.*
] www.cherokeeheritage.org

## )klahoma City 39

*444,700.* *189 W eridan, (800) 225-5652.*
] www.visitokc.com

)KLAHOMA CITY was built and founded in a single ıy, April 22, 1889, as part of .e first Oklahoma Territory land rush. Over 10,000 land claims were filed on that day, creating a city out of thin air. The city became the state capital in 1910 and saw its first oil strike in 1928. Today, there are more than 2,000 still-active oil wells, including one on the grounds of the Oklahoma State Capitol, within the city limits.

The **Oklahoma State Museum of History** chronicles the state's intimate relationship with oil, as well as its pre-settlement history. The **National Cowboy Museum** contains one of the country's most comprehensive collections of Western art. Among its exhibits are works by such artists as Charles Russell, and Albert Bierstadt. It also features a giant statue of the famed Wild West figure Buffalo Bill and a collection of Western actor John Wayne memorabilia. On a more somber note, the city has paid homage to the 168 people killed in the tragic 1995 Federal Building bombing incident *(see p438)* with the dignified **Oklahoma City National Memorial**. The 3.3-acre (1.3-ha) downtown memorial includes a museum, a reflecting pool, and a 60-year-old American elm tree.

**National Cowboy Museum**
1700 NE 63rd St. *(405) 478-2250.* *9am–5pm daily.* *Jan 1, Thanksgiving, Dec 25.*
W www.nationalcowboymuseum.com

**Oklahama State Museum of History**
2100 Lincoln Blvd. *(405) 521-2491.* *8am–5pm Mon–Sat.* *public hols.*
W www.ok-history.mus.ok.us

**The reflecting pool at the Oklahoma City National Memorial**

### OLD ROUTE 66: THE HISTORIC "MOTHER ROAD"

Route 66 has been immortalized as the "mother road" traveled by the migrant Oklahoma family in author John Steinbeck's 1939 novel, *The Grapes of Wrath*, as they fled the drought-stricken Dust Bowl on the way to California. This historic highway, charted in 1926, was the first to link Chicago to Los Angeles. Old Route 66 heads southwest from the state's northeastern corner to its western border with Texas, meandering along the original two-lane alignment much of the way, frequently within sight of the modern interstates, I-44 and I-40 that parallel its original route. West of Oklahoma City, the route runs alongside I-40, with several sections of old road veering off the Interstate. The **Oklahoma Route 66 Museum** in Clinton sits across from a Best Western Motel where Elvis Presley slept on four separate occasions. The recently renovated museum has one of the country's best Route 66 collections. The **National Route 66 Museum** in Elk City (30 miles/48 km west of Clinton) sports a smaller but equally engaging array of exhibits, including a pickup truck modeled after the one used in director John Ford's 1940 film adaptation of *The Grapes of Wrath*. Other sights along the route include the **Totem Pole Park** (about 4 miles/6 km east of Foyil), and the **Will Rogers Memorial Museum** at Claremore (27 miles/43 km east of Tulsa). Oklahoma's favorite son, humorist Will Rogers, was born in a log cabin in nearby Oologah. The museum relates the life story of this colorful actor and newspaper columnist, and screens several of his films.

**Totem Pole Park**

# Practical Information

UP-TO-DATE INFORMATION is essential when planning an itinerary across the Great Plains, where cities and attractions are often separated by miles and miles of rolling prairie. A region of small towns, wide-open spaces, and distant horizons, the beautiful landscape of the Great Plains draws visitors searching for a taste of wholesome Americana. The best time to plan a trip is from mid-April through late October, but bear in mind that many of the historical sights are open only from Memorial Day (end May) to Labor Day (end August).

## Tourist Information

TRAVELERS ENTERING the Great Plains via a principal Interstate Highway are greeted with signs advertising a state "Welcome Center." These centers provide a full range of tourist information, as well as clean restrooms and free coffee. Most of the region's major airports and train stations have information desks stocked with free brochures and maps. All of the larger cities and smaller towns operate Convention & Visitors' Bureaus, which provide free directories of events, attractions, accommodations, and restaurants, both in print and online.

## Natural Hazards

TORNADOES USUALLY occur during summer, particularly in the eastern portions of Kansas and Oklahoma, called "Tornado Alley." In the event of a tornado warning, travelers should first seek shelter in the basement of a solidly constructed building and then tune into a local radio station for additional information.

## Getting Around

MOST OF THE major cities in the Great Plains have public bus systems that provide affordable but limited service. However, the convenient St. Louis Metrorail system is the only public rail transit system in the region.

## Driving in the Great Plains

DRIVING IS THE best way to explore the region, since most sights are usually situated far away from each other. Thus certain precautions are necessary to ensure a safe journey. Seat belts are a must for drivers and front-seat passengers in all the states. Most states also require seat belts for back-seat passengers. Child seats are also mandatory, but age restrictions may vary from one state to another. Motorcyclists are required to wear helmets in all of the states except Iowa which has no restrictions.

Speed limits vary but are usually between 70–75 mph (112–120 km/h) on Interstat Highways, which are locate outside crowded urban area Radar detectors are permitte in all the states.

## Etiquette

GREAT PLAINS residents ten to be friendly and polit Drivers on the empty back roads usually acknowledge oncoming car or truck by raising one or two fingers o of the steering wheel in a modified version of a wave. The polite response is to of the same in return.

## Festivals

THE GREAT PLAINS states stag a wide range of annual community, regional, and sta festivals. The largest of the region's many fairs is the **Iow State Fair**, held in August in Des Moines, while one of th country's friendliest Independence Day celebrations takes place in historic Independence, Missouri. All through summer, Native Americans in South Dakota hold several traditional "pow wow" get-togethers. Other summertime events are the historical productions staged by the Great Plains Chautauqua Society.

Musical festivals also abou in the region, with summer blues festivals in Kansas City, St. Louis, and Lincoln vying f top billing. The Walnut Valle bluegrass festival in Winfield, Kansas, and **Woody Guthrie Free Folk Festival** in his hometown Okemah, Oklahoma, are also very popular. Polka music, beer, and German food end the festiva season at Missouri's **Oktoberfest**, in the Missouri River community of Herman

## Sports

MISSOURI HAS a monopoly on professional sports teams in the region, with Kansas City and St. Louis operating the region's only pro baseball (Kansas City

## The Climate of The Great Plains

This is a region of extremes, with hot summers and cold winters, especially in North and South Dakota. The southern states – Kansas, Missouri, and Oklahoma – have a more temperate climate, with milder winters. With its cooler nights and sunny days, June is perfect for touring the region's historic sites. Wildflowers are most colorful in May and September, while October's changing colors make it ideal for scenic drives through the wooded Ozark Mountains.

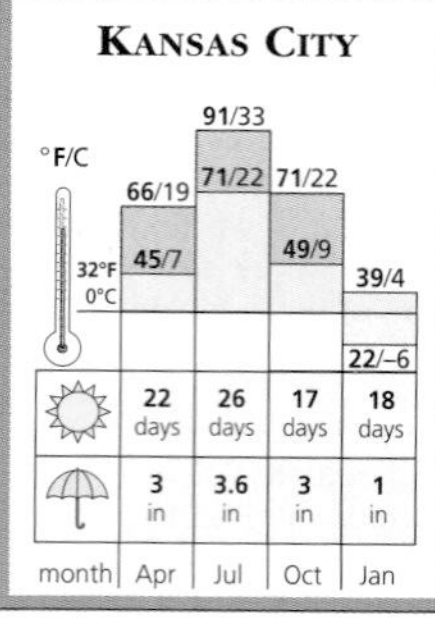

›yals and St. Louis ›rdinals) and football ansas City Chiefs and St. ›uis Rams) franchises. Many the states have minor ague baseball teams as well, oviding travelers with pportunities to watch up-d-coming players in cozier ttings. Iowa is a mecca for inor league fans, with A-vel teams in Burlington, edar Rapids, Clinton, and avenport, and the AAA filiate of the Chicago Cubs Des Moines.

College football and basket-ll are also very popular, rticularly in the southern ains states. The annual **ansas–Kansas State** foot-ll game is the seasonal max to one of college otball's most colorful rastate rivalries.

## Outdoor Activities

N defiance of the stereo-typical image of the Great ains as flat and devoid of pography, hikers, cyclists, d mountain bikers flock to e region's hilly areas. ebraska's Pine Ridge untry, South Dakota's dlands and Black Hills, and e Kansas Flint Hills are vens for campers and kers. The 200-mile (320-km) **aty Trail** bike path winds ong the Missouri River for much of its route. Iowa's seven-day 500-mile **RAGBRAI** cycling event is one of the world's largest, while the August motorcycle rally and race in Sturgis, draws thousands of participants and spectators. Fishing and boat-ing enthusiasts can choose from a range of mainly man-made lakes, such as Nebraska's Lake McConaughy. Streams and rivers in the Missouri Ozarks near Branson provide opportunities to fish and canoe. Visitors should contact the state tourist offices for lists of outfitters for a particular region.

## Entertainment

The busiest live music and theatrical venues in the Great Plains are in Kansas City and St. Louis, with an array of clubs and theaters sprinkled in cities such as Tulsa, Lawrence, Lincoln, Omaha, Grand Forks, and Des Moines. The region's most spectacular outdoor performance venues include **The Muny** in Forest Park in St. Louis, Kansas City's **Starlight Theater**, in the city's bucolic Swope Park; and North Dakota's **Medora Musical**, featuring live Wild West musical programs on summer nights against the backdrop of the Theodore Roosevelt National Park bad-lands. A dizzying array of rides and activities awaits those who are more adventurous at the region's largest amusement parks, Kansas City's Worlds of Fun and Six Flags St. Louis.

## Shopping

The region's premier retail destination is Kansas City's elegantly designed **Country Club Plaza**. This 1920s urban shopping district has several higher-end specialty shops and department stores. A popular suburban shopping destination is the upscale **Galleria** mall in Clayton.

Iowa's Amana Colonies offer some of the best locally made products at the **Amana Woolen Mill** and **Millstream Brewing Company**. The best place to visit for Native American crafts and other merchandise is South Dakota. The **Native American Educational and Cultural Center** at the Crazy Horse Memorial in the Black Hills, and the **Red Cloud Heritage Center** on the Pine Ridge Reservation offer a wide selection of handmade rugs, apparel, and other items. For Wild West souvenirs, travelers should visit **Wall Drug**, in Wall, located in South Dakota, for the widest selection.

## Directory

### Tourist Offices

**Iowa**
(888) 472-6035.
www.traveliowa.com

**Kansas**
(800) 252-6727.
www.travelks.org

**Missouri**
(800) 877-1234.
www.missouritourism.org

**Nebraska**
(800) 228-4307.
www.visitnebraska.org

**North Dakota**
(800) 435-5663.

**Oklahoma**
(800) 652-6552.
www.travelok.com

**South Dakota**
(605) 773-3301; (800) 732-5682.
www.travelsd.com

### Road Conditions

**Iowa**
(800) 288-1047.

**Kansas**
(800) 585-7623.

**Nebraska**
(402) 479-4512.

**Oklahoma**
(405) 425-2385.

**South Dakota**
(866) 697-3511.

### Festivals

**Woody Guthrie Free Folk Festival**
Okemah Industrial Park, Okemah, OK.
(918) 623-2440. www.woodyguthrie.com

### Entertainment

**The Muny**
Forest Park, St. Louis, MO.
(314) 361-1900.

**Starlight Theater**
4600 Starlight Rd, KC, MO.
(800) 776-1730.
www.kcstarlight.com

**Medora Musical**
Burning Hills Amphitheater, Medora, ND
(800) 633-6721.
www.medora.com

### Shopping

**Amana Woolen Mill**
800 48th Ave, Amana, IA.
(800) 222-6430.
www. amana woolenmill.com

**Red Cloud Heritage Center**
US 18, Pine Ridge, SD.
(605) 867-5491.

# Where to Stay

THIS REGION'S UNIQUE NATURAL features and vibrant cities make it worth one's while to seek out interesting places to stay. There are a variety of historic hotels, chain hotels, and luxurious bed-and-breakfast inns in larger centers, while guest ranches, mountain lodges, and state park cabins provide comfortable accommodations in spectacular natural settings.

## NORTH DAKOTA

**MANDAN:** *Fort Abraham Lincoln State Park* $
4480 Fort Lincoln Rd, Mandan. *(701) 667-6340.* FAX *(701) 667-6349.*
W www.state.nd.us/ndparks
Relax in the historical shadows of Lewis & Clark in clean, simply furnished cabins overlooking a beautiful, unspoiled section of the Missouri River. P

**MEDORA:** *Dahkotah Lodge* $$
4456 West River Rd, 20 miles S of Medora. *(701) 623-4897.*
W www.dahkotahlodge.com
Guests can take part in trail rides and annual livestock branding in this ranch that stands on the edge of the North Dakota badlands. P

## SOUTH DAKOTA

**BADLANDS NATIONAL PARK:** *Cedar Pass Lodge* $$
1 Cedar Pass Lodge. *(605) 433-5460.* FAX *(605) 433-5560.*
W www.cedarpasslodge.com These rustic cabins are conveniently located in the heart of Badlands National Park, providing convenient access for hikers and motorists eager to explore the park. P

**CUSTER:** *State Game Lodge* $$$
HC 83, US 16A. *(605) 255-4541.* FAX *(605) 255-4706.*
W www.custerresorts.com
Built in 1920, this stately stone-and-wood lodge overlooks a picturesque Black Hills valley. The structure served as President Calvin Coolidge's "Summer White House" in 1927. P TV

**CUSTER:** *Sylvan Lake Lodge & Resort* $$$
At Hwy 89-87 Junction. *(605) 574-2561.* FAX *(605) 574-4943.*
W www.custerresorts.com
This deluxe Black Hills mountain resort features a rustic lodge with cozily furnished guest rooms, as well as private cabins with fireplaces and kitchenettes. P TV

**DEADWOOD:** *Bullock Hotel* $$$
633 Main St. *(800) 336-1876.* FAX *(605) 578-1382.*
W www.bullockhotel.com
The popular 1895 sandstone Bullock Hotel has been impeccably restored with wet bars and jacuzzi tubs in its spacious guest rooms. P TV

**INTERIOR:** *Circle View Guest Ranch* $$
20055 E Hwy 44. *(605) 433-5582.* FAX *(605) 433-5581.*
W www.circleviewranch.com
On the edge of Badlands National Park and the Pine Ridge Reservation, this guest ranch provides comfortable, affordable accommodations with easy access to hiking trails through the rugged badlands. P

**PIERRE:** *Governor's Inn* $$
700 W Sioux Ave. *(605) 224-4200.* FAX *(605) 224-4200.*
W www.govinn.com
Located just minutes from the State Capitol and downtown Pierre, the rooms in this remodeled hotel are furnished with microwaves and refrigerators. Guests are served Continental breakfast. P TV

**RAPID CITY:** *Alex Johnson Hotel* $$
523 6th St. *(605) 342-1210.* FAX *(605) 342-7436.*
W www.alexjohnson.com
Known in its heyday as "The Showplace of the West," this downtown, 1928 Rapid City gem is ornately decorated with Native American motifs and artwork, and Germanic Tudor designs. P TV

| | Credit Cards | Number of Rooms | Restaurant | Children's Facilities | Garden or Terrace |
|---|---|---|---|---|---|
| Fort Abraham Lincoln State Park | | 2 | | ● | |
| Dahkotah Lodge | ■ | 8 | ■ | ● | ■ |
| Cedar Pass Lodge | ■ | 22 | ■ | | |
| State Game Lodge | ■ | 66 | ■ | | ■ |
| Sylvan Lake Lodge & Resort | ■ | 66 | ■ | | ■ |
| Bullock Hotel | ■ | 36 | ■ | | |
| Circle View Guest Ranch | ■ | 7 | | | ■ |
| Governor's Inn | ■ | 82 | | | |
| Alex Johnson Hotel | ■ | 143 | ■ | | |

| | | | | | |
|---|---|---|---|---|---|
| **rice categories** for a standard<br>ouble room per night,<br>clusive of service charges,<br>nd any additional taxes:<br>$ under $50<br>$$ $50–$100<br>$$$ $100–$150<br>$$$$ $150–$200<br>$$$$$ over $200 | **CREDIT CARDS**<br>Major credit cards accepted.<br>**RESTAURANT**<br>Hotel restaurant or dining room usually open to nonresidents unless otherwise stated.<br>**CHILDREN'S FACILITIES**<br>Cribs and a baby-sitting service available. Some hotel restaurants have children's portions and high chairs.<br>**GARDEN OR TERRACE**<br>Hotels with a garden, courtyard, or terrace. | | | | |

## NEBRASKA

| | CREDIT CARDS | NUMBER OF ROOMS | RESTAURANT | CHILDREN'S FACILITIES | GARDEN OR TERRACE |
|---|---|---|---|---|---|
| **IADRON:** *Olde Main Street Inn* $$<br>5 Main St. (308) 432-3380.<br>www.chadron.com/memberspages/oldemain<br>iis 1890s hotel offers a rustic High Plains saloon, home-cooked meals, d convenient access to the downtown business district. | ■ | 9 | ■ | | |
| **RAWFORD:** *Fort Robinson State Park* $<br>20, 3 miles (5 km) W of Crawford. (308) 665-2900. FAX (308) 665-2906.<br>www.ngpc.state.ne.us<br>oused in a historic US Army fort, the horseback rides, cookouts, and king trails make this stay an essential Great Plains' experience. | ■ | 22 | ■ | | |
| **NCOLN:** *Cornhusker Hotel* $$$<br>3 S 13th St. (402) 474-7474, (800) 793-7474. FAX (402) 474-1847.<br>www.thecornhusker.com<br>iis deluxe urban hotel provides convenient access to the historic aymarket District, downtown museums, shops, and the University of ebraska campus. | ■ | 290 | ■ | | |
| **EBRASKA CITY:** *Lied Lodge & Conference Center/At Arbor Day Farm* $$$<br>00 Sylvan Rd. (402) 873-8733. FAX (402) 873-4999.<br>www.liedlodge.org<br>iis hotel offers a good restaurant, wooden beam construction and scenic ews of the surrounding parks and orchards. | ■ | 144 | ■ | | ■ |
| **MAHA:** *Best Western Redick Plaza Hotel* $$<br>04 Harney St. (402) 342-1500, (888) 342-5339. FAX (402) 342-2401.<br>www.redickplazahotel.com<br>iis Art Deco hotel offers downtown accommodations within walking stance of the antique shops, bookstores, and restaurants of the lively ld Market warehouse district. | ■ | 89 | ■ | | |
| **COTTS BLUFF:** *Barn Anew B&B* $$<br>'0549 County Rd L. (308) 632-8647. FAX (308) 632-5518.<br>www.prairieweb.com/barnanew<br>ocated on the old Oregon Trail, in the shadow of Scotts Bluff National onument, this renovated 1907 barn provides relaxing accomodations on e site of an original Nebraska homestead. | ■ | 4 | | | ■ |

## IOWA

| | CREDIT CARDS | NUMBER OF ROOMS | RESTAURANT | CHILDREN'S FACILITIES | GARDEN OR TERRACE |
|---|---|---|---|---|---|
| **MANA COLONIES:** *Die Heimat Country Inn B&B* $<br>34 V St, Homestead #10. (319) 622-3937.<br>www.dheimat.com<br>eep in an authentic canopy bed in this historic 1850s former stagecoach op and communal kitchen in the heart of Homestead village. Keeping ith Amana traditions, the rooms are simply decorated with Amana walnut nd cherry furniture. | ■ | 18 | | | ■ |
| **ES MOINES:** *Hotel Fort Des Moines* $$$<br>00 Walnut St. (515) 243-1161. FAX (515) 243-4317.<br>www.hotelfortdesmoines.com<br>iis stately 1919 downtown hotel has hosted John F. Kennedy, Elvis resley, and Elizabeth Taylor. | ■ | 240 | ■ | | |
| **UBUQUE:** *The Redstone Inn & Suites* $$$<br>04 Bluff St. (563) 582-1894. FAX (563) 582-1893.<br>www.theredstoneinn.com<br>iis 1894 private residence and tavern has been convererted into an inn. he Redstone Inn overlooks downtown Dubuque and the Mississippi iver. | ■ | 15 | ■ | | |

For key to symbols see back flap

**Price categories** for a standard double room per night, inclusive of service charges, and any additional taxes:
- $ under $50
- $$ $50–$100
- $$$ $100–$150
- $$$$ $150–$200
- $$$$$ over $200

**CREDIT CARDS**
Major credit cards accepted.

**RESTAURANT**
Hotel restaurant or dining room usually open to nonresidents unless otherwise stated.

**CHILDREN'S FACILITIES**
Cribs and a baby-sitting service available. Some hotel restaurants have children's portions and high chairs.

**GARDEN OR TERRACE**
Hotels with a garden, courtyard, or terrace.

| | | Credit Cards | Number of Rooms | Restaurant | Children's Facilities | Garden or Terrace |
|---|---|---|---|---|---|---|
| **MISSOURI** | | | | | | |
| **KANSAS CITY:** *Quarterage Inn*<br>560 Westport Rd. (816) 931-0001. FAX (816) 931-8891.<br>www.quarteragehotel.com<br>In the heart of Old Westport, this inn offers reasonably priced accommodations in one of the city's most central locations. | $$$ | ■ | 123 | | | |
| **KANSAS CITY:** *Raphael Hotel*<br>325 Ward Pkwy. (816) 756-3800. FAX (816) 802-2131.<br>www.raphaelkc.com<br>Built in 1927 as an upscale apartment house, the Raphael was intended to complement the adjacent Country Club Plaza shops. This Spanish-influenced boutique hotel provides excellent service and European-style accommodations. | $$$ | ■ | 123 | ■ | | |
| **KANSAS CITY:** *Southmoreland on the Plaza*<br>116 E 46th St. (816) 531-7979. FAX (816) 531-2407.<br>www.southmoreland.com<br>An elegant, discreet urban oasis, this inn serves wine and hors d'oeuvres every night in the lobby. | $$$$ | ■ | 13 | | | ■ |
| **KANSAS CITY:** *Hotel Phillips*<br>106 W 12th St. (816) 221-7000. FAX (816) 221-3477.<br>www.hotelphillips.com<br>Recently renovated, this 1931 Art Deco hotel combines historic ambience and modern convenience in the heart of Kansas City's bustling downtown business district. | $$$$ | ■ | 217 | ■ | | |
| **ST. LOUIS:** *Napolean's Retreat B&B*<br>1815 Lafayette Ave. (314) 772-6979. FAX (314) 772-7675.<br>www.napoleonsretreat.com<br>Overlooking the lovely Lafayette Square park, this 1880 Victorian B&B offers deluxe accommodations in an elegant, refined atmosphere just minutes from downtown St. Louis. | $$$ | ■ | 5 | | | ■ |
| **ST. LOUIS:** *Seven Gables Inn*<br>26 N Meremac. (314) 863-8400. FAX (314) 863-8846.<br>www.sevengablesinn.com<br>This Prince Tudor-style inn features sophisticated lodging, excellent service, and three top-notch restaurants. | $$$ | ■ | 32 | ■ | | ■ |
| **ST. LOUIS:** *WS on Washington*<br>400 Washington Ave. (314) 231-1100. FAX (314) 231-1199.<br>www.wshotels.com<br>Strikingly furnished suites and a top-notch spa and fitness center are among the features of this luxury hotel in the vibrant, downtown warehouse and loft district. | $$$$ | ■ | 78 | ■ | | |
| **KANSAS** | | | | | | |
| **COTTONWOOD FALLS:** *1874 Stonehouse B&B*<br>Mulberry Hill, Rte 1, Flint Hills. (620) 273-8481. FAX (620) 273-8481.<br>www.stonehousebandb.com<br>Plush guest rooms and a relaxing tallgrass prairie and Cottonwood River nature trail make this 19th-century farmhouse inn the premier lodging destination in the Flint Hills. | $$ | ■ | 4 | | | ■ |
| **COTTONWOOD FALLS:** *Grand Central Hotel*<br>215 Broadway. (620) 273-6763. FAX (620) 273-8381.<br>www.grandcentralhotel.com<br>Built in 1884 and renovated in 1995, the historic Wild West Grand Central Hotel is noted for its plush, oversized guest rooms. | $$$$ | ■ | 10 | ■ | | |

**OUNCIL GROVE:** *Cottage House Hotel & Motel* $$$
5 N Neosho. (620) 767-6828. FAX (620) 767-6414.
www.cotthouse.com
ocated on the Santa Fe Trail, this historic lodging establishment features eriod furnishings and unique guest rooms, including an ornate turret oom and private honeymoon cottage.

| | | | | |
|---|---|---|---|---|
| ■ | 40 | | | |

**AWRENCE:** *Eldridge Hotel* $$
h & Massachusetts St. (785) 749-5011. FAX (785) 749-4512.
www.eldridgehotel.com
tastefully renovated hotel built in 1926 lies just a short distance way from downtown Lawrence's sophisticated restaurants and opping area.

| | | | | |
|---|---|---|---|---|
| ■ | 48 | ■ | | |

**AWRENCE:** *Circle S Ranch & Country Inn* $$$$
325 Circle S Ln. (785) 843-4124. FAX (785) 843-4474.
www.circlesranch.com
st minutes north of downtown Lawrence, this luxurious retreat offers weeping views and imaginatively themed guest rooms – including the owboy Room and its longhorn headboard and bucket-shaped shower ead.

| | | | | |
|---|---|---|---|---|
| ■ | 12 | ■ | | ■ |

**OPEKA:** *Senate Luxury Suites* $$$
)0 SW Tyler. (785) 233-5050. FAX (785) 233-1614.
www.senatesuites.com
uilt in 1928 and recently refurbished, this downtown Victorian hotel ffers individually decorated suites, each with ornate woodwork and rivate balconies.

| | | | | |
|---|---|---|---|---|
| ■ | 52 | | | |

**OPEKA:** *Capitol Plaza Hotel* $$$
717 SW Topeka Blvd. (785) 431-7200. FAX (785) 431-7206.
www.jqhhotels.com
n elegant, 5,000 sq-foot (465 sq-m) ballroom, lush garden atrium, and eated indoor pool make the Capitol Plaza Hotel Topeka's premier usiness and luxury hotel.

| | | | | |
|---|---|---|---|---|
| ■ | 224 | ■ | | |

**VICHITA:** *Hotel at Old Town* $$$
30 E 1st St. (316) 267-4800. FAX (316) 267-4840.
www.hotelatoldtown.com
uilt in 1906, this former warehouse structure now houses a deluxe uites hotel in the heart of Wichita's Old Town neighborhood. Each uite features a fully equipped kitchen and CD player.

| | | | | |
|---|---|---|---|---|
| ■ | 115 | | | |

**VICHITA:** *Inn at the Park* $$$
751 E Douglas Ave. (316) 652-0500. FAX (316) 652-0525.
www.innatthepark.com
his romantic getaway in the heart of Wichita's stately, early 20th century eighborhood provides elite accomodations for business travelers and acationers seeking to unwind in an opulent mansion.

| | | | | |
|---|---|---|---|---|
| ■ | 12 | | | ■ |

## OKLAHOMA

**BARTLESVILLE:** *Hotel Phillips* $$
21 S Johnstone. (918) 336-5600. FAX (918) 336-0350.
www.hotelphillips66.com
favorite haunt of petroleum executives, Hotel Phillips offers large, omfortable rooms and the very good Grill 66 restaurant, right in owntown Bartlesville.

| | | | | |
|---|---|---|---|---|
| ■ | 157 | ■ | | |

**CLINTON:** *Best Western Tradewinds Courtyard Inn* $
128 Gary Blvd. (580) 323-2610. FAX (580) 323-4655.
www.bestwestern.com
lvis Presley fans can rent a suite where "The King" stayed several times uring his visits here in the 1960s. The suite contains original furnishings om Presley's last visit – including the bed and vanity.

| | | | | |
|---|---|---|---|---|
| ■ | 76 | ■ | | |

**TULSA:** *Hotel Ambassador* $$$
324 S Main St. (918) 587-8200. FAX (918) 587-8208.
www.hotelambassador-tulsa.com
his upscale 1929 hotel is known to be favored by Tulsa's swashbuckling il barons and has been lovingly renovated, with beautiful marble-topped anities and stone tile baths in luxurious rooms.

| | | | | |
|---|---|---|---|---|
| ■ | 55 | ■ | | |

For key to symbols see back flap

# Where to Eat

THE GREAT PLAINS IS the United States's largest cattle-producing area. As a result, red meat is a staple at most of the region's small-town cafés and big-city steakhouses. However, healthier, less hearty dining alternatives are also available in plenty. The opening times of restaurants are indicated by a "B" for breakfast, "L" for lunch, and "D" for dinner.

## North Dakota

**BISMARCK:** *Fiesta Villa Restaurant & Lounge* $
411 E Main St. *(701) 222-8075.*
Located in Bismarck's mission-style, Northern Railroad Depot building, this downtown Mexican favorite serves spicy South-of-the-Border cuisine in a lively, welcoming atmosphere. *L, D.*

**BISMARCK:** *Bistro 1100* $$
1103 E Front Ave. *(701) 224-8800.*
A three-cheese penne pasta and creatively prepared American cuisine combine with a casually elegant decor to make Bistro 1100 Bismarck's most refined dining establishment. *L, D.* ● *Sun.*

**EAST GRAND FORKS:** *Whitey's Café and Lounge* $$
121 DeMers Ave. *(218) 773-1831.*
This onetime bootleggers' bar was rebuilt following the 1997 flood, re-opening three doors down, with its horseshoe-shaped bar still intact. The tender, pan-fried walleye entrée is as good as ever. *L, D.*

**GRAND FORKS:** *Sanders 1907 Dakota Cuisine* $$
22 S 3rd St. *(701) 746-8970.* W www.sanders1907.com
Impeccable service and haute cuisine are the trademarks of this cozy downtown tradition, famous locally for its "Dakota cuisine" specialties, such as walleye, lamb chops, and grilled salmon. *D.* ● *Sun, Mon.*

## South Dakota

**CUSTER:** *The Pheasant Dining Room* $$
State Game Lodge, US 16A. *(605) 255-4541.* W www.custerresorts.com
This historic restaurant is housed in a stately 1920 lodge building and overlooks a ponderosa pine forest and a scenic mountain valley. It is known for its delectable buffalo, elk, venison, pheasant, and trout dishes. *B, L, D.*

**DEADWOOD:** *Jakes Atop the Midnight Star* $$$
677 Main St. *(605) 578-1555.*
Owned by *Dances With Wolves* actor Kevin Costner, this restaurant is located atop The Midnight Star casino in historic downtown Deadwood. Jakes serves up South Dakota's most adventurous gourmet cuisine. *D.*

**PIERRE:** *La Minestra* $$$
106 E Dakota Ave. *(605) 224-8090.*
Tucked away in quiet downtown Pierre, La Minestra prepares a delectable range of Italian specialties and innovative fish, meat, and poultry dishes, including a pan-fried, pistachio-crusted walleye entrée. *L Mon–Fri, D.* ● *Sun.*

**RAPID CITY:** *Firehouse Brewing Company* $$
610 Main St. *(605) 348-1915.* W www.firehousebrewing.com
South Dakota's first brewpub is located in a 1915 firehouse in downtown Rapid City. Its baked pasta with three cheeses and homemade desserts complement an array of handcrafted ales. *L, D.*

**SPEARFISH:** *Bay Leaf Café* $
126 W Hudson. *(605) 642-5462.*
This delightful, vegetarian-friendly downtown café features several unusual dishes on its menu. Among these are a spicy gazpacho soup and jerk-seasoned Jamaican salad. *L, D.* ● *Sun (Sep–May).*

| Restaurant | Credit Cards | Outdoor Tables | Vegetarian | Good Wine List | Regional Cuisine |
|---|---|---|---|---|---|
| Fiesta Villa Restaurant & Lounge | ■ | | ■ | ● | ■ |
| Bistro 1100 | ■ | | ■ | ● | ■ |
| Whitey's Café and Lounge | ■ | | ■ | ● | ■ |
| Sanders 1907 Dakota Cuisine | ■ | | ■ | ● | ■ |
| The Pheasant Dining Room | ■ | | ■ | ● | ■ |
| Jakes Atop the Midnight Star | ■ | | ■ | ● | ■ |
| La Minestra | ■ | | ■ | ● | ■ |
| Firehouse Brewing Company | ■ | ● | ■ | ● | ■ |
| Bay Leaf Café | ■ | ● | ■ | ● | ■ |

**rice categories** include a ıree-course meal for one, a ·lass of house wine, and all navoidable extra charges such s sales tax and service.

$ under $25
$$ $25–35
$$$ $35–50
$$$$ $50–70
$$$$$ over $70

**CREDIT CARDS**
Major credit cards accepted.

**OUTDOOR TABLES**
Garden, courtyard, or terrace with outside tables.

**VEGETARIAN**
A good selection of vegetarian dishes available.

**GOOD WINE LIST**
Extensive list of good wines, both domestic and imported.

**REGIONAL CUISINE**
The menu contains some regional specialties.

## NEBRASKA

**NCOLN:** *Green Gateau* $$
0 S 10th St. (402) 477-0330.
ıis cozy restaurant has an old European-inn ambience, and the gourmet ening menu features favorites such as veal parmesan and beef ellington. *B, L, D.*

**NCOLN:** *La Paz Mexican Restaurant* $$
1 N Cottner Blvd. (402) 466-9111.
ıis family-oriented restaurant with a South-of-the-Border atmosphere, is e of Lincoln's best restaurants. Do try the cream and chicken chiladas and the margaritas. *L, D.*

**MAHA:** *Gorat's Steak House* $$
17 Center St. (402) 551-3733.
longtime favorite of Omaha financier Warren Buffet, Gorat's is a classic uth Omaha steakhouse, complete with cantankerous waiters, a colorful netele, and some of the nation's best filet mignon and chateaubriand. *D.*

**MAHA:** *McFoster's Natural Kind Café* $$
2 S 38th St. (402) 345-7477.
unky waiters, a varied menu, and live folk and blues music make is vegetarian café one of Omaha's best. The vegan enchiladas are ceptional. *L, D.*

**MAHA:** *Flatiron Café* $$$
th & Howard. (402) 344-3040.
edged into the historic Flatiron building, this is an imaginative gourmet staurant with a varied menu and house specialties such as grilled salmon th strawberry balsamic vinaigrette. *L Mon–Fri, D. ● Sun.*

## IOWA

**MANA COLONIES:** *Ox Yoke Inn* $$
20 220th Trail. (319) 622-3441.
sitors can enjoy German and American cuisine, as well as homemade sserts in family-style Amana tradition at this 1940 country restaurant. e bar offers Amana-brewed Millstream beers on tap. *L, D.*

**EDAR RAPIDS:** *Hacienda las Glorias* $
45 Blairs Ferry Rd. (319) 294-2101.
tasty array of authentic Mexican entrées, seasoned with a zesty home-ade salsa or rich mole sauce, and a delightful dessert selection, stinguish this family-owned eatery. *L, D.*

**LIVE:** *Cosi Cucina* $$$
75 NW 86th St. (515) 278-8148.
ıis upscale Clive establishment is known for its Italian and French ısine and ever-changing specials, which have included ostrich, emu, ako shark, and buffalo. *L, D.*

**AVENPORT:** *Duck City Bistro* $$
5 E 3rd St. (563) 322-3825.
ıis bustling downtown Quad Cities bistro's French and Continental fare augmented by an adventurous array of Asian, Cajun, and Italian ıtrées. *D. ● Sun.*

**ES MOINES:** *Sage* $$$
87 University Ave. (515) 255-7722. www.sagetherestaurant.com
ıis calm, intimate Des Moines bistro lets its contemporary American eations do the talking. Be sure to sample the blue-cheese polenta, veet potato purée, and Iowa pork loin. *D. ● Sun, Mon.*

| Restaurant | Credit Cards | Outdoor Tables | Vegetarian | Good Wine List | Regional Cuisine |
|---|---|---|---|---|---|
| Green Gateau | ■ | | ■ | | ■ |
| La Paz Mexican Restaurant | ■ | | ■ | | ■ |
| Gorat's Steak House | ■ | | | ● | ■ |
| McFoster's Natural Kind Café | ■ | ● | ■ | ● | ■ |
| Flatiron Café | ■ | ● | ■ | ● | ■ |
| Ox Yoke Inn | ■ | | | ● | ■ |
| Hacienda las Glorias | ■ | ● | ■ | | ■ |
| Cosi Cucina | ■ | | ■ | ● | |
| Duck City Bistro | ■ | ● | ■ | ● | ■ |
| Sage | ■ | ● | | ● | ■ |

**Price categories** include a three-course meal for one, a glass of house wine, and all unavoidable extra charges such as sales tax and service.
$ under $25
$$ $25–35
$$$ $35–50
$$$$ $50–70
$$$$$ over $70

**CREDIT CARDS**
Major credit cards accepted.

**OUTDOOR TABLES**
Garden, courtyard, or terrace with outside tables.

**VEGETARIAN**
A good selection of vegetarian dishes available.

**GOOD WINE LIST**
Extensive list of good wines, both domestic and imported.

**REGIONAL CUISINE**
The menu contains some regional specialties.

**DUBUQUE:** *Rafters* $$$
2728 Asbury Rd, Suite 1000. *(563) 556-4800.*
Steaks, chops and seafood presented with sophisticated creativity. Entrées include Hawaiian ribeye, Pistachio-crusted mahi mahi, and chicken and brie quesadillas. *L, D.* *Sun D, Dec 24, 25.*

**IOWA CITY:** *Devotay* $$
117 N Linn St. *(319) 354-1001.*
This cozy downtown tapas restaurant offers a full range of cold and hot tapas, sandwiches, and other entrées. *L, D.* *Sun L.*

## MISSOURI

**KANSAS CITY:** *Bluebird Bistro* $$$
1700 Summit St. *(816) 221-7559.*
This colorful West Side bistro has expanded its wide-ranging vegetarian menu to include a succulent range of meat dishes, including organic beef, bison, and free-range chicken. *B, L, D.* *Sun (except brunch).*

**KANSAS CITY:** *Garozzo's Ristorante* $$$
526 Harrison St. *(816) 221-2455.*
Garozzo's Ristorante offers an authentic Italian dining experience, complete with intimate lighting, wisecracking waiters, homemade pastas, excellent tiramisu, and a hearty wine list. *L, D.* *Sun L.*

**KANSAS CITY:** *Hereford House Restaurant* $$$$
2 E 20th St. *(816) 842-1080.*
This classic 1950s steak house offers thick Kansas City steaks with oven-roasted tilapia, cedar-planked salmon, and mouthwatering Caesar salads. *L Mon–Fri, D.*

**ST. LOUIS:** *Cunetto House of Pasta* $$$
5453 Magnolia Ave. *(314) 781-1135.*
Located in the Italian neighborhood known as The Hill, Cunetto offers a dizzying array of pastas and entrées, as well as a hearty toasted ravioli appetizer. *L Mon–Fri, D.* *Sun.*

**ST. LOUIS:** *Café Balaban* $$$$
405 N Euclid Ave. *(314) 361-8085.*
Since 1972, this Central West End institution has served a wide range of entrées, ranging from its signature beef Wellington to glazed salmon, jerk chicken, and bison carpaccio. *L, D.*

**ST. LOUIS:** *Sidney Street Café* $$$$
2000 Sidney St. *(314) 771-5777.*
Exposed brick, hardwood floors, and intimate lighting provide a romantic backdrop for this cozy restaurant's trademark staples, including steak wasabi, Tuscan sea bass, and Asian salmon. *D.* *Sun, Mon.*

## KANSAS

**COTTONWOOD FALLS:** *Grand Central Hotel Grill* $$$
215 Broadway. *(620) 273-6763.*
Located on the first floor of a restored 1884 hotel, this bustling gem serves up a wide range of tender steaks in addition to vegetarian-friendly pastas and entrées. *L, D.* *Sun.*

**COUNCIL GROVE:** *Hays House Restaurant Tavern* $
112 W Main St. *(620) 767-5911.*
Built in 1857 on the old Santa Fe Trail, the oldest continuously operating restaurant west of the Mississippi is famous for its pan-fried chicken, cranberry-strawberry pie, and handmade ice cream. *B, L, D.* *Sun D, Mon.*

| Restaurant | Credit Cards | Outdoor Tables | Vegetarian | Good Wine List |
|---|---|---|---|---|
| Rafters | ■ | | ■ | |
| Devotay | ■ | | ■ | ● |
| Bluebird Bistro | ■ | | ■ | ● |
| Garozzo's Ristorante | ■ | | ■ | ● |
| Hereford House Restaurant | ■ | | | ● |
| Cunetto House of Pasta | ■ | | ■ | ● |
| Café Balaban | ■ | | ■ | ● |
| Sidney Street Café | ■ | | ■ | ● |
| Grand Central Hotel Grill | ■ | | ■ | ● |
| Hays House Restaurant Tavern | ■ | | | |

**WRENCE:** *Teller's* $$
Massachusetts St. (785) 843-4111.
used in a former bank building, this comfortable downtown Lawrence orite specializes in imaginatively prepared Italian cuisine, using fresh, ally grown produce. *L, D.*

**WRENCE:** *Pachamama's* $$$
51 Quail Creek Dr. (785) 841-0990. www.pachamamas.com
is eclectic, upscale-casual establishment tucked away on the southwest e of town features an evolving array of regional, Asian, and Italian ights, with at least one flavorful vegetarian special every evening. *D.*

**ANHATTAN:** *Harry's Uptown Supper Club* $$$
3 Poyntz Ave. (785) 537-1300.
is beautifully designed, high-ceilinged restaurant serves pastas and ceptionally prepared American dishes on the first floor of downtown nhattan's stately Wareham Hotel. *D.* ● *Sun.*

**PEKA:** *New City Café* $$
)5 S, Gage Center Dr. (785) 271-8646.
ie of Topeka's true finds, New City Café offers a constantly changing of salads, internationally inspired entrées, and homemade desserts for asually elegant dining experience. *L Mon–Fri, D.* ● *Sun.*

**ICHITA:** *Olive Tree Bistro* $$$
49 N. Rock Rd. (316) 636-1100.
is excellent bistro offers continental cuisine in an elegant and gracious nosphere. The menu features fresh ingredients and there's a lengthy list wines to complement dinner. *D, Sun brunch.* ● *Sun D.*

## OKLAHOMA

**TOOSA:** *Molly's Landing* $$
)0 N Hwy 66. (918) 266-7853.
is Route 66 roadside tradition features thick steaks and homemade eads and desserts, in a rustic log cabin furnished with leather, rawhide airs, and Wild West decor. *L, D.* ● *Sun.*

**LAHOMA CITY:** *Bricktown Brewery Restaurant & Pub* $$
Oklahoma. (405) 232-2739. www.bricktownbrewery.com
ormer warehouse and candy factory, this busy brewpub features ndcrafted beers, live music, and a variety of regional dishes, including 3Q ribs and chicken-fried steak. *L, D.*

**KLAHOMA CITY:** *Mickey Mantle's Steakhouse* $$$
Mickey Mantle Dr. (405) 272-0777.
eat steaks and Mickey Mantle baseball memorabilia are the main draws re. The menu includes a good selection of salads, seafood, pasta, cken, and a variety of desserts. *D.*

**KLAHOMA CITY:** *The Coach House* $$$$
37 Avondale Dr. (405) 842-1000.
orld-renowned Chef Kurt Fleischfresser prepares a delicious variety of contemrary American dishes, including a roasted rack of pork with huckleberry sauce, this elegant, fine-dining restaurant. *L Mon–Fri, D.* ● *Sun.*

**ILSA:** *Casa Bonita* $
20 S Sheridan. (918) 836-6464.
is restaurant entices over 10,000 patrons a week to experience its olling mariachi musicians and out-of-this-world decor, which includes erupting volcano, 30-foot (9-m) waterfall, and Victorian carousel. ).

**ILSA:** *Garlic Rose* $$$
)9 S Peoria. (918) 746-4900.
cated in the heart of Tulsa's Brookside restaurant and retail district, the rlic Rose offers succulent pastas and Italian main courses in a lively town setting. *L, D.* ● *Sun, Mon L.*

**ILSA:** *The Chalkboard* $$$
24 S Main St. (918) 582-1964.
oused in the historic Hotel Ambassador, The Chalkboard's flavorful lian, American, and regional creations, along with its romantic atmosere, make this one of Tulsa's long-standing favorites. *B, L, D.*

# TEXAS

# TEXAS

BY ALMOST ANY STANDARD *Texas is big. Stretching nearly 1,00 miles (1,600 km) across, and even longer north to south, it by far the largest of the "Lower 48" states and also among th most populous, with 20 million residents. While its size has inspired love of all things large, its past as an independent nation has give Texans a sense of pride and spirit of freedom, as is evident by the sta flag that still carries the Lone Star, emblem of the Republic.*

The huge scale of Texas seems to have encouraged a culture of exaggeration, and according to residents, everything about the state is bigger, better, and brasher than anywhere else. The horns on the emblematic longhorn cattle, the great fortunes made from the state's supplies of oil, and even the one-time role of the Dallas Cowboys football team as "America's Team" – almost every aspect of life is imbued with a sense of superiority. Whether this is deserved or not is a matter of opinion, but contradiction is not what many Texans want to hear. As signs and songs all over the state say: "Don't Mess With Texas."

**Dome of Texas State Capitol, Austin**

### HISTORY

In Texas, history begins at the Alamo, a former Spanish mission and Mexican fort. "Remember the Alamo" wa the battle cry of the Texas wa of independence from Mexic In December 1835, a band rebellious American settle commandeered the fort. Tw months later, the vanquishe Mexican army retaliated b attacking the fort for 13 day until all the 189 American inside were killed. Despite th setback, the freelance Americans und General Samual Houston defeated th Mexicans in 1836 and declared th independent Republic of Texas. Th Republic, which included parts of wh are now New Mexico, Oklahom Colorado, and Wyoming, was annexe by the US in 1845. This move ignite the Mexican War, and after two years sporadic fighting Mexico was forced t accept the loss of Texas, and the rest the West, in 1848.

**Plaque depicting a scene from the Texas War of Independence, the Alamo complex, San Antonio**

◁ **Cowboy boots on display at M.L. Leddy's Boots and Saddlery in San Angelo, southwest of Abilene**

ulpture of longhorn cattle outside the Dallas onvention Center

he second half of the 19th century 'as the heyday of the great cattle rives of the Wild West. Huge herds of exas longhorn cattle, descendants of nimals introduced by the Spanish olonists centuries before, roamed the pen range. Rounded up and driven by owboys to towns such as Fort Worth nd Dallas, these cattle were loaded nto trains and shipped to different arkets located in the eastern US. After 'orking on the range for weeks at a me, the cowboys' arrival into town 'as often heralded by a frenzy of unplay and general debauchery.

## Key Dates in History

**1519** Spanish explorer Alonso Alvarez de Pineda sets foot in what is now Texas

**1528** Cabeza de Vaca and a black African slave spend six years traveling across Texas

**1685** Rene-Robert Cavelier, Sieur de la Salle, establishes a short-lived French colony on the Gulf of Mexico at Matagorda Bay

**1716** Spain establishes Catholic missions in southern Texas

**1822** American immigrant Stephen F. Austin establishes a settlement along the Brazos River

**1836** Battle of the Alamo; Texas becomes a Republic

**1845** Texas becomes a state

**1870** Texas readmitted to the Union

**1900** Hurricane hits Galveston, killing 6,000

**1901** Oil is discovered at Spindletop

**1962** NASA's "Mission Control" in Houston

**1963** President John F. Kennedy assassinated in Dallas; Texas native Vice President Lyndon B. Johnson assumes leadership

**1986** Crude oil prices fall, damaging economy

**2001** Texas Governor George W. Bush is named as 43rd president, despite losing the popular vote

## Economy & Culture

Though Texas has one of the nation's most diversified economies, historically it has been dependent upon two main industries, oil and agriculture. Since the discovery of oil in the early 1900s, the state has remained the center of the US petroleum industry, producing one-third of the nation's output and controlling most of the vast quantities imported from overseas. In fact, it is hard to think of Texas without reference to the oil industry, thanks to images of gushers, "Texas Tea," and the machinations of the Ewing family on the 1980s TV show *Dallas*.

Agriculture, too, is very important. The livestock industry is still big business, so identified with its "cowboy culture" roots that boots, jeans, and a Stetson hat seem to be the official state costume. However, Texas also produces other crops such as cotton and citrus. The state's high-tech industry is led by Texas Instruments and Austin-based Dell Computer, while the huge military presence supports a major aeronautical engineering industry, particularly at NASA's "Mission Control" in Houston.

These frequently booming and often busting industries have created many fortunes. Texan wealth supports not only glitzy shops and fancy restaurants but has also endowed several excellent museums in Houston, Fort Worth, and other cities. However, the most authentic images of Texas are not of urban sophistication but of the down-home informality and vast open spaces of its rural reaches. Perhaps the best way to find its heart is to follow a dusty country road, stopping for coffee in a small-town café, with its parking lot full of pickup trucks, or watching the sun set over the ever-distant horizon.

**Cowboys relaxing on a Texas ranch at sunset**

# Exploring Texas

Texas is so large that it is a challenge to see all of it. Public transportation is negligible in this fossil-fueled state, where driving is an essential part of life. Many visitors fly between the main cities of Dallas, Austin, and Houston, and then rent a car to get around. About 90 percent of the state's 20 million residents live in the cities, which are equipped with restaurants, hotels, and visitor attractions. Out in the countryside, where the "real" Texas lives, facilities are few and far between. Even in the more popular areas such as the Hill Country outside Austin, hotels and restaurants tend to be basic, and distances are so great that travel time can take up a large portion of the day.

## Sights at a Glance

*Dallas pp478–9* 1
*Fort Worth pp480–81* 2
Austin 3
Fredericksburg 4
Kerrville 5
New Braunfels 6
*San Antonio pp484–5* 7
*Houston pp486–7* 8
Big Thicket National Preserve 9
Galveston 10
Aransas National Wildlife Refuge 11
Corpus Christi 12
Padre Island National Seashore 13
Laredo 14
Rio Grande Valley 15
Big Bend National Park 16
Fort Davis 17
El Paso 18
Guadalupe Mountains National Park 19
Lubbock 20
Canyon 21
Amarillo 22
Abilene 23

## Key

- Airport
- Highway
- Major road
- Railroad
- State border
- International border

**Sparkling glass office towers, dominating the Dallas skyline**

**SEE ALSO**

- ***Practical Information*** pp494-5
- ***Where to Stay*** pp496-7
- ***Where to Eat*** pp498-9


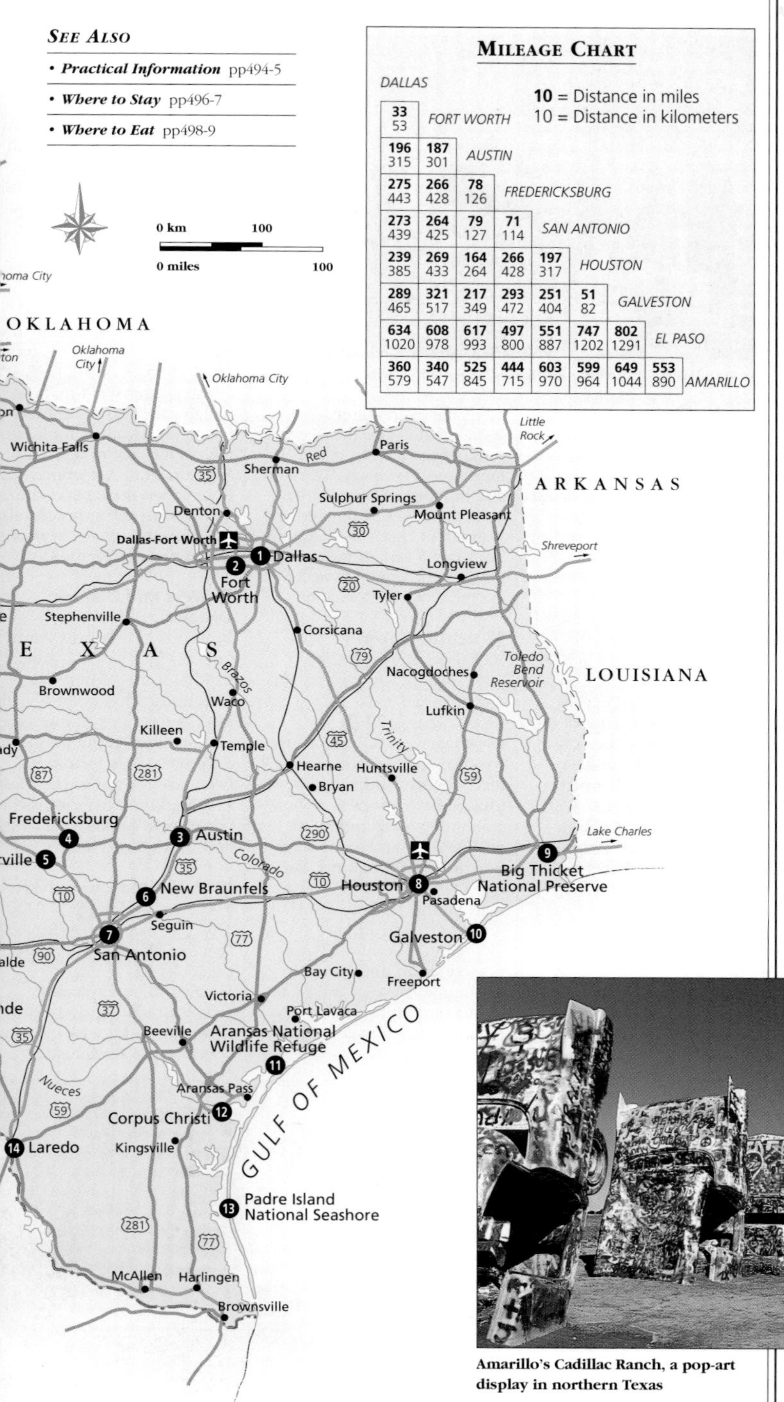


**MILEAGE CHART**

**10** = Distance in miles
10 = Distance in kilometers

| | DALLAS | FORT WORTH | AUSTIN | FREDERICKSBURG | SAN ANTONIO | HOUSTON | GALVESTON | EL PASO |
|---|---|---|---|---|---|---|---|---|
| FORT WORTH | **33** / 53 | | | | | | | |
| AUSTIN | **196** / 315 | **187** / 301 | | | | | | |
| FREDERICKSBURG | **275** / 443 | **266** / 428 | **78** / 126 | | | | | |
| SAN ANTONIO | **273** / 439 | **264** / 425 | **79** / 127 | **71** / 114 | | | | |
| HOUSTON | **239** / 385 | **269** / 433 | **164** / 264 | **266** / 428 | **197** / 317 | | | |
| GALVESTON | **289** / 465 | **321** / 517 | **217** / 349 | **293** / 472 | **251** / 404 | **51** / 82 | | |
| EL PASO | **634** / 1020 | **608** / 978 | **617** / 993 | **497** / 800 | **551** / 887 | **747** / 1202 | **802** / 1291 | |
| AMARILLO | **360** / 579 | **340** / 547 | **525** / 845 | **444** / 715 | **603** / 970 | **599** / 964 | **649** / 1044 | **553** / 890 |

**Amarillo's Cadillac Ranch, a pop-art display in northern Texas**

**View of Dallas from the Reunion Tower Observation area**

# Dallas ❶

*1,100,000.* ✈ *Union Station, 400 S Houston St.* *Greyhound, 205 S Lamar St.* *100 S Houston St, (214) 571-1300.* *Cotton Bowl Parade (Jan 1); Dallas Blooms (mid-Mar–mid-Apr); Texas State Fair (Sep–Oct).* W www.visitdallas.com

When most people think of Texas, they think of Dallas, even though it is neither the state capital nor the biggest city. Located in the northeastern corner of the state, this is where the cotton fields and oil wells of East Texas meet the wide-open West Texas rangelands. With a forest of sparkling glass office towers dominating the downtown area, Dallas is the commercial and financial center of the "Lone Star" state, a role it has played since its days as the junction between the two main southwestern railroads. This fast-growing metropolis devoted to business has a huge concentration of technology firms, corporate headquarters, and wholesale markets. Infamous as the place where President Kennedy was assassinated, Dallas is nonetheless an energetic, enjoyable city, home to many prestigious museums, restaurants, and cultural venues.

Dallas is a sprawling city, merging into neighboring Fort Worth *(see pp480–81)*. The nation's eighth-largest city features a lively downtown, where most of the visitor attractions are located. A square-mile grid of streets centering on Main Street holds the main commercial district that is also the home of some of the country's best museums. The lively West End and hip Deep Ellum districts lie at the edges of downtown. Walking in Dallas is an option, but a car, a cab, or the new DART trams can help make the most of a visitor's time.

### Reunion Tower

300 Reunion Blvd E. *(214) 651-1234.* *10am–10pm Sun–Thu, 10am–midnight Fri–Sat.* *may close for special events.*

Looking over Dallas from the western edge of downtown, this 50-story landmark is topped by a geodesic sphere containing a restaurant, a cocktail bar, and an observation area. Although not the city's tallest building, a title held by the 72-story Bank of America Tower located on Main Street, Reunion Tower does offer an unforgettable panoramic view of Dallas and its surrounding suburbs, and remains one of the city's most distinctive landmarks.

### Sixth Floor Museum

411 Elm St. *(214) 747-6660.* *9am–6pm daily.* *Dec 25.*

At the west end of downtow Dallas, this private museum meticulously re-creates the context while describing the controversial events of November 22, 1963, when President Kennedy was assassinated. Located in the former warehouse from which Lee Harvey Oswald shot and killed Kennedy, the exhibition concentrates on th life and times of Kennedy.

The corner window from which the shots were fired has been rebuilt to look like did on the day of the assassination. A portion of th floor space documents the many conspiracy theories th question the official version of the president's murder.

### West End Historic District

Bounded by highways and railroad tracks, this compact district of the century-old warehouses has been revitalized as the city's prime recreation center. At the north en a former candy factory has been resurrected as the West End Marketplace, a four-stor complex of shops, nightclub and movie theaters.

### Dallas Museum of Art

1717 N Harwood St. *(214) 922-1200.* *11am–5pm Tue–Sun (unti 9pm Thu).* *Jan 1, Thanksgiving, Dec 25.*

Housed in an expansive modern building north of downtown, the wide-ranging collection of this museum

**Modernist façade of the Dallas Museum of Art**

ves a fine overview of art story. The main galleries e arranged by continent, th works shown in chrono- gical order. Noteworthy nong these is the Art of e Americas gallery, display- g treasures from ancient aya and Inca civilizations rough paintings by such nerican artists as Frederic urch and Thomas Hart nton, with a special focus Texas-made art of the ild West.

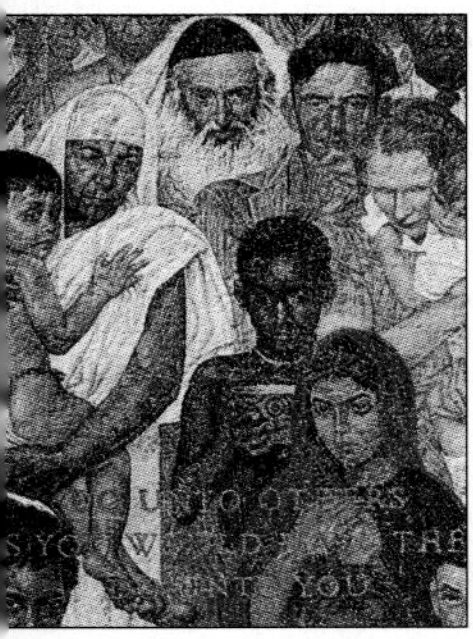

saic mural in downtown's anks-giving Square

The European Sculpture and Painting gallery traces the evolution of art from Greek and Roman antiquities through the Renaissance, ending with a fine display of Modernist paintings. The world's most extensive collection of works by influential Dutch artist Piet Mondrian (1872–1944) is also on display.

THE BONE

**Sign from a Deep Ellum nightclub**

### Thanks-giving Square

Pacific Ave. *(214) 969-1977.*

A peaceful and quiet oasis in bustling downtown, this pocket-sized park is packed with waterfalls, gardens, a belltower, and a chapel. A small museum traces the history of the American custom of Thanksgiving and expresses gratitude for life in all its myriad forms.

### Fair Park

First Ave. *(214) 421-9600.*

This 277-acre (111-ha) exhibition center is the site of the annual Texas State Fair. It hosts the famous annual Cotton Bowl football game as well as many concerts and theater festivals. Alongside an aquarium, a natural history museum, and an African-American history museum, a highlight here is the Hall of State, a huge Art Deco repository of exhibits tracing all things Texan with customary bravado.

### Deep Ellum

Main & Commerce Sts. *(214) 748-4332.* www.deepellumtx.com

Long known as Deep Ellum (a corruption of Elm Street), this is one of the centers of historic Dallas. During Prohibition *(see p49)* the neighborhood flourished as secret "speakeasy," with nightclubs providing alcohol and entertainment. Seminal jazz and blues musicians have performed here over the years. Today, the neighborhood is a combination of industrial premises, stylish restaurants, and avant-garde nightclubs.

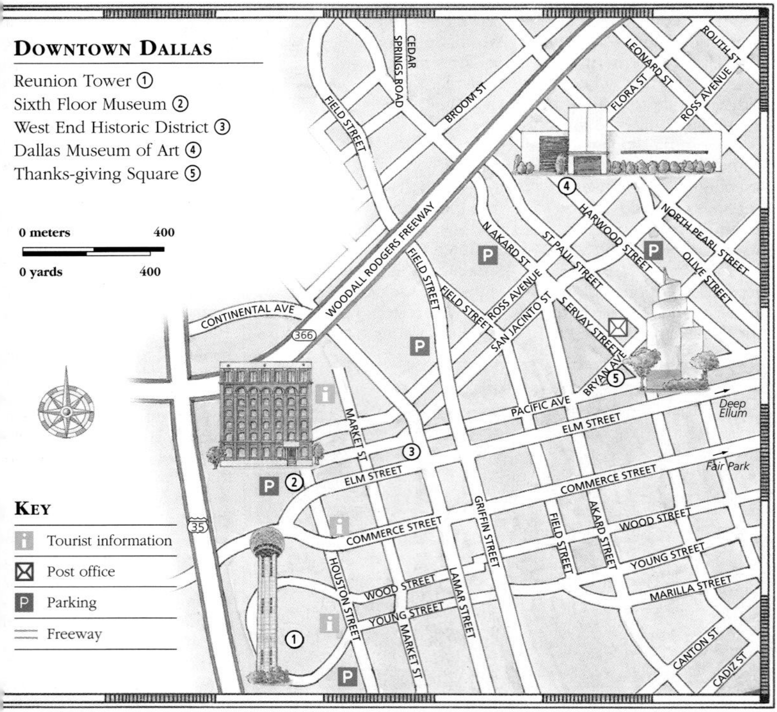

## Downtown Dallas

Reunion Tower ①
Sixth Floor Museum ②
West End Historic District ③
Dallas Museum of Art ④
Thanks-giving Square ⑤

0 meters 400
0 yards 400

**Key**

Tourist information
Post office
Parking
Freeway

# Fort Worth ❷

*492,000. ✈ 🚌 Greyhound Lines, 901 Commerce St. ℹ 415 Throckmorton St, (817) 336-8791. 🎪 Fort Worth Stock Show & Rodeo (late Jan–early Feb); Van Cliburn International Piano Competition (Jun).* W www.fortworthgov.org

UNLIKE ITS FLASHY neighbor, Dallas, 25 miles (40 km) to the east, Fort Worth is smaller, much calmer, and more down-to-earth. In many ways it is also truer to its Texas roots. Founded in 1849 as a US Army outpost, Fort Worth boomed after the Civil War, when Chisholm Trail cattle drives made the city one of the country's largest livestock markets. Although cowboy culture lives on in the Stockyards District and the Amon Carter Museum, Fort Worth is also a capital of "high" culture, with some of the nation's finest performing arts spaces and organizations.

Fort Worth has three main areas of interest. Downtown Fort Worth revolves around Sundance Square, comprising more than a dozen blocks of historic buildings at the center of the city. To the north is the Stockyards District, where the Wild West culture is alive and well. About 2 miles (3 km) to the west, the Fort Worth Cultural District has some of the country's best museums. These are centered around the landmark Kimbell Art Museum, which along with the Amon Carter Museum traces the highpoints of European and American art. Other museums include the excellent Modern Art Museum, and the Museum of Science and History, which also houses a planetarium.

**The Water Gardens, designed by the architect Philip Johnson**

While walking is enjoyable in and around downtown, a car is essential to get around the rest of city.

### Sundance Square

(817) 255-5700.

The heart of downtown Fort Worth, Sundance Square's name is a reminder of the city's Wild West past, when Chisholm Trail cattle drives used to come right through town, and cowboys and outlaws such as Butch Cassidy and the Sundance Kid frequented the city's many saloons. Filled with well-restored commercial buildings dating from the turn of the 20th century, the bric paved streets of Sundance Square are now lined with theaters, shops, and restaurants. The city's symphony, ballet, and opera companies are all housed here. An important museum in this area is the **Sid Richardson Collection of Western Art** on Main Street. Housed in a replica of an 1895 building, the museum exhibits 60 paintings of the famed artist Frederic Remington and Charles M. Russell. Also on Main Street is the trompe l'oeil mural of the Chisholm Trail by Richard Haas.

### Water Gardens

Houston & Commerce Sts.

(817) 871-7275.

Located on the site of Fort Worth's historic red-light district of Wild West saloons this 5-acre (2-ha) park features a variety of waterfal cascades, stream and fountains. Constructed in concrete and designed by architect Philip Johnson, the Wa Gardens provide welcome relief c hot summer days

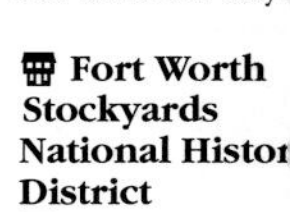


**Advertisement for Western wear in the Stockyards District**

### Fort Worth Stockyards National Histor District

(817) 626-7921.

With its cobblestoned street raised wooden sidewalks, and streetlights designed to resemble old-fashioned gas lights, this small but engagir 10-block neighborhood is located 2 miles (3 km) nort of downtown. Known as the Stockyards District, it developed alongside the sprawling Fort Worth Stockyards, where each day more than a million head of cattle were sold and shipped to markets in the eastern Unite States. Though the stockyar ceased to be commercially viable many years ago, the complex preserves the old wooden pens and holds da livestock auctions.

Today, the neighborhood offers a glimpse of what life in Texas was like a century

**View of Stockyards District with its many saloons**

…nghorn cattle being led through Stockyards National Historic District

…go. A number of lively …owboy-themed saloons and …onky-tonk nightclubs, many …aturing live music, are also …cated here. The oldest and …ost atmospheric of these is …e White Elephant Saloon. …lso nearby are the Longhorn …loon and **Billy Bob's Texas** *(…ee p495)*. Said to …e the largest …ghtclub in the …orld, Billy Bob's …exas is housed … a huge building …nd boasts …2 bar areas. …ve bull-riding …emonstrations …so take place here …n weekend nights. …he district includes a small …useum and a steam train. …ther attractions include …eekend rodeos and a daily …arade of longhorn cattle …own Exchange Avenue. …oday, this is an up-and-…oming area, where trendy …ars and cafés spring up …most every day.

Sign for Billy Bob's Texas nightclub

### Kimbell Art Museum

3333 Camp Bowie Blvd. *(817) 332-8451.* *10am–5pm Tue–Thu, noon–8pm Fri, 10am–5pm Sat, noon–5pm Sun.* *Jan 1, Jul 4, Thnksg., Dec 25.* *exhibitions only.*

One of the most unforgettable museums and art collections in the United States, the Kimbell Museum is an architectural masterpiece, designed by Louis Kahn in 1971 as a series of vaulted roofs that seem to hover in mid-air. The gallery spaces are bathed in natural light, showing off the varied beauty of the diverse collections, which include pre-Columbian Mayan pottery, and jewelry, as well as rare ancient Asian bronzes. Paintings on display range from Renaissance and Baroque masterpieces by Rubens, Rembrandt, Tiepolo, and Tintoretto to a world-class collection of Post-Impressionist and early Modernist paintings by such celebrated masters as Cezanne, Picasso, and others.

### Amon Carter Museum

3501 Camp Bowie Blvd. *(817) 738-1933.* *10am–5pm Tue, Wed, Fri & Sat, 10am–8pm Thu, noon–5pm Sun.* *Jan 1, Jul 4, Thanksg., Dec 25.* www.cartermuseum.org

Along with the Kimbell Art Museum across the street, the Amon Carter Museum anchors Fort Worth's much-vaunted Cultural District, which is located 2.5 miles (4 km) west of downtown. In contrast to its neighbor, however, the Amon Carter Museum concentrates entirely on American art of the Wild West, housing seminal paintings, drawings, and sculptures by Thomas Moran, Frederic Remington, Charlie Russell, and Georgia O'Keeffe among others. Said to be one of the foremost collections of cowboy art, the Amon Carter Museum also has the distinction of possessing the world's most extensive library. It has more than 100,000 photographs documenting the discovery, exploration, and settlement of the country's western frontier.

The Amon Carter Museum, which features cowboy art

Magazine cover depicting cowboy in action, 1913

## Cowboys

The romanticized image of the cowboy, as portrayed by Hollywood Westerns, was far removed from reality. During the 1880s, the demand for beef in the East and Midwest led to the Texas cattle trails, which linked the open ranges with railroads. Of these, the most famous was the Chisholm Trail to Abilene, Kansas. Cowboys traveled across the country on trail drives that were often fraught with danger. These poorly paid young men mostly rode the flanks of a herd to prevent cattle from wandering off. Those at the rear faced even more difficult conditions: Indian attacks, choking dust, long hours, and outlaw hustlers. From this tough life emerged the myth of the cowboy, celebrated in films, literature, music, and fashion. The first cowboy star was Buffalo Bill *(see p582)*. Since then, the rugged roles played by John Wayne and Clint Eastwood fashioned popular perceptions of cowboys and life in the Wild West.

Exterior of the Texas State Capitol in Austin

## Austin ❸

575,000. 209 E 6th St; (512) 478-0098, (800) 926-2282. www.ci.austin.tx.us

THE CAPITAL CITY of Texas, Austin is also home to a thriving high-tech industry as well as the state's main university. However, it is best known for hosting one of the liveliest popular music scenes in the country since the 1960s. Musicians as diverse as Janis Joplin and Willie Nelson achieved prominence in Austin, and the city still abounds in live music venues, concert halls, and nightclubs that host scores of young musicians aspiring to fame.

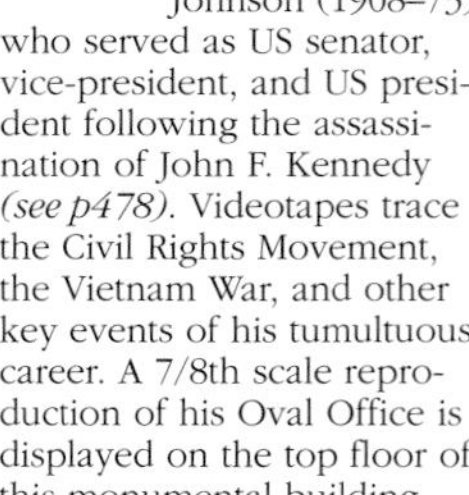


Nightclub sign, Austin

Showcasing the Texan love of all things large, the **Texas State Capitol**, in the heart of downtown, is the largest such structure in the US. Built in 1888, it has 500 rooms covering some 8.5 acres (3.5 ha) of floor space. With its over 300-ft (92-m) high pink granite dome dominating the downtown skyline, the building is taller than the US Capitol in Washington *(see pp198–9)*. In the rotunda beneath the dome, the floor contains the official seals of the six nations – Spain, France, Mexico, the Republic of Texas, the Confederacy, and the US – whose flags have all flown over Texas.

North of the Capitol complex, the expansive campus of the **University of Texas** spreads east from Guadalupe Street. Centering on a landmark tower, the campus holds a number of museums and libraries. The new **Blanton Museum of Art** has over 13,000 works of art, from the Renaissance to Abstract Expressionism, many of which were donated by novelist James Michener. The **Lyndon Baines Johnson Presidential Library**, at the northeast edge of the campus, is a repository for all official documents of the Texas-born Johnson (1908–73), who served as US senator, vice-president, and US president following the assassination of John F. Kennedy *(see p478)*. Videotapes trace the Civil Rights Movement, the Vietnam War, and other key events of his tumultuous career. A 7/8th scale reproduction of his Oval Office is displayed on the top floor of this monumental building.

### Texas State Capitol

11th St & Congress Ave. *(512) 463-0063. 7am–10pm Mon–Fri, 9am–8pm Sat–Sun. Jan 1, Easter, Thanksgiving, Dec 24–25.*

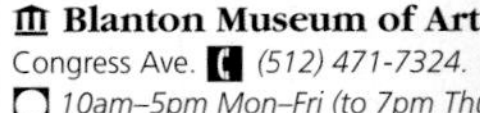

### Blanton Museum of Art

Congress Ave. *(512) 471-7324. 10am–5pm Mon–Fri (to 7pm Thu), 1–5pm Sat–Sun. public hols.*

## Fredericksburg ❹

*8,400. 302 E Austin St, (830) 997-6523.* www.fredericksburg.texas.com

ONE OF THE loveliest small towns in Texas, and centerpiece of the rolling Hill Country that spreads over 25,000 sq miles (64,749 sq km) west of Austin, Fredericksburg was first settled by German immigrants in 1846. The town's strong Germanic heritage is kept alive by a number of biergartens and Bavarian-style buildings such as the reconstructed Vereinskirche (community or union church) in the Marktplatz, off Main Street.

The town is also home to the **National Museum of the Pacific War**, which traces the history of US military activities in the South Pacific during World War II. The museum is housed in the steamboat-shaped Nimitz Hotel. The hotel was built in the 1850s by the family of US Admiral Chester Nimitz, the commander-in-chief of US forces, who was born in Fredericksburg. It operated as a hotel until the early 1960s and opened as a museum in 1967. The museum has been greatly expanded since, but the appearance of the old hotel has been preserved. The tranquil Japanese Peace Garden, gifted by the Japanese government, is at the back.

Located midway between Fredericksburg and Austin, the boyhood home of the Vietnam War-era, 36th US president has been preserved

Tank display in the National Museum of the Pacific War, Fredericksburg

the **Lyndon B. Johnson tional Historical Park**. ner features of the park, ich includes some sites ead out over the surround- area, are Johnson's one- om rural school, the ranch t served as his "Texas nite House," and his grave.

**National Museum of the cific War**
E Main St. (830) 997-4379. m–5pm daily. Dec 25.
www.nimitz–museum.org

**Lyndon B. Johnson tional Historical Park**
290 in Johnson City. (830) 3-7128. 8:45am–5pm daily. Jan 1, Thanksg., Dec 25.
www.nps.gov/lyjo

## errville 5

21,000. 2108 Sidney er St, (830) 896-1155.
www.kerrvilletx.com

PICTURESQUE RESORT and retirement community ated in the rugged hills ove the Guadalupe River, rrville is one of the largest vns in the Texas Hill untry. This friendly town is nous for the 18-day folk isic festival it hosts annu- y at the Quiet Valley Ranch t south of town, starting ursday before Memorial y. While the festival now racts singers and fans from over the world, it still ains the homey, intimate nosphere of the early years. Another highlight in town the **Museum of Western t**, which showcases con- nporary painting and lpture depicting the working life of cowboys. The many galleries within the museum display everything from illustrations made for Western novels to more workaday aspects of cowboy life such as saddles and spurs.

**German-style architecture in New Braunfels**

**Museum of Western Art**
1550 Bandera Hwy. *(830) 896-2553.* *9am–5pm Tue–Sat, 1–5pm Sun.* *Jan 1, Easter, Thanksgiving, Dec 25.*
www.caamuseum.com

## New Braunfels 6

*28,000.* *390 S Seguin St, (830) 625-2385.*
www.nbcham.org

A POPULAR DAY-TRIP from San Antonio *(see pp484–5)*, New Braunfels was one of many towns settled by German immigrants in the tumultuous 1840s, when Texas was an independent republic offering land grants to Anglo-Saxon settlers. The German heritage still thrives in local architecture, cuisine, language, and festivals. Many historic and restored German-style buildings can be seen across the town. However, German influence is most evident in the numerous annual festivals celebrated here, such as the sausage and beer festivals and the Polka Festival, all of which help preserve the town's strong German roots.

Built on the site that the town's aristocratic founder Prince Carl of Solms-Braunfels, Germany, chose for his castle (it was never built), the **Sophienburg-New Braunfells Archives and Museum of History** documents the town's history. Exhibits include several local artifacts and re-creations of pioneers' homes and shops, an early bakery, a doctor's office, and a pharmacy.

**Sophienburg-New Braunfells Archives & Museum of History**
401 W Coll St. *(830) 629-1572.* *10am–5pm Mon–Sat, 1–5pm Sun.* *public hols.*

**llery inside Kerrville's Museum of Western Art, displaying paintings and lptures exemplifying the life of cowboys.**

# San Antonio ❼

Detail, Alamo Memorial

THE MOST HISTORIC CITY in Texas, San Antonio is also the most popular, both for its pivotal historic role and its natural beauty. Once home to the Comanche Indians, the riverside site drew the attention of Spanish missionaries, who founded Mission San Antonio de Valero in 1718. Later converted into a military outpost and renamed the Alamo, it was the site of the most heroic episode of the Texan revolution. Predominantly Hispanic and Mexican in character, San Antonio balances a thriving economy with a careful preservation of its past. Most of the historic sites lie within a block of the pedestrian-friendly Riverwalk in the downtown core.

Hertzberg Circus Museum

**★ Riverwalk (Paseo del Rio)**

*This tree-shaded path along the San Antonio River was built as a flood-control project during the Depression-era New Deal. Now a horseshoe-shaped, open-air promenade lined with shops, Riverwalk is a peaceful oasis in the middle of the city.*

Hertzberg Circus Museum

**★ La Villita**

*It was in this early 19th-century "little village," that the Mexicans officially surrendered to the Republic of Texas. The quaint village of stone and adobe buildings now houses craft workshops.*

Mission San Jose

## Missions National Historical Park

This 819-acre (331-ha) historic park preserves four Spanish frontier missions, which, along with the Alamo, formed the northern edge of Spain's North American colonies in the 18th century. Still in use as Catholic parish churches, the former missions such as Missions San Jose, San Juan, Espada, and Concepcion spread south from downtown San Antonio along the 9-mile (14-km) "Mission Trail." The finest of the group, Mission San Jose, is known for the intricately carved stonework of the Rose Window adjacent to the sacristy.

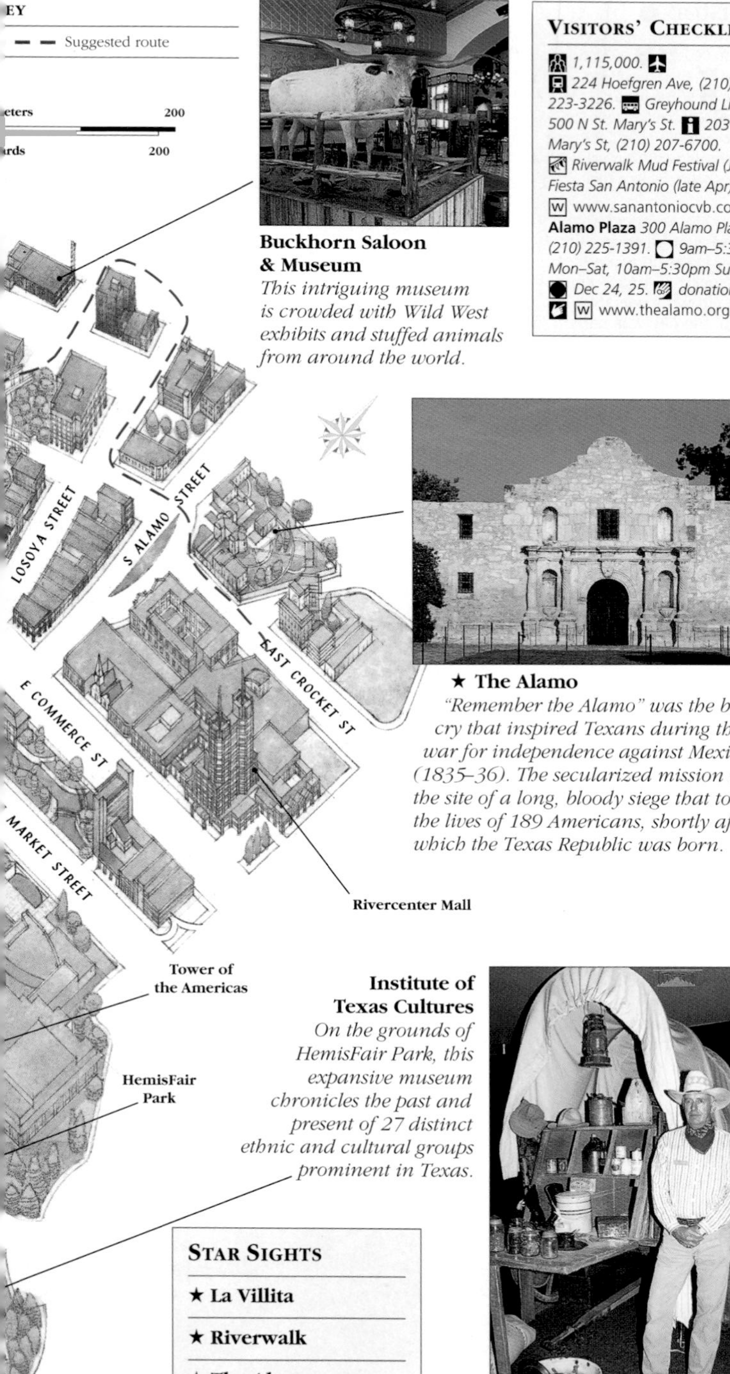


**Buckhorn Saloon & Museum**
*This intriguing museum is crowded with Wild West exhibits and stuffed animals from around the world.*

## Visitors' Checklist

1,115,000. 224 Hoefgren Ave, (210) 223-3226. Greyhound Lines, 500 N St. Mary's St. 203 S St. Mary's St, (210) 207-6700. Riverwalk Mud Festival (Jan), Fiesta San Antonio (late Apr). www.sanantoniocvb.com

**Alamo Plaza** 300 Alamo Plaza, (210) 225-1391. 9am–5:30pm Mon–Sat, 10am–5:30pm Sun. Dec 24, 25. donation. www.thealamo.org

**★ The Alamo**
*"Remember the Alamo" was the battle cry that inspired Texans during their war for independence against Mexico (1835–36). The secularized mission was the site of a long, bloody siege that took the lives of 189 Americans, shortly after which the Texas Republic was born.*

Rivercenter Mall

Tower of the Americas

HemisFair Park

**Institute of Texas Cultures**
*On the grounds of HemisFair Park, this expansive museum chronicles the past and present of 27 distinct ethnic and cultural groups prominent in Texas.*

## Star Sights

- ★ La Villita
- ★ Riverwalk
- ★ The Alamo

## Houston ❽

*1,800,000.* *902 Washington Ave.* *Greyhound Lines, 2121 S Main St.* *901 Bagby St, (713) 437-5200.* *Houston Livestock Show (late Feb–early Mar); Art Car Parade (May); Thanksgiving Day Parade (Nov).* www.houston-guide.com

A CITY OF constant change and great diversity, the story of Houston is a typical Texas success story. Founded in 1836 in what was then a swamp, the city was named in honor of Texas hero General Sam Houston *(see p474)* and served as capital of the Texas Republic until 1839. A center for shipping cotton, Houston's fortunes faded after the Civil War, but it developed into a major port following the construction of a shipping channel to the Gulf of Mexico. The discovery of oil turned the city into a major petrochemical producer, and in recent years it has grown into the biggest city in Texas and the fourth-largest in the US. Free enterprise rules Houston, the home of the now-defunct Enron, but a long tradition of community pride has also endowed the city with some of the world's finest art museums.

A huge, sprawling city that has grown to cover over 600 sq miles (1554 sq km), Houston is a thoroughly confusing place, lacking in an overall plan. The absence of zoning codes or any real visual order, the frequent changes in street names and directions, and the lack of public transportation and often heavy road traffic, can make matters worse.

In short, to see Houston visitors should be prepared to drive, and to get lost more than once. The main attractions for visitors lie southwest of downtown, on and around the Rice University campus.

**Expansive gardens surrounding Ima Hogg's mansion, Bayou Bend**

### Menil Collection

1515 Sul Ross. *(713) 525-9400.* *11am–7pm Wed–Sun.* *Jan 1, Easter, Jul 4, Thanksgiving, Dec 25.*

One of the world's better assemblies of painting and sculpture, this collection was endowed by the family of Houston philanthropist Dominque de Menil, who died in 1997. It is housed in a striking modern building designed by Italian architect Renzo Piano, one of the designers of the Pompidou Center in Paris. The most extensive display here is of Surrealist paintings, notably by Rene Magritte and Max Ernst. The museum also has a world-class collection of Cubist painting by Picasso and Braque in particular, as well as a full survey of 20th-century American paintings by Jackson Pollock, Jasper Johns, Robert Rauschenberg, and Cy Twombly. Separate galleries display ancient and medieval art of the Mediterranean. Also on view is a show of works by Native peoples of Africa, the South Pacific, and the Pacific Nort west region of North Americ

A short walk east from the main museum stands the ecumenical **Rothko Chapel**, spare concrete space designe around a series of large, dark colored abstract paintings by the American artist Mark Rothko. Commissioned by th de Menil family and complet by architect Philip Johnson in 1971, the chapel is open during museum hours. Two blocks to its south lies the Menil-sponsored **Byzantine Fresco Chapel Museum**, a detailed replica of a 13th-century Eastern Orthodox chapel, which displays the only Byzantine frescos on vie in the Western Hemisphere.

### Museum of Fine Arts

1001 Bissonnet St. *(713) 639-73* *Tue–Sun.* *Jan 1, Thnksg., De 25.* www.mfah.org

The oldest art museum in Texas, and one of the larges in the US, the collections here range from Greek and Roman antiquities to Wild West sculptures by Frederic Remington. The striking new Beck Building has European art of the late 19th and early 20th century, with a survey works by Manet, Pisarro, Renoir, and other masters.

### Bayou Bend

1 Wescott St. *(713) 639-7750.* *10–11:30am, 1–2.45pm Tue–Fri, 10–11:15am Sat.* *Jan 1, Thanksgiving, Dec 25.*

The largest public gardens in Houston surround the pink stucco mansion of oil heires Ima Hogg (1882–1975), who survived her somewhat unfo tunate name to become one

**A view of downtown Houston and Memorial Park**

›n signs light up the lively Montrose District

Houston's greatest
ıefactors. The wealthy
ilanthrope was not only
ıous as a patron of the
s but was also passionately
ıcerned with the well-
ing of the city. Now run by
: Museum of Fine Arts, her
me displays a collection of
corative arts, highlighted by
ugar bowl crafted by Colo-
l hero Paul Revere *(see
42)*, and 5,000 pieces of
niture, ceramics, and
tiles. Also on display are
rtraits by early American
ists John Singleton Copley
d Charles Willson Peale.

### Montrose District

ontrose" is a catch name › the lively collection of countercultural-flavored galleries, shops, nightclubs, cafés, and restaurants that can be found along Montrose Street and its intersection with Westheimer Road. Apart from the shopping malls and downtown business district, Montrose District is one of the few walkable neighborhoods in Houston and is especially popular on weekend nights.

### Space Center Houston

1601 Nasa Rd 1. (281) 244-2100. *times vary. Call to check.* Dec 25. www.spacecenter.org

Adjacent to the Johnson Space Center, the mission control for all manned US explorations of space since 1965, this visitor-friendly attraction traces the full story of the Space Race. Hands-on exhibits let visitors try on space helmets, touch moon rocks, or peer into actual spaceships such as those from the Mercury, Gemini, and Apollo programs. Computer simulations let visitors fly the space shuttle or land on the moon. But the major attraction of the Space Center is the tour of the still-in-use mission control facilities, where the historic missions to the moon and back were guided.

### San Jacinto Battleground

Hwy 134, 21 miles (34 km) SE of downtown. *(281) 479-2431. May–Sep: 8am–7pm daily; Oct–Apr: 8am–9pm daily.*

The vast plains of Texas can be seen for miles from the foot of this 605-ft (184-m) tall monument, claimed to be one of the tallest in the world. It marks the site of the final battle for the independence of the Texas Republic in 1836. The slim shaft is topped by a massive "Lone Star." A museum at the base traces the history and culture of the state, while an adjacent theater hosts a popular 42-projector, multi-image slide show.

San Jacinto tower

## Downtown Houston

Menil Collection ①
Museum of Fine Arts ②
Bayou Bend ③
Montrose District ④

### Key

Post Office
Freeway

0 meters 250
0 yards 250

**Dense cypress swamp in the Big Thicket National Preserve**

## Big Thicket National Preserve ⑨

Junction of US 69 & Hwy 420, 7 miles (11 km) N of Kountze. *(409) 246-2337.* *9am–5pm daily.* *Jan 1, Dec 25.* www.nps.gov/bith

MAINTAINING A unique mixture of mountains, plains, swamps, and forests, the Big Thicket National Preserve protects 15 distinct biologically diverse areas (nine land units and six water corridors) encompassing over 97,000 acres (39,255 ha) along the Texas–Louisiana border.

Although much of the preserve is relatively inaccessible, the area once served as a hideout for runaway slaves and outlaws. Today, it is best known for housing a wide range of plants and animals. A series of short hiking trails offer close-up views of dense groves of resident oaks, cactus, carnivorous "pitcher plants," and millions of mosquitoes.

## Galveston ⑩

*60,000.* *2428 Seawall Blvd, (409) 763-4311.*

THOUGH comparatively smaller than other Texas cities, Galveston rivals the rest of the state for historical significance and character. Originally a notorious hideout for slave-trading Gulf Coast pirate Jean Lafitte *(see p350)*, Galveston was burned to the ground by US forces in 1821. But by the 1890s the port had grown to be the largest and wealthiest city in Texas. The economy soon declined following a devastating hurricane in 1900, which killed as many as 6,000 people. The subsequent rise of Houston also contributed to Galveston's fading fortunes.

In recent years, many of the city's grand Victorian mansions and 19th-century storefronts have been restored to their original glory. Many exuberantly designed buildings from that period survive in the Strand National Historic Landmark District, near the waterfront. The superbly restored **Ashton Villa** offers a glimpse of an era of wealth and prosperity as well as disaster and change.

Often hailed as one of the state's best resorts on the Gulf of Mexico, the charming island city features more than 30 miles (48 km) of pristine, sandy beaches. Visitors can also indulge in the family-friendl fun of **Moody Gardens**, wi its waterpark pools, a 10-stc Rainforest Pyramid offering incredible tropical environment, and a series of massiv aquariums showcasing life from the world's oceans.

**Ashton Villa**
2328 Broadway. *(409) 762-3933.* *noon–4pm daily; summer 10am–4pm Mon–Sat, noon–4pm S* *Thanksgiving, Dec 25.*

**Moody Gardens**
1 Hope Blvd. *(409) 744-4673.* *Apr–Oct: 10am–9pm daily; Nov–Mar: 10am–6pm Sun–Fri, 10am–8p Sat.* *Dec 25.*

## Aransas National Wildlife Refuge ⑪

Hwy 239. 65 miles (105 km) NE of Corpus Christi. *(361) 286-3559.* *dawn–dusk.* *Dec 25.*

WHILE SUN worshipers flock to the Gulf Coast beaches throughout winter, birds and bird-watchers congregate slightly inland at the 70,000-acre (28,328-ha) Aransas National Wild life Refuge. Established in 1937 to protect the vanishin wildlife of coastal Texas, Aransas is today home to alligators, armadillo, boars, javelinas, coyotes, white-tailed deer, and many other species of wildlife. The most famous visitors here are the endangered whooping cranes, the tallest birds native to North

**Bird-watching in Aransas**

**Pyramid-shaped greenhouse in Moody Gardens, Galveston**

adre Island National Seashore – a popular vacation destination

merica. Standing 5 ft (1.5 m) ll, with white bodies, black-pped wings, and red heads, e cranes migrate here from anada between November nd March, making the salt-ater marshes their winter eding grounds.

Ringed by tidal marshes nd broken by long, narrow onds, Aransas is an ever-hanging land that is still eing shaped by the irquoise blue waters of San ntonio Bay and the storms f the Gulf of Mexico. Grass-nds, live oaks, and red bay hickets that cover deep, andy soils provide spectac-lar background scenery.

## Corpus Christi ⓬

*325,000. 1201 N horeline, (361) 881-1888.*

THE DEEPEST commercial port in Texas and an xtensive US military pres-nce have made Corpus hristi one of the fastest-rowing cities in the state. Its ilitary importance is marked y the famous 910-ft (277-m) ong aircraft carrier, the USS *exington*, moored along the -mile (3-km) downtown aterfront. To its south, the **exas State Aquarium** xplores the sea life of the ulf of Mexico with whales, ays, and sharks, and re-reations of reefs similar to hose that have grown around he Gulf's many offshore oil igs. Texas river otters and the emp's Ridley sea turtle are lso found here.

"Corpus," as residents call the city, looks out across the harbor to **Mustang Island State Park**, where over 5 miles (8 km) of sandy beach stretch along the Gulf of Mexico. At the park's north end, modern condominium resorts detract from the natural scene, overshadowing the historic community of Port Aransas at the island's northern tip.

**Texas State Aquarium**
2710 N Shoreline Blvd. *(361) 881-1200. Memorial Day–Labor Day: 9am–6pm daily; 9am–5pm daily rest of year. Thanksg., Dec 25.*

## Padre Island National Seashore ⓭

*Malaquite Visitor Center, (361) 949-8068.* www.nps.gov/pais

BORDERED BY a pair of tourist resorts at its north and south ends, Padre Island is a slender sandbar that stretches for more than 110 miles (177 km) between Corpus Christi and the Mexican border. The central 65 miles (105 km) have been preserved as the Padre Island National Seashore, which, with few roads and no commercial development, is among the longest wild stretches of coastline in the country. The park is open throughout the year for camping, beachcombing, surfing, swimming, hiking, fishing, and various other activities. Coyotes and other native wild animals still roam the heart of the island.

This is one of the nation's most popular vacation spots. It receives an average of 800,000 visitors per year, especially during the Spring Break, when university students from colder climes in the northern Midwest flock here to unwind and party. South Padre Island marks the southern end of the Gulf Coast of Texas.

A view of the Corpus Christi waterfront

**Republic of the Rio Grande Museum, San Augustin Plaza, Laredo**

## Laredo ⓮

*200,000.* *501 San Augustin St, (956) 795-2200.*

LOCATED ON THE north bank of the legendary Rio Grande (or Rio Bravo, as it is known in Mexico), Laredo is often referred to as the "Gateway to Mexico." It operates two international bridges to Mexico and is hence one of the principal US ports of entry into Mexico.

Located north of the Rio Grande, the original center of Laredo has been well preserved around the historic San Augustin Plaza. Here, the intriguing **Republic of the Rio Grande Museum** is housed in a building that once served as the Capitol of the short-lived independent republic that in 1840 included southern Texas and the three northernmost states of Mexico. The museum traces Laredo's role under six different national flags.

**Republic of the Rio Grande Museum**
1005 Zaragoza St. *(956) 727-3480.* *9am–4pm Tue–Sat, 1–4pm Sun.* *public hols.*

## Rio Grande Valley ⓯

*FM 1015 Expressway 83, Welasco, (956) 968-3141.*

STRETCHING ALONG the Rio Grande for 200 miles (322 km) between Laredo and the Gulf of Mexico, the Rio Grande Valley is a bustling corridor of agricultural, commercial, and retirement communities all jumbled together in a complicated sprawl. Linked by east-west US 83, which becomes increasingly busy as it gets closer to the Gulf, the valley feels very different from the rest of Texas, thanks in part to the lush, temperate climate softened by moisture-laden breezes. Numerous roadside stands sell bags of grapefruits and bunches of red chili peppers, while convoys of trucks lumber past between warehouses and factories on both sides of the river.

The region's story from border banditry to bilateral trade is traced with permanent and changing exhibits at the **Rio Grande Valley Museum**, while numerous parks try to protect the region's varied natural heritage. The 525-acre (212-ha) **Sabal Palm Audubon Sanctuary** preserves the last stand of the stumpy native Sabal palm trees, which once lined the river for miles upstream.

**Rio Grande Valley Museum**
24–25 Boxwood & Raintree Sts, Harlingen. *(956) 430-8500.* *10am–4pm Wed–Sat, 1–4pm Sun.* *by appointment.*

**Sabal Palm Audubon Sanctuary**
International Blvd, 6 miles (10 km) SE of Brownsville. *(956) 541-8034* *7am–5pm daily.* *Jan 1, Thanksgiving, Dec 25.*

## Big Bend National Park ⓰

*Panther Junction, (432) 477-1158* www.nps.gov/bibe

ONE OF THE wildest and most isolated corners of the US, this diverse park cover 801,000 acres (324,154 ha) of southwest Texas. The name "Big Bend" comes from the 90 degree turn made by the Rio Grande as it carves its way toward the Gulf of Mexico through the volcanic rock of the San Vicente and Sierra de Carmen Mountains. Ranging from 1,500-ft (457-m) deep river canyons along the Rio Grande to the pine-forested Chisos Mountains, Big Bend offers a complete experience of the rivers, mountains, canyons, and deserts that define the American Southwest. These contrasts in topography have created a unique

**Fascinating rock formations at Big Bend National Park**

liversity of plant and animal habitats. Coyotes, roadrunners, and javelinas roam freely amid blossoms of spring wildflowers and cacti.

## Fort Davis ⓱

600. Town Square, (432) 426-3015. www.ftdavis.com

SITUATED IN THE scenic Davis Mountains at a height of 4,900 ft (1,494 m), Fort Davis is a popular destination for visitors seeking relief from a typical Texas summer. A key site during the Indian Wars of the 19th century, it was originally established in 1854 as a US Army fort along the main road between El Paso and San Antonio *(see pp484–5)*. Today, it has been preserved as the **Fort Davis National Historic Site**. In summer, costumed interpreters help visitors on self-guided tours through some of the site's restored structures.

Guide dressed as an 1880s cavalry soldier in Fort Davis

The area's high altitude and isolation from large cities has also made it a fine location for astronomical research. Located atop the 6,791-ft (2,070-m) Mount Locke, 17 miles (27 km) northwest of town, the **McDonald Observatory** gives visitors the opportunity to see stars and planets. The Hobby-Eberle spectroscope here has a 430-inch (1,092-cm) mirror, the world's largest.

Catholic Ysleta Mission in El Paso

**Fort Davis National Historic Site**
*Hwy 17. (432) 426-3224. 8am–5pm daily. major public hols.*

**McDonald Observatory**
*Hwy 118. (432) 426-3640. Sep–Apr: 9am–5pm daily; May–Aug: 9am–5pm daily; 8pm–11pm Tue, Fri, Sat. Jan 1, Thnksg., Dec 25.*

## El Paso ⓲

*560,000. 1 Civic Center Plaza, (915) 534-0600.* www.visitelpaso.com

LOCATED ON THE northern bank of the Rio Grande, at one of the river's safest natural crossing places, El Paso has long been part of the largest and liveliest international community along the US–Mexico border. In 1598, Spanish explorer Juan de Onate crossed the river from Mexico and named the place "El Paso del Rio del Norte." It took another 80 years before the city was established with a trio of Catholic missions at Ysleta, Socorro, and San Elizario. Still in operation, the missions are among the oldest communities in Texas. The story of the varying course of the Rio Grande, which frequently shifted its course (and the international border) until a concrete channel was built in 1963, is detailed in a museum at the **Chamizal National Memorial**, a 55-acre (22-ha) park on the US side. Outside, a 1.8 mile (2.9 km) walking trail circles the park.

**Chamizal National Memorial**
800 S San Marcial St. *(915) 532-7273. 8am–5pm daily. Jan 1, Thanksgiving, Dec 25.*

### VISITING MEXICO

A short, easy walk over the "International Bridge" from San Augustin Plaza, Laredo, leads visitors across the border in the typical Mexican border town of Nuevo Laredo. This trip gives visitors a deeper appreciation of the interdependence of these two very different yet increasingly similar countries. There is so much shared culture that, in the border areas at least, the differences between the US and Mexico are less striking than the similarities. Thanks mainly to the "Mexicanization" of the American side, where the population is more than 80 percent Latino, the food, music, and language is much the same. Nuevo Laredo, Juarez, and other Mexican cities are far larger and busier than their American counterparts, with a huge array of shops, restaurants, and bars offering a taste of Mexico. Elsewhere, along the more than 1,000-mile (1,609-km) border, dozens of small towns and villages are less frenetic, letting visitors sample a taco while soaking up some south-of-the-border ambience. For US citizens, a trip across the border requires proof of identity and citizenship. For non-citizens, however, it is vital to confirm their legal status and ensure that they can return to the US. For all travelers, it is far easier and usually quicker to cross the border on foot.

"International Bridge" across the river to Nuevo Laredo, Mexico

Towering El Capitan in Guadalupe Mountains

## Guadalupe Mountains National Park 19

US 62/180, (915) 828-3251. www.nps.gov/gumo

An almost road-free region on the Texas–New Mexico border, this national park covers 85,000 acres (34,398 ha) of rugged mountains that make up portions of the world's most extensive Permian limestone fossil reef, El Capitan, and the 8,749-ft (2,667-m) Guadalupe Peak, the highest point in Texas. Formed as part of the same prehistoric limestone that makes up the nearby (and more popular) Carlsbad Caverns National Park *(see p552)*, the Guadalupe Mountains reward visitors with lofty peaks, spectacular views, unusual flora and fauna, and a colorful record of the past.

A short trail from the visitor center leads to the remains of a stone wall and foundations of a former frontier stagecoach station. This was built as part of the **Butterfield Trail**, which first established a link between St. Louis and California in 1858.

A few miles northeast of the visitor center, a forest of hardwood trees lines the trail of **McKittrick Canyon**. Here lies the site's most famous attraction, the spectacular red-and-orange foliage in October and November. The hiking trails between the canyon walls that shelter a perennial stream are also very popular.

## Lubbock 20

195,000. 1301 Broadway, (806) 747-5232.

Home to 30,000 sports-crazy students at Texas Tech University, Lubbock is a cattle-ranching and cotton-growing city that is perhaps best known for its musical progeny. Local musicians including Roy Orbison, Joe Ely, Waylon Jennings, and Tanya Tucker are all honored in Lubbock's guitar-shaped **Buddy Holly Center**, a musical Hall of Fame named for the city's favorite son, Charles Hardin Holley. A statue of Buddy Holly, one of rock 'n' roll's most enduring icons, stands along 8th Street and Avenue Q.

Other aspects of Lubbock history are covered in the Texas Tech University's **Ranching Heritage Center**, an outdoor assembly of historic structures collected from all over Texas. On display are more than 30 original ranch buildings, from cowboy huts to stately overseers' mansions.

**Buddy Holly Center**
1801 Ave G. *(806) 767-2686.*
*10am–6pm Tue–Fri, 11am–6pm Sat. Jan 1, Easter, Jul 4, Thanksgiving, Dec 25.*

**Ranching Heritage Center**
3121 4th St. *(806) 742-0498.*
*10am–5pm Mon–Sat, 1–5pm Sun. Jan 1, Thanksg., Dec 24–25.*

## Canyon 21

*12,000. 1518 5th Ave, (806) 655-7815.*

Taking its name from the beautifully sculpted geology of nearby Palo Duro Canyon, this medium-sized Texas town is also home to the largest and best-known historical museum in the state. **The Panhandle-Plains Historical Museum**, housed in a stately 1930s complex on the campus of West Texas A&M University, holds over three million exhibits tracing the history of north-central Texas. Flint arrowheads from the Alibates quarry, north of Amarillo, highlight the culture of the region's prehistoric people, while geology and paleontology come together in exhibits exploring prehistoric dinosaurs and their relation to the region's prime industry, petroleum. The story of another great Texas tradition, cattle ranching, is explored through the life of Wild West rancher Charles Goodnight, who owned a

### Buddy Holly (1936–59)

Buddy Holly's statue, Lubbock

Singer, instrumentalist, and songwriter, Buddy Holly was one of the first major rock 'n' roll music performers. Deeply influenced by local blues and country music, he began to sing in country groups while still in high school. By the mid-1950s, Holly was playing in small clubs throughout the Southwest. Drawn increasingly to rock music as exemplified by Elvis Presley, he recorded both alone and as lead performer with the Crickets. The group's energetic style, combining elements of country music and a strong background rhythm, together with Holly's unique hiccoughing vocals, quickly made them a success. Songs such as "Maybe Baby" and Holly's solo hit "Peggy Sue" became runaway hits. Holly's phenomenal career came to an abrupt end in 1959 when he died in a plane crash in Iowa.

·w of Palo Duro Canyon, the "Grand Canyon of Texas"

·0,000-acre (202,344-ha) ıch, and later led the fight save native bison from tinction. Goodnight's home now preserved in the joyable "Pioneer Town," cated behind the museum. About 12 miles (19 km) east town, **Palo Duro Canyon ate Park** protects the 60- le (97-km) long, 1,100-ft 35-m) deep red and yellow ndstone gorge also known the "Grand Canyon of xas." A number of scenic ives and hiking routes run tween the rim and the nyon floor, offering views such geological oddities as e 300-ft (91-m) tall stone ighthouse." Palo Duro is so home to a wide variety flora and fauna, including ring wildflowers, mule deer, d wild turkeys. In summer, e of the canyon's 600-ft 83-m) cliffs forms the backdrop for the pageantry of *Texas*, a popular play on the history of the state.

sculpturally implanted Cadillac r at Cadillac Ranch, Amarillo

**Panhandle-Plains Historical Museum**
2503 4th Ave. *(806) 651-2244.* *Jun–Aug: 9am–6pm Mon–Sat, 1– 6pm Sun; Sep–May: 9am–5pm Mon–Sat, 1–6pm Sun.* *Jan 1, Thanksgiving, Dec 24–25.*

**Palo Duro Canyon State Park**
Hwy 217. *(806) 488-2227.* *8am–10pm daily.*

## Amarillo 22

*176,000.* *4th & Buchanan Sts, (806) 374-1497.*
www.visitamarillotx.com

The commercial heart of the sprawling Texas Panhandle region, and a key center for agriculture as well as oil, natural gas, and nuclear power industries, Amarillo was first settled in 1887 along the Santa Fe Railroad. The city later thrived thanks to its location along the legendary Route 66 *(see p40)*. The route is now immortalized by **Cadillac Ranch**, a Pop Art work created from 10 classic Cadillac cars planted nose-down in a pasture west of downtown. Another more typically Texas experience is the **Amarillo Livestock Auction**, where modern-day cowboys buy and sell their cattle.

**Cadillac Ranch**
S side of I-40 between Hope Rd & Arnot Rd exits. *24 hours.*

## Abilene 23

*110,000.* *1101 N 1st St, (325) 676-2556.*

Although named for the notorious Wild West town in Kansas, Abilene evolved from a frontier settlement to a solid, stable community. Also known as the "Buckle of the Bible Belt," thanks to its predominantly Christian colleges where 8,000 students study, Abilene's past is kept alive at **Buffalo Gap Historical Village**, 14 miles (23 km) southwest of downtown. Founded in 1878, Buffalo Gap maintains over a dozen old buildings such as a courthouse, a train station, and a schoolhouse. Exhibits include Paleo-Indian artifacts and a frontier weapons collection.

**Buffalo Gap Historical Village**
Hwy 89. *(325) 572-3365.* *Mar 15–Nov 15: 10am–6pm Mon–Sat, noon–6pm Sun; Nov 16–Mar 14: 10am–5pm Thu–Sat, noon–5pm Sun.* *Thnksg., Dec 25.*

Cowboy in Buffalo Gap Historical Village, Abilene

# Practical Information

IN A STATE AS VAST AS TEXAS, it helps greatly that information for travelers is readily accessible. Images of oil and cattle ranches immediately spring to mind, and while this is true for much of the state, Texas has much variety to offer. Stretching for nearly 800 miles (1,287 km) from east to west, the state offers everything from bayous and forests to prairies, bare windswept plains, and beautiful beaches. The dynamic, bustling big cities of Dallas and Houston are a contrast to the laid-back charm of the capital city of Austin with its lush riverside parks, and historic San Antonio with its predominantly Hispanic cultural ambience.

## Tourist Information

ALONG MOST major highways in Texas, there are "Welcome Centers," operated by the **Travel Division** of the Texas Department of Transportation. Open between 8am and 5pm daily, these centers offer a full range of tourist information, including details of weather and road conditions, attractions and accommodations. Texas also publishes a magazine called *Texas Monthly* with travel stories and photographic essays on the wonders of the "Lone Star" state.

Most airports have information desks, and all major towns and cities have tourist-oriented Visitors' Bureaus or Chambers of Commerce.

## Natural Hazards

TEXAS HAS ITS fair share of natural hazards. Winter blizzards block roads and strand drivers under heavy snows, while in spring, torrential rains that occur along with tornadoes and severe thunderstorms flood towns and cities located along streams and rivers. The most dangerous hazards are hurricanes, which can strike the Gulf Coast from June till December. Hurricane winds reach speeds of 75 to 150 mph (121 to 241 km/hr) or more, but even more dangerous than the high winds is the storm surge, a dome of ocean water that can cause severe flooding along coastal rivers and bays. Fortunately, sophisticated warning systems are in place to give visitors plenty of time to get out of harm's way. Radio and TV stations broadcast storm watches and evacuation warnings.

## Getting Around

PUBLIC TRANSPORTATION is almost negligible in this state, although a few **Greyhound** routes cover some major cities. A single **Amtrak** route also shuttles along the southern part of t state. There is an excellent network of airports across t state, and many visitors fly between the major cities, a then rent a car to get aroun the surrounding region.

Driving is essential in Texas and the low price of gas makes it a cheap and convenient option. Seat bel are required for drivers and front seat passengers, as well as back seat passenge under 15 years of age. Chil seats are mandatory for all occupants aged 2 and unde Motorcyclists under 21 year of age must wear helmets, while riders over 21 years. must have proof of health insurance before they ride without a helmet. Radar detectors are permitted.

Speed limits for vehicles vary in Texas, with a statewide maximum of 70 mph (113 km/hour) allowed on Interstate Highways during daylight hours.

## Annual Events & Festivals

ONE OF THE BEST ways for visitors to get a feel fo Texas is to take part in one of the state's huge range of annual events and festivals. Soon after the New Year se in, the annual cleaning of the Riverwalk Canal in San Antonio launches the Mud Week, a 10-day festival of a and entertainment. In Marc Austin hosts the youthful South by Southwest festival of popular music.

But the festival season really gets going in summer starting at the end of May with the nationally acclaime **Kerrville Folk Festival**. Many other local festivals, fairs and events take place i towns all over the state, winding up with the massiv **Texas State Fair**. This is or of the largest state fairs in the country, and is held in October in Dallas' extensive Fair Park. In addition to the national holidays, Texas als celebrates Confederate Herc Day (Jan 19), Emancipation Day (June 19), and Lyndon Johnson's Birthday (Aug 27)

## The Climate of Texas

Despite its generally mild climate, weather across the vast state tends to vary greatly. Spring is ideal for travel, when the days are cool and wildflowers are in full bloom. Summer can be very hot and humid, with severe rains often causing floods along rivers and in low-lying areas. October is also good for travel, as temperatures are mild and the skies clear. In winter, snow storms blow down from the Great Plains, and hurricanes hit the Gulf Coast.

**Dallas**

| month | Apr | Jul | Oct | Jan |
|---|---|---|---|---|
| °F/C (high) | 75/24 | 95/35 | 79/26 | 57/14 |
| °F/C (low) | 55/13 | 75/24 | 56/13 | 36/2 |
| sunshine | 21 days | 25 days | 23 days | 21 days |
| rainfall | 3.5 in | 2.3 in | 3.5 in | 1.8 in |

32°F 0°C

## ORTS

PRINGTIME IN Texas is synonymous with baseball, ich is played at a variety of els all over the state. Major gue baseball is represented e by the Houston Astros d the Texas Rangers, both whom play in state-of-the- stadiums, though the ros no longer play in the rodome – once the world's gest indoor space. Tickets major league baseball nes, however, can be pensive and hard to come In any case, a better sense the game and its impor- ce to Texas can be perienced by attending a xas League baseball game, ich may not be as slick, is often more fun. Played smaller arenas in front of a se-knit crowd of enthusi- ic fans, the main Texas gue teams include the El so Diablos and the San tonio Missions.

s summer fades into fall, American football season gins. A number of intense astate rivalries, such as that ween the University of xas and Texas A&M iversity, enliven the college tball season. At the pro- sional National Football gue (NFL) level, the pride Texas is the Dallas Cowboys, self-proclaimed "America's Team." The New Year kicks off in Dallas with the Cotton Bowl, a championship football game played between two of the top universities in the country.

Winter is also basketball season, and games are played at all levels throughout the state. At the professional National Basketball Association level, Texas has the Houston Rockets, the Dallas Mavericks, and the San Antonio Spurs.

## OUTDOOR ACTIVITIES

VISITORS CAN participate in a vast range of outdoor activities all over Texas. From golf to fishing, river rafting to cycling, Texas has something for everyone at all levels and abilities. There are golf courses all over the state, most of them open to the public. Fishing, in a variety of freshwater lakes and in the Gulf of Mexico, is regulated by the **Texas Parks Department**. River rafting along the Rio Grande through **Big Bend National Park** draws people from all over the world, so advance reservations are essential. Biking is also a popular activity, and bicycles can easily be rented from shops in most Texas towns.

## ENTERTAINMENT

LOCATED IN Fort Worth's lively Stockyard District, **Billy Bob's**, the world's largest honky-tonk, is just one of hundreds of nightclubs and performance venues all over this music-loving state. More upscale and refined music can also be enjoyed, thanks to the many orchestras in Texas. Fort Worth has one of the finest music venues, the **Bass Performance Hall**, home to the city's symphony, opera, and ballet.

## SHOPPING

VISITORS WANTING to bring home a souvenir of Texas should try cowboy boots. Western wear shops all over the state may have the perfect pair, but some visitors may wish to take advantage of the discounts offered close to the source at El Paso-based **Tony Lama's**, one of the country's largest and most famous boot makers. For more upscale needs, nothing beats **Neiman-Marcus**, one of the nation's most exclusive department stores, which started in Dallas and is still in business downtown. The sales tax in Texas is 6.25 percent, and cities and counties may impose an additional tax of 2 percent.

## DIRECTORY

### OURIST NFORMATION

**ravel Division**
ept. of Transportation,
O Box 149248,
ustin, TX 78714.
(512) 486-5800.
oad Conditions
(800) 452-9292.

### NATURAL HAZARDS

**National Hurricane enter**
(305) 229-4470.

### GETTING AROUND

**mtrak**
(800) 872-7245.

**Greyhound**
(800) 231-2222.

### ANNUAL EVENTS & FESTIVALS

**Kerrville Folk Festival**
www.kerrville-music.com

**Texas State Fair**
www.bigtex.com

### SPORTS

**Dallas Cowboys**
(972) 556-9900.

**Dallas Mavericks**
(214) 747-6287.

**El Paso Diablos**
(915) 755-2000.

**Houston Astros**
(877) 927-8767.

**Houston Rockets**
(713) 627-3865.

**San Antonio Missions**
(210) 675-7275.

**San Antonio Spurs**
(210) 554-7787.

**Texas Rangers**
(817) 273-5100.

### OUTDOOR ACTIVITIES

**Big Bend Nat'l Park**
(432) 477-2251.

**Texas Parks Dept.**
(512) 389-4800.

### ENTERTAINMENT

**Bass Performance Hall**
525 Commerce St, Fort Worth.
(817) 212-4200.

**Billy Bob's**
Texas Rodeo Plaza, Fort Worth.
(817) 624-7117.

### SHOPPING

**Neiman-Marcus**
1618 Main St, Dallas.
(214) 741-6911.
www.neimanmarcus.com

**Tony Lama Boots**
7156 E Gateway, El Paso.
(915) 772-4327.

# Where to Stay

TRAVELERS TO TEXAS CAN CHOOSE from a wide variety of places to stay, from anonymous highway motels to atmospheric lodgings in historic buildings. Larger cities such as San Antonio and Dallas offer the best range of options. The Gulf Coast has many beach resorts, and there are also unique rural accommodations, many of which pay homage to the state's ranching traditions.

**AMARILLO:** *Big Texan Motel* $
7701 E I-40. *(806) 372-5000, (800) 657-7177.* FAX *(806) 371-0099.*
W www.bigtexan.com
Part of the famous "Big Texan" steak house restaurant complex, this standard highway motel, with all the modern amenities, is designed to look like a Wild West town.

**AUSTIN:** *Carrington's Bluff* $$
1900 David St. *(512) 479-0638.* FAX *(512) 478-2009.*
W www.carringtonsbluff.com
A charming B&B inn, Carrington's Bluff lies within walking distance of downtown and the university campus.

**AUSTIN:** *Driskill Hotel* $$$$$
604 Brazos St. *(512) 474-5911.* FAX *(512) 474-2214.* W www.driskillhotel.com
This distinctive, 1886 landmark features stylized heads of longhorn steers amid an opulent Neo-Classical decor.

**BIG BEND NATIONAL PARK:** *Chisos Mountains Lodge* $
*(432) 477-2291.* W www.chisosmountainslodge.com
A large, modern motel with a few historic stone cottages and excellent views, this complex offers the only indoor accommodations in the park. Advance reservations are essential.

**DALLAS:** *Adolphus Hotel* $$$$
1321 Commerce St. *(214) 742-8200.* FAX *(214) 651-3561.*
W www.hoteladolphus.com
Built by beer baron Adolphus Busch in 1912, this opulent hotel has since become a Baroque-style showcase.

**DALLAS:** *The Mansion on Turtle Creek* $$$$$
2821 Turtle Creek Blvd. *(214) 559-2100.* FAX: *(214) 528-4187.*
W www.mansiononturtlecreek.com
This Marriott-affiliated property has spacious and tastefully appointed rooms, furnished with all modern amenities.

**EL PASO:** *Camino Real Hotel* $$
101 S El Paso St. *(915) 534-3000.* FAX: *(915) 534-3024.*
W www.caminoreal.com
A downtown landmark, this grand hotel's elegant dining area features a huge Tiffany stained-glass dome.

**FORT DAVIS:** *Historic Prude Ranch* $$
Hwy-118. *(432) 426-3202, (800) 458-6232.* FAX *(432) 426-4401.*
W www.prude-ranch.com
The most popular "dude ranch" in Texas, this hotel offers a wide range of activities to its guests including horseback riding, bird-watching, swimming, and taking part in ranching activities.

**FORT DAVIS:** *Indian Lodge* $$
P O Box 1707, Fort Davis 79734. *(432) 426-3254.* FAX *(432) 426-2022.*
W www.tpwd.state.tx.us/park/indian
Backed by the rugged foothills of Davis Mountain State Park, this historic 1930s lodge has an evocative ambience. Advance reservations are essential.

**FORT WORTH:** *Stockyards Hotel* $$$
109 E Exchange Av. *(817) 625-6427.* FAX *(817) 624-2571.*
W www.stockyardshotel.com
This stylish hotel in the heart of the lively Stockyards District is a historic landmark. Room 305, where bank robbers Bonnie and Clyde stayed in 1933, is now the "Bonnie and Clyde Suite."

| Hotel | Credit Cards | Number of Rooms | Recommended Restaurant | Children's Facilities |
|---|---|---|---|---|
| Big Texan Motel | ■ | 54 | ■ | |
| Carrington's Bluff | ■ | 8 | | ● |
| Driskill Hotel | ■ | 188 | ■ | ● |
| Chisos Mountains Lodge | ■ | 72 | ■ | |
| Adolphus Hotel | ■ | 433 | ■ | ● |
| The Mansion on Turtle Creek | ■ | 141 | ■ | |
| Camino Real Hotel | ■ | 359 | ■ | ● |
| Historic Prude Ranch | ■ | 41 | ■ | ● |
| Indian Lodge | ■ | 39 | ■ | ● |
| Stockyards Hotel | ■ | 52 | | ● |

'rice categories for a standard louble room per night, inclusive f breakfast, service charges, nd any additional taxes:

- $) under $100
- $)$ $100–$150
- $)$)$ $150–$200
- $)$)$)$ $200–$250
- $)$)$)$)$ over $250

**CREDIT CARDS** Major credit cards accepted.

**NUMBER OF ROOMS** Number of rooms in the hotel.

**RECOMMENDED RESTAURANT** Good restaurant within the hotel.

**CHILDREN'S FACILITIES** Hotel has various facilities for young children.

**GARDEN OR TERRACE** Hotel has a garden, courtyard, or terrace.

| | Credit Cards | Number of Rooms | Recommended Restaurant | Children's Facilities | Garden or Terrace |
|---|---|---|---|---|---|
| **ORT WORTH:** *Etta's Place* $$$<br>0 W 3rd St. (817) 255-5760. FAX (817) 878-2560. W www.ettas-place.com<br>his comfortable and atmospheric B&B inn has a large library, and a usic room for guests. | ■ | 10 | | | ■ |
| **REDERICKSBURG:** *Inn on Barons Creek Spa & Conference Center* $$<br>8 S Washington St. (830) 990-9202. FAX (830) 990-2582.<br>] www.innonbaronscreek.com<br>pened in 2005, this elegant inn is located close to Main St. Amenities clude a day spa, with a full range of treatments. | ■ | 78 | | | ■ |
| **ALVESTON:** *Tremont House* $$$<br>00 Ship's Mechanic Row. (409) 763-0300. FAX (409) 763-0300.<br>www.wyndham.com<br>modern hotel in a Victorian-era building, Tremont House's rooftop terrace erlooks the Gulf Coast and Galveston harbor. | ■ | 119 | ■ | ● | ■ |
| **ARLINGEN:** *La Quinta Inn* $<br>02 S Expressway 83. (956) 428-6888. FAX (956) 425-5840.<br>] www.laquinta.com<br>comfortable motel with great service, La Quinta is conveniently located the heart of the Rio Grande Valley. | ■ | 130 | | ● | |
| **OUSTON:** *Lovett Inn* $$<br>1 Lovett Blvd. (713) 522-5224. FAX (713) 528-6708. W www.lovettinn.com<br>cated on a tree-lined street near Montrose District, this friendly inn is own for its genteel Southern hospitality. | ■ | 10 | | ● | ■ |
| **OUSTON:** *Warwick Hotel* $$$<br>01 Main St. (713) 526-1991. FAX (713) 526-0359.<br>] www.warwickhotelhouston.com<br>ithin walking distance of the Museum of Fine Arts, this well-restored 20s hotel feels like a luxury resort. | ■ | 308 | ■ | | ■ |
| **AREDO:** *La Posada Hotel* $$$<br>00 Zaragoza St. (956) 722-1701, (800) 444-2099. FAX (956) 722-4758.<br>] www.laposadahotel.com<br>iilt in 1916, this adobe-style building with all modern conveniences fers a very pleasant overnight stay. | ■ | 208 | ■ | ● | ■ |
| **JBBOCK:** *La Quinta Inn* $$<br>1 Avenue Q. (806) 763-9441. FAX: (806) 747-9325.<br>] www.laquinta.com<br>cated on the musical "Walk of Fame," across from the statue of Buddy Holly, is inn is a convenient base for enjoying the city. | ■ | 137 | ■ | ● | |
| **ARATHON:** *Gage Hotel* $$$<br>1 W US-90. (432) 386-4205, (800) 884-4243. FAX (432) 386-4510.<br>www.gagehotel.com<br>ch room in this low-key but distinctive 1920s hotel has period furniture d many accoutrements of cowboy life. | ■ | 43 | ■ | ● | |
| **N ANTONIO:** *Hampton Inn Riverwalk* $$<br>4 Bowie St. (210) 225-8500. FAX (210) 225-8526.<br>www.hamptoninn.com<br>cated in downtown San Antonio, this family-friendly lodge has large oms and a free breakfast buffet. | ■ | 169 | | ● | ■ |
| **N ANTONIO:** *Menger Hotel* $$$$<br>4 Alamo Plaza. (210) 223-4361. FAX (210) 228-0022.<br>www.mengerhotel.com<br>iilt in an unbeatable location, this 1859 hotel offers four-star facilities th a deep sense of Texas heritage. | ■ | 315 | ■ | ● | ■ |

For key to symbols see back flap

# Where to Eat

THE BEST PLACES TO EAT in Texas are those that offer variations within the state's traditional cuisines. "Tex-Mex" is the predominant food style, mixing Mexican dishes with large quantites of Texas beef. Beef also features prominently in the steakhouses and barbecue restaurants. Opening times of restaurants are indicated by a "B" for breakfast, "L" for lunch, and "D" for dinner.

**ABILENE:** *Perini Ranch* $$$
Hwy-89 in Buffalo Gap. *(325) 572-3339.*
One of many contenders for "Best Steakhouse in Texas," Perini's draws customers with juicy steaks. *L Fri–Sun, D Wed–Sun.* *Mon, Tue.*

**AMARILLO:** *Golden Light Café* $
2908 W 6th St. *(806) 374-0097.*
For some of the best burgers, crispiest fries, coldest beers, and coolest live music along historic Route 66, stop at this place – in business since 1946. *D Tue–Sat.*

**AMARILLO:** *Big Texan Steak Ranch* $$$
7701 E I-40. *(806) 372-6000.*
The Big Texan offers a unique test of appetites – if you can eat an entire 72-oz steak, plus accompaniments, within an hour, the meal is free. (If you don't manage to finish, and nine out of ten people don't, the price is around $60). *B, L, D.*

**AUSTIN:** *Hoover's Cooking* $
2002 E Manor Rd. *(512) 479-5006.*
Described as "Texas Comfort Food," the offerings in this boisterous east Austin barn range from okra and black-eyed peas to smoky ribs, chicken, and sausage links. The place also serves great desserts. *L, D.*

**AUSTIN:** *Threadgill's* $
6416 N Lamar Blvd. *(512) 451-5440.*
All-American diner food with a Texas twist is served in a reincarnation of one of Austin's landmark nightclubs – a former gas station. The huge collection of neon signs alone is well worth a visit. *L, D.*

**CORPUS CHRISTI:** *City Diner* $$
622 N Water St. *(361) 883-1609.*
This friendly, retro-1950s diner offers fresh Gulf Coast seafood and a delectable array of seasonal shellfish. *B, L, D.*

**CORPUS CHRISTI:** *Republic of Texas Steakhouse* $$$
900 N Shoreline. *(361) 887-1600.*
With a staggering view of the Gulf Coast, thanks to its position atop the 20-story Omni Hotel, this wonderfully cozy restaurant serves Texas-style steak, chicken, and seafood. *D.*

**DALLAS:** *Gennie's Bishop Grill* $
321 N Bishop Ave. *(214) 946-1752.*
Line up in this 1970s cafeteria to load your plate with an array of fresh vegetables, cornbread muffins, and delicious garlic chicken. But save room for dessert, as the pies are fantastic. *L Mon–Fri.*

**DALLAS:** *Ciudad* $$$
3888 Oak Lawn Ave. *(214) 219-3141.*
Modern Mexico City-style food that goes far above the standard fare. Clever and well-executed dishes served in a sophisticated dining room. *D Mon–Sat, Sun Brunch.*

**DALLAS:** *Zodiac Restaurant* $$
1618 Main St. *(214) 573-5800.*
Take a break from shopping and enjoy a soup, sandwich, or salad at this delectable café, located on the sixth floor of the legendary Neiman-Marcus department store. *Sun.*

**DALLAS:** *Mansion on Turtle Creek Restaurant* $$$$$
2821 Turtle Creek Blvd. *(214) 559-2100.*
This top-rated, elegant restaurant specializes in gourmet versions of traditional Texas and Southwestern food. *(optional)*

| Restaurant | Credit Cards | Outdoor Tables | Vegetarian | Good Wine List | Children's Facilities |
|---|---|---|---|---|---|
| Perini Ranch | ■ | ● | ■ | ● | ■ |
| Golden Light Café | ■ | ● | ■ | | ■ |
| Big Texan Steak Ranch | ■ | | | | ■ |
| Hoover's Cooking | ■ | | ■ | | ■ |
| Threadgill's | ■ | | ■ | | ■ |
| City Diner | ■ | | | | ■ |
| Republic of Texas Steakhouse | ■ | | | ● | ■ |
| Gennie's Bishop Grill | ■ | | ■ | | ■ |
| Ciudad | ■ | ● | ■ | | |
| Zodiac Restaurant | ■ | | ■ | ● | ■ |
| Mansion on Turtle Creek Restaurant | ■ | | | ● | |

**'rice categories** include a hree-course meal for one, a glass of house wine, and all unavoidable extra charges such s sales tax and service.
$ under $25
$$ $25–35
$$$ $35–50
$$$$ $50–70
$$$$$ over $70

**Credit Cards**
Major credit cards accepted.

**Outdoor Tables**
Garden, courtyard, or terrace with outside tables.

**Vegetarian**
A good selection of vegetarian dishes available.

**Good Wine List**
Extensive list of good wines, both domestic and imported.

**Children's Facilities**
Various facilities for young children.

| | Price | Credit Cards | Outdoor Tables | Vegetarian | Good Wine List | Children's Facilities |
|---|---|---|---|---|---|---|
| **L Paso:** *H&H Coffee Shop*<br>1 E Yandell Ave. (915) 533-1144.<br>though basic, the fare here has drawn admiration from such culinary ghts as the *Gourmet* magazine and Julia Child. *B, L.* *Sun.* | $ | | | ■ | | ■ |
| **L Paso:** *Forti's Mexican Elder*<br>1 Chelsea St. (915) 772-0066.<br>ne of the oldest and largest "Tex-Mex" restaurants, this hacienda-style ace serves fine food enlivened by the strolling bands of mariachi usicians. *L, D.* *Thanksgiving, Dec 25.* | $$ | ■ | ● | ■ | | ■ |
| **ort Worth:** *Joe T. Garcia's*<br>01 N Commerce St. (817) 626-4356.<br>is large Mexican restaurant offers all the usual favorites – tacos, chiladas, and fajitas. *L, D.* | $ | | | ■ | | ■ |
| **ort Worth:** *Cattlemen's Steak House*<br>58 N Main St. (817) 624-3945.<br>ith walls covered in life-size portraits of beloved bovine breeds, and a lection of sirloin, rib eye, strip, and filet steaks ready to be grilled over charcoal fire, there's no doubt that beef is the draw here. *L, D.* | $$$ | ■ | | ■ | | ■ |
| **redericksburg:** *Altdorf Biergarten*<br>1 W Main St. (830) 997-7865.<br>r a taste of the German heritage that animates this Hill Country town, it hard to beat this massive *biergarten*, with its sausages, schnitzels, and uerkraut. *L, D.* *Tue.* | $$ | ■ | ● | | | ■ |
| **alveston:** *Gaido's*<br>00 Seawall Blvd. (409) 762-9625.<br>cated right on the Gulf of Mexico, this family-run landmark has been rving fresh-caught fish and shrimp for generations. *L, D.* | $$$ | ■ | ● | ■ | | ■ |
| **ouston:** *T'afia*<br>01 Travis St. (713) 524-6922.<br>astal Mediterranean cuisine made with local ingredients and served in casual, small and intimate dining room. *D Tue–Sat.* | $$$ | ■ | ● | ■ | ● | |
| **ouston:** *Americas*<br>00 Post Oak Blvd. (713) 961-1492.<br>ne of the city's most popular restaurants, Americas looks like a rain- rest and specializes in Carribean cuisine. Try the Gulf Coast snapper ired with a fresh corn on the cob. *L, D.* *Sun.* | $$$ | ■ | | ■ | ● | ■ |
| **ubbock:** *Chez Suzette*<br>23 50th St, Lubbock. (806) 795-6796.<br>is is the most romantic dining spot in Lubbock. Italian cuisine, with French influence with pasta, seafood, veal, and excellent desserts. | $$ | ■ | | ■ | ● | |
| **arathon:** *Café Cenizo*<br>1 W US-90. (432) 386-4437.<br>is atmospheric place in the middle of the lonesome West Texas cattle untry offers eclectic versions of Texas fare. | $$$ | ■ | | ■ | | ■ |
| **an Antonio:** *Mi Tierra Café*<br>8 Produce Row. (210) 225-1262.<br>ell-prepared "Tex-Mex" food is served at this café 24-hours a day. rolling "travatore" musicians add to the experience. | $ | ■ | | ■ | | ■ |
| **an Antonio:** *Boudro's*<br>21 E Commerce St. (210) 224-8484.<br>is waterfront restaurant mixes Texas beef with Mexican and Louisiana ajun specialties. *L, D.* | $$$ | ■ | ● | ■ | ● | ■ |

For key to symbols see back flap

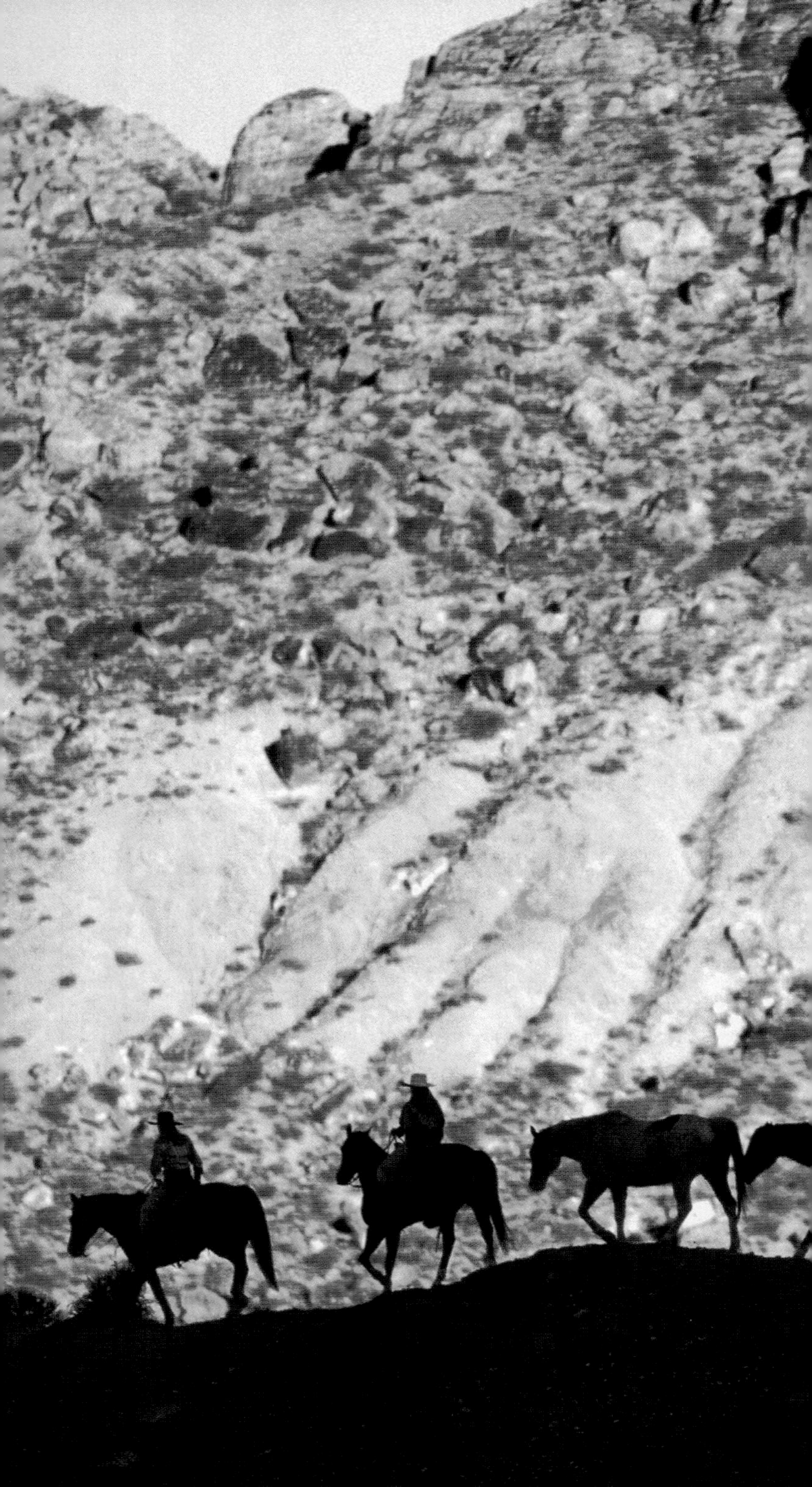

# The Southwest

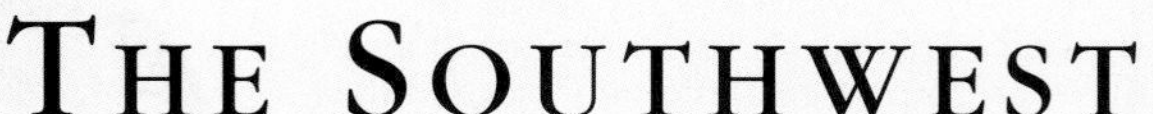

# The Southwest at a Glance

America's southwest is made up of the states of Nevada, Utah, Arizona, and New Mexico. It also includes the Four Corners area, the only place in the US where four states – parts of Utah, Arizona, New Mexico, and Colorado – meet at a central point. The region boasts spectacular landscapes, dominated by desert, deep canyons, and high mesas. Equally fascinating is its multicultural heritage, influenced by Native American, Hispanic, and Anglo-American settlers. Today, this region offers visitors a range of sights, most of which are concentrated in the cities of Phoenix, Tucson, Albuquerque, and Las Vegas.

**Hopi-made coiled basket made of willow or yucca leaves**

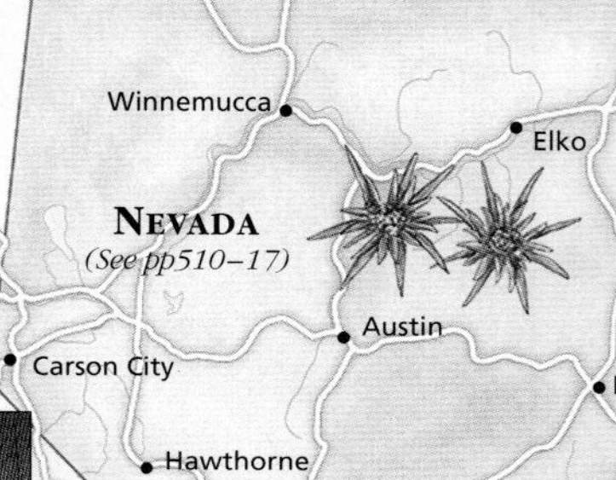

***Las Vegas*** (see pp510–15) *in Nevada draws more than 37 million visitors each year. Its unique attractions are its fantastic, palace-like hotels and casinos with their promise of million-dollar jackpots.*

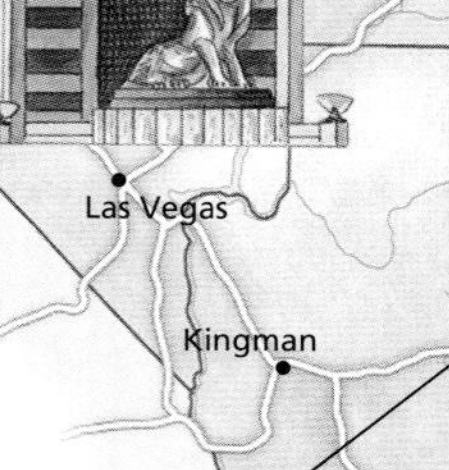

*The* ***Grand Canyon*** (see pp536–9) *in Arizona is the second most-visited national park in the country. This is, however, one of the many natural wonders in a state well-known for its stunning landscapes of pristine deserts, forested hills, and fertile meadows.*

◁ **Horseback riders negotiating a steep trail along a canyon, southern Utah**

i and dried chilies adorning a flower shop, Tucson

**Locator Map**

***Arches National Park*** (see pp520-21) *is just one of the many geological wonders in Utah, a state with the highest concentration of national parks in the United States. The dramatic and unpromising landscape of Utah also became the spiritual and worldly base of the Mormons. Salt Lake City, the state capital, is located northwest of the park.*

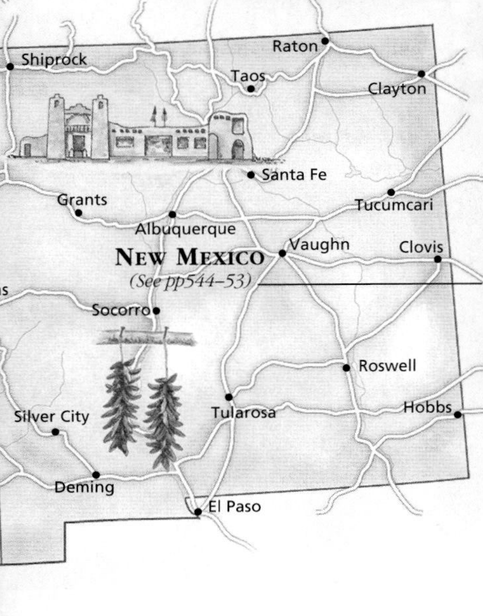


***New Mexico*** (see pp544–53) *is one of the Southwest's most popular destinations. Its scenic beauty and rich cultural heritage have lured generations of artists, who have made Santa Fe and Taos vibrant creative centers. Albuquerque, the largest city, has many fine museums.*

IERA
"SHOW OF THE YEAR"
Splash
VOTED SHOW
OF THE YEAR

# THE SOUTHWEST

DISTINGUISHED BY ITS DRAMATIC LANDSCAPE, *the Southwest is a land of twisting canyons, cactus-studded deserts, and rugged mountains. For more than 15,000 years, the region was inhabited by Native Americans, but by the 20th century Anglo-American traditions had mingled with those of the Hispanic and Native peoples to create the region's multicultural heritage.*

The states of Nevada, Utah, Arizona, and New Mexico make up America's Southwest. Perceptions of this region are influenced by the landscape – the red sandstone mesas of Monument Valley, the tall saguaro cacti of Arizona's Sonoran Desert, the staggering scale of the Grand Canyon, and New Mexico's adobe architecture. At its heart is its defining geological feature – the Colorado Plateau – a rock tableland rising more than 12,000 ft (3,660 m) above sea level and covering a vast area of around 130,000 sq miles (336,700 sq km). The plateau was created by the same geological upheavals that formed the Rocky Mountains. Subsequent erosion by wind, water, and sand molded both hard and soft rock to form the mesas, canyons, and mountains. Many of these natural wonders have been preserved as national parks.

The region's main city, Las Vegas, has been synonymous with glamor and entertainment ever since Nevada legalized gambling in 1931. Mobster Bugsy Siegel opened the first luxury hotel, the Flamingo, in 1946, and soon there was a proliferation of casinos. Some of the biggest names in show business, such as Frank Sinatra and Elvis Presley, as well as eccentric millionaire Howard Hughes, have all contributed to Vegas's image as the fun city of limos, showgirls, and glitzy lifestyles. This city of megaresorts and casinos is as popular for its wedding chapels, where more than 100,000 couples get married each year.

## HISTORY

The first Native American people were a society of hunters who inhabited the region between 10,000 and 8,000 BC. The introduction of new farming techniques and crops, especially corn from Mexico, saw the start of settled farming communities in around 800 BC. By AD 500 an agrarian society

**The desert floor dotted with sagebrush and ponderosa pines, Monument Valley, Arizona**

**Sparkling neon stars of the Riviera Hotel in Las Vegas, Nevada**

was well established, and large villages or pueblos began to develop. By 700 the three main cultures in the region were the Hohokam, the Mogollon, and the Ancestral Puebloan. Ancestral Puebloan people constructed elaborate dwellings that grew into large cities such as Chaco Canyon. However, in the 12th and 13th centuries, these settlements were mysteriously abandoned. It is thought that the people migrated to the Pueblo Indian settlements along the Rio Grande Valley and northwest New Mexico, where their descendants still live. The 15th century saw the arrival of the Navajo, who were hunters, and the fierce Apache warriors from Canada.

In the 1500s, the Spanish quest for wealth, particularly gold, led to the establishment of a permanent colony called New Mexico, which included all of the present-day states of New Mexico and Arizona, as well as parts of Colorado, Utah, Nevada, and California. Mexican independence from Spain was declared in 1821, paving the way for Anglo-American traders. The first Anglos (non-Spanish people of Eur pean descent) in the Southwest we "mountain men" or fur trapper who helped open up the tra routes to the west. With th establishment of the O Spanish and the Santa Fe Trai this remote region becan more accessible.

**Ancient pottery bowl**

The US government's vigoro expansion led to conflict wi Mexico, and the region became a pa of the United States in 1848. Soon, th settlers began to forcibly acquire Nati land, and more than 8,000 Navajo we made to march "The Long Walk" to reservation in New Mexico in 186 Resentment against the Anglos ins gated the Indian Wars, which fina ended with the surrender of Apac leader Geronimo in 1886.

At the same time, rich lodes of go silver, and copper were discovered Arizona, and mining camps such Bisbee and Tombstone became boo towns. This was the Wild West mining prospectors, ranch cowbo and notorious outlaws, such as Bi the Kid, whose exploits form part American folklore

### Key Dates in History

**800 BC** Corn brought from Mexico

**AD 800** Chaco Canyon under construction

**1400** Migrations of the Navajo and Apache

**1540–42** Francisco Vasquez de Coronado leads the search for gold in New Mexico

**1610** Santa Fe established as capital of New Mexico

**1680** The Pueblo revolt against the Spanish

**1821** Santa Fe Trail opened

**1848** Treaty of Guadalupe-Hidalgo cedes Mexican territory to the US

**1868** Navajo reservation founded in Four Corners region

**1869** The coming of the railroad

**1912** New Mexico and Arizona become 47th and 48th states of the United States

**1931–36** Hoover Dam constructed in Arizona

**1945** First atomic bomb tested in New Mexico

**1974** Central Arizona Project begins to extract water from the Colorado River

**1996** President Clinton signs Navajo-Hopi Land Dispute Settlement Act

**2000** Forest fires devastate large parts of northern New Mexico and Arizona

### Society & Culture

The Southwest is a crossroads of t three great cultures that shap America – Native American, Hispan and Anglo-American. The Spani language is prominent, not only in lingual New Mexico but also Arizona. A host of Native Americ languages are also spoken, reflecti the far longer history of the regio Native inhabitants. The Hopi and oth Pueblo peoples trace their ancest back to the Ancestral Puebl peoples, while the Navajo occupy t country's largest reservation, stretchi across the northern ends of bo Arizona and New Mexico. The Apac and many other tribes have land he as well. Today, Native populations ha a hand in governing their own lan and many have diversified their bu ness interests to regenerate th economy and are involved in touris running casinos, and the production such crafts as pottery and rugs.

olorful Navajo rug

A trinity of religious activity is dominant in the Southwest. The most visible is Roman Catholicism, which was introduced in the 16th century by the Spanish colonists. It is today the main ligion, although several Protestant :nominations exist as well. Utah's sidents, however, are predominantly ormon. Native American spiritual ·liefs are complex, as each tribe has own practices.

One of the region's most famous :ributes is the quality of light found in e hills of northern New Mexico. eorgia O'Keeffe's paintings of e local landscape in the ·40s helped to make the area ound Santa Fe a mecca for tists. Today, the city has the untry's second largest art ıde. The smaller resort town Taos is also famous for its sident painters and sculptors. ınta Fe, as well as Phoenix, ıcson, and Albuquerque also offer pera, ballet, classical music, and major eatrical productions. The Pheonix mphony and New Mexico Symphony rchestra, based in Albuquerque, are :st known for their concerts, while zz and country music can be heard in most every city and major town.

Route 66 Flagstaff sign

### Economics & Tourism

oday, New Mexico and Arizona are e country's fifth and sixth largest ates. Despite the fact that the region's pulation is increasing, it remains one the least populated in the United ates. The cities of Phoenix, Tucson, ınta Fe, and Albuquerque account for ·ound 60 percent of the region's pulation. Such intense urbanization ıs put tremendous pressure on the gion's resources, particularly water, hich has become one of the Southest's most pressing issues.

The legacy of the two World Wars ıanged the Southwest's economic course. In the 1940s, New Mexico's sparsely populated and remote desert area of Los Alamos was chosen as the location for the top secret Manhattan Project, which developed the world's first atomic bomb. Since then, the region has been a major center for national defense research and development of nuclear weapon technology, as well as for research into space travel, with both state and federal governments as major employers. Today, other research projects, including biotechnology, especially the Genome Project (which maps all human genes) and computer technology, attract scientists to the Southwest.

Tourism is another of the region's principal employers. Vast wilderness areas and a warm climate make outdoor leisure popular in the Southwest. Its national parks, established in the early 1900s, draw ever-increasing numbers of tourists each year as well. There are also miles of hiking trails, rivers for whitewater rafting, lakes for water sports, ski resorts, and some of the nation's finest golf courses. One of the best ways to experience the landscape is on a trail ride, while armchair cowboys can attend that great Southwestern event – the rodeo.

The Southwest is as much a state of mind as it is a geographical region. The attractions of the landscape and a romantic sense of the past combine to conjure up the idealized legends of the "Wild West." For many visitors, the Southwest offers the chance to indulge that bit of cowboy in their souls.

Horseback riding, a popular pastime in the Sonoran Desert near Tucson, Arizona

# Exploring the Southwest

The four states of the Southwest encompass many natural wonders, such as the Grand Canyon and Monument Valley in Arizona, and Zion National Park in Utah. Beyond the scenic are the pueblo villages along the Rio Grande in New Mexico and the glitter of Las Vegas, Nevada's fastest growing city. Above all, the region conjures up images of the Wild West, as portrayed by Hollywood and preserved by the myths around old mining towns, such as Bisbee and Tombstone.

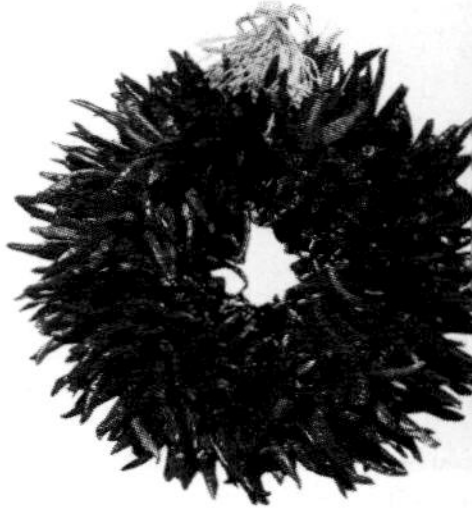

**Chili wreath, Santa Fe**

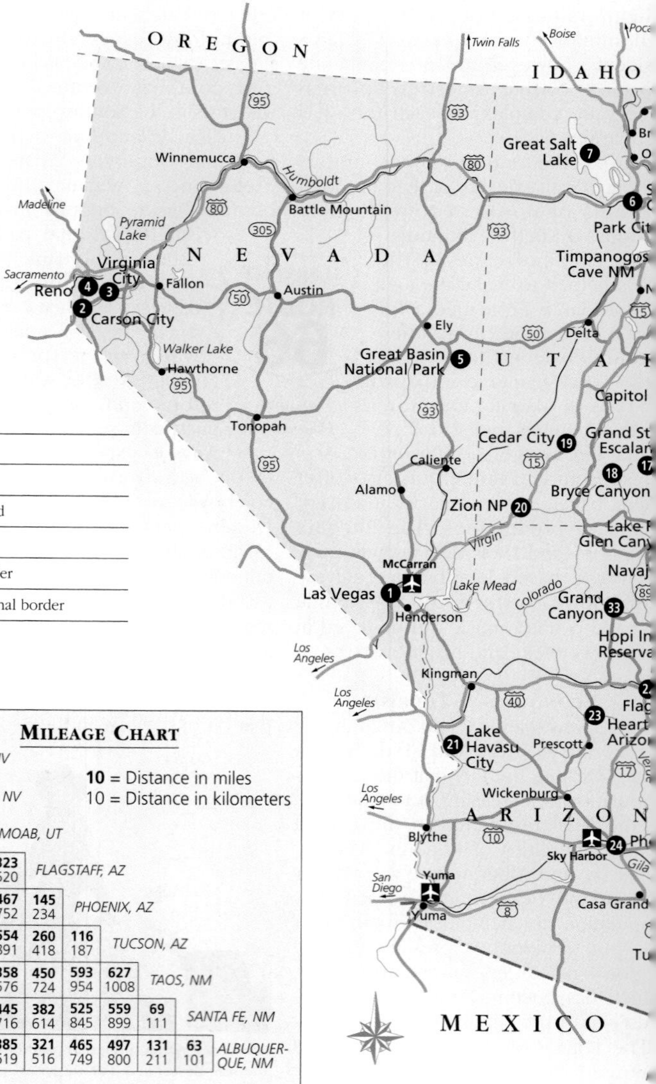

OREGON
IDAHO
NEVADA
UTAH
ARIZONA
MEXICO
Twin Falls
Boise
Winnemucca
Humboldt
Battle Mountain
Madeline
Pyramid Lake
Virginia City
Sacramento
Reno
Fallon
Austin
Carson City
Walker Lake
Hawthorne
Ely
Great Basin National Park
Tonopah
Caliente
Alamo
Cedar City
Zion NP
Virgin
McCarran
Las Vegas
Henderson
Lake Mead
Colorado
Grand Canyon
Los Angeles
Kingman
Lake Havasu City
Prescott
Wickenburg
Blythe
Sky Harbor
Yuma
San Diego
Casa Grand
Great Salt Lake
Park Cit
Timpanogos Cave NM
Delta
Capitol
Grand St Escalan
Bryce Canyon
Lake P
Glen Cany
Navaj
Hopi In Reserva
Flag
Heart
Arizo
Gila
Tu
95
93
80
305
50
15
40
17
10
8
89

**Key**

- Airport
- Highway
- Major road
- Railroad
- State border
- International border

**Mileage Chart**

**10** = Distance in miles
10 = Distance in kilometers

| | | | | | | | | |
|---|---|---|---|---|---|---|---|---|
| LAS VEGAS, NV | | | | | | | | |
| **447** 719 | RENO, NV | | | | | | | |
| **458** 737 | **750** 1207 | MOAB, UT | | | | | | |
| **251** 404 | **697** 1121 | **323** 520 | FLAGSTAFF, AZ | | | | | |
| **286** 460 | **888** 1429 | **467** 752 | **145** 234 | PHOENIX, AZ | | | | |
| **506** 814 | **1003** 1614 | **554** 891 | **260** 418 | **116** 187 | TUCSON, AZ | | | |
| **701** 1128 | **1375** 2213 | **358** 576 | **450** 724 | **593** 954 | **627** 1008 | TAOS, NM | | |
| **633** 1018 | **1307** 2103 | **445** 716 | **382** 614 | **525** 845 | **559** 899 | **69** 111 | SANTA FE, NM | |
| **572** 920 | **1246** 2005 | **385** 619 | **321** 516 | **465** 749 | **497** 800 | **131** 211 | **63** 101 | ALBUQUERQUE, NM |

## SIGHTS AT A GLANCE

**Nevada**

*Las Vegas pp510–15* **1**
Carson City **2**
Virginia City **3**
Reno **4**
Great Basin National Park **5**

**Utah**

Salt Lake City **6**
Great Salt Lake **7**
Park City **8**
Timpanogos Cave National Monument **9**
*Arches National Park pp520–21* **10**
Moab **11**
*Canyonlands National Park p522* **12**
Green River **13**
Hovenweep National Monument **14**
Lake Powell & Glen Canyon National Recreation Area **15**
Capitol Reef National Park **16**
Grand Staircase–Escalante National Monument **17**
*Bryce Canyon National Park pp526–7* **18**
Cedar City **19**
*Zion National Park p525* **20**

**Arizona**

Lake Havasu City **21**
Flagstaff **22**
*Heart of Arizona Tour p529* **23**
*Phoenix pp530–31* **24**
Tucson **25**
Nogales **26**
Bisbee **27**
Amerind Foundation **28**
Petrified Forest National Park **29**
Window Rock **30**
Hopi Indian Reservation **31**
Tuba City **32**
*Grand Canyon pp536–9* **33**
Navajo National Monument **34**
*Monument Valley pp540–41* **35**
*Canyon de Chelly National Monument pp542–3* **36**

**New Mexico**

Chaco Culture National Historical Park **37**
Taos **38**
*Northern Pueblos Tour p545* **39**
*Santa Fe pp546–7* **40**
*Albuquerque pp548–50* **41**
Roswell **42**
Carlsbad Caverns National Park **43**
White Sands National Monument **44**
Gila Cliff Dwellings National Monument **45**

### *SEE ALSO*


- ***Practical Information*** pp554–5
- ***Where to Stay*** pp556–9
- ***Where to Eat*** pp560–63

**Mummy Cave Overlook in Canyon de Chelly, Arizona**

# Las Vegas ❶

THE HEART OF LAS VEGAS, Nevada's most famous city, lies along Las Vegas Boulevard, a sparkling vista of neon known simply as "the Strip." The southern stretch of this 3.5-mile (6-km) long street that runs northeast through the city is home to a cluster of lavishly themed hotels, with their own shops, restaurants, and gaming casinos. They lure almost 37 million visitors every year, making Vegas the entertainment capital of the world. When the lights come on in the evening, these new megaresorts become a fantasyland with riotous design and architecture, such as that of the Luxor's striking pyramid with its sphinx. The exotically themed Aladdin Hotel is evidence of the city's ability to reinvent itself quickly – it took only two years to build.

**A dazzling nighttime view of the Strip**

**New York New York**
*A replica of the Statue of Liberty forms part of the façade of this hotel, whic is composed of a ho of such Manhattan landmarks as the Empire State Building.*

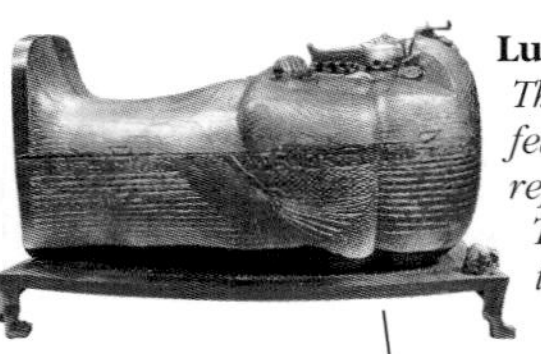

**Luxor**
*The hotel's Egyptian features include a reproduction of Tutankhamun's tomb in the King Tut Museum.*

**The Boardwalk Casin** is a Holiday Inn hotel a features a roller coaster facing the Strip.

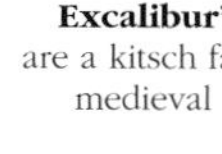

**Mandalay Bay's** interior, with its palm trees and bamboo, re-creates a 19th-century tropical paradise.

**Excalibur's** towers are a kitsch fantasy of medieval England.

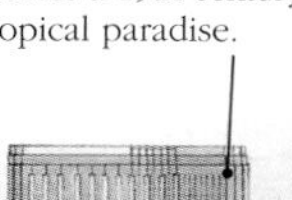

**Showcase Mall** a striking buildi with its giant ne Coca-Cola bottle A huge games arcade makes th mall very popul with families.

**Tropicana**
*This casino was rebuilt in the late 1970s with a stunning Art Nouveau-style stained-glass ceiling and glass lamps.*

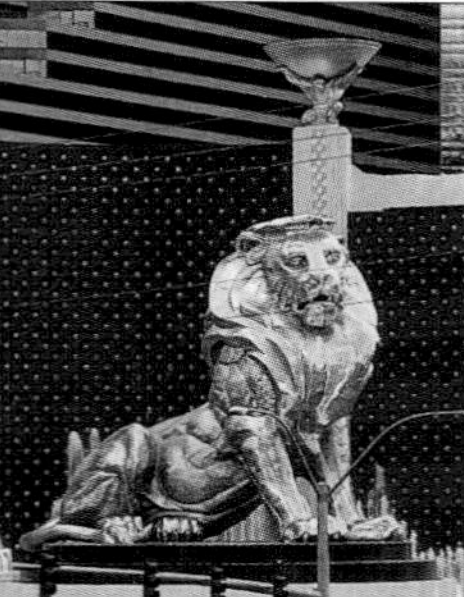

**MGM Grand Hotel**
*The largest hotel in the US with more than 5,000 rooms, the Grand displays 45-ft (15-m) high statue o Leo, symbol of the Holly-wood film studio, MGM.*

**Caesars Palace**
*Reproduction Roman statuary adorns the grounds of Caesars Palace. One of the Strip's oldest and most glamorous hotels, Caesars was ›uilt in 1966. Inside, the lavish Forum Shops mall features moving statues.*

**Imperial Palace**
*A pagoda fronts this Asian-themed hotel, famous for its classic car collection, which is open to all visitors.*

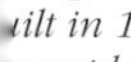

**:llagio**
*ıilt in 1998, this luxury resort's ·gant lobby is hung with sculpted ıss flowers, designed by glass artist ıle Chihuly* (see p628).

**ris**, with its half-scale ›lica of the Eiffel Tower, is ;760-million resort mod-·d on the French capital.

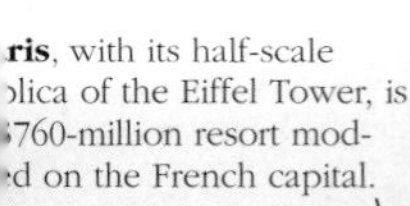

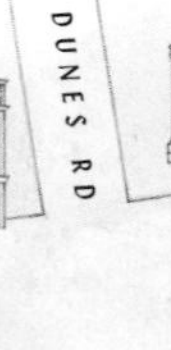

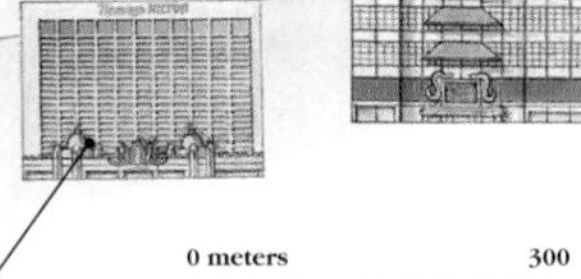

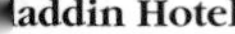

**laddin Hotel**
*›ened in 1963, Aladdin's reputation as one ' the glitziest Strip hotels was sealed when Elvis ·esley married Priscilla here in 1967. The old ıilding was imploded in 1998, and a new ·abian Nights-themed resort opened in 2000.*

**Flamingo**
*The flaming pink and orange neon flower of the Flamingo hotel's façade is a famous Strip icon. New York City Gangster Bugsy Siegel created the hotel and casino in 1946. He was killed, just a year later, by fellow investors.*

# Las Vegas (The Strip Continued)

The legalization of gambling in Nevada paved the way for Las Vegas' casino-based growth. The first casino resort, the El Rancho Vegas Hotel-Casino, opened in 1941 and was located on the northern section of the Strip. A building boom followed in the 1950s, resulting in a plethora of resorts. The Sands, Desert Inn, Sahara, and Stardust hotels began the process that transformed the Strip into a high-rise adult theme park. Although many of these north Strip resorts remain, they are now unrecognizable, thanks to million-dollar rebuilding programs.

**Roulette is very popular in Vegas – gambli was legalized in Nevada in 1931**

**Treasure Island**

*Treasure Island's skull and crossbones sign lures passers-by to the battling pirate ship show, held each evening on the hotel's Strip-side lagoon.*

**The Fashion Show Mall** is currently the largest shopping destination in Vegas, with mo than 200 stores, an entertainm complex, and a food court serving both fast and fresh fo

**The Mirage** is both stylish and tacky – its beautiful, Strip-facing gardens feature an "erupting" volcano.

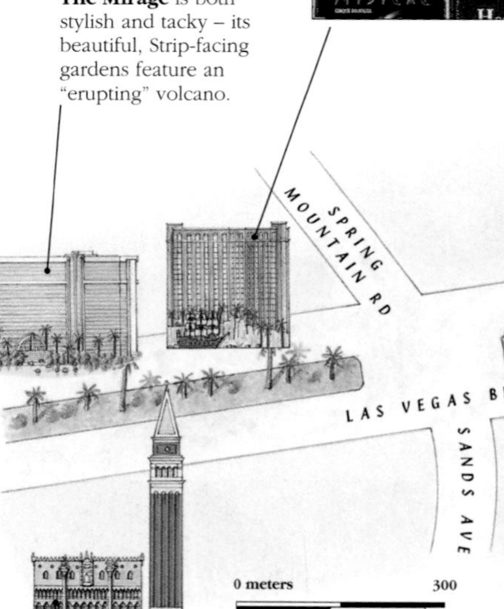

**Wynn Las Vegas**

*This hotel has it all: a casino, an exclusive golf course, oversized luxurious room restaurants with award-winning chefs, nightclubs, and dozens of designer shop*

**Venetian**

*One of the world's most luxurious hotels, this has mock canals flowing through its shopping area. Madame Tussaud's Wax Museum is located inside the hotel.*

**Stardust**
*This famous sign, with its twinkling neon colors, is a noted Strip landmark. Originally made in 1968, today's hotel sign was altered in 1991.*

**Stratosphere Tower**
*An observation deck at the top of this 1,149-ft (350-m) tower offers fine views of the city and the ring of mountains that rise from the desert.*

**Circus Circus**
*Lucky the Clown beckons visitors to this resort, which offers circus acts and traditional carnival games on the mezzanine floor above the casino.*

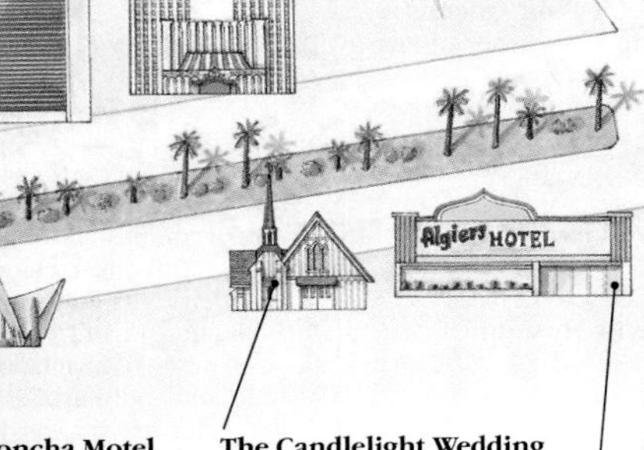

**a Concha Motel** s a rare remnant of tylish old Vegas. It vas built in 1961.

**The Candlelight Wedding Chapel** is located next to the Algiers Hotel. It is possible to get married here at any time of the day or night.

**lgiers Hotel**
*3uilt in 1953, this is the oldest intact hotel left on he Strip. Despite extensive redecoration, it retains he low-rise motel style of Vegas's original resorts, vith its pink and blue exterior and elegant neon.*

**Neon lights at the Riviera Hotel**

## LAS VEGAS NEON

The twinkling, flashing neon sign remains the dominant icon of Las Vegas, even though several of the new themed megaresorts here have opted for a more understated look. Neon is a gas discovered by British chemist Sir William Ramsey in 1898. But it was a French inventor, Georges Claude, who, in 1910, discovered that an electric current passed through a glass tube of neon emitted a powerful, shimmering light. In the 1940s and 50s the craft of neon sign-making was elevated to the status of an art form in Las Vegas.

### Exploring Las Vegas

Rising like a mirage out of Nevada's beautiful southern desert, Las Vegas is a fascinating wonderland that promises fun to all its visitors. Beyond the allure of the Strip are the glittering malls and museums in the downtown area. For those who can tear themselves away from the city, the surrounding canyons, mountains, deserts, and parks offer a wealth of natural beauty and outdoor pleasures. Apart from tourism and gaming, Las Vegas is also famous for wedding chapels that offer a wide range of customized ceremonies.

### Liberace Museum

1775 E Tropicana Ave. (702) 798-5595. *10am–5pm Mon–Sat; noon–4pm Sun.* www.liberace.org

This museum, founded in 1979, celebrates the life and work of one of Las Vegas's best-loved performers, Liberace (1919–87). It displays 18 of his 39 pianos, his lavish costumes, trademark capes, and stage jewelry. The costumes worn at his final 1986 performance took six seamstresses, wearing protective sunglasses against the glare of the stones, several months to make. The customized cars include a rare Rolls Royce covered with mirror tiles, in which the flamboyant artist would arrive at his show. Collections of objects from around the world include a piano-shaped ring, set with 260 diamonds.

### Fremont Street Experience

**Light Shows** *6pm–midnight daily.* www.vegasexperience.com
**Binion's Horseshoe** 128 E Fremont St. *(702) 382-1600.* *24 hours.* www.binions.com
**Four Queens** 202 E Fremont St. *(702) 385-4011.* *24 hours.* www.fourqueens.com

Known as "Glitter Gulch," Fremont Street was where the first casinos with neon signs and illuminated icons were located. However, during the 1980s and 1990s as the Strip became more glamorous, this street went into decline. To reverse the process, an ambitious $70-million project was initiated by the city in 1994 to revitalize the area. It was further enhanced in 1994 and the street is now a colorful, bustling pedestrian mall, covered by a vast steel canopy, extending for five blocks, and from which the spectacular sound-and-light shows are projected every night. Gaze upward to experience high-resolution images presented by more than 12 million LED modules with concert-quality sound.

**Façade of Binion's Horseshoe**

Established by Dallas bootlegger and gambler Benny Binion, the landmark **Binion's Horseshoe** retains an old-style Vegas atmosphere. Now managed by Harrah's Casinos, the legend continues with table games, slots, keno, and poker. Another historic casino along the Street is **Four Queens**. Named for the owner's four daughters, the casino has chandeliers and gilt mirrors, reminiscent of 19th-century New Orleans. It also claims to have the largest slot machine in the world.

### Lied Discovery Children's Museum

833 Las Vegas Blvd. *(702) 382-3445.* *10am–5pm Tue–Sun.* *Mon (except school hols), Jan 1, Thanksgiving, Dec 25.* www.ldcm.org

A conical, concrete teepee forms part of this striking museum devoted to interactive exhibits. Children can stand inside a gigantic bubble, freeze their shadows on a wall, or even work in th in-house television studio.

### The Las Vegas Natural History Museum

900 Las Vegas Blvd. *(702) 384-3466.* *9am–4pm daily.* *Jan Thanksgiving, Dec 25.* www.lvnhm.org

A popular choice with famili who need a break from the Strip resorts, this museu has an appealing range of exhibits. Dioramas re-create the African savann complete with leop ards, cheetahs, and antelopes. The marine exhibit offe a chance to view live sharks and eels at close quarters. Animatroni dinosaurs and the hands-on discovery room, where visito can dig fossils and operate a robotic baby dinosaur, are popular with children.

### Boulder City & Hoover Dam

*12,500.* *(702) 597-5970.*

Named after Herbert Hoover, the 31st president, the histor Hoover Dam lies about 30 miles (48 km) east of Las Vegas. Before its constructio the Colorado River frequentl flooded acres of farmland in Mexico and southern California. After much consideration, the dam was built between 1931 and 1935 across the Colorado River's Black Canyon. Hailed as an engineering marvel, it gave this desert region a reliable water supply and provided inexpensive electricity to Nevada, Arizona, and California. This colossus c

**An animatronic *Tyrannosaurus rex* in roaring form at the Las Vegas Natural History Museum**

iew of the Hoover Dam

oncrete is today a huge ›urist attraction. Guided ›urs take visitors into the epths of the dam. The top of ıe visitor center offers superb iews of the dam.

Just 8 miles (13 km) vest of the dam, 3oulder City was built › house the dam's onstruction workers. Vith its neat yards and uburban streets, it is ne of Nevada's most ttractive well-ordered ›wns. Several of its 1930s uildings remain, including ıe historic Boulder Dam lotel, which houses the loover Dam Museum.

### Lake Mead National ecreation Area

*Las Vegas.* *(702) 293-8906, '02) 293-8990.* *8:30am–4:30pm aily.* *Jan 1, Thanksgiving, ec 25.* *limited.* www.nps.gov/lame

ıfter the completion of loover Dam, the waters of the Colorado River filled the deep canyons, which once towered above the river, to create Lake Mead. This huge reservoir is the largest man-made body of water in the US. Its 700-mile (1,130-km) shoreline is home to forests, canyons, and flower-rich meadows. Dotted with beaches, marinas, and campgrounds, the reservoir area offers water sports such as sailing, waterskiing, swimming, and fishing. Striped bass and rainbow trout are popular catches.

### Valley of Fire State Park

*Las Vegas.* *(702) 397-2088.* *partial.* www.state.nv.us/stparks **Lost City Museum of Archaeology** 721 S Moapa Valley Blvd, Overton. *(702) 397-2193.* *8:30am–4:30pm daily.* *Thnksg., Dec 25.*

**Hoover Dam sign**

This spectacularly scenic state park is in a remote desert location some 60 miles (97 km) northeast of Las Vegas. It derives its name from the red sandstone formations that began as huge, shifting sand dunes about 150 million years ago. The extreme summer temperatures mean that spring or fall are the best times to explore the wilderness. Of the four well-maintained trails, the Petroglyph Canyon Trail is an easy half-mile (0.8 km) loop, which takes in several fine prehistoric Ancestral Puebloan rock carvings. One of the most famous depicts an *atlatl*, a notched stick used to add speed and distance to a thrown spear. Ancestral Puebloan people settled in the nearby town of Overton along Muddy River, around 300 BC. They left some 1,500 years later, perhaps because of a long drought. Archaeologists have discovered hundreds of prehistoric artifacts in the area, many of which are housed in Overton's **Lost City Museum of Archaeology**, just outside the town. Its large collection includes pottery, beads, woven baskets, and delicate turquoise jewelry, which was a local specialty.

### Red Rock Canyon

*Las Vegas.* *(702) 515-5350.* *8am–5pm daily.* *public hols.* *limited.* www.redrockcanyon.blm.gov

From downtown Las Vegas it is a short, 10-mile (16-km) drive west to the low hills and steep gullies of the Red Rock Canyon National Conservation Area. Here, baked by the summer sun, a gnarled escarpment rises out of the desert, its gray limestone and red sandstone the geological residue of an ancient ocean and the huge sand dunes that succeeded it. The canyon is easily explored on a 13-mile (21-km) long scenic road that loops off Hwy 159 providing a good overview and great picnic spots, but the best way to explore these steep winding canyons is on foot. Watch for the bighorn sheep and desert tortoises when hiking.

Extraordinary rock formations in the Valley of Fire State Park

# Nevada

NEVADA WAS KNOWN AS THE "Silver State" mainly because of the immense wealth that came out of the late 19th-century silver mines of the Comstock Lode, east of Reno. Today, it is synonymous with adult fun, thanks to the presence of the world's largest gambling and entertainment mecca at glittering Las Vegas *(see pp510–15)*. Away from its few cities, Nevada is mostly uninhabited desert, with ridge after ridge of rugged mountains dividing the endless sagebrush plains.

**Façade of the impressive State Capitol in Carson City**

## Carson City ❷

*55,000. 1900 S Carson St Suite 100, (775) 687-7410.* www.visitcarsoncity.com

THE STATE CAPITAL and third largest city in Nevada, Carson City was named in honor of the Wild West explorer Kit Carson. Nestled at the base of the eastern escarpment of the Sierra Nevada, the city was founded in 1858, a year before the discovery of the Comstock Lode mines. It still retains a few old-fashioned casinos in its downtown core.

The excellent **Nevada State Museum**, down the street from the impressive State Capitol, is housed inside the 1870 US Mint building, where coins were made from Comstock silver. The museum holds a full-scale replica of a working mine, as well as displays on the natural history of Nevada and the Great Basin.

On the south side of Carson City, the **Nevada State Railroad Museum** preserves 60 steam engines and freight cars from the old Virginia & Truckee Railroad, which carried ore from the Comstock Lode between 1869 and the 1930s. Later used in Hollywood films, the trains also offer excursions on summer weekends.

**Nevada State Museum**
600 N Carson St. *(775) 687-4810.*
*8:30am–4:30pm daily. Jan 1, Thanksgiving, Dec 25.*

**Nevada State Railroad Museum**
2180 S Carson St. *(775) 687-6953.*
*8:30am–4:30pm daily. Jan 1, Thanksgiving, Dec 25.*

## Virginia City ❸

*1,000. 86 S C St, (775) 847-0311.* www.virginiacity–nv.org

PROSPECTORS following the gold deposits up the slopes of Mount Davidson discovered one of the world's richest strikes, the Comstock Lode, in 1859. Almost overnight, the bustling camp of Virginia City grew into the largest settlement between Chicago and San Francisco. It had over 100 saloons and 25,000 residents, among whom was a journalist from Missouri who later became famous under the pseudonym Mark Twain.

**Old timers in a Wild West-themed saloon in Virginia City**

Over the next 20 years, tons of gold and silver were mined here, but by the turn of the 20th century the town had begun to fade. However, the popular 1960s TV show *Bonanza* has given the city a new lease on life as one of Nevada's most enjoyable destinations. A National Historic Landmark, the city is located at an elevation of 6,220 ft (1,896 m); its steep streets offer fine views of the surrounding mountains. The old main street, **C Street**, is packed with historic sites dotted alongside Wild West-themed saloons and souvenir shops. Up the hill along B Street, the elegant **Castle** is the state's best-preserved mansion. It was built in 1863–68 and in it's heyday it was considered to be one of the finest mansions in the west. Although the interior is now closed to the public, you can still gain a glimpse of the amount of wealth that flowed through here in the 1860s.

The city's main historical museum fills the old **Fourth Ward School**, the Victorian Gothic landmark at the south end of C Street. It showcases the city's lively history with exhibits ranging from mining tools to Mark Twain, who began his career at the city's *Territorial Enterprise*. An intact classroom is preserved as it was in 1936, when the last class graduated.

**Fourth Ward School**
C St. *(775) 847-0975.*
*mid-May–Oct: 10am–5pm daily.*
*Nov–late May.*

## Reno ❹

*190,000. 4590 S Virginia St, (800) 367-7366.* www.visitrenotahoe.com

SELF-PROCLAIMED "The Biggest Little City in the World," Reno was Nevada's main gambling destination until it was surpassed by glitzy Las Vegas in the 1950s. The city

chway over Virginia Street in downtown Reno

›o achieved national promi- nce in the 1930s as a center : quick divorces. Although ıaller than Las Vegas, Reno s a similar array of 24-hour- day casino-fueled fun. At the **berty Belle Saloon and staurant** south of down- wn, visitors can see the first ›t machine, the seductive vice that led to the gam- ng mania. Exhibits here tell complete story of auto- ıted gambling, starting with invention of the three-reel ›t machine by the immigrant ıarlie Fey in San Francisco 1885. More than 75 old slot d fortune-telling machines, well as penny arcade mes are on view.

The **National Automobile useum**, on the south bank the Truckee River, has one the country's most extensive r collections. From early ıssics to 1960s hot rods, museum – styled like a e-1940s Chrysler – show- ses the cars in stage-set reets" that provide evoca- e period backgrounds.

**Liberty Belle Saloon & staurant**
*50 S. Virginia St. (775) 825- 76. 11am–9pm Mon–Fri, n–10pm Sat, 4pm–10pm Sun. Thanksg., Dec 25.*

**National Automobile useum**
*S Lake St. (775) 333-9300. 9:30am–5:30pm Mon–Sat, 10am– n Sun. Thanksgiving, Dec 25.* www.automuseum.org

**VIRONS:** West of Reno, the rtling beauty of **Lake Tahoe** *(see p718)* greets visitors at the vada/California border.

Surrounded by summer resorts and winter ski areas, this is one of the most popular destinations in western US.

## Great Basin National Park ❺

*100 Great Basin Hwy, Baker, (775) 234-7331. 8am–5pm daily (extended summer hours). Jan 1, Thanksgiving, Dec 25. limited.* www.nps.gov/grba

TRAVELERS DRIVING along the "Loneliest Road in America" are beckoned by the towering silhouette of the 13,063-ft (3,982-m) Wheeler Peak which stands at the center of Great Basin National Park. Below the peak lies the park's centerpiece, the **Lehman Caves**, discovered when homesteader Absalom Lehman stumbled upon their small entrance in 1885. Their fantastic limestone formations, including thousands of stalactites and shields, can be seen on various guided tours that take place at intervals all through the day.

Tours start from the park visitor center, which offers hiking and camping details, along with exhibits on Great Basin's wildlife. The well-maintained **Wheeler Peak Scenic Drive** starts near the visitor center and passes through all the major Great Basin climate zones while climbing from 6,500 ft (1,982 m) to over 10,000 ft (3,048 m) in 12 steep miles (19 km). Great Basin National Park's remote location has made it one of the least-visited national parks in the country, so hikers and campers can find immense solitude among the limestone caves, alpine forests, ancient bristlecone pines, and glacial lakes.

Picturesque Wheeler Peak at Great Basin National Park

### THE LONELIEST ROAD IN AMERICA

One of the country's most compelling drives, the Nevada portion of transcontinental US 50, stretching between Lake Tahoe in the west and Great Basin National Park on the Utah border, traverses over 400 miles (644 km) of corrugated country. Early explorers mapped this region, Pony Express riders raced across it, and the long-distance Lincoln Highway finally tamed it. But US 50 has long played second fiddle to busy I-80, the more popular route across the state. The Nevada Commission on Tourism now sponsors a tongue-in-cheek promotion where travelers on US 50 can get a certificate saying "I Survived the Loneliest Road in America."

Sign on US 50 highway

# Utah

BEST KNOWN AS world headquarters for the Mormon Church, Utah is also home to some of the most remarkable landscapes in the US. The inhospitably rugged sandstone canyons of the Colorado Plateau, which covers the southern half of the state, have been preserved within a series of unforgettably beautiful national parks, forests, and monuments. The towering snow-capped peaks of the Wasatch Mountains in the northern half of the state, a haven for skiers worldwide, played host to the 2000 Winter Olympics. West of the mountains sits the Mormon-dominated state capital Salt Lake City, Utah's only major city, bordered by its namesake lake.

## Salt Lake City 6

*175,000. 90 South West Temple St, (801) 534-4902.*

PLEASANT AND FRIENDLY Salt Lake City makes a great stopover for weary travelers between Denver and San Francisco. Although its name derives from the undrinkable alkaline Great Salt Lake that spreads to the west, the city actually has abundant fresh water, thanks to the rain and snowmelt of the Wasatch Range, which rises to the east. Founded and controlled by the Mormons since 1847, the city spreads for miles and miles along the base of the snowcapped peaks.

Apart from its spectacular natural setting, Salt Lake City is known as the spiritual base of the Mormon church, which has its worldwide headquarters in Temple Square downtown. Here, the six spires of the main Mormon temple and the famous oblong auditorium of the **Mormon Tabernacle**, built in 1867, stand side by side. The temple is closed for renovations until 2007, but the Mormon Tabernacle choir still performs pipe organ recitals in its temporary location at the Convention Center nearby.

To the west of Temple Square, the amazing **Family History Library** holds records of Mormon family trees dating back to the mid-16th century. Eastward, the 1850 Beehive House has been preserved as it was when Mormon leader Brigham Young lived here. At its entrance stands the stately 76-ft (23-m) Eagle Gate, capped by a 4,000-pound eagle with an impressive wingspan of 20 ft (6 m). To the north, the domed **Utah State Capitol**, modeled after the US Capitol, features a series of exhibits on Utah's history.

**Mormon Tabernacle**
Temple Square. *(801) 240-2534.*
*closed for renovation until 2007.*

**Family History Library**
35 NW Temple St.
*(801) 240-2331 8am–5pm Mon, 8am–9pm Tue–Sat.*
*Sun, Jul 4, Dec 25, 26.*

View of "Eagle Gate" looking toward the Utah State Capitol

Visitors enjoying the view from the Great Salt Lake shore

## Great Salt Lake 7

Great Salt Lake State Park, I-80 exit 104. *(801) 250-1898. Apr–Oct: 7am–8pm daily; Nov–Mar 8am–5pm daily. limited.*

THE LARGEST salt lake in North America, the Great Salt Lake is a shallow remna of the prehistoric Lake Bonneville. Depending on th weather, the lake covers an area ranging from 1,000 sq miles (2,590 sq km) to 2,500 sq miles (6,477 sq km). The salt flats stretching west fron the lake to the Nevada bord are so hard and expansive that they have long been use as a proving ground for auto mobile racers. Apart from some algae and microscopic brine shrimp, the lake itself supports almost no life. How ever, the **Antelope Island State Park**, located in the middle of the lake, is home t resident herds of bighorn sheep, mule deer, bison, and its namesake, the pronghorn antelope. Access to the island lying about 40 miles (64 km) northwest of Salt Lake City, i by way of a 7-mile (11-km) long causeway. Visitors can camp or swim along the sho or take guided lake cruises.

West from Salt Lake City, toward the lake's south shor the **Great Salt Lake State Park** offers a broad, sandy beach with a marina and observation deck.

**Antelope Island State Park**
I-15 exit 335. *(801) 773-2941.*
*7am onward, hours vary.*
*limited.*

## ark City 8

7,300. Cnr Olympic Blvd &
y 224, (435) 649-6100.
www.parkcityinfo.com

N HOUR'S drive east from downtown Salt Lake City, rough the Wasatch Mounns, leads to this popular sort. The city started life in e 1860s as a silver mining mp and still retains several rn-of-20th-century buildings ong its photogenic Main eet. In recent years, it has come world-famous as the me of the prestigious **ndance Film Festival**. unded by actor and direcr Robert Redford in 1981, e annual festival focuses on dependent and documeny films and has become nerica's foremost venue for novative cinema. The fesal's popularity is linked to rk City's excellent skiing cilities, showcased in the 00 Winter Olympics. A nse of the town's history can be obtained at **Park City Museum** in the old City Hall.

### Park City Museum

528 Main St. *(435) 649-6100.*
*May & Nov: 11am–5pm Mon–Sat, noon–6pm Sun; rest of the year: 10am–7pm Mon-Sat, noon–6pm Sun.*
*Jan 1, Thanksgiving, Dec 25.*
*limited.*

## Timpanogos Cave National Monument 9

Rte 3, American Fork. *(801) 756-5238.* *mid-May–mid-Oct: 7am–5:30pm daily* *Nov–mid-May*
W www.nps.gov/tica

ONE OF THE the most popular destinations around Salt Lake City, the Timpanogos Cave National Monument lies deep beneath the 11,750-ft (3,581-m) summit of Mount Timpanogos. The site preserves a trio of massive limestone caverns stretching nearly 1,800 ft (549 m) deep into the mountain. Reached by way of a steep, 1.5 mile (2 km) uphill hike from the visitor center, and linked by man-made tunnels, the three caves are very cool (43° F/6° C), very damp, and full of spectacular limestone formations. Electric lights showcase the sundry stalactites, stalagmites, crystalline helictites, and other water-sculpted formations, all of which are still being formed. Only a limited number of people are allowed inside, so visitors should come early in the day or during the week to avoid the worst crowds.

Timpanogos Cave is one of the many highlights of the drive along the 40-mile (64-km) **Alpine Loop**, which follows Highway 92 around the landmark mountain. Many campgrounds, picnic spots, scenic views, and hiking trails can be enjoyed by trekkers along the way.

**Scenic view along Alpine Loop following Highway 92**

**storic houses lining Main Street in Park City**

### The Mormons

The Church of Jesus Christ of Latter Day Saints, a large Christian denomination, was founded by Joseph Smith (1805–44), a farm worker from New York State. In 1820 Smith claimed to have seen visions of the Angel Moroni, who led him to a set of golden tablets, which he translated and later published as the *Book of Mormon*, thus establishing the Mormon Church. Although this new faith grew rapidly, it attracted hostility because of its political and economic beliefs, and the practice of polygamy. Seeking refuge, the Mormons moved to Illinois in 1839, where Smith was killed by an angry mob. Leadership passed to Brigham Young, who led the members on an arduous journey west, in the hope of escaping persecution and setting up a safe haven in the unpromising landscape of Salt Lake Valley. The pioneers traveled across bleak prairies and mountains in primitive wagons, braving the fierce weather. Young's followers finally established successful farming communities across Utah's wilderness. Today, Mormons form 70 percent of Utah's population.

**Portrait of Brigham Young (1801–77)**

# Arches National Park ⑩

Wildflowers in the park

ARCHES NATIONAL PARK has the the highest concentration of natural sandstone arches in the world. More than 80 of these natural wonders have formed over millions of years. The park "floats" on a salt bed, which once liquefied under the pressure exerted by the rock above it. About 300 million years ago, this salt layer bulged upward, cracking the sandstone above. Over time the cracks eroded, leaving long "fins" of rock. As these fins eroded, the hard overhead rock formed arches, which range today from the solid looking Turret Arch to the graceful Delicate and Landscape Arches.

**Devil's Garden**
*This area contains several of the park most beautiful arches, including Landscape Arch, a slender curve of sandstone more than 300 ft (91 m) long, which is thought to be the longe natural arch in the world.*

**Sunset Watch at Delicate Arch**
*A natural amphitheater surrounds the arch, creating seating from which vistas of the La Sal Mountains are framed.*

### The Windows Section

In the park's Windows Section, a one-mile loop trail leads to Turret Arch, then the North and South Windows Arches, located side by side. With excellent viewing spots available, many visitors photograph the North and South arches framed by the sandstone Turner Arch, as seen here.

### Exploring the Park

The scenic drive to these spectacular arches starts at the visitor center at the park's south end, just off Highway 191. Several easy trails start from parking lots at the road's viewpoints. The loop at Balanced Rock is a suitable trail for children, and the Delicate Arch Viewpoint Trail has disabled access. Although permitted, camping is not popular because of the heat and water scarcity in the area.

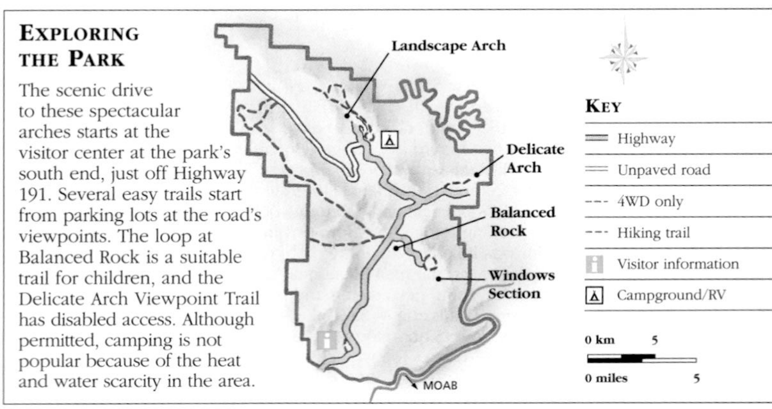

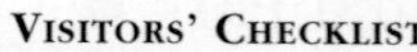

**Visitors' Checklist**

(435) 259-8161. Mar 9–Oct 11: 7:30am–6:30pm; Oct 12–Nov 1: 7:30am–5:30pm; Nov 2–Mar 8: 8am–4.30pm. (campground, Park Avenue Viewpoint, Delicate Arch Viewpoint Trail & Balanced Rock Trail.) www.nps.gov/arch

**elicate Arch**
*he most celebrated of all the rches here, and a state symbol, Delicate Arch appears on any Utah license plates. It reached by a moderate 45-inute walk over sandstone.*

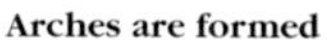

**Arches are formed** through a process that takes millions of years; today's arches continue to erode and will eventually collapse.

**Balanced Rock**
*This precariously balanced boulder atop a sandstone spire is one of the park's landmarks. Good views are available from the trail as well as the scenic road route.*

**ark Avenue and the Courthouse Towers**
*he large, rock monoliths known as Courthouse Towers ear an uncanny resemblance to city skyscrapers. They an be seen from Park Avenue, an easy, short trail.*

**Western-style, timber-clad gift store on Main Street, Moab**

## Moab ⓫

6500. Main & Center Sts, (435) 259-8825.
www.discovermoab.com

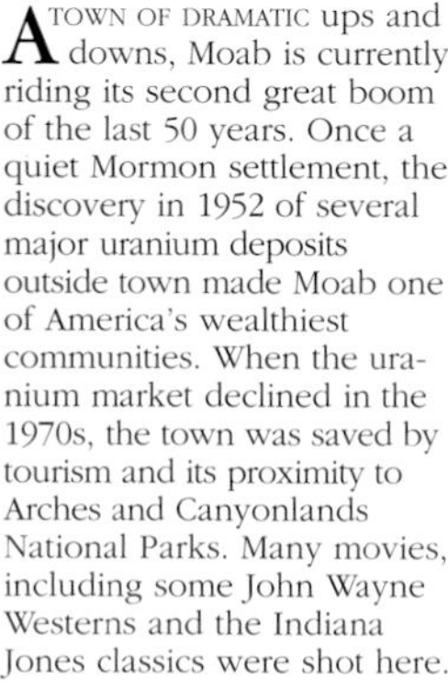

A town of dramatic ups and downs, Moab is currently riding its second great boom of the last 50 years. Once a quiet Mormon settlement, the discovery in 1952 of several major uranium deposits outside town made Moab one of America's wealthiest communities. When the uranium market declined in the 1970s, the town was saved by tourism and its proximity to Arches and Canyonlands National Parks. Many movies, including some John Wayne Westerns and the Indiana Jones classics were shot here.

Today, Moab is a top destination for lovers of the outdoors. Mountain bikers come here for the challenging ride from Moab Rim, reached by Moab Skyway, a scenic tram ride offering panoramic views of the area. Numerous hiking trails and 4WD routes take in some of this region's fabulous landscapes. Moab is also a major center for whitewater rafting on the Colorado River. **Matheson Wetlands Preserve** off Kane Creek Boulevard has 2 miles (3 km) of hiking trails along a riverside wetland, home to birds and indigenous wildlife.

### Matheson Wetlands Preserve

Off Kane Creek Blvd. (435) 259-4629. dawn–dusk daily.

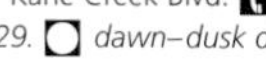

# Canyonlands National Park ⓬

MILLIONS OF YEARS AGO, the Colorado and Green Rivers cut winding paths deep into rock, creating a labyrinth of rocky canyons that form the heart of this stunning wilderness. At its center, the rivers' confluence divides the park's 527 sq miles (1,365 sq km) into three districts – the Needles, the Maze, and the grassy plateau of the Island in the Sky. Established as a national park in 1964, Canyonlands is growing in popularity. Most wilderness travel here requires a permit.

**VISITORS' CHECKLIST**

*2282 South West Resource Blvd, Moab, (435) 719-2313. visitor center: 8am–4:30pm daily (longer during spring & fall). Jan 1, Thanksgiving, Dec 25.*

www.nps.gov/cany

**Mesa Arch**
*An easy and rewarding 500-yard (455-m) trail leads to Mesa Arch, a long, low curve of stone that perfectly frames the snowcapped La Sal Mountains in the distance.*

**KEY**

- Highway
- 4WD only
- Hiking route
- Campground/RV
- Picnic area
- Visitor information
- National Park boundary
- Viewpoint

**White Rim Road** is a 100-mile (160 km) trail accessed via the exhilaratin Shafer Road, a 4WD track down a steep cliff.

**Horseshoe Canyon** contains 6,000-year-old petroglyphs, said to be some of the oldest in existence.

**Needles Distric**
*The most interestin features in th remote distric are the hundrec of red rock spire or needles, fo which was name*

**The Maze** canyons, where outlaw Butch Cassidy hid out in the late 1800s, offer a challenge to skilled hikers.

0 km 5
0 miles

**Island in the Sky**
*Easy access by car makes this the most visited district of the park. A popular stop here is the Grandview Overlook, which offers panoramic views of the rocky canyons of the Green and Colorado Rivers.*

ıe deep crevices of the canyons in the wide valley around Green River

## ıreen River ⓭

▮ 1,000. ℹ 885 E Main St, (435) ı4-3526. ◯ Apr–Oct: 8am–8pm; ɔv–Mar: 8am–5pm daily.

OCATED IN A broad, bowl-‿ shaped valley, the town ·ew around a ford of the ild Green River in the 19th ıd early 20th centuries. ɔday, it is a launching spot ·r whitewater rafting on the reen and Colorado Rivers. American geologist and eth-ɔlogist John Wesley Powell 834–1902) began his explo-.tion of the Colorado River ıd Grand Canyon from here ı 1871. The **John Wesley ɔwell River History ɩuseum** at Green River has ),000 sq ft (1,860 sq m) of isplays tracing the history of ıe area's exploration.

**John Wesley Powell ɩver History Museum**
35 E Main St. ☎ (435) 564-3427. ◯ Apr–Oct: 8am–8pm daily; ɔv–Mar: 8am–5pm daily. public hols.

## ɪovenweep ɴational ɩonument ⓮

of Hwy 191. ☎ (970) 562-4282. ◯ 8am–5pm daily (to 6pm May–Oct). Jan 1, Thanksgiving, Dec 25. W www.nps.gov/hove

THE SIX SEPARATE sets of ruins at this Ancestral Puebloan te were discovered by W.D. ɩuntington, leader of a ɩormon expedition, in 1854. he culture at Hovenweep, a 'te word meaning "Deserted alley," reached its peak etween 1200 and 1275. Little is known of the Utes beyond the clues found in the round, square, and D-shaped towers, and pottery and tools that they left behind.

Researchers have speculated that the towers might have been built as defensive fortifications, astronomical observatories, storage silos, or as religious structures for the entire community.

## Lake Powell & Glen Canyon National Recreation Area ⓯

2 miles (3 km) N of Page on Hwy 98, off Hwy 160. ✈ ℹ Carl Hayden Visitor Center, (928) 608-6404. ◯ Apr–Oct: 8am–7pm daily; Nov– Mar: 8am–5pm daily. ♿ visitor center only. Page & Wahweap only. W www.nps.gov/glca, www.lakepowell. com

THE GLEN CANYON National Recreation Area (NRA), established in 1972, covers more than one million acres of dramatic desert and canyon country around the 185-mile (298-km) long Lake Powell, named after John Wesley Powell. The lake was created by damming the Colorado River and its tributaries to supply electricity to the region's growing population.

The construction of the Glen Canyon Dam, completed in 1963, was controversial from the start. The spirited campaign, led by the environmentalist Sierra Club, continues to argue for the restoration of Glen Canyon, believing that ancient ecosystems are being ruined. Pro-dam advocates, however, firmly believe in its ability to store water, generate power, and provide recreation.

The "Y"-shaped recreation area follows the San Juan River east almost to the town of Mexican Hat, and heads northeast along the Colorado toward Canyonlands National Park. Within the area is the **Antelope Canyon**, a famously deep "slot" canyon. Other highlights include Lees Ferry, a 19th-century Mormon settlement that now offers tourist facilities, and the **Rainbow Bridge National Monument**. Rising 309 ft (94 m), this is the largest natural bridge in the world.

Today, the lake is busy with water sports enthusiasts and houseboat parties, exploring the myriad sandstone side canyons. Glen Canyon is also one of the most popular hiking, biking, and 4WD destinations in the country.

Rose-colored sandstone of Antelope Canyon, in Glen Canyon NRA

## Capitol Reef National Park 16

10 miles (16 km) E of Torrey, Hwy 24. (435) 425-3791. 8am–4:30pm daily. Dec 25.
www.nps.gov/care

Covering 378 square miles (980 sq km), this spectacular park encloses a 100-mile (160-km) long, colorful wall of rock that was thrust up by the earth 65 million years ago. The strata that buckled upward folded back on itself, trapping water in the process. Around 100 years ago, prospectors crossing the desert were forced to stop at this wind-carved Waterpocket Fold. They likened the rock barrier to an ocean reef and thought its round white domes looked just like the US Capitol building, hence the park's name.

An adventurous drive along the partly unpaved Notom-Bullfrog Road provides a good overview of the area. Cars can negotiate the road in dry weather, but extra gas and water are essential. Capitol Gorge, to the north, can be reached via a scenic route, extending about 10 miles (16 km) into the heart of the park. Guided walking tours are available during summer, but be aware that only experienced hikers should attempt to explore the back country here.

To the north lies the 1908 **Gifford Farmhouse**. Now a cultural center, it is dedicated to the 1880s Mormon settlement that once flourished here. Fremont Canyon, on its right, features the famous Fremont Petroglyphs, created by the Ancestral Puebloans between 700 and 1250. Farther north, is the Cathedral Valley, named for the rock monoliths that tower over the desert.

## Grand Staircase-Escalante National Monument 17

755 W Main St, Escalante, (435) 826-5499. Mar–Oct: 7:30am–5:30pm daily; Nov: 8am–4:30pm daily; Dec–Apr: 8am–4:30pm Mon–Fri.
www.ut.blm.gov/monument

Established by President Clinton in 1996, this monument encompasses 1.9 million acres (769,000 ha) of pristine rock canyons, mountains, and high desert plateaus. It was named for its four 12-million-year-old cliff faces that rise in tiered steps across the Colorado Plateau. To preserve its wild state, no new roads, facilities, or campgrounds are being built here. This vast untamed area is best explored on scenic drives combined with daylong hikes. About 9 miles (14 km) south of Highway 12 stands **Kodachrome Basin State Park**, a distinctive landscape noted for its 67 free-standing sand pipes or rock chimneys, formed millions of years ago as geyser vents.

**Kodachrome Basin State Park**
(435) 679-8562; (800) 322-377
dawn–dusk daily.

## Bryce Canyon National Park 18

*See pp526–7.*

## Cedar City 19

15,750.
286 N Main St, (435) 586-5124

Founded by Mormons in 1851, Cedar City develop as a center for mining and smelting iron. The Iron Missi State Park and Museum offer a glimpse of this pioneering spirit and features a large collection of early vehicles. The town offers a choice of hotels within an hour's drive of Zion National Park. Cedar City is popular for its annual Shakespeare Festival, staged a replica of London's Globe Theatre. East of tow the spectacular **Cedar Breaks National Monu ment** features limestone cliffs and a lake topped by a deep green forest. In winter, the area is a popular skiing resort.

**Vintage wagon outside Cedar City's museum**

**Cedar Breaks National Monument**
(435) 586-9451. daily.
**Visitor Center** Jun–Labor Day: 8am–6pm daily; Labor Day–mid-Oct 9am–5:30pm daily.
www.nps.gov/cebr

**Fishing in the lake at Cedar Breaks National Monument, near Cedar City**

# :ion National Park ⓴

AT THE HEART OF THIS beautiful national park lies Zion Canyon, perhaps the most popular of all of Utah's natural wonders. It was carved by the powerful waters of the Virgin River and then widened, sculpted, and reshaped by wind, rain, and ice. Its majestic walls rise up to 2,000 ft (600 m) and are shaped into jagged peaks and formations in shades of red and white. Wild meadows and luxuriant foliage along the river account for the area's abundant wildlife. The park ıuttle is the only way into the canyon. A number of ıort walks, beginning at the shuttle stops, follow ·arked trails to the tough 16-mile (26-km) hike through ıe canyon and involves wading through the river.

**Wild-**
**ıowers**

### VISITORS' CHECKLIST

Hwy 9, near Springdale. *Zion Canyon Visitor Center, (435) 772-3256. late Mar–early Nov: 8am–8pm daily; early Nov–late Mar: 8am–5pm daily.* partial. www.nps.gov/zion

**The spectacular Zion–Mt. Carmel Highway**

### ZION CANYON

The Virgin River meanders quietly through banks of wildflowers, cottonwood, oak, and willow trees, which grow beneath the sloping walls of the canyon. Be aware that sudden summer rainstorms may cause floods, so visitors are advised to check conditions first.

**iking**

*ımerous guided walking ıd biking tours of Zion's ·ology and history leave ıily from the visitor center. ·nerald Pools Trail and ınyon Overlook Trail are ırticularly popular trails.*

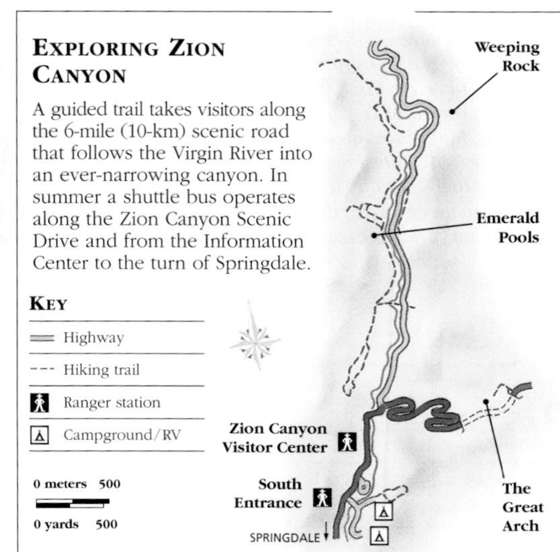

### EXPLORING ZION CANYON

A guided trail takes visitors along the 6-mile (10-km) scenic road that follows the Virgin River into an ever-narrowing canyon. In summer a shuttle bus operates along the Zion Canyon Scenic Drive and from the Information Center to the turn of Springdale.

# Bryce Canyon National Park ⓲

A SERIES OF DEEP AMPHITHEATERS filled with flame-colored rock formations called hoodoos are the hallmark of Bryce Canyon National Park. Bryce is high in altitude, reaching elevations of 6,000–8,000 ft (1,829–2,438 m), with a 18-mile (30-km) scenic road running along the rim of Paunsaugunt Plateau. Highlights include views of vast fields of pink, orange, and red spires; the Paiute Indians, once hunters here, described them as "red rocks standing like men in a bowl-shaped recess." The canyon's maze of pillars and channels is best appreciated on foot.

**Sunrise Point**
*From this lookout it is easy to see why early settler and Mormon farmer Ebenezer Bryce, after whom the park is named, called it "a helluva place to lose a cow."*

12

PINK CLIFFS

63

Fairyland Point

Queen's Garden Trail

Navajo Loop Trail

**Thor's Hammer**
*Carved into the pink cliffs of the highest "step" of the Grand Staircase* (see p524), *this unusual landscape consists of eroded sandstone. Hoodoos such as Thor's Hammer are formed as rain and wind erode "fins" of harder rock that become columns, then further erode into strangely shaped hoodoos. The high altitude, ice, and wind continue the "carving" process today.*

**Sunset Point** is one of the major lookouts in Bryce Canyon. Inspite of its name it faces east, so while sunrises can be spectacular here, sunsets can be a little anticlimactic.

**KEY**

- Highway
- Hiking route
- Ranger station
- Campground/RV
- Picnic area
- Visitor information
- Viewpoint

**Navajo Loop**
*This 1.4-mile (2-km) round-trip trail zigzags sharply down the cliff face for 500 ft (150 m) to finish in a slow meander among slot canyons and rock stands. The climb back up the trail is particularly strenuous.*

**yce Amphitheater**
*his panoramic vista f snow-covered rock spires is among the ost popular views of e park. In both winter and summer the amphitheater is best seen from Inspiration Point.*

**VISITORS' CHECKLIST**

Hwy 63 off Hwy 12. *PO Box 170001, (435) 834-5322. regular shuttle service between the entrance & Bryce Point from Memorial Day to Labor Day. daily. Jan 1, Thanksg., Dec 25.* **Visitor Center** *mid-Apr–Jun: 8am–6pm; Jun–Oct: 8am–8pm; Oct–Apr: 8am–4:30pm. limited.* www.nps.gov/brca

**Natural Bridge**
*This graceful natural bridge is located a few yards from the park's scenic highway. It frames a picturesque view of the distant valley below. Officially, it is a natural arch and not a bridge, as it was formed not by a river but by the same natural forces (of wind, rain, and ice) that created the park's hoodoos.*

**Agua Canyon**
*This overlook features some of the most delicate and beautiful of the park's formations, as well as a good view of the layered pink sandstone cliffs typical of the Paunsaugunt Plateau.*

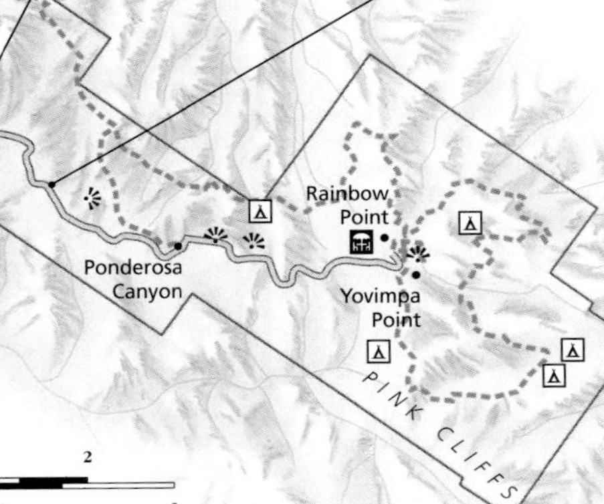

**Utah Prairie Dog**
*Now threatened, the Utah prairie dog lives only in southern Utah; those living in the park today constitute the largest remaining group.*

# Arizona

OFTEN REFERRED TO AS the Grand Canyon State after its most famous sight, Arizona offers a range of stunning natural beauty. Its southwest corner features the hostile but eerily beautiful Sonoran Desert, bordered by the state's economic hub, Phoenix, and the city of Tucson. To the north, the landscape changes, rising through high desert plateaus, toward canyons and mountains, the romanticized "Wild West" of cowboy films. Here, the city of Flagstaff and the picturesque towns of Sedona and Jerome attract thousands of visitors. Over 25 percent of Arizona is Native American reservation land. The state also houses several Ancient Puebloan ruins.

**London Bridge spanning a man-made waterway in Lake Havasu City**

## Lake Havasu City 21

*45,000. 314 London Bridge Rd, (928) 453-3444.*
www.golakehavasu.com

CALIFORNIA businessman Robert McCulloch founded Lake Havasu City in 1964. The resort city he built on the Colorado River was popular with the landlocked citizens of Arizona. His real brainwave, however, came four years later when he bought London Bridge and painstakingly transported it stone-by-stone from England to Lake Havasu. Some mocked McCulloch, suggesting that he had thought he was buying London's Gothic Tower Bridge, not this more ordinary one. There was more hilarity when it appeared that there was nothing in Havasu City for the bridge to span. Undaunted, McCulloch simply created the waterway he needed by digging a channel to divert water from Lake Havasu. The bridge and its adjoining mock-Tudor village complex have since become one of Arizona's most popular tourist attractions.

## Flagstaff 22

*58,000. Amtrak Flagstaff Station, 1 E Rte 66. Flagstaff bus station, 399 S Malpais Lane. Amtrak depot, 1 E Rte 66, (928) 774-9541. 8am–5pm daily. public hols. Flagstaff Festival of the Arts (early Jul–mid-Aug).*

NESTLING AMONG the pine forests of northern Arizona's San Francisco Peaks, Flagstaff is one of the region's most attractive towns. Its historic downtown, an attractive ensemble of red-brick buildings housing bars and restaurants, dates from the 1890s, when the town developed as a lumber center.

Flagstaff's lively café society owes much to the students of the **Northern Arizona University**, home to two campus art galleries. The Beasley Gallery holds temporary exhibitions and student work, while the Old Main Art Museum and Gallery has the permanent Weiss collection, which includes works by the Mexican artist Diego Rivera.

Situated on Mars Hill is the 1894 **Lowell Observatory**, named for its benefactor, Percival Lowell, a member c one of Boston's wealthiest families. Lowell wanted to look for life on Mars and although he did not succeec the observatory earned repute with its documented evidence of an expanding universe, along with the discovery of Pluto by astronomer Clyde Tombaug

A few miles northwest of downtown, set picturesquel in a pine forest, is the **Museum of Northern Arizona**. It holds one of the Southwest's most comprehensive collections of South western archaeological artifacts, as well as fine art and natural science exhibits. The museum presents an excelle overview of Anasazi history and contemporary Navajo, Hopi, and Pai cultures.

The collections are arrange in a series of galleries aroun a central courtyard. The Archaeology Gallery provide a fine introduction to the region's historic cultures. The award-winning anthropology exhibition in the Ethnology Gallery documents 12,000 years of Hopi, Zuni, Navajo, and Pai tribal cultures on the Colorado Plateau. The museum shop sells Native Americ arts and crafts. A section has exhibits that focus on the variety of plants and animals found on the Colorado Plateau through the ages.

**Museum of Northern Arizona**
3101 N Fort Valley Rd. *(928) 774 5213. 9am–5pm daily. public hols.*
www.musnaz.org

**Native American exhibits, Museu of Northern Arizona in Flagstaff**

# Heart of Arizona Tour 23

THE VERDE RIVER passes through the wooded hills and fertile meadows of central Arizona, before opening into a wide, green valley between Flagstaff and Phoenix. The heart of Arizona is full of charming towns such as Sedona, hidden away among stunning scenery, and the former mining town of Jerome. Over the hills lies Prescott, once the state capital and now a busy, likable little town with a center full of dignified Victorian buildings. The area's ancient history can be seen in its two beautiful pueblo ruins, Montezuma Castle and Tuzigoot.

### Tips for Drivers

**Recommended route:** *From Sedona, take Hwy 89A to Tuzigoot, Jerome, & Prescott. Hwy 69 runs east from Prescott to Interstate Hwy 17, which connects to Camp Verde, Fort Verde, & Montezuma Castle.*
**Tour length:** *85 miles (137 km).*
**When to go:** *Spring & fall are delightful; summer is very hot.*

**Sedona** ①
Set among dramatic red rock hills, Sedona is a popular resort, known for its New Age stores and galleries as well as for its friendly ambience.

### Key

Tour route
Other road

FLAGSTAFF
Sedona
Cottonwood
Verde River
Prescott Valley
Prescott
89A
179
260
69
17
0 km 10
0 miles 10
PHOENIX

**Tuzigoot National Monument** ②
Stunning views of the Verde River Valley are seen at this ruined hilltop pueblo, occupied until 1425.

**Jerome** ③
A popular relic of Arizona's mining boom, Jerome is known for its 1900s brick buildings, which cling to the slopes of Cleopatra Hill.

**Prescott** ④
This cool hilltop town is set among the rugged peaks and lush woods of Prescott National Forest, making it a popular center for many outdoor activities.

**Montezuma Castle National Monument** ⑥
The Ancestral Puebloan ruins here date from the 1100s and occupy one of the loveliest sites in the Southwest.

**Camp Verde** ⑤
A highlight of this little town is Fort Verde. Built by the US Army in 1865, this stone fort is manned by costumed guides.

## Phoenix 24

*1,300,000 (city only). Greyhound Bus, 2115 E Buckeye Rd. 50 North 2nd St, (602) 254-6500. The PGA's Phoenix Golf Open (Jan).*

STRETCHING ACROSS the entire Salt River Valley, Arizona's capital, Phoenix, started out as a farming town in the 1860s and soon developed into the economic hub of the state. As it grew, it gradually absorbed the surrounding towns of Scottsdale, Mesa, and Tempe, and now has over a million people within the city and almost three million in Metropolitan Phoenix. Downtown Phoenix has many historic attractions while the metropolitan area, famed for the design studio Taliesin West, is also popular with tourists for its spas and resorts during the warm winter months.

### Exploring Downtown Phoenix

Downtown, where the city began in the 19th century, covers a few blocks east and west of Central Avenue and north and south of Washington Street. Washington Street houses the copper-domed **Arizona State Capitol Museum**, originally the state legislature. Among the exhibits are a series of sepia photographs documenting the city's political history. To its west is the **Arizona Mining and Mineral Museum** that traces Arizona's colorful mining history, which made millionaires of some and destitutes of many. Exhibits include photographs, historic tools, and quarried rocks.

More glimpses of the city's history can be seen in the attractive restored Victorian houses on the tree-lined **Heritage Square**, some of which have been converted into tearooms and small museums. Visitors can get a better impression of the city's early history at the inventive **Phoenix Museum of History** across the street. It features unusual artifacts, such as a steam-powered bicycle, and re-creates the city's first jail.

**Cash register at the Museum of History**

In between these historic attractions stands the ultra-modern **Arizona Science Center**, with over 300 interactive science exhibits offering virtual reality trips through the human body.

A short drive north of downtown leads to the highly acclaimed **Phoenix Art Museum**, renowned for its stimulating temporary exhibitions. The museum's second floor houses works by 18th- and 19th-century American artists, particularly those painters connected with the Southwest. Among the exhibits are works by Georgia O'Keeffe and Gilbert Stewart, whose celebrated *Portrait of George Washington* (1796) is seen on every dollar bill.

The **Heard Museum**, farther north, was founded in 1929 by Dwight Heard, a wealthy rancher and newspaper tycoon, whose wife, Maie, amassed an extraordinary collection of Native Southwestern American art. The museum exhibits over 30,000 works, bu its star attraction is the displa of more than 500 *kachina* dolls. Apart from dolls, there an award-winning display of Native American pottery, jewelry, and textiles called Home: Native Peoples In The Southwest. Other interesting galleries are the Sandra Day O'Connor Gallery, which documents the museum's history and showcases the Heard family's early collection, and the Freeman Gallery, with its interactive hands-on display, which shows how artists interpret their environment through ar

The 1900 façade of the Arizona State Capitol Building, Phoenix

**Heard Museum**

2301 North Central Ave.
*(602) 252-8840. (602) 252-8848. 9:30am–5pm daily. public hols.*
www.heard.org

**ENVIRONS:** About 12 miles (19 km) northeast of downtown lies the former town of **Scottsdale**, founded in the late 19th century. Replete with air-conditioned malls, designer stores, hotels, cafés, and restaurants, it is also famous for its world-clas golf courses. Scottsdale's quiet, tree-lined streets and desert setting attracted the visionary architect Frank Lloyd Wright *(see p396)* to establish his winter studio **Taliesin West** here in 1937. The 600-acre (240-ha) complex is now an architecture school and a working design studio. The muted tones of its low-

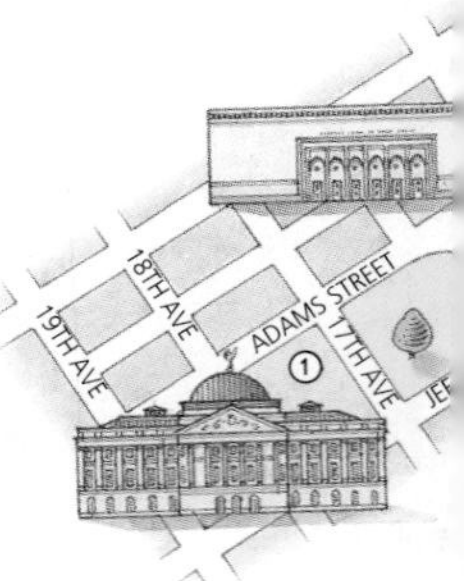

…iesin West façade, designed to blend with the desert landscape

**…ights at a Glance**

…izona State Capitol Museum ①
…izona Mining and Mineral Museum ②
…eritage Square ③
…izona Science Center ④
…oenix Museum of History ⑤
…oenix Art Museum ⑥

lying buildings and use of local stone for irregular walls reflects Wright's enthusiasm for the desert setting.

The **Cosanti Foundation**, 4 miles (6 km) west of Taliesin West, was established by the Italian architect and student of Wright, Paolo Soleri (b.1919), to further his study of what he termed "arcology": a combination of architecture and ecology to create new urban habitats. Today, the site consists of simple, low structures, housing studios, a gallery, and craft workshops, where Soleri and his workers make and sell their trademark wind-bells and cast bronzes.

South of the Cosanti Foundation is the **Camelback Mountain**, named for its humped shape. One of the city's most distinctive landmarks, the mountain is a granite and sandstone out-crop formed by prehistoric volcanic forces. A steep climb, covering 1,300 ft (390 m) in the space of a mile, leads to the summit.

More glimpses of the Native American past can be at the **Pueblo Grande Museum.** It displays an ancient Hohokam ruin, as well as artifacts such as cooking utensils and pottery. Many of these pieces come from the adjacent Archaeological Park, the site of a Hohokam settlement from the 8th to the 14th centuries. The site was originally excavated in 1887, and today has an easy-to-follow path, which guides visitors through the ruins.

Innovative design of the Cosanti Foundation gift shop, Scottsdale

## Tucson 25

750,000. Amtrak Station, 400 E Toole Ave. Greyhound Lines, 2 S 4th Ave. 110 S Church Ave, (520) 624-1817, (800) 638-8350. *La Fiesta de los Vaqueros (late Feb); Tucson Folk Music Festival (May).* www.visittucson.org

THE SECOND largest city in Arizona, Tucson (pronounced too-sahn) is located on the northern boundary of the Sonoran Desert, in a basin surrounded by five mountain ranges. The town's Colonial past dates to the 1770s, when strong resistance from the local Tohono O'odham and Pima Native tribes forced the Spanish to move their regional fortress, or presidio, from nearby Tubac to Tucson.

The city's main sights are clustered around the University of Arizona campus and the historic downtown area. The **Barrio** and **El Presidio** historic districts are located here. El Presidio occupies the area where the original Spanish fortress was built. Today, many of the historic buildings have been converted into restaurants, shops, and offices. Five of El Presidio's oldest dwellings, including the J. Knox Corbett House, are located in the Historic Block. They form a part of the **Tucson Museum of Art**, with its excellent collection of pre-Columbian artifacts, and exhibitions of contemporary American and European work. Southeast of the museum, the Pima County Courthouse, built in 1927, is a fine example of Spanish Colonial Revival Style.

The **St. Augustine Cathedral**, with its imposing sandstone façade, is southwest of El Presidio. Begun in 1896, the cathedral is modeled after the Spanish Colonial style of the Cathedral of Querétaro in central Mexico. The Barrio Historic District, farther south, was once a business district. Today, its quiet streets are lined with brightly painted adobe houses. On nearby Main Street is the "wishing shrine" of El Tiradito, where a young man was killed as a consequence of a lovers' triangle. The locals believe that if a candle lit here burns through a night, their wishes will come true.

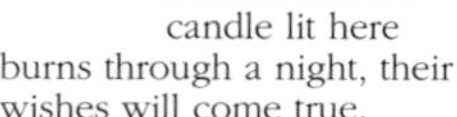

**Stained-glass window in the Cathedral**

The University of Arizona campus houses several museums. The most notable is the **Arizona State Museum**, renowned for its collections of artifacts covering 2,000 years of Native history. Beyond downtown, Metropolitan Tucson extends into the surrounding mountain ranges. **Mount Lemmon** (9,157 ft/2,790 m), the highest peak, is to the north, while to the west is one part of the Saguaro National Park (the other is to the east), where vistas of the tall saguaro cacti can be seen.

About 14 miles (22 km) west of the university, lies the fascinating **Arizona-Sonora Desert Museum**. Covering more than 21 acres (8.5 ha), it includes a botanical garden, zoo, and natural history museum with displays describing the history, geology, and flora and fauna of the Sonoran Desert.

Nearby is the **Old Tucson Studios**, a Wild West theme park originally built as a set for a Western movie in 1939. Some of Hollywood's most famous Westerns, such as *Gunfight at the OK Corral* (1957) and *Rio Bravo* (1958), were filmed here.

The Southwest's oldest and best preserved Mission church lies south of Tucson. The **San Xavier del Bac Mission**, completed in 1797 by Franciscan missionaries, is built of adobe brick and is considered the finest example of Spanish Colonial architecture in the US. Its highlights include an ornate Baroque façade decorated with carved figures of saints, a glorious painted ceiling, and a spectacular main altar.

**San Xavier del Bac Mission**
1950 W San Xavier Rd, 10 miles (16 km) S of Tucson on I-19. *(520) 294-2624. 8am–5pm daily.*

### SOUTHWEST ARCHITECTURE

The Southwest has been witness to a range of architecture styles from Ancestral Puebloan adobe to Spanish Colonial, and 19th- and early 20th-century Mission and Pueblo Revival. Colonizers brought their own forms that mingled with the Native, creating a unique plethora of multicultural styles.

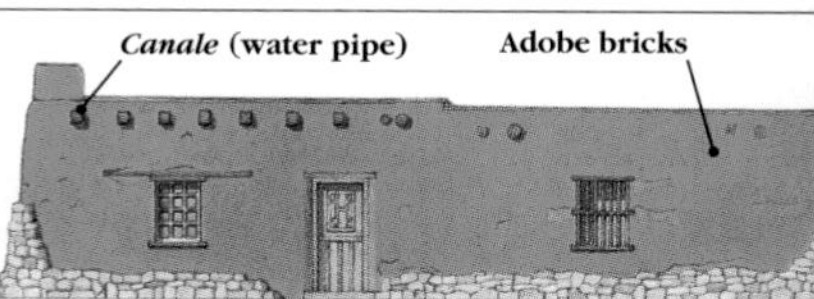


***This adobe home** in El Rancho de las Golondrinas Museum in Santa Fe is made of adobe (sun-baked bricks that are a mixture of mud, sand, and straw), cemented with similar material, and replastered with mud.*

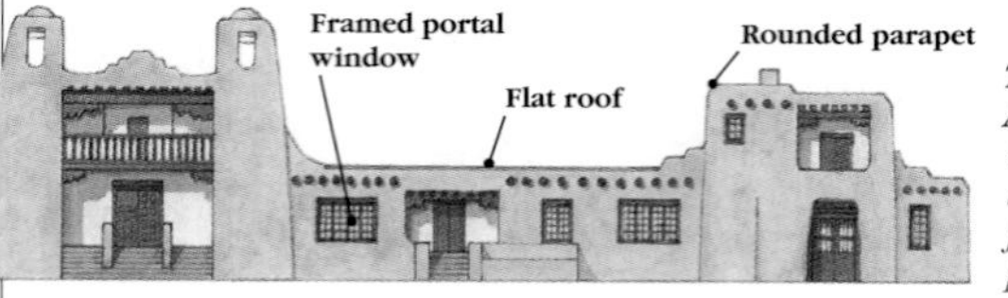


***The Santa Fe Museum of Fine Arts** was the city's first building in Pueblo Revival style, with adobe walls, rounded parapets, framed portal windows, and pueblo-style multitiered stories.*

atue of Virgin Mary at the San ıvier del Bac Mission, Tucson

## ɿogales 26

ɿ 19,500. 123 W Kino rk, (520) 287-3685.

THE BIRTHPLACE of jazz star Charles Mingus, Nogales really two towns that raddle the US border with exico. It is a busy port of ıtry, handling huge amounts freight, including 75 ercent of all winter fruit and egetables sold in North merica. The town attracts rge numbers of visitors search of bargains at ıopping districts on both des of the border. here is a profound ontrast between the uiet, ordered streets the US side, and e ramshackle ouses and bustling, rge-scale street arket across e border.

Visas are required only for visitors traveling beyond town limits. US citizens should carry a passport or birth certificate for identification, while foreign nationals should carry their passport and make sure that their visa status enables them to re-enter the US.

## Bisbee 27

*6,500. Bisbee Chamber of Commerce, 1 Main St, (520) 432-5421.*

THE DISCOVERY of copper here in the 1880s sparked a mining rush, and by the turn of the century Bisbee was the largest city between St. Louis and San Francisco. Today, this is one of the Southwest's most atmospheric mining towns. Victorian buildings such as the landmark Copper Queen Hotel still dominate the historic town center, while attractive clusters of houses cling to the sides of the surrounding mountains. Visitors can tour the mines that once flourished here. The Bisbee Mining and Historical Museum illustrates the realities of mining and frontier life.

Mexican pottery from Nogales

**ENVIRONS:** Some 25 miles (40 km) north of Bisbee is **Tombstone**, one of the wildest towns in the West. Founded by a prospector in 1877, its name derives from the warning he received that "all you'll find out there is your tombstone." Instead, the silver he found led to a silver rush. Today, Tombstone is a living legend, famous as the site of the 1881 gunfight at OK Corral between the Earp brothers and the Clanton gang. The OK Corral is now a museum, where the infamous gunfight is re-enacted. The old seat of justice, Tombstone Courthouse, is a historic site.

## Amerind Foundation 28

*(520) 586-3666. Oct–May: 10am–4pm daily. Jun–Sep: Mon & Tue; public hols.*
*www.amerind.org*

THE AMERIND Foundation is one of the country's most important private archaeological and ethnological museums. The name Amerind is a contraction of "American Indian," and this collection depicts all aspects of Native American life through thousands of artifacts of different cultures. The displays include Inuit masks, Cree tools, and sculpted effigy figures from Mexico's Casas Grandes.

The adjacent Amerind Art Gallery has a fine collection of Western art by such artists as William Leigh and Frederic Remington. The delightful pink buildings, designed in the Spanish Colonial Revival style, are also interesting.

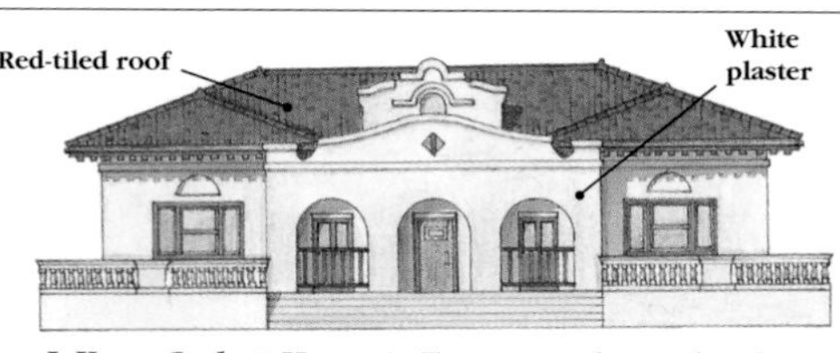


***J. Knox Corbett House** in Tucson was designed in the 20th-century Mission Revival style by the Chicago architect David Holmes in 1906. It is characterized by white stucco walls, flat roofs, courtyards, and minimal ornamentation.*

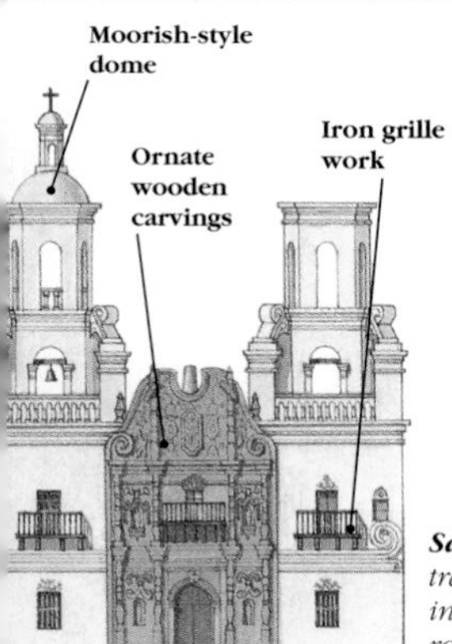


***San Xavier del Bac Mission** is a fine example of the Baroque tradition of Spanish Colonial churches. The style saw a resurgence in the 20th century as Spanish Colonial Revival, with red-tiled roofs, ornamental terra-cotta, iron grille work, and white walls.*

## Petrified Forest National Park ㉙

Off I-40. (928) 524-6228. *summer: 7am–7pm; winter: 8am–5pm.* *Dec 25.* *partial.* www.nps.gov/pefo

THIS FOSSILIZED prehistoric forest is one of Arizona's most unusual attractions. Millions of years ago, rivers swept trees downstream into a vast swamp that once covered this whole area. Groundwater transported silica dioxide into downed timber, eventually turning it into the quartz stone logs seen today, with colored crystals preserving the shape and structure of the trees.

Running the entire length of the forest is the famous Painted Desert. This is an area of colored bands of sand and rock that change from blues to reds throughout the day as the shifting light catches the different mineral deposits.

A 28-mile (45-km) scenic road starting at the visitor center travels the length of the park. There are nine overlooks along the way, including Kachina Point, where the Painted Wilderness trailhead is located. A permit is required to camp in the wilderness area. Near the south end of the road is the fine **Rainbow Forest Museum**.

**Rainbow Forest Museum**
Off Hwy 180 (S entrance). *(928) 524-3138.* *8am–5pm daily.*

**Eroded sandstone opening of Window Rock, near Highway 12**

## Window Rock ㉚

*4,500.* *Hwy 264, (928) 871-6436.*

WINDOW ROCK is the capital of the Navajo Nation, the largest Native American reservation in the Southwest. The town is named for the natural arch found in the sandstone cliffs located about a mile north of the main strip on Highway 12.

The **Navajo Nation Museum** located in Window Rock is one of the largest Native American museums in the country. Opened in 1997, the huge *hogan*-shaped building houses displays that cover the history of the Ancestral Puebloans and the Navajo.

**Navajo Nation Museum**
Hwy 264 & Post Office Loop Rd, *(928) 871-7941.* *8am–5pm Mon, 8am–8pm Tue–Fri, 9am–5pm Sat.* *Sun.*

## Hopi Indian Reservation ㉛

*10,000.* *Hwy 264, Second Mesa, (928) 734-2401.* *May–S… 6am–9pm daily; Oct–Apr: 7am–8p… daily.* *Jan 1, Thanksgiving, Dec*

BELIEVED TO be direct descendants of the Ancestral Puebloans, the Hopi Indians have lived in and cultivated this harsh and barren reservation area for almost a thousand years. They worship through the *kachina*, the living spirits of plants and animals, believed to visit the tribe during the growing season. Most Hopi villages are located on or near one of three mesas (fla… topped elevations), named First, Second, and Third Me… Artisans of each mesa specialize in particular crafts.

Visitors can take a guided walking tour of the impressive pueblo, **Walpi**, on the

**Historic pueblo town of Walpi on First Mesa at the Hopi Indian Reservation**

ıcestral Puebloan ruins of Keet Seel at the Navajo National Monument

:st Mesa. Inhabited in the :th century, it was built to : easily defended against ›ssible Spanish or Navajo :acks. It straddles a dramatic ıife-edge of rock, extending ›m the tip of the First Mesa. places, Walpi is less than ›0 ft (33m) wide with a drop several hundred feet on ›th sides. The Walpi tour includes several stops where visitors can purchase *kachina* figurines, distinctive hand-crafted pottery, rugs, and baskets, or sample the Hopi *piki* bread. A wider range of Hopi arts and crafts are available in the galleries and stores of the Second Mesa. The Hopi Cultural Center here has a restaurant and the only hotel for miles around, as ell as a museum that has an :cellent collection of photo-aphs depicting various pects of Hopi life.

On the Third Mesa, Old raibi pueblo, thought to have :en founded in the 12th ntury, is fascinating because claims that it is the oldest ntinually occupied human ttlement in North America.

ıchina doll

**Walpi**

(928) 737-2262.

**alking Tours** *9:30am–3pm daily.*

## Tuba City ㉜

*17,300. Tuba City Trading Post, (928) 283-5441.*

NAMED FOR TUUVI, a Hopi Indian who converted to the Mormon faith, Tuba City is best known for the 65-million-year-old dinosaur tracks found just off the main highway, 5 miles (8 km) southwest of the town. This is also the largest community in the western section of the Navajo Reservation and is a good spot from which to explore both the Navajo National Monument and the Hopi Reservation.

## Grand Canyon ㉝

*See pp536–9.*

## Navajo National Monument ㉞

*(928) 672-2700. 8am–5pm daily. Jan 1, Thanksgiving, Dec 25.* www.nps.gov/nava

ALTHOUGH NAMED because of its location on the Navajo Reservation, this monument is actually known for its Ancestral Puebloan ruins. The most accessible ruin here is the beautifully preserved, 135-room pueblo of Betatakin, which fills a vast, curved niche in the cliffs of Tsegi Canyon. An easy, 1-mile (1.6-km) trail from the visitor center, along piñon pines and juniper trees, leads to an overlook, which provides a captivating view of Betatakin. For a closer look at these ancient houses, visitors can take the daily six-hour hiking tours held from late May to early September.

A more demanding 17-mile (27-km) hike leads to **Keet Seel**, a more impressive ruin. Only a limited number of permits to visit the ruin are issued each day. This hike requires overnight camping at a campsite with the most basic facilities. Keet Seel was a larger and more successful community than Betatakin. Construction began here in about 1250, but the site is thought to have been abandoned by 1300.

The Keet Seel ruins at the Navajo National Monument

# Grand Canyon ㉝

One of the world's great natural wonders, the Grand Canyon is an instantly recognizable symbol of the Southwest. Running through Grand Canyon National Park *(see pp538–9)*, it is 217 miles (349 km) long, about 4 to 18 miles (6 to 29 km) wide, and over 5,000 ft (1,500 m) deep. It was formed over a period of six million years by the Colorado River, whose fast-flowing waters sliced their way through the Colorado Plateau, which includes the gorge, most of northern Arizona, and the Four Corners region. The plateau's geological vagaries have defined the river's course, and exposed vast cliffs are ringed by rocks of different color, variegated hues of limestone, sandstone, and shale. By any standard, the canyon, with its vast scale, is spectacular. But its special beauty is in the ever-shifting patterns of light and shadow and the colors of the rock, bleached white at midday, but bathed in red and ocher at sunset.

**Mule Trip Convoy**
*A mule ride is a popular method of exploring the canyon's narrow trails.*

**Havasu Canyon**
*Since 1300 Havasu Canyon has been home to the Havasupai Indians. A population of around 500 Indians lives on the Havasupai Reservation, making a living from the tourist trade.*

**Grandview Point**
*At 7,400 ft (2,250 m), this is one of the highest places on the South Rim, the canyon's southern edge. It is one of the stops along the breathtaking Desert View Drive* (see p538). *The point is thought to be the spot from where the Spaniards had their first glimpse of the canyon in 1540.*

**North Rim**

*The North Rim receives roughly one-tenth the number of visitors of the South Rim. While less accessible, it is a more peaceful destination offering a sense of unexplored wilderness. Hikes include the North Kaibab Trail, a steep descent down to Phantom Ranch, the only lodge on the canyon floor.*

## Visitors' Checklist

*Canyon View Information Plaza, S of Mather Point, Arizona, (928) 638-7888. Grand Canyon Airport, Tusayan. Grand Canyon Railway from Williams daily. From Flagstaff & Williams. South Rim: year-round: daily. North Rim: summer only. North Rim: late Nov–mid-May: closed because of snow.*

partial.

www.nps.gov/grca

**Bright Angel Trail**

*Used by both Native Americans and early settlers, the Bright Angel Trail follows a natural route along one of the canyon's enormous fault lines. It is an appealing option for day-hikers; unlike some other trails in the area, it offers plenty of shade and several seasonal water sources.*

## Yavapai Point at the South Rim

Situated 5 miles (8 km) north of the canyon's South Entrance, along a stretch of the Rim Trail, is Yavapai Point. Its observation station offers superb views, and a viewing panel identifies several of the central canyon's landmarks.

## How the Canyon was Formed

While the Colorado River, which changed course four million years ago, accounts for the canyon's depth, its width and formations are the work of even greater forces. Wind rushing through the canyon erodes the limestone and sandstone a few grains at a time, and rain pouring over the rim cuts deep side canyons through the softer rock. Perhaps the greatest force is ice. Water from rain and snowmelt works into cracks in the rock. When frozen, it expands, forcing the rock away from the canyon walls. Soft layers erode quickly into sloped faces, while harder rock resists erosion, leaving sheer vertical faces.

**Cracks formed by water erosion**

# Exploring Grand Canyon National Park

**Bell near Hermits Rest**

A WORLD HERITAGE SITE, Grand Canyon National Park covers 1,904 sq miles (4,930 sq km), and consists of the canyon itself, which starts where the Paria River empties into the Colorado, and stretches from Lees Ferry to Lake Mead *(see p515)*. The park has two main entrances, on the North and South Rims of the canyon. Its main roads, Hermit Road and Desert View Drive, both accessible from the south entrance, overlook the canyon. Visitors can also enter the park from the north, although this route (Hwy 67) is closed during winter. Walking trails along the North and South Rims offer staggering views but to experience the canyon at its most fascinating, the trails that head down toward the canyon floor should be explored. The Bright Angel Trail on the South Rim and the North Kaibab Trail on the North Rim descend to the canyon floor and are tough hikes involving an overnight stop.

**Adobe, Pueblo-style architecture of Hopi House, Grand Canyon Village**

### Grand Canyon Village

Grand Canyon National Park.
*(928) 638-7888.* *partial.*

Grand Canyon Village has its roots in the late 19th century. The extensive building of visitor accommodations started after the Santa Fe Railroad opened a branch line here from Williams in 1901, although some hotels had been built in the late 1890s. The Fred Harvey Company constructed a clutch of well-designed, attractive buildings. The most prominent is the El Tovar Hotel *(see p562)*. Opened in 1905, it is named after Spanish explorers who reached the gorge in 1540. The Hopi House also opened in 1905 – a rendition of a traditional Hopi dwelling, where locals could sell their craftwork as souvenirs. It was built by Hopi craftsmen and designed by Mary E.J. Colter, an ex-schoolteacher and architect, who drew on Southwestern influences, mixing both Native American and Hispanic styles. She is responsible for many of the historic structures that now grace the South Rim, including the 1914 Lookout Studio and Hermits Rest, and the rustic 1922 Phantom Ranch *(see p562)* on the canyon floor.

Today, Grand Canyon Village has a wide range of hotels, restaurants, and stores. It can be surprisingly easy to get lost here since the buildings are spread out and discreetly placed among wooded areas. The village is the starting point for most of the mule trips through the canyon. It is also the terminus for the Grand Canyon Railway, restored steam trains that make the 64-mile (103-km) journey from Williams.

### The South Rim

Most of the Grand Canyon's 4.3 million annual visitors come to the South Rim, since unlike the North Rim, it is open year-round and is easily accessible along Highway 180/64 from Flagstaff *(see p528)* or Williams. **Hermit Road** and **Desert View Drive** (Hwy 64) start at Grand Canyon Village and include some of the best views of the gorge. Hermit Drive is closed to private vehicles from March to November, but there are free shuttle buses, and Desert View Drive is open all year.

From the village, Hermit Road meanders along the South Rim, extending for 8 miles (13 km). Its first viewpoint is **Trailview Overlook** which provides an overview of the canyon and the winding course of the Bright Angel Trail. Moving on, **Maricopa Point** offers especially panoramic views of the canyon but not of the Colorado River, which is more apparent from nearby **Hopi Point**. At the end of Hermit Road lies **Hermits Rest**, where a gift shop, decorated in rustic style is located in yet another Mary Colter-designed building. The longer Desert View Drive runs in the opposite direction, and covers 26 miles (42 km). It winds for 12 miles (20 km) before reaching **Grandview Point**, where the Spaniards may have had their first glimpse of the canyon in 1540.

**The interior of the Hermits Rest gift store with crafts for sale lining the walls**

esert View's stone Watchtower n Desert View Drive

## California Condors

America's largest bird, the California condor, has a wingspan of over 9 ft (2.7 m). Nearly extinct in the 1980s, the last 22 condors were captured for breeding in captivity. In 1996, the first captive-bred birds were released in Northern Arizona. Today, about 50 condors fly the skies over Northern Arizona. They are frequent visitors to the South Rim, though visitors should not approach or attempt to feed them.

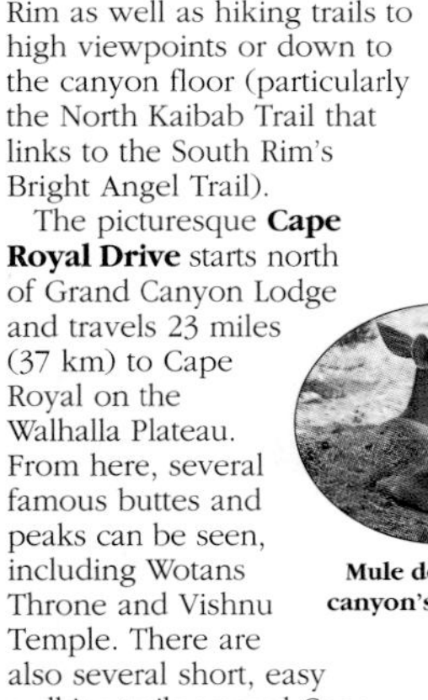



**A pair of California condors**

en miles (16 km) farther on e the pueblo remains of usayan Ruin, where there is small museum with exhibits n Ancestral Puebloan life. he road finally ends at the tunning overlook of **Desert iew**. The Watchtower here vas Colter's most fanciful reation, its upper floor ecorated with early 20th-entury Hopi murals.

Just east of Grand Canyon 'illage is **Yavapai Point** from vhere it is possible to see hantom Ranch. This is the nly roofed accommodation vailable on the canyon floor, cross the Colorado River.

### he North Rim

tanding at about 8,000 ft 2,400 m), the North Rim is igher, cooler, and greener nan the South Rim, with ense forests of ponderosa ine, aspen, and Douglas fir. 'isitors are most likely to spot vildlife on the North Rim. Iule deer, Kaibab squirrel, nd wild turkey are among ne most common sights. he North Rim is reached ia Highway 67, off Highway 9A, ending at **Grand anyon Lodge** *(see p558)* vhere there are visitor services, campground, a gas station, estaurant, and a general store. Jearby there is a National Park ervice information center, vhich offers maps of the area. he North Rim and all its acilities are closed between nid-October and mid-May, vhen it is often snowed in. he North Rim is twice as far from the river as the South Rim, and the canyon really stretches out from the overlooks giving a sense of its 10-mile (16-km) width. There are about 30 miles (45 km) of scenic roads along the North Rim as well as hiking trails to high viewpoints or down to the canyon floor (particularly the North Kaibab Trail that links to the South Rim's Bright Angel Trail).

The picturesque **Cape Royal Drive** starts north of Grand Canyon Lodge and travels 23 miles (37 km) to Cape Royal on the Walhalla Plateau. From here, several famous buttes and peaks can be seen, including Wotans Throne and Vishnu Temple. There are also several short, easy walking trails around Cape Royal, along the top. A 3-mile (5-km) detour leads to **Point Imperial**, the highest point on the canyon rim, while along the way the **Vista Encantada** has delightful views and picnic tables overlooking the gorge.

**Mule deer on the canyon's North Rim**

### The Bright Angel Trail

This is the most popular of all Grand Canyon hiking trails. The Bright Angel trailhead is at Grand Canyon Village on the South Rim. The trail begins near the Kolb Studio at the western end of the village. It then switches dramatically down the side of the canyon for 9 miles (13 km). The trail crosses the river over a suspension bridge, ending a little farther on at Phantom Ranch. There are two rest-houses and a fully equipped campground along the way. It is not advisable to attempt the whole trip in one day. Many walk from the South Rim to one of the rest stops and then return up to the rim. Temperatures at the bottom of the canyon can reach 110°F (43°C) or higher during the summer. Day-hikers should therefore carry a quart (just under a liter) of water per person per hour for summer hiking. Carrying a first-aid kit is also recommended.

**Hikers taking a break on the South Rim's Bright Angel Trail**

# Monument Valley ㉟

FROM SCENIC HIGHWAY 163, which crosses the border of Utah and Arizona, it is possible to see the famous buttes and mesas of Monument Valley. These ancient rocks, soaring upward from a seemingly boundless desert, have come to symbolize the American West, since they have been used as a backdrop for countless movies and TV shows.

The area's visitor center sits within the boundary of Monument Valley Tribal Park, but many of the valley's spectacular rock formations and other sites are found just outside the park boundary.

**Guided Tours**
*A row of kiosks at the visitor center offer Navajo-guided 4WD tours of the valley. The marketing tactics can be aggressive, but the tours offer an excellent way to see places in the park that are otherwise inaccessible.*

**Three Sisters**
*One of several distinctive pinnacle rock formations at the valley, the closest view of the Three Sisters can be seen from John Ford's Point, and is one of the most photographed sights here.*

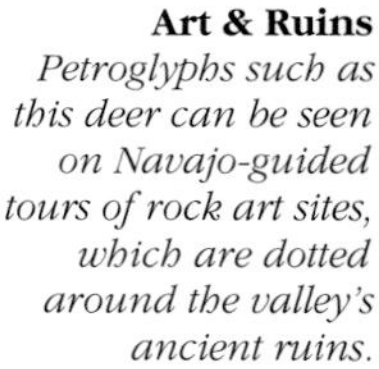

**Art & Ruins**
*Petroglyphs such as this deer can be seen on Navajo-guided tours of rock art sites, which are dotted around the valley's ancient ruins.*

**MONUMENT VALLEY**
Monument Valley is not really a valley. The tops of the mesas mark what was once a flat plain. Millions of years ago, this plain was cracked by upheavals within the earth. The cracks widened and eroded, leaving the formations rising from the desert floor.

## EXPLORING THE VALLEY

The awe-inspiring beauty of Monument Valley's buttes and mesas can be viewed by travelers from Highway 163. Visitors can also pay a fee to travel on a 17-mile (27-km) self-guided drive along a well-marked dirt road. (Fees are collected at the visitor center.) Alternatively, Navajo guides may be hired for hiking, horseback, or 4WD tours to fascinating and less-visited parts of the valley.

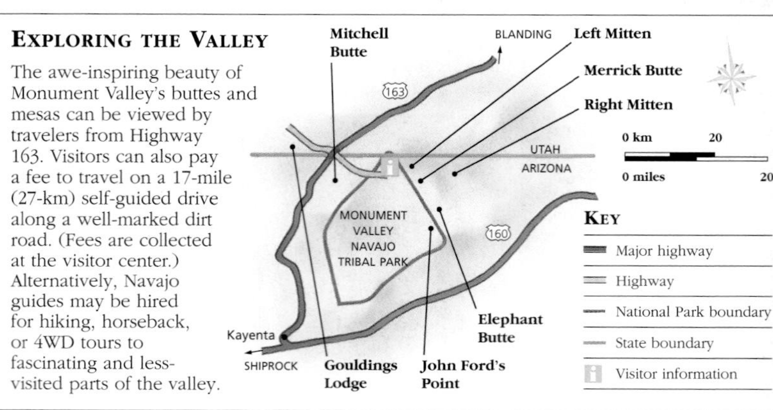

**ɔhn Ford's Point**
*ɔe most popular stop along the valley drive is John Ford's ɔint, which is said to be the film director's favorite view ˚ the valley. Various stands offer a range of Navajo crafts. nearby native* hogan *(Navajo dwelling) serves as a gift ɔop where Navajo weavers demonstrate their craft.*

## Visitors' Checklist

*PO Box 360289, Monument Valley, (435) 727-5870.*
*sunrise–sunset daily.*
*Dec 25.*
*visitor center only.*
www.navajonationparks.org

**Navajo Weaver**
*Navajo women are usually considered to be the finest weavers in the Southwest. One rug can take months to complete and sell for thousands of dollars. Using the natural colors of the land, the weavers often add a "spirit line" to their work to prevent their spirit being "trapped" within the rug.*

## The Wild West

Romanticized in cowboy movies, the "Wild West" conjures up images of tough men herding cattle across the country before living it up in a saloon. But frontier life was far from romantic. Settlers arriving in this wilderness were caught up in a first-come first-served battle for land and wealth, fighting Native Americans and each other for land. The rugged life of the mining prospectors and ranch cowboys helped to create the idea of the American West. Today, visitors can still see former mining towns such as Bisbee or enjoy re-enacted gunfights on the streets of Tombstone *(see p533),* the site of one of the Wild West's most famous tales. In the late 19th-century, however, such survival skills as good shooting often co-existed with a kill-or-be-killed ethos. Guided trail rides, offered at many dude ranches, are a great way to explore the contemporary Wild West.

**Guided trail rides, conducted to explore the Wild West**

# Canyon de Chelly National Monument 36

**Flowering cactus**

THE AWESOME thousand-foot cliffs of the Canyon de Chelly boast of a long and eventful history of human habitation. Archaeologists have found evidence of four periods of Native culture, starting with the Basketmaker people around AD 300, followed by the Great Pueblo Builders, who created the cliff dwellings in the 12th century. They were succeeded by the Hopi, who lived here seasonally for around 300 years, taking advantage of the canyon's fertile soil. Today, the canyon is the cultural and geographic heart of the Navajo Nation, where Navajo farmers still live tending the sheep, introduced by the Spanish, and women weave rugs at outdoor looms. Pronounced "d'Shay," de Chelly is a Spanish corruption of the Native name *tsegi*, meaning rock canyon.

**Yucca House Ruin**
*Perched on the mesa top, this ruin of an Ancestral Puebloa[n] house sits in a rock hollow, pr[ec]iously overhanging a sheer dr[op to] the valley floor.*

**Canyon Vegetation**
*Within the canyon, cottonwood and oak trees line the river washes; the land itself is a fertile oasis of meadows, alfalfa and corn fields, and fruit orchards.*

**Stone and adobe** cliff dwellings were home to the Ancestral Puebloans from the 12th to the 14th centuries and were built to face south toward the sun, with cooler areas within.

**Navajo Fortress**
*This imposing rock tower was the site of a three-month siege in 1863, when a group of Navajos reached the summit via pole ladders. They were trying to escape a US government patrol led by Kit Carson* (see p544) *to settle the Navajo raids. Carson's persistence finally led them to surrender an[d] they were marched to a camp in New Mexic[o]*

**Hiking in the Canyon**
*'anyon de Chelly is a popular destination for hikers, but apart from the White ouse Ruins Trail, isitors can enter he canyons only with a Navajo guide.*

### VISITORS' CHECKLIST

2 miles (3.5 km) E of Chinle & Hwy 191. *PO Box 588, Chinle, (928) 674-5500.* *8am–5pm daily.* *Dec 25.* *guided tours are obligatory within the canyon except at the White House.*
www.nps.gov/cach

**The pale walls** of the White House cliff drop 550 ft (160 m) to the canyon floor.

***Hogan* Interior**
*The* hogan *is the center of Navajo family life. Made of horizontal logs, a smoke hole in the center provides contact with the sky, while the dirt floor gives contact with the earth. A door faces east to greet the rising sun.*

## WHITE HOUSE RUINS

This group of rooms, tucked into a tiny hollow in the cliff, seem barely touched by time. The dwellings were originally situated above a larger pueblo, much of which has now disappeared. It is the only site within the canyon that can be visited without a Navajo guide, reached via a steep 2.5-mile (5-km) round-trip trail that winds to the canyon floor and offers magnificent views.

## MASSACRE CAVE

The canyon's darkest hour was in 1805, when a Spanish force under Lieutenant Antonio Narbona entered the area. The Spanish wanted to subdue the Navajo, claiming they were raiding their settlements. While some Navajo fled by climbing to the canyon rim, others took refuge in a cave high in the cliffs. The Spanish fired into the cave, and Narbona boasted that he had killed 115 Navajo including 90 warriors. Navajo accounts are different, claiming that most of the warriors were absent (probably hunting) and those killed were mostly women, children, and the elderly. The only Spanish fatality came when a Spaniard attempting to climb into the cave was attacked by a Navajo woman and both plunged over the cliff, gaining the Navajo name "Two Fell Over." The Anglo name is "Massacre Cave."

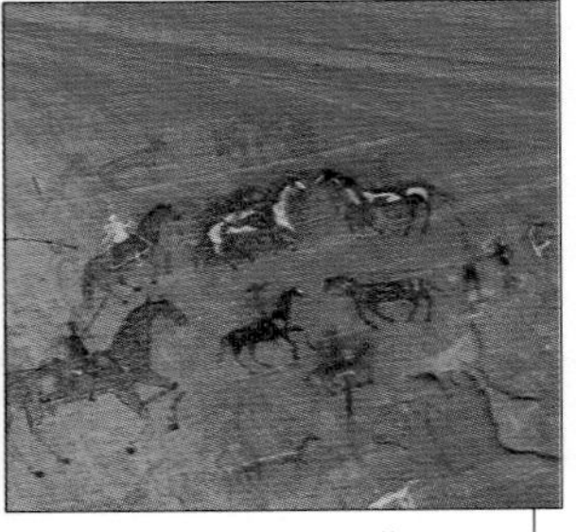

**Pictograph on a canyon wall showing invading Spanish soldiers**

# New Mexico

NEW MEXICO'S RICH CULTURAL HERITAGE and unique mix of Native American, Hispanic, and Anglo American people make it a fascinating place to visit. The forested peaks of the Rocky Mountains offer ski resorts in winter and cool retreats in summer. Northern New Mexico, with its soft colors and vivid desert landscapes, has attracted generations of artists to the creative centers of Santa Fe and Taos. In the vast, wild south visitors can explore ancient Native ruins at Bandelier National Monument and the fascinating cave systems of Carlsbad Caverns.

**Fajada Butte in Chaco Culture National Historical Park**

## Chaco Culture National Historical Park 37

*3 miles (5 km) SE of Nageezi off US 550. (505) 786-7014. 8am–5pm daily. public hols. www.nps.gov/chcu*

ONE OF THE Southwest's most impressive cultural sites, Chaco Canyon reflects the sophistication of the Ancestral Puebloan civilization that existed here. With its six "great houses" (pueblos that contained hundreds of rooms) and many lesser sites, the canyon was once the political, religious, and cultural center for settlements that spread across much of the Four Corners.

Visitors can access the site via a 16-mile (26-km) dirt road that is affected by flash floods in wet weather. A paved loop road in the site passes several of Chaco's highlights. The major stop is **Pueblo Bonito**, the largest of the "great houses," a D-shaped, four-story structure with more than 600 rooms, and 40 *kivas*, round, pit-like rooms used for religious ceremonies. Begun around AD 850, it was built in stages over the course of 300 years. **Casa Riconada**, the largest religious chamber at Chaco, measuring 62 ft (19m) in diameter, lies to the southeast.

A short trail from Pueblo Bonito leads to another great house, **Chetro Ketl**, covering 3 acres (2 ha). The masonry used to build the later portions of this structure is among the most sophisticated found in any Ancestral Puebloan site. A two-hour hike northward leads to **Pueblo Alto**, built atop the mesa at the junction of many ancient Chacoan roads.

**Finely wrought stonework at Chaco Canyon**

## Taos 38

*6,000. Greyhound, Taos Bus Center, Hwy 68. 1139 Paseo de Pueblo Sur (505) 758-3873, (800) 732-8267.*

THE CITY OF TAOS, home to Indians for around 1,000 years, is now a vibrant artistic center. In 1898, artists Ernest Blumenschein and Bert Phillips stopped here to repai a wagon wheel and never lef In 1915 they established the Taos Society of Artists, which continues to promote the work of local artists. Some o these are exhibited at the **Harwood Museum of Art**, located in a tranquil, 19th-century adobe compound. More works by the society's artists are housed in the **Blumenschein Home and Museum**, nearby.

The tree-lined, old Spanish **Plaza** at the heart of Taos makes for a pleasant stroll. T its east is the **Kit Carson Home and Museum**. A fur trapper and soldier, Carson's (1809–68) remarkable life is the focus of this museum.

A few miles north of the town center, Taos' main street, Paseo del Pueblo Norte, leads to the **Millicent Roger Museum**, with its brilliant collection of Native arts and crafts, and black-on-black pottery of Puebloan artist Maria Martinez. This road leads to the dramatic Ri Grande Gorge Bridge, the country's second-highest suspension bridge, built in 1965 It offers awesome views of the gorge and the surroundin stark, sweeping plateau.

**Taos Pueblo** is north of th city. It features two multistor communal adobe houses still inhabited by villagers, makin it one of the oldest communities in the country.

The Hacienda Martinez *(see p551)* at **Rancho de Taos**, south of the city, is a well-preserved Spanish Colonial house with thick adobe walls and heavy gates The 18th-century adobe church of San Francisco de Asis, was often painted by Georgia O'Keeffe, the most distinguished member of the Taos Society of Artists.

# Northern Pueblos Tour 39

**Redware pottery**

THE FERTILE VALLEY of the Rio Grande between Santa Fe and Taos is home to eight pueblos of the 19 Native American pueblos in New Mexico. Although geographically close, each pueblo has its own government and traditions, and many offer attractions to visitors. Nambe gives stunning views of the surrounding mountains, mesas, and high desert. San Idelfonso is famous for its fine pottery, and other villages produce handcrafted jewelry or rugs.

### Tips for Drivers

***Starting point:*** *Tesuque Pueblo, N of Santa Fe on Hwy 84.*
***Length:*** *45 miles (70 km). Local roads leading to pueblos are often dirt tracks, so allow extra time.*
***Note:*** *Visitors are welcome, but respect their laws & etiquette* *(see p554).* *Indian Pueblo Cultural Center, (505) 843-7270.*
www.indianpueblo.org

**Santa Clara Pueblo ⑤**
This small pueblo is known for its artisans and their work. As in many pueblos, it contains a number of craft shops and small studios, often run by the Native artisans themselves.

**Puye Cliff Dwellings ⑥**
Now deserted, this site contains over 700 rooms, complete with stone carvings, which were home to Native peoples until 1500.

**San Juan Pueblo ⑦**
Declared the first capital of New Mexico in 1598, this village is now a center for the visual arts and has an arts cooperative.

**San Ildefonso Pueblo ④**
Occupied since AD 1300, this pueblo is best known for its etched black pottery, the proceeds of which saved its people from the Depression of the 1930s.

**Nambe Pueblo ③**
Set in a beautiful fertile valley, this village is bordered by a lakeside hiking trail with waterfall views and a buffalo ranch.

**Pojoaque Pueblo ②**
The new Peoh Cultural Center and Museum here is an excellent introduction to the pueblo way of life in these small communities.

**Tesuque Pueblo ①**
The Tewa people here have concentrated on farming and pottery-making for centuries.

**Key**

Tour route

Other road

# Santa Fe ⓴

THE OLDEST STATE CAPITAL in North America, Santa Fe was founded by the Spanish conquistador Don Pedro de Peralta, who established a colony here in 1610. This colony was abandoned in 1680 after the Pueblo Revolt, but was later recaptured. When Mexico gained independence in 1821, traders and settlers from Missouri poured into the area via the Santa Fe Trail. Perched on a high plateau, this beautiful city is surrounded by mountains. Its heart, since its founding, is the central Plaza, and there is no better place to begin exploring the city. Today, it houses a Native American market under the portal of the Palace of the Governors, and the square is lined with shops, cafés, and several galleries.

**★ Museum of Fine Arts**
*Built of adobe in 1917, this museum focuses on the paintings and sculpture of Southwestern artists.*

**★ Palace of the Governors**
*This single-story adobe building, built in 1600, was the seat of regional government for 300 years. Now part of the Museum of New Mexico, it houses displays on the city's history.*

SHERIDAN
LINCOLN
PALACE AVENUE
PLAZA
BURRO ALLEY
W SAN FRANCISCO STREET
DON GASPAR AVENUE
GALISTEO STREET
WATER STREET

0 meters 100
0 yards 100

**KEY**

- - - Suggested route

**STAR SIGHTS**

**★ Museum of Fine Arts**

**★ Palace of the Governors**

**Original Trading Post** sells Hispanic art, antiques, and Native American crafts.

**The Plaza**
*The obelisk at the center of this main square commemorates Santa Fe's war veterans. The Plaza is lined with old Colonial buildings, including the Palace of Governors.*

**aint Francis Cathedral**
*his colorful, carved wooden 'atue of the Virgin stands in side chapel belonging to the riginal 17th-century church n which the present athedral was built in 1869.*

**VISITORS' CHECKLIST**

65,000. *Santa Fe Municipal Airport, 10 miles (16 km) SW of Santa Fe.* *Lamy, 18 miles (29 km) S of city.* *858 St. Michael's Drive.* *201 W. Marcy St, (505) 955-6200, (800) 777-2489.* *Spanish Market (Jul); Santa Fe Opera Season (Jul & Aug); Indian Market (Aug); Fiestas de Santa Fe (Sep).* www.santafenm.org

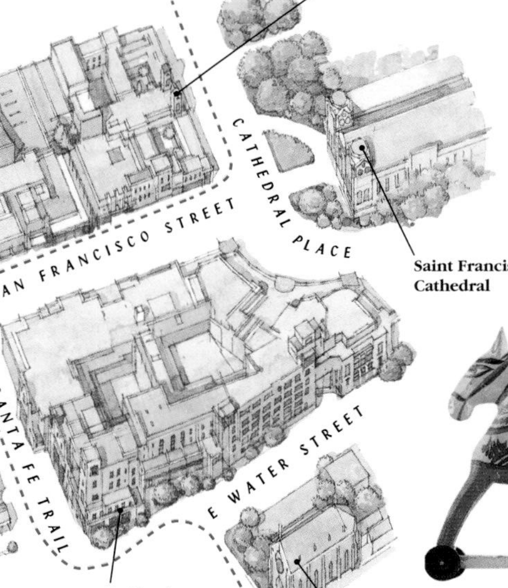


**Institute of American Indian Arts Museum**

**Saint Francis Cathedral**

**La Fonda Hotel**

**Girard Collection toy, Museum of International Folk Art**

**Loretto Chapel**
*Built in Gothic style by French architects in the 1870s, the Loretto Chapel was modeled on the Sainte-Chappelle in Paris. Its elegant spiral staircase has no nails or center support, and its perfect craftsmanship is all that keeps it aloft.*

**Exploring Santa Fe**

This city's rich history and beautiful architecture have made it one of the country's most popular destinations. It is famous for its adobe buildings, art galleries, and the Museum of New Mexico's four museums. In addition to the Palace of the Governors and Museum of Fine Arts, there is the **Georgia O'Keeffe Museum**, northwest of the Plaza. This has the world's largest collection of O'Keeffe's works, including several of her best-loved paintings such as *Jimson Weed* (1932), *Purple Hills II*, and *Ghost Ranch, New Mexico* (1934).

Across the Santa Fe River is the fourth museum, the **Museum of International Folk Art**, with its stunning collection of folk art from all over the world. Alongside, on Museum Hill, the **Museum of Indian Art and Culture** is dedicated to traditional Native American arts and culture. Its main exhibit, "Here, Now and Always," tells the story of the region's oldest communities, in the words of Pueblo, Navajo, and Apache people.

Running parallel to the river, the gallery-lined **Canyon Road** was originally an Indian track between the Rio Grande and Pecos pueblo. To its west, on the Old Santa Fe Trail, is the **San Miguel Mission**, built in 1610. To the northwest, the 1795 **Santuario de Guadelupe**, dedicated to the Virgin of Guadelupe, patron saint of Mexican and Pueblo peoples, marked the end of Camino Real, the main trade route from Mexico. About 15 miles (24 km) south of Santa Fe, **El Rancho de las Golondrinas**, now a living history museum, was a historic stopping-off point on the Camino Real.

**Museum of International Folk Art**

706 Camino Lejo. *(505) 476-1200.* *10am–5pm Tue–Sun.* *public hols.*

## Albuquerque ㊶

*580,000. 401 2nd St NW, (505) 842-9918, (800) 284-2283.*

Occupied by Native peoples from 1100 to 1300, Albuquerque's first inhabitants were a small group of Colonial pioneers who settled by the Rio Grande in the wake of late 16th-century Spanish explorers. In 1706, a band of 18 families won formal approval for their town from the Spanish crown by naming the city after the Spanish Duke of Alburquerque, (the first "r" in the name was later dropped). Albuquerque's Old Town, today, still has many original adobe buildings dating from the 1790s, while downtown, to its east, is much more contemporary. Many of the city's shops, museums, and high-tech industries are located here.

**Modern sculpture**

### Exploring Albuquerque

Dominating the historic Old Town is the Plaza, which was the center of Albuquerque for over 200 years. Today, this charming square is a pleasant open space where both locals and visitors relax on benches, surrounded by lovely adobe buildings. Opposite is the imposing **San Felipe de Neri Church**. Completed in 1793, this was the city's first civic structure. Despite many renovations, the church retains its original adobe walls. The nearby streets are lined with museums, colorful craft shops, and restaurants, such as the Church Street Café *(see p563)*. Said to occupy the oldest house in the city, this café serves excellent New Mexican cusine. Beyond is a craft store, the Agape Pueblo Pottery, which stocks a wide selection of handcrafted pueblo pottery.

**San Felipe de Neri Church, at th north end of Old Town Plaza**

### Albuquerque BioPark

2601 Central Ave NW. *(505) 764-6200. 9am–5pm daily. Thanksgiving, Dec 25.*

The park encompasses the Albuquerque Aquarium and the Rio Grande Botanic Garden. The Rio Grande Zoological Park is located nearby. The botanic garden occupies 10 acres (4 ha) of woodland along the Rio Grande and has a wide variety of rare plants and gardens.

The aquarium focuses on the marine life of the Rio Grande, one of America's great rivers, and features a fascinating walk-through eel cave containing moray eels. There is also an impressive 285,000-gallon (1,078,842-liter), floor-to-ceiling shark tank.

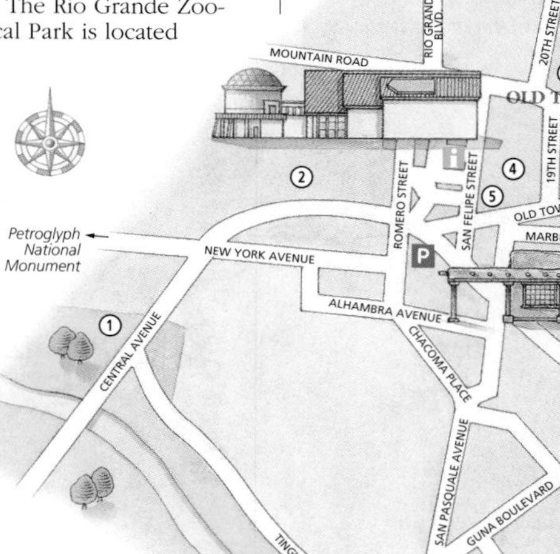


### Turquoise Museum

2107 Central Ave NW. *(505) 247-8650. 9:30am–5pm Mon–Fri, 9:30am–4pm Sat. Thanksgiving, Dec 25.*

The fascinating displays in this museum focus on consumer education, helping visitors to judge the quality of turquoise gemstones. The entrance is a replica mine tunnel that leads to the "vault," which contains an unsurpassed collection of rare and varied turquoise specimens from around the world.

**Glasshouse at Rio Grande Botanic Garden, Albuquerque BioPark**

**New Mexico Museum Natural History & ience**

)1 Mountain Rd NW. (505) 1-2800. 9am–5pm daily. Jan & Sep: Mon, public hols. www.nmnaturalhistory.org

is entertaining museum has series of interactive exhibits. sitors can stand inside a nulated live volcano or plore an ice cave. The volator" is a ride through 38 llion years of the region's olution using the latest leo technology. Replica nosaurs, a state-of-the-art anetarium, and a large-reen film theater are all ghly popular with children.

**Albuquerque Museum Art & History**

)0 Mountain Rd NW. (505) 2-4600. 9am–5pm Tue–Sun. public hols. www.cabq.gov/museum

is excellent museum depicts ur centuries of history in e middle of Rio Grande lley. The well-chosen ifacts are expertly arranged maximum impact. Exhibits focus on the Spanish Colonial period (1598–1821) and include a reconstructed 18th-century house and chapel. From March to December, the museum organizes walking tours of the Old Town.

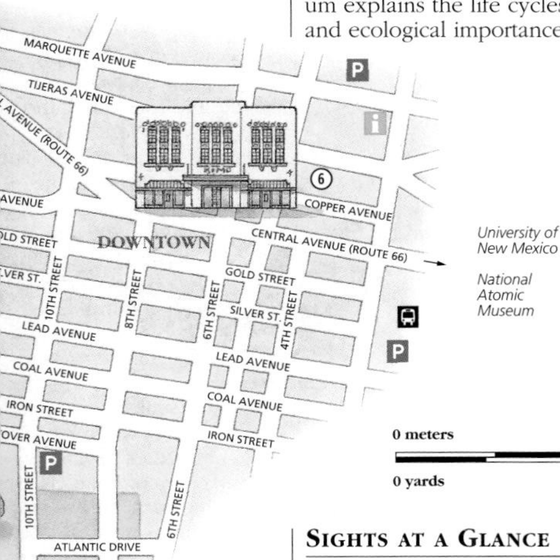


**KEY**

Bus station

Parking

Visitor information

Colorful tiles decorating the Art Deco-style façade of the KiMo Theater

**American International Rattlesnake Museum**

202 San Felipe Ave N. (505) 242-6569. *10am–6pm Mon–Sat, 1–5pm Sun; winter: 11:30am–5.30pm Mon–Fri, 10am–6pm Sat, 1–5pm Sun.* *public hols.* www.rattlesnakes.com

This animal conservation museum explains the life cycles and ecological importance of some of Earth's most misunderstood creatures. It contains the world's largest collection of live rattlesnakes, including natives of North, Central, and South America. The snakes are displayed in glass tanks that simulate their natural habitat as closely as possible and are accompanied by explanatory notices suitable for both adults and children. The museum also features other much-maligned venomous animals such as tarantulas and the Gila monster lizard.

## Sights at a Glance

Albuquerque BioPark ①
Turquoise Museum ②
New Mexico Museum of Natural History and Science ③
Albuquerque Museum of Art and History ④
American International Rattlesnake Museum ⑤
KiMo Theater ⑥
Rio Grande Zoological Park ⑦

**KiMo Theater**

423 Central Ave NW. (505) 768-3522. *call for program.* www.cabq.gov/rimo

Built in 1927, the KiMo Theater was one of many entertainment venues constructed in the city during the 1920s and 30s. The building's distinctive design was inspired by that of the nearby Native American pueblos and created a fusion of Pueblo Revival and Art Deco styles. Today, the KiMo Theater presents an eclectic range of musical and theatrical performances.

**Rio Grande Zoological Park**

903, 10th St SW (505) 764-6200. *9am–5pm daily (to 6pm Sat–Sun in summer).* *Thnksg, Dec 25.*

The Rio Grande Zoo forms part of the Albuquerque BioPark. The zoo is noted for its imaginative layout with enclosures designed to simulate the animals' natural habitats, including the African savanna. Among the most popular species here are lowland gorillas and white Bengal tigers.

Indian Pueblo Cultural Center courtyard

## Albuquerque: Farther Afield

New Mexico's largest city, Albuquerque, has grown to fill the valley that stretches westward from the foothills of the Manzano and Sandia Mountains and across the banks of the Rio Grande. The coming of the railroad during the 1880s brought increasing numbers of settlers and greater prosperity. Today, the best way to explore the city is by car. The major sights, including the historic Old Town *(see p548)*, are all located near highway exits. Two Interstate Highways cross the center of the city. I-25 travels north to south across downtown, while I-40 cuts west to east. At the eastern end of this lies the University of New Mexico campus with its museums and galleries.

### Indian Pueblo Cultural Center

2401 12th St NW. (505) 843-7270. *daily. Jan 1, Thanksgiving, Dec 25.* www.indianpueblo.org

This impressive museum and cultural center is run by the 19 Indian pueblos that lie along the Rio Grande around Albuquerque and Santa Fe. It traces the Puebloan peoples' complex history and varied culture through their oral history and presents it from their viewpoint.

The building is designed to resemble the layout of a pueblo dwelling, and is set around the Puebloan Central Courtyard. This large courtyard, with its red adobe walls decorated with murals and hung chilies, emulates the layout of a Pueblo dwelling. Each weekend exuberant dance performances are held here. The center also contains a restaurant serving Pueblo Indian cooking, and an excellent group of gift shops offering high-quality pottery, jewelry, and other crafts from each pueblo.

### University of New Mexico & Art Museum

*2401 Redondo Dr, (505) 277-1989.* www.unm.edu **University Art Museum** *(505) 277-4001. 9am–4pm Tue–Fri, 5–8pm Tue, 1–4pm Sun. Mon, Sat, University holidays.* **Maxwell Museum of Anthropology** *(505) 277-4405. 9am–4pm Tue–Fri, 10am–4pm Sat. Mon, Sun.*

The campus of New Mexico's largest university (UNM) is known for its Pueblo Revival-style architecture and its museums. The **University Art Museum** has one of the state's largest fine arts collection, including paintings and sculpture by Old Masters, and other works from the 17th to the 20th centuries.

Horse at Museum of Anthropology, UNM

The **Maxwell Museum of Anthropology**, one of the finest of its kind in the US, emphasizes the culture of the Southwest, with an important collection of art and artifacts. The musuem also has traveling exhibits on regional and international themes, as well as a permanent exhibition entitled "Ancestors," which traces human development.

### National Atomic Museum

1905 Mountain Rd NW. *(505) 245-2137. daily. public hols.* www.atomicmuseum.co

This museum recently relocated from Kirkland Air Force Base to near Old Town Albuquerque. Its displays are devoted to the history of nuclear weapons and atomic energy in the US, from the time when Los Alamos was chosen as the location of the Manhattan Project *(see p507)*. This top-secret project resulted in the world's first nuclear explosion in 1945.

Artifacts range from Einstein's letter to President Roosevelt suggesting the possibility of an atom bomb to the casings of bombs themselves. There are replicas of Little Boy and Fat Man, the bombs dropped on Hiroshima and Nagasaki in 1945.

### Petroglyph National Monument

*4735 Unser Blvd NW, (505) 899-0205. 8am–5pm daily. public hols. limited.* www.nps.gov/petr

This site, on the western outskirts of Albuquerque, was established in 1990 to preserve nearly 20,000 images carved into rock along the 17 mile (27-km) West Mesa escarpment. The earliest date back to 1,000 BC, but the most prolific period is thought to be between 1300 and 1680. The pictures range from human figures such as musicians and dancers to animals, including snakes, birds, and insects. Spirals and other geometric symbols are common, as are hands, feet, and animal tracks. The meanings of some petroglyphs have been lost over time, but others have great cultural significance to today's Puebloan population.

Hundreds of petroglyphs are accessible along Boca Negra Canyon, 2 miles (3 km) north of the park visitor center, where three trails wind past them. Visitors should not touch the petroglyphs; they are easily damaged.

# Hispanic Culture in New Mexico

THE HEART OF Hispanic culture in the Southwest is found in New Mexico. Here, the Hispanic population, descendants of the original Spanish colonizers of the 16th century, outnumbers that of the Anglo-Americans. The Spanish introduced sheep and horses to the region, as well as bringing Catholicism with its saints' festivals and colorful church decorations.

**Chili *ristras*, garlands of dried red chilies**

Centuries of mixing with both the Southwest's Native and Anglo cultures have also influenced every aspect of modern Hispanic society, from language and cooking to festivals and the arts. Contemporary New Mexican residents bear the Hispanic surnames of their ancestors, and speak English with a Spanish accent. Even English speakers pepper their speech with Spanish terms.

## Spanish Influence

The restored El Rancho de las Golondrinas *(see p547)* is today a living museum, centered on the hacienda, pioneered in the Southwest by Spanish colonists. In a hacienda, a large number of rooms (approximately 20) would be set around one or two courtyards, reflecting the extended family style of living favored by the Spanish.

**Wells** were located in the middle of the main courtyard to be easily accessible.

**Adobe beehive ovens** *(hornos)* were introduced by the Spanish for baking bread. They were originally of Moorish design.

***Hacienda Martínez*** (see p544) *was built south of Taos in 1804 by Don Antonio Martínez, an early mayor of the town. It is one of the few Spanish haciendas to be preserved in more or less its original form. Today, it is open to visitors who can watch local artisans demonstrating a variety of traditional folk arts.*

**Navajo rug**

**Carved wooden *bulto* of St. Joseph**

## Crafts

Navajo rugs are considered a Native handicraft, but their designs also show signs of Moorish patterns brought by colonizers from Spain. Other folk art forms include artistic pottery, intricate silverwork, and carved wooden figures known as *bultos*, which combine religious beliefs and artistic expression.

***Corn****, the region's staple food since pre-Columbian times, is used to make tortilla chips, which are served with* guacamole *(avocado dip).*

## Roswell 42

50,000. 426 N Main St, (505) 624-7704. 8:30am–5:30pm Mon–Fri, 10am–3pm Sat & Sun. www.roswellcvb.com

THIS SMALL ranching town is a byword for aliens and UFOs since the night of July 4, 1947, when an unidentified airborne object crashlanded here. Jim Ragsdale, camping nearby, later claimed in 1995 to have seen a flash and a craft, hurtling through the trees and the bodies of four "little people," with skin like snakeskin. The US Air Force issued a statement that a flying saucer had been recovered, and despite a denial later on, the story caught people's imagination.

Witnesses were allegedly sworn to secrecy, fueling rumors of a cover-up and alien conspiracy theories to this day. The **International UFO Museum and Research Center** features a collection of newspaper clippings and photographs of the crash site, and a film with over 400 interviews of various people connected to the incident.

Roswell's **Museum and Art Center** houses a large collection of artifacts on the history of the American West. The fascinating Robert H. Goddard Collection details 11 years of experiments by the famous rocket scientist.

**Roswell's Alien Zone symbol**

**Limestone columns in the Big Room at Carlsbad Caverns**

## Carlsbad Caverns National Park 43

3225 National Parks Hwy, Carlsbad. to Carlsbad. to White's City. (505) 785-2232, (800) 967-2283 (tour reservations). May–Aug: 8:30am– 5pm daily; Sep–mid-May: 8:30am–3:30pm (Natural Entrance). Call for last entry times. Dec 25. partial. www.nps.gov/cave

LOCATED IN THE state's remote southeastern corner, this park protects one of the world's largest cave systems. Geological forces carved out this complex of chambers, and their decorations began to be formed around 500,000 years ago when dripping water deposited drops of the crystalized mineral calcite. Native pictographs near the Natural Entrance indicate that they had been visited by Native peoples, but it was cowboy Jim White who brought them to national attention in 1901. Concrete trails and electric lights have been laid out through this underground gallery of limestone caves. From the visitor center, elevators drop 750 ft (229 m) down to the **Big Room**. This space can also be reached via the **Natural Entrance Route**, which involves a half-hour walk over a steep, paved trail.

A self-guided tour leads to the Big Room, 25 stories hig and 8.2 acres (3.3 ha) in are festooned with stalagmites, stalactites, and flowstone formations. The adjoining ranger-led **King's Palace Tour** takes in the deepest cave open to the public, 830 ft (250 m) below groun To its right, a paved section serves as the popular **Underground Lunchroom** a diner and souvenir shop.

The caverns' recesses are the summer abode of almos a million free-tailed bats. They emerge at dusk to cro the desert in search of food

## White Sands National Monument 44

(505) 679-2599. 8am–5pm daily. Dec 25. www.nps.gov/whsa

THE GLISTENING dunes of the White Sands Nationa Monument rise up from the Tularosa Basin at the northe end of the Chihuahuan Dese It is the world's largest gypsu

### DESERT FLORA AND FAUNA

**Desert scorpion**

Most of the Southwest is covered by four deserts, yet it is not an arid wasteland. The Sonoran Desert, with its rich array of flora and fauna, is famed for its saguaro cactus. The climatic extremes of the Chihuahuan Desert support hardy agaves and coyotes. The cooler Great Basin is home to many grasses and desert animals. The winter rain in the Mojave Desert results in a spectacular display of wildflowers in spring.

***Prickly pear cacti** flower in spring and are among the largest of the many types of cacti that flourish in the Sonoran Desert.*

***Bighorn sheep** are shy, elusive creatures and are not easily spotted. Now a protecte species, they are being gradually reintroduced throughout the desert areas.*

aptree yucca plant in the White Sands National Monument

ne field, covering around 0 sq miles (800 sq km). ypsum is a water soluble neral, rarely found as sand. it here, with no drainage tlet to the sea, the sediment ashed by the rain into the sin becomes trapped. As e rain evaporates, dry lakes m and strong winds blow e gypsum up into the vast lds of rippling dunes.

Visitors can explore White nds by car on the Dunes ive, a 16-mile (26-km) loop. ur clearly marked trails lead m points along the way, in-ading the wheelchair-acces-ble Interdune Boardwalk. ar-round ranger-led walks roduce visitors to the dunes' ra and fauna. Only plants at grow quickly enough not be buried survive, such as e hardy soaptree yucca. ost of the animals are noc-rnal and include foxes, yotes, and porcupines.

The park is surrounded by e White Sands Missile Range, a military testing site. For safety, the park and the road leading to it (Hwy 70) may close for up to two hours when testing is underway. The **White Sands Missile Range Museum** displays many of the missiles tested here, as well as the V-2 rockets used in World War II.

## Gila Cliff Dwellings National Monument ㊺

*(505) 536-9461. late May–early Sep: 8am–6pm daily; mid-Sep–mid-May: 9am–4pm daily. Jan 1, Dec 25.* www.nps.gov/gicl

THE GILA (pronounced hee-la) Cliff Dwellings are one of the most remote archaeological sites in the Southwest, situated among the piñon, juniper, and ponderosa evergreens of the Gila National Forest. The dwellings occupy five natural caves in the side of a sandstone bluff high above the Gila River.

Hunter-gatherers and farmers called the Tularosa Mogollon established their 40-room village here in the late 13th century. The Mimbres Mogollon people, famous for their abstract black-and-white pottery designs on hand-coiled earthenware, also lived in this area. The cliff dwellers hunted the local wildlife, including whitetail and mule deer. They probably farmed the fields alongside the Gila River, growing corn and squash. A granary still holds a dessicated reserve of tiny corn. The ruins are accessed by a 1-mile (1.6-km) round-trip hike from the footbridge crossing the Gila River's West Fork. Allow two hours to navigate the 40-mile (64-km) road to the site from Silver City as it winds and climbs through the mountains and canyons of the forest.

*e **Joshua tree** was med by Mormons who v the upraised arms of hua in its branches.*

***Yucca plants** have been gathered for centuries and have many uses: their fruit can be eaten, and the roots make shampoo.*

***The javelina** is a strange pig-like mammal that wanders the Chihuahuan and Sonoran Deserts in small packs.*

***Golden eagles** can be seen high in the sky in daytime as they hunt for prey across the Great Basin Desert.*

# Practical Information

DOTTED WITH DRAMATIC rock formations, canyons, ancient sites, and wild deserts, the Southwest offers visitors a range of outdoor pleasures. The cities feature superb museums, good dining, and accommodations, along with a laid-back culture. A major draw for visitors are the casinos of Las Vegas. The Southwest is a year-round destination. The high-lying areas of Arizona, New Mexico, and Utah have cold, snowy winters, making them popular for skiing, while the states' southern areas offer warm and sunny winters. But the less-crowded and milder spring and fall are the ideal seasons to visit.

## Tourist Information

EACH STATE and major towns and cities have departments of tourism. Many of the Southwest's attractions on Indian reservation lands are managed by Native American tribal councils. For advice on these contact the local **Bureau of Indian Affairs** or the **Navajo Tourism Department**.

## Personal Security

MOST TOURIST AREAS in the Southwest are friendly and unthreatening, but it is wise to be cautious. Find out which parts of town are unsafe at night. Never carry too much cash, and lock your valuables in the hotel safe.

## Natural Hazards

RAPID WEATHER changes in the Southwest often present dangerous situations. In parts of southern Utah and Arizona, sudden summer storms can cause flash floods. Visitors often underestimate the dry heat of the region's summers. Hikers must carry at least a gallon (4 liters) of drinking water per person for each day of walking.

The Southwest's wilderness harbors venomous creatures such as scorpions, snakes, and the Gila monster lizard; but it is unlikely you will be bitten if you avoid their habitats. Insect bites may hurt but are rarely fatal to adults. But, if bitten, seek medical help.

## Getting Around

THOUGH SLOWER than car and plane travel, trains and buses are enjoyable means of exploring the region. Visitors can take special railroad trips to enjoy some of the Southwest's most delightful scenery. The Grand Canyon Railway's diesel and steam rail trips from Williams to Grand Canyon feature packages that include Western entertainments.

Long-distance buses are the least expensive mode of travel. A bus tour is often the most convenient way of seeing both major city sights and some of the more remote scenery of the Southwest. In major cities, local bus routes cover most attractions. Taxis are also an efficient way of traveling around cities.

## Driving in the Southwest

A CAR IS OFTEN the only means of reaching remote areas. There are car rental agencies all over the region, but it is best to arrange a fly-drive deal for cities such as Las Vegas. Pay attention to road signs especially in remote areas where they may issue warnings about local hazards. Check your route to see if a Four-Wheel Drive (4WD) vehicle is required. Most backcountry areas now have roads that can carry conventional cars, but a 4WD is essential in some wild areas. When traveling between remote destinations, inform someone of your plans. Be wary of seasonal dangers such as flash floods in Utah's canyonlands. Carry plenty of food and water, and a cell phone as a precaution.
If your vehicle breaks down stay with it since it offers protection from the elements and telephone for help.

## Etiquette

DRESS IN THE Southwest is informal, practical, and dependent on the climate. Some of the region's most famous sights are located on reservation land. Visitors are welcome but must be sensitive as to what may cause offense. It is illegal to bring alcohol onto reservations – even a bottle visible in a locked car will land you in trouble. Ask before photographing anything, especially ceremonial dances or Native homes, and bear in mind that a fee may be requested. Do not wander off marked trails as this is forbidden.

## The Climate of the Southwest

The weather in this region ranges from the heat of the desert to the ice and snow of the mountains. Temperatures usually vary with altitude. As a result the higher elevations in the north, especially Utah, northern Arizona, and New Mexico, experience cold, snowy winters. The southern areas, on the other hand, have mild, sunny winters and hot, dry summers. Summer temperatures in the desert often reach more than 100°F (38°C), but can drop to almost 30°F (10°C) after sunset. Except for violent summer storms, rainfall is scarce in the Southwest.

**Las Vegas**

| month | Apr | Jul | Oct | Jan |
|---|---|---|---|---|
| °F/C (high) | 81/27 | 103/40 | 84/29 | 60/16 |
| °F/C (low) | 45/7 | 68/20 | 47/8 | 29/–2 |
| sunshine | 26 days | 27 days | 26 days | 24 days |
| rainfall | 0.3 in | 0.5 in | 0.3 in | 0.7 in |

## )utdoor Activities

W ITH THOUSANDS of miles of rock canyons, spec- ıcular deserts, and snow- apped peaks, the Southwest ; a magnet for climbers, ikers, mountain bikers, 4WD rivers, and skiers. All ational parks have well- ıarked trails and ranger-led ikes, focusing on the local ora, fauna, and geology.

Utah considers itself the ⁄orld's mountain bike capital, nd Moab is a pilgrimage site ɔr such bikers. **Poison Spider ɜicycles** sells and repairs ikes as well as runs Nichols ours, which leads groups ırough wilderness areas.

The Green, San Juan, and ɔlorado Rivers are ideal for ⁄hitewater rafting. A thrilling 2–20 day rafting trip along ıe Colorado River through ıe Grand Canyon is offered y many outfitters, including **;anyon Explorations**. Water ports, such as powerboating, ɜtskiing, and fishing, are opular in the artificial lakes.

Air tours are a good option ɔr time-restricted travelers ⁄ho wish to see the remote ttractions. **Slickrock Air ɜuides of Moab** offer three- our tours that cover Canyon- ınds, Lake Powell, Capitol eef National Park, and the ɜrand Canyon's North Rim. Iowever, helicopter tours of ıe Grand Canyon have a ɜputation for bad safety.

Arizona's 275 golf courses make the Southwest a golfer's paradise. Scottsdale, considered America's premier golf spot, is famous for its **Boulders Resort**. The ski season runs from November to April. Utah has some of the best skiing in the region, while New Mexico's **Taos Ski Valley** includes world-class slopes.

## Entertainment

THE SOUTHWEST's blend of cultures has made the region a lively center for arts and entertainment. The cities of Phoenix, Santa Fe, Tucson, and Albuquerque offer opera, ballet, classical music, and theatrical productions. The small resort towns of Sedona and Taos, famed for their resident artists, regularly host touring productions and theater and musical shows. Most cities and major towns have a lively nightlife that includes country music, jazz, and rock as well as dinner theater and standup comedy.

The Southwest is a mecca for Western-style entertainment such as rodeo contests. Historic frontier towns such as Tombstone also stage mock gunfights. Check with the **Tombstone Visitor Center** for details. For sports fans, there are major league and college football, baseball, and basketball games.

## Gambling in Las Vegas

DESPITE ITS GROWING fame as the entertainment capital of the world, Las Vegas is popular mainly for its casinos. They can seem daunting at first, but with a basic understanding of the rules, most games are relatively easy. Some hotels have gaming guides on their in-house TV channels, and many casinos give free lessons at the tables. If you are winning, it is customary to tip the dealers.

## Shopping

THE SOUTHWEST's exciting range of Indian, Hispanic, and Anglo-American products make shopping a cultural adventure. Native crafts, including rugs and jewelry, can be bought in reservation posts or Pueblo stores.

Santa Fe is famous for its galleries selling Georgia O'Keeffe-inspired landscapes, contemporary art, and bronze cowboy sculptures.

Across the region, specialty grocery stores stock local products such as hot chili sauces and blue corn chips.

The big cities offer a choice of air-conditioned malls. The biggest concentration is in Phoenix, and its **Metrocenter Mall** is the region's largest. Las Vegas' fantasy themed malls make shopping one of its many attractions.

## Directory

### Tourist Offices

**Arizona**
*(602) 364-3700, (866) 298-3795.*
www.arizonaguide.com

**Colorado**
*(800) 265-6723.*
www.colorado.com

**New Mexico**
*(505) 827-7400; (800) 545-2070.*
www.newmexico.org

**Utah**
*(801) 538-1030.*
www.utah.com

**Bureau of Indian Affairs**
PO Box 10, Phoenix, AZ 85001.
*(602) 379-4511.*

**Navajo Tourism Department**
PO Box 663, Window Rock, AZ 86515.
*(928) 871-6436.*

### Mountain Biking

**Poison Spider Bicycles**
497 N Main St, Moab, UT 84532.
*(800) 635-1792, (435) 259-7882.*

### Whitewater Rafting

**Canyon Explorations**
PO Box 310, Flagstaff, AZ 86002.
*(928) 774-4559.*

### Air Tours

**Slickrock Air Guides of Moab**
*(435) 259-6216.*

### Skiing

**Taos Ski Valley**
PO Box 90 Taos Ski Valley, NM 87525
*(505) 776-2291.*

### Golf

**Boulders Resort**
34631 N. Tom Darlington Dr, Carefree, AZ 85377.
*(800) 553-1717.*

### Rodeos & Wild West Shows

**Tombstone Visitor Center**
*(520) 457-3421, (800) 457-3423.*

### Shopping

**Metrocenter Mall**
9617 Metro Pkwy, Phoenix, AZ 85051.
*(602) 997-2641.*

# Where to Stay

THE SOUTHWEST HAS A LONG HISTORY of hospitality that is reflected in the wide variety of accommodations on offer. There is a wealth of options for visitors, ranging from luxurious five-star resorts to simple rustic lodges. Las Vegas hotels are noted for their themes and size. Across the region prices tend to vary according to the season.

## NEVADA

**DOWNTOWN LAS VEGAS:** *Binion's Horseshoe* $
128 E Fremont St, NV 89101. *(702) 382-1600* FAX *(702) 384-1574.*
W www.binions.com
Known for hosting the world series poker championship, all rooms have been remodeled in shades of pink. TV P

**DOWNTOWN LAS VEGAS:** *Four Queens Hotel & Casino* $$
202 E Fremont St, NV 89109. *(800) 634-6045.* FAX *(702) 387-5160.*
W www.fourqueens.com
With its impressive, glittering façade this hotel retains the glamorous atmospere of Old Las Vegas. 24 TV P

**LAS VEGAS – THE STRIP:** *Tropicana* $$$
3801 Las Vegas Blvd S, NV 89109. *(800) 634-4000.* FAX *(702) 739-2492.*
W www.tropicanalv.com
Noted for the lush gardens and waterfalls around its delightful pool area, the Tropicana is a popular Vegas institution. 24 TV P

**LAS VEGAS – THE STRIP:** *Caesars Palace* $$$$
3570 Las Vegas Blvd S, NV 89109. *(800) 634-6001.* FAX *(702) 9671-3890*
W www.caesarspalace.com
This Vegas institution is world-famous for its luxurious rooms, all with marble bathrooms. 24 TV P

**LAS VEGAS – THE STRIP:** *Treasure Island* $$$$
3300 Las Vegas Blvd S, NV 89109. *(800) 288-7206.* FAX *(702) 894-7446.*
W www.treasureisland.com
This hotel is a popular choice with families because of its pirate theme. 24 TV P

**LAS VEGAS – THE STRIP:** *Venetian* $$$$
3355 Las Vegas Blvd S, NV 89109. *(888) 283-6423.* FAX *(702) 414-4805.*
W www.venetian.com
All rooms are luxury suites with a minibar, two TVs, fax, and three telephone lines, set among palatial splendor. 24 TV P

**LAS VEGAS – THE STRIP:** *Bellagio* $$$$$
3600 Las Vegas Blvd S, NV 89109. *(888) 987-6667.* FAX *(702) 693-8546.*
W www.bellagio.com
The rooms in this highly sophisticated resort are decorated with imported Carrara marble bathrooms and silk furnishings. 24 TV P

**CARSON CITY:** *Best Western Piñon Plaza Resort* $$$
2171 Hwy 50E, NV 89701. *(775) 885-9000, (887) 519-5567*
W www.pinonplaza.com
This hotel in Nevada's capital city is popular for its delightful pool area and spa, as well as its full-service casino/resort. TV P

**GREAT BASIN NATIONAL PARK:** *Hotel Nevada* $
501 Aultman St, Ely, NV 89301. *(775) 289-6665, (888) 406-3055*
W www.hotelnevada.com
Located in downtown Ely, this landmark hotel was built in 1929. It has a full-service casino-resort, and a restaurant that serves breakfast, lunch, and dinner 24-hours a day. P

**RENO:** *Peppermill Reno* $$
2707 S Virginia St, NV 89502. *(775) 826-2121, (800) 282-2444*
W www.peppermillreno.com
This high-rise resort is located close to the airport, shopping, downtown, and Lake Tahoe. Housing seven restaurants, this totally full-service casino-resort offers everything from a barber to a spa to business facilities to pools, and outdoor activities. 24 TV P

| Hotel | Number of Rooms | Restaurant | Children's Facilities | Garden or Terrace | Swimming Pool |
|---|---|---|---|---|---|
| Binion's Horseshoe | 366 | ● | ■ | | ■ |
| Four Queens Hotel & Casino | 690 | ● | | | ■ |
| Tropicana | 1,874 | ● | | ● | ■ |
| Caesars Palace | 2,454 | ● | | ● | ■ |
| Treasure Island | 2,885 | ● | | | ■ |
| Venetian | 4,000 | ● | | ● | ■ |
| Bellagio | 4,000 | ● | ■ | ● | ■ |
| Best Western Piñon Plaza Resort | 148 | ● | ■ | ● | ■ |
| Hotel Nevada | 65 | ● | | | |
| Peppermill Reno | 1,070 | ● | | ● | ■ |

Price categories for a standard double room per night, inclusive of service charges and any additional taxes:
$ under $50
$$ $50–100
$$$ $100–150
$$$$ $150–200
$$$$$ over $200

**RESTAURANT**
Hotel restaurant or dining room usually open to nonresidents unless otherwise stated.

**CHILDREN'S FACILITIES**
Cribs and a baby-sitting service available. Some hotel restaurants have children's portions and high chairs.

**GARDEN OR TERRACE**
Hotels with a garden, courtyard, or terrace.

**SWIMMING POOL**
Hotel with an indoor or outdoor swimming pool.

| | Number of Rooms | Restaurant | Children's Facilities | Garden or Terrace | Swimming Pool |
|---|---|---|---|---|---|
| **UTAH** | | | | | |
| **RYCE CANYON:** *Bryce Canyon Lodge* $$$<br>yce Canyon National Park, UT 84717. *(435) 834-5361; (303) 297-757 (central reservations).* FAX *(303) 297-3175.* W www.brycecanyonlodge.com<br>his Western classic, just 100 yds (30 m) from the canyon rim, has egant period decor, rooms with Southwestern themes, and fireplaces. *Nov 1–Mar 31.* P | 115 | ● | | ● | |
| **EDAR CITY:** *Crystal Inn Cedar City* $$<br>575 W 200 North, UT 84720. *(888) 787-6661.* FAX *(435) 586 1010.* W www.crystalinns.com<br>ully renovated and redecorated in 2002, this is still one of Cedar City's est hotels. TV P | 100 | | ■ | | ■ |
| **INOSAUR NATIONAL PARK:** *Best Western Dinosaur Inn* $$$<br>51 E Main St, Vernal, UT 84078. *435-789-2662, (800) 780-7234* W www.bestwestern.com<br>reasonably priced, comfortable inn located near Dinosaur National ark, with its own pool and a restaurant. TV P | 60 | | ■ | ● | ■ |
| **SCALANTE:** *Prospector Inn* $$<br>30 W Main St, UT 84726. *(435) 826-4653.* FAX *(435) 826-4285.* W www.prospectorinn.com<br>his is one of Escalante's nicer family hotels. The spacious rooms are omfortable, and all have two beds. TV P | 50 | ● | | | |
| **OAB:** *The Landmark Motel* $$<br>58 N Main St, UT 84532. *(800) 441-6147.* FAX *(435) 259-5556.* W www.landmarkinnmoab.com<br>downtown Colonial building with spacious rooms. A bargain for large milies. TV P | 36 | | ■ | | ■ |
| **ALT LAKE CITY:** *Carlton Hotel*<br>40 E S Temple, UT 84111. *(801) 355-3418, (800) 633-3500.*<br>his family-run hotel is near the Mormon temple and genealogical library nd caters mainly to genealogists. | 40 | ● | | | |
| **ORREY:** *Wonderland Inn* $$<br>75 E Hwy 24, UT 84775. *(877) 854-0184.* FAX *(435) 425-3212.* W www.capitolreefwonderland.com<br>bright, cheerful property with pleasant rooms located close to Capitol eef National Park. TV P | 50 | ● | | ● | ■ |
| **ION NATIONAL PARK:** *Zion Lodge* $$$<br>pringdale, UT 84767. *(435) 772-3213.* FAX *(435) 772-2001.* W www.zionlodge.com<br>spacious lodge in Zion National Park, offering comfortable rooms and abins surrounded by natural beauty. P | 121 | ● | ■ | ● | |
| **ARIZONA** | | | | | |
| **ISBEE:** *Copper Queen Hotel* $$$<br>Howell Ave, AZ 85603. *(520) 432-2216; (800) 247-5829.* FAX *(520) 432-4298.* W www.copperqueen.com<br>late 19th-century hotel, decorated in the period style. A comprehensive list sightings of various resident ghosts is also available! TV P | 48 | ● | | ● | ■ |
| **HINLE:** *Thunderbird Lodge* $$<br>anyon De Chelly, AZ 86503. *(800) 679-2473.* FAX *(928) 674-5844.* W www.tbirdlodge.com<br>his lodge is part of the excellent complex that lies at the mouth of the enic and beautiful Canyon de Chelly. Rooms are tastefully decorated. TV P | 72 | ● | | | |

For key to symbols see back flap

**Price categories** for a standard double room per night, inclusive of service charges and any additional taxes:
- $ under $50
- $$ $50–100
- $$$ $100–150
- $$$$ $150–200
- $$$$$ over $200

**RESTAURANT**
Hotel restaurant or dining room usually open to nonresidents unless otherwise stated.

**CHILDREN'S FACILITIES**
Cribs and a baby-sitting service available. Some hotel restaurants have children's portions and high chairs.

**GARDEN OR TERRACE**
Hotels with a garden, courtyard, or terrace.

**SWIMMING POOL**
Hotel with an indoor or outdoor swimming pool.

| Hotel | Price | Number of Rooms | Restaurant | Children's Facilities | Garden or Terrace | Swimming Pool |
|---|---|---|---|---|---|---|
| **FLAGSTAFF:** *Hotel Monte Vista*<br>100 San Fransisco St, AZ 86001. *(928) 779-6971.* FAX *(928) 779-2904.*<br>Many of the rooms in this unique 1920s hotel are named after some of the most famous guests who stayed here, such as Bob Hope. | $$ | 50 | ● | | | |
| **FLAGSTAFF:** *Hotel Weatherford*<br>23 N Leroux St, AZ 86001. *(928) 779-1919.* FAX *(928) 773-8951.*<br>W www.weatherfordhotel.com<br>The 1890s Weatherford is one of Flagstaff's most distinctive hotels. Its better rooms are decorated with antiques. | $$ | 10 | ● | | | |
| **GRAND CANYON:** *Bright Angel Lodge*<br>Grand Canyon South Rim, AZ 86023. *(303) 297-2757.* FAX *(303) 297-3175.*<br>W www.grandcanyonlodges.com<br>Popular with hikers, Bright Angel offers frugal rooms in its 1930s lodge as well as appealing log cabins. | $$ | 89 | ● | | ● | |
| **GRAND CANYON (NORTH RIM):** *Grand Canyon Lodge*<br>Bright Angel Point, Grand Canyon, AZ 86052. *(303) 297-2757.* FAX *(928) 638-2554.*<br>W www.grandcanyonnorthrim.com<br>The only hotel on the canyon's North Rim, this lodge has cabins and motel-style rooms. *Oct–May.* | $$ | 205 | ● | | | |
| **GRAND CANYON VILLAGE:** *Maswik Lodge*<br>Grand Canyon South Rim, AZ 86023. *(303) 297-2757.* FAX *(303) 297-3175.*<br>W www.grandcanyonlodges.com<br>Popular with families, this lodge is located at the west end of the village close to the South Rim. | $$$ | 278 | ● | ● | ● | |
| **GREEN VALLEY:** *Best Western Green Valley*<br>111 S La Cañada, AZ 85614 *(800) 344-1441.* FAX *(520) 625-0215.*<br>This hotel serves as a great base for exploring San Xavier Mission and Madera Canyon. It features a heated pool and spa. | $$ | 107 | ● | | ● | ● |
| **JEROME:** *Ghost City Inn*<br>541 N Main St, AZ 86331. *(928) 634-4678.*<br>W www.ghostcityinn.com<br>In a handsome Victorian villa, this well-maintained inn has tastefully decorated bedrooms and fabulous views. | $$$ | 6 | | | ● | |
| **LAKE HAVASU CITY:** *Ramada Inn*<br>271 S Lake Havasu Ave, AZ 86403. *(928) 855-1111.* FAX *(928) 855-6228.*<br>Recently revamped, this stylish hotel offers spacious elegant rooms and is a short walk from London Bridge. | $$ | 193 | ● | ● | | ● |
| **MONUMENT VALLEY:** *Gouldings Lodge*<br>Off Hwy 163, UT 84536. *(800) 874-0902.* FAX *(435) 727-3344.*<br>W www.gouldings.com<br>This inn has hosted movie stars and directors from almost every film made here. Rooms offer superb views of Monument Valley. | $$$$ | 62 | ● | | | ● |
| **PHOENIX:** *Pointe At South Mountain Resort*<br>7777 S Pointe Parkway, AZ 85044. *(602) 438-9000.* FAX *(602) 431-6535.*<br>W www.pointesouthmtn.com<br>In the hills south of Phoenix, this resort offers every amenity, including golf and four restaurants. | $$$$$ | 640 | ● | ● | ● | ● |
| **SCOTTSDALE:** *Scottsdale Princess*<br>7575 E Princess Dr, AZ 85255. *(480) 585-4848.* FAX *(480) 585-0086.*<br>W www.fairmont.com<br>A first-rate resort-hotel in a handsome setting with all amenities and several award-winning restaurants. | $$$$$ | 651 | ● | ● | ● | ● |

| | Rooms | | | | |
|---|---|---|---|---|---|
| **ECOND MESA, HOPI RESERVATION:** *Hopi Cultural Center Hotel* $$<br>.te 264, AZ 86043. (928) 734-2401. FAX (928) 734-6651.<br>W www.hopiculturalcenter.com<br>'his renovated hotel with an adobe look and pastel interior is the best ccommodation for miles around. TV P | 33 | ● | | | |
| **EDONA:** *Star Motel* $$<br>95 Jordan Rd, AZ 86336. (928) 282-3641.<br>:onveniently located in the center of Sedona, this unassuming ıotel offers some of the most reasonably priced rooms in town.<br>TV P | 11 | | | | |
| **'UCSON:** *Hacienda del Sol Guest Ranch Resort* $$$$<br>601 N Hacienda del Sol Rd, AZ 85718. (520) 299-1501; (800) 728-6514. FAX<br>520) 299-5554. W www.haciendadelsol.com<br>)verlooking desert landscape, this luxury retreat in the hills above town as been popular since the 1940s, when such stars as Katherine Hepburn sed to visit. TV P | 30 | ● | | ● | ■ |
| **VINDOW ROCK:** *Quality Inn* $$<br>8 W Hwy 264, AZ 86515. (800) 662-6189. FAX (928) 871-5466.<br>'his attractive, comfortable hotel is one of the Navajo reservation's howpieces. Rooms are immaculately clean. TV P | 56 | ● | | | |
| **NEW MEXICO** | | | | | |
| **LBUQUERQUE:** *Albuquerque Doubletree Hotel* $$$<br>01 Marquette Ave, NW, NM 87102. (888) 223-4113. FAX (505) 247-7025.<br>W www.doubletreehotels.com<br>'ery comfortable, friendly, well-appointed hotel in the heart of owntown. TV P | 295 | ● | | | ■ |
| **LBUQUERQUE:** *Albuquerque Hilton* $$$<br>901 University Blvd, NE, NM 87102. (800) 274-6835. FAX (505) 880-1196.<br>W www.hilton. com<br>esort-like facility in the heart of downtown, with courtyard gardens, and ı- and outdoor pools. TV P | 263 | ● | | ● | ■ |
| **LBUQUERQUE:** *Casas de Sueños* $$$$<br>10 Rio Grande Blvd, SW, NM 87104. (505) 247-4560. FAX (505) 842-8493.<br>W www.casasdesuenos.com<br>his "House of Dreams" was a 1930s artists' colony. Charming cottages ırround a lovely courtyard. TV P | 21 | | | ● | |
| **:HAMA:** *The Gandy Dancer Bed & Breakfast* $$$<br>99 Maple Ave, NM 87520. (505) 756-2191. FAX (505) 756-2649.<br>W www.gandydancerbb.com<br>)ne block from the Cumbres and Toltec Scenic Railroad, this delightful &B is in a Victorian mansion. TV P | 7 | | | ● | |
| **ANTA FE:** *El Rey Inn* $$<br>862 Cerrillos Rd, NM 87505. (800) 521-1349. FAX (505) 989-9249.<br>W www.elreyinnsantafe.com<br>et among lush gardens, this pleasant hotel has rooms decorated in outhwestern style. TV P | 86 | | | ● | ■ |
| **ANTA FE:** *Inn of the Turquoise Bear* $$$<br>42 E Buena Vista St, NM 87505. (800) 396-4104. FAX (505) 988-4225.<br>W www.turquoisebear.com<br>&B in an adobe villa set in acres of gardens, rock terraces, and tall ines. Great rooms and delicious breakfast. TV P | 11 | | | ● | |
| **ANTA FE:** *La Fonda Hotel* $$$$$<br>00 E San Francisco, NM 87501. (800) 523-5002. FAX (523) 982-6367.<br>W www.lafondasantafe.com<br>Santa Fe landmark, this newly renovated 1920s hotel stands on the site f an original 1610 adobe. TV P | 167 | ● | | | ■ |
| **'AOS:** *Taos Inn* $$$<br>25 Paseo del Pueblo Norte, NM 87571. (888) 461-8267. FAX (505) 758-5776.<br>W www.taosinn.com<br>his historic inn just north of the Plaza has rooms in adobe buildings ating from the 1800s, decorated with Mexican tiles, locally made ırniture, and hand-woven bedspreads. TV P | 36 | ● | | ● | ■ |

For key to symbols see back flap

# Where to Eat

The Southwest offers a top-class regional cuisine, as well as a diverse range of other eating experiences, especially in the larger cities. Mexican food is often best at local restaurants in New Mexico and Arizona, while Utah favors American fare. Hotel restaurants often serve the best food in small towns. "L" indicates lunch and "D" indicates dinner in the listings below.

## Nevada

| Restaurant | Price | Credit Cards | Outdoor Tables | Vegetarian | Bar Area | Children's Facilities |
|---|---|---|---|---|---|---|
| **Downtown Las Vegas:** *California Pizza Kitchen*<br>At the Mirage, 3500 Las Vegas Blvd S, NV 89109. *(702) 791-7111.*<br>California Pizza Kitchen features an enormous range of gourmet woodfired pizzas, as well as a choice of pastas, salads, and delicious desserts. | $$ | ■ | | ■ | ● | |
| **Downtown Las Vegas:** *Ranch Steakhouse*<br>At Binion's Horseshoe, 128 E Fremont St, NV 89101. *(702) 382-1600.*<br>Classic American steakhouse fare includes prime rib as well as seafood at reasonable prices in this venerable Las Vegas casino. ● *L.* | $$$$ | ■ | | | ● | |
| **Las Vegas – The Strip:** *Diego*<br>MGM Grand, 3799 Las Vegas Blvd S, NV 89109. *(702) 891-3200.*<br>This vibrant and modern restaurant features the bold flavors of Mexico. Authentic dishes are steeped in tradition but served with a twist. Favorites include slow-roasted goat and chicken mole. | $$$ | ■ | | ■ | ● | |
| **Las Vegas – The Strip:** *Top of the World*<br>Stratosphere Tower, 2000 Las Vegas Blvd S NV89104. *(702) 380-7711.*<br>Panoramic views are available from this restaurant 833 ft (255 m) above the Strip. The menu is European with great meat, steak, and seafood. | $$$ | ■ | | | ● | |
| **Las Vegas – The Strip:** *Emeril's New Orleans Fish House*<br>At MGM Grand, 3799 Las Vegas Blvd S, NV 89109. *(702) 891-7374.*<br>One of the most popular restaurants in Las Vegas, noted for its unique fusion of Creole and Cajun cooking. Some great snacks are available at the Seafood Bar. | $$$$ | ■ | | ■ | ● | |
| **Las Vegas – The Strip:** *Rosewood Grille*<br>3339 Las Vegas Blvd S, NV 89109. *(702) 792-5965.*<br>This is one of Las Vegas' landmark restaurants, famous for its good seafood, especially the Maine lobsters, and extensive wine list. | $$$$ | ■ | | | ● | |
| **Las Vegas – The Strip:** *Spago*<br>At Caesars Palace, 3570 Las Vegas Blvd S, NV 89109. *(702) 369-6300.*<br>Spago's contemporary interior echoes its famous sister restaurant in Los Angeles. Fusion cooking mixes Asian and American dishes with Italian styles in such dishes as baked red snapper. | $$$$ | ■ | ● | ■ | ● | |
| **Las Vegas – The Strip:** *Trattoria del Lupo*<br>At Mandalay Bay, 3950 Las Vegas Blvd S, NV 89109. *(702) 740-5522.*<br>Owned by famous chef, Wolfgang Puck, who is credited with combining classic Italian cooking with contemporary California cuisine. | $$$$ | ■ | ● | ■ | ● | |
| **Carson City:** *Bugsy's Deli*<br>At the Flamingo, 3555 Las Vegas Blvd S, NV 89109. *(702) 733-3111.*<br>One of the few remaining signs of Bugsy Seigel's involvement in the hotel are the black and white photos of the gangster on the walls. This place serves New York-style deli food at reasonable prices. | $ | ■ | | ■ | | ■ |
| **Carson City:** *Red's Old 395 Grill*<br>1055 S Carson St, NV 89701. *(775) 887-0395.*<br>Popular with locals for all kinds and sizes of steaks and seafood specials. It has a full bar that serves wine. | $$ | | ● | ■ | ● | ■ |
| **Great Basin National Park (Baker):** *The Border Inn Restaurant*<br>Hwys 50 & 6, Baker, NV 89311. *(775) 234-7300.*<br>Good American food – hearty steaks, chicken, and burgers – is the specialty at this lively, 24-hour restaurant, near the Great Basin National Park. | $ | ■ | | | | ■ |

ice categories include a
ree-course meal for one, a
ass of house wine, and all
navoidable extra charges such
sales tax and service.
) under $20
)$ $20–30
)$$ $30–45
)$$$ $45–60
)$$$$ over $60

**CREDIT CARDS**
Major credit cards accepted.

**OUTDOOR TABLES**
Garden, courtyard, or terrace with outside tables.

**VEGETARIAN**
A good selection of vegetarian dishes available.

**BAR AREA**
There is a bar area or cocktail bar within the restaurant, available for drinks and/or bar snacks.

**CHILDREN'S FACILITIES**
Small portions and/or high chairs available on request.

| | Price | Credit Cards | Outdoor Tables | Vegetarian | Bar Area | Children's Facilities |
|---|---|---|---|---|---|---|
| **UTAH** | | | | | | |
| **YCE CANYON NATIONAL PARK:** *Bryce Canyon Lodge*<br>ce Canyon National Park, UT 84717. *(435) 834-5361.*<br>is is the best fine dining establishment in the area, serving Continental isine in an elegant setting. It serves meals that are traditional and well ne. *Nov 1–Mar 31.* | $$ | ■ | ● | ■ | | ■ |
| **RYCE CANYON NATIONAL PARK:** *Foster's Family Steakhouse*<br>50 Hwy 12, Bryce, UT 84759. *(435) 834-5227.*<br>is family oriented steakhouse that also serves prime rib, Utah trout, d western chilli, as well as sandwiches that are made with bread baked the premises daily. *B, L D.* *Jan: Mon–Thu.* | $$ | ■ | | ■ | | ■ |
| **EDAR CITY:** *Rusty's Ranch House*<br>75 E Hwy 14, UT 84720. *(435) 586-3839.*<br>is barn surrounded by mountain views houses a comfortably elegant untry steakhouse specializing in hearty meals like slow-roasted baby ck ribs and broiled salmon with garlic, basil, and butter. *D.* *Sun.* | $$ | ■ | | ■ | | ■ |
| **OAB:** *Eddie McStiff's*<br>S Main St, UT 84532. *(435) 259-2337.*<br>zza, pasta, and McStiff's own award-winning beer are the specialties re. Another favorite is skewered steak and chicken satay. | $ | ■ | ● | | ● | ■ |
| **OAB:** *Center Café*<br>N 100 W, UT 84532. *(435) 259-4295.*<br>ternational cuisine featuring specialties such as pan-seared lamb loin ith roasted garlic flan. Specials can include exotic, tasty dishes featuring trich or bison. *Winter: Mon–Wed.* | $$ | ■ | ● | | | |
| **ALT LAKE CITY:** *Lion House Pantry*<br>E South Temple, UT 84150. *(801) 363-5466.*<br>oused in the historic Brigham Young house (1856), this restaurant rves authentic Mormon cuisine in cafeteria style. | $ | ■ | ● | ■ | | |
| **ALT LAKE CITY:** *Market Street Grill*<br>Market St, UT 84101. *(801) 322-4668.*<br>is popular place serves steaks, seafood, and a great hearty breakfast in informal setting. | $$$ | | | | ● | |
| **ORREY:** *Capitol Reef Café*<br>0 W Main St, UT 84775. *(435) 425-3271.*<br>cated near Capitol Reef National Park, this unusual find features locally rmed smoked or grilled trout, stir fries, vegetarian entrées, and a host of aginative dishes. It serves delicious homemade soups and salads. | $ | ■ | | ■ | | ■ |
| **ION NATIONAL PARK:** *Zion Lodge*<br>on National Park, UT 84767. *(435) 772-3213.*<br>etter than average tourist fare, with a very good breakfast buffet d dinners that include steak and trout. | $$ | ■ | ● | | ● | ■ |
| **ARIZONA** | | | | | | |
| **HINLE:** *Thunderbird Lodge*<br>anyon De Chelly, AZ 86503. *(928) 674-5841.*<br>afeteria-style place serving large portions of classic American diner food om breakfast through dinner. Excellent value and tasty. | $ | ■ | | | | |
| **LAGSTAFF:** *Charly's Pub & Grill*<br>3 N Leroux, AZ 86001. *(928) 779-1919.*<br>his fast-moving restaurant is a popular spot, serving an enticing range f burgers and sandwiches, as well as Mexican specialties. | $ | ■ | | ■ | ● | |

For key to symbols see back flap

**Price categories** include a three-course meal for one, a glass of house wine, and all unavoidable extra charges such as sales tax and service.
$ under $20
$$ $20–30
$$$ $30–45
$$$$ $45–60
$$$$$ over $60

**CREDIT CARDS**
Major credit cards accepted.

**OUTDOOR TABLES**
Garden, courtyard, or terrace with outside tables.

**VEGETARIAN**
A good selection of vegetarian dishes available.

**BAR AREA**
There is a bar area or cocktail bar within the restaurant, available for drinks and/or bar snacks.

**CHILDREN'S FACILITIES**
Small portions and/or high chairs available on request.

**FLAGSTAFF:** *Cottage Place Restaurant* $$$
126 W Cottage Ave, AZ 86001. *(928) 774-8431.*
One of Flagstaff's best eating places with an imaginative menu that includes vegetarian dishes and a good selection of seafood and meats. *D.* ● *Mon.*

**GRAND CANYON:** *Bright Angel Restaurant* $$
Bright Angel Lodge, AZ 86023. *(928) 638-2631.*
A bustling café-restaurant that serves light meals and salad as well as full meals. Reservations are not accepted, so you may have to line up.

**GRAND CANYON:** *Phantom Ranch* $$
Grand Canyon, AZ 86023. *(928) 638-2631.*
Situated on the canyon floor and accessible only by hiking or mule trail, Phantom Ranch has a canteen providing meals by advance reservation only. The house specialty is the "Hiker's Stew."

**GRAND CANYON VILLAGE:** *El Tovar Hotel* $$$$
Grand Canyon South Rim, AZ 86023. *(928) 638-2631.*
El Tovar has a large dining room overlooking the South Rim of the Grand Canyon. The menu is wide-ranging and portions are large. Reservations for dinner are essential.

**JEROME:** *English Kitchen* $
119 Jerome Ave, AZ 86331. *(928) 634-2132.*
This café serves standard but well-prepared breakfast and lunch in premises that once served as an opium den in Jerome's wild past. *L.* ● *Mon.*

**JEROME:** *Flatiron Café* $
416 N Main St, AZ 86331. *(928) 634-2733.*
Great salads are a specialty of this amiable café in the center of Jerome. Also try the tasty scrambled eggs at breakfast. *L.*

**LAKE HAVASU CITY:** *Mud Shark Brewing Co* $$
210 Swanson Ave, AZ 86403. *(928) 453-2981.*
Located close to London Bridge, this place brews its own beer. Food is a cut above the usual pub fare.

**PHOENIX:** *Sam's Café* $
2566 E Camelback Rd, AZ 85016. *(602) 954-7100.*
Good food and good value for Southwestern, vegetarian and Tex-Mex cuisine. Some hand-crafted specials, such as applewood-smoked salmon.

**PHOENIX:** *Aunt Chilada's at Squaw Peak* $$
27330N Dreamy Draw Dr, AZ 85020. *(602) 944-1286.*
Mexican food is the specialty of this popular restaurant, which occupies an imaginatively modernized, 19th-century general store.

**PHOENIX:** *Vincent's on Camelback* $$$$$
3930 E Camelback Rd, AZ 85251. *(602) 224-0225.*
This classy restaurant offers an imaginative menu blending French and Southwestern cuisine. Reservations recommended. ● *mid-May–Sep: Mon & Sun.*

**SCOTTSDALE:** *The Squash Blossom* $$$
Hyatt Regency at Gainey Ranch, 7500 E Doubletree Ranch Rd, AZ 85258. *(480) 991-3388.*
The emphasis of this excellent café is on Southwest cuisine.

**SECOND MESA, HOPI RESERVATION:** *Hopi Cultural Center Restaurant* $$
Rte 264, AZ 86043. *(928) 734-2401.*
Traditional dishes like Hopi stew can be interesting, although standard Mexican and American fare is also served. ● *Thanksgiving, Dec 25.*

| Restaurant | Credit Cards | Outdoor Tables | Vegetarian | Bar Area | Children's Facilities |
|---|---|---|---|---|---|
| Cottage Place Restaurant | ■ | | ■ | | |
| Bright Angel Restaurant | ■ | | ■ | | ■ |
| Phantom Ranch | ■ | ● | ■ | | |
| El Tovar Hotel | ■ | | ■ | ● | |
| English Kitchen | ■ | ● | ■ | | |
| Flatiron Café | ■ | ● | ■ | | |
| Mud Shark Brewing Co | ■ | ● | ■ | ● | |
| Sam's Café | ■ | | ■ | | ■ |
| Aunt Chilada's at Squaw Peak | ■ | ● | ■ | ● | ■ |
| Vincent's on Camelback | ■ | | ● | ■ | |
| The Squash Blossom | ■ | ● | ■ | ● | ■ |
| Hopi Cultural Center Restaurant | ■ | | | | ■ |

**EDONA:** *Shugrue's Hillside Grill* $$$
illside Courtyard, 671 Hwy 179, AZ 86336. (928) 282-5300.
rguably the best steaks in town can be enjoyed at this brisk, modern estaurant. The service is excellent – both efficient and courteous.

**UBA CITY:** *Hogan Restaurant* $
O Box 247, AZ 86045. (928) 283-5260.
ocated next to the Quality Inn, Hogan's offers a full Mexican/American nenu, which is a cut above average diner fare.

**UCSON:** *El Charro Café* $
11 N Court Ave, AZ 85701. (520) 622-1922.
ucson's oldest Mexican restaurant is critically acclaimed as serving some f the best traditional Mexican food in the country. Try the famous *carne eca* (sun-dried beef), a Tucson specialty.

**UCSON:** *Janos* $$$$$
Vestin La Paloma, 3770 E Sunrise Dr, AZ 85718. (520) 615-6100.
One of Tucson's most elegant restaurants, Janos blends French cooking echniques with Southwestern ingredients. The menu changes seasonally nd the extensive wine list is chosen to match. *Sun, public hols.*

**OMBSTONE:** *Big Nose Kate's* $
17 E Allen St, AZ 85638 (520) 457-3107.
his restaurant has a great old-fashioned saloon atmosphere, with an riginal cowboy bar and loads of Western memorabilia.

**VINDOW ROCK:** *Navajo Nation Inn Dining Room* $
8 West Hwy 264, AZ 86515. (928) 871-4108.
his is where the Navajo businessmen and politicians eat. Traditional ishes are served in a room decorated with Native art. *Sat & Sun D.*

## NEW MEXICO

**LBUQUERQUE:** *Church Street Café* $
111 Church St NW, NM 87124. (505) 247-8522.
ocated in the Old Town just behind San Felipe de Neri church, this tmospheric restaurant is found in one of the oldest buildings in the tate. Highly acclaimed for its authentic Hispanic fare.

**LBUQUERQUE:** *Monte Vista Fire Station* $$$
201 Central Ave NE, NM 87106. (505) 255-2424.
Now a National Historic Site, this Art Deco Pueblo Revival building was nce a fire station. A local favorite, it serves creative Southwestern food.

**LBUQUERQUE:** *The Artichoke Café* $$$
24 Central Ave SE, NM 87102. (505) 243-0200.
his relaxed but stylish downtown restaurant serves French-American bistro are. You can eat outside in good weather. *Sat & Sun L.*

**CARLSBAD:** *The Flume* $$
329 S Canal St, NM 88220. (505) 887-2851.
This casual restaurant is one of the best in Carlsbad. It is famous for its rime rib, but steaks, chicken, and seafood are also served.

**ANTA FE:** *Dave's Not Here* $
115 Hickox St, NM 87501. (505) 983-7060.
popular eatery featuring good-sized portions of New Mexican favorites, ncluding *chili rellenos* (stuffed chilies) and tacos.

**ANTA FE:** *Maria's New Mexican Kitchen* $
55 W Cordova Rd, NM 87501. (505) 983-7929.
This very busy local restaurant serves authentic old Sante Fe-style ooking. Margaritas are a specialty of the house.

**ANTA FE:** *Old House Restaurant* $$$$
09 W San Francisco St, NM 87501. (505) 988-4455.
This is in the Eldorado Hotel and is one of Sante Fe's finest restaurants. pecialties include pepper-crusted salmon.

**TAOS:** *Doc Martin's Restaurant* $$$
25 Paseo del Pueblo Norte, NM 87571. (505) 758-1977.
ocated in the historic Taos Inn, dating from 1600, this perennial favorite erves New American and northern New Mexican cuisine.

For key to symbols see back flap

# The Rockies

# The Rockies at a Glance

THE FOUR STATES OF Montana, Idaho, Wyoming, and Colorado form the heart of the Rockies, the mountain range that dominates the landscape of North America. This beautiful but sparsely populated region encompasses a wealth of natural wonders such as the geysers of Wyoming's Yellowstone National Park, the varied landscapes of Montana's Glacier National Park, and the cliff dwellings of Colorado's Mesa Verde National Park. Colorado is also celebrated as the skiing capital of the United States. The area's human history lends itself to superlatives as much as the land does. Throughout the Rockies there are tangible signs of such legendary 19th-century Native Americans and cowboys as Sitting Bull and "Buffalo Bill" Cody.

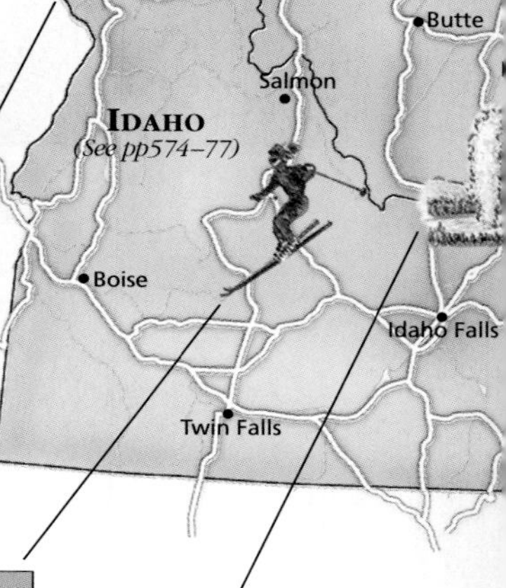

***Coeur d'Alene*** (see p574) *in Idaho is located along Lake Coeur d'Alene. This popular vacation destination is famous for its unique floating golf green on the 14th hole.*

***Sun Valley*** (see p576), *in southern Idaho, is one of the oldest and most exclusive winter resorts in the country. Its picturesque environs also offer many recreational options.*

***Yellowstone National Park*** (see pp584–5) *is perhaps one of the country's most visited parks. The highlights of this wild wonderland are the hot springs, particularly Old Faithful Geyser and its steaming plume.*

◁ **Mountain summit reflected in the placid waters of Lake Josephine, Glacier National Park, Montana**

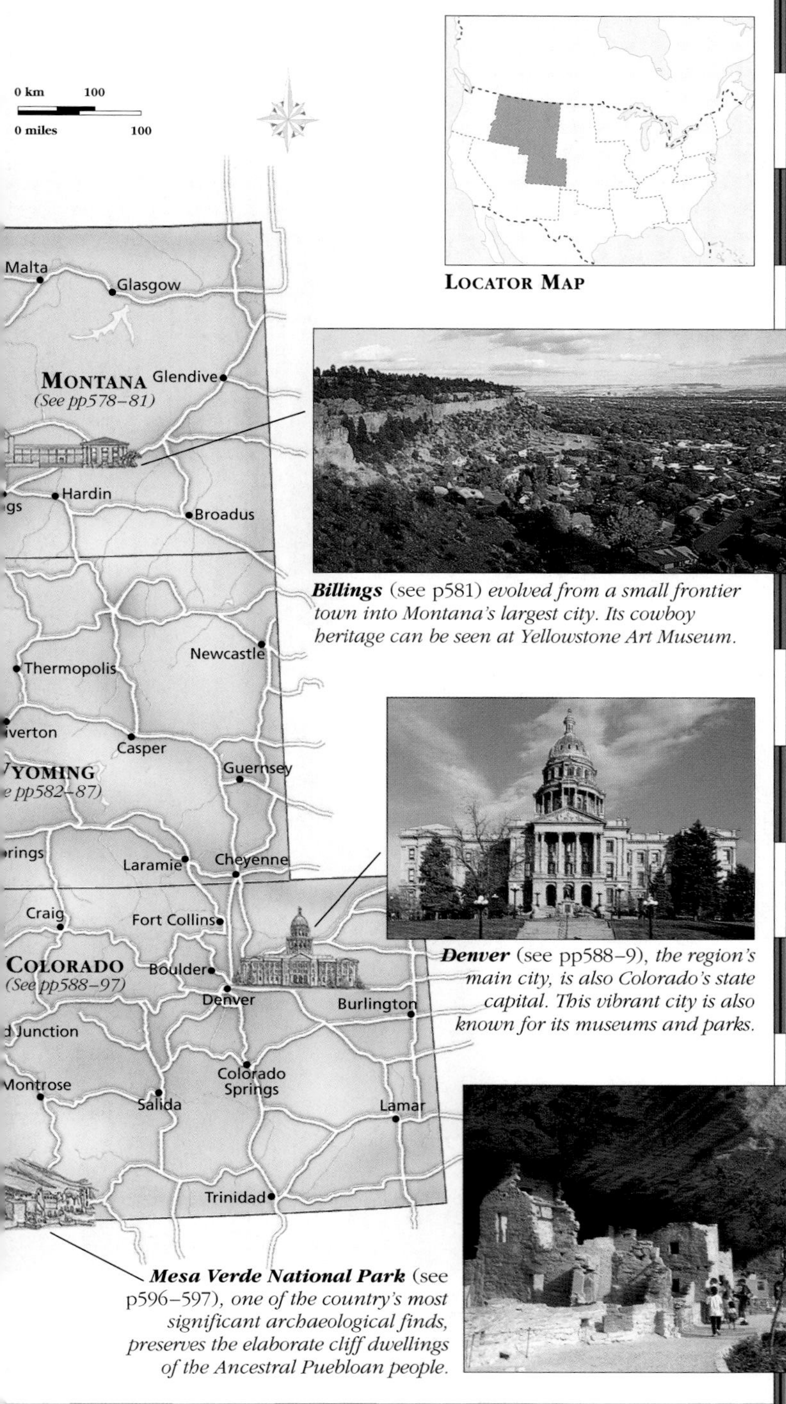


**Billings** (see p581) *evolved from a small frontier town into Montana's largest city. Its cowboy heritage can be seen at Yellowstone Art Museum.*

**Denver** (see pp588–9), *the region's main city, is also Colorado's state capital. This vibrant city is also known for its museums and parks.*

**Mesa Verde National Park** (see p596–597), *one of the country's most significant archaeological finds, preserves the elaborate cliff dwellings of the Ancestral Puebloan people.*

# The Rockies

One of the world's great outdoor regions, *the Rockies offer a variety of experiences not found anywhere else. The sheer scale of the landscape is breathtaking, and words can hardly express the thrill of seeing firsthand the broad expanses of the Wyoming plains, Idaho's deep river canyons, the towering peaks of Colorado, or the rugged vastness of Montana.*

The underlying geology of the Rocky Mountains is ancient, with some of the country's oldest rocks forming the highly stratified Precambrian peaks and valleys of Glacier National Park. The rest of the range is varied, with mineral-rich granite batholiths sharing space with the vast red-rock mesas of the Colorado Plateau. Evidence of volcanic activity, forming and reforming the landscape from deep beneath the surface, is also omnipresent, most prominently in Idaho's Craters of the Moon National Monument, and most famously in the geysers, mudpots, and hot springs of Yellowstone National Park in Wyoming.

This region has also been shaped by some of North America's mightiest rivers. Beside the terrifying whitewater rapids of the Snake and other tumultuous rivers, the Rockies form the headwaters of many major western rivers, including the Colorado, the Missouri, the Columbia, and the Rio Grande. These rivers and their many tributaries offer some of the finest fishing in the world. Wildflowers are abundant, especially in the alpine meadows, while the dense forests are the habitat of a wide range of wildlife. Moose, elk, and bald eagles are spotted frequently along trails and roads, and the backwoods areas hold some of the nation's last wild populations of carnivores, including mountain lions, wolves, and massive grizzly bears.

## History

The history of the Rockies is as wild and larger-than-life as the land itself. From the late 18th century, intrepid "mountain men" – French-Canadian and American fur trappers – traveled throughout the Rockies, trapping beavers and other animals for their valuable skins. After the Louisiana Purchase in 1803, the fledgling country acquired control of the Rockies, and the first official American

**Pool along the Firehole Lake Drive, Yellowstone National Park, Wyoming**

**Cross-country skiing at Steamboat Springs, one of Colorado's popular ski resorts**

presence was established between 1803 and 1806 by explorers Meriwether Lewis and William Clark. These daring men were accompanied by a "Corps of Discovery" made up of 29 soldiers and fur trappers, and joined by the legendary Indian guide Sacagawea and her baby son. They followed the Missouri upstream from the frontier outpost of St. Louis, traveling by boat and later by foot across Montana and Idaho on an epic 5,000-mile (8,047-km) journey to the Pacific Ocean and back. Also in 1806, Zebulon Pike led an expedition to Colorado, following the Arkansas River and spotting the majestic mountain that bears his name.

**Lewis & Clark National Historic Trail Interpretive Center, Great Falls, Montana**

These explorers' published accounts, describing the sublime landscape and its wealth of wildlife, attracted increasing numbers of trappers and hunters, and by the 1830s several commercial outposts had been established, usually at the confluence of major rivers. Their routes across what had once been seen as an impenetral barrier slowly but surely paved the w for transcontinental travelers. By t mid-1800s, thousands of pionee following the Oregon Trail and otl routes crossed the Rocky Mountaii bound for the Pacific Northwest, t California gold fields, a the Mormon lands Utah. As a result, conflic between immigrants a Native Americans increas dramatically. In t mountains, the N Percé and other sm tribes lived comparative peaceful and sedenta lives, while east of t mountains were migratory bands Plains Indians, including such diver and often rival tribes as the Siou Cheyenne, Crow, Arapahoe, a Shoshone. Most of these eastern trib were themselves recent arrivals. Livi in mobile encampments of tepee they had mastered the art of ridi horses and hunting buffalo. As co boys and ranchers moved into the ri grazing lands, some 50 million nati bison were all but eradicated, a the tribes whose entire culture w based on these mighty herds can under desperate threat.

By the beginning of the 20th centur all the tribes had been contained in small reservations, far from the previous homelands. Ironically, one the country's greatest Native Americ cultural repositories is in Wyoming Buffalo Bill Historical Center, a mem rial to the man who, as buffalo hunt and Indian fighter, contributed great to their destruction.

## Key Dates in History

**1200** Ancestral Pueblo Indians abandon their cliff dwellings at Mesa Verde, Colorado

**1700–1800** French-Canadian fur trappers explore the Rockies

**1803** The US acquires much of this region through the Louisiana Purchase

**1803** The Lewis and Clark expedition begins

**1806** Zebulon Pike explores the Arkansas River in southern Colorado

**1843** The Oregon Trail is opened

**1858** Gold is discovered outside Denver

**1869** Wyoming gives women the vote

**1872** US Congress establishes the world's first national park at Yellowstone

**1876** Battle of Little Bighorn

**1915** The Lincoln Highway, the first transcontinental route from New York City to San Francisco, runs across southern Wyoming

**1951** Warren Air Force Base in Cheyenne is declared the base of operations for all US Intercontinental Ballistic Missiles (ICBMs)

**1988** Forest fires across the Rockies cause serious damage to Yellowstone National Park

**2003** Memorial commemorating the Native American victory at the Battle of Little Bighorn is dedicated at the site of the battle in Montana

**Tepees, Buffalo Bill Historical Center, Wyoming**

ıe former silver-mining town of Wallace, near Coeur d'Alene, Idaho

### Progress & Development

he first transcontinental railroad ossed southern Wyoming in the late 360s, followed in the 1870s and 1880s other railroads, such as the Northern acific and Great Northern. Carrying ttle to eastern markets, and bringing eapons and supplies to the Wild 'est, it was these railroads that actually onsolidated American settlement.

The search for and discovery of luable minerals, mainly gold, silver, ıd copper, was another primary ıpetus to settlement. Because of the gion's expansive forests, the lumber dustry, too, had been an economic ainstay since pioneer times, and over ıe previous century oil and coal eposits have been the source under-ing numerous booms and busts, pecially in Colorado and Wyoming.

### Tourism & the Economy

atural resource-based industries are ill active all over the Rockies, though ıe main economic force today is urism. These four states contain the ghest mountains, the densest forests, ıe wildest rivers, and the most rugged ınyons in the "Lower 48" states. onsequently, the Rockies is a magical ace offering sublime scenery as well a wide variety of attractions, such as istoric train rides, summer "dude ranches," and historic sites. Many places also feature music festivals, Plains Indian pow-wows, or theatrical re-creations of Wild West shootouts.

This is also the best place to appreciate the great outdoors. Intrepid guides offer unforgettable trips such as whitewater rafting or fly-fishing for trout. The proliferation of ski resorts has also added to the state's tourism potential. When gold was discovered outside Denver in 1850, several mining camps sprang up at such evocatively named places as Silverton and Cripple Creek in Colorado and "Last Chance Gulch," now Helena, Montana. Many of these erstwhile mining centers are now deluxe winter resorts, such as Crested Butte, Telluride, and Aspen in Colorado, and Idaho's Sun Valley.

Neon sign for the Cowboy Bar, Jackson, Wyoming

# Exploring the Rockies

THE SHEER VASTNESS OF THE Rocky Mountains landscape and the relative shortness of the tourism season means that visitors need to plan well ahead. Many attractions on this 1,000-mile (1,609-km) long swath of mountains are on such high elevations that they are inaccessible during the long winter, with snow blocking roads from late October until June. The heavy snowfalls, however, enhance the region's phenomenal winter sports, and Denver, the main city, is a prime starting point for most visitors. Driving is the best way to explore the area, because public transportation is limited, and the national parks and most of the other attractions are far away.

**KEY**

- Airport
- Highway
- Major road
- Railroad
- State border
- International border

## SIGHTS AT A GLANCE

**Idaho**

Coeur d'Alene 1
Hells Canyon National Recreation Area 2
Salmon 3
Sawtooth National Recreation Area 4
Boise 5
Sun Valley 6
Three Island Crossing State Park 7
Bruneau Dunes State Park 8
Twin Falls 9
Craters of the Moon National Monument 10
Idaho Falls 11

**Montana**

Big Hole National Battlefield 12
Missoula 13
Flathead Valley 14
*Glacier National Park p579* 15
Great Falls 16
Helena 17
Butte 18
Bozeman 19
Billings 20
Little Bighorn Battlefield National Monument 21

**Wyoming**

Cody 22
*Yellowstone National Park pp584–5* 23
Jackson 24
*Grand Teton National Park p583* 25
Bighorn Mountains 26
Devil's Tower National Monument 27
Casper 28
Guernsey 29
Laramie 30
Cheyenne 31

**Colorado**

*Denver pp588–9* 32
Boulder 33
Golden 34
Idaho Springs & Georgetown 35
Rocky Mountain National Park 36
Manitou Springs 37
Colorado Springs 38
Cripple Creek 39
Cañon City 40
*Colorado Ski Resorts pp594–5* 41
Great Sand Dunes National Monument & Preserve 42
Durango 43
Mesa Verde National Park 44
Ouray 45
Black Canyon of the Gunnison National Park 46
Colorado National Monument 47

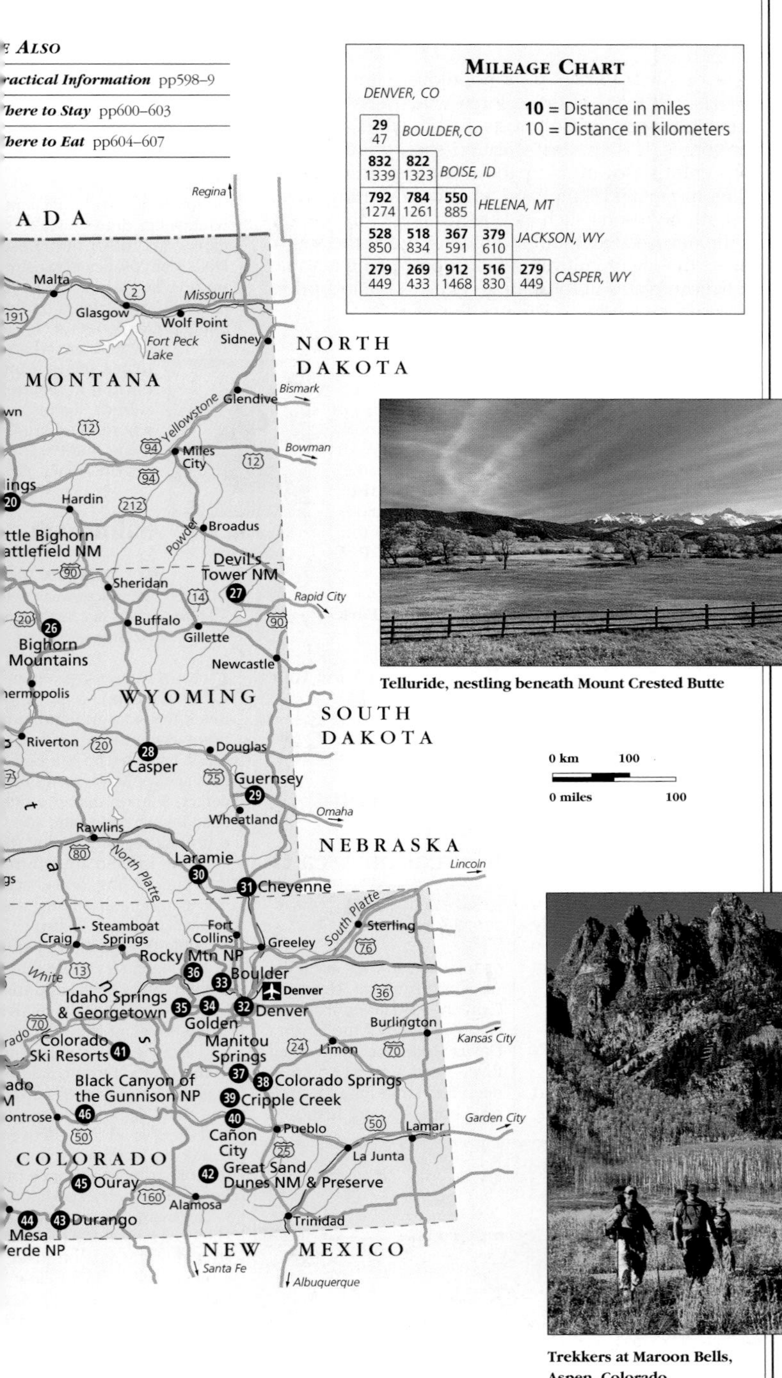


| DENVER, CO | BOULDER, CO | BOISE, ID | HELENA, MT | JACKSON, WY | |
|---|---|---|---|---|---|
| **29** 47 | | | | | BOULDER, CO |
| **832** 1339 | **822** 1323 | | | | BOISE, ID |
| **792** 1274 | **784** 1261 | **550** 885 | | | HELENA, MT |
| **528** 850 | **518** 834 | **367** 591 | **379** 610 | | JACKSON, WY |
| **279** 449 | **269** 433 | **912** 1468 | **516** 830 | **279** 449 | CASPER, WY |

**Telluride, nestling beneath Mount Crested Butte**

**Trekkers at Maroon Bells, Aspen, Colorado**

# Idaho

One of the country's least populous states, Idaho has vast tracts of unexplored wilderness – remote mountain ranges, dense forests, frozen lakes, and deep river gorges. It is an ideal vacation spot for adventure sports enthusiasts, offering abundant opportunities for hiking, mountain biking, and whitewater rafting. To the north lie resorts such as Coeur d'Alene; the center has the majestic Sawtooth Mountains; while the south consists mainly of cultivated fields, prompting automobile license plates in the state to declare Idaho's pride in its primary product, "Famous Potatoes."

## Coeur d'Alene ❶

*38,000. 1621 N 3rd St, (208) 664-3194.* www.coeurdalene.org

A major vacation destination, Coeur d'Alene was founded in the 1870s as a US Army outpost. Its present "four star" status refers to the luxury available at the town's world-famous **Coeur d'Alene Resort** *(see p600)*. Located along the shore of the beautiful Lake Coeur d'Alene, this exclusive resort is well known for its unique floating golf green on the 14th hole. On the resort's east side, the 120-acre (49-ha) **Tubbs Hill Park** is a nature preserve with hiking trails, dense pine forests, and great views. Lake Coeur d'Alene is also home to one of the country's largest populations of ospreys and bald eagles, which can be seen frequently in winter diving for salmon in the waters of Wolf Lodge Bay.

A century ago, Coeur d'Alene was a busy service center for the prosperous silver mines in mountains east of the lake. A number of Victorian-era towns still stand in the former mining districts, and museums and mine tours offer a glimpse into this lost world. The town of Wallace, 52 miles (84 km) east, offers the **Sierra Silver Mine Tour**, which guides visitors through the workings of an 1890s silver mine.

**Tubbs Hill Park**
*(208) 769-2252.*
*dawn–dusk daily.*

**Sierra Silver Mine Tour**
420 5th St, Wallace. *(208) 752-5151. May–Sep: daily. First tour at 9am, then every half hour.*

## Hells Canyon National Recreation Area ❷

PO Box 832, Riggins. *(208) 628-3916.* www.fs.fed.us/hellscanyon

The deepest river gorge in North America, Hells Canyon was carved from the craggy granite of the Seven Devils Mountains by the Snake River. Over a mile (1.6 km) deep and straddling the three-state border where Idaho, Washington, and Oregon meet, the canyon and its surroundings are now a rec ational area that includes so 215,000 acres (87,008 ha) o wilderness where no motor vehicles are permitted. Nea 100 miles (161 km) of undeveloped and turbulent whitewater draws kayakers, rafters, and other thrillseeke Hells Canyon lies downstre from Hells Canyon Dam. Th main visitor center is on the Oregon *(see pp640–41)* side of the dam, while Idaho, the best intr duction to the area is from Riggins, where there are many outfitters wh provide rental gea

**Kayaking, Hells Canyon**

## Salmon ❸

*3,120. 200 Main (208) 756-2100.* **Sacajawea Cente** May–Oct: Sat–Sun; daily in sum mer. www.salmonidaho.com

Situated along the banks the wild and scenic Salm River, this was an important point along the Lewis and Clark Trail *(see p570)*. Essen tially a supply town and res center, Salmon makes a fine base for exploring the surrounding region. Among the activities offered are raft trip kayaking, skiing, horseback riding, mountain biking, an snowmobiling. It is also possible to hike along parts of the legendary route that the explorers Lewis and Cla followed in the early 1800s while traveling from Illinois find a navigable water route to the Pacific Ocean. Salmo was the birthplace of Lewis and Clark's guide, Sacajawe and there is an interpretive center on Main Street that explores the significance of her role in their expedition.

The main highway, scenic US 93, winds along the mai stream of the Salmon River, while smaller roads follow tributaries into the wild. At t hamlet of North Fork, Salmo River Road turns west from t highway, heading downstrea along impassable rapids tha Lewis and Clark aptly dubb the "River of No Return."

**A view of the scenic Lake Coeur d'Alene, near the resort**

view of the Sawtooth Mountains, from the shores of Redfish Lake

## awtooth National ecreation Area ❹

vy 75. (208) 737-3200. **Camp-ound.** *year-round.*

HIS SUPERB destination for . hiking and camping compasses 765,000 acres 09,586 ha) of rivers, ountain meadows, forests, d jagged peaks of the wtooth Range. For visitors iving up Hwy 75 from Sun lley *(see p576)*, the best troduction to the area is at e 8,701-ft (2,652-m) high **alena Summit**, where a ectacular panorama looks orth over the Salmon River. At an elevation of 6,200 ft ,890 m), surrounded by the wtooth Mountains, the tiny amlet of **Stanley** (popula-on 75), has one of the most eautiful settings of any town the US. The unpaved reets and wood-fronted ontier-style buildings make sitors feel like they have, at st, arrived in the Wild West, espite the fact that the glitzy sort of Sun Valley is barely n hour away to the south. nother attraction is **Redfish ake**, 10 miles (16 km) south f Stanley, where rustic Red-sh Lake Lodge is found near e foot of Mount Heyburn.

## Boise ❺

185,787. 312 S 9th St, uite 100, (800) 635-5240.

FRENCH TRAPPERS in the 19th-century named this outpost Boise," meaning wooded. ven today, this homespun, slow-paced city presents a picture-postcard image of America. Locals and visitors walk, ride bicycles, or enjoy an afternoon picnic on the grass in the vast Greenbelt parkland that adjoins the Boise River in the heart of downtown.

Boise is also the state capital and the largest city in rural Idaho. Its focal point is the domed **State Capitol**, which was completed in 1920 after 15 years of construction. The building's main distinction is that it is the only US capitol to be heated by naturally occurring geothermal water. It was built of sandstone blocks quarried by inmates at the **Old Idaho Penitentiary**, 2 miles (3 km) east of the capitol.

Now open to visitors, the state penitentiary was in use from 1870 to 1970. Apart from the prison, the grounds also house a series of museums dedicated to such subjects as transportation, the uses of electricity, and mining.

The city's historic center is three blocks south of the capitol. Here a dozen late-Victorian commercial buildings have been restored and house a lively set of coffee houses, bars, restaurants, and boutiques. Boise's oldest building, completed in 1864, now houses the **Basque Museum and Cultural Center**, which traces the presence of Basque sheepherders in Boise and across western US, and is also known for celebrating Basque culture with frequent events. A cluster of museums and cultural centers lie in **Julia Davis Park**, a 40-acre (16-ha) green area that straddles the Boise River at the heart of the Greenbelt.

A 15-minute drive by car away from the city is the **Peregrine Fund World Center for Birds of Prey**. One of the most successful organizations for breeding as well as studying raptors, the world center has been instrumental in recovering endangered populations of peregrine falcons in the US, a species that was nearly wiped out by lethal pesticides in the 1970s. Visitors also have the rare opportunity to see a variety of birds including eagles, condors, and falcons while enjoying a hilltop view of the surrounding sagebrush plains.

**Peregrine Fund World Center for Birds of Prey**

5668 West Flying Hawk Lane. *(208) 362-3716.* *Mar–Oct: 9am–5pm daily; Nov–Feb: 10am–4pm Tue–Sun.* *Jan 1, Thanksgiving, Dec 25.*

The beautiful exterior of the Idaho State Capitol in Boise

**Skaters outside Sun Valley Lodge, Sun Valley**

## Sun Valley ❻

*251 Washington Ave, Ketchum, (208) 726-3423.*
www.visitsunvalley.com

DEVELOPED IN the late 1930s by the Union Pacific Railroad baron Averell Harriman, Sun Valley is one of the oldest and highest-profile winter resorts in the US. The construction of the Tyrolean-style **Sun Valley Lodge** *(see p600)* and the adjacent ski area was completed in 1936, after which Harriman was inspired to invite Hollywood movie stars and other members of the glitterati to enjoy his facilities. Sun Valley's fame was thus ensured by the presence of celebrities such as Errol Flynn, Gary Cooper, Clark Gable, and Ernest Hemingway. Since then, the Olympic-quality skiing on the well-groomed slopes of the 9,151-ft (2,789-m) Bald Mountain has continued to draw an exclusive clientele during the season between November and April. The resort also commissioned the world's first ski-lift.

Before the 1930s, however, the area was a mining and sheep-ranching center, based in the adjacent town of Ketchum. This town still retains many of its rugged frontier characteristics, despite the influx of multi-million-dollar vacation homes. The region's history is on view in the **Ketchum Sun Valley Heritage & Ski Museum**. Although most visitors never stray beyond Sun Valley and Ketchum, the surrounding landscape is filled with other recreational options. Bicyclists can follow the 20-mile (32-km) **Wood River Trail**, along the old Union Pacific Railroad right-of-way. The Wood River is also a prime trout-fishing stream, while to the north, the majestic Sawtooth National Recreation Area *(see p575)* offers pristine hiking and camping country.

**Ketchum Sun Valley Heritage & Ski Museum**
180 1st Ave E. *(208) 726-8118.*
*11am–3:30pm Mon–Fri, 1–4pm Sat.*

## Three Island Crossing State Park ❼

Off I-84, Glenns Ferry Exit. *Glenns Ferry, (208) 366-2394.* ***Campground.***
www.idahoparks.org/parks/threeisland.html

ONE OF THE most evocative sights along the historic Oregon Trail *(see p450)* is the famous Three Islands Crossing, which provided one of the few safe places for emigrants to cross the dangerous Snake River. The ford was in use until 1869, when Gus Glenn constructed a ferry 2 miles (3 km) upstream. Not all attempts at crossing, however, were successful. Depending on the time of year and the level of the water, it sometimes proved fatal to the pioneers in the westward-bound wagons. Some pioneers balked at the dangers involved and did no attempt the crossing. Instead they would continue along the river's barren south bank before rejoining the main tra west of Boise.

**The Hemingway Memorial, Sun Valley**

Today, the park offers a campground and numerous picnic areas. Visitors can stil experience the dangers of th 1800s if they visit the park in mid-August, when the ford crossing is re-created by history enthusiasts wearing period costumes and driving replica wagons.

## Bruneau Dunes State Park ❽

Hwy 78 (off State Hwy 51).
*Mountain Home, (208) 366-791*
***Campground.***

IMMEDIATELY south of the Snake River, at the foot of the high-desert Owyhee Mountains, a surprising sight arises from the surrounding sagebush plains. Some of the largest sand dunes in North America, the Bruneau Dunes rise to heights of nearly 500 (152 m). They are protected from the destructive impacts of cars, motorcycles, and dune buggies within one of Idaho's largest state parks.

A visitor center explains how these quartz and feldsp sand dunes were formed, and why they are not blown away. The reason for this phe nomenon is simple: prevailin winds blow from opposite directions for roughly equal amounts of time, which keep the dunes fairly stable. There are also specimens of local wildlife on display, including a short-eared owl. A small astronomical observatory is often open to the public.

The park encompasses a variety of habitats such as marsh, prairie, and desert. Wildlife includes snakes and lizards, and birds such as ow and eagles. A few small lakes lie at the foot of the dunes where visitors can go fishing in canoes or rubber rafts. Other activities offered are camping and horseback riding

ake River Gorge, Twin Falls

## win Falls 9

36,000. 858 Blue
es Blvd N, (208) 733-3974.
www.twinfallschamber.com

HE FALLS FOR which the city was named have en diminished by dams d irrigation, but Twin Falls still home to a splendid aterfall. Called the "Niagara the West," the 212-ft (65-m) gh and 1,000-ft (305-m) de **Shoshone Falls** is an pressive sight, especially in ring when the water flows at their peak.

Located 5 miles (8 km) rtheast of the city, the falls framed by the deep **Snake ver Gorge**, famous for the fated attempt by motor-cle daredevil Evel Knievel leap across it in 1974. He rvived, but with many uries. The city stretches ong the level plains to the uth of the gorge, and is the nter for potato-growing ms and cattle ranches.

## raters of the Moon National Monument 10

20. (208) 527-3257.
(Campground only).
www.nps.gov/crmo

PRAWLED ACROSS 83 sq miles (215 sq km) in central aho, the Craters of the oon National Monument owcases one of the most extraordinary landscapes in the country. The most accessible section can be explored via the numerous short trails that lead through rippling, jagged, lava fields, strewn with cones and craters. They range from 15,000 to 2,000 years of age. The fields were formed by molten lava, which seeped out from gaps in the earth's crust over a period of 13,000 years. Despite their forbidding, blackened appearance, the lava fields harbor more than 50 species of mammals, 170 species of birds, and millions of resplendent wildflowers, which bloom in summer each year. Numerous caves and lava tubes also run beneath the surface.

The name "Craters of the Moon" was coined in the 1920s, when the monument was established. The visitor center near the entrance recounts the park's geological and natural history. Visitors can also improve their Hawaiian lava vocabulary, learning the scientific terms for sharp lava *(a'a)*, layered lava *(kipukas)*, and smooth lava *(pa'hoe'hoe)*.

In the 1960s, astronauts from the *Apollo 14* space mission visited the monument to learn more about volcanic geology that was similar to that of the moon.

Camping is also available in the park during the summer, and the main loop road draws crowds of cross-country skiers during winter.

## Idaho Falls 11

50,730. 630 W Broadway, (866) 365-6943.
www.visitidahofalls.com

SET ALONG THE banks of the Snake River, with Wyoming's Grand Teton Mountains rising to the east, Idaho Falls is a charming and predominantly agricultural city with a large Mormon population *(see p519)*. Dominated by the towering Mormon temple, the city has a vast "Greenbelt" area where people can jog and inline skate. Although the Idaho Falls, which lent their name to the city, have now been dammed, they still provide a scenic setting to the parkland. The main attraction here is the **Idaho National Engineering and Environmental Laboratory** (INEEL), located 50 miles (80 km) west of the city. Established in 1949 to design, build, and test nuclear reactors for military and civilian purposes, the 890-sq-mile (2,305-sq-km) site now holds the largest concentration of nuclear reactors in the world. The world's first reactor, the EBR-1, was built here in 1951 and is now open for viewing. On July 17, 1955, INEEL was the site of the world's first peaceful use of atomic power, when INEEL engineers sent 2,000 kilowatts (2 megawatts) of electricity to light up the nearby town of Arco.

**Idaho National Engineering & Environmental Lab**
Hwy 20/26. (800) 708-2680. May–Sep: 8am–4pm daily. Jul 4.

**Blackened volcanic cones, Craters of the Moon National Monument**

# Montana

THE NORTHERNMOST OF THE Rocky Mountain states, Montana abounds in tall, rugged mountains, snowcapped peaks, lush valleys, and seemingly endless plains stretching beneath its trademark "big sky." The sheer scale and majesty of its wide open spaces and the larger-than-life character of its inhabitants, past and present, prompted Nobel Prize-winning novelist John Steinbeck to write "Montana seems to me to be what a small boy would think Texas is like from hearing Texans. Of all the states it is my favorite and my love."

**Big Hole National Battlefield, surrounded by mountains**

## Big Hole National Battlefield ⓬

*Hwy 43 near Wisdom. (406) 689-3155. May–Sep: 9am–6pm; Oct–Apr: 9am–5pm daily. Jan 1, Thanksgiving, Dec 25. (free in winter).*

LOCATED NEAR the Idaho border at an altitude of some 7,000 ft (2,134 m) in the Bitterroot Mountains, this battlefield site sits at the head of the lush Big Hole Valley, famed for its cattle ranches and trout-fishing opportunities. This serene pastoral scene is far removed from the suffering experienced here on August 9, 1877. On that day, the flight north by 750 Nez Perce Indians, mostly women and children, was cut short by a surprise attack by US Army soldiers and civilian volunteers, leading to the death of nearly 100 Indians. The tribe continued their journey toward Canada, traveling another 1,500 miles (2,414 km) before finally surrendering in October, just 30 miles (48 km) short of the Canadian border.

## Missoula ⓭

*58,000. 825 E Front St, (406) 543-6623.*

NESTLING IN the Rocky Mountains of western Montana, Missoula is still dependent upon traditional Montana industries, such as timber and transportation. This lively city is also home to the University of Montana.

Surrounded by acres of magnificent wilderness, this picturesque city formed the backdrop of the book and subsequent movie *A River Runs Through It*. The city also houses the **Smokejumpers Base**, a national center for fighting forest fires in the Rockies. Exhibits explore fire-fighting techniques and equipment, and depending on the time of the year (summer is forest-fire season), guests are able to tour the airplanes and meet fire-fighters.

To the south, the Bitterroot Valley has ranches and small towns, hemmed in by a pair of towering mountain ranges.

### Smokejumpers Base Visitor Center

Aerial Fire Depot, Missoula Int'l Airport, Hwy 93. *(406) 329-4934. Memorial Day–Labor Day: daily; Labor Day–Memorial Day: by appt.*

## Flathead Valley ⓮

*Bigfork Chamber of Commerce, 8155, Hwy 35, (406) 837-5888.* **Salish & Kootenai Tribal Council** *(406) 675-2700.*

MOST OF THE valley's land which stretches betwe the 40-mile (64-km) long an 15-mile (24-km) wide Flathead Lake and Missoula, is part of the Flathead India Reservation. Since 1855 this has been home to descendants of the region's Salish, Kootenai, and Pend D'Oreil Indian tribes. In summer, communities such as Elmo and Arlee celebrate Native traditions in numerous pow wows, which are traditional gatherings featuring rodeo competitions, craft demonstrations, and sales.

The **People's Center** in Pablo traces the history of t Flathead region from a Nati American perspective. To th west, some 18,500 acres (7,487 ha) of rolling ranchland were set aside in 1908 the National Bison Range, housing bison, deer, bighor sheep, and pronghorn.

The largest natural freshwater lake west of the Missi sippi River, Flathead Lake is deep-blue jewel at the west ern foot of the Rocky Moun tains. Cherry orchards and towns like Bigfork line Hwy 35 on the lake's eastern sho while to the west the busier US 93 hugs the water for ov 35 miles (56 km). Rent bike or kayaks, or take guided b tours into the scenic lake.

### People's Center

53253 Hwy 93, Pablo. *(406) 88 5344. 9am–5pm Mon–Fri; also 10am–5pm Sat–Sun from Memoria Day to Labor Day only.*

**Flathead Lake, nestling at the foot of the Rocky Mountains**

# Glacier National Park ⓯

North of W Glacier. (406) 888-5800. most visitor facilities open late May–mid-Sep. www.nps.gov/glac

SPREADING NEARLY a million acres (404,690 ha) over the northern Rocky Mountains, Glacier National Park holds some of the world's most sublime scenery. With elevations ranging from 3,200 ft (975 m) along the Flathead River to summits topping 10,000 ft (3,048 m), the park contains a wide variety of landscapes. Alongside four dozen glaciers (which gave the park its name) and ancient limestone cliffs, there are lakes, waterfalls, and abundant wildlife, including moose, wolves, and bears. The flora ranges from high grassy plains to alpine tundra. In July, the park's higher altitudes are ablaze with meadows of blue gentians, yellow lillies, pink heathers, and feathery white Bear Grass.

**Hiking, a popular activity in Glacier National Park**

**Avalanche Creek** drops through dense forests down a red rock gorge. A boardwalk nature trail runs along its length.

**Going-to-the-Sun Mountain Road** runs past St. Mary's Lake. This 50-mile (80-km) road is the main access for touring the park, joining the park headquarters to the east entrance.

**Swiftcurrent Lake** sits at the foot of deeply glaciated valleys. Its shores offer rustic lodgings.

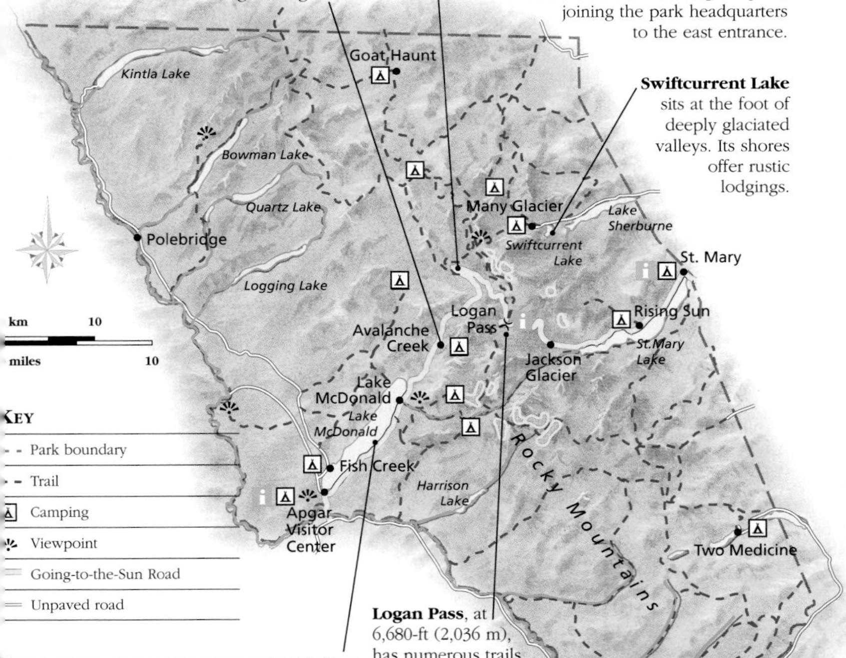

Goat Haunt
Kintla Lake
Bowman Lake
Quartz Lake
Polebridge
Logging Lake
Many Glacier
Lake Sherburne
Swiftcurrent Lake
St. Mary
Logan Pass
Rising Sun
Avalanche Creek
Jackson Glacier
St. Mary Lake
Lake McDonald
Lake McDonald
Fish Creek
Harrison Lake
Rocky Mountains
Apgar Visitor Center
Two Medicine

km 10
miles 10

**KEY**

- Park boundary
- Trail
- Camping
- Viewpoint
- Going-to-the-Sun Road
- Unpaved road

**Logan Pass**, at 6,680-ft (2,036 m), has numerous trails that lead from the road to alpine lakes and wildflower-rich meadows.

**Lake McDonald**

*Surrounded by dense conifer forests and a circle of high peaks, this 10-mile (16-km) long glacier-carved lake is the largest in the park.*

## Great Falls 16

56,700. 710 1st Ave N, (406) 761-4434. www.greatfallsonline.net

NESTLING picturesquely between the majestic Rocky Mountains to the west and Little Belt Mountains to the east, this rural city owes its name to its location along the Missouri River. As the river cuts through the city, it drops over 500 ft (152 m) in a series of rapids and five breathtaking waterfalls, first noted by explorers Lewis and Clark *(see p570)* in 1805.

The city is best known for its two excellent museums. One, the **Charles M. Russell Museum**, traces the history of the American West, focusing on the life and work of resident cowboy and prolific Wild West artist "Charlie" Russell, who gave the city much of its cultural flavor. His home and log cabin studio are next to the expansive museum.

On a bluff overlooking the Missouri River, 2 miles (3 km) northeast of downtown, is the **Lewis and Clark National Historic Trail Interpretive Center**. This museum details the epic explorations of the Corps of Discovery, the cross-country expedition led by Meriwether Lewis and William Clark from 1803 to 1806.

For 45 miles (72 km) downstream from the center, the Missouri River runs as a "Wild and Scenic" river on one of its virgin stretches, a route paralleled by a bike trail and driving tour along US 87. The route ends at Fort Benton, historic head of navigation on the Missouri River.

**Charles M. Russell Museum**
400 13th St N. (406) 727-8787. *May–Sep: 9am–6pm Mon–Sat, noon–5pm Sun; Oct–Apr: 10am–5pm Tue–Sun.* *Jan 1, Easter, Thanksgiving, Dec 25.*

**Lewis & Clark National Historic Trail Interpretive Center**
4201 Giant Springs Rd. *(406) 727-8733.* *Memorial Day–Sep: 9am–6pm daily; Oct–Memorial Day: 9am–5pm Tue–Sat, noon–5pm Sun.* *Jan 1, Thanksgiving, Dec 25.*

**Lewis and Clark National Historic Trail Interpretive Center, Great Falls**

## Helena 17

*27,500. 225 Cruse Ave, (406) 442-4120.*

THE STATE capital, Helena makes a fine base for exploring Montana. Originally known as "Last Chance Gulch," Helena was founded as a gold-mining camp in the 1860s. Fortunately much of the wealth generated here remained, as is evident from the number of mansions built by mining millionaires. Many of these exuberantly designed Victorian-era homes have been converted into B&B inns. The centerpiece of Helena is the copper-domed **Montana State Capitol**, decorated with several fine historical murals, including one of explorers Lewis and Clark painted by Charlie Russell. A statue on the grounds portrays Helena resident Jeanette Rankin, who in 1917 was the first woman to be elected to the United States Congress.

**Statue of Jeanette Rankin, Montana State Capitol**

## Butte 18

*34,000. 1000 George St, (406) 723-3177, (800) 735-6814.*

LOCATED IN THE heart of the Rocky Mountains, Butte is named for the prominent conical hill, Big Butte, which guards its northwest corner. That Butte has some of the world's richest mineral reserves is evident by the extensive signs of the gold, silver, and copper mining industry that thrived here from the 1870s through the first half of the 20th century. Glimpses of Butte's multi-ethnic, immigrant culture are also visible in such events as the St. Patrick's Day celebration by the town's Irish Catholic population. Of Butte's many fine museums, the **World Museum of Mining** occupies the site of an early gold mine. Its superb collection of mineral specimens, mining machinery, and mementos of the town's proud industrial heritage, also includes displays on Butte's leading role in the development of mine-workers unions. Outside, some 30 historic buildings dating from 1880 to 1910 re-create an early mining camp, complete with a church, a schoolhouse, bordellos, and boarding houses.

Sites such as the **Granite Mountain Mine Memorial** commemorate the 168 men killed in a 1917 mine disaster. High above the city, the 90-ft (27-m) statue of "Our Lady of the Rockies" stands as a proud symbol of Butte's strength and endurance.

**World Museum of Mining**
155 Museum Way, off Park St. *(406) 723-7211.* *Apr–Oct: 9am–5:30pm daily (to 9pm Jun–Aug).*

xterior of the Museum of the Rockies, Bozeman

## 3ozeman ⓲

27,500. 2000 ommerce Way, (406) 586-5421.

SITUATED IN THE heart of the Gallatin Valley, Bozeman es in the middle of a sacred ioux Indian hunting ground, vhich is now the state's most roductive agricultural region. ounded in the 1860s, the city ; one of the few Montana owns where the economy nd history are not based on nining or railroads. Its pre- ent prominence is due nainly to the Montana State Iniversity. Established in 893, it is the state's largest niversity and houses the **luseum of the Rockies**. 'he museum takes visitors nrough four billion years of arth's history, delving into verything from displays of inosaurs and dinosaur eggs nearthed in Montana Plains, o pioneer history, Indian rtifacts, and Western art. A lanetarium presents astron- my and laser light shows.

Downtown's tree-lined treets are pleasant to stroll nrough. Visitors can also earn about local history t the **Gallatin Pioneer luseum**, housed in the ormer county jail.

Bozeman is also a base for arious activities based in the urrounding countryside. The eadwaters of the Missouri River, the longest river in he US, are formed by the onfluence of the Jefferson, Madison, and Gallatin Rivers, vhich come together 40 miles 64 km) northwest of 3ozeman. All three smaller ivers are famous for fishing nd whitewater rafting.

**Museum of the Rockies**
600 W Kagy Blvd on the Montana State University Campus. *(406) 994-2251. May–Sep: 8am–8pm daily; Oct–Apr: 9am–5pm Mon–Sat, 12:30–5pm Sun. Thnksg., Dec 25.*

**Gallatin Pioneer Museum**
317 W Main St. *(406) 522-8122. mid-May–mid-Sep: 10am–4:30pm Mon–Sat; mid-Sep–mid-May: 11am–4pm Tue–Fri, 1–4pm Sat. public hols.*

## Billings ⓴

*90,000.*
*815 S 27th St, (406) 245-4111.*
www.billingschamber.com

FOUNDED BY the Northern Pacific Railroad in 1882, and now Montana's largest city, Billings was named after the railroad company's president. In just a few months, Billings grew into a bustling community of 2,000 people. Visitors can get a feel of the town's frontier days, and of Montana's proud cowboy traditions, from the Wild West paintings and sculptures displayed in the **Yellowstone Art Gallery**. The gallery is located in the old county jail.

However, the most striking feature of Billings is the Rimrocks, a 400-ft (122-m) high sandstone wall that runs the length of the city along the Yellowstone River.

Outside the city the scenery is even more spectacular, especially along the Beartooth Highway that runs southwest toward Yellowstone National Park *(see pp584–5)*. The 65-mile (105-km) section of highway between Red Lodge and the Wyoming border has been rated among the country's most breathtaking driving routes.

**Yellowstone Art Museum**
401 N 27th St. *(406) 256-6804. 10am–5pm Tue–Sat (until 8pm on Thu), noon–5pm Sun. public hols.*

## Little Bighorn Battlefield National Monument ㉑

*Exit 510 off I-90, Hwy 212, Crow Agency. (406) 638-3204.*
www.nps.gov/libi

LOCATED ON the Crow Indian Reservation, this battlefield preserves the site of a key moment in American history, known as "Custer's Last Stand." In June 1876, the impetuous US Army Lieutenant Colonel George Armstrong Custer *(see p446)* led his troop of 210 soldiers of the 7th Cavalry in an attack on a large Indian encampment along the Little Bighorn River. Almost immediately they were surrounded by more than 2,000 combined Sioux and Cheyenne Indian warriors under the leadership of legendary Chief Sitting Bull. Custer's soldiers were wiped out. A sandstone marker stands above the soldiers' mass grave, and a small museum describes the disastrous battle.

**Memorial to Custer's Last Stand, Little Bighorn Battlefield**

# Wyoming

THE WYOMING STATE INSIGNIA, an image of a cowboy waving his Stetson hat while riding on the back of a bucking horse, says it all. This is classic cowboy country, a land of wide-open grasslands stretching for miles in every direction, where fewer than a half-million people inhabit an area of nearly 100,000 sq miles (260,000 sq km). For visitors, the main draws of Wyoming lie in its northwestern corner, where the twin spectacles of Yellowstone and Grand Teton National Parks attract some three million visitors annually.

**Buffalo Bill Historical Center, Cody**

## Cody 22

*9,000. 836 Sheridan Ave, (307) 587-2777.*

CODY WAS FOUNDED by Wild West impresario "Buffalo Bill" Cody in 1896. Long the symbol of the American West, the city maintains its frontier look and is home to two museums that document this unique era. The smaller of these is **Trail Town**, a homespun collection of artifacts and buildings assembled on the original site of Cody. One highlight here is a log cabin reputedly used as a hideout by outlaws Butch Cassidy and the Sundance Kid.

Cody's main attraction, however, is the **Buffalo Bill Historical Center**, a 240,000-sq-ft (22,300-sq-m) complex of galleries that trace the natural, cultural, and military history of the Wild West. It holds more than 500 weapons, a superb collection of Western art, and Plains Indians artifacts, as well as a museum on Buffalo Bill himself.

In keeping with Buffalo Bill's pursuit of public spectacle, Cody's other great attraction is the **Cody Night Rodeo**, the nation's longest-running rodeo, held daily between late June and August.

### Buffalo Bill Historical Center

*720 Sheridan Ave. (307) 587-4771. Jun–Sep 15: 7am–8pm; Sep 16–Oct: 8am–5pm; Nov–Mar: 10am–3pm Tue–Sun; Apr: 10am–5pm daily; May: 8am–8pm daily. Jan 1, Thanksgiving, Dec 25.*

## Yellowstone National Park 23

*See pp584–5.*

## Jackson 24

*9,000. 532 N Cache St, (307) 733-3316.*

A POPULAR STOP since the days of the fur-trapping mountain men, Jackson is perhaps Wyoming's most visited city. Located at the southern entrance to Grand Teton and Yellowstone National Parks, much of its natural beauty is giving way to vacation homes and ski resorts. But Jackson retains its Wild West ambience despite the boutiques and art galleries that surround its tree-lined central square, and the congested summer traffic.

Alongside the national parks, dude ranches, and Wild West re-enactments, the main attraction is wildlife. The 25,000-acre (10,120-ha) **National Elk Refuge**, stretching between Jackson and the Grand Teton National Park, is home to some 7,500 native elk that congregate here in winter. Its entrance lies one mile (1.6 km) northeast of Jackson. Guided tours on horse-drawn sleighs are offered between November and April. In summer, the main gondola at Jackson Hole Ski Area (rated as one of the country's most challenging) lifts sightseers over 4,000 ft (1,219 m) to the top of Rendezvous Peak for a grand panorama.

### National Elk Refuge

*E Broadway at Elk Refuge Rd. (307) 733-9212. 8am–5pm daily (until 7pm Memorial Day–Labor Day). Thnksg., Dec 25. sleigh rides.*

### BUFFALO BILL

One of the most colorful Wild West figures, William Frederick Cody (1846–1917) started out as a teenage rider for the Pony Express. He then served as US Army scout during the Indian Wars. When the war ended in 1865, he began supplying buffalo meat to workers of the transcontinental railroad, earning himself the nickname "Buffalo Bill." Cody was the model for a series of newspaper stories and "dime novels" written by Ned Buntline. The real-life Buffalo Bill soon parlayed his credentials into worldwide fame and fortune. Star of a spectacular circus in which historical scenes were acted out by cowboys and Indians, including such figures as Chief Sitting Bull, Cody toured the world between 1883 and World War I. Despite his fortune, by 1913 he was bankrupt, and died four years later in Denver *(see pp588–9)*.

**Statue of Buffalo Bill**

# Grand Teton National Park ㉕

Moose. Grand Teton National Park Headquarters, (307) 739-3300.
www.nps.gov/grte

THE YOUNGEST peaks in the Rockies, the Grand Tetons are among the sharpest and most dramatic mountains in the world. Their silver granite peaks rise over a mile above the lush Snake River Valley of Jackson Hole, all of which has been protected within the boundaries of the 485-sq-mile (1,256-sq-km) Grand Teton National Park. There are miles of hiking trails that lead to numerous glaciers and lakes. Wildlife, such as elk, bison, and bears, abound. In summer, kayakers and rafters float the Snake River, while powerboats and canoes take more leisurely cruises on Jackson and Jenny Lakes. In winter, all hiking trails are open to skiers who make their way through the wilderness.

**A view of the Grand Teton summits and fall colors**

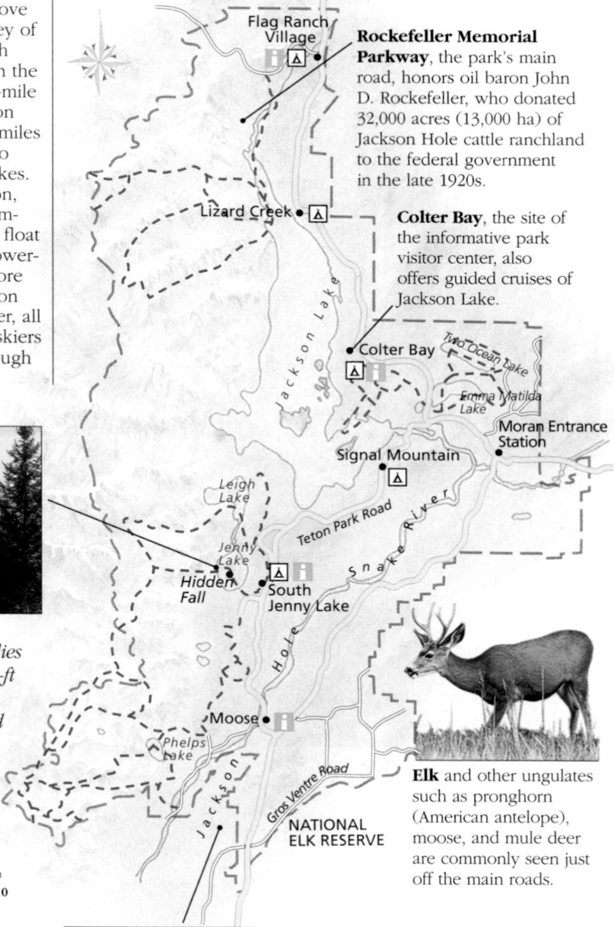

**Rockefeller Memorial Parkway**, the park's main road, honors oil baron John D. Rockefeller, who donated 32,000 acres (13,000 ha) of Jackson Hole cattle ranchland to the federal government in the late 1920s.

**Colter Bay**, the site of the informative park visitor center, also offers guided cruises of Jackson Lake.

**Jenny Lake**
*The popular Jenny Lake lies at the base of the 13,770-ft (4,197-m) Grand Teton. Trails lead along forested shores to quiet beaches, with the mountains reflecting in the distance.*

**Elk** and other ungulates such as pronghorn (American antelope), moose, and mule deer are commonly seen just off the main roads.

km 10

miles 10

**KEY**

- Park boundary
- Trail
- Camping
- Major road
- Unpaved road

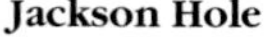

**Jackson Hole**
*Frontier fur trappers referred to a large valley ringed by mountains as a "hole." This valley of the Snake River runs between the Grand Teton and Gros Ventre Mountains, upstream from Jackson.*

# Yellowstone National Park ㉓

Official park sign

One of the marvels of the world, and the country's oldest national park, this wild wonderland spreads across the three states of Wyoming, Montana, and Idaho. Its heart is a volcanic plateau at an average elevation of 8,000 ft (2,438 m), housing over 10,000 hot springs and geysers – more than half of the world's total. Alongside the spectacular shows of geothermal activity, it has dense forests, towering peaks, deep river canyons, and enough outdoor recreation to last a lifetime. The 175-mile (282-km) Grand Loop Road does a full circuit of the main sights. Lodging is often booked solid, so visitors should reserve in advance.

An elk crossing the road in the park

Mammoth Hot Springs
Gardiner
Roaring
Steamboat Geyser
West Entrance
Madison
Madison
20
89
Great Fountain Geyser
Grand Prismatic Spring
MT
ID
Old Faithful
Lone Star Geyser
Firehole
Shoshone Lake
Approximate Caldera Boundary

**★ Mammoth Hot Springs**
*Hundreds of geothermal springs bubble up in Yellowstone, forming colored pools of boiling hot, mineral-rich water. The mineral content drapes delicate curtains of marble-like travertine over the cascading terraces of stone.*

**Grand Prismatic Spring**
*The 370-ft (113-m) wide Grand Prismatic Spring lies close to Old Faithful. The rainbow-colored hot spring, lining the bank of the Firehole River, is one of the world's largest.*

**★ Old Faithful Geyser**
*Named for its precise 90-minute eruption cycle, Old Faithful is the park's icon. Its steaming plume shoots as high as 120–180 ft (36–55 m) and lasts 2 to 5 minutes. Visitors line up on the wooden boardwalk to watch it spurt nearly 8,400 gallons (31,797 liters) of water per eruption.*

**Bison**
*With over 3,000 bison, Yellowstone has the world's largest herd. They roam freely across the park, often even disrupting traffic. Despite their docile appearance, bison can be dangerous, so visitors should avoid contact with them or any other wild animal.*

### VISITORS' CHECKLIST

US 26 in Moose. *YNP Headquarters, Mammoth Hot Springs, (307) 344-7381.* *year-round, but most facilities & roads are closed from October to May due to winter snows. The only open road is US 212, along the northern edge, between Gardiner & Cooke City, Montana.* www.nps.gov/yell

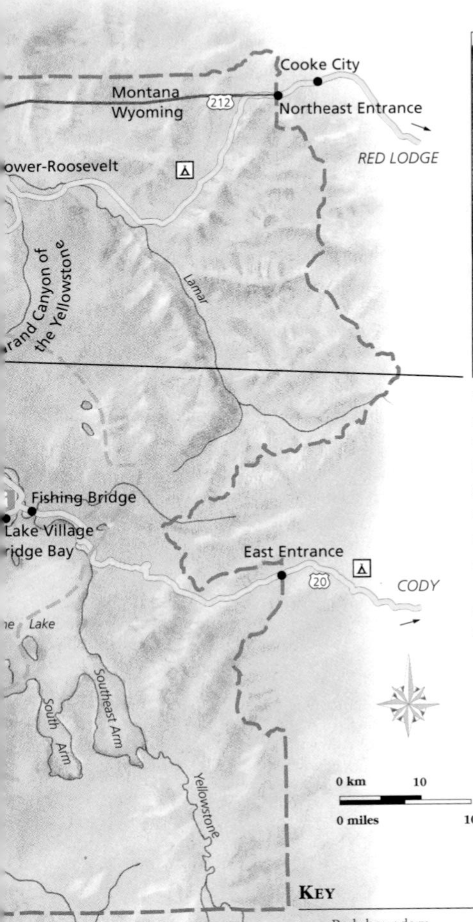

**★ Grand Canyon**
*Plunging 500 ft (152 m) in a pair of falls – Upper and Lower Falls – the Yellowstone River has carved this 20-mile (32-km) long canyon into the mineral-rich yellow and orange rhyolite rock. Many trails along its rim offer splendid vistas. "Uncle Tom's Trail" drops down a steep staircase on to a platform, offering a close-up view of the falls.*

### KEY

- Park boundary
- Park information
- Camping
- Ferry
- Geyser
- Major road
- State border

### STAR SIGHTS

★ **Grand Canyon**

★ **Mammoth Hot Springs**

★ **Old Faithful Geyser**

**Bears**
*Bears are plentiful in the park. Black bears are the most common, and more than 200 grizzlies inhabit its wilder reaches. Most animals avoid contact with humans, and rangers advise that humans should avoid any contact with bears.*

The Medicine Wheel on Medicine Mountain, the Bighorn Scenic Byway (US 14)

## Bighorn Mountains 26

**Bighorn National Forest** (307) 674-2600.

STANDING AT the western edge of the historic plains of the Powder River Basin, the Bighorn Mountains were named for the bighorn sheep that were once abundant here. Crowned by the 13,175-ft (4,016-m) Cloud Peak, the mountains are crossed by a pair of very scenic highways, US 16 in the south (the old Yellowstone Trail) and US 14 in the north, which divides into two forks. The northernmost section of US 14 climbs past one of the country's most enigmatic archaeological sites, the **Medicine Wheel**, an 80-ft (24-m) diameter stone circle, which is located 27 miles (43 km) east of Lovell. This ancient circle is held sacred by Native Sioux and Cheyenne Indians, and offers a vast panorama from its 10,000-ft (3,048-m) elevation.

## Devil's Tower National Monument 27

(307) 467-5283.
www.nps.gov/deto/home.htm

RISING OVER 1,200 ft (366 m) above the surrounding plains, Devil's Tower is a flat-topped volcanic plug that looks like a giant tree stump. Featured in the 1977 Steven Spielberg movie *Close Encounters of the Third Kind*, this geological landmark is located in Wyoming's north-eastern corner, looming over the banks of the Belle Fourche River. Set aside as a national monument by President Theodore Roosevelt in 1906, Devil's Tower (also known as Bear's Lodge) is a sacred site of worship for many Native Americans. The rolling hills of this 1,347-acre (545-ha) park are covered with pine forests, deciduous wood-lands, and prairie grasslands, and abound in deer, prairie dogs, and other wildlife. The site's vertical rock walls and scenic trails are a magnet for rock-climbers and hikers.

## Casper 28

50,000. 330 S Center St, (307) 234-5362.
www.casperwyoming.info

LOCATED IN the heart of Wyoming, Casper has been the center of the state's large petroleum industry since 1890. Surrounded by miles of broad, flat plains, this large, busy city grew up around the 1860s Fort Caspar, now a historical site and museum, known as the **Fort Caspar Museum**. Many of the fort buildings have been reconstructed at the point where the historic Oregon Trail *(see p450)* crossed the North Platte River, west of downtown. The museum features a variety of cultural and natural history exhibits pertaining to central Wyoming.

North and west of Casper lie miles of arid badlands, including such sites as the legendary "Hole in the Wall," where outlaws such as Butch Cassidy had hideouts. More accessible to visitors is the weirdly eroded forest of figures known as "Hell's Half Acre," located 35 miles (56 km) west of town on the south side of US 20.

**Fort Caspar Museum**
4001 Fort Caspar Rd. (307) 235-8462. *daily, hours vary.*

A view of the exterior of Fort Caspar Museum, Casper

## ‹uernsey 29

‹ 1,150. 90 S Wyoming St, (307) ‹6-2715.

‹ET ALONG THE banks of the ‹ North Platte River, this is a ‹nall town whose size belies ‹wealth of historical interest. ‹st south of town are two of ‹e most palpable reminders ‹the pioneer migrations ‹estward along the Oregon ‹ail. The **Oregon Trail Ruts ‹ate Historic Site** preserves ‹set of 4–6-ft (1–1.8-m) deep ‹ouges carved by wagon ‹heels into the soft riverside ‹ndstone. A mile south, the ‹egister Cliff has been ‹scribed with the names of ‹undreds of explorers, fur ‹appers, and Oregon Trail ‹oneers who crossed the ‹ea in the mid-1800s.

Evocative as these sights are, ‹uernsey's most important ‹storic spot is the **Fort ‹aramie National Historic ‹te**, a reconstruction of a fur-‹apping and US cavalry out-‹ost. Between its founding in ‹e 1830s and its abandonment ‹1890s, the fort was a prime ‹oint of contact between ‹uropeans, Americans, and ‹ative Americans. Many of the ‹uildings have been restored, ‹nd costumed interpreters act ‹ut roles from the fort's history.

**‹ Fort Laramie National ‹istoric Site**

‹ 26. (307) 837-2221.

‹ May–Sep: 8am–7pm daily; Oct–‹r: 8am–4:30pm daily. Jan 1, ‹anksgiving, Dec 25.

## ‹aramie 30

‹ 27,200. 800 S 3rd St, ‹07) 745-7339.

HOME TO THE main state university campus, the ‹nall city of Laramie exudes ‹ infectious youthful vitality, ‹hich is rare in other ‹yoming cities. Located east ‹f downtown at an elevation ‹f 7,200 ft (2,195 m), the ‹niversity of Wyoming is ‹e highest college in the ‹ountry. The campus is ‹ominated by the strikingly ‹odern **American Heritage ‹enter**, an art museum and library documenting Wyoming history and culture. The town also housed Wyoming's first prison, now restored to its 1880s condition, when Butch Cassidy and other outlaws served time here. Located west of downtown, the old prison is now the centerpiece of the **Wyoming Territorial Prison State Historic Park**, which includes a re-creation of a frontier town.

The area around Laramie is rich historically and scenically. The 50-mile (80-km) stretch of the Lincoln Highway between Laramie and Cheyenne preserves part of the first transcontinental road in the US. To the west of Laramie, Hwy 130 follows the Snowy Range Scenic Byway through the beautiful Medicine Bow Mountains.

**Statue of cowboy, Old West Museum, Cheyenne**

**American Heritage Center**

22nd St & Willett Dr. (307) 766-2570. 7:30am–4:30pm daily; Labor Day–Memorial Day: 8am–5pm Mon–Fri, 11am–5pm Sat. public hols.

**Wyoming Territorial Prison State Historic Park**

975 Snowy Range Rd. (307) 745-6161. May–Sep: 10am–5pm daily.

## Cheyenne 31

55,000. 121 W 15th St, Suite 202, (307) 778-3133.

FOUNDED IN 1867 as a US Army fort along the newly constructed Union Pacific Railroad, Cheyenne later matured from a typical Wild West town into Wyoming's state capital and the largest city in the area.

The 10-day Cheyenne Frontier Days festival, held every summer, brings to life the old days with parades, Indian pow-wows, horse races, and the world's largest outdoor rodeo. Visitors can also get a sense of Cheyenne heritage at the **Frontier Days Old West Museum**, which displays hundreds of antique saddles and wagons, such as the historic Deadwood Stage. During the 1870s and 1880s, this coach made a three-day trip between Cheyenne and the gold mines at Deadwood in South Dakota *(see p446)*.

Downtown Cheyenne features two landmark buildings – the 1917 State Capitol and the former Union Pacific Depot, an elaborate Romanesque-style structure that has been restored to its original 1886 splendor. The western edge of Cheyenne features Warren Air Force Base, the primary command center of the US arsenal of nuclear-tipped intercontinental ballistic missiles, which are known as ICBMs.

**Frontier Days Old West Museum**

Frontier Park on N Carey Ave. (307) 778-7290. 9am–5pm Mon–Fri, 10am–5pm Sat–Sun. public hols.

**The prison in Wyoming Territorial Park, Laramie**

# Colorado

THE NAME "COLORADO" dates back to the 16th century, when Spanish explorers first used the moniker in reference to the red rock formations that skirt the Front Range of the Rocky Mountains. Over 400 years later, the term conjures images of majestic peaks and snow-clad ski slopes, with good reason. Colorado is the most mountainous state in the US, with 54 summits that measure more than 14,000 ft (4,267 m) above sea level. Officially a state since 1876, during the past century Colorado has evolved from a sparsely inhabited mining and trapping country to become the most populous business center for the Rocky Mountain region.

**Denver skyline with the Rockies forming a backdrop**

## Denver 32

*554,600.* *1555 California St, Suite 300.* *(303) 892-1112.* www.denver.org

FOUNDED AT THE junction of the Platte River and Cherry Creek as a supply base for miners in 1858, Denver's mild climate attracted settlers. Soon after, it emerged as the region's primary trade and population center, and eventually became the state capital in 1876.

In the new millennium, abundant parklands, a vibrant downtown, and a number of well-known museums define this growing city. Denver is set picturesquely at the foot-hills of the Rocky Mountains.

### Civic Center Park

Between Colfax Ave & 14th Ave Pkwy, Broadway & Bannock St. **Colorado History Museum** 1300 Broadway. *(303) 866-3682.* *10am–5pm Mon–Sat, noon–5pm Sun.* www.coloradohistory.org **Denver Art Museum** 100 W 14th Ave Pkwy. *(720) 865-5000.* *10am–5pm Tue–Sat (until 9pm Wed), noon–5pm Sun.* *public hols.* www.denverartmuseum.org

The geographical, cultural, and political heart of Denver, the Civic Center Park is dominated by the gold-domed **Colorado State Capitol**. This ornate structure houses the state legislature and governor's office. To the south stands the **Colorado History Museum**, where a comprehensive, wall-mounted timeline traces the state's history. Rotating exhibits also focus on varied aspects of Colorado's past. Continuing clockwise around the park is the tiled, seven-story high **Denver Art Museum**. This is one of the city's best museums and has impressive collections of both Western as well as Native American objects. Its latest addition is the ultra-modern landmark Frederic C. Hamilton Building. Finally, a block west of the park is the **Denver Mint**, one of four mints in the country, which presses more than ten billion coins in a year.

### Molly Brown House

1340 Pennsylvania St. *(303) 832-4092.* *10am–4pm Tue–Sat, noon–4pm Sun (& Mon Jun–Aug).*

This restored mansion, now a museum, was the home of "The Unsinkable Molly Brown," so-called for her survival of the *Titanic* in 1912. Margaret Tobin Brown was a flamboyant and persistent woman whose life story exemplifies the boom-and-bust backdrop that is Colorac history. Born in 1867 in Hannibal, Missouri, she cam west to the boomtown of Leadville, Colorado, in 1886, where she married a well-known mining man, J.J. Brown. When the silver mark collapsed, J.J. persevered unt he laid claim to one of Colorado's richest veins of gold in 1893. The couple the moved to Denver, where the lived in luxury, despite not being accepted by the city's elite. Her courageous rescue efforts during the sinking of the *Titanic* made her a nation celebrity. With this came the society approval that had pre-viously eluded her. However, she died in New York in 193 penniless and alone. Later, in the 1960s, she was immor-talized on stage and screen.

### Larimer Square & Lowe Downtown (LoDo)

**Larimer Square** Larimer St betweer 14th & 15th Sts. *(303) 685-814* www.larimersquare.com **LoDo District** Bordered by Market & Wynkoop St. *(303) 628-5428.*

The birthplace of Denver, Larimer Square remains a commercial and cultural hub for the city. Lying adjacent to Confluence Park, where the Platte River and Cherry Creel meet, this was the site where white settlers first set up camp. The square bustles with activity both day and night, mainly because of its many boutiques, galleries, bars, and restaurants.

After a disastrous fire in 1863, wooden structures wer prohibited. As a result, red-brick Victorian architecture dominates both the square and the neighboring Lower Downtown area (nicknamed

**Larimer Square, the birthplace of Denver**

LoDo"). Centered on Union tation, LoDo experienced a enaissance of sorts in the 990s, thanks to the arrival of he city's professional baseball eam and their Coors Field tadium. Today, this is a avorite club-hopping district, vell known for its smoky jazz oints, dance clubs, and amous microbreweries.

### City Park

etween 17th & 26th Avenues from ork St to Colorado Blvd. *(303) 64-2500.* *24 hours daily.*
**enver Zoo** 2300 Steele St. *(303) 76-4800.* *Apr–Sep: 9am–6pm aily; Oct–Mar: 10am–5pm daily.* www.denverzoo.org
**enver Museum of Nature & cience** 2001 Colorado Blvd. *(303) 370-8339.* *9am–5pm aily.* *Dec 25.* www.dmns.org

.bout 2 miles (3 km) east f downtown is Denver's argest park, which offers a vide range of activities. It has well-stocked fishing lake, unning trails, a golf course, hady picnic areas, and sports elds. The park also contains ne city's two most popular ttractions – the **Denver Zoo** nd the **Denver Museum of Nature and Science**. The oo, the seventh largest in the ountry, is noted especially for its innovative animal habitats, which include the world's largest indoor Komodo dragon exhibit. The Denver Museum of Nature and Science, on the eastern edge of the City Park, features a wide range of exhibits.

### Black American West Museum & Heritage Center

3091 California St.
*(303) 292-2566.*
*Jun–Aug: 10am–5pm daily; Sep–May: 10am–2pm Wed–Fri, 10am–5pm Sat & Sun.* *Jan 1, Easter, Thanksgiving, Dec 25.*

A hidden gem in the Five Points neighborhood, this fascinating museum is housed in a Victorian home, previously the abode of Justina Ford. In 1902 she became Denver's first female African-American doctor. The museum's founder, Paul Stewart, opened the museum in 1971 to commemorate Ford's life and to educate people about the African-American contribution to the American West. The museum's collection includes letters, photographs, and assorted memorabilia that effectively re-create the incredible stories of African Americans in pioneer times.

**Black American West Museum and Heritage Center**

### Museo de las Americas

861 Santa Fe Dr. *(303) 571-4401.*
*10am–5pm Tue–Sat.* *Jan 1, July 4, Thanksgiving, Dec 25.*

Founded in the early 1990s, the Museo de las Americas is a touchstone for Denver's sizable Hispanic population. The first such museum in the region, it relates Mexican and Latin American history, as well as offers fascinating glimpses of their artistic and cultural traditions. The permanent collections are dedicated to the pre-Colombian Aztec as well as the Colonial period. Among the exhibits on display are a replica of an Aztec Sun Stone and a wall-size mural of the Aztec metropolis Tenochtitlán.

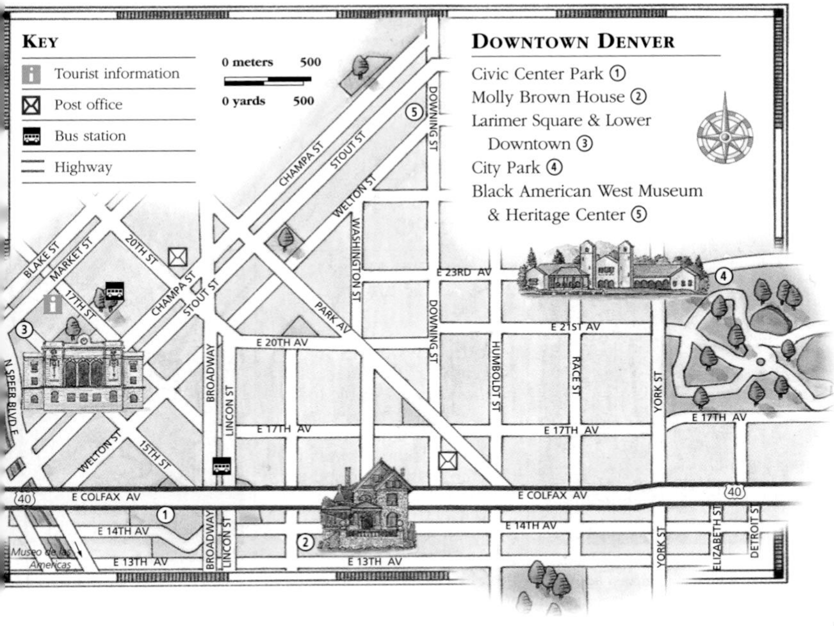

**The attractive University of Colorado, Boulder**

## Boulder 33

*95,000. 2440 Pearl St, (303) 442-2911.*

An idyllic college town set at the foot of the Rockies, Boulder is best known for its bohemian culture, liberal politics, and thriving high-tech industry. The city was founded in 1858 as a commercial hub for the miners and farmers who settled nearby. After Colorado gained statehood, the **University of Colorado** (CU) was established here, at an altitude of 5,400 ft (1,646 m). Since then, the attractive Victorian-era campus and its coinciding vibrant culture have defined Boulder, attracting intellectuals, radicals, and individualists.

Northwest of the campus, the pedestrian-only Pearl Street Mall, lined with lively restaurants, bars, and shops, is the stage for many street performers. Nearby, the Hill District forms the center of Boulder's energetic nightlife and music scene. The I.M. Pei-designed **National Center for Atmospheric Research** is to the southeast. The center also features an art gallery and is a start-off point for some lovely nature trails.

**Cycling across Boulder Canyon, minutes from downtown Boulder**

West of Boulder, the jagged and forested crags of the Rockies provide a scenic backdrop to the city below. The nearby Flatiron Range, Eldorado Canyon, and Indian Peaks Wilderness Area are popular with climbers, hikers, and backpackers.

**National Center for Atmospheric Research**
1850 Table Mesa Dr. *(303) 497-1174. 8am–5pm Mon–Fri, 9am–4pm Sat–Sun.*

**Indian Peaks Wilderness Area**
70 miles (113 km) W of Boulder, US Forest Service. *(303) 444-6600. 24 hours daily.*

## Golden 34

*18,000. 1010 Washington Ave, (303) 279-3113, (800) 590-3113.*

Golden's history as an early nexus of trade and politics remains visible today. Its origins date to the early 1840s, when hunter Rufus Sage, one of the first Anglos to camp in this area, spotted flakes of gold in the waters of Clear Creek. His findings led to an influx of Easterners in the 1850s, and by the 1860s the city emerged as a regional railroad hub and was declared the capital of the newly formed Colorado Territory. The original Territorial Capitol in the Loveland Building, which forms the center of downtown, dates from that period.

Golden's past is also visible at the impeccably restored **Astor House Museum.** Several rooms here recreate the 1867–1908 era when it served as a boarding house. The Old Armory nearby is the largest cobblestone building in the US. The 3-acre (1.2-ha) **Clear Creek History Park** houses many historic structures such as a 1876 schoolhouse. The town is also home to **Coors Brewery** where visitors can glimpse the malting, brewing, and packaging processes and sample the famous beer.

The gravesite and museum of William "Buffalo Bill" Cody *(see p582)* overlooks the city on Lookout Mountain. An observation deck here offers beautiful panoramic views.

**Astor House Museum**
822 12th St. *(303) 278-3557. 10am–4:30pm Tue–Sat. Jan 1, Jul 4, Nov 27, Dec 24–25.*
www.astorhousemuseum.org

**Clear Creek History Park**
11th St between Arapahoe & Cheyenne St. *(303) 277-2337. May & Sep: 10am–4:30pm Sat; Jun–Aug: 10am–4:30pm Tue–Sat; Oct–Apr: by appointment only.*
www.clearcreekhistorypark.org

**Cobblestone exterior of the armory, near Astor House, Golden**

## daho Springs & Georgetown 35

2,000. 2060 Miner St, '03) 567-4382.

SITUATED WITHIN an hour's drive from downtown enver, the well-preserved 360s mining towns of Idaho prings and Georgetown are est known for their unblemhed Victorian architecture, unning mountains, and ome excellent museums.

Idaho Springs was founded 1 1859 and quickly emerged s a mining center when the urrounding streams and iountains were found to be xceptional sources of gold. he town's mining history is aced through exhibits that iclude equipment, payroll ecords, receipts, and photoraphs at the **Argo Gold line, Mill, and Museum**.

Georgetown, another minig town set up during the iid-19th century Gold Rush, 15 miles (24 km) west of laho Springs. It is a vision of ictorian elegance tucked into n alpine valley 8,500 ft 2,591 m) above sea level.

One of the attractions here the **Hamill House Museum**, vhich was built in 1867. It vas enlarged in 1879 and ow presents the public with ie elegant, spacious lifestyle f a silver-mining magnate. here's also a carriage house, ffice building, and privy.

South from Idaho Springs, ımmer drivers can wind ieir way up the highest road 1 the United States. The lount Evans Scenic Byway pllows Hwy 103 and Hwy 5 through the Pike National Forest toward the 14,264-ft (4,347-m) high summit of Mount Evans.

**Victorian architecture in downtown Georgetown**

### Argo Gold Mine, Mill, & Museum

Just W of Idaho Springs, S of I-70, exit from 241A. *(303) 567-2421.* *mid-Apr–mid-Oct: 9am–6pm daily.* www.historicargotours. com

### Hamill House Museum

305 Argentine St. *(303) 569-2840.* *summer: 10am–4pm daily; Sep–Dec 25: noon–4pm Sat–Sun.* www.historicgeorgetown.org

## Rocky Mountain National Park 36

1000 US Hwy 36. *(970) 586-1206.* *24 hours daily. (Trail Ridge Road closed between Nov–May).* www.nps.gov/romo

THIS NATIONAL PARK offers some of the most spectacular mountain views in the United States. Established in 1915, the park spreads across 416 sq miles (1,077 sq km) and includes 114 named peaks that measure more than 10,000 ft (3,048 m). The tallest of these, Longs Peak, is 14,255 ft (4,345 m) high. Snaking through the alpine scenery is the Continental Divide, which separates the western part of the US from the east, and where snowmelt flows down and eventually empties into the Atlantic and Pacific Oceans. Almost 150 lakes originate here, some occupying pastoral, forested settings, while others are perched on almost inaccessible shelves, high in the wilderness.

The majority of the two million annual visitors to the park drive 50 miles (80 km) on **Trail Ridge Road**, a spectacular stretch of highway that showcases the park's brilliant panoramas. After leaving the resort environment of Estes Park, the road climbs to its highest point of 12,183 ft (3,713 km) near the center of the park, before descending into a scenic valley north of the small town of Grand Lake. The tundra in the park's high country is an island of arctic vegetation surrounded by plants of lower latitudes. Wildlife watchers are likely to see elk, moose, black bear, and bighorn sheep.

Popular summer activities within the park include hiking, biking, backpacking, and fishing, while winter attracts snowshoers and skiers. Although there are no hotels inside the park, there are five fee-based campgrounds and numerous accommodations in both Estes Park and Grand Lake.

**view of the myriad peaks from the pinnacle of Trail Ridge Road, Rocky Mountain National Park**

Pikes Peak Cog Railway atop the mountain, Manitou Springs

## Manitou Springs 37

*5,500.* *354 Manitou Ave, (800) 642-2567.*
www.manitousprings.org

THIS CHARMING Victorian community attracts weekend visitors who come to explore its art galleries, shops, and restaurants. A product of the Gold Rush of the 1850s, it later became a popular spa town because of the natural mineral springs found here. Manitou (meaning "Full of Spirit" in Native Algonquian) is one of the largest national historic districts in the country. It is famous for two attractions that predate it by centuries, the **Cave of the Winds**, an impressive limestone cavern (now with light shows and tours) and the **Manitou Springs Cliff Dwellings**, dating from 1100 to 1300.

Manitou Springs is also the gateway to Pikes Peak *(see p570)*. The **Pikes Peak Cog Railway**, a historic train that climbs to the summit of the 14,110-ft (4,300-m) mountain, has its depot here.

**Cave of the Winds**
US 24, exit 141. *(719) 685-5444.*
*May–Sep: 9am–9pm daily; Oct–Apr: 10am–5pm daily.*
www.caveofthewinds.com

**Pikes Peak Cog Railway**
515 Ruxton Ave. *(719) 685-5401.*
*Apr–Oct: several departures daily; Nov–Dec: limited schedule.* *Jan–Mar.* www.cograilway.com

**Manitou Springs Cliff Dwellings**
3 Kreg Lane. *(800) 354-7791.*
*check for times.*
www.cliffdwellingsmuseum.com

Clocktower, Manitou Springs

## Colorado Springs 38

*380,000.* *515 S Cascade Ave, (719) 635-7506.*

ESTABLISHED BY railroad baron William Jackson Palmer in 1871, Colorado Springs nestles below the looming beauty of Pikes Peak. The first resort town in the western US, it was initially nicknamed "Little London" because of the scores of English tourists that it attracted. The **Garden of the Gods** on the west side of town lures hikers and climbers with its awe-inspiring red sandstone formations, rife with arches, overhangs, stately walls, and precarious balancing rocks. One of the most recognizable – and most photographed – formations is Kissing Camels, so named for its resemblance to a pair of lip-locked dromedaries. Also located here is the Rock Ledge Ranch Historic Site, a preserved ranch that dates to the 1880s. The Italian Renaissance-style **Broadmoor Resort** *(see p603)* on Lake Circle, initially opened in 1918, epitomizes this era.

In the 1950s, Colorado Spring was chosen to be the home of the prestigious **US Air Force Academy** and the National Missile Defense Headquarters (NORAD). The latter is situated on the city's southwestern fringe, deep within the bomb-proof Cheyenne Mountain.

Culturally more conservativ than Denver *(see pp588–9)*, modern-day Colorado Springs is one of the fastest-growing cities in the US, with rows of houses extending into the foothills to the west, and the vast plains to the east. However, the town continues to retain many aspects of its pas The spirit of the Wild West remains alive even today at the **Pro Rodeo Hall of Fame** which documents the origins of rodeo as well as the storie of prominent American rodeo stars through the ages. The **Colorado Springs Pioneers Museum** presents the area's history in the restored 1903 E Paso County Courthouse.

**Garden of the Gods**
1805 North 30th St. *(719) 634-6666.* *Jun–Aug: 8am–8pm daily; Sep–May: 9am–5pm daily.* *Jan 1, Thnksg., Dec 25.* *only for Rock Ledge Ranch Historic Site.*

**Broadmoor Resort**
1 Lake Dr. *(719) 634-7711.*
*daily, but can vary. Call ahead to check.* www.broadmoor.con

**Pro Rodeo Hall of Fame**
101 Pro Rodeo Dr. *(719) 528-4764.* *9am–5pm daily.* *Jan 1, Easter, Thanksgiving, Dec 25.*
www.prorodeo.org

**Colorado Springs Pioneers Museum**
215 S Tejon St. *(719) 385-5990.*
*Sep–May: 10am–5pm Tue–Sat; Jun–Aug: 10am–5pm Tue–Sat, 1–5pr Sun.* www.cspm.org

Kissing Camels formations, Garden of the Gods in Colorado Springs

e magnifient view over the Royal Gorge Bridge and Park located in Cañon City

## ripple Creek 39

1,200. 513 E Bennett Ave, 9) 689-3315.

NOWN AS "Poverty Gulch" before a gold strike in 90 transformed it, this is e of the best-preserved th-century mining towns in e entire state. The fasci- ting **Mollie Kathleen Gold ine** is the best place to plore the town's mining story. Discovered by Mollie thleen Gortner in 1891, this ld mine on the southwest ce of Pikes Peak is the untry's only vertical-shaft ne that offers tours. Even ough mining operations ded in 1961, gold veins are ll visible on its walls.

The town is anomalous, as e surrounding area is still ned for gold though mining s ceased in most other lorado boomtowns. Its aint charm has faded after w-stakes gambling was galized here in 1990. This, however, is tempered by the fact that most of the casinos are housed in atmospheric storefronts that resemble the sets of a Hollywood Western.

terior of Mollie Kathleen Gold ne, Cripple Creek

### Mollie Kathleen Gold Mine

N Colorado Hwy 67. *(719) 689-2466.* *Apr–Oct: 8am–6pm daily; Nov–Mar: 10am–4pm daily.* www.goldminetours.com

## Cañon City 40

*16,000.* *403 Royal Gorge Blvd, (719) 275-2331, (800) 876-7922.*

A COLORFUL place, blessed with clear skies, sunshine, and spectacular scenery, Cañon City, surprisingly, is also the "Prison Capital of Colorado." It acqired this title in 1876, after it chose to house the state prison instead of the state university. Today, prisons remain a key component of the regional economy. The **Museum of Colorado Prisons**, housed in a former correctional facility, was established in 1871. Just 12 miles (19 km) west of the city stands the well-known **Royal Gorge Bridge & Park**. Etched into the granite bedrock for three million years by the Arkansas River, this beautiful, breathtaking gorge is over 1,000 ft (305 m) from rim to river at its deepest, but only 40 ft (12 m) wide at its base. Traversed by the world's highest suspension bridge and 12 miles (19 km) of railroad – the **Royal Gorge Route Railroad** – the park also attracts whitewater rafters to the challenging stretch of the river raging and foaming below.

### Museum of Colorado Prisons

201 N 1st St. *(719) 269-3015.* *May–Aug: 8:30am–6pm daily; Sep–Apr: 10am–5pm Fri–Sun.* www.prisonmuseum.org

### Royal Gorge Bridge & Park

US Hwy 50. *(888) 333-5597.* *Apr–early Oct: 10am–7pm daily; mid-Oct–Mar: 10am–5pm daily.* www.royalgorgebridge.com **Royal Gorge Route Railroad** *(303) 569-2403.* *Jun–Sep: daily; Oct–Dec & Feb–May: Sat–Sun.* *Jan.*

### WHITEWATER RAFTING IN COLORADO

The best way to enjoy the pristine Colorado wilderness is to take a whitewater rafting trip on the Arkansas River. The picturesque towns of Salida and nearby Buena Vista, 26 miles (42 km) to the north, are hubs for outfitters who offer guided river trips. With about 100 rafting companies in operation, this is the most intensively rafted river in the US. The Colorado River Outfitters Association (303-280-2554), is one of the best sources of information on rafting trips.

Rafting on the Arkansas River, Colorado

# Colorado Ski Resorts 41

One of Colorado's most enduring symbols is of pristine white mountains dotted with skiers. The state's recreational ski industry dates to 1935 when Berthoud Pass, northwest of Denver, became the destination ski resort for pioneering skiers. As the sport's economic potential developed after World War II, many old mining towns emerged as popular ski resort towns. Today the state is undoubtedly the country's skiing capital, with more than 24 resorts. In recent years, other winter sports, such as snowboarding, have become very popular, and most ski mountains now allow snowboarders.

***Steamboat Springs**, the cowboy cousin to the conservative luxury of Aspen, wears its rambunctious Western spirit as a badge of honor. It has some of the state's best snow (a dry, feathery powder), a 3,668-ft (1,118-m) vertical drop, and a total of 142 runs.*

**Max altitude:** *10,564 ft (3,220 m)*

**Geared to:** *all levels*

**Ski level:** 13% 56% 31%

***Aspen**, a favorite of the rich and famous, has more than 200 different runs on three striking mountains. It developed when the Aspen Skiing Company opened its first lift in 1947. Sleek restaurants and boutiques housed behind Victorian-era storefronts complement the splendid ski terrain. Aspen also has a vibrant art and culture scene.*

**Max altitude:** *11,675 ft (3,559 m)*

**Geared to:** *all levels*

**Ski level:** 16% 61% 23%

**Snowmass**, just a 30-minute drive from Aspen, is a complete resort in itself. Larger than all three of Aspen's ski areas combined, it has plenty of wide-open runs.

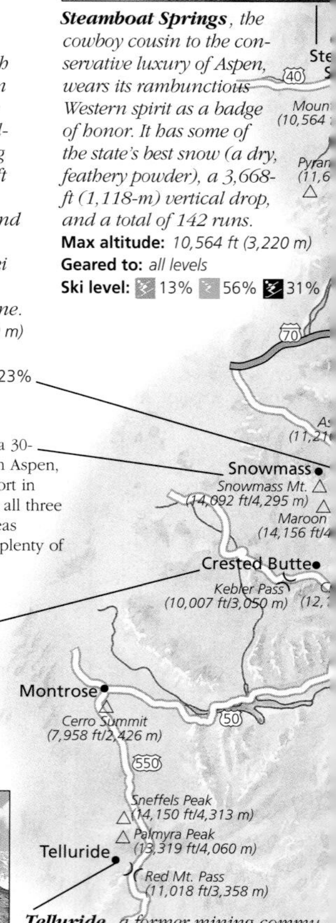

0 km 50

0 miles 50

**Crested Butte** draws serious skiers to its unparalleled expert terrain. The town sits at the base of Mount Crested Butte, with a vertical drop of 2,775 ft (846 m) and 824 acres (333 ha) for "extreme" skiing.

Snowmass

Snowmass Mt. (14,092 ft/4,295 m)

Crested Butte

Kebler Pass (10,007 ft/3,050 m)

Montrose

Cerro Summit (7,958 ft/2,426 m)

Sneffels Peak (14,150 ft/4,313 m)

Palmyra Peak (13,319 ft/4,060 m)

Telluride

Red Mt. Pass (11,018 ft/3,358 m)

***Telluride**, a former mining community, opened as a ski resort in 1971. The nearby valley was once a hideout for outlaw Butch Cassidy. The town is also known for its bohemian politics, lively nightlife, and trails that lead to such scenic areas as Bridal Veil Falls.*

**Max altitude:** *12,255 ft (3,736 m)*

**Geared to:** *all levels*

**Ski level:** 22% 38% 40%

***Winter Park**, Colorado's oldest full-service ski resort, is linked to Denver by the Ski Train – 67 miles (108 km) of track that connect the slopes with LoDo's Union Station. The resort's three ski mountains offer downhill terrain for every skill level, and there are also numerous cross-country trails nearby.*
**Max altitude:** *12,060 ft (3,676 m)*
**Geared to:** *experts*
**Ski level:** 9% 21% 70%

**Keystone**, with its 12-hour ski day, is now famous for being Colorado's best night-skiing resort. Open eight months a year, it has three ski mountains and offers a variety of activities such as snowboarding, ice skating, sleigh rides, and indoor tennis.

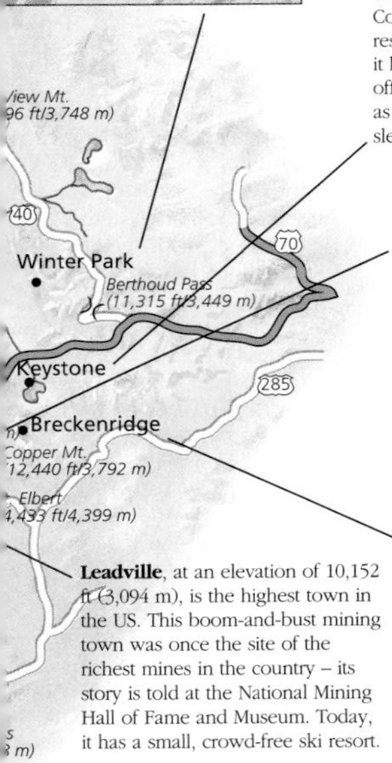

**Copper Mountain** offers some of the most advanced skiing and snowboarding terrain in Colorado, as well as areas for novice and intermediate skiers. Once maligned, the newly re-designed village now brims with shops, bars, and restaurants.

*View Mt.*
*96 ft/3,748 m)*
40
Winter Park
*Berthoud Pass*
*(11,315 ft/3,449 m)*
70
Keystone
285
Breckenridge
*Copper Mt.*
*12,440 ft/3,792 m)*
*Elbert*
*4,433 ft/4,399 m)*

**Leadville**, at an elevation of 10,152 ft (3,094 m), is the highest town in the US. This boom-and-bust mining town was once the site of the richest mines in the country – its story is told at the National Mining Hall of Fame and Museum. Today, it has a small, crowd-free ski resort.

## Ski Resorts & Companies

**Aspen Skiing Company (Aspen-Snowmass)**
*(970) 925-1220, (800) 308-6935. Dec–mid-Apr: 9am–4pm daily.* www.aspensnowmass.com

**Breckenridge Ski Resort**
*(970) 453-6118. late Oct–May: 8:30am–4pm daily.* www.breckenridge.com

**Keystone** *(800) 427-8308. mid-Oct–Apr: 8:30am– 8:30pm daily.* www.keystoneresort.com

**Steamboat Ski Corp.**
*(970) 879-6111. mid-Nov–mid-Apr: 8:30am–4pm daily.* www.steamboat.com

**Telluride Ski Company**
*(800) 801-4832. late Nov–mid-Apr: 8:30am–4pm daily.* www.telski.com

**Vail Mountain** *(800) 404-3535, (970) 476-5601. mid-Nov–Apr: 8:30am–4pm daily.* www.vail.com

**Winter Park** *(970) 726-5514. mid-Nov–late Apr: 8:30am–4pm daily.* www.skiwinterpark.com

**Ski Train** *(303) 296-4754.* ***See also pp598–9.***

***Breckenridge** boasts an interesting history, recreation facilities including ice skating* (above)*, and nightlife. The resort is spread across four peaks on the west side of town.*
**Max altitude:** *12,998 ft (3,962 m)*
**Geared to:** *all levels*
**Ski level:** 13% 32% 55%

***Vail**, the largest single-mountain ski resort in the US, attracts skiers and snowboarders alike. The domain of Native tribes until the 1870s mining boom, the town actually developed when Vail Mountain opened to skiers in 1962. It has more than 2,000 trails and a 3,450-ft (1,052-m) vertical drop.*
**Max altitude:** *11,570 ft (3,527 m)*
**Geared to:** *all levels*
**Ski level:** 18% 29% 53%

### Key

- Major road
- Minor road
- Good for beginners
- Good for intermediate skiers
- Good for advanced skiers
- Peak
- Pass

Great Sand Dunes National Monument & Preserve

## Great Sand Dunes National Monument & Preserve ㊷

11500 Colorado Hwy 150, NE of Alamosa. *(719) 378-6399.* *24 hrs daily.* www.nps.gov/grsa

Named after North America's tallest sand dunes, this unique place will soon become Colorado's newest national park, following the resolution of a long legal battle over water rights in 2002. The dunes sit at the foot of the gnarled Sangre de Cristo Mountains, their sand long since carried to this scenic spot by melting glaciers and the Rio Grande River. This unusual ecosystem is home to several equally unusual animals and insects, such as a species of kangaroo rat that never drinks water, and the Great Sand Dunes tiger beetle.

The park has a campground and a mix of long and short trails. Many visitors scale the dunes, which sometimes measure up to 700 ft (213 m).

## Durango ㊸

*16,000.* *111 South Camino del Rio, (888) 414-0835, (970) 247-0312.*

Once described by American humorist Will Rogers as "out of the way and glad of it," Durango was established in the Animas River Valley in 1881 as a rail station for the mines in the nearby San Juan Mountains. After the mining boom ended, Durango emerged as a major tourism center and cultural symbol of the West. This modern city is today a model of historic preservation, with late-19th-century saloons and hotels lining Main Avenue, and elegant mansions from the same era on Third Street. One thing, however, has changed – diehard mountain bikers, entrepreneurs, and artists have replaced the rugged miners.

Many visitors take a day trip on the **Durango & Silverton Narrow Gauge Railroad**. A fully functional 1882 steam engine, it follows a scenic 50-mile (80-km) journey, traveling from the valley floor to rock ledges en route to the erstwhile mining town of Silverton. Durango's other prime attraction is the great outdoors of the **San Juan National Forest**, where mountain biking is the top sport. Other popular activities are hiking, horseback riding, backpacking, rock-climbing, and river rafting.

**Durango & Silverton Narrow Gauge Railroad & Museum**
479 Main Ave. *(970) 247-2733.* *daily. Hours may vary, call for detail* www.durangotrain.con

**San Juan National Fore**
15 Burnett Court. *(970) 247-48* *24 hrs daily.*

## Mesa Verde National Park ㊹

East of Cortez via US Hwy 160. *(970) 529-4465.* *8am–5pm dail open 5pm to sunset in summer.* www.nps.gov/meve

When it was established 1906, Mesa Verde became the first archaeological site in the US to receive national park status. Tucked into the recesses of canyon walls, the park's defining fea tures are 500 fascinating cliff dwellings last inhabited by tl indigenous Puebloan people before they abandoned them in 1300. The dwellings range from small houses to the 200 room **Cliff Palace** and are some of the most significant archaeological finds in the U.

Park rangers lead tours between April and Novembe to some of the most importa dwellings, including Cliff Palace. Visitors can also explore several structures on their own, including the well preserved Spruce Tree House and Square Tower House, th park's tallest ruin. The **Chap Mesa Archaeological Museum** displays a fascinati collection of pottery and oth artifacts used by Puebloan people in their daily life.

There are also 18 miles (29 km) of hiking trails within th park. One of them, the

Durango & Silverton Narrow Gauge Railroad

troglyph Loop Trail, ers visitors a chance to w ancient rock art. Camp- ; and wildlife viewing cluding foxes, mountain ns, and elk) are among the ıer activities. In winter, ›ss-country skiing and ›wshoeing are popular.

**Chapin Mesa chaeological Museum**
*(970) 529-4631. 8am–5pm daily.*

**ıare Tower House, Mesa Verde tional Park**

## uray ㊺

*800. Adjacent to Ouray Hot ings Pool on North US Hwy 550, 0) 325-4746, (800) 228-1876.*

NICKNAMED THE "Switzerland of America" for its semblance to a village in e Alps, Ouray is located 80 les (128 km) north of ırango. It was named after e Ute chief whose people nted in the area before ld and silver prospectors tablished the town in 1876. oday the entire town is listed the National Register of storic Places, a testament to e number of well-main- ned 19th-century structures ll in existence. Two natural onders – the massive geo- ermal-powered **Ouray Hot rings Pool**, and the stun- ng **Box Canyon Falls**, ıich cascades 285 ft (87 m) wn a natural cliff-side ute – are easily accessible m the town center.

Ouray is also on the **San an Skyway**, a 236-mile 80-km) loop that includes e "Million Dollar Highway" Silverton. Its surrounding wild-lands lure rock- and ice-climbers, four-wheel-drive enthusiasts, and other out-doors adventurers.

**Ouray Hot Springs Pool**
US Hwy 550, at the northern end of Ouray. *(970) 325-7073. May–Sep: 10am–10pm daily; Oct–Apr: noon–9pm daily.*

**Box Canyon Falls & Park**
S of Ouray via US Hwy 550. *(970) 325-4464. May 15–Oct 15: 8am–8pm daily. Oct 16–May 14.*

## Black Canyon of the Gunnison National Park ㊻

E of Montrose via US Hwy 50.
*(970) 641-2337. 24 hrs daily.*
www.nps.gov/blca

THOUGH NOT AS vast as Arizona's Grand Canyon *(see pp536–9)*, the Black Canyon is strikingly deep with steep sides. The canyon was created by the Gunnison River as it slowly sliced through solid stone for two million years. Its north and south rims have completely different ecosystems and are separated by a crevice 2,400 ft (732 m) at its deepest point and just 40 ft (12 m) at its narrowest point.

The **South Rim Road** meanders for about 7 miles (11 km) past several over-looks, including a fantastic vista of a multihued rock face known as Painted Wall, which is twice the height of New York's Empire State Building *(see p73)*. Although the park's northern edge is more isolated, it has a campground and offers magnificent sunset views.

Climbing is a popular sport in the park, as is hiking, camp-ing, and fishing. Among the many trails is one particularly difficult one that descends to the canyon's floor.

The park's varied and abundant wildlife includes a variety of birds such as the peregrine falcons who nest on the canyon's sheer walls. Wildcats and bears also roam the vast park.

## Colorado National Monument ㊼

W of Grand Junction via I-70 or 7 miles (11 km) S of Fruita on US Hwy 340. *(970) 858-3617. 24 hrs daily.* www.nps.gov/colm

CARVED BY WIND and water over the last 225 million years, this immense 20,500-acre (8,296-ha) national monu-ment has been molded into an eeire high desert landscape of spectacular canyons, and red sandstone arches. A driving tour on the 22-mile (35-km) **Rim Rock Drive** offers several splendid panoramas, while numerous trails lead visitors right into the heart of the landscape. The park's two geological highlights are the incredible sandstone arches of Rattlesnake Canyon, and Miracle Rock, which is consid-ered to be the largest balanced rock in the world.

**The eerie high desert landscape of Colorado National Monument**

# Practical Information

EXPLORING THE FOUR Rocky Mountain states requires some advance planning, simply because of the sheer size and diversity of the region's landscape. The boundaries of this mountainous region stretch from the Canadian border in the north to New Mexico in the south. To the west, the area is bordered by the plateaus and basins of the Intermontane region. The breath-taking scenery, rugged terrain, scanty resources, and sparse population of the Rockies are spread across elevations that range from under 1,000 ft (305 m) to over 14,000 ft (4,267 m) above sea level.

## TOURIST INFORMATION

TRAVELERS ENTERING the Rocky Mountain states via an Interstate Highway are greeted with signs advertising a state "Welcome Center." These centers provide a full range of tourist information as well as clean restrooms and free coffee. Denver's International Airport (DIA), and most of the region's other major airports and train stations have information desks, stocked with free brochures and maps. Most larger cities and smaller towns operate **Convention & Visitors Bureaus** or **Chambers of Commerce**, which provide free travel information.

## NATURAL HAZARDS

THE SHORT SUMMERS of the Rockies region are warm and glorious, but can bring sudden thunderstorms, especially in the mountains. Rock slides, bugs, and wildlife are other hazards. Elevation across the four states can vary from under 1,000 ft (305 m) to over 14,000 ft (4,267 m) above sea level. At higher elevations, in areas such as Yellowstone National Park, roads may be closed by snow between late October and early June. The Interstate Highways and access routes to the region's many ski areas are kept open all year round.

Winters are long and often bitterly cold with heavy winter and spring snows, and travelers should take sensible precautions. Drivers should make sure that they possess, and know how to install, snow chains or other traction devices, which are required by law. Be especially careful while driving on icy surfaces, which are treacherous.

In remote areas, hikers should be prepared for all weather conditions in winter as well as summer. Carry basic emergency supplies, including food and water, and extra clothing in case the weather changes for the worse.

## THE CLIMATE OF THE ROCKIES

Weather across the Rocky Mountain region is marked by long, snowy winters, short springs and fall, and hot summers. The main factor determining weather is elevation – temperatures are cooler and snowfalls heavier the higher you go. Visitors should be prepared for winter conditions at any time of year. Yet, months like October offer crisp days, ideal for scenic drives through the mountains when you can enjoy the fall colors of the aspens.

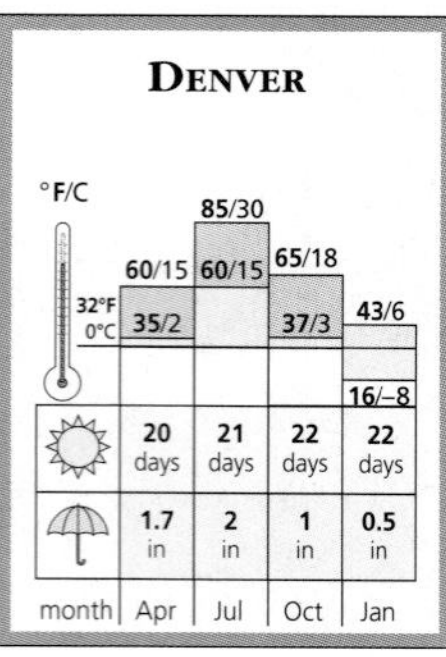


## GETTING AROUND

FOR VISITORS coming from t East or West Coast, Denv is a prime starting point. Smaller regional cities throug out the Rockies have airport such as the Missoula, (MT) County International Airport Other than organized bus tours, public transportation i limited. Denver has city buse a light-rail system, and free shuttle buses. Having a car i essential in this region since most national parks and oth sights are located at great distances from the major citi

Seat belts are required for drivers and front seat passe gers in all four states. Child seats are compulsory for all passengers aged eight ar under. Helmets are requirec for all motorcyclists under the age of 18.

Speed limits vary but are usually 70–75 mph (112–12 km/hr) on Interstate Highways outside the populated urban areas. Radar detector are permitted in the entire Rocky Mountain region.

## ETIQUETTE

VISITORS TO THIS part of th West should wear clothi appropriate to the weather. Guests at dude ranches, ski areas, and other vacation spots need to dress comfortably, depending on the outdoor sport they pursue.

Some of the region's most famous sights are located o Native American reservation land. Visitors are welcome b must be sensitive as to what may cause offense. It is illeg to bring alcohol onto reserv tions, and taking photograp may not be allowed.

## FESTIVALS

SUMMER IN THE ROCKIES bring a deluge of outdoor even including community and st fairs, in addition to regional and national music, and art festivals. Fireworks, bands, and festivals abound for the July 4th celebrations, while the region's strong Native American heritage is also cel brated with a number of pow wows in July and August on elected reservations. Music nd various cultural events, uch as the ever popular **elluride Bluegrass estival**, the world-famous **spen Music Festival & chool** (970-925-3254), and ne **Big Sky Arts Festival** ake place throughout the ummer months.

### PORTS

THE ROCKY MOUNTAIN states all offer a wide variety of ports throughout the year. Denver is home to many of he region's professional eams. The **Colorado Rockies** lay baseball all summer at the ld-fashioned Coors Field owntown. The **Denver Broncos** play professional ootball in the fall, and winter ees the **Denver Nuggets** on he basketball court. Many of he region's universities and olleges play seasonal games, ften with heated regional ivalries, and if you're lucky, ou can take in a local ummer softball game.

One spectator sport characeristic of the Rockies is the odeo, and many national ompetitions are held here. vents such as bull- and ronco-riding, calf roping, and teer wrestling showcase a owboy's skill. Cheyenne, Wyoming, hosts the "World's argest Outdoor Rodeo" when nore than 250,000 fans flock here during **Frontier Days** at the end of July (800-227-6336). Dude ranches often offer special rodeos for guests.

### OUTDOOR ACTIVITIES

THE MOST POPULAR outdoor activity is downhill skiing, which draws many participants and billions of dollars to the region's world-class resorts. Colorado has many of the biggest and most highly regarded resorts in the United States, but there is also excellent skiing at Idaho's Sun Valley, Wyoming's Jackson Hole, and at smaller resorts throughout the region. Snowboarding is also popular, and cross-country skiing can be enjoyed in the stunning landscape of the region's many parks and forests. The ski season is from December to March, but many resorts are open until May or June depending on the weather.

Montana is home to such famous trout-fishing spots as the Madison and Yellowstone Rivers, while Idaho, Wyoming, and Colorado all offer excellent fly-fishing. Licenses are required, and catch-and-release is encouraged. Visitors can contact the **Montana Fish, Wildlife & Parks Department** or the **Idaho Fish & Game Department** for details.

Other popular warm-weather activities include hiking, mountain biking, and rafting. Rafting the Snake River through Grand Teton National Park is extremely popular, as is the wilder Salmon River in Idaho. The **Colorado River Outfitters Association** is one of the best sources of information on guided river-rafting trips. **Lewis & Clark Trail Adventures** lead whitewater raft trips through miles of Idaho rivers. **Snow King Ski Resort** near Jackson, Wyoming also offers historical hiking and rafting trips. Bicycle and motorcycle riding is gaining as much popularity as hiking, fishing, and skiing. **Open Road Bicycles** in Missoula, Montana, rents bikes for a day or by the week (406-549-2453). They will also help outfit and plan trips.

### ENTERTAINMENT

THE SKI RESORTS and dude ranches in the area offer evening entertainment from cabaret and local theater productions to first-run movies. However, many evenings at these resorts are spent in hot tubs, relaxing around the bar, or at in-house casinos. College towns, such as Bozeman and Missoula, Montana, have many of the amenities that the backcountry lacks: good bookstores, brew pubs, museums, and events that appeal to both urban and cowboy culture.

## DIRECTORY

### TOURIST INFORMATION

**Colorado**
1675 Broadway, Suite 1700 Denver, CO 80202.
*(800) 265-6723.*
www.colorado.com

**Idaho**
700 W State St, Boise.
*(208) 334-2470, (800) 847-4843.*
www.visitid.org

**Montana**
301 S Park Ave, Helena.
*(800) 847-4868.*
www.visitmt.com

**Wyoming**
I-25 at College Dr, Cheyenne. *(800) 225-5996.* www.wyomingtourism.org

### ROAD CONDITIONS

**Idaho**
*(888) 432-7623.*

**Montana**
*(800) 226-7623.*
www.mdt.state.mt.us/travinfo

### FESTIVALS

**Colorado State Fair**
*(719) 561-8484.*
www.coloradostatefair.com

**Eastern Idaho State Fair**
*(208) 785-2480.* www.idaho-state-fair.com

**Montana State Fair**
*(406) 727-8900.* www.mtexpopark.com

**Telluride Bluegrass Festival**
*(800) 624-2422.*
www.bluegrass.com

**Wyoming State Fair**
*(307) 358-2398.*
www.wystatefair.com

### SPORTS

**Colorado Rapids**
*(303) 405-1100.*

**Colorado Rockies**
*(303) 292-0200.*

**Denver Broncos**
*(303) 649-9000.*

**Denver Nuggets**
*(303) 405-1100.*

### FISHING

**Idaho Fish & Game Dept.**
600 S Walnut St
Boise, ID 83712.
*(208) 334-3700.*

**Montana Fish, Wildlife & Parks Department**
1420 E 6th Ave
Helena, MT 59620.
*(406) 444-2535.*

# Where to Stay

PLACES TO STAY IN THE Rocky Mountains region are as varied as the landscape. In towns, visitors can choose from historic hotels and quaint B&B inns, but in rural areas the choice is usually limited to highway motels. Most national parks have large rustic lodges, and there are also several "dude ranches" where guests can play cowboy while enjoying luxurious all-inclusive accommodations.

| Idaho | Credit Cards | Number of Rooms | Recommended Restaurant | Children's Facilities | Garden or Terrace |
|---|---|---|---|---|---|
| **BOISE:** *Idaho Heritage Inn* $<br>109 W Idaho St. *(208) 342-8066; (800) 342-8455.* FAX *(208) 343-2325.*<br>W www.idheritageinn.com<br>Within walking distance of the State Capitol and the historic downtown area, this inn was built for Governor Chase Clark in 1904. It retains its period character but has all modern facilities. | ● | 6 | | ● | ■ |
| **BOISE:** *Owyhee Plaza Hotel* $$<br>1109 Main St. *(208) 343-4611; (800) 233-4611.* FAX *(208) 336-3860.*<br>W www.owyheeplaza.com<br>Located downtown, this grand old-fashioned hotel has character to spare plus full services and modern conveniences. | ● | 100 | ■ | ● | |
| **COEUR D'ALENE:** *Coeur d'Alene Resort* $$$$$<br>PO Box 7200, 115 South 2nd St. *(208) 765-4000, (800) 688-5253.*<br>FAX *(208) 664-7276.* W www.cdaresort.com<br>Located on the lovely Lake Coeur d'Alene, this deluxe golf, ski, and spa resort is famous for its floating golf green, and offers a range of activities such as lake cruises, jet skiing, and parasailing. | ● | 338 | ■ | ● | ■ |
| **IDAHO FALLS:** *Best Western Driftwood Inn* $$<br>575 River Parkway. *(208) 523-2242, (800) 939-2242.* FAX *(208) 523-0316.*<br>W www.bestwestern.com<br>Located within walking distance of the Snake River and downtown Idaho Falls, this inn is a comfortable base for exploring eastern Idaho. | ● | 74 | | ● | ■ |
| **KETCHUM:** *Best Western Tyrolean Lodge* $$<br>260 Cottonwood St. *(208) 726-5336, (800) 333-7912.* FAX *(208) 726-2081.*<br>W www.bestwestern.com<br>Located at the south end of town, off the main highway, this Austrian-style lodge is convenient for visits to the Sun Valley region. | ● | 56 | | ● | |
| **RIGGINS:** *Best Western Salmon Rapids Lodge* $$<br>1010 S Main St. *(208) 628-2743, (877) 957-2743.* FAX *(208) 628-3834.*<br>W www.salmonrapids.com<br>Located at the confluence of the Salmon and Little Salmon Rivers, this hotel is ideal for rafters and visitors to Hells Canyon. | ● | 55 | ■ | ● | |
| **SALMON:** *Twin Peaks Ranch* $$$$$<br>Twin Peaks. *(208) 894-2290, (800) 659-4899.* FAX *(208) 894-2429.*<br>W www.twinpeaksranch.com<br>Located on 3,000 acres (1,214 ha) in the rugged mountains above the Salmon River, this guest ranch offers deluxe cabins and a range of outdoor activities, from fly-fishing to horseback riding. Minimum stay is three nights. | ● | 24 | ■ | ● | ■ |
| **STANLEY:** *Salmon River Lodge* $<br>Hwy-75. *(208) 774-3422.* W www.mywildidaho.com<br>Across the river from the main highway, this quiet, peaceful, 8-acre (3 ha) resort offers four cabins, one with a kitchen. *Oct–Memorial Day.* | ● | 4 | | ● | ■ |
| **STANLEY:** *Redfish Lake Lodge* $$$<br>Hwy-75. *(208) 774-3536; (208) 644-9096.* FAX *(208) 774-3546.*<br>W www.redfishlake.com An old-fashioned, unpretentious lodge with two dozen rustic log cabins fronting a beautiful lake, and surrounded by dense forests and sublime mountains. The ideal Idaho experience. *Oct–Memorial Day.* | ● | 40 | ■ | ● | ■ |
| **SUN VALLEY:** *Sun Valley Lodge* $$$$$<br>Sun Valley. *(208) 622-2151, (800) 786-8259.* FAX *(208) 622-2030.*<br>W www.sunvalley.com<br>Rustic luxury is the hallmark of this deluxe lodge, built as the centerpiece of the country's most exclusive downhill ski resort. | ● | 148 | ■ | ● | ■ |

**Price categories** for a standard double room per night, inclusive of breakfast, service charges, and any additional taxes:

- ($) under $100
- ($)($) $100–$150
- ($)($)($) $150–$200
- ($)($)($)($) $200–$250
- ($)($)($)($)($) over $250

**CREDIT CARDS**
Major credit cards accepted.

**NUMBER OF ROOMS**
Number of rooms in the hotel.

**RECOMMENDED RESTAURANT**
Good restaurant within the hotel.

**CHILDREN'S FACILITIES**
Hotel has various facilities for young children.

**GARDEN OR TERRACE**
Hotel has a garden, courtyard, or terrace.

## MONTANA

| Hotel | Credit Cards | Number of Rooms | Recommended Restaurant | Children's Facilities | Garden or Terrace |
|---|---|---|---|---|---|
| **UTTE:** *Copper King Mansion* ($)<br>19 W Granite St. (406) 782-7580.<br>his 1884 mansion is packed with so much opulent Victoriana that it oubles as a museum, with guided tours between May and October. | ● | 5 | | ● | ■ |
| **LATHEAD VALLEY:** *Best Western KwaTaqNuk Resort* ($)($)<br>03 E US-93, Polson. (406) 883-3636. FAX (406) 883-5392. W www.kwataqnuk.com<br>ocated on the shores of Flathead Lake, this large modern hotel (whose alish Indian name means "Where the Water Leaves the Lake") is part of a esort and casino complex run by the local Indian tribes. | ● | 112 | ■ | ● | ■ |
| **LACIER NATIONAL PARK:** *Glacier Park Lodge* ($)($)($)<br>S-2, East Glacier Park. (406) 892-2525. FAX (406) 892-1375.<br>W www.bigtreehotel.com<br>uilt by the Great Northern Railroad in 1913, this rustic landmark is emarkable for the massive 50-ft (15-m) high Douglas fir trees supporting he roof over the spacious lobby. *Oct–Memorial Day.* | ● | 151 | ■ | ● | ■ |
| **LACIER NATIONAL PARK:** *Izaak Walton Inn* ($)($)($)<br>S-2, Essex. (406) 888-5700. FAX (406) 888-5200. W www.izaakwaltoninn.com<br>uilt as a lodging house for railroad crews in the early 1900s, this inn has raditional rooms and a few cabooses for train enthusiasts. In winter, the in is a mecca for cross-country skiers. | ● | 33 | ■ | ● | ■ |
| **LACIER NATIONAL PARK:** *Lake McDonald Lodge* ($)($)($)<br>ake McDonald. (406) 888-5431, (406) 892-2525. FAX (406) 892-1375.<br>W www.lakemcdonaldlodge.com<br>he most intimate of the park lodges, the Lake McDonald Lodge features huge fireplace in the lobby and grand views over sublime Lake IcDonald. *Oct–Memorial Day.* | ● | 100 | ■ | ● | ■ |
| **LACIER NATIONAL PARK:** *Many Glacier Hotel* ($)($)($)<br>Iany Glacier. (406) 892-2525. FAX (406) 892-1375.<br>W www.glacierparkinc.com he largest and most stunningly sited of the ark's lodges, it overlooks Swiftcurrent Lake against a backdrop of laciated peaks. *mid-Sep–mid Jun.* | ● | 215 | ■ | ● | ■ |
| **REAT FALLS:** *Best Western Heritage Inn* ($)($)<br>700 Fox Farm Rd. (406) 761-1900, (800) 548-8256. FAX (406) 761-0136.<br>W www.bestwestern.com/heritageinngreatfalls<br>his large, comfortable motel features a large indoor pool and an atrium arden, perfect for those long Montana winters. | ● | 234 | ■ | ● | |
| **REAT FALLS:** *Pine Butte Guest Ranch* ($)($)($)($)($)<br>C 58 Box 34C. (406) 466-2158. FAX (406) 466-5462.<br>W http://nature.org/wherewework/northamerica/states/montana/travel/<br>his 1930s dude ranch, now operated by the Nature Conservancy, lets isitors hike mountain trails, ride horses, or just read a good book by the eated pool. The hotel requires a minimum one-week stay. | ● | 10 | ■ | ● | ■ |
| **IELENA:** *Sanders Bed & Breakfast* ($)($)<br>28 N Ewing St. (406) 442-3309. FAX (406) 443-2361. W www.sandersbb.com<br>uilt in 1875 by Montana's first US senator, this lavish home is filled with eriod furnishings but has been thoroughly outfitted with modern onveniences. | ● | 7 | | | ■ |
| **IISSOULA:** *Goldsmith's Inn* ($)($)<br>09 E Front St. (406) 728-1585; (866) 666-9945. FAX (406) 543-0045.<br>W www.missoulabedandbreakfast.com<br>ocated on the banks of Clark Fork River, within walking distance of owntown, this 1911 home offers the best in comfort. | ● | 7 | ■ | ● | ■ |

For key to symbols see back flap

**Price categories** for a standard double room per night, inclusive of breakfast, service charges, and any additional taxes:

- $ under $100
- $$ $100–$150
- $$$ $150–$200
- $$$$ $200–$250
- $$$$$ over $250

**Credit Cards**
Major credit cards accepted.

**Number of Rooms**
Number of rooms in the hotel.

**Recommended Restaurant**
Good restaurant within the hotel.

**Children's Facilities**
Hotel has various facilities for young children.

**Garden or Terrace**
Hotel has a garden, courtyard, or terrace.

## Wyoming

| Hotel | Price | Credit Cards | Number of Rooms | Recommended Restaurant | Children's Facilities | Garden or Terrace |
|---|---|---|---|---|---|---|
| **Bighorn Mountains:** *Tensleep Preserve*<br>1095B Rd 56, Ten Sleep. *(307) 366-2674.* FAX *(307) 366-2262.*<br>This Nature Conservancy guest ranch offers luxurious tent cabins. Meals are served on the deck overlooking canyons and pine-forested uplands in the foothills of the Bighorn Mountains. Book in advance. ● *Oct–Apr.* | $ | ● | 12 | ■ | ● | ■ |
| **Cheyenne:** *Nagle Warren Mansion Bed & Breakfast*<br>222 E 17th St. *(307) 637-3333, (800) 811-2610.* FAX *(307) 638-6879.*<br>W www.naglewarrenmansion.com<br>This late-Victorian stone mansion offers contemporary luxury and historic ambience within walking distance of downtown. TV | $$$ | ● | 12 | | | ■ |
| **Cody:** *Hotel Irma*<br>1192 Sheridan Ave. *(307) 587-4221, (800) 745-4762.* FAX *(307) 587-1775.*<br>W www.irmahotel.com<br>Built in 1902 by Wild West impresario "Buffalo Bill" Cody, and named for his daughter, this unpretentious hotel is a historic landmark. The cherry-wood bar in its restaurant was a gift from England's Queen Victoria. P | $$ | ● | 40 | ■ | ● | |
| **Grand Teton National Park:** *Flagg Ranch Resort*<br>US-89, Moran Junction. *(307) 543-2861, (800) 443-2311.* FAX *(307) 543-2356.*<br>W www.flaggranch.com<br>Located in a beautiful setting midway between Grand Teton and Yellow-stone National Parks. ● *mid-Oct–mid-May.* P | $$ | ● | 92 | ■ | ● | ■ |
| **Grand Teton National Park:** *Jenny Lake Lodge*<br>Jenny Lake. *(307) 543-2811, (800) 628-9988.* FAX *(307) 543-3358.*<br>W www.gtlc.com<br>A romantic retreat in the heart of the park, this deluxe inn has a rustic ambience but luxurious amenities. P | $$$$$ | ● | 37 | ■ | ● | ■ |
| **Jackson:** *Wort Hotel*<br>50 N Glenwood St. *(307) 733-2190, (800) 322-2727.* FAX *(307) 733-2067.*<br>W www.worthotel.com<br>Located at the heart of downtown, the Wort lets you sample the Wild West flair of Jackson, while savoring all creature comforts. P TV | $$$$ | ● | 60 | ■ | ● | |
| **Laramie:** *Vee-Bar Guest Ranch*<br>2091 Hwy-130, Centennial. *(307) 745-7036, (800) 483-3227.* FAX *(307) 745-7433.*<br>W www.ranchweb.com/veebar With log cabins set along a rushing stream, this "dude ranch" in the Medicine Bow Mountains is one of the country's most popular. There is a minimum stay of three nights. P | $$$$$ | ● | 9 | ■ | ● | |
| **Yellowstone National Park:** *Lake Yellowstone Hotel*<br>Lake Yellowstone. *(307) 344-7311.* FAX *(307) 344-7456.*<br>W www.travelyellowstone.com<br>A romantic retreat in the heart of the park, this deluxe inn has a rustic ambience but luxurious amenities. P | $$ | ● | 300 | ■ | ● | ■ |
| **Yellowstone National Park:** *Old Faithful Inn*<br>Old Faithful. *(307) 344-7311.* FAX *(307) 344-7456.*<br>W www.travelyellowstone.com<br>Built in 1903–04, now with a modern annex, this hotel has an unbeatable location near Old Faithful geyser. The rustic lobby and dining room ceiling soaring nearly 100 ft (31 m) overhead is spectacular. ● *mid-Sep–Jun.* P | $$ | ● | 327 | ■ | ● | ■ |
| **Yellowstone National Park:** *Bill Cody Ranch*<br>2604 Yellowstone Hwy. *(307) 587-6271, (800) 615-2934.* FAX *(307) 587-6272.*<br>W www.billcodyranch.com Located at the east entrance to Yellowstone, this rustic lodge offers several private cabins and a full range of "Wild West" activities. ● *Oct–mid-May.* P | $$$ | ● | 14 | ■ | ● | ■ |

## COLORADO

**SPEN:** *Hotel Jerome* $$$$$ — 91
30 E Main St. (970) 920-1000. FAX (970) 925-2784. W www.hoteljerome.com
uilt at the height of Colorado's silver boom, this downtown landmark exudes xury in its rooms and amenities. TV P

**OULDER:** *Hotel Boulderado* $$$$ — 160
15 13th St. (303) 442-4344. FAX (303) 442-4378. W www.boulderado.com
pened in 1909, Boulder's oldest and best hotel retains a level of Victorian andeur along with its many modern amenities. P TV

**OLORADO SPRINGS:** *Broadmoor* $$$$$ — 700
Lake Ave. (719) 577-5775. FAX (719) 577-5738. W www.broadmoor.com
ocated near Cheyenne Lake, this hotel offers superb rooms, a full-service pa, three golf courses, and fine restaurants. TV P

**ENVER:** *Queen Anne B&B* $$ — 14
47-51 Tremont Pl. (303) 296-6666. FAX (303) 296-2151. W www.queenannebnb.com
romantic getaway, Denver's best B&B features a pair of Victorian mansions. Rates include breakfast and complimentary wine. P

**ENVER:** *Adam's Mark Hotel* $$$$ — 1,225
550 Court Pl. (303) 893-3333. FAX (303) 626-2542. W www.adamsmark.com/denver
his 18th-century resort offers spacious, country-style rooms, and activities such as golf, falconry, and off-road driving. TV P

**ENVER:** *Brown Palace Hotel* $$$$$ — 241
21 17th St. (303) 297-3111. FAX (303) 321-5900. W www.brownpalace.com
ocated in downtown Denver, this hotel is best known for its nine-story rium lobby and lavish presidential suites. TV P

**URANGO:** *Strater Hotel* $$$ — 93
99 Main Ave. (970) 247-4431, (800) 247-4431. FAX (970) 259-2208.
W www.strater.com One of the few Colorado hotels to have been open ontinuously since the 1880s, the Strater retains a historic ambience but ffers all modern conveniences. TV P

**STES PARK (ROCKY MOUNTAIN NATIONAL PARK):** *Stanley Hotel* $$$$$ — 135
33 Wonderview Ave. (970) 586-3371, (800) 976-1377. FAX (970) 586-4964.
W www.stanleyhotel.com
pened by steam engine pioneer F.O. Stanley in 1909, the hotel combines ately elegance with spectacular mountain views. TV P

**ANITOU SPRINGS:** *Cliff House* $$$ — 55
06 Canon Ave. (719) 685-3000, (888) 212-7000. FAX (719) 685-3913.
W www.thecliffhouse.com
ne of the state's oldest hotels, the Cliff House is a fine example of Rocky ountain Victorian architecture in a splendid setting. TV P

**ESA VERDE NATIONAL PARK:** *Far View Lodge* $$ — 150
ile Marker 15, Mesa Verde. (970) 529-4422, (800) 449-2288. FAX (970) 529-4411.
W www.visitmesaverde.com
he only indoors accommodation in Mesa Verde National Park, this lodge ffers standard rooms with amazing views, as well as immediate access the park and its stunning cliff dwellings. P

**TEAMBOAT SPRINGS:** *Sheraton Steamboat Resort* $$$$ — 325
200 Village Inn Ct. (970) 879-2220. FAX (970) 879-7686. W www.sheraton.com/steamboat
his full-service resort offers a nice mix of hotel rooms and larger condominium units, as well as a shopping arcade, a top-rated golf course, and even rooftop spas with splendid mountain views. TV P

**ELLURIDE:** *New Sheridan Hotel* $$$ — 32
31 W Colorado Ave. (970) 728-4351, (800) 200-1891. FAX (970) 728-5024.
W www.newsheridan.com
ebuilt after an 1891 fire, this hotel has the comforts of a B&B and the skiriented amenities common to Telluride's larger resorts. TV P

**AIL:** *Vail Cascade* $$$$$ — 399
300 Westhaven Dr. (970) 476-7111. FAX (970) 479-7020.
W www.vailcascade.com
ne of the most complete ski-oriented lodgings in Colorado, this foureason resort has a spa and full range of amenities. TV P

For key to symbols see back flap

# Where to Eat

Restaurants in the Rockies reflect the rugged character of the region and are often decorated to evoke the region's Wild West heritage. Most eateries are unpretentious and tend to close by 9pm, but in cities they often aspire to cosmopolitan sophistication. Opening times are indicated by a "B" for breakfast, "L" for lunch, and "D" for dinner.

## Idaho

**Boise:** *Brick Oven Bistro* $

801 Main St. *(208) 342-3456.*

Located right on the Grove in downtown Boise, this restaurant has been serving homemade American regional fare since 1984. Enjoy dishes from New England, the Southwest and, Cajun-style cuisine. There's also, fresh soups. and salads as well as old favorites from the soda fountain *L, D.*

**Boise:** *Guido's Original New York Pizza* $

235 N 5th St. *(208) 345-9011.*

Rated as the best pizza place in Boise, Guido's is a great little restaurant to eat cheaply and take in the pulse of this youthful, energetic city at the same time. *L, D.*

**Coeur d'Alene:** *Iron Horse Bar & Grill* $$

407 Sherman Ave. *(208) 667-7314.*

Historic photos and artifacts from Idaho's mining and railroad heritage set the stage at the Iron Horse Bar & Grill, with its range of hamburgers, steaks, and fish. *B, L, D.*

**Coeur d'Alene:** *The Wine celler* $$

313 Sherman Ave. *(208) 644-9463*

There's a great combination here, of Mediterranean cuisine, candle-lit tables, an award-winning wine list and live music, usually jazz or blues played on Tuesday to Saturday nights. *D.*

**Coeur d'Alene:** *Cedars Floating Restaurant* $$

N-1 Marina Dr. *(208) 664-2922.*

Its hard to imagine a better view than one you get from your table here. Cedars offers a huge menu featuring fresh and deep-sea fish from all over the world. There is also a floating deck with boat parking available for visitors. *D.*

**Idaho Falls:** *Rutabaga's* $$$

415 River Parkway. *(208) 529-3990.*

An unexpected treat for visitors, this small Idaho Falls restaurant has been serving adventurous food for more than a decade, mixing various influences from all over the world. *L (Tue–Fri in summer, Fri only rest of year), D Mon–Sat, Sun (on;y brunch).*

**Ketchum:** *Sawtooth Club* $$

231 N Main St. *(208) 726-5233.*

Steaks and seafood, grilled over a mesquite fire, are the stars of the menu here. *D.*

**Sun Valley:** *The Ram Restaurant* $$$$

Sun Valley Village. *(208) 622-2225.*

After a grueling day on the resort's challenging ski slopes, treat yourself to a delicious meal of French bistro fare. The Ram Restaurant's sample dishes include cheese fondue, veal, trout, and halibut, as well as a range of seafood and beef specialties. *D.*

**Twin Falls:** *Buffalo Café* $

218 W 4th Ave. *(208) 734-0271.*

Start the day with an enormous, stomach-stretching breakfast at this tiny, ever-popular café. Don't forget to try their signature dish – the Buffalo Chip – which is a hefty omelet of eggs, bacon, cheese, and fried potatoes. *B, L.*

**Twin Falls:** *Rock Creek* $$

200 Addison Ave W *(208) 734-4154.*

For good steak or seafood, and the state's largest salad bar, come to this long-standing local favorite. *D.*

| Restaurant | Credit Cards | Outdoor Tables | Vegetarian | Good Wine List | Children's Facilities |
|---|---|---|---|---|---|
| Brick Oven Bistro | ■ | ● | ■ | | ■ |
| Guido's Original New York Pizza | | ● | ■ | | ■ |
| Iron Horse Bar & Grill | ■ | ● | ■ | | ■ |
| The Wine celler | ■ | | | ● | |
| Cedars Floating Restaurant | ■ | ● | ■ | ● | ■ |
| Rutabaga's | ■ | ● | ■ | ● | |
| Sawtooth Club | ■ | ● | ■ | ● | ■ |
| The Ram Restaurant | ■ | ● | ■ | ● | ■ |
| Buffalo Café | ■ | | ■ | | ■ |
| Rock Creek | ■ | ● | | ● | ■ |

?rice categories include a hree-course meal for one, a glass of house wine and all unavoidable extra charges such as sales tax and service.
$ under $25
$$ $25–35
$$$ $35–50
$$$$ $50–70
$$$$$ over $70

**Credit Cards**
Major credit cards accepted.

**Outdoor Tables**
Garden, courtyard, or terrace with outside tables.

**Vegetarian**
A good selection of vegetarian dishes available.

**Good Wine List**
Extensive list of good wines, both domestic and imported.

**Children's Facilities**
Restaurant has various facilities for young children.

## Montana

| | Credit Cards | Outdoor Tables | Vegetarian | Good Wine List | Children's Facilities |
|---|---|---|---|---|---|
| **IGFORK:** *Swan River Café* $$<br>50 Grand Ave. (406) 837-2220.<br>his friendly local favorite serves a wide array of seafood, fresh fish, and eaks. Their popular Sunday night buffet includes shrimp appetizers, rime rib, salmon, salads, vegetables, and desserts. *B, L, D.* | ■ | ● | ■ | ● | ■ |
| **IGFORK:** *Bigfork Inn* $$$$<br>04 Electric Ave. (406) 837-6680.<br>ne of the main proponents of regional Rocky Mountain cuisine, this ng-standing favorite is famous for wild game, venison, and duck served ith a local cherry-and-blackcurrant sauce. *D.* *(Fri & Sat only).* | ■ | ● | ■ | ● | ■ |
| **ILLINGS:** *Walkers Grill* $$<br>700 1st Ave N. (406) 245-9291.<br>odern decor in a historic setting, Walker's Grill offers local meat and fish ishes along with pizzas and pastas. *D.* *(Sun only).* | ■ | | ■ | ● | ■ |
| **OZEMAN:** *Mackenzie River Pizza Company* $<br>32 E Main Street. (406) 587-0055.<br>xcellent pizza, pasta, and a wide range of local micro-brewed beers, in e heart of downtown Bozeman. *L, D.* | ■ | | ■ | | ■ |
| **UTTE:** *Matt's Place* $<br>orner of Rowe Rd & Montana St. (406) 782-8049.<br>ne of the original "drive-ins" in the Rockies, this Butte landmark has een serving burgers and milk shakes since the 1930s. An all-American assic. *L, D.* | | | | | ■ |
| **UTTE:** *Uptown Café* $<br>7 E Broadway. (406) 723-4735.<br>formal bistro serving upscale but not expensively priced fish, meat, iicken and pasta dishes. *L, D.* | ■ | | ■ | ● | ■ |
| **LACIER NATIONAL PARK:** *Izaak Walton Inn* $<br>5-2 in Essex. (406) 888-5700.<br>uilt for railroad workers, this unpretentious dining room serves big por-ons of inexpensive, hearty food with a railroad theme. *B, L, D.* | ■ | ● | ■ | ● | ■ |
| **LACIER NATIONAL PARK:** *Lake McDonald Lodge* $$$<br>oing-to-the-Sun Rd. (406) 888-5431.<br>he meals served in this rustic hunting lodge setting in Russell's Fireside inning Room are as memorable as the scenery outside *B, L, D.* | | | ■ | | ■ |
| **REAT FALLS:** *Dante's Creative Cuisine* $$<br>325 8th Ave N. (406) 453-9599.<br>ocated in a former iron foundry, this innovative restaurant offers a range Southwestern, Mexican, and Italian-inspired pastas and salads. *L, D.* | ■ | | ■ | ● | ■ |
| **ELENA:** *Windbag Saloon & Grill* $<br>9 S Last Chance Gulch. (406) 443-9669.<br>his local favorite serves Western fare, including handcut steaks and ourmet burgers. Large portions and microbrews. *L, D.* *Sun.* | ■ | | | | ■ |
| **IISSOULA:** *The Shack* $$<br>22 W Main St. (406) 549-9903.<br>business since the 1950s, this bustling place draws workers, students, nd families for breakfast omelets and other filling fare. *B, L, D.* | ■ | | ■ | | ■ |
| **IISSOULA:** *Guy's Lolo Creek Steakhouse* $$<br>600 W US-12. (406) 273-2622.<br>ocated in the southern foothills of Missoula, this massive log cabin erves excellent steaks and fresh fish grilled over an open fire. *D.* | ■ | | | ● | ■ |

For key to symbols see back flap

**Price categories** include a three-course meal for one, a glass of house wine and all unavoidable extra charges such as sales tax and service.
($) under $25
($)($) $25–35
($)($)($) $35–50
($)($)($)($) $50–70
($)($)($)($)($) over $70

**CREDIT CARDS**
Major credit cards accepted.

**OUTDOOR TABLES**
Garden, courtyard, or terrace with outside tables.

**VEGETARIAN**
A good selection of vegetarian dishes available.

**GOOD WINE LIST**
Extensive list of good wines, both domestic and imported.

**CHILDREN'S FACILITIES**
Restaurant has various facilities for young children.

| Restaurant | Price | Credit Cards | Outdoor Tables | Vegetarian | Good Wine List | Children's Facilities |
|---|---|---|---|---|---|---|
| **WYOMING** | | | | | | |
| **BIGHORN MOUNTAINS:** *Colonel Bozeman's*<br>655 E Hart St, Buffalo. *(307) 684-5555.*<br>Located in the historic cowboy town of Buffalo, this friendly restaurant serves local specialties like buffalo steaks in a room full of Wild West memorabilia. *L, D.* | ($)($) | ■ | ● | ■ | ● | ■ |
| **CASPER:** *Poor Boy's Steakhouse*<br>739 N Center St. *(307) 237-8325.*<br>Popular, family-friendly American-style restaurant, with checkered tablecloths and large portions of steak, chicken, and fish. *L, D.* | ($)($) | ■ | | ■ | ● | ■ |
| **CODY:** *Cassie's Supper Club*<br>214 Yellowstone Ave. *(307) 527-5500.*<br>Steaks and hamburgers are the favorite foods at this friendly, unpretentious restaurant. There's also a chuckwagon dinner buffet in summer. Late at night, Cassie's turns into Cody's most popular dance hall. *L, D.* | ($) | ■ | ● | ■ | ● | ■ |
| **GRAND TETON NATIONAL PARK:** *Dornan's Chuck Wagon*<br>100 Moose Rd. *(307) 733-2415.*<br>Open since 1948, and located near the park's main visitor center in Moose, this family restaurant is unique, to say the least. Eating inside tepees, or at tables along the Snake River, visitors can enjoy pancake breakfasts, lunchtime sandwiches and burgers, or chuckwagon barbecue buffets at dinner. *B, L, D.* *Oct–May.* | ($) | ■ | ● | ■ | ● | ■ |
| **GRAND TETON NATIONAL PARK:** *Jenny Lake Lodge Dining Room*<br>Inner Park Rd. *(307) 733-4647.*<br>Set amid pine trees near a wildflower meadow, this exclusive restaurant serves some of the finest cuisine in the Rockies. Reservations are required. *B, L, D.* *Oct–May.* | ($)($)($)($)($) | ■ | | ■ | ● | |
| **JACKSON:** *Jedediah's Original House of Sourdough*<br>135 E Broadway. *(307) 733-5671.*<br>Located in a historic log cabin, this informal favorite is usually surrounded by lines of hungry patrons waiting for their pancake breakfasts. Lunch choices include a range of sandwiches and burgers. *B, L.* | ($) | ■ | ● | ■ | | ■ |
| **JACKSON:** *Granary Restaurant*<br>1800 Spirit Dance Rd. *(307) 733-8833.*<br>Set atop Gros Ventre Butte in the luxurious Spring Creek Ranch resort, this fine restaurant has a view of the Grand Tetons that complements the array of fresh fish and meat dishes on the menu. *B, L, D.* | ($)($)($) | ■ | ● | ■ | ● | ■ |
| **YELLOWSTONE NATIONAL PARK:** *Old Faithful Inn Dining Room*<br>Old Faithful Bypass. *(307) 545-4999.*<br>Served in a massive room with a 50-ft (15-m) fireplace and a soaring timber ceiling, the food here is secondary to the setting, which is an architectural landmark of the Rockies. *B, L, D.* *mid-Sep–Jun.* | ($)($)($) | ■ | | ■ | | ■ |
| **COLORADO** | | | | | | |
| **BOULDER:** *John's Restaurant*<br>2328 Pearl St. *(303) 444-5232.*<br>John's is a testament to culinary skill. The menu blends classical Mediterranean traditions with those of the Far East and the Southwest, with an emphasis on Colorado game meats. *D.* *Sun, Mon.* | ($)($)($) | ■ | ● | ■ | ● | ■ |
| **BOULDER:** *Flagstaff House*<br>1138 Flagstaff Rd. *(303) 442-4640.*<br>Long considered one of the area's most romantic restaurants, Flagstaff House has an excellent Continental menu to match. *D.* | ($)($)($)($)($) | ■ | ● | ■ | ● | ■ |

For key to symbols see back flap

**RECKENRIDGE (SUMMIT COUNTY):** *Café Alpine* $$$
6 E Adams Ave. *(970) 453-8218.*
1e popular Café Alpine eatery features a tapas bar and terrific wine
st. The restaurant's eclectic menu changes seasonally, with everything
om ostrich to beef, duck, and seafood. Afternoon tapas is served from
om in summer. *D.*

**OLORADO SPRINGS:** *Blue Star* $$$
45 S Tejon St. *(719) 632-1086.*
hip restaurant and bar, the Blue Star restaurant serves an eclectic
enu with a variety of Mediterranean, Asian, and Southwestern
shes. *L (Mon–Fri), D.*

**ENVER:** *Tosh's Hacienda* $
90 Downing St. *(303) 295-1861.*
longtime standout Mexican restaurant, Tosh's Hacienda has staked
reputation since it opened in the 1940s on its zesty family recipes,
hich include a top-notch enchilada and relleno. The restaurant also
rves succulent margaritas as accompaniment. *Brunch (11am onwards), L, D.*

**ENVER:** *Wynkoop Brewing Company* $$
34 18th St. *(303) 297-2700.*
1e Wynkoop is the city's best and oldest microbrewery, housed
a redbrick structure. It offers its patrons pub fare, steaks, poultry,
d seafood alongside its standout beers. *L, D.*

**ENVER:** *Buckhorn Exchange* $$$
00 Osage St. *(303) 534-9505.*
proud possession of Denver's first liquor license, this 1893 restaurant
pointed with taxidermy of all descriptions, now serves gargantuan
eaks as well as elk, buffalo, and other game dishes. *L (Mon–Fri), D.*
*(Wed–Sat).*

**URANGO:** *Randy's* $$
2 College Dr. *(970) 247-9083.*
urango's most intimate restaurant, Randy's features an attractive
erry-wood bar, and serves beef and fresh seafood with attractive
esentations. The restaurant is known for its delicious prime rib
nners. *D.*

**STES PARK (ROCKY MOUNTAIN NATIONAL PARK):** *Dunraven Inn* $$
70 Colorado Hwy 66. *(970) 586-6409.*
1is Italian restaurant, decorated with reproductions of Leonardo
a Vinci's *Mona Lisa*, serves pasta and steak dishes to a boisterous
entele. *D.*

**ANITOU SPRINGS:** *Briarhurst Manor* $$$$
4 Manitou Ave. *(719) 685-1864.*
oused in the 1876 manor built by the founder of Manitou Springs, the
iarhurst is a landmark restaurant that is known for its wide selection
beef, poultry, seafood, and game, as well as its innovative sauces.
*Jan–Mar: Mon, Tue..*

**ORRISON:** *The Fort* $$$
12 Colorado Hwy 8. *(303) 697-4771*
oused in a replica of a historic Colordao fort, this restaurant specializes
wild game and offers excellent cuisine, service, and atmosphere. *D.*
*(occasionally).*

**NOWMASS:** *Krabloonik* $$$$
50 Divide Rd. *(970) 923-3953.*
ocated in a charming log building, Krabloonik is known for its
ouse-smoked game and its homemade soups and breads. The
oprietors also operate dogsled trips in winter from an onsite
ennel. *D (Summer); L & D (Winter).* *(Visitors must call in advance if they
quire wheelchair access).*

**AIL:** *Sweet Basil* $$$
3 E Gore Creek Dr. *(970) 476-0125.*
ne of Vail's culinary trendsetters since it opened in 1977, Sweet
asil infuses Pacific Rim touches in contemporary cuisine. The
enu changes seasonally, using the freshed available ingredients.
*D.*

| | | | | | |
|---|---|---|---|---|---|
| Café Alpine | ■ | ● | ■ | ● | ■ |
| Blue Star | ■ | | ■ | ● | ■ |
| Tosh's Hacienda | ■ | ● | ■ | | ■ |
| Wynkoop Brewing Company | ■ | ● | ■ | | ■ |
| Buckhorn Exchange | ■ | ● | | ● | ■ |
| Randy's | ■ | | ■ | ● | ■ |
| Dunraven Inn | ■ | | ■ | ● | ■ |
| Briarhurst Manor | ■ | ● | ■ | ● | ■ |
| The Fort | ■ | ● | ■ | ● | ■ |
| Krabloonik | ■ | | ■ | ● | ■ |
| Sweet Basil | ■ | ● | ■ | ● | ■ |

# The Pacific Northwest

# THE PACIFIC NORTHWEST

SOME OF NORTH AMERICA'S MOST RUGGED *and spectacular terrain unfolds across the Pacific Northwest. Native cultures have lived here for thousands of years, while European settlement is as recent as the early 19th century. The region is now home to two of North America's most sophisticated cities, Portland and Seattle, surrounded by soaring mountains, dense forests, and sparkling water.*

The call of the wild is what draws visitors to Oregon and Washington, the states that comprise the Pacific Northwest. This region's vast landscapes bear the imprint of the geological forces that carved deep gorges and thrust up soaring mountain peaks. Despite urban development, the wilderness areas retain a certain pristine quality, especially when one encounters the 800-year-old Sitka spruce trees in a coastal rainforest or the lava fields flanking Mount St. Helens, formed during the volcano's eruption in 1980.

The weather in this region is as varied as its topography. West of the mountains, the north Pacific Ocean currents ensure pleasant summers and wet, mild winters. On the eastern plateaus, however, temperatures dip to well below freezing in the winter, often accompanied by heavy snow, and in the summer they soar. In the central mountain region, inland deserts usually experience harsh winters with frequent road closures and dry hot summers.

## HISTORY

The region's Native peoples have lived in harmony with the land since their ancestors migrated here almost 15,000 years ago. The abundance of food and resources, west of the Cascade Mountains and along the coast, enabled many tribes to live in well-established settlements, hunting and fishing. Those tribes, living in the harsher landscapes east of the mountains, pursued more nomadic lifestyles, migrating across the high-desert hunting grounds in search of bison and deer. In spring and

**Mount Rainier towering above Tacoma's Commencement Bay and its industrial tideflats, Washington**

◁ **The Pinnacles, spires of volcanic ash inside the caldera, at Crater Lake National Park, Oregon**

summer, they moved up the mountain slopes to pick berries and dig roots. This tranquil existence was abruptly disturbed with the arrival of European traders and settlers.

The quest to discover the Northwest Passage – a quick ocean route linking Europe with the Far East – lured early European explorers to this region in the 16th century. The first was Spanish explorer Juan Rodriguez, who sailed from Mexico to southern Oregon in 1543. He was followed by Britain's Sir Francis Drake, who ventured as far north as the Strait of Juan de Fuca in 1592.

Portland, City of Roses

Britain's next major expedition was in the 1770s, when Captain James Cook, accompanied by George Vancouver and Peter Puget, sailed up the coasts of Oregon and Washington. In 1791, Vancouver and Puget also charted what is now Puget Sound in Washington. Their explorations coincided with those of an American fur trader from the East Coast, Captain Robert Gray, who discovered the Columbia River in 1792, naming it after his ship. Soon, othe American vessels arrived in search c animal pelts and other bounty.

The battle to control the Pacifi Northwest was waged by the Britisl and Americans with trade, not gunfire The 1803–06 Lewis and Clark expe dition opened up the region tc American fur traders, who wer determined to wrest this ver lucrative trade from the British At that time, the dominan player was Britain's Hudsoı Bay Company (HBC), whicl continued to more or less rul the region until the middle o the 19th century.

Between 1843 and 1860 thousands of American settler migrated westward on the 2,000 mile (3,218-km) Oregon Trail. As a result, America and Britain divided th region in 1846, using the 49th paralle as the new boundary between Britisl Columbia to the north and Orego to the south. Oregon, which include the present-day states of Oregon Washington, and Idaho, became a U territory two years later. In 1852, thi territory was further divided int Washington and Oregon.

Those who profited least from th division of spoils were the Nativ peoples. Diseases had already deci mated many tribes, but now, those wh survived were removed from thei lands and moved to reservations.

### Key Dates in History

**1543** Spanish explorer Juan Rodriguez Cabrillo sails to the coast of southern Oregon

**1765** Robert Rogers maps the vast territory he refers to as Oregon

**1792** Robert Gray crosses the Columbia River

**1829** Oregon City is the first town west of the Rocky Mountains

**1846** US acquires Oregon and Washington

**1848** Oregon Territory established

**1851** Portland is incorporated

**1852** Washington Territory is formed

**1859** Oregon becomes 33rd state

**1865** Seattle is incorporated

**1897** Klondike Gold Rush brings prosperity to Seattle

**1889** Washington becomes 42nd state

**1905** Portland hosts World's Fair with Lewis & Clark Exposition

**1916** Boeing Air Company founded in Seattle

**1949** Seattle earthquake

**1980** Mt. St. Helens erupts in Washington

**1995** Amazon.com launched from Seattle

**2002** Seahawks stadium opens in Seattle

### People & Politics

Nearly ten million people call th Pacific Northwest region their home The nationwide spurt in growth of th Hispanic population in the 1990s i visible in this region as well. Hispanics

**Romantic interpretation of the Oregon Trail's westward trek, painted c.1904**

owboarding at Mount
ood, Oregon

today, constitute the largest ethnic group in the state of Oregon, representing 8 percent of the state's population. Hispanics also form 7.5 percent of Washington's local population. Native Americans have a significant presence here as well, having recovered from the ecline that took place after European ettlement. Many of the tribes continue live in traditional communities, reserving their cultural identites.

Portland and Seattle are among the ntinent's fastest-growing cities. Though oth tend to be liberal in their olitics, other areas in the acific Northwest region main conservative. Even , a unique political climate as emerged in the area. regonians are the first in the S to have approved assisted suicide for e terminally ill, while Washingtonians ave the distinction of electing the ountry's first Asian-American governor. ulturally, the region has cultivated a ch tradition of excellence in the arts, iences, public services, and creative ntrepreneurship. Some of the region's est creative talents include Dale hihuly (b. 1941), one of the world's ading glass sculpturists, rock legend mi Hendrix (1942–70), Matt Groening . 1954), creator of the popular TV ow *The Simpsons*, and Linus Pauling 901–94), winner of two Noble Prizes, r chemistry in 1954 and peace in 1962.

### Economy & Industry

n recent years, the region's economy ad undergone great changes. While traitional industries such as fishing, ining, and logging struggle for survival, ose based on services and technology ourish. Since the 1980s, when Bill ates, the founder of Mircosoft, the orld's foremost computer software mpany, established his headquarters in attle, there has been a proliferation of igh-tech companies. Some 3,000 software and e-commerce businesses operate in the Seattle area alone. Jeff Bezos, another Seattle-based entrepreneur, set up Amazon.com, the world's largest online retailer. Among the other major companies with interests here are computer industry giants Intel, Epson, and Hewlett-Packard, the aerospace leader Boeing, which operates several plants in western Washington, and the sportswear chain Nike. Starbucks, the coffee house that first opened in Seattle's Pike Place Market in the 1970s, now has coffee bars all over the world.

Amid this economic transformation, one industry has done consistently well. Increasingly, tourists are spending healthy sums to enjoy what the locals have long considered their greatest resource – the Pacific Northwest's natural beauty. The region not only offers great opportunities for some of the world's finest adventure sports such as whitewater rafting, kayaking, hiking, skiing, and rockclimbing, but for those who prefer more placid pastimes, the opportunities for sitting next to a mountain stream, or strolling along a remote beach are seemingly endless.

Fresh

Neon sign at Seattle's Pike Place Market

Portlanders relaxing at one of the city's local cafés and wine bars

# Exploring the Pacific Northwest

THE PACIFIC NORTHWEST, comprising Oregon and Washington, is a region of great natural beauty. Its lofty mountains, deep canyons, crystal clear lakes, mighty rivers, and rugged shoreline offer visitors a chance to enjoy a wide range of outdoor activities. Equally alluring are its two principal cities – Portland and Seattle, with their excellent museums and vibrant cultural scene. Both cities are well-connected by air, road, and rail. However, the best way to explore the region, especially remote areas, such as Oregon's Hell Canyon and Washington's Olympic Peninsula, is by car.

**The Space Needle, dominating the Seattle skyline**

## Sights at a Glance

**Washington**
- *Seattle pp616–19* 1
- Olympic Peninsula 2
- Port Townsend 3
- Bellingham 4
- *San Juan Islands pp622–3* 5
- North Cascades Highway 6
- Lake Chelan 7
- Leavenworth 8
- Spokane 9
- Walla Walla 10
- Yakima Valley 11
- Maryhill 12
- *Mount Rainier National Park pp626–7* 13
- Tacoma 14
- Olympia 15
- Mount St. Helens National Volcanic Monument 16
- Fort Vancouver 17

**Oregon**
- *Portland pp630–31* 18
- Columbia River Gorge 19
- Mount Hood 20
- Astoria 21
- Oregon Coast 22
- Salem 23
- Eugene 24
- Madras & Warm Springs 25
- Sisters 26
- Bend 27
- Newberry National Volcanic Monument 28
- *Crater Lake National Park pp636–7* 29
- Oregon Caves National Monument 30
- Ashland 31
- Steens Mountain 32
- Malheur National Wildlife Refuge 33
- John Day Fossil Beds National Monument 34
- Pendleton 35
- Wallowa Mountains 36
- *Hell's Canyon National Recreation Area pp640–41* 37

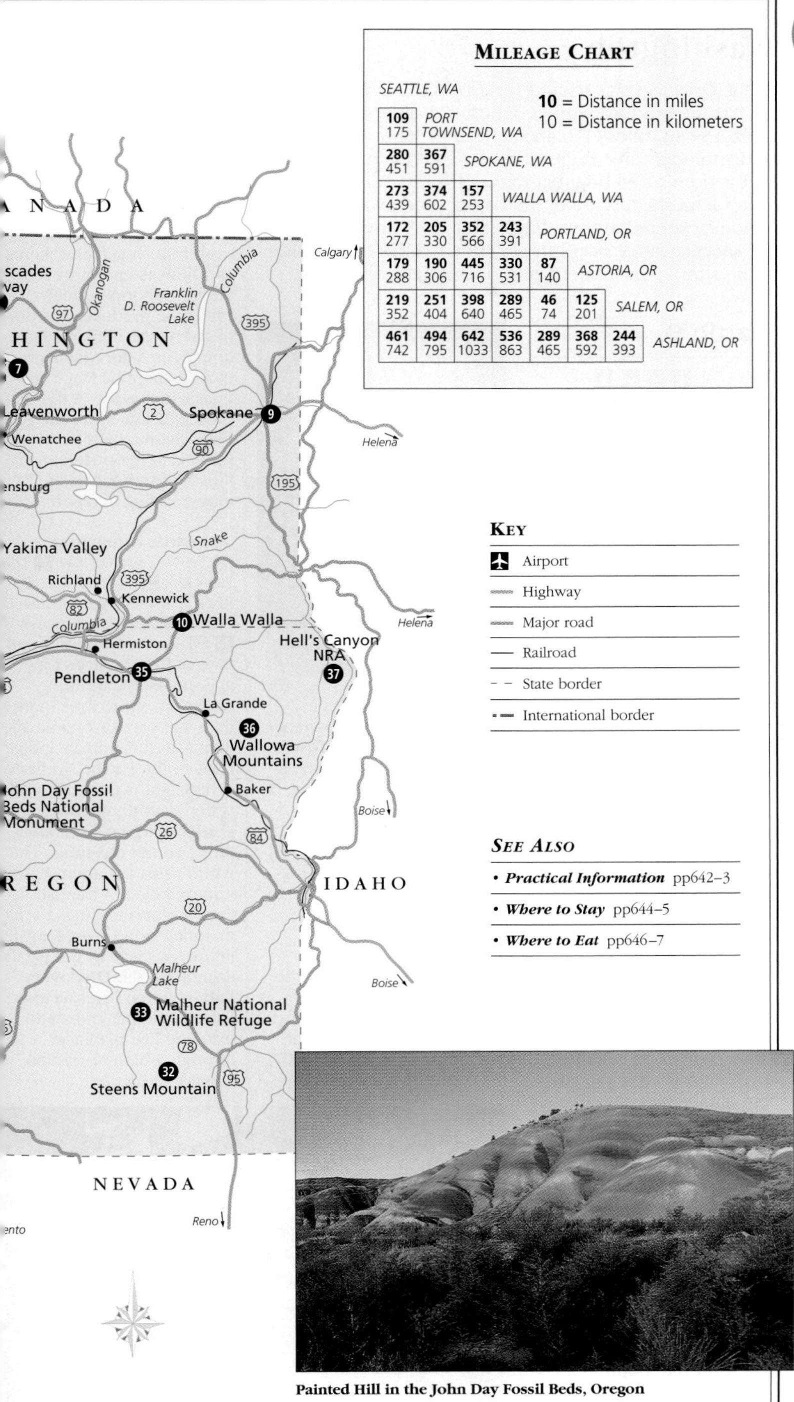

**Mileage Chart**

**10** = Distance in miles
10 = Distance in kilometers

| | Seattle, WA | Port Townsend, WA | Spokane, WA | Walla Walla, WA | Portland, OR | Astoria, OR | Salem, OR |
|---|---|---|---|---|---|---|---|
| Port Townsend, WA | **109** 175 | | | | | | |
| Spokane, WA | **280** 451 | **367** 591 | | | | | |
| Walla Walla, WA | **273** 439 | **374** 602 | **157** 253 | | | | |
| Portland, OR | **172** 277 | **205** 330 | **352** 566 | **243** 391 | | | |
| Astoria, OR | **179** 288 | **190** 306 | **445** 716 | **330** 531 | **87** 140 | | |
| Salem, OR | **219** 352 | **251** 404 | **398** 640 | **289** 465 | **46** 74 | **125** 201 | |
| Ashland, OR | **461** 742 | **494** 795 | **642** 1033 | **536** 863 | **289** 465 | **368** 592 | **244** 393 |

**Key**

- Airport
- Highway
- Major road
- Railroad
- State border
- International border

***See Also***


- ***Practical Information*** pp642–3
- ***Where to Stay*** pp644–5
- ***Where to Eat*** pp646–7




Painted Hill in the John Day Fossil Beds, Oregon

# Washington

THE ONLY US STATE named for a president, Washington has an extraordinary geographical diversity within its 68,139 sq miles (176,466 sq km) of land. Of its three distinct geographic regions, the coastal Olympic Peninsula is dominated by great tracts of forest. Most of the state's largest cities are in the damp, green western region, scattered around Puget Sound. A drive through the spectacular peaks of the North Cascades takes visitors to the sunny, dry eastern part of the state.

## Seattle ❶

*534,700.* *800 Convention Place, Galleria Level, (206) 461-5840.* www.cityofseattle.net

NESTLED BETWEEN Puget Sound and Lake Washington, with Mount Rainier in the background, Seattle has a spectacular setting. The home of Microsoft and Boeing, the city's growth since the Klondike Gold Rush of 1897 *(see p737)* has been vigorous. Its prime geographic location, enviable lifestyle, and flourishing film and music scene make Seattle one of America's most attractive cities.

### Pioneer Square

Bounded by Alaskan & Yester Ways, 2nd Ave & S King St. *15, 18, 21, 22, 56.* *Occidental Park.* **Klondike National Historical Park** 319 2nd Ave S. *(206) 220-4240.* *9am–5pm daily.* *Jan 1, Thanksg., Dec 25.*

Seattle's first downtown and later a decrepit skid row, Pioneer Square is now a revitalized business neighborhood and National Historic District with a thriving art scene. Many of its buildings were constructed in the years between the two pivotal events in Seattle's history – the Great Fire of 1889 and the Klondike Gold Rush of 1897–98. The handsome Pioneer Building on 1st Avenue, for instance, was completed three years after the fire.

The story of Seattle's role in the Gold Rush is told in the **Klondike National Historical Park** on South Jackson Street. A Seattle institution, the **Elliott Bay Book Company** nearby, occupies the site of the city's first hospital and stocks around

**A display in Klondike Gold Rush National Historical Park**

150,000 titles. Opened in 1914, Seattle's first skyscraper, the terra-cotta **Smith Tower**, offers superb views from its wraparound observation deck.

### Pike Place Market

Bounded by Pike & Virginia Sts, from 1st to Western Aves. *(206) 682-7453.* *15, 18.* *8am–9pm Mon–Sat, 11am–5pm Sun; may vary.* *public hols.* www.pikeplacemarket.org

Said to be the soul of Seattle, Pike Place Market is known as much for its colorful personality as for its abundant local produce. Established in 1907, the country's oldest continuously operating farmers' market is now a historic district bustling with farmers artists, and street performers Rachel, an enormous piggy bank, stands at the main entrance to the market, whc heart is the **Main Arcade** ar the adjacent **North Arcade**. Here, low counters display fresh fruit, vegetables, herbs and flowers grown by local farmers. Shoppers get to "meet the producer," as promised by the market's signature green sign. Attractions include the Pike Place Starbucks, birthplace of the omı present chain, and **Pike Pla Fish**, the market's best-knov seafood vendor. Here, fish-flinging fishmongers are a long-standing tradition.

### Seattle Aquarium

Pier 59, 1483 Alaskan Way. *(20 386-4320.* *15, 18, 21, 22, 56. Pike.* *10am–7pm daily; Labor D –Memorial Day: 10am–5pm daily.* www.seattleaquarium.org

One of the country's top aquariums, the Seattle Aquarium showcases more than 400 species of animals, plants, and mammals indige nous to the Pacific Northwe A highlight is the huge und water glass dome, filled wit sharks, octopus, and other Puget Sound creatures. The world's first aquarium-basec salmon ladder – the fish jumping up the rungs to the maturing pond – explains tl entire life cycle of the Pacifi salmon. In the **Discovery Lab**, children can touch star fish and hermit crabs and examine live plankton through a high-resolution video microscope.

**Pike Place Fish in Pike Place Market, which offers both fish and fun**

**I Odyssey Maritime ɩiscovery Center**

ɘll St Pier 66, 2205 Alaskan Way. (206) 374-4000. *15, 18, 21, 2, 56. Bell. 10am–5pm Tue–ɪt, noon–5pm Sun. Mon, Jan 1, ɜy before Thanksgiving, Thanks-ving, Dec 24–25.* *ɛhibits, lectures, films.* www.ody.org

ocated on Seattle's historic ɾorking waterfront, the )dyssey is the country's first ɪaritime discovery center. It ses interactive exhibits and ɪort films to explain how ɪe maritime and fisheries ɪdustries contribute to the ɾell-being of the region. In **haring the Sound**, visitors an paddle kayaks through irtual waters, dock a small ɪnker, and learn about Puget ound. Interactive exhibits in ɪe **Harvesting the Sea** allery invite visitors to xperience the lives of rabbers and salmon shermen. The hands-n exhibits are eared toward eople of all ages, ɾho enjoy this leverly designed ɪuseum.

Inside Odyssey Maritime Discovery Center

**Seattle Art Museum**

100 University St. *(206) 654-3100.* *174. closed for renovation until spring 2007. Some of the collection will be displayed at the Seattle Asian Art Musuem. (free 1st Thu of month).* www. seattleartmuseum.org

**Benaroya Hall** 200 University St. *(206) 215-4700. 174. noon & 1pm Tue & Fri.* www.benaroyahall.com

At the entrance of the Seattle Art Museum stands the giant *Hammering Man*, a 48-ft (15-m) animated steel sculpture created as a tribute to workers. The bold limestone-and-sandstone museum building is as impressive. Its permanent collection includes 23,000 objects ranging from ancient Egyptian reliefs and wooden African sculptures to Old Master paintings and contemporary American art. Traveling exhibits are on the second floor. Also part of the museum are the Seattle Asian Art Museum in Volunteer Park in Capitol Hill *(see p618)*, and the Olympic Sculpture Park, which is located on Seattle's waterfront.

**The *Hammering Man* sculpture at the entrance of Seattle Art Museum**

Across the street, **Benaroya Hall**, home of the Seattle Symphony, occupies an entire city block. Of its two performing halls, Taper Auditorium, acclaimed for its fine acoustics, has 2,500 seats. The multilevel Grand Lobby, dramatic at night when lit, offers stunning views of the city skyline. Benaroya Hall has some excellent tools and an impressive private art collection.

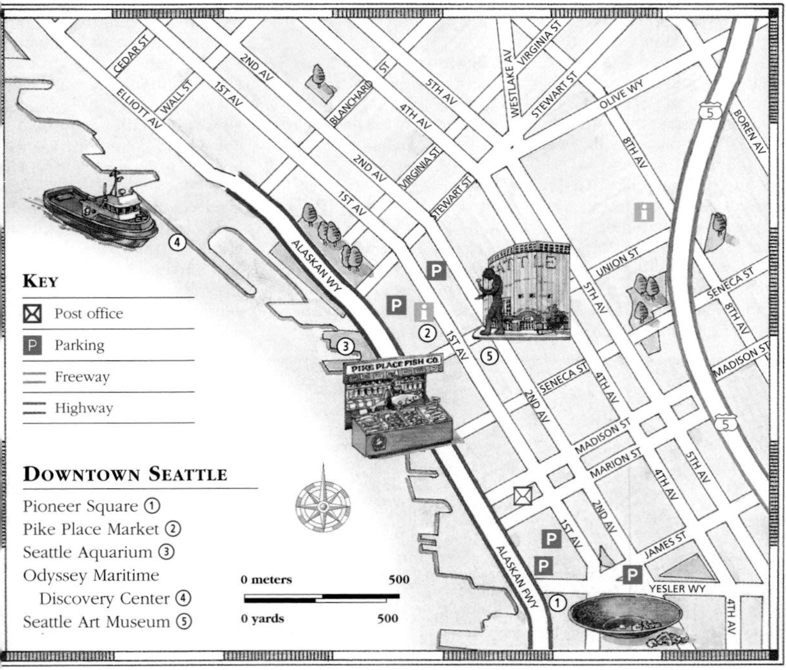

**KEY**

- Post office
- Parking
- Freeway
- Highway

**DOWNTOWN SEATTLE**

Pioneer Square ①
Pike Place Market ②
Seattle Aquarium ③
Odyssey Maritime Discovery Center ④
Seattle Art Museum ⑤

0 meters 500
0 yards 500

## Seattle: Beyond Downtown

This extensive city offers plenty of opportunities for exploration and recreation. Immediately north of downtown are the prime cultural venues of Seattle Center, while to its northeast is the prominent Capitol Hill. Farther afield are the lively University District, Woodland Park Zoo, and the characterful neighborhoods of Fremont and Ballard.

### Seattle Center

Bounded by Denny Way & 1st Ave N, Mercer & Broad Sts. *(206) 684-7200.* *Seattle Center.* *2, 3, 4, 16, 19, 24, 33.* www.seattlecenter.com **Space Needle** 400 Broad St. *(206) 905-2100.* *check for times.* www.spaceneedle.com **Experience Music Project** 325 5th Ave N. *(206) 367-5483.* *10am–8pm daily.* *Thanksgiving, Dec 25.* www.emplive.com

The proud legacy of the city's second World's Fair in 1962, this 74-acre (30-ha) urban park contains several innovative structures, cultural venues, and excellent museums. Among the most striking is the **Space Needle**. Supported by three curved steel legs, the needle's glass-enclosed tophouse features an observation deck and a revolving restaurant. At the base of the Space Needle, the exuberant Frank Gehry-designed **Experience Music Project** celebrates music with rare memorabilia, interactive exhibits, and live performance space. The Jimi Hendrix Gallery here has been recently revamped. Also in the Seattle Center, the **Pacific Science Center** features six buildings of white pre-cast concrete surrounding five arches that soar over reflecting pools and fountains. Its hands-on science and math exhibits are especially appealing to kids.

The center is best reached by the **Seattle Monorail**. It covers the 1.2-mile (2-km) distance between the downtown station (5th Avenue at Pine Street) and the Seattle Center in 90 seconds.

**Space Needle, Seattle's best-known landmark and prime tourist attraction**

### Belltown

Bounded by Denny Way, Virginia St, Elliot Ave, & Broad St. *15, 18, 21, 22, 56.* **Austin A. Bell Building** 2326 1st Ave. **Virginia Inn** 1937 1st Ave. *(206) 728-1937.* *11:30am–midnight Sun–Thu, 11:30am–2am Fri–Sat.*

South of the Seattle Center lies trendy Belltown. With its broad avenues lined with hip clubs, chic restaurants, and eclectic shops, it has been compared to Manhattan's Upper West Side. Earlie an unremarkable area filled with labor union halls, car lots, and sailors' taverns, its iden tity began to change in the 1970s when artists, attracted by cheap rent and abundant studio space, moved in. Belltown experienced a building boom during the software explosion of the 1990s and now bears little resemblance to its early days. The handsome four-story brick **Austin A. Bell Building** is one of the few remaining original structures. Commissioned in 1888 by Austin Americus Bell, the wealthy son of Seattle pionee William M. Bell, for whom Belltown is named, it is listec on the National Register of Historic Places. The building now houses pricey condominiums, a coffee shop, and an upscale restaurant. The brick-and-tile **Virginia Inn** *(see p646)*, on the southern boundary of Belltown, is another historic building. A popular watering hole for more than a century, it is no Seattle's hottest art bar, with rotating exhibits by local artists adorning the walls.

**The Experience Music Project building, in Seattle Center**

### Capitol Hill

Bounded by Montlake Blvds E & NE, E Pike & E Madison Sts, 23rd Ave E & I-5. *7, 9, 10.*

Lively Capitol Hill is a colorfu neighborhood where no one blinks at spiked purple hair and multiple body piercings. Broadway, the district's major avenue, is lined with shops and ethnic restaurants. Bronz footsteps, to teach passersby the tango and fox trot, are embedded in the sidewalk of Broadway.

While people-watching is a major source of entertainment, Capitol Hill also features two vintage movie houses: the **Egyptian** on East Pine Street and the **Harvard Exit** on Eas Roy Street. The hill is also home to **St. Mark's Episcopal Cathedral** on 10th Avenue Street, known for its magnificent Flentrop organ, consisting of 3,944 pipes.

chard Beyer's aluminium sculpture in Fremont

**Fremont**

ounded by N 50th St, Lake ashington Ship Canal, Stone Way ve N, & 8th Ave NW. *26, 28.*

his funky district declared self an "artists' republic" in e 1960s, one consisting of udents, artists, and bohe- ians attracted here by low nts. By the late 1990s, its naracter began to change, ter a high-tech firm set up ffice here. However, Fremont as managed to hold on to erished traditions, such as e Summer Solstice Parade nd an outdoor film series.

Public art is a fixture of remont. A 13.5-ft (4-m) tall atue of Lenin towers above edestrians at Fremont Place, nd a 15-ft (4.5-m) tall olkswagen-eating troll lurks nder the north end of the urora Bridge. On 34th Street, culptor Richard Beyer's *People Vaiting for the Interurban* is egularly clothed by locals. he dog's face in the culpture is modeled after an onorary mayor, with whom e artist had a dispute.

**University District**

ounded by NE 55th St, Portage Bay, ontlake Blvd NE, & I-5. *4014 niversity Way NE, (206) 543-9198. 7, 25, 43, 70, 71, 72, 73. 8am–5pm Mon–Fri.* **Washington ark Arboretum** 2300 Arboretum r E. *(206) 543-8800.* **isitor Center** *10am–4pm.* **rounds** *7am–dusk. to apanese Garden.* ww.depts.washington.edu/wpa

he hub of the energetic -District is the University f Washington, the premier nstitute of higher learning in he Northwest. Located on the ite of the 1909 World's Fair, the lovely 693-acre (280-ha) parklike campus is home to more than 35,000 students and 218 buildings in a mix of architectural styles. Just inside the main campus entrance is the **Burke Museum of Natural History and Culture**, featuring dinosaur fossils and Northwest Native art. On the western edge of the campus sits the **Henry Art Gallery**, the first public art museum in the state. The university's main avenue **University Way Northeast**, just west of the campus, is lined with bookstores, pubs, and inexpensive restaurants. University Village, east of the campus, offers an upscale shopping and dining experience.

A must-see is the **Washington Park Arboretum**, a 230-acre (93-ha) garden and living plant museum, with 4,600 species. Its Japanese Garden has carp-filled ponds and an authentic teahouse that is open for ceremonies once a month.

**Woodland Park Zoo**

5500 Phinney Ave N. *(206) 684-4800. 5. check for times.* www.zoo.org

Designed in 1899, this is one of the oldest zoos on the West Coast and a major Seattle attraction. The nearly 300 animal species residing at the 92-acre (37-ha) zoo are grouped together in ecosystems rather than by species, in habitats designed to resemble their natural habitats. A visitor center at the main entrance provides maps and other information, such as animal feeding times. Among the excellent naturalistic habitats are the **Elephant Forest** – with its enormous elephant pool and Thai logging camp replica – and the **Trail of Vines**, which includes the first open-forested canopy for orangutans to be created within a zoo. The **Family Farm** features a popular petting zoo; a recent addition here is the Bug World exhibit. Indigenous North American animals can be viewed in their natural habitats along the **Northern Trail**.

**Ballard**

Bounded by Salmon Bay, Shilshole Bay, & Phinney Ridge. *15, 17, 18.* **Hiram M. Chittenden Locks** 3015 NW 54th St. *(206) 783-7059.* **Grounds** *7am–9pm daily.* **Visitor Center** *check for times. May–Sep: daily, Oct–Nov & Mar–Apr: Thu–Mon.*

Located in northwest Seattle, Ballard's distinct Scandinavian accent dates to its settlement by Scandinavian fishermen and loggers in 1853. At the turn of the 19th century, Ballard was a mill town, producing an impressive three million wooden shingles a day. North of the shingle mills, **Ballard Avenue** was the commercial center of this area and is now a historic district, which features a wide array of ethnic cafés and lively music clubs.

Historic belltower in Ballard

The area's Scandinavian heritage is celebrated at the annual Norwegian Constitution Day Parade on May 17, at the excellent **Nordic Heritage Museum** on Northwest 67th Street.

Located at the west end of Ballard, the **Hiram M. Chittenden Locks** allow boats to travel between salt-water Puget Sound and freshwater Lake Union and Lake Washington. Its grounds include 7 acres (3 ha) of botanical gardens.

# The Olympic Peninsula ❷

**Olympic National Park Headquarters** *3002 Mt Angeles Rd, 1 mile S of Port Angeles, (360) 452-0330.*
www.nps.gov/olym/home.htm

BORDERED BY THE Pacific Ocean, the Strait of Juan de Fuca, and Puget Sound, Washington's Olympic Peninsula is an extraordinary piece of land. Its coastline, etched with bays and inlets, is peppered with majestic sea stacks – portions of wave-eroded headlands that remain as offshore mounds. Some of the country's most pristine mountains, beaches, and forestlands can be found in this remote region.

Sitting on the northwest tip of the peninsula, historic **Port Townsend** is known for its Victorian architecture and vibrant arts community. To its south, **Port Gamble**, a former logging town on the Kitsap Peninsula, has retained its original New England Victorian-style homes, country store, and church. The 1982 movie, *An Officer and a Gentleman*, was filmed here.

The centerpiece of the peninsula is the sprawling **Olympic National Park** *(p34)*, a UNESCO biosphere reserve and World Heritage Site. Encompassing 923,000 acres (373,540 ha), this biologically diverse park is a treasure-trove of snowcapped mountain peaks, lakes, waterfalls, rivers, and rainforests. Running through the center of the park are the jagged, glacier-covered Olympic Mountains. With its West Peak rising to a height of 7,965 ft (2,428 m), the three-peaked Mount Olympus is the highest mountain in the range.

The peninsula's Lake Crescent Lodge

The park headquarters are located in Port Angeles, a working port town. Sitting in the rain shadow of the Olympic Mountains, Sequim (pronounced "Squim") features an elk viewing site and the Olympic Game Farm, home to endangered animals. Southwest of Sequim, **Hurricane Ridge** offers panoramic views of the Olympic Mountains, the Strait of Juan de Fuca, and Vancouver Island from its 5,230-ft (1,594-m) high summit. In spring, the ridge is covered with wildflowers.

To the west, is the picturesque Lake Crescent area. Trout fishing is the main draw in this 625-ft (190-m) deep freshwater lake whose crystal clear waters also make it a favorite with divers. The historic resort, **Lake Crescent Lodge** *(see p644)*, located on the lake's southern shore, is a lovely place to stay. Farther west, the 4-mile (6.5-km) long **Rialto Beach** offers superb views of the Pacific Coast, with its tide pool sea stacks, rocky islands and the Hole in the Wal a tunnel carved by waves into a cliff.

The coastline receives the highest rainfall in the state. As a result, rainforests carpet much of the region. The **Ho Rainforest**, with its annual rainfall of 14 ft (4 m), is a magical place, lush with Sitka spruce, Douglas fir, yew, and red cedar, draped with moss. Ancient trees here tower to nearly 300 ft (91 m) in height and even the ferns grow talle than the hikers. Rainforests also surround the shores of Lake Quinalt. Snowcapped mountains encircle this glacia lake, which attracts fishermen and swimmers alike.

Wildlife is plentiful in the Olympic Peninsula – deer and bear abound, and the Olympic National Park has the country's largest herd of Roosevelt elk. The peninsula offers a wide range of outdoor recreation activities; among the most popular pursuits are fly- and deep-sea fishing, kayaking, whitewater rafting, mountain biking, hiking, and bird-watching. Skiing and snowshoeing are popular winter activities.

The majestic Olympic Mountains in Olympic National Park

ɪint Wilson Lighthouse, in Port Townsend's Fort Worden State Park

## ort Townsend ❸

8,000. from Keystone on ɦidbey Island & from Edmonds. 2437 E Sims Way, (888) 365-78. www.ptguide.com

ᴛHIS SEAPORT, a National Historic Landmark, is one only three seaports on the ıtional Registry. A building ɔom in the late 1800s left e town with several grand ctorian mansions, which ɔw form the cornerstone of thriving tourism industry. Downtown's Romanesque **fferson County Court-ɔuse** with its 124-ft (38-m) l clock tower, is claimed to the jewel of Port Town-ɴd's Victorian architecture. rther away, the old City ıll is now the **Jefferson ɔunty Historical Society**, ɔme to the city council, as ell as an excellent museum. her famous buildings clude the Ann Starrett Man-ɔn and the Rothschild House. The **Fire Bell Tower**, on e bluff overlooking down-wn, was built to summon e town's voluntary fire ɦters. The tower now ads the country's list of the n Most Endangered Historic easures. **Point Wilson ghthouse**, in Fort Worden ıte Park, first lit in 1879, is l in operation.

Port Townsend is also an cellent base from which to ıke whale-watching, kayak-ɡ, and cycling day-trips.

**Jefferson County ɔurthouse**
20 Jefferson St. (360) 385-ɔ0. 8am–5pm Mon–Fri. public hols.

## Bellingham ❹

71,000. 904 Potter St, (800) 487-2032. www.bellingham.org

OVERLOOKING Bellingham Bay and many of the San Juan Islands *(see pp622–3)*, this town consists of four original towns – Whatcom, Sehome, Bellingham, and Fairhaven – consolidated into a single entity in 1904. The town's historic architecture includes Old Whatcom County Courthouse on East Street, the first brick building north of San Francisco, built in 1858, and the majestic City Hall. Built in 1892 in the Victorian Second Empire style, the City Hall is now the heart of the **Whatcom Museum of History and Art**. This four-building campus includes a children's museum. Among the highlights here are exhibits on the Northwest Coast Native Americans and the birds of the Pacific Northwest.

Tower of Bellingham's former City Hall

The downtown area has several restaurants, art galleries, and specialty shops. South of downtown, the historic Fairhaven district is an artsy enclave of Victorian buildings housing galleries, restaurants, and bookstores.

Just up the hill from downtown sits the campus of **Western Washington University**, with its famous collection of outdoor sculptures, including artworks by noted American artists Richard Serra, Mark di Suvero, and Richard Beyer.

From Bellingham's ports, passenger ferries leave for whale-watch cruises and tours to Vancouver Island and the San Juan Islands. Near the city are several waterfront parks, hiking and biking trails, and recreational areas. South of the city, Chuckanut Drive (Hwy 11) is a scenic 21-mile (34-km) loop. Some 55 miles (88.5 km) east of Bellingham is the 10,778-ft (3,285-m) high Mount Baker, popular for skiing and snowboarding.

**Whatcom Museum of History & Art**
121 Prospect St. (360) 676-6981. noon–5pm Tue–Sun. **Children's Museum** Tue–Wed, 10am–5pm Thu–Sat, noon–5pm Sun.

**Western Washington University**
S College Dr & College Way. (360) 650-3424. **Visitor Center** mid-Sep–mid-Jun: 7:15am–8pm Mon–Fri; mid-Jun–mid-Sep: 7:15am–5pm Mon–Fri. public hols. www.wwu.edu

Crab traps on a boat ready to set out from Bellingham Harbor

# San Juan Islands ❺

**A Washington State ferry sailing from the mainland to the islands**

SCATTERED BETWEEN the Washington mainland and Vancouver Island, the San Juan archipelago consists of over 700 islands, 172 of them named. Ferries sail from Anacortes to the four largest islands – Lopez, Shaw, Orcas, and San Juan. Affectionately called "Slopez" because of its laid-back nature, Lopez's gently rolling roads, numerous stopping points, and friendly drivers make it a popular destination for cycling. Horseshoe-shaped Orcas, the hilliest island in the chain, offers breathtaking views from atop 2,409-ft (734-m) Mount Constitution. The best destination for walk-on passengers, San Juan Island is home to Friday Harbor, the largest town in the archipelago. The nationally renowned Whale Museum is located here. Primarily residential, Shaw Island does not offer any visitor facilities.

**Sailboats in the Channel**
*Sailors love the many harbors and good winds in the San Juan Channel.*

**★ Roche Harbor**
*A charming seaside village, Roche Harbor features a marina, Victorian gardens, a chapel, and the historic Hotel de Haro, built in 1886.*

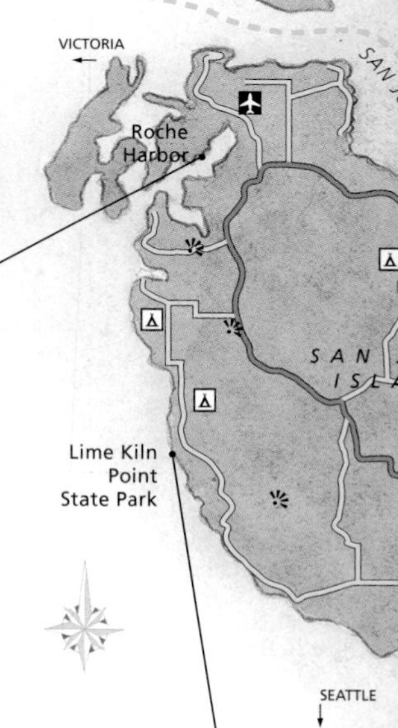


0 km 2
0 miles 2

**Lime Kiln Point State Park**
*This state park, with its picturesque lighthouse, is the only park in the country dedicated to whale-watching.*

**STAR SIGHTS**

- ★ **Deer Harbor**
- ★ **Friday Harbor**
- ★ **Lopez**
- ★ **Roche Harbor**

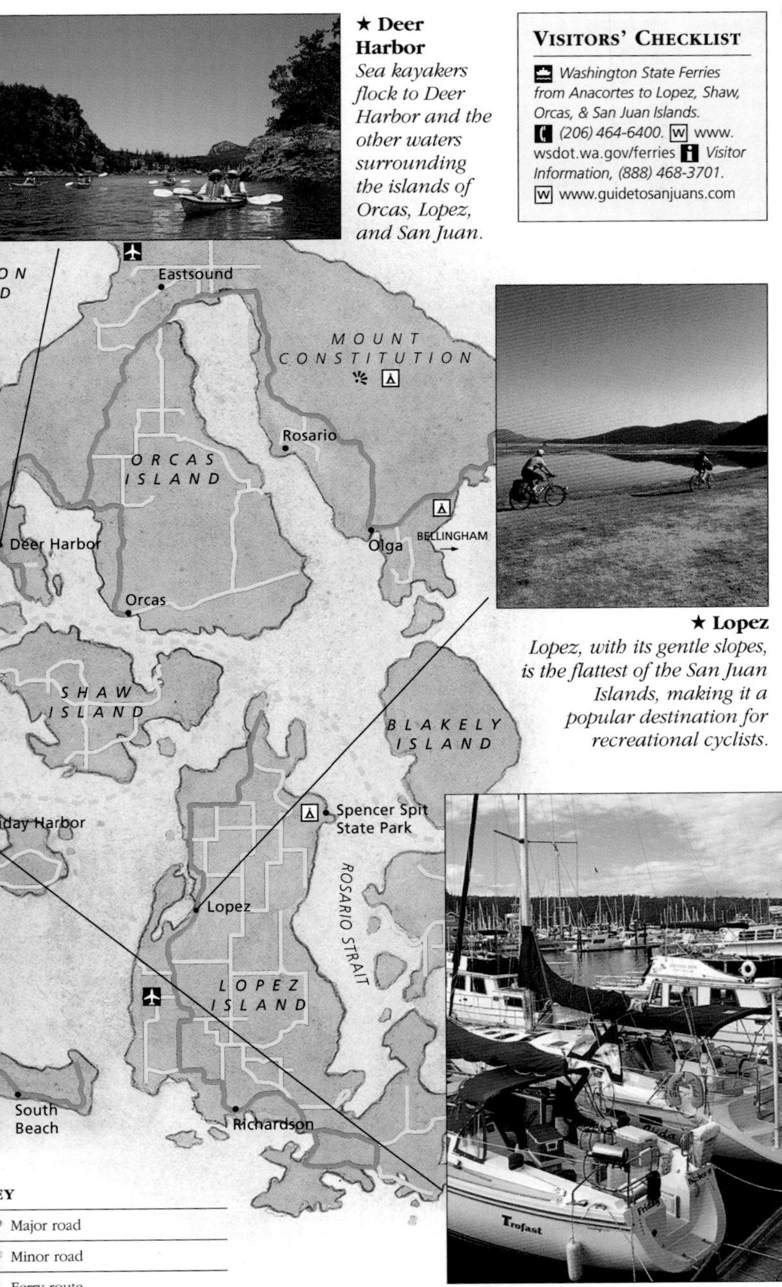


**★ Deer Harbor**
*Sea kayakers flock to Deer Harbor and the other waters surrounding the islands of Orcas, Lopez, and San Juan.*

**★ Lopez**
*Lopez, with its gentle slopes, is the flattest of the San Juan Islands, making it a popular destination for recreational cyclists.*

**★ Friday Harbor**
*The largest town in the San Juans, Friday Harbor offers a number of restaurants, inns, galleries, and shops – all within easy walking distance of the ferry dock.*

### Visitors' Checklist

*Washington State Ferries from Anacortes to Lopez, Shaw, Orcas, & San Juan Islands.* *(206) 464-6400.* www.wsdot.wa.gov/ferries *Visitor Information, (888) 468-3701.* www.guidetosanjuans.com

**Turquoise-colored Diablo Lake in North Cascades National Park**

## North Cascades Highway ❻

State Rte 20.

The scenic North Cascades Highway is the northernmost mountain pass route in Washington. It is the 132-mile (213-km) section of Highway 20 between Winthrop in the east and I-5 to the west. Bisecting the **North Cascades National Park**, it offers access to the many wonders of this breathtakingly beautiful eco-system of jagged snowcapped peaks, forested valleys, and cascading waterfalls. The entire route is open from mid-April to mid-October.

The road follows the Skagit River, passing Gorge Creek Falls, Lake Diablo, and Ruby Creek. Along the way, the Ross Lake Overview is an ideal spot to view the scenic lake. At 5,477 ft (1,669 m), **Washington Pass Overlook** provides heart-pounding vistas of the steep pass up Liberty Bell Mountain. A dominant feature of the park, **Mount Shuksan** at the height of 9,131 ft (2,783 m), is one of the state's highest mountains.

The heavily glaciated park is home to a variety of animals – bald eagles, gray wolves, and bears. Many hiking trails link the highway to the quiet town of Stehekin at the northernmost tip of Lake Chelan.

**North Cascades National Park**
*SR 20, near milepost 120 & Newhalem, (206) 386-4495.*
www.ncascades.org

## Lake Chelan ❼

*102 E Johnson Ave, (509) 682-3503.* www.lakechelan.com

Magnificent Lake Chelan, in the remote northwest end of the Cascades, claims the distinction of being the country's third-deepest lake, reaching 1,500 ft (457 m) at its deepest point. Fed by 27 glaciers and 59 streams, the lake, which is less than 2 miles (3 km) wide, stretches for 55 miles (89 km). In summer, it buzzes with activity – boating, fishing, snorkeling, water-skiing, and wind surfing. The resort town of **Chelan** at the southeastern end of the lake has been a popular summer vacation destination for generations of Western Washingtonians seeking the sunny, dry weather on the eastern side of the state. Basking in the rain shadow of the Cascade Mountains, the town enjoys 300 days of sunshine each year. The town's vintage **Ruby Theatre** on East Woodin Avenue is one of the oldest continuously running movie theaters in the Northwest. Chelan's other highlights are the murals on buildings, which depict the history of the Lake Chelan Valley.

About 9 miles (14 km) from downtown Chelan is the town of **Manson**, whose main attraction is the Scenic Loop Trail. It offers easy exploration of the nearby orchards and hill countryside. Farther north, the lakeside town of **Stehekin** can be reached by ferry.

**Sign welcoming visitors to Lake Chelan**

## Leavenworth ❽

*2,500.* *220 9th St, (509) 54 5807.* www.leavenworth.o

Once a logging town, Leavenworth, at the foo of the Cascade Mountains in central Washington, is now a quaint little Bavarian-style town seemingly straight out of a fairy tale. This theme w consciously developed in th 1960s to help revitalize the town and, today, every commercial building in town Starbucks and McDonald's included, looks as though it belongs in the Alps.

The town now bustles wit festivals, art shows, and summer theater productions attracting more than a millio visitors each year. Among its popular festivals are Faschin a classic Bavarian carnival held in February; Maifest, with its 16th-century costumes, maypole dances, and jousting; and Oktoberfest *(se p30)*, the traditional celebrati of German foo beer, and musi Teeming with Bavarian specialt shops and restaurants, the town also ha the fascinating **Leavenwort Nutcracker Museum**, whic showcases 4,500 nutcrackers from 38 countries, some dating back 500 years.

**Leavenworth Nutcrack Museum**
735 Front St. *(509) 548-4573.*
*May–Oct: 2–5pm daily; Nov–Apr 2–5pm Sat–Sun.* *for groups by appt.*

**A traditional horse-drawn 13-barrel beer wagon in Leavenworth**

## pokane 9

195,000. 301–801 W erside Ave, (800) 248-3230. www.visitspokane.com

WASHINGTON'S largest inland city, this is the land Northwest's commer- al and cultural center. The y was rebuilt in brick and rra-cotta after a disastrous e in 1889 – its many hand- me buildings are reminders that building boom. Spokane is the smallest city host a world's fair (Expo 4). The fair site is now the rawling **Riverfront Park**, a 0-acre (40-ha) expanse in e heart of the city. Of the wn's two museum's, the **orthwest Museum of Arts Culture** showcases region- history, while **Campbell ouse** (1898) nearby is an teractive museum. Other tractions are an IMAX® neater and a 1909 carousel. 37-mile (60-km) trail con- ects the city with Riverside ate Park, located 6 miles 0 km) to the northwest.

**Northwest Museum of rts & Culture**
16 W 1st Ave. (509) 456-3931.
*11am–5pm Tue–Sun.*
*public hols.*
www.northwestmuseum.org

## Valla Walla 10

30,000. 29 E Sumac St, (509) 25-0850. www.wallawalla.org

LOCATED IN THE southeast corner of the state, Walla Walla is a green oasis in the midst of an arid landscape. he town features several ational Register buildings, lovely parks, and a wealth of public art. The attractive campus of **Whitman College**, one of the nation's top-rated liberal arts colleges, is three blocks from downtown.

A popular destination for wine connoisseurs, the Walla Walla Valley has more than 35 wineries – several right in the heart of downtown. Among the town's other claims to fame are its delicious sweet Walla Walla onions and its annual Hot Air Balloon Stampede, a rally of some 45 pilots, held in May. The stampede also features live music, arts-and-crafts booths, and various events.

**Fort Walla Walla Museum**, on Myra Road, consisting of original and replica pioneer buildings, gives a historical perspective of the area. The **Whitman Mission National Historic Site**, about 7 miles (11 km) west of town, is a memorial to pioneer missionaries Marcus and Narcissa Whitman who were massacred by Cayuse Indians. On weekends, the Living History Company honors the area's history through music and dance.

**Fort Walla Walla Museum**
755 Myra Rd. (509) 525-7703.
*Apr–Oct: 10am–5pm daily.*
*(call ahead).* *by arrangement.*
www.fortwallawallamuseum.org

**Whitman Mission National Historic Site**
Hwy 12. (509) 522-6360.
*Jun–Sep: 8am–6pm daily; Oct–May: 8am–4:30pm daily.* *Jan 1, Thanksgiving, Dec 25.*
*(except Monument Hill).*
www.nps.gov/whmi

alloons over Walla Walla during the annual Hot Air Balloon Stampede

## Yakima Valley 11

10 N 8th St, Yakima, (509) 575-3010. www.visityakima.com

WITH ITS RICH volcanic soil, abundance of irrigation water, and 300 days of annual sunshine, the Yakima Valley is the fifth largest producer of fruits and vegetables in the US, and home to more than 30 regional wineries. Yakima, the valley's largest community and commercial hub, is a good base for visiting the valley's award-winning wineries.

Grapes from Yakima Valley

A 40-minute drive away is White Pass and Chinook Pass, where you can hike, fish or go mountain bike riding and white water rafting. Otherwise, soak up some native culture at the Yakama Nation Cultural Center.

## Maryhill 12

100. *Klickitat County Visitor Information Center, (509) 773-4395.*

A REMOTE SAGEBRUSH bluff overlooking the Columbia River is where entrepreneur Sam Hill chose to build his palatial residence. In 1907, he purchased 7,000 acres (2,833 ha) here, with the vision of creating a utopian colony for Quaker farmers. He called the community Maryhill, in honor of his daughter, Mary. The ideal community did not materialize, and Hill turned his unfinished mansion into a museum. The treasures of the **Maryhill Museum of Art** include the throne and gold coronation gown of his friend Queen Marie of Romania, 87 sculptures and drawings by Auguste Rodin, and an impressive collection of Native American art. The beautifully landscaped grounds include a picnic area.

**Maryhill Museum of Art**
35 Maryhill Museum Dr, Goldendale.
(509) 773-3733.
*Mar 15–Nov 15: 9am–5pm daily.*

# Mount Rainier National Park ⓭

**Jeep with outdoor equipment**

ESTABLISHED IN 1899, Mount Rainier National Park encompasses 337 sq miles (872 sq km), of which 97 percent is designated wilderness. Its centerpiece is Mount Rainier, an active volcano towering 14,410 ft (4,392 m) above sea level. Surrounded by old-growth forest and wildflower meadows, Mount Rainier was named in 1792 by Captain George Vancouver *(see p612)* for fellow British naval officer Peter Rainier. Designated a National Historic Landmark District in 1997, the park, which features 1920s and 30s National Park Service rustic architecture, attracts two million visitors a year. The summer draws hikers, mountain climbers, and campers; the winter lures snowshoers and cross-country skiers.

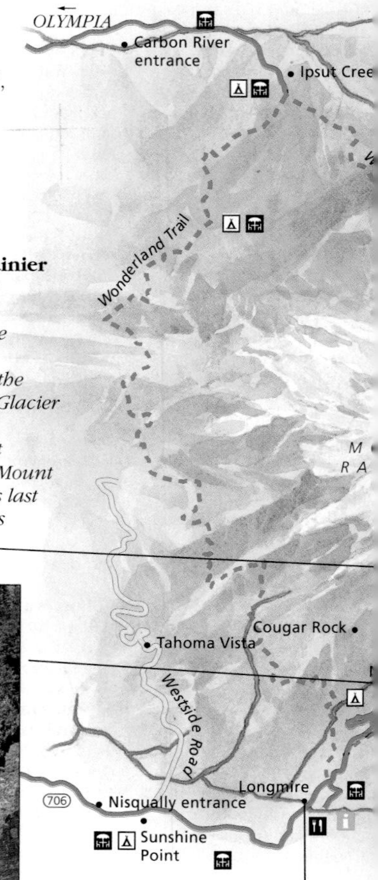

**Mount Rainier Nisqually Glacier**
*Close to the Paradise entrance, the Nisqually Glacier is one of the most visible on Mount Rainier. Its last retreat was 1985–91.*

**Mount Rainier Narada Falls**
*One of the more spectacular and easily accessible cascades along the Paradise River, Narada Falls is just a short, steep hike from Route 706. The falls plummet 168 ft (51 m).*

OLYMPIA
Carbon River entrance
Ipsut Cree
Wonderland Trail
Cougar Rock
Tahoma Vista
Westside Road
706
Nisqually entrance
Longmire
Sunshine Point

**STAR SIGHTS**

- ★ **Emmons Glacier**
- ★ **Paradise**
- ★ **Sunrise**

**National Park Inn**
*This small, cozy inn, located in Longmire and open year round, is a perfect spot from which to enjoy stunning views of Mount Rainier.*

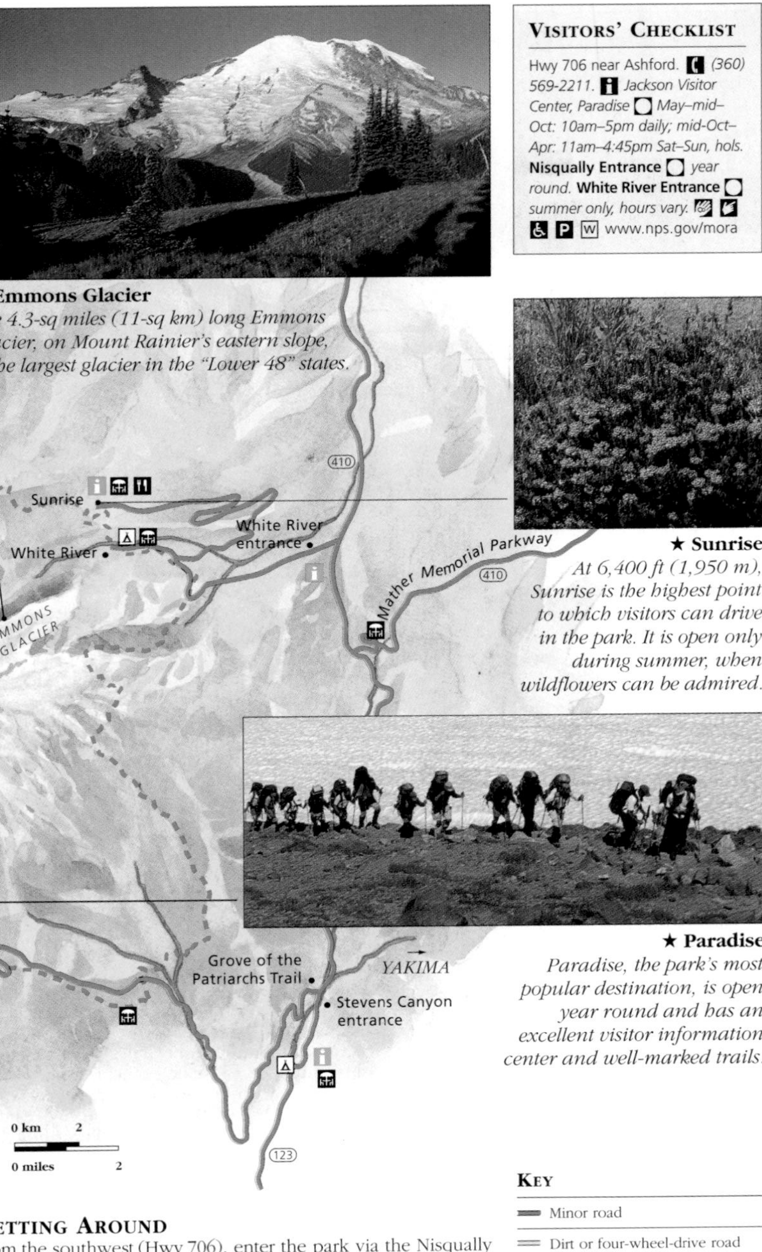


**Emmons Glacier**
*e 4.3-sq miles (11-sq km) long Emmons acier, on Mount Rainier's eastern slope, he largest glacier in the "Lower 48" states.*

**★ Sunrise**
*At 6,400 ft (1,950 m), Sunrise is the highest point to which visitors can drive in the park. It is open only during summer, when wildflowers can be admired.*

**★ Paradise**
*Paradise, the park's most popular destination, is open year round and has an excellent visitor information center and well-marked trails.*

### Visitors' Checklist

Hwy 706 near Ashford. (360) 569-2211. *Jackson Visitor Center, Paradise* *May–mid-Oct: 10am–5pm daily; mid-Oct–Apr: 11am–4:45pm Sat–Sun, hols.* **Nisqually Entrance** *year round.* **White River Entrance** *summer only, hours vary.* www.nps.gov/mora

### Key

- Minor road
- Dirt or four-wheel-drive road
- Hiking trail
- Camping
- Picnic area
- Tourist information
- Restaurant

### etting Around

om the southwest (Hwy 706), enter the park via the Nisqually te. Open year round, this is the primary entrance in winter. ive 6 miles (10 km) to Longmire, where facilities include an n and museum, and the Wilderness Information Center, open om late May to October. The 12-mile (19-km) road between radise and Longmire is steep; drive carefully. Carry chains hen traveling by car during winter. Ashford Mountain Center uttle (tel. 360/569-2604) offers a seasonal shuttle service to, d tours of, Mount Rainier.

**The modern stainless steel exterior of the Tacoma Museum of Glass**

## Tacoma ⓮

*195,000.* *1119 Pacific Ave, (253) 627-2836.*
www.traveltacoma.com

WASHINGTON'S third-largest city, located south of Seattle, Tacoma was founded as a sawmill town in the 1860s. It prospered with the arrival of the railroad in the late 1880s, becoming a major shipping port for important commodities such as lumber, coal, and grain. Many of the Pacific Northwest's railroad, timber, and shipping barons settled in Tacoma's Stadium District. This historic area, with its stately turn-of-the-20th-century mansions, is named for the French château-style **Stadium High School**, also known as the "Castle."

The undisputed star of the city's revitalized waterfront is the striking **Museum of Glass**. The 75,000-sq-ft (6,968-sq-m) landmark building showcases contemporary art, with a focus on glass. A dramatic 90-ft (37-m) metal-encased cone houses a spacious glass-blowing studio.

The stunning Chihuly Bridge of Glass serves as a pedestrian walkway linking the museum to downtown Tacoma and the innovative **Washington State History Museum**. The museum features interactive exhibits, high-tech displays, and theatrical storytelling by actors in period costume, who relate stories of the state's past history.

The 50,000-sq-ft (4,645-sq-m), stainless-steel-wrapped **Tacoma Art Museum** was designed to be a dynamic cultural center and a show-piece for the city. Its growing collection of works, from the 18th century to the present day, include a large assembly of Pacific Northwest art, European Impressionist pieces, Japanese wood-block prints, and Tacoma artist Dale Chihuly's *(see p613)* glassworks. In keeping with its vision of creating a place that "builds community through art," the museum's facilities include the Bill and Melinda Gates Resource Center, providing visitors with access to a range of state-of-the-art research equipment. Children of all ages can also make use of the in-house, interactive art-making studio, ArtWORKS.

**Sign denoting the old town of Tacoma**

Tacoma's most popular attraction is **Point Defiance Park**, ranked among the 20 largest urban parks in the US. Encompassing 700 acres (285 ha), its grounds include Fort Nisqually, the first Euro-pean settlement on Puget Sound and a major fur-tradi[ng] establishment. Also in the park are seven specialty gar-dens, a scenic drive, hiking and biking trails, beaches, a boat marina, and a picnic are[a].

Highlighting a Pacific Rim theme, the **Point Defiance Zoo and Aquarium** on Pea[rl] Street features more than 5,000 animals. A vantage point at the park's west end offers superb views of Moun[t] Rainier *(see p626–7)*, Puget Sound, and the Tacoma Narrows Bridge, famous as one of the longest suspensi[on] bridges in the world.

The fishing village of **Gig Harbor**, 11 miles (17 km) south of Tacoma, has shops and restaurants that reflect t[he] Scandinavian and Croatian heritage of its 6,500 inhabitan[ts].

**Museum of Glass**
1801 E Dock St. *(253) 284-4750, (866) 468-738[6]* *10am–5pm Wed–Sat, noon–5p[m] Sun.* *Mon, Tue, Jan 1, Thanks-giving, Dec 25.*
www.museumofglass.org

**Washington State History Museum**
1911 Pacific Ave. *(888) 238-437[3]* *10am–5pm Mon–Sat, noon–5p[m] Sun.* *public hols.* *for groups.* www.wshs.org

## Olympia ⓯

*43,000.* *1600 4th Ave E, (360) 357-3362.*
www.thurstonchamber.com

NAMED FOR ITS magnificent view of the Olympic Mountains, Washington's state capital is located at t[he] southern tip of Puget Sound. The city's **State Capitol Campus** is dominated by the 2[8]-story Legislative Building (the Capitol), whose

**The Romanesque Legislative Building on the State Capitol Campus, Olymp[ia]**

7-ft (87-m) brick-and-ndstone dome is one of the lest masonry domes in the orld. One of the most impres-e in the nation, the campus compasses superb buildings, veral fountains, and monu-ents. Its landscaped grounds ere designed in 1928 by the msted Brothers, sons of ederick Olmsted, one of the eators of New York City's entral Park *(see p78)*.

The **State Capital Museum** ovides a historical perspec-e of Washington's early oneer settlements, through collections of early photo-aphs and documents. The **ate Archives**, with its storical records and artifacts, another institution related the state's past. Visitors can cess such unique treasures documents from the Canwell ommittee, which blacklisted ispected Communists ıring the 1950s *(see p50)*.

Tree-lined streets, old omes, a picturesque water-ont, and a thriving cultural ommunity all contribute to lympia's charm. Tucked nong downtown's historic ıildings are several shops, staurants, and galleries. /ithin walking distance are tractions such as the lively **lympia Farmers Market,** ffering local produce, sea-ood, and crafts, along with ining and entertainment.

**Percival Landing**, a 1.5-ıile (2.5-km) boardwalk long Budd Inlet, offers views f the Olympic Mountains, ıe Capitol dome, Puget ound, and ships in port.

**State Capitol Campus**
*409 13th Ave SW, (360) 586-687. Jan 1, Thanksgiving, ec 25.* **Legislative Building** *Iemorial Day–Labor Day: 8am–5pm Ion–Fri, 9am–4pm Sat–Sun; Labor ay–Memorial Day: 8am–5pm Ion–Fri. Campus: hourly 0am–3pm daily; Temple of Justice: am–5pm Mon–Fri.*

**State Capital Museum**
*11 21st Ave SW. (360) 753-580. 10am–4pm Tue–Sat. public hols.*
www.washingtonhistory.org

**State Archives**
*129 Washington St SE. (360) 586-1492. :30am–4:30pm Mon–Fri.*

**Mount St. Helens and the surrounding area after the 1980 explosion**

## Mount St. Helens National Volcanic Monument 16

*(360) 449-7800.*
www.fs.fed.us/gpnf/mshnvm

ON THE MORNING of May 18, 1980, Mount St. Helens literally exploded. Triggered by a powerful earthquake, the peak erupted, spewing one cubic mile (4.17 cubic km) of rock into the air and causing the largest recorded avalanche in history. In the blink of an eye, the mountain lost 1,314 ft (400 m), and 234 sq miles (606 sq km) of forestlands were destroyed. The eruption also claimed 57 human lives and those of millions of animals and fish.

The 110,000-acre (44,000-ha) monument was created in 1982 to allow the environment to recover naturally while encouraging research, recreation, and education. Roads and trails allow visitors to explore this fascinating region by car and foot. On the mountain's west side, Hwy 504 leads to five visitor centers, which document the disaster and recovery efforts. Mount St. Helens National Volcanic Monument Visitor Center, at milepost 5, features interpretative exhibits of the mountain's history. The visitor center at Hoffstadt Bluffs, at milepost 27, gives visitors their first full view of Mount St. Helens and offers helicopter tours into the blast zone from May to September. **Johnson Ridge Observatory**, at the end of the road, offers panoramic views.

## Fort Vancouver 17

*(360) 696-7655. May–Oct: 9am–5pm daily; Nov–Apr: 9am–4pm daily. Thanksgiving, Dec 24, 25, & 31. partial.*
www.nps.gov/fova

BETWEEN 1825 and 1849, Fort Vancouver was an important trading outpost for the British-based Hudson's Bay Company, the giant fur-trading organization. Located close to major tributaries and natural resources, it was the center of political and commercial activities in the Pacific Northwest during these years. During the 1830s and 1840s, the fort also provided essential supplies to settlers.

A National Historic Site, Fort Vancouver features accurate reconstructions of nine of the original buildings, including the jail, fur store, and wash house, all on their original sites. Guided tours and re-enactments offer a window into the fort's past. Over a million artifacts have been excavated from this site.

**The three-story bastion, dating from 1845, at Fort Vancouver**

# Oregon

OREGON IS BEST KNOWN FOR ITS many scenic wonders – snowcapped mountains, flowing rivers, verdant forests, and desert vistas are just some of the attractions in this incredibly diverse state. This rugged landscape was first settled by pioneers who migrated along the Oregon Trail *(see p450)*. Today, the state is known not only for its scenic beauty but also for its cosmopolitan pleasures. Portlanders are eager to claim their city as one of the most sophisticated and cultured anywhere.

**Evening view of the Portland skyline and the Willamette River**

## Portland ⓲

*536,240.* *26 SW Salmon St, (503) 222-2223.*

KNOWN AS THE City of Roses, Portland was founded in 1843, on the west bank of the Willamette River. It grew into a major port, but later, with the arrival of the railroad and decline in river trade, the city center moved inland. This area, with its steel-framed buildings, is now the city's downtown, while Old Town encompasses the former port and riverfront quarter. Portland's beautiful parks and gardens and well-preserved historic landmarks are a tribute to foresight and successful urban planning.

### Pioneer Courthouse Square

SW Broadway & Yamhill St.
*(503) 223-1613.*
**Pioneer Courthouse** 701 SW 6th Ave. *(503) 326-2115.* *9am–5pm Mon–Fri.* *public hols.*
www.pioneercourthousesquare.org

This one-block, brick-paved pedestrian square, in eastern downtown, is the heart of Portland, where Portlanders gather for free lunchtime concerts, flower shows, and other events, or simply for a chance to sit and enjoy their beautiful city. Underground spaces next to the square accommodate offices and businesses, which include the Portland Visitors Association Information Center, a coffee shop, and a branch of Powell's City of Books, a well-known store specializing in travel books.

Opposite is the **Pioneer Courthouse**, the first federal building to be built in the Pacific Northwest region. The US Court of Appeals and a US post office branch are housed here. Its octagonal tower has been a fixture of the Portland skyline from 1873.

### South Park Blocks

Bounded by SW Salmon St & I-405, SW Park & SW 9th Aves.
**Oregon Historical Society**
1200 SW Park Ave. *(503) 222-1741.* *10am–5pm Tue–Sat, until 8pm Thu.* *public hols.*
www.ohs.org
**Portland Art Museum** 1219 SW Park Ave. *(503) 226-2811.* *10am–5pm Tue–Wed & Sat, 10am–8pm Thu–Fri, noon–5pm Sun.* *Dec 25.*
www.pam.org

A green ribbon of elm-shaded lawns laid out by frontier businessman and legislator Daniel Lownsdale in 1852, the so-called South Park Blocks is a 12-block stretch running through the central city. Among its distinctive features are statuary and some 40 ornamental fountains. South Park Blocks is also the venu[e] for a colorful local market, held every Saturday, where farmers sell their wares to locals and visitors alike.

The **Oregon Historical Society** to the south of the park has huge murals on its façades that depict scenes from the Lewis and Clarke expedition *(see p570)* and other significant moments in the state's history. On display in the galleries, which extend through three buildings, are paintings, photographs, maps and historical documents that make this museum the largest repository of Oregon's historical artifacts.

The **Portland Art Museum** opposite South Park Blocks in Southwest Park Avenue, is the oldest museum in the Pacific Northwest. Its sizable collection of European works, includes paintings by Picasso, Van Gogh, and Monet, and sculpture by Rodin and Brancusi. Its new Grand Ronde Center for Native American Art displays masks, jewelry, and totem poles created by the indigenous peoples of North America. It is undergoing a program of expansion, including the renovation and restoration of the North Building, and the creation of an underground gallery linking the museum's two main buildings.

### Governor Tom McCall Waterfront Park

Bounded by SW Harrison & NW Glisa[n] Sts, SW Naito Pkwy & Willamette Rive[r]

Buried beneath an expressway from the 1940s to the 1970s, this 1.5-mile- (2.5-km-) long

**The Saturday Farmers Market in South Park Blocks**

ain gateway to Portland's Saturday Market

retch of Willamette River vaterfront was reclaimed nd transformed into a park. amed after Tom McCall, regon's environmentally ninded governor from 1967 1975, the park is now a equently used riverside romenade and the venue for nany local festivals, including he annual Rose Festival, held etween May and June.

One of its most popular ttractions is **Salmon Street prings**, a fountain whose 00 jets splash water directly nto the pavement, providing elief on a hot day. Another ighlight is the **Battleship regon Memorial**, at its outhern end. Built in 1956, he memorial honors an 1893 JS Navy ship. A time capsule ealed in its base in 1976 is to e opened in 2076.

**RiverPlace Marina** at the outhwest end of Tom McCall ark offers many amenities ncluding restaurants, one of he city's higher-end hotels – he RiverPlace Hotel *(see 645)*, upscale shops, sloping awns, riverside walks, and a arge marina.

### Old Town & Chinatown

Bounded by SW Naito Pkwy & NW Glisan St, NW 3rd Ave & SW Pine St.

Elegant brick façades and quiet streets belie Old Town's raucous, 19th-century frontier-town past. A National Historic Landmark today, this river-front district once drew dockworkers, shipbuilders, and traders from all over the world during its heyday as a major port and the city's commercial center. Old Town is now a trendy, colorful neighborhood, especially during weekends, when vendors gather for the **Portland Saturday Market**, America's largest handicrafts bazaar. Chinatown Gate, a five-tiered, dragon-festooned gateway leads to Chinatown, home to the city's many Asian immigrants, who first arrived in Portland more than 135 years ago. The neighborhood's tranquil **Classical Chinese Garden** is a 15th century Ming-style walled enclave, with waterways and pavilions.

### Pearl District

W Burnside to NW Lovejoy Sts, from NW 8th to NW 15th Aves.

**Portland Streetcar** East- & southbound on NW Lovejoy St & 11th Ave, north- & westbound on 10th Ave & NW Northrup St. *every 15 mins, 5:30am–11pm Mon–Thu, 5:30am–1am Fri, 7:30am–1am Sat, 7:30am–11pm Sun.*

www.shopthepearl.com

Often called Portland's "newest" neighborhood, Pearl District actually occupies an old industrial area on the north side of Burnside Street. Many former warehouses and factories have been refurbished to house chic galleries, designer shops, design studios, clubs, cafés, restaurants, and breweries. A good time to visit Pearl District is during a First Thursday event, which takes place the first Thursday of every month. At this time, the many art galleries in the area remain open until late, usually 9pm. The district has a calendar of events, from small-dog playgroups, to a regular Farmers' Market held every Thursday in summer. The website has details.

A quaint way to travel between Pearl District and Nob Hill, a gracious, late-19th-century neighborhood, is to take the **Portland Streetcar**. These low-slung Czech-built trams are not only a convenient way to get around but are also free within the city center.

### Washington Park

SW Park Pl.

*(503) 823-2223.*

*24 hrs daily (not all sights).*

*to some exhibits.*

www.parks.ci.portland.or.us

Washington Park, a popular outdoor playground, is surrounded by the city on all its sides. Its attractions include the Hoyt Arboretum, which has more than 8,000 trees and shrubs, the Japanese Garden, the International Rose Test Garden, and the popular **Oregon Zoo**, which has the largest number of elephants bred in captivity.

### Oregon Museum of Science and Industry

1945 SE Water Ave.

*(503) 797-4000.*

*Labor Day–mid-Jun: 9:30am–5:30pm Tue–Sun; mid-Jun–Labor Day: 9:30am–7pm daily.*

*public hols.*

*of submarine.*

www.omsi.edu

Sign at Oregon Zoo

**Eastbank Esplanade**

Bounded by Willamette River & I-5, Steel & Hawthorne Bridges.

East of the river, the Oregon Museum of Science and Industry (OMSI) is a top US science museum. A favorite among the hundreds of interactive exhibits is the earthquake simulator, in which visitors are shaken and rattled while learning about the tectonic plates that still shift beneath Portland.

Nearby, the **Eastbank Esplanade** is a pedestrian and bicycle path following the east bank of the Willamette River. A 1,200-ft (365-m) section floats on water, while a cantilevered portion is suspended above one of the city's original commercial piers, providing unobstructed river views.

**Columbia River Gorge and the Cascade Mountains**

## Columbia River Gorge ⓳

*775 Summer St NE, Salem, (800) 547-7842.*

THIS MAGNIFICENT fir- and maple-covered river canyon cuts through the Cascade Mountains, forming a boundary between the states of Washington and Oregon. The best way to explore the area is to take the **Historic Columbia River Highway**. Blasted out of narrow cliffs, this road was designed to maximize viewing pleasure while minimizing environmental damage as much as possible. Along the route are the spectacular **Multnomah Falls**, tumbling 620 ft (186 m) in two picturesque cascades, and the cosy, rustic Timberline Lodge dating from the 1930s *(see p645)*.

## Mount Hood ⓴

*775 Summer St NE, Salem, (800) 547-7842.*

THE SPECTACULAR snow-covered peak of Mount Hood, the tallest of Oregon's Cascade peaks, rises south of the Columbia River Gorge. Home to year-round skiing and snowboarding, the valleys below are famous for their produce of apples, apricots, pears, and peaches. The **Mount Hood Loop** is a good way to explore the area; the highest point on the loop, known as **Barlow Pass**, is so steep that at one time, wagons had to be lowered down the hillsides with ropes. The Hood River Valley offers blossoming fruit trees in season and lovely views of the majestic Mount Hood throughout the year. **Hood River**, a riverside town called the "Windsurfing Capital of the World," also offers great opportunities for other sports such as mountain biking.

## Astoria ㉑

*10,000. 111 W Marine Dr. (800) 875-6807.*
www.oldoregon.com

THE OLDEST American settlement west of the Rocky Mountains, Astoria was established when John Jacob Astor sent fur traders around Cape Horn to establish a trading post at the mouth of the Columbia River in 1811. Earlier, explorers Lewis and Clark *(see p570)* spent the winter of 1805–1806 at a crude stockade near Astoria, making moccasins, preserving fish, and recording in their journals accounts of bear attacks and the almost continual rain. The stockade has since been rebuilt at Fort Clatsop National Memorial.

These days, the town is a bustling port; its old Victoria homes climb a hillside abov the river. One such home, th stately **Captain George Flavel House Museum**, retains the cupola from whic the captain and his wife onc watched river traffic. An eve better view can be enjoyed from atop the 164-step spiral staircase of the **Astoria Column**, encircled with friez paying homage to the history of the Pacific Northwest. The town honors its seafaring past at the **Columbia River Maritime Museum**, wher riverside galleries house fishing dories as well as Native American dugout canoes and other river-oriented artifacts. The lightship *Columbia*, berthed in front, once guided ships across the treacherous area at the mouth of the river.

**Astoria Column**

**Captain George Flavel House Museum**
441 8th St. *(503) 325-2203. May–Sep: 10am–5pm daily; Oct–Apr: 11am–4pm daily. Jan 1, Thanksg., Dec 24–25.*

**Columbia River Maritime Museum**
1792 Marine Dr. *(503) 325-2323. 9:30am–5pm daily. Thanksgiving, Dec 25.*
www.crmm.org

**The majestic peak of Mount Hood as seen from Hood River Valley**

a stacks rise off Bandon coast, with houses in the background

## )regon Coast ㉒

*PO Box 74, 137 NE 1st St, Newport, 'egon 97365, (541) 265-2188.*
] www.visittheoregoncoast.com

HUNDREDS OF miles of pristine beaches make ıe Oregon Coast one of the ıe state's best-loved tourist estinations. The developed orthern part has some of regon's most popular esorts, while the southern art is more wild and rugged. he coast is ideal for a range f recreational activities such s driving, cycling, hiking, amping, shell-fishing, and hale- or bird-watching.

Oregon's favorite beach own, **Cannon Beach**, south f Astoria, retains a quiet harm. Haystack Rock, one of ıe tallest coastal monoliths in ıe world, towers 235 ft (72 m) bove a long beach and tidal ools. Ecola State Park, at the each's north end, carpets illamook Head, a basalt eadland, with verdant orests. Viewpoints look cross raging surf to Tillamook Rock Lighthouse, which was built in 1880.

icturesque house on Hemlock treet, Cannon Beach

Nature is the main attraction along the 35-mile (56-km) **Three Capes Scenic Route**, farther south. The rocks below Cape Meares State Scenic Viewpoint and Cape Meares Lighthouse are home to one of the largest colonies of nesting seabirds in North America. The Cape Lookout State Park is a good place to spot migrating gray whales. The Oregon State Parks Association provides detailed information about the sights along this stunning route.

The **Cape Perpetua Scenic Area** has the highest viewpoint on the coast. A road ascends to the top at 800 ft (240 m), and an easy hike along the Giant Spruce Trail leads to a majestic, 500-year-old Sitka spruce. From Cape Perpetua, Hwy 101 leads to Heceta Head State Park, with its ocean views – birds nest on rocks and sea lions and gray whales swim offshore. Rising high above the surf, the Heceta Head Lighthouse was first lit in 1894. Steller's sea lions inhabit the Sea Lion Caves, the only wild sea lion rookery on the North American mainland.

Dune buggy, Oregon Dunes National Recreation Area

The massive sand dunes of the **Oregon Dunes National Recreation Area** stretch south from Florence for 40 miles (64 km). Towering sand formations, lakes, pine forests, grasslands, and open beaches attract a variety of recreation enthusiasts. Boardwalks make it easy to enjoy stunning vistas from Oregon Dunes Overlook, about 20 miles (32 km) south of Florence, while the mile-long Umpqua Scenic Dunes Trail, 30 miles (48 km) south of Florence, skirts the tallest dunes.

**Bandon**, near the mouth of the Coquille River, is so small and weathered that it is difficult to imagine that it was once a major port. Craggy rock formations rise from the ocean just off the beach. These wind-sculpted shapes include Face Rock, allegedly an Indian maiden who was frozen into stone by an evil spirit. A wild landscape of dunes and sea grass can be seen at the Bullards Beach State Park, which lies across the marshy, bird-filled Coquille Estuary.

**Three Capes Scenic Route**
*Oregon State Parks Association*
*(800) 551-6949.*
www.oregonstateparks.org

**Cape Perpetua Scenic Area**
*Interpretive Center (541) 547-3289. Memorial Day–Labor Day: 9am–5pm daily; Labor Day–Memorial Day: reduced hours, call for times. public hols.*

**Oregon Dunes National Recreation Area**
*855 Highway Ave, Reedsport. (541) 271-3611. dawn–dusk daily.* www.fs.fed.us/r6/siuslaw/oregondunes

Local arts and crafts on display at the Saturday Market in Eugene

## Salem ㉓

121,000. 1313 Mill St SE, (800) 874-7012. www.scva.org

Once a thriving trading and lumber port on the Willamette River, Salem became the capital of the Oregon Territory in 1851.

At the edge of Bush's Pasture Park stand **Asahel Bush House**, an 1878 home with a conservatory said to be the first greenhouse west of the Mississippi River, and the historic **Deepwood Estate**. The **Mission Mill Museum** preserves some of the state's earliest structures. These include the 1841 home of Jason Lee, who helped found Salem, and the Kay Woolen Mill, where waterwheels from the 1890s are still intact.

Asahel Bush House, Salem

The state's history is also in evidence around the **Oregon State Capitol**. A gilded pioneer stands atop the rotunda, marble sculptures of Lewis and Clark *(see 570)* flank the entrance, and the murals inside depict Captain Robert Gray's discovery of the Columbia River *(see p612)*.

**Waller Hall**, built in 1867, houses the **Hallie Ford Museum of Art** with its outstanding collection of 20th-century Native American basketry and paintings.

### Mission Mill Museum

1313 Mill St SE. *(503) 585-7012.* *10am–5pm Mon–Sat.* *major hols.*

## Eugene ㉔

*130,000.* *754 Olive St, (541) 484-5307.* www.visitlanecounty.org

The University of Oregon brings culture and distinction to Eugene, which straddles the banks of the Willamette River at the south end of the river valley. The glass-and-timber **Hult Center for the Performing Arts**, is regarded as one of the best-designed performing arts complexes in the world. The **University of Oregon Museum of Natural History** counts among its holdings some ancient shoes – a pair of sagebrush sandals dating from as early as 9500 BC.

Local artisans sell their wares at the **Saturday Market**, in downtown Park Blocks. The **Fifth Street Public Market**, an assemblage of shops and restaurants in a converted feed mill, bustles with locals and university students.

## Madras & Warm Springs ㉕

**Madras** *274 SW 4th St, (541) 4 2350.* www.madraschamber.cc
**Warm Springs** *1233 Veterans (541) 553-3333.* www.warmsprings.com

Madras is a desert ranchi town surrounded by rimrock and vast tracts of wilderness recreation lands. **Crooked River National Grassland** provides endless vistas as well as fishing and rafting opportunities on two US National Wild and Scenic Rivers – the Deschutes and the Crooked – that weave through thousands of acres c juniper and sage brush. **Cov Palisades State Park** surrounds the deep waters of Lake Billy Chinook, a popula destination for boaters.

The Treaty of 1855 betwee the US government and the Wasco, Walla Walla, and Paiute tribes established land for the tribes located on the 640,000-acre (256,000-ha) Warm Springs Reservation in central Oregon. Today, these Confederated Tribes preserve their cultural heritage at the **Museum at Warm Springs** with a stunningly beautiful collection of basketry and beadwork, haunting historic photographs, and videotapes of tribal ceremonies. The tribes also manage a casino and a resort, where a large pool is heated by hot springs

### Museum at Warm Springs

Hwy 26, Warm Springs. *(503) 553-3331.* *10am–5pm daily.* *Jan 1, Thanksgiving, Dec 25.* www.ctws.org/museum

Swimming pool fed by hot springs at the Warm Springs Reservation resort

alloping horses near Sisters, the peaks of the Three Sisters Mountains visible in the distance

## isters 26

9000. 164 N Elm St, 41) 549-0251.
www.sisterschamber.com

THIS WILD-WEST style ranching town is surrounded by ısh pine forests, alpine ıeadows, and rushing :reams. The peaks of the hree Sisters, each above 0,000 ft (3,000 m), rise ıajestically in the background.

**NVIRONS:** The McKenzie ass climbs from Sisters to a -mile (1.6-km) summit amid massive lava flow. The **Dee Vright Observatory** rovides panoramic views of ıore than a dozen Cascade Iountain peaks, buttes, and weeping lava fields.

**Dee Wright Observatory**
wy 242, 15 miles (24 km) west of isters. *mid-Jun–Oct: dawn–dusk aily. Oct–mid-Jun.*

Bend's High Desert Museum, which howcases life in the region

## Bend 27

63,000. 777 NW Wall St, 541) 382-8048.
www.bendchamber.org

BUSY BEND, once a sleepy lumber town, is alluringly close to the ski slopes, lakes, streams, and many other natural attractions. While unsightly development is quickly replacing the juniper- and sage-covered grazing lands on the outskirts, the old brick business district retains its small-town charm. Drake Park is a grassy downtown retreat on both banks of the Deschutes River, and **Pilot Butte State Scenic Viewpoint**, atop a volcanic cinder cone that rises from the center of town, overlooks the High Desert and snow-capped Cascade peaks.

The **High Desert Museum** celebrates life in the rugged terrain that covers much of central and eastern Oregon. Walk-through dioramas use dramatic lighting and sound effects in authentic re-creations of Native American dwellings. A trail leads to replicas of a settler's cabin and a sawmill, and to natural habitats, including a trout stream and an aviary full of hawks and other raptors.

**High Desert Museum**
59800 S Hwy 97. *(541) 382-4754. 9am–5pm daily. Jan 1, Thanksgiving, Dec 25.*
www.highdesertmuseum.org

**ENVIRONS:** The best way to explore the magnificent South Cascades Mountains is to take the **Cascade Lakes Highway**, a 95-mile (153-km) long loop, starting from Bend. Southward, the route passes Lava Butte, which offers fine mountain views. Also located along the highway is Elk Lake, popular for sailing, fishing, and windsurfing. Another interesting sight is Mount Bachelor, 12 miles (20 km) west of Bend. It offers some of the best skiing and snowboarding in the region. An enormous, 45-sq-mile (117-sq-km) lava flow – Devil's Garden – lies northwest of Mount Bachelor. Astronauts used it to train on foot and in moon buggies for their historic 1969 moonwalk.

## Newberry National Volcanic Monument 28

*Apr–Oct: dawn–dusk daily.* www.fs.fed.us *Lava Lands Visitor Center, 11 miles S of Bend on US 97, (541) 593-2421.*

ENCOMPASSING EERIE and bleak landscapes of black lava, as well as sparkling mountain lakes, waterfalls, hemlock forests, and snow-capped peaks, the Newberry National Volcanic Monument occupies an area of 55,000 acres (22,000 ha). Exhibits at the **Lava Lands Visitor Center** explain how the volcano has been built by thousands of eruptions which, seismic activity suggests, may begin again. Other exhibits here highlight central Oregon's cultural history.

At Lava River Cave, a passage extends for almost one mile (0.8 km) into a lava tube, through which molten lava once flowed. The Lava Cast Forest has a trail that transverses a forest of hollow molds, formed by hot, molten lava that created casts around the tree trunks.

A jagged outcrop at the Newberry National Volcanic Monument

# Crater Lake National Park ㉙

OREGON'S ONLY NATIONAL PARK surrounds Crater Lake. At 1,943 ft (592 m), this lake is the deepest in the country and the seventh deepest in the world. Its creation began about 7,700 years ago when Mount Mazama erupted and then collapsed, forming the caldera in which the lake now sits. The rim of the crater rises to an average of 1,000 ft (300 m) above the lake. On the drive encircling the lake, 90 miles (144 km) of trails, various overlooks, and a beautiful lodge offer magnificent views.

**KEY**

- Tour route
- Other road
- Viewpoint
- Information

**Merriam Point** ④
This is an excellent spot from which to admire the west side of the lake, with the cone-shaped Wizard Island and the black volcanic blocks that surround it.

**The Watchman** ③
Named for its historic fire tower, the Watchman can be reached after a moderate climb. It is the nearest lookout to Wizard Island.

**Wizard Island** ②
A 300-ft (90-m) wide crater sits at the summit of this small cone-shaped volcanic island that juts 764 ft (233 m) above the surface of the lake.

0 km 2

0 miles 2

Rim Vill

Mazama Village

**Crater Lake Lodge** ①
Perched on top of the caldera rim, this rustic hotel *(see p645)* has been welcoming guests since 1915. Extensive renovations have restored the structural integrity of the building, which was once at risk of collapsing under its own weight and of the snow that could accumulate in winter. Magnificent views can be enjoyed from this lodge.

**Rim Drive** ⑤
Spectacular views of the lake, the islands, and the surrounding mountains unfold at every turn of this 33-mile (53-km) circuit.

### Tips for Drivers

***Tour length:*** *33 miles (53 km).*
***Starting point:*** *Steel Information Center, on Rim Drive 4 miles (6.5 km) north of Rte 62.*
***When to go:*** *Rim Drive is open from the end of June to mid-October, weather permitting.*
***Stopping-off points:*** *Breakfast, lunch, and dinner are offered at Crater Lake Lodge; snacks are sold in Rim Village. Two-hour narrated boat trips (late Jun–mid-Sep: 10am–4pm daily) depart from Cleetwood Cove, at the bottom of a steep 1-mile (1.6-km) trail.*

**Cleetwood Trail** ⑥
This 1-mile (1.6-km) strenuous trail, which drops a steep 700 ft (210 m), is the only access to the lake. In summer, a boat tour departs from the dock at the base of the trail.

**Mount Scott** ⑦
When the weather allows, views from the peak extend as far as Mount Shasta in California.

**The Pinnacles** ⑧
Pumice spires, also known as fossil fumaroles, rise from the caldera's eastern base and form this eerie landscape. Many of the spires are hollow.

**Sinnott Memorial Overlook** ⑨
Beautiful views reward the intrepid traveler who attempts the short descent to Sinnott Memorial Overlook just below the caldera rim. Here, knowledgeable park rangers give geology talks.

**A park ranger with tourists in the Oregon Caves National Monument**

## Oregon Caves National Monument ㉚

*19000 Caves Hwy, Caves Junction, (541) 592-3400. mid-Mar–mid-Jun & mid-Oct–Nov: 10am–4pm daily; mid-Jun–Aug: 9am–6pm daily; Sep–mid-Oct: 9am–5pm daily. Dec–Feb.* www.nps.gov/orca

Visitors on the 70-minute guided tours of these vast underground caverns follow lighted trails past strange formations, cross underground rivers, squeeze through giant ribs of marble, and clamber up and down staircases into huge chambers hung with stalactites. Discovered in 1874 by a hunter chasing his dog into a dark hole in the side of Elijah Mountain, the caves have been formed by the steady trickling of water over hundreds of thousands of years.

## Ashland ㉛

*20,000. 110 E Main St, (541) 482-3486.*

Every year, some 350,000 theatergoers descend on this amiable town. The major draw is the **Oregon Shakespeare Festival**, which annually presents a schedule of 11 plays by Shakespeare as well as by classical and contemporary playwrights. Theater buffs can also see props and costumes from past performances and take detailed backstage tours of the festival's three venues – Elizabethan Theatre, Angus Bowmer Theatre, and the modern New Theatre.

**Oregon Shakespeare Festival**
15 S Pioneer St. *(541) 482-2111.*
www.orshakes.org

## Steens Mountain ㉜

**Steens Mountain Loop Rd** (for 58 miles/93.5 km), starting North Loop Rd in Frenchglen. *PO Box 1645, Medford, Oregon 97501, (800) 448-4856.*

SCENERY DOES NOT get much grander than it does here on this 9,700-ft (2,910-m) mountain in southeastern Oregon. The west slope rises gradually from sagebrush country, while the eastern slope drops more steeply. Antelope, bighorn sheep, and wild horses roam gorges and alpine tundra carpeted with wildflowers; eagles and falcons soar overhead.

The **Steens Mountain Loop Road** traverses this remarkable landscape. Lovely, marsh-fringed Lily Lake, on the west side of the Warner Mountains, is slowly silting up. However, it is popular with anglers because of its trout-fishing opportunities. The nearby Donner and Blitzen River was named "Thunder and Lightning" by an army officer attempting to cross it during a thunderstorm in 1864. Kiger Gorge to the east affords views of four immense gorges scooped out from the mountainside by massive glaciers. **East Rim Viewpoint** is a full mile (1.6 km) above the alkali flats of the Alvord Desert. Sitting in the mountain's rain shadow, this desert receives a mere 6 inches (15 cm) of rain a year.

**Resting mule deer in the Malheur National Wildlife Refuge**

## Malheur National Wildlife Refuge ㉝

*(541) 493-2612.* **Refuge & Museum** *dawn–dusk daily.* *public hols.*
**Visitor Center**
*7am–4:30pm Mon–Thu, 7am–3:30pm Fri (some weekends in spring & summer).* *public hols.*
www.malheur.fws.gov

ONE OF THE nation's largest wildlife refuges, Malheur spreads across 186,500 acres (74,600 ha) of the Blitzen Valley floor. More than 320 species of birds and 58 species of mammals are found here. Sandhill cranes, tundra swans, snowy white egrets, white-faced ibis, pronghorn antelope, mule deer, and redband trout are among the most numerous of the refuge's denizens.

Spring and fall are the best times to view birds, which alight in the refuge on their annual migrations up and down the Pacific Flyway, a major north–south route for migrating North American waterfowl. A small museum houses specimens of birds commonly seen in the refuge

**ENVIRONS:** From the refuge, the 69-mile (110.5-km) **Diamond Loop National Back Country Byway** heads into sage-covered hills and red rimrock canyons. Along the route are Diamond Craters, a volcanic landscape; the Round Barn, a distinctive 19th-century structure; and Diamond, a small, poplar-shaded ranch town.

**Diamond Loop National Back Country Byway**
*28910 Hwy 20 W, Hines, (541) 573-4400.*

## John Day Fossil Beds National Monument ㉞

Hwy 19, 40 miles (64 km) W of John Day. *(541) 987-2333.* *dawn–dusk daily.*
**Visitor Center (Sheep Rock Unit)**
*8:30am–4:30pm daily.* *public hols between Thanksgiving & Presidents Day.*
www.nps.gov/joda

PREHISTORIC FOSSIL beds litter the John Day Fossil Beds National Monument, where sedimentary rocks preserve the plants and animals that

**View of the Steens Mountain from the East Rim Viewpoint, above the alkali flats of the desolate Alvord Desert**

Formations at John Day Fossil Beds National Monument's Sheep Rock unit

flourished in jungles and savannas for 40 million years, between the extinction of the dinosaurs and the start of the most recent Ice Age. The monument's 14,000 acres (5,600 ha) comprise three units – Sheep Rock, Painted Hills, and Clarno. At all three, trails provide opportunities for the close-up observation of the fossil beds. Painted Hills presents the most dramatic landscapes – vol-canic rock formations in vivid hues of red, pink, bronze, tan, and black. Clarno contains some of the oldest formations, dating back 54 million years and including some of the finest fossil plant remains on earth. At Sheep Rock, the visitor center displays many important finds from the beds.

## Pendleton ㉟

120,000. 501 S Main St, (541) 276-7411.

PENDLETON'S OUTSIZED reputation for raucous cowboys and lawless cattle rustlers is matched by the fact that it is eastern Oregon's largest town. But visitors may be disappointed to learn that these colorful days belong to the past. However, cowboy lore comes alive during the Pendleton Round-Up each September, when rodeo stunt performers and some 50,000 spectators crowd into town. Previous rodeos are honored in the photographs and other memorabilia at the **Round-Up Hall of Fame**.

The town's biggest business, the **Pendleton Woolen Mills**, is known for its warm clothing and blankets, particularly its "legendary" blankets whose designs are a tribute to Native American tribes. The mill wove its first Indian trade blanket in 1895.

The **Pendleton Underground Tours** begin in a subterranean labyrinth of opium dens, gaming rooms, and Prohibition-era drinking establishments and include stops at a bordello and the cramped 19th-century living quarters of Chinese laborers.

The **Tamástslikt Cultural Institute** commemorates local history by displaying re-creations of historic structures, exhibits of war bonnets, and other artifacts.

**Pendleton Woolen Mills**

1307 SE Court Pl.
*(541) 276-6911.*
**Salesroom** *8am–5pm Mon–Sat, 11am–3pm Sun.* *Jan 1, Thanksgiving, Dec 25.* *9am, 11am, 1:30pm, 3pm Mon–Fri.*
www.pendleton-usa.com

**Round-Up Hall of Fame**

1205 SW Court Ave. *(541) 276-2553.* *May–Sep: 10am–5pm Mon–Sat; Oct–Apr: by appointment.* *public hols.*

A rodeo rider at the popular Pendleton Round-Up

## Wallowa Mountains ㊱

**Elkhorn Drive National Scenic Byway** (for 83 miles/134 km), starting at Baker City.

THE WALLOWA Mountains form a 10,000-ft (3,050-m) high, 40-mile (64-km) long wall of granite in northeastern Oregon. Driving through the region takes in some of the finest scenery in the state.

The best way to explore the Wallowa Mountains is to take the **Elkhorn Drive National Scenic Byway**, a two-lane paved road, which begins from Baker City. Nestled between the Wallowa Mountains and the Elkhorn Range, the town has some lovely downtown blocks and fine Victorian houses. Farther north, the National Historic Oregon Trail Interpretive Center displays replicas of pioneer scenes. Surrounded by dense wilderness, the sleepy town of **Joseph** lies to the east of the Wallowa Mountains. Named after Chief Joseph, leader of the Nez Percé peoples, Joseph is a popular destination for recreation enthusiasts and artisans. One of Joseph's main attractions is the **Wallowa County Museum**, which is devoted to Chief Joseph's famous retreat, and to the history of both Indians and settlers of the area.

Wallowa Lake

The crystal-clear waters of the **Wallowa Lake** sparkle at the foot of the Wallowa Mountains. The Wallowa Lake Lodge, a log building dating from the 1920s, still provides accommodations and meals. The popular Wallowa Lake Tramway whisks riders up to the summit of Mount Howard to enjoy spectacular views of the sparkling lake below and majestic peaks rising up.

**Wallowa County Museum**

110 S Main St, Joseph.
*(541) 432-6095 or (541) 432-4834 out of season.* *Memorial Day–late-Sep: 10am–5pm daily.*

# Hells Canyon National Recreation Area ㊲

**Local prickly pear cactus**

SOME OF THE WILDEST terrain in North America clings to the sides of craggy, 9,400-ft (2,865-m) peaks at Hells Canyon before plunging to the famed basin far below. Here, the Snake River rushes through the world's deepest river-carved gorge. Visitors revel in the massive canyon walls rising 6,000 ft (1,830 m), the upland pine forests, and the delicate wildflower-covered alpine meadows – 652,000 wilderness acres (264,000 ha) in all. Much of the terrain is too rugged to cross, even on foot, making long sections of the Snake River accessible only by boat. Many visitors settle for the stunning views from several lookouts, and no one is disappointed.

**Hells Canyon National Recreation Area Viewpoint**

**Buckhorn Lookout** ①
One of several scenic overlooks situated in the Hells Canyon area, superb views of the Wallowa-Whitman National Forest and the Imnaha River canyon are afforded from this remote spot.

**Nee-Me-Poo Trail** ②
Visitors hiking along this National historic trail follow in the footsteps of the famous Chief Joseph and 700 Nez Percé Indians who, in 1877, embarked on an 1,800-mile (2,897-km) trek toward freedom in Canada.

**Hells Canyon Reservoir** ⑥
This 25-mile- (40-km-) long reservoir, part of a huge power-generating complex on the Snake River, is formed by Oxbow Dam to the south and Hells Canyon Dam to the north. A private road along the east shore provides access to the river.

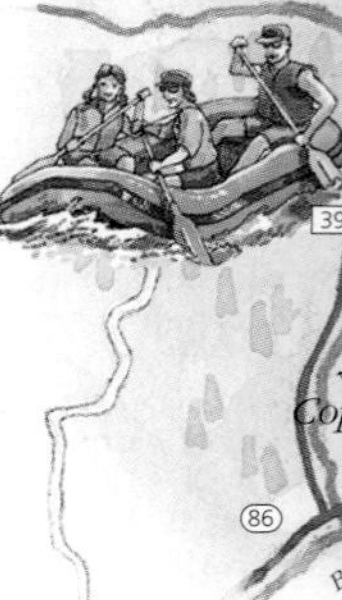

## Tips for Drivers

***Tour length:*** *214 miles (344 km), including all turnoffs.*
***Starting point:*** *Oregon SR 350, 8 miles (13 km) east of Joseph.*
***When to go:*** *Summer months only. Some roads are not suitable for every type of vehicle. For information, call the area's visitor center at (541) 426-5546.*
***Stopping off points:*** *Picnic areas are widely available. Imnaha offers restaurants and lodging.*

**Imnaha River ③**
A road from the town of Imnaha follows this frothy river through a pine-scented valley, isolated ranches, and a fish weir where Chinook salmon, having migrated from the Pacific Ocean, can be seen swimming upstream.

## Key

Tour route
Other road
Information
Viewpoint

**Hat Point Road ④**
A steep, dizzying, 23-mile (37-km) gravel road takes visitors up to Hat Point, located at an elevation of 7,000 ft (2,100 m).

0 km 10
0 miles 10

Pittsburg Landing
493
4240
Snake River
Seven Devils Mountains
⑤ Hells Canyon Dam
454
ig Bar

**Wild and Scenic River ⑤**
A 31.5-mile (50.5-km) stretch of the Snake River, from Hells Canyon Dam to Upper Pittsburg Landing, is designated a Wild River. Experienced guides pilot rafters over the many stretches of rapids, but searing temperatures, bears, rattlesnakes, poison ivy, and generally inhospitable terrain discourage overland treks.

**A boat negotiating rapids on the Snake River**

# Practical Information

THE STUNNING SCENERY OF THE Pacific Northwest attracts visitors from around the world. Booming tourism – and in more recent years, ecotourism – has spawned a vast network of facilities and services: internationally acclaimed restaurants and accommodations abound, and efficient transportation by air, land, and water takes travelers virtually anywhere they want to go. The peak tourist season extends from mid-May through September. Winter is also a great time to visit the region as it is ideal for skiing and other snow sports.

## Tourist Information

MAPS AND information about sights, events, accommodations, and tours are available free of charge from **Washington State Tourism** and the **Oregon Tourism Commission**. These agencies also provide either free reservations services for a wide range of accommodations or referrals to these services. Most Pacific Northwest communities operate visitor centers or tourism booths, offering information about local activities, lodgings, and restaurants.

## Personal Security

THE PACIFIC NORTHWEST prides itself on its safe cities and its welcoming attitude toward visitors. Street crime is rare, and the police are a visible presence in all major cities. However, it is wise to be careful and find out which parts of town are less safe than others. Your hotel or a tourist information center will provide information about which areas are best to stay away from. In the country, wildlife and natural dangers can be avoided by heeding local warnings and advice.

In an emergency, call 911 for the fire department, police, or an ambulance; if you are not in a major city, dial 0. The call can be placed from any phone free of charge. Hospitals are listed in phone books, and each has an emergency room that can be accessed 24 hours a day.

## Natural Hazards

BEFORE HEADING out on a hike or going camping, check in with the forest service for information on the conditions in the surrounding area and recommended safety precautions. Skiers and snowboarders should always heed warning signs and stay on groomed runs.

Insects can be annoying while hiking or camping – blackflies in the spring or mosquitoes in the summer. Ticks, which can be carriers of Lyme disease, are found in dry, wooded areas. Protect yourself by using tick repellant and wear long trousers, long sleeves, and socks. In case of a rash or flu-like symptoms, contact a doctor immediately.

On the beach, heed the red tide warnings that alert shellfish collectors to contamination. When camping, beware of cougars, wolves, coyotes, and bears. Be advised that leaving any food or garbage out will attract dangerous wildlife.

Potential safety hazards for drivers include gravel roads, which may become very slippery with rain, heavy snowfalls, black ice, and fog. To be safe, always carry a spare tire, and salt or sand in winter, also a flashlight, jumper cables, blankets, water emergency food, and a shovel. Always carry a cell phone.

## Getting Around

VISITORS TO the Pacific Northwest have a wide range of transportation options. **United Airlines** offers flights to the major cities of the Pacific Northwest while **Alaska Airlines** and **Horizon Airlines** fly to these and regional destinations.

Although the bus may be the slowest way of getting to the Pacific Northwest, it is probably the most economical. **Greyhound** has bus routes throughout the region; **Gray Line**, **Maverick**, and **Pacific Coach Lines** offer sightseeing tours. Discounts are available for children, students, and senior citizens. The train is a good way to get to the Pacific Northwest and to travel within it. **Amtrak** offers daily service to Oregon and Washington from the Midwest and California and has daily runs between Seattle, Portland, and Eugene. **American Orient Express Railway** offers scenic trips in the Pacific Northwest aboard luxury cars.

Driving is by far the best mode of transport in the region, especially to enjoy the spectacular beauty of more

## The Climate of the Pacific Northwest

Rain is a distinctive presence in only half the Pacific Northwest – the part west of the mountains that divide the region. The weather in this western, coastal region remains mild throughout the year, and snow is rare in all but the higher elevations. The mountains see heavy winter snowfall, much to the delight of skiers. East of the mountains, the summers are hot, dry, and sunny, and winters more severe than west of the mountains.

**Seattle**

| °F/C | Apr | Jul | Oct | Jan |
| --- | --- | --- | --- | --- |
| High | 58/14 | 72/22 | 59/15 | 45/7 |
| Low | 43/6 | 54/12 | 47/8 | 36/2 |
| Sunshine | 16 days | 20 days | 13 days | 9 days |
| Rainfall | 2.5 in | 0.8 in | 3.2 in | 5.3 in |
| month | Apr | Jul | Oct | Jan |

32°F 0°C

remote areas. Remember to tune into local television and radio news channels for regular reports on traffic and road conditions, particularly during the winter.

### Etiquette

Dress in the Pacific Northwest tends to be casual, practical, and dependent on the weather. Stricter clothing requirements apply in theaters, high-end restaurants, and other more formal places. Designated beaches allow topless and nude sunbathing. The legal drinking age is 21. Smoking in public places is prohibited.

### Laws

The Seattle and Portland Police Departments are a visible presence, either on foot, bicycle, or squad car. There are also neighborhood security teams made up of citizen volunteers, which patrol on foot. Outside the metropolitan areas, there are county police and sheriff's offices to assist you.

It is illegal and insensitive to comment on or joke about bombs, guns, and terrorism in places such as airports. Drunk driving is also taken seriously; remember that open alcohol containers in a car are illegal. Narcotics users can face criminal charges and severe penalties.

### Sports & Outdoor Activities

The dramatically varied terrain and beautiful landscape of the Pacific Northwest make this the ideal region for a wide variety of outdoor activities. Both Washington and Oregon provide great conditions for adventure sports such as hang gliding and paragliding. Whitewater rafting is also popular, especially in the waters of the Cascades Range. Skiing and snowboarding are other popular activities.

For those interested in more placid pastimes, the **Oregon Department of Fish and Wildlife** or the **Washington Department of Fish and Wildlife**, provide information on freshwater fishing.

One of the most excting ways to explore the scenic Pacific Northwest is by foot. Visitor centers and the **American Hiking Society** provide information about hiking; and the **Pacific Northwest Trail Association** offers details about the beautiful 1,200-mile (1,931-km) trail, which runs from the Continental Divide to the Pacific Ocean.

In summer, the region's many beaches are ideal for relaxing and offer refreshing waters to swim in. The coasts are also a delight for bird-watchers who can catch sight of gulls, sandpipers, plovers, and ducks. Canoeing and kayaking provide environmentally friendly ways of seeing the region's beautiful waters and abundant marine life. Washington's Puget Sound and San Juan Islands are the most popular destinations for sea kayaking, while Olympic National Park is the hot spot for canoeists. In Oregon, the Columbia River provides stretches of calmer water for paddling.

Cycling and inline skating are inexpensive ways of traveling. Several companies offer long-distance cycling tours in the region; **Bicycle Adventures** offers tours through the two states.

### Shopping

Downtown districts in the Pacific Northwest provide everything from luxury goods offered by exclusive stores to flea market bargains. Outdoor gear manufactured by world-famous local companies such as REI are popular with tourists interested in adventure sports. Other items to shop for are antiques, books, and music from both the chain stores and independents, first-class wines (Pinot Noirs, Chardonnays, Rieslings, and dessert wines), and smoked Pacific salmon. Native American jewelry, carvings, paintings, and other handicrafts are also available throughout the region.

## Directory

### Tourist Information

**Oregon Tourism Commission**
775 Summer St NE, Salem, OR 97301-1282.
*(503) 986-0000, (800) 547-7842.*
www.traveloregon.com

**Washington State Tourism**
P.O. Box 42500. Olympia, WA 98504-2500.
*(800) 544-1800.*
www.tourism.wa.gov

### Travel

**Alaska Airlines**
*(800) 252-7522.*

**Horizon Airlines**
*(800) 547-9308.*

**United Airlines**
*(800) 864-8331.*

**Gray Line**
*In Portland: (800) 422-7042. In Seattle: (800) 426-7532.*

**Greyhound**
*(800) 229-9424.*
www.greyhound.com

**American Orient Express Railway**
*(888) 759-3944.*

**Amtrak**
*(800) 872-7245.*

### Freshwater Fishing

**Oregon Dept of Fish and Wildlife**
*(503) 872-5268.*
www.dfw.state.or.us

**Washington Dept of Fish & Wildlife**
*(360) 902-2200.*
www.wa.gov/wdfw

### Hiking

**American Hiking Society**
*(301) 565-6704.*
www.americanhiking.org

**Pacific Northwest Trail Association**
*(877) 854-9415.*
www.pnt.org

### Bird-watching

**Malheur National Wildlife Refuge**
*(541) 493-2612.*
pacific.fws.gov/malheur

# Where to Stay

WHETHER YOU ARE LOOKING for a relaxing oceanside inn, a small B&B, a low-key hostel, a convenient motel, or a perfectly appointed hotel in the heart of the city, the Pacific Northwest offers accommodations to suit every taste and budget. In addition, rustic lodges and guest ranches, usually near scenic areas, provide lodgings and unforgettable outdoor experiences.

## Washington

| | Credit Cards | Number of Rooms | Restaurant | Children's Facilities | Garden or Terrace |
|---|---|---|---|---|---|
| **CHELAN:** *Campbell's Resort* $$$<br>104 W Wooden Ave. (509) 682-2561, (800) 553-8225. FAX (509) 682-2177.<br>W www.campbellsresort.com<br>Enjoying a prime beachfront location, this long-time local favorite offers a host of on-site facilities including a spa and a beach bar. Rooms are spacious and unfussy; a few have kitchens. | ■ | 175 | ■ | ● | ■ |
| **LEAVENWORTH:** *Pine River Ranch* $$$<br>19668 Hwy 207. (800) 669-3877. FAX (509) 763-2073. W www.prranch.com<br>At this small B&B set in the Cascade Mountains, there's a full breakfast served each morning, and all rooms have a fireplace and whirlpool tub. | ■ | 6 | | | ■ |
| **PORT ANGELES:** *Lake Crescent Lodge* $$$<br>416 Lake Crescent Rd. (360) 928-3211. FAX (360) 928-3253.<br>W www.lakecrescentlodge.com<br>Set on the shores of a fjord, this lodge makes a fine base for exploring Olympic National Park's northern areas. Nov–Mar. | ■ | 52 | ■ | ● | ■ |
| **PORT TOWNSEND:** *Manresa Castle Hotel & Inn* $$<br>7th & Sheridan St. (360) 385-5750, (800) 732-1281. FAX (360) 385-5883.<br>W www.manresacastle.com<br>Built for the city's first mayor, the Manresa Castle has been a hotel since the 1960s. The restaurant-lounge has been beautifully restored. | ■ | 40 | ■ | ● | ■ |
| **QUINAULT:** *Lake Quinault Lodge* $$$<br>PO Box 7, Quinault. (360) 288-2900, (800) 562-6672. FAX (360) 288-2901.<br>W www.visitlakequinault.com<br>Styled along the lines of a grand park lodge, this 1926 property offers rooms retaining their original charm, without intrusive modern amenities; only a few rooms have TVs. | ■ | 92 | ■ | ● | ■ |
| **SEATTLE:** *Ace Hotel* $$<br>2423 1st Ave, Seattle. (206) 448-4721. FAX (206) 374-0745. W www.acehotel.com<br>Groovy, minimalist decor and friendly service are the hallmarks of this modern hotel in Belltown. The hotel and its Cyclops Bar are popular with visiting musicians and artists. Most rooms share bathrooms. | ■ | 28 | | ● | |
| **SEATTLE:** *Pensione Nichols* $$<br>1923 1st Ave. (206) 441-7125, (800) 440-7125. FAX (206) 441-7125.<br>W www.pensionenichols.com<br>Located near Pike Place Market, two suites in this B&B offer amenities such as kitchen, private bathroom, and balcony; the other rooms share bathrooms. | ■ | 12 | | | |
| **SEATTLE:** *MarQueen Hotel* $$$<br>600 Queen Anne Ave N. (206) 282-7407, (888)-3076. FAX (206) 283-1499.<br>W www.marqueen.com<br>This quaint brick hotel close to the Seattle Center is small but classic. Each spacious room has a kitchenette and is richly appointed with hardwood floors, area rugs, and upscale amenities. | ■ | 56 | | ● | |
| **WALLA WALLA:** *Best Western Walla Walla Suites Inn* $<br>7 E Oak St. (509) 525-4700. FAX (509) 525-2457. W www.bestwestern.com<br>This modern, comfortable all-suites inn is handy for nearby wineries and restaurants, with rooms that are well appointed. | ■ | 78 | | ● | |
| **YAKIMA:** *Birchfield Manor Country Inn* $$$<br>2018 Birchfield Rd. (509) 452-1960, (800) 375-3420. FAX (509) 452-2334.<br>W www.birchfieldmanor.com<br>This quaint inn offers accomodations in the original manor house and the guest cottage, in a gracious pastoral setting. All rooms have private baths; some with jacuzzis and fireplaces. | ■ | 11 | | ● | ■ |

**Price categories** for a standard double room per night, including tax and service charges. (Prices may fluctuate depending on arrival date and availability.)

$ under $100
$$ $100–$150
$$$ $150–$200
$$$$ over $200

**CREDIT CARDS**
Major credit cards accepted.

**RESTAURANT**
Hotel restaurant or dining room also open to nonresidents.

**CHILDREN'S FACILITIES**
Child cots and a baby-sitting service available. Some hotel restaurants provide children's portions and highchairs.

**GARDEN OR TERRACE**
Hotels with a garden, courtyard, or terrace.

## OREGON

| Hotel | Credit Cards | Number of Rooms | Restaurant | Children's Facilities | Garden or Terrace |
|---|---|---|---|---|---|
| **ASTORIA:** *Rose River Inn Bed and Breakfast* $$<br>1510 Franklin Ave. *(503) 325-7175, (888) 876-0028.* FAX *(503) 325-7188.*<br>W www.roseriverinn.com<br>This lovely B&B is furnished with country antiques and art. Some rooms have views and one suite has its own Finnish sauna. Wake up to a gourmet breakfast, served in a dining room overlooking the Columbia River. TV | ■ | 4 | | ● | ■ |
| **BEND:** *Mount Bachelor Village Resort* $$$<br>19717 Mt Bachelor Dr. *(800) 457-5204.* FAX *(541) 388-7401.*<br>W www.mtbachelorvillage.com<br>Myriad activities are accessible from this upscale, full-service resort: on-site tennis courts and spa; hiking, running, and biking trails; skiing at Mount Bachelor. Choose from a selection of well-appointed condominiums. TV | ■ | 130 | ■ | ● | ■ |
| **COLUMBIA RIVER GORGE:** *Timberline Lodge* $$$<br>Timberline, Mount Hood. *(503) 622-7979, (800) 547-1406.* FAX *(503) 622-0710.*<br>W www.timberlinelodge.com<br>This celebrated 1930s-era lodge, set midway up Mount Hood, was built using local stone and rough-hewn timber, adding greatly to its rustic ambience. Highlights include the handsome main staircase with animal carvings, and the atrium's huge rock fireplace. | ■ | 70 | ■ | ● | ■ |
| **CRATER LAKE NATIONAL PARK:** *Crater Lake Lodge* $$$<br>565 Rim Village Dr. *(541) 830-8700.* FAX *(541) 830-8514.*<br>W www.craterlakelodges.com<br>This splendid 1915 lodge sits poised to take in spectacular lake views. Its magnificent Great Hall, detailed with Art Deco flourishes, is a reminder of a bygone era. The rooms are fully refurbished, some with old-fashioned claw-foot bathtubs. *mid-Oct–mid-May.* | ■ | 71 | ■ | ● | ■ |
| **PORTLAND:** *Heathman Hotel* $$$<br>1001 SW Broadway. *(503) 241-4100, (800) 551-0011.* FAX *(503) 790-7110.*<br>W www.heathmanhotel.com<br>The award-winning Heathman Restaurant is a major draw, but guests also appreciate the comforts offered by this stylish hotel with a distinct European flavor. On display are the great city views and works by local artisans in each well-appointed room. TV | ■ | 150 | ■ | | |
| **PORTLAND:** *RiverPlace Hotel* $$$<br>1510 SW Harbor Way, Portland. *(800) 227-1333.* FAX *(503) 295-6160.*<br>W www.riverplacehotel.com<br>This recently refurbished property is decorated in northwest Craftman style, with natural wood and tiles in muted earth tones. Room decor is soft and intimate. Complimentary on-site spa services. TV | ■ | 84 | ■ | ● | ■ |
| **PORTLAND:** *Embassy Suites* $$$$<br>319 SW Pine St. *(503) 279-9000, (800) 362-2779.* FAX *(503) 497-9051.*<br>W www.embassysuites.citysearch.com<br>Centrally located, this family- and business-friendly hotel provides spacious rooms and the convenience of many on-site amenities, including a day spa. TV | ■ | 276 | ■ | ● | |
| **PORTLAND:** *Governor Hotel* $$$$<br>614 SW 11th Ave. *(503) 224-3400, (800) 554-3456.* FAX *(503) 241-2122.*<br>W www.govhotel.com<br>This stately hotel, found on the National Register of Historic Places, is adorned with local Native art and murals depicting the Lewis and Clark expedition era. Some of its elegantly furnished rooms feature fireplaces and balconies. TV | ■ | 100 | ■ | | |

For key to symbols see back flap

# Where to Eat

KNOWN FOR ITS VAST RANGE of local seafood, the Pacific Northwest also boasts a large number of coffee bars. Seattle and Portland are in the midst of a culinary revolution – small restaurants popping up on every block with a variety of fare ranging from wildberry pancakes to pumpkin soup. "B" indicates breakfast, "L" lunch, and "D" dinner in the listings below.

## WASHINGTON

**BELLINGHAM:** *Pepper Sisters* $$$
1055 N State St. ☎ *(360) 671-3414.*
Centrally located in a historic commercial building, this cheerful bistro presents imaginative Southwestern fare, such as cilantro grilled salmon and spicy eggplant *tostada*. *D.* ● *Mon.*

**LEAVENWORTH:** *Echo Bistro* $$$
911 Commercial St. ☎ *(509) 548-9685.*
This cheery restaurant, located in a turn-of-the-19th-century home, is popular for its mixed grill items and handmade German sausage. A good selection of German brews is served in the large outdoor *biergarten*.

**PORT TOWNSEND:** *Sentosa Sushi* $$
218 Polk St. ☎ *(360) 385-2378.*
A great place to dine on a variety of sushi and Pan-Asian noodle dishes in a funky but relaxing setting. Some vegan menu choices also offered.

**SEATTLE:** *Jack's Fish Spot* $
1514 Pike Place. ☎ *(206) 467-0514.*
This no-nonsense eatery is a must-try for some of the best fish-and-chips and chowder in the city. Open until 5pm.

**SEATTLE:** *Virginia Inn and Tavern* $$
1937 1st Ave. ☎ *(206) 728-1937.*
This local centenarian, an atmospheric spot for dining on tasty fare, such as tapenade and chicken gumbo, is also a popular watering hole.

**SEATTLE:** *Elliott's Oyster House* $$$
1201 Alaskan Way. ☎ *(206) 623-4340.*
This convivial seafood house on the waterfront has an interior distinguished by teak, copper, and rough-hewn timber. Locals and tourists alike sit at the 21-foot (7-m) bar for local brews and raw oysters on the half shell.

**SEATTLE:** *Peso's* $$$
605 Queen Anne Ave N. ☎ *(206) 283-9353.*
This popular Mexican restaurant, decorated in kitsch style, fills up on weekends. The food packs a spicy punch, and is consistently good. Highlights include the meat dishes and the award-winning margaritas.

**SPOKANE:** *Paprika* $$$$$
1228 S Grand Blvd. ☎ *(509) 455-7545.*
Paprika prides itself on its creative, seasonally changing menu, with highlight dishes such as braised rabbit with chestnuts. The artwork displayed here was created by the restaurant's sous-chef. ● *Sun, Mon.*

**TACOMA:** *El Gaucho* $$$$$
2119 Pacific Ave. ☎ *(253) 272-1510.*
This stylish steakhouse attracts a sophisticated crowd, with a menu that features sirloin steaks and seafood dishes. The cigar lounge is popular for martinis and after-dinner drinks. ♫

**WALLA WALLA:** *Merchants LTD* $
21 E Main St. ☎ *(509) 525-0900.*
A great spot for healthy and hearty breakfasts and lunches, this eatery covers the space of three red-brick storefronts along Main Street. It also has a bakery and a gourmet groceries section. ● *Sun D.*

**YAKIMA:** *Birchfield Manor Restaurant* $$$$
2018 Birchfield Rd. ☎ *(509) 452-1960.*
This charming Victorian inn prides itself on the fine French country cuisine offered in the cozy dining room. Its European-trained chef presents six main dishes with well-considered wine choices.

| | Credit Cards | Vegetarian | Outdoor Seating | Children's Facilities | Late Opening |
|---|---|---|---|---|---|
| Pepper Sisters | ■ | ● | | | |
| Echo Bistro | ■ | ● | ■ | ● | |
| Sentosa Sushi | ■ | ● | | | |
| Jack's Fish Spot | | ● | | ● | |
| Virginia Inn and Tavern | ■ | ● | ■ | | ■ |
| Elliott's Oyster House | ■ | ● | ■ | ● | |
| Peso's | ■ | ● | | ● | ■ |
| Paprika | ■ | ● | | | |
| El Gaucho | ■ | ● | | ● | ■ |
| Merchants LTD | ■ | ● | ■ | ● | |
| Birchfield Manor Restaurant | ■ | ● | | ● | |

**Price categories** for a three-course meal and a glass of house wine, including taxes and service:
- $ under $25
- $$ $25–$35
- $$$ $35–$50
- $$$$ $50–$70
- $$$$$ over $70

**CREDIT CARDS**
Major credit cards accepted.

**VEGETARIAN**
A selection of vegetarian dishes available.

**OUTDOOR SEATING**
Garden, terrace, or courtyard with outside seating available.

**CHILDREN'S FACILITIES**
Children's menu or portions; highchairs available.

**LATE OPENING**
Full meals or light menu served after 11pm.

## OREGON

| Restaurant | Price | Credit Cards | Vegetarian | Outdoor Seating | Children's Facilities | Late Opening |
|---|---|---|---|---|---|---|
| **STORIA:** *Wet Dog Café and Brew Pub*<br>44 11th St. (503) 325-6975.<br>friendly and casual place on the Columbia River waterfront to grab urgers, sandwiches, and other hearty American fare. On weekends, the rew pub becomes a popular spot featuring live music. | $$ | ■ | ● | ■ | ● | |
| **STORIA:** *Baked Alaska*<br>12th St. (503) 325-7414.<br>he nautical decor suggests the mood for fresh seafood and assorted game neats served at this pier-side restaurant. Great views of the Columbia River an be enjoyed by visitors from the floor-to-ceiling windows in the airy lining room. | $$$$ | ■ | ● | ■ | ● | |
| **BEND:** *Merenda Restaurant and Wine Bar*<br>00 NW Wall St. (541) 330-2304.<br>Rustic French and Italian dishes, grilled on a wood fire, are the specialties t this charming restaurant, popular for its stellar list of spirits and local vines – 80 selections by the glass and 700 by the bottle. | $$$ | ■ | ● | | ● | |
| **UGENE:** *Oregon Electric Station Restaurant and Lounge*<br>7 E 5th Ave. (541) 485-4444.<br>ocated inside a 1912 train depot, this charming red-brick restaurant serves op-notch steak, fish, and pasta entrées and offers a lengthy wine list. Guests can dine in antique train cars, or *al fresco* on the front patio. | $$$$ | ■ | ● | ■ | ● | |
| **ORTLAND:** *Fong Chong*<br>01 NW 4th Ave. (503) 228-6868.<br>his Chinatown restaurant makes up for its well-worn interior by serving vhat is arguably the city's best *dim sum*. | $ | ■ | ● | | ● | |
| **ORTLAND:** *Good Dog/Bad Dog*<br>08 SW Alder St. (503) 222-3410.<br>his fun and funky hangout, with photos of four-legged stars adorning the valls, has all types of low-fat hot dogs, including the Oregon Smokey, local favorite made with blackstrap molasses. All sausages are homemade. | $ | ■ | ● | ■ | ● | |
| **ORTLAND:** *San Felipe Taqueria*<br>221 SE Milwaukie Ave, Portland. (503) 235-8158.<br>favorite lunch spot with locals, this unassuming *taqueria* (no-fuss eatery erving mainly burritos, tacos, etc) offers tasty Mexican fare. The *gorditas* puck-shaped tarts filled with a choice of meats) and *tortas* (Mexican andwiches) are particularly good. *Sun, Mon.* | $ | ■ | ● | | ● | |
| **ORTLAND:** *Pazzo Ristorante*<br>27 SW Washington St. (503) 228-1515.<br>With a menu that changes seasonally, this urban, casual restaurant serves good seafood and regional Italian cuisine. You'll find it in the Hotel Vintage Plaza in downtown. *B, L, D.* | $$ | ■ | | ■ | ● | |
| **ORTLAND:** *Heathman Restaurant and Bar*<br>001 SW Broadway. (503) 790-7752.<br>his award-winning, special-occasion restaurant features a menu of Pacific Northwest cuisine, which changes seasonally. Standout dishes nclude the *foie gras* cappucino and tuna Rossini. Live jazz Wednesday o Saturday. | $$$$ | ■ | ● | ■ | ● | |
| **ALEM:** *Original Roadhouse Grill*<br>81 Lancaster Dr NE. (503) 375-0942.<br>t must be the mix of well-presented American classics such as steaks, hops, and grilled chicken, plus the line dancing every evening that keep atrons, both locals and tourists, coming back to this easy-going restaurant. | $$$ | ■ | ● | | ● | |

For key to symbols see back flap

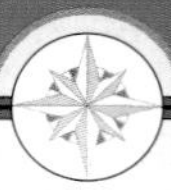

# California

# California at a Glance

SITUATED ON THE Pacific Coast, California is 800 miles (1,300 km) long and 250 miles (400 km) wide, covering an area of 158,710 sq miles (411,060 sq km). An area of startling contrasts, the scorching deserts and snowcapped mountains of the south lead to the vast wilderness areas of the north. Los Angeles and San Francisco are the state's two major cities, and the state capital is Sacramento.

***Sacramento*** (see p717) *in Gold Country is California's capital city. Its primary landmark is the California State Capitol, completed in 1874. In the old city, along the river, are many historic buildings built for the gold miners of 1849.*

***Napa Valley*** (see p712), *a long, sliver of land, lies in the heart of Northern California's Wine Country. Hundreds of wineries dot the entire length of the valley; most offer tours and wine tastings.*

***San Francisco's*** (see pp694–711) *Golden Gate Bridge connects the city with Marin County. This famous landmark was opened in 1937.*

***Santa Barbara*** (see p686), *on the Central Coast, is a repository of the region's Spanish heritage. Its legendary mission, referred to as the "Queen of Missions," was built four years after the city was established as an important garrison in 1782.*

◁ **Rocks and crashing surf at Big Sur, Central Coast**

**Locator Map**

'osemite National Park (see p718) *in the Iigh Sierras is an unforgettable wilderness f forests, alpine meadows, breathtaking vaterfalls, and imposing granite rocks. The iant sequoia trees here were California's irst tourist attraction.*

**Death Valley National Park** (see pp684–5) *shows the California desert at its harshest and most awe-inspiring. The Native Americans called the valley Tomesha, "the land where the ground is on fire," an apt name for this extremely hot place.*

**Los Angeles** (see pp658–77) *is a city dominated by wealth, fame, and glamor, as perceived by Hollywood. Its popular beaches along the Pacific Ocean attract more than 30 million people a year.*

**San Diego** (see p678) *was the site of the first Spanish mission. Today, it is a major commerical and military port, where aircraft carriers, cruise ships, fishing boats, and pleasure craft are a common sight.*

# CALIFORNIA

IMPRESSIVE FOR BOTH ITS SIZE *and its sway over modern culture, California symbolizes the United States' diversity and sense of prosperity. Here can be found towering forests, high mountain peaks, deserts within half a day's drive of ocean beaches, and two of the world's foremost cities, San Francisco and Los Angeles.*

Perceptions of California vary so greatly that some people now joke that there are two states. The first is geographic – California is the Union's third-largest state (after Alaska and Texas). It claims some high mountain peaks such as Mount Whitney as well as the country's lowest expanse of dry land – Death Valley. Roughly one in every eight Americans is a Californian, making this the most populous of the 50 states, represented by the largest Congressional delegation.

State Seal

The other California is a realm of romance, formed by flickering celluloid images. Think "California" and pictures are immediately conjured up of bikini-clad beachcombers, middle-class suburban families in sprawling ranch houses, and glamorous film stars emerging from limousines before hordes of autograph seekers. These stereotypes are perpetuated by the tourism and entertainment media, especially Hollywood. The earlier Spanish legends had glorified Califorina as exotic, while the later Gold Rush elevated it to a land of fortune and opportunity. Whatever the truth may be, such were the eulogies that created California's colorful and seductive image.

### HISTORY

Although the Spanish first "discovered" California in 1542, they colonized the area only in the 18th century. Their rule was enforced through three institutions – the mission (church), the presidio (fort), and the pueblo (town). Of these the mission was the most influential, and Franciscan friars set up 21 missions at

**Window-shopping along Ocean Avenue, Carmel's most exclusive street**

◁ **The Los Angeles skyline with snowy Mount Baldy in the background, a view from Baldwin Hills**

approximately 30-mile (48-km) intervals along El Camino Real ("the Royal Road") from San Diego to Sonoma. Still, the territory remained remote until 1848 when Mexico ceded California to the US, and gold was found in the Sierra Nevada foothills. The Gold Rush of 1849 drew hordes of prospectors, known as "Forty-Niners" after the year of their arrival. The discovery of silver deposits in the western Sierras, as well as the completion of the transcontinental railroad in 1869, brought greater prosperity. But along with the changes came racial tensions, ignited by the influx of Chinese immigrants, who were brought to help build the railroad. Immigrants have since contributed to the state's cultural richness as well as its overpopulation and social tensions.

**The popular Third Street Promenade, Santa Monica**

On April 18, 1906, San Francisco was struck by the country's worst ever earthquake, and many believed that California's heyday was over. However the state's subsequent revival was linked to Hollywood's lucrative film industry. Movies and the new medium of television made California the symbol of America's postwar resurgence – suddenly everybody wanted the prosperous middle-class existence they believed was common here. At the same time racial discrimination and violence persisted, state schools lacked funds, and Hollywood found itself attacked by politicians as a hotbed of Marxist Communism.

Since the 1960s, however, California has been the birthplace of some of the country's most significant social movements. The University of California at Berkeley was home to the Free Speech Movement, and Haight Ashbury in San Francisco was the mecca for "hippies." Today, Silicon Valley is a leading center of the computer industry, and many world-class high-tech firms are based here. Yet, despite progress and prosperity, California is still earthquake prone.

### Key Dates in History

**1542** Spanish explorer Juan Rodríguez Cabrilho discovers California

**1769** The first mission is set up at San Diego

**1776** New presidio set up in San Francisco

**1781** Pueblo of Los Angeles founded

**1848** US annexes California. Gold discovered

**1853** Levi Strauss lands in the Bay Area and begins selling his canvas trousers

**1854** Sacramento becomes the state capital

**1869** Transcontinental railroad completed

**1891** Stanford University opens

**1893** San Andreas Fault discovered

**1906** Earthquake strikes San Francisco

**1911** *The Law of the Range* is the first film made in Hollywood

**1929** Actor Douglas Fairbanks Sr. hosts the first Academy Awards presentation

**1945** UN Charter signed in San Francisco

**1968** Senator Robert F. Kennedy assassinated

**1978** Apple Computer's first personal computer

**1984** Los Angeles hosts its second Olympics

**1992** Statewide racial riots

**2001** Energy crisis; rolling blackouts conserve electricity

## Society & Politics

If the US as a whole is a melting pot of people, California is an ethnic microcosm. It receives the highest number of immigrants (more than 200,000 every year), and its racial makeup is the nation's most diverse. The percentage of whites and African Americans is lower than the national average, but the Asian population is more than triple the national level. Hispanics too, account for more than a quarter of all Californians. This ethnic cocktail is nost visible in such cities as San Diego, .os Angeles, and San Francisco. Popuation growth has inevitably disturbed he balance between rural and urban ectors. Since the 1950s, farmlands ave declined as the need for housing as arisen. Today, the fast-expanding ob markets are in the service industries nd in the Silicon Valley.

Most visitors usually come to see California's two main cities – San rancisco and Los Angeles. In he north and south of the tate respectively, they define he opposing sides of its charcter. San Francisco is more compact, and prides itself on ts nonconformity and openmindedness. It has evolved into a pro-labor hotbed, with a history of activism (the Bay Area led he anti-Vietnam War movement). It also has one of the world's largest concentrations of gays and lesbians. Los Angeles, in contrast, is a sprawling city without a focal point, where illusions of wealth, fame, and glamor have created a dimensionless image of bright lights and conservative politics. The conflicting power that the two cities exert on the politics of the state and the nation explains why California may appear a little schizophrenic.

Beat writer Jack Kerouac

### Culture & the Arts

For most people, California's contributions to culture are Hollywood blockbusters or televised sitcoms. But another creativity reveals itself through its history of landscape painting, portraiture, and 20th-century avant-garde art. Modern artists such as John McLaughlin and Elmer Bischoff, and such pioneers of photographic art as Imogen Cunningham and Ansel Adams, have all achieved international recognition. British artist David Hockney lived here for many years, capturing the state's sun-soaked image on canvas. California is also home to some of the world's finest art museums, including the Los Angeles County Museum of Art, the San Francisco Museum of Modern Art, and the J. Paul Getty Museum. The Bay Area's Victorian architecture has always been a major tourist attraction, and visiting designers Frank Lloyd Wright and Daniel Burnham have left their mark here as well. Recent influential architects include residents Frank Gehry and Joe Esherick.

Over the years, California has been home to scores of successful writers, including Nobel Prize-winner John Steinbeck and Beat authors Jack Kerouac and Allen Ginsburg. The tradition continues with Amy Tan *(The Joy Luck Club)*, and detective novelist Sue Grafton, among others. Pop music also plays a major role, for this is where the Beach Boys, Janis Joplin, the Grateful Dead, and the Red Hot Chili Peppers launched their careers.

Californians love to eat out, and chefs Wolfgang Puck and Alice Waters have achieved fame promoting "California cuisine" – a blend of local ingredients and Asian techniques. This, combined with a selection of world-class local wines, is proof that Californians take good care of their palates. They are generally body-conscious and frequent gyms, or participate enthusiastically in sports and a wide range of activities. Luckily, surrounded by some of the nation's most beautiful countryside and the gentlest climate, they don't have to go far to enjoy a satisfying outdoor experience.

San Francisco's cable car, a good way to get around

# Exploring California

Beyond Los Angeles and San Francisco are other interesting towns and sights to visit. Highlights include San Diego and the Death Valley National Park in the south, and Monterey, Sacramento, and the Yosemite National Park in the north. Most visitors arrive at airports in Los Angeles and San Francisco. Both cities are linked to the rest of the state by an extensive road and rail network.

Shelter Island yacht harbor in San Diego Bay

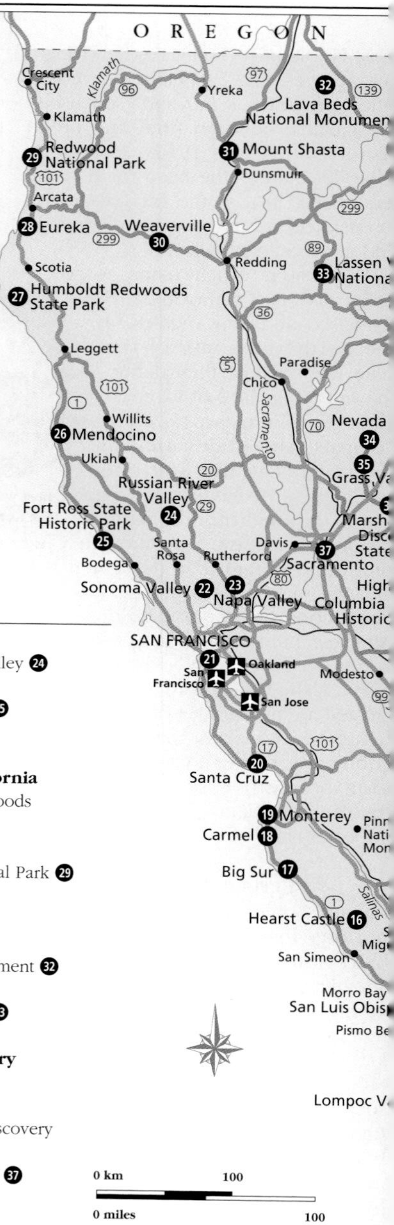

## Sights at a Glance

*Los Angeles pp658–77* 1

**San Diego County**
San Diego 2
Sea World 3
La Jolla 4
Tijuana, Mexico 5

**The Deserts**
Palm Springs 6
Anza-Borrego Desert State Park 7
Salton Sea 8
Joshua Tree National Park 9
Mojave Desert 10
*Death Valley National Park pp684–5* 11

**Central Coast**
Santa Barbara 12
Channel Islands National Park 13
Lompoc Valley 14
San Luis Obispo 15
*Hearst Castle™ pp688–9* 16
*Big Sur pp690–91* 17
Carmel 18
Monterey 19
Santa Cruz 20

*San Francisco pp694–711* 21

**The Wine Country**
Sonoma Valley 22
Napa Valley 23
Russian River Valley 24
Fort Ross State Historic Park 25
Mendocino 26

**Northern California**
Humboldt Redwoods State Park 27
Eureka 28
Redwood National Park 29
Weaverville 30
Mount Shasta 31
Lava Beds National Monument 32
Lassen Volcanic National Park 33

**The Gold Country**
Nevada City 34
Grass Valley 35
Marshall Gold Discovery State Park 36
*Sacramento p717* 37
Highway 49 38
Columbia State Historic Park 39

**The High Sierras**
Lake Tahoe 40
Yosemite National Park 41
Eastern Sierras 42
Sequoia & Kings Canyon National Parks 43

OREGON
Crescent City
Klamath
Yreka
Lava Beds National Monumen
Mount Shasta
Dunsmuir
Redwood National Park
Arcata
Eureka
Weaverville
Redding
Lassen National
Scotia
Humboldt Redwoods State Park
Leggett
Paradise
Chico
Sacramento
Willits
Mendocino
Ukiah
Nevada
Grass Va
Russian River Valley
Fort Ross State Historic Park
Marsh Disc State
Davis
Santa Rosa
Rutherford
Bodega
Sonoma Valley
Napa Valley
High
Columbia Historic
SAN FRANCISCO
Oakland
San Francisco
Modesto
San Jose
Santa Cruz
Monterey
Carmel
Big Sur
Hearst Castle
San Simeon
Morro Bay
San Luis Obis
Pismo Be
Lompoc V

0 km 100
0 miles 100

### See Also

• **Practical Information** pp720–21
• **Where to Stay** pp722–5
• **Where to Eat** pp726–9

Giant sequoia trees in Yosemite National Park

## Mileage Chart

**10** = Distance in miles
10 = Distance in kilometers

| | Los Angeles | San Diego | Palm Springs | Santa Barbara | Monterey | Santa Cruz | San Francisco | Sonoma |
|---|---|---|---|---|---|---|---|---|
| San Diego | **121** 195 | | | | | | | |
| Palm Springs | **107** 172 | **138** 222 | | | | | | |
| Santa Barbara | **95** 153 | **220** 354 | **202** 325 | | | | | |
| Monterey | **320** 515 | **468** 753 | **425** 684 | **250** 402 | | | | |
| Santa Cruz | **363** 584 | **492** 792 | **467** 752 | **272** 438 | **43** 69 | | | |
| San Francisco | **380** 612 | **556** 895 | **485** 781 | **337** 542 | **112** 180 | **73** 117 | | |
| Sonoma | **409** 658 | **599** 964 | **513** 826 | **380** 612 | **158** 254 | **118** 190 | **45** 72 | |
| Sacramento | **384** 618 | **504** 811 | **488** 785 | **404** 650 | **195** 314 | **156** 251 | **87** 140 | **69** 111 |

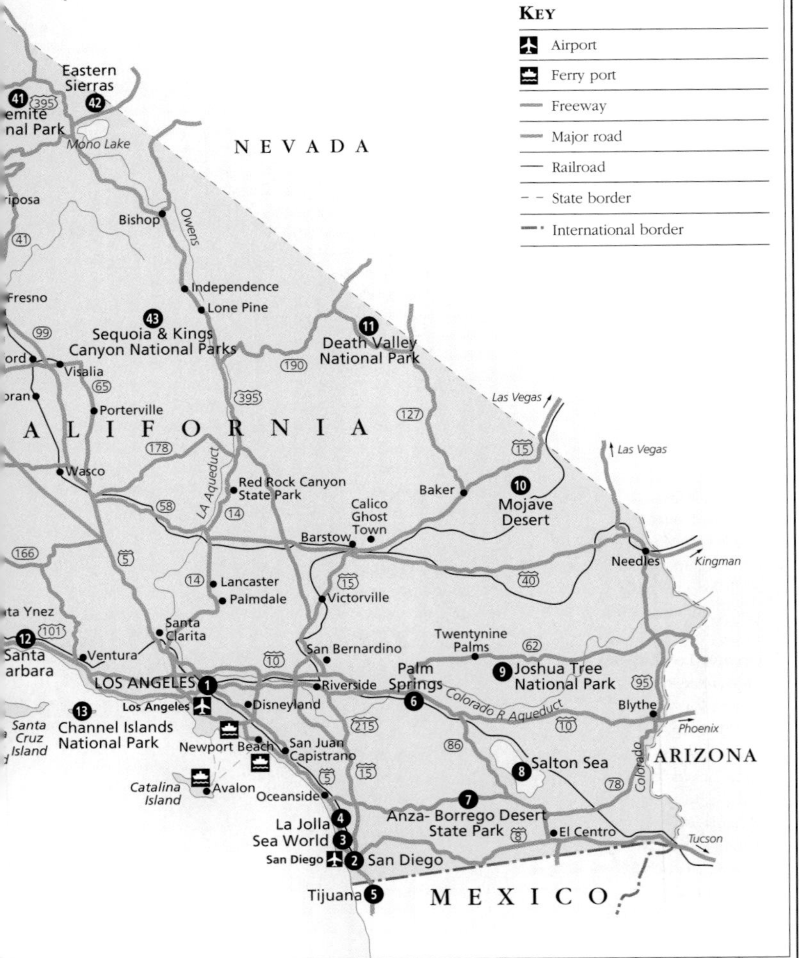

## Key

- Airport
- Ferry port
- Freeway
- Major road
- Railroad
- State border
- International border

NEVADA

CALIFORNIA

ARIZONA

MEXICO

Eastern Sierras 42
41 Yosemite National Park
Mono Lake
Bishop
Owens
Independence
Lone Pine
Fresno
43 Sequoia & Kings Canyon National Parks
11 Death Valley National Park
Visalia
Porterville
Las Vegas
Wasco
Red Rock Canyon State Park
LA Aqueduct
Baker
10 Mojave Desert
Calico Ghost Town
Barstow
Needles
Kingman
Lancaster
Palmdale
Victorville
Santa Clarita
12 Santa Barbara
Ventura
San Bernardino
Twentynine Palms
LOS ANGELES 1
Riverside
Palm Springs 6
9 Joshua Tree National Park
Blythe
Los Angeles
Disneyland
Colorado R Aqueduct
Phoenix
13 Channel Islands National Park
Santa Cruz Island
Newport Beach
San Juan Capistrano
8 Salton Sea
Colorado
Catalina Island
Avalon
Oceanside
7 Anza-Borrego Desert State Park
La Jolla 4
Sea World 3
El Centro
Tucson
San Diego 2 San Diego
Tijuana 5

# Los Angeles ❶

SITTING IN A BROAD, flat basin, surrounded by beaches, mountains, and deserts, the 467-sq-mile (1,200-sq-km) city of Los Angeles has a population of 3.7 million. The city's celluloid self-image, with its palm trees, shopping malls, and opulent lifestyles, has been idealized as the ultimate "American Dream." While known for its museums and galleries, it is still the fantasy worlds of Hollywood and Disneyland that draw most people to Los Angeles.

**Waterskiing, a popular activity along the south Los Angeles coastline**

## SIGHTS AT A GLANCE

Getty Center ①
Santa Monica ②
Venice ③
Museum of Tolerance ④
Westwood & UCLA ⑤
The Golden Triangle ⑥
*Sunset Boulevard pp664–5* ⑦
Mulholland Drive ⑧
Hollywood Boulevard ⑨
Hollywood Bowl ⑩
Farmers Market ⑪
Miracle Mile ⑫
Exposition Park & University of Southern California ⑬
Los Angeles Central Library ⑭
Los Angeles City Hall ⑮
Music Center ⑯
Grand Central Market ⑰
Little Tokyo ⑱
Museum of Contemporary Art ⑲
El Pueblo ⑳
Lummis House ㉑
Southwest Museum ㉒
Griffith Park ㉓
Hollywood Sign ㉔
Universal Studios ㉕

**Greater Los Angeles**
***(see inset map)***
Malibu ㉖
Pasadena ㉗
Watts Towers ㉘
Long Beach ㉙
Knott's Berry Farm ㉚
Mission San Juan Capistrano ㉛
Newport Beach ㉜
*Disneyland® Resort pp674–5* ㉝

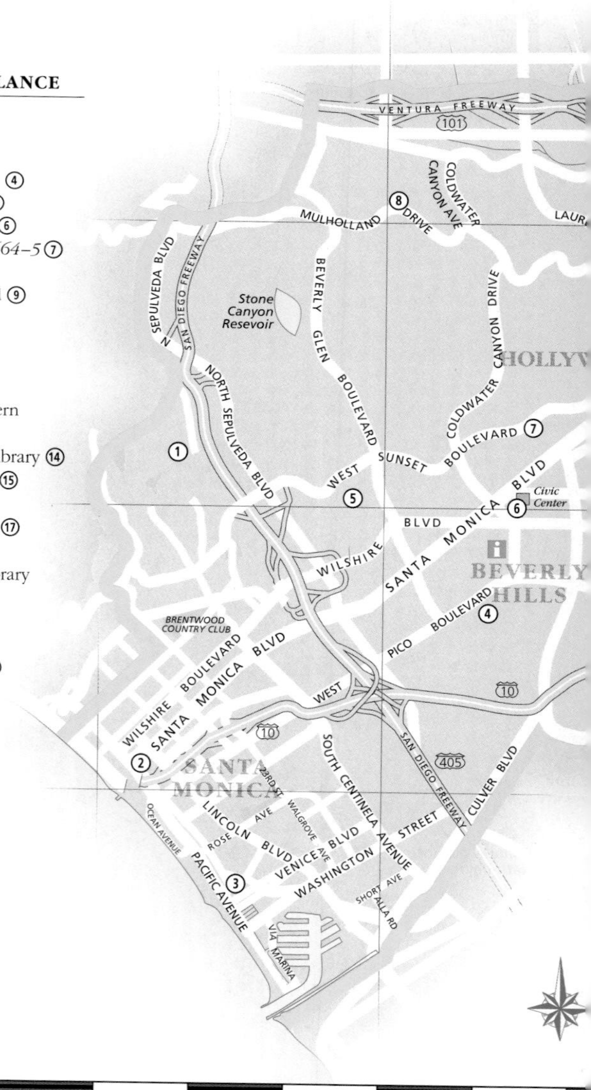

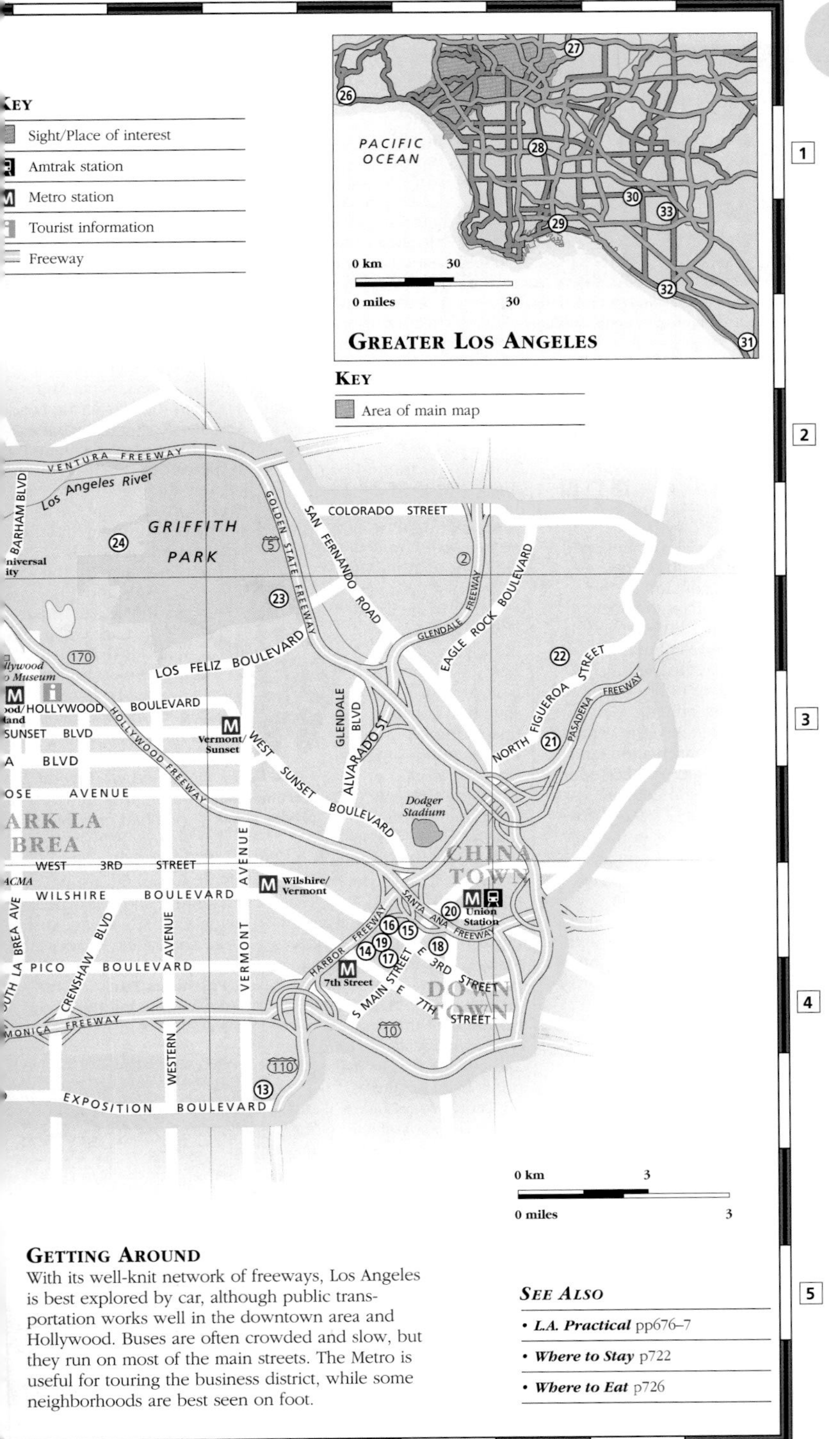


## Getting Around

With its well-knit network of freeways, Los Angeles is best explored by car, although public transportation works well in the downtown area and Hollywood. Buses are often crowded and slow, but they run on most of the main streets. The Metro is useful for touring the business district, while some neighborhoods are best seen on foot.

### See Also


- ***L.A. Practical*** pp676–7
- ***Where to Stay*** p722
- ***Where to Eat*** p726

***Adoration of the Magi* (c.1495–1505) by Andrea Mantegna, Getty Museum**

## Getty Center ①

**Map** B3. 1200 Getty Center Dr. *(310) 440-7300.* *10am–6pm Tue–Thu & Sun, 10am–9pm Fri–Sat. No parking reservations needed Sat–Sun.* *public hols.* www.getty.edu

SITUATED AMID the untamed beauty of the Santa Monica Mountains in the Sepulveda Pass, the Getty Center holds a commanding physical and cultural position in the area. Opened in 1997, the 110-acre (45-ha) complex houses not only the Getty Museum but also the center's research, conservation, and grant programs, dedicated to art and cultural heritage.

J. Paul Getty (1892–1976) made his fortune in the oil business and became an ardent collector of art. He amassed a remarkable collection of European art works, focusing on pre-20th-century artistic movements, from the Renaissance to Post-Impressionism. A bold collector, Getty enjoyed the pursuit of an object almost more than the possession of it. He wanted his collection to be open to the public free of charge. His original home, the Getty Villa in Malibu, was the site of the first Getty Museum. The villa, now undergoing remodeling, will house Greek and Roman antiquities when it reopens in fall 2006.

Since Getty's death, the Trust has purchased works of the highest quality to complement the existing collection. New departments such as manuscripts and drawing have also been added.

From below, the center may look like a fortress, but once inside, the scale is intimate, with fountains, walkways, courtyards, and niches. An electric tram brings visitors from the parking lot to the complex. The museum has a tall, airy foyer that opens onto a central courtyard. Facing this courtyard are the five two-story pavilions that feature the varied art collections. European paintings in the museum date from the 13th to the late 19th centuries and include masterpieces such as Andrea Mantegna's *Adoration of the Magi* (c.1495–1505), Rembrandt's *The Abduction of Europa* (1632), Paul Cézanne's *Still Life with Apples* (1900), and Vincent Van Gogh's *Irises* (1889). The last was painted by the artist when he was in the asylum at St-Remy. The Getty's collection of sculpture contains fine examples of Baroque and Neo-Classical works, including François Girardon's *Pluto Abducting Proserpine* (c.1693–1710) and statues – *Venus, Juno,* and *Minerva* (1773) – by Joseph Nollekens.

The museum's photography department features works of many of the pioneers of photography, such as Louis-Jacques-Mande Daguerre (inventor of the daguerreotypes) and William Henry Fox Talbott (the first to make prints from negatives).

Decorative arts were Getty's first love as a collector, after he rented a New York penthouse furnished with 18th-century French and English antiques. The museum holds a superb collection of ornate French furniture and decorative arts, with coffers, chandeliers, wall-lights, and tapestries, dating from the reign of Louis XIV to the Napoleonic era (1643–1815).

The museum traces the development of handwritten and illuminated manuscripts from the sixth to the 16th century, and holds an impressive collection of masterpiece from different historical periods such as the Byzantine, Ottoman, Romanesque, Gothic, and the Renaissance.

## Santa Monica ②

**Map** B4. *90,000.* *1400 Ocean Ave, (310) 393-7593* *Santa Monica Festival (Apr).*

WITH ITS FRESH sea breezes mild climate, and friendly streets, Santa Monica has been the star of the Los Angeles coastline since the 1890s, when trolleys linked it to the city, and beach parties became the rage. In the early days, it lived a dual life as a sleepy coastal town and the headquarters for offshore gambling ships. In the 1920s and 30s, movie stars such as Cary Grant and Mary Pickford bought land here, creating "the Gold Coast." Following the success of the television series *Baywatch*, the popular beach and pier gained worldwide fame. But the city, perched on a high yellow cliff overlooking Santa Monica Bay, is also noted for its restaurants, shopping areas, and vibrant arts scene. Lush parks dot the city's landscape, with none quite as beautiful as **Palisades Park**, on the bluff overlooking the ocean. Stretching 1.5 miles (2.5 km)

**Street entertainer playing guitar**

**Tall palm trees lining the road in Palisades Park, Santa Monica**

The Chiat Day Mojo Advertising Agency, designed by Frank Gehry

along the cliff's edge, this narrow, well-manicured park is one of the best spots to watch the sun set. For the quintessential California experience, take a walk or jog along the paths, with the ocean as a backdrop and the towering palms overhead. At the northern end, the aptly named Inspiration Point has great views of the bay, stretching from Malibu to Palos Verdes.

Inland, between Wilshire Boulevard and Broadway, is **Third Street Promenade**. Once a decaying shopping street, this boulevard has undergone a major face-lift and is now one of the liveliest places in Los Angeles. Its three pedestrian blocks are lined with shops, cafés, bookstores, and theaters. At night the mood is especially festive, with street performers entertaining visitors with music, dance, and magic tricks.

Santa Monica's other important shopping area is Main Street, which runs south toward Venice. It abounds in a wide range of shops, restaurants, and galleries. Many examples of public art are displayed along the street, such as Paul Conrad's *Chain Reaction*, a stainless-steel and copper-link chain statement against nuclear war. The Frank Gehry-designed **Chiat Day Mojo Advertising Agency** building, shaped like a pair of binoculars, dominates the street. Main Street also features the California Heritage Museum, which has the distinction of showcasing various periods in the state's history.

Northeast of the beach, the 1908 **Santa Monica Pier** is the West Coast's oldest amusement pier, with bumper cars, roller coasters, and a giant Ferris wheel. There is also the 1922 carousel that featured in Paul Newman's 1973 film, *The Sting*. **Bergamot Station** is a large, sprawling 5.5-acre (2-ha) arts complex that stands on the site of an abandoned trolley station. The crude buildings are constructed out of aluminum siding, but with an added touch of elegant high-tech styling. More than 20 galleries display the latest in contemporary as well as radical art. The Santa Monica Museum of Art, within the Bergamot Station, focuses on the work of contemporary artists, particularly those who are involved in performance and multimedia art.

**Santa Monica Pier**

Colorado & Ocean Aves. *(310) 458-8900, 260-8744 Pacific Park information. daily.* **Carousel** *May–Sep: 10am–5pm Tue–Sun; Oct–Apr: 10am–5pm Sat–Sun. (310) 395-4248.*

**Bergamot Station**

2525 Michigan Ave. *(310) 829-5854. 10am–5pm Tue–Fri, 11am–5pm Sat. Sun, public hols.*

## Venice ③

**Map** B5. *2904 Washington Blvd, Suite 100, (310) 396-7016.* www.venice.net

Founded by tobacco tycoon Abbot Kinney, as a US version of Venice (Italy), this lively beach town was a swampland little more than 100 years ago. Hoping to spark a cultural renaissance in California, Kinney built a system of canals, and imported gondolas to punt along the waterways. Today, only a few of the original canals remain, the rest having been filled in. The best place to see the canals is on **Dell Avenue**, where old bridges, boats, and ducks grace the waterways.

However, the town is best known for the bustling, circus atmosphere of its beach. On the boardwalk during weekends, men and women whiz past on bicycles and skates, while a zany array of jugglers, acrobats, and one-man bands captivate the crowds. Muscle Beach, where Arnold Schwarzenegger used to work out, still attracts body builders.

Man-made canal in Venice

### Raymond Chandler

American novelist Raymond Chandler (1888–1959) set several of his works in Santa Monica, a city that he loathed and thinly disguised as sleazy Bay City in *Farewell, My Lovely*. Corruption, vice, and the city's offshore gambling circuit of the 1920s and 1930s are well documented in his portrayal of Santa Monica. His novels, such as *The Big Sleep, The High Window, and The Long Goodbye,* depicting the dark side of L.A., were made into films. A leading figure of the so-called hard-boiled school of detective writing of the period, Chandler's famous detective Philip Marlowe epitomized a tough, unsentimental point of view.

Raymond Chandler

## Museum of Tolerance ④

**Map** C4. 9786 W Pico Blvd. *(310) 553-8403.* *11:30am–4pm Mon–Thu, 11:30am–1pm Fri, 11am–5pm Sun.* *Sat, Jan 1, Thanksgiving, Dec 25, & all major Jewish hols.* www.wiesenthal.com/mot

Dedicated to the promotion of respect and understanding among all people, this museum focuses on the history of racism and prejudice in the United States, and on the European Holocaust experience.

The museum tour begins in the **Tolerancenter**, where visitors are challenged to confront racism and bigotry through interactive exhibits. A computerized wall map locates more than 250 known racist groups in the US, while a 16-screen video wall depicts the 1960s Civil Rights struggle in the country. Interactive videos also pose questions of responsible citizenship and social justice. They offer footage and interviews of the 1992 L.A. race riots, in which 26 people were killed and 3,000 homes destroyed. In the **Whisper Gallery** visitors actually hear racial and sexual taunts so that they can experience these themselves. The Holocaust section has a re-creation of the Wannsee Conference, in which Third Reich leaders decide on the "The Final Solution of the Jewish Question," outlined right down to its harrowing implementation in a reproduced gas chamber. Some of the exhibits may not be suitable for children under the age of 10.

Exhibition on racial prejudice at the Museum of Tolerance

## Westwood & UCLA ⑤

**Map** B4. **UCLA Campus** *(310) 825-4321.* **Westwood Village** *10779 W Pico Blvd, Westside, (310) 475-8806.*

With its wide range of academic departments and professional schools, boasting a strength of over 35,000 students, the 419-acre-(170-ha) University of California Los Angeles (UCLA) is a city within a city. The original campus was designed in 1925 to resemble the Romanesque towns of Europe. But as the university expanded, more modern architecture was favored. The disappointing mix of bland structures that resulted is redeemed by the beautiful landscaped grounds. The four red-brick buildings that make up the **Royce Quadrangle** are the oldest on UCLA's campus. Built in the Italian Romanesque style, Royce, Kinsey, and Haines Halls and Powell Library far surpass the other buildings at UCLA in beauty.

Since it was first developed in 1928, Westwood Village with its pleasant, pedestrian-friendly streets has been one of the most successful shopping districts in Southern California. It remains the most densely packed movie-theater district in the US, with some theaters offering sneak previews of the latest films. South of Westwood, the **Armand Hammer Museum of Art and Culture** holds the art collection of businessman Armand Hammer (1899–1990). The Hammer collection includes a variety of Impressionist and Post-Impressionist works by such artists as Claude Monet, Camille Pissarro, and Vincent Van Gogh. Southeast of the museum, the tranquil **Westwood Memorial Park** marks the final resting place of several celebrities such as Dean Martin, Peter Lorre, Natalie Wood, and most famously, Marilyn Monroe.

Entrance to UCLA at the Armand Hammer Museum of Art

Tucked away in a shady canyon northeast of Westwood, the serene **Mildred E. Mathias Botanical Garden** contains a wide variety of plants – almost 4,000 rare and native species that include sub-tropical and tropical varieties.

Farther north, UCLA's **Fowler Museum of Cultural History** holds exhibitions that focus on the prehistoric, historic, and contemporary societies of Africa, Asia, the Americas, and Oceania. The collection consisting of 750,000 artifacts makes it one of the nation's leading university museums.

**Armand Hammer Museum of Art & Culture**
10899 Wilshire Blvd. *(310) 443-7000.* *11am–7pm Tue, Wed, Fri, Sat; 11am–9pm Thu; 11am–5pm Sun.* *Jul 4, Thanksgiving, Dec 25.* *(free 11am–9pm Thu).* www.hammer.ucla.edu

**Fowler Museum of Cultural History**
*(310) 825-4361.* *noon–5pm Wed–Sun (until 8pm Thu).* *public hols.* *(free Thu).*

## The Golden Triangle ⑥

Map C4.

THE AREA BORDERED by Santa Monica Boulevard, Wilshire Boulevard, and North Crescent Drive is the business district of Beverly Hills, known as the "Golden Triangle." The shops, restaurants, and art galleries lining the streets are some of the most luxurious in the world. Cutting through the middle is **Rodeo Drive**, one of the most celebrated shopping streets. It derives its name from El Rancho Rodeo de las Aguas ("the Ranch of the Gathering of Waters"), the name of an early Spanish land grant that included Beverly Hills. Today, Rodeo Drive's wide, tree-lined sidewalks house Italian designer boutiques and the best names in fashion, such as Gucci and Christian Dior, world-class jewelers, and many leading L.A. retailers. The place is also a prime area for celebrity-spotting.

Next to it, on Wilshire Boulevard, the cream of American department stores offer a heady mix of style and opulence. Around the corner, **2 Rodeo**, developed in 1990 as a mock-European shopping street, is one of the most expensive retail centers ever built.

At the eastern end of the Golden Triangle lies the MGM Building. Built in 1920, it was the headquarters of the newly formed Metro-Goldwyn-Mayer film studios.

**Façade of the Beverly Hills Civic Center in Los Angeles**

To the north are the beautifully manicured Beverly Gardens and the elegant **Beverly Hills Civic Center**, with its landmark Spanish Colonial **City Hall**. Designed in 1932 by local firm Koerner and Gage, the hall's majestic tower, capped by a tiled cupola, has now become a symbol of the European-inspired city of Beverly Hills. In 1990, architect Charles Moore linked the building to a new Civic Center by a series of pedestrianized courtyards. On the upper levels, balconies and arcaded corridors continue the Spanish Colonial theme. The modern section houses a beautiful public library as well as the local fire and police stations. Billboards are banned in the area, and a height restriction of three stories is imposed on any new buildings, leaving City Hall to dominate the skyline.

The latest addition to the Golden Triangle, the **Museum of Television and Radio** on North Beverly Drive, holds a collection of 75,000 television and radio programs and offers a comprehensive history of broadcasting. Visitors can watch and listen to news and a collection of entertainment and sports programs from the earliest days of radio and television to the present. Pop music fans can see footage of the early Beatles or of a young Elvis Presley making his television debut, while sports enthusiasts can relive classic Olympic competitions. The museum also hosts exhibitions, seminars, and screenings on specialized topics and selected actors or directors.

North of Golden Triangle, above Sunset Boulevard *(see pp664–5)*, lie the palatial estates, the famed **Hollywood Actors' Homes** that have made Beverly Hills the symbol of success for those in the entertainment industry. When, in 1920, Mary Pickford and Douglas Fairbanks Sr. built their mansion, **Pickfair**, at the top of Summit Drive, everyone else followed – and stayed. Sunset Boulevard divides the haves from the have-nots: people who live south of it may be rich, but those who live to the north of the road are considered to be the super-rich. Houses come in almost every architectural style; some are ostentatious, others surprisingly modest. They can be toured along a 5-mile (8-km) drive, maps for which are available from street vendors. Visitors must remember that film stars' homes are private residences; please do not tresspass.

**Cushion on display in the Gucci boutique**

**Faye Dunaway's house at No. 714 Palm Drive, Beverly Hills**

**Beverly Hills Civic Center**
455 N Rexford Dr. *(310) 285-1000.* *7:30am–5:30pm Mon–Thu, 8am–5pm Fri.* *public hols.*

**Museum of Television & Radio**
465 N Beverly Dr. *(310) 786-1000.* *noon–5pm Wed–Sun (until 9pm Thu).* *public hols.*

**2 Rodeo**
268 N Rodeo Dr. *(310) 247-7040.*
www.2rodeo.com

# Sunset Boulevard ⑦

Sunset Boulevard has been associated with the movies since the 1920s, when it was a dirt track linking the burgeoning Hollywood studios with the hillside homes of the screen stars. Its liveliest and most historically rich stretch, Sunset Strip, is filled with restaurants, luxury hotels, and nightclubs. Once a magnet for gamblers and bootleggers, this 1.5-mile (2.4-km) stretch held famous nightclubs such as Ciro's and Mocambo – where legend says Margarita Cansino met studio boss Harry Cohen, who renamed her Rita Hayworth. While the Strip remains at the center of L.A.'s nightlife, the other section of the Boulevard, the Old Studio District, once the hub of the film industry, is now a mostly run-down, decrepit area frequented by drug dealers and prostitutes.

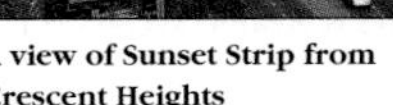

A view of Sunset Strip from Crescent Heights

**The Rainbow Bar & Grill,** formerly the Villa Nova, has walls lined with wine casks and gold records. Vincente Minnelli proposed to Judy Garland here and, eight years later in 1953, Marilyn Monroe met Joe DiMaggio here on a blind date.

**The Comedy Store**, *a world-famous spot for stand-up comedy, occupies the site of the 1940s' nightclub Ciro's.*

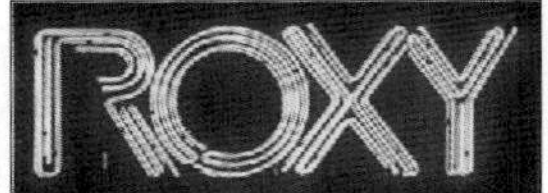



**The Roxy**
*This trendy nightclub stands on the site of the old Club Largo.*

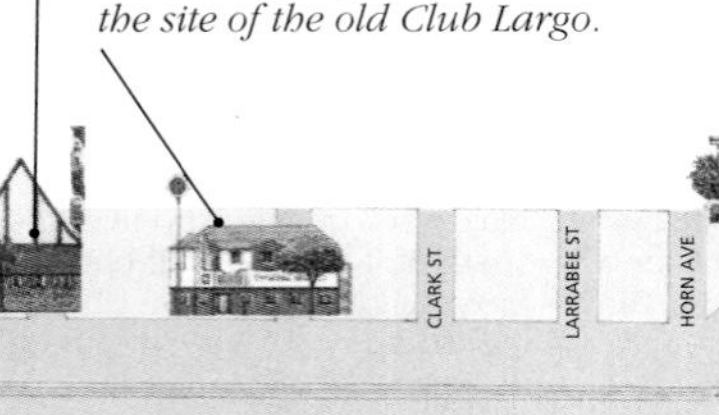



**Sunset Plaza**

**The Viper Room** is a popular live music club, part-owned by Johnny Depp. In 1993 actor River Phoenix, having taken a lethal cocktail of drugs, collapsed and died on the sidewalk outside.

**The Original Spago** was celebrity Chef Wolfgang Puck's first restaurant. Many Oscar night parties were hosted here by legendary Hollywood agent Irving "Swifty" Lazar, in the 1970s and 80s.

**Sunset Plaza**
*Lined with chic stores and cafés, this area is best explored on foot.*

**Hyatt Hotel**
*Visiting rock stars regularly frequent this hotel. Jim Morrison stayed here when he played with The Doors at the nearby Whisky A Go Go.*

**Argyle Hotel**
*An apartment complex in Hollywood's heyday, this Art Deco high-rise was once home to luminaries such as Jean Harlow and Clark Gable.*

**Chateau Marmont**
*The hotel was modeled on a Loire Valley château. When it opened in 1929, it attracted actors such as Errol Flynn and Greta Garbo. Among today's regulars are Christopher Walken and Winona Ryder.*

N LAUREL AVE
N FAIRFAX AVE
LA BREA AVE
N LAUREL AVE

**A & M Records** was built by Charlie Chaplin as homes for workers at his studio.

**The Trocadero** nightclub had Nat "King" Cole as its pianist in its heyday. Only three steps remain of the old building.

**Directors' Guild of America**
*This is one of the many offices on the Strip connected with the film industry.*

**The Roxbury Club**, west of the Chateau Marmont hotel, is popular with the stars of teenage TV shows. It stands on the site of the 1940s Players Club, owned by movie director Preston Sturges.

**Schwab's**
*Now a Virgin Megastore, this former drugstore was a popular meeting place for film stars and columnists. Facing it, the legendary Garden of Allah apartment complex once held such residents as Scott Fitzgerald and Dorothy Parker.*

**The House of Blues**
*This tin-roofed blues bar has been transported from Clarksdale, Mississippi. It is part-owned by the actor Dan Aykroyd, who co-starred with John Belushi in the 1980 cult movie* The Blues Brothers.

**Billboards**
*Huge billboards, handpainted by Hollywood's finest artists to promote new films or personalities, are landmark symbols of Sunset Strip.*

## Mulholland Drive ⑧

**Map** C2. Off Hwys 1 & 27, from Hollywood Fwy to Leo Carrillo State Beach. *23805 Stuart Ranch Rd, Ste 100, (310) 456-9025.*

MULHOLLAND DRIVE, one of the most famous roads in Los Angeles, runs for nearly 50 miles (80 km) from north Hollywood to the Malibu Coast. As it winds along the ridge of the Santa Monica Mountains, the route has spectacular views of the city and the San Fernando Valley.

The road was named for William Mulholland (1855–1935), who designed a series of aqueducts to channel water into Los Angeles. He oversaw the completion of Mulholland Drive in 1924.

## Hollywood Boulevard ⑨

**Map** D3.

ONE OF THE most famous streets in the world, Hollywood Boulevard's name is still redolent with glamor. Despite its recent run-down look, many of its landmark sights retain the original appeal and charisma.

Perhaps the only pavement in the city to be cleaned six times a week, the **Walk of Fame** is set with more than 2,000 polished marble stars. Since 1960, luminaries from the worlds of film, radio, television, theater, and music have been immortalized on the boulevard and on Vine Street. However, stardom does not come easily: each personality must be sponsored and approved by the Chamber of Commerce, and pay a $7,500 installation fee.

**Façade of the well-known Mann's Chinese Theatre**

The famed **Mann's Chinese Theatre** on the north side of the boulevard has changed little since its opening in 1927, with the premiere of Cecil B. de Mille's *King of Kings*. The theater's creator, Sid Grauman, is also credited with one of Hollywood's longest-running publicity stunts: its famed autograph patio with hand- and footprints of stars. Legend has it that the custom began when silent screen star Norma Talmadge accidentally stepped on the wet cement. Grauman then invited her, along with Mary Pickford and Douglas Fairbanks Sr. to legitimately leave their imprints. Across the road stands the **Clarion Hotel Hollywood Roosevelt**, frequented by famous figures such as Marilyn Monroe, Clark Gable, and Ernest Hemingway. It was the locale of the first Academy Awards ceremony in 1929. Nearby, the restored **El Capitan Theater** was the venue for many movie openings. Neon lights draw visitors to this theater that now has premiers of Disney animations. To its west, **Ripley's Believe It or Not!®** is devoted to the bizarre. Farther along, **Frederick's of Hollywood** is the flagship store of Fredrick Mellinger's famous mail-order lingerie business launched in 1946. Its Celebrity Lingerie Hall of Fame includes Marilyn Monroe's bra from the film *Let's Make Love* (1960), Tony Curtis's black lace bra from *Some Like It Hot* (1959), and Madonna's black bustier.

MARILYN MONROE

**Star in Walk of Fame**

**Walk of Fame**
*6541 Hollywood Blvd, (323) 461-2804.* *(323) 469-8311.*

**Mann's Chinese Theatre**
6925 Hollywood Blvd. *(323) 461-3331.* *(323) 464-8111.* *daily.* www.mannmoviefone.com

## Hollywood Bowl ⑩

**Map** D3. 2301 N Highland Ave. *(323) 850-2000.* *late Jun–late Sep* **Box office** *10am–6pm Tue–Sun.* www.hollywoodbowl.com

SITUATED IN A natural amphitheater that was once revered by the Cahuenga Pass Gabrielino Indians, the 60-acre (24-ha) Hollywood Bowl has now become sacred to Angelenos. The summer home of the L.A. Philharmonic since 1922, the site attracts thousands of people on warm evenings to listen to the orchestra.

Much altered over the years, the shell-shaped stage was first designed in 1929 by Lloyd Wright, son of architec

### THE RISE OF HOLLYWOOD

In 1887, prohibitionist Harvey Henderson Wilcox and his wife, Daeida, set up a sober, Christian community in an L.A. suburb and called it Hollywood. Ironically, over the next several decades the movie business with all its decadence came to replace their Utopia. The takeover started in 1913 with the filming of Cecil B. deMille's *The Squaw Man*. Silent film stars such as Charlie Chaplin and Mary Pickford were succeeded by icons of a more glamorous Hollywood, such as Errol Flynn and Mae West. Wall Street bankers soon realized their potential and invested heavily in the film industry.

**Oscar statuette**

'rank Lloyd Wright. Rumor ays that material for the building was taken from the et of Douglas Fairbanks Sr's novie *Robin Hood*.

The Edmund D. Edelman Hollywood Bowl Museum xplores the site's rich history hrough videos, old programs nd posters, and memorabilia of the artists who have come ere, from violinist Jascha Heifetz to the Beatles.

'ollywood Bowl, nestling in the ollywood Hills

## 'armers Market ⑪

lap D3. 6333 W 3rd St. (323) 33-9211. 9am–9pm Mon–Fri, am–8pm Sat, 10am–7pm Sun. Jan 1, Thanksgiving, Dec 25. www.farmersmarketla.com

DURING the Great Depression in 1934 a group of armers began selling their roduce directly to the public n a field at the edge of town. ince then, Farmers Market as been a favorite meeting lace for Angelenos. Bustling ith stalls and shops selling verything from fresh roduce to antiques and T-hirts, the market also has ome of the best cafés and estaurants in the city.

## Miracle Mile ⑫

lap D4. Wilshire Blvd between Brea & Fairfax Aves. 685 Figueroa St, (213) 689-8822; 6801 ollywood Blvd, (323) 467-6412.

DEVELOPER A.W. Ross bought 18 acres (7.2 ha) of land ong Wilshire Boulevard in 920 and built an upscale hopping district, with wide reets meant for cars and Art eco buildings, earning it the ame "Miracle Mile." Today, dotted with grocery stores, this stretch is a shadow of its former self. The western end of the Miracle Mile has fared better. With its five museums, including the **Los Angeles County Museum of Art** (LACMA), the area is now known as Museum Row.

The largest encyclopedic art museum west of Chicago, LACMA offers a comprehensive survey of the history of world art, with a collection of over 100,000 objects dating from the prehistoric to contemporary times. Collections include pre-Columbian stone objects, Islamic art, and a wide selection of European and American decorative arts, paintings, and sculpture. Especially impressive are its collection of scrolls and ceramics from the Far East.

Nearby, the **George C. Page Museum** showcases over one million fossils discovered at the La Brea Tar Pits. The tar, formed some 42,000 years ago, entrapped and killed animals who came here to drink water. Their bones were then fossilized. For centuries the tar was used by the Native Americans, Mexicans, and Spanish to waterproof baskets and roofs. In 1906, geologists discovered the largest collection of fossils of mammals, birds, reptiles, plants, and insects from the Pleistocene Epoch ever found in one place. The only human skeleton found in the pits is that of the "La Brea Woman." A hologram changes her from a skeleton to a fully fleshed person and back again. The **Peterson Automotive Museum** traces the evolution of the nation's car culture with detailed displays of vintage cars, old showrooms, and cars of filmstars, such as Rita Hayworth's 1953 Cadillac and Clark Gable's Mercedes-Benz. Its other exhibits include a 1920s garage; an opulent 1930s car showroom; and a 1950s drive-in restaurant.

Farther along, the **Craft and Folk Art Museum**, houses more than 3,000 folk art and craft objects from around the world. These range from objects as diverse as 19th-century American quilts to contemporary furniture and African masks.

Los Angeles County Museum of Art (LACMA), Miracle Mile

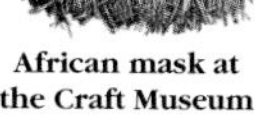

African mask at the Craft Museum

**LACMA**
5905 Wilshire Blvd. (323) 857-6000. noon–8pm Mon–Tue & Thu (until 9pm Fri), 11am–8pm Sat–Sun. Wed, Thanksgiving, Dec 25. (free 2nd Tue of month & after 5pm). www.lacma.org

**George C. Page Museum of La Brea Discoveries**
5801 Wilshire Blvd. (323) 934-7243. 9:30am–5pm daily. Jan 1, Jul 4, Thanksgiving, Dec 25. (free first Tue of month).

Model of La Brea Tar Pits in the George C. Page Museum

## Exposition Park & University of Southern California ⑬

**Map** E4. *DASH Shuttle C from Business District.* *81.* **Natural History Museum of L.A. County** *(213) 763-3466.* **L.A. Memorial Coliseum** *(213) 748-6136.* **University of Southern California** *(213) 740-5371.* www.usc.edu

LOCATED SOUTHWEST of downtown, Exposition Park began life in the 1880s as an area of open-air markets, carnivals, and horse-racing. By the end of the century, the district was rife with drinking, gambling, and prostitution. When Judge William Miller Bowen's Sunday school pupils began skipping church to enjoy local temptations, he pushed for the transformation of the area into a cultural landmark that today includes three museums. The **Natural History Museum of Los Angeles County**, at the heart of the park, displays a variety of specimens and artifacts, alongside an insect zoo and a hands-on Discovery Center. A short drive southeast leads to the **California Museum of Science and History**, with its interactive exhibits aiming to make science accessible to all.

Farther east lies the **California Afro-American Museum** that is a record of Afro-American achievements in various fields. The park is also home to the **Los Angeles Memorial Coliseum**, which was the site of the 1932 and 1984 Olympics, and was also home to the University's Trojan football team. Across the street, stands the 152-acre (62-ha) **University of Southern California** that houses about 28,000 students.

**Natural History Museum at Exposition Park**

**Rotunda of Los Angeles City Hall**

## Los Angeles Central Library ⑭

**Map** E4. 630 W 5th St. *(213) 228-7000.* *10am–8pm Mon–Thu, 10am–6pm Fri–Sat, 1–5pm Sun.* *public hols.* www.lapl.org

BUILT IN 1926, this civic treasure was struck by an arson attack in 1986. Seven years later, after a $213.9 million renovation program sympathetic to the original architecture, the library's capacity was doubled to more than 2.1 million books.

The original building combines Beaux Arts grandeur with Byzantine, Egyptian, and Roman architectural elements. The library is also a popular venue for prose and poetry readings, and concerts.

The **First Interstate World Center** across the street is a 73-story office block designed by I.M. Pei. At 1,017 ft (310 m), it is the tallest building in the city.

## Los Angeles City Hall ⑮

**Map** E4. 200 N Spring St. *(213) 485-2121.* *8am–5pm Mon–Fri.* *public hols.* *from Main St.* *advance reservations required.*

WHEN IT WAS BUILT in 1928, sand from every county in California and water from each of the state's 21 missions was added to the City Hall's mortar. The tower of this 28-story structure is still one of L.A.'s most familiar landmarks. It served as the Daily Planet building in the television serie *Superman.* Inside, the rotunda has a inlaid-tile dome and great acoustics. The **Los Angeles Children's Museum** across the street is guided by the principle that children learn best by doing. Some 20 hands-on activities are linked by a series of ramps. Called the Discovery Maze, the system was designed by architect Frank Gehry.

## Music Center ⑯

**Map** E4. 135 N Grand Ave. *(213) 972-7211.* **Dorothy Chandle Pavilion box office** *noon–6pm Tue–Sat, noon–4pm Sun.* **Mark Tape Forum & Ahmanson Theater box offices** *noon–8pm Tue–Sun.* www.musiccenter.org

**Music Center Plaza and Fountain**

THIS PERFORMING arts complex is situated at the northern end of Bunker Hill. The Dorothy Chandler Pavilio is named after the wife o the former publisher of the *Los Angeles Times.* It is home to the L.A. Music Center Opera, the L.A. Master Chorale, and from fall to spring, the L.A. Philharmonic. The Ahmanso Theater has movable walls to adjust the auditorium size, and it stages Broadway plays The Mark Taper Forum has won almost every theatrical prize in the US. It presents first-class plays such as Tony Kushner's *Angels in America* The Walt Disney Concert Ha opened here in October 200 it is the new home of the L.A Philharmonic Master Chorale

## Grand Central Market ⑰

**Map** E4. 317 S Broadway. *(213) 624-2378.* *9am–6pm daily.* *Jan 1, Thanksgiving, Dec 25.*

ANGELENOS have been coming to this vibrant indoor bazaar since 1917. Today, over 40 stallholders operate inside the marketplace, selling fruit, vegetables, meat, and herbs. The market's Latin American clientele come here to buy exotic products from their home countries, such as fresh Nogales cacti and beans from El Salvador.

Billed as the "shortest railway in the world," the adjacent **Angels Flight** funicular transported riders between Hill Street and Bunker Hill for almost 70 years. By 1969, Bunker Hill had degenerated, and the city dismantled the funicular, promising to reinstall it once the area had been redeveloped. It fulfilled that vow in 1996, some 27 years later.

**Angels Flight**
Between Grand, Hill, 3rd & 4th Sts. *(213) 626-1901. Closed for the foreseeable future.*

## Little Tokyo ⑱

**Map** F4. *244 S San Pedro St, (213) 628-2725.*

SITUATED SOUTHEAST of the City Hall, Little Tokyo attracts more than 200,000 visitors to its Japanese markets and temples. The first Japanese settled here in 1884. Today, the heart of the area is the Japanese American Cultural and Community Center, from which cultural activities are organized. Nearby, the Japanese Village Plaza is a lively place to shop. Housed in a former Buddhist Temple, the **Japanese American National Museum** traces the history of Japanese-American life in the US.

To its east, on Central Avenue the **Geffen Contemporary at MOCA**, once an old police garage,

**Japanese American Art Museum, Little Tokyo**

was used as an exhibition space for MOCA. Redesigned by Frank Gehry, the warehouse is a permanent fixture of the L.A. arts scene, hosting exhibitions often including highlights from MOCA.

**Japanese American National Museum**
369 E 1st St. *(213) 625-0414.* *10am–5pm Tue–Sun (until 8pm Thu).* *Jan 1, Thanksgiving, Dec 25.* www.janm.org

## Museum of Contemporary Art ⑲

**Map** E4. 250 S Grand Ave. *(213) 621-2766.* *11am–5pm Tue–Sun (until 8pm Thu).* *Jan 1, Jul 4, Thanksgiving, Dec 25.* *(free 5–8pm Thu).* www.moca.org

RATED AS ONE OF the ten best works of architecture in the United States, the Museum of Contemporary Art (MOCA), designed by Japanese architect Arata Isozaki, presents an intriguing combination of pyramids, cylinders, and cubes. It holds a respectable selection of post-1940 art, including Pop Art and Abstract Expressionist works by artists as diverse as Mark Rothko, Robert Rauschenberg, and Claes Oldenburg.

## El Pueblo ⑳

**Map** F4. Downtown L.A. between N Main St & Olvera St & N Alamenda St.

THE OLDEST PART of the city, El Pueblo de la Reina de Los Angeles was founded in 1781 by Felipe de Neve, the Spanish governor of California. Today, El Pueblo is a State Historic Monument, housing some of the city's oldest buildings, such as the Old Plaza Church and the Avila Adobe, the city's oldest existing house, furnished as it would have been in the 1840s. Olvera Street, preserved as a Mexican marketplace in the 1920s, abounds in shops selling colorful Mexican dresses, leather sandals, *piñatas* (clay or paper-mâché animals), and snacks like *churros*, a Spanish-Mexican fried bread. During festivals, such as the Blessing of the Animals, Cinco de Mayo *(see p28)*, and the Mexican independence Day fiesta (September 13–15), El Pueblo is ablaze with color and sound.

Nearby, the 1939 grand passenger terminal, **Union Station**, is a blend of Spanish Mission, Moorish, and Streamline Moderne architectural styles. Stars of 1940s films were photographed here. Recently it has been the location for several movies, such as Sydney Pollack's *The Way We Were* (1973).

**The distinctive façade of Union Station, El Pueblo**

## Lummis House ㉑

**Map** F3. 200 E Ave 43. *(323) 222-0546.* *8:30am–5pm Mon–Fri.* ***Donation.***

ALSO KNOWN AS "El Alisal," Spanish for "Place of the Sycamore," this house was the home of journalist, photographer, artist, and historian Charles Fletcher Lummis (1859–1928). The structure, which Lummis built with his own hands, displays various design elements – Native American, Mission Revival, and Arts and Crafts – revealing the dominant influences in his life.

Today, Lummis House is the headquarters of the Historical Society of Southern California. It exhibits Native American artifacts from the owner's collection, and its impressive interiors include a grand Art Nouveau fireplace.

The garden, originally planted with vegetables and fruit trees, was redesigned in 1985. It now grows drought-tolerant and native southern California plant species.

**Restored interior of the 19th-century Lummis House**

## Southwest Museum ㉒

**Map** F3. 234 Museum Dr. *(323) 221-2164.* *10am–5pm Tue–Sun.* *Jan 1, Easter Sun, Thanksgiving, Dec 25.* www. southwestmuseum.org

WITH ONE OF the nation's richest collections of Native American art and artifacts, this museum was the brainchild of Charles Fletcher

**Mission Revival-style Southwest Museum**

Lummis, who donated many of his personal holdings to start the collection. During his cross-country trek from Ohio to L.A. in the late 19th century, Lummis spent a long time in the Southwest, becoming one of the first whites to appreciate the history and culture of Native Americans.

The museum displays tribal artifacts from prehistoric times to the present day, providing an excellent overview of Native American heritage. The collection of 11,000 baskets is particularly impressive. Tepees, storytelling, and workshops help to involve children at the museum.

Set atop Mount Washington, the Mission Revival building offers excellent views of downtown L.A. to the south.

**Sequoyah Indian relief**

## Griffith Park ㉓

**Map** E3. 96. *6am–10pm daily.* *4730 Crystal Springs Dr, (213) 485-5027.* www.laparks.org

GRIFFITH PARK is a 4,000-acre (1,600-ha) wilderness of rugged hills, forested valleys, and green meadows in the center of L.A. The land was donated to the city in 1896 by Colonel Griffith J. Griffith, a Welshman who emigrated to the US in 1865 and made a fortune speculating in mining. Today, people come to Griffith Park to escape from the city crowds, visit the sights, picnic, hike, or go horseback riding.

The **Griffith Observatory**, currently closed for renovation until June 2006, is located on Mount Hollywood and commands stunning views of the L.A. basin below. Inside, the Hall of Science explains important scientific concepts with exhibits such as the Foucault Pendulum, demon-strating the earth's rotation. Visitors are taken on a journey through space and time, as some 9,000 stars and planets are projected onto the ceiling at the Planetarium Theater. On the roof, the Zeiss Telescope is open to the public on clear nights.

Northeast of the observatory lies the **Greek Theater**. Styled after an ancient Greek amphitheater, this open-air music venue has excellent acoustics. On summer nights, more than 6,000 people sit under the stars and enjoy popular and classical music performances. Farther north, in the hills just off Griffith Park Drive, is a 1926 merry-go-round. Adults and children can still ride on its 66 horses and listen to its giant band organ.

A short drive north leads to the 113-acre (46-ha) hilly compound of **Los Angeles Zoo**, housing more than 1,200 mammals, reptiles, and birds living in simulations of their natural habitats. Many newborn creatures can be seen in the Animal Nursery, including some from the zoo's respected breeding program for rare and endangered species. The zoo also hosts several animal shows, aimed at a young audience.

Opposite the zoo, the **Autry Museum of Western Heritage** explores the many

**View of the Griffith Observatory on Mount Hollywood, Griffith Park**

ultures that have shaped the merican West. Exhibits nclude a replica of a 19th-entury Mexican-American anch from Arizona. Founded y the film star Gene Autry, the Singing Cowboy," the nuseum also houses a superb ollection of movie and elevision memorabilia.

At the northwestern end of he park, **Travel Town** resents an outdoor collec-ion of vintage trains and cars. hildren and adults can climb board freight cars and ailroad carriages, or ride n a small train. To its east, n Zoo Drive, miniature team trains take people on ides during weekends.

**Griffith Observatory**
800 Observatory Rd. *(323) 664-181.* *Planetarium.* *limited.* www.griffithobs.org
*urrently closed for renovation ntil June 2006.*

## Hollywood Sign ㉔

**Map** D2. Mount Cahuenga, above ollywood. *Hollywood Visitors nformation Center, 6801 Hollywood lvd, (323) 467-6412.*

THE HOLLYWOOD SIGN is an internationally recognized ymbol of the movie business. et high up in the Hollywood ills, it is now a protected istoric site. Though visible or miles from many parts of os Angeles, it is not possible or the public to reach the ign itself, since there is no egitimate trail leading up to he tall 45-ft (13-m) letters.

Erected in 1923, it originally dvertised the Hollywoodland ousing development of the ormer *L.A. Times* publisher arry Chandler. The "land" was removed in 1949. Nearly 0 years later, donors pledged 27,000 per letter for a new ign. It has been the scene of ne suicide – that of disap-ointed would-be actress Peg ntwhistle, who jumped ff the "H" in 1932 – and umerous prank spellings, uch as "Hollyweed," cknowledging the more enient marijuana laws of the 970s; and "UCLA" during a ootball game.

## Universal Studios ㉕

**Map** D2. 100 Universal City Plaza, Universal City. *1-800-UNIVERSAL.* *424.* *Jun–Sep: 8am–10pm daily; Oct–May: 9am–7pm daily.* *Thanksgiving, Dec 25.* www.universalstudioshollywood.com

SPREAD OVER 415 acres (168 ha), the world's largest working movie and television studio and theme park, Universal Studios Hollywood started out as a poultry farm. In 1915, Carl Laemmle bought a chicken ranch on this site and moved his film studio here from Hollywood. He charged visitors 25 cents to see films being made, and guests could also buy fresh eggs. With the advent of the "talkies" in 1927, the sets needed quiet and the visits stopped.

Jurassic Park sign

In 1964, Universal Studios Hollywood launched its **Studio Tour** tram ride, a behind-the-scenes view of Hollywood movie making. Boarded from the Entertainment Center, which has the new **Spiderman Rocks!** show with dazzling pyrotechnics and stunts, the Studio Tour takes guests through movie sets in trams, outfitted with state-of-the-art audio and video systems. Celebrity hosts, such as actor Jason Alexander and director Ron Howard, narrate the inner workings of the real Hollywood. Passengers experience an earthquake, encounter King Kong and Jaws, and survive a collapsing bridge, a flash flood, and an avalanche. If they are lucky, visitors can even see a film being made.

Another popular attraction is **CityWalk Promenade**, designed by architect Jon Jerde. With its festive assortment of façades for the shops, restaurants, bars, and theaters, Universal's CityWalk is being hailed as the entertainment mecca of Southern California. It is also one of the prime areas for visitors to buy Hollywood memorabilia. Universal's Entertainment Center and the lower portions of the studio lots give an insight into the special effects and stunts used to make a film, and offer some of the park's most spectacular thrill rides. The audience becomes part of the wild jetskiing in the sea water spectacular, **WaterWorld**, they are terrified by monsters at the **Terminator 2:3D** show, and panicked in the heat of the blazing inferno in a re-creation of the final scene of the fire-fighting film *Backdraft*. The ride **Jurassic Park**, literally recaptures the thrill of the movie, while **Shrek 4-D**, reunites the talents of Eddie Murphy, Mike Myers, and Cameron Diaz in an all-new animated saga based on the Oscar-winning film *Shrek*. Another new blockbuster ride, **The Mummy Returns – Chamber of Doom**, takes visitors through hair-raising adventures in the labyrinth of the mummy's tomb, past Egyptian burial chambers and waterfalls of scorpions.

**Terrifying the audience at the Terminator 2:3D show, Universal Studios**

# Greater Los Angeles

FROM THE FREEWAYS, it is hard to appreciate the many treasures that lie within Los Angeles's sprawl. But a short drive beyond the central sights to nearby areas can be surprisingly rewarding. Upscale Pasadena with its delightful old town has some excellent museums and galleries. Farther south, Orange County offers visitors a wide range of attractions, from sandy beaches to cultural sites and museums. For visitors seeking family fun and roller-coaster thrills, there are the homey Knott's Berry Farm, and the fantasy kingdom of Disneyland.

## Malibu ㉖

**Malibu Colony** (310) 456-5737. **Malibu Lagoon State Beach** (818) 880-0367. *8am–sunset daily.* **Adamson House** (310) 456-8432. *11am–3pm Wed–Sat.* **Malibu Creek State Park** *(818) 880-0350; for camp bookings (800) 444-7275. 8am–sunset.*

TWENTY MILES NORTH of Santa Monica Bay, the Rancho Topanga Malibu Sequit was bought in 1887 by Fredrick and May Rindge. The Rindge family fought with the state for many years to keep their property secluded. Eventually failing, they had to sell much of Malibu to film stars such as Bing Crosby and Gary Cooper. Today the **Malibu Colony** is a private, gated compound still favored by people from the entertainment industry.

A few miles east, the **Malibu Lagoon State Beach**, the largest village of Chumash people in the 16th century, is now a natural preserve and bird refuge. To its east, Surfrider County Beach is considered by many to be the surfing capital of the world.

Nearby, the Spanish Colonial **Adamson House** with vivid tiles and opulent decor, houses a museum showcasing the history of Malibu.

To the north, the 10,000-acre (4,000-ha) **Malibu Creek State Park** features forests, meadows, waterfalls, picnic areas, and hiking trails. Much of the park was owned by 20th Century Fox until 1974. *M*A*S*H*, *Butch Cassidy and the Sundance Kid*, and *Tarzan* were all filmed here.

## Pasadena ㉗

*135,000. 79 from downtown. 171 S Los Robles Ave, (626) 795-9311. Tournament of Roses Parade (Jan 1); Pasadena Spring Art Festival (mid-Apr).* www.pasadenacal.com

WITH THE completion of the Santa Fe Railroad in 1887, wealthy people from the East Coast, along with artists and bohemians, settled in Pasadena to savor the warm winters of Southern California. This mix of creativity and wealth has resulted in a city with a splendid cultural legacy.

The historic district of **Old Town Pasadena**, at the heart of the city, underwent a recent face-lift ushering in a spate of upscale shops, restaurants, and cafés in restored historic buildings. The highlights of the area include the **Norton Simon Museum** featuring one of the finest collections of Old Masters and Impressionist paintings in the country.

To the north, local architect Charles and Henry Greene's sprawling **Gamble House** is considered a consummate craftsman bungalow by many.

A few miles east of Old Town, opulent San Marino is home to the **Huntington Library, Art Collections, and Botanical Gardens**. Once the estate of railroad tycoon Henry E. Huntington (1850–1927), the Beaux Arts mansion holds one of the most important libraries and collections of 18th-century British and French art in the world. Rare books in the library's collection include priceless objects such as a Gutenberg bible, a Chaucer manuscript, and Benjamin Franklin's handwritten autobiography. The botanical gardens are made up of 15 theme areas: the most popular are the Desert, Japanese, and Shakespearean Gardens.

**Mausoleum at Huntington, designed by John Russell Pope**

### Huntington Library, Art Collections, & Botanical Gardens

1151 Oxford Rd. *(626) 405-2100. Jun–Aug: 10:30am–4:30pm Tue–Sun; Sep–May: noon–4:30pm Tue–Fri, 10:30am–4:30pm Sat–Sun. public hols.* www.huntington.org

## Watts Towers ㉘

1727 E 107th St, Watts. *(213) 847-4646. 10am–4pm Tue–Sat, noon–4pm Sun. (Towers). Arts Center only.* www.wattstower.net

WATTS TOWERS embodies the perseverance and vision of Italian folk artist Simon Rodia. Between 1921 and 1954, the tile-worker sculpted steel rods and pipes,

**View across Malibu Lagoon to the Santa Monica Mountains**

into a huge skeletal framework, adorning it with shells, tiles, and broken glass. He never gave a reason for building the towers and, upon finishing, deeded the land to a neighbor and left L.A. The towers, standing 100 ft (30 m) at their tallest, are now a State Historic Site. Next to the monument, the Watts Towers Arts Center is well known for holding temporary exhibitions of work by African-American artists. It also hosts workshops for artists of all ages.

The *Queen Mary*, Long Beach's most famous hotel

## Long Beach ㉙

*Metro Blue Line from downtown Los Angeles.*

WITH PALM TREES and ocean as a backdrop, downtown Long Beach is a mixture of carefully restored buildings and modern glass high-rises. At its heart, **Pine Avenue**, lined with stores, cafés, and restaurants, retains the early Midwestern charm that gave the city its nickname, "Iowa by the Sea."

Along the ocean, the restaurants and shops in Shoreline Village offer views of the ocean liner *Queen Mary (see p722)*. The Cunard flagship from 1930s to the 1960s, this luxury liner was converted into a troopship during World War II. It carried more than 80,000 soldiers during its wartime career. At the end of the war, it transported more than 22,000 war brides and children to the US during "Operation Diaper." It was permanently docked for use as a hotel and tourist attraction in 1967. Today, visitors can view part of the original Engine Room, examples of the different accommodations, and an exhibition on the war years.

Nearby, the **Aquarium of the Pacific** is one of the largest aquariums in the United States. It holds 550 species in 17 major habitats, offering visitors a fascinating exploration of marine flora and fauna from the Pacific Ocean's three distinct regions: Southern California/Baja; the Tropical Pacific, and the Northern Pacific.

**Queen Mary**
Pier J, 1126 Queens Hwy. *(562) 435-3511.* *Mon–Sat.*
www.queenmary.com

**Aquarium of the Pacific**
100 Aquarium Way. *(562) 590-3100.* *9am–6pm daily.* *Dec 25, weekend of the Toyota Grand Prix.*
www.aquariumofpacific.org

## Knott's Berry Farm ㉚

8039 Beach Blvd, Buena Park. *(714) 827-1776.* *(714) 220-5200.* *29, 38, 42.* *hours vary per season & day. Call to verify park hours.* *Dec 25.*
www.knotts.com

LOCATED IN Buena Vista in Orange County, Knott's Berry Farm has grown from a 1920s boysenberry farm to a 21st-century multi-day entertainment complex. Offering more than 165 different rides and attractions, its main charm lies in its emphasis on authenticity. The **Old West Ghost Town**, in the heart of the park, has original ghost town buildings. America's very first theme park, Knott's offers six themed areas, dozens of live-action stages, thrill rides, shopping, and dining, as well as a full-fledged resort.

Statues of cowboys on a Ghost Town bench

Cloisters framing Mission San Juan Capistrano's central courtyard

## Mission San Juan Capistrano ㉛

Camino Capistrano & Ortega Hwy. *(949) 234-1300.* *8:30am–5pm daily.* *Good Fri pm, Thanksg., Dec 25.* *Swallow Festival (Mar).* www.missionsjc.com

THIS "Jewel of the Missions" was founded in 1776, and its chapel is the only surviving building in California where Fr. Junípero Serra preached. One of the largest in the chain, the mission was built as a self-sufficient community. Its Great Stone Church was destroyed by an earthquake in 1812, leaving a rambling complex of adobe and brick buildings. A recent restoration program re-creates the mission's former glory.

## Newport Beach ㉜

Hwy 1, S from Los Angeles.

FAMOUS FOR ITS million-dollar homes and lifestyles to match, Newport Beach has a 3-mile (5-km) stretch of wide sand and two piers along Orange County's coast. Fresh fish, caught by the historic Dory fishing fleet, is sold beside Newport Pier at the northern end of the beach. Farther inland, the coastal wetland of **Upper Newport Bay Ecological Preserve** is a refuge for wildlife and migratory birds. It also offers a bike path, fishing, and guided tours on foot and by kayak.

# Disneyland® Resort ㉝

Disney's "Magic Kingdom" in Anaheim is not only the top tourist attraction in California, it is part of the American Dream. Now encompassing the original Disneyland Park, Disney's California Adventure, Downtown Disney, plus three enormous hotels, the Resort has become the model for theme parks around the globe. Visitors to "The Happiest Place on Earth" find fantasy, thrill rides, glittering shows, and shopping in a brightly orchestrated land of lines, fireworks, and Mickey Mouse, which is as American as apple pie.

**Exploring the Resort**

Spread over 85 acres (34 ha), the original Disneyland Park is divided into eight theme areas or "lands." Transportation around the park is provided by Disneyland Railroad and monorail. Disney's newest venture, Disney's California Adventure Park, is smaller than Disneyland Park and can easily be covered on foot. With three theme areas, it is more suited to teenagers, as the attractions may be too intense for toddlers. At the heart of the Resort, Downtown Disney is a lively area full of restaurants, shops, and entertainment venues.

It takes at least three days to explore the theme parks. Both parks stay open late during the peak seasons. The **Fireworks Show** in Disneyland and in Downtown Disney are fantastic.

## Disneyland Park

Main Street USA is a colorful street lined with historic buildings. Central Plaza is the venue for the daily "Parade of the Stars," featuring Disney characters and scenes from Disney's most famous movies. Guests can meet with famous Disney characters and will find ample opportunities for photographs. City Hall offers maps, dining, and entertainment schedules, while the Main Street Cinema screens early Disney silent films. There is also a large selection of shops and eateries.

Visions of the future inspire the rides in Tomorrowland, where sights change regularly to keep one step ahead of real-life technology. One of the first attractions in 1955 was **Autopia**, that has since been updated and now takes visitors on a ride into a parallel universe. **Star Tours** was redesigned in collaboration with the *Star Wars* genius George Lucas. Its fabulous use of flight-simulator technology makes it one of the park's most realistic rides. Visitors board a StarSpeeder spaceship and are transported through outer space strewn with starships, comets, and asteroids. **Space Mountain** is a Disneyland favorite that offers a high speed roller-coaster ride, 118 ft (36 m) above the ground. Conducted almost entirely in darkness, the ride has sudden meteoric flashes and celestial showers, and is not suitable for very young children.

The colorful architecture of cartoons comes to life in Mickey's Toontown – a three-dimensional cartoon world where all Disney's favorite animated characters reside. The most popular residences are Mickey's house and Minnie's cottage. Most of the attractions are geared toward kids from age three up. **Chip 'n Dale Treehouse**, a mini-roller coaster; **Goofy's Bounce House**; and a floating bumper-boat ride offer gentle thrills. **Roger Rabbit's Car Toon Spin** is the favorite. Its spinning cars take visitors on a madcap drive through a surreal cartoon world.

Fantasyland, dominated by the pink and gold towers of **Sleeping Beauty's Castle** and a replica of the **Matterhorn**, is a shrine to children's dreams. Nursery heroes such as Peter Pan and Snow White provide the themes for gentle fairytale rides. The historic **Matterhorn Bobsleds** offers "icy" roller-coaster rides down the slopes of a replica of Switzerland's famous peak. Bobsleds climb to its summit, then drop into a high-speed descent, passing glacier caves and waterfalls as they go. **It's a Small World** creates a Utopian vision of global harmony, with almost 300 singing-and-dancing Audio-Animatronics® dolls dressed in national costumes.

Inspired by the Wild West, Frontierland features a skirt-lifting song and dance on the **Golden Horseshoe Jamboree**. Every weekend night, the skies above Frontierland are lit up with the spectacular **Fantasmic!** fireworks show, complete with sound effects and live performers. Thrill-seekers should not miss the **Big Mountain Thunder Railroad** roller-coaster ride, where a runaway train speeds through the cavernous interior of Big Thunder Mountain, narrowly escaping boulders and waterfalls.

## Tickets & Tips

Each theme park (except for Downtown Disney) has a separate admission ticket that covers all the rides and shows, and includes a park map and schedule of events. Parking is extra, as are certain shows, food, and arcades. Multi-day tickets for three to four days and Annual Passports allow unlimited admission and access to attractions. A Fastpass lets guests obtain a voucher with a computer-assigned boarding time for specific attractions or rides. This eliminates waiting in long lines. Guests can also save time at the front gate by buying tickets in advance.at any Disney store or online at www.disney.com. To help plan your day, there is updated information on showtimes, waiting times, and ride closures at the information board at the end of Main Street opposite the Plaza Pavillion.

Critter Country is built in a rustic style, based on the rugged American Northwest. It is home to **Splash Mountain**, one of Disneyland's most popular attractions. This watery ride in hollowed-out logs features singing characters from the 1946 film *Song of the South* such as Brer Rabbit and Brer Fox, and ends in a plummet down a steep waterfall.

The charming New Orleans Square is modeled on the French Quarter in New Orleans as it was during the city's heyday in the 19th century. Quaint wrought-iron balconies adorn buildings housing French-style shops. One of its top attractions, **Haunted Mansion**, promises "999 ghosts and ghouls," and some visitors are so familiar with its introductory commentary that they join in as they descend into its spooky world of mischievous spirits and grave-diggers. The ethereal figures, including a talking woman's head in a crystal ball, are extremely realistic. Another favorite, **Pirates of the Caribbean** provides a floating ride through a yo-ho-ho world of ruffians who have the gifts of song, dance, and heavy drinking with the use of Audio-Animatronics®. This technique, which brings models to life using electronic impulses to control sounds and actions, was perfected at Disneyland. **The Disney Gallery** shows visitors the art behind the world of Disney, and some of the original artworks and designs for Disney's elaborate projects are on display here.

The exotic atmosphere in Adventureland offers dark, humid waterways lined with tropical plants. This is the smallest, but perhaps most adventuresome, "land" in the park. The **Enchanted Tiki Room** showcases mechanical singing birds in a zany, musical romp through the tropics. Inspired by the 1982 film trilogy, the **Indiana Jones™ Adventure** sets off on a jeep-style drive through the Temple of the Forbidden Eye. Theatrical props and scenery, a realistic soundtrack, superb film images, and the sensation of a roller coaster make this the ultimate experience in Disneyland. The safari-style **Jungle Cruise** boat ride leads visitors through a jungle full of rampant apes and blood-thirsty headhunters, accompanied by a real-life captain.

## Downtown Disney

Located between the entrances to Disneyland Park and Disney's California Adventure, Downtown Disney® is a garden paradise, offering visitors some 300,000 sq ft (27,870 sq m) of innovative restaurants, shops, and entertainment venues. The fact that this area has no admission fee makes Downtown Disney® one of the more popular – but crowded – spaces. A 12-screen AMC Theatre®, ESPN Zone™, and a LEGO Imagination Center® are its top attractions. The snack shops, restaurants, vast range of retail and specialty shops, and a travel center create a total Disney experience.

## Shopping

The Disneyland shops, particularly those along Main Street USA, are often busy late in the day, especially at closing time. If you can, it is worth making your purchases earlier in the day and then collecting them later from the Redemption Center. Although many of the goods on sale in the theme park bear the faces of Disney characters, each of the eight lands adds its own variations to what is available. In Adventureland, for example, you can buy Indiana Jones-style clothing, while Native American Crafts are on sale in Frontierland. The Disney Gallery in New Orleans Square sells limited-edition lithographs by the Disney cartoonists. The largest of all the shops within the Magic Kingdom is the Emporium in Main Street.

## Visitors' Checklist

1313 Harbor Blvd, Anaheim. *(714) 781-7290.* *24 hrs a day, (714) 781-4565.* *from LAX.* *435.* *Jun–Aug: 8am–midnight daily; Sep–May: 9am–6pm daily.* www.disneyland.com

## Disney's California Adventure

The newest star in Anaheim is Disney's California Adventure, lying adjacent to Disneyland. It is divided into three "lands," each offering themed experiences that celebrate the California dream. The emphasis is on adults and older teens, but there are still plenty of rides available for all ages.

Hollywood Pictures Backlot offers a tongue-in-cheek view of the motion picture industry. The two blocks of façades and fakery give the visitor a Disney-eye view of Hollywood. The **Hyperion Theater** features staged live musical shows, and at Jim Henson's **Muppet*Vision 3-D** visitors can see Miss Piggy, Kermit, and all the lovable Muppet characters in a tribute to movie making. Golden State features California's topography and agriculture. The star ride is **Soarin' Over California**, a simulated hang-glider ride that portrays the beauties of California's landscape on a huge wrap-around screen. Guests can feel the wind currents and smell the scent of orange blossoms as they soar 40 feet (12 m) high. **Bountiful Valley** features healthy snacks and a 3-D film starring Flik from *A Bug's Life*. Smell-o-Vision and touchy-feelies make this a completely buggy experience for all.

Considerably lower key than the thrills in the original park, Paradise Pier is the place where roller coasters, Ferris wheels, and parachute rides rule. **California Screamin'**, the giant **Sun Wheel**, and **King Triton's Carousel** are reminiscent of seaside recreation parks as they used to be years ago.

# Los Angeles Practical Information

Los Angeles offers a wealth of entertainment and outdoor pleasures to its visitors. At the center of the film industry, L.A. dominated the world stage for most of the 20th century. It is therefore not surprising that L.A. sees itself as the "Entertainment Capital of the World." But the glamor of the movies is just one aspect of the city that manufactures the American Dream. This year-long vacation spot is also famous for its long beaches, mountain ranges, and some of the world's best museums.

## Tourist Information

The main branch of the **Los Angeles Convention and Visitors' Bureau** is in downtown L.A., and it offers multilingual assistance. Its visitors' guide, *Destination Los Angeles*, gives listings of restaurants, coffee houses, hotels, shops, and other attractions. There is also a 24-hour events hotline. The city's two other main information centers are the **Hollywood Visitors' Information Center** and the **Beverly Hills Visitors' Bureau**. Various publications can help sift through the city's entertainment riches. The *L.A. Weekly* – a free paper available at bars, clubs, and corner markets across Los Angeles – has the most comprehensive entertainment and arts listings.

## Getting Around

The sprawling 467 sq miles (1,200 sq km) city of Los Angeles may seem a bit daunting to navigate. The most cost-effective method of getting around is by car. A network of freeways provides a convenient, if crowded, means of traveling in the area. It is advisable to avoid the freeways during rush hours (8am to 9:30am and 4am to 6:30pm). Some freeways are busy regardless of the hour, and it can be less stressful to take one of the city's major streets. When parking, read the posted signs for limitations, and carry plenty of quarters for the parking meters. At nights, it is safer to valet park.

Although the city is spread out, many of its districts are pedestrian-friendly. Third Street Promenade and the beach in Santa Monica are best explored on foot. Other such areas include Old Pasadena, downtown, and the Golden Triangle in Beverly Hills. Visitors should avoid walking at night unless the street is well lit and populated.

Greater Los Angeles is served by the **Metropolitan Transportation Authority (MTA)**. Bus stops display an MTA sign, and buses run on the main thoroughfares. The **DASH** shuttle provides travel within small areas, such as downtown and Hollywood, for a quarter. Bus tickets are sold at most grocery stores.

L.A.'s growing subway system, the **Metro**, serves parts of the city well. It is made up of three lines, red, blue, and green, which serve different areas. The Green Line is useful for the airport.

Other ways to get around include the somewhat expensive taxis, which have to be called by phone. Two reliable taxi companies are **Yellow Cab** and the Independent Cab Co. Visitors can also rent a limousine for a luxurious alternative. Private bus lines, such as **L.A. Tours**, offer package tours of the city.

## Outdoor Activities

Each year more than 30 million people visit the beaches around Los Angeles, making them the most popular vacation destinations on the West Coast. The Malibu headland, from Point Dume to Malibu Lagoon, alternates between rocky shorelines and beaches. Farther along, the shoreline becomes a long sandy strand leading to the renowned beaches of Santa Monica and Venice. Inland, the pristine and rugged terrain of the Santa Monica Mountains offer plenty of hiking trails with panoramic views of the Pacific Ocean. L.A.'s beaches are a great natural resource and offer great swimming and volleyball opportunities. The waters off the Malibu Pier and Topanga State Beach are considered to be the best for surfing.

Griffith Park offers miles of hiking trails, opportunities for horseback riding, and cycling. But the best place for cyclists is the coastal bike path that runs for 25 miles (40 km) along Santa Monica Bay (bicycles are not allowed on the freeways). Bicycles can be rented from **Sea Mist Skate Rentals** (Santa Monica Pier) and at the local pizza stands (Santa Monica Beach). Sports include baseball at the famed Dodger Stadium, and college football at Pasadena's Rose Bowl. Basketball and ice hockey, at the Great Western Forum, are popular draws, as are horse racing at the Hollywood Park Racetrack and polo at the Will Rogers State Historic Park.

## Entertainment

Los Angeles's large and successful artistic community guarantees that there is always plenty to do in the city, although only small areas tend to be lively after dark.

Most visitors don't spend a lot of time seeing movies in Los Angeles, even though all the current releases and countless classics are always being shown. The movie palaces themselves, however, draw the crowds, with Mann's Chinese and El Capitan theaters on Hollywood Boulevard being the best known. Multiplexes, such as those in **Universal City** and the Beverly Center, offer state-of-the-art facilities.

Stage productions are also plentiful and diverse, with L.A. putting up over a 1,000 professional plays each year. Pantages in Hollywood is a leading venue for touring Broadway musicals. Housed in beautiful Mediterranean-style theaters, the **Pasadena Playhouse** and the **Geffen**

**Playhouse** both put on new works as well as old favorites.

The city has a well-respected symphony orchestra, the L.A. Philharmonic, and an opera company, the **L.A. Opera**. In the summer there are outdoor concerts in places such as the Hollywood Bowl.

Naked ambition and unbridled youth fuel the rock clubs that line Sunset Strip. The venerable **Whiskey a Go Go** and **The Roxy** compete with relative newcomers such as the Viper Room and the Key Club. L.A.'s jazz scene is exemplified by cozy joints such as **The Baked Potato**.

Whether it's house or hiphop at The Century Club, or hipster big beats at The Garage, the L.A. club scene runs all types of dance music. With its large gay population, West Hollywood has several discos. A current favorite is **The Factory**.

Many of L.A.'s television and film studios offer behind-the-scenes tours as well as tickets to tapings of popular shows. In the high-tech **CBS-TV** studios, soap operas, such as *The Bold and the Beautiful*, and game shows are taped before live audiences. The popular **Warner Bros** tour is probably the truest look at modern-day filmmaking.

Most of the areas within L.A. have local festivals, particularly in the summer, which feature food, live music, arts, and crafts.

## Shopping

Whatever money can buy can be found in Los Angeles, from Cartier necklaces to everyday items. While indoor shopping malls are the norm for much of the US, L.A.'s temperate climate allows for a range of pleasant outdoor alternatives. Melrose Avenue and Santa Monica's Third Street Promenade are both young, lively areas, while upscale Rodeo Drive is probably the most famous. One of the more pleasant shopping areas in L.A. is Old Pasadena, which has a range of unique shops in late 19th-century buildings.

L.A.'s favorite and best known department stores are **Bloomingdales** and **Macy's**, and Nordstrom's popular shoe department draws cutomers especially in January and June during its half-price sales.

Fashion styles are casual in L.A. but couture clothes are available in Beverly Hills. Todd Oldham and Tyler Trafficante are two of the hottest women's fashion labels in town, while Bernini and Mark Michaels have some of the best fashions for men.

Antique shops are centered around Melrose Place, close to Melrose Avenue, while some of L.A.'s leading art galleries are located at Bergamot Station.

Hollywood memorabilia is on sale as well. Two good shops are Fantasies Come True and **Larry Edmund's Cinema Bookshop**. There is a selection of Latin American arts and crafts, popular in Los Angeles, at The Folk Tree.

The California fresh produce and wines have representation in L.A. Grand Central Market, and Farmers Market overflows with a wide range of fresh fruit and vegetables. Trader Joe's, cited as one of the finest reasons to live in the city, sells a vast array of gourmet foods and wines.

## Directory

### Tourist Offices

**Beverly Hills**
(310) 248-1015.

**Hollywood**
(323) 461-9520.

**Los Angeles Visitors' Bureau**
(213) 689-8822.

### Public Transportation

**DASH**
(800) 266-6883.

**L.A. Tours**
(323) 460-6490.

**MTA**
(800) 266-6883.
www.mta.net

**Yellow Cab**
(800) 200-1085.

### Cycling

**Sea Mist Skate Rentals**
1619 Ocean Front Walk, Santa Monica, CA 90401.
(310) 395-7076.

### Cinemas

**Cineplex Odeon Universal City Cinemas**
Universal City, CA 91608.
(818) 508-0588. www.enjoytheshow.com

### Theaters

**Geffen Playhouse**
10886 Le Conte Ave. (310) 208-5454. www.geffenplayhouse.com

**Pasadena Playhouse**
39 S El Molino Ave, Pasadena, CA 91101.
(626) 356-7529.

### Opera

**L.A. Opera**
135 N Grand Ave.
(213) 972-8001.

### Rock, Jazz, Blues, & Clubs

**Baked Potato**
3787 Cahuenga Blvd W, Studio City, CA 91105.
(818) 980-1615.

**Key Club**
9041 W Sunset Blvd.
(310) 274-5800.

**The Factory**
652 N La Peer Dr.
(310) 659-4551.

**The Roxy**
9009 W Sunset Blvd.
(310) 276-2222.

**Whiskey a Go Go**
8901 W Sunset Blvd.
(310) 652-4202.

### Studio Tours

**CBS-TV**
7800 Beverly Blvd.
(323) 575-2624.

**Warner Bros**
4000 Warner Blvd, Burbank.
(818) 977-1744.

### Shopping

**Bloomingdales**
Beverly Center, 8500 Beverly Blvd.
(310) 360-2700.
www.bloomingdales.com

**Larry Edmund's Cinema Bookshop**
6644 Hollywood Blvd.
(323) 463-3273.
www.larryedmunds.com

**Macy's**
8500 Beverly Blvd.
(310) 854-6655.
www.macys.com

# San Diego County

SAN DIEGO'S CHARACTER has always been determined by the sea. Its magnificent natural harbor attracted the Spanish as well as gold prospectors and whalers. The US Navy arrived in 1904, and today San Diego has become one of the largest military establishments in the world. Extending to the Mexican border, its coastline has 70 miles (112 km) of stunning beaches, rocky cliffs, coves, and seaside resorts, with plentiful opportunities for leisure activities.

**The Gaslamp Quarter, the star of downtown San Diego**

## San Diego ❷

*1,500,000. 1050 Kettner Blvd. 120 W Broadway. Horton Plaza, 1st & F Sts, (619) 236-1212. Street Scene Festival (Sep).*

THE MUSEUMS and art venues of **Balboa Park** *(see pp 680–81)* are the prime cultural attractions of San Diego, California's second largest city. San Diego's growth as a modern city began with the waterfront development initiated by San Francisco businessman, Alonzo Horton, in the 1870s. He also designed the plan of the **Gaslamp Quarter**, which is now the centerpiece of downtown, and the best place to shop and dine. The wealth of period buildings ranges from a pie bakery to ornate offices and grand Victorian hotels. The district is particularly attractive at night, when it is illuminated by graceful gaslamps. Close by is **Horton Plaza**, an innovatively designed shopping center built in 1985.

At the western end of Broadway is the **Santa Fe Depot**, a Spanish Colonial-style railroad station dating from 1915. The towering America Plaza houses the **Museum of Contemporary Art**, whose galleries display work by new artists and selections from its large permanent collection.

The promenades and piers of the **Embarcadero** waterfront pathway lead to the Maritime Museum and its three historic ships. Of these, the highlight is the *Star of India*, an 1863 merchantman. To the south is Broadway Pier, where visitors can take a harbor excursion.

North of downtown is **Old Town**, site of the original Spanish settlement near the San Diego River. Today, more than 20 historic buildings have been restored to form the Old Town San Diego State Historic Park. The Plaza, at its center, was where parades and fiestas once took place. The old Spanish presido and mission is now part of Presido Park. Crowning the hill the **Junípero Serra Museum** is named after the founder of California's missions *(see p692)*. On display are archaeological finds as well as exhibits on San Diego's successive Native American, Spanish, Mexican, and American communities.

To the west of Old Town is the **Point Loma Peninsula**, at the southern tip of which is the Cabrillo National Monument, named after the city's discoverer, Juan Rodríguez Cabrillo; his statue overlooks the Bay. Between December and March, the nearby Whale Overlook is a popular spot to watch gray whales on their annual migration south.

The peninsula of Coronado has the city's most exclusive boutiques and hotels. The **Hotel del Coronado**, or "Del," opened in 1888 and is a lovely Victorian seaside hotel *(see p722)*. Its guest list reads like a Who's Who of 20th-century US history, including Presidents Franklin D. Roosevelt and Bill Clinton, and film star Marilyn Monroe. It has been the setting for several films, including *Some Like It Hot*, the 1959 classic starring Marilyn Monroe, Jack Lemmon, and Tony Curtis. The Coronado Ferry ride is enchanting at dusk, when the sun's last rays illuminates the skyscrapers of downtown.

**Junípero Serra Museum**
*2727 Presidio Dr. (858) 297-3258. 10am–4:30pm Fri–Sun. Dec 25.*

**Impressive turrets and gables of the Hotel del Coronado, San Diego**

## Sea World ❸

500 Sea World Dr. (619) 226-3901. 9. daily. www.seaworld.com

San Diego's Sea World covers 150 acres (60 ha) of Mission Bay. The ride up the Skytower, a 320-ft (98-m) column, offers splendid views. Another fabulous ride is the 100-ft (30-m) Bayside Skyride, where gondola cars make an enormous loop over the waters of Mission Bay.

The stars of Sea World are the performing whales and dolphins. One performance reveals the intelligence of dolphins and pilot whales, while another demonstrates the virtuosity of killer whales. Other attractions include the shark and otter pools, and opportunities to feed killer whales and seals. Shamu's Happy Harbor is an aquatic adventure park for children.

Sea World's staff are devoted to animal rescue and rehabilitation, and run educational and conservation programs.

**Killer whales performing acrobatic feats for the crowd at Sea World**

## La Jolla ❹

32,000. from San Diego. 1055 Wall St, Suite 110, (858) 454-1444. www.lajollabythesea.com

Set amid cliffs and coves, La Jolla is an elegant coastal resort. Its streets are lined with gourmet chocolatiers and jewelers, and visitors come to enjoy the art galleries and the restaurants that promise a "Mediterranean" view. The town is home to the University of California at San Diego and the **Salk Institute for Biological Studies**, founded by Dr. Jonas Salk, who developed the polio vaccine. The Scripps Institution of Oceanography has the **Birch Aquarium at Scripps**. It provides an insight into the world of oceanography. The **Museum of Contemporary Art** occupies a prime oceanfront location. A companion to the gallery in San Diego, it displays works of post-1950 art and houses a bookstore and café.

## Tijuana, Mexico ❺

Mexico. *San Diego Trolley to San Ysidro, then bus or walk.* **Tourist Office** *Ave Revolución y Calle.* *(011-52-66) 88-05-55.* *daily.*

The international border crossing at Tijuana is one of the busiest in the world. Thousands of Americans come here every year, for the inexpensive shopping and exuberant nightlife – Mexican laws permit anyone over 18 to drink alcohol.

The futuristic **Centro Cultural Tijuana**, built on the banks of the Tijuana River in 1982, has an OMNIMAX theater, which screens films on Mexico. Exhibitions on Mexican themes are also held here. The open-air Mexitlán rooftop exhibition re-creates the country's architectural treasures in miniature.

The best shopping is in the quiet bazaars located on both sides of the lively Avenida Revolución. Painted pottery, leather boots, silver jewelry, and tequila are some favorite buys. Visitors rarely need to change money, as US dollars and major credit cards are accepted widely. The Tourist Office provides maps and has an English-speaking staff.

**Centro Cultural Tijuana**
Paseo de los Héroes. *(011-52-66) 84-11-11.* *daily.*

**The beautiful rocky shoreline of La Jolla Cove**

# Balboa Park

Statue of El Cid in Balboa Park

Located in the heart of San Diego *(see p678)*, Balboa Park is one of the city's most popular attractions. Founded in 1868, its lush beauty owes much to the horticulturalist Kate Sessions, who planted trees throughout its 1,200 acres (485 ha). In 1915, the park was the site of the Panama-Pacific Exposition, which celebrated the opening of the Panama Canal. Many of the Spanish Colonial-style pavilions built in that year survive along El Prado (the park's main street); the animals gathered for the exhibition formed the nucleus of the renowned San Diego Zoo. Today, Balboa Park has one of the country's richest concentrations of museums and performance spaces.

**Plaza de Panama**
*This plaza was at the heart of the famous 1915 Exposition.*

**★ San Diego Museum of Man**
*Housed in the historic 1915 Spanish Colonial California Building, this anthropological museum traces the early history of mankind.*

**El Prado**

**Aerospace Museum**
*This A-12 Blackbird, built in 1962, is beside a museum devoted to flight history. Over 60 original and reconstructed aircrafts are on display here.*

**San Diego Automotive Museum**

**Pan-American Plaza**

**Spreckels Organ Pavilion**

0 meters 100

0 yards 100

**★ San Diego Museum of Art**
*This fine museum, displaying American and European works, is the main art museum in the park.*

**★ San Diego Zoo**
*Orangutans are among the 4,000 animals that inhabit the enclosures of this world-famous zoo.*

**Botanical Building**
*Constructed from thin strips of redwood, this shaded sanctuary is full of tropical and sub-tropical plants.*

**San Diego Automotive Museum**
*Dream cars and motorcycles from the US and Europe shine on in this nostalgic museum.*

### Visitors' Checklist

Park Blvd, Laurel & 6th Sts. 🚌 *7.* **Visitor Center** Plaza de Panama. ☎ *(619) 239-0512.* ◯ *9am–4pm daily.* ● *Jan 1, Thanksgiving, Dec 25.* **Spreckels Organ Pavilion** *Free concerts Jun–Sep: 7:30pm Mon, 2–3pm Sun.* **San Diego Zoo** ☎ *(619) 234-3153.* ◯ *early Sep–Jun: 9am–4pm daily; Jul–Aug: 9am–5pm daily.* 
W www.sandiegozoo.org

### Star Sights

- ★ **California Building/San Diego Museum of Man**
- ★ **San Diego Museum of Art**
- ★ **San Diego Zoo**

**Exploring Balboa Park**

Most of the park's museums lie along the central El Prado, while some are located to the south. The pleasant grounds, shady picnic groves, and traffic-free promenades are usually crowded with joggers, cyclists, and street artists.

The **San Diego Museum of Man**, at the western end of El Prado, is an anthropological museum about the early history of mankind. Exhibits cover the cultures of ancient Egypt and the Mayans, and Native American crafts. Close by, the **San Diego Museum of Art's** large and varied collection is boosted by special exhibitions. It displays a vast range of European and American art from 1300 to the 20th century, as well some fine exhibits from South Asia, Japan, and China.

The **Timken Museum of Art**, lying east of the Museum of Art, displays a handful of splendid works by European masters such as Frans Hals, Rembrandt, and Paul Cézanne. It also has a collection of Russian icons.

Farther east along El Prado, the **Natural History Museum** features its own giant-screen film, *Ocean Oasis*, taking visitors on an incredible journey through Baja California and the Sea of Cortes. The main attraction at the **Reuben H. Fleet Science Center**, just across the plaza, is the IMAX® cinema in the Space Theater, where films are projected onto an enormous tilting screen. Laser and planetarium shows are also staged here.

Just north of the museums, the **San Diego Zoo** is one of the best in the world and is famous for its conservation programs. Spread over 100 acres (40 ha), it houses 800 animal species in enclosures designed to closely resemble their natural habitat. A 35-minute narrated bus tour covers most of the zoo, while the aerial Skyfari ride offers an exciting trip across the south of the park in gondola cars that run 180 ft (55 m) up. There is also a Children's Zoo. The zoo is open in summer for nocturnal exploration.

# The Deserts

National park sign

THE SEARING DESERTS of Southern California have a haunting beauty all their own, with jagged canyons, steep hills, and carpets of wildflowers in spring. At the heart of the Low Desert is Palm Springs, the region's most sought-after resort, with hotels and golf courses. The stark Joshua Tree National Park lies to the east. Farther north, the Mojave Desert is the state's greatest secret, all too often missed by visitors. Its main draw, Death Valley National Park, has some of the highest temperatures in the Western Hemisphere.

## Palm Springs ❻

*42,000.* *Indio.* *3111 N Indian Ave.* *2781 N Palm Canyon Drive, (800) 347-7746, (760) 778-8418.* *Palm Springs International Film Festival (early–mid-Jan).* www.palm–springs.com

THE LARGEST OF the desert cities, Palm Springs was first sighted in 1853 when a survey party came across a grove of palm trees surrounding a freshwater spring pool in the Coachella Valley. The first hotel was constructed in 1886, and by the turn of the century, Palm Springs was a thriving health spa. Soon after, it became a fashionable winter resort for the rich and famous. Today, its population doubles each winter, when visitors come to enjoy the relaxing, outdoor lifestyle. First-class hotels such as the Marriot and Givenchy abound, and a number of celebrities live here. The area around Palm Springs has numerous resort cities, such as Rancho Mirage, Indian Wells, and La Quinta, and more than 80 luxury golf courses.

Downtown's two main shopping streets are Palm Canyon and Indian Canyon Drives; both are lined with restaurants, boutiques, and art galleries. The **Village Green Heritage Center**, in the heart of the shopping area, has a few historic buildings, including Ruddy's 1930s General Store Museum, a replica of the original, with authentic packaged goods ranging from licorice to patent medicines. The Agua Caliente Cultural Museum displays the heritage of the area's Cahuilla people.

The state-of-the-art **Oasis Water Resort** has 13 waterslides, including a 70-ft (20-m) free-fall slide. An enormous wave-action pool creates 4-ft (1.2-m) high waves suitable for surfing and boogie boarding. The resort also has a hotel, heated spas, health clubs, and restaurants.

Oasis Water Resort in Palm Springs

The **Palm Springs Aerial Tramway** covers a 2.5-mile (4-km) trip via cable car, which ascends 5,900 ft (1,790 m) over spectacular scenery to the Mountain Station in the Mount San Jacinto Wilderness State Park. Visitors travel through five distinct ecosystems, ranging from desert to alpine forest, where the weather becomes icy cold. At the top, there are 54 miles (85 km) of hiking trails, a ski center, campsites, and a cafeteria. Observation decks offer terrific views of the Coachella Valley, Palm Springs, and the San Bernardino Mountains to the north. On a clear day, it is possible to see the Salton Sea, 50 miles (80 km) away.

Sculpture Garden in the Palm Springs Desert Museum

The **Palm Springs Desert Museum** focuses on art, natural science, and the performing arts. The galleries contain paintings from the 19th century to the present day, as well as Native American artifacts and natural history exhibits. Modern sculpture adorns the gardens. About 5 miles (8 km) south of Palm Springs are the **Indian Canyons**, four spectacular natural palm oases, set in rocky gorges. Clustered along streams fed by mountain springs, Murray, Tahquitz, Andreas, and Palm Canyons are located on the land of the Agua Caliente Cahuilla people. Rock art and other traces of these early inhabitants can still be seen. Palm and Andreas Canyons have many trails that are popular for either hiking or driving.

### Palm Springs Aerial Tramway

Tramway Rd. *(760) 325-1391.* *daily.*

## Anza-Borrego Desert State Park ❼

*Escondido.* **Visitor Center** *(760) 767-4205.* *Jun–Sep: Sat & Sun; Oct–May: daily.* www.anzaborregostatepark.org

DURING THE Gold Rush of 1849 *(see p654)*, tens of thousands of miners passed through the Anza-Borrego

Desert. Today, this former gateway to San Diego County is a remote and pristine park, offering an insight into the unique desert environment, with its steep ravines and rocky badlands.

The visitor center is in **Borrego Springs**, the park's only significant town. Nearby, the Palm Canyon Nature Trail leads to an oasis where endangered bighorn sheep can often be seen. From the **Box Canyon Historical Monument**, lying southwest of the visitor center, there are views of the old road once used by miners en route to the goldfields, which lay 500 miles (800 km) to the north.

The desert bursts into bloom between March and May. Cacti and desert flowers such as desert poppies and dune primroses produce a riot of color.

Much of the park, including its campsites, is accessible via the 100 miles (160 km) of roads. Four-wheel drive vehicles are recommended, however, for the 500 miles (800 km) of unsurfaced roads.

## Salton Sea 8

*Mecca.* *Indio.* **Visitor Center** *(760) 393-3052.* *daily.*

THE SALTON SEA was created by accident in 1905 when the Colorado River flooded and flowed into a newly dug irrigation canal leading to the Imperial Valley. By the time the flow was stemmed two years later, a 35-mile (55-km) inland sea had formed in the Salton Sink, 230 ft (70 m) below sea level.

Despite the high salinity, saltwater game fish live here, with 10-lb (4.5-kg) orange-mouth corvina being caught regularly. Waterskiing, windsurfing, and boating are other popular activities. The area off Mecca Beach has the best spots for swimming. The adjoining marshlands are a refuge for migrating birds such as geese, blue herons, and egrets. On the eastern side, there are hiking trails and camp sites within the State Recreation Area.

**Spiny-leaved Joshua trees in Joshua Tree National Park's western half**

## Joshua Tree National Park 9

*Desert Stage Lines from Palm Springs to Twenty-nine Palms.* **Oasis Visitors' Center** 74485 National Park Dr, Twenty-nine Palms. *(760) 367-5500.* *8am–4:30pm daily.* *Dec 25.*

THE JOSHUA TREE National Park was established to protect the unique Joshua tree. The tree was named by early Mormon travelers, who saw the upraised arms of the biblical Joshua in its twisted branches. The species can grow up to 30 ft (9 m) and live for about 1,000 years.

The 630,800-acre (255,300-ha) park, with its formations of pink and gray rocks, abandoned mines, and oases, is a climber's and hiker's paradise. A popular trail begins close to the **Oasis Visitors' Center**. South of here, the gigantic boulders in **Hidden Valley** form corrals, which were hideouts for cattle rustlers in the days of the Wild West. Farther south, **Key's View** offers sweeping vistas of the valley, desert, and mountains. Close to Key's View, the **Lost Horse Mine** was the historic mine where over $270,000 in gold was extracted in its first decade of operation.

A variety of animals, which have specially adapted to this environment, thrive here. The kangaroo rat gets its food and water from seeds alone, and the jackrabbit has a coat of muted fur to camouflage it from predators such as the coyote, bobcat, and eagle.

## Mojave Desert 10

Barstow. *831 Barstow Rd, (760) 252-6000.*

LYING AT AN altitude of 2,000 ft (600 m), the Mojave or High Desert was the gateway to California for traders in the 19th century. **Barstow**, the largest town, is a stop-over between L.A. and Las Vegas. In the 1870s, gold and silver were discovered in this area, and towns such as Calico sprang up. They were soon abandoned and became ghost towns when the mines became exhausted. Many of Calico's buildings are intact, and visitors can even take a ride in a mine train. To the west, Edwards Air Force Base is famous for its space shuttle landings. The **Red Rock Canyon State Park** nearby has red sandstone and pink volcanic rock, while the **Mitchell Caverns** have limestone formations. Northern Mojave is dominated by the **Death Valley National Park** *(see pp684–5)*.

**Rock formations in the Mitchell Caverns, Mojave Desert**

# Death Valley National Park ⓫

THE NATIVE AMERICANS CALLED the valley Tomesha, "the land where the ground is on fire," an apt name for Death Valley, which has the highest mean temperature on earth – the highest ever recorded was 134° F (57° C) in the shade in 1913. This is a land of wrenching extremes, a sunken trough in the earth's crust that reaches the lowest point in the Western Hemisphere. The park stretches 140 miles (225 km) and is guarded on two sides by some of the highest mountains on the continent. Its unique landscape includes delicate rock formations, polished canyons, and burning salt flats. Although always inhospitable, it is one of the most popular tourist destinations in California.

**Dante's View, taking in jagged peaks and the entire valley floor**

**Exploring Death Valley National Park**

Death Valley was once an insurmountable barrier to miners and emigrants. Today, it is accessible by car, and visitors can take short walks from the roads to spectacular viewpoints. The best time to visit is between October and April, when temperatures average 65° F (18° C). Avoid the period between May and September, when the ground temperatures can exceed a searing 100º F (38º C).

There is a surprising amount of plant life, and for a few weeks each year wildflowers appear amid the rocks. An array of animals such as foxes and tortoises have evolved to survive in this harsh climate.

**Furnace Creek**, with its visitors' complex, is located in the heart of Death Valley. Millennia of winter floods have carved a gateway into the Valley through the eastern hills. The springs here are some of the desert's few freshwater sources and are thought to have saved the lives of hundreds of gold prospectors crossing the desert. Today, the same springs make Furnace Creek a desert oasis shaded by date palms. There are a variety of restaurants and motels, and the **Death Valley Museum and Visitor Center** has exhibits and slide shows explaining the area's natural and human history. In winter, ranger programs and guided walks are available. The world's lowest golf course, lying at 214 ft (65 m) below sea level, and the 1920s Furnace Creek Inn *(see p723)*, which runs bus tours in winter, are also located here.

On Hwy 190, close to the visitor center, the eerie ruins of the **Harmony Borax Works** can still be seen. Borax was discovered here in 1873, but mining did not begin until the 1880s, when crystallized borate compounds were taken to be purified. They were then loaded onto wagons and hauled 165 miles (265 km) to Mojave Station. Used for producing heat-resistant glass, borax is commonly used today as an ingredient in detergents. The Borax Museum has exhibits of mining tools and transport machinery used at the 19th-century refinery.

**Salt Creek**, lying near the Borax Museum, supports the hardy pupfish. Endemic to Death Valley, the pupfish can live in water almost four times as salty as the sea and can withstand temperatures of up to 111° F (44° C). The fish attract other wildlife, including great blue herons. Walkways allow visitors to explore this unique site.

Some of the Valley's most breathtaking natural features lie south of Furnace Creek. About 3 miles (5 km) south, on Hwy 178, a short hike leads into **Golden Canyon**. The mustard-colored walls after which the canyon was named, are best seen in the afternoon sun. Native Americans used the red clay at the mouth of the canyon for face paint. The layers of rock were originally horizontal, but geological activity has now tilted them to an angle of 45°. The roads are often in bad condition due to flash floods. **Zabriskie Point** offers great views of the mud hills of Golden Canyon. Made famous by Antonioni's eponymous 1960s film, the point was named after a general manager of the Valley's borax operations.

**Dante's View** lies 5, 475 ft (1,650 m) above sea level at Death Valley's southern end. Its name was inspired by Dante's *Inferno*. The best time

**Multicolored hills of the Artist's Palette**

›alt formations at the Devil's Golf Course

## VISITORS' CHECKLIST

**Death Valley Museum & Visitor Center** Rte 190, Furnace Creek. *(760) 786-2331.* *daily.* *Jan 1, Thanksgiving, Dec 25.* **Emergency** *For Park Rangers, call up 911 or (760) 786-2331.* www.nps.gov/deva

o see the view, which takes n the entire floor of Death's 'alley, is in the morning.

**Badwater**, to the west, is he lowest point in the West-ern Hemisphere. It lies 282 ft 85 m) below sea level and is one of the world's hottest places. The air can reach 120° (49° C), and as the ground emperature is 50 percent higher than the air temper-ture, it really is possible to ry an egg on the ground. The vater here is not poisonous, out it is unpalatable, filled vith sodium chloride and sul-ates. In spite of the extreme conditions, Badwater is home o several species of insect nd to the endangered Death Valley snail.

**Devil's Golf Course** is an xpanse of salt pinnacles, ocated 12 miles (19 km) outh of Furnace Creek, off Hwy 178. Until about 2,000 ears ago, a succession of akes covered the area. When he last lake evaporated, it eft behind alternating layers of salt and gravel, some 1,000 t (305 m) deep and covering 200 sq miles (520 sq km). The ground is 95 percent salt, and isitors can actually hear the salt expand and contract with he continual change of tem-perature. New salt crystals identified by their whiter hue) continue to form. The multicolored hills known as he **Artist's Palette** are to the north. Created by mineral deposits and volcanic ash, heir hues are at their most ntense in the late afternoon.

Located northwest of the visitor center, the village of **Stovepipe Wells**, founded in 1926, was the valley's first resort. According to legend, a lumberjack traveling west struck water here and stayed on. An old stovepipe, similar to the ones that were used to form the walls of wells, marks the site, which is the Valley's second-largest outpost.

A walk along the 14 sq miles (36 sq km) of undulating **Sand Dunes**, north of Stovepipe Wells, is one of the greatest experiences of Death Valley. Shifting winds blow the sand into the classic crescent dune shape. Mesquite trees dot the lower dunes. A variety of wildlife feeds on the seeds of these trees, such as kangaroo rats and lizards. Among the region's other, mainly nocturnal, creatures are animals that are as diverse as the rattlesnake, the chuckwalla lizard, and the coyote.

Northern Death Valley has the 3,000-year-old **Ubehebe Crater**, where few tourists venture, despite the beauty of the landscape. This is only one of the dozen volcanic craters in the Mojave area; it is 900 yds (800 m) wide and 500 ft (150 m) deep).

East of the crater, lies the Moorish-style **Scotty's Castle**. It was commissioned by Albert Johnson at a cost of $2.4 million in 1922, and covers about 30,000 sq ft (2,800 sq m). "Death Valley Scotty," a friend of Johnson's, lived here until his death in 1948. In 1970 it was bought by the National Park Service which gives guided tours.

**Scotty's Castle**
Hwy 267. *(760) 786-2392.* **Castle** *daily.* **Grounds** *daily.*

## DEATH VALLEY SCOTTY

Walter Scott, would-be miner, beloved charlatan, and sometime performer in Buffalo Bill's Wild West Show, liked to tell visitors that his wealth lay in a secret gold mine. That "mine" was, in fact, his friend Albert Johnson, a Chicago insurance executive, who paid for the castle where Scott lived and received visitors. Built in the 1920s by European craftsmen and Native American labor, the castle has a Moorish feel. Scott never owned the building, and Johnson paid all his bills. "He repays me in laughs," said Johnson. Although Johnson died in 1948, Scott was allowed to remain here until his death in 1954. The edifice is still known as Scotty's Castle.

The grandiose, Moorish-style Scotty's Castle

# Central Coast

CALIFORNIA'S SPANISH HERITAGE is highly visible in this pleasant coastal area. Several of the 21 missions, established by Franciscan friars in the 18th and early 19th centuries, are located here. These, as well as the Spanish Colonial capital at Monterey, preserve vestiges of the state's rich Colonial past. Besides historic sights, the rugged shoreline along the Pacific Ocean harbors beach resorts and large areas of natural beauty.

**The 1929 Spanish Colonial-style County Courthouse, Santa Barbara**

## Santa Barbara ⓬

*90,200. 209 State St. 1020 Chapala St. 34 W Carrillo. Stearns Wharf. 12 E Carrillo St, (805) 965-3023. I Madonnari Italian Street Painting Festival (May); Fiesta (Aug).*

SANTA BARBARA IS a Southern Californian rarity: a city with a single architectural style. Following a devastating earthquake in 1925, the entire center was rebuilt according to strict rules that dictated Mediterranean-style architecture. Santa Barbara is today a quiet administrative center with a sizable student population, which lends the city an informal flavor.

Often called the "Queen of the Missions," **Santa Barbara Mission** is the most visited in the state. The tenth mission built by the Spanish, it was founded in 1786 on the feast day of St. Barbara – four years after the colonists established a garrison here. The present structure took shape after the third adobe church on the site was destroyed by an earthquake in 1812. Its twin towers and the blend of Roman, Moorish, and Spanish styles, were the inspiration for what came to be known as Mission Style. This is the only California mission that has been in continuous use since it was founded.

The beautifully landscaped Sacred Gardens were once a working area for Native Americans. The surrounding living quarters now display a rich collection of mission artifacts. The church's Classical façade was designed by Padre Antonio Ripoll, who was influenced by the Roman architect Vitruvius Pollio (around 27 BC). Its Neo-Classical interior has imitation marble columns, while the reredos has a painted canvas backdrop and carved wooden statues.

The **County Courthouse** on Figueroa Street is still in use. In the Assembly Room are murals depicting California history. The **Museum of Art**, close by, has an outstanding collection that includes Asian and American art, antiquities, and photographs. To its south is the **Lobero Theater**. This graceful 1924 structure stands on the site of the city's original theater. Farther east is the **Presidio**. Built in 1782, this was the last in a chain of four Spanish forts erected along the coast. Other sights include the **Paseo Nuevo**, a colorful outdoor shopping center, and the Historical Museum, housed in two adobe buildings. Among the many artifacts on display here is a statue of the 4th-century martyr St. Barbara.

**Santa Barbara Mission**
2201 Laguna St. *(805) 682-4713. 22. 9am–5pm daily.* ***Donation.***

**Museum of Art**
*(805) 963-4364. 11am–5pm Tue–Sun.*

## Channel Islands National Park ⓭

*Ventura. Island Packers, 1867 Spinnaker Dr, (805) 642-1393.* **Visitor Center** *(805) 658-5730. daily.* www.nps.gov/chis

THE UNPOPULATED volcanic islands of Santa Barbara, Anacapa, San Miguel, Santa Cruz, and Santa Rosa, together comprise the Channel Islands National Park. Access is strictly monitored by park rangers, who issue landing permits from the visitor center. Camping is allowed on all the islands, but visitors must book two weeks in advance. They must also bring their own food and water supplies, since none is available on any of the five islands.

Day trips to Anacapa Island, nearest the mainland, offer an insight into this unique coastal ecosystem. All the islands' rock pools are rich in marine life, and the surrounding kelp forests provide shelter for more than 1,000 plant and animal species. The islands' many sea caves make sea kayaking an exciting experi-

**Statue of the 4th-century martyr St. Barbara**

ence. The snorkeling and scuba diving here are considered to be among the best on the entire Pacific Coast.

Wildlife on these islands is plentiful and includes sea lions, elephant seals, cormorants, and gulls. Depending on the time of year, visitors can spot gray whales, dolphins, and California brown pelicans on the passage across the Santa Barbara Channel.

La Purísima Concepción Mission in Lompoc Valley

## Lompoc Valley 14

Lompoc. 111 S I St, Lompoc, (805) 736-4567).
www.lompoc.com

One of the world's major producers of flower seed, Lompoc Valley is surrounded by hills and flower fields, and is a blaze of color between late spring and mid- summer each year. Marigolds, sweet peas, asters, lobelia, larkspur, nasturtiums, and cornflowers are just some of the varieties grown here. A map of the area's flower fields is distributed by Lompoc town's Chamber of Commerce. The Civic Center Plaza, between Ocean Avenue and C Street, has a display garden where all the varieties of flowers are labeled and identified.

California's 11th mission, **La Purísima Concepción**, located 3 miles (5 km) north-east of Lompoc, was declared a State Historic Park during the 1930s. The early 19th-century buildings have now been perfectly reconstructed, and the entire complex provides a real insight into the missionary way of life. Visitors can view the priests' living quarters, furnished with authentic pieces in the elegant residence building. The simple, narrow church is decorated with colorful stencilwork. The adjacent workshops at one time produced cloth, candles, leather goods, and furniture for the mission.

The mission's gardens also have been faithfully restored. The numerous varieties of fruit, vegetables, and herbs that are now grown here were all common in the 19th century. Visitors can also view the system that provided the mission with water.

**La Purísima Concepción Mission**
2295 Purísima Rd, Lompoc. *(805) 733-3713.* *9am–5pm daily.* *Jan 1, Thanksgiving, Dec 25.*

## San Luis Obispo 15

*43,000.*
*1037 Mill St, (805 541-8000).*
www.sanluisobispo.com

This small city, situated in a valley in the Santa Lucia Mountains, developed around the **San Luis Obispo Mission de Tolosa**, founded on September 1, 1772, by Father Junípero Serra *(see p692)*. Fifth in the chain of 21 missions, and also one of the wealthiest, it is still in use as a parish church. Beside the church, the mission's museum displays Chumash Indian artifacts such as baskets, vessels, and jewelry, the padre's bed, and the mission's original altar.

In front of the church is Mission Plaza, a landscaped public square bisected by the tree-lined San Luis Creek. During the 1860s, bullfights and bear-baiting took place here; today it hosts many of the city's less bloody events.

Just west of the Plaza, is the Ah Louis Store. Founded in 1874 by a Chinese cook, and railroad laborer, it became the center of a then thriving Chinatown and served as a post office, bank, and store. The property is still owned by the Louis family, but it is now a gift shop.

**San Luis Obispo Mission de Tolosa**
751 Palm St. *(805) 781-8220.* *9am–5pm Mon–Fri.* *Jan 1, Easter, Thanksgiving, Dec 25.*

### Mission Architecture

Santa Barbara Mission

The 21 missions established along El Camino Real were adaptations of Mexican Baroque architecture. Designed by friars, these provincial versions were built of adobe bricks and wood by unskilled Native Americans. Over the years they decayed or were shaken by earthquakes, but many have been carefully restored. Distinctive features include massive walls covered with white lime cement, small window openings, rounded gables, and tiered bell towers. The early 20th-century Mission Revival style is a more elegant version of the original. Today, most missions offer public tours.

# Hearst Castle™ ⓰

Tile detail

PERCHED ON a hill above the village of San Simeon, Hearst Castle™ was the private playground and museum of media tycoon William Randolph Hearst. One of California's top tourist attractions, its three guest houses are superb buildings in their own right, but the highlight of the tour is the twin-towered Casa Grande (the "Big House"). Designed by the Paris-trained architect Julia Morgan and built in stages from 1922 to 1947, its 115 rooms hold numerous artworks and epitomize the glamor of the 1930s and 40s.

**Casa Grande**
*Casa Grande's "poured concrete" façade is in the Mediterranean Revival style. It is embellished with ancient architectural fragments.*

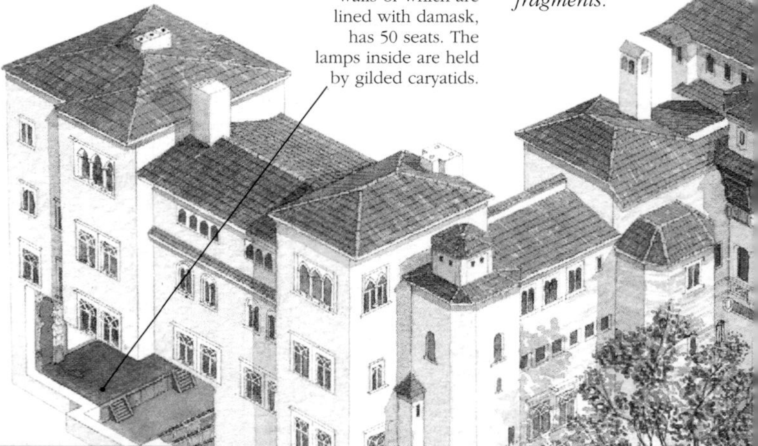

**The Theater**, the walls of which are lined with damask, has 50 seats. The lamps inside are held by gilded caryatids.

★ **Billiard Room**
*This room features an early 16th-century millefleurs tapestry of a stag hunt.*

## Star Features

- ★ The Assembly Room
- ★ Billiard Room
- ★ Gothic Study
- ★ Refectory

## William Randolph Hearst

The son of a multimillionaire, W.R. Hearst (1863–1951) was an ebullient personality who made his own fortune in magazine and newspaper publishing. He married Millicent Willson, an entertainer from New York, in 1903. On his mother's death in 1919, Hearst inherited the San Simeon property. He began to build the castle and grounds as a tribute to his mother, and then lived there with his mistress, the actress Marion Davies. The couple entertained royally at San Simeon over the next 20 years. When Hearst suffered problems with his heart in 1947, he moved to a house in Beverly Hills, where he died in 1951.

**Portrait of Hearst, age 31**

**★ Gothic Study**
*Hearst ran his media empire from the Gothic Study. His most prized books and manuscripts were kept behind grilles.*

**★ The Assembly Room** features a 16th-century French fireplace. Italian choir stalls line the walls, which are hung with Flemish tapestries.

**★ Refectory**
*Tapestries and choir stalls cover the walls of the massive dining hall. Its long, medieval table has cathedral seats and is decorated with silver candlesticks.*

**VISITORS' CHECKLIST**

750 Hearst Castle Rd. *(805) 927-2020, (800) 444-4445.* *8am–4pm daily.* *Jan 1, Thanksgiving, Dec 25.* *call ahead.* *obligatory.* www.hearstcastle.org

**Exploring Hearst Castle**

Visitors must take one of the four guided tours, of which Tour One is best for first-timers. In spring and autumn, evening tours feature actors or "guests" in 1930s costume.

**La Casa Grande** was built from reinforced concrete to withstand California's earthquakes. This gilded playhouse for Hearst's many famous guests has scores of bedrooms, an Assembly Room, a Billiard Room, two pools, and a theater, where up to 50 guests could watch film premieres. Hearst himself lived in the sumptuous, third-floor Gothic Suite. The exquisite heated indoor **Roman Pool** was entirely covered with mosaics of hammered gold and Venetian glass.

The magnate transformed the California hillside into a veritable Garden of Eden, laying 127 acres (51 ha) of gardens. Fan palms, Italian cypresses, and huge 200-year-old oaks were hauled up at great expense. Five greenhouses and 4,000 fruit trees supplied plants and fruit. Ancient and modern statues were collected to adorn the terraces. Among the finest are four statues of Sekhmet, the Egyptian goddess of war, dating from 1350 to 1200 BC. The 104-ft (32-m) white marble **Neptune Pool** is flanked by colonnades and the façade of a reproduction Greek temple.

A great lover of the outdoors, Hearst had a covered bridlepath built, so that he could ride in all weather. There was also a private zoo on Camp Hill that once had lions, bears, elephants, leopards, and pumas. Zebras, giraffes, ostriches, and even a baby elephant were free to wander the grounds. The three guesthouses – Casa del Mar, Casa del Sol, and Casa del Monte – are luxurious mansions in their own right.

# Big Sur ⓱

CALIFORNIA'S WILDEST LENGTH of coastline was named El Pais Grande del Sur, the "Big Country to the South," by Spanish colonists at Carmel *(see p692)* in the late 18th century, and since then, Big Sur has been attracting hyperbole. The novelist Robert Louis Stevenson called it "the greatest meeting of land and sea in the world," and the 100 miles (160 km) of breathtaking mountains, cliffs, and rocky coves still leave visitors groping for adjectives.

The scenic Highway 1 was constructed across this rugged landscape during the 1930s, but otherwise Big Sur has been preserved in its natural state. There are no large towns and very few signs of civilization in the area. Most of the shore is protected in a series of state parks that offer dense forests, broad rivers, and crashing surf, all easily accessible within a short distance of the road.

**Crashing surf and rocky cliffs, typical of the Big Sur coastline**

**Point Lobos State Reserve**
*This is the habitat of the Monterey cypress, the only tree to survive the region's mixture of fog and salt spray. Its branches are shaped by the strong sea winds.*

**Point Sur Lighthouse** sits atop a volcanic cone. It was manned until 1974 but is now automated.

**Bixby Creek Bridge**
*This picturesque arched bridge was built in 1932. For many years it was the world's largest single-arch span, standing 260 ft (79 m) tall and 700 ft (213 m) long. Hwy 1 was named the state's first scenic highway here in 1966.*

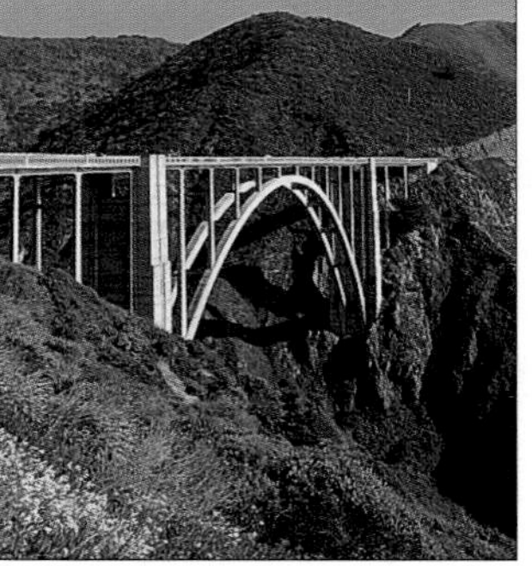

**Nepenthe** is a lovely resort hidden from the road by oak trees. It has long been frequented by Hollywood movie stars.

**KEY**

- Minor road
- Scenic route
- Hiking trail
- National park boundary
- River or lake
- Camping
- Viewpoint

**Andrew Molera State Park**
*Opened in 1972, this park includes 10 miles (16 km) of hiking trails and 2.5 miles (4 km) of quiet, sandy beach.*

**ulia Pfeiffer Burns State Park**
*1 tunnel under Hwy 1, accessible only on foot, leads o a 100-ft (30-m) high bluff, from which the McWay Creek vaterfall spills into the Pacific Ocean.*

**Visitors' Checklist**

1,500. Nepenthe Park. (831) 667-2100.

**Ventana Wilderness**
*Many of the steep ridges of this beautiful wilderness, a part of the Los Padres National Forest, are accessible only to experienced hikers. Campsites cover the lower reaches.*

**The Esalen Institute** was set up in the 1960s to hold New Age seminars. Its hot springs were first frequented by Native Americans and still attract visitors.

**San Simeon Point** is a natural harbor that was used by William Randolph Hearst to ship in materials for his estate, Hearst Castle™, located on the inland hilltop *(see pp688–9)*.

**Jade Cove**
*This beautiful cove can be reached only by way of a steep path down the cliff face. The removal of jade above the high tide level is prohibited.*

**The beautiful Gothic arch of the main altar, Carmel Mission**

## Carmel 18

*24,000. Monterey-Salinas Transit (MST), (831) 899-2555. 137 Crossroads Blvd, (831) 626-1424. Carmel Bach Festival, Monterey (Sep–Mar). www.carmelmission.org*

THIS WEALTHY RESORT, with its art galleries and shops, has one of the area's most spectacular beaches. Among the town's many cultural events is a Bach Festival.

A short drive from town is the **Carmel Mission**, founded in 1770 by the father of California's mission chain, Junípero Serra. The most important of the 21 missions, it served as the administrative center for the state's northern missions. Father Serra, who lived here until his death in 1784, is buried at the foot of the altar. The sarcophagus, one of the finest in the US, depicts Father Serra recumbent in death, surrounded by three mourning priests.

Carmel Mission was abandoned in 1834, and restoration work began in 1924, following the original plans. It now functions as a Catholic church. Its beautiful altar, with a Gothic arch and ornate decoration, is the only one of its kind among the 21 missions in California. The reconstructed living quarters evoke 18th-century mission life; the kitchen still has its original oven from Mexico.

**Carmel Mission**

3080 Rio Rd, Carmel. *(831) 624-3600. daily upto 4:30pm. Thanksgiving, Dec 25.*

## Monterey 19

*35,000. Tyler, Pearl & Munras Sts, (831) 899-2555. 401 Camino el Estero, (831) 648-5350. Monterey Blues Festival (Jul); Monterey Jazz Festival (Sep); Laguna Seca Races (May–Oct).*

THE NAVIGATOR Sebastián Vizcaíno landed here in 1602 and named the bay after his patron, the Count of Monterrey. But it was not until the Spanish captain Gaspar de Portolá and Father Serra arrived in 1770, establishing a church and presidio, that Monterey grew into a pueblo. It served as the Spanish Colonial capital of California until the Gold Rush of 1848, when it lost its status to San Francisco.

Monterey still retains its unique character as a fishing port and market town. Today visitors come to tour its carefully restored historic sites and attend the famous annual jazz festival in September.

In the center of town, a cluster of old buildings form the Monterey State Historic Park. The stately **Colton Hall** was where the California State Constitution was first signed in 1849. It now houses a museum commemorating the event. A short distance to the north, **Larkin House** was built in 1837 by an East Coast merchant, Thomas Larkin. Its architectural style, with two stories of adobe brick, wooden porticoes, and symmetry of plan and elevation, has become representative of the Monterey style. Farther east, **Stevenson House** is where Robert Louis Stevenson lived in 1879. It is now a museum. The Royal Presidio Chapel on Church Street was built in 1794 and is the town's oldest building. To the north are the Old Whaling Station, where mementos of the whaling industry are displayed and the Custom House, preserved as it was in the 1830s and 40s.

**Street sign in Cannery Row**

Close by, **Fisherman's Wharf**, once the center of the fishing and whaling industries, is now well known for its seafood restaurants.

**Cannery Row**, a six-block harbor-front street celebrated by John Steinbeck in his ribald novels *Cannery Row* and *Sweet Thursday*, was once the site of more than 20 fish-packing plants that processed fresh sardines. The canneries thrived in the early 20th century. In 1945 the sardines disappeared, and the canneries were abandoned. The buildings that remain house a collection of electic restaurants and shops. One notable building, at No. 800, is the old laboratory of "Doc" Ricketts, noted marine biologist, beer drinker, and Steinbeck's best friend. It is now a private club.

The **Monterey Bay Aquarium**, at the end of

### THE 17-MILE DRIVE

The Monterey Peninsula has a spectacular coastline, best explored via a toll road, the 17-Mile Drive. The road offers superb views of crashing surf, coastal flora, and the Del Monte Forest. The drive begins at Spanish Bay, a popular picnicking area at the edge of Pacific Grove. Sights include the Carmel Mission; the striking Tor House, built in rock by the poet Robinson Jeffers; Lone Cypress, perhaps the most photographed tree in the world; and Spyglass Hill, a golf course named after a site in Robert Louis Stevenson's novel, *Treasure Island*. Among the other attractions are the exculsive country clubs and championship golf courses.

**Spanish Bay, a picnicking area**

annery Row, is the largest in ıe US. More than 570 species nd 350,000 specimens ortray Monterey Bay's rich ıarine environment. Among ıe exhibits are an enclosed elp forest, a rock pool, and display of live jellyfish. The ɔuter Bay Wing has a one ıillion-gallon (4.5 million-ter) tank, which re-creates ıe conditions of the ocean. It ɔntains yellowfin tuna, cean sunfish, and barracuda. he Research Institute offers isitors a chance to watch ıarine scientists at work, hile the Splash Zone is a ands-on aquarium for kids.

The wealthy resort of **acific Grove**, at the end of ıe peninsula, was originally ɔunded in 1889 as a religious etreat. Today, it is best nown for its quaint wooden ouses, many now converted ıto inns, coastal parks, and ıe beautiful migratory ıonarch butterflies that arrive etween October and April.

**Monterey Bay Aquarium**
36 Cannery Row. *(831) 648-388.* *daily.* *Dec 25.*
www.montereybayaquarium.org

## anta Cruz 20

*252,000. 920 Pacific Ave.*
*701 Front St, (831) 425-1234.*
*Santa Cruz Fungus Fair (Jan); am Chowder Cook-Off (Feb).*

ERCHED AT THE northern tip of Monterey Bay, Santa ruz is a lively beach town, acked by densely forested ıountains. Surrounded by ırmland, it evokes an agri-ultural rather than suburban eel. The town's cosmopolitan haracter is due to the pres-nce of the large University of alifornia campus, with its udents and professors from ll over the world.

Much of the downtown rea was badly damaged by ıe Loma Prieta earthquake in 989. It has recovered since ıen, and many good book-tores, art galleries, and cafés ow line the streets.

The town's highlight is the aterfront, particularly the **anta Cruz Beach Board-walk**, the last surviving old-style amusement park on the West Coast. Its main attraction is the Giant Dipper roller coaster, built by Arthur Looff in 1924 and now a National Historic Landmark. The car travels along the 1-mile (1.6-km) wooden track at 55 mph (88 km/h). The carousel near-by has horses and chariots hand-carved by Looff's father, craftsman Charles Looff, in 1911. The ride is accompan-ied by a 100-year-old pipe organ. The park also has 27 other modern rides and an Art Deco dance hall.

**Eroded archway at the Natural Bridges State Park, Santa Cruz**

The **Museum of Art and History at the McPherson Center**, on Front Street, is a 20,000 sq ft (1,858 sq m) cul-tural center, which opened in 1993. The Art Gallery shows works primarily by local north central artists, while the History Gallery displays vari-ous aspects of Santa Cruz County's past.

Standing on a hill to the northeast of town is a replica of the **Mission Santa Cruz**, founded in 1791. All traces of the original were destroyed by frequent earthquakes, and the present structure was built in 1931. It now houses a small museum.

The scenic Cliff Drive along the coast takes in the **Natural Bridges State Beach**, named for the archways that were carved into the cliffs by ocean waves. One of the original arches still remains, through which waves roll into a small sandy cove. The park also preserves a eucalyptus grove and a nature trail, which shows the stages in the life cycle of the monarch butter-fly. Also along the coast is the Surfing Museum, housed in a lighthouse. The museum has artifacts from every era of Santa Cruz surfing history. Surfboards range from 1930s redwood planks to today's high-tech laminates.

East of downtown, Mystery Spot is a redwood grove, which has been drawing visitors for decades due to various strange events here. Balls roll uphill, parallel lines converge, and the laws of physics seem to be suspend-ed. Part tourist trap, part genuine oddity, this attraction has to be seen to be believed.

**Santa Cruz Beach Boardwalk**
400 Beach St. *(831) 423-5590.*
*call ahead for opening times.*

### Surfing in California

Surfing was originally practiced by the Hawaiian nobility as a religious ceremony; it was introduced to California by Hawaiian George Freeth in 1907. The sport evolved into a truly California pursuit with the Beach Boys' hit song "Surfin" in 1961. Films such as *Ride the Wild Surf* (1964), and *Beach Blanket Bingo* (1965) helped to establish its cultural allure, and beach parties in the style of these films were highly popular in the 1960s. Today, surf culture determines fashion as well as speech.

**Surfers on fiberglass boards**

# San Francisco ㉑

SAN FRANCISCO IS, after New York, the second most densely populated city in the US, with 750,000 people crowded into 47 sq miles (122 sq km). It is located at the tip of a peninsula, with the Pacific Ocean to the west and San Francisco Bay to the east. To the north, Golden Gate Bridge links it to the Marin Headlands. The Greater San Francisco area includes the cities of Oakland and Berkeley. San Francisco is a compact city, and most of the area can be explored on foot. The estimated 43 hills give many of the streets near impossible gradients but offer superb views.

A panoramic view of San Francisco from a penthouse bar on Nob Hill

**KEY**

- Sight/Place of interest
- Airport
- Cable car terminal
- Streetcar station
- BART station
- Ferry terminal
- Tourist information
- Parking
- Church
- Synagogue
- Freeway

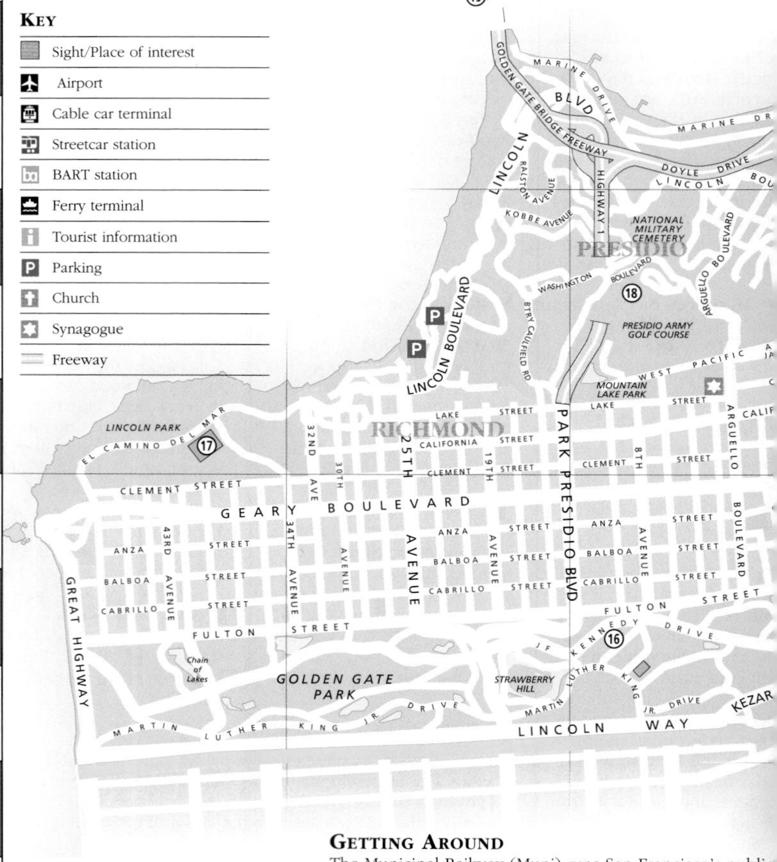

0 meters 750

0 yards 750

**GETTING AROUND**

The Municipal Railway (Muni) runs San Francisco's public transportation system. Visitors can use one pass – the Muni Passport – to travel on buses, Metro streetcars (electric trams), and the three cable car lines. Buses and streetcars serve all areas, while the high-speed BART (Bay Area Rapid Transit) rail system links the suburbs and outlying regions. Taxis are advised for traveling at night. Ferries run regularly east and north across the bay.

## IGHTS AT A GLANCE

inancial District ①
Vells Fargo History Museum ②
erba Buena Center for the Arts ③
ın Francisco Museum of Modern Art ④
nion Square ⑤
hinatown ⑥
*ob Hill p701* ⑦
isherman's Wharf ⑧
orth Beach ⑨
*lcatraz Island p703* ⑩

Pacific Heights ⑪
Asian Art Museum ⑫
*Mission Dolores p705* ⑬
Haight Ashbury ⑭
California Academy of Sciences ⑮
de Young Museum ⑯
Legion of Honor ⑰
The Presidio ⑱
Golden Gate Bridge ⑲

**Greater San Francisco**
***(see inset map)***
San Jose ⑳
Palo Alto ㉑
Oakland ㉒
Berkeley ㉓
Sausalito ㉔
Muir Woods ㉕

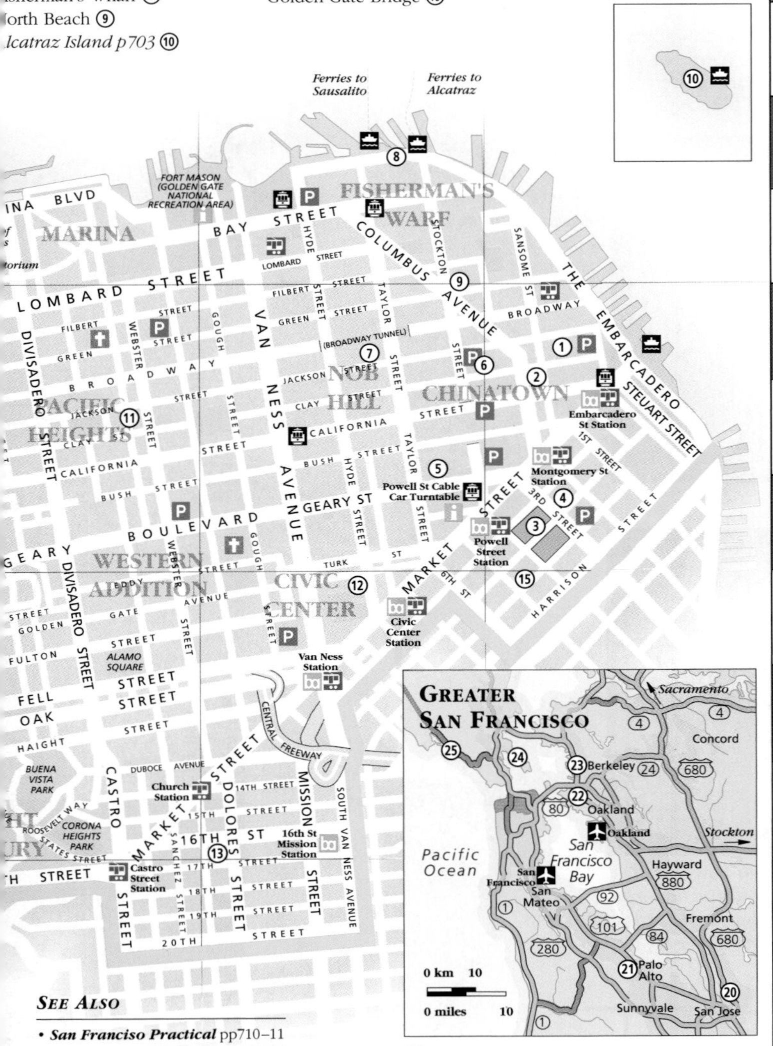

*Ferries to Sausalito*
*Ferries to Alcatraz*
FORT MASON (GOLDEN GATE NATIONAL RECREATION AREA)
MARINA
FISHERMAN'S WHARF
PACIFIC HEIGHTS
NOB HILL
CHINATOWN
WESTERN ADDITION
CIVIC CENTER
Powell St Cable Car Turntable
Embarcadero St Station
Montgomery St Station
Powell Street Station
Civic Center Station
Van Ness Station
Church Station
Castro Street Station
16th St Mission Station
ALAMO SQUARE
BUENA VISTA PARK
CORONA HEIGHTS PARK

## GREATER SAN FRANCISCO

Sacramento
Concord
Berkeley
Oakland
Stockton
San Francisco Bay
Pacific Ocean
San Francisco
San Mateo
Hayward
Fremont
Palo Alto
Sunnyvale
San Jose
0 km 10
0 miles 10

**KEY**

Area of main map



***SEE ALSO***

- ***San Francisco Practical*** pp710–11
- ***Where to Stay*** p724
- ***Where to Eat*** pp728–9

# The 49-Mile Scenic Drive

**Official sign**

Linking the city's most intriguing neighborhoods, fascinating sights, and spectacular views, the 49-Mile Scenic Drive (79 km) provides a splendid overview of San Francisco. Keeping to the well-marked route is easy: just follow the blue-and-white seagull signs. Some of these are hidden by overhanging vegetation, so you need to be alert. Set aside a whole day for this trip; there are plenty of places to stop to take photographs or admire the views.

**The Palace of Fine Arts & the Exploratorium**
*The grand Neo-Classical buildin and its modern science museum stand near the entrance to the Presidio.*

**Stow Lake ⑤**
*There is a waterfall and a Chinese pavilion on the island in this picturesque lake, where you can also rent boats.*

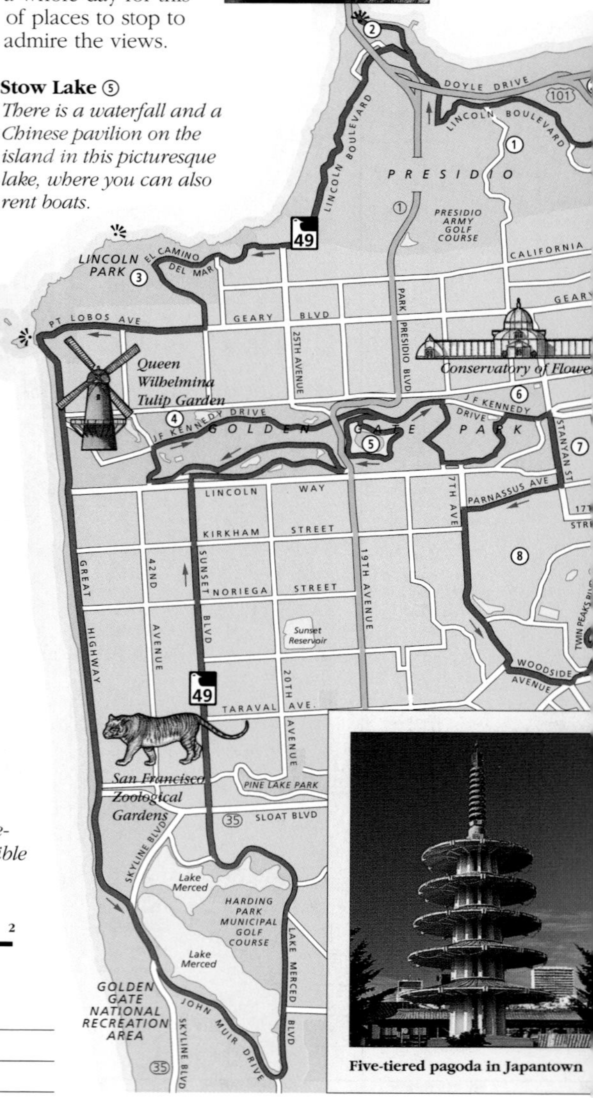

**Sutro Tower ⑧**
*This distinctive orange-and-white tower is visible from all over the city.*

0 km 2

0 miles 1

**Key**

— 49-Mile Scenic Drive

Viewpoint

**Five-tiered pagoda in Japantown**

**Coit Tower** ⑳
*Overlooking North Beach, Telegraph Hill is topped by this tower, which has fine murals and an observation deck.*

**San Francisco National Maritime Museum** ㉑
*Resembling a beached ocean liner, this 1939 building houses a collection of nautical bric-a-brac.*

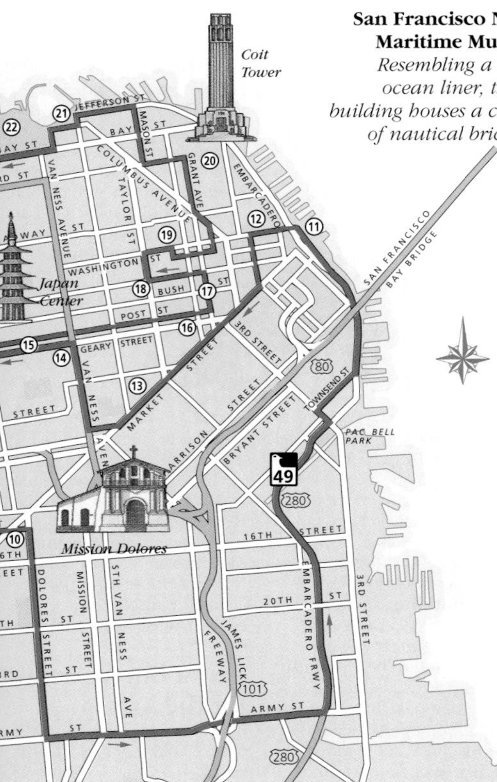

**Grace Cathedral** ⑱
*This impressive cathedral, based on Notre Dame in Paris, dominates the summit of the city's steepest hill, Nob Hill.*

## Tips for Drivers

***Starting point:*** *Anywhere. The circuit is designed to be followed in a counterclockwise direction starting and ending at any point.*
***When to go:*** *Avoid driving during rush hours: 7–9am, 4–7pm. Most of the views are as spectacular by night as by day.*
***Parking:*** *Use the parking lots that are located around the Financial District, the Civic Center, Japantown, Nob Hill, Chinatown, North Beach, and Fisherman's Wharf. Elsewhere, street parking is usually easily available.*

## Finding the Sights

① Presidio *p707*
② Fort Point *p707*
③ Legion of Honor *p706*
④ Queen Wilhelmina Tulip Garden
⑤ Stow Lake
⑥ Conservatory of Flowers
⑦ Haight Street
⑧ Sutro Tower
⑨ Twin Peaks
⑩ Mission Dolores *p705*
⑪ Ferry Building *p698*
⑫ Embarcadero Center *p698*
⑬ Civic Center
⑭ St. Mary's Cathedral
⑮ Japan Center
⑯ Union Square *p699*
⑰ Chinatown Gateway *p700*
⑱ Grace Cathedral *p701*
⑲ Cable Car Barn *p701*
⑳ Coit Tower *p702*
㉑ San Francisco National Maritime Museum *p702*
㉒ Fort Mason
㉓ Marina Green
㉔ Palace of Fine Arts and the Exploratorium *p704*

**Transamerica Pyramid, the tallest building on the city's skyline**

## Financial District ①

**Map** F3. *Between Washington & Market Sts.* *1, 12, 15, 32, 42, 83.* *F, J, K, L, M, N.* *California St.* **Embarcadero Center** *1, 32, 42.* *J, K, L, M, N.* *California St.*

San Francisco's economic engine is fueled by the Financial District, lying at the heart of downtown. The district stretches from the imposing skyscrapers and plazas of the **Embarcadero Center** to staid Montgomery Street, called the "Wall Street of the West." All the main banks, brokers, and law offices are located here.

Completed in 1981 after a decade of construction, the vast Embarcadero Center stretches from Justin Herman Plaza to Battery Street and houses a large number of commercial outlets and offices. A shopping arcade occupies the first three tiers of its four high-rise towers. The splendid foyer of the Hyatt Regency Hotel, located here, has a 17-story atrium.

North of Washington Street, the **Jackson Square Historical District** was once the heart of the business community. Renovated in the early 1950s, this area contains brick, cast-iron, and granite façades dating from Gold Rush days. From 1850 to 1910 it was known as the Barbary Coast, notorious for its brothels and squalor. Today, the buildings are used as showrooms, law offices, and antique shops; some of the best ones can be seen in Jackson and Montgomery Streets.

Standing adjacent is a soaring San Francisco landmark, the **Transamerica Pyramid**. Capped with a spire on top of its 48 stories, it reaches 853 ft (260 m) and is the tallest building in the city. Its 3,678 windows take cleaners an entire month to wash. Designed by William Pereira, the building stands on what was earlier the site of the historic Montgomery Block, which contained many important offices. Numerous artists and writers took up residence in the block, including the writer Mark Twain, who often visited the Exchange Saloon, located in the building's basement. Farther south, the granite **Bank of America** was originally the Bank of Italy, founded by A.P. Giannini in San Jose. Its 52 floors make it one of the city's tallest skyscrapers, with incredible views from the top. At the district's northeastern corner lies the **Ferry Building**, built in 1903. In the early 1930s, over 50 million passengers a year passed through here, to and from the transcontinental railroad in Oakland or homes across the bay. Its clock tower was inspired by the Moorish bell tower of Seville Cathedral in Spain. With the opening of the Bay Bridge in 1936, it began to deteriorate. A few ferries still cross to Tiburon, Sausalito, and Oakland. On the building's east side stands the Gandhi Monument (1988). Designed by K.B. Patel and sculpted by Z. Pounov and S. Lowe, it bears an inscription of Gandhi's words.

**Transamerica Pyramid**
600 Montgomery St. *8:30am–4:30pm Mon–Fri.* *public hols.*

**Bank of America**
555 California St. *(415) 433-7500 (Camelian Room).*
www.camelianroom.com

## Wells Fargo History Museum ②

**Map** F3. 420 Montgomery St. *(415) 396-2619.* *1, 12, 15, 42.* *Montgomery St.* *9am–5pm Mon–Fri.* *public hols.*
www.wellsfargohistory.com

Founded in 1852, Wells Fargo & Co. became the greatest banking and transportation company in the West. The company moved people, goods, gold, and mail. The Pony Express was one of their mail ventures. The museum displays splendid stagecoaches – famous for the legendary stories of their heroic drivers and the bandits who robbed them. The best known bandit was Black Bart, who left poems at the scene of his crimes. He was later identified as the mining engineer Charles Boles. Exhibits include a simulated stagecoach ride, Pony Express mail, photographs, gold nuggets, and the imperial currency of the eccentric Joshua Norton, who proclaimed himself Emperor of the United States in 1854.

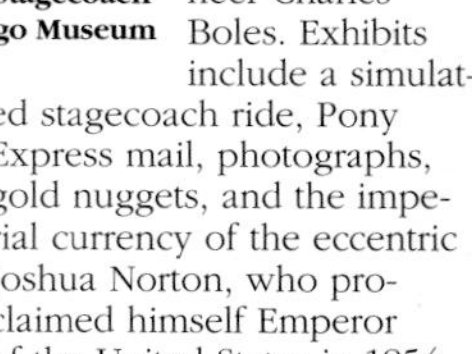

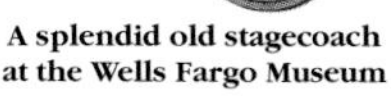

**A splendid old stagecoach at the Wells Fargo Museum**

## Yerba Buena Center for the Arts ③

**Map** F3. Mission, 3rd, Folsom & 4th Sts. *(415) 978-2787.* *9, 14, 15, 30, 45, 76.* *J, K, L, M, N.* **Center for the Arts Galleries & Forum** *11am–5pm Tue–Sun (until 8pm first Thu of month).* *public hols.* *(free first Thu of month).* **Zeum** *(415) 777-2800.* *11am–5pm Sat & Sun.* *Dec 25.* *open 11am–5:30pm daily.*
www.yerbabuenaarts.org

The construction of the underground Moscone Center, San Francisco's largest venue for conventions, heralded the beginning of ambitious plans for Yerba Buena Gardens, now the Yerba Buena Center for the Arts. New housing, hotels,

splanade Gardens in the Yerba Buena Center for the Arts

ıuseums, and shops have prung up. The center is ituated at the heart of SoMa South of Market), an area ıat has become the city's artists' quarter," with its varehouses-turned-studios, ars, and avant-garde theaters. 'he **Esplanade Gardens** ;ive visitors a chance to wan- er along paths or relax on enches. Close by, the Martin uther King Jr. Memorial has vords of peace in several ınguages. The adjacent **Cen- er for the Arts Galleries nd Forum** have visual arts alleries and a screening oom featuring contemporary rt and films. The **Center for he Arts Theater** presents erforming arts that reflect ıe cultural diversity of the ity in a 755-seat indoor ıeater. **Zeum**, located at the 'erba Buena Rooftop, has an ngoing program of events nd provides opportunities or youngsters and artists to ollaborate in the design and reation of anything from obots to sculptures.

## San Francisco Museum of Modern Art ④

**Map** F3. 151 Third St. *(415) 357-4000.* *5, 9, 12, 14, 15, 30, 38, 45.* *J, K, L, M, N.* *11am–9pm Thu, 11am–6pm Fri–Tue. Times may change, please call to confirm.* *Wed, Jan 1, Thanksgiving, Dec 25.* *(free first Tue of month; half-price admission Thu 6–9pm).* www.sfmoma.org

THIS DRAMATIC museum forms the nucleus of San Francisco's reputation as a leading center of modern art. Created in 1935 with the aim of displaying works by 20th-century artists, it moved into its new quarters in 1995. The focus of Swiss architect Mario Botta's Modernist building is the 125-ft (38-m) cylindrical skylight, which channels light down to the first floor atrium court. More than 17,000 works of art are housed in its 50,000 sq ft (4,600 sq m) of gallery space, and it offers a dynamic schedule of changing exhibits from around the world.

The galleries display paintings, sculptures, architecture, design, photography, and media art. Among the highlights are works by Dali, Matisse, and Picasso; Diego Rivera's mural *The Flower Carrier*, a powerful irony on the human cost of luxury, painted in oil and tempera on Masonite in 1935; and Richard Shaw's sculpted figure *Melodius Double Stop* in the California Art section.

**Victory Monument in Union Square**

## Union Square ⑤

**Map** E3. *2, 3, 4, 30, 38, 45.* *J, K, L, M, N.* *Powell–Mason, Powell–Hyde.*

UNION SQUARE, lined with palm trees, is at the heart of the city's main shopping district and has a wealth of fine department stores. It was named after the pro-Union rallies held here during the Civil War of 1861–65. The original churches, gentlemen's clubs, and a synagogue were eventually overtaken by shops and offices. Some of the main stores include Macy's, Saks, and Gump's. The area also houses many antiquarian bookshops and smaller boutiques. Union Square marks the edge of the **Theater District** and is bordered on the west side by the luxurious Westin St. Francis Hotel. At the center of the square there is a bronze statue of the Goddess of Victory, sculpted by Robert Aitken in 1903 to commemorate Admiral Dewey's victory during the Spanish–American War (1898). The **Circle Gallery Building** at 140 Maiden Lane is an art gallery designed by Frank Lloyd Wright. It was the precursor to his Guggenheim Museum in New York *(see p82)*.

### CALIFORNIA'S EARTHQUAKES

The San Andreas Fault extends some 600 miles (965 km) along California's coastline and is one of the few sites on Earth where an active plate boundary occurs on land. Each year, the Pacific Plate moves 1–1.6 inches (2.5–4 cm). The terrible fire of 1906 that destroyed San Francisco was caused by an earthquake estimated at 7.8 on the Richter Scale. More recently, the earthquake of October 1989, south of San Francisco, killed 62 people and caused at least $6 billion worth of damage. In 1994, the Northridge quake, magnitude 6.7, rocked Los Angeles. Scientists predict that the next major earthquake, the "Big One," will hit Southern California.

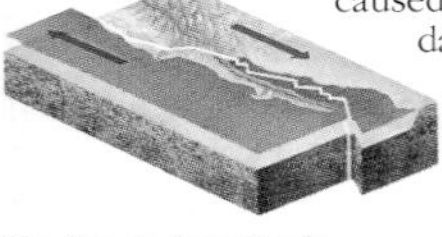

**The San Andreas Fault**

**Colorful oriental architecture along Grant Avenue, Chinatown**

## Chinatown ⑥

**Map** F3. *1, 2, 3, 4, 15, 30, 45.* *all three lines go to Chinatown.*

An estimated 25,000 Chinese migrants settled in the plaza on Stockton Street during the Gold Rush era of the 1850s *(see p654)*. Today, the district evokes the atmosphere of a bustling southern Chinese town, although the architecture and customs are distinctly American hybrids on a Cantonese theme. This densely populated neighborhood has been called the "Gilded Ghetto," because its colorful façades screen a harsher world of sweatshops and cramped living quarters. Cable cars run down two sides of the district.

The ornate Chinatown Gateway, marking the southern entrance to Chinatown, was designed by Clayton Lee as an arch over the start of the main tourist street, **Grant Avenue**. The three-arched structure was inspired by the ceremonial entrances of traditional Chinese villages. It is capped with green roof tiles and a host of propitiatory animals in glazed ceramic.

Dragon lampposts, upturned roofs, and stores selling everything from kites and cooking utensils to antiques, embroidered silks, and gems line Grant Avenue. Most of the buildings were erected after the 1906 earthquake in an Oriental Renaissance style. In the 1830s and 40s it was the main thoroughfare of Yerba Buena, the village that preceded San Francisco. A plaque at No. 823 marks the site of the first dwelling, a canvas tent that was built in 1835.

To the east of Grant Avenue is the city's original town square, **Portsmouth Plaza**, which was laid out in 1839. In 1846 marines raised the American flag above the plaza, officially seizing the port as part of the United States. Two years later, it was here that Sam Brannan announced the discovery of gold in the Sierra Nevada Mountains *(see pp718–19)*. It soon became the hub of the new booming city in the 1850s. Today, Portsmouth Plaza is the social hub of Chinatown. In the morning people practice t'ai chi, and from noon to evening gather to play cards.

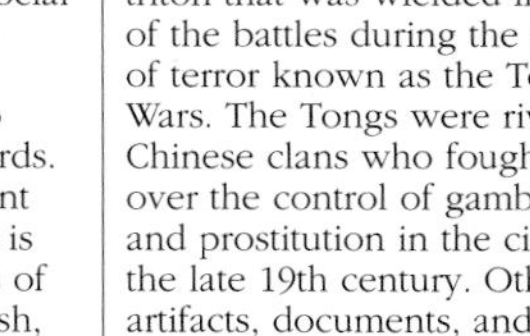
**Dragon's Head at the Chinese Historical Society**

Running parallel to Grant Avenue, **Stockton Street** is where locals shop. Boxes of the freshest vegetables, fish, and other produce spill over onto crowded sidewalks. The Kong Chow Temple, located here, features fine Cantonese wood carvings.

Chinatown's busy alleys, located between Grant Avenue and Stockton Street, echo with authentic sights and sounds of the Orient. The largest of the four narrow lanes is Waverly Place, also known as the "Street of Painted Balconies." Watch for the Tin How Temple, which is brightly decorated with hundreds of gold and red lanterns. Nearby, Ross Alley has the tiny Fortune Cookie Factory, where visitors can see how the famous San Francisco creation is made. The alleys have many old buildings as well as laundries and old-fashioned herbalist shops, displaying elk antlers, sea horses, snake wine, and other exotic wares. Numerous small restaurants, above and below street level, serve cheap and delicious food.

The newly renovated **Chinese Historical Society** has a range of fascinating exhibits including a ceremonial dragon costume and a "tiger fork," a triton that was wielded in one of the battles during the reign of terror known as the Tong Wars. The Tongs were rival Chinese clans who fought over the control of gambling and prostitution in the city in the late 19th century. Other artifacts, documents, and photographs illuminate the daily life of Chinese immigrants in San Francisco. Among these is a yearbook written in Chinese.

**Chinese Historical Society**
965 Clay St. *(415) 391-1188.*
*1, 30, 45.* *Powell St.*
*11am–4pm Tue–Fri & Sun.*
*public hols.*

### Cable Cars

**One of the city's cable cars**

The cable car system was launched in 1873, with its inventor Andrew Hallidie riding in the first car. He was inspired to tackle the problem of transporting people up the city's steep slopes after seeing an accident, where a horse-drawn tram slipped down a hill. His system was a success, and by 1889 cable cars were running on eight lines. Before the 1906 earthquake, over 600 cars were in use. With the advent of the internal combustion engine, however, they became obsolete, and in 1947 attempts were made to replace them with buses. After a huge public outcry, the present three lines were retained.

# Nob Hill ⑦

**Map** E3. 🚌 *1, 12, 30, 45, 83.* 🚋 *California St, Powell–Mason, Powell–Hyde.*

NOB HILL IS the highest summit of the city itself, rising 338 ft (103 m) above the bay. It is San Francisco's most celebrated hilltop, famous for its cable cars, plush hotels, and views. The steep slopes kept prominent citizens away until the opening of the California Street cable car line in 1878. The rich then flocked to build homes here, including the "Big Four" railroad barons, who were among its richest tenants. The name "Nob Hill" is thought to come from the Indian word *nabob*, meaning chieftain. Sadly, all the grand mansions were leveled in the great earthquake and fire of 1906. The only building that survived was the home of James C. Flood, which is now the Pacific Union Club.

Nob Hill still attracts the affluent to its hotels, which recall the opulence of the Victorian era and offer fine views of the city.

**Grace Cathedral** is the main Episcopal church in San Francisco. Designed by Lewis P. Hobart, this building was inspired by Notre Dame in Paris. Preparatory work began in 1928, but the cathedral was not completed until 1964. Its entrance doors are cast from molds of Ghiberti's "Doors of Paradise," made for the Baptistry in Florence.

A short distance north of Nob Hill is the **Cable Car Barn**, erected in 1909, which garages cable cars at night. It is a repair shop, museum, and powerhouse of the cable car system. Anchored to the ground floor are the engines and wheels that wind the cables through the system of channels and pulleys beneath the city's streets. Visitors can observe them from the mezzanine, then walk down to look under the street. The museum also houses an early cable car and the mechanisms that control individual cars.

**Grace Cathedral**
1100 California St. *(415) 749-6300. Choral evensong 5:15pm Thu, 3pm Sun; Choral Eucharist 6am, 7:30am, 8:15am, 11am Sun.*

**Cable Car Barn**
1201 Mason St. *(415) 474-1887. summer: 10am–6pm daily; winter: 10am–5pm daily. Jan 1, Thanksgiving, Dec 25. mezzanine only.*
***Video show.***
www.cablecarmuseum.com

## GRACE CATHEDRAL

The interior of this Gothic-style cathedral is replete with marble and beautiful stained glass. The leaded windows were designed by Charles Connick, using the blue glass of Chartres as his inspiration. The rose window has thick faceted glass, which is illuminated from the inside at night. Other windows are by Henry Willet and Gabriel Loire, and include depictions of Albert Einstein and astronaut John Glenn. The cathedral also features a 13th-century Catalonian crucifix and a 16th-century Brussels tapestry, and is popular for its choral evensong, held every Thursday and Sunday.

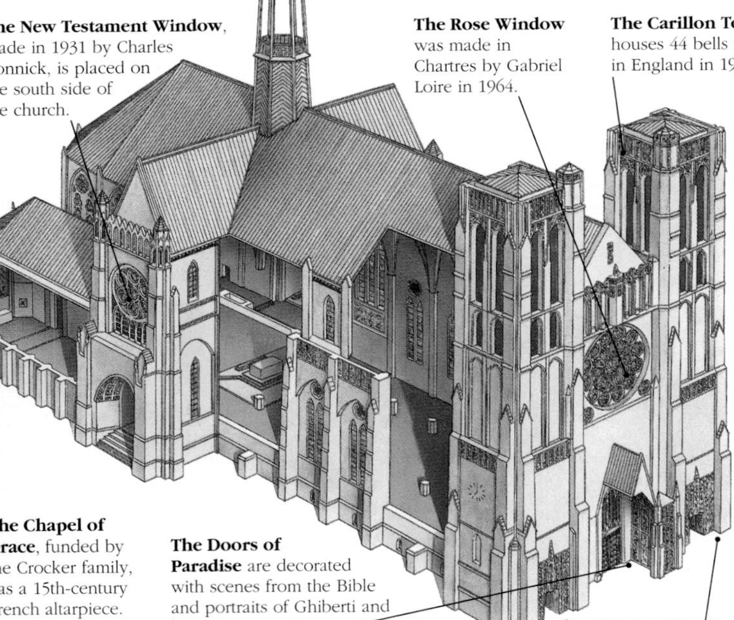

**The New Testament Window**, made in 1931 by Charles Connick, is placed on the south side of the church.

**The Rose Window** was made in Chartres by Gabriel Loire in 1964.

**The Carillon Tower** houses 44 bells made in England in 1938.

**The Chapel of Grace**, funded by the Crocker family, has a 15th-century French altarpiece.

**The Doors of Paradise** are decorated with scenes from the Bible and portraits of Ghiberti and his contemporaries.

**Entrances**

Shops and amusements at Pier 39, Fisherman's Wharf

## Fisherman's Wharf ⑧

**Map** E2. Between the coastline & Beach St. 🚌 *15, 19, 25, 30, 32, 39, 42, 45, 47.* 🚋 *Powell–Mason, Powell–Hyde.*

ITALIAN SEAFOOD restaurants have replaced fishing as the primary focus of Fisherman's Wharf. Fishermen from Genoa and Sicily first arrived here in the late 19th century and founded San Francisco's fishing industry. Since the 1950s, the area has given way to tourism, although brightly colored boats still set out to sea early each morning. The specialty here is the delicious Dungeness crab.

**Pier 39** is the Wharf's hub, with restaurants, shops, and specialty stores, set against a backdrop of stunning bay views. Refurbished in 1978 to resemble a quaint wooden fishing village, the pier is also home to groups of sea lions that bask on the docks.

Docked at Pier 45 is the World War II submarine **USS *Pampanito***, which fought several battles in the Pacific, sinking six enemy ships. Visitors can tour the torpedo room, galley, and officer's quarters. To its south on Jefferson Street is **Ripley's Believe It Or Not! Museum**, which displays the cartoonist's collection of curiosities – one of which is a cable car built of 275,000 matchsticks. Farther along Jefferson Street, **The Cannery**, earlier a fruit processing factory, now houses a mall with restaurants, museums, and shops. The **San Francisco National Maritime Museum** on Beach Street, displays ship models, nautical instruments, and photographs illustrating nautical history. A large collection of old ships are moored at the nearby **Hyde Street Pier**. Among the finest is the *C.A. Thayer*, a three-masted schooner built in 1895.

## North Beach ⑨

**Map** E2. 🚌 15, 30, *39, 45.* 🚋 *Powell–Mason, Powell–Hyde.*

SOUTH OF Fisherman's Wharf is North Beach, also known as "Little Italy." Settlers from Chile, China, and Italy brought their enthusiasm for nightlife to the area, earning North Beach its vibrant reputation and attracting bohemians and writers, including the leading chronicler of the "Beat generation," Jack Kerouac. At the junction of Broadway and Columbus Avenue, the **City Lights Bookstore**, once owned by the Beat poet Lawrence Ferlinghetti, was the first bookshop in the US to sell only paperbacks. **Vesuvio**, south of City Lights, was one of the most popular Beat bars. Welsh poet Dylan Thomas was a patron here, and it is still a favorite with poets and artists. The former **Condor Club** is located on a stretch of Broadway known as The Strip, noted for its "adult entertainment." This landmark establishment was where the area's first topless show was staged in June 1964. **Caffè Trieste**, on the corner of Vallejo Street, is the oldest coffee house in San Francisco and a genuine Beat rendezvous since 1956. Very much a part of Italian-American culture, it offers live opera on Saturday afternoons.

**Lombard Street**, a little to the north, is renowned as "the crookedest street in the world." Banked at a natural incline of 27 degrees, this hill proved too steep for vehicles to climb. In the 1920s the section close to the summit of Russian Hill was revamped, and eight tight curves were added. There are spectacular views of San Francisco from the summit, especially at night. Close by, the **San Francisco Art Institute** is famous for its Diego Rivera Gallery, which contains an outstanding mural by the famous Mexican muralist created in 1931.

The 210-ft **Coit Tower** lies at the top of Telegraph Hill. The lobby has many Depression-era murals.

### San Francisco's Murals

Coit Tower's mural of Fisherman's Wharf in the 1930s

San Francisco's cosmopolitan heritage comes alive in the bright murals that decorate walls and public places in several parts of the city. Life in the metropolis is one of the major themes. The Mission District has over 200 murals showing every aspect of daily life on the walls of restaurants, banks, and schools. Many of these were painted in the 1970s, when the government paid rebellious young people to create public works of art. One of the best is the *Carnaval Mural* on 24th Street. The city also has three murals by Diego Rivera, the Mexican artist who revived fresco painting in the 1930s and 40s.

Cars negotiating Lombard St, "the crookedest street in the world"

## Alcatraz Island ⑩

ALCATRAZ MEANS "pelican" in Spanish and refers to the first inhabitants of this rocky, steep-sided island. In 1859, the US Army established a fort here that guarded San Francisco Bay until 1907, when it became a military prison. From 1934 to 1963 it served as a maximum-security federal penitentiary. Dubbed "The Rock" by prisoners, it housed an average of 264 of the country's most infamous criminals, who were transferred here for disobedience while serving time in prisons elsewhere in the US. Today, Alcatraz is part of the Golden Gate National Recreation Area.

### VISITORS' CHECKLIST

*(415) 705-5555 for tickets & schedules.* *from Pier 41.* *daily: first ferry 9:30am; last ferry 2:15pm (4:15pm in summer).* *Jan 1, Dec 25.* **Night Tours** *(415) 561-4926.* *accessible in places.* **Film presentation** *Buy tickets in advance.* www.nps.gov/goga

**The Cell Block**
*Prisoners spent between 16 and 23 hours every day alone in stark cells, equipped with only a toilet and bunk. Many cells measured 5 ft by 9 ft (1.5 m by 2.7 m).*

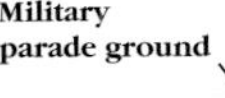

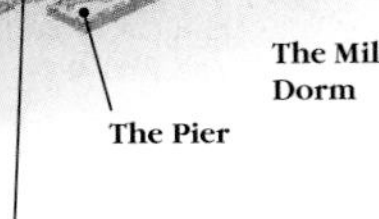


**The Visitor Center** is in the barracks building behind the jetty. It houses an information center, bookstore, exhibits, and a multimedia show providing a historical overview of Alcatraz.

**Alcatraz from the Ferry**
*Looming ominously out of the ocean, "The Rock" promised its inmates strict discipline and constant vigilance.*

**Exercise Yard**
*Meals and a walk around the exercise yard were the highlights of a prisoner's day. This walled yard appeared in films that were shot here.*

### FAMOUS INMATES OF ALCATRAZ ISLAND

**Al Capone**
Al Capone was convicted in 1934 for income tax evasion and spent much of his five-year sentence at Alcatraz in an isolation cell. He left the prison mentally unstable.

**Robert Stroud**
Stroud spent most of his 17 years here in solitary confinement. Despite assertions to the contrary in the film *The Birdman of Alcatraz* (1962), he was forbidden from keeping birds in his cell.

**Anglin Brothers**
John and Clarence Anglin and Frank Morris chipped through the walls of their cells, hiding the holes with cardboard grates. They made a raft to escape and were never caught. Their story was dramatized in the film *Escape from Alcatraz* (1979).

**George Kelly**
George "Machine Gun" Kelly was the prison's most dangerous inmate and has the singular distinction of serving 17 years for kidnapping and extortion.

**Haas-Lilienthal House in Pacific Heights, an 1886-Queen Anne mansion**

## Pacific Heights ⑪

**Map** D3. 🚌 *1, 3, 12, 19, 22, 24, 27, 28, 29, 30, 42, 43, 45, 47, 49, 83.* 🚋 *California St.*

The steep blocks between **Alta Plaza** and **Lafayette Park** are set in the heart of the exclusive Pacific Heights district. After cable cars linked it with the downtown area in the 1880s, it quickly became a desirable place to live, and many palatial Victorian houses line its quiet streets. Some date from the late 19th century, while others were built after the devastating earthquake and fire of 1906.

The **Haas-Lilienthal House**, an elaborate Queen Anne-style mansion, was built in 1886 for the merchant William Haas. Furnished in Victorian style, it is the only intact private home of the period and houses the headquarters of the Architectural Heritage Foundation. The impressive **Spreckels Mansion** on Washington Street, constructed on the lines of a French Baroque palace, is now home to best-selling novelist Danielle Steele. Close by, Lafayette Park is one of San Francisco's loveliest hilltop gardens, lined with pine and eucalyptus trees. It offers excellent views of the numerous Victorian houses in the surrounding streets. Located across the street from the park, **2151 Sacramento Street** is an ornate French-style mansion, which has a plaque commemorating a visit by the famous author Sir Arthur Conan Doyle in 1923.

At the center of Pacific Heights is Alta Plaza, a landscaped urban park, where the San Franciscan elite come to relax. Set up in the 1850s, this hilltop green has tennis courts and a playground. The stone steps rising from Clay Street on the south side offer overall views of Haight Ashbury.

North of Pacific Heights, the streets drop steeply down to the Marina District, which was created from reclaimed land for the 1915 Panama-Pacific Exposition. The Expo's only surviving monument is the grand **Palace of Fine Arts**. This Neo-Classical building has a large rotunda with allegorical paintings on its dome. It houses the entertaining Exploratorium Science Museum and hosts events such as the May Film Festival.

**🏛 Haas-Lilienthal House**
2007 Franklin St. ☎ *(415) 441-3004.* 🕐 *noon–3pm Wed & Sat, 11am–4pm Sun.* 🎫 🛍 W www.sfheritage.org

## Asian Art Museum ⑫

**Map** E4. Larkin at Grove St. ☎ *(415) 581-3500.* 🚌 *5, 8, 19, 21, 26, 42, 47, 49.* 🚋 *F, J, K, L, M, N.* 🕐 *9am–5pm Tue–Sun (until 9pm Thu).* 🎫 ♿ 📖 🛍 ☕ W www.asianart.org

The new Asian Art Museum is located on Civic Center Plaza in a building that was the crown jewel of the Beaux Arts movement. The former Main Library, built in 1917, has undergone seismic strengthening and adaptive reuse of space to create the largest museum outside Asia devoted exclusively to Asian art. The new museum's exhibits include 12,000 art objects spanning 6,000 years of history and representing over 40 Asian nations. There are also performance venues and a hands-on discovery center. The terrace café overlooks the Civic Center and Fulton Street Mall.

**The grand staircase at the Asian Art Museum**

### The Sounds of 1960s San Francisco

During the late 1960s, and most notably during the 1967 "Summer of Love," young people from all over the country flocked to the Haight Ashbury district. They came not just to "turn on, tune in, and drop out," but also to listen to rock bands such as Janis Joplin's Big Brother and the Holding Company, Jefferson Airplane, and the Grateful Dead, all of whom emerged out of the thriving music scene. Impresario Bill Graham put unlikely pairs such as Miles Davis and the Grateful Dead on the same bill at Fillmore Auditorium. He also brought in big-name performers such as Jimi Hendrix and The Who, making "the Haight" the focus of the rock world.

**A 1960s street scene in Haight Ashbury**

## Mission Dolores ⑬

**Map** E4. 16th St & Dolores St. *22. J.* *(415) 621-8203.* *daily.* *Thanksgiving, Dec 25.* www.missiondolores.org

PRESERVED INTACT since it was built in 1791, Mission Dolores, after which the surrounding Mission District is named, is the oldest building in the city and an embodiment of San Francisco's Spanish Colonial roots. Founded by Father Junípero Serra as the sixth California mission, it is formally known as the Mission of San Francisco de Asis. The name Dolores reflects its proximity to Laguna de los Dolores (Lake of Our Lady of Sorrows), an ancient swamp. The building is modest by mission standards, but its 4-ft (1.2-m) thick walls have survived.

**Figure of saint in the mission**

Paintings by Native Americans adorn the restored ceiling. There is a fine Baroque altar and reredos, and a display of historical documents in the small museum. Most services are held in the basilica, built adjacent to the mission in 1918. The cemetery contains graves of San Franciscan pioneers, as well as a mass grave of 5,000 Native Americans, who died in the measles epidemics of 1804 and 1826.

**The altarpiece of Mission Dolores, imported from Mexico in 1780**

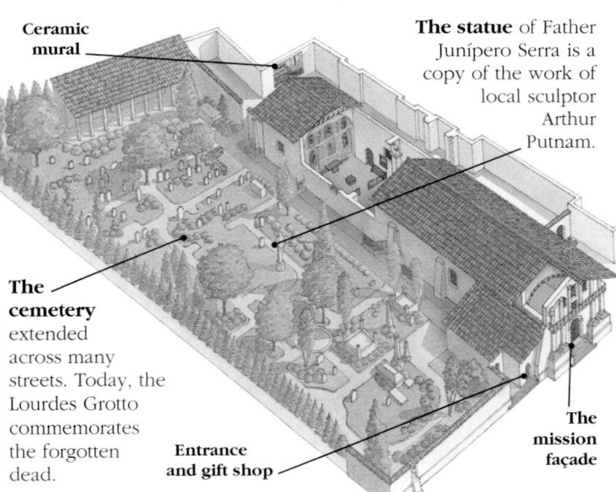


## Haight Ashbury ⑭

**Map** D4. *6, 7, 33, 37, 43, 66, 71.* *N.* **Lower Haight** *6, 7, 22, 66, 71.* *K, L, M.*

STRETCHING FROM Buena Vista Park to Golden Gate Park, Haight Ashbury was the center of the hippie world in the 1960s. Originally a quiet, middle class suburb – hence the dozens of elaborate Queen Anne-style houses – it changed dramatically into the mecca of a free-wheeling, bohemian community that defied social norms and conventions. In 1967, the "Summer of Love," fueled by the media, brought some 75,000 young people in search of free love, music, and drugs, and it became the focus of a worldwide youth culture. Thousands lived here, and there was even a free clinic to treat hippies without medical insurance.

Today, "the Haight" retains its radical atmosphere and has settled into being one of the liveliest and most unconventional places in San Francisco, with an eclectic mix of people, second-hand clothing shops, excellent music and book stores, and a variety of excellent cafés.

Buena Vista Park on its eastern fringe has a mass of knotted trees and offers magnificent views of the city. The grand (Richard) Spreckels Mansion on Buena Vista Avenue (not to be confused with the one on Washington Street), is a typical late-Victorian home. It was once a guest house, and its visitors included writer Jack London and journalist Ambrose Bierce. The **Red Victorian Hotel**, affectionately dubbed the "Jeffrey Haight" in 1967, was a favorite among hippies. It now caters to a New Age clientele and offers rooms with transcendental themes.

**The Red Victorian Hotel in Haight Ashbury, a relic of the hippie era**

Halfway between City Hall and Haight Ashbury, the **Lower Haight** marks the border of the predominantly African-American Fillmore District, which is one of the liveliest parts of the city. Unusual art galleries, boutiques, inexpensive cafés, and bars serve a largely bohemian clientele. It also has dozens of houses known as "Victorians," built from the 1850s to the 1900s, including cottages such as the Nightingale House at 201 Buchanan Street. Although safe during the day, the Lower Haight can be unnerving after dark.

## California Academy of Sciences ⑮

**Map** F3. 875 Howard St near 5th St. *(415) 750-7145.* *5, 9.* *J, K, L.* *call for times.* www.calacademy.org

THE ACADEMY is temporarily located on Howard Street while the building at the southern end of Golden Gate Park undergoes extensive refurbishment; the renovated building is slated to reopen in 2008. Founded in 1853, this is San Francisco's oldest and most popular science museum. It has an outstanding natural history collection, an anthropology section, an aquarium, and a planetarium. The **African Hall**, with its displays of realistic models of animals from Africa's jungles in lifelike dioramas, provides an opportunity to examine big game at close range. The diorama of a watering hole in the African savanna features the changing light and sounds of an African day, compressed into a 20-minute cycle. One of the museum's star exhibits, in its Earth and Space section, is **The Earth Quake!**, where visitors experience earth tremors and learn about their destructive power. The **Morrison Planetarium** has one of the world's most precise star projectors, which transforms the ceiling into the night sky. Popular planetarium shows include "The Sky Tonight" and "Worlds Unseen."

A small percentage of the museum's sizable collection relating to American Indian, Polynesian, Asian, Melanesian, and other cultures is on display at any one time. Navajo and Pueblo artworks are well represented in the superb **Elkus Collection of Native American Art**. Evolutionary history is the subject of the **Life Through Time** section, which has life-sized models of Velociraptors and of a Quetzalcoatlus, the largest flying creature that ever lived. A popular draw is the skeleton of a *Tyrannosaurus rex*.

***Tyrannosaurus rex* skeleton**

The enchanting **Steinhart Aquarium**, the oldest and one of the most diverse aquariums in the US, houses more than 8,000 specimens of tide-pool animals, sea mammals, and other aquatic creatures. Prime attractions here include the Giant Pacific octopus and the Sharks of the Tropics tank. The **Gem and Mineral Hall** contains more than 1,000 specimens of gemstones and minerals, including a 1,350-lb (612-kg) quartz crystal from Arkansas. A special exhibition shows how gemstones are set to make jewelry. In **Wild California**, naturalistic dioramas portray the landscapes and animals of California, with recorded commentaries helping to explain the scenes.

**Lifelike dioramas in the African Hall of the California Academy of Sciences**

## de Young Museum ⑯

**Map** C4. 50 Tea Garden Dr. *(415) 863-3330.* *44.* *9:30am–5:15pm Tue–Sun (until 8:45pm Fri).* *Mon.* *(free 1st Tue of month).* www.thinker.org

THE DE YOUNG museum was founded in 1895 and has been an integral part of Golden Gate Park for more than 100 years. In 1989 the building suffered irreparable damage from an earthquake and the old building closed to make way for a new, seismically stable one. The new museum, which opened in 2005, has double the exhibition space of the old one, but returns nearly two acres of open space to the Park.

The de Young's permanent collection comprises American art from the 17th to the 20th centuries as well as work from nearly 30 countries. There are also special exhibitions held regularly, and outside, there's a sculpture garden and terrace, and a children's garden.

## Legion of Honor ⑰

**Map** C4. 34th Ave & Clement, Lincoln Park. *(415) 750-3600.* *18.* *(415) 863-3330.* *9:30am–5pm Tue–Sun.* *Mon.* *(free on Tue).* *Appointment required to see the Achenbach Collection.* www.thinker.org

INSPIRED BY THE Palais de la Légion d'Honneur in Paris, Alma de Bretteville Spreckels built this museum in the 1920s to promote French art in California. Designed by the architect George Applegarth, it displays European art from the last eight centuries, with paintings by Rembrandt, Monet, and Rubens, and more than 70 sculptures by Rodin. The Achenbach Foundation, a well-known collection of graphic works, occupies a part of the gallery.

The museum's collection of European art is displayed in the galleries on the first floor. The portrait *The Impresario* (1877) by Edgar Degas emphasizes the subject's size by making him appear too large for the frame. Claude Monet's beautiful *Waterlilies* (1914–17) is one of a series depicting the lily pond in his gardens in Giverny, near Paris. The original bronze casting of Rodin's *Le Penseur* (1904), better known as *The Thinker*, is located at the center of the colonnaded Court of Honor. It is one of the 11 castings of the statue in collections around the world. The oil-on-canvas *The Tribute Money* (1612) shows the Flemish artist Peter Paul Rubens' typical use of primary colors.

## The Presidio ⑱

**Map** C3. **Visitor Center** *102 Montgomery St.* ☎ *(415) 561-4323.* ◯ *9am–5pm daily.* ● *public hols.* ♿

To the north of Golden Gate Park, overlooking San Francisco Bay, the Presidio was established as an outpost of Spain's New World empire in 1776. For many years it was a military base but in 1994 it became a national park, with acres of woodland full of wildlife. Remnants of its military past, including the barracks, artillery emplacements, and museum, can be seen. There are also many hiking trails, bike paths, and beaches. The coastal path is one of the city's most popular walks and picnic areas.

The Presidio Museum is part of the new **Mott Visitor Center** in the Main Post area. It houses artifacts relating to the Presidio's long history. Close by, the **Officers' Club** was built over the adobe remains of the original 18th-century Spanish fort, still preserved inside the building. A 19th-century cannon from the Spanish–American War lies across the adjoining parade ground. To the north, close to the bay, is the large, grassy **Crissy Field**, that was reclaimed from marshland for the 1915 Panama-Pacific Exposition. The **Military Cemetery**, east of the visitor center, holds the remains of

**Detail of the 19th-century cannon located on the Presidio grounds**

15,000 American soldiers killed during various wars. At the park's southeast corner, the decorative **Arguello Gate** has military symbols on its surface and marks the entrance to the former army base, now open to the public.

At the northwestern tip of the Presidio, **Fort Point** is an impressive brick fortress that once guarded the Golden Gate during the Civil War and also survived the 1906 earthquake. The fort was built in 1861 to protect San Francisco Bay from attack, and to defend ships carrying gold from the California mines. It is a good place from which to view Golden Gate Bridge and there is also a museum displaying military uniforms and arms.

**Detail, Arguello Gate**

## Golden Gate Bridge ⑲

**Map** B2. Hwy 101, Presidio. ☎ *(415) 923-2000.* 🚌 *2, 4, 8, 10, 18, 20, 28, 29, 50, 72, 76, 80. Pedestrians & cyclists allowed 5am–9pm daily, east walkway only.* ♿ *observation area only.* 🛍

Named after the part of San Francisco Bay called "Golden Gate" by John Frémont in 1844, the Golden Gate Bridge opened in 1937, connecting the city with Marin County. It took just over four years to build, at a cost of $35 million. This world-famous landmark offers breathtaking views; the bridge has six lanes for vehicles plus a free pedestrian walkway. Each year, more than 40 million vehicles cross it, averaging a daily count of about 118,000. It is the world's third largest single-span bridge, stretching 1.7 miles (2.7 km). When it was built, it was the world's longest and tallest suspension structure, rising 746 ft (227 m) above the water.

Designed by Chicago-based engineers Joseph Strauss and Leon Moisseiff, the bridge is a remarkable feat of engineering. The mammoth structure was built to withstand 100 mph (160 km/h) winds. Its south pier was sunk 100 ft (30 m) into the seabed, while each pier supports a 44,000-ton steel tower. The original coat of paint lasted for 27 years, but since 1965 it has needed continuous painting. The two 7,650-ft (2,332-m) cables are more than 3 ft (1 m) thick and contain 80,000 miles (128,744 km) of steel wire, enough to circle the earth at the equator three times. The best views are available from the Marin County side.

**The Golden Gate Bridge, with a single span of 4,200 ft (1,280 m)**

## Greater San Francisco

Many of the settlements encircling San Francisco Bay were once summer retreats for the city's residents, but today they are sprawling suburbs or cities in their own right. Two popular destinations in the East Bay are Oakland's museum and Berkeley's famous university. The landmark San Francisco–Oakland Bay Bridge stretches 4.5 miles (7.2 km) and is crossed by 250,000 vehicles a day – even more than the Golden Gate. Farther south, San Jose combines the technology of Silicon Valley with fine museums and Spanish Colonial architecture. To the north is the rocky coastline of the Marin Headlands, with its abundant wildlife.

### San Jose ⑳

*846,000.* *65 Cahill St.* *70 Almeden St.* *180 S Market St, (888) 726-5673.* *Festival of the Arts (Sep).* www.sanjose.org

The only other original Spanish Colonial town in California apart from Los Angeles, San Jose was founded in 1777 by Felipe de Neve and has become the state's third largest city. It is now the commercial and cultural center of South Bay and the civic heart of Silicon Valley.

The **Mission Santa Clara de Asis**, on the campus of the Jesuit University of Santa Clara, is a modern replica of the adobe original, first built in 1777. Relics include bells given to the missionaries by the Spanish monarchy. The large **Rosicrucian Egyptian Museum and Planetarium** has an extensive collection of ancient Egyptian artifacts. Displays include mummies, burial tombs, and toys, some of which date to 1500 BC. There are replicas of the sarcophagus in which Tutankhamen was discovered in 1922, and the Rosetta Stone.

At the heart of San Jose, the fascinating **Tech Museum of Innovation** is crowded with hands-on exhibits, encouraging visitors to discover how technological inventions work. Here, the focus is on understanding the workings of computer hardware and software.

The **Winchester Mystery House**, on the outskirts of town, has a remarkable history. Sarah Winchester, widow and heiress of the Winchester Rifle fortune, was told by a medium that the expansion of her farmhouse would exorcise the spirits of those killed by the rifle. She kept builders working 24 hours a day, 7 days a week, for 38 years, until her death in 1922. The result is a bizarre complex of 160 rooms, including stairs that lead nowhere and windows set into floors. The total cost amounted to $5.5 million.

**Organ, Winchester Mystery House**

The center of the computer industry, **Silicon Valley** covers about 100 sq miles (260 sq km) from Palo Alto to San Jose. The name refers to myriad businesses rather than a specific location. The seeds of the hardware and software industries were sown in the 1980s at Stanford University, at the Xerox Palo Alto Research Center, and in the garages of pioneers William Hewlett, David Packard, and later Steve Jobs and Stephen Wozniak, who invented the Apple personal computer. Many world-class firms are based here.

#### Winchester Mystery House

525 S Winchester Blvd. *(408) 247-2000.* *check for times.* *Dec 25.* *gardens only.*

***The Thinker* by Auguste Rodin at the Stanford Museum of Art**

### Palo Alto ㉑

**Stanford University** *(650) 723-2053.* **Visitor Center** *11am–3:15pm except during winter break.* *university hols; call ahead.*

Among the most pleasant of the Bay Area suburbs, Palo Alto grew up to serve Stanford University, one of the most reputed centers of education in the US. It was founded in 1891 by the railroad tycoon Leland Stanford in honor of his son who died at the age of 16. The campus covers 8,200 acres (3,320 ha), and is larger than the downtown district of San Francisco. Designed in a mixture of Romanesque and Mission styles, its sandstone buildings are capped by red-tiled roofs. The Memorial Church is decorated with gold-leaf and tile mosaic. The **Stanford Museum of Art** holds one of the largest collections of sculptures by Auguste Rodin, including the impressive *Gates of Hell.*

### Oakland ㉒

*387,000.* *1245 Broadway St.* *(510 874-4800).* *Festival at the Lake (Jun).*

At one time a small, working-class suburb of San Francisco, Oakland grew into a flourishing city when it became the West Coast terminus of the transcontinental railroad. Many of the African Americans who worked on the railroad settled here, later followed by the Hispanics, giving Oakland a multicultural atmosphere that continues to this day. Its literary associations, including Jack London and Gertrude Stein, have also enhanced the area as a cultural center.

**Jack London Square** on the waterfront was named after author Jack London who grew up in Oakland in the 1880s and frequently visited the area. Today, it is a bright promenade of shops, restaurants, and pleasure boats. The Jack London Museum contains books, photographs, and memorabilia. To the east, the **Oakland Museum of California** is dedicated to documenting California's art, history, and ecology. The Cowell Hall of California History has a large collection of Californian artifacts, while the Gallery of California Art is famous for early oil paintings of San Francisco.

To the north, the two blocks of **Old Oakland** (also known as Victorian Row) attract crowds of shoppers. Northern California's only **Mormon Temple**, situated on a hilltop on the eastern edge of the city, offers great views of the Bay Area. Its central ziggurat is surrounded by four towers, all clad with white granite and capped by golden pyramids.

**Oakland Museum of California**
*Oak & 10th Sts.* *(510) 238-2200.* *10am–5pm Wed–Sat, noon–5pm Sun.* *Jan 1, Thanksgiving, Dec 25, Mon & Tue.* *(free 2nd Sun).* www.museumca.org

## Berkeley ㉓

*104,900.* *2160 Shattuck Ave.* *1834 University Ave, (800) 847-4823* *Fourth of July Fireworks; Telegraph Ave Book Fair (Jul).*

Berkeley began to boom after the earthquake of 1906, when many San Franciscans fled their city and settled on the East Bay. It was the seat of the student uprisings against the Vietnam War in the 1960s, earning itself the nickname "Beserkeley." Many

**Model of DNA at the Lawrence Hall of Science, UC Berkeley**

stores still hark to the hippie era with psychedelic merchandise, but in recent years Berkeley has begun to change its profile. Stylish restaurants have emerged, as well as a reputation for fine food; it was here that the popular California cuisine was born.

Berkeley is essentially a university town. The **University of California at Berkeley's** reputation for countercultural movements sometimes eclipses its academic reputation, yet with its student body of 30,000, it is one of the country's most prestigious institutions. Founded in 1868, it has at least ten Nobel laureates among its professors. There are many museums, cultural amenities, and noteworthy buildings to visit. The **University Art Museum** includes works by Piccasso and Cézanne among its exhibits. The main campus landmark, the 307-ft (94-m) **Sather Tower** and the splendid **Lawrence Hall of Science** are all outstanding.

To the south, the **Telegraph Avenue** was the center of student protest in the 1960s. Today, this fascinating street swarms with students, musicians, street vendors, and eccentrics. There is also a plethora of bookstores, coffee houses, and cheap eateries. North of the University, **Shattuck Avenue**, nicknamed "Gourmet Ghetto," is known for its restaurants.

**University of California at Berkeley**
*(510) 642-6000.* **University Art Museum** *(510) 642-0808.* *Wed–Sun.* *public hols.*

## Sausalito ㉔

*7,300.* *777 Bridgeway Ave, 4th floor, (415) 332-0505.*

In this small town, Victorian bungalows cling to hills rising from San Francisco Bay. Bridgeway Avenue along the waterfront serves as a promenade for crowds that patronize the restaurants and shops and enjoy the views. The **Bay Model Visitor Center** is a fascinating model simulating the tides in San Francisco Bay.

**Bay Model Visitor Center**
2100 Bridgeway Ave. *(415) 332-3871.* *Sep–May: Tue–Fri; Jun–Aug: Tue–Sun.* *public hols.*

## Muir Woods ㉕

*Mill Valley.* **Visitor Center** *Hwy 1, Mill Valley, (415) 388-2595.* *8am–5pm daily*

Nestling at the foot of Mount Tamalpais is Muir Woods National Monument, one of the few remaining stands of old-growth coastal redwoods. Before the 19th-century lumber industry boom, these tall trees (the oldest is 1,000 years old) covered the Californian coastline. The woods were named in honor of John Muir, the naturalist responsible for turning Yosemite into a national park *(see p718)*. Muir Beach nearby is a wide expanse of sand, usually crowded during the summer weekends.

**Muir Woods, the last remaining redwood forest in the Bay Area**

# San Francisco Practical Information

San Francisco occupies a compact area, making it a sightseer's dream. Its efficient transportation system has cable cars, buses, Muni Metro, and BART lines. The city prides itself on its variety of cultural and entertainment opportunities, which make it one of the most enjoyable vacation spots in the world. The Civic Center is the main venue for classical music, opera, and ballet, while pop music – in particular jazz and blues – is where the city really excels. There are also diverse theater companies and specialty movie houses.

## Tourist Information

Visitors planning a trip will find the *San Francisco Book*, published twice yearly by the **San Francisco Convention and Visitors' Bureau**, very helpful. It is available free at the **Visitor Information Center** at Hallidie Plaza. Complete listings of what's on are given in the *San Francisco Chronicle* and *Examiner* newspapers; the *Chronicle's* Sunday edition is very useful. Other sources are the weekly newspapers, such as the *San Francisco Weekly* or the *San Francisco Bay Guardian*. These give both listings and reviews, especially of live music, films, and nightclubs. For details on events, call the visitors' bureau's Events Line.

## Getting Around

The best way to explore San Francisco is on foot, although the hills can be strenuous. The city's main sights all lie within 15 to 20 minutes of each other. City taxis are licensed and operate 24 hours a day. **City Cab** and Yellow Cab are good bets.

The San Francisco Municipal Railway or **Muni**, runs the city's transportation system. The Muni Passport, valid for 1, 3, or 7 days can be used for unlimited travel on Muni buses, Muni Metro streetcars, as well as San Francisco's three cable car lines. These are available at the Visitor Information Center.

Buses and streetcars serve all areas. Buses stop only at designated places, every few blocks, and route numbers are printed on the buses. Muni Metro streetcars and BART trains both use the same underground terminals on Market Street. The high-speed BART trains stop at five downtown stations: Van Ness, Civic Center, Powell, Montgomery, and Embarcadero.

San Francisco's famous cable cars operate from 6:30am to 12:30am daily, at 15-minute intervals. Cars run on three routes; the popular Powell–Hyde line, the Powell–Mason line, and the California line.

Boats and passenger ferries are also a fun way to get around the city's shoreline. The Ferry Building is the terminal for the **Golden Gate Ferries**. Bay sightseeing cruises from Fisherman's Wharf are operated by the **Blue & Gold Fleet**. **Hornblower Dining Yachts** offer lunch on Friday, brunch on weekends, and dinner daily on their cruises.

Other modes of travel include bicycles, which can be rented for around $25 a day or $125 a week. Details of scenic routes are available from the **Start to Finish** rental. Pedicabs and horse-drawn cabs are found on the Embarcadero. Sightseeing bus tours are also available.

## Sports & Outdoor Activities

The city has plenty of options for sports fans. The home ground of the San Francisco 49ers is 3-Com Park. Other football teams are supported by local colleges, UC Berkeley, and Stanford University. Two professional baseball teams play in the Bay Area, the National League San Francisco Giants (in Pacific Bell Park) and the American League Oakland Athletics (in the McAfee Coliseum).

Golfers have a range of courses to choose from, including the municipal links in **Lincoln Park**. Most of the public swimming pools are located in the suburbs; for details contact the **City of San Francisco Recreation and Parks Department**. To swim in the chilly ocean, head out to China Beach. There are tennis courts in almost all the public parks, with the largest ones in Golden Gate Park. **Claremont Resort Spa and Tennis Club** in Berkeley offers fine courts with unlimited playing time even to non-guests.

## Entertainment

San Francisco offers visitors an unending variety of high-quality entertainment. It has an avid film-going community, and one of the best movie houses is the **AMC Kabuki**, an eight-screen complex in the Japan Center, which also hosts the San Francisco **International Film Festival** each May. The main venue for first-run foreign films is the **Opera Plaza**. For theater goers, major shows are staged at Theater District venues, the two largest being the **Curran Theater** for Broadway shows; and the Geary Theater, now home to the **American Conservatory Theater (ACT)**, which performs October through May.

The **San Francisco Opera Association** season runs from September to December; tickets can cost more than $100, but there is a summer season with less expensive tickets. The **Civic Center** complex on Van Ness Avenue offers opera, classical music, and dance. The **San Francisco Ballet** season runs from February to April, while the Yerba Buena Center for the Arts is home to the **LINES Contemporary Ballet**.

Two of the best rock clubs, **Slim's** and **Paradise Lounge**, are opposite one another in the SoMa district. Another popular place is the **Fillmore Auditorium**, the legendary birthplace of psychedelic rock during the 1960s. There are a number of places to hear live jazz, such as **Jazz at Pearl's**, and live blues is played in bars such as **The Saloon**. The annual **San Francisco Blues Festival** attracts blues bands from all over the country.

The **Bambuddha Lounge** has some of San Francisco's best DJs. The clientele here is mainstream, but some of the most popular clubs are primarily, though rarely exclusively, gay. These include **Rawhide II**, which has square dancing every night.

Piano bars all have nightly live music. One of the best is the Art Deco-style **Top of the Mark** at the top of the Mark Hopkins InterContinental Hotel. **Cobb's Comedy Club** stages a great comedy show.

San Francisco also has a number of free concerts that are regularly staged all over the city. Watch for the San Francisco Symphony Orchestra in late summer at Stern Grove. The San Francisco Opera performs in Golden Gate Park in the "Opera in the Park" event. The summer Shakespeare Festival is also held here.

## SHOPPING

SHOPPING IN SAN FRANCISCO is a complete experience that allows a glimpse into the city's culture. The diversity of San Francisco makes buying anything here an adventure. An enormous range of goods is available, from the practical to the more eccentric, but you can take your time in choosing, since browsers are made to feel welcome, particularly in the many small specialty shops and boutiques. Guided shopping tours are available for those who want to be directed to the best shops.

For visitors who want convenience, the numerous shopping centers, such as the Embarcadero Center and Japan Center, are excellent.

Similarly, huge retail department stores such as **Macy's** and **Neiman Marcus** offer an outstanding selection of goods and services.

The city's innovative entrepreneurial spirit is evident in its specialty shops, such as the humorous art at **Smile–A Gallery with Tongue in Chic** or the non-electric toys at **Gamescapes**.

A mecca for designer wear, the city is home to the famous **Levis Strauss & Co**, which has been making jeans since 1853 and offers factory tours on Tuesdays and Wednesdays to visitors. For discount designer wear, head to the trendy SoMa district.

Book lovers should head for **A Clean Well-Lighted Place for Books**, or the famous Beat hideout **City Lights Bookstore**, which stays open late and is a famous San Francisco institution.

Art lovers will find something to their liking in the city's hundreds of galleries, featuring works by emerging and more established artists as well as expressions of Native American folk artists.

The city is also home to many dedicated "foodies," gastronomes whose liking for fine wine and gourmet meals have resulted in unusual and delicious grocery stores. Regular farmers' markets, held in the center of the city, abound in locally grown fruit and vegetables, while seafood and wines from **Napa Valley Winery Exchange** figure among the city's best buys.

## DIRECTORY

### TOURIST OFFICES

**San Francisco Convention & Visitors' Bureau**
(415) 974-6900.

**Visitor Information Center**
(415) 391-2000.
sfvisitor.org

### PUBLIC TRANSPORTION

**Blue & Gold Fleet**
(415) 773-1188.

**City Cab**
(415) 920-0700.

**Golden Gate Ferries**
(415) 923-2000.

**Muni Information**
(415) 673-6864.
www.sfmuni.com

### FILM & THEATER

**American Conservatory Theater (ACT)**
(415) 749-2228.

**AMC Kabuki**
(415) 346-3243.

### OPERA, CLASSICAL MUSIC, & DANCE

**LINES Contemporary Ballet**
Yerba Buena Center for the Arts, 700 Howard St.
(415) 978-2787.

**San Francisco Opera Assn.**
301 Van Ness Ave.
(415) 861-4008.

**San Francisco Symphony Assn.**
201 Van Ness Ave.
(415) 864-6000.

### JAZZ

**Jazz at Pearl's**
256 Columbus Ave.
(415) 291-8255.

### CLUBS

**Bambuddha Lounge**
601 Eddy St.
(415) 885-5088.

### SPORTS & OUTDOOR ACTIVITIES

**Recreation & Parks Department**
Tennis Information.
(415) 831-6302.
Swimming Information.
(415) 831-2747.

### SHOPPING

**City Lights Bookstore**
261 Columbus Ave.
(415) 362-8193.

**A Clean Well-Lighted Place for Books**
601 Van Ness Ave.
(415) 441-6670.

**Gamescapes**
333 Divisadero St.
(415) 621-4263.

**Levi Strauss & Co**
250 Valencia St.
(415) 565-9159.

**Macy's**
Stockton & O'Farrell Sts.
(415) 397-3333.

**Napa Valley Winery Exchange**
415 Taylor St.
(415) 771-2887.

**Neiman Marcus**
150 Stockton St.
(415) 362-3900.

**Smile–A Gallery with Tongue in Chic**
500 Sutter St.
(415) 362-3437.

# The Wine Country

BORN IN THE SONOMA VALLEY in 1823, when Franciscan priests planted grapes to make sacramental wines, California's wine industry was taken to new heights by the flamboyant Hungarian Count Agoston Haraszthy in 1857. Known as the "Father of California Wine," he planted European grapes in the state's first big vineyard at the revered Buena Vista Winery. Today, in addition to its superb wines and vineyards, the Wine Country is known for its mild climate, rocky landscapes, secluded beaches, redwood groves, and impressive architecture.

**View of vineyards in the Sonoma Valley, famous for wineries**

## Sonoma Valley 22

*8,600.* *90 Broadway & W Napa Sts, Sonoma Plaza.* *453 1st St E, (707) 996-1090.* *Valley of the Moon Vintage Festival (late Sep).* www.sonomavalley.com

NESTLING IN THE crescent-shaped Sonoma Valley are 6,000 acres (2,400 ha) of beautiful vineyards. At the foot of the valley lies the tiny town of Sonoma. This town has had a colorful past, as it was here on June 14, 1846, that about 30 American farmers captured Mexican General Mariano Vallejo and his men, to protest the fact that land ownership was reserved for Mexican citizens. They seized control of Sonoma, declared California an independent republic, and flew their own flag, with a crude drawing of a grizzly bear. Although the republic was annulled 25 days later when the United States annexed California, the Bear Flag design was adopted as the official state flag in 1911.

Sonoma's main attractions are its world-famous wineries and meticulously preserved historical sites lining the Spanish-style plaza. Many of the adobe buildings house wine shops, boutiques, and restaurants serving excellent local cuisine. East of the plaza is the restored **Mission San Francisco Solano de Sonoma**, the last of California's 21 historic Franciscan missions (founded by Father José Altimira of Spain in 1823). Today, all that survives of the original building is the corridor of his quarters. The adobe chapel was built by General Vallejo in 1840.

A short drive northward leads to the **Jack London State Historic Park**. In the early 1900s, London, the famous author of *The Call of the Wild* and *The Sea Wolf*, abandoned his hectic lifestyle to live in this tranquil 800-acre (325-ha) expanse of oaks, madrones, and redwoods. The park retains eerie ruins of London's dream home, the Wolf House, mysteriously destroyed by fire just before completion. After London's death, his widow, Charmian Kittredge, built a magnificent home on the ranch, called the House of Happy Walls. Today, the house has been made into a museum, worth a visit for its display of London memorabilia.

**Mission San Francisco Solano de Sonoma**
E Spain St. *(707) 938-9560.* *daily.* *Jan 1, Thanksg., Dec 25.*

**Jack London Historic State Park**
London Ranch Rd, Glen Ellen. *(707) 938-5216.* **Park & Museum** *daily.* *Jan 1, Thanksgiving, Dec 25.* *museum only.*

## Napa Valley 23

*115,000.* *1310 Town Center Mall, Napa, (707) 226-7459.* *Napa Valley Mustard Festival (Feb–Apr).*

LYING AT the heart of California's wine industry, the 35-mile (56-km) sliver of land known as Napa Valley encompasses the towns of Yountville, Oakville, St. Helena, Rutherford, and Calistoga. More than 250 wineries are scattered across its hillsides and valleys, some dating from the early 19th century. Prominent among these is the **Mumm Napa Valley** winery, partly owned by French champagne producer G.H. Mumm, where wines are made in the classic tradition. To its north, the **Rutherford Hill Winery** features caves dug into the hillsides, for aging wines. Farther north, the modern **Clos Pegase** winery is famed for its distinctive art collection and superior wines.

**Statue at Clos Pegase**

For a bird's-eye view of the valley, visitors can take hot-air balloon trips over the Wine Country from Yountville or a three-hour luxury tour in the Napa Valley Wine Train, enjoying gourmet cuisine. But the best way to explore the valley is along a scenic 40-mile (64-km) drive, stopping along the way at the B&B inns in the towns of St. Helena and Calistoga. The latter is popular for its spa treatments and good Wine Country cuisine, prepared with the freshest ingredients. A few miles north of Calistoga, the Old Faithful Geyser spouts jets of boiling mineral water 60 ft (18 m) into the sky, once every 40 minutes. To the west lies the **Petrified Forest**, home of the largest petrified trees in the world – huge redwoods which were turned to stone by a volcanic eruption that took place more than three million years ago.

**Petrified Forest**
4100 Petrified Forest Rd. *(707) 942-6667. daily. Thanksgiving, Dec 25. limited.*

**The Clos Pegase winery designed by Michael Graves, Napa Valley**

## Russian River Valley 24

*from Healdsburg. 16209 1st St, Guerneville, (707) 869-9000.*
www.russianriverchamber.com

Bisected by the Russian River and its tributaries, this valley contains many smaller valleys, dotted with vineyards, apple orchards, redwood groves, family farms, and sandy river beaches. At its hub is the town of **Healdsburg**, with a splendid Spanish-style town square lined with shops, restaurants, and cafés.

Southwest of Healdsburg lies **Guerneville**, a summer haven for San Francisco's gay population. Every September, the town hosts the famous Russian River Jazz Festival at Johnson's Beach, where visitors can take a canoe or raft down the gentle Russian River. Otters and blue herons can be often be seen here.

Hikers and equestrians also flock to Guerneville to visit the 805-acre (330-ha) **Armstrong Redwoods State Reserve**, one of the few remaining old-growth redwood forests in California. Among its redwoods is a 308-ft (94-m) giant – a 1,400-year-old tree named Colonel Armstrong.

**Armstrong Redwoods State Preserve**
17000 Armstrong Woods Rd, Guerneville. *(707) 869-2015, 865-2391. daily.*

## Fort Ross State Historic Park 25

*(707) 847-3286. from Point Arena. sunrise–sunset daily. Thanksgiving, Dec 25.*
www.mcn.org/one/rrparks/fortress

On a windswept headland north of Jenner stands this well-restored Russian trading outpost, founded in 1812 (the name "Ross" is a derivative of the Russian word "Rossyia," meaning Russia). The Russians were the first Europeans to visit the region, serving as representatives of a Russian-American Company, established in 1799. They never tried to expand their territory in California and abandoned the fort after 30 years of peaceful trading.

Built in 1836, the house of the fort's last manager, Alexander Rotchev, is still intact. Within the wooden palisade are several other reconstructed buildings. The most impressive is the 1824 Russian Orthodox chapel. Every July, a living history day is held, in which costumed actors recreate life at the outpost.

**Town of Mendocino perched on the rocky Mendocino headlands**

## Mendocino 26

*1,200. 332 N Main St, Fort Bragg, (707) 961-6300.*
www.mendocinocoast.com

The founders of this fishing village came to California from New England in 1852, building their new homes to resemble those they had left behind. The Mendocino coastline is thus often referred to as "California's New England Coast." Perched on a rocky promontory above the Pacific Ocean, Mendocino retains the picturesque charm of its days as a fishing center. Its heather-covered bluffs, migrating gray whales, and stunning ocean vistas make it a popular tourist center, yet the town seems untarnished by commercialism. It is a thriving arts center with a large number of resident artists and writers. Visitors can stroll around the many exclusive boutiques, art galleries, bookshops, and cafés.

### California Wines

With over 327,000 acres (132,000 ha) of land under viticulture, California produces 90 percent of the nation's wine. Its latitude, proximity to the ocean, and sheltered valleys create a mild climate, ideal for growing grapes. Half the grapes grown here are harvested from the fertile stretch of land bordered by the Sacramento Valley to the north and San Joaquin Valley to the south. The north coast, home to most of the state's 800 wineries, accounts for less than a quarter of California's wine-growing acreage, but produces many of the country's best Sauvignon Blanc, Cabernet Sauvignon, Merlot, and Chardonnay grapes. Chardonnay and Pinot Noir grapes are the mainstays of the central coast region, which extends from the San Francisco Bay Area to Santa Barbara.

**Sparkling Cuvee Napa by Mumm**

# Northern California

RUGGED AND SPARSELY populated, Northern California has a diverse landscape of dense forests, volcanic mountains, and arid plains. It also has the world's largest concentration of giant redwood trees, now protected by national parks. Scenic routes in the parks offer visitors a chance to view their awesome beauty. To experience the full immensity of the trees, however, it is best to walk around in these majestic groves.

Avenue of the Giants in the Humboldt Redwoods State Park

## Humboldt Redwoods State Park 27

US Hwy 101. Garberville. **Visitor Center** Weott (707) 946-2263. *Apr–Oct: 9am–5pm; Nov–Mar: 10am–4pm.* *Thanksg., Dec 25.*

THIS PARK HAS the world's tallest redwood trees and the most extensive primeval redwood groves. The tallest individual specimen, the 364-ft (110-m) Dyersville Giant, was blown over by a storm in 1991. Now seen lying on its side, its size appears even more astounding.

The serpentine 33-mile (53-km) **Avenue of the Giants** runs through the 52,000-acre (21,053-ha) park. The visitor center is halfway along the road.

To the north is the town of **Scotia**, built in 1887 to house the workers of the Pacific Lumber Company's massive redwood mill. Scotia is the only complete lumber community still in existence in California. Its small museum traces the history of the town, and of the lumber industry, as well as offers self-guided tours of the lumber mill.

## Eureka 28

*27,600.* *2112 Broadway, (707) 442-3738.*

FOUNDED BY gold miners in 1850, Eureka was named after the state's ancient Greek motto, meaning "I have found it." Today, it is the northern coast's largest industrial center, with extensive logging and fishing operations surrounding the state-protected natural harbor. Its Old Town's many restored 19th-century buildings have been converted into fashionable cafés, bars, and restaurants.

Eureka also houses the 1885 Carson Mansion, home of the millionaire lumber baron William Carson, and now a private club. Its Gothic design is enhanced by its redwood construction, painted to resemble stone.

## Redwood National Park 29

Arcata to Crescent City is 78 miles (125km). US Hwy 101 is the quickest route. www.nationalpark.com/redwood

SOME OF THE largest original redwood forests in the world are preserved in this national park. Stretching along the coastline, the 58,000-acre (23,500-ha) park includes many smaller state parks and can be explored along a day-long drive. A two-day trip, however, allows time to walk away from the roads and experience the tranquility of the stately groves, or spot one of the world's last remaining herds of Roosevelt elk.

The park's headquarters are in **Crescent City**, a few miles north of which lies the 9,200-acre (3,720-ha) Jedediah Smith Redwoods State Park, with the most awe-inspiring coastal redwoods. Named after the fur trapper Jedediah Smith, the first white man who walked across the US, it has excellent campground facilities. South from Crescent City, the **Trees of Mystery** grove features unusual looking fiberglass statues of

### REDWOODS & THE LUMBER INDUSTRY

The tallest tree on earth, the coniferous coastal redwood *(Sequoia sempervirens)* is unique to the northwest coast. It can live for 2,000 years and reach 350 ft (105 m), with roots that grow up to 200 ft (60 m) horizontally but only 4–6 ft (1–2 m) deep. Its fast growth and resistance to disease makes it ideal for commercial use. By the 1920s, however, logging had destroyed 90 percent of the groves. The Save the Redwoods League was formed, buying land now under state park protection. Lumber firms still own some groves, and their future remains a major environmental issue, both locally and nationally.

Redwood lumber

the mythical lumberjack Paul Bunyan and his faithful ox, Babe *(see p419)*. The park's main attraction is the world's tallest tree, a 368-ft (112-m) giant, standing in the **Tall Trees Grove**. Farther south is Big Lagoon, a freshwater lake stretching for 3 miles (5 km) and two other estuaries. Together, they form the **Humboldt Lagoons State Park**. The headlands at Patrick's Point State Park, at the southern end, are a good place to watch for migrating gray whales in winter.

## Weaverville ㉚

*3,500.* *317 Main St, (530) 623-6101.* www.trinitycounty.com

THIS SMALL RURAL town has changed little since it was founded by gold prospectors 150 years ago. The **Jake Jackson Museum**, in the heart of the small commercial district, traces the history of the town and its surrounding gold mining and lumber region. Next door, the **Joss House State Historic Site** is the country's oldest and best-preserved Chinese temple. Built in 1874, it is a reminder of the many Chinese immigrants who came to the US to mine gold, and stayed on as cheap labor to build the California railroads.

North of Weaverville, the Trinity Alps rise up at the center of beautiful mountain wilderness. The mountains are popular with hikers and backpackers in summer and with cross-country skiers during the winter months.

## Mount Shasta ㉛

*Dunsmuir.* *Siskiyou.* *Shasta.* **Visitor Center** *(530) 926-4865.* *daily.* www.mtshastachamber.com

AT A HEIGHT of 14,162 ft (4,316 m) Mount Shasta is the second highest of the Cascade Mountains, after Mount Rainier in Washington *(see pp626–7)*. Visible more than 100 miles (160 km) away and usually covered with

**Mount Shasta, towering over the town of Shasta below**

snow, the summit is a popular destination for adventure sports enthusiasts such as mountaineers. At its foothills lies the picturesque town of **Shasta**, which was once one of the state's largest gold mining camps. Today, Shasta makes a welcome base with plenty of good places to stay.

## Lava Beds National Monument ㉜

*(530) 667-2282.* *Klamath Falls.* *daily.*

SPREADING OVER 46,500 acres (18,800 ha) of the Modoc Plateau, this eerie landscape of lava flows has over 200 caves and lava tubes – those cylindrical tunnels created by exposed lava turning to stone. Most of the volcanic caves lie near the visitor center, where visitors can take ranger-led or self-guided tours down into the caves. To visit any of the caves, wear sturdy shoes, carry a flashlight, and check first with the visitor center.

The park is also notable as the site of the 1872–73 Modoc War, one of the many conflicts between the US and the Native Americans. For six months a group of Modoc Indians, under the command of "Captain Jack," evaded the US Cavalry from a natural fortress of passageways along the park's northern border. The captain was eventually hanged, and the rest were forced into a reservation in what is now Oklahoma.

## Lassen Volcanic National Park ㉝

*Chester, Red Bluff.* **Visitor Center** *(530) 595-4444.* *daily.*

BEFORE THE eruption of Mount St. Helens in Washington in 1980 *(see p629)*, the 10,457-ft (3,187-m) high Lassen Peak was the last volcano to erupt on mainland US. In nearly 300 eruptions between 1914 and 1917, it laid 100,000 acres (40,500 ha) of the surrounding land to waste.

Lassen Peak is considered to be still active. Numerous areas on its flanks show clear signs of the geological processes. The boardwalk trail of Bumpass Hell (named for an early guide, who lost his leg in a boiling mudpot in 1865) leads past a series of steaming sulfurous pools of boiling water, heated by molten rock deep underground. In summer, visitors can take the winding road through the park, climbing more than 8,500 ft (2,590 m) high to Summit Lake. The road continues winding its way through the so-called Devastated Area, a bleak gray landscape of rough volcanic mudflows, which terminates at the Manzanita Lake, and the **Loomis Museum**.

### Loomis Museum

Lassen Park Rd, N Entrance. *(530) 595-4444.* *late Jun–mid-Sep: daily.*

**Sulfur springs in Lassen Volcanic National Park**

# The Gold Country

LOCATED AT THE HEART of California, the Gold Country was once a real life El Dorado, where a thick vein of gold sat waiting to be discovered. Once home of the Miwok and Maidu peoples, the Gold Rush turned this quiet region into a lawless jamboree of gold miners from all over the world. But the boom went bust by 1860. A few years later, the area saw another short-lived boom, when the transcontinental railroad was constructed through the Sierra Nevada Mountains by low-paid laborers, many of whom were Chinese.

**Firehouse #1 Museum, a Nevada City landmark**

## Nevada City 34

*2,855. 132 Main St, (530) 265-2692.*

LOCATED AT THE northern end of the Mother Lode gold fields, this picturesque city deserves its reputation as the "Queen of the Northern Mines." But the once thriving city faded into oblivion after the Gold Rush subsided. It was resurrected as a tourist destination a century later with galleries, restaurants, and inns re-creating Gold Rush themes. The town boasts one of the region's most photographed façades in the **Firehouse #1 Museum**, with its dainty balconies and white cupola. It is now a local history museum. Antique mining devices are displayed across the street. Other historic buildings include the Nevada Theater, a performance venue since 1865, and the National Hotel. One of California's oldest hotels, it first opened in the mid-1850s.

## Grass Valley 35

*9,000. 248 Mill St, (530) 273-4667.*

ONE OF THE largest and busiest gold mining towns, Grass Valley employed workers from the tin mines of Cornwall in England. It was their expertise that enabled local mines to stay in business long after the others had fallen quiet. At the entrance to the town's **North Star Mining Museum** are the giant Pelton wheel that increased production in underground mines. Also on view are a stamp mill (for crushing ore) and a Cornish pump which was used to filter out water.

**A nugget of gold set inside quartz crystal**

Grass Valley also served the nearby **Empire Mine**, the state's richest and longest surviving gold mine. Now a state park, the mine had recovered almost six million ounces of gold when it closed in 1956. Mining equipment and artifacts can be seen in the park and in the museum, but it is Empire Cottage, the mine's owner home that embodies the mine's riches.

**North Star Mining Museum**
*Mill St at Allison Ranch Rd. (530) 273-4255. Apr–Oct: daily.*

**Empire Mine State Park**
*(530) 273-8522. daily. Jan 1, Thanksgiving, Dec 25.*

## Marshall Gold Discovery State Park 36

*(530) 622-3470. from Placerville. 8am–5pm daily. Jan 1, Thanksg, Dec 25.*

THIS PEACEFUL park protects the site where gold was first discovered in 1848. James Marshall spotted shiny flakes in the water channel of a sawmill he and other workers were building for the Swiss entrepreneur John Sutter. Gold miners soon took over Sutter's land leaving him penniless. Within a year, Coloma had turned into a thriving city but then declined, with news of richer deposits elsewhere.

A replica of **Sutter's Mill** stands on the original site, and a statue of Marshall marks his grave. The park's Gold Country Museum features Native American artifacts, films, and other exhibits on the discovery of gold.

**Reconstructed Sutter's Mill, Marshall Gold Discovery State Park**

## Sacramento 37

*30, 31, 32.* *(916) 442-7644.* www.oldsacramento.com

FOUNDED BY John Sutter in 1839, California's capital city preserves many historic buildings along the waterfront in Old Sacramento. Most of the structures date from the 1860s, when it became the supply point for miners. Both the transcontinental railroad and Pony Express had their western terminus here, with riverboats providing passage to San Francisco. The **California State Railroad Museum**, at the northern edge of the old town, houses some immaculately restored locomotives. A little away from the old city, the State Capitol stands in a landscaped park. To its east, Sutter's Fort is a re-creation of the town's original settlement.

**California State Railroad Museum**
111 I St. *(916) 445-6645.* *10am–5pm daily.* *Jan 1, Thanksgiving, Dec 25.*

**CALIFORNIA STATE CAPITOL**

Designed in 1860 in grand Renaissance Revival style, this building was completed in 1874. Housing the office of the governor and the state senate chambers, the Capitol also serves as a museum of the state's political and cultural history.

**The Capitol Rotunda** was restored to its original 19th-century splendor in 1975.

**Original 1860 statuary**

**Entrance**

**The Historic Offices** on the first floor contain a few government offices restored to their turn-of-the-century appearance.

## Highway 49 38

*542 Main St, Placerville, (530) 621-5885.*

THE GOLD COUNTRY offers one of California's best scenic drives, through rocky ridges and flowing rivers, along Highway 49. Many of the towns it passes through, such as **Sutter Creek**, have survived unchanged since the Gold Rush. Named after John Sutter, this scenic town grew up to service the Old Eureka Mine, owned by Hetty Green, the "Richest Woman in the World." Leland Stanford, the railroad baron, made his fortune here, by investing in the town's Lincoln Mine. He used the money to become a railroad magnate and then the governor of California.

A short drive southeast leads to **Jackson**, a bustling gold mining community that has continued to thrive as a lumber mill town since 1850. The Amador County Museum, located on a hill above the town, features a range of old mining equipment.

Northward, Highway 49 passes through **Placerville**. Once a busy supply center for the area's mining camps, the town is still a major transportation center. Of interest here are the Placerville History Museum and the El Dorado County Historical Museum, which displays a replica of a 19th-century general store, artifacts from the Chinese settlement, and other local historical exhibits.

**Parrots Ferry Bridge along Highway 49**

## Columbia State Historic Park 39

Hwy 49. *22708 Broadway, (209) 532-0150.*

AT THE HEIGHT of the Gold Rush, Columbia was one of the most important towns in the Gold Country. Most of the state's mining camps disintegrated once the gold ran out in the late 1850s. But Columbia was kept intact by its residents until 1945, when it was turned into a state historic park. Many of the town's buildings are preserved in their original state, like its transportation office, the **Wells Fargo Express Office**, and the restored **Columbia Schoolhouse**. Visitors can buy pans of sand to try panning gold.

**Wells Fargo Express Office & Columbia Schoolhouse**
*10am–4pm daily, Jun–Aug: until 6pm.* *Thanksgiving, Dec 25.*

# The High Sierras

FORMING A TOWERING WALL AT THE eastern side of central California, the densely forested, 14,000-ft (4,270-m) high Sierra Nevada Mountains were formed 3 million years ago. Known as the High Sierras, these rugged mountains make up one of the state's most popular recreation areas, preserved by a series of national parks.

Skiing at Lake Tahoe's Alpine Meadows Resort

## Lake Tahoe 40

*South Lake Tahoe, (800) 288-2463*

THE DEEP, EMERALD waters of this beautiful lake are set within an alpine valley at the highest point of the High Sierras. For over a century, Lake Tahoe has been a year-round recreational haven, offering water sports, hiking, and camping. South Lake Tahoe, the largest town here, caters to visitors headed for Nevada's casinos. To its west, the inlet of Emerald Bay State Park is the most photographed part of the lake. To the north is the D.L. Bliss State Park with its 1903 Ehrman Mansion. The surrounding peaks are also famous for their ski resorts. The world-class Alpine Meadows and Squaw Valley are well-known because the Winter Olympics were held here in 1960.

## Yosemite National Park 41

*from Merced.* *Yosemite Valley.* *from Merced.* *PO Box 577, Yosemite, (209) 372-0200.* *daily.* www.nps.gov/yose

A WILDERNESS of evergreen forests, high meadows, and sheer granite walls, the 1,170 sq mile (3,030 sq km) Yosemite National Park (established in 1890) protects some of the world's most beautiful mountain terrain. Soaring cliffs, rugged canyons, valleys, gigantic trees, and waterfalls all combine to lend Yosemite its incomparable beauty. Each season offers a different experience, from the swelling waterfalls of spring to the russet colors of fall. Numerous roads, bus tours, bike paths, and hiking trails lead visitors from one awe-inspiring panoramic view to another.

Yosemite Valley is a good base from which to explore the park. **Yosemite Museum**, in the village, displays the history of the Native Miwok and Paiute people, along with works by local artists. Nearby is the **Ahwanee Hotel** *(see p725)*. Built in 1927, this is one of the country's best-known hotels. Just to the south of the Valley Visitor Center, the tiny wooden **Yosemite Chapel** (1879) is the sole reminder of the park's Old Village, dating from the 19th century.

Standing nearly 1 mile (1.6 km) above the valley floor, the silhouette of the **Half Dome** cliff has become the symbol of Yosemite. Geologists believe that it is now three-quarters of its original size, rather than a true half. It is thought that 15,000 years ago glacial ice floes moved across the valley, scything off rock, depositing it downstream. A formidable trail leads to the 8,840-ft (2,695-m) summit, offering panoramic views of the valley. The other major cliff, **El Capitan**, standing guard at the valley's western entrance, attracts rock-climbers, who spend days on its sheer face

El Capitan, the world's largest piece of exposed granite, Yosemite NP

o reach the top. But the great Yosemite panorama is best experienced from the 3,215-ft (980-m) high **Glacier Point**. It can be reached only in summer, because snow blocks the road during winter.

Among the park's most recognizable features are the cascading Yosemite waterfalls, the highest in North America. Tumbling from a height of 2,425 ft (740 m) in two great leaps, **Upper** and **Lower Yosemite Falls** are at their peak in May and June, when the snow melts. By September, however, the falls often dry up.

In summer, when the wildflowers are in full bloom, the park's striking landscape is best explored in the subalpine **Tuolumne Meadows** along the Tuolumne River at the Yosemite's eastern edge.

A few miles past Yosemite's southern entrance, **Mariposa Grove** features over 500 giant sequoia trees *(Sequoiadendron gigantea)*, some more than 3,000 years old.

The 1879 Yosemite Chapel, Yosemite National Park

## Eastern Sierras 42

**Bodie State Historic Park** *from Bridgeport.* *End of Hwy 270, (760) 647-6445.* *daily.* **Mono Lake** *(760) 647-3044.* *Merced.*

HIGH UP IN the foothills of the eastern Sierras lies **Bodie State Historic Park**, the largest ghost town in California. It was named after the prospector Waterman S. Bodey, who discovered surface gold here in 1859. The town thrived in the mid-1870s but declined when the gold ran out in 1882. Now protected as a state historic park, Bodie's 170 buildings have been maintained in a state of "arrested decay." The result is an experience of empty streets lined by deserted wooden buildings. The Miner's Union Hall has been converted into a visitor center and a museum.

Tufa spires rising out of Mono Lake, Eastern Sierras

Nearby **Mono Lake**, covering 60-sq miles (155-sq km), lies at the eastern foot of the Sierra Nevada Mountains and presents an eerie sight of limestone towers rising from the water. Set between two volcanic islands, the lake has no natural outlet, but evaporation and water diversion to Los Angeles, through aqueducts, have caused it to shrink to one-fifth of its size. The lake's water has turned brackish and alkaline, putting the local wildlife and ecosystem in grave danger. In recent years, Mono Lake has been the subject of much environmental debate.

## Sequoia & Kings Canyon National Parks 43

Ash Mountain, Three Rivers. *(559) 565-3341.* *daily.* *call ahead.* *summer only.* www.nps.gov/seki

THESE TWIN national parks preserve lush green forests, magnificent glacier-carved canyons, and granite peaks. America's deepest canyon, the south fork of the Kings River, cuts a depth of 8,200 ft (2,500 m) through Kings Canyon. Roads serve the western side of the parks; the rest is accessible only to hikers or rented pack-trains of horses or mules.

The parks embrace 34 separate groves of the sequoia tree, the earth's largest living species. **Giant Forest**, at the southern end of Sequoia National Park, is one of the world's largest groves of living sequoias. A 3-mile (5-km) trail from here leads to Moro Rock, a granite monolith affording a 360-degree view of the High Sierras and the Central Valley. To its east lies the marshy Crescent Meadow, bordered by sequoias. Another short trail leads to **Tharp's Log**, a hollowed-out sequoia, home to Hale Tharp, a 19th-century farmer who was introduced to the area by Native Americans.

North of Giant Forest is the world's largest living thing, the 275-ft (84-m) **General Sherman's Tree**. It still grows 0.4 inches (1 cm) every ten years and is rivaled by the third largest sequoia, **General Grant Tree** in Kings Canyon Park. This park also features the Big Stump Trail, lined with tall stumps, left by loggers in the 1880s.

Along the eastern boundary of Sequoia is the 14,496-ft (4,420-m) **Mount Whitney**, one of the highest peaks on the US mainland. A steep trail leads from Whitney Portal Road to the summit, offering a panorama over the High Sierras. The mountain, named in honor of geologist Josiah Whitney, was first climbed in 1873. The lovely green alpine meadows around it are ideal for backpacking in the summer months.

# Practical Information

California is a vibrant and diverse vacation destination. The spirit of the state can be felt in the busy cities of San Francisco, Los Angeles, and San Diego as much as in the quiet wilderness of the Sierra Nevada Mountains. At the center of the film industry, Los Angeles prides itself as the entertainment capital of the world. All over the state visitors needs' are well tended. The state's major tourist spots see a rush of visitors from mid-April to September. But the winter months are equally popular, either for the warm climate of the south or the ski slopes of Lake Tahoe.

## Tourist Information

Advance information can be obtained from the **California Division of Tourism** or the nearest US Consulate. Local Visitors' and Convention Bureaus supply maps, guides, event listings, and discount passes for public transportation and tourist destinations.

## Personal Security

San Francisco is one of the safest large cities in the US. Problems are more visible in Los Angeles, although the notorious gangs of the city generally do not bother visitors. Still, as in every big city, visitors can be victims of petty thefts or car crime. Although police patrol regularly in the tourist areas, it is good to be cautious. Safety rules for pedestrians are strictly observed – jay-walking, or crossing the road anywhere except at an intersection, can result in a fine.

## Natural Hazards

In the event of an earthquake, it is most important not to panic. Most injuries occur from falling material. Stand in a doorway, or crouch under a table. In a car, slow down and pull over.

When hiking in the wilderness, be wary of occasionally dangerous wildlife. Also be careful of rapid climatic changes in deserts, where temperatures can drop to below freezing points at high elevations. The Pacific Ocean can often be rough, with a strong undertow.

## Getting Around

Although often more time-consuming, traveling by train, bus, and ferry is an inexpensive way of getting around the state. Within the major cities of San Francisco, Los Angeles, and San Diego, the public transportation network serves parts of the city very well, with shuttle buses, trams, Metro trains, ferries, taxis, and cable cars.

The network of Amtrak railroad lines and connecting bus services serves the state's populous areas. Guided bus tours are a convenient way of sightseeing. Express boat services provide a fast link from Los Angeles to Santa Catalina Island, while others sail more leisurely across San Francisco Bay. Most ferries carry foot passengers and bicycles.

## Driving in California

Driving is the best way to travel around the state. It is best to arrange a fly-drive package before leaving for California. Find out exactly what is included and whether any extra payments may arise when the car is returned. These additions – which may include collision damage waiver, drop-off charges, and rental tax – can double the original fee. Litigation is common in California, so it is best to be fully insured.

In the US, cars are driven on the right side of the road. Seat belts are compulsory. The maximum speed limit is generally 65 mph (104 km/h) In cities, the speed limits are restricted as marked and may vary within a few miles. These controls are rigorously enforced by the Highway Patrol. Drunk driving is a serious offense and carries very heavy penalties. You can turn right on red at traffic lights if there is nothing coming the other way. The first vehicle to reach a stop-sign junction has the right of way.

Parking in California cities is strictly controlled and can be somewhat expensive. In remote areas, drivers should be wary of wildlife that may stray onto the roads.

## Outdoor Activities

California is practically synonymous with the great outdoors. The deserts, redwood forests, alpine meadows, mountains, lakes, and white beaches all welcome visitors. The state

## The Climate of California

Apart from the extremes of the north and the deserts, the state's climate is neither oppressive in summer, nor too cold in winter. The Northern Coastal Range is temperate, although wet in winter. To the east, rain turns to snow on the Sierra Nevada Mountains. Central California and the Central Valley have a Mediterranean climate, characterized by seasonal changes in rainfall – a dry summer and a rainy winter – but only moderate changes in temperature. The weather becomes drier and warmer toward the south with soaring temperatures in the desert in summer.

### Los Angeles

| month | Apr | Jul | Oct | Jan |
|---|---|---|---|---|
| °F/C (high) | 70/21 | 81/27 | 76/24 | 65/18 |
| °F/C (low) | 50/10 | 60/16 | 54/12 | 46/8 |
| sunshine | 21 days | 25 days | 23 days | 21 days |
| rainfall | 1 in | 0.01 in | 0.3 in | 2.9 in |

32°F 0°C

has a culture rich with physical activity, and wilderness is never far from any city.

With more than 250 places classified as state parks, wilderness areas, or historic sites, California is a hikers' and campers' paradise. For camping, reserve a site with **State Park Reservations** or **Yosemite Reservations**. There are more than 1 million miles (1.6 million km) of trails in California, the longest being the Pacific Crest Trail, stretching from Canada to Mexico. The **Sierra Club** organizes guided outings and provides detailed maps. Many state parks also allow cyclists on their hiking trails. Outfitters such as **Backroads** lead groups of cyclists on tours of rolling countrysides.

Equestrians find a wide variety of riding trails here. California's 900-mile (1,450-km) coastline offers various beaches. Some have rough waves and rocky shores; others, with white sand, arching waves, and warm water, are ideal for surfing. The best beaches include the **Leo Carrillo State Beach** in Orange County, **Windansea Beach** in La Jolla, and **Corona del Mar** in Newport.

The lakes, rivers, and beaches of California offer a variety of watersports, from slow cruises on houseboats to parasailing and whitewater rafting. Most outfitters that offer river rafting also provide kayak and canoe trips. For more information, contact **American River Touring Association**. The rivers and coastline are feeding grounds for migrating birds. In autumn, ducks, geese, and other shorebirds can be spotted here. The state is also an angler's haven. The rivers and streams of the Sierra Nevada Mountains have plenty of trout. Bass fishing in California's lakes and reservoirs is plentiful throughout the year.

From December through April, gray whales travel 7,000 miles (11,260 kms) from the California coast to Mexico. Ocean cruises offer views of the impressive mammals.

California's great outdoors list also includes island hopping. Five volcanic islands off the coast of Southern California form the Channel Islands National Park, ideal for hiking, exploring rock pools, and spotting whales and dolphins. **Island Packers** is only one of the many outfits that offer island tours.

California is famed for its special interest vacations, the most popular being the tours of the state's missions along El Camino Real. Resident writers often give readings at local writers' workshops such as the **Santa Barbara Writers' Conference**. Institutes such as **Tante Marie's Cooking School** provide lodging, cooking classes, shopping tours, and visits to the Wine Country during week-long intensive courses in summer.

## Shopping

A MAJOR PLAYER in the global economy, California is known for its casual clothing as well as the best in cutting-edge fashion. It is the largest producer of children's clothing in the US, with Sara's Prints and **Levi Strauss** being among the best. It is equally famous for its sportswear and swimwear, designed by names such as **California Wave**.

Fresh fruit, nuts, and vegetables from the San Joaquin Valley feeds the entire nation. The fine wines of Napa and Sonoma Valleys are available in wineries across the state. Some, such as **Viansa Winery** and **Sebastiani Vineyards**, also sell a wide range of wine related products.

Aside from the shopping districts of L.A. and San Francisco, the state's smaller towns offer a wide range of merchandise and local produce in roadside food stands, wineries, antique shops, and flea markets, where prices tend to be cheaper than in cities.

## Directory

### Tourist Offices

**California Division of Tourism**
(800) 862-2543.
FAX (916) 322-2881.

### Special Interest Vacations

**California Office of Tourism**
PO Box 9278,
Van Nuys, CA 91409.
(800) 862-2543.

**Santa Barbara Writers' Conference**
PO Box 304,
Carpinteria, CA 93014.
(805) 684-2250.

**Tante Marie's Cooking School**
271 Francsico St,
San Francisco, CA 94133.
(415) 788-6699.
W www.tantemaries.com

### Camping

**State Park Reservations**
(800) 444-7275.
W www.parks.ca.gov

**Yosemite Reservations**
(559) 252-4848.
W www.yosemitepark.com

### Hiking

**Sierra Club**
730 Polk St, San Francisco.
(415) 977-5500.

### Mountain Biking

**Backroads**
801 Cedar St, Berkeley.
(510) 527-1555.

### Whitewater Rafting & Kayaking

**American River Touring Association**
24000 Casa Loma Rd,
Groveland, CA 95321.
(209) 962-7873.
W www.arta.org

### Island Hopping

**Island Packers**
1867 Spinnaker Dr,
Ventura, CA 93001.
(805) 642-1393.

### Shopping

**California Wave**
1250 E Slavsen Ave, L.A.
(323) 233-0077.

**The Original Levi Strauss**
1155 Battery,
San Francisco.
(415) 501-6000.

### Wineries

**Sebastiani Vineyards**
389 Fourth St E,
Sonoma, CA 95476.
(707) 938-5532.

**Viansa Winery**
Arnold Dr, Sonoma.
(707) 935- 4700.

# Where to Stay

FRAMED BY RUGGED COASTAL mountains, forested hills, sophisticated urban centers, and a long coastline, California is one of the premier vacation destinations in the world. From budget inns to five-star resorts, there is a wealth of options for travelers to the state. Hotels here have been selected across a wide price range for their excellent facilities and locations.

| Hotel | Number of Rooms | Restaurant | Children's Facilities | Garden or Terrace | Swimming Pool |
|---|---|---|---|---|---|
| **LOS ANGELES** | | | | | |
| **ANAHEIM:** *Disneyland Hotel* $$$$ <br> 1150 W Cerritos, CA 92802. *(714) 778-6600.* FAX *(714) 956-6597.* <br> W www.disneyland.com This large hotel with guest rooms or cottages is linked to Disneyland by monorail. The emphasis is on entertainment. TV P | 990 | ● | ■ | ● | ■ |
| **BEVERLY HILLS:** *Peninsula Beverly Hills* $$$$$ <br> 9882 S Santa Monica Blvd, CA 90212. *(310) 551-2888, (800) 462-7899.* <br> FAX *(310) 788-2319.* W www.peninsula.com <br> Celebrities come to this luxurious five-star hotel. 24 TV P | 196 | ● | ■ | ● | ■ |
| **DOWNTOWN:** *Miyako Inn and Spa* $$ <br> 328 E 1st St, CA 90012. *(213) 617-2000, (800) 228-6596.* FAX *(213) 617-2700.* <br> W www.miyakola.com <br> This hotel in Little Tokyo has a karaoke lounge and separate spa facilities for men and women. Children under 12 stay free. TV P | 174 | ● | | | |
| **HOLLYWOOD:** *The Ramada Hollywood* $$ <br> 1160 N Vermont, CA 90029. *(323) 660-1788, (800) 272-6232.* FAX *(323) 660-8069.* <br> W www.ramadahollywood.com This chain hotel near Universal Studios has suites and rooms with Internet, free breakfast, and a jacuzzi. TV P | 140 | | ■ | | ■ |
| **LONG BEACH:** *Hotel Queen Mary* $$$ <br> 1126 Queen's Hwy, CA 90802. *(562) 435-3511, (800) 437-2934.* FAX *(562) 437-4531.* <br> W www.queenmary.com The famous ocean liner's first-class staterooms have been updated and restored. Breakfast is included. TV P | 365 | ● | ■ | ● | |
| **MALIBU:** *Casa Malibu Inn on the Beach* $$ <br> 22752 Pacific Coast Hwy, CA 90265. *(310) 456-2219, (800) 831-0858.* <br> FAX *(310) 456-5418.* This hotel is built on its own private beach. TV P | 21 | | | ● | |
| **PASADENA:** *Ritz Carlton Huntingdon Hotel* $$$$ <br> 1401 S Oak Knoll Ave, CA 91106. *(626) 568-3900, (800) 241-3333.* FAX *(626) 568-3700.* <br> W www.ritzcarlton.com This luxury hotel has elegant rooms and a wooden bridge between the two wings overlooking Japanese gardens. 24 TV P | 392 | ● | ■ | ● | ■ |
| **SANTA MONICA:** *Sheraton Delfina* $$$ <br> 530 W Pico Blvd, CA 90405. *(310) 399-9344, (800) 325-3535.* <br> FAX *(310) 399-2504.* W www.sheraton.com <br> Offers jacuzzis, a free airport shuttle, and tours. TV P | 314 | ● | ■ | | ■ |
| **VENICE BEACH:** *The Cadillac* $ <br> 8 Dudley Ave, CA 90291. *(310) 399-8876.* FAX *(310) 399-4536.* <br> W www.thecadillachotel.com This gorgeous Art Deco hotel is right on the beach, with a sauna, pool tables, and sun terrace. TV P | 41 | | | ● | |
| **WEST HOLLYWOOD:** *Argyle Hotel* $$$$$ <br> 8358 Sunset Blvd, CA 90069. *(323) 654-7100, (800) 225-2637.* FAX *(323) 654-1004.* <br> W www.argylehotel.com Originally built as apartments for film stars, the rooms here are Italian Art Deco in style. 24 TV P | 64 | ● | ■ | ● | ■ |
| **SAN DIEGO COUNTY** | | | | | |
| **CORONADO:** *Hotel del Coronado* $$$$$ <br> 1500 Orange Ave, CA 92118. *(619) 435-6611, (800) 468-3533.* FAX *(619) 522-8238.* <br> This grand Victorian hotel on the beach has been updated with modern annexes and a spa. 24 TV P | 700 | ● | ■ | ● | ■ |
| **LA JOLLA:** *Embassy Suites Hotel* $$$ <br> 4550 La Jolla Village Dr, CA 92122. *(858) 453-0400, (800) 362-2779.* <br> FAX *(858) 453-4226.* W www.embassysuites.com <br> This modern hotel with two-room suites is perfect for families. It offers breakfast and a game room. TV P | 335 | ● | ■ | | ■ |

**Price categories** for a standard double room per night, inclusive of breakfast, service charges, and any additional taxes:

- $ under $100
- $$ $100–$150
- $$$ $150–$200
- $$$$ $200–$250
- $$$$$ over $250

**Restaurant**
Hotel restaurant or dining room usually open to nonresidents unless otherwise stated.

**Children's Facilities**
Indicates cribs and/or a baby-sitting service available. A few hotels also provide children's portions and high chairs in the restaurant.

**Garden or Terrace**
Hotels with a garden, courtyard, or terrace, often with tables for eating outside.

**Swimming Pool**
Hotel with indoor or outdoor swimming pool.

| Hotel | Number of Rooms | Restaurant | Children's Facilities | Garden or Terrace | Swimming Pool |
|---|---|---|---|---|---|
| **San Diego:** *Marriott Hotel* $$$$<br>333 W Harbor Dr, CA 92101. (619) 234-1500, (800) 228-9290. FAX (619) 234-8678.<br>W www.marriott.com A 25-story luxury hotel next to San Diego Bay with exceptional outdoor landscaping and facilities. 24 TV P | 1,362 | ● | ■ | | ■ |
| **Tijuana:** *Grand Hotel Tijuana* $$<br>4500 Blvd Agua Caliente, CP 22420. (011-52-66) 81-70-00. FAX (011-52-66) 81-70-16.<br>This is a large hotel complex with twin towers. Facilities include tennis courts and Jacuzzis. 24 TV P | 423 | ● | ■ | ● | ■ |

## The Deserts

| Hotel | Number of Rooms | Restaurant | Children's Facilities | Garden or Terrace | Swimming Pool |
|---|---|---|---|---|---|
| **Death Valley:** *Furnace Creek Inn* $$$$<br>1 Main St, CA 92328. (760) 786-2345. FAX (760) 786-2514.<br>W www.furnacecreekresort.com This marvelous, historic resort is one of the most stylish in the desert, with spring-fed pools, tennis, and golf. 24 TV P | 68 | ● | ■ | ● | ■ |
| **Palm Springs:** *The Palm Springs Hilton Resort* $$$$<br>400 E Tahquitz Canyon Way, CA 92262. (760) 320-6868, (800) 522-6900. FAX (760) 320-2126. W www.hilton.com<br>Near downtown, this hotel's sports facilities include tennis courts and access to local golf courses. TV P | 260 | ● | ■ | ● | ■ |
| **Palm Springs:** *The Parker Palm Springs* $$$$$<br>4200 E Palm Canyon Dr, CA 92264. (760) 770-5000. FAX (760) 324-7280.<br>This hotel is the epitome of understated elegance. Facilities include a golf course, tennis courts, and a spa. 24 TV P | 98 | ● | | ● | ■ |
| **Twentynine Palms:** *Best Western Gardens Inn & Suites* $<br>71487 Twenty Nine Palms Hwy, CA 92277. (760) 367-9141. FAX (760) 367-2584.<br>W www.bestwestern.com This lushly landscaped hotel is conveniently located near the main entrance to the Joshua Tree National Park. TV P | 84 | | ■ | ● | ■ |

## Central California

| Hotel | Number of Rooms | Restaurant | Children's Facilities | Garden or Terrace | Swimming Pool |
|---|---|---|---|---|---|
| **Big Sur:** *Post Ranch Inn* $$$$$<br>PO Box 219, Hwy 1, CA 93920. (831) 667-2200, (800) 527-2200. FAX (831) 667-2824.<br>W www.postranchinn.com Buildings at this extraordinary resort with spa facilities include tree houses and earth shelters built into the hillside. P | 30 | ● | | ● | ■ |
| **Carmel:** *Highlands Inn and Restaurant* $$$$$<br>Pacific Coast Hwy 1, CA 93923. (831) 624-3801, (800) 682-4811. FAX (831) 626-1574.<br>This rustic hotel is set in woodland on a bluff overlooking the coast. The inn offers excellent ocean views. TV P | 142 | ● | ■ | ● | ■ |
| **Monterey:** *Monterey Plaza Hotel and Spa* $$$$<br>400 Cannery Row, CA 93940. (831) 646-1700, (800) 334-3999. FAX (831) 646-5937.<br>W www.montereyplaza.com Some rooms have balconies with views of Monterey Bay. The hotel is near all the city sights. 24 TV P | 290 | ● | ■ | | |
| **Santa Barbara:** *Four Seasons Biltmore* $$$$$<br>1260 Channel Dr, CA 93108. (805) 969-2261, (800) 332-3442. FAX (805) 565-8323.<br>W www.fshr.com A luxury resort since the 1920s, the rooms, suites, and cottages are set in coastal gardens. 24 TV P | 213 | ● | ■ | ● | ■ |
| **Santa Cruz:** *Sunset Inn* $$<br>2424 Mission St, CA 95060. (831) 423-7500. FAX (831) 423-7595.<br>This hotel has microwaves and refrigerators in all rooms. Close to excellent restaurants and all corporate businesses. TV P | 32 | | ■ | | |
| **San Luis Obispo:** *The Madonna Inn* $$$<br>100 Madonna Rd, CA 93405. (805) 543-3000, (800) 543-9666. FAX (805) 543-1800.<br>W www.madonnainn.com All the rooms have themes – for example, the Caveman Room is made entirely out of rock. Book in advance. TV P | 109 | ● | ■ | ● | |

For key to symbols see back flap

**Price categories** for a standard double room per night, inclusive of breakfast, service charges, and any additional taxes:

- $ under $100
- $$ $100–$150
- $$$ $150–$200
- $$$$ $200–$250
- $$$$$ over $250

**RESTAURANT**
Hotel restaurant or dining room usually open to nonresidents unless otherwise stated.

**CHILDREN'S FACILITIES**
Indicates cribs and/or a baby-sitting service available. A few hotels also provide children's portions and high chairs in the restaurant.

**GARDEN OR TERRACE**
Hotels with a garden, courtyard, or terrace, often with tables for eating outside.

**SWIMMING POOL**
Hotel with indoor or outdoor swimming pool.

| | NUMBER OF ROOMS | RESTAURANT | CHILDREN'S FACILITIES | GARDEN OR TERRACE | SWIMMING POOL |
|---|---|---|---|---|---|
| **SAN FRANCISCO** | | | | | |
| **BERKELEY:** *Claremont Resort, Spa, & Tennis Club* $$$$<br>41 Tunnel Road, Oakland, CA 94623. (510) 843-3000, (800) 843-7924. FAX (510) 549-8582. W www.claremontresort.com<br>At the foot of the Berkeley Hills, this is the area's grandest hotel. | 239 | ● | ■ | ● | ■ |
| **CHINATOWN & NOB HILL:** *Hotel Triton* $$$$$<br>342 Grant Ave, CA 94108. (415) 394-0500, (800) 433-6611. FAX (415) 394-0555. W www.hoteltriton.com Small but stylish, this is the newest hip place to stay. You might even run into a rock star or two. | 140 | ● | | | |
| **DOWNTOWN:** *Clift Hotel* $$$$$<br>495 Geary St, CA 94102. (415) 775-4700, (800) 652-5438. FAX (415) 441-4621. W www.morganshotelgroup.com Well-appointed rooms, old-world elegance, and gracious service characterize this fine hotel. | 363 | ● | | | |
| **FISHERMAN'S WHARF:** *Sheraton at Fisherman's Wharf* $$$<br>2500 Mason St, CA 94133. (415) 362-5500, (800) 325-3535. FAX (415) 956-5275. W www.sheratonatthewharf.com This family-oriented tourist hotel is also popular with business people and has easy access to many attractions. | 525 | ● | ■ | | ■ |
| **HAIGHT ASHBURY:** *Red Victorian Bed & Breakfast* $$<br>1665 Haight St, CA 94117. (415) 864-1978. FAX (415) 863-3293. W www.redvic.com This unique hotel offers New Age accommodation in themed rooms such as the Flower Child Suite; no radios, TVs, or smoking. | 18 | | | | |
| **MUIR BEACH:** *The Pelican Inn* $$$<br>10 Pacifica Way, CA 94965. (415) 383-6000. FAX (415) 383-3424. W www.pelicaninn.com Roaring fireplaces, British beers, and gorgeous rooms, some with four-poster beds, are all within walking distance of Muir Woods. | 7 | ● | ■ | ● | |
| **OAKLAND:** *Waterfront Plaza Hotel* $$$$<br>10 Washington St, CA 94607. (510) 836-3800; (800) 729-9338. FAX (510) 832-5695. W www.waterfrontplazahotel.com Many rooms have fireplaces and views across the bay at this well-appointed hotel at the edge of Jack London Square. | 145 | ● | ■ | ● | ■ |
| **PACIFIC HEIGHTS:** *Edward II Inn & Suites* $$$<br>3155 Scott St at Lombard, CA 94123. (415) 922-3000, (800) 473-2846. FAX (415) 931-5784. W www.edwardii.com<br>This 1949 house offers free breakfasts and afternoon sherry. | 39 | | | | |
| **SAN JOSE:** *San Jose Hilton & Towers Hotel* $$$<br>300 Almaden Blvd, CA 95110. (408) 287-2100, (800) 445-8667. FAX (408) 947-4489. W www.hilton.com This chain hotel is well equipped for the business traveler. Each floor has its own concierge. | 354 | ● | ■ | ● | ■ |
| **WINE COUNTRY** | | | | | |
| **MENDOCINO:** *MacCallum House* $$$<br>45020 Albion St (PO Box 206), CA 95460. (707) 937-0289, (800) 609-0492. W www.maccallumhouse.com Not all rooms have private baths at this 19th-century inn. Ask for one of the annexes, many of which also have fireplaces. | 19 | ● | ■ | ● | |
| **NAPA:** *Silverado Country Club Resort* $$$$<br>1600 Atlas Peak Rd, CA 94558. (707) 257-0200, (800) 532-0500. FAX (707) 257-5425. W www.silveradoresort.com Luxurious guest bungalows surround an old mansion set in 1,200 acres (485 ha). Fabulous recreational facilities are also available for guests staying here. | 280 | ● | ■ | ● | ■ |
| **SONOMA:** *Victorian Garden Inn* $$$<br>316 E Napa St, CA 95476. (707) 996-5339. FAX (707) 996-1689. W www.victoriangardeninn.com This peaceful Greek Revival farmhouse offers the perfect antidote to a hectic tour of the region's wineries. | 5 | | | ● | ■ |

| | | | | | |
|---|---|---|---|---|---|
| **THE NORTH** | | | | | |
| **EUREKA:** *Quality Inn* $<br>1209 4th St, CA 95501. *(707) 443-1601.* FAX *(707) 444-8365.*<br>W www.qualityinneureka.com Along with a prime location at the heart of Eureka's Old Town, this hotel offers spacious rooms and suites, plus a sauna. TV P | 60 | ● | ■ | | ■ |
| **MOUNT LASSEN:** *Mineral Lodge* $<br>PO Box 160 Mineral, CA 96063. *(530) 595-4472.* FAX *(530) 595-4452.*<br>W www.minerallodge.com This rustic lodge offers motel-style rooms, and a tavern. It is on the southern fringes of Lassen Volcanic National Park. TV P | 20 | ● | ■ | ● | |
| **MOUNT SHASTA:** *Mountain Air Lodge* $<br>1121 S Mount Shasta Blvd, CA 96067. *(530) 926-3411, (800) 727-3704.*<br>This simple lodge-style hotel is in a wonderful mountain setting. Ski slopes and water-sports facilities are just a short drive away. TV P | 30 | | | | |
| **SHELTER COVE:** *The Ashbrook Inn* $$$<br>578 Hillside Dr, CA 95589. *(707) 986-7109.* W www.ashbrookinn.com<br>This bed & breakfast inn has great views from its rooms. There's also internet access and a gourmet breakfast. Massage therapist on site. | 3 | | | | |
| **WEAVERVILLE:** *Motel Trinity* $<br>1112 Main St, CA 96093. *(530) 623-2129.* FAX *(530) 623-6007.*<br>Accommodations in this small motel range from single rooms to two-bedroom suites with kitchenettes. Some rooms have jacuzzis. TV | 25 | ● | | ● | ■ |
| **GOLD COUNTRY & THE CENTRAL VALLEY** | | | | | |
| **GRASS VALLEY:** *Holbrooke Hotel & Restaurant* $$$<br>212 West Main St, CA 95945. *(530) 273-1353, (800) 933-7077.* FAX *(530) 273-0434.*<br>W www.holbrooke.com Rooms in this downtown hotel – a California Historic Landmark – are named after famous guests. TV P | 27 | ● | ■ | ● | |
| **NEVADA CITY:** *National Hotel* $<br>211 Broad St, CA 95959. *(530) 265-4551.* FAX *(530) 265-2445.*<br>W www.thenationalhotel.com This historic building surrounded by pine trees has been a hotel since 1855. All the rooms have Victorian furnishings. TV P | 42 | ● | ■ | ● | ■ |
| **SACRAMENTO:** *Marriott Hotel* $$$$<br>1211 Point E Dr, Rancho Cordova, CA 95742. *(916) 638-1100, (800) 228-9290.*<br>FAX *(916) 638-5803.* W www.marriott.com<br>This hotel is perfect for the business traveler and the tourist. TV P | 262 | ● | ■ | ● | ■ |
| **SONORA:** *Sonora Days Inn & Café* $$<br>160 S Washington St, CA 95370. *(209) 532-2400, (800) 580-4667.* FAX *(209) 532-4542.*<br>W www.sonoradaysinn.com Housed in an 1890s Spanish-style buildingin old downtown Sonora; there is a motel annex at the back. TV P | 64 | ● | ■ | ● | ■ |
| **SUTTER CREEK:** *Sutter Creek Inn* $$<br>75 Main St, CA 95685. *(209) 267-5606.* FAX *(209) 267-9287.* W www.suttercreekinn.com<br>This English-style country inn has swinging beds that hang by chains from the ceiling. Some rooms have fireplaces and private patios. P | 17 | | | ● | |
| **THE HIGH SIERRAS** | | | | | |
| **KINGS CANYON NATIONAL PARK:** *Montecito Lodge* $$<br>PO Box 858, Grant Grove, CA 93633. *(559) 565-3388; (800) 227-9900.*<br>FAX *(559) 565-3223.* W www.montecitolodge.com<br>Set amid groves of giant sequoias, this is a family-oriented lodge. P | 52 | ● | ■ | ● | ■ |
| **LEE VINING:** *Best Western Lake View Lodge* $<br>PO Box 345, CA 93541. *(760) 647-6543, (800) 528-1234.* FAX *(760) 647-6325.*<br>W www.bestwestern.com Set on the western shore of Mono Lake, this motel makes an excellent base for exploring the area. Some rooms have kitchens. TV P | 46 | | ■ | ● | |
| **TRUCKEE:** *Donner Lake Village Resort* $$<br>Suite 101, 15695 Donner Pass Rd, CA 96161. *(530) 587-6081, (800) 621-6664.*<br>FAX *(530) 587-8782.* W www.donnerlakevillage.com With its own beach and marina , this resort has two-bedroom suites. TV P | 49 | | ■ | | |
| **YOSEMITE NATIONAL PARK:** *Ahwahnee Hotel* $$$$<br>Yosemite Valley, CA 95389. *(209) 372-1407.* FAX *(209) 372-1403.*<br>W www.yosemitepark.com This is the most stylish of Yosemite's hotels. Rental bikes and horseback riding are available. P | 123 | ● | ■ | ● | ■ |

For key to symbols see back flap

# Where to Eat

Of all the states in the country, California has perhaps the widest variety of places to eat. "California cuisine" – light food prepared in a range of international styles using locally grown ingredients – is now internationally recognized. The many ethnic cuisines reflect the state's many cultures. In the listings below, "L" indicates lunch and "D" stands for dinner.

## Los Angeles

**Beverly Hills:** *Nate 'n' Al's Deli* $
414 N Beverly Dr, CA 90210. *(310) 274-0101.* Everyone comes here for fabulous sandwiches, deli items, and dinners. Breakfast is served all day.

**Beverly Hills:** *Mr. Chow* $$$$$
344 N Camden Dr, CA 90210. *(310) 278-9911.*
Celebritites come to this stylish restaurant for delicious Peking-style cuisine. Favorites include drunken fish and gamblers' duck. *Sat & Sun L.*

**Downtown:** *Cicada* $$$$
617 S Olive St, CA 90014. *(213) 488-9488.*
The contemporary Italian cuisine packs in the customers at this beautiful Art Deco restaurant in the Oviatt Hotel. *D.* *Sun.*

**Hollywood:** *Canter's Deli* $
419 N Fairfax Ave, CA 90036. *(323) 651-2030.*
This 24-hour deli has superb sandwiches and diner-style meals.

**Hollywood:** *The Gumbo Pot* $
Farmers Market, 6333 W 3rd St, CA 90036. *(323) 933-0358.*
Try gumbo stew and enormous po' boys (foot-long sandwiches) at this Cajun fast-food bar, with occasional live Cajun bands.

**Hollywood:** *Mandalay* $$$$
611 N La Brea Ave, CA 90036. *(323) 933-0717.*
This French-Vietnamese restaurant's eclectic menu includes sushi, dumplings, and traditional Vietnamese dishes such as spicy beef salad. *D.*

**Long Beach:** *New York Bryan's* $$
213A Pine Ave at Broadway St, CA 90802. *(562) 437-1234.*
A fusion of Mediterranean and Latin flavors highlights the cuisine at this trendy café with rotating art exhibits and good live bands. *Sat & Sun L.*

**Malibu:** *Gladstone's 4 Fish* $$$
17300 Pacific Coast Hwy, CA 90272. *(310) 454-3474.*
This oceanside seafood restaurant is great fun for families. Portions are huge, but you can take home the leftovers in an aluminum foil sculpture.

**Pasadena:** *Yujean Kang's* $$$
67 N Raymond Ave, CA 91103. *(626) 585-0855.*
Presentation is everything at this very elegant Chinese restaurant.
Try the "lobster with strange flavors." Lunch is a bargain. *Tue.*

**Santa Monica:** *Schatzi on Main* $$
3110 Main St, CA 90405. *(310) 399-4800.*
Hollywood star Arnold Schwarzenegger owns this pleasant restaurant serving Austrian specialties and healthy California cuisine.

**Venice:** *Café 50s Diner* $
838 Lincoln Blvd, CA 90291. *(310) 399 1955.*
This tiny 1950s café serves sandwiches, salads, hamburgers, milkshakes, and "blue plate special" dinners, such as pot roast, in the evenings.

**West Hollywood:** *The Rainbow Bar and Grill* $
9015 Sunset Blvd, CA 90069. *(310) 278-4232.*
This high-energy hangout for the entertainment industry serves Continental food with Italian flair. It is also a nightclub in the evenings. *Sat & Sun.*

**Westwood/West L.A.:** *Bombay Café* $$
12021 W Pico Blvd, CA 90025. *(310) 473-3388.*
One of the best Indian restaurants in the city, this place serves homecooked dishes from the owner's native city. Busy but worth it.

| Restaurant | Outdoor Eating | Vegetarian Specialties | Bar Area/Cocktail Bar | Fixed-Price Menu | Children's Facilities |
|---|---|---|---|---|---|
| Nate 'n' Al's Deli | | | | | ■ |
| Mr. Chow | | ● | ■ | ● | ■ |
| Cicada | | ● | ■ | ● | |
| Canter's Deli | | ● | ■ | | ■ |
| The Gumbo Pot | ■ | ● | | | |
| Mandalay | | ● | ■ | | ■ |
| New York Bryan's | ■ | ● | | | ■ |
| Gladstone's 4 Fish | ■ | ● | ■ | | ■ |
| Yujean Kang's | | ● | | ● | ■ |
| Schatzi on Main | ■ | ● | ■ | | ■ |
| Café 50s Diner | | ● | | | ■ |
| The Rainbow Bar and Grill | ■ | ● | ■ | | ■ |
| Bombay Café | | ● | | | ■ |

**Price categories** include a three-course meal for one, a glass of house wine, and all unavoidable extra charges such as sales tax and service.
$ under $20
$$ $20–30
$$$ $30–45
$$$$ $45–60
$$$$$ over $60

**OUTDOOR EATING**
Some tables on a patio or terrace.
**VEGETARIAN SPECIALTIES**
One menu always includes a selection of vegetarian dishes.
**BAR AREA/COCKTAIL BAR**
There is a bar area or cocktail bar within the restaurant.
**FIXED-PRICE MENU**
A fixed-price menu offered at lunch, dinner or both, usually with three courses.
**CHILDREN'S FACILITIES**
Small portions and/or high chairs available on request.

## SAN DIEGO COUNTY

**CORONADO:** *Poebe's* $$$
1201 1st St, Old Ferry Landing Plaza. *(619) 437-4474.*
There are lovely views of downtown San Diego from this restaurant, which serves creative Polynesian cuisine. The setting is very Hawaiian, with waterfalls and tropical plants every place you look.

**LA JOLLA:** *Top O' The Cove* $$$$$
1216 Prospect St, CA 92037. *(858) 454-7779.*
Fabulous coastal views, celebrity customers, and delicious food guarantee the success of this famous restaurant. The cuisine is contemporary French with a Pacific Rim influence. Dress up.

**SAN DIEGO:** *Big Kitchen* $
3003 Grape St, CA 92102. *(619) 234-5789.*
The best breakfast intown and rumored to be where Whoopi Goldberg washed dishes. The staff is good humored, the place is kid friendly, and it's very, very popular. *L.*

**SAN DIEGO:** *Humphrey's* $$$$$
2241 Shelter Island Dr, CA 92106. *(619) 224-3577.*
Named after Humphrey Bogart and decorated in the style of *Casablanca,* this seafood restaurant serves lobster fresh from the tank.

## THE DESERTS

**BARSTOW:** *Slash X Ranch Café* $$
28040 Barstow Rd, CA 92311. *(760) 252-1197.*
A Barstow staple for 50 years, this café offers all manner of homestyle cooking, including hamburgers and barbeque favorites. *D Sun–Wed.*

**DEATH VALLEY:** *Wrangler Steakhouse* $$
Furnace Creek Ranch, CA 92328. *(760) 786-2345 (ext. 250).*
This classic steak house offers steaks, chops, chicken, and seafood in a Southwestern setting. There is also a well-stocked salad bar.

**DEATH VALLEY:** *Inn Dining Room* $$$
Furnace Creek Inn, CA 92328. *(760) 786-2345 (ext. 253).*
There are wonderful mountain views from this popular Continental restaurant set in the Furnace Creek Inn. *Mon.*

**PALM SPRINGS:** *Flower Drum* $$
424 S Indian Canyon Dr, CA 92262. *(760) 323-3020.*
Five chefs serve five regional styles of Chinese cooking. There is a stream filled with fish running through the center of the restaurant. *L.*

## CENTRAL CALIFORNIA

**BIG SUR:** *Nepenthe* $$
Hwy 1, CA 93920. *(831) 667-2345.*
Originally a honeymoon retreat for Orson Welles and Rita Hayworth, this restaurant offers panoramic views of the coastline. The emphasis is on basic American cuisine.

**CARMEL:** *The French Poodle* $$$
Junipero & 5th Ave, CA 93921. *(831) 624-8643.*
This intimate restaurant was selected as one of the best French restaurants in the US by the International Restaurant Rating Bureau. *D. Sun.*

**MONTEREY:** *Fresh Cream* $$$$
99 Pacific St, Suite 100C, Heritage Harbor, CA 93940. *(831) 375-9798.*
This award-winning restaurant, with its harbor views, offers some of the best French food in Northern California. *D.*

| Restaurant | Outdoor Eating | Vegetarian Specialties | Bar Area/Cocktail Bar | Fixed-Price Menu | Children's Facilities |
|---|---|---|---|---|---|
| Coronado: Poebe's | ■ | ● | ■ | | ■ |
| La Jolla: Top O' The Cove | ■ | ● | | ● | ■ |
| San Diego: Big Kitchen | | ● | | | ■ |
| San Diego: Humphrey's | | | ■ | | ■ |
| Barstow: Slash X Ranch Café | | | | | |
| Death Valley: Wrangler Steakhouse | | ● | ■ | | ■ |
| Death Valley: Inn Dining Room | | ● | ■ | | ■ |
| Palm Springs: Flower Drum | | ● | ■ | ● | ■ |
| Big Sur: Nepenthe | ■ | ● | ■ | ● | ■ |
| Carmel: The French Poodle | | ● | | | |
| Monterey: Fresh Cream | | ● | ■ | | ■ |

For key to symbols see back flap

**Price categories** include a three-course meal for one, half a bottle of house wine, and all unavoidable extra charges such as sales tax and service.

- $ under $20
- $$ $20–30
- $$$ $30–45
- $$$$ $45–60
- $$$$$ over $60

**Outdoor Eating**
Some tables on a patio or terrace.

**Vegetarian Specialties**
One menu always includes a selection of vegetarian dishes.

**Bar Area/Cocktail Bar**
There is a bar area or cocktail bar within the restaurant.

**Fixed-Price Menu**
A fixed-price menu offered at lunch, dinner or both, usually with three courses.

**Children's Facilities**
Small portions and/or high chairs available on request.

| Restaurant | Outdoor Eating | Vegetarian Specialties | Bar Area/Cocktail Bar | Fixed-Price Menu | Children's Facilities |
|---|---|---|---|---|---|
| **Santa Barbara:** *Something's Fishy* $$<br>502 State St, CA 93101. *(805) 966-6607.*<br>The crowd is mixed at this lively Japanese restaurant. Sit at the all-you-can-eat sushi bar or have a Benihana-style dinner cooked and served at your table. | | | | | ■ |
| **Santa Barbara:** *The Wine Cask* $$$<br>813 Anacapa St, CA 93101. *(805) 966-9463.*<br>Mediterranean cuisine is offered here and one of the best wine lists in the US. Eat inside under the decoratively painted ceiling or outside in the courtyard. *L.* | ■ | ● | ■ | | ■ |
| **Santa Cruz:** *Crows Nest* $$<br>2218 E Cliff Dr, CA 95062. *(831) 476-4560.*<br>Perched on Santa Cruz harbor jetty, this restaurant serves fresh seafood, steaks, and pastas. The house specialty is Alderwood smoked salmon. | ■ | ● | ■ | | ■ |
| **San Luis Obispo:** *Tio Alberto's* $<br>1131 Broad St, CA 93401. *(805) 546-9646.*<br>The specialty is *carne asada* (grilled beef) at this popular, old-style Mexican restaurant. No alcohol is served or allowed. | | | | | |

## San Francisco

| Restaurant | Outdoor Eating | Vegetarian Specialties | Bar Area/Cocktail Bar | Fixed-Price Menu | Children's Facilities |
|---|---|---|---|---|---|
| **Berkeley:** *Chez Panisse Restaurant* $$$$$<br>1517 Shattuck Ave, CA 94709. *(510) 548-5525.*<br>One of the country's top restaurants, founder Chef Alice Waters is credited with having invented California cuisine here. *Sun.* | | ● | ■ | ● | |
| **Chinatown & Nob Hill:** *Fornou's Oven* $$$<br>905 California St, Stanford Court Hotel, CA 94108. *(415) 989-1910.*<br>The name comes from the large Portuguese tile oven in the center of this Mediterranean-style restaurant. The rack of lamb is wonderful. | | | ■ | | ■ |
| **Downtown:** *House of Nan King* $<br>919 Kearny St, CA 94133. *(415) 421-1429.*<br>Many consider this the best budget Chinese restaurant in the country. There is an extensive Shanghai menu of braised meats and vegetable dishes. *Sun L.* | | ● | | | |
| **Downtown:** *Cypress Club* $$$$$<br>500 Jackson St, CA 94133. *(415) 296-8555.*<br>There is no more attractive combination of good food, great style, and indefinably San Franciscan "buzz" than in this popular haunt. *L.* | | ● | ■ | | |
| **Fisherman's Wharf:** *Alioto's* $$$$<br>Pier 45, CA 94133. *(415) 673-0183.*<br>Fresh seafood has been served here by the Alioto family since 1930. Fine views of the Golden Gate Bridge. | | ● | ■ | | ■ |
| **Golden Gate Park & the Presidio:** *New Eritrea Restaurant* $$<br>907 Irving St, CA 94122. *(415) 681-1288.*<br>This family-owned Eritrean and Ethiopian restaurant has the best all-you-can-eat weekday buffet lunch in the city. The full bar offers African beers. | | ● | ■ | | |
| **Haight Ashbury:** *Cha Cha Cha* $<br>1801 Haight St, CA 94133. *(415) 386-5758.*<br>You will have to wait for a table at this very popular tapas bar. The menu changes daily and mixes Caribbean, Cajun, and Mexican influences. | | | ■ | | |
| **North Beach:** *Little Joe's & Baby Joe's* $<br>2550 Van Ness, CA 94133. *(415) 433-4343.*<br>One of the best cheap Italian eating places in the city, Little Joe's is very lively, and the food is good. The garlic squid is particularly popular. *limited.* | | ● | | | ■ |

**PACIFIC HEIGHTS:** *Café Marimba* $$
2317 Chestnut St, CA 94123. *(415) 776-1506.*
The brightly painted café in the Marina district makes a perfect backdrop for the innovative southern Mexican specialties served here. *Mon.*

**SAN JOSE:** *Tied House Café and Brewery* $$
65 N San Pedro St, CA 95112. *(408) 295-2739.*
Best known for its beers, which are made on the premises, this lively, airy restaurant features especially good seafood dishes. *Sun L.*

**THE MISSION DISTRICT:** *El Nuevo Frutilandia* $
3077 24th St, CA 94110. *(415) 648-2958.*
The authentic Cuban and Puerto Rican specialties are complemented by a casual Caribbean atmosphere. Serves tropical fruitshakes. *Mon.*

## WINE COUNTRY

**NAPA:** *Napa Valley Wine Train* $$$$
1275 McKinstry St, CA 94559. *(800) 427-4124.* www.winetrain.com
Gourmet California cuisine is served on this luxury diesel train as you enjoy the views of the beautiful Wine Country. *Mon & Tue D.*

**SONOMA:** *Ristorante Piatti* $$
405 1st St West, CA 94576. *(707) 996-2351.*
This bustling Italian bistro is part of a small California chain. The risotto of the day is always delicious, as are the signature pizzas, pasta dishes, and chicken.

## THE NORTH

**EUREKA:** *Samoa Cookhouse* $
59 Cookhouse Lane, CA 95501. *(707) 442-1659.*
For a taste of the North Coast woods as they used to be, nothing beats this century-old dining hall, which still serves mountains of good food.

**MOUNT SHASTA:** *Michael's* $$
313 N Mount Shasta Blvd, CA 96067. *(530) 926-5288.*
Delicious sandwiches, light lunches, and Italian dinners have made this restaurant in the Mount Shasta area a favorite for many years. *Sun, Mon.*

**WEAVERVILLE:** *La Grange Café* $$
226 N Main St, CA 96093. *(530) 623-5325.*
Adventurous Californian health food is offered here at moderate prices, including oganic salads and a wide range of vegetarian dishes. *Sun.*

## GOLD COUNTRY & THE CENTRAL VALLEY

**NEVADA CITY:** *Country Rose Café* $$
300 Commercial St, CA 95959. *(530) 265-6248.*
This busy bistro-style café, housed in an 1860s brick building, specializes in French country cuisine, such as sautéed chicken. A classical guitarist often plays on weekends. Reservations are recommended.

**SACRAMENTO:** *The Firehouse* $$$
1112 2nd St, CA 95814. *(916) 442-4772.*
The original fire pole still stands in this converted fire station, built in the 1850s. The fare is superb with dishes such as glazed duck and filet mignon. *Sun, Mon D, Sat L.*

**SONORA:** *Banny's Café* $$
83 S Stewart St, Suite 100, CA 95370. *(209) 533-4709.*
An eclectic mixture of California, Italian, Mediterranean, and Thai cuisine is served from the seasonal menu at this pleasant café.

## THE HIGH SIERRAS

**SOUTH LAKE TAHOE:** *Chevys* $
3678 Lake Tahoe Blvd, CA 95731. *(530) 542-1741.*
Huge portions of traditional Mexican food and inexpensive cocktails are the main attractions of this popular, casual restaurant.

**YOSEMITE NATIONAL PARK:** *Ahwahnee Dining Room* $$$$
Yosemite Valley, CA 95389. *(559) 252-4848.*
The soaring ceiling of this beautiful hotel dining room makes up for rather bland food. Steaks and other simple dishes are a safe bet.

For key to symbols see back flap

# Alaska & Hawai'i

# ALASKA

FOR MOST VISITORS, *familiar images of Alaska include pristine waterways, towering snowcapped peaks, glaciers calving to form icebergs, and massive grizzly bears feasting on salmon. All this and much more can still be found here on North America's "Last Frontier," where less than one percent of the state's 375 million acres (150 million ha) shows any sign of human habitation.*

Situated at the top of the North American continent and separated from the rest of the country by Canada, Alaska is more than twice the size of Texas, the next largest state. Alaska can be divided into three regions, both geographically and for the purpose of travel. Southeast Alaska, commonly called the Inside Passage, is a long, narrow stretch of islands and channels sandwiched between the Pacific Ocean and Canada's Coast Mountains. Picture-postcard coastal towns, including the state capital Juneau, are linked conveniently by an efficient state-run ferry system.

The bulk of Alaska's land mass, however, lies in the continent's extreme northwest corner, closer to Russia than the "Lower 48" states. The modern city of Anchorage is a good base for exploring the Kenai Peninsula and Denali National Park, or as a jumping-off point for more adventurous destinations such as Kodiak Island and the Alaska Peninsula. To the west of the mainland, the windswept volcanic archipelago of the Aleutian Islands stretches 1,200 miles (1,932 km) west into the Bering Sea.

**Russian doll on sale in Juneau**

### HISTORY

Alaska's southeast corner is 500 miles (805 km) from the rest of the US, but its farthest reaches a mere 50 miles (80 km) from Russia. As a result, the state's history reflects its role as a bridge and buffer between these two powerful nations. Human history here goes back much farther, since Alaska was the point of entry for some of the first people to set foot in North America, who crossed a land bridge over the Bering Strait 13,000 to 30,000 years ago. While some groups continued their migrations southward, a few remained for millenia, hunting and fishing until the arrival of Western Europeans. The original Alaskans' descendants today include the island-dwelling Aleut, the coastal Tlingit, the Athabascans of the interior, and the Eskimos of artic and western Alaska.

**A panoramic view of North America's highest peak, Mount McKinley in Denali National Park**

**◁ Hawai'i's Makapu'u Beach on southeast O'ahu, backed by the peaks of the Ko'olau Range**

**A brown bear fishing for salmon at Brooks Camp, Katmai National Park, Alaska Peninsula**

The first non-Native settlements were outposts built by Russian fur traders in the late 18th century. Although their far-flung colony stretched as far south as California, it declined as trappers decimated once-huge populations of seals and sea otters. Seen as a liability, Alaska was sold by Russia in 1867 to the US Secretary of State William Seward. The purchase was popularly considered a waste of money and dubbed "Seward's Folly"; however, doubts vanished when the first of many deposits of gold was found near Juneau. More mineral discoveries, including gold in 1898 at distant Nome, as well as vast quantities of copper, and oil at Prudhoe Bay, have all proved the wisdom of Seward's purchase.

## Alaska Today

Alaska is home to 635,000 people. Of the population, 16 percent are of Native descent, while the remainder come from diverse backgrounds (only 34 percent of the total are born in the state). It has a population density of just one person per square mile (compared to over 1,000 in New Jersey).

**Visitors at Aialik Glacier, one of the main attractions at Kenai Fjords National Park**

Alaska's economy depends upon oil from the North Slope, but government jobs, seafood processing, and tourism are also important. Anchorage is a major international hub for air cargo shipments. Over time, there has been a growing awareness to preserve and protect Alaska's unique wilderness from the commercial pressures arising from the state's natural wealth. The vast majority of Alaska is owned by the government, and much of this is protected in national parks and other undeveloped areas stretching from Glacier Bay to the Gates of the Arctic.

## Key Dates in History

**13,000–30,000 years ago** Migratory peoples cross from present-day Siberia into Alaska

**1741** Working for the Czar of Russia, Danish explorer Vitus Bering and his crew are the first Europeans to visit Alaska

**1867** To ease an economic recession, the Czar of Russia sells Alaska to the US for $7.2 million

**1880** Gold is discovered near Juneau

**1897** The Klondike Gold Rush hits Skagway

**1912** Alaska becomes a US Territory

**1942** US Army builds the 1,442-mile (2,322-km) Alaska Highway as an overland link

**1959** Alaska becomes the 49th state

**1964** Good Friday earthquake destroys much of Anchorage

**1968** Oil discovered at Prudhoe Bay

**1977** Trans-Alaska pipeline completed

**1989** *Exxon Valdez* runs aground on Bligh Reef, spilling 11 million gallons (50 million liters) of oil into Prince William Sound

**2001 onwards** Alaska is a resource-dependent state, and the potential extraction of oil from the Arctic National Wildlife Refuge continues to stir a national debate

# Exploring Alaska

A VAST WILDERNESS OF VIRGIN rivers, towering mountain peaks, abundant wildlife, and calving glaciers, Alaska is by far the largest state in the United States. Its sheer size means that travel takes up a fair proportion of a visitor's time. However, the state has an excellent transportation and tourism infrastructure, which caters to a million visitors each year, most of whom arrive during the brief summer season from late May to early September. Good roads connect Anchorage, Fairbanks, and other cities, but much of Southeast Alaska – including the capital city of Juneau – are inaccessible by road. Ferries, planes, and cruise ships connect coastal towns, while remote bush villages are accessed only by air.

**King Salmon Antler's Inn, outside Katmai NP, Alaska Peninsula**

## Sights at a Glance

Ketchikan 1
Sitka 2
Juneau 3
Glacier Bay National Park 4
Skagway 5
Anchorage 6
Valdez 7
Seward 8
Homer 9
Kodiak Island 10
Alaska Peninsula 11
Aleutian Islands 12
Nome 13
Fairbanks 14
*Denali National Park pp742–3* 15

### *See Also*

• ***Practical Information*** p756

• ***Where to Stay*** pp758–9

• ***Where to Eat*** p762

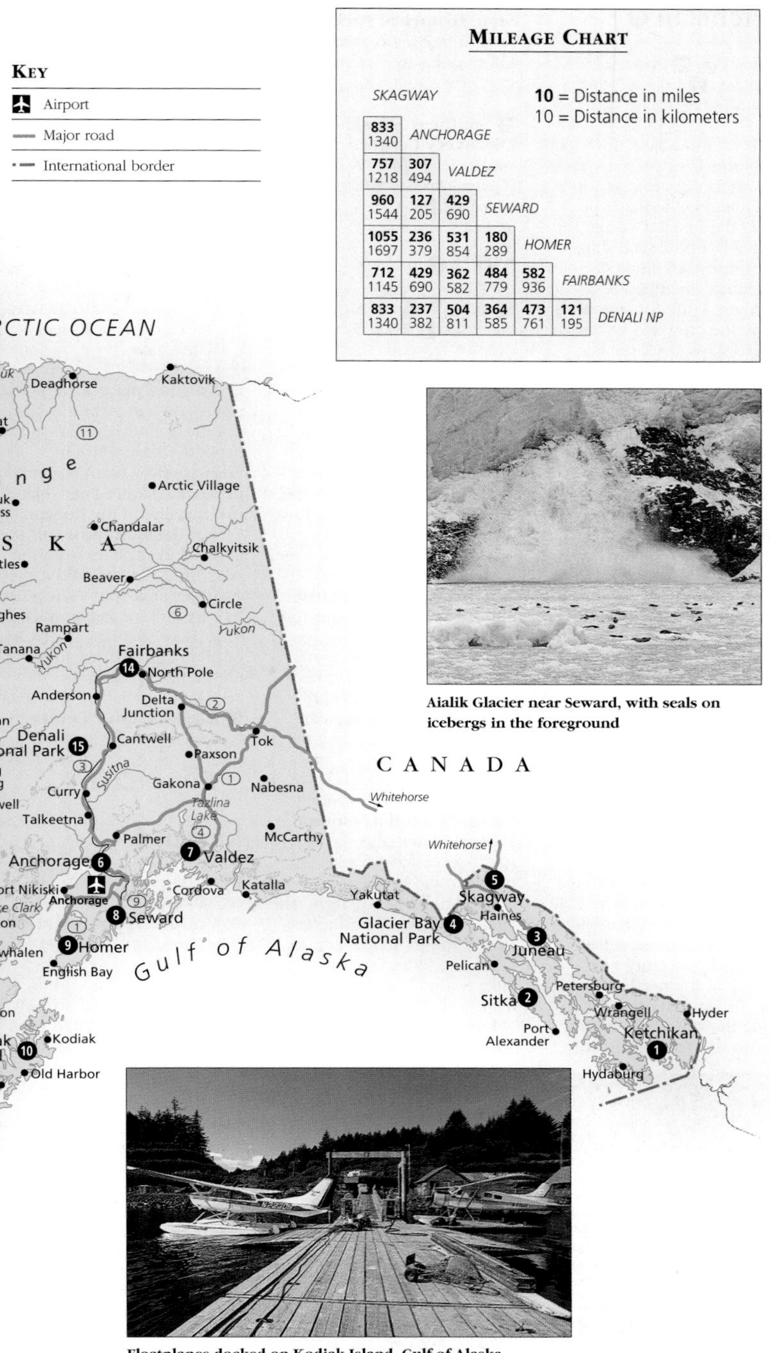


**Mileage Chart**

**10** = Distance in miles
10 = Distance in kilometers

| SKAGWAY | | | | | | |
|---|---|---|---|---|---|---|
| **833** 1340 | ANCHORAGE | | | | | |
| **757** 1218 | **307** 494 | VALDEZ | | | | |
| **960** 1544 | **127** 205 | **429** 690 | SEWARD | | | |
| **1055** 1697 | **236** 379 | **531** 854 | **180** 289 | HOMER | | |
| **712** 1145 | **429** 690 | **362** 582 | **484** 779 | **582** 936 | FAIRBANKS | |
| **833** 1340 | **237** 382 | **504** 811 | **364** 585 | **473** 761 | **121** 195 | DENALI NP |

Aialik Glacier near Seward, with seals on icebergs in the foreground

Floatplanes docked on Kodiak Island, Gulf of Alaska

## Ketchikan ❶

*9,000. 2 miles (3 km) S of downtown. 131 Front Street, (907) 225-6166.*

STRUNG OUT ALONG the waters of the Tongass Narrows and backed by forested hills, Ketchikan is the first stop along the Inside Passage for Alaska-bound cruise ships and ferries. All kinds of watercraft, floatplanes, and kayakers jostle for space along the crowded waterfront. Cruise ships dock outside downtown, providing passengers with easy access to local attractions such as the **Creek Street** precinct. Formerly the heart of a red-light district, the street is lined with colorfully restored wooden houses built on pilings over the water and linked by a boardwalk. The creek below fills up with spawning salmon in late summer.

Even for those who are not planning a trip into the wilderness, the **Southeast Alaska Discovery Center** is definitely worth a visit. Exhibits here relate the human and natural history of the southeast region of Alaska, and also include a fabulous re-creation of a rainforest. Ketchikan's **Totem Heritage Center** displays an incredible collection of more than 30 original totems poles, many more than a century old.

Lying to the north of the city, Tongass Avenue runs along the waterfront all the way to the **Totem Bight State Historical Park**. From here, a trail leads past huge totem poles to a reconstruction of a Native clan house.

### Southeast Alaska Discovery Center

50 Main Street. *(907) 228-6220. 8am–5pm daily. Oct–Apr: Sun & Mon.*

## Sitka ❷

*8,900. 7 miles (11 km) N of downtown. 303 Lincoln St, (907) 747-5940. Alaska Day (Oct 18).*

FOUNDED BY Russian entrepreneur Alexander Baranof in 1799, Sitka was the capital of Russian America until Alaska was sold to the United States in 1867. Even now, a strong Russian influence survives here. The center of town is dominated by **St. Michael's Cathedral**, a Russian Orthodox cathedral that was rebuilt after the original 1848 structure burned down in 1966. It preserves many Russian artifacts, including the Sitka Madonna, supposedly blessed with healing powers. Beyond St. Michael's is **Sitka National Historic Park**, the site of a fierce week-long battle between the Russians and local Tlingit tribe in 1804. The area is sprinkled with totem poles, and its shores are gently lapped by the waters of Sitka Sound. Native workers display their craft skills at a cultural center throughout the warm summer. The park is also a good place to view the town's natural setting. Islands dot the Sound, and the snow-capped volcano Mount Edgecumbe – often compared to Japan's Mount Fuji – sits majestically on the horizon.

Totem pole, Sitka

The Russian-style St. Michael's Cathedral, Sitka

The **Alaska Raptor Center**, across Indian River from the park, rehabilitates bald eagles, owls, and falcons. Visitors are free to walk or join a guided tour. Sitka also has a network of hiking and biking trails for the more adventurous.

### Alaska Raptor Center

1000 Raptor Way. *(907) 747-8662. May–Sep: 8am–4pm Mon–Fri. Oct–Apr.*

## Juneau ❸

*31,000. Auke Bay, 14 miles (22 km) NW of downtown, (907) 465-3940. Centennial Hall Visitor Center, 101 Egan Dr, (907) 586-2201.*

JUNEAU IS POSSIBLY the most spectacularly located capital city in the US. It is also the most remote, with no road access to the outside world or even to the rest of Alaska. With its large resident population, as well as the 700,000 visitors who arrive during the short summer (late May–early Sep), Juneau is the busy hub of the Inside Passage. Sandwiched between steep-sided forested peaks and the Gastineau Channel, the heart of the city is an intriguing mix of modern high-rise buildings and historic gems such as the **Red Dog Saloon**, and the **Alaskan Hotel**.

Ketchikan's Creek Street, with restored buildings linked by a boardwalk

The best way to appreciate the town's wonderful location is by taking the tramway up **Mount Roberts**, from where the panorama extends across Gastineau Channel. The downtown **Alaska State Museum** contains a fine collection of Russian artifacts as well as Native crafts such as Eskimo masks. Its natural history section exhibits a re-creation of a bald eagle's nest. Located at the northern end of the city, 13 miles (21 km) from downtown, **Mendenhall Glacier** is an impressive attraction. A part of the massive Juneau Icefield, this slowly retreating 1.5-mile (2.4-km) wide glacier is calving icebergs into Mendenhall Lake. A lakeside visitor center offers interpretive panels describing the forces behind glacial movement. This is the starting point for hiking trails that provide close-up views of the glacier. Rafting is also offered here for adventure seekers.

**Alaska State Museum**
395 Whittier St. *(907) 465-2901.* *mid-May–mid-Sep: daily; mid-Sep–mid-May: Tue–Sun.* *major public hols.*

**Mendenhall Glacier**
Off Mendenhall Loop Rd. *(907) 789-0097.* *May–Sep: 8am–6:30pm daily; Oct–Apr: 10am–4pm Thu–Sun.*

## Glacier Bay National Park ❹

*from Juneau.* *(907) 697-2230.* **Glacier Bay Cruiseline** *Departures: Jun–mid-Sep: daily (times vary).* *(800) 451-5952.*

GLACIER BAY HAS changed greatly since the British explorer Captain George Vancouver *(see p612)* found his way through Icy Strait in 1794. During the ensuing 200 years, the glaciers have retreated almost 100 miles (160 km), creating a magnificent waterway indented by long bays and protected by the 5,156-sq-mile (13,354-sq-km) national park. Six glaciers reach the sea and break up into massive chunks of ice, which float into a bay inhabited by humpback whales, porpoises, and seals.

Most visitors to Glacier Bay arrive aboard cruise ships. Travelers can also come by way of the hamlet of Gustavus from Juneau, making the short overland trip to Bartlett Cove and Glacier Bay Lodge *(see p758)* by taxi. From Bartlett Cove, it is 40 miles (64 km) to the nearest glacier in a high-speed catamaran. An onboard park naturalist describes the bay's natural history. The tidewater glaciers are the main highlight of the trip to Glacier Bay National Park.

The scenic White Pass & Yukon Route Railroad near Skagway

## Skagway ❺

800. *SW end of Broadway.* *Broadway at 2nd Ave, (907) 983-2854.*

THE FINAL NORTHBOUND stop for travelers on the Inside Passage is this little tourist town surrounded by towering peaks. In 1897, thousands of fortune seekers heading for the Klondike goldfields arrived here only to be faced with an almost insurmountable obstacle – the 33-mile (53 km) **Chilkoot Trail**. This trail traversed a harrowing 45-degree slope nicknamed the "Golden Staircase" over the White Pass to the headwaters of the Yukon River. In the following years, Skagway became a lawless outpost, unofficially ruled by the notorious businessman "Soapy" Smith, who died in a famous shootout with a local surveyor outside the City Hall.

Today, Skagway's fortunes rely largely on promoting its colorful history. The whole of the downtown district is protected as the **Klondike Gold Rush National Historic Park**, encompassing false-fronted buildings, old-time saloons, as well as the distinctive Arctic Brotherhood Hall, whose interesting façade is decorated with about 20,000 pieces of driftwood. The **White Pass & Yukon Route Railroad**, which was originally built over the White Pass as an alternative to the Chilkoot Trail, now operates purely for tourists on a scenic three-hour long round-trip to the pass and back.

### ALASKA MARINE HIGHWAY

Logo, Alaska Marine Highway

The state-operated ferry service links towns that are inaccessible by road throughout southeast and south central Alaska, extending service as far south as Prince Rupert (British Columbia) and Bellingham (Washington). En route, visitors pass magnificent fjords, towering glaciers, and virgin forests. The comfortable and well-equipped vessels carry vehicles, and feature cabins, dining areas, and onboard naturalists. It is possible to even pitch tents on the outer deck. Bookings should be made well in advance *(see p756)*.

Clan house in the Alaska Native Heritage Center, Anchorage

## Anchorage 6

*270,000.* *4th Ave at F St, (907) 274-3531.* *Alaska State Fair (late Aug).*

LYING BETWEEN Cook Inlet and the Chugach Mountains, Anchorage is Alaska's largest city. Although this coastal urban sprawl is often described as being un-Alaskan, it is still worth spending a little time in this northern metropolis, soaking up the wealth of sights and taking advantage of its many services. It also serves as Alaska's financial and transportation hub. Most of downtown was destroyed by the 1964 Good Friday earthquake *(see p733)*, when the north side of 4th Avenue sank 10 ft (3 m). Interpretive displays at **Earthquake Park**, west of downtown toward the airport, tell the story of the Big One. The park offers superb views over the downtown skyline to the Chugach Mountains.

One of Alaska's finest museums, the **Anchorage Museum of History and Art** displays an impressive collection of Alaska-themed paintings, and an Alaska Gallery with creative dioramas that chronicle prehistoric times through the present day. At the **Alaska Native Heritage Center**, costumed actors provide visitors with a glimpse of Native culture through dance. An entire section has been dedicated to a re-created Native village set beside a pond. Located 50 miles (80 km) southeast of the city, **Portage Glacier** is steadily retreating and is now out of sight from the visitor center. A tour boat plies the lake close to the glacier.

**Anchorage Museum of History & Art**
121 W 7th Ave. *(907) 343-6173.* *mid-May–mid-Sep: 9am–6pm daily; mid-Sep–mid-May: 10am–6pm Wed–Sat, noon–5pm Sun.*

**Alaska Native Heritage Center**
8800 Heritage Center Dr. *(907) 330-8000.* *May–Sep: 9am–6pm daily; Oct–Apr: 10am–5pm Sat.*

## Valdez 7

*4,000.* *downtown.* *200 Chenega St, (800) 770-5954.* **Prince William Sound Cruises & Tours** *Departures: late Jun–early Sep: daily, (877) 777-2805.* *limited.*

THE PICTURESQUE town of Valdez nestles below snowcapped peaks along an arm of Prince William Sound, a vast bay encompassing islands, glaciers, and icy waters teeming with wildlife. This is North America's northernmost ice-free port. The **Trans-Alaska Pipeline**, which runs above ground for 800 miles (1,288 km) across the state from Prudhoe Bay on the Arctic Ocean, ends here, from where it is transferred to oil tankers. The *Exxon Valdez*, the best known tanker, infamously ran aground in 1989, spilling millions of gallons of oil into the Sound. A huge cleanup effort has attempted to restore the Sound, and although there are no obvious signs of the spill today, its adverse effect on birds, fish, and marine mammals persists. A cruise of the Sound passes the **Columbia Glacier**, which is more than 3 miles (4.8 km) wide at its 250-ft (75-m) high face, and continously calves icebergs into the sea. Check with the vistor center for summer tours. The town's **Valdez Museum** explores the Native culture, the importance of oil for the local economy, the *Exxon Valdez* oil spill, and the devastating 1964 Good Friday earthquake, whose epicenter lay less than 60 miles (97 km) from Valdez. The town also offers great hiking, sea kayaking, and rafting opportunities.

Bronze sculpture, Valdez Museum

**Valdez Museum**
217 Egan Dr. *(907) 835-2764.* *mid-May–Sep: 9am–6pm daily; Oct–mid-May: 1pm–5pm Mon–Fri, noon–4pm Sat.*

Re-creation of a traditional miner's cabin, Valdez Museum

The magnificent Exit Glacier in the Kenai Fjords National Park, north of Seward

## Seward 8

4,000. downtown. 3rd St, (907) 224-8051.

One of the only large towns on the Kenai Peninsula, Seward is a charming fishing port at the head of Resurrection Bay, surrounded by the snow-capped Kenai Mountains. One of its main attractions is the **Alaska SeaLife Center**, which exhibits the marine life of the surrounding ocean. The centerpiece is a string of three huge aquariums holding colorful puffins, seals, and sea lions. Smaller tanks provide a home for crabs and octopuses, while a "touch tank" encourages a hands-on approach to exploring sessile life along the tidal zone.

Seward is encircled by the **Kenai Fjords National Park**, a 906-sq-mile (2,347-sq-km) glaciated coastal wilderness. From the gigantic Hardy Icefield, glaciers radiate in all directions, eight of which are "tidewater glaciers," which extend to sea level. Seward's downtown dock is the departure point for boat trips along the park's coastline. These day cruises also provide excellent opportunities for viewing whales, seals, sea lions, porpoises, and large concentrations of photogenic puffins perched on rocky outcrops. The park's most accessible glacier is Exit Glacier, located off the highway, 4 miles (6.4 km) north of Seward. From the end of the access road, a short trail leads through a forest of stunted trees, suddenly emerging at the improbable sight of a deep-blue river of ice running through the trees.

**Alaska SeaLife Center**
Railway Ave. *(907) 224-6300.* *mid-Apr–mid-Sep: 8am–7pm daily; mid-Sep–mid-Apr: 10am–5pm daily.* *Thanksgiving, Dec 25.*

**Kenai Fjords National Park**
**Park** **Visitor Center** *(907) 224-7500.* *mid-Apr–Sep: daily; Oct: Mon–Fri.*

## Homer 9

*4,000.* *Homer Spit.* *201 Sterling Hwy, (907) 235-7740.* **Central Charters Booking Agency** *Departures: Jun–Sep, (907) 235-7847.* *limited.*

At the end of the Sterling Highway lies Homer, a delightful little hamlet by the water. It was discovered by Homer Pennock, a gold-prospector who arrived here in 1896. Today, this town has become a popular destination for visitors. Its main focus is **Homer Spit**, a 4-mile (6.4-km) finger of land that juts into Kachemak Bay, with the rugged Kenai Mountains glistening across the water. A busy road traverses the entire Spit, passing beaches strewn with driftwood, a colorful collection of dry-docked boats, fishing-supply stores, and lively restaurants. Known as the "Halibut Capital of the World," fishing is its main attraction. Charter operators and their boats line the Spit; day trips include tackle and bait as well as instruction. Those who manage to hook a 200-lb (90-kg) halibut can arrange to have it frozen and shipped home. The **Fishing Hole** on the Spit is a man-made waterhole stocked with salmon for an easy catch.

The magnificent wilderness of the **Kachemak Bay State Park**, on the bay's opposite shore, can be explored through a number of hiking trails. The best-known of these leads the visitor to the Grewingk Glacier.

Fishermen with a halibut "weigh-in" on Homer Spit

The northern end of Kodiak Island, covered with thick spruce forests

## Kodiak Island ⓾

*14,000. downtown.*
*100 Marine Way, (907) 486-4782.*

THE SECOND-LARGEST island in the United States, Kodiak extends for 100 miles (160 km) across the Gulf of Alaska. Most of the island is an inaccessible stretch of wilderness protected by the 2,969-sq-mile (7,690-sq-km) **Kodiak National Wildlife Refuge**. Kodiak Island is famous as the habitat of about 2,500 Kodiak bears – the world's largest brown bear – some of which stand 10 ft (3 m) tall and weigh up to 1,500 lb (675 kg). The visitor center provides details on charter flights to the best viewing spots.

Most of the island's residents live in the town of Kodiak, home of the country's largest Coast Guard station and its third-largest fishing fleet. North America's oldest Russian building, a storehouse dating to 1808, is now the excellent **Baranof Museum**. A repository of Kodiak's history, the museum's highlights include a superb samovar (urn) collection, Aleut kayaks, and photographs of the town after it was hit by a *tsunami* (massive tidal wave), triggered by the 1964 Good Friday earthquake *(see p733)*. To explore the local fishing industry, follow Shelikof Street past the harbor to the canneries, one of which was converted from a 1945 troop ship.

### Baranof Museum

*101 Marine Way. (907) 486-5920.*
*Jun–Aug: 10am–4pm Mon–Sat; noon–4pm Sun; reduced hours for the rest of the year. Feb.*

## Alaska Peninsula ⓫

*King Salmon Airport, (907) 246-4250.*

DOMINATED BY the Alaska Range, this remote part of the state attracts visitors for its intriguing wilderness and wildlife viewing opportunities. In 1912, the second-largest blast in recorded history occurred when the peninsula's Mount Novarupta erupted, covering a 400-sq-mile (1,036-sq-km) area with ash and pumice up to a height of 700 ft (210 m). The blast was heard as far away as Seattle, and the ash that erupted stayed in the atmosphere for an entire year, changing weather patterns worldwide.

Samovar, Baranof Museum

The 6,250-sq-mile (16,187-sq-km) **Katmai National Park** encompasses the area where the volcano was most active. A remnant is the Valley of 10,000 Smokes, where hot gases and ash continue to spew across a lunar-like landscape. Bears and other wildlife abound in the park, most famously at Brooks Falls.

Adjacent to Katmai, photographers from around the world gather at the **McNeil River State Game Sanctuary** to photograph brown bears catching salmon as they struggle up to McNeil River Falls. Access to the falls is by air taxi from King Salmon or Homer *(see p739)*.

### McNeil River State Game Sanctuary

*Best viewing: Jul–mid-Aug.*
***Permit required** from Department of Fish & Game, (907) 267-2182.*

A brown bear at Katmai National Park, Alaska Peninsula

## Aleutian Islands ⓬

14,000. Unalaska. Unalaska Visitors' Bureau, Broadway, Unalaska, (907) 581-2612.

BEYOND THE Alaska Peninsula, the summits of the Aleutian Range have created a string of islands that extend 1,200 miles (1,932 km) into the Pacific Ocean. Originally settled by hardy Aleut seal hunters, the islands were occupied for more than a year by the Japanese during World War II. Today, over half the archipelago's population live in the town of **Unalaska**, set around a picturesque Dutch Harbor. This town is North America's number one seafood producer. The catch includes crab, halibut, cod, and pollock. Its harbor is lined with fishing boats, container cranes, and processing plants, all catering to this industry. The **Russian Orthodox Church of the Holy Ascension**, built in 1827, dominates the foreshore.

## Nome ⓭

3,600. 301 Front St, (907) 443-6624.

FEW WOULD ARGUE with the local catchphrase that "there's no place like Nome." Perched on the edge of the Bering Sea, closer to Russia than to Anchorage, the town was named after an early cartographer marked this location as "Name?" on a map. Later another mapmaker misread the annotation as "Nome." Gold was discovered in nearby **Anvil Creek** around the same time that prospectors were moving on from the played-out Klondike *(see p733)* goldfields, and by the year 1900 approximately 20,000 miners had descended on this remote outpost.

Although Nome is now a shadow of its former self, it is still a fascinating and popular destination. Friendly staff at the tourist information office obligingly indicate historic relics such as the **Last Train to Nowhere**, and the rusting hulks of dredges that have long since been abandoned. There are many hiking trails stretching across the treeless tundra. Panning for gold along the beach is another unique activity.

**View of the aurora borealis, or northern lights, Alaska**

## Fairbanks ⓮

35,400. 550 1st Ave, (907) 456-5774.

SURROUNDED BY sub-arctic wilderness, Fairbanks is Alaska's second-largest city and has one of the largest populations at this latitude anywhere in the world. Located just 150 miles (241 km) south of the Arctic Circle, the sun barely dips below the horizon at the time of the summer solstice (Jun 21). The long hours of darkness through winter make it a good place to view the aurora borealis, or northern lights, a phenomenon of dazzling sheets of light produced in the sky by electron and proton particles of the solar wind. Fairbanks is also known for its extremes in temperature, which often soar well above 90° F (32° C) in summer, but dip below -60° F (-15° C) in winter. The city's many unique attractions include the **Ice Museum**, where a huge walk-in freezer holds impressive ice sculptures. Another museum on the University of Alaska grounds provides a home for a 36,000-year-old mummified bison. At **Pioneer Park**, historic buildings collected from around the state help to recreate a Gold Rush-era town on the banks of the Chena River. One of its main highlights is a restored sternwheeler, the *Nenana*, claimed to be the world's second largest wooden hulled vessel. Each summer evening, Pioneer Park plays host to a musical revue, with dancers who are dressed in period costume.

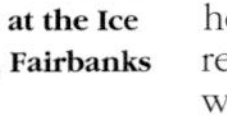

**Caribou at the Ice Museum, Fairbanks**

**Pioneer Park**

Airport Way. (907) 459-1087. daily. **Gold Rush Town** Memorial Day–Labor Day: 11am–9pm daily.

**The Iditarod Trail Sled Dog Race**

### THE IDITAROD

In March each year, depending on the snowfall, dog mushers from around the world gather in Anchorage for the Iditarod Trail Sled Dog Race, one of the world's most grueling races. After an outbreak of diphtheria in Nome in 1925, a relay of mushers and their dogs took just six days to cover 670 frozen miles (1,078 km), delivering a vaccine that saved hundreds of lives. Today, the race is a professional production, with top competitors; the racers become household names, and images of the sled dogs fighting the elements are beamed worldwide.

# Denali National Park ⓯

ALASKA'S TOP ATTRACTION, Denali National Park encompasses 9,375 sq miles (24,281 sq km). The 20,320-ft (6,194-m) high Mount McKinley, North America's highest peak, dominates the landscape, rising 10,000 ft (3,048 m) above the surrounding peaks. The park is home to abundant wildlife, including grizzly bears, moose, and caribou, and wildflowers explode with color across the tundra in July. Only one road penetrates Denali, traversing varied landscapes that include lowlands and high mountain passes. Several hiking trails can be enjoyed in the vicinity of the visitor center. Other activities include sled dog demonstrations, rafting on the Nenana River, and flight-seeing around Mount McKinley.

**The Alaska Railroad**
*Many travelers opt for rail travel when it comes to visiting Denali.*

**★ Wonder Lake**
*On a clear day, Mount McKinley is visible from various locations within Denali National Park.*

**★ Mount McKinley**
*View of the snow clad Mount McKinley from Park Road, en route to Wonder Lake. Originally called Denali, "the Great One," by Athabascan Natives, many Alaskans still continue to refer to Mount McKinley by its old name.*

**★ Whitewater Rafting**
*Thrills and spills abound on the Nenana River, which flows along the eastern boundary of the national park.*

## Visitors' Checklist

**Park** ◯ *daily.* **Visitor Center** ◯ *mid–end May: 9am–5pm daily; Jun–mid-Sep: 9am–9pm daily; mid-Sep–mid-May 10am–4pm daily.* ☎ *(907) 683-2294.* **Park shuttle buses:** *Reserve seats in advance. Some buses return from the Eielson Visitor Center, which has great views of Mount McKinley; others continue to Wonder Lake 25 miles (40 km) from the peak. The 90-m/150-km round trip takes 13 hours.* **Departures:** *mid-May–mid-Sep: daily from 6am to 2pm at regular intervals. Check website for schedule.* ☎ *(907) 272-7275.* W www.nps.gov/dena

Sanctuary River
Teklanika River
Savage River
Riley Creek
Igloo Creek
Toklat
Nenana River
Alaska Range
Cantwell
Eielson Visitor Center
Glacier
Eldridge Glacier
Alaska Railroad

**Tourists on a park shuttle bus trip**

**Key**

- - Park boundary
Camping
Alaska railroad
Major road
Unpaved road

## Wildlife Viewing

**Mountain goat**

One of the major attractions in Alaska is wildlife viewing, and Denali National Park provides great opportunities to see a wide variety of the state's largest and most impressive animals. Grizzly bears, moose, Dall sheep, and caribou are routinely sighted by visitors from the park shuttle buses, with drivers stopping to allow viewing and photography. The park is also home to wolves, and while they are not as commonly sighted as many other mammals, spotting these magnificent creatures in the wild is a memorable experience for visitors.

**Grizzly bear feeding on berries**

**Moose wading in water**

**Caribou are a common sight**

## Star Sights

- ★ **Mount McKinley**
- ★ **Whitewater Rafting**
- ★ **Wonder Lake**

# HAWAI'I

A TROPICAL ISLAND PARADISE *of golden sand beaches, waterfalls, and lush forests, the Aloha State attracts more than 6 million visitors a year. An isolated archipelago in the middle of the Pacific Ocean, the islands' exotic landscape and luxurious hospitality offer a wealth of experiences from volcanic eruptions and world-class surfing to glimpses of the fascinating cultural heritage of Polynesia.*

Located in the middle of the Pacific Ocean, 2,500 miles (4,000 km) southwest of Los Angeles, the Hawaiian Islands are volcanic in origin. In fact, the islands are still evolving, as is evident from the lava flows on the slopes of 13,796-ft (4,205-m) Mount Kīlauea on the island of Hawai'i or the "Big Island."

Polynesian dancer, a popular attraction

The next largest island, Maui, was formed by the dormant volcano Haleakalā. This, the fastest-growing of the islands, still retains some significant history, especially in the former whaling port of Lahaina. The next island along in the chain, Moloka'i, is well off the tourist trail. Formerly a pineapple ranching center, Moloka'i is famous for the towering cliffs that line its northern coast. Lāna'i, another small island, is also offshore from Maui.

The most popular and developed island is O'ahu, where three-quarters of the population lives and most of the visitors congregate. The center of O'ahu is Honolulu, the state capital and only big city. Across the ocean from O'ahu sits magical Kaua'i, known as the "Garden Isle" for its verdant rainforests, kept moist by more than 400 inches (10 m) of annual rainfall.

The summit of Maui's Mount Haleakalā

### HISTORY

Hawai'i's historical connections to the US mainland are both distant and contentious. Originally colonized by Polynesians, Hawai'i was a group of independent kingdoms when it was discovered by English sailor Captain James Cook in 1778. Initially welcomed by the natives, Cook was killed by them a year later. Other explorers followed, bringing new, often fatal diseases. By the end of the 18th century, however, the islands had been united into a respected monarchy under the revered monarch, King Kamehameha the Great (ruled 1795–1819).

During the early 19th century, European traders introduced fundamental changes. Christianity was introduced by Puritan missionaries from Boston in 1820, while economically, forestry and whaling gained importance. These proved destabilizing to Native culture, and by the 1880s, white American entrepreneurs, mainly sugar cane and pineapple farmers, acquired control, and the monarchy was overthrown in 1893. After a series of highly complicated political maneuvers, Hawai'i became part of the US in 1898. Much later, in 1993, the US issued a formal apology to the people of Hawai'i for its leading role in the "illegal overthrow of the Kingdom of Hawai'i."

**Canoeing and swimming, some of the most popular water activities in Hawai'i**

Powerful American plantation owners dominated the first half of the 1900s, and all attempts to unionize the low-paid, mostly Japanese labor force were firmly squelched. Ironically, it took the threat of invasion to make the feudal institutions democratic. On December 7, 1941, Japan attacked Pearl Harbor, instigating America's entry into World War II, and changing Hawai'i forever.

## Hawai'i Today

Located midway between mainland US and the Far East, Hawai'i has a diverse population. Of its 1.1 million residents, roughly one-third are non-Asian, one-third are of Japanese descent, and the rest a wide-ranging mix of Filipinos, Chinese, Koreans, and Samoans. Only a few thousand full-blooded indigenous Hawaiians survive today, but the native spirit of "Aloha," a Hawaiian word that simultaneously means hello, goodbye, welcome, and love, is still alive.

The introduction of air travel in 1959 brought Hawai'i within easy reach of the West Coast. As tourism became the chief industry, resort developments proliferated, signaling a new era for island economy. At the same time, a resurgence in Native culture, language, and crafts has softened the harsher edges of the commercial development, so that no matter where you go in the islands, Polynesian roots grow very close to the surface.

**Cyclist on a scenic bike ride, away from the crowded beach Waikīkī**

### Key Dates in History

**AD 400** Polynesians migrate to the Hawaiian Islands from the Marquesas Islands

**1778** James Cook is the first European to the islands, which he names the Sandwich Islands after his benefactor, the Earl of Sandwich

**1795** Reign of Kamehameha begins

**1893** With the support of the US Navy, American businessmen overthrow the Kingdom of Hawai'i, declaring an independent republic

**1898** Hawai'i is annexed as a US Territory

**1941** Japanese bombers attack Pearl Harbor on December 7

**1959** Hawai'i becomes the 50th state

**1983** Mount Kīlauea begins its present eruption

**1993** US government issues a formal apology on the 100th anniversary of the overthrow of the Kingdom of Hawai'i

**1996** Citizens vote to convene on the issue of sovereignty

# Exploring Hawai'i

THE WORLD'S MOST isolated archipelago, Hawai'i lies 2,500 miles (4,000 km) from the West Coast. The five main islands – O'ahu, Moloka'i, Maui, Hawai'i, and Kaua'i – stretch across over 500 miles (805 km) of the Pacific Ocean. Although most of its six million annual visitors arrive by air in Honolulu, the state capital, travel from one island to another is mainly by inter-island flights. A handful of ferry services and some luxury cruises also link the islands. The most reliable way to explore individual islands is by car, as public transportation is minimal, except on O'ahu.

A secluded swimming spot on the rocky coast of the Ke'anae Peninsula

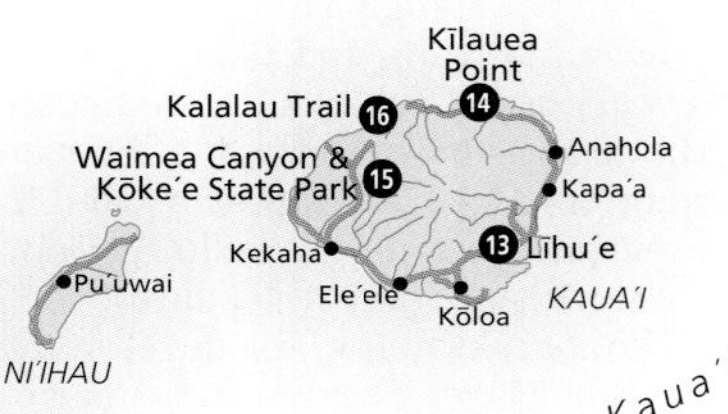



## SIGHTS AT A GLANCE

**O'ahu**
Honolulu 1
Byodo-In Temple 2
Hawai'i's Plantation Village 3
North Shore 4

**Moloka'i & Maui**
Kaunakakai 5
Kalaupapa National Historical Park 6
Lahaina 7
Haleakalā National Park 8
Hāna 9

**Hawai'i Island**
*Hawai'i Volcanoes National Park p752* 10
Hilo 11
Pu'uhonua O Hōnaunau National Historical Park 12

**Kaua'i**
Līhu'e 13
Kīlauea Point 14
Waimea Canyon & Kōke'e State Park 15
Kalalau Trail 16

Windsurfers in action at Ho'okipa Beach County Park, near the beach town of Pā'ia on Maui's north shore

**Dramatic Honomanū Bay with its clear blue waters, surrounded by lushly forested cliffs**

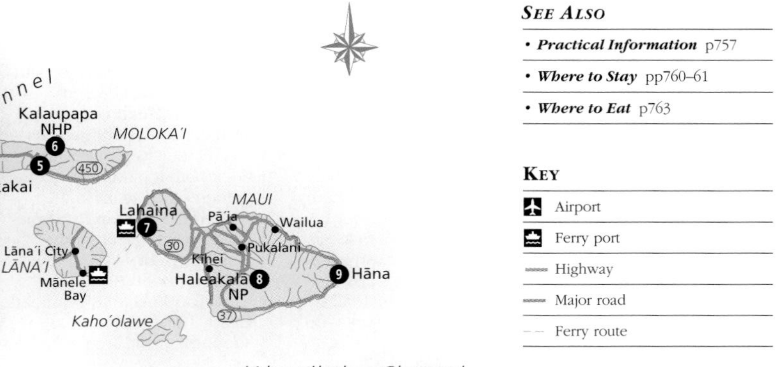


### SEE ALSO

- ***Practical Information*** p757
- ***Where to Stay*** pp760–61
- ***Where to Eat*** p763

### KEY

- Airport
- Ferry port
- Highway
- Major road
- Ferry route

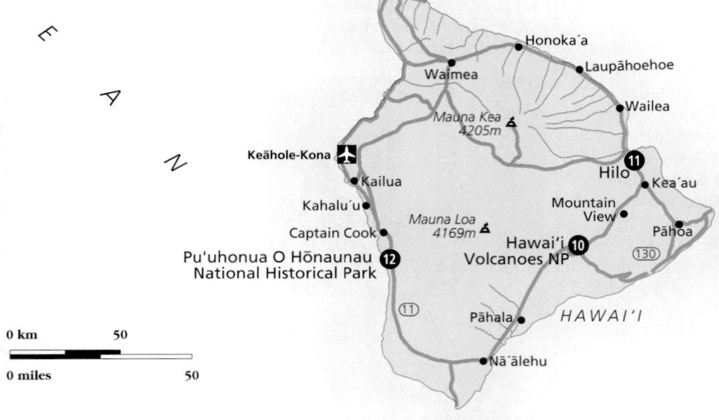

# O'ahu

THE THIRD LARGEST ISLAND in the archipelago, with an area of 600 sq miles (1,550 sq km), O'ahu is Hawai'i's most visited and most populous island. Three-quarters of the state's million residents live here, most of them in the Greater Honolulu area. Outside the urban areas, with their cultural attractions, O'ahu offers spectacular scenery, with lush plantations, tropical beaches, and a surfers' paradise on the North Shore.

## Honolulu ❶

*371,657. HVCB-Honolulu, (808) 923-1811; O'ahu VB, 733 Bishop St, Honolulu, (808) 524-0722. www.gohawaii.com*

HAWAI'I'S CAPITAL city has two focal points – the historic and business district of downtown Honolulu, and the world famous resort of Waikīkī, 3 miles (5 km) to its east. The downtown area, which first gained prominence as a trading port in the early 19th century, today manages to squeeze together towering skyscrapers, a royal palace, Japanese shrines, New England-style missionary houses, a bustling Chinatown, strip joints, and fish markets in a relatively small and compact area.

Dominating downtown's Capitol District is the magnificent Victorian-style **'Iolani Palace**, completed in 1882. The only royal palace in the US, it was designed and first lived in by King David Kalākaua, followed by his sister Queen Lili'uokalani, who reigned for only two years before the monarchy was overthrown in 1893 *(see p744)*. Recently used as a movie set, the palace has luxurious interiors and a *koa*-wood staircase.

**'Iolani Palace crest**

To its south is the New England-style **Kawaiaha'o Church**, constructed of coral blocks. It was built in 1842, by which time American missionaries had gained many influential local converts to Christianity. The upper gallery has portraits of Hawaiian monarchs, most of whom were baptized, married, and crowned here. Adjacent to the church is the **Mission Houses Museum**, which contains the oldest timber frame house in Hawai'i, built in 1821 by the New England missionary Reverend Hiram Bingham. Housed in three buildings, the museum has a printing house and lovingly preserved interiors.

Nearby is the bronze **Statue of King Kamehameha**, Hawai'i's most revered monarch, who ruled from 1795 to 1819 *(see p744)*. The statue, with its feathered cloak and an arm extended in a welcome, is one of Hawai'i's most famous sights.

North of the Capitol District is **Chinatown**, with two marble lions guarding its entrance. The area is an exotic neighborhood of open-air markets, *lei* (flower garland) stands, eateries, and herbal medicine shops. Hawai'i's first Chinese arrived on merchant ships in 1789, followed in 1852 by larger numbers who came to work on O'ahu's sugar plantations. Chinatown's buildings include the Art Deco **Hawai'i Theatre** and the state's oldest Japanese Shinto shrine, the **Izumo Taisha Shrine**, built in 1923.

**Statue of King Kamehameha, his hand extended in welcome**

At Honolulu Harbor, the fascinating **Hawai'i Maritime Center** displays antique canoes and exhibits tracing the exploits of Polynesian navigators. Moored next to it are the *Hōkūle'a*, a modern replica of an ancient Polynesian canoe with sails, and the restored 1878 *Falls of Clyde*, the world's last surviving full-rigged four-masted sailing ship.

**Waikīkī**, originally a place of taro patches and fish ponds, now has one of the world's famous beaches – a sliver of people-packed sand against the backdrop of **Diamond Head** crater. Waikīkī bustles with some 65,000 tourists a day who flock here to sunbathe on the golden sand, swim in the sheltered water, and surf the gentle waves. The sandy beach stretches for 2.5 miles (4 km), from the Hilton Hawaiian Village to Diamond Head. The streets and shopping malls are packed with beachwear vendors, honeymooners, Japanese matrons, and boys carrying surfboards. Conspicuous amid the glass and concrete skyscrapers are two stately

**The Waikīkī Beach front, lined with high-rise hotels**

old hotels – the coral pink **Royal Hawaiian Hotel** and the Colonial-style **Moana Hotel**, Waikīkī's oldest.

Several interesting sights are also located in Greater Honolulu. Considered the world's finest museum of Polynesian culture, **Bishop Museum** was created by American businessman Charles Bishop to preserve royal heirlooms left by his wife, a Hawaiian princess. Its priceless exhibits include fabulous ceremonial feather standards, rare *tamate* costumes made of shredded fiber, sacred images, and a *hale* (traditional house) thatched with *pili* grass.

The **National Memorial Cemetery of the Pacific**, located in Punchbowl, the crater of an extinct volcano, has over 33,000 graves. Among those buried here are victims of Pearl Harbor and those killed in the Korean and Vietnam wars.

**Pearl Harbor**, a place of pilgrimage for many visitors, houses warships, military museums, and memorials. Most significant among these is the **USS *Arizona* Memorial**, which stands perched above the ship of the same name that was sunk during the Japanese bombing on December 7, 1941. Some of the volunteer guides that you will meet here happen to be survivors of that fateful attack, which killed more than 2,000 US officers and men, and destroyed 18 battleships, bringing the United States into World War II *(see p745)*.

**Hawai'i Maritime Center**
Pier 7, Honolulu Harbor. *(808) 536-6373. 19, 20. 8:30am–8pm daily. Dec 25.*

**Bishop Museum**
1525 Bernice St. *(808) 847-3511. 2. 9am–5pm daily. Dec 25. Craft demonstrations, music & dance recitals: daily.* www.bishopmuseum.org

**Pearl Harbor**
7 miles (11 km) NW of downtown Honolulu. *20, 42.* **USS *Arizona* Memorial** 1 Arizona Memorial Drive. *(808) 422-0561. 7:30am–5pm daily. Jan 1, Thanksgiving, Dec 25.* www.nps.gov/usar

## Byodo-In Temple ❷

47-200 Kahekili Hwy (Hwy 83), Kāne'ohe. *(808) 239-8811. on Kahekili Hwy (Hwy 83), then 10-min walk. 8:30am–4:30pm daily. Dec 25.*

This replica of a 900-year-old Japanese temple in a tranquil and secluded spot is O'ahu's hidden treasure, its bright red walls framed against the backdrop of fluted green cliffs. A curved vermilion footbridge and a three-ton bell lead to the Byodo-In Temple, which houses a beautiful 9-ft (3-m) Buddha. Sunset here is a magical experience, with the cliffs giving off pink and mauve hues.

**Sign for Hale'iwa, O'ahu's surf town**

## Hawai'i's Plantation Village ❸

94-695 Waipahu St, Waipahu. *(808) 677-0110. Waipahu. 10am–4:30pm Mon–Sat. public hols.*

This three-million dollar restored village portrays a hundred years of sugar plantation culture, from 1840 to 1943. It also contains various re-created buildings from the major ethnic groups that worked in the plantations – Korean, Puerto Rican, and Japanese homes – as well as a Shinto shrine. Personal objects placed in the houses give the impression that the occupants have just left, soon to return. The small on-site museum runs informative walking tours for visitors.

## North Shore ❹

*2,500. HVCB, Waikīkī, (808) 924-0266. O-Bon Buddhist Festival (Jul or Aug).*

The hub for the North Shore surfing community is **Hale'iwa**. The town's picturesque harbor is flanked by well-appointed public beaches. **Ali'i Beach** is famous for big waves and surfing contests. The adjacent **Hale'iwa Beach Park** is one of the few North Shore spots where it is usually quite safe to swim in winter. At the enchanting annual O-Bon Festival, thousands of floating lanterns are released into the ocean here.

Another popular North Shore spot is the **Waimea Valley Audubon Center**. The valley is a botanical paradise, with 36 gardens, thousands of rare tropical plants, and 30 species of birds. There are no longer the commercial shows that Waimea Valley was once famous for, such as hula, and cliff-diving. Instead, the center provides an important educational resource and is a beautiful and unspoilt environment. Visitors can tour the valley, but bring binoculars as the park has great opportunities for bird watchers. Afterwards, swim or snorkel at the Waimea Beach Park across the street from the center.

**Waimea Valley Audubon Center**
59-864 Kamehameha Hwy (Hwy 83), Waimea. *(808) 638-9199. 9:30am–5pm daily.*

**The enchanting Byodo-In Temple, a Buddhist shrine**

# Moloka'i & Maui

THE SMALL ISLAND OF Moloka'i, between O'ahu and Maui, is much less developed for tourism than its neighbors. The gentle pace of life, and the spectacular scenery of its flower-decked south coast and of the Kalaupapa National Historical Park, backed by the world's highest sea cliffs, enchant most visitors. Maui, Hawai'i's second largest island, offers lively resorts with a range of water sports, as well as lush plantations and the awesome grandeur of the Haleakalā Volcano.

**Moloka'i's isolated Kalaupapa Peninsula, backed by towering cliffs**

## Kaunakakai 5

*3,500. Ala Malama St & Kamehameha V Hwy (Hwy 450), (808) 553-3876. Ka Moloka'i Makahiki (cultural festival, late Jan).*

MOLOKA'I'S MAIN town, Kaunakakai, was built in the 19th century as a port for the local sugar and pineapple plantations. Today, commercial agriculture has all but disappeared from the island, and Kaunakakai looks its age. The main street, with its wooden boardwalk, is lined with false-fronted stores. A short distance from the town center, local fishermen throng **Kaunakakai Harbor**, its long stone jetty jutting out into the ocean. About 2 miles (3 km) west of town is the **Kapuāiwa Coconut Grove**, whose 1,000 soaring trees are a majestic sight, silhouetted against the setting sun.

**ENVIRONS:** East of Kaunakakai begins the **Kamehameha V Highway**, which is among the most beautiful coastal drives in Hawai'i. The 27-mile (44-km) highway takes in ancient sites, picturesque churches, pristine beaches, and sleepy villages tucked away amid tropical flowers and luxuriant rainforests. The road finally twists to a halt at the stunningly beautiful **Hālawa Valley** which, with its soaring walls, lush vegetation, idyllic beaches, and shimmering waterfalls, is Moloka'i's most scenic spot.

## Kalaupapa National Historical Park 6

Reached by foot or mule on Kalaupapa Trail: trailhead on Hwy 470, 3 miles (5 km) N of Kualapu'u, between the mule stables & Kalaupapa Overlook. *compulsory. Father Damien Tours, (808) 567-6171. Book well in advance. Visitors must be 16 years of age or older. For Moloka'i Mule Ride, (808) 567-6088, book in advance.*

THE ISOLATED Kalaupapa Peninsula, sealed off from the rest of Moloka'i by a mighty wall of cliffs, is home to the **Kalaupapa National Historical Park**. In 1865, when the imported disease of leprosy seemed to threaten the survival of the Hawaiian people, the peninsula was designated a leper colony, and those afflicted were exiled here. The park now serves as a memorial. The main settlement was at the village of Kalaupapa, on the sheltered western side of the peninsula. The last patients arrived in 1969, when the policy of enforced isolation ended. Kalaupapa's small population today includes a few aging patients who chose to live out their lives here.

South of the village is the precipitous **Kalaupapa Trail**, a favorite with hikers and mule riders who enjoy stupendous views during the 2-mile (3-km) trip. At the center of the peninsula is the **Kauhakō Crater**, with an 800-ft (245-m) deep lake.

On the peninsula's eastern shore is **St. Philomena Church**, in the original leprosy settlement of Kalawao. Shipped out from Honolulu in 1872, the church was later modified by the Belgian priest Father Damien (1840–89), who dedicated his life to caring for the leprosy patients. Father Damien succumbed to leprosy in 1889 and has been beatified by the Pope. His right hand is interred in the church. From the peninsula's eastern side, small islands poke out of the waters of the ocean, next to staggering 2000-ft (600-m) cliffs – the tallest sea cliffs in the world.

**St. Philomena Church, where Father Damien's hand is buried**

**Locals demonstrating their courage at Keka'a Point, Kā'anapali**

## Lahaina 7

9,500. Lahaina Harbor. 648 Wharf St, (808) 667-9193. *A Taste of Lahaina (food festival, mid-Sep); Halloween Mardi Gras of the Pacific (Oct 31).* www.visitlahaina.com

One of Maui's most popular attractions, this small harbor town was the capital of the Kingdom of Hawai'i until 1845 and a major center of the whaling trade. The area around Front Street has a wealth of well-restored historic sites, evocative of Lahaina's past. Among them is the **Baldwin Home**, Maui's oldest Western-style dwelling, dating from the 1830s, with original furnishings and artifacts. Nearby is the **Chinese Wo Hing Temple**, built in 1912. A favorite landmark is Lahaina's first hotel, the charming 1901 **Pioneer Inn**, still a tourist mecca and hotel.

Docked in the harbor, beside the lighthouse, is the *Carthaginian II*, a 1920s German schooner transformed to look like the kind of small freighter that brought cargo and people to the islands in the 1800s. It has a fascinating museum in the hold, devoted to whales and the whale trade.

Just 6 miles (10 km) north of Lahaina is Maui's biggest resort, **Kā'anapali**, its long white beach lined with hotels. **Pu'u Keka'a**, better known as Black Rock, towers above the beach and overlooks one of Maui's best snorkeling spots. Vintage steam locomotives make the short and scenic trip here from Lahaina. A 20-minute drive north of Kā'anapali is Maui's other major resort, **Kapalua**, with its exquisite crescent bays, blue waters, luxury hotels, golf courses, and beautiful pineapple plantations.

## Haleakalā National Park 8

Haleakalā Crater Road (Hwy 378). *24 hrs daily.* **Park Headquarters** *(808) 572-4400. 7:30am–4pm daily.* **Visitor Center** *sunrise–3pm daily.* **Cabins** *To enter lottery for reservations, write to: Cabins, Haleakalā National Park, Box 369, Makawao, HI 96768.*

The land mass of East Maui is really the top of an enormous volcano that begins more than 3 miles (5 km) below sea level. Haleakalā last spewed molten lava some 200 years ago and is still considered to be active, although not currently erupting. Its summit depression is 7.5 miles (12 km) long and 2.5 miles (4 km) wide. This natural wonder is preserved as part of the national park. The 2-hour drive to the 10,023-ft (3,055-m) **Pu'u 'Ula'ula Summit**, the highest point in Maui, offers a breathtaking view of the entire volcano, with its cinder cones and brightly colored ashes.

The best way to appreciate Haleakalā's scale and varied terrain is to descend 3,000 ft (900 m) into the volcano. The 10-mile (16-km) **Sliding Sands Trail** takes you from the visitor center through scenery that ranges from barren cinder desert to alpine shrubland. Also worth exploring is the **Silversword Loop** where one of the world's rarest plants, the Haleakalā Silversword, thrives. It takes up to 50 years to flower, when it raises a spectacular spike of purplish flowers.

## Hāna 9

*700. MVB, Wailuku, (808) 244-3530. East Maui Taro Festival (Mar/Apr).*

Often called Hawai'i's most Hawaiian town, Hāna continues to lag lazily behind modernity. Its perfect round bay and dreamy climate have made it a prized settlement since ancient times. **Ka'uiki Head**, the large cinder cone on the right flank of the bay, served as a natural fortification.

The **Hāna Cultural Center** presents a *kauhale* (residential compound) in the precontact style once unique to this area and exhibits artifacts that give a sense of local history. **Wānanalua Church**, constructed from blocks of coral in 1838, was built by missionaries on top of an existing *heiau* (temple), thus symbolizing the triumph of Christianity over paganism.

The scenic **Hāna Belt Road** twists along the coast to Pā'ia, with views of waterfalls, gulches choked with vegetation, taro fields, botanical gardens, rocky cliffs, and the dramatic Honomanū Bay with its black sand beach.

**Pu'u 'Ula'ula Summit in Haleakalā National Park, Maui's highest point**

# Hawai'i Island

SPREADING OVER 4,035 SQ MILES (10,450 sq km), Hawai'i Island, also known as the Big Island, is more than twice the size of all the other islands combined. Its natural wonders include the earth's most massive mountain, Mauna Loa, which rises over 30,000 ft (9,150 m) from the ocean floor, and Kīlauea, the most active volcano on earth, both of which form part of the Hawai'i Volcanoes National Park. Equally fascinating are the island's well-preserved cultural sites within the Pu'uhonua O Hōnaunau National Historical Park.

## Hawai'i Volcanoes National Park ⑩

Hawai'i Belt Road (Hwy 11).
*24 hours daily.* **Kīlauea Visitor Center** *(808) 985-6000. 7:45am–5pm daily.* **Jaggar Museum** *(808) 985-6049. 8:30am–5pm daily.* **Volcano Art Center** *(808) 967-7565. 9am–5pm daily. Dec 25.* **Volcano House Hotel** *(808) 967-7321.* www.nps.gov/havo

ENCOMPASSING about a quarter of a million acres, this national park includes the 13,677-ft (4,169-m) summit of Mauna Loa, 150 miles (240 km) of hiking trails, and vast tracts of wilderness that preserve some of the world's rarest species of flora and fauna. But it is Kīlauea Caldera and the lava flows of its furious East Rift Zone that draw most visitors. Two roads – **Crater Rim Drive**, which loops around the caldera, and **Chain of Craters Road**, which descends through the recent outpourings – form a gigantic drive-through museum. The present eruption started in 1983 and produces slow-moving lava, which poses no threat to visitors. However, you should stay out of closed areas; no one knows how long the flow will continue or where it will next erupt.

East of the park, the **Kīlauea Iki Overlook** gives a view of the crater, which in 1959 filled with bubbling lava,

**Lava fountains spewing from Kīlauea during the 1983 eruption**

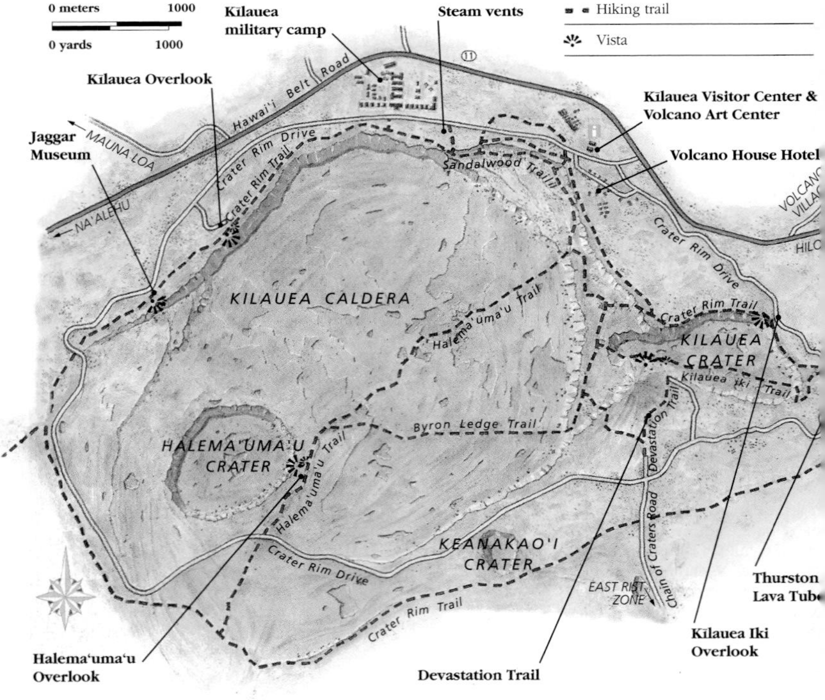

**KEY**

Major road
Minor road
Hiking trail
Vista

0 meters 1000
0 yards 1000

Kīlauea military camp
Steam vents
Kīlauea Overlook
Jaggar Museum
Kīlauea Visitor Center & Volcano Art Center
Volcano House Hotel
Thurston Lava Tube
Kīlauea Iki Overlook
Devastation Trail
Halema'uma'u Overlook

Thurston Lava Tube, formed by the hardening of a lava stream

shooting fire fountains 1,900 ft (580 m) into the air. Across the road from the crater, at the eastern edge of the park, lies the Thurston Lava Tube. This huge tunnel was left behind when a subterranean river of lava drained away. An easy trail runs through the tube and a grove of giant ferns. Nearby, the short Devastation Trail features ghostly remains of a rainforest, wiped out by ash falling from Kīlauea Iki's 1959 eruption. Farther west, the Halema'uma'u Overlook affords views of the once boiling lake of lava. The crater below still steams with sulfurous fumes. This is the home of Pele, the fiery-tempered volcano goddess, who migrated from Kahiki (Tahiti) seeking a dry place for her eternal fires.

## Hilo ⓫

*38,000. Kamehameha Ave, near Mamo St, (808) 961-8744. BIVB, 250 Keawe St, (808) 961-5797. Merrie Monarch Festival (Mar or Apr).*

ALTHOUGH IT IS the state's second city, "rainy old Hilo" is a contrast to sunny, urban Honolulu. The city's progress has been checked by nature – rain falls 278 days of the year, and two destructive *tsunamis* pounded Hilo in 1946 and 1960. The city has since retreated from the sea, turning the waterfront area into enormous parks, while the rain has made it a natural garden, full of orchids and anthuriums. Hilo's population is largely Japanese and Filipino in ancestry.

The downtown business district, with its restored buildings, is worth exploring on foot. The **Lyman Museum and Mission House** vividly evokes a bygone era – it is preserved as it was in the 1830s, with Victorian furnishings and artifacts.

On the Waiākea Peninsula, jutting into Hilo Bay, is the 30-acre (12-ha) **Lili'uokalani Gardens**, landscaped in Japanese style, while east of downtown are the 80-ft (24-m) high **Rainbow Falls**. The morning sun, filtering through the mist of the waterfall, often creates beautiful rainbows.

The east side of Hilo Bay offers fine snorkeling and swimming at the **James Kealoha Beach Park**; and at the **Richardson Ocean Park**.

### PROFESSOR JAGGAR (1871–1953)

Thomas A. Jaggar was a pioneer in the young science of volcanology. A professor of geology at Massachusetts Institute of Technology, he founded the Hawaiian Volcano Observatory at Kīlauea Caldera in 1912. Four years later, he and Honolulu publisher Lorrin Thurston persuaded Congress to preserve the area as a national park. Professor Jaggar developed techniques for collecting volcanic gases and measuring ground tilt, seismic activity, and lava temperatures. The work he initiated has made Kīlauea one of the world's best understood volcanoes.

Professor Jaggar on a boat trip

## Pu'uhonua O Honaunau National Historical Park ⓬

Hwy 160, off Hawai'i Belt Rd (Hwy 11). *(808) 328-2326. 6am–8pm Mon–Thu, 6am–11pm Fri–Sun.* **Visitor Center** *8am–5pm. Daily orientation talks.* www.nps.gov/puho

FROM THE 11th century on, social interactions were regulated by the *kapu* (taboo) system, and even minor infractions, such as stepping on a chief's shadow, were punished by violent death. Lawbreakers could, however, escape punishment by reaching a *pu'uhonua* (place of refuge). The greatest of these was at **Hōnaunau**, a 6-acre ( 2-ha) temple compound dating from the 16th century, which offered absolution to all those who could swim or run past the chief's warriors. The sanctuary was stripped of power in 1819, after the fall of the *kapu* system. Now partly restored, it provides a glimpse into precontact Hawai'i.

Located on a peninsula of black lava, whose jagged shoreline made it difficult for *kapu*-breakers to approach from the sea, the *pu'uhonua's* focal point is the 1650 **Hale O Keawe Heiau**, the temple that once held the bones and therefore the *mana* (sacred power) of great chiefs. Outside it stand Ki'i – wooden images of gods. As impressive is the great drystone wall, 10 ft (3 m) high and 17 ft (5 m) wide. Built around 1550, it separated the *pu'uhonua* from the palace area inland.

The Hale O Keawe Heiau, a place of spiritual power

# Kaua'i

WIND AND WATER HAVE HAD six million years to transform Kaua'i, the oldest of the major Hawaiian islands, into a stunning array of pleated cliffs and yawning chasms, cloaked with a mantle of emerald green vegetation. Also known as the "Garden Island," Kaua'i is Hawai'i's most beautiful and irresistible destination. Its highlights include Kīlauea Point's glorious beaches, the dramatic Waimea Canyon, and the soaring cliffs of the Kalalau Trail on the Nā Pali Coast. You can drive anywhere in Kaua'i in three hours or less.

**The shady *koa*-wood veranda at Grove Farm Homestead**

## Līhu'e ⓭

*5,500. Rice St, (808) 241-6410. KVB, 4334 Rice St, Suite 101, (808) 245-3971. Kaua'i-Tahiti Fete (mid-Aug).*

ALTHOUGH LĪHU'E happens to be the administrative and business center of Kaua'i, it is actually little more than a plantation village. It was built in the 19th century to serve the Līhu'e Sugar Mill, whose rusting machinery still dominates the downtown area. Lihu'e's oceanfront district, with the beautiful Kalapakī Beach, is especially appealing, and the outskirts of town offer such delights as grand plantation mansions and a stunning waterfall.

Within the town, **Kaua'i Museum** displays a splendid collection of traditional artifacts, including huge *koa*-wood bowls, royal feather standards, and old weapons. It also has exhibits on the island's history and geology. The imposing **Grove Farm Homestead** on Nāwiliwili Road is an early 20th-century mansion, paneled in dark, heavy *koa* wood. A guided tour, which must be reserved in advance, covers the rather formal house, the cramped servants' quarters, and the beautifully scented orchard.

**Kalapakī Beach**, with gently sloping beautiful white sands and sheltered inshore waters, is the safest beach in the area and especially suitable for families with small children. On its far side, the scenic palm-fringed **Nāwiliwili Beach County Park** is ideal for picnics.

The grand 1930s house known as **Kilohana Plantation**, 1.5 miles (2.5 km) west of Līhu'e, resembles an English country estate. Visitors can tour the house, which has a restaurant and some shops, and explore the cane fields in old-fashioned horse-drawn carriages. The mansion commands superb views of the Kilohana mountain inland.

**ENVIRONS:** Just 5 miles (8 km) north of Līhu'e, a winding road through cane fields leads to the twin cascades of the 80-ft (24-m) **Wailua Falls**. They are best viewed from the roadside parking lot, as the path down the hillside can be slippery. **Menehune Fish Pond** 1.5 miles (2.5 km) south of Līhu'e, is located in idyllic pastoral landscape. With its ancient stonemasonry, the pond was used to fatten mullet for the royal table.

## Kīlauea Point ⓮

Kīlauea Road, off Kūhiō Hwy (Hwy 56), 10 miles (16 km) NW of Anahola. *Kīlauea. KVB, Līhu'e, (808) 245-3971.*

THE NORTHERNMOST spot on the Hawaiian archipelago, Kīlauea Point is a rocky promontory pounded by mighty waves. The windswept clifftop has been set aside as the **Kīlauea Point National Wildlife Refuge**, where bird-watcher's can spot frigatebirds, Laysan albatrosses, and many other species. A short walk beyond the visitor center leads to the red and white **Kīlauea Lighthouse**, erected in 1913. Approaching the tip of the headland, there are splendid views westward to the fabled **Nā Pali** cliffs. Half a mile (800 m) west of the Kīlauea turn-off on Kalihiwai Road, a red dirt

**The twin cascades of Wailua Falls near Līhu'e**

The Pu'u O Kila Lookout, with views of the Kalalau Valley

track leads to the vast but little-visited shelf of glorious yellow sand known as **Secret Beach**. The ocean can be rough for swimming here, but it is a beautiful place to walk, with its dramatic views of the lighthouse and a glorious waterfall at the far end.

Official marker

**Kīlauea Point National Wildlife Refuge**

Kīlauea Point. *(808) 828-1413.* *10am–4pm Mon–Fri.* *Jan 1, Thnksg, Dec 25.*

## Waimea Canyon & Koke'e State Park 15

Kōke'e Road (Hwy 550). *Kaua'i Division of State Parks, (808) 274-3444.* **Kōke'e State Park** *daily.* **Kōke'e Museum** *(808) 335-9975. Donation.* *10am–4pm daily.* **Kōke'e Lodge** *(808) 335-6061.* *Cabins available for rent.*

No visitor should leave Kaua'i without taking in the rugged grandeur of Waimea Canyon and the breathtaking views from Kōke'e State Park. Waimea Canyon, known as the "Grand Canyon of the Pacific," was created by an earthquake that almost split Kaua'i in two. The gorge, now 3,000 ft (915 m) deep, is still eroding as landslides and the Waimea River continue to carry away tons of soil. Of the several lookouts dotted along the rim, the **Waimea Canyon Lookout**, despite being the lowest of the lookouts, offers the best canyon views. The more adventurous can take hiking trails to explore in greater depth. The **Kukui Trail** heads sharply down into the canyon as far as the Waimea River – a relatively easy and rewarding trip. At the North End of Waimea Canyon is **Kōke'e State Park**, laced through with more hiking trails. From the park's **Pu'u O Kila Lookout**, the majestic amphitheater of the Kalalau Valley opens out; another view is from the nearby **Kalalau Lookout**. A highlight of the park is the **Alaka'i Swamp**, a bowl-like depression drenched by nearly 42 ft (13 m) of rain every year. Part rainforest, part bog, the area boasts some of Hawai'i's rarest birds, such as the *'i'iwi* or honey-creeper, and the tiny yellow *'anianiau*. A hiking trail leads to the more accessible part of the swamp. Information, hiking advice, and maps are all available at the Kōke'e State Park headquarters.

## Kalalau Trail 16

Visitors must obtain permission in advance from the State Parks office. **State Parks office** *3060 'Eīwa St, Līhu'e, HI 96766, (808) 274-3444.*

The precipitous cliffs of the Nā Pali Coast make it impossible for the road to continue west of Kē'ē Beach on Kauai's north shore. But hardy hikers can follow the narrow Kalalau Trail for another 11 miles (18 km) to isolated Kalalau Valley. One of the most dramatic hikes in the world, it covers a landscape of almost primeval vastness and splendor. While this is not an expedition to undertake lightly, a half-day round trip to Hanakāpī'ai Valley is within most capabilities and provides an unforgettable wilderness experience.

The trail begins at the end of **Kūhiō Highway**, climbing steeply to **Makana Peak** and affording spectacular views of the rugged coastline. It continues on to **Ke Ahu A Laka**, which was once Hawai'i's most celebrated school for *hula* dancing. The next stop is **Hanakāpī'ai Valley** where in summer a pristine sandy beach replaces the pebbles found at the valley mouth in winter. Wading and swimming here are unsafe, due to dangerous rip currents.

The more challenging part of the trail continues through an abandoned coffee plantation to the **Hanakāpī'ai Falls**, and then to **Pā Ma Wa'a**, an 800-ft (240-m) cliff, which is the highest point on the trail. The trail then dips into several hanging valleys where the streams have still to cut their way down to sea level, before reaching the beautiful campsite at **Hanakoa Valley**, set amid the ruins of ancient taro terraces. For the last 5 miles (8 km), the trail clings perilously to a sandstone cliff. The magical view of **Kalalau Valley** is the trail's reward. Note that there is no food or safe drinking water *en route*.

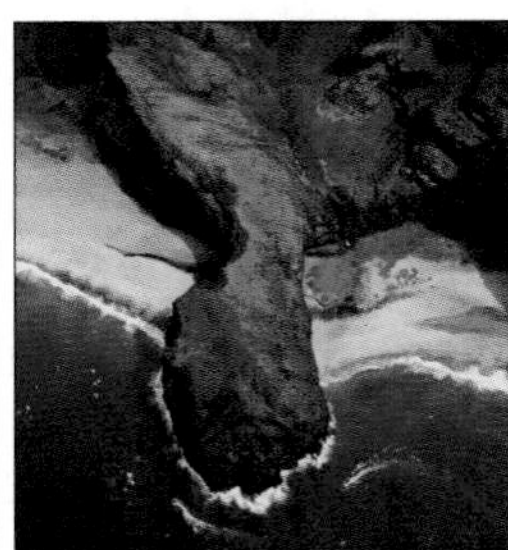

The soaring, pleated cliffs of the Nā Pali Coast, Kalalau Trail

# Alaska Practical Information

TRAVELING AROUND THE LARGEST state in the US requires a great deal of advance planning. From endless snowfields, towering mountains, majestic rainforests, sweeping tundra, active volcanoes, and the spectacular "northern lights" to some of the world's most abundant wildlife preserves, Alaska has much to offer its visitors. Although traveling in Alaska is more expensive than in other parts of the country, visitors on a small budget can also have a memorable trip.

## Tourist Information

THE BEST SOURCE of travel information is the very comprehensive Alaska Vacation Planner, published by the **Alaska Travel Industry Association** (ATIA). The ATIA is run jointly by the state and various travel businesses. Many regional tourism councils also publish brochures on travel in their areas.

## Getting Around

VISITORS HAVE A number of transportation options. **Alaska Airlines** flights link larger cities and towns, while smaller "bush" planes take visitors to more remote areas. The state-run **Alaska Railroad** connects Fairbanks, Anchorage, Seward, and Denali National Park. The main intercity bus service, **Alaska Direct BusLine**, has year-round service.

A government-operated ferry service, the **Alaska Marine Highway System** links towns throughout southeast and south central Alaska, with service extending as far south as Prince Rupert in British Columbia and Bellingham, Washington. The large, comfortable, and well-equipped ships carry hundreds of vehicles and feature cabins, multiple dining areas, and onboard naturalists. The pace is relaxed and the atmosphere is very casual; some travelers even sleep under the stars on the outer deck. Book well in advance for this popular ferry service. However, driving within Alaska involves long distances; be especially careful of collisions with Alaska's wildlife.

## Natural Hazards

MOST TRAVELERS visit Alaska in the milder summer season between late May and early-September. Even so, bring a jacket and warm clothes for chilly nights. Summer also brings the worst of Alaska's insects, mainly mosquitoes and blackflies. Backcountry travelers also need to take precautions in bear country. **Park Service** or **Forest Service** rangers can provide safety tips.

## The Climate of Alaska

Although situated near the Arctic Circle, weather patterns vary a great deal in Alaska. Winters are cold and dark, but summer with its warm weather and long days is the prime season for visitors. In the state's northern tier, the sun does not set for two months of the year, and there is daylight for as many as 22 hours each day in June at Fairbanks. July is the rainiest month. Most coastal cruises take place in the summer.

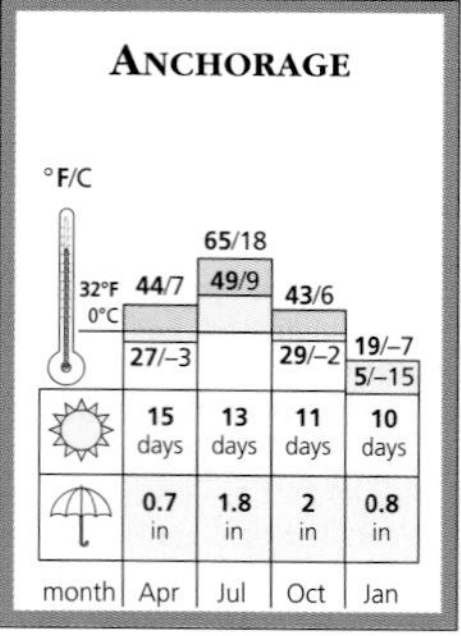


## Directory

### Tourist Information

**Alaska Travel Industry Association (ATIA)**
*(907) 929-2842,*
(800) *862-5275.*
www.travelalaska.com

### Travel

**Alaska Airlines**
*(206) 433-3100.*
www.alaskaair.com

**Alaska Direct Busline**
*(907) 277-6652,*
*(800) 770-6652.*

**Alaska Marine Highway System**
*(907) 465-3941.*
www.dot.state.ak.us/amhs

**Alaska Railroad**
*(907) 265-2494.*
www.akrr.com

## Festivals

THERE ARE A number of special events taking place in Alaska at different times of the year. Starting in spring, the famous **Iditarod Trail Sled Dog Race** runs between Anchorage and Nome. April sees the **Alaska Folk Festival** held in Juneau. The **Alaska State Fair** (August) in Palmer is famous for its pumpkins and cabbages, which grow to world-record sizes under the state's 24-hour sunshine. On October 18th, the **Alaska Day Celebration**, the day Alaska was bought from Russia by the US, livens up the Colonial town of Sitka.

## Outdoor Activities

THE VAST MAJORITY of Alaska is set aside as public land, making the state a paradise for hikers, fishermen, and other outdoor enthusiasts. Trekking, mountain climbing, skiing, rafting, kayaking, and whale-watching are some of the activities that visitors can enjoy here. Most tourist offices provide information and details of outdoor pursuits that Alaska has to offer.

# Hawai'i Practical Information

TOURISM IS HAWAI'I'S most important industry. From the bright lights of Waikīkī and Honolulu to the remote waterfalls of Maui's Hāna district, the islands offer something to suit all budgets. The cost of living in Hawai'i is about 40 percent higher than that in the rest of the US; even so, Hawai'i is a year-round destination. However, visitors will enjoy better prices in the off-season, between April and December.

## Tourist Information

VISITOR INFORMATION desks at all airports provide maps and guides, and all major hotels have a guest services desk. All islands have a branch of the **Hawai'i Visitors' and Convention Bureau** (HVCB), or some other visitors' bureau.

## Getting Around

DRIVING IS THE best way to get around, since public transportation is limited. Seat belts are mandatory, and children under three must sit in approved car seats. Distances between gas stations can be long, so keep the tank at least half full. Always check the weather – many roads wash out during or after heavy rains.

Allow plenty of time for any trip. The locals move at a leisurely pace, seldom using horns. On narrow roads, pull over to let cars pass.

## Natural Hazards

VISITORS SHOULD be aware of certain potential dangers that the sun and the ocean pose to health. Thus, wear a hat and sunglasses, use sunblock cream, and drink plenty of fluids as a protection against the harsh sun.

Ask the lifeguard about ocean conditions, as some beaches can be safe in summer but very dangerous in winter. Swim facing away from the beach, as sudden rogue waves can sweep you out to sea. If you get carried out by a rip current, try to swim with it until it dissipates. Always check for rocks and corals below the surface, and wear protective foot gear. If you cut yourself on coral, clean the cut thoroughly with antiseptic. If you step on a sea urchin, or are stung by a jellyfish, apply a paste of vinegar and meat tenderizer. Although shark encounters are rare, it's best that you check with the lifeguard before swimming.

## Outdoor Activities

HAWAI'I OFFERS A plethora of outdoor activities, many focused on the ocean, such as surfing, swimming, fishing, scuba diving, and snorkeling. In addition, sports enthusiasts have a variety of opportunities such as horseback riding, hiking, and playing golf on some of the world's best courses.

## Entertainment

MUSIC AND DANCE are as important to Hawaiians as the air they breathe. Most islands offer extravagant Polynesian shows, with *lū'au*-style meals, and music and dance from other Pacific islands such as Tahiti and Fiji. You can dance the night away in nightclubs in Honolulu and Maui, but also be prepared for earlier nights in other parts of the state.

## Festivals

A DIVERSE RANGE of festivals and events take place all through the year. The onset of summer sees **Lei Day** with everyone donning flowered garlands. The **King Kamehameha Day** honors the chief who united the islands. All summer long, there are cultural, music, and food festivals, as well as sports events, from rodeos to canoe races and the grueling **Ironman Triathlon**. Summer draws to a close with the grand **Aloha Week Festivals**.

Winters offer sports and cultural events such as the **Triple Crown of Surfing**, and the **Merrie Monarch Festival** which culminates with the "Olympics" of *hula*.

## Directory

### Tourist Information

**Hawai'i Visitors' & Convention Bureau**
(808) 923-1811.
www.gohawaii.com

### Snorkeling

**Snorkel Bob's**
700 Kapahulu Ave, Honolulu, O'ahu. (808) 735-7944.
www.snorkelbob.com

### Scuba Diving

**Bubbles Below**
PO Box 157, Eleele, Kaua'i.
(808) 332-7333. www.bubblesbelowkauai.com

## The Climate Of Hawai'i

Hawai'i has two distinct seasons, summer and winter. May to October is hot and dry, while November through April is cooler and wetter. Happily for visitors, there are very few days when Hawai'i's beaches do not beckon. Sudden rains or storms mean the onset of winter, as do the big waves that surfers eagerly await. However, Hawai'i is not all sunshine, and residents in the cooler upcountry areas spend Christmas Eve gathered around the fireplace.

### Honolulu

| month | Apr | Jul | Oct | Jan |
|---|---|---|---|---|
| °F/C (high) | 78/25 | 82/28 | 82/28 | 76/24 |
| °F/C (low) | 68/20 | 73/22 | 73/22 | 68/20 |
| sunshine | 21 days | 24 days | 22 days | 20 days |
| rainfall | 1.5 in | 0.6 in | 2.3 in | 3.5 in |

32°F 0°C

# Where to Stay

These hotels have been selected across a wide price range for their excellent facilities and locations. While Hawai'i is a year-round destination, Alaska's accommodations fill fast during the short and busy summer. This chart lists hotels by region and within this by price category. In the Hawai'i section, figures in parentheses indicate the number of suites available.

| Alaska | Credit Cards | Number of Rooms | Restaurant | Breakfast Included | Summer Only |
|---|---|---|---|---|---|
| **Alaska Peninsula:** *Brooks Lodge* $$$$$<br>Katmai National Park. (907) 243-5448, (800) 554-0551. FAX (907) 243-0649.<br>W www.bear–viewing.com<br>A famous hunting lodge located within walking distance of bear-viewing platforms. Has a package that includes the flight from Anchorage and three meals per day. *mid-Sep–May.* | ■ | 16 | ■ | ● | ■ |
| **Anchorage:** *Hostelling International Anchorage* $<br>700 H St. (907) 276-3635. FAX (907) 276-7772. W www.alaska.net<br>Visitors can walk to downtown and the long-distance bus terminal from this centrally located hostel. There are private rooms in addition to male and female dormitories. The check-in time is 8am–noon and 1–5pm. | ■ | 95 beds | | | |
| **Anchorage:** *Hotel Captain Cook* $$$$$<br>4th Avenue at K St. (907) 276-6000, (800) 843-1950. FAX (907) 343-2298.<br>W www.captaincook.com<br>Located in the heart of downtown, this is Alaska's largest hotel with rooms in three towers. An understated elegance pervades the building. TV | ■ | 547 | ■ | | |
| **Denali National Park:** *Westmark Denali Sourdough Cabins* $$$<br>Parks Hwy. (907) 683-2773, (800) 764-0015. FAX (907) 683-2357.<br>W www.westmarkhotels.com/sourdough<br>The park visitor center is only a 10-minute walk from this scattering of functional cabins spread throughout the forest. *mid-Sep–mid-May.* TV | ■ | 45 | ■ | | ■ |
| **Denali National Park:** *Kantishna Roadhouse* $$$$$<br>Park Rd Kantishna. (907) 459-2120, (800) 942-7420. FAX (907) 459-2160.<br>W www.kantishnaroadhouse.com<br>This hotel has an upscale, rustic ambience that extends from the inviting guest cabins to the comfortable communal area of the main lodge. Access is by private bus from the park entrance. *mid-Sep–May.* | ■ | 32 | ■ | ● | ■ |
| **Fairbanks:** *Springhill Suites* $$$<br>575 1st Ave. (907) 451-6552, (888) 287-9400. FAX: (907) 451-6553.<br>W www.springhillsuites.com<br>The standard suite at this Marriott-affiliated property is unequaled in Fairbanks. Its rooms are spacious and tastefully appointed. TV | ■ | 140 | ■ | ● | |
| **Fairbanks:** *Sophie Station Hotel* $$$$<br>1717 University Ave. (907) 479-3650, (800) 528-4916. FAX: (907) 479-7951.<br>W www.fountainheadhotels.com<br>This all-suites hotel features comfortable rooms with kitchenettes, and is close to the airport. TV | ■ | 148 | ■ | | |
| **Glacier Bay National Park:** *Glacier Bay Lodge* $$$$<br>Bartlett Cove. (888) 229-8687. FAX (907) 258-3668.<br>W www.visitglacierbay.com/lodging<br>This lodge is set in a forest at the departure point for cruises into Glacier Bay. Most visitors stay as part of a package tour. *mid-Sep–mid-May.* TV | ■ | 56 | ■ | ● | ■ |
| **Homer:** *Land's End Resort* $$$<br>4786 Homer Spit Rd. (907) 235-0400, (800) 478-0400. FAX (907) 235-0420.<br>W www.lands–end–resort.com<br>Named for its location at the tip of Homer Spit, this hotel offers splendid views over the ocean from its comfortable rooms. TV | ■ | 80 | ■ | | |
| **Juneau:** *Alaskan Hotel* $<br>167 S Franklin St. (907) 586-1000, (800) 327-9347. FAX (907) 463-3775.<br>W www.ptialaska.net/~akhotel<br>This inexpensive downtown hotel has been popular since it opened in 1913. The old-fashioned rooms here are clean and comfortable. TV | ■ | 40 | | | |

**Price categories** for a standard double room per night in peak season, and inclusive of all taxes:

- $ under $75
- $$ $75–$125
- $$$ $125–$185
- $$$$ $185–$250
- $$$$$ over $250

**CREDIT CARDS**
Major credit cards accepted.

**NUMBER OF ROOMS**
Number of rooms in the hotel. Hostels offer dormitory-style accommodations; number of beds are indicated in the column.

**RESTAURANT**
Hotel restaurant or dining room, also open to non residents.

**BREAKFAST INCLUDED**
Cooked or Continental breakfast included in rates.

**SUMMER ONLY**
Opens in May or June and is closed by early October.

| | Credit Cards | Number of Rooms | Restaurant | Breakfast Included | Summer Only |
|---|---|---|---|---|---|
| **JUNEAU:** *Juneau International Hostel* $<br>614 Harris St. (907) 586-9559. www.juneauhostel.org<br>Visitors can check in between 8am and 9am and after 5pm at this friendly and homey hotel. There are separate dormitories for men and women, a kitchen, but no TV. There is also a midnight curfew. | | 46 beds | | | |
| **JUNEAU:** *Westmark Baranof* $$$<br>127 N Franklin St. (907) 586-2660, (800) 544-0970. FAX (907) 586-8315.<br>www.westmarkhotels.com<br>This is the grand dame of Juneau hotels. This nine-story downtown gem has beautiful pressed tin ceilings and polished wood furnishings in the lobby. However, the rooms of the Westmark Baranof are modern and well-equipped. | ■ | 196 | ■ | | |
| **KETCHIKAN:** *Blueberry Hill B&B* $$$<br>500 Front St. (907) 247-2583, (877) 449-2583. FAX (907) 247-2584.<br>www.blueberryhillbb.com<br>A budget B&B, within walking distance of downtown. Rooms are brightly decorated and two feature water views. | ■ | 4 | | | |
| **KETCHIKAN:** *Cedars Lodge* $$$$<br>1471 Tongass Ave. (907) 225-1900, (800) 813-4363. FAX (907) 225-8604.<br>www.cedarslodge.com<br>With its waterfront setting, this hostelry is preferred by anglers, who head out on guided trips from the lodge's private marina. Some of the units of Cedars Lodge have attached kitchens. *Oct–Apr.* | ■ | 13 | ■ | ● | ■ |
| **KODIAK ISLAND:** *Kodiak Inn* $$$<br>236 Rezanof Dr, Kodiak. (907) 486-5712. FAX (907) 486-3430.<br>www.kodiakinn.com<br>Affiliated with the Best Western chain, this is the largest and most modern hotel on Kodiak Island. | ■ | 80 | ■ | | |
| **NOME:** *Chateau de Cape Nome* $$$<br>E 4th Avenue at East N St. (907) 443-2083.<br>This is the family home of a descendant of one of the original Klondike Gold Rush miners. The atmosphere here is exceptionally warm and friendly. | | 3 | | ● | |
| **SEWARD:** *Seward Windsong Lodge* $$$$<br>Exit Glacier Rd, mile 12.5. (907) 224-7116, (877) 777-2805. FAX (907) 224-7118.<br>www.sewardwindsong.com<br>Overlooking Resurrection River north of Seward, this lodge takes advantage of its delightful surroundings. *mid-May–mid-Sep.* | ■ | 108 | ■ | | ■ |
| **SITKA:** *Sitka Hotel* $<br>118 Lincoln St. (907) 747-3288. FAX (907) 747-8499.<br>www.sitkahotel.com<br>This attractive yet economical hotel with comfortable rooms has been restored to its 1930s grandeur. The bar is popular with locals. | ■ | 60 | ■ | | |
| **SKAGWAY:** *Skagway Inn* $$$<br>655 Broadway. (907) 983-2289, (888) 752-4929. FAX (907) 983-2713.<br>www.skagwayinn.com<br>Built in 1897, this charming B&B was originally a bordello for gold miners. Guests enjoy the Victorian ambience and a cozy downstairs bistro. | ■ | 12 | ■ | | |
| **VALDEZ:** *Aspen Hotel Valdez* $$$<br>100 Meals Ave. (907) 835-4445. FAX (907) 835-2437.<br>www.aspenhotelsak.com<br>A well-maintained hotel in the center of town. Each room is equipped with a microwave, small refrigerators, and voice-mail. | ■ | 102 | ■ | ● | |

For key to symbols see back flap

**Price categories** for a standard double room for one night in tourist season (Dec–Apr), including taxes:

- $ under $85
- $$ $85–$150
- $$$ $150–$250
- $$$$ $250–$400
- $$$$$ over $400

**Credit Cards**
Major credit cards accepted.

**Number of Rooms**
Number of rooms in the hotel (suites shown in parentheses).

**Recommended Restaurant**
Good restaurant within the hotel.

**Children's Facilities**
Hotel has various facilities for young children.

**Ocean View**
Ocean-front guestrooms or rooms with spectacular ocean views are available.

## Hawai‘i

| Hotel | Credit Cards | Number of Rooms (Suites) | Recommended Restaurant | Children's Facilities | Ocean View |
|---|---|---|---|---|---|
| **Honolulu (O‘ahu):** *Doubletree Alana Waikīkī Hotel* $$$<br>1956 Ala Moana Boulevard, HI 96815. Tel (808) 941-7275. FAX (808) 941-7423.<br>W www.alana–doubletree.com<br>A favorite with islanders, this is one of the best small hotels and is located near the shoppers' mecca known as the Ala Moana Center. It offers attractively appointed, functional rooms. | ■ | 268 (45) | ■ | | ■ |
| **Waikīkī (O‘ahu):** *Radisson Waikīkī Prince Kūhiō* $$$<br>2500 Kūhiō Ave, HI 96815. Tel (808) 922-0811, (800) 333-3333. FAX (808) 921-5507.<br>W www.radisson.com/waikikihi<br>Located a block away from the beach and two blocks from Kapi‘olani Park, this hotel still seems a long way from the Waikīkī crowds. It offers lovely rooms with marble baths. | ■ | 620 (6) | ■ | | ■ |
| **Waikīkī (O‘ahu):** *Royal Garden at Waikīkī* $$$<br>440 ‘Olohana St, HI 96815. Tel (808) 943-0202, (800) 367-5666. FAX (808) 945-7407.<br>W www.royalgardens.com<br>This boutique hotel is truly a breath of fresh air. Half a block from the Ala Wai Canal, it is fairly quiet with beautifully appointed rooms and baths, and an excellent restaurant, the Cascada. | ■ | 201 (19) | ■ | ● | |
| **Waikīkī (O‘ahu):** *Halekūlani* $$$$<br>2199 Kālia Rd, HI 96815. Tel (808) 923-2311, (800) 367-2343. FAX (808) 926-8004.<br>W www.halekulani.com<br>The Halekūlani is the epitome of elegance. Everything is perfect, from the manicured tropical grounds and the tasteful decor to the superb cuisine at La Mer and the beautiful, orchid-design pool. | ■ | 412 (44) | ■ | | ■ |
| **Waikīkī (O‘ahu):** *The Royal Hawaiian* $$$$<br>2259 Kalākaua Ave, HI 96815. Tel (808) 923-7311, (866) 500-8313. FAX (808) 924-7098.<br>W www.starwood.com/luxury.com<br>This elegant Waikīkī landmark, built in 1927, is affectionately known as the Pink Palace of the Pacific. | ■ | 526 (54) | ■ | ● | ■ |
| **Waikīkī (O‘ahu):** *Sheraton Moana Surfrider* $$$$<br>2365 Kalākaua Ave, HI 96815. Tel (808) 922-3111, (800) 325-3535. FAX (808) 923-0308.<br>W www.sheraton.com<br>The splendid "First Lady of Waikīkī" combines modern comforts with high elegance and grandeur. Don't on any account miss the tea on the popular Banyan Veranda. | ■ | 791 (46) | ■ | ● | ■ |
| **Kaunakakai (Moloka‘i):** *Hotel Moloka‘i* $$<br>Mile Marker 2, Kamehameha V Hwy, PO Box 1020, HI 96748. Tel (808) 553-5347.<br>FAX (808) 553-5047. W www.hotelmolokai.com<br>This oceanfront, Polynesian-style hotel is a favorite with islanders, offering simple, comfortable lodgings and warm service. Enjoy seaside dining at the Holo Holo Kai restaurant. | ■ | 45 | | | |
| **Kaunakakai (Moloka‘i):** *Moloka‘i Shores Suites* $$$<br>Mile Marker 1, Kamehameha V Hwy, PO Box1037, HI 96748. Tel (808) 553-5954, (800) 535-0085. FAX (800) 553-3241. W www.marcresorts.com<br>These one-and-two-bedroom condos lie just minutes from the main town. This hotel also offers whale-watching opportunities during winter. | ■ | (102) | | | ■ |
| **Hāna (Maui):** *Josie's Hāna Hideaway* $$$<br>PO Box 265, HI 96713. Tel (808) 248-7727. FAX (808) 248-8418.<br>W www.hanahideaway.com<br>Each of the houses in this complex has its own special charm and is close to the peaceful village of Hāna. Some have beautiful ocean views, others are surrounded by coconut, banana, and papaya groves. | ■ | 12 | | | ■ |

| | | | | | |
|---|---|---|---|---|---|
| **KĀ'ANAPALI (MAUI):** *Kā'anapali Beach Hotel* $$$<br>2525 Kā'anapali Parkway, HI 96761. *(808) 661-0011, (800) 262-8450.*<br>FAX *(808) 667-5978.* W www.kbhmaui.com<br>Great hospitality has earned this low-rise property a reputation as Maui's most Hawaiian hotel. Authentic foods, craft classes, and free children's programs are also available. | ■ | 416 (14) | ■ | ● | ■ |
| **KĀ'ANAPALI (MAUI):** *Sheraton Maui* $$$$$<br>2605 Kā'anapali Parkway, HI 96761. *(808) 661-0031, (866) 500-8313.*<br>FAX *(808) 661-0458.* W www.sheraton–maui.com<br>Perched on top of Black Rock high above the beach, this hotel has the distinction of having furnishings made from *koa* wood, and a variety of native plants. | ■ | 510 (45) | ■ | ● | ■ |
| **LAHAINA (MAUI):** *Lahaina Inn* $$<br>127 Lahainaluna Rd, HI 96761. *(808) 661-0577, (800) 669-3444.*<br>FAX *(808) 667-9480.* W www.lahainainn.com<br>Lovingly restored to Victorian elegance, this small inn has individually decorated rooms with private *lānai* on which breakfast is served every morning. David Paul's "Lahaina Grill" is downstairs. | ■ | 9 (3) | | | ■ |
| **LAHAINA (MAUI):** *Lahaina Shores Beach Resort* $$$<br>475 Front St, HI 96761. *(808) 661-4835, (800) 642-6284.* FAX *(808) 661-4696.*<br>W www.lahainashores.com<br>This seven-story plantation-style resort with fully equipped kitchens is the only beachfront hotel in town. It is also close to the local shops. | ■ | 184 (15) | | | ■ |
| **HILO (HAWAI'I ISLAND):** *Hawai'i Naniloa Hotel* $$<br>93 Banyan Dr, HI 96720. *(808) 969-3333, (800) 367-5360.* FAX *(808) 969-6622.*<br>W www.naniloa.com<br>Located on the lovely Banyan Drive, the Naniloa is as luxurious as it gets in Hilo. There are two pools, a health spa, and a restaurant on the property, and a nine-hole golf course across the street. | ■ | 318 (7) | ■ | | ■ |
| **HILO (HAWAI'I ISLAND):** *Uncle Billy's Hilo Bay Hotel* $$<br>87 Banyan Dr, HI 96720. *(808) 935-0861, (800) 367-5102.* FAX *(808) 935-7903.*<br>W www.unclebillys.com<br>A low-rise, family-style Polynesian resort with a nightly *hula* show, where visitors are welcome to experience Hilo as local residents do. | ■ | 143 | ■ | | ■ |
| **VOLCANO VILLAGE (HAWAI'I ISLAND):** *Kīlauea Lodge* $$<br>Old Volcano Rd, PO Box 116, HI 96785. *(808) 967-7366.* FAX *(808) 967-7367.*<br>W www.kilauealodge.com<br>Built as a YMCA camp in 1938, the refurbished lodge is a mile (1.5 km) from Volcanoes National Park. It also has a fine restaurant. ***Cottages:*** *2* | ■ | 11 | ■ | | |
| **LĪHU'E (KAUA'I):** *Kaha Lani Resort* $$$<br>4460 Nehe Rd, HI 96766. *(808) 822-9331, (800) 367-5004.*<br>FAX *(808) 822-2828.* W www.castleresorts.com<br>A few minutes north of town, this low-rise complex offers a range of condos in a quiet setting beside the beach. The attractive units have fully-equipped kitchens. Free tennis and outdoor barbeques. | ■ | 74 units | | | ■ |
| **LĪHU'E (KAUA'I):** *Kaua'i Beach Marriott Resort & Beach Club* $$$$<br>3610 Rice St, HI 96766. *(808) 245-5050, (800) 228-9290.*<br>FAX *(808) 245-5049.* W www.marriott.com<br>Facing the ocean, this luxury resort enjoys a quarter-mile of white-sand beach and the largest pool in the state. Restaurants include the casual Duke's Canoe Club. | ■ | 345 (11) | ■ | | ■ |
| **PRINCEVILLE:** *Hanalei Bay Resort & Suites* $$$<br>5380 Honoiki Rd, HI 96722. *(808) 826-6522; (800) 827-4427.*<br>FAX *(808) 826-6680.* W www.hanaleibayresort.com<br>Perched above Hanalei Bay, this gem of a resort is rated in the Condé Nast Traveler Magazine Top 30 Tropical Resorts worldwide. There's a lagoon pool with waterfalls, tennis courts, and superb golf nearby. | ■ | 182 | | | ■ |
| **WAIMEA (KAUA'I):** *Waimea Plantation Cottages* $$$<br>9400 Kaumuali'i Hwy, PO Box 367, HI 96796. *(808) 338-1625.* FAX *(808) 338-2338.*<br>W www.aston–hotels.com<br>Step back into old Hawai'i at these wonderfully restored plantation cottages set in coconut groves at the gateway to the Waimea Canyon. Ceiling fans and period furniture. | ■ | 50 | | | |

For key to symbols see back flap

# Where to Eat

BOTH ALASKA AND HAWAI'I OFFER an enormous choice of places to eat. Restaurants have been selected across a wide range of price categories for their good value, excellent food, atmosphere, and location. Restaurants are listed by area and within these by price. Opening times are indicated by a "B" for breakfast, "L" for lunch, and "D" for dinner.

## Alaska

| Restaurant | Price | Credit Cards | Outdoor Tables | Vegetarian | Good Wine List | Late Opening |
|---|---|---|---|---|---|---|
| **ANCHORAGE:** *Club Paris*<br>417 W 5th Ave. (907) 277-6332.<br>The filet mignon with blue cheese stuffing is legendary. Save room for a slice of just-as-delicious cheesecake. *L, D.* P | $$$ | ■ | | ■ | ● | |
| **ANCHORAGE:** *Marx Bros Cafe*<br>627 W 3rd Ave. (907) 278-2133.<br>An intimate restaurant with an Alaska-sized reputation for presentations of Alaskan seafood and game. Reservations required. *D.* ● *Sun & Mon.* | $$$$ | ■ | | ■ | ● | |
| **DENALI:** *Perch Restaurant*<br>13 miles S of Visitor Center. (907) 683-2523.<br>An informal place offering tender cuts of beef and seafood. It has great views of the Alaska Range. *B, L, D.* ● *Oct–Apr: Mon–Thu.* P | $$$ | ■ | ● | ■ | ● | |
| **FAIRBANKS:** *Pike's Landing*<br>4438 Airport Way W. (907) 479-6500.<br>Reserve a table by the window or dine outdoors, overlooking the Chena River. The wide-ranging menu and casual atmosphere mirror its clientele. *L, D.* P | $$$ | ■ | ● | ■ | ● | |
| **HOMER:** *Boardwalk Fish & Chips*<br>Homer Spit Rd. (907) 235-7749.<br>The best halibut and chips in the "Halibut Capital of the World." Also try a bowl of creamy clam chowder with a side of scallops. *L, D.* ● *Oct–Apr.* P | $ | | | | | |
| **JUNEAU:** *Gold Creek Salmon Bake*<br>Basin Rd. (907) 789-0052, (800) 323-5757.<br>Salmon, ribs, and chicken grilled outdoors in traditional style. The set price includes entertainment and hotel transfers. *L, D.* ● *Oct–Apr.* P | $$$ | ■ | ● | ■ | | |
| **JUNEAU:** *Fiddlehead Restaurant & Di Sopra*<br>429 W Willoughby Ave. (907) 586-3150.<br>Offers earthy dishes like fisherman's pie. Upstairs, Di Sopra presents local seafood with an Italian twist. *B, L, D.* P | $$$$ | ■ | | ■ | ● | |
| **KETCHIKAN:** *Annabelle's Keg & Chowder House*<br>326 Front St. (907) 225-6009.<br>Authentic Alaskan food served in the elegant surroundings. Good seafood, fish, and king crab is on offer here, as well as sandwiches and burgers. *L, D.* | $$$ | ■ | | ■ | ● | |
| **KODIAK ISLAND:** *Second Floor Restaurant*<br>116 W Rezanof Dr. (907) 486-8555.<br>Good Japanese cuisine is available at this eatery, which uses local seafood in the tempura and "Kodiak Rolls." *L, D.* ● *Sat–Sun L.* P | $$$$$ | ■ | | | | |
| **SEWARD:** *Ray's Waterfront*<br>Small Boat Harbor, 1316 4th Ave. (907) 224-5606.<br>Views to snowcapped peaks and walls adorned with trophy fish for a classic Alaskan ambience. Cedar plank salmon and Thai-style seafood are favorites here. ● *Oct–Mar.* P | $$ | ■ | | ■ | ● | |
| **SITKA:** *Van Winkle & Sons*<br>205 Harbor Dr. (907) 747-7652.<br>A popular place, it is best known for the fresh halibut and chips, but also has a full seafood menu. *L, D.* P | $$ | ■ | | ■ | ● | |
| **SKAGWAY:** *Stowaway Café*<br>2nd Ave. (907) 983-3463.<br>Well-spaced tables, perfectly grilled fish, and water views make this a romantic place to enjoy dinner. It is just a few steps from the cruise ship dock. ● *Oct–Apr.* P | $$$ | ■ | | | ● | |

**Price categories** include a three-course meal for one, a glass of house wine, and all unavoidable extra charges such as sales tax and service:
$ under $20
$$ $20–30
$$$ $30–45
$$$$ $45–60
$$$$$ over $60

**CREDIT CARDS**
Major credit cards accepted.

**OUTDOOR TABLES**
Garden, courtyard, or terrace with outside tables.

**VEGETARIAN**
A good selection of vegetarian dishes available.

**GOOD WINE LIST**
Extensive list of good wines, both domestic and imported.

**LATE OPENING**
Full menu or light meals served after 11pm.

## HAWAI'I

| Restaurant | Credit Cards | Outdoor Tables | Vegetarian | Good Wine List | Late Opening |
|---|---|---|---|---|---|
| **HALE'IWA (O'AHU):** *Kua 'Aina Sandwich* $<br>66-214 Kamehameha Hwy (Hwy 83). *(808) 637-6067.*<br>If you love burgers and fries, try this humble surfer hangout on O'ahu's North Shore. A local landmark, it has the best food in town. | | ● | | | |
| **HONOLULU (O'AHU):** *Ono Hawaiian Foods* $<br>726 Kapahulu Ave. *(808) 737-2275.*<br>Second only to a *tūtū's* (grandmother's) kitchen, this small eatery is great for Hawaiian dishes such as *poi, laulau,* and *lomi-lomi* salmon. *Sun.* | | | | | |
| **HONOLULU (O'AHU):** *Kincaid's Fish, Chop & Steakhouse* $$$<br>1050 Ala Moana Boulevard (at Ward Warehouse). *(808) 591-2005.*<br>Kincaid's offers excellent food and first rate service. It is a terrific place to take a break from shopping, but it tends to get extremely busy around noon. | ■ | | | ● | ■ |
| **WAIKĪKĪ (O'AHU):** *Duke's Canoe Club* $$$<br>2335 Kalākaua Ave (in the Outrigger Waikīkī). *(808) 922-2268.*<br>Just steps from Duke Kahanamoku's favorite surfing spot, this is part restaurant, part bar, part museum, and one of the most popular hangouts in town. A varied menu of steak, fish, and salads. | ■ | ● | | ● | |
| **KAUNAKAKAI (MOLOKA'I):** *Kanemitsu Bakery* $<br>79 Ala Malama St. *(808) 553-5855. Meals until 11:30am; bakery open until 6:30pm.*<br>Locals say if you haven't been to this bakery, you haven't been to this region at all. Sweet breads are baked daily. Local-style breakfast and lunch. | | | | | |
| **HĀNA (MAUI):** *Hāna Ranch Restaurant* $$<br>Hāna Ranch Center, off Hāna Hwy (Hwy 360). *(808) 248-8255.*<br>Whether in the light-wood dining room or outside amid the serenity of Hāna, the food is superb, prepared simply with local ingredients. | ■ | ● | | | |
| **LAHAINA (MAUI):** *Longhi's* $$$<br>888 Front St. *(808) 667-2288.*<br>Created by "a man who loves to eat" (Bob Longhi), this is a Maui institution. The orange juice and coffee alone are worth the trip for breakfast. Specials include *'ahi* (tuna) torino and shrimp amaretto. | ■ | | | ● | |
| **LAHAINA (MAUI):** *David Paul's Lahaina Grill* $$$$$<br>127 Lahainaluna Rd. *(808) 667-5117.*<br>Voted "Best Maui Restaurant" ten times by *Honolulu* magazine readers, try Lahaina Grill's superb *kālua* duck, Tequila shrimp, or triple berry pie. | ■ | | | ● | |
| **HILO (HAWAI'I ISLAND):** *Nihon Restaurant & Cultural Center* $$<br>123 Lihiwai St. *(808) 969-1133.*<br>Japanese in design, Nihon gives you culture with your sushi. The upstairs dining room offers a beautiful view of Hilo Bay and Lili'uokalani Gardens. The food here is authentic and delicious. *Sun.* | ■ | ● | | ● | |
| **LĪHU'E (KAUA'I):** *Hamura Saimin Stand* $<br>2956 Kress St. *(808) 245-3271.*<br>Many feel this restaurant makes Hawai'i's best noodles. Customers sit at a counter, and even on the hottest day, the *saimin* is absolutely delicious. | | | | | |
| **LĪHU'E (KAUA'I):** *Gaylord's at Kilohana* $$$<br>3-2087 Kaumuali'i Hwy (Hwy 50). *(808) 245-9593.*<br>Located at Kaua'i's legendary plantation estate, Gaylord's offers visitors open-air dining with a varied menu that ranges from pasta to prime rib. | ■ | ● | | ● | |

For key to symbols see back flap

# General Index

Page numbers in **bold** type refer to main entries.

## A

## C

## N

# O

# P

## S

## Y



## Z

# Acknowledgements

## Proof Reader & Indexer
Glenda Fernandes.

## DK London Editorial & Design Assistance
Brigitte Arora, Sherry Collins, Jo Cowen, Caroline Evans, Madeline Farbman, Jacky Jackson, Pamela Marmito, Ros Walford.

## Factcheckers
D. Clancy, Jerry Dean, Paul Franklin, Jill Metzler, Don Pitcher, Mike Rogers.

## Senior DTP Designer
Jason Little.

## Senior Cartographic Editor
Casper Morris.

## DK Picture Library
Mark Dennis.

## Production Controllers
Sarah Dodd, Melanie Dowland.

## Managing Art Editor
Jane Ewart.

## Publishing Manager
Helen Townsend.

## Publisher
Douglas Amrine.

Dorling Kindersley would like to thank the following people whose contributions and assistance have made the preparation of this book possible.

## Additional Contributors
Ruth & Eric Bailey, Jyl Benson, Eleanor Berman, Jeremy Black, Lester Brooks, Patricia Brooks, Tom Bross, Susan Burke, Rebecca Carman, Richard Cawthorne, Brett Cook, Donna Dailey, Bonita Halm, Michelle de Larrabeiti, David Dick, Susan Farewell, Rebecca Poole Forée, Paul Franklin, Donald S. Frazier, Bonnie Friedman, Rita Goldman, Patricia Harris, Ross Hassig, Carolyn Heller, Pierre Home-Douglas, Lorraine Johnson, Penney Kome, Esther Labi, Philip Lee, Helga Loverseed, David Lyon, Clemence McLaren, Guy Mansell, Fred Mawer, Nancy Mikula, Melissa Miller, Kendrick Oliver, Barry Parr, Ellen Payne, J. Kingston Pierce, Alice L. Powers, Jennifer Quasha, George Raudzens, Juliette Rogers, John Ryan, Alex Salkever, Litta W. Sanderson, Kem Sawyer, Emma Stanford, Brett Steel, Arvin Steinberg, Phyllis Steinberg, Nigel Tisdall, Brian Ward, Greg Ward, John Wilcock, Ian Williams, Marilyn Wood, Paul Wood, Stanley Young.

## Additional Illustrators
Ricardo Almazan, Ricardo Almazan Jr, Arcana Studios, Robert Ashby, William Band, Gilles Beauchemin, Richard Bonson, Joanne Cameron, Stephen Conlin, Gary Cross, Richard Draper, Dean Entwhistle, Eugene Fleurey, Chris Forsey, Martin Gagnon, Vincent Gagnon, Stephen Gyapay, Stéphane Jorisch, Patrick Jougla, Nick Lipscombe, Claire Littlejohn, Luc Normandin, Lee Peters, Mel Pickering, Robbie Polley, Kevin Robinson, Hamish Simpson, Mike Taylor, Pat Thorne, Chris Orr & Associates, Jean-François Vachon, John Woodcock.

## Additional Photographers
Max Alexander, Peter Anderson, Jaime Baldovinos, Alan Briere, Demetrio Carrasco, Philippe Dewet, Philip Dowell, Neil Fletcher, Bruce Forster, John Heseltine, Ed Homonylo, Philip C. Jackson, Eliot Kaufman, Alan Keohane, Dave King, Andrew Leyerle, Neil Lukas, David Lyons, Norman McGrath, Andrew McKinney, Tim Mann, Gunter Marx, Neil Mersh, Howard Millard, Michael Moran, Sue Oldfield, Scot Pitts, Rob Reichenfeld, Julio Rochon, Kim Sayer, Neil Setchfield, Mike Severns, Chris Stevens, Clive Streeter, Giles Stokoe, Scott Suchman, Matthew Ward, Stephen Whitehorne, Linda Whitwam, Francesca Yorke.

## Photographic & Artwork Reference
Madeline Farbman; Emily Hovland; Independence National Historic Park: Phil Sheridan; National Park Service: Tom Patterson; Philadelphia Convention & Visitors Bureau:

Danielle Cohn, Ellen Kornfield, Marissa Philip, San Antonio Convention & Visitors Bureau: Angela McClendon; M&A Design: Ajay Sethi, Mugdha Sethi; AirPhoto USA: Brian Garcia, Shannon Kelley.

## Photography Permissions

DORLING KINDERSLEY would like to thank the following for their assistance and kind permission to photograph at their establishments (the establishments are listed in chapter order):

Old Merchant's House, East Village, NY; American Museum of Natural History, NY; Museum of American Folk Art, NY; Studio Museum in Harlem, NY; The Cloisters, NY; Columbia University, NY; Rockefeller Group, NY; Massachusetts State House, Boston; Nichols House Museum, Boston; Trinity Church, Boston; Museum of Fine Arts, Boston; Sackler Museum, Boston; New England Aquarium, Boston; Salem Witch Museum, MS; Plimoth Plantation, MS; Mark Twain House, CT; Florence Griswold Museum, CT; Currier Gallery of Art, Manchester; National Air and Space Museum, Washington, DC; National Museum of Natural History, Washington, DC; National Museum of African Art, Washington, DC; National Museum of American History, Washington, DC; Kenmore House, VA; Library of Congress, Washington, DC; South Carolina State Museum, SC; Stone Mountain Park, GA; Shaker Village of Pleasant Hill, Harrodsburg, KY; Graceland, TN; Historic New Orleans Voodoo Museum, New Orleans, LA; Nottoway Plantation, LA; National Voting Rights Museum and Institute, Selma, AL; Elvis Presley Park, Tupelo CVB; Spertus Museum of Jewish Studies, Chicago; Field Museum, Chicago; Oriental Institute Museum, Chicago; Museum of Broadcast Communications, Chicago; University of Notre Dame, IN; Eiteljorg Museum, IN; Franklin Park Conservatory and Botanical Gardens, OH; Detroit Metro CVB, MI; The Detroit Institute of Arts, MI; Circus World Museum, Baraboo, WI; Walker Art Center, MN; The Mammoth Site of Hot Springs, South Dakota Inc., SD; The Nelson Atkins Museum of Art, MO; City Manager, Vince Capell, St. Joseph, MO; Woolaroc Ranch Museum, OK; Oral Roberts University, OK; Cowboy Artists of America Museum, Kerville,TX; Museum of Indian Arts and Culture, Santa Fe; Millicent Rogers Museum, Taos, NM; Las Vegas Natural History Museum; Cedar City Museum, UT; Museum of Northern Arizona, Flagstaff, AZ; Phoenix Museum of History, Phoenix, AZ; Hopi Learning Center, AZ; New Mexico Museum of Natural History and Science, Albuquerque, NM; Albuquerque Museum of Art and History, Albuquerque; Maxwell Museum of Anthropology, Albuquerque, NM; Hubbell Trading Post, NM; Odyssey Maritime Discovery Center, WA; Seattle Art Museum, WA; National Park Service, OR; Museum of Tolerance, Los Angeles, CA; Balboa Park, San Diego; Hearst Castle, San Simeon; Huntington Library, San Marino; Knotts Berry Farm, Buena Park; Museum of Contemporary Art, LA; *Queen Mary*, Long Beach; Sacramento State Capitol; San Diego Aerospace Museum; San Diego Automotive Museum; San Diego Museum of Art; San Diego Zoological Society; Santa Barbara Mission, CA; Wells Fargo History Museum, San Francisco, CA; San Francisco History Center, San Francisco Public Library, CA; University of California, Berkeley; University of California, LA; Winchester Mystery House, San Jose; Valdez Museum, Valdez, AK; Baranof Museum, Kodiak Island, AK; Ice Museum, Fairbanks, AK; as well as all the other churches, museums, hotels, restaurants, shops, galleries and sights too numerous to thank individually.

## Picture Credits

t = top; tl = top left; tlc = top left centre; tc = top centre; tr = top right; cla = centre left above; ca = centre above; cra = centre right above; cl = centre left; c = centre; cr = centre right; clb = centre left below; cb = centre below; crb = centre right below; bl = bottom left; b = bottom; bc = bottom centre; bcl = bottom centre left; br = bottom right.

Every effort has been made to trace the copyright holders and we apologize in advance for any unintentional omissions. We would be pleased to insert the appropriate acknowledgements in any subsequent edition of this publication.

Works of art have been reproduced with the permission of the following copyright holders:

© ALBUQUERQUE MUSEUM OF ART AND HISTORY: Museum Purchase, 1993 General Obligation Bond Estella Loretto *Earth Mother, Offerings for a Good Life (No Wa Mu Stio)*, 1994, 548tl; BELL ATLANTIC BUILDING: *Telephone Men & Women at Work* by Dean Cornwell, 140tl; COLUMBIA UNIVERSITY: 84cla; Courtesy COMMONWEALTH OF MASSACHUSETTS ART COMMISSION: *Civil War Army Nurses Memorial* Bela Pratt, 1911, 138tr; Stained glass window, Main Stair Hall, 1900/details: *Magna Carta seal 43, Seal of the Commonwealth* (pre-1898) 138cl; *Return of the Colours to the Custody of the Commonwealth*, December 22, 1986, mural by Edward Simmons 1902: 139cbl. © Denman Fink: Detail from *Law Guides Florida's Progress*, 1940, 287tl; HISTORIC NEW ORLEANS VOODOO MUSEUM: *Marie Laveau* by Charles M. Gandolfo, 348br; Courtesy FLORENCE GRISWOLD MUSEUM: *The Harpist, A Portrait of Miss Florence Griswold*, by Alphonse Jongers, 1903, 159br; © Georg John Lober: *Hans Christian Anderson*, 1956, 78br. MILLICENT ROGERS MUSEUM: 507tl; HENRY MOORE FOUNDATION: *Reclining Figure: Hand* (1979), the work illustrated on page 76bl has been reproduced by permission of the Henry Moore Foundation; SACKLER MUSEUM, Cambridge, Boston: 149tc; Courtesy KENNETH TREISTER HOLOCAUST MEMORIAL: © Kenneth Treister, *A Sculpture of Love and Anguish*, 1990, 293cl. Courtesy THE SEATTLE ARTS COMMISSION © Jonathan Borofsky: *Hammering Man*, 1988, 617tr. © Victor Arnautoff, *City Life*, Coit Tower, 1934, 702bl. COLLECTION OF SPERTUS MUSEUM: *Flame of Hope* by Leonardo Nierman, 1995, 392crb.

The publisher would like to thank the following individuals, companies and picture libraries for permission to reproduce their photographs:

ALAMY: Joseph Sohm 652; THE AFRICAN AMERICAN MUSEUM IN PHILADELPHIA: 100cla; ATLANTA–FULTON PUBLIC LIBRARY FOUNDATION, INC. COURTESY THE ATLANTA HISTORY CENTER: 260cr;

© RICHARD BEYER: *People Waiting for the Interurban* 619tl; THE BROOKLYN MUSEUM OF ART: 87bc; CAESARS ENTERTAINMENT: 511br; BRUCE COLEMAN INC., NEW YORK: Jeff Foott 122-123; BRUCE COLEMAN, LONDON: Raimund Cramm GDT 303br; COLORADO HISTORICAL SOCIETY: William Henry Jackson Collection: *Westward HO!* 1904, 612bl; CONVENTION AND VISITORS ASSOCIATION OF LANE COUNTY, OR: 634tl; CORBIS: 32br, 34br, 38tr, 38cl, 39br, 47b, 49t, 53cra, 95tl, 95b, 127b, 166br, 189tl, 335 (inset), 376-377, 394bl, 433 (inset), 565 (inset), 688br, 730 (inset), 741tr; 752cra, 753bl; AFP 53br; James L. Amos 57tl; Craig Aurness 204bl, 688tr (Hearst Castle, CA Park Service), 692tl; Dave Bartruff 101br, 450tc; Tom Bean 35tl, 41br, 527br; Nathan Benn 56cl; Corbis-Bettman 28br, 43b, 44br, 45t, 46tl, 50tl, 50br, 53tl, 53tc, 53tr, 60cl, 90bl, 94bl, 187 (inset), 193bl, 225cl, 225bc, 226cla, 349br, 393crb, 421cla, 450cla, 511bl, 655ca, 661br; Richard Bickel 108cr; Kristi J. Black 689tl; © Carnegie Museum of Art, Pittsburgh, photo by W. Cody 108bc; Steve Chenn 102bl; L. Clarke 54-55; Jerry Cooke 92cr, 243b; Richard A. Cooke 109b, 188bl, 221b; Lake County Museum 9 (inset), 519br; Richard Cummins 30bc, 103tc, 107tr, 338, 339b, 485tc; Jeff Curtes 595bl; Corcoran Gallery of Art, Washington, D.C.; 2003: *Washington Before Yorktown*, 1824-25, by Rembrandt Peale, 42; *George Washington*, 1796, by Gilbert Stuart, 52clb; Dennis Degnan 105tl; Hulton–Deutsch Collection 140 cr; Jay Dickman 219br; Henry Dittz 665br; Duomo 29br; Peter Finger 90tr, 91tr; Kevin Fleming 189cr, 192t, 225tr, 226br, 227br, 238-239, 407br; Owen Franken 29cl; Michael Freeman 198cl; Raymond Gehman 527tc; Mark E. Gibson 194br; Tod A. Gipstein 189br; Farell Grehan 97br, 165bl; Bob Gomes 29tr; The Solomon R. Guggenheim Foundation, NY: (*Man with Arms Crossed*, 1895-1900, by Cézanne, photo by Francis G. Mayer) 82tr; Liz Haymans 593br; Robert Holmes 104bc, 334-

335; Dave G. Houser 712cla; George H. H. Huey 503ca; Swim Ink 48ca; Woolfgang Kaehler 34cl; Catherine Karnow 101tc, 512crb; Steve Kaufman 579tr; Layne Kennedy 109tr, 380, 421tr; Dave King 552clb; Bob Krist 61bl, 98tr, 103cl, 352bl, 688clb, 689bl; Owaki-Kulla 242, 353bl; Robert Landau 93tl; Larry Lee 32tr; Danny Lehman 35tr; George D. Lepp 39tr; Craig Lovell 32cl; Georgia Lowell 706bl; James Marshall 517bc, 741bl; Francis G. Mayer 44tl, 60tr, 81tl, 94crb; Buddy Mays 91cr, 475br; Joe McDonald 65b; Louis K. Meisel Gallery 8-9; Kelly-Mooney Photography 31tr, 96br, 97tl, 199cr; David Muench 33tl, 56bl, 64, 92bc, 106cla, 126, 188tr, 218br, 219cla, 220cla, 224tr, 436, 527cbr, 755tl; Marc Muench 594tr, 595tl, 595crb; Walley McNamee 53crb; © National Portrait Gallery, Smithsonian Institution, Washington, DC, acquired as a gift to the nation through the generosity of the Donald W. Reynolds Foundation, 2003; 203br (*Lansdowne portrait of George Washington*, 1796, by Gilbert Stuart, photo by Archivo Iconografico, S. A.); Richard T. Nowitz 104tl, 191b, 220br, 221tl; Pat O'Hara 610; Douglas Peebles 33bl, 594cl; The Phillips Collection, Washington, D.C.: (*The Luncheon of the Boating Party*, 1881, by Pierre Auguste Renoir (1841-1919), photo by Francis G. Mayer) 210tl; Charles Philip 35bl; Philadelphia Museum of Arts: 105crb; Neil Preston 269bl; Greg Probst 564-565; Carl & Ann Purcell 94tc; Roger Ressmeyer 286br, 608-609, 629tr; Jim Richardson 33cr; Bill Ross 38bl, 63br; Ron Sanford 437b; Paul A. Souders 224b; Kevin Schafer 56tr; Alan Schein 57br, 92tl, 108tl; Phil Schermeister 378cb, 516bc; Flip Schulke 51tr; Michael T. Sedam 34tr, 611b, 750cla; Leif Skoogfors 102cla, 107clb; Lee Snider 61ca, 91bl, 96clb, 100tr, 101cr, 101cb, 106br, 198tr, 218tl, 227tl; Joseph Sohm; ChromoSohm Inc. 39tl, 41tl, 57cra, 217cra; 486b; Ted Spiegel 57crb; Mark L Stephenson 31crb, 755br; David Stoecklein 500-501; Bequest of Mrs. Benjamin Ogle Tayloe, Collection of the Corcoran Art Gallery: 52ctl; Underwood & Underwood 93bl, 264cla, 381b; Ron Watts 32bl, 33tr, 62tr, 93br; David H. Wells 105b; Nick Wheeler 669bcl; Oscar White 53cb; Michael S. Yamashita 96cla, 421b; Bo Zaunders 472-473, 481tl; Paul Franklin: 539tr; The Frick Collection: *Lady Meux* by James Abbot McNeill Whistler, 1881, 80bl;

Getty Images: Jack Dykinga 26-27; Robert Glusic 648-649; Chris Noble 568; © J Paul Getty Trust: *Adoration of the Magi*, 1495-1505, by Andrea Mantegna, 660tl; Granger Collection, New York: 52tc, 52clb, 52bl, 52bc, 52br, 53bl, 501 (inset);

Courtesy of Harley Davidson Motor Company: 107bl; Hells Canyon Adventures: 641crb, 641bl; Historic New Orleans Collection: 351cb; Historic New Orleans Voodoo Museum: *Portrait of Marie Laveau* 348br; Lincoln Park Zoo, Chicago: 396cl;

Mary Evans Picture Library: 27 (inset), 55 (inset), 123 (inset), 239 (inset), 283 (inset), 377 (inset), 473 (inset), 481bl; 609 (inset); 649 (inset); Masterfile: Garry Black 432-433; Bill Brooks 40tr; Gail Mooney 35crb; Randy Lincks 41cr; Museum of Fine Arts, Boston: HU–MFA Expedition *Shawabtis of Tabarka* 147tl; Egypt Exploration Fund *Inner Coffin of Nes-mut-aat-neru* 147cl; Ruth & Carl J. Shapiro Colonnade and Vault *John Singer Sargent Murals* 147br; Museum of International Folk Art, a unit of the Museum of New Mexico: Girard Foundation Collection, Photo Michel Monteaux *Toy Horse* Bangladesh, Indian. C. 1960. 547cb;

© 2003 Board of Trustees, National Gallery of Art, Washington, DC: *The Alba Madonna*, 1510, by Raphael (Raffaello Sanzio of Urbino, 1483–1520), Andrew W. Melon Collection: 201tl; NHPA: David Middleton 553 br; National Museum of American Jewish History: Collection of Congregation Mikveh Israel: 100clb; National Museum of Natural History, Washington/© Smithsonian Institution: Dane Penland 202cr; National Park Service, OR: 637tr; The Nature Conservancy: Rich Franco Photography 313b; Nelson-Atkins Museum of Art, Kansas City, Missouri: *Shuttlecocks* by Claes Oldenburg and

Coosje van Bruggen, 1994: 457tl; New Orleans Metropolitan Convention & Visitors Bureau: Ann Purcell 344bl; Carl Purcell 346tl;

Odyssey Maritime Discovery Center, WA: 617cl; Pedro E. Guerrero © 2002, Talesin Preservation Inc.: 415tl; © Courtesy of the Pennsylvania Academy of Fine Arts; Philadelphia: Joseph E. Temple Fund, 2003: *The Fox Hunt,* 1893, by Winslow Homer 103br;

Redferns Music Picture Library: 49bc; The Ronald Grant Archive: 666bl; Mae Scanlan: 202tl; John G. Shedd Aquarium, Chicago: © Edward G. Lines 393tr; Superstock: 174tl;

Terra Galleria Photography: 624tl;

Courtesy of Universal Orlando Resort: 308tl; © 2002 Universal Studios, Inc.: 308br, 309tl, 309br;

Viewfinders: Bruce Forster 623cra, 637ca, 637bl, 639bc; Trevor Graves 613tl; Rich Iwasaki 620tc; Pefley 622tr; Bob Poole 632br; Greg Vaughn 620b, 623tl, 628br, 632cra, 633t, 633crb, 635br, 636cla, 636 br, 638b, 640bl, 641tl;

Walla Walla Chamber of Commerce: 625bl; Walker Art Center, Minneapolis: *Spoonbridge and Cherry* by Claes Oldenburg and Coosje van Bruggen, 1987-1988, Gift of Frederick R. Weisman in honor of his parents, William and Mary Weisman, 1988: 416tr; © White House Historical Association (White House Collection) 206cla, 206bc, 207tc, 207cr, 207bl (653, 579, 656, 140, 663) Bruce White 195tr (3074); Words and Pictures: 334bl, 346tl; World Pictures: 653b, 730-731.

Back Endpaper: Corbis: Tom Bean, Jan Butchofsky-Houser, Charles Krebs, Owaki-Kulla, Robert Landau, Lester Lefkowitz.

Jacket
Front - DK Picture Library: Matthew Ward bc; Getty Images: Joseph Pobereskin cl; Ken Reid cr; Robert Harding Picture Library: main image. Back - Corbis: Dallas and John Heaton tl; David Muench br. Spine - Robert Harding Picture Library

All other images © Dorling Kindersley. For further information see **www.dkimages.com**

**SPECIAL EDITIONS OF DK TRAVEL GUIDES**

DK Travel Guides can be purchased in bulk quantities at discounted prices for use in promotions or as premiums.
We are also able to offer special editions and personalized jackets, corporate imprints, and excerpts from all of our books, tailored specifically to meet your own needs.

To find out more, please contact:
(in the United States) **SpecialSales@dk.com**
(in the UK) **Sarah.Burgess@dk.com**
(in Canada) DK Special Sales at **general@tourmaline.ca**
(in Australia) **business.development@pearson.com.au**

# Further Reading

**Fiction**

*Winesburg, Ohio* Anderson, Sherwood, Random House, 1995.

*I Know Why the Caged Bird Sings* Angelou, Maya, Random House, 1983.

*Midnight in the Garden of Good and Evil* Berendt, John, Random House, 1994.

*Dandelion Wine* Bradbury, Ray, Random House, 1985.

*A Walk in the Woods* Bryson, Bill, Random House, 1999.

*Breakfast at Tiffany's* Capote, Truman, Penguin, 1988.

*The Awakening* Chopin, Kate, Random House, 1985.

*The Last of the Mohicans* Cooper, James Fenimore, Penguin, 1984.

*The Red Badge of Courage* Crane, Stephen, Penguin, 1994.

*Time and Again* Finney. Jack, Simon & Schuster, 1995.

*The Great Gatsby* Fitzgerald, F. Scott, Penguin, 1994.

*The Little Shepherd of Kingdom Come* Fox, Jr, John, University Press of Kentucky, 1987.

*The Scarlet Letter* Hawthorne, Nathaniel, Penguin, 1994.

*Farewell to Arms* Hemingway, Ernest, Simon & Schuster, 1995.

*The Legend of Sleepy Hollow* Irving, Washington, Penguin, 1999.

*On the Road* Kerouac, Jack, Penguin, 1998.

*To Kill a Mockingbird* Lee, Harper, Warner Books, 1988.

*Call of the Wild and Other Stories* London, Jack, Penguin, 1995.

*A River Runs Through It and Other Stories* Maclean, Norman, University of Chicago Press, 2001.

*Lonesome Dove* McMurtry, Larry, Simon & Schuster, 1986.

*Gone With the Wind* Mitchell, Margaret, Warner Books, 1993.

*Beloved* Morrison, Toni, Penguin, 1998.

*The Octopus* Norris, Frank, Penguin, 1994.

*Catcher in the Rye* Salinger, JD, Penguin, 1994.

*The Jungle* Sinclair, Upton, Penguin, 1985.

*Uncle Tom's Cabin* Stowe, Harriet Beecher, Penguin, 1981.

*The Grapes of Wrath* Steinbeck, John, Penguin, 2001.

*The Adventures of Tom Sawyer*, Twain, Mark, Penguin, 1986.

*The Color Purple* Walker, Alice, Pocket Books, 1990.

*Our Town and Other Plays* Wilder, Thornton, Penguin, 2000.

*A Streetcar Named Desire* Williams, Tennessee, Signet, 1989.

*Look Homeward Angel* Wolfe, Thomas, Simon & Schuster, 1995.

**History & Politics**

*One Nation: America Remembers September 11, 2001* Life Magazine/ Giuliani, Rudolph W, Little Brown & Company, 2001.

*The Penguin History of the USA* Brogan, Hugh, Penguin, 2001.

*An Hour Before Daylight* Carter, Jimmy, Simon & Schuster, 2001.

*The Civil War: A Narrative* Foote, Shelby, Vintage, 1986.

*1939: The Lost World of the Fair* Gelertner, David, Free Press, 1999.

*Dispatches* Herr, Michael, Vintage, 1991.

*Benjamin Franklin: An American Life* Isaacson, Walter, Simon & Schuster, 2003.

*Writings* Jefferson, Thomas, Library of America, 1984.

*Profiles in Courage* Kennedy, John F, Perennial Press, 2000.

*Profiles in Courage for Our Time* Kennedy, Caroline, Hyperion, 2003.

*The Columbia Historical Portrait of New York* Kouwenhoven, John, Icon, 1972.

*John Adams* McCollough, David, Simon & Schuster, 2002.

*Collected Writings* Paine, Thomas, Library of America, 1995.

*American Colonies* Taylor, Alan, Penguin, 2002.

*Civil Disobedience* Thoreau, Henry David, Dover, 1993.

*Democracy in America* Tocqueville, Alexis de, Alfred A. Knopf, 1994.

*Writings from The New Yorker* White, E.B., Perennial Press, 1991.

*All the President's Men* Woodward, Bob, and Bernstein, Carl, Simon & Schuster, 1994.

**Natural History & Travel**

*National Audubon Society Field Guide to North American Mammals* Whitaker Jr, John O, Alfred A. Knopf, 1996.

*North American Wildlife: Wildflowers* Reader's Digest Association, 1998.

*North American Wildlife: Trees & Non-Flowering Plants* Reader's Digest Association, 1998.

*America's National Parks* Tehabi Books/ Dorling Kindersley, 2001.

*National Geographic on Assignment USA* National Geographic, 1997.

*The Mississippi and the Making of a Nation* National Geographic, 2002.

*Route 66 Main Street USA* Freeth, Nick, Taylor, Paul, Motorbooks Intl, 2001.

*Bayou Farewell* Tidwell, Mike, Pantheon, 2003.

**Art**

*Twentieth Century American Art* Lee Doss, Erika, Oxford University Press, 2002.

*Framing America: A Social History of American Art* Pohl, Frances K., Thames & Hudson, 2002.

## DK Eyewitness Travel Guides

**Boston**
0-7894-9559-7 $20.00 (US) $30.00 (Canada)
0-7513-6864-4 £10.99 (UK) $32.00 (Australia)

**California**
0-7894-1451-1 $29.95 (US) $40.00 (Canada)
0-7513-4841-4 £16.99 (UK) $45.00 (Australia)

**Chicago**
0-7894-9562-7 $20.00 (US) $30.00 (Canada)
0-7513-4825-2 £10.99 (UK) $32.00 (Australia)

**Florida**
0-7894-9564-3 $25.00 (US) $34.95 (Canada)
0-7513-4831-7 £14.99 (UK) $39.95 (Australia)

**Hawaii**
0-7894-9732-8 $29.95 (US) $20.00 (Canada)
0-7513-4823-6 £12.99 (UK) $32.00 (Australia)

**New England**
0-7894-9570-8 $25.00 (US) $34.95 (Canada)
0-7513-6866-0 £14.99 (UK) $39.95 (Australia)

**New Orleans**
0-7894-9737-9 $20.00 (US) $29.95 (Canada)
0-7513-1317-3 £12.99 (UK) $32.00 (Australia)

**New York**
0-7894-9382-9 $25.00 (US) $35.00 (Canada)
0-7513-6860-1 £14.99 (UK) $39.95 (Australia)

**Pacific Northwest**
0-7894-9680-1 $25.00 (US) $35.00 (Canada)
0-7513-6997-7 £15.99 (UK) $42.00 (Australia)

**San Francisco**
0-7894-9420-5 $20.00 (US) $30.00 (Canada)
0-7513-4842-2 £12.99 (UK) $35.00 (Australia)

**Southwest USA & Las Vegas**
0-7894-9565-1 $20.00 (US) $30.00 (Canada)
0-7513-6871-7 £14.99 (UK) $39.95 (Australia)

**Washington, DC**
0-7894-9576-7 $20.00 (US) $29.95 (Canada)
0-7513-2739-5 £9.99 (UK) $32.00 (Australia)

## DK Top 10 Guides

**Boston**
0-7894-9193-1 $10.00 (US) $15.00 (Canada)
0-7513-4851-1 £6.99 (UK) $19.95 (Australia)

**Maui, Moloka'i & Lana'i**
0-7566-0032-4 $10.00 (US) $15.00 (Canada)
1-4053-0274-7 £6.99 (UK) $19.95 (Australia)

**Miami & the Keys**
0-7894-9185-0 $10.00 (US) $15.00 (Canada)
0-7513-4848-1 £6.99 (UK) $19.95 (Australia)

**Orlando**
0-7894-8435-8 $10.00 (US) $15.00 (Canada)
0-7513-3762-5 £6.99 (UK) $19.95 (Australia)

**New York**
0-7894-8351-3 $10.00 (US) $15.00 (Canada)
0-7513-3571-1 £6.99 (UK) $19.95 (Australia)

**San Francisco**
0-7894-9190-7 $10.00 (US) $15.00 (Canada)
0-7513-4853-8 £6.99 (UK) $19.95 (Australia)

**Washington, DC**
0-7894-9186-9 $10.00 (US) $15.00 (Canada)
0-7513-4850-3 £6.99 (UK) $19.95 (Australia)

**Chicago**
0-7566-0031-6 $10.00 (US) $15.00 (Canada)
1-4053-0272-0 £6.99 (UK) $19.95 (Australia)

**Las Vegas**
0-7894-8354-8 $10.00 (US) $15.00 (Canada)
0-7513-3825-7 £6.99 (UK) $19.95 (Australia)

## Upcoming Titles

**Top 10 Honolulu & O'ahu**

**Top 10 Los Angeles**

**Top 10 Virgin Islands**

**Eyewitness Orlando & the Space Coast**

**Eyewitness Arizona & the Grand Canyon**

EYEWITNESS TRAVEL INSURANCE

FOR PEACE OF MIND ABROAD,
**WE'VE GOT IT COVERED**

**DK INSURANCE** PROVIDES YOU WITH QUALITY WORLDWIDE INSURANCE COVER

**For an instant quote**
go to **www.dk.com/travel-insurance**

Organised by Columbus Travel Insurance Services Ltd, 17 Devonshire Square, London EC2M 4SQ, UK.
Underwritten by certain underwriters at Lloyd's and Professional Travel Insurance Company Ltd.

# Highlights of the USA

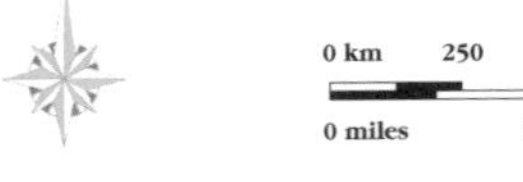

**Mount Rainier National Park, Washington's prime outdoor destination**

**Las Vegas neon lightening up the Strip**

**The luxurious Beverly Hills Hotel, a landmark in Los Angeles**

**Sandstone formations, Zion National Park, Utah**

**Key**

- Great Cities
- Charming Cities
- Fun Places to Visit
- National Parks